HIPPOCRENE STANDARD DICTIONARY

DUTCH-ENGLISH
ENGLISH-DUTCH

Arseen Rijckaert

HIPPOCRENE BOOKS
New York

Originally published as Nederlands-Engels/Engels-Nederlands Zakwoordenboek
Copyright© 1979, 1993 by Standaard Uitgeverij n.v. Antwerpen.

Hippocrene Dutch-English/English-Dutch Standard Dictionary, 1997.
Second printing, 1999.

For information, address:
Hippocrene Books, Inc.
171 Madison Avenue
New York, NY 10016

Library of Congress Cataloging-in-Publication Data
Rijckaert, Arseen.
        Dutch-English, English-Dutch / Arseen Rijckaert.
          p.   cm.
        ISBN 0-7818-0541-4
        1. English language--Dictionaries--Dutch. 2. Dutch language-
-Dictionaries--English.   I. Title.   II. Series.
PF640.R48   1997
439.31'321--dc21   96-54647
                                      CIP

Printed in the United States of America.

HIPPOCRENE STANDARD DICTIONARY

DUTCH-ENGLISH
ENGLISH-DUTCH

Contents

AFKORTINGEN

aanw. vnw.	aanwijzend voornaamwoord.	*ong.*	ongunstige betekenis.
aardk.	aardkunde	*onp.*	onpersoonlijk.
aardr.	aardrijkskunde.	*ontleedk.*	ontleedkunde.
adj.	adjective.	*on. w.*	onovergankelijk werkwoord.
adv.	adverb.	*o. w*	overgankelijk werkwoord.
alg.	algemene betekenis.	*pers. vnw.*	persoonlijk voornaamwoord.
Am.	Amerikanisme.	*Pl.*	Plantkunde.
beeldh.	beeldhouwkunst.	*pop.*	populaire, volkstaal.
betr. vnw.	betrekkelijk voornaamwoord	*pron.*	pronoum.
bez. vnw.	bezittelijk voornaamwoord.	*prot.*	protestants.
Bijb.	Bijbel.	*rek.*	rekenkunde.
bijv.	bijvoeglijk.	*sb.*	substantive
bilj.	biljart.	*Sc.*	Scottish.
b.n.	bijvoeglijk naamwoord.	*sch.*	scheepvaart.
boekh.	boekhouden.	*scheik.*	scheikunde.
bouwk.	bouwkunde.	*scherts.*	schertsend.
burgerl.	burgerlijk.	*schild.*	schilderkunst.
bw.	bijwoord.	*sl.*	slang.
cj.	conjunction.	*sp.*	sport.
conj.	conjunction.	*spoorw.*	spoorwegen.
dial.	dialect	*stelk.*	stelkunde.
dicht.	dichterlijk.	*sterr.*	sterrenkunde.
Dk.	Dierkunde.	*taalk.*	taalkunde.
drukk.	drukkersterm.	*tel.*	telefonie, telegrafie.
E. I.	Engels-Indië	*telw.*	telwoord.
eig.	eigenlijke betekenis.	*tn.*	techniek.
el.	elektriciteit.	*ton.*	toneel.
Eng.	Engels.	*t.t.*	tegenwoordige tijd.
fam.	familiaar.	*tuinb.*	tuinbouw.
fig.	figuurlijk.	*tw.*	tussenwerpsel.
fot.	fotografie.	*v.*	vrouwelijk.
gen.	geneeskunde.	*vb.*	verb.
gesch.	geschiedenis.	*v.d.*	verleden deelwoord.
godsd.	godsdienst.	*vi.*	intransitive verb.
gram.	grammaticaal.	*visv.*	visvangst.
gymn.	gymnastiek.	*vl.*	vliegwezen.
H.	handel.	*vnw.*	voornaamwoord.
ij.	interjection.	*vnw. bw.*	voornaamwoordelijk bijwoord.
Ir.	Irish.		
kaartsp.	kaartspel.	*voetb.*	voetbal.
kath.	katholiek.	*vr.*	reflexive verb.
klankl.	klankleer.	*vr. vnw.*	vragend voornaamwoord.
landb.	landbouw.	*vt.*	transitive verb.
lett.	letterkunde.	*v.t.*	verleden tijd.
lidw.	lidwoord.	*v.v.*	voorvoegsel.
m.	mannelijk.	*vw.*	voegwoord.
mar.	marine.	*vz.*	voorzetsel.
meetk.	meetkunde.	*w.*	werkwoord.
mil.	militaire term.	*wap.*	wapenkunde.
muz.	muziek.	*w.t.*	wetenschappelijke term.
mv.	meervoud.	*wijsb.*	wijsbegeerte.
myth.	mythologie.	*wisk.*	wiskunde.
Nat.	natuurkunde.	*w. vnw.*	wederkerend voornaamw.
Nederl.	Nederlands.	*w.w.*	wederkerend werkwoord.
N.N.	Noord Nederlands.	*Z.A.*	Zuid-Afrikaans.
o.	onzijdig.	*zelfst.*	zelfstandig.
onbep.	onbepaald.	*Z.N.*	Zuid-Nederlands.
onb. vnw.	onbepaald voornaamwoord.	*z.n.*	zelfstandig naamwoord.

VERKLARING VAN DE UITSPRAAKTEKENS

â   als a in *far, part, fast* — ongeveer als aa in het Nederl. *paar*.

ɒ   als u in *but* — ongeveer als de ö in het Duitse *Löffel*, doch gaat meer naar de korte a.

ə: als ur in *burst, turn* — ongeveer als de eu van het Franse *leur* en de toonloze e.

ae   als a in *fat, man* — tussen de a van het Nederlands *kan* en de e van *wet*.

ai   als i in *line, wine* — ongeveer als ei in het Duitse *Wein*.

au   als ou in *house, mouse* — ongeveer als de verkorte a -klank van *maken* gevolgd door een lichte oe-klank.

e   als e in *men, melt* — lijkt enigszins op de i van *winnen*.

ê   als a in *care* — lijkt op de è in het Franse *mère*.

ə   als a in *ago*, als r in *care*, er in *driver, letter*.

êə   als ere in *there* — ê ongeveer als de Franse è in *zèle*.

ei   als a in *fate, table* — ongeveer als de Nederlandse klank *ee*.

i   als i in *will* — ongeveer als de i in het Duitse *bitte*.

f   als ee in *tree* — als ie in *zien*, doch iets langer.

ɔ   als o in *not* — ongeveer als de o in het Nederlands *lot*.

o: als o in *for* en aw in *law* — ongeveer als oa in het Oostvlaams dialekt *proaten*.

ɔi   als oy in *boy* — de ɔ is hierbij een verkorte o:.

ou   als o in *home, stone* — ongeveer als de Nederlandse klank *oo*.

u   als oo in *foot* of u in *full*. — ongeveer als de aangehouden oe-klank in *voet*.

ù   als oo in *food* of u in *rule* — ongeveer als de oe in *moed*, doch langer aangehouden.

g   als g in *good* — als de g in het Franse *guerre*.

j   als y in *yes, yell* — als j in het Nederlands *jager*.

ʌ   als ng in *long, song* — als ng in het Nederlands *ring*.

ʒ   als si in *occasion* — als g in het Franse *plage*.

ʃ   als sh in *sharp, ship* — als ch in het Franse *chasse*.

θ   als th in het Engelse *this, father*.

δ   als th in het Engels *thin, thing*.

w   als w in het Engelse *way, water*.

x   als ch in het Nederlandse *lach, och*.

De klemtoon wordt aangeduid door het teken ' voor de beklemtoonde lettergreep.

DUTCH-ENGLISH

A

aai *m.* caress, stroke; (*onder de kin*) chuck; (*fig.: tik, gevoelige* —) whisk, slap.

aaien *o. w.* caress, stroke; chuck.

aak *v.* (*sch.*) ake, (Rhine-)barge.

aal *m. en v.* (*Dk.*) eel.

aalbes *v.* currant.

aalfuik *v.* eel-basket, eel-pot.

aalmoes *v.* alms; charity.

aalmoezenier *m.* almoner; **leger—**, army chaplain.

Aalst *o.* Alost.

aalt *v. en o.* stale, liquid manure, dung.

aalvijver *m.* eel-pond.

aambeien *v. mv.* hemorrhoids, piles.

aamborstigheid *v.* asthma.

aan *voorz.* at; on, upon; bij (*omschrijving v. datief*) to. [tump.

aanaarden *o. w.* earth up, hill up.

aanbakken *on. w.* stick to the pan.

aanbeeld *o.* (*in smederij*) anvil; (*in oor*) anvil, incus.

aanbeeldsblok *o.* anvil-block.

aanbelangen *on. w.* zie **aangaan**.

aanbellen *on. w.* ring (the bell).

aanbesteden *o. w.* put out to contract, let out in contract, ask (invite) tenders for.

aanbesteding *v.* putting (letting) out to contract, contract, public tender; **bij —**, by contract.

aanbevelen *o. w.* recommend, commend; *w. w.* **zich —**, recommend oneself.

aanbevelenswaardig *b. n.* (re)commendable.

aanbeveling *v.* (re)commendation; introduction; **op — van**, at (on, through) the recommendation of.

aanbiddelijk *b. n.* adorable; *bw.* adorably.

aanbidden *o. w.* adore, worship.

aanbidder *m.* **aanbidster** *v.* worshipper, adorer.

aanbidding *v.* worship, adoration.

aanbieden *o. w.* (*v. goederen, diensten, enz.*) offer; (*v. wissel, enz.*) present; (*v. geld, diensten, enz.*) tender; (*v. telegram*) hand in, tender; *w. w.* **zich —**, (*v. persoon*) offer (oneself); (*vrijwillig*) volunteer; (*v. gelegenheid*) present itself, offer (itself).

aanbieder *m.*offerer;presenter;tenderer.

aanbieding *v.* offer, tender; (*v. wissel*) presentation.

aanbinden *o. w.* fasten, tie on, put on, bind.

aanblazen *o. w.* (*v. vuur; fig.*) blow; fan; (*v. twist, tweedracht*) fan, foment; (*v. hartstochten*) blow up, stir up, rouse; (*v. letter*) aspirate.

aanblik *m.* sight, look, view, aspect.

aanbod *o.* offer; (*H.: offerte*) tender; (*tegenover vraag*) supply; **vast —**, firm offer; **vrijblijvend —**, offer without engagement.

aanbouw *m.* annex(e); (*v. huizen, schepen*) construction, building; (*v. grond*) cultivation; (*v. gewassen*) growth.

aanbouwen *o. w.* (*v. vleugel aan gebouw*) add; (*v. huizen, schepen*) build; (*v. grond*) cultivate; (*v. gewassen*) grow.

aanbreken *on. w.* (*v. dag*) break, dawn; (*v. avond, nacht*) fall, descend, close in; *o. w.* (*v. fles*) open, tap; (*v. voorraad*) break into.

aanbrengen *o. w.* carry, bring; (*plaatsen*) fit, fix; (*v. versieringen*) place, put up; (*v. veranderingen*) make, introduce; (*v. voordeel, geluk*) bring; (*oververtellen*) tell, reveal; (*aanklagen*) denounce, delate, accuse; *werven: v. leden, enz.*; *v. kapitaal*) bring in.

aanbrenger *m.* (*aanklager*) denouncer, denunciator, informer; (*klikker*) telltale.

aandacht *v.* attention.

aandachtig *b. n.* (*bw.*) attentive(ly).

aandeel *o.* share; portion, part, quota.

aandeelbewijs *o.* share(-certificate), share-warrant.

aandeelhebber *m.* partner, participant.

aandeelhouder *m.* shareholder.

aandenken *o.* memory, remembrance; (*voorwerp*) souvenir, keepsake, memento.

aandienen *o. w.* announce.

aandoen *o. w.* (*v. kleren: aantrekken*) put on; (*veroorzaken*) cause, give; (*v. haven*) touch at; (*v. station*) call at.

aandoening *v.* (*v. lichaamsdeel*) affection; (*ontroering*) emotion.

aandoenlijk *b. n.* affecting, moving, touching, pathetic; (*v. gemoed, enz.*) sensitive, impressionable, easily affected.

aandraaien *o. w.* (*v. schroef, ook fig.*) turn on, tighten; (*aanzetten*) fix on, fasten; (*v. el. licht*) turn on, switch on.

aandrang *m.* (*het aandringen*) pressure, insistence, urgency; (*innerlijk*) impulse; (*v. volk: opeenhoping*) crowd, concourse; (*v. bloed*) congestion, afflux (of blood).

aandrift *v.* impulse; instinct.

aandrijven *o. w.* prompt, incite, press (on); (*v. vee, enz.*) drive on; *on. w.* be washed ashore; **komen —**, come floating along.

aandrijver *m.* driver; (*fig.*)stimulator, instigator.

aandringen *on. w.* press the point (the matter), pursue the point; **— op**, insist on; *z. n., o.* insistence; **op — van**, at the instance of.

aandruisen *on. w.* **— tegen**, clash with, be contrary to, be in conflict (in discordance) with.

aanduiden *o. w.* (*wijzen*) point out, show, indicate; (*uitdrukken, getuigen van*) denote, indicate, argue; (*betekenen*) signify, mean; (*door teken —*) mark, indicate.

aandurven *o. w.* dare.

aaneen *bw.* together; consecutively.

aaneengroeien *on. w.* grow together.

aaneenhangen *on. w.* hang together.
aaneenknopen *o. w.* tie together.
aaneennaaien *o. w.* sew together.
aaneenschakelen *o. w.* link together.
aaneenschakeling *v.* concatenation, consecution.
aaneenschrijven *o. w. (v. woord)* write in one; *(v. letters)* join.
aangaan *on. w. (v. vuur, enz.)* burn, light, catch, take fire; *(beginnen)* begin, commence; *(v. huwelijk)* enter into, contract; *(v. schulden)* contract, incur; *(v. overeenkomst)* conclude; *(v. weddenschap, enz.)* lay, make; *(betreffen)* concern, regard, touch.
aangaande *vz.* concerning, relative to, as for, as to.
aangebonden *b. n.* **kort —,** short-tempered, choleric.
aangeboren *b. n.* innate, inborn, native; *(v. gebrek)* congenital.
aangedaan *b. n.* touched, moved, affected.
aangeklaagde *m.* accused; defendant.
aangelegenheid *v.* matter, concern, affair.
aangenaam *b. n.* agreeable, pleasant; pleasing; *(v. huis, enz.)* comfortable.
aangenomen *b. n.* accepted; *(v. kind)* adoptive; *(v. werk)* contract; *(v. naam)* assumed; **— dat,** assuming that, supposing that, on the supposition that.
aangeschoten *b. n. (v. vogel)* winged; *(licht dronken)* slightly disguised, half seas over, tipsy.
aangesloten *b. n.* connected; *(v. vereniging, bij partij, enz.)* affiliated.
aangetekend *b. n.* registered; **— verzenden,** send by registered post.
aangeven *o. w. (aanreiken)* give, hand, pass, reach; *(aanwijzen: richting, op landkaart, enz.)* indicate, mark; *(v. geboorte)* give notice of, register; *(v. ziekte)* notify; *(v. thermometer, enz.)* register, record; *(v. bagage)* register; *(aan douane)* declare; *(bij gerecht)* denounce, delate, inform against; *(muz.: v. maat)* mark, give; *w. w.* **zich —,** *(voor examen, wedstrijd)* enter one's name, enter; *(mil.)* report oneself.
aangever *m. (bij gerecht)* denunciator, informer; *(v. goederen)* declarant.
aangezicht *o.* face, countenance.
aangezien *vw.* seeing (that), since, whereas.
aangifte *v. (v. geboorte, enz.)* notification; *(v. goederen)* declaration; *(voor belasting)* return, declaration; *(bij gerecht)* information.
aangorden *o. w.* gird on.
aangrenzend *b. n.* adjacent, adjoining, contiguous.
aangrijpen *o. w.* seize, take hold of; *(v. gelegenheid)* take, fasten upon; *(v. voorwendsel)* seize upon, fasten upon; *(aanvallen)* attack, assail; *(v. gezondheid, krachten)* tell upon, try.
aangrijpend *b. n.* moving, touching.

aangroei *m.* growth, increase, accretion, augmentation.
aangroeien *on. w.* grow, increase, accrue, augment; *(v. geluid, aantal)* swell; **doen —,** swell.
aanhaken *o. w.* hook on, hitch on.
aanhalen *o. w. (gaan halen)* fetch, bring; *(aantrekken, toetrekken)* pull (draw) tighter; *(v. koord, enz.)* haul, set up; *(in beslag nemen)* seize, detain, confiscate; *(citeren)* quote, cite, instance; adduce, bring forward; *(liefkozen)* caress, fondle, love; *(bij deling)* bring down; *on. w. (v. wind)* brisk up, freshen (up).
aanhalig *b. n.* affectionate, caressive, cajoling, coaxing.
aanhalingstekens *o. mv.* inverted commas, quotation marks.
aanhang *m.* adherents, followers, hangers-on, partisans.
aanhanger *m.* adherent, follower; partisan.
aanhangig *b. n.* pending; *(recht, ook:)* sub judice.
aanhangsel *o.* appendix; appendage; *(v. document, wissel)* rider; *(v. polis, enz.)* slip; *(v. testament)* codicil.
aanhankelijk *b. n.* attached, affectionate.
aanhankelijkheid *v.* attachment.
aanhebben *o. w.* have on, wear.
aanhechten *o. w.* affix, attach.
aanhechting *v.* affixion, attachment; *(v. grondgebied)* annexation; *(v. zegel)* apposition.
aanhef *m. (v. redevoering)* exordium; *(v. brief)* beginning; *(muz.)* intonation.
aanhitsen *o. w.* incite, excite, set on, egg on, instigate.
aanhitser *m.* inciter, instigator.
aanhitsing *v.* incitement, instigation.
aanhoren *o. w.* listen to.
aanhorigheid *v.* appurtenance.
aanhouden *o. w. (arresteren)* arrest, apprehend; *(staande houden)* stop, hold on; *(v. goederen)* seize, detain; *(v. briefwisseling, vriendschap, enz.)* keep up; *(v. noot, toon)* hold, sustain; *(v. kleren)* keep on; *(v. kachel, enz.)* keep burning, keep in; *(v. voorstel, enz.)* hold over; *(op veiling)* withdraw; *on. w. (blijven duren)* hold, continue; *(volharden, volhouden)* persevere; *(hardnekkig volhouden)* persist.
aanhoudend *b. n.* continual; *(hardnekkig)* persistent.
aanhouder *m.* perseverer, sticker.
aanhouding *v. (arrestatie)* arrestation, apprehension; detention; *(v. goederen)* seizure, detainment; *(v. schip)* holding up, embargo.
aankijken *o. w.* look at.
aanklacht *v.* accusation, charge, information.
aanklagen *o. w.* accuse.
aanklager *m. (alg.)* accuser; *(recht)* plaintiff.
aanklampen *o. w. (v. schip)* board; *(v. persoon)* accost, buttonhole.

aankleden *o. w.* dress; (*v. kamer*) fit up; (*v. toneelstuk*) stage; *w. w.* **zich** —, dress (oneself).
aankleding *v.* dressing, clothing; fitting up; staging, stage-setting.
aankloppen *on. w.* knock (rap) at the door.
aanknopen *o. w.* tie on to; (*v. gesprek, onderhandelingen*) enter into.
aankomeling *m.* (*nieuweling*) newcomer; (*beginner*) beginner, novice.
aankomen *on. w.* arrive, come; (*v. trein, boot, enz.*) come in, arrive; (*aanraken, betasten*) touch; (*v. slag*) go home; (*in gewicht toenemen*) gain; put on weight, put on flesh.
aankomst *v.* arrival; coming in.
aankondigen *o. w.* (*officieel*) notify; (*adverteren*) advertise, announce, publish; (*voorspellen*) herald, harbinger; betoken, spell.
aankondiger *m.* announcer; herald, harbinger; reviewer.
aankondiging *v.* notification; advertisement, announcement; review, notice, press-notice.
aankoop *m.* purchase, acquisition.
aankopen *o. w.* purchase, acquire, buy.
aankoper *m.* purchaser, buyer.
aankweken *o. w.* grow, raise, cultivate.
aanlanden *on. w.* land, arrive.
aanlaten *o. w.* (*v. kleren*) keep on; (*v. licht, enz.*) keep lit, keep burning; (*v. deur*) leave ajar; (*v. radio*) leave (turned) on.
aanleg *m.* (*v. wegen, straten*) laying-out; (*v. el. licht*) installation; (*v. gas, waterleiding*) laying-on; (*v. spoorweg*) construction; (*v. stad*) planning; (*wijze v. aanleggen*) design, plan; (*natuurlijke geschiktheid*) (natural) disposition, aptitude, natural ability, talent, turn; (*vatbaarheid: voor ziekte, enz.*) tendency, predisposition; (*recht*) instance.
aanleggen *o. w.* (*v. verband, pleister, enz.*) apply; (*v. el. licht*) put in; (*v. gas, waterleiding*) lay-on; (*v. spoorweg*) construct, lay down; (*v. stad*) build, plan; (*v. tuin, park, enz.*) lay-out; (*v. verzameling, lijst*) make; (*v. vuur*) build up, make up; *on. w.* (*stilhouden, stoppen*) stop, bait, fetch up; (*v. geweer*) level one's gun.
aanleghaven *v.* port of call.
aanlegplaats *v.* landing-stage.
aanleiding *v.* occasion, inducement, motive; *naar* — *van uw schrijven,* referring to your letter, with reference to your letter.
aanleren *o. w.* (*v. taal, vak, enz.*) learn; (*v. gewoonte, enz.*) acquire; *on. w.* improve.
aanleunen *on. w.* — *tegen,* lean against; (*mil.*) lean upon.
aanlokkelijk *b. n.* alluring, seducing, tempting, inviting; charming, attractive.
aanlokkelijkheid *v.* alluringness, seducingness; charm, attraction.

aanlokken *o. w.* allure, tempt, entice.
aanloop *m.* run; (*mil.*) rush, assault; (*fig.: inleiding*) preamble.
aanloophaven *v.* port of call.
aanlopen *on. w.* (*ergens*) call in, call round, drop in; (*duren*) last; (*v. wiel*) be out of truth; (*v. rem*) drag.
aanmaning *v.* exhortation; dun, dunning letter; (*recht*) monition.
aanmatigen (**zich**) *w. w.* arrogate to oneself.
aanmatigend *b. n.* arrogant, presumptuous, assuming.
aanmatiging *v.* arrogance, presumption, assumingness.
aanmelden *o. w.* announce; *zie ook* **aandienen**; *w. w.* **zich** —, (*voor betrekking*) apply; (*voor examen*) enter (one's name); (*bij politie*) come forward.
aanmelding *v.* announcement, notice; (*voor betrekking*) application.
aanmerkelijk *b. n.* considerable, notable.
aanmerken *o. w.* (*beschouwen*) consider; (*opmerken*) remark, observe.
aanmerking *v.* consideration; remark, observation.
aanminnig *b. n.* lovely, sweet, amiable; charming.
aanmoedigen *o. w.* encourage; countenance.
aanmoediging *v.* encouragement; countenance.
aanmonsteren *o. w.* engage, enlist; *on. w.* sign on, sign the articles.
aannaaien *o. w.* sew (on).
aannemelijk *b. n.* credible; acceptable, admissible.
aannemen *o. w.* (*het aangebodene, uitnodiging, enz.*) accept; (*v. boodschap, geld, enz.*) take; (*v. goederen*) take acceptance; (*als lid*) admit; (*v. houding, kind, naam*) adopt; (*prot.*) confirm; (*in dienst nemen*) take on, engage; (*v. wetsontwerp*) pass. (*v. motie*) carry, adopt; (*veronderstellen*) suppose; (*v. werk*) contract for; (*v. godsdienst*) embrace.
aannemer *m.* receiver; contractor; (*in bouwvak*) (master) builder, (building) contractor.
aanneming *v.* acceptance; adoption; admission; (*v. wetsontwerp*) passage; (*v. motie*) carriage; (*prot.: kerkelijk*) confirmation.
aanpakken *o. w.* seize, lay (take) hold of; (*v. onderwerp*) tackle.
aanpassen *o. w.* (*v. kleren, enz.*) try on; *w. w.* **zich** — *aan,* adapt (adjust, accommodate) oneself to.
aanpassing *v.* adaptation, adjustment, accommodation.
aanpassingsvermogen *o.* adaptive power, adaptability.
aanplakbil et *o.* placard, poster.
aanplakken *o. w.* paste (up); (*v. officiële bekendmaking*) post (up).
aanprijzen *o. w.* recommend, commend highly.

aanpunten *o. w.* point, make a point to, sharpen.

aanraden *o. w.* advise, counsel; *(aanbevelen)* recommend.

aanraken *o. w.* touch.

aanraking *v.* touch, contact.

aanranden *o. w.* assail, assault; *(met beroving)* hold up; *(fig.: v. vrijheid, enz.)* attack.

aanrander *m.* assailant, assaulter.

aanranding *v.* assailing, assault; holdup; attack.

aanrekenen *o. w.* charge; count... to.

aanrichten *o. w.* *(v. schade)* cause, do, effect; *(v. onheil)* do; *(v. verwoesting)* make, work, commit; *(v. slachting, bloedbad)* perpetrate.

aanrijding *v.* collision, smash.

aanroepen *o. w.* *(v. God)* invoke; *(v. persoon, taxi)* call, hail; *(mil.)* challenge.

aanroeping *v.* invocation; *(mil.)* challenge.

aanrukken *on. w.* advance, march on.

aanschaffen *o. w.* procure, buy; *w. w.* **zich —,** procure, buy, purchase.

aanschaffing *v.* procuring, buying, purchase; acquisition.

aanschijn *o.* *(gelaat)* face, countenance; *(schijn, voorkomen)* appearance, look.

aanschouwelijk *b. n.* clear, graphic; *bw.* clearly; graphically.

aanschouwen *o. w.* behold; see.

aanschouwing *v.* beholding, observation; *(innerlijke —)* intuition.

aanschrijven *o. w.* *(v. persoon: berichten)* notify; *(met circulaire)* circularize; *(oproepen)* summon.

aanschrijving *v.* notification; order; summons.

aanslaan *o. w.* *(v. snaar, toets)* touch; *(v. noot)* strike; *(in belasting)* assess; *(in beslag nemen)* seize, confiscate; *(sch.)* sling, bend; *on. w.* *(mil.)* salute; *(groeten)* touch one's cap; *(v. kogel)* ricochet; *(v. motor)* start (up); *(v. ruiten)* get steamy; *(v. spiegel)* get dim; *(v. metaal)* tarnish, get tarnished.

aanslag *m.* *(het aanslaan)* striking; *(v. toetsen)* touch; *(in belasting)* assessment; *(v. kogel)* impact; *(op 't leven)* attempt, attack; *(op ruit)* moisture.

aanslagbiljet *o.* notice of assessment.

aanslibben *on. w.* accrete.

aansluiten *o. w.* connect, joint; *(tel.)* put on, put through **(met,** to), connect **(met,** with); *(radio)* take over; *on. w.* *(v. treinen)* correspond; *(v. wegen)* join; *w. w.* **zich —,** *(fig.: verenigen)* unite, join hands.

aansluiting *v.* connection; *(tel.)* connection, communication; *(v. trein)* correspondence; association; union.

aansnellen *on. w.* **komen —,** come running on (along).

aanspannen *o. w. en on. w.* put (the horses) to; *(mil.)* limber up.

aanspoelen *o. w.* wash ashore, drift ashore; wash up; *on. w.* be washed ashore.

aansporen *o. w.* *(v. paard)* spur (on), urge on; *(v. persoon)* incite, excite, stimulate, animate, urge (on).

aansporing *v.* incitement, excitation, stimulation; **op — van,** at the instance of; *(ong.)* at the instigation of.

aanspraak *v.* right, title, pretension; claim; **— maken op,** lay claim to.

aansprakelijk *b. n.* responsible, liable, answerable; **— stellen voor,** hold responsible (liable) for.

aansprakelijkheid *v.* responsibility, liability, answerableness.

aanspreken *o. w.* *(v. persoon)* speak to, address; *(op straat)* accost; *(v. menigte)* harangue.

aanstaan *on. w.* *(behagen, bevallen)* please.

aanstaande *b. n.* *(volgende)* next; *(te verwachten)* (forth)coming; *(v. schoonmoeder, enz.)* prospective; *(v. moeder)* expectant; *z. n., m. en v.* **zijn (haar) —,** his (her) future, his (her) intended; his fiancée (her fiancé).

aanstalten *v. mv.* preparations, preparatives.

aanstekelijk *b. n.* infectious, contagious, catching.

aansteken *o. w.* *(v. lamp, sigaar, enz.)* light; *(v. vuur)* kindle, light; *(v. vat)* broach, tap.

aanstellen *o. w.* appoint; *(installeren)* instate; *w. w.* **zich —,** pose, attitudinize; *(te keer gaan)* take on, carry on.

aanstellerig *b. n.* affected, posturing, stag(e)y, attitudinizing.

aanstelling *v.* appointment; *(mil.: als officier)* commission.

aanstippen *o. w.* tick off, check off.

aanstoking *v.* incitation, incitement.

aanstonds *bw.* directly, forthwith.

aanstoot *m.* *(schok)* shock, collision; *(fig.: schandaal, ergernis)* offence, scandal.

aanstormen *on. w.* **komen —,** come rushing (tearing) along, come on full tear, come on full speed.

aanstotelijk *b. n.* offensive, objectionable, scandalous, obnoxious, shocking.

aanstoten *o. w.* *(v. persoon: als teken)* nudge; jog; *on. w.* bump up against, strike against.

aantal *o.* number.

aantekenen *o. w.* *(optekenen)* note down, write down; *(aanduiden)* mark; *(v. brief, enz.: inschrijven)* register.

aantekening *v.* note, annotation; memorandum; *(v. brief)* registration; *(op school)* bad mark; *(v. huwelijk)* *(kerk.)* publication of the banns; *(burgerl.)* notice of marriage.

aantijgen *o. w.* impute.

aantijging *v.* imputation.

aantocht *m.* **in — zijn,** *(v. onweer, enz.)* be coming on, be approaching, be drawing near; *(v. leger)* be advancing, be marching on.

aantonen *o. w.* show; *(bewijzen)* demonstrate, prove; *—de wijs,* indicative mood.
aantrekkelijk *b. n.* attractive, attract.
aantrekkelijkheid *v.* attractiveness.
aantrekken *o. w. (naar zich halen)* draw, pull, attract; *(vaster trekken)* draw tighter, tighten; *(sch.)* tauten; *(v. kleren)* put on; *(v. schoenen)* put on, pull on; *(v. handschoenen)* put on, draw on; *w. w. zich iets —,* take something to heart, take offence at something.
aantrekkingskracht *v.* attractive power, (power of) attraction.
aanvaarden *o. w. (v. wissel, gevolgen, voorwaarden, enz.)* accept; *(v. bewind, bevel, verantwoordelijkheid)* assume; *(v. nalatenschap, eigendom, enz.)* take possession of; *(v. ambt)* enter upon, take up; *(v. gevolgen)* face, abide, accept.
aanvaarding *v.* acceptance; *(v. eigendom, enz.)* taking possession; *(v. ambt)* entering.
aanval *m. (mil.)* attack, onset, charge, assault; *(v. koorts, enz.)* access, attack.
aanvallen *o. w. en on. w.* attack, assault, assail; *(met de bajonet)* charge.
aanvallend *b. n.* offensive; aggressive.
aanvaller *m.* attacker, assailant, aggressor.
aanvallig *b. n.* lovely, sweet, charming.
aanvalsoorlog *m.* war of aggression.
aanvalsplan *o.* plan of attack.
aanvalstroepen *m. mv.* shock troops.
aanvalswagen *m.* tank.
aanvang *m.* beginning, commencement, start; *(v. wedstrijd)* start.
aanvangen *on. w.* begin, commence; *o. w.* do.
aanvangssalaris *o.* commencing salary.
aanvankelijk *b. n.* initial, original; *(v. onderwijs)* elementary; *bw.* in the beginning, at (the) first, at the outset.
aanvaren *o. w.* bring (convey) in ships.
aanvaring *v.* collision.
aanvatten *o. w.* seize, take (catch) hold of.
aanvechting *v.* temptation.
aanverwant *m. en v. zie* **verwant.**
aanvoegen *o. w.* add, join; *—de wijs,* subjunctive mood.
aanvoer *m.* supply; *(v. goederen ook:)* arrival(s).
aanvoerbuis *v.* supply-pipe, feedpipe; *(v. gas, water)* service-pipe.
aanvoerder *m.* commander, leader; *(sp.)* captain, skipper.
aanvoeren *o. w. (aanbrengen)* supply; *(v. redenen, argumenten)* advance, put forward; *(v. feiten, argumenten)* allege; *(v. bezwaren)* raise; *(mil.)* command, be in command of.
aanvraag *v. (vraag)* demand; *(verzoek)* request, application; *(v. goederen)* inquiry.
aanvragen *o. w.* apply for, ask for, solicit.
aanvrager *m.* applicant.
aanvullen *o. w. (v. verlies, tekort)* make up, make good, supply; *(v. leemte)* fill; *(v. opening, bres)* fill up; *(v. lijst, verhaal, enz.)* amplify; *(volledig maken)* complete, supplement.
aanvullingsbegroting *v.* supplementary estimates.
aanvuren *o. w.* fire, stimulate, excite.
aanwakkeren *o. w. (v. persoon: aansporen)* animate, stimulate; *(v. moed, hartstochten)* rouse; *(v. nieuwsgierigheid, vijandschap)* stir up; *(v. onenigheid, tweedracht)* foment; *on. w.* increase; *(v. wind)* freshen (up).
aanwakkering *v.* animation, stimulation; stirring up; fomentation.
aanwas *m. (toeneming: v. bevolking, enz.)* increase, growth; *(vergroting; v. grond, enz.)* accretion; *(v. rivier)* rise.
aanwenden *o. w. (v. middel)* use, employ, apply; *(v. moeite)* take; *(v. geld: gebruiken tot)* appropriate.
aanwending *v.* use, employment, application, appliance; *(v. geneesmiddel)* adhibition.
aanwensel *o.* (acquired) habit, trick.
aanwerven *o. w.* recruit, enlist.
aanwerving *v.* recruiting, recruitment, enlistment.
aanwezig *b. n.* present; *(bestaand)* extant, existing; *(v. voorraad)* on hand.
aanwezigheid *v.* presence; existence.
aanwijzen *o. w. (wijzen)* show, indicate, point out; *(v. thermometer, enz.)* mark, register; *(toewijzen: v. aandeel, geld)* assign, allocate; *(v. plaats, enz.)* allot; *(voor bijzonder doel)* designate, tell off.
aanwijzend *b. n.* indicant; *(v. voornaamw.)* demonstrative.
aanwinst *v. (winst)* gain; *(in bibliotheek, museum, enz.)* acquisition.
aanwrijven *o. w. en on. w. — tegen,* rub against.
aanzeggen *o. w.* announce, notify, give notice of.
aanzetten *o. w. (v. stuk)* fit on; *(v. knoop, enz.)* sew on; *(v. motor)* start (up), crank up; *on. w. (v. wijn)* crust; *(v. spijzen)* stick to the pan; *(v. paard)* begin to draw.
aanzien *o. w.* look at, see; *(beschouwen)* consider, regard.
aanzien *o. (aanblik)* look, aspect, sight; *(achting)* consideration, esteem, respect, regard.
aanzienlijk *b. n. (belangrijk)* considerable; *(voornaam)* respectable; of high standing.
aanzijn *o.* existence.
aanzitten *on. w.* sit at table.
aanzoek *o.* request, solicitation; *(huwelijks—)* offer, proposal.
aanzoeken *o. w. en on. w.* request, petition; apply.
aanzoeker *m.* petitioner; applicant; *(ten huwelijk)* suitor, aspirant.
aap *m.* monkey; *(staartloos)* ape.
aar *v. (v. koren)* ear; *(ader)* vein.
aard *m. (natuur, karakter)* nature,

disposition, character; (*soort*) kind, sort.
aardappel *m.* potato.
aardappelloof *o.* potato-leaves, (potato-)haulm; (*Sc.*) shaws.
aardappelmeel *o.* potato-flour.
aardappelrooier *m.* potato-lifter.
aardappelschil *v.* potato-peel, potato-skin.
aardas *v.* axis of the earth, earth's axis.
aardbaan *v.* orbit of the earth.
aardbei *v.* strawberry.
aardbeving *v.* earthquake.
aardbodem *m.* earth, surface of the earth.
aarde *v.* earth; (*teelaarde*) mould.
aardewerk *o.* earthenware, crockery, pottery.
aardgordel *m.* zone.
aardig *b. n.* (*bevallig*) pretty, nice; (*geestig*) witty, smart; (*grappig*) funny; (*vrij groot*) fair; *bw.* nicely; smartly.
aardigheid *v.* niceness, prettiness; wittiness, smartness; (*grap*) joke, jest.
aardklomp *m.* **aardkluit** *v.* clod of earth.
aardkorst *v.* crust of the earth, earth's crust.
aardkunde *v.* geology.
aardmannetje *o.* gnome, goblin.
aardmuis *v.* field-mouse.
aardnoot *v.* earth-nut.
aardolie *v.* petroleum, rock-oil.
aardrijkskunde *v.* geography.
aardrijkskundig *b. n.* geographical.
aards *b. n.* terrestrial, earthly; wordly.
aardslak *v.* slug.
aardstorting *v.* earthfall, fall of earth, landfall.
aardwerker *m.* navvy, digger.
aardworm *m.* earth-worm.
aars *m.* arse.
aartsbedrieger *m.* arrant-cheat, regular cheat.
aartsbisdom *o.* archbishopric, archdiocese.
aartsbisschop *m.* archbishop.
aartsbisschoppelijk *b. n.* archi-episcopal.
aartsbroederschap *v.* archconfraternity.
aartsdeken *m.* archdean.
aartsdeugniet *m.* arrant knave.
aartsdom *b. n.* fearfully stupid, as stupid as an ass.
aartsengel *m.* archangel.
aartsgierigaard *m.* arrant niggard.
aartshertog *m.* archduke.
aartshertogdom *o.* archduchy.
aartsleugenaar *m.* arrant liar, archliar, consummate liar.
aartslui *b. n.* bone-lazy.
aartsluiaard *m.* inveterate idler, regular lazy-bones.
aartspriester *m.* archpriest.
aartsvader *m.* patriarch.
aartsvijand *m.* arch-enemy.
aarzelen *on. w.* hesitate, waver, vacillate, hang back.

aarzeling *v.* hesitation, wavering, vacillation.
aas *o.* (*lokaas*) bait; (*kreng*) carrion; (*kaartsp.*) ace.
aaskever *m.* carrion-beetle, horse-beetle.
aasvlieg *v.* blue-bottle, flesh-fly, meat-fly.
abces *o.* abscess.
abdij *v.* abbey.
abdis *v.* abbess.
abnormaal *b. n.* abnormal.
abonnee *m.* (*op dagblad, telefoon, enz.*) subscriber; (*op spoor, enz.*) seasonticket holder.
abonnement *o.* subscription.
abonneren *w. w. zich — op,* subscribe to (for).
abrikoos *v.* apricot.
absolutie *v.* absolution.
absolutisme *o.* absolutism.
absoluut *b. n.* (*bw.*) absolute(ly).
abstract *b. n.* abstract; (*verstrooid*) abstracted, distrait.
abt *m.* abbot.
abuis *o.* mistake, error, slip, blunder.
academicus *m.* university graduate.
academie *v.* academy.
accent *o.* accent.
accept *o.* (*H.*) acceptance; (*promesse*) promissory-note.
acceptant *m.* acceptor.
acceptatie *v.* acceptance.
accepteren *o. w.* accept.
acces *o.* access.
accijns *m.* excise, accise.
accijnsbiljet *o.* excise-notice.
accijnsplichtig *b. n.* excisable.
accijnsvrij *b. n.* free from excise.
accountant *m.* accountant.
accrediteren *o. w.* (*bij hof, enz.*) accredit; (*H.: bij bank*) open a credit.
accumulator *m.* (*el.*) accumulator, storage-battery.
accuraat *b. n.* exact, precise.
acetyleen *o.* acetylene.
ach! *tw.* ah! alas! alack!
Achillespees *v.* tendon of Achilles.
acht *telw.* eight.
acht *v.* attention, care.
achtbaar *b. n.* estimable, honourable, respectable; (*voor titel*) honourable.
achtbaarheid *v.* respectability.
achteloos *b. n.* careless, negligent; (*onoplettend*) inattentive.
achteloosheid *v.* carelessness, negligence; inattention.
achten *o. w.* (*achting toedragen*) esteem, respect; (*denken, menen*) think, judge, esteem, count.
achtenswaardig *b. n.* estimable, respectable, honourable, worthy of esteem (respect).
achtenswaardigheid *v.* respectability.
achter *vz.* behind; after, at the back of; (*sch.*) abaft; *bw.* behind. [back.
achteraan *bw.* behind, in the rear, at the

achteraf *bw.* in the rear; out of the way; after all.

achteras *v.* rear axle-tree.

achterbaks *bw.* underhand, secretly, behind one's back; *b. n.* underhand, backdoor, backstairs.

achterband *m.* back tyre, hind tire.

achterblijven *on. w.* stay behind, remain behind; *(iem. niet bijhouden)* drop behind; lag behind; *(op school)* be backward.

achterblijver *m.* straggler, laggard.

achterbuurt *v.* back-street, low quarter, slum.

achterdeur *v.* back-door.

achterdocht *v.* suspicion.

achterdochtig *b. n.* *(bw.)* suspicious(ly).

achtereen *bw.* *(achtereenvolgens)* successively, consecutively, in succession.

achtereenvolgens *bw.* successively, consecutively, in succession.

achteren *bw.* **naar —,** backward(s); **van — naar voren,** backward(s); **ten —,** behindhand, in arrears.

achtergrond *m.* back-ground; *(toneel)* back-scene.

achterhalen *o. w.* overtake; *(v. misdadiger, enz.)* hunt down.

achterhoede *v.* rear(-guard); *(sp.: voetb.)* defence, backs.

achterhouden *o. w.* keep back, hold back, withhold; *(recht)* detain.

achterhoudend *b. n.* reserved, close, secretive.

achterhouding *v.* keeping back; *(recht)* detention.

achterin *bw.* *(in boek, enz.)* at the back; *(in tuin, enz.)* at the back.

Achter-Indië *o.* Further India.

achterkamer *v.* back-room.

achterkant *m.* back(-part), rear side; *(verkeerde kant)* reverse side.

achterkeuken *v.* back-kitchen.

achterklap *m.* backbiting, scandal, slander, calumny.

achterkleinkind *o.* great-grandchild.

achterland *o.* hinterland.

achterlap *m.* heel-piece.

achterlaten *o. w.* leave; *(bij overlijden)* leave behind.

achterlicht *o.* tail-light, rear-light, backlamp. [abdomen.

achterlijf *o.* hind-part; *(v. insekt)*

achterlijk *b. n.* *(in ontwikkeling, groei)* backward; *(bij tijd)* behind the times.

achterlijkheid *v.* backwardness.

achtermast *m.* aftermast.

achterna *bw.* behind, after; *(naderhand, later)* afterwards.

achternazitten *o. w.* look sharp after.

achterneef *m.* great-nephew; second cousin.

achteronder *o.* *(sch.)* afterhold.

achterop *bw.* behind, at the back.

achterover *bw.* backward(s), on one's back.

achterpoot *m.* hindfoot, hindpaw, hindleg.

achterschip *o.* aftership, stern.

achterstaan *on. w.* **— bij,** *(minder zijn dan)* be inferior to; *(achtergesteld worden bij)* be neglected for.

achterstallig *b. n.* standing out; overdue.

achterstand *m.* arrears, arrearage.

achterste *b. n.* hindmost, hind; *z. n., o* back-part, hind-part; *(zitvlak)* posterior(s): *(pop.)* backside, bottom.

achtersteven *m.* stern-post.

achteruit *bw.* backwards, back; *(sch.)* abaft, aft; **—!** stand back! *z. n., o.* back-yard, back-premises.

achteruitboeren *on. w.* go downhill.

achteruitgaan *on. w.* go backwards; *(v. inkomsten, gezondheid, ijver, enz.)* fall off, decline; *(v. zieke)* go downhill, go back, decline, be on the decline; *(in kwaliteit)* deteriorate, decay; *(more l)* retrograde, retrogress, degenerate.

achteruitgang *m.* going down; decline; fall; retrogression.

achteruitgang *m.* back-door, back-exit, rear-exit.

achteruitkrabbelen *on. w.* back out of it, cry off, climb down.

achteruitslaan *on. w.* *(v. paard)* lash out, plunge, kick; *(v. schip, machine)* reverse.

achteruitzetten *o. w.* *(v. klok)* put back, set back, retard; *(in vermogen, rang, enz.)* throw back; *(verongelijken)* slight.

achtervoegsel *o.* suffix.

achtervolgen *o. w.* run after, pursue, chase; *(vervolgen)* persecute; *(v. gedachte)* haunt.

achtervolging *v.* pursuit; persecution.

achterwaarts *bw.* backwards, back; *b. n.* backward, retrograde.

achterwege *bw.* **— blijven,** fail to come, fail to appear; **— laten,** omit, drop; **— houden,** keep back.

achterwiel *o.* hind-wheel, back-wheel.

achterzak *m.* *(v. jas)* tail-pocket, back-pocket; *(v. broek)* hip-pocket.

achterzijde *v.* zie **achterkant.**

achthoek *m.* octagon.

achting *v.* esteem, respect, regard, consideration.

achtkantig *b. n.* eight-sided, octagonal.

achtste *b. n.* eighth; **— noot,** *(muz.)* quaver; *z. n., o.* eighth, eighth part.

achttal *o.* number of eight.

achttien *telw.* eighteen.

achtvlak *o.* octahedron.

actief *b. n.* active, diligent, energetic; in active service; *(v. handelsbalans)* favourable; *z. n., o.* assets.

actieradius *m.* *(vl.)* radius of action.

activiteit *v.* activity.

actrice *v.* actress.

actualiteit *v.* actuality.

acuut *b. n.* *(bw.)* acute(ly).

adder *v.* viper, adder.

addergebroed *o.* viperous brood, brood of vipers.

adel *m.* nobility.
adelaar *m.* eagle.
adelborst *m.* midshipman, naval cadet.
adeldom *m.* nobility.
adelen *o. w.* ennoble, raise to the peerage.
adellijk *b. n.* (*v. persoon*) noble; nobiliary; (*r. wild*) high; (*v. vlees*) gamy, high.
adelstand *m.* nobility.
adem *m.* breath.
ademen *o. w. en on. w.* breathe.
ademhalen *on. w.* breathe, draw breath.
ademhaling *v.* breathing, respiration.
ademhalingswerktuigen *o. mv.* respiratory organs.
ademtocht *m.* breath, respiration, gasp of breath.
ader *v.* (*in lichaam; in hout, enz.*) vein; (*v. erts*) vein, lode, seam.
aderbreuk *v.* rupture of a blood-vessel, phleborrhage.
aderlaten *o. w.* let blood, bleed.
aderlating *v.* bleeding, blood-letting; (*fig.*) bleeding, drain.
aderspat *v.* varix, varicose vein.
aderverkalking *v.* arteriosclerosis.
adjudant *m.* adjutant; (*v. vorst, generaal*) aide-de-camp.
adjunct *m.* assistant, deputy.
administrateur *m.* (*alg.*) administrator; (*beheerder*) manager.
administratie *v.* administration.
admiraal *m.* admiral.
admiraalsschip *o.* flagship, admiral's ship.
adres *o.* (*op brief*) address, direction; (*verzoekschrift*) petition, memorial; **per —,** care of, c/o.
adresboek *o.* directory.
adressant *m.* (*H.: afzender*) sender; (*v. verzoekschrift*) applicant, petitioner.
adresseren *o. w.* (*v. brief*) direct, address; (*met verzoekschrift*) memorialize; *w. w.* **zich — aan,** apply to.
adresstrook *v.* label.
advertentie *v.* advertisement, notice.
advertentiebureau *o.* advertising-office, advertising agency.
advies *o.* advice.
adviesjacht *o.* (*sch.*) advice-boat.
adviseur *m.* adviser.
advocaat *m.* barrister (-at-law), counsel; lawyer, solicitor; (*Sc.*) advocate; (*drank*) advocaat, egg-punch.
af off; down.
afbakenen *o. w.* (*v. terrein*) mark out, stake out; (*v. weg, enz.*) trace (out); (*v. vaarwater*) beacon; (*v. gebied, land*) delimit; (*fig.*) map out, define.
afbeelden *o. w.* represent, picture, paint, portray.
afbeelding *v.* representation, picture, painting, portrait(ure).
afbeeldsel *o.* image, portrait.
afbestellen *o. w.* cancel; countermand.
afbetalen *o. w.* pay off, pay up.

afbetaling *v.* payment.
afbeulen *o. w.* (*v. paard*) override; (*v. personeel*) fag out, overdrive; *w. w.* **zich —,** work oneself to the bone, work oneself to death.
afbinden *o. w.* (*v. schaatsen*) bind off, take off, untie; (*v. ader*) ligature, tie up, ligate; (*v. wrat*) string; *on. w.* untie one's skates.
afblijven *on. w.* keep one's hands off, leave alone, let alone; **— !** hands off!
afborstelen *o. w.* (*v. stof, enz.*) brush off; (*v. kleren*) brush; (*v. persoon*) brush, give a brush up; *w. w.* **zich —,** brush oneself up.
afbraak *v.* old materials, rubbish; (*handeling*) demolition, pulling down.
afbranden *o. w.* (*v. huis, enz.*) burn down; (*v. verf*) burn off; *on. w.* be burnt down.
afbreken *o. w.* (*v. huis, enz.*) demolish, pull down; (*v. tak, bloem*) break; (*v. brug*) break down; (*v. reis, gesprek, relaties, enz.*) break off; (*v. machine*) break up; (*v. el. stroom*) cut; (*v. verhaal*) interrupt; (*v. woord*) divide; (*v. vriendschap, diplomatieke betrekkingen*) sever; (*v. steiger, boot*) take down; (*v. schrijver, enz.*) run down, cry down, pull to pieces; *on. w.* (*v. draad*) break; (*in gesprek*) stop, make a pause; *z. n., o.* (*v. huis, enz.*) demolition; (*v. diplom. betrekkingen, enz.*) rupture, severance; (*v. onderhandelingen*) break-down.
afbreker *m.* demolisher; destructionist.
afbrengen *o. w.* (*naar beneden*) bring off; (*v. schip*) get off, get afloat.
afbreuk *v.* detriment, derogation, damage; **— doen aan,** prejudice, derogate, be detrimental to, be derogatory to.
afbrokkelen *on. w.* crumble down, crumble off.
afdak *o.* pent-house, shed.
afdalen *o. w. en on. w.* descend, go down.
afdammen *o. w.* dam up.
afdamming *v.* damming up.
afdanken *o. w.* (*v. personeel*) dismiss; (*v. troepen*) disband; (*v. kleren*) cast off; (*v. schip*) scrap, lay up; (*v. ambtenaar: wegens leeftijd*) superannuate; (*aan de dijk zetten*) shelve, lay upon the shelf.
afdanking *v.* dismissal; disbandment, disbanding; shelving.
afdeling *v.* division, classification; (*v. zaak, bestuur*) department; (*compartiment*) compartment; (*v. boek, vergadering*) section; (*onderdeel*) division, section, part.
afdelingschef *m.* head of department, departmental chief, **—** manager.
afdingen *on. w.* bargain, haggle, higgle; beat down the price; *o. w.* beat down.
afdoen *o. w.* (*v. kledingstuk, enz.*) take off, put off; (*afmaken: v. zaak, enz.*) finish, end, settle.
afdoend *b. n.* (*v. bewijs, argument*) conclusive; (*v. maatregel: doeltreffend*)

efficacious, effective, effectual; (v. be-sluit) final.

afdoening v. (v. zaken) dispatch; (v. schuld) payment, settlement.

afdokken on. w. come down, pay down, stump up, cash up.

afdragen o. w. (v. trap, enz.) carry down; (v. kleren) wear out; (v. schuld) pay off.

afdreigen o. w. (geld) extort; (persoon) blackmail.

afdreiging v. blackmail, chantage.

afdrijvend b. n. purging, purgative, repellent; abortive, abortifacient; — middel, repellent.

afdrijving v. leeway; expulsion; (criminal) abortion.

afdrogen o. w. wipe off, dry.

afdruipen on. w. (in droppels afvallen) trickle down, drip down; (v. afwas) drain; (v. kaars) gutter; (stil weggaan) slink off, slink away.

afdruk m. (v. boek,. enz.) copy, impression; (overdruk: v. artikel, enz.) off print; (fot.) print; (in druk) print, imprint.

afdwalen on. w. stray off, stray from the path, lose one's way; (fig.: v. onderwerp) wander (deviate, stray) from one's subject; (ong.) go astray.

afdwaling v. straying, wandering; (ong.) deviation, aberration; (sterr.) aberration.

afdwingen o. w. (v. eerbied, bewondering, enz.) command, compel; (v. geld, belofte, enz.) extort; (v. rechten, enz.) enforce; (v. bekentenis, geheim, enz.) wring.

affaire v. (zaak) affair, business; (handelszaak) business; (transactie) transaction.

affronteren o. w. affront.

affuit o. gun-carriage.

afgaan o. w. (trap) go down; (heuvel, enz.) walk down; on. w. (v. boot) start (off),set off; (v.getij) recede,ebb,go out.

afgang m. (stoelgang) motion, stool; (uitwerpselen) excrements, faeces, motions, stools; (helling) declivity.

afgebroken (v. woorden) broken.

afgelasten o. w. countermand, cancel, counter-order, order off, call off.

afgeleefd b. n. decrepit, worn with age, used up.

afgeleefdheid v. decrepitude.

afgelegen b. n. remote, distant, out-of-the-way.

afgemat b. n. weary, worn out, tired out, exhausted.

afgematheid v. weariness, exhaustion.

afgemeten b. n. measured; (stijfdeftig) dignified, stately, stiff, formal.

afgepast b. n. (v. geld) exact; (v. gordijnen, enz.) edged.

afgericht b. n. (v. paard) broke(n) to the rein (to the saddle); trained, drilled; (mil.) off the square.

afgesloofd b. n. worked out, worn out, fagged (out).

afgesproken b. n. pre-arranged.

afgestorven b. n. deceased, dead; z. n., m. en v. de —e, the deceased, the departed.

afgevaardigde m. (Kamerlid) deputy, representative, Member of Parliament; (op vergadering) delegate.

afgevallene m. en v. apostate, renegade.

afgeven o. w. (boodschap, goederen, enz.) deliver; (kaarten, enz.) issue; (telegram, pakje, enz.) tender, hand in; (H.: v. stukken) surrender; (v. reuk warmte) give out; on. w. (v. kleur) come off, rub off; (v. stof) stain; — op, cry down, run down; w. w. zich — met, (inter)meddle with, take up with, have, intercourse with.

afgezaagd b. n. sawn off; (fig.) stale, trite, time-worn, well-worn.

afgezant m. ambassador, messenger.

afgezonderd b. n. retired, solitary, secluded, sequestered.

afgieten o. w. pour off; (door vergiet) strain off; (v. beeld, in vormen) cast.

afgietsel o. (plaster) cast, copy.

afgietseldiertjes o. mv. infusoria.

afgifte v. delivery; (v. kaartjes, enz.) issue.

afgod m. idol.

afgodendienaar m. idolater.

afgrijselijk b. n. horrible, horrid, hideous, ghastly.

afgrijselijkheid v. horribleness, horridness, horror, ghastliness.

afgrijzen o. horror, abhorrence.

afgrond m. abyss, gulf; (steil; fig.) precipice.

afgunst v. envy, jealousy.

afgunstig b. n. envious, jealous (op, of).

afhaken o. w. (v. spoorwagen) uncouple; (mil.: v. kanon) unlimber; (tel.) unhitch; unhook, unclasp.

afhalen o. w. (naar beneden) fetch down, bring down; (v. goederen) fetch, collect; (v. persoon) call for (a person); (in auto, rijtuig) take up, pick up.

afhandelen o. w. settle, conclude, terminate, dispatch.

afhandig b. n. iem. iets — maken, filch something of a person, trick one out of a thing.

afhangen o. w. unhang, take down; on. w. hang down; depend (on).

afhangend b. n. hanging; (Pl.: v. takken) drooping.

afhankelijk b. n. dependent; van elkaar —, interdependent.

afhankelijkheid v. dependence.

afhaspelen o. w. reel off, unreel; (fig.) bungle, scamp.

afhelpen o. w. help down, help off; (v. kwaal, enz.) relieve (from).

afhouden o. w. keep off; (v. geld: korten) deduct; on. w. (sch.) bear away, bear off.

afhouding v. keeping off; (korting) deduction.

afhouwen o. w. cut off, chop off, lop off.

afjakkeren o. w. (r. paard) override, overdrive; (v. personeel) overwork, jade, drive hard.

afkappen o. w. cut off, chop off, lop off; (afknotten) truncate; (v. woord) apostrophize.

afkappingsteken o. apostrophe.

afkeer m. aversion (van, to, from, for), repugnance (to, against), dislike (of, to), antipathy (to, against).

afkeren o. w. (v. gelaat, hoofd, enz.) turn away, turn aside, avert; (v. gevaar) avert; (r. slag) parry, ward off; w. w. **zich** —, turn away, turn aside.

afkerig b. n. averse (van, to, from).

afkerigheid v. aversion, averseness.

afketsen v. t. (v. voorstel, enz.) reject; (v. plannen, enz.) defeat, frustrate; on. w. fall through, drop through.

afkeuren o. w. (laken, misprijzen) blame, disapprove, condemn; (sterk —) denounce; (als onbruikbaar afwijzen) condemn, declare unfit for use; (v. schip) scrap; (r. persoon) reject; (v. film) ban.

afkeurenswaardig b. n. objectionable, blamable, censurable, condemnable.

afkeuring v. disapproval, disapprobation, condemnation, censure; (mil.) rejection; (op school) bad mark.

afkijken o. w. **iets van iem.** —, learn something by watching a person; on. w. copy, scrib (van, from).

afkloppen o. w. beat off; on. w. (bijgeloof) touch wood.

afkluiven o. w. gnaw off, pick.

afknippen o. w. (v. bloem, enz.) cut (off), snip (off); (v. sigaar) clip; (v. as v. sigaar) flick off; (v. haar, lamp) trim.

afknipsel(s) o. (mv.) clipping(s), cutting(s).

afknotten o. w. (v. boom) lop off, top; (v. boom, kegel) truncate.

afkoelen o. w. cool (down); (tegen bederf) refrigerate; on. w. cool (down), calm down.

afkoeling v. cooling down; refrigeration; (v. atmosfeer) fall in temperature.

afkomen o. w. (kamer, weg) come down; on. w. (afstammen) come from, be descended from; **er met de schrik** —, get off for the fright.

afkomst v. descent, origin, birth, extraction; (r. woord) derivation.

afkomstig b. n. sprung, descended; native of; (v. woord) derived (from).

afkondigen o. w. (v. wet, besluit) promulgate; (v. staking, enz.) proclaim, declare; (v. huwelijk) publish.

afkondiging v. promulgation; proclamation; publication.

afkooksel o. decoction.

afkoop m. buying off; (loskoping) redemption; (r. polis) surrender.

afkopen o. w. (kopen van) buy from, purchase from; (v. verplichting, enz.) buy

off, redeem; (loskopen) ransom, redeem; (v. polis) surrender; (v. pensioen) commute.

afkorten o. w. (v. woord, enz.) shorten, abbreviate; (v. verhaal) abridge.

afkorting r. shortening, abbreviation; abridgment; **op** —, on account.

afkrabben o. w. scrape off, scratch off.

aflaat m. indulgence.

afladen o. w. (lossen) unload, discharge, (verzenden) ship, forward.

aflaten o. w. let down; (v. hoed, enz.) leave off; on. w. — **van,** cease from, desist from, leave off.

afleggen o. w. (r. kleren) lay aside, put off, take off; (voor goed: afdanken) cast off, discard; (v. wapens, last, enz.) lay down; (v. lijk) compose, lay out; (v. afstand) cover; **het** —, have (get) the worst of it; (bij examen) fail, be ploughed; (het onderspit delven) go to the wall.

aflegger m. (v. lijk) layer-out; (v. plant) layer; (kledingstuk) cast-off (coat, trousers.

afleiden o. w. (naar beneden) lead down; (in andere richting) turn off, divert; (v. aandacht, enz.) distract, divert; (v. verdenking) avert; (v. woord) derive; (besluiten, gevolgtrekking maken) conclude, deduce, infer; (vermaken) divert.

afleiding v. (v. aandacht, enz.) diversion; (vermaak, ontspanning) distraction, diversion; (v. woord) derivation; (afgeleid woord) derivative; (gevolgtrekking) deduction.

afleidingsbuis v. conduit-pipe.

afleidingskanaal o. channel.

afleren o. w. (gewoonte, enz.) unlearn; **iem. iets** —, break a person of; correct a person of.

afleveren o. w. deliver.

aflevering v. (v. goederen) delivery; (v. boek) part, number.

aflezen o. w. (v. vruchten) gather, pick; (v. akker) glean; (v. thermometer, enz.) read (off); (v. naamlijst, enz.) call over.

afloeren o. w. spy out.

afloop m. (v. termijn, enz.) expiration, expiry; (uitslag) result, issue, event; (v. gebeurtenis: einde) end, close; (afvoerpijp, buis) drain, dischargepipe, outlet; (helling) descent, declinvity, slope.

aflopen on. w. (eindigen) turn out, end; result, conclude; (v. contract, termijn, enz.) expire, extinguish, terminate, run out; (hellen) slope, decline; (naar beneden lopen) run down; (v. schip) be launched, leave the ways; (v. getij) ebb, go out; (v. kaars) gutter, run; (r. wekker) go off; (v. klos) run out; o. w. (r. straat, heuvel, enz.) run down, go down; (r. schoenen) wear out; (v. school) pass through; (v. cursus) finish off.

aflosbaar b. n. redeemable, repayable.

aflossen o. w. (v. persoon, wacht) relieve; (v. schuld, enz.: afbetalen) pay off, discharge; (*v. obligatie, hypotheek*) redeem; pay off.

aflossing *v.* (*v. wacht, enz.*) relief; (*v. lening, hypotheek*) redemption; (*v. schuld*) discharge.

afluisteren *o. w.* overhear, learn by listening.

afmaken *o. w.* (*v. brief, enz.: eindigen*) finish, complete; (*v. verloving*) break off; (*v. zaak*) settle; (*v. boek, enz.: afkammen*) slate, run down, cut up, rend to tatters; (*doden*) kill, slaughter; (*v. vijand*) dispatch, finish off; *w. w.* **er zich met een grapje van —,** pass off the matter with a joke.

afmatten *o. w.* wear out, fatigue, harass.

afmatting *v.* weariness, fatigue, lassitude.

afmeten *o. w.* measure (off).

afmeting *r.* (*het afmeten*) measurement; (*grootte*) dimension.

afmonsteren *o. w.* pay off, discharge; *on. w.* sign off.

afnemen *o. w.* (*wegnemen*) take away, (*v. verband, enz.*) take off; (*v. gordijnen; schilderij*) take down; (*kopen*) buy; (*v. kaarten*) cut; (*afzetten*) take off, pull off; *on. w.* decrease, diminish; (*v. wind*) go down, subside, abate; (*v. krachten*) decline; (*v. koorts*) remit, subside; (*v. invloed: maan*) wane, be on the wane; (*v. storm*) abate; (*v. voorraad*) get low; (*v. dagen*) draw in.

afnemer *m.* (*klant*) customer, client; (*koper*) purchaser, buyer.

afpassen *o. w.* (*v. terrein, afstand*) pace; (*v. kostuum*) try the last fit(ting).

afpersen *o. w.* (*r. geld, enz.*) extort, pinch; (*v. belofte*) wrest, wring; (*c. tranen, enz.*) force.

afperser *m.* extorter, extortioner.

afpersing *r.* extortion, exaction; (*geld-afdreiging*) blackmail; wresting.

afplukken *o. w.* pluck (off), gather, pick.

afpraten *o. w.* **heel wat —,** talk quite a lot, talk quite a good deal.

afraden *o. w.* **iem. iets —,** dissuade a person from something.

afraken *on. w.* (*v. verloving, enz.*) go off, break off, be broken off; **— van,** get away from, get off, get clear of; (*kwijtraken*) get rid of.

afranselen *o. w.* thrash, whack, drub, lick.

afreis *v.* departure.

afreizen *on. w.* depart, set out, leave; *o. w.* travel.

afrekenen *on. w.* settle (square) accounts; *o. w.* take off, count off, deduct.

afrekening *r.* settlement; (*nota*) account, statement (of account).

africhten *o. w.* (*alg.*) train; (*voor examen*) coach; (*v. paard*) break.

africhting *v.* training; coaching; dressing.

afroepen *o. w.* (*v. namen*) call over; (*v. treinen*) call out; (*iem. van werk, enz.*) call away (from).

afroeping *v.* proclamation; (*appèl*) roll-call, call-over.

afrollen *o. w.* (*afwinden*) unroll, unreel; *on. w.* **— van,** roll down.

afromen *o. w.* cream, take the cream off.

afroming *v.* creaming, skimming.

afronden *o. w.* round (off).

afronding *v.* rounding off.

afrossen *o. w.* thrash, drub, lick.

afrukken *o. w.* tear off, tear away, snatch away.

afschaafsel *o.* shavings.

afschaffen *o. w.* (*alg.*) abolish; (*v. wetten, enz.*) repeal, abrogate; (*r. misbruiken*) reform, redress, do away with; (*r. personeel, enz.*) do away with; (*v. auto, enz.*) put down, give up, part with.

afschaffer *m.* abolisher.

afschaffing *v.* abolition; repeal, abrogation; redress; putting down.

afschaven *o. w.* (*v. plank, enz.*) plane (off); (*v. huid*) graze, abrade, bark.

afscheid *o.* leave, farewell.

afscheidbaar *b. n.* separable.

afscheiden *o. w.* separate; (*met geweld*) sever; (*v. vochten: uitscheiden*) excrete, secrete; (*afzonderen*) segregate; *w. w.* **zich —,** separate (oneself); (*v. partij*) secede, break away.

afscheiding *v.* separation; (*tussenschot*) partition; (*v. partij*) secession, separation; (*v. vocht*) secretion, excretion.

afscheppen *o. w.* (*v. melk*) skim, cream; (*v. metalen*) skim, scum, scoop off; (*verwijderen*) take off, skim (off).

afscheuren *o. w.* tear off; *w. w.* **zich — van,** separate from, sever connections with.

afscheuring *v.* tearing off; (*in kerk*) schism.

afschieten *o. w.* (*v. wapen*) fire, discharge, shoot; (*v. pijl*) shoot, let fly; (*v. vuurpijl*) send up, fire; (*r. vogel*) shoot down; (*v. kamer, enz.*) partition off, board off; *on. w.* **op iem. —,** rush at a person.

afschilferen *on. w.* scale, peel off, exfoliate; (*v. huid*) peel; (*v. hout*) whittle.

afschrappen *o. w.* scrape (off); (*v. vis*) scale.

afschrift *o.* copy, duplicate.

afschrijven *o. w.* (*overschrijven*) copy, transcribe; (*v. bestelling*) cancel, countermand; (*v. bedrag, kapitaal*) write down; (*als waardevermindering, verlies: v. schuld*) write off.

afschrijver *m.* copier; plagiarist.

afschrik *m.* horror; (*afschuw*) abhorrence.

afschrikken *o. w.* deter; discourage; (*v. vogels, wild*) scare.

afschroeven *o. w.* unscrew, screw off.

afschudden *o. w.* shake off.

afschuimlepel *m.* skimmer.

afschuiven *o. w.* push off; (*v. grendel*) remove, push back **van zich —,** shif) off, get one's self excused; *on. w.* slide down; (*sl.*) come down.

afschutting *v.* partition, fence; (*tralie-werk*) railing. [ination.

afschuw *m.* horror, abhorrence, abomination.

afschuwelijk *b. n.* abominable, horrible, execrable, odious; *bw.* abominably, horribly, execrably, odiously.

afschuwelijkheid *v.* abomination, horribleness, execrableness, odiousness.

afslaan *o. w.* (*hoed, enz.*) knock off, strike off; (*v. vijand, aanval*) beat off, repulse, repel; (*v. aanbod, uitnodiging*) decline; (*v. prijs*) knock down; reduce; (*v. voorstel: verwerpen*) reject; (*v. stof, as v. sigaar*) flick off; *on. w.* (*v. prijzen*) go down; (*muz.*) make the down-beat.

afslag *m.* (*v. prijs*) abatement, reduction; (*veiling*) Dutch auction; (*muz.*) down-beat.

afslager *m.* auctioneer.

afslijten *o. w. en on. w.* wear off, wear down; (*fig.*) wear off, wear out.

afsloven (zich) *w. w.* drudge, slave, toil and moil.

afsluiten *o. w.* (*v. deur, enz.: op slot doen*) lock; (*v. kamer, huis, enz.*) lock up; (*v. gas, water*) turn off; (*v. el. stroom: uitschakelen*) put out of circuit, disconnect; (*v. stoom, toevoer*) cut off; (*v. weg, enz.*) close; (*v. lening*) contract; (*v. verzekering*) effect, take out; (*v. rekening*) close; (*v. boeken*) balance, close; (*v. contract, overeenkomst*) conclude, make; (*v. tijdperk*) close.

afsluiting *v.* (*alg.*) closing; locking up; (*v. gas*) obturation; (*v. kraan*) shutting off, turning off; (*v. contract, enz.*) conclusion, negotiation; (*v. rekening*) closing; (*v. boeken*) balancing; (*v. tijdperk*) termination; (*wat afsluit*) partition, enclosure, fence.

afsmeken *o. w.* implore, beseech, invoke.

afsmeking *v.* imploration, invocation.

afsnauwen *o. w.* snap at, snarl at, snub.

afsnijden *o. w.* (*v. bloem, enz.*) cut; (*v. sigaar*) clip; (*v. nagels*) pare; (*takken v. vruchtbomen*) prune off; (*van andere bomen*) lop off; (*v. gas, terugtocht, enz.*) cut off.

afsnijding *v.* cutting off.

afspannen *o. w.* (*uit juk: v. ossen*) unyoke; (*v. paard*) unharness; (*v. viool, boog*) unstring; (*met hand meten*) span.

afspanning *v.* unteaming; taking out; baiting-place.

afspelen *o. w.* (*v. spel*) finish, play to a finish; (*muz.*) play to the end; (*v. instrument*) play out, wear out; (*v. biljartbal*) save; *w. w.* **zich —,** be enacted.

afspiegelen *o. w.* reflect, mirror; *w. w.* **zich —,** be reflected, be mirrored.

afspiegeling *v.* reflection.

afspraak *v.* agreement; (*overeenkomst*) arrangement, agreement; (*voor samenkomst*) appointment, engagement.

afspreken *o. w.* agree upon, arrange.

afspringen *on. w.* (*v. muur, enz.*) jump off, leap down; (*v. knoop*) burst off; (*v. glazuur*) chip off; (*v. koop*) go off, come to nothing; (*v. onderhandelingen*) collapse, be broken off, break down; (*v. verloving*) go off.

afstaan *o. w.* (*v. gebied*) cede; (*v. bezit, plaats*) yield; (*v. recht, bezit, enz.*) resign, relinquish; (*v. voorrecht*) surrender; (*v. opbrengst*) hand over; *on. w.* **— van,** stand away from, stand back from.

afstammeling *m.* descendant.

afstammen *on. w.* **— van,** be descended from, spring from; (*v. woord*) be derived from.

afstamming *v.* (*v. persoon*) descent, extraction; (*v. woord*) derivation.

afstand *m.* (*ruimte*) distance; (*v. gebied, bezit, recht*) cession; (*v. recht, vordering, enz.*) relinquishment, renunciation, surrender; (*v. de troon*) abdication; (*v. boedel*) renunciation; **— doen van,** (*v. gebied, bezit, recht*) cede; (*v. recht, vordering*) relinquish; (*v. d. troon*) abdicate, vacate; (*v. geloof, wereld*) renounce.

afstandsmeter *m.* odometer; (*v. taxi*) taximeter; (*mil.*) range-finder.

afstappen *on. w.* step down; (*v. paard*) get off, alight; (*v. fiets*) get off, dismount; *o. w.* (*v. weg, enz.*) pace.

afsteken *o. w.* cut (off); (*met beitel*) chisel off, bevel; (*afbakenen*) lay out, mark out; (*v. vuurwerk*) let off; (*v. wijn*) draw off; (*v. speech*) deliver, make; (*v. toast*) propose; (*v. bezoek*) pay; *on. w.* (*van wal*) push off; **— bij,** contrast with.

afstellen *o. w.* (*v. motor*) tune up.

afstemmen *o. w.* (*v. motie*) negative, reject; (*v. wet*) throw out; (*v. voorstel*) vote down, outvote; (*v. radio, enz.*) tune in.

afstemming *v.* rejection; tuning (in).

afstempelen *o. w.* (*v. postzegels*) obliterate; (*v. aandelen, enz.*) stamp.

afsterven *on. w.* (*overlijden*) die, depart this life; (*v. lichaamsdeel*) mortify; (*v. vee*) die off; (*v. plant*) die down, die back, die off; (*v. vriendschap*) die out.

afstijgen *on. w.* (*v. paard, fiets*) get off, dismount; (*v. ladder, enz.*) go down; (*in hotel*) put up, alight.

afstorten *o. w.* hurl down, precipitate; *w. w.* **zich — van,** hurl (throw) oneself from (down).

afstoten *o. w.* (*v. persoon*) repel, repulse; rebuff; (*v. voorwerp*) knock off (down), push off (down), thrust off (down); (*sch.*) shove off, push off; (*nat.*) repel; *on. w.* repel.

afstrijken *o. w.* (*v. maat*) level, strike; (*v. lucifer*) strike, light, scratch; (*v. kleren*) strike off, slip off; (*v. was*) iron, finish ironing.

afstromen *on. w.* stream down, flow down.

afstropen *o. w. (v. huid, enz.)* peel off, strip (off); *(v. paling)* skin; *(v. haas)* strip; *(v. konijn)* uncase; *(fig.: v. streek)* ravage, ransack, pillage, harry.

afstuiten *on. w.* rebound, recoil; *(v. wapen)* glance off.

aftakelen *o. w. (v. schip)* unrig, dismantle; *(v. huis, enz.)* strip; *on. w.* be on the decline, lose one's strength.

aftakeling *v.* unrigging, dismantling; stripping; *(fig.)* decay.

aftappen *o. w.* draw (off); *(op flessen)* bottle; *(v. bloed, rubber, enz.)* tap; *(bij pleuris, enz.)* draw off, drain.

aftellen *o. w. (tellen)* count off; *(aftrekken)* subtract; *(bij spel)* count out.

aftobben (zich) *w. w.* weary oneself out.

aftocht *m.* retreat.

aftrap *m. (sp.: voetb.)* kick-off.

aftreden *on. w. (naar beneden komen)* step down, descend; *(zijn ambt neerleggen)* retire (from office), resign (office); *(v. koning)* abdicate; *z. n. o.* resignation, retirement.

aftreding *v.* resignation, retirement.

aftrek *m. (mindering)* deduction, abatement; *(bij belasting)* rebate, allowance; *(H.: vraag naar koopwaren)* sale, demand.

aftrekken *o. w. (v. bedrag)* deduct; *(neertrekken)* draw off (down, away), pull off, tear off; *(rek.: v. getal)* subtract; *(v. vuurwapen)* pull, press (the trigger); *(v. kruiden)* infuse; *(v. aandacht, enz.: afleiden)* divert; *on. w. (weggaan)* withdraw, march off, draw off; *(mil.)* retreat; *(v. wacht)* go off, be relieved; *(v. onweer)* blow over; *(rek.)* subtract.

aftrekker *m.* subtrahend.

aftrekking *v.* deduction; *(rek.)* subtraction.

aftreksel *o.* infusion, extract.

aftroeven *o. w.* trump; *(fig.)* trim, give a dressing-down.

aftroggelaar *m.* wheedler. [out of.

aftroggelen *o. w.* wheedle out of, trick

afvaardigen *o. w.* delegate, depute; *(naar parlement)* return.

afvaardiging *v.* delegation, deputation.

afvaart *v.* departure, sailing.

afval *o. (alg.)* refuse (matter), rubbish, waste; *(v. dieren, slacht—)* garbage, offal; *(bij bewerking: v. metaal, enz.)* clippings, cuttings; *(v. eten)* scraps, leavings; *(afgevallen fruit)* windfall; *m. (godsd.)* apostasy; *(pol.)* defection.

afvallen *on. w. (naar beneden vallen)* fall off, tumble down; *(ontrouw worden: godsd.)* apostatize; *(pol.)* secede; *(bij spel)* drop out; *(lichamelijk achteruitgaan, vermageren)* fall away, lose flesh, decay, waste; *(sch.)* pay off.

afvallig *b. n. (alg.)* disloyal, unfaithful; *(godsd.)* apostate, apostatical.

afvallige *m. en v. (godsd.)* apostate, renegade; *(v. partij)* deserter.

afvalligheid *v. (v. geloof)* apostasy; *(v. partij)* desertion, defection.

afvaren *on. w. (wegvaren)* sail, depart, start, put to sea; *o. w. (strooma/waarts varen)* sail down, steam down (the river).

afvegen *o. w.* wipe off; *(v. stof)* dust; *(v. brilleglazen)* polish; *(v. tranen)* dry.

afvoer *m. (v. goederen)* transport, removal, conveyance; *(v. water, enz.)* carrying off, drawing off, discharge, outlet; *(riool)* sewer, catch-drain.

afvoerbuis *v.* outlet-pipe, eductionpipe; *(in machine)* exhaust-pipe; *(v. gaskachel)* flue.

afvoeren *o. w. (v. goederen)* transport, convey; *(v. water, enz.)* drain away, carry off; *(afschrijven)* write off; scrap; *(mil.)* remove from the list; *(v. spier)* abduce.

afvragen *o. w.* ask (for), demand; *(op school)* hear (the lessons); *w. w.* **zich —,** ask oneself.

afvuren *o. w.* fire (off), discharge.

afwaaien *o. w. en on. w.* blow off.

afwaarts *b. n., bw.* downward.

afwachten *o. w.* await, wait for, stay for; *(v. gevolgen)* abide; *on. w.* wait, await developments.

afwachting *v.* expectation; **in — van uw antwoord,** awaiting your reply.

afwas *m.* washing-up.

afwassen *o. w. (v. vaatwerk)* wash up; *(v. handen, enz.)* wash, wash off.

afwateren *o. w. en on. w.* drain.

afweer *m.* defence.

afweergeschut *o.* anti-aircraft guns.

afwegen *o. w. (v. goederen)* weigh out; *(fig.: v. woorden, enz.)* weigh.

afwenden *o. w. (v. ogen, gelaat)* turn away, turn aside; *(v. gevaar, slag, enz.)* avert; *(v. slag)* parry, ward off; *(v. nederlaag, faillissement, gevaar)* stave off; *(v. aandacht)* divert.

afwennen *o. w.* **iem. iets —,** disaccustom a person from, wean a person from; *w. w.* **zich iets —,** break oneself of a habit, get out of a habit.

afweren *o. w. (v. gevaar, enz.)* avert, keep off; *(v. slag)* parry, ward off; *(v. aanval)* repel.

afwering *v.* keeping off; parrying, warding off; repulse; defence.

afwerken *o. w.* finish, finish off, complete; *(v. programma)* work off, get through, conclude; *(v. schip)* float.

afwerking *v.* finish, finishing.

afwerpen *o. w.* cast off, throw off, throw down; *(naar beneden storten)* precipitate; *(v. winst)* yield.

afwezig *b. n.* absent.

afwezigheid *v.* absence; *(recht)* nonappearance.

afwijken *on. w. (v. koers, weg, enz.)* deviate, deflect; *(v. lijnen, stralen)* diverge, be divergent; *(v. kompasnaald, kogel)* deviate; *(fig.: v. gewoonte, waarheid, enz.)* depart; *(v. 't rechte pad)* deviate, wander from; *(v. spoor)* digress from; *(in mening)* differ, dissent; *(v. monster: verschillen)* differ; *(v. algemene regel)* derogate from.

afwijking *v.* deviation; deflection, divergence, declination; (*v. gebruik, enz.*) departure; (*in tekst, enz.*) difference, variation; (*v. licht, verstand*) aberration.

afwijzen *o. w.* (*v. persoon*) refuse admittance (to); (*v. verzoek, kandidaat, minnaar*) refuse; (*v. aanbod, uitnodiging*) decline; (*v. aanvraag, eis*) reject; (*v. vordering*) disallow, dismiss.

afwijzend *b. n.* declinatory.

afwijzing *v.* refusal, denial; rejection; disclaimer.

afwikkelen *o. w.* (*v. koord, enz.*) unroll, unwind, wind off, uncoil; (*fig.: v. zaken*) wind up, settle; (*langzamerhand doen aflopen*) liquidate; (*v. contract*) fulfil, complete.

afwinden *o. w.* wind off; unreel, unwind.

afwisselen *o. w.* (*v. zaken*) alternate, interchange; (*v. persoon*) **iem. —,** relieve a person, take a person's place; (*afwisseling geven*) vary, diversify; *on. w.* (*beurtelings vervangen worden*) alternate; (*verschillen*) vary.

afwisselend *b. n.* (*veranderlijk, elkaar opvolgend*) alternate; (*afwisseling biedend*) varied, variegated, varying, diversified; *bw.* alternately, by turns, in turn.

afwisseling *v.* (*opeenvolging*) alternation, succession; (*verscheidenheid*) variety, diversity; (*verandering*) change, variation.

afwissen *o. w.* wipe (off).

afzakken *on. w.* (*v. kleren*) come down, slip down; (*v. kousen*) sag (down); *o. w.* **de rivier —,** drop (sail, float) down the stream.

afzakkertje *o.* settler, top-up.

afzeggen *o. w.* (*v. bestelling, uitnodiging*) countermand, cancel; (*v. persoon, vergadering*) put off.

afzegging *v.* countermand, counterorder; excuse.

afzenden *o. w.* send off; (*H.*) despatch, ship, forward.

afzender *m.* sender; consignor, despatcher, shipper.

afzending *v.* sending; despatch(ing), forwarding, shipment.

afzet *m.* (*H.*) sale; (*sp.*) take-off.

afzetbaar *b. n.* removable, deposable.

afzetbaarheid *o.* removability.

afzetgebied *o.* market, outlet, opening, débouché.

afzetsel *o.* (*Pl.: loot, stek*) layer, cutting, offshoot; (*aan kleed: strook*) trimming; (*neerslag*) sediment, deposit.

afzetten *o. w.* (*v. hoed*) put off, take off; (*v. arm, been*) amputate, cut off; (*ontslaan*) (*v. ambtenaar, enz.*) dismiss, remove; (*v. officier*) cashier; (*v. koning*) depose, dethrone; (*afsluiten, met soldaten*) line off; (*afbakenen*) peg out, stake out; (*v. straat: afpalen*) close off; (*als versiering: omboorden*) set off; (*passagier, uit rijtuig*) set down, put down; (*v. goederen*) sell, dispose of;

(*bedriegen, overvragen*) swindle, cheat, victimize; (*v. motor*) shut off, stop; (*v. telefoon*) disconnect, switch off.

afzetter *m.* swindler, sharper, cheat.

afzetterij *v.* swindling, swindle, sharping; (*sl.*) ramp.

afzetting *v.* (*v. lichaamsdeel*) amputation; (*v. ambtenaar*) dismissal, removal, deposition, deposal.

afzichtelijk *b. n.* (*bw.*) hideous(ly), ghast(ly). [liness.

afzichtelijkheid *v.* hideousness, ghast-

afzien *o. w.* (*v. straat, weg*) look down; (*v. stad, museum*) go over; (*fam.*) do; *on. w.* (*eig.*) look away from; (*afkijken*) copy (from); (*opgeven: v. plan, poging*) abandon, give up; (*afstand doen van: recht, vordering*) relinquish, renounce, waive.

afzienbaar *b. n.* to be overlooked; **in afzienbare tijd,** in the near future.

afzijdig *b. n.* **zich — houden,** hold (keep) aloof, stand aside.

afzoeken *o. w.* search, beat; (*v. zeeën, enz.*) scour.

afzonderen *o. w.* separate, set (put) apart, put aside; (*v. patiënt*) isolate, segregate; *w. w.* **zich —,** (*van samenleving*) seclude oneself; (*van de wereld*) retire, sequester oneself.

afzondering *v.* separation; isolation, segregation; seclusion; retirement.

afzonderlijk *b. n.* (*v. kamer, tafel*) separate; (*v. ingang, enz.*) private; (*v. draad, bloem*) single; (*v. geval*) individual; *bw.* separately, singly; individually.

afzwering *v.* abjuration; renunciation; falling off by ulceration.

afzwoegen *w. w.* **zich —,** toil and moil, drudge.

agaat *o.* **—steen** *m.* agate.

agent *m.* (*H.*) agent, transactor; (*politie—*) policeman, constable; (*vooral bij aanspraak*) officer; (*sl.*) bobby, copper.

agentschap *o.* agency; (*v. bank*) branch.

ahorn(boom) *m.* maple(-tree).

air *o.* air; appearance, seeming.

ajuin *m.* onion.

akelei *v.* (*Pl.*) columbine.

akelig *b. n.* dreary, dismal; (*v. verschijning, enz.*) ghastly; (*v. verhaal*) lugubrious; (*van gil, enz.*) horrid.

akeligheid *v.* dreariness, dismalness; (*persoon*) nasty fellow.

akker *m.* field.

akkerbouw *m.* agriculture, tillage.

akkerland *o.* arable land.

akkerman *m.* husbandman, ploughman.

akkoord *z. n., o.* (*overeenkomst*) agreement, arrangement; (*schikking*) settlement; (*H.: met crediteuren*) composition; (*muz.*) chord; *b. n.* correct.

akkoordbevinding *v.* **bij —,** if found correct.

akte *v.* document; deed; instrument; (*kath.*) act; diploma, certificate; (*voor jacht*) licence; (*bedrijf*) act.

al, alle *telw.* all; every; *bw.* already, yet; *vw.* though, although, even if, even though.

alarm *o.* alarm; alert.

alarmklok *v.* alarm-bell, tocsin.

albast *o.* alabaster.

albedrijf *m.* factotum, busy-body, Jack of all trades.

album *o.* (*alg.*) album; (*foto—*) photograph-book, album; (*voor uitknipsels, enz.*) scrap-book.

alcohol *m.* alcohol.

aldaar *bw.* there, at that place.

aldoor *bw.* all the time, all along, continuously, incessantly.

aldra *bw.* ere long, before long, soon.

aldus *bw.* (*alzo, op die manier*) thus, in this way (manner); (*dus*) so, therefore.

aleer *vw.* before, ere.

algemeen *b. n.* universal; general; common, general; indefinite, vague; public; *bw.* universally; generally; *z. n., o.* **in het —**, in general, generally, in (on) the whole.

algemeenheid *r.* universality, generality; commonness.

Algerië *o.* Algeria.

Algiers *o.* Algiers.

alhier *bw.* here, at this place.

alhoewel *vw.* (al)though.

alk *v.* (*Dk.*) auk, razor-bill.

alkoof *v.* alcove bedroom.

allebei(de) both (of them).

alledaags *b. n.* everyday, workaday; daily; quotidian; plain, ordinary; stale, trivial, trite; common, commonplace.

alledaagsheid *v.* triviality, triteness, staleness; commonness.

alleen *b. n.* alone, by oneself, single; (*eenzaam*) lonely; *bw.* only.

alleenhandel *m.* monopoly.

alleenheerschappij *v.* absolute power, — monarchy.   [autocrat.

alleenheerser *m.* absolute monarch,

alleenspraak *v.* monologue, soliloquy.

alleenstaand *b. n.* single, solitary, detached, isolated.

alleenverkoop *m.* (*H.*) monopoly, sole agency, sole sale.

alleenvertegenwoordiger *m.* (*H.*) sole agent.

allemaal *telw* all, one and all, the whole lot; altogether.

alleman *vnw.* everybody.

allengs (kens) *bw.* gradually, by degrees, insensibly.

aller— of all, very, most.

allereerst *b. n.* very first; *bw.* first of all.

allerhande *b. n.* of all sorts, all sorts of, all kinds of.

Allerheiligen *m.* Allsaints(-day), All-Hallows.

allerheiligst *b. n.* most holy, sacrosanct; **het A—e,** (*kath.*) the Eucharist.

allerhoogst *b. n.* very highest, highest of all; supreme; **de A—e,** the Most High.

allerlaatst *b. n.* very last, last of all; ultimate.

allerlei *b. n.* all kinds of, of all sorts; *z. n., o.* (*allerlei dingen*) all sorts of things; (*in dagblad*) miscellaneous; (*lett.*) miscellanea, miscellany.

allerminst *b. n.* very least; least of all.

allerwegen *bw.* everywhere.

Allerzielen *m.* All Souls' day.

alles *onb. vnw.* all, everything; anything.

allesbehalve *bw.* anything but.

alleszins *bw.* in every respect, in all respects, in every way, everyway.

allicht *bw.* (most) probably, in all probability, perhaps.

allooi *o.* alloy.

almacht *r.* omnipotence.

almachtig *b. n.* almighty, omnipotent; all-powerfull; *bw.* mighty, almighty.

almanak *m.* almanac, calendar.

alom *bw.* everywhere.

alomtegenwoordig *b. n.* omnipresent, ubiquitous.

alomtegenwoordigheid *v.* omnipresence, ubiquity.

aloud *b. n.* ancient, antique.

Alpen *m. mv.* **de —,** the Alps.

alreeds *bw.* already.

als *vw.* (*gelijk*) like; (*in de hoedanigheid van*) as; (*zoals: opsomming*) as; (*bij wijze van*) by way of; (*wanneer*) when; (*indien*) if; (*alsof*) as if.

alsdan *bw.* (*op die tijd*) then, at that time; (*in dat geval*) in that case.

alsem *m.* wormwood, absinth.

alsmede *vw.* and also, as well.

alsof *vw.* as if, as though.

alt *v.* alto; contralto.

altaar *o.* altar.

altegader, altemaal *bw.* all, one and all, altogether.

altemet *bw.* perhaps; now and then.

alteratie *v.* agitation, emotion, commotion.

althans *bw.* at least, anyway, anyhow.

altijd *bw.* always, ever.

altijddurend *b. n.* everlasting.

aluin *v.* alum.

alvast *bw.* meanwhile.

alvermogend *b. n.* omnipotent, all-powerful.

alvleesklier *v.* pancreas.

alvorens *vw.* before.

alwetend *b. n.* omniscient, all-knowing.

alwetendheid *v.* omniscience.

alziend *b. n.* all-seeing.

alzijdig *b. n.* all-sided, many-sided, universal; versatile.

alzo *bw.* (*aldus, op die wijze*) thus, in this way; (*dus*) consequently, so.

amandel *r.* (*vrucht*) almond; (*in neuskeelholte*) tonsil, amygdal.

amaril *v.* emery.

ambacht *o.* trade, craft, handicraft.

ambachtsman *m.* artisan, mechanic.

ambachtsschool *v.* technical school.

amber *m.* (*grijze —*) ambergris; (*gele —*) amber; (*hars*) styrax.

ambitie v. diligence, assiduity; (eerzucht) ambition.
ambrozijn o. ambrosia.
ambt o. (alg.) office, place, charge, employment, function; (kerkelijk) dignity.
ambtelijk b. n. (bw.) official(ly).
ambteloos b. n. out of office, retired.
ambtenaar m. official, public servant, functionary.
ambtgenoot m. colleague.
ambtsbezigheden v. mv. official duties; (v. advocaat, enz.) professional duties.
ambtshalve bw. officially, by (in) virtue of one's office, ex officio.
amechtig b. n. breathless, out of breath, panting for breath.
amechtigheid v. breathlessness.
amen o. amen.
Amerika o. America.
amethist m. amethyst.
ammoniak m. (liquid) ammonia.
ammunitie v. (am)munition.
ammunitiewagen m. ammunition-waggon, caisson.
amnestie v. amnesty.
amortisatie v. amortization, sinking, redemption.
amper bw. scarcely, hardly, barely.
anarchist m. anarchist.
Andalusië o. Andalusia.
ander (bijv.) other; (zelfst.) **een —,** another man.
anderdeels bw. on the other hand.
anderhalf telw. one and a half.
anders bw. (op andere wijze) otherwise, in another manner, differently; (zo niet) else, otherwise.
andersdenkend b. n. of another opinion, different(ly)-minded; (godsd.) dissenting; heterodox.
andersom bw. the other way about.
anderszins bw. otherwise.
andijvie v. endive.
angel m. (v. bij) sting, stinger; (vis —) hook, fish-hook; (v. pijl) barb.
Angelsakser m. Anglo-Saxon.
angst m. fear, terror, fright; (ziels—) anguish, agony.
angstig b. n. (bw.) fearful(ly).
angstkreet m. cry of distress.
angstvallig b. n. (nauwgezet) scrupulous, conscientious; (vreesachtig, beschroomd) timid, timorous.
angstwekkend b. n. alarming.
angstzweet o. cold perspiration.
anijs m. anise.
anjelier, anjer v. (Pl.) pink, carnation.
anker o. (sch.) anchor; (v. muur) brace, cramp-iron; (v. magneet) armature, keeper; (maat) anker.
ankeren on. w. (sch.) anchor, cast anchor.
ankerhaak m. (sch.) cat(-hook).
ankertouw o. cable.
annalen v. mv. annals.
annexatie v. annexation.
anno anno, in the year.

ansjovis v. anchovy.
antecedent o. (vroeger feit) precedent; (gram.) antecedent.
antenne v. aerial, antenna.
antikrist m. Antichrist.
Antillen v. mv. **de —,** The Antilles.
antilope v. antelope.
anti-semiet m. anti-Semite.
antraciet o. anthracite, blind-coal, glance-coal.
Antwerpen o. Antwerp.
antwoord o. (op vraag, enz.) answer, reply; (scherp —) retort; (gevat —) repartee; (op antwoord) rejoinder; (liturgisch: beurtzang) response; **in — op,** in reply to.
antwoorden o. w. en on. w. answer, reply; rejoin; (scherp) retort; (liturgisch) respond.
apart b. n. separate, apart; bw. apart, separately; in separate form.
apekool v. rubbish, fiddle-faddle, gammon and spinach.
Apennijnen v. mv. Apennines.
apenootje o. monkey-nut, pea-nut, pignut.
apin v. she-monkey, she-ape.
apostel m. apostle.
apotheek r. chemist's (shop); dispensary.
apotheker m. (pharmaceutical) chemist, pharmacist.
apothekersflesje o. dispensing-bottle.
apparaat o. apparatus.
appèl o. (recht: beroep) appeal; (naamafroeping) roll-call, call-over; (mil.) roll-call, parade, muster; (bij schermen) alarm.
appel m. (Pl.) apple; (v. degen) pommel; (v. oog) apple, ball, pupil.
appelboom m. apple-tree.
appeldrank m. cider.
appelflauwte v. fit of hysterics.
appelmoes o. en v. apple-sauce.
appelsien v. orange.
appetijt m. appetite.
applaudisseren on. w. applaud, cheer, clap.
april v. April.
aprilgrap v. April-fooljoke, April-trick.
apropos bw. en tw. apropos; by the bye, by the way.
aquarel r. water-colour, aquarelle.
ar r. sleigh, sledge.
Arabië o. Arabia.
arbeid m. labour, work; (zware —) toil.
arbeiden on. w. labour, work; toil.
arbeider m. labourer, workman, hand; worker.
arbeidersklasse v. working-class(es).
arbeiderspartij v. Labour party.
arbeiderswoning v. artisan's dwelling, working-class house.
arbeidscontract o. labour-contract.
arbeidskracht v. labour power.
arbeidsvermogen o. energy, working-power.
arbeidzaam b. n. laborious, industrious.

arbeidzaamheid v. laboriousness, industry.
arceren o. w. hatch, shade.
archief o. archives, records; Rolls; (gebouw) record-office, record-rooms.
architect m. architect.
archivaris m. archivist, keeper of the records.
arduin o. —**steen** m. free-stone, ashlar.
are v. are.
arend m. eagle.
arendsjong o. eaglet.
arendsnest o. eagle's nest, aerie, eyry.
arendsneus m. aquiline nose.
argeloos b. n. harmless, inoffensive; (aan geen kwaad denkend) unsuspecting; (onschuldig) innocent.
argeloosheid v. harmlessness, inoffensiveness; unsuspectingness; innocence.
Argentinië o. the Argentine, Argentina.
arglist v. craft, craftiness, guile, cunningness.
arglistig b.n. crafty, guileful, cunning.
argument o. argument, plea.
argwaan m. suspicion, mistrust.
argwanend b. n. (bw.) suspicious(ly).
aria v. air, aria, tune, song.
Ariër m. Aryan.
ark v. ark.
arm m. arm.
arm b. n. poor.
armband m. (sieraad om pols) bracelet; (band om arm) armlet, brassard.
armbestuur o. public assistance committee.
arme m. en v. poor man (woman); (bedeelde) pauper.
Armenië o. Armenia.
armenkas v. fund for the poor.
armenzorg v. poor relief.
armhuis o. alms-house, workhouse.
armleuning v. arm-rest, elbow-rest.
armoede v. poverty; penury, indigence; (schaarste) paucity.
armoedig b. n. poor, beggarly, needy, shabby; bw. poorly.
armvol m. armful.
armzalig b. n. poor, miserable, pitiful, pitiable; beggarly.
arreslede v. zie **ar.**
arrest o. (verzekerde bewaring) arrest, custody, detention; (beslaglegging) attachment, seizure; (uitspraak, vonnis) judgment, decision, decree.
arrestant m. arrested person, prisoner.
arresteren o. w. (aanhouden) arrest, take into custody; (v. notulen) confirm.
arrondissement o. district.
arrondissementsrechtbank v. district-court, county-court.
arsenaal o. arsenal, armoury.
artikel o. (alg.) article; (H.: koopwaar) article, commodity; (v. wet, enz.) article, clause, section.
artillerie v. artillery; (geschut, ook :) ordnance.   [gunner.
artillerist m. artillerist, artillery-man,

artisjok v. (Pl.) artichoke.
arts m. physician, doctor, medical man.
artsenij v. medicine, medicament; (fam.) physic.
as v. (v. wagen) axle, axle-tree; (v. planeet) axis; (tn.) spindle, shaft; (muz.) A flat; (alf.) ashes, ash; (gloeiende —) embers; cinders; (stoffelijk overschot) ashes.
asbak m. ash-pan.
asbelt v. ash-pit, ash-hole, refuse-tip, refuse-dump.
asbestpapier o. asbestos paper.
Asdag m. Ash-Wednesday.
asfalt o. asphalt, bitumen.
asgrauw b.n. ashen (-grey), ash-coloured, ashy pale.
asiel o. asylum.
askar v. dust-cart.
asperge v. asparagus.
aspirant m. aspirant, candidate, applicant.
aspunt o. pole.
Assepoester v. Cinderella.
assistent m. assistant; (v. hoogleraar) demonstrator.
assistente v. assistant, lady-help.
assuradeur m. assurer.
assurantie v. insurance; assurance.
aster v. (Pl.) aster.
astma o. asthma.
aswenteling v. rotation.
aterling m. wretch, miscreant.
Athene o. Athens.
Atlantisch b. n. Atlantic; —**e Oceaan,** Atlantic (Ocean).
atlas m. atlas.
atlas o. (stof) satin.
atleet m. athlete.
atletiek v. athletics, athleticism.
atmosfeer v. atmosphere.
atoom o. atom.
attent b. n. (opmerkzaam) attentive; (gereed om dienst te bewijzen) considerate, thoughtful.
attentie v. attention; consideration, thoughtfulness; —**s,** attentions, assiduities.
attest o. certificate, testimonial.
auctie v. auction, (public) sale.
audiëntie v. audience.
auditeur-militair m. judge-advocate.
augurk v. gherkin.
augustus m. August.
Australië o. Australia.
auteur m. author.
auteursrecht o. copyright.
auto v. motor-car, automobile.
autobus v. motor-bus.
autogarage v. (motor-)garage.
automaat m. automaton; (verkoop—) automatic-machine, vending-machine; (in station) ticket-machine.
autoped m. autoped, scooter.
autoriteit v. authority.
autotocht m. motor(ing) tour.
aval o. (H.) guarantee.
avegaar m. (tn.) auger, wimble.

averechts *bw.* invertedly; (*fig.*) wrongly, (in) the wrong way; preposterously; *b. n.* inverted; wrong; preposterous.
averij *v.* (*sch.*) (*geldelijk*) average; (*materiële schade*) damage.
avond *m.* evening, night; (*dicht*) even.
avondblad *o.* evening-paper.
avondgebed *o.* evening-prayer.
avondklok *v.* curfew; evening-bell.
avondmaal *o.* supper, evening-meal.
avonturen *o. w.* risk, venture, hazard.

avontuur *o.* adventure.
avontuurlijk *b. n.* adventurous; (*r. verhaal*) romantic, marvellous; (*gewaagd, riskant*) risky.
axioma *o.* axium.
azen *on. w.* — **op,** (*als prooi zoeken*) prey on, feed on; (*streven naar, loeren op*) covet, lie in wait for.
Azië *o.* Asia.
azijn *m.* vinegar.
azijnzuur *o.* acetic acid.
azuur *o.* azure, sky-blue.

B

baadster *v.* (fair) bather.
baai *v.* (*golf, inham*) bay; (*stof*) baize; (*tabak*) Maryland; (*wijn*) red wine, claret.
baak *v.* beacon.
baal *v.* (*zak: v. rijst, suiker, enz.*) bag; (*v. katoen*) bale; (*v. papier*) ten reams.
baan *v.* (*pad*) path, way; (*sp.: v. tennis, cricket*) court; (*ren—*) course, (running-) track; (*ijs—*) (skating-)rink; (*op vliegveld*) runway; (*v. planeet*) orbit; (*r. projectiel*) trajectory; (*r. spoorweg*) track; (*v. stof, enz.: strook*) breadth, width; (*lijn—*) ropewalk.
baanbreker *m.* pioneer, path-cleaver.
baantjesjager *m.* place-hunter, office-seeker.
baanwachter *m.* signal-man, flagman, line-keeper; (*bij overweg*) crossing-keeper.
baar *v.* (*golf*) wave, billow; (*lijkbaar*) bier; (*draagbaar*) litter; (*staaf*) bar, ingot; (*zandbank: wap.*) bar; (*jongensspel*) prisoner's bar; *m.* (*nieuweling, groentje*) novice, newcomer, greenhorn; (*op school*) freshman; *b. n.* — **geld,** ready money, cash, hard cash.
baard *m.* (*v. mens, dier, enz.*) beard; (*v. kat*) whiskers; (*v. sleutel*) bit; (*v. veer*) vane.
baardeloos *b. n.* beardless, unbearded; (*fig. ook:*) callow.
baarkleed *o.* pall.
baars *m. en v.* perch, bass.
baas *m.* master; (*bij aanspreking*) governor; (*meesterknecht*) foreman.
baat *v.* profit, benefit; avail.
baatzucht *v.* selfishness, egoism, self-interest.
baatzuchtig *b. n.* selfish, egoistic(al), self-interested.
babbelaar *m.* (*persoon*) chatterer, babbler; (*vrouw ook:*) chatterbox, gossip; (*stroopballetje*) bull's eye; (*klikker*) telltale.
babbelen *on. w.* (*praten*) chatter; (*keuvelen*) chat; (*kwaadspreken*) gossip; (*in klas*) talk; (*klikken*) blab, tell tales; (*v. kind*) prattle, babble.
babbelkous *v.* chatterbox, gossip.

bacil *r.* bacillus (*mr.: bacilli*).
bad *o.* bath.
baden *o. w. en on. w.* bathe; *w. w.* **zich —,** bathe.
bader *m.* bather.
badgast *m.* bather.
badhanddoek *m.* bath towel.
badkamer *v.* bath-room.
badkostuum *o.* bathing-costume.
badkuip *v.* bathing-tub, bath.
badmantel *m.* bath(ing)-wrap, bath-cloak.
badplaats *v.* (*aan zee*) seaside-place, seaside-resort, coast-resort, watering-place; (*in binnenland*) watering-place, spa, (German) bath.
bagage *v.* luggage; (*mil.; Am.*) baggage.
bagagebureau *o.* luggage-office.
bagagewagen *m.* (*v. trein*) luggage-van; (*mil.*) baggage-waggon.
bagatel *v. en o.* trifle, bagatelle.
baggeren *o. w.* dredge (out).
baggermachine *v.* dredging-machine.
baggermolen *m.* dredger, dredging-machine, dredging-mill.
bajonet *v.* bayonet.
bak *m.* (*voor water, enz.*) cistern, tank, reservoir; (*v. kalk, enz.*) hod, trough; (*v. koffer, enz.*) tray; (*v. rijtuig*) body; (*r. auto*) locker; (*r. baggermachine*) bucket; (*matrozentafel*) mess.
bakboord *o.* (*sch.*) port.
baken *o.* beacon, seamark; (*boei*) buoy.
bakenen *on. w.* beacon, erect beacons.
baker *v.* (dry-) nurse.
bakeren *o. w.* swaddle; *on. w.* drynurse.
bakermat *v.* cradle, birth-place; nurse.
bakerspeld *r.* swaddling-pin.
bakfiets *v.* carrier cycle.
bakhuis *o.* bake-house.
bakkebaard *m.* whisker(s); (*fam.*) mutton-chops.
bakken *o. w.* (*brood*) bake; (*vis, enz.*) fry; *on. w.* make bread; bake; (*v. sneeuw*) bind, ball; (*bij examen*) fail.
bakker *m.* baker.
bakkerij *v.* bake-house, bakery; baker's trade, baker's business.
bakkersknecht *m.* baker's man.
bakkes *o.* mug, phiz.

bakoven *m.* oven.
baksel *o.* batch, baking.
baksteen *m.* brick.
bakvis *v.* (*eig.*) frying-fish, frier, fryer; (*fig.: meisje*) flapper, bread-and-butter miss.
bal *m.* ball; bowl.
bal *o.* ball.
balanceerstok *m.* balancing-pole.
balans *v.* (*weegschaal*) balance, (pair of) scales; (*tn.*) beam; (*H.*) balancesheet.
baldadig *b. n.* (*bw.*) wanton(ly).
baldadigheid *v.* wantonness, mischief.
balein *o. en v.* (*v. walvis*) baleen, whalebone; (*v. korset*) busk; (*v. paraplu*) rib.
balie *v.* (*rechtbank*) bar; (*v. kantoor*) counter; (*leuning*) railing, balustrade, parapet; (*kuip*) tub.
baljuw *m.* bailiff.
balk *m.* beam; (*ruw geschaafd*) balk; (*dak—*) rafter; (*vloer—*) joist; (*muz.: noten—*) staff, stave; (*wap.*) bend; (*op check, enz.*) bar.
Balkanschiereiland *o.* Balkan peninsula.
balken *on. w.* bray; (*fig.*) bawl, squall.
balkon *o.* balcony; (*v. tram, trein*) platform.
ballast *m.* ballast; (*fig.*) lumber encumbrance, rubbish.
ballen *on. w.* (*tot een bal worden*) ball; (*met de bal spelen*) play at (with a) ball; *o. w.* **de vuist —,** clench the fist, double the fist.
balling *m. en v.* exile; outlaw.
ballingschap *v.* exile, banishment.
ballon *m.* (*luchtbal*) balloon; (*v. lamp*) globe.
balloteren *on. w.* vote by ballot, ballot.
balorig *b. n.* refractory, unruly, untractable, cross, bad-tempered.
balsem *m.* balm, balsam.
balsemen *o. w.* embalm.
balspel *o.* playing at ball.
Baltisch *b. n.* Baltic.
balzaal *v.* ball-room.
bamboe *v. en o.* bamboo.
ban *m.* (*kerkelijk*) excommunication; (*wereldlijk*) ban; proscription; (*mil.*) levy, draft; (*rechtsgebied*) jurisdiction.
banaan *v.* banana.
banbliksem *m.* anathema.
band *m.* (*om te binden*) tie; (*v. muts, schort, enz.*) string; (*lint*) ribbon; (*verband*) bandage; (*om af te binden*) ligature; (*om arm, hoed*) band; (*breuk—*) truss; (*v. vat, enz.*) hoop; (*v. fiets*) tire, tyre; (*v. boek*) cover, binding; (*boekdeel*) volume; (*bilj.*) cushion; (*draagband*) sling; (*voor documenten, enz.*) tape; (*fig. : v. bloed, vriendschap*) tie; (*v. liefde*) bond.
bandiet *m.* bandit, brigand, ruffian.
banen *o. w.* **een weg —,** break (clear, open) a way.
bang *b. n.* afraid (*alleen predikatief*); (*vreesachtig*) fearful, timorous, timid; (*laf*) cowardly; (*angstig: v. dagen, uren*) anxious; (*ongerust, bezorgd*) uneasy.

banier *v.* banner, standard.
banier *m.* banneret; (*sl.*) toff, swell.
bank *v.* (*zitbank*) bench; (*in tuin, rijtuig*) seat; (*school—: met lessenaar*) desk; (*lang, zonder leuning*) form; (*kerk—*) pew; (*geld—, speel—, enz.*) bank.
bankbiljet *o.* banknote.
bankbreuk *v.* bankruptcy.
banket *o.* (*feestmaal*) banquet; (*gebak*) fine pastry, fancy-cake(s), almond pastry; (*mil.*) banquette, firing-step, foot-bank.
banketbakker *m.* confectioner.
bankhouder *m.* (*bij spel*) banker; (*houder v. pandhuis*) pawn-broker.
bankier *m.* banker.
bankroetier *m.* bankrupt.
bankschroef *v.* bench-vice.
bankwerker *m.* fitter, engine-turner.
banneling *m.* exile.
bannen *o. w.* (*verbannen*) exile, banish, expel; (*v. geesten: verdrijven*) exorcize.
banvloek *m.* anathema, ban.
bar *v.* bar.
bar *b. n.* (*v. land: kaal, onvruchtbaar*) barren; (*v. weer: guur*) raw, inclement; (*v. gelaat: nors, stuurs*) grim, stern; (*v. koude: scherp*) severe, biting.
barak *v.* (*voor zieken*) shed; (*mil.*) hut; (*fig.*) hovel.
barbaars *b. n.* barbarous, barbaric.
barbier *m.* barber.
bard *m.* bard.
baren *o. w.* bear, give birth to; (*v. verwondering, enz.*) cause, occasion.
barensnood *m.* labour, travail.
barensweeën *o. mv.* labour-pains, pains of child-birth.
baret *v.* (*v. priester*) barret, biretta; (*v. student*) cap.
bargoens *b. n.* (*dieventaal*) thieves flash; (*fig.*) jargon, gibberish, double Dutch, lingo.
barheid *v.* barrenness; inclemency; grimness; severity.
bark *v.* bark, barque.
barmhartig *b. n.* charitable, merciful.
barmhartigheid *v.* charity, mercifulness, mercy.
barnsteen *o.* amber.
barometer *m.* barometer.
baron *m.* baron.
barones *v.* baroness.
barrevoeter *m.* barefooted friar.
barrevoets *bw.* barefooted.
bars *b. n.* (*v. blik, gelaat*) stern; (*v. stem*) harsh, gruff, rough.
barsheid *v.* sternness; harshness, gruffness, roughness.
barst *v.* crack, flaw, burst.
barsten *on. w.* (*v. glas, ijs, enz.*) crack, burst, be (get) cracked; (*v. hout*) split; (*v. huid*) chap, be (get) chapped; (*uiteen—*) burst, explode.
bas *v.* (*muz.*) bass.
baseren *o. w.* base, found, ground (**op, on**).

basis v. (meetk., mil.) base; (fig.) basis.
bassen on. w. bay, bark.
bast m. (tussen schors en spint) bast, inner bark; (schors) rind, bark; (v. peulvrucht) shell, husk, pod.
bastaard z. n., m. bastard; (Dk., Pl.) mongrel; (Pl.; v. woord, vorm) hybrid; b. n. bastard; mongrel; hybrid.
bastaardwoord o. hybrid (word).
bataljon o. battalion.
baten v. mv. profits; (activa) assets.
baten o. w. avail.
batig b. n. — saldo, (H.) credit balance.
batist o. batiste, lawn, cambric.
baviaan m. baboon.
bazelen on. w. twaddle, drivel, talk rot, talk nonsense.
bazin v. mistress (of the house); (fig.) virago.
bazuin v. (muz.) trombone; (Bijb.) trumpet.
beambte m. functionary, official, officer.
beamen o. w. assent to, say yes to, say amen to.
beaming v. assent.
beangst b. n. uneasy, anxious, alarmed.
beantwoorden o. w. en on. w. (v. brief, vraag, enz.) answer, reply to; (v. groet, bezoek, liefde) return.
bebloed b. n. bloody, blood-stained, blood-covered.
beboeten o. w. fine, mulct, amerce.
bebouwbaar b. n. arable, tillable, cultivable.
bebouwen o. w. (v. land) cultivate, till; (v. bouwgrond) build upon.
bed o. bed.
bedaagd b. n. aged, elderly.
bedaard b. n. (bw.) calm(ly), tranquil (ly), quiet(ly), composed(ly).
bedaardheid v. calmness, quietness, composure.
bedacht, — op, mindful of, studious of, alive to; niet — op, unsuspicious of.
bedachtzaam b. n. (met overleg te werk gaande) thoughtful; (niet overijld) deliberate; (voorzichtig; omzichtig) cautious, circumspect.
bedachtzaamheid v. thoughtfulness; deliberateness; cautiousness, circumspection.
bedanken o. w. thank; dismiss, discharge; throw over; on. w. render (return) thanks; decline; resign; withdraw one's subscription.
bedankje o. acknowledgement; (note of polite) refusal.
bedaren o. w. quiet, tranquillize, pacify; soothe; appease; still; mitigate, assuage, allay; on. w. calm (down), quiet (down), compose oneself; abate, subside; die down.
bedauwen o. w. bedew.
beddegoed o. bedding, bed-clothes.
beddesprei v. bed-spread, coverlet, counter-pane.
bedding v. (v. rivier, enz.) bed; (aardk.: laag) layer, stratum; (mil.) platform.

bede v. (gebed) prayer; (smeekbede) entreaty, supplication; (verzoek) request, solicitation; (gesch.) benevolence.
bedeesd b. n. timid; bashful, timorous.
bedeesdheid v. timidity, bashfulness, timorousness.
bedekken o. w. cover (up).
bedektelijk bw. covertly, stealthily.
bedelaar m. beggar; (dicht.) mendicant.
bedelarij v. begging, beggary, mendicancy.
bédelen o. w. beg; on. w. beg, beg alms, beg (ask) charity.
bedélen o. w. (begiftigen) endow; (v. armen) bestow alms on (upon).
bedelstaf m. beggar's staff.
bedelven o. w. burry, entomb.
bedelzak m. (beggar's) wallet.
bedenkelijk b. n. (gevaarlijk) critical; (gewaagd) hazardous, risky; (zorgelijk) precarious; (ernstig) serious, grave; (twijfelachtig) doubtful; (verdacht) suspicious.
bedenken o. w. (uitdenken, verzinnen) think of, devise, contrive, invent; (overdenken) consider, weigh, reflect; (onthouden, niet vergeten) remember, bear in mind; (een fooi geven) remember, tip; w. w. zich —, (over iets nadenken) reflect, take thought; (van gedachte veranderen) change one's mind, think better of it.
bedenking v. consideration; (bezwaar) objection.
bedenktijd m. time to consider, time for reflection (consideration).
bederf o. (rotting) putrefaction, decay; (achteruitgang, v. kwaliteit) deterioration; (v. zeden) depravation, depravity, corruption; (bedervende invloed) taint.
bederfwerend b. n. antiseptic.
bederven o. w. (v. kind, ogen, werk, enz.) spoil; (v. lucht) deteriorate, vitiate, taint; (v. zeden) corrupt, deprave; (v. taal, enz.) corrupt; (v. maag) derange, disorder; (v. goederen) damage; (v. effect, vreugde, enz.) mar; on. w. (v. eetwaren) spoil, taint, go bad; (v. goederen) deteriorate; (v. melk) turn sour.
bedevaart m. pilgrimage.
bedevaartganger m. pilgrim.
bediende m. (in huis) servant, domestic; (lakei) footman; (in hotel, enz.) waiter, attendant; (in zaak) employee; (kantoor—) clerk; (winkel—) shop-assistant.
bedienen o. w. (v. klanten, enz.) serve, attend to; (aan tafel, enz.) wait upon; (mil.) serve, work; (v. machine) operate, tend, mind; (kath.: v. zieke) administer the last sacraments; w. w. zich —, help oneself; on. w. (aan tafel) wait, do the waiting; (in winkel) serve.
bediening v. (in hotel, winkel) service, attendance; (aan tafel) waiting; (ambt) office, function; (mil.) service; (kath.: v. zieke) administration of the last sacraments.

bedillen *o. w.* censure, cavil at, carp at.
bediller *m.* censurer.
beding *o.* condition, stipulation, proviso.
bedingen *o. w.* (*bepalen*) condition, stipulate; (*verkrijgen*) obtain.
bedlegerij *b. n.* bed-ridden, laid-up, confined to (one's) bed.
bedoeld *b. n.* intended.
bedoelen *o. w.* (*menen, willen zeggen*) mean, mean to say; (*beogen*) purpose, have in view.
bedoeling *v.* (*voornemen, oogmerk*) intention, design, purpose, intent; (*betekenis*) purport, meaning; (*plan*) intention.
bedompt *b. n.* close, stuffy; (*v. atmosfeer: drukkend, zwoel*) sultry, close.
bedotten *o. w.* trick, gull, diddle, befool, take in.
bedrag *o.* amount.
bedragen *o. w.* amount to, come to.
bedremmeld *b. n.* confused, perplexed, put out.
bedreven *b. n.* skilful, skilled, adept; practised, expert, experienced.
bedrevenheid *v.* skilfulness, skill; expertness.
bedriegen *o. w.* deceive, cheat, dupe, trick, take in, swindle, impose upon; *on. w.* cheat; *w. w.* **zich —,** deceive (delude) oneself; (*zich vergissen*) be mistaken.
bedrieger *m.* deceiver, impostor.
bedrieglijk *b. n.* (*v. persoon*) deceitful; (*v. praktijken, enz.*) fraudulent, sharp; (*misleidend*) deceptive, deceiving, fallacious; (*v. argumenten, enz.*) specious, delusive.
bedrijf *o.* (*handeling*) deed, action; (*beroep*) business, trade; (*zaak*) business, concern; (*exploitatie*) working; (*v. toneelstuk*) act.
bedrijfsbelasting *v.* trade-income tax.
bedrijfsinkomsten *v. mv.* revenue.
bedrijfskapitaal *o.* working-capital.
bedrijven *o. w.* commit, perpetrate.
bedrijvig *b. n.* active, bustling, busy, industrious.
bedrijvigheid *v.* (*drukte*) activity, stir; (*beweging*) bustle; (*werkzaamheid, vlijt*) industry.
bedrinken *o. w.* drink (to); *w. w.* **zich —,** fuddle oneself.
bedroeven *o. w.* afflict, grieve, distress; *w. w.* **zich — over,** be grieved at.
bedroevend *b. n.* sad, sorrowful, pitiable, pitiful, distressing.
bedrog *o.* deceit, cheat.
bedrukt *b. n.* printed; (*fig. : bedroefd, neerslachtig*) dejected, down, depressed, melancholy.
bedruktheid *v.* dejectedness, dejection, depressedness, depression.
bedstede *v.* cupboard-bed, closet-bed.
beducht *b. n.* afraid.
beduiden *o. w.* (*betekenen*) signify, mean; (*aanduiden, aanwijzen*) indicate, point out; (*voorspellen*) portend, betoken;

(*voorstellen*) represent; (*uitleggen, duidelijk maken*) make clear.
bedwang *o.* restraint, control; repression.
bedwelmd *b. n.* stunned, stupefied; (*door bedwelmend middel*) drugged; (*door drank*) intoxicated.
bedwelmen *o. w.* stun, stupefy; (*door bedwelmend middel*) drug; (*door drank*) intoxicate.
bedwelming *v.* (*handeling*) stunning; (*toestand*) stupefaction, stupor; (*narcose*) narcosis.
bedwingen *o. w.* (*in bedwang houden*) restrain, control, check; (*v. land*) conquer, subdue; (*v. oproer*) repress, suppress, quell; (*v. toorn*) contain, keep down; (*v. tranen*) keep back, command; (*v. hartstochten*) govern, master, control, subdue; *w. w.* **zich —,** restrain oneself, contain oneself.
beëdigd *b. n.* confirmed by oath, given on oath, sworn; (*v. persoon*) sworn.
beëdigen *o. w.* (*v. persoon: ambtenaar*) swear (in), swear into office; (*v. getuige, enz.*) swear, administer the oath to; (*v. verklaring, enz.*) confirm on oath, swear to.
beëindigen *o. w.* terminate; bring to an end, finish, conclude.
beek *v.* brook, rill, rivulet.
beeld *o.* (*alg.*) image; (*standbeeld*) statue; (*afbeelding, portret*) likeness, picture, portrait; (*spiegelbeeld*) reflection; (*zinnebeeld*) emblem, symbol; (*redefiguur*) figure (of speech), metaphor.
beeldend *b. n.* **—e kunsten,** plastic arts, arts of design.
beeldenstormer *m.* iconoclast, image-breaker.
beeldhouwer *m.* sculptor, statuary; wood-carver.
beeldhouwkunst *v.* sculpture.
beeldhouwwerk *o.* sculpture, statuary (work); (*in hout*) carved wood, carving.
beeldrijk *b. n.* ornate, flowery, full of images.
beeldschrift *o.* figurative writing, picture writing; (*Egyptisch*) hieroglyphics.
beeldspraak *v.* metaphorical (figurative) language; metaphor.
beeldwerk *o.* imagery; statuary.
beeltenis *v.* image, portrait, likeness, effigy.
beemd *m.* meadow, pasture, field; (*dicht.*) lea.
been *o.* (*lichaamsdeel: v. passer, enz.*) leg; (*deel v. geraamte; stofnaam*) bone; (*v. hoek*) side.
beenachtig *b. n.* bony; osseous.
beenbreuk *v.* fracture of the leg (of a bone).
beeneter *m.* caries, necrosis.
beensplinter *m.* splinter of a bone.
beenvlies *o.* periosteum.
beenvliesontsteking *v.* periostitis.
beer *m.* (*roofdier*) bear; (*mannetjes-*

varken) boar; (*stenen waterkering*) dam, weir, buttress; (*muurstut*) buttress, counterfort; (*schuld*) debt; (*schuldeiser*) dun, creditor; (*heiblok*) rammer, monkey; (*uitwerpselen*) night-soil, dung, muck.

beerput *m.* cess-pool, cesspit.

beest *o.* (*alg.*) animal; (*v. paard, koe, ook:*) beast; (*wild* —) brute; (*fig.*) beast, brute; (*bilj.*) fluke, scratch.

beestachtig *b. n.* beastly, bestial, brutal, brutish.

beestenspel *o.* menagerie.

beet *m.* (*het bijten*) bite; (*v. slang*) sting; (*hapje*) bit, morsel, mouthful.

beetje *o.* little, little bit; **lekker** —, tit-bit, dainty.

beetwortel *m.* beet(root).

bef *v.* band, (pair of) bands.

befaamd *b. n.* famous, famed, noted, renowned; (*ong.: berucht*) notorious.

begaafd *b. n.* gifted, talented.

begaafdheid *v.* giftedness, talents, ability, parts.

begaan *o. w.* (*v. weg: lopen over*) walk (upon), tread; (*v. misdaad, enz.: bedrijven*) commit, perpetrate; *on. w.* **laten** —, leave to.

begaan *b. n.* (*v. pad, weg*) trodden, beaten; — **zijn met,** pity, have pity on.

begaanbaar *b. n.* practicable, passable.

begeerlijk *b. n.* desirable, eligible; (*begerig*) eager, greedy.

begeerte *v.* desire, wish; (*sterker*) avidity.

begeleiden *o. w.* (*v. persoon: vergezellen; muz.*) accompany; (*geleiden*) conduct; (*mil.*) escort; (*v. schip*) convoy.

begeleider *m.* companion, guide; (*muz.*) accompanist.

begeleiding *v.* accompanying; (*muz.*) accompaniment; (*mil.*) escort; (*v. schip*) convoy.

begeren *o. w.* desire, wish (for), covet.

begerig *b. n.* desirous, eager; (*inhalig, hebzuchtig*) greedy, covetous.

begeven *o. w.* (*v. ambt, enz.: schenken*) bestow, confer; (*verlaten, in de steek laten*) forsake; *w. w.* **zich** — (**naar**), go; repair, resort (to).

begieten *o. w.* water, wet.

begiftigen *o. w.* (*v. persoon, instelling, enz.*) endow.

begiftiging *v.* endowment, donation.

begin *o.* beginning, commencement, outset; start, inception, opening.

beginneling *m.* beginner, commencer, novice, tiro, tyro.

beginnen *o. w.* begin, commence; *on. w.* begin; (*v. winter, dooi, enz.*) set in; (*v. school*) open, begin; (*sp.*) start.

beginsel *o.* (*grondregel*) principle; (*Bijb. : begin*) beginning; **de** (**eerste**) —**en,** the rudiments, the elements.

beginselvast *b. n.* firm of principle.

begoochelen *o. w.* (*betoveren*) bewitch, fascinate; (*bedriegen, misleiden*) delude, beguile.

begoocheling *v.* bewitchment, fasci-nation, glamour, spell; delusion, beguilement.

begraafplaats *v.* cemetery, burying-place, burial-place, churchyard, graveyard.

begrafenis *v.* interment, inhumation, burial, funeral.

begraven *o. w.* bury; (*dicht.*) inter, inhume.

begrenzen *o. w.* (*v. land, enz.*) bound, border; (*beperken*) limit, circumscribe.

begrijpelijk *b. n.* (*te begrijpen, verstaanbaar, duidelijk*) comprehensible, understandable, intelligible, easily understood; (*denkbaar*) conceivable; (*vlug van begrip*) intelligent, understanding.

begrijpen *o. w.* (*vatten, verstaan*) understand, conceive, comprehend; (*inhouden*) contain; (*insluiten*) include, imply.

begrip *o.* (*denkbeeld, voorstelling*) idea, notion, conception; (*het begrijpen, bevatting*) comprehension, apprehension; (*wet.*) concept.

begroeten *o. w.* salute, greet; welcome.

begroeting *v.* salutation, greeting.

begroting *v.* estimate; (*v. Staat, enz.*) estimates, budget.

begunstigen *o. w.* favour; (*beschermen, steunen*) support, countenance.

begunstiger *m.* favourer, patron; (*klant*) customer, patron.

behaaglijk *b. n.* (*aangenaam*) pleasant; (*gemakkelijk*)comfortable; (*gezellig,knus*) snug.

behaaglijkheid *v.* pleasantness; comfort, comfortableness; snugness.

behaagziek *b. n.* coquettish.

behaagzucht *v.* coquetry.

behaard *b. n.* hairy, hirsute, covered with hair; (*Pl.*) pilose.

behagen *o. w.* please; *z. n., o.* pleasure.

behalen *o. w.* gain, win, obtain, get.

behalve *vz.* (*uitgezonderd*) except, but; (*benevens*) besides.

behandelen *o. w.* (*v. persoon*) treat; deal (with, by); handle, manage; (*v. patient*) attend, treat; (*v. zaken*) handle, manipulate; (*v. rechtszaak*) try, hear.

behandeling *v.* treatment; attendance; handling, manipulation; trial, hearing; (*v. wetsontwerp*) discussion.

behangen *o. w.* hang; paper; drape.

behanger *m.* paper-hanger, paperer; (*stoffeerder*) upholsterer.

behangsel *o.* (wall-)paper, (paper)hangings.

behangselpapier *o.* (wall-)paper.

behartigen *o. w.* have at heart, promote, serve.

beheer *o.* management, direction, administration.

beheerder *m.* manager, director, administrator; (*in faillissement*) trustee.

beheersen *o. w.* command, control, master; be master of; dominate; rule, govern, sway; *w. w.* **zich** —, govern oneself, control (command, master.

possess) oneself, keep (command) one's temper.

behelpen (zich) *w. w.* make shift, manage.

behelzen *o. w.* contain.

behendig *b. n. (bw.)* dexterous(ly), adroit(ly), deft(ly), skilful(ly).

behendigheid *r.* dexterity, adroitness, deftness, skill.

behept *b. n.* — **met,** affected (afflicted) with; subject to, liable to; loaded with.

beheren *o. w.* manage, administer, conduct.

behoeden *o. w.* guard, watch over; — **voor,** preserve (protect, guard) from.

behoeder *m.* protector, preserver, defender.

behoedzaam *b. n.* cautious, wary, prudent.

behoefte *v.* want, need, necessity.

behoeftig *b. n.* indigent, necessitous, needy, destitute, penurious.

behoeftigheid *r.* indigence, neediness, destitution, penury.

behoeven, ten — van, in behalf of, for the benefit of.

behoeven *o. w.* want, need, require.

behoren *on. w. (toebehoren)* belong to, appartain to; (passen, betamen) be fit, be proper; z. n., o. **naar —,** properly, duly, as it should be.

behoud *o. (r. gezondheid, vrede, enz.)* preservation, maintenance; (redding) salvation; (tegend. v. afschaffing) retention: (politiek) conservatism.

behouden *o. w.* keep, retain, preserve, maintain.

behouden *b. n.* safe, safe and well, safe and sound.

behoudens *rz.* except; barring.

behulp, met — van, by means of; with the help (assistance, aid) of.

behulpzaam *b. n.* helpful, ready to help.

behulpzaamheid *r.* helpfulness, readiness to help.

beiaard *m.* chimes, carillon.

beiaardier *m.* carillon player, carillonneur.

beide(n) *telw.* both.

beiden *on. w. (talmen)* tarry, linger; *o. w. (afwachten)* wait for, bide.

beijveren (zich) *w. w.* do one's utmost (one's best), lay oneself out, exert oneself.

beitel *m.* chisel: **holle —,** gouge.

beitelen *o. w.* chisel.

bejaard *b. n.* aged, elderly, advanced in years.

bejammeren *o. w.* deplore, lament; (bewenen) bewail, bemoan.

bejegenen *o. w.* treat, use.

bek *m. (v. paard, enz.)* mouth; (v. vogel) beak, bill; (v. pen) nib; (r. nijptang) bit, jaws; (v. bankschroef) jaws, sides, cheeks; (v. gaspijp) burner; (v. dakgoot) lip, spout; (pop. : v. mens) snout.

bek-af *b. n.* dead tired, knocked up, done lup, fagged out.

bekampen *o. w.* zie **bestrijden.**

bekeerling *m. en r.* convert, convertite.

bekend *b. n.* known; (welbekend) well-known, noted; (ong. : berucht) notorious; — **maken,** announce, make known, publish; (r. geheim) divulge.

bekende *m. en r.* acquaintance.

bekendheid *r.* name, reputation, notoriety; (ong.) notoriety.

bekendmaking *r.* announcement, publication, notification, notice; (officieel) proclamation; (r. rerkiezingsuitslag) declaration.

bekennen *o. w. (v. zonde, misdrijf)* confess; avow, own; (erkennen) admit, acknowledge; (bemerken, bespeuren) see; on. w. (kaartsp.) follow suit; (recht : r. gerangene) plead guilty.

bekentenis *r.* confession, avowal; acknowledgment.

beker *m.* cup, goblet, bowl, beaker; (bij dobbelspel) dice-box.

bekeren *o. w. (tot andere godsdienst)* convert; (r. zondaar) reclaim; w. w. **zich —,** be converted; (r. zondaar) reform, repent, mend one's ways.

bekering *v.* conversion; (r. zondaar) reform, reclamation.

bekeuren *o. w.* summon, fine, amerce.

bekijken *o. w.* look at, view.

bekijven *o. w.* scold, chide.

bekken *o. (kom, schotel)* basin; (muz.) cymbal; (ontleedk.) pelvis; (r. rivier) catchment-basin, catchment-area.

beklaagde *m. en v.* accused, prisoner; (in burgerl. zaak) defendant.

bekladden *o. w.* blot, blotch, daub, bespatter; (fig.) daub, stain, defame.

beklagen *o. w. (v. persoon)* pity, commiserate; (v. zaak : betreuren) lament, deplore; w. w. **zich —,** lament, complain.

beklagenswaardig *b. n.* lamentable, deplorable, pitiable, to be pitied.

bekleden *o. w. (bedekken)* clothe; (stoelen) cover, upholster; (beeld) drape, dress; (wand) plank; (tn.) (stoomketel) lag; (scheepswand) metal, plate, sheathe; (kabel) serve; (mil. : v. wal, loopgraaf) revet; (met hout) wainscot, panel; (r. ambt) hold, fill, occupy.

beklemd *b. n. (benauwd)* oppressed; (met klemtoon) accented, stressed; (r. breuk) strangulated.

beklemdheid *v.* oppression, oppressiveness; strangulation.

beklemmen *o. w.* oppress.

beklimmen *o. w. (v. trap)* climb; (r. berg) climb, ascend; (v. troon) ascend, mount; (v. kansel) mount, go into; (mil.) scale, escalade.

beklimming *r.* climbing; ascent; mounting; escalade.

beknellen *o. w.* pinch, pin; (fig.) oppress

beknibbelen *o. w.* skimp, scrimp.

beknopt *b. n.* brief; compendious; (verhaal) succinct; (handboek) concise; (ver-

slag) condensed; (*uitdrukking : gedrongen, pittig*) terse.
beknoptheid *v.* briefness, brevity; succinctness; compendiousness; conciseness; compression; terseness.
beknorren *o. w.* chide, scold.
bekomen *o. w.* (*krijgen*) get, obtain, receive; (*v. spijzen, enz.*) agree with, suit; *on. w.* come to, recover.
bekommerd *b. n.* concerned, anxious, uneasy, solicitous.
bekommeren *w. w.* **zich — om** (*over*), be anxious about, trouble (one's head) about, be solicitous about, care for.
bekommering *v.* **bekommernis** *v.* anxiety, trouble, solicitude, care.
bekoorlijk *b. n.* charming, enchanting.
bekoorlijkheid *v.* charm, enchantment. [tempt.
bekoren *o. w.* charm, enchant; (*kath.*)
bekoring *v.* charm, enchantment, fascination; (*kath.*) temptation.
bekorten *o. w.* shorten, curtail; (*v. boek, enz.*) abridge, condense; (*v. verhaal*) abbreviate; *w. w.* **zich —,** be brief. make it short.
bekostigen *o. w.* pay the expenses of, defray the cost of.
bekrachtigen *o. w.* (*v. verklaring, vonnis, enz.*) confirm; (*v. verdrag*) ratify; (*v. gebruik, wet*) sanction; (*v. overeenkomst*) validate.
bekrachtiging *v.* confirmation; ratification; sanction; validation.
bekrimpen *o. w.* reduce, retrench; *w. w.* **zich —,** stint oneself, pinch oneself, skrimp.
bekrompen *b. n.* (*kleingeestig : v. persoon*) narrow-minded; (*v. beginselen*) hide-bound; (*v. ruimte*) confined; (*v. omstandigheden*) straitened; *bw.* **— wonen,** live in cramped quarters.
bekrompenheid *v.* narrow-mindedness, narrowness.
bekronen *o. w.* (*de kroon zetten op*) crown; (*de prijs toekennen*) award the (a) prize.
bekroning *v.* crowning, coronation.
bekwaam *b. n.* able, capable, competent, apt, clever.
bel *v.* (*schel*) bell; (*v. tram, ook :*) gong; (*bobbel, waterblaasje*) bubble; (*oorbel*) ear-drop.
belachelijk *b. n.* ridiculous, ludicrous; (*lachwekkend*) laughable.
belagen *o. w.* waylay, lay snares for.
belager *m.* waylayer.
belanden *on. w.* land, arrive.
belang *o.* (*voordeel*) interest, concern; (*gewicht, belangrijkheid*) importance.
belangeloos *b. n.* (*bw.*) desinterested(ly).
belangeloosheid *v.* desinterestedness.
belanghebbende *m. en v.* party concerned, person interested.
belangrijk *b. n.* important, of importance; (*aanmerkelijk*) considerable; *bw.* considerably.

belangrijkheid *v.* importance.
belangstelling *v.* interest; (*deelneming*) sympathy.
belangwekkend *b. n.* interesting.
belastbaar *b. n.* (*v. goederen, bij invoer*) dutiable; (*v. inkomen*) assessable; (*v. bezittingen, waarde, enz.*) taxable, ratable, assessable; (*voor accijns*) excisable.
belasten *o. w.* (*last opleggen*) burden; (*tn.*) load; (*belasting opleggen*) tax; impose a tax, impose duties on; (*opdragen*) charge, commission; *w. w.* **zich — met,** charge oneself with.
belasteren *o. w.* calumniate, defame, slander, asperse, backbite, traduce.
belasting *v.* (*handeling*) burdening; taxation; (*gewicht*) load, weight; (*rijks—*) tax, taxes; (*indirecte —*) duty.
beledigen *o. w.* offend; affront, insult; (*grof —*) outrage; (*kwetsen*) injure.
beledigend *b. n.* offensive, insulting, injurious.
belediger *m.* offender, insulter.
belediging *v.* (*v. persoon*) affront, insult; (*v. gevoelens*) offence, outrage, hurt; (*kwetsuur*) lesion, injury.
beleefd *b. n.* (*bw.*) polite(ly), civil(ly), courteous(ly).
beleefdheid *v.* politeness, civility, courteousness.
beleg *o.* siege.
belegeraar *m.* besieger.
belegeren *o. w.* besiege, lay siege to.
belegering *v.* siege.
beleggen *o. w.* (*bedekken met*) cover, overlay; (*bijeenroepen : v. vergadering*) convene, convoke; (*op rente uitzetten*) invest, lay out; (*sch.*) belay.
belegsel *o.* covering; trimming(s); (*v. uniform*) facings.
beleid *o.* (*overleg, omzichtigheid*) prudence, discretion, tact, generalship; (*bestuur, leiding*) conduct, management.
belemmeren *o. w.* hinder, impede; (*v. uitzicht, plannen*) obstruct; (*in groei*) stunt.
belemmering *v.* hindrance, impediment; obstruction.
belet *o.* hindrance.
beletsel *o.* hindrance, impediment, obstacle.
beletten *o. w.* (*iets*) prevent, put a stop to; obstruct; (*met infinitief*) prevent (hinder) from, preclude from.
beleven *o. w.* live to see; (*doormaken*) go through.
belezen *o. w.* (*bezweren*) exorcize; (*overhalen*) persuade; *b. n.* well-read, bookread.
belezenheid *v.* reading.
Belg *m.* Belgian.
belgen *w. w.* **zich — over,** be angry at, be incensed at (by), take offence at.
belhamel *m.* bell-wether; (*fig.*) ringleader; (*schelm*) rascal.
belichten *o. w.* (*v. feit, enz.*) illuminate, illustrate, elucidate; (*v. schilderij*) light; (*fot.*) expose.

belichting *v.* illumination, elucidation; lighting, light; exposure.
believen *o. w.* please; **als het u belieft,** (if you) please; *z. n., o.* **naar —,** at will, at pleasure.
belijden *o. w.* (*bekennen*) confess, avow; (*v. godsdienst*) profess.
belijdenis *v.* confession, avowal; profession; (*prot.*) confirmation; (*kerkgenootschap*) denomination.
bellen *on. w.* ring (the bell); (*met drukknop*) press the button, pull (touch) the bell; (*v. trambestuurder*) sound the gong.
belofte *v.* promise; (*recht : in plaats v. eed*) affirmation.
beloken *b. n.* — **Pasen,** Low Sunday, Quasimodo.
belommerd *b. n.* shady.
belonen *o. w.* reward; recompense, remunerate; requite.
beloning *v.* reward; recompense, remuneration; requital.
belonken *o. w.* ogle at.
beloop *o.* (*gang, loop*) course, way; (*bedrag*) amount; (*sch.*) sweep.
belopen *o. w.* walk, tread; *on. w.* (*bedragen*) amount to, come to.
belopen *b. n.* bloodshot.
beloven *o. w.* promise.
beluisteren *o. w.* listen to; (*gen.*) auscultate, auscult.
belust *b. n.* — **op,** eager for, longing for, keen about.
bemachtigen *o. w.* seize, take possession of, make oneself master of; (*v. plaats, bestelling, enz.*) secure; (*wederrechtelijk*) usurp.
bemannen *o. w.* (*v. schip, loopgraaf*) man; (*v. vesting*) garrison.
bemanning *v.* (*v. schip*) crew, ship's company; (*v. vesting*) garrison.
bemantelen *o. w.* (*eig.*) cloak, cover with a cloak; (*fig.*) cloak, veil, palliate, disguise, gloss over, gloze over.
bemerken *o. w.* perceive, observe, notice, remark.
bemerking *v.* observation, remark.
bemesten *o. w.* manure, dung.
bemesting *v.* manuring, dunging.
bemiddelaar *m.* mediator, interposer, intercessor, intermediary, go-between.
bemiddeld *b. n.* in easy circumstances, well-off, well-to-do.
bemiddelen *o. w.* mediate; (*v. geschil*) adjust, settle.
bemiddeling *v.* mediation, intercession.
bemind *b. n.* loved, beloved.
beminde *m. en v.* lover, sweetheart, well-beloved.
beminnelijk *b. n.* lovable, lovely, amiable.
beminnelijkheid *v.* lovableness, loveliness, amiability. [cherish.
beminnen *o. w.* love, like, be fond of.
bemoedigen *o. w.* encourage, cheer, hearten.
bemoeien *w. w.* **zich — met,** meddle with, interfere in.

bemoeizucht *v.* meddlesomeness.
bemonsteren *o. w.* (*H.*) sample.
bemorsen *o. w.* soil, dirty, begrime.
benadelen *o. w.* hurt, harm; prejudice, injure.
benadeling *v.* hurting, harming; prejudice, injury.
benaderen *o. w.* (*beslag leggen op*) confiscate, seize; (*schatten*) estimate, compute roughly; (*nabijkomen*) approximate.
benadering *v.* (*beslaglegging*) confiscation, seizure; (*v. getallen, enz.*) approximation; **bij —,** approximately, by approximation.
benaming *v.* name, denomination, appellation.
benard *b. n.* critical, perilous.
benardheid *v.* distress; stringency.
benauwd *b. n.* (*bedompt*) stuffy, poky; (*beklemd*) oppressed, tight in the chest; (*drukkend*) close, sultry; (*eng, nauw*) tight; (*bang*) fearful, timid, afraid; (*angstig*) anxious; (*v. droom*) bad.
benauwdheid *v.* (*beklemming op de borst*) oppression, breathing spasm; closeness, sultriness; (*angst*) anxiety, fear.
bende *v.* (*v. soldaten*) troop, body; (*v. dieven, enz.*) band, gang, set; (*v. bedelaars*) horde; (*v. oproerlingen*) band.
beneden *vz.* under, below, beneath; (*in huis*) downstairs, down.
benedenhuis *o.* lower maisonnette, lower half-house; ground-floor, downstairs house.
benedenverdieping *v.* ground-floor.
benemen *o. w.* take away; *w. w.* **zich het leven —,** make away with oneself, take one's (own) life.
benepen *b. n.* (*v. ruimte : klein*) confined, poky, cramped; (*v. gelaat*) pinched; (*kleinzielig*) small-minded, pusillanimous, petty.
beneveld *b. n.* foggy, misty, hazy; (*v. verstand*) muzzy, muddled; (*licht dronken*) fuddled, muzzy.
benevelen *o. w.* fog; (*v. verstand, oordeel*) befog, cloud; (*door drank*) fuddle, bemuse.
benevens *vz.* (together) with, besides, in addition to.
bengel *m.* pickle, urchin, naughty boy.
bengelen *on. w.* (*luiden*) ring; (*slingeren*) dangle; swing.
benieuwen *o. w.* **het zal mij — of,** I wonder if.
benig *b. n.* bony; osseous.
benijdbaar *b. n.* enviable.
benijden *o. w.* envy, be envious of.
benijdenswaardig *b. n.* enviable.
benijder *m.* envier, envious (jealous) person.
benodigdheden *v. mv.* requisites; requirements, necessaries; (*toneel*) properties.
benoemd *b. n.* — **getal,** concrete number.

benoeming *r.* appointment, nomination.

benutten, benuttigen *o. w.* utilize, avail oneself of, make use of, make the most of.

benzine *v.* benzine; (*v. motoren*) petrol, motor-spirit.

beoefenaar *m.* (*v. taal, kunst*) practiser, student; (*liefhebber: v. sport, enz.*) votary, amateur; (*v. kunst, enz.*) cultivator.

beoefenen *o. w.* (*v. wetenschap, kunst*) study, cultivate; (*v. beroep*) follow, practise, exercise; (*v. deugd*) practise.

beoefening *v.* study, cultivation; practice.

beogen *o. w.* have in view, aim at, contemplate.

beoordeling *v.* judgment; (*v. boek; enz.*) review, criticism.

bepaald *b. n.* (*vastgesteld*) fixed; (*stellig, beslist: v. antwoord, weigering, enz.*) positive, absolute, definite; (*duidelijk omschreven*) well-defined; distinct, determinate, definite; (*gram.*) definite; *bw.* fixedly; positively, absolutely; distinctly, determinately, definitely.

bepalen *o. w.* (*vaststellen*) (*v. prijs*) fix; (*r. tijd*) fix, appoint; (*v. voorwaarden*) stipulate; (*berekenen*) determine, ascertain; (*voorschrijven*) provide; (*v. wet*) ordain, prescribe; (*regelen*) arrange, determine; (*omschrijven*) define; *w. w.* **zich — tot,** restrict (confine) oneself to.

bepaling *v.* fixing; stipulation; regulation, prescription, provision; determination, ascertainment; definition; adjunct.

bepantsering *r.* armouring, armour-plating.

bepeinzen *o. w.* meditate on, ruminate on, muse on.

beperken *o. w.* limit, confine, set bounds to; (*v. uitgaven, enz.*) reduce, retrench; (*r. rechten*) restrict; (*r. brand*) keep down, keep within bounds; (*betekenis v. woord*) modify, qualify; *w. w.* **zich — tot,** restrict (confine) oneself to.

beperkt *b. n.* limited; narrow; confined.

bepraten *o. w.* (*iets: praten over*) talk about, talk over, discuss; (*iemand: bepraten*) talk... over, talk... round, persuade.

beproefd *b. n.* well-tried; (*r. methode*) approved; (*r. middel*) approved, efficacious.

beproeven *o. w.* (*onderzoeken, proberen*) try, endeavour, attempt; (*op de proef stellen*) try, test; (*met ziekte, tegenspoed*) visit, afflict.

beproeving *r.* trial, test; visitation, affliction.

beraad *o.* deliberation; consideration.

beraadslagen *on. w.* deliberate (**over,** on, upon); **— met,** consult with, confer with.

beraadslaging *r.* deliberation, consultation.

beraden *b. n.* well-considered, well-advised, considerate, deliberate; resolute; *w. w.* **zich —,** consider, think it over; change one's mind, think better of it.

beramen *o. w.* (*v. middelen, plannen: bedenken*) devise, project, contrive; (*v. complot*) concoct, lay; (*v. aanval, enz.*) conspire, plot; (*schatten*) estimate.

beraming *r.* projection; concoction; conspiration, plotting; estimate, estimation.

berechten *o. w.* (*kath.: bedienen*) administer the last sacraments to; (*recht: behandelen*) try; (*uitspraak doen*) adjudicate, adjudge.

berechting *v.* administration of the last sacraments; trial; adjudication, adjudment.

beredderen *o. w.* arrange, put in order.

bereden *b. n.* (*v. politie, enz.*) mounted; (*v. paard*) broken(-in).

bereid *b. n.* (*gereed*) ready, prepared; (*geneigd*) disposed, willing.

bereiden *o. w.* (*r. maaltijden, enz.*) prepare; (*v. leer*) dress, curry; (*r. onthaal*) give.

bereidvaardig, bereidwillig *b. n.* ready, willing; *bw.* readily, willingly, with alacrity.

bereidwilligheid *v.* readiness, willingness.

bereik *o.* reach, range.

bereikbaar *b. n.* attainable, within-reach.

bereiken *o. w.* reach, attain.

bereisd *b. n.* (*v. persoon*) (much-)travelled; (*v. streek, land*) much-travelled, much-frequented.

berekend *b. n.* calculating.

berekenen *o. w.* (*uitrekenen*) calculate, compute; (*in rekening brengen*) charge.

berekening *r.* calculation, computation; charge.

berg *m.* mountain, mount.

bergachtig *b. n.* mountainous.

bergaf *bw.* downhill.

bergbewoner *m.* mountaineer; (*in Schotland*) highlander.

bergen *o. w.* (*opslaan, wegleggen*) store, warehouse; (*plaatsen*) put, store; (*v. gestrand schip*) salve; (*verbergen*) hide, conceal; (*bevatten*) hold, contain; (*sch.: v. zeil*) take in; (*r. lijk*) recover; *w. w.* **zich —,** save oneself, get out of the way.

Bergen *o.* (*België*) Mons; (*Noorwegen*) Bergen.

bergengte *r.* narrow pass, mountain-pass, defile.

bergkloof *r.* ravine, gorge, cleft, gully.

bergland *o.* mountainous country, highlands.

bergop *bw.* uphill.

bergpas *m.* mountain-pass, defile.

bergrat *v.* dormouse, marmot.

bergstroom *m.* mountain-stream, torrent.

bergzout *o.* rock-salt.

bericht *o.* (*nieuws*) news, tidings; (*kennisgeving*) notice, intimation, communication; (*H.*) advice, report, communication; (*dagblad*—) paragraph, newspaper report; (*nieuwtje*) piece of information, piece of intelligence.

berichten *o. w.* let know, inform, send word, write word; (*H., ook:*) advise; (*kennis geven van*) give notice of.

berichtgever *m.* informant; (*v. dagblad: verslaggever*) reporter.

berijdbaar *b. n.* (*v. weg*) practicable, passable; (*voor fiets, ook:*) ridable, rideable; (*v. dier, fiets*) rideable.

berijden *o. w.* (*v. weg*) ride over; (*v. paard*) ride.

berin *v.* she-bear.

berispelijk *b. n.* blamable, reprovable, reprehensible, censurable.

berispen *o. w.* blame, reprove, reprehend, censure.

berisping *v.* blame, reproof, reprimand, reprehension, rebuke.

berk, berkeboom *m.* birch.

berm *m.* (*v. weg*) border; (*mil.*) berm.

beroemd *b. n.* famous, celebrated, illustrious, renowned.

beroemdheid *v.* fame, celebrity, illustriousness, renown.

beroemen *w. w. zich — op,* pride oneself on, glory in; (*bluffen*) boast of, brag of.

beroep *o.* (*werkkring*) occupation, calling; (*ambacht*) trade; (*in vrije beroepen*) profession; (*zaak*) business; (*recht*) appeal; (*prot.: v. predikant*) call, invitation.　　　　　　　　[profession.

beroepshalve *bw.* by virtue of one's

beroepsspeler *m.* professional (player).

beroerd *b. n.* miserable, pitiful, unpleasant; (*v. weer, enz.*) rotten, beastly.

beroeren *o. w.* stir, disturb, perturb, trouble.

beroering *v.* disturbance, perturbation, trouble; agitation, commotion.

beroerte *v.* (paralytic) stroke, (apoplectic) fit, stroke of apoplexy.

berokkenen *o. w.* cause, give.

berouw *o.* repentance, contrition; (*spijt*) compunction; (*wroeging*) remorse.

berouwen *o. w.* repent (of), regret.

beroven *o. w.* rob, spoliate; deprive, bereave.

beroving *v.* robbery, spoliation, deprivation.

berrie *v.* barrow, handbarrow, stretcher; (*lijkbaar*) bier.

berucht *b. n.* (*v. inbreker, enz.*) notorious; (*v. persoon, huis*) disreputable, illfamed, of ill fame.

beruchtheid *v.* notoriousness, notoriety; disreputableness, disrepute.

berusten *on. w. — bij,* (*v. stukken, enz.*) be deposited with, rest with; (*v. rechten, enz.*) be vested in; — *in,* acquiesce in, submit to, reconcile oneself to, resign oneself to; (*in behandeling, belediging, enz.*) put up with.

berusting *v.* acquiescence, submission, resignation.

bes *v.* berry; (*aalbes*) currant; (*muz.*) B flat.

beschaafd *b. n.* (*v. volk*) civilized; (*welgemanierd*) well-bred, polite, refined, polished; (*ontwikkeld*) cultivated; educated, cultured.

beschaamd *b. n.* ashamed, feeling shame; abashed, shame-faced.

beschaamdheid *v.* shame, shamefacedness, bashfulness.

beschadigen *o. w.* damage, hurt.

beschadiging *v.* damage, hurt.

beschamen *o. w.* put to shame, shame, abash, confound; (*v. hoop, verwachtingen*) disappoint, falsify.

beschaming *v.* confusion, shame; disappointment.

beschaven *o. w.* plane; (*fig.*) polish, refine; (*v. wilden*) civilize.

beschaving *v.* civilization, culture.

bescheid *o.* (*inlichting*) information; (*antwoord*) answer, reply; —en, documents, records, papers.

bescheiden *o. w.* (*ontbieden*) summon, order to appear, send for; appoint; (*toebedelen*) allot, apportion; *b. n.* (*bw.*) modest(ly), unassuming(ly), unpretending(ly), unpretetious(ly), unobtrusive(ly).

beschermeling *m. en v.* protégé(e).

beschermen *o. w.* protect, screen, shelter.

beschermer *m.* protector; patron.

beschermheilige *m. en v.* patron, patron saint.

bescherming *v.* protection; (*beschutting*) shelter, cover, protection; (*steun*) patronage.

beschieten *o. w.* (*mil.*) fire upon (at), cannonade, bombard, shell; (*bekleden*) case, line; (*met hout*) board, wainscot, plank.

beschieting *v.* bombardment, firing cannonade, shelling.

beschijnen *o. w.* shine upon, light up; (*verlichten*) illuminate, illumine.

beschikbaar *b. n.* available, at a person's disposal.

beschikbaarheid *v.* availability.

beschikken *o. w.* arrange, manage, order, dispose; *on. w. — over,* have the disposal of, have at one's disposal; (*soms:*) dispose of.

beschikking *v.* disposal, disposition, command; (*regeling*) arrangement; (*besluit*) decree, ordinance.

beschilderen *o. w.* paint.

beschimmelen *on. w.* grow (get) mouldy, mildew.

beschimpen *o. w.* revile, taunt, rail at, scoff at, jeer (at).

beschimper *m.* reviler, scoffer, jeerer.

beschoeien *o. w.* campshed, camp-sheet.

beschonken *b. n.* drunk, tipsy, intoxicated.

beschouwen *o. w.* consider, regard; (*bezien*) view, look at, contemplate.

beschouwing v. contemplation, consideration; contemplation, reflection, speculation; view, way of thinking; observation; dissertation.

beschrijven o. w. (vol schrijven) write all over, cover with writing; (schrijven op) write upon; (meetk.) describe, construct; (te boek stellen) describe; (v. vergadering: bijeenroepen) convoke, convene.

beschrijvend b. n. descriptive.

beschrijving v. description.

beschroomd b. n. timid, timorous, fearful, bashful, diffident, shy.

beschroomdheid v. timidity, timorousness, bashfulness, diffidence, shyness.

beschuit v. rusk, biscuit.

beschuldigde m. en v. **de —,** the accused.

beschuldigen o. w. accuse (of), incriminate, charge (**van,** with); (gerechtelijk) indict (**van,** for); (v. staatsmisdrijf) impeach (**van,** of).

beschuldiger m. accuser.

beschuldiging v. accusation, charge; indictment; impeachment.

beschut b. n. sheltered; protected.

beschutten o. w. shelter, protect screen.

besef o. (begrip) notion, idea, sense; (bewustzijn) realization, consciousness.

beseffen o. w. realize.

beslaan o. w. (v. paard) shoe; (v. wiel) tire; (v. vat) hoop; (met zilver, enz.) mount; (met leder, enz.) cover; (met nagels) stud, set; (sch.: bodem v. schip) sheathe; (v. zeil) make up, furl; (v. beslag) beat up; (v. ruimte: innemen) take up, occupy; on. w. (v. glas, enz.: door waterdamp) get dim, become dimmed (steamed); (v. metaal: dof worden) tarnish; (v. vloeistoffen) chill.

beslag o. (als versiering) mount, mounting; (v. deur) iron work; (v. vat) bands, hoops; (v. stok) tip, ferrule; (v. wiel) tire; (v. paard) (horse-)shoes; (v. schip) sheathing; (voor gebak) batter; (op tong) fur, coating; (voor brouwsel) mash; (recht: beslaglegging) attachment, seizure, distraint, distrainment, distress; (op schip) embargo; — **leggen op,** attach, seize, distrain on; (op schip) lay (put) an embargo on.

beslaglegging v. seizure, attachment, distraint, distress.

beslechten o. w. settle, arrange, compose, make up.

beslissen o. w. decide (**over,** on); (scheidsrechterlijk) arbitrate.

beslissend b. n. decisive; determining, determinant; critical; final; conclusive; casting; bw. decisively; determinately.

beslissing v. decision, determination, resolution.

beslist b. n. decided; resolute, peremptory, firm; bw. decidedly; peremptorily.

beslommering v. care, trouble, worry.

besloten b. n. resolved, resolute,

determined; (v. vergadering, terrein) private.

besluit o. (slotsom, gevolgtrekking) conclusion; (einde, afloop) conclusion, close, end, termination; (beslissing) resolve, resolution, determination, decision; (v. vergadering) resolution; (v. overheid) decree; **Koninklijk —,** Order in Council, Royal Warrant.

besluiteloosheid v. indecision, irresolution, wavering.

besluiten o. w. (een besluit nemen) resolve, decide, determine; (een gevolgtrekking maken) conclude, infer; (eindigen) end, conclude; (omsluiten, omvatten) contain, enclose, include.

besmetten o. w. contaminate, infect; (fig.) pollute, taint, stain.

besmetting v. contagion, infection, contamination; pollution, taint.

besnijdenis v. circumcision.

besnoeiing v. lopping, pruning; clipping; curtailment, retrenchment, cut, cutting-down.

bespannen o. w. (v. viool, raket, enz.) string; (v. paarden: inspannen) put to.

besparen o. w. save, economize; (v. moeite, leed) save, spare.

besparing v. saving, economization.

bespeuren o. w. perceive, discover, descry, observe.

bespieden o. w. spy on (upon), watch.

bespieder m. spy, watcher.

bespiegelend b. n. **—e wijsbegeerte,** speculative philosophy; **een — leven,** a contemplative life.

bespoedigen o. w. accelerate, hasten, expedite, forward; precipitate.

bespottelijk b. n. ridiculous, ludicrous, laughable; bw. ridiculously, ludicrously, laughably.

bespotten o. w. ridicule, deride, mock.

bespreken o. w. (spreken over) talk about, speak about, discuss; (vooruit huren, enz.) book, engage, secure, reserve; (v. boek, enz.) review; (aankondigen) notice; (v. legaat, bij testament) bequeath.

bespreking v. discussion; (v. plaats) booking; (v. boek) review; notice.

besproeien o. w. (v. bloemen, enz.) water; (v. land) irrigate; (met tranen) moisten, wet.

best b. n. best; very good; dear; bw. very well; best; z. n., o. best.

bestaan on. w. exist, be; — **in,** consist in; — **uit,** consist of, be composed of; z. n., o. (het zijn) being, existence; (kostwinning) subsistence.

bestand b. n. — **tegen,** proof against; (opgewassen tegen) equal to.

bestand o. truce.

bestanddeel o. element, component part, constituent part, ingredient.

bestedeling m. en v. pauper; almsman, almswoman; charity-child.

besteden o. w. (v. geld) spend, lay out; (v. prijs) pay; (v. tijd) spend; (v. aan-

dacht) give, devote; (*in de kost doen*)
put out to board (*bij*, with).
bestek *o.* (*bouwk.*) specification, speci-
fications and conditions, estimate;
(*sch.*) reckoning; (*ruimte*) space, compass.
bestelen *o. w.* rob, plunder.
bestelfiets *v.* carrier-cycle.
bestelgoed *o.* parcels.
bestellen *o. w.* order; (*bezorgen*) deliver;
(*regelen*) order, arrange; (*v. persoon:
ontbieden*) appoint.
bestelling *v.* (*v. post*) delivery; (*H.*)
order, commission; (*bestelde goederen*)
goods (articles) ordered.
bestemmen *o. w.* destine; (*v. geld*)
earmark, set apart; (*v. dag, enz.*)
appoint, fix.
bestemming *v.* destination; (*lot*)
destiny, (appointed) lot.
bestendig *b. n.* (*duurzaam*) durable,
constant, lasting; (*vast, niet veranderend*) continuous, continual, incessant;
(*v. weer*) settled; (*v. barometer*) set fair;
(*v. karakter*) steady, steadfast, firm.
bestendigen *o. w.* continue, perpetuate;
confirm, continue.
bestijgen *o. w.* (*v. berg*) climb, ascend;
(*v. paard*) mount; (*v. troon*) mount,
ascend. [ing.
bestijging *v.* climbing, ascent; mount-
bestoken *o. w.* (*v. vijand*) harass; (*van
vesting*) shell, cannonade, batter.
bestormen *o. w.* (*v. vesting*) storm,
assault, rush; (*met vragen, enz.*) assail,
bombard; (*met verzoeken, enz.*) besiege.
bestorming *v.* storming, assault, rush;
(*v. bank*) run.
bestoven *b. n.* covered with dust, dusty;
(*Pl.*) pollinated.
bestraffen *o. w.* punish, chastise; (*berispen*) reprimand.
bestrating *v.* paving; pavement.
bestrijden *o. w.* fight (against), combat; (*betwisten*) dispute, contest, con-
trovert; (*v. voorstel, vordering*) oppose;
(*v. onkosten*) defray, cover, bear; (*v.
misbruiken, enz.*) battle with.
bestrijken *o. w.* stroke, pass one's hand
over; cover, spread (over); command;
cover, sweep, enfilade, flank.
besturen *o. w.* (*v. land, enz.*) govern,
rule; (*v. goed, enz.*) manage, administer;
(*v. zaak*) conduct; run; (*v. auto, wagen*)
drive; (*v. schip*) steer; (*v. vliegtuig*) pilot.
bestuur *o.* government, rule; reign;
administration, management, direction; board (of directors, of managers);
executive; committee.
bestuurbaar *b. n.* manageable, direct-
able, navigable, steerable; (*v. ballon*)
dirigible.
bestuurder *m.* governor; manager,
administrator, director; (*v. tram*) driver,
motorman; (*v. vliegtuig*) pilot.
betaalbaar *b. n.* payable.
betaaldag *m.* day of payment; pay-
day; quarter-day.

betaalmiddel *o.* tender, circulating
medium.
betalen *o. w.* pay.
betaling *v.* payment.
betamelijk *b. n.* proper, decent, becoming, seemly; *bw.* properly &c.
betamen *on. w.* become, behove, be
becoming, be seemly.
betekenen *o. w.* (*willen zeggen*) signify,
mean; (*voorspellen*) spell, betoken, forebode, signify; (*recht: v. dagvaarding*)
serve.
betekenis *v.* signification, meaning,
sense; (*gewicht, belang*) importance,
consequence, significance.
beter *b. n. en bw.* better.
beteren *on. w.* become better, get
better, improve; (*v. zieke, ook:*) recover
(one's health); *o. w.* **ik kan het niet
—,** I cannot help it; *w. w.* **zich —,**
mend one's ways, reform.
beterschap *v.* improvement, change for
the better; amendment; recovery.
beteugelen *o. w.* bridle, curb, rein in,
check, restrain.
beteuterd *b. n.* confused, perplexed.
betichten *on. w.* **iem. van iets —,**
accuse a person of something, impute
something to a person.
betichting *v.* accusation, imputation.
betitelen *o. w.* title, entitle, style, address.
betogen *o. w.* demonstrate, argue.
betoger *m.* demonstrator.
betoging *v.* demonstration.
beton *o.* concrete.
betonen *o. w.* show; manifest.
betoog *o.* demonstration, argument,
argumentation.
betoveren *o. w.* bewitch, enchant;
(*fig. ook:*) fascinate, charm.
betovering *v.* enchantment, bewitchment, fascination, spell, (magic) glamour.
betrappen *o. w.* (*trappen op*) tread
(upon); (*fig.*) catch, detect.
betreffen *o. w.* concern, touch, regard,
affect; **wat mij betreft,** as for me, for
my part.
betreffende *vz.* concerning, regarding,
with regard to, respecting, relative to.
betrekkelijk *b. n.* comparative; (*v.
voornaamwoord, enz.*) relative; *bw.*
comparatively, relatively.
betrekken *o. w.* (*v. goederen*) get,
order, obtain; (*v. huis, enz.*) move
into, take possession of; (*v. winterkwar-
tieren*) go into, move into, take up;
(*v. wacht*) mount; *on. w.* (*v. lucht*)
become overcast, cloud over; (*v. gelaat*)
cloud over, fall.
betrekking *v.* (*verhouding*) relation;
(*ambt, plaats*) place, situation, position;
met — tot, in relation to, with regard
to, in respect of.
betreuren *o. w.* regret; deplore, lament,
bewail; (*overledene*) mourn for.
betrokken *b. n.* (*v. lucht*) cloudy overcast; (*v. gelaat*) clouded; drawn.
betrokkene *m.* (*H.: v. wissel*) drawee

the person in question, the person concerned; **de —n,** the parties (persons) involved.
betrouwbaar *b. n.* reliable, trustworthy, dependable.
betrouwen *o. w.* trust, confide.
betten *o. w.* (*v. wond*) bathe; (*v. ogen*) dab, bathe; (*warm —*) stupe.
betuigen *o. w.* testify; attest, declare, certify.
betwijfelen *o. w.* doubt, question, call in question.
betwistbaar *b. n.* contestable, disputable, challengeable; (*v. gebied, enz.*) debatable; (*twijfelachtig*) questionable.
betwisten *o. w.* contest, dispute, challenge; (*v. vordering*) resist; (*ontkennen*) deny.
beu *b. n.* tired (of), disgusted (with).
beugel *m.* ring, strap, clip, bow; (*v. beurs*) clasp, frame; (*v. fles*) wire stople-holder, clasp; (*v. sabel*) guard, sword-guard; (*v. tram*) bow, contact-bow, overhead-arm; (*v. mand*) handle; (*v. hangslot*) shackle; (*sch.: v. kompas*) gimbal(s); (*v. riem*) chape; (*bij 't vissen*) trawl-head; (*voor been*) leg-iron.
beuk *m.* (*v. kerk: midden—*) nave; (*zij—*) aisle.
beuk *m.* **beukeboom** *m.* beech.
beukenoot *v.* beech-nut.
beul *m.* executioner, hangman, headsman; (*fig.*) brute, tyrant.
beuling *v.* sausage, (black) pudding.
beunhaas *m.* interloper, pettifogger; dabbler; (*op effectenbeurs*) outside broker.
beurs *v.* (*voor geld*) purse; (*studie—*) scholarship, exhibition; (*Sc.*) bursary; (*gebouw*) Exchange; (*buiten Engeland ook:*) Bourse; (*kath.*) bursa; (*Pl.*) volva.
beursnotering *v.* stock-exchange quotation(s), official list, stock-list.
beursstudent *m.* exhibitioner, foundationer; (*Sc.*) bursar.
beurt *v.* turn.
beurtelings *bw.* by turns, turn (and turn) about, in turn, in rotation, alternately.
beuzelachtig *b. n.* trifling, fiddling, futile, trivial, paltry.
bevaarbaar *b. n.* navigable.
bevallen *o. w.* (*behagen*) please, suit; (*voldoen*) give satisfaction; *on. w.* be confined, be delivered (*van,* of).
bevallig *b. n.* charming, graceful, amiable.
bevalling *v.* confinement, delivery, accouchement.
bevangen *o. w.* seize.
bevattelijk *b. n.* (*v. persoon: vlug v. begrip*) intelligent, teachable; (*v. zaak: gemakkelijk te begrijpen*) comprehensible, intelligible, lucid, clear; *bw.* intelligibly, comprehensibly.
bevatten *o. w.* (*inhouden*) contain, hold, comprise; (*begrijpen*) comprehend, grasp, conceive.

bevechten *o. w.* figt (against), combat.
beveiligen *o. w.* protect, safeguard, secure (*tegen,* against), shelter (*tegen,* from).
bevel *o.* order, command; (*recht*) injunction; (*dicht.*) behest.
bevelen *o. w.* (*gebieden, gelasten*) order, command, charge; (*toevertrouwen*) commend, recommend.
bevelhebber *m.* commander.
bevelschrift *o.* warrant; mandate.
beven *on. w.* (*van angst, enz.*) tremble; (*van koude*) shiver, shake, quake; (*van ouderdom*) dodder; (*v. stem*) quiver, quaver.
bever *m. en o.* (*dier; bont*) beaver.
bevestigen *o. w.* (*vastmaken*) fix, fasten, attach; (*mil.: v. stad*) fortify; (*v. macht, enz.*) consolidate; (*v. vriendschap, verbond, enz.*) cement; (*v. bericht, gerucht*) confirm; (*v. verklaring, mening, enz.*) corroborate, fortify, bear out; (*prot.: v. lidmaat*) confirm; (*v. predikant*) induct, institute.
bevestiging *v.* fastening; fortification; consolidation; cementing; confirmation; corroboration; induction.
bevinden *o. w.* find; *w. w.* **zich —,** be; (*het maken*) be, feel.
bevinding *v.* experience; (*v. commissie, enz.*) finding.
bevlekken *o. w.* spot, stain, soil; defile, pollute.
bevochtigen *o. w.* moisten; damp, wet.
bevoegd *b. n.* (*door wet, gezag*) competent; (*door kennis, na examen*) qualified; (*gemachtigd*) authorized, entitled.
bevoegdheid *v.* competence, competency; qualification; authority; power.
bevolken *o. w.* people; populate.
bevolking *v.* (*handeling*) peopling; (*bewoners*) population.
bevolkt *b. n.* populated.
bevooroordeeld *b. n.* prejudiced, prepossessed, bias(s)ed.
bevoorrechten *o. w.* privilege, favour.
bevorderen *o. w.* (*v. zaak, wetenschap, enz.*) promote, advance; further; (*v. eetlust*) stimulate; (*v. spijsvertering*) aid; (*v. gezondheid*) benefit, be beneficial to; (*tot ambt*) prefer; (*in rang*) promote; (*v. leerling*) move up to a higher form (class).
bevrachten *o. w.* freight, charter; (*laden*) load.
bevrachting *v.* freighting, chartering.
bevragen *o. w.* **te — bij,** apply to, inquire of (at).
bevredigen *o. w.* (*v. persoon*) pacify, conciliate; (*v. wensen, enz.*) gratify; (*v. hartstochten*) indulge; (*v. honger, enz.*) appease, satisfy; (*bevrediging geven*) satisfy, give satisfaction.
bevredigend *b. n.* satisfactory.
bevreemden *o. w.* **het bevreemdt mij,** I wonder at it, I am surprised at it.
bevreesd *b. n.* afraid.

bevriend *b. n.* friendly; on friendly terms, intimate.

bevriezen *on. w.* freeze (over), congeal; (*v. aardappelen, enz.*) become frosted; (*dooàvriezen*) freeze to death; *o. w.* freeze, congeal.

bevrijden *o. w.* free (**van,** from, of), deliver (**van,** from); (*in vrijheid stellen*) set free, set at liberty, release, liberate; (*r. gevaar*) rescue; (*vrijmaken: v. slaven, enz.*) emancipate.

bevrijding *v.* deliverance, delivery; release, liberation; rescue; emancipation.

bevroeden *o. w.* (*begrijpen, inzien*) understand, realize, apprehend; (*vermoeden*) suspect, presume.

bevruchten *o. w.* fecundate, fructify, impregnate; (*Pl.*) fertilize.

bevuilen *o. w.* dirty, foul, befoul, soil.

bewaarder *m.* keeper, guardian, custodian; (*in gevangenis*) warder; (*huis—*) care-taker.

bewaarkluis *v.* safe deposit vault.

bewaarplaats *v.* depository, storehouse; (*kinder—*) day-nursery.

bewaarschool *r.* infant school, kindergarten.

bewaken *o. w.* watch; (keep) watch over, guard.

bewaker *m.* keeper, guard, watcher; (*in gevangenis*) warder.

bewapenen *o. w.* arm.

bewaren *o. w.* (*v. vlees, vruchten, enz.* preserve, conserve; (*r. geheim, stilzwijgen, enz.*) keep; (*v. ernst, waardigheid*) maintain, keep up; (*besparen*) save, spare.

bewaring *v.* preservation, conservation; keeping; custody; **in — geven,** (*r. bagage, geld*) deposit.

beweegbaar *b. n.* movable.

beweeglijk *b. n.* (*beweegbaar*) movable; (*v. trekken, enz.*) mobile; (*levendig*) lively, mercurial; (*onrustig*) fidgety; (*licht geroerd*) susceptible.

beweegreden *v.* motive, reason.

bewegen *on. w.* move; stir; *o. w.* (*in beweging brengen*) move; budge; (*overhalen, overreden*) move, induce, prevail upon, persuade; (*ontroeren*) move, affect; *w. w.* **zich —,** move, stir; (*verroeren*) budge.

beweging *r.* motion, movement, stir; (*met hand, arm, enz.*) motion; (*lichaams—*) exercise; (*gemoeds—*) emotion; (*opwinding*) commotion, excitement; (*drukte*) agitation, stir; (*fam.*) bustle.

bewenen *o. w.* mourn over (for), weep over (for), deplore, lament, bewail.

beweren *o. w.* assert, maintain, contend, claim; (*wat nog niet bewezen is*) allege; (*voorgeven*) pretend.

bewering *v.* assertion, contention; allegation.

bewerken *o. w.* (*met werktuigen, bearbeiden*) work, dress; (*v. grond*) till, cultivate; (*v. ijzer*) hammer, beat; (*v. deeg, boter,*

enz.) work; (*vervaardigen*) manufacture; (*vormen*) fashion, model; (*v. onderwerp*) work up; (*v. woordenboek, enz.*) compile; (*opnieuw —*) rewrite, revise; (*omwerken*) remodel; (*veroorzaken, tot stand brengen*) cause, effect, operate, bring about; (*v. persoon: beïnvloeden*) influence, operate upon, manage.

bewerker *m.* author, originator; (*v. onheil, enz.*) worker; (*v. boek, enz.*) compiler; reviser; adapter; artificer.

bewerking *v.* working; tillage, cultivation; compilation; revision; manipulation; adaptation; dramatization; orchestration, arrangement; (*afwerking, wijze v. bewerken*) workmanship; (*rek.*) operation.

bewieroken *o. w.* incense; (*fig.*) praise (laud) to the skies, incense.

bewijs *o.* proof, evidence; (*bewijsvoering, het bewijzen*) demonstration; argumentation; (*bewijsgrond*) argument; (*bewijsstuk*) voucher, (piece of) evidence; certificate; (*attest*) certificate, testimonial, testimony; (*blijk*) mark, vidence, token.

bewijsbaar *b. n.* demonstrable, provable, capable of proof.

bewijzen *o. w.* (*juistheid v. iets: aantonen*) prove, demonstrate; evidence; establish, make out; (*betonen*) (*gunst, weldaad*) confer; (*dienst*) render; (*vriendschap, dankbaarheid*) show.

bewilligen *on. v.* **— in,** grant, concede, consent to, agree to, acquiesce in.

bewind *o.* government, administration, management.

bewindvoerder *m.* director, manager, administrator; (*in faillissement*) trustee.

bewogen *b. n.* moved, agitated; (*fig.*) moved; affected.

bewolken *o. w.* cloud; *on. w.* cloud over (up), become cloudy, become overcast.

bewonderen *o. w.* admire.

bewondering *v.* admiration.

bewonen *o. w.* inhabit, live in, occupy, reside in.

bewoner *m.* (*r. land, stad, enz.*) inhabitant; (*v. huis*) occupant, occupier, tenant, inmate; (*v. kamer*) occupant; (*v. bos, water, enz.*) denizen.

bewoonbaar *b. n.* inhabitable.

bewoording(en) *v.* (*mv.*) wording, terms.

bewust *b. n.* (*besef hebbend van*) conscious; (*bekend, bedoeld*) in question.

bewusteloos *b. n.* unconscious, senseless, insensible.

bewustzijn *o.* consciousness, (full) knowledge.

bezadigd *b. n.* sober-minded, soberblooded, sedate, staid, cool-headed.

bezegelen *o. w.* seal; (*fig.*) seal, put (set) the seal to.

bezem *m.* broom; (*r. twijgen*) besom.

bezeren *o. w.* hurt, injure; *w. w.* **zich —,** hurt oneself.

bezet *b. n.* (*v. plaats: in beslag genomen*) taken, engaged; (*r. persoon, tijd, enz.*)

engaged, occupied; (*mil.: v. stad, enz.*) occupied, under occupation; (*met diamanten, enz.*) set, stuck.
bezeten *b. n.* possessed.
bezetene *m. en v.* one possessed.
bezetsel *o.* trimming.
bezetten *o. w.* (*v. post, vacature*) fill; (*mil.: v. stad, enz.*) occupy; (*v. plaats*) take; (*met diamant, enz.*) set; (*v. rol, toneelstuk*) cast; (*v. loopgraven*) garrison, mount.
bezetting *v.* (*v. post*) filling; (*v. stad*) occupation; (*garnizoen*) garrison; (*v. orkest*) strength; (*v. toneelstuk*) cast.
bezichtigen *o. w.* view, inspect, (have) a look at; *te* —, on view.
bezichtiging *v.* view, inspection; examination.
bezield *b. n.* animated, inspired.
bezielen *o. w.* inspire, inspirit, animate.
bezieling *v.* animation, inspiration.
bezienswaardig *b. n.* worth seeing, worth being looked at.
bezig *b. n.* busy, occupied, engaged.
bezigheid *v.* occupation, employment, business. [busy.
bezighouden *o. w.* keep at work, keep
bezijden *bw.* beside, at the side of.
bezingen *o. w.* sing (of); (*dicht.*) chant.
bezinksel *o.* deposit, deposition, sediment, dregs, lees; (*scheik.*) residuum.
bezinnen *on. w.* reflect; *w. w. zich* —, (*overdenken*) think, reflect, consider; (*van gedachten veranderen*) change one's mind, think better of it.
bezinning *v.* consciousness.
bezit *o.* possession; (*v. effecten*) holding(s); (*tegenover schulden*) assets; (*fig., ook:*) asset.
bezitten *o. w.* possess, own, have.
bezitter *m.* possessor, proprietor, owner.
bezoedelen *o. w.* soil, stain; (*fig.*) tarnish, besmirch, bespatter, sully; defile, contaminate, pollute.
bezoek *o.* visit; (*kort, beleefdheids—*) call; (*personen*) visitors, company guests; (*v. school, enz.*) attendance; (*inspectie—*) visitation.
bezoeken *o. w.* visit; see, go to see, call on; (*v. school, kerk, enz.*) frequent; (*Bijb.*) visit; (*beproeven*) afflict, try.
bezoeker *m.* visitor, caller, guest; (*v. schouwburg*) theatre-goer; frequenter; (*v. concert*) concert-goer.
bezoldiging *v.* pay, salary, stipend.
bezondigen *w. w. zich* —, sin.
bezorgd *b. n.* anxious, solicitous, uneasy, apprehensive.
bezorgdheid *v.* anxiety, solicitude, uneasiness, apprehension.
bezorgen *o. w.* (*bestellen*) deliver, carry; (*verschaffen*) procure, get; (*veroorzaken*) cause, give, present; (*zorgen voor*) attend to, effect.
bezuinigen *o. w.* economize, retrench, reduce.
bezuinigingsmaatregel *m.* measure of economy.

bezwaar *o.* difficulty, objection; (*gewetens—*) scruple; (*grief*) grievance.
bezwaarlijk *b. n.* hard, difficult, onerous; *bw.* hardly, with difficulty.
bezwaren *o. w.* load, weight; (*fig.*) burden, oppress.
bezwarend *b. n.* aggravating; damaging; burdensome, onerous; damning.
bezweet *b. n.* perspiring, sweating, in a perspiration, in a sweat.
bezwering *v.* swearing; exorcism, conjuration; adjuration, conjuration.
bezwijken *on. w.* succumb.
bezwijmen *on. w.* faint (away), swoon, fall into a swoon.
bezwijming *v.* swoon, fainting fit, faint.
bibberen *on. w.* shiver; (*v. schrik*) tremble.
bidbankje *o.* praying-desk, praying-stool.
biddag *m.* day of prayer.
bidden *on. w.* pray, say one's prayers; *o. w.* pray; (*iem.*) entreat, implore, beg.
biecht *v.* confession.
biechteling *m.* confessant, penitent.
biechtstoel *m.* confessional.
biechtvader *m.* confessor.
bieden *o. w.* (*aanbieden*) offer, present; (*op verkoping*) bid, offer; *on. w.* bid.
biefstuk *m.* rumpsteak.
bier *o.* beer, ale.
bierglas *o.* beer-glass, tumbler.
bierwagen *m.* brewer's cart, dray-cart, dray.
bies *v.* (*Pl.*) rush, bulrush; (*op kleren*) piping; (*rand*) border.
biet *v.* beet.
big *v.* piglet, pigling.
bij *v.* bee.
bij *vz.* (*plaats*) by, with, near; *bw. hij is goed* —, he is all there, he has (all) his wits about him.
bijaldien *vw.* in case.
bijbaantje *o.* by-employment, by-job.
bijbedoeling *v.* by-end, by-design, by-purpose, be-intent, by-motive.
bijbehorend *b. n.* accessory, belonging to it; *met* —..., with... to match.
bijbel *m.* bible.
bijbelverklaring *v.* exegesis.
bijbetalen *o. w.* pay in addition, pay extra.
bijbetaling *v.* additional payment, extra payment.
bijblad *o.* supplement; extra sheet, supplementary sheet; (*Pl.*) stipule.
bijblijven *on. w.* (*gelijke tred houden*) keep pace; (*niet vergeten worden*) remain, stick in a person's memory.
bijbrengen *o. w.* (*bewijzen, argumenten*) bring forward, produce, adduce, allege; (*na bezwijming*) bring round, restore to consciousness; (*v. kennis, enz.*) impart, infuse; (*inprenten*) incalculate (upon a person).
bijdehand *b. n.* smart, bright, quickwitted, spry.
bijdraaien *on. w.* (*sch.*) heave to, bring to; (*fig.*) come round, swing round

bijdrage v. contribution.
bijeen bw. together.
bijeenbrengen o. w. bring together; (v. geld) collect.
bijeenkomen on. w. (bij elkaar komen) come together, meet (together), assemble; (bij elkaar passen) match, go together.
bijeenkomst v. meeting, assemblage, assembly.
bijeenroepen o. w. (v. Parlement) call together; (v. vergadering) convoke, convene, summon, call.
bijenhouder m. bee-keeper, bee-master, apiarist, hiver.
bijenteelt v. bee-culture, apiculture.
bijenwas o. en v. beeswax.
bijgaand b. n. enclosed, annexed.
bijgeloof o. superstition.
bijgenaamd b. n. surnamed, nicknamed.
bijgevolg bw. in consequence, consequently.
bijhouden o. w. (v. glas, enz.) hold out, reach out; (iem., iets) keep up, keep (pace) with; (Frans, Duits, enz.) keep up; (H.: v. boeken) keep up to date.
bijkaart v. (in atlas) inset, inset-map; (in spel) plain card, non-trump cards.
bijkantoor o. branch-office; (v. post) sub-office.
bijkomen on. w. (tot zich zelf komen) come to (oneself), come round, regain consciousness; (na ziekte, aankomen) put on flesh, put on weight, gain weight; (bijgevoegd worden) be added, be extra.
bijkomend b. n. (v. kosten) extra, incidental; (v. omstandigheden) attendant.
bijkomstigheid v. a mere accident, incidental, accidental circumstance.
bijl v. axe, hatchet; (dissel) adze.
bijlage v. annex, appendix, enclosure, accompanying paper, supplementary report.
bijleggen o. w. (er bij doen) add; (v. twist, geschil) accommodate, arrange, settle, compose.
bijna bw. almost, nearly, next to all but.
bijnaam m. (toenaam, tweede naam) surname, by-name; (spotnaam) nickname, sobriquet, by-name.
bijpassen o. w. pay in addition, supply; on. w. pay extra, pay the difference, pay the deficiency.
bijpassend b. n. to match.
bijrekenen o. w. add, include.
bijrivier v. affluent, tributary stream.
bijslag m. extra allowance.
bijstaan o. w. assist, help, succour, render assistance (to).
bijstand m. assistance, help, aid, succour.
bijster b. n. **het spoor — zijn**, have lost one's way; (fig.) be off one's have, be at fault, be at sea; bw. exceedingly; extremely.
bijt v. (in ijs) gap, hole; (voor brand) fire-hole.

bijten o. w. en on. w. bite.
bijtend b. n. biting, caustic, corrosive; (fig.) biting, caustic, cutting, poignant, trenchant, mordant.
bijtijds bw. (niet te laat, op tijd) in good time, in due time; (vroegtijdig) betimes, in good time.
bijvak o. subsidiary branch, side-subject.
bijval m. approval, approbation, applause.
bijverdienste v. extra profit, accidental profits, accessory revenue.
bijvoegen o. w. add; annex, append; (opmerkingen) subjoin; (insluiten) enclose.
bijvoeging v. addition.
bijvoeglijk b. n. adjectival; — **naamwoord**, adjective; bw. — **gebruikt**, used adjectively.
bijvoegsel o. addition; supplement, appendix, appendage.
bijvoorbeeld, for instance, for example.
bijwerken o. w. (v. boeken) write up, enter up; bring up to date; (v. schilderij, enz.) touch up, retouch; (v. achterstand) get up, overtake; (v. leerling) coach up.
bijwijlen bw. once in a while, now and then, at times.
bijwonen o. w. be present at, assist at; (v. vergadering, kerkdienst, enz.) attend.
bijwoord o. adverb.
bijwoordelijk b. n. (bw.) adverbial(ly).
bijzaak v. accessory-matter, subordinate matter, matter of secondary importance.
bijzetten o. w. (zetten bij) place near(er), put near; (begraven) inter, entomb, deposit (in the family vault); (sch.) set.
bijzetting v. deposition, interment.
bijziend b. n. near-sighted, myopic.
bijziendheid b. near-sightedness, myopy.
bijzijn o. presence.
bijzin m. subordinate clause.
bijzit v. concubine, mistress.
bijzonder b. n. (eigen, speciaal) particular, special; (privaat, niet openbaar) private; (eigenaardig) peculiar, strange; bw. particularly, specially; peculiarly; (buitengewoon) uncommonly, exceedingly.
bijzonderheid v. (abstract) particularity; (concreet) particular, detail; (eigenaardigheid) peculiarity.
bikhamer m. pick(-hammer).
bikkel m. knuckle-bone.
bil v. buttock; (v. dier) rump.
biljart o. (spel) billiards; (tafel) billiard-table.
biljartbal m. billiard-ball.
biljet o. (kaartje, v. spoor, enz.) ticket; (strooi—) handbill; (aanplak—) poster.
billijk b. n. just, equitable, reasonable; (v. prijs) moderate; (v. oordeel, behandeling) fair.
billijkerwijze bw. in equity, in reason, in justice, in fairness.
billijkheid v. equity, reasonableness; moderateness; fairness.

binden *o. w. (v. boek, schoven, enz.)* bind; *(v. lint, schoenen)* tie; *(v. zak, pak, enz.)* tie up; *(v. saus, soep, enz.)* thicken; *w. w.* **zich —,** tie one's own hands, bind oneself, commit oneself.

bindsel *o.* bandage, tie; *(sch.)* seizing.

bindtouw *o.* string; *(voor schoven)* binder twine.

binnen *vz.* within; **— het uur,** within an hour; *bw.* **—!** come in! *naar* **— gaan,** go in; **—in,** inside.

binnenband *m.* (inner) tube, inner tyre.

binnenbrengen *o. w.* bring in, take in; *(v. schip)* bring into port.

binnendeur *v.* inner door.

binnendijk *m.* inner dike.

binnengaan *o. w. en on. w.* enter, go in; go into.

binnenhalen *o. w.* gather (in); bring in, fetch in.

binnenhaven *v.* inner harbour; inland port.

binnenkamer *v.* inner room.

binnenkort *bw.* before long, shortly, at an early date.

binnenland *o.* interior, inland.

binnenleiden *o. w.* usher (in).

binnenlopen *o. w. (v. trein)* run in, draw in; *(v. schip)* put into port, put in; *o. w. (v. huis)* run into; *(v. haven)* put into.

binnenplaats *v.* **binnenplein** *o.* inner court. [tion.

binnenscheepvaart *v.* inland naviga-

binnensmokkelen *o. w.* smuggle (in,) run.

binnensmonds *bw.* under one's breath, inwardly, mumblingly.

binnenste *b. n.* inmost, inner(most); *z. n., o.* inside, interior.

binnenwaarts *bw.* inward(s).

binnenweg *m.* by-path, short cut.

binnenzak *m.* inside pocket.

binnenzijde *v.* inside, inner side.

binocle *v.* binocular, opera-glass.

bioscoop *m.* bioscope, cinema(tograph), picture-theatre.

Birma *o.* Burma.

bis *encore;* *(muz.)* B sharp.

bisdom *o.* diocese, bishopric.

bisschop *m.* bishop.

bisschoppelijk *b. n.* episcopal.

bits *b. n.* snappish, snappy, acrimonious, acerb, tart.

bitsheid *v.* snappishness, acrimony, acerbity, tartness.

bitter *b. n.* bitter; acerb, acrid; *bw.* bitterly; *z. n., o.* bitters.

bitterappel *m.* bitter-apple, bitter-gourd, colocynth.

bitterheid *v.* bitterness; acerbity, acrimony.

bivak *o.* bivouac.

blaadje *o.* *(papier)* sheet, leaf; *(bedrukt)* leaflet; *(dagblad)* paper; *(ong.)* rag; *(bloem—)* petal; *(v. samengesteld blad)* leaflet, foliole; *(presenteer—)* salver, tray

blaam *v.* blame, censure, reproach, reprehension; *(smet)* blemish.

blaar *v. (blein)* blister, plain; *(v. dier: bles)* blaze, white spot.

blaartrekkend *b. n.* raising blisters; *(wet.)* epispastic, vesicant, vesicatory.

blaas *v.* bladder; *(in water, enz.)* bubble

blaasbalg *m.* (pair of) bellows.

blaasinstrument *o. (muz.)* wind-instrument; *de* **—en,** the wind(s).

blaaskaak *m.* gasbag, windbag, bladder, braggart, swaggerer.

blaasorkest *o.* wind-band.

blaaspijp *v. (tn.)* blow-pipe, blast-pipe; *(v. glasblazer)* blow-tube, blow-pipe, blowing-iron; *(voor kogeltjes, erwten, enz.)* pea-shooter, blow-gun, blow-tube, sarbacane.

blad *o. (v. boom, boek)* leaf; *(dagblad)* newspaper; *(v. papier, metaal)* sheet; *(thee—, presenteer—)* tray; *(v. tafel)* top; *(uittrekbaar)* leaf; *(neerhangend)* flap; *(v. zaag)* blade.

bladeren *on. w.* **in een boek —,** turn over (the leaves of) a book.

bladerrijk *b. n.* leafy, full of leaves.

bladertooi *m.* foliage.

bladgroen *o.* leaf-green; *(wet.)* chlorophyll.

bladknop *m.* leaf-bud.

bladluis *v.* plant-louse, tree-louse, green fly.

bladrups *v.* canker-worm.

bladwijzer *m. (inhoudsopgave)* index, table of contents; bookmark.

bladzijde *v.* page.

blaffen *on. w.* bark.

blaken *on. w. (v. zon)* blaze.

blakend *b. n.* burning, ardent.

blaker *m.* flat candlestick.

blanco *b. n.* (in) blank.

blank *b. n.* white; *(v. huid)* clear, fair, white; *(blinkend)* bright; *(fig.)* pure; *z. n., m. (domino)* blank.

blanke *m. en v.* a white man (woman).

blanketsel *o.* pearl-powder, (facial) paint, rouge.

blankheid *v.* whiteness, fairness.

blaten *on. w.* bleat.

blauw *b. n.* blue; *z. n., o.* blue.

Blauwbaard *m.* Blue-beard.

blauwbes *v.* bilberry.

blauwborstje *o.* blue-throat.

blauwsel *o.* blue, powder-blue.

blazen *on. w.* blow; *(v. kat)* spit, swear; *(v. locomotief)* snort; *(damspel)* huff; *o. w.* blow; *(v. instrument)* blow, play.

blazer *m.* blower; *(muz.)* windblower; *(pocher)* braggart.

blazoen *o.* blazon.

bleek *b. n.* pale, pallid, wan.

bleek *v.* bleach-field, bleach(ing)-ground, bleach-green.

bleekheid *v.* paleness, pallor.

bleekneus *m.* tallow-face.

bleekwater *o.* bleaching-liquor.

bleekzucht *v.* chlorosis, green-sickness.

bleken *o. w.* bleach, whiten.

blekerij *r*. bleachery, bleach-works.
bles *r*. (*witte plek*) blaze; *m*. (*paard*) blazed horse, horse with a blaze.
bleu *b*. *n*. timid, shy, bashful.
blij(de) *b*. *n*. joyful, joyous, pleased, glad, cheerful.
blijdschap *r*. joy, gladness.
blijheid *r*. joy, joyfulness, gladness.
blijk *o*. mark, token, sign, proof.
blijkbaar *b*. *n*. (*bw*.) apparent(ly), evident(ly), obvious(ly), manifest(ly).
blijken *o*. *w*. *en* *on*. *w*. be evident, be obvious.
blijmoedig *b*. *n*. joyful, cheerful, merry, jovial.
blijspel *o*. comedy.
blijven *on*. *w*. (*ergens*) remain, stay; (*in toestand*) remain, keep, continue; (*overblijven*) remain, be left; (*doorgaan met*) continue; keep; (*omkomen*) perish, be killed, be left (on the field).
blijvend *b*. *n*. (*v*. *indruk*, *verbetering*, *vrede*, *enz*.) lasting; (*v*. *waarde*) enduring, abiding; (*v*. *woonplaats*, *enz*.) permanent; (*v*. *kleur*) fast; (*v*. *goederen: duurzaam*) durable.
blik *m*. look, gaze, regard, view; (*vluchtig*) glance, glimpse; (*heimelijk*) peep.
blik *o*. (*metaal*) tin, tin-plate, white iron, tinned-iron; (*vuilnis—*) dust-pan.
blikken *b*. *n*. (of) tin.
blikken *on*. *w*. look, glance.
blikopener *m*. tin-opener.
bliksem *m*. lightning.
bliksemafleider *m*. lightning-conductor, lightning-rod.
bliksemen *on*. *w*. lighten; (*v*. *ogen*) flash; (*pop*.: *uitvaren*) fulminate, thunder, storm and swear.
bliksemsnel *b*. *n*. with lightning speed, quick as lightning.
blikslager *m*. tinman, tinsmith, tinner, white smith.
blikwerk *o*. tinware.
blind *o*. (*vensterluik*) shutter; (*sch.: boegsprietzeil*) spritsail.
blind *b*. *n*. blind; **—e darm,** blindgut; (*wet*.) caecum; **—e passagier,** stowaway.
blinddoek *m*. bandage; (*fig*.) blind.
blinde *m*. *en* *v*. blind man, blind woman; (*kaartsp*.) dummy.
blindheid *v*. blindness; (*wet*.) cecity.
blinken *on*. *w*. shine, gleam, glitter.
blo(de) *b*. *n*. bashful, timid.
bloed *o*. blood.
bloed *m*. simpleton.
bloedaandrang *m*. congestion, rush of blood.
bloedarmoede *v*. anaemia, poorness of blood, bloodlessness.
bloedbad *o*. carnage, massacre, slaughter, blood-bath, bath of blood.
bloeddorstig *b*. *n*. bloodthirsty.
bloeden *on*. *w*. bleed.
bloedhond *m*. bloodhound.
bloedig *b*. *n*. bloody, sanguinary, sanguine.

bloedlichaampje *o*. blood-corpuscle, globule.
bloedneus *m*. bloody nose.
bloedraad *m*. (*gesch*.) Council of Blood.
bloedrood *b*. *n*. blood-red, scarlet.
bloedschande *r*. incest.
bloedsomloop *m*. circulation of (the blood).
bloedspuwing *v*. spitting of blood, haemoptysis.
bloeduitstorting *v*. effusion of blood, haemorraghe.
bloedval *o*. blood-vessel.
bloedvergiftiging *v*. blood-poisoning; (*wet*.) sepsis.
bloedverwant *m*. *en* *v*. (blood-)relation, relative, kinsman, kinswoman.
bloedzuiger *m*. blood-sucker, sanguisuge; (*fig*.) vampire, extortioner.
bloedzuiverend *b*. *n*. depurative, abstergent, abluent.
bloedzweer *v*. boil, bloody-tumour.
bloei *m*. blossom, bloom, flower; (*het bloeien*) florescence, flowering; (*fig*.) bloom, flower; flourishing, efflorescence.
bloeien *on*. *w*. bloom, flower; blossom; (*fig*.) flourish, prosper, thrive.
bloeitijd *m*. flowering-time, blossom time, time of flowering; (*fig*.) flowering-age, flourishing-period.
bloeiwijze *v*. inflorescence.
bloem *v*. flower; (*v*. *meel*) flour; (*frisheid*) bloom.
bloemblad *o*. petal.
bloemdek *o*. perianth.
bloemenmeisje *o*. flower-girl.
bloemist *m*. flower-grower, florist, floriculturist.
bloemisterij *v*. cultivation of flowers; floriculture; floricultural garden.
bloemkelk *m*. flower-cup, calyx.
bloemknop *m*. flower-bud.
bloemkool *v*. cauliflower.
bloemkroon *v*. corolla.
bloemlezing *v*. anthology.
bloempot *m*. flowerpot.
bloemscherm *o*. umbel.
bloemsteel *m*. **bloemstengel** *m*. flower-stalk; (*wet*.) peduncle.
bloesem *m*. blossom, bloom, flower.
bloheid *v*. bashfulness, timidity.
blok *o*. block; (*v*. *brandhout*) billet; (*v*. *lood*, *tin*) pig; (*speelgoed*) brick, (building-)block; (*aan been*) clog, hobble; *m*. (*Z*. *N*.: *klomp*) clog, wooden shoe.
blokhuis *o*. blockhouse, loghouse; (*spoorw*.) singal-box.
blokkade *v*. blockade.
blokken *on*. *w*. sap, plod, swot, mug, grind (**op,** at).
blokschaaf *v*. smoothing-plane.
blond *b*. *n*. blond, fair, light.
blonde *v*. blonde, blond-lace.
bloodaard *m*. coward, dastard, faint-heart, poltroon.
bloot *b*. *n*. (*onbedekt*) bare, naked; (*enkel*, *zonder meer*) mere, bare; *bw*. barely, merely.

blootleggen *o. w.* bare, lay bare, lay open, open; (*fig.*) lay open; (*v. plan*) expose.
blootshoofds *bw.* bareheaded.
blootstellen *o. w.* expose; *w. w. zich — aan*, (*gevaar, enz.*) expose oneself to; (*blaam, kritiek, enz.*) lay oneself open to.
blootsvoets *b. n.* barefooted.
blos *m.* (*v. verlegenheid*) blush; (*v. opwinding*) flush; (*v. gezondheid*) bloom.
blozen *on. w.* blush, flush, colour (up).
bluf *m.* brag(ging), boast(ing), bounce; swank(ing).
bluffen *on. w.* brag, boast, bounce, swagger; (*sl.*) swank.
bluffer *m.* braggart, boaster, swaggerer; (*sl.*) swanker.
blussen *o. w.* extinguish, put out.
blussing *v.* extinction.
blutsen *o. w.* bruise.
bobijn *v.* bobbin.
bochel *m.* hump, hunch; (*v. persoon ook:*) humpback, hunchback.
bocht *v.* (*v. weg, rivier, enz.*) bend, turn(ing), winding; (*v. lijn*) curve, flexion; (*v. touw*) bight; (*v. de kust*) trend; (*baai*) bay; bight; *o.* (bad) stuff, trash, rubbish.
bochtig *b. n.* tortuous, sinuous, winding.
bod *o.* offer; (*op verkoping*) bid.
bode *m.* messenger; (*post—*) letter-carrier; (*vrachtrijder*) carrier; (*dienstpersoneel*) servant, domestic; (*gemeente —*) beadle.
bodem *m.* (*v. ton, mand, enz.*) bottom; (*grondgebied, land*) soil, ground, territory; (*schip*) ship, vessel, bottom.
bodemerij *v.* bottomry.
bodemerijbrief *m.* bottomry-bond; (*op lading*) respondentia-bond.
bodemgesteldheid *v.* nature of the soil.
boedel *m.* (personal) estate, property, movables.
boedelbeschrijving *v.* inventory; (*ceel*) schedule of property.
boedelscheiding *v.* division of an estate.
boef *m.* (*schurk, schavuit*) knave, rogue, villain; (*tuchthuis—*) convict, jail-bird.
boeg *m.* (*sch.*) bow(s); (*v. paard*) counter, chest, shoulders.
boeganker *o.* (*sch.*) bower, bow-anchor.
boeglijn *v.* (*sch.*) bowline, bower-cable.
boegspriet *v.* (*sch.*) bowsprit; (*sp.*) greasy pole.
boei *v.* (*voetbeugel*) shackle, fetter; (*aan handen*) handcuff; (*sch.: baken*) buoy.
boeien *o. w.* fetter, shackle, put in irons; handcuff; (*fig.*) captivate, enthrall
boeiend *b. n.* captivating, enthralling; (*v. roman, enz.*) enchaining, absorbing; (*v. onderwerp*) engaging.
boek *o.* book; (*papiermaat*) quire.
boekband *m.* binding (of a book).
boekbeoordeling *v.* review, criticism.
boekbinder *m.* bookbinder.
boekbinderij *v.* bookbinding.

boekdeel *o.* volume, tome.
boekdrukker *m.* printer, typographer.
boekdrukkerij *v.* printing-office, printing-establishment.
boekdrukkunst *v.* (art of) printing, typography.
boeken *o. w.* enter (in the books); (*v. order*) book; (*fig.: v. succes, enz.*) score.
boekenkast *v.* book-case.
boekenliefhebber *m.* book-lover, lover of books, bibliophile.
boekenrek *o.* book-rack, book-shelves.
boekentas *v.* book-bag, book-carrier; (*op rug*) satchel.
boekenwurm *m.* book-worm.
boekhandel *m.* book-trade, book-selling; (*winkel*) bookseller's shop, book-shop.
boekhandelaar *m.* bookseller.
boekhouden *on. w.* (*H.*) keep the books; (*in huishouding*) keep accounts; *z. n. o.* book-keeping.
boekhouder *m.* book-keeper.
boekhouding *v.* book-keeping, accountancy.
boekjaar *o.* financial year.
boekje *o.* booklet.
boekweit *v.* buckwheat.
boekwerk *o.* book, work, volume.
boel *m. zie boedel*; a lot.
boeman *m.* bug-bear, ogre, bugaboo, bogey(-man).
boemelen *on. w.* knock about, loaf about.
boemeltrein *m.* slow train, stopping train.
boenen *o. w.* scrub; rub; polish, beeswax.
boenwas *o.* beeswax.
boer *m.* (*landbouwer*) farmer, husbandman; (*buitenman*) peasant, countryman, rustic; (*lomperd, kinkel*) boor, yokel; (*kaartsp.*) bower, knave, jack; (*oprisping*) belch.
boerderij *v.* farm, farmery.
boeren *on. w.* farm.
boerenbedrijf *o.* farming.
boerenbedrog *o.* flat-catching, humbug, quackery.
boerendorp *o.* rural village, country village.
boerenjongen *m.* peasant-boy, country-lad, rustic; **—s,** (*likeur*) brandy and raisins.
boerenkiel *m.* smock-frock.
boerenknecht *m.* farm-hand.
boerenkost *m.* country-fare.
boerenkrijg *m.* peasants' war.
boerenmeisje *o.* country-girl, country-lass; **—s,** (*likeur*) brandy and apricots.
Boerenoorlog *m.* Boer War.
boerenschuur *v.* barn.
boerin *v.* farmer's wife; country-woman, peasant woman.
boers *b. n.* boorish, rustic, clownish, countrified.
boert *v.* joke, pleasantry, bantering, jest.

boertig b. n. (bw.) jocular(ly), comical-(ly).

boete v. (geldstraf) penalty, fine, forfeit; (boetedoening) penance, penitence.

boetekleed o. hair-shirt, penitential garment.

boeteling (e) m. (v.) penitent.

boeten o. w. (v. zonden) expiate; (v. misdrijf) atone; (v. lusten) gratify; (v. netten, enz.) mend, repair; on. w. make amends.

boetprediker m. preacher of penitence.

boetpsalm m. penitential psalm.

boetseren o. w. model.

boetvaardig b. n. penitent, repentant, contrite.

boetvaardigheid v. penitence, repentance, contrition.

boevenstreek m. (piece of) knavery, villainy.

boezelaar m. apron.

boezem m. bosom, breast; (v. hart) auricle; (v. zee) bay; (v. polder) catch-water basin.

boezemvriend m. bosom friend.

bof m. (doffe slag, plons) thud, bump; (buitenkansje) fluke, piece of luck; (gen.) mumps; (wet.) parotitis.

boffen on. w. be lucky, be in luck, have a (run of) luck, turn up trumps.

boffer m. lucky bird, lucky dog, flukist.

bogen on. w. — op, glory in, boast.

Bohemen o. Bohemia.

bok m. (Dk.) goat, he-goat; (v. gems, hert, enz.) buck; (hijstoestel) gin, derrick, (fitting) jack; (v. rijtuig) box; (gymn.) vaulting-buck; (bilj.) rest, jigger; (fout, flater) blunder; (sl.) bloomer; (nors man) cross-patch.

bokaal v. goblet, beaker, cup; (vol) bumper.

bokje o. (Dk.) kid; (vogel) jack-snipe, small-snipe; (Pl.) hayband.

bokkesprong m. caper, capriole.

bokkig b. n. surly, sulky.

bokking m. (vers) bloater, bloated herring; (gerookt) red herring.

boksen on. w. box.

bokser m. boxer, pugilist, prize-fighter.

boksleder o. goatskin.

bokspartij v. boxing-match, prize-fight, pugilistic contest.

bol z. n., m. ball, sphere, globe; (v. lamp) globe; (meetk.) sphere; (v. plant, thermometer) bulb; (v. hoed) crown; (fam.: hoofd) noddle, pate; b. n. (v. lens, enz.) convex; (v. wangen) chubby, bulging; (bol staand: v. zeil, enz.) bulging, bulgy.

bolgewas o. bulbous plant.

bolrond b. n. convex; spherical, bulbous.

bolsjewisme o. bolshevism.

bolster m. (v. vrucht) shell, husk; (peluw) bolster.

bolvormig b. n. spherical, globe-shaped.

bolwerk o. bastion, rampart; (fig.) bulwark, stronghold. [it off.

bolwerken o. w. het —, manage, bring

bom v. (mil.) bomb; (v. vat) bung.

bomaanslag m. bomb-outrage.

bombardement o. bombardment.

bombarderen o. w. bomb, bombard, shell; (fig.) bombard.

bombast m. bombast; (fig.) fustian claptrap, bombast, high-faluting(g).

bomen on. w. (have a) chat, yarn, spin a yarn.

bomgat o. bung-hole; (v. toren) sound-hole.

bommenwerper m. (vl.) bomber.

bomvrij b. n. bomb-proof, shell-proof.

bon m. ticket, check, voucher; (voor levensmiddelen) ticket, coupon.

bonbon o. bonbon, sweet, goody.

bond m. alliance, league, confederacy; (v. staten) confederation; (vak—) union, association.

bondgenoot m. ally, confederate.

bondig b. n. (bw.) concise(ly), succinct-(ly); (v. stijl) terse.

bondsstaat m. federal state.

bondstroepen m. mv. federal troops.

bonestaak m. bean-stick, bean-pole; (fig.) hop-pole, maypole, lamp-post, bean-pole.

bons v. thump, bump, bounce, thud.

bont b. n. party-coloured, many-coloured; (v. bloemen, enz.) variegated; (v. paard) piebald, pied; (v. koe) spotted; (v. gezelschap, enz.) motley; (v. kleding, kleuren) gay.

bont o. fur; (gekleurde katoenen stof) printed cotton.

bontjas v. fur coat.

bontmuts v. fur cap.

bontwerk o. furriery, peltry.

bontwerker m. furrier.

bonzen on. w. thump, bump; (v. hart) throb, thump, pound.

boodschap v. message, errand.

boodschappen o. w. announce, bring (send) word.

boodschapper m. messenger, announcer.

boog m. (schietwapen) bow; (v. cirkel) arc; (bouwk.: v. wenkbrauwen) arch; (bocht) curve, bend; (muz.) tie, bind.

boogbrug v. arched bridge.

booglamp v. (electric) arc-lamp.

boogpees v. bowstring.

boogschieten o. archery.

boogschutter m. archer; (sp.) toxophilite.

boom m. (Pl.) tree; (tn.) beam, arbor; (sch.: vaar—) punting-pole, quant; (zeil—) boom; (dissel) pole; (v. lamoen) shaft; (ter afsluiting) bar, barrier; (haven—) boom; (v. kippen) perch.

boomgaard m. orchard.

boomkever m. may-bug, cockchafer.

boomkweker m. nursery-man, arborist, arboriculturist.

boomkwekerij v. (handeling) arboriculture; (plaats) tree-nursery.

boompje o. little tree, treelet; (jong —) sapling.

boomrijk *b. n.* wooded, well-timbered, abounding in trees.
boomschors *v.* tree-bark.
boomstam *m.* tree-trunk, tree-stem.
boomzwam *v.* agaric.
boon *v.* bean.
boor *v.* (*omslagboor*) brace-and-bit; (*drilboor*) drill; (*grote* —) auger, gimlet; (*voor rots*) borer.
boord *m.* (*rand: v. tapijt, enz.*) border; (*v. bos*) edge; (*v. rivier*) bank; (*v. glas*) brim; (*v. schip*) board; (*hals*—) collar.
boordevol *b. n.* full to the brim, brimfull.
boormachine *v.* boring-machine.
boort *o.* bort.
boortoren *m.* derrick.
boorwater *o.* boracic water, boric lotion.
boorzuur *o.* boracic acid.
boos *b. n.* (*nijdig, kwaad*) angry, cross; (*slecht*) bad, evil; (*kwaadaardig: v. geest, enz.*) malign, evil; (*v. invloed*) malefic, malicious.
boosaardig *b. n.* malicious, malign; (*v. ziekte*) malignant.
boosdoener *m.* malefactor, evil-doer.
boosheid *v.* anger; malignity; wickedness.
booswicht *m.* malefactor, criminal, wretch.
boot *v.* boat; (*stoom*—) steamer; (*sieraad*) brooch, pendant, clasp.
bootshaak *m.* boat-hook.
bootsman *m.* boatswain.
boottocht *m.* boat-excursion.
bootwerker *m.* docker, dock-worker.
bord *o.* (*om te eten*) plate; (*school*—) (black-)board; **plat** —, meat-plate; **diep** —, soup-plate.
bordenwasser *m.* plate-washer.
bordes *o.* flight of steps.
bordpapier *o.* pasteboard, cardboard.
borduren *o. w. en on. w.* embroider; (*fig.*) embroider, romance.
boren *o. w.* bore; drill; (*v. tunnel*) bore, drive, burrow; (*v. put*) sink; (*door*—) perforate, pierce.
borg *m.* (*persoon*) surety, guarantee, guarantor; (*zaak*) security, guaranty, pledge; (*recht*) bail, bailsman.
borgen *on. w.* give credit; (*op borg kopen*) buy on credit; (*ontlenen*) borrow.
borgstelling *v.* surety, security, guarantee.
borgtocht *m.* surety, bail, pledge.
borrel *m.* drop, dram, nip, wet.
borst *v.* breast, bosom; (*borstkas*) chest; (*v. dier*) brisket, breast.
borst *m.* lad.
borstbeeld *o.* bust; (*op munt*) effigy.
borstbeen *o.* breastbone; (*wet.*) sternum.
borstel *m.* brush; (*stijve haren: v. varken, enz.*) bristle.
borstelig *b. n.* bristly, bristling.
borstholte *v.* cavity of the chest, chest-cavity, thoracic cavity.

borstkas *v.* chest; (*wet.*) thorax.
borstlijder(es) *m.* (*v.*) pulmonary sufferer, consumptive (patient).
borstrok *m.* (under)vest, singlet.
borstvlies *o.* pleura.
borstvliesontsteking *v.* pleuritis, pleurisy.
bos *m.* (*radijs, veren, sleutels*) bunch; (*hooi*) bottle; (*stro*) bundle, truss; (*haar*—) shock, tuft.
bos *v.* wood; (*woud*) forest.
bosbewoner *m.* woodsman, forester, forest-dweller.
bosbouw *m.* forestry, sylviculture.
bosduif *v.* wood-pigeon, ring-pigeon.
bosje *o.* grove, spinney; (*struikgewas*) bush, bosquet.
bosmier *v.* wood-ant, red ant.
bosrijk *b. n.* woody, wooded.
bosuil *m.* long-eared owl, tawny owl.
boswachter *m.* forester.
boswezen *o.* forest service, forestry.
bot *z. n., v.* (*vis*) flounder; (*Pl.: knop*) bud; *z. n., o.* (*been, knook*) bone; (*eind touw*) end of a rope; *b. n.* (*stomp*) blunt; (*dom*) dull, obtuse, stupid; (*vierkant, ronduit*) flat.
botanie *v.* botany.
boter *v.* butter.
boterbloem *v.* buttercup; butter-flower.
boteren *o. w.* (*met boter besmeren*) butter; *on. w.* (*boter maken, karnen*) make butter, churn; come.
boterham *v.* (slice of) bread and butter.
boterkoek *m.* butter-cake.
boterpot *m.* butter-pot, butter-crock.
botervlootje *o.* butter-dish, butter-boat.
botheid *v.* bluntness; dul(l)ness, obtuseness, stupidity.
botsen *on. w.* — **tegen,** strike against, dash against, impinge on.
botsing *v.* collision, clash; impact.
bottelarij *v.* bottling establishment; bottling room.
bottelen *o. w.* bottle.
botten *on. w.* bud.
botterik *m.* blockhead, dunderhead, dunce.
botvieren *on. w.* **zijn hartstochten—,** give rein to one's passions.
botweg *bw.* bluntly, flatly, point-blank.
bouillon *m.* broth, beef-tea, clear soup.
bout *m.* (*tn.*) bolt; (*soldeer*—) iron; (*v. strijkijzer*) heater, box-iron; (*v. geslacht dier*) quarter; (*schape*—) leg (of mutton); (*v. vogel*) drumstick.
bouw *m.* (*v. huizen*) building, construction, erection; (*gebouw*) building, edifice; (*samenstelling*) structure, frame; (*het verbouwen*) cultivation, culture.
bouwbedrijf *o.* building-trade, building-industry.
bouwdoos *v.* box of (building-)bricks.
bouwen *o. w.* (*v. huis, enz.*) build; (*ineenzetten: v. machine, enz.*) construct; (*verbouwen*) grow, cultivate; *on. w.* build.

bouwgrond *m.* building-ground.
bouwkosten *m. mv.* building-expenses, cost of construction.
bouwkunde *r.* architecture.
bouwkundige *m.* architect.
bouwland *o.* arable land.
bouwsteen *m.* building-stone, building-brick.
bouwstoffen *r. mv.* materials.
bouwvak *o.* building-trade.
bouwvallig *b. n.* ruinous, tumble-down, crazy; (*fig.*) dilapidated.
boven *rz.* (*hoger dan*) above; (*meer dan*; *vlak boren*) over; *bw.* above; aloft, on high; (*in huis*) upstairs.
bovenaan *bw.* at the head, at the top.
bovenal *bw.* above all, above all things.
bovenarm *m.* upper arm.
bovendek *o.* (*sch.*) upper deck, main deck.
bovendien *bw.* besides, moreover, in addition.
bovendrijven *on. w.* float on the surface; (*fig.*) prevail, predominate.
bovengemeld, bovengenoemd *b. n.* above-mentioned.
bovengoed *o.* upper clothes.
bovengrond *m.* top-soil.
bovenhand *r.* back of the hand; (*fig.*) upper hand.
bovenhuis *o.* upper part of a house; flat, upstairs house.
bovenkant *m.* upper side.
bovenleer *o.* upper leather, uppers.
bovenlichaam *o.* upper part of the body.
bovenloop *m.* upper course, upper reaches.
bovenmate *bw.* extremely, exceedingly, beyond measure.
bovenmenselijk *b. n.* superhuman.
bovennatuurlijk *b. n.*-supernatural.
bovenop *bw.* on (the) top, at the top, atop.
bovenverdieping *r.* upper storey, upper floor, top floor.
boycotten *o. w.* boycott.
braadoven *m.* roaster, Dutch oven.
braadrooster *m.* grid-iron, grill.
braadspit *o.* spit.
braadworst *r.* roast-sausage, German sausage.
braaf *b. n.* honest, good, virtuous; *bw.* well.   [ity.
braafheid *r.* honesty, goodness, prob-
braak *b. n.* fallow; *z. n., v.* (*inbraak*) (house-)breaking, burglary; (*werktuig*) brake.
braakland *o.* fallow (land).
braakmiddel *o.* vomitory, emetic.
braam *v.* (*r. mes*) wire-edge, burr; (*vis*) ray's bream; (*Pl.*) blackberry.
braambes *r.* blackberry.
braambos *o.* blackberry-brake.
braamstruik *m.* blackberry bush, bramble.
Brabander *m.* Brabantine, Brabant man.

Brabant *o.* Brabant.
brabbeltaal *v.* jabber, gibberish.
braden *o. w. en on. w.* (*in pan*) fry; (*in oven*) bake, roast; (*op ruur, rooster*) grill, broil; (*aan spit*) roast.
brak *b. n.* brackish, saltish, briny; *z. n., m.* (*Dk.*) beagle; (*bengel*) little rogue, brat, urchin.
braken *o. w. en on. w.* vomit; (*r. vlas*) break.
braking *r.* vomiting.
bramzeil *o.* top-gallant-sail.
brand *m.* fire; (*grote —*) conflagration; (*brandstof*)fuel, firing, firewood; (*uitslag*) eruption; (*in 't koren*) dustbrand, black rust, burn, blight.   [mable.
brandbaar *b. n.* combustible, inflam-
brandbom *v.* incendiary bomb.
brandemmer *m.* fire-bucket.
branden *on. w.* burn, be on fire; *o. w.* (*hout, kalk, houtskool*) burn; (*v. koffie*) roast; (*v. sterke drank*) distil; (*v. vee*) brand-mark, brand; (*met hete vloeistof*) scald; (*r. wond*) cauterize; (*r. glas*) stain.
brandend *b. n.* burning; (*v. kaars, lucifer*) lighted; (*v. zuur: bijtend*) caustic; (*v. verlangen, liefde*) ardent; *bw.* — **heet,** burning hot, roasting hot.
branderig *b. n.* (*v. lucht, smaak*) burnt; (*r. gevoel*) burning, tingling; (*v. koren*) smutty, smutted.
brandewijn *m.* (French) brandy.
brandglas *o.* burning-glass, sun-glass.
brandhout *o.* fire-wood, burning-wood.
branding *r.* breakers, surf, surge.
brandkast *v.* safe, strong-box.
brandkogel *m.* fire-ball, incendiary bullet.
brandmerken *o. w.* brand; (*fig.*)brand, stigmatize.
brandnetel *r.* stinging-nettle.
brandpunt *o.* focus; (*fig.*)focus; centre.
brandschade *v.* damage by fire.
brandschatten *o. w.* hold (put) to ransom, lay under contribution.
brandsignaal *o.* fire-signal.
brandslang *v.* fire-hose, hose pipe.
brandspiritus *m.* methylated spirit.
brandspuit *r.* fire-engine.
brandstapel *m.* (funeral) pile.
brandstichter *m.* incendiary, fire-raiser.
brandstichting *v.* arson, fire-raising.
brandstof *v.* fuel, firing.
brandverf *v.* enamel.
brandverzekering *v.* fire-insurance.
brandvrij *b. n.* fire-proof.
brandweer *v.* fire-brigade.
brandweerman *m.* fireman.
brandwond *r.* burn; (*door vloeistof*) scald.
branie *b. n.* bold, daring, plucky; *z. n., m.* daring, pluck; (*fat, grote mijnheer*) swell; (*bluf, opschepperij*) swank, swagger.
brasem *m.* bream.
braspartij *o.* orgy, debauchery, debauch, revel, carouse.

brassen *on. w.* revel, carouse, feast; *o. w. (sch.)* brace.
Brazilië *o.* Brazil.
breed *b. n.* broad, wide.
breedsprakig *b. n.* prolix, diffuse, verbose.
breedte *v.* breadth, width; *(aardr.)* latitude.
breedtecirkel *m.* parallel of latitude.
breedtegraad *m.* degree of latitude.
breedvoerig *b. n.* circumstantial, detailed; ample, large; *bw.* in detail, at length, amply, at large, fully.
breekbaar *b. n.* breakable, fragile, brittle.
breekijzer *o.* crowbar, crow; jemmy.
breidel *m.* bridle; *(fig.)* check, curb, bridle.
breidelen *o. w.* bridle, check, curb.
breien *o. w. en on. w.* knit.
breigaren *o.* knitting-yarn, knitting-cotton.
brein *o.* brain, intellect.
breinaald *v.* knitting-needle.
breister *v.* knitter.
breiwerk *o.* knitting(-work).
breken *o. w. (v. glas, enz.)* break; *(v been)* fracture; *(v. licht)* refract; *(verbrijzelen)* smash, shatter; *on. w.* break, be broken; go to pieces.
breker *m.* breaker.
breking *v.* breaking; *(v. licht)* refraction.
brem *v. (pekel)* pickle, brine; *(Pl.)* broom, genista.
Bremen *o.* Bremen.
brengen *o. w. (naar spreker toe)* bring; *(van spreker af)* take; *(van een plaats naar een andere)* carry, convey.
brenger *m.* bearer.
bres *v.* breach.
Bretagne *o.* Brittany.
bretels *v. mv.* braces, suspenders.
breuk *v. (barst, scheur)* crack, burst, flaw; *(v. arm, been)* fracture; *(v. ingewand: uitzakking)* hernia; *(tussen vrienden)* rupture; *(wisk.)* fraction; *(H.)* breakage.
breukband *m.* truss.
brevet *o.* brevet, patent, certificate.
brevier *o. (getijdenboek)* breviary; *(lettersoort)* brevier.
brief *m.* letter, epistle.
briefkaart *v.* postcard.
briefomslag *m. en o.* envelope.
briefport *o.* postage.
briefwisseling *v.* correspondence.
bries *v.* (brisk) wind, breeze.
briesen *on. w. (v. paard)* snort; *(v. leeuw)* roar.
brievenbesteller *m.* letter-carrier, postman.
brievenbus *v.* letter-box; *(op straat)* pillar-box.
brieventas *v.* pocket-book, lettercase.
brigade *v.* brigade.
brigadier *m. (mil.)* brigade-commander, brigadier; *(v. politie)* police-sergeant.

brij *v.* porridge; *(fig.)* pulp.
briket *v.* (coal-)briquette.
bril *m.* (pair of) spectacles; *(auto—, stof—)* goggles; *(v. W. C.)* seat.
briljant *b. n. (bw.)* brilliant(ly).
brilleglas *o.* spectacle-glass.
brillekoker *m.* spectacle-case.
brillen *on. w.* wear spectacles.
brilslang *v.* spectacle(d) snake, cobra.
brisantgranaat *v.* high explosive shell.
Brit *m.* Briton.
brits *v.* plank bed, wooden bed.
Brits *b. n.* British.
brodeloos *b. n.* breadless.
broedei *o.* brood egg.
broeden *on. w.* brood, hatch, sit (on eggs); *o. w.* brood, hatch.
broeder *m.* brother; *(in klooster)* brother, friar; *(in ridderorde)* companion. [love.
broederliefde *v.* fraternal (brotherly)
broederlijk *b. n.* brotherly, fraternal.
broedermoord *m.* fratricide.
broederschap *v.* fraternity, brotherhood; *(kerkelijke vereniging)* confraternity, brotherhood.
broedhen *v.* brood-hen, sitter.
broedmachine *v.* incubator, hatcher, hatching-apparatus.
broedsel *o.* brood, hatch.
broedtijd *m.* brooding-time, breeding-time; *(v. vogels ook:)* nesting-season.
broeien *on. w. (v. vogels)* brood, hatch, sit; *(v. hooi)* heat, get heated, get hot; *(v. de lucht)* be sultry; *o. w. (v. varken)* scald.
broeikas *v.* hot-house, glass-house, forcing-house.
broeinest *o.* hot-bed, seed-bed.
broek *v. (lang)* (pair of) trousers; *(Am.)* pantaloons; *(kort)* (pair of) breeches; *(sport—, jongens—)* knickerbockers; shorts; *(pof—; sl.)* plus fours; *(v. kanon)* breech.
broek *o.* marsh, swamp.
broekspijp *v.* trouser-leg, trouser.
broekzak *m.* trouser(s)-pocket, breeches-pocket.
broer *m. zie* **broeder.**
brok *m. en o.* piece, bit, fragment, morsel, lump.
brokkelen *o. w. en on. w.* crumble.
brokstuk *o.* piece, fragment, scrap.
brombeer *m.* growler, grumbler, grouser.
brommen *on. w. (v. insekt)* hum, buzz, drone; *(v. persoon)* growl, grumble, grouse; *(mompelen)* mutter; *(gevangen zitten)* do time.
bromtol *m.* humming-top.
bromvlieg *v.* meat-fly, drone-fly, blue-bottle.
bron *v. (v. rivier)* source; *(in bodem)* well, spring; *(fig.)* source, fountain, spring, cause, origin.
bronchitis *v.* bronchitis.
brons *o.* bronze.
bronsttijd *m.* rutting-season, rutting-time.

bronwater o. spring-water, well-water; mineral water.

brood o. bread; **een —,** a loaf (of bread).

broodbakker m. baker.

broodbakkerij v. bakery, baker's business; (gebouw) bakehouse, bakery.

broodkorf m. bread-basket.

broodkruim (el) v. (bread)-crumb.

broodmes o. bread-knife.

broodnodig b. n. highly necessary.

broodsuiker v. loaf-sugar.

broodwinning v. subsistence, means of subsistence, bread-winning.

broodzak m. bread-bag; (mil.) haver-sack.

broos v. (toneellaars) buskin.

broos b. n. frail, fragile, brittle.

bros b. n. crisp, brittle, shivery.

brosheid v. crispness, brittleness.

brouwen o. w. brew; (fig.) brew, concoct, hatch; on. w. speak with a burr.

brouwer m. brewer.

brouwerij v. brewery.

brouwersknecht m. brewer's man, drayman.

brouwkuip v. brewing-vat, brewing-tub.

brouwsel o. brew, brewage, brewing, concoction; (fig.) brewage, concoction, tap.

brug v. bridge; (op stoomboot) bridge, bridge-deck; (loopplank) gangway; (gymn.) parallel bars.

Brugge o. Bruges.

bruggehoofd o. abutment of a bridge; (mil.) bridge-head.

brugleuning v. parapet, railing.

brugwachter m. bridgeman, tollman.

bruid v. bride elect; (op trouwdag) bride.

bruidegom m. bridegroom.

bruidsbed o. bride-bed, bridal bed, nuptial couch.

bruidsdagen m. mv. bridal days.

bruidsjapon v. bridal gown, wedding-dress.

bruidsjonker m. (v. bruid) bride's page, bridal page; (v. bruidegom) groomsman, bridesman.

bruidsmeisje o. bridesmaid.

bruidspaar o. bridal pair, bride and bridegroom; (op huwelijksdag) newly-wedded pair.

bruidsschat m. dowry, dower, dot.

bruidstooi m. bridal attire.

bruikbaar b. n. serviceable, usable, useful.

bruikleen o. loan.

bruiloft v. wedding, wedding-party; (dicht.) nuptials.

bruiloftsmaal o. wedding-banquet.

bruin b. n. brown; (v. paard: rood —) bay; z. n., o. brown.

bruinachtig b. n. brownish.

bruinharig b. n. brown-haired.

bruinkool b. brown coal, lignite.

bruinsteen m. brown-stone, manganese.

bruinvis v. porpoise, sea-hog.

bruisen on. w. (v. dranken) effervesce, fizz; (v. zee) seethe, roar; (v. bloed) seethe, rush.

brulaap m. howling-monkey, howler.

brullen on. w. roar.

Brussel o. Brussels.

brutaal b. n. (vrijpostig) forward, cheeky, pert, saucy; bold, cool; (onbeschaamd) impertinent, impudent, insolent; (vermetel) audacious, daring; bw. forwardly; coolly; impertinently.

bruto b. n. (H.) gross.

buffel m. buffalo.

buffer m. buffer.

bufferstaat m. buffer-state.

buffet o. (meubel) buffet, side-board; (tapkast) bar; (in station, enz.) refreshment bar, buffet.

buffetjuffrouw v. bar-maid.

bui v. (v. regen, hagel) shower; (wind en regen, sneeuw—) squall; (v. hoesten, lachen) fit; (gril) freak, whim.

buidel m. bag, pouch; (beurs) purse, pouch.

buidelrat v. pouched rat, opossum.

buigen o. w. bend, bow; (v. stralen) diffract; (fig.) submit, give in; on. w. bend; bow; (zich krommen) curve; w. w. **zich —,** bend, bow; (bukken) stoop; (v. rivier, enz.) curve, make a bend; (zich onderwerpen) submit, yield.

buiging v. (als groet) bow; (v. dames: nijging) curts(e)y; (v. stem) modulation, inflexion; (gram.) declension. [ing.

buigingsuitgang m. inflexional end-**buigingsvorm** m. inflexional form.

buigzaam b. n. flexible, pliant, supple; (fig.) yielding, pliant, supple.

buigzaamheid v. flexibility, pliancy, suppleness.

buik m. belly; (eufemistisch) stomach; (v. schip, ton, enz.) bulge; (v. zeil) bunt.

buikholte v. abdomen, abdominal cavity.

buikloop m. diarrhœa, flux.

buikpijn v. stomach-ache, abdominal pain, belly-ache.

buikpotig b. n. gastropodous; **— dier,** gastropod.

buikriem m. belly-band, girth.

buikspreker v. ventriloquist.

buiktyfus m. enteric (fever).

buikvlies o. peritoneum.

buikvliesontsteking v. peritonitis.

buil v. lump, bruise, swelling.

buil m. (zakje) paper bag; (meelzeef, builmolen) bolter, bolting-machine, bolting-mill.

builen o. w. bolt.

builenpest v. bubonic plague.

buis o. jacket.

buis v. tube, pipe, conduit; (in lichaam) duct; (v. granaat) fuse; (sch.) herring-boat.

buit m. booty, spoil(s), loot, prize, capture.

buitelen on. w. tumble, fall head over heels; (v. vliegtuig) loop the loop.

buiteling v. tumble; (v. vliegtuig) looping the loop; (v. acrobaat) somersault.
buiten rz. outside; out of; beyond; without; bw. outside; out of doors, outdoors, out; z. n., o. country-seat, country-house.
buitenband m. (r. fiets) (cycle) cover, outer cover, outer tyre.
buitendeur v. outer door; street-door, front-door.
buitendien bw. besides, moreover.
buitengewoon b. n. extraordinary; bw. extraordinarily.
buitenkans(je) v. (o.) stroke of (good) luck, windfall.
buitenland o. foreign country (countries): in het —, abroad, in foreign parts.
buitenlander m. foreigner.
buitenlands b. n. foreign; (uitheems: v. planten, enz.) exotic.
buitenleven o. country-life.
buitenlucht v. country-air.
buitenmate bw. beyond measure, extremely.
buitenshuis bw. out of doors, outdoors, out of the house.
buitensluiten o. w. lock out, shut out; (fig.) exclude, shut out.
buitenspeler m. (voetb.) winger.
buitensporigheid v. extravagance, excessiveness, exorbitance.
buitenstaander m. outsider.
buitenstad v. suburb.
buitenwereld v. outer world.
buitenwijk v. suburb; mv. ook: outskirts.
buitmaken o. w. seize, capture, prize.
buizerd m. buzzard, puttock.
bukken o. w. (v. hoofd) bend, stoop; on. w. duck; stoop; w. w. zich —, stoop; duck.
buks v. rifle.
buks m. (Pl.) box.
bul m. (stier) bull; v. (pauselijke brief) bull; (diploma) diploma.
bulderen on. w. (v. wind, kanon, enz.) roar; (v. donder, kanon, enz.) boom, bellow; (v. persoon) roar, rant, bluster, storm.
Bulgarije o. Bulgaria.
bulken on. w. low, bellow, roar.
bullebak m. bully, bear, bugbear, browbeater.
bult m. (buil, bobbel) lump, bump, boss; (bochel) hump, hunch.
bultenaar m. hunchback, humpback.
bundel m. (v. kleren, enz.) bundle;

(v. brieven, bankbiljetten, pijlen) sheaf; (v. gedichten) collection.
bunder o. hectare.
bunker m. bunker.
burcht m. castle, citadel, stronghold.
burchtheer m. (gesch.) chatelain.
burchtvrouw v. (gesch.) chatelaine.
bureau o. (meubel) writing-table, writing-desk; (lokaal) bureau, office; (mil.) orderly-room.
burg m. castle, citadel, stronghold.
burgemeester m. burgomaster; (in Engeland) mayor.
burger m. citizen; (niet-mil.) civilian; (niet edelman) commoner.   [citizens.
burgerij v. commonalty, middle classes;
burgerkeuken v. plain cooking, bourgeois cookery.
burgerkleding v. **burgerkleren** o. mv. plain clothes, civilian clothes.
burgerleven o. private life, civil(ian) life.
burgerlijk b. n. (niet-mil.)civil,civilian; (v. de staatsburger) civil, civic; (v. de burgerstand) middle-class, bourgeois; (eenvoudig; niet voornaam) middle-class, bourgeois, plain; —e stand, registration service, civil registration.
burgeroorlog m. civil war.
burgerpakje o. (mil.) suit of civics.
burgerrecht o. civic (civil) right, citizenship; (v. stad) freedom of a city.
burgertwist(en) m. (mr.) civil strife.
burgerwacht v. citizen guard, civic guard.
burggraaf m. burg(g)rave, viscount.
burggravin v. viscountess.
bus v. (voor brieven, geld, enz.) box; (voor groenten, enz.) tin; (voor koffie, thee) canister; (v. wiel) box; (geweerloop) barrel; (ziekenfonds) (sick-)club; (begrafenisfonds) (burial-)club; (autobus) bus.
busdokter m. club-doctor.
buskruit o. gunpowder.
buslichting v. collection.
bustehouder m. bust supporter.
buur m. neighbour.
buurman m. neighbour.   [talk.
buurpraatje o. gossip, neighbourly
buurschap v. neighbourhood.
buurt v. neighbourhood, vicinity; (wijk) quarter; (gehucht) hamlet.
buurten on. w. pay a visit to a neighbour, visit one's neighbours.
buurtspoor o. **buurtspoorweg** m. local railway.
buurvrouw v. neighbour.

C

cacao v. cocoa.
cacaoboon v. cocoa-nib.
cachet o. (voorwerp) seal, signet; (merk, onderscheid) cachet, stamp, impress.

cachot m. (mil.)military prison, (punishment) cell.
cactus m. cactus; (mv.) cacti.
cadeau o. present.

cadettenschool *r.* military school, cadet school.
café-chantant *o.* cabaret, music-hall; café chantant.
cafetaria *v.* (*m.*) cafetaria.
Calvarieberg *m.* (Mount) Calvary.
camera *v.* (*m.*) camera.
campagne *r.* (*m.*) campaign.
Canarische eilanden *o. mv.* the Canaries, the Canary Islands.
canon *m.* (*deel der Mis, geloofsregel, enz.*) canon; (*rente bij erfpacht*) rent-charge, ground-rent; (*kettingzang*) catch.
canonisatie *v.* canonization.
caoutchouc *o.* caoutchouc, india-rubber.
cape *v.* cape.
capitulatie *v.* capitulation.
capituleren *on. w.* capitulate.
capsule *v.* (*m.*) capsule.
carambole *v.* (*bilj.*) cannon.
carbol *o. en m.* carbolic acid (solution).
carburator *m.* carburetter.
cargadoor *m.* ship-broker.
caroussel *v.* merry-go-round, giddy-go-round.
cassatie *v.* cassation, appeal.
casueel *b. n.* casual, accidental, fortuitous; *bw.* casually, accidentally, fortuitously.
catacombe *v.* catacomb.
catalogus *m.* catalogue.
Catalonië *o.* Catalonia.
catechisatie *v.* (*het onderricht*) catechizing; (*de lessen*) catechumen classes, confirmation classes.
catechismus *m.* catechism.
categorie *v.* category.
causerie *v.* talk.
cautie *v.* bail, security, caution.
cavalerie *v.* cavalry, horse.
cavalerist *m.* cavalry-man, cavalry-soldier, horse-soldier, trooper.
cedel *v.* schedule, bill; (*lijst*) list.
ceder *m.* cedar.
cederboom *m.* cedar(-tree).
cederhout *o.* cedar-wood, cedar.
ceintuur *v.* belt, sash; (*sjerp*) scarf.
ceintuurbaan *v.* belt-railway, circular railway.
cel *v.* cell; (*telefoon—*) (call-)box.
celebrant *m.* celebrant, officiating priest.
celebreren *o. w.* celebrate.
cellebroeder *m.* cellite.
cello *v.* cello.
celluloid *o.* celluloid.
celstraf *v.* solitary confinement.
celwagen *m.* prisoner's van.
cement *o.* cement.
censor *m.* censor, licenser.
censuur *v.* censorship, censure, stricture.
cent *m.* cent.
centenaar *m.* hundredweight, quintal.
centenbak *m.* collecting-box; (*sl.*) latch-pan.
centigram *o.* centigramme.
centiliter *m.* centilitre.
centimeter *m.* centimetre.

centrale *v.* (*el.*) generating-station, power-station; (*tel.*) central-exchange, (telephone) exchange.
centraliseren *o. w.* centralize.
centrum *o.* centre.
ceremonie *v.* ceremony.
ceremoniemeester *m.* Master of the Ceremonies.
certificaat *o.* certificate.
cervelaatworst *v.* saveloy.
cesuur *v.* caesura.
chagrijn *o.* chagrin, grief.
charteren *o. w.* (*H. en sch.*) charter.
chaufferen *on. w.* drive.
chauffeur *m.* chauffeur, motor(-car) driver.
chef *m.* chief; (*patroon*) employer, principal; (*directeur*) manager; (*afdelings—*) department-head; (*eerste bediende*) chief clerk; (*v. station*) station-master; (*— van exploitatie*) (*spoorw.*) traffic manager; (*kok*) chef.
chemicaliën *v. mv.* chemicals.
chemie *v.* chemistry.
cheque *v.* (*H.*) check, cheque.
chertepartij *v.* charter-party.
chic *b. n.* chic, smart, stylish; *z. n. m. en v.* chicness, smartness.
chijl *v.* chyle.
China *o.* China.
Chinees *m.* Chinaman, Chinese.
chirurg *m.* surgeon.
chloor *o.* chlorine.
chloroform *v.* chloroform.
chocolade *v.* chocolate.
chocoladefabriek *v.* chocolate-mill.
cholera *v.* cholera.
christelijk *b. n.* (*bw.*) Christian(ly).
Christen *m.* Christian.
Christendom *o.* Christianity.
Christenmens *m.* Christian.
Christus *m.* Christ.
chronologisch *b. n.* (*bw.*) chronological(ly).
chronometer *m.* chronometer.
ciborie *v.* ciborium.
cichorei *v.* (*plant*) chicory; (*suikerij*) chicory, succory.
cider *m.* cider.
cijfer *o.* figure, cipher; (*in geheimschrift*) cypher; (*op school*) mark.
cijferen *on. w.* cipher, cypher.
cijferschrift *o.* (*muz., enz.*) numerical notation; (*geheimschrift*) cipher, code.
cijns *m.* tribute, tribute-money.
cijnsplichtig *b. n.* tributary.
cilinder *m.* cylinder; (*hoed: fam.*) top-hat, chimney pot hat.
cilindrisch *o.* cylindric(al).
cimbaal *v.* cymbal.
cinema *v.* picture-theatre, picture-house, picture-palace.
cipier *m.* jailer, gaoler, gaol-keeper, turnkey.
cipres *v.* cypress.
circa *bw.* circa, about.
circus *o.* circus; (*sl.*) ring.
cirkel *m.* circle.

cirkelboog m. arc of a circle.
cirkelomtrek m. circumference of a circle.
cirkelsegment o. segment of a circle.
cirkelvormig b. n. circular.
citaat o. quotation.
citadel v. citadel, fortress.
citer v. cither(n), zither(n).
citeren o. w. (gezegde, passage) quote; (boek, schrijver) cite; (dagvaarden) cite, summon.
citroen m. lemon; (grote —) citron.
citroenlimonade v. (siroop) lemon-syrup; (drank) lemon-drink, lemon-squash.
citroensap o. lemon-juice.
civetkat v. civet(-cat).
civiel b. n. (burgerlijk) civil; (billijk) cheap, moderate, reasonable.
clandestien b. n. clandestine, secret.
clausule v. clause, proviso, stipulation.
cliché o. (stereotype) plate, block; (fot.) negative.
cliënt m. client; (H.) (klant) customer, client.
cliëntele v. clientele, clientage, customers.
club v. club.
coalitie v. coalition.
codetelegram o. code telegram, code message.
codex m. codex.
codicil o. codicil.
coëfficiënt o. coefficient.
cognac m. cognac, brandy.
cognossement o. (H.) bill of lading.
cohesie v. cohesion.
cokes v. mv. coke.
collecte v. collection.
collectie v. collection.
collega m. colleague.
college o. (bestuurslichaam) college; (raad) board; (v. hoogleraar) lecture, college course; (gymnasium) (Z. N.) grammar-school.
collegegeld o. lecture fee, tuition fee.
collegiaal b. n. fraternal, brotherly; bw. as a good colleague, in a brotherly spirit.
Coloradokever m. Colorado-beetle.
comfort o. comfort; (in hotel, enz.) conveniences.
comfortabel b. n. comfortable, commodious, with every comfort.
commandant m. commander; (v. vesting, enz.) commandant; (sch.) captain, master, commander; (brand-weer—) chief officer of the fire-brigade.
commandeur m. commander.
commanditair b. n. — vennoot, sleeping partner, limited partner, silent partner; —e vennootschap, limited partnership.
commando o. (word of) command.
commandobrug v. navigating-bridge.
commies m. custom-house officer, revenue-man; (op ministerie, enz.) clerk.

commiesbrood o. (mil.) ammunition bread, army bread, ration bread.
commissaris m. commissioner; (v. politie) superintendent of police, Chief Constable; (v. maatschappij) director; (v. orde) steward.
commissie v. committee, board; (op-dracht, order) commission, order; (com-missieloon) commission.
commissieloon o. (H.) commission.
commissionair m. (H.) commission-agent; (aan station) commissionaire, porter.
committent m. principal, mandator.
communiceren on.w. communicate.
communie v. (Holy) Communion.
communiebank v. communion rails.
communist m. communist.
compagnie v. company.
compagnon m. partner.
compensatie v. compensation.
competent b. n. competent.
compliment o. compliment.
complimenteren o. w. compliment.
componeren o. w. en on. w. compose.
componist m. composer.
compositie v. composition.
compromis o. compromise.
compromitteren o. w. compromise.
comptabiliteit v. (rekenplichtigheid) accountability; (boekhouding-afdeling) accountancy department; (vak) accountancy.
concaaf b. n. concave.
concentratie v. concentration.
concert o. concert; (van één persoon of één componist) recital; (muziekstuk) concerto.
concessie v. concession; (mijn—) claim.
concierge m. door-keeper, hall-porter; janitor.
concilie o. council.
concurrent z. n., m. competitor, rival; b. n. —e schuldeisers, unsecured creditors.
concurrentie v. competition, rivalry.
concurreren on. w. compete (with...).
conditioneren o. w. stipulate, condition.
condoleren o. w. condole.
conducteur m. (v. trein) guard; (v. tram) conductor.
confectie v. ready-made clothes (clothing).
conferentie v. conference, parley.
confisqueren o. w. confiscate.
confrontatie v. confrontation.
confronteren o. w. confront.
congregatie v. congregation; (kath. ook:) sodality.
congres o. congress.
congreslid o. member of the congress.
connossement o. bill of lading.
consciëntie v. conscience.
consecratie v. consecration.
conservatief b. n. en z. n., m. conservative.

conservenfabriek v. preserving-factory, tinning factory; (*Am.*) canning, canning-factory.
consideratie v. consideration.
consignatie v. (*H.*) consignment.
consignatiegever m. (*H.*) consignor.
consignatienemer m. consignee.
consigneren o. w. (*H.*) consign; (*mil.*) confine to barracks.
consortium o. (*H.*) combine, syndicate.
consternatie v. consternation.
constructie v. construction, structure.
consul m. consul.
consulaat o. consulate.
consult o. consultation.
consulteren o. w. consult.
consumptie v. consumption.
contact o. contact, touch.
contactbord o. switch-board.
contant b. n. en bw. cash.
contingent o. contingent, quota.
conto o. (*H.*) account.
contrabande v. contraband (goods).
contract o. contract, agreement.
contracteren on. w. en o. w. contract.
contramine v. *in de — zijn*, (*H.*) speculate for a fall, buy short; (*fig.*) be contrary.
contrapunt o. (*muz.*) counterpoint.
contributie v. (*voor lidmaatschap*) subscription; (*belasting*) contribution, tax.
controle v. check, supervision; inspection.
controleren o. w. check, verify; (*kaartjes, enz.*) examine, inspect.
controleur m. controller, checker; (*v. kaartjes*) inspector, ticket-examiner.
conversatie v. conversation.
convocatiebiljet o. notice of meeting.
convoceren o. w. call, summon.
coöperatie v. co-operation.
coöperatief b. n. co-operative.
coördinatie v. co-ordination.
copieus b. n. plentiful.
corps o. corps, body; (*mil.*) corps.
correct b. n. (*bw.*) correct(ly).
correctie v. correction; (*als tuchtiging ook:*) punishment.
corrector m. proof-reader.
correspondent m. correspondent.
correspondentie v. correspondence.
corresponderen on. w. correspond; (*v. kamers, enz.*) connect; (*v. treinen, enz.*) correspond, run in connection.

corrigeren o. w. en on. w. correct; read (proofs).
corrupt b .n. corrupt.
corruptie v. corruption.
corsage o. bodice, corsage.
Corsica o. Corsica.
corvee v. (*mil.*) (*werk*) fatigue-duty; (*troep*) fatigue-party; (*karwei*) tough job.
coulant b. n. (*H.*) accommodating, business-like, easy to deal with.
coulisse v. side-scene.
coupé m. (*v. trein*) compartment; (*rijtuig*) brougham, coupé. [cutting.
coupon v. coupon; (*stof*) remnant.
couponblad o. coupon-sheet.
courant b. n. current, marketable.
courant v. (*dagblad*) (news) (paper), journal.
couvert o. (*briefomslag*) envelop, eover; (*tafelgereedschap*) cover.
credit o. (*H.*) credit.
crediteren o. w. *iem. — voor*, credit a person's account with, credit a person for, carry to a person's credit.
crediteur m. creditor.
creditnota v. credit-note.
creditpost m. credit-post.
creditsaldo o. credit-balance.
creditzijde v. credit-side.
crematie v. cremation.
crème v. cream.
cricketen o. w. play cricket.
cricketveld o. cricket-ground, —field.
crisis v. crisis; (*kritiek ogenblik*) critical stage; (*keerpunt*) turning-point.
criterium o. criterion, test.
cultus m. cult.
cultuur v. culture, cultivation.
cultuurgeschiedenis v. history of civilization, social history.
cultuurvolk o. civilized nation.
curatele v. guardianship, curatelle.
curator m. guardian; (*in faillissement*) (official) receiver, trustee; (*v. krankzinnige*) committee; (*v. museum, enz.*) curator, custodian.
curieus b. n. curious, odd, queer.
curiositeit v. curiosity.
cursief b. n. in italics, italicized.
cursus m. course; (*schooljaar*) school-year.
cycloon m. cyclone.
cyclus m. cycle.
cynisch b. n. cynic; cynical.
cynisme o. cynicism.

D

daad v. deed, act, action; (*roemrijke —, prestatie*) achievement, exploit.
daadwerkelijk b. n. (*bw.*) actual(ly), real(ly).
daags bw. by day, on the day, in the daytime.

daags b. n. *—e kleren*, every-day clothes.
daar bw. there; vw. as, because.
daaraan (*— aan dat*), at (by, to) it; thereat, thereto.
daarachter bw. behind it, there behind.

daarbeneden *bw.* under it, beneath it; down there.

daarbij *bw.* near it; *(daarnevens)* besides, over and above that, moreover.

daarbinnen *bw.* within, in there.

daarboven *bw.* above it, over it; up there.

daarbuiten *bw.* outside (of it); without (it).

daardoor *bw.* *(plaats)* through it (this, that); *(oorzaak)* by that, by these means.

daarenboven *bw.* besides, moreover.

daarentegen *bw.* on the contrary, on the other hand.

daareven *bw.* just now.

daarginds *bw.* over there.

daarheen *bw.* there.

daarin *bw.* in it (this, that), in there.

daarlangs *bw.* by it, along that road.

daarlaten *bw.* **nog daargelaten dat,** let alone that.

daarmede *bw.* with that (this).

daarna *bw.* after that, then.

daarnaast *bw.* beside it, next to it, by the side of it.

daarnevens *bw.* besides, over and above that.

daarom *bw.* therefore, for that reason, on that account.

daarop *bw.* on (upon) it (that); thereupon, after this.

daarover *bw.* over it, across it (that); about that, concerning that, on that point (subject).

daartegenover *bw.* opposite; on the other hand.

daartoe *bw.* for that, for it, for that purpose.

daartussen *bw.* between that, between (them), among them.

daarvan *bw.* of that; from that.

daarvoor *bw.* for that (purpose); for it; *(tijd)* before that (it); *(plaats)* in front of that (it, them).

dadel *v.* date.

dadelijk *b. n.* *(onmiddellijk)* immediate, direct; *(v. genade, enz.)* actual; *bw.* immediately, directly, instantly, on the instant.

dader *m.* doer, perpetrator, author; *(v. misdrijf)* offender, culprit.

dag *m.* day; *(daglicht)* daylight.

dagblad *o.* daily paper, newspaper.

dagbladpers *v.* daily press.

dagboek *o.* diary, journal; *(kladboek)* waste-book; *(boekhouding)* day-book.

dagdief *m.* idler, dawdler, time-thief.

dagelijks *bw.* every day, daily; *b. n.* daily, everyday; *(voor hemellichamen)* diurnal.

dagen *on. w.* dawn; *vt.* summon, summons.

dageraad *m.* dawn, day-break.

daggeld *o.* daily pay; daily wages.

daglicht *o.* day-light, day.

dagloner *m.* day-labourer.

dagloon *o.* day's wages, daily wages.

dagmars *m.* day's march.

dagorde *v.* order of the day.

dagreis *v.* day's journey.

dagtaak *v.* day's work.

dagtekenen *o. w. en on. w.* date.

dagtekening *r.* date.

dagvaarden *o. w.* summon(s), cite, serve a process on.

dagvaarding *r.* summons, citation, warrant to appear, writ.

dagwerk *o.* day-work, daily work.

dak *o.* roof.

dakbalk *m.* roof-beam.

dakgoot *r.* gutter.

dakkamertje *o.* attic, garret, room under the leads.

dakloos *b. n.* roofless, homeless.

dakpan *r.* roofing-tile, (pan-)tile.

dakstro *o.* thatch.

dakvenster *o.* dormer-window, garret-window, attic-window.

dal *o.* valley; *(dicht.)* vale, dale; *(nauw —; Sc.)* glen.

dalen *on. w.* *(r. ballon, vliegtuig)* descend; *(v. zon)* sink, go down; *(v. barometer, temperatuur, enz.)* fall, drop; *(v. prijzen)* fall, go down; *(r. stem)* sink, drop; *(fig.: in achting)* sink.

daling *v.* descent; fall, drop.

dam *m.* dam, dike; causeway; *(in rivier)* weir; *(in 't groot)* barrage; *v. (in damspel)* king, crowned man.

damast *o.* damask.

dambord *o.* draught-board.

dame *v.* lady; *(bij dans, enz.)* partner.

damescoupé *m.* ladies' compartment.

damestasje *o.* lady's bag, vanity-bag.

damhert *o.* fallow-deer.

dammen *on. w.* play at draughts.

damp *m.* vapour, steam, smoke, fume.

dampen *on. w.* steam, smoke; puff (away) at one's pipe.

dampig *b. n.* *(nevelig)* vaporous, vapoury, hazy; *(kortademig, v. paard)* broken-winded, short-winded, pursy.

dampkring *m.* atmosphere.

damschijf *v.* draughtsman.

damspel *o.* draughts, game of (at) draughts; draught board and men.

dan *bw.* then; *vw.* than.

danig *b. n.* thorough, tremendous; *bw.* thoroughly, tremendously, very much, greatly.

dank *m.* thanks, acknowledgment.

dankbaar *b. n.* *(bw.)* thankful(ly), grateful(ly).

dankbaarheid *v.* thankfulness, gratitude.

dankbetuiging *v.* expression of thanks, thanksgiving.

danken *o. w.* thank; give thanks; *on. w.* give (render, return) thanks; *(na maaltijden)* say grace.

dankgebed *o.* prayer of thanks; *(na maaltijden)* grace.

danklied *o.* song of thanksgiving.

dankzegging *v.* thanksgiving.

dans *m.* dance.

dansen *on. w.* dance.

danser *m.* dancer, partner.
danskunst *v.* art of dancing.
dansles *v.* dancing-lesson.
danswoede *v.* dancing-mania.
dapper *b. n.* (*bw.*) brave(ly), valiant(ly), gallant(ly), valorous(ly).
dapperheid *v.* bravery, gallantry, valour.
dar *m.* drone.
darm *m.* intestine, gut; **—en,** *ook:* bowels, entrails.
darmbloeding *v.* intestinal hemorrhage.
darmkanaal *o.* intestinal canal, intestinal tube.
darmontsteking *v.* enteritis.
darmvlies *o.* peritoneum.
dartel *b. n.* frisky, frolicsome, playful, rompish; (*ong.*) skittish.
dartelen *on. w.* frisk, frolic, dally.
dartelheid *v.* friskiness, playfulness.
das *m.* badger; *v.* neck-cloth, cravat; (neck-)tie.
dashond *m.* badger-dog, badgerer.
dat *aanw. vnw.* that; *betr. vnw.* that, which; *vw.* that.
data *o. mv.* data.
dateren *o. w.* date.
datgene *vnw.* that.
dato *bw.* dated...
datum *m.* date.
dauw *m.* dew.
dauwdroppel *m.* dew-drop.
dauwen *on. w.* dew.
daveren *on. w.* boom, shake.
de *lidw.* the.
debat *o.* debate, discussion.
debatteren *on. w.* debate, discuss.
debet *z. n., o.* (*H.*) debit.
debetnota *v.* debit-note.
debetsaldo *o.* debit-balance.
debiet *o.* sale.
debiteren *o. w.* (*op debetzijde boeken*) debit; (*verkopen*) sell; (*in 't klein*) retail.
debiteur *m.* debtor.
debuteren *on. w.* make one's debut.
debuut *o.* debut, first appearance.
december *m.* December.
decigram *o.* decigram(me).
deciliter *m.* decilitre.
decimaal *b. n.* decimal; *z. n., v.* decimal (place).
decimeter *m.* decimetre.
declaratie *v.* declaration; (*v. douane*) entry; (*v. onkosten*) voucher.
decor *o.* scenery.
decreet *o.* decree, enactment.
deeg *o.* dough; (*v. gebak*) paste; (*gerezen*) sponge.
deegrol *v.* rolling-pin.
deel *v.* (*plank*) deal, board, plank; (*dorsvloer*) treshing-floor.
deel *o.* part, portion; (*aandeel*) share; (*v. boek*) volume.
deelachtig *b. n.* **— worden** (**zijn**), participate in, share; **— maken,** impart to.
deelbaar *b. n.* divisible.

deelgenoot *m.* sharer, partner; (*H.: compagnon*) partner; (*aandeelhouder*) shareholder.
deelnemen *on. w.* **— aan,** take part in, participate in, join in; (*komplot, enz.*) be a party to; (*maaltijd*) partake of.
deelnemer *m.* participator, partner; (*bij verg. examen*) competitor; (*bij wedstrijd*) competitor, contestant; (*aan komplot, enz.*) participant.
deelneming *v.* (*het meedoen*) participation; (*het medegevoelen*) sympathy; compassion, commiseration.
deelsom *v.* division sum.
deelstreepje *o.* hyphen.
deeltal *o.* dividend.
deelteken *o.* diaeresis; (*rek.*) division sign, double point.
deelwoord *o.* participle.
deemoed *m.* humility, meekness, submissiveness.
deerlijk *b. n.* (*bw.*) sad(ly), grievous(ly), piteous(ly), pitiful(ly).
deern(e) *v.* girl, wench, damsel.
deernis *v.* pity, commiseration, compassion.
defect *z. n., o.* defect, deficiency; (*tn.*) fault; breakdown; *b. n.* (*v. rem*) defective; (*v. klep, band, enz.*) faulty; (*v. machine*) out of order.
defensief *b. n.* (*bw.*) defensive(ly).
deficit *o.* deficit, deficiency.
deftig *b. n.* (*v. gelaat*) grave; (*v. gebouw, voorkomen, enz.*) stately; (*v. taal, stijl*) dignified; (*v. stadswijk*) aristocratic.
deftigheid *v.* gravity; stateliness; portliness; dignity; (air of) distinction.
degelijk *b. n.* (*v. persoon, hoedanigheid, enz.*) sterling; (*v. opvoeding, kennis*) sound; (*v. werk, enz.*) thorough; (*v. voedsel*) substantial; (*v. argument, enz.*) solid; *bw.* soundly; thoroughly.
degelijkheid *v.* sterling character, sterling qualities; soundness; thoroughness; solidity.
degen *m.* sword; (*scherm—*) foil.
degene *vnw.* he, she; **—n die,** those who.
degenstok *m.* sword-stick.
deining *v.* heave, roll, swell.
dek *o.* (*bedekking*) cover; covering; (*v. bed*) bed-clothes; (*v. paard*) horse-cloth; (*sch.*) deck.
dekblad *o.* (*Pl.*) bract; (*v. sigaar*) wrapper.
deken *v.* blanket; (*gewatteerde —*) quilt, coverlet; *m.* dean; (*v. diplomatiek corps*) doyen.
dekken *o. w.* cover; (*v. huis: met pannen*) tile; (*met stro, riet*) thatch; (*met leien*) slate; (*v. kosten*) cover, defray; (*v. schade, enz.*) cover, make good; (*v. verzekering*) cover; (*sch.*) damp down; *w. w.* **zich —,** cover oneself, put on one's hat; secure oneself; shield oneself; (*mil.*) take cover.
dekking *v.* cover; covering; (*mil.*) cover; (*fig.*) protection, guard, shield.
dekkleed *o.* cover, horse-cloth.

dekmantel *m.* cloak; (*fig.*) cloak, disguise, mask.
deksel *o.* cover; lid.
deksteen *m.* cap-stone; (*v. muur*) coping-stone.
dekstoel *m.* deck-chair.
dekverf *v.* body-colour.
dekzeil *o.* tarpaulin.
delen *o. w. en on. w.* divide; (*v. mening, enz.*) share.
deler *m.* (*v. persoon*) divider; (*v. getal*) divisor.
delfstof *v.* mineral.
delfstoffenrijk *o.* mineral kingdom.
delfstofkunde *v.* mineralogy.
delgen *o. w.* (*v. schuld*) pay off, clear off, discharge, amortize; (*v. lening*) extinguish, redeem.
delging *v.* payment, discharge, amortization; redemption.
delicatesse *v.* delicay; (*v. lekkernij ook:*) dainty (bit).
deling *v.* (*rek.*) division; (*verdeling: v. eigendom, enz.*) partition.
delven *on. w.* dig, scoop.
demobilisatie *v.* demobilization.
democratie *v.* democracy.
dempen *o. w.* (*v. gracht, enz.*) fill up; (*v. geluid*) deaden; (*muz.*) mute; (*v., licht*) subdue, dim; (*v. oproer*) quell crush, stamp out; (*v. vuur*) quench, extinguish.
demping *v.* filling up; quenching, extinguishment, extinction.
den *m.* fir(-tree).
Denemarken *o.* Denmark.
denkbaar *b. n.* imaginable, conceivable, thinkable.
denkbeeld *o.* idea, notion.
denkelijk *b. n.* likely, probable.
denken *o. w. en on. w.* think; (*van plan zijn*) intend, think of.
denker *m.* thinker.
denkvermogen *o.* thinking-faculty; intellectual capacity; intellectual power.
denkwijze *v.* way of thinking, habit of thought, mentality.
denneboom *m.* fir-tree.
dennenbos *o.* fir-wood.
deposito *o.* deposit.
depothouder *m.* stocker, manager of a branch-establishment.
derde *telw.* third.
derdemachtswortel *m.* cube root.
deren *o. w.* hurt, harm, injure.
dergelijk *vnw.* such, such-like, similar.
derhalve *bw.* therefore, consequently, so.
dermate *bw.* in such a manner, to a degree, to such an extent, so much.
dertien *telw.* thirteen.
dertiende *telw.* thirteenth.
dertig *telw.* thirty.
derven *o. w.* be deprived of, lack.
derving *v.* privation, lack.
derwaarts *bw.* thither, that way.
derwijze *bw.* in such a way.
des *bw.* of the; — *te beter,* so much the

better, all the better; — *te meer,* so much the more.
desbetreffend *b. n.* relating to this matter, — to the matter in question.
desem *m.* leaven.
deserteren *on. w.* desert (the colours), run away.
deserteur *m.* deserter, runaway.
deskundige *m.* expert.
desnoods *bw.* if need be, in case of need, at a pinch.
desondanks *bw.* nevertheless.
dessert *o.* dessert.
destijds *bw.* at the (that) time.
deswege *bw.* on that account, for that reason, therefore.
detail *o.* detail; (*H.*) retail.
detailhandel *m.* retail trade.
detailprijs *m.* retail price.
detective *m.* detective.
detectiveverhaal *o.* detective story.
deugd *v.* virtue; (good) quality.
deugdelijk *b. n.* (*betrouwbaar*) reliable; (*duurzaam*) durable; (*v. bewijs, argument*) valid; (*v. reden*) solid.
deugdelijkheid *v.* reliableness, reliability; durability, good quality; validity; solidity.
deugdzaam *b. n.* virtuous. [tue.
deugdzaamheid *v.* virtuousness; virdeugen *on. w.* be good, be fit.
deugniet *m.* good-for-nothing, never-do-well, rascal, rogue, scamp.
deuk *v.* dent, dint.
deuken *o. w.* dent, indent.
deukhoed *m.* soft felt hat, squash hat.
deun *m.* tune, air; (*eentonig*) sing-song.
deur *v.* door.
deurbel *v.* door-bell.
deurknop *m.* door-handle, (door-)knob.
deurlijst *v.* door-frame.
deurwaarder *m.* process-server, warrant-officer, sheriff's officer; (*in rechtszaal*) usher, crier.
devies *o.* device, motto.
devoot *b. n.* devout, pious.
dewijl *vw.* because, as, since.
deze *vnw.* this; (*mv.*) these; (*de laatstgenoemde*) the latter.
dezelfde *vnw.* the same.
diaconie *v.* poor-relief board.
diagnose *v.* diagnosis.
diaken *m.* deacon.
dialect *o.* dialect.
dialoog *m.* dialogue.
diamant *o. en m.* diamond.
diamanthandelaar *m.* diamond-broker, diamond-merchant.
diamantslijper *m.* (*slijper*) diamond-polisher; (*alg.: bewerker*) diamond-cutter.
diamantzetter *m.* diamond-setter.
dicht *b. n.* (*gesloten: v. deur, enz.*) closed, shut; (*v. bevolking, woud, enz.*) dense; (*v. massa*) compact; (*niet lek*) tight; (*v. mist, haar, enz.*) thick; (*v. weefsel*) close; *bw.* (*bevolkt*) densely; (*begroeid*) thickly; (*geschreven*) closely.

dicht *o.* poetry.
dichtbij *b. n. bw. vz.* close by, hard by, near.
dichtdoen *o. w.* shut, close.
dichten *o. w. en on. w.* make verses, write poetry, write verses; *o. w.* (*dicht maken*) stop, close up.
dichter *m.* poet.
dichterlijk *b. n.* (*bw.*) poetic(ally).
dichtgooien *o. w.* (*v. deur, enz.*) slam, bang, throw to; (*v. gracht, enz.*) fill up.
dichtheid *v.* density; compactness; thickness.
dichtknopen *o. w.* button up.
dichtkunst *v.* (art of) poetry, poetic art.
dichtmaat *v.* metre; *in —,* in verse.
dichtplakken *o. w.* seal (up), gum (stick) down.
dichtregel *m.* line of poetry.
dichtstuk *o.* poem, piece of poetry.
dictaat *o.* dictation.
dictator *m.* dictator.
die *aanw. vnw.* that; those; *betr. vnw.* who, which, that.
dieet *o.* diet; regimen.
dief *m.* thief, robber.
diefachtig *b. n.* thievish, thieving.
diefstal *m.* theft, robbery; (*recht*) larceny.
diegene *vnw.* he, she; *—n,* those.
dienaangaande *bw.* with respect (reference) to that.
dienaar *m.* servant; (*buiging*) bow.
dienares *v.* servant; (*buiging*) curtsey.
diender *m.* policeman, constable.
dienen *o. w.* serve; *on. w.* serve; be in service; (*soldaat zijn*) be in the army.
dienovereenkomstig *bw.* accordingly.
dienst *m.* service.
dienstbaar *b. n.* subservient (*aan,* to).
dienstbaarheid *v.* servitude; subserviency; (*Bijb.*) bondage.
dienstbetoon *o.* service(s) rendered.
dienstbode *m. en v.* servant, domestic (servant).
dienstdoend *b. n.* (*v. beambte, mil.*) on duty; (*aan 't hof*) in waiting; (*waarnemend*) acting.
dienstig *b. n., bw.* serviceable, useful, expedient; fit.
dienstjaar *o.* (*v. ambtenaar, enz.*) year of service; (*boekjaar*) fiscal year, financial year.
dienstknecht *m.* servant, man-servant.
dienstmaagd *v.* (maid-)servant; (*Bijb.*) hand-maid.
dienstmeisje *o.* servant-girl.
dienstplicht *m.* liability to service; (*mil.*) compulsory (military) service.
dienstregeling *v.* time-table, service-table. [able.
dienstvaardig *b. n.* obliging, service-
dienstvaardigheid *v.* obligingness, serviceableness.
dienstweigering *v.* refusal to obey an orders; (*mil.*) refusal of (military) service; (*te velde*) disobedience in the field.

dientengevolge *bw.* in consequence, therefore.
dienvolgens *bw.* accordingly, consequently.
diep *b. n.* deep; (*fig. vooral*) profound; *bw.* deeply; profoundly; sink deep; (*fig.*) fall very low; *z. n., o.* (*diepte, diep water*) deep; (*vaargeul*) canal.
diepgaand *b. n.* sinking deep; (*fig.*) (deep-)searching, penetrating; (*v. geschil*) deep-lying; (*v. verandering*) radical.
diepgang *m.* (*sch.*) (depth of) draught.
dieplood *o.* deep-sea lead, sounding-lead, sounding-line.
diepte *v.* depth; (*zee, enz.*) deep; (*fig.*) deepness, profoundness.
diepzinnig *b. n.* deep, profound, abstruse.
diepzinnigheid *v.* depth, profoundness, abstruseness.
dier *o.* animal, beast.
dierbaar *b. n.* dear, beloved.
dierenarts *m.* animal doctor.
dierenbescherming *v.* protection of animals.
dierenepos *m.* beast epic.
dierenhuid *v.* skin of an animal.
dierentemmer *m.* (wild) beast tamer.
dierentuin *m.* zoological garden(s); (*fam.*) zoo.
dierkunde *v.* zoology.
dierlijk *b. n.* animal; (*beestachtig*) bestial; (*v. lust, begeerte*) brutal, brutish.
dierlijkheid *v.* animality; bestiality; brutality, brutishness.
diersoort *v.* species of animals.
diets *b. n.* *iem. iets — maken,* make one believe something.
Diets *o.* (mediaeval) Dutch.
dievegge *v.* (female) thief.
dievengespuis *o.* pack of thieves.
dievenhol *o.* thieves' den.
dievenlantaarn *v.* dark lantern, bull's eye.
dieventaal *v.* thieves' patter, thieves' slang.
dievenwagen *m.* prisoner's van.
dij *v.* thigh.
dijbeen *o.* thigh-bone; (*wet.*) femur.
dijk *m.* dike, bank, dam, embankment.
dijkbreuk *v.* rupture of a dike, dike-burst.
dijkwerker *m.* diker.
dijkwezen *o.* dikes.
dik *b. n.* thick; (*dicht: v. haar, mist*) thick, dense; (*opgezet: v. wang, enz.*) swollen; (*zwaarlijvig*) stout; (*log*) bulky; (*v. melk*) curdled; *bw.* thickly, densely; *z. n., o.* thick (part); (*v. koffie*) grounds, dregs.
dikbuik *m. en v.* pot-belly, fatguts.
dikbuikig *b. n.* pot-bellied, big-bellied, corpulent.
dikhuidig *b. n.* thick-skinned; (*wet.*) pachyderm.
dikkop *m.* thick-skull; (*larve v. kikvors*) tadpole.
dikte *v.* thickness, etc. [ly.
dikwerf, dikwijls *bw.* often, frequent-

dilettant(e) *m.* (*v.*) dilettante, amateur.
ding *o.* thing.
dingen *on. w.* haggle, higgle, chaffer, bargain.
dinsdag *m.* Tuesday.
diocees *o.* diocese.
diploma *o.* certificate, diploma; (*v. schouwburg*) season-ticket.
diplomaat *m.* diplomat, diplomatist.
directeur *m.* (*r. maatschappij*) director, managing-director; (*v. fabriek, zaak, schouwburg*) manager; (*v. school*) head-master,principal;(*v.gevangenis*)governor; (*v. ziekenhuis*) superintendent; (*r. zangvereniging*) choir-master.
directie *r.* managing board, board of directors; management.
dirigeerstok *m.* baton, conductor's wand.
dirigent *m.* (musical, orchestral) conductor; (*r. koor*) choir-master.
dirigeren *o. w.* direct; (*r. orkest*) conduct.
dis *v.* (*muz.*) D sharp.
dis *m.* table, board.
disagio *o.* discount.
discipel *m.* disciple.
disconteren *o. w.* discount.
disconto *o.* (rate of) discount; (*bank—*) bankrate.
discontobank *v.* discount-bank.
discontovoet *m.* rate of discount.
discreet *b. n.* (*kies*) considerate; (*bescheiden*) modest; (*geheimen kunnende bewaren*) close, secret.
discus *m.* discus, disc, disk.
discuswerper *m.* discobolus.
disgenoot *m.* fellow-guest; neighbour at table.
disharmonie *r.* disharmony, discord.
dissel *m.* (*r. wagen*) pole, shaft; (*bijl: r. wagenmaker*) adze.
disselboom *m.* pole.
disselpaard *o.* pole-horse.
dissertatie *v.* (*verhandeling*) dissertation; (*v. doctoraat*) thesis.
distel *r.* thistle.
distelvink *m.* gold-finch.
distilleerderij *r.* distillery.
distilleertoestel *o.* still.
district *o.* district.
dit *aanw. vnw.* this.
ditmaal, this time.
divan *m.* divan.
dividend *o.* dividend.
divisie *v.* division.
divisiegeneraal *m.* division general.
dobbelaar *m.* dicer, gambler.
dobbelen *on. w.* (play at) dice, gamble.
dobbelsteen *m.* die (*mr.:* dice); (*fig.*) cube, die.
dobber *m.* (*drijver, boei*) buoy; (*r. hengelsnoer*) float.
doch *vw.* but, yet, still.
dochter *v.* daugther.
dochtermaatschappij *r.* subsidiary company, affiliated company, daughter-company.

doctor *m.* doctor; (*geneeskunde*) doctor (of medicine), physician; (*rechten*) doctor of laws, graduate in law; (*theologie*) doctor of divinity.
doctores *v.* lady-doctor.
document *o.* document.
dode *m. en v.* dead person, dead man (woman).
dodelijk *b. n.* (*v. angst, wonde, enz.*) mortal; (*v. vergif, slag, wapen*) deadly; (*v. ongeluk*) fatal; (*v. dosis*) lethal; *bw.* mortally, deadly.
doden *o. w.* kill; slay; (*fig.*) mortify.
dodenakker *m.* God's acre, cemetery.
dodend *bw.* deadly.
dodendans *m.* death-dance, danse macabre.
dodenhuis *o.* ossuary.
dodenlijst *r.* death-roll, obituary.
dodenmars *m.* dead march.
dodijnen *on. w.* dandle.
doedelzak *m.* bagpipe(s).
doek *m.* (*opneemdoek, keukendoek, enz.*) cloth; (*omslagdoek*) shawl, wrap; (*handdoek*) towel; *o.* cloth, linen; (*v. schilder*) canvas; (*v. toneel*) curtain; (*v. film*) screen; (*sch.*) rag, sail.
doekje *o.* cloth; (*om vinger*) rag.
doel *o.* (*doeleinde, oogmerk*) aim, object, purpose, end, design; (*mikpunt*) target, butt; (*eindpunt; voetb.*) goal.
doelbewust *b. n.* purposeful.
doeleinde *o.* end, purpose.
doelen *on. w.* — **op,** aim at; (*fig.*) allude to, aim at.
doelloos *b. n.* (*bw.*) aimless, purpose-less, objectless; (*nutteloos*) useless.
doelmatig *b. n.* appropriate (suitable, adapted) to the purpose, fit for the purpose, practical efficient.
doelmatigheid *r.* appropriateness, suitability, efficiency.
doelpunt *o.* goal.
doeltreffend *b. n.* efficient, efficacious; effective.
doelverdediger, doelwachter *m.* goal-keeper.
doen *o. w. en on. w.* (*alg.*) do; (*v. poging, keus, verzoek, enz.*) make; (*v. stap, sprong, wandeling*) take; (*vóór infinitief*) make; (*wegbergen, steken*) put; (*kosten*) be worth; *z. n., o.* doing(s).
does *m.* (*Dk.*) barbet.
doezelaar *m.* stump.
doezelig *b. n.* fuzzy, hazy, blurred.
dof (*v. kleur, licht, klank*) dull, dull-toned; (*v. goud, koper*) dead; (*v. ogen*) lack-lustre, dim; (*v. licht*) dim; (*lusteloos, onverschillig*) dull.
dof *m.* (*slag, bons*) thud, buffet; (*duw, stoot*) push.
doffer *m.* (*Dk.*) cock-pigeon, male-pigeon.
dofheid *r.* dullness; dimness; lack of lustre.
dog *m.* mastiff, bulldog.
dogma *o.* dogma.
dok *o.* dock.

dokgelden *o. mv.* dock dues, dockage.
dokter *m.* doctor, physician, medical man.
doktersrekening *v.* doctor's bill.
dokwerker *m.* dock-labourer, docker.
dol *m.* (*sch.*) thole(-pin), thowl.
dol *b. n.* (*gek*) mad; (*woedend*) delirious, frantic, wild; (*v. schroef*) drunken; (*v. kompas*) whirling; *bw.* madly; deliriously.
dolen *on. w.* wander (about), roam (about), ramble.
dolfijn *m.* dolphin.
dolgraag *bw.* —*!* with the greatest pleasure !
dolheid *v.* madness, frenzy, wildness.
dolik *v.* (*Pl.*) cockle, darnel.
dolk *m.* dagger, poniard, dirk, stiletto.
dolksteek *m.* dagger-stroke, (dagger-)-stab.
dollekervel *v.* hemlock.
dolleman *m.* madman, madcap.
dollen *on. w.* sport, frolic.
dom *m.* (*domkerk*) cathedral (church); (*koepel*) dome.
dom *b. n.* stupid, dull, slow; (*onnozel*) silly.
domein *o.* domain, crown-land, demesne; (*fig.*) domain.
domheid *v.* stupidity, dullness.
domicilie *o.* domicile.
domiciliëren *o. w.* domicile, domiciliate; (*v. wissel ook:*) make payable.
dominee *m.* clergyman; minister; (*ong.*) parson.
dominosteen *m.* domino.
domkop *m.* blockhead, dunderhead, blunderhead, dunce, dolt, numskull.
dommekracht *v.* jack-screw, jack.
dommelen *on. w.* doze, drowse.
dommelig *b. n.* dozy, drowsy.
dommeligheid *v.* doziness, drowsiness.
dommerik, domoor *m. zie* **domkop.**
dompelaar *m.* (*Dk.*) diver.
dompelen *o. w.* plunge, dive, dip, duck; (*fig.*) plunge.
dompeling *v.* immersion.
dompen *o. w.* extinguish, put out.
domper *m.* extinguisher; (*fig.*) obscurant(ist).
dompig *b. n.* close; stuffy musty.
domtoren *m.* cathedral tower.
Donau *m.* Danube.
donder *m.* thunder. [shower.
donderbui *v.* thunderstorm, thunder-
donderdag *m.* Thursday.
donderen *on. w.* thunder; (*uitvaren*) thunder, fulminate; (*vallen*) tumble.
donderend *b. n.* thundering, thunderous.
donderkop *m.* thunder-cloud.
dondersteen *m.* thunder-stone; (*fig.*) bully, thundering blackguard.
donderweer *o.* thundery weather.
donderwolk *v.* thunder-cloud.
donker *b. n.* dark, obscure; (*v. weer*) gloomy, dull; (*fig.*) murky, dusky; (*dicht.*) darksome, darkling; *bw.* darkly; *z. n., o.* dark, darkness.

donkerheid *v.* darkness, obscurity.
dons *o.* down, fluff.
donsachtig *b. n.* downy, fluffy.
dood *b. n.* dead.
doodaf *b. n.* dead-beat, knocked-up, dog-tired.
doodarm *b. n.* very poor, as poor as Job, as poor as a church-mouse.
doodbedaard *b. n.* quite calm, as cool as a cucumber.
doodbidder *m.* undertaker's man, mute.
doodbloeden *on. w.* bleed to death; (*fig.*) fizzle out, blow over.
doodeenvoudig *b. n.* as easy as lying, ever so simple.
doodgaan *on. w.* die.
doodgeboren *b. n.* dead-born, still-born.
doodgraver *m.* grave-digger; (*Dk.*) burying-beetle, sexton-beetle.
doodkist *v.* coffin.
doodmoe *b. n.* dead-tired, tired to death.
doodop *b. n. zie* **doodaf.**
doods *b. n.* deathlike, deathly, dead.
doodsakte *v.* certificate of death.
doodsangst *m.* mortal agony, pangs of death; (*fig.*) mortal fear, agony of fear.
doodsbed *o.* death-bed.
doodsbenauwd *b. n.* suffocating; (*fig.*) mortally afraid, in an agony of fear.
doodsbleek *b. n.* deathly pale, dead white, livid.
doodsbrief *m.* mortuary letter.
doodschieten *o. w.* shoot (dead).
doodsengel *m.* angel of death.
doodsgerochel *o.* death-rattle, ruckle.
doodsgevaar *o.* danger of life, deadly peril.
doodsheid *v.* deadness, deathliness.
doodshemd *o.* shroud, winding-sheet.
doodshoofd *o.* death's head, skull.
doodskleed *o.* shroud, winding-sheet.
doodskleur *v.* death-colour.
doodslaan *o. w.* kill; (*fig.: bij twistgesprek*) silence.
doodslaap *m.* sleep of death.
doodslag *m.* manslaughter, homicide.
doodsnik *m.* last gasp, death-sob.
doodsstrijd *m.* agony, death-struggle.
doodsteek *m.* death-blow, finishing-stroke.
doodstil *b. n.* stock-still, as still as death.
doodstraf *v.* capital punishment.
doodsverachting *v.* contempt of death.
doodsvijand *m.* mortal enemy.
doodszweet *o.* sweat of death, death-sweat.
doodverven *o. w.* dead-colour.
doodvonnis *o.* sentence of death, death-sentence.
doodziek *b. n.* dangerously (mortally) ill, sick to death.
doodzonde *v.* mortal sin, deadly sin.

doof *b. n.* deaf.
doofheid *v.* deafness.
doofpot *m.* extinguisher.
doofstom *b. n.* deaf-mute, deaf and dumb.
dooi *m.* thaw.
dooien *on. w.* thaw.
dooier *m.* yolk.
doolhof *m.* labyrinth, maze.
doolweg *m.* wrong way, wrong path.
doop *m.* baptism, christening.
doopakte *v.* certificate of baptism.
doopceel *v.* certificate of baptism.
doopgelofte(n) *v.* (*mv.*) baptismal vow(s).
doopkapel *v.* baptistery.
doopnaam *m.* Christian name.
doopsel *o.* baptism.
doopvont *v.* baptismal font.
doopwater *o.* baptismal water.
door *vz.* (*v. tijd, plaats*) through; (*v. oorzaak, middel*) by; *bw.* through.
doorbakken *o. w.* bake through.
doorbladeren *o. w.* (*v. boek*) turn over the leaves of, run over, skim.
doorboren *o. w.* (*met puntig voorwerp*) pierce, perforate; (*met dolk*) stab; (*met bajonet*) transfix; (*met kogels*) riddle; (*met blikken*) transfix, look daggers at.
doorbraak *v.* (*v. dijk*) burst, bursting; breaking(-through); (*mil.*) break-through.
doorbreken *o. w.* (*v. brood, stok, enz.*) break; (*mil.: v. vijand*) break through; (*v. blokkade*) run; *on. w.* (*v. zon*) break through, come out; (*v. dijk, abces*) burst.
doorbrengen *o. w.* (*v. tijd*) pass; (*v. dagen, geld*) spend; (*ong.: v. geld, fortuin*) run through.
doorbrenger *m.* spendthrift.
doordacht *b. n.* duly (well) considered, well-thought out.
doordat *vw.* because.
doordien *vw.* because, as, since.
doordraaien *on. w.* continue turning, keep on turning; (*fam.*) be on the spree.
doordraaier *m.* fast fellow, gay fellow, loose fish.
doordraver *m.* rattle(-box).
doordrijven *o. w.* **zijn zin —,** carry one's point.
doordrijver *m.* headstrong (persistent) person.
doordringbaar *b. n.* (*voor kogel, oog, enz.*) penetrable; (*voor warmte, vocht, enz.*) permeable, pervious.
doordringbaarheid *v.* penetrability; permeability, perviousness.
doordringen *on. w.* penetrate; (*door-sijpelen*) ooze through.
doordringen *o. w.* pierce, penetrate; permeate, pervade.
dooreen *bw.* together, pell-mell, confusedly, in confusion, higgledy-piggledy.
dooreenhaspelen *o. w.* mix up, muddle up, middle together.

dooreenlopen *on. w.* flow together; run together.
doorgaan *on. w.* (*zijn weg vervolgen*) walk on, go on; (*v. trein, enz.*) go through; (*plaats hebben*) come off, take place; *o. w.* (*doorlopen: v. straat, rekening, enz.*) go through; (*v. schoenen*) walk through.
doorgaans *bw.* generally, commonly, usually.
doorgang *m.* passage; (*v. planeet*) transit.
doorgestoken *b. n.* pierced.
doorgronden *o. w.* (*v. plan, enz.*) penetrate; (*v. karakter, mysterie*) fathom; (*v. zaak, geheim*) get to the bottom; (*v. persoon*) see through.
doorhakken *o. w.* cut (through), cleave, split.
doorhalen *o. w.* (*doorstrepen*) strike (cross, scratch) out, strike through, cancel; (*hekelen*) take up roundly, haul over the coals; (*v. boek, enz.*) cut up; (*v. linnen: door blauwsel*) blue; (*door stijfsel*) starch; (*v. wetsontwerp*) carry through.
doorhaling *v.* erasure, cancellation, deletion.
doorheen *bw.* through.
doorhelpen *o. w.* help through, get out of a scrape.
doorkijken *o. w.* look through, look over, glance through, skim.
doorklieven *o. w.* cleave (through).
doorkneden *o. w.* knead thoroughly.
doorknippen *o. w.* cut (through), snip (through).
doorkomen *o. w.* get through, pass; (*v. winter, enz.*) live through; (*door ziekte*) pull through, survive; *on. w.* (*v. zon*) break through, burst through; (*v. tanden*) erupt.
doorkruisen *o. w.* (*v. straten, in alle richtingen*) traverse; (*v. zee, woud*) range, scour.
doorlaat *m.* culvert, sluice, floodgate.
doorliggen *w. w.* **zich —,** become bedsore.
doorloop *m.* passage, gateway.
dóórlopen *on. w.* go (walk, run) on; keep going (walking, running); (*v. kleuren*) run; (*v. molen*) run away; *onw.* (*lopen door*) go (walk, run) through, traverse; (*v. krant*) glance one's eye over; (*v. inhoud*) run over; (*v. schoenen*) walk through, wear out by walking.
doorlópen *o. w.* (*v. school, enz.*) pass through.
doorlopend *b. n.* continuous; *bw.* continuously.
doorluchtig *b. n.* illustrious.
doorluchtigheid *v.* illustriousness.
doormaken *o. w.* go through, pass through.
doorn *m.* thorn, prickle, spine; (*v. mes, enz.*) tang.
doornachtig *b. n.* thorny, spinous.
doornappel *m.* thornapple.

doornat *b. n.* wet through, wet to the skin, soaked; (*v. zweet*) wet all over.
doornenkroon *v.* crown of thorns.
Doornik *o.* Tournai.
doorregen *b. n.* (*v. spek*) streaky, streaked; (*v. vlees*) marbled.
doorregenen *on. w.* rain on, keep on raining; rain through.
doorreis *v.* passage through, journey through.
doorrijden *on. w.* ride on, drive on; *o. w.* (*v. stad, streek, enz.*) ride (drive) through; wear through by riding.
doorroken *on. w.* smoke on, go on smoking; *o. w.* smoke thoroughly; (*v. pijp*) colour.
doorschieten *o. w.* shoot through; (*met kogels*) riddle; (*v. boek*) interleave.
doorschijnen *on. w.* shine (show) through.
doorschijnend *b. n.* diaphanous, transparent, translucent.
doorschrappen *o. w.* scratch (cross, strike) out, cancel.
doorschudden *o. w.* shake (up); (*v. kaarten*) shuffle.
doorsijpelen *on. w.* ooze through; (*v. dak*) let in water; (*fig.*) filter in, percolate through.
doorslaan *o. w.* (*v. spijker, enz.*) drive through; (*v. metaal, leder*) punch; (*in tweeën slaan*) knock in two; *on. w.* (*v. balans*) dip, kick the beam; (*v. paard*) break into a gallop; (*v. schroef, enz.*) race; (*v. papier*) blot, run; (*v. wiel*) skid; (*v. muur*) sweat; (*fig.: v. persoon*) run on.
doorslaand *b. n.* **een — bewijs,** a conclusive (convincing) proof.
doorslag *m.* (*vergiettest*) colander, strainer; (*drevel*) punch, drift; (*v. brief*) carbon (copy); (*H.: overwicht*) overweight, turn in the scale.
doorslikken *o. w.* swallow (down).
doorsnede *v.* diameter; section; (*fig.*) on an average. [in two.
dóórsnijden *o. w.* cut (through), cut **doorsnijden** *o. w.* (*v. rivier, spoorweg, enz.*) intersect, cross, traverse.
doorsnuffelen *o. w.* rummage, ransack, forage in, search through.
doorstaan *o. w.* (*v. aanval, beleg*) stand, sustain; (*v. kritiek, onderzoek*) bear; (*v. ziekte, gevaar*) pull through; (*v. pijn*) endure.
doorstappen *on. w.* go on, walk on.
dóórsteken *o. w.* (*v. dijken*) pierce, cut; (*v. abces*) lance; (*v. blaar*) prick.
doorstéken *o. w.* run through, pierce, transfix.
doorstoten *o. w.* push (thrust)through; (*bilj.*) run through.
doorstromen *o. w.* stream (flow, run) through.
doortastend *b. n.* (*v. persoon*) energetic, thorough(-going); (*v. maatregel*) drastic; *bw.* energetically; drastically.
doortintelen *o. w.* thrill.
doortocht *m.* passage, march through.

doortrapt *b. n.* consummate, thoroughpaced, out-and-out, unmitigated.
doortraptheid *v.* cunning, craft.
dóórtrekken *o. w.* (*stuk trekken*) pull to pieces, pull in two; (*v. lijn*) continue, extend; (*meetk.*) produce; (*v. spoorweg*) extend; (*de straten, enz.*) go (march) through.
doortrékken *o. w.* penetrate, permeate, pervade, soak.
doorvaart *v.* passage.
doorvaren *o. w.* (*v. kanaal*) pass through, sail through.
doorvoer *m.* (*H.*) transit.
doorvoeren *o. w.* (*H.: v. goederen*) pass (convey) in transit; (*v. hervorming, princiep*) carry through, follow out.
doorvoerhandel *m.* transit(-trade).
doorvoerrechten *o. mv.* transit duties.
doorwaadbaar *b. n.* fordable.
doorwandelen *on. w.* walk on; *o. w.* walk through, walk all over.
doorweekt *b. n.* soaked, soppy, sodden.
doorweken *o. w.* soak, steep, sodden.
dóórwerken *on. w.* work on, keep working, go on with one's work; *o. w.* work through.
doorwerken *o. w.* elaborate, work (up) thoroughly; (*met goud, zilver, enz.*) interweave work.
doorworstelen *o. w.* struggle through.
doorzakken *on. w.* sag.
doorzenden *o. w.* send on, forward (on); (*v. brief*) (re-)forward; (*v. rekwest*) transmit, send up.
doorzetten *o. w.* carry through, see through; (*v. wil*) assert; *on. w.* persist, persevere.
doorzettingsvermogen *o.* persistence, perseverance.
doorzicht *o.* penetration, perspicacity, discernment, insight.
doorzichtig *b. n.* transparent; (*v. exuus, enz. ook:*) thin.
dóórzien *o. w.* (*doorkijken*)look through, glance through, glance over.
doorzien *o. w.* (*v. persoon, plannen, enz.*) see through; (*v. geheim*) see into; (*v. waarheid, gedachten, enz.*) penetrate.
doorzoeken *o. w.* (*v. kast, lessenaar, kamer*) rummage; (*v. huis*) search, ransack.
doorzwelgen *o. w.* swallow.
doos *v.* box, case.
doosvrucht *v.* capsule, capsular fruit.
dop *m.* (*v. ei, noot*) shell; (*v. sommige zaden*) husk; (*v. bonen, erwten*) pod; (*v. vulpen, enz.*) cap, top; (*v. fles*) capsule; (*v. pijp*) cover; (*hoed*) tile; (*stijve—*) bowler, pot-hat.
dopeling *m. en v.* child (person) to be baptized (receiving baptism).
dopen *o. w.* baptize, christen; (*v. schip, enz.*) name; christen; (*indopen*) dip, immerse.
doper *m.* baptizer.
doperwt *v.* green pea; (*mv.:* green peas(e)).

dor *b. n. (v. land)* barren; *(v. woestijn)* arid; *(fig.: v. onderwerp)* dry, arid; *(verdord)* withered.

dorheid *v.* barrenness; aridity; dryness.

dorp *o.* village.

dorpel *m.* threshold.

dorpeling *m. en v.* villager.

dorps *b. n.* countrified, rustic, village-like.

dorpskermis *v.* country-fair.

dorpsplein *o.* village-green.

dorsen *o. w. en on. w.* thresh, thrash.

dorsmachine *v.* threshing-machine.

dorst *m.* thirst.

dorstig *b. n.* thirsty.

dorsvlegel *m.* flail.

dorsvloer *m.* threshing-floor.

dos *m.* attire, dress; *(dicht.)* raiment.

dosis *v.* dose, quantity.

dot *m. (v. haar, enz.)* knot; *(v. gras)* tuft.

douane *v.* custom-house, the Customs.

douanebeambte *m.* custom-house officer, customs-officer.

dove *m.* deaf person, deaf man.

doven *o. w.* extinguish, put out; *(v. as)* quench.

dovenetel *v. (witte)* dead nettle; *(gele)* yellow archangel.

dozijn *o.* dozen.

dra *bw.* soon.

draad *m.* thread; *(vezel)* fibre; *(elek. lamp)* filament; *(v. mes, enz.)* wire-edge; *(metaal—)* wire; *(v. boon, erwt)* string.

draadbericht *o.* wire, cable, telegram.

draadloos *b. n.* wireless.

draadnagel *m.* wire-nail.

draadtrekkerij *v.* wire-drawing mill.

draadversperring *v.* (barbed) wire entanglement.

draadwerk *o.* wire-work; *(v. goud, enz.)* filigree.

draagbaar *b. n.* bearable; *(v. vracht)* portable; *(v. kleren)* wearable.

draagbaar *v.* stretcher, litter.

draagblak *m.* supporting-beam.

draagkracht *v.* bearing power, strength to bear; *(v. geweer, kanon)* range; *(v. brug, schip, enz.)* carryingcapacity; *(v. stem)* port; *(v. balk)* working-load; *(v. fundering)* supporting power.

draaglijk *b. n.* tolerable; *(tamelijk)* passable, tolerable; *bw.* tolerably.

draagriem *m.* strap; *(v. kijker, enz.)* lanyard.

draagvlak *o. (v. vliegtuig)* plane.

draagwijdte *v. (v. vuurwapen)* range; *(v. woorden)* bearing.

draai *m.* turn; *(v. weg)* turning, winding; *(v. touw)* twist.

draaibank *v.* lathe.

draaiboom *m.* turnpike, turnstile.

draaibrug *v.* swing-bridge, swivel-bridge.

draaideur *v.* revolving door, turnstile door.

draaien *on. w.* turn; *(om as)* turn, revolve, rotate; *(in cirkel)* whirl, gyrate; *(snel)* spin (round); *(v. wind)* shift; *(fig.)* shuffle, prevaricate, tergiversate; *(kronkelen)* turn, wind; *(aan autom. telefoon)* dial; *o. w.* turn; *(v. schip)* wind; *w. w. zich —,* turn.

draaier *m. (v. hout, ivoor)* turner; *(fig.)* shuffler, prevaricator.

draaierig *b. n.* dizzy, giddy, vertiginous.

draaierij *v.* turnery, turning (turner's) shop; *(fig.)* shuffling, prevarication.

draaihek *o.* turnstile, tourniquet.

draaikolk *m.* whirlpool, eddy.

draaikrukje *o.* revolving-stool.

draaimolen *m.* round-about, merry-go-round, whirligig.

draaiorgel *o.* barrel-organ.

draaischijf *b. (v. pottenbakker)* potter's wheel; *(v. spoorw.)* turn(ing)-table, turning-plate. [ligig.

draaitol *m.* (spinning-)top; *(fig.)* wihr-

draak *m. (Dk.)* dragon; *(toneel)* gallery-hit, blood-and-thunder play.

drab *v.* dregs, lees: sediment.

drabbig *b. n.* turbid, muddy, dreggy.

dracht *v. (last)* load, charge; *(kleder—)* dress, costume; *(draagwijdte: v. kanon)* range; *(v. dier)* gestation; *(v. wond)* discharge, matter, pus.

drachtig *b. n.* with young; pregnant.

draf *m.* trot; *(afvalprodukt, varkensvoer)* swill, draff.

dragen *o. w.* bear; *(aan 't lichaam: kleren, ringen, enz.)* wear; *(bij zich hebben)* carry; *(verdragen)* support; *on. w. (v. wapen, stem)* carry; *(v. ijs)* bear, hold; *(v. wond)* discharge, suppurate.

drager *m.* bearer, carrier, porter; *(fig.: v. beginselen)* exponent.

dragonder *m.* dragoon; *(fig.: manwijf)* horse-godmother, grenadier.

dralen *on. w.* linger, tarry, delay; *(treuzelen)* loiter, dawdle.

drama *o.* drama.

drang *m.* pressure; urgency, impulse; *(innerlijke —)* urge, craving.

drank *m.* drink, beverage; *(medicijn)* draught, potion.

drankverbruik *o.* drink-consumption

drankverkoper *m.* liquor-seller.

drankzucht *v.* dipsomania, drink-craving.

dras *z. n., v.* mire, marshy land.

drasland *o.* marsh-land, swamp.

drassig *b. n.* marshy, swampy, soppy, spongy.

drastisch *b. n. (bw.)* drastic(ally).

draven *on. w.* trot.

draver *m.* trotter.

draverij *v.* trotting-match.

dreef *v.* alley, lane.

dreggen *o. w.* drag, dredge, creep.

dreigbrief *m.* menacing (threatening) letter.

dreigen *o. w. en on. w.* menace, threaten.

dreigend *b. n.* menacing, threatening; *(v. gevaar, ongeluk)* imminent, impending; *(v. gebaren)* minatory; *(v. lucht)* menacing, lowering.

dreiging *v.* menace, threat.
drek *m.* dirt, muck, excrement(s); (*slijk*) mire, dirt.
drempel *m.* threshold, doorstep; (*v. sluis*) sill.
drenkeling *m. en v.* drowning person; drowned person.
drenken *o. w.* (*v. vee, paarden*) water; (*v. aarde*) drench.
drenkplaats *v.* watering-place.
drentelen *on. w.* saunter.
dresseren *o. w.* (*v. paard*) break (in); (*v. hond*) train, teach; (*v. leerling*) drill, coach.
dreumes *m.* little nipper, toddler.
dreunen *on. w.* (*v. geschut*) boom, roar; (*v. donder*) rumble, roar; (*bij lezen*), drone.
drevel *m.* (*tn.*) drift, driver, punch.
drie *telw.* three.
driedekker *m.* (*sch.*) three-decker; (*vl.*) triplane; (*fig.*) virago, horse-godmother
driedubbel *b. n.* treble, triple, threefold.
Drieëenheid *v.* Trinity.
driehoek *m.* triangle.
driehoeksmeting *v.* trigonometry.
driehoofdig *b. n.* three-headed.
driejaarlijks *b. n.* triennial.
driejarig *b. n.* triennal; three years old.
driekleur *v.* tricolour.
Driekoningen *m.* Epiphany, Twelfth Night.
drieledig *b. n.* tri-merous.
drieling *m.* triplets.
drieluik *o.* triptych.
driemaandelijks *b. n.* quaterly, threemonthly.
driemanschap *o.* triumvirate.
driesprong *m.* three-forked road, trifurcation.
driest *b. n.* audacious, bold, reckless.
driestheid *v.* audacity, boldness, recklessness.
drietalig *b. n.* trilingual.
drietallig *b. n.* ternary.
drietand *m.* trident.
Drievuldigheid *v.* (Holy) Trinity.
driewieler *m.* tricycle.
drift *v.* (*hartstocht*) passion; (*haast, ongeduld*) haste, precipitation; (*opvliegendheid*) passion, heat; (*troep: v. dieren*) drove; (*kudde: v. schapen*) flock; (*v. schip*) drift; (*v. wolken*) scud, drift.
driftig *b. n.* passionate; choleric, irascible; hasty, hurried; (*sch.*) adrift, afloat.
driftkop *m.* hothead, spitfire.
drijfanker *o.* (*sch.*) drift-anchor.
drijfas *v.* driving-shaft.
drijfijs *o.* drift-ice, floating-ice.
drijfkracht *v.* (*tn.*) propelling-force; (*fig.*) driving-force, moving power.
drijfriem *m.* (*tn.*) driving-band, driving-belt.
drijfveer *v.* moving spring, mainspring; (*fig. ook:*) incentive, motive.
drijfzand *o.* quicksand, drift-sand.
drijven *on. w.* (*zich aan oppervlakte*

bewegen) swim; (*niet zinken*) float; (*v. schip: met stroom mee*) drift, be drifted; (*zeer nat zijn*) be soaking (sopping) wet; be dropping water; *o. w.* (*v. vee, enz.*) drive; (*v. machine*) drive, propel; (*v. goud, zilver*) chase, enchase; (*fig.*) drive, actuate, prompt.
drijver *m.* (*v. vee*) driver, drover; (*bij jacht*) beater; (*v. metalen*) chaser; embosser; (*v. vliegboot*) float; (*fig.*) zealot, fanatic.
dril *m.* drill; (*gelei*) jelly, gelatine.
drilboor *v.* drill, wimble.
drillen *o. w.* (*v. soldaten, enz.*) drill; (*voor examen*) coach, cram; (*boren*) drill, bore.
dringen *on. w.* push, crowd, throng, hustle; *o. w.* (*van plaats*) push; (*in hoek, enz.*) crowd; (*ergens tegen aan*) press; (*fig.*) urge, actuate.
dringend *b. n.* (*v. verzoek, bericht, gesprek*) urgent; (*v. vraagstukken, verplichtingen*) pressing; (*v. nood*) crying.
drinkbaar *b. n.* drinkable, potable.
drinkbak *m.* (*v. paard*) water(ing)-trough; (*v. hond, enz.*) water-bowl, drinking-trough.
drinkbeker *m.* cup, goblet.
drinken *o. w. en on. w.* drink; *z. n., o.* drinking; (*concreet*) beverage.
drinkgelag *o.* drinking-bout, potation, carouse.
drinkgeld *o.* drink-money; gratuity, tip.
drinkwater *o.* drinking-water.
droef *b. n.* sad, afflicted.
droefenis *v.* sorrow, grief, affliction, distress.
droefgeestig *b. n.* melancholy, mournful, gloomy.
droefgeestigheid *v.* melancholy, mournfulness, gloominess.
droefheid *v.* sadness, sorrow, affliction.
droes *m.* (*kwade*) glanders; (*goedaardige*) strangles; (*huid—*) farcy.
droesem *m.* dregs, lees, draff, sediment.
drogen *o. w.* dry; wipe dry; (*v. fruit*) dry, evaporate; *on. w.* dry.
drogerij *v.* drying-place, drying-room; **—en,** drugs, druggist's wares.
drogreden *v.* sophism.
drom *m.* throng, crowd, multitude.
dromen *o. w. en on. w.* dream.
dromer *m.* dreamer, visionary.
dromerij *v.* day-dream(ing), reverie.
drommel *m.* deuce, devil.
dronk *m.* draught, drink.
dronkaard *m.* drunkard, inebriate.
dronken *b. n.* (*predikatief*) drunk; (*attributief*) drunken, intoxicated, inebriated, tipsy.
dronkenschap *v.* drunkenness, inebriety, intoxication.
droog *b. n.* dry; (*dor: v. grond, onderwerp, enz.*) arid; (*v. verhaal, enz.*) dusty, dry as dust; (*v. weer*) fine, dry.
droogdok *o.* dry-dock, graving-dock.
droogjes *bw.* drily, with dry humour.

droogleggen *o. w. (v. grond, moeras)* drain; *(v. Zuiderzee)* reclaim; *(verkoop van sterke drank verbieden)* make dry.
droogmiddel *o.* siccative.
droogpruim(er) *m.* dry (old) stick, dry file.
droogstoppel *m. zie* **droogpruimer.**
droogte *v.* dryness, drought; shoal, sand-bank.
droogvoets *bw.* dry-shod.
droom *m.* dream.
droombeeld *o.* illusion, vision, phantasm.
drop *v.* licorice; *m. (drup)* drop, bead; *(het druppelen)* drip.
druif *v.* grape.
druifluis *v.* vine-pest, phylloxera.
druilen *on. w.* mope, pout; *(v. weer)* drizzle, mizzle.
druilerig *b. n.* moping, mopish; drizzling, mizzling.
druipen *on. w.* drip, drop; *(v. kaars)* run, gutter; *(bij examen)* be ploughed, be plucked.
druipnat *b. n.* dripping (wet), soaked.
druipneus *m.* running nose; *(v. persoon)* sniveller.
druipsteen *m.* sinter (deposits); *(hangend)* stalactite; *(staand)* stalagmite.
druisen *on. w.* roar, swish.
druivenat *o.* grape-juice, juice of grapes.
druivenoogst *m.* grape-harvest, vintage.
druiventros *m.* bunch of grapes.
druiverank *v.* tendril (of a vine).
druk *b. n. (v. straat, toneel, verkeer, enz.)* busy; *(v. stad)* bustly; *(v. winkel, cafe: druk bezocht)* much frequented; *(v. handel, gesprek, enz.: levendig)* brisk, lively; *(v. persoon)* busy, bustling; *(zenuwachtig —)* fussy; *(v. kleuren, versieringen)* busy, noisy, loud, gaudy; *bw.* busily; bustily.
druk *m. (alg.)* pressure; *(v. hand)* squeeze, pressure; *(drukkend gevoel)* oppression; *(v. boek)* print(ing); *(uitgave)* impression.
drukfout *v.* misprint, printer's error, typographical error.
drukken *o. w.* press; squeeze; *(v. boek, katoen, enz.)* print; *(fig.: terneerslaan)* oppress; *(v. belasting, zorgen, enz.)* weigh (heavy) upon; *(v. markt, prijzen)* depress; *on. w.* press; *(knellen)* pinch.
drukkend *b. n. (v. belasting)* onerous; *(v. last, warmte, gevoel)* oppressive; *(v. weer: zwoel)* close, sultry, stifling, muggy.
drukker *m.* printer; *(tn.)* presser.
drukkerij *v.* printing-office; press-room.
drukkersjongen *m.* printer's devil.
drukking *v.* pressure; weight.
drukknop *m. (el.)* push-button, bell-push.
drukletter *v.* type; *(tegenst. van schrijfletter)* print-letter, Roman letter.

drukproef *v.* proof(-sheet).
drukte *v. (herrie, opschudding)* bustle, noise; *(ophef)* fuss; *(v. zaken, bezigheden)* rush (press) of business.
druktemaker *m.* noisy-fellow.
drukwerk *o.* printed matter, printed papers.
druppel *m.* drop.
druppelen *on. w.* drop, drip, trickle.
druppelflesje *o.* dropping-bottle.
dubbel *b. n.* double; *(tweevoudig)* twofold, bifold; *(v. huis)* double-fronted; *bw.* doubly; *z. n., m. (v. postzegel)* doublet, duplicate; *(v. domino)* double.
dubbelen *o. w. (verdubbelen: v. getal, enz.)* double; *(tn.: v. schip)* sheathe.
dubbelganger *m.* double.
dubbelpunt *o.* colon.
dubbelspoor *o.* double track (line).
dubbelzinnig *b. n.* ambiguous; *(niet onverdacht)* equivocal; *(schuin)* double-meaning, indecent.
dubbelzinnigheid *v.* ambiguity; equivocalness, equivocality; double-entendre, double-meaning.
duchten *o. w.* fear, dread.
duchtig *b. n.* sound, strong, thorough; *bw.* soundly, strongly, thoroughly, terribly.
duel *o.* duel, single, combat.
duf *b. n.* fusty, stuffy, earthy; *(fig.)* fusty, musty, flat, stale, dull.
dufheid *v.* fustiness, stuffiness; *(fig.)* flatness, dullness.
duidelijk *b. n. (klaar, helder)* clear, plain; *(v. uitspraak: goed te verstaan)* distinct; *(klaarblijkelijk, voor de hand liggend)* obvious, patent; *(uitdrukkelijk)* explicit.
duidelijkheid *v.* clearness, plainness; distinctness; obviousness.
duiden *on. w. — op,* point to, hint at; *o. w.* interpret.
duif *v.* pigeon, dove.
duighout *o.* clapboard, stave-wood.
duikboot *v.* submersible, submarine; *(Duits)* U-boat.
duikelen *on. w. (buitelen)* turn somersaults; *(tuimelend vallen)* tumble, fall head over heels; *(v. vliegtuig)* loop (the loop); *(duiken)* dive; *(bij examen)* be ploughed; *(fig.)* come to grief.
duikeling *v.* somersault; tumble; looping the loop.
duiken *on. w.* dive, dip, plunge.
duiker *m. (v. persoon)* diver; *(Dk.)* diver, diving-bird; *(tn.: onder dijk, enz.)* culvert, sluice; *(Pl.)* buurreed.
duikerklok *v.* diving-bell.
duikerpak *o.* diving-dress, diving-suit.
duim *m.* thumb; *(Eng. maat)* inch; *(tn.: v. deur)* hinge; *(haak)* hook.
duimhandschoen *m.* mitten.
duimschroef *v.* thumb-screw.
duimstok *m.* (folding-)rule, inch-rule.
duin *o.* dune.
Duinkerken *o.* Dunkirk.

duister *b. n.* dark, obscure; *(schemerig)* dim; *(pikdonker)* murky; *(somber)* gloomy; *(fig.)* mysterious, cryptic; dark, obscure; *z. n., o.* **het** —, the dark.
duisternis *v.* darkness, dark, obscurity.
duit *m.* doit; farthing.
duitendief *m.* scrape-penny, pinch-penny.
Duits *b. n.* German.   [manophil.
Duitsgezind *b. n.* pro-German, Ger-
Duitsland *o.* Germany.
duiveboon *v.* horse-bean, tick-bean.
duivel *m.* devil, demon, satan; *(fam.)* Old Nick, Old Scratch.
duivelbezwering *v.* exorcism.
duivels *b. n.* devilish, diabolical, demoniac(al).
duivelskind *o.* child of Satan, child of the devil, imp (of Satan).
duivenhok, duivenkot *o.* pigeon-house, pigeonry, dovecot.
duivenhouder, duivenmelker *m.* pigeon-fancier.
duivenslag *m.* pigeon-loft.
duiventil *v.* pigeon-house, dovecot.
duizelen *on. w.* grow-dizzy (giddy).
duizelig *b. n.* dizzy, giddy.
duizeligheid *v.* dizziness, giddiness, swimming in the head.
duizeling *v.* dizziness, vertigo.
duizelingwekkend *b. n.* dizzy, giddy, vertiginous.
duizend *telw.* a (one) thousand.
duizendpoot *m.* millipede, centipede; *(sl.: dienstmeisje)* slavey.
duldbaar *b. n.* bearable, tolerable, supportable.
dulden *o. w.* *(v. persoon)* bear, tolerate; *(v. handelingen)* stand, tolerate; *(v. pijn)* suffer, endure; *(toestaan)* allow.
dun *b. n.* *(alg.)* thin; *(v. middel, stam, enz.)* slender; *(v. bier)* small; *(v. haar)* scanty; *(v. dampkring)* rare; *(v. bevolking)* thin, sparse.   [sparseness.
dunheid *v.* thinness; rareness, tenuity;
dunk *m.* opinion.
dunken *on. w.* think.
dunlijvig *b. n.* lank.   [thin.
dunnen *o. w.* thin out; tin; *on. w.*
duozitting *v.* pillion(-seat).
dupe *m. en v.* dupe, victim.
duplicaat *o.* duplicate.
duren *on. w.* last; *(aanhouden)* continue; *(in stand blijven)* endure.
durf *m.* daring; *(fam.)* pluck.
durfal *m. en v.* dare-all, dare-devil.
durfniet *m. en v.* dare-nought, coward.
durven *o. w.* dare.
dus *bw.* *(aldus)* thus; *vw.* *(derhalve)* consequently, therefore, so.
dusdanig *b. n.* such.
dutten *on. w.* doze, snooze, (take a) nap.
duur *m.* duration; *(looptijd: v. contract, enz.)* currency; *(voortduring)* continuance.
duur *b. n.* dear; *(v. kleren, dokter, hotel, enz.)* expensive; *(kostbaar)* costly; *bw.* dear(ly).

duurtetoeslag *m.* cost-of-living bonus, extra allowance for dear living.
duurzaam *b. n.* *(v. stof)* that wears well, hard-wearing; *(v. vrede)* durable, lasting.
duw *m.* push; *(por)* thrust, shove, poke; *(met elleboog)* nudge.
duwen *o. w. en on. w.* push; thrust.
dwaalgeest *m.* wandering (erring) spirit.
dwaalleer *v.* false doctrine, heresy.
dwaallicht *o.* will-o'-the-wisp, jack-o'-lantern, ignis fatuus.
dwaalspoor *o.* wrong track (way, path), erroneous way; *(fig.)* put off the scent, lead into error, lead astray.
dwaalster *v.* planet, wandering star.
dwaas *b. n.* foolish, silly; *(ongerijmd)* absurd; *z. n., m.* fool.
dwaasheid *v.* folly, foolishness.
dwalen *on. w.* wander, rove, roam; *(fig.)* err.
dwaling *v.* error, mistake.
dwang *m.* compulsion, constraint, coercion.
dwangarbeid *m.* forced labour; penal servitude.
dwangarbeider *m.* convict.
dwangbevel *o.* *(recht)* warrant, writ; *(v. belasting)* distress-warrant, warran of distress.
dwangbuis *o.* strait waistcoat.
dwangmiddel *o.* means of coercion.
dwarrelen *on. w.* whirl (round), flutter.
dwarrelwind *m.* whirlwind, tornado.
dwars *b. n.* transverse, transversal, diagonal; *(fig.)* cross-grained, wrong-headed, contrary, perverse, pig-headed.
dwarsbalk *m.* cross-beam; *(wapenk.)* fesse.
dwarsbomen *o. w.* cross, thwart.
dwarsdoor *vz. en bw.* straight through; right across.
dwarsdrijven *on. w.* cross, thwart.
dwarsdrijver *m.* cross-patch, thwarter, cross-grained fellow.
dwarsdrijverij *v.* contrariness, perverseness, cussedness.
dwarshout *o.* cross-beam.
dwarskijker *m.* spy; *(bij examen)* invigilator.
dwarslijn *v.* cross-line, transversal line.
dwarsstraat *v.* cross-street, side-street, by street.
dweepachtig *b. n.* *(bw.)* enthusiastic-(ally); *(fam.)* gushing(ly); *(fanatiek)* fanatic(ally).   [swab.
dweil *v.* floor-cloth, house-flannel; *(sch.)*
dwepen *on. w.* be fanatical.
dweper *m.* fanatic, zealot; enthusiast.
dweperij *v.* fanaticism; extravagant enthusiasm, dream-enthusiasm.
dwerg *m.* dwarf, pigmy, pygmy.
dwingeland *m.* tyrant.
dwingelandij *v.* tyranny.
dwingen *o. w.* force, compel, constrain; *on. w.* *(v. kind)* whine, pule, be tyranically insistent.
dynamiet *o.* dynamite.

E

eb, ebbe v. ebb, ebb-tide.
ebbehout o. ebony.
echo v. echo.
echt b. n. (niet vervalst: koffie, boter, enz.) genuine; (v. brieven, documenten) authentic; (wettig) legitimate; (v. zijde, haar, enz.) real; (zeer prettig, leuk) tophole, first-rate, ripping; bw. really, fearly.
echt m. marriage, matrimony, wedlock.
echtbreekster v. adulteress.
echtbreken on. w. commit adultery.
echtbreker m. adulterer.
echtelijk b. n. conjugal; matrimonial, connubial.
echter bw. however, nevertheless.
echtgenoot m. husband.
echtgenote v. wife, spouse.
echtheid v. genuineness; authenticity; legitimacy.
echtpaar o. married couple.
echtscheiding v. divorce.
economie v. economy.
edel b. n. noble; (v. stenen, metalen) precious; bw. nobly; z. n., m. mv. de —en, the nobility; (gesch.) the nobles.
edelachtbaar b. n. worshipful, honorable.
edelgesteente o. precious stone, gem, gemstone.
edelknaap m. page.
edellieden m. mv. noblemen, nobles.
edelmoedig b. n. generous, magnanimous.
edelmoedigheid v. generosity, magnanimity.
edelvalk m. great northern falcon.
edelvrouw v. noblewoman.
editie v. edition; (v. krant) edition, issue.
edoch vw. however, still, but.
eed m. oath.
eedaflegging v. taking an oath.
eedbreuk v. perjury, oath-breaking, violation of one's oath.
eekhoorn m. squirrel.
eelt o. callosity.
eeltig b. n. horny, callous.
eeltknobbel m. **eeltplek** v. callosity; (aan grote teen) bunion.
een lidw. a, an.
één, een telw. one.
eend v. (Dk.) duck; (fig.) goose, ass.
ééndagsvlieg v. ephemerid, ephemeron.
ééndekker m. monoplane.
eendekroos o. (Pl.) duck-weed.
eender b. n. equal, the same; bw. equally.
eendracht v. concord, union, harmony.
eendrachtig b. n. united, harmonious, unanimous; bw. in concord, in union, in harmony.
eenheid v. (rek.) unit; (eigenschap: het een zijn) oneness, unity; (deugd) unity, unanimity, harmony.
eenheidsfront o. united front.
eenheidsprijs m. unit price.

eenhoevig b. n. one-hoofed, soliped.
eenhoofdig b. n. (Dk., Pl.) monocephalous; (v. staatsbestuur) monarchical.
eenhoorn m. (Dk.) unicorn.
eenjarig b. n. (v. kind) of one year, one year old; (v. plant) annual.
eenlettergrepig b. n. monosyllabic.
eenmaal bw. once; (eens, te eniger tijd) one day.
eenoog m. one-eyed person.
eenparig b. n. unanimous; (v. beweging) uniform; bw. unanimously, by common consent, with one accord (consent).
eenparigheid v. unanimity, uniformity.
eenrichtingverkeer o. one-way traffic.
eens bw. (eenmaal) once; (in zekere tijd) once, one day; (in de toekomst) one day.
eensgezind b. n. unanimous, in harmony, at one.
eensgezindheid v. unanimousness, unanimity, harmony.
eensklaps bw. suddenly, (all) at once, of a sudden.
eensluidend b. n. of the same tenor; verbally identical.
eenstemmig b. n. (muz.) for one voice; (fig.: eenparig) unanimous; bw. with one voice; unanimously.
eentonig b. n. monotonous.
eentonigheid v. monotony.
eenvoud m. simplicity.
eenvoudig b. n. (v. kleding, stijl, enz.) simple; (v. spijzen, woorden, enz.) plain; (v. mensen) middle class; bw. simply; plainly.
eenzaam b. n. solitary, lonely; (verlaten, doods) desolate; (afgezonderd) retired, secluded; bw. solitarily.
eenzaamheid v. solitariness, solitude; retirement, seclusion.
eenzelvigheid v. solitariness, self-containment.
eenzijdig b. n. (v. inzicht, denkbeeld, enz.) one-sided; (v. overeenkomst) unilateral; (partijdig) partial; bw. onesidedly; partially.
eer bw. before, sooner, rather; vw. before.
eer v. honour; (verdienste) credit.
eerbaar b. n. virtuous, modest, chaste, honest.
eerbaarheid v. virtue, modesty, chastity, honesty.
eerbied m. respect, reverence, veneration.
eerbiedig b. n. respectful, reverent, reverential, deferential.
eerbiedigen o. w. respect, reverence; defer to.
eerbiedwaardig b. n. respectable, venerable; (aloud: v. gebruiken, enz.) time-honoured.
eerder b. n. zie **eer**.
eergierig b. n. (bw.) ambitious(ly).

eergisteren *bw.* the day before yesterday.

eerlang *bw.* before long, shortly.

eerlijk *b. n.* (*v. persoon*) honest; (*v. persoon, bedoelingen, enz.*) honourable; (*v. uiterlijk*) honest-looking; (*v. strijd, kans, enz.*) fair: *bw.* honestly; fairly.

eerlijkheid *v.* honesty, probity, fairness

eerloos *b. n.* infamous, dishonourable.

eerroof *m.* defamation.

eerst *b. n.* (*alg.*) first; (*voornaamste*) leading, chief; (*v. firma*) first-class; (*v. minister, meridiaan*) prime; (*v. bewoners*) primeval; *bw.* first; firstly, at first; (*pas, slechts*) only.

eerstdaags *bw.* one of these days, in a few days.

eersteling *m. en r.* (*v. kind*) first-born; (*v. dier*) firstling; (*Bijb.*) first-fruit; (*fig.*) first-fruit, first-work.

eerstkomend, eerstvolgend *b. n.* next, following.

eertijds *bw.* formerly, in former times.

eervol *b. n.* honourable: *bw.* honourably.

eerwaard *b. n.* reverend; **uw —e,** Your Reverence.

eerzaam *b. n.* respectable, honourable, honest.

eerzucht *v.* ambition.

eerzuchtig *b. n.* (*bw.*) ambitious(ly).

eetbaar *b. n.* eatable, edible.

eetbaarheid *v.* eatableness, edibility.

eetgerei *o.* dinner-things.

eethuis *o.* eating-house.

eetketeltje *o.* (*mil.*) mess-tin, canteen.

eetlepel *m.* table-spoon.

eetlust *m.* appetite, stomach.

eetwaren *v. mv.* eatables, victuals.

eetzaal *v.* (*in huis*) dining-room; (*in kazerne*) mess-room; (*in klooster, pensionaat*) refectory; (*op schip*) dining-saloon.

eeuw *v.* century; (*tijdperk*) age.

eeuwfeest *o.* centenary.

eeuwig *b. n.* eternal, perpetual; everlasting; *bw.* for ever.

eeuwigheid *v.* eternity.

effect *o.* effect; (*bilj.*) side.

effectenmakelaar *m.* stock-broker.

effectenrekening *v.* stock-account.

effectief *b. n.* effective, real; *bw.* really; *z. n., o.* (*mil.*) effective.

effen *b. n.* smooth, level, even; (*v. grond, ring, enz.*) plain; (*v. stoffen*) plain, unfigured; (*v. rekening*) settled, balanced.

effenen *o. w.* smooth, level, make even.

effenheid *v.* smoothness, evenness.

eg *v.* harrow, drag.

egel *m.* hedge-hog.

eggen *o. w. en on. w.* harrow, drag.

Egypte *o.* Egypt.

Egyptenaar *m.* Egyptian.

Egyptisch *b. n.* Egyptian.

ei *tw.* ah!, indeed!

ei *o.* egg.

eierdop *m.* egg-shell.

eierkoek *m.* egg-cake.

eierkolen *v. mv.* ovoid coals, ovoids.

eierleggend *b. n.* egg-laying, oviparous.

eierstok *m.* ovary, ovarium.

eigen *b. n.* (*toebehorend aan*) own, private; (*aangeboren*) innate, natural; (*gemeenzaam, vertrouwelijk*) familiar, intimate; (*kenmerkend*) proper to, specific to.

eigenaar *m.* (*v. boek, land, enz.*) owner; (*v. land, huis, enz.*) proprietor.

eigenaardig *b. n.* peculiar, singular.

eigenaardigheid *v.* peculiarity; (*geestelijke —*) idiosyncracy.

eigenbelang *o.* self-interest, personal interest.

eigendom *o.* property, possession.

eigendunk *m.* self-conceit.

eigendunkelijkheid *v.* arbitrariness.

eigenhandig *b. n.* with one's own hands; autographic; (*op brief*) by hand; *bw.* by hand.

eigenliefde *v.* self-love, love of self.

eigenlijk *b. n.* proper; properly so called; *bw.* properly; properly speaking.

eigenmachtig *b. n.* arbitrary, high-handed; *bw.* arbitrarily, high-handedly.

eigennaam *m.* proper name.

eigenschap *v.* (*v. persoon*) quality; (*v. zaken*) property; (*rek.*) law, rule.

eigenwaan *m.* self-conceit, conceitedness, presumption.

eigenwijsheid *v.* self-conceit, conceitedness, opinionatedness.

eigenzinnig *b. n.* self-willed, wilful, obstinate.

eigenzinnigheid *v.* self-will, wilfulness, obstinacy.

eik *m.* oak.

eikel *m.* (*Pl.*) acorn; gland.

eikeloof *o.* oak-leaves.

eiland *o.* island; isle.

eilandbewoner *m.* islander.

eind *o.* end; termination, conclusion, close; (*uiteinde*) end, extremity; (*stuk*) piece; length; (*afstand*) distance; way; (*v. overeenkomst, enz.*) expire.

eindbeslissing *v.* final decision.

einddiploma *o.* (*school—*) leaving certificate.

einddoel *o.* ultimate object, final purpose.

eindelijk *bw.* at last, finally, in the end; *b. n.* ultimate.

eindeloos *b. n.* endless, interminable, infinite; *bw.* infinitely, without end.

eindexamen *o.* school leaving examination, final examination.

eindigen *o. w.* end, finish, conclude, terminate; *on. w.* end, finish, conclude, terminate, come to an end.

eindje *o.* end; (*v. sigaar*) end, butt, stub; (*v. potlood, enz.*) stub. .

eindklank *m.* final sound.

eindpaal *m.* limit, bound, goal; (*sp.*) winning-post.

eindpunt *o.* end, terminal point; (*v. spoorweg, tram*) terminus.

eindstation *o.* terminal station, terminus.

eirond *b. n.* egg-like, eg-shaped, oval.
eis *m.* demand, claim; (*gestelde* —, *voor examen, enz.*) requirement; (*vereiste*) exigency; (*recht: v. Op. Min.*) requisitory.
eisen *o. w.* demand, require, claim.
eiser(es) *m.* (*v.*) claimer, claimant, demandant; (*recht*) plaintiff, prosecutor.
eiwit *o.* white of egg, glair; (*gen.*) albumen.
eiwitstof *v.* albumen.
ekster *m.* magpie, pie.
eksteroog *o.* corn.
el *v.* ell; (*Engelse* —) yard.
elders *bw.* elsewhere.
elegant *b. n.* (*bw.*) elegant(ly), stylish-(ly).
elektricien *m.* electrician.
elektriciteit *v.* electricity.
elektrisch *b. n.* (*bw.*) electric, electrical-(ly).
elektriseren *o. w.* electrify, electrize.
elektrode *v.* electrode.
element *o.* element; (*el.*) cell.
elevatie *v.* elevation (of the Host).
elf *m.* elf.
elf *telw.* eleven.
elfde *b. n.* eleventh.
elft *m.* shad.
elftal *o.* (number of) eleven; (*sp.*) eleven.
elk *onb. vnw.* every, each, any; *zelfst.* everybody, each.
elkaar, elkander *vnw.* each, other, one another.
elkeen *onb. vnw.* every man, everybody, every one.
elleboog *m.* elbow. [ness.
ellende *v.* misery, distress, wretched-
ellendeling *m.* wretch, miscreant, villain.
ellendig *b. n.* miserable, wretched.
els *v.* (*priem*) awl, brad-awl.
els *m.* (*Pl.*) alder.
Elzasser *m.* Alsatian.
email *o.* enamel.
embargo *o.* embargo.
eminentie *v.* eminence.
emissie *v.* emission; (*v. aandelen*) issue.
emissiekoers *m.* price of issue.
emmer *m.* pail, bucket.
en *vw.* and; *n... n...*, both... and...
encyclopedie *v.* (en)cyclopaedia.
endeldarm *m.* rectum.
endossant *m.* (*H.*) endorser.
endossement *o.* (*H.*) endorsement.
endosseren *o. w.* (*H.*) endorse.
enenmale *bw.* **ten** —, entirely, utterly, altogether, absolutely.
energie *v.* energy.
energiek *b. n.* (*bw.*) energetic, energetical(ly).
eng *b. n.* (*niet wijd, nauw*) narrow; (*v. kleren*) tight; (*naar, onaangenaam*) creepy, weird, uncanny; *bw.* closely.
engagement *o.* engagement.
engageren *o. w.* engage; *w. w.* **zich** —, become engaged.

engel *m.* angel.
Engeland *o.* England; (*dicht.*) Albion.
engelbewaarder *m.* guardian angel.
engelenbak *m.* upper gallery; (*de personen*) the gods.
Engels *b. n.* English; *z. n., o.* English.
Engelsgezind *b. n.* Anglophile.
Engelsman *m.* Englishman.
engheid *v.* narrowness; tightness.
engte *v.* narrow; (*zee*—) strait; (*berg*—) defile; (*land*—) isthmus.
enig *b. n.* (*waarvan geen tweede is: v. kind*) only; (*v. erfgenaam, enz.*) sole; (*ongeëvenaard*) unique; *bw.* — **mooi,** extremely beautiful; *vnw.* some, any.
enigermate *bw.* in some degree, in a measure, to some extent, somewhat.
enigszins *bw.* somewhat, in some degree, in some sort, a little.
enkel *m.* ankle.
enkel *b. n.* single; *bw.* only, merely, simply.
enkeling *m.* individual.
enkelvoud *o.* singular (number).
enorm *b. n.* (*bw.*) enormous(ly).
ent *v.* graft.
enten *o. w.* graft, inoculate.
enterbijl *v.* (*sch.*) boarding-axe.
enteren *o. w.* (*sch.*) board.
enterhaak *m.* (*sch.*) grappling-iron, grappler.
enting *v.* grafting, inoculation.
entrée *v.* (*ingang*) entrance; (*het binnenkomen*) entrance, entry; (*toelating*) entrance, admission; (*toegangsprijs*) entrance-fee; admission, door-money; (*gerecht*) entree.
entrepot *o.* (*H.*) bonded-warehouse.
enveloppe *v.* envelope, cover.
epidemie *v.* epidemy, epidemic.
epistel *o.* epistle.
epos *o.* epic, epic poem, epopee.
equator *m.* equator.
er *bw.* there; *vnw.* **wat is** — ? what is it?
erbarmelijk *b. n.* pitiable, pitiful, lamentable, wretched.
erbarmen *w. w.* **zich** — **over,** have pity on, have compassion on, have mercy upon, compassionate.
erbarming *v.* pity, compassion.
ereburger *m.* freeman.
eredienst *m.* public worship, cult.
erekruis *o.* cross of honour, cross of merit.
erelid *o.* honorary member.
eren *o. w.* honour, reverence; revere.
ereplaats *v.* place of honour.
ereprijs *m.* prize; (*Pl.*) veronica, speedwell.
ereteken *o.* mark of honour; (*ordeteken*) badge of honour.
erewacht *v.* guard of honour.
erewoord *o.* word of honour; (*mil.*) parole (of honour).
erf *o.* yard; patrimony.
erfdeel *o.* heritage, (hereditary) portion; *vaderlijk* —, patrimony.

erfdochter v. heiress.
erfelijkheid v. heredity.
erfenis v. inheritance, heritage.
erfgenaam m. heir.
erflater m. testator, legator.
erflating v. testation, legacy.
erfprins m. hereditary prince.
erfstuk o. heirloom.
erftante v. legacy aunt.
erfzonde v. original sin.
erg b. n. bad; (v. zieke) bad, ill, poorly; (v. pijnen, enz.) severe; bw. badly; severly; very (much, bad); z. n., o. suspicion.
ergens bw. somewhere, anywhere.
erger b. n. worse.
ergeren o. w. (ontstemmen) annoy, vex; (aanstoot geven) scandalize, shock, give umbrage (offence); w. w. **zich —**, take offence, be scandalized, be shocked.
ergerlijk b. n. annoying, vexatious, provoking; scandalous, shocking, offensive.
ergernis v. annoyance, vexation; scandal, umbrage, offence.
ergst b. n. worst.
erkennen o. w. acknowledge; (openlijk —) avow, confess; (toegeven) admit.
erkenning v. acknowledg(e)ment, recognition; admission.
erkentelijk b. n. thankful, grateful.
erkentelijkheid v. thankfulness, gratitude.
erker m. (vierkant) bay-window; (rond) bow-window; (v. bovenverdieping) oriel window.
ernst m. earnest(ness), seriousness, gravity.
ernstig b. n. (v. ziekte, ongeval, persoon) serious; (v. persoon) serious-minded; (v. fout, enz.) grave; (v. gelaatsuitdrukking) stern.
eronder bw. under it (them).
erop bw. on it (them).
erts o. ore.
ervaren o. w. experience; b. n. experienced, expert, skilled, practised.
ervaring v. experience; practice.
erven o. w. inherit; on. w. come into money, inherit.
erwt v. pea.
erwtensoep v. pea-soup.
es m. ash, ash-tree.
eskader o. (sch.) squadron.
esp m. (Pl.) asp, asp-tree.
espeboom m. asp, asp-tree.
estafette v. estafette, dispatch-rider.
Estland o. Esthonia.
etalage v. (uitstalling) display; (raam) show-window, shop-window.
etappe v. (afstand) stage; (rustpunt) halting-place; (mil.) supply-depot.
eten o. w. eat; on. w. eat; dine, have dinner; z. n., o. (voedsel) food; (maaltijd) meal; dinner; supper.
etensbakje o. trough.
etenstijd m. meal-time; dinner-time.
etensuur o. dinner-hour.

ether m. ether.
Ethiopië o. Ethiopia.
etiket o. label.
etmaal o. day of 24 hours, space of 24 hours, (natural) day.
ets v. etching.
etsen o. w. en on. w. etch.
etsnaald v. etching-needle.
ettelijk b. n. some, several.
etter m. (purulent) matter, pus, discharge.
etteren on. w. suppurate, ulcerate, discharge, fester.
Europa o. Europe.
Europeaan m. European.
euvel o. evil, fault.
euveldaad v. evil dead, crime, misdeed.
evacuatie v. evacuation.
evangelie o. gospel.
evangelist m. evangelist.
even b. n. even; bw. (gelijk) equally; (eventjes) just, only.
evenaar m. equator.
evenals b. n. (just) as, (just) like.
evenaren o. w. equal, be a match for.
evenbeeld o. image, likeness; counterpart.
eveneens bw. as well, also, likewise.
evenknie m. equal, compeer.
evenmens m. fellow-man.
evenmin bw. no more (than).
evennaaste m. fellow-man.
evennachtslijn v. equinoctial line.
evenredig b. n. (v. getal, vertegenwoordiging, enz.) proportional; (v. deel) aliquot.
evenredigheid v. proportion.
evenveel telw. as much. [still.
evenwel bw. however, nevertheless, yet,
evenwicht o. balance, equilibrium.
evenwijdig b. n. parallel.
evenzeer bw. as much, so much.
evenzo bw. likewise.
everzwijn o. wild boar.
ex vz. ex, late, sometime.
examen o. examination.
examinandus m. examinee.
excellent b. n. (bw.) excellent(ly).
excellentie v. excellency.
excentriek b. n. eccentric, odd; bw. eccentrically; z. n., o. (tn.) eccentric.
excommuniceren o. w. excommunicate.
excuus o. excuse, apology; pardon.
executie v. execution; (v. hypotheek) foreclosure.
exemplaar o. exemplar, specimen, sample; (v. boek, enz.) copy; (v. wissel) via.
exercitie v. (mil.) drill.
exercieveld o. (mil.) drill-ground, parade(-ground).
expediteur m. forwarding-agent, shipping-agent.
expeditie v. (mil.) expedition; (H.) dispatch, forwarding, shipping.
expeditiekorps o. (mil.) expeditionary corps.

experiment o. experiment.
exploitatie v. working, exploitation.
exploitatiekosten m. mv. workingexpenses, working-cost(s), cost of working.
exploot o. writ.
export m. export, exportation.
exporteur m. exporter.
exporthandel m. export trade.
expres b. n. express.
extase v. ecstasy, rapture.
extra (bijzonder) extra, special; (boven het gewone) additional.

extract o. extract; (v. boek) excerpt.
extratrein m. special train.
ezel m. (Dk.) ass, donkey; (v. schilder) easel.
ezelen on. w. drudge, slave, work like a horse.
ezelin v. she-sass, jenny-ass.
ezelskop| m. ass's head; (fig.) dunce, ass, blockhead.
ezelsoor o. ass's ear; (v. boek) dog's ear.
ezelstrap m. ass's kick.

F

faam v. fame; (reputatie, (goede) naam) reputation, repute.
fabel v. fable; (fig.) fable, myth; (verzinsel, ook:) fabrication.
fabeldichter m. fabulist.
fabriek v. factory, manufactory; works; mill.
fabrieksarbeider m. factory-hand, mill-hand, factory-worker.
fabrieksgebouw o. factory-building.
fabrieksprijs m. manufacturer's price; (kostende prijs) cost-price.
fabrikaat o. manufacture, make.
fabrikant m. manufacturer; (fabriekseigenaar) factory-owner, mill-owner.
factor m. (H.: factoor) factor; (rek.) factor.
factureren o. w. (H.) invoice.
factuur v. invoice.
factuurbedrag o. invoice-amount.
factuurprijs m. invoice-price.
faecaliën v. mv. faeces, night-soil.
failliet o. (faillissement) bankruptcy, failure; m. (persoon) bankrupt.
faillissement o. bankruptcy, failure; (onmacht om te betalen) insolvency.
fakkel v. torch; (fig.: lichtgevend lichaam, voorlichter) luminary.
falanx v. phalanx.
falen on. w. (missen) miss; (het mis hebben) make a mistake; (mislukken) fail.
familie v. (gezin, kinderen, geslacht) family; (bloedverwanten) relations.
familiebetrekking v. relationship, kindred; (bloedverwant) relation.
familiekring m. (leden v. gezin) domestic circle; (leden v. familie) family circle.
familieleven o. domestic life; family-life.
familielid o. member of the family; (bloedverwant) relation, relative.
familienaam m. surname; (vooral v. adellijke familie) family-name.
familiestuk o. family piece.
familietrek m. (gelijkenis) family likeness; (v. karakter) characteristic.
familietrots m. family-pride.
familietwist m. family-quarrel.

familiewapen o. family arms. [ly
fanatiek b. n. fanatic(al); bw. fanatical-
fantaseren o. w. (verzinnen) invent; (improviseren) improvise; on. w. romance, indulge in fancies; (muz.) play extempore.
fantasie v. phantasy, fancy; (muz.) voluntary; fantasia.
fantasieartikel o. fancy-article.
fantastisch b. n. (bw.) fantastic(ally).
Farizeeër m. Pharisee; (fig.) Pharisee, hypocrite.
fascist m. fascist.
fat m. dandy, knut, buck, fop, exquisite.
fataal b. n. fatal.
fatsoen o. (vorm, model) fashion, form; (leest) shape; (v. kleren) cut; (goede manieren) decorum, good form, good breeding; (fatsoenlijkheid) decency.
fatsoenlijk b. n. (achtenswaardig) respectable; (welvoeglijk: persoon, houding) decent; (v. buurt, omgeving) reputable; (deftig, meestal ironisch) genteel.
fatsoenlijkheid v. respectability; decency; gentility.
fatterig b. n. dandified, knutty, foppish; bw. foppishly.
fazant m. pheasant.
februari m. February.
fee v. fairy.
feeks v. virago, vixen, shrew, termagant.
feest o. feast, festivity; (feestviering) festival; (traktatie, schoolfeest) treat.
feestdag m. festive day, feast, feast-day; (kerkelijk) holyday.
feestdos m. festive attire.
feestelijk b.n. (bw.) festive(ly), festal(ly).
feestmaal o. banquet, festive entertainment.
feeststemming v. festive mood.
feestvieren on. w. feast, make merry.
feestvreugde v. festive joy, festive mirth.
feil v. (gebrek) fault; (vergissing, misslag) error, mistake.
feilbaar b. n. fallible, liable to error.
feilbaarheid v. fallibility, liability to error.
feilen on. w. make a mistake, err.
feilloos b. n. (bw.) faultless(ly).

feit *o.* fact; (*daad*) deed.
feitelijk *b. n.* factual, actual; *bw.* (*in feite*) in fact, in point of fact; (*eigenlijk*) virtually; (*praktisch*) practically.
fel *b. n.* (*bw.*) fierce(ly), grim(ly).
felicitatie *v.* congratulation.
femelaar *m.*, **—ster** *v.* bigot, canter, sniveller.
femelen *on. w.* cant, snivel.
ferm *b. n.* (*H.: v. markt*) steady, firm.
fiche *v.* counter, fish.
fielt *m.* rogue, rascal, scoundrel.
fier *b. n.* proud, high-spirited, haughty.
fierheid *v.* pride, high-spiritedness, haughtiness.
fiets *v.* cycle, bicycle; (*fam.*) bike.
fietsband *m.* (cycle-)tyre.
fietsbel *v.* (bi)cycle-bell.
fietsen *on. w.* bike, cycle.
fietser *m.* cyclist.
fietspad *o.* cycling-track.
figuur *o. en v.* figure; (*ter versiering*) diagram.
figuurlijk *b. n.* (*bw.*) figurative(ly).
figuurzaag *v.* fret-saw.
fijn *b. n.* fine; (*v. hoedanigheid: uitgelezen*) choice, exquisite; (*heerlijk*) delicate; lovely; (*chic, elegant*) smart; (*v. kleren*) swagger; (*voornaam: omgeving, wijk, enz.*) swell; (*v. onderscheid: subtiel*) subtle; (*nauwgezet, orthodox*) precise, punctilious; (*femelend, schijnheilig*) sanctimonious; *z. n., o.* **het —e van de zaak**, the quintessence of the matter.
fijngevoelig *b. n.* (*bw.*) delicate(ly), sensitive(ly).
fijngevoeligheid *v.* delicacy, sensitiveness.
fijnheid *v.* fineness; choiceness; delicacy; subtlety; *v.* (*onderscheiding: v. taal, enz.*) nicety.
fijnmalen *o. w.* grind fine, pulverize.
fijnproever *m.* gastronomer; (*fig.*) connoisseur.
fijt *v.* whitlow.
fiks *bw.* soundly, thoroughly; *b. n.* sound, thoroug.
filiaal *v. en o.* branch-establishment; (*kantoor*) branch-office.
film *v. en o.* film.
filmster *v.* film-star.
filosoof *m.* philosopher.
filter *m. en o.* filter, percolator; (*fot.*) screen, filter; (*v. waterleiding*) filter-bed.
Fin *m.* Finn.
finaal *b. n.* final; *bw.* absolutely, utterly.
finale *v.* (*muz.*) finale; (*sp.*) final.
financiën *v. mv.* finance(s).
Finland *o.* Finland.
firma *v.* firm; house (of business).
firmament *o.* firmament, sky.
firmant *m.* partner, member of the firm.
fiscus *m.* **de —**, the exchequer, the treasury.
fistel *v.* fistula.
fitter *m.* fitter.
fladderen *on. w.* (*v. vleermuis, enz.*) flitter, flit; (*klapwieken*) flutter; (*wap-*

peren, heen en weer bewegen) stream, flow; (*vliegen, zweven*) hover.
flakkeren *on. w.* flicker, waver, flare.
flambouw *v.* torch, flambeau.
flanel *o.* flannel.
flank *v.* flank, side.
flankaanval *m.* (*mil.*) flank-attack.
flankdekking *v.* flank-covering; flank-company.
flankvuur *o.* (*mil.*) flank-fire.
flansen *o. w.* **in elkaar —**, knock together.
flapuit *m. en v.* blabber.
flarden *m. mv.* rags, tatters.
flater *m.* blunder.
flauw *b. n.* (*v. spijzen*) insipid, savourless; (*zwak: v. weerstand, begrip, enz.*) weak, faint; (*niet helder: v. kleur, geluid*) dim, faint; (*v. markt*) flat, weak, dull, inactive; (*fig.: smakeloos*) insipid; (*v. grap*) silly, mild; (*v. gesprek: geesteloos*) vapid.
flauwheid *v.* insipidity; weakness, faintness; silliness; vapidity.
flauwte *v.* faint, swoon.
flegmatiek *b. n.* (*bw.*) phlegmatic(ally), stolid(ly).
flemen *on. w.* coax, cajole.
flemer *m.* coaxer, cajoler.
flens *v.* (*tn.*) flange.
flensje *o.* thin pancake.
fles *v.* bottle.
flessentrekker *m.* swindler, sharper.
flets *b. n.* pale, faded; (*v. ogen*) dim; (*v. bloemen*) wilted; (*v. persoon, ook:*) off-colour.
fleur *m.* bloom, flower, prime; *v.* (*vistuig*) angling-rod.
flikflooien *o. w. en on. w.* coax, cajole, flatter, fawn.
flikflooierij *v.* coaxing, cajolery, fawning.
flikje *o.* chocolate-drop.
flikken *o. w.* cobble, patch.
flikkeren *on. w.* (*v. kaars*) flicker; (*v. sterren*) twinkle; (*fonkelen, schitteren*) glitter.
flikkerlicht *o.* flickering light; (*v. vuurtoren*) flash(ing)-light.
flink *b. n.* (*krachtig, sterk*) vigorous, robust, sound; (*wilskrachtig*) energetic, pushing; (*v. jongen*) fine; (*v. vrouw: knap*) comely; (*inhuishouding*) managing; (*dapper, kranig*) plucky; (*levendig, pittig*) spirited; (*v. hoeveelheid*) considerable; (*aantal*) goodly; (*v. omvang: boekdeel, bedrag, enz.*) substantial; (*stevig: v. dosis, wandeling, enz.*) stiff; (*grondig, degelijk*) thorough; (*v. pas, slag, houding*) smart; *bw.* vigorously, soundly; energetically.
flinkheid *v.* thoroughness, push, nerve.
flits *m.* (*pijl, schicht*) arrow, dart; (*bliksem—*) flash.
flodderen *on. w.* (*ploeteren*) flounder, splash through the mud; (*v. kleren*) hang flapping, flop, bag.
floers *o.* (black) crape; (*fig.*) veil.

floret *o.* silk-ferret.
floret *v. (schermdegen)* (fencing-)foil.
flottielje *v.* flotilla.
fluisteren *o. w. en on. w.* whisper.
fluisterend *b. n.* whisperingly, in a whisper, in whispers.
fluit *v.* flute.
fluiten *on. w. (op vingers, v. wind, kogel)* whistle; *(v. vogel)* flute, pipe; *(in schouwburg, enz.: uitfluiten)* hiss; *(op fluit)* flute, play (on) the flute.
fluitist *m.* flute-player, flutist, flautist.
fluks *bw.* quickly; *b. n.* quick.
fluweel *o.* velvet.
fluweelachtig *b. n.* velvet-like, velvety.
fluwijn *o. (Dk.)* polecat; *(Z. N. oorkussen)* pillow.
fnuiken *o. w.* clip.
foedraal *o.* case; *(schede: v. vaandel, enz.)* sheath; *(omslag)* cover.
foerage *v. (mil.)* forage.
foerier *m. (mil.)* quartermaster.
fok *v. (sch.)* foresail.
fokkemast *m.* foremast.
fokken *o. w.* breed, rear.
fokker *m.* breeder, stock-breeder, cattle-breeder.
fokkerij *v. (v. vee)*stock-breeding, cattle-breeding.
folio *o.* folio.
folteraar *m.* torturer, tormentor.
folterbank *v.* rack, torture.
folteren *o. w.* put to the rack; *(fig. ook:)* torture, torment.
foltering *v.* torture, torment.
fondament *o. (grondslag)* foundation(s); *(scherts: zitvlak)* fundament.
fonds *o. (H.)* fund; *(zieken—, enz.)* club; *(kapitaal)* funds; **—en,** *(effecten)* funds, stocks, securities.
foneticus *m.* phonetician.
fonkelen *on. w.* sparkle, scintillate.
fonkeling *v.* sparkling, scintillation.
fonkelnieuw *b. n.* brand-new, spick-and-span new.
fontein *v.* fountain.
fooi *v.* gratuity, drink-money, tip.
foppen *o. w.* fool, hoax; *(bedriegen)* cheat, take in.
fopspeen *v.* comforter, (baby) soother.
forel *v.* trout.
formaat *o.* format, size.
formatie *v.* formation; *(mil.: legersterkte)* establishment.
formeel *b. n. (bw.)* formal(ly).
formulier *o. (ter invulling)* form, blank; *(kerkelijk)* formulary.
fornuis *o.* furnace, kitchen-range, kitchener.
fors *b. n. (stoer, krachtig)* robust, stalwart; *(v. wind, stem)* strong; *(luid: v. stem)* loud; *(v. taal, stijl)* vigorous; *(v. klap, slag)* smart; *bw.* strongly; vigorously.
forsheid *v.* robustness, vigour.
fort *o.* fort, fortress.
fortificatie *v.* fortification.
fortuin *v. en o.* fortune.

fortuinlijk *b. n.* lucky.
fortuinzoeker *m.* fortune-hunter, adventurer.
fossiel *b. n. en z. n., o.* fossil.
fout *v.* error, mistake; *(moreel)* fault; *(grove —)* blunder.
foutief *b. n.* wrong, faulty.
fraai *b. n.* beautiful, nice, pretty, handsome; *(ironisch)* nice.
fraaiheid *v.* beauty, prettiness, handsomeness.
fractie *v.* fraction.
frak *v.* dress-coat.
framboos *v.* raspberry.
Franciscaner *m.* Franciscan.
franco *b. n. en bw. (p. post)* post-paid, postage-paid, post-free; *(v. goederen)* carriage paid.
frank *m.* franc.
frank *b. n. (bw.)* frank(ly).
frankeerkosten *m. mv. (v. brief)* postage; *(v. pakket)* carriage.
frankeren *o. w.* prepay, post-pay; *(zegel opplakken)* stamp.
Frankrijk *o.* France.
Frans *b. n. en z. n., o.* French.
Fransgezind *b. n.* Francophil, pro-French.
frater *m.* brother.
fratsen *v. mv.* caprices, whims.
frees *v. (tn.)* fraise.
fregat *o.* frigate.
fret *o. (Dk.)* ferret; *(tn.)* gimlet.
freule *v.* honourable miss; *(in aanspraak)* Miss.
fries *v. en o.* frieze.
Fries *m.* Frisian.
Friesland *o.* Friesland.
frikadel *v.* minced-meat ball.
fris *b. n. (alg.)* fresh; *(v. drank)* refreshing; *(v. kamer, ochtend)* cool; *(gezond, in goede conditie)* fit; *bw.* freshly, fresh.
frisheid *v.* freshness, coolness.
frommelen *o. w.* rumple, ruffle, crumple.
frons(el) *v.* ruffle, frown, wrinkle.
fronsen *o. w.* ruffle, frown, wrinkle.
front *o. (alg.)* front; *(v. gebouw)* façade, front; *(frontbreedte)* frontage.
frontaanval *m. (mil.)* frontal attack.
fruit *o.* fruit.
fruitboom *m.* fruittree.
fruitschaal *v.*, **fruitschotel** *m.* fruit-dish. [shop.
fruitwinkel *m.* fruit-shop, fruiterer's
fuif *v.* spree, spread, beano, blow-out, jamboree.
fuik *v.* bow-net, fish-trap; *(aalfuik)* eel-basket.
fuiven *on. w.* feast, make merry; *o. w. iem.* **—,** feast a person.
fuiver *m.* feaster.
functie *v.* function.
furie *v.* fury.
fusilleren *o. w.* shoot (down).
fust *o.* cask, barrel.
fut *v.* spunk; spirit.
futloos *b. n.* spunkless, spiritless.
futselwerk *o.* trifling-work.

G

gaaf *b. n.* sound, whole, entire.
gaafheid *v.* soundness, woleness.
gaai *m.* (*Dk.*) jay; (*houten vogel*) popinjay.
gaan *on. w.* go; (*voor infinitief*) go to, go and; *z. n., o.* going, walking.
gaande *b. n.* going.
gaandeweg *bw.* gradually, little by little, by degrees.
gaar *b. n.* (*v. vlees, enz.*) done; (*fig.*) clever, knowing, wide-awake.
gaarkeuken *v.* cook-shop, eating-house, chop-house.
gaarne *bw.* willingly, readily, gladly; with pleasure.
gaas *o.* gauze.
gade *m.* husband; *v.* wife; consort; (*dicht.*) spouse.
gadeslaan *o. w.* observe, watch.
gading *v.* liking.
gaffel *v.* (*alg.*) fork; (*tweetandig*) two-pronged fork; (*hooivork*) prong, pitch-fork; (*sch.*) gaff.
gal *v.* gall, bile; (*wet.*) choler; (*v. paard*) wind-gall.
gala *o.* gala; (*kleding*) full dress.
galachtig *b. n.* bilious; (*fig.*) choleric, bilious.
galafscheiding *v.* secretion of bile.
galanterie *v.* gallantry; —**ën,** fancy-goods, fancy-articles.
galblaas *v.* gall-bladder.
galei *v.* (*sch.*) galley.
galeiboef *m.* galley-convict.
galerij *v.* gallery.
galg *v.* gallows; gallows-tree, gibbet.
galgebrok *m.* gallows-bird, scape-gallows.
galgehumor *m.* hempen humour, sardonic humour.
galgemaal *o.* last meal, parting meal, fare-well dinner.
galjoen *o.* (*sch.*) galleon.
galkoorts *v.* billious fever.
gallen *o. w.* gall.
galm *m.* sound, boom, reverberation.
galmen *on. w.* sound, resound.
galnoot *v.* gall-nut.
galop *m.* gallop; (*dans*) galop.
galsteen *m.* gall-stone, bile-stone.
galvaniseren *o. w.* galvanize.
galwesp *v.* gall-fly, gall-insect.
galziekte *v.* billious complaint.
gang *v.* (*v. huis, onderaards, enz.*) passage; (*v. huis, vooral lange, brede* —) corridor; (*steeg, slop*) alley; (*v. mijn*) gallery, level.
gang *m.* (*v. persoon*) gait, walk; (*v. paard*) pace; (*v. zaak*) progress; (*v. ziekte, geschiedenis, enz.*) course; (*v. machine*) running, working; (*bij schermen*) pass; (*aan tafel*) course.
gangbaar *b. n.* current.
gangbaarheid *v.* currency.
gangmaker *m.* (*sp.*) pace-maker.
gans *v.* goose.

gans *b. n.* whole, all; *bw.* wholly, entirely.
ganzebloem *v.* ox-eye (daisy).
ganzeleverpastei *v.* gooseliver pie.
ganzenbord *o.* (royal) game of goose.
ganzevoet *m.* (*Pl.*) goose-foot, pigweed.
gapen *on. w.* (*geeuwen*; *v. afgrond*) yawn; (*v. wond, enz.*) gape.
gapend *b. n.* (*v. afgrond*) yawning; (*v. wond, enz.*) gaping.
gaper *m.* yawner, gaper.
gaping *v.* gap, hiatus.
gappen *o. w. en on. w.* (*sl.*) pinch, nim, nab, pilfer, bag, sneak.
garage *v.* garage.
garderobe *v.* wardrobe; (*in station, enz.*) cloak-room.
gareel *o.* harness, (horse-)collar.
garen *o. w.* gather, collect.
garen *o.* thread, yarn.
garen *b. n.* thread.
garen- en bandwinkel *m.* haberdashery, fancy-woolshop.
garenklos *m.* cotton-bobbin.
garenspinner *m.* yarn-spinner.
garf *v.* sheaf.
garnaal *v.* shrimp; (*steurgarnaal*) prawn.
garnizoen *o.* garrison.
garstig *b. n.* rancid.
gas *o.* gas.
gasbek *m.* gas-jet.
gasbrander *m.* gas-burner.
gasfitter *m.* gas-fitter.
gaskraan *v.* gas-tap, gas-cock.
gaslantaarn *v.* gas-light.
gasmasker *o.* gas-mask, gas-helmet.
gasmeter *m.* gas-meter.
gasstel *o.* gas-stove.
gast *m. en v.* guest, visitor.
gastheer *m.* host.
gasthuis *o.* hospital.
gastmaal *o.* feast, banquet, entertainment.
gastvrij *b. n.* hospitable; *bw.* hospitably.
gastvrijheid *v.* hospitality.
gastvrouw *v.* hostess.
gasvormig *b. n.* gasiform, gaseous.
gat *o.* hole, opening, gap; (*v. broek*) seat; (*achterste*) bottom; backside; (*zee*—, *vaargeul*) pass, channel, inlet; (*v. dorp, enz.*) dog-hole, nest, wretched hole of a place.
gauw *b. n.* quick, swift, agile; *bw.* quickly, swiftly; (*spoedig*) soon.
gauwdief *m.* pilferer, sneak-thief, snatch-thief, pickpocket.
gave *v.* gift, donation, endowment.
gazel *v.* gazelle.
gazon *o.* lawn, (green)sward.
geaardheid *v.* disposition, nature, temper, composition.
geacht *b. n.* respected, esteemed; —**e Heer,** Dear Sir.
gebaar *o.* gesture, gesticulation.
gebabbel *o.* prattle, tattle, chatter, chit-chat, gossip.

gebak o. pastry, cake.

gebalk o. braying, bray.

gebarenkunst v. mimic art.

gebarenspel o. gestures, gesticulation, mimicry; pantomine, dumbshow.

gebarentaal v. gesture language, sign-language, conversation by gestures.

gebazel o. twaddle, empty talk.

gebed o. prayer.

gebedel o. begging.

gebedenboek o. prayer-book.

gebeente o. bones.

gebergte o. (chain of) mountains, mountain-range.

gebeten b. n. bit(ten).

gebeuren on. w. happen, occur, come about, chance, come to pass; befall.

gebeurlijk b. n. possible, contingent, what may happen.

gebeurlijkheid v. possibility, contingency, eventuality.

gebeurtenis v. event, occurrence.

gebeuzel o. trifling, dawdling, toying.

gebied o. (grond—) territory, dominion; (rechts—) jurisdiction; (fig.) domain, field, department, territory, sphere, realm.

gebieden o. w. en on. w. command, order.

gebiedend b. n. (v. toon) commanding, imperative, compelling; (v. eis, noodzaak, enz.) imperative; (v. persoon) imperious.

gebieder m. ruler, lord, master.

gebint o. cross-beams.

gebit o. (echt) teeth, set of teeth; (kunst—) artificial set of teeth, denture; (ijzeren —, v. toom) bit, mouth-bit.

gebladerte o. foliage, leaves.

geblaf o. barking, bark, baying.

gebod o. command, injunction, order; (goddelijk) commandment.

gebogen b. n. (v. stok) bent; (v. spiegel, enz.) curved; (v. neus) arched.

gebonden b. n. (v. boek) bound; (v. warmte) latent; (v. saus) thick; (v. handen, enz.: niet vrij) tied; (muz.: v. noten) syncopated; (v. stijl) poetic.

gebondenheid v. lack of freedom, state of being tied down; thickness; latency.

geboomte o. trees, timber.

geboorte v. birth; (v. Christus, O. L. Vrouw) nativity.

geboortecijfer o. birth-rate, natality.

geboortedag m. birth-day.

geboorteland o. native country.

geboortig b. n. — uit B., born at B., a native of B.

geboren b. n. born.

gebouw o. building; edifice, structure; (fig.) fabric; edifice, structure.

gebraad o. roast, roast-meat.

gebrabbel o. gibberish, jabbering, jargon.

gebreid b. n. knitted.

gebrek o. (armoede) want, indigence, need; (schaarste) shortage, shortness, scarcity; (tekort, gemis) want, lack;

(fout) fault, defect, imperfection, deficiency, failing; (lichamelijk) defect; (in wet, enz.) defect, flaw.

gebrekkelijk b. n. infirm, crippled, disabled.

gebrekkelijkheid v. infirmity, crippleness.

gebrekkig b. n. (v. persoon) invalid, infirm, crippled, deformed; (door ouderdom) decrepit; (v. uitspraak, toestel, werkwoord) defective; (v. uitdrukking, taal) faulty; (v. argument) poor; (v. verpakking) insufficient; bw. haltingly.

gebroed o. brood; (v. vissen, ook:) fry.

gebroeders m. mv. brothers.

gebroken b. n. broken; — getal, fraction, fractional number.

gebrom o. buzz(ing), humming, murmur; (v. persoon) grumbling, growling; (v. hond) growl(ing).

gebruik o. (v. koffie, bier, wijn, wapens, enz.) use; (verbruik) consumption; (gewoonte) usage, custom, habit, practice.

gebruikelijk b. n. usual, habitual, customary.

gebruiken o. w. use, employ, make use of; (v. spijzen, drank, enz.) take, partake of; (verbruiken) consume.

gebruiker m. user; (verbruiker) consumer.

gebruiksaanwijzing v. directions for use.

gebulder o. rumbling, booming, roar(ing).

gebuur m. en v. neighbour.

gedaagde m. en v. defendant; (bij echtscheiding) respondent.

gedaan b. n. done, finished.

gedaante v. shape, form, figure.

gedaanteverandering v., **gedaanteverwisseling** v. metamorphosis, transformation, shape-shifting.

gedachte v. thought, idea, notion, conception; (het nadenken) reflection; (mening) opinion; (herinnering) memory.

gedachteloos b. n. (bw.) thoughtless(ly), inconsiderate(ly).

gedachtengang m. current (line, train) of thought.

gedachtenis v. (abstract: herinnering) memory, remembrance; (concreet: voorwerper herinnering) memento, keepsake.

gedachtenwisseling v. exchange of thoughts.

gedaver o. booming, shaking.

gedeelte o. part, section; instalment; (aandeel) share.

gedeeltelijk b. n. partial; bw. partly, in part.

gedegen b. n. native.

gedenkboek o. memorial volume; annals, records?

gedenkdag m. anniversary; memorial day.

gedenken o. w. remember, commemorate.

gedenknaald v. memorial column (needle), obelisk.

gedenkpenning *m.* commemorative medal.
gedenkschrift *o.* memoir.
gedenkteken *o.* monument, memorial.
gedicht *o.* poem.
gedienstig *b. n. (bw.)* obliging(ly), attentive(ly).
gedienstigheid *v.* obligingness, complaisance.
gedierte *o. (dieren)* animals, beasts; *(ongedierte)* vermin.
gedijen *on. w.* thrive, prosper, flourish.
geding *o. (recht)* lawsuit, action, case; *(fig.)* quarrel.
gedoe *o.* doings, bustle, goings-on.
gedogen *o. w.* permit, suffer, tolerate, allow.
gedraal *o.* lingering, loitering, tarrying, delay.
gedrag *o. (uiterlijk: manieren, optreden)* demeanour, behaviour, deportment, bearing; *(zedelijk)* conduct.
gedragen (zich) *w. w.* behave, conduct oneself.
gedragslijn *v.* line of conduct, line of action, course (of action).
gedragsregel *m.* rule of conduct.
gedrang *o.* crowd, throng, crush.
gedrentel *o.* lounging, sauntering.
gedrocht *o.* monster, monstrosity.
gedrongen *(v. stijl)* terse, compact; *(v. gestalte)* thick set.
gedruis *o.* rush, roar(ing), noise.
gedrukt *b. n. (v. boek, enz.)* printed; *(zwaarmoedig, neerslachtig)* depressed, dejected, in low spirits, low(-spirited); *(v. handel)* depressed, dull, weak.
gedruktheid *v.* depression, depressedness, dejection.
geducht *b. n.* formidable; *(enorm)* enormous, tremendous; *bw.* formidably; tremendously; soundly.
geduld *o.* patience, forbearance.
geduldig *b. n. (bw.)* patient(ly).
gedurende *vz.* during, for.
gedurig *b. n.* continual, incessant; *bw.* continually, incessantly, continuously.
gedwee *b. n.* pliable, pliant, submissive, docile, meek.
gedweeheid *v.* pliability, pliancy, submissiveness, docility, meekness.
gedwongen *b. n. (v. lach, lening, enz.)* forced; *(v. werkloosheid, enz.)* enforced; *(v. dienst, verkoop)* compulsory; *(v. houding)* constrained; *bw.* forcedly.
gedwongenheid *v.* forcedness, constraint.
geëerd *b. n.* honoured.
geel *b. n.* yellow; *z. n., o.* yellow; *(v. ei)* yolk.
geelkoper *o.* brass.
geelzucht *v.* jaundice.
geen *vnw. (bijvoegl.)* no, not a, not any; *(zelfst.)* none, not one, not any.
geenszins *bw.* not at all, by no means.
geest *m. (tegenover lichaam)* spirit; *(denkvermogen, verstand)* mind, intellect; *(ziel; schim; spook)* spirit, ghost spectre,

phantom, apparition; *(geestigheid)* wit.
geestdrift *v.* enthusiasm, ardour.
geestdriftig *b.n. (bw.)* enthusiastic(ally).
geestelijk *b. n. (niet stoffelijk)* spiritual, immaterial; *(verstandelijk)* intellectual, mental; *(niet werelds, kerkelijk)* spiritual, ecclesiastical; religious, sacred; *(v. de geestelijkheid)* clerical, sacerdotal, ecclesiastical.
geestelijke *m.* clergyman.
geestelijkheid *v.* clergy.
geestenbanner *m.* exorcist.
geestesgesteldheid *v.* mentality, mental condition.
geestig *b. n.* witty, smart.
geestigheid *v.* wit, wittiness; *(aardigheid)* witticism.
geestrijk *b. n.* witty, spirited.
geestverheffend *b. n.* exalting, noble, sublime.
geestverrukking *v.* rapture, exaltation, ecstasy, trance.
geestverschijning *v.* apparition, phantom.
geestverwant *b. n.* congenial; *z. n., m. (gelijkgezinde)* congenial spirit, kindred spirit; *(partijgenoot, aanhanger)* supporter, adherent.
geestverwantschap *v.* congeniality of mind (spirit).
geeuwen *on. w.* yawn, give a yawn.
geeuwhonger *m.* canine hunger; *(wet.)* bulimy.
gefluister *o.* whisper(ing).
gefluit *o.* whistling; *(v. vogel)* warbling, singing.
gegadigde *m.* party interested, person interested; *(bij koop)* intending (prospective) purchaser, intending buyer; *(bij inschrijving)* intending subscriber; *(sollicitant)* candidate, applicant.
gegil *o.* scream(ing), yell(ing).
gegoed *b. n.* well-to-do, well-off, in easy circumstances.
gegoedheid *v.* ease, competency, wealth.
gegons *o. (v. insekt)* buzz(ing), hum; *(v. rad, wiek)* whirr(ing).
gegoten *b. n. (v. ijzer, staal)* cast.
gegrinnik *o.* grinning.
gegrond *b. n.* (well-)founded, (well-)-grounded.
gegrondheid *v.* foundedness, soundness, justness.
gehaast *b. n.* hurried.
gehakt *b. n.* minced meat; *(varkens—)* sausage meat.
gehalte *o. (alg.)* quality, standard; *(v. alcohol)* proof; *(v. bier)* gravity; *(v. erts)* grade; *(v. goud, zilver)* alloy, fineness; *(v. water, zuren, enz.)* percentage.
gehardheid *v.* hardiness, inurement.
gehavend *b. n.* battered, dilapidated.
gehechtheid *v.* attachment.
geheel *b.n.* whole, entire, total, complete; *bw.* wholly, entirely, totally, completely; *z. n., o.* whole.

geheelonthouder *m.* total abstainer, teetotaller.

geheim *b. n.* secret; *(ongeoorloofd)* clandestine; *(v. wetenschap)* occult; *(v. zitting, stemming, enz.)* private, secret; *(v. leer, enz.)* cryptic; *z. n., o.* secret, mystery.

geheimhoudend *b. n.* secret, secretive, close.

geheimhouding *v.* secrecy.

geheimschrift *o.* cipher, cryptogram; cryptography.

geheimzinnig *b. n.* mysterious.

geheimzinnigheid *v.* mysteriousness.

gehekel *o.* cavilling, fault-finding, criticizing.

gehemelte *o.* *(v. mond)* palate; *(v. troon)* canopy.

geheugen *o.* memory, remembrance.

gehijg *o.* panting, gasping.

gehinnik *o.* neighing, whinnying.

gehoor *o.* *(het horen)* hearing; *(de toehoorders)* audience, auditory, hearers; *(v. predikant)* congregation; *(geluid)* sound.

gehoorzaal *v.* audience-chamber; auditory, auditorium.

gehoorzaam *b. n.* *(bw.)* obedient(ly), dutiful(ly).

gehoorzaamheid *v.* obedience, dutifulness.

gehoorzamen *o. w.* obey; *on. w.* obey, be obedient; *(mil.)* obey orders.

gehoorzenuw *v.* auditory (auditive, acoustic) nerve.

gehucht *o.* hamlet.

geijkt *b. n.* *—e maten,* legally stamped measures; *—e uitdrukking,* current expression, standing phrase.

geil *b. n.* *(v. grond)* rank; *(wulps, wellustig)* lascivious, lecherous, salacious, lustful.

geilheid *v.* rankness; lasciviousness, lecherousness, salacity, lust.

geiser *m.* geyser.

geit *v.* goat.

geiteleer *o.* goatskin.

geitje *o.* kid, goatling, little (young) goat.

gejaagd *b. n.* hunted; *(fig.)* agitated, nervous, flurried, flustered.

gejaagdheid *v.* agitation, hurry, flurry, fluster.

gejammer *o.* lamentation(s), lamenting.

gejouw *o.* hooting.

gejubel *o.* shouting, shouts, cheering, jubilation.

gejuich *o.* shouting, shouts, rejoicing, exultation.

gek *b. n.* *(krankzinnig)* mad, crazy, lunatic, crack-brained; *(dwaas)* foolish, mad, silly; *(bespottelijk)* funny, queer; *(vreemd)* curious, odd, funny, queer; *bw.* madly, foolishly, funnily, oddly; like a madman; *z. n., m.* *(krankzinnige)* madman, lunatic; *(dwaas)* fool; *(modegek)* fop; *(schoorsteenkap)* cowl, turncap, chimneyjack.

gekakel *o.* cackle, cackling; *(fig.)* chitchat, title-tattle, cackle, cackling.

gekant *b. n.* *— tegen,* set against, hostile to.

gekarteld *b. n.* *(v. munt)* milled; *(Pl.)* crenate(d).

gekerm *o.* groaning, moaning, moans, lamentation(s).

gekeuvel *o.* chat(ting), chitchat, talk, gossip.

gekheid *v.* *(dwaasheid)* folly, foolishness, madness, foolery; *(scherts)* joke, joking; *(lol)* fun, lark(s).

gekir *o.* cooing.

gekkenhuis *o.* madhouse, lunatic asylum, bedlam.

gekkenpraat *m.* nonsense, foolish talk, the talk of a madman.

gekleed *b. n.* dressed.

geklets *o.* banging, smacking, clashing; *(fig.: kletspraat)* twaddle, rot, rubbish.

gekletter *o.* clattering, clashing, clanging.

geklik *o.* tale-telling.

geklok *o.* *(v. hen)* clucking; *(v. fles)* gluck-gluck.

geknars *o.* *(v. tanden)* gnashing; *(v. scharnier, enz.)* grating; *(v. wiel, ook:)* grind(ing).

geknetter *o.* crackle, crackling.

geknies *o.* fretting.

geknoei *o.* botching, bungling; *(gekonkel)* intriguing, plotting, jobbery.

gekonkel *o.* intriguing, plotting, jobbery.

gekoppeld *b. n.* coupled.

gekraak *o.* creaking.

gekrab *o.* scratching.

gekrakeel *o.* wrangling, bickering(s).

gekreun *o.* groaning, groans, moaning, moans.

gekriebel *o.* tickling, itching; *(v. geschrift)* scribbling, niggling, writing.

gekscheren *on. w.* jest, joke, banter.

gekuip *o.* intriguing, intrigues, plotting.

gekuist *b. n.* chaste, pure.

gekunsteld *b. n.* artificial, mannered, affected.

gekunsteldheid *v.* artificiality.

gekwetste *m.* wounded, (injured)person.

gelaarsd *b. n.* booted.

gelaat *o.* countenance, face; *(dicht.)* visage.

gelaatskleur *v.* complexion.

gelaatstrek *m.* feature.

gelaatsuitdrukking *v.* facial expression, countenance.

gelag *o.* score.

gelagkamer *v.* tap-room, bar-room.

gelang *bw.* *naar — van,* in proportion to, according to.

gelasten *o. w.* order, command, charge, instruct.

gelastigde *m.* mandatory, delegate, deputy, proxy.

gelaten *b. n.* *(bw.)* resigned(ly).

gelatenheid *v.* resignation.

geld *o.* money.

geldadel *m*. moneyed aristocracy.

geldafpersing *v*. extortion (of money), blackmail.

geldbelegging *v*. investment.

geldboete *v*. money-fine, money-penalty.

geldduivel *m*. demon of money, mammon.

geldelijk *b. n.* (*nadeel, beloning, enz.*) monetary; (*v. moeilijkheden*) pecuniary, financial; (*v. steun, enz.*) financial; *bw.* financially.

gelden *on. w.* (*kosten, waard zijn*) cost, be worth; (*van kracht zijn*) be in force, be valid, obtain, carry; (*betrekking hebben op*) concern, apply to.

geldgebrek *o*. want of money, penury, impecuniosity, lack of funds.

geldig *b. n.* valid.

geldigheid *v*. validity; (*v. kaartje, ook:*) availability.

geldkist *v*. strong-box.

geldlade *v*. cash-drawer, till.

geldnood *m*. famine of money.

geldschieter *m*. money-lender.

geldsom *v*. sum of money.

geldstuk *o*. coin.

geldverlegenheid *v*. pecuniary embarrassment, monetary difficulties.

geldverspilling *v*. waste of money.

geldwezen *o*. finance.

geldwolf *m*. money-grubber, money-bug, money-catcher.

geldzorgen *v. mv.* money-cares, money-troubles, financial worries.

geldzucht *v*. money-lust, money-grubbing, love of money.

geleden *b. n.* past; ago, since.

geleding *v*. (*Dk., Pl.*) articulation, joint, juncture; (*tn.*) joint; (*v. kust*) indentation.

geleerd *b. n.* learned.

geleerde *m*. learned man, scholar, savant.

geleerdheid *v*. learning, erudition.

gelegen *b. n.* (*liggende*) lying, situated; (*van pas*) convenient.

gelegenheid *v*. occasion; (*gunstige —*) opportunity; (*ruimte, plaats*) accommodation, place.

gelei *v*. (*v. vruchten*) marmalade, jam, jelly, preserves; (*voor vlees, enz.*) jelly.

geleibiljet *o*. (*voor vervoer per as*) way-bill; (*voor vervoer te water*) shipping-bill; (*voor douane*) permit.

geleibrief *m*. (*vrijgeleide*) safe-conduct.

geleide *o*. attendance, guard, care, guidance; (*mil.*) escort; (*v. vloot*) convoy.

geleidelijk *b. n.* gradual, gradational; *bw.* gradually, by degrees.

geleiden *o. w.* (*v. persoon*) lead, conduct, accompany; (*mil.*) escort; (*sch.*) convoy; (*el.*) conduct; (*tn.*) guide.

geleider *m*. leader, guide, conductor; (*el.*) conductor.

geleiding *v*. leading, conducting, guiding; (*el.*) conducting-wire, electric wiring; (*v. warmte, enz.*) conduction; (*v. waterleiding*) conduit-pipes.

geleischip *o*. tender.

geletterde *m*. man of letters, literary person.

gelezen *b. n.* read; *z. n., o. het —e,* the things (books) read.

gelid *o*. (*geleding, gewricht*) joint; (*mil.*) rank, file.

geliefde *m*. lover; *v*. lady-love, sweetheart, love, beloved, dearest.

gelieven *m. mv.* lovers.

gelieven *o. w.* please.

gelijk *b. n.* (*hetzelfde, niet verschillend*) similar, identical; equal, alike; (*gelijkwaardig*) equivalent; (*effen*) even, smooth, level; *bw.* (*eender*) alike, similarly; (*evenmatig*) equally; (*tegelijk, tegelijkertijd*) at the same time, simultaneously; *z. n., o.* right; *vw.* as.

gelijkaardig *b.n.* similar, homogeneous.

gelijke *m*. equal.

gelijken *o. w. en on. w.* resemble, be like, look like.

gelijkenis *v*. (*overeenkomst*) likeness, resemblance, similarity, similitude; (*Bijb.: afbeelding*) likeness; (*zinnebeeldig verhaal, parabel*) parable.

gelijkheid *v*. equality; (*gelijkenis*) similarity; (*v. oppervlakte, enz.*) evenness, smoothness.   [good time.

gelijklopen *on. w.* (*v. uurwerk*) keep

gelijkluidend *b. n.* (*v. woorden*) homonymous; (*muz.*) unisonous, consonant; (*v. document, enz.*) of same tenor, like-worded.

gelijkluidendheid *v*. homophony; unisonance, consonancy; conformity.

gelijkmaken *o. w.* equalize, make equal; (*effenen*) level, smooth; *on. w.* (*sp.*) equalize.

gelijkmatig *b. n.* (*v. temperatuur, enz.*) equable, equal; (*v. beweging, versnelling*) uniform; (*v. toon, enz.*) even; (*el.*) continuous; *bw.* equably, equally; uniformly; evenly.

gelijknamig *b. n.* (*v. personen*) of the same name; (*v. breuken*) having the same denominator; (*el.*) analogous, like, similar; (*v. woorden*) homonymous.

gelijkslachtig *b. n.* homogeneous.

gelijkslachtigheid *v*. homogeneity, homogeneousness.

gelijkstaan *on. w.* be equal; (*sp.*) be (draw) level.

gelijkstellen *o. w.* put on a par, put on a level; equalize.

gelijkstroom *m*. continuous current, direct current.

gelijktijdig *b. n.* simultaneous, synchronous; (*v. schrijvers, enz.*) contemporary.

gelijkvloers *b. n.* (*fig.*) plain, pedestrian, homely.

gelijkvormig *b. n.* of the same form, similar, conformable.

gelijkwaardig *b. n.* equivalent; of the same value.

gelijkzijdig *b. n.* equilateral.   [ing.

geloei *o*. lowing, bellowing; roar, roar-

gelofte v. vow, promise.

geloof o. belief, credit, credence, faith; (godsdienstig) belief, faith; (geloofsbelijdenis) creed.

geloofsartikel o. article of faith.

geloofsbelijdenis v. confession of faith.

geloofsbrieven m. mv. (v. gezant) credentials, letters of credence; (v. kamerlid) documentary proof of one's election.

geloofsijver m. religious zeal.

geloofspunt o. doctrinal point, point of doctrine.

geloofsverzaking v. apostasy.

geloofwaardig b. n. credible, veridical, reliable; bw. credibly.

geloofwaardigheid v. credibleness, credibility, reliability, veracity.

geloop o. running.

geloven o. w. en on. w. believe, credit; (menen, denken) believe, think.

gelovig b. n. believing, faithful.

geluid o. sound, noise, voice.

geluidgevend b. n. sounding.

geluidloos b. n. soundless.

geluidsfilm v. sound-film.

geluimd b. n. humoured, in a temper.

geluk o. (gevoel) happiness; (groot —) felicity; (gunstig toeval) luck, good luck, fortune, chance; (gunstige loop v. omstandigheden) fortune; (succes) success; (zegen) blessing.

gelukken on. w. succeed.

gelukkig b. n. (gevoel) happy; (toevallig) lucky; (door omstandigheden) fortunate; (goed gevonden, enz.) felicitous; bw. happily, luckily, fortunately, by good luck.

geluksbode m. bearer of good news.

gelukskind o. spoilt child of fortune, fortune's favourite.

geluksster v. lucky star.

gelukwensen o. w. congratulate, offer one's congratulations, wish joy, wish good luck.

gelukzalig b. n. blessed.

gelukzaligheid v. bliss, blessedness, beatitude.

gelukzoeker m. adventurer, fortune-hunter.

gemaakt b. n. (v. kleren) ready-made, ready-to-wear; (v. manieren, enz.) affected, finical, prim; bw. affectedly, in a finical way, primly.

gemaaktheid v. affectation, primness.

gemaal m. spouse, husband; (vooral in titels) consort.

gemaal o. (het malen) grinding; (te malen graan) multure; (belasting) duty on flour; (toestel) pumping-engine; (fig.: gezeur, gezanik) worry, bother.

gemachtigde m. proxy, delegate, deputy; (in proces) attorney; (v. postwissel) endorsee.

gemak o. (gemakkelijkheid) ease, facility; (gerief) comfort; convenience, commodity; (behaaglijkheid) ease; (beste kamer) (place of) convenience.

gemakkelijk b. n. easy; (v. huis) com-

modious, convenient; (v. leunstoel, enz.) comfortable; bw. easily, with ease, conveniently; comfortably.

gemakshalve bw. for convenience (' sake).

gemakzucht v. love of ease.

gemalin v. spouse, consort.

gemanierd b. n. well-mannered, well-bred, mannerly.

gemanierdheid v. good breeding, mannerliness.

gematigd b. n. (v. persoon, temperatuur, enz.) moderate; (v. woorden, enz.) measured; (v. luchtstreek) temperate.

gematigdheid v. moderation; temperateness.

gemeen b. n. (algemeen) common, public, general; (gewoon) common, ordinary, usual; (gemeenschappelijk) common, joint; (slecht) bad, vile; (min, laag, verachtelijk) mean, base, low, dirty; (vuil, plat) obscene, foul, smutty, scurrilous, filthy; (ordinair) common, vulgar, low; bw. commonly; ordinarily, usually; meanly, lowly; vulgarly; z. n., o. rabble, mob, vulgar, populace.

gemeengoed o. common property.

gemeenheid v. meanness, baseness, shabbiness, etc.

gemeenschap v. (aanraking, verbinding) connection, communication; (fig.: omgang) commerce, intercourse; (maatschappij, enz.) community; (gemeenschappelijkheid) community.

gemeenschappelijk b. n. (v. vriend, kamer) common; (v. eigendom, belangen) joint; bw. commonly; jointly, conjointly, in common.

gemeente v. (burgerlijk) municipality; (kerkelijk) parish; (prot.: gehoor v. predikant) congregation.

gemeenteambtenaar m. municipal, official.

gemeentebestuur o. municipality, (municipal) corporation, municipal authority.

gemeentehuis o. municipal hall, town-hall.

gemeentereiniging v. municipal scavenging system.

gemeenzaam b. n. familiar, intimate.

gemeenzaamheid v. familiarity, intimacy.

gemeld b. n. above, above-mentioned, above-said.

gemelijk b. n. peevish, fretful, sullen, morose, cross, crusty.

gemelijkheid v. peevishness, fretfulness, etc.

gemenebest o. commonwealth, republic.

gemengd b. n. mixed, miscellaneous, mingled.

gemiddeld b. n. (v. getal, prijs, enz.) average; (v. tijd, afstand) mean; bw. on an average, averagely.

gemijmer o. musing, reverie, meditation.

gemijterd *b. n.* mitred.
gemis *o.* lack, want.
gemoed *o.* mind, heart.
gemoedelijk *b. n.* (*v. persoon*) kind-(-hearted), good-natured, jovial, kindly disposed; (*v. woorden*) feeling, sympathising.
gemoedelijkheid *v.* kind-heartedness, good nature.
gemoedsaandoening *v.* emotion.
gemoedsbezwaar *o.* conscientious scruple (objection).
gemoedsrust *v.* tranquillity (peace) of mind, serenity, inward peace.
gemok *o.* sulking, pouting.
gemompel *o.* murmuring, murmur, grumbling.
gemopper *o.*, **gemor** *o.* murmuring, grumbling; (*sl.*) grousing.
gems *v.* chamois.
gemurmel *o.* murmur(ing), gurgle, gurgling, purling.
genaakbaar *b. n.* accessible, approachable, of easy access.
genaakbaarheid *v.* accessibility, approachableness. [nated.
genaamd *b. n.* named, called; denomi-
genade *v.* (*v. God*) grace; (*barmhartigheid*) mercy; (*begenadiging, vergiffenis*) pardon.
genadebrood *o.* bread of charity, bread of dependence.
genademiddel *o.* means of grace.
genadeoord *o.* (*kath.*) place of pilgrimage.
genadeslag *m.* finishing stroke, death-blow; knock-out (blow).
genadig *b. n.* (*v. God, enz.*) merciful, gracious; (*neerbuigend*) gracious, condescending; *nw.* mercifully, graciously, condescendingly.
genaken *o. w.* approach; *on. w.* approach, draw near.
gene *aanw. vnw.* that, the former.
geneesheer *m.* doctor, physician.
geneeskrachtig *b. n.* healing, curative; medicinal, officinal.
geneeskunde *v.* medical science, medicine, healing art, therapeutics.
geneesmiddel *o.* remedy, medicine.
genegen *b. n.* (*neiging hebbende tot*) inclined, disposed, willing; (*gunstig gezind*) favourably (friendly, kindly) disposed.
genegenheid *v.* inclination, affection, attachment.
geneigd *b. n.* — *te* (*tot*), inclined to, disposed to.
geneigdheid *v.* inclination, disposition; proneness, propensity.
generaal *b. n.* general.
generaal *m.* (*mil.*) general.
generen *o. w.* inconvenience, incommode, discommode, embarrass; *w. w.* **zich** —, feel embarrassed, be shy.
generhande, generlei *b. n.* of no kind; no manner of; **op** — **wijs,** in no wise; in no manner whatever.

geneugte *v.* pleasure, delight, joy.
genezen *o. w.* cure; restore; (*v. wond*) heal.
genezing *v.* cure, recovery, healing.
genie *o.* genius; (*v. mil.*) engineering.
geniep *o.* **in het** —, in secret, secretly, furtively, by stealth, stealthily.
geniepig *b. n.* sneaky, sneaking, malicious; *bw.* sneakily, sneakingly, in a sneaky way, in an underhand way.
genieten *o. w.* enjoy; *on. w.* enjoy oneself.
genieter *m.* epicurean, sensualist.
genodigde *m.* person invited, guest.
genoeg *onbep. telw.* enough, sufficient-(ly).
genoegdoening *v.* satisfaction, reparation, atonement.
genoegen *o.* pleasure, delight, joy, enjoyment; satisfaction, contentment.
genoeglijk *b. n.* pleasant, pleasurable, agreeable, enjoyable.
genoeglijkheid *v.* pleasantness, pleasurableness, agreeableness.
genoegzaamheid *v.* sufficiency.
genoemd *b. n.* named, called; (*zo even genoemd*) just mentioned, above-said.
genoot *m.* fellow, companion, associate, partner.
genootschap *o.* society, association.
genot *o.* pleasure, joy, delight; (*het genieten*) delectation, enjoyment; (*vruchtgebruik*) usufruct.
genotmiddel *o.* luxury.
genotzucht *v.* love of pleasure.
Gent *o.* Ghent.
Gentenaar *m.* native of Ghent.
geoefend *b. n.* practised, trained; expert.
geoefendheid *v.* expertness.
geoorloofd *b. n.* lawful, allowed, admissible, permitted.
gepantserd *b. n.* armoured, armour-clad, iron-clad.
gepastheid *v.* propriety, suitability, suitableness, becomingness, fitness.
gepeperd *b. n.* peppered, peppery; (*fig.: v. stijl, enz.*) peppery; (*pikant*) highly seasoned; (*v. rekening*) salt, exorbitant.
gepeupel *o.* mob, populace, rabble, riff-raff.
gepieker *o.* brooding, puzzling.
gepiep *o.* chirping, squeaking.
geploeter *o.* drudging, plodding, toiling.
gepoch *o.* boasting, brag(ging), swagger-(ing).
gepraat *o.* talk, tattle, tittle-tattle.
geprikkeld *b. n.* irritated.
gepruil *o.* pouting, sulkiness.
geraakt *b. n.* touched; (*fig.*) piqued, offended, nettled, sore.
geraaktheid *v.* irritation, pique; (*Z.N.: beroerte*) apoplexy.
geraamte *o.* (*v. mens, dier*) skeleton; (*v. huis*) shell, carcass; (*v. vliegtuig*) fuselage; frame, frame-work.
geraken *on. w.* get, arrive, come to, attain.

gerecht b. n. just, condign, righteous, due.

gerecht o. (gang) course; (schotel) dish; (court of) justice, tribunal.

gerechtelijk b. n. (v. verkoop, moord, enz.) judicial; (v. raadsman, stappen, enz.) legal; bw. judicially; legally.

gerechtigd b. n. qualified, entitled; authorized.

gerechtigheid v. justice.

gerechtsdienaar m. law-officer, police-officer.

gerechtshof o. court (of justice).

gerechtszaal v. hall of justice.

geredelijk b. n. readily.

gereed b. n. ready; (af) finished, done.

gereedheid v. readiness.

gereedschap o. tools, instruments, utensils, implements.

geregeld b. n. regular, orderly, fixed, set, settled; bw. regularly.

geregeldheid v. regularity.

gerei o. tackle; implements.

gereutel o. (geklets) twaddle, rot; (v. stervende) death-rattle.

geriefelijk b. n. commodious, comfortable, convenient.

geriefelijkheid v. accommodation, convenience, commodity.

gerieven o. w. (v. persoon) accommodate, oblige; (Z. N.: v. klanten) serve.

gering b. n. small, scant, scanty, slight, trifling, low.

geringschatten o. w. depreciate, have a low opinion of, disparage.

geringschatting v. depreciation, disdain, disregard, slight.

geroffel o. roll, rub-a-dub.

gerokt b. n. (v. vrouw) skirted; (v. heer) dress-coated; (Pl.) tunicated.

gerommel o. rumbling; (v. donder) roll.

geronk o. (v. persoon: in slaap) snoring; (v. machine) snorting.

geronnen b. n. (v. melk) curdled; (v. bloed) clotted.

gerst v. barley.

gerucht o. rumour, report; (geluid) noise.

geruchtmakend b. n. sensational.

geruis o. (v. wat beweegt) noise; (v. kleren, bladeren) rustling; (v. bergstroom) rushing; (v. rivier) murmur; (v. rok, zijde) swish; (in de oren) tingling.

geruisloos b. n. (bw.) noiseless(ly), silent(ly).

gerust b. n. easy; (rustig) quiet, peaceful; bw. quietly, easily.

geruststellen o. w. reassure, set at ease, tranquillize.

geruststellend b. n. reassuring, tranquillizing.

geruststelling v. relief, tranquillisation, assurance.

geschater o. burst (peals, shout) of laughter.

geschenk o. present, gift; (schenking) donation.

geschermutsel o. (mil.) skirmishing.

gescherts o. joking, jesting.

geschieden on. w. happen, occur, come to pass, chance; take place, befall.

geschiedenis v. history; (verhaal) story, tale.

geschiedschrijver m. historian, historiographer.

geschikt b. n. proper, suitable, fit, suited; (bekwaam) able, capable, efficient; (v. gereedschap, enz.) apt; (v. tijd, weg) proper; (v. kandidaat) eligible; (schappelijk) decent, obliging; (passen) appropriate.

geschiktheid v. propriety, suitability, fitness; ability, capability; aptness.

geschil o. difference, dispute, quarrel, controversy.

geschooi o. begging.

geschoold b. n. schooled, practised, trained; (v. arbeider) skilled.

geschreeuw o. cries, shrieks, shouts.

geschrift o. writing.

geschrijf o. scribble, scribbling, writing.

geschut o. (mil.) artillery, guns, cannon, ordnance.

gesel m. scourge, lash, whip.

geselen o. w. whip, flog, flagellate; (fig.) scourge, lash.

geseling v. scourging, lashing, flogging; flagellation.

geselroede v. scourge, lash.

gesjacher o. bartering, haggling.

geslaagd b. n. successful.

geslacht o. butchered meat, slaughtered meat.

geslacht o. (ras, familie) race, family, lineage; (generatie) generation; (soort: v. dieren, planten) species; (kunne) sex; (gram.) gender.

geslachtelijk b. n. (bw.) sexual(ly).

geslachtloos b. n. sexless, asexual; (gram.) genderless.

geslagen b. n. beaten.

geslepen b. n. whetted, sharp(ened); (v. glas) cut; (fig.) sly, cunning.

geslepenheid v. slyness, cunning.

geslinger o. swinging, dangling; (v. schip) rolling.

gesloten b. n. (v. deur, enz.) closed, shut; (op slot) locked; (mil.: v. geledeten) serried; (fig.) close, uncommunicative, reticent.

gesmeek o. supplication(s), entreaty, pleading.

gesmul o. feasting, banqueting, guzzling.

gesnap o. small talk, tittle-tattle; (v. kind) prattle.

gesnater o. chattering, jabbering.

gesnuffel o. snuffling, sniffing; ferreting, rummaging.

gespan o. team.

gespierd b. n. muscular, brawny, sinewed, sinewy; (fig.: v. taal, enz.) nervous, sinewy.

gespierdheid v. muscularity; (fig.) nervousness, nerve.

gespin o. spinning; (v. kat) purring.

gesprek o. conversation, talk; (dicht.) discourse.

gespronqen b. n. (v. band) punctured; (v. glas, enz.) burst; (v. snaar) snapped; (v. handen) chopped.

gestadigheid v. steadiness, continuance, constancy, settledness; (volharding) perseverance.

gestalte v. figure, stature, shape, size.

gestamp o. stamping, trampling; (v. machine) thud; (v. schip) pitching.

gesteente o. (precious) stones; stone, rock.

gestel o. constitution, system, structure.

gesteld b. n. set; established; vw. suppose, supposing.

gesteldheid v., **gesteltenis** v. state, condition; (v. bodem, enz.) nature, character, constitution.

gesternte o. star; stars, constellation.

gesticht o. institution, establishment, edifice; (toevluchtsoord, tehuis) asylum, home.

gestoelte o. seat, chair.

gestommel o. cluttering, stumbling.

gestoot o. pushing.

gestotter o. stammering, stuttering.

gestrekt b. n. stretched.

gesukkel o. bungling, muddling, botching; (ziekelijkheid) ailing.

getal o. number.

getalsterkte v. numerical strength.

getier o. clamour, noise.

getij o. tide.

getijden o. mv. (kath.) de —, the hours.

getimmerte o. structure, building.

getintel o. sparkling, twinkling; (v. koude) tingling.

getob o. (met zorgen) bother, worry; (gezwoeg) toiling, drudgery.

getouw o. gear, loom.

getreuzel o. lingering, loitering, dawdling, dallying.

getroosten (zich) w. w. bear patiently, put up with.

getrouw b. n. faithful, true, loyal, trusty; (nauwkeurig) accurate, exact.

getrouwheid v. faithfulness, fidelity, loyalty.

getuige m. en v. (recht) witness, evidence; (bij huwelijk) best man; (bij tweegevecht) second.

getuigen o. w. testify, witness, bear witness, attest; on. w. depose, give evidence, appear as a witness; (godsd.) bear testimony, testify.

getuigenis o. en v. evidence, testimony, witness.

getuigenverhoor o. examination of the witnesses.

getuigschrift o. certificate, testimonial, attestation; (v. dienstbode) character.

getwist o. quarrelling, wrangling.

geul v. channel, gully.

geur m. odour, smell, fragrance, perfume, scent, aroma, flavour.

geuren on. w. (geur verspreiden) smell, exhale odours, give forth scent; (ijdel pronken) swank, swagger, cut a dash.

Geus m. (gesch.) Beggar; Protestant.

geus v. (sch.) jack(-flag).

gevaar o. danger, risk, peril.

gevaarlijk b. n. dangerous, risky, perilous, hazardous.

gevaarte o. colossus, monster.

gevaarvol b. n. perilous, hazardous.

geval o. case.

gevangen b. n. caught, captive, imprisoned.

gevangenbewaarder m. jailer, warder, turnkey.

gevangene m. en v. prisoner, captive.

gevangenis v. (gebouw) prison, jail, gaol; (straf) captivity, imprisonment.

gevangennemen o. w. take prisoner, arrest, capture, apprehend; (mil.) take captive, take prisoner.

gevangenschap v. imprisonment, confinement; captivity.

gevat b. n. quick-witted, ready-witted, quick at repartee, smart, clever.

gevatheid v. quick-wittedness, ready wit, quickness at repartee, smartness, cleverness.

gevecht o. fight, battle, combat, action, engagement.

gevechtsvliegtuig o. fighting-plane, fighter, battle-plane.

gevederte o. feathers.

geveinsd b. n. simulated, feigned, dissembled, dissembling, hypocritical.

geveinsdheid v. simulation, hypocrisy.

gevel m. front, façade; (scherts: neus) conk, proboscis.

gevelspits v. gable.

geven o. w. give, make a gift of; present with; (opleveren, verschaffen) afford, produce, yield; (v. warmte, geur, enz.) give out; (verlenen) confer, grant, bestow; (v. kaarten in kaartsp.) deal; on. w. give; (kaartsp.) deal; w. w. zich **gewonnen —,** yield the point.

gever m. giver, donor.

gevest o. hilt.

gevestigd b. n. fixed, established.

gevierd b. n. fêted; (v. held, enz.) celebrated; (v. toneelspeler, enz.) popular.

gevlei o. flattering, coaxing, wheedling.

gevoeglijk bw. decently, properly, conveniently, appositely.

gevoeglijkheid v. decency, propriety, convenience, appositeness.

gevoel o. (gewaarwording) feeling, sensation, sentiment; (gevoelszin) feeling, touch.

gevoelen o. w. feel; zie **voelen;** z. n., o. (gemoedsbeweging) feeling, sentiment; (mening) opinion, idea, thought.

gevoelig b. n. (vatbaar voor aandoeningen) feeling, impressionable, impressible, sensitive; (lichtgeraakt) touchy, sensitive; susceptible; (pijnlijk: v. voet, enz.) tender; (v. instrument; fot.) sensitive; bw. feelingly; severely.

gevoeligheid v. feelingness, impressibility, sensitiveness; touchiness; tenderness; severity.

gevoelloos b. n. unfeeling, apathetic, impassive; insensible; (v. lichaamsdeel) numb.

gevoelloosheid v. unfeelingness, apathy; insensibility; (dicht.) anaesthesia.

gevoelsleven o. inner life.

gevoelsmens m. man of feeling, emotional person.

gevoelszenuw v. sensory (sensorial, sensitive) nerve.

gevoelvol b. n. (full of) feeling, tender; bw. feelingly.

gevogelte o. birds, fowls, poultry.

gevolg o. (uitvloeisel, resultaat) consequence, result; (v. personen) suite, train, retinue, following.

gevolgtrekking v. conclusion, deduction, consequence, inference.

gevolmachtigde m. (gemachtigde) proxy, attorney; (v. land, regering) plenipotentiary.

gevreesd b. n. dreaded.

gewaad o. garment, attire, garb, dress.

gewaarworden o. w. become aware of, perceive, notice, experience; (te weten komen) find out.

gewaarwording v. (aandoening) sensation; (vermogen) perception.

gewag o. — **maken van,** mention, make mention of.

gewagen on. w. — **van,** mention, make mention of.

gewapend b. n. (mil.) armed; (v. beton) reinforced, armoured, steel.

gewapenderhand bw. by force of arms, with the armed hand.

gewas o. vegetation, growth; (plant) plant, herb; (oogst) crop, harvest.

geween o. weeping, crying.

geweer o. rifle; (jacht—) gun.

geweerkolf v. butt-end.

geweerriem m. rifle-sling.

geweerschot o. rifle-shot, gun-shot.

geweervuur o. rifle-fire, fusillade, musketry.

gewei o. (getakte horens) antlers, horns; (ingewand v. wild) entrails, intestines, bowels.

geweld o. (kracht) force, violence; (lawaai) noise, racket.   [outrage.

gewelddaad v. (act of) violence,

gewelddadigheid v. (act of) violence, outrage.

geweldig b. n. (bw.) violent(ly); vehement(ly), powerful(ly), mighty(-ily).

geweldpleging v. violence.

gewelf o. vault, arch, arched roof.

gewennen o. w. accustom, habituate; on. w. — **aan,** accustom to, get accustomed to, get used to; w. w. **zich — aan,** accustom oneself to, become (get) used to.

gewenst b. n. (wenselijk) desirable, advisable; (verlangd) desired, desiderated, wished for.

gewest o. region; (provincie) province.

gewestspraak v. dialect.

geweten o. conscience.

gewetensangst v. pangs (qualms, anguish) of conscience.

gewetensvol b. n. conscientious.

gewetenswroeging v. compunctions, twinges (stings) of conscience.

gewezen b. n. late, former; ex-.

gewicht o. weight; (fig.) importance, weight, moment.

gewichtig b. n. weighty, important, momentous.

gewiekst b. n. knowing, sharp, cunning.

gewijd b. n. consecrated; sacred.

gewild b. n. (in trek, gezocht) in demand, in request, in favour, favoured, called for, popular; (gemaakt) studied, affected.

gewillig b. n. willing, tractable, docile, ready, compliant.

gewin o. gain, profit.

gewis b. n. (bw.) certain(ly), sure(ly).

gewoel o. bustle, stir.

gewonde m. wounded person.

gewoon b. n. (gebruikelijk) usual, habitual, customary, accustomed; (niet buitengewoon) ordinary, common, plain; (gewend) habituated, accustomed, used; (ordinair) common; bw. commonly, usually, habitually; simply.

gewoonlijk bw. usually, ordinarily, commonly, generally, as a rule.

gewoonte v. (aangenomen gebruik) custom, usage, use; (persoonlijke handeling) habit, custom, practice; (aanwensel) habit, habitude, wont; trick.

geworden on. w. come to hand.

gewricht o. joint, articulation; (wet.) arthrosis.

gewrichtsknobbel m. condyle.

gewrocht o. production, creation, work.

gezag o. authority, power; (fig.) influence, prestige, credit.

gezaghebbend b. n. authoritative.

gezaghebber m. administrator, manager, director.   [captain.

gezagvoerder m. master (of a ship),

gezalfde m. anointed.

gezamenlijk b. n. collective, joint, conjunct, combined; bw. collectively, jointly, conjunctively; completely; together.

gezang o. (het zingen) singing; (lied) song; (kerk—) hymn; (v. vogels) warbling.

gezanik o. bother, botheration.

gezant m. ambassador; (gevolmachtigd minister) minister(-resident); (afgezant) envoy.

gezantschap o. embassy.

gezegde o. saying, expression, dictum, phrase; (gram.) predicate.

gezel m. (makker, kameraad) companion, mate, fellow; (handwerksgezel) journeyman, workman.

gezellig b. n. (v. persoon) companionable, sociable, convivial, social; (v. kamer, enz.) snug, cosy; (v. dieren: gezellig levend) social, gregarious.

gezelligheid v. companiableness, sociability, conviviality; snugness, cosiness.

gezellin v. companion.

gezelschap o. company, society.

gezet b. n. (zwaarlijvig, dik) corpulent, stout, stocky, stubby; (geregeld, bepaald, vast) set, definite, fixed.

gezicht o. (aangezicht) face; (dicht.) visage; (uitdrukking) countenance, looks; (het zien) sight; (het geziene) view, sight, spectacle; (gezichtsvermogen) sight, eyesight; (visioen) vision.

gezichtsbedrog o. optical illusion.

gezichtseinder m. horizon.

gezien b. n. visa, visé; (geacht, in aanzien) esteemed, respected.

gezin o. family, household.

gezindheid v. disposition, inclination; (godsdienstig) persuasion, religious conviction.

gezinshoofd o. head of the family; householder.

gezinsleven o. family-life.

gezocht b. n. (in trek, gewild) in demand, in request, sought-after; (verzonnen) got-up, trumped-up; (gekunsteld, onnatuurlijk) affected, studied, laboured; (v. stijl) forced; (ver —) farfetched.

gezochtheid v. (great) demand, being in request; (gekunsteldheid, onnatuurlijkheid) affectation, affectedness, studiedness; forcedness; farfetchedness.

gezond b. n. (alg.) healthy; (v. lucht, klimaat, enz.) salubrious; (gezondheidbevorderend) healthful, healthgiving; (v. spijs, drank) wholesome; (gaaf) sound; (fig.) sane; bw. healthily; soundly.

gezondheid v. health, healthfulness; salubrity; soundness; sanity, saneness.

gezondheidsleer v. hygiene, sanitary science, hygienics.

gezusters v. mv. sisters.

gezwel o. swelling, tumour, growth.

gezwind b. n. (bw.) swift(ly), quick(ly).

gezwollen b. n. (v. wangen, gezicht) swollen, bloated; (v. lichaamsdelen) tumid, tumescent; (fig.) bombastic, stilted, pompous, turgid.

gezworen b. n. sworn.

gezworene m. juror, juryman.

gids m. guide.

giechelen o. w. giggle, snigger, titter.

gier m. (Dk.) vulture; (gil) scream, screech; (sch.: draai, zwenking) sheer; v. (mestvocht) stale, muck-water.

gierbrug v. flying-bridge.

gieren on. w. (gillen) scream, screech; (v. wind) howl; (sch.) yaw, sheer off; o. w. dress (feed) with liquid manure.

gierig b. n. avaricious, niggardly, miserly, stingy.

gierigaard m. miser, niggard, skinflint.

gierigheid v. avarice, miserliness, niggardliness, stinginess.

gierzwaluw v. martin, swift.

gieten o. w. en on. w. (v. water, regen) pour; (v. metalen) cast, found; (v. ka-

nonnen) found; (v. kaarsen, enz.) mould; (fig.) mould.

gieter m. watering-pot, watering-can; (v. metalen) founder, caster; moulder.

gieterij v. foundry, foundry works.

gietvorm m. casting-mould, matrix.

gif, gift o. (alg.) poison; (dierlijk) venom; (v. ziekte: smetstof) virus, toxin; (fig. ook:) bane.

gift v. present, gift, donation, gratuity; (dosis) dose.

giftig b. n. poisonous, venomous; (fig.) envenomed, venomous, virulent.

giftmenger m., **giftmengster** v. poisoner.

gij pers. vnw. you; (dicht.) ye.

gijzelaar m. hostage; (voor schuld) prisoner for debt.

gil m. yell, scream, shriek.

gild(e) o. guild, corporation, craft.

gildebroeder m. guild-brother, member of a guild, brother of the craft.

gillen on. w. yell, scream, shriek.

ginder, ginds bw. over there, yonder.

gips o. gypsum, gyps; (gebrand) plaster.

gipsafgietsel o. plaster-cast; (v. dode) death-mask.

gipsverband o. plaster of Paris bandage; plaster (of Paris) dressing, plaster-jacket.

giro v. clearing, transfer.

girobank v. clearing-bank, transfer bank.

giroverkeer o. clearing system, transfer system.

gis v. guess, conjecture.

gispen o. w. blame, censure, castigate; (onbarmhartig hekelen) scarify.

gisping v. blame, censure, castigation; scarification.

gissen o. w. guess, conjecture.

gissing v. guessing, conjecture; (schatting) estimation.

gist v. yeast, barm.

gisten on. w. ferment, work, rise.

gisteren bw. yesterday.

gisting v. ferment, fermentation, working.

gistkuip v. fermenting-vat.

git o. jet.

gitaar v. guitar.

glad b. n. (v. oppervlakte, zee, tong) smooth; (v. huid) smooth, sleek; (v. straat, enz.: glibberig) slippery; (v. ring) plain; (fig.: slim) clever, cunning, artful, cute; bw. smooth, smoothly.

gladheid v. smoothness; slipperiness.

gladmaken o. w. polish, smooth.

glans m. gloss, lustre, effulgence; (v. schoenen) polish, shine; (v. haar, zijde, enz.) gloss; (v. kolen) glance; (v. ogen, metalen) lustre; (v. goud) glitter; (fig.) splendour, brilliancy, gleam, lustre.

glansperiode v. heyday, golden age, noonday of its glory.

glanspunt o. acme, height; crowning event.

glansrijk b. n. glorious, brilliant,

resplendent, splendid, radiant; *bw*, gloriously, brilliantly.
glanzen *on. w.* gleam, shine, shimmer.
glisten; *o. w. (v. zijde, enz.)* gloss; *(v. leer, papier, schilderij)* glaze; *(v. metaal)* furbish, brighten; burnish; *(v. marmer, enz.)* polish.
glas *o.* glass; *(v. lamp)* chimney; *(ruit)* (window-)pane; *(v. bril)* glass, lens; *(sch.)* bell.
glasblazer *m.* glass-blower.
glasblazerij *v.* glass-works.
glashelder *b. n. en bw.* clear as glass (as crystal), crystalclear.
glasraam *o.* window(-frame), glazed window, frame.
glasscherf *v.* fragment of glass, glass splinter, piece of broken glass.
glassnijder *m.* glass-cutter.
glaswaren *v. mv.* glassware, glass articles, glass-work.
glaswerk *o. zie glaswaren; (v. gebouw)* glazing.
glazenkast *v.* glazed cabinet; *(keukenkast)* kitchen-dresser.
glazenmaker *m. (persoon)* glazier; *(Dk.: insekt)* dragon-fly.
glazuur *o. (v. aardewerk)* glazing, glaze; *(v. tanden)* enamel.
gletsjer *m.* glacier.
gleuf *v.* groove; *(lange opening)* slot, slit.
glijbaan *v.* slide.
glijboot *v.* hydroplane.
glijden *on. w. (op glijbaan, enz.)* slide; *(uitglijden, afglijden)* slip; *(v. boot, enz.)* glide; *(v. vliegtuig)* plane, glide.
glijvlucht *v.* volplane, glide.
glimlach *m.* smile.
glimlachen *on. w.* smile *(tegen,* at, on).
glimmen *on. w.* glimmer, gleam, shine.
glimp *m.* glimpse, show.
glimworm *m.* glow-worm, fire-fly.
glinsteren *on. w.* glitter, glint, glisten, sparkle, twinkle.
glinstering *v.* glittering, glint, glistering, sparkle, sparkling.
glippen *o. w.* slip.
globaal *b. n.* rough; *bw.* roughly, in the gross.
gloed *m.* glow, blaze; *(fig.)* ardour, fervour, verve, fervency, fire.
gloeidraad *m.* filament.
gloeien *on. w. (v. metaal)* glow, be red-hot; *(fig.: v. ogen, wangen)* glow, be aglow, burn; *(v. oren)* burn, tingle; *o. w.* make red-hot, heat to whiteness; *(uitgloeien)* anneal.
gloeiend *b. n.* glowing, red-hot, burning; *(fig.)* ardent, fervid; *bw.* — *heet,* *(v. water, enz.)* burning hot, scalding hot; *(v. metaal)* red-hot.
gloeihitte *v.* red heat, white heat; intense heat; incandescent heat.
gloeilamp *v.* incandescent lamp.
gloeioven *m.* annealing furnace, calcinating furnace.
glooiing *v.* slope.

gloor *m.* glow; *(fig.)* splendour, lustre.
gloren *on. w.* glimmer, gleam; *(v. dag)* dawn, break.
glorie *v.* glory, lustre, splendour.
gluiper (d) *m.* sneak, skulk.
glunder *b. n.* cheerful, cheery, blithe, jovial, buxom.
gluren *on. w.* peep, peer, spy, pry; *(ong.)* leer.
gnoe *o.* gnu.
goal *m.* goal.
God *m.* God.
goddelijk *b. n.* divine, heavenly, god-like.
goddelijkheid *v.* divineness, divinity.
goddeloos *b. n.* godless, ungodly, impious, unholy, wicked.
godendienst *m.* idolatry.
godenleer *v.* mythology. [gods.
godenspijs *v.* ambrosia, food of the
godgeleerde *m.* theologian, divine.
godheid *v. (abstract)* divinity, godhead; *(concreet)* deity.
godin *v.* goddess.
godsdienst *m.* religion.
godsdiensthaat *m.* religious hatred.
godsdienstigheid *v.* religiousness, piety, devotion.
godsdienstplechtigheid *v.* religious ceremony.
godsgericht *o.* ordeal.
godshuis *o. (kerk, tempel)* house of God, place of worship, church, temple; *(liefdegesticht)* charitable institution, alms-house.
godslastering *v.* blasphemy.
godspenning *m.* earnest-money.
godsspraak *v.* oracle.
godsvrucht *v.* piety, devotion.
godvruchtig *b. n.* pious, devout.
goed *b. n. (niet slecht)* good; *(goedaardig)* kind, good-natured; *(juist)* right; *(niet bedorven)* sweet; *bw.* well; *(juist)* right.
goed *o. (het goede)* good; *(koopwaar)* goods, wares; *(bezit)* goods, property, possession; *(kleding)* clothes, things; *(reisgoed, bagage)* luggage, things; *(stof)* stuff, material; *(landgoed)* estate; *(gerei)* things.
goedaardig *b. n. (v. persoon)* good-natured, benignant, kind-hearted; *(v. ziekte)* benign, benignant, mild.
goedaardigheid *v. (v. persoon)* good-nature, kind-heartedness; *(v. ziekte)* benign character, mildness, non-malignity.
goeddunken *on. w.* think fit, think proper; *z. n., o.* approbation, pleasure.
goedendag *m.* good day; *(bij afscheid)* good bye; *(wapen)* morning-star, morgenstern, mace.
goederenkantoor *o.* goods-office; parcel's delivery.
goederenstation *o.* goods-station.
goederentrein *m.* goods-train, freight-train.
goederenverkeer *o.,* **goederenvervoer** *o.* goods-traffic, carrying-traffic.

goederenvliegtuig *o.* cargo-plane.
goederenvoorraad *m.* stock (of goods), stock-in-trade.
goedertieren *b. n.* merciful, clement.
goedertierenheid *v.* mercy, clemency.
goedgelovig *b.n.* (lichtgelovig) credulous, trustful; (zuiver in de leer) orthodox.
goedgelovigheid *v.* credulity, trustfulness; orthodoxy.
goedgunstig *b. n.* favourable, kind, obliging.
goedhartig *b. n.* good-natured, kind-hearted.
goedheid *v.* goodness, kindness.
goedkeuren *o. w.* approve; consent to, agree to; (v. notulen, verslag) adopt; (mil.: voor dienst) pass fit; (v. vliegtuig) certify as airworthy; (v. film) pass.
goedkeuring *v.* approbation, approval; (v. notulen, verslag) adoption; (op school) good mark.
goedkoop *b. n.* cheap; inexpensive.
goedmaken *o. w.* (inhalen, herstellen) make good; make up for; (v. vergissing, fout, enz.) repair, redeem.
goedschiks *bw.* with a good grace, willingly.
goedsmoeds *bw.* (welgemoed, opgeruimd) of good cheer, cheerful; (koelbloedig) in cold blood, deliberately.
goedvinden *o. w.* think fit (proper); (goedkeuren) approve of; z. n., o. approbation, consent.
goedzak *m.* (goedhartig persoon) good-natured chap, kind soul, good fellow; (lobbes, sul) softy, soft Johnny simpleton.
golf *v.* (baar) wave; (grote —) billow; (inham) gulf, bay.
golf *o.* (sp.) golf.
golfbreker *m.* breakwater, groyne.
golflengte *v.* wave-length.
golfspeler *m.* golf-player, golfer.
golfstok *m.* golf-stick, golf-club.
Golfstroom *m.* Gulf-stream.
golven *o. w. en on. w.* wave, undulate.
golving *v.* waving, undulation.
gom *v.* gum.
gommen *o. w.* gum.
gondel *v.* gondola; (v. luchtschip, ook:) car.
gong *v.* gong, tam-tam.
gonzen *on. w.* buzz, hum, drone.
goochelaar *m.* juggler, conjurer, prestidigitator, illusionist.
goochelen *on. w.* juggle, conjure, do tricks.
goochelkunstje *o.* juggling-trick, conjuring-trick, sleight of hand.
gooi *v.* throw, cast; toss.
gooien *o. w.* throw, fling, cast.
goor *b. n.* (onfris, vuil) dingy; sallow; (bedorven, onsmakelijk) nasty.
goot *v.* gutter; (straatgoot, ook:) kennel, drain.
gootpijp *v.* water-pipe.
gootsteen *m.* sink, sink-stone, slop-sink.
gordel *m.* (om middel) girdle, waist-

band, belt; (v. forten) circle, ring, girdle; (dicht.) zone.
gordeldier *o.* armadillo.
gorden *o. w.* gird.
gordijn *o. en v.* curtain; (rol-) blind; (v. bed) (bed-)hangings, curtains.
gordijnroede *v.* curtain-rod, curtain-pole.
gordijnvuur *o.* (mil.) curtain-fire, barrage.
gorgel *m.* throat, throttle.
gorgelen *on. w.* gargle; (v. vogel: rollend kwelen) warble.
gort *r.* (grutten) groats, grits; v. en o. (varkensziekte) measles.
gortebrij *r.*, **gortepap** *r.* barley-gruel.
goud *o.* gold.
goudader *v.* vein of gold, gold-vein, gold-lode.
goudbedding *v.* deposit of gold.
goudbrasem *m.* goldney, gilthead.
gouddekking *v.* gold-cover.
gouden *b. n.* gold, golden.
goudfazant *m.* golden pheasant.
goudgehalte *o.* gold-grade, percentage of gold, fineness.
goudhaantje *o.* (vogel) gold-crest, gold-crested wren; (insekt) rose-chafer.
goudklomp *m.* nugget of gold.
Goudkust *r.* Gold Coast.
goudmijn *v.* gold-mine; (fig.) gold-mine, mine of wealth.
goudsmid *m.* goldsmith.
goudstuk *o.* gold-piece.
goudvink *m.* (Dk.) bull-finch; (fig.: goudstuk) goldfinch; (mil.) officer.
goudvis *m.* (Dk.) gold-fish; (fig.) rich heiress, oofy girl.
goudvlies *o.* gold-beater's skin.
goudvoorraad *m.* gold-stock(s), stock of bullion.
goudvos *m.* golden fox; (paard) bay horse, light chestnut.
goudzoeker *m.* gold-seeker, gold-finder, gold-hunter.
gouvernement *o.* government.
gouverneur *m.* governor; (huisonderwijzer) house-tutor.
gouw *v.* district, province.
graad *m.* (rang) degree, grade, rank; (v. thermometer, hoek, enz.) degree; (v. verwantschap) degree, remove.
graadboog *m.* graduated arc, protractor.
graadverdeling *v.* graduation, division into degrees.
graaf *m.* count; (in Engeland) earl.
graafschap *o.* (gebied) county, shire; (waardigheid) countship, earldom.
graafwerk *o.* excavation, digging, earth-work.
graag *b. n.* (begerig) eager; (hongerig) hungry; bw. gladly, willingly, readily.
graagheid *v.* eagerness, appetite.
graan *o.* corn; grain.
graangewassen *o. mv.* cereals.
graankorrel *m.* grain of corn.
graanoogst *m.* grain-crop, cereal crop.
graanzolder *m.* corn-loft.

graat v. fish-bone.
grabbelen on. w. scramble (for).
gracht v. (in stad) canal; (straat langs gracht) quay; (om vesting, slot) ditch, moat.
graf o. grave; (dicht., hogere stijl) tomb, sepulchre.
grafheuvel m. grave-mound, burial mound; (gesch.) tumulus, barrow.
grafkelder m. family-vault.
grafkrans m. mortuary crown, funeral wreath.
grafkuil m. grave. [robber.
grafschender m. grave-robber, tomb-
grafschennis v. violation of tombs (of a tomb).
grafschrift o. epitaph.
grafsteen m. grave-stone, tomb-stone.
graftombe v. tomb.
grafzuil v. sepulchral column, memorial column.
gram o. gram, gramme.
gram b. n. wrathful, wrath.
grammofoon v. gramophone.
gramschap v. anger, wrath, ire.
granaat m. (edelsteen) garnet; v. (mil.) shell, shrapnel; (hand—) grenade.
granaatappel m. pomegranate.
granaatvuur o. shell fire.
graniet o. granite.
grap v. joke, jest, fun.
grapjas m. joker, buffoon, wag.
grappenmaker m. joker, buffoon, wag, fun-maker.
grappig b. n. funny, comic, droll, facetious.
gras o. grass.
grasboter v. grass-butter, May-butter.
grashalm m. grass-blade, blade of grass.
grasland o. grass-land, grassy land, pasture-land.
grasmaand v. grass-month, April.
grasmus v. hedge-sparrow, white-throat.
grasperk o. lawn, grass-plot.
graszode v. (turf) sod.
gratie v. (bevalligheid; gunst) grace; (ontheffing v. straf) pardon; (v. doodstraf) reprieve.
gratis b. n. gratis, free of cost, free (of charge), gratuitous; bw. gratis, free of charge, without charge.
grauw m. (snauw) snarl, grumble, growl.
grauw o. rabble, mob.
grauw b. n. gray, grey; (fig.) drab.
grauwtje o. donkey.
grauwvuur o. fire-damp.
graveelsteen m. (renal, urinary) calculus, (urinary) stone.
graveerijzer o. engraving-tool.
graven o. w. en on. w. (v. put, kanaal, enz.) dig; (v. mijn, enz.) sink; (v. konijnen, enz.) burrow.
graver m. digger.
graveren o. w. en on. w. engrave; (v. stempels) sink.
gravin c. countess.
grazen on. w. graze, feed, pasture.

greb v. furrow, trench.
greep m. (het grijpen) grip, grasp, clutch; (handigheid) knack; (muz.) touch; v. (handvat) grip, handle, haft, hilt; (handvol) handful; (vork) fork.
grein o. (korreling; gewicht) grain; (stof) camlet.
grendel m. bolt; (v. geweer) loading-bolt.
grenehout o. (red) deal, pine-wood.
grens v. (grenslijn, uiterste lijn) limit; (v. land, landgoed, enz.) boundary; (rand, zoom) border; (staatkundig) frontier.
grensdorp o. frontier village.
grensgebied o. borderland, confines.
grensgeschil o. boundary quarrel (dispute), frontier dispute.
grenslijn v. frontier-line; (fig.) line of demarcation, boundary line, limit-line.
grenspaal m. boundary-post, boundary-mark, landmark.
grenswacht v. frontier guard.
grenzeloos b. n. boundless, limitless, unlimited.
grenzen on. w. — aan, border on, confine on (with), adjoin; (fig.) border on, verge on.
greppel v. furrow, trench, ditch.
gretig b. n. eager, greedy, avid, desirous; bw. eagerly, greedily, avidly.
gretigheid v. eagerness, greediness, avidity.
grief v. grievance; (krenking, belediging) offence, wrong; (vore, rimpel) furrow.
Griekenland o. Greece.
griep v. influenza.
griesmeel o. semolina, semola.
griet m. (vogel) godwit; v. (vis) brill.
grieven o. w. grieve, hurt, offend.
grievend b. n. grievous, offending.
griezelen on. w. shiver, shudder.
griezelig b. n. grisly, shuddery, creepy, gruesome, curdling.
griezeligheid v. gruesomeness.
grif bw. readily, promptly.
griffel v. slate-pencil; (boom-ent) graft.
griffie v. registry, record-office, office of the rolls.
griffier m. clerk (of the court), recorder, [registrar.
grifheid v. readiness.
grijns v. grin, grimace, sneer.
grijnslach m. grin, sneer, sneering, laugh, sardonic smile.
grijnslachen on. w. grin, sneer, laugh sardonically.
grijnzen on. w. grin, sneer, (make a) grimace.
grijpen o. w. (pakken) seize, catch, grasp; (naar zich toe) snatch; (in klauw) clutch; on. w. — naar, grab (grasp, clutch, snatch) at, make a grab at.
grijpgier m. kite, hawk, vulture.
grijs b. n. gray, grey, grey-headed; (eerwaardig, v. ouderdom) hoary.
grijsaard m. gray-haired man, old man; graybeard.

grijzen *on. w.* grey, become (get) grey, grow grey, grizzle.

gril *v* caprice, frak, fancy, crotchet, whim, whimsy.

grillig *b. n.* capricious, freakish, fanciful, crotchety, whimsical, fantastic.

grilligheid *v.* capriciousness, fancifulness, whimsicalness, fantasticalness.

grimmen *on. w.* be angry, be furious.

grimmig *b. n.* grim, furious, truculent.

grimmigheid *v.* grimness, fury, truculence.

grind *o. en v.* gravel, gritstone; (*vooral op strand*) shingle.

grindweg *m.* gravel-road, gravelled road.

grinniken *on. w.* grin, snigger; (*van genoegen*) chuckle, chortle.

groef *v.* groove, channel; (*in zuil*) flute; (*in molensteen*) trench; (*in gelaat, huid*) furrow.

groei *m.* growth.

groeien *on. w.* grow.

groeikracht *v.* vegetative faculty, vegetative force, growing faculty, vitality.

groeizaam *b. n.* favourable to vegetation.

groeizaamheid *v.* (*v. weer*) growthiness.

groen *b. n.* green; (*fig.*) fresk, verdant, green; (*onrijp*) unripe; *z. n., o.* (*kleur*) green; (*planten*) greenery, verdure; *m.* greenhorn, novice; (*stud.*) freshman, fresher, greeny.

groenheid *v.* greenness, verdancy.

groente *v.* (*vers*) greens, (green) vegetables, green stuff; (*bereid, als toekruid*) potherbs, vegetables.

groentetuin *m.* kitchen-garden.

groentewinkel *m.*, **groentezaak** *v.* greengrocer's (shop), vegetable shop.

groep *v.* group.

groet *m.* greeting, salute, salutation; bow.

groeten *o. w.* greet, salute; *on. w.* salute, take off one's hat.

grof *b. n.* (*niet fijn; niet glad*) coarse rough; (*v. gelaatstrekken*) large, coarse; (*v. taal*) coarse, vulgar; (*v. stem: laag*) gruff; *bw.* coarsely, roughly.

grofheid *v.* coarseness, roughness.

grommen *o. w.* (*v. vis*) gut.

grommen *on. w.* (*brommen*) growl, grumble, snarl; (*v. donder*) growl, rumble.

grompot *m.* growler, grumbler.

grond *m.* (*aarde*) ground, earth; soil; (*land*) land; (*grondvlak, bodem*) ground, bottom; (*grondslag*) base, ground, foundation, substratum; (*reden*) ground, reason.

grondbeginsel *o.* basic (fundamental) principle, root-principle; **de —en,** (*v. wetenschap, enz.*) the elements, the rudiments.

grondbelasting *v.* land-tax, ground-tax.

grondbestanddeel *o.* fundamental part (ingredient), primary component.

gronden *o. w.* (*grondverven*) ground; (*grondvesten, stichten*) found, lay the foundations of; (*fig.*) ground, found, base.

grondgebied *o.* territory.

grondgedachte *v.* root (basic) idea, leading thought.

grondgesteldheid *v.* nature (character, condition) of the soil.

grondgetal *o.* base.

grondig *b. n.* (*v. smaak*) earthy, muddy; (*fig.*) thorough; (*v. studie, onderzoek*) profound; (*v. verandering*) fundamental; (*v. onderzoek*) exhaustive; (*v. genezing*) radical.

grondlaag *v.* first layer, bottom layer.

grondlegging *v.* foundation.

grondlijn *v.* base, basis.

grondoorzaak *v.* original (prime, first, root) cause.

grondregel *m.* principle, maxim.

grondslag *m.* foundation(s), groundwork; (*fig.*) base, basis, groundwork.

grondstof *v.* raw material, element.

grondtoon *m.* (*muz.*) key-note, fundamental tone; (*fig.*) ground-note, dominant note, key-note, prevailing tone.

grondverf *v.* ground-colour, priming prime colour, first coat (of paint).

grondvest *v.* foundation; base.

grondvesten *o. w.* found, lay the foundations of.

grondvesting *v.* foundation.

grondvlak *o.* (*meetk.: basis*) base; (*v. plan*) ground-plane.

grondwerker *m.* navvy.

grondwet *v.* constitution, fundamental [law.

grondwettelijk *b. n.* constitutional.

grondwettig *b. n.* constitutional.

groot *b. n.* (*omvangrijk*) big, large, large-sized; (*uitgestrekt*) great, large; vast; (*volwassen*) grown-up; (*v. gestalte*) tall; (*van belang*) great; (*belangrijk*) great, grand; *bw.* large.

grootbedrijf *o.* big industry, large-scale industry.

grootboek *o.* ledger.

grootbrengen *o. w.* bring up, rear, raise.

Groot-Brittannië *o.* Great Britain.

groothandel *m.* wholesale trade.

groothandelaar *m.* wholesale dealer.

grootheid *v.* greatness, largeness, tallness, magnitude; (*wisk.*) quantity

grootheidswaanzin *m.* megalomania.

groothertog *m.* grand duke.

groothertogdom *o.* grand duchy.

groothertogin *v.* grand duchess.

grootmeester *m.* grand-master.

grootmoeder *v.* grandmother.

grootmoedig *b. n.* large-hearted, magnanimous, high-minded, generous.

grootouders *m. mv.* grandparents.

groots *b. n.* (*prachtig, heerlijk*) grand, grandiose, majestic, noble; (*fier, trots*) high, proud, haughty.

grootscheeps *bw.* in grand style, on the grand scale; *b. n.* grand, princely, lordly.

grootspraak *r.* bluff, brag, boasting, boast, bravado.

grootspreker *m.* bragger, braggart, boaster.

grootte *v.* greatness, largeness, bigness, size, bulk, extent; (*v. ster*) magnitude; (*v. schip*) burden; (*v. persoon: lengte*) height.

grootvader *m.* grandfather.

grootvorst *m.* grand duke.

grootvorstin *v.* grand-duchess.

gros *o.* (*grote hoop, merendeel*) gross, mass, main body; (*12 dozijn*) gross.

grot *v.* grotto, cave; (*dicht.*) grot.

grotelijks *bw.* greatly, largely, to a great (large) extent, to a high degree.

grotendeels *bw.* for the greater part, for the most part.

gruis *o.* (*v. kolen*) coal-dust, culm; (*v. stenen*) grit; (*aardk.*) waste.

gruizelementen *o. mv.* **aan —**, (in)to smithereens, to shivers, to atoms, to nieces.

grut *o.* **het kleine —**, the small fry.

grut (ten) *v.* (*mv.*) groats, grits.

gruwel *m.* (*gevoel*) abomination, horror; (*daad*) atrocity.

gruweldaad *v.* atrocity.

gruwelijk *b. n.* abominable, horrible, atrocious; *bw.* abominably, horribly, atrociously.

gruwen *on. w.* shudder.

guerrilla-oorlog *m.* guerilla warfare.

guit *m.* wag, scamp, rogue; (*ong.*) rogue.

guitenstreek *m.* **guitenstuk** *o.* roguish trick.

gul *v.* (*Dk.: vis*) codling.

gul *b. n.* (*zacht, mul*) loose; (*vrijgevig*) generous, liberal, open-handed; (*hartelijk, gulhartig*) cordial, openhearted, frank, genial.

gulden *z. n., m.* guilder, Dutch florin; *b. n.* golden.

gulhartig *b. n.* open-hearted, cordial, frank, genial.

gulhartigheid *v.* open-heartedness, cordiality, frankness, geniality.

gulp *v.* (*golf: v. bloed, enz.*) gulp; (*split*) trousers-fly, trousers-slit.

gulweg *bw.* openly, frankly, genially.

gulzig *b. n.* gluttonous, greedy.

gulzigaard *m.* glutton.

gulzigheid *r.* gluttony, greediness.

gummi *o.* (india-)rubber.

gunnen *o. w.* (*verlenen, toewijzen*) allow, grant, award; (*niet misgunnen*) not envy, not grudge.

gunst *z. n., v.* favour; (*H.*) favour, custom, goodwill; *tw.* goodness gracious!

gunsteling *m.* favourite.

gunstig *b. n.* favourable, auspicious, propitious; *bw.* favourably.

gutsen *o. w.* (*tn.*) gouge; *on. w.* (*v. bloed, enz.*) gush, spout.

guur *b. n.* bleak, raw, inclement, rough.

guurheid *v.* bleakness, rawness, inclemency.

gymnasium *o.* grammar-school.

gymnastiek *v.* gymnastics.

gymnastiekzaal *v.* gymnasium (-room), drill-hall.

H

Haag, Den —, *o.* The Hague.

haag *v.* hedge, hedge-row; (*v. personen*) lane.

haai *m.* (*Dk.*) shark; (*fig.*) kite, vulture.

haak *m.* (*om vast te houden, op te hangen, enz.*) hook; (*winkel—*) square; (*zethaak*) composing-stick; (*v. telefoon*) clamp; (*v. raam, deur*) catch, clasp; (*om slot open te maken*) pick(-lock).

haaknaald *v.* crochet-needle.

haakpen *v.* crochet-needle, crochet-hook.

haaks *b. n.* square(d).

haakwerk *o.* crochet-work, crocheting.

haal *m.* (*aan sigaar, enz.*) pull; (*met pen*) stroke; dash.

haan *m.* (*Dk.*) cock; (*v. geweer*) cock, cocking-piece.

haar (*bez. vnw.*) her; (*mv.*) their; (*pers. vnw.*) her; (*mv.*) them.

haar *o.* hair.

haarbos *m.* (*haarbundel*) tuft of hair; (*al het haar*) shock of hair.

haarbreed (te) *v.* hair-breadth.

haard *m.* hearth, fire-place; (*kachel*) stove; (*v. ziekte*) nidus, focus; (*fig.*) hotbed.

haardijzer *o.* (*ijzer rondom de haard*) fender; (*waarop het hout ligt*) fire-dog.

haardscherm *o.* fire-screen.

haardstede *v.* hearth; fireside.

haardvuur *o.* grate-fire.

haarfijn *b. n.* as fine as hair; (*fot.*) dead sharp; (*fig.*) subtle, minute; *bw.* minutely, to a nicety, in great detail.

haarkam *m.* hair-comb.

haarkloven *on. w.* split hairs, quibble.

haarklover *m.* hair-splitter, seed-splitter, word-splitter.

haarkloverij *v.* hair-splitting, quibbling.

haarlint *o.* hair-ribbon, hair-lace, fillet.

haarlok *v.* lock of hair.

haarpijn *v.* next-morning headache.

haarspeld *v.* hair-pin.

haartooi *m.* head-dress.

haas *m.* hare; (*fam.*) puss; (*osse—*) fillet of beef, undercut.

haast *v.* haste, speed; (*grote —*) hurry.

haast *bw.* nearly, almost.

haasten *o. w.* hurry; *w. w.* **zich** —, hasten, make haste.
haastig *b. n.* hasty, speedy, hurried; *bw.* hastily, speedily, hurriedly, in a hurry.
haastigheid *v.* hastiness, speed, hurry.
haat *m.* hatred.
haatdragend *b. n.* resentful, rancorous, vindictive.
hachelijk *b. n. (gevaarlijk)* dangerous, perilous; *(gewaagd)* hasardous; *(netelig)* precarious, critical.
hachje *o. (flinke jongen, waaghals)* daredevil.
hagedis *v.* lizard; *(kleine* —) newt, swift.
hagedoorn *m.* hawthorn.
hagel *m.* hail; *(om te schieten)* shot, hail-shot.
hagelbui *v.* hail-storm, shower of hail.
hagelen *onp. w.* hail.
hagelkorrel *m. (hagelsteen)* hail-stone; *(v. schiethagel)* grain of shot.
hagelwit *b. n.* white as snow.
hagepreek *v.* hedge-sermon.
hak *v.* heel; *(werktuig)* hoe, pick-axe, pick; *m. (houw)* cut.
hakbijl *v.* chopping-knife, chopper, hatchet.
hakblok *o.* chopping-block.
haken *o. w. (met haak vastmaken)* hook; *(v. weefsel)* crochet; *on. w. (blijven hangen of steken)* catch; *(handwerken)* crochet; *(reikhalzen, heftig verlangen naar)* hanker for (after), hunger after.
hakenkruis *o.* swastika.
hakkelen *on. w.* stammer, stutter.
hakken *o. w. en on. w.* chop, cut, mince; *(kloven)* cleave, chop.
hakmes *o.* chopping-knife, chopper, cleaver.
hal *v.* hall.
halen *o. w.* fetch, draw, pull; *on. w. (sch.)* pull; *(toneel)* draw (raise) the curtain.
half *b. n.* half; *bw.* half; half-an-half; *z. n., o.* half.
halfbakken *b. n.* half-baked.
halfbloed *z. n., m.* half-breed, half-blood, half-caste; *b. n.* half-bred, half-blooded.
halfbroeder *m.* half-brother.
halfdonker *o.* semi-darkness.
halfhemdje *o.* front, dickey.
halfluid *b. n.* in an undertone.
halfrond *o.* hemisphere.
halfslachtig *b. n. (van gemengd ras)* half-bred, mongrel; *(amfibisch)* amphibious; *(fig.)* half-hearted.
halfstok *bw.* half-mast high, half-masted.
halfvasten *v.* mid-lent.
halfweg *bw.* half-way.
halfzuster *v.* half-sister.
halm *m.* stalk, straw, blade.
halmstro *o.* threshed stalks, straw.
hals *m.* neck.
halsader *v.* jugular (vein).
halsband *m.* collar.

halsboord *m.* neck-band.
halsbrekend *b. n.* breakneck.
halsdoek *m.* neck-cloth, neck-handkerchief.
halsstarrig *b. n.* obstinate, stubborn, headstrong.
halsstarrigheid *v.* obstinacy, stubbornness.
halster *m.* halter, head-collar.
halswervel *m.* cervical vertebra.
halt *v.* halt.
halte *v.* stopping-place, stop; *(v. spoorweg)* halting-place, wayside station.
halvemaan *v.* half-moon; *(mil.)* demilune; *(broodje)* crescent (roll).
ham *v.* ham.
hamel *m.* wether.
hamer *m.* hammer; *(houten* —) mallet, hammer.
hameren *on. w.* hammer.
hamerslag *m. (slag v. hamer)* stroke (blow) of a hammer, hammer-blow; *o. (afspringende deeltjes v. gloeiend ijzer)* hammer-scale, iron-scale.
hamsteraar *m.* food-hoarder.
hamsteren *o. w. en on. w.* hoard (food); *z. n., o.* food-hoarding.
hand *v.* hand.
handboeien *v. mv.* handcuffs, manacles; *(sl.)* bracelets.
handboek *o.* manual, hand-book.
handboog *m.* hand-bow.
handboor *v.* gimlet.
handdoek *m.* towel; *(op rol)* roller, jacktowel.
handdruk *m.* hand-pressure, handshake, hand-grasp.
handel *m. (tn.: v. machine)* handle.
handel *m.* trade, commerce; *(zaak)* business; *(ong.)* traffic.
handelaar *m.* merchant, dealer, trader.
handelbaar *b. n.* tractable, manageable, docile, pliable.
handelen *on. w. (te werk gaan, doen)* act, do; *(handel drijven)* trade, deal.
handeling *v.* action, act; *(in toneelspel)* operation, action.
handelsagent *m.* commercial agent.
handelsartikel *o.* article of commerce.
handelsbediende *m.* clerk.
handelsbedrijf *o.* trade, business.
handelsbetrekkingen *v. mv.* commercial relations.
handelsbrief *m.* business letter.
handelscorrespondentie *v.* commercial correspondence.
handelsfirma *v.* trading-firm.
handelsgeest *m.* commercial spirit.
handelshaven *v.* shipping-port.
handelskringen *m. mv.* trade circles, commercial circles.
handelsonderneming *v.* commercial undertaking, — enterprise.
handelspapier *o.* commercial paper.
handelsrecht *o.* commercial law, law merchant.
handelsreiziger *m.* commercial traveller.

handelsrekenen *o.* commercial arithmetic.
handelsterm *m.* business term.
handelsverdrag *o.* commercial treaty.
handelsverkeer *o.* commercial intercourse, traffic.
handelsvloot *v.* merchant fleet, mercantile marine.
handelswereld *v.* commercial (business) community, world of commerce.
handelswetenschappen *v.mv.* science of business.
handelszaak *v.* business concern, business.
handelwijze *v.* proceeding, manner (way) of acting, method.
handenarbeid *m.* manual labour.
handgebaar *o.* gesture, motion with the hand.
handgeld *o.* earnest-money, handsel.
handgemeen *z. n., o.* hand-to-hand fight, mêlée; *b. n.* — *worden,* come to blows, come to close quarters.
handgranaat *v.* grenade.
handgreep *v.* grip, grasp; (*kunstgreep*) knack; (*truc*) trick, dodge.
handhaven *o. w.* maintain; (*verdedigen*) vindicate; (*hooghouden, verdedigen:* v. *eer, wet, enz.*) uphold; *w. w.* **zich** —, maintain one's position; hold one's own.
handhaving *v.* maintenance, vindication.
handig *b. n.* (*bedreven, vaardig*) handy, adroit, clever, deft, skilful; (*gemakkelijk te hanteren*) handy; *bw.* adroitly, cleverly, deftly, skilfully.
handigheid *v.* handiness, adroitness, cleverness, skill.
handkar *v.* hand-cart, push-cart, barrow.
handkoffer *m.* hand-bag.
handkus *m.* kiss on the hand.
handlanger *m.* helper; (*ong.:* medeplichtige) accomplice.
handleiding *v.* manual, guide.
handoplegging *v.* laying on (imposition) of hands.
handpalm *v.* palm of the hand.
handschoen *m.* glove; (*voor werk, sport, enz.*) gauntlet.
handschoenwinkel *m.* glove-shop.
handschrift *o.* manuscript; (*manier van schrijven*) handwriting.
handtasje *o.* hand-bag.
handtastelijk *b. n.* palpable, obvious, evident.
handtastelijkheden *v. mv.* assault, physical violence.
handtekening *v.* signature.
handvat *o.* handle.
handvol *v.* handful.
handwerk *o.* trade, handicraft; (*geen machine-werk*) handwork.
handwerker *m.* artisan.
handwijzer *m.* hand-post, sign-post, guide-post.
handwoordenboek *o.* hand-lexicon, (pocket) dictionary.

hanekam *m.* cock's comb; (*Pl.*) rattle-grass, cock's comb.
hanepoot *m.* cock's foot; (*bij 't schrijven*) pot-hook, scrawl; (*Pl.*) panic-(-grass).
hangbrug *v.* suspension-bridge.
hangbuik *m.* swag-belly.
hangen *o. w.* hang; *on. w.* hang.
hangend *vz.* hanging, pending.
hangklok *v.* hanging clock.
hangmat *v.* hammock.
hangslot *o.* padlock.
hansworst *m.* buffoon, clown, Jack Pudding.
hanteren *o. w.* handle, manipulate.
hantering *v.* handling, manipulation.
Hanzestad *v.* Hanse(atic) town.
hap *m.* (*daad*) bite; (*beet, stuk*) bite, bit, morsel; (*mondvol*) mouthful.
haperen *on. w.* (*blijven steken, bij spreken, enz.*) falter, stammer; (*v. machine*) miss, stick; (*ontbreken*) falter, wave.
hapering *v.* faltering, hitch; hesitation.
happen *on. w.* bite, snap.
hard *b. n.* (*alg.*) hard; (*v. stem*) loud; (*v. kleur*) glaring, glary; (*v. werk: inspannend*) strenuous; (*v. staal*) tempered; *bw.* hard, hardly; (*regenen, enz.*) heavily; (*luid*) loud; (*snel: lopen*) fast.
harddraverij *v.* trotting-match.
harden *o. w.* harden; (*v. staal*) temper; (*uithouden, volhouden*) stand.
hardhandig *b. n.* (*bw.*) hardhanded(ly), violent(ly), rough(ly).
hardheid *v.* hardness.
hardhorig *b. n.* dull (thick, hard) of hearing.
hardlijvig *b. n.* costive, constipated.
hardlijvigheid *v.* costiveness, constipation.
hardlopen *o.* running.
hardloper *m.* runner, racer; (*op korte afstand*) sprinter; (*v. schip*) fast sailer.
hardnekkig *b. n.* (*v. persoon*) obstinate; (*v. ziekte*) rebellious, obstinate; (*v. verkoudheid, strijd, weerstand*) stubborn; (*aanhoudend: v. hoest, praatjes, warmte, enz.*) persistent; *bw.* obstinately; stubbornly.
hardnekkigheid *v.* obstinacy; stubbornness, persistency.
hardop *bw.* loud, aloud.
hardvochtig *b. n.* hard-hearted.
hardvochtigheid *v.* hardheartedness.
harem *m.* harem, haram, seraglio.
harent, ten —, at her house; **van** —**wege,** in her name; **om** —**wil,** for her sake.
harerzijds *bw.* on her part, on her behalf.
harig *b. n.* hairy; (*ruig*) hirsute; (*wet.*) pilose.
haring *m.* (*Dk.*) herring; (*v. tent*) tent-peg.
harington *v.* herring-tub, herring-barrel.
hark *v.* rake; (*fig.: v. persoon*) (*stijve* —) muff, poker.

harken *o. w. en on. w.* rake.
harlekijn *m.* harlequin, buffoon.
harmonie *v.* harmony.
harmonika *v.* accordion; (*mond*—) harmonica.
harmonisch *b. n.* (*bw.*) harmonic(ally).
harnas *o.* armour; (*borstharnas*) cuirass.
harp *v.* (*muz.*) harp; (*zeef*) riddle.
harpoen *m.* harpoon, toggle-iron.
harpspeler *m.*, **harpspeelster** *v.* harper, harpist.
hars *o. en v.* resin; rosin.
harsboom *m.* resiniferous tree.
harslak *o.* resinous lac.
harst *m.* sirloin.
hart *o.* heart; (*fig.: kern*) heart, core.
hartaandoening *v.* cardiac affection, affection of the heart.
hartader *v.* great artery, aorta; (*fig.*) artery.
hartedief *m. en v.* darling.
harteleed *o.* heart-grief, heart-break, heart-sore.
hartelijk *b. n.* (*bw.*) hearty(-ily), cordial(ly).
hartelijkheid *v.* heartiness, cordiality.
harteloos *b. n.* (*bw.*) heartless(ly).
harteloosheid *v.* heartlessness.
hartenaas *o.* ace of hearts.
hartenboer *m.* knave of hearts.
hartenheer *m.* king of hearts.
hartenvrouw *v.* queen of hearts.
hartig *b. n.* (*flink, ferm*) hearty; (*goed gezouten, pittig*) salt, well-seasoned.
hartklep *v.* valve of the heart, heart valve, cardiac valve; (*tn.: v. pomp*) suction-valve, suction-clack.
hartklopping *v.* palpitation of the heart.
hartstocht *m.* passion. [(ly).
hartstochtelijk *b. n.* (*bw.*) passionate-
hartverlamming *v.* paralysis of the heart, heart-failure.
hartverscheurend *b. n.* heart-rending, heart-piercing.
hartvlies *o.* endocardium.
haspel *m.* (*tn.*) reel, windlass.
haspelen *on. w.* reel, wind; (*fig.: knoeien*) bungle, muddle; (*kibbelen*) bicker, wrangle.
hatelijk *b. n.* spiteful, malicious, invidious, odious.
hatelijkheid *v.* spitefulness, invidiousness, malice.
haten *o. w.* hate.
hauw *v.* (*Pl.*) silique.
have *v.* property, goods, stock; — **en goed,** good and chattels.
haveloos *b. n.* ragged, shabby.
haveloosheid *v.* raggedness, shabbiness.
haven *v.* harbour, port; (*fig.*) port, haven; (*stad*) port.
havenarbeider *m.* dock-worker, docker.
havendam *m.* jetty, mole.
havenen *o. w.* batter, handle, roughly, ill-treat.

havengelden *o. mv.* harbour-dues, dock-dues.
havenloods *m.* harbour-pilot.
havenmeester *m.* harbour-master.
havenstad *v.* port, seaport town.
haver *v.* oats.
havergort *v.* grits, (oat-)groats.
havermeel *o.* oat-meal.
havermout *o. en v.* rolled oats; (*pap*) oatmeal porridge.
havik *m.* hawk, goshawk.
havikskruid *o.* hawk-weed.
haviksneus *m.* hawk-nose, aquiline nose.
hazelaar *m.* hazelnut-tree, hazel.
hazeleger *o.* form of a hare.
hazelip *v.* hare-lip.
hazelmuis *v.* common dormouse.
hazelnoot *v.* (hazel-)nut; filbert.
hazelworm *m.* blind-worm, slow-worm.
hazemond *m.* rabbit-mouth, hare-lip.
hazepeper *v.* jugged hare.
hazewind(**hond**) *m.* greyhound.
he *tw.* o! oh! hey! I say! (*sch.*) ahoy!
hebben *o. w.* have.
hebzucht *v.* cupidity, covetousness, greed (of gain).
hebzuchtig *b. n.* acquisitive, covetous, greedy (of gain).
hecht *o.* handle, haft; (*v. zwaard*) hilt.
hecht *b. n.* firm, solid, strong.
hechten *o. w.* (*vastmaken, vastbinden*) attach, affix, fasten; (*v. wond*) suture, stitch up; (*fig.*) attach; *on. w.* — **aan iets,** be attached to a thing; *w. w.* **zich** — **aan,** attach oneself to, get attached to. [finement.
hechtenis *v.* custody, detention, con-
hechtheid *v.* firmness, solidity, strength.
hechtpleister *v.* sticking-plaster, court-plaster.
hectogram *o.* hectogram(me).
hectoliter *m.* hectolitre.
hectometer *m.* hectometre.
heden *bw.* to-day; — **avond,** this evening, to-night; **tot op** —, up to the present; — **ten dage,** nowadays; — **over acht dagen,** this day week.
hedendaags *b. n.* modern, present, contemporary.
heel *b. n.* whole, entire; *bw.* quite; — **wat,** a great deal, a good deal; — **en al,** entirely, quite, altogether.
heelal *o.* universe.
heelhuids *bw.* with a whole skin, scot-free, unscathed, without injury.
heelkunde *v.* surgery, healing-art.
heelmeester *m.* surgeon.
heelster *v.* zie **heler.**
heen *bw.* away; **waar gaat ge** —? where are you going? **nergens** —, nowhere; — **en terug,** there and back; **overal** —, everywhere; — **en weer lopen,** walk to and fro, walk up and down.
heengaan *on. w.* go away, walk off; (*v. minister*) go out; (*sterven*) go, pass away.

heenkomen *on. w.* get away, escape; *z. n., o.* **een goed — zoeken,** seek safety in flight; make one's escape.

heenlopen *on. w.* run away; *loop heen!* get you gone, get along with you!

heenreis *v.* out-journey, voyage out, outward voyage.

heenstappen *o. w.* stride off, march off; **— over,** step across; *(fig.)* pass over.

heer *m.* gentleman; *(meester, baas)* master; *(gebieder)* lord; *(in kaartspel)* king.

heerbaan *v.* high-road, military road.

heerlijk *b. n.* *(van de heer)* manorial, seigneurial; *(prachtig)* glorious; *(v. voedsel, drank, geur)* delicious.

heerlijkheid *v.* *(adellijk goed)* manor, seigniorage; magnificence, glory; deliciousness.

heerschap *o.* master, lord.

heerschappij *v.* mastery, dominion, empire, lordship.

heersen *on. w.* *(v. persoon: heerschappij voeren)* rule, reign, govern, sway; *(v. ziekte, enz.)* reign, be prevalent.

heersend *b. n.* ruling, reigning; dominant, prevailing; *(v. godsdienst, regeringsvorm)* established.

heerser *m.* ruler, governor.

heerszucht *v.* lust of power, ambition (for power).

heerszuchtig *b. n.* ambitious, imperious.

hees *b. n.* *(bw.)* hoarse(ly).

heesheid *v.* hoarseness.

heester *m.* shrub.

heet *b. n.* hot; *(v. luchtstreek)* torrid; *bw.* hotly.

heetgebakerd *b. n.* hot-tempered, hot-blooded, hasty.

heethoofd *m.* hot-head, hot-spur.

heethoofdig *b. n.* hot-headed, hot-brained.

hefboom *m.* lever.

heffen *o. w.* *(optillen)* raise, lift; *(innen)* levy; *(opleggen)* impose.

heft *o.* *zie* **hecht.**

heftig *b. n.* *(bw.)* violent(ly), vehement(ly), impetuous(ly).

heftigheid *v.* violence, vehemence.

heg *v.* hedge.

hei *tw.* hey! hallo!

hei *v.* *(heiblok)* beetle, rammer, pile-driver.

heide *v.* heath, moor; *(plant)* heather, heath.

heidebloem *v.* heath-flower, flower of the heath.

heiden *m.* heathen, pagan; *(zigeuner)* gipsy.

heidendom *o.* heathendom, paganism, heathenism.

heien *o. w.* ram, pile.

heil *o.* welfare, good, prosperity; *(geestelijk: v. d. ziel)* salvation.

Heiland *m.* Saviour.

heilbot *v.* halibut.

heildronk *m.* toast, health.

heilig *b. n.* holy; sacred; *bw.* sacredly.

heiligdom *o.* *(plaats)* sanctuary; *(reliek)* *(sacred)* relic.

heilige *m. en v.* saint.

heiligen *o. w.* sanctify; *(v. zondag)* keep holy.

heiligheid *v.* holiness, sacredness, sanctity.

heiligmaking *v.* sanctification.

heilloos *b. n.* *(slecht)* impious; *(noodlottig)* fatal, disastrous.

heilsleger *o.* salvation army.

heilwens *m.* congratulation, felicitation, benediction.

heilzaam *b. n.* salutary, beneficial, salubrious; *(doeltreffend, probaat)* efficacious.

heilzaamheid *v.* salutariness, beneficial (salutary) influence.

heimelijk *b. n.* secret, private; clandestine; *(v. gedachte, gevoelen)* sneaking; *(onderhands, stiekem: v. overeenkomst, enz.)* hole-and-corner; *bw.* secretly, privately, in secret, in private, clandestinely.

heimwee *o.* homesickness, nostalgia.

heining *v.* enclosure, fence.

heirbaan *v.* *zie* **heerbaan.**

hek *o.* *(toegangs—)* gate; *(ijzeren —)* railing; *(omheining)* fence, paling; *(sp.)* hurdle, fence.

hekel *m.* *(werktuig)* hackle; *(tegenzin, afkeer)* dislike; **een — hebben aan,** dislike, hate.

hekelen *v.* hackle; *(fig.)* satirize; criticize.

hekelschrift *o.* satire.

heks *v.* hag, witch; *(fig.: feeks)* vixen, shrew, hell-cat.

heksendans *m.* witches' dance.

hekserij *v.* sorcery, witchcraft.

hekwerk *o.* railing, trellis-work.

hel *v.* hell.

hel *b. n.* clear, bright, glaring.

held *m.* hero.

heldendaad *v.* heroic deed (action), act of heroism, exploit.

heldendood *m.* heroic death.

helder *b. n.* *(v. licht, water, enz.)* clear; *(v. kleur, ogen, lucht)* bright; *(v. klank)* clear, sonorous; *(v. stijl, enz.: duidelijk)* clear, lucid; *(zindelijk)* clean.

helderheid *v.* clearness; brightness; sonority; lucidity; cleanness.

helderziende *m. en v.* clairvoyant.

helderziendheid *v.* clearsightedness; clairvoyance, second sight.

heldhaftig *b. n.* *(bw.)* heroic(ally).

heldhaftigheid *v.* heroism.

heldin *v.* heroine.

helen *o. w.* receive, fence, secrete.

helen *o. w.* heal, cure; *on. w.* heal, cicatrize.

heler *m.* receiver, fence.

helft *v.* half; **tegen de — van de prijs,** at half the price.

heling *v.* receiving, fencing, secretion.

hellen *on. w.* incline, slant, slope.

hellend *b. n.* inclined, slanting, sloping.
helleveeg *v.* hell-cat, virago, shrew.
helling *v.* inclination, incline; declivity; (*v. berg*) versant; (*v. spoorweg*) gradient; (*sch.*) slip, slipway.
helm *r.* (*Pl.*) beach-grass, lyme-grass; *m.* (*v. soldaat, enz.*) helmet; (*dicht.*) casque; (*v. duiker*) headpiece.
helmhoed *m.* sun-helmet, pith-helmet.
helmkruid *o.* fig-wort, brown wort.
helpen *o. w. en on. w.* (*hulp verlenen, bijstaan*) help, aid, assist, succour; (*baten*) avail, be of avail, be of use; (*in winkel: bedienen*) attend to, serve.
helper *m.*, **helpster** *v.* helper, assistant, aid.
hels *b. n.* hellish, infernal, devilish, diabolic.
hem *pers. rnw.* him.
hem *tw.* hem!
hemd *o.* shirt; (*vrouwen—*) chemise.
hemdbroek *v.* combination.
hemdsmouw *v.* shirt-sleeve.
hemel *m.* heaven; (*uitspansel*) sky, firmament, heavens; (*v. troon*) canopy, baldachin; (*v. bed*) tester.
hemelgewelf *o.* vault of heaven, celestial vault, firmament.
hemellichaam *o.* heavenly body, celestial body.
hemellicht *o.* celestial luminary, — light.
hemelrijk *o.* kingdom of Heaven.
hemelsbreed *b. n.* wide.
hemels *b. n.* heavenly, celestial.
hemeltergend *b. n.* crying to heaven.
hemelvaart *v.* Ascension.
hemelvuur *o.* lightning.
hen *v.* hen.
hen *pers. rnw.* them.
Henegouwen *o.* Hainault.
hengel *m.* angling-rod, fishing-rod.
hengelen *on. w.* angle; *o.* **het —**, line-fishing, rod-fishing, angling.
hengsel *o.* handle, bail; (*scharnier*) hinge.
hengst *m.* stallion.
hennep *m.* hemp.
hennepbraak *v.* hemp-brake.
hennepbraker *m.* hemp-brake.
hennepzaad *o.* hempseed.
herademen *on w.* breathe again, respire.
herberg *v.* inn, public-house.
herbergen *o. w.* lodge, house, accommodate; (*v. vluchteling, enz.*) harbour.
herbergier *m.* inn-keeper, host, landlord.
herbergzaam *b. n.* hospitable.
herbergzaamheid *v.* hospitableness.
herboren *b. n.* born again, regenerate.
herdenken *o. w.* commemorate; (*zich herinneren*) remember.
herdenking *v.* commemoration; remembrance.
herder *m.* shepherd; (*fig.: v. geestelijke*) shepherd, pastor.
herderin *v.* shepherdess.

herderlijk *b. n.* pastoral.
herderslied *o.* pastoral song.
herdersstaf *m.* sheep-hook, (shepherd's) crook; (*v. bisschop*) crosier, pastoral staff.
herdruk *m.* reprint, new edition.
hereboer *m.* gentleman-farmer.
herenhuis *o.* genteleman's house.
herenigen *o. w.* re-unite.
herenknecht *m.* footman, livery servant.
herfst *m.* autumn; (*Am.*) fall.
herfstdag *m.* autumnal day, day in autumn.
herfstdraden *m. mv.* gossamer, airthreads.
herfstmaand *v.* autumn month, September.
herhaald *b. n.* repeated; **—e malen**, repeatedly.
herhalen *o. w.* repeat, reiterate; **in 't kort —**, summarize, recapitulate.
herhaling *v.* repetition, reiteration; recapitulation.
herinneren *o. w.* **iem. aan iets —**, remind a person of a thing; *w. w.* **zich —**, remember, recollect, (re)call to mind.
herinnering *v.* (*het zich herinneren*) recollection, remembrance, reminiscence; (*aandenken*) souvenir, memento, memorial, keepsake; (*wat helpt onthouden*) reminder, remembrancer; **ter — aan**, in remembrance of, in memory of.
herkauwen *o. w. en on. w.* ruminate, chew the cud.
herkauwer *m.* ruminant, cud-chewer.
herkennen *o. w.* recognize, know (again).
herkenning *v.* recognition.
herkenningsteken *o.* mark (sign) of recognition.
herkiezing *v.* re-election; (*herstemming*) second ballot.
herkomst *v.* (*v. persoon*) origin, extraction, derivation; (*v. zaak*) origin, provenance.
herleiden *o. w.* reduce, convert.
herleiding *v.* reduction, conversion; (*v. breuken*) simplification, conversion.
herleven *on. w.* revive, return to life; **doen —**, revive, revivify.
herleving *v.* revival, renascence.
hermelijn *m. en o.* ermine; (*bruin*) stoat.
hernemen *o. w.* take again; (*mil.*) retake, recapture; (*hervatten*) resume, reply.
herneming *v.* retaking, recapture.
hernieuwen *o. w.* renex, renovate.
hernieuwing *v.* renewal.
heropenen *o. w.* re-open.
heropening *v.* re-opening.
herrie *v.* (*drukte, opschudding, lawaai*) noise, din, racket, pother, hullabaloo; (*twist*) row; **— maken (schoppen)**, kick up a row, raise a dust.
herroepen *o. w.* recall, revoke; (*v. belofte*) revoke, retract; (*v. wet*) repeal

annul; (v. order) countermand; (v. ver-klaring) recant.

hersenen, hersens v. mv. brain; (verstand) brains; (wet.) cerebrum.

hersenkas v. brain-box. [brained.

hersenloos b. n. brainless, shallow-

hersenontsteking v. inflammation of the brain, encephalitis.

hersenschim v. chimera, phantasm.

hersenschudding v. concussion of the brain.

hersenvlies o. cerebral membrane.

hersenvliesontsteking v. meningitis.

hersmelten o. w. remelt, refound, smelt again.

herstel o. (reparatie) reparation, repair; (v. gezondheid) recovery, reestablish-ment; (v. grieven) redress; (v. schade, enz.) recuperation; (v. wet, monarchie, enz.) restoration.

herstelbaar b. n. curable, reparable, restorable, remediable, retrievable.

herstellen o. w. (repareren: v. kleren, enz.) repair, mend; (v. grieven) redress; (v. fout, schade, enz.) retrieve; (v. mo-narchie, enz.) restore; (v. verzuim, enz.) remedy; **in zijn eer —,** rehabilitate; on. w. (v. ziekte) recover; w. w. **zich —,** recover oneself.

herstellende m. en v. reconvalescent.

herstelling v. repairing, repair, mend-ing; restoration; recovery.

herstellingsoord o. (voor zieken) health-resort, sanatorium; (voor herstel-lenden) convalescent home.

herstemming v. second ballot.

hert o. deer; (mannetjeshert) stag, hart; **vliegend —,** stag-beetle.

hertog m. duke.

hertogdom o. duchy.

hertogelijk b. n. ducal.

hertogin v. duchess.

heruitzenden o. w. (radio) relay.

heruitzending v. relay.

hervatten o. w. (v. werk, enz.) resume; (v. bezoek) repeat.

hervatting v. resumption; repetition.

hervormde m. en v. member of the Reformed Church, protestant.

hervormen o. w. reform, reshape, amend.

hervormer m. reformer.

hervorming v. reform; (v. kerk) reformation.

herwinnen o. w. regain, recover; (v. geld) win back; (v. eer, fortuin) retrieve.

herzien o. w. (v. boek, wet) revise; (v. mening, enz.) reconsider, review; (v. systeem) overhaul.

herziening v. revision; reconsideration, review; overhauling.

hesp v. knuckle of a ham; (Z. N.) ham.

het lidw. the; vnw. it; he, she, they.

heten o. w. (heet maken) heat, make hot.

heten o. w. (noemen) name, call; on. w. (genoemd worden) be named, be called.

hetgeen vnw. what, that which; (betr. vnw.) which.

hetwelk vnw. which.

hetzelfde vnw. the same.

hetzij vgw. (nevenschikkend) either... or; (onderschikkend) whether... or.

heugenis v. remembrance, memory, recollection.

heuglijk b. n. (verheugend, verblijdend) joyful, pleasant; (gedenkwaardig) memorable.

heul m. (Pl.) poppy; o. (hulp, bijstand, troost) comfort, aid; v. (duiker onder een weg) culvert; (brug) bridge.

heulen on. w. **— met,** collude with, tamper with.

heulzaad o. mawseed.

heup v. hip; (v. dier) haunch.

heupgewricht o. hip-joint.

heupjicht v. hip-gout, sciatica.

heus b. n. (beleefd) courteous, polite, kind; (werkelijk) real; bw. courteously, politely, kindly; really, truly, indeed.

heuvel m. hill.

heuveltop m. hill top.

hevel m. siphon.

hevig b. n. (v. pijn, storm) violent; (v. wind, gevecht) sharp; (v. regen, onweer) heavy; (v. protest, verzet) vehement.

hevigheid v. violence; vehemence; intensity.

hiaat o. en m. hiatus, gap.

hiel m. heel.

hier bw. here.

hierachter bw. behind; (in boek, enz.) here (in) after.

hiërarchie v. hierarchy.

hierbij bw. herewith; (toegevoegd) annexed; (ingesloten) enclosed; (vlak bij) hard by.

hierboven bw. up here, above.

hierin bw. in here, in this.

hierlangs bw. past here, this way.

hiermede bw. with this.

hierna bw. after this, hereafter.

hiernaast bw. next door.

hiernamaals bw. hereafter, in the beyond; z. n., o. **het —,** the hereafter; the beyond.

hieromtrent bw. about this, on this subject.

hieronder bw. below, underneath, under here; (v. bladzijde) at foot; (te midden van) among these; **als — op-gegeven,** as stated below.

hiertegen bw. against this.

hiertegenover bw. opposite, over the way.

hiertoe bw. for this purpose; **tot —,** so far, thus far.

hiervoor bw. for this, in return (for this); before, this.

hij vnw. he.

hijgen on. w. pant; (snakken) gasp.

hijsen o. w. (v. zeil) hoist; (v. vlag) hoist, run up, heave out; on. w. (stevig drinken) tipple, booze, hoist, lift the elbow.

hikken on. w. hiccough.

hinde v. hind, doe.

hinder *m.* hindrance, impediment, obstacle.
hinderen *o. w.* (*belemmeren*) hinder, hamper, impede, incommode, inconvenience; (*ergernis, verdriet veroorzaken*) annoy; *on. w.* hinder, be a hindrance.
hinderlaag *v.* ambush, ambuscade.
hindernis *v.* obstacle, hindrance, encumbrance.
hinderwet *v.* nuisance act.
hinkelen *on. w.* play at hop-scotch.
hinkelspel *o.* (game of) hop-scotch.
hinniken *on. w.* neigh.
historisch *b. n.* (*bw.*) historical(ly).
hit *m.* pony, nag.
hitte *v.* heat.
hittegolf *m.* heat-wave.
hobbelig *b. n.* rugged, rough, uneven, bumpy.
hobbelpaard *o.* rocking-horse.
hoe *bw.* how.
hoed *m.* (*v. heren*) hat; (*v. dames*) hat; bonnet.
hoedanigheid *v.* quality; *in zijn — van,* in his capacity of.
hoede *v.* guard; care, protection.
hoeden *o. w.* (*v. schapen, vee*) tend, watch, keep; (*behoeden, beschermen*) guard, protect; *w. w. zich — voor,* guard against, beware of.
hoedenfabriek *v.* hat-manufactory.
hoedenmaakster *v.* bonnet-maker, milliner.
hoedenmaker *m.* hatter.
hoedenwinkel *m.* hat-shop.
hoeder *m.* guardian, keeper; (*v. vee*) herdsman, herder.
hoef *v.* hoof.
hoefbeslag *o.* (horse-)shoeing.
hoefgetrappel *o.* hoof-beats, clatter of hoofs.
hoefijzer *o.* horseshoe.
hoefijzersmederij *v.* farrier's shop, farriery.
hoefsmid *m.* shoeing-smith, farrier.
hoek *m.* (*v. straat, kamer, enz.*) corner; (*meetk.*) angle; (*deel v. beurs*) market; section; (*haak, vishaak*) hook, fishhook.
hoekig *b. n.* angular; (*fig.*) rugged, angular.
hoekpunt *o.* angular-point.
hoeksteen *m.* corner-stone, key-stone.
hoen *o.* hen, fowl.
hoenderachtig *b. n.* gallinaceous.
hoenderhof *m.* poultry-yard, fowl-yard.
hoenderhok *o.* poultry-house, chicken-house.
hoenderpark *o.* poultry-farm, chicken-farm.
hoenderrek *o.* hen-roost.
hoenderteelt *v.* poultry-farming, chicken-farming, chicken-raising.
hoepel *m.* hoop.
hoepelen *on. w.* trundle (bowl) a hoop, play with a hoop.
hoepelrok *m.* hoop-petticoat, crinoline.
hoes *v.* (chair) cover, dust sheet.
hoest *m.* cough.

hoestbui *v.* fit of coughing, coughing-fit, coughing-spell.
hoesten *on. w.* cough.
hoestmiddel *o.* cough-medecine, pectoral.
hoeve *v.* farm, farmstead.
hoeveel *telw.* (*enk.*) how much; (*mv.*) how many.
hoeveelheid *v.* quantity.
hoeveelste *rangtelw. de — (van de maand) hebben wij ?* what day of the month is it ? *de — is hij ?* what is his number ? *de — maal ?* the how-many-eth time ?
hoeven *o. w.* need.
hoever *bw.* how far, to what extent.
hoewel *vgw.* though, although.
hoezeer *vgw.* how much; *— ook,* however much, much as.
hof *m.* garden; *o.* court.
hofdame *v.* court-lady, lady in waiting; (*ongehuwd*) maid of honour.
hoffelijk *b. n.* courteous, courtly.
hoffelijkheid *v.* courteousness, courtesy.
hofjonker *m.* page.
hofleverancier *m.* purveyor to H. M. the King (the Queen).
hofmeester *m.* (*sch.*) steward.
hofprediker *m.* court-chaplain.
hofraad *m.* privy council; (*persoon*) privy councellor.
hofstede *v.* zie **hoeve.**
hogepriester *m.* highpriest, pontiff.
hoger *b. n.* higher.
hogerhuis *o.* House of Lords.
hogeschool *v.* university.
hok *o.* (*v. honden*) kennel; (*v. schapen, kippen, enz.*) pen; (*v. varkens*) sty; (*v. wilde dieren*) cage; (*v. konijnen*) hutch; (*bergplaats*) shed; (*gevangenis*) quod.
hokken *on. w.* (*v. machine, enz.*) come to a standstill.
hol *o.* cavern, cave; (*holte*) cavity; (*v. dier*) hole; (*v. wild dier*) den; (*v. rovers, enz.*) den, haunt.
hol *m. iem. het hoofd op — brengen,* turn a person's head; *op — gaan (slaan),* bolt, run away.
hol *b. n.* (*v. boom, wangen, stem, enz.*) hollow; (*v. lens, spiegel*) concave; (*v. ogen*) sunken, cavernous; (*v. vertrek*) gaunt, cavernous; (*fig.: v. woorden, hoofd, enz.*) hollow, empty.
holderdebolder *tw.* head over heels, helter-skelter.
Holland *o.* Holland.
Hollander *m.* Dutchman; *vliegende —,* Flying Dutchman; (*speelgoed*) racer, cycle car; *de —s,* the Dutch.
hollen *on. w.* run, scamper.
holrond *b. n.* concave.
holsblok *o.* wooden shoe.
holte *v.* cavity; (*v. hand, grond, enz.*) hollow; (*v. oog*) socket; (*v. maag*) pit.
hom *v.* milt, soft-roe.
hommel *m.* (*dar*) drone; bumblebee.
homp *v.* hunch, hunk, lump, chunk.
hond *m.* dog; (*jacht—*) hound.

hondebaantje *o.* dog's berth, rotten job. [dogs.
hondekar *v.* dog-cart, cart drawn by
hondeleven *o.* dog's life.
honderas *o.* canine race.
honderd *telw.* hundred; **vier ten —,** four per cent.
honderdjarig *b. n.* a hundred years old, centenary, centennial.
honderdman *m. (gesch.)* centurion.
honderdvoud *o.* centuple.
hondeweer *o.* beastly weather.
hondsdagen *m. mv.* dog-days, canicular days.
hondsdolheid *v.* rabies, canine madness; *(bij mens)* hydrophobia.
hondsgras *o.* dog's tooth.
honen *o. w.* insult, taunt.
Hongarije *o.* Hungary.
honger *m.* hunger.
hongerig *b. n.* hungry, starving.
hongerlijder *m.* hungerer, starveling.
hongerloon *o.* starvation wages, starvation salary.
hongersnood *m.* famine.
hongerstaking *v.* hunger-strike.
honi(n)g *m.* honey.
honi(n)graat *v.* honey-comb.
honorarium *o. (v. dokter, enz.)* fee; *(v. schrijver)* copy-fee, author's fee.
honoreren *o. w. (H.: v. wissel)* honour, protect, give due protection to; **niet —,** dishonour; *(v. schrijver)* pay.
hoofd *o.* head; *(v. gezin, school, enz.)* head; *(chef, leider)* chief, leader; *(v. brief, artikel, enz.)* heading.
hoofdader *v.* cephalic vein; *(fig.)* main artery, chief artery.
hoofdagent *m.* general agent, principal agent; *(v. politie)* head police-constable, police sergeant.
hoofdaltaar *o.* high altar.
hoofdarbeid *m.* brain-work.
hoofdartikel *o.* leading article, leader.
hoofdbegrip *o.* fundamental (principal) notion.
hoofdbestanddeel *o.* chief ingredient, main constituent.
hoofdbewerking *v. (rek.)* elementary operation, fundamental operation.
hoofdbreken *o.* trouble, care, racking of one's brains.
hoofddeksel *v.* covering for the head, head-gear.
hoofddeugd *v.* cardinal virtue.
hoofddoek *m.* head-kerchief.
hoofdelijk *b. n. (per hoofd)* per capita; *(v. onderwijs)* individual.
hoofdgebouw *o.* main-building.
hoofdgedachte *v.* leading (principal) idea.
hoofdgetal *o.* cardinal (number).
hoofdingang *m.* principal (main) entrance.
hoofdkantoor *o.* head-office; *(v. posterijen)* general post-office.
hoofdkerk *v.* cathedral.
hoofdknik *m.* nod (of the head).

hoofdkussen *o.* pillow.
hoofdkwartier *o. (mil.)* headquarters.
hoofdleiding *v. (bestuur)* general management, supreme direction; *(r. gas, enz.)* main (-line).
hoofdletter *r.* capital (letter); *(beginletter)* initial.
hoofdmacht *r. (v. leger)* main body.
hoofdonderwijzer *m.* head-master, head-teacher.
hoofdpeluw *r.* bolster.
hoofdpersoon *m.* principal person; *(r. roman)* principal character, hero.
hoofdpijn *v.* headache.
hoofdprijs *m.* great prize.
hoofdregel *m.* principal (cardinal) rule.
hoofdrekenen *o.* mental arithmetic.
hoofdrol *r.* principal part, leading part.
hoofdschotel *m.* principal dish, staple dish; *(fig.)* staple feature.
hoofdschuldige *m. en r.* chief culprit (offender).
hoofdstad *r.* capital; metropolis.
hoofdstraat *r.* principal street, main street.
hoofdstuk *o.* chapter.
hoofdtelwoord *o.* cardinal (number).
hoofdtoon *m.* principal stress; *(grondtoon)* fundamental tone.
hoofdtrek *m.* principal trait, main (essential) feature; **in'—ken,** in outline.
hoofdverkeersweg *m.* main road, arterial road, highway of traffic.
hoofdwindstreken *v. mr.* cardinal points (of the compass).
hoofdzakelijk *b. n.* principally, chiefly, mainly.
hoofdzetel *m.* principal seat, main seat.
hoofdzin *m. (gram.)* principal sentence.
hoofdzonde *r.* capital (deadly, mortal) sin.
hoofs *b. n.* courtly.
hoofsheid *r.* courtliness.
hoog *b. n.* high; *(v. stem, gewelf, enz.)* high-pitched; *(r. kamer)* high-ceilinged; *(v. gewelf: fig.: ideaal, enz.)* lofty.
hoogachten *o. w.* respect, esteem highly.
hoogachting *r.* respect, esteem, regard.
hoogdravend *b. n.* high-stepping; *(fig.)* high-sounding, stilted, bombastic, grandiloquent.
hoogdravendheid *v.* high-sounding-ness, grandiloquence.
hooggedelgeboren, hooggedelge-streng *b. n.* right honourable.
hoogeerwaard(e) *b. n.* right (most) reverend.
hooggaand *b. n.* high, running, high, heavy.
hooggebergte *o.* high mountains.
hooghartig *b. n.* high-spirited; *(ong.)* haughty, proud.
hooghartigheid *r.* hauteur, haughtiness.
hoogheid *v.* highness, grandeur.
hooghouden *o. r.* uphold, maintain, sustain.
Hooglanden *o. mr.* Highlands.
hooglopend *b. n.* zie **hooggaand.**

hoogmis v. high mass.
hoogmoed m. pride; haughtiness.
hoogmoedig b. n. proud, haughty.
hoogoven m. blast-furnace.
hoogspanning v. high tension.
hoogst b. n. highest, sovereign, supreme; bw. highly, very, greatly, extremely.
hoogsteigen b. n. *in — persoon,* in his own proper person.
hoogstwaarschijnlijk b. n. highly (most) probable; bw. most probable.
hoogte v. height; *(verhevenheid)* height, elevation, eminence; *(meetk.: v. hemellichaam)* altitude; *(H.: v. prijzen)* highness; *(r. kamer, dak; toon; fig.)* pitch.
hoogtemeter m. altimeter, hypsometer.
hoogtepunt o. culminating point, acme, zenith, height.
hoogterecord o. *(vl.)* altitude record, height record.
hoogteroer o. *(vl.)* elevator, horizontal rudder; *(v. duikboot)* diving-rudder.
hoogtijd m. festival, feast, high-day.
hoogveen o. peat-moor.
hoogverheven b. n. lofty, sublime.
hoogverraad o. high-treason.
hoogvlakte v. plateau, upland plain, tableland.
hoogwaardigheid v. eminence.
hoogwaardigheidsbekleder m. dignitary.
hooi o. hay.
hooiberg m. hay-stack, hay-rick.
hooien on. w. make hay, hay.
hooier m. hay-maker.
hooimaand v. hay-mouth, July.
hooimijt v. zie *hooiberg.*
hooischuur v. hay-barn.
hooivork v. hay-fork.
hooiwagen m. hay-cart; *(Dk.: spin, mug)* daddy-long-legs, father-long-legs.
hoon m. insult, taunt, scorn, contumely.
hoongelach o. scornful laughter.
hoop m. *(stapel)* heap, pile; *(menigte)* heap, multitude.
hoop v. hope, hopes.
hoorbaar b. n. audible; bw. audibly.
hoorder m. hearer, auditor.
hoorn m. *(v. koe, enz.: v. instrument)* horn; *(mil.)* bugle; *(v. auto)* horn, hooter; *(r. telefoon)* receiver.
hoornbeesten o. mv. horned cattle.
hoornblazer m. horn-blower; *(mil.)* bugler, trumpeter.
hoornvee o. horned cattle.
hoornvlies o. horny coat of the eye, cornea.
hoos o. water-spout.
hoosvat o. bailer, scoop.
hop v. *(Pl.)* hop; hops.
hop m. *(Dk.)* hoopoe.
hop tw. gee-up ! gee-ho !
hopeloos b. n. *(bw.)* hopeless(ly), desperate(ly).
hopeloosheid v. hopelessness, desperateness.
hopen o. w. en on. w. hope.

hopveld o. hop-field.
horde v. horde, troop, band; *(vlechtwerk)* hurdle.
horen on. w. zie *behoren.*
horen o. w. en on. w. hear; *(vernemen)* hear, learn.
horizon m. horizon, sky-line.
horizontaal b. n. *(bw.)* horizontal(ly).
horloge o. watch.
horlogemaker m. watch-maker.
horlogezakje o. watch-pocket.
horrelvoet m. club-foot, stump-foot.
hort m. jerk, jolt, push.
horten on. w. jerk, jolt; *(haperen)* hitch.
horzel v. horse-fly, gad-fly, hornet.
hospes m. landlord; innkeeper.
hospitaal o. hospital, infirmary.
hospitaaldoek, hospitaallinnen o. waterproof bed sheeting.
hostie v. host.
hotel o. hotel.
hotelhouder m. hotel-keeper.
hotelrat v. hotel-thief; *(sl.)* hotel-mouse.
houdbaar b. n. tenable, maintainable.
houden o. w. *(vasthouden)* hold; *(behouden)* keep, retain; *(inhouden)* hold, contain; *(v. belofte, woord: er op nahouden)* keep; *(v. redevoering)* deliver, hold, make; *(v. winkel, herberg, enz.)* keep; *(vieren: v. feest, enz.)* celebrate, keep, observe; on. w. hold, keep; w. w. *zich —,* pretend to be, feign, sham.
houder m. keeper; *(v. wissel, effecten, enz.)* holder; *(v. brief, enz.)* bearer.
houding v. *(lichaams—)* carriage; *(gedrag)* deportment; attitude; *(optreden)* bearing; attitude.
hout o. wood; *(timmerhout)* timber.
houtachtig b. n. woody, wood-like.
houtas v. wood-ashes.
houtazijn m. wood-vinegar, wood-acid.
houterig b. n. wooden.
houtgewas o. wood.
houthakker m. wood-cutter.
houtkever m. death-watch.
houtlijm v. joiner's glue.
houtmijt v. wood-stack.
houtskool v. charcoal.
houtsnee, houtsnede v. wood-cut, wood-engraving.
houtsnip v. wood-cock.
houtspaander m. chip of wood.
houtstapel m. wood-stack, pile of wood.
houtteer v. wood-tar.
houtvester m. forester.
houtvezel v. woody fibre.
houtvlot o. raft.
houtvuur o. wood-fire.
houtworm m. wood-worm.
houtzagerij v. saw-mill.
houvast o. handhold; *(fig.)* holdfast, support, mainstay; *geen — hebben,* have nothing to go by.
houw m. cut, gash.
houweel o. pickaxe, mattock.
houwen on. w. hew, cut, hack.
houwitser m. *(mil.)* howitzer.

hovaardig *b. n. (bw.)* proud(ly), haughty(—ily).

hovaardigheid *v.* **hovaardij** *v.* pride, haughtiness.

hoveling *m.* courtier.

hovenier *m.* gardener.

hovenieren *on. w.* garden.

hozen *on. w.* scoop, bail.

huichelaar(ster) *m. (v.)* hypocrite, dissembler, double-dealer.

huichelarij *v.* hypocrisy, dissembling, dissimulation, duplicity, sanctimoniousness.

huichelen *o. w.* simulate, feign, sham; *on. w.* dissemble, play the hypocrite.

huid *v. (v. mens, of dier)* skin; *(v. dier)* hide; *(met haar)* fell; *(v. pels)* pelt; *(v. schip)* sheathing, (iron) plating.

huidig *b. n.* present-day, modern.

huidklier *v.* skin-gland.

huiduitslag *m.* eruption (of the skin), cutaneous inflammation.

huif *v. (hoofddeksel)* coif; *(bedekking v. wagen)* hood, tilt, awning.

huifkar *v.* tilt-cart, hooded cart.

huig *v.* uvula.

huik *v. (gesch.)* hooded cloak.

huilen *on. w. (schreien)* cry, weep; *(v. dier)* howl; *(klagend —)* whine; *(v. wind)* howl, whistle.

huilerig *b. n.* cryish, whining, lachrymose.

huis *o.* house; *(te —)* home; *(handels—)* house, firm.

huisbaas *m.* landlord.

huisbewaarder *m.* **huisbewaarster** *v.* care-taker.

huisdier *o.* domestic animal.

huisdokter *m.* family doctor.

huisduif *v.* house-dove, domestic pigeon.

huiselijk *b. n. (v. het huis)* domestic, house-hold; *(gezellig; aan huis gehecht)* domesticated, home-loving; *bw.* homishly.

huiselijkheid *v.* domesticity, hominess, homeliness.

huisgenoot *m.* inmate; house-mate.

huisgezin *o.* family, household.

huishoudboek *o.* housekeeping book.

huishoudelijk *b. n.* household, domestic; *(spaarzaam)* economical.

huishouden *on. w.* keep house; *z. n., o.. (gezin)* household, family; *(bestuur v. huis)* housekeeping.

huishoudgeld *o.* housekeeping-money, housekeeping-allowance.

huishoudkunde *v.* (domestic) economy.

huishoudschool *v.* housewifery school, school for household training.

huishoudster *v.* housekeeper.

huishuur *v.* house-rent.

huisjesslak *v.* shell-snail.

huiskamer *v.* sitting-room, living-room.

huisknecht *m.* servant, domestic; *(in hotel)* boots.

huiskrekel *m.* house-cricket, cricket on the hearth.

huismeester *m.* major-domo, steward.

huismiddeltje *o. (fig.)* palliative, makeshift.

huismoeder *v.* mother of a family; *(vrouw des huizes)* mistress of the house.

huisnaaister *v.* visiting seamstress.

huisonderwijzer *m.* private teacher.

huisraad *o.* (house-)furniture, household effects. [familias.

huisvader *m.* father of a family, pater

huisvesten *o. w.* house, lodge, take in, accommodate.

huisvesting *v.* lodging, accommodation, house-room.

huisvriend *m.* family friend, friend of the house.

huisvrouw *v.* housewife, mistress of the house; *(echtgenote)* wife.

huiswaarts *bw.* homeward.

huiswerk *o.* house-work, household work; *(v. school)* home-work, home-tasks.

huiszoeking *v.* house-search, domiciliary search.

huiveren *on. w. (v. schrik)* shudder; *(v. koude, schrik)* shiver.

huivering *v.* shives; shudder.

huiveringwekkend *b. n.* horrible.

huizen *on. w.* house, be housed, lodge.

hulde *v.* homage.

huldigen *o. w.* pay (do, render) homage to; *(fig.: v. beginsel)* recognize.

huldiging *v.* homage.

hullen *o. w.* wrap (up), envelop; *(fig.)* wrap, shroud; *w. w.* **zich —,** wrap oneself.

hulp *v.* help, aid, assistance; *(in nood, ook:)* succour, relief; *(redding)* rescue.

hulpbehoevend *b. n.* wanting assistance, requiring help; *(behoeftig)* needy, destitute indigent; *(lichamelijk: sukkelend, hulpeloos)* invalid, helpless; *(door zwakte, ouderdom)* infirm.

hulpbetoon *o.* assistance.

hulpboek *o. (H.)* auxiliary book.

hulpbron *v.* resource.

hulpeloos *b. n. (bw.)* helpless(ly).

hulpeloosheid *v.* helplessness.

hulpgeroep *o.* cry for help.

hulplijn *v. (meetk.)* auxiliary line, artificial line; *(v. spoorweg)* subsidiary line, — railway; *(muz.)* ledger line.

hulpmiddel *o.* expedient, makeshift, remedy.

hulpvaardig *b. n.* willing (ready) to help, helpful.

hulpvaardigheid *v.* willingness (readiness) to help, helpfulness.

hulpwerkwoord *o.* auxiliary (verb).

huls *v. (Pl.)* pod, cod, hull, shell, case; *(v. patroon)* cartridge-case; *(v. stro, enz.)* straw-case, envelope.

hulst *m.* holly.

humeur *o.* temper, humour, mood.

humor *m.* humour.

humus *m.* humus, vegetable mould.

hun *bez. vnw.* their; *pers. vnw.* them.

hunkeren *o. w.* hanker *(naar,* after), hunger *(naar,* for, after).

hunnentwil *bw. om* —, for their sake(s), in their behalf.
huppelen *on. w.* hop, skip.
hups *b. n. (beleefd, voorkomend)* obliging, courteous, kind; *(flink)* strapping.
hupsheid *v.* obligingness, courtesy, kindness.
huren *o. w. (alg.)* hire; *(v. huis)* rent, hire; *(v. dienstbode)* engage, hire; *(v. schip)* charter.
hurken *on. w.* squat.
hut *v.* hut, hovel; *(klein huisje)* cottage; *(dicht.)* cot; *(v. schip)* cabin.
hutspot *v.* hotchpotch, hodge-podge.
huur *v.* (house-)rent, rental, hire; *(v. dienstbode: loon)* wages; *(huurtijd)* lease.
huurbordje *o.* board ,,to let'', ,,to let'' board, ,,to let'' sign.
huurder *m. (alg.)* hirer; *(v. huis)* tenant, lessee.
huurgeld *o.* rent, hire.
huurkazerne *v.* tenement house.
huurkoets *v.* hackney-coach.
huurkoetsier *m.* hackney-coachman, cabman.
huurling *m.* hireling, mercenary.
huurprijs *m.* rent.
huurwaarde *v.* rental value, rent-value.
huurwet *v.* rent act, rent restriction act.
huwbaar *b. n.* marriageable; *(v. meisje ook :)* nubile.

huwelijk *o.* marriage, wedding; *(toestand)* marriage, matrimony, wedlock.
huwelijksaankondiging *v.* notification of marriage.
huwelijksaanzoek *o.* offer (of marriage), proposal (of marriage).
huwelijksafkondiging *v. (op stadhuis)* public notice of marriage; *(kerkelijk)* banns.
huwelijksbootje *o.* hymen's boat.
huwelijksgeluk *o.* conjugal bliss, wedded (connubial) happiness. [ry.
huwelijksgift *v.* marriage-portion, dow-
huwelijksleven *o.* married life.
huwelijksreisje *o.* wedding-trip, wedding-journey, honeymoon(-trip).
huwelijksvoorwaarden *v. mv.* marriage settlement.
huwelijkszegen *m.* nuptial benediction, nuptial blessing; *(kinderen)* offspring.
huwen *o. w. en on. w.* marry, wed.
huzaar *m.* hussar.
hyacint *v.* hyacinth.
hyena *v.* hyena.
hygiëne *v.* hygiene, hygenics, sanitary science.
hypotheek *v.* mortgage.
hypotheekgever *m.* mortgager, mortgagor.
hypotheekhouder *m.* mortgagee.
hypotheeknemer *m.* mortgagee.

I

ideaal *b. n.* ideal; *bw.* ideally; *z. n., o.* ideal.
idealist *m.* idealist.
idealistisch *b. n.* idealistic.
idee *v.* idea; notion; *(mening)* opinion.
identiteit *v.* identity.
identiteitskaart *v.* card of identity.
idioot *b. n.* idiotic, imbecile; *(fig.)* idiotic, foolish, silly; *bw.* idiotically, foolishly; *z. n., m.* idiot, fool.
ieder *vnw. (bijv.)* every; each; *een* —, every one, everybody; *(zelfst.)* everyone, everybody; anyone; each. [body.
iedereen *onbep. vnw.* everyone, every-
iemand *onbep. vnw.* somebody, some one; any body; a man.
iep *m.* elm, elm-tree.
Ier *m.* Irishman.
Ierland *o.* Ireland; *(dicht.)* Erin, Hibernia.
iet *zie niet.*
iets *vnw.* something, anything; *bw. (bevestigend)* a little, somewhat, slightly; *(vragend of ontkennend)* any.
ijdel *b. n.* vain; *(ledig; nietswaardig)* idle; *(hersenschimmig)* illusive.
ijdelheid *v.* vanity, vainness; *(vergeefsheid)* futility.
ijk *m.* gauge, verification of weights and measures.

ijken *o. w.* gauge; *een geijkte uitdrukking,* a standing phrase.
ijker *m.* gauger; inspector of weights and measures.
ijkgewicht *o.* standard weight.
ijl *b. n. (v. lucht, bos, enz.)* thin; *(v. lucht, gas)* rare, rarefied, tenuous.
ijl *v.* haste, speed; *in aller* —, in great haste, at the top of one's speed, with all speed.
ijlbode *m.* courier, express-messenger.
ijlen *on. w. (zich haasten, spoeden)* hasten, hurry (on), speed.
ijlen *on. w. (in koorts)* rave, wander, be delirious.
ijlgoed *o.* speed-goods, express (dispatch) goods.
ijlheid *v.* thinness; rarity, tenuity.
ijlhoofd *o.* rattle-brain, rattle-pate.
ijlhoofdig *b. n. (licht van hoofd)* light-headed; delirious; *(leeghoofdig, onbesuisd)* rattle-brained, rattle-pated, empty-headed, feather-brained.
ijlhoofdigheid *v.* light-headedness; deliriousness; rattle-brainedness, thoughtlessness.
ijlings *bw.* hastily, in hot haste.
ijs *o.* ice; *(room—)* ice-cream, ice.
ijsbank *v.* ice-bank.
ijsbeer *m.* white bear, polar bear.

ijsberg m. iceberg.
ijsbloemen v. mv. frost-flowers.
ijsbreker m. ice-breaker.
ijselijk b. n. horrible, terrible; (af-grijselijk) gruesome.
ijsfabriek v. ice-factory, ice-works.
ijsgang m. ice-drift, breaking up of the ice.
ijskast v. refrigerator, ice-safe, ice-box.
ijskegel m. icicle.
ijskelder m. ice-house.
ijskoud b. n. icy-cold, frigid.
IJsland o. Iceland.
ijsveld o. ice-field.
ijsvogel m. kingfisher; (dicht.) halcyon.
ijsvorming v. glaciation, formation of ice.
ijsvos m. arctic fox.
ijswafel v. iced-wafer, ice-cream wafer.
ijszee v. ice-sea, polar sea; **de IJszee,** the Arctic Sea.
ijver m. (vurige ijver) zeal, ardour, fervour; (onverdroten ijver) assiduity; (vlijt) diligence, industry.
ijveraar m. zealot; devotee.
ijveren on. w. be zealous.
ijverig b. n. zealous, fervent; assiduous; diligent, industrious; bw. zealously, etc.
ijverzucht v. jealousy, envy.
ijzel m. glazed frost.
ijzelen onp. w. **het ijzelt,** there is a glazed frost.
ijzen on.w. shudder, shiver (with horror).
ijzer o. iron; (v. slee) runner; (v. schaats) blade.
ijzerachtig b. n. iron-like; ferruginous.
ijzerdraad o. iron-wire.
ijzerdraadtrekker m.iron-wiredrawer.
ijzergieterij v. iron-foundry, iron works.
ijzerhandel m. iron-trade, ironmongery.
ijzerhoudend b. n. ferriferous, ferruginous.
ijzerkruid o. (Pl.) verbena, vervain.
ijzersterk b. n. strong as iron.
ijzervijlsel o. iron-filings.
ijzerwaren v. mv. ironwares, hardware, ironmongery.
ijzerwerk o. ironwork.
ijzig b. n. (kil als ijs) icy, as cold as ice; (ijzingwekkend) gruesome.
ijzingwekkend b. n. gruesome, grewsome.
ik pers. vnw. I; **— zelf,** I myself.
illusie v. illusion.
illustratie v. illustration; (tijdschrift) illustrated paper.
imaginair b. n. imaginary.
imitatie v. imitation.
imitatieleer o. imitation leather.
imker m. bee-farmer, apiarist.
immer bw. ever.
immermeer bw. ever, evermore.
immers bw. indeed.
imperatief b. n. imperative; bw. imperatively; z. n., m. imperative.
imperiaal b. n. imperial.
import m. (H.) import.

importeren o. w. (H.) import.
importeur m. (H.) importer.
importhandel m. (H.) import trade.
in vz. en bw. (binnen zekere grenzen) in; (buiten grenzen, van ene plaats naar andere) into; (vóór namen v. grote steden en plaats van inwoning) in; (vóór andere plaatsnamen) at.
inachtneming v. observance.
inademen o. w. breathe, inspire, inhale; on. w. inhale.
inbaar b. n. collectable, collectible.
inbeelden w. w. zich —, imagine, fancy.
inbeelding v. imagination, fancy; (verwaandheid) selfconceit, presumption.
inbegrepen b. n. alles —, all found, no extras; **kosten —,** charges included, inclusive of charges; **vracht —,** cost and freight; **invoerrechten —,** duty paid; custom free.
inbeslagname, inbeslagneming v. seizure, attachment; (v. schip) seizure, embargo; (v. tijd) taking up.
inbezitneming v. taking possession (of); (bezetting) occupation.
inbezitstelling v. handing over; (recht) delivery.
inbijtend b. n. corrosive, mordant.
inbinden o. w. (v. boek) bind; (sch.: v. zeil) reeve; on. w. (sch.) shorten sail; (fig.) climb down, take in reef.
inblazen o. w. blow into; (fig.) prompt, suggest.
inblazer m. prompter, suggester, instigator.
inblazing v. insufflation; (fig.) prompting, suggestion, instigation.
inboezemen o. w. inspire with; strike into.
inboorling m. native, indigene.
inborst v. character, nature; (aard, aanleg) disposition.
inbraak v. burglary, housebreaking.
inbreken on. w. break into a house, commit burglary.
inbreker m. burglar, housebreaker.
inbrengen o. w. bring in; (bij spaarbank, enz.) deposit; **— tegen,** object to; oppose; bring against. [vendor.
inbrenger m. depositor; (in N.V.)
inbreuk v. (schending) violation; (overtreding) transgression, infraction; **— maken op,** encroach upon, infringe.
inburgeren o. w. naturalize; w. w. zich —, (v. woorden, enz.) become naturalized, be generally adopted.
incasseren o. w. (v. schuld) collect; (verzilveren: cheque, enz.) cash.
incasso o. (H.) collection.
incassokosten m. mv. collecting-charges.
incident o. incident.
inclusief b. n. (bw.) inclusive(ly).
incognito bw. incognito; (fam.) incog.
indachtig b. n. mindful of.
indelen o. w. (in hoofdstukken, enz.) divide; (groeperen) group; (mil.: inlijven) incorporate; (in graden) graduate.

indeling v. division; grouping; incorporation; graduation.

indenken o. w. (bedenken, overdenken) consider (of), think (of); w. w. **zich —in,** try to realize, enter into the spirit of.

inderdaad bw. indeed, really.

inderhaast bw. in a hurry, hurriedly, in haste.

indertijd bw. at the time.

index m. (v. boek) index, table of contents; (kath.) index.

indexcijfer o. index number, index-figure.

indien vgw. if, in case.

indienen o. w. (wetsontwerp, begroting) present, introduce, bring in; (klacht) lodge; (verzoekschrift) present; (vordering) put in (a claim); **zijn ontslag —,** tender one's resignation.

Indiër m. Indian.

indijken o. w. dike in, dam in, endike, embank.

indijking v. endiking, diking in, damming in, embankment.

indommelen on. w. doze off, drop off.

indompeling v. immersion.

indringen on. w. push into, press into; (binnendringen) penetrate (into), enter by force; (v. vloeistof) soak in; w. w. **zich —,** obtrude oneself (upon).

indringer m. obtruder, intruder.

indringerig b. n. (bw.) intrusive(ly), obtrusive(ly).

indruisen on. w. **— tegen,** clash with, jar with, interfere with; run counter to.

indruk m. impression; imprint.

indrukken o. w. (induwen) press in, push in; (stempel, merk, enz.) impress, imprint; (plat drukken) crush, squash.

indrukwekkend b. n. impressive, imposing; (v. persoon) commanding.

inductiestroom m. (el.) induced current.

industrie v. industry.

indutten on. w. doze off, drop off; (fig.) go to sleep.

ineengedrongen b. n. close together; (v. gestalte) thick-set.

ineenkrimpen on. w. shrink, writhe.

ineenslaan o. w. strike together; (dicht.) smite together; (in elkaar zetten) knock together.

ineenstorten on. w. crumble (come, go) down, fall to the ground; (met geraas: v. dak, enz.) crash in, fall in; (fig.) collapse.

ineenstorting v. crash; collapse.

ineenzakken on. w. collapse.

inenten o. w. (v. boom) ingraft, inoculate; (v. kind) vaccinate.

inenting v. inoculation; vaccination.

infanterie v. infantry, foot. [dier.

infanterist m. infantry-man, foot-sol-

infectie v. infection.

infectiehaard m. nidus.

influisteren o. w. whisper; prompt, suggest.

informatie v. (inlichting) information;

(navraag) inquiry; **—s inwinnen,** make inquiries.

informeren on. w. inquire, make inquiries.

ingaan on. w. (intreden, binnengaan) enter, go (walk) into; (beginnen, van kracht worden) take effect; (v. rente) accrue; o. w. enter.

ingaand b. n. **—e rechten,** import duties.

ingang m. entrance, entry, ingress; (als opschrift) way in.

ingebeeld b. n. (denkbeeldig) imaginary, fancied; (verwaand) (self) conceited, presumptuous.

ingeboren b. n. innate.

ingelegd b. n. (ingemaakt) preserved; (in zuur) pickled; (met hout, metaal, enz.) inlaid.

ingemaakt b. n. (v. groenten, enz.) preserved; (v. bonen, ook:) potted; (in zuur) pickled.

ingenaaid b. n. sewed, stitched.

ingenieur m. engineer.

ingenomen b. n. taken; (fig.) charmed, pleased (met, with).

ingenomenheid v. sympathy; (voldoening) satisfaction.

ingesloten b. n. enclosed; (inbegrepen) included, inclusive.

ingetogen b. n. modest, retiring.

ingetogenheid v. modesty.

ingeving v. suggestion; inspiration, prompting.

ingewanden o. mv. bowels, entrails; intestines.

ingewijde m. adept; (fam.) insider.

ingewikkeld b. n. intricate, complicated.

ingewikkeldheid v. intricacy, complicacy.

ingezetene m. inhabitant, resident.

ingezonden b. n. sent in; **— stuk,** letter (to the editor).

ingooien o. w. throw in, cast in; (v. ruiten) smash, break.

ingraven o. w. dig in; w. w. **zich —,** (mil.) dig in, entrench oneself; (v. konijn, enz.) burrow.

ingrijpen on. w. (tn.) grip; (in gezag, enz.) encroach; (tussenbeide komen) intervene, interfere, take action.

inhalen o. w. (naar binnen halen) fetch in, bring in; (v. oogst) get in, gather (in); (v. zeilen) take in; (v. vlag) strike; (feestelijk ontvangen) receive in state; (bereiken door lopen, rijden, enz.) overtake, come up with, catch up; (v. vaartuig) overhaul.

inhalig b. n. greedy, covetous, grasping.

inhaligheid v. greed, covetousness.

inham m. creek, bay.

inhebben o. w. hold, contain; (sch.) carry.

inhechtenisneming v. arrestation, apprehension, imprisonment.

inheems b. n. (v. voortbrengselen) native, indigenous; (v. ziekte) endemic; (v. goe-

deren) domestic; (*v. vee*) home-born, home-bred.

inhoud *m.* (*inhoudsruimte*) capacity; (*kubieke* —) content, cubic capacity; (*v. boek, brief, enz.*) contents; (*inhoudsopgave*) table of contents; (*strekking*) tenor, purport; (*v. dagblad*) contents bill; **korte —,** summary.

inhouden *o. w.* (*bevatten*) contain, hold; (*tegenhouden*) contain, check; (*v. adem*) hold, catch; (*niet uitbetalen*) stop, dock; (*afhouden*) deduct; (*op veiling*) withdraw, buy in; (*v. voedsel*) retain; (*v. verlof*) stop, cancel; *w. w.* **zich —,** contain oneself; restrain oneself.

inhoudsmaat *v.* measure of capacity, cubic measure.

inhoudsopgave *v.* (*v. boek*) table of contents; (*v. dagblad*) contents-bill.

inhuldigen *o. w.* inaugurate, install.

inhuldiging *v.* inauguration, installation.

injectiespuit *v.* injection syringe, hypodermic syringe.

inkankeren *on. w.* eat into, corrode; become inveterate.

inkeer *m.* repentance; **tot — komen,** repent.

inkepen, inkerven *o. w.* notch, nick, indent.

inkeping, inkerving *v.* notch, nick, indentation.

inklaren *o. w.* (*H.*) clear (in).

inklaring *v.* (*H.*) clearing(-in), clearance (inwards).

inkleden *o. w.* clothe.

inkomen *on. w.* come in, enter; *z. n., o.* income.

inkomst *v.* entrance, entry; **—en,** income, earnings; (*v. bedrijf, staat, enz.*) revenue; **—en en uitgaven,** receipts and expenditure.

inkomstenbelasting *v.* income-tax.

inkoop *m.* purchase.

inkoopfactuur *v.* invoice.

inkoopsprijs *m.* cost price, purchase price, buying price.

inkopen *o. w.* buy, purchase; (*terugkopen*) buy in.

inkorten *o. w.* shorten, curtail.

inkrimpen *on. w.* shrink, contract; (*fig. ook:*) dwindle; *w. w.* **zich —,** retrench (reduce, curtail) one's expenses.

inkrimping *v.* shrinking, contraction; dwindling; retrenchment, curtailment.

inkt *m.* ink.

inktkussen *o.* inking-pad.

inktpot *m.* inkpot, ink-well; inkstand.

inktpotlood *o.* copying-pencil.

inktvis *m* ink-fish, cuttle-fish, squid.

inkuilen .. *w.* (*v. aardappelen*) put in pits; (*v. veevoeder*) ensilage, ensile, store in a silo.

inkwartiering *v.* billeting, quartering.

inladen *o. w.* (*v. goederen*) load; ship; (*mil.: v. soldaten*) entrain.

inlander *m.* native.

inlands *b. n.* (*v. voortbrengselen*) home;

(*v. artikelen*) home-made; native, indigenous; (*v. vee*) homebred; (*v. spek*) home-fed.

inlassen *o. w.* insert, intercalate, introduce; (*tn.*) let in, mortise.

inlassing *v.* insertion, intercalation; interpolation.

inlaten *o. w.* let in, admit; *w. w.* **zich — met,** have dealings with.

inleg *m.* (*bij spaarbank*) deposit; (*bij spel*) stakes; (*voor lidmaatschap*) entrance money, entrance fee; (*inslag v. kledingstuk*) tuck; (*binnenste v. sigaar*) filling.

inleggen *o. w.* put in, lay in; (*geld inzetten bij spel*) stake; (*bij bank*) deposit; (*inmaken*) preserve; (*in 't zuur*) pickle; (*met koper, ivoor, enz.*) inlay; (*v. kledingsukt*) take in; (*v. trein*) put on.

inlegsel *o.* tuck.

inleiden *o. w.* introduce, usher in; (*fig.: in wetenschap*) initiate; (*v. debat*) open, initiate.

inleidend *b. n.* introductory; preliminary; (*v. studie*) propaedeutic.

inleiding *v.* introduction; (*v. rede*) preamble, exordium.

inleveren *o. w.* (*goederen, wapens*) deliver up; (*lijst, enz.*) send in, hand in; (*huiswerk*) give in, hand in.

inlichten *o. w.* inform, give information.

inlichting *v.* information; **—en vragen,** make inquiries, inquire.

inliggend *b. n.* enclosed.

inlijven *o. w.* incorporate; annex.

inlijving *v.* incorporation; annexation.

inlopen *o. w.* drop in, run into; *on. w.* drop in, run in.

inlossen *o. w.* redeem, take out of pawn.

inluiden *o. w.* ring in. [pickling.

inmaak *m.* preservation; (*in 't zuur*)

inmaken *o. w.* preserve; pickle; (*in blik*) tin.

inmenging *r.* meddling, interference.

inmiddels *bw.* meanwhile, in the meantime.

innaaien *o. w.* (*v. kledingstuk*) take in; (*v. boek*) sew, stitch; (*met metaaldraad*) wire-stitch.

innemen *o. w.* (*mil.: veroveren*) take capture; (*naar binnen halen*) take in, bring in; (*v. geneesmiddel, enz.*) take; (*v. schip: lading*) take in, load; (*v. ruimte: beslaan*) take up, occupy; (*v. kledingstuk: innaaien*) take in, tuck in; (*v. kaartjes, enz.*) collect; (*fig.: bekoren*) charm, captivate.

innemend *b. n.* taking, winning; charming, captivating; prepossessing; attractive; (*v. hoedanigheden*) endearing.

inneming *v.* taking, capture.

innen *o. w.* collect; (*v. check*) cash.

innerlijk *b. n.* (*v. leven*) inner; (*v. krachten, enz.*) internal; (*v. deugd*) intrinsic; (*binnenwaarts*) inward.

innig *b. n.* hearty, earnest; (*v. genegenheid, samenwerking*) close; (*v. liefde*) fond, ardent; (*v. gebed, godsvrucht*) fervent.

innigheid *v.* heartiness, earnestness; closeness; fondness; fervour.
inning *v.* collection; cashing.
inpakken *o. w.* pack, pack up; (*in balen*), bale: *w. w.* **zich —,** wrap (oneself) up.
inpalmen *o. w.* haul in.
inpompen *o. w.* pump in; (*fig.*) cram.
inprenten *o. w.* imprint, impress, inculcate, instill.
inproppen *o. w.* cram in(to); (*v. voedsel*) bolt.
inrekenen *o. w.* rake up, bank up; (*arresteren*) run in, take up.
inrichten *o. w.* (*ordenen, regelen*) arrange, regulate; (*v. huis, enz.*) fit up, furnish: *w. w.* **zich —,** set up house, settle in; (*in zaak*) set up in business.
inrichting *v.* (*regeling*) arrangement, disposition; (*meubilering*) furnishing, fitting up; (*stichting, instelling*) institution, establishment.
inrij *m.* way in, entrance.
inroepen *o. w.* (*persoon*) call in; (*hulp, enz.*) invoke, implore.
inruilen *o. w.* barter, exchange (**tegen,** for).
inrukken *o. w.* (*in stad*) march into; *on. w.* break ranks, dismiss; (*v. brandweer*) withdraw.
inschakelen *o. w.* (*aaneenschakelen*) connect up; (*el.*) switch on, put in circuit; (*mach.*) throw into gear; (*inlassen*) insert.
inschenken *o. w.* pour out, pour in.
inschepen *o. w.* ship, embark, put on board; *w. w.* **zich —,** embark, take ship.
inscheping *v.* embarkation, embarkment.
inscheppen *o. w.* put in.
inschieten *o. w.* shoot in; (*mil.*) range; *w. w.* **zich —,** (*mil.*) find (obtain) the range.
inschikkelijk *b. n.* complying, obliging, compliant, complaisant, accommodating.
inschikkelijkheid *v.* obligingness, compliancy, complaisance.
inschrift *o.* inscription.
inschrijven *o. w.* (*namen, enz.*) inscribe, book, register, enrol; (*leerlingen*) enter, matriculate; *on. w.* (*bij aanbesteding*) tender, send in a tender; (*op lening, boek*) subscribe (to); (*op aandelen*) apply (for).
inschrijver *m.* tenderer; (*op lening*) subscriber; (*op aandelen*) applicant.
inschrijving *v.* (*in register*) registration, enrolment; (*v. studenten*) matriculation; (*bij aanbesteding*) tender; (*op lening*) subscription; (*op aandelen*) application; (*op grootboek*) inscribed stock.
inschuiftafel *v.* telescope-table.
inschuiven *o. w.* push in, shove in.
insekt *o.* insect.
insektenkunde *v.* entomology.
insgelijks *bw.* likewise, in the same way.
inslaan *o. w.* (*door slaan indrijven: spijker, enz.*) drive in; (*stuk maken, vernietigen*) beat in, batter in, bash in,

knock in; (*opdoen, inkopen*) lay in, stock; (*verkleinen, verkorten*) take in, tuck in; (*v. weg: opgaan, opwandelen*) take, turn into; *on. w.* (*v. bliksem*) strike; (*v. boek, toneelstuk, enz.*) take, catch on; (*v. rede, enz.*) go home; (*v. les, waarschuwing*) sink in.
inslag *m.* (*v. weefsel*) woof; (*v. kledingstuk*) turning; (*voorraad*) provisions, supply.
inslapen *on. w.* fall asleep, drop off to sleep; (*fig.*) pass away.
inslikken *o. w.* swallow; (*letters, woorden*) clip.
insluipen *on. w.* steal in, sneak in; (*fig.*) creep in.
insluiten *o. w.* (*opsluiten, binnen sluiten*) lock in; (*afsluiten, begrenzen; v. brief*) enclose; (*mil.: v. stad*) invest; (*omvatten*) include, comprise; (*meetk.*) contain.
insluiting *v.* enclosure; investment; inclusion.
insmeren *o. w.* grease, oil, smear.
insnijden *o. w.* cut in (into), incise.
inspannen *o. w.* (*v. paarden*) put; (*fig.: v. krachten*) exert; *w. w.* **zich —,** exert oneself, bestir oneself.
inspanning *v.* exertion, effort.
inspiratie *v.* inspiration.
inspreken *o. w.* **moed —,** inspire with courage, hearten.
inspringen *on. w.* leap in (into); (*drukk.: v. regels*) indent; (*v. huis*) stand back from the street; (*v. hoek*) re-enter; **—de regel,** receding line.
inspuiten *o. w.* inject.
inspuiting *v.* injection.
instaan *o. w.* **— voor,** (*waarborgen: kwaliteit, echtheid*) guarantee; (*v. verklaring, waarheid, enz.*) vouch (for); (*v. persoon*) answer (for).
instandhouding *v.* maintenance, upkeep, preservation.
instantie *v.* instance, resort.
instappen *on. w.* step in; (*in rijtuig, enz.*) get in; **—;** (take your) seats please!
insteken *o. w.* put in; (*fig.*) prompt suggest.
instellen *o. w.* (*inrichten*) establish; (*onderzoek, vervolging, enz.*) institute; (*camera, microscoop*) focus; (*instrument*) adjust; (*commissie*) set up; (*vordering*) bring, put in.
instelling *v.* establishment; institution; adjustment.
instemmen *on. w.* **— met,** agree with, fall in with, accede to; (*goedkeuren*) approve of.
instemming *v.* agreement; (*goedkeuring*) approval; concurrence.
instituut *o.* institute, institution; boarding-school.
instorten *on. w.* fall down, tumble down, fall in, collapse; (*v. zieke*) relapse; (*v. grond*) cave in; *o. w.* pour into; (*fig.*) infuse.

instorting v. down-fall; falling down, collapse; relapse; infusion.
instructie v. (onderricht, enz.) instruction; (dienstorder) order; (recht) (judicial) inquiry, preliminary inquiry.
instrument o. (muz.) (musical)instrument; (werktuig) instrument, implement.
insturen o. w. send in.
integendeel bw. on the contrary.
intekenen o. w. subscribe (to, for).
intekening v. subscription.
intelligent (v. persoon) intelligent; (v. uiterlijk) intellectual.
interest m. interest.
interneren o. w. intern.
internering v. internment.
interpelleren o. w. interpellatie; (in Eng.) (ask a) question.
interpreteren o. w. interpret.
intiem b. n. intimate.
intijds bw. (in good) time.
intimiteit v. intimacy.
intocht m. entry.
intomen o. w. (v. paard) curb, rein in, bridle in, pull up; (fig.) curb, check, restrain.
intrede v. entrance; entry.
intreden o. w. enter.
intrek m. zijn — nemen, put up (at).
intrekken o. w. draw in, draw back, retract; (v. wet, motie, voorrecht; munt) withdraw; (decreet) revoke; (bestelling, verlof) cancel; (vergunning) discontinue; (bankbiljetten, obligaties) retire; (besluit, bevel) reverse, countermand; (v. stad) march into; on. w. (in huis) move in.
intrekking v. withdrawal; revocation; cancellation; discontinuation; retractation.
intrige v. intrigue, machination, scheming; (v. drama, enz.) plot.
introducé m. guest.
intussen bw. meanwhile.
inval m. (het plotseling binnendringen) invasion, irruption; (met plundering) incursion, inroad; (v. politie, enz.) raid; (gril) conceit, fancy.
invalide b. n. invalid, disabled; (v. arbeider) broken-down; z. n., m. invalid, disabled soldier.
invallen on. w. (vallen in) fall in, drop in (into); (instorten) tumble down, collapse; (v. licht) enter; (v. vorst, enz.) set in; (v. duisternis) fall; (in rede, bij spel) cut in; (bij zang) join in; (in land) invade; (voor iem.) deputize; (v. wangen) fall in.
invalshoek m. angle of incidence; (v. projectiel) angle of descent.
inventaris m. inventory; (v. goederen ook:) stock-in-trade.
invloed m. influence, interest.
invloedrijk b. n. influential.
invoegen o. w. insert, put in, intercalate.
invoer m. importation, import; (de goederen) imports.

invoerder m. importer; (r. nieuwe methode, enz.) introducer.
invoeren o. w. import; introduce; (v. gebruik) set up.
invoerhandel m. import trade.
invoerrechten o. mv. import duties, duties of entry.
invoervergunning v. import permit.
invorderen o. w. collect; (v. schuld) recover.
invreten on. w. bite in, corrode.
invrijheidstelling v. liberation, discharge, release.
invullen o. w. (naam, enz.) fill in; (cheque, stembiljet, enz.) fill up, fill in.
invulling v. filling in (up).
inwendig b. n. internal, inward, interior; bw. internally, inwardly; z. n., o. het —e, the interior.
inwerken on. w. — op, act (operate) upon, affect, influence; w. w. zich ergens —, post oneself up, get thoroughly acquainted with.
inwerpen o. w. throw in; smash.
inwijden o. w. (v. kerk) consecrate; (v. gebouw) inaugurate; (bekend maken met) initiate.
inwijding v. consecration; inauguration; initiation.
inwikkelen o. w. wrap (up), fold up, cover up.
inwilligen o. w. comply with, grant, concede, agree.
inwilliging v. compliance, consent.
inwinnen o. w. (herwinnen, inhalen) regain, win back; iemands raad —, take a person's advice.
inwisselen o. w. change.
inwonen on. w. live in.
inwoner m. inhabitant; (v. huis) occupant, inmate; (v. kamer) lodger.
inzage v. inspection, examination; ter — ontvangen, receive on approval; — nemen van, inspect, examine.
inzamelen on. w. collect, gather.
inzameling v. collection gathering.
inzegenen o. w. (v. huwelijk, enz.) bless; (v. kerk, enz.) consecrate.
inzegening v. blessing; consecration.
inzenden o. w. send in; (in krant) contribute.
inzender m. (op tentoonstelling) exhibitor, exhibitant; (in krant) contributor.
inzending v. sending in; (op tentoonstelling) exhibit; (in krant) contribution.
inzepen o. w. (bij het wassen) soap; (bij 't scheren) lather.
inzet m. (bij spel, enz.) stake(s); (bij veiling) upset-price.
inzetten o. w. (bij spel) stake; (bij veiling) start, put up; (inlassen) insert; (ruiten, enz.) set in, put in; (edelgesteenten, enz.) set; (gezang, psalm) start; (beginnen te spelen, te zingen) intone, intonate; on. w. (spel) stake; (muz.) intone; set in. [opinion.
inzicht o. insight; (mening) view,

inzien *o. w. (brief, dagblad)* glance over; *(fout, gevaar)* see, recognize, realize; *(verslag, enz.)* skim; *z. n., o.* **mijns —s,** in my opinion, in my view, to my thinking.
inzittenden *mr.* occupants.
inzonderheid *bw.* especially.

inzwelgen *o. w.* swallow (up), gulp down.
iris *v.* iris, rainbow.
isolator *m.* insulator.
Italiaans *b. n.* Italian; *z. n., o.* Italian.
Italië *o.* Italy; *(dicht.)* Italia.
ivoor *o.* ivory.

J

ja *bw.* yes; *(versterking)* yea, nay; *(aarzeling)* h'm-yes.
jaaglijn *v.* towing-line, track-rope.
jaagpad *o.* tow(ing)-path.
jaar *o.* year; twelvemonth.
jaarbeurs *v.* industries fair.
jaardienst *m. (voor overledene)* annual mass.
jaarfeest *o. (jaarlijks feest)* annual feast; *(verjaardag)* anniversary.
jaargang *m. (oude —)* file; *(alle nummers van 't jaar)* volume; *(sedert oprichting)* year of publication; *(v. wijn)* vintage.
jaargeld *o. (toelage)* annual allowance, annuity; *(pensioen)* pension.
jaargetij (de) *o. (tijd van 't jaar)* season; *(jaardienst)* annual mass.
jaarkring *m. (12 maanden)* annual cycle; *(ring in boom)* annual ring.
jaarlijks *bw.* every year, yearly, annually; *b. n.* yearly, annual.
jaartal *o. (in chronologische tabel)* year; *(in datum, enz.)* date.
jaartelling *v.* era.
jaarwedde *v.* (annual) salary.
jacht *o. (sch.)* yacht.
jacht *v. (alg.)* chase; *(op vogels, enz.)* shooting; *(op groot wild)* hunting; *(fig.)* pursuit; *(haast)* haste.
jachtakte *v.* shooting-licence; game-licence.
jachtclub *v.* hunting-association; *(sch.)* yachtclub.
jachtgeweer *o.* sporting-gun, shot-gun.
jachthond *m.* sporting-dog, hound.
jachtmes *o.* hunting-knife.
jachtstoet *m. (jachtpartij)* hunting-party, shooting-party; *(jachtgevolg)* hunting-train.
jachtvliegtuig *o.* hunter, chaser plane.
jagen *o. w. (groot wild)* hunt; *(hazen, patrijzen)* shoot; *(nazitten)* chase; *(fig.)* drive, hurry (on); *on. w. (snellen)* rac, scud, tear; *(jachten)* rush; *(v. pols, hart)* race; *(op jacht zijn)* hunt, shoot; *(op hazen)* course.
jager *m.* hunter, sportsman; *(pikeur)* huntsman; *(mil.)* rifleman; *(vl.)* chaser, hunter; *(v. schuit)* towing-horse driver; *(zeil)* flying-jib; *(Dk.)* skua.
jagerslatijn *o.* sportman's yarn.
jagerstas *v.* game-bag; hunter's bag.
jak *o.* jacket; *(korte (uniform)jas)* coatee; *(Dk.) m.* yak.

jakhals *m.* jackal.
jaloers *b. n.* jealous, envious.
jaloersheid *v.* jealousy.
jam *v.* jam; *(aardappelsoort)* yam, potato.
jammer *m.* misery; **het is—,** it is a pity; **hoe —!** the pity of it ! what a — !
jammeren *on. w.* lament, wail.
jammerklacht *v.* lamentation.
jammerlijk *b. n.* miserable, pitiable, pitiful, piteous, wretched; *bw.* miserably, piteously, wretchedly.
janhagel *v.* kind of biscuit; *o. (gepeupel)* rabble, mob.
januari *m.* January.
Japanees *m.* Japanese.
japon *v.* dress, gown.
jarig *b. n. (één jaar oud)* a year old; *(van één jaar)* of a year; **hij is vandaag —,** it is his birth-day to-day.
jarige *m. en v.* the person whose birth-day it is, — celebrating his (her) birth-day; *(op verjaardagsfeest ook:)* the hero (heroine) of the feast.
jas *v.* coat; **geklede —,** frock-coat.
jasmijn *v.* jessamine.
jassen *o. w.* peel (potatoes); *on. w.* play „jas".
jaszak *m.* coat-pocket.
jawoord *o.* consent.
je *pers. vnw.* you; *bez. vnw.* your.
jegens *vz.* towards, to.
jekker *m.* jacket, jersey.
jenever *v.* gin, Hollands.
jeneverneus *m.* bottle-nose, drunkard's nose.
jeneverstoker *m.* gin-distiller.
jeneverstruik *m.* juniper.
jeugd *v.* youth.
jeugdig *b. n. (bw.)* youthful(ly).
jeugdigheid *v.* youthfulness, youth.
jeuken *on. w.* itch; *o. w.* scratch; *w. w.* **zich —,** scratch oneself.
jeuking *v.* itching.
Jezuïet *m.* Jesuit.
jicht *v.* gout.
jichtlijder *m.* gouty patient, sufferer from gout.
jij *pers. vnw.* you.
jockey *m.* jockey.
jodenbuurt *v.* Jew's quarter, ghetto.
jodendom *o. (Joodse leer)* Judaism; *(al de Joden)* Jewry, Jews.
jodenhaat *m.* Jew-hatred.
jodin *v.* Jewess.

joelen on. w. shout, cheer; (brullen) bawl.
jokken on. w. fib, tell fibs, tell stories; (schertsen) joke.
jol v. (sch.) yawl, jolly-boat; (kleine —) dingey.
jolig b. n. jolly, merry.
joligheid v. jolliness.
jong b. n. young; z. n., o. young one; (v. beer, ros, enz.) cub.
jongedochter v. (young) girl; (ongehuwde vrouw) spinster.
jongeheer m. young gentleman; (gevolgd door eigennaam) — **A.**, Master A.
jongeling m. young man; youth; (knaap) lad.
jongelingschap v. (leeftijd) youth, adolescence; (de jongelingen) young men, youths.
jongelingsjaren o. mv. years of adolescence.
jongen m. boy, lad.
jongensachtig b. n. (bw.) boyish(ly); (v. meisje) boy-like.
jongensgek v. girl fond of boys, a regular flirt.
jongensjaren o. mv. (years of) boyhood.
jongensstreek m. boyish trick.
jonggeborene m. en v. new-born child, baby.
jonggehuwden, jonggetrouwden m. en v. mv. newly-married couple.
jonggezel m. bachelor, single man.
jongstleden b. n. last.
jonk v. (sch.) junk.
jonker m. (young) nobleman.
jonkheer m. ,,jonkheer''.
jonkheid v. youth.
jonkvrouw v. maid; (freule) honourable [miss.
jood m. Jew, Hebrew.
journaal o. (H.) journal; (sch.) log-book; (dagboek) diary.
journalist m. journalist, pressman.
jouwen on. w. hoot. [joy.
jubelen on. w. jubilate, exult, shout for

jubeljaar o. jubilee year; (kath.) Holy Year, Jubilee.
jubellied o. song of rejoicing.
jubilaris m. jubilarian, person celebrating his jubilee; (op het feest) hero (heroine) of the feast.
jubileum o. jubilee.
juchtleer o. Russia leather, yuft.
Judaspenning v. (Pl.) Judas money, satin-flower.
juffer v. young lady, girl, miss; (sch.) beam, pole; (straatstamper) rammer, paving-beetle.
juffrouw v. miss, young lady; (bij aanspreking: ongehuwd) Miss; (gehuwd) Mrs.; (zonder eigennaam) Madam.
juichen on. w. jubilate, shout.
juichkreet m. shout of joy.
juist b. n. (waarde, balans, enz.) exact; (reden, enz.) precise; (v. definitie) correct; (vermoeden; tijd; hoeveelheid) right; (v. thermometer, enz.) accurate; (v. schatting, verhouding) just; bw. exactly; correctly; rightly; just.
juistheid v. exactness, exactitude, correctness, precision; (v. opmerking, enz.) justness.
juk o. yoke, cross-beam; (v. balans) beam.
jukbeen o. yoke-bone, cheek-bone; (wet.) zygoma.
juli m. July.
juni m. June.
junior b. n. junior.
juridisch b. n. (bw.) juridical(ly).
jurist m. (rechtsgeleerde) jurist, barrister, lawyer; (student in de rechten) law-student.
jurk v. frock, gown, dress.
jurylid o. member of the jury; (recht) juror.
justitie v. justice; (rechterl. macht, rechtspleging) judicature.
juweel o. jewel, gem.
juweelkistje o. jewel-box, jewel-case.
juwelier m. jeweller.

K

kaai v. (open) quay; (afgesloten) wharf.
kaaigeld o. quayage, quay-dues, wharfage.
kaaiman m. caiman, alligator.
kaak v. jaw; (v. vis) gill.
kaakbeen o. jaw-bone.
kaakslag m. slap in the face.
kaal b. n. (v. persoon) bald; (v. vogel) callow, unfledged; (v. boom) leafless, bare; (v. veld, muur) naked, bare; (v. kleren) threadbare.
kaalheid v. (v. hoofd) baldness, calvity; (v. kleren) threadbareness, shabbiness.
kaalhoofdig b. n. baldheaded.
kaalkop m. baldhead, baldpate.
kaap v. cape, headland, promontory.
Kaapstad v. Cape-town.

kaapstander m. capstan. [teasel·
kaarde v. (werktuig) wool card; (Pl.)
kaarden o. w. card, tease (wool).
kaarder m. **kaardster** v. carder.
kaardwol v. card wool.
kaars v. candle; (Pl.) blowball; vet —, tallow-candle.
kaarsedief m. candle-waster.
kaarsenfabrikant, kaarsenmaker m. candle-maker.
kaarsepit v. candle-wick.
kaarsesnuiter m. (pair of) snuffers, candle-snuffer.
kaarsvet o. tallow.
kaart v. (speel—) card; (land—) map; (spoor—, toegangs—) ticket; (zee—) chart.

kaarten *on. w.* play at cards.
kaartje *o.* (*naamkaartje*) card; (*voor spoor, enz.*) ticket.
kaartspel *o.* card-playing; (*spelletje*) game at cards; (*spel kaarten*) pack of cards.
kaartsysteem *o.* card index system.
kaas *v.* cheese.
kaasachtig *b. n.* cheesy, cheese-like; (*wet.*) caseous.
kaasboer *m.* cheese-maker.
kaasstof *v.* casein(e).
kaasstremsel *o.* rennet.
kaatsbaan *v.* fives-court, Dutch hand-tennis court.
kaatsbal *m.* hand-ball; (*speelgoed*) ball, bouncer.
kaatsen *on. w.* play at ball.
kaatser *m.* hand-ball player, hand-tennis player.
kaatsnet *o.* racket.
kabaal *o.* noise, clamour, hubbub, racket, row.
kabbelen *on. w.* ripple, babble, lap, purl, murmur.
kabbeling *v.* rippling, ripple, babble purl, murmur.
kabel *m.* cable.
kabelbaan *v.* cable-way.
kabelballon *m.* captive balloon.
kabelbericht *o.* cable-message, cable, cablegram.
kabelen *o. w.* cable.
kabeljauw *m. en v.* cod, cod-fish.
kabinet *o.* (*meubel, vertrek*) cabinet; (*kamertje*) closet; (*W. C.*) water-closet; (*galerij voor kunstvoorwerpen*) picture-gallery, museum; (*ministerie*) cabinet, ministry.
kabouter (mannetje) *m.* (*o.*) elf, gnome.
kabuiskool *v.* headed cabbage.
kachel *v.* stove.
kachelglans *m.* stove-polish.
kachelgruis *o.* coal-dust, small-coals.
kachelpijp *v.* stove-pipe; (*hoed*) stove-pipe (hat), topper.
kachelsmid *m.* stove-maker.
kadaster *o.* land registry, register of real property, cadastre; (*kantoor*) land registry office.
kade *v.* quay, wharf.
kader *o.* (*mil.*) skleton (of a regiment) (regimental) cadre.
kaderschool *v.* (*mil.*) cadre school.
kadet *m.* (*mil., sch.*) cadet.
kadetje *o.* roll.
kaduuk *b. n.* crazy, rickety; (*v. persoon*) knocked up.
kaf *o.* chaff.
Kaffer *m.* Caffre, Kaf(f)ir; (*fig.*) boor.
kajuit *v.* cabin.
kajuitsjongen *m.* cabin-boy.
kakelen *on. w.* cackle; (*fig.*) cackle, chatter, gabble.
kakkerlak *m.* cockroach, black-beetle.
kalander *v.* calender; *m.* (*insect*) corn-weevil, calander.
kalender *m.* calendar.

kalenderjaar *o.* calendar year.
kalf *o.* (*Dk.*) calf; (*bovendrempel*) lintel; (*dwarshout*) cross-beam; (*fig.*) calf.
kalfaten, kalfateren *o. w.* (*sch.*) caulk; (*fig.*) patch up.
kalfslapje *o.* veal collop, veal-steak.
kalfsoog *o.* calf's eye; **kalfsogen,** (*fig.*) goggle-eyes, saucer-eyes.
kalfsribbetje *o.* veal-cutlet.
kalfsschenkel *m.* knuckle of veal.
kalfsvel *o.* calf's skin, calfskin.
kalfszwezerik *m.* (calf's) sweetbread.
kaliber *o.* caliber, calibre, (size of) bore.
kalium *o.* potassium.
kalk *v.* lime; **gebluste** —, slaked lime; **ongebluste** —, quick lime.
kalkbak *m.* mason's hod.
kalkbranderij *v.* lime-burning; (*oven*) lime-kiln.
kalkgrond *m.* limy soil, calcareous soil.
kalkoen *m.* turkey.
kalm *b. n.* calm, quiet, composed, collected; (*v. markt*) quiet; *bw.* calmly, quietly, composedly.
kalmte *v.* calm, calmness, composure.
kalverliefde *v.* calf-love.
kam *m.* (*haar*—) comb; (*v. haan*) crest, comb; (*v. vogel, helm*) crest; (*v. viool*) bridge; (*v. rad*) cam, cog; (*v. berg, heuvel*) ridge, crest.
kameel *m.* camel.
kamelot *o.* camlet.
kamenier *v.* lady's maid, waiting-maid, waiting-woman.
kamer *v.* room, chamber; (*v. sluis, torpedo, enz.*) chamber; (*v. hart*) ventricle; **donkere** —, dark room.
kameraad *m.* comrade, companion, mate, fellow.
kamerarrest *o.* confinement (to one's room); (*met toegang*) open arrest; (*zonder toegang*) close arrest.
kamerdienaar *m.* valet, (waiting-)-man; (*aan het hof*) groom of the chamber, chamberlain.
kamerheer *m.* chamberlain; (*v. Paus*) chamberlain, camerlingo.
kamerjapon *v.* dressing-gown.
kamerlid *o.* member of the Chamber, member of Parliament.
kamerwacht *v.* (*mil.*) orderly man.
kamfer *v.* camphor.
kamferspiritus *m.* camphorated spirits, spirits of camphor.
kamgras *o.* (*Pl.*) dog's-tail grass.
kamhagedis *v.* iguana.
kammen *o. w.* comb; (*v. wol*) card, comb; *w. w.* **zich** —, comb one's hair.
kamp *o.* camp, encampement; (*partij*) camp; *m.* (*afgepaald stuk grond*) enclosed field, parcel, lot; (*strijd, worsteling*) fight, combat, struggle.
kampen *on. w.* fight, combat, struggle.
kamperen *o. w.* camp, encamp; *on. w.* camp, camp out, go to camp, be encamped.   [bine.
kamperfoelie *v.* honeysuckle, wood-
kampernoelie *v.* mushroom.

kampioen *m.* champion.
kampioenschap *o.* championship.
kamprechter *m.* umpire.
kampvuur *o.* camp-fire.
kamrad *o.* cog-wheel, cam-wheel.
kan *v.* can, jug, mug; *(maal)* litre.
kanaal *o.* *(natuurlijk: vaargeul)* channel; *(gegraven)* canal; *(buis; fig.)* channel.
kanalje *o.* rabble, mob, canaille.
kanarie *m.* canary.
kandelaar *m.* candle-stick.
kandidaat *m.* candidate; *(sollicitant)* applicant; *(v. predikant, enz.)* postulant, aspirant; *(graad)* bachelor.
kandidatuur *v.* candidature, candidateship, nomination.
kandijsuiker *v.* sugar-candy.
kaneel *o. en v.* cinnamon. [canker.
kanker *m.* cancer; *(v. plant; fig.)*
kankeren *on. w.* cancer; *(fig.)* canker; *(mopperen)* grouse, grumble.
kankergezwel *o.* cancerous tumour, cancerous growth.
kannibaal *m.* cannibal.
kano *v.* canoe.
kanon *o.* gun, cannon.
kanonneerboot *v.* gunboat.
kanonnevlees *o.* cannon-fodder.
kanonnier *m.* gunner, gun-server, artillerist.
kanonvuur *o.* gun-fire, cannonade.
kans *v.* chance, opportunity.
kansel *m.* pulpit.
kanselarij *v.* chancery.
kanselier *m.* chancellor. [sermon.
kanselrede *v.* pulpit oration, homily,
kansspel *o.* game of chance, hazard.
kant *v.* lace.
kant *m.* *(zijde)* side; *(rand, zoom)* border; *(v. water; scherpe —)* edge; *(v. biadzijde)* margin; *(v. afgrond)* brink.
kant *b. n.* neat; **— en klaar,** cut and dried, trim and tight.
kantelen *o. w.* cant, tilt; *(omkantelen)* turn over; *on. w.* turn over, topple over; capsize.
kanten *b. n.* lace, of lace.
kanten *o. w.* cant, square; *(v. schip)* careen; *w. w.* **zich — tegen,** make a stand against, set one's face against, oppose.
kanton *o.* canton.
kantongerecht *o.* police-court.
kantonrechter *m.* justice of the peace; cantonal judge.
kantoor *o.* office; *(soms:)* countinghouse.
kantoorbediende *m.* office-clerk.
kantoorbehoeften *v. mv.* office-appliances; *(schrijfbehoeften)* stationery.
kantoorkruk *v.* office-stool.
kantoorloper *m.* collecting-clerk, runner.
kantoorwerk *o.* **kantoorwerkzaamheden** *v. mv.* office-work, clerical work, desk work.
kanttekening *v.* marginal note.
kantwerk *o.* lace-work, lace.

kantwerkster *v.* lace-worker, lace-maker.
kanunnik *m.* canon, prebendary.
kap *v.* *(hoofddeksel)* cap, coif; *(v. huis)* roof(ing); *(v. schoorsteen)* cowl; *(v. muur)* coping; *(v. rijtuig, auto)* hood; *(v. lamp)* shade; *(v. molen)* cap; *(v. kajuit)* hatch; *(v. monnik)* cowl, hood; *(v. kloosterzuster)* wimple; *(v. laars)* top.
kapblok *o.* chopping-block.
kapel *v.* *(bedehuis)* chapel; *(muziekkorps)* band; *(vlinder)* butterfly.
kapelaan *m.* chaplain.
kapelmeester *m.* bandmaster.
kapen *o. w.* *(sch.)* capture; *(wegnemen, stelen)* pilfer, pinch, purloin; *on. w.* *(sch.)* privateer; pilfer, filch.
kaper *m.* privateer, raider; pilferer.
kaperschip *o.* privateer, raider.
kapitaal *b. n.* capital; *z. n., o.* capital.
kapitaalbelegging *v.* investment (of capital).
kapitaalkrachtig *b. n.* well-provided with capital.
kapitaalvlucht *v.* flight of capital.
kapitalist *m.* capitalist, moneyed man.
kapiteel *o.* capital, head (of a column).
kapitein *m.* captain; *(sch.)* captain, master; **— ter zee,** (naval) captain.
kapittel *o.* chapter.
kaplaars *v.* top-boot.
kapmantel *m.* capuchin, hooded cloak; *(bij het kappen)* dressing-jacket.
kapmes *o.* chopper, chopping-knife.
kapokboom *m.* capoc-tree.
kapot *b. n.* broken, all to pieces; *(v. sokken)* holey, in holes; *(v. slot, enz.)* out of order; *(v. verdriet)* broken-hearted.
kapot *v.* capote, greatcoat.
kapotjas *v.* capote, greatcoat.
kappen *o. w.* *(v. bomen)* fell, cut down; *(v. hout)* chop; *(v. kabel)* cut; *(v. haar)* dress; *w. w.* **zich —,** dress one's hair.
kapper *m.* hairdresser.
kaproen *v.* hood, cap.
kapseizen *on. w.* capsize, keel round, turn turtle, be upset.
kapsel *o.* head-dress, hair-dress, coiffure.
kapstok *m.* *(aan muur)* peg; *(staand)* hat-stand, coat-stand, hall-stand.
kapucijner *m.* Capuchin(-friar).
kapucijner *m.* *(erwt)* marrow-pea, grea pea, marrow-fat.
kar *v.* cart; *(auto)* car; *(fiets)* machine; *(hand—)* hand-cart, barrow; *(v. snelpers)* coffin.
karabijn *v.* carbine, carabine.
karaf *v.* carafe, water-bottle; *(voor wijn)* decanter.
karakter *o.* character; *(teken)* mark, sign, character.
karakteristiek *b. n.* *(bw.)* characteristic(ally).
karakterloos *b. n.* characterless; *bw.* with characterlessness.
karavaan *v.* caravan.
karbonade *v.* chop, cutlet.

kardinaal *m.* cardinal.
kardoes *m.* (*poedelhond*) water-spaniel; *v.* cartridge, cartouche.
Karel *m.* Charles; (*fam.*) Charley, Charlie; — *de Grote,* Charlemagne.
karig *b. n.* (*schraal*) scanty, meagre, slender; (*v. maaltijd*) frugal; (*schriel*) parsimonious; *bw.* scantily; frugally.
karikatuur *v.* caricature; (*fam.*) take-off.
karkas *o.* carcass, skeleton.
karkiet *m.* reed-bird, reed-warbler.
Karmeliet *m.* Carmelite.
karn *v.* churn.
karnemelk *v.* buttermilk, churn-milk.
karnen *o. w.* churn.
karnton *v.* churn.
karper *m.* carp.
karpet *o.* (square of) carpet.
karrespoor *o.* cart-rut.
karrevracht *v.* cart-load.
kartel *o.* cartel.
kartel *m.* (milled) notch. [shot.
kartets *v.* grape-shot cartridge, canister-
karton *o.* cardboard, pasteboard; (*doos*) cardboard box, carton.
karwats *v.* riding-whip, horsewhip, hunting-crop.
karwei *v.* job.
karwijzaad *o.* caraway-seed.
kas *v.* (*geld*) cash; (*kantoor*) pay-office, cash-office; (*kassa*) pay-desk, cash-desk, cashier's desk; (*broeikas*) hothouse, glass-house; (*v. horloge*) (watch-)case; (*v. ring*) bezel; (*v. oog, enz.*) socket.
kasboek *o.* cash-book. [bank-keeper
kashouder *m.* cashier, cash-keeper,
kassa *v.* (*kas, geld*) cash; (*kassa*) cash-desk; (*in bioscoop, enz.*) box-office.
kassier *m.* (*kashouder*) cashier; (*bankier*) banker.
kassiersloon *o.* bank commission.
kast *v.* (*alg.*) cupboard; (*boeken*—) book-case; (*kleer*—) wardrobe; (*linnen*—) linen-cupboard; (*voor porselein, enz.*) cabinet; (*v. viool*) body; (*horloge*—) watch-ease.
kastanje *v.* chestnut.
kastanjebruin *b. n.* chestnut, auburn bay.
kasteel *o.* castle; (*mil.*) citadel; (*schaaksp.*) castle, rook; (*v. schip*) poop, forecastle.
kastekort *o.* deficit, deficiency.
kastijden *o. w.* chastise, castigate, punish.
kastpapier *o.* shelf-paper.
kastrol *v.* casserole, saucepan, stewpan, stewing-pan.
kasvoorraad *m.* cash in hand.
kat *v.* cat; tabby-cat; (*sch.*) cat-head; (*mil.*) cavalier; (*fig.*) cat, scratch-cat, shrew.
katachtig *b. n.* cat-like, feline.
katafalk *v.* catafalque.
katapult *m.* catapult.
kater *m.* male cat, tom-cat.
katheder *m.* (*leerstoel*) chair; (*v. bis-schop*) cathedra.

kathedraal *v.* cathedral (church).
katholiek *b. n. en z. n., m.* Roman Catholic.
katoen *o.* cotton.
katoendrukkerij *v.* calico-printing works (or: factory).
katoog *m.* (*steen*) cat's-eye.
katrol *v.* pulley.
kattekwaad *o.* mischief, waggish tricks.
katterigheid *v.* chippiness, next-morning headache.
kattestaart *m.* cat's tail; (*Pl.*) purple loosestrife; willow-herb. [owl.
katuil *m.* wood-owl, screech-owl, brown
katvis *m.* small fry.
katzwijm *o.* fainting fit, pretended swoon.
Kaukasus *m. de —,* the Caucasus.
kauw *v.* (*Dk.*) jackdaw.
kauwen *o. w. en on. w.* chew, masticate.
kauwgom *v.* chewing gum.
kauwmiddel *o.* masticatory.
kavel *m.* lot, parcel.
kavelen *o. w.* (*in delen splitsen*) lot, parcel out, set out, divide into lots; (*nauwkeurig berekenen*) compute.
kaveling *v.* lotting (out), laying out to lots; lot, parcel.
kazemat *v.* casemate.
kazerne *v.* barracks.
kazuifel *v.* chasuble.
keel *v.* throat; gullet.
keelgat *o.* gullet.
keelholte *v.* pharynx.
keelklank *m.* guttural (sound).
keelontsteking *v.* (*bij mens*) inflammation of the throat, laryngitis; (*bij dieren*) garget.
keelspiegel *m.* laryngoscope.
keeltering *v.* laryngealphthisis, laryngophthisis.
keep *v.* notch, nick, score, indent, indentation.
keer *m.* (*wending*) turn, change; (*maal*) time; **geen enkele —,** never once; **één enkele —,** only once; **twee —,** twice; **— op —,** time after time; **voor één —,** for this once; once in a way; **voor deze —,** this time.
keerkring *m.* tropic.
keerpunt *o.* turning-point.
keerzijde *v.* other side, reverse (side); (*v. stof*) wrong side; (*fig.*) seamy side, dark side, reverse.
keeshond *m.* Pomeranian dog, Dutch barge-dog.
keet *v.* (*zoutziederij*) salt-works; (*loods*) shed, hut, shanty.
keffen *on. w.* yap, yelp; (*kijven*) wrangle, squabble.
keffer *m.* yapper; wrangler.
kegel *m.* (*meetk.*) cone; (*in kegelspel*) skittle, ninepin; (*ijs*—) icicle.
kegelspel *o.* (game of) skittles, ninepins.
kegelvormig *b. n.* conic, conical, cone-shaped.
kei *m.* boulder; (*straatkei*) paving-stone; (*ronde* —) cobble(-stone).

keilen o. w. fling, pitch; on. w. (kis-kassen) make ducks and drakes.
keizer m. emperor.
keizerin v. empress.
keizerrijk o. empire.
keizersnede v. caesarian operation.
kelder m. cellar.
kelderen o. w. cellar, lay up, store (in a cellar); on. w. (v. effecten, enz.) slump, tumble (down).
keldergat o. air-hole, vent-hole; (v. kolenkelder) man-hole.
kelderkamer v. (boven een kelder) room over (above) a cellar; (beneden begane grond) basement-room.
kelderkeuken v. basement-kitchen.
keldermeester m. cellarman; (in klooster) cellarer.
kelen o. w. cut the throat of, kill (off).
kelk m. cup, chalice; (v. bloem) calyx; (v. aronskelk) sheath.
kelkblad o. calyx-leaf, sepal.
kelkdoek m. purificatory. [like.
kelkvormig b. n. cup-shaped, calyx-
kemel m. camel.
Kempen v. mv. de —, the Campine.
kemphaan m. fighting-cock, game-cock; (mannetje) ruff; (wijfje) reeve; (fig.) bantam cock.
kenmerk o. mark of identification, distinguishing mark; (fig.) character-istic.
kenmerken o. w. characterize, mark; w. w. zich — door, be characterized by.
kennelijk b. n. (herkenbaar) recogniz-able; (zichtbaar) visible; (blijkbaar) apparent, evident, obvious.
kennen o. w. know, be acquainted with.
kenner m. connoisseur, judge.
kennis v. knowledge, acquaintance; (persoon) acquaintance; (bewustzijn) consciousness.
kennisgeving v. information, intima-tion, notice; notification; (v. verloving, enz.) announcement.
kennismaking v. acquaintance.
kennisneming v. (taking) cognizance, examination, inspection; perusal.
kenschetsen o. w. characterize.
kenspreuk v. motto.
kenteken o. distinctive mark, distinc-tive, badge, token.
kentekenen o. w. characterize.
kenteren on. w. turn, cant.
kenterhaak m. (sch.) cant-hook.
kentering v. turn, turning (of the tide); (v. moesson) change, transition, turn.
keper v. twill; (Z. N.: balk) beam; (wap.) chevron.
kerel m. fellow, chap.
keren o. w. (omkeren) turn; (v. hooi) make, ted, toss; (tegenhouden, tegen-gaan) stop, check, arrest, make a stand against; on. w. turn; per —de post, by return of post; w. w. zich —, turn (round).
keren o. w. sweep, clean.

kerf v. notch, nick.
kerfstok m. tally, tally-stick; hij heeft veel op zijn —, he has a great score.
kerk v. church; (v. afgescheidenen) chapel.
kerkban m. excommunication.
kerkbesluit o. ecclesiastical decree.
kerkbestuur o. church government.
kerkboek o. church-book, prayer-book; parish register, parochial register, church-register.
kerkdienst m. divine service, church service.
kerkedienaar m. beadle, verger, sexton.
kerkelijk b. n. ecclesiastical.
kerker m. prison, jail, gaol; (onderaards) dungeon.
kerkeren o. w. imprison, incarcerate.
kerkfabriek v. church-fabric.
kerkgang m. going to church, church-going; (na bevalling) churching.
kerkganger m. **kerkgangster** v. church-goer.
kerkhof o. churchyard, cemetery, grave-yard.
kerkleraar m. teacher of the church.
kerkscheuring v. schism.
kerkstoel m. prie-dieu (chair).
kerktoren m. church-steeple; (zonder spits) church-tower.
kerkvergadering v. council; synod, church-meeting.
kerkvoogd m. (kath.) prelate; (prot.) churchwarden.
kerkzwaluw v. church-martin.
kermen on. w. moan, groan.
kermis v. (pleasure) fair, kermis.
kermiswagen m. caravan.
kern v. (v. noot) kernel; (v. perzik, kers) stone; (v. boom) heart; (v. hout) pith; (v. komeet) nucleus; (fig.) kernel, marrow, pith, gist.
kernachtig b. n. pithy, terse.
kernachtigheid v. pithiness, terseness.
kerngezond b. n. healthy to the core, hale and hearty.
kers v. (vrucht) cherry; (Pl.) cress.
kerseboom m. cherry-tree.
Kerstavond m. (avond vóór Kerstmis) Christmas-Eve; (avond van Kerstmis) Christmas evening.
Kerstdag m. Christmas-day.
kerstenen o. w. christianize.
Kerstlied o. Christmas carol.
Kerstmis v. Christmas, Xmas.
Kerstnacht m. Christmas night.
kervel v. (Pl.) chervil.
kerven o. w. carve, notch, slash; (v. tabak) cut.
ketel m. (in keuken) kettle; (was—brouw—) cauldron, copper; (v. stoom-machine) boiler.
ketelbikker m. scaler.
keteldal o. basin valley, circus, cirque.
ketellapper m. tinker.
ketelmuziek v. rough music, tin-kettl-ing.
keten v. chain; (fig.) bond, chain.

ketenen *o. w.* chain, enchain, shackle.
ketsen *on. w.* (*v. geweer*) miss fire, misfire, give a miss; (*bilj.*) miscue; *o. w.* (*v. voorstel, enz.*) reject, defeat; (*v. plan*) turn down.
ketter *m.* heretic.
ketterij *v.* heresy.
ketting *m.* chain; (*wererij*) warp, chain.
kettingbreuk *v.* continued fraction.
kettingbrug *v.* chain-bridge, suspension-bridge.
kettingganger *m.* chained convict.
kettingkast *v.* gear-case, chain-cover.
kettingregel *m.* chain-rule, compound rule of three.
kettingschakel *v.* link.
kettingsteek *m.* chain-stitch, lock-stitch.
kettingzijde *v.* organzine, thrown silk.
keuken *v.* kitchen.
keukenafval *o.* kitchen-waste.
keukengereedschap *o.*, **keukengerei** *o.* kitchen-utensils.
keukenkast *v.* kitchen-cupboard, kitchen-cabinet.
keukenmeid *v.* cook; kitchen-maid.
keukenpiet *m.* kitchen-hunter, cotquean.
Keulen *o.* Cologne.
Keuls *b. n.* Cologne.
keur *v.* (keuze) choice; selection; (*het puik*) flower, pick; (*merk*) hall-mark; (*gesch.: handvest*) charter; (*stedelijke verordening*) regulation, by-law.
keurder *m.* examiner; essayer.
keuren *o. w.* (*alg.*) examine, judge, test; (*v. goud, zilver*) assay; (*v. eetwaren*) inspect; (*v. wijn, enz. : proeven*) taste; (*geneeskundig*) examine.
keurig *b. n.* exquisite, choice, trim, nice; *bw.* exquisitely, nicely.
keurigheid *v.* choiceness, trimness, exquisiteness, nicety.
keuring *v.* (*v. monsters, geneeskundig, enz.*) examination; (*v. metalen*) assay; (*v. eetwaren*) inspection; tasting; testing.
keurkorps *o.* picked body, crack regiment.
keurprins *m.* electoral prince.
keurs *v.*, **keurslijf** *o.* bodys, stays; (*fig.*) shackles, trammels.
keurtroepen *m. mv.* picked men.
keus *v.* choice, selection; **naar uw —,** at your option.
keuterboer *m.* small farmer, crofter, cottier.
keuvelen *on. w.* chat; (*v. kind*) prattle.
kever *m.* beetle, chafer.
kibbelen *on. w.* bicker, wrangle, squabble.
kibbelpartij *v.* squabble.
kiek *v.* snapshot, view.
kieken *o. w.* snapshot, take a view (a snapshot) of.
kieken *o.* chicken.
kiekendief *m.* (*Dk.*) kite.
kiel *m.* blouse, smock(-frock).
kiel *v.* (*sch.*) keel.
kielgang *m.* garboard strake.

kielwater *o.* wake, dead water.
kiem *v.* germ; (*fig.*) germ, seed.
kiemdodend *b. n.* germicidal.
kiemen *on. w.* germinate, shoot; (*fig.*) germ, germinate.
kieming *v.* germination.
kiemkracht *v.* germinative power.
kiemvrij *b. n.* germ-free, sterile.
kier *m.* chink, jar; **op een —,** ajar.
kies *v.* double-tooth, molar-tooth, grinder.
kies *o.* (*mineraal*) pyrites.
kies *b. n.* delicate, considerate.
kiesbaar *b. n.* eligible.
kiesbevoegdheid *v.* right to vote.
kiesdistrict *o.* constituency, borough.
kieskauwen *on. w.* eat reluctantly, nibble at one's food.
kiespijn *v.* toothache.
kiesplicht *m.* compulsory suffrage.
kiesvereniging *v.* electoral association.
kieswet *v.* electoral law, ballot act.
kietelen *o. w. en on. w.* tickle.
kieuw *v.* gill.
kievit *m.* lapwing, pewit; (*fam.*) plover.
kiezel *o.* gravel; (*scheik.*) silicon.
kiezelaarde *v.* siliceous earth.
kiezelzand *o.* gravel.
kiezen *o. w.* choose, select; (*tot voorzitter, enz.*) elect; *on. w.* choose; (*stemmen*) vote.
kiezer *m.* constituent, voter, elector.
kiezerslijst *v.* list of voters, electoral register, electoral roll.
kijf *v.* **buiten —,** beyond dispute, beyond controversy, indisputably.
kijk *m.* look, aspect.
kijken *on. w.* look.
kijker *m.* (*persoon*) looker-on, spectator; (*optisch instrument*) spy-glass, telescope; (*toneel—*) opera-glass.
kijven *on. w.* quarrel, wrangle.
kik *m.* **hij gaf geen —,** he did not utter a sound, he did not raise a squeak.
kikvors *m.* frog.
kil *v.* channel.
kil *b. n.* chilly, frigid, shivery.
killig *b. n.* chilly, shivery.
kilo *o.*, **kilogram** *o.* kilogramme.
kilometervreter *m.* road-hog, milestone monger, mile-hunter, speeder.
kim *v.* (*gezichtseinder*) horizon; (*v. vat*) chimb, chime; (*v. schip*) bilge.
kin *v.* chin.
kinawijn *m.* quinine wine.
kind *o.* child; baby, babe, infant.
kinderachtig *b. n.* childish, puerile, silly.
kinderachtigheid *v.* childishness, puerility, silliness.
kinderarts *m.* children's specialist.
kindergoed *o.* baby-clothes, baby-linen, child's clothes.
kinderjaren *o. mv.* (years of) childhood, infancy.
kinderjuffrouw *v.* nursery-governess.
kinderliefde *v.* (*v. ouders voor kin-*

deren) love of one's children; *(r. kin-deren voor ouders)* filial love.
kinderlijk *b. n.* childly, childlike, childish; *(v. zoon, dochter)* filial.
kinderloos *b. n.* childless, without family.
kindermeel *o.* infants' food.
kindermeid *v.*, **kindermeisje** *o.*, nurse-maid, nurse-girl.
kindermoord *m.* infanticide, child-murder.
kinderpokken *r. mr.* smallpox.
kinderpraat *m.* childish prattle, childish talk; *(fig.)* childish talk.
kindersprookje *o.* nursery tale.
kindersterfte *v.* infant mortality.
kindertaal *v.* child's language.
kindertuin *m.* child's (children's) garden.
kinderverlamming *v.* infantile paralysis.
kinderwagen *m.* baby-car, baby-carriage, perambulator.
kinderziekte *v.* children's complaint, infant disease.
kinds *b. n.* doting, in one's second childhood.
kindsheid *r.* dotage, second childhood; childhood.
kinine *v.* quinine.
kinkel *m.* lout, boor; clown.
kinketting *m.* curb-chain.
kinkhoest *m.* hooping-cough.
kinnebak *v.* mandible, jaw-bone.
kip *v.* hen, fowl, chicken; *(op tafel)* chicken.
kipkar *v.* tip-cart, dumping-cart.
kippeborst *v.* pigeon-breast.
kippenhok *o.* hen-house, chicken-house, poultry-house.
kippevel *o.* hen-skin; *(fig.)* goose-flesh.
kippig *b. n.* short-sighted, near-sighted, beetle-eyed.
kirren *on. w.* coo.
kiskassen *on. w.* make ducks and drakes.
kist *v.* case; *(voor thee, enz.)* chest; *(voor sigaren, enz.)* box; *(grote koffer)* trunk; *(doodkist)* coffin; *(sl.: vliegtuig)* bus.
kisten *o. w. (v. lijk)* coffin; *(v. dijk)* strengthen by means of a coffer-dam; *(in kisten verpakken)* pack in cases.
kisting *v.* coffer-dam.
kit *v. (kan)* jug; *(voor kolen)* coalhod, (stove-)filler; *(opiumkit)* (opium-)den; *(kleefmiddel)* lute.
kittelachtig *b. n.* ticklish.
kittelen *o. w. en on. w.* tickle, titillate.
kittelorig *b. n.* touchy, ticklish, thinskinned.
kittelorigheid *v.* touchiness, ticklishness, thin-skinnedness.
klaaglied *o.* mourning-song, elegy, dirge, threnody; (song of) lamentation.
klaagmuur *m.* Wailing-Wall.
klaagster *v.* complainter, lamenter.
klaar *b. n. (helder)* clear, limpid; *(dui-*

delijk) clear, evident, manifest; *(gereed)* ready; *(af)* finished.
klaarblijkelijk *b. n. (bw.)* clear(ly), evident(ly), obvious(ly), manifest(ly).
klaarblijkelijkheid *v.* clearness, evidence, obviousness.
klaarheid *r.* clearness, clarity, limpidity.
klaarkomen *o. w.* get ready; get done.
klaarleggen *o. w.* put ready, put in readiness; *(v. kleren, enz.)* lay out.
klaarlicht *b. n.* **op —e dag,** in broad daylight; **het is —e dag,** it is bright day.
klaarmaken *o. w.* get ready, prepare; *(r. middagmaal)* cook; *(v. sla)* dress; *(v. drank)* mix, prepare; *(v. recept)* make up, dispense; *w. w. zich —,* get ready.
klaarspelen *o. w.* **het —,** manage it, pull it off, work it.
klaarziend *b. n.* clear-sighted, shrewd.
klacht *v.* complaint; *(recht)* plaint; *(jammer—)* lamentation; **een — indienen,** send in a complaint.
klad *r. (vlek)* stain, smudge, blot, blotch, spot; *(ontwerp, schets)* rough draught.
kladboek *o.* *(H.)* waste-book.
kladden *on. w.* stain, blot; *(v. papier)* blot; *(krabbelen)* scribble, scrawl; *(fig.)* daub, smear; *(H.)* undersell, undercut, sell under the value.
kladpapier *o.* scribbling-paper, scribble-paper; *(vloeipapier)* blotting-paper.
kladschilder *m.* dauber, flinger of paint.
kladschrift *o.* *(knoeierig schrift)* shoddy hand-writing; *(schrijfboek v. h. klad)* rough-copy book.
klagen *on. w.* complain, make complaint; *(weeklagen)* lament; *o. w.* **iem. zijn nood —,** tell one's cause of trouble to a person.
klager *m.* complainer; *(recht)* plaintiff.
klak *v. (klap, slag)* smack, crack, slap; *(vlak, spat)* blot, smudge; *(Z. N.: pet)* cap.
klakkeloos *b. n.* groundless; *bw. (plotseling, onverhoeds)* suddenly; *(onredelijk)* without rhyme or reason, without any motive.
klam *b. n.* moist, damp, clammy.
klandizie *v.* custom, customers, clientele; *(als deel van de activa)* goodwill.
klank *m.* sound, ring.
klankbodem *m.* sound-board.
klankbord *o.* sound-board, sounding-board.
klankfilm *v. en o.* sound-film.
klankleer *v.* phonetics.
klankloos *b. n.* toneless.
klanknabootsing *v.* onomatopoeia.
klankrijkheid *v.* sonority, sonorousness.
klankverschuiving *v.* sound-shifting, shifting of sound; permutation of consonants.
klant *m.* customer, client.
klap *m.* smack, slap, blow, clap; *(met*

zweep) lash, stroke; (*Z. N.: gepraat, gesnap*) gossip, tittle-tattle.
klapbes *v.* gooseberry.
klapdeur *v.* swing-door.
klapekster *v.* grey shrike; (*fig.*) gossip.
klaplopen *on. w.* sponge, cadge.
klaploper *m.* sponger, cadger, parasite; (*sch.*) (double-)whip.
klappei *v.* gossip.
klappen *on. w.* clap, smack; (*oververtellen*) tell tales, blab.
klapper *m.* (*klikker*) tell-tale, informer; (*babbelaar*) prattler, tattler; (*register, op boek, enz.*) index, register; (*v. vuurwerk*) cracker, squib; (*v. molen*) clap, clapper, clacker; (*Pl.*) cocoa-nut.
klapperen *on. w.* rattle; (*v. tanden*) chatter; (*v. deur, zeil, enz.*) flap.
klappernoot *v.* coco(a)-nut.
klappertanden *on. w.* **hij klappertandt,** his teeth chatter.
klaproos *v.* corn-poppy, cock-rose.
klapstoel *m.* folding-chair; (*in schouwburg*) tip-up seat, flap-seat.
klaptafel *v.* leaf-table, folding-table.
klapvlies *o.* valve, valvule.
klapwieken *on. w.* clap (flap) the wings.
klaren *o. w.* (*zuiveren*) clear, purify, clarify, fine; (*v. goederen, schip, anker*) clear; *on. w.* clear, settle; zie ook **opklaren.**
klaroen *v.* clarion.
klasse *v.* (*alg.*) class; (*school*) class, form, standard; (*klaslokaal*) class-room; (*v. schepen*) rate, class.
klassebewustzijn *o.* class-consciousness.
klassenhaat *m.* class-hatred.
klassiek *b. n.* classic, classical; **de —en,** the classics; *bw.* classically.
klateren *on. w.* (*v. donder, metaal*) rattle; (*v. water*) splash.
klatergoud *o.* tinsel, brassfoil, leaf-brass; (*fig.*) tinsel.
klauteren *on. w.* clamber, climb.
klauw *m.* (*v. dier; ong.: v. mens*) paw; (*v. roofdier*) claw; (*v. roofvogel*) talon, claw; (*v. anker*) fluke; (*gereedschap*) weeding-hook, rake; (*v. auto; fig.*) clutch.
klauwen *on. w.* claw.
klauwzeer *o.* blackleg, blackquarter.
klaver *o.* clover, trefoil, shamrock.
klaverblad *o.* clover-leaf, trefoil-leaf; (*fig.*) trio.
klaveren *v. mv.* clubs.
klavier *o.* piano; (*toetsenbord*) keyboard.
kleden *o. w.* dress; clothe; *w. w.* **zich —, dress.
klederdracht *v.* costume, dress.
kleding *v.* clothes, clothing, dressing, vesture; (*dicht.*) raiment, attire, apparel.
kleed *o.* garment, garb, dress; (*vloer—*) (floor-)carpet; (*tafel—*) table-cover.
kleedje *o.* (*vloer—*) carpet, rug; (*tafel—*) table-centre; (*Z. N.: jurkje*) frock.
kleedkamer *v.* dressing-room; (*voor publiek in schouwburg*) cloak-room.

kleefdeeg *o.* lute.
kleefmiddel *o.* agglutinant.
kleefpleister *v.* sticking-plaster, adhesive plaster.
kleerkast *v.* clothes-press, wardrobe, clothes-cupboard.
kleermaker *m.* tailor.
kleerwinkel *m.* outfitter's shop.
kleiaarde *v.* clay-soil, clay-ground.
klein *b. n.* little, small; (*gering*) slight; (*v. gestalte*) short, undersized.
Klein Azië. *o.* Asia Minor, Lesser Asia.
kleindochter *v.* grand-daughter.
Klein duimpje *o.* Tom Thumb.
kleineren *o. w.* belittle, disparage.
kleingeestig *b. n.* narrow-minded, small-minded.
kleingoed *o.* (*kinderen*) small fry, youngsters; (*koekjes*) all sorts; (*andere artikelen*) runts.
kleinhandelaar *m.* retail dealer.
kleinheid *v.* smallness, littleness.
kleinigheid *v.* trifle, small thing; **dat is voor mij een —,** I make nothing of that.
kleinkind *o.* grandchild.
kleinkrijgen *o. w.* **iem. —,** subdue (break in) a person, bring a person to his knees.
kleinsteedsheid *v.* provincial manners, parochialism.
kleintje *o.* little one, baby; **de —s,** (*fam.*) the small fry.
kleinzerig *b. n.* touchy, easily touched, over-sensitive.
kleinzerigheid *v.* touchiness, over-sensitiveness.
kleinzoon *m.* grandson.
klem *v.* (*val*) catch, (man-)trap; (*tn.*) bench-clamp; (*ziekte: kramp*) lock-jaw, tetanus; (*v. paard*) stag-evil; (*el.*) terminal; (*nadruk*) stress, accent, emphasis; (*moeilijkheid, verlegenheid*) scrape, fix.
klemmen *o. w.* (*vinger, voet*) pinch, jam; (*tanden*) clench; (*in de armen*) clasp; *on. w.* (*v. deur*) stick, jam.
klemmend *b. n.* conclusive, cogent, forcible.
klemschroef *v.* clamping-screw; (*el.*) terminal (screw).
klemtoon *m.* stress, accent.
klep *v.* (*tn.*) valve, stopper; (*v. zak, tafel, enz.*) flap; (*v. pet*) peak; (*v. vizier*) leaf; (*v. blaasinstrument*) key; (*v. kachel*) damper; (*v. molen*) clap, clapper; (*v. pomp*) sucker.
klepel *m.* (*v. bel*) clapper; (*v. ooievaar*) bill.
kleppen *on. w.* (*v. klok*) toll; clack, clap.
klepper *m.* (*nachtwacht*) watchman; (*paard*) steed; **—s,** castanets, (rattle-)-bones.
klepperen *on. w.* clapper, rattle; (*v. ooievaar*) clatter.
klerenhanger *m.* clothes hanger, hat-and-coat rack, coat-hanger.
klerk *m.* clerk.

klets v. (slag, klap) smack, clash, slap; (dwaas gebabbel) twaddle, talkee-talkee, slosh, (tommy-)rot.
klets! tw. smack! flap! bang!
kletsen on. w. (met zweep) crack; (v. regen) splash; (babbelen; bazelen) chatter; talk nonsense, talk rot.
kletskop m. env. scald head, moist tetter.
kletskous v. chatterbox, chatter-pie.
kletsnat b. n. soaking wet, sopping wet, soaked to the skin. [tattle.
kletspraat (je) m. (o.) small talk, gossip,
kletteren on. w. (v. regen, hagel) clatter, patter; (v. wapens) clash, clang.
kleur v. (alg.) colour; (tint) hue; (v. gelaat) complexion; (kaartsp.) suit; (wap.) tincture, enamel; (fig.) colour, colouring, complexion; (muz.) colour, timbre.
kleuren o. w. colour, paint; (fot.) tone; on. w. (blozen) colour, blush; (kaartsp.) (play at) commerce.
kleurenblindheid v. colour-blindness, daltonism.
kleurendruk m. chromolithography, colour-printing; in —, in colours, printed in colour.
kleurenpracht v. colorific splendour, orgy (feast) of colour(s).
kleurig b. n. many-coloured, bright-coloured, colourful.
kleurling m. coloured man, man of colour.
kleurloos b. n. colourless, achromatic; (fig.) drab, colourless.
kleurmiddel o. colorant, pigment.
kleurpotlood o. coloured-chalk, colour-chalk.
kleurschakering v. colour-variation, shade, nuance, tinge.
kleurstof v. colouring matter, pigment.
kleuter m. tot, toddler, kid.
kleven on. w. cleave, adhere, stick, cling.
kleverig b. n. adhesive, sticky, viscous, gluey.
kleverigheid v. stickiness, viscosity.
kliek v. clique, coterie, junto.
klier v. gland.
kliergezwel o. scrofulous tumour, struma.
klierziekte v. scorfulous disease, scrofula.
klieven o. w. cleave.
klik m. (sch.) afterpiece (backpiece) of the rudder; (v. uurwerk) warning, clack; (met tong) click.
klikken on. w. tell tales, tell; (sl.) peach; o. w. tell.
klikker m. tell-tale, tale-bearer; (sl.) peach, sneak.
klikspaan m. zie **klikker.**
klimaat o. climate; **aan het — gewennen,** acclimate, acclimatize.
klimboon v. runner bean.
klimmen on. w. climb, mount, ascend.
klimmend b. n. climbing; (Pl.) scandent; (wap.) rampant; saltant; salient.

klimmer m. climber.
klimop o. en m. ivy.
klimpartij v. scramble.
klimtouw o. climbing-rope.
klimvogel m. climber.
klingelen on. w. jingle, tinkle.
kliniek v. clinic.
klink v. (v. deur) latch, catch, click; (v. kous) clock.
klinkdicht o. sonnet.
klinken on. w. (een klank geven) sound, ring, clink; (hard metaalachtig) clang; (aanstoten) clink glasses, touch glasses; o. w. rivet, clinch.
klinker m. (letter) vowel; (tn.) riveter, (steen) brick, clinker.
klinkerbestrating v. brick-pavement, clinker-pavement.
klinkhamer m. riveting-hammer.
klinknagel m. rivet, riveting-nail; clinch.
klip v. rock, crag, reef, cliff; (fig.) rock, snag.
klipgeit v. chamois.
klipper m. (sch.) clipper.
klipzout o. rock-salt.
klipzwaluw v. edible nest swift.
klis v. (Pl.) bur; (v. haar, enz.) tangle.
klodder v. clot, blob, blotch, dab.
kloek b. n. brave, stout, bold, strong.
kloek v. zie **klokhen.**
klok v. (uurwerk) clock; (bel) bell; (stolp) bell-glass, bell-jar; (v. luchtpomp) receiver, vacuum chamber.
klokhen v. clucker, clucking-hen, mother-hen.
klokhuis o. core.
klokje o. small clock, little clock; (Pl.) bell-flower, harebell, blue-bell, Canterbury bell; (v. luchtpomp) receiver.
klokken on. w. cluck, chuckle, glug.
klokkenist m. chimer, chime-player.
klokkenspel o. chimes, carillon.
klokslag m. stroke of the clock.
klokspijs v. bell-metal.
klokzeel o. bell-rope.
klomp m. (kluit, klont) lump; (holsblok) clog, wooden shoe.
klompenmaker m. clog-maker.
klompvoet m. club-foot.
klont v. clod; lump.
klonteren on. w. clot, curdle.
kloof v. cleft, chasm, crevice, fissure, rift, gap; (in huid) chap; (fig.) gap, rift, gulf.
klooster o. (alg.) cloister; (voor mannen) monastery; (voor vrouwen) convent, nunnery.
kloosterbroeder m. friar; (lekebroeder) lay-brother.
kloostercel v. monastery cell, convent cell.
kloostergang v. cloister, ambulatory.
kloostergelofte v. monastic vow; **de —n afleggen,** take the vows.
kloosterlatijn o. monk's Latin.
kloosterleven o. monastic life, convent life, cloister-life.

kloosterling *m.* monk; (*non*) nun.
kloosterzuster *v.* nun.
klop *m.* knock, tap, rap; (*v. hart*) throb — **krijgen**, be drubbed, get a drubbing, be licked, be beaten.
klopjacht *v.* battue.
kloppartij *v.* scrap, scuffle, tussle.
kloppen *on. w.* (*op deur, enz.*) knock, tap, rap; (*op schouder*) tap; (*v. hart*) beat; (*hevig*) throb, palpitate; *o. w.* (*v. tapijt*) beat; (*v. stenen, kolen*) break; (*v. eieren*) beat up, whip (up).
klopper *m.* (*deur—*) knocker; (*telegr.*) sounder; (*bij jacht*) beater.
klos *m.* bobbin, spool, reel, spindle; (*el.*) coil.
klotsen *on. w.* (*v. golven*) dash; (*bilj.*) counter.
kloven *o. w.* cleave, split, chop.
klucht *v.* farce; farcical comedy.
kluchtig *b. n.* comical, farcical, droll, funny, odd.
kluif *v.* chunk, bone (to pick), knuckle of pork.
kluis *v.* (*v. kluizenaar*) hermitage; (*v. bank*) strong-room, safe-deposit; (*sch.*) hawse-hole.
kluister *v.* fetter, shackle **—s**, (*fig.*) shackles, trammels. [mel.
kluisteren *o. w.* fetter, shackle tram-
kluit *m.* (*Dk.*) avocet.
kluit *v.* clod, lump.
kluitenbreker *m.* clod-crusher.
kluiven *o. w. en on. w.* pick; gnaw, nibble, mumble.
kluiver *m.* picker; gnawer; (*sch.: fok*) (middle-)jib.
kluizenaar *m.* hermit, recluse, anchoret.
kluts *v.* clutch.
klutsen *o. w.* beat up, whip.
kluwen *o.* clew; ball.
knaagdier *o.* rodent, gnawer.
knaap *m.* (*jongen*) boy, lad, fellow; (*klerenstander*) coat-hanger; (*dommekracht*) jack.
knabbelen *o. w. en on. w.* nibble, gnaw, munch.
knagen *on. w.* gnaw; (*v. geweten*) prick.
knaging *v.* gnawing.
knak *m.* crack, snap; (*fig.*) blow, injury.
knakken *o. w.* (*v. stengel, enz.*) break; crack; (*v. gezondheid*) injure, shake, impair; break; *on. w.* (*v. bloem*) snap; (*v. vingers*) crack.
knakworst *v.* small German sausage, ham sausage.
knal *m.* (*v. kanon*) report; (*v. donder*) peal; (*v. kurk*) pop; (*ontploffing*) detonation, explosion.
knalgas *o.* detonating gas, fulminating gas, oxyhydrogen.
knallen *o. w.* (*v. geweer, zweep*) crack; (*v. kanon*) bang; (*v. kurk*) pop; (*v. goud, kwik, enz.*) fulminate.
knalpot *m.* dash-pot, silencer.
knap *m.* crack, snap.
knap *b. n.* (*v. uiterlijk: mooi, welgevormd*) handsome, good-looking, comely

(*v. verstand: bekwaam*) clever, able, capable (*fatsoenlijk*) decent, respectable (*net, keurig*) spruce, smart; (*krap*) tight; *bw.* cleverly, ably, etc.
knapheid *v.* good looks; cleverness, ability, skill, skilfulness.
knapkoek *m.* crisp cake, snap.
knappen *on. w.* crack; (*v. vuur*) crackle; (*v. touw, enz.*) snap; **doen —**, crack; *o. w.* crack.
knapzak *m.* knapsack, haversack, wallet.
knarsen *on. w.* creak, grate, gnash, grind.
knarsetanden *on. w.* gnash (grind, grit) one's teeth.
knauwen *o. w. en on. w.* gnaw, munch.
knecht *m.* servant; (*huis—*) footman.
knechten *o. w.* enslave.
kneden *o. w.* knead; (*fig.*) mould, fashion, knead.
kneedbaar *b. n.* kneadable; (*fig.*) mouldable, plastic.
kneep *v.* pinch; mark of a pinch; (*fig.*) dodge, trick, wrinkle, catch.
knel *v. in de — zitten*, be in a cleft stick, be in a fix, be in a scrape.
knellen *o. w.* pinch, squeeze; (*fig.*) oppress; *on. w.* pinch, press.
knetteren *on. w.* crackle, crepitate, sputter; (*v. radio*) crackle; (*v. donder*) crash.
kneukel *m.* knuckle.
kneuzen *o. w.* bruise; (*gen.*) contuse; *w. w.* **zich —**, be bruised, get bruised, get contused.
kneuzing *v.* bruise; (*gen.*) contusion.
knevel *m.* (*v. man*) moustache; (*v. dier*) whiskers; (*mondprang*) gag; (*handboei*) handcuff; (*sch.*) toggle.
knevelarij *v.* extortion.
knevelen *o. w.* (*met koord*) pinion, tie, truss up; (*met prop*) gag; (*fig.*) (*onderdrukken*) oppress; (*afpersen*) extortion, extortionate, extort money from.
knibbelen *on. w.* higgle, haggle; play at spillikins.
knie *v.* knee.
knieband *m.* knee-string; (*v. vee*) knee-halter.
kniebroek *v.* knickerbockers, knee-breeches, smalls.
kniebuiging *v.* genuflexion; (*gymn.*) knee-crooking. [stool.
knielbank *v.* kneeling-stool, praying-
knielen *on. w.* kneel; bend the knee, go down on one's knee(s).
knieschijf *v.* knee-cap; (*wet.*) patella.
knieval *m.* prostation.
kniezen *on. w.* mope, fret.
knijpbril *m.* folders, pince-nez.
knijpen *o. w.* pinch; (*fig.*) squeeze; *on. w.* pinch; (*sch.*) hug the wind, keep close to the wind.
knijper *m.* (*persoon*) pincher, pinchpenny; (*voorwerp*) clip, fastener; (*v. kreeft*) pincer.
knijptang *v.* (*groot*) pincers; (*klein*) nippers.

knikkebenen *on. w.* give at the knees.
knikkebollen *on. w.* niddle-noddle.
knikken *on. w.* nod.
knikker *m.* marble; *(grote* —) taw; *(albasten* —) ally; *(fig.)* pate, head.
knikkeren *on. w.* play at marbles.
knip *m. (met wijsvinger en duim)* fillip; *v. (insnijding: met schaar)* cut, snip; *(v. deur)* catch, spring-bolt; *(v. raam)* catch, sash-fastener; *(v. beurs)* snap; *(v. armband)* spring-catch, snap; *(vogelknip)* trap, spring, snare.
knipmes *o.* clasp-knife; *(groot* —) jack-knife.
knipogen *on. w.* wink, blink (one's eyes).
knippen *o. w. (v. haar)* cut; *(v. kleed)* cut out; *(v. kaartjes)* clip, punch; *(v. coupons)* clip; *(v. nagels)* cut, trim, pare; *(v. dief, enz.: vangen)* trap; *(sl.)* pinch, nab; *on. w. (met vingers)* fillip, snap (one's fingers); *(v. oogleden)* flicker; *(v. ogen)* blink.
kniptang *v.* nippers.
kniptor *v.* snap(ping)-beetle, click-beetle.
knobbel *m.* bump, knob, knot; nodosity, protuberance; *(ziekteknobbel)* tubercle.
knobbelziekte *v.* rickets.
knoeien *on. w. (morsen)* mess, make a mess; *(fig.)* boggle, bungle, blunder.
knoeier *m.* boggler, bungler, blunderer; dabbler, botcher; swindler, cheat.
knoeierij *v.* mess, messing, bungle, bungling; *(fig.)* jobbery; *(geldelijk)* malversation(s).
knoeiwerk *o.* bungling work, bungle, botchery, patch-work, scamped work.
knoest *m.* knot, knag, gnarl.
knoestig *b. n.* knotty, knaggy, gnarly, gnarled.
knoflook *o.* garlic.
knokig *b. n.* bony, knuckly.
knol *m. (raap)* turnip; *(v. aardappel, enz.)* tuber; *(paard)* jade, hack, screw.
knolgewas *o.* tuberous plant. [celery.
knolselderij *v.* celeriac, (turnip-rooted)
knoop *m. (aan kleren, enz.)* button; *(sch.: in touw)* knot; *(Pl.)* node, joint; *(sterr.)* node; *(vloek)* expletive, oath.
knoopsgat *o.* button-hole.
knop *m.* knob; *(v. stok)* head, knob, top; *(v. degen, zadel)* pommel; *(v. el. bel)* button, push; *(v. el. licht)* (light-)switch; *(v. deur)* knob, handle; *(v. plant)* bud, gemma.
knopen *o. w.* tie, knot; button; *(v. beurs)* net; *(v. visnet)* make.
knorhaan *m.* gurnet, gurnard.
knorren *on. w. (v. varken)* grunt; *(fig.: brommen)* grumble, growl.
knorrepot *m.* grumbler, growler, grouser.
knorrig *b. n.* grumbling, growling, grumpy, peevish, testy.
knots *v.* club, cudgel, bludgeon; *(gymn.)* Indian club.
knotten *o. w. (v. boom)* head, top; *(v. wilg)* pollard, poll; *(v. kegel)* truncate; *(fig.)* clip, curtail, cut down.

knotwilg *m.* pollard-willow.
knuist *m.* fist, paw.
knul *m. (lomperd)* lout; *(lummel)* dolt, duffer, booby, mug.
knuppel *m.* club, cudgel, bludgeon; *(v. vliegtuig)* (joy-)stick; *(fig.: lomperd)* lout.
knusjes *bw.* snugly.
knutselaar *m.* trifler, niggler, potterer.
knutselen *on. w.* do some trifling (piffling) work, niggle, potter.
koddig *b. n.* droll, comical, odd.
koe *v.* cow.
koedrijver *m.* cow-driver, (cattle-) drover.
koek *m.* gingerbread; *(gebak)* cake.
koekbakkerij *v.* confectionner's shop.
koekdeeg *o.* gingerbread paste.
koekeloeren *on. w.* peer, look absently.
koekoek *m. (Dk.)* cuckoo; *(dakvenster, bovenlicht)* attic-window, sky-light.
koekoeksbloem *v.* ragged robin; red campion; bachelor's buttons.
koel *b. n.* cool; cool, cold; *bw.* coolly.
koelbak *m.* cooler.
koelbloedig *b. n.* cold, indifferent, cold-blooded; *bw.* in cold blood, cold-bloodedly.
koelbloedigheid *v.* cold-bloodedness.
koelen *o. w.* cool; *(in ijs)* ice, cool; *on. w.* cool (down); *(v. wind)* freshen up.
koelheid *v.* coolness; *(fig.)* coldness, coolness.
koelkelder *m.* cooling-cellar, refrigerating-cellar.
koelte *v.* coolness.
koeltjes *bw.* coolly, coldly.
koen *b. n.* bold, daring, hardy.
koenheid *v.* boldness, daringness, hardihood, hardiness.
koepel *m. (bouwk.)* dome, cupola; *(tuinhuisje)* summer-house.
koepeldak *o.* dome-shaped roof.
koepelgewelf *o.* dome(-shaped vault).
koepokinenting *v.* vaccination.
koepokstof *v.* vaccine(lymph), vaccine matter, calf-lymph.
koers *m. (sch.)* direction, course; *(H.: v. geld)* rate (of exchange); *(v. effecten)* (market-)quotation, price; *(fig.)* course, tack, line of action.
koersdaling *v.* fall in prices; depreciation of currency values.
koersen *on. w.* shape (steer) one's course.
koershoudend *b. n.* steady, firm.
koersinzakking *v.* collapse of prices.
koersschommeling *v.* fluctuation.
koersverbetering *v.*, **koersverhoging** *v.* rise in the exchange, advance, improvement (in prices).
koersverschil *o.* difference in price.
koest *b. n.* quiet; **zich — houden,** keep mum, keep quiet, lie low.
koestal *m.* cow-house, cow-shed, byre.
koesteren *o. w.* cherish; *(v. gevoelens, enz.)* entertain; *w. w.* **zich —,** bask.
koeterwaals *o.* gibberish, double Dutch, jargon.

koets *v.* coach, carriage.
koetshuis *o.* coach-house.
koetsier *m.* coachman; driver.
koevoet *m.* crow-bar.
koffer *m.* box, trunk; (*voor geld*) coffer; (*hand—*) bag, handbag.
koffie *v.* coffee; *— zetten*, make coffee; *— drinken,* take coffee; (*lunchen*) lunch.
koffieboon *v.* coffee-bean, coffee-nib.
koffiebranderij *v.* coffee-roasting factory.
koffiedik *o.* coffee-grounds.
koffiemolen *m.* coffee-mill, coffee-grinder.
koffiepot *m.* coffee-pot.
koffietafel *v.* **aan de —,** at lunch.
kogel *m.* (*v. geweer*) bullet; (*v. kanon*) ball.
kogelas *v.* ball-bearing.
kogelbaan *v.* trajectory.
kogelgewricht *o.* ball-and-socket joint.
kogellager *o.* ball-bearing.
kogelstoten *on. w.* (*sp.*) put the shot; *z. n., o.* shot-put(ting).
kogelvanger *m.* (*mil.*) practise-butt, stop-butt, bullet-catcher.
kogelvrij *b. n.* bullet-proof, shot-proof.
kohier *o.* assessment list, valuation list.
kok *m.* cook.
koken *o. w.* (*v. water*) boil; (*v. spijzen*) cook; *on. w.* boil; (*de spijzen bereiden*) do the cooking; (*v. zee; fig.*) seethe, boil.
koker *m.* boiler, cooker.
koker *m.* case, sheath, tube; (*voor pijlen*) quiver.
kokhalzen *on. w.* retch, keck, heave (the gorge).
kokosmat *v.* coco-mat.
kokosnoot *v.* coco-nut.
kokosolie *v.* coco-nut oil.
kokospalm *m.* coco(-nut) palm.
kokosvet *o.* (hard) coco-oil.
koksmaat *m.* cook's mate.
kolder *m.* (*gesch.*) jerkin; (*paardeziekte*) (blind) staggers.
kolen *v. mv.* coal, coals.
kolenbekken *o.* coal basin, coal-field.
kolendamp *m.* coal-vapour; (*wet.*) carbonic oxide, carbon monoxide.
kolenemmer *m.* coal-scuttle.
kolengruis *o.* coal-dust.
kolenhok *o.* coal-hole, coal-shed.
kolenmijn *v.* coal-mine, coal-pit, colliery.
kolenruim *o.* coal-hold, bunker.
kolenschop *v.* coal-shovel, coal-scoop.
kolenwagen *m.* coal-truck, coal-wagon; (*v. locomotief*) tender.
kolf *v.* bat, club; (*v. kolfspel*) kolf-stick; (*v. geweer*) butt-end; (*distilleer—*) receiver; (*Pl.*) spadix.
kolffles *v.* retort.
koliek *v.* colic.
koliekpijn *v.* gripes, gripings.
kolk *v.* (*put, diepte*) pit, pool; (*afgrond*) abyss, gulf; (*v. sluis*) (lock-)chamber; (*draai—*) eddy, whirl-pool.
kolom *v.* column.

kolonel *m.* colonel.
koloniaal *b. n.* colonial; **koloniale waren,** colonial produce; groceries; *z. n., m.* (*mil.*) colonial soldier.
kolonie *v.* colony, settlement.
kolonist *m.* colonist, settler.
kolossaal *b. n.* colossal, huge, enormous, gigantic; (*prijs*) immense.
kom *v.* basin, bowl.
kombuis *v.* (*sch.*) caboose, cook's galley.
komedie *v.* (*spel, stuk*) comedy, play; (*gebouw*) theatre; (*fig.*) comedy, play-acting.
komediespel *o.* theatrical performance; (*blijspel*) comedy.
komen *on. w.* come.
komfoor *o.* chafing-dish, brazier.
komiek *b. n.* comical, droll, funny; *z. n., m.* low comedian, funny-man, clown.
komkommer *v.* cucumber.
komkommertijd *m.* dull (silly, dead) season.
komma *v.* comma; (*in breuk*) decimal, point.
kommapunt *o.* semicolon.
kommer *m.* affliction, distress, trouble, grief, sorrow.
kommerlijk *b. n.* needy, scanty, indigent, distressed.
kompas *o.* compass.
kompasnaald *v.* needle (of a compass), compass-needle.
kompasroos *v.* compass-card, rhumb-card.
komplot *o.* plot, intrigue, conspiracy.
kompres *z. n., o.* compress, pledget; *b. n.* compact, close; *bw.* **— gedrukt,** closely printed.
komst *v.* coming, arrival.
kondschappen *o. w.* notify, inform (of) send word.
konijn *o.* rabbit, cony; bunny.
konijnehok *o.* rabbit-hutch.
koning *m.* king; (*bij kegelspel*) king-pin.
koningin *v.* queen.
koningsgezindheid *v.* royalism.
koningshuis *o.* royal house.
koningsmoord *m.* regicide.
koninkje *o.* petty king, kinglet, kingling.
koninkrijk *o.* kingdom.
konkelaar *m.* intriguer, plotter, schemer.
konkelen *on. w.* intrigue, plot, scheme, machinate.
konvooi *o.* (*sch.*) convoy.
konvooiloper *m.* (*sch.*) ship-broker, customs broker.
kooi *v.* (*v. vogels, enz.*) cage; (*v. schapen*) fold, pen; (*v. eenden*) (duck-)decoy; (*sch.*) berth, bunk.
kookboek *o.* cookery book.
kookkunst *v.* culinary art, art of cooking, cookery.
kookpan *v.* saucepan; (*v. steen*) casserole.
kool *v.* (*Pl.*) cabbage.
kool *v.* coal; (*houtskool*) charcoal; (*scheik.*) carbon.

koolblad *o.* cabbage-leaf.
koolmees *v.* titmouse, coal-mouse.
kooloxyde *o.* carbonic oxide.
koolraap *v.* Swedish turnip.
koolstof *v.* carbon.
koolwitje *o.* (*vlinder*) cabbage butterfly.
koolzaad *o.* rape-seed, cole-seed, colza.
koolzuur *o.* carbonic acid.
koon *v.* cheek.
koop *m.* bargain, purchase.
koopakte *v.* purchase-deed, deed of purchase, title-deed, deed of sale.
koopdag *m.* day of sale, public sale.
koophandel *m.* commerce, trade.
koopje *o.* bargain, dead bargain.
koopkracht *v.* purchasing power, buying-power.
koopman *m.* merchant; dealer.
koopmansgeest *m.* commercial (mercantile) spirit.
koopvaardij *v.* commercial navigation, mercantile marine, merchant service.
koopvaardijschip *o.* merchantman, trading-ship, trading-vessel.
koopvaardijvlag *v.* merchant flag.
koopwaar *r.* merchandise, commodity.
koopzucht *v.* eagerness to buy.
koor *o.* (*zangers*) choir; (*tegenover solo*) chorus; (*in kerk*) choir, chancel.
koord *o.* cord, string, rope.
koorddanser *m.*, **—es** *r.* rope-dancer, rope-walker.
koorde *r.* (*meetk.*) chord.
koordje *o.* bit (piece) of string.
koorgestoelte *o.* choir stalls.
koorheer *m.* canon, prebendary.
koorhemd *o.* surplice, alb.
koorkap *v.* pluvial.
koorts *r.* fever. [fit.
koortsaanval *m.* attack of fever, fever-
koortsdrank *m.* fever-draught, febrifuge potion.
koortsig *b. n.* feverish, feverous.
koortsuitslag *m.* rash; (*op lip*) fever-spot.
koorzang *m.* choral song, choral singing.
koorzanger *m.* choralist; (*in kerk*) chorister.
koot *v.* (*v. mens*) knuckle-bone; (*v. paard*) pastern.
kop *m.* head; (*r. pijn*) bowl; (*v. golf*) crest; (*r. wolk*) thundercloud; (*voor koffie, thee*) cup; (*v. vliegtuig*) head, nose; (*gen.*) cupping-glass; (*v. dagbladartikel*) headline; (*fig.*) head, headpiece.
kopen *o. w.* buy, purchase.
koper *o.* copper; **geel —**, brass; **rood —**, copper; **geslagen —**, hammered copper.
koper *m.* buyer, purchaser.
koperdraad *o.* brass-wire; copper-wire.
koperdruk *m.* copper-plate; copper-plate printing.
kopergroen *o.* verdigris, acetate of copper.
koperhoudend *b. n.* (*v. bodem*) copper-bearing, cupriferous; (*scheik.*) cupric, cuprous.

koperrood *b. n.* copper-red, cupreous red, copper-coloured; *z. n., o.* copper-as.
koperslager *m.* copper-smith, brazier.
koperwaren *v. mv.*, **koperwerk** *o.* copper-ware, brass-ware.
kopieerinkt *m.* copying-ink.
kopiëren *o. w.* copy; (*akte*) engross (a deed).
kopij *r.* copy.
kopijrecht *o.* copyright.
kopje *o.* head; cup.
koppel *o.* (*paar*) couple; brace; (*stel, menigte*) (*v. patrijzen, enz.*) covey; (*v. vee*) herd.
koppel *m.* (*voor sabel*) belt; (*voor honden*) leash; (*wap.*) fesse.
koppelaar *m.* match-maker, marriage-broker; (*strafbaar*) pander, bawd procurer, pimp.
koppelen *o. w.* (*v. honden*) couple, leash; (*v. wagens, enz.*) couple; (*r. woorden*) join; *on. w.* couple; (*v. huwelijk*) make a match; (*ong.*) pander, procure, pimp; (*sch.*) calculate the traverses.
koppeling *r.* coupling; joining.
koppelkoers *r.* (*sch.*) traverse.
koppelriem *m.* (*mil.*) belt.
koppelstang *v.* (*tn.*) coupling-rod.
koppelteken *o.* (*gram.*) hyphen.
koppelwerkwoord *o.* copula.
koppelwoord *o.* (*gram.*) copulative.
koppensneller *m.* head-hunter.
koppig *b. n.* obstinate, headstrong, stubborn, pig-headed; (*v. drank*) heady.
koppigheid *r.* obstinacy; headiness.
kopstation *o.* terminus, terminal station.
kopstuk *o.* head-piece; (*v. persoon, ook:*) head-johnny.
koptelefoon *r.* headphone, earphone.
koraal *m.* (*muz.*) (*koorzanger, koorknaap*) chorister; choir-boy, singing-boy; *o.* (*zang*) choral song, chorale.
koraal *o.* coral; (*v. kraal*) bead.
koraaldier *o.* coral-polyp.
koraalvisser *m.* coral-fisher, coral-diver.
koralen *b. n.* coral, coralline.
kordaat *b. n.* resolute, bold, stout-hearted, brave, firm.
kordaatheid *v.* resoluteness, boldness, stout-heartedness.
koren *o.* corn, grain.
korenaar *r.* ear of corn.
korenakker *m.* corn-field.
korenbloem *r.* cornflower, bluebottle.
korengarf *v.* sheaf of corn.
korenhalm *m.* corn-stalk.
korenschoof *r.* sheaf of corn.
korenschuur *r.* granary.
korenveld *o.* corn-field.
korenwan *r.* winnow, corn-fan.
korf *m.* basket, hamper; (*bijen—*) hive.
korfbal *m.* basket-ball.
korhaan *m.* woodcock.
korhen *r.*, **korhoen** *o.* grey-hen, wood-hen.

kornet *m. en r.* cornet.
kornis *v.* cornice.
kornuit *m.* comrade, companion, crony.
korporaal *m.* corporal.
korps *o.* corps.
korrel *v.* grain; *(op geweer)* bead.
korrelen *on. w.* grain, granulate.
korrelig *b. n.* granular, grainy.
korreling *v.* granulation, graining.
korrelsuiker *v.* granulated sugar.
korset *o.* corset, (pair of) stays.
korst *v. (alg.; v. brood)* crust; *(v. kaas)* rind; *(op wond)* scab.
kort *b. n.* short, brief; *bw.* shortly, briefly.
kortademig *b. n.* short-breathed, short of breath, short-winded, asthmatic.
kortaf *b. n.* short, curt; *bw.* shortly, curtly.
kortelings *bw.* recently, lately, short time ago.
korten *o. w.* shorten, make short; *(v. vleugels)* clip; *(v. haar)* trim, clip; crop; *(v. loon, enz.)* deduct from; *on. w.* grow short(er); **de dagen —,** the days are drawing in (are shortening).
korting *v. (v. loon, enz.)* deduction, reduction, stoppage; *(H.) (vooraf bedongen)* discount; *(later toegestaan, voor beschadiging, enz.)* allowance; *(op grote partij, rabat)* rebate.
kortom *bw.* in short, in a word, in brief.
Kortrijk *o.* Courtray.
kortschrift *o.* shorthand, stenography.
kortsluiting *v.* short-circuit(ing).
kortstondig *b. n.* of short duration, short-lived, short, brief.
kortweg *bw.* shortly, in short, briefly, summarily.
kortwieken *o. w.* clip the wings of.
kortzicht *o. (H.)* short date; **op —,** at short sight.
kortzichtig *b. n.* near-sighted, short-sighted.
kortzichtigheid *v.* near-sightedness, short-sightedness.
kortzichtwissel *m.* short-bill, short-dated bill.
korvet *v.* corvette.
korzeligheid *v.* crabbedness.
kost *m.* food, victuals, board, fare; *(bestaan, levensonderhoud)* living, livelihood.
kostbaar *b. n. (veel geld kostende, duur)* expensive; costly; *(veel waard)* valuable, precious; *(weelderig)* sumptuous.
kostbaarheid *v.* expensiveness; costliness; sumptuousness; **kostbaarheden,** valuables.
kostelijk *b. n.* costly, exquisite; *(v. weer, enz.)* splendid; *bw.* exquisitely; splendidly.
kosteloos *b. n.* free, gratis, gratuitous; *bw.* gratis, free of charge, gratuitously.
kosten *o. w.* cost; **wat kost dit?** what do you charge for this? what price is this? what is the price?
kosten *m. mv.* cost; *(uitgaven)* expense(s),

outlay; *(recht)* costs; *(wat in rekening gebracht wordt, onkosten)* charges.
koster *m.* sexton, sacristan.
kostganger *m.* boarder.
kosthuis *o.* boarding-house.
kostprijs *m. (H.)* cost-price.
kostschool *v.* boarding-school.
kostuum *o. (v. vrouw)* costume, suit; *(v. man)* suit; *(voor gec. bal)* fancy dress.
kostuumpop *v.* dress-stand, lay figure.
kostwinner *m.* bread-winner.
kostwinning *v.* livelihood.
kot *o. (v. honden)* kennel; *(r. schapen)* cot, pen; *(v. varkens)* sty.
kotter *m.* cutter.
koud *b. n.* cold; frigid.
koude *v.* cold, coldness.
koudegolf *v.* cold wave, arctic wave.
koudvuur *o.* gangrene.
kous *v.* stocking.
kouseband *m.* garter.
kousenhandel *m.* hosier's business.
kousje *o. (lamp—)* wick; *(gloei—)* mantle.
kout *m.* chat, talk.
kouten *on. w.* chat, talk, coze.
kouter *m.* talker, conversationalist.
kouter *o. (v. ploeg)* coulter.
kouwelijk *b. n.* chilly.
kozijn *o.* window-frame.
kozijn *m. (Z. N.: neef)* cousin.
kraag *m.* collar; *(v. bont, enz.)* tippet; *(v. vogel, enz.)* ruff.
kraai *v. (Dk.)* crow; *(sl.: aanspreker)* undertaker's man.
kraaien *on. w. (v. haan)* crow; *(v. kind)* crow, goo-goo; *o. w.* **victorie —,** cry victory, be cock-a-hoop.
kraakamandel *v.* shell-almond, soft-shelled almond.
kraakbeen *o.* cartilage, gristle.
kraakzindelijk *b. n.* very clean, scrupulously (studiously, rigidly) clean.
kraal *v.* coral; *(bouwk.)* bead; *(Z.A.)* kraal.
kraam *v.* booth, stall, stand.
kraambed *o.* childbed.
kraaminrichting *v.* maternity home, lying-in hospital.
kraamvrouw *o.* lying-in woman, woman in childbed.
kraan *v. (v. vat, enz.)* tap, cock; *(hijstuig)* crane, derrick; *m. (vogel)* crane; *(persoon)* dab, nailer.
kraanvogel *m.* crane.
krab *v. (Dk.)* crab(-fish); *(schram)* scratch.
krabbelaar *m.,* **—ster** *v.* scratcher; scrawler.
krabbelen *o. w. en on. w.* scrawl, scribble; **weer overeind —,** scramble up.
krabben *on. w. (met nagels)* scratch; *(v. paard)* paw; *o. w.* scratch, scrape; *w. w.* **zich —,** scratch (oneself).
krabber *m.* scratcher; *(voetschrabber)* scraper.
kracht *v.* force, strength, vigour, power; *(v. wind, enz.)* force, intensity; *(v. ge-*

neesmiddel) efficacy, potency, virtue; **van — zijn,** be in force; **van — worden,** take effect.
krachtdadig *b. n. (bw.)* energetic-(ally), powerful(ly), vigorous(ly); effectual(ly), efficacious(ly).
krachtdadigheid *v.* energy, powerfulness, vigour; efficacy.
krachteloos *b. n. (v. persoon)* powerless, impotent, effete, strengthless; *(v. wet, enz.)* invalid, ineffectual; **— maken,** *(v. bepaling, wet, enz.)* make null and void, invalidate, annul.
krachtens *vz.* in (by) virtue of, on the strength of.
krachtig *b. n. (v. lichaam)* strong, robust; *(v. voedsel, enz.)* strong, forceful, potent; *(v. argumenten)* cogent, forcible; *(v. pogingen)* strenuous; *(v. maatregelen, enz.)* energetic, drastic, strong; *(v. weerstand)* stout; *bw.* strongly, energetically.
krachtinstallatie *v.* (electric) power plant.
krak *z. n., m. en r.; tw.* crack.
Krakau *o.* Cracow.
krakelen *on. w.* quarrel, wrangle.
krakeling *m.* cracknel; *(zoute —)* pretzel.
kraken *on. w.* crack; *(v. nieuwe schoenen, enz.)* creak, squeak; *(v. sneeuw)* crackle; *o. w.* crack.
kram *r.* cramp(-iron), clamp, clasp, stapple.
kramp *v.* cramp, spasm.
kranig *b. n.* brave, clever, bold, smart; *bw.* in dashing style.
kranigheid *v.* cranerie, dash.
krankheid *v.* sickness, illness.
krankzinnig *b. n.* insane, lunatic, crazy, mad.
krankzinnigengesticht *o.* lunatic asylum, mental hospital, madhouse.
krankzinnigheid *v.* insanity, lunacy, craziness, madness.
krans *m.* wreath, garland, crown.
krant *v.* (news)paper.
krantenjongen *m.* news-boy.
krap *v. (meekrap)* madder; *(v. boek)* clasp; *(varkensrib)* spare rib, pork-cutlet.
krap *b. n.* tight, narrow, skimpy; *bw.* **zij hebben het —,** they are in straitened circumstances.
kras *b. n. (v. persoon)* strong, vigorous; *(v. maatregel, enz.)* drastic, strong; *(v. bewering, enz.)* steep, stiff; *bw.* strongly, vigorously.
kras *v.* scratch.
krassen *on. w.* scratch; scrape; *(v. stem)* grate; *(v. raaf)* croak, caw; *(v. uil)* hoot, screech.
krat *o. (v. wagen)* tail-board; *(H.)* crate, skeleton case; luggage-frame.
krater *m.* crater.
kratervormig *b. n.* crater-shaped, craterlike, crateriform.
krediet *o.* credit.

kredietbrief *m.* letter of credit (L/C).
kreeft *m. (zeekreeft)* lobster; *(rivierkreeft)* crawfish, crayfish; *(sterr.)* cancer.
kreeftskeerkring *m.* tropic of cancer.
kreek *v.* creek.
kreet *m.* cry, scream, shriek.
kregeligheid *v.* peevishness; spiritedness, gameness.
krekel *m.* (house-)cricket.
kreng *o.* carrion, carcass; *(fig.)* beast, rotter, pig, blighter.
krenken *o. w.* injure, offend; hurt, wound.
krenking *r.* injury, offence, hurt; *(v. verstand)* derangement.
krent *v.* currant.
krenterigheid *r.* meanness, niggardliness, niggling, cheese-paring.
kreuk, kreukel *r.* crease, wrinkle, rumple, crumple, pucker.
kreuk(el)en *o. w.* crease, wrinkle, rumple, crumple, pucker (up).
kreunen *on. w.* groan, moan.
kreupel *b. n.* lame, cripple; **— lopen,** halt, limp, walk with a limp.
kreupelhout *o.* underwood, undergrowth.
krib(be) *r. (voederbak)* manger, crib; *(slaapstede)* cot, crib; *(dam, waterkering)* etty, groyne.
kribbebijter *m. (paard)* crib-biting horse, crib-biter; *(fig.)* crib-biter.
kribbig *b. n.* peevish, crusty, fractious, testy, querulous, petulant.
kriebelen *on. w.* tickle, itch; *o. w.* tickle; scrawl.
kriek *r.* black cherry.
krieuwelen *o. w. en on. w.* tickle.
krijg *m.* war.
krijgen *o. w.* get; *(bekomen)* receive, obtain; *(verkrijgen)* acquire, obtain; *(v. ziekte, enz.)* catch.
krijger *m.* warrior.
krijgertje *o.* (game of) tag; **— spelen,** play at tag, play at tig. [of arms.
krijgsbedrijf *o.* military exploit, feat
krijgsbeleid *o.* military skill, military talent.
krijgsgevangene *m.* prisoner of war.
krijgshaftig *b. n.* martial, warlike, soldierly.
krijgshaftigheid *v.* martial spirit, martiality, valour, warlike appearance.
krijgsheld *m.* military hero.
krijgskunde *v.,* **krijgskunst** *v.* military science, art of war, strategy.
krijgslist *r.* stratagem, ruse of war.
krijgsmacht *r.* (military) forces.
krijgsmakker *m.* fellow-soldier, brother-officer.
krijgsraad *m.* council of war; *(militaire rechtbank)* court-martial.
krijgstucht *r.* military discipline.
krijgsverrichtingen *r. mv.* military operations.
krijgsvolk *o.* soldiers, soldiery, military.
krijgszuchtig *b. n.* bellicose, warlike.
krijsen *o. w. en on. w.* scream, shriek, cry.

krijt o. (om te schrijven) chalk; (om te tekenen) crayon, chalk.
krijten on. w. cry, weep; o. w. cry, scream.
krijtgroeve v. chalk-pit, chalk-working.
krijtrots v. chalk-cliff.
krijtwit b. n. as white as chalk, chalk-white; z. n., o. chalk-dust.
krik tw. crack!
Krim, de —, the Crimea.
krimp b. n. crimp; — snijden, (v. vis) crimp; z. n., v. (krimping) shrinkage; (gebrek) want.
krimpen on. w. (v. stof) shrink; (v. wind) back; o. w. shrink.
krimping v. shrinkage.
krimpvrij b. n. unshrinkable, non-shrinkable.
kring m. circle; ring.
kringloop m. circular course; (fig.) circle, cycle.
kringvormig b. n. circular, spherical.
krioelen on. w. swarm; — van, swarm with, crawl with.
kristal o. crystal.
kristalhelder b. n. crystal-clear, (as clear as) crystal.
kristalvorming v. crystallization.
kritiek b. n. critical; z. n., v. criticism; (kunst, letterkunde, ook:) critique.
Kroatië o. Croatia.
krocht v. crypt, cavern.
kroeg v. public-house, pot-house, tavern.
kroegbaas m. publican.
kroegloper m. pub-loafer, tavern-haunter.
kroep v. croup.
kroes m. (drink—) cup, mug, noggin; (smelt—) crucible.
kroes b. n. frizzy, frizzled, fuzzy, crisped, woolly. [haired.
kroesharig b. n. crisp-haired, woolly-
krokodil m. crocodile.
krokus m. (Pl.) crocus.
krom b. n. crooked, curved, bent; (v. neus) hooked.
krombenig b. n. bandy-legged, bow-legged; (met X-benen) baker-legged.
kromgroeien on. w. grow crooked.
krommen o. w. en on. w. bow, bend, curve; w. w. zich —, bend, curve.
kromming v. curvation, curvature; curve, bend, turn, winding.
kromstaf m. crook, crosier, pastoral staff
kromtrekken on. w. warp, become warped, cast.
kromzwaard o. scimitar; (kort) falchion.
kronen o. w. crown.
kroniek v. chronicle.
kroniekschrijver m. chronicler.
kroning v. crowning, coronation.
kronkel m. twist(ing), coil, crinkle; (wet.) torsion.
kronkeldarm m. ileum.
kronkelen on. w. (w. w. zich —), wind, twist, meander.

kronkeling v. winding, twisting, coil.
kronkelpad o., **kronkelweg** m. winding path (road), tortuous path; (fig.) devious (circuitous) way, crooked path.
kroon v. crown; (v. hoofd, boom) crown, top; (v. hoef) coronet; (Pl.: v. bloem) corolla; (licht) crown, lustre, chandelier; gaselier.
kroonjuwelen o. mv. crown-jewels.
kroonlijst v. cornice.
kroonraad m. Privy Council.
kroos o. (Pl.: eenden—) duck-weed; (Z. N.: interest) interest; v. (v. duig) croze.
kroost o. issue, progeny, offspring.
krop m. (v. vogel) crop, gizzard, craw; (gezwel) goitre.
krop v. (v. sla, kool, enz.) head.
kropduif v. cropper(-pigeon), pouter-(-pigeon).
kropgezwel o. goitre, Derbyshire neck, bronchocele.
kroppen on. w. (v. sla, enz.) heart, go to head; o. w. (v. vogel) cram.
kropsla v. cabbage-lettuce.
krot o. cot, coot, hovel, kennel, dog-hole.
krottenbuurt v. slum.
kruid o. herb; (gen.) medicinal herb, herbal medicine.
kruiden o. w. season, spice; sterk gekruid, highly seasoned (spiced); (fig.) spicy.
kruidenier m. grocer.
kruidenierswaren v. mv. groceries.
kruidenierswinkel m., **kruidenierszaak** v. grocery, grocer's shop.
kruidenlezer m., **kruidenzoeker** m. herbalist.
kruidje-roer-me-niet o. (Pl.) sensitive plant; (fig.) touch-me-not.
kruidkoek m. spiced gingerbread.
kruidkunde v. botany.
kruidkundig b. n. botanical.
kruidkundige m. botanist, herbalist.
kruidnagel m. clove.
kruidnoot v. nutmeg.
kruidtuin m. botanical garden.
kruien o. w. wheel away, remove; on. w. trundle a wheel-barrow; (v. ijs) drift; (v. rivier) be full of drift-ice.
kruier m. (met kruiwagen) barrow-man; (v. bagage) porter, commissionaire.
kruik v. stone bottle, jar, pitcher.
kruim v. crumb.
kruimel v. crumb.
kruimelen on. w. crumble, crumb.
kruin v. (v. hoofd) skull; crown; (v. boom) top; (v. berg, dijk) crown, top; (v. golf) crest.
kruinschering v. tonsure.
kruipen on. w. creep, crawl; (Pl.) trail, creep; (v. tijd) drag, crawl; (fig.) cringe, crawl, grovel, truckle.
kruipend b. n. creeping, crawling; (Pl.) reptant; repent; (Dk.) reptile, reptilian; (fig.) cringing; — dier, reptile.

kruiperig *b. n.* cringing, crawling, truckling, fawning.
kruis *o.* (*alg.*) cross; (*muz.*) sharp; (*v. dier*) croup; (*v. paard*) croup, crupper; (*v. mens*) small of the back; (*v. broek*) seat, slack; (*v. anker*) cross, crown; (*fig.*) cross.
kruisafneming *v.* descent from the Cross.
kruisband *m.* (postal) wrapper; **onder —,** by bookpost, under wrapper.
kruisbeeld *o.* crucifix.
kruisberg *m.* (Mount) Calvary.
kruisbes *v.* gooseberry.
kruisbloemig *b. n.* cruciferous; **—en,** *ook:* cruciferae.
kruisboog *m.* cross-bow, arbalest; (*bouwk.*) groined arch, ogive.
Kruisdagen *m. mv.* Rogation-days.
kruisdrager *m.* crucifer, cross-bearer.
kruiselings *bw.* crosswise, crossways.
kruisen *o. w.* cross; (*v. dieren*) cross, interbreed; (*v. planten*) cross-fertilize, cross; (*kruisigen*) crucify; *on. w.* (*sch.*) cruise.
kruiser *m.* cruiser.
kruishout *o.* cross-beam; **het —,** (*v. Christus*) the Cross.
kruisigen *o. w.* crucify.
kruising *v.* (*v. dieren*) cross-breeding; (*v. wegen*) crossing.
kruispunt *o.* (point of) intersection; (*v. spoorwegen*) crossing, junction.
kruisridder *m.* knight of the Cross.
kruissnelheid *v.* (*vl.*) cruising speed.
kruisteken *o.* sign of the cross.
kruistocht *m.* (*gesch.*) crusade; (*v. schip*) cruise.
kruisvaart *v.* crusade.
Kruisverheffing *v.* Exaltation of the Cross.
kruisverhoor *o.* cross-examination, cross-questioning.
kruisvuur *o.* cross-fire.
kruisweg *m.* (*kruising v. wegen*) cross-road; (*kath.*) Way of the Cross.
kruiswoordraadsel *o.* cross-word puzzle.
kruit *o.* powder, gunpowder.
kruitkamer *v.* (*v. schip*) powder-room; (*v. kanon*) powder-chamber.
kruitvat *o.* powder-barrel.
kruiwagen *m.* wheelbarrow.
kruk *v.* (*v. kreupele*) crutch; (*v. deur*) handle; (*tn.*) winch, crank; (*v. vogel*) perch; (*stoel*) stool, tabouret; *m.* (*knoeier, broddelaar*) crock, bungler, spoon.
krukas *v.* (*tn.*) crank-shaft.
krukboor *v.* (*tn.*) auger, wimble, breast-drill.
krul *v.* (*alg., in haar, enz.*) curl; (*v. hout*) shaving; (*bij 't schrijven*) flourish, quirk; (*krulversiering*) scroll; (*Pl.: ziekte*) curl.
krulhaar *o.* curly hair.
krulijzer *o.* curling-iron, waving-iron, curler.

krullen *on. w.* curl; *o. w.* (*alg.*) curl; (*v. haar*) curl, crisp, friz(z), wave.
kubiek *b. n.* cubic, cubical; **—e inhoud,** solid content, cubic content; *z. n., o.* cube.
kubiekwortel *m.* cube root.
kuch *v.* cough; *o.* (*mil.*) ammunition bread.
kuchen *on. w.* cough.
kudde *v.* herd; (*v. schapen, geiten*) flock.
kuieren *on. w.* stroll, walk, saunter.
kuif *v.* (*v. vogel*) tuft, crest; (*v. man*) forelock.
kuiken *o.* (*Dk.*) chicken; (*fig.*) dolt, simpleton, ninny.
kuil *m.* pit, hole; (*sch.*) waist; (*v. visnet*) cod-end.
kuilen *o. w.* pit; ensilage, silo.
kuip *v.* tub, barrel; (*voor gisten, enz.*) vat.
kuiper *m.* cooper; (*fig.*) intriguer.
kuiphout *o.* staves.
kuis *b. n.* chaste, pure.
kuisen *o. w.* chasten, purify.
kuisheid *v.* chasteness, chastity.
kuit *v.* (*v. been*) calf; (*v. vis*) spawn, roe.
kunde *v.* knowledge, learning.
kundig *b. n.* able, capable, clever, skilful.
kundigheid *v.* knowledge, learning, skill; **kundigheden,** accomplishments, acquirements.
kunne *v.* sex.
kunnen be able.
kunst *v.* art; (*toer*) trick, feat; (*kunstje*) trick, knack; **zwarte —,** necromancy; **de vrije —en,** the liberal arts; **de beeldende —en,** the plastic arts; **de schone —en,** the fine arts.
kunstacademie *v.* academy of arts.
kunstbloem *v.* artificial flower.
kunstboter *v.* artificial butter, margarine.
kunstbroeder *m.* fellow-artist, brother-artist.
kunstenaar *m.,* **kunstenares** *v.* artist.
kunstenmaker *m.* acrobat; (*goochelaar*) juggler.
kunstgebit *o.* set of artificial teeth, denture.
kunstgewrocht *o.* product of art.
kunstgreep *m.* artifice, trick, knack.
kunstig *b. n.* artful, ingenious.
kunstlicht *o.* artificial light.
kunstliefhebber *m.* art-lover.
kunstmatig *b. n.* artificial.
kunstmest *m.* artificial (chemical) manure.
kunstrijder *m.* circus-rider, equestrian; figure-skater.
kunstschilder *m.* painter, artist.
kunstsmaak *m.* artistic taste.
kunststuk *o.* masterpiece; clever trick.
kunstvaardigheid *v.* skilfulness.
kunstvoorwerp *o.* object of art, art-object.
kunstwaarde *v.* artistic value.

kunstwerk *o.* work of art.
kunstwol *v.* artificial wool, synthetic wool, shoddy.
kunstzijde *v.* artificial silk.
kuras *o.* cuirass.
kurassier *m.* cuirassier.
kurk *o. en v.* cork.
kurketrekker *m.* corkscrew; *(gekrulde lok)* corkscrew curl.
kus *m.* kiss.
kushandje *o.* hand(-blown) kiss.
kussen *o. w.* kiss.
kussen *o.* cushion; *(v. bed)* pillow.
kussensloop *v.* pillow-slip, pillow-case.
kust *v.* coast, shore.
kustland *o.* coast-land.
kustvaarder *m.* coasting-vessel, coaster.
kustvisserij *v.* inshore fishery, coast-fishing.
kustwachter *m.* coast-guard, coast-guard man.
kuur *v.* *(gril, nuk)* caprice, freak, whim; *(v. paard)* vice; *(geneeswijze)* cure.
kwaad *b. n.* *(slecht)* bad, ill, evil, wicked; *(kwaadaardig)* malignant; *(v. paard, hond)* vicious, nasty; *(boos)* angry; *bw.* badly; *z. n., o.* *(het slechte, verkeerde)* wrong, evil; *(nadeel, letsel)* injury, harm, wrong.
kwaadaardig *b. n.* malicious, vicious, ill-natured; *(v. ziekte, enz.)* malignant, virulent.
kwaadaardigheid *v.* malice, ill-nature, viciousness; malignancy, virulence.
kwaaddoener *m.,* **kwaaddoenster** *v.* malefactor, evil-doer.
kwaadgezindheid *m.* malevolence.
kwaadheid *v.* anger.
kwaadspreken *on. w.* throw mud, sling mud; *— van,* speak ill of, slander.
kwaadspreker *m.* slanderer, calumniator, backbiter, scandal-monger.
kwaadwillig *b. n.* malevolent, malignant, ill-disposed, ill-affected.
kwaadwilligheid *v.* malevolence.
kwaal *v.* complaint, disease, trouble, malady, evil.
kwab *v.* lobe; *(v. koe)* dewlap.
kwadraat *o.* quadrate, square.
kwadrant *o.* quadrant.
kwajongen *m.* mischievous (naughty) boy.
kwajongensstreek *m.* boy's trick, monkey-trick, practical joke.
kwaken *on. w.* *(v. eend)* quack; *(v. kikvors)* croak; *(fig.)* quack.
kwakkel *m.* *(Dk.)* quail.
kwakzalver *m.* quack; *(fig.)* quack, charlatan, mountebank.
kwakzalverij *v.* quackery, charlatanry.
kwal *v.* jelly-fish, slobber.
kwalijk *b. n.* sick, queasy, qualmish; *bw.* ill, amiss; *(nauwelijks)* hardly, scarcely; *— nemen,* take ill, take amiss.
kwalijkgezind *b. n.* evil-minded; ill-disposed.

kwaliteit *v.* quality, character; *in zijn — van...,* in his capacity as a...
kwanselaar *m.* barterer, trucker.
kwanselen *on. w.* barter, truck.
kwansuis *bw.* for form's sake, for the look of the thing; in pretence.
kwant *m.* fellow, chap, blade.
kwantiteit *v.* quantity.
kwart *o.* fourth part, quarter; *(muz.: noot)* crotchet; *(interval)* fourth; *— over vijf,* a quarter past five; *— voor vijf,* a quarter to five.
kwartaal *o.* quarter (of a year), three months.
kwartel *m.* quail.
kwartier *o.* quarter (of an hour); *(v. maan)* quarter (of the moon); *(mil.)* quarters, billet; *(v. stad; wap.)* quarter.
kwartierarrest *o.* confinement to barracks (to quarters).
kwartiermeester *m.* *(mil.)* pay-master; *(sch.)* quartermaster.
kwartnoot *v.* crotchet.
kwarts *o.* quartz.
kwast *v.* *(drank)* lemon-squash; *m.* *(knoest in hout)* knot, knarl, knag; *(borstel)* brush; *(sieraad)* tassel; *(fig.: persoon)* zie **kwibus**.
kweeappel *m.* quince(-apple).
kweek *v.* couch-grass, dog-grass.
kweekschool *v.* normal school, training college, (teacher's) seminary; *(fig.)* nursery.
kweekvijver *m.* nurse-pond.
kwekeling *m. en v.* *(alg.)* pupil; *(bij onderwijs)* pupil-teacher.
kweken *o. w.* *(v. planten)* grow, cultivate; *(v. groenten, enz.: verbouwen)* raise, cultivate; *(v. vee)* breed, rear; *(fig.)* breed.
kweker *m.* grower, nurseryman.
kwekerij *v.* nursery.
kwelduivel *m.,* **kwelgeest** *m.* tormentor, torturer, teaser.
kwelen *o. w. en on. w.* warble, carol.
kwellen *o. w.* torment, tease, vex, trouble, worry, plague.
kwelling *v.* torment, vexation, trouble.
kwelwater *o.* ooze.
kwestie *v.* question, matter; *buiten — stellen,* rule out; *de zaak in —,* the point at issue; the matter in question.
kwetsbaar *b. n.* vulnerable.
kwetsbaarheid *v.* vulnerability.
kwetsen *o. w.* wound, hurt, injure; *(v. vrucht)* bruise; *(fig.)* wound, hurt, outrage, offend.
kwetsuur *v.* wound, hurt, injury.
kwetteren *on. w.* *(v. vogel)* twitter, chatter, chirp, chirrup; *(v. persoon)* chatter, tattle.
kwezel *v. en m.* bigot, devotionalist, canter.
kwezelarij *v.* bigotry.
kwibus *m.* fop, fool, coxcomb, prig.
kwiek *b. n.* spry, brisk, bright, sprightly, alert.
kwijl *v.* drivel, slobber, slaver.

kwijnen on. w. (v. persoon) languish, linger (away), pine (awayl); (v. planten) droop, wilt; (v. gesprek) flag, drag; (v. handel) languish.
kwijnend b. n. languishing.
kwijt b. n. — **raken,** (verliezen) lose; (afkomen van) get rid of; **ik ben het —,** (verloren) I have lost it; (vergeten) it has slipped my memory.
kwijtbrief m. receipt, acquittance.
kwijten w. w. zich — **van,** acquit oneself of.
kwijting v. discharge; (v. schuld) payment, acquittance; — **verlenen,** discharge.
kwijtschelden o. w. (v. straf, schuld) remit, let off; (v. vordering) relinquish; (v. zonde) forgive.
kwijtschelding v. remission, remittal;

(amnestie) amnesty, (free) pardon; (v. zonde) absolution.
kwik o. quicksilver; (wet.) mercury.
kwikstaart m. wagtail.
kwikzilver o. quicksilver, mercury.
kwinkslag m. witticism, quibble, jest, joke.
kwint v. quint, fifth.
kwispel m. brush, tuft (of hair); (wijwaterkwast) sprinkler.
kwispelen on. w. wag the tail, wag.
kwispelstaarten on. w. wag the tail.
kwistig b. n. (bw.) lavish(ly), liberal(ly); (sterker) prodigal(ly).
kwistigheid v. lavishness, liberality; prodigality.
kwitantie v. receipt.
kwitantiezegel o. receipt-stamp.
kwiteren o. w. receipt.

L

la v. (muz.) la; (lade) drawer.
laadboom m. (sch.) derick, cargoboom.
laadbrief m. bill of lading.
laadhaven v. port of loading.
laadperron o. loading-platform.
laadplaats v. loading-berth.
laadruim o. (sch.) cargo-hold.
laadstok m. ramrod, gun-rod.
laadvermogen o. (sch.) carrying-capacity, cargo-capacity; (vl.) charge-capacity.
laag b. n. low; (v. kamer, enz.) low-pitched, low-ceiled; (fig.) base, mean, abject; bw. lowly; basely, meanly, abjectly.
laag v. layer; (wet.) stratum; (v. stenen, enz.) course; (v. verf) coat; (hinderlaag) ambush, snare, trap.
laaghartigheid, laagheid v. baseness, vileness, meanness.
laagspanning v. (el.) low tension.
laagte v. lowness; (diepte, in bodem) depression.
laagtij o. ebb, low tide.
laagvlakte o. low-lying plain.
laakbaar b. n. blamable, blameful, blameworthy, reprehensible, condemnable.
laan v. avenue.
laars v. boot; **hoge —,** jack-boot.
laarzeknecht m. boot-jack.
laarzetrekker m. boot-jack.
laat b. n. en bw. late; **hoe — is het?** what o'clock is it? what time is it? what's the time?
laatdunkendheid v. self-conceit, conceitedness, arrogance.
laatst b. n. (in volgorde) last; (v. tijd) latest, last; most recent; bw. lately, the other day; z. n. **de —e,** the last-named, the latter; **ten —,** at last; lastly, in the last place.

laatstgenoemd b. n. last-named, last-mentioned, latter.
laatstleden b. n. last.
labberdaan m. salt cod.
lach m. laugh, laughter; (glim—) smile.
lachduif v. (Dk.) laughing-dove, laugher.
lachen on. w. laugh; (glim—) smile.
lachend b. n. laughing; smiling; bw. laughingly, with a laugh.
lacher m. laugher.
lachgas o. laughing-gas, nitrous oxide.
lachlust m. inclination to laugh, risibility, hilarity.
lachwekkend b. n. laughter-moving, laughter-stirring; (belachelijk) ridiculous, risible.
lachziek b. n. laughsome, given to laughing, giggling.
ladder v. ladder.
laddersport v. step (rung) of a ladder.
ladderwagen m. (v. brandweer) ladder-truck, tender; (v. boer) rack-wag(g)on.
lade v. drawer; (geld—) till; (v. geweer) stock.
ladelichten o. till-robbing.
laden o. w. (v. wagen) load; (v. schip) load, lade, freight; (v. vuurwapen) load, charge; (v. accu, enz.) charge; on. w. load, take in cargo.
lader m. loader, charger.
lading v. (v. wagon) load; (v. schip) cargo, freight; (v. vuurwapen; el.) charge.
laf b. n. (flauw, zouteloos) insipid; (v. weer: zwoel, drukkend) muggy; (lafhartig, blood) cowardly, chicken-hearted, pusillanimous.
lafaard m. coward, poltroon.
lafenis v. refreshment, relief, comfort.
lafhartig b. n. cowardly, chicken-hearted pusillanimous.
lafhartigheid v. cowardice, cowardliness, pusillanimity.

lafheid v. (smakeloosheid) insipidity, insipidness; zie **lafhartigheid.**
lager b. n. lower, inferior.
lager(bier) o. lager(beer).
Lagerhuis o. Lower House, House of Commons.
lagerwal m. (sch.) lee-shore.
lak o. (om te vernissen) lac, lacquer; (zegellak) sealing-wax; (zegel van lak) seal.
lakei m. lackey, footman; (ong.) flunkey.
laken o. w. blame, censure, find fault with.
laken o. (stof; tafel—) cloth; (bedde—; fig.: v. sneeuw, enz.) sheet.
lakenfabriek v. cloth-manufactory.
lakken o. w. (vernissen, glanzen) lacker, lacquer, varnish, japan; (v. brief, enz.) seal.
lakmoes o. Dutch blue, litmus.
laks b. n. lax, indolent, slack.
lakschoen m. patent-leather shoe.
laksheid v. laxness, laxity, indolence, slackness.
lam o. lamb.
lam b. n. (verlamd) paralytic, paralysed, palsied; (beroerd, onaangenaam) tiresome, awkward, provoking.
lamheid v. paralysis, palsy.
lamlendig b. n. miserable.
lammeling m. miserable fellow, blighter.
lammergier m. lammergeyer.
lamp v. lamp; (radio—) valve.
lampekap v. lamp-shade; reflector.
lampion v. Chinese lantern.
lampzwart o. lamp-black, smoke-black.
lanceren o. w. (v. torpedo, plan, enz.) launch; (v. bericht, gerucht) start.
land o. (vaste bodem) land; (aardr.: staat) country; (dicht.) land; (bouwland, akker) field; (grondbezit) land, estate; (platte—) country.
landaard m. (nationaliteit) nationality; (volksaard) character of a nation, national character.
landarbeider m. agricultural labourer.
landbewoner m. countryman.
landbouw m. agriculture.
landbouwer m. farmer, agriculturist.
landbouwgereedschappen o. mv. agricultural implements.
landbouwkundige m. agriculturist.
landbouwonderneming v. planting enterprise.
landbouwprodukten o. mv. agricultural produce.
landbouwschool v. school of agriculture, agricultural college.
landdag m. diet.
landedelman m. country gentleman, — nobleman.
landelijk b. n. rural; rustic.
landen o. w. land, disembark; on. w. land, disembark, go ashore; (vl.) land, descend, come to earth.
landengte v. isthmus.
land-en-zeemacht v. Army and Navy.

landerig b. n. blue, in the dumps, in the blues.
landgenoot m. (fellow-)countryman, compatriot.
landgenote v. (fellow-)countrywoman.
landgoed o. country-seat, estate.
landheer m. landowner, landed proprietor.
landhoeve v. farm.
landhoofd o. land-abutment, jetty.
landhuis o. country-house, villa; (klein —) cottage.
landhuur v. landrent.
landing v. landing, disembarkation; (vl.) landing, descent.
landingsplaats v. landing-place.
landingstoestel o. (vl.) undercarriage.
landingstroepen m. mv. landing-forces.
landkaart v. map.
landleger o. land-forces, land-army.
landleven o. country-life, rural life.
landlieden m. mv. country-people, country-folk.
landloper m. vagabond, vagrant, tramp.
landman m. countryman, peasant.
landmeter m. (persoon) surveyor; (Dk.: rups) geometer, looper.
landontginning v. land reclamation.
landouw v. field, region.
landrat v. (Dk.) land-rat; m. (fig.) land-lubber, landsman.
landschap o. landscape.
landschapschilder m. landscape-painter, landscapist.
landstaal v. vernacular language.
landstreek v. region, district, quarter.
landsverdediging v. defence of the realm, national defence.
landverhuizer m. emigrant.
landverhuizing v. emigration.
landverraad o. high treason.
landverrader m. traitor of (to) one's country.
landvoogd m. governor (of a country).
landwaarts bw. landwards; **meer —,** more inland.
landweer v. territorial army, — force.
landweg m. (door land) country road; (niet over zee) overland route.
landwinning v. land-reclamation, reclaiming of land.
lang b. n. long; (v. gestalte) tall, high; bw. long; **— geleden,** long ago.
langarmig b. n. long-armed.
langdradig b. n. long-winded, prolix.
langdurig b. n. (v. vriendschap, ziekte, enz.) long, lasting; (v. relaties) long-established; (v. verblijf, afwezigheid) prolonged; (v. twist, enz.) long-standing.
langgerekt b. n. long-drawn (out); (v. onderhandelingen, verhoor, enz.) protracted.
langoor m. en v. longear(s).
langpoot m. long-legs.
langs vz. along; **— mijn huis,** past my house; bw. **hij ging —,** he went past.
langtong m. en v. long-tongue, backbiter.

langverwacht *b. n.* long-expected, long looked-for.
langvingerig *b. n.* long-fingered; *(fig.)* sticky-fingered, light-fingered.
langwerpig *b. n.* oblong.
langzaam *b. n.* slow, tardy, lingering; *bw.* slowly; *(sch.)* easy.
langzamerhand *bw.* by degrees, gradually, little by little.
lankmoedig *b.n.* long-suffering, patient.
lankmoedigheid *v.* long-suffering, patience.
lans *v.* lance.
lansier *m.* lancer.
lantaarn *v.* lantern; *(v. fiets: straat—)* lamp; *(v. dak, lichtkoepel)* sky-light; glass-roof.
lantaarnpaal *m.* lamp-post.
lanterfanten *on. w.* idle, loaf, loiter.
lap *m.* *(stuk goed: afgescheurd)* rag, tatter; *(afgeknipt)* cutting; *(overgebleven stuk)* remnant; *(op kleding)* patch, piece; *(slordig)* botch; *(wrijflap)* cloth; *(zeem)* shammy, leather; *(v. grond: stuk)* patch; *(v. vlees)* slice; *(sp.: baanronde)* lap; *(sl.: klap)* slap, box.
lapmiddel *o.* remedial measure, patch-work measure, palliative, makeshift.
lappen *o. w.* *(v. kleren, enz.)* patch, piece, mend; *(v. ramen: zemen)* shammy; *(sp.)* lap; *(fig.)* manage.
lappenmand *v.* remnant-basket.
lapwerk *o.* patchwork; cobbler's work; *(fig.)* patchwork, tinkering, botchery.
larie *v.* nonsense, humbug, fudge, fiddle-faddle; *—!* fiddlesticks!
larve *v.* larva, grub.
las *m.* joint, groin, weld, seam, scarf.
lasijzer *o.* welding-iron.
lasplaat *v.* *(v. rails)* fish-plate.
lassen *o. w.* *(v. ijzer)* weld; *(v. hout, leder)* scarf; *(v. draad)* joint.
lasser *m.* welder.
last *m.* *(vracht)* load, burden; *(lading)* charge, load; *(v. schip)* cargo, freight; *(zwaartedruk)* load, weight; *(hinder, overlast)* trouble, nuisance, bother; *(bevel, opdracht)* order, charge, command, mandate; *(recht)* injunction; **—en,** duties, rates and taxes, charges.
last *o.* *(scheeps—)* 2 tons, last; *(maat)* 30 hectolitres.
lastdier *o.* beast of burden.
lastdrager *m.* porter.
laster *m.* calumny, defamation, slander, back-biting.
lasteraar(ster) *m.* *(v.)* calumniator, defamer, slanderer, backbiter.
lasteren *o. w.* calumniate, defame, slander, backbite, vilify.
lasterpraatje *o.* (piece of) scandal; **—s,** scandal, slanderous talk.
lastgever *m.,* **lastgeefster** *v.* principal, mandator.
lastig *b. n.* *(last of zorg veroorzakend)* troublesome, burdensome; *(moeilijk)* difficult, hard; embarrassing; *(ongelegen)* inconvenient, awkward; *(vervelend)* an-

noying; *(netelig)* delicate, ticklish; *(veeleisend)* exacting; *(v. kind: moeilijk te regeren)* unruly, troublesome, difficult; *bw.* with difficulty.
lastpost *m.* *(v. persoon)* nuisance, pest; pickle; *(v. zaak)* nuisance, trouble, troublesome business.
lastwagen *m.* carrying-van.
lat *v.* lath; *(v. jaloezie)* slat, lath; *(mil. sl.: sabel)* poker, skewer.
laten *o. w.* *(in een toestand —)* leave, let be; *(toelaten)* permit, let, suffer, allow; *(gelasten)* order, command, tell; *(nalaten, verzuimen)* omit, forbear; *(ophouden met: roken, drinken, enz.)* leave off, stop; *(toewijzen)* let have; *(zorgen, dat iets gebeurt)* make, have, get, cause.
later *b. n.* later; *bw.* later; *(naderhand)* later on, afterwards.
Latijn *o.* Latin.
latuw *v.* lettuce.
latwerk *o.* lath-work, lathing.
lauw *b. n.* tepid, lukewarm; *(fig.)* lukewarm, half-hearted.
lauwerkrans *m.* laurel-wreath, wreath of laurels.
lauwheid *v.* tepidness, lukewarmness; half-heartedness.
laven *o. w.* refresh; *w. w.* **zich —,** refresh oneself, slake one's thirst.
lavendelolie *v.* oil of lavender, lavender-oil.
laveren *on. w.* tack (about), hover, beat up against the wind; *(fig.)* tack, hover, steer a middle course.
lawaai *o.* noise, tumult, uproar, din, hubbub.
lawaaimaker *m.* noise-maker, noise-monger; *(fig.)* blusterer, swanker.
lazaret *o.* lazaretto, lazaret.
leb, lebbe *v.* rennet.
ledematen *o. mv.* limbs; members.
ledenpop *v.* lay figure, manikin; *(fig.)* puppet, pawn.
leder *o.* leather; *zie ook* **leer.**
lederbereider *m.* leather-dresser, currier.
ledergoed *o.* leather-work, leathers.
lederhuid *v.* corium, true skin.
ledig *b. n.* empty; *(nietsdoend)* idle; *(leegstaand: v. huis, enz.)* vacant, unoccupied; *(fig.: v. hoofd, leven, enz.)* empty.
ledigen *o. w.* empty.
ledigheid *v.* *(het ledig zijn)* emptiness; *(nietsdoen)* idleness.
ledikant *o.* bedstead.
leed *o.* *(lichamelijk. leed)* harm, injury, hurt; *(smart)* affliction, grief, sorrow.
leed *b. n.* **met lede ogen,** with envious eyes, with regret.
leedvermaak *o.* resentful pleasure (at another's misfortune).
leedwezen *o.* regret.
leefregel *m.* regimen, diet, rule of life.
leeftijd *m.* *(levensduur)* lifetime; *(ouderdom)* age.
leeghoofd *o.* empty head, rattle-brain.

leeglopen *on. w. (v. vat, enz.)* empty (out), become empty; *(v. fietsband)* run down, become deflated; *(nietsdoen)* idle (about), loaf; *laten —, (v. bad)* drain; *(v. ballon, band, enz.)* deflate.
leegloper *m.* idler, loafer.
leek *m.* layman, secular.
leem *o.* loam, clay.
leemachtig *b. n.* loamy, clayey.
leemte *v.* gap, lacuna, flaw, blank, hiatus, void.
leen *o.* fief, feudal tenure; *in — hebben,* have borrowed, have the loan of.
leenbank *v.* loan-office.
leengoed *o.* feudal estate, feudal holding, fief.
leenheer *m.* feudal lord, liege lord.
leenroerig *b.n.* feudal, feudatory.
leenstelsel *o.* feudal system.
leep *b. n.* sly, shrewd, cunning, deep.
leepheid *v.* slyness, cunning.
leer *v.* ladder.
leer *v. (lering, les)* lesson; *(leerstelsel)* doctrine; *(theorie)* theory; *(het leerling zijn)* apprenticeship.
leer *o.* leather; *van — trekken,* draw the sword; give it one.
leergang *m.* course of instruction, educational method.
leergeld *o. (schoolgeld)* school-money, school-fee, tuition-fee; premium; — *betalen,* learn something to one's cost; pay for one's schooling.
leergierig *b. n.* studious, eager to learn.
leerjaar *o.* year's course; class.
leerjongen *m.* apprentice.
leerling *m.* pupil, disciple; *(leerjongen)* apprentice.
leerlooier *m.* tanner.
leerlooierij *v.* tannery.
leermeester *m.* teacher, master, preceptor.
leermeesteres *v.* teacher, mistress.
leermeisje *o.* apprentice, apprenticed girl.
leerplicht *m.* compulsory education, obligatory education.
leerplichtig *b. n.* of school-age, liable to compulsory education.
leerrijk *b. n.* instructive, informative informing.
leerstelling *v.* theorem, tenet; *(kerkelijk)* tenet, dogma.
leerstelsel *o.* system.
leerstoel *m.* chair.
leertijd *m.* time of learning, time to learn; pupilage; *(v. leerjongen)* (term of) apprentice-ship.
leervak *o.* subject (of instruction).
leervertrek *o.* school-room.
leerzaam *b. n. (v. persoon)* studious, teachable, docile; *(v. boek, enz.)* instructive, informative; *bw.* instructively.
leerzaamheid *v.* studiousness, teachableness, docility; instructiveness.
leesbaar *b. n. (v. geschrift)* legible, readable; *(v. boek, enz.)* readable, worth reading.

leesbaarheid *v.* legibility; readableness.
leesboek *o.* reading-book, reader.
leeslust *m.* love of reading, eargerness to read.
leesoefening *v.* reading-exercise.
leest *v. (v. schoenmaker)* last, boot-tree; *(vorm. v. lichaam)* waist, figure.
leesteken *o.* sign of punctuation, punctuation-mark, stop.
leeszaal *v.* (public) reading-room, public library.
leeuw *m.* lion.
leeuwebek *m.* lion's mouth; *(Pl.)* snap-dragon, dragon's head.
leeuwedeel *o.* lion's share.
leeuwekuil *m.* lion's den.
leeuwerik *m.* (sky)lark.
leeuwin *v.* lioness.
lef *o.* spunk, pluck, nerve, grit; *(bluf, opsnijderij)* swank.
legaat *o.* legacy, bequest; *m. (pauselijk —)* legate.
legatie *v.* legation, embassy.
leger *o. (mil.)* army; *(fig.)* army, host; bed; *(v. haas)* form; *(v. wild dier)* lair; *(v. wolf)* haunt.
legeraalmoezenier *m.* army chaplain.
legerbericht *o.* army bulletin.
legering *v.* alloy.
legermacht *v.* army forces, army.
legerstede *v.* couch, bed.
leggen *o. w.* lay, put, place; *(sp.)* throw, lay out, knock out.
legger *m. (persoon)* layer; *(register)* register; *(balk)* ledger; *(bij spoorrails: dwarslegger)* sleeper; *(onderste molensteen)* bed-stone.
leghen *v.* layer, laying hen.
legioen *o.* legion.
legitimatiebewijs *o.*, **legitimatiekaart** *v.* identification paper, certificate of identity.
legitimeren *o. w.* legitimate; *w. w. zich —,* prove one's identity.
legpenning *m.* counter.
legtijd *m.* laying-season.
lei *v.* slate.
leiband *m.* leading-string.
leiboom *m.* espalier (tree), trellised tree, wall tree.
leidak *o.* slated roof.
leidekker *m.* slater.
leiden *o. w. (v. persoon, partij, enz.)* lead; *(v. bezoekers, dienst, vergadering enz.)* conduct; *(v. zaak)* manage; *(v. werk, enz.)* direct; *(v. stappen, karakter, enz.)* guide.
leider *m.* leader; conductor; guide.
leiding *v.* leading; leadership; conduct; management, direction; guidance; *(muz.)* conductorship; *(v. waterleiding, enz.)* conduct-pipe, conduct, conduit-pipe(s).
leidsel *o.* rein. [mentor.
leidsman *m.* guide, leader, monitor,
leidstar *v.* guiding-star.
lek *b. n.* leaky; *(v. fietsband)* punctured; *z. n., o.* leak, leakage; *(v. gas)* escape, leakage; *(v. fietsband)* puncture.

lekbakje o. drip-cup.
lekken on. w. leak, be leaky, have a leak; (v. schip) make water; (likken) lick.
lekker b. n. (van smaak: eten, enz.) delicious, nice, dainty, good, tasty, toothsome; (v. geur) nice, sweet; (v. weer) nice, genial; (kieskeurig) dainty, fastidious, nice.
lekkerbek m. en v. gourmet, epicure, sweet-tooth, dainty feeder.
lekkernij v. titbit, dainty, delicacy.
lel v. (v. oor) lobe; (huig) uvula; (v. haan) gill; (slet) slut.
lelie v. lily; (wap.) flower-de-luce.
lelijk b. n. ugly; (v. persoon) plain, homely; bw. uglily.
lelijkerd m. en v. ugly fellow, ugly person; (fig.) scamp.
lemmer o. blade.
lemmet o. zie **lemmer.**
lende v. loin.
lendepijn v. lumbər pain, lumbago.
lendestuk o. loin.
lenen o. w. (geven) lend (to); (ontvangen) borrow (of, from).
lener m. lender; borrower.
lengen o. w. lengthen; (aanlengen: v. saus, enz.) dilute; on. w. (v. dagen) become longer, draw out, lengthen.
lengte v. length; (v. persoon) height, size; (aardr.) longitude.
lengtecirkel m. circle of longitude, meridian.
lengtemaat v. linear measure, measure of length.
lenig b. n. pliant, lithe, supple, limber.
lenigen o. w. alleviate, mitigate, assuage, relieve, allay.
lenigheid v. pliantness, litheness.
leniging v. alleviation, relief, assuagement, mitigation.
lening v. loan.
lens v. lens.
lens b. n. empty.
lente v. spring.
lepel m. (eet—) spoon; (om te scheppen) ladle; (druip—) baster; (v. haas) ear.
lepelen on. w. use one's spoon.
leperd m. slyboots, shrewd (cunning) fellow.
leproos m. leper.
leraar m. (secondary school) teacher; (predikant) minister.
lerares v. (secondary)teacher, mistress, (secondary) schoolmistress.
leren b. n. leather.
leren on. w. learn; o. w. (v. persoon: onderwijzen) teach; (v. lessen, enz.) learn; **van buiten —,** learn by heart, commit to memory.
lering v. instruction; lesson, learning; (kath.: catechismus) catechism.
les v. lesson; (berisping) lecture; (uit H. Schrift) lection.
lessen o. w. quench, allay, slake.
lessenaar m. desk; writing-desk, reading-desk.

lesuur o. lesson; lesson hour.
Letland o. Latvia.
letsel o. hurt, harm, damage, injury.
letten on. w. **let wel!** observe! mind (you)! mark you! — **op,** pay attention to; observe, mind, attend to.
letter v. letter, character; (lettertype) type.
letteren o. w. mark, letter.
lettergreep v. syllable.
letterkast v. (op school) letter-box; (op drukkerij) type-case, letter-case.
letterkunde v. literature.
letterkundige m. en v. man of letters, literary man (woman).
letterlijk b. n. literal; bw. literally, to the letter.
letterzetten on. w. compose, set up type.
letterzetter m. compositor, type-setter.
letterzetterij v. composing-room.
leugen v. lie, falsehood.
leugenaar (ster) m. (v.) liar, untruther.
leugentaal v. lies, lying.
leuk b. n. (doodkalm) cool, dry; (aardig, grappig) funny, amusing, droll; (prettig) nice, pleasant, jolly.
leukerd m. droll fellow.
leukweg bw. coolly, drily, in his dry way.
leunen on. w. lean (**op,** on; **tegen,** against).
leuning v. rail; (v. trap) banisters, balusters, handrail; (v. brug) parapet; (v. stoel) back.
leuningstoel m. arm-chair, elbow-chair, easy-chair.
leurder m. hawker.
leuren on. w. hawk.
leus v. watch-word, catch-word, device, (rallying-)cry.
leut v. fun.
leuteraar m. (kletser) twaddler, driveller; (talmer) loiterer, lingerer, dawdler, slow-coach.
leuteren on. w. (kletsen) twaddle, drivel, talk rot; (talmen) loiter, linger, dawdle.
Leuven o. Louvain.
leven o. life; (drukte, lawaai) noise, tumult, racket; (het levend vlees) the quick.
leven on. w. live.
levend b. n. living, alive.
levendig b. n. (v. persoon) lively, vivacious; (v. kleur, enz.) vivid, lively; (v. gesprek, handel) brisk; (v. belangstelling) keen, lively; (v. discussie) animated; bw. livelily, etc.
levendigheid v. liveliness, vivacity, briskness, animation, brightness.
levenloos b. n. lifeless, inanimate.
levensader v. fountain of life; (fig.) life artery, life-string.
levensbehoeften v. mv. necessaries of life.
levensbehoud o. preservation of life.
levensbeschrijver m. biographer.
levensbeschrijving v. biography.
levensdrang m. life-impulse.

levensgeesten *m. mr.* vital spirits.
levensgevaar *o.* peril (danger) of life.
levensgevaarlijk *b. n.* perilous, dangerous to life.
levensgezel (lin) *m. (v.)* companion of life, partner for life.
levensjaar *o.* year of one's life.
levenskracht *v.* vital energy (power, force, strength), vitality.
levenslang *b. n.* for life, lifelong.
levenslicht *o.* life, birth.
levensloop *m.* course of life, career.
levenslust *m.* animal spirits, love of life.
levenslustig *b. n.* full of life, enjoying life, cheerful.
levensmiddelen *o. mr.* provisions victuals.
levensmiddelenvoorziening *v.* victualling.
levensmoe *b. n.* life-weary, weary of, life, world-weary.
levensmoeheid *v.* weariness of life.
levensonderhoud *o.* livelihood, subsistence, sustenance.
levensstandaard *m.* standard of living, subsistence level.
levenstaak *v.* life-work, life-task.
levensverzekering *v.* life-insurance (assurance). [cy.
levensverzekeringspolis *v.* life-policy
levensvoorwaarde *v.* condition of life; *(fig.)* vital condition.
levenswandel *m.* conduct in life, life-conduct.
levensweg *m.* path of life.
levenswijsheid *v.* wordly wisdom.
levenswijze *v.* manner of living (life), way of living.
leventje *o.* life.
lever *v.* liver.
leveraandoening *v.* liver-trouble.
leverancier *m.* furnisher, purveyor, supplier, dealer; *(v. leger, vloot)* contractor; *(v. eetwaren)* caterer, provider.
leveren *o. w. (afleveren)* deliver; *(voorzien van)* furnish, supply, purvey.
levering *v. (alg.)* supply; *(aflevering)* delivery; **op** —, for future delivery, forward; *(effectenbeurs)* for the account.
leveringstermijn *m.* term of delivery.
leverontsteking *v.* inflammation of the liver; *(wet.)* hepatitis.
levertraan *v.* cod-liver oil.
leverworst *v.* liver sausage.
lexicon *o.* lexicon.
lezen *o. w. en on. w. (v. boek, enz.)* read; *(v. aren)* glean, gather; *(v. bloemen, kruiden)* gather; *(v. hop)* pick.
lezer *m.* reader; gleaner, gatherer.
lezeres *v.* reader.
lezing *v. (voorlezing)* lecture; *(het lezen)* reading; *(voorstellingswijze)* version; *(v. aren, enz.)* gleaning, gathering.
lias *v. (v. papieren)* file; *o. (gesteente)* lias.
liberaal *b. n. (bw.)* liberal(ly); *z. n., m.* liberal.
lichaam *o.* body; frame; **naar — en ziel (geest)**, in body and mind.

lichaamsbouw *m.* build, stature, frame.
lichaamsgebrek *o.* physical (of: bodily) defect.
lichaamskracht *v.* bodily strength, physical strength, force.
lichaamsoefening *v.* bodily exercise, physical exercise.
lichamelijk *b. n.* bodily, corporal; *(stoffelijk)* corporeal, material.
licht *b. n. (niet donker)* light; *(v. dag, enz.)* bright; *(v. kleur)* light-coloured; *(v. haar)* fair; *(v. bier)* blond; *(niet zwaar)* *(v. gewicht, werk, slaap, enz.)* light; *(v. koude, wond, enz.)* slight; *(v. tabak, bier, enz.)* mild; *(gering)* slight; *bw.* lightly; brightly; slightly; *(gemakkelijk)* easily.
licht *o.* light; *(fig.)* light, luminary.
lichtbaak *v.* light beacon.
lichtbeeld *o.* lantern view.
lichtbreking *v.* refraction of light.
lichtbundel *m.* pencil of rays, beam of light.
lichtekooi *v.* light-o'-love, prostitute, light-skirts.
lichtelaaie *bw. in —*, in a blaze, ablaze.
lichtelijk *bw.* slightly.
lichten *o. w. (oplichten)* lift, raise; *(v. geladen schip)* lighten; *(v. gezonken schip)* raise; *(v. brievenbus)* clear; *on. w. (licht geven)* give light, shine; *(licht worden)* lighten, get light; *(aanbreken, dagen)* dawn; *(v. zee)* phosphoresce; *(weerlichten)* lighten.
lichtend *b. n.* luminous; shining bright; phosphorescent.
lichter *m. (sch.)* lighter; *(tn.)* lifter.
lichtgas *o.* illuminating-gas, coal-gas, light-gas.
lichtgelovig *b. n. (bw.)* credulous(ly).
lichtgelovigheid *v.* credulousness, credulity.
lichtgeraakt *b. n.* touchy, thin-skinned, quick to take offence.
lichtgevend *b. n.* luminous.
lichtheid *v.* lightness; easiness.
lichting *v. (v. leger)* levy, draft; *(v. brieven)* collection, gathering; *(v. schip)* raising; lightening.
lichtkogel *m.* fire ball, luminous ball.
lichtkrans *m.* luminous circle; *(om hoofd)* halo, glory; *(om zon)* corona, sun-glow.
lichtmis *m.* libertine, devauchee, rake.
Lichtmis *v. (2 februari)* Candlemas.
lichtpunt *o.* luminous point, point of light; *(el.)* connection, lighting connection; *(fig.)* bright spot, ray of hope.
lichtscherm *o.* shade, screen.
lichtschip *o.* lightship.
lichtsterkte *v.* light-intensity, intensity of light; *(in kaarssterkte)* candle-power.
lichtvaardig *b. n.* rash, light-minded, inconsiderate, thoughtless.
lichtvaardigheid *v.* rashness, light-mindedness, inconsideratness.

lichtzinnig b. n. light, frivolous, light-minded.

lichtzinnigheid v. levity, frivolity, light-mindedness.

lid o. (v. lichaam) limb; (v. vinger, teen) phalanx; (v. insekt, enz.) articulation; (gewricht) joint; (v. stengel, stam) internode; (persoon: v. vereniging, enz.) member; (v. vergelijking) term; (v. wetsartikel) paragraph.

lidmaat m. en v. member.

lidmaatschap o. membership.

lidwoord o. article.

lied o. song; (kerk—) hymn; (v. minstreel) lay.

lieden m. mv. people, folk.

liederavond m. song recital.

liederboek o. book of songs, songbook.

liederlijk b. n. debauched, dissolute, raffish; (slordig, armoedig) miserable, wretched.

liederlijkheid v. debauchery, dissoluteness. [song.

liedje o. ditty, (street-)ballad, tune,

liedjeszanger m. ballad-singer.

lief b. n. (bemind) dear, beloved; (aanminnig, innemend) lovely, sweet, pretty; (beminnelijk) lovely, amiable; (vriendelijk) kind; (aardig) nice; bw. amiably, sweetly, kindly, nicely; — doen, do the agreeable, do the amiable;; z. n., m. en v. zijn —, his sweetheart, his best girl; haar —, her best boy.

liefdadig b. n. charitable, beneficent.

liefdadigheid v. charity, beneficence.

liefdadigheidsinstelling v. charitable institution, charity.

liefde v. love; (naasten—) charity.

liefdeband m. tie of love, love-tie.

liefdeloos b. n. loveless, uncharitable, unloving.

liefdeloosheid v. lovelessness.

liefdesgeschiedenis v. love-affair, affair of the heart; (verhaal) love-story.

liefdoenerij v. demonstrative affection, feline amenities.

liefelijk b. n. lovely, sweet, charming; bw. lovelily, in a lovely manner, sweetly, charmingly.

liefelijkheid v. loveliness, sweetness, charm.

liefhebben o. w. love, cherish.

liefhebbend b. n. loving, affectionate.

liefhebber m. lover, amateur; (H.: gegadigde) purchaser, buyer.

liefhebberij v. favourite pursuit, favourite occupation, amateur work, fad, hobby.

liefkozen o. w. caress, fondle, stroke.

liefkozing v. caress; (handeling) caressing, fondling.

liefste m. lover, best boy; v. sweetheart, best girl, beloved.

lieftallig b. n. lovable, lovely, amiable, sweet.

lieftalligheid v. lovableness, loveliness, amiability, sweetness.

liegen on. w. lie, tell lies, tell fibs; o. w. gij liegt het, that is a lie; hij liegt het, he is a liar.

lier v. (muz.) lyre; (draaiorgel) hurdy-gurdy, barrel-organ; (sch.) winch, lifting crab.

lierzang m. lyric poem, lyric.

lies v. groin; o. (Pl.) float-grass.

liesbreuk v. inguinal rupture, groin rupture.

lieveheersbeestje o. lady-bird.

lieveling m. en v. darling, dear, favourite, pet.

lieverlede bw. van —, gradually, by degrees, little by little.

lievevrouwebedstro o. (Pl.) (sweet-scented) woodruff.

lift v. lift, elevator.

ligdagen m. mv. (sch.) lay-days.

liggeld o. dock dues; harbour dues, port-charges.

liggen on. w. lie; (v. stad, enz.) be situated, lie.

liggend b. n. lying; recumbent; (v. boord) lie-down, turn-down; (Pl.) prone; (wap.) couchant.

ligger m. (v. artikel: in winkel) shopkeeper; (spoorw.: dwars—) sleeper; zie ook legger.

ligging v. (v. gebouw, enz.) situation, position; (v. land, enz.) lie; (v. soldaten, enz.: slaapplaats) bedding.

ligplaats v. (v. schip) berth.

ligstoel m. reclining-chair, lounge-chair.

lijboord o. (sch.) leeside.

lijdelijk b. n. (bw.) passive(ly).

lijden o. w. (v. pijn, koude, enz.) suffer; (doorstaan) bear, endure; z. n., o. suffering(s).

lijdend b. n. suffering; (gram.) passive.

lijdensbeker m. cup of bitterness, cup of misery.

lijdensgeschiedenis v. (v. Christus) Passion; (fig.) tale of woe (of misery).

lijdenspreek v. passion-sermon.

lijdensweek v. Passion week, Holy week.

lijder(es) m. (v.) sufferer, patient.

lijdzaam b. n. patient, meek, long-suffering.

lijdzaamheid v. patience, meekness, long-suffering.

lijf o. body; (v. japon) bodice.

lijfarts m. physician in ordinary, court-physician.

lijfgoed o. body linen, wearing-apparel.

lijfje o. bodice.

lijfknecht m. valet, body-servant.

lijfrente v. life-rent (life-)annuity.

lijfsdwang m. constraint, imprisonment (arrest) for debt.

lijfspreuk v. device, motto, favourite maxim.

lijfstraf v. corporal punishment.

lijfstraffelijk b. n. criminal.

lijfwacht v. life-guard, body-guard.

lijk o. corpse, dead body; (ontl.) cadaver;

(sch.: v. zeil) leech, bolt-rope; *(sl.: lege fles)* dead man.

lijkbaar *v.* bier.

lijkbidder *m.* undertaker's man.

lijkdienst *m.* funeral service.

lijken *on. w. (gelijken)* be like, look like, resemble; *(schijnen)* seem, appear; *(aanstaan)* suit, please.

lijken *o. w. (sch.)* bolt.

lijkenhuis(je) *o.* dead-house, mortuary, morgue.

lijkgewaad *o.* winding-sheet, shroud.

lijkkist *v.* coffin.

lijkkleed *o.* pall.

lijkplechtigheden *v. mv.* funeral ceremonies, exequies, obsequies, funeral rites.

lijkrede *v.* funeral oration.

lijkschouwing *v.* post-mortem examination, autopsy.

lijkstaatsie *v.*, **lijkstoet** *m.* funeral procession. ation.

lijkverbranding *v.* cremation, incinerlijm *v.* gluc; *(vogel)* bird-lime.

lijmen *o. w.* glue; *iem. —,* talk a person over, rope a person in; *on. w. (bij 't spreken)* drawl, speak with a drawl.

lijmerig *b. n.* sticky; *(bij 't spreken)* drawling.

lijmpot *m.* glue-pot, gum-pot.

lijn *v. (streep, spoor—)* line; *(koord)* cord, rope, string, line.

lijnbaan *v.* rope-walk, rope yard, ropery.

lijnboot *v.* liner.

lijnkoek *m.* linseed-cake, oil-cake.

lijnolie *v.* linseed oil.

lijnrecht *b. n.* straight, perpendicuₐr, diametrical.

lijntekenen *o.* geometrical drawing, linear drawing.

lijntrekker *m.* dawdler, slacker, shirker; *(sl.)* lead-swinger.

lijnwaad *o.* linen.

lijnzaad *o.* linseed.

lijst *v.* list, register; *(rand)* edge, border; *(om schilderij, enz.)* frame; *(bouwk.)* cornice.

lijster *v.* thrush; *(dicht.)* throstle.

lijsterbes *v.* service-berry, mountain-ash berry; *m. (boom)* mountain-ash; rowan(-tree).

lijvig *b. n.* corpulent, voluminous, bulky, substantial.

lijvigheid *v.* corpulency, voluminousness, bulkiness.

lijzig *b. n.* drawling, slow.

likdoorn *m.* corn.

likdoornsnijder *m.* corn-cutter, chiropodist.

likeur *v.* liqueur.

likeurstoker *m.* liqueur-distiller.

likhout *o.* polishing-stick, sleeking-stick.

likken *o. w.* lick; *(glad maken)* polish, sleek.

lil *o.* jelly, gelatine.

linde *v.* lime-tree, lime, linden-tree, linden.

liniaal *v. en o.* ruler.

linie *v.* line.

linker *b. n.* left; *(wap.)* sinister.

linkerd *m.* gauche man.

linkerzijde *v.* left side; left-hand side.

links *bw.* at (to, on) the left; at the left hand side; *(fig.)* in a left-handed way, awkwardly; *b. n.* left-handed; *(fig.)* gauche, awkward, left-handed; *(in politiek)* left.

linksheid *v.* left-handedness; *(fig. ook:)* gaucherie, awkwardness.

linksom *bw.* to the left; *(mil.)* left turn!

linnen *o.* linen; **grof —,** canvas; — **band,** cloth (binding); *in —, (v. boek)* (bound) in cloth; — **stoffen,** linens.

linnengoed *o.* linen.

linnenmand *v.* (soiled) linen-basket, clothes-basket.

linnennaaister *v.* seamstress.

linnenwinkel *m.* linen-draper's shop.

lint *o.* ribbon, riband; *(band)* tape.

lintworm *m.* tape-worm. [saw.

lintzaag *v.* ribbon-saw, belt-saw, band-

linze *v.* lentil.

linzenmeel *o.* lentil flour.

lip *v.* lip; *(v. anker)* bill.

lipbloemig *b. n.* labiate.

lipletter *v.* labial letter, labial.

lippenstift *v.* lipstick.

liquidatie *v.* liquidation, winding-up; *(effectenbeurs)* settlement.

liquideren *o. w.* liquidate, wind up; *on. w.* go into liquidation.

lis *v.* zie **lus.**

lis(bloem) *v.* iris, flag.

lispelen *on. w.* lisp.

list *v.* artifice, trick, ruse, craft; *(krijgs—)* stratagem.

listig *b. n.* artful, sly, cunning, crafty, wily, subtle.

listigheid *v.* artfulness, slyness, cunning, craftiness, subtlety.

litanie *v.* litany.

Litauen *o.* Lithuania.

liter *m.* litre.

literatuur *v.* literature.

litteken *o.* scar, cicatrice.

liturgie *v.* liturgy.

livrei *v.* livery.

lob *v.* lobe.

loco *(H.)* spot, on (the) spot.

loco-burgemeester *m.* deputy-mayor, acting-mayor.

locogoederen *o. mv.* spot goods.

locomotief *v.* (locomotive) engine, locomotive.

lodderig *b. n.* drowsy.

loden *b. n.* leaden, lead; *o. w. (sch.: peilen)* sound, plumb, heave the lead; *(bouwk.: v. muur)* plumb; *(in lood zetten)* lead; *(van gemerkte loden voorzien)* lead.

loeder *m. en v.* shunk, scurf (of a fellow); beast (of a woman).

loef *v. (sch.)* luff, windward side.

loeien *on. w. (v. koe)* low, moo; *v. (stier)* bellow; *(v. wind)* roar.

loer *r.* **op de — liggen,** lie in wait, lie on the look-out.
loeren *on. w.* peer, spy, pry, lurk.
lof *m.* praise, laud, laudation, encomium, commendation.
lof *o.* (*kath.*) benediction.
lof *o.* leaves.
loffelijk *b. n.* laudable, commendable, praiseworthy.
loffelijkheid *v.* laudableness, praiseworthiness.
loflied *o.* hymn of praise.
lofrede *v.* laudatory oration (speech), panegyric, eulogy.
lofspraak *v.* praise, laudation, eulogy, commendation.
lofzang *m.* hymn (song) of praise, panegyric; (*ter ere van God*) hymn, doxology.
log *b. n.* unwieldy; (*v. gang*) heavy; (*v. zaak, massa, enz.*) cumbersome, cumbrous, unmanageable.
log *v.* (*sch.*) log.
loge *v.* (*v. vrijmetselaar*) lodge; (*in schouwburg*) box.
logé *m.* guest, visitor.
logegebouw *o.* masonic hall, free mason's hall.
logement *o.* inn, hotel.
logenstraffen *o. w.* give the lie to.
logeren *on. w.* stay; (*fam.*) stop; **bij iem. —,** stay at a person's house, stay with a person; *o. w.* give houseroom, put up.
logger *m.* lugger, drifter.
logies *o.* lodging, accommodation; (*mil.*) lodgement; (*sch.*) crew space, forecastle.
logisch *b. n.* (*bw.*) logical(ly), rational-(ly).
lok *v.* lock, curl.
lokaal *o.* room, hall.
lokaalspoorweg *m.* suburban railway, district railway, light-railway.
lokaaltrein *m.* local (train).
lokaas *o.* bait, decoy, allurement.
lokaliteit *v.* locality; room, hall.
lokeend *v.* decoy(-duck).
loket *o.* (*v. postkantoor*) counter, (stamp-)window; (*v. station*) ticket-window; (*v. schouwburg*) office, (window of the) box-office, (window of the) office-window; (*in bank, winkel*) pay-desk; (*in kluis*) locker, safe; (*in loketkast*) pigeon-hole.
lokfluit(je) *v.* (*o.*) bird-call.
lokken *o. w.* bait, decoy, allure, entice, tempt; **iem. naar een plaats —,** lure a person to a place.
lokspijs *v.* bait, decoy; (*fig.*) lure.
lokstem *v.* enticing (tempting) voice, siren voice.
lol *v.* fun, spree, lark.
lolletje *o.* spree, lark.
lommer *v. en o.* (*schaduw*) shade; (*gebladerte*) foliage.
lommerd *m.* pawnshop, pawnbroker's shop.

lommerdhouder *m.* pawnbroker.
lommerig, lommerrijk *b. n.* shady, shaded, shadowy.
lomp *b. n.* (*onhandig*) clumsy, awkward; (*plomp, log*) unwieldy, ponderous; (*ruw, ongemanierd*) rude, rough, unmannerly; (*v. vorm: onbehouwen*) inelegant.
lomp *v.* rag, tatter.
lomperd *m.* boor, churl, clodhopper, lout.
lompheid *v.* clumsiness, awkwardness; unwieldiness, ponderousness; rudeness, roughness.
lonen *o. w.* pay, repay.
lonend *b. n.* paying, remunerative.
long *v.* lung.
longaandoening *v.* pulmonary affection, affection of the lungs.
longlijder *m.* consumptive, pulmonic (consumptive) patient.
longontsteking *v.* pneumonia.
longtering *v.* pulmonary consumption, consumption of the lungs, phthisis.
lonken *on. w.* ogle.
lont *v.* (slow) match, fuse; (*v. granaat*) fuse; **— ruiken,** smell a rat.
loochenbaar *b. n.* deniable.
loochenen *o. w.* deny, disavow.
loochening *v.* denial, disavowal.
lood *o.* (*metaal*) lead; (*dieplood*) sounding-lead, plumb, plummet; (*schietlood*) plumb(ing)-line; (*gewicht*) decagram.
loodgieter *m.* plumber.
loodlijn *v.* perpendicular (line); (*sch.*) sounding-line.
loodrecht *b. n.* (*bw.*) perpendicular(ly).
loods *v.* (*keet, bergplaats, enz.*) shed, booth, shanty; *m.* (*sch.*) pilot.
loodsen *o. w.* pilot.
loodsschuit *v.* pilot-bark.
loodswezen *o.* pilotage (service).
loodwit *o.* white lead; (*wet.*) ceruse.
loodzekering *v.* lead-fuse.
loof *o.* foliage, leaves.
loofdak *o.* foliage, roof of foliage; (*in tuin*) garden-arch.
loofhut *v.* tabernacle.
loofwerk *o.* (*bouwk.*) leaf-work, festoon-work.
loog *v.* lye; (*wet.*) lixivium.
loogzout *o.* alkali, alkaline salt, lixivial salt.
looi *v.* oak-bark, tanbark.
looien *o. w.* tan.
looier *m.* tanner.
looierij *v.* tannery, tan-yard, tan-works; tanner's trade.
looiersmes *o.* grainer, fleshing-knife.
look *o.* garlic, leek.
loom *b. n.* slow, heavy; (*mat*) languid; (*v. markt*) inactive, dull; (*v. weer*) muggy, slack, oppressive, close.
loomheid *v.* slowness, heaviness; languor, lassitude; inactivity, dulness; mugginess, slackness, closeness.
loon *o.* wages, salary, pay; (*beloning*) reward, recompense; (*verdiende —*) deserts.

loonactie *v.* agitation (campaign) for higher (better) wages.

loonarbeid *m.* wage-work, hired labour.

loonarbeider *m.* wage-worker, wage-earner, hired labourer.

loonbederver *m.* blackleg, knobstick, rat.

loonstandaard *m.* wage-rate, rate of wages.

loonstrijd *m.* wage-struggle, wage-war.

loontrekkend *b.n.* wage-earning, wage-paid.

loontrekker *m.* wage-earner.

loop *m.* (*het lopen*) run; (*gang: v. persoon, dier*) walk, gait; (*v. zaken, gebeurtenissen*) course; (*v. geweer*) barrel; (*buik—*) diarrhoea; **rode —,** bloody flux, dysentery.

loopbaan *v.* career; (*v. hemellichaam*) orbit, track.

loopbrug *v.* foot-bridge; (*sch.*) gangway.

loopgraaf *v.* trench.

loopjongen *m.* errand-boy, messenger-boy.

looppas *m.* (*mil.*) double-quick (time).

loopplank *v.* (*sch.*) gangway, gangboard, shore plank; (*v. auto, wagon, enz.*) foot-board, running-board.

loopvogel *m.* courser, walker.

loor *v.* **te — gaan,** be lost, get lost.

loos *b. n.* (*sluw, listig*) sly, crafty, cunning; (*niet echt: v. deur, muur*) dummy, blind, blank; (*vals: v. bodem, alarm*) false; (*ledig: v. noot, enz.*) deaf.

loot *v.* (*Pl.*) shoot, cutting; (*fig.*) offspring, scion.

lopen *on. w.* (*gaan*) walk; (*hard —*) run; (*v. machine, enz.*) go, run; (*v. rivier, schip, trein, enz.*) run; *z. n., o.* **onder het —,** while walking.

lopend *b. n.* running; (*v. maand, jaar, enz.*) current.

loper *m.* (*alg.*) runner; (*trap—*) staircarpet; (*tafel—*) table-centre; (*in gang*) carpet-slip; (*in schaakspel*) bishop; (*sleutel*) pass-key, master-key, lockpicker; (*v. bank, kantoor, enz.*) messenger; (*kranten—*) newsboy.

lor *v.* rag.

lorkeboom *m.* larch(-tree).

los *m.* (*Dk.*) lynx.

los *b. n.* (*niet vast, slap*) loose; (*losstaand, onsamenhangend*) detached; (*v. zeden*) lax, loose; (*losgegaan: v. das, pakje, enz.*) undone; (*losgeknoopt*) unbuttoned; (*v. brood, enz.*) light, spongy; *bw.* loosely.

losbandig *b. n.* licentious, dissipated, dissolute.

losbandigheid *v.* licentiousness, dissipation, dissoluteness, libertinism, licence.

losbarsten *on. w.* break out, burst (forth), explode.

losbarsting *v.* outbreak, burst, explosion.

losbladig *b. n.* loose-leaf.

losbol *m.* loose liver, rake, libertine, debauchee.

losbranding *v.* discharge. [away.

losbreken *on. w.* break loose, break

losdraaien *o. w.* unscrew, untwist, twist off, turn in.

losgaan *on. w.* get loose, come loose; (*v. strik, enz.*) come undone, come untied.

losgeld *o.* (*losprijs*) ransom; (*H : losloon*) charges for unloading.

losgespen *o. w.* unbuckle.

losgooien *o. w.* throw open, unloosen; (*sch.*) cast off.

loshaken *o. w.* unhook, unhitch.

loshangen *on. w.* hang loose.

losheid *v.* looseness; (*v. stijl*) fluency, ease.

losknopen *o. w.* unbutton; untie.

loskomen *on. w.* get loose, be set free; (*fig.*) let oneself go, expand, come out of one's shell.

loskopen *o. w.* ransom, redeem, buy off.

loskrijgen *o. w.* get loose, unloosen; undo.

loslaten *o. w.* let loose, release, set free; *on. w.* loose hold; (*v. verf, enz.*) come off.

loslippig *b. n.* loose, loose-tongued, flippant.

loslopen *on. w.* be at liberty, be at large.

losmaken *o. w.* loosen; (*v. knoop, enz*) untie, undo; (*v. jas, enz.*) unbutton; (*v. kleed, enz.*) unhook; (*v. steen, enz.*) dislodge; (*fig.: v. geld*) disengage; *w. w.* **zich —,** disengage oneself, free oneself.

losplaats *v.* (*sch.*) discharging-berth.

losraken *on. w.* get loose, loosen, get detached.

losrukken *o. w.* pull loose, tear open.

lossen *o. w.* (*v. schip*) unload, uncharge, discharge, unship; (*v. lading*) land, unload; (*v. pand*) redeem; (*v. wapen*) discharge; (*v. schot*) fire; *on. w.* break bulk.

losser *m.* unloader.

lossing *v.* unloading, discharge; landing; redemption.

lossingshaven *v.* port of discharge.

losslaan *o. w.* knock (strike) loose (open); *on. w.* (*sch.*) break adrift.

lossnijden *o. w.* cut loose; (*v. gehangene*) cut down.

lostrekken *o. w.* tear loose, pull loose.

loswerken *o. w. en on. w.* work loose; *w. w.* **zich —,** disengage oneself, work loose.

loswikkelen *o. w.* unwrap, unswaddle.

lot *o.* (*levens—*) lot; (*nood—*) fate, destiny, fortune; (*loterijbriefje*) lottery-ticket; (*prijs*) prize.

loterij *v.* lottery; (*fig.*) gamble.

lotgenoot *m.* partner in adversity, companion in misfortune, fellow-sufferer.

lotgeval *o.* adventure.

Lotharingen *o.* Lorraine.

loting *v.* drawing of lots, draw, ballot; (*mil.*) conscription, drawing for the militia.

lotsbestemming v. destiny.
lotsverbetering v. improvement in one's lot; betterment.
lotswisseling v. vicissitude, turn of fate. [bare.
louter b. n. en bw. pure, mere, sheer,
louteren o. w. purify, refine.
loutering v. purifying, purification, refin ng.
louwmaand v. January.
loven o. w. praise, laud, glorify, commend.
lover o. foliage.
lucht v. air; (uitspansel) sky; (reuk) small, scent.
luchtaanval m. air-attack, air-raid.
luchtafweergeschut o. anti-aircraft guns.
luchtballon m. balloon.
luchtband m. pneumatic tire.
luchtbel v. air-bubble, air-bell.
luchtblaasje o. air-bladder.
luchtbombardement o. aerial bombardment.
luchtdicht b. n. air-tight, hermetic(al); bw. hermetically.
luchtdruk m. atmospheric pressure; air-pressure.
luchtdrukmachine v. pneumatic engine, air-compressor.
luchtgat o. (in muur, enz.) air-hole; (luchtkoker) funnel; (muz.) vent-hole; (vl.) air-hole, air-pocket; (v. insekt) stigma, spiracle.
luchtgesteldheid v. climate; condition of the air, atmosphere.
luchtgevecht o. air-fight, aerial battle.
luchthartig b. n. light-hearted, light-spirited.
luchthartigheid v. light-heartedness, light-spiritedness.
luchthaven v. air-port.
luchtig b. n. (fris, aan de lucht blootgesteld) well aired, well ventilated; (v. kleren, kamer, enz.) airy; (v. brood, gebak) light; bw. airily; lightly.
luchtkasteel o. airy castle.
luchtkoker m. air-shaft, ventilating-shaft.
luchtledig b. n. void of air, airless, exhausted (of air); — maken, exhaust.
luchtlijn v. air-line.
luchtmacht v. air-force.
luchtpijp v. wind-pipe; (wet.) trachea.
luchtpomp v. air-pump.
luchtpost v. air mail, aerial mail.
luchtreiziger m. air-traveller, air-passenger; aeronaut, balloonist.
luchtruim o. atmosphere, air, space.
luchtsprong m. caper, gambol.
luchtstoringen v. mv. (radio) atmospherics, strays; atmospheric disturbances.
luchtstreek v. climate, zone.
luchtstroom m. air-current.
luchttorpedo v. aerial torpedo.
luchtvaart v. air-navigation, aviation, aeronautics.

luchtvaartmaatschappij r. aerial navigation company.
luchtverkeer o. air-traffic, aerial traffic, air-navigation.
luchtverschijnsel o. atmospheric phenomenon.
luchtverversing r. ventilation.
luchtweg m. air-route, air-way; de — en, the bronchial tubes.
luchtziek b. n. airsick.
lucifer v. match.
lui m. mv. people, folk.
lui b. n. lazy, idle.
luiaard m. (persoon) sluggard, lazybones, lazy body; (Dk.) ai, sloth.
luid b. n. (bw.) loud(ly).
luid o. naar — van, according to.
luiden on. w. sound, ring; (kleppen) toll; (v. brief, telegram, enz.) read, run; o. w. ring, peal; toll.
luidens vz. according to.
luidkeels bw. aloud, at the top of one's voice.
luidruchtig b. n. clamarous, noisy, loud, tumultuous.
luidruchtigheid v. clamorousness, noisiness, loudness, tumultuousness.
luidspreker m. loud speaker.
luier v. napkin; diaper; —s, swaddling-clothes.
luiermand v. (mandje) baby-linen basket; (kleertjes) baby-linen, baby-clothes, layette.
luierstoel m. easy chair, lounge-chair.
luiheid v. idleness, laziness, sloth.
luik o. (v. raam) shutter; (in vloer: val—) trap-door; (sch.) hatch, hatch-cover.
Luik o. Liege.
luilekkerland o. Lubberland, (land of) Cockaigne, fools' paradise.
luim v. (stemming) humour, temper, mood; (gril) caprice, freak, whim.
luimig b. n. humorous; (grillig, nukkig) capricious.
luimigheid v. humorousness, humour.
luipaard m. leopard.
luis v. louse (mv.: lice).
luister m. lustre, splendour, resplendence; —bijzetten, grace, add lustre (to).
luisteraar(ster) m. (v.) listener; (luistervink) eavesdropper, listener; (radio) listener(-in).
luisteren on. w. listen; (radio) listen (in); (gehoorzamen) obey.
luisterpost m. (mil.) listening-post.
luisterrijk b. n. splendid, glorious, magnificent.
luistervink m. eavesdropper; (radio) listener(-in).
luitenant m. lieutenant.
luk o. — of raak, hit or miss, at random, at adventure, hitty-missy.
lukken on. w. succeed.
lukraak bw. zie luk; b. n. haphazard wild.
lummel m. lout, lubber, booby.
lunch m. lunch, luncheon.

lurven *r. mr.* **iem. bij de — pakken,** collar a person.

lus *r. (r. touw)* noose; *(r. jas, schoen, enz.)* tab, tag; *(in tram)* hand-strap; *(als versiering, voor knoop, enz.)* loop; *(sch.)* slipknot, running-noose.

lust *m. (neiging, zin)* inclination, mind, liking; *(verlangen, begeerte)* desire, appetite; *(genot)* delight; *(eet—)* appetite; *(zinnelijke —)* lust.

lusteloos *b. n.* listless, languid; *(v. markt)* dull, flat, languid.

lusteloosheid *v.* listlessness, apathy; dullness, languor.

lusten *o. w.* like, fancy.

luster *m.* lustre, chandelier.

lusthof *m.* pleasure garden, pleasure ground; *(fig.)* Eden, garden of Eden.

lusthuis *o.* pleasure-house, country-seat.

lustig *b. n.* merry, cheerful; *bw.* merrily, cheerfully.

lustigheid *v.* merriment, cheerfulness, gaiety, joviality.   [delight.

lustoord *o.* pleasure ground, abode of

luttel *b. n.* little, small; few.

luwen *on. w. (v. wind)* abate, fall, lull, drop; *(v. vriendschap, enz.)* cool down; *(v. ijver)* flag; *(v. opwinding enz.)* die down, calm down, quiet down.

luxeartikel *o.* article of luxury; **—en,** *ook:* fancy articles, fancy goods.

luxepaard *o.* fancy horse.

lyceum *o.* lyceum.

lynx *m.* lynx.

lyriek *v.* lyric poetry, lyrics; lyricism.

lyrisch *b. n.* lyric(al); *bw.* lyrically.

M

ma *r.* mamma.

maag *r.* stomach; *(v. dier)* maw, stomach; *(v. vogel ook:)* gizzard.

maag *m. en v.* kinsman; kinswoman.

maagbitter *o.* stomachic bitters.

maagd *v.* maid(en), virgin; *(sterr.)* Virgo.

maagdelijk *b. n.* virginal, maidenly, virgin.

maagdelijkheid *v.* virginity.

maagdenpalm *m. (Pl.)* periwinkle.

maagdenroof *m.* rape, ravishment.

maagkramp *v.* spasm of the stomach.

maaglijder *m.* stomachic patient.

maagpijn *v.* stomach-ache; *(wet.)* gastrodynia.

maagsap *o.* gastric juice.

maagschap *o.* kindred, kindship, consanguinity; *v.* relations.

maagstreek *v.* gastric region.

maagzweer *v.* stomach ulcer, gastric ulcer, ulcer in the stomach.

maaien *o. w. en on. w. (v. gras)* mow, cut (down); *(v. koren)* cut (down), reap.

maaier *m.* mower; reaper.

maaitijd *m.* mowing-time.

maak *v.* **in de —,** making; *(om te herstellen)* under repair.

maakloon *v.* charge for making, cost of making.

maaksel *o.* make, manufacture, fashion.

maal *v. (brieven—)* mail, letterbag; *(keer)* time; **een—,** once; **twee—,** twice; **drie—,** three times; *(vlek)* spot; *o. (maaltijd)* meal, repast.

maalderij *v.* mill-house.   [vortex,

maalstroom *m.* whirlpool, maelstrom,

maaltand *m.* molar (tooth), grinder.

maaltijd *m.* meal, repast.

maan *v.* moon; *(satelliet)* satellite.

maanbrief *m.* dunning-letter.

maand *v.* month.

maandag *m.* Monday.

maandblad *o.* monthly (paper, review).

maandelijks *bw.* monthly, every month; *b. n.* monthly.

maandrekening *v.* monthly account.

maandstaat *m.* monthly return, — report

maankop *v. (plant)* poppy; *m. (vrucht)* poppy-head.

maanziek *b. n.* moon-struck, lunatic.

maar *vw.* but; *bw.* but, only, merely; *z. n., o.* but.

maarschalk *m.* marshal.

maart *m.* March.

maarts *b. n.* (of) March; **—e bui,** April shower.

maas *v. (v. netwerk)* mesh; *(v. breiwerk: steek)* stitch.

Maas *v.* **de —,** the Meuse, the Maas.

maat *v. (voorwerp om te meten)* measure; *(afmeting, grootte)* measure, size; *(verskunst)* measure, metre; *(muz.)* measure, time.

maat *m.* mate, comrade, companion; *(bij spel)* partner.

maatjesharing *v.* matie, maty.

maatregel *m.* measure.

maatschappelijk *b. n.* social; **— kapitaal,** nominal capital, registered capital.

maatschappij *v. (samenleving, gemeenschap)* society; *(vereniging, genootschap)* society; *(handelsvereniging)* company.

maatstaf *m.* measuring stick, measuring-staff, measuring-rod; *(fig.)* measure; standard, gauge.

maatstok *m. (muz.)* baton, conductor's baton; *(v. schoenmakerij)* size-stick; *(v. timmerman)* rule.

machinaal *b. n. (bw.)* mechanical(ly), automatical(ly).

machine *v.* machine, engine; *(als beweegkracht)* engine; *(fig.)* machine.

machinefabriek *v.* engineering-works.

machinegeweer *o.* machine-gun.

machinekamer *v.* engine-room.

machineschrijven *o.* type-writing.
machinist *m.* (*v. trein*) engine-driver; (*op schip*) engineer; (*v. schouwburg*) scene-shifter.
macht *v.* (*sterkte, kracht*) power; (*v. ouders*) authority; (*heerschappij*) dominion; (*menigte, groot aantal*) power, heaps, lots; (*mil.: strijd—*) force(s).
machteloos *b. n.* powerless, impotent.
machtgever *m.* principal.
machthebbende, machthebber *m.* man in power, authority.
machtig *b. n.* (*beschikkend over macht*) powerful, mighty; (*v. voedsel: krachtig, zwaar*) rich; (*overweldigend*) stupendous, tremendous; *bw.* powerfully.
machtigen *o. w.* authorize, empower.
machtiging *v.* authorization.
machtmiddel *o.* means of power; powerful weapon.
machtsmisbruik *o.* abuse of power.
machtsverheffing *v.* involution.
machtsvertoon *o.* display (parade) of power, show of force.
made *v.* maggot, grub, cheese-mite; (*visaas*) gentle.
madeliefje *o.* daisy.
magazijn *o.* warehouse, storehouse; (*mil.*) magazine.
magazijnmeester *m.* store-keeper.
mager *b. n.* (*v. persoon*) thin, lean; (*v. vlees*) lean; (*v. kost, grond*) meagre; (*v. kaas, grond*) poor.
magerheid *v.* leanness, thinness.
magertjes *bw.* poorly.
magistraat *m.* magistrate.
magneet *m.* magnet; (*in motor*) magneto.
magneetanker *o.* magnetic armature.
magneetijzer *o.* magnetic iron.
magneetnaald *v.* magnetic needle, compass-needle.
magnesia *v.* magnesia.
mahonie (hout) *o.* mahogany.
mailboot *v.* mail-steamer.
mais *m.* maize, Indian corn.
majesteit *v.* majesty.
majesteitsschennis *v.* lese-majesty, lèse-majesté.
majoor *m.* major.
mak *b. n.* tame, meek, gentle, manageable.
makelaar *m.* broker.
maken *o. w.* (*vervaardigen, voortbrengen*) make; (*met b. n.*) make, render; (*herstellen*) mend, repair; (*v. vertaling, rekensom*) do; (*v. tegenwerpingen, bezwaren, enz.*) make, raise; (*vormen: v. gedachte, voorstelling*) form.
maker *m.* maker, author.
makheid *v.* tameness, meekness, gentleness.
makker *m.* mate, comrade, companion.
makreel *m.* mackerel.
mal *b. n.* foolish, mad; (*met pers. of zaak*) fond; *bw.* foolishly.
mal *m.* (*model, patroon, vorm*) model, gauge, mould.
malaria *v.* malaria, malaria fever.

malariamug, malariamuskiet *v.* (malaria(l) mosquito, anopheles.
malen *o. w.* (*v. koren, koffie*) grind; (*schilderen*) paint, picture.
malheid *v.* foolishness.
maling *v. iem. in de — nemen,* make a fool of a person; pull a person's leg; *— hebben aan iets,* not care a button (straw, a damn) for a thing.
mals *b. n.* (*v. vlees*) tender; (*v. vrucht*) mellow; (*v. regen*) soft; (*v. gras, weide*) lush.
malsheid *v.* tenderness; mellowness; softness.
man *m.* man; (*echtgenoot*) husband.
manchet *v.* (*los*) cuff; (*vast*) wristband.
manchetknoop *m.* sleeve-link, cuff-link, cuff-stud, wrist-stud.
manco *o.* (*H.*) shortage; short weight, short measure; short delivery.
mand *v.* basket, hamper; (*draag—*) pannier.
mandaat *o.* mandate; (*volmacht*) proxy, power of attorney; (*betalings—*) pay-warrant.
mandefles *v.* wicker-bottle; (*groot*) demijohn; (*v. gekleurd glas*) carboy.
mandenmaken *o.* basket-making.
mandewerk *o.* basket-work, basketware.
manen *o. w.* dun, press for payment.
manen *v. mv.* (*v. paard*) mane.
maneschijn *m.* moonshine, moonlight.
mangel *o.* (*gebrek*) want, lack, default; *m.* mangling-machine, mangle.
mangelen *o. w.* (*v. linnen*) mangle; *on. w.* be wanting, lack, be in want of.
manhaftig *b. n.* manly, manful, virile, brave.
manhaftigheid *v.* manliness, manfulness, bravery.
maniak *m.* (*gek*) maniac; (*zonderling*) faddist.
manier *v.* manner, fashion, way.
manifest *o.* manifesto; (*scheeps—*) manifest.
manifestatie *v.* manifestation, demonstration.
maniok *m.* manioc.
mank *b. n.* lame, crippled; *— gaan,* halt, limp, have a limp in one's galt.
mankeren *on. w.* fail, be absent; *o. w. de trein —,* miss the train.
manmoedig *b. n.* manful, manly, brave, valorous.
manmoedigheid *v.* manfulness, manliness, valour.
manna *o.* manna.
mannelijk *b. n.* (*eigen aan de man*) masculine; (*kloek, flink*) manly; (*v. mann. geslacht*) male; (*gram., rijm*) masculine.
mannelijkheid *v.* masculinity; manliness, virility.
mannenklooster *o.* monastery.
mannenkoor *o.* male voice choir; men's choral society.
mannentaal *v.* manly language.

mansarde *v*. garret. [roof.
mansardedak *o*. curb-roof, mansard
manschap *v*. (*mil*.) men; (*sch*.) crew.
manslag *m*. manslaughter.
mantel *m*. coat, jacket; cloak, mantle; (*tn*.: *v. kogel*) jacket; (*om kachel*) fire-screen.
mantelkostuum *o*. coat and skirt.
manufacturen *v. mv*. drapery, drapery goods, piece-goods, soft goods, soft wares.
manuscript *o*. manuscript.
map *v*. portfolio.
marcheren *on. w*. march.
marconist *m*. wireless operator.
mare *v. news*, tidings, report.
marechaussee *v*. military police, constabulary; *m*. member of the military police.
maretak *m*. mistletoe.
margriet *v*. (*Pl*.) ox-eye daisy.
Maria-Boodschap *v*. Visitation of the Virgin Mary, Annunciation-day.
Maria-Hemelvaart *v*. Assumption.
Maria-Lichtmis *v*. Candlemas.
marine *v*. navy.
marineblauw *o*. navy blue.
marineofficier *o*. naval officer.
marinier *m*. marine (soldier).
marionettenspel *o*. puppet-show, marionette show.
mark *v*. (*grensland*) march, border-land; (*munt*) mark.
marketenter *m*. sutler.
marketentster *v*. canteen-woman.
markgraaf *m*. margrave.
markgravin *v*. margravine.
markies *m*. marquis, marquess.
markiezin *v*. marchioness; (*in Fr*.) marquise.
markt *v*. (*plaats*) market, market-place; (*prijs*) market, market-price.
marktbezoek *o*. attendance at the market.
marktdag *m*. market-day.
markten *on. w*. market, go to the market, go marketing.
marktgangers *m. mv*. market-people.
marktgeld *o*. market-dues, stallage.
markthal *r*. market-hall, covered market.
marktkraam *v*. market-stall, booth.
marktkramer *m*. market-man.
marktplaats *r*. market-place, market-square; (*stad*) market-town.
marktschreeuwer *m*. quack, mounte-bank.
marmelade *v*. marmalade.
marmer *o*. marble.
marmerbeeld *o*. marble statue.
marmeren *b. n*. marble; *o. w*. grain.
marmerpapier *o*. marbled paper.
marmerzaag *v*. marble-saw. [pig.
marmot *v*. (*Dk*.) marmot; guinea-
marokijn *o*. morocco(-leather).
Marokko *o*. Morocco.
mars *v*. (*r. marskramer*) wallet; (*sch*.) top; (*v. oorlogsschip*) fightingtop.

mars *m*. march.
marskramer *m*. pedlar, hawker.
marsorder *v*. marching orders.
marsroute *v*. march-line.
marstenue *o*. (light) marching-kit, marching-order.
marsvaardig *b. n*. ready to march.
marszeil *o*. (*sch*.) top-sail.
martelaar *m*. martyr.
martelaarsboek *o*. martyrology.
martelaarschap *o*. martyrdom.
martelares *v*. martyr.
martelen *o. w*. torture, torment, martyr.
marteling *v*. torture; martyrdom.
marteltuig *o*. torturing instruments, instruments of torture.
marter *m*. marten.
masker *o*. mask; (*fig*.) disguise, mask; (*bij chloroformeren*) face-piece; (*bij schermen*) face-guard; (*v. insekt*) larva.
massa *v*. mass; (*menigte*) crowd; (*H.: in faillissement*) bankrupt's estate.
massamoord *m*. wholesale murder.
massaproductie *v*. mass production.
masseren *o. w*. massage.
massief *b. n*. (*v. goud, zilver, enz*.) solid; (*v. gebouw*) massive.
mast *m*. (*sch*.) mast; (*by gymnastiek*) (climbing-)pole.
mastboom *m*. pine.
mastbos *o*. fir-wood; (*fig*.) forest of masts.
mat *v*. mat; (*v. stoel*) (rush-)-bottom; (*voor vijgen*) frail, tap.
mat *b. n*. (*krachteloos, uitgeput*) languid, weary, tired; (*dof: v. goud*) mat; (*v. kleur, klank*) dull, dead; (*v. licht*) dim; (*v. ogen*) dull, lustreless; (*in schaakspel*) check mate; (*v. markt*) dull, weak, flat.
mate in gelijke —, in the same measure.
mateloos *b. n*. measureless, unlimited; (*fig*.) immense.
materiaal *o*. material(s).
materie *v*. matter.
matglas *o*. ground glass, milk-glass, dull-glass; (*fot*.) focussing-screen.
matheid *v*. weariness, languor, lassitude.
matig *b. n*. (*niet overdreven, middel-matig*) moderate; (*sober: v. eten*) frugal; (*v. drinken*) temperate, sober; (*v. prijs*) reasonable, moderate; *bw*. moderately, soberly, etc.
matigen *o. w*. (*v. verlangens, enz*.) moderate; (*temperen, verzachten*) temper; mitigate; (*v. genoegens, enz*.: *wijzigen*) modify; *w. w. zich —*, compose oneself, restrain oneself.
matigheid *v*. moderation; frugality; temperance, sobriety.
matje *o*. mat.
matras *v*. mattress.
matrijs *v*. matrix, matrice.
matroos *m*. sailor.
matrozenpak(je) *o*. sailor suit.
matteklopper *m*. carpet-beater.
matten *o. w*. mat, cane, rush, bottom; *b. n*. cane-bottomed, rush-bottomed.
mattenvlechten *o*. mat-plaiting.

maximum *o.* maximum.
maximumsnelheid *v.* (*hoogste snelheid*) maximum speed; (*beperkte snelheid: in stad, dorp*) speed limit.
mazelen *v. mv.* measles.
mazen *o. w.* darn.
mechaniek *v. en o.* mechanism.
Mechelen *o.* Mechlin.
medaille *v.* medal.
mede *v.* (*Pl.: meekrap*) madder; (*drank*) mead.
mede *bw.* also, too; with me, with him, etc.
medearbeider *m.* co-operator; fellow-worker, fellow-labourer.
medebeklaagde *m. en v.* co-accused; co-defendant.
medebelanghebbende *m.* co-partner, sharer.
medebezitter *m.* joint-proprietor.
medebrengen *o. w.* bring, bring along, bring with one; (*fig.*) (*gevaar, vertraging*) involve; (*werk, kosten*) entail; (*in huwelijk*) bring (in).
medebroeder *m.* (*ambtgenoot*) colleague; (*evenmens*) fellow-man, brother.
medeburger *m.* fellow-citizen.
mededader *m.* accomplice.
mededeelbaar *b. n.* communicable.
mededeelzaam *b. n.* (*geneigd tot geven*) liberal, open-handed; (*spraakzaam*) expansive, communicative.
mededelen *o. w.* communicate; (*berichten*) inform.
mededeling *v.* communication; information.
mededingen *on. w.* compete (*naar,* for.)
mededinger *m.* rival, competitor.
mededinging *v.* rivalry, competition; *buiten* —, hors concours, not competing.
mededoen *on. w.* (*bij spel, sport, enz.*) join; (*bij uitvoering, enz.*) take part; (*aan wedstrijd*) compete; (*met gezelschap, enz.*) be of the party.
mededogen *o.* compassion, pity.
mededogend *b. n.* (*bw.*) compassionate(ly).
mededogendheid *v.* compassion.
medeëigenaar *m.* joint-proprietor, part-owner.
medeërfgenaam *m. en v.* joint heir(ess).
medeërven *on. w.* come in for a share, be joint heir (heiress).
medeëter *m.* (*persoon*) commensal, boarder; (*in huid*) comedo.
medegaan *on. w.* accompany (a person); go with (a person).
medegeven *o. w.* give along with, give; (*bij huwelijk*) give as a dowry; *on. w.* yield, give (way).
medegevoel *o.* sympathy, fellow-feeling.
medehelpen *on. w.* assist, lend (bear) a hand.
medehelper *m.*, **medehelpster** *v.* assistant.
medehulp *v.* assistance.
medeklinker *m.* consonant.

medekomen *on. w.* come along with.
medekrijgen *o. w.* get along with one; (*bij huwelijk*) receive for one's portion.
medeleven *on. w.* — *met,* enter into the life (the spirit) of.
medelijden *o.* compassion, pity, commiseration; *uit* —, out of pity.
medelijdend *b. n.* (*bw.*) compassionate(ly).
medelopen *on. w.* accompany (a person), run (walk) along with.
medemens *m.* fellow-man.
medeminnaar *m.*, **medeminnares** *v.* rival.
medenemen *o. w.* take away, take (along) with.
medeondertekenaar *m.* cosignatory.
medeplichtig *b. n.* accessary.
medeplichtige *m. en v.* accessary, accomplice.
medeplichtigheid *v.* complicity.
medepraten *on. w.* join in the conversation, take part in the conversation.
medereken *o. w.* include (in the reckoning), count (in).
medereijden *on. w.* ride along with.
medeslepen *o. w.* drag along; carry along (away); (*verleiden*) seduce; (*in ondergang, verderf*) involve (in).
medespelen *on. w.* join in a game, take part in a game; (*v. toneelspeler*) play.
medespeler *m.* play-fellow, partner.
medespreken *on. w.* join (take part) in the conversation.
medetrekken *o. w.* pull too; pull (drag) along.
medevoelen *on. w.* *met iem.* —, sympathize (feel) with a person.
medevoeren *on. w.* carry along with.
medewerken *on. w.* co-operate; (*v. kunst, letterkunde*) collaborate.
medewerker *m.* co-operator, co-worker; (*v. schrijver, enz.*) collaborator; (*v. dagblad, tijdschrift*) contributor; (*v. toneel*) performer.
medewerking *v.* co-operation; collaboration; contribution.
medeweten *o.* knowledge.
medezeggenschap *v.* right of say; (*in bedrijf*) co-partnership; — *hebben,* have a say, have a voice in the matter.
mediaan *o.* (*papier*) middle-sized paper, medium-paper.
mediaanletter *r.* pica.
medicament *o.* medicament, medicine.
medicijn *v.* medicine; *student in de* —*en,* medical student.
medicus *m.* medical man, doctor physician; (*student*) medical student.
medisch *b. n.* (*bw.*) medical(ly).
meditatie *v.* meditation.
mediteren *on. w.* meditate.
mee *z. n., v. en bw.* zie **mede**
meedogenloos *b. n.* (*bw.*) pitiless(ly), relentless(ly), merciless(ly), remorseless(ly).

meegaand *b. n.* accommodating, yielding, pliable, complaisant.
meekrap *r.* madder.
meel *o.* (*ongebuild*) meal; (*gebuild*) flour.
meelbuil *r.* bolter.
meeldraad *m.* (*Pl.*) stamen.
meelfabriek *r.* flour-mill.
meelkist *v.* meal-hutch, meal-chest, flour-chest.
meeloper *m.* supernumerary; hanger-on.
meelsuiker *r.* powder-sugar.
meelworm *m.* meal-worm, meal-beetle.
meer *o.* lake; (*Ierl.*) lough; (*Schotl.*) loch.
meer *bw.* more; **des te —**, so much the more; **niet —**, no more, no longer; **hoe langer hoe —**, more and more; **wat — is**, what is more; **min of —**, more or less.
meerdere *m.* superior.
meerderen *on. w.* augment, increase; (*bij het breien*) increase.
meerderheid *v.* (*groter aantal*) majority, plurality; (*geestelijk overwicht*) superiority.
meerderjarig *b. n.* of age.
meerderjarigheid *v.* majority, full age.
meerderjarigverklaring *v.* emancipation.
meergegoeden *m. mv.* **de —**, the better-class people.
meerkol *v.* jay.
meermalen *bw.* more than once, frequently, repeatedly.
meermin *v.* mermaid.
meerschuim *o. en b. n.* meerschaum.
meerstemmig *b. n.* (*muz.*) arranged for several voices; sung in parts.
meertouw *o.* mooring-cable.
meerval *m.* (*Dk.*) sheat-fish.
meervoud *o.* (*gram.*) plural.
meervoudsvorm *m.* plural form.
mees *v.* titmouse, tomtit.
meesmuilen *on. w.* smirk, simper.
meest *b. n.* most; *bw.* most; (*meestal*) mostly; *z. n., o.* most; **de —en**, most of them; most people.
meestal *bw.* mostly, usually.
meestbegunstigd *b. n.* most favoured.
meestbiedende *m. en v.* highest bidder.
meestendeels *bw.* for the most part.
meester *m.* master; (*onderwijzer*) teacher.
meesterachtig *b. n.* (*bw.*) magisterial(ly); (*bazig, heerszuchtig*) masterful(ly), imperious(ly).
meesteres *v.* mistress.
meesterknecht *m.* foreman.
meesterschap *o.* mastership, mastery; (*over de zee, taal, enz.*) command.
meesterstuk, meesterwerk *o.* masterpiece.   [point.
meet *v.* trig, starting-line, starting-
meetbaar *b. n.* measurable, mensurable.
meetbrief *m.* (*sch.*) certificate of registry, measuring-bill.
meetkunde *r.* geometry.

meetkundige *m.* geometrician.
meetronen *o. w.* coax away, coax along.
meetstok *m.* measuring-yard, measuring-rod.
meeuw *v.* sea-gull, sea-mew.
meevallen *on. w.* exceed expectation.
meevaller *m.*, **—tje** *o.* piece of good luck, windfall.
mei *m.* May.
meibloem *v.* may-lily.
meid *v.* servant, maid, maid-servant; (*fam.: meisje*) girl.
meidoorn *m.* (*Pl.*) hawthorn, may-tree, may-flower.
meier *m.* farmer; (*gesch.*) sheriff, bailiff.
meierij *r.* (*gesch.*) jurisdiction of a sheriff, bailiwick.
meikever *m.* cock-chafer, May-bug.
meinedigheid *v.* perjury.
meineed *m.* perjury; **een — doen,** forswear (perjure) oneself.
meisje *o.* girl; (*verloofde*) fiancée; (*fam.*) sweetheart; best girl.
meisjesjaren *o. mv.* girlhood, years of girlhood.
meisjesnaam *m.* girl's name; (*v. gehuwde vrouw*) maiden name.
meiviering *v.* May-day celebration.
mejuffrouw *v.* (*ongehuwd*) Miss; (*gehuwd*) Madam; (*met naam*) Mrs., mistress.
melaatse *m. en v.* leper.
melancholie *v.* melancholy.
melden *o. w.* mention, inform (of), report, announce; (*bij kaartspel*) call; *w. w.* **zich —**, report oneself.
meldenswaardig *b. n.* worth mentioning.
melding *v.* mention.
melig *b. n.* mealy; (*v. aardappelen*) floury, mealy; (*v. peer*) woolly, mealy.
melk *v.* milk.
melkader *v.* lacteal vein.
melkafscheiding *v.* lactation.
melkbaard *m.* milksop, greenhorn.
melkbeest *o.* milking beast, milker.
melkboer *m.* milkman; dairy-farmer.
melkchocolade *v.* milk-chocolate.
melkdistel *m.* (*Pl.*) sow-thistle.
melken *o. w. en on. w.* milk.
melker *m.* milker.
melkerij *v.* dairy, dairy-farm.
melkfles *v.* milk-bottle.
melkinrichting *v.* dairy.
melkkan *v.* milk-jug.
melkkoe *v.* milch-cow, milking-cow.
melksap *o.* milky juice; (*Pl.; wet.*) latex.
melkster *v.* milker.
nelktand *m.* milk-tooth.
melkvee *o.* milch-cattle, dairy-cattle.
melkwagen *m.* milk-cart.
melkweg *m.* (*sterr.*) Milky Way, galaxy.
melodie *v.* melody, tune, air.
melodrama *o.* melodrama.
meloen *v.* melon.

memorandum o. memorandum.
memorie v. (geheugen) memory; (geschrift) memorial.
men onbep. vnw. one, people, a man, they, we, you; (wordt ook dikwijls vertaald door lijdende vorm).
menen o. w. (denken) think, suppose; (bedoelen) mean; (van plan zijn) intend, mean.
mengbaar b. n. mixable, miscible.
mengbaarheid v. mixability, miscibility.
mengelen o. w. mingle, mix.
mengeling v. mixture.
mengelmoes o. medley, jumble, hodge-podge, mishmash.
mengelwerk o. miscellany.
mengen o. w. mix, mingle; (v. koffie, thee, enz.) blend; (v. metalen) alloy; (verdunnen, vervalsen) dilute; w. w. **zich — in**, meddle with; interfere in; (in gesprek) join in.
menging v. mixing, mixtion, mixture, blending.
mengsel o. mixture.
menie v. red lead.
menig onbep. telw. many, several.
menigmaal bw. frequently, repeatedly, many times.
menigte v. multitude, crowd, great number.
menigvuldig b. n. manifold, frequent, abundant.
menigvuldigheid v. multiplicity, frequency, abundance.
mening v. opinion.
meningsverschil o. difference (divergence) of opinion.
mennen o. w. en on. w. drive.
menner m. driver.
mens m. (v. vrouw ook: o.) man; **—en**, men, people; **geen —**, nobody, no man, not any body, not a living soul; **alle —en**, every body; all the world; **de grote —en**, grown-up people.
mensdom o. mankind.
menselijk b. n. human.
menseneter m. man-eater, cannibal.
mensengedaante v. human shape.
mensenhaat m. misanthropy.
mensenhater m. misanthrope, man-hater, hater of mankind.
mensenkennis v. knowledge of human nature (character), experience of the world.
mensenleven o. human life.
mensenliefde v. philanthropy.
mensenoffer o. human sacrifice.
mensenras o. human race.
mensenschuw b. n. shy, unsociable.
mensenvriend m. philanthropist.
mensheid v. (menselijke natuur) human nature, humanity; (mensdom) mankind, human race.
menslievend b. n. (bw.) humane(ly), philanthropic(ally).
menslievendheid v. humanity, philanthropy.

mensonterend b. n. unworthy of man.
menswaardig b. n. worthy of a human being.
menswording v. incarnation.
mentaliteit v. mentality.
menu o. menu (card), bill of fare.
mep m. slap, blow, crack, bang.
merel v. blackbird, ouzel.
meren o. w. (sch.) moor.
merendeel o. **het —**, the greater part, the greater number, the generality.
merg o. (in been) marrow; (wet.) medulla; (Pl.) vegetable marrow, pith; (fig.) pith.
mergel v. marl.
mergelgroeve v. marl-pit.
mergpijp v. marrow-bone.
meridiaan m. meridian.
merk o. (soort: v. sigaren, fietsen, enz.) brand; (kenteken) mark; (op goud, zilver: keur) hall-mark; (handelsmerk) trade-mark.
merkbaar b. n. perceptible, noticeable, appreciable; bw. perceptibly, noticeably.
merkelijk b. n. considerable, remarkable.
merken o. w. (v. merk voorzien) mark; (bemerken) perceive, notice.
merkijzer o. marking-iron.
merklap m. sampler.
merkteken o. mark, sign, token.
merkwaardig b. n. remarkable, noteworthy, curious.
merkwaardigheid v. remarkableness, curiosity.
merrie v. mare.
mes o. knife.
messelegger m. knife-rest.
messenmaker m. cutler.
messenmakerij v. cutlery.
messenslijper m. grinder.
Messias m. Messiah.
messing o. brass.
mest m. dung, manure.
mestaarde v. (vegetable) mould.
mestdier o. fatting animal.
mesten o. w. (v. grond) dung, manure; (v. dier) fatten.
mestgaffel v. dung-fork.
mesthoop m. dung-hill, manure-heap.
mestkar v. dung-cart.
mestput m. dung-pit.
meststof v. manure, fertilizer.
mestvarken o. fatting pig, store-pig.
met vz. with.
metaal o. metal.
metaalachtig b. n. metallic.
metaalbewerker m. metal-worker, metallurgist.
metaalbewerking v. metal-working.
metaaldraad m. (tn.) metallic wire; (v. el. lamp) metal filament.
metaalgieterij v. (metal-)foundry.
metaalindustrie v. metallurgic industry.
metaalschuim o. dross.
metaalslak v. (metal) slag, scoria.
metaalwaren v. mr. metal wares.

metaalzaag *v.* hacksaw.
metalen *b. n.* metal; metallic.
meteen *bw. (tegelijkertijd)* at the same time; *(onmiddellijk)* immediately.
meten *o. w.* measure; *(peilen, roeien)* gauge; *w. w. zich met iem.* —, compete with a person.
meteoorsteen *m.* meteoric stone.
meteoroloog *m.* meteorologist.
meter *v.* godmother.
meter *m. (maat)* metre; *(persoon)* measurer, gauger; *(gas—)* meter.
metgezel *m.,* —**lin** *v.* companion, mate.
methode *v.* method.
methodisch *b. n. (bw.)* methodic(ally).
meting *v.* measuring; *(H.)* admeasurement.
metriek *b. n.* metric; — **stelsel,** metric system; *z. n., v.* metric(s), prosody.
metselaar *m.* bricklayer.
metselarij *v.* masonry.
metselen *on. w.* mason, lay bricks; *o. w.* build. [mortar.
metselkalk *v.,* **metselspecie** *v.*
metselsteen *m.* brick.
metselwerk *o.* brick-work, masonry.
metten *v. mv.* matins; *korte* — *maken met,* make no ceremony of; make short work of; give short shrift to.
metterdaad *bw.* indeed, in fact.
mettertijd *bw.* in course of time, in due course.
metworst *v.* German sausage.
meubel *o.* piece (article) of furniture.
meubelen *o. w.* furnish.
meubelfabriek *v.* cabinet-making works.
meubelmagazijn *o.* furniture-store.
meubelmaker *m.* cabinet-maker, joiner.
meubelwinkel *m.* furniture-shop.
meubilair *o.* furniture.
meubileren *o. w.* furnish, fit up.
meubilering *v. (het meubileren)* furnishing; *(meubilair)* furniture.
mevrouw *v. (vóór eigennaam)* Mrs.; *(zonder naam)* lady; *(aanspreking zonder naam)* Madam.
Mexico *o.* Mexico.
miauwen *on. w.* miaow, mew.
mica *o.* mica.
microbe *v.* microbe.
microfoon *m.* microphone.
microscoop *m. en o.* microscope.
middag *m.* midday, noon; *voor de* —, in the morning, before noon; *na de* —, in the afternoon; *van* —, this afternoon.
middagdutje *o.* siesta, afterdinner nap.
middagmaal *o.* midday-meal, dinner.
middagmalen *on. w.* dine.
middaguur *o.* noontide, noon.
middel *o. (om tot doel te geraken)* means, expedient; *(genees—)* remedy; *(v. lichaam)* waist, middle.
middelaar *m.* mediator.
middelares *v.* mediatrix.
middelbaar *b. n.* middle, medium, intermediate.

middeleeuwen *v. mv.* middle ages.
middelerwijl *bw.* meanwhile, in the meantime.
middelevenredig (e) *bn. en z. n., v.* mean proportional.
middelgewicht *o. (sp.)* middle-weight.
middelhand *v.* metacarpus.
middelklasse *v.* middle class, intermediate class.
middellands *b. n.* mediterranean; *de M—e zee,* the Mediterranean.
middellijn *v.* middle-line; central line; diameter.
middelmaat *v.* medium, medium size, mean.
middelmatig *b. n.* middle-sized; moderate; *(niet bijzonder, tamelijk slecht)* mediocre, indifferent; *bw.* moderately; indifferently, in a mediocre way.
middelmatigheid *v.* mediocrity.
middelpunt *o.* centre, central point.
middelpuntvliedend *b. n.* centrifugal.
middelst *b. n.* middle, middlemost.
middelvinger *m.* middle-finger.
middelvoet *m.* metatarsus.
middelweg *m.* midway, middle course, middle way, mean.
midden *z. n., o.* middle; *(v. stad, land)* centre; *bw.* — *in de kamer,* in the middle of the room (of the floor).
Midden-Europa *o.* central Europe.
middenrif *m.* midriff, diaphragm.
middenstand *m.* middle class(es).
middernacht *m.* midnight.
midscheeps *bw.* amidship.
mier *v.* ant, pismire.
miereneter *m.* ant-eater.
mierenhoop *m.* ant-heap, ant-hill.
mierenleeuw *m.* ant-lion.
mierennest *o.* ant-hill, nest of ants.
mierikswortel *m.* horse-radish.
miezerig *b. n. (v. persoon)* measly, scrubby; *(v. weer)* drizzly, dull.
mij (to) me; *van* — *(het mijne),* mine.
mijden *o. w.* avoid, shun, fight shy of.
mijl *v. (Eng.* —) mile (1609 m.); league *(te land: ± 4800 m.; op zee: ± 5600 m).*
mijlpaal *m.* milestone; *(fig. ook:)* landmark.
mijmeren *on. w.* dream, muse.
mijmering *v.* day-dreaming, musing.
mijn *vnw.* my.
mijn *v.* mine.
mijnarbeid *m.* miner's work, mining.
mijnbedrijf *o.* mining-industry.
mijnbouwkundig *b. n.* mining.
mijnbouwschool *v.* school of mines.
mijnent, te —, at my house.
mijnenthalve, mijnentwege *bw.* as for me; from me, in my name.
mijnentwil, om —, for my sake.
mijnerzijds *bw.* on my part.
mijngas *o.* fire-damp, black-damp.
mijnheer *m.* gentleman; *(vóór eigennaam)* Mr.; *(bij aanspreking, zonder naam)* sir.
mijnhout *v.* pit-timber.

mijningenieur m. mining-engineer.
mijnlamp v. safety-lamp, mine-lamp, Davy (lamp).
mijnramp v. mining-disaster, mine-disaster.
mijnwerker m. miner.
mijt v. (insekt) mite; (stapel) stack.
mijter m. mitre.
mik v. white bread; (tn.) fork; (sch.) boom-crutch.
mikken on. w. (take) aim.
mikpunt o. aim; (fig.) butt, target.
mild b. n. (zacht: v. weer, enz.) soft, genial; (vrijgevig, gul) liberal, generous, free-handed; (overvloedig) generous bountiful, plentiful.
milddadig b. n. (vrijgevig) liberal, generous, free-handed; (weldoende) charitable.
mildheid v. liberality, generosity; bounty.
milicien m. conscript, recruit.
militair b. n. military; z. n., m. military man, soldier.
militie v. militia.
militieplichtig b. n. liable to military service.
miljard o. milliard.
miljoen o. million.
milt v. milt, spleen.
miltvuur o. anthrax, splenic fever.
mimiek v. mimicry, mimic art.
min v. (liefde) love.
min v. (voedster) nurse, wet-nurse.
min b. n. (gering) little; (laag, gemeen) mean, base; (slecht) poor, bad; (v. zieke) poorly; bw. less; — of meer, more or less.
minachten o. w. disdain, disregard, slight, hold in contempt.
minachtend b.n. disdainful, slighting, contemptuous.
minachting v. disdain, disregard, contempt.
minder b. n. en bw. less, inferior.
minderbroeder m. Franciscan (friar), Minorite.
mindere m. inferior; (mil.) private.
minderen on. w. (afnemen) diminish, decrease; (bij breien) narrow; o. w. (v. zeil) take in, reduce.
minderheid v. minority; (in kracht) inferiority.
mindering v. (v. hoeveelheid) diminishing, diminution; (bij breien) narrowing.
minderjarige m. en v. minor, person under age; (recht) infant.
minderjarigheid v. minority, non-age; (recht) infancy.
minderwaardig b. n. inferior; geestelijk —, mentally deficient.
minderwaardigheid v. inferiority.
mineraal o. mineral.
mineraalwater o. mineral water.
miniatuurschilder m. miniature painter.
minimum o. minimum (mv.: minima).

minister m. minister, secretary (of State); Eerste —, Prime Minister, Premier.
ministerie o. ministry, department, Office.
ministerraad m. cabinet council, council of ministers.
minnaar m. lover.
minnares v. love, mistress.
minne v. love.
minnekozen on. w. make love, bill and coo.
minnelijk b. n. amicable, friendly; bij —e schikking, amicably.
minnen o. w. en on. w. love.
minnezanger m. minstrel, troubadour.
minst b. n. least, fewest; (geringst) least, slightest, smallest; (slechtst) worst; bw. least; z. n. de —e zijn, yield, give way; in het — niet, not in the least; op zijn —, at least; at the least.
minstens bw. at least, at the least.
minteken o. minus sign, negative sign.
minuut r. minute.
minzaam b. n. affable, suave, friendly.
minzaamheid v. affability, suavity, friendliness.
mirabel v. mirabelle.
miraculeus b. n. (bw.) miraculous(ly).
mirakel o. miracle.
mirre v. myrrh.
mis v. mass; (jaarmarkt) fair.
mis bw. (soms als b. n.) amiss, wrong(ly).
misbaar o. uproar, clamour, hubbub; groot — maken, take on terribly.
misbaksel o. monstrosity, abortion.
misboek o. missal.
misbruik o. abuse, misuse.
misbruiken o. w. misuse, abuse.
misdaad v. crime, misdeed, misdoing.
misdadig b. n. criminal; guilty.
misdadiger m. criminal, malefactor.
misdeeld b. n. poor, destitute.
misdienaar m. server, acolyte.
misdoen o. w. do wrongly.
misdóen o. w. offend, sin.
misdrijf o. crime, offence, misdemeanour.
misdruk o. macule, mackle.
miserabel b. n. miserable, wretched.
miserie v. misery.
misgaan on. w. go wrong.
misgewaad o. mass vestments.
misgewas o. failure of crops, bad crop.
misgreep m. mistake; blunder, slip.
misgrijpen on. w. fail to catch, miss in catching.
misgunnen o. w. grudge, envy.
mishagen onp. w. displease; z. n., o. displeasure.
mishandelen o. w. maltreat, mishandle, ill-treat, ill-use.
mishandeling v. maltreatment, ill-treatment, ill-usage.
miskelk m. chalice.
miskennen o. w. fail to appreciate, undervalue, misjudge, misprize.
miskenning v. want of appreciation, misappreciation, misprision.

misleiden *o. w.* mislead, misguide, deceive.
misleider *m.* deceiver, impostor.
misleiding *v.* misleading, deception, deceit, imposture.
mislopen *on. w.* go wrong; *(fig.)* miscarry, go wrong, fail, turn out ill; *o. w.* miss.
mislukkeling *m.* failure, misfit.
mislukken *on. w.* fail, miscarry; *(v. onderhandelingen)* break down.
mislukking *v.* failure, miscarriage.
mismaakt *b. n.* deformed, misshapen.
mismaaktheid *v.* deformity.
mismaken *o. w.* deform, disfigure.
misnoegd *b. n.* displeased, discontented, dissatisfied.
misnoegdheid *v.*, **misnoegen** *o.* displeasure, discontentedness.
misoffer *o.* (sacrifice of the) mass.
mispel *v.* *(vrucht)* medlar; *m. (boom)* medlar-tree.
misplaatst *b. n.* out of place; *(fig.: v. handeling, vertrouwen, enz.)* misplaced; *(v. ijver, medelijden)* mistaken.
misprijzen *o. w.* disapprove of, condemn.
mispunt *o. (bilj.)* miss, miss-cue; *(fam.: v. persoon)* bad fellow, good-for-nothing, rotter.
misrekenen *o. w.* miscalculate; *w. w. zich —*, be out in one's reckoning.
misrekening *v.* miscalculation, misreckoning.
missaal *o.* missal.
misschien *bw.* perhaps.
misselijk *b. n.* sick, qualmish; *(fig.)* sickening, disgusting, horrid.
misselijkheid *v.* sickness, nausea.
missen *o. w.* *(niet treffen, niet raken)* miss; *(v. trein, boot)* lose; *(niet hebben)* lack, miss; *(het gemis voelen)* miss; *(verzuimen: v. les, enz.)* lose; *on. w.* miss, fail; *(sp.)* give a miss; *dat kan niet —*, it is bound to happen.
missie *v.* mission.
missiehuis *o.* mission-house.
missiewerk *o.* missionary work.
missionaris *m.* missionary.
misslaan *o. w. en on. w.* miss; *(sp.)* give a miss.
misslag *m.* miss; *(fig.)* fault, error.
misstaan *on. w. (v. kleding)* not become, not suit, suit ill; *(fig.)* be unbecoming.
misstap *m.* false step, wrong step, misstep; *(fig.)* slip, lapse, faux pas.
misstappen *on. w.* make a false step, miss one's footing.
mist *m.* fog; *(nevel)* mist.
mistbank *v.* fog bank.
mistellen *o. w. en on. w.* miscount, count wrong.
misthoorn *m.* foghorn, siren, syren.
mistig *b. n.* foggy; misty.
mistroostig *b. n.* disconsolate, dejected.
mistrouwen *o. w.* distrust, mistrust; *z. n., o.* distrust, mistrust.

mistrouwend, mistrouwig *b. n.* distrustful.
misverstaan *o. w.* misunderstand, misapprehend.
misverstand *o.* misunderstanding; misapprehension, misintelligence.
misvormd *b. n.* deformed, disfigured, misshapen.
misvormen *o. w.* deform, disfigure.
misvorming *v.* malformation, disfigurement.
miswijn *m.* sacramental wine.
mitrailleur *m.* machine-gunner.
mitrailleursnest *o.* group of machine-guns.]gun.
mitrailleuse *v.* mitrailleuse, machine-
mits *vw.* provided (that), on the understanding that, on condition that; *z. n., m. er is een — bij,* there is a condition connected with it; there is a proviso.
mitsdien *bw.* consequently, therefore.
mitsgaders *bw.* together with.
mobiel *b. n.* mobile.
mobilisatie *v.* mobilization.
mobiliseren *on. w.* mobilise.
modaliteit *v.* modality.
modder *v.* mud, mire, ooze.
modderachtig *b. n.* muddy, miry, oozy.
modderig *b. n.* muddy, miry, oozy.
moddermolen *m.* dredging-machine.
modderpoel *m.* slough, quagmire.
mode *v.* fashion, mode.
modeartikel *o.* fancy article, novelty; fashionable article; *—en,* fancy articles, fancy goods; millinery.
modeblad *o.* fashion paper.
modegek *m.* dandy, fop.
modegril *v.* freak of fashion.
model *o.* model, pattern, cut.
modelhoeve *v.* model farm.
modemaakster *v.* milliner.
modenaaister *v.* dress-maker.
modepop *v.* doll, fashion-doll.
modern *b. n.* modern; *(ong.)* modernist.
modeshow *v.* dress parade, dress show.
modewinkel *m.,* **modezaak** *v.* milliner's shop; *(voor heren)* gentlemen's outfitter's shop.
modiste *v.* milliner, dress-maker.
moe *b. n.* tired, fatigued, weary; *— maken,* tire, fatigue.
moed *m.* courage, heart, spirit.
moedeloos *b. n.* out of heart, fainthearted, dejected, desponding.
moedeloosheid *v.* dejection, despondency, dejectedness.
moeder *v.* mother; *(v. gesticht)* matron.
moederhuis *o.* mother-house.
moederland *o.* mother country, home country.
moederliefde *v.* maternal love.
moederlijk *b. n.* maternal, motherly.
moederloos *b. n.* motherless.
moedermelk *v.* mother's milk.
moedermoord *m.* matricide.
moederschap *o.* motherhood, maternity.

moederschip *o.* mother-ship, depot ship; (*v. vliegt.*) aircraft carrier.
moedertaal *r.* mother-tongue, native tongue.
moedervlek *v.* mole, birthmark, mother-spot.
moedig *b. n.* courageous, brave, valiant.
moedwil *m.* wantonness, petulance; *uit —,* wantonly.
moedwillig *b. n.* (*bw.*) wanton(ly), petulant(ly).
moeheid *v.* fatigue, weariness, lassitude.
moeial *m. en v.* busybody.
moeien *o. w.* trouble, give trouble.
moeilijk *b. n.* (*v. werk, taal, enz.*) difficult; (*v. tijden, lot, enz.*) hard; (*v. taak*) arduous, difficult; *bw.* with difficulty; hardly.
moeilijkheid *v.* difficulty, trouble; (*verlegenheid, ook:*) scrape.
moeite *v.* (*inspanning*) trouble, labour, pains; (*last*) trouble, difficulty.
moeke *r.* mummy, mammy.
moer *v.* (*bezinksel*) sediment, lees, dregs; (*v. schroef*) nut.
moeras *o.* marsh, swamp, morass.
moeraskoorts *v.* paludal fever, malaria.
moerassig *b. n.* marshy, boggy, swampy.
moerbei, moerbezie *v.* mulberry.
moerbout *m.* (*tn.*) nut-bolt.
moerkonijn *o.* doe-rabbit.
moerschroef *v.* nut, female screw.
moes *v.* (*moeder*) mums; *o.* mash, jelly, pulp; stewed vegetables or fruit.
moesgroente *v.,* **moeskruid** *o.* greens, vegetables, pot-herbs.
moestuin *m.* kitchen-garden, vegetable garden.
moeten *o. w. en on. w.* be obliged, be forced, be compelled; must, should.
mof *v.* (*voor handen*) muff; (*tn.*) sleeve, socket.
moffelen *o. w.* muffle, enamel.
mogelijk *b. n.* possible; *bw.* possibly; (*wellicht*) possibly, perhaps; *z. n., o. al het —e,* all that is possible.
mogelijkheid *v.* possibility.
mogen *hulpw.* be allowed, be permitted; (*onv. teg. t.*) may; *o. w.* (*houden van*) like.
mogendheid *v.* power.
moker *m.* maul; (*v. smid*) sledge.
mokken *on. w.* sulk.
mol *m.* (*Dk.*) mole.
mol *v.* (*muz.*) flat, minor key.
molen *m.* mill.
molenaar *m.* miller; (*meikever*) may-bug.
molenrad *o.* mill-wheel.
molensteen *m.* millstone.
molenvang *v.* stay of a mill.
molest *o.* molest.
molesteren *o. w.* molest, annoy.
molestpremie *v.* war-risk premium.
molleval *r.* mole-trap.

mollig *b. n.* plump, chubby; (*muz.*) mellow.
molligheid *v.* plumpness, chubbiness; mellowness.
molm *m. en o.* mould; (*turf—*) peatdust.
molmachtig *b. n.* worm-eaten.
molshoop *m.* mole-hill.
mom *v.* mask, show.
moment *o.* moment.
momentopname *v.* instantaneous photograph, snapshot.
mompelen *o. w.* mutter, mumble.
monarch *m.* monarch.
monarchie *v.* monarchy.
mond *m.* (*alg.*) mouth; (*v. maag, enz.*) orifice; (*v. kanon, geweer*) muzzle; (*v. haven, ook:*) entrance.
mondarts *m.* surgeon-dentist.
mondbehoeften *v. mv.* provisions, victuals.
mondeling *b. n.* oral, verbal; *bw.* orally, verbally, by word of mouth.
mond- en klauwzeer *o.* foot-and-mouth disease.
mondharmonica *v.* mouth-organ.
mondig *b. n.* of age.
mondigheid *v.* majority, full age.
monding *v.* mouth.
mondklem *r.* lock-jaw.
mondprop *m.* gag.
mondstuk *o.* mouth-piece; (*v. kanon*) chase; (*v. muziekinstrument*) mouthpiece, embouchure.
mondvol *m.* mouthful.
mondvoorraad *m.* provisions.
monitor *m.* monitor.
monnik *m.* monk, friar.
monnikenklooster *o.* monastery.
monnikenwerk *o.* monkish work, useless work, labour lost.
monnikskap *v.* cowl; (*Pl.*) monk's hood, aconite.
monnikspij *v.* monastic (monk's) frock.
monogram *o.* monogram.
monopolie *o.* monopoly.
monster *o.* monster; (*H.*) (trade-) sample, specimen; pattern; *als — verzenden,* send by sample post.
monsterachtig *b. n.* (*bw.*) monstrous-(ly).
monsterachtigheid *v.* monstrosity.
monsteren *o. w.* muster; call over the muster-roll.
monstering *r.* (*mil.*) muster, review.
monstrans *v.* monstrance.
monter *b. n.* brisk, lively, game, gay.
monteren *o. w.* (*v. machine, enz.*) mount, assemble, erect, adjust; (*v. schilderij, juweel, enz.*) mount; (*v. toneelstuk*) stage, mount, get up.
montering *v.* mounting, erection, adjusting; staging, mounting.
monteur *m.* mounter, erector; (*v. toneelstuk*) stager.
montuur *v.* frame, mount; (*v. steen*) setting.
monument *o.* monument.

mooi *b. n.* handsome, pretty, fine, beautiful; *bw.* handsomely, prettily, finely, beautifully; **zich — maken,** dress oneself up, trick oneself out.
mooiprater *m.* flatterer, fawner, coaxer.
Moor *m.* Moor, blackamoor.
moord *m.* murder.
moorddadig *b. n.* murderous, slaughterous; *(fig.)* cut-throat.
moorden *on. w.* commit murder, kill.
moordenaar *m.* murderer.
moordenares *v.* murderess.
moordgeroep, moordgeschreeuw *o.* cry of murder.
moordhol *o.* cut-throat den.
moot *v. (v. vis)* fillet.
mop *m. (Dk.: hond)* pug(-dog); *v. (grap, geestigheid)* joke; *(gebakken metselsteen)* brick; *(hard koekje)* biscuit; *(inktvlek)* blot.
mopneus *m.* pug-nose.
moppentapper *m.* joker.
mopperen *on. w.* grumble; grouse.
moraal *v.* moral.
moreel *b. n. (bw.)* moral(ly); *z. n., o.* morale.
morel *v.* morel, morello.
morgen *z. n., m.* morning; *bw.* to morrow.
morgengebed *o.* morning-prayer.
morgenrood *o.* red of dawn; *(dicht.)* morning-red.
morgenschemering *v.* morning-twilight, (early) dawn.
morgenstond *m.* morning dawn, morning-time, early morning.
morgenwijding *v. (per radio)* daily service.
mormel *o.* monster, freak.
mormeldier *o.* marmot, dormouse.
morren *on. w.* grumble, murmur.
morsdood *b. n.* stone-dead.
morsen *on. w.* mess, make a mess; *o. w. (v. water, thee, enz.)* slop; *(v. melk, wijn)* spill.
morsesleutel *m.* Morse key.
morsig *b. n.* dirty, grubby.
morsigheid *v.* dirtiness, grubbiness.
morspot *m. en v.* mucker, messer.
mortel *v.* mortar.
mortier *m.* mortar.
mortierstamper *m.* pestle.
mos *o.* moss.
mosachtig *b. n.* mossy, moss-like.
moskee *v.* mosque.
mossel *v.* mussel.   [bed.
mosselbank *v.* mussel-bank, mussel-
mosterd *m.* mustard.
mot *v.* (clothes-)moth.
mot *o. (turfmolm)* peat-dust.
motie *v.* motion, vote.
motief *o. (beweegreden)* motive; *(in de kunst)* motif, motive.
motor *m. (alg.)* motor; *(v. auto, vliegtuig)* engine.
motorboot *r.* motor-boat, motor-launch.

motorfiets *v.* motor-cycle, moto-cycle.
motorpech *o.* engine trouble.
motregen *m.* drizzling rain, drizzle, mizzle.
motregenen *onp. w.* drizzle, mizzle.
motto *o.* motto, device.
mout *o.* malt.
mouterij *v.* malt-house.
mouw *v.* sleeve.
mozaïek *o.* mosaic work, mosaic.
Mozes *m.* Moses.
mud *v. en o.* hectolitre.
muf *b. n. (v. kamer, enz.)* fuggy, stuffy; *(fig.)* musty, fusty.
mufheid *v.* fug; mustiness, fustiness.
mug *v.* gnat, midge.
muggebeet *m.* gnat-bite.
muggengordijn *o.* mosquito-curtain, mosquito-net.
muggeziften *on. w.* split hairs.
muil *m. (Dk.)* mule; *(bek)* mouth, snout, muzzle; *v. (pantoffel)* mule; *(met hiel)* slipper.
muilband *m.* muzzle.
muildier *o.* mule.
muilezel *m.* hinny.
muilkorf *m.* muzzle.
muilpeer *v.* box on the ear, slap (in the face).
muis *v.* mouse *(mr.: mice)*; *(v. hand)* ball of the thumb, muscle of the hand; *(rookvlees)* smoked fillet.
muisstil *b. n.* mouse-still, as still (silent, quiet) as a mouse.
muit *v.* mew.
muiteling *m.* mutineer, rebel.
muiten *on. w.* mutiny, rebel.
muiter *m.* zie **muiteling.**
muiterij *v.* mutiny, rebellion, sedition.
muizenissen *v. mv.* **— in het hoofd hebben,** have maggots (cobwebs) in one's brain.
muizenvalk *m.* buzzard.
mul *b. n.* loose, sandy; *z. n., v.* mould.
mulat *m.* mulatto.
mummie *v.* mummy.
munitie *v.* (am)munition.
munitiekist *v.* ammunition-chest, caisson.
munt *v. (geldstuk)* coin; *(geld)* money; *(gebouw)* Mint; *(Pl.)* mint.
munten *o. w.* coin, mint.
munter *m.* coiner, minter.
muntgehalte *o.* alloy of coins.
muntstelsel *o.* monetary system.
muntstuk *o.* coin, piece of money.
murik *v. (Pl.)* chickweed.
murmelen *on. w.* murmur; *(v. beekje)* babble, purl, murmur.
murw *b. n.* soft, tender, mellow; **— slaan,** marrow; beat to a jelly.
mus *v.* sparrow.
museum *o.* museum.
musicus *m.* musician.
muskaat *v. (noten)* nutmeg; *m. (wijn)* muscadel.
muskaatnoot *v.* nutmeg.
muskaatwijn *m.* muscadel.

musket o. (gesch.) musket.
musketier m. (gesch.) musketeer.
muskiet v. mosquito.
muskus v. musk.
muskusdier o. musk-animal.
mussenhagel m. dust shot, small shot.
muts v. cap; (Schotse —) bonnet; (kinderbaret) tam (o'shanter).
mutsaard m. faggot.
mutsenmaakster v. milliner.
muur m. wall; v. (Pl.) chickweed.
muuranker o. (bouwk.) cramp-iron, brace.
muurbloem v. (Pl.) wall-flower.
muurtapijt o. hangings.
muze v. muse.

muziek v. music; **op — zetten,** set to music.
muziekboek o. music-book:
muziekinstrument o. musical instrument.
muziekkorps o. band (of musicians).
muzieksleutel m. clef, key.
muziektas v. music-carrier.
muziektent v. band-stand.
muzikaal b. n. musical.
muzikant m. musician, bandsman.
mysterie o. mystery.
mystiek b. n. mystic(al); bw. mystically; z. n., v. mysticism.
mythologie v. mythology.

N

na vz. after; — **elkaar,** in succession, one after the other; **tweemaal — elkander,** twice consecutively, twice running; bw. near; (dicht.) nigh.
naad m. (v. kleed, hout, enz.) seam; (v. wond) suture.
naaf v. nave, hub; (v. schroef) (propeller) boss.
naaien o. w. sew; (v. wond) sew up, stitch; on. w. sew, do needlework.
naaigaren o. sewing-thread.
naaikistje o. work-box.
naaikussen o. sewing-cushion.
naaimachine v. sewing-machine.
naaister v. needle-woman, sewing-woman, seamstress.
naakt b. n. naked, bare, nude.
naaktheid v. nakedness, bareness, nudity.
naald v. needle.
naaldboom m. needle-leaved tree.
naaldvis m. (Dk.) needle-fish, pipe-fish.
naam m. name; (faam) name, reputation.
naambord o. name-board; (aan deur) name-plate, door-plate.
naamdag m. name-day, saint's day.
naamdicht o. acrostic.
naamgenoot m. en v. namesake.
naamkaartje o. card, visiting-card.
naamloos b. n. nameless, anonymous.
naamstempel m. signature stamp, stamped signature.
naamval m. case.
naamvalsuitgang m. case ending.
naamwoord o. noun, substantive.
naäpen o. w. ape, mimic, imitate.
naar vz. (plaats) to; (in de richting van) towards; (volgens) according to; (evenals) after; vw. — **men zegt,** as they say; it is said; bw. **dat is er —,** that depends.
naar b. n. unpleasant, disagreeable; (v. geluid) dismal; (v. reuk, smaak) nasty; (droevig) dreary; (onlekker) unwell, queer.
naargelang vz. according as.

naarheid v. unpleasantness; dismalness; dreariness.
naarmate vw. according to, in proportion to.
naarstig b. n. (bw.) assiduous(ly), diligent(ly), industrious(ly), sedulous(ly).
naarstigheid v. assiduity, diligence, industry, sedulity.
naast vz. next (to), beside; alongside of; b. n. next, nearest, next-door; bw. nearest.
naaste m. en v. fellow-creature, fellow-man, neighbour.
naastenliefde v. love of one's neighbour, love of one's fellow-creatures.
nabericht o. postscript.
nabij bw. near; close to; **van —,** from close by.
nabijgelegen b. n. neighbouring, adjacent.
nabijheid v. neighbourhood, vicinity, proximity, nearness.
nablijven on. w. stay on, remain behind; (op school) stay in, be kept in.
nabloei m. second bloom.
nabloeien on. w. bloom later.
nabootsen o. w. imitate; (spottend) mimic, take off.
nabootsing v. imitation; minicry, take-off.
naburig b. n. neighbouring, near-by; (aangrenzend) adjacent. ty.
nabuurschap v. neighbourhood, vicinity.
nacht m. night; **'s —s,** at night; **van —,** (afgelopen) last night; (komende —) to-night.
nachtasiel o. night-shelter.
nachtbel v. night-bell.
nachtbraken on. w. revel by night, lucubrate, make a night of it.
nachtbraker m. night-reveller.
nachtegaal m. nightingale.
nachtelijk b. n. nightly; nocturnal.
nachtevening v. equinox.
nachtkastje o. night-stand, pedestal cupboard.

nachtkroeg *v.* night-house, night pub.

nachtleger *o.* bed, lodging(-place); (*mil.*) bivouac.

nachtmerrie *v.* nightmare.

nachtploeg *v.* night-shift.

nachtraaf *v.* (*Dk.*) common owl; *m.* (*fig.*) night-reveller, fly-by-night, nightbird.

nachtrust *v.* night's rest.

nachtschade *v.* (*Pl.*) nightshade, banewort.

nachtschone *v.* (*Pl.*) pretty by night, four o'clock flower, marvel of Peru.

nachtslot *o.* double lock; **op het — doen,** double-lock.

nachtuil *m.* screech-owl, owlet.

nachtvlinder *m.* night-moth; *v.* nightbird, fly-by-night.

nachtwaker *m.* night-watchman.

nadat *vw.* after.

nadeel *o.* (*schade*) injury, hurt, prejudice, detriment; (*geldelijk* —) loss; (*verlies*) disadvantage; (*schaduwzijde*) drawback; **ten nadele van,** at the expense (cost) of; to the detriment (prejudice) of.

nadelig *b. n.* injurious, hurtful, prejudicial, detrimental; disadvantageous.

nadenken *on. w.* think, reflect; **— over,** meditate on (upon), reflect on (upon), think about; **zonder —,** thoughtlessly, unthinkingly, without thinking.

nader *b. n.* (*korter: v. weg, enz.*) nearer, shorter; (*uitvoeriger*) further; *bw.* nearer.

naderen *on. w.* approach, draw near; *o. w.* approach, draw near to, come up to.

naderhand *bw.* afterwards, later on.

nadering *v.* approach, drawing near.

nadien *vw.* since, subsequently.

nadoen *o. w.* imitate; (*spottend*) mimic.

nadruk *m.* (*klem, kracht*) emphasis, energy, accent, stress; (*v. boek, enz.*) reprint; (*zonder toestemming*) pirated edition, piratical publication; **de — leggen op,** accent, stress; (*fig.*) accentuate, emphasize, stress, lay stress on.

nadrukkelijk *b. n.* (*bw.*) emphatic(ally), express(ly).

nadrukken *o. w.* reprint; (*zonder toestemming*) pirate, reprint piratically.

nagaan *o. w.* (*volgen*) follow; (*gadeslaan*) keep an eye on, keep track of; (*controleren*) control; (*nasporen*) trace; (*onderzoeken*) examine, verify; (*v. politie*) dog, watch; (*zich voorstellen*) imagine; (*bedenken*) consider; *on. w.* (*v. uurwerk*) be slow.

nagalmen *on. w.* resound, reverberate, echo.

nagapen *o. w.* gape after.

nagedachtenis *v.* memory, remembrance; (*herdenking*) commemoration; **ter — van,** in memory of, in commemoration of.

nagel *m.* nail; (*klinknagel*) rivet; (*Pl.: v. bloemblad*) claw; (*kruid—*) clove.

nagelbloem *v.* gilly-flower.

nagelen *o. w.* nail.

nagelkruid *o.* (*Pl.*) avens.

nageltang *v.* nail-clippers.

nagelvast *b. n.* fixed with nails.

nagemaakt *b. n.* counterfeit, imitation; (*v. cheque, enz.*) forged; (*v. bloemen, enz.*) artificial; (*onecht, schijn*) mock.

nagenoeg *bw.* almost, nearly, all but.

nagerecht *o.* dessert.

nageslacht *o.* posterity, progeny, issue.

naherfst *m.* late autumn.

nahooi *o.* aftermath.

naijver *m.* (*wedijver*) emulation; (*jaloezie*) jealousy, envy.

najaar *o.* autumn.

najaarsstormen *m. mr.* equinoctia gales, blasts of autumn.

najagen *o. w.* (*wild, enz.*) chase, pursue; (*fig.: genoegens, enz.*) pursue; (*kennis, rijkdom, effect*) hunt after, strain after.

naken *o. w.* approch, draw near.

nakijken *o. w.* (*v. persoon*) look after; (*lessen*) look over; (*schoolwerk, oefeningen: verbeteren*) correct; (*drukproef*) revise; (*nauwkeurig —: document, enz.*) examine, peruse.

naklank *m.* resonance, resound, echo.

nakomeling *m. en v.* descendant.

nakomelingschap *v.* posterity, progeny, issue.

nakomen *on. w.* follow, come later on, come afterwards; *o. w.* (*v. belofte, enz.*) perform, fulfil, make good; (*v. verplichting*) meet, honour, discharge; (*naleven: v. wet, enz.*) observe; (*volgen*) come after, follow; (*v. instructies*) execute.

nalaten *o. w.* (*achterlaten bij overlijden*) leave (behind); (*laten varen, niet meer doen*) leave off; (*niet doen*) omit; (*verzuimen*) neglect.

nalatenschap *v.* estate; (*erfenis*) inheritance.

nalatig *b. n.* negligent, neglectful, remiss, careless.

nalatigheid *v.* negligence, remissness, carelessness; (*recht*) non-feasance, laches; (*plichtverzuim*) dereliction of duty.

naleven *o. w.* (*beginsel, stelregel*) live up to; (*overeenkomst*) perform, fulfil; (*wet, reglement*) observe.

naleving *v.* living up to; performance; fulfilment; observance.

nalopen *o. w.* run after, follow; *on. w.* (*v. uurwerk*) be slow.

namaak *v.* imitation, counterfeit(ing), forgery.

namaaksel *o.* imitation, counterfeit.

namaken *o. w.* (*model, enz.*) imitate, copy; (*geld*) counterfeit; (*bankbiljetten, handtekening*) forge.

namelijk *bw.* (*te weten*) namely, to wit; (*immers*) for, because.

Namen *o.* Namur.

namens *vz.* in the name of, on behalf of; **— mij,** *ook:* from me.

nameten *o. w.* measure (again); *(controleren)* check the measure of.

namiddag *m.* afternoon.

naogen *o. w.* eye, watch, follow (with the eye).

nap *m.* cup, bowl, basin.

napraten *o. w.* parrot, repeat; *on. w.* remain talking.

nar *m.* fool, jester.

narede *v.* epilogue.

narekenen *o. w.* check, verify; *(uitrekenen)* calculate.

narigheid *v.* misery.

narijden *o. w.* ride after, drive after.

narrenkap *v.* foolscap.

narwal *m.* *(Dk.)* narwhal, unicorn fish.

naschrift *o.* postscript.

naschrijven *o. w.* copy; *(v. schrijver overnemen)* plagiarize.

naslaan *o. w.* *(woord, enz.)* look up, look out; *(v. woordenboek, enz.)* consult, turn up.

nasleep *m.* train (of consequences); *(v. ziekte, oorlog, enz.)* aftermath.

nasmaak *m.* after-taste, taste, tang.

naspel *o.* *(ton.)* after-piece, after-play; *(muz.)* postlude; *(fig.)* sequel.

nastreven *o. w.* *(v. geluk, macht, enz.)* strive after, aspire to; *(v. doel)* pursue.

nat *b. n.* wet; *(vochtig)* damp, moist; — **maken,** wet; *z. n., o.* wet, liquid.

natellen *o. w.* count over, count again, check.

natheid *v.* wetness, dampness, moistness.

natie *v.* nation.

nationaal *b. n.* national.

nationaliteit *v.* nationality.

nationaliteitsgevoel *o.* national feeling.

natrium *o.* sodium.

naturaliseren *o. w.* naturalize.

natuur *v.* nature; *(landschap)* (natural) scenery; *(aard)* temper, temperament.

natuurdrift *v.* instinct.

natuurgetrouw *b. n.* true to nature.

natuurkenner *m.* naturalist, natural philosopher.

natuurkunde *v.* physics, natural science.

natuurkundige *m.* physicist, natural philosopher.

natuurlijk *b. n.* natural; *bw.* naturally; —! of course!

natuurmens *m.* natural man.

natuurschoon *o.* natural beauty, beautiful scenery.

natuurverschijnsel *o.* natural phenomenon.

natuurwetenschap *v.* natural science.

nauw *b. n.* *(smal: v. weg, enz.)* narrow; *(v. kleding, schoenen)* tight; *(v. ruimte)* confined; *(fig.)* close; *bw.* narrowly; tightly; closely.

nauw *o.* *(zeestraat)* strait; *(fig.)* pinch, scrape.

nauwelijks *bw.* scarcely, hardly.

nauwgezet *b. n.* conscientious; *(angstvallig)* scrupulous, painstaking; *(stipt)* punctual, exact.

nauwgezetheid *v.* conscientiousness; painstaking; punctuality, exactitude.

nauwheid *v.* harrowness; tightness; closeness.

nauwkeurig *b. n.* accurate, exact, punctual.

nauwkeurigheid *v.* accuracy, exactness, punctuality.

nauwsluitend *b. n.* close-fitting.

nauwte *v.* defile, narrow pass; *(op zee)* strait(s), narrows.

navel *m.* navel; *(wet.)* umbilicus; *(Pl.)* hile.

navelband *m.* umbilical bandage.

navertellen *o. w.* repeat.

navolgen *o. w.* follow, imitate.

navolger *m.* follower, imitator.

navolging *v.* imitation.

navorsen *o. w.* investigate, search into, inquire into, explore.

navraag *v.* inquiry; *(H.)* demand, request; — **doen naar,** inquire after (about), make inquiries about.

navragen *o. w.* inquire, make inquiries.

naweeën *o. mv.* after-pains; *(fig.)* after-effects, evilconsequences, aftermath.

nawerken *on. w.* work overtime; produce after-effects.

nawerking *v.* after-effect.

nazaat *m.* descendant.

nazeggen *o. w.* repeat.

nazenden *o. w.* send after, forward.

nazien *o. w.* *(volgen met de ogen)* look after, follow with one's eyes; *(nagaan, onderzoeken)* examine, go through; *(v. rekening)* check; *(voor reparatie)* overhaul; *(verbeteren: v. werk, oefeningen)* correct.

ne(d)er *bw.* down.

nederdalen *on. w.* go down, come down, descend.

nederdaling *v.* descent.

nederig *b. n.* humble, modest, low, lowly.

nederigheid *v.* humbleness, humility, modesty, lowliness.

nederlaag *v.* defeat, overthrow; **de — lijden,** be defeated, suffer defeat.

Nederland *o.* The Netherlands, Holland.

Nederlands *b. n.* Dutch.

ne(d)erlaten *o. w.* let down, lower; *(loodlijn)* erect, let fall.

ne(d)erleggen *o. w.* lay down, put down; *w. w.* **zich —,** lie down; **zich er bij —,** acquiesce in it, put up with it.

nederzetting *v.* settlement.

neef *m.* *(kind v. oom of tante)* cousin; *(oomzegger)* nephew.

neen *bw.* no.

neerhaal *m.* downstroke.

neerhalen *o. w.* pull down; lower.

neerschieten *o. w.* *(v. persoon)* shoot dead; *(v. vogel, enz.)* shoot down; *(v. vliegtuig)* bring down; *on. w.* dart down, dash down.

neerslaan *o. w.* *(v. persoon)* strike down, knock down; *(v. ogen)* cast down, lower; *(v. kap, enz.)* lower, let down; *(scheik.)* precipitate; *(fig.)* deject; *on. w.* be

struck down, fall down; (scheik.) precipitate, be precipitated.
neerslachtig b. n. dejected, depressed, downcast, low-spirited.
neerslachtigheid v. dejection, dejectedness, depression of spirits, low spirits.
neerslag m. (muz.) down-beat; (regen) down-fall; o. (scheik.) precipitation; (bezinksel) deposit, sediment.
neerstorten on. w. fall down; (vl.) crash; o. w. fling down.
neerstorting v. falling down; (vl.) crash.
neervlijen o. w. lay down; w. w. **zich —,** lie down.
negatief b. n. (bw.) negative(ly); z. n., o. negative.
negen telw. nine.
negende b. n. ninth; **ten —,** ninthly.
negenhoek m. nonagon, enneagon.
negenoog r. (Dk.) lamprey; (gen.) furuncle.
negentien telw. nineteen.
negentig telw. ninety.
negentiger m., **negentigjarige** m. en v. nonagenarian.
neger m. negro; (fam.) nigger.
negerij r. negro-village; (fig.) (dog-) hole.
negerin r. negress.
neigen o. w. incline, bend; on. w. incline, bend; w. w. **zich —,** bend, bow.
neiging v. inclination, leaning (towards).
nek m. neck, nape of the neck.
nekken o. w. kill, break the neck of, slay.
nekkramp v. cerebro-spinal fever (of: meningitis).
nemen o. w. take, accept; (mil.: vesting, enz.) take, carry; (bespreken: plaats, enz.) take, engage.
nemer m. taker; (koper) buyer; (v. wissel) payee.
nerf v. rib, vein, nerve; (v. hout, leer) grain.
nergens bw. nowhere.
nering v. trade, retail trade; (klandizie) custom, goodwill.
neringdoende m. shopkeeper, tradesman.
nest o. (alg.) nest; (v. jonge honden) litter; (v. plaats) dog-hole; (v. roofvogel) eyrie; (fig.: meisje) minx, chit, horrid little piece.
nestel m. lace, shoulder-knot; (veter) lace.
nestelen on. w. nestle, make a nest; w. w. **zich —,** sconce oneself; o. w. lace up.
nestkuiken o. nestling; (fig.: v. kind) pin-basket.
nestvogel m. nestling.
net o. (alg.) net; (in trein) rack; (spoorweg—) network; (boodschappen—) net bag, string bag.
net b. n. (proper, zindelijk) tidy, clean; (deftig, fatsoenlijk) decent, respectable, nice; (aardig) trim, neat, dainty; (v.

aard) cleanly; bw. neatly; decently; (juist, precies) just, exactly, precisely; z. n., o. fair copy.
netel v. (Pl.) nettle.
neteldoek o. muslin.
netelig b. n. thorny, spinous; (v. zaak) ticklish; (v. vraagstuk) vexed; (hachelijk) critical, difficult.
neteligheid v. thorniness, spinality; ticklishness; criticalness, difficulty.
netelkoorts, netelroos v. nettle-rash.
netheid v. tidiness, cleanness; respectability; neatness, daintiness; cleanliness.
netto b. n. en bw. (H.) net; **— gewicht,** net weight; **— contant,** net cash.
netvlies o. retina.
netvliesontsteking v. retinitis.
neuriën o. w. en on. w. hum.
neus m. nose; (v. schoen) toe-cap, point; (aan lamp) snuff; (v. geweerkolf) heel; (v. dakpan) knob, nib; (v. schaaf) handle.
neusdoek m. handkerchief; (Z. N. ook:) shawl, wrap.
neusgat o. nostril.
neushoorn m. rhinoceros.
neusklank m. nasal sound, nasality.
neusring m. nose-ring; (v. vee, varken) nose-ring, snout-ring.
neusverkoudheid v. snivels.
neutraal b. n. neutral; (v. school, onderwijs) secular, unsectarian.
neutraliteit v. neutrality.
neuzen on. w. nose; **— in,** pry into.
nevel m. mist, haze; (zware —) fog.
nevelachtig b. n. misty, hazy, nebulous; foggy.
nevelbank v. fog-bank.
nevelbeeld o. mirage, looming, aerial image.
nevenschikkend b. n. co-ordinative.
nicht v., **—je** o. (dochter v. oom of tante) cousin; (oomzegster) niece.
niemand onbep. vnw. nobody, no one, none; **— minder dan,** no less a man than.
niemendal o. nothing at all.
nier v. kidney.
nierlijder m. nephritic sufferer, nephrytic patient.
nierontsteking v. nephritis.
nierpijn v. nephritic (pain).
niersteen m. (gen.) renal calculus; gravel; (delfstof) nephrite, jade.
nierziekte v. renal disease, nephritic disease.
nieskruid o. (Pl.) hellebore.
niesmiddel o. sternutatory, sternutative powder.
niespoeder o. sneezing-powder.
niet bw. not; **— eens,** not even; never; **— meer,** not more, no more; z. n., o. nothing, nought, naught; v. (in loterij) blank; **te — doen,** nullify, annul, override, abolish.
niet v. (tn.) rivet, clench.
nieteling m. nullity, nonentity.

nietig *b. n. (gering, onbeduidend)* paltry, beggarly, miserable, insignificant; *(v. persoon)* puny, diminutive; *(ongeldig)* void, null (and void).

nietigheid *v. (ongeldigheid)* nullity; *(geringheid, kleinigheid)* insignificance.

nietigverklaring *v.* nullification.

niets *vnw.* nothing, naught.

nietsdoener *m.* idler, do-nothing.

niettegenstaande notwithstanding, in spite of.

niettemin *bw.* nevertheless, for all that.

nieuw *b. n. (alg.)* new; *(v. groenten, haring, enz.: vers)* fresh; *(v. de laatste tijd)* recent; *(v. geschiedenis, schrijvers, enz.)* modern.

nieuwbakken *b. n.* new, new-made; *(fig.)* new, new-fangled, new-made.

nieuweling *m. en v.* novice, beginner, new-comer; *(op school)* new boy; *(aan universiteit)* freshman.

nieuwheid *v.* newness.

nieuwigheid *v.* novelty, innovation.

nieuwjaar *o.* New-Year.

nieuws *o.* news, tidings; *(nieuwtje)* piece of news; *(nieuw artikel)* novelty.

nieuwsbericht *o. (in dagblad)* news item; *(nieuwtje)* piece of news, piece of intelligence.

nieuwsblad *o.* newspaper.

nieuwsgierig *b. n.* inquisitive, curious.

nieuwsgierigheid *v.* inquisitiveness, curiosity.

niezen *on. w.* sneeze.

nijd *m.* envy.

nijdig *b. n.* angry; *(sl.)* stuffy, shirty; — **worden,** get angry, lose one's temper; *bw.* angrily.

nijdigaard *m.* cross-patch.

nijdigheid *v.* anger; *(sl.)* stuffiness, shirtiness.

nijgen *on. w.* bow, make a bow, curtsy.

nijging *v.* bow, curtsy.

nijlpaard *o.* hippopotamus.

nijpen *on. w.* nip, pinch.

nijpend *b. n.* nipping; *(v. wind, koude, enz.)* nipping, biting, sharp; *(v. armoede, gebrek)* grinding; *(v. honger)* pinching.

nijptang *v.* (pair of) pincers.

nijverheid *v.* industry.

nikkel *o.* nickel.

nikker *m. (neger)* nigger; *(duivel)* fiend.

nimf *v.* nymph.

nimmer *bw.* never.

nippertje *o.* nip; **op het —,** in the (very) nick of time, at the very nick.

nis *v.* niche.

nobel *b. n.* noble.

noch *vw.* neither... nor.

nochtans *bw.* nevertheless, yet, still.

node *bw.* reluctantly, unwillingly.

nodeloosheid *v.* needlesness.

nodig *b. n.* necessary, needful; — **hebben,** want, need, be in want of, be in need of; *bw.* necessarily; *z. n., o.* **het —e,** what is necessary; necessaries of life.

nodigen *o. w.* invite.

noemen *on. w. (een naam geven)* name; call, term, style, denominate; *(vermelden)* name, mention; *w. w.* **zich —,** call oneself.

noemenswaardig *b. n.* worth mentioning; **niet —,** *(ook:)* negligible.

noemer *m.* denominator.

noen *m.* noon.

noenmaal *o.* midday-meal, lunch(eon).

noest *b. n.* diligent, laborious, industrious, indefatigable.

noestheid *v.* diligence, laboriousness, industry, indefatigableness.

nog *bw.* yet, still, further; — **eens,** again, once again, once more; — **enige,** a few more; — **niet,** not yet, not just yet; — **steeds niet,** still not; **tot — toe,** up to now; — **iets,** something else.

nogal *bw.* rather, fairly, pretty.

nogmaals *bw.* again, once again, once more.

nok *v. (v. gewelf)* ridge; *(sch.)* nock, yard-arm; *(tn., v. projectiel, enz.)* stud.

nok *m. (snik)* sob.

nokbalk *m.* ridge-purlin, ridge-pole.

nominatief *m.* nominative.

non *v.* nun.

nonactief *b. n.* not in active service; on half-pay.

nonnenklooster *o.* nunnery, convent.

nonsens *m.* nonsense; *(sl.)* rot; —*!* fiddle-sticks!

nood *m.* need, necessity, distress, want.

noodanker *o. (sch.)* sheet-anchor, spare-anchor, anchor of distress.

noodbrug *v.* temporary bridge.

nooddruft *v. (levensbehoeften, voedsel)* necessaries of life, food, provisions; *(armoede)* indigence, poverty, want.

nooddruftig *b. n.* indigent, necessitous.

noodgedwongen *b. n. en bw.* by force, perforce, compelled by necessity.

noodklok *v.* alarm-bell, tocsin.

noodkreet *m.* cry of distress.

noodlanding *v.* forced landing, emergency landing; *(vl. ook)* forced descent.

noodlijdend *b. n. (v. gemeente, streek)* necessitous, distressed; *(v. persoon, volk)* indigent, poor, destitute.

noodlot *o.* fate, destiny.

noodlottig *b. n. (bw.)* fatal(ly).

noodrem *v.* safety-brake, danger-brake.

noodroer *o. (sch.)* jury-rudder.

noodtoestand *m.* state of necessity (emergency).

nooduitgang *m.* emergency exit.

noodweer *o. (onweer)* heavy (severe) weather, tempestuous weather; *v. (tegenweer)* self-defence.

noodwendigheid *v.* necessity.

noodwoning *v.* emergency dwelling.

noodzaak *v.* necessity.

noodzakelijk *b. n.* necessary; *bw.* necessarily, needs, of necessity.

noodzakelijkheid *v.* necessity.

noodzaken *o. w.* force, oblige, compel contrain, necessitate.

nooit *bw.* never.
noord *v. en o.* north.
noordelijk *b. n.* northern; arctic; (*v. wind*) northerly; (*v. richting*) northward; *bw.* northerly; northward(s).
noorden *o.* north.
noordenwind *m.* north wind.
noorderlicht *o.* northern lights, aurora borealis.
noordpool *v.* north pole.
noordpoolgebied *o.* arctic regions.
noordpoolreiziger *m.* arctic explorer.
noordster *v.* North star, polar star.
Noordzee *v.* North Sea, German Ocean.
Noorwegen *o.* Norway.
noot *v.* (*Pl.*) nut; (*muz.*) note; (*aantekening*) note. [incite.
nopen *o. w.* induce, compel, prompt,
nopens *vz.* concerning, with regard to.
normaalschool *v.* normal school.
nors *b. n.* gruff, surly.
norsheid *v.* gruffness, surliness.
nota *v.* note; (*rekening*) account, bill.
notabele *m. en v.* notable (man), notability, leading man (person).
nota bene nota bene, mind.
notariaat *o.* notaryship; office of notary.
notaris *m.* notary.
noteboom *m.* walnut-tree.
notedop *v.* nut-shell; (*fig.: bootje*) cockle-shell boat.
notekraker *m.* (pair of) nutcrackers; (*Dk.*) nut-cracker.
notenbalk *m.* (*muz.*) staff, stave.
notenpapier *o.* (*muz.*) music-paper.
notenschrift *o.* (*muz.*) notation.
noteren *o. w.* (*aantekenen*) note, note down, jot (down), make a note of;(*H.: v. prijzen*) quote; (*v. bestelling*) book.
notering *v.* noting, notation; (*H.*) quotation; (*v. effecten*) price.
notitie *v.* notice; (*aantekening*) note, jotting.

notulen *v. mv.* minutes.
novelle *v.* short story, novelette; (*recht*) amending bill, amendment act.
november *m.* November.
novice *m.* novice, probationer.
nu *bw.* now, at present; — **nog niet,** not yet; **van** — **af,** from this moment; **tot** — **toe,** hitherto, up to now; — **eerst,** only now, not until now; *z. n., o.* **het** —, the present; *vw.* now that.
nuchter *b. n.* sober, jejune; (*fig.*) greenhorn, simpleton; (*onnozel*) green; (*v. kalf*) new(ly) born.
nuchterheid *v.* sobriety; soberness, jejuneness; simplicity.
nuf *v.* prude, Miss Pert.
nuk *v.* freak, whim, caprice.
nukkig *b. n.* freakish, whimsical, capricious.
nul *v.* nought, naught, cipher; zero.
nulpunt *o.* zero.
nummer *o.* number; (*v. handschoenen, enz.*) size; (*op programma*) item; (*sp.*) event; (*v. auto*) registration number.
nummerbord *o.* (*v. auto*) number plate; (*el.*) indicator, annunciator.
nummeren *o. w.* number; *w. w.* **zich** —, number off.
nuntius *m.* nuncio.
nut *o.* use, benefit, profit, utility; **van** — **zijn,** be useful.
nutteloos *b. n.* (*zonder nut*) needless, useless; (*fig.: vruchteloos*) fruitless; *bw.* needlessly, uselessly; in vain.
nutteloosheid *v.* uselessness.
nutten *on. w.* be of use, avail.
nuttig *b. n.* useful, of use, profitable.
nuttigen *o. w.* take, partake.
nuttigheid *v.* utility.
nuttiging *v.* consumption; (*v. de Mis*) Communion.
nylon (*stofnaam*) *o. en m.,* (*kous*) *v.* (*m.*) nylon

O

oase *v.* oasis.
obelisk *v.* obelisk.
oblaat *m.* oblate; *v.* (*Prot.: avondmaalsofferbrood*) oblation, host.
obligatie *v.* bond, debenture; — **op naam,** registered debenture.
obligatiehouder *m.* bond-holder.
obligo *o.* **zonder ons** —, without our prejudice.
observatiepost *m.* observation-post.
observatorium *o.* observatory.
obstinaat *b. n.* (*bw.*) obstinate(ly).
oceaan *m.* ocean.
oceaanvlucht *v.* transoceanic flight.
ochtend *m.* morning.
ochtendgloren *o.* day-break, peep of day.
ochtendjapon *v.* morning gown.
octaaf *v. en o.* octave.

octrooi *o.* (*patent*) patent; (*handelsmachtiging, vergunning*) charter; (*belasting*) octroi.
oculeren *o. w.* inoculate, graft.
oefenen *o. w.* exercise, practise, train; *on. w.* practise, train; *w. w.* **zich** —, practise, exercise oneself.
oefening *v.* exercise, practice; (*godsdienstige* —) prayer-meeting.
oefenplaats *v.* practice-ground, practising-ground; (*mil.*) drill-ground.
oefentijd *m.* time for practising, period of instruction.
oerdier *o.* protozoan (*mv.: protozoa*).
oermens *m.* primitive man, prehistoric man.
oeros *m.* (*Dk.*) aurochs.
oerwoud *o.* virgin (native) forest.
oester *v.* oyster.

oever m. (v. zee) shore; (v. rivier) bank; (v. meer) margin, shore.
oeverbewoner m. riverain.
oeverkruid o. shore-weed.
oeverloper m. (Dk.) strand-snipe.
oeverzwaluw v. bank-martin, sand-martin.
of vw. or; (onderschikkend) if, whether.
offensief b. n. (bw.) offensive(ly); z. n., o. offensive.
offer o. offering, sacrifice, immolation; (slachtoffer) victim.
offerande r. offering, sacrifice, oblation; (v. de Mis) offertory.
offerblok o. offertory-box.
offeren o. w. offer (up), sacrifice, offer in sacrifice, immolate.
offergave v. offering.
offerlam o. sacrificial lamb; Lamb of God.
offerte v. offer; **een — doen,** make an offer.
offervaardigheid v. willingness (readiness) to make sacrifices; open-handedness, liberality.
offerwijn m. libatory wine.
officie o. office.
officieel b. n. official.
officier m. (military) officer.
officieus b. n. (bw.) semi-official(ly).
ofschoon vw. although, though.
ogenblik o. moment, instant, twinkling of an eye.
ogenblikkelijk b. n. (v. gevaar, enz.) immediate; (v. indruk, enz.) momentary; bw. immediately, instantly, directly, at the moment, on the instant.
ogenschouw v. inspection; **in — nemen,** inspect, review, examine, have a look at.
ogief o. (bouwk.) ogee, ogive.
oker v. ochre.
okergeel b. n. ochreous; z. n., o. yellow ochre.
okkernoot v. walnut.
oksaal o. organ-loft.
oksel m. arm-pit; (Pl.) axil, axilla.
okshoofd o. hogshead.
oktober m. October.
olie v. oil.
oliehoudend b. n. oleiferous.
oliekoek m. dough-nut; (voor vee) oil-cake.
oliën o. w. oil; (tn.) lubricate.
olienoot(je) v. (o.) peanut, ground-nut.
oliepit v. (floating) wick.
oliepot m. lubricator, oil-box.
oliesel o. **het H. —,** (kath.) the extreme unction.
olieslagerij v. oil-mill.
olievlek v. oil-stain.
olifant m. elephant.
olifantsziekte v. elephantiasis.
olijf v. olive.
Olijfberg m. Mount of Olives.
olijfboom m. olive-tree.
olijk b. n. (bw.) roguish(ly), playful(ly), arch(ly).

olijkerd m. rogue.
olijkheid v. roguishness, archness.
olm(boom) m. elm.
om vz. (— heen) round; about; (omstreeks) about; (tijdstip: te) at; (regelmatig, telkens na) every; (wegens) on account of, because of, for; (tegen, voor) for; at; bw. **— en —,** alternately; **beurt — beurt,** turn and turn about.
omarmen o. w. embrace, take in one's arms.
omber v. (aardsoort) umber; o. (kaartspel) ombre.
ombervis m. maigre, bar.
omblad o. (v. sigaar) binder, wrapper.
ombouwen o. w. reconstruct, rebuild.
ombrengen o. w. (doden) kill, dispatch, do to death, make away with.
ombuigen o. w. bend (down), turn back (down, up); on. w. bend, double (up).
omdat vw. because, as.
omdoen o. w. (v. kleren) put on; (v. touw, papier, enz.) put round.
omdraai m. (v. weg) turn, turning, bend; (v. wiel, enz.) turn.
omdraaien o. w. turn, turn round; on. w. (v. wind) turn, go round; (v. partij, v. richting wisselen) change one's mind; w. w. **zich —,** turn round; turn on one's heel; (liggend: in bed) turn over.
omdraaiing v. turning, rotation, circumrotation.
omeggen o. w. harrow.
omfloersen o. w. mufle; (fig.) shroud; **omfloerst vaandel,** draped colours.
omgaan on. w. (rondgaan) go round, go about; (voorbijgaan) pass; (gebeuren) happen, take place.
omgang m. (verkeer) (social) intercourse, companionship; (galerij) gallery; (rondgang) round, circuit; (v. wiel) rotation; (ommegang, processie) procession.
omgangstaal v. colloquial language.
omgekeerd b. n. turned, turned up; (v. doos, kist, enz.) turned upside down; (v. blad) turned over; (v. orde, verhouding, enz.) inverted; bw. upside down; **— evenredig,** inversely proportional; z. n., o. **het —e,** the reverse.
omgeven o. w. surround, encircle, encompass.
omgeven o. w. (rond geven) distribute, hand round, deal (round).
omgeving v. (v. stad, enz.) surroundings, environs, environment; (v. persoon) surroundings, entourage.
omgooien o. w. turn over, overturn, throw over, upset; (tn.: v. machine) reverse; (sch.) swing round; (v. mantel, enz.) throw on.
omgorden o. w. gird on, gird round; (fig.) gird, engirdle.
omgrenzen o. w. bound, border, limit; (fig.) circumscribe.
omgroeien o. w. grow round, grow about.

omhaal *m.* ceremony; fuss; (*v. woorden*) verbiage, verbosity; wordiness; (*krul, v. letter*) flourish; **zonder veel —,** without much ado; (*v. woorden*) without circumlocution; **met veel —,** with much circumstance.

omhakken *o. w.* cut down, hew down, fell.

omhalen *o. w.* (*v. muur*) pull down; (*v. grond*) break up; hoe up; (*v. schip*) put about.

ómhangen *o. w.* put on; hang otherwise; (*mil.*) sling; *on. w.* hang about, lop about, loiter.

omhángen *o. w.* hang (about), cover.

omheen *bw.* about, round, about.

omheinen *o. w.* fence in, fence round, hedge in, enclose.

omheining *v.* fence, enclosure.

omhelzen *o. w.* embrace; (*fig.*) embrace, espouse.

omhelzing *v.* embrace; (*fig.: v. leer, enz.*) embracement, espousal.

omhoog *bw.* on high, aloft; **handen —!** hands up!

omhoogbrengen *o. w.* raise.

omhullen *o. w.* envelop, wrap round, enwrap; (*fig.*) shroud, enshroud.

omhulsel *o.* envelope, envelopment.

omkantelen *on. w.* turn over, topple over, fall over, cant over.

omkeer *m.* change, turn, reversal; revolution; (*reactie*) revulsion; (*omverwerping*) subversion.

omkeren *o. w.* (*v. hoofd, kussen, enz.*) turn; (*v. kaart*) turn up, turn; (*v. blad, hooi*) turn over; (*v. kist, enz.*) turn upside down; (*v. stelling*) convert; (*v. volgorde, enz.*) reverse; (*omverwerpen*) subvert; *on. w.* return, turn back; (*veranderen*) change; *w. w.* **zich —,** turn (round); (*vlug*) wheel round; (*in bed*) turn over, turn round.

omkering *v.* turning; (*v. verhouding, woordschikking*) inversion; conversion; reversal; subversion.

omkijken *on. w.* look back; (*rondkijken*) look round.

ómkleden *w. w.* **zich —,** change (one's clothes); *o. w.* clothe, invest.

omkleedsel *o.* clothing, envelope.

omkneden *o. w.* knead again; give a new fashion to.

omkomen *on. w.* (*sterven*) perish; (*v. tijd*) end, come to an end.

omkoopbaar *b. n.* corruptible, venal.

omkopen *o. w.* corrupt, buy over.

omkoper *m.* corrupter, briber.

omkoperij *v.,* **omkoping** *v.* corruption, bribery, subornation.

omkransen *o. w.* wreathe.

omkrullen *o. w. en on. w.* curl up.

omlaag *bw.* below, down.

omleggen *o. w.* (*v. wissel*) shift; (*v. beugel*) reverse; (*sch.: v. roer*) shift, put over; (*v. schip*) careen; (*v. verband*) apply; (*v. weg*) divert; (*andersom leggen*) put about.

omlegsel *o.* border, edging; binding.

omliggend *b. n.* circumjacent, surrounding, neighbouring.

omlijsten *o. w.* frame.

omlijsting *r.* frame; (*handeling*) framing; (*fig.*) setting.

omloop *m.* (*v. bloed, geld*) circulation; (*v. planeet*) revolution; (*v. toren*) gallery; (*v. molen*) platform; (*v. dier*) pluck; (*v. vinger*) whitlow.

omlopen *on. w.* (*rondlopen*) walk about; (*lopen om*) go (walk) round; (*v. hoek*) turn; (*v. wind*) shift; (*v. gerucht*) be abroad, be current; (*v. tijd*) pass; (*omverlopen*) run down, knock down, upset.

ommantelen *o. w.* (*met mantel omhangen*) mantle; (*v. stad: versterken*) fortify, wall (in).

ommezien *o.* **in een —,** in a twinkle, in the twinkling of an eye, in a trice.

ommuren *o. w.* wall in, enclose with walls.

omploegen *o. w.* plough (up).

ompraten *o. w.* talk round, talk over.

omranden *o. w.* border, edge, rim.

omrasteren *o. w.* fence in, rail in, pale in.

omrastering *v.* railing.

omreis *r.* roundabout journey.

omréizen *o. w.* travel about.

ómreizen *on. w.* go (travel) by a roundabout way.

omrekenen *o. w.* convert.

omrekeningstabel *v.* conversion table.

omringen *o. w.* surround, encircle, encompass.

omroep *m.* (*radio*) broadcast(ing).

omroepen *o. w.* cry (about); (*radio*) broadcast.

omroeper *m.* (town-)crier, public crier, common crier, bell-man; (*radio*) announcer.

omroeren *o. w.* stir.

omruilen *o. w.* exchange, change.

omschakelaar *m.* (*el.*) change-over switch.

omschakelen *o. w.* (*el.*) change over; (*v. machine*) reverse.

omschansing *v.* intrenchment, circumvallation.

omschrift *o.* legend, circumscription.

omschrijven *o. w.* (*v. woord*) define; (*taalk.*) periphrase; (*nauwkeurig aangeven: rechten, plichten, enz.*) circumscribe; (*beschrijven*) describe; (*meetk.*) circumscribe.

omschrijving *v.* definition; periphrase, periphrasis; circumscription; description; (*H.*) specification.

omsingelen *o. w.* ring round, surround, encircle; (*v. vesting*) invest.

omsingeling *v.* encirclement; (*v. vesting*) investment.

omslaan *o. w.* (*omverslaan*) knock down, beat down; (*neerslaan: v. kraag, enz.*) turn down; (*v. broekspijp*) turn up; (*v. mantel, enz.*) throw on, put on;

(v. sjaal, enz.) wrap about; (v. blad) turn over; (v. kosten, enz.: gelijkelijk verdelen) apportion; on. w. (omvallen, omkantelen) be upset, overturn, be overset, turn turtle, capsize; (vl.) be blown over; (v. weer) break, change; (v. wind) shift, turn; **rechts (links)** —, turn to the right (to the left).

omslachtig b. n. (v. methode, systeem) cumbersome, cumbrous; (langdradig) digressive, prolix, long-winded; (omstandig) circumstantial.

omslachtigheid v. cumbersomeness, prolixity; circumstantiality.

omslag m. (v. mouw) cuff, turn-back; (v. broek) turn-up; (v. boek) cover, wrapper; (v. brief) envelope; (v. kosten) apportionment; (v. belasting) tax; (tn.: v. boor) brace; (gen.: natte —) compress, (wet.) pack; (warme —) (hot) fomentation; (fig.: omhaal) fuss, ado, ceremony; (moeite) trouble, bother.

omslagboor v. hand-brace, brace and bit.

omslagdoek m. shawl, wrap.

omsluieren o. w. veil, cover.

omsluiten o. w. encircle, enclose, surround; (vast omklemmen) clasp; (v. vesting: insluiten) invest.

omspitten o. w. dig (up), break up.

omspringen on. w. jump about, hop about; (omverspringen) upset; — **met,** manage, treat.

omstander m. bystander.

omstandig b. n. circumstantial, detailed; bw. circumstantially, in detail.

omstandigheid v. (alg.) circumstance; (uitvoerigheid) circumstantiality.

omstoten o. w. push down, push over, overthrow, overturn, upset.

omstralen o. w. shine about, irradiate.

omstreek v. surrounding country, neighbourhood, vicinity.

omstrengelen o. w. enlace, entwine, twine about, wind about, embrace.

omstrengeling v. entwinement, twisting about, embrace.

omtrek m. (alg.: v. voorwerp, enz.) outline, contour; (v. cirkel) circumference; (v. veelhoek) perimeter, periphery; (schets) outline; (v. stad enz.: omgeving) environs, neighbourhood, vicinity.

omtrekken o. w. (omvertrekken) pull down; (trekken om) march about, march round; (omsingelen) turn, outflank, envelop.

omtrent vz. (ongeveer) about; (nopens, ten opzichte van) about, concerning, respecting, with regard to; bw. about, near.

omtuimelen on. w. tumble down, topple over, purl.

omvang m. circumference, extent; (v. boek) size; (muz.: v. stem, instrument) range, compass; (v. borst) width; (v. onderzoek) scope, ambit; (v. werk) scope; (v. boom) girth; (grootte; belangrijkheid)

magnitude; (v. begrip, enz.) latitude; (volume) volume, bulk.

omvangrijk b. n. extensive, voluminous; (lijvig) extended, bulky, voluminous; (v. stem) of great compass.

omvatten o. w. enclose, close round, embrace; (omspannen) span; (fig.) include, comprise, embrace.

omver bw. down, over.

omvormen o. w. transform, remodel.

omweg m. roundabout way, circuitous road (route); detour.

omwenden o. w. turn (round); (v. schip) put about; w. w. **zich** —, turn (round).

omwentelen on. w. revolve, rotate, gyrate.

omwenteling v. revolution, rotation, gyration; (fig.) revolution.

omwentelingsas v. axis of rotation.

omwerken o. w. reconstruct, remodel, refashion; (v. boek) recast, rewrite; (v. grond) dig up, plough, turn up.

omwerking v. reconstruction, remodelling; recasting; (concreet) recast; turning up.

omwinden o. w. wind (twine) about (round), entwine, envelop.

omwindsel o. wrapper, bandage; (Pl.) involucrum.

omwisselen o. w. change, exchange; on. w. alternate, change.

omzendbrief m. circular letter; (kerkelijk) pastoral letter.

omzet m. turnover, returns.

omzetbelasting v. turnover tax.

omzetten o. w. (v. voorwerp) place (arrange) differently; (v. woord, getal, muz.) transpose; (v. machine) reverse; (el.: stroom) commute; (H.) turn over; sell.

omzetting v. transposition; (v. woordorde) inversion; (tn.) reversal; (el.) commutation; (v. lening, effecten, enz.) conversion; (in daden) translation.

omzichtig b. n. circumspect, cautious, wary; bw. circumspectly, cautiously, warily, with circumspection.

omzichtigheid v. circumspection, cautiousness, caution, wariness.

omzien on. w. look back.

omzomen o. w. hem; border, fringe.

omzwachtelen o. w. swathe, bandage; (v. kind) swaddle.

omzweven o. w. hover about, flit (float) about.

onaangediend b. n. unannounced.

onaangegeven b. n. unentered.

onaangenaam b. n. disagreeable, unpleasant; (v. smaak) offensive.

onaangenaamheid v. disagreeableness, unpleasantness.

onaangeroerd b. n. untouched, intact; (v. spijs, ook.) untasted.

onaannemelijk b. n. (v. voorstel, voorwaarden, enz.) unacceptable; (ongeloofwaardig) incredible.

onaannemelijkheid v. unacceptableness; incredibility.

onaantastbaar *b. n.* unassailable; (*fig.*) unassailable; unimpeachable; unchallengeable; indisputable; inviolable.
onaantastbaarheid *v.* unassailableness, unassailability.
onaanzienlijk *b. n.* (*v. bedrag, enz.*) inconsiderable; (*onbeduidend*) insignificant; (*v. geboorte, stand*) humble.
onaardig *b. n.* unpleasant, ungraceful; unkind.
onachtzaam *b. n.* inattentive, careless, negligent.
onachtzaamheid *v.* inattention, carelessness, negligence.
onafgebroken *b. n.* uninterrupted, unintermitted, continuous; *bw.* uninterruptedly, continuously, without interruption.
onafgehandeld *b. n.* not terminated, unsettled.
onafgewend *b. n.* unaverted; *bw.* fixedly, steadily.
onafgewerkt *b. n.* unfinished.
onafhankelijk *b. n.* independent.
onafhankelijkheid *v.* independence.
onaflosbaar *b. n.* irredeemable.
onafwendbaarheid *v.* inevitableness, unavoidableness.
onafzienbaar *b. n.* beyond the reach of the eye, not to be overseen; endless, interminable, immense.
onafzienbaarheid *v.* immensity, immenseness.
onbaatzuchtig *b. n.* (*bw.*) disinterested-(ly), unselfish(ly).
onbaatzuchtigheid *v.* disinterestedness, unselfishness.
onbarmhartig *b. n.* merciless, pitiless.
onbarmhartigheid *v.* unmercifulness, pitilessness.
onbeantwoord *b. n.* (*v. brief*) unanswered; (*v. liefde, vriendschap*) unreturned, unrequited; (*v. vraag, kwestie*) open.
onbebouwd *b. n.* (*v. land*) uncultivated, untilled, waste; (*v. ruimte, terrein*) unbuilt(on), vacant.
onbedaarlijk *b. n.* ungovernable, inextinguishable.
onbedacht(zaam) *b. n.* thoughtless, rash, inconsiderate.
onbedachtzaamheid *v.* thoughtlessness, inconsiderateness.
onbedorven *b. n.* undeteriorated, not spoiled; (*fig.*) undepraved, uncorrupted, innocent.
onbedreven *b. n.* inexperienced, unskilled, unskilful.
onbedrevenheid *v.* inexperience, unskilfulness. [ling.
onbeduidend *b. n.* insignificant; trif-
onbedwongen *b. n.* untamed, unsubdued; unconquered.
onbeëdigd *b. n.* unsworn.
onbegaanbaar *b. n.* impracticable, impassable.
onbegonnen *b. n.* not yet begun; **een — werk,** a bootless affair.

onbegrensd *b. n.* unlimited, unbounded.
onbegrepen *b. n.* not understood.
onbegrijpelijk *b. n.* incomprehensible; (*ondenkbaar*) inconceivable; (*v. woorden, enz.*) unintelligible.
onbegrijpelijkheid *v.* incomprehensibility; inconceivableness.
onbehaaglijk *b. n.* disagreeable, unpleasant; (*onlekker*) out of sorts; (*niet op zijn gemak*) uncomfortable.
onbehaaglijkheid *v.* disagreeableness, unpleasantness; uncomfortableness, discomfort.
onbeheerd *b. n.* unowned, ownerless; **—e goederen,** unclaimed goods.
onbeholpen *b. w.* awkward, clumsy, shiftless, helpless.
onbeholpenheid *v.* awkwardness, clumsiness, shiftlessness.
onbehoorlijk *b. n.* unseemly, unbecoming, improper, indecent.
onbehoorlijkheid *v.* unseemliness, impropriety, indecency.
onbehouwen *b. n.* unhewn, undressed; (*fig.*) ungainly, unwieldy; (*vlegelachtig*) unmannered.
onbekend *b. n.* unknown.
onbekende *m. en v.* stranger; (*wisk.*) unknown.
onbekendheid *v.* (*het niet kennen*) ignorance, unacquaintance, unacquaintedness. [less.
onbekommerd *b. n.* unconcerned, care-
onbekommerdheid *v.* unconcern, carelessness.
onbekrompen *b. n.* (*mild, royaal*) unstinted, open-handed, liberal, lavish; (*niet kleingeestig*) open-minded, liberal.
onbekrompenheid *v.* unstintedness, open-handedness, liberality; open-mindedness.
onbekwaam *b. n.* incapable, unable, incompetent, inefficient; (*beschonken*) drunk and incapable.
onbeleefd *b. n.* impolite, uncivil, discourteous, ill-mannered.
onbeleefdheid *v.* impoliteness, incivility, discourtesy.
onbelemmerd *b. n.* unhindered, unimpeded, unhampered, unobstructed.
onbelezen *b. n.* illiterate, unread.
onbemerkt *b. n.* unperceived, unobserved, unnoticed.
onbemiddeld *b. n.* without means, impecunious.
onbemind *b. n.* unbeloved, unloved, unpopular.
onbenoemd *b. n.* unappointed; (*niet genoemd*) unnamed.
onbenullig *b. n.* inane, fatuous, dullheaded; (*v. verhaal, rede*) feeble.
onbenulligheid *v.* inanity, fatuousness, dull-headedness.
onbenut *b. n.* unused.
onbepaald *b. n.* indefinite, unlimited, vague; (*onzeker*) uncertain; **—e wijs,** infinitive.

onbepaaldheid *v.* indefiniteness, unlimitedness; uncertainty.
onbeperkt *b. n.* unlimited, boundless, unrestrained.
onbeproefd *b. n.* untried, untested.
onberaden *b. n.* thoughtless, inconsiderate, unadvised, ill-advised, ill-considered.
onbereden *b. n. (v. paard)* unbroken, unridden; *(mil.)* unmounted, not mounted; *(v. weg)* unfrequented.
onbereikbaar *b. n.* unreachable; inaccessible, unapproachable; *(fig.)* unattainable.
onberekenbaar *b. n.* in alculable.
onberispelijk *b. n.* irreproachable, impeccable, blameless, faultless, flawless, above reproach, irreprehensible.
onberoerd *b. n.* unmoved, unperturbed, untouched.
onbeschaafd *b. n.* impolite, rude, unmannerly, uneducated; *(v. volk)* uncivilized, uncultivated, uncultured, barbarous.
onbeschaafdheid *v.* impoliteness, rudeness, unmannerliness; uncultivatedness, barbarism.
onbeschaamd *b. n.* impudent, insolent, impertinent, brazen-faced.
onbeschaamdheid *v.* impudence, insolence, impertinence.
onbescheiden *b. n.* indiscreet, immodest.
onbescheidenheid *v.* indiscretion, immodesty.
onbeschreven *b. n. (v. papier, enz.)* not written upon, blank; *(v. wet: ongeschreven)* unwritten.
onbeschrijfelijk *b. n.* indescribable, beyond description.
onbeschroomd *b. n.* fearless, undaunted, unawed, unabashed. [etc.
onbeschroomdheid *v.* fearlessness,
onbeslist *b. n.* undecided.
onbesmet *b. n.* uninfected, uncontaminated; stainless, spotless, undefiled.
onbesproken *b. n. (v. plaats)* unbooked, unreserved, unengaged; *(v. onderwerp)* undiscussed; *(fig.: v. gedrag)* reproachless, blameless, unimpeached.
onbestaanbaar *b. n.* impossible.
onbestelbaar *b. n.* undeliverable.
onbestemd *b. n.* undeterminate, undetermined, vague.
onbestendig *b. n.* unstable, unsteady, inconstant, variable, changeable, unsettled.
onbestendigheid *v.* instability, inconstancy, changeability, unsettledness.
onbestorven *b. n. (v. vlees)* too fresh; *(v. metselwerk)* fresh.
onbesuisd *b. n.* hot-headed, hotbrained, rash, foolhardy.
onbetaald *b. n.* unpaid, unsettled.
onbetamelijk *b. n.* unbecoming, improper, unseemly, indecent.

onbetamelijkheid *v.* unbecomingness, impropriety, unseemliness, indecency.
onbetrouwbaar *b. n.* unreliable, untrustworthy.
onbetwist *b. n.* uncontested, undisputed, unchallenged.
onbevangen *b. n. (zonder vooroordeel, onpartijdig)* unprejudiced, unbias(sed), open-minded; *(vrijmoedig)* unconcerned.
onbevaren *b. n. (v. zee)* unexplored, unnavigated; *(v. matroos)* unexperienced.
onbevlekt *b. n.* unstained, unspotted.
onbevoegd *b. n.* incompetent, unqualified.
onbevredigd *b. n.* unsatisfied, ungratified.
onbevreesd *b. n.* unafraid, fearless, undaunted.
onbevreesdheid *v.* fearlessness.
onbevrucht *b. n.* unimpregnated.
onbewaakt *b. n.* unguarded; not watched.
onbeweegbaar *b. n.* immovable.
onbeweegbaarheid *v.* immovableness, immovability.
onbeweeglijk *b. n.* immobile, immovable, motionless.
onbewimpeld *b. n.* undisguised, open, frank.
onbewogen *b. n.* unmoved, untouched, unconcerned; *(v. gelaat)* impassive; *(v. oppervlakte)* unruffled.
onbewoonbaar *b. n.* uninhabitable.
onbewoond *b. n.* uninhabited; *(v. huis)* untenanted, unoccupied, uninhabitated.
onbewust *b. n. (v. handeling)* unconscious; *(v. zonde, enz.)* unwitting; *bw.* unconsciously, unwittingly.
onbewustheid *v.* unconsciousness.
onbezet *b. n. (v. leerstoel)* unoccupied, not occupied, disengaged; *(v. zitplaats)* free; *(v. ambt)* vacant; *(mil.)* unoccupied, ungarrisoned.
onbezoldigd *b. n.* unsalaried, unpaid.
onbezonnen *b. n.* thoughtless, inconsiderate, rash, giddy, unthinking.
onbezonnenheid *v.* thoughtlessness, etc.
onbezorgd *b. n.* careless, unconcerned, light-hearted, care-free.
onbezorgdheid *v.* carelessness, unconcern, light-heartedness.
onbezwaard *b. n. (v. eigendom: zonder hypotheek)* unmortgaged; unencumbered; *(v. gemoed, geweten)* unburdened, unencumbered. [(ly).
onboetvaardig *b. n. (bw.)* impenitent-
onboetvaardigheid *v.* impenitence.
onbruik *o.* disuse, desuetude; *in — geraken,* go out of use, fall into desuetude (disuse).
ondank *m.* ingratitude, thanklessness.
ondankbaar *b. n.* ungrateful, unthankful, thankless.
ondankbaarheid *v.* ingratitude, unthankfulness, thanklessness.

ondanks *vz.* in spite of, notwithstanding.

onder *vz. (plaats, lager dan)* under; *(dicht.)* underneath, beneath; *(te midden van)* among; *(tijdens, gedurende)* during; *bw.* below.

onderaan *vz.* at the bottom (foot) of; *bw.* below, at the bottom.

onderaandeel *o.* sub-share.

onderaannemer *m.* sub-contractor.

onderaards *b. n.* subterranean, subterraneous, underground.

onderarm *m.* fore-arm.

onderblijven *on. w.* remain under water; stay downstairs.

onderbouw *m.* substructure, infrastructure; *(v. spoorweg)* roadbed.

onderbreken *o. w.* break, break off, interrupt.

onderbreking *v.* break, interruption.

onderbroek *v.* (pair of) drawers, pants.

onderbuik *m.* abdomen.

onderdaan *m.* subject.

onderdak *o.* shelter, accommodation, home.

onderdanig *b. n.* submissive; humble.

onderdanigheid *v.* submissiveness, submission; humility.

onderdeel *o. (onderste deel)* lower part; part, inferior part; *(onderverdeling)* subdivision; *(v. wetenschap)* branch.

onderdirecteur *m.* sub-director, sub-manager, assistant manager.

onderdoen *o. w. (v. schaatsen)* tie on, put under; *on. w.* **niet — voor,** not yield to, be a match for; **voor niemand —,** be second to none, yield to none.

onderdompeling *v.* immersion, submersion, plunge, ducking.

onderdrukken *o. w. (v. volk)* oppress; *(v. opstand, zucht, enz.)* suppress; *(v. angst)* keep down; *(v. snik)* stifle; *(v. tranen, ontroering)* force back.

onderdrukker *m. (v. volk)* oppressor; *(v. opstand)* suppressor.

onderdrukking *v.* oppression; suppression.

onderduiken *on. w. (v. vogel, enz.)* dive, duck, plunge; *(v. zon)* sink (dip) below the horizon.

ondereen *bw.* together, pell mell.

ondergaan *on. w.* go down, sink, perish; *(v. zon, enz.)* set, go down.

ondergáán *o. w.* undergo, suffer, endure.

ondergang *m. (v. zon)* setting; *(fig.)* decline, fall, downfall, ruin, ruination, destruction.

ondergeschikte *m.* subordinate, inferior.

ondergetekende *m. en v.* undersigned.

ondergoed *o.* underclothes, undergarments, underwear.

ondergrond *m.* underground, subsoil; foundation, groundwork.

ondergronds *b. n.* underground.

onderhandelaar *m.* negotiator.

onderhandelen *on. w.* negotiate, treat.

onderhandeling *v.* negotiation; *(mil.)* parley.

onderhands *b. n. (v. akte, overeenkomst, enz.)* private; *(ong.)* underhand, backstairs; *(v. verkoop)* private, by private contract.

onderhavig *b. n.* **in het —e geval,** in the present case, in the case in question.

onderhevig *b. n.* **— aan,** liable to, subject to; **aan twijfel —,** open to question.

onderhorig *b. n.* dependent, subordinate, belonging (to).

onderhorige *m. en v.* subordinate.

onderhoud *o. (v. persoon: levensonderhoud)* maintenance, support, sustenance, keep; *(v. weg, gebouw, enz.)* upkeep, maintenance; *(v. auto, enz.)* upkeep; *(gesprek)* conversation, interview.

ónderhouden *o. w.* keep under.

onderhóuden *o. w. (v. huis, enz.)* keep in repair; *(v. briefwisseling, taal, enz.)* keep up; *(v. gezin, enz.)* provide for, support, maintain; *(aangenaam bezighouden)* entertain; amuse; *w. w.* **zich(zelf) —,** provide for oneself, support oneself; **zich — met iem.,** converse with a person.

onderhoudskosten *m. mv.* cost of maintenance, upkeep expenses.

onderhuid *v.* cutis, corium, derm; *(sch.)* inner planking, dead works.

onderkin *v.* double chin.

onderkleed *o.* undergarment.

onderkomen *on. w.* find (get) shelter, find accommodation, find a lodging; *z. n., o.* shelter, accommodation, lodging.

onderkoning *m.* viceroy.

onderkruipen *o. w. (v. persoon)* undercut, undersell; supplant; *(v. zaak)* spoil a person's trade; *(bij staking)* blackleg, rat.

onderkruiper *m.* undercutter, underseller, price-cutter; spoil-trade; *(bij staking)* blackleg, rat, scab.

onderlaag *v.* substratum, under-layer.

ónderleggen *o. w.* put under, lay under, underlay.

onderlegger *m.* blotting-pad; *(balk)* girder; *(v. traploper)* stair-pad.

onderlijf *o.* lower part of the body, abdomen.

onderlijfje *o.* bodice, underbodice, camisole.

onderling *b. n.* mutual; *bw. (wederkerig)* mutually; *(samen)* together.

onderlip *v.* lower lip, under lip.

ondermaans *b. n.* sublunary.

ondermelk *v.* skimmed milk.

ondermijnen *o. w.* undermine, sap.

ondernemen *o. w.* undertake, attempt.

ondernemer *m.* undertaker.

onderneming *v.* undertaking, enterprise; *(bedrijf)* concern; *(waagstuk)* venture.

onderofficier *m.* non-commissioned officer; *(mar.)* petty officer.

onderonsje *o.* family party, small intimate party; private affair, private business.

onderpacht *v.* sublease.

onderpand *o.* pledge, guarantee, security.

onderpastoor *m.* chaplain.

onderricht *o.* instruction, tuition.

onderrichten *o. w.* instruct, teach.

onderrichting *v.* instruction; (*inlichting*) information.

onderrok *m.* underskirt, petticoat.

onderschatten *o. w.* undervalue, underestimate, underrate.

onderscheid *o.* (*verschil*) difference; (*het maken v. onderscheid*) distinction.

onderscheiden *o. w.* distinguish, discriminate, discern; (*fig.*) distinguish, single out; *w. w.* **zich —,** distinguish oneself; **zich — van,** be distinguished from.

onderscheiden *b. n.* different, distinct; (*allerlei*) various; (*verscheiden*) several.

onderscheiding *v.* distinction.

onderscheidingsteken *o.* distinguishing mark, mark of distinction, badge.

onderscheppen *o. w.* intercept.

onderschepping *v.* interception.

onderschrift *o.* subscription; (*bij plaat*) letterpress; (*v. film*) caption; (*v. brief*) signature, subscription.

onderschrijven *o. w.* sign; (*fig.*) subscribe to, endorse.

onderschuiven *o. w.* foist in, shove under; (*fig.*) substitute, surreptitiously.

onderspit *o.* **het — delven,** be worsted, have the worse, go to the wall.

ónderstaan *on. w.* be flooded.

onderstáán *o. w.* dare, presume, venture.

onderstaand *b. n.* subjoined, undermentioned.

onderstand *m.* assistance, relief; (*recht*) subsistence pay, maintenance, allowance.

onderste *o.* undermost; **het — boven,** upside down, face down; topsy-turvy; **het —,** the bottom part.

onderstel *o.* under-carriage, underframe; (*v. auto, ook:*) chassis; (*v. locomotief*) bogie.

onderstellen *o. w.* suppose, presume.

onderstelling *v.* supposition; hypothesis.

ondersteunen *o. w.* support; (*fig.*) succour, support; (*v. armen*) relieve.

ondersteuning *v.* support; relief.

onderstrepen *o. w.* underline.

onderstuk *o.* lower part, bottom piece.

ondertekenen *o. w.* sign; **mede —,** countersign.

ondertekening *v.* signature.

ondertrouw *m.* publication of the banns; notice of marriage; betrothment.

ondertussen *bw.* meanwhile, in the mean time.

onderverdelen *o. w.* subdivide.

onderverdeling *v.* subdivision.

ondervinden *o. w.* experience.

ondervinding *v.* experience.

ondervoed *b. n.* underfed, undernourished.

ondervoorzitter *m.* vice-president, deputy-chairman, vice-chairman.

ondervragen *o. w.* interrogate, question, examine; (*recht: verhoren*) try.

ondervraging *v.* interrogation, examination.

onderwereld *v.* underworld, nether world.

onderwerp *o.* subject, theme, topic; (*gram.*) subject.

onderwerpen *o. w.* subject, subdue; *w. w.* **zich —,** submit.

onderwerping *v.* subjection; submission; resignation.

onderwijs *o.* instruction, tuition; (*met opvoeding*) education.

onderwijzen *o. w.* instruct, teach; *on. w.* teach.

onderwijzer *m.* (elementary school, primary) teacher, master.

onderwijzeres *v.* teacher.

onderworpen *b. n.* (*onderdanig*) submissive; (*gelaten, berustend*) resigned.

onderworpenheid *v.* submissiveness, submission; resignation; subjection.

onderzoek *o.* inquiry, investigation, examination; (*wetenschappelijk*) research; (*scheikundig*) analysis.

onderzoeken *o. w.* inquire, investigate, examine; (*wet.*) research into, make researches into; (*scheik.*) analyse; (*v. land, enz.*) explore; (*keuren: v. ogen, goud, enz.*) test; (*v. redenen, enz.*) probe.

ondeugd *v.* vice; (*v. kind*) (little) rogue (rascal), naughty boy (girl).

ondeugdelijk *b. n.* (*v. voedsel, enz.*) unsound; (*v. stoffen, enz.*) flimsy.

ondeugend *b. n.* (*v. kind*) naughty; (*v. dier*) vicious, wicked.

ondeugendheid *v.* naughtiness; wickedness.

ondienst *m.* bad service, ill turn.

ondiepte *v.* shallowness; (*concreet*) shoal, shallow.

ondier *o.* brute, monster.

onding *o.* absurdity, non-entity.

ondoelmatig *b. n.* unsuitable, inexpedient, inappropriate.

ondoeltreffend *b. n.* ineffective, ineffectual.

ondoordringbaar *b. n.* impenetrable; (*voor water, enz.*) impervious, impermeable.

ondoordringbaarheid *v.* impenetrability; imperviousness.

ondoorschijnend *b. n.* opaque, untransparent.

ondoorzichtig *b. n.* untransparent, not transparent.

ondoorzichtigheid *v.* untransparency.

onduidelijk *b. n.* (*v. uitspraak, enz.*) indistinct; (*v. omtrekken, enz.*) illdefined, indistinct; (*v. tekst, betekenis*)

unclear, not clear; (*v. telegram*) unintelligible.

onduidelijkheid *v.* indistinctness; unintelligibility.

onduldbaar *b. n.* unbearable, insufferable, intolerable.

onecht *b. n.* not genuine, falsified, bogus, sham, counterfeit; (*v. document, enz.*) spurious, unauthentic; (*v. munt*) false, spurious; (*v. diamant*) imitation; (*v. kleur*) not fast, fading; (*v. kind*) illegitimate, natural, born out of wedlock; (*fig.: gevoelens*) sham; (*v. adel*) bogus.

onechtheid *v.* spuriousness, unauthenticity; illegitimacy.

onenig *b. n.* disagreeing, discordant, at issue, at variance.

onenigheid *v.* disagreement, discord, dissension; — *krijgen,* quarrel, fall out.

oneens *b. n.* **het — zijn met iem.,** be at issue with a person, disagree with a person.

oneer *v.* dishonour, disgrace. [ful.

oneerbiedig *b. n.* irreverent, disrespect-

oneerbiedigheid *v.* irreverence, disrespect.

oneerlijk *b. n.* (*bw.*) dishonest(ly), unfair(ly).

oneffen *b. n.* uneven, rugged, rough.

oneffenheid *v.* unevenness, ruggedness, roughness.

oneindig *b. n.* endless, unending, infinite; *bw.* infinitely.

oneindigheid *v.* infinity.

onervaren *b. n.* inexperienced.

oneven *b. n.* odd.

onevenredig *b. n.* disproportional, disproportionate, out of (all) proportion; inadequate; *bw.* disproportionately, out of (all) proportion.

onevenredigheid *v.* disproportion; inadequacy.

onfatsoenlijk *b. n.* indecent, improper.

onfatsoenlijkheid *v.* indecency, impropriety.

onfeilbaar *b. n.* infallible, unfailing.

onfeilbaarheid *v.* infallibility.

ongaar *b. n.* (*v. vlees*) underdone, not done enough; (*v. brood*) slackbaked, under-baked.

ongaarne *bw.* unwillingly, reluctantly, with a bad grace.

ongeacht *b. n.* unesteemed; *vz.* irrespective of; in spite of, notwithstanding; apart from.

ongebonden *b. n.* unbound; (*in losse vellen*) in sheets; (*fig.*) unrestrained; (*losbandig*) dissolute, licentious, loose; — *stijl,* prose; *bw.* dissolutely, licentiously, loosely.

ongebondenheid *v.* dissoluteness, licentiousness, looseness, debauchery.

ongedaan *b. n.* undone, unperformed; — *maken,* undo, live past; (*H.: v. koop, enz.*) cancel, cry off.

ongedeerd *b. n.* unhurt, hurtless, uninjured, unharmed.

ongedekt *b. n.* uncovered; (*v. krediet*) open; (*v. lening, bankbiljetten*) fiduciary.

ongedierte *o.* vermin.

ongeduld *o.* impatience.

ongeduldig *b. n.* (*bw.*) impatient(ly).

ongedurig *b. n.* inconstant, restless.

ongedurigheid *v.* inconstancy, restlessness.

ongedwongen *b. n.* unconstrained, unrestrained, natural; unforced, uncompelled; (*v. stijl*) unlaboured.

ongedwongenheid *v.* unconstrainedness, unconstraint, abandon(ment).

ongeëvenaard *b. n.* unequalled, matchless, unmatched.

ongegrond *b. n.* unfounded, ungrounded, groundless, without foundation.

ongehoord *b. n.* unheard; (*fig.*) unheard of, unprecedented.

ongehoorzaam *b. n.* disobedient.

ongehoorzaamheid *v.* disobedience.

ongehuwd *b. n.* unmarried.

ongekookt *b. n.* unboiled, raw.

ongekunsteld *b. n.* artless, ingenuous, unstudied, unaffected, natural.

ongekunsteldheid *v.* artlessness, ingenuousless, etc.

ongeldig *b. n.* non valid, invalid, void, null and void; — *maken,* invalidate, nullify.

ongeldigheid *v.* invalidity, nullity.

ongeldigverklaring *v.* annulment, nullification, invalidation.

ongeleerd *b. n.* (*v. persoon*) untaught, ignorant, unlettered, unlearned, illiterate; (*v. les*) unlearned, unlearnt.

ongelegen *b. n.* inconvenient, unseasonable, inopportune.

ongelijk *b. n.* (*oneffen*) unequal, uneven; (*verschillend*) different, dissimilar, unequal; (*ongelijkmatig: v. pas, enz.*) unequal; (*v. gewas, enz.*) patchy; *bw.* unequally, unevenly; *z. n., o.* wrong; — *hebben,* be wrong; be in the wrong.

ongelijkbenig *b. n.* (*v. driehoek*) scalene.

ongelijkheid *v.* inequality, unevenness; difference, dissimilarity, disparity.

ongelijksoortig *b. n.* dissimilar, incongruous, heterogeneous.

ongelijkvormig *b. n.* dissimilar.

ongelikt *b. n.* unlicked.

ongeloof *o.* unbelief, disbelief. [ous.

ongelovig *b. n.* unbelieving, incredul-

ongelovige *m. en v.* unbeliever, infidel.

ongelovigheid *v.* incredulity.

ongeluk *o.* (*ongeval*) accident, casualty; (*lichter*) mishap; (*ongelukkig toeval*) ill-luck; (*door omstandigheden*) misfortune; (*innerlijk*) unhappiness; (*met machine, motor*) breakdown.

ongelukkig *b. n.* (*door omstandigheden*) unfortunate; (*innerlijk*) unhappy; (*door toeval*) unlucky; (*noodlottig*) ill-fated; (*gebrekkig*) crippled; *bw.* unfortunately.

ongelukkige *m.* (*gebrekkige*) cripple.

ongeluksdag *m.* black(-letter) day, unlucky (fatal) day, ill-fated day.

ongeluksvogel *m.* bird of ill omen.

ongemak *o.* inconvenience, discomfort; *(euvel, gebrek)* trouble, infirmity; *(last, ontbering)* hardship.

ongemakkelijk *b. n. (v. stoel, enz.)* uneasy, not easy, uncomfortable; *(v. kleding)* uncomfortable; *(v. persoon)* hard to please; *(lastig, ongelegen)* inconvenient; *bw.* not easily; roundly, unmercifully.

ongemanierd *b. n.* unmannerly, ill-mannered, ill-bred, mannerless, rude, unpolished.

ongemanierdheid *r.* unmannerliness, ill-breeding.

ongemeen *b. n.* uncommon, out of the common, extraordinary, singular, out of the way; *bw.* uncommonly, extraordinarily.

ongemerkt *b. n. (zonder bemerkt te worden)* unperceived; *(zonder merkteken)* unmarked, unlettered; *bw.* without being perceived; *(geleidelijk)* gradually.

ongenaakbaar *b. n.* unapproachable, inaccessible.

ongenade *v.* disgrace, disfavour, displeasure.

ongenadig *b. n.* merciless, pitiless, unmerciful; *bw.* mercilessly, pitilessly.

ongeneeslijkheid *v.* incurableness, incurability.

ongenodigd, ongenood, *b. n.* uninvited, unasked, unbidden.

ongeoorloofd *b. n.* unpermitted, unallowed, illicit, unlawful.

ongepast *b. n.* inappropriate, unbecoming, improper, unsuitable, unseemly, unfitting.

ongepastheid *v.* inappropriateness, unsuitableness, impropriety, unseemliness, unfittingness.

ongerechtigheid *v.* iniquity, injustice.

ongeregeld *b. n.* irregular, disorderly, inordinate.

ongeregeldheid *v.* irregularity; inordinacy; **ongeregeldheden,** riots, disturbances.

ongerept *b. n.* untouched, intact; *(v. sneeuw, enz.)* virgin; *(rein)* inviolate, pure, undefiled, untainted.

ongeriefelijk *b. n.* inconvenient; *(v. huis, enz.)* uncomfortable, incommodious.

ongeriefelijkheid *v.* inconvenience; uncomfortableness.

ongerijmd *b. n.* absurd, preposterous, non-sensical.

ongerijmdheid *v.* absurdity.

ongerust *b. n.* uneasy, anxious, worried.

ongerustheid *v.* uneasiness, anxiety.

ongeschikt *b. n.* unsuitable, unfit, improper, inapt, inefficient; *(ongelegen)* inconvenient.

ongeschiktheid *v.* unsuitability, unfitness, impropriety, inaptitude, inefficiency, incapacity.

ongeschonden *b. n.* undamaged, intact; *(v. eer, wet, enz.)* inviolate, inviolated.

ongeschondenheid *v.* intactness, undamaged condition; inviolacy.

ongeschoold *b. n.* unschooled; untrained, unpractised; *(v. arbeid, arbeider)* unskilled.

ongesteld *b. n.* indisposed, unwell.

ongesteldheid *v.* indisposition.

ongestoord *b. n.* undisturbed; uninterrupted; *bw.* undisturbedly, without being disturbed; uninterruptedly.

ongestraft *b. n.* unpunished; *bw.* with impunity.

ongetekend *b. n.* not signed, unsigned, anonymous.

ongetwijfeld *bw.* undoubtedly, doubtless, no doubt, without doubt.

ongevaarlijk *b. n.* undangerous.

ongeval *o.* accident.

ongeveer *bw.* about, somewhere about, in the neighbourhood of; *(bijna)* nearly, almost.

ongeveinsdheid *v.* sincerity, unfeignedness.

ongevraagd *b. n. (v. persoon)* uninvited, unbidden, unasked; *(v. zaak:* advies, opmerking, enz.*)* unsolicited, uncalled for, unasked (for).

ongewapend *b. n.* unarmed; *(v. oog)* naked, unaided, unarmed.

ongewenst *b. n.* unwished for, undesirable, not wished.

ongewerveld *b. n.* invertebrate.

ongewijd *b. n.* unhallowed, unconsecrated; *(v. muziek)* secular.

ongewoon *b. n.* unusual, uncommon, unwonted, unfamiliar, novel.

ongewoonheid *r.* unusualness, uncommonness, novelty.

ongewoonte *v.* unwontedness, unfamiliarity, want of practice.

ongezellig *b. n. (v. persoon)* uncompanionable, unsociable, unclubbable; *(v. kamer, enz.)* cheerless.

ongezelligheid *v.* unsociableness.

ongezocht *b. n.* unsought; natural, unaffected, unstudied.

ongezond *b. n. (v. voeding)* unwholesome; *(v. persoon, gelaatskleur, enz.)* unhealthy; *(v. lucht, klimaat, enz.)* insalubrious, unhealthy.

ongodsdienstig *b. n.* irreligious.

ongunst *v.* disfavour, disgrace.

ongunstig *b. n.* unfavourable; *(v. wisselkoers, rapport, enz.)* adverse; *(v. voorteken)* inauspicious, unfavourable; *bw.* adversely.

onguur *b. n. (v. weer)* inclement, rough, rude; *(v. persoon)* repulsive, sinister, forbidding; *(v. taal)* coarse.

onhandig *b. n. (v. persoon)* clumsy, awkward, unhandy; *(v. zaak)* unwieldy, unhandy. [ness.

onhandigheid *v.* clumsiness, awkward-

onheil *o.* calamity, disaster, mischief.

onheilspellend *b. n.* ominous, portentous, inauspicious.

onherbergzaam *b. n.* inhospitable.

onherroepelijk *b. n. (v. besluit, enz.)*

irrevocable; (v. wet) unrepealable; (v. vonnis) irreversible; bw. irrevocably.
onheuglijk b. n. immemorial.
onheus b. n. discourteous, uncourteous, ungracious, disobliging.
oninbaar b. n. irrecoverable.
oningewijd b. n. uninitiated; **de —en,** the uninitiated, the outsiders.
onjuist b. n. inexact, incorrect, inaccurate.
onjuistheid v. inexactness, incorrectness, inaccuracy; falsity; (fout) error.
onkenbaar b. n. unknowable; unrecognizable.
onkies b. n. indelicate, immodest.
onkiesheid v. indelicacy, immodesty.
onkosten m. mv. expenses, charges.
onkruid o. weeds.
onkuis b. n. unchaste.
onkuisheid v. unchastity.
onkunde v. ignorance.
onkundig b. n. ignorant.
onkwetsbaar b. n. invulnerable.
onkwetsbaarheid v. invulnerability.
onlangs bw. the other day, recently, lately.
onleesbaar b. n. (v. geschrift) illegible, unreadable; (v. boek, enz.) unreadable.
onloochenbaar b. n. undeniable, incontestable, not to be denied.
onlusten m. mv. disturbances, troubles, riots.
onmacht v. (machteloosheid, onvermogen) impotence, inability; (flauwte, bezwijming) swoon, fainting-fit, faint.
onmachtig b. n. impotent, powerless; (niet in staat tot) unable (to).
onmatig b. n. immoderate, intemperate.
onmatigheid v. immoderateness, intemperance, insobriety.
onmeedogend b. n. pitiless, merciless, ruthless.
onmens m. en o. brute, monster.
onmenselijk b. n. inhuman, brutal.
onmenselijkheid v. inhumanity, brutality.
onmerkbaar b. n. imperceptible; unperceivable; bw. imperceptibly, insensibly.
onmetelijk b. n. immeasurable, immense.
onmetelijkheid v. immeasurableness, immensity.
onmiddellijk b. n. immediate, direct; bw. immediately, directly, at once.
onmin v. discord, disagreement, dissension; **in — leven met.** be at variance with.   [tial.
onmisbaar b. n. indispensable, essen-
onmisbaarheid v. indispensableness, indispensability.
onmogelijk b. n. impossible; bw. not possibly.
onmogelijkheid v impossibility
onmondig b. n. minor, under age; — **blijven,** (fig.) remain in tutelage.
onmondigheid v. minority, non-age; (recht) infancy; (fig.) tutelage.

onnatuurlijk b. n. unnatural, not natural; (gemaakt, ook:) affected; bw. unnaturally.
onnatuurlijkheid v. unnaturalness; affectation.
onnavolgbaar b. n. inimitable.
onneembaar b. n. impregnable.
onnodig b. n. unnecessary, needless; bw. unnecessarily, needlessly, without necessity.
onnozel b. n. silly, simple; (onschuldig) innocent, harmless.
Onnozele-kinderendag m. Innocents' Day.
onnozelheid v. silliness, simplicity; innocence.
onomwonden b. n. (bw.) explicit(ly), frank(ly), unreserved(ly).
onontbeerlijk b. n. indispensable.
onontkoombaar b. n. ineluctable, inevitable, inescapable.
onontwikkeld b. n. undeveloped, not developed; (fig.: v. persoon) uneducated.
onooglijk b. n. unsightly, ungraceful, unlovely.
onooglijkheid v. unsightliness, ungracefulness, unloveliness.
onopgemerkt b. n. unobserved, unnoticed, unnoted, undetected.
onopgesierd b. n. unadorned, unvarnished, uncoloured; (v. verklaring, verslag, enz.) bald; (v. waarheid) sober, plain.
onophoudelijk b. n. unceasing, neverceasing, incessant; bw. incessantly.
onoprecht b. n. (bw.) insincere(ly), disingenious(ly).
onoprechtheid v. insincerity.
onopzettelijk b. n. (bw.) unintentional-(ly), undesigned(ly), inadvertent(ly).
onordelijk b. n. disorderly, unruly.
onordelijkheid v. disorderliness; unruliness.
onovergankelijk b. n. intransitive.
onovertrefbaar b. n. unsurpassable.
onovertroffen b. n. unsurpassed.
onoverwinnelijkheid v. invincibility.
onoverwonnen b. n. unconquered.
onoverzienbaar b. n. not to be overseen; interminable, immense.
onpaar b. n. odd.
onpas te —, unseasonably, out of season.
onpasselijk b. n. indisposed, unwell.
onpasselijkheid v. indisposition.
onraad o. danger, trouble.
onrecht o. injustice, wrong.
onrechtmatig b. n. unlawful, illegal.
onredelijk b. n. unreasonable, irrational.
onredelijkheid v. unreasonableness; irrationality.
onregelmatigheid v. irregularity.
onrein b. n. unclean, impure.
onreinheid v. uncleanness, impurity.
onrijm o. prose.
onrijp b. n. unripe; (fig.) immature, unripe.

onrijpheid *v.* unripeness, immaturity.
onroerend *b. n.* immovable.
onrust *v.* unrest, disquiet; (*rusteloosheid*) unrest, restlessness; (*ongerustheid*) uneasiness; (*tn.: in uurwerk*) fly, balance; (*persoon*) fidget.
onrustbarend *b. n.* alarming.
onrustig *b. n.* restless, unquiet; (*v. slaap*) troubled, uneasy; (*zenuwachtig*) fidgety.
onruststoker *m.* agitator, mischiefmaker, firebrand.
ons *pers. vnw.* us; *van* —, ours; *bez. vnw.* our; *de onze,* ours.
ons *o.* ounce; hectogram.
onschadelijk *b. n.* inoffensive, harmless, innocuous, innoxious.
onschadelijkheid *v.* inoffensiveness, harmlessness, innocuity.
onschatbaar *b. n.* invaluable, inestimable, priceless.
onschendbaar *b. n.* inviolable.
onschendbaarheid *v.* inviolability.
onschuld *v.* innocence.
onschuldig *b. n.* innocent; guiltless, harmless; inoffensive.
onsmakelijk *b. n.* unsavoury, unpalatable, unappetizing.
onsmakelijkheid *v.* unsavouriness, etc.
onstandvastig *b. n.* unstable; inconstant.
onstandvastigheid *v.* instability; inconstancy.
onsterfelijk *b. n.* immortal, undying, deathless.
onstuimig *b. n.* (*v. zee, wind*) tempestuous, boisterous, turbulent; (*fig.: v. persoon*) impetuous.
onstuimigheid *v.* tempestuousness, boisterousness, turbulence; (*fig.*) impetuosity.
ontaard *b. n.* degenerate.
ontaarden *on. w.* degenerate, deteriorate.
ontaarding *v.* degeneration, deterioration.
ontberen *o. w.* lack, be in want of.
ontbering *v.* want, privation, hardship.
ontbieden *o. w.* send for, summon, order to appear.
ontbijt *o.* breakfast.
ontbinden *o. w.* (*losmaken*) untie, undo, loose; (*scheik.*) decompose; (*v. parlement, vennootschap, huwelijk*) dissolve; (*v. leger*) disband; (*v. optocht*) break up, dissolve; (*v. krachten, enz.*) resolve.
ontbinding *v.* untying; decomposition; dissolution; disbandment; resolution.
ontbladeren *o. w.* strip off the leaves.
ontbloot *b. n.* naked, bare.
ontbloten *o. w.* bare, denude; (*v. hoofd*) uncover, bare; (*fig.*) lay bare; *w. w. zich* —, divest oneself.
ontboezemen *o. w.* unbosom; *zich* —, unbosom oneself, pour out one's heart.
ontboezeming *v.* effusion, outpouring.

ontbolsteren *o. w.* shell, unhusk; (*fig.*) polish.
ontbranden *on. w.* ignite, take fire.
ontbranding *v.* ignition, combustion.
ontbreken *on. w.* fail, be wanting, be missing; *het —de,* the deficiency.
ontdaan *b. n.* disconcerted, discomposed, upset, haggard.
ontdekken *o. w.* (*hoofd*) uncover; (*v. land, enz.*) discover; (*v. fout, vergissing*) detect; (*v. waarheid, enz.*) find out; (*v. goud, petroleum*) strike.
ontdekker *m.* discoverer.
ontdekking *v.* discovery.
ontdekkingsreis *v.* voyage of discovery, exploring, expedition.
ontdoen *o. w.* undo; — *van,* strip of; *w. w. zich — van,* part with; dispose of.
ontdooien *on. w.* thaw; (*fig.*) melt, come out of one's shell, thaw.
ontduiken *o. w.* (*duikende ontwijken*) duck away from, elude; (*v. wet, bepalingen*) get round, evade; (*v. voorwaarden, belasting, enz.*) dodge; (*v. moeilijkheid, plicht, enz.*) shirk; (*v. vraag, contract, enz.*) evade.
ontduiking *v.* elusion; evasion; (*recht*) fraud.
onteren *o. w.* dishonour, degrade; (*verkrachten*) violate, deflower, dishonour, ravish; (*v. kerk, enz.: ontheiligen*) desecrate.
ontering *v.* dishonouring, degradation; violation, defloration, rape; desecration.
ontegensprekelijk *b. n.* incontestable, undeniable, unquestionable; *bw.* incontestably, undeniably, unquestionably.
onteigenen *o. w.* (*v. eigenaar*) dispossess; (*v. eigendom*) expropriate.
onteigening *v.* dispossession; expropriation
ontelbaar *b. n.* innumerable, numberless, countless.
ontembaar *b. n.* untamable, indomitable.
onterven *o. w.* disinherit.
ontevreden *b. n.* discontented, dissatisfied; (*mopperig*) disgruntled; *de —en,* the malcontents.
ontevredenheid *v.* discontent, discontentedness, dissatisfaction.
ontfermen *w. w. zich — over,* take pity on, have mercy on, commiserate.
ontferming *v.* pity, commiseration.
ontfutselen *o. w. iem. iets —,* pilfer (filch) something from a person.
ontgaan *on. w.* escape, elude, get away from; *o. w. moeilijkheden —,* obviate difficulties.
ontgelden *o. w.* pay for, suffer for.
ontginnen *o. w.* (*v. land, in cultuur brengen*) reclaim; (*v. grond*) break up; (*v. bos*) clear; (*v. mijn*) work; (*v. koolmijn*) exploit.
ontginning *v.* reclaiming, reclamation; clearing; working; exploitation.

ontgoochelen *o. w.* disillusion(ize), disenchant, undeceive.
ontgoocheling *v.* disillusionment, disenchantment.
onthaal *o.* (*ontvangst*) entertainment, treat; (*fig.: v. voorstel, enz.*) reception.
onthalen *o. w.* entertain, treat, regale.
ontheffen *o. w.* (*v. verplichting*) discharge, dispense, exempt, exonerate.
ontheffing *v.* discharge, dispensation, exemption, exoneration; (*v. ambt*) removal, discharge, supersession; (*v. belasting*) remission.
ontheiligen *o. w.* desecrate, profane.
ontheiliger *m.* desecrator, profaner.
ontheiliging *v.* desecration, profanation.
onthoofden *o. w.* behead, decapitate.
onthoofding *v.* decapitation.
onthouden *o. w.* (*niet vergeten*) retain, keep in remembrance; (*niet geven, achterhouden*) keep from, withhold; *w. w.* **zich — van,** abstain from, refrain from.
onthouder *m.* abstainer.
onthouding *v.* abstinence, abstemiousness; (*v. stemming*) abstention.
onthullen *o. w.* (*v. gedenkteken*) unveil; (*v. geheim*) reveal, disclose.
onthulling *v.* unveiling; revelation, disclosure.
onthutst *b. n.* confused, disconcerted, perplexed, discomfited, dismayed.
ontijdig *b. n.* unseasonable, untimely; (*te vroeg*) premature; *bw.* unseasonably, untimely; prematurely, before one's time.
ontkennen *o. w.* deny; (*v. schuld: niet erkennen*) disown; *on. w.* (*recht*) deny the charge.
ontketenen *o. w.* unchain, unshackle.
ontkiemen *on. w.* germinate; (*fig. ook:*) germ.
ontkieming *v.* germination.
ontkleden *o. w. en w. w.* **zich —,** undress.
ontknopen *o. w.* untie, undo; (*v. jas, enz.*) unbutton; (*fig.*) unravel.
ontkomen *on. w.* escape, get off.
ontladen *o. w.* (*v. schip, kanon, enz.*) unload; (*v. schip, el.*) discharge.
ontlading *v.* (*v. schip*) unloading, discharge; (*el.*) discharging, discharge.
ontlasten *o. w.* unburden; *w. w.* **zich —,** (*v. rivier*) discharge (oneself), disembogue; (*v. onweer*) burst, break; (*v. persoon*) have (do) a motion.
ontlasting *v.* discharge, relief; (*stoelgang*) motion, evacuation.
ontleden *o. w.* analyse, reduce to its elements; (*v. dier, plant, enz.*) dissect, anatomize; (*redekundig*) analyse; (*taalkundig*) parse.
ontleder *m.* dissector.
ontleding *v.* analysis; parsing; dissection.
ontleedkunde *v.* anatomy.
ontlenen *o. w.* **— aan,** borrow from, adopt from; derive from.

ontlening *v.* borrowing, adoption; derivation.
ontloken *b. n.* (*v. bloem*) blown, full-blown, opened; (*fig.: v. talent, enz.*) full-blown.
ontlokken *o. w.* elicit from, draw from.
ontlopen *o. w.* run away from, escape; (*mijden*) avoid, shun.
ontluiken *on. w.* open, expand.
ontluiking *v.* opening.
ontmoedigen *o. w.* discourage, dishearten, dispirit.
ontmoediging *v.* discouragement, disheartenment.
ontmoeten *o. w.* (*opzettelijk*) meet; (*toevallig*) meet with, come across; (*fig.: weerstand, enz.*) encounter.
ontmoeting *v.* meeting; encounter.
ontnemen *o. w.* take (away) from, deprive of.
ontnuchteren *o. w.* sober; (*fig.*) disillusion, disenchant, undeceive.
ontoegankelijk *b. n.* inaccessible, unapproachable.
ontoereikend *b. n.* insufficient; inadequate.
ontoerekenbaar *b. n.* (*v. persoon*) irresponsible, of unsound mind, unaccountable; (*recht*) non compos (mentis); (*v. daad*) not imputable.
ontplofbaar *b. n.* explosive.
ontploffen *on. w.* explode, detonate.
ontploffing *v.* explosion, detonation.
ontplooien *o. w.* unfurl, unfold; (*fig.*) unfold, develop, put forth; *w. w.* **zich —,** unfurl, unfold; (*mil.*) deploy; (*fig.*) unfold, develop, expand.
ontpoppen *w. w.* **zich — als,** turn out to be, blossom out as, reveal oneself as,
ontraden *o. w.* dissuade, discourage, advise against.
ontrafelen *o. w.* unravel.
ontredderen *o. w.* disable, shatter, cripple, throw out of gear, put out of joint.
ontreddering *v.* disorganization, disorder confusion.
ontrieven *o. w.* deprive of; *w. w.* **zich —,** put up with privations.
ontroeren *o. w.* move, affect, touch; *on. w.* be moved, be affected.
ontroering *v.* emotion.
ontrollen *o. w.* unroll, unfurl, unfold.
ontromen *o. w.* skim, cream.
ontroostbaar *b. n.* inconsolable, disconsolate.
ontrouw *b. n.* untrue, unfaithful, disloyal; *z. n., v.* unfaithfulness, disloyalty; infidelity.
ontroven *o. w.* steal from, rob of.
ontruimen *o. w.* (*v. huis*) vacate; (*v. straten, enz.*) clear; (*mil.: v. stad, enz.*) evacuate.
ontruiming *v.* vacation; clearance, clearing; evacuation.
ontrukken *o. w.* wrest from, tear from, snatch away from.

ontschepen *o. w.* (*v. passagier*) disembark; (*v. goederen*) discharge, unship; *w. w.* **zich** —, disembark.
ontscheping *v.* disembarkation, disembarkment; discharge.
ontschieten *on. w.* slip from.
ontsieren *o. w.* disfigure, deface.
ontslaan *o. w.* discharge, dismiss.
ontslag *o.* discharge, dismissal; (*vrijwillig*) resignation.
ontslapen *on. w.* pass away, expire.
ontsluieren *o. w.* unveil; (*fig.: v. geheim, enz.*) reveal, disclose, unveil.
ontsluiten *o. w.* open; unlock; (*fig.*) open, unseal; *w. w.* **zich** —, open.
ontsmetten *o. w.* disinfect, deodorize.
ontsmetting *v.* disinfection, deodorization.
ontsmettingsmiddel *o.* disinfectant, deodorant.
ontsnappen *on. w.* escape, evade.
ontsnapping *v.* escape.
ontspannen *o. w.* (*v. boog*) unbend, unstring; (*v. geest*) unbend; (*v. trommel*) unbrace; (*v. vuisten*) unclench; (*v. spieren*) relax; *w. w.* **zich** —, (*v. persoon*) relax, unbend, recreate, divert oneself; (*v. spieren*) relax.
ontspanning *v.* relaxation; (*fig.: vermindering v. spanning*) relief (of tension); (*verpozing*) relaxation, distraction, diversion, recreation.
ontsporen *on. w.* run off the rails, be derailed; **doen** —, throw off the rails, derail.
ontsporing *v.* derailment.
ontstaan *on. w.* come into existence, arise, take its rise; (*v. brand, enz.*) originate; **doen** —, cause, occasion, give rise to; — **uit,** arise from, proceed (spring) from; *z. n., o.* origin.
ontsteken *o. w.* kindle, light, ignite; (*Z. N.: v. vat*) pierce, broach; *on. w.* (*v. wond*) inflame.
ontsteking *v.* ignition; (*v. wond*) inflammation.
ontsteld *b. n.* alarmed, frightened.
ontstellen *o. w.* alarm, frighten, startle; *on. w.* be frightened, be startled, become alarmed.
ontsteltenis *v.* agitation, consternation, alarm, dismay.
ontstemmen *o. w.* (*muz.*) put out of tune; (*fig.*) put out, displease, put out of temper.
onttrekken *o. w.* withdraw, withhold; *w. w.* **zich** — **aan,** withdraw from.
onttronen *o. w.* dethrone.
onttroning *v.* dethronement.
ontucht *v.* lewdness, fornication, prostitution.
ontuchtig *b. n.* lewd, lascivious, unchaste.
ontvangbewijs *o.* receipt.
ontvangen *o. w.* receive; (*H.: v. goederen*) take delivery of; (*v. salaris*) draw; *on. w.* receive, hold reception.
ontvanger *m.* (*v. belasting*) receiver,

tax-collector; (*ontvangtoestel*) receiver; (*v. brief, enz.*) recipient; (*H.: v. goederen*) consignee; (*v. zegelrechten*) stamp collector.
ontvangst *v.* (*v. persoon, radio*) reception; (*v. brief, geld, enz.*) receipt.
ontvangtoestel *o.* (*radio*) receiver, receiving-set.
ontveinzen *o. w.* dissemble, conceal.
ontvetten *o. w.* ungrease.
ontvlambaar *b. n.* inflammable.
ontvlammen *on. w.* inflame, kindle.
ontvlezen *o. w.* strip of the flesh.
ontvlieden *o. w.* flee (fly) from, fly away.
ontvluchten *o. w. en on. w.* fly, flee, escape.
ontvluchting *v.* flight; escape.
ontvoeren *o. w.* carry off, abduct; (*v. kind*) kidnap.
ontvoering *v.* adduction; kidnapping.
ontvolken *o. w.* depopulate; (*fig.*) empty.
ontvolking *v.* depopulation.
ontvouwen *o. w.* unfold, develop.
ontvouwing *v.* unfolding, development.
ontvreemden *o. w.* steal; embezzle.
ontvreemding *v.* theft; embezzlement.
ontwaken *on. w.* awake, get awake, wake up.
ontwapenen *o. w.* disarm.
ontwapening *v.* (*v. soldaat, enz.*) disarming; (*als doel, beweging*) disarmament.
ontwaren *o. w.* perceive, descry.
ontwennen *o. w.* disaccustom, lose the habit of.
ontwerp *o.* project, plan; (*v. wet*) bill; (*v. document*) draft; (*tekening*) design.
ontwijden *o. w.* desecrate, profane, defile, violate.
ontwijken *o. w.* (*v. slag, moeilijkheid, enz.*) dodge, evade; (*v. persoon, plaats*) avoid, shun; (*v. kwestie*) fence with, blink; (*onaangenaamheden*) shy away from; (*v. plicht, enz.*) shirk.
ontwijking *v.* evasion.
ontwikkeld *b. n.* developed; (*fig.*) educated, well-informed.
ontwikkelen *o. w.* develop; (*v. warmte*) generate, engender; (*v. theorieën*) evolve, unfold; (*v. kracht*) put forth; *w. w.* **zich** —, develop.]tion.
ontwikkeling *v.* development; educa-
ontwortelen *o. w.* uproot, unroot, tear up by the roots, eradicate.
ontwrichten *o. w.* dislocate, disjoint, put out.
ontwrichting *o.* dislocation; (*fig.*) dislocation, unsettlement; disruption.
ontzag *o.* awe, respect, veneration.
ontzaglijk *b. n.* awful, stupendous; (*v. menigte, enz.*) vast; *bw.* awfully.
ontzagwekkend *b. n.* awe-inspiring; formidable.
ontzeggen *o. w.* deny; refuse, forbid; *w. w.* **zich iets** —, deny oneself something.

ontzenuwen *o. w.* enervate, unnerve; (*fig.*) invalidate, refute, disprove.

ontzet *b. n.* appalled, aghast, horrified; (*v. rails*) out of alignment.

ontzet *o.* (*mil.: v. stad, resting*) relief, delivery; (*v. aangevallene*) rescue.

ontzettend *b. n.* appalling, terrible, dreadful; (*fam.*) awful; *bw.* terribly, dreadfully; awfully.

ontzetting *r.* (*schrik*) appalment, aghastness, horror; (*mil.*) relieving, relief; (*v. persoon*) rescue; (*uit ambt*) deprivation, dismissal.

ontzield *b. n.* inanimate, exanimate, lifeless.

ontzien *o. w.* (*vrezen*) stand in awe of; (*eerbiedigen*) respect, look up to; (*sparen*) spare, save; *w. w.* **zich —,** take care (be careful) of oneself, spare oneself.

ontzinken *on. w.* sink away from; (*fig.: v. moed, krachten, enz.*) give way, fail.

onuitgegeven *b. n.* unpublished.

onuitgesproken *b. n.* unspoken.

onuitputtelijk *b. n.* inexhaustible, unfailing.

onuitstaanbaar *b. n.* intolerable, insufferable, unbearable.

onuitwisbaar *b. n.* indelible, ineffaceable, unerasable.

onvast *b. n.* (*v. grond*) infirm, soft; (*v. gang, hand, enz.*) unsteady; (*v. karakter*) unstable, unsteady, irresolute; (*v. weer*) unsettled; (*v. toestand*) unsettled; uncertain; (*r. markt*) fluctuating, unsteady; (*v. slaap*) light.

onvastheid *v.* instability, unstableness, etc.

onvatbaar *b. n.* **— voor,** (*ziekte, besmetting*) immune from; (*rede*) impervious to, insensible to; (*medelijden*) inaccessible to; (*verbetering*) incapable of; (*lijden*) impassible.

onveilig *b. n.* unsafe, unsecure.

onveranderd *b. n.* unchanged, unaltered.

onverantwoordelijk *b. n.* (*niet verschoonbaar, onvergeeflijk*) inexcusable, unjustifiable, unwarrantable; (*niet aansprakelijk*) irresponsible, unaccountable.

onverbasterd *b. n.* undegenerate, uncorrupted.

onverbeterlijk *b. n.* incorrigible.

onverbiddelijk *b. n.* inexorable, relentless.

onverbogen *b. n.* (*gram.*) undeclined

onverbreekbaar, onverbrekelijk *b. n.* unbreakable, indissoluble.

onverdacht *b. n.* unsuspected, above suspicion.

onverdeeld *b. n.* undivided, entire; (*v. goedkeuring*) unqualified; (*v. succes*) unmixed; (*v. winst*) accumulated; *bw.* wholly, whole-heartedly.

onverdeeldheid *v.* state of undividedness.

onverderfelijk *b. n.* imperishable, incorruptible.

onverdiend *b. n.* (*v. lof, enz.*) undeserved, unmerited; (*r. geld*) unearned.

onverdorven *b. n.* undepraved, unspoiled.

onverdraagzaam *b. n.* intolerant.

onverdraagzaamheid *v.* intolerance.

onverdroten *b. n.* indefatigable, unwearied, unwearying, unflagging.

onverenigbaar *b. n.* (*v. ambten*) incapable of being together; **— met,** incompatible with, inconsistent with, irreconcilable with.

onvergankelijk *b. n.* imperishable, undying, everlasting.

onvergeeflijk *b. n.* unpardonable, unforgivable, irremissible.

onvergetelijk *b. n.* unforgettable, ever memorable.

onverhinderd *b. n.* unhindered, unimpeded.

onverhoeds *bw.* unawares, unexpectedly, suddenly.

onverhoeds *b. n.* unexpected, sudden.

onverholen *b. n.* unconcealed, undisguised, open; *bw.* undisguisedly, openly, frankly.

onverhoopt *b. n.* unexpected, unhoped for, unlooked for.

onverklaarbaar *b. n.* inexplicable.

onverkocht *b. n.* unsold.

onverkort *b. n.* unabridged, uncurtailed.

onverlaat *m.* miscreant, wretch, brute.

onverlet *b. n.* unhindered, unimpeded; (*ongedeerd*) uninjured.

onvermengd *b. n.* unmixed, unalloyed, undiluted, unqualified, pure.

onvermijdelijk *b. n.* inevitable, unavoidable; inescapable.

onverminderd *b. n.* undiminished, unabated; *rz.* (*behoudens*) without prejudice to, without detriment to.

onvermoeibaar *b. n.* indefatigable, untirable.

onvermogen *o.* impotence, incompetency, inability, disability, incapacity; (*behoeftigheid*) indigence.

onvermurwbaar *b. n.* unrelenting, relentless, inflexible, inexorable.

onverplicht *b. n.* not obligatory, not compulsory; (*v. leervak*) optional.

onverpoosd *b. n.* uninterrupted, unintermitted, unremitting; *bw.* uninterruptedly, unceasingly.

onverricht *b. n.* undone; **—er zake,** without having effected one's object.

onversaagd *b. n.* intrepid, undaunted, dauntless, unflinching.

onversaagdheid *v.* intrepidity, undauntedness.

onverschillig *b. n.* indifferent, careless, insouciant; *bw.* indifferently, insouciantly, carelessly.

onverschilligheid *v.* indifference, insouciance, unconcern.

onverschoonbaar *b. n.* inexcusable, unpardonable.

onverschrokken *b. n.* undaunted, dauntless, intrepid.

onverschrokkenheid *v.* undauntedness, intrepidity.
onverslijtbaar *b. n.* not to be worn out, indestructible, imperishable, everlasting.
onverstaanbaar *b. n.* unintelligible.
onverstand *o.* unwisdom.
onverstandig *b. n.* unwise, ill-judged.
onverstoorbaar *b. n.* imperturbable, indisturbable; (*b. ernst*) invincible.
onvervaard *b. n.* undaunted, fearless, undismayed.
onvervalst *b. n.* unadulterated, unalloyed, unqualified, genuine.
onvervreemdbaar *b. n.* inalienable; (*v. recht, ook:*) indefeasible.
onvervulbaar *b. n.* unrealizable.
onverwacht *b. n.* unexpected, unlooked for.
onverwijld *b. n.* immediate; *bw.* immediately, without delay.
onverzadigd *b. n.* unsatiated, not satiated, unsatisfied; (*v. stoom*) unsaturated.
onverzoenlijk *b. n.* irreconcilable, implacable.
onverzoenlijkheid *v.* irreconcilableness, implacability, irreconcilability.
onverzorgd *b. n.* (*v. zieke, enz.*) not attended to, unattended to, untended to; (*v. tuin, enz.*) unkempt, uncared for; (*v. haar, enz.*) untidy.
onverzwakt *b. n.* not enfeebled, not weakened, unweakened; (*fig.*) unimpaired, unremitting.
onvindbaar *b. n.* unfindable, not to be found.
onvoldaan *b. n.* unsatisfied, dissatisfied; (*v. rekening*) unpaid, unsettled.
onvoldoend *b. n.* (*niet toereikend*) insufficient, inadequate; (*v. kwaliteit, enz.; onbevredigend*) unsatisfactory; *bw.* insufficiently.
onvolmaakt *b. n.* (*bw.*) imperfect(ly), defective(ly).
onvolmaaktheid *v.* imperfection, deficiency, defectiveness.
onvolprezen *b. n.* beyond praise, transcendent.
onvoltallig *b. n.* incomplete.
onvoltooid *b. n.* unfinished, incomplete; (*gram.*) imperfect.
onvoorwaardelijk *b. n.* (*bw.*) unconditional(ly), implicit(ly).
onvoorzichtig *b. n.* imprudent, unwary, incautious.
onvoorzichtigheid *v.* imprudence.
onvoorzien *b. n.* unforeseen.
onvoorziens *bw.* unexpectedly.
onvriendelijk *b. n.* unkind, unfriendly; ungracious.
onvriendelijkheid *v.* unkindness, unfriendliness.
onvrij *b. n.* not free.
onvrijwillig *b. n.* not voluntary, compulsory, forced; *bw.* on compulsion, under coercion.
onvruchtbaar *b. n.* infertile, sterile,

barren, unfruitful; (*vruchteloos*) fruitless; — **maken,** sterilize.
onvruchtbaarheid *v.* infertility, sterility, barrenness; fruitlessness.
onwaar *b. n.* untrue, false.
onwaarde *v.* invalidity, nullity.
onwaardig *b. n.* unworthy.
onwaarheid *v.* untruth, falsehood.
onwaarschijnlijk *b. n.* improbable, unlikely.
onwankelbaar *b. n.* unshakable, unshaken, unwavering. [etc.
onwankelbaarheid *v.* unshakableness,
onweder, onweer *o.* thunder-storm, storm.
onwe(d)erlegbaar *b. n.* irrefutable, indisputable, unanswerable, irrefragable.
onwederroepelijk *b. n.* irrevocable; *bw.* irrevocably.
onweersbui *v.* thunder-storm.
onwel *b. n.* indisposed, unwell.
onwelkom *b. n.* unwelcome.
onwellevend *b. n.* impolite, discourteous, ill-mannered.
onwelvoeglijk *b. n.* (*bw.*) indecent(ly).
onwelvoeglijkheid *v.* indecency.
onwetend *b. n.* ignorant.
onwetendheid *v.* ignorance.
onwettig *b. n.* unlawful, illegal; (*v. kind*) illegitimate.
onwijs *b. n.* (*bw.*) unwise(ly), foolish(ly).
onwil *m.* unwillingness, obstinacy.
onwillekeurig *b. n.* involuntary; *bw.* involuntarily, in spite of oneself.
onwillig *b. n.* unwilling; (*weerspannig*) recalcitrant, refractory.
onwrikbaar *b. n.* immovable; (*fig. v. persoon*) unflinching, steadfast, unyielding; (*v. overtuiging, enz.*) unshaken, unshakable, unwavering.
onwrikbaarheid *v.* immovability; unshakableness, etc.
onzacht *b. n.* rough, rude, ungentle.
onzachtheid *v.* roughness, rudeness, ungentleness.
onze *bez. vnw.* our; *de —,* ours.
onzedelijk *b. n.* immoral, obscene.
onzedig *b. n.* (*bw.*) immodest(ly).
onzedigheid *v.* immodesty.
onzeker *b. n.* uncertain, doubtful, problematic; (*onvast: v. hand.*) shaky, unsteady; (*v. pas*) unsure, unsteady; (*v. weer, toestand*) unsettled.
onzekerheid *v.* uncertainty, doubt; unsettledness; insecurity.
onze-lieve-heersbeestje *o.* lady-bird.
onze-lieve-vrouwebedstro *o.* woodruff.
onzentwege *van —,* on our part, on our behalf.
onzevader, het —, the Lord's prayer.
onzichtbaar *b. n.* invisible.
onzichtbaarheid *v.* invisibility.
onzijdig *b. n.* neutral; (*gram.*) neuter.
onzijdigheid *v.* neutrality.
onzin *m.* nonsense, rot, fudge.
onzindelijkheid *v.* uncleanliness, dirtiness.

onzuiver *b. n.* impure, unclean; (*v. weegschaal*) unjust; (*muz.*) flat, out of tune, false; (*fig.*) unchaste, lewd.

onzuiverheid *v.* impurity, uncleanliness.

ooft *o.* fruit.

oog *o.* (*alg.*) eye; (*op dobbelsteen*) point, spot; (*v. schaar*) bow; (*in brood, kaas*) hole; **in 't — houden,** bear in mind; keep an eye upon.

oogappel *m.* apple of the eye, eyeball; (*fig.*) the apple of one's eye.

oogarts *m.* oculist, eye-doctor, eye-surgeon.

ooggetuige *m. en v.* eyewitness.

oogglas *o.* (*monocle*) eye-glass; (*v. kijker*) eye-piece, ocular; (*kijker*) spy-glass.

oogholte *v.* orbit, eye-socket.

oogje *o.* (little) eye.

oogklep *v.* eye-flap, blinker.

ooglid *o.* eyelid.

oogmerk *o.* object in view, aim, intention.

oogpunt *o.* point of view, view-point.

oogspiegel *m.* ophthalmoscope.

oogst *m.* harvest; crop(s).

oogsten *o. w.* reap, harvest, gather; (*fig.*) reap, earn.

oogsttijd *m.* harvest-time, reaping-time.

oogverblindend *b. n.* dazzling, blinding.

oogvlies *o.* tunic of the eye; (*hard*) cornea.

oogwater *o.* eyewater, eye-wash.

oogzenuw *v.* optic nerve.

ooi *v.* ewe.

ooievaar *m.* stork.

ooit *bw.* ever.

ook *bw.* also, too, as well, likewise; **— niet,** neither; **hoe dan —,** anyhow.

oom *m.* uncle.

oor *o.* ear; (*in boek*) dog's ear; (*v. mand, enz.*) handle.

oorarts *m.* aurist, aural surgeon, ear-specialist. [proper.

oorbaar *b. n.* becoming, decent, seemly,

oord *o.* place, region, country.

oordeel *o.* (*mening, gevoelen*) judgment, opinion; (*recht*) judgment, sentence; (*v. jury*) verdict.

oordelen *on. w.* judge, deem; **te — naar,** judging from.

oorhanger *m.* ear-drop, pendant.

oorheelkunde *v.* otology.

oorkonde *v.* charter, deed, document, record.

oorkussen *o.* pillow.

oorlel *v.* ear-lobe, ear-lap.

oorlog *m.* war; **in — zijn met,** be at war with.

oorlogsbehoeften *v. mv.* ammunition(s), necessaries of war, military stores.

oorlogsbuit *m.* spoils of war.

oorlogshaven *v.* naval port.

oorlogsmolestverzekering *v.* war-risk insurance.

oorlogsschip *o.* war-ship, man-of-war.

oorlogsverklaring *v.* declaration of war.

oorlogsvloot *v.* navy fleet.

oorlogszuchtig *b. n.* bellicose, warlike, eager for war.

oorontsteking *v.* inflammation of the ear; (*wet.*) otitis.

oorring *m.* ear-ring.

oorschelp *v.* auricle, concha.

oorsprong *m.* origin, source, rise, spring, fountain-head.

oorspronkelijk *b. n.* original, primitive; *bw.* originally; *z. n., o.* **het —e,** the original.

oorspronkelijkheid *v.* originality.

oorveeg *m.* box on the ear; **iem. een — geven,** smack a person's head, box a person's ears.

oorworm *m.* ear-wig.

oorzaak *v.* cause; origin.

oorziekte *v.* ear disease.

oost east.

Oost-Afrika *o.* East Africa.

oostelijk *b. n.* eastern, easterly.

oosten *o.* east; **het O—,** the East, the Orient.

Oostenrijk *o.* Austria.

oosterlengte *v.* eastern longitude.

oosterling *m.* Eastern, Oriental.

Oostzee *v.* **de —,** the Baltic.

ootmoed *m.* meekness, humility, submission.

ootmoedig *b. n.* meek, humble, submissive; *bw.* meekly, humbly, submissively.

op *vz.* on, upon, at, in; *bw.* up.

opbellen *o. w.* ring up; (*telef.*) ring up, call up.

opbeuren *o. w.* lift up; (*fig.*) cheer up, comfort, hearten up.

opbeuring *v.* lifting up; (*fig.*) comfort.

opbiechten *o. w.* confess.

opbieden *on. w.* make a higher bid; **— tegen,** bid against, try to outbid.

opbinden *o. w.* bind up, tie up.

opblazen *o. w.* blow up, inflate.

opbod *o.* advance bidding; **bij — verkopen,** sell by auction.

opbouw *m.* building, construction; (*fig.*) upbuilding; (*stichting*) edification.

opbouwen *o. w.* build up; **weer —,** rebuild, reconstruct.

opbreken *o. w.* (*openbreken*) break up, break open; (*v. straat*) tear up, dig up; (*v. tenten, kramen*) take down, strike; *on. w.* break up, strike camp; (*oprispen*) repeat.

opbrengen *o. w.* (*omhoogbrengen*) raise; (*opdienen, op tafel zetten*) bring up, serve (up); (*opvoeden, grootbrengen*) bring up, rear; (*opleveren*) bring in, realize; (*winst*) yield; (*betalen: v. belasting, enz.*) pay; (*v. schip*) seize, capture; (*aanhouden*) run in; (*v. huur, enz.*) produce.

opbrengst *v.* (*geldelijk*) proceeds; (*produktie*) produce, output, outturn; (*v. oogst, belasting, enz.*) yield.

opcenten *m. mv.* additional percentage (on taxes), surtax.

opdagen *on. w.* turn up, show up, appear arrive.

opdat *vw.* that, in order that; — *niet*, lest.

opdienen *o. w.* serve up, dish up.

opdoemen *on. w.* loom (up).

opdoen *o. w.* (*kopen, inslaan*) lay in, get in; (*opdissen*) serve up, dish up; (*krijgen*) gain, obtain, get; (*v. ziekte*) contract, catch, take; (*v. kennis, enz.*) acquire, pick up, gather; *w. w. zich* —, arise.

opdraaien *o. w.* turn up, turn open; *on. w. iem. voor de kosten laten* —, let a person in for the cost.

opdracht *v.* (*last,taak*) charge, mandate, order, instruction, commission; (*zending*) mission; (*v. boek, enz.*) dedication; *in* — *handelen,* act under orders.

opdreunen *o. w.* rattle off, roll out, patter out, chant.

opdrijven *o. w.* (*v. wild*) start; (*v. prijzen*) force up, push up, run up, inflate; (*v. effecten*) boom, bull.

opdrijving *v.* forcing up, inflation.

opdringen *o. w. iem. iets* —, thrust (press, force) something upon a person; *on. w.* press on, push on; *w. w. zich* — *aan,* intrude upon, obtrude (thrust, press, force) oneself upon.

opduikelen, opduiken *on. w.* emerge; (*fig.*) emerge, turn up, crop up; *o. w.* unearth, disentomb.

opeen *bw.* together, one upon another.

opeenhoping *v.* accumulation; congestion; (*v. volk*) crowd, mass.

opeenvolgen *on. w.* follow (succeed) each other.

opeenvolgend *b. n.* successive, consecutive.

opeenvolging *v.* succession, sequence.

opeisen *o. w.* demand; (*v. stad*) summon; (*v. geld*) claim.

opeising *v.* demand; summons.

open *b. n.* (*alg.*) open; (*v. betrekking*) vacant; (*v. stad*) open, unfortified; *bw.* openly.

openbaar *b. n.* public; — *maken,* publish, disclose, make known, make public; (*v. vonnis*) promulgate; *bw.* publicly, in public.

openbaarmaking *v.* publication, disclosure; promulgation.

openbaren *o. w.* reveal; (*bekend maken*) divulge, disclose, reveal; *w. w. zich* —, reveal itself, manifest itself.

openbaring *v.* revelation, disclosure.

openbreken *o. w.* (*v. deur, enz.*) break open, burst, force (open); (*v. slot, pakkist*) prize open.

openen *o. w.* open; (*v. brief*) unclose.

openhartig *b. n.* open-hearted, frank, plain, straight.

openhartigheid *v.* open-heartedness, frankness, straightness.

opening *v.* opening; aperture; interstice.

openingsrede *r.* inaugural address, opening speech.

openlaten *o. w.* (*v. deur, enz.*) leave open; (*v. ruimte: niet invullen*) leave blank.

openlijk *b. n.* open, public.

openluchtspel *o.* (*v. kinderen*) open-air game, outdoor game; (*v. toneel*) open-air play.

openmaken *o. w.* open, unlock; (*v. pakje*) undo.

openslaan *o. w.* (*v. boek*) open; (*v. bed*) turn down.

opensnijden *o. w.* cut open; (*v. boek*) cut.

openspalken, opensperren *o. w.* open wide, distend.

openstaan *on. w.* (*v. deur, enz.*) be open, stand open; (*r. betrekking*) be vacant; (*v. rekening*) be unpaid, be unsettled.

openvallen *on. w.* fall open; (*fig.*) fall vacant, become vacant.

openvouwen *o. w.* unfold, open out.

operatie *v.* operation.

operatiekamer *v.* operation room, operating room.

operazanger(es) *m.* (*v.*) opera-singer.

opeten *o. w.* eat up, eat; *zich* —, eat one's heart out.

opflikken *o. w.* vamp up.

opflikkeren *on. w.* flare up; blaze up.

opflikkering *v.* flare-up.

opfrissen *o. w.* (*fris maken, verkwikken*) refresh, revive; (*v. kennis, enz.*) brush up, rub up, polish up; *on. w.* freshen (up); *w. w. zich* —, freshen oneself up.

opfrissing *r.* refreshment.

opgaaf *v.* (*mededeling, lijst*) statement, report; (*officieel*) returns; (*voor belasting*) return; (*taak*) task; (*op school: oefening*) exercise; (*op examen*) paper, question.

opgaan *on. w.* (*opwaarts gaan*) go up, rise; (*v. zon*) rise; (*v. deling: geen rest overlaten*) terminate; (*v. vergelijking*) hold good; (*voor examen*) go up, go in; (*opraken*) run out; (*v. berg, heuvel*) ascend, mount; (*v. trap*) go up.

opgaand *b. n.* (*v. lijn*) ascending, rising; (*v. zon*) rising; (*r. deling*) terminating.

opgang *m.* (*r. zon*) rise; (*v. heuvel*) ascent, slope; (*fig.*) rise, growth, success.

opgeblazen *b. n.* blown out, blown up; (*v. wangen*) puffed; (*fig.*) puffed up, swollen, bloated; bumptious.

opgeblazenheid *v.* puffiness; bloatedness; bumptiousness.

opgeld *o.* agio; — *doen,* be in great demand; find a ready market.

opgepropt *b. n.* — *met,* crammed with, cram-full of, packed.

opgeruimd *b. n.* cheerful, cheery, good humoured, in high spirits.

opgeruimdheid *v.* cheerfulness, good humour, high spirits.

opgeschoten *b. n. een* — *jongen,* a

strapping lad; (*ong.*) a overgrown boy, a weedy boy.

opgesmukt *b. n.* ornate, embellished; showy, gaudy.

opgetogen *b. n.* ravished, elated, enraptured.

opgetogenheid *v.* ravishment, elation, rapture, ecstasy.

opgeven *o. w.* (*afgeven*) give up, hand over; (*aanreiken*) hand up; (*vermelden: v. naam, leeftijd, reden, enz.*) give, state; (*voor belasting*) return; (*v. taak, enz.*) set; (*v. tekst, lied, enz.*) give out; (*laten varen*) give up, abandon, drop; (*v. zieke*) give up, give over; (*v. raadsel*) propose, propound, ask; *on. w.* expectorate; *w. w.* **zich** —, forward one's name, apply.

opgewassen *b. n.* — **zijn tegen**, be a match for, be equal to.

opgewekt *b. n.* (*v. persoon*) cheerful, cheery, in high spirits; (*v. gesprek, enz.*) animated.

opgewektheid *v.* cheerfulness, high spirits.

opgewonden *b. n.* excited, heated.

opgraven *o. w.* (*v. voorwerp*) dig up, dig out; (*v. lijk*) exhume, disentomb, unbury, disinter.

opgraving *v.* digging up, excavation; exhumation, disinterment.

opgroeien *on. w.* grow up.

ophaal *m.* (*v. letter*) upstroke, hair-line.

ophaalbrug *v.* draw-bridge, lift-bridge, bascule-bridge.

ophalen *o. w.* (*omhoog halen*) draw up, pull up; (*v. anker*) weigh; (*hoger maken: v. muur*) raise, run up; (*v. kleur*) exalt; (*inzamelen*) collect, gather; (*goedmaken: v. verlies*) repair, make up; (*lijk uit het water*) recover.

ophanden *bw.* at hand, approaching, near.

ophangen *o. w.* hang, hang up; (*v. lamp, enz.: aan plafond*) suspend; *w. w.* **zich** —, hang oneself.

ophef *m.* fuss.

opheffen *o. w.* (*optillen*) lift (up); (*v. hostie: in de mis*) elevate; (*v. ogen*) raise, elevate; (*fig.: beter maken*) lift, raise (up); (*afschaffen: v. wet, enz.*) abolish, abrogate, repeal; (*v. zaak, enz.*) discontinue, close; (*v. school*) close; (*v. kloosters*) dissolve; (*v. faillissement, vonnis*) annul; (*v. twijfel*) remove, clear up; (*v. invoerrechten, storing, enz.*) remove; (*v. embargo*) take off, lift; (*v. beleg, blokkade, enz.*) raise; (*v. misbruiken*) do away with; *w. w.* **zich** —, raise oneself.

opheffing *v.* lifting (up); elevation; raising; abolition; abrogation, repeal; discontinuance, closing; dissolution; annulment; removal; withdrawal; neutralization; (*v. staking*) termination.

ophelderen *o. w.* clear up, explain, elucidate; *on. w.* (*v. weer, gelaat*) clear (up), brighten (up).

opheldering *v.* explanation; elucidation; clearing (up), brightening (up).

ophemelen *o. w.* extol (to the skies), cry up, write up.

ophijsen *o. w.* hoist (up).

ophitsen *o. w.* (*v. hond*) set on; (*fig.*) incite, instigate, stir up, egg on, set on.

ophogen *o. w.* heighten, raise.

ophopen *o. w.* heap up, pile up, bank up, accumulate; *w. w.* **zich** —, accumulate.

ophouden *o. w.* (*omhooghouden*) hold up; (*uitsteken: v. hand*) hold out; (*op het hoofd houden*) keep on; (*hooghouden: v. traditie, stand, enz.*) keep up, maintain; (*v. eer*) uphold; (*v. reputatie*) live up to, sustain, uphold; (*inhouden: v. adem*) retain; (*tegenhouden: v. werk, verkeer, enz.*) hold up; (*v. persoon*) detain, keep; (*bij verkoping*) withdraw, buy in; *on. w.* cease, stop, come to an end; **houd op!** stop ! (*wacht even: fam.*) hold on ! *w. w.* **zich** —, keep, stay; (*sl.*) hang out; *z. n., o.* **zonder** —, incessantly, continually, continuously, without intermission, without cessation.

opinie *v.* opinion.

opium *o.* opium.

opiumschuiver *m.* opium-smoker.

opjagen *o. w.* drive up, send up; (*v. wild*) start, rouse; (*v. vogels, ook:*) flush, spring; (*v. hert*) unharbour; (*v. konijn*) bolt out; (*v. vijand*) dislodge; (*fig.: v. prijzen*) force up, run up, drive up.

opkikkeren *o. w. en on. w.* perk up, cheer up.

opklapbed *o.* convertible bed, folding bedstead.

opklaren *o. w.* make clear; (*fig.*) elucidate, clear up; *on. w.* (*v. weer, gezicht*) clear (up), brighten (up); (*v. gezicht, ook:*) light up.

opklimmen *on. w.* ascend, mount, climb (up); (*fig.*) rise, get on in the world.

opklimming *v.* ascent, graduation, progression, climax.

opknappen *o. w.* (*opschikken, netjes maken*) (*v. kamer*) tidy up, make tidy, clean up; (*v. kind*) smarten up; (*v. huis*) do up, brush up; (*v. kleren*) touch up, patch up, do up, (*v. zaak, enz.*) manage, put right; (*v. zieke*) put right, bring round; *on. w.* (*v. zieke*) recuperate (one's health), pick up; (*v. uiterlijk*) improve; *w. w.* **zich** —, tidy (smarten) oneself up, have a brush up.

opknopen *o. w.* tie up, truss up, string up; (*ophangen*) string up, strap up.

opkomen *on. w.* (*v. zon, maan*) rise; (*opgroeien, opschieten*) come up; (*overeind komen, zich oprichten*) get up, recover one's legs; (*verschijnen: voor examen, vergadering, enz.*) present oneself; (*mil.*) join the colours; (*recht*) appear; (*toneel*) come on; (*v. wind; deeg*) rise; (v. onweer, mist; koorts) come on; (v. stad) arise, spring up.

opkomst v. rise, origin; (v. vergadering, enz.) attendance, turn-up; (v. zon, maan) rising; (onder de wapenen) joining the colours.

opkopen o. w. buy up; engross, forestall.

opkoper m. buyer-up; (gesch.) engrosser, forestaller.

opkroppen o. w. bottle up, cork up.

oplaag v. (v. boek) impression, edition; (v. dagblad) circulation.

opladen o. w. load (up), lade.

oplappen o. w. patch up, piece up, vamp up; (fig. ook:) tinker up.

opleggen o. w. (op iets leggen) lay on; (v. handen) impose; (v. straf) inflict; (v. belasting) impose, lay on; (v. boete) impose, inflict; (v. zwijgen) command, impose; (v. geheimhouding) enjoin; (v. schip) lay up; (v. goederen, in pakhuis) store; (v. tafel, enz.: inleggen met) veneer.

oplegging v. laying on; imposition; infliction.

oplegsel o. (v. meubel) veneer; (v. japon) trimming.

opleiden o. w. lead up; (ten dans) lead out, take out; (fig.) bring up, educate.

opleiding v. training, education.

opletten on. w. pay attention, attend, be attentive.

oplettend b. n. (bw.) attentive(ly).

oplettendheid v. attention, attentiveness.

opleveren o. w. (voortbrengen, opbrengen) produce, bring in; (afleveren) deliver (up), give delivery of.

oplichten o. w. (optillen) lift up, lift, raise; (ontvoeren) carry off, kidnap; (bedriegen, afzetten) swindle, defraud.

oplichter m. swindler, sharper.

oplichterij v. swindling, swindle, fraud.

oploop m. tumult, riot, row.

oplopen on. w. (v. weg, enz.: stijgen) rise, ascend, slope up; (v. kosten) mount up; (opzwellen) swell (up); (vooruitlopen) walk on.

oplopend b. n. rising, sloping, upwards; (fig.: v. prijzen) advancing.

oplosbaar b. n. soluble, solvable, dissolvable.

oplossen o. w. (in vloeistof) dissolve; (v. raadsel, vraagstuk) solve; (v. vergelijking) resolve; (v. kruiswoordraadsel) work out; (v. geheim) unriddle; on. w. dissolve.

oplossing v. solution; (v. vergelijking) resolution.

opluisteren o. w. add lustre to, grace, adorn.

opmaken o. w. (verbruiken, verteren) eat, use up; (v. geld) spend; (verkwisten, doorbrengen) dissipate, squander; (v. haar) dress, do (up); (v. hoed) trim (up); (v. bed) make; (v. rekening, polis, lijst, enz.) make out; (drukk.) draw up; (v.

verslag, inventaris, contract) draw up; (v. rekening) cast up; (v. vogel) truss; (v. plan) lay down; w. w. **zich — voor de reis,** get ready for the journey.

opmars m. advance, march forward.

opmerken o. w. (waarnemen, zien) mark, remark, notice, observe; (een opmerking maken) observe, remark.

opmerker m. observer.

opmerking v. observation, remark.

opmerkzaam b. n. (bw.) attentive(ly).

opmerkzaamheid v. attention, attentiveness

opmeten o w. measure; (v. landmeter) survey.

opname v. taking, adoption; (mil.) survey.

opnemen o. w. (in handen nemen: boek, krant, enz.) take up; (oprapen) pick up; (optillen) take up, lift; (v. japon) gather up, pick up; (tot zich nemen; v. voedsel, enz.) digest, assimilate; (v. geld) take up, borrow; (v. vloerkleed, enz.) take up, raise; (op grammofoon) record; (v. artikel in dagblad, enz.) insert; (in woordenboek) enter; (meten: v. land) survey; (v. gas) read, take; (v. kas) check; (v. temperatuur, enz.) take; (v. stemmen) collect, count; (v. schade) ascertain; (bekijken) survey, take stock of; on. w. catch on, meet with success; prosper.

opneming v. survey; (v. gasmeter, enz.) reading; (in ziekenhuis, enz.) admission; (v. artikel, in dagblad) insertion; (v. temperatuur) taking; (v. stemmen) count; (v. voedsel) ingestion; (v. vocht, enz.) absorption.

opnieuw bw. anew, again, once more, a second time.

opnoemen o. w. name, mention; (opsommen) enumerate.

opofferen o. w. offer up, sacrifice.

opoffering v. sacrifice.

oponthoud o. stay, stoppage, stop; (gedwongen) detention; (vertraging) delay.

oppassen o. w. (verzorgen: v. zieke, enz.) take care of, wait on; attend to; (passen: v. hoed) try on; on. w. take care, be careful; (opletten) attend, pay attention.

oppassend b. n. well-behaved, well-conducted, steady, steady-going.

oppasser m. (bewaker) watcher; (in dierentuin, enz.) attendant, keeper; (v. huis) caretaker; (verzorger) nurse; (mil.) officer's servant, soldier-servant; (bij cavalerie) batman.

opper m. hay-cock, hay-rick.

opperbevel o. supreme command, chief-command.

opperbevelhebber m. commander-in-chief.

opperen o. w. (v. hooi) cock; (v. plan) propose, suggest, put forward; (v. bezwaren) raise; (v. mening) advance.

oppergezag o. supreme authority.

opperhoofd o. chief, chieftain, head.

oppermacht *v.* supremacy, supreme power.
opperman *m.* hodman, hod-carrier.
opperpriester *m.* high-priest.
oppervlak *o.* (*bovenvlak*) upper surface; (*oppervlakte*) surface.
oppervlakkig *b. n.* superficial; (*fig.*) shallow, superficial; *bw.* superficially.
oppervlakte *v.* surface; (*grootte*) area, superficies.
opperwachtmeester *m.* sergeant-major.
oppikken *o. w.* (*door vogel*) peck up; (*inrekenen*) run in; (*op de kop tikken*) pick up, snap up.   [up.
oppoetsen *o. w.* polish, clean up, brush
oprakelen *o. w.* (*v. vuur*) poke up, stir up; (*fig.*) rake up, dig up, resuscitate, disinter.
oprapen *o. w.* pick up, take up, gather up.
oprecht *b. n.* sincere, straightforward, straight, upright.
oprechtheid *v.* sincerity, straightforwardness, uprightness.
oprichten *o. w.* (*omhoogheffen, overeindzetten*) raise, set up; (*v. hoofd*) lift up; (*v. standbeeld*) erect, set up; (*v. zaak, school, enz.*) establish, found, set up; (*v. vereniging, filiaal*) start; (*v. maatschappij*) form, found; *w. w.* **zich —,** erect (straighten) oneself, stand up; (*in bed*) sit up.
oprichter *m.* erector; establisher, founder; (*v. maatschappij*) promotor.
oprichting *v.* erection; establishment, foundation; formation.
oprijlaan *v.* (carriage) drive.
oprispen *on. w.* repeat; (*boeren*) belch.
oprisping *v.* belch, eructation.
oprit *m.* ascent, slope, up-hill road; (*oprijlaan*) drive.
oproep *m.* summons; (*fig.*) call.
oproepen *o. w.* (*v. leden, voor vergadering, enz.*) summon, convoke; (*v. soldaten*) call up; (*v. geesten*) conjure up, raise; (*v. verleden, enz.*) evoke.
oproeping *v.* summoning, summons, convocation; (*mil.*) calling-up notice; conjuring-up, raising.
oproer *o.* rebellion, revolt, insurrection; (*muiterij*) mutiny.
oproerig *b. n.* rebellious, insurgent; mutinous; seditious.
oproerling *m.* rebel, insurgent, insurrectionary, insurrectionist.
oprollen *o. w.* roll up.
opruien *o. w.* incite, instigate, stir up.
opruier *m.* inciter, instigator, seditionist.
opruiing *v.* incitement, instigation, sedition.
opruimen *o. w.* (*wegruimen, wegdoen*) clear away; (*uitverkopen*) make away with, clear off; (*afschaffen*) do away with, abolish; (*v. kamer, enz.*) tidy up; (*tn.: ruimer maken*) ream.
opruiming *v.* clearing away; (*H.*) selling-off, clearance-sale.

oprukken *on. w.* advance; **— tegen,** march upon, march against.
opscheppen *o. w.* ladle out, serve up; *on. w.* brag, swank, boast.
opschepper *m.* braggart, swanker, swankpot, swaggerer.
opschieten *on. w.* shoot up; (*fig.*) make headway, make way, make progress, proceed, get on.
opschik *m.* finery, trappings, frills.
opschilderen *o. w.* paint anew.
opschrift *o.* superscription, inscription; (*v. artikel, enz.*) heading; (*v. film, plaat, enz.*) caption, heading; (*v. munt*) legend; (*v. brief, pakket: adres*) direction.
opschrikken *on. w.* start, be startled; **doen —,** startle.
opschroeven *o. w.* screw up; (*fig.*) cry up, puff up.
opschudden *o. w.* shake up.
opschudding *v.* commotion, tumult, agitation, bustle, sensation.
opslaan *o. w.* (*in de hoogte slaan*) strike up; (*v. kraag, enz.*) turn up; (*v. mouwen*) tuck up, roll back; (*v. ogen, blik: omhoogrichten*) elevate, raise, turn up; (*openen: v. boek*) open; (*v. bladzijde*) turn up; (*v. prijzen, lonen*) raise; (*inslaan, opdoen*) lay in; (*in pakhuis*) store, warehouse; (*v. tent, enz.*) pitch, set up; *on. w.* (*duurder worden*) advance, rise, go up.
opslag *m.* up-stroke; (*v. uniform*) facing; (*v. mouw*) cuff; (*v. oog*) look; (*verhoging*) rise, advance, augmentation; (*in pakhuis*) storage, warehousing; (*muz.*) up-beat; (*Pl.*) wild shoots; **iem. — geven,** raise a person's wages.
opslagkosten *m. mv.* storage, warehouse rent, warehouse charges.
opslagplaats *v.* store, storage building, storage yard.
opslorpen *o. w.* slobber, sip up; absorb.
opsluiten *o. w.* lock up, shut up; (*v. misdadiger*) confine, incarcerate; (*v. krankzinnige*) place under restraint; *on. w.* (*mil.*) close, close up, take up, close order.
opsluiting *v.* locking up; confinement, incarceration.
opsmuk *m.* finery, trappings frills.
opsmukken *o. w.* trim, trick out, embellish; (*fig.: verhaal*) dress up, embellish; (*v. waarheid*) adorn, varnish.
opsnij(d)en *o. w.* cut up, cut open, carve; *on. w.* (*fig.*) brag, swank, swagger, vapour.
opsnij(d)er *m.* braggart, swanker, vapourer, boaster.
opsnuiven *o. w.* snuff in, inhale.
opsommen *o. w.* enumerate, sum up, count up.
opsomming *v.* enumeration, summing up.
opspelen *on. w.* (*muz.*) strike up; (*kaartsp.*) lead, play first; (*fig.*) kick up a row, cut up rough.

opsporen o. w. trace, run down, seek out, find out.

opsporing r. tracing, running down; (mijnbouw: r. goud, enz.) exploration, prospecting.

opspraak r. scandal.

opspringen on. w. jump up, start up; (v. bal) bounce.

opstaan on. w. (recht gaan staan) stand up; (v. stoel, uit bed, enz.) get up, rise; (in opstand komen) rebel, revolt.

opstand m. (oproer) rising, rebellion, revolt, insurrection; (bouwk.: tekening v. gebouw) (vertical) elevation; (r. winkel) fixtures.

opstandeling m. rebel, insurgent.

opstanding r. resurrection.

opstapelen o. w. heap up, pile up, stack (up), accumulate; w. w. zich —, accumulate; bank up.

opsteken o. w. (in de hoogte steken) hold up, put up, lift; (r. haar) do up, turn up; put up; (v. sigaar, lamp: aansteken) light; (r. rat: opensteken) pierce, broach; (v. geld) pocket; on. w. (v. wind, storm) rise; (plotseling) spring up.

opstel o. composition, essay, theme, paper.

opstellen o. w. (v. brief, verslag, enz.) draw up, draft; (r. machine, enz.: in elkaar zetten) mount, erect, fit up, set up; (v. wet, verzoekschrift, enz.: ontwerpen) frame; (r. kanon) mount, place in position; (v. troepen, enz.) draw up, line up.

opsteller m. (v verslag) author; (r. wet, enz.) framer; (v. document) draftsman; (r. dagblad, enz.) redactor.

opstelling r. erection; framing; (mil.) drawing up, formation; disposition.

opstijgen on. w. mount, ascend, rise; (v. vliegtuig, ook:) take off, fly off, take the air.

opstoken o. w. (r. kachel, enz.) poke up, stir; (v. kolen, hout: verbranden) burn; (fig.) incite, instigate.

opstootje o. disturbance, riot, tumult, rising.

opstopper m. slap, punch, cuff, dig.

opstrijken o. w. (v. linnen) iron; (r. hoed) brush up; (r. snor) twirl up; (r. geld) pocket, sweep off, scoop in.

opstropen o. w. (r. mouwen) tuck up, strip up, roll back.

opstuiven on. w. fly up; (fig.) fly out, bristle up, flare up.

opsturen o. v. send up, despatch.

optekenen o. w. note down, note, write (take, jot) down.

optellen o. w. add (up), cast up, count up; (opnoemen) enumerate.

optelling v. (rek.) addition; enumeration.

optica r. optics.

optie r. option; in — hebben, have the refusal of.

optillen o. w. lift up, raise, elevate.

optocht m. procession.

optooien o. w. adorn, decorate, trim.

optrede v. curtail-step; (stoep) steps; (r. rijtuig) foot-board.

optreden on. w. make one's appearance, appear; (ten tonele verschijnen) enter, go on; (fig.: handelend —) act, take action; (zich laten gelden) assert oneself; z. n., o. appearance; (fig.) action, way of acting, proceeding, attitude.

optrekje o. cottage, country-box.

optrekken o. w. (omhoogtrekken) draw up, pull up; (r. gordijn) raise; (v. schouders) shrug, hunch up; (bouwen) raise; (hoger maken) run up; (optellen) add (up), count up; on. w. (r. mist, enz.) lift; (marcheren) march.

opvallen on. w. strike.

opvallend b. n. (bw.) striking(ly), conspicuous(ly).

opvaren o. w. sail up, go up, steam up; on. w. ascend.

opvatting r. idea, conception, opinion, view.

opvegen o. w. sweep up.

opvissen o. w. fish up; (fig.) hunt up, fish up.

opvliegen on. w. fly up; (fig.) fly out, flare up, explode.

opvliegend b. n. short-tempered, quick-tempered, irascible.

opvoeden o. w. bring up, rear, educate.

opvoeding r. education, bringing-up.

opvoedkunde r. pedagogy.

opvoedkundige m. educationalist, pedagogue.

opvoeren o. w. (hoger brengen) carry up; (v. prijzen, enz.: opdrijven) raise, force up; (v. toneelstuk) perform, produce, act.

opvoering r. performance.

opvolgen o. w. (v. persoon) succeed; (r. bevel, raad: opvolgen) obey, follow.

opvolger m. successor.

opvolging v. succession.

opvorderen o. w. claim.

opvouwbaar b. n. folding, foldable; (r. boot, enz.) collapsible.

opvouwen o. w. fold up.

opvrolijken o. w. brighten (up), cheer (up), liven up.

opvullen o. w. fill up; (r. kleding, enz.) pad; (r. dier: opzetten) stuff; (larderen) lard.

opvulsel o. filling; padding; stuffing.

opwaarts bw. upward(s).

opwachten o. w. wait for; (met kwade bedoelingen) waylay.

opwachting r. zijn — maken bij, pay one's respects to, wait upon.

opwarmen o. w. warm up, heat up; (fig.: r. oud verhaal, enz.) rehash.

opwegen on. w. — tegen, balance, counterbalance, equipoise.

opwekken o. w. awake, rouse; (fig.) stir up, awake, rouse; (r. nieuwsgierigheid, verontwaardiging, enz.) provoke;

(v. eetlust) stimulate, quicken; (v. elektriciteit) generate; (v. gevoelens, enz.) excite.

opwekkend b. n. exciting, stimulating, inspiring; (v. lucht) bracing.

opwekking v. awaking; stimulation; generation; excitement; resuscitation.

opwelling v. welling-up.

opwerpen o. w. throw up; cast up; (v. barricade) erect; (fig.: v. vraag, bezwaar) raise; w. w. **zich — als,** set up for, constitute oneself the...

opwinden o. w. (v. horloge, enz.) wind up; (fig.) excite; w. w. **zich —,** get excited, work oneself up.

opwinding v. winding up; excitement, agitation.

opzadelen on. w. saddle (up).

opzakken o. w. bag.

opzegbaar b. n. withdrawable; (v. contract, enz.) terminable.

opzeggen o. w. (v. les, gedicht, enz.) say, repeat, recite; (v. overeenkomst, enz.) terminate, denounce; (v. kapitaal) recall, withdraw; (v. koop) cancel.

opzegging v. termination, denunciation; withdrawal; notice.

opzeggingstermijn m. term of notice.

opzenden o. w. send (up), dispatch, forward; (nazenden) forward, redirect; (v. stukken) send in.

opzet o. (plan, voornemen) design, intention; (recht) malice, intent; **met —,** by design, designedly, on purpose, purposely, intentionally, deliberately; **zonder —,** unintentionally, undesignedly; m. (v. boek) framework, plan; (mil.: v. kanon) tangent sight.

opzettelijk b. n. intentional, wilful, premeditated; (v. leugen, enz.) deliberate, calculated; bw. zie **met opzet.**

opzetten o. w. (v. hoed, enz.) put on; (overeind zetten) place upright, set up, put up; (v. zaak: oprichten) set up, establish, start; (v. dieren) stuff; (bij breien, haken) cast on, set on; (bij spel: inzetten) stake; (fig.: aanhitsen: opstoken) set on, instigate, incite; on. w. (oplopen, zwellen) swell (up); (naderen, komen —) come on; (v. persoon) turn up, make one's appearance.

opzicht o. (toezicht) supervision; (betrekking, aanzien) respect; **in alle —en,** in all respects, in every respect; **te zijnen —e,** in regard to him; with respect to him.

opzichter m. overseer, superintendent; (v. bouwwerk) surveyor, clerk of the works.

opzichtig b. n. showy, garish, gaudy, noisy.

opzien on. w. look up; z. n., o. — **baren,** make (cause, create) a sensation, make a stir.

opzienbarend b. n. sensational, startling.

opzitten on. w. sit up; (v. hond) beg.

opzoeken o. w. (zoeken) seek look

for; (woord, trein) look up; (bezoeken) call on, give a call, call to see.

opzwellen on. w. swell (up), tumefy, bloat, expand.

opzwelling v. swelling, tumefaction.

opzwepen o. w. whip up; (fig.) whip up, work up, stir up, incite.

orakel o. oracle.

oranje b. n. orange.

oranjeappel m. orange.

orde v. order.

ordebroeder m. brother, friar.

ordelievend b. n. orderly.

ordeloos b. n. disorderly.

ordeloosheid v. disorderliness.

ordenen o. w. order, regulate, arrange; (kath.: in een orde opnemen, wijden) ordain.

ordening v. regulation; arrangement; ordination.

order v. order, command; (H.) order.

orderbriefje o. note of hand, promissory note; order-form.

ordeteken o. order, badge of an order, decoration; (mv. ook:) insignia.

ordonnans m. orderly, runner; (officier) galloper, aide-de-camp; soms: orderly-officer.

orgaan o. organ.

organisatie v. organization.

organist m. organist, organ-player.

orgel o. organ.

orgeldraaier m. organ-bellows.

oriënteren w. w. **zich —,** take one's bearings, find one's latitude.

origineel b. n. (bw.) original(ly); z. n., o. original.

orkaan m. hurricane.

orkest o. orchestra, band.

os m. ox, bullock; (fig.) ass, blockhead.

ossegebraad o. roast beef.

ossehaas m. fillet of beef, undercut.

ossenweider m. grazier, neat-herd.

ossetong v. ox-tongue, neat's tongue; (Pl.) bugloss, alkanet.

otter m. otter.

oud b. n. (in jaren) old, aged; (van de oude tijd) ancient; (antiek) antique; z. n.; **de O—en,** the ancients.

oudbakken b. n. stale.

oude m. (v.) old man (old woman).

oudejaarsavond m. New Year's eve.

ouder b. n. older; elder; z. n., m. en v. parent.

ouderdom m. (leeftijd) age; (hoge leeftijd) old age.

ouderdomspensioen o., **ouderdomsrente** v. old-age pension.

ouderhuis o. parental home.

ouderling m. elder.

ouderloos b. n. parentless, without parents, orphaned.

ouderwets b. n. old-fashioned, ancient, antique.

oudewijvenpraat m. old wives tale(s), gossip.

oudgediende m. veteran; (uit wereld-

oorlog) ex-Serviceman; (*fig.*) old compaigner, old-timer, old hand.
oudheid *v.* antiquity, oldness.
oudheidkenner *m.* antiquarian.
oudje *o.* old man; old woman; **de —s,** the old folks.
ouds van —, of old, from of old, formerly.
oudstrijder *m.* veteran, ex-combatant.
ouwel *m.* wafer; (*gen.: voor poeders, enz.*) cachet.
ovaal *b. n.* (*bw.*) oval(ly); *z. n., o.* oval.
ovatie *v.* ovation.
oven *m.* oven; (*kalk—*) klin; (*v. fabriek*) furnace, oven.
over *vz.* (*boven*) over; (*over... heen, dwars —*) over, across; (*aan de overzijde van*) beyond; (*tegenover*) opposite; (*meer dan*) over, above, upwards of; (*via*) by way of, via; (*na*) in; (*omtrent*) about, concerning.
overal *bw.* everywhere.
overbekend *b. n.* generally known; (*meestal ongunstig*) notorious.
overbelasten *o. w.* overburden; (*tn.: v. machine*) overload; (*v. belastingen*) overtax.
overbevolking *v.* over-population; (*het 'eveel*) surplus population.
overbevolkt *b. n.* over-populated.
overblijfsel *o.* remainder, remnant; rest, relic, remains.
overblijven *o. w.* (*overschieten*) be left, remain; (*'s nachts*) stay the night; (*op school*) stay at school.
overbluffen *o. w.* bluff, run a bluff on, put out of countenance, face down.
overbodig *b. n.* superfluous, redundant.
overboeken *o. w.* transfer.
overboord *bw.* overboard.
overbrengen *o. w.* (*naar andere plaats*) transport, transfer, remove; (*v. nieuws, warmte, enz.*) transmit; (*v. geluid*) convey; (*v. boodschap*) take; (*afgeven*) deliver; (*in andere taal*) translate; (*v. ziekte*) transmit, transplant, carry; (*verklappen*) tell, blab, repeat; (*bij optelling*) carry; (*algebra*) transpose.
overbrenging *v.* (*v. goederen*) transport, transportation, conveyance; (*v. zaak, bedrag*) transfer; (*tn., v. kracht, enz.*) transmission; (*in andere taal*) translation; (*v. bloed*) transfusion; removal.
overbrieven *o. w.* tell, repeat.
overbruggen *o. w.* bridge over.
overbuur *m.* neighbour over the way, opposite neighbour.
overdaad *v.* excess, superabundance.
overdadig *b. n.* (*bw.*) superabundant(ly); excessive(ly).
overdekt *b. n.* covered in, roofed in.
overdenking *v.* consideration, reflection, meditation.
overdonderen *o. w.* bounce, bully, browbeat.
overdracht *v.* transfer, conveyance; assignment; delegation.

overdragen *o. w.* carry over; (*v. bezit*) transfer, make over, convey; (*v. rechten*) assign; (*v. gezag, ambt*) delegate; (*v. taak*) depute; (*endosseren*) endorse.
overdreven *b. n.* (*vergroot: v. beweringen, enz.*) exaggerated, overdone; (*buitensporig: v. eis, prijs, enz.*) excessive, extravagant, immoderate, exorbitant.
overdrijven *on. w.* (*v. onweer, enz.*) blow over.
overdrijven *o. w.* exaggerate, overdo.
overdrijving *v.* exaggeration.
overdruk *m.* (*v. artikel, enz.*) offprint, separate (copy); (*op postzegel*) overprint, surcharge; (*tn.*) effective pressure, overpressure.
overdrúk *b. n.* too busy, overbusy, too much occupied.
overeenkomen *on. w.* agree (with a person, on a thing), harmonize; **— met,** (*overeenstemmen*) agree with; (*beantwoorden aan*) correspond with; (*gelijken op*) ressemble; (*van gelijke waarde zijn*) be equivalent to; *o. w.* (*prijs, enz.*) agree on.
overeenkomst *v.* (*gelijkenis*) ressemblance, similarity; (*overeenstemming*) conformity; agreement; (*contract*) contract; (*verdrag*) treaty, convention; **volgens —,** as agreed upon, as per agreement; **bij onderlinge —,** by mutual consent.
overeenkomstig *b. n.* conformable, agreeable.
overeenstemmen *on. w.* agree, concur, accord, harmonize.
overeenstemming *v.* agreement, concurrence; consonance; harmony, unison; (*gram.*) concord; **tot — komen,** come to an agreement, come to terms.
overeind *bw.* on end, upright, erect, endwise.
overerven *o. w.* inherit; *on. w.* be transmitted (by inheritance).
overerving *v.* inheritance.
overgaan *on. w.* (*v. bel*) ring, go; (*ophouden: v. pijn, enz.*) pass off, wear off; (*v. bui*) blow over; (*bevorderd worden*) be removed, be moved up, get one's remove; *o. w.* (*straat, enz.*) cross.
overgang *m.* crossing; transition, change; (*v. godsdienst*) conversion; (*sterr.: v. Venus*) transit; (*muz.*) modulation; (*in politiek*) change of sides, desertion.
overgangsexamen *o.* promotion trial, test examination.
overgangsrecht *o.* right of transfer.
overgankelijk *b. n.* (*bw.*) (*gram.*) transitive(ly).
overgave *v.* delivery, handing over; (*v. macht, enz.*) transmission; (*overdracht*) transfer; (*v. stad, vesting, documenten*) surrender; (*afstand*) cession.
overgeven *o. w.* (*aangeven, overreiken*) hand over, hand, reach, pass; (*afstaan*) give over, deliver up, surrender, yield;

(v. ambt, waardigheid) resign; (v. bloed: braken) spit, fetch up; on. w. vomit; w. w. **zich** —, surrender, give oneself up.
overgevoelig b. n. over-sensitive, too sensitive; (v. zenuwen) hyperaesthetic.
overgrootmoeder v. great-grandmother.
overgrootvader m. great-grandfather.
overhaastig b. n. precipitate, rash, overhasty.
overhaasting v. precipitation, precipitancy, over-haste.
overhalen o. w. (van de ene plaats naar een andere) fetch over; (in veerboot) ferry over; (v. bel) pull; (v. geweer) cock; (v. schip: omleggen) careen; (distilleren) refine, clarify, distil; (v. hefboom) pull over.
overhand v. **de — hebben,** have (hold) the upper hand; have the mastery, be in the ascendant; prevail. [deliver.
overhandigen o. w. hand (over),
overhandiging v. handing over, delivery; presentation.
overhands bw. overhand.
overhebben o. w. have left.
overheen bw. over, across.
overheerlijk b. n. delicious, exquisite, choice.
overheersen o. w. domineer, overdominate; on. w. predominate.
overheersend b. n. dominant, predominant, prevailing.
overheerser m. ruler, tyrant, despot.
overheersing v. rule, domination.
overheid v. **de —,** the authorities.
overheidspersoon m. magistrate.
overhellen on. w. hang over, lean over, incline; (sch.) list, lie over.
overhemd o. shirt, day-shirt; (met stijf front) dress-shirt.
overhoeks b. n. diagonal, oblique, transversal.
overhoop bw. in a heap, all of a heap, in disorder, in confusion, pell-mell.
overhouden o. w. save; have left.
overig b. n. remaining; **het —e,** the rest, the remainder.
overigens bw. for the rest; otherwise.
overijlen w. w. **zich —,** hurry, rush things, be precipitant.
overijling v. hurry, precipitation, precipitance, hastiness.
overjas v. overcoat, greatcoat, top-coat.
overkant m. other side, opposite side; **aan de —,** over the way.
overkoken on. w. boil over.
óverkomen on. w. overcome; (radio) come through, come over.
overkómen o. w. befall, happen to.
overkomst v. coming (over), visit.
óverladen o. w. (v. trein, schip, enz.) tranship; (v. wagon in wagon) transfer; (opnieuw laden) re-load.
overláden o. w. overload, overburden; (fig.: met eerbewijzen) overload; (met geschenken, enz.) smother; (markt) overstock, flood.

overláden b. n. overloaded, overcharged; (v. markt) overstocked, glutted; (v. kaart, programma, agenda) overcrowded, overloaded; (v. maag) surfeited.
overladingskosten m. mv. transhipment charges.
overlangs bw. lengthwise, longitudinally.
overlast m. overweight, surcharge; inconvenience, importunity, nuisance; molestation.
overlaten o. w. leave.
overleden b. n. deceased.
overledene m. en v. deceased, departed.
óverleer o. upper leather, vamp.
overleg o. deliberation, judgment, consideration, forethought; (met een ander) deliberation, consultation; (verstandig beleid) management.
óverleggen o. w. (ter zijde leggen, oversparen) lay by, lay up, put aside; (overgeven, inleveren) hand in (over), produce.
overléggen o. w. deliberate, consider; **met iem. —,** consult a person.
overleven o. w. survive, outlive.
overlevende m. en v. survivor, longest liver.
overlevering v. tradition.
overliggeld o. demurrage.
overlijden on. w. decease, die, pass away, depart this life; z. n., o. decease, death, demise.
óverlopen on. w. (v. vloeistof) run over, overflow; (naar vijand) go over, desert.
óverloper m. deserter, turn-coat; (politiek) ratter, rat.
overmaat v. over-measure; (fig.) excess, surplus.
overmacht v. superior power, superior forces, superiority; (noodzaak) force majeure.
overmaken o. w. (opnieuw maken) do over again; remake; (v. geld) remit; (overdragen: v. bezittingen) make over, transfer.
overmannen o. w. overpower, overmatch, overcome.
overmatig b. n. (bw.) excessive(ly).
overmeesteren o. w. overmaster, overpower, conquer.
overmoed m. over-boldness, recklessness; (verwaandheid, zelfoverschatting) presumption.
overmorgen bw. the day after to-morrow.
overnachten on. w. pass the night.
overname v. taking over.
overnemen o. w. (v. zaak, praktijk, enz.) take over; (kopen) buy; (van schrijver) borrow, copy; (v. gedachte, woord uit vreemde taal) adopt; (v. gewoonte, enz.) catch up.
overpeinzen o. w. meditate on, reflect on.
overpeinzing v. meditation, reflection.
overplaatsen o. w. remove, put in

another place; (*v. ambtenaar, enz.*) transfer.
overplanten *o. w.* transplant.
overproduktie *v.* over-production.
overreden *o. w.* persuade, prevail on, talk over.
overreding *v.* persuasion.
overreiken *o.w.* hand (over), reach, pass.
overrijden *o. w.* (*v. persoon*) run over; (*v. paard*) override, overdrive.
overrok *m.* over-skirt.
overrompelen *o. w.* surprise, take by surprise.
overrompeling *v.* surprise.
overschatten *o. w.* overrate, overestimate.
overschepen *o. w.* tranship.
overscheppen *o. w.* scoop, ladle, transfuse.
overschieten *o. w.* (*overblijven*) remain (over), be left.
overschoen *m.* overshoe, galosh.
overschot *o.* remainder, rest; (*het meerdere*) surplus; (*H.*) balance.
overschrijden *o. w.* cross, step across, overstep; (*fig.*) exceed, surpass, overstep.
overschrijven *o. w.* write out, copy, transcribe; (*in 't net*) copy fair; (*v. wissel*) endorse; (*in de boeken*) transfer.
overschrijving *v.* copy, transcript; transfer. [wire.
overseinen *o. w.* transmit, telegraph,
overslaan *o. w.* (*v. persoon*) pass over; (*v. woorden, enz.*) omit, miss (out); (*weglaten: v. bijzonderheden, woord, enz.*) skip; (*verzuimen*) miss; *on. w.* (*v. golven*) curl over; (*v. motor*) misfire; (*v. stem*) crack; have a catch in one's voice.
overspannen *o. w.* (*met hand, enz., overreiken*) span; (*te sterk spannen*) overstrain, overstretch; *w. w.* **zich —**, over-exert oneself; *b. n.* overstrained, overstrung, overexcited, overwrought.
overspanning *v.* (*v. brug*) span; overstrain, overstraining, overexertion, overexcitement, surexcitation.
overspel *o.* adultery.
overstaan *on. w.* stand over; **ten — van,** in the presence of, before.
overstaand *b. n.* opposite.
overstapkaartje *o.* correspondence-ticket, transfer (ticket).
overstappen *o. w.* step over, cross, go across; (*v. trein, tram, enz.*) change.
overste *m.* chief, captain, governor; (*mil.*) colonel-in-chief; (*mil.*) lieutenant-colonel; (*in klooster*) prior, superior.
overstelpen *o. w.* overwhelm.
overstelping *v.* overwhelming.
overstemmen *o. w.* (*v. instrument*) tune again; *on. w.* vote again.
overstémmen *o. w.* (*geluid, iemands stem*) drown, deafen; (*bij verkiezing*) out-vote.
overstromen *on. w.* overflow.
overstrómen *o. w.* flood, overflood, inundate.

overstroming *v.* inundation, flood.
overstuur *b. n. en bw.* out of order, in disorder, upset.
overtocht *m.* passage; (*korter*) crossing.
overtollig *b. n.* (*bw.*) superfluous(ly).
overtreden *o. w.* transgress, infringe, contravene, break.
overtreder *m.* transgressor, infringer, breaker.
overtreding *v.* transgression, infringement, breach.
overtreffen *o. w.* surpass, excel, exceed, outdo, outvie; **in aantal —,** outnumber.
óvertrekken *o. w.* (*v. rivier, enz.*) cross; (*v. tekening: natrekken*) trace, transfer; *on. w.* (*v. onweer*) blow over.
overtrékken *o. w.* (*v. meubelen*) cover, upholster; (*v. paraplu*) recover.
overtuigen *o. w.* convince, convict, satisfy, persuade; *w. w.* **zich —,** convince (satisfy) oneself.
overtuiging *v.* conviction. [time.
overuren *o. mv.* overtime hours, over-
overval *m.* surprise attack, surprise; (*door politie*) raid; (*v. bank, enz.*) hold-up.
overvleugelen *o. w.* (*overtreffen*) surpass; (*mil.*) outflank.
overvloed *m.* abundance, plenty, profusion; **— hebben van,** abound in, abound with; **ten —e,** moreover.
overvloedig *b. n.* abundant, plentiful, profuse, copious.
overvloeien *on. w.* overflow, run over.
overvragen *o. w.* overcharge, ask too much.
óverweg *m.* cross-over-road; (*spoorw.*) level crossing.
overwég *bw.* **goed met elkaar — kunnen,** get on well together.
óverwegen *o. w.* reweigh, weigh (over) again.
overwégen *o. w.* weigh, consider, contemplate; *on. w.* preponderate, turn the scale.
overwegend *b. n.* preponderating, preponderant; **van — belang,** of paramount importance, all-important.
overweging *v.* consideration, reflection; (*recht*) preamble.
overweldigen *o. w.* (*v. persoon*) over-power; (*v. troon, enz.*) usurp.
overweldigend *b. n.* (*v. meerderheid*) overwhelming; (*v. schouwspel*) thrilling; (*v. overwinning, enz.*) sweeping, smashing.
overweldiger *m.* usurper.
overweldiging *v.* usurpation; overpowering.
overwelven *o. w.* vault, overarch.
overwerk *o.* overwork, extra work.
óverwerken *on. w.* do overwork, work overtime.
overwérken *o. w.* overdrive; *w. w.* **zich —,** overwork (oneself).
overwicht *o.* overweight; (*fig.*) preponderance, ascendancy.
overwinnaar *m.* conqueror, victor.

overwinnen *o. w.* conquer, vanquish, overcome; (*fig.*) conquer, surmount, overcome.
overwinning *v.* victory.
overwintering *v.* wintering, hibernation.
overwonnene *m.* vanquished person (party).
overzees *b. n.* oversea(s), beyond sea(s), transmarine.
overzetboot *v.* ferry-boat.

overzetten *o. w.* (*met boot*) ferry (over, across), take across; (*vertalen*) translate.
overzetter *m.* ferryman; translator.
overzetting *v.* translation.
overzicht *o.* survey, (general) view, summary, synopsis.
óverzien *o. w.* look over, go through.
overzien *o. w.* overlook, oversee, survey.
overzijde *v.* opposite side, other sid.

P

pa *m.* pa, papa, father.
paaien *o. w.* appease, soothe; (*sch.*) grave; *on. w.* (*v. vissen*) spawn, mate.
paal *m.* (*heipaal*) pile; (*v. telegraaf, enz.*) pole; (*mil.*) palisade; (*wapenk.*) pale; (*Z. N.: ovenpaal*) oven-peel; (*staak*) stake. [dwelling.
paalwoning *v.* pile-dwelling, lake-
paar *o.* pair; (*koppel*) couple.
paard *o.* (*Dk.*) horse; (*v. schaakspel*) knight; (*gymn.*) (vaulting-)horse.
paardebloem *v.* (*Pl.*) dandelion.
paardeboon *v.* (*Pl.*) horse-bean.
paardekracht *v.* horse-power, H. P.
paardemiddel *o.* horse-physic; (*fig.*) kill or cure remedy, heroic remedy.
paardenarts *m.* veterinary surgeon, horse-doctor.
paardenkoper *m.* horse-dealer.
paardenstamboek *o.* stud-book.
paardenvoeder *o.* forage, fodder.
paardestaart *m.* horse-tail.
paardewerk *o.* horse-work, horse-labour; (*fig.*) drudgery.
paardrijden *o.* horse-riding, riding (on horseback).
paardrijder *m.* horseman, equestrian; (*kunstrijder*) horse-rider.
paarlemoer *o.* mother of pearl, nacre, pearl-shell.
paars *b. n.* purple, violet.
paartijd *m.* pairing-time, pairing-season, mating-season.
paasbest *o.* Easter-best, Sundaydress.
paasbloem *v.* (*Pl.*) moonwort, primrose; (*fig.*) girl in her Easter-best.
paasdag *m.* Easter-day.
paasfeest *o.* Easter; (*v. d. joden*) Passover.
paaslam *o.* paschal lamb.
pacht *v.* (*pachtsom*) rent, rent-money; (*contract*) lease; (*monopolie, enz.*) farm; *in — geven,* let out, farm out.
pachten *o. w.* rent; (*v. tol, enz.*) farm.
pachter *m.* (*alg.*) lessee, renter; (*v. tol, boerderij*) farmer.
pachthoeve *v.* farm.
pachtsom *v.* rent.
pachtstelsel *o.* farming-system.
pad *o.* path; (*breed —*) walk; *v.* (*Dk.*) toad.

paddestoel *m.* toad-stool; (*eetbaar*) mushroom.
padvinder *m.* path-finder; boy scout.
pagaai *v.* paddle.
pagaaien *on. w.* paddle.
page *m.* page, footboy; (*schildknaap*) squire.
pagina *v.* page.
pak *o.* pack; (*H.*) package; (*klein —*) parcel; (*in doek, enz.; bundel*) bundle; (*kleren*) suit (of clothes).
pakezel *m.* pack-donkey, pack-mule, packing mule.
pakgoed *o.* package.
pakhuis *o.* warehouse.
pakijs *o.* pack-ice.
pakjesdrager *m.* porter, commission-naire.
pakken *o. w.* (*inpakken*) pack; (*grijpen*) catch, seize, grip, grasp, take hold of; (*omhelzen*) hug, cuddle; (*v. kou*) catch; (*fig.: v. publiek, lezer*) take hold of, fetch.
pakket *o.* packet, parcel.
pakketboot *v.* packet-boat.
pakketpost *v.* parcel-post.
paklinnen *o.* packing-cloth, canvas.
pakpapier *o.* packing-paper.
pakzadel *o.* pack-saddle.
pal *m.* click, catch, pawl; (*v. bajonet*) pusher.
pal *b. n.* (*bw.*) firm(ly).
paleis *o.* palace.
palen *on. w. — aan,* confine upon.
palet *o.* palette, pallet; (*kaatsplankje*) battledore.
paling *m.* eel.
palingvel *o.* eel-skin.
paljas *m.* buffoon, clown, merry andrew, Jack Pudding; *v.* (*stromatras*) pallet, palliasse.
palm *v.* (*v. hand*) palm; (*maat*) decimeter; *m.* (*boom, tak*) palm.
palmboom *m.* palm-tree.
palmhout *o.* box-wood.
palmtak *m.* palm-branch.
Palmzondag *m.* Palm Sunday.
pamflet *o.* lampoon, libel.
pamfletschrijver *m.* lampoonist, pamphleteer.
pan *v.* (*braad—*) pan, frying-pan; (*dak—*)

tile; (*herrie*) row, shindy, bean-feast.
pand *o.* (*onderpand*) security, pledge; (*huis*) house, building; (*huis en erf*) premises; (*v. jas of rok*) tail, flap.
pandbeslag *o.* mortgage security, distraint.
pandbrief *m.* mortgage bond.
pandgever *m.* pawner.
pandhouder *m.* pawnee.
pandjeshuis *o.* pawnshop.
pandjesjas *v.* tail-coat.
pandnemer *m.* pledger.
paneel *o.* panel.
paneelwerk *o.* panelling, wainscoting.
paneermeel *o.* bread-crumbs.
panharing *m.* fresh herring.
paniek *v.* panic.
pannekoek *m.* pan cake.
pannenbakker *m.* tile-maker.
pannenbakkerij *v.* tile-works.
panorama *o.* panorama.
panter *m.* panther, leopard.
pantoffel *v.* slipper.
pantoffelheld *m.* henpecked husband.
pantser *o.* (*mil.*) armour; cuirass; (*v. schip*) armour-plating.
pantserauto *o.* armoured car.
pantserdek *o.* armoured deck, deck armour.
pantserplaat *v.* armour-plate.
pantserschip *o.* iron-clad.
pap *v.* pap, porridge; (*gen.*) cataplasm, poultice; (*voor katoen, enz.*) dressing; (*v. papierbereiding*) pulp.
papaver *v.* (*Pl.*) poppy.
papegaai *m.* (*Dk.*) parrot; (*houten* —) popinjay.
paperassen *v. mv.* (*papieren*) papers; (*prulpapieren*) waste paper.
papier *o.* paper.
papieren *b. n.* paper.
papierfabriek *v.* paper-mills, paper-factory.
papiermand *v.* waste-paper basket.
papiermerk *o.* water-mark.
papkom *v.* porridge-basin.
papzak *m.* pot-belly.
paraaf *v.* (*pennetrek achter handtekening*) paraph; (*verkorte naamtekening*) initials.
paraat *b. n.* ready, prepared; (*v. executie*) summary.
parabel *v.* parable.
parabool *v.* (*wisk.*) parabola.
parachutist *m.* parachutist.
parade *v.* (*mil.*) parade, review; (*bij schermen*) parade, parry; (*fig.*) parade show, display.
parademars *m.* parade-march.
paradepas *m.* parade-step.
paradijs *o.* paradise.
paradijsvogel *m.* bird of paradise.
paraferen *o. w.* paraph; initial.
paraffine *v.* paraffin.
paraplu *v.* umbrella.
parasiet *m. en v.* parasite; (*fig.*) parasite, toady.
parasol *v.* sun-shade, parasol.

pardon *o.* pardon; —*!* sorry!
parel *v.* pearl.
parelduiker *m.* (*visser*) pearl-diver, pearl-fisher; (*Dk.: vogel*) black-throated diver.
parelen *on. w.* pearl, sparkle.
parelgort *v.* pearl-barley.
parelhoen *o.* guinea-fowl, pearl-hen.
parelsnoer *o.* pearl-necklace.
parelvisser *m.* pearl-fisher.
paren *o. w.* pair, couple; (*fig.*) unite, combine.
parenthese *v.* parenthesis.
pari (*H.*) par; à —, at par.
paring *r.* copulation.
park *o.* park, (pleasure-)grounds.
parket *o.* (*recht*) parquet, office of Counsel for the prosecution; (*in schouwburg*) parquet; (*fig.*) scrape.
parketvloer *m.* parquet-floor.
parkiet *m.* parakeet, paroquet.
parlement *o.* parliament.
parlementslid *o.* member of parliament.
parmantig *b. n.* (*bw.*) pert(ly), smart-(ly), perky (perkily), jaunty (jauntily).
parochiaan *m. en v.* parishioner.
parochie *v.* parish.
parochiekerk *v.* parish church.
part *o.* part, share, portion; *voor mijn —*, as for me; for my part.
part *v.* trick.
parterre *o.* (*v. schouwburg*) pit; (*v. huis*) ground-floor.
particulier *b. n.* (*niet voor allen*) particular; (*niet publiek*) private; *z. n., m.* private person.
partij *v.* party; (*v. spel*) game; (*v. huwelijk*) match; (*v. goederen*) parcel, lot; (*muz.*) part.
partijbelang *o.* party interest.
partijdig *b. n.* (*bw.*) partial(ly).
partijgenoot *m.* partisan.
partituur *v.* (music-)score.
parvenu *m.* parvenu, upstart, mushroom.
pas *m.* (*schrede, stap*) pace; step; (*bergengte*) pass, defile; (*paspoort*) passport.
Pasen *v.* Easter; (*v. de Joden*) Passover.
pasgeboren *b. n.* new-born.
pasgehuwd *b. n.* newly married.
pasgeld *o.* change, small money.
paslood *o.* plummet.
paspoort *o.* passport; (*mil.*) discharge papers.
passage *v.* (*doorgang*) passage; (*galerij*) arcade; (*sch.: overtocht*) passage, voyage; (*v. boek*) passage; (*verkeer*) traffic.
passagier *m.* passenger.
passagiersboot *v.* passenger-steamer.
passen *on. w.* (*v. kleren*) fit; (*bij kaartspel*) pass; (*betamen*) become, befit; (*schikken*) suit, be convenient; *o. w.* fit on, try on.
passend *b. n.* (*v. klederen, enz.*) fitting; (*fig.*) fit, suitable; (*v. tekst, gelegenheid, enz.*) appropriate.
passer *m.* (pair of) compasses.

passeren *on. w.* pass, pass by; *o. w.* (*voorbijgaan*) pass (by); (*bij benoeming*) pass over; (*r. akte*) execute; (*overgaan*) cross; (*doorbrengen: v. tijd*) pass.
passie *r.* (*alg.*) passion; (*liefhebberij, ook:*) craze, mania.
passief *b. n.* (*bw.*) passive(ly); *z. n., o.*
actief en —, assets and liabilities.
passiespel *o.* passion-play.
pasta *v.* paste.
pastei *v.* pastry, pie.
pasteibakker *m.* pastry-cook; (*Z. N.*) confectioner, pastry-cook.
pasteibakkerij *r.* confectioner's shop.
pastel *o.* pastel.
pastoor *m.* (parish) priest.
pastoraal *b. n.* pastoral.
pastorie *v.* (*kath.*) (parochial) presbytery; (*prot.*) rectory, vicarage, parsonage.
pateen *r.* paten.
patent *b. n.* capital, excellent, first-rate; *bw.* capitally.
patent *o.* (*voor uitvinding*) patent; (*voor bedrijf*) licence.
patenthouder *m.* patentee.
pater *m.* father.
paternoster *o.* paternoster.
patiënt *m.* patient.
patriarch *m.* patriarch.
patrijs *m.* patridge.
patrijspoort *v.* (*sch.*) port-hole.
patrijzennet *o.* tunnel-net.
patriot *m.* patriot.
patrones *v.* patron saint, patroness.
patroon *m.* (*heilige*) patron saint, patron; (*meester, baas*) employer, master, principal, patron; *v.* cartridge; *losse* —, blank cartridge; *scherpe* —, ball cartridge. *o.* (*model*) pattern, model; (*tekening*) design.
patroonhouder *m.* (*v. geweer*) clip; (*r. machinegeweer*) feed-band.
patroonhuls *v.* cartridge-case.
patroonriem *m.* cartridge-belt.
patroontas *v.* cartridge-box.
patrouille *v.* patrol.
pauk *v.* (kettle)drum.
paukenist, paukeslager *m.* kettledrummer.
paus *m.* pope.
pauselijk *b. n.* papal, pontifical.
pauw *m.* peacock.
pauwachtig *b. n.* (*Dk.*) pavonine; (*fig.*) peacockish.
pauze *v.* pause; (*in schouwburg, enz.*) interval, wait; (*muz.*) rest.
paviljoen *o.* pavillion, tent, marquee; (*v. inrichting, rusthuis, enz.*) cottage.
pech *o.* bad luck, ill-luck; — *hebben,* be down on one's luck; have a run (a streak) of bad luck.
pedaal *o.* pedal.
pedant *z. n., m.* pedant; *b. n.* (*bw.*) pedantic(ally); (*verwaand*) conceited(ly).
peddelen *on. w.* pedal.
pedel *m.* bedel, beadle, mace-bearer.
peen *r.* carrot; (*witte* —) parsnip.

peer *r.* pear; (*r. el. lamp*) bulb.
pees *r.* tendon, sinew, string; (*v. boog*) string.
peetoom *m.* godfather.
peettante *r.* godmother.
peil *o.* gauge, (water-)mark; (*fig.*) standard, level.
peilen *o. w.* (*inhoud v. vat, enz.*) gauge; (*sch.*) sound; (*v. zon*) take the sun's altitude; (*r. wond*) probe; (*fig.: v. persoon*) sound; (*v. ellende, enz.*) fathom, plumb.
peiler *m.* gauger, sounder.
peiling *r.* gauging, sounding.
peillood *o.* sounding-lead, plummet.
peilloos *b. n.* fathomless, unfathomable, plumbless.
peilstok *m.* (*sch.*) sounding-rod; (*v. wijnroeier*) gauging-rod.
peinzen *on. w.* meditate, ponder, muse.
peinzer *m.* meditator, muser.
pek *o.* pitch; (*voor schoenmakers*) wax.
pekdraad *m.* wax-end, waxed thread.
pekel *v.* pickle, brine.
pekelharing *m.* pickled herring, salt herring.
pekelzonde *v.* (*oude zonde*) old sin; (*kleine zonde*) peccadillo, venial sin.
pekken *o. w.* pitch.
pekketel *m.* pitch-kettle.
pel *v.* (*v. vrucht*) skin; (*v. ei*) shell; (*v. peulen*) hull.
pelgrim *m.* pilgrim, palmer.
pelgrimsstaf *m.* pilgrim's staff.
pelgrimstas *r.* pilgrim's scrip.
pelgrimstocht *m.* pilgrimage.
pelikaan *m.* pelican.
pellen *o. w.* (*v. noten, amandelen, enz.*) peel; (*v. rijst, maïs*) husk, hull; (*v. peulen, noten*) shell; (*v. eieren*) chip.
peloton *o.* platoon.
pels *m.* fur; fur coat.
pelshandelaar *m.* furrier.
pelsjager *m.* (fur-)trapper.
pelsjas *v.* fur coat.
pelswerk *o.* furriery, peltry.
peluw *v.* bolster, pillow.
pen *v.* (*alg.*) pen; (*losse* —) nib; (*slag*—) pinion; (*pin*) peg, pin; (*ganzepen*) quill; (*brei*—, *haak*—) needle; (*v. gloeikous*) prop; (*voor de neus*) cavesson.
penarie *v. in de* — *zitten,* be in a scrape, be in the soup.
penitentie *v.* penance; (*fig.*) affliction.
pennelikker *m.* quill-driver.
pennemes *o.* penknife.
pennestrijd *m.* pen combat, pen polemics, paper war.
penning *m.* (*munt*) penny, farthing; (*metalen plaatje, gedenk*—) medal.
penningmeester *m.* treasurer.
pens *v.* (*deel v. maag der herkauwers*) paunch, rumen; (*buik*) paunch; (*als voedsel*) tripe.
penseel *o.* (*fijn*) pencil; (*groot* —) (paint-)brush.
pensioen *o.* (retiring) pension; (*mil.*) retired pay.

pensioenfonds o. pension fund.
pension o. boarding-house.
pensioneren o. w. pension off, grant a pension; (mil.) place on the retired list.
pentekening v. pen-drawing.
peper m. pepper.
peperbus v. pepper-box.
peperen o. w. pepper.
peperkoek m. gingerbread.
pepermunt v. (Pl.) peppermint; (tabletje) peppermint lozenge.
pepermuntje o. peppermint lozenge.
per per; via; by.
perceel o. (kaveling, partij) lot, parcel; (v. grond ook:) allotment, plot; (pand, huis) building, house; (huis en erf) premises.
percent o. percentage, percent.
pereboom, perelaar m. pear-tree.
perfect b. n. (bw.) perfect(ly).
perfectie v. perfection.
periode v. period; (v. ziekte, enz.) stage.
periodiek b. n. (bw.) periodical(ly); z. n., o. periodical.
periscoop m. periscope.
perk o. (v. bloemen) bed; (grens) limit, bound(s).
perkament o. parchment, vellum.
permissie v. permission; (mil.) leave (of absence); met —, by your leave.
permissiebiljet o. permit, pass; (H.: om te bezichtigen, enz.) order-to-view, inspection-order.
perron o. platform.
perronkaartje o. platform-ticket.
Pers m. Persian.
pers v. press.
persbericht o. press-report.
persen o. w. press, squeeze.
perser m. presser.
persgas o. high-pressure gas.
persgesprek o. interview.
persing v. pressing, pressure.
perskaart v. press-ticket.
personeel b. n. personal; z. n., o. staff, servants, domestics, personnel.
persoon m. en v. person.
persoonlijk b. n. personal; (particulier: v. schulden, enz.) private; (individueel) individual; bw. personally, in person.
persoonsbeschrijving v. personal description.
persoverzicht o. press review, review of the press.
Perzië o. Persia.
perzik v. peach.
pest v. plague, pest, pestilence; (fig.) pest, pestilence.
pestachtig b. n. pestilential.
pesten o. w. nag, tease, badger.
pestlijder m. plague-patient.
pet v. cap.
petekind o. godchild.
peter m. godfather.
peterselie v. parsley.
petitie v. petition, memorial.
petroleum v. petroleum, oil.

petroleumlamp v. paraffin-lamp.
petroleumveld o. oil-field.
peukje o. cigar-end.
peul v. husk, shell.
peulerwt v. green pea.
peulvrucht(en) v. (mv.) pulse, leguminous plant(s).
peuteren on. w. potter, niggle, fumble, finger.
peuterwerk o. piddling-work, pernickety work.
peuzelen on. w. munch.
pezerik m. pizzle.
pezig b. n. sinewy, wiry.
pianist m., **pianiste** v. pianist.
piano v. piano.
pianokrukje o. piano-stool, music-stool.
piccolo v. (muz.) piccolo; m. buttons, page-boy.
picknicken on. w. picnic.
piek v. (spies, lans) pike; (sch.: bergtop) peak.
piekdrager m. pikeman.
piekfijn b. n. smart, natty, spick and span.
pienter b. n. clever, bright, smart, sharp, brainy.
piepen on. w. (v. vogel) peep, chirp; (v. muis) squeak; (v. scharnier, enz.) creak.
pier v. (worm) earth-worm; m. (in zee) pier, jetty.
pierewaaier m. fast fellow, rake.
pieterman m. (Dk.) weever.
pij v. cowl.
pijl m. arrow; (korte, stompe —) bolt; (fig.) shaft; (vuurpijl) rocket.
pijler m. pillar, column; (v. brug) pier.
pijlkruid o. (Pl.) arrow-grass.
pijlwortel m. (Pl.) arrowroot.
pijn v. pain; (aanhoudende —) ache; (stekende —) smart; m. (pijnboom) pine, pine-tree.
pijnappel m. fire-cone, pine-cone.
pijnbank v. torture, rack.
pijnboom m. pine-tree.
pijnigen o. w. torture, torment, rack.
pijniging v. torture.
pijnlijk b. n. (bw.) painful(ly).
pijnloos b. n. (bw.) painless(ly).
pijnstillend b. n. pain-deadening, pain-killing, anodyne; — **middel,** anodyne.
pijp v. pipe; (v. broek) leg; (v. blaasbalg) noze, nozzle; (buis) tube, spout, conduit; (v. lak, kaneel, enz.) stick; (fluit) fife.
pijpedop m. lid of a pipe-bowl.
pijpekop m. pipe-bowl.
pijpenrek o. pipe-rack.
pijporgel o. pipe-organ.
pik m. (wrok) grudge, pique; (met bek, enz.) peck.
pik v. (houweel) pick, pickaxe.
pikant b. n. piquant, pungent, spicy, (highly) seasoned; (fig.) piquant.
pikdonker b. n. pitch-dark.
pikhouweel o. pickaxe.
pikken on. w. (v. vogel) peck, pick; (prikken) prick.

pil *v.* pill.
pilaar *m.* pillar, column, post.
pilaarbijter *m.* hypocrite.
piloot *m.* pilot.
pimpernel *v.* (*Pl.*) salad-burnet, bennet.
pimpernoot *v.* pistachio-dut, bladdernut.
pin *v.* peg, pin.
pindakaas *v.* pea-nut cheese.
pingelen *on. w.* higgle, haggle, chaffer.
pink *v.* (*sch.*) pink; *m.* little finger; (*Dk.:* jong rund) heifer.
pinken *on. w.* wink, pink.
Pinksteren *v.* Whitsun(tide); (*v. de Joden*) Pentecost.
pinksterbloem *v.* (*Pl.*) cuckoo-flower; (*pop.*) girl in her Whitsunbest.
pint *v.* pint.
pioen(roos) *v.* peony.
pionier *m.* pioneer, path-finder.
piot *m.* footslogger.
piraat *m.* pirate.
pisang *v.* banana.
pissebed *v.* (*Dk.*) sow-bug; (*Pl.*) dandelion.
pistool *v. en o.* (*wapen*) pistol; *v.* (*oude munt*) pistole.
pit *v.* (*eetbaar: v. noot, amandel, enz.*) kernel; (*steen: v. kers, perzik, enz.*) stone; (*v. appel, peer, enz.*) pip; (*wiek: v. kaars, lamp*) wick; (*fig.*) pith, spirit; (*v. wijn, roman, enz.*) body.
pittig *b. n.* pithy; (*fig.*) nutty; (*v. stijl*) crisp.
pittigheid *v.* pithiness.
plaag *v.* plague; (*kwelling*) vexation; (*onaangenaamheid, last*) nuisance; (*plaaggeest*) tease, teaser.
plaaggeest *m.* tease, teaser.
plaagziek *b. n.* (fond of) teasing.
plaat *v.* (*v. glas, metaal, deur, enz.*) plate; (*geplet metaal*) sheet; (*v. marmer, enz.*) slab; (*wijzer*) dial; (*grammofoon—*) record; (*gravure, prent*) picture, engraving, print; (*ondiepte*) shallow, shoal, sands.
plaatijzer *o.* sheet-iron.
plaats *v.* (*alg.*) place; (*ruimte*) space, room, place; (*bij huis*) yard; (*zitplaats*) seat, place; (*v. schip: positie*) position; (*betrekking*) situation, office; (*in boek*) place, passage; **in — van,** instead of.
plaatsbekleder *m.* substitute, (*v. dokter, enz.*) locum tenens.
plaatsbepaling *v.* localisation, determination of a place; (*gram.*) adjunct of place.
plaatsbespreking *v.* booking.
plaatsbewijs *o.* ticket.
plaatsbureau *o.* (*in station*) booking-office; (*in schouwb.*) box-office; (*mil.*) town-major's office.
plaatselijk *b. n.* (*bw.*) local(ly).
plaatsen *o. w.* (*een plaats geven*) seat; (*zetten*) put, place; (*v. geld: beleggen*) invest; (*v. advertentie*) insert; (*H.: v. koopwaren*) dispose off, sell, find a

market for; (*v. machine*) put up, set up; (*in betrekking*) place, get a place; (*v. lening, orders, enz.*) place; (*v. soldaten*) station, locate; (*v. officieren*) quarter; (*aanstellen*) appoint.
plaatsgebrek *o.* want of space.
plaatsing *v.* placing; investment; insertion; disposal; appointment.
plaatsruim:te *v.* room space; (*in hotel, enz.*) accommodation.
plaatsvervanger *m.* (*alg.*) substitute; (*v. dokter, enz.*) locum tenens; (*v. bisschop*) surrogate; (*gevolmachtigde*) deputy; (*v. toneelspeler*) understudy.
plaatsvervanging *v.* substitution.
pladijs *v.* plaice, flat fish.
plafond *o.* ceiling.
plagen *o. w.* (*uit scherts*) tease, chaff; (*kwellen, hinderen*) vex; (*sarren*) nag, badger.
plager *m.* teaser; vexer.
plagerij *v.* teasing; vexation.
plaggensteker *m.* turf-cutter, sod-cutter.
plak *v.* (*v. ham, kaas, enz.*) slice; (*v. ham*) rasher; (*v. chocolade*) cake, bar.
plakboek *o.* scrap-book.
plakbrief *m.* placard, posting-bill.
plakkaat *o.* placard, poster; (*gesch.*) edict, proclamation.
plakken *o. w.* paste, stick, glue; *on. w.* stick; **blijven —,** (*fig.*) stick on, sit on.
plakzegel *o.* receipt-stamp, revenue-stamp.
plamuur(sel) *o.* priming.
plan *o.* (*tekening, schets*) plan, design; (*ontwerp, uitgewerkt schema*) project, scheme, plan, design; (*opzet, voornemen*) project, intention, plan; (*plattegrond*) (ground-)plan.
planeet *v.* planet.
planeetbaan *v.* orbit (of a planet).
planeren *o. w.* (*v. metaal*) planish; (*v. papier*) size, planish; *on. w.* (*v. vliegtuig*) plane, glide.
plank *v.* (*dik*) plank; (*dun*) board; (*in kast, enz.*) shelf; (*sch.: loopplank*) gangway.
plankenkoorts *v.* stage-fright.
plankenvloer *m.* boarded floor.
plant *v.* plant.
plantaarde *v.* (vegetable) mould.
plantaardig *b. n.* vegetable.
plantage *v.* plantation, estate.
planten *o. w.* plant.
plantenetend *b. n.* plant-eating, herbivorous.
plantengroei *m.* plant-growth, vegetation.
plantenkenner *m.* botanist.
plantenrijk *o.* vegetable kingdom.
plantentuin *m.* botanic(al) garden.
planter *m.* planter.
plantsoen *o.* plantation; ornamental grounds, pleasure park.
plas *m.* pool, puddle.
plasregen *m.* downpour, pelting rain, splashing rain.

plassen *on. w.* splash, plash.
plat *b. n.* (*r. neus, dak*) flat; (*effen*) even; (*horizontaal*) level; (*fig.*) broad, vulgar, trivial, coarse; *bw.* flat; broadly, vulgarly, trivially, coarsely; *z. n., o.* (*v. dak*) leads, flat; (*v. degen, hand, enz.*) flat.
platbodemd *b. n.* (*sch.*) flat-bottomed.
plateel *o.* pottery, faience.
platform *o.* platform.
platheid *v.* flatness; (*fig.*) broadness, vulgarity, trivialness, coarseness.
platkop *m.* flat-head.
platliggen *on. w.* lie flat.
platluis *v.* crab-louse.
platneus *m.* flat-nose.
plattegrond *m.* (*v. gebouw*) ground-plan, floor-plan; (*v. schouwburg*) seat-plan; (*v. stad*) map, plan.
platteland *o.* country.
plattelandsbewoner *m.* rural resident, countryman.
platvoet *m.* flat-foot.
platweg *bw.* flatly.
platzak *b. n.* out of cash.
plavei *v.* paving-stone.
plaveien *o. w.* pave.
plaveisel *o.* pavement.
plecht *v.* (*sch.*) half-deck, forward deck, after-deck.
plechtanker *o.* sheet-anchor.
plechtig *b. n.* ceremonial, ceremonious, solemn; stately; imposing.
plechtigheid *v.* solemnity, ceremony, rite.
pleegouders *m. mv.* foster-parents, adopted parents.
plegen *o. w.* (*v. misdaad, enz.*) commit, perpetrate; (*v. bedrog*) practise; (*gewoon zijn*) use, be accustomed.
pleidooi *o.* pleading, plea, defence; **een — houden,** make a plea.
plein *o.* square, public place.
pleister *v.* plaster; *o.* (*pleisterkalk, gips*) plaster, stucco.
pleisterbeeld *o.* plaster-cast.
pleisteren *o. w.* plaster, stucco; *on. w.* (*in herberg, enz.*) stop; bait.
pleisterkalk *v.* plaster, stucco, parget.
pleisterplaats *v.* baiting-place, bait-house, stage.
pleit *o.* (*recht*) suit, plea.
pleitbezorger *m.* solicitor, counsel; attorney, lawyer; (*fig.*) intercessor, advocate.
pleiten *on. w.* plead, argue; (*fig.*) tell.
pleiter *m.* pleader; (*advocaat*) counsel.
pleitgeding *o.* law suit.
pleitziek *b. n.* litigious, contentious.
plek *v.* (*plaats*) place, spot; (*vlek*) stain, spot.
plekken *on. w.* stain, fleck.
plengen *o. w.* (*v. tranen, bloed*) shed; (*v. wijn*) spill, pour out; (*gesch.: als offer*) offer as a libation.
plenging *v.* shedding; spilling, pouring out.

pletten *o. w.* planish, flatten, roll out, laminate.
pletterij *v.* flatting-mill, rolling-mill.
pleuris *v.* pleurisy.
plezier *o.* pleasure.
plezierboot *v.* excursion steamer.
plezierig *b. n.* pleasant.
pleziermaker *m.* merry-maker, reveller.
plezierreis *v.* pleasure-trip, pleasuring-tour, excursion for pleasure.
pleziertochtje *o.* pleasure-trip, jaunt.
plicht *m.* duty, obligation.
plichtmatig *b. n.* dutiful, conformable to one's duty.
plichtsbetrachting *v.* devotion to duty.
plichtshalve *bw.* dutifully, in duty; (*ambtelijk*) officially.
plichtverzaking *v.*, **plichtverzuim** *o.* neglect (dereliction, faillure) of duty.
ploeg *m.* (*landbouwwerktuig*) plough; *v.* (*groep werklieden*) gang, shift; (*afdeling kandidaten, bij examen*) batch; (*sport*) team.
ploegbaas *m.* ganger, foreman, gaffer.
ploegboom *m.* plough-beam.
ploegen *o. w.* (*v. land, zee*) plough; (*tn.*) groove.
ploegijzer, ploegkouter, ploegmes *o.* coulter.
ploegvoor *v.* furrow.
ploert *m.* cad, sweep; (*sl.*) townee, snob; (*studententaal*) landlord.
ploertendoder *m.* bludgeon, life-preserver.
ploertenstreek *m.* mean trick, scurvy trick.
ploeteren *on. w.* (*in water*) dabble, splash; (*fig.: zwoegen*) drudge, plod, toil (and moil).
plof *z. n., m.* thud, dump, plump; *tw.* plump! flop! plop!
plomberen *o. w.* fill with lead, fill; (*H.*) lead, seal (with lead).
plomp *z. n., m.* (*waterlelie*) white waterlily; (*gele —*) brandy-bottle; *b. n.* (*onhandig, lomp*) clumsy, awkward; (*zwaar, log*) unwieldy; cumbersome; (*ruw*) rude, blunt, coarse.
plompheid *v.* clumsiness; lumpishness.
plonzen *on. w.* (*plassen*) splash, dabble; (*duiken*) plunge.
plooi *v.* fold; (*in broek, enz.*) crease; (*rimpel: in voorhoofd*) wrinkle.
plooibaar *b. n.* pliable, pliant, flexible.
plooien *o. w.* fold; crease; wrinkle; *w. w. zich —,* fold.
plootwol *v.* fell-wool.
ploten *o. w.* shear.
plots, plotseling *b. n.* sudden; *bw.* suddenly, all of a sudden.
pluim *v.* plume, feather; (*Pl.*) panicle; (*fig.*) compliment.
pluimen *o. w.* plume.
pluimstaart *m.* bushy (plumy) tail.
pluimstrijken *o. w.* fawn upon, cajole, stroke down.

pluimstrijker *m.* fawner, adulator, wheedler.

pluis *z. n., v.* fluff; *(pluche)* plush; *b. n.* **niet —,** not as it should be; not trustworthy.

pluizen *o. w.* fluff, pick; *on. w.* fluff, give off fluff.

pluk *m.* gathering, picking, plucking; *(handvol)* handful.

plukharen *on. w.* (have a) tussle, be at loggerheads.

plukken *o. w.* *(v. bloemen, vruchten)* gather, pick, pluck; *(v. vogel)* pluck, plume; *(fig.)* fleece, pluck, milk.

plukker *m.* gatherer, picker, reaper.

pluksel *o.* lint.

plunderaar *m.* plunderer, robber, pillager.

plunderen *o. w.* *(v. stad)* plunder, pillage, sack; *(v. persoon)* rob, plunder; *(v. huis)* rifle.

plundering *v.* plundering, pillage.

plunje *v.* togs, toggery.

plutocraat *m.* plutocrat.

pluvier *m.* *(Dk.)* plover.

pochen *on. w.* boast, brag.

pocher *m.* boaster, braggart.

pocherij *v.* boasting, bragging, brag.

podium *o.* podium, platform.

poedel *m.* *(Dk.)* poodle; *(bij kegelspel: misworp)* boss, miss.

poedelnaakt *b. n.* stark naked.

poeder *o.* powder.

poederkwast *m.* powder-puff.

poedervorm *m.* **in —,** pulverized, in powder form.

poëet *m.* poet.

poel *m.* pool; *(kleine —)* puddle; *(modder—)* slough.

poelier *m.* poulterer.

poen *m.* *(persoon)* vulgarian, snob, cad, bounder; *(geld)* tin, rhino.

poes *v.* puss, cat; *(bont)* boa, furtippet.

poeslief *b. n.* suave; silky; all smiles and graces.

poespas *m.* hotch-potch, hode-podge.

poets *v.* trick, prank.

poetsen *o. w.* polish, clean.

poetser *m.* polisher, cleaner.

poetskatoen *o.* cotton waste.

poezelig *b. n.* plump, chubby.

poezeligheid *v.* plumpness, chubbiness.

poëzie *v.* poetry.

pofbroek *v.* plus fours, knickerbockers; *(oudtijds)* trunk-hose.

poffen *on. w.* *(op krediet kopen)* buy on tick; *(v. kastanjes, aardappelen: braden)* roast; *(mil.: schieten)* puff; *o. w.* *(krediet geven)* give credit.

poffertje *o.* fritter.

pofmouw *v.* puffed sleeve, puff sleeve, balloon sleeve.

pogen *o. w.* endeavour, try, attempt.

poging *v.* endeavour, effort, attempt.

pointeren *o. w.* *(mil.)* lay.

pokdalig *b. n.* pock-marked.

poken *on. w.* poke the fire.

pokken *on. w.* get small pox

pokstof *v.* vaccine, (vaccine-)lymph.

polder *m.* polder.

polderland *o.* polder-land.

polemiek *v.* polemic(s), controversy.

Polen *o.* Poland.

poliep *v.* *(Dk.)* polyp; *(gezwel)* polypus.

polijsten *o. w.* polish, burnish.

polijststeen *m.* polishing-stone.

polikliniek *v.* policlinic.

polis *v.* policy.

polishouder *m.* policy-holder.

politicus *m.* politician.

politie *v.* police.

politieagent *m.* police-man, police-officer; *(fam.)* bobby.

politiecommissaris *m.* police-commissioner, chief constable.·

politiek *z. n., v.* *(alg.)* politics; *(gedragslijn)* policy, line of policy; *(burgerkleding)* plain clothes; *b. n.* *(bw.)* political(ly); *(fig.)* politic(ly), diplomatic(ally).

politiemacht *v.* police-force, body of police.

politiemuts *v.* *(mil.)* foraging-cap, fatigue-cap.

politoer *o.* polish.

politoeren *o. w.* polish, burnish.

pollepel *m.* ladle.

polospel *o.* polo.

pols *m.* *(gewricht)* wrist; *(polsslag)* pulse; *(springstok)* pole, leaping-pole.

polsader *v.* radial vein, artery.

polsen *o. w.* feel the pulse; *(fig.)* sound.

polsslag *m.* pulsation, pulse.

polsstok *m.* leaping-pole, jumping-pole.

pomerans *v.* *(Pl.)* bitter orange; *(bilj.)* leather-tip, cue-tip.

pommade *v.* pomatum, pomade.

Pommer (**aan**) *m.* Pomeranian.

Pommeren *o.* Pomerania.

pompbak *m.* pump-box, pump-cistern.

pompelmoes *v.* shaddock, pommelmoose; *(kleine —)* grape-fruit.

pompen *on. w.* pump.

pompier *m.* engine-man.

pompoen *m.* pumpkin, gourd.

pompstation *o.* pumping-station.

pompwater *o.* pump-water.

pon *v.* nighty, night-dress.

pond *o.* pound.

ponjaard *m.* poniard, dagger.

pons *v. en m.* punch.

pont *v.* ferry-boat, pontoon.

pontificaat *o.* pontificate.

pontonbrug *v.* pontoon-bridge.

pony *m.* *(Dk.)* pony, Shetland (pony).

pook *v.* poker.

Pool *m.* Pole, Polander.

pool *v.* *(lange overjas)* greatcoat; *(aspunt)* pole.

poolijs *o.* polar ice.

poollanden *o. mv.* polar regions.

poollicht *o.* polar lights, aurora borealis.

Pools *b. n.* Polish.

poolshoogte *v.* elevation of the pole, latitude; **— nemen,** take (find out) one's bearings, see how the land lies.

poolster *v.* polar star, pole-star.

poolvos m. arctic fox.
poolzee v. polar (arctic; antarctic) sea (ocean).
poort v. gate, gateway, doorway.
poorter m. (gesch.) citizen, freeman, burgher.
poos v. while, time.
poot m. (v. dier) paw, foot, leg; (v. meubel) leg; (fam.: hand) hand, fist, fin, paw.
poot v. (v. plant: stekje, lootje) slip, shoot, layer; (v. vis) fry.
pootaardappel m. seed-potato.
pop v. (speelgoed) doll; (in poppenspel, marionet) puppet; (v. insekt) pupa, nymph; (v. vogel) hen; (in kaartspel) pictorial card, picture card; m. (sl.: gulden) bob, guilder.
popelen on. w. quiver, throb; — van vreugde, leap up for joy.
poppenkast v. Punch-and-Judy show, puppet-show.
poppenkraam v. booth for dolls and toys; (fig.) puppetry.
populier m. poplar.
por m. thrust, dig; (steek) stab.
poreus b. n. porous.
poreusheid v. porosity.
porren o. w. (v. vuur) poke, stir; (v. persoon) poke, prod; (wekken) knock up, call up; (aanzetten) spur on, rouse.
porselein o. porcelain, china, china ware.
port o. postage.
portaal o. porch, portal; (trap—) landing.
portefeuille v. (brieventas, zak—) pocket-book, letter-case; (v. minister; map, voor tekeningen, enz.) portfolio; (voor tijdschriften) reading-case.
portie v. portion, part, share; (v. maaltijd) helping; (rantsoen) allowance; (fig.: v. geduld, enz.) dose.
portiek v. portico, porch.
portier m. door-keeper; hotel-porter, hall-porter; o. carriage-door.
portierswoning v. porter's lodge.
portret o. portrait; (foto) photo(graph); (beeltenis, gelijkenis) likeness.
portvrij b. n. post-paid, (postage) free.
portzegel o. due stamp.
positie v. (stelling, plaats) position; (betrekking) position, situation; (maatschappelijke —) status; (bij vioolspel) shift.
positief b. n. positive; (zelfbewust) cocksure; bw. decidedly.
post m. (v. deur, enz.) post; jamb; (mil.: standplaats) post; (schildwacht) sentry; (bij staking) picket; (betrekking, ambt) post-office, place; (H.: in boek) entry; (v. rekening) item; (v. de staatsbegroting) vote; (postbode) postman; v. (brievenpost) post, mail; (postkantoor) post-office, post.
postbeambte m. postal worker, postal servant.
postbode m. letter-carrier, postman.

postbus v. post-office box, post-box.
postcheque v. postal cheque.
postdirecteur m. postmaster.
postduif v. carrier-pigeon, messenger-pigeon.
postelein v. (Pl.) purslane, purslain.
posten o. w. (v. brief) post; (bij werkstaking) picket.
poste-restante to be called for, to wait arrival, poste restante.
posterijen v. mv. de —, the Post Office, the postal service.
postkantoor o. post-office.
postkwitantie v. postal collection order.
postmerk o. post mark.
postpakket o. postal parcel.
postpapier o. note-paper, letter paper.
poststempel o. postmark.
posttarief o. rates of postage, postal rates.
postulant m. postulant.
postuur o. shape, figure; (houding) posture, attitude.
postverkeer o. postal traffic.
postwissel m. money-order, post-office order.
postzegel m. en o. (postage) stamp.
postzegelverzamelaar m. stamp-collector, philatelist.
pot m. pot; (voor inmaak) jar, pot; (v. kachel) fire-pot; (nacht —) chamber-pot; (bij spel: inzet) stakes, pool, stock of money.
potas v. potash.
potdeksel o. pot-lid.
potdicht b. n. very close, perfectly closed; (fig.) as close as wax.
poten o. w. (v. planten) plant; (v. vis) set.
potentaat m. potentate.
potig b. n. robust, strong, raw-boned.
potje o. (little) pot.
potlood o. (schrijfvoorwerp) pencil, lead-pencil; (poetsmiddel) black-lead, plumbago.
pots v. (poets, grap) prank, farce; (Z. N.: kinderbaret) tam (o'shanter).
potscherf v. potsherd.
potsenmaker m. wag, buffoon.
potsierlijk b. n. grotesque, droll, comic(al).
potten o. w. (v. plant) pot, put in pots; (v. geld) hoard up; on. w. salt down money; make a stocking.
pottenbakker m. potter, ceramist.
potvis m. cachelot.
pover b. n. poor, shabby; (v. uitslagen) meagre.
praaien o. w. (sch.) hail, speak.
praal m. pomp, magnificence, splendour.
praalgraf o. mausoleum.
praalvertoon o. pomp, ostentation.
praalzucht v. ostentation, fondness (love) of display.
praat m. talk, tattle.
praatje o. talk, chat; (kletspraatje) idle story; (gerucht) rumour.

praatjesmaker *m.* chatterer; (*opsnijder*) blusterer, braggart.
pracht *v.* splendour, magnificence, pomp.
prachtig *b. n.* magnificent, splendid, superb; (*weelderig*) sumptuous.
practicus *m.* practical person.
praktijk *v.* practice.
pralen *on. w.* shine, sparkle, glitter; (*fig.: ong.*) flaunt.
praler *m.* parader, swaggerer.
pralerij *v.* ostentation swagger, show.
prangen *o. w.* press, squeeze; (*beklemmen*) oppress.
pranger *m.* barnacles.
prat *b. n. en bw.* proud; — **gaan op,** pride oneself on, glory in.
praten *on. w.* talk; chat; (*ong.: vervelend praten*) prate.
prater *m.* talker, chatterer; (*ong.*) prater.
prauw *v.* proa(h).
precies *b. n.* (*bw.*) precise(ly), exact(ly).
predikaat *o.* (*ambts- of eretitel*) title; (*gram.: gezegde*) predicate; (*beoordeling, cijfer*) mark.
predikant *m.* (*kath.*) preacher; (*prot.*) clergyman, minister, pastor.
predikheer *m.* Dominican.
prediking *v.* preaching.
preek *v.* sermon; (*fig.*) preachment, sermon.
preekstoel *m.* pulpit.
prefatie *v.* preface.
prefect *m.* prefect.
preferent *b. n.* preferential; (*v. schuld, aandelen*) preferred.
prei *v.* leek.
prelaat *m.* prelate.
premie *v.* premium; (*uitvoer—*) bounty; (*H.*) option.
premieaffaire *v.* option.
premiegeld *o.* option money.
premielening *v.* lottery loan.
premier *m.* prime minister, premier.
prent *v.* print, picture, engraving.
prentbriefkaart *v.* picture post-card.
prenten *o. w.* imprint, impress.
prentenkabinet *o.* gallery of prints.
president *m.* president; (*voorzitter*) chairman, president; (*v. jury*) foreman.
presidentschap *o.* presidency, presidentship, chairmanship.
preskop *m.* brawn, pressed hog's head.
pressen *o. w.* press.
prestatie *v.* performance, achievement.
presteren *o. w.* achieve.
pret *v.* pleasure, fun; — **maken,** enjoy oneself, make merry, have a good time.
pretbederver *m.* kill-joy.
pretendent *m.* pretender, claimant; (*minnaar*) suitor.
pretentie *v.* (*aanmatiging*) pretension; (*aanspraak, vordering*) claim, pretension.
pretmaker *m.* merrymaker, reveller.
prettig *b. n.* pleasant, amusing, nice.
preuts *b. n.* prudish, squeamish, prim.

preutsheid *v.* prudishness, squeamishness, primness, prudery.
prevelen *o. w. en on. w.* mutter.
prieel *o.* arbour, bower, summer-house.
priem *m.* piercer, pricker, awl; (*breinaald*) knitting-needle; (*dolk*) dagger; (*kleine dolk, stilet*) stiletto.
priemen *o. w.* pierce, prick.
priester *m.* priest.
priestergewaad *o.* sacerdotal vestments.
priesterlijk *b. n.* priestly.
priesterschap *o.* sacerdocy.
priesterwijding *v.* ordination.
prij *v.* (*aas*) carrion; (*boos wijf*) virago, shrew, vixen.
prijken *on. w.* shine, glitter, blaze.
prijs *m.* (*waarde in geld*) price; (*beloning; in loterij, enz.*) prize.
prijsbederver *m.* underseller, spoiltrade.
prijscourant *v.* (*H.*) price-current, price-list.
prijsdaling *v.* (*H.*) fall in price(s).
prijsgeven *o. w.* abandon, give up; (*aan de vlammen*) commit; (*aan de vergetelheid*) consign.
prijshoudend *b. n.* (*H.*) firm, steady.
prijskamp *m.* competition.
prijslijst *v.* price-list.
prijsopdrijving *v.* (*H.*) inflation of prices.
prijsschommeling *v.* price fluctuation.
prijsverhoging *v.* increase, rise (of prices).
prijsverlaging *v.* abatement, reduction.
prijsvraag *v.* prize subject, prize question.
prijzen *o. w.* (*loven, roemen*) praise, commend; extol, glorify; (*dicht.*) laud; (*van prijscijfer voorzien*) price, ticket.
prijzenswaardig *b. n.* praiseworthy, laudable, commendable.
prik *m.* prick, stab, sting.
prikkel *m.* (*priem, prikstok*) goad; (*stekel: v. insekt, enz.*) sting; (*v. egel, plant*) prickle; (*fig.*) stimulus, spur, incentive.
prikkelbaar *b. n.* irritable, excitable.
prikkeldraad *o.* barbed wire.
prikkelen *o. w.* prickle, tickle, titillate; (*fig.: v. persoon*) irritate; (*opwekken*) excite, stimulate; (*v. nieuwsgierigheid*) prick, pique, excite.
prikkeling *v.* prickling, tickling; irritation; stimulation, excitation.
pril *b. n.* —**le jeugd,** early youth.
prima *b. n.* first class, first rate, prime.
primaat *m.* primate.
primaatschap *o.* primateship, primacy.
primo *bw.* first(ly), in the first place.
principaal *m.* master; (*H.*) principal.
prins *m.* prince.
prinsdom *o.* principality.
prinses *v.* princess.
prinsessenbonen *v. mv.* French beans, butter-beans.
prins-gemaal *m.* prince consort.

prior *m.* prior.
prioriteit *v.* priority.
privaat *b. n. (bw.)* private(ly); *z. n., o.* privy, water closet; *(in openb. instellingen)* latrine.
privé *o.* private, personal.
pro *bw. en vz.* pro.
probaat *b. n.* approved, efficacious, excellent, sure.
proberen *o. w. (toetsen, keuren, op de proef stellen)* try, test; *(beproeven)* attempt.
probleem *o.* problem.
procent *o.* percent, percentage.
proces *o. (rechtsgeding)* action, lawsuit; *(ontwikkelingsgang)* process.
processie *v.* procession.
proces-verbaal *o. (verslag)* record, official report; *(bekeuring)* warrant.
proclamatie *v.* proclamation.
procuratie *v.* procuration, power of attorney, proxy.
procuratiehouder *m.* proxy, confidential clerk, managing clerk.
procureur *m.* attorney, solicitor.
procureur-generaal *m.* attorney-general.
produkt *o.* product; *(opbrengst)* produce; *(v. letterkunde, enz.)* production.
produktief *b. n.* productive; *(winstgevend)* remunerative; — **maken,** make pay.
proef *v. (toets, onderzoek)* trial, test, experiment; *(v. foto)* proof, copy; *(drukproef)* proof; *(natuurk., scheik.)* experiment.
proefbalans *v.* trial balance, pro-forma balance.
proefballonnetje *o.* pilot-balloon; *(fig.)* (trial) kite.
proefdruk *m.* proof, first impression.
proefflesje *o.* sample bottle.
proefgewicht *o.* standard weight.
proefhoudend *b. n.* proof, standard.
proefkonijn *o.* laboratory rabbit; experimental guinea-pig.
proeflezer *m.* corrector of the press, proof-reader.
proefneming *v.* experiment; *(handeling)* experimentation.
proefondervindelijk *b. n. (bw.)* experimental(ly).
proefrit *m.* trial ride, trial run.
proefschrift *o.* thesis, act.
proefstation *o.* experiment station, testing station.
proefstuk *o.* trial piece, sample piece, specimen.   [ciate.
proeftijd *m.* time of probation; novi-
proefwerk *o.* test paper, examination paper.
proesten *on. w.* sneeze.
proeven *o. w.* taste; *(als keuring ook:)* sample; *(v. goud)* assay; *on. w.* taste.
proever *m.* taster.
profeet *m.* prophet.
professor *m.* professor.
profetes *v.* prophetess.

profetie *v.* prophecy.
profijt *o.* profit, gain.
profijtelijk *b. n. (voordelig)* profitable; *(winstgevend)* lucrative.
pro forma for form's sake.
projectiedoek *o.* screen.
projectiel *o.* projectile.
proletariër *m.* proletarian.
proloog *m.* prologue, proem.
promesse *v. (H.)* promissory note.
promotie *v. (bevordering)* promotion, rise, advancement; *(aan universiteit)* graduation.
promotor *m.* promotor, company-promotor.
prompt *b. n. (bw.)* prompt(ly).
promptheid *v.* promptness, promptitude, readiness.
pronken *on. w.* make a parade, make a show, show off, cut a dash.
pronker *m.* showy fellow, beau, dandy.
pronkerig *b. n.* fond of show, showy, ostentatious.
pronkerwt *v. (Pl.)* sweet-pea.
pronkstuk *o.* show-piece.
prooi *v.* prey.
proost *m.* dean.
prop *v. (op fles)* stopple, stopper, stop; *(gen.: v. watten)* swab, pledget; *(v. kanon)* wad; *(in de mond)* gag; *(v. vat)* bung; *(om te gooien)* pellet; *(in de keel)* lump; *(v. persoon)* dump.
propaganda *v.* propaganda.
proper *b. n.* neat, clean, tidy.
proportie *v.* proportion.
proppeschieter *m.* pop-gun.
propvol *b. n.* crammed (full), chock-full.
protectoraat *o.* protectorate.
protest *o.* protest, protestation.
protestakte *v.* deed of protest.
Protestant *m.* Protestant.
protesteren *on. w.* protest.
proviand *o.* provisions, victuals, stores.
proviandering *o.* provisionment, provisioning, victualling.
provinciaal *b. n.* provincial; *z. n., m.* provincial (resident); *(v. kloosterorde)* provincial.
provincie *v.* province.
provinciestad *v.* provincial town, country town.
provisie *v. (voorraad)* stock, provision, supply; *(loon, v. makelaars, enz.)* commission.
provisiekamer *v.* pantry, larder.
provisiekast *v.* pantry, larder, store-cupboard.
provoost *v. (mil.)* detention-room; black-hole; *(straf)* close arrest.
proza *o.* prose.
prozaïst, prozaschrijver *m.* prose-writer, prosaist.
pruik *v.* wig, periwig, peruke.
pruilen *on. w.* pout, sulk.
pruilmondje *o.* pout.
pruim *v.* plum; *(gedroogd)* prune; *(reine claude)* greengage; *(v. tabak)* quid, plug; chew.

pruimeboom *m.* plum-tree.
pruimen *o. w. (tn.: v. stoomketel)* prime; *(v. tabak)* chew; *on. w.* chew (tobacco); *(smakelijk eten)* eat heartily.
pruimer *m.* (tobacco-)chewer.
pruimtabak *v.* chewing-tobacco.
Pruisen *o.* Prussia.
Pruisisch *b. n.* Prussian.
prul *o.* bauble, bawble, gimcrack; trashy novel; catch-penny publication.
pruldichter *m.* poetaster, versifier.
prullaria *o. mv.,* **prullenboel** *m.* trash, stuff, rubbish, gewgaws.
prullenkamer *v.* lumber-room.
prullenmand *v.* waste-paper basket.
prullerig, prullig *b. n.* trashy, rubbishy, trumpery.
prulschrijver *m.* paltry writer, scribbler.
prulwerk *o.* trash, rubbish.
prutsen *on. w.* potter, fiddle, tinker.
prutser *m.* potterer, tinker.
prutswerk *o.* pottering work.
pruttelen *on. w. (borrelend koken)* simmer; *(fig.: mopperen)* grumble, sputter.
psalm *m.* psalm.
psalter *o. (instrument)* psaltery; *(psalmboek)* psalter.
pseudoniem *z. n., o.* pseudonym, penname; *b. n.* pseudonymous.
psychiater *m.* psychiater.
publiciteit *v.* publicity.
publiek *b. n.* public; *bw.* publicly, in public; *z. n., o.* public; *(gehoor)* audience.
puddelen *o. w.* puddle.
pui *v. (v. winkel, enz.)* shop-front, underfront (lower front) of a building; *(v. stadhuis)* flight of steps.
puik *b. n.* choice, excellent, first rate; *bw.* to perfection, beautifully.
puilen *on. w.* swell, bulge; *(v. ogen)* start (from).

puimen *o. w.* pumice.
puimsteen *m.* pumice-stone.
puin *o.* rubbish, debris, ruins; *(afbraak)* rubble.
puinhoop *m.* rubbish-heap, heap of rubbish; *(ruïne)* (heap of) ruins.
puist *v.* tumour.
puistig *b. n.* blotchy, pimply.
puistje *o.* pimple, pustule.
puitaal *m.* eel-pout.
pul *v.* jug, vase.
pulp *v.* pulp.
pulver *o.* powder, gun-powder.
pulveriseren *o. w.* pulverize, powder.
pummel *m.* yokel, boor, lout, bumpkin.
punt *v. (v. naald, pen, enz.)* point; *(v. neus, tong)* tip; *(van i)* dot; *(v. asperge)* top; *(sch.: v. anker)* peak; *(leesteken)* full stop; **dubbele —,** colon; **komma —,** semi-colon; *o.* point; *(v. agenda, programma, enz.)* item; *(bij koersnotering)* unit; *(v. bespreking, enz.)* point.
puntbaard *m.* pointed beard.
puntdicht *o.* epigram.
puntgevel *m.* gable.
puntig *b. n.* pointed, sharp.
pupil *m. en v.* pupil, ward; *v. (v. oog)* pupil.
puree *v.* purée.
puren *o. w.* suck.
purgatie *v.* purge, purgation.
purgeermiddel *o.* purgative, purge.
purgeren *on. w.* take a purgative.
purper *o.* purple.
purperrood *b. n. en z. n., o.* purple.
put *m. (waterput)* well; *(kuil)* pit, hole; *(v. mijn)* shaft, pit.
putten *o. w.* draw.
putter *m.* water-drawer; *(Dk.)* goldfinch, thistle-finch.
puur *b. n. (bw.)* pure(ly).
puzzel *v.* puzzle.

Q

quadrille *v.* quadrille, square dance.
quadrilleren *on. w.* play quadrille.
quadrupel *b. n.* quadruple.
quantum *o.* quantum, amount.
quarantaine *v.* quarantine.
quasi *bw.* quasi; *(voorgevend)* pretended; *(ogenschijnlijk)* seeming.
quatertemper *m.* ember fast.
quatertemperdag *m.* ember-day.
quatre-mains *m., à —,* for four hands; **een —,** a duet.
queue *v. (v. biljart)* cue; *(v. japon)* dress-improver, bustle.

quidam *m.* queer bird, odd fish, rummy chap.
quitte *b. n.* quits.
qui vive *tw. en z. n., o.* who goes there ? **op zijn — zijn,** be on the qui vive (on the alert).
quota *v.* quota, contingent, share, part.
quotatie *v.* assessment.
quoteren *o. w.* assess.
quotiënt *o.* quotient.
quotum *o.* quota, share.

R

ra *v.* (*sch.*) yard.

raad *m.* (*raadgeving*) advice, counsel; (*raadgevend college*) council; (*persoon*) counsel, counsellor; — **van beroep,** board of appeal; — **van State,** Privy Council; State Council; — **van commissarissen,** — **van beheer,** (*H.*) board of directors; *iem.* — **geven,** advise a person; — **inwinnen,** ask (a person's) advice; — **schaffen,** devise ways and means.

raadgevend *b. n.* (*v. lichaam*) advisory; (*v. commissie*) consultative.

raadgever *m.* adviser, counsellor.

raadgeving *v.* advice, counsel.

raadhuis *o.* town hall.

raadplegen *o. w.* (*v. advocaat, dokter, enz.*) consult; (*v. vriend, enz.*) take counsel with.

raadpleging *v.* consultation.

raadsbesluit *o.* (*v. gemeenteraad*) decision, decree; (*v. God*) ordinance, decree.

raadsel *o.* riddle, enigma, puzzle.

raadsheer *m.* councillor, senator; (*in gerechtshof*) justice; (*in schaakspel*) bishop; (*Dk.: duif*) jacobin.

raadslid *o.* councillor, member of the (town-)council.

raadsverslag *o.* town-council report.

raadszitting *v.* sitting (session) of the town-council.

raadzaal *v.* council-chamber, council-room.

raadzaam *b. n.* advisable.

raaf *v.* raven.

raak *b. n.* hit; home.

raaklijn *v.* tangent.

raam *o.* (*v. huis*) window; (*het schuivende gedeelte*) sash; (*lijst, omlijsting*) frame; (*v. pers*) chase; *m.* (*raming*) estimate, rough calculation.

raap *v.* turnip; (*veevoeder*) rape; (*knol—*) swede.

raapkool *v.* turnip-cabbage.

raapzaad *o.* rapeseed.

raar *b. n.* (*ongewoon*) unusual, extraordinary; (*vreemd, zonderling*) queer, strange, odd; (*zeldzaam*) rare; *bw.* strangely.

raaskallen *on. w.* rave, talk nonsense.

raat *v.* honeycomb.

rabarber *v.* rhubarb.

rabat *o.* (*H.: korting*) reduction, discount; (*rand, zoom*) border; (*smal bloembed*) platband.

rabbijn, rabbi *m.* rabbi, rabbin.

race *v.* race.

racebaan *v.* race-course.

rad *z. n., o.* wheel; *b. n.* (*vlug*) quick, glib, nimble; (*v. spraak*) voluble, glib.

radbraken *o. w.* (*v. veroordeelde*) break upon the wheel; (*fig.: v. taal*) murder.

radeloos *b. n.* desperate, at one's wit's end.

radeloosheid *v.* desperation.

raden *o. w.* (*raad geven, aanraden*) counsel, advise; (*gissen*) guess; *on. w.* guess.

raderwerk *o.* wheel-work.

radheid *v.* quickness, glibness, nimbleness; (*v. tong*) volubleness, volubility.

radicaal *b. n.* radical; *z. n., o.* (*diploma, bul*) certificate, diplomae; , titl (*v. pers.: scheik.*) radical.

radijs *v.* radish.

radio *v.* radio.

radio-actief *b. n.* radio-active.

radio-omroep *m.* broadcast(ing).

radio-ontvangtoestel *o.* wireless receivingset.

radiostation *o.* radio-station.

radiotelegrafist *m.* wireless operator.

radium *o.* radium.

radiumhoudend *b. n.* radium-bearing.

radius *m.* radius, radial line.

rafactie *v.* (*H.*) allowance for damage.

rafel *v.* fray.

rafelen *o. w. en on. w.* fray, ravel out.

rafelig *b. n.* frayed.

rafelkant *m.* fag-end.

raffinaderij *v.* refinery, sugar-refinery, refining-works.

rag *o.* cobweb.

ragfijn *b. n.* cobwebby, gossamer, as fine as gossamer.

rakelen *o. w.* rake.

rakelijzer *o.* rake, oven-fork.

rakelings *bw.* *iets* — *voorbij gaan,* brush past a thing.

raken *o. w.* (*treffen*) hit; (*betreffen*) concern, affect; (*aanraken*) touch; *on. w.* get.

raket *o.* (*v. tennis, enz.*) racket; (*v. pluimbal*) battledore; *v.* (*vuurpijl*) rocket; (*Pl.*) hedge-mustard.

raketbom *v.* rocketbomb.

rakker *m.* rascal, rogue, scapegrace.

ram *m.* (*Dk.*) ram; (*sterr.*) Aries.

ramen *o. w.* estimate.

ramenas *v.* black radish.

raming *v.* estimate; (*sch.*) dead-reckoning.

rammel *m.* rattle; (*afranseling*) dusting, drubbing.

rammelaar *m.* (*speelgoed; babbelaar*) rattle; (*Dk.: konijn*) buck-rabbit.

rammelen *on. w.* (*praten*) rattle; (*v. geld*) jingle; (*v. ketenen*) clank.

rammeling *v.* shaking, drubbing.

rammelkast *v.* (*v. rijtuig*)rattletrap, rumble-tumble; (*v. auto*) crock of a car, ramshackle čar; (*v. piano*) tin-kettle.

ramp *v.* disaster, calamity.

rampspoed *m.* adversity.

rampspoedig *b. n.* disastrous, calamitous.

rampzalig *b. n. (jammerlijk)* miserable, wretched; *(noodlottig)* fatal.
rand *m. (v. hoed, glas)* brim; *(v. papier, boek)* margin; *(v. handdoek, kleed)* edging; *(v. tafel, bed, enz.)* edge; *(v. bos)* skirt, edge; *(v. afgrond)* brink; *(v. put)* parapet; *(fig.: v. ondergang)* verge.
randgebergte *o.* border mountains.
randgemeenten *v. mv.* satellite towns.
randversiering *v.* ornamental border.
rang *m.* rank, degree, grade.
rangeerlijn *v.* shunt line.
rangeren *o. w. (in orde brengen, ordenen)* arrange, order; *(v. spoorwagens)* shunt; *on. w.* shunt.
ranggetal *o.* zie **rangtelwoord**.
ranglijst *v.* list; *(mil.: v. officieren)* army list; list of candidates.
rangnummer *o.* number (in the list).
rangorde *v.* order.
rangschikken *o. w. (ordenen)* arrange, range; *(v. argumenten, feiten, enz.)* marshal; *(volgens bevoegdheid, enz.)* grade; *(tabellarisch)* tabulate; *(classificeren)* class, classify.
rangschikking *v.* arrangement; classification.
rangtelwoord *o.* ordinal number.
rank *z. n., v.* tendril; vine; *b. n. (v. gestalte)* slender; *(v. schip)* crank, cranky.
rankheid *v.* slenderness; crankness.
ranonkel *v.* ranunculus.
ransel *m.* knapsack, rucksack; *(mil.)* knapsack, pack; *(slaag)* flogging, drubbing.
ranselen *o. w.* thrash, whop, wallop, drub.
rantsoen *o. (afgepaste hoeveelheid)* ration, portion, allowance; *(losprijs)* ransom.
rantsoeneren *o. w.* ration, allowance, put on rations.
rantsoenering *v.* rationing.
ranzig *b. n.* rancid.
rap *b. n.* quick, agile, nimble.
rapen *o. w. en on. w.* pick up, gather, collect.
rapheid *v.* quickness, agility, nimbleness.
rapier *o.* rapier.
rapport *o. (verslag)* statement; report; *(op school)* report; *(betrekking, verband)* connection.
rariteit *v.* curiosity, curio.
ras *o. (v. mensen)* race; *(v. dieren)* breed, stock.
rasecht *b. n.* pure-bred, true-bred.
rasheid *v.* quickness, swiftness.
rasp *v.* rasp, grater.
raspen *o. w.* rasp, grate.
rassehaat *m.* race-hatred.
raster *m.* lath.
rastering *v.* railing.
rasterwerk *o.* lattice(-work), grillage, railing.
rat *v.* rat.
ratel *m.* rattle; *(v. tong)* clack, clapper.
ratelpopulier *m.* trembling poplar, mountain-ash.

ratelslang *v.* rattle-snake.
ratjetoe *v. (mil.)* hodge-podge, hotchpotch; *(fig. ook:)* farrago, olio, olla podrida.
rato rate; *naar —,* in proportion.
rattenkruit *o.* arsenic.
rattenvanger *m.* rat-catcher; *(hond)* ratter.
ratteval *v.* rat-trap.
rauw *b. n. (niet gekookt)* raw, uncooked; *(v. geluid)* hoarse, raucous; *(v. huiden)* raw, untanned.
rauwheid, rauwigheid *v.* rawness; harshness.
ravijn *o.* ravine.
ravotten *on. w.* romp.
razen *on. w.* rage, rave.
razend *b. n.* raving, furious, mad; *(v. honger)* ravenous; *(v. hoofdpijn)* splitting, raging; *bw.* ravingly, furiously.
razernij *v.* rage, frenzy, madness; *(gen.)* rabies.
reactie *v.* reaction, reflex action; *(fig.)* revulsion (of feeling).
reageren *on. w.* react.
realist *m.* realist.
rebel *m.* rebel, mutineer.
rebellie *v.* rebellion, mutiny.
rebus *m.* rebus.
recensie *v.* criticism, critique, review.
recept *o. (v. dokter)* prescription; *(voor keuken)* recipe, receipt.
receptenboek *o.* prescription-book; receipt-book.
recherche *v.* detective force, criminal investigation department.
recht *o. (alg.)* right; *(aanspraak, bevoegdheid)* right, claim, title; *(rechtsgeleerdheid, wetten)* law; *(gerechtigheid)* right, justice; *(geheven recht, belasting)* duty, custom; *(op postwissel)* poundage.
recht *b. n. (juist: v. woord, enz.)* right; *(niet krom: v. lijn, enz.)* straight; *bw.* rightly; straightly.
rechtbank *v.* court of justice, lawcourt; *(fig.)* tribunal, bar.
rechten *o. w. (recht maken)* right, straighten; *(recht spreken)* administer justice to.
rechter *m.* judge, justice.
rechter *b. n.* right; *(v. paard, rijtuig, enz.)* off.
rechterarm *m.* right arm.
rechterlijk *b. n.* judicial, justiciary.
rechterzijde *v.* right side.
rechthebbende *m. en v.* rightful claimant.
rechthoek *m.* rectangle.
rechthoekig *b. n. (v. vorm)* rectangular; *(met rechte hoek)* right-angled.
rechtlijnig *b. n.* rectilinear.
rechtmatig *b. n.* rightful, lawful, legal, legitimate.
rechtop *bw.* upright, straight, erect.
rechtover *bw.* just opposite.
rechts *bw.* to (on) the right.
rechtsbegrip *o.* sense of justice.
rechtsbevoegd *b. n.* competent.

rechtsbevoegdheid *v.* jurisdiction, competence.
rechtschapen *b. n.* upright, honest.
rechtschapenheid *v.* honesty, uprightness, probity.
rechtsgebied *o.* jurisdiction.
rechtsgeding *o.* lawsuit.
rechtsgeldigheid *v.* validity, legality.
rechtsgeleerde *m.* lawyer, jurist, jurisconsult.
rechtsgrond *m.* principle of justice.
rechtsingang *m.* — *verlenen*, find a (true) bill.
rechtskosten *m. mv.* legal expenses.
rechtskundig *b. n.* legal, juridical.
rechtsom *bw.* to the right.
rechtsomkeert *tw* right about... turn! (*fig.*) turn tail.
rechtspersoon *m.* corporate body, corporation.
rechtspersoonlijkheid *v.* incorporation; — *verkrijgen* (*hebben*), be incorporated.
rechtspleging *v.* administration of justice, (exercise of) judicature.
rechtspraak *v.* administration of justice; (*verzameling v. vonnissen, enz.*) jurisprudence.
rechtspreken *on. w.* administer justice.
rechtstandig *b. n.* perpendicular.
rechtstreeks *bw.* directly.
rechtsvervolging *v.* prosecution.
rechtsvordering *v.* action, (legal) claim.
rechtswege *bw.* *van* —, in justice, by right.
rechtszaak *v.* law suit, cause.
rechtszitting *v.* sitting of the court.
rechtuit *bw.* straight on; (*fig.*) straight out, frankly.
rechtvaardig *b. n.* just, righteous.
rechtvaardigen *o. w.* justify.
rechtvaardigheid *v.* righteousness, justice.
rechtzinnig *b. n.* (*bw.*) orthodox(ly).
reclame *v.* (*beklag*) complaint; (*vordering*) claim; (*bezwaarschrift: tegen belasting*) appeal; (*in dagblad, enz.*) advertising, advertisement; puff; — *maken,* advertise.
reclameartikel *o.* sale article.
reclamebureau *o.* publicity agency.
reclameren *o. w.* claim back, reclaim; *on. w.* protest (object) to.
record *o.* record.
rector *m.* (*v. gymnasium, enz.*) headmaster, principal; (*v. seminarie, enz.*) rector; (*v. klooster*) rector, director; — *Magnificus,* Vice-Chancellor.
reçu *o.* (*v. bagage, vestiaire*) ticket, check; (*kwitantie*) receipt; (*v. post*) certificate of posting.
redactie *v.* (*v. dagblad*) editorship; (*gezamenlijke redacteuren*) editoral staff, the editors; (*v. artikel, zin, enz.*) wording; *onder* — *van,* edited by.
reddeloos *b. n* past recovery, past hope,

irrecoverable, irretrievable; *bw.* irrecoverably, irretrievably.
redden *o. w.* save, rescue; *w. w. zich* —, save oneself; pay one's own way; roll one's own log.
redder *m.* saver, rescuer; (*v. land, zielen*) saviour.
redderen *o. w.* arrange, put (bring) in order.
redding *v.* saving, rescue; salvation; (*bevrijding*) deliverance.
redding(s)boei *v.* life-buoy.
reddingsgordel *m.* life-belt.
reddingsmiddel *o.* life-saving appliance.
reddingswerk *o.* rescue-work; (*bij brand, enz.*) salving-operations.
rede *v.* (*denkvermogen, oordeel*) reason, sense; (*redevoering, toespraak*) speech, discourse, oration.
rede *v. zie* **ree.**
redekavelen *on. w.* argue, reason, talk, palaver.
redekunst *v.* rhetoric.
redelijk *b. n.* (*met rede begaafd*) rational; (*verstandelijk*) reasonable; (*billijk, niet overdreven*) reasonable, moderate; (*tamelijk*) passable; *bw.* reasonably; moderately; passably.
redelijkheid *v.* reasonableness.
redeloos *b. n.* void of reason, irrational.
reden *v.* (*beweeggrond, oorzaak*) reason, cause; (*verhouding*) ratio.
redenaar *m.* orator.
redenaarsgave *v.*, **redenaarstalent** *o.* oratorial talent, oratorical endowments.
redeneren *on. w.* reason.
redenering *v.* reasoning.
reder *m.* (ship-)owner.
rederij *v.* ship-owners society, shipping company, ownery.
rederijker *m.* (*gesch.*) rhetorician; member of a dramatic club.
rederijkerskamer *v.* guild of rhetoric, society of rhetoricians; dramatic club.
redetwist *m.* dispute, disputation, controversy.
redetwisten *on. w.* dispute; (*ruzie maken*) wrangle.
redevoering *v.* speech, address; (*plechtig*) oration.
ree *v.* (*Dk.*) roe, hind; (*sch.*) road(s), roadstead.
reebout *m.* haunch of venison.
reeds *bw.* already.
reëel *b. n.* (*werkelijk: v. waarde, enz.*) real; (*degelijk*) sound.
reef *o.* (*sch.*) reef.
reegeit *v.* roe.
reeks *v.* series; (*v. woorden, vragen*) string; (*v. bergen*) chain; (*v. gebeurtenissen, gevolgen, enz.*) train; (*wisk.*) progression.
reep *v.* (*touw*) rope, cord, line, string; (*strook*) strip; (*v. chocolade*) bar.
reet *v.* cleft, crack, crevice, fissure, chink; (*werktuig*) flax-brake.

referentiën *r. mv.* references.
referte *r.* reference; **onder — aan** referring to.
reflexbeweging *v.* reflex (action).
reformatie *r.* reformation.
refrein *o.* burden (of a song), chorus, refrain.
refter *m.* refectory.
regel *m.* rule; *(lijn)* line; *(v. spel)* rule, law.
regelaar *m.* regulator.
regelen *o. w. (schikken, ordenen)* arrange, order; *(v. prijzen, enz.)* order, regulate; *(v. verkeer)* direct; *(tn.: v. uurwerk, kompas, enz.)* regulate, adjust.
regeling *r.* arrangement, order; regulation, adjustment.
regelmaat *r.* regularity.
regelmatig *b. n. (bw.)* regular(ly).
regelmatigheid *r.* regularity.
regelrecht *bw.* right, straight, straightway.
regen *m.* rain; **blauwe —,** *(Pl.)* wistaria; **gouden —,** *(Pl.)* laburnum.
regenachtig *b. n.* rainy.
regenbak *m.* cistern, tank.
regenboog *m.* rain-bow.
regenboogvlies *o.* iris.
regenbui *r.* shower of rain.
regendicht *b. n.* rain-proof, rain-tight.
regendroppel *m.* drop of rain.
regenen *onp. w.* rain.
regenjas *r.* rain-coat, mackintosh.
regenscherm *o.* umbrella.
regent *m.* regent, governor; *(v. weeshuis, enz.)* trustee; *(v. gevangenis)* (prison) commissioner.
regentes *r.* regent, lady governor.
regenwater *o.* rain-water.
regeren *o. w.* reign over, rule; *(v. ministers)* govern; *(v. paard)* manage; *on. w.* reign, rule, govern.
regering *v. (v. vorst)* reign, rule; *(bestuur)* government.
regeringloosheid *v.* anarchy.
regeringsbesluit *o.* decree, ordinance.
regeringskringen *m. mv.* government circles.
regeringswege *bw.* **van —,** from the government, officially.
regie *v. (v. toneel: spelleiding)* staging; *(monopolie: van tabak, enz.)* regie, state (government) monopoly.
regime *o. (regeerstelsel)* regime; *(leefregel)* regimen.
regiment *o.* regiment.
regimentsarts *m.* regimental surgeon.
register *o. (boek)* register; *(inhoudsopgave)* index, table of contents; *(muz.: v. orgel)* (organ-)stop.
registratie *v.* registration.
registratiekosten *m. mv.* registry fees.
registreren *o. w.* register.
reglement *o.* regulation(s), rules; *(v. maatschappij)* by-law.
rei *m.* chorus; dance.
reiger *m.* heron.

reiken *on. w.* reach; extend, stretch; *o. w.* reach.
reikhalzen *on. w.* **— naar,** long for, yearn for, hanker after.
rein *b. n. (bw.)* pure(ly), clean(ly); *(kuis)* chaste(ly).
reinheid *r.* purity, cleanness.
reinigen *o. w.* clean; *(zuiveren: r. bloed, enz.)* purify.
reiniging *r.* cleaning; purification.
reinigingsdienst *m.* (public) cleaning department.
reis *v. (alg.)* journey; *(rondreis)* tour, trip; *(op zee)* voyage; *(overtocht)* passage.
reisbenodigdheden *r. mv.* travelling requisites.
reisbureau *o.* travel-bureau, tourists' agency.
reisdeken *v.* railway rug.
reisduif *v.* homing pigeon, passenger pigeon.
reisgeld *o.* journey-money, travellingmoney.
reisgids *m.* guide-book, travellers' guide; *(v. spoorweg, enz.)* time-table.
reisgoed *o. (bagage)* luggage.
reiskosten *m. mv.* travelling-expenses.
reisroute *v.* route, itinerary.
reistas *v.* travelling-bag.
reisvaardig *b. n.* ready to set out.
reizen *on. w.* travel, journey, voyage.
reiziger *m.* traveller.
rek *v. (v. elastiek)* elasticity, spring; *(v. gymnastiek)* horizontal bar.
rek *o. (in keuken, voor pannen, enz.)* rack; *(voor handdoeken)* towel-horse; *(voor kleren)* clothes-horse; *(voor kippen)* roost.
rekbaar *b. n.* extensible, elastic, ductile, malleable.
rekbaarheid *v.* extensibility, elasticity, ductility, malleability.
rekel *m. (vlegel; hond)* cur; *(vos)* male fox.
rekenboek *o.* arithmetic book, sum book, ciphering-book.
rekenen *on. w.* cipher, count, calculate, reckon; **— op,** *(v. persoon)* depend upon; *(v. zaak)* count upon; *o. w.* reckon, count; *(in rekening brengen)* charge; *(schatten)* estimate, value; **bij elkaar —,** count up, sum up.
rekening *v. (nota)* bill, account; *(berekening)* calculation, reckoning; **in — brengen,** charge; **— houden met,** take into account, reckon with, take account of.
rekening-courant *v.* account current, current account. [customer.
rekeninghouder *m.* current account
rekenkunde *v.* arithmetic.
rekenles *v.* arithmetic lesson.
rekenmachine *v.* calculatingmachine.
rekenmunt *v.* money of account.
rekenraam *o.* abacus.
rekenschap *v.* account; **— geven van,** render an account of; **iem. — vragen,** call a person to account.

rekest o. petition, memorial.
rekken o. w. (v. metaaldraad) draw out; (v. stof, schoenen) stretch; (v. hals) crane; (v. bezoek, tijd, enz.) protract; (v. redevoering) spin out; (v. woorden) draw out, trail; (v. preek) lengthen out; (v. tijd) prolong; on. w. (v. vogels) roost.
rekruteren o. w. recruit.
rekruut m. recruit.
rekstok m. horizontal bar.
rekwest o. petition, memorial.
rekwestrant m. petitioner, memorialist.
relaas o. relation, account, story.
relatie v. relation.
reliëf o. relief.
reliek v. relic.
religieus b. n. religious.
reling v. (sch.) rail.
relletje o. row, disturbance.
rem v. brake, break, (wheel-)drag; (fig.) drag.
remblok o. brake-block, drag.
rembours o. cash on delivery.
remedie v. remedy.
remise v. (v. geld) remittance; (bij spel) draw, drawn game; (koetshuis) coach-house, carriage-house, car-shed.
remmen o. w. brake; (fig.) check; on. w. turn on the brake, put on the drag.
rempedaal o. brake pedal.
remschoen m. brake-shoe, skid, drag.
remtoestel o. brake, break.
ren m. (snelle loop) course, run; (galop) gallop, trot; v. chicken-run.
renbaan v. race-ground.
renbode m. courier.
rendier o. reindeer.
rennen on. w. race, run, gallop.
renner m. racer.
renpaard o. race-horse.
rensport v. racing, the turf.
renstallen m. mv. racing-stables.
rente v. interest; **op — zetten,** put out at (upon) interest.
rentegevend b. n. interest-bearing.
rentenier m. rentier, retired tradesman.
rentevoet m. rate of interest.
rentmeester m. steward, treasurer.
rentmeesterschap o. stewardship.
reorganisatie v. reorganization.
rep m. **in — en roer,** alarmed; in commotion; in a stir.
reparatie v. repair(s), reparation.
repareren o. w. repair, mend.
repertorium o. repertory.
repetitie v. (alg.) repetition; (v. toneelstuk, enz.) rehearsal.
repliek v. counter-plea, rejoinder retort.
reppen on. w. **— van,** mention, make mention of; w. w. **zich —,** hurry, make haste.
represaillemaatregel m. reprisal.
reproduceren o. w. reproduce.
reptiel o. reptile.
republiek v. republic.
republikein m. republican.
reputatie v. reputation.

requiem-mis r. requiem.
reserve v. (H.) reserve; (mil.) reserve (troops), reserves.
reservedelen o. mv. spare parts, renewal parts.
reservefonds o. reserve fund.
reservist m. reservist.
residentie v. residence, royal residence, court-capital.
resolutie v. resolution.
respect o. respect, esteem, regard.
respijt o. (H.) respite, delay, grace.
rest v. rest; remainder.
restant o. remainder, remnant; (saldo) balance.
restauratie v. (herstel) restoration, renovation; (restaurant) restaurant.
restauratiewagen m. dining-car.
resteren on. w. remain, be left.
resultaat o. result, outcome.
resumeren o. w. sum-up, summarize, resume.
retort v. retort.
retourbiljet, retourkaartje o. return ticket.
retraite v. retreat.
reu m. male dog.
reuk m. smell; (geur) smell, odour, scent; (v. hond, enz.) scent.
reukflesje o. smelling bottle.
reukorgaan o. organ of smell, olfactory organ.
reukwater o. perfumed water.
reukwerk o. perfume(s), perfumery.
reukzenuw v. olfactory nerve.
reumatiek v. rheumatism.
reus m. giant, colossus.
reusachtig b. n. gigantic; (v. huis, bedrag) huge, colossal.
reutel m. rattle in the throat.
reutelen on. w. rattle.
reuzel m. lard.
reuzengeslacht o. race of giants, giant race.
reuzengestalte v. gigantic stature.
reuzenschrede v. giant's stride.
reuzenslang v. python, boa constrictor.
reveil o. revival.
revisie v. (alg.) revision; (v. drukwerk) revise, clean proof.
revolutie v. revolution.
revolutiebouw m. jerry building.
revolutionnair b. n. revolutionary; z. n., m. revolutionist.
revolver m. revolver.
revue v. (mil.; tijdsch.) review; (toneel) revue.
rib v. (alg.) rib; (v. kubus) edge.
ribbenkast v. body, carcass.
ribbestuk o. rib of beef.
richel v. border, edge, ridge.
richten o. w. (alg.) direct; (v. wapen) point, level; (v. kanon) lay, train, point; (v. brief) direct, address; w. w. **zich — tot iem.,** apply to, address oneself to a person.
richting v. direction, set; (v. kust; fig.) trend; (mil.) alignment, dressing; (over-

tuiging) persuasion; (*gezindheid*) school of thought.
richtingsbord *o.* (*v. tram*) route indicator.
richtingzoeker *m.* (*vl.*) direction-finder.
richtlat *v.* (*v. metselaar*) jointing-rule.
richtlijn *v.* (*mil.*) line of sight; (*schietlood*) plumb-line; (*fig.*) dirigent, directess.
richtsnoer *o.* line of conduct, directive, rule (of conduct).
ricinusolie *v.* castor-oil.
ridder *m.* knight.
ridderkruis *o.* cross of knighthood.
ridderlijk *b. n.* (*bw.*) knightly; chivalrous(ly).
ridderlijkheid *v.* chivalrousness, chivalry.
ridderorde *v.* order of knighthood.
ridderslag *m.* accolade
riek *v.* pitch-fork, three-pronged fork.
rieken *on. w.* smell.
riem *m.* (*v. leer*) strap; (*gordel*) girdle; (*roeispaan*) oar; (*v. geweer, kijker, enz.*) sling; (*drijf—*) (driving-)belt; (*papier*) ream; (*scheer—*) strop.
riet *o.* reed; (*bamboe*) cane; (*bies*) rush; (*voor daken*) thatch; (*voor limonade*) straw.
rieten *b. n.* reed; (*v. dak*) thatched; (*v. stoel*) cane.
rietfluit *v.* reed-pipe.
rietgans *v.* bean goose.
rietgors *v.* (*Dk.*) reed-bunting.
rietsuiker *v.* cane-sugar.
rif *o.* (*klip*) reef; (*geraamte*) carcass, skeleton; (*v. zeil*) reef.
rij *v.* row, range, series, line, file.
rijbaan *v.* riding-ground, riding-track; (*voor schaatsen*) (skating-)rink, skating ground.
rijbewijs *o.* (driving) licence, motor driver's licence.
rijbroek *v.* riding-breeches.
rijden *on. w.* (*op fiets, in trein, tram, enz.*) ride; (*in rijtuig, auto*) drive; (*schaatsen—*) skate; (*mennen*) drive; *o. w.* drive; (*v. kind, zieke, enz.*) wheel.
rijder *m.* rider, horseman; skater.
rijdier *o.* riding-animal, mount.
rijf *v.* (*rasp*) grater, rasp; (*hark*) rake.
rijgen *o. w.* (*met veters:* *v. schoenen, korset*) lace; (*met spelden, steken*) tack; (*met steken*) baste; (*v. kralen*) string, thread; (*v. papieren*) file.
rijglaars *v.* lace-up boot.
rijgnaald *v.* lacing-needle.
rijgsnoer *o.* (stay-)lace.
rijk *b. n.* (*v. persoon, volk*) rich, wealthy, opulent; (*v. maaltijd*) copious, sumptuous; (*v. kleding, versiering*) rich, sumptuous; (*v. verzameling: uitgebreid*) ample; *bw.* richly; copiously; amply.
rijk *o.* state; empire, kingdom, realm; (*gebied*) domain.
rijkaard *m.* rich man, rich fellow, plutocrat, Croesus.

rijkdom *m.* riches, wealth; (*fig.*) abundance, copiousness, wealth.
rijkelijk *bw.* richly, abundantly, copiously, amply.
rijkelui *m. mv.* rich people.
rijknecht *m.* groom, jockey.
rijkostuum *o.* riding-suit, riding-dress, riding-kit.
rijksarchief *o.* Public Record(s) Office.
rijksarchivaris *m.* Master of the Rolls.
rijksbeheer *o.* **onder —,** under State control.
rijksdaalder *m.* rixdollar.
rijksdag *m.* diet.
rijksmunt *v.* coin of the realm; (*gebouw*) Royal Mint.
rijkunst *v.* horsemanship.
rijlaars *v.* riding-boot.
rijm *m.* *zie* **rijp**; *o.* rhyme, rime.
rijmelaar *m.* rhymer, verse monger, poetaster.
rijmelen *on. w.* write doggerel.
rijmen *o. w. en on. w.* rhyme, rime.
rijmpje *o.* rhyme, short rhyme.
Rijn *m.* Rhine.
rijp *m.* hoar-frost; (*dicht.*) rime.
rijp *b. n.* ripe; (*fig.*) mature.
rijpen *o. w. en on. w.* (*v. fruit, enz.*; *fig.*) ripen, mature; *on. w.* (*licht vriezen*) rime, freeze with a hoar-frost.
rijpheid *v.* ripeness, maturity.
rijping, rijpwording *v.* ripening, maturation.
rijs *o.* twig, sprig, osier, birch.
rijschaaf *v.* trying-plane.
rijschool *v.* riding-school.
rijshout *o.* osiers, twigs, sprigs.
Rijsel *o.* Lisle, Lille.
rijst *v.* rice.
rijstepap *v.* rice-milk.
rijstetaart *v.* rice-cake.
rijstkorrel *m.* rice-grain.
rijstveld *o.* rice-field, paddy-field.
rijswerk *o.* osiery, osier-work; (*mil.*) fascine-work.
rijtuig *o.* carriage, coach; vehicle; (*huur—*) cab.
rijtuigfabriek *v.* carriage-works, coach-works.
rijweg *m.* carriage-road, carriage-way; (*voor ruiters*) bridle-path.
rijwiel *o.* bicycle, cycle.
rijwielpad *o.* cycle-track.
rijwielplaatje *o.* licence tab.
rijzen *on. w.* (*v. persoon, zon, deeg, enz.*) rise; (*v. prijzen*) rise, go up; (*zich voordoen: v. moeilijkheden, enz.*) arise.
rijzig *b. n.* tall.
rijzweep *v.* horse-whip, riding-whip.
rillen *on. w.* shiver (with), shudder (at).
rilling *v.* shivering, shiver, shudder.
rimpel *m.* (*in huid*) wrinkle; (*diepe —*) furrow; (*in kleed, blad, enz.*) rumple; (*v. water*) ripple, ruffle.
rimpelen *on. w.* wrinkle; (*v. water*) ruffle, ripple; *o. w.* wrinkle; (*v. water:* *doen —*) ruffle, ripple.
rimram *m.* balderdash, slush, rigmarole.

ring m. (alg.) ring; (om maan) circle
halo; (v. boom) circle.
ringbaan v. belt-railway.
ringdijk m. ring-dike, enclosing-dike.
ringelmus v. tree-sparrow.
ringeloren o. w. bully, order about.
ringen o. w. (v. varken) ring, nuzzle;
(v. paard) infibulate; (v. boom) girdle.
ringrijden on. w. tilt at the ring.
ringrups v. lackey caterpillar, ring-
straked caterpillar.
ringslang v. ring-snake, grass-snake.
ringvormig b. n. ring-shaped, annular.
ringworm m. annelid; (huiduitslag)
ring-worm.
rinkel m. jingling-bell.
rinkelen on. w. jingle.
rins b. n. sourish, tart.
riolering v. sewerage.
riool o. sewer, drain.
rioolbuis v. sewer-pipe, draining-tube.
rioolnet o. sewerage.
risico o. risk.
riskeren o. w. hazard, risk.
rist v. (v. uien, enz.) rope, string; (v.
bessen) bunch; (fig.) string.
rit m. ride.
ritje o. ride.
ritme o. rhythm.
ritmeester m. cavalry captain.
rits tw. crack! pop!
rits v. groove.
ritselen on. w. rustle.
ritseling v. rustling.
ritsen o. w. (tn.) groove.
ritueel b. n. (bw.) ritual(ly).
ritus m. rite.
rivaliteit v. rivalry, competition.
rivier v. river.
rivierkreeft m. crayfish.
rivieroever m. riverside.
rivierpaard o. hippopotamus.
rivierschip o. river-vessel; (mv. ook:)
river-craft.
rob m. (Dk.) seal.
robbedoes m. en v. romping boy, rowdy boy; rowdy girl, tomboy.
robijn o. en m. ruby.
robuust b. n. robust.
rochel v. phlegm.
rochelen on. w. expectorate; (vooral v.
stervende) rattle, ruckle.
roebel m. rouble.
roede v. rod, switch; (voor kastijding)
birch, birchrod; (maat) decametre; (staf)
verge.
roeibootje v. rowing-boat, row-boat.
roeien o. w. en on. w. (sch.) row, pull;
(peilen) gauge.
roeier m. (sch.) rower, oarsman; (peiler) gauger.
roeipen v. thole.
roeiriem m., **roeispaan** v. (voor één
hand) scull; (voor twee handen) oar.
roeisport v. rowing, boating.
roeitochtje o. row.
roeiwedstrijd m. rowing-match, boat-
race.

roek m. (Dk.) rook.
roekeloos b. n. (bw.) rash(ly), reckless-
(ly).
roekeloosheid v. rashness, recklessness.
roem m. glory, renown; celebrity.
roemen o. w. praise; on. w. boast.
roemer m. (persoon) boaster; (glas)
rummer.
roemrijk b. n. glorious, renowned,
illustrious.
roemzuchtig b. n. ambitious; vain-
glorious.
roep m. call, cry; (gerucht) rumour.
roepen on. w. call, cry; (schreeuwen)
cry, shout.
roeping v. call, calling; vocation.
roepstem v. call, voice.
roer o. (v. schip, roerblad) rudder;
(roerpen) helm; (v. pijp) stem; **aan 't
— komen,** come into office.
roereieren o. mv. scrambled eggs.
roeren o. w. (v. koffie, enz.) stir; (fig.)
touch; move; on. w. move, stir; **— aan,**
touch; w. w. **zich —,** stir, move.
roerganger m. helmsman.
roerig b. n. (druk, levendig) active,
restless, stirring, bustling; (oproerig)
turbulent.
roerigheid v. activity, restlessness,
bustle; turbulence.
roering v. (beweging) stir, motion; (opschudding) commotion.
roerloos b. n. (v. schip) rudderless;
(onbeweeglijk) motionless; (fig.) unmoved.
roerpen v. (sch.) tiller, helm(-stock).
roerspaan v. stirrer, spatula.
roervink m. stirrer up, decoy-bird;
(fig.) firebrand.
roes m. drunken fit, intoxication.
roest v. en o. (voor hoenders) roost,
perch.
roest o. rust; **oud —,** refuse iron, scrap
iron; v. (plantenziekte) dustbrand, smut.
roesten on. w. (v. hoenders) perch,
roost; (v. ijzer, enz.) rust, get rusty.
roestig b. n. rusty.
roestkleurig b. n. rust-coloured, ru-
biginous.
roestvlek v. spot of rust; (op wasgoed)
iron-mould.
roestvrij b. n. rust proof.
roet o. soot.
roetachtig b. n. sooty.
roetkleurig b. n. soot-coloured, of a
sooty colour.
roetlucht v. sooty smell, smell of sooty.
roetvlek v. smut.
roetzwart b. n. black as soot; z. n., o.
bistre.
roffel m. (mil.) roll, ruffle.
roffelen on. w. (mil.) roll (the drum),
beat a roll (ruffle); (knoeien) bungle;
o. w. (met schaaf) rough-plane.
roffelschaaf v. trying-plane.
roffelvuur o. drum-fire.
roffelwerk o. shoddy work.

rog *m.* thorn-back, ray.
rogge *v.* rye.
roggebloem *v.* rye-flour.
roggebrood *o.* rye-bread, black bread.
rok *m.* (*v. vrouw*) skirt; (*onder—*) petticoat; (*v. heer*) dress-coat; *in —,* in dress-clothes, dress-coated.
rokbeschermer *m.* dress-guard.
rokbroek *v.* divided skirt.
roken *o. w. en on. w.* smoke.
roker *m.* smoker.
rokerig *b. n.* smoky.
rol *v.* (*alg.*) roll; (*tn.*) roller, cylinder; (*deeg—*) rolling-pin; (*v. toneel*) part, role, character; (*v. papier, perkament*) scroll; (*recht: v. rechtszaken*) cause-list; (*v. aangeklaagden*) calendar; (*katrol*) pulley.
rolbrug *v.* roller-bridge.
rolfilm *v.* (*phot.*) roll-film.
rollen *on. w.* roll; tumble; *o. w.* (*v. papier, enz.*) roll; (*sl.*) pick; *iemands zakken —,* pick a person's pockets.
rolletje *o.* (*v. papier, geld, enz.*) roll; (*onder stoel, tafel, enz.*) castor, caster; (*v. schaats*) roller.
rolluik *o.* rolling shutter.
rolmops *v.* roll-herring.
rolprent *v.* film.
rolschaats *v.* roller-skate.
rolschaatsenbaan *v.* skating-rink.
rolstoel *m.* wheel-chair.
rolstok *m.* rolling-pin.
roltabak *v.* twist, roll-tobacco.
roltrap *v.* escalator, moving staircase.
rolvast *b. n.* word-perfect, letter-perfect.
rolverdeling *v.* cast.
rolwagen *m.* (*voertuig*) truck, trundle; (*soort porseleinen vaas*) roll-waegen.
rolwagentje *o.* lorry.
roman *m.* novel.
romance *v.* romance.
romein *v.* (*letter*) Roman type.
Romeins *b. n.* Roman.
romen *o. w.* cream, skim.
rommel *m.* lumber, rubbish, litter, raffle, jumble.
rommelen *on. w.* (*in boeken, papieren*) rummage; (*in koffer, enz.*) poke about; (*v. donder*) rumble.
rommelig *b. n.* littery, disorderly.
rommelkamer *v.,* **rommelzolder** *m.* lumber-room.
rommelpot *m.* rumbler, rumbling-pot.
romp *m.* (*lichaamsdeel*) trunk; (*v. schip*) hull; (*v. vliegtuig*) fuselage, body.
rond *b. n.* round, rotund, circular, globular; *vz.* round; *z. n., o.* round; *in het —,* around; round about.
rondachtig *b. n.* roundish.
rondbazuinen *o. w.* trumpet forth, blaze abroad.
rondboog *m.* (*bouwk.*) round arch, Roman arch.
rondborstig *b. n.* frank, candid, open-hearted.
rondborstigheid *v.* frankness, open-heartedness, candour.

rondbrengen *o. w.* take round, hand round.
rondbrenger *m.* (*v. brood, enz.*) rounds-man.
rondbrieven *o. w.* spread about, rumour about.
ronddelen *o. w.* deal round, distribute, give out.
ronddolen *on. w.* rove (wander, gad) about.
ronddraaien *on. w.* turn (round, about), wheel round; rotate, gyrate; *o. w.* turn round; swing round; (*snel*) whirl round.
ronddragen *o. w.* carry about.
ronddraven *on. w.* trot about.
ronddwalen *on. w.* wander (roam, ramble) about.
ronde *v.* round, circuit, tour; (*mil.*) round; (*v. politieagent*) beat; (*sp.*) heat; (*op wielerbaan, enz.*) lap.
rondedans *m.* round dance, ring-dance.
ronden *o. w.* (*rond maken*) round, make round; (*afronden*) round off; *on. w.* round, become round.
rondfladderen *on. w.* flutter about.
rondgaan *on. w.* go about, go round; *laten —,* pass round, hand about, put about, circulate.
rondgang *m.* perambulation, tour, circuit.
rondgeven *o. w.* pass round, hand about.
rondheid *v.* roundness, rotundity; (*fig.*) frankness, openness, candour.
ronding *v.* rounding; (*v. weg, dek, enz.*) camber.
rondje *o.* round.
rondkijken *on. w.* look about.
rondkomen *on. w.* make (both) ends meet.
rondkuieren *on. w.* stroll about.
rondleiden *o. w.* lead about.
rondlopen *on. w.* walk about; (*fam.*) knock about.
rondneuzen *on. w.* nose about.
rondreis *v.* round trip, (*circular*) tour; (*sch.*) round voyage.
rondreizen *on. w.* travel about.
rondrijden *on. w.* ride about; *o. w.* drive about.
rondrit *m.* tour, circuit.
rondschrift *o.* round hand, round text.
rondschrijven *o.* circular letter.
rondslenteren *on. w.* lounge about.
rondslingeren *o. w.* fling about; *on. w.* lie about.
rondsnuffelen *on. w.* mouse about.
rondstrooien *o. w.* strew about; (*fig.*) put about, blow about.
rondsturen *o. w.* send round, send out.
rondtasten *on. w.* grope about.
rondtrekken *on. w.* wander about.
rondtrekkend *b. n.* vagrant.
ronduit *b. n.* plain-spoken, straight (forward), frank; *bw.* plainly, frankly, roundly.

rondvertellen *o. w.* spread, blare about, buzz round.
rondvliegen *on. w.* fly about, fly round.
rondvlucht *v.* circuit.
rondvraag *v. iets in — brengen,* put the question.
rondwandelen *on. w.* walk about.
rondweg *bw.* roundly.
rondzwerven *on. w.* wander (rove, roam) about, vagabondize.
ronken *on. w. (v. persoon)* snore; *(v. machine)* snort, whirr; *(v. wagen)* stake.
ronselaar *m.* crimp.
ronselen *o. w. en on. w.* crimp.
rood *b. n.* red.
roodachtig *b. n.* reddish, ruddy.
roodborstje *o. (Dk.)* (robin) red-breast.
roodharig *b. n.* red-haired.
roodheid *v.* redness.
roodhuid *m.* redskin, red-Indian.
roodkapje *v.* Little Red Riding-hood.
roodkleurig *b. n.* red-coloured, ruddy.
roodsel *o.* ruddle; *(blanketsel)* rouge.
roodvonk *o.* scarlatina, scarlet fever.
roof *v.* scab, scurf; *m.* plunder, robbery.
roofdier *o.* beast of prey.
roofgierig *b. n. (bw.)* rapacious(ly).
roofgierigheid *v.* rapacity.
roofmoord *m.* murder with robbery.
roofschip *o.* pirate-ship, pirate.
rooftocht *m.* predatory (marauding) expedition.
roofvogel *m.* bird of prey.
roofziek *b. n.* rapacious.
roofzucht *v.* rapacity.
rooien aim; *(uitgraven, uitdoen: v. aardappelen)* dig up, lift, raise; *(v. bomen)* pull up, stub.
rooilijn *v.* alignment, building-line.
rook *v. (hooistapel)* (hay-)cock; *m.* smoke.
rookartikelen *o. mv.* smokers' requisites.
rookgordijn *o. en v.* smoke-screen.
rookspek *o.* smoke-dried pork.
rooktabak *v.* smoking-tobacco.
rookvang *m.* chimney-flue.
rookwolk *v.* cloud of smoke, smoke-cloud.
rookworst *v.* smoked sausage.
rookzolder *m.* smoking-loft.
room *m.* cream.
roomboter *v.* dairy-fresh.
roomijs *o.* ice-cream.
roomkaas *v.* cream-cheese.
Rooms *b. n.* Roman Catholic, Roman.
roomvla *v.* cream-custard.
roos *v. (Pl.)* rose; *(op hoofd)* dandruff, scurf; *(huidziekte)* erysipelas; St. Anthony's fire; *(v. kompas)* card; *(mil.: v. schietschijf)* bull's eye.
rooskleurig *b. n.* rose-coloured, rosy.
rooster *m. (in kachel)* grate; *(om te braden)* grill, gridiron; *(lijst)* list, roster; *(op school, kantoor, enz.)* time-table; *(elektrische —)* grid.
roosteren *o. w.* grill, roast, broil.
roosterwerk *o.* grate, grating.

root *v. (voor vlas)* retting, retting-place.
ros *o. (dicht.)* steed, courser.
ros *b. n.* red, reddish, ruddy.
rosachtig *b. n.* reddish, russet.
rosbief *v.* roast beef.
rosharig *b. n.* red-haired.
roskam *m.* curry-comb.
roskammen *o. w.* curry; *(fig.)*criticize severely.
rossig *b. n.* reddish, ruddy.
rot *o. (mil.: v. soldaten)* squad, file; *(v. geweren)* stack.
rot *b. n.* rotten, putrid, putrefied.
rotatiepers *v.* rotary press.
roten *o. w.* ret.
rotgans *v. (Dk.)* wild goose.
rotheid *v.* rottenness.
rots *v.* rock; *(steil)* crag; *(vooral aan de kust)* cliff.
rotsachtig *b. n.* rocky.
rotsachtigheid *v.* rockiness.
rotsblok *o.* boulder; piece of rock.
rotsgevaarte *o.* mass of rocks.
rotsketen *v.* chain of rocks.
rotskloof *v.* rocky cleft.
rotsspleet *v.* chasm.
rotsvast *b. n.* firm as a rock.
rotswoning *v.* cave-dwelling.
rotten *on. w.* rot, putrefy.
rotting *v.* putrefaction.
rotting *m.* cane.
routine *v.* routine, (daily) round.
rouw *m.* mourning; *— dragen,* mourn.
rouwband *m.* mourning band.
rouwbeklag *o.* condolence.
rouwbrief *m.* death-circular.
rouwdienst *m.* memorial service.
rouwen *m. w.* go (be) in mourning, mourn.
rouwfloers *o.* crape.
rouwgewaad *o.* mourning; *(v. weduwe)* weeds.
rouwkapel *v.* funeral chapel.
rouwklacht *v.* lamentation.
rouwkleding *v.* mourning-wear, mourning(-clothes).
rouwkleed *o.* mourning-dress.
rouwkoets *v.* mourning-coach, funeral [coach.
rouwkoop *m.* smart money, rue-bargain.
rouwkrans *m.* funeral wreath.
rouwmoedig *b. n.* contrite.
rouwmoedigheid *v.* contrition.
rouwrand *m.* black border.
rouwsluier *m.* weeper, crêpe veil, widow's veil.
rouwtijd *m.* period of mourning.
roven *o. w. en on. w.* rob, plunder.
rover *m.* robber, brigand; *(struik—)* foot-pad.
roverbende *v.* gang of robbers.
roverij *v.* robbery, brigandage.
rovershol, roversnest *o.* den (haunt) of robbers.
royaal *b. n. (v. persoon: vrijgevig, mild)* liberal, free-handed, munificent; *(v. beloning, gift, enz.)* handsome, generous; *(ruim)* ample.

rozeboom, rozelaar *m.* rose-tree.
rozegeur *m.* scent of roses, perfume of roses.
rozeknop *m.* rosebud.
rozenhoedje *o.* chaplet.
rozenkrans *m.* rosary; chaplet.
rozenperk *o.* rose-bed, rosary.
rozet *v.* rosette; *(knoop)* rose-knot; *(v. lint, enz. ook:)* favour.
rozig *b. n.* rosy, roseate.
rozijn *v.* raisin.
rozijnenbrood *o.* plum-loaf.
rubber *m.* rubber.
rubberaanplant, rubberplantage *v.* rubber plantation.
rubberband *m.* rubber-tyre.
rubriek *v.* rubric; *(in dagblad)* column; *(afdeling)* division, category; *(hoofd, titel)* head, heading.
ruchtbaar *b. n. (bekend, openbaar)* known, public.
ruchtbaarheid *v.* publicity.
rug *m. (ook v. hand, boek)* back; *(v. berg)* ridge.
ruggegraat *v.* vertebral column, spine, backbone; *(fig.)* backbone.
ruggegraatsverkromming *v.* spinal curvature.
ruggelings *bw.* backwards, back to back.
ruggemerg *o.* spinal marrow.
ruggemergsontsteking *v.* inflammation of the spinal marrow; *(wet.)* myelitis.
ruggespraak *v.* consultation.
ruggesteun *m.* backing, support.
rugleuning *v.* back.
rugslag *m. (bij zwemmen)* back-stroke.
rugvin *v.* dorsal fin.
rugwaarts *bw.* backward(s).
rugzak *m.* rucksack.
rui *m.* moulting(-time).
ruien *on. w.* moult.
ruif *v.* rack.
ruig *b. n. (harig)* hairy, shaggy, bushy; *(ruw)* rude, rough; *(Pl.)* villous.
ruigheid *v.* hairiness, shagginess; roughness; villosity.
ruiken *o. w.* smell, scent; *on. w.* smell; *naar rook —,* smell of smoke.
ruiker *m.* nosegay, bouquet.
ruil *m.* exchange, barter, truck.
ruilen *o. w.* exchange, barter, truck.
ruilhandel *m.* barter, truck.
ruiling *v.* exchange, change.
ruilmiddel *o.* medium of exchange.
ruilverdrag *o.* treaty of barter.
ruilverkeer *o.* traffic.
ruim *o. (v. schip)* hold; *(v. Prot. kerk)* nave.
ruim *b. n.* large, wide; *(v. kamer, enz.)* spacious; *(v. kleed, voorraad, middelen)* ample; *(v. kledingstuk, zetel, huis)* roomy; *(v. salaris)* liberal; *(v. zak, huis)* capacious; *bw.* largely; amply; liberally; above; beyond.
ruimen *o. w.* empty, evacuate; *on. w. (sch.)* veer aft, free.

ruimschoots *bw.* amply, abundantly, plentifully, copiously.
ruimte *v.* room, space, capacity; *(tussen—)* interval, distance.
ruimtemaat *v.* measure of capacity.
ruimtevrees *v.* agoraphobia.
ruin *m. (Dk.)* gelding.
ruïne *v.* ruins; *(fig.)* wreck.
ruïneren *o. w.* ruin.
ruisen *on. w.* rustle; *(v. beek)* murmur, purl.
ruit *v. (v. glas)* pane; *(figuur)* diamond, lozenge; *(wisk.)* rhomb; *(wapenk.)* lozenge; *(v. stof)* check; *(Pl.)* rue.
ruiten *o. w.* lozenge, chequer; *v. mv.* diamonds.
ruiter *m.* rider, horseman; *(mil.)* trooper.
ruiterij *v. (mil.)* cavalry.
ruiterstandbeeld *o.* equestrian statue.
ruitewisser *m.* windscreen wiper.
ruitijd *m.* moulting-time.
ruitje *o. (v. raam)* pane; *(figuur)* diamond; *(op goed)* check.
ruitvormig *b. n.* lozenge-shaped, diamond-shaped, lozenged.
ruk *m.* pull, tug, jerk, wrench.
rukken *o. w. en on. w.* pull, tug, jerk.
rukwind *m.* gust of wind.
rumoer *o.* noise, clamour, uproar.
rumoerig *b. n.* noisy, uproarious, tumultuous.
run *v.* tan, bark, tanning-bark.
rund *o.* horned beast: bull, ox, cow.
rundergebraad *o.* roast beef.
runderhaas *m.* chine.
runderharst *m.* sirloin, loin of beef.
runderpest *v.* cattle-plague.
runderstal *m.* stable for cattle.
rundvee *o.* bovine cattle, (horned) cattle.
rundvet *o.* beef fat.
rundvlees *o.* beef.
runmolen *m.* tan-mill, bark-mill.
runnen *on. w.* curdle.
rups *v.* caterpillar.
rupsband *m.* caterpillar.
rupsband-tractor *m.* crawler-tractor.
rupsendoder *m. (Dk.)* ichneumon-fly.
rupsklaver *v. (Pl.)* snail clover.
rus *m. (Pl.)* rush.
Rusland *o.* Russia.
rust *v.* rest, repose, quiet, calm, tranquillity; *(mil.)* fall out; *(muz.)* rest; *(tn.: v. vuurwapen)* safety-catch; *(voetb.)* half-time.
rustaltaar *o.* wayside altar.
rustbank *v.* couch.
rustbed *o.* couch.
rustdag *m.* day of rest, holiday, off-day.
rusteloos *b. n. (bw.)* restless(ly).
rusteloosheid *v.* restlessness.
rusten *on. w.* rest, repose.
rustend *b. n.* retired; *(v. priester, predikant, enz.)* emeritus.
rusthuis *o.* rest home, home of rest.
rustiek *b. n. (v. brug, enz.; ong.)* rustic; *(v. eenvoud, enz.)* rural.

rustig *b. n.* quiet, tranquil, still, restful; *bw.* quietly, in quiet.
rustkuur *v.* rest-cure.
rustoord *o.* retreat.
rustpauze *v.* rest, pause.
rustplaats *v.* resting place.
rustpunt *o.* (point of) rest, pause.
ruststoel *m.* rest-chair
rustteken *o* (*muz.*) rest.
rusttijd *m.* resting-time, (time of) rest.
rustuur *o.* hour of rest, — of repose.
rustverstoorder *m.* disturber of the peace, peace-breaker.

rustverstoring *v.* disturbance, breach of the peace.
ruwigheid *o.* roughness.
ruw *b. n.* (*oneffen*) rugged, rough; (*onbewerkt:* *v. katoen, suiker, enz.*) raw; (*v. olie*) crude; (*v. diamant, enz.*) rough; (*grof*) coarse; (*fig.*) rude, coarse, crude, rough; *bw.* roughly.
ruzie *v.* quarrel, squabble, brawl, fray; — **hebben,** have a quarrel, be quarreling, be at odds; — **krijgen,** fall out, quarrel, fall at odds, get into a row.
ruzieachtig *b. n.* quarrelsome.
ruziemaker, ruziezoeker *m.* brawler quarrelsome person.

S

saai *v. en o.* serge.
saai *b. n.* dull, slow; (*v. persoon*) flat; (*v. dag, rede*) tedious; (*v. leven*) drab; (*v. boek, enz.*) heavy.
saaien *b. n.* serge.
saaiheid *v.* dullness, etc.
saam *bw.* together.
sabbat *m.* Sabbath.
sabel *o.* sable.
sabel *v.* sword; (*cavalerie*—) sabre.
sabelbont *o.* sable (fur), sabeline.
sabeldier *o.* sable.
sabelen *on. w.* sabre.
sabelgekletter *o.* sabre-rattling.
sabelhouw *m.* sabre-cut, sword-cut.
sabelkling *v.* blade of a sword.
sabelschede *v.* scabbard.
sabotage *v.* rattening.
saboteren *o. w.* ratten.
saboteur *m.* saboteur.
sacrament *o.* sacrament.
sacramentaliën *o. mv.* sacramentals.
sacramenteel *b. n.* sacramental.
Sacramentsdag *m.* Corpus-Christi-day.
sacristie *v.* sacristy, vestry.
safeloket *o.* safe, safe deposit box.
saffiaan *o.* morocco (leather).
saffier *m. en o.* sapphire.
saffraan *v.* saffron.
sage *v.* legend, tradition, myth.
sago *v.* sago.
sajet *o.* wool.
salade *v.* salad.
saladekrop *m.* salad-head.
salariëren *v.* salary, pay.
salaris *o.* salary, pay.
saldo *o.* balance.
salmiakgeest *m.* liquid ammonia.
salon *o.* drawing-room; (*v. kapper, enz.*) saloon.
salontafeltje *o.* fancy table.
salonwagen *m.* saloon-carriage, drawing-room car, Pullman (car).
salpeter *o.* saltpetre, nitre.
salpeterzuur *o.* nitric acid.
salto *m.* caper, leap; — **mortale,**

sensation header, sensation somersault, break-neck leap.
salueren *o. w. en on. w.* salute.
saluut *o.* salute, salutation.
saluutschot *o.* salute.
salvo *o.* (*mil.*) volley, salvo.
samen *bw.* together.
samenbinden *o. w.* bind together, tie up, connect.
samenbrengen *o. w.* bring together, throw together.
samendoen *o. w.* put together; *on. w.* be partners, go shares, act in common.
samendrukbaar *b. n.* compressible.
samendrukken *o. w.* press together, compress.
samenflansen *o. w.* knock together, patch up.
samengaan *on. w.* go together; (*fig.*) go together, pair off, agree; — **met,** go with, accompany; stand it with.
samengesteld *b. n.* (*v. blad, rente*) compound; (*v. zin*) complex, compound; (*ingewikkeld*) complicated.
samengesteldheid *v.* complexity.
samenhang *m.* cohesion, coherence, connection; (*v. zin*) context.
samenhangen *on. w.* cohere, be connected.
samenhangend *b. n.* coherent, connected, cohesive.
samenhorigheid *v.* oneness, solidarity.
samenklank *m.* unison, consonance.
samenklinken *o. w.* (*tn.*) rivet together; *on. w.* (*muz.*) harmonize, chime together.
samenkomen *on. w.* come together, assemble, meet, gather.
samenkomst *v.* meeting, assembly, conference.
samenleving *v.* (*maatschappij*) society; (*samenwoning*) cohabitation.
samenloop *m.* concourse, concurrence; (*v. rivieren*) confluence; **een—van omstandigheden,** a conjunction (coincidence, concurrence) of circumstances.

samenlopen *on. w.* run together, concur; *(te hoop lopen)* flock together; *(v. lijnen, enz.)* converge.

samenpersen *o. w.* press together, compress.

samenpersing *v.* compression.

samenraapsel *o.* hotch-potch, hodgepodge.

samenroepen *o. w.* call together; *(v. vergadering)* convoke, convene.

samenroeping *v.* convocation.

samenscholen *on. w.* assemble, gather, flock together.

samenscholing *v.* gathering, riotous assemblage; *(recht)* (unlawful) assembly.

samensmelten *o. w. en on. w.* melt together, fuse; *(v. maatschappijen, enz.)* amalgamate.

samensmelting *v.* melting together, fusion; amalgamation, fusion.

samenspannen *on. w.* conspire, plot.

samenspanning *v.* conspiracy, plot.

samenspel *o.* ensemble acting; *(muz.)* ensemble playing, ensemble; *(sp.)* combined action, combined play, teamwork.

samenspraak *v.* dialogue.

samenstel *o.* construction, structure.

samenstellen *o. w.* compose, compile, compound, make up.

samensteller *m.* composer, compiler.

samenstelling *v.* composition, structure; texture; *(gram.)* compound word, compound.

samenstroming *v.* confluence; concourse.

samentellen *o. w.* add (up).

samentreffen *on. w.* meet; *(toevallig gelijktijdig plaatshebben)* coincide; *z. n., o.* meeting; coincidence.

samentrekken *o. w.* draw together; *(v. wenkbrauwen)* contract; *(v. weefsel)* astringe; *(v. troepen)* concentrate; *on. w.* contract; *w. w. zich —,* contract.

samentrekkend *b. n.* astringent.

samentrekking *v.* contraction; astriction; concentration.

samentrekkingsteken *o.* circumflex

samenvallen *on. w. (alg.)* coincide; *(v. tijd)* synchronize; *(v. plaats)* be conterminous.

samenvatten *o. w.* take together; resume, sum up, summarize, recapitulate.

samenvatting *v.* résumé, summing up, summary, recapitulation.

samenvloeien *on. w.* unite; *(fig.)* merge *(met,* in); *(v. kleuren)* blend.

samenvloeiing *v.* confluence, junction.

samenvoegen *o. w.* join, conjoin, unite.

samenvoeging *v.* junction, conjunction, union.

samenvouwen *o. w. (v. blad, enz.)* fold up; *(v. handen)* fold.

samenweefsel *o.* texture, web, tissue; *(fig.)* tissue.

samenwerken *on. w.* act (work) together, cooperate, collaborate.

samenwerking *v.* cooperation, collaboration; team-work.

samenwonen *on. w.* live together; cohabit.

samenwoning *v.* living together; cohabitation.

samenzang *m.* community singing; *(in school, enz.)* combined singing.

samenzijn *on. w.* be together; *z. n., o.* gathering, assembly, being together.

samenzweerder *m.* conspirator, plotter.

samenzweren *on. w.* conspire, plot.

samenzwering *v.* conspiracy, plot.

sanatorium *o.* health-resort, sanatorium.

sanctie *v.* sanction.

sandelhout *o.* sandal-wood.

's anderendaags *bw.* the following day.

sanitair *b. n.* sanitary.

sap *o. (v. plant)* sap; *(v. vruchten, groenten; in lichaam)* juice.

sappeur *m. (mil.)* sapper.

sappig *b. n.* sappy; juicy; *(fig.)* luscious, spicy.

sappigheid *v.* juiciness; succulence.

sarcasme *o.* sarcasm.

sarcastisch *b. n. (bw.)* sarcastic(ally).

sardine *v., sardientje* *o.* sardine.

sardineblikje *o.* sardine-tin.

sarren *o. w.* tease, vex, nag, bait.

sas *v. (mil.)* composition; *o. (schutsluis, kolk)* sluice, lock-chamber.

satan *m.* satan, devil.

satanisch *b. n.* satanic(al); *bw.* satanically.

satelliet *m.* satellite; *(fig.)* satellite, myrmidon.

sater *m.* satyr.

satijn *o.* satin.

satire *v.* satire.

satiriek *b. n.* satiric(al); *bw.* satirically.

saucijs *v.* sausage.

saus *v.* sauce, relish; *(v. vlees)* gravy.

sausen *o. w.* sauce.

sauskom *v.* sauce-boat.

sauslepel *m.* sauce-ladle, gravy-spoon.

sauspan *v.* saucepan.

's avonds *bw.* in the evening.

savooiekool *v.* savoy (cabbage).

scalp *m.* scalp.

scandaleus *b. n.* scandalous.

scandaliseren *o. w.* give offence.

Scandinavië *o.* Scandinavia.

scapulier *o.* scapulary.

scepticisme *o.* scepticism.

schaaf *v.* plane; *(voor groenten)* slicer, shredder.

schaafbank *v.* carpenter's bench, joiner's bench.

schaafbeitel *m.* bit.

schaafmachine *v.* planing-machine.

schaafmes *o.* plane-iron.

schaafsel *o.* shavings.

schaak *o.* check; **— spelen,** play at chess.

schaakbord *o.* chess-board.

schaakmat *b. n.* checkmate; **— zetten,**

(*eig.*) mate; (*fig.*) checkmate, stale-mate.

schaakpartij *v.* game of chess.

schaakspel *o.* (game of) chess; chess-board and men, set of chessmen.

schaal *v.* (*v. dier, ei*) shell; (*schotel*) dish; (*weegschaal*) (pait of) scales; (*deel v. weegschaal*) scale; (*voor collecte*) plate; (*drink—*) cup; (*graadverdeling*) scale; (*toon—*) scale, gamut.

schaaldier *o.* crustacean, crustaceous animal; **—en,** shell-fish, crustacea.

schaalverdeling *v.* scale division, graduation; (*v. camera*) focussing-scale.

schaambeen *o.* shame-bone, pubis.

schaamdelen *o. mv.* genitals, pudenda.

schaamrood *b. n.* blushing with shame; *z. n., o.* blush (of shame).

schaamte *v.* shame.

schaamtegevoel *o.* sense of shame.

schaamteloos *b. n.* shameless, bare-faced, impudent.

schaamteloosheid *v.* shamelessness, impudence.

schaap *o.* sheep; (*fig.*) sheep, mutton-head.

schaapachtig *b. n.* sheepish, sheep-like.

schaapherder *m.* shepherd.

schaapsvacht *v.* sheepskin.

schaar *v.* scissors, pair of scissors; (*snoei—*) shears; (*ploeg—*) share; (*v. kreeft*) pincer(s).

schaars *b. n.* scanty, scarce; (*v. geld*) scarce, tight.

schaarsheid, schaarste *v.* scarcity, scantiness; (*v. geld, enz.*) tightness, dearth.

schaats *v.* skate.

schaatsenrijden *on. w.* skate; *z. n., o.* skating.

schaatsenrijder *m.* skater.

schabel *v.* (*m.*) footstool.

schacht *v.* (*v. anker*) shank; (*v. mijn, lift, enz.*) shaft; (*v. veer*) quill; (*v. laars*) leg; (*v. pijl, veer*) stem.

schade *v.* damage, injury, harm; (*nadeel*) detriment; (*verlies*) loss; (*averij*) average.

schadelijk *b. n.* noxious, harmful, hurtful, nocuous, injurious, detrimental, prejudicial; (*onvoordelig*) unprofitable.

schadelijkheid *v.* noxiousness, harm-fulness, etc.

schadeloos *b. n.* harmless.

schadeloosstelling *v.* indemnification, compensation, recoupment, reparation.

schaden *o. w.* damage, harm, hurt, injure; *on. w.* do harm, be hurtful.

schadepost *m.* loss.

schaderegeling *v.* settlement of damages.

schadevergoeding *v.* indemnification, compensation.

schadeverhaal *o.* redress.

schaduw *v.* shade; (*met bepaalde omtrek*) shadow.

schaduwbeeld *o.* silhouette, shadow-graph.

schaduwen *o. w.* shade.

schaduwkant *m.* (*v. straat*) shade(d) (shady) side.

schaduwloos *b. n.* shadeless.

schaduwrijk *b. n.* shady, shadowy.

schaduwzijde *v.* shade(d) (shady) side; (*fig.*) drawback, dark side.

schaffen *o. w.* give, procure.

schaften *on. w.* eat; knock off for one's meal.

schafttijd *m.* off-time, half-time, knock-ing-off time, meal-time.

schaftuur *o.* meal-hour, off-hour.

schakel *m.* link.

schakering *v.* variegation, gradation.

schakelaar *m.* switch.

schakelbord *o.* switch-board.

schakelen *o. w.* link; (*el.*) switch, connect.

schakeling *v.* linking; connection.

schakelrad *o.* (*in uurwerk*) balance-wheel.

schaken *on. w.* play at chess; *o. w.* run away with, carry off, abduct.

schaker *m.* (*schaakspeler*) chessplayer; abductor.

schaking *v.* abduction, elopement.

schal *m.* sound.

schalie *v.* (*Z. N.*) slate.

schaliedekker *m.* (*Z. N.*) slater.

schalks *b. n.* waggish, roguish, arch.

schalksheid *v.* waggishness, roguishness, archness.

schallen *on. w.* sound, resound.

schalmei *v.* shawn, reed-pipe.

schamel *b. n.* poor, humble, mean.

schamelheid *v.* poverty, humbleness.

schamen *w. w.* **zich —,** be ashamed, feel shame.

schampen *on. w.* graze.

schampschot *o.* graze, grazing shot, glance, glancing shot.

schandaal *o.* scandal, shame.

schandalig *b. n.* (*bw.*) scandalous(ly); shameful(ly); disgraceful(ly).

schanddaad *v.* infamous deed, infamy, deed of infamy.

schande *v.* shame, infamy, disgrace; scandal.

schandelijk *b. n.* (*bw.*) shameful(ly), infamous(ly) ignominious(ly) disgrace-ful(ly); outrageous(ly).

schandmerk *o.* mark of infamy, stigma.

schandpaal *m.* pillory.

schandvlek *v.* stain, stigma.

schandvlekken *o. w.* disgrace, dis-honour, defame.

schans *v.* (*mil.*) entrenchment, sconce, redoubt; (*sch.*) quarter-deck.

schansgraver *m.* sapper, pioneer.

schapebout *m.* leg of mutton, gigot.

schapemelk *v.* sheep's milk.

schapenteelt *v.* sheep-breeding.

schapestal *m.* sheep-fold.

schapevacht *v.* fleece.

schapevlees *o.* mutton.

schapewol *v.* sheep's wool.

schapewolkjes *o. mv.* fleecy clouds.

schappelijk *b. n.* moderate, tolerable, reasonable, fair; (*v. persoon*) decent; *bw.* moderately, tolerably, reasonably, fairly.

schappelijkheid *v.* moderateness, tolerableness, fairness.

schar *v.* dab.

schare *v.* (*menigte*) crowd, multitude; (*leger—*) host.

scharen *o. w.* range, draw up; *w. w. zich —*, range oneself, place oneself.

scharenslijper *m.* scissors-grinder, knife-grinder.

scharlaken *b. n. en z. n., o.* scarlet.

scharlakenkoorts *v.* scarlatina, scarlet fever.

scharminkel *m.* scrag, skeleton.

scharnier *o.* hinge.

scharniergewricht *o.* hinge-joint.

scharrelaar *m.* (*op schaatsen*) potterer, wobbler, scrambler, beginner; (*knoeier*) botcher, bungler; (*schacheraar*) petty dealer.

scharrelen *on. w.* (*op schaatsen*) potter about, muddle along; (*knoeien*) bungle, muddle; (*schacheren*) deal, job; (*v. kippen*) scratch; (*flirten*) philander.

schat *m.* treasure.

schatbewaarder *m.* treasurer.

schateren *on. w. — van 't lachen,* shout (roar) with laughter.

schaterlach *m.* loud laugh, burst of laughter.

schatkamer *v.* treasury, treasure-chamber; (*fig.*) storehouse, treasure-house, treasure-room.

schatkist *v.* (public) treasury, exchequer.

schatkistbiljet *o.* exchequer bill, treasury-bill.

schatkistobligatie *v.* treasury bond.

schatplichtig *b. n.* tributary.

schatrijk *b. n.* very rich, wealthy.

schatten *o. w.* (*v. onkosten, enz.*) estimate; (*v. goederen*) value; (*voor belasting*) appraise, value, assess; (*mil.: v. afstand*) gauge; *naar waarde —,* appreciate, prize; *te hoog —,* overestimate, overvalue; *te laag —,* underestimate, undervalue.

schatter *m.* appraiser, valuer, valuator; (*voor belasting, ook:*) assessor.

schattig *b. n.* sweet, dinky.

schatting *v.* estimation, estimate, valuation.

schaven *o. w.* plane, dress; (*huid*) abrade, graze.

schavot *o.* scaffold.

schavuit *m.* rascal, rogue, scapegrace.

schavuitenstreek *m.* rascally trick, roguery.

schede *v.* (*alg.*) sheath; (*v. zwaard*) scabbard, sheath; (*Pl., ontleedk.*) vagina.

schedel *m.* skull, brain-pan, cranium.

schedelboor *v.* trepan, trephine.

schedelboring *v.* trepanation.

schedelbreuk *v.* fracture of the skull, cranial fracture.

scheef *b. n.* (*v. lijn, hoek*) oblique; (*v.*

gezicht, hals) wry; (*schuin: v. hak, enz.*) slanting, sloping; (*v. muur*) out of truth; (*v. schoorsteen, toren*) leaning; *bw.* obliquely, etc.

scheefheid *v.* wryness, obliqueness, slantingness.

scheel *b. n.* squinting, squint-eyed, cross-eyed, cock-eyed.

scheelheid *v.* squintingness, strabismus.

scheeloog *m.* squint-eye.

scheelzien *on. w.* squint, have a squint; *z. n., o.* squinting, strabismus.

scheen *v.* shin.

scheep — gaan, go on board, embark.

scheepsbemanning *v.* ship's crew.

scheepsberichten *o. mv.* shipping-intelligence.

scheepsbevrachter *m.* chartering-broker.

scheepsbouw *m.* ship-building.

scheepsdek *o.* deck.

scheepsdokter *m.* ship's surgeon.

scheepsgeschut *o.* naval guns.

scheepsjongen *m.* ship's boy, cabin-boy.

scheepsjournaal *o.* ship's journal.

scheepskapitein *m.* ship-captain, sea-captain, master (of a ship).

scheepskeuken *v.* galley, caboose.

scheepskost *m.* sea-fare.

scheepsladder *v.* Jacob's ladder.

scheepslading *v.* ship-load, cargo.

scheepsmaat *m.* ship-mate.

scheepsmakelaar *m.* shipbroker.

scheepsproviand *v.* ship's stores.

scheepsramp *v.* shipping-disaster.

scheepsruimte *v.* tonnage, shipping, cargo space.

scheepston *v.* (register) ton.

scheepswant *o.* rigging.

scheepvaart *v.* navigation.

scheepvaartaandelen *o. mv.* shipping-shares.

scheepvaartbedrijf *o.* shipping-trade, shipping.

scheepvaartverkeer *o.* shipping-traffic, shipping.

scheerbekken *o.* shaving-basin.

scheerder *m.* barber; (*v. schapen*) shearer.

scheergereedschap *o.,* **scheergerei** *o.* shaving-tackle, shaving-things.

scheerkwast *m.* shaving brush, lather-brush.

scheerling *v.* (*Pl.*) hemlock.

scheermes *o.* razor.

scheerriem *m.* strop.

scheerwinkel *m.* barber's shop.

scheerwol *v.* fleece wool.

scheerzeep *v.* shaving-soap.

scheidbaar *b. n.* separable.

scheiden *o. w.* (*alg.*) separate, divide, disunite, disjoin, disconnect; (*v. haar*) part; (*scheik.*) decompose; (*v. huwelijk*) divorce; *on. w.* (*uiteengaan*) part, separate.

scheiding *v.* separation, division, disjunction; parting; decomposition;

divorce; *(tussenschot, enz.)* partition.
scheidingslijn *v.* line of demarcation.
scheidsgerecht *o.* court of arbitration, arbitration board.
scheidsmuur *m.* partition-wall, party-wall; *(fig.)* barrier.
scheidsrechter *m.* arbiter, arbitrator; *(sp.)* umpire, referee.
scheidsrechterlijk *b. n.* arbitral; *bw.* by arbitration.
scheikunde *v.* chemistry.
scheikundig *b. n. (bw.)* chemical(ly).
scheikundige *m.* chemist; *(v. voedingsstoffen)* analyst.
schel *b. n. (v. geluid)* shrill, strident, piercing; *(v. licht)* glaring, vivid; *z. n., v.* bell.
Schelde *v.* Scheldt.
schelden *on. w.* call names; — **op,** abuse, inveigh against, decry; — **als een viswijf,** scold like a fishwife; *o. w.* **iem. voor een verrader —,** call a person a traitor.
scheldnaam *m.* nickname.
scheldpartij *v.* slanging-match.
scheldwoord *o.* abusive word, abusive term, term of abuse.
schelen *on. w. (verschillen)* differ; *(ontbreken)* want; **wat scheelt u toch ?** what is the matter with you? **het kan me niet —,** I don't care.
schelf *v.* stack, rick.
schellak *o.* shellac.
schellen *on. w.* ring (the bell).
schelm *m.* rascal, rogue, knave.
schelmstuk *o.* roguish trick, piece of roguery (of knavery).
schelp *v.* shell; *(bij diner)* scallop.
schelpdier *o.* shell-fish; *(wet.)* testacean.
schelpvis *m.* shell-fish.
schelvis *m.* haddock.
schema *o.* diagram, scheme, outline, skeleton.
schemer *m.* twilight; *(sterker)* dusk.
schemerachtig *b. n.* dim, dusky; *(fig.)* dim.
schemeravond *m.* twilight.
schemerdonker *o.* twilight.
schemeren *on. w. ('s avonds)* grow dusk; *('s morgens)* dawn; *(v. licht)* gleam, glimmer; *(v. persoon)* sit in the twilight.
schemerig *b. n.* dim, crepuscular; — **worden,** grow dim.
schemering *v.* twilight, dusk, dimness, crepuscule.
schemerlamp *v.* twilight lamp, floor-lamp; *(op tafel)* table-lamp.
schemerlicht *o.* twilight; dim light.
schenden *o. w. (beschadigen)* damage; *(v. gelaat, enz.: verminken)* disfigure, mutilate; *(v. eed, verdrag, enz.)* violate; *(v. wet: overtreden)* infringe, transgress; *(v. moraal enz.)* outrage; *(ontheiligen)* profane, desecrate.
schender *m.* violator; transgressor; profaner, desecrator.
schending *v.* damaging; disfigurement, mutilation; violation; infringement,

transgression; profanation, desecration.
schenkblad *o.* tray.
schenkel *m.* shank; *(wet.)* femur.
schenken *o. w. (uitgieten: koffie, water)* pour; *(presenteren: likeuren, enz.)* serve; *(verkopen)* sell, retail; *(geven)* give, grant; *on. w.* serve drinks.
schenker *m.* cup-bearer; *(gever)* donor.
schenking *v.* donation, grant, gift.
schennis *v.* violation; transgression; outrage.
schep *m. (voorwerp)* scoop, shovel; *(hoeveelheid)* spoonful, shovelful.
schepbord *o.* float-board, float; *(v. molenrad, stoombootrad)* paddle.
schepel *o.* bushel, decalitre.
schepen *m.* sheriff, alderman, magistrate.
schepen *o. w.* ship.
scheplepel *m.* ladle.
schepnet *o.* dip-net, landing-net.
scheppen *o. w.* scoop; ladle; *(v. papier)* dip; *(vormen)* create, make; **orde —,** establish order.
schepper *m.* creator, maker; *(voorwerp)* scoop, scooper; *(papier—)* dipper.
schepping *v.* creation.
scheppingskracht *v.* creative power.
scheprad *o.* paddle-wheel, scoop-wheel.
schepsel *o.* creature.
scheren *o. w. (v. persoon)* shave; *(v. schaap)* shear, clip; *(v. laken)* shear; *(v. haag)* trim *(sch.)* reeve *(fig.: afzetten)* fleece; *w. w.* **zich —,** shave; **zich laten —,** get shaved, have a shave; *on. w.* **langs het watervlak —,** skim the water.
scherf *v.* potsherd; *(v. glas)* splinter, fragment; *(v. granaat)* splinter.
scherfvrij *b. n. (mil.)* splinter-proof.
schering *v. (v. schaap)* shearing; *(v. weefsel)* warp, chain; — **en inslag,** warp and woof.
scherm *o. (voor haard, enz.)* screen; *(toneel)* curtain; *(Pl.)* umbel; *(fig.)* fence.
schermbloemigen *v. mv.* umbelliferae.
schermdegen *m.* foil.
schermen *on. w.* fence.
schermer *m.* fencer.
schermkunst *v.* art of fencing, swordsmanship.
schermutseling *v.* skirmish.
schermzaal *v.* fencing-room.
scherp *b. n. (alg.)* sharp; *(v. gezicht, verstand, reuk)* keen *(v. hoek, oordeel)* acute; *(v. taal, zwaard)* trenchant; *(v. toon)* edgy; *(v. antwoord)* tart, cutting; *(gram.: v. medeklinker)* voiceless; *(fig.: v. tong)* caustic; *(v. pen)* pungent; *(v. concurrentie)* close, keen; fierce; *bw.* sharply, keenly; *z. n., o. (v. mes)* edge.
scherpen *o. w. (scherp maken)* sharpen; *(v. potlood)* point, sharpen; *(v. scheermes)* strop, whet; *(fig.)* sharpen.
scherpheid *v.* sharpness; keenness; acuteness; trenchancy; tartness; causticity; pungency; *zie* **scherp.**
scherphoekig *b. n.* acute-angled.
scherpklinkend *b. n.* shrill.

scherprechter *m.* executioner.
scherpschutter *m.* sharp-shooter, marksman.
scherpsnijdend *b. n.* keen-edged.
scherpte *v.* sharpness, edge; (*v. foto, kijker, enz.*) definition.
scherpziend *b. n.* sharp-sighted, keen-sighted; (*fig. ook:*) penetrating, perceiving, perspicacious.
scherpzinnig *b. n.* acute, sharp (-witted), keen (-witted), penetrating, sagacious.
scherpzinnigheid *v.* acuteness, acumen, sharpness, penetration, sagacity.
scherts *v.* pleasantry, badinage, banter, raillery; jest, joke.
schertsen *on. w.* jest, joke; *ik schertste maar,* I said it only for fun.
schets *v.* draught, sketch, (sketchy) outline.
schetsen *on. w.* sketch, outline.
schetteren *on. w.* (*v. trompet, enz.*) blare, bray; (*v. spreker*) rant, vapour; (*bluffen*) brag, swagger.
scheur *v.* crack, fissure, cleft; (*in stof, enz.*) tear, rip.
scheurbuik *v.* scurvy.
scheuren *o. w.* (*in stukken*) tear up; (*toevallig*) tear; (*vrijwillig, uit droefheid, enz.*) rend; (*v. weiland*) break up, plough up, open; *on. w.* tear.
scheuring *v.* (*v. weiland*) breaking up; (*fig.*) rupture, split; (*kerkelijk*) schism.
scheurkalender *m.* tear-off calendar, block-calendar.
scheurmaker *m.* schismatic.
scheut *m.* (*Pl.*) shoot, sprig; (*pijn*) twinge, stab; (*kleine hoeveelheid vloeistof*) dash.
scheutig *b. n.* open-handed, free-handed, liberal.
schicht *m.* arrow, dart; flash.
schichtig *b. n.* shy, skittish; — *worden,* shy, take fright.
schichtigheid *v.* shyness, skittishness.
schielijk *b. n.* (*bw.*) sudden (ly), prompt- (ly), swift (ly).
schielijkheid *v.* suddenness, promptness, swiftness.
schier *bw.* almost, nearly, all but.
schiereiland *o.* peninsula.
schietbaan *v.* rifle-range.
schieten *on. w.* fire, shoot; *o. w.* (*afschieten*) fire; (*neerschieten*) shoot; (*v. geld*) lend.
schieter *m.* shooter; (*v. bakker*) peel, (bread-)shovel; (*v. slot*) bolt; (*kleermot*) clothes-moth.
schietgat *o.* embrasure, loop-hole.
schietgebed *o.* ejaculatory prayer.
schietgeweer *o.* fire-arm.
schietkatoen *o.* gun-cotton.
schietlood *o.* plumb, plummet.
schietoefeningen *v. mv.* target-practice, firing-exercise(s), artillery practice.
schietpartij *v.* shooting-affray, shooting-affair.
schietschijf *v.* target, mark.
schietspoel *v.* shuttle.

schiften *o. w.* sort; separate; (*doorexamen, enz.*) eliminate; *on. w.* (*v. melk*) curdle, run.
schifting *v.* sorting; curdling.
schijf *v.* (*alg.*) disk; (*schiet—*) mark, target; (*werp—*) quoit; (*v. damspel*) man; (*v. wiel, enz.*) disk, disc; (*v. telefoon, radio*) dial; (*v. katrol*) sheave; (*plakje: v. ham, enz.*) slice; (*runder—*) round.
schijn *m.* (*schijnsel*) shine, sheen, glimmer; (*fig.: voorkomen*) appearance, semblance, seeming; pretext, pretence, show.
schijnaanval *m.* feigned attack.
schijnbaar *b. n.* (*bw.*) seeming (ly), apparent (ly).
schijnbeeld *o.* phantom, simulacrum, illusion.
schijnbeweging *v.* feint.
schijndood *b. n.* apparently dead, in a state of suspended animation; *z. n., m.* apparent death, suspended animation.
schijnen *on. w.* (*licht verspreiden*) shine; (*lijken*) seem, look; *naar het schijnt,* it appears, to all appearance.
schijnheilig *b. n.* (*bw.*) hypocritical (ly), sanctimonious (ly).
schijnheilige *m.* hypocrite.
schijnheiligheid *v.* hypocrisy, sanctimoniousness.
schijnsel *o.* glimmer, sheen, glow.
schijnvrede *m.* false (hollow) peace.
schijnwerper *m.* (*zoeklicht*) searchlight, floodlight; (*v. auto*) dazzle lamp, dazzle headlight.
schik *m. in zijn — zijn,* be in high spirits, be pleased.
schikken *o. w.* (*ordenen*) arrange, order; (*in orde brengen: v. kleren, enz.*) adjust; (*bijleggen: v. twist*) settle, make up; *onp. w.* (*gelegen komen*) suit; *schikt het u?* is it convenient to you? *w. w. zich —,* (*v. zaken*) come right; *zich — in zijn lot,* resign oneself to one's fate.
schikking *v.* arrangement; settlement; agreement, accommodation.
schil *v.* (*v. bananen, bessen, enz.*) skin; (*v. sinaasappel*) peel; (*v. appel, peer*) paring; (*schors; korst*) rind.
schild *o.* shield; (*beukelaar*) buckler; (*wap.*) scutcheon; (*v. schildpad*) shell; (*v. insekt*) wing-case.
schilddrager *m.* shield-bearer; (*wap.*) supporter.
schilder *m.* (*kunst—*) painter, artist; (*huis—*) painter, house-painter.
schilderachtig *b. n.* (*bw.*) picturesque- (ly), pictorial (ly).
schilderen *o. w.* paint; (*fig.*) paint, picture, delineate, depict; *on. w.* (*mil.: v. schildwacht*) do sentry go, stand sentry; (*staan wachten*) cool one's heels.
schilderes *v.* paintress, woman-painter.
schilderij *v. en o.* painting, picture.
schilderkunst *v.* art of painting.
schildersezel *m.* (painter's) easel.

schildersgereedschap *o.* painter's tools.

schilderskwast *m.* paint-brush.

schilderstuk *o.* picture, painting.

schildkever *m.* tortoise-beetle, helmet-beetle.

schildknaap *m.* shield-bearer, squire.

schildluis *v.* scale insect, coccus (insect).

schildpad *v.* (*land—*) tortoise; (*zee—*) turtle; *o.* (*stof*) tortoise-shell.

schildvleugelig *b. n.* sheath-winged.

schildwacht *m.* sentinel, sentry.

schildwachthuisje *o.* sentry-box.

schilfer *v.* scale; *—s op het hoofd,* dandruff.

schilferen *on. w.* scale (off), peel (off).

schilfersteen *m.* schist.

schillen *o. w.* (*aardappelen, sinaasappelen*) peel; (*appelen, peren*) pare; *on. w.* peel.

schim *v.* shadow, shade, ghost.

schimmel *m.* (*paard*) grey horse, grey; *v.* mould, mildew.

schimmelen *on. w.* mould, grow mouldy, grow mildewy.

schimp *m.* contumely, scoff, scorn, taunt.

schimpdicht *o.* satire.

schimpdichter *m.* satirist.

schimpen *on. w.* scoff, revile, gibe.

schimper *m.* scoffer.

schimperij *v.* scoffing, abuse, taunt.

schimpnaam *m.* nickname, abusive name.

schimprede *v.* abusive speech, invective.

schimpwoord *o.* abusive word, abusive term.

schip *o.* ship, vessel; (*v. kerk*) nave.

schipbreuk *v.* shipwreck.

schipbreukeling *m. en v.* shipwrecked person, castaway.

schipbrug *v.* bridge of boats, boat-bridge.

schipper *m.* bargeman, boat-man, skipper.

schipperen *on. w.* trim, temporize, tergiversate.

schippershaak *m.* boat-hook.

schippersknecht *m.* bargeman's mate.

schisma *o.* schism.

schismatiek *b. n.* (*bw.*) schismatic(ally); *z. n., m.* schismatic.

schitteren *on. w.* (*v. licht*) shine; (*v. ogen*) glitter; (*v. diamant*) sparkle.

schitterend *b. n.* radiant, sparkling, brilliant, glorious, splendid.

schittering *v.* glittering; sparkling, sparkle; lustre, splendour.

schlager *m.* hit, song-hit.

schminken *o. w.* make up; *w. w. zich —,* make up, paint one's face.

schobbejak, schobberd *m.* scalawag, scallywag, scamp, rogue.

schoeien *o. w.* shoe; *zie* **beschoeien.**

schoeisel *o.* shoeing, shoes; (*H.*) footwear.

schoen *m.* (*alg.*) shoe; (*hoog*) boot.

schoenaantrekker *m.* shoe-lift, shoe-horn.

schoenborstel *m.* shoe-brush, blacking-brush.

schoener *m.* (*sch.*) schooner.

schoenlapper *m.* cobbler; (*vlinder*) tortoise-shell.

schoenleer *o.* shoe-leather, boot-leather.

schoenmaker *m.* shoe-maker.

schoenpoetser *m.* (*op straat*) shoe-black; (*in hotel*) boots.

schoensmeer *o.* blacking, boot-polish, boot-cream.

schoentrekker *m.* shoe-lift.

schoenveter *m.* boot-lace, boot-string.

schoenwinkel *m.* shoe-shop, boot-shop.

schoffel *v.* hoe.

schoffelen *o. w.* hoe.

schoft *v.* (*v. paard*) withers; (*werktijd*) shift; *m.* rascal, scamp, knave.

schok *m.* (*alg.*) shock; (*hevig*) concussion; (*v. rijtuig, bus, enz.*) jolt, jerk; (*fig.*) shock.

schokbreker *m.* shock absorber, bumper.

schokken *o. w.* shake, convulse, concuss, jerk; (*fig.*) shake, convulse.

schokschouderen *on. w.* shrug one's shoulders.

schol *v.* (*Dk.*) plaice; (*ijs—*) floe.

scholekster *v.* oyster-catcher.

scholier(ster) *m.* (*v.*) pupil, scholar.

schommel *m.* swing.

schommelen *on. w.* (*v. slinger*) swing, oscillate; (*op schommel*) swing; (*v. trein, op een stoel*) rock; (*v. schip*) roll; (*v. prijzen*) fluctuate, oscillate; (*waggelen*) roll, wobble; *o. w.* swing, rock.

schommeling *v.* swinging; oscillation, fluctuation; (*bij aswenteling*) nutation.

schommelstoel *m.* rocking-chair.

schone *v.* beauty, fair one.

schoof *v.* sheaf.

schooien *on. w.* beg, go a-begging.

schooier *m.* beggar; (*landloper*) tramp, vagrant; (*schoelje*) scallywag; (*haveloze kerel*) ragamuffin.

school *v.* school; (*opleidings—, kost—*) college; (*v. haringen*) shoal.

schoolarts *m.* school medical officer.

schoolbank *v.* school-desk; (*zonder leuning*) form.

schoolbehoeften *v. mr.* school-necessaries, educational appliances.

schoolbezoek *o.* (*v. leerlingen*) school-attendance; (*v. inspectie*) inspection.

schoolblijven *on. w.* stay in (after school-hours), be kept in; *z. n., o.* detention, staying-in.

schoolboek *o.* school-book, class-book, lesson-book.

schoolbord *o.* black-board.

schoolgaan *on. w.* go to school.

schoolgeld *o.* school-fee.

schoolhoofd *o.* school-head, head of a school, headmaster.

schooljaar *o.* scholastic year, school-year.

schooljeugd *v.* school-children.

schooljongen *m.* school-boy.

schooljuffrouw *v.* school-mistress, school-teacher.

schoolkameraad *m.* school-fellow, school-mate.

schoollokaal *o.* class-room.

schoolmeester *m.* schoolmaster; *(fig.)* pedant.

schoolmeubelen *o. mv.* school-furniture.

schoolonderwijs *o.* school-teaching.

schoolopziener *m.* school-inspector.

schoolplicht *m.* compulsory attendance at school.

schoolplichtig *b. n.* of school-age.

schoolrapport *o.* school-report.

schools *b. n.* scholastic.

schooltas *v.* school-bag; *(op rug)* satchel.

schooltijd *m.* school-hours; class-time; *(schooljaren)* school-time.

schooltoezicht *o.* school inspection.

schooltucht *v.* school-discipline.

schoolwerk *o.* school-work, home-task.

schoolwet *v.* education act.

schoolwezen *o.* school-affairs, educational matters, public education.

schoon *vw.* though, although.

schoon *b. n.* *(mooi)* beautiful, handsome, fine; *(zindelijk)* clean; *(zuiver)* pure; *bw.* beautifully, handsomely; cleanly.

schoonbroeder *m.* brother-in-law.

schoondochter *v.* daughter-in-law.

schoonheid *v.* beauty, handsomeness, fairness.

schoonheidsgevoel *o.* sense of beauty, aesthetic sense.

schoonheidsleer *v.* aesthetics.

schoonklinkend *b. n.* melodious; *(fig.)* fine-sounding.

schoonmaak *v.* clean-up, (house-) cleaning.

schoonmaken *o. w.* clean; *(v. vis)* gut; *(v. gevogelte)* draw; *(v. sla)* pick.

schoonmoeder *v.* mother-in-law.

schoonouders *m. mv.* father-and-mother-in-law, parents-in-law, *(fam.)* in-laws.

schoonschrift *o.* calligraphic writing; *(schrijfboek)* copy-book.

schoonvader *m.* father-in-law.

schoonvegen *o. w.* sweep clean.

schoonzuster *v.* sister-in-law.

schoonzoon *m.* son-in-law.

schoor *m.* *(bouwk.)* buttress, shore, support; *(sch.)* feather.

schoorbalk *m.* summer.

schoorhout *o.* prop, shoring timber.

schoormuur *m.* buttress.

schoorsteen *m.* chimney; *(v. stoomboot, locomotief)* funnel.

schoorsteenkleed *o.* mantelpiece covering.

schoorsteenmantel *m.* mantelpiece. mantel-shelf, chimney-shelf.

schoorsteenveger *m.* chimney-sweep-(er).

schoorsteenwissel *m.* accommodation bill.

schoorvoeten *on. w.* hesitate.

schoorvoetend *b. n.* hesitatingly, reluctantly.

schoot *m.* lap; *(fig.)* womb; *(sch.: v. zeil)* sheet; *(v. slot)* bolt.

schoothondje *o.* lap-dog, toy-dog.

schootslijn *v.* *(mil.)* line of fire.

schootsvel *o.* apron.

schop *v.* shovel, spade; *(voor graan, enz.)* scoop; *m.* kick.

schoppen *v. mv.* spades.

schoppen *on. w.* kick; *(naar, at)*; *o. w.* **herrie —**, kick up a row (a dust)

schoppenaas *o.* ace of spades.

schor *v.* salting(s), muddy flat, haugh.

schor *b. n.* hoarse, husky.

schoren *o. w.* shore up, buttress, support, prop.

schorheid *v.* hoarseness, huskiness.

schorpioen *m.* *(Dk.)* scorpion; *(sterr.)* Scorpio.

schors *v.* bark.

schorsen *o. w.* *(betalingen, vijandelijkheden, enz.)* suspend; *(v. vergadering)* adjourn; *(v. geestelijke)* inhibit, interdict.

schorseneel *v.*, **schorseneer** *v.* scorzonera.

schorsing *v.* suspension; adjournment; inhibition, interdict.

schort *v. en o.* apron; *(kinder—)* pinafore.

schot *o.* *(v. geweer, enz.)* shot, report; ₃*(sein—)* signal-gun; *(in kamer: tussen—)* partition; *(sch.: waterdicht —)* bulkhead.

Schot *m.* Scotchman, Scot.

schotel *m.* dish.

schoteldoek *m.* dish-cloth.

schotelrek *o.* dish-rack, dish-stand.

schoteltje *o.* dish; *(voor kopje)* saucer.

Schotland *o.* Scotland.

schots *v.* floe (flake) of ice, ice-floe.

schots *bw.* rudely; roughly.

schotschrift *o.* lampoon, libel.

schotwond *v.* shot-wound, bullet-wound.

schouder *m.* shoulder.

schouderband *m.* shoulder-belt; *(v. schort)* strap; *(v. onderlijfje)* shoulder-band.

schouderblad *o.* shoulder-blade; *(wet.)* scapula.

schouderen *o. w.* **het geweer —**, shoulder the rifle.

schoudergewricht *o.* shoulder-joint.

schoudermantel *m.* cape, mantlet, tippet.

schouderriem *m.* baldric.

schouderstuk *o.* *(alg.)* shoulder-piece; *(mil.)* shoulder-strap; *(v. hemd, enz.)* yoke; *(v. rund, schaap, enz.)* shoulder.

schout-bij-nacht *m.* rear-admiral.

schouw v. (schoorsteen) chimney, fire) place; (sch.) scow, punt; (het schouwen-inspection, survey.
schouwburg m. theatre, play-house.
schouwburgbezoeker m. theatregoer, playgoer.
schouwen o. w. inspect, survey.
schouwing v. inspection, survey.
schouwspel o. spectacle, scene, sight, view.
schouwtoneel o. stage, scene, theatre.
schoven o. w. sheave.
schraag v. trestle; support.
schraal b. n. (v. persoon) thin, spare, gaunt; (v. inkomen, hoop) slender; (v. weer, wind) bleak; (v. grond, oogst) poor; (v. kost) scanty, spare, poor, meagre; bw. poorly, scantily.
schraalhans m. miser, niggard.
schraalheid v. thiness, spareness; slenderness; bleakness; poorness, poverty; zie **schraal**.
schraapachtig b. n. scraping, covetous, stingy.
schraapachtigheid v. covetousness, stinginess, scrapingness.
schraapzucht v. scrapingness, covetousness, stinginess.
schraapzuchtig b. n. scraping, covetous, stingy.
schrabben o. w. scratch, scrape.
schragen o. w. support, shore (up), stay, buttress (up).
schram v. scratch, scrape, graze.
schrammen o. w. scratch, graze.
schrander b. n. sagacious, intelligent, ingenious, discerning, clever.
schranderheid v. sagacity, intelligence, ingenuity, discernment, cleverness.
schransen on. w. gormandize, gorge.
schrap z. n., v. scratch, stroke; bw. **zich — zetten**, put one's back to the wall; take a firm stand.
schrapen o. w. scrape.
schrappen o. w. (v. aardappelen, enz.) scrape; (v. vis) scale; (doorhalen: van naam, enz.) strike out, delete; (v. schuld) cancel; (v. passage) expunge.
schrapping v. striking out; striking off; deletion; cancellation; expunction.
schrapsel o. scrapings.
schrede v. pace, step, stride.
schreef v. line, stroke, scratch.
schreeuw m. cry, shout; scream.
schreeuwen on. w. cry, shout; (gillen) scream.
schreeuwend b. n. crying; (v. kleuren, enz.) loud, shouting, blatant; (v. onrecht) glaring.
schreeuwer m. bawler, screamer; (fig.) bragger, ranter, windbag, mouther.
schreeuwerig b. n. (v. stem, enz.) screaming; (v. persoon) clamorous; loud-voiced; (v. kleuren) shouting; (v. spreker) ranting; (v. rede) vociferous.
schreien on. w. weep; (huilen) cry.

schreier m. weeper, crier.
schrift o. (het geschrevene) writing, writ; (schrijfboek) writing-book, note-book; **de Heilige S—**, the Holy Scriptures.
schriftelijk b. n. written, in writing; bw. in writing, on paper, by letter; z. n., o. **het —**, (deel v. examen) the written work.
schriftgeleerde m. scribe.
schriftkundige m. handwriting expert.
schriftuitlegging v. exegesis.
schriftuur v. (geschreven stuk) document, writing; (H. Schrift) Scripture.
schriftvervalser m. forger.
schriftvervalsing v. forgery.
schrijden on. w. stride.
schrijfboek o. writing-book, exercise-book; (met voorbeelden) copy-book.
schrijfbureau o. writing-desk, writing-table.
schrijffout v. clerical error, slip of the pen.
schrijfletter v. script-letter.
schrijfmachine v. typewriter.
schrijfpapier o. writing-paper.
schrijfster v. authoress, (woman) writer.
schrijftaal v. written language.
schrijftrant m. style (manner) of writing.
schrijfwerk o. writing, clerical work.
schrijfwijze v. (schrijftrant) style (manner) of writing; (v. getal, enz.) notation.
schrijlings bw. astride, astraddle, stride-legs.
schrijn m. en o. box, chest.
schrijnen o. w. graze, abrade, fret; on. w. (v. wond; fig.) smart.
schrijnwerker m. joiner, cabinet-maker.
schrijven o. w. write; on. w. write; z. n., o. (schrift) writing, handwriting; **uw laatste —**, your last respects; **uw van 15e dezer**, your favour of the 15th inst.
schrijver m. (v. brief, enz.) writer; (v. boek, enz.) author; (op kantoor) (copying-)clerk, copyist.
schrik m. fright, terror, dread.
schrikaanjagend b. n. terrifying, scaring, fear-inspiring.
schrikachtig b. n. easily frightened; nervous; (fam.) jumpy.
schrikbarend b. n. frightful, dreadful, terrific.
schrikbewind o. (Reign of) Terror; terrorism.
schrikkeldag m. intercalary day.
schrikkeljaar o. leap year, bissextile year.
schrikken on. w. be frightened, take fright; (opschrikken) start; **iem. doen —**, frighten a person, give a person a fright.
schrikwekkend b. n. terrifying, terrific, appalling.

schril b. n. (v. stem, klank) shrill, reedy; (v. licht, kleuren) glaring; (v. tegenstelling) violent.

schrobben o. w. (v. vloer) scrub, scour; (sch.) hog.

schrobber m. scrubbing-brush, scrubber.

schroef v. screw; (bank—) vice; (sch.) screw, propeller; (v. vliegtuig) propeller, screw-propeller; (v. snaarinstrument) peg, tuning-peg.

schroefbank o. vice-bench, file-bench.

schroefboor v. screw-auger, spiral drill.

schroefbout m. screw-bolt.

schroefmoer v. nut, female screw.

schroefsleutel m. screw-wrench.

schroefvormig b. n. screw-shaped, spiral; helical.

schroeien o. w. (v. gras, enz.) scorch; (v. haar, gevogelte) singe; (v. varken) scald; (v. wond) cauterize; on. w. be singed, get singed.

schroevedraaier m. screw-driver, turn-screw.

schroeven o. w. screw.

schrokken o. w. en on. w. gorge, guzzle, gobble.

schrokkig b. n. gluttonous, greedy.

schromelijk b. n. terrible, gross.

schromen o. w. fear, dread.

schrompelig b. n. shrivelled, wrinkled.

schroom m. diffidence, scruple, dread, fear.

schroomvallig b. n. diffident, timorous, timid.

schroomvalligheid v. diffidence, timorousness, timidity.

schroot o. (mil.) grape-shot, canister-shot; (hagel) shot.

schrootvuur o. grape-fire.

schub v. scale.

schubdier o. (gordeldier in Amerika) armadillo; (in Indonesië) pangolin.

schubvleugelig b. n. scaly-winged; (wet.) lepidopterous.

schuchter b. n. timid, timorous, bashful, coy shy.

schuchterheid v. timidity, timorousness, bashfulness, coyness, shyness.

schuddebollen on. w. niddle-noddle, nid-nod.

schudden o. w. shake; (n. kaarten) shuffle; on. w. (alg.) shake; (v. hoofd: schuddebollen) niddle-noddle, nid-nod; (v. rijtuig) jolt.

schudding v. shaking, shock, concussion.

schuieren o. w. brush.

schuif v. (alg.) slide; (v. doos) sliding-lid; (v. kachel) damper; (grendel) bolt.

schuifblad o. sliding-board.

schuifdeur v. sliding-door, folding-door.

schuifelen on. w. (met voeten) shuffle, shamble; (v. slang) hiss.

schuifgordijn v. en o. curtain.

schuifkast v. steam-chest.

schuiflade v. drawer.

schuifraam o. sash-window, lift-up window.

schuiftrompet v. trombone, slide-trumpet.

schuilen on. w. take shelter; (zich verbergen) hide (oneself).

schuilgaan on. w. (v. zon, enz.) hide (itself).

schuilhoek m. hiding-place.

schuilhouden w. w. zich —, be in hiding, keep in the shade.

schuilnaam m. penname, pseudonym.

schuilplaats v. hiding-place, place of concealment, shelter; refuge, asylum.

schuim o. (v. zeep) lather; (op bier, enz.) froth; (op golven, enz.) foam; (v. metalen) dross; (v. soep, enz.) scum; (fig.) scum, off-scum, off-scourings, dregs.

schuimen on. w. (v. zeep) lather; (v. bier, enz.) froth; (v. golven, mond) foam; (v. soep) scum; (v. wijn) sparkle, bead; (klaplopen) sponge; (op zee) scour (the seas); o. w. scum.

schuimer m. (klaploper) sponger; (zee—) pirate.

schuimlepel m. skimmer.

schuimspaan v. skimmer.

schuin b. n. (v. muur, enz.) slanting, sloping; (v. richting, lijn, enz.) oblique; (v. vlak) inclined; (v. rand) bevel(led); (fig.) obscene, smutty, blue; bw. slantingly, etc.; aslant, awry; askew.

schuit v. boat, barge.

schuitje o. (sch.) (little) boat; (v. ballon) car, basket; (tn.) pig.

schuiven o. w. push, shove; (ring aan vinger) slip; (v. deur) slide; on. w. slide.

schuld v. (te betalen bedrag) debt; (fout) fault, guilt.

schuldbekentenis v. confession of guilt; (H.) I O U (= I owe you), bond.

schuldbelijdenis v. confession of guilt.

schuldbesef o. consciousness of guilt.

schuldbrief m. debenture.

schulddelging v. debt-redemption.

schuldeiser m. creditor.

schuldeloos b. n. guiltless, blameless, faultless, innocent.

schuldenaar m. debtor.

schuldig b. n. guilty, culpable; — zijn, (moeten betalen) owe; (schuld hebben) be guilty.

schuldige m. en v. culprit, delinquent.

schuldinvordering v. recovery of a debt.

schuldregeling v. debt settlement, scurvy.

schuldvordering v. claim.

schulpen o. w. scallop.

schunnig b. n. shabby, shady, mean.

schuren o. w. (v. vloer) scrub; (v. ketel, enz.) scour; (v. huid) chafe, graze, gall; on. w. over het zand —, grate over the sand.

schurft v. (v. mens) itch; (v. schaap) scab, scabies; (v. paard, hond) mange; (Pl.) scab; (wet.) psora.

schurftig *b. n.* scabby, mangy.

schurk *m.* rogue, rascal, villain, scoundrel, knave.

schurkachtig *b. n.* roguish, rascally, villainous, scoundrelly, knavish.

schurkenstreek *m.,* **schurkerij** *v.* roguery, roguish trick, scoundrelism, (piece of) villainy, knavish trick, piece of knavery.

schut *o.* *(scherm)* screen; *(schutting)* fence, hoarding; *(schot)* partition.

schutblad *o.* *(v. boek)* fly-leaf; *(v. plant)* bract.

schutbord *o.* *(v. auto)* dash-board, dash; *(sch.)* hatch.

schutsengel *m.* guardian angel.

schutsheilige *m.* patron saint.

schutsluis *v.* sash-lock.

schutspatroon *m.* patron saint.

schutsvrouw *v.* patroness.

schutten *o. w.* *(v. schip)* lock through; *(v. water)* dam up; *(v. vee)* pound.

schutter *m.* *(hij die schiet)* marksman, firer, shot; *(gesch.: lid v. de schutterij)* soldier of the Civic guard, militiaman; *(sterrenbeeld)* Sagittarius.

schutterij *v.* *(gesch.)* National guard, Civic guard, militia.

schutting *v.* fence, hoarding.

schuur *v.* barn.

schuurlinnen *o.* emery-cloth, abrasive cloth.

schuurpapier *o.* emery-paper, glasspaper, abrasive paper.

schuw *b. n.* shy, timid, timorous, bashful.

schuwen *o. w.* shun, fight shy of.

schuwheid *v.* shyness, timidity, bashfulness.

scrupuleus *b. n.* scrupulous, conscientious.

secondant *m.* assistant-master; *(in duel)* second; *(bij boksen)* bottle-holder.

seconde *v.* second.

secondewijzer *m.* seconds hands.

secreta *v.* secret, secreta.

secretariaat *o.* secretaryship, secretariat(e).

secretaris *m.* *(alg.)* secretary; *(v. gemeente)* town-clerk.

secretaris-generaal *m.* (permanent) undersecretary.

sectie *v.* *(afdeling)* section; *(v. lijk)* dissection, autopsy, post-mortem (examination); *(mil.)* section; platoon; *(in parlement)* (sessional) committee.

sector *m.* sector.

secunda *v.* *(H.)* second (of exchange).

sedert *vz.* *(tijdstip)* since; *(tijdruimte)* for; *bw. en vw.* since.

segment *o.* segment.

sein *o.* signal.

seinen *o. w. en on. w.* signal; *(telegraferen)* telegraph, wire, cable.

seingever *m.* *(tel.)* transmitter, sender.

seinhuisje *o.* signal-box, signal-cabin.

seinhuiswachter *m.* signal-man.

seinlantaarn *v.* signal-lamp, signallight.

seinmast *m.* signal-post.

seinpaal *m.* signal-post, semaphore.

seinschot *o.* signal-gun, signal-shot.

seintoestel *o.* signalling apparatus; *(radio)* transmitting-apparatus.

seinvlag *v.* signal-flag.

seismograaf *m.* seismograph.

seizoen *o.* season.

seizoenarbeider *m.* seasonal worker.

seizoenopruiming *v.* spring (summer) clearance sale.

sekreet *o.* privy, water-closet.

sekse *v.* sex.

sekte *v.* sect.

selderij *v.* celery.

selectief *b. n.* selective.

semester *o.* semester, six months.

seminarie *o.* seminary.

senaat *m.* senate.

senior *m.* senior.

sensatie *v.* sensation, stir; thrill.

sensatiepers *r.* sensational press, yellow press.

sensatieroman *m.* sensational novel, thriller, (shilling-)shocker.

sensatiestuk *o.* sensational play, thriller, hair-raiser.

sensueel *b. n.* sensual.

sentimenteel *b. n.* sentimental.

september *m.* September.

serenade *v.* serenade.

sergeant *m.* sergeant.

sergeant-majoor *m.* sergeant-major.

serie *v.* *(alg.)* series; *(bilj.)* break, sequence.

sering *v.* lilac.

sermoen *o.* sermon; *(fig.)* lecture.

serpent *o.* serpent; *(fig.)* virago, viperess.

serpentijn *o. en v.* serpentine.

serre *v.* *(voor planten, broeikas)* conservatory; hot-house, green-house; *(glazen veranda)* glazed verandah.

servet *o.* napkin, table-napkin, serviette.

servetring *m.* napkin-ring, serviettering.

Servië *o.* Serbia.

servies *o.* dinner-service; tea-set.

servituut *o.* easement, servitude, charge.

sfeer *v.* sphere, orbit; *(fig.)* sphere, domain, province.

sfinx *v.* sphinx.

sidderen *on. w.* tremble, thrill, quake, shudder.

siddering *v.* trembling, thrill, shudder.

sidderrog *m.* electric rayfish.

sier *v.* **goede — maken,** make good cheer.

sieraad *o.* ornament.

sieren *o. w.* adorn, ornament, decorate, embellish; *w. w.* **zich —,** adorn oneself.

sierheester *v.* ornamental shrub.

sierlijk *b. n.* graceful, elegant.

siësta *v.* siesta, nap.

sigaar *v.* cigar.

sigarenfabriek *v.* cigar-factory, cigarworks.

sigarenkist *v.* cigar-box.
sigarenmaker *m.* cigar-maker.
sigaret *v.* cigarette.
sigarettenkoker *m.* cigarette-case.
signaal *o.* (*alg.*) signal; (*mil.*) call, bugle-call.
signalement *o.* (personal, official) description.
signatuur *v.* signature.
sijpelen *on. w.* ooze, trickle, percolate, filter.
sijs(je) *m.* (*o.*) siskin.
sik *v.* (*geit*) goat, goatling; (*baard v. geit*) goat's beard; (*v. man*) chintuft, chin-beard.
sikkel *v.* sickle, reaping-hook; (*v. maan*) crescent, sickle.
sikkepit(je) *v.* (*o.*) bit, mite.
silhouet *v.* silhouette.
silo *v.* (*afgedekte kuil*) silo; (*pakhuis*) silo, (grain) elevator, grain warehouse.
simpel *b. n.* simple, mere; (*onnozel*) silly.
sinaasappel *m.* orange.
sinds *bw. en vz.* since.
sindsdien *bw.* since.
singel *m.* (*gordel*) girdle; (*v. priester*) cingulum; (*buikriem v. paard*) girth; (*stadsgracht*) moat, ring canal; (*weg langs stadsgracht*) boulevard, promenade; (*onder stoel, enz.*) web.
sinjeur *m.* fellow.
sint *b. n. en z. n., m.* saint.
Sint-Andrieskruis *o.* St. Andrew's cross.
sintel *m.* cinder; **—s,** cinders; slag.
Sint-Pieterspenning *m.*Peter'spence.
sip *b. n. en bw.* — **kijken,** look blue, look glum.
sirene *v.* siren.
siroop *v.* treacle; (*vruchten—*) syrup.
sissen *on. w.* hiss; (*bij 't braden*) sizzle, frizzle.
sisser *m.* (*persoon*) hisser; (*vuurwerk*) squib.
sits *o.* chintz.
situatie *v.* situation.
sjaal *v.* shawl.
sjacheraar *m.* barterer, chafferer.
sjacheren *on. w.* barter, chaffer.
sjalot *v.* shallot, eschalot.
sjees *v.* gig.
sjerp *v.* sash, scarf.
sjilpen *on. w.* chirp, cheep.
sjofel *b. n.* shabby, seedy.
sjorren *o. w.* lash, gammon.
sjortouw *o.* (*sch.*) lanyard, lashing.
sjouwen *o. w.* carry; (*sleuren*) drag, lug; *on. w.* (*zwaar werken*) drudge, toil, fag.
sjouwer *m.* porter, dock-hand.
skelet *m.* skeleton; (*v. dier*) carcass.
ski *v.* ski.
slaaf *m.* slave, bondman.
slaafs *b. n.* slavish, servile.
slaafsheid *v.* slavishness, servility.
slaags *bw.* — **raken,** come to close

quarters, join battle; — **zijn,** be fighting, be engaged.
slaan *o. w.* (*éénmaal*) strike; (*herhaaldelijk*) beat; (*ranselen*) thrash, lick, flog; *on. w.* (*v. hart*) beat; (*v. klok*) strike; (*v. nachtegaal*) jug; (*v. paard*) kick; (*v. zeil*) flap; (*in damspel*) take, capture.
slaap *m.* sleep; (*v. hoofd*) temple; *in* — **wiegen,** rock asleep; (*fig.*) put to sleep, lull to sleep.
slaapdrank *m.* sleeping-draught.
slaapdronken *b. n.* overcome with sleep, sleep drunk, sleep-charged, drowsy.
slaapkamer *v.* bedroom.
slaapliedje *o.* lullaby.
slaapmiddel *o.* opiate, narcotic.
slaapmuts *v.* night-cap.
slaapplaats *v.* sleeping-place, sleeping-accommodation.
slaapstede *v.* cupboard-bed, closet-bed (stead).
slaaptijd *m.* bedtime.
slaapvertrek *o.* sleeping-apartment, bed-chamber, sleeping-chamber.
slaapwandelaar(ster) *m.* (*v.*) sleep-walker, somnambulist.
slaapzaal *v.* dormitory.
slaapzak *m.* sleeping-bag.
slaapziekte *v.* (*tropisch*) sleeping sickness, sleep. disease; (*Europees*) sleepy sickness, encephalitis lethargica.
slabakken *on. w.* (*talmen, treuzelen*) dawdle; (*verflauwen, verslappen*) slacken; (*luieren*) idle, slack.
slabben, slabberen *o. w.* lap.
slabbetje *o.* bib, feeder.
slachtafval *m. en o.* garbage.
slachtblok *o.* slaughtering-block.
slachten *o. w.* kill, slaughter.
slachten *o. w.* (*gelijken*) favour, be like, resemble.
slachter *m.* butcher.
slachterij *v.* butcher's shop; slaughter-house.
slachthuis *o.* slaughter-house, abattoir.
slachting *v.* slaughter, butchery.
slachtmaand *v.* November.
slachtoffer *o.* victim.
slag *o.* sort, kind, type, class; *van allerlei* —, of every sort and kind.
slag *m.* (*met hand*) blow, box, cuff; (*in gelaat*) slap, smack; (*met vuist, enz.*) blow; (*met zweep, enz.*) stroke, lash; (*v. vleugels*) beat, stroke; (*v. hart, pols*) pulsation, beat; (*v. donder*) clap; (*muz.*) beat; (*v. klok*) stroke; (*plof*) thud, thump; (*v. vogel*) warble; (*v. nachtegaal*) jug; (*v. wiel*) turn; (*in kaartspel*) trick; (*veldslag*) battle; (*tegenspoed, enz.*) blow; (*handigheid*) knack.
slagader *v.* artery; *grote* —, aorta.
slagaderverkalking *v.* arteriosclerosis
slagboom *m.* barrier.
slagen *on. w.* succeed; (*voor examen*) pass.
slager *m.* butcher.
slagersknecht *m.* butcher's man.

slagerswinkel m. butcher's shop.
slaghamer m. mallet.
slaghoedje o. percussion-cap.
slaglinie v. (mil.) line of battle.
slagnet o. clap-net, fowling-net, drop-down net.
slagorde v. order of battle, battle-array.
slagpen v. flight-feather, quill-feather.
slagregen m. down-pour, driving rain, heavy shower.
slagroom v. whipped cream.
slagschip o. battle-ship, capital ship.
slagtand m. (v. hond, wolf) fang; (v. olifant) tusk.
slagvaardig b. n. ready for battle, ready for the fray; (fig.) quick at repartee, quick-witted.
slagveld o. battle-field, field of battle.
slagwerk o. (v. klok) striking-work, striking-parts; (v. orkest) instruments of percussion.
slagzwaard o. broadsword.
slak v. (met huisje) snail; (zonder huisje) slug; (v. metaal) slag, scoria.
slaken o. w. (v. zucht) heave, fetch, utter; (v. boeien) break.
slakkegang m. snail's pace, snail's gallop.
slakkesteker m. (bajonet) cheese-toaster, cheese-knife, cat-stabber.
slang v. (Dk.) snake, serpent; (v. brandspuit, tuin—) hose; (buis) tube; (v. distilleerketel) worm; (fig.) serpent, viper.
slangebroedsel o. brood of snakes.
slangegift o. snake-poison.
slangemens m. contortionist, distortionist, serpent-man.
slangenbezweerder m.snake-charmer
slank b. n. slender, svelte, slim.
slap b. n. (v. zaken, koord, enz.) slack; (v. boord, hoed) soft; (v. benen) supple; (v. wangen, karakter) flabby; (v. vlees) flaccid; (v. dranken) weak, thin, sloppy; (v. voeding) unsubstantial; (v. markt) dull, weak; (v. tucht) lax; (v. persoon) weak; (lusteloos) limp; (v. fietsband) flat, slack, soft; bw. flabbily; limply.
slapeloos b. n. sleepless.
slapen on. w. sleep, be asleep.
slaper m. sleeper; (slaapgast) lodger.
slaperig b. n. sleepy, drowsy.
slapheid v. slackness; weakness, etc.; zie **slap**; (v. tucht) laxity.
slaven on. w. slave, drudge.
slavenarbeid m. slavery, slaves work; (fig.) drudgery.
slavenhandel m. slave-trade, slaving.
slavenhandelaar m. slave-trader, slave-dealer.
slavenjacht v. slave-hunting.
slavernij v. slavery, servitude, bondage, thraldom.
slavin v. (female) slave, bondwoman.
slecht b. n. bad; bw. badly.
slechten o. w. level (with the ground), raze, demolish.
slechtheid v. badness; wickedness.

slechts bw. only, but, merely.
slede v. (voertuig) sledge, sleigh; (v. affuit) sledge; (v. draaibank) carriage, slide; (op scheepshelling) cradle.
slee v. (Pl.) sloe.
slee b. n. (wrang) tart; (stomp, bot) blunted, blunt; (v. tanden) on edge.
sleep m. train.
sleepboot v. tug-boat, tow-boat, steam-tug.
sleepdrager m., **sleepdraagster** v. train-bearer.
sleepkabel m. (v. ballon) guide-rope.
sleeploon o. cartage; (sch.) towage.
sleepnet o. drag-net, trailing-net, trawl-net.
sleeptouw o. tow-rope, towing-rope; (v. ballon) guide-rope; **op — hebben,** have in tow; **op — nemen,** take in tow.
sleeptros m. tow-line, towing-rope, hawser.
sleet v. wear and tear.
sleets b. n. (v. goed) wearing away very soon; (v. persoon) wearing out one's clothes in a short time (very quickly).
slem o. slam.
slemppartij v. carousal.
slenteren on. w. saunter, lounge.
slepen on. w. drag, trail.
slepen o. w. drag, haul; (met sleepboot) tow; (muz.: v. noten) slur; w. w. **zich naar huis —,** drag oneself home.
sleper m. carter, carman; (sch.) tug-boat; (in mijn) haulier.
slet v. slut, drab, trull, strumpet.
sleuf v. groove, slot, slit.
sleur v. routine, routinism, rut.
sleuren o. w. drag, trail; on. w. trail.
sleutel m. key; (v. kachel) damper, register, regulator; (muz.) clef; **Engelse —,** monkey-wrench, monkey-spanner, shift-key.
sleutelbaard m. key-bit.
sleutelbeen o. collar bone, clavicle.
sleutelbloem v. primula, primrose.
sleutelgat o. key-hole.
sleutelring m. key-ring.
slib v. ooze, mud, silt, slime, mire.
slibberen on. w. slide, slip, slither.
slibberig b. n. slippery, slithery.
slier m. (rij) string; (streep) streak, smear.
slierbaan v. slide.
slieren on. w. slide, glide.
sliert m. string, trail.
slijk o. mud, mire, dirt, slime.
slijkbord o. (over wiel) mud-guard; (vóór aan voertuig) dash-board; (v. auto) wing, mud-guard.
slijkerig b. n. muddy, miry, slimy, oozy.
slijm o. slime, phlegm, mucus.
slijmachtig b. n. slimy, mucous.
slijmvlies o. mucous membrane.
slijpen o. w. grind, whet, sharpen; (v. diamant) cut; polish.
slijper m. (v. messen, enz.) grinder; (v. diamant) cutter, polisher.
slijpmolen m. grinding-mill.

slijpsteen *m*. grindstone, whetstone.
slijten *o. w*. (*v. kleren*) wear out; (*v. schoenen*) wear down; (*doorbrengen*) pass, spend; (*verkopen*) retail; *on. w*. wear away, wear out, get used up.
slijter *m*. retailer, retail-dealer; (*v. dranken*) licensed victualler.
slijterij *v*. gin-shop, licensed victualler's shop.
slikken *o. w*. swallow; *on. w*. swallow, make a gulp.
slim *b. n*. sly, artful, crafty, cunning.
slimheid *v*. sliness, craft, craftiness, cunning, cunningness.
slimmerd *m*. slyboots, sly dog.
slinger *m*. (*v. klok*) pendulum; (*v. pomp: zwengel*) handle; (*werptuig*) sling; (*v. auto*) crank, starting-handle; (*versiering*) garland, festoon; (*slingerende beweging*) lurch.
slingeraap *m*. spider-monkey.
slingeren *on. w*. (*alg.*) swing, oscillate; (*v. pad, enz.: kronkelen*) wind, meander; (*v. schip*) roll; (*v. rijtuig*) lurch, sway; (*v. dronkaard*) reel, lurch; (*ordeloos liggen*) lie about; *o. w*. (*gooien*) fling, hurl.
slingerpad *o*. winding-path.
slingerplant *v*. climber, climbing plant, trailer, trailing plant.
slingeruurwerk *o*. pendulum clock.
slinken *on. w*. shrink; (*door koken*) boil down; (*v. gezwel*) go down, subside.
slinks *b. n*. cunning, artful, crafty, sly.
slinksheid *v*. cunning, artfulness.
slip *v*. lappet; tail, coat-tail, flap.
slippen *on. w*. (*v. persoon*) slip; (*v. auto*) skid, side-slip.
slipper *m*. **een —(tje) maken,** take French leave, slip away.
slobkous *v*. (*lang*) gaiter; (*kort*) spat.
slodderachtig *b. n*. slovenly, grubby, sloppy.
slodderkous *v*. draggletail, slattern.
sloddervos *m. en v*. sloven, grub.
sloep *v*. sloop, shallop, boat.
slof *v*. (*pantoffel*) slipper; (*v. strijkstok*) nut, heel; (*remschoen*) skid, skid-pan.
slof *b. n*. slack, lax, negligent.
slok *m*. draught, swallow.
slokdarm *m*. gullet; (*wet.*) esophagus.
slokje *o*. (small) draught, sip; (*borrel*) dram, drop, nip.
slokken *on. w*. guzzle, swallow.
slons *v*. slattern, sloven, slut, draggletail.
sloof *v*. (*voorschoot*) apron; (*persoon*) drudge.
sloop *v*. pillow-slip, pillow-case.
sloot *v*. ditch.
slop *o*. slum, blind alley.
slopen *o. w*. (*v. huis*) pull down; (*v. gebouwen*) demolish; (*v. vesting*) demolish, dismantle; (*v. schip*) break up; (*fig.*) sap, undermine.
sloping *v*. demolition, breaking-up.
slordig *b. n*. slovenly, careless, dowdy, sloppy.
slordigheid *v*. slovenliness, carelessness, dowdiness.

slot *o*. (*v. deur, enz.*) lock; (*v. boek, enz.*) clasp; (*v. armband*) snap; (*einde, besluit*) end, conclusion; (*v. redevoering*) peroration; (*kasteel*) castle.
slotenmaker *m*. lock-smith.
slotklinker *m*. final vowel.
slotkoers *m*. closing price; closing quotation.
slotrede *v*. peroration; conclusion.
slotsom *v*. result, conclusion.
slotstuk *o*. concluding piece, finale.
slotvoogd *m*. castellan.
slotwoord *o*. final word, concluding word(s), peroration.
sloven *on. w*. drudge, toil.
sluier *m*. veil; (*op foto*) fog.
sluieren *o. w*. veil; (*fotoplaat*) fog.
sluik *b. n*. (*v. haar*) lank, straight; **ter-—(s),** on the sly, underhand.
sluikhandel *m*. smuggling; **— drijven,** smuggle.
sluikhandelaar *m*. smuggler.
sluimeren *on. w*. slumber, doze; (*fig.*) slumber.
sluimering *v*. slumber, doze.
sluipen *on. w*. steal, slink, sneak.
sluipmoord *m*. assassination.
sluis *v*. sluice, lock.
sluisbalk *m*. lock-beam.
sluisdeur *v*. lock-gate, flood-gate.
sluiskolk *v*. lock-chamber, sluice-chamber.
sluiswachter *m*. lock-keeper, lock-master, locksman.
sluitband *m*. belly-band, bandage.
sluitboom *m*. (*v. spoorweg*) swing-gate; (*v. haven*) boom.
sluiten *o. w*. (*deur, boek, enz.*) shut, close; (*op slot doen*) lock; (*v. winkel, beurs, enz.: tijdelijk*) close; (*voor goed*) shut up, close down; (*v. debat, enz.*) close, terminate; (*v. verdrag*) conclude, make; (*v. overeenkomst, koop*) close, strike, conclude; (*v. lening, huwelijk*) contract; (*v. verzekering*) effect; (*v. rekening, vergadering*) close; (*v. vrede*) conclude, make; *on. w*. **de markt sloot vast,** the market closed firm; *w. w*. **zich —,** (*v. wond, ogen*) close; (*v. bloem*) shut, close (up).
sluitend *b. n*. (*v. deur, enz.*) closing, shutting; (*v. kleren*) close-fitting; (*v. begroting*) balanced.
sluiting *v*. shutting, closing; locking; (*v. debat, enz.*) closure; (*met feestdagen*) break-up; (*v. fles*) stopper.
sluitingstijd *m*., **sluitingsuur** *o*. closing-time,closing-hour,shutting-up hour.
sluitmand *v*. hamper.
sluitrede *v*. syllogism.
sluitsteen *m*. key-stone.
sluitstuk *o*. (*v. kanon*) breech-piece, breech-block.
sluitzegel *o*. poster stamp.
slungel *m*. lout, hobbledehoy, hobbadehoy.
slurf *v*. (*v. olifant*) trunk, proboscis; (*v. insekt*) proboscis.

slurpen *o. w.* sip, lap, gobble up.
sluw *b. n.* sly, cunning, crafty, astute.
sluwheid *v.* slyness, cunningness, craftiness, astuteness.
smaad *m.* indignity, revilement, contumely, obloquy; *(recht)* libel.
smaadschrift *o.* libel, lampoon.
smaak *m.* taste; savour, relish; *(smaak en geur)* flavour; *(zin, lust)* liking.
smaakje *o.* **er is een — aan,** it has a taste, there is a tang about it.
smaakvol *b. n.* tasteful, in good taste.
smachten *on. w.* languish, pine, long.
smachtend *b. n.* languishing.
smadelijk *b. n.* scornful, contumelious, humiliating, ignominious.
smaden *o. w.* revile, vilify, vilipend.
smak *m.* *(met lippen)* smacking, smack; *(bons, harde plof)* heavy fall, (dull) thud.
smak *v.* *(Pl.)* sumac(h).
smakelijk *b. n.* savoury, tasteful, tasty, relishable, palatable, toothsome; *bw.* savourily.
smakeloos *b. n.* *(v. spijs of drank)* tasteless, without taste, savourless; insipid; *(fig.)* out of taste, in bad taste.
smakeloosheid *v.* tastelessness; insipidity.
smaken *on. w.* taste; *o. w.* **genoegens —,** enjoy pleasures.
smakken *on. w.* *(met de lippen)* smack; *(met een smak vallen)* fall with a thud; *o. w.* dash, fling, cast.
smal *b. n.* narrow.
smaldeel *o.* *(sch.)* squadron.
smalen *on. w.* rail.
smalend *b. n.* scornful, contumelious.
smalheid *v.* narrowness.
smaragd *o.* emerald.
smart *v.* pain, grief, affliction, sorrow.
smartelijk *b. n.* painful, grievous.
smartelijkheid *v.* painfulness, grievousness.
smarten *o. w.* cause pain, give pain, grieve; *(v. wonden)* smart; *(sch.)* parcel.
smeden *o. w.* forge; *(wellen)* weld; *(fig.: v. komplot)* lay, plan; *(v. plannen)* hatch, devise.
smeder *m.* forger, deviser.
smederij *v.* smithy, forge.
smeedbaar *b. n.* malleable.
smeedhamer *m.* sledge-hammer, forging hammer.
smeedijzer *o.* wrought iron.
smeekbede *v.* supplication, entreaty, obsecration.
smeekgebed *o.* supplication, humble prayer.
smeekschrift *o.* petition.
smeer *o.* grease, fat; *(voor schoenen)* dubbing, grease; *(talk)* tallow.
smeerachtig *b. n.* greasy.
smeerlap *m.* *(eig.)* greasing-clout; *(fig.)* dirty fellow, skunk, blighter, blackguard.
smeerolie *v.* lubricating oil.
smeerpot *m.* grease-pot, lubricator.

smeken *o. w.* supplicate, entreat, implore, beseech.
smeker *m.* suppliant.
smeltbaar *b. n.* fusible, liquefiable.
smeltbaarheid *v.* fusibility.
smelten *o. w.* melt, fuse, liquefy; *(v. vet)* render; *(v. erts)* smelt; *on. w.* melt, fuse; *(v. boter)* melt, oil.
smelterij *v.* melting-house, smelting-works.
smeltkroes *m.* melting-pot, crucible.
smeltoven *m.* smelting-furnace.
smeltpunt *o.* melting-point, fusing-point.
smeren *o. w.* grease, oil, lubricate, smear; *(met boter)* butter.
smerig *b. n.* dirty; *(vettig)* greasy; *(fig.)* dirty; *(v. handeling, streek)* sordid; *(v. behandeling)* shabby; *(v. weer)* dirty, greasy, foul.
smet *v.* spot, stain; *(fig.)* stain; slur, blemish, taint.
smetstof *v.* virus, infectious matter.
smetteloos *b. n.* stainless, spotless, impeccable, immaculate.
smetten *o. w.* stain, soil; *on. w.* *(v. huid)* be chafed, get sore; *(v. stoffen, enz.)* soil.
smeulen *on. w.* smoulder; *(fig.)* simmer, smoulder.
smid *m.* smith.
smidse *v.* forge, smithy.
smijdig *b. n.* supple, malleable, pliant.
smijdigheid *v.* suppleness, malleability, pliancy.
smijten *o. w.* throw, fling, cast, dash; *on. w.* **met het geld —,** throw (fling) one's money about.
smoel *m.* mug, gob.
smoesje *o.* pretext, dodge, poor excuse.
smokkelaar *m.* smuggler; *(v. drank, geweren)* runner.
smokkelen *o. w.* *(alg.)* smuggle; *(v. drank, geweren)* run; *on. w.* smuggle; *(bij spel)* play false, trick, cheat.
smokkelhandel *m.* smuggling, contraband trade.
smokkelwaar *v.* contraband (goods).
smook *m.* smoke.
smoordronken *b. n.* dead drunk, as thigt as a drum.
smoorheet *b. n.* sweltering, suffocating, broiling.
smoorlijk *bw.* **— verliefd,** over head and ears in love, dead in love.
smoren *o. w.* smother, strangle, suffocate; *(v. vlees)* braise, stew; *(fig.)* stifle, choke (down); **in de kiem —,** nip in the bud; crush in the germ; *on. w.* smother; stifle.
smous *m.* *(persoon)* smouch; *(hond)* griffon.
smout *o.* grease, lard.
smoutwerk *o.* table-work, tabular work.
smukken *o. w.* trim, deck out, adorn.
smullen *on. w.* feast, guzzle, banquet.
smulpaap *m.* free-liver, gastronomer, gastronomist, epicure.
smulpartij *v.* banquet, feasting-party.

snaak *m.* wag, droll.
snaaks *b. n.* waggish, droll.
snaaksheid *v.* waggishness, drollery.
snaar *r.* string, chord.
snakken *on. w.* — *naar,* languish for, yearn for.
snappen *o. w.* (*grijpen, vatten*) snatch; (*betrappen*) catch out, catch in the act, spot; (*begrijpen*) grasp, understand; *on. w.* prattle, tattle, chat.
snars *r.* **geen —,** not a bit, not the least bit.
snater *m.* clack.
snateren *on. w.* (*v. eend*) chatter; (*v. persoon*) chatter, jabber.
snauwen *on. w.* snarl.
snavel *m.* bill; beak.
snede *v.* (*wonde*) cut; (*groter*) gash, slash; (*insnijding*) incision; (*brood, vlees*) slice; (*spek*) rasher; (*v. mes, enz.: scherp*) edge; (*v. versregel*) caesura, section.
snedig *b. n.* witty, smart.
sneeuw *v.* snow.
sneeuwbal *m.* snowball; (*Pl.*) guelderrose, snowball.
sneeuwblind *b. n.* snow-blind.
sneeuwbui *r.* snow-shower, snowsquall.
sneeuwen *onp. w.* snow.
sneeuwen *b. n.* snow; snowwhite.
sneeuwjacht *r.* snow-drift, drivingsnow.
sneeuwman *m.* snow-man.
sneeuwval *m.* snow-fall; (*lawine*) snowslide, avalanche.
sneeuwvlaag *v.* snow-shower.
sneeuwvlok *v.* snow-flake, flake of snow.
Sneeuwwitje *o. en r.* Little Snow-white.
snel *b. n.* quick, swift, rapid, fast, speedy.
snelblusser *m.* fire-extinguisher.
snelheid *v.* rapidity, swiftness, quickness, speed, velocity.
snelheidsmeter *m.* speed indicator, tachometer, speedometer.
snellen *on. w.* hasten, rush, hurry.
snelschrift *o.* shorthand, stenography.
sneltrein *m.* fast train, express (train).
snelverkeer *o.* fast traffic.
snelwerkend *b. n.* quick-acting, speedy, rapid.
snerpend *b. n.* (*v. koude*) biting, piercing; (*r. wind*) cutting, searching, rasping.
snert *r.* pea-soup; (*fig.*) trash, muck.
sneuvelen *on. w.* be killed (in battle), be slain, perish.
snibbig *b. n.* (*bw.*) snappish(ly.)
snibbigheid *v.* snappishness.
snijboon *v.* French bean, haricot bean.
snijden *o. w.* cut; (*aan stukken*) cut up; (*vlees; figuren in hout, enz.*) carve; (*v. dier: castreren*) castrate, geld; (*fijn—*) mince; (*in repen —*) shred; (*fig.: afzetten*) fleece, shear; *on. w.* cut; (*kaartspel*) finesse; *w. w.* **zich —,** cut oneself.
snijdend *b. n.* cutting; (*fig.*) sharp, biting; (*meetk.*) secant, intersecting.

snijder *m.* cutter, carver; (*graveur*) engraver; (*kleermaker*) tailor.
snijkamer *v.* dissecting-room.
snijlijn *v.* secant, intersecting line.
snijmachine *v.* cutting-machine; slicing-machine; (*drukkerij*) guillotine, plough; (*fot.*) table.
snijtand *m.* incisor, cutting-tooth.
snijwerk *o.* carved work, carving(s).
snik *m.* gasp, sob; *b. n.* **hij is niet goed —,** he is not all there.
snikheet *b. n.* broiling, suffocatingly hot.
snikken *on. w.* sob.
snip *v.* snipe.
snipper *v.* cutting, clipping, scrap, shred, snip, chip.
snippermand *v.* waste-paper basket.
snippertje *o.* snippet, chip, shred.
snipperuur(tje) *o.* spare hour, leisurehour.
snipperwerk *o.* trifling work.
snit *v.* cut.
snoeien *o. w.* (*alg., v. boom*) lop; (*v. vruchtbomen, rozestruiken, enz.*) prune; (*v. haag*) clip, trim; (*v. munten*) clip.
snoeimes *o.* pruning-knife; hedge-bill.
snoeischaar *v.* lopping-shears, pruningshears, garden-shears.
snoek *m.* pike.
snoekbaars *m.* pike-perch.
snoepachtig *b. n.* sneaky; fond of sweets.
snoepen *on. w.* eat sweets; (*heimelijk*) sneak.
snoeperig *b. n.* lovely, charming, nice, pretty, ducky.
snoeperij *v.,* **snoepgoed** *o.* sweets, goodies, nicies, lollipops.
snoeplust *m.* fondness for sweets.
snoepwinkeltje *o.* sweet-shop.
snoer *o.* cord, lace, line; (*v. paarlen*) string, rope; (*elektrisch*) flex.
snoes *m.* darling, duck, ducky, dink, peach.
snoet *m.* snout, muzzle; (*gezicht*) mug.
snoeven *on. w.* brag, boast, bluster, swagger.
snoever *m.* braggart, boaster, blusterer, swaggerer.
snoezig *b. n.* lovely, sweet, ducky, dinky.
snood *b. n.* base, vile, heinous, sinister, wicked.
snoodaard *m.* villain, miscreant, rascal.
snoodheid *v.* baseness, wickedness, heinousness.
snor *m.* moustache.
snorken *on. w.* snore, snort; (*fig.*) brag, boast.
snorker *m.* snorer; (*fig.*) braggart, boaster.
snorren *on. w.* (*v. machine, enz.*) whir, drone; (*zacht —*) hum, purr; (*v. kachel*) roar; (*v. taxi*) crawl, ply for hire.
snot *o.* mucus; (*fam.*) snot; *v.* (*snotziekte*) chicken coryza.
snotaap *m.* snotty, brat, whipper-snapper.

snotneus *m*. snotty nose; *(lamp)* slush-lamp.

snuffelen *on. w*. *(met neus)* sniff, nose; *(fig.)* ferret, nose, rummage, root, pry.

snufje *o*. *het nieuwste* —, the latest novelty, the latest thing.

snugger *b. n*. bright, clever, sharp, brainy.

snuggerheid *v*. brightness, cleverness, sharpness.

snuif *v*. snuff.

snuifdoos *v*. snuff-box.

snuifje *o*. pinch of snuff.

snuisterijen *v. mv*. knick-knacks, trinkets, bric-a-brac.

snuit *m*. *(v. varken, enz.)* snout, muzzle; *(v. olifant)* trunk; *(v. insekt)* proboscis; *(v. schip)* beak, rostrum, nozzle; *(gezicht)* mug.

snuiten *o. w*. *(kaars)* snuff; *on. w*. blow one's nose.

snuiter *m*. (pair of) snuffers; chap, fellow.

snuiven *on. w*. sniff, snuffle; *(v. paard)* snort; *(snuif gebruiken)* take snuff.

snurken *on. w*. snore, snort.

sober *b. n*. sober, frugal; *(schraal)* scanty.

soberheid *v*. soberness, sobriety, frugality; scantiness.

sociaal-democraat *m*. social-democrat.

socialisme *o*. socialism.

sociëteit *v*. club-house, club.

soda *v*. soda.

sodawater *o*. soda-water.

soep *v*. soup; *(bouillon)* broth.

soepelheid *v*. suppleness.

soepgroente *v*. soup-greens, pot-herbs.

soepketel *m*. soup-kettle.

soeplepel *m*. *(om te scheppen)* soup-ladle; *(eetlepel)* soup-spoon.

soes *v*. *(gebak)* puff, cream puff, puff-cake; *m*. *(dommel)* doze, drowse.

soezen *on. w*. doze, drowse.

sok *v*. sock, half-stocking; *(tn.)* socket; *(persoon)* muff, duffer, (old) fogey.

sokophouder *m*. sock-suspender.

soldaat *m*. soldier.

soldatenbrood *o*. ammunition bread.

soldatenmuts *v*. forage-cap.

soldeerbout *m*. soldering-boit, soldering-iron. [lamp.

soldeerlamp *v*. soldering-lamp, blow-

soldeersel *o*. solder.

soldenier *m*. mercenary.

solderen *o. w*. solder.

soldij *v*. pay.

solfer *v*. sulphur, brimstone.

solidariteit *v*. solidarity; *(H.)* joint liability.

solide *b. n*. *(stevig)* solid, substantial, strong; *(v. persoon)* steady; *(H.: v. firma, enz.)* substantial, respectable; *(vertrouwbaar)* trustworthy, reliable; *(in staat tot betalen)* solvent; *(v. belegging)* sound, safe.

solist *m*. soloist, solist.

sollen *o. w*. toss, haul about; *on. w*. romp; — *met*, *(fig.)* make fun of.

sollicitant *m*. candidate, applicant, postulant.

solliciteren *on. w*. apply; — *naar een betrekking*, apply for a situation.

solospel *o*. solo performance.

solovlucht *v*. solo flight, lone flight.

solvent *b. n*. solvent.

som *v*. *(bedrag)* sum, (total) amount; *(vraagstuk)* sum, problem.

somber *b. n*. gloomy, sombre; *(v. weer)* dull; *(fig.)* gloomy, sombre, sad, dark, dejected.

somberheid *v*. gloom, sombreness; dulness, darkness; dejection.

sommige *onbep. telw. mv*. some; —*n*, some.

soms *bw*. sometimes, now and then.

somtijds, somwijlen *bw*. sometimes.

soort *v. en o*. *(alg.)* kind, sort; *(merk)* brand; *(nat. hist.)* species.

soortelijk *b. n*. specific.

soortgelijk *b. n*. similar, suchlike.

soortgenoot *m*. congener.

soortnaam *m*. generic name, class-name.

sop *o. en v*. broth.

soppen *on. w*. sop, soak, dip, steep.

sopraan *v*. soprano, treble.

sorbet *o*. sorbet, sherbet.

sorteren *o. w*. sort, assort.

souffleur *m*. prompter.

soutane *v*. soutane.

souverein *b. n*. sovereign; *z. n., m*. sovereign; *(tn.: boor)* countersink.

sovjetrepubliek *v*. Soviet Republic, Soviet Union.

spa zie **spade**.

spaak *v*. spoke; *(v. stoel)* rung.

spaan *v*. *(v. hout)* chip; *(boter—)* scoop, pat, blade; *(schuim—)* skimmer.

Spaans *b. n*. Spanish; *z. n., o*. Spanish.

spaarbank *v*. savings-bank.

spaarbankboekje *o*. deposit book, savings-bank book.

spaarder *m*. saver, economizer; *(inlegger)* depositor.

spaarduiten *m. mv*. savings.

spaarkas *v*. savings-bank.

spaarpenningen *m. mv*. savings.

spaarpot *m*. money-box, savings-box.

spaarzaam *b. n*. saving, economical, thrifty.

spaarzaamheid *v*. economy, thrift.

spade *v*. spade.

spade *b. n*. late.

spalk *v*. splint.

span *o*. *(v. hand)* span; *(gespan)* team, yoke; set.

spanbroek *v*. (pair of) tights, tight trousers.

Spanjaard *m*. Spaniard.

Spanje *o*. Spain.

spankracht *v*. tensile force, tension; *(v. gas, enz.)* expansive force, expansibility.

spannen *o. w*. *(v. touw)* stretch; *(strakker —)* tighten; *(v. net)* spread; *(v. strik)*

lay; (v. boog) draw, bend, stretch; (v. trommel) brace; (haan v. geweer) cock; (spieren, zenuwen) strain; on. w. (v. kleren) be tight; (te nauw) drag; w. w. **zich ervoor —**, take it up, take the matter in hand.
spannend b. n. (v. kleren) tight; (v. verhaal, wedren) thrilling; (v. toneel) exciting, tense.
spanner m. spanner, nut-key; (Dk. vlinder, rups) geometer.
spanning v. (alg., v. spieren, enz.) tension; (nat.) tension, strain; (el.) tension, voltage; (druk) pressure, stress; (v. brug, enz.) span; (fig.) tension; (onzekerheid) uncertainty, suspense.
spanraam o. stretcher-frame, tenter-frame, stretcher, tenter.
spanriem m. knee-strap, kicking-strap.
spanschroef v. tightening-screw, stretching-screw; (sch.) rigging screw.
spanwijdte v. span.
spanzaag v. span-saw, frame-saw.
spar m. (boom) spruce-fir; v. (v. dak) rafter; (v. schip) spar.
sparen o. w. (geld, enz.: overleggen) save, save up; (ontzien) spare; on. w. save (up), lay by, economize.
spartelen on. w. sprawl, struggle, flounder, squirm.
spat v. (vlek) stain, spot, speck, fleck; (aderspat) spavin.
spatader v. varicose vein, varix.
spatbord o. splash-board, mudguard.
spatie v. space.
spatten on. w. splash, spatter; (v. pen) splutter; o. w. spurt; **vonken —**, emit sparks, sparkle.
specerij v. spice.
specht m. woodpecker.
speciaal b. n. (bw.) special(ly).
specialiseren o. w. specialize.
specialist m. (gen.) consulting physician, specialist.
specie v. (gemunt geld) specie, ready money, hard money, cash; (mortel) mortar.
specifiek b. n. (bw.) specific(ally).
speculatie v. speculation; stock-jobbing.
speculeren on. w. speculate; **— op,** trade on, take advantage of.
speeksel o. saliva, spittle, sputum.
speekselklier v. salivary gland.
speelbal m. (bilj.) playing-ball, player's ball, cue-ball; (fig.) toy, plaything, sport.
speeldoos v. musical box.
speelgoed o. playthings, toys.
speelgoedwinkel m. toy-shop.
speelhol o. gaming-den, gambling-den, gambling-hell. [house.
speelhuis o. gaming-house, gambling-
speelkaart v. playing-card.
speelpenning m. counter, fish.
speelplaats v. playground.
speelpop v. (fig.) puppet, doll, toy.
speels b. n. playful, gamesome, sportive.

speelseizoen o. play-season; (v. toneel) theatrical season.
speelsheid v. playfulness, gamesomeness, sportiveness.
speeltafel v. gaming-table, gambling-table, play-table; card-table.
speelterrein o. playing-field, playground, recreation-ground.
speeltijd m. playtime.
speeltuig o. (musical) instrument.
speelziek b. n. playful, gamesome.
speen v. teat, nipple; (fop—) comforter.
speenvarken o. sucking-pig.
speer v. spear; (werp—) javelin.
speervormig b. n. spear-shaped; (Pl.) hastate.
speerwerpen o. javelin throwing.
spek o. (vers) pork; (gezouten, gerookt) bacon.
spekslager m. pork-butcher.
speksteen m. soap-stone, steatite.
spektafel o. hubbub, racket.
spekvet o. bacon fat, lard.
spel o. play; performance; (ton.) acting; (op instrument) playing, execution; (aan speeltafel) gambling; (kaarten, enz.) pack; (volgens spelregels) game; (op foor, kermis) show, booth.
spelbederver m. mar-game, spoil-sport, kill-joy.
speld v. pin.
speldenkoker m. needle-case, pin-case.
speldenkussen o. pin-cushion.
speldenwerk o. lace-work.
speldeprik m. pin-prick.
spelen on. w. (alg.) play; (voor geld) game, gamble; o. w. play.
speler m. player; (gokker) gambler, gamester; (muz.) fiddler, musician; (ton.) performer, actor.
spelevaren on. w. **gaan —,** go out boating, go out for a sail.
spelfout v. spelling-mistake.
speling v. play, tolerance.
spelkunst v. orthography.
spelleider m. games master, games teacher, game-instructor.
spellen o. w. en on. w. spell.
spelling v. spelling, orthography.
spelonk v. cave, cavern, grotto.
spelregel m. (v. spelling) spelling-rule, rule for spelling; (v. een spel) rule of the game, playing-rule.
spenen o. w. wean, ablactate.
sperboom m. barrier, bar.
sperren o. w. bar, block up.
spervuur o. barrage, curtain-fire.
sperwer m. sparrow-hawk.
speurder m. sleuth.
speuren o. w. trace, track.
speurzin m. flair, nose.
spichtig b. n. lank, weedy; (v. haar) spiky.
spichtigheid v. lankness; weediness.
spie v. pin, peg, wedge; o. (cent) cent; (geld) oof.
spieden on. w. spy.
spiegel m. glass, looking-glass; (groot)

mirror; (gen.) speculum; (sch.) stern, escutcheon; (v. zee: oppervlak) surface, level.

spiegelei o. fried egg.

spiegelen on. w. shine; reflect; w. w. **zich —**, look in a looking-glass, look at oneself in the glass.

spiegelfabriek v. looking-glass factory.

spiegelgevecht o. sham-fight, mock-fight, mimic battle.

spiegelhars o. en v. colophony.

spiegeling v. reflection.

spiegelkast v. mirrored cupboard, mirror-fronted wardrobe.

spiegelzaal v. hall of mirrors, mirrored room.

spier v. muscle; (Pl.) spire, shoot, blade; (Dk.: vogel) martlet; (sch.) boom, spar.

spiering v. smelt.

spierkracht v. muscular strength, muscle, muscularity.

spierkramp v. muscular spasm.

spiernaakt b. n. stark naked, naked to the buff.

spierpijn v. muscular pain(s).

spierstelsel o. muscular system.

spierverrekking v. sprain.

spies v. spear, lance, javelin, pike.

spijbelen on. w. play truant, play the wag.

spijker m. nail.

spijkerboor v. gimlet

spijkeren o w. nail.

spijkerkist v. nail-box.

spijkerschrift o. cuneiform characters (writing), nail headed characters.

spijkervast b. n. nailed.

spijs v. food; fare.

spijshuis o. restaurant.

spijskaart v. menu, bill of fare.

spijskamer v. pantry.

spijsvertering v. digestion.

spijt v. regret; **— hebben van,** regret, be sorry for.

spijten onp. w. **het spijt mij,** I am sorry (for it).

spijtig b. n. (bw.) spiteful(ly); **het is — dat...,** it is a pity that, it is to be regretted that.

spijzen o. w. feed, give to eat.

spijziging v. feeding, giving to eat.

spikkel m. spot, speck, stain.

spikkelig b. n. speckled.

spiksplinternieuw b. n. spick-and-span-new, brand-new.

spil v. spindle, pivot; (as) axis, axle; (v. wenteltrap) newel; (sp.: voetb.) centre; o. (sch.: windas) capstan, windlass.

spillebeen m. en v spindle-leg, spindle-shank; (persoon) spindle-legged person, spindle-shanks

spilziek b. n. wasteful, prodigal, extravagant, thriftless.

spilzucht v. prodigality, extravagance.

spin v. spider.

spinazie v. spinage, spinach.

spinnen o. w. spin; (v. tabak) twist;

on. w. (op spinmachine) spin; (v. kat) purr.

spinnerij v. spinning-mill.

spinneweb o. cobweb.

spinnewiel o. spinning-wheel.

spint o. sap-wood; (wet.) alburnum.

spion m. spy; (spiegeltje) spy-mirror, spying-mirror.

spionage v. spying, espionage.

spioneren on. w. spy, play the spy.

spiraal v. spiral, spiral line, helix.

spiraalboor v. twist drill.

spiraaldaling v. (v. vliegtuig) spiral-dive.

spiritist m. spiritist, spiritualist.

spiritualiën v. mv. (ardent) spirits, spirituous liquors, alcoholic liquors.

spiritus m. spirits.

spirituslampje o. spirit lamp.

spit o. (braadspit) spit; (reumatische pijn) lumbago, crick (in the back); (spadevol) spadeful.

spits b. n. pointed, sharp, spiry; bw. pointedly.

spits v. point; (v. toren) spire; (spits torentje) pinnacle; (v. leger) point, van-guard; (v. berg) top, summit, peak; (v. speer) point, (spear)head.

spits o. **het — afbijten,** bear the brunt of the battle (of the fight, of the fighting).

spits m. (hond) spitz, Pomeranian dog.

spitsboef m. rascal, rogue, scoundrel.

spitsboog m. pointed arch, Gothic arch, ogive.

spitsbroeder m. brother in arms, comrade.

spitsen o. w. point, sharpen; **zijn oren —,** prick one's ears; w. w. **zich — op,** set one's heart on, look forward to, be agog on.

spitsheid v. pointedness, sharpness.

spitsmuis v. shrew-mouse, shrew.

spitsneus m. pointed nose.

spitsroede v. gantlope.

spitsvondig b. n. subtle, cavilling, hair-splitting, quibbling.

spitsvondigheid v. subtleness, quibble, subtilization, trifling, distinction; **spitsvondigheden,** subtleties, quiddities.

spitszuil v. obelisk.

spitten o. w. en on. w. dig, spade.

spleet v. cleft, fissure, chink, crevice.

splijten o. w. split, cleave, rend, rive; on. w. split, fissure, get slit up.

splijting v. cleavage, split.

splijtzwam v. fission fungus; (wet.) schizomycete; (fig.) disintegrant, seed(s) of disruption.

splinter m. splinter, shiver, spall.

splinteren on. w. splinter, shiver.

splinternieuw b. n. spick-and-span-new, brand-new.

spliterwten v. mv. split peas(e).

splitsen o. w. split (up), divide; (v. touw) splice; w. w. **zich —,** split (up), divide; (v. weg, enz. ook:) bifurcate.

splitsing v. splitting (up), division;

bifurcation; (v. touw) splicing; (fig.) dis-integration, disruption, split.

spoed m. (haast) speed, speediness, haste, expedition; (tn.: v. schroef) pitch, travelling; (mil.: v. vuurwapen) twist.

spoedbestelling v. (post) express delivery; (H.) rush order, short notice order.

spoedeisend b. n. urgent, pressing.

spoeden on. w. en w. w. **zich —,** speed, hasten, hurry.

spoedig b. n. speedy, quick; bw. soon, speedily, quickly; **zo — mogelijk,** as soon as possible.

spoel v. spool, shuttle, bobbin; (radio) coil; (v. veer) quill.

spoelbak m. rinsing-tub, washing-tub, wash-up; (fot.) washer, washing-trough.

spoeldrank m. gargle.

spoelen o. w. (op klossen winden) spool; (reinigen, wassen) wash, rinse.

spoeling v. hog-wash, pig-wash, draff, swillings.

spoelwater o. wash, slops, dish-water.

spoken on. w. haunt, walk.

sponde v. couch, bed, bedside.

sponning v. rabbet, groove; (v. schuif-raam) runway.

spons v. sponge.

spook o. ghost, phantom, spectre; (persoon) freak, toad, horror; (fig.) bogey.

spookachtig b. n. ghostly, spectral, spooky.

spookgestalte v. spectre, phantom.

spookhuis o. haunted house.

spookschip o. spectre-ship.

spoor v. (v. ruiter) spur; (v. haan) ergot; (v. bloem) calcar, spur; (bij bedekt-bloeienden) spore; (v. affuit) spade; (v. mast) step.

spoor o. (v. voet) footmark, footprint, trace, track; (v. wild) scent; (v. haas) prick; (v. hert) slot; (v. wagen) rut, track; (overblijfsel) trace, vestige; (trein, spoorweg) railway, rails, track; (sch.: v. mast) step.

spoorbaan v. railway, railroad.

spoorboekje o. (railway) time-table, railway-guide.

spoordijk m. railway-embankment.

spoorkaartje o. railway-ticket.

spoorloos b. n. trackless; bw. trackless-ly, without a trace, leaving no trace.

spoorslag m. spur, incitement, incentive, stimulus.

spoorslags bw. at full speed, in full galop, hot foot.

spoorstaaf v. rail.

spoorweg m. railway, railroad.

spoorwegbeambte m. railway official, railway employee.

spoorweggids m. railway-guide, (railway) time-table.

spoorwegligger m. (railway-)sleeper.

spoorwegnet o. railway-system, net-work of railways.

spoorwegovergang m. level crossing.

spoorwegrijtuig o. railway-carriage.

spoorwegverkeer o. railway-traffic.

spoorwegwachter m. signal-man, gate-keeper; (wisselwachter) pointsman.

spoorwegwerker m. surface-man.

sporen on. w. go by rail(way), rail it, train it.

sport v. (v. stoel) rail, rundle; (v. ladder) rung, round.

sport v. sport.

sporthemd o. sports-shirt.

sportnieuws o. sporting-news.

sportterrein o. sports-ground, sports-field.

sporttrui v. sweater, jersey.

spot m. mockery, derision, ridicule, scoff.

spotachtig b. n. mocking, scoffing, derisive.

spotgoedkoop b. n. dirt-cheap, dog-cheap; bw. dirt-cheap, at a derisory price.

spotlach m. mocking laugh, jeering laugh, jeer.

spotprent v. caricature.

spotprijs m. nominal price, laughter price, rockbottom price.

spotten on. w. mock, scoff, jeer.

spotter m. mocker, scoffer.

spotternij v. mockery, derision, jeering, taunt.

spotvogel m. (Dk.) mocking-bird; (fig.) mocker, scoffer.

spotwoord o. derisive word, scoff, taunt.

spraak v. speech, language.

spraakkunst v. grammar.

spraakleer v. grammar.

spraakvermogen o. power of speech.

spraakverwarring v. confusion of tongues, babel (of tongues).

spraakwending v. turn of speech.

spraakzaam b. n. talkative, loquacious, conversable, gossipy.

spraakzaamheid v. talkativeness, lo-quacity.

sprake v. **daarvan kan geen — zijn,** that is out of the question; **ter — brengen,** bring forward.

sprakeloos b. n. speechless, dumb, tonguetied.

sprakeloosheid v. speechlessness, dumbness.

sprank v. spark.

spreekbeurt v. turn to speak; speaking engagement, lecture.

spreekbuis v. speaking-tube, con-versation-tube; (fig.) mouth-peice, channel of communication.

spreekhoorn m. (roeper, spreektrompet) speaking-trumpet; (voor hardhorenden) ear-trumpet.

spreekkamer v. (bij particulier) parlour; (bij dokter, enz.) consulting-room, con-sultation-room; (in klooster) parlour, visiting parlour, locutory.

spreektaal v. spoken language.

spreekuur o. (v. dokter) consulting-hour; (v. advocaat, hoofd v. school) office-hour.

spreekwoord *o.* proverb, adage.
spreeuw *m.* starling.
sprei *v.* bed-spread, coverlet, counterpane.
spreiden *o. w.* spread.
spreiding *v.* (*mil.*) dispersion.
spreken *o. w. en on. w.* speak; talk; *z. n., o.* **onder het —,** while talking.
sprekend *b. n.* speaking.
spreker *m.* (*alg.*) speaker; (*redenaar*) orator.
sprengen *o. w.* sprinkle.
sprenkel *v.* (*vlekje, spat*) speck; (*vonk*) spark, sparkle.
sprenkelen *o. w.* sprinkle; (*v. strijkgoed*) damp.
sprenkeling *v.* sprinkling.
spreuk *v.* motto, aphorism, maxim, apothegm; (*spreekwoord*) proverb.
spriet *m.* (*Pl.*) blade; (*Dk.: vogel*) corn-crake, land-rail; (*v. insekt*) feeler, antenna; (*sch.*) sprit.
springbok *m.* tupping-ram; (*gymnastiek*) vaulting-buck.
springbron *v.* spring, fountain.
springen *on. w.* (*v. mens, dier*) spring, bound, jump, leap; (*v. handen*) chap; (*uiteenspringen: v. granaat, enz.*) burst, explode; (*v. band*) burst; (*v. fontein*) spout; (*v. glas*) crack, burst, spring; (*v. snaar*) break, snap; (*fig.: v. handelshuis*) burst up, go smash.
springer *m.* leaper, jumper, springer.
springgranaat *v.* high-explosive shell.
springlading *v.* (*mil.: in granaat*) bursting-charge; (*voor rots*) blasting-charge.
springlevend *b. n.* fully alive, alive and kicking.
springpaard *o.* jumper, jumping-horse; (*bij gymnastiek*) vaulting-horse; (*sch.*) stirrup of the foot-ropes.
springplank *v.* spring-board, jumping-board.
springslot *o.* spring-lock, snap-lock.
springstof *v.* explosive.
springstok *m.* leaping-pole, jumping-pole.
springtij *o.* spring-tide, spring.
springtouw *o.* skipping-rope.
springveren *b. n.* **— matras,** spring mattress, spring-bed.
springzeil *o.* safety-sheet, jumping-sheet.
sprinkhaan *m.* grass-hopper, locust.
sproeien *o. w.* sprinkle, water.
sproeiwagen *m.* water-cart, hydraulic van, street-sprinkler.
sproet *v.* freckle.
sprokkelen *o. w.* gather, pick (up).
sprokkelhout *o.* dead wood, dry sticks.
sprokkeling *v.* gathering of dead wood, wood-gathering, wood-picking; **—en,** (*fig.*) gleanings.
sprokkelmaand *v.* February.
sprong *m.* leap, jump, spring, bound, gambol, caper; (*fig.*) leap, jump, skip; (*muz.*) skip; (*beentje: hazesprong*) hock.

sprookje *o.* fairy-tale, nursery-tale.
sprookjesachtig *b. n.* fairy-like.
sprot *v.* sprat.
spruit *v.* sprout, shoot, offshoot, scion, sprig; (*fig.*) offshoot, scion, sprig.
spruiten *on. w.* sprout, shoot.
spruitjes *o. mv.* sprouts.
spruitkool *v.* sprouts, sprout-cabbage.
spruw *v.* thrush, aphta.
spuien *on. w.* sluice; (*fig.*) ventilate, let in fresh air; *o. w.* (*H.*) unload.
spuigat *o.* scupper, scupper-hole.
spuit *v.* syringe, squirt; (*brand—*) fire-engine; (*voor naaimachine, enz.*) oiler; (*sl.: paraplu*) brolly, gamp; (*mil.: geweer*) shooting-iron, gas-pipe.
spuiten *o. w. en on. w.* spout, squiet, spurt, spirt.
spuitgast *m.* hose-man, fire-man, engine-man.
spuitwater *o.* aerated water, soda-water.
spul *o.* (*goedje*) stuff; (*kermistent*) booth, show; (*last, moeite*) trouble.
spurrie *v.* spurry.
spurten *on. w.* spurt, sprint.
sputteren *on. w.* sputter, splutter.
spuwbak *m.* spittoon, spitbox.
spuwen *o. w.* (*uitspuwen*) spit; (*braken*) vomit; spew, spue; *on. w.* spit; vomit, spew, spue.
staaf *v.* (*v. ijzer*) bar; (*v. goud*) ingot; (*v. hout*) stick, stave.
staafgoud *o.* gold in bars, bar-gold.
staak *m.* stake, pole, picket.
staal *o.* (*metaal*) steel; (*gen.*) steel, iron; (*monster*) sample, specimen, pattern.
staalboek *o.* (*H.*) sample-book, pattern-book, design-book, sampler.
staalfabriek *v.* steel-works.
staalhard *b. n.* (*as*) hard as steel.
staalpil *v.* steel pill.
staaltje *o.* sample, specimen; (*fig.*) sample, specimen, piece.
staan *on. w.* stand, be; (*staan blijven, stilstaan*) stop; (*v. kleren, enz.: passen*) become, fit; **laten —,** let alone.
staand *b. n.* standing; (*v. boord*) stand-up.
staangeld *o.* (*waarborg*) deposit; (*op markt*) stallage.
staanplaats *v.* stand; (*voor taxi's, rijtuigen*) cab-stand; standing-room.
staar *v.* cataract; **zwarte —,** amaurosis.
staart *m.* (*v. dier, vlieger, enz.*) tail; (*v. konijn, haas*) scut, tail; (*v. Chinees: vlecht*) pigtail, queue; (*v. affuit*) trail.
staartster *v.* comet.
staartstuk *o.* (*v. rund*) rump(-piece); (*v. viool*) tail-piece; (*v. kanon*) breech-piece.
staartvlak *o.* (*vliegt.*) tail-plane.
staat *m.* (*land*) state; (*toestand*) state, condition; (*rang*) rank; (*lijst*) list, statement, tabular statement.
staathuishoudkunde *v.* political economy.

staatkunde *v. (alg.)* politics; *(bepaald beleid)* policy.
staatsambt *o.* public office, government employment.
staatsbank *v.* national bank.
staatsbegroting *v.* budget.
staatsbetrekking *v.* government-office.
staatsblad *o.* Statute Book.
staatsburger(es) *m. (v.)* citizen.
staatsexamen *o.* government examination.
staatsfondsen *o. mv.* government securities, government stock.
staatsgreep *m.* coup d'état.
staatsie *v.* state, pomp, ceremony; *(plechtige optocht, stoet)* procession, cortège.
staatsiekleed *o.* state-robes, robes of state, court-dress.
staatsinkomsten *v. mv.* public revenue.
staatskas *v.* public exchequer, (public) treasury.
staatslening *v.* state loan, public loan.
staatsman *m.* statesman.
staatsminister *m.* minister of state.
staatsmisdadiger *m.* political offender.
staatsraad *m. (raad van State)* Privy Council; *(lid van die raad)* Privy Councillor.
staatsrecht *o.* constitutional law.
staatsregeling *v.* constitution.
staatsschuld *v.* public debt, national debt.
staatsuitgaven *v. mv.* public expenditure.
staatsverraad *o.* high treason.
stabiel *b. n.* stable, stationary, steady.
stabiliteit *v.* stability.
stad *v. (alg.)* town; *(grote —)* city.
stadgenoot *m.* fellow-citizen, fellow-townsman.
stadhouder *m. (gesch.)* stadtholder.
stadhuis *o.* town hall, city hall.
stadhuiswoord *o.* official term, learned word.
stads *b. n.* townish.
stadsbestuur *o.* municipality.
stadsleven *o.* town-life, urban life.
stadsmensen *m. mv.* townsfolk, townspeople.
stadsnieuws *o.* town-news, local news.
stadsreiniging *v.* (municipal) scavengering.
stadswijk *v.* quarter of a (the) town, ward.
staf *m.* staff; *(teken v. waardigheid)* mace, staff; *(v. bisschop)* crosier; *(fig.)* staff, prop.
stafofficier *m.* staff-officer, officer on the staff.
stafrijm *o.* alliteration.
stag *o. (sch.)* stay; **over — gaan,** *(sch.)* stay, go about; *(fig.)* change one's tack, try another tack.
staken *o. w. (v. betaling, enz.)* stop,

suspend; *(v. werk)* strike; *on. w.* cease, stop, leave off; *(in staking gaan)* go on strike; be out on strike.
staker *m.* striker.
staketsel *o.* palisade, fence, trellis-fence, railing.
staking *v. (v. werk)* cessation; *(bij werkstaking)* strike; *(v. betaling)* suspension, stoppage; *(v. rechtsgeding, enz.)* discontinuance; **in — zijn,** be out (on strike).
stakker(d) *m.* poor devil, poor fellow; *(v. vrouw, kind)* poor thing, poor creature.
stal *m. (paarden—)* stable; *(vee—)* cow-house, cow-shed, byre; *(varkens —)* sty; *(schapen—)* fold.
stalen *o. w.* steel, steelify; *(fig.)* steel, harden, brace.
stalen *b. n.* steel, of steel; *(fig.)* steel, steely, iron.
staljongen *m.* stable-boy, stable-man.
stalknecht *m.* stableman, groom.
stallen *o. w. (v. paarden, enz.)* stable; *(v. vee)* house, stall; *(v. auto, enz.)* garage, stable, put up.
stalles *v. mv.* stalls.
stalling *v.* stable, stabling; *(het stallen)* stabling.
stalmeester *m.* master of the horse, equerry.
stalmest *m.* stable-dung, stable-manure, farmyard-manure.
stalwacht *v.* stable-guard.
stam *m. (alg.: v. boom, woord, enz.)* stem; *(v. boom)* trunk, bole; *(afstamming, geslacht)* stock, race; *(onder één hoofd)* tribe.
stamboek *o. (v. persoon)* book of genealogy, genealogical register; *(mil.)* regimental roll; *(v. paarden)* stud-book; *(v. vee)* herd-book; *(v. schapen)* flock-book.
stamboeknummer *o. (mil.)* regimental number.
stamboom *m.* family tree, genealogical tree, pedigree.
stamelen *on. w.* stammer, stutter; *o. w.* stammer (out), stutter (out), falter.
stamgast *m.* regular customer, habitué.
stamhout *o.* trunk-wood, standing timber.
stamhuis *o.* dynasty.
stamklinker *m.* radical vowel.
stammen *on. w. — van,* descend from, be descended from.
stampen *on. w. (met voet)* stamp, tramp; *(v. schip)* pitch, plunge; *(v. machine)* thud; *o. w. (aardappelen)* mash; *(fijn—)* pound, bruise, bray; *(v. goud)* crush.
stamper *m. (persoon, voorwerp)* stam, per; *(v. vijzel)* pounder, pestle; *(v. kanon)* rammer; *(straatstamper)* rammer; paving-beetle; *(v. bloem)* pistil.
stamppot *m.* hotchpot.
stampvol *b. n.* crowded, crammed, chockfull, packed (to suffocation).

stamtafel v. genealogical table; (in café, enz.) habitués' table.

stamverwant b. n. cognate; (gram.) paronymous, cognate; **—e woorden,** paronyms; z. n., m. congener.

stamwapen o. family arms.

stamwoord o. primitive word, radical word, stem.

stand m. (houding) attitude, posture, pose; (bij gymnastiek) position; (bij golf, biljart, enz.) stance; (hoogte: r. barometer, water, enz.) height; (ligging) position, situation, location; (toestand) condition, situation, state; (rang in de maatschappij) standing, position, station, rank; (v. maan) phase; (v. partijen bij verkiezing) state; (bij spel) scores; **de burgerlijke —,** the registrar's office; **de hogere —en,** the higher classes, the upper classes.

standaard m. standard; (sch.) board pendant.

standbeeld o. statue.

standje o. (berisping, verwijt) blow-up, blowing-up, scolding, rowing; (herrie) scene, row, shindy, riot, affray.

standplaats v. (alg.) standing-place, stand; (v. ambtenaar) station, post (of duty); (v. taxi, huurrijtuig) stand, cabstand; (v. venter, enz.) pitch.

standpunt o. point of view, standpoint.

standrecht o. summary justice, drumhead court-martial.

standvastig b. n. steadfast, firm, constant.

standvastigheid v. steadfastness, firmness, constancy.

stang v. (tn.) bar, rod, pole; (v. tramwagen, enz.) stanchion; (voor vogels, enz.) perch; (aan gebit v. paard) bridlebit.

stank m. stink, stench, bad smell.

stap m. step; pace, stride.

stapel m. (hoop) pile, stack, heap; (sch.) stocks; launching-berth; (v. strijkinstrument) sound; (stapelplaats) staple.

stapelen o. w. pile (up), heap, stack.

stapelgek b. n. stark mad, raving mad, as mad as a hatter, as mad as a March hare.

stapelhuis o. warehouse.

stapelplaats v. emporium, mart.

stappen on. w. step; (met grote passen) stride, stalk.

stapvoets bw. at a foot-pace, at a walking-pace; (stap voor stap) step by step, pace for pace.

starogen on. w. stare.

startbaan v. runway.

starten on. w. start.

statenbond m. confederation (of states).

Staten-Generaal m. mv. States General.

statie v. (kruiswegstatie) Station of the Cross; (Z. N.: station) station.

statig b. n. stately, solemn, grave,

dignified; bw. in a stately manner, solemnly

statigheid v. stateliness, solemnity, gravity.

station o. station.

stationschef m. station-master.

statistiek v. statistics.

statuut o. statute.

staven o. w. (v. mening) confirm, bear out; (v. beschuldiging) substantiate; (v. eis, enz.) support, authenticate.

staving v. confirmation, substantiation.

stede v. (dicht.) stead, place.

stedeling m. townsman, town-dweller, city-dweller; **—en,** townspeople citizens.

stedenaanleg m. town-planning.

steeds bw. always, ever, continually; **nog —,** still; **— meer,** ever more.

steeg v. lane, alley.

steeg b. n. restive.

steek m. (met speld, enz.) prick; (v. breiwerk) stitch; (v. zwaard) thrust; (v. dolk) stab; (v. wesp) sting; (v. pijn) stitch, twitch, pang; (hoed) cocked hat, three-cornered hat; (fig.: hatelijke toespeling) dig, gird, prod.

steekbeitel m. paring-chisel, ripping-chisel.

steekhoudend b. n. valid, sound, solid.

steekpenning m. hush-money, bribe.

steekvlam v. blow-torch, blow-pipe flame, thin flame.

steel m. (handvat) handle; (r. bloem, vrucht) stalk; (v. bloem, pijp) stem; (v. bijl) helve, shaft.

steelsgewijze bw. stealthily, by stealth.

steen m. (alg.) stone; (bak—) brick; (v. vrucht) stone, kernel; (in dominospel) stone, piece, domino; (dobbel—) die; (gen.: ziekte) stone, calculus.

steenachtig b. n. stony; (wet.) petrous.

steenbakker m. brick-maker.

steenbakkerij v. brick-works, brickyard, brick-field.

steenbok m. ibex; (Z. A.) stone-bock; (sterr.) Capricorn.

steendruk m. lithography.

steeneik m. holm-oak.

steengroeve v. stone-quarry, stonepit.

steenhouwer m. stone-cutter, stonemason, stone-dresser.

steenkolen v. mv. coal, pit-coal.

steenkolengruis o. coal-dust.

steenkolenmijn v. coal-mine, coalworks, colliery.

steenpuist v. boil, phlegmon.

steenrots v. rock.

steentijdperk o. stone-age.

steenuil m. church-owl, barn-owl.

steenvalk m. stone-falcon, stone-hawk.

steenvrucht v. stone-fruit, drupe.

steenweg m. paved road, causeway.

steenworp m. stone's throw, stone-cast.

steenzout o. rock-salt.

steenzwaluw v. swift.

steiger m. (aan huis) scaffolding, scaffold, staging, stage; (aanlegplaats) pier, jetty, landing-stage, landing-bridge.

steigeren *on. w.* rear, rear and plunge, prance.

steil *b. n.* (*naar boven*) steep; (*naar beneden*) bluff; (*loodrecht*) sheer; (*zeer steil, loodrecht en vlak*) precipitous; (*sch.: v. kust*) steep-to; (*fig.: star, vasthoudend*) dogmatic, rigid, uncompromising, hard-shell; stiff-necked.

steilheid *v.* steepness, etc.

stek *v.* (*Pl.*) slip, cutting, set.

stekeblind *b. n.* stone-blind, bat-blind, stark blind.

stekel *m.* (*v. distel, insekt, enz.*) prick, prickle, sting; (*v. doorn*) point; (*v. egel*) spine, quill.

stekelbaars *v.* stickleback.

stekelbes *v.* gooseberry.

stekelhuidigen *m. mv.* echinoderms.

stekelvarken *o.* porcupine.

stekelvinnigen *m. mv.* spiny-finned fishes.

steken *o. w.* (*met speld, angel, enz.*) sting, prick; (*met zwaard, enz.*) thrust; (*met dolk*) stab; (*H.: monsters*) draw; (*ergens in*) put, stick; *on. w.* (*v. insekt*) sting; (*v. brandnetel, enz.*) prick; (*v. wond*) smart, tingle; (*v. likdoorn*) shoot; (*v. zon*) burn; *w. w.* **zich in schulden** —, run in the debt.

stekend *b. n.* stinging; smarting; shooting; burning.

stekken *o. w.* slip, set.

stekker *m.* (*el.*) plug, wall-plug.

stel *o.* set; (*v. wagen*) undercarriage.

stelen *o. w.* steal; (*gappen*) pilfer; *on. w.* steal, thieve.

stelkunde *v.* algebra.

stellen *o. w.* (*plaatsen*) place, put; (*regelen*) adjust, regulate; (*v. prijs: vaststellen*) fix; (*richten: v. camera*) focus; (*v. kanon*) lay, train; (*v. vraag*) pose, put; (*veronderstellen, aannemen*) suppose; (*v. kandidaten: voordragen*) put forward; *on. w.* compose; *w. w.* **zich** —, place (put) oneself, take one's stand.

stellig *b. n.* (*v. antwoord, bewijs*) positive; (*v. verklaring*) explicit; (*v. hoop, verwachting*) sure and certain; *bw.* positively; explicitly.

stelling *v.* (*te bewijzen waarheid: thesis*) theorem; thesis; (*wisk.*) proposition; (*steiger, stellage*) scaffolding; (*mil.: plaatsing, opstelling*) position; (*vesting*) fortifications.

stellingoorlog *m.* position warfare, war of positions, trench war(fare).

steloefening *v.* exercise in correct writing.

stelpen *o. w.* staunch, stanch, stop.

stelregel *m.* maxim, precept, (fixed) rule.

stelsel *o.* system.

stelselmatig *b. n.* (*bw.*) systematical(ly).

stelt *v.* stilt.

steltloper *m.* (*persoon*) stilt-walker,

stilter; (*vogel*) stilt-bird, stilt-walker, stilter, grallatorial bird.

stem *v.* voice; (*bij stemming, verkiezing*) vote; (*v. muziekstuk*) part.

stembanden *m. mv.* vocal chords.

stembiljet *o.* voting-paper, ballot-paper.

stembuiging *v.* modulation, intonation, inflection.

stembus *v.* ballot-box, poll.

stemgerechtigd *b. n.* entitled to a (the) vote, qualified to vote, enfranchised.

stemgerechtigde *m.* person entitled to the vote; voter, elector.

stemmen *o. w.* (*v. kandidaat*) vote; (*v. viool*) tune; (*v. orgelpijpen*) voice, key up; *on. w.* vote, poll, ballot; (*v. orkest*) tune up; attune; (*v. instrumenten*) accord, be in tune.

stemmig *b. n.* (*v. persoon*) grave, sedate, demure, staid; (*v. kleding, enz.*) quiet, sober.

stemmigheid *v.* gravity, sedateness, demureness; quietude, sobriety.

stemming *v.* voting, vote; ballot; (*in parlement*) division; (*muz.*) tuning; (*v. beurs, markt*) tone; (*gemoeds—*) disposition, mood, frame of mind, humour; (*v. publiek*) general sentiment.

stemopnemer *m.* (*bij verkiezing*) polling-clerk, scrutineer; (*in parlement*) teller.

stemopneming *v.* counting of votes.

stempel *m.* (*voor naam, datum, enz.*) stamp, mark; (*voor munten, enz.*) die; (*afdruk*) impress, imprint, stamp; (*post—*) postmark; (*v. bloem*) stigma; (*keur*) hall-mark.

stempelband *m.* cloth binding.

stempelen *o. w.* stamp, mark; postmark; hall-mark; *on. w.* (*v. werkloze*) sign the (unemployment) register.

stempelkussen *o.* stamp pad, inking pad.

stemplicht *m.* compulsory voting.

stemrecht *o.* (*bij verkiezing*) suffrage, vote, franchise; (*in vergadering, enz.*) right to vote, vote.

stemverandering *v.* breaking of the voice, mutation.

stemvork *v.* tuning-fork.

stenen *on. w.* moan, groan.

stengel *m.* stalk, stem; (*v. blad, ook:*) petiole.

stenigen *o. w.* stone (to death), lapidate.

steniging *v.* stoning, lapidation.

stenograaf *m.* stenographer, shorthand-writer.

stenotypist(e) *m.* (*v.*) shorthand typist.

steppe *v.* steppe.

ster *v.* star.

sterfbed *o.* death-bed, dying-bed.

sterfelijk *b. n.* mortal.

sterfelijkheid *v.* mortality.

sterfgeval *o.* death, decease.

sterfhuis *o.* house of a deceased person, house of mourning.

sterfte v. mortality.
sterftecijfer o. (rate of) mortality, death-rate.
steriliseren o. w. sterilize.
sterk b. n. strong, robust, firm; (v. el. stroom, bril, enz.) powerful; (v stijging of daling) sharp; (v. wind) high; (v. boter: ranzig) strong, rancid.
sterken o. w. strengthen, fortify, invigorate.
sterkte v. strength; (v. lens) power; (bolwerk, vesting) stronghold, fortress.
sterkwater o. aqua fortis, spirits.
sterrebaan v. orbit (course) of a star.
sterrenbeeld o. constellation.
sterrenhemel m. starry sky.
sterrenkijker m. (instrument) telescope; (persoon) star-gazer.
sterrenkunde v. astronomy.
sterrenkundige m. astronomer.
sterrenwacht v. (astronomical) observatory.
sterrenwichelaar m. astrologer.
sterretje o. little star; asterisk, star; (mil.) pip.
sterveling m. mortal.
sterven on. w. die, expire; o. w. **duizend doden —,** taste death a thousand times.
stervend b. n. dying, sinking, moribund.
stervensuur o. dying-hour, hour of death.
steun m. support, prop; (fig.) stay, stand-by, support, prop.
steunbalk m. supporting beam, summer.
steuncomité o. relief committee.
steunen o. w. support, prop; (fig.: v. persoon) support, uphold, stand by; (moed geven) bear up; (v. zaak, instelling: kunstmatig staande houden) bolster up, buttress; (moreel steunen) countenance; (motie in parlement) second, support; on. w. support oneself, lean.
steunfonds o. relief-fund.
steunpilaar m. pillar; (fig.) pillar, supporter, stand-by.
steunpunt o. point of support; (v. hefboom) fulcrum; (mil.) supporting-point.
steur m. sturgeon; (kleine) sterlet.
steven m. prow, stem.
stevenen on. w. steer, sail, set sail.
stevig b. n. (v. persoon) strong, sturdy, well-knit, well set-up; (v. zaken) solid, strong; (v. voeding, maaltijd, enz.) substantial; (v. karton, plank, enz.) stout; (v. paal, enz.) firm; bw. strongly, solidly, etc.
stevigheid v. strongness; solidity; substantiality; stoutness; firmness; sturdiness.
sticht o. bishopric; (klooster) convent.
stichtelijk b. n. edifying; devout.
stichten o. w. (v. zaak, kerk) found, establish; (v. kolonie) plant, found; (v. fonds) raise, start; (v. keizerrijk) build up; (toehoorders, in kerk, enz.) edify; (v. vrede) make; on. w. edify.
stichting v. (oprichting) foundation;

(inrichting) institution, institute, foundation, alms-house; (v. hoorders, enz.) edification.
stiefbroeder m. step-brother.
stiefmoeder v. step-mother.
stiefmoederlijk b. n. step-motherly.
stiefvader m. step-father.
stiefzoon m. step-son.
stiefzuster v. step-sister.
stiekem b. n. underhand; bw. on the sly, stealingly, on the quiet, in secret, secretly.
stier m. (Dk.) bull; (sterr.: in Dierenriem) Taurus.
stierenvechter m. bull-fighter.
stift v. peg, pin, point; (hoofdpijn—) pencil; (graveer—) burin.
stijf b. n. stiff; (v. luchtschip) rigid; (fig.) stiff, starchy, starched; (v. markt) firm; bw. stiffly.
stijfheid v. stiffness; rigidity; starchiness.
stijfhoofdig b. n. obstinate, headstrong, opiniative, mulish. [ness.
stijfhoofdigheid v. obstinacy, mulish-
stijfkop m. obstinate person, mule.
stijfsel v. starch; (om te plakken) paste.
stijfselen o. w. starch.
stijfselfabriek v. starch-factory.
stijfte v. stiffness.
stijgbeugel m. stirrup.
stijgen on. w. (v. weg, barometer, enz.) rise; (v. prijzen, enz.) rise, advance, go up, tend upwards; (v. vliegtuig) rise, climb.
stijging v. rise, rising, advance.
stijl m. (schrijfwijze, bouwtrant, tijdrekening) style; (v. deur, raam) post, jamb; (v. vliegtuig) strut; (v. lening) baluster.
stijloefening v. stylistic exercise, exercise in composition.
stijven o. w. (alg.) stiffen; (v. linnen) starch; (fig.) stiffen, harden, back up; on. w. stiffen.
stijving v. stiffening.
stikbom v. asphyxiating bomb.
stikdonker b. n. pitch-dark; pitchy; z. n., o. pitch darkness.
stikgas o. (mil.) asphyxiating-gas; (in mijn) choke-damp.
stikheet b. n. suffocating, sweltering.
stikken on. w. stifle, be stifled, choke, suffocate, be suffocated.
stikken o. w. (met garen, enz.) stitch.
stikstof v. nitrogen.
stil b. n. (zonder geluid) silent, still; (onbeweeglijk) still; (rustig) quiet; (v. zaken) slack; (v. markt) quiet, dull, flat; bw. silently; quietly.
stilhouden on. w. stop, come to a stop; (v. auto, trein, enz., ook:) pull up, draw up; o. w. **het —,** keep it quiet, hush it up; w. w. **zich —,** be quiet, keep quiet; keep silent.
stillen o. w. (v. pijn) quiet, relieve, allay, alleviate; (v. honger) appease, satisfy, check; (v. dorst) quench, allay; (v. kind) quiet, silence, still, hush; (v.

toorn) pacify; (*v. angst, geweten*) quiet.
stilletjes *bw.* silently; secretly, on the sly.
stilleven *o.* still life.
stilliggen *o. w.* (*in bed, enz.*) lie still; (*v. fabriek*) be idle, have close down; (*v. schepen*) lie idle; lie up.
stilstaan *on. w.* stand still; (*v. fabriek*) be idle; (*v. handel, enz.*) be at a stand-still, stand still; (*gestremd zijn*) stagnate.
stilstaand *b. n.* (*v. water*) stagnant, dead; (*v. klok*) stopped; (*v. trein*) standing, stationary.
stilstand *m.* standstill, stoppage; (*in zaken, enz.*) stagnation, stagnancy; (*in groei, ontwikkeling*) arrest; (*v. werk, enz.*) cessation.
stilte *v.* silence, stillness, quiet.
stilzitten *on. w.* sit still; (*fig.*) stand idle, sit still (and do nothing).
stilzwijgen *o.* silence, reticence.
stilzwijgend *b. n.* (*v. persoon*) silent, taciturn; (*v. toestemming, afspraak*) tacit; (*v. voorwaarde, verbintenis*) implied; *bw.* tacitly.
stilzwijgendheid *v.* silence, taciturnity; (*geheimhouding*) secrecy.
stinkbom *v.* stink-bomb.
stinken *on. w.* stink, smell (bad), reek.
stinkend *b. n.* stinking, reeking, evil-smelling, fetid.
stinkgranaat *v.* stink-shell.
stip *v.* point, dot.
stippelen *o. w.* stipple, point, dot, speckle.
stippellijn *v.* dotted line.
stipt *b. n.* punctual, precise, exact, accurate, prompt; *bw.* punctually, precisely, exactly.
stiptheid *v.* punctuality, precision, exactness, accuracy, promptness.
stoeien *on. w.* romp, have a game of romps.
stoel *m.* chair, seat; (*v. bisschop*) see; (*Pl.*) stool; (*v. torenklok*) frame.
stoelenzetster *v.* pew-opener.
stoelgang *m.* stool(s), motion(s).
stoelleuning *v.* chair-back.
stoep *v.* (flight of) steps, door-step; (*trottoir*) footway, pavement.
stoer *b. n.* sturdy, hardy, stalwart, strong.
stoet *m.* cortege, train, procession, retinue.
stoeterij *v.* stud, haras; stud-farm.
stof *v.* (*weefsel*) stuff, material; (*grondstof, materie*) matter; (*onderwerp*) subject-matter, theme.
stof *o.* dust, powder.
stofbezem *m.* duster, hair-broom.
stofbril *m.* goggles.
stofdoek *m.* duster, dust-cloth.
stoffelijk *b. n.* material.
stoffen *o. w.* (*stof afnemen*) dust; *on. w.* (*bluffen*) boast, brag; *b. n.* of Denmark satin.
stoffer *m.* duster, hair-broom, dusting-brush.

stofferen *o. w.* furnish, upholster, garnish; (*v. schilderij*) fill in.
stofferig, stoffig *b. n.* dusty.
stofgoud *o.* gold-dust.
stofjas *v.* dust-coat.
stofnaam *m.* (*gram.*) name of material, material noun.
stofregenen *on. w.* drizzle, mizzle.
stofvrij *b. n.* dust-proof.
stofwisseling *v.* metabolism.
stofwolk *v.* cloud of dust, dust-cloud.
stofzuiger *m.* vacuum cleaner, suction cleaner.
stok *m.* (*alg.*) stick, staff; (*wandelstok*) cane, walking-stick; (*v. vogels*) perch; (*v. kippen*) roost, perch; (*v. vlag; bij bonen, enz.*) pole; (*v. politie*) truncheon, baton; (*v. anker*) stock; (*golf—*) club, stick; (*v. kaarten*) talon; (*v. zweep*) crop; (*v. cheque, enz.*) counterfoil.
stokdoof *b. n.* stone-deaf, as deaf as a post.
stoken *o. w.* (*kolen, hout, enz.*) burn; (*v. fornuis, machine, enz.*) stoke; (*v. vuur*) make; (*v. dranken*) distil; (*fig.: kwaad; onheil*) brew; stir up; *on. w.* make a fire, have a fire in the room; (*v. stoker*) stoke; (*fig.*) stir up trouble.
stoker *m.* stoker, fireman; (*v. dranken*) distiller; (*fig.*) fire-brand.
stokerij *v.* (*v. dranken*) distillery; (*fig.*) mischief-making.
stokoud *b. n.* very old, stricken in years.
stokpaardje *o.* hobby-horse; (*fig.*) hobby, crotchet.
stokroos *v.* hollyhock, rose-mallow.
stokvis *m.* (*herring*) hake; (*gedroogde kabeljauw*) stockfish, hard fish.
stola *v.* stole.
stollen *on. w.* coagulate, congeal, curdle, set, clot.   [curdling.
stolling *v.* coagulation, congelation,
stolp *v.* cover, glass-bell, glass-shade.
stom *b. n.* (*sprakeloos*) mute, speechless, dumb; (*dom*) stupid, dull, dense.
stomen *on. w.* steam; (*walmen*) smoke; *o. w.* (*in stoom koken*) steam; (*drillen*) cram.
stomer *m.* steamer, steamship.
stomheid *v.* muteness, speechlessness, dumbness; stupidity.
stomme *m. en v.* dumb person.
stommelen *on. w.* clump, clutter, bustle, jumber.
stommerik *m.* stupid, blockhead, fat-head, dullard.
stommigheid *v.*, **stommiteit** *v.* (*abstract*) stupidness, stupidity, density; (*concreet*) stupidity, blunder, bloomer, folly.
stomp *b. n.* blunt, dull; (*v. neus*) flat, snub; (*v. hoek*) obtuse; (*fig.*) obtuse, dense; *z. n., m.* dig, punch, thump, push, bluff; *z. n., v.* (*kort, afgeknot deel*) stump, stub.
stompen *o. w.* pummel, punch, thump, push, buff.
stomphoekig *b. n.* obtuse-angled.

stompje o. (v. sigaar, potlood, enz.) stump, stub; (v. sigaar, ook:) fag-end.

stompvoet m. club-foot, stump-foot.

stompzinnig b. n. obtuse, blunt, dull.

stompzinnigheid v. obtuseness, bluntness, dullness.

stond v time, moment, hour.

stoof v. foot-warmer, foot-stove; (Z. N.: kachel) stove.

stoofpan v. stewing-pan, stew-pan, sauce-pan.

stookplaats v. fire-place, hearth; (sch.) stoke-hole, stoke-hold.

stool v. stole.

stoom m. steam.

stoomboot v. steamboat, steamer, steamship.

stoomketel m. boiler, steam-boiler.

stoomklaar b. n. under steam, in steam.

stoomschip o. steamship, steamer.

stoomwals v. steam-roller.

stoomwasserij v. steam-laundry.

stoop v. stoup.

stoornis v. disturbance, disorder.

stoot m. (duw) push; (met zwaard, enz.) thrust; (met dolk) stab; (bij schermen) lunge; (bilj.) shot, stroke; (botsing) impact; (op hoorn, enz.) blast.

stootkar v. push-cart.

stoottroepen m. mv. shock troops.

stootwapen o. thrust-weapon.

stop v. (v. fles, enz.) stopper; stopple; (in wasbekken, enz.) plug; (v. rat) bung; (in kous, enz.) darn; (el.) plug.

stopcontact o. plug-connection, plug-contact.

stopfles v. stoppered bottle, (glass-) jar.

stopgaren o. mending-cotton, darning-thread.

stopnaald v. darning-needle, darner.

stoppel m. stubble.

stoppen o. w. (een opening dichtmaken) stop (up); (met stop) plug up; (v. kousen, enz.) darn, mend; (v. lek) stop; (v. pijp) fill, load; (v. worst) fill; (met stopverf) putty (up); (wegbergen, indoen) put, on. w. (v. tram, trein, enz.) stop, halt, pull up, come to a stop; (v. spijzen) bind, constipate, make costive.

stoppend b. n. binding, constipating, astringent, obstructive.

stopverf v. putty.

stopwoord o. expletive, stop-gap.

stopzetten o. w. (v. werk, enz.) stop, put a stop to; (v. machine) shut off; (v. fabriek) close down, shut down, throw idle.

stopzetting v. stopping; (v. fabriek) stoppage, closing down, shutting down.

store v. roller blind, Venetian blind.

storen o. w. disturb; (verstoren, in de war brengen) derange, perturb; (onderbreken: v. les, verbinding, enz.) interrupt; (radio) cause interference; w. w. zich niet — aan, disregard, ride roughshod over.

storing v. disturbance, derangement, perturbation; interruption; intrusion; (v. radio) interference, jamming.

storm m. storm, gale, blast; (hevig) tempest.

stormaanval m. assault.

stormachtig b. n. stormy, tempestuous, tumultuous.

stormband m. hat-guard; (v. helm) chin-strap, cheek-strap.

stormen on. w. storm.

stormenderhand bw. by storm.

stormhoed m. (gesch.) morion.

stormklok v. alarm-bell, tocsin.

stormloop m. rush, assault, onslaught; (fig.) rush; (op bank) run.

stormlopen on. w. — op (tegen), storm, rush, assault.

stormpas m. double-quick step (pace).

stormram m. battering-ram.

stormschade v. storm-damage, gale-damage.

stormtroepen m. mv. shock-troops, storm-troops.

stormweer o. stormy weather, tempestuous weather.

stort v. tinned sheet-iron; (stortplaats) shoot, dumping-ground.

stortbad o. shower bath.

stortbui v. heavy shower, downpour, deluge of rain.

storten o. w. (ruilnis, puin) shoot, dump, tip; (bloed, tranen) shed; (melk, enz.) spill; (geld) pay in; on. w. tumble; fall down; pay in; w. w. zich — in, plunge into.

storting v. shedding; spilling; payment, deposit, contribution.

stortkar v. tumbrel, tumbril, tilt(ing)-cart.

stortplaats v. shoot, rubbish-tip, dumping ground.

stortregenen on. w. come pouring down, pour (with rain), rain cats and dogs.

stortvloed m. torrent, flood, deluge.

stortzee v. head-sea, topping sea.

stoten on. w. (alg.) push; (v. geweer) kick, recoil; (schokken) jolt, bump; (met horens) butt; (bilj.) cue; o. w. (duwen) push; (aan —) nudge; (stuk—, fijnstampen) pound; iem. van zich —, repudiate a person, cast a person off; w. w. zich —, bump oneself, knock oneself; strike one's foot; zich — aan, take offence at, be offended at, be shocked at, be scandalized by.

stotteren on. w. stammer, stutter.

stout o. stout.

stout b. n. (stoutmoedig, onversaagd) bold, daring, audacious; (ondeugend) naughty.

stoutmoedig b. n. bold, daring, undaunted.

stoutmoedigheid v. boldness, daring, temerity, courage.

stoutweg bw. boldly.

stouwen o. w. (goederen) stow; (het ruim) trim; on. w. stew, be stewing.

stoven *o. w.* stew, braise; *on. w.* stew; *w.w. zich — in de zon,* bask in the sun.
straal *m.* (*v. licht*) ray, beam; (*v. bliksem*) flash; (*v. water, enz.*) spout, jet, squirt, spurt; (*v. cirkel*) radius; (*v. paardehoef*) frog.
straalbrekend *b. n.* refractive.
straalbreking *v.* refraction.
straalbundel *m.* pencil of rays.
straat *v.* street; road; (*zee—*) straits.
straatbengel *m.* mud lark.
straatbordje *o.* name-plate (of a street).
straatcollecte *v.* street collection.
straatjongen *m.* street-boy, street-arab, gutter-snipe.
straatliedje *o.* street-song.
straatorgel *o.* street-organ, barrel-organ.
straatreiniger *m.* scavenger, street-cleaner, street-orderly.
straatsteen *m.* paving-stone.
straatveger *m.* road-sweeper, street-sweeper, scavenger.
straatventer *m.* street-vendor, street-trader, (street-)hawker.
straatvuil *o.* street-refuse, town-refuse.
straatweg *m.* highroad.
straatwerker *m.* road-maker, street-maker.
straf *b. n.* severe, stern, austere; (*v. bries, drank, enz.*) stiff, strong; *bw.* severely, sternly, austerely.
straf *v.* punishment, penalty; (*op school: strafwerk*) imposition.
strafbaar *b. n.* punishable, liable to punishment; actionable, indictable.
strafbepaling *v.* penal prescription, penal provision; (*clausule*) penalty-clause.
straffeloos *b. n.* unpunished, with impunity.
straffen *o. w.* punish; (*tuchtigen*) chastise.
strafgevangenis *v.* (criminal) prison, house of correction.
strafinrichting *v.* penal establishment, penitentiary.
strafkolonie *v.* penal settlement, convict settlement; (*voor landlopers*) tramp colony.
strafmaatregel *m.* punitive measure.
strafpeleton *o.* punishment squad.
strafplaats *v.* place of execution.
strafport(o) *o.* surcharge, additional postage.
strafportzegel *o.* (postage) due stamp.
strafrecht *o.* criminal law.
strafrechtelijk *b. n.* criminal, penal.
strafschop *m.* penalty kick.
straftijd *m.* term of imprisonment.
strafvordering *v.* criminal procedure, penal proceedings.
strafwerk *o.* imposition; (*in school te maken*) detention-work.
strafwet *v.* criminal law, penal law.
strak *b. n.* tight, stiff, taut; (*v. gelaat*) set; (*v. blik*) fixed, hard; *bw.* taut; hard, fixedly.

strakjes, straks *bw.* (*aanstonds*) presently, by and by; (*zoëven*) just now, a little while ago; *tot —!* so long!
stralen *on. w.* beam, shine, radiate; (*bij examen*) be plucked, be ploughed.
stralend *b. n.* (*bw.*) radiant(ly); (*el.*) radiating(ly).
stralenkrans *m.* nimbus, aureole.
stram *b. n.* stiff, rigid.
stramien *o.* catgut.
strand *o.* beach, sands, strand, shore.
strandbewoner *m.* inhabitant of the coast, coaster.
stranddief *m.* strand-robber, wrecker.
stranden *on. w.* strand, run aground, run ashore.
strandgoed *o.* stranded goods, wrecked goods, wreck, flotsam.
stranding *v.* stranding, grounding.
strandrecht *o.* right of wreck, right of salvage, shore-rights.
strandstoel *m.* beach-chair, (wicker) dome-chair, beehive-chair.
strategie *v.* strategy, strategics.
strategisch *b. n.* strategic(al); *bw.* strategically.
streek *v.* (*uitgestrektheid, gewest, oord*) region, district, tract, part of the country; (*v. kompas*) point, rhumb; (*met pen, potlood, enz.*) stroke; (*op viool*) bowing; (*v. penseel*) touch, stroke; *m.* (*list*) trick, artifice; (*poets*) prank, trick.
streep *v.* stripe, streak, stroke, line; (*aandachtstreep, in telegram, enz.*) dash; (*bilj.*) balk.
strekken *o. w.* stretch, extend; *on. w.* stretch, extend, reach; *w. w. zich —,* stretch oneself.
strekking *v.* tendency, purport, tenor, drift.
strelen *o. w.* stroke, caress, fondle; (*fig.*) flatter; tickle, titillate.
streling *v.* stroking, caress.
stremmen *o. w.* (*v. melk*) curdle, coagulate; (*v. bloed*) congeal; (*v. verkeer*) stop, block, obstruct, hold up; *on. w.* (*v. melk*) curd, curdle, coagulate; (*v. bloed*) congeal, coagulate.
stremsel *o.* coagulant; (*kaas—*) rennet.
streng *v.* (*v. garen*) skein; (*v. touw*) strand; (*voor paard: trektouw*) trace.
streng *b. n.* (*alg.*) severe; (*v. uiterlijk*) stern, severe; (*v. wetten*) rigid, rigorous; (*v. examen*) stiff, rigorous; (*v. controle, bewaking*) close; (*in godsdienst*) rigid, strict, observant; (*v. tucht*) strict, rigid; (*v. moraal*) austere; *bw.* severely, rigidly, strictly, etc.
strengelen *o. w.* twist, twine; *w. w. zich —,* twist, twine, wreathe; (*zich*) *in elkaar —,* intertwine.
strengheid *v.* severity; sternness; rigour; austerity.
streven *on. w.* strive; *— naar,* strive for (after), aspire to (after), aim at; *z. n., o.* ambition, aspiration, endeavour(s), efforts.

striemen o. w. weal, wale, castigate, lash.

strijd m. fight, battle, combat, struggle, conflict.

strijden on. w. fight, battle, combat, struggle, contend; dispute; — *tegen,* fight against, be opposed to, be at variance with; — *met,* fight with (against); (*fig.*) be contrary to; o. w. *de goede strijd* —, fight the good fight.

strijdend b. n. fighting, contending.

strijder m. fighter, combatant, warrior.

strijdig b. n. conflicting, contending; (*fig., ook:*) contrary, contradictory, discordant, incompatible; — *met,* contrary to, in defiance of, incompatible with, inconsistent with, clashing with.

strijdkrachten v. mv. (military) forces.

strijdlust m. combativeness, bellicosity, pugnacity, fighting spirit.

strijdlustig b. n. combative, bellicose, pugnacious, desirous of fighting.

strijdmacht v. force.

strijdmakker m. brother in arms, companion in arms.

strijdperk o. lists, arena.

strijdvaardig b. n. ready to fight, in fighting trim.

strijdvaardigheid v. readiness to fight.

strijdwagen m. chariot.

strijkbord o. (*v. ploeg*) breast-board, mould-board; (*v. metselaar*) float.

strijkconcert o. concert for strings.

strijken o. w. (*v. linnen*) iron; (*glad—*) smooth; (*v. vlag*) strike, haul down; (*v. boot, zeil*) lower; (*uitspreiden*) spread; on. w. (*met hand*) stroke; (*met voet*) shuffle; (*linnen*) iron.

strijkijzer o. smoothing-iron, flat-iron; box-iron.

strijkkwartet o. string(ed) quartette.

strijknet o. sweep-net, drag(-net).

strijkorkest o. string-band, string-orchestra. [table.

strijkplank v. ironing-board, ironing-

strijkster v. ironer.

strijkstok m. (*voor viool*) bow, fiddle-stick; (*voor maat*) strickle, strike.

strijkvuur o. (*mil.*) raking fire.

strik m. (*v. lint*) knot; (*dasje*) bow, bow-tie; (*om te vangen*) snare, wire, noose.

strikken o. w. (*v. das, enz.*) tie; (*v. vogels*) snare; (*v. hazen*) wire, gin, springe, snare; (*fig.*) ensnare, snare.

strikt b. n. strict, rigorous, exact; bw. strictly.

strikvraag v. catch-question, poser.

strippen o. w. strip, stem.

stro o. straw

strodak o thatched roof.

stroef b. n. (*v. scharnier, enz.*) stiff; (*op het gevoel*) rough, unsmooth; (*v. uiterlijk, gelaatstrekken*) harsh, rugged; (*v. manieren*) stiff; (*v. gedicht*) jerky; bw. stiffly.

strohalm m. straw, blade of straw.

strohoed m. straw-hat.

strohut v. thatched hut.

stroken on. w. — *met,* tally with, square with, agree with.

stroleger o. bed of straw, litter.

stromat v. straw mat.

stromatras v. straw mattress, paillasse.

stromen on. w. stream, flow; (*snel—*) rush.

stroming v. current; (*fig.*) drift, trend current.

strompelen on. w. stumble, hobble, totter, dodder.

stronk m. (*v. boom*) stump, stub; (*v. kool*) stalk; (*v. andijvie*) head.

strooibiljet o. handbill, throw-out, throw-away.

strooien b. n. straw.

strooien o. w. (*v. zand, as*) sprinkle; (*v. bloemen*) strew; (*v. zaad*) scatter; (*v. suiker, meel*) dredge.

strook v. (*v. land, stof, enz.*) strip; (*v. papier*) slip; (*v. kleed*) flounce, band, furbelow; (*v. postwissel, enz.*) counterfoil; (*telegr.*) tape.

stroom m. (*het stromen*) stream, current; (*rivier*) stream, river; (*el.*) current; (*berg—*) torrent; (*fig.*) flood, flow, flux, stream.

stroomafwaarts bw. downstream, down the river.

stroombreker m. (*in zee*) breakwater; (*v. brug*) starling; (*el.*) circuit-breaker, contact-breaker, interruptor.

stroomgebied o. (river-)basin.

stroomlijn v. (*v. auto, enz.*) streamline.

stroomopwaarts bw. up the river, upstream.

stroomsterkte v. strength of current.

stroomversnelling v. rapid.

stroomwisselaar m. (*el.*) commutator, switch.

stroop v. treacle; (*vruchten—*) syrup; (*suiker—*) molasses; (*fig.*) butter.

strooptocht m. predatory incursion, depredation; raid, marauding-expedition.

strop m. (*om iem. op te hangen*) halter, rope; (*voor wild*) snare, gin; (*sch.*) strop; (*stropdas*) stock; (*tn.*) link; (*v. laars*) strap.

stropen o. w. (*v. paling, enz.*) skin; (*bast v. boom, bladeren v. tak*) strip; (*v. wild*) poach; on. w. (*v. rover*) maraud, pillage; (*v. wilddief*) poach.

stropen o. w. (*met stroop*) treacle, smear with treacle.

stroper m. poacher; marauder.

strot m. throat.

strotader v. jugular vein.

strotklep v. epiglottis.

strozak m. straw-mattress, pallet.

struif v. omelet(te).

struik m. bush, shrub.

struikelblok o. stumbling-block, obstacle.

struikelen on. w. stumble, trip; *iem. doen* —, trip a person.

struikgewas o. bushes, shrubs, brushwood, scrub.

struikrover m. highwayman, footpad.

struis v. ceruse, white lead.

struis m. ostrich.

struis b. n. robust, sturdy, well set-up.

struisvogel m. ostrich.

studeerkamer v. study.

student m. student, undergraduate, college man.

studeren on. w. study, read; (aan universiteit) be at college; (muz.) practise.

studie v. (alg.) study; (op school) preparation time.

studiebeurs v. scholarship, studentship, exhibition.

studieboek o. study-book, text-book, manual.

studiefonds o. foundation, endowment, scholarship fund.

studiejaar o. year of study. [tour.

studiereis v. study-tour, instructional

studieverlof o. (mil.) study leave.

stug b. n. stiff; (nors) surly, gruff, scowling.

stugheid v. stiffness; surliness, gruffness.

stuifmeel o. pollen.

stuifzand o. drift-sand, blowing sand.

stuip v. convulsion, fit; (fig.) freak.

stuiptrekking v. convulsion, convulsive movement, twitching.

stuitbeen o. coccyx, tail-bone.

stuiten o. w. (v. hollend paard) stop; (v. vijand) check; (v. opmars) stem; (v. vuur, enz.) arrest; (v. bal) bound, bounce; (fig.) shock, offend; on. w. — op, encounter, meet with.

stuitend b. n. offensive, shocking, obnoxious, revolting.

stuiven on. w. be dusty; (v. vonken, enz.) fly (about); (snellen) tear, rush, dash, fly.

stuiver m. penny.

stuk z. n., o. (alg.) piece; (v. geheel) piece, fragment, splinter; (lap) piece; (op kledingstuk) patch; (v. brood, kaas: homp) chunk; (deel) part; (effect) security; (document) document, paper; (geschut) gun, piece; (v. schaakspel) man, piece; (toneelstuk) play, piece; (schilderstuk) piece, picture; (artikel) paper; (aantal: v. vee) head; b. n. broken, out of order, in pieces.

stukadoor m. plasterer, stucco-worker, stuccoer.

stukgoed(eren) o. (mv.) (manufacturen) piece-goods; (tapijthandel) body goods; (per trein) parcels; (sch.) general goods.

stukloon o. piece-wage(s).

stukslaan o. w. smash (up), smash (knock, beat) to pieces; on. w. be dashed to pieces.

stukvallen on. w. fall to pieces; smash.

stukwerk o. piece-work.

stukwerker m. piece-worker, piece-workman.

stumper(d) m. bungler, lubber, duffer, crock.

sturen o. w. (zenden) send; (besturen: v. schip, motor, enz.) steer; (v. paard) guide, drive, manage; on. w (sch.) steer; (sp.) cox.

stut m. support, prop, stay; (tegen muur, boom, enz.) shore; (sch.) pillar, stanchion; (in geraamte, v. vliegtuig) strut; (onder drooglijn) prop, clothes-prop.

stutbalk m. supporting beam, summer.

stutten o. w. prop, support, shore (up), buttress up, underpin.

stuur o. (v. schip) helm, rudder, tiller; (v. auto) wheel; (v. fiets) handle-bar.

stuurboord o. starboard.

stuurinrichting v. steering-gear; (v. vliegtuig) controls; (v. torpedo) gyroscope.

stuurlastig b. n. (sch.) down by the stern, too much by the stern.

stuurlieden, stuurlui m. mv. steersmen.

stuurloos b. n. out of control.

stuurman m. (alg.) steersman; (op boot) mate, navigating officer; (roerganger) helms-man, man at the helm; (v. reddingboot, luchtschip) coxswain; (v. oorlogsschip) lieutenant-commander; (sp.) cox.

stuurs b. n. sour, surly, sullen, gruff, glum.

stuurstang v. (v. auto) steering connecting rod; (v. fiets) handle-bar; (sch.) steering-rod; (v. vliegtuig) control lever.

stuwdam m. weir, barrage, retaining dam.

stuwkracht v. propelling force, propulsive force; (opwaarts) lift, lifting-power; (fig.) driving-power, driving-force.

subjectief b. n. subjective.

subsidie o. en v. subsidy, subvention, grant (-in-aid).

substituut m. substitute, deputy.

substituut-griffier m. Deputy Registrar.

subtiel b. n. subtle.

succes o. success; **veel —!** good luck! **veel — hebben,** score a great success, score heavily, have a great run.

successie v. succession.

successierechten o. mv. death-duties, legacy-duties, succession-duties.

successiewet v. inheritance act, law of settlement.

suf b. n. dull, dull-headed, sleepy; (in hoofd) dazed, hazed; (v. blik) muzzy; (v. oud mens) doting.

suffen on. w. doze, drowse, dote, moon, be in the clouds.

suffer(d) m. dotard; (fig.) duffer, dullard, muff.

suggestie v. suggestion.

suiker v. sugar.

suikerbakker m. confectioner.

suikerbiet v. sugar-beet, beetroot.

suikerboon *r.* (*Pl.*) butter-bean; (*snoepgoed*) sugar-plum.
suikeren *o. w.* sugar, sweeten.
suikerfabriek *v.* sugar-factory, sugarworks, sugar-mill.
suikergoed *o.* confectionery, sweetmeats.
suikeroom *m.* legacy uncle, gold uncle.
suikerpot *m.* sugar-basin, sugar-bowl.
suikerraffinaderij *v.* sugar-refinery.
suikerriet *o.* sugar-cane.
suikerstok *m.* sugar-stick.
suikerziekte *r.* diabetes; *lijder aan —,* diabetic.
suikerzoet *b. n.* as sweet as sugar, sugary; (*fig.*) sugared, sugary, honeyed.
suite *v.* suite (of rooms); (*kaartsp.*) sequence, run (of cards); (*muz.*) suite.
suizen *on. w.* buzz; (*r. wind*) sigh, sough; (*r. boom, regen*) rustle; (*v. kogel*) whizz.
sukade *r.* candied peel, succade.
sukkelaar(ster) *m.* (*v.*) ailing man (woman), invalid, valetudinarian; crock, mopstick.
sukkelachtig *b. n.* ailing, cranky; (*stumperig*) bungling.
sukkeldraf *m.* egg-trot, jog-trot, market-trot.
sukkelen *on. w.* be ailing, be in poor health.
sul *m.* soft Johnny, softy, noodle, muff,
mug, simpleton, flat, dolt, dunce, juggings.
sulfaat *o.* sulphate.
sulfer *o. en v.* sulphur.
sullig *b. n.* soft, softy, goody-goody, silly, oafish.
sultan *m.* sultan.
supplement *o.* supplement.
suppoost *m.* door-keeper, usher, hall-attendant; (*v. gevangenis*) turnkey, warder, gaoler.
surplus *o.* surplus, excess, overspill; (*H.: dekking*) cover, margin.
surrogaat *o.* substitute, succedaneum.
surseance *v.* surcease.
sussen *o. w.* (*v. kind*) hush; quiet; (*v. persoon*) soothe, pacify; (*v. geweten*) quiet, salve, ease, pacify.
symbolisch *b. n.* symbolic(al), emblematic(al); *bw.* symbolically, emblematically.
symbool *o.* symbol, emblem.
symfonie *v.* symphony.
symmetrie *v.* symmetry.
sympathie *v.* sympathy, fellow-feeling, congeniality.
symptoom *o.* symptom.
synagoge *v.* synagogue.
syndicaat *o.* syndicate, pool, ring.
synoniem *b. n.* synonymous; *z. n., o.* synonym.
Syrië *o.* Syria.
systeem *o.* system.

T

taai *b. n.* (*v. vlees, enz.*) tough, leathery; (*v. persoon, dier*) wiry; (*v. vloeistof*) viscous, tenacious; (*fig.: v. persoon, gestel*) tough, wiry; (*v. studie*) stiff; (*v. volharding, rasthoudendheid*) dogged; (*v. geheugen, leven*) tenacious; (*v. boek, werk, enz.: saai*) tedious, dull.
taaiheid *r.* toughness; wiriness; viscosity; tenacity.
taak *r.* task; (*v. school*) work, lesson(s).
taal *v.* language, tongue, speech.
taalbegrip *o. geen — hebben,* have no idea of grammar.
taalboek *o.* grammar, language-book.
taalfout *v.* grammatical mistake, offence (mistake) against the language.
taalgeleerde *m.* linguist, philologist.
taalgrens *v.* language, boundary.
taalkunde *v.* philology.
taalkundig *b. n.* grammatical, linguistic, philological; *bw. — juist,* grammatically correct.
taaloefening *r.* grammatical exercise.
taalregel *m.* grammatical rule, rule of grammar.
taalschat *m.* vocabulary.
taalstrijd *m.* language struggle.
taalwet *v.* linguistic law.
taalwetenschap *v.* science of language, linguistics, philology.
taalzuiveraar *m.* purist.
taan *r.* tan.
taankleurig *b. n.* tan-coloured, tawny.
taart *r.* tart, cake.
taart(e)schep *v.* tart-server.
tabak *v.* tobacco.
tabaksblad *o.* tobacco-leaf.
tabaksdoos *v.* tobacco-box.
tabakszak *m.* tobacco-pouch.
tabbaard, tabberd *m.* tabard, robe, gown.
tabel *v.* table, index, list, schedule.
tabernakel *o.* tabern-.cle.
tablet *v. en o.* tablet; lozenge, square.
tachtig *telw.* eighty.
tachtiger *m.* octogenarian, man of eighty; (*schrijver*) writer of the eighties.
tact *m.* tact.
tactiek *r.* tactics.
tactvol *b. n.* (*bw.*) tactful(ly).
taf *v.* taffeta.
tafel *r.* table.
tafelbier *o* table-beer.
tafeldekken *o.* laying a (the) table.
tafeldienen *o.* waiting at table.
tafelkleed *o* table-cover.
tafellinnen *o.* table-linen.

tafelschuier *m.* crumb-brush, table-brush.
tafelschuimer *m.* sponger, smell-feast.
tafeltennis *o.* table-tennis, ping-pong.
tafereel *o.* scene, picture.
tak *m. (alg.)* branch; *(zware* —) bough; *(v. gewei)* tine.
takel *m.* pulley, tackle.
takelen *o. w. (sch.)* tackle, rig; *(ophijsen)* hoist (up).
takeling *v.* tackling, cordage.
takkenbos *m.* faggot.
taks *m. (vk.)* dachs-hund, (German) badger-dog; *v. (vereiste hoeveelheid)* complement; *(aandeel, rantsoen)* portion, share, rate.
tal *o.* number; — *van,* numerous, a (great) number of.
talent *o.* talent.
talentvol *b. n.* talented, gifted.
taling *m. (Dk.)* teal.
talisman *m.* talisman, amulet, charm.
talk *v. (vet)* tallow; *(delfstof)* talc.
talloos *b. n.* numberless, unnumbered, without number.
talmen *on. w.* loiter, linger, delay.
talrijk *b. n.* numerous, multitudinous.
talud *o.* talus
tam *b. n.* tame, tamed, domesticated; *(fig.)* tame.
tamarinde *v.* tamarind.
tamboer *m.* drummer.
tamelijk *b. n.* tolerable, fair, passable; *bw.* tolerably, fairly, passably.
tamheid *v.* tameness.
tand *m.* tooth; *(v. vork, eg)* prong, tine; *(v. wiel)* tooth, cog.
tandarts *m.* dentist.
tandeloos *b. n.* toothless.
tandenborstel *m.* tooth-brush.
tandengeknars *o.* gnashing of teeth.
tandenkrijgen *o.* dentition.
tandentrekker *m.* tooth-drawer.
tandestoker *m.* tooth-pick.
tandglazuur *o.* enamel.
tandheelkundige *m.* dentist, dental surgeon.
tandkas *v.* tooth-socket; *(wet.)* alveolus.
tandletter *v.* dental (letter).
tandpasta *o.* tooth-paste.
tandpijn *v.* toothache; *(wet.)* odontalgy.
tandrad *o.* cog-wheel, toothed wheel.
tandradbaan *v.* rack railway.
tandvlees *o.* gums.
tandvulling *v.* filling, stopping.
tanen *o. w.* tan; *on. w.* tan; *(fig.)* fade, tarnish, pale; *(v. populariteit)* wane.
tang. *v* (pair of) tongs; *(nijptang)* pincers, nippers; *(v. tandarts)* dental forceps; *(v. heelkundige)* forceps; *(fig.)* shrew, virago.
tanig *b. n.* tawny.
tank *v.* tank.
tankschip *o.* tank-boat, tank-steamer, tanker.
tankwagen *m.* tank-car.
tante *v.* aunt.
tap *m. (kraan)* tap; *(spon)* bung; *(v.*

kanon, stoommachine) trunnion; *(tn.: bij timmerwerk, enz.)* tenon; *(ijskegel)* icicle.
tapijt *o.* carpet.
tapijtweverij *v.* carpet-weaving factory.
tappen *o. w.* tap, draw; **moppen** —, cut (crack) jokes; *on. w.* keep a bar, keep a public-house.
tapper *m.* tavern-keeper, ale-house keeper.
taptemelk *v.* skim-milk.
taptoe *v.* tattoo, last post.
tarbot *v.* turbot.
tarief *o.* tariff; *(v. huurrijtuigen)* (legal) fare.
tarra *v. (H.)* tare.
tarten *o. w.* challenge, defy, set at defiance, dare.
tarwe *v.* wheat.
tarwebloem *v.* flour of wheat, wheat-flour.
tarwebrood *o.* wheaten bread, white bread.
tas *m. (hoop)* heap, pile; *v. (Z. N.: kopje)* cup.
tas *v.* pouch, (hand-)bag; *(school—)* satchel.
tassen *o. w.* heap up, pile up.
tastbaar *b. n.* tangible, palpable.
tasten *o. w.* touch, feel; *on. w.* feel, grope, fumble.
tastzin *m.* touch, tactile sense.
tateren *on w.* prattle.
taxatie *v.* appraisement, appraisal, valuation.
taxeren *o. w.* appraise, value, estimate.
taxi *v.* taxi, taxi-cab.
taxis(boom) *m.* yew-tree.
te *vz.* at, in, to; *bw. (vóór b. n.)* too; *(vóór infinitief)* to.
techniek *v.* technics, technical skill, technical science; *(v. kunstenaar)* technique.
technisch *b. n. (bw.)* technical(ly).
teder *b. n. (bw.)* tender(ly).
tederheid *v.* tenderness.
teef *v.* bitch, female dog.
teek *v.* tick.
teelaarde *v.* vegetable earth, mould, humus.
teelgewas *o.* cultivated plant(s).
teelt *v.* cultivation, culture.
teemachtig *b. n.* whining, drawling.
teems *v.* sieve, strainer.
teen *v.* osier(-twig), withe.
teen *m.* toe.
teenganger *m. (Dk.)* digitigrade.
teenwilg *m.* osier(-willow).
teer *b. n.* zie **teder.**
teer *o.* tar.
teergevoelig *b. n.* tender, delicate, sensible, sensitive.
teergevoeligheid *v.* tenderness, delicacy, sensitiveness.
teerhartig *b. n.* tender-hearted.
teerhartigheid *v.* tender-heartedness.
teerkost *m.* provisions.
teerling *m.* die, cube.

teerspijze v. (kath.) viaticum.
tegel m. tile.
tegelbakker m. tile-maker.
tegelbakkerij v. tile-works.
tegelijk(ertijd) bw. at the same time, at once; (samen) together; — **met,** simultaneously with, along with.
tegemoetgaan o. w. go to meet.
tegemoetkomen o. w. come to meet; (fig.) go to meet, meet.
tegemoetkomend b. n. accommodating, compliant.
tegemoetkoming v. accommodating spirit; (vergoeding) allowance, compensation.
tegen vz. (alg.) against; (v. tijd) by, towards; (v. prijs) at; (jegens) to, with; (vergeleken bij) to; (recht) versus; z. n., o. **het voor en —,** the pro(s) and con(s).
tegenaanval m. counter-attack.
tegenantwoord o. rejoinder.
tegenargument o. counter-argument.
tegenbericht o. contrary message; (H.) advice to the contrary.
tegenbetoog o. counter-argumentation, counter-demonstration.
tegenbod o. counter-bid.
tegendeel o. contrary; reverse; **in —,** on the contrary.
tegendraads bw. against the grain.
tegengaan o. w. go to meet; (fig.) oppose, check, counteract.
tegengesteld b. n. opposite, contrary.
tegengif o. antidote.
tegenhanger m. counterpart; (fig.) set-off.
tegenhouden o. w. stop, arrest; (v. vooruitgang, enz.) retard, restrain.
tegenkanting v. opposition.
tegenkomen o. w. (v. persoon) meet, meet with; (v. persoon, woord, enz.) come across.
tegenlist v. counter-stratagem.
tegenmaatregel m. counter-measure.
tegenover bw. opposite (to), over against.
tegenovergelegen b. n. opposite.
tegenovergesteld b. n. opposite, contrary; opposed.
tegenoverliggend, tegenover-staand b. n. opposite.
tegenpartij v. en m. adversary, other party, opponent.
tegenpruttelen on. w. grumble, protest.
tegenslag m. reverse, set-back, check.
tegenspartelen on. w. struggle (against), resist.
tegenspeler m. (sport) opponent; (toneel) opposite number.
tegenspoed m. adversity, ill-luck.
tegenspraak v. contradiction.
tegenspreken o. w. (logenstraffen, ontkennen) contradict, deny; (bestrijden) answer back; w. w. **zich —,** contradict oneself.
tegenstaan on. w. resist, cause disgust.
tegenstand m. resistance, opposition.
tegenstander m. adversary, opponent.

tegenstellen o. w. oppose.
tegenstelling v. contrast, opposition, contradistinction, antithesis; (in redenering) contraposition.
tegenstemmen on. w. vote against, vote negatively.
tegenstreven o. w. resist, oppose; on. w. resist, recalcitrate.
tegenstrever m. adversary. [trate.
tegenstribbelen on. w. resist, recalci-
tegenstrijdig b. n. (v. berichten, enz.) contradictory; (v. belangen) clashing; (v. inzichten, meningen) conflicting.
tegenstrijdigheid v. contradiction; inconsistency; contrariety; discrepancy.
tegenstroom m. (op rivier of zee) counter-current, reflux; (el.) reverse (inverse) current.
tegenvallen on. w. fall short of one's exspectations, not come up to the expectations, be disappointing.
tegenvaller m. disappointment; (fam.) come-down.
tegenvergif o. antidote.
tegenvoeter m. antipode.
tegenvoorstel o. counter-proposal.
tegenwaarde v. counter-value.
tegenwerken o. w. work against, cross, counteract, obstruct.
tegenwerking v. crossing, opposition, obstruction.
tegenwerpen o. w. object.
tegenwerping v. objection.
tegenwicht o. counterpoise, counter-weight, counterbalance.
tegenwind m. adverse wind, counter-wind, head-wind.
tegenwoordig b. n. present; bw. at present, nowadays.
tegenwoordigheid v. presence.
tegenzang m. antistrophe, antiphon.
tegenzee v. backwash.
tegenzin m. dislike, antipathy, aversion, repugnance; **met —,** with a bad grace, reluctantly, unwillingly.
tegoed bw. to the good.
tehuis z. n., o. home; (onderdak: voor daklozen, enz.) shelter; bw. at home.
teil v. basin.
teisteren o. w. harass, ravage, visit; (v. ziekte, ongedierte, enz.) infest.
teken o. sign, token, mark; (v. ziekte) symptom; (vastgesteld —) signal; (lees—) stop, mark of punctuation.
tekenaap m. pantograph.
tekenaar m. drawer, draughtsman.
tekenboek o. sketch-book, drawing-book.
tekenen o. w. draw, delineate, sketch; (ondertekenen) sign; (merken) mark; (intekenen) subscribe; on. w. draw; sign.
tekenend b. n. characteristic.
tekenfilm v. film-cartoon. [square.
tekenhaak m. drawing-square, T-
tekening v. drawing, sketch; (ontwerp, schets) design; (ondertekening) signature; (het ondertekenen) signing.
tekenkrijt o. crayon, drawing chalk.

tekenles r. drawing-lesson.
tekenpapier o. drawing-paper.
tekenpen v. crayon-holder, porte-crayon.
tekort o. (alg.) shortage, deficiency; (v. geld) deficit, deficiency.
tekortkoming v. shortcoming, failing; (gebrek) imperfection.
tekst m. text; (bijschrift: bij plaat, enz.) letterpress; (verband, samenhang) context; (bij muziek) words.
tekstuitlegger m. exegete.
tekstverklaring v. textexegesis.
tel m. count, counting.
telaatkomer m. late comer.
telastlegging v. imputation, charge, accusation.
telbaar b. n. countable, numerable.
telefoneren o. w. en on. w. telephone.
telefoon v. telephone.
telefoonboek o. telephone-book, telephone-directory.
telefooncentrale v. telephone-exchange, central exchange.
telefoongesprek o. telephone-call; conversation over the telephone.
telefoonjuffrouw v. telephonist, telephone-girl; (fam.) phone-girl.
telefoonnet o. telephone-system.
telefoontoestel o. telephone set.
telegraaf v. telegraph; **per —,** by wire.
telegrafie v. telegraphy.
telegrafist m. telegraphist, telegrapher.
telegram o. telegram, wire; (kabel—) cablegram.
telegramadres o. telegraphic address.
telegrambesteller m. telegraph messenger, telegram-carrier.
telen o. w. (v. groenten, enz.: verbouwen) grow, cultivate; (v. dieren) breed, rear.
teler m. grower, cultivator; breeder.
teleurstellen o. w. disappoint.
teleurstelling v. disappointment.
televisie v. television.
telg v. (v. plant) sprout, shoot, scion; m. en v. (v. mens) descendant, shoot.
telganger m. ambler, ambling horse.
teling v. growing, cultivation; breeding.
teljoor v. (Z. N.) plate.
telkenmale, telkens bw. again and again, at every turn, every moment; **— als,** whenever.
tellen o. w. count; (bedragen) number; on. w. count.
teller m. teller, counter, numberer; (v. breuk) numerator; (bij volkstelling) enumerator.
telling v. count, counting; (volks—) enumeration, census.
teloorgaan on. w. be lost, be wasted.
telpas m. amble.
telraam o. ball-frame.
telwoord o. numeral; **hoofd—,** cardinal (number); **rangschikkend —,** ordinal (number).
temmen o. w. tame.
temmer m. tamer.
tempel m. temple.

temperatuur v. temperature.
temperen o. w. (matigen: v. vuur, ijver, enz.) temper, damp; (v. geluid) damp, deaden, soften; (v. licht, kleur) soften; (v. metaal) temper; (v. pijn, strengheid, enz.) mitigate.
tempo o. (muz.) time, movement; (alg. pace.
ten vz. **— westen van,** to the west of.
tendensroman m. novel with a purpose, purpose novel.
tendentieus b. n. tendentious.
tender m. tender.
tenen b. n. osier, wicker-work.
tenger b. n. slight, slender, slim.
tengerheid v. slightness, slenderness, slimness.
tengevolge bw. **— van,** in consequence of.
tenietdoening v. annulment, nullification, cancelling.
tenminste bw. at least.
tennis o. lawn-tennis.
tennisnet o. tennis-net.
tennisveld o. tennis-field, tennis-ground.
tenor m. tenor.
tent v. (alg.) tent; (kermis—) booth; (sch.: op dek) awning.
tentdoek o. (tent-)canvas.
tentoonstellen o. w. exhibit, show.
tentoonstelling v. exhibition, show.
tentpaal m. tent-pole.
tenue o. (mil.) dress, uniform.
tenware vgw. unless.
tenzij vgw. unless.
tepel m. nipple; (v. dier) teat.
ter vz. at (the), in, into (the); **— vergelijking,** for comparison.
teraardebestelling v. burial, interment, funeral.
terdege bw. soundly, thoroughly.
terdoodbrenging v. execution.
terecht b. n. **— zijn,** be found; bw. justly, rightly, truly.
terechtbrengen o. w. (in orde brengen) arrange, put to rights; (op de goede weg brengen) reclaim.
terechtkomen on. w. be found again; (in orde komen) come out (all) right.
terechtstaan on. w. stand one's trial, be committed for trial, be put on trial.
terechtstellen o. w. (voor de rechter roepen) put on trial; (de doodstraf voltrekken) execute.
terechtstelling v. trial; execution.
terechtwijzen o. w. set right, put right; (vermanen, berispen) reprimand, reprove.
terechtwijzing v. reprimand, reproof, correction.
terechtzitting v. session, sitting.
teren o. w. tar.
teren on. w. **op eigen kosten —,** live at one's own expense; pay one's own way.
tergen o. w. provoke, irritate, tease, aggravate.

terhandstelling v. handing over, delivery.

tering v. (ziekte) pulmonary consumption, phthisis; (verteer) expense.

teringlijder m. consumptive (patient).

terloops bw. incidentally, casually, in passing.

term m. term.

termijn m. (tijdruimte) term, time; (gedeeltelijke betaling) instalment.

termijnhandel m. dealing in futures, (business in) futures.

ternauwernood bw. scarcely, hardly, barely.

terneergeslagen b. n. cast down, dejected.

terpentijn v. turpentine.

terras o. terrace.

terrein o. ground; (bouw—) building-site; (stuk grond) plot; (mil.) terrain, ground; (fig.) domain, field, ground, department.

terreur v. terror.

terroriseren o. w. terrorize, intimidate.

tersluiks bw. on the sly, stealthily, by stealth.

terstond bw. at once, immediately, directly.

terug bw. back, backward.

terugbetaalbaar b. n. repayable.

terugbetalen o. w. pay back, repay, refund.

terugbetaling v. repayment, refund; (v. bank) withdrawal.

terugblik m. retrospective view, retrospect.

terugbrengen o. w. bring back; (verminderen) reduce (to).

terugdeinzen on. w. shrink back; — voor, shrink from.

terugdenken on. w. — aan, recall (to mind, to memory); w. w. zich — in, carry oneself back to.

terugdrijven o. w. drive back, repulse, repel. [back.

terugeisen o. w. reclaim, demand

teruggaan on. w. go back, return; (v. prijzen, enz.) go down, decline, fall.

teruggetrokken b. n. retiring, self-centred, self-contained.

teruggeven o. w. give back, return; (v. ontvreemd goed) restore; on. w. give change.

terugkaatsen o. w. (v. bal, enz.) strike ~, throw back; (v. geluid, licht) reflect; on. w. rebound, be thrown back; reflect, be reflected; (v. geluid) reverberate.

terugkeer m. return, coming back.

terugkeren on. w. return; (omkeren) turn back.

terugkomen on. w. return, come back; (v. ziekte) recur.

terugkomst v. return, coming back.

terugkopen o. w. repurchase, buy back; (bij verkoping) buy in.

terugkrabbelen on. w. hark back, cry off, back out (of it).

terugkrijgen o. w. get back.

teruglopen on. w. (alg.) run back, walk back; (H.: v. prijzen) recede; (v. water) flow (run) back.

terugnemen o. w. take back; (fig.) retract, withdraw.

terugneming v. taking back; retractation.

terugreis r. return, journey-back. (v. schip) voyage home.

terugroepen o. w. call back, recall.

terugslaan o. w. beat back, repulse; (v. bal) strike back, return; on. w. strike (hit) back; (v. motor) back-fire.

terugslag m. recoil, repercussion; (v. motor) back-fire; (fig.) reaction, revulsion.

terugstoten o. w. push back; (fig.) repel.

terugtocht m. retreat.

terugtraprem v. coaster-brake, back-pedalling brake.

terugtrekken o. w. draw (pull) back; (v. klauwen; fig.: belofte) retract; on. w. (mil.) retreat, withdraw; w. w. zich —, retreat; (uit zaken, politiek, enz.) retire; (bij examen) withdraw.

terugvinden o. w. find again.

terugvoeren o. w. carry back.

terugvorderen o. w. claim (ask, demand) back; (bij bank) withdraw, draw out.

terugwerken on. w. react.

terugwerkend b. n. retroactive, reacting.

terugwerking v. retroaction.

terugwijken on. w. (alg.) recede; (mil.) retreat.

terugzenden o. w. send back, return.

terwijl vw. (v. tijd) while, whilst; (v. tegenstelling) whereas, while; bw. (in the) meanwhile, in the mean time.

terzelfdertijd at the same time.

terzijde aside.

terzijdestelling v. putting aside, disregard.

test v. fire-pan; (proef) test, trial; (sl.) nob, nut.

testament o. last will, testament; Testament.

testamentmaker m. testator.

teug v. draught.

teugel m. rein, bridle.

teugelloos b. n. unbridled, unrestrained.

tevens bw. at the same time.

tevergeefs bw. in vain, vainly.

tevreden b. n. (voldaan) satisfied; (v. karakter) contented; (genoegen nemend met: predikatief) content.

tevredenheid v. satisfaction; contentedness; contentment; content.

tevredenstellen o. w. satisfy; content; zich — met, be satisfied with, content oneself with.

tewaterlating v. launch, launching.

teweegbrengen o. w. bring about, cause, occasion, effect.

tewerkstellen o. w. make to work.

textielfabriek *v*. textile works.
textielgoederen *o. mv.* textile goods.
tezamen *bw.* together.
thans *bw.* at present, now, by this time.
theater *o.* theatre.
thee *v.* tea.
theekopje *o.* tea-cup.
theelepeltje *o.* tea-spoon.
theemuts *v.* tea cosy.
theepot *m.* tea-pot.
theeschoteltje *o.* saucer.
thema *v.* exercise; *o.* theme.
theologant *m. (godgeleerde)* theologian; *(student in godgel.)* divinity student, student of theology.
theoloog *m.* zie **theologant.**
thermometer *m.* thermometer.
thermosfles *v.* thermos (flask), vacuum flask.
thesaurie *v.* treasury.
thesis *v.* thesis.
thuis *bw.* at home; *z. n., o.* home.
thuisbrengen *o. w. (naar huis brengen)* see home; *(weten wie iem. is)* locate, identify.
thuiskomst *v.* home-coming, return (home).
thuiszittend *b. n.* stay-at-home.
tien *telw.* ten.
tiende *b. n.* tenth; *z. n., o.* tenth part; tenth.
tiendelig *b. n.* consisting of ten parts; *(v. breuk, stelsel)* decimal.
tiendplichtig *b. n.* tithable.
tiental *o.* ten, decade.
tientje *o.* ten-guilder piece; *(v. rozenkrans)* decade (of the rosary).
tienvoud *o.* decuple.
tienvoudig *b. n.* tenfold.
tierelieren *on. w.* warble, twitter, sing.
tieren *on. w. (razen)* rage, rant, storm, bluster.
tieren *on. w. (gedijen, welig groeien)* thrive, get on well; *(fig.)* flourish.
tij *o.* tide.
tijd *m. (alg.)* time; *(periode)* season, period; *(gram.)* tense.
tijdbepaling *v.* computation of time; *(gram.)* adjunct of time.
tijdelijk *b. n.* temporary; *(wereldlijk)* temporal; *bw.* temporarily.
tijdens *vz.* during.
tijdgeest *m.* spirit of the age, spirit of the time, time-spirit.
tijdgenoot *m.* contemporary.
tijdig *b. n.* timely, seasonable, early; *bw.* in good time, betimes.
tijding *v.* news, tidings, intelligence.
tijdje *o.* time, (little) time; **voor een —** for a while; **een — geleden,** some time ago, lately.
tijdkring *m.* period.
tijdmeter *m.* chronometer.
tijdopname *v. (sp.)* timing; *(v. foto)* time-exposure.
tijdperk *o.* period.
tijdrekening *v.* chronology.
tijdruimte *v.* space of time, period.

tijdsbestek *o.* space of time.
tijdschrift *o.* periodical (paper), magazine.
tijdstip *o.* point of time, epoch.
tijdsverloop *o.* course of time; **een — van,** a lapse of.
tijdsverschil *o.* difference in time.
tijdvak *o.* period.
tijdverdrijf *o.* pastime, recreation.
tijdverlies *o.* loss of time.
tijdvorm *m. (gram.)* tense-form.
tijger *m.* tiger.
tijgerin *v.* tigress.
tijk *o.* tick.
tik *m.* touch, pat; *(op deur)* tap, rap.
tikken *on. w. (v. klok, enz.)* tick; *(aan deur, raam)* tap; *(typen)* typewrite; *o. w.* tap; *(v. brief, enz.)* type, type-write.
tiktak *o. (geluid)* tick-tack; *(spel)* backgammon, trick-track.
til *m.* lift, lifting (up); **op — zijn,** be approaching; **er is wat op —,** there is something in the wind.
tillen *o. w.* lift, heave.
timmeren *on. w.* carpenter.
timmerhout *o.* timber.
timmerman *m.* carpenter.
timmerwerk *o.* carpenter's work, carpentering, carpentry.
tin *o.* tin; pewter.
tinne *v.* pinnacle, battlement, crenel.
tint *v.* tint, tinge, hue.
tintelen *on. w. (flikkeren: v. sterren, enz.)* twinkle, sparkle, scintillate; *(v. ogen)* twinkle, dance; *(v. geest; v. wijn)* sparkle; *(v. kou)* tingle; *(v. oren)* burn.
tinteling *v.* twinkling; sparkling.
tinten *o. w.* tinge, tint.
tinwerk *o.* tin-ware, pewter.
tip *m.* tip; *(v. zakdoek, sluier)* corner.
tip *m. (inlichting)* tip.
tiptop tiptop, top-hole, first rate
tiran *m.* tyrant.
titel *m.* title; *(v. hoofdstuk, enz.)* heading, title.
titelblad *o.* title-leaf, title-page.
titelen *o. w.* title.
titelplaat *v.* frontispiece.
titelrol *v.* title-rôle, title-part, name-part.
titularis *m.* holder (of an office), functionary; *(kerkelijk)* incumbent.
tjilpen *on. w.* chirp, twitter, cheep.
toast *m.* toast.
tobbe *v.* tub.
tobben *on. w. (zwaar werken)* toil, drudge, plod; *(vol zorg zijn)* worry (about), brood (over).
toch *(evenwel, niettegenstaande dat)* yet, still, for all that, nevertheless, all the same, though; *(zeker)* surely, to be sure; *(werkelijk)* really; *(ongeduld)* ever.
tocht *m. (trek, zuigwind)* draught; *(reis)* march, expedition, journey.
tochtband *o.* list; **van — voorzien,** list.
tochten *on. w.* **het tocht hier,** there is a draught here, it is draughty here.

tochtig b. n. draughty; (loops) bullish, ruttish.

toe b. n. en bw. to; towards; (dicht) shut.

toebehoren on. w. belong to; z. n., o. **met** —, with appurtenances, with accessories.

toebereiden o. w. prepare; (met specerijen) season; (v. sla) dress.

toebereiding v. preparation; seasoning; dressing.

toebereidselen o. mv. preparatives, preparations.

toebinden o. w. bind up, tie up.

toebrengen o. w. (v. verlies, wond, enz.) inflict; (v. slag) deal, strike; (v. letsel, schade) do.

toedienen o. w. (v. geneesmiddel, laatste sacramenten) administer; (straf, enz.) mete out, measure out; (v. klap, enz.) deal, give.

toediening v. administration; dealing.

toedoen o. w. shut, close; z. n , o. **door uw** —, through your intermediary, through you; **zonder uw** —, but for you.

toedraaien o. w. turn off; close (lock) by turning.

toedracht v. **de juiste — van de zaak,** the rights of the matter; the ins and outs of the affair.

toedragen o. w. bear; **achting** —, esteem; w. w. **zich** —, happen; come to pass.

toeëigenen o. w. **zich iets** —, appropriate something.

toeëigening v. appropriation.

toefluisteren o. w. **iem. iets** —, whisper something in a person's ear.

toegaan on. w. (dichtgaan) close, shut; (gebeuren, voorvallen) happen, come to pass.

toegang m. access, (road of) approach; (ingang) entrance; (toelating) admission, admittance.

toegangsbewijs o., **toegangskaart** v. admission ticket, ticket of admission, permit.

toegangsprijs m. admission-fee, entrance-money, (price of) admission.

toegankelijk b. n. accessible, approachable; **— voor het publiek,** open to the public.

toegedaan b. n **iem. — zijn,** be attached to a person; **een mening — zijn,** hold an opinion (a view).

toegeeflijk b. n. indulgent, lenient.

toegeeflijkheid v. indulgence, leniency.

toegenegen b. n. affectionate; **Uw —,** yours affectionately.

toegenegenheid v. affection, affectionateness, inclination.

toegeven o. w. (geven boven het bedongene) give into the bargain; (fig.: erkennen) admit, grant, concede; on. w. give in, cave in, yeld.

toegevend b. n. indulgent.

toegeving v compliance

toegift v. addition; makeweight; **als** —, into the bargain.

toegrendelen o. w. bolt.

toegrijnzen o. w. grin at.

toehalen o. w. draw closer, tie (draw) tighter.

toejuichen o. w. applaud, cheer, acclaim.

toejuiching v. applause, cheer, shout.

toekennen o. w. (v. prijs, straf)adjudge, award; (v. waarde) attach; (v. titel, enz.) confer.

toekenning v. adjudication, award, grant.

toekijken on. w. look on.

toekijker m. looker-on, onlooker.

toekomen on. w. (rondkomen) make both ends meet; (toebehoren) belong, be due; **doen** —, send, hand.

toekomend b. n. future, next; **—e tijd,** (gram.) future (tense).

toekomst v. future.

toekomstdroom m. dream of the future.

toekomstig b. n. future.

toekrijgen o. w. (dicht krijgen) get shut; (als toegift, bijkrijgen) get into the bargain.

toelaatbaar b. n. admissible, allowable.

toelachen o. w. smile at; (fig.) smile on.

toelage v. gratification, allowance; extra salary (pay, wages).

toelaten o. w. (veroorloven) permit; allow, tolerate; (toegang verlenen) admit; (doorlaten) pass.

toelating v. permission; admission, admittance.

toelatingsexamen o. entrance examination; (tot hogeschool) matriculation.

toelatingskaart v. pass, order.

toeleg m. intention, purpose, design, attempt.

toeleggen o. w. (dichtdoen) cover up; (toewijzen) allow; **het er op — om,** be bent upon... ing; w. w. **zich — op,** apply oneself to.

toelichten o. w. clear up, elucidate, explain; (met voorbeelden) illustrate.

toelichting v. elucidation, explanation.

toeloop m. concourse, confluence.

toelopen on. w. come running on; **op iem.** —, go up to a person.

toeluisteren on. w. listen.

toemaat v. overmeasure, extra measure.

toemaken o. w. (v. deur, enz.) close, shut; (v. brief) fold up; (v. jas) button up.

toemetselen o. w. wall up.

toen bw. then, at that time; **van — af,** from then, from that time; vw. when, as.

toenaaien o. w. sew up.

toenaam m. (bijnaam) nickname; (familienaam) family name.

toenadering v. approach; (fig.) rapprochement.

toenemen on. w. increase, grow, augment; (v. wind) freshen, gather strength.

toeneming v. increase, growth; rise, progress.

toenmaals bw. then, at the (that) time.

toenmalig b. n. then, of the time.

toepasselijk b. n. appropriate, applicable, apposite, suitable; — **geval,** case in point; — **zijn op,** apply to, be relevant to.

toepassen o. w. (v. regel, kunstmatige ademhaling, enz.) apply; (v. wet) administer; (in praktijk brengen) practise, put into practice; **verkeerd —,** misapply.

toepassing v. application; **in — brengen,** practise.

toeplakken o. w. paste up, glue up; (v. brief) close, seal (up).

toer m. (reis, tocht) tour, excursion, trip; (wandeling) turn; (ritje) drive; ride; (beurt) turn; (kunststuk) feat, trick; (v. breiwerk) round.

toereiken o. w. (aangeven) reach, pass, hand; on. w. (voldoende zijn) suffice, be sufficient.

toereikend b. n. sufficient, enough.

toerekenbaar b. n. (v. persoon) responsible, accountable; (v. daad) imputable.

toerekening r. imputation.

toeren on. w. take a drive; (in auto) motor.

toerenteller m. (tn.) revolution-counter.

toerist m. tourist, excursionist.

toeristenverkeer o. tourist traffic.

toeroepen o. w. call to, cry to.

toerusten o. w. equip, prepare, fit out; w. w. **zich —,** equip oneself, prepare, get (make) ready.

toerusting v. equipment, preparation, fitting out.

toeschietelijk b. n. complaisant, accommodating, responsive.

toeschietelijkheid v. complaisance, accessibility, responsiveness.

toeschijnen on. w. seem, appear.

toeschouwer m. spectator, looker-on, onlooker.

toeschrijven o. w. ascribe, attribute; (ong.) impute.

toeslaan o. w. (dichtslaan: v. deur, enz.) slam, bang; (v. boek) shut; on. w. (dichtslaan) be slammed; (er op slaan) lay it on.

toeslag m. (bijslag) extra allowance; (mil.) field allowance; (wat moet bijbetaald worden) additional charge; (op vrachtprijs) surcharge; (bij verkoop) knocking down.

toesluiten o. w. close, shut, lock.

toesnauwen o. w. snarl at.

toesnellen on. w. rush on.

toesnoeren o. w. lace up.

toespeling v. allusion, insinuation, hint; (hatelijke —) innuendo; **—en maken op,** allude to.

toespijs v. condiment.

toespraak v. address, speech, allocu-

tion; **een — houden,** give an address, deliver a speech.

toespreken o. w. speak to; address.

toestaan o. w. (toelaten) allow, permit; (inwilligen) grant, concede, allow; (verlenen) accord.

toestand m. state of affairs, condition, situation, position; (geval) case; (omstandigheden) circumstances.

toestel o. apparatus, appliance, machine, instrument.

toestemmen o. w. (goedkeuren) consent; (toegeven) admit, assent (to), grant; on. w. assent; — **in,** accede to, grant, agree to.

toestemming v. consent, assent, permission.

toestoppen o. w. (v. opening) stop up; (v. oren) stop; (v. kind, in bed) tuck in; (in 't geheim geven) give secretly, give on the sly.

toestromen on. w. stream (flow, rush) towards, come flocking on.

toesturen o. w. send, forward, remit.

toetakelen o. w. (v. schip) rig; (opdirken) accoutre, dress out; (mishandelen) manhandle, knock about, mangle.

toetasten on. w. (nemen: v. eten) help oneself, fall to; (bij aanbod) jump at an offer.

toeten on. w. toot, tootle, honk.

toeter m. tootling horn.

toetreden on. w. — **tot,** join, enter into.

toetreding v. joining (up), accession.

toets m. (beproeving v. metalen) assay, test; (v. piano) key; (penseelstreek) touch; (fig.) test.

toetsen o. w. (v. metalen) assay, test; (fig.) test, try.

toetssteen m. touchstone.

toeval o. accident, incident; chance; (ziekte) fit of epilepsy.

toevallig b. n. accidental, casual, fortuitous; bw. accidentally, by accident, by chance.

toeven on. w. (blijven) stay; (dralen) tarry, linger.

toeverlaat m. stay, refuse, support.

toevertrouwen o. w. **iem. iets —,** commit something to a person's charge, entrust a person with something.

toevloed m. affluence.

toevlucht v. (steun, hulp) recourse; (wijkplaats, schuilplaats) refuge, shelter.

toevluchtsoord o. (heaven of, house of) refuge.

toevoegen o. w. (bij iets voegen) add (to), join (to); (zeggen) say; (v. woorden, bemerkingen) address; (ten dienste stellen) place at a person's disposal.

toevoeging v. addition.

toevoegsel o. supplement, addition, adjunct, appendix.

toevoer m. supply; (v. gas, lucht) flow.

toevoeren o. w. supply.

toevoerkanaal o. feeder.

toevouwen o. w. fold up.

toevriezen on. w. freeze over (up).

toewenken *o. w.* beckon to.
toewensen *o. w.* wish.
toewijden *o. w.* dedicate; *w. w. zich —*
aan, devote oneself to.
toewijding *v.* devotion, application.
toewijzen *o. w. (v. prijs, enz.)* assign,
award; *(v. aandeel)* allot; *(op veiling)*
knock down.
toewijzing *v.* assignment, award;
allotment; adjudication.
toezeggen *o. w.* promise.
toezegging *v.* promise.
toezenden *o. w.* send, forward; *(v. geld)*
remit.
toezending *v.* sending, forwarding; *(v. geld)* remittance.
toezicht *o.* surveillance, inspection,
superintendence, supervision.
toezien *on. w. (toekijken)* look on; *(op-zicht houden)* survey; superintend; *(op-letten, oppassen)* take care, be careful.
toezwaaien *o. w.* wave to, sway to;
lof —, praise, extol.
toga *v.* gown, toga, robe.
toilet *o.* toilet, toilette; *(kleding)* dress;
(kaptafel) toilet, toilet-table, dressing-table; *(privaat)* lavatory.
toiletspiegel *m.* toilet-mirror, dressing
glass.
tol *m. (doortochtgeld, op weg, enz.)* toll;
(schatting) toll, tribute; *(tolboom)* turn-pike; *(tolhuis)* turnpike-house; *(belasting)* customs, duties; *(speelgoed)* top.
tolbeambte *m.* custom-house officer.
tolgaarder *m.* toll-gatherer, toll-keeper.
tolgeld *o.* toll.
tolhuis *o.* toll-house, turnpike-house.
tolk *m.* interpreter; *(fig.)* mouth-piece.
tollen *on. w.* spin a top, play with a
top.
tollenaar *m. (tolgaarder)* toll-gatherer;
(Bijb.) publican.
tolplichtig *b. n.* liable (subject) to toll.
tolverbond *o.* customs-union.
tolvrij *b. n.* toll-free, free of duty, duty-free.
tomaat *v.* tomato.
ton *v. (vat, kuip)* cask, barrel, tun;
(maat) ton; *(sch.: boei)* buoy.
tondeldoos *v.* tinder-box.
tondeuse *v.* (hair-)clipping machine.
toneel *o.* stage; *(deel v. bedrijf)* scene;
(fig.) theatre, scene.
toneelgezelschap *o.* theatrical company, troupe, company of actors
(players); *(v. amateurs)* dramatic club.
toneelkijker *m.* opera-glass, binocular.
toneelscherm *o.* (stage-)curtain, (act-)
drop; *(coulisse)* side-scene.
toneelschikking *v.* mise en scene,
stage-setting.
toneelspeelster *v.* actress.
toneelspel *o.* play; acting.
toneelspeler *m.* actor, player.
toneelstuk *o.* (stage-)play, dramatic
piece.
tonen *o. w.* show; *(aantonen)* prove,
demonstrate.

tong *v.* tongue; *(vis)* sole; *(muz.: v.*
orgelpijp) languet.
Tongeren *o.* Tongres.
tongletter *v.* lingual (letter).
tongval *m.* dialect; accent.
tonijn *m.* tunny.
tonnemaat *v.* tonnage, burden.
tonnen *o. w.* barrel (up).
tonsuur *v.* tonsure.
toog *v.* cassock, soutane; *m. (Z. N.:*
toonbank) (shop-)counter.
tooi *m.* attire, ornament, decoration;
(opschik) finery.
tooien *o. w.* adorn, decorate, deck, dress
out.
toom *m.* bridle, reins.
toon *m.* tone; *(klemtoon)* accent; stress;
(klank) sound; *(fig.)* tone, note.
toonaangevend *b. n.* giving the tone,
leading.
toonaard *m. (muz.)* tonality; *(majeur of*
mineur) key.
toonbank *v.* (shop-)counter.
toonbeeld *o.* model, paragon, example.
toonder *m.* bearer.
toondichter *m.* (musical) composer.
toonhoogte *v.* pitch.
toonkunst *v.* music.
toonkunstenaar *m.,* **toonkunste-
nares** *v.* musician, composer.
toonladder *v.* scale, gamut.
toonloos *b. n. (v. stem)* toneless; *(v.*
klank, lettergreep) atonic, unaccented.
toonteken *o. (gram.)* accent, stress-mark.
toonzetter *m.* musical composer.
toonzetting *v.* musical composition;
tonality.
toorn *m.* anger, wrath choler; *(dicht.)* ire.
toornig *b. n.* angry, wrathful.
toorts *v.* torch; link; *(Pl.)* mullein.
top *m. (v. berg)* top, summit; *(v. boom,*
enz.) top; *(v. vinger)* tip; *(v. driehoek,*
kegel) apex; *(tol)* top.
top *tw.* done! agreed! taken! I am on!
topaas *m.* topaze.
toplicht *o. (sch.)* top-light, top-lantern,
mast-head light.
toppen *o. w. (v. bomen)* top, head.
toppunt *o. (alg.)* top, summit; *(meetk.)*
apex, vertex; *(sterr.)* culminating point;
(fig.) top, culminating point, pinnacle,
acme, summit, climax, apogee, height,
zenith.
tor *v.* beetle; scarab.
toren *m.* tower; *(met spits)* steeple;
(slottoren) donjon; *(schaaksp.)* castle.
torengebouw *o.* sky-scraper.
torenspits *v.* spire.
torenuurwerk *o.* tower-clock.
torenvalk *m.* staniel, kestrel, wind-hover.
tornen *o. w.* rip (up, open), unsew,
unstitch; *on. w.* come unsewed, come
unstitched.
torpederen *o. w.* torpedo.
torpedo *v. (mil.)* torpedo; *(Dk.: vis)*
torpedo, numb-fish, cramp-fish.

torpedojager *m.* (torpedo-boat) destroyer
torsen *o. w.* bear, carry.
tortel *m. en v.* turtle(-dove).
tortelduif *v.* turtle-dove.
tot *vz.* (*v. plaats*) to, as far as; (*v. tijd*) till, until, to; *vw.* till, untill.
totaal *b. n.* total, entire; *bw.* totally, entirely, altogether, utterly; *z. n., o.* total, total amount, sum total; *in —,* in the aggregate.
touw *o.* (*dun*) string, twine; (*iets dikker*) cord; (*dik*) rope; *op — zetten,* set on foot, take in hand; put on the stocks; launch.
touwladder *v.* rope-ladder.
touwwerk *o.* cordage, ropes; (*sch.*) rigging.
tovenaar *m.* sorcerer, magician, enchanter, wizard.
toverachtig *b. n.* magic(al), enchanting, charming, fairy-like.
toverboek *o.* conjuring-book.
toveren *on. w.* practise magic (sorcery), work (practise) charms; (*goochelen*) conjure, juggle.
toverfluit *v.* magic flute.
toverheks witch.
toverij *v.* magic, sorcery, witchcraft; (*goochelarij*) conjuring, jugglery.
toverkracht *v.* witchcraft, magic power.
toverroede *v.,* **toverstaf** *m.* magic wand.
toverslag *m. als bij —,* as by magic, by the wave of the wand.
traag *b. n.* (*bw.*) slow(ly), indolent(ly), suggish(ly), tardy(-ily).
traagheid *v.* slowness, indolence, sluggishness, tardiness, dullness; (*nat.*) inertia.
traan *m.* tear.
traan *v.* train-oil, fish-oil.
traanbom *v.* tear-shell, tear-bomb, lachrymatory bomb.
traangas *o.* (*mil.*) tear-gas.
traanklier *v.* lachrymal gland.
trachten *o. w.* try, attempt, endeavour; *— naar,* strive after.
tractor *m.* tractor.
traditie *v.* tradition.
tragedie *v.* tragedy.
trainen *o. w.* train; *w. w. zich —,* train.
traject *o.* stretch; (*afstand*) distance; (*overtocht, overvaart*) passage.
traktaat *o.* treaty.
traktement *o.* salary, pay.
tralie *v.* bar; lattice, trellis, grate, grating.
traliehek *o.* grille; (*rond gebouw*) railings.
traliewerk *o.* lattice-work, trellis(-work).
tram *v.* tramway, tram(-car).
trambestuurder *m.* tram-driver, motorman.
tramhalte *v.* stopping-place, stop.

tramlijn *v.* tram(way) line.
tramwissel *m.* tramway switch(es) (*wisselplaats*) tramway siding.
transactie *v.* transaction.
transatlantisch *b. n.* transatlantic.
transformator *m.* (*el.*) transformator, transformer.
transito *o.* (*H.*) transit.
transitohandel *m.* transit-trade.
transport *o.* (*verroer*) transport, carriage; (*boekh.*) amount carried over (forward).
transportschip *o.* transport-ship, troop-ship.
transportvliegtuig *o.* (*mil.*) troop-carrying plane, troop-plane.
trant *m.* manner, way, custom, method.
trap *m.* (*schop*) kick; (*trede*) degree; *de —pen van vergelijking,* the degrees of comparison; *stellende —,* positive; *vergrotende —,* comparative; *overtreffende —,* superlative.
trap *v.* (*al de treden te zamen*) stairs, staircase, flight of stairs; (*trapladder*) step-ladder.
trapas *r.* (*v. fiets*) pedal-shaft, crank axle.
trapezium *o.* (*meetk.*) trapezium; (*gymn.*) trapeze, trapezium.
trapgans *v.* bustard.
trapgevel *m.* stepped gable, (crow-)step gable.
trapladder *v.* step-ladder.
trapleuning *v.* banisters; (*voor de hand*) handrail.
traploper *m.* stair-carpet.
trappelen *on. w.* (*v. ongeduld*) stamp; trample.
trappen *o. w.* tread; (*v. orgel*) blow; (*schoppen*) kick; *on. w.* tread, trample; kick; (*op fiets*) pedal.
trapper *m.* treadle; (*v. fiets*) pedal, treadle.
trapportaal *o.* landing.
traproede *v.* stair-rod.
trapsgewijze *b. n.* gradual; *bw.* stepwise, step by step; (*fig.*) gradually, by degrees.
trasraam *o.* trass-layer.
trassaat *m.* (*H.*) drawee.
trassant *m.* (*H.*) drawer, giver.
trawant *m.* moon, satellite; (*fig.*) satellite, henchman.
trawler *m.* trawler.
trechter *m.* funnel, hopper; (*v. granaat*) crater.
tred *m.* tread, pace, step.
trede *v.* (*stap*) step, pace; (*v. trap, rijtuig*) step; (*v. ladder*) rung; (*v. naaimachine*) treadle.
treden *on. w.* tread, step, walk, pace; *in bijzonderheden —,* enter into detail(s); *naar voren —,* come forward, come to the front; *o. w.* tread.
tredmolen *m.* tread-mill; (*fig.*) jog-trot, tread-mill.
treeplank *v.* foot-board; (*v. auto, enz.*) running-board.
treffelijk *b. n.* (*bw.*) excellent(ly).

treffelijkheid v. excellence.
treffen o. w. (raken) hit, strike; (fig.) touch, strike; (aantreffen) meet (with); on. w. **dat treft gelukkig,** that is a lucky hit; that is a happy coincidence; z. n., o. fight, conflict, encounter.
treffend b. n. (v. gelijkenis) striking; (aandoenlijk) moving, touching.
treffer m. (mil.) hit, hitting shot; (fig.) hit, lucky hit.
trefkans v. (mil.) striking-chance, probability of hitting.
trefzekerheid v. (mil.) accuracy of fire.
trein m. (spoorw.: mil.) train; (gevolg) retinue, suite, following, train.
treinreis v. train-journey.
treiteraar m. pesterer, teaser, nagger.
treiteren o. w. pester, tease, nag, vex.
trek m. (ruk) pull, haul, tug; (aan pijp) pull, whiff; (v. schoorsteen; tocht) draught; (v. gelaat) feature; (v. karakter) trait; (penne—) stroke, dash; (eetlust) appetite; (lust, neiging) mind, inclination; (in kaartspel) trick; (v. vogels: het trekken) migration, roading.
trekgat o. air-hole, vent-hole.
trekken o. w. (v. lijn, figuur, besluit, enz.) draw; (v. voorwerp, drukproef, enz.) pull; (sleuren) drag, lug; (v. planten) force; (v. tand) draw, pull out, extract; on. w. (rukken) draw, pull; (v. koffie, thee, schoorsteen, enz.) draw; (v. scheermes) pull, scratch; (tochten) be draughty; (gaan, reizen) go, march, travel; (krom trekken) warp, become warped; (fig.) draw.
trekker m. (v. wissel) drawer; (v. vuurwapen) trigger; (v. laars) tab; (sp.) hiker.
trekking v. (v. loterij) drawing, draw; (zenuw—) convulsion, twitch.
treklade v. drawer.
trekpaard o. draught-horse.
trekpad o. towing-path.
trekpen v. drawing-, tracing-, bow-pen.
trekpleister v. vesicatory, blister(ing)-plaster; (fig.) sweetheart.
trekschuit v. draw-boat, tow-boat.
trekvogel m. bird of passage, migrating bird, migrant.
tremmen o. w. trim.
trens v. (lus) loop; (toom) bridle-bit, snaffle-(bit), bridoon.
tres v. braid, lace; (v. haar) tress.
treurdicht o. elegy.
treuren on. w. mourn, grieve, sorrow; (fig.: kwijnen) languish.
treures m. weeping ash.
treurig b. n. sad, mournful, sorrowful.
treurlied m. mourning-song.
treurmars m. funeral march, dead march.
treurspel o. tragedy.
treurwilg m. weeping-willow.
treuzelaar m. dawdler, slacker, loiterer.
treuzelen on. w. dawdle, loiter, linger.
tribune v. (v. spreker) tribune, plat-

form; (voor publiek) gallery; (sp.: bij wedrennen) stand.
tricot o. (stof) tricot, stockinet; (v. kunstenmaker, enz.) tights; (v. kind) jersey.
triest(ig) b. n. gloomy, melancholy; (v. weer) dreary; (somber: v. dag, enz.) murky, dismal.
trilgras o. quaking-grass.
trilharen o. mv. vibrissae.
triljoen o. trillion.
trillen on. w. (alg.) tremble; (v. stem) vibrate, quaver, tremble; (nat.) vibrate; **doen —,** vibrate, set vibrating; (v. gras) quake, dither; (v. film) flicker; (v. vliegtuig) flutter.
triller m. (muz.) trill, shake, quaver.
trilling v. vibration, quiver, quivering, trill.
trilogie v. trilogy.
trilplaat v. diaphragm.
trilpopulier m. trembling poplar.
trimester o. three months; (op school) term.
triomf m. triumph.
triomfboog m. triumphal arch.
triomftocht m. triumphal procession.
triplex o. triplex, three-ply.
trippelen on. w. trip.
triptiek v. triptych; (voor auto's) triptyque.
troebel b. n. troubled, turbid, cloudy, thick, muddy.
troebelen m. mv. disturbances, riots.
troef v. trump, trumps, trump-card.
troep m. (menigte, aantal) crowd, troop; (v. spelers) troupe, company; (bende: dieven, enz.) band, gang; (v. honden, wolven) pack; (kudde) flock, drove; **—en,** (mil.) troops, forces.
troepenmacht v. force, military forces.
troetelen o. w. coddle, pet, fondle.
troetelkind o. spoiled child, pet, fondling, mother's darling.
troetelnaam m. pet-name.
troffel m. (Z. N.) trowel.
trog m. trough.
trom v. drum.
trommel v. (trom) drum; (tn.) drum; barrel; (blikken doos) box, case.
trommelaar m. drummer; (mil.) drum.
trommelen on. w. drum; (op piano) drum, strum.
trommelvlies o. tympanum.
trommelvuur o. drum fire.
trommelzucht v. hoove, blast; (wet.) tympanites.
tromp v. (v. olifant) trunk; (muziekinstrument) trump, trumpet, horn; (v. vuurwapen) mouth, muzzle.
trompet v. trumpet.
trompetvogel m. trumpeter, trumpet-bird.
tronen on. w. throne, sit on the throne; reign.
tronen o. w. allure, entice, decoy.
tronie v. visage, face; (fam.) phiz, mug.

tronk *m.* (*stam*) trunk; (*stronk*) stump, stub.

troon *m.* throne.

troonhemel *m.* canopy, baldachin.

troonopvolger *m.* heir to the throne.

troonrede *v.* speech from the throne, royal speech, King's (Queen's) speech.

troonsafstand *m.* abdication.

troonsbestijging *v.* accession to the throne.

troost *m.* comfort, consolation.

troosteloos *b. n.* disconsolate, inconsolable; (*v. aanblik, landschap, enz.*) disconsolate, comfortless, dreary.

troosteloosheid *v.* disconsolateness, inconsolableness.

troosten *o. w.* comfort, console.

troostend *b. n.* comforting, consoling, consolatory.

troostprijs *m.* consolation prize.

troostrijk, troostvol *b. n.* comforting, consolatory.

tropen *m. mv.* tropics.

tropenkoorts *v.* dengue.

tros *m.* (*v. bloemen, vruchten*) cluster; (*v. druiven, bananen*) bunch; (*bloeiwijze*) raceme; (*sch.: touw*) hawser; (*mil.*) camptrain.

trosvormig *b. n.* (*Pl.*) racemose.

trots *z. n., m.* pride, haughtiness; *vw.* in spite of, in defiance of; *bw.* proudly, haughtily.

trots *b. n.* proud, haughty.

trotseren *o. w.* defy, bid defiance to, brave, face.

trotsering *v.* defiance.

trottoir *o.* footway, pavement; (*Am.*) side-walk.

trouw *b. n.* (*alg.*) faithful; (*v. vriend*) true, trusty; (*v. onderdanen*) loyal; (*v. bezoeker: geregeld*) regular; *bw.* faithfully, loyally; *z. n., r.* faithfulness; loyalty; fidelity; (*huwelijk*) marriage.

trouwakte *v.* marriage-certificate.

trouwdag *m.* wedding-day.

trouweloos *b. n.* (*bw.*) faithless(ly), disloyal(ly), perfidious(ly).

trouweloosheid *v.* faithlessness, disloyalty, perfidy.

trouwen *on. w. en o. w.* marry; wed.

trouwens *bw.* indeed, for that matter, after all.

trouwhartig *b. n.* true-hearted, candid, cordial; *bw.* candidly, cordially.

trouwhartigheid *v.* true-heartedness, candour, cordiality.

trouwkleed *o.* wedding-dress.

trouwlustig *b. n.* desirous of marrying.

trouwplechtigheid *v.* nuptial ceremony, wedding (ceremony).

trouwring *m.* wedding-ring.

truffel *v.* truffle.

trui *v.* jersey, guernsey; (*sport—*) sweater.

trust *v.* (*H.*) trust, pool.

truweel *o.* trowel.

Tsaar *m.* Czar, Tsar.

Tsarina *v.* Czarina, Tsarina.

Tsjechoslovakije *o.* Czechoslovakia.

tuberculeus *b. n.* tuberculous, tubercular.

tuberculose *v.* tuberculosis.

tucht *v.* discipline.

tuchteloos *b. n.* undisciplined, undisciplinable, insubordinate; (*losbandig*) dissolute, licentious.

tuchteloosheid *v.* indiscipline, insubordination; licence, licentiousness, dissoluteness.

tuchthuis *o.* house of correction, convict prison.

tuchthuisboef *m.* convict, jail-bird.

tuchthuisstraf *v.* imprisonment.

tuchtigen *o. w.* punish, chastise, correct.

tuchtiging *v.* punishment, chastisement, correction. [sure.

tuchtmaatregel *m.* castigatory measure

tuchtroede *v.* rod (of correction), chastening rod.

tuchtschool *v.* reformatory (school).

tuffen *on. w.* motor; (*fam.*) mote.

tuig *o.* (*gereedschap*) tools, utensils; (*sch.*) rigging, tackle; (*v. paard*) harness; (*slecht goed, prullen*) stuff, trash, rubbish; (*fig.: gemeen volk*) riff-raff, rabble, scum, vermin.

tuigen *o. w.* (*v. paard*) harness; (*v. schip*) rig.

tuil *m.* (*ruiker*) bunch (of flowers), nosegay; (*bloeiwijze*) corymb.

tuimelaar *m.* (*persoon; duif*) tumbler; (*Dk.: vis*) porpoise; (*v. geweer*) nut, tumbler; (*glas*) tumbler.

tuimelen *on. w.* tumble, topple over.

tuimeling *v.* tumble; (*v. paard, fiets*) spill; (*duikeling*) somersault.

tuimelraam *o.* flap-window, bascule window.

tuin *m.* garden.

tuinbed *o.* garden-bed.

tuinboon *v.* broad bean, horse-bean.

tuinbouw *m.* horticulture.

tuinbouwgereedschap *o.* horticultural implements.

tuinbouwkundige *m.* horticulturist.

tuinbouwschool *v.* school of gardening, horticultural college.

tuingereedschap *o.* gardener's tools.

tuingewassen *o. mv.* garden-plants.

tuinier *m.* gardener.

tuinieren *on. w.* garden, do gardening, do garden work.

tuinslang *v.* garden-hose.

tuit *v.* spout, nozzle.

tuitkan *v.* spouted pitcher.

tuk keen; — **op,** keen on; eager for, fond of.

tulband *m.* (*hoofddeksel*) turban; (*gebak*) raisin cake.

tule *v.* tulle.

tulp *v.* tulip.

tumult *o.* tumult.

tuniek *v.* tunic.

tunnel *v.* tunnel; (*v. station*) subway.

turen *on. w.* peer, stare, gaze.

turf *m.* peat; turf.

turfaarde v. peat-mould.
turfboer m. peat-man, peat-dealer.
turfstrooisel o. peat-litter, moss-litter.
Turkije o. Turkey.
turkoois m. en o. turquoise.
turnen on. w. do gymnastics, gymnasticize.
turngebouw o. gymnastic hall.
tussen vz. between; (te midden van) among, amidst.
tussenbedrijf o. interval, interact, interlude.
tussenbeide bw. (nu en dan) now and then, once in a while, between whiles; (tamelijk) middling, passable, so so.
tussenbeidekomen on. w. intervene, interfere, interpose.
tussendek o. (sch.) between decks; (3e klas) steerage.
tussendeur v. communicating-door, connecting door.
tussengevoegd b. n. interpolated, intercalary.
tussenhandel m. intermediate trade, commission-business.
tussenhaven v. intermediate port.
tussenkomend b. n. intervenient.
tussenkomst v. intervention; (bemiddeling) intermediary; (voorspraak) mediation, intercession.
tussenlanding v. vlucht zonder —, non stop flight.
tussenlassen o. w. interpolate.
tussenpersoon m. intermediary, agent, middleman.
tussenpoos v. interval, intermission; bij tussenpozen, at intervals.
tussenruimte v. intervening space, interspace, interstice, interval.
tussenschot o. partition; (Dk., Pl.) septum.
tussenspel o. interlude, interact, intermezzo.
tussentijds bw. between times, between whiles.
tussentijds b. n. —e verkiezing, by-election.
tussenvoegen o. w. insert, interpolate, intercalate.
tussenvoeging v. intercalation, interpolation. [tion.
tussenwerpsel o. (gram.) interjec-
tussenzin m. parenthesis, parenthetic clause.
twaalf telw. twelve.
twaalfde b. n. twelfth.
twaalftal o. twelve, dozen.
twaalfvingerig b. n. —e darm, duodenum.
twee telw. two; (op kaart, dobbelsteen) deuce.
tweebenig b. n. two-legged.
tweebladig b. n. two-leaved, bifoliate.
tweede b. n. second.
tweedekker m. (vl.) biplane, two-decker.
tweedracht v. discord.

tweedrachtig b. n. discordant, disunited.
tweegesprek o. dialogue.
tweegevecht o. duel, single combat.
tweehoevig b. n. cloven-footed; (wet.) bisulcate.
tweehoofdig b. n. two-headed; (wet.) bicephalous, bicipital.
tweejarig b. n. of two years, biennal.
tweeklank m. (gram.) diphthong.
tweeledig b. n. (v. betekenis, strekking) double; (dubbelzinnig) ambiguous, equivocal.
tweeling m. en v. (pair of) twins; de T—en, (sterr.) the Twins, Geminy.
tweelingbroeder m. twin-brother.
tweelobbig b. n. (Pl.) dicotyledonous.
tweemotorig b. n. twin-engined.
tweepersoons b. n. for two, double; (v. bed) double; (v. kamer) two-bedded; (sch.: v. hut) for two, two-bedded.
tweeslachtig b. n. bisexual, hermaphroditic; (amfibisch) amphibious; (fig.) ambiguous; — dier, amphibian.
tweespalt v. discord, dissension.
tweespan o. two-horse team.
tweespraak v. dialogue.
tweesprong m. cross-road, cross-way, bifurcation.
tweestrijd m. duel; (fig.) inward conflict, internal combat; in — staan, be in two minds.
tweetakkig b. n. bifurcate.
tweetal o. two, pair.
tweetalig b. n. bilingual, bilinguous.
tweevoud o. double; in —, in duplicate.
tweewieler m. two-wheeler, bicycle.
tweezaadlobbig b. n. (Pl.) bilobate.
tweezijdig b. n. two-sided; bilateral.
twijfel m. doubt.
twijfelaar (ster) m. (v.) doubter, sceptic.
twijfelachtig b. n. doubtful, dubious, questionable.
twijfelen on. w. doubt.
twijfeling v. doubt, hesitation.
twijfelzucht v. scepticism.
twijg v. twig, spray; (fig.: telg) scion.
twijn m. twine, twist.
twijnen o. w. twine, twist.
twintig telw. twenty.
twintigste b. n. twentieth (part).
twintigtal o. score, twenty.
twist m. quarrel, dispute, altercation.
twist o. (garen) twist.
twistappel m. apple of discord, bone of contention.
twisten on. w. quarrel, dispute, contend, wrangle.
twistgeding o. lawsuit, contentious issue.
twistgesprek o. disputation, dispute.
twistpunt o. disputed point, matter in dispute, controversial question (issue).
twiststoker m. fire-brand, mischiefmaker.
twistziek b. n. quarrelsome; contentious, disputatious.

twistzoeker *m.* quarrelsome person (fellow).
tyfus *m.* (*buik—*) typhoid (fever), enteric fever; (*vlek—*) typhus (fever).
type *o.* (*en r.*) type.

typen *o. w.* type (write).
typisch *b. n.* (*bw.*) typical(ly).
typist(**e**) *m.* (*v.*) typewriter, typist.
typograaf *m.* typographer.

U

U *v.* U.
U *vnw.* you; (*dicht.*) thee.
Ued. you, Your Honour.
ui *m.* (*Pl.*) onion; (*mop*) joke.
uientapper *m.* joker.
uier *m.* udder.
uil *m.* (*Dk.*) owl; (*domkop*) ninny, blockhead.
uilachtig *b. n.* owlish.
ulenspiegel *m.* Owlglass, Howleglass.
uilskuiken *o.* owl, goose, ninny, numskull.
uiltje *o.* owlet; (*vlinder*) owl-moth.
uit *rz.* out of; from; *bw.* out.
uitademen *on. w.* expire; *o. w.* expire, breathe out; (*fig.*) exhale.
uitbannen *o. w.* banish, expulse, exile; (*v. geesten*) exorcise.
uitbanning *v.* banishment, expulsion; exorcism, exorcization.
uitbarsten *on. w.* burst out, break out, explode; (*v. vulkaan*) erupt, break out.
uitbarsting *v.* explosion; eruption; outbreak; (*v. toorn, gelach*) burst; (*v. oproer, enz.*) outbreak.   [abroad.
uitbazuinen *o.w.* trumpet forth, blazon
uitbeelden *o. w.* (*afbeelden, afschilderen*) depict; (*voorstellen*) personate (*v. rol*) render.
uitbenen *o. w.* bone.
uitbesteden *o. w.* (*r. kind*) put out to nurse, board out; (*v. werk*) contract out, put out to contract.
uitbesteding *v.* putting out to board, boarding-out; contract, putting out to contract.
uitbetalen *o. w.* pay, pay out; (*v. check*) cash (up).
uitbetaling *v.* payment.
uitblazen *o. w.* (*v. licht*) blow out; (*v. ei*) blow; *on. w.* **even —,** breathe (oneself), have a breathing-spell.
uitblijven *on. w.* stay away, stop out; (*v. onweer, regen, enz.*) hold off.
uitblinken *on. w.* shine, excel.
uitbloeien *on. w.* cease blossoming.
uitblussen *o. w.* extinguish.
uitborstelen *o. w.* brush.
uitbotten *on. w.* bud (forth), sprout.
uitbouw *m.* annex, wing, extension.
uitbouwen *o. w.* extend, enlarge (by building).
uitbraaksel *o.* vomit.
uitbraken *o. w.* vomit, bring up, spew out; (*fig.*) belch forth (out).
uitbranden *o. v.* burn out; (*r. wond*) cauterize; *on. w.* be burned out.

uitbrander *m.* scolding, dressing-down, wigging.
uitbreiden *o. w.* (*uitstrekken: armen*) spread; (*v. zaken, werk, enz.*) enlarge; (*v. zaken, gebied*) extend; *w. w.* **zich —,** (*v. gebied, oppervlakte*) enlarge, extend, expand; (*v. ziekte, beweging, brand*) spread.
uitbreiding *v.* enlargement, extension, expansion; spreading.
uitbreken *o. w. en on. w.* break out; (*v. oorlog, ziekte, ook:*) burst out; (*uit gevangenis*) break (out of) prison, break jail; *z. n., o.* **het —,** (*v. oorlog, enz.*) the outbreak.   [er.
uitbreker *m.* jail-breaker, prison-break-
uitbrengen *o. w.* (*v. woorden*) bring out; (*v. geluid*) emit; (*v. stem*) give; (*v. verslag*) deliver; (*sch.*) run out; (*v. toast*) submit; (*aan 't licht brengen*) disclose, bring to light; (*v. geheim*) betray.
uitbroeden *o. w.* (*eieren, vogels*) hatch; (*kuikens, boze plannen*) brood.
uitbrullen *o. w.* roar (out).
uitbuiten *o. w.* (*v. persoon*) exploit, sweat, grind down; (*v. zaak*) exploit.
uitbundig *b. n.* (*bovenmatig*) exuberant; (*buitengewoon*) enthusiastic, excessive; *bw.* exuberantly; enthusiastically, excessively.
uitbundigheid *v.* exuberance; excess.
uitdagen *o. w.* (*tot gevecht*) challenge, call out; (*fig.*) defy, challenge.
uitdagend *b. n.* (*bw.*) defiant(ly).
uitdager *m.* challenger.
uitdaging *v.* challenge; provocation.
uitdelen *o. w.* (*geld, enz.*) distribute, deal out; (*aalmoezen*) dispense; (*straffen*) hand out, measure out.
uitdeler *m.* distributor; dispenser.
uitdeling *v.* distribution; (*H.: bij faillissement*) dividend.
uitdoen *o. w.* (*r. vuur, licht*) put out, extinguish; (*v. kleren: uittrekken*) take off, put off; (*doorhalen: v. schuld, enz*) cross out, cancel.
uitdossen *o. w.* attire, dress up, trim out; *w. w.* **zich —,** attire oneself.
uitdoven *o. w.* extinguish; (*fig.*) extinguish, quench; *on. w.* go out.
uitdoving *v.* extinguishment.
uitdraaien *o. w.* (*lamp, gas*) turn out; (*el. licht, ook:*) switch off (out); *on. w.* **op niets —,** come to nothing, fizzle out.
uitdragen *o. w.* carry out.
uitdrager *m.* second-hand dealer.

uitdrijven *o. w.* drive out, expel; (*v. geesten*) cast out, exorcize.

uitdrijving *v.* expulsion; casting out exorcization.

uitdrinken *on. w.* finish, empty; (*inééns*) drink off, toss off.

uitdrogen *o. w.* desiccate, exsiccate, dry up; (*v. pan, enz.*) wipe out; *on. w.* dry up.

uitdrukkelijk *b. n.* (*bw.*) express(ly), explicit(ly), positive(ly).

uitdrukken *o. w.* squeeze out, press out; (*fig.*) express.

uitdrukking *v.* expression, locution, term; (*bewoordingen: v. brief, enz.*) wording; **vol —**, expressive.

uiteen *bw.* asunder.

uiteengaan *on. w.* separate, part, disperse; (*v. vergadering, enz.*) break up; (*op reces gaan: v. Kamers, enz.*) rise.

uiteenlopen *on. w.* diverge.

uiteenlopend *b. n.* divergent, different.

uiteenspreiden *o. w.* spread out, un-fold.

uiteenvallen *on. w.* fall apart, fall to pieces; (*v. verbond, enz.*) break up.

uiteinde *o.* end, extremity, extreme point; (*fig.*) end.

uiten *o. w.* utter, express, give utterance to; *w. w.* **zich —**, express oneself.

uiteraard *bw.* naturally, of its very nature.

uiterlijk *b. n.* outward, external; *bw.* outwardly, externally; (*op zijn meest*) at the utmost; (*op zijn laatst*) at the latest; *z. n., o.* (outward) appearance, exterior.

uiterst *b. n.* (*v. plaats*) outmost, farthermost, extreme; (*fig.*) utmost, outside, utter, extreme; *bw.* extremely, in the extreme, supremely, highly.

uiterste *o.* extreme, extremity.

uitfluiten *o. w.* hiss, catcall.

uitgaaf *v.* (*v. geld*) expenditure, expense; (*v. boek, enz.*) publication; (*druk*) edition.

uitgaan *on. w.* (*v. persoon, vuur, licht, enz.*) go out. [day.

uitgaansdag *m.* day out, day off, off-

uitgang *m.* egress, issue, way out, exit; (*v. woord*) ending, termination.

uitgangspunt *o.* starting-point.

uitgebreid *b. n.* (*bw.*) extensive(ly), comprehensive(ly).

uitgebreidheid *v.* extensiveness, extent.

uitgehongerd *b. n.* famished, famishing, ravenous, starved, starving.

uitgelaten *b. n.* elated, exultant, exuberant, rollicking.

uitgelatenheid *v.* elation, exuberance, exuberant joy.

uitgeleefd *b. n.* decrepit.

uitgeleide *o.* conduct; **— doen,** show out; (*aan trein, enz.*) see off, give a send-off.

uitgelezen *b. n.* (*v. wijn, gezelschap*) select; (*v. vruchten, sigaren*) choice; (*v. boek: gelezen*) read, finished.

uitgenomen *b. n.* except, excepted.

uitgeslapen *b. n.* (*fig.*) wide-awake, knowing, shrewd.

uitgestorven *b. n.* (*v. dieren*) extinct; (*v. plaats*) deserted.

uitgestrekt *b. n.* extensive, vast.

uitgestrektheid *v.* extent, extension, expanse.

uitgeven *o. w.* (*v. geld*) spend; (*v. bankbiljetten, lening, enz.*) issue; (*v. bankbiljetten, ook:*) emit; (*uitdelen*) distribute; (*v. boek, enz.*) publish; (*voor de druk verzorgen*) edit; *w. w.* **zich — voor,** give oneself out as, pass oneself off as (for).

uitgever *m.* publisher.

uitgeversfirma *v.* publishing-firm.

uitgewekene *m. en v.* emigrant, refugee.

uitgewezene *m.* exile, banished person.

uitgezocht *b. n.* zie **uitgelezen.**

uitgezonderd *b. n.* except, excepted, save.

uitgifte *v.* issue, emission; (*v. nieuw kapitaal*) output.

uitglijden *on. w.* slip, slide.

uithalen *o. w.* (*schoonmaken*) (*v. kamer*) turn out; (*v. vis*) gut; (*v. pijp, enz.*) clean; (*uittrekken*) draw out, pull out; (*bij breien, enz.*) unpick; (*bij 't zingen*) draw out; (*v. zakken, enz.*) turn out, clear out; (*streken, grappen*) play, perpetrate; (*sch.*) track, haul; *on. w.* (*uitwijken*) pull out, fetch out; (*feestelijk onthalen*) make a grand set-out.

uithangbord *o.* sign-board, shop-sign.

uithangen *o. w.* hang out; (*fig.*) play; *on. w.* **waar zou hij —?** where can he hang out (stick)?

uitheems *b. n.* (*v. woorden, voortbrengselen*) foreign; (*v. planten*) exotic; (*vreemd, zonderling: v. gewoonten, enz.*) strange.

uithoek *m.* out-of-the-way place (corner), remote corner.

uithongeren *o. w.* famish, starve (out).

uithoren *o. w.* draw (out), pump.

uithouden *o. w.* hold out; (*fig.*) bear, suffer, stand.

uithoudingsvermogen *o.* staying-power; enduringness.

uithuizig *b. n.* gadabout, from home.

uiting *v.* utterance, uttering, expression.

uitjouwen *o. w.* hoot at.

uitkeren *o. w.* pay, share out.

uitkering *v.* payment, share out; (*bij faillissement*) dividend; (*bij verzekering*) benefit; (*bij staking*) strike-pay; (*aan werklozen*) unemployment dole (allowance, benefit).

uitkiezen *o. w.* choose, select.

uitkijken *on. w.* look out; **— naar,** look out for, watch for; *o. w.* **zich de ogen —,** stare one's eyes out.

uitkijkpost *m.* observation-post, look-out.

uitkijktoren *m.* conning-tower, watch-tower.

uitklaring *v.* clearing, clearance.

uitkleden *o. w.* undress, strip; *w. w.* **zich —,** undress, strip.
uitkloppen *o. w.* (*tapijten, enz.*) beat; (*pijp*) beat out; knock out.
uitknippen *o. w.* cut out, clip out.
uitkoken *o. w.* boil.
uitkomen *on. w.* (*ergens uit komen*) come out, come forth; (*v. bomen: uitlopen*) come out, bud out; (*v. kuiken, enz.*) hatch (out), come out of the shell; — of the egg; (*v. boek, enz.*) come out, appear, be published; (*v. droom, voorspelling*) come true; (*bekend worden*) get out, come out, become known; (*v. misdaad*) come out, come to light, be brought to light; (*bij kaartspel*) lead, play first; (*v. som*) come out, work out, come right; (*in 't oog vallen*) show, come out; (*rondkomen, toekomen*) make both ends meet; **doen —,** accentuate, bring out; (*voordeel, enz.*) set off; **— op,** (*v. kamer, enz.*) open into (on, on to); (*v. straat, enz.*) debouch on to.
uitkomst *v.* (*afloop, uitslag*) result, issue; (*v. vraagstuk*) result; (*redding*) relief, deliverance.
uitkrabben *o. w.* scratch out.
uitlaat *m.* exhaust; (*v. riool*) outfall.
uitlachen *o. w.* laugh at; *on. w.* laugh one's fill.
uitladen *o. w.* unlade, unload.
uitlaten *o. w.* (*v. persoon, hond, enz.*) let out; (*v. bezoeker*) see out; (*weglaten: v. woord, enz.*) leave out, omit; (*v. kleding*) leave off; (*v. stoom*) let off; (*v. gas: uit ballon, enz.*) release; *w. w.* **zich — over iets,** let on about it.
uitlating *v.* (*weglating*) letting out, omission; (*gram.*) elision; (*uiting, gezegde*) utterance; (*uit toneelstuk*) cut.
uitleg *m.* (*verklaring*) explanation, interpretation; (*v. iemands woorden*) construction; (*v. stad, enz.*) extension, enlargement.
uitleggen *o. w.* (*verklaren*) explain, make clear, expose, expound; (*v. wet, droom*) interpret; (*v. stad, enz.*) extend; (*v. kledingstuk*) let out.
uitlegger *m.* explainer; expounder; interpreter.
uitlegging *v.* explanation, exposition; interpretation; (*v. d. Bijbel*) exegesis.
uitlekken *on. w.* leak out; (*fig., ook:*) trickle out, transpire.
uitlenen *o. w.* lend out.
uitleveren *o. w.* deliver up, hand over; (*v. misdadiger*) extradite.
uitlevering *v.* extradition.
uitlokken *o. w.* (*twist, oorlog, enz.*) provoke; (*antwoord, verklaring*) elicit; (*kritiek*) invite, evoke; (*protest, vinnig antwoord*) bring forth; **— tot,** entice to.
uitloop *m.* (*v. water*) outlet.
uitlopen *on. w.* (*v. persoon*) run out, go out; (*uitbotten*) bud, shoot, sprout, come out; (*v. schip*) sail, put out; (*v. vliegtuig*) taxi.
uitloper *m.* (*v. persoon*) gadabout,

gadder; (*v. planten*) offshoot, sucker; (*v. gebergte*) spur.
uitloting *v.* drawing.
uitloven *o. w.* offer, promise.
uitmaken *o. w.* (*v. boek, spel, enz.*) finish; (*v. verloving, enz.*) break off; (*beslissen, beslechten*) decide, settle; (*vormen*) form, constitute; (*uitdoven*) put out; call names.
uitmergelen *o. w.* exhaust.
uitmeten *o. w.* (*meten*) measure; (*in 't klein verkopen*) measure out.
uitmonden *on. w.* **— in,** debouch into.
uitmonding *v.* debouchment, embouchure.
uitmunten *on. w.* excel (in, at); **— boven,** excel, surpass.
uitmuntend *b. n.* (*bw.*) excellent(ly); eminent(ly); **—e cijfers,** (*op school*) top-marks.
uitmuntendheid *v.* excellence; eminence.
uitnemen *o. w.* take out.
uitnodigen *o. w.* invite.
uitnodiging *v.* invitation.
uitoefenen *o. w.* (*beroep, invloed, recht*) exercise; (*vak*) practise, carry on, prosecute; (*ambt*) hold, occupy.
uitpakken *o. w.* unpack; *on. w.* pour out (unpack) one's heart, unpack one's soul; (*opsnijden*) fling (sling, throw) the hatchet.
uitpluizen *o. w.* pick; sift (out).
uitplunderen *o. w.* plunder, pillage sack, ransack.
uitproesten *o. w.* **het —,** burst out laughing.
uitpuilen *on. w.* protrude, bulge, protuberate; (*v. aderen*) stand out.
uitputten *o. w.* draw out, exhaust; *w. w.* **zich —,** exhaust oneself.
uitputting *v.* exhaustion; (*door ondervoeding, ook:*) inanition.
uitrafelen *o. w.* ravel out, fray.
uitreiken *o. w.* distribute, give, deliver; (*kaartjes, enz.*) issue.
uitreiking *v.* distribution, delivery; issue.
uitrekbaar *b. n.* extensible, elastic.
uitrekenen *o. w.* calculate, compute; (*v. vraagstuk*) work out.
uitrekken *o. w.* stretch (out); *w. w.* **zich —,** stretch oneself.
uitrichten *o. w.* perform, do.
uitroeien *o. w.* (*eig. en fig.*) root out, eradicate, extirpate; (*fig. ook:*) exterminate; (*v. onkruid*) weed out; (*v. ratten, enz.*) destroy.
uitroep *m.* exclamation, shout, cry.
uitroepen *o. w.* exclaim, cry out, call out; (*tot koning, veldheer, enz.*) proclaim.
uitroep(ings)teken *o.* note of exclamation.
uitrukken *o. w.* pull out, pluck out; (*haar*) tear; *on. w.* (*mil.*) march (out); (*v. brandweer, wacht*) turn out.
uitrusten *on. w.* rest, take rest, repose, repose oneself.

uitrusten *o. w.* (*r. persoon, leger, schip*) equip; (*r. persoon, vloot*) fit out; (*r. paard: optuigen*) caparison.

uitrusting *r.* equipment; fitting out; caparison; (*voor reis, enz.*) outfit.

uitschakelaar *m.* (*el.*) circuit-breaker, cut-out.

uitschakelen *o. w.* (*el.*) switch off, cut out, put out of circuit; (*fig.*) eliminate, exclude.

uitschakeling *r.* switching-off, putting out of circuit; elimination.

uitscheiden *on. w.* stop, leave off; *o. w.* excrete.

uitschelden *o. w.* call names, abuse.

uitschilderen *o. w.* paint, portray.

uitschot *o.* rejects, refuse, returns, cullings, throw-outs; (*bocht*) rubbish, trash; (*v. personen*) trash, rubbish, riff-raff, dregs (of the gutter, of the people).

uitschrappen *o. w.* scrape (out); (*doorhalen*) scratch out, erase.

uitschrijven *o. w.* write out; (*r. rekening, enz.*) make out, draw out; (*r. lening*) issue; (*v. vergadering*) call, convene.

uitschudden *o. w.* shake (out); (*v. persoon*) clean out, strip to the skin.

uitslaan *o. w.* beat out, strike out; (*v. spijker*) drive out; (*r. tapijten, enz.*) shake, beat; (*v. tafelkleed, enz.*) unfold; (*v. armen, vleugels*) stretch out, spread; (*v. klauwen*) put forth; (*H.*) release; *on. w.* (*v. vlammen*) break out (forth); (*r. mazelen*) come out; (*v. uitslag*) break out; (*v. muur*) sweat, give.

uitslag *m.* (*afloop*) result, issue, event; (*op huid*) eruption, rash; (*schimmel*) mouldiness; (*salpeter*) efflorescence.

uitslapen *o. w. en on. w.* sleep one's fill.

uitsluiten *o. w.* (*v. persoon*) exclude; (*r. twijfel, misverstand, enz.*) preclude; (*buiten sluiten*) shut out, lock out; (*v. werklieden*) lock out.

uitsluitend *b. n.* (*bw.*) exclusive(ly).

uitsluiting *v.* exclusion; preclusion; lock out.

uitsnijden *o. w.* cut out, excise; (*v. hout*) carve (out).

uitsnijding *v.* cutting out, excision.

uitspannen *o. w.* (*v. paard*) take out, unharness; (*uitstrekken*) stretch out, extend; (*v. net, zeil, enz.*) spread; *on. w.* unteam; *w. w.* **zich —**, unbend, recreate.

uitspanning *v.* (*pleisterplaats*) baiting-place; garden-restaurant, garden-café, tea-garden; (*fig.*) recreation, relaxation; (*op school*) break time.

uitspansel *o.* firmament, sky, heavens.

uitsparen *o. w.* save, economize.

uitspatting *r.* dissipation, debauch(ery).

uitspelen *o. w.* (*r. kaart, enz.*) play, lead; (*v. spel*) finish.

uitspraak *v.* (*wijze van spreken*) pronunciation; (*uitlating*) utterance, pronouncement; (*recht*) judg(e)ment,

sentence; (*r. jury*) verdict; (*r. scheidsrechter*) award.

uitspraakleer *v.* phonetics, orthoepy.

uitspreiden *o. w.* spread (out).

uitspreken *o. w.* (*woord, oordeel, enz.*) pronounce; (*mening, wens, dank*) express; *on. w.* finish (speaking).

uitspruiten *on. w.* (*Pl.*) sprout, shoot up.

uitstaan *o. w.* endure, suffer, bear; *on. w.* be put out at interest, stand out.

uitstalkast *r.* show-case.

uitstallen *o. w.* expose for sale.

uitstalling *v.* (shop-window) display; (*handeling*) window-dressing.

uitstapje *o.* excursion, tour, trip, jaunt.

uitstappen *on. w.* get out, step out, alight.

uitstedig *b. n.* absent from town.

uitsteeksel *o.* projection; protuberance; (*r. been*) process.

uitstek *o.* projection; **bij —**, par excellence, pre-eminently.

uitsteken *o. w.* (*r. hand, enz.*) hold out, stretch out, extend; (*r. tong, vlag*) put out; *on. w.* (*in elke richting*) stick out; (*horizontaal*) jut out, project, protrude.

uitstekend *b. n.* excellent, eminent; first-rate; (*v. werk, enz.*) high-class; *bw.* excellently, eminently, extremely well.

uitstel *o.* delay, postponement, respite; **— van betaling,** extension (deferment) of payment.

uitstellen *o. w.* delay, defer, put off, postpone.

uitstelling *v.* (*v. 't H. Sacrament*) exposition (of the Blessed Sacrament).

uitsterven *on. w.* die out; become extinct.

uitstomen *on. w.* steam out; *o. w.* dry-clean.

uitstorten *o. w.* pour out, pour forth, shed; *w. w.* **zich —**, discharge itself, disgorge itself; (*fig.*) unbosom oneself.

uitstralen *o. w.* give out, send out, beam forth, radiate.

uitstraling *v.* radiation, emanation.

uitstrekken *o. w.* stretch, stretch out, stretch forth, reach out; *w. w.* **zich —**, (*v. land, enz.*) extend, stretch (out); (*r. persoon, dier*) stretch (out), extend, reach.

uitstrooien *o. w.* strew, spread, disseminate; (*fig.*) spread, disseminate, circulate, put about.

uitstrooisel *o.* (false) rumour, false report.

uitsturen *o. w.* send out.

uitteren *on. w.* pine (waste) away, waste.

uittocht *m.* departure, exodus.

uittreden *on. w.* step out; (*mil.*) fall out; (*uit zaken, firma, enz.*) retire.

uittrekken *o. w.* (*r. tand, kruiden, enz.*) extract, draw; (*r. kleren*) take off, strip off; (*v. schoenen, handschoenen*) pull off; (*v. lade, enz.*) pull out; (*r. tafel, ook:*) extend; (*v. bedrag*) appropriate.

uittreksel *o.* (*beknopt overzicht, korte*

inhoud) abridgment, abstract, epitome; (*passage*) extract, excerpt; (*afkooksel*) extract.
uitvaagsel *o.* sweepings, off-scourings, dregs, scum (of the people).
uitvaardigen *o. w.* (*v. bevel, enz.*) issue; (*v. wet, decreet*) promulgate.
uitvaart *v.* funeral, obsequies.
uitval *m.* (*mil.*) sally, sortie; (*bij schermen*) thrust, lunge; (*fig.*) outburst, sally.
uitvallen *on. w.* (*alg.*) fall out; (*v. haar*) come out, fall out; (*mil.*) make a sally, sally out; (*bij een mars*) fall out; (*bij schermen*) lunge; (*fig.*) fly out, flare up; (*gebeuren, uitkomen*) turn out.
uitvechten *o. w. het —*, fight it out, battle it out.
uitvegen *o. w.* sweep out; (*v. woord, enz.*) wipe out, efface.
uitverkocht *b. n.* (*v. boek*) out of print; (*v. artikel*) sold out (off), out of stock; (*v. schouwburg, enz.*) house full.
uitverkoop *m.* selling off, clearance sale.
uitverkopen *o. w. en on. w.* sell off, clear, hold a clearance sale.
uitverkoren *b. n.* chosen, elect, select; *—e*, sweetheart, favourite. [find out.
uitvinden *o. w.* invent; (*opsporen*)
uitvinder *m.* inventor.
uitvinding *v.* invention.
uitvissen *o. w.* fish out; (*fig.*) fish out, ferret out, nose out, scent out.
uitvloeisel *o.* outcome, consequence, result.
uitvlucht *v.* pretext, evasion, subterfuge, prevarication.
uitvoer *m.* export, exportation; *ten — brengen*, execute, carry into effect.
uitvoerder *m.* executor; (*H.*) exporter.
uitvoeren *o. w.* (*v. bevel, plan, enz.*) execute; (*v. plan, bedreiging, enz.*) carry into execution; (*v. besluit, overeenkomst, bevel*) carry into effect, carry out; (*v. bestelling*) execute, fill; (*v. goederen*) export; (*operatie, taak*) perform.
uitvoerend *b. n.* executive.
uitvoerhandel *m.* export trade.
uitvoerig *b. n.* ample, copious, full, circumstantial, minute, detailed; *bw.* amply, copiously, fully, minutely, in detail.
uitvoerigheid *v.* ampleness, copiousness, circumstantiality.
uitvoering *v.* (*v. bevel, enz.*) execution; (*v. boek*) get-up, make up; (*voorstelling*) performance; (*afwerking*) finish.
uitvoerrechten *o. mv.* export-duties.
uitvoervergunning *v.* licence to export goods, export licence.
uitvorsen *o. w.* find out, ferret out.
uitvragen *o. w.* interrogate; catechize.
uitwas *o.* outgrowth, excrescence.
uitwaseming *v.* exhalation; evaporation.
uitwassen *o. w.* wash out; (*v. wond*) bathe.
uitweg *m.* way-out, escape; (*v. vloeistof*)

outlet; (*fig.*) way-out, outlet, expedient.
uitweiden *on. w.* digress; *— over*, expatiate on, enlarge on (upon), digress on.
uitwendig *b. n.* external, outward; *bw.* externally, outwardly; on the outside.
uitwerken *o. w.* (*v. plan, enz.*) work out; (*v. schema, enz.*) elaborate; (*v. gedachte*) develop; (*tot stand brengen*) bring about, effect; *on. w.* work; (*uitgisten*) cease fermenting.
uitwerking *v.* working-out; elaboration; (*resultaat*) effect, result; *geen — hebben*, be ineffective, produce no effect; *— hebben*, be effective.
uitwerpen *o. w.* throw out, cast out, eject; (*v. ballast*) empty; (*uitbraken*) vomit.
uitwerpselen *o. mv.* excrements, excreta.
uitwijken *on. w.* (*op zij gaan*) step aside, turn aside, give way; (*v. auto, enz.*) pull out; (*naar buitenland*) emigrate; (*v. muur*) sag, bulge (out); *niet —, (sch.*) stand on.
uitwijzen *o. w.* (*tonen*) show; (*beslissen*) decide; (*uit het land*) expel, banish.
uitwijzing *v.* expulsion.
uitwinnen *o. w.* save.
uitwisselen *o. w.* exchange; interchange.
uitwissen *o. w.* blot out, wipe out, expunge, efface.
uitwringen *o. w.* wring out, extort.
uitzenden *o. w.* send out, dispatch; (*radio*) broadcast, radiate.
uitzending *v.* sending out, dispatch; (*radio*) broadcasting, radiation.
uitzet *m.* outfit; (*v. bruid*) trousseau.
uitzetbaar *b. n.* expansive, dilatable.
uitzetten *o. w.* (*in omvang doen toenemen*) expand, extend, enlarge; (*nat.*) expand, dilate; (*v. geld*) invest, put out; lay out; (*sch.: v. boot*) put out, get out, lower; (*mil.: v. schildwacht*) post; (*uit land*) expel, banish; (*recht: uit huis*) evict; *on. w.* (*alg.*) expand, dilate, swell; (*nat.*) expand, dilate; *w. w. zich —*, expand.
uitzicht *o.* view; (*eig. en fig.*) outlook, prospect, perspective.
uitzien *on. w.* look out; *er —*, look; *— naar*, look out for; (*trachten*) look forward to.
uitziften *o. w.* sift (out); (*fig.*) sift out, thrash out.
uitzinnig *b. n.* distracted, demented.
uitzinnigheid *v.* distraction, dementia.
uitzitten *o. w.* sit out.
uitzoeken *o. w.* select; choose; (*sorteren*) sort (out); (*v. was*) look out.
uitzondering *v.* exception; *bij —*, exceptionally, by way of exception.
uitzonderingstarief *o.* exceptional rate, preferential tariff.
uitzuigen *o. w.* suck (out); (*fig.*) sweat, extort.

uitzweten *o. w.* exude, ooze out, sweat out.
ultimatum *o.* ultimatum.
unicum *o.* single copy; unique thing.
unie *v.* union.
uniform *b. n.* uniform; *z. n., v. (alg.)* uniform; *(mil.)* uniform, regimentals.
universiteit *v.* university, college.
urine *v.* urine.
urn *v.* urn.
usantie *v.* usage, custom; *(H.)* uso, usance.
uso *o. (H.)* usance.
usowissel *m.* bill at usance.

ut *v. (muz.)* ut, do.
uur *o.* hour.
uurloon *o.* hourly pay.
uurwerk *o.* clock, watch, timepiece.
uurwerkmaker *m.* clock-maker, watch-maker.
uw *bez. vnw.* your, thy; **de —e, het —e,** yours, thine.
uwent *bw.* **ten —,** at your home; at your place.
uwentwege *bw.* **van —,** in your name, on your behalf.
uwentwil om —, for your sake.
uwerzijds *bw.* on your part.

V

vaag *b. n.* vague; *(v. ideeën)* hazy, foggy, vague; *(v. verslag, enz.)* loose; *(onbepaald)* indefinite.
vaak *m.* sleepiness; **— hebben,** be sleepy.
vaak *bw.* often, frequently.
vaal *b. n. (v. gelaatskleur)* sallow; *(v. kleur)* ashen; *(fig.)* drab.
vaalbleek *b. n.* sallow, muddy.
vaalheid *v.* sallowness.
vaan *v.* flag, banner, standard.
vaandel *o.* standard, colour(s), ensign.
vaandrig *m.* standard-bearer; *(v. ruiterij)* cornet.
vaardig *b. n.* adroit, clever; *(gereed)* ready.
vaardigheid *v.* cleverness, dexterity, proficiency; readiness; fluency.
vaargeul *v.* channel; *(in het ijs)* lane, ice-lane.
vaars *v.* heifer.
vaart *v. (scheepvaart)* navigation; *(snelheid)* speed, headway; *(kanaal)* canal, waterway.
vaartuig *o.* vessel.
vaarwater *o.* fairway, channel, waterway.
vaarwel *tw.* farewell, good-bye, adieu; *z. n., o.* farewell.
vaas *v.* vase.
vaatdoek *m.* dish-cloth, dish-towel, clout.
vaatje *o.* little (small) barrel (cask), keg.
vaatwerk *o.* casks and tubs; (plates and) dishes.
vacatie *v.* sitting.
vacatiegeld *o.* fee.
vacature *v.* vacancy; vacant place.
vacht *v.* fleece, pelt, fell.
vadem *m.* fathom.
vader *m.* father.
vaderland *o.* (native) country, fatherland.
vaderlander *m.* patriot.
vaderlandlievend *b. n. (bw.)* patriotic-(ally).
vaderlandsliefde *v.* love of country, patriotism.

vaderschap *o.* paternity, fatherhood.
vadsig *b. n.* lazy, inert, indolent.
vadsigheid *v.* laziness, inertness, indolence.
vagebond *m.* vagabond, tramp.
vagevuur *o.* purgatory.
vak *o. (v. studie)* branch, subject; *(beroep)* trade, line; *(v. dokter, leraar, enz.)* profession; *(hokje: v. kast, enz.)* partition, compartment, pigeon-hole; *(v. muur)* bay; *(v. beschot, enz.)* panel; *(v. begraafplaats)* plot.
vakantie *v.* holiday(s); *(vooral v. rechtbank en universiteit)* vacation.
vakantiereis(je) *v. (o.)* holiday-trip.
vakarbeider *m.* skilled labourer.
vakbond *m.* trade-union.
vakkundig *b. n.* competent, skilled.
vakman *m.* expert; *(handwerksman)* skilled labourer; *(niet-handwerksman)* professional man.
vakschool *v.* professional school, trade school, vocational school.
vakvereniging *v.* trade-union; *(v. dokters, enz.)* professional union.
val *m.* fall; *(fig.)* fall, overthrow, downfall; **een — doen,** have a fall; **ten — brengen,** *(v. persoon)* ruin, bring to ruin; *(v. regering)* overthrow, bring down.
val *v.* trap; **een — zetten,** set a trap.
val *o. (sch.)* halyard.
valbijl *v.* guillotine.
valbrug *v.* draw-bridge.
valdeur *v.* trap-door; *(v. sluis)* penstock.
valies *o.* portmanteau, carpet-bag, travelling-bag, valise.
valk *m.* falcon, hawk.
vallei *v.* valley; *(nauw en begroeid)* dell; *(dicht.)* vale, dale.
vallen *on. w.* fall; drop, go down; *z. n., o. (v. avond)* nightfall; *(v. water)* fall.
vallend *b. n.* **—e ster,** shooting star, falling star.
valling *v. (helling)* slope; *(sch.: v. mast,*

steven) rake; (*Z. N.: verkoudheid*) cold (in the head).
valluik *o.* hatch; trapdoor; (*op toneel*) vampire; (*v. galg*) drop.
vals *b. n.* (*niet echt*) false; (*niet oprecht*) false, perfidious, treacherous, guileful; (*boosaardig: v. paard, hond, enz.*) vicious; (*v. bankbiljet, enz.*) forged, bad, false; (*v. getuigschrift*) spurious; *bw.* falsely.
valsaard *m.* false (perfidious, treacherous) person.
valscherm *o.* parachute.
valschermspringer *m.* parachutist.
valsheid *v.* falseness, falsehood, perfidy, treachery; — *in geschrifte*, forgery.
valstrik *m.* gin, snare, trap; (*fig.*) snare, trap, pitfall.
valuta *v.* value; (*koers*) exchange, rate of exchange; (*geld*) currency.
van *vz.* (*bezit*) of; (*ook uitgedrukt door* 2e *naamval*); (*afkomst*) of; (*scheiding*) from; (*oorzaak*) with, from, for; (*vóór stofnaam*) of; (*eigenschap, datum*) of; *z. n., m.* family-name.
vanaf *vz.* from.
vanavond *bw.* this evening, to-night.
vandaag *bw.* to-day.
vandaan *bw.* **daar** —, from that place.
vandaar *bw.* (*oorzaak*) hence; (*plaats*) from there.
vangen *o. w.* catch, capture; (*snappen*) catch, trap, entrap.
vangst *v.* catch, capture; bag.
vanille *v.* vanilla.
vanillestokje *o.* vanilla-pod, stick of vanilla.
vanouds *bw.* of old.
vanwaar *bw.* from where, whence, from what place.
vanwege *vz.* on account of, because of, by reason of; (*namens*) in the name of, on behalf of.
vanzelf *bw.* of itself, of its own accord.
varen *v.* (*Pl.*) fern, bracken, brake.
varen *on. w.* navigate, sail; *o. w.* **iem. over de rivier** —, take (row) a person across the river.
variëteit *v.* variety.
varken *o.* pig, swine, hog (*ook fig.*); (*gemest* —) porker; (*borstel*) scrubber, carpet brush; (*watervat*) breaker; (*student*) outsider.
varkensgehakt *o.* sausage meat.
varkenshok *o.* piggery, pig-pen, pigsty.
varkenstrog *m.* pig-tub, hog-trough.
varkensvlees *o.* pork.
vast *b. n.* fast; firm; fixed; steady; permanent; (*niet vloeibaar*) solid; *bw.* fast; firm, firmly; (*alvast*) just as well.
vastberaden *b. n.* resolute, firm, determined.
vastberadenheid *v.* resoluteness, resolution, firmness, determination.
vasteland *o.* continent; mainland.
vasten *v.* lent.
vasten *on. w.* fast.

vastenavond *m.* Shrove Tuesday.
vastenavondgek *m.* carnaval buffoon, Merry Andrew.
vastenbrief *m.* Lenten pastoral (letter).
vastendag *m.* fast-day, fasting-day.
vasthechten *o. w.* attach, fasten, fix; *w. w.* **zich** — **aan,** attach oneself to, cling to.
vastheid *v.* firmness, fixity, fixedness, solidity; stability.
vasthouden *o. w.* hold, hold fast; (*v. goederen: niet verkopen*) hold up, hang on to; (*gevangen houden*) detain; (*mil.: v. vijand*) contain, hold; *on. w.* — **aan,** stick to; be tenacious of; cling to; *w. w.* **zich** —, hold fast, hold tight.
vasthoudend *b. n.* tenacious; (*behoudend*) conservative; (*gierig*) tight-fisted, stingy, close, niggardly.
vastleggen *o. w.* fix, fasten; (*v. hond*) chain up, tie, fasten; (*v. boot*) moor; (*fig.: v. kapitaal*) tie up, lock up; (*betekenis v. woord*) fasten down; (*in de geest*) fixe, file.
vastlopen *on. w.* (*v. machine*) jam, get stuck; (*v. schip*) run aground; (*fig.*) get stuck, stick fast; (*v. onderhandelingen, enz.*) end in a deadlock.
vaststaan *on. w.* stand firm, stand fast, be steady; **dat staat vast,** that is a fact.
vaststellen *o. w.* (*v. feit*) establish, ascertain; (*v. dag, tijdstip*) appoint, fix; (*v. bedrag, betekenis v. woord*) determine; (*v. schade*) assess, place; (*v. dividend*) declare; (*v. voorwaarden*) stipulate; (*v. identiteit, doodsoorzaak, enz.*) establish; (*v. ziektegeval*) diagnose; (*v. grenzen*) fix, delimit, settle.
vaststelling *v.* establishment; appointment, fixation; determination; declaration; delimitation, settlement.
vastzetten *o. w.* fasten, set fast, set tight; (*v. geld*) tie up, lock up; (*v. wiel*) chock; (*v. wekker*) stop; (*v. venster*) wedge; (*in gevangenis*) commit to prison, put into prison; (*door redenering*) corner, stump, pose, gravel.
vat *o.* cask, barrel, butt, tun; (*Pl.; Dk.*) vessel.
vat *m.* hold, grip; **geen** — **op iem. hebben,** have no hold on a person.
vatbaar *b. n.* — **voor,** capable of, accessible to, susceptible to, liable to, amenable to, pervious to, open to.
Vatikaan *o.* Vatican.
vatten *o. w.* catch, seize, grasp; (*begrijpen*) understand, comprehend; (*diamant, enz.*) set, mount.
vechten *on. w.* fight, combat.
vechtersbaas *m.* fighter, scrapper, game-cock.
vechtjas *m.* slasher, soldier.
vechtpartij *v.* fight, scrap, scuffle, tussle.
veder *v.* feather; zie **veer**.
vederbos *m.* tuft, crest, plume; (*op helm*) panache, plume.
vederwolk *v.* cirrus (*mv.: cirri*).

vee *o.* cattle; live-stock.
veearts *m.* veterinary surgeon.
veeartsenijkunde *v.* veterinary art.
veefokker *m.* cattle-breeder, stock-breeder, stock-raiser.
veeg *b. n.* fated, doomed; (*noodlottig*) fatal, ominous.
veeg *m.* (*met bezem*) whisk; (*met doek, enz.*) wipe; (*klap: in gezicht*) slap; (*om de oren*) wipe, swipe, box.
veegsel *o.* sweepings.
veehoeder *m.* herdsman, cattle-herd.
veekoek *m.* cattle-cake, cattle-feeding cake, oil-cake, linseed-cake.
veel *telw.* (*vóór enkelv.*) much, a good deal, a great deal; (*vóór mv.*) many; *te* —, too much; too many; — *te* —, much too much; far too many; *bw.* much, far; (*dikwijls*) often, frequently.
veelal *bw.* often, many times, as a rule.
veelbetekenend *b. n.* significant, meaning; *bw.* significantly, meaningly, with meaning.
veelbewogen *b. n.* very agitated, eventful, convulsive, stirring, chequered.
veeleer *bw.* rather, sooner.
veeleisend *b. n.* exacting, exigent.
veelhoek *m.* polygon.
veelkleurig *b. n.* many-coloured, multi-coloured, variegated, polychrome.
veelomstreden *b. n.* much disputed, vexed.
veelomvattend *b. n.* much embracing, wide.
veelsoortig *b.n.* manifold, multifarious.
veelstemmig *b. n.* many-voiced; (*muz.*) polyphonous, polyphonic.
veelvoud *o.* multiple.
veelvraat *m.* (*Dk.*) wolverine; (*fig.*) glutton.
veelvuldig *b. n.* frequent; manifold, multifarious.
veelwijverij *v.* polygamy.
veelzeggend *b. n.* significant, pregnant.
veelzijdig *b. n.* many-sided, multi-lateral; (*fig.*) versatile, many-sided, varied, wide.
veem *o.* dock-company, warehouse-company, storage-company.
veemarkt *v.* cattle-market.
veen *o.* peat-soil, peat-moor, turf-moor, peat, bog.
veengrond *m.* peat ground, boggy ground, bog-land.
veepest *v.* cattle-plague, rinderpest.
veer *v.* (*v. vogel*) feather; (*v. uurwerk, enz.*) spring; (*v. bril*) ear-piece.
veer *o.* (*overzetplaats*) ferry; (*pont*) ferry-boat, floating bridge; (*veerdienst*) ferry-service.
veerboot *v.* ferry-boat, ferry-steamer.
veerhuis *o.* ferry-house.
veerkracht *v.* elasticity, resilience, spring.
veerkrachtig *b. n.* elastic, resilient, springy.
veerman *m.* ferryman.

veerpont *v.* ferry-boat, ferry-steamer; (*voor trein*) ferry-bridge.
veerslot *o.* spring-lock.
veertien *telw.* fourteen; — *dagen,* a fortnight.
veertig *telw.* forty.
veestal *m.* cow-house, byre.
veestapel *m.* stock of cattle, live stock.
veeteelt *v.* cattle-breeding, stock-breeding, stock-raising.
veevoeder *o.* cattle-fodder, forage.
vegen *o. w.* (*v. vloer, schoorsteen*) sweep; (*v. tapijt, enz.*) brush; (*v. voeten, neus*) wipe; *on. w.* (*v. drukinkt*) slur, cloud.
vegetariër *m.* vegetarian.
veil *o.* (*Pl.*) ivy.
veil *b. n.* venal, corruptible, mercenary.
veilen *o. w.* (*door eigenaar*) auction, bring to the hammer, offer for sale; (*door veiler*) auctioneer.
veilheid *v.* venality, corruptibility, mercenariness.
veilig *b. n.* safe, sure, secure; *bw.* safely, with safety.
veiligheid *v.* safety, security; (*el.*) fuse, safety-fuse, cut-out.
veiligheidsdienst *m.* service of security.
veiligheidsklep *v.* safety-valve.
veiligheidslamp *v.* safety-lamp, davy (-lamp).
veiligheidsmaatregel *m.* measure of precaution, precautionary measure.
veiligheidsslot *o.* safety-lock.
veiligheidsspeld *v.* safety-pin, shield-pin.
veiling *v.* public sale, auction, sale by auction; *in* — *brengen,* bring to the hammer, put up for auction, sell by auction, submit to auction.
veinzen *o. w.* feign, simulate, affect; *on. w.* feign, dissemble; simulate.
veinzer *m.* dissembler, hypocrite.
vel *o.* skin, hide; (*op melk*) film, (bit of) skin; (*papier*) sheet.
veld *o.* field; (*v. vuurwapen*) land.
veldarbeid *m.* field-work, field-labour, labour in the fields.
veldbed *o.* field-bed, camp-bed.
veldfles *v.* case-bottle, travelling-flask; (*mil.*) soldier's bottle, water-bottle, canteen.
veldheer *m.* general.
veldhospitaal *o.* ambulance, field-hospital.
veldkijker *m.* field-glasses.
veldloop *m.* cross-country run.
veldmuis *v.* field-mouse, vole.
veldslag *m.* battle.
veldtent *v.* (army) tent.
veldtenue *o.* field-service uniform, marching-order.
veldvruchten *v. mv.* produce of the fields, fruits of the earth.
veldwachter *m.* rural constable, county constable, rural policeman, village policeman.
veldweg *m.* field-track, cart-track.

velen *many; zie* **veel.**
velen *o. w.* stand.
vellen *o. w. (v. boom)* fell, cut down; *(v. lans)* couch, lay in rest; *(fig.: v. oordeel, vonnis)* pass, pronounce.
ven *c.* fen.
vendel *o.* colour(s); *(vroeger: troepenafdeling)* company.
venijn *o.* venom.
venijnig *b. n.* venomous; *(fig.)* vicious, virulent, venomous.
vennoot *m.* partner.
vennootschap *v.* partnership, company.
venster *o.* window.
vensterblind *o.* shutter, window-shutter.
vensterenveloppe *v.* outlook envelope.
vensterglas *o.* window-glass; *(ruit)* window-pane.
vensterraam *o.* window-frame.
vent *m.* fellow, chap, johnny.
venten *o. w.* hawk, peddle; *(luid)* cry; shout.
venter *m.* hawker, pedlar, street-trader, street-vendor; *(met fruit, groenten, vis)* coster-monger.
ventiel *o. en m. (tn.)* valve; *(v. orgel)* ventil.
ventje *o.* little fellow, little man; *(in aanspreking)* boysey, little man.
ver *b. n. (v. afstand)* far; distant; remote; *(v. bloedverwantschap)* distant, remote; *bw.* far; **op —re na niet,** not by far, not by a long chalk.
verachtelijk *b. n. (verachting opwekkend, laag)* contemptible, despicable; *(verachting uitdrukkend)* contemptuous, disdainful; *bw.* contemptuously, with contempt.
verachten *o. w.* despise, contemn, hold in contempt, have contempt for, scorn.
verachting *v.* contempt, disdain, scorn.
verademen *on. w.* breathe again.
veraf *bw.* far (away), at a great distance.
verafgelegen *b. n.* far, remote, distant, outlying.
verafgoden *o. w.* idolize.
verafschuwen *o. w.* abhor, detest, loathe.
veranderen *o. w. (alg.)* change; *(wijzigen)* alter; *(geheel anders maken)* transform; *on. w.* change, alter.
verandering *v.* change; alteration; transformation; commutation; conversion.
veranderlijk *b. n.* changeable, variable, unsettled; *(wispelturig)* inconstant; *(dicht.)* changeful.
veranderlijkheid *v.* changeableness, changeability, variableness, alterability; inconstancy; instability.
verantwoordelijk *b. n.* responsible, answerable, accountable.
verantwoordelijkheid *v.* responsibility, answerableness.
verantwoorden *o. w.* answer for,

account for; *(rechtvaardigen)* justify; *w. w.* **zich —,** justify oneself.
verantwoording *v. (verantwoordelijkheid)* responsibility, accountability; *(rekenschap, rechtvaardiging)* account, justification.
verassen *o. w.* cremate, incinerate.
verbaasd *b. n.* surprised, astonished; *(hoogst —)* amazed; *bw.* wonderingly, in wonder, in surprise.
verbaasdheid *v.* surprise, astonishment, amazement.
verband *o. (omwinding, zwachtel)* bandage, dressing; *(voor ader)* ligature; *(samenhang)* connection; *(betrekking)* relation, connection; *(zinsverband)* context; *(verbintenis, verplichting)* lien, obligation, charge, bond, engagement; *(mil.)* liaison.
verbandkist *v.* dressing-case.
verbandstoffen *v. mv.* wound-dressing requisites.
verbannen *o. w.* exile, banish, expel, proscribe.
verbanning *v.* exile, banishment, expulsion, proscription.
verbasteren *on. w.* degenerate.
verbastering *v.* degeneration; *(v. woord)* corruption.
verbazen *o. w.* surprise, astonish; *(ten hoogste —)* amaze; *w. w.* **zich —,** be surprised, be astonished; be amazed **(over,** at).
verbazend *b. n.* surprising, astonishing; amazing, prodigious, marvellous; *bw.* surprisingly, astonishingly, prodigiously, marvellously.
verbeelden *o. w.* represent; *w. w.* **zich —,** imagine, fancy.
verbeelding *v. (verbeeldingskracht)* imagination, fancy; *(inbeelding, verwaandheid)* conceit, conceitedness.
verbeiden *o. w.* wait for, await.
verbergen *o. w.* hide, conceal; *w. w.* **zich —,** hide, conceal oneself, secrete oneself.
verbeten *b. n.* **— woede,** pent-up fury.
verbeteraar *m.* corrector; mender; rectifier; improver; reformer.
verbeteren *o. w. (beter maken)* better, make better, ameliorate, improve, mend; *(r. fouten)* correct, rectify; *(v. gebreken)* remedy; *(v. wet, enz.)* amend; *(r. tekst)* emend; *(zedelijk —)* reform, reclaim; *on. w.* correct; *w. w.* **zich —,** *(v. conditie)* better one's condition (position), better oneself; *(v. gedrag)* amend, reform oneself, mend one's ways, turn over a new leaf.
verbeterhuis *o.* house of correction.
verbetering *v.* change for the better, amelioration, improvement; correction, rectification; amendment; emendation; reformation, reclamation.
verbeurdverklaren *o. w.* confiscate forfeit, seize.
verbieden *o. w.* forbid, prohibit, interdict, veto.

verbijsterd *b. n.* bewildered, perplexed, dazed.

verbijsteren *o. w.* bewilder, perplex, daze.

verbijstering *v.* bewildering, bewilderment, perplexity.

verbinden *o. w.* (*verenigen, samenvoegen*) connect, join, link, link up; (*tel.*) connect, put through, put on; (*gen.*) bind up, bandage, dress; (*anders binden*) rebind, tie (bind) otherwise; (*v. kleuren; scheik.*) combine; *w. w.* **zich —**, (*v. personen*) ally oneself, enter into an alliance; (*tot iets*) commit (bind, pledge) oneself, undertake; (*v. kleuren, elementen*) combine; (*el.: met de aarde*) earth ground.

verbinding *v.* (*v. twee punten; v. treinen*) connection; (*v. spoorw.*) junction; (*band*) attachment; (*gemeenschap*) communication; (*v. personen*) union; (*scheik.*) combination; (*el.*) connection; (*v. woorden in uitspraak*) liaison; (*v. wond*) dressing, bandaging.

verbindingskanaal *o.* junction canal.

verbindingsteken *o.* (*gram.*) hyphen.

verbintenis *v.* (*overeenkomst*) contract, agreement; (*belofte, verplichting*) commitment, undertaking, engagement, bond; (*verbond*) alliance.

verbitterd *b. n.* embittered; exasperated.

verbitteren *o. w.* embitter; exasperate, exacerbate.

verbittering *v.* embitterment, bitterness; exasperation.

verbleken *on. w.* (*v. persoon*) pale, grow pale, turn pale, go white; (*v. kleur*) pale, fade; **doen —**, pale.

verblijden *o. w.* rejoice, delight, cheer, gladden; *w. w.* **zich —**, rejoice, be rejoiced.

verblijf *o.* (*het verblijven*) residence, stay; (*tijdelijk*) sojourn, stay; (*verblijfplaats*) residence, abode; home.

verblijfplaats *v.* abode, residence.

verblijven *on. w.* remain, stay; (*tijdelijk, ook:*) sojourn.

verblinden *o. w.* blind, dazzle; (*fig. ook:*) infatuate.

verblinding *v.* blinding, blindness, dazzle, dazzlement.

verbloemen *o. w.* disguise, veil, gloze over, palliate, camouflage, smooth over, varnish.

verbluffen *o. w.* confound, dumbfound, stagger, face down.

verbluft *b. n.* confounded; dumbfounded, staggered, struck all of a heap.

verbod *o.* prohibition, interdiction; (*v. dagblad*) suppression.

verboden *b. n.* forbidden.

verbolgen *b. n.* angry, incensed, wrathful, irate.

verbolgenheid *v.* anger, wrath, ire.

verbond *o.* alliance, league, union; confederation, coalition; (*verdrag*) treaty, pact; covenant.

verbonden *b. n.* allied.

verborgenheid *v.* secrecy; mystery.

verbouwen *o. w.* (*v. huis, enz.*) rebuild, newbuild, alter; (*telen*) grow, cultivate; (*uitgeven om te bouwen*) spend in building.

verbranden *o. w.* (*v. hout, papier, enz.*) burn; (*v. martelaar*) burn to death; (*v. lijk*) cremate, incinerate; (*v. afval*) incinerate; *on. w.* be burnt; (*door zon*) tan.

verbranding *v.* (*alg.*) combustion, burning; (*snelle —*) deflagration; burning to death; (*v. lijk*) cremation.

verbrandingsoven *m.* incinerator; (*voor lijkverbranding, ook:*) crematorium.

verbrassen *o. w.* dissipate, squander.

verbreden *o. w.* widen, broaden, enlarge; *w. w.* **zich —**, widen (out), broaden (out).

verbreiden *o. w.* (*v. nieuws, enz.*) spread; (*v. leer*) propagate; *w. w.* **zich —**, spread.

verbreken *o. w.* (*v. zegel, belofte, contract*) break; (*v. gelofte, eed*) violate; (*v. ketenen*) burst, break; (*v. schakel, relaties, enz.*) sever; (*v. verbindingen*) cut, interrupt; (*v. blokkade*) run.

verbreking *v.* breaking; violation; interruption, severance.

verbrijzelen *o. w.* break to pieces, smash (up), shatter.

verbroederen *on. w.* (*en w. w.: zich —*) fraternize.

verbrokkelen *o. w.* crumble; (*fig.*) disrupt, dismember; *on. w.* crumble (to pieces).

verbruik *o.* (*v. voedingswaren, stroom, enz.*) consumption; (*v. energie*) expenditure; (*overmatig —, slijtage*) waste, wastage.

verbruiken *o. w.* consume; (*v. krachten, reserve, enz.*) use up.

verbruiker *m.* consumer.

verbruiksartikel *o.* article of consumption.

verbuigen *o. w.* bend, twist (out of shape), distort; (*tn.*) buckle; (*gram.*) decline.

verbuiging *v.* bending, twisting out of shape; declension.

verdacht *b. n.* suspect, suspected; suspicious; (*v. zaken*) questionable; *bw.* suspectly, suspectedly, suspiciously.

verdachte *m.* **de —**, the suspected person, the suspect; (*recht*) the accused.

verdachtmaking *v.* insinuation; reflection.

verdagen *o. w.* adjourn, prorogue.

verdampen *o. w. en on. w.* evaporate.

verdamping *v.* evaporation.

verdedigen *o. w.* (*alg.*) defend; (*zijn rechten*) stand up for; *w. w.* **zich —**, defend oneself.

verdediger *m.* defender; (*recht*) counsel for the defendant (for the defence), defending counsel.

verdediging *v.* defence.

verdedigingswerken *o. mv.* defensive works, defence works, defences.

verdeeld *b. n.* divided.

verdeeldheid *v.* dissension, discord, division.

verdelen *o. w.* divide, distribute, parcel out, portion out.

verdelgen *o. w.* destroy, exterminate, extirpate.

verdelging *v.* destruction, extermination, extirpation.

verdelgingsoorlog *m.* war of extermination, exterminatory war.

verdeling *v.* division, distribution, partition.

verdenken *o. w.* suspect.

verdenking *v.* suspicion.

verder *b. n. (afstand)* farther, further; *(bijkomend, later)* further; *bw.* farther, further.

verderf *o.* ruin, destruction, perdition; undoing.

verderfelijk *b. n.* pernicious, ruinous, mischievous, noxious, vicious, baleful, baneful.

verderven *o. w.* pervert, corrupt.

verdichtsel *o.* invention, fiction, fabrication, fable, figment, story.

verdienen *o. w. (v. geld)* gain, earn; *(v. straf, enz.)* deserve, merit, be deserving of.

verdienste *v. (loon)* wages, earnings; *(winst)* profit, gain; *(verdienstelijkheid)* merit, desert(s).

verdienstelijk *b. n.* deserving, meritorious.

verdiepen *o. w.* deepen; *w. w. zich — in,* lose oneself in; indulge in.

verdieping *v.* deepening; *(v. huis)* story, floor; *(in muur)* recess.

verdierlijken *o. w.* bestialize, brutalize, imbrute; *on. w.* get brutalized, become a brute, grow brutal.

verdikken *o. w. en on. w.* thicken; *(v. vloeistof)* thicken, condense, inspissate.

verdisconteren *o. w.* discount, negotiate.

verdoemde *m.* damned, doomed.

verdoemen *o. w.* damn.

verdoen *o. w.* dissipate, squander, waste; *w. w. zich —,* make away with oneself.

verdonkeren *o. w.* darken, obscure, dim; *(fig. ook:)* obfuscate.

verdoold *b. n.* strayed, straying, stray; *(fig.)* misguided, mistaken, deluded.

verdord *b. n.* withered; *(v. landstreek)* parched, arid.

verdorren *on. w.* wither.

verdorven *b. n.* depraved, corrupt, perverse, perverted.

verdorvenheid *v.* depravity, depravation, corruption, perversion, perversity, perverseness.

verdoven *o. w. (doof maken)* deafen, make deaf; *(v. geluid)* deafen, deaden, dull; *(v. stem)* drown; *(v. licht, glans)* tarnish, dull; *(v. persoon: bedwelmen)* stun, stupefy; *(door kou)* benumb;

(gen.) render insensible, anaesthetize; *on. w. (v. glans)* tarnish.

verdoving *v.* deafening; stupefaction, stupor; numbness; anaesthetization, anaesthesia.

verdovingsmiddel *o.* narcotizer, narcotic, anaesthetic.

verdraagzaam *b. n.* tolerant, forbearing.

verdraagzaamheid *v.* toleration, tolerance, forbearance.

verdraaid *b. n.* distorted, contorted, twisted; *(v. handschrift)* disguised; *bw.* deuced, devilish.

verdraaien *o. w.* distort, contort, twist; *(v. slot)* spoil, force; *(fig.: v. woorden, feiten)* pervert.

verdrag *o.* treaty, pact, compact, agreement.

verdragen *o. w. (dulden, verduren)* suffer, endure, bear, tolerate, stand; *(zich laten welgevallen)* put up with; *(verplaatsen, wegdragen)* remove, shift.

verdragend *b. n. (v. geluid: stem, enz.)* carrying; *(mil.: v. kanon)* wide-range, long-range.

verdriet *o.* grief, sorrow; **— hebben,** be in trouble, be in grief; be distressed; **— aandoen,** afflict, grieve.

verdrijven *o. w. (v. plaats)* drive out, drive away, chase out, chase away, expel, oust; *(v. zorgen, angst, verdriet)* dissipate, dispel, chase away; *(v. tijd)* pass away, while away, beguile; *(wisk.)* eliminate.

verdringen *o. w.* push away, push aside, crowd out, elbow out; *(fig.)* crowd out, cut out, supplant, supersede, oust; *w. w. zich —,* crowd.

verdrinken *o. w. (door drinken verspillen)* drink away, spend on drink, drink up, guzzle away; *(v. dier, enz.)* drown; *(v. verdriet, zorgen)* drink down, drown; *(v. land)* inundate; *on. w.* be drowned, drown; *w. w. zich —,* drown oneself.

verdrinking *v.* drowning.

verdrukken *o. w.* oppress.

verdrukking *v.* oppression.

verdubbelen *o. w.* double; *(gram., fig.)* redouble.

verduidelijken *o. w.* elucidate, explain, make clear.

verduisteren *o. w. (duister maken)* darken, obscure, dim; *(fig.)* obfuscate, darken, obscure, eclipse; *(v. geld: achterhouden)* embezzle, peculate; *on. w.* darken, grow dark, get dark.

verduistering *v.* darkening, obscuration; *(fig.)* obfuscation; *(v. zon, maan)* eclipse; *(v. geld)* embezzlement, peculation, defalcation.

verdunnen *o. w.* thin, attenuate; *(v. vloeistoffen, dranken, enz.)* dilute; *(v. lucht)* rarefy.

verduren *o. w. (verdragen, dulden, doorstaan)* bear, endure, suffer, hold out; *(duurder maken)* make dearer, make more expensive

verduurzamen *o. w.* preserve, cure, pot.

verdwaasd *b. n.* infatuated, besotted, foolish.

verdwalen *on. w.* lose one's way, go astray, get lost.

verdwijnen *en. w.* disappear; (*plotseling*) vanish; (*geleidelijk*) fade away, melt away.

verdwijning *v.* disappearance; vanishing; (*v. geld, enz.*) leakage.

veredelen *o. w.* (*v. vruchten*) improve, meliorate; (*v. geest, smaak, metalen*) refine; (*fig.*) ennoble, elevate.

vereelt *b. n.* callous, horny, hornyhanded; (*fig.*) callous, obdurate.

vereenvoudigen *o. w.* simplify.

vereenzelvigen *o. w.* identify.

vereffenen *o. w.* (*v. rekening*) balance, settle, square; (*v. schuld*) clear off, square; (*v. geschil*) adjust, settle.

vereisen *o. w.* require, demand.

vereiste *v.* requirement, requisite.

verenigd *b. n.* united, combined, joined, conjoined.

verenigen *o. w.* unite, join, combine; (*verbinden*) connect, link, join; (*verzamelen*) assemble, collect, gather together; *w. w.* **zich —,** unite, combine, join forces, become one; (*zich verzamelen,* assemble; **zich — met,** join; (*het eens zijn met*) agree to.

vereniging *v.* (*handeling*) union, joining, junction, combination, association, amalgamation; (*genootschap, bond, enz.*) society, club, association, union.

vereren *o. w.* respect, honour, venerate, revere, adore.

verergeren *o. w.* make worse, worsen, aggravate; exacerbate; *on. w.* become worse, worsen, change for the worse, deteriorate, exacerbate.

verering *v.* veneration, reverence, adoration, worshipping.

veretteren *on. w.* fester, suppurate.

verf *v.* paint; (*voor schilderij*) colour, paint; (*voor stoffen*) dye.

verfijnen *o. w.* refine.

verflauwen *on. w.* (*v. geluid*) faint; (*v. kleur*) fade; (*v. ijver, belangstelling, enz.,* flag, dull, slacken; (*v. snelheid*) slacken (*H.*) slacken, droop, flag, become dull; (*v. wind*) abate.

verfoeien *o. w.* detest, abominate, abhor, execrate.

verfraaien *o. w.* embellish, beautify.

verfraaiing *v.* embellishing, embellishment, beautification.

verfrissen *o. w.* refresh; *w. w.* **zich —,** refresh (oneself), take some refreshment.

verfrissing *v.* refreshment.

verfwaren *v. mv.* oils and colours, paints and colours.

verfwinkel *m.* colour-shop.

vergaan *on. w.* (*alg.*) perish, pass away; (*v. schip*) perish, be wrecked, founder; (*verteren*) decay, waste (away); (*v. vlieg-* *tuig*) crash, be lost, be wrecked; *z. n., o.* passing away; (*v. schip*) loss, wreck; (*v. vliegtuig*) crash; (*het verteren*) decay.

vergaarbak *m.* reservoir, receptacle.

vergaderen *o. w.* (*vergaren*) gather, assemble, collect; *on. w.* assemble, meet, sit.

vergadering *v.* assembly, meeting; conference.

vergallen *o. w.* break the gall of; (*fig.*) embitter, sour, gall.

vergankelijk *b. n.* perishable, transitory, transient, fleeting.

vergankelijkheid *v.* perishableness, transitoriness, transiency, instability.

vergasser *m.* carburettor.

vergassing *v.* gasification; (*bij motor*) carburation, vaporization.

vergasten *o. w.* treat (**op,** to), regale (**op,** with); *w. w.* **zich — aan,** feast upon, take delight in.

vergeefs *b. n.* vain, idle, useless, fruitless.

vergeetachtigheid *v.* forgetfullness, aptness to forget, obliviousness.

vergeet-mij-niet *v.* (*Pl.*) forget-me-not.

vergelden *o. w.* repay, requite, reward.

vergelding *v.* requital, reward, return, retribution, retaliation.

vergeldingsmaatregel *m.* retaliatory measure.

vergelijk *o.* agreement, accommodation, compromise, settlement.

vergelijken *o. w.* compare.

vergelijking *v.* comparison; (*wisk.*) equation; (*redefiguur*) simile.

vergemakkelijken *o. w.* facilitate, make easy (easier).

vergen *o. w.* require, demand, ask.

vergenoegen *o. w.* content, satisfy; *w. w.* **zich — met,** content oneself with, be content with, rest contented with.

vergeten *o. w.* forget; *w. w.* **zich —,** forget oneself; *b. n.* forgotten.

vergeven *o. w.* (*vergiffenis schenken*) forgive, pardon; (*vergiftigen*) poison; (*v. ambt, enz.*) give away; (*bij kaartsp.:* verkeerd geven) deal wrong, misdeal, make a misdeal.

vergevensgezind *b. n.* forgiving, placable.

vergeving *v.* (*v. zonden*) remission, pardon; (*v. predikantsplaats*) collation.

vergewissen *w. w.* **zich — van,** ascertain, make sure of.

vergezellen *o. w.* accompany; (*v. meerderen*) attend. [vista.

vergezicht *o.* perspective, prospect,

vergiet *o.* strainer, colander, cullender.

vergieten *o. w.* (*v. bloed, tranen*) shed; (*v. melk, wijn, enz.*) spill; (*v. metalen*) recast.

vergiffenis *v.* pardon, forgiveness; (*v. zonden*) remission.

vergift *o.* poison; (*dierlijk*) venom, poison.

vergiftigen *o. w.* poison, envenom, intoxicate.

vergiftiging r. poisoning, intoxication.
vergissen w. w. **zich —,** mistake, be mistaken; commit a mistake (an error).
vergissing r. mistake, error, slip, oversight; **bij —,** by mistake, mistakenly, in error; unintentionally.
verglazen o. w. (van buiten) glaze, enamel; (in glas veranderen) vitrify.
vergoeden o. w. make good, compensate, defray; (terugbetalen) reimburse; (v. verlies) recoup, make good.
vergoeding r. compensation, reimbursement, indemnification, indemnity; (fig.) amends.
vergoelijken o. w. (v. fouten, enz.) gloss over, smooth over; (v. vergrijp) palliate, extenuate; (v. verdrag) excuse; (v. onrecht, enz.) explain away.
vergooien o. w. throw away, chuck away; w. w. **zich —,** throw oneself away.
vergramd b. n. angry; (dicht.) wrathful.
vergrijp o. transgression; offence; (sterker) outrage.
vergrootglas o. magnifying-glass.
vergroten o. w. (v. macht, rijkdom, enz.) aggrandize; (v. gebouw, portret, enz.) enlarge; (v. kennis, voortbrengst) augment, increase; (v. getallen) augment, amplify; (met vergrootglas; overdrijven) magnify; (v. voorraad) increase.
vergruizen o.w. grind, pound, triturate pulverize, powder, crush; (v. erts) mill.
verguizen o. w. revile, vilify, vituperate, abuse, libel.
verguizing v. revilement, vilification, vituperation, abuse.   [edged.
verguld b. n. gilt; **— op snee,** glit-
vergulden o. w. gild.
vergulder m. gilder.
vergunning v. allowance, permission, leave; (voor drankverkoop, enz.) licence; (concessie) concession.
verhaal o. story, narration, narrative, relation, account; (recht) redress, (legal) remedy, recourse.
verhaasten o. w. hasten, accelerate, quicken, precipitate; expedite.
verhakking v. (mil.) abat(t)is.
verhalen o. w. (vertellen) narrate, relate, tell, recount; (sch.) shift, warp.
verhaler m. narrator, relater, story-teller.
verhandelen o. w. (handelen in) deal in; (verkopen) sell, dispose of; (v. wissel) negotiate; (bespreken) discuss, debate.
verhandeling v. treatise, essay, lecture, discourse, dissertation.
verharden o. w. harden, indurate; (v. weg) metal, ballast; (fig.) harden, obdurate, steel; on. w. (eig. en fig.) become hard, harden, indurate.
verharding v. hardening, obduration, induration; (v. weg) metalling, ballasting; (vereelting) callosity.
verheerlijking o. w. glorify, magnify, extol.
verheerlijking v. glorification.

verheffen o. w. (v. ogen, stem, enz.) raise; (v. hoofd) lift; (v. persoon: prijzen) exalt, extol; (v. geest) lift up, uplift, elevate; w. w. **zich —,** rise.
verheffing v. raising; exaltation; elevation; uplift.
verhelen o. w. conceal, hide, keep secret, disguise, dissemble.
verhelpen o. w. remedy, redress, rectify, correct, straighten (out).
verhemelte o. (v. mond) palate; (v troon) canopy.
verheugd b. n. pleased, glad, happy.
verheugen o. w. gladden, make glad, rejoice, delight; w. w. **zich —,** rejoice, be glad, enjoy.
verheven b. n. (fig.) exalted, elevated, lofty, sublime, august; (v. beeldwerk) in relief, raised, embossed.
verhevenheid v. elevation, rise; (fig. elevation, loftiness, sublimity.
verhinderen o. w. hinder, prevent.
verhitten o. w. heat; (fig.) fire, inflame, heat; w. w. **zich —,** heat (overheat) oneself.
verhitting v. heating, calefaction; (fig.) heating, excitement, inflammation.
verhoeden o. w. prevent, avert, ward off.
verhogen o. w. (hoger maken: v. muur, dijk, enz.) heighten; (v. prijs) raise, put up, advance; (v. loon, salaris, weg, enz.) raise; (muz.) raise, elevate; (v. eetlust) provoke; (v. som, bod) increase; (v). waarde, contrast) - enhance; (v. lasten) advance, put up; (v. bekoorlijkheid, vreugde) add to; (bevorderen) promote; (v. leerling) move up (remove) to a higher class.
verhoging v. (handeling) heightening; raising; elevation; enhancement; promotion; (v. loon, salaris, prijs, enz.) increase, advance, rise, raise; (v. grond) elevation, eminence, rise; (verhoog) (raised) platform; (op school) remove; (bevordering) advancement, promotion.
verholen b. n. concealed, secret, hidden.
verhongeren on. w. famish, starve (to death), die of hunger, perish of starvation, die of famine; o. w. famish, starve.
verhoor o. hearing, trail, examination, interrogation, interrogatory.
verhoren o. w. (v. gebed) hear, answer; (v. wens) grant; (v. getuige) interrogate, hear, examine; (v. gevangene) try, hear; (v. les) hear.
verhouding v. (tussen personen) relation; (tussen getallen, enz.) proportion; ratio.
verhuisboedel m. furniture to be removed.
verhuiskosten m. mv. removal-expenses, moving-expenses, expenses of (re-)moving.
verhuizen on. w. remove, move, move house; o. w. remove.
verhuizing v. removal, move, shift, flit.

verhuren *o. w. (v. kamers, enz.)* let; *(v. fietsen, paarden, enz.)* let out (on hire), hire out; *(v. land)* lease out, farm; *(v. huis)* let out on lease, rent; *(v. schip)* freight; *w. w.* **zich — als,** hire oneself out as.

verhuring *v.* letting (out), hiring (out) location.

verhuurkantoor *o. (voor huizen)* house-agent's office; *(voor personeel)* registry office, employment agency.

verijdelen *o. w.* frustrate, baffle, foil, defeat, baulk.

verjaard *b. n.* superannuated, statute-barred; nullified (barred) by the statute of limitations; extinguished by limitation.

verjaardag *m. (geboortedag)* birthday; *(v. gebeurtenis)* anniversary.

verjagen *o. w. (v. dieren)* hunt away, hunt out; *(v. vogels, enz.)* drive away, chase away, frighten away, shoo away; *(v. persoon)* expel; *(v. vijand)* dislodge, turn out; *(v. angst, zorgen)* dispel.

verjaren *on. w.* celebrate one's birthday; become extinguished by lapse of time, become superannuated, become statute-barred, become prescriptive.

verjongen *o. w.* rejuvenate, rejuvenize, make young again; *on. w.* become (grow) young again, rejuvenate, rejuvenize.

verkalken *on. w.* calcine, calcify; *(v. bloedvaten)* harden.

verkalking *v.* calcination, calcification.

verkavelen *o. w.* lot out, parcel out.

verkeer *o.* traffic; commerce; *(omgang)* intercourse.

verkeerd *b. n.* wrong, bad; *bw.* wrong, wrongly, amiss.

verkeersagent *m.* point-policeman, traffic-policeman.

verkeersongeval *o.* street accident, traffic accident.

verkeersvliegtuig *o.* passenger plane.

verkeersweg *m.* communication road; *(grote —)* arteral road.

verkennen *o. w.* reconnoitre, scout.

verkenner *m.* scout.

verkenning *v.* reconnoitring, scouting.

verkenningsvliegtuig *o.* scouting aeroplane, scout-plane, reconnaissance plane.

verkeren *on. w. (omgaan)* have intercourse, associate; *(veranderen)* change, turn; *(zich bevinden)* be.

verkering *v.* courtship.

verkiesbaar *b. n.* eligible.

verkiesbaarheid *v.* eligibility.

verkieslijk *b. n.* preferable **(boven,** to).

verkiezen *o. w. (de voorkeur geven)* prefer **(boven,** to); *(kiezen)* choose; *(bij stemming)* elect; *(voor parlement)* return.

verkiezing *v. (keus)* choice; *(voorkeur)* preference; *(bij stemming)* election; *(tot kamerlid)* return, election.

verkiezingsstrijd *m.* election-contest, electoral struggle.

verkikkerd *b. n.* — **zijn op iets,** be keen on something.

verklaarbaar *b. n.* explicable, explainable, accountable.

verklappen *o. w.* blab out, let out; *w. w.* **zich —,** give oneself away.

verklaren *o. w. (zeggen)* declare; *(uitleggen, duidelijk maken)* explain, elucidate, interpret, make clear, clear up; *(getuigen)* depose, testify; *(betuigen verzekeren)* certify.

verklaring *v.* declaration, statement; *(uitleg)* explanation, elucidation; *(attest.* certificate; *(recht: v. getuige)* deposition, evidence.

verkleden *o. w. (anders kleden)* put into another dress, dress otherwise; *(vermommen)* disguise; *w. w.* **zich —,** *(zich anders kleden)* change one's clothes (dress); *(zich vermommen)* disguise oneself, dress (oneself) up.

verkleding *v.* change of clothes, change of dress; disguise, make-up.

verkleefd *b. n.* attached, devoted.

verkleefdheid *v.* attachment, devotion, affection.

verkleinen *o. w. (in omvang, enz.)* reduce; *(verminderen)* diminish, lessen, reduce; *(v. kleding)* cut down; *(fig.)* disparage, belittle, derogate from.

verkleining *v.* reduction; diminution; disparagement, belittlement; *(v. breuk)* simplification, reduction (to its lowest terms).

verkleinwoord *o.* diminutive.

verkleumd *b. n.* benumbed, numb.

verklikken *o. w. (v. zaak)* tell, disclose; *(v. persoon)* peach upon.

verklikker *m. (persoon)* tell-tale, tale-bearer, peacher; *(v. luchtpomp)* tell-tale *(apparatus);* *(v. stoomketel)* indicator, detector, vacuum-gauge.

verkneukelen *w. w.* **zich —,** hug oneself with joy (delight), rub one's hands with joy, chuckle; **zich — in,** revel in, chuckle over. [tion.

verknochtheid *v.* attachment, devo-

verknoeien *o. w. (bederven)* spoil, bungle, botch, muddle, muck, muff; *(verspillen)* waste, muddle away, fritter away.

verkoelen *o. w.* cool (down); *(tegen bederf)* refrigerate, chill; *(v. champagne)* ice; *on. w.* cool (down), become cold.

verkoeling *v.* cooling; *(fig.)* coolness, chill, cooling.

verkolen *o. w.* carbonize; char; *on. w.* become (get) carbonized, char, get charred.

verkond(ig)en *o. w.* proclaim, announce.

verkoop *m.* sale.

verkoopboek *o.* sales-book, book of sales.

verkoophuis *o.* auction-room, sale-room, mart, repository.

verkoopprijs *m.* selling-price.

verkopen *o. w.* sell; *(van de hand doen:*

huis, paard, enz.) dispose of; (*v wissel*) negotiate.
verkoper *m.* seller, vendor; (*in zaak*) salesman.
verkoping *v.* sale, public sale, auction.
verkorten *o. w.* shorten; abridge; (*v. woord, verhaal, naam*) abbreviate; (*v. tijd*) beguile, while away; (*v. bericht, verslag*) condense; (*v. tekening*) foreshorten; (*v. iemands rechten*) encroach upon, abridge.
verkorting *v.* shortening, abridgement; abbreviation; foreshortening.
verkouden *b. n.* — *zijn,* have a cold; — *worden,* catch cold.
verkrachten *o. w.* violate, deflower, ravish, outrage, rape; (*v. wet, recht*) violate.
verkrachting *v.* violation, defloration, ravishment, outrage, rape; violation.
verkreukelen *o. w.* rumple, crumple (up), crush.
verkrijgbaar *b. n.* obtainable, to be had, to be got, procurable.
verkrijgen *o. w.* obtain, gain, acquire get; (*v. stemmen bij verkiezing*) poll.
verkroppen *o. w.* swallow, digest, bottle up.
verkwanselen *o. w.* barter away, bargain away, make a market of, fritter away.
verkwijnen *on. w.* pine away, languish.
verkwikken *o. w.* refresh, freshen up, comfort; *w. w. zich* —, refresh oneself.
verkwikking *v.* refreshment, comfort.
verkwisten *o. w.* squander, dissipate, waste, throw away. [thrift.
verkwister *m.* prodigal, waster, spend-
verkwisting *v.* dissipation, wasting, wastefulness, prodigality, thriftlessness.
verlagen *o. w.* lower; (*v. prijs*) reduce, lower; (*v. loon*) cut down; (*muz.*) flatten, flat, lower; (*v. leerling*) put in a lower form, put back into a lower class; *w. w. zich* —, lower (degrade, debase, demean) oneself (*tot,* to).
verlak *o.* varnish, lacquer, japan.
verlamd *b. n.* paralysed, palsied.
verlammen *o. w.* paralyse; (*fig.*) cripple, paralyse; *on. w.* become paralysed.
verlamming *v.* paralysis, palsy.
verlangen *o. w.* desire, want; *on. w.* long, be longing; — *naar,* long for, look forward to; *z. n., o.* desire; longing; *op* —, (*op aanvraag*) on application.
verlaten *o. w.* leave; (*voor langere tijd of voorgoed*) quit; (*in de steek laten*) abandon, desert, forsake; (*ontruimen*) vacate; *w. w. zich* — *op,* rely on, depend on, trust to.
verlaten *w. w. zich* —, be belated, outstay one's time.
verlaten *b. n.* (*niet bewoond: eiland, enz.*) abandoned, deserted; (*v. schip*) derelict; (*v. persoon*) lonely; forlorn; (*in de steek gelaten*) forsaken; (*afgelegen*) lonely solitary; (*beurs*) neglected.

verlatenheid *v.* abandonment, desertion; loneliness, forlornness.
verleden *b. n.* last; past; — *tijd,* past tense; *z. n., o.* past.
verlegenheid *v.* timidity, bashfulness, shyness; confusion, embarrassment, perplexity; (*moeilijkheid*) trouble, scrape, embarrassment.
verleidelijk *b. n.* tempting, seductive, alluring; *bw.* temptingly, seductively, seducingly, alluringly.
verleiden *o. w.* (*verlokken*) tempt, allure; (*tot kwaad brengen*) seduce; (*v. meisje*) seduce, debauch, betray.
verleider *m.* seducer, tempter.
verleiding *v.* seduction, temptation.
verlekkerd *b. n.* keen (*op,* on).
verlenen *o. w.* (*pensioen, krediet, uitstel*) grant; (*hulp, steun*) afford, lend, render; (*korting, krediet*) allow; (*toelating*) give; (*diploma*) grant (*aan,* to), confer (*aan,* on); (*titel*) confer, bestow (on).
verlengen *o. w.* lengthen, make longer; (*meetk.: v. lijn*) produce; (*v. termijn, krediet*) extend; (*v. wissel*) prolong, renew; (*v. paspoort, enz.*) renew; (*v. verblijf, bezoek*) protract, prolong.
verlenging *v.* lengthening; production; extension; prolongation; renewal; protraction.
verlengstuk *o.* lengthening-piece.
verleppen *on. w.* fade, wither.
verlet *o.* hindrance, delay.
verlevendigen *o. w.* revive, vivify, quicken, enliven.
verlichten *o. w.* (*helder maken*) light, light up, illuminate; (*v. geest*) enlighten; (*minder zwaar maken*) lighten; (*fig.*) relieve, alleviate, ease.
verlichting *v.* lightning, illumination; enlightenment; lightening; relief, alleviation, ease.
verliefd *b. n.* enamoured, amorous, in love.
verlies *o.* loss; (*door dood*) bereavement, loss.
verliezen *o. w.* lose.
verlof *o.* (*veroorloving*) permission, leave; (*vakantie*) leave (of absence); (*mil.*) furlough; (*v. bierslijter*) licence.
verlofganger *m.* soldier on furlough; leave-man.
verlokken *o. w.* tempt, allure, entice, seduce.
verloochenen *o. w.* deny, disown, disavow, renounce, repudiate; *w. w. zich* —, deny oneself, practise self-denial; belie one's nature.
verloochening *v.* denial, disavowal, renouncement, repudiation.
verloofde *m. en v.* fiancé(e), affianced, betrothed, intended; *de* —*n,* the engaged couple.
verloop *o.* (*v. ziekte, enz.*) course, progress; (*v. tijd*) process, course, lapse, expiration; (*verval, achteruitgang*) decay, decline, falling off.
verlopen *on. w.* (*v. tijd*) pass, pass away,

go by, elapse; (*v. zaak*) go down, run to seed; (*v. pas, enz.*) expire; (*bilj.: v. bal*) run into the pocket, pocket itself; (*tn.: v. boor*) run out.

verlopen *b. n.* (*v persoon*) seedy-looking, seedy, raffish

verloren *b. n.* lost; *de — zoon,* the prodigal son. [tocology.

verloskunde *v.* obstetrics, midwifery,

verloskundige (*mann.*) obstetric surgeon, obstetrician, accoucheur; (*vrouw.*) midwife, accoucheuse.

verlossen *o. w.* (*vrij maken, redden*) deliver, liberate, rescue, release; (*door Christus*) redeem; (*helpen bij bevalling*) deliver.

verlosser *m.* deliverer, liberator; *de V—,* the Redeemer.

verlossing *v.* (*bevrijding*) deliverance, redemption, rescue; (*bevalling*) delivery, accouchement, confinement.

verloven *o. w.* betroth, affiance, promise in marriage; *w. w. zich —,* become engaged.

verloving *v.* betrothal, betrothing, engagement.

verluchten *o. w.* (*uitluchten*) air, ventilate; (*illustreren*) illuminate.

verlustigen *o. w.* divert, amuse; *w. w. zich —,* disport oneself; *zich — in,* delight in, take delight in, take pleasure in.

vermaak *o.* diversion, pleasure, amusement, delight.

vermaard *b. n.* famous, celebrated, renowned, illustrious.

vermageren *o. w.* make lean, emaciate, waste, attenuate; *on. w.* grow lean, lose flesh, become thin, waste.

vermagering *v.* emaciation.

vermaken *o. w.* (*verlustigen*) amuse, divert; (*veranderen, herstellen*) make over, alter, refashion, repair; (*bij testament schenken*) bequeath, leave by will; *w. w. zich —,* amuse oneself, enjoy oneself.

vermaledijen *o. w.* curse, damn.

vermanen *o. w.* admonish, exhort, warn.

vermaning *v.* admonition, exhortation, warning.

vermannen *w. w. zich —,* summon up one's courage, pull oneself together, brace (nerve) oneself, steel oneself.

vermeend *b. n.* fancied, supposed, pretended, would-be.

vermeerderen *o. w.* augment, add to, increase, enlarge; *on. w.* increase (*met,* by); *w. w. zich —,* (*r. zaken, getallen, enz.*) augment, increase; (*v. personen,* multiply.

vermeerdering *v.* augmentation, increase, enlargement, addition.

vermelden *o. w.* mention, state, record.

vermelding *v.* mention, record.

vermengen *o. w.* mix, mingle; (*v. thee, koffie, enz.*) blend; (*v. metalen*) alloy; *w. w. zich —,* mix, mingle.

vermenigvuldigen *o. w.* multiply (*met,* by); (*verveelvoudigen*) manifold; *w. w. zich —,* multiply.

vermenigvuldiging *v.* multiplication.

vermetelheid *v.* audacity, temerity, recklessness, boldness.

vermeten *w. w. zich —,* (*zich in het meten vergissen*) measure wrong; (*fig.: zich verstouten*) presume, make bold, dare.

vermijden *o. w.* avoid; (*schuwen*) shun; (*ontwijken*) evade.

verminderen *o. w.* lessen, diminish, decrease, cut down; *on. w.* lessen, diminish, decrease, fall off; (*v. wind*) fall, abate; (*v. pijn, enz.*) remit, abate.

vermindering *v.* diminution, decrease, falling-off; reduction; slackening; abatement; decline.

verminken *o. w.* mutilate, maim; (*fig.*) mutilate, disfigure, garble, tamper with.

verminkte *m.* cripple, crippled person, maimed person.

vermist *b. n.* missing.

vermits *vw.* whereas, since, as.

vermoedelijk *b. n.* presumable, probable, presumptive; *bw.* presumably, probably.

vermoeden *o. w.* suspect; presume, suppose, conjecture, surmise; *z n, o.* supposition, presumption, surmise; (*verdenking*) suspicion.

vermoeidheid *r.* fatigue, weariness, tiredness.

vermoeien *o. w.* tire, weary, fatigue; *w. w. zich —,* get tired, tire oneself, fatigue oneself.

vermogen *o. w.* be able; *z. n., o.* (*geschiktheid*) faculty, ability; (*macht*) power; (*fortuin*) fortune, wealth, riches; (*werkvermogen*) capacity, power.

vermogend *b. n.* (*rijk*) rich, wealthy; substantial; (*machtig, invloedrijk*) influential.

vermolmen *on. w.* moulder (away), fall to dust.

vermoorden *o. w.* murder, kill.

vermorsen *o. w.* muddle away, waste, squander, trifle away, idle away.

vermorzelen *o. w.* crush, smash (up), pulverize.

vermurwen *o. w.* soften, make soft, mollify.

vernagelen *o. w.* (*v. kanon*) spike; (*v. paard*) prick; (*v. deur*) nail up.

vernederen *o. w.* humble, humiliate, mortify, abase; *w. w. zich —,* humble (humiliate, abase) oneself.

vernedering *v.* humiliation, mortification, abasement.

vernemen *o. w.* hear, learn, understand; *on. w. — naar,* inquire after (about).

vernielal *m.* destroyer, destructionist, vandal.

vernielen *o. w.* destroy, smash (up).

vernieling *v.* destruction.

vernielzucht *r.* love of destruction, destructiveness, vandalism.

vernietigen *o. w. (vernielen)* destroy, smash (up), innihilate, wreck; *(te niet doen, nietig verklaren)* nullify, annul, sed aside, reverse, quash.

vernietiging *v.* destruction, smash up, annihilation; *(recht: nietigverklaring)* nullification, annulment, quashing.

vernieuwen *o. w.* renew, renovate.

vernieuwing *v.* renewal, renovation.

vernikkelen *o. w.* nickel, nickel-plate, plate with nickel.

vernis *o.* varnish; veneer, top-dressing.

vernuft *o.* genius, ingenuity, ingeniousness; *(geestigheid)* wit; *(persoon)* genius.

vernuftig *b. n.* ingenious; *(geestig)* witty.

veronachtzamen *o. w.* neglect; disregard; *(me topzet)* slight put a slight on.

veronachtzaming *v.* neglect, negligence, disregard; slight, slighting.

veronderstellen *o. w.* suppose; presume, assume.

veronderstelling *v.* supposition.

verongelijken *o. w.* wrong, do wrong, injure.

verongelijking *v.* wrong, injury, injustice.

verongelukken *on. w. (v. persoon)* meet with an accident, come to grief; perish; *(v. schip)* be wrecked, be lost, founder, perish; *(v. vliegtuig)* be wrecked, be lost, crash; *(v. zaak: mislukken)* miscarry, fail.

verontreinigen *o. w.* defile, soil, sully, pollute, foul, befoul.

verontrusten *o. w.* disquiet, disturb, perturb, alarm, discompose; *w. w.* **zich —,** be alarmed *(over,* at, about).

verontschuldigen *o. w.* excuse; *w. w.* **zich —,** apologize, excuse oneself.

verontschuldiging *v.* excuse; apology, indignation.

verontwaardigen *o. w.* make indignant, rouse the indignation of; *w. w.* **zich —,** be indignant, be filled with indignation.

verontwaardiging *v.* indignation.

veroordeelde *m.* condemned person.

veroordelen *o. w. (alg.)* condemn; *(recht)* sentence, pass sentence on, condemn; *(in burgerlijke zaak)* give judgment against; *(afkeuren)* condemn, censure.

veroordeling *v.* condemnation; *(recht)* conviction; *(afkeuring)* condemnation, censure; *(openlijke —)* denunciation.

veroorloven *o. w.* permit, allow, give leave.

veroorzaken *o. w.* cause, occasion, bring about, give rise to.

verootmoedigen *o. w.* humble, humiliate, mortify, chasten.

verootmoediging *v.* humiliation, mortification.

verordening *v.* order, ordinance, regulation(s); *(v. gemeente, enz.)* by-law.

verouderd *b. n.* out of date, antiquated, archaic, obsolete; *(v. kwaal, gewoonte)* inveterate.

verouderen *on. w. (v. persoon)* grow (become, get) old, age; *(v. woord, enz.)* become obsolete; *o. w.* age, make older.

veroveren *o. w.* conquer, capture.

verovering *v.* conquest, capture.

verpachten *o. w.* lease, let on lease, put out to lease; *(v. belasting, monopolie, enz.)* farm out.

verpachting *v.* lease, leasing; farming out.

verpakken *o. w. (inpakken)* pack, put up, wrap up; *(anders pakken)* repack, pack otherwise.

verpakking *v.* packing.

verpanden *o. w.* pawn; *(v. huis, goederen)* mortgage, hypothecate; *(v. woord, eer)* pledge, plight.

verpersoonlijken *o. w.* personify, impersonate.

verpesten *o. w.* infect; *(fig.)* infect, poison, corrupt, taint, contaminate.

verplaatsen *o. w.* move, remove, displace; *(v. woord, letter)* transpose; *(v. zaak, ambtenaar)* transfer; *(v. leerling)* give a new place to, shift; *(bevorderen)* move up to a higher class.

verplaatsing *v.* move, movement, removal, displacement; transposition; transfer; shift, shifting.

verpleegster *v.* nurse, sick-nurse.

verplegen *o. w.* nurse, tend, attend.

verpleging *v.* nursing; *(onderhoud)* maintenance, sustenance; *(mil.)* supply; *(inrichting)* nursing home; *(mil.)* supplying.

verpletteren *o. w.* crush, crash, smash, shatter, dash to pieces.

verplichten *o. w.* oblige, compel, force; *(door een dienst)* oblige; *w. w.* **zich — te,** bind (pledge) oneself to.

verplichtend *b. n.* obliging; *(niet facultatief)* obligatory.

verplichting *v.* obligation, debt of obligation; commitment, engagement, undertaking.

verpozen *w. w.* **zich —,** take a rest, rest, unbend.

verpozing *v.* rest, recreation.

verpoppen *w. w.* **zich —,** pupate.

verraad *o.* treason, treachery, betrayal.

verraden *o. w.* betray, go back on; *(fig.)* betray, show, bespeak; *w. w.* **zich —,** betray oneself.

verrader *m.* betrayer, traitor.

verraderlijk *b. n.* treacherous, traitorous, treasonous, perfidious.

verrassen *o. w.* surprise, take by surprise.

verrassing *v.* surprise; *(mil.)* surprise attack.

verregaand *b. n.* extreme, excessive; *bw.* excessively, exceedingly.

verrekenen *o. w.* settle, reckon up; *w. w.* **zich —,** miscalculate, misreckon; make a mistake in one's calculations.

verrekening *v. (vereffening)* settle-

ment; (*door 't clearing-house*) clearance; (*misrekening*) miscalculation.

verrekijker *m.* telescope, glass, spyglass.

verrekken *o. w.* (*v. spier*) strain, wrench; (*v. arm*) wrench, sprain, dislocate; (*v. kaak*) crick; (*v. heup*) put out of joint; *w. w. zich* —, overreach oneself.

verrichten *o. w.* do, execute, perform, effect, carry out, conduct.

verrichting *v.* (*handeling*) action, operation, transaction; (*volvoering*) execution, performance; (*functie*) function.

verrijken *o. w.* enrich.

verrijzen *on. w.* rise; (*ontstaan: v. stad, enz.*) spring up.

verrijzenis *v.* resurrection, rising from the dead.

verroeren *o. w.* (*en w. w. zich* —), stir, move, budge. [rusty.

verroesten *on. w.* rust, grow rusty, get

verrotten *on. w.* rot, putrefy, decay.

verruilen *o.* exchange, barter.

verrukkelijk *b. n.* delightful, ravishing, enchanting, charming, topping, delectable; (*vooral v. smaak, geur*) delicious.

verrukken *o. w.* delight, ravish, enchant, enrapture.

verrukking *v.* delight, ravishment, rapture, transport, ecstasy.

vers *o.* (*gedicht*) poem; (*versregel; bijb.*) verse; (*couplet*) stanza; couplet.

vers *b. n.* (*alg.*) fresh; (*v. brood, melk, enz.*) new; (*v. eieren*) new-laid.

versagen *on. w.* despond, despair, grow faint-hearted.

verschaald *b. n.* flat, stale, vapid.

verschaffen *o. w.* procure, furnish, provide, supply; *w. w. zich* —, provide (furnish, supply) oneself with, procure.

verschalen *on. w.* get (go, grow) flat (stale, vapid).

verschalken *o. w.* outwit, outmanœuvre, overreach.

verschansen *o. w.* entrench; *w. w. zich* —, entrench oneself, ensconce oneself.

verschansing *v.* (*mil.*) entrenchment; (*sch.*) bulwarks.

verscheiden *on. w.* depart this life, pass away, pass over; *z. n., o.* decease, death, expiration, passing away (over).

verscheiden *b. n. en telw.* (*verschillend*) various, different, diverse; (*meerdere*) several, sundry.

verscheidenheid *v.* variety, diversity; difference.

verscherpen *o. w.* sharpen, make sharper, whet; (*fig.*) sharpen, strengthen, stiffen; (*verergeren*) aggravate.

verscherping *v.* sharpening, strengthening, stiffening; aggravation; tightening up; accentuation; intensification.

verscheuren *o. w.* (*aan stukken scheuren*) tear, tear up, tear to pieces; (*van eenrijten: kleren, enz.*) rend; (*verslinden*)

lacerate, mangle, devour, tear to pieces; (*fig.*) rend, lacerate.

verschiet *o.* distance, perspective; (*fig.*) prospect, perspective.

verschieten *o. w.* shoot; (*al schietende verbruiken*) use up, consume; (*voorschieten, lenen*) advance, lend; (*omzetten: v. graan*) stir (about); (*v. kaarten*) shuffle; *on. w.* (*v. persoon*) change colour, turn pale; (*v. ster*) shoot; (*v. kleur*) fade; (*v. stof*) lose colour, discolour; *niet* —, (*v. stof*) be sun-proof, be fast-dyed.

verschijnen *on. w.* (*alg.*) appear; (*v. persoon, zaak: zich vertonen*) make one's appearance, put in an appearance; turn up, show up; (*v. rente, enz.*) fall due; (*verstrijken v. termijn*) expire; (*v. boek*) appear, be published, come out; (*recht*) appear, enter an appearance.

verschijning *v.* appearance; (*v. boek*) appearance, publication; (*geest*—) apparition, ghost, vision, phantom; (*persoon*) figure; (*v. rente, enz.*) falling due; (*v. termijn*) expiration.

verschijnsel *o.* phenomenon; (*symptoom*) symptom, sign.

verschil *o.* difference, disparity; (*onderscheid*) distinction; (*verscheidenheid*) variety, diversity; (*twist, onenigheid*) dispute, quarrel, difference.

verschillen *on. w.* differ, be different, vary.

verschillend *b. n.* different, differing, distinct; (*allerlei*) various; (*verscheiden*) several.

verschonen *o. w.* put on clean things, put on clean linen; (*fig.: verontschuldigen, vergoelijken*) excuse, whitewash, blanch over; extenuate; (*door de vingers zien*) overlook; (*ontzien*) spare; *w. w. zich* —, change one's linen; (*fig.*) excuse oneself; extenuate oneself.

verschoning *v.* change of linen, change, clean linen; (*fig.*) excuse; pardon. [pariah.

verschoppeling *m.* outcast, castaway,

verschoppen *o. w.* kick away; (*fig.*) spurn.

verschot *o.* (*ruime sortering*) assortment, choice; (*het voorgeschotene*) advanced money, outlays, disbursement, out-of-pocket expenses.

verschoten *b. n.* faded.

verschrikkelijk *b. n.* (*bw.*) frightful(ly), dreadful(ly), terrible(-bly).

verschrikken *o. w.* frighten, terrify, startle; (*v. vogels*) scare (away); *on. w.* zie *schrikken*.

verschrikking *v.* (*het verschrikken*) fright, terror, start; (*wat doet schrikken*) horror, terror.

verschroeien *o. w.* scorch, singe; *on. w.* be scorched, be singed.

verschrompeld *b. n.* shrivelled (up), wizened, shrunken; (*v. appel*) withered, shrivelled.

verschrompelen *on. w.* shrivel (up), wizen, wither, shrink.

verschuilen *o. w.* hide, conceal, shelter; *w. w.* **zich —,** hide, conceal oneself.

verschuiven *o. w.* shove (away), remove, shift, slide; *(uitstellen)* put off, postpone, defer, remit; *on. w.* shift.

verschuldigd *b. n.* indebted, due.

versieren *o. w.* *(met bloemen, vlaggen, enz.)* decorate, ornament, deck; embellish, beautify; *(v. kleed)* trim; *(v. tafel)* garnish; adorn; *w. w.* **zich —,** adorn oneself.

versiering *v.* decoration, ornament, ornamentation, embellishment; adornment.

verslaafd *b. n.* — **aan,** addicted to, given to, enslaved to, a slave to.

verslaan *o. w.* defeat, beat; *(sp. ook:)* outplay; *(v. dorst)* quench; *on. w.* *(v. warme dranken)* cool; *(v. koude dranken)* have the chill taken off.

verslag *o.* report, account.

verslagen *b. n.* defeated, beaten; *(fig.)* dismayed, dejected, prostrate, crushed.

verslagenheid *v.* dismay, dejection, dejectedness, prostration, consternation.

verslaggever *m.* reporter.

verslapen *o. w.* sleep away; sleep off; *w. w.* **zich —,** oversleep oneself, oversleep.

verslappen *o. w.* relax, slacken; *(v. klimaat)* enervate; *on. w.* *(v. touw, spieren, ijver, enz.)* relax, slacken; *(v. ijver, ook:)* flag; *(v. belangstelling)* weaken.

verslapping *v.* relaxation, slackening; enervation; flagging.

versleten *b. n.* worn (out), threadbare, dilapidated, the worse for wear; *(v. persoon)* worn out.

verslijten *o. w.* wear out; *(v. tijd)* while away; *on. w.* wear out, wear off, wear away.

verslikken *w. w.* **zich —,** choke, swallow (something) the wrong way.

verslinden *o. w.* devour; *(fig.)* devour, gobble up, gobble down, swallow up, consume.

verslingerd *b. n.* — **op,** keen on; mashed on.

versmachten *on. w.* *(v. dorst)* be parched with thirst; *(fig.)* languish, pine away.

versmaden *o. w.* disdain, despise, scorn.

versmading *v.* disdain, despising, scorn.

versmelten *o. w.* *(v. boter)* melt; *(v. metalen)* melt, fuse; *(v. erts)* smelt; *(samensmelten)* melt together; *(v. maatschappijen)* amalgamate; *(omsmelten)* remelt, melt down; *on. w.* melt, melt away.

versnapering *v.* dainty bit, dainty, titbit, refreshment.

versnellen *o. w. en on. w.* accelerate.

versneller *m.* accelerator.

versnelling *v.* *(v. beweging)* acceleration; *(v. fiets, enz.)* gear, gearing, speed.

versnipperen *o. w.* cut into (little) bits; *(v. grond)* split up; *(v. stemmen,*

enz.) split; *(v. tijd, krachten)* fritter away, disperse.

versnippering *v.* cutting up; splitting up; dispersion.

verspelen *o. w.* play away, gamble away, lose in playing.

versperren *o. w.* block, block up, bar, obstruct; *(v. straat)* barricade.

versperring *v.* blocking(-up), barring, obstruction; *(barricade)* barricade; *(mil.)* entanglement.

verspieden *o. w.* spy out, reconnoitre, scout.

verspieder *m.* spy, scout.

verspillen *o. w.* *(v. geld)* squander; *(v. krachten, geld)* dissipate, waste, spend; *(v. melk, enz.)* spill.

versplinteren *o. w. en on. w.* splinter, break into splinters, shiver, break to shivers, shatter, sliver.

verspreid *b. n.* *(v. bevolking)* sparse; *(v. huizen)* scattered; *(v. dorp)* straggling; *(v. aantekeningen)* stray; *(mil.)* extended, loose.

verspreiden *o. w.* *(v. geruchten, nieuws)* spread, circulate, put about; *(v. ziekte)* spread; *(v. menigte)* disperse, scatter; *(nieuws per radio)* broadcast; *(v. leerstellingen)* disseminate; *(v. godsdienst)* propagate; *(v. geur; geluk, enz.)* diffuse; *(v. leugens)* circulate; *w. w.* **zich —,** *(v. ziekte, leer, mening, enz.)* spread; *(v. gerucht)* spread, get abroad; *(v. menigte)* disperse, scatter (away).

verspreider *m.* spreader, circulator; disseminator; propagator.

verspreiding *v.* spreading, circulation; *(v. ziekte, beschaving)* spread; dispersion, scattering; dissemination; propagation; *(v. kennis)* diffusion, spread; *(v. dieren, planten, enz.)* distribution.

verstaan *o. w.* understand; *(dicht.)* comprehend; *w. w.* **zich — met,** come to an understanding with.

verstaanbaar *b. n.* understandable, intelligible; **zich — maken,** make oneself understood; *bw.* understandably, intelligibly.

verstalen *o. w.* steel, harden; *w. w.* **zich —,** steel (harden) one's heart.

verstand *o.* understanding, intellect, intelligence, mind, sense.

verstandhouding *v.* understanding.

verstandig *b. n.* *(met verstand begaafd)* understanding, intelligent; *(v. verstand getuigend)* sensible, wise, reasonable; *bw.* sensibly, wisely, reasonably.

versteend *b. n.* petrified, turned to stone, fossil, fossilized, stony; *(fig.)* petrified, turned to stone.

verstek *o.* *(recht)* default; *(v. timmerman)* mitre.

verstekeling *m.* stowaway.

versteken *o. w.* hide, conceal; put away; *w. w.* **zich —,** hide, conceal (oneself); *(aan boord)* stow away.

versteld *b. n.* *(v. kleren)* repaired, mended; patched; — **staan,** be taken aback, be staggered, be startled, be perplexed.

verstellen *o. w. (herstellen: v. kleren, enz.)* repair, mend, patch; *(v. instrument,enz.)*adjust; *(verplaatsen)*transpose.

versteller *m.* mender.   [into stone.

verstenen *o. w. en on. w.* petrify, turn

versterken *o. w.* strengthen, invigorate; *(v. stad, lichaam, enz.)* fortify; *(v. licht, geluid)* intensify; *(v. positie)* consolidate; *(radio)* amplify; *(fot.)* intensify; *(v.leger,partij,muz.)*reinforce.

versterking *v.* strengthening; fortification; intensification; consolidation; amplification; reinforcement.

versterven *on. w. (overlijden)* die, die out, decease; *(bij erfenis overgaan)* devolve upon; *w. w.* **zich —,** mortify the flesh.

versterving *v.* mortification.

verstijfd *b. n. (alg.)* stiff; *(v. koude)* benumbed.

verstikken *o. w.* suffocate, stifle, strangle, smother, choke, throttle, asphyxiate; *on. w.* zie **stikken.**

verstoken *o. w.* burn; consume.

verstoken *b. n.* **— van,** deprived of, devoid of, destitute of.

verstokt *b. n. (v. hart, geweten)* obdurate; *(v. zondaar)* hardened, casehardened; *(v. vrijgezel)* confirmed, determined, inveterate, incarnate; *(v. dronkaard, roker)* confirmed; *(v. speler)* seasoned.

verstomd *b. n.* struck dumb, speechless.

verstommen *o. w.* strike dumb, silence; *on w* be struck dumb, be speechless, become silent.

verstompen *o. w.* blunt, dull, make blunt, make dull; *(fig.)* blunt, dull, hebetate, stupefy, obtund; *on. w.* blunt, dull, grow dull.

verstoord *b. n.* disturbed; *(fig.: ontstemd)* offended, vexed, annoyed, cross, ruffled.

verstoppen *o. w. (dichtstoppen)* choke (up), stop up, clog, plug; *(v. ingewanden)* constipate, obstruct, confine; *(verbergen)* hide, conceal, put away.

verstopping *v. (v. verkeer, enz.)* stoppage, obstruction, hold-up; *(v. ingewanden)* constipation, obstruction, costiveness; *(v. bloedvat)* embolism.

verstoptheid *v. (gen.)* constipation, obstruction, costiveness, obstipation.

verstoren *o. w. (v. stilte)* disturb; *(v. geluk)* disturb, perturb, trouble; *(v. plannen)* interfere with, upset; *(ontstemmen)* offend, annoy, vex, ruffle.

verstoten *o. w. (v. kind)* disown; *(v. vrouw)* repudiate.

verstouten *w. w.* **zich —,** *(het wagen)* make bold, presume; *(moed vatten)* take heart.

verstrekken *o. w.* furnish, procure, provide, supply.

vérstrekkend *b. n.* far-reaching.

verstrijken *on. w.* expire; elapse.

verstrijking *v.* expiration, expiry.

verstrooid *b. n. (verspreid)* scattered, dispersed; *(fig.)* distracted, absentminded, preoccupied, distrait.

verstrooidheid *v.* absent-mindedness, absence of mind, wool-gathering.

verstuiken *o. w.* sprain, wrick; *w. w.* **zich —,** sprain one's ankle.

verstuiking *v.* spraining, sprain.

verstuiven *o. w.* pulverize, spray, atomize, nebulize; *on. w.* be blown away; be scattered, be dispersed.

versuft *b. n.* dull, dazed, muffish; *(v. oud mens)* doting.

vertaalwerk *o.* translations, translation work.

vertakking *v.* branching, ramification

vertalen *o. w.* translate.

vertaler *m.* translator.

vertaling *v.* translation; *(v. de bijbel)* version; *(woordelijke — van klassieken)* crib.

verte *v.* distance.

vertederen *o. w.* soften, mollify; *on. w.* soften, mellow.

vertedering *v.* softening, mollification

verteerbaar *b. n.* digestible; **licht —,** easy of digestion.

vertegenwoordigen *o. w.* represent; be representative of.

vertegenwoordigend *b. n.* representative.

vertegenwoordiger *m.* representative; *(H. ook:)* agent.

vertegenwoordiging *v.* representation; *(H. ook:)* agency.

vertellen *o. w.* tell, narrate, relate; *on. w.* tell a story; *w. w.* **zich —,** miscount, make a mistake in counting.

vertelling *v.* narration, story, tale.

verteren *o. w (v geld)* spend; *(v voedsel)* digest; *(door vuur, enz)* consume; *(door hartstocht)* eat up, burn out; *on. w. (v. voedsel)* digest; *(vergaan, enz.)* waste (away).

vertering *v. (v. voedsel)* digestion; *(verbruik)* consumption; *(gelag)* score; *(uitgaven)* expenses.

vertier *o. (drukte, bedrijvigheid)* activity; *(verkeer)* traffic.

vertikken *o. w.* **het —,** refuse (flatly); **hij vertikte het,** he just would not do it.

vertinnen *o. w.* tin, coat with tin.

vertoeven *on. w.* sojourn, stay, reside.

vertolken *o. w.* interpret; *(fig.)* voice; *(muz.)* interpret, render, read.

vertolker *m.* interpreter; *(fig.)* exponent; mouth-piece.

vertolking *v.* interpretation; voicing; rendering, reading.

vertonen *o. w. (laten zien)* show, exhibit, produce; *(v. kunstwerk: tentoonstellen)* expose, exhibit, show; *(ton.)* produce, present, perform; *(in bioscoop)* screen, show, feature, present.

vertoning *v.* show, exposition; *(opvoering)* representation, performance; *(v.*

film) exhibition, show; (*schouwspel*) spectacle.

vertoog *o.* remonstrance, representation; (*betoog*) demonstration.

vertoon *o.* (*het vertonen*) presentation; demonstration, exhibition; (*praal, bluf*) show, ostentation.

vertoornen *o. w.* incense, make angry, infuriate; *w. w. zich —,* become angry.

vertragen *o. w.* retard, delay, slacken; *on. w.* slacken, slow down.

vertraging *v.* retardation, retardment, delay.

vertrapt *b. n.* trodden under foot; (*fig.*) down trodden.

vertrek *o.* departure, start; (*v. boot*) sailing, departure; (*kamer*) room, apartment.

vertrekken *on. w.* depart, start, leave; (*v. boot, ook:*) sail; (*v. vliegtuig, ook:*) take off; *o. w.* (*v. tafel, stoel*) move, remove; (*v. gelaat*) contort, distort.

vertroetelen *o. w.* pamper, cocker (up), spoil, coddle, pet, cosset.

vertrouwelijk *b. n.* familiar, intimate, confidential; (*geheim*) confidential; *bw.* confidentially, in confidence; intimately.

vertrouwelijkheid *v.* confidentiality, confidentialness; familiarity, intimacy.

vertrouweling *m.* confidant, intimate.

vertrouwen *o. w.* trust; *iem. iets —,* trust a person with something; *on. w. — op,* rely on; *z. n., o.* confidence, trust, faith.

verwijfeling *v.* despair, desperation.

vervaard *b. n.* alarmed, afraid, frightened.

vervaardigen *o. w.* make, manufacture, construct.

vervaardiging *v.* making, manufacture, construction.

vervagen *on. w.* fade (away), become obscured, become blurred.

verval *o.* (*achteruitgang*) decline, decay, deterioration, falling-off; (*v. gebouw, enz.*) dilapidation; (*v. rivier*) fall, slope, grade, difference in the levels; (*v. wissel*) expiration, maturity; (*fooien*) perquisites, vails.

vervaldag *m.* due date, day of maturity, day of payment.

vervallen *on. w.* (*in verval raken*) decay, fall into decay, go to ruin; (*v. gebouw, ook:*) fall into disrepair; (*v. wet*) lapse, be abrogated; (*v. polis, recht, pas, wet, enz.*) lapse; (*v. termijn, contract*) expire, terminate, run out; (*v. wissel, enz.*) fall due, become due, mature, arrive at maturity; (*v. coupons*) be payable, become payable; (*v. trein*) be taken off; (*v. wedstrijd, enz.*) be abandoned, be dropped.

vervallen *b. n.* (*v. gebouw, enz.*) dilapidated, out of repair, crazy, ruinous; (*v. wissel*) due, overdue, matured; (*v. coupons*) payable; (*v. termijn, contract*) expired; (*v. wet*) abrogated; (*v. recht*) lapsed; (*v. persoon*) worn (out), wasted.

vervalsen *o. w.* (*v. voedingswaren*) adulterate; fake; (*v. documenten*) falsify, forge, cook, fake; (*v. bankbiljetten, handschrift*) counterfeit; (*v. munt*) debase; (*v. melk, tekst, enz.*) sophisticate; (*v. wijn*) doctor; (*v. dobbelstenen*) load; (*v. rekening*) falsify, cook.

vervalser *m.* adulterator, faker; falsifier, forger; counterfeiter.

vervalsing *v.* adulteration; falsification, forging, cooking; counterfeiting; sophistication.

vervangen *o. w.* (*alg.*) take the place of, supply the place of, replace; (*aflossen*) relieve; (*voor goed, ook:*) supersede.

vervangstuk *o.* spare part.

vervelen *o. w.* bore, tire, weary; (*ergeren*) annoy; *on. w.* bore, tire, become a bore; *w. w. zich —,* be bored, feel bored.

vervelend *b. n.* boring, tiresome; (*v. plaats, spel, enz.*) dull, slow; (*v. taak*) irksome; (*langdradig*) tedious; (*hinderlijk*) annoying.

verveling *v.* boredom, tiresomeness, weariness; tedium, tediousness, ennui.

vervellen *on. w.* peel, skin, desquamate; (*v. slang*) cast (shed) the skin, slough.

verven *o. w.* paint; (*v. stoffen, haar*) dye; *w. w. zich —,* paint.

ververij *v.* dye-house, dye-works.

verversen *o. w.* refresh; renew; *w. w. zich —,* refresh oneself, take some refreshment.

verversing *v.* refreshment.

vervlaamsen *o. w.* Flemish.

vervliegen *on. w.* fly, fly away; (*verdampen, vervluchtigen*) evaporate, volatilize; (*fig.*) evaporate; (*v. hoop, enz.*) melt (vanish) in the air.

vervloeken *o. v.* (*alg.*) curse, damn, execrate; (*door banvloek*) anathematize, excommunicate.

vervloeking *v.* curse, imprecation, malediction; anathema.

vervoegen *o. w.* (*v. werkwoord*) conjugate; *w. w. zich — bij,* apply to.

vervoeging *v.* conjugation.

vervoer *o.* transport, conveyance, carriage; transit.

vervoeren *o. w.* transport, convey, carry (away).

vervoering *v.* transport, rapture, ravishment, exaltation, ecstasy.

vervolg *o.* continuation, sequel; *in het —,* in future.

vervolgen *o. w.* (*voortzetten*) continue, proceed on; pursue; (*achternazetten*) pursue, be in pursuit of; (*kwellen, plagen*) persecute; (*recht*) prosecute; proceed against.

vervolgens *bw.* then, further, thereupon, next; (*naderhand*) afterwards.

vervolging *v.* pursuit; persecution; prosecution.

vervolgingswaanzin *m.* persecution mania, persecutory paranoia.

vervormen *o. w.* (*een andere vorm*

geven) transform, refashion, remodel, recast; (*misvormen*) deform.

vervreemden *o. w.* (*v. eigendom*) alienate; (*v. persoon*) alienate, estrange (*van*, from); *w. w. zich — van*, become a stranger to, get estranged from.

vervreemding *v.* alienation, estrangement.

vervroegen *o. w.* fix at an earlier time (hour, date); *een datum —*, advance a date.

vervullen *o. w.* (*v. plaats, vacature, rol*) fill; (*v. taak*) accomplish; (*v. plicht*) carry out, discharge; (*v. belofte*) fulfil, keep, redeem, make good; (*iemands wens*) comply with; (*v. plaats*) occupy; (*v. vacature*) supply.

vervulling *v.* fulfilment, performance; discharge; realization.

verwaand *b. n.* conceited, presuming, bumptious, arrogant, cocky.

verwaardigen *o. w. iem. met geen blik —*, not deign to look at a person; *w. w. zich — te,* condescend to, deign to.

verwaarlozen *o. w.* neglect.

verwachten *o. w.* expect; look (forward) to, anticipate.

verwachting *v.* expectation.

verwant *b. n.* allied, related, kindred, congenial; (*v. talen, woorden, enz.*) cognate; (*predikatie*) akin.

verwantschap *v.* (*alg.*) relatedness, relationship, relation, connection, affinity; (*v. aard, karakter*) congeniality; (*bloed—*) consanguinity, kinship; (*scheik.*) affinity.

verward *b. n.* (*in de war*) entangled, tangled, disordered, disarranged, tumbled, tousled, confused; (*ingewikkeld*) intricate, tangled; (*fig.*) confused, entangled; (*verlegen*) confused, perplexed; *bw.* confusedly.

verwardheid *v.* confusion, disorder; (*verlegenheid*) confusion, perplexity.

verwarmen *o. w.* warm, heat.

verwarming *v.* warming, heating; calefaction; *centrale —*, steam heating.

verwarren *o. w.* entangle, tangle, ravel, snarl; (*fig.*) confuse, muddle up, mix up, confound; *w. w. zich —*, get entangled, entangle, get confused.

verwedden *o. w.* bet, wager, lay; (*door wedden verliezen*) bet away, lose in betting.

verweer *o.* (*verdediging*) defence, vindication; (*tegenstand*) resistance.

verweerd *b. n.* (*v. gelaat, enz.*) weathered, weather-beaten; (*v. muur*) weatherworn, weather-stained.

verweerder *m.* defender; (*recht*) defendant.

verweerschrift *o.* (written) defence, apology, vindication.

verwekken *o. w.* (*v. kinderen*) beget, generate, procreate; (*fig.: v. toorn, verontwaardiging*) rouse; (*v. angst*) inspire; (*v. slaap*) induce; (*v. ontevredenheid*) cause, excite, raise; (*v. dorst, wanorde, enz.*) create; (*v. afgunst*) provoke; (*v. tumult, oproer, enz.*) breed, raise.

verwelken *on. w.* fade, wither, wilt.

verwelkomen *o. w.* welcome, bid welcome.

verwelkoming *v.* welcoming, welcome.

verwennen *o. w.* spoil, indulge, over-indulge, indulge too much; (*vertroetelen*) coddle, pamper; *w. w. zich —*, coddle oneself.

verwenning *v.* over-indulgence; coddling.

verwensen *o. w.* curse, execrate.

verwensing *v.* curse, execration; malediction.

verweren *o. w.* defend; *w. w. zich —*, defend oneself, speak up for oneself, act defensively; (*tegenspartelen*) struggle, resist.

verwerken *o. w.* (*v. grondstoffen*) work up, put into work; (*v. voedsel; fig.*), digest, assimilate.

verwerpelijk *b. n.* reprehensible, rejectable, objectionable, condemnable.

verwerpen *o. w.* reject; (*sterker*) repudiate, scorn; (*bij stemming: v. wet, motie, enz.*) reject, defeat, negative.

verwerven *o. w.* obtain, acquire, win, gain; *w. w.* win, gain.

verwezenlijken *o. w.* realize, actualize, effectuate; *w. w. zich —*, be realized, materialize; (*v. vermoedens, enz., ook:*) become certainty.

verwezenlijking *v.* realization, actualization.

verwijden *o. w.* widen; let out; *w. w. zich —*, widen; (*v. ogen*) dilate.

verwijderen *o. w.* remove, put out of the way; (*van sportveld*) send off; (*van school*) expel; (*uit de klas*) send out of class; (*v. vlekken*) remove, take out; (*alg.*) eliminate; *w. w. zich —*, go away, turn away, retire, withdraw; (*v. voetstappen, enz.*) recede.

verwijdering *v.* removal; expulsion; elimination; (*vervreemding*) alienation, estrangement.

verwijfd *b. n.* (*bw.*) effeminate(ly,) womanish(ly).

verwijl *o.* delay.

verwijt *o.* reproach, blame, reproof.

verwijten *o. w.* reproach, blame, upbraid.

verwijzen *o. w.* refer.

verwijzing *v.* reference; (*in boek, ook:*) cross-reference; (*naar ander hof*) remittal.

verwikkelen *o. w.* complicate, embroil, make intricate; *verwikkeld zijn in,* be mixed up (implicated, involved) in.

verwikkeling *v.* complication, entanglement.

verwilderd *b. n.* (*v. tuin*) overgrown, weedgrown, unkempt; (*v. plant, dier*) run wild; (*v. landerij*) fallen out of cultivation; (*v. blik, uitdrukking*) haggard; (*moreel*) brutified, brutalized.

verwisselen *o. w. (omruilen)* change, exchange, interchange; *(v. letters in woord)* transpose; *(v. termen)* alternate, commute; *on. w. — van kleur,* change colour.

verwisseling *v.* change, exchange, interchange; *(verwarring)* mistake; *(in volgorde)* permutation; *(v. letters in woord)* transposition.

verwittigen *o. w.* inform, notify, advise, send word, warn.

verwittiging *v.* information, notice, communication, warning.

verwoed *b. n.* furious, enraged, fierce.

verwoesten *o. w.* destroy, lay waste, devastate, ruin, ravage.

verwoesting *v.* destruction, devastation, ravage, havoc.

verwonderen *o. w.* surprise, astonish; *w. w. zich — (over),* be surprised (at), be astonished (at), wonder (at), marvel (at).

verwondering *v.* astonishment, surprise, wonder.

verworgen *o. w.* strangle, throttle.

verworging *v.* strangulation.

verworpeling *m.* outcast, reprobate.

verworpen *b. n.* rejected; thrown out; *(fig.)* cast out, reprobate, depraved.

verwringen *o. w.* distort, contort, twist, wrench; *(fig.)* distort, twist.

verzachten *o. w.* soften; *(fig.)* soften, soothe, allay, alleviate, mitigate, relieve, ease; *(v. wet)* relax, mollify.

verzadigd *b. n.* satiated, satisfied, filled; *(scheik., nat.)* saturated.

verzadigen *o. w.* satiate; *(scheik., nat.)* saturate; *w. w. zich —,* eat one's fill, satisfy oneself.

verzaken *o. w. (alg.)* renounce, forsake; *(kaartsp.)* revoke.

verzaking *v.* renouncement, renunciation, forsaking; *(kaartsp.)* revoke; neglect.

verzamelaar *m.* collector, gatherer, compiler.

verzamelen *o. w. (v. geld, zegels, enz.)* collect; *(v. honig)* gather, harvest; *(v. fortuin, inlichtingen)* accumulate; *(v. aanhangers, vrienden)* assemble; *(v. kracht, kennis, enz.)* store up; *(v. aantekeningen, verhalen)* compile; *(v. voorwerpen, menigte)* congregate; *on. w. (mil.)* close; *w. w. zich —, (v. personen)* assemble, meet, congregate; rally; *(v. stof, enz.)* collect, congregate.

verzameling *v.* collection; gathering; accumulation; assemblage; compilation.

verzamelnaam *m.* collective noun.

verzanden *on. w.* sand up, silt up, get silted with sand.

verzegelen *o. w.* seal (up); *(recht)* put under seal, put seals upon, place seals on, affix seals to.

verzeilen *on. w. (wegzeilen)* sail (away); *(verkeerd zeilen)* sail out of the course; *(op een bank)* run aground.

verzekeren *o. w. (betuigen, met klem*

verklaren) assure; *(waarborgen)* ensure, assure; *(assureren) (eigendommen)* insure; *(leven)* insure, assure; *(zeeverzekering, ook:)* underwrite; *(vastmaken, beveiligen)* secure; *w. w. zich —,* take out an insurance, insure *(tegen,* against); *(op 't leven)* take out a life-policy; *zich — van,* ascertain, make sure of.

verzekering *v.* assurance; *(assurantie)* insurance.

verzekeringsmaatschappij *v.* insurance company.

verzekeringspolis *v.* policy of insurance, insurance-policy.

verzenden *o. w. (v. goederen)* send, send off, dispatch, forward, ship; *(v. geld)* remit; *(v. telegram)* send, transmit; *(v. uitnodigingen)* send out.

verzender *m.* sender; *(H.)* sender; shipper, consignor.

verzending *v.* sending; dispatch, forwarding, shipment; remittance; transmission.

verzendingskosten *m. mv.* forwarding-charges.

verzengen *o. w.* scorch, singe, torrefy.

verzet *o. (tegenstand)* resistance, opposition; *(recht)* refractory conduct; *(verpozing, ontspanning)* diversion, recreation.

verzetten *o. w. (verplaatsen: anders zetten)* move, remove, transpose, shift; *(v. werk)* manage, handle; *(ontspannen)* divert, distract; *w. w. zich —, (weerstand bieden)* resist, offer resistance; *(in verzet komen)* make opposition, withstand; *(zich schrap zetten)* recalcitrate, be refractory, turn restive, offer resistance; *(tegen verdriet)* bear up; *(zich ontspannen)* take some recreation, be taken out of oneself, unbend.

vérziendheid *v.* far-sightedness, long-sightedness, presbyopia.

verzinken *o. w. (met een laagje zink overdekken)* zinc.

verzinken *on. w.* sink, sink down, become submerged; *o. w. (tn.)* countersink.

verzinnen *o. w.* invent, devise, contrive, fabricate *(v. leugen, beschuldiging)* trump up.

verzinsel *o.* invention, fabrication, fiction, figment.

verzoek *o.* request; *(aan overheid)* petition.

verzoeken *o. w. (uitnodigen)* ask, invite; *(beleefd vragen)* request, beg; *(in verzoeking brengen)* tempt.

verzoeking *v.* temptation.

verzoekschrift *o.* petition, memorial.

verzoenen *o. w.* reconcile; *(gunstig stemmen)* conciliate, propitiate; *w. w. zich —,* become reconciled.

verzoening *v.* reconciliation, reconcilement, atonement.

verzoeten *o. w.* sweeten, dulcify; *(fig.)* sweeten.

verzorgen *o. w.* care for, take care of, provide for, attend to, look after; *(v.*

handen, nagels) manicure; *(v. paard)* groom; *w. w.* **zich —,** take care of oneself.

verzorging *v.* care, provision, providing, nurture.

verzot *b. n.* **— op,** fond of, doting upon, enamoured of.

verzuchting *v.* sigh, sighing; *(klacht)* lamentation.

verzuim *o.* neglect, negligence, omission, oversight; *(op school)* non-attendance; *(recht)* default.

verzuimen *o. w.* *(niet nakomen, verwaarlozen)* neglect; *(niet doen)* omit, **fail;** *(niet waarnemen, onbenut laten)* lose, miss, let slip; *(niet bijwonen: school, vergadering, enz.)* miss, stay away from; *on. w.* stay (stop) away (from school, from church, etc.).

verzuren *o. w.* sour, make sour; *on. w.* sour, grow (become) sour, turn sour, turn.

verzwakken *o. w.* weaken; enfeeble; enervate; debilitate; *(fot.)* reduce; *on. w.* weaken, grow weak.

verzwakking *v.* weakening; enfeeblement; debilitation.

verzwaren *o. w.* make heavier, aggravate; *(v. straf)* make more severe; *(v. dijk)* strengthen.

verzwelgen *o. w.* swallow up, gobble up, gorge (down), guzzle down.

verzweren *on. w.* fester, ulcerate, suppurate.

verzwijgen *o. w.* conceal, keep a secret, suppress.

vesper *v.* vespers, evensong.

vest *o.* waistcoat; *(winkelterm)* vest.

vest *v.* *(vesting)* fortress, stronghold; *(gracht)* moat; *(muur)* wall, rampart.

vestigen *o. w.* establish, set up, settle, found; *w. w.* **zich —,** settle, settle down, establish oneself.

vesting *v.* fortress, stronghold.

vestingoorlog *m.* siege war.

vestingstraf *v.* detention (confinement, imprisonment) in a fortress, fortress-detention.

vest(jes)zak *m.* waistcoat-pocket.

vet *z. n., o.* *(alg.)* fat; *(smeer)* grease; *(reuzel)* lard; *(wet.)* adipose; *b. n.* fat; *(vuil)* greasy.

vete *v.* fend, enmity, rancour.

veter *m.* *(v. schoen)* boot-lace, shoestring; *(v. korset)* corset-lace, stay-lace.

veteraan *m.* veteran, old campaigner; *(fig. ook:)* old stager.

veterbeslag *o.* tag.

vetgans *v.* penguin.

vetkaars *v.* dip, tallow-dip.

vetmesten *o. w.* fat off, fatten (up), feed; *w. w.* **zich — met,** batten on.

vetvlek *v.* grease spot, greasy mark (spot).

vetweider *m.* grazier, stock-feeder.

veulen *o.* foal; *(hengst)* colt, colt foal; *(merrie)* filly, filly foal.

vezel *v.* fibre, filament, thread.

vezelachtig *b. n.* fibrous, fibroid.

via via, by the way of, by the route of.

viaduct *v. en o.* viaduct, archway, railway-arch.

vicaris *m.* vicar.

vier *telw.* four.

vierde *b. n.* fourth; *z. n., o.* fourth (part); **ten —,** fourthly, in the fourth place.

vieren *o. w.* celebrate; keep; *(v. Sabbat, zondag)* observe, keep holy; *(v. touw)* veer out, veer away, ease off, slack off; *on. w.* veer, give line.

vierendelen *o. w.* quarter.

vierhoek *m.* quadrangle, rectangle.

viering *v.* celebration; *(v. zondag)* observance.

vierkant *b. n.* *(v. figuur)* square, quadrangular; *(v. getallen)* square; *(fig.)* four-square; *bw.* squarely; *z. n., o.* square.

vierkantig *b. n.* square, quadrangular.

vierkantswortel *m.* square root.

viermaal *bw.* four times.

vierschaar *v.* tribunal, court of justice.

viersprong *m.* cross-road, cross-way, ourway.

viertal *o.* four, number of four, set of four.

viervoeter *m.* quadruped, four-footer.

viervoetig *b. n.* four-footed, quadruped.

vies *b. n.* *(vuil, smerig)* dirty, grubby; *(v. weer)* nasty, foul, muggy; *(walglijk)* filthy, nasty; *(gemeen: v. verhaal, enz.)* obscene, smutty, filthy; *(v. stank)* offensive, nauseating, noisome, sickening; *(kieskeurig)* particular, dainty, fastidious, nice; *bw.* nastily.

viesneus *m.* particular (fastidious) fellow, sniffer.

viezerik *m.* dirty fellow, dirty pig.

vigilie *v.* vigil.

vijand *m.* enemy; *(dicht.)* foe.

vijandelijk *b. n.* *(van de vijand)* enemy, of the enemy, hostile; *(v. daad, enz.: als van een vijand)* hostile, inimical.

vijandelijkheid *v.* hostility.

vijandschap *v.* enmity, animosity.

vijf *telw.* five.

vijfhoek *m.* pentagon.

vijfling *m.* (set of) quintuplets; *(één hiervan)* quintuplet.

vijftien *telw.* fifteen.

vijftiende *b. n.* *(z. n., o.)* fifteenth (part).

vijftig *telw.* fifty.

vijftiger *m. en v.* man (woman) of fifty (in the fifties).

vijfvingerkruid *o.* cinquefoil, cinqfoil, five-finger grass.

vijg *v.* fig.

vijgeboom *m.* fig-tree.

vijl *v.* file.

vijlen *o. w.* file; *(fig.)* file, polish.

vijver *m.* pond.

vijzel *m.* *(stampvat)* mortar; *v. (dommekracht)* jack-screw, jack.

vilder *m.* skinner, flayer, (horse-)-knacker.

villapark *o.* villa park.
villen *o. w.* flay, fleece, skin.
vilt *o.* felt.
vilthoed *m.* felt-hat, felt, castor, beaver.
vin *v.* (*v. vis*) fin; (*puist*) acne, pustule.
vinden *o. w.* find; (*aantreffen*) come across, meet with, light upon; (*van mening zijn*) think.
vinding *v.* invention, discovery, device.
vindingrijk *b. n.* inventive, ingenious; resourceful.
vindingrijkheid *v.* inventiveness, ingenuity; resourcefulness.
vinger *m.* finger.
vingerafdruk *m.* finger-print, finger-mark.
vingerhoed *m.* thimble.
vingerhoedskruid *o.* fox-glove.
vingerlid *o.* finger-joint.
vingervlug *b. n.* light-fingered, nimble-fingered.
vingerwijzing *v.* hint, indication.
vink *m.* finch.
vinkeslag *m.* finch-trap.
vinnig *b. n.* (*v. toon, antwoord*) sharp, biting, snappish, cutting; (*v. koude*) biting, cutting; (*v. strijd*) sharp, fierce, keen; (*v. woorden*) mordant; (*v. toon*) caustic, trenchant; (*v. twist*) acrid.
vinnigheid *v.* sharpness, bitingness, etc.; causticity, trenchancy.
violet *b. n. en z. n., o.* violet.
violier *v.* stock-gillyflower.
violist *m.* violinist, violin-player.
viool *v.* (*muz.*) violin; (*fam.*) fiddle; (*Pl.*) violet.
vioolhars *v. en o.* colophony, violin-rosin.
viooltje *o.* (*Pl.*) (*welriekend*) violet; (*driekleurig*) pansy, heartsease, love-in-idleness.
virtuoos *m.* virtuoso (*mv.:* virtuosi).
vis *m.* fish.
visaas *o.* fish-bait.
visarend *m.* orsprey, ossifrage, fish-hawk.
viseren *o. w.* visé, visa; (*mikken*) (take) aim.
visgraat *v.* fish-bone; (*tn.*) herring-bone.
vishaak *m.* fish-hook.
visie *v.* vision.
visioen *o.* vision.
visitatie *v.* (*v. schip*) visitation, visit; (*v. bagage, enz.*) examination, inspection; (*huiszoeking*) search; (*kath.*) visitation.
visitekaartje *o.* visiting-card.
viskuit *v.* (hard) roe, spawn; milt.
vislijm *v.* fish-glue, isinglass.
vissen *on. w.* fish.
visser *m.* (*van beroep*) fisherman; (*hengelaar*) angler.
vissersboot *v.* fishing-boat.
vissershaven *v.* fishing-port.
vissersring *m.* (*v. paus*) Fisherman's ring.
visvangst *v.* fishing, fishery.

visvrouw *v.* fishwife, fish-woman.
vitten *on. w.* find fault, cavil, carp; — **op,** find fault with, cavil at, carp at.
vitter *m.* fault-finder, caviller.
vivisectie *v.* vivisection.
vizier *m.* vizi e)r.
vizier *o.* (*v. helm*) visor; (*mil.: v. vuurwapen*) (back-)sight. [bead.
vizierkorrel *v.* foresight, aim-sight,
vizierlijn *v.* line of sight.
vla *v.* custard.
vlaag *v.* (*v. regen, enz.*) shower; (*v wind*) squall, gust (of wind); (*fig.*) fit; burst.
Vlaams *b. n.* Flemish; *z. n., o.* Flemish.
Vlaanderen *o.* Flanders.
vlag *v.* flag; (*mil.*) colours; (*fig.*) standard; (*Pl.: v. vlinderbloem*) vexillum, standard; (*v. veer*) vane, web.
vlaggen *on. w.* put out (hang out, display, hoist) the flag(s).
vlaggestok *m.* flag-staff, flag-pole.
vlak *b. n.* (*v. land, enz.*) flat, level; (*zonder oneffenheden*) smooth; *bw.* flatly; (*precies*) exactly, right; *z. n., o.* level; (*meetk., enz.*) plane; (*v. meetkundig lichaam*) face; (*v. water, ijs, enz.*) sheet.
vlakgom *v.* India rubber, eraser.
vlakken *o. w.* flatten, level.
vlakte *v.* plain, level; (*v. water, ijs, enz.*) sheet.
vlaktemaat *v.* superficial measure.
vlam *v.* flame; (*grote — *) blaze; (*v. hout*) grain.
Vlaming *m.* Fleming.
vlammen *on. w.* flame, be aflame, blaze (up), be in a blaze; *o. w.* (*v. zijde, enz.*) wave, water.
vlammenwerper *m.* (*mil.*) flame-thrower, flame-projector.
vlas *o.* flax.
vlasbaard *m.* flaxen beard, downy beard; (*melkmuil*) beardless boy, milksop.
vlasbraak *v.* flax-breaker, brake.
vlashekel *m.* flax-hackle.
vlasspinnerij *v.* flax-mill.
vlasteelt *v.* flax-growing.
vlasvink *m.* linnet.
vlaszaad *o.* flax-seed, linseed.
vlecht *v.* braid, tress, plait, plaited hair.
vlechten *o. w.* (*v. haar*) plait, braid; (*v. krans*) wreathe, plait; (*v. matten*) pleat, weave, plait; (*v. manden*) make; (*v. touw, enz.*) twist, twine; (*v. takken, rijs*) wattle; *on. w.* plait, pleat.
vlechtwerk *o.* wicker-work, basket-work, wattle-work; (*fröbelwerk*) mat-plaiting.
vle(d)ermuis *v.* bat.
vlees *o.* (*alg.*) flesh; (*als voedsel*) meat; (*v. vruchten*) pulp, flesh.
vleesetend *b. n.* flesh-eating, carnivorous.
vleesextract *o.* meat (beef) extract, extract of meat, essence of beef.
vleeshouwer *m.* butcher.

vleeshouwerij v. butchery.
vleesnat o. (jus) gravy; (bouillon) broth; (v. rauw vlees) meat-juice.
vleeswaren v. mv. meats, meat-products.
vleeswording v. incarnation.
vleet v. herring-net; **bij de —**, in plenty, plenty of, lots of, heaps of.
vlegel m. flail; (fig.) boor, churl, bounder.
vlegeljaren o. mv. years of indiscretion, awkward age.
vleien o. w. flatter, coax, wheedle, cajole; (kruiperig) fawn upon, cringe to; w. w. **zich — met de hoop, dat,** indulge a hope that.
vleier m. flatterer, coaxer, adulator.
vleierij v. flattery, adulation.
vleitaal v. flattering words, flattery.
vlek o. market-town, borough.
vlek v. spot, stain, soil, blot; (smeer) splotch, smudge, daub; (op fruit, enz.) speck; (fig.) stain, blot, blemish.
vlekkeloos b. n. spotless, stainless, speckless, immaculate, blameless.
vlekkenwater o. cleansing-drops, scouring-drops, detergent.
vlektyfus m. typhus (fever).
vlerk v. wing.
vleugel m. (v. vogel, gebouw, leger, enz.) wing; (dicht.) pinion; (v. deur) leaf; (v. molen, schroef) vane; (piano) grand piano.
vleugeladjudant m. aide-de-camp, wing-adjutant.
vleugelman m. file-leader, leader of the file, marker, guide
vleugelmoer v (tn.) butterfly-nut, winged nut.
vlezig b. n. fleshy; meaty; (v. vruchten) pulpy.
vlieden o. w. flee, fly, eschew, shun; on. w. flee, fly.
vlieg v. fly.
vliegboot v. flying-boat.
vliegen on. w. (alg.) fly; (in vliegtuig, ook:) plane, aviate.
vliegenier m. flying-man, airman, aviator, flier.
vliegenkast v. meat-safe, wire-gauze safe.
vliegensvlug bw. at top-speed, as quick as lightning, in less than no time.
vliegenvanger m. fly-catcher, fly-trap; (Pl.) fly-trap; (Dk.: vogel) fly-catcher, catch-fly.
vlieger m. kite.
vlieghaven v. air-port.
vliegmachine v. flying-machine, aeroplane.
vliegterrein o. aviation ground, flying-ground, aerodrome.
vliegtocht m. flying-expedition.
vliegtuigschip o. aircraft carrier.
vliegwezen o. flying.
vliegwiel o. fly-wheel.
vlier v. elder; **wilde —**, danewort.
vliering v. loft, garret, attic.

vlierstroop v. elder-syrup.
vlies o. (in lichaam) membrane; (op vloeistof, oog, enz.) film; (zeer dun), pellicle; (vacht) fleece; (Pl.: om zaadlobben) cuticle; (v. goud, enz.: op melk) skin.
vliet m. rill, brook, watercourse.
vlieten on. w. flow, run.
vlijen o. w. lay down, stow, arrange; w. w. **zich — in het gras,** nestle down in the grass.
vlijmend b. n. lancinating, sharp; (v. koude) biting; (v. wind) sharp, cutting; (v. pijn) excruciating; (v. smart) poignant.
vlijt v. diligence, application, industry, assiduity.
vlijtig b.n. diligent, industrious, assiduous.
vlinder m. butterfly; (avondvlinder) moth.
vlinderbloemigen v. mv. papilionaceous flowers.
vlo v. flea.
vloed m. (tegenover eb) flood tide, high tide, flood, tide, flux; (rivier) flood, river, stream; (fig.) flood, flow, torrent.
vloeibaar b. n. liquid, fluid; **— maken (worden),** liquefy.
vloeibaarheid v. liquidity, fluidity, liquid state.
vloeien on. w. (stromen) flow, stream; (v. inkt) run, blot, spread; o. w. blot.
vloeiend b. n. flowing, fluent; bw. fluently.
vloeipapier o. (poreus papier) blotting paper; (zijdepoort) tissue paper.
vloeistof v. liquid.
vloek m. (godslastering) oath, swearword, curse, blasphemy; (vervloeking) malediction, imprecation, curse.
vloeken on. w. swear, curse, curse and swear, use strong language; o. w. curse.
vloer m. floor.
vloeren o. w. floor.
vloerkleed o. carpet.
vloermat v. floor-mat.
vloersteen m. paving-stone, paving-tile, floor-tile.
vlok v. (v. sneeuw flake; (v. wol), enz.) flock; (v. haar)tuft.
vlooienspel o. tiddlywinks.
vloot v. fleet, navy.
vlootbasis v. naval base.
vlot o. raft, float.
vlot b. n. (drijvend) afloat, adrift; (fig.: vlug)fluent; (vloeiend: v. stijl, enz.) flowing, fluent, smooth; bw. fluently.
vlotbrug v. raft bridge, floating bridge
vlotten on. w. float; (fig.) go smoothly; o. w. (v. hout) raft.
vlotter m. (persoon) raftsman, rafter; (toestel) float, floating-gauge.
vlucht v. (het vluchten) flight, escape; (het vliegen) flight; (troep vogels) flock, flight; (afstand tussen vleugeluiteinden) wing-span, wing-spread, spread of wing; (v. deur, enz.) reveal.
vluchteling m. fugitive; (uitgewekene) refugee.

vluchten *on. w.* fly (away), flee; *o. w.* fly, flee, shun, eschew.

vluchthaven *v.* port (harbour) of refuge, safe harbour, port of distress.

vluchtig *b. n. (v. persoon)* volatile, superficial, scatter-brained; *(v. stoffen)* volatile; *(v. blik)* cursory, hasty; *(v. bezoek)* flying, hasty; *(v. beeld)* evanescent; *(v. schets)* hasty; *(v. genoegens)* transient, transitory, fleeting, fugacious.

vlug *b. n. (snel)* quick, rapid, fast; *(lenig, handig)* nimble, agile; *(geestelijk)* quick, nimble, smart; *bw.* quickly; nimbly; smartly.

vlugheid *v.* quickness, rapidity; nimbleness; smartness; promptness, promptitude.

vlugschrift *o.* pamphlet.

vlugzout *o.* sal volatile.

vocht *o. (vloeistof)* fluid, liquid; *(nat)* moisture, damp; *(sap)* juice.

vochtig *b. n.* moist, damp; *(onaangenaam —)* dank; *(wet.)* humid; **— worden,** become moist (damp, &c.), moisten; **— maken,** misten, damp, wet.

vochtigheid *v.* moistness, dampness; dankness; humidity; *(concreet)* moisture, damp.

vod *v.* rag, tatter.

voddenmarkt *v.* rag-market, rag-fair.

vodderij *v.* trash, trumpery.

voeden *o. w. (v. persoon, pomp, kanaal, enz.)* feed; *(v. persoon, dier, hoop, enz.)* nourish; *(fig.)* foster, cherish, nourish, entertain, nurse; *on. w.* feed; *w. w.* **zich —,** feed *(met,* on).

voeder *m. (persoon)* feeder, nourisher; *o.* fodder, forage, provender.

voeding *v. (handeling)* feeding, alimentation, nourishment; *(voedsel)* food, nourishment, nutrition; *(mil.)* subsistence.

voedingsgewassen *o. mv.* food-plants.

voedingsproces *o.* process of nutrition.

voedingswaarde *v.* food-value, feeding value, nutritive value.

voedsel *o.* food, nutrition, nutriment, nourishment; *(rantsoen)* dietary.

voedselvoorziening *v.* food-supply, feeding.

voedster *v.* nurse, foster-mother; *(haas, konijn)* doe.

voedzaam *b. n.* nourishing, nutritious, nutritive.

voeg *v.* joint, seam.

voegen *on. w. (betamen)* become, behove; *w. w.* **zich — naar,** comply with, acede to; conform to.

voegen *o. w. (bijvoegen)* add; *(v. metselwerk)* joint, point, flush; *(onp.: schikken)* suit; **— bij,** add to; *on. w.* joint, point, do pointing-work; *w. w.* **zich — bij,** join.

voegijzer *o.* jointer, pointing-iron, pointing-trowel.

voelbaar *b. n.* perceptible, sensible; *(tastbaar)* palpable, tangible, tactile.

voelen *o. w.* feel; *(met duim)* thumb;

(v. belediging, enz.) be alive to; *on. w. het voelt hard,* it is hard to the touch; *w. w.* **zich —,** feel; feel oneself.

voelhoorn *m.* feeler, tenter, tentacle, antenna.

voeling *v.* feeling, touch.

voeren *o. w. (voederen)* feed, give a feed; *(brengen)* bring, lead, take; *(vervoeren)* convey; carry, transport; *(hanteren)* handle, wield.

voeren *o. w. (van binnen bekleden)* line.

voering *v.* lining.

voerman *m.* driver; *(vrachtrijder)* waggoner, carrier; *(koetsier)* coachman; *(sterr.)* Waggone.

voertaal *v.* medium (of instruction), vehicle, vehicular language.

voertuig *o.* vehicle, carriage, conveyance.

voet *m.* foot; *(fig.)* foot, footing.

voetbal *m.* football; **— spelen,** play (at) football.

voetballer *m.* football-player, footballer.

voetbank(je) *v. (o.)* foot-stool.

voetboog *m.* cross-bow.

voetganger *m.* foot-passenger, walker, pedestrian.

voetlicht *o.* footlights.

voetmat *v.* foot-mat.

voetpad *o.* foot-path, pathway.

voetschrapper *m.* door-scraper, foot-scraper, boot-scraper.

voetspoor *o.* foot-print, foot-mark, track.

voetstap *m.* step, footstep.

voetstuk *o.* pedestal, foot.

voetval *m.* prostration.

voetvolk *o.* foot-soldiers, infantry, foot.

voetwortel *m.* tarsus.

voetzoeker *m.* squib, (fire-)cracker, jumping cracker.

vogel *m.* bird; *(gevogelte)* fowl.

vogelhandelaar *m.* bird-fancier, bird-seller.

vogelknip *v.* bird-trap.

vogelkooi *v.* bird-cage.

vogellijm *v. (hars)* bird-lime; *(Pl.)* mistletoe.

vogelvanger *m.* bird-catcher, fowler.

vogelverschrikker *m.* scarecrow.

vogelvlucht *v.* bird's eye view.

vogelvrij *b. n.* outlawed.

vogelvrijverklaarde *m. en v.* outlaw.

vol *b. n.* full; filled.

volbloed *b. n.* thoroughbred, full-blood(ed); *(fig.)* out-and-out.

volbrengen *o. w.* fulfil, accomplish, execute, achieve, perform.

voldaan *b. n. (tevreden)* satisfied, content; *(betaald)* paid, settled; *(onder rekening)* received.

vóldoen *o. w.* fill (up).

voldóen *o. w. (tevreden stellen)* satisfy, give satisfaction to, content, please; *(betalen)* pay, settle; *(kwiteren)* receipt; *on. w. (voldoening schenken)* satisfy, give satisfaction.

voldoening v. satisfaction, content; (betaling) payment, settlement; (voor onrecht, enz.) reparation, atonement.

voldongen b. n. een — feit, an accomplished fact.

voleinden o. w. finish, complete, end, accomplish, bring to a close.

volgaarne bw. right willingly.

volgeling m. follower, adherent, votary, disciple.

volgen o. w. follow; (v. leidraad, spoor) follow up; (v. plan, enz.) pursue; on. w. follow, ensue.

volgend b. n. following, next; succeeding; subsequent.

volgens bw. according to; (in overeenstemming met) in accordance with.

volgkoets v. mourning-coach.

volgnummer o. serial number, reference number, consecutive number.

volgorde r. order (of succession), sequence.

volgwagen m. (v. tram) trailer, tow-car; zie **volgkoets.**   [amenable.

volgzaam bl n. docile, tractable,

volgzaamheid v. docility, tractability, amenableness.

volharden o. w. persevere, persist.

volharding r. perseverance, persistence, persistency, tenacity.

volhardingsvermogen o. perseverance, persistency.

volheid v. fulness.

volhouden o. w. maintain; (v. pogingen, rol, enz.) sustain; (v. strijd, enz.) keep up; on. w. persevere, persist, hold on, hold out.

volk o. (mensen) people; (natie) nation, people; (arbeiders) hands, work-people.

volkenbond m. League of Nations.

volkenkunde v. ethnology.

volkomen b. n. perfect; complete; bw. perfectly; completely.

volkrijk b. n. populous.

volksbelang o. public interest.

volksbuurt v. popular neighbourhood, low quarter.

volksdracht v. national costume, national dress.

volksfeest o. national feast; popular fête; public amusement.

volksgeloof o. popular belief.

volksgezondheid v. public health.

volksgunst v. public favour, popular favour, popularity.

volkslied o. national song, national air, national anthem; popular song, folksong.

volksmond m. in de —, in popular language, in the language of the people, in the mouths of the people.

volksoploop m. street-crowd.

volksoproer o. popular rising.

volkspartij v. people's party, party of the people, democratic faction (party).

volksplanting v. colony, settlement.

volksregering v. democracy, popular government, government by the people.

volksstam m. tribe, race.

volkstaal v. language of the people, popular language, vulgar tongue; national idiom, vernacular.

volkstelling v. census.

volksuitgave v. popular edition.

volksvertegenwoordiger m. representative (of the people).

volkswoede v. popular fury.

volledig b. n. complete, full; bw. completely, fully.

volledigheidshalve bw. for the sake of completeness.

volleerd b. n. finished, accomplished, consummate, proficient.

volmaakt b. n. (bw.) perfect(ly).

volmaaktheid v. perfection.

volmacht v. plenary power, full powers, power of attorney, general authority; (procuratie) procuration, proxy.

volmondig b. n. frank, unconditional, unqualified; bw. frankly, unconditionally, outright.

volop bw. plenty (of), in plenty, in abundance.

volslagen b. n. complete, absolute, full, total, utter, perfect; bw. completely, absolutely, &c.

volstaan on. w. suffice, be sufficient.

volstorten o. w. pay up (in full).

volstrekt b. n. (bw.) absolute(ly).

voltallig b. n. complete, full, plenary; — maken, complete, make a round number of, make up the number.

voltooien o. w. complete, finish; voltooid, (gram.) perfect.   [ment.

voltooiing r. completion, accomplish-

voltreffer m. (mil.) direct hit.

voltrekken o. w. (v. vonnis) execute; (v. huwelijk) consummate; (v. huwelijksplechtigheid) solemnize, perform.

voltrekking v. execution; consummation; solemnization.

voluit bw. in full, fully out.

volvet b. n. full-cream, whole-fat.

volwassen b. n. full-grown, grown-up, adult.

volwassene m. en v. adult, grown-up; —n, grown people.

volzin m. sentence, period.

vondeling m. en v. foundling.

vondst v. find, discovery.

vonk v. spark, sparkle.

vonken on. w. sparkle, spark, emit sparks.

vonnis o. sentence, judgment; (v. jury) verdict.

vonnissen o. w. sentence, condemn.

voogd (es) m. (v.) guardian.

voogdij v. guardianship.

voor v. furrow.

voor vz. (tijd: eerder dan) before; (geleden) ago; (gedurende, voor de duur van) for; (ten behoeve van, ten gunste van) for; (in plaats van) for, instead of; (plaats) in front of, before; (fig.: niet tegen) for, in favour of; bw. in front; vw. before; z. n., o. het — en tegen, the pro(s) and con(s), the merits and demerits.

vooraanstaand *b. n.* standing in front; *(fig.)* prominent, leading, foremost; of note and standing.
vooraf *bw.* beforehand, previously.
voorafgaan *o. w.* precede, go before.
voorafgaand *b. n.* preceding, foregoing; *(v. opmerkingen, enz.)* preliminary, introductory, prefatory, preambulatory.
vooral *bw.* especially, above all (things).
voorarm *m.* fore-arm.
voorarrest *o.* preliminary imprisonment, imprisonment before trial, detention on remand.
vooravond *m. (begin van de avond)* first part of the evening; *(de avond van te voren)* eve.
voorbaat *v.* **bij —,** in anticipation, beforehand, in advance.
voorbarig *b. n.* premature, hasty, overhasty, rash; *(fam.)* previous.
voorbedacht *b. n.* premeditated; **met —en rade,** with premeditation; of (with) malice prepense.
voorbedachtheid *v.* premeditation.
voorbedingen *o. w.* condition, stipulate (beforehand).
voorbeeld *o. (ter navolging)* example, model, pattern; *(ter illustratie)* example, instance, specimen; *(in schrijfboek,* copy-book heading; copy-slip; **bij —)** for example, for instance.
voorbeeldig *b. n.* exemplary.
voorbehoud *o.* reserve, reservation, restriction, proviso.
voorbehouden *o. w.* reserve.
voorbereiden *o. w.* prepare, make ready; *w. w.* **zich —,** prepare oneself.
voorbereiding *v.* preparation.
voorbereidsel *o.* preparative.
voorbericht *o.* preface, foreword.
voorbestemmen *o. w.* predestine, predestinate.
voorbij *vz.* beyond, past, on the other side of; *bw.* past; over, out.
voorbijgaan *o. w.* pass (by), go past; *on. w. (v. persoon)* go by, pass by, pass, move past; *(v. tijd, enz.)* pass, pass away, wear away, go by; *z. n., o.* **in 't —,** in passing; by the way, incidentally.
voorbijganger *m.* passer-by.
voorbijstreven *o. w.* outstrip, distance.
voorbode *m.* forerunner, precursor; *(dicht.)* harbinger.
voordat *vw.* before.
voordeel *o.* advantage, benefit; *(geldelijk: winst)* profit, gain.
voordelig *b. n.* profitable, advantageous, gainful; *bw.* profitably, advantageously, to advantage.
voordek *o. (sch.)* foredeck, forward deck.
voordeur *v.* front door, street-door.
voordoen *o. w.* do first; put before, put on; *w. w.* **zich —,** *(v. gelegenheid)* offer, present itself; *(v. moeilijkheid, enz.)* arise, emerge, crop up.
voordracht *v. (wijze v. voordragen)* diction, delivery, utterance; *(hetgeen*

men voordraagt) discourse, lecture, address, speech; *(v. gedicht)* recitation, recital; *(muz.)* execution, rendering, style of playing; *(kandidatenlijst)* select list, recommendation, nomination.
voordragen *o. w. (v. gedicht, enz.)* recite, say; *(v. muziekstuk)* execute, render; *(v. kandidaat)* propose, nominate; recommend; present.
voordrager *m.* reciter.
vooreerst *bw. (in de eerste plaats)* in the first place, for one thing, to begin with; *(voorlopig, in de eerste tijd)* for the present, for the time being, for some time to come.
voorgaan *on. w. (alg.)* go before; *(fig.: het voorbeeld geven)* set an example; *(de leiding nemen)* take the lead; *(de voorrang hebben)* take precedence, take the pas; *(v. horloge)* be fast, go too fast, gain; *o. w. (de weg wijzen)* lead the way; precede.
voorgaand *b. n.* preceding, last; *(v. term)* antecedent.
voorganger *m. (in ambt, enz.)* predecessor; *(dicht.)* foregoer; *(leider)* leader; *(prot.: predikant)* pastor, minister; *(sch.)* foreganger.
voorgeborchte *o.* **— der hel,** limbo, limbus patrum.
voorgenomen *b. n.* intended, proposed, purposed, contemplated.
voorgerecht *o.* entrée, first course.
voorgevel *m.* front, fore-front, facade.
voorgeven *o. w. (beweren)* pretend, profess; *(bij spel)* give odds, give points.
voorgevoel *o.* presentiment, anticipation; *(dicht.)* forefeeling.
voorgift *v.* odds; handicap.
voorgrond *m.* foreground, front; **op de — treden,** come (be) to the fore, come to the front, come into prominence.
voorhamer *m.* sledge-hammer.
voorhanden *b. n. (in voorraad)* on hand, in stock, in store; *(beschikbaar)* available; *(bestaande)* existing, extant; **niet meer —,** sold out, exhausted, out of stock.
voorhang *m.* curtain; *(Bijb.)* veil.
voorhaven *v.* outport.
voorheen *bw.* before, formerly, in former times.
voorhistorisch *b. n.* prehistoric.
voorhoede *v.* advance guard, vanguard, van; *(fig. ook:)* forefront.
voorhof *o.* fore-court; *(v. oor)* vestibule.
voorhoofd *o.* forehead; *(dicht.)* front.
voorhuis *o.* hall, vestibule, porch.
vooringenomen *b. n.* prepossessed, partial, prejudiced, biassed.
vooringenomenheid *v.* prepossession, prejudice, bias.
voorjaar *o.* spring.
voorkamer *v.* front room.
voorkant *m.* foreside, fore-part, front side, front, face.
voorkeur *v.* preference, choice; *(recht van —)* priority, preference, first claim;

bij —, for (by) preference, for (by) choice, preferably.

vóórkomen *on. w. (gebeuren)* happen, occur; *(lijken, toeschijnen)* seem to, appear to; *(recht: v. persoon)* appear in court, be brought up; *(v. zaak)* come on, come up; *(v. rijtuig)* come round; *(opendoen)* answer the door; *(bij wedstrijd)* get ahead, get the start, draw out in front; *z. n., o. (uiterlijk)* appearance, aspect, look(s); occurrence.

voorkómen *o. w. (beletten, verhinderen)* prevent, obviate, preclude, save; *(afwenden)* stave off, avert; *(vlugger zijn dan, vóór zijn)* anticipate, forestall.

vóórkomend *b. n.* occurring.

voorkómend *b. n.* obliging, complaisant, attentive.

voorkomendheid *v.* obligingness, complaisance.

voorlaatst *b. n.* last but one; penultimate.

voorleggen *o. w.* put (lay, place) before, submit, propound.

voorlezen *o. w.* read to; read out.

voorlichten *o. w.* light, light out, carry a light before; *(fig.)* enlighten, illuminate, instruct, advise.

voorliefde *v.* predilection, liking, partiality.

voorliegen *o. w.* lie to.

voorlopen *on. w. (vooraflopen)* lead the way, go (walk) in front; *(v. uurwerk)* gain, go too fast.

voorloper *m.* forerunner; precursor; *(tn.: blokschaaf)* jack-plane; *(schoolboekje)* primer.

voorlopig *b. n.* provisional, preliminary; *bw.* provisionally; for the present, for the time being.

voormalig *b. n.* former, late.

voorman *m. (v. werklieden)* foreman; *(mil.)* front-rank man; *(H.: bij wissel)* preceding endorsee; preceding holder; *(fig.)* leader, leading man.

voormeld *b. n.* above-mentioned, forementioned, forecited.

voormiddag *m.* morning, forenoon.

vóórnaam *m.* Christian name, first name.

voornáám *b. n.* distinguished, of distinction; prominent, eminent; *(deftig)* fashionable, of gentle birth; *(belangrijk)* important.

voornaamheid *v.* distinction, prominence.

voornaamwoord *o. (gram.)* pronoun.

voornamelijk *b. n.* principally, especially, chiefly, mainly.

voornemen *w. w. zich —,* determine, resolve, intend, purpose, make up one's mind; *z. n., o.* intention.

vooroordeel *o.* prejudice; bias; prejudgment.

voorop *bw.* on the fore part; in front.

vooropstellen *o. w.* premise, postulate.

voorouders *m. mv.* ancestors, forefathers; forbears.

vorooverhellen *on. w.* incline forward, lean over.

vooroverlijden *o.* predecease.

vooroverlópen *on. w.* stoop, walk with a stoop.

voorplecht *v. (sch.)* forecastle.

voorplein *o.* castle-yard, front-yard, fore-court.

voorpoot *m.* foreleg, forepaw.

voorpost *m. (mil.)* outpost.

voorproefje *o.* foretaste, taste.

voorraad *m. (v. levensmiddelen)* provision; *(v. goederen, enz.)* stock, store, supply.

voorraadkamer *v.* store-room, pantry.

voorrang *m.* precedence, priority.

voorrecht *o.* privilege; prerogative.

voorrede *v.* preface; *soms:* foreword.

voorschieten *o. w.* advance, lend.

voorschijn *bw.* **te — brengen,** produce, bring forth, bring out; **te — komen,** appear, make one's appearance, come out; emerge.

voorschip *o.* fore-part of the ship.

voorschoot *m.* apron; *(v. kind, voorspelder)* pinafore.

voorschot *o.* advance, advanced money, loan.

voorschrift *o. (opdracht)* instruction, direction; *(v. dokter, enz.)* prescription; *(voor gedrag)* precept; *(v. reglement, enz.)* regulation.

voorschrijven *o. w. (eig.)* write (for), set a writing-copy, show how to write; *(fig.)* prescribe.

voorslag *m.* first stroke; *(v. klok)* warning; *(voorstel)* proposal, proposition; *(muz.)* grace-note, grace.

voorsmaak *m.* foretaste, taste.

voorsnijmes *o.* carving-knife.

voorspel *o. (muz.)* prelude, overture; *(ton.)* introduction, introductory part, prologue; *(fig.)* prelude.

vóórspellen *o. w.* spell to.

voorspéllen *o. w.* presage, prognosticate, predict, foretell, prophesy; *(uit tekenen)* augure.

voorspelling *v.* prediction, presage, prognostication, prophecy.

voorspiegelen *o. w.* **iem. iets —,** hold out false hopes to a person.

voorspoed *m.* prosperity.

voorspoedig *b. n.* prosperous, successful.

voorspraak *v. (handeling)* intercession, mediation; *(persoon)* intercessor, mediator; advocate.

voorspreken *o. w.* speak in favour of.

voorsprong *m.* start; *(bij wedren, enz.)* law, start.

voorstaan *o. w. (verdedigen, bevorderen)* defend, advocate; champion, stand for; *on. w. (vooraanstaan)* stand in front; *(buiten staan wachten: v. rijtuig, auto)* be at the door; *(voor de verbeelding staan)* be present to one's mind.

voorstad *v.* suburb.

voorstander *m.* defender, advocate supporter, champion, partisan.

voorste *b. n.* foremost, first.

voorstel *o.* (*voorslag*) proposal; (*v. bestuur, ook:*) resolution; (*v. leden der vergadering*) motion; (*wets—*) bill; (*v. wagen*) forecarriage; (*som, vraagstuk*) problem.

voorstellen *o. w.* (*een voorstel doen*) propose, suggest, propound; (*ter kennismaking*) present, introduce; (*ton.*) represent; (*verbeelden*) represent, stand for; *w. w.* **zich —,** introduce oneself; (*zich verbeelden*) imagine, conceive, fancy, figure to oneself, picture to oneself; (*zich voornemen, van plan zijn*) purpose, propose, intend.

voorstelling *v.* (*v. personen*) introduction; presentation; (*begrip*) idea, conception, notion; (*wijze van voorstellen*) representation; (*in schouwburg, enz.*) performance.

voorsteven *m.* (*sch.*) prow, head; stem.

voorstuk *o.* front-piece; (*v. schoen*) front; (*ton.*) curtain raiser.

voortaan *bw.* in future, henceforward, henceforth.

voortbewegen *o. w.* move forward, propel; *w. w.* **zich —,** move (on), go on.

voortbrengen *o. w.* produce, bring forth, progenerate, procreate, create.

voortbrenger *m.* producer, generator, procreator.

voortbrengsel *o.* product, production; **—en,** produce.

voortduren *on. w.* continue, last.

voortdurend *b. n.* (*steeds herhaald*) continual; (*zonder onderbreking*) continuous, lasting, permanent; *bw.* continually; continuously.

voorteken *o.* presage, sign, omen, augury, indication; (*muz.*) accidental.

voortgaan *on. w.* go on, continue, proceed; (*vooruitgaan*) progress.

voortgang *m.* progress.

voortmaken *on. w.* make haste, hurry (up); *w. w.* **zich —,** get away, run off.

voortplanten *o. w.* (*v. planten, dieren, ziekte, licht, geluid, enz.*) propagate; (*v. licht, geluid, ziekte*) transmit; *w. w.* **zich —,** propagate, breed; multiply; (*Pl., Nk.*) propagate itself; (*v. licht, geluid, enz.*) travel, be transmitted.

voortplanting *v.* propagation, multiplication; transmission.

voortreffelijk *b. n.* excellent, firstrate; *bw.* excellently.

voortrekken *o. w.* **iem. —,** favour a person.

voortrukken *o. w.* pull forward, pull along; *on. w.* march on, press on, push forward.

voorts *bw.* further, besides, moreover; **en zo —,** and so on, etcetera.

voortsnellen *on. w.* rush on, hurry on, hasten along.

voortspruiten *on. w.* **— uit,** result from, proceed from, arise from.

voortstuwen *o. w.* press forward, push along, propel.

voortstuwing *v.* propulsion.

voortvarend *b. n.* energetic, pushful.

voortvluchtig *b. n.* fugitive; **de —e,** the fugitive, the runaway.

voortzetten *o. w.* continue, proceed on, pursue.

voortzetting *v.* continuation.

vooruit *bw.* forward; (*van te voren*) before, beforehand, in advance.

vooruitbetalen *o. w.* prepay, pay in advance.

vooruitbetaling *v.* prepayment, payment in advance, payment by anticipation.

vooruitgang *m.* progress, improvement; (*v. prijzen*) advance.

vooruitkomen *on. w.* (*eig. en fig.*) advance, get on, make headway.

vooruitspringen *on. w.* jump forward; (*v. muur, enz.*) project, jut out.

vooruitstrevend *b. n.* progressive.

vooruitzicht *o.* prospect, outlook.

vooruitzien *o. w.* foresee; *on. w.* look ahead.

vooruitziend *b. n.* far-seeing, forwardlooking, provident.

voorval *o.* event, incident, occurrence.

voorvoegsel *o.* prefix.

voorwaar *bw.* indeed, truly, in truth; (*Bijb.*) verily.

voorwaarde *v.* condition, stipulation; **—n, ook:** terms.

voorwaardelijk *b. n.* conditional; *bw.* conditionally.

voorwaarts *bw.* forward(s), onward(s); *b. n.* forward, onward.

voorwenden *o. w.* pretend, affect, feign, simulate, sham.

voorwendsel *o.* pretext, pretence, blind.

voorwerp *o.* object, article; (*gram.*) object.

voorweten *o.* (fore)knowledge, prescience.

voorwiel *o.* front-wheel, forewheel.

voorzaat *m.* ancestor, forefather, progenitor.

voorzanger *m.* precentor, chanter.

vóórzeggen *o. w.* prompt, ditacte.

voorzéggen *o. w.* predict, presage, prophesy.

voorzeker *bw.* certainly, to be sure, surely, no doubt.

voorzetsel *o.* preposition.

voorzetten *o. w.* place in front; (*v. klok*) put forward, put ahead.

voorzichtig *b. n.* prudent, careful, cautious.

voorzichtigheid *v.* prudence, care, caution.

voorzichtigheidshalve *bw.* by way of precaution.

voorzien *o. w.* (*vooruitzien*) foresee; **— van,** provide with, furnish with, supply with; *on. w.* **— in,** supply, meet, fill, cover.

voorzienigheid *v.* providence.

voorzijde *v.* (*v. huis, enz.*) front, foreside; (*v. medaille*) obverse face, obverse; (*v. wissel*) face.

voorzitten *on. w.* preside, be in the chair.

voorzitter *m.* president, chairman; (*v. stembureau*) presiding officer.

voorzorg *v.* precaution, provision, care, providence.

voorzorgsmaatregel *m.* precautionary measure, precaution.

voorzover *bw.* in so far as.

voos *b. n.* spongy, woolly; (*fig.*) rotten, unsound.

vorderen *on. w.* advance, progress, make progress, make headway; *o. w.* demand, claim, exact; (*vereisen*) require, demand.

vordering *v.* (*voortgang*) advance progress, improvement; (*eis*) demand, claim.

voren *m.* roach, rudd.

voren *bw.* **als —,** as heretofore; *van te* **—,** beforehand.

vorig *b. n.* former, previous, preceding, last.

vork *v.* fork.

vorm *m.* form; (*tn.: gietvorm*) mould, matrix; (*drukk.*) forme; (*gedaante*) shape, form; (*gram.*) form; voice; (*plichtpleging, formaliteit*) form, formality, ceremony.

vormelijk *b. n.* formal, conventional, ceremonious.

vormeling *m.* (*kath.*) confirmee.

vormen *o. w.* (*een vorm geven*) form fashion, frame, shape, model, mould; (*v. regering, commissie, enz.*) form, constitute, create; (*v. fonds*) start, set up, build up; (*uitmaken*) constitute; (*kath.*) confirm.

vorming *v.* forming, formation, shaping, moulding; (*fig.*) education, cultivation.

vormsel *o.* (*kath.*) confirmation.

vors *m.* frog.

vorsen *on. w.* inquire, search, investigate.

vorst *v.* (*v. dak: nok*) ridge; (*het vriezen*) frost; *m.* monarch, sovereign, prince.

vorstendom *o.* principality.

vorstenhuis *o.* dynasty.

vorstin *v.* monarch, queen, empress, sovereign, princess.

vos *m.* fox; (*paard*) sorrel (horse), bay (horse); (*vlinder*) tortoise-shell (butterfly); (*bont*) fox stole.

vouw *v.* (*alg.*) fold; (*in kleed, enz.*) crease, plait, pleat, ply.

vouwbeen *o.* folder, paper-knife; (*drukk.*) stroker.

vouwen *o. w.* fold.

vouwstoel *m.* folding-chair, camp-stool.

vraag *v.* question; query; (*om iets*) request; (*H.: tegenover aanbod*) demand; (*recht*) interrogatory.

vraaggesprek *o.* interview.

vraagstuk *o.* question, problem.

vraagteken *o.* note (point) of interrogation, interrogation-mark.

vraatzuchtig *b. n.* voracious, ravenous, gluttonous.

vracht *v.* freight; (*sch.*) cargo; (*v. wagon*) load; (*vrachtprijs*) (*te water*) freight, freight charges; (*te land*) carriage; (*voor personen*) fare.

vrachtauto *v.* motor-truck, motorlorry.

vrachtboot *v.* cargo-boat, cargo-steamer, freighter, freight-steamer.

vrachtbrief *m.* (*per spoor*) consignment note; (*per schip*) bill of lading.

vrachtgoed *o.* goods; (*per schip*) cargo.

vrachtrijder *m.* carrier.

vrachtvrij *b. n.* (*per spoor*) carriage paid; (*per schip*) freight paid; (*per post*) post-paid.

vragen *o. w.* ask; (*in rekening brengen*) charge; *on. w.* ask; (*kaartsp.*) call, declare; **— naar iem.,** ask after a person, inquire for a person.

vragenlijst *v.* questionnaire.

vrede *m.* peace.

vredegerecht *o.* (*Z. N.*) district-court.

vredelievend *b. n.* peace-loving, peaceful, peaceable, pacific; *bw.* peacefully, peaceably, pacifically.

vrederechter *m.* justice of the peace.

vredescongres *o.* peace congress.

vredesverdrag *o.* treaty of peace, peace-treaty.

vredig *b. n.* (*bw.*) peaceful(ly), quiet(ly).

vreedzaam *b. n.* peaceable; *bw.* peaceably in peace.

vreemd *b. n.* (*niet bekend; aan anderen toebehorende*) strange; (*buitenlands*) foreign; extraneous; (*uitheems: v. planten, bomen, enz.*) exotic; (*raar*) singular, queer, odd, funny, strange; *bw.* strangely.

vreemde *m. en v.* (*onbekende*) stranger; (*buitenlander*) foreigner.

vreemdeling *m. en v.* (*onbekende*) stranger; (*buitenlander*) foreigner; alien.

vreemdelingenverkeer *o.* tourist traffic, tourism.

vreemdenlegioen *o.* foreign legion.

vrees *v.* fear; (*sterk*) dread.

vreesachtig *b. n.* timid, timorous, fearful.

vrek *m.* miser, niggard, pincher, skinflint.

vrekkigheid *v.* miserliness, stinginess, avarice.

vreselijk *b. n.* dreadful, frightful, fearful, terrible, horrible; *bw.* dreadfully, &c.

vreten *o. w.* (*v. dier*) eat, feed on; *on. w.* (*v. dier*) feed; (*v. mens*) feed, guttle, gorge, stuff.

vreugde *v.* joy, gladness.

vreugdedag *m.* day of rejoicing.

vreugdekreet *m.* shout of joy, whoop of delight.

vrezen *o. w.* fear, be afraid of; (*sterker*) dread; *on. w.* be in fear.

vriend *m.* friend.

vriendelijk *b. n.* friendly, affable

kind; *bw.* affably, kindly, in a friendly way.

vriendelijkheid *r.* friendliness, affability, kindness.

vriendenkring *m.* circle of friends.

vriendin *r.* (lady, woman) friend.

vriendschap *v.* friendship, amity.

vriendschapsbetuiging *v.* profession of friendship.

vriespunt *o.* freezing-point.

vriezen *on. w.* freeze.

vrij *b. n.* free; (*in vrijheid*) free, at liberty; (*onbezet, niet besproken*) disengaged, not engaged, not bespoken; (*met vrije tijd, geen werk hebbend*) free, at liberty, at leisure, disengaged; (*onbelemmerd; v. uitzicht, enz.*) free, unobstructed; (*ongedwongen*) free, unconstrained, easy; (*zonder hypotheek*) free; *bw.* (*vrijelijk*) freely; (*tamelijk*) rather, pretty, fairly; (*gratis*) free (of charge).

vrijaf *o.* holiday, half-holiday, day off, off-day.

vrijbiljet *o.* free ticket; (*r. schouwburg, trein, enz.*) free pass.

vrijblijven *on. w.* remain free; —*d,* (*H.*) without engagement.

vrijdag *m.* Friday.

vrijdenker *m.* free-thinker.

vrijdom *m.* franchise, freedom, immunity, exemption.

vrijen *on. w.* court; make love, sweetheart, cuddle, bill and coo; *o. w.* court, woo.

vrijgeleide *o.* safe-conduct.

vrijgevig *b. n.* liberal, open-handed, free-handed, generous.

vrijgevigheid *v.* liberality, open-handedness, free-handedness, generosity.

vrijgezel *m.* (old) bachelor.

vrijhandel *m.* free trade.

vrijhaven *v.* free port, free harbour.

vrijheid *v.* liberty, freedom.

vrijheidsoorlog *m.* war of independence.

vrijkorps *o.* volunteer corps.

vrijlating *v.* release; liberation, emancipation, manumission.

vrijmaken *o. w.* (*v. persoon*) free, set at liberty, emancipate; (*v. slaven*) liberate, emancipate, manumit; *w. w. zich* —, disengage oneself, free oneself.

vrijmetselaar *m.* freemason.

vrijmoedig *b. n.* (*bw.*) free(ly),frank(ly), outspoken(ly), bold(ly).

vrijmoedigheid *v.* freeness, frankness, boldness.

vrijpleiten *o. w.* exculpate, exonerate; plead free; *w. w. zich* —, exculpate oneself.

vrijpostig *b. n.* free, forward, sancy.

vrijspraak *v.* acquittal.

vrijspreken *o. w.* (*recht*) acquit.

vrijstellen *o. w.* exempt.

vrijstelling *v.* exemption, freedom; certificate of exemption.

vrijster *v.* sweetheart, young woman;

(*ongehuwde vrouw*) maid, spinster.

vrijwaren *o. w.* — *voor (tegen),* safeguard against, guarantee from, protect (guard, secure) from (against).

vrijwel *b. n.* pretty good; *bw.* rather well, rather, fairly.

vrijwillig *b. n.* voluntary, free; *bw.* voluntarily, freely, of one's own free will.

vrijwilliger *m.* volunteer.

vrijzinnig *b. n.* liberal; (*in godsdienstzaken, ook:*) latitudinarian, modernist.

vroed *b. n.* wise, prudent, cautious; *de* —*e vaderen,* the City Fathers, the elder fathers.

vroedschap *v.* town-council.

vroedvrouw *v.* midwife, accoucheuse.

vroeg *b. n.* early *bw.* early at an early hour; betimes — *of laat,* sooner or later.

vroeger *b. n.* earlier; (*vorig, enz.*) former, previous; late; *bw.* earlier, sooner; (*in vroeger tijd*) formerly, in former times (days), before now; on former occasions.

vroegmis *v.* early mass.

vroegrijp *b. n.* early-ripe, precocious, premature.

vrolijk *b. n.* merry, gay, cheerful; *bw.* merrily, gaily, cheerfully.

vrolijkheid *v.* mirth, gaiety, cheerfulness; merriment.

vroom *b. n.* pious, devout.

vroomheid *v.* piety, devoutness, devotion.

vrouw *v.* (*alg.*) woman; (*echtgenote*) wife; (*dicht.*) spouse; (*kaartsp.*) queen.

vrouwelijk *b. n.* (*v. geslacht, plant, dier, enz.*) female; (*een vrouw passend*) womanly; (*van een vrouw*) feminine; (*gram.*) feminine.

vrouwenarts *m.* gynaecologist.

vrouwenbeweging *v.* women's rights movement, feminist movement.

vrouwengek *m.* dangler after women, philanderer.

vrouwenhaar *o.* woman's hair; (*Pl.*) maidenhair.

vrouwenhater *m.* woman-hater, misogynist.

vrouwenlist *v.* female (woman's) cunning; woman's craft, woman's stratagem.

vrucht *v.* fruit; — *dragen,* bear fruit, fructify.

vruchtafdrijving *v.* abortion.

vruchtbaar *b. n.* fruitful, fertile, fecund, prolific; — *maken,* fertilize, fecundate.

vruchtbaarheid *v.* fruitfulness, fertility, fecundity.

vruchtbeginsel *o.* ovary.

vruchteloos *b. n.* fruitless, ineffectual, vain; futile; *bw.* fruitlessly, ineffectually, vainly, in vain.

vruchtgebruik *o.* usufruct.

vruchtkiem *v.* germ, embryo.

vuig *b. n.* vile, base, sordid, mean.

vuil *b. n.* dirty, filthy, grimy, grubby,

smudged, squalid; (*fig.*) dirty, filthy, nasty, smutty, obscene; z. *n., o.* dirt, ordure.
vuilbek *m.* talker of smut, foul-mouthed fellow.
vuilnisbak *m.* dust-bin, refuse-bin; (*op straat*) orderly-bin.
vuilnisbelt *v.* refuse dump, rubbish-dump.
vuilnisblik *o.* dustpan.
vuilniskar *v.* dust-cart, refuse-cart.
vuist *v.* fist; *voor de* —, off-hand, extempore.
vuistgevecht *o.* fist-fight; pugilistic fight, boxing-match.
vuistslag *m.* blow with the fist.
vulkaan *m.* volcano.
vulkachel *v.* slow-combustion stove, base-burner.
vullen *o. w.* (*v. gias, enz.*) fill; (*v. dieren, gans, enz.*) stuff; (*v. kies*) stop, plug, fill; (*v. ballon, luchtschip*) inflate; (*el.: v. accu*) fill, charge; (*v. sofa*) wad; (*r. tijd*) fill (up).
vulling *v.* (*alg.*) filling; (*v. dieren, enz.*) stuffing; (*v. kies*) stopping, plug, filling; (*v. ballon*) inflation; (*v. sofa*) wadding.
vulpenhouder *m.* fountain-pen.
vulsel *o.* (*v. dieren, gans, enz.*) stuffing; (*vlees*—) force-meat; (*v. pasteitje*) mince-meat; (*v. kies*) stopping; (*v. sofa*) wad.
vuns *b. n.* musty, fusty, frowzy.
vunsheid *v.* mustiness, fustiness, frowziness.
vurehout *o.* deal-wood, deal.

vuren *on. w.* fire (**op,** at, on), shoot; (*v. zee*) phosphoresce; z. *n., o.* firing.
vuren *b. n.* deal.
vurig *b. n.* fiery; (*v. ijver, verlangen, liefde, enz.*) ardent; (*v. paard*) spirited, high-mettled, fiery; (*v. gebed, haat*) dervent; (*v. wens* fervid; (*v. hoop, bewonderaar*) devout; (*v. huid*) red, inflamed; *bw.* fierily; ardently; fervently; fervidly; devoutly.
vurigheid *v.* fieriness; ardency, ardour; spirit, mettle; fervency; (*v. huid*) redness, inflammation; (*in koren*) blight.
vuur *o.* (*alg.*) fire; (*fig.*) ardour, fire; (*ontsteking*) gangrene; (*in hout*) dry rot; (*in koren*) blight.
vuurdoop *m.* (*mil.*) baptism of fire, fire-baptism.
vuurhaard *m.* hearth, fire-place.
vuurkogel *m.* (*mil.*) fire-ball.
vuurpijl *m.* rocket; (*Pl.*) flame-flower.
vuurpoel *m.* sea of fire.
vuurrood *o.* red as fire, fiery red.
vuurslag *o.* strike-a-light, (flint and) steel.
vuurspuwend *b. n.* fire-splitting, emitting (spitting) fire.
vuursteen *m.* flint, fire-stone.
vuurtoren *m.* lighthouse, light-tower-pharos.
vuurvast *b. n.* fire-proof, fire-resisting, incombustible.
vuurwapen *o.* fire-arm.
vuurwerk *o.* fireworks; pyrotechnic display.

W

waadbaar *b. n.* fordable.
waag *v.* (*toestel*) balance; (*plaats*) weigh-house.
waaghals *m.* venturer, risker, dare-devil, venturesome fellow.
waagschaal *v.* scale; (*fig.*) balance.
waagstuk *o.* risky thing, risky enterprise, hazardous undertaking.
waaien *on. w.* (*v. wind*) blow; (*v. vlag, enz.*) flutter (fly, float) in the wind.
waaier *m.* fan. [farm-dog.
waakhond *m.* watchdog, house-dog.
waakzaam *b. n.* vigilant, wakeful, watchful.
waakzaamheid *v.* vigilance, wakefulness, watchfulness.
Waal *v.* (*rivier*) Waal.
Waal *m.* Walloon.
waan *m.* erroneous opinion, (idea, conjecture), delusion, fancy.
waangeloof *o.* superstition.
waanvoorstelling *v.* delusion, hallucination.
waanwijs *b. n.* (self-)conceited, opinionated, presumptuous.
waanzin *m.* insanity, madness; dementia; (*razernij*) frenzy.

waar *v.* wares, goods, commodity, merchandise, stuff.
waar *b. n.* true; (*wezenlijk*) veritable.
waar *bw.* where; — *naartoe ?* where ? — *vandaan,* from where, whence; *vw.* where; (*aangezien*) since, as.
waarachtig *b. n.* true, real, veritable; *bw.* truly, really; —*!* surely, certainly!
waarborg *m.* guarantee, guaranty, warrant, security.
waarborgen *o. w.* guarantee, warrant.
waarborgsom *v.* caution money, security.
waard *m.* host, landlord; innkeeper; (*Dk.*) drake.
waard *v.* (*uiterwaard*) foreland, fore-shore; (*ingedijkt land*) polder.
waard *b. n.* worth; —*e vriend,* dear friend.
waarde *v.* value, worth.
waardeloos *b. n.* worthless.
waarderen *o. w.* (*waarde bepalen*) value, estimate; (*door taxateur*) appraise; (*op prijs stellen*) appreciate, value, esteem.
waardering *v.* valuation, estimation; appraisal; appreciation.

waardevermeerdering *v.* increase in value.

waardevermindering *v.* fall in value, depreciation; devaluation.

waardevol *b. n.* valuable, of value.

waardig *b. n.* worthy; (*deftig*) dignified.

waardigheid *v.* (*verdienste*) worthiness; (*uiterlijk*) dignity; dignified manners; (*ambt*) dignity.

waardigheidsbekleder *m.* dignitary.

waardin *v.* hostess, landlady.

waardoor *vnw. bw.* (*vragend*) through what? by what? (*betr.*) through which, by which.

waarheen *vnw. bw.* where, where to, to what place.

waarheid *v.* truth.

waarheidlievend, waarheidminnend *b. n.* truthful, truthloving; veracious.

waarlijk *bw.* truly, in truth, really, indeed.

waarmerk *o.* stamp; (*op goud, enz.*) hall-mark.

waarmerken *o. w.* stamp, attest, certify, authenticate; (*v. goud, enz.*) hall-mark; (*v. doorhaling, enz.*) confirm.

waarnemen *o. w.* (*zien, bemerken*) observe; perceive; (*v. plicht, enz.: in acht nemen*) perform, attend to; (*gebruik maken, partij trekken*) avail oneself of, make use of; (*v. zaken, belangen: behartigen*) look after.

waarnemend *b. n.* acting, temporary.

waarneming *v.* observation; perception; deputizing, substitution.

waarnemingspost *m.* observation post.

waarom *vw.* why; (*dicht.*) where-fore.

waarop *vnw. bw.* (*vragend*) on what? for what? (*betr.*) upon which, after which, whereupon.

waarschijnlijk *b. n.* probable, likely; *bw.* probably.

waarschuwen *o. w.* warn, admonish, caution.

waarschuwing *v.* warning, caution, admonition; (*v. belasting*) demand-note, default notice.

waaruit *vnw. bw.* (*vragend*) from what? (*betr.*) from which; (*dicht.*) whence.

waarvan *vnw. bw.* (*vragend*) of what? (*betr.*) of which, of whom? (*dicht.*) where-of.

waarzegger *m.* fortune-teller, soothsayer; (*uit de hand*) palmist.

waas *o.* (*over veld*) haze; (*op vruchten*) bloom; (*fig.: zweem, schijn*) air.

wacht *m.* (*schildwacht*) sentry; (*waker*) watchman; *v.* (*mil.*) guard; (*sch.*) watch; (*toneel*) cue.

wachten *on. w.* wait; *o. w.* wait for, await; (*verwachten*) expect; *w. w. zich — voor,* be on one's guard against.

wachter *m.* watchman, watchkeeper; (*sterr.: bijplaneet, satelliet*) satellite.

wachtkamer *v.* (*in station, enz.*) waiting-room; (*mil.*) guard-room.

wachtmeester *m.* sergeant major.

wachttoren *m.* watch-tower.

wachtwoord *o.* (*alg.*) password; (*mil.*) password, countersign; (*r. officier ook:*) parole; (*fig.*) catchword.

wad *o.* mud-flat, tidal marsh.

waden *on. w.* wade, ford.

wafel *v.* wafer, waffle, wafer-cake.

wagen *o. w.* venture, hazard, risk; *w. w. zich — aan,* venture on (upon).

wagen *m.* (*voertuig*) vehicle; (*rijtuig*) carriage, coach; (*auto, tram—*) car; (*vracht*) wag(g)on.

wagenas *v.* axle-tree.

wagenmaker *m.* coach-builder; wagon-builder, cart-wright. [park.

wagenpark *o.* (*mil.*) wagon-park, field-

wagensmeer *o.* axle-grease, wheel-grease, cart-grease.

wagenspoor *o.* (wheel-)rut, track.

waggelen *on. w.* stagger, totter, reel; (*v. kind*) toddle; (*v. eend, enz.*) waddle; (*v. tafel*) wobble.

waken *on. w.* wake, watch.

wakker *b. n.* (*niet slapend*) awake; (*waakzaam*) vigilant, watchful, on the alert; (*flink, levendig*) spry; smart; brisk.

wal *m.* (*sch.: oever*) bank, shore, coast; (*kade*) quay, embankment; (*v. vesting*) rampart; (*onder de ogen*) bag.

walg *m.* loathing, disgust, aversion, abomination.

walgen *on. w.* loathe, nauseate.

walging *v.* loathing, nausea, disgust.

walm *m.* smoke.

walmen *on. w.* smoke.

walrus *m.* walrus, sea-horse, sea-cow.

wals *v.* (*dans*) waltz; (*tn.*) roller, cylinder.

walsen *on. w.* (*dansen*) waltz; *o. w.* (*v. weg, enz.*) roll.

walstro *o.* (*Pl.*) bedstraw.

walvis *m.* whale.

walvisachtig *b. n.* whalelike; (*wet.*) cetaceous.

wambuis *o.* jacket.

wan *z. n., v.* (*werktuig*) winnow, van; (*H.*) ullage; *b. n.* slack.

wanbedrijf *o.* misdemeanour, crime.

wanbegrip *o.* false notion.

wand *m.* wall.

wandalmanak *m.* wall-calendar, block-calendar, sheet-almanac.

wandelaar(ster) *m.* (*v.*) walker, lounger, pedestrian.

wandelen *on. w.* walk, take a walk.

wandelgang *v.* lobby.

wandelhoofd *o.* promenade pier.

wandeling *v.* walk, stroll.

wandelstok *m.* walking-stick.

wandeltocht *m.* walking-tour.

wandgedierte *o.* bugs.

wandversiering *v.* wall-decoration, mural ornament.

wanen *o. w.* fancy, imagine, think.

wang *v.* cheek.

wangedrag *o.* bad conduct, misconduct, misbehaviour.

wangedrocht *o.* monster, monstrosity.
wangeluid *o.* dissonance, cacophony.
wanhoop *v.* despair.
wanhoopskreet *m.* cry of despair (desperation).
wanhopen *on. w.* despair.
wanhopig *b. n. (bw.)* despairing(ly), desperating(ly).
wankel *b. n. (v. meubel, enz.)* unstable, unsteady; *(v. trap, enz.)* rickety, shaky; *(v. pas)* faltering; *(v. gezondheid)* delicate.
wankelen *on. w.* totter, stagger; *(fig.: aarzelen)* waver, vacillate.
wankelmoedig *b. n.* wavering, wavery, vacillating.
wanmolen *m.* winnowing-mill.
wanneer *bw.* when; *vw. (v. tijd)* when; *(v. voorw.: indien)* if.
wanorde *v.* disorder.
wanschapen *b. n.* misshapen, deformed, malformed, monstrous.
wansmaak *m.* bad taste.
want *v.* mitten, fingerless glove.
want *o. (sch.)* rigging, shrouds; *(netten)* fishing-) nets.
want *vw.* for.
wantoestand *m.* abuse.
wantrouwen *o. w.* distrust; suspect; *z. n., o.* distrust; *(achterdocht)* suspicion.
wapen *o.* weapon, arm; *(afdeling v. leger)* arm (of service); *(wap.)* (coat of) arms; **te —!** to arms!
wapenbroeder *m.* brother in arms, companion (comrade) in arms.
wapenen *o. w.* arm; *(v. beton)* armour, reinforce; *w. w.* **zich —,** arm oneself, arm.
wapenmagazijn *o.* arsenal.
wapenrusting *v.* armour.
wapenschild *o.* escutcheon, armorial bearings.
wapenschouwing *v.* review.
wapensmid *m.* armourer.
wapenstilstand *m.* armistice, suspension of hostilities.
wapperen *on. w.* wave, stream, flutter, fly (out), float **(boven,** over).
war *v.* **in de — brengen (maken),** *(v. persoon)* confound, confuse, put out; *(v. plannen, kamer)* derange, disarrange; *(v. haar)* rumple, tangle, untidy; *(v. bed, kleren)* tumble.
warboel *m.* muddle, mess, confusion, tangle, huddle, hugger-mugger.
warenhuis *o.* department store(s); *(broeikas)* greenhouse.
wargeest *m.* muddle-head, scatter-brain, mar-all; *(rustverstoorder)* agitator.
warm *b. n.* warm, hot; *(v. bron)* thermal, hot; *bw.* warmly, hotly.
warmen *o. w.* warm, heat, make hot; **zich —,** warm oneself.
warmoes *o.* pot-herbs, vegetables, greens.
warmoez(en)ier *m.* kitchen-gardener.
warmte *v.* warmth; *(nat.)* heat; *(fig.)* ardour, warmth.

warmtebron *v.* source of heat.
warmte-eenheid *v.* thermal unit, calorie.
warmtegolf *v.* heat-wave.
warmtevoortbrenging *v.* thermogenesis.
warmwaterkruik *v.* hot-water bottle.
warnet *o.* tangle, maze, labyrinth.
warrelen *on. w.* whirl, swirl.
warrelwind *m.* whirlwind.
wars *b. n.* **— van,** averse to (from).
wartaal *v.* incoherent talk, jargon, gibberish.
was *m. (groei)* growth; *(v. rivier)* rise; *o.* wax.
was *v.* wash, laundry, washing.
wasdoek *o.* oil-cloth.
wasdom *m.* growth.
wasecht *b. n.* washable, fast-dyed, washing.
wasemen *on. w.* steam.
wasgoed *o.* wash, washing, things for the wash.
wasinrichting *v.* laundry.
waskaars *v.* wax-candle, taper.
waskuip *v.* wash(ing)-tub.
wasmand *v.* laundry-basket.
wassen *o. w. en on. w.* wash; *(v. borden, schotels: afwassen)* wash up; *(v. kaarten: doorschudden)* make, shuffle; *(v. stenen v. dominospel)* mix; *(v. melk)* water; *w. w.* **zich —,** wash oneself.
wassen *on. w. (groeien, opschieten)* grow; *(v. rivier)* rise.
wassen *o. w.* wax; *b. n.* waxen, wax.
wasserij *v.* laundry.
wastafel *v.* wash-stand, wash-hand stand.
wasvrouw *v.* washerwoman, laundress.
wat *vr. vnw.* what; **— is er?** what is the matter? what is it? *betr. vnw.* what; which; that; *onb. vnw. (zelfst)* something; *(bijvoegl.)* some, any; *bw. (een weinig)* a little; *(zeer veel, heel erg)* very, quite.
water *o. (vloeistof)* water; *(waterzucht)* dropsy.
waterachtig *b. n.* watery, waterish.
waterafvoer *m.* water-drainage, draining.
waterbel *v.* bubble.
waterblaas *v.* urinary bladder; *(blaar)* blister; *(bel)* (water-)bubble.
waterbloem *v. (Pl.)* water-flower, aquatic flower.
waterbouwkunde *v.* hydraulics, hydraulic engineering.
waterbreuk *v.* hydrocele.
waterdamp *m.* (water-)vapour, steam.
waterdicht *b. n.* impermeable (imperveous) to water; *(v. kleren, materiaal, enz.)* water-proof; *(v. schoenen, kelder, enz.)* watertight; *(v. huis)* weatherproof.
wateren *o. w.* water; *on. w.* make water, urinate; *(v. ogen)* run.
waterhoen *o.* water-hen.
waterhoofd *o.* hydrocephalus.
waterhoos *v.* waterspout.

waterhoudend *b. n.* aquiferous, hydrous, water-bearing.

waterjuffer *v.* dragon-fly, damsel-fly.

waterkering *v.* dam, weir.

waterkuur *v.* water-cure, hydropathic cure.

waterlaarzen *v. mv.* wading-boots, waders.

waterleiding *v.* waterworks; (*bovengronds*) aqueduct.

waterloop *m.* watercourse.

watermerk *o.* watermark.

watermolen *m.* water-mill; (*in polder*) drainage mill.

waternimf *v.* water-nimph, naiad.

waterpas *b. n.* level; **niet —,** out of level; *z. n., o.* water-level, levelling-instrument.

waterpeil *o.* watermark; (*toestel*) water-gauge.

waterpers *v.* hydraulic press.

waterplaats *v.* urinal; (*voor schepen* watering-place.

waterplant *v.* aquatic plant, water-plant.

waterplas *m.* puddle, plash.

waterproef *b. n.* zie **waterdicht;** *z. n., v.* (*godsgerecht*) water-ordeal.

waterput *m.* (draw-)well.

waterrat *v.* (*Dk.*) water-vole, water-rat; (*fig.*) water-dog.

waterscheiding *v.* watershed, water-parting, divide.

waterschuw *b. n.* hydrophobic, hydrophobous, afraid of water.

watersnip *v.* snipe.

watersnood *m.* inundation, flood.

waterspiegel *m.* water-level, water-line, surface of the water.

waterstand *m.* height of the water, water-level.

waterstof *v.* hydrogen.

waterval *m.* water-fall, fall(s); (*klein*) cascade.

watervliegtuig *o.* hydroplane, sea-plane, water-plane.

watervloed *m.* great flood, inundation.

watervogel *m.* water-bird, aquatic bird.

watervrees *v.* hydrophobia.

waterwild *o.* water-fowl, aquatic game.

waterzonnetje *o.* watery sun.

watten *z. n., v. mv.* wadding; (*gen.*) cotton-wool; *b. n.* wadded, quilted.

web *o.* web.

wed *o.* (*drenkplaats*) horse-pond, watering-place; (*waadbare plaats*) ford.

wedde *v.* salary, pay.

wedden *on. w.* bet, wager, lay a wager.

weddenschap *v.* bet, wager.

weder *z. n., o.* weather; *bw.* zie **weer.**

wederdienst *m.* service in return, reciprocal service.

wedergeboorte *v.* re-birth, regeneration, new birth.

wederhelft *m. en v.* better half; spouse; consort, wife.

wederinstorting *v.* relapse.

wederkerend *b. n.* (*gram.*) reflexive.

wederkerig *b. n.* mutual, reciprocal.

wederleggen *o. w.* refute, confute; disprove.

wederliefde *v.* returned love, return of love, love in return.

wederom *bw.* again, anew, once again.

wederopbouw *m.* rebuilding, reconstruction.

wederrechtelijk *b. n.* (*bw.*) illegal(ly), unlawful(ly).

wedervaren *o. w.* befall, happen to; **recht laten —,** do justice to; *z. n. o.,* adventure(s), experience(s).

wedervergelding *v.* retaliation; requital, recompense, reward.

wederwaardigheid *v.* vicissitude.

wederzijds *b. n.* mutual, reciprocal.

wedijver *m.* emulation, competition, rivalry.

wedijveren *on. w.* vie, compete.

wedloop *m.* running-match, foot-race; (*fig.*) race.

wedstrijd *m.* match, competition, contest.

weduwe *v.* widow.

weduwnaar *m.* widower.

wee *z. n., o.* woe, pain, grief; *tw.* **— hem!** woe is him!; *b. n.* (*v. smaak*) sickly; (*flauw*) faint, qualmish.

weefgetouw *o.* (weaving-)loom.

weefgoederen *o. mv.* textiles, hosiery.

weefsel *o.* tissue, texture, fabric; weave.

weefspoel *v.* shuttle.

weegbaar *b. n.* weighable, ponderable.

weegbree *v.* (*Pl.*) plantain, way-bread.

weegbrug *v.* weigh-bridge.

weegschaal *v.* pair of scales, balance; (*sterr.*) Libra, the Scales.

week *v.* week.

week *b. n.* soft; (*fig.*) soft, tender, weak; **— maken, — worden,** soften; *z. n., v.* **in de — zetten,** put in soak.

weekblad *o.* weekly (paper).

weekdier *o.* pulpy animal; (*wet.*) mollusc.

weekgeld *o.* (*weekloon*) weekly pay, weekly wages; (*huishoudgeld, zakgeld, enz.*) weekly allowance.

weekhartig *v. n.* soft-hearted, tender-hearted.

weekheid *v.* softness.

weeklacht *v.* lamentation, lament, wailing.

weelde *v.* (*alg.*) luxury; (*overvloed*) abundance, profusion, opulence; (*v. plantengroei*) luxuriance; (*dartelheid*) luxuriousness, exuberance.

weemoed *m.* melancholy, sadness.

weemoedig *b. n.* sad, melancholy.

weer *o.* weather.

weer *v.* defence, resistance.

weer *bw.* again.

weerbaar *b. n.* (*verdedigbaar*) defensible; (*strijdbaar*)capable of bearing arms.

weerbaarheid *v.* defensibility; ability to defend oneself.

weerbarstig *b. n.* unruly, refractory, recalcitrant, obstinate.

weerbarstigheid v. unruliness, refractoriness, recalcitrance.

weerbericht o. weather-report.

weerga v. equal, match, peer.

weergalm m. echo, reverberation.

weergalmen on. w. resound, reverberate, re-echo.

weergaloos b. n. unequalled, matchless, peerless, unrivalled, unexampled.

weergeven o. w. restore, return, give back; (fig.: muz.; in andere vorm, enz.) render; (inhoud van boek, brief, enz.; stem) reproduce; (iems. mening) give; (openbare mening) voice.

weerglas o. weather-glass, barometer.

weerhaak m. barb, barbed hook.

weerhaan m. weather-vane, weathercock; (fig. ook:) time-server, time-pleaser.

weerkaatsen o. w. (v. licht, geluid, warmte) reflect; (v. geluid) re-echo; on. w. rebound.

weerklinken on. w. resound, re-echo, ring again.

weerkunde v. meteorology.

weerlicht o. sheet lightning, heat lightning, summer lightning.

weerlichten on. w. lighten.

weerloosheid v. defencelessness.

weermacht v. military forces.

weerschijn m. reflex, reflection.

weersgesteldheid v. state of the weather; (v. land, streek) weather conditions.

weerskanten bw. van —, from (on) both sides, from either side; aan — van, on either side of.

weerspannig b. n. refractory, recalcitrant, rebellious.

weerstaan o. w. resist, withstand, oppose.

weerstandsvermogen o. power of resistance, resisting-power; endurance; (uithoudingsvermogen) staying-power.

weerstreven o. w. (v. persoon) oppose; (v. bevelen, enz.) struggle against.

weerwil m. in — van, in spite of, notwithstanding, despite of.

weerwolf m. wer(e)wolf, man-wolf, wolf-man.

weerzien o. w. see again; z. n., o. meeting again; tot —s, till we meet again; (fam.) so long.

weerzin m. aversion, repugnance, reluctance.

wees m. en v. orphan.

weeshuis o. orphan-house, orphanage.

weetal m. en v. wiseacre, know-all.

weetgierig b. n. eager to learn, desirous of knowledge.

weg m. way, road, roadway; path; (sch.) route; (fig.) way, road, course, avenue, channel.

weg bw. (vertrokken) gone; (verloren) gone, lost; (verwijderd, afwezig) away; — ermee! away with it!

wegblijven on. w. stay away; (v. werk, school) absent oneself.

wegbrengen o. w. carry away, take away; (v. persoon) see off; (v. schip) sink, scuttle, cast away.

wegdragen o. w. carry away, carry off; (v. prijs) bear away.

wegen o. w. weigh; (fig.: v. woorden) weigh, measure; (op de hand) poise; on. w. weigh.

wegenbouw m. road-making, road-construction.

wegens vz. on account of, because of.

weggaan on. w. go away, leave.

weggeven o. w. give away.

weggooien o. w. (v. voorw.) throw away, chuck away; (v. geld) throw (chuck) away, waste; (fig.) pooh-pooh; w. w. zich —, throw oneself away, make oneself cheap.

weghalen o. w. take away, fetch away remove.

weging v. weighing.

wegjagen o. w. (v. personen, dieren) drive away (off), chase away (off); (v. vogels) shoo away; (v. personeel) send packing; (v. school) expel; (v. student) rusticate, send down; (mil.) dismiss the service; (voor 't front) drum out.

wegkomen on. w. get away.

wegkwijnen on. w. languish, waste away, pine away.

weglaten o. w. leave out, miss out, omit; (v. naam, enz.) suppress; (v. titel) dispense with.

weglating v. leaving out, omission; suppression.

weglopen on. w. run away (off); make off.

wegnemen o. w. take away; remove; (fig.: v. moeilijkheid) obviate; (v. verdenking) allay; (stelen) pilfer, steal.

wegraken on. w. get away, get (be) lost, be mislaid, miscarry.

wegruimen o. w. clear away, remove; (v. moeilijkheden) smooth away.

wegruiming v. removal.

wegrukken o. w. tear away, snatch away.

wegscheren o. w. shave off, shear off; w. w. zich —, make oneself scarce, decamp.

wegspoelen o. w. wash away, rinse away; on. w. be washed away.

wegsteken o. w. put away, pocket.

wegsterven on. w. die away, die down; (v. lawaai, rumoer) fade out.

wegsturen o. w. send away; (v. bediende) dismiss; (v. leerling v. school) turn out; (v. student) rusticate.

wegtrekken o. w. pull away; on. w. (v. troepen, enz.) march away (off); (v. wolken, bui) blow over, pass over; (v. mist) lift; (v. pijn) diminish.

wegvagen o. w. sweep away; wipe out; (fig.) blot out.

wegvallen on. w. fall off, drop off; (fig.) be left out, be omitted.

wegvoeren o. w. carry away (off), lead away; (ontvoeren) abduct, kidnap.

wegwedstrijd *m.* road race, long-distance race.
wegwerker *m.* roadman, roadmender; *(bij de spoorwegen)* surface-man.
wegwijzer *m. (persoon)* guide; *(handwijzer)* guide-post, direction-post, handpost; *(gids, handleiding)* manual, handbook; *(reisgids)* guide(-book).
wegzenden *o. w. (verzenden)* send away; *(ontslaan)* dismiss, send away.
wei *v. (v. melk)* whey; *(v. bloed)* serum.
weide *v.* meadow.
weidegrond *m.* pasture-ground, meadow-land, grass-land.
weiden *on. w.* graze, feed; *o. w. (hoeden)* tend.
weids *b. n. (statig, groots)* stately; *(klinkend: v. titel, enz.)* sonorous, high-sounding.
weifelaar *m.* waverer, wobbler.
weifelen *on. w.* waver, vacillate.
weifeling *v.* wavering, vacillation, hesitation.
weigeren *o. w. (niet toestaan)* refuse; *(afwijzen)* refuse, decline; *on. w. (v. rem, enz.)* fail (to act), refuse to act; *(v. vuurwapen)* miss fire.
weigering *v.* refusal; miss-fire.
weiland *o. (alg.)* meadow-land, grass-land; *(stuk —)* pasture.
weinig *telw. (enk.)* little; *(mv.)* few; *bw.* little.
weitas *v.* game-bag.
wekelijk *b. n.* soft, tender, weak, effeminate.
wekelijks *b. n.* weekly, hebdomadal.
weken *o. w.* soften; *(in melk, koffie, enz.)* soak; *on. w.* soften; soak.
wekken *o. w.* (a)wake; (a)waken, rouse, call; *(fig.: v. belangstelling)* excite; *(v. nieuwsgierigheid, verontwaardiging, enz.)* provoke; *(v. verdenking)* create, engender; *(v. herinneringen)* call up, evoke.
wekker *m. (persoon)* awaker, knocker-up, window-tapper; *(klok)* alarum-(-clock).
wel *v.* spring, fountain, well-head.
wel *bw. (en b. n.) (goed)* well; rightly; *(zeer)* very (much); *(versterkend)* indeed, truly; *(vermoeden, geruststelling)* surely; *(uitroep)* why well, *(vragend)* are you, have you; &c., **— ?** well? *(als beleefdheidsvorm)* kindly; *(getal, maat, enz.)* no less than, quite, as much as, as many as; *z. n., o.* welfare, well-being.
welaan *tw.* well then, very well.
welbehagen *o.* pleasure, complacency.
welbespraakt *b. n.* fluent, voluble, well-spoken.
welbespraaktheid *v.* fluency, volubility, readiness of speech, eloquence.
weldaad *v.* benefit, benefaction.
weldoen *on. w. (goed doen)* do good, do well; *(helpen, ondersteunen)* do almsdeeds.
weldoener *m.* benefactor.
weldra *bw.* soon, shortly, before long.
Weledelgeboren *b. n.* honourable.

weleer *bw.* formerly, in olden times, of old.
weleerwaard *b. n.* reverend; *Uw W—e,* Your Reverence.
welfsel *o.* vault.
welgesteld *b. n.* well-to-do, well off, in easy circumstances.
welgesteldheid *v.* prosperity, easy circumstances.
welgevallen *z. n., o.* pleasure, complacency, satisfaction; *naar —,* at pleasure, at will; *o. w. zich iets laten —,* put up with a thing, submit to a thing.
welgevallig *b. n.* pleasing, agreeable.
welig *b. n.* luxuriant.
weliswaar *bw.* it is true.
welk *vr. vnw.* what; *(v. bepaald aantal)* which; *betr. vnw. (v. persoon)* who, that; *(v. zaak)* which, that.
welkom *b. n.* welcome; *iem. — heten,* bid (make) a person welcome, welcome a person; *z. n., o.* welcome.
wellen *on. w.* well (up); *o. w. (v. boter, enz.)* draw.
wellevendheid *v.* good breeding, courtesy, politeness.
wellicht *bw.* perhaps.
welluidend *b. n.* melodious, harmonious, euphonious.
wellust *m. (gunstig)* delight, bliss; *(ong.)* voluptuousness, sensuality, luxury, lust; sensual enjoyment (gratification).
welnemen *o. met uw —,* by your leave.
welnu *tw.* well then, well, now.
welp *o.* cub.
welput *m.* well.
welriekend *b. n.* sweet-smelling, sweet-scented, odoriferous, fragrant.
welslagen *o.* success.
welsprekend *b. n.* eloquent.
welsprekendheid *v.* eloquence.
welstand *m. (voorspoed)* welfare, prosperity, well-being; *(gezondheid)* (good) health.
welvaart *v.* prosperity; *(welzijn)* welfare.
welvaren *on. w.* prosper, thrive, be prosperous; be in good health, be quite well; *z. n., o.* welfare.
welvarend *b. n. (voorspoedig)* prosperous, thriving; *(gezond)* healthy, in good health.
welven *o. w.* vault, arch; *w. w. zich —,* vault, arch.
welving *v.* vaulting; vault; *(v. weg)* camber.
welvoeglijk *b. n.* well-becoming, seemly, decent.
welvoeglijkheid *v.* seemingness, decency, propriety.
welwillend *b. n.* benevolent, obliging, kind.
welwillendheid *v.* benevolence, kindness.
welzijn *o.* welfare, well-being, prosperity; *voor het algemeen —,* for the public (common) good.

wemelen *on. w.* — **van,** swarm (teem) with; (*v. ongedierte*) crawl with; (*v. fouten, ook:*) bristle with.

wenden *o. w.* turn; (*sch.*) put about; *on. w.* turn; (*sch.*) go about, put about; *w. w.* **zich** —, turn; **zich** — **tot,** (*fig.*) apply to.

wending *v.* turn, turning.

wenen *on. w.* weep, cry.

Wenen *o.* Vienna.

wenk *m.* wink, hint, nod.

wenkbrauw *v.* eyebrow.

wenken *o. w.* beckon.

wennen *o. w.* accustom, habituate (**aan,** to), familiarize (**aan,** with); *on. w.* **het zal wel** —, you will get used to it.

wens *m.* wish, desire.

wenselijk *b. n.* desirable.

wensen *o. w.* wish; (*verlangen*) desire, want, wish.

wentelen *o. w.* turn about (over), roll, revolve; *on. w.* en *w. w.* **zich** —, (*v. planeten, enz.*) revolve; rotate; (*in modder, enz.*) welter, wallow, roll (about).

wenteling *v.* revolution; rotation.

wenteltrap *v.* (*trap*) winding staircase, winding-stairs, spiral-stairs; (*Dk.*) wentletrap.

wereld *v.* world, universe.

wereldbeschrijving *v.* cosmography.

wereldbol *m.* globe.

wereldburger *m.* citizen of the world, cosmopolitan, cosmopolite.

werelddeel *o.* part of the world, continent.

wereldlijk *b. n.* (*niet geestelijk*) secular; (*v. macht*) temporal; (*v. goederen*) worldly.

wereldling *m.* en *v.* worldling.

wereldmacht *v.* world-power.

wereldrijk *o.* world-empire.

werelds *b. n.* wordly, mundane; (*niet geestelijk*) secular; (*tijdelijk*) temporal.

wereldstad *v.* metropolis.

wereldtentoonstelling *v.* international exhibition, world's fair.

wereldwijsheid *v.* worldly wisdom; philosophy of life.

wereldzee *v.* ocean.

weren *o. w.* avert; prevent; (*v. persoon*) exclude; *w. w.* **zich** —, (*zich inspannen, zijn best doen*) exert oneself; (*zich verdedigen*) defend oneself.

werf *v.* ship-yard; ship-building yard; (*v. marine*) dockyard; (*kaai*) quay, wharf.

werfbureau *o.* (*mil.*) recruiting-office.

wering *v.* prevention; exclusion.

werk *o.* oakum, tow.

werk *o.* work, labour; (*v. uurwerk, enz.*) works.

werkbroek *v.* overalls, working-trousers.

werkdadig *b. n.* efficacious, active, effective.

werkdag *m.* (*geen zondag*) work-day, working-day, week-day.

werkelijk *b. n.* real, actual; (*v. dienst*) active; *bw.* really, actually; indeed.

werkelijkheid *v.* reality.

werkeloosheid *v.* inaction, idleness.

werken *on. w.* work; (*v. machine, enz.*) work, function; (*v. vulkaan*) work, be in eruption; (*v. geneesmiddel*) act, operate, work, take effect, be effective; (*v. schip*) labour; (*v. lading*) shift; (*v. hout*) warp, get warped, work; *o. w.* **zich dood** —, work oneself to death (to the bone).

werkend *b. n.* working; (*v. vulkaan; vennoot, lid, enz.*) active; (*v. geneesmiddel, enz.*) efficacious, effective.

werker *m.* worker.

werkgever *m.* employer.

werkhuis *o.* work-house; (*v. werkvrouw*) place.

werking *v.* action, working, operation; (*v. vulkaan*) activity; (*uitwerking, gevolg*) effect; (*werkdadigheid*) efficacy.

werkkracht *v.* (*arbeidsvermogen*) power of work, working-faculty, energy; (*arbeider*) hand, workman.

werkkring *m.* sphere of action, sphere of activity, field of activity.

werkloon *o.* wage(s), pay.

werkloos *b. n.* out of work, out of employment, unemployed, workless.

werkloosheid *v.* unemployment.

werkloze *m.* out-of-work, unemployed workman.

werkman *m.* workman, operative; (*handwerksman*) working-man, artisan.

werknemer *m.* employee.

werkplaats *v.* workshop.

werkster *v.* (woman, girl, female) worker; (*werkvrouw*) charwoman.

werktafel *v.* work-table.

werktuig *o.* tool, instrument; (*v. gehoor, gezicht, enz.*) organ.

werktuigkunde *v.* mechanics.

werktuigkundige *m.* mechanician, instrument-maker, practical engineer.

werktuiglijk *b. n.* (*bw.*) mechanical(ly).

werkverschaffing *v.* provision of work, procuring of employment.

werkvolk *o.* workmen, work-people, labourers.

werkwoord *o.* verb.

werkzaam *b. n.* laborious, active, industrious.

werkzaamheid *v.* laboriousness, activity, industry.

werpen *o. w.* throw, cast, fling, toss, hurl.

werpnet *o.* cast-net.

werpschijf *v.* quoit, coit; (*gesch.*) discus.

werpspeer *v.* javelin.

wervel *m.* vertebra (*mv.:* vertebrae).

werveldier *o.* vertebrate (animal).

wervelkolom *v.* spinal (vertebral) column, spine.

wervelstorm *m.* cyclone, tornado.

werven *o. w.* en *on. w.* recruit, enlist; enrol; (*v. stemmen, klanten*) canvass for; (*v. leden*) bring in.

werving *v.* recruitment, enlistment; enrolment; canvassing.

weshalve *vw.* wherefore, for which reason.
wesp *v.* wasp.
wespennest *o.* wasp's nest, vespiary; *(fig.)* hornet's nest.
west *o.* west.
westelijk *b. n.* westerly, western.
westen *o.* west, occident.
westerlengte *v.* west(ern) longitude.
westers *b. n.* western, occidental.
wet *v. (alg.)* law; *(bepaald)* act.
wetboek *o.* code (of law).
weten *o. w. (alg.)* know; *(bekend zijn met)* be aware of; *on. w.* know; *hij weet ervan,* he is in the know; *z. n., o.* knowledge.
wetenschap *v.* science; *(het weten)* knowledge.
wetenswaardig *b. n.* worth knowing, interesting.
wetenswaardigheid *v.* thing worth knowing.
wetgeleerde *m.* jurist, legist.
wetgevend *b. n.* legislative, law-making, law-giving.
wethouder *m.* alderman.
wetsontwerp *o.* bill.
wetsovertreder *m.* law-breaker.
wetstaal *o.* (whetting-)steel.
wetstaal *v.* law-language, legal language.
wetsteen *m.* whetstone; *(v. zeis)* strickle.
wettelijk *b. n.* legal; *(— voorgeschreven)* statutory.
wettelijkheid *v.* legality.
wetten *o. w.* whet, sharpen.
wettig *b. n.* lawful, legitimate, legal; *— maken,* legalize; *bw.* lawfully, legitimately, legally.
wettigheid *v.* legitimacy.
weven *o. w. en on. w.* weave.
wever *m.* weaver; *(Dk.)* weaver-bird.
weverij *v.* weaving-mill.
weverskam *m.* reed, slay.
wezel *v.* weasel.
wezen *on. w.* be; *zie ook: zijn; z. n., o. (schepsel)* being, creature; *(bestaan)* being, existence; *(aard)* nature, character; *(wezenlijkheid)* essence, substance; *(voorkomen, uiterlijk)* countenance, aspect.
wezenlijk *b. n. (werkelijk)* real; *(hoofdzakelijk)* essential, substantial, fundamental.
wezenlijkheid *v.* reality; essentiality.
wezenloos *b. n.* vacant, blank, vacuous; expressionless.
wezenstrek *m.* feature.
wichelaar(ster) *m. (v.)* augurer.
wichelroede *v.* divining-rod; dowsing-rod, twig.
wichelroedeloper *m.* dowser.
wicht *o. (kind)* baby, child.
wicht *o. (gewicht)* weight.
wie *vr. vnw.* who? *van — is het?* whose is it? *— van hen?* which of them? *onb. vnw. — ook,* who(so)ever; *betr. vnw.* he who.

wieden *o. w. en on. w.* weed.
wieder *m.* weeder.
wieg *v.* cradle.
wiegelen *on. w.* rock, wobble.
wiegelied *o.* cradle-song, lullaby.
wiegen *o. w.* rock; *zie ook: slaap.*
wiek *v. (vlerk, vleugel)* wing; *(molen—)* sail, wing, sweep; *(pit v. lamp)* wick.
wiel *o.* wheel.
wielerbaan *v.* cycling-track, cycle-track.
wielersport *v.* cycling.
wielerwedstrijd *m.* cycle race.
wielewaal *m. (Dk.)* (golden) oriole.
wielrennen *o.* cycle-racing.
wielrijder *m.* cyclist, wheelman.
wier *o.* sea-weed; *(wet.)* alga.
wierook *m.* incense, frankincense; *(fig.)* incense.
wierookvat *o.* censer, incensory, thurible.
wig *v.* wedge; *(tn.)* key.
wigvormig *b. n.* wedge-shaped.
wij *pers. vnw.* we.
wijd *b. n.* wide; spacious, large, ample; *bw.* wide(ly); *— en zijd,* far and wide; *—er maken,* widen.
wijdbeens *bw.* straddle-legged.
wijden *o. w. (v. priester)* ordain; *(v. kerk, voorwerp, enz.)* consecrate; *— aan,* dedicate to; *(v. tijd, krachten)* devote to; *w. w. zich — aan,* devote oneself to.
wijding *v.* ordination; consecration; devotion.
wijdte *v.* width, breadth, space; *(v. spoor)* gauge.
wijf *o.* woman, female; *(ong.: kwaad —)* virago, shrew, vixen.
wijfje *o.* little wife, wifey; *(v. dier)* female.
wijk *v.* quarter, district; *(v. melkboer, enz.)* round, walk.
wijken *on. w.* give way, give ground, yield.
wijkplaats *v.* asylum, refuge.
wijkverpleegster *v.* district-nurse.
wijl *v.* while, time.
wijl *vw.* since, because, as.
wijlen *b. n.* late, deceased.
wijn *m.* wine.
wijnappel *m.* wine-apple.
wijnberg *m.* vineyard.
wijnbouw *m.* vine-culture, viniculture.
wijnbouwer *m.* vine-grower.
wijndruif *v.* grape.
wijnfles *v.* wine-bottle.
wijngaard *m.* vineyard.
wijngaardenier *m.* vine-dresser, vintager.
wijngaardluis *v.* vine-pest, phylloxera.
wijngeest *m.* spirit of wine, alcohol.
wijnglas *o.* wine-glass.
wijnkan *v.* wine-tankard.
wijnkelder *m.* wine-cellar, wine-vault(s).
wijnlezer *m.* vintager.
wijnmaand *v.* October.
wijnoogst *m.* vintage.
wijnpers *v.* winepress.
wijnsteen *m.* wine-stone, tartar.
wijnsteenzuur *o.* tartaric acid.

wijnstok m. vine.

wijs v. (manier) manner, way; (muz.) tune, melody; (gram.) mood.

wijs b. n. wise; bw. wisely.

wijsbegeerte v. philosophy.

wijsgeer m. philosopher.

wijsheid v. wisdom.

wijsmaken o. w. iem. iets —, make a person believe something, impose upon a person.

wijsneus m. wiseacre, pedant, prig.

wijsvinger m. forefinger, index.

wijten o. w. iets — aan, impute something to; het is te — aan, it is owing to.

wijting v. (Dk.) whiting.

wijwater o. holy water.

wijwaterkwast m. holy-water sprinkler, aspergillum.

wijwatervat o. holy-water font.

wijze v. zie wijs.

wijze m. sage, wise man.

wijzen o. w. point out, show; (recht: v. vonnis) pronounce; on. w. point.

wijzer m. (v. uurwerk) hand; (tn.) indicator; (handwijzer) finger-post; (v. barometer, enz.) pointer.

wijzerbord o., **wijzerplaat** v. dial-plate, clock-face.

wijzigen o. w. modify, alter, change; (v. wetsontwerp: amenderen) amend.

wijziging v. modification, alteration, change.

wikkelen o. w. wrap (up), envelop; (in zwachtel, enz.) swathe (in); (fig.: in moeilijkheden, enz.) involve (in); (in gesprek) draw (into); w. w. zich in zijn mantel —, wrap one's cloak about one.

wikken o. w. weigh.

wil m. will, desire, wish.

wild b. n. (dieren, planten) wild; (v. dieren ook:) ferine; (onbeschaafd, woest) savage; (v. kind) wild, unruly; (v. drift, enz.) fierce; bw. wildly; z. n., o. game; (gejaagd —) quarry; (wildbraad) venison.

wilde m. savage; (v. kamerlid) independent; (extremist) wild man.

wildebras m. (v. jongen) wild monkey, wild boy, romping boy; (v. meisje) tomboy, romp.

wildernis v. wilderness, waste.

wildstroper m. poacher.

wildzang m. (v. vogels) warbling; (dicht.) wood-notes; zie wildebras.

wilg m. willow.

willekeur v. arbitrariness, high-handedness; naar —, at pleasure, at one's own sweet will.

willekeurig b. n. (eigendunkelijk) arbitrary, high-handed; (v. beweging, enz.) voluntary.

willen o. w. en on. w. will; (wensen) wish to, want to; (genegen zijn) be willing; z. n., o. volition.

willens bw. on purpose, wilfully; — of onwillens, willynilly; — en wetens, knowingly (and willingly).

willig b. n. willing, docile, biddable; (H.: v. markt) firm, animated.

willoos b. n. will-less.

willoosheid v. will-lessness.

wilsbeschikking v. last will (and testament).

wilskracht v. will-power, will-force, energy.

wimpel m. pennon, pendant, streamer; (v. jacht) burgee.

wimper v. (eye) lash.

wind m. wind; (gen.) wind, flatulence.

windas v. (tn.) windlass.

windbrekend b. n. carminative.

windbuil v. windbag, gas-bag. [egg.

windei o. wind-egg, sheer-egg, shell-less

winden o. w. (v. garen, enz.) wind, twist; (met windas, enz.) wind up.

winderig b. n. (alg.) windy; (v. weer) windy, blowy, blustery; (fig. opgeblazen) flatulent.

winderigheid v. windiness; flatulence.

windhaan m. weathercock, vane.

windhond m. greyhound; (ruigharige Schotse —) deer-hound.

windmolen m. windmill.

windpokken v. mv. wind-pox, chicken-pox.

windroos v. (sch.) compass-card, rhumb-card; (Pl.) anemone, wind-flower.

windscherm o. wind-screen.

windsel o. band, bandage, swathing-band, swathe.

windstilte v. calm.

windstoot m. gust of wind.

windstreek v. point of the compass, point of the wind.

windwijzer m. weathercock, weather-vane.

winkel m. shop; (werkplaats) work-shop.

winkelbediende m. shop-assistant, shop-hand.

winkeldochter v. shop-girl, sales-woman; (fig.) shopkeeper.

winkelhaak m. (werktuig) square; (scheur) trapdoor.

winkelier m. shopkeeper, shopman.

winkelkast v. show-window, shop-window.

winkelprijs m. retail-price, selling-price.

winkelraam o. shop-window.

winkelwaar v. shop-wares, shop-goods.

winket o. wicket.

winnaar m. winner.

winnen o. w. en on. w. win; gain; (verkrijgen) gather, harvest; make; (v. land) gain, reclaim.

winner m. winner.

winning v. (v. erts, enz.) winning, production, extraction.

winst v. gain, profit(s), benefit, return(s); (bij spel) winnings.

winstbejag o. pursuit of gain.

winst-en-verliesrekening v. profit and loss account.

winstgevend b. n. remunerative, lucrative, profitable.

winstuitkering *v.* distribution of profits.
winter *m.* (*jaargetijde*) winter; (*aandoening v. handen, enz.*) chilblain.
winteravond *m.* winter-evening.
winterhulp *v.* winter-relief.
winterkoninkje *o.* (*Dk.*) wren.
wintermaand *v.* December.
winterslaap *m.* winter sleep; hibernation.
wintersport *v.* winter-sports.
wip *v.* (—*plank, schommel*) seesaw; (*v. brug*) swipe, bascule; *m.* (*sprong*) skip; *tw.* whip!
wipbrug *v.* drawbridge, bascule-bridge, balance-bridge.
wipkar *v.* tilt-cart.
wippen *on. w.* whip, skip; (*v. tafel, enz.: waggelen*) wobble; (*op wipplank*) (play at) seesaw; *o. w.* (*v. ambtenaar, enz.*) turn out; (*sl.*) fire; (*v. minister, regering*) unseat.
wipplank *v.* seesaw.
wirwar *m.* tangle.
wis *b. n.* certain, sure.
wis *v.* wisp.
wiskunde *v.* mathematics.
wiskundige *m.* mathematician.
wispelturig *b. n.* inconstant, changeable, fickle.
wissen *o. w.* wipe; (*mil.: v. kanon*) sponge.
wissel *m.* (*H.*) bill of exchange, draft; (*v. spoor*) points; (*toestel*) switch.
wisselagent *m.* exchange-broker, bill-broker.
wisselbeker *m.* challenge cup.
wisselen *o. w.* (*v. geld*) change, give change for; (*v. brieven, woorden, enz.*) exchange; (*v. complimenten, klappen, enz.*) bandy; (*v. tanden*) shed; *on. w.* change, give change; (*veranderen*) vary.
wisselgeld *o.* (small) change.
wisselhandel *m.* bill-broking.
wisseling *v.* (*ruil*) exchange; change, variation, fluctuation.
wisselkantoor *o.* exchange office.
wisselkoers *m.* rate of exchange.
wisselrekening *v.* exchange-account.
wisselspoor *o.* side-rails, siding, shunt-line.
wisselstand *m.* position of the points.
wisselstroom *m.* (*el.*) alternating current.
wisselstuk *o.* spare piece.
wisselvallig *b. n.* precarious, uncertain, chancy.
wisselvalligheid *v.* precariousness, uncertainty.
wisselwachter *m.* pointsman, switchman.
wit *b. n.* white; — *maken,* whiten, blanch; *z. n., o.* white.
witgloeiend *b. n.* white hot, incandescent.
witgoud *o.* platinum.
witheid *v.* whiteness.
witkalk *v.* whitewash.

witkiel *m.* (luggage-)porter railway-porter.
witloof *o.* succory.
wittebrood *o.* white bread.
wittebroodsweken *v. mv.* honeymoon.
wittekool *v.* white cabbage.
witten *o. w.* whitewash.
witvis *m.* whiting, whitebait.
woede *v.* rage, fury.
woeden *on. w.* rage; *z. n.* raging.
woedend *b. n.* furious, raging, infuriated; — *worden,* fly (fall) into a passion, become enraged; *iem.* — *maken,* enrage (infuriate) a person.
woeker *m.* usury.
woekeraar *m.* usurer.
woekerdier *o.* parasite.
woekeren *on. w.* practise usury; (*v. planten*) be (grow) rank; (*v. kwaad*) be (grow) rampant.
woekerhandel *m.* usurious trade.
woekerplant *v.* parasitic plant, parasite.
woekerrente *v.* usurious interest, usury.
woekerwinst *v.* exorbitant profit (gain), usury.
woelen *on. w.* (*in bed*) toss about, turn and toss; (*wroeten*) burrow, grub, root; *o. w.* **uit de grond** —, grub out.
woelgeest *m.* turbulent spirit (fellow); agitator.
woelig *b. n.* (*v. kind*) restless; (*v. tijd, enz.*) turbulent; (*v. weder*) broken, lumpy.
woeligheid *v.* restlessness; turbulence.
woeling *v.* agitation, turbulence.
woensdag *m.* Wednesday.
woerd *m.* (*Dk.*) drake.
woest *b. n.* (*v. grond: onbebouwd*) waste; (*onbewoond*) desolate, desert; (*nijdig*) wild, savage; (*ruw: v. jongen, weer, enz.*) wild; (*v. blik*) fierce; (*v. kreten*) tumultuous.
woestaard, woesteling *m.* savage, brute.
woestheid *v.* wildness, savagery; fierceness.
woestijn *v.* desert.
wol *v.* wool.
wolf *m.* wolf; (*insekt: koren*—) weevil; (*in tanden*) caries; (*tn. in weverij: duivel, snar*) devil, gin, willow; (*muz.: v. piano, enz.*) wolf.
wolfshond wolf-dog, wolf-hound.
wolfskers *v.* deadly nightshade.
wolfsklauw *m.* wolf's claw; *v.* (*Pl.*) club-moss, wolf's foot.
wolfsklem *v.* wolf-trap.
wolk *v.* cloud.
wolkbreuk *v.* cloud-burst, rain-burst.
wolkenkrabber *m.* sky-scraper.
wollen *b. n.* woollen; — **stoffen,** woollens.
wollig *b. n.* woolly.
wolspinnerij *v.* wool mill.
wolvee *o.* wool-producing cattle.
wolvin *v.* she-wolf.
wond *z. n., v.* wound; *b. n.* sore.
wonder *o.* wonder, marvel; **prodigy;** (*bovennatuurlijk*) miracle.

wonderbaar b. n. wonderful; miraculous.

wonderbaarlijk b. n. (bw.) marvellous-(ly), miraculous(ly).

wonderdoener m. wonder-worker, miracle-worker.

wonderdokter m. wonder-doctor, quack, unrecognized practitioner.

wonderkind o. wonder-child, infant prodigy, infant phenomenon.

wondermens m. prodigy, human wonder.

wonderolie v. castor-oil.

wonderteken o. miraculous sign, miracle.

wondnaad m. suture.

wonen on. w. live, reside; (lett.) dwell.

woning v. dwelling, house, residence, habitation.

woningbureau o. house agent's office, house-agency.

woningnood m. house famine.

woonachtig b. n. resident, living.

woonhuis o. dwelling-house.

woonkamer v. living-room, sitting-room.

woonplaats v. dwelling-place, residence, domicile.

woonstad v. residential town.

woonwagen m. caravan, living-wagon.

woord o. word, term.

woordafleiding v. etymology, derivation of words.

woordbreuk v. breach of faith, breach of promise.

woordelijk b. n. literal, verbal; (v. verslag) verbatim; bw. literally, verbally; verbatim; word for word.

woordenboek o. dictionary.

woordenlijst v. word-list, list of words, vocabulary.

woordenrijk b. n. (v. taal) rich in words; (breedsprakig) wordy, verbose; (rad v. tong) voluble.

woordenschat m. store of words, vocabulary.

woordenwisseling v. passage of words, altercation, dispute.

woordenzifter m. verbalist, quibbler, word-catcher.

woordomzetting v. (gram.) transposition (of words), inversion.

woordontleding v. parsing.

woordraadsel o. logogriph.

woordschikking v. order of words.

woordspeling v. play upon words, pun, quibble.

woorduitlating v. (gram.) ellipsis.

woordvoerder m. spokesman, speaker, mouth-piece.

worden on. w. become, grow, get, go, turn, fall.

wording v. origin, genesis; **in —,** nascent, in gestation.

wordingsgeschiedenis v. genesis.

worgen o. w. strangle, throttle.

worging v. strangling, strangulation, throttling.

worgkoord o. gar(r)otte, strangling-cord.

worm m. worm; (made) grub, maggot; (regen—) grub.

wormkruid o. (Pl.) tansy; (guldenroede) golden rod.

wormstekig b. n. worm-eaten, wormed, wormy.

worp m. throw; (v. biggen, enz.) litter.

worst v. sausage.

worstelaar m. wrestler.

worstelen on. w. wrestle; (fig.) struggle, wrestle.

worsteling v. wrestling, wrestle; (fig) struggle, wrestle.

wortel m. (v. plant, enz.) root; (peen.) carrot; (v. getal) root.

wortelgrootheid v. radical quantity.

wortelknol m. (Pl.) tuber.

wortelschieting v. (Pl.) radication.

wortelteken o. radical sign.

worteltrekking v. extraction of roots, evolution.

woud o. wood, forest.

wouw m. (Dk.) kite, glede.

wouw v. (Pl.) weld, wolds.

wraak v. revenge, vengeance.

wraakbaar b. n. blamable, objectionable; (recht) challengeable.

wraakgevoel o. feeling of revenge.

wraakgierig b. n. revengeful, vindictive.

wraakneming v. retaliation, revenge, vengeance.

wrak b. n. rickety; crazy; (sch.) cranky.

wrak o. wreck, derelict.

wraken o. w. (afkeuren) disapprove of, take exception to; (recht) challenge, rule out of court; on. w. (sch.) make leeway.

wrakgoederen o. mv. wreck, flotsam and jetsam.

wrakhout o. wreckage.

wraking v. (recht) challenge; (sch.) leeway, drift.

wrang b. n. acid, acerb; (in de mond) harsh, tart; (v. wijn) rough.

wrangheid v. acidness, acerbity; harshness, tartness.

wrat v. wart; (wet.) verruca.

wreed b. n. cruel; ferocious; bw. cruelly.

wreedaard m. cruel man, brute.

wreedheid v. cruelty; ferocity.

wreef v. instep.

wreken o. w. revenge; avenge; w. w. **zich —,** revenge oneself, avenge oneself, be revenged.

wrevel m. spite, resentment, rancour; (knorrigheid) peevishness.

wrevelig b. n. spiteful, resentful, rancorous; peevish, crusty, testy.

wrijfdoek m. rubbing-cloth, polishing-cloth, rubber.

wrijfhout o. (sch.) fender, wood fender.

wrijfsteen m. rubbing-stone.

wrijfwas o. en v. beeswax, French polish.

wrijven o. w. rub; (boenen) polish, beeswax, rub; (v. verf) bray, grind.

wrijving *v.* rubbing, friction; *(fig.)* friction.

wrikken *on. w.* jerk at; *o. w. (sch.)* scull.

wrikriem *m.* scull.

wringen *o. w. (v. wasgoed, enz.)* wring (out); *(v. handen)* wring; *w. w.* **zich —,** twist oneself, wriggle.

wringing *r.* wringing, twist(ing).

wringmachine *v.* (clothes-)wringer.

wroeging *v.* remorse, compunction, contrition.

wroeten *on. w.* root, rout, grub; *(v. mol, enz.)* burrow.

wrok *m.* grudge, rancour, resentment.

wrokken *on. w.* grudge, chafe, fret.

wrokkig *b. n.* rancorous.

wrong *v. (alg.)* roll, twist; *(v. haar)* knot, chignon; *(wap.)* wreath, torse; *(tulband)* turban; *(ruk)* wrench.

wuft *b. n.* fickle, frivolous, volatile; *bw.* frivolously.

wuftheid *v.* fickleness, frivolity, volatility.

wuiven *on. w.* wave.

wulps *b. n.* wanton, lascivious, lewd.

wulpsheid *v.* wantonness, lasciviousness, lewdness.

wurm *m. (Dk.)* worm; *m. en o.* **het (arme) —,** the poor mite.

X

x-benen *o. mv.* turned-in (knock-kneed) legs, baker legs.

x-stralen *m. mv.* x-rays, Röntgen-rays.

xylofoon *v.* xylophone.

Y

yaleslot *o.* Yale lock.

yankee *m.* yankee.

yen *m.* yen.

yoghurt *m.* yoghourt.

Z

zaad *o.* seed; *(dierlijk)* semen, sperm; *(v. vis)* spawn; *(fig.)* seed.

zaadbakje *o.* seed-box.

zaadhuisje *o. (Pl.)* seed-vessel, capsule.

zaadkorrel *v.* grain of seed.

zaadlob *v. (Pl.)* seed-lobe.

zaadvlies *o. (Pl.)* seed-coat.

zaag *v.* saw; *(fig.: v. persoon)* bore.

zaagbok *m.* saw-horse, trestle.

zaagmachine *v.* sawing-machine.

zaagmeel *o.* saw-dust.

zaagvis *m. (Dk.)* saw-fish.

zaaibed *o.* seed-bed.

zaaien *o. w.* sow.

zaaier *m.* sower.

zaaigoed *o.* sowing-seed.

zaailand *o.* sowing-land.

zaaimachine *v.* sowing-machine, sower.

zaaitijd *m.* sowing-time.

zaak *v. (voorwerp)* thing; *(aangelegenheid)* matter, affair, business, case; *(handel, bedrijf)* business, concern, trade; *(transactie)* transaction; *(recht)* case, (law)suit; *(winkel)* business.

zaakgelastigde *m.* commissioner, agent, deputy.

zaakwaarnemer *m.* solicitor, commissioner, law-agent.

zaal *v.* hall, room; *(in ziekenhuis)* ward; *(v. vergadering, dans, enz.)* saloon; *(v. schouwburg)* auditorium.

zaalwachter *m.* usher.

zaan *v.* curds of milk.

zacht *b. n. (niet hard, week)* soft; *(v. behandeling)* gentle; *(v. straf)* mild; *(niet luid: v. geruis, gemurmel, muziek)* soft; *(v. toon)* mellow; *(v. klimaat, winter)* mild; *(niet ruw)* smooth; *(niet schel: v. kleur, tint)* soft; *(v. licht)* soft, mellow, subdued; *(niet pijnlijk)* easy; *(niet snel)* slow; *(geleidelijk: v. helling)* gentle; *bw.* softly, *enz.*

zachtaardig *b. n.* gentle, sweet, mild.

zachtheid *v.* softness; gentleness; mildness; smoothness.

zadel *m. en o.* saddle.

zadelen *o. w.* saddle.

zadelknop *m.* pommel.

zadelmaker *m.* saddler.

zadelmakerij *v.* saddlery; *(werkplaats)* saddler's shop.

zadelriem *m.* saddle-strap, saddle-girth.

zadeltas *v.* saddle-bag; *(aan fiets)* tool-bag.

zagen *o. w.* saw; *on. w. (ong.: op viool)* scrape; **over iets —,** harp on a subject.

zager *m.* sawyer; scraper.

zagerij *v.* sawing; sawing-mill.

zak *m. (alg.)* bag; *(groot: voor kolen, aardappelen, enz.)* sack; *(v. kledingstuk)* pocket; *(leren —, tabaks— enz.)* pouch;

(v. papier) bag; (Dk., Pl.) sac; (slop) blind alley.

zakalmanak m. pocket-almanac.

zakboekje o. note-book; (mil.) account-book.

zakdoek m. (pocket-)handkerchief.

zakelijk b. n. (wezenlijk: v. verschil) essential; (v. uiteenzetting, enz.) matter-of-fact; (degelijk: v. artikel, enz.) well-informed; (v. beheer) business-like; (niet persoonlijk) objective; (beknopt) concise, succinct; (zaakrijk: v. studie, enz.) matterful.

zakelijkheid v. essentialness; business-like character; objectivity; conciseness; matterfulness.

zakenman m. business-man.

zakenreis v. business-tour.

zakformaat o. pocket-size.

zakgeld o. pocket-money.

zakje o. (small) bag (pocket, &c.); paper bag, cornet.

zakken on. w. (v. water) sink; (v. barometer) fall; (v. muur, deur, enz.) sag; (v. aandelen) fall; (bij examen) fail, be plucked; (bij 't zingen) lose the key, go flat; (v. vliegtuig) lose height.

zakken o. w. (in zakken doen) bag, sack, put in sacks.

zakkenroller m. pickpocket.

zaklantaarn v. pocket-lantern; (elektr.) electric lamp, — torch.

zakmes o. pocket-knife.

zakuurwerk o. watch.

zakvormig b. n. sack-shaped, bag-shaped; (Pl.) saccate.

zakwoordenboek o. pocket dictionary.

zalf v. ointment, unguent, salve

zalig b. n. blessed, blissful; (heerlijk, verrukkelijk) divine, heavenly, delicious; (v. weer) glorious.

zaliger b. n. late, deceased; — gedachtenis, of blessed memory.

zaligheid v. salvation, bliss, beatitude.

zaligmakend b. n. beatific, saving, soul-saving.

Zaligmaker m. Saviour.

zaligmaking v. salvation.

zaligverklaring v. beatification.

zalm m. en v. salmon.

zalven o. w. (bij wijding) anoint; (gen.: v. wond, enz.) rub with ointment.

zalvend b. n. unctuous.

zalving v. anointing; (fig.) unction, unctuousness.

zand o. sand.

zandbank r. sand-bank, shallow; (in haven- of riviermond) bar, sand-bar.

zandblad o. (v. tabak) sand-leaf.

zandhaas m. white hare; (mil.) foot-slogger.

zandkoker m. sand-box.

zandlaag v. layer of sand.

zandloper m. hour-glass, sand-glass.

zandman m. sand-hawker, sand-vendor.

zandplaat v. sand-bank, flat, shoal.

zandruiter m. unhorsed rider, unseated horseman.

zandsteen o. sandstone.

zandvlo v. sand-flea, earth-flea.

zang m. (het zingen) singing, song; (lied, zangstuk) song; (v. gedicht) canto.

zanger m. singer, vocalist; (dichter) singer, songster, bard, poet; (vogel) (feathered) songster.

zangeres v. (female, lady) singer.

zangerig b. n. melodious.

zangkoor o. choir.

zangoefening v. singing-exercise.

zanguitvoering r. choral (vocal) concert.

zangvereniging v. choral (vocal) society.

zangvogel m. singing-bird, song-bird.

zaniken on. w. bother, nag.

zat b. n. satiated, satisfied; (dronken) fuddled, tight.

zaterdag m. Saturday.

zavel o. sabulous clay.

ze pers. vnw. she, her; they, them.

zebra m. zebra.

zede v. custom, usage.

zedelijk b. n. (bw.) moral(ly).

zedelijkheid v. morality.

zedeloos b. n. (bw.) immoral(ly), profligate(ly).

zedenbederf o. demoralization, corruption, depravity.

zedenleer v. moral philosophy, ethics.

zedenles v. moral (lesson).

zedenpreek v. moralizing sermon.

zedig b. n. modest; (meestal gemaakt —) demure.

zedigheid v. modesty; damureness.

zee v. sea, ocean; (dicht.) main.

zeeassurantie m. marine-insurance.

zeebad o. sea-bath.

zeebeer m. ursine seal.

zeeboezem m. gulf, bay.

zeebonk m. sea-dog, old salt.

zeedijk m. sea-bank, sea-dike, sea-wall.

zeedrift v. flotsam, floatage.

zeeduivel m. (Dk.) sea-devil, devil-fish, frog-fish.

zeeëngte v. strait(s), narrow(s).

zeef v. sieve, strainer; (voor koren, enz.) riddle; (voor kolen, enz.) screen.

zeegolf v. sea-wave, ocean-wave; (inham) gulf.

zeegras o. seaweed.

zeehaven v. port, harbour; (stad) sea-port.

zeehond m. seal.

zeehoofd o. pier, jetty.

zeekreeft m. lobster.

zeekwal v. jelly-fish.

zeel o. cord, rope, strap, trace.

zeelieden m. mv. seamen, sailors, mariners.

zeelt v. tench.

zeem o. shammy.

zeemacht v. naval forces.

zeemanshuis o. sailor's home.

zeemeermin v. mermaid.

zeemeeuw v. (sea-)gull, seamew.

zeemijl v. nautical mile, sea-mile.

zeemlap *m.* shammy (chamois) leather, wash-leather.
zeemogendheid *v.* naval (maritime) power.
zeenatie *v.* maritime nation.
zeep *v.* soap.
zeepaling *m.* sea-eel; conger.
zeepbakje *o.* soap-dish.
zeepfabriek *v.* soap-works.
zeepsop *o.* soap-suds.
zeepzieder *m.* soap-boiler.
zeepziederij *v.* soap-works, soap-house.
zeer *o.* sore, ache; — **doen,** ache, burt; (*iem.*) hurt, pain.
zeer *b. n.* sore.
zeer *bw. (alg.: met b. n. en bw.)* very; (*met w. w.*) (very) much; *ook:* highly, greatly; **al te —,** too much.
zeeroof *m.* piracy.
zeerover *m.* pirate, corsair.
zeeschuim *o.* foam of the sea, sea-foam.
zeespiegel *m.* sea-level, surface of the sea.
zeester *v.* star-fish, sea-star.
zeestraat *v.* strait(s).
zeevaarder *m.* navigator.
zeevaardig *b. n.* ready to sail.
zeevaart *v.* navigation.
zeewaardig *b. n.* seaworthy.
zeewezen *o.* maritime (nautical) affairs.
zeewier *o.* sea-weed, varec.
zeeziek *b. n.* seasick.
zeezout *o.* sea-salt.
zefier *m.* zephyr.
zege *v.* victory, triumph.
zegel *o. (v. lak, op document)* seal; (*v. post, belasting*) stamp; (*gezegeld papier*) stamped paper; (*voorwerp*) seal; stamp; **op —,** on stamped paper.
zegelafdruk *m.* seal; impressed stamp.
zegelen *o. w.* seal; (*recht*) place under seal; (*stempelen*) stamp.
zegellak *o.* sealing-wax.
zegelrecht *o.* stamp-duty.
zegelring *m.* seal-ring, signet-ring.
zegen *m.* blessing, bliss, benediction; *v.* (*visnet*) drag-net, seine.
zegenen *o. w.* bless.
zegening *v.* blessing, benediction.
zegenrijk *b. n.* salutary, most blessed.
zegepraal *v.* victory.
zegepralend *b. n.* triumphant, victorious.
zegetocht *m.* triumphal march.
zegevieren *on. w.* triumph.
zegge *v. (Pl.)* sedge; *zie* **zeggen.**
zeggen *o. w.* say; tell; *z. n., o.* saying.
zegsman *m.* informant, authority.
zegswijze *v.* saying, expression, (standing) phrase.
zeil *o. (sch.)* sail; (*op boot, enz.*) awning; (*dekkleed*) tarpaulin.
zeilboot *v.* sailing-boat.
zeildoek *o.* sail-cloth, canvas.
zeilen *on. w.* sail.
zeiler *m. (persoon)* yachtsman, sailing-man; (*schip*) sailer, sailing-ship.
zeilklaar *b. n.* ready to sail.

zeilsport *v.* yachting.
zeilwedstrijd *m.* sailing-match, regatta.
zeis *v.* scythe.
zeker *b. n. en onb. vnw. (veilig, buiten gevaar)* safe, secure; (*betrouwbaar*) sure; (*vaststaand*) certain; (*overtuigd*) certain, sure; (*ongenoemd, niet aan te duiden*) certain; *bw. (stellig)* certainly, surely, positively; for certain.
zekerheid *v. (het zeker zijn)* certainty; (*beslistheid*) decision; (*veiligheid*) safety, security; (*waarborg*) security.
zekerheidshalve *bw.* for security('s-sake), for safety('s sake).
zekering *v. (el.)* cut-out fuse.
zelden *bw.* seldom, rarely.
zeldzaam *b. n.* rare; (*schaars*) scarce; (*buitengewoon*) singular; *bw.* rarely; singularly, exceptionally.
zeldzaamheid *v.* rarity; scarceness; singularity; curiosity.
zelf *aanw. vnw.* self.
zelfbedrog *o.* self-deception, self-deceit.
zelfbegoocheling *v.* self-delusion.
zelfbehagen *o.* self-complacency.
zelfbeheersing *v.* self-command, self-control, self-possession.
zelfbehoud *o.* self-preservation.
zelfbeschikkingsrecht *o.* right of self-determination.
zelfbestuur *o.* self-government, autonomy.
zelfbewust *b. n.* self-assured, self-confident.
zelfkant *m.* selvage, selvedge, list; (*fig.*) outskirts.
zelfmoord *m.* suicide, self-murder.
zelfmoordenaar *m.* self-murderer.
zelfopoffering *v.* self-sacrifice, self-immolation.
zelfs *bw.* even.
zelfstandig *b. n.* independent; (*in eigen behoeften kunnende voorzien*) self-supporting; (*gram.*) substantive; *bw.* independently; substantively.
zelfstandigheid *v.* independence; (*samenstellend bestanddeel*) substance; (*zelfregering*) autonomy.
zelfverdediging *v.* self-defence.
zelfverloochening *v.* self-denial, self-renunciation, self-abnegation.
zelfvertrouwen *o.* self-confidence, self-reliance.
zelfvoldoening *v.* self-satisfaction.
zelfwerkend *b. n.* self-acting, automatic.
zelfzucht *v.* egoism, egotism, selfishness.
zeloot *m.* zealot; fanatic.
zemelen *v. mv.* bran.
zemen *b. n.* (of) shammy; *o. w.* leather, clean with wash-leather.
zendeling *m.* missionary.
zenden *o. w.* send; (*verzenden*) forward, dispatch.
zender *m.* sender; (*radio—*) transmitter.
zending *v. (het zenden)* sending, for-

warding, dispatch; (*het gezondene*) sending, consignment, shipment; (*opdracht*; *roeping*) mission; (*missie*) mission; mission-work.

zendtoestel *o.* transmitting set.

zengen *o. w. en on. w.* (*v. kleding, gras, enz.*) scorch; (*v. veren, haar, enz.*) singe.

zenging *v.* scorching; singeing.

zenuw *v.* nerve; (*fig.: ziel*) sinew.

zenuwaanval *m.* attack of nerves, nervous attack.

zenuwachtig *b. n.* nervous; (*fam.*) nervy, jumpy; (*opgewonden*) flurried, flustered.

zenuwachtigheid *v.* nervousness.

zenuwarts *m.* nerve doctor, nerve specialist, neurologist.

zenuwgestel *o.* nervous system.

zenuwknoop *m.* ganglion, nerve-knot, bundle of nerves; (*fig.*) bundle of nerves.

zenuwlijder *m.* nervous sufferer, neuropath.

zenuwlijdersinrichting *v.* mental home.

zenuwpijn *v.* neuralgia.

zenuwtrekking *v.* nervous spasm, — twitch; (*vooral v. gezicht*) tic.

zenuwziekte *v.* nervous disease, — complaint, neurosis.

zerk *v.* slab; (*op graf*) tombstone.

zes *telw.* six.

zesdaags *b. n.* six days'.

zesde *b. n.* sixth (part).

zeshoek *m.* hexagon.

zestal *o.* six, half a dozen.

zestien *telw.* sixteen.

zestiende *b. n.* sixteenth.

zestig *telw.* sixty.

zesvlak *o.* hexahedron.

zet *m.* (*duw, stoot*) push, shove; (*bij spel, fig.*) move.

zetel *m.* seat; (*v. bisschop*) chair; (*ambt*) see; (*v. regering, in parlement, enz.*) seat; (*v. maatschappij*) registered office.

zetelen *on. w.* sit, reside.

zetfout *v.* printer's (typographical) error, misprint.

zethaak *m.* (*sch.*) boat-hook; (*drukk.*) composing-stick.

zetmachine *v.* composing-machine.

zetmeel *o.* amyl, starch, farina.

zetsel *o.* (*drukk.*) matter; (*treksel: v. thee, enz.*) brew.

zetten *o. w.* (*plaatsen*) set, put, place; (*v. thee, koffie*) make; (*drukk.*) set up, compose; (*v. arm, been*) set; (*v. edelgesteenten*) set, mount; *w. w. zich —,* (*v. persoon*) sit down, take a seat; (*v. vrucht*) set.

zetter *m.* (*drukk.*) compositor; (*v. belasting*) assessor.

zetterij *v.* composing-room.

zeug *v.* sow.

zeur(der) *m.* bore.

zeuren *on. w.* worry, tease, bother; (*kletsen*) jaw, prose; (*drensen*) pule, whine.

zeven *o. w.* sieve; (*v. kolen*) screen; (*v. grint, enz.*) riddle.

zeven *telw.* seven.

zevende *b. n.* seventh (part).

zeventien *telw.* seventeen.

zeventig *telw.* seventy.

zeveren *on. w.* drivel, slobber, slaver.

zich *w. vnw.* oneself, himself, herself, themselves.

zicht *v.* reaping-hook, sickle.

zicht *o.* sight; (*op zee, enz.*) visibility; (*Z. N.: uitzicht*) view.

zichtbaar *b. n.* visible; (*merkbaar*) perceptible; (*blijkbaar, klaarblijkelijk*) manifest.

zichtbaarheid *v.* visibility; perceptibility.

zichtzending *v.* consignement on approval, goods sent on approval.

ziedaar *tw.* there; there is, that is.

zieden *o. w.* boil; *on. w.* seethe, boil.

ziehier *tw.* look here; (*bij aanbieding*) here you are.

ziek *b. n.* (*predikatief*) ill, diseased; (*attributief*) sick; — **worden,** fall ill.

zieke *m. en v.* sick person, patient, invalid.

ziekelijk *b. n.* sickly, ailing; (*fig.*) morbid, sickly.

ziekenauto *v.* (*motor*) ambulance.

ziekenhuis *o.* hospital, infirmary.

ziekenrapport *o.* sick-parade.

ziekentransport *o.* ambulance service.

ziekenverpleger *m.* (male, man) nurse, hospital attendant; (*mil.*) hospital orderly.

ziekenzaal *v.* hospital ward; (*in school, gesticht, enz.*) infirmary.

ziekte *v.* (*het ziek zijn*) illness, sickness; (*ernstige, langdurige —*) disease; (*kwaal*) complaint; (*v. maag, lever, enz.*) disorder; (*aandoening*) affection.

ziektetoestand *m.* state of disease, diseased condition.

ziekteverlof *o.* sick-leave.

ziel *v.* soul; spirit; (*v. kanon*) bore; (*v. fles*) kick.

zieleheil *o.* salvation.

zieleleed *o.* agony of the soul, agony of mind, mental suffering.

zielig *b. n.* (*treurig, beklagenswaardig*) piteous, pitiable; (*eenzaam, verlaten*) forlorn.

zielkunde *v.* psychology.

zielkundige *m.* psychologist.

zielloos *b. n.* (*zonder ziel*) soulless; (*dood*) inanimate, lifeless.

zielsangst *m.* anguish, mental agony.

zielsrust *v.* tranquillity of soul (of mind), peace of mind.

zielsverhuizing *v.* migration of souls, metempsychosis.

zieltogen *on. w.* be dying, be expiring, agonize.

zieltogend *b. n.* dying, expiring, moribund.

zielzorg *v.* cure of souls, spiritual charge.

zien *o. w.* (*alg.*) see; (*bemerken*) see, perceive; *on. w.* see; (*kijken*) look; *z. n., o.* seeing; sight.

zienderogen *bw.* visibly, perceptibly.
zienswijze *r.* opinion, view, judgment, way of thinking.
zier *r.* whit, atom.
ziezo *tw.* well, so; all right.
zift *v.* sieve.
ziften *o. w.* sift.
zifter *m.* sifter; *(fig.: ritter)* fault-finder, hair-splitter. [ing.
zifterij *r.* cavilling criticism, fault-find-
Zigeuner *m.* Zingaro, gipsy.
zigzagvormig *b. n.* zigzag.
zij *(enk.)* she; *(mr.)* they.
zij *v.* zie **zijde**.
zijaanval *m.* flank attack.
zij (de) *v. (alg.)* side; *(v. leger)* flank.
zijde *v.* silk.
zijdeachtig *b. n.* silky.
zijdelings *b. n. (r. blik, enz.)* lateral; *(r. verwantschap)* collateral; *(r. invloed, enz.)* indirect; *bw.* sideways, sidelong, indirectly.
zijderups *v.* silk-worm.
zijgebouw *o.* annex(e), wing.
zijkant *m.* side.
zijn *bez. vnw.* his, its; one's.
zijn *ww. (zelfstandig ww. en koppelww.)* be; *(hulpww.)* have; *z. n., o.* being.
zijnent *bw.* **te —,** at his house; at his place.
zijnentwege *bw.* **van —,** in his name; as for him. [river.
zijrivier *r.* affluent, confluent, tributary
zijspoor *o.* siding, side track.
zijstraat *v.* side-street, by-street, off-street.
zijtak *m. (r. boom)* side-branch, lateral branch; *(v. rivier)* affluent, tributary river, branch; *(v. gebergte)* spur, branch; *(v. familie)* collateral branch.
zijwaarts *bw.* sideward(s), side-ways.
zijweg *m.* side-way, by-way, by-road.
zilt, —ig *b. n.* saltish, briny.
ziltheid *v.* saltishness, brininess.
zilver *o.* silver; *(—en voorwerpen)* silver, plate, silver-plate; *(in staven)* bullion, bar-silver; *(wap.)* argent.
zilverachtig *b. n.* silvery, argentine.
zilverling *m. (Bijb.)* piece of silver, silverling.
zilverpapier *o.* silver-paper, tin-foil.
zilversmid *m.* silversmith.
zilverwerk *o.* silver-ware, silver-work, plate.
zin *m. (verstand, zielsvermogen)* sense; *(betekenis)* sense, meaning; *(lust, begeerte)* mind, desire; *(gram.: volzin)* sentence.
zindelijkheid *v.* cleanness, neatness, tidiness, cleanliness.
zingen *o. w. en on. w. (alg.)* sing; *(dicht.)* chant; *(v. vogels)* sing, carol, warble.
zingenot *o.* sensual pleasure(s).
zink *o.* zinc; *(H.)* spelter.
zinken *b. n.* zinc.
zinken *on. w.* sink.
zinklood *o. (dieplood)* sounding-lead; *(metaalsoort)* zinc-lead.

zinledig *b. n.* meaningless, devoid of sense.
zinledigheid *v.* meaninglessness, vacuity.
zinnebeeld *o.* emblem, symbol.
zinnelijk *b. n. (van de zinnen)* of the senses, sensuous; *(de zinnen strelend;* wellustig) sensual.
zinnelijkheid *v.* sensuality, sensualism.
zinneloos *b. n.* insane, mad, deranged.
zinneloosheid *v.* insanity, madness, alienation of mind.
zinsbedrog *o.,* **zinsbegoocheling** *v.* illusion, delusion.
zinsnede *r.* period; passage.
zinsontleding *r. (gram.)* analysis.
zinspelen *on. w.* **— op,** allude to, hint at.
zinspeling *v.* allusion.
zinspreuk *v.* motto, device; *(kernspreuk)* aphorism.
zinsverbijstering *v.* mental derangement, mental alienation.
zintuig *o.* organ of sense, sense-organ.
zinverwant *b. n.* synonymous.
zit *m.* seat.
zitbad *o.* sitz-bath, hip-bath.
zitbank *v.* bench, seat; *(meubel)* settee; *(in kerk)* pew.
zitplaats *v.* seat; *(in kerk)* sitting.
zitten *on. w.* sit; *(op tak: v. vogel)* be perched; *(v. kleding)* fit, sit.
zittend *b. n.* seated, sitting; *(v. leven)* sedentary; *(Pl.)* sessile.
zitting *v. (v. raad, commissie, enz.)* session; *(een enkele —, gewoonlijk:)* sitting; *(v. stoel)* seat, bottom.
zitvlak *o.* seat, sit-upon; *(iron.)* seat of honour.
zo *bw.* so, such, like that; *(zoëven)* just now, just; *(terstond)* presently, directly; *(op die manier)* thus, so, in this manner; *vw. (v. vergelijking)* as; *(v. voorwaarde; v. veronderstelling)* if.
zoals *vgw.* as; like.
zodanig *b. n.* such; **als —,** as such, in that capacity; *bw.* so, so much, in such a way, in such a manner.
zodat *vgw.* so that.
zode *v.* sod, turf.
zodoende *bw. (op die wijze)* thus, in that way (manner); *(bijgevolg)* so, consequently.
zodra *bw.* as soon as.
zoek *bw.* **het is —,** it has been mislaid, it is not to be found; **— raken,** get lost; **op — naar,** in search of.
zoeken *o. w. (voorwerp, persoon, enz.)* look for; *(woord)* look up; *(hulp, voordeel, enz.)* seek; *on. w.* seek, search; *z. n., o.* search, quest, hunt.
zoeklicht *o.* searchlight.
zoel *b. n.* balmy, mild.
zoemen *on. w.* buzz, hum.
zoen *m. (kus)* kiss; *(verzoening)* atonement, expiation, reconciliation.
zoenen *o. w. en on. w.* kiss.

zoenoffer *o.* expiatory sacrifice, sin-offering, peace offering.
zoet *b. n.* sweet; (*v. kind*) good.
zoetemelk *v.* sweet-milk.
zoetheid *v.* sweetness.
zoethout *o.* (*Pl.*) liquorice; (*wortel*) stick-liquorice.
zoetigheid *v.* sweetness; (*snoepgoed*) sweets, sweet stuff.
zoetwater *o.* fresh water.
zoetzuur *b. n.* sour-sweet; *z. n., o.* sweet pickles.
zoëven *bw.* just now, a moment (minute) ago.
zog *o.* (mother's) milk; (*sch.*) wake.
zogen *o. w.* suckle, nurse.
zogenaamd *b. n.* so-called, would-be, pretended.
zolder *m.* loft, garret; (*zoldering*) ceiling.
zoldering *v.* ceiling.
zolderkamertje *o.* garret, attic.
zolderraam *o.* garret-window; (*loodrecht*) dormer-window.
zolderverdieping *v.* attic-floor.
zomen *o. w.* hem; (*tn.*) seam.
zomer *m.* summer.
zomerachtig *b. n.* summerlike.
zomersproeten *v. mv.* freckles.
zon *v.* sun.
zondaar *m.* sinner.
zondag *m.* Sunday.
zondags *bw.* on Sunday, every Sunday.
zondagsrust *v.* Sunday rest.
zondares *v.* sinner.
zonde *v.* sin.
zondebok *m.* scapegoat.
zonder *vz.* without.
zonderling *b. n.* singular, queer, odd, eccentric; *z. n., m.* original, eccentric; (person), odd fellow.
zondig *b. n.* sinful.
zondigen *on. w.* sin.
zondvloed *m.* deluge.
zonnebaan *v.* ecliptic.
zonnebad *o.* sun-bath, insolation.
zonneblind *z. n., o.* Persian blind; *b. n.* sun-blind.
zonnebloem *v.* sunflower.
zonnebril *m.* sun-glasses, sun-goggles.
zonnecirkel *m.* solar cycle.
zonnedak *o.* awning.
zonnegloed *m.* heat (glow) of the sun.
zonnescherm *o.* parasol, sunshade; (*jaloezie*) sun-blind; (*voor winkelvenster*) (sun-shade) awning.
zonneschijn *m.* sunshine.
zonnestand *m.* (*hoogte*) height of the sun; (*stilstand*) solstice.
zonnesteek *m.* sun-stroke, heat-stroke.
zonnestelsel *o.* solar system.
zonnestraal *m.* sunbeam, ray of the sun.
zonnevlek *v.* sun-spot, solar spot.
zonnewijzer *m.* sun-dial.
zonnig *b. n.* sunny, sunshiny.
zonsondergang *m.* sunset, sundown.
zonsopgang *m.* sunrise.

zoogdier *o.* mammal.
zool *v.* sole.
zoölogie *v.* zoology.
zoom *m.* (*v. kleed, handdoek, enz.*) hem; (*v. bos, stad, enz.*) edge, border, skirt; (*v. rivier*) bank; (*tn.: koperslagerij*) seam.
zoon *m.* son.
zorg *v.* (*zorgzaamheid; verzorging*) care; (*bezorgdheid*) solicitude; (*ongerustheid, kommer*) anxiety, trouble; (*kopzorg*) worry; (*zorgstoel*) easy chair.
zorgeloos *b. n.* careless, light-hearted, improvident.
zorgeloosheid *v.* carelessness, improvidence.
zorgen *on. w.* care; — *voor,* take care of; (*van 't nodige voorzien*) provide for; *voor zichzelf* —, fend (provide) for oneself.
zorgvuldig *b. n.* (*bw.*) careful(ly).
zorgwekkend *b. n.* alarming; critical.
zot *b. n.* foolish; *z. n., m.* fool.
zotteklap, zottepraat *m.* foolish talk, nonsense, stuff and nonsense.
zottin *v.* fool.
zout *o.* salt; *b. n.* salt, saltish, briny.
zouten *o. w.* salt.
zoutgehalte *o.* salt-content.
zoutkeet *v.* salt-house, salt-works.
zoutmijn *v.* salt-mine.
zoutvaatje, zoutvat *o.* salt-cellar.
zoutzieder *m.* salt-maker.
zoutzuur *o.* muriatic acid, hydrochloric acid; *b. n.* muriatic, hydrochloric.
zoveel *onb. telw.* so much; — *als,* as much as.
zoveelste *n'th.*
zover *bw.* so far, as far as.
zowaar *bw.* really; sure enough.
zucht *m.* sigh; (*v. begeerte*) desire; (*naar kennis, macht*) appetite (for); (*ziekte*) dropsy.
zuchten *on. w.* sigh; (*kermen*) moan, groan; (*v. wind*) sigh, sough, moan.
zuid south.
zuidelijk *b. n.* southern; (*v. wind*) southerly; *bw.* southward.
zuiden *o.* south; *ten* — *van,* (to the) south of.
zuiderbreedte *v.* south(ern) latitude.
zuiderkruis *o.* Southern Cross.
zuiderlicht *o.* southern lights, aurora australis.
Zuiderzee *v.* Zuyder (Zuider) Zee.
zuidkust *v.* south coast.
zuidpool *v.* south pole, antarctic pole.
zuidvruchten *v. mv.* semi-tropical fruit, sub-tropical fruit.
Zuidzee *v. Stille* —, South-Sea, Pacific Ocean.
zuigeling *m.* baby, suckling, sucking child.
zuigen *o. w. en on. w.* suck.
zuiger *m.* (*persoon*) sucker; (*v. pomp, enz.*) sucker, piston; (*v. zuigfles*) sucker, mouthpiece; (*stof* —) aspirator.
zuigfles *v.* feeding-bottle, nursing-bottle.

zuigpomp v. sucking-pump; aspiring pump.

zuil v. pillar, column.

zuilengalerij v., **zuilengang** v. colonnade, arcade.

zuinig b. n. economical; careful; (*spaarzaam*) sparing; (*schraal*) sparing, frugal; bw. economically, carefully, frugally.

zuinigheid v. economy, sparingness, frugality, carefulness.

zuipen on. w. guzzle, booze, tipple, swill, soak; o. w. drink, quaff, guzzle.

zuiper m. toper, tippler, soaker, boozer.

zuivel o. dairy-products, butter and cheese.

zuivelfabriek v. dairy-factory, butter-and-cheese factory.

zuiver b. n. (*schoon:* v. handen, enz.) clean; (*helder, rein:* v. water, lucht, enz.) pure; (*zonder bijmengsels, niet vermengd*) pure, inadulterated; (v. geweten) clear; (*kuis*) pure, chaste; (*H.:* v. winst) net, clear; (*muz.:* v. klank, toon) pure; (v. stem) true; (v. uitspraak) correct; (*louter:* v. onzin, vooroordeel, enz.) pure, sheer, mere; bw. purely.

zuiveren o. w. (v. vuil) clean; (v. bloed, lucht, metaal, enz.) purify; (v. suiker, metalen) refine; (v. wond) deterge, absterge; (*ontsmetten*) disinfect; (*fig.:* v. zonden) cleanse; (v. lucht, atmosfeer) clear; w. w. **zich** —, clean oneself.

zuiverheid v. cleanness, purity; (*fig.*) pureness.

zuivering v. cleaning; purification; refinement; cleansing; clearing; purgation.

zuiveringszout o. aperient salt.

zulk such.

zullen (*toekomst*) 1e pers.: shall, 2e en 3e pers.: will; (*vragend*) 1e en 2e pers.: shall; 3e pers.: will; (*vermoeden, waarschijnlijkheid*) will; (*belofte; bevel; bedreiging*) shall; (*afspraak*) are to.

zurig b. n. sourish.

zurigheid v. sourishness.

zuring v. (*Pl.*) sorrel.

zus bw. (*zodanig, op zulk een wijze*) so, thus, in that manner.

zus v. sister.

zusterschool v. convent school.

zuur b. n. (*alg.*) sour; (*wrang*) sour, tart, acid; (v. smaak, uiterlijk) acid; (*scheik.*) acid, acetous; — **worden,** sour, turn sour; bw. sourly; z. n., o. (*scheik.*) acid; (*ingemaakt*) pickles.

zuurdeeg o. **zuurdesem** m. leaven.

zuurheid v. sourness; acidity.

zuurkijker m. sour-face, sour-faced fellow, crab.

zuurkool v. sourcrout, sauerkraut.

zuurstof v. oxygen.

zuurzoet b. n. sour-sweet.

zwaai m. (*met arm*) swing, sweep; (*met wapen, enz.*) flourish.

zwaaien o. w. (v. scepter) sway, wield; (v. hamer, zwaard, enz.) swing; (v. wapen: lans, enz.) brandish, flourish; (v.

vlag) wave, flourish; on. w. (v. dronken man) reel, make indents; (v. takken, enz.) sway, swing; (v. schip) swing, round, lurch.

zwaan m. swan; **jonge** —, cygnet.

zwaar b. n. (*alg.*) heavy; (*fors, zwaargebouwd*) heavily-built, massive, robust; (*log, plomp*) ponderous; (v. ziekte, straf) severe; (v. taak: moeilijk) heavy, difficult; (v. belasting) onerous; (v. examen) stiff, severe; (v. stem) deep; (v. kanon) heavy; (v. drank, tabak) strong; bw. heavily; etc.

zwaard o. (*mil.*) sword; (v. vaartuig) lee-board.

zwaardlelie v. (*Pl.*) sword-lily, gladiole.

zwaardvis m. sword-fish.

zwaargewicht o. (*sp.*) heavy-weight.

zwaarlijvig b. n. corpulent, obese, stout.

zwaarlijvigheid v. corpulence, obesity, stoutness.

zwaarmoedig b. n. melancholy, melancholic, spleeny.

zwaarte v. weight, heaviness.

zwaartekracht v. gravitation.

zwaartepunt o. centre of gravity; (*fig.*) main point, pith of the matter.

zwabber m. (*borstel*) swab, swabber, mop; (*scheepsjongen*) swabber; (*zwierbol*) loose fish.   [swathe.

zwachtel m. bandage, roller-bandage,

zwachtelen o. w. bandage, swathe; (*inbakeren*) swaddle.

zwager m. brother-in-law.

zwak b. n. (*alg.*) weak; (v. kind, plant, gezondheid*) delicate; (v. kreet, klank, kleur, weerstand) faint; (v. oude man) frail; ook: infirm; (*zedelijk* —) weak, weak-willed, weak-natured; (v. kandidaat) weak, shaky; bw. weakly, &c.; z. n., o. weakness.

zwakheid v. (*lichamelijk*) weakness; feebleness, debility; (v. wil) feebleness; (*zedelijk*) frailty.

zwakkeling m. en v. weakling.

zwakzinnigheid v. feeble-mindedness.

zwalken on. w. drift about, wander about.

zwaluw v. swallow.

zwaluwstaart m. swallow-tail; (*tn.*) dovetail; (*rok*) claw-hammer, swallow-tailed coat.

zwam v. fungus (*mv:* fungi) agaric; (*bij paarden*) spavin.

zwang m. **in** — **komen,** become the fash on (the vogue), come into vogue.

zwanger b. n. pregnant, enceinte, expecting.

zwangerschap v. pregnancy, gestation.

zwarigheid v. difficulty, objection; (*gewetensbezwaar*) scruple.

zwart b. n. black; z. n., o. **in het** — (**gekleed**), (dressed) in black; **de —en,** the blacks.

zwartgallig b. n. atrabilious, melancholy.

zwartgalligheid v. atrabiliousness, melancholy.

zwartmaking v. blackening.
zwavel v. sulphur.
zwaveligzuur o. sulphurous acid.
zwavelzuur b. n. sulphuric, sulpha-
tic; z. n., o. sulphuric acid, (oil of)
vitriol.
Zweden o. Sweden.
zweefbaan v. hanging railway, aerial
railway; (voor goederen) telpher line,
telpher way.
zweefmolen m. giant's stride.
zweefrek o. trapeze.
zweefvliegtuig o. glider, sailplane.
zweefvlucht v. volplane, glide.
zweem m. (v. vrees, waarheid, enz.)
semblance (v. spot, ijdelheid) touch; (v.
verschil) shade; (v. hoop; v. glimlach)
flicker.
zweep v. whip.
zweepslag m. lash; (knal) whip-
crack.
zweer v. ulcer, boil, sore.
zweet o. perspiration; sweat; (op muur)
moisture, sweat.
zweetdoek m. sweat-cloth.
zweetdrank m. sudorific.
zweetvoeten m. mv. sweating feet,
perspiring feet.
zwelgen o. w. swill, quaff; on. w.
(drinken) carouse, guzzle; (eten) guttle,
gormandize.
zwelgerij, zwelgpartij v. orgy.
zwellen on. w. swell.
zwelling v. swelling, tumour.
zwembad o. swimming-bath.
zwemblaas v. swimming-bladder, sound.
zwembroek v. bathing-drawers, swim-
ming-trunks.
zwemgordel m. swimming-belt.
zwemkunst v. art of swimming.
zwemmen on. w. swim.
zwemmer m. swimmer.
zwemvogel m. web-footed-bird, swim-
ming-bird.
zwendel m. swindling, fraud.
zwendelaar m. swindler, sharper.
zwendelen on. w. swindle.
zwengel m. (v. pomp) pump-handle,
sweep, lever; (v. wagen) splinter-bar,
wiffle-tree, swingle-tree; (v. molen)
wing; (draaikruk) crank; (v. vlegel)
swipple.
zwenken on. w. turn about, wheel
about, swing round; (mil.) wheel; (fig.)
change front.
zwenking v. swing, turn, wheel, swerve;

(mil.) wheel; (fig.) change of front, volte
face.
zweren on. w. (r. wond) ulcerate, fester;
(een eed doen) swear; o. w. swear.
zwerftocht m. wandering, ramble, pere-
grination.
zwerk o. welkin, firmament.
zwerm m. swarm.
zwerveling m. wanderer, vagabond,
tramp, rambler. [roma.
zwerven on. w. wander, ramble, rove,
zweten on. w. perspire; sweat; o. w.
sweat.
zwetsen on. w. boast, brag, talk big.
zweven on. w. (in de lucht) float; (in
vloeistof) be suspended, be in suspension; (v. vogel, enz.) hover; (over 't ijs)
glide.
zwezerik m. sweetbread
zwichten o. w. (sch.) swift; on. w. yield,
give way, give in.
zwier m. (draai, zwaai) flourish; (opschik) finery; (gratie) elegance; (luchtige
—) jauntiness, dash; (staatsie) pomp.
zwieren on. w. (v. dronken man) reel.
zwierig b. n. jaunty, dashing, stylish.
zwierigheid v. dashism, stylishness.
zwijgen on. w. (niet spreken) be silent;
(opeens —) fall silent; z. n., o. silence.
zwijgend b. n. silent; (v. karakter)
taciturn, silent; bw. silently, in silence.
zwijger m. taciturn (silent) person.
zwijgzaam b. n. taciturn, reticent, uncommunicative.
zwijm v. swoon, fainting-fit.
zwijmelen on. w. be dizzy, become dizzy.
zwijn o. pig, hog; (fig.) swine, pig,
hog.
zwijnenhoeder m. swine-herd.
zwijnenstal m. piggery, pigsty.
zwijntje o. piggy, porket; (sl.: fiets)
bike.
zwikboor v. auger, gimlet.
zwikken on. w. sprain.
zwikking v. sprain.
zwingel m. swingle.
zwingelen o. w. swingle; scutch.
Zwitserland o. Switzerland.
zwoegen on. w. toil, drudge, slave, slog
(away).
zwoeger m. drudge, toiler.
zwoel b. n. sultry, muggy, close.
zwoelheid v. sultriness, mugginess,
closeness.
zwoerd, zwoord o. pork-rind, bacon-
rind, rind of bacon.

ENGLISH-DUTCH

LIJST
VAN ONREGELMATIGE WERKWOORDEN
List of irregular verbs

to abide (by)	{ abode { abided	{ abode { abided	*blijven bij, zich houden aan*
to arise	arose	arisen	*ontstaan, verrijzen.*
to awake	{ awoke { awaked	{ awoke [1] { awaked [1]	*ontwaken, wekken.*
to be	was	been	*zijn.*
to bear	bore	borne	*dragen.*
		to be born	*geboren worden.*
to beat	beat	beaten	*slaan, verslaan.*
to become	became	become	*worden.*
to befall	befell	befallen	*gebeuren, overkomen.*
to begin	began	begun	*beginnen.*
to behold	beheld	beheld	*aanschouwen*
to bend	bent	bent	*buigen.*
to bereave	{ bereft { bereaved	{ bereft { bereaved	*beroven.*
to beseech	besought	besought	*smeken.*
to bet	{ bet { betted	{ bet { betted	*wedden.*
to bid	bade	bidden	*gelasten, gebieden, verzoeken.*
to bind	bound	bound	*binden.*
to bite	bit	bitten	*bijten.*
to bleed	bled	bled	*bloeden.*
to blend	blent	blent	*mengen.*
to blow	blew	blown	*blazen, waaien.*
to break	broke	broken	*breken.*
to breed	bred	bred	*kweken, fokken, opvoeden.*
to bring	brought	brought	*brengen.*
to build	built	built	*bouwen.*
to burn	{ burnt { burned	{ burnt { burned	*branden.*
to burst	burst	burst	*barsten.*
to buy	bought	bought	*kopen.*
to cast	cast	cast	*werpen*
to catch	caught	caught	*vangen.*
to chide	chid	{ chid { chidden	*bekijven, berispen.*
to choose	chose	chosen	*kiezen.*
to cleave	cleft	cleft	*klieven.*
to cling	clung	clung	*zich vastklemmen.*
to clothe	{ clothed { clad	{ clothed { clad	*kleden.*
to come	came	come	*komen.*
to cost	cost	cost	*kosten.*
to creep	crept	crept	*kruipen.*
to crow	{ crew { crowed	crowed	*kraaien.*
to cut	cut	cut	*snijden.*
to dare	{ durst { dared	dared	*durven.*
to deal	dealt	dealt	*handelen, uitdelen.*

1. Het verl. deelw. *awoke* (*awaked*) wordt meestal vervangen door *awakened* of door *woke*.

to dig	dug	dug	*graven.*
to do	did	done	*doen.*
to draw	drew	drawn	*trekken, tekenen.*
to dream	{ dreamt { dreamed	{ dreamt { dreamed	*dromen.*
to drink	drank	drunk	*drinken.*
to drive	drove	driven	*rijden, drijven.*
to dwell	dwelt	dwelt	*wonen.*
to eat	ate	eaten	*eten.*
to fall	fell	fallen	*vallen.*
to feed	fed	fed	*(zich) voeden.*
to feel	felt	felt	*voelen.*
to fight	fought	fought	*vechten.*
to find	found	found	*vinden.*
to flee	fled	fled	*vlieden, vluchten.*
to fling	flung	flung	*werpen, slingeren.*
to fly	flew	flown	*vliegen.*
to forbear	forbore	forborne	*nalaten.*
to forbid	forbade	forbidden	*verbieden.*
to forget	forgot	forgotten	*vergeten.*
to forgive	forgave	forgiven	*vergeven.*
to forsake	forsook	forsaken	*verlaten, in de steek laten.*
to freeze	froze	frozen	*vriezen.*
to get	got	got	*krijgen.*
to gild	{ gilt { gilded	{ gilt { gilded	*vergulden.*
to gird	{ girt { girded	{ girt { girded	*omgorden.*
to give	gave	given	*geven.*
to go	went	gone	*gaan.*
to grind	ground	ground	*malen, slijpen.*
to grow	grew	grown	*groeien.*
to hang	hung	hung	*hangen.*
to have	had	had	*hebben.*
to hear	heard	heard	*horen.*
to hew	hewed	{ hewn { hewed	*houwen.*
to hide	hid	{ hidden { hid	*verbergen.*
to hit	hit	hit	*treffen.*
to hold	held	held	*houden.*
to hurt	hurt	hurt	*bezeren.*
to keep	kept	kept	*houden, bewaren.*
to kneel	{ knelt { kneeled	{ knelt { kneeled	*knielen.*
to knit	{ knitted { knit	{ knitted { knit	*breien.*
to know	knew	known	*wen kennen.*
to lay	laid	laid	*leggen.*
to lead	led	led	*leiden.*
to lean	{ leant { leaned	{ leant { leaned	*leunen.*
to leap	{ leapt { leaped	{ leapt { leaped	*springen.*
to learn	{ learnt { learned	{ learnt { learned	*leren.*
to leave	left	left	*verlaten, laten.*
to lend	lent	lent	*lenen.*
to let	let	let	*laten.*
to lie	lay	lain	*liggen.*
to light	{ lighted { lit	{ lighted { lit	*aansteken.*
to lose	lost	lost	*verliezen.*

to make	made	made	*maken.*
to mean	meant	meant	*menen, bedoelen, betekenen.*
to meet	met	met	*ontmoeten.*
to mow	mowed	mown	*maaien.*
to overcome	overcame	overcome	*overwinnen.*
to pay	paid	paid	*betalen.*
to put	put	put	*leggen, plaatsen, zetten.*
to read	read	read	*lezen.*
to rend	rent	rent	*scheuren, verscheuren.*
to rid	rid	rid	*bevrijden.*
to ride	rode	ridden	*rijden.*
to ring	rang	rung	*bellen, luiden.*
to rise	rose	risen	*opstaan, opgaan, stijgen.*
to run	ran	run	*hard lopen, hollen.*
to saw	sawed	{ sawn / sawed	*zagen.*
to say	said	said	*zeggen.*
to see	saw	seen	*zien.*
to seek	sought	sought	*zoeken.*
to sell	sold	sold	*verkopen.*
to send	sent	sent	*zenden.*
to set	set	set	*zetten.*
to sew	sewed	{ sewn / sewed	*naaien.*
to shake	shook	shaken	*schudden.*
to shear	sheared	{ shorn / sheared	*scheren (v. schapen)*
to shed	shed	shed	*storten, vergieten.*
to shine	shone	shone	*schijnen.*
to shoe	shod	shod	*beslaan.*
to shoot	shot	shot	*schieten.*
to show	showed	shown	*tonen, laten zien.*
to shred	shred	shred	*aan repen snijden.*
to shrink	shrank	shrunk	*terugdeinzen.*
to shut	shut	shut	*sluiten.*
to sing	sang	sung	*zingen.*
to sink	sank	sunk	*zinken.*
to sit	sat	sat	*zitten.*
to slay	slew	slain	*doden, doodslaan.*
to sleep	slept	slept	*slapen.*
to slide	slid	slid	*glijden.*
to sling	slung	slung	*werpen (met een slingerende beweging).*
to slink	slunk	slunk	*sluipen.*
to slit	slit	slit	*splijten.*
to smell	{ smelt / smelled	{ smelt / smelled	*ruiken.*
to smite	smote	smitten	*slaan, treffen.*
to sow	sowed	{ sown / sowed	*zaaien.*
to speak	spoke	spoken	*spreken.*
to speed	sped	sped	*(zich) spoeden.*
to spell	{ spelt / spelled	{ spelt / spelled	*spellen.*
to spend	spent	spent	*uitgeven.*
to spill	{ spilt / spilled	{ spilt / spilled	*morsen, storten.*
to spin	spun	spun	*spinnen.*
to spit	{ spit / spat	{ spit / spat	*spuwen.*
to split	split	spilt	*splijten.*
to spoil	{ spoilt / spoiled	{ spoilt / spoiled	*bederven.*

to spread	spread	spread	*verspreiden.*
to spring	sprang	sprung	*springen.*
to stand	stood	stood	*staan.*
to steal	stole	stolen	*stelen, sluipen.*
to stick	stuck	stuck	*blijven steken, steken, plak-ken.*
to sting	stung	stung	*steken, prikken.*
to stink	{ stank { stunk	stunk	*stinken.*
to strew	strewed	{ strewn { strewed	*strooien.*
to stride	strode	stridden	*schrijden.*
to strike	struck	struck	*slaan; staken.*
to string	strung	strung	*aanrijgen; besnaren.*
to strive	strove	striven	*streven.*
to strow	strowed	{ strowed { strown	*strooien.*
to swear	swore	sworn	*zweren.*
to sweat	{ sweat { sweated	{ sweat { sweated	*zweten.*
to sweep	swept	swept	*vegen.*
to swell	swelled	{ swelled { swollen	*zwellen.*
to swim	swam	swum	*zwemmen.*
to swing	swung	swung	*zwaaien.*
to take	took	taken	*nemen.*
to teach	taught	taught	*onderwijzen.*
to tear	tore	torn	*scheuren.*
to tell	told	told	*vertellen.*
to think	thought	thought	*denken.*
to thrive	throve	thriven	*voorspoed hebben.*
to throw	threw	thrown	*werpen.*
to thrust	thrust	thrust	*stoten.*
to tread	trod	{ trodden { trod	*betreden.*
to understand	understood	understood	*verstaan, begrijpen.*
to wake	{ woke { waked	{ woke { waked	*ontwaken, wekken.*
to wear	wore	worn	*dragen (aan 't lichaam).*
to weave	wove	woven	*weven.*
to weep	wept	wept	*wenen.*
to win	won	won	*winnen.*
to wind	wound	wound	*winden.*
to withdraw	withdrew	withdrawn	*(zich) terugtrekken.*
to withhold	withheld	withheld	*onthouden, terughouden.*
to withstand	withstood	withstood	*weerstaan.*
to wring	wrung	wrung	*wringen.*
to write	wrote	written	*schrijven.*

A

a een.

abandon [ə'bændn] *vt.* verlaten, aan
zijn lot overlaten; opgeven, prijsgeven;
(*H.*) afstand doen van, abandonneren.

abandoned [ə'bændənd] *adj.* verlaten;
opgegeven, prijsgegeven; verdorven,
losbandig.

abase [ə'beis] *vt.* vernederen; verlagen;
vr. — *oneself,* zich vernederen.

abash [ə'bæʃ] *vt.* beschamen, verlegen
maken.

abate [ə'beit] *vt.* verminderen, verlagen;
uit de weg ruimen, verwijderen, wegnemen; afschaffen; (*recht*) vernietigen; verzachten, lenigen; *vi.* verminderen, afnemen, bedaren; (*recht*) ongeldig worden.

abatement [ə'beitmənt] het verminderen *o.*; het verwijderen *o.*, verwijdering
v.; afschaffing *v.*; vernietiging *v.*; verzachting, leniging *v.*; korting *v.*, afslag
m., rabat *o.*

abat(t)is [ə'bæti] (*mil.*) verhakking *v.*

abattoir [æbə'twâ] slachthuis *o.*

abbess ['æbis] abdis *v.*

abbey ['æbi] abdij *v.*; abdijkerk *v.*

abbot ['æbət] abt *m.*

abbreviate [ə'briivieit] *vt.* afkorten, verkorten; bekorten; (*v. breuk*) herleiden;
[ə'briiviit] *adj.* verkort, afgekort.

abbreviation [əbriivi'eiʃən] afkorting,
verkorting *v.*; (*v. breuk*) herleiding *v.*

abdicate ['æbdikeit] *vi.* & *vt.* afstand
doen (van), aftreden, de regering (de)
kroon) neerleggen.

abdication [æbdi'keiʃən] afstand (van
de troon), troonsafstand *m.*

abdomen [æb'doumən, 'æbdomən] onderbuik *m.*, buikholte *v.*; (*v. insekt*)
achterlijf *o.*

abduct [æb'dəkt] ontvoeren, wegvoeren; afvoeren; wegtrekken.

abduction [æb'dəkʃən] ontvoering,
wegvoering *v.*; afvoering *v.*; onttrekking *v.*; (*v. spier*) afwending *v.*

abet [ə'bet] aanzetten, aanhitsen, ophitsen; opstoken, aanstoken; steunen,
bevorderen (*v. misdrijf, enz.*).

abeyance [ə'beiəns] (tijdelijke) onbe-
heerdheid *v.*; toestand van onzekerheid,
onbesuisheid *v.*; tijdelijke opschorting *v.*

abhor [əb'ho:] verfoeien, verafschuwen,
gruwen van, een afschuw hebben van.

abhorrence [əb'hərəns] afschuw *m.*,
afgrijzen *o.*, gruwel *m.*

abide [ə'baid] verblijven, vertoeven, verblijf houden, wonen; volharden; vasthouden (aan); verdragen, uitstaan;
blijven bij, zich houden aan; doorstaan;
onder de ogen zien.

ability [ə'biliti] bekwaamheid, bevoegdheid *v.*; vermogen *o.*; (*H.*) solventie,
solvabiliteit *v.*; *mv.:* **abilities,** talenten,
begaafdheden, natuurlijke gaven.

abject [æbdʒikt] *adj.* laag, verachtelijk,

gemeen; ellendig, diepgezonken; *sb.*
laaghartige *m.*; verachtelijk wezen *o.*;
verworpeling *m.*

abjure [æb'dʒûə] afzweren; bij ede herroepen.

ablactate [æ'blakteit] spenen.

ablaze [ə'bleiz] brandend, in prand,
vlammend, in vlammen; in lichterlaaie;
gloeiend (*with,* van); vol vuur; opgewonden.

able ['eibl] bekwaam, in staat; bevoegd,
knap, handig, bedreven; (*v. matroos*) vol;
be —, kunnen, vermogen, in staat zijn.

abloom [ə'blûm] in (volle) bloei.

ablush [ə'bləʃ] blozend.

ablution [ə'blûʃən] reiniging, wassing;
ablutie; ablutiewater *o.*

abnegate ['æbnigeit] verloochenen; opgeven, prijsgeven; zich ontzeggen.

abnormal [əb'no:məl] abnormaal, onregelmatig, afwijkend.

aboard [ə'bo:d] aan boord; aan boord
van.

abode [ə'boud] verblijf *o.*, verblijfplaats
v.; woning, woonplaats *v.*

abolish [ə'bəliʃ] afschaffen, opheffen,
een einde maken aan; buiten werking
stellen; vernietigen.

abolition [æbə'liʃən] afschaffing *v.*;
vernietiging *v.*

abominable [ə'bəminəbl] afschuwelijk,
verfoeilijk.

abomination [əbəmi'neiʃən] afschuw,
gruwel *m.*; afschuwelijkheld *v.*

abortion [ə'bo:ʃən] ontijdige bevalling,
miskraam *v.*; vruchtafdrijving *v.*; mis-
lukte plant of bloem *v.*; (*fig.*) mislukking *v.*

abound [ə'baund] vol zijn van, in overvloed aanwezig zijn, in overvloed voorkomen; — *in* (*with*), overvloeien van,
overvloed hebben van; wemelen van.

about [ə'baut] *prep.* om, rondom, in de
buurt van; ongeveer, zowat; omstreeks,
omtrent; over, betreffende, met betrekking tot; aan, bij; wegens; *adv.* om; in
't rond; in omloop; in de buurt; ongeveer; op 't punt; op de been.

above [ə'bəv] *prep.* boven, boven...
uit, boven... verheven; meer dan; *adv.*
boven; hierboven; *adj.* bovengenoemd;
bovenvermeld; bovenstaand.

above-mentioned [ə'bəv'menʃənd] bovenvermeld, bovengenoemd.

above-said [ə'bəv'sed] bovengenoemd,
bovenvermeld.

abrade [ə'breid] schaven, afschaven, af-
schuren.

abreast [ə'brest] naast elkander, op een
rij; (*sch.*) dwars.

abridge [ə'bridʒ] verkorten, bekorten;
besnoeien, beperken, verminderen; vereenvoudigen; — *of,* beroven van, ver
korten in.

abroach [ə'broutʃ] (r. vat) aangestoken.

abroad [ə'broːd] naar alle kanten, in 't rond, alom; (r. gerucht) in omloop; ruchtbaar; buitenslands; (soms:) van huis, buitenshuis.

abrogate ['æbrəgeit] afschaffen, opheffen, intrekken.

abrogation [æbrə'geiʃən] afschaffing, opheffing, intrekking v.; herroeping r.

abrupt [ə'brɒpt] steil; plotseling, haastig, schielijk; (r. stijl) afgebroken; hortend; (Pl.) afgeknot.

abscess ['æbsis] gezwel, ettergezwel, abces o.

abscond [əb'skɒnd] zich verbergen, zich verschuilen; zich (stilletjes) uit de voeten maken.

absence ['æbsəns] afwezigheid v.; gebrek, gemis o., ontstentenis v.; (mil.) appèl o.

absent ['æbsənt] afwezig; verstrooid, afgetrokken.

absent-minded(ly) ['æbsənt'maindid(li)] adj. (adv.) verstrooid, afgetrokken.

absolute ['æbsəl(j)ût] adj. absoluut, volstrekt, volslagen; volmaakt, volkomen; onbeperkt; onvoorwaardelijk.

absolution [æbsə'l(j)ûʃən] vrijspraak v.; (r. zonden) absolutie, vergiffenis r.; ontheffing v.

absolve [əb'zɒlv] vrijspreken; (kath.) de absolutie geven; (r. belofte, enz.) ontslaan.

absorb [əb'soːb] opzuigen, opslorpen, (in zich) opnemen; (fig.) verslinden, verzwelgen; geheel in beslag nemen.

absorption [əb'soːpʃən] opslorping, absorptie r.

abstain [əb'stein] zich onthouden (from, van).

abstainer [əb'steinə] onthouder m.

abstemiousness [əb'stîmiəsnis] matigheid v.

abstention [əb'stenʃən] onthouding v.

absterge [əb'stə:dʒ] afwissen; reinigen, zuiveren.

abstergent [əb'stə:dʒənt] adj. zuiverend, reinigend· sb. zuiverend (reinigend) middel o.

abstinence ['æbstinəns] onthouding v.· wapenschorsing v.

abstract ['æbstrækt] adj. abstract, afgetrokken; diepzinnig; theoretisch; (r. getallen) onbenoemd.

abstract ['æbstrækt] sb. afgetrokken begrip o.; abstractie v.; overzicht, uittreksel, kort begrip o.

abstruse(ly) [əbs'trûs(li)] adj. (adv.) diepzinnig, duister, onverstaanbaar.

absurd [əb'sə:d] ongerijmd, dwaas, onzinnig, belachelijk.

absurdity [əb'sə:diti] ongerijmdheid, dwaasheid, onzinnigheid, absurditeit v.

abundance [ə'bɒndəns] overvloed m.; (grote) menigte r.

abundant [ə'bɒndənt] overvloedig; rijk (in, aan).

abuse [ə'bjûz] rt. misbruiken, misbruik maken van; mishandelen; uitschelden, beschimpen; beledigen.

abuse [ə'bjûs] sb. misbruik o., misstand m.; beschimping r., scheldwoorden o. mr.; belediging v.

abusive [ə'bjûsiv] verkeerd; beledigend.

abut [ə'bɒt] grenzen aan, palen aan.

abutment [ə'bɒtmənt] belending r.; aanrakingspunt o.; steunpilaar, steun m.; beer, schoor m.; bruggenhoofd o.

abyss [ə'bis] afgrond m.; peilloze diepte r.; (r. ellende) poel m.; hel v.

academy [ə'kædəmi] academie, hogeschool r.

accede [æk'sîd] toetreden (to, tot), toestemmen (to, in), instemmen (to, met).

accelerate [æk'seləreit] verhaasten, bespoedigen; versnellen; vervroegen; te vroeg dateren.

acceleration [ækselə'reiʃən] bespoediging v.; versnelling v.

accent ['æksənt] sb. accent o., klemtoon, nadruk m.; klankteken, toonteken o.; stembuiging, uitspraak r.; toon m.

accent [æk'sent] rt. accentueren, de nadruk leggen op; accenten plaatsen op.

accept [æk'sept] aannemen; aanvaarden; (H.) accepteren.

acceptable [æk'septəbl] aannemelijk; aangenaam, welkom.

acceptance [æk'septəns] aanneming r., het aannemen; (gunstige) ontvangst v.; (H.) accept o., acceptatie r.

access ['ækses, æk'ses] toegang m.; nadering v.; (v. ziekte) aanval m.; vlaag, opwelling v.; toeneming, vermeerdering, aangroeiing r.; genaakbaarheid r.

accessible [æk'sesibl] toegankelijk; genaakbaar; vatbaar, ontvankelijk.

accessory [æk'sesəry] adj. bijkomstig, bijkomend, bijbehorend; ondergeschikt, van ondergeschikt belang; medeplichtig.

accident ['æksidənt] toeval o., toevalligheid v.; ongeluk, ongeval o.; toevallige omstandigheid r.; bijkomstigheid v.; (v. terrein, enz.) ongelijkheid, onregelmatigheid v.

accidental [æksi'dentəl] adj. toevallig; bijkomstig, bijkomend.

acclaim [ə'kleim] vt. toejuichen, begroeten (als).

acclimatize [ə'klaimətaiz] acclimatiseren.

acclivity [ə'kliviti] schuinte, (opwaartse) helling v.

accommodate [ə'kɒmədeit] aanpassen (to, aan); bijleggen, vereffenen, verzoenen; schikken, voegen; voorzien (with, van).

accommodation [əkɒmə'deiʃən] aanpassing v.; schikking r., vergelijk o., akkoord o.; inschikkelijkheid v.; gerief, gemak o.

accompaniment [ə'kɒmpənimənt] begeleiding v., accompagnement o.

accompany [ə'kɒmpəni] vergezellen, begeleiden; (muz.) begeleiden, accompagneren; (fig.) vergezeld doen gaan (**with**, met); gepaard gaan, samengaan (**with**, met).

accomplice [ə'kɔmplis] medeplichtige m. & v.

accomplish [ə'kɔmpliʃ] volbrengen, tot stand brengen; vervullen, ten uitvoer brengen; voltooien, volmaken; (v. contract) nakomen; (v. afstand) afleggen; (volledig) uitrusten.

accomplished [ə'kɔmpliʃt] beschaafd; talentvol, welonderlegd; (v. feit) voldongen.

accomplishment [ə'kɔmpliʃmənt] vervulling r.; voltooiing v.; uitvoering v.; volmaaktheid r.; kennis, bekwaamheid v., (verworven) talent o.

accord [ə'kɔ:d] ri. overeenstemmen, overeenkomen.

accordance [ə'kɔ:dəns] overeenstemming v.; **in — with**, overeenkomstig.

according [ə'kɔ:diŋ] adj. overeenstemmend; prep. **— as,** naarmate, naargelang, al naar; **— to,** naar gelang van; overeenkomstig, volgens.

accordingly [ə'kɔ:diŋli] adv. diensvolgens, dienovereenkomstig; bijgevolg.

accordion [ə'kɔ:diən] harmonika v., accordeon o.

accost [ə'kɔst] rt. aanspreken, het woord richten tot; aanklampen.

accouchement [ə'kûʃmo:ŋ] bevalling v.

accoucheur [ækû'ʃə] verloskundige m.

account [ə'kaunt] rt. rekenen, houden voor, beschouwen als, achten; ri. **— for,** rekenschap geven van, verantwoorden; verklaren; (v. wild) voor zijn rekening nemen, neerleggen, doden; (sp.: cricket) maken; nemen; sb. rekening, berekening v.; afrekening v.; rekenschap, verklaring v.; bericht, verslag, verhaal, relaas o.; schatting r.; betekenis v., belang, gewicht o.; voordeel, profijt o.; (H.) rescontre v.; tijdrekening v.

accountability [əkauntə'biliti] verantwoordelijkheid r.; toerekenbaarheid v.

accountable [ə'kauntəbl] verantwoordelijk; toerekenbaar; **— (for),** verklaarbaar.

accountant [ə'kauntənt] (hoofd)boekhouder; administrateur m.; accountant m.

account current [ə'kaunt'kərənt] rekening-courant v.

accredit [ə'kredit] geloof schenken aan; ingang doen vinden; accrediteren; machtigen; krediet verschaffen; toeschrijven (**to,** aan).

accrescence [æ'kresns] aanwas m.

accrete [æ'krît] vi. samengroeien; zich hechten (**to,** aan).

accretion [ə'krîʃən] groei, aangroei.

accrue [ə'krû] aangroeien, toenemen, oploonen; voortspruiten (**from,** uit).

accumulate [ə'kjûmjuleit] vt. opeenstapelen, opeenhopen, ophopen; bijeenbrengen.

accumulation [əkjûmju'leiʃən] op-

eenstapeling, ophoping v.; vermeerdering v.; hoop, stapel m.

accumulator [ə'kjûmjuleitə] (el.) accumulator m.

accuracy ['ækjurəsi] nauwkeurigheid, nauwgezetheid, stiptheid.

accurate(ly) ['ækjurit(li)] adj. (adv.) nauwkeurig, nauwgezet, stipt, accuraat.

accusation [ækju'zeiʃən] aanklacht, beschuldiging v.

accuse [ə'kjûz] beschuldigen, aanklagen.

accuser [ə'kjûzə] beschuldiger, aanklager m.

accustom [ə'kɔstəm] vt. gewennen (**to,** aan); vr. **— oneself to,** zich gewennen aan.

accustomed [ə'kɔstəmd] gewoon, gewend; gebruikelijk.

ace [eis] (spel) aas, één; kleinigheid v.

acerbate ['æsəbeit] verzuren, verbitteren.

acervate [ə'sə:vit] bij elkaar groeiend.

acetylene [æ'setilîn] acetyleen(gas) o.

ache [eik] (voortdurende) pijn v.

achieve [ə'tʃîv] volbrengen, voleinden; tot stand brengen; verwerven; bereiken; behalen.

achievement [ə'tʃîvmənt] volbrenging, voleinding v.; verrichting v.; verwerving r.; (roemrijke) daad v., wapenfeit o.; succes o.

acid ['æsid] adj. zuur, scherp.

acknowledge [ə'knɔliɔʒ] erkennen, toegeven, bekennen; erkentelijk zijn voor, bedanken voor; (v. groet) beantwoorden.

acknowledg(e)ment [ək'nɔlidʒmənt] erkenning v.; bekentenis v.; (bewijs van) erkentelijkheid v., dank m.; (v. groet) beantwoording v.; bericht o. van ontvangst.

acme ['ækmi] toppunt, hoogtepunt o.; (fig.) glanspunt o.

acne ['ækni] puist, gezichtspuist v.

acock [ə'kɔk] (v. hoed) scheef, schuinstaand, op één oor; tartend.

acolyte ['ækəlait] misdienaar, acoliet m.; helper m.

acorn ['eikɔ:n] eikel m.

acquaintance [ə'kweintəns] bekendheid v.; kennismaking v.; bekende m., kennis(sen) m. (mv.).

acquainted [ə'kweintid] bekend (**with,** met); op de hoogte (**with,** van).

acquiesce ['ækwi'es] berusten (**in,** in), zich neerleggen (**in,** bij); toestemmen (**in,** in).

acquirable [ə'kwaiərəbl] verkrijgbaar.

acquire [ə'kwaiə] verkrijgen, verwerven; **—d,** aangeleerd.

acquisition [ækwi'ziʃən] verkrijging, verwerving v.; aanschaffing v.; aanwinst v., (het) verworvene o.; talent o.

acquit [ə'kwit] vrijpraten; ontslaan; **— oneself of,** zich kwijten van.

acquittal [ə'kwitəl] vrijspraak v.; ontslag o.; ontheffing r.

acquittance [ə'kwitəns] vrijspraak v.; ontslag o.; kwijting, vereffening; kwitantie v.

acrid ['ækrid] scherp, bijtend, bitter, wrang, bits.

acrimonious(ly) [ækri'mouniəs(li)] adj. (adv.) scherp, bits.

acrobat ['ækrəbæt] acrobaat m.

across [ə'krɔ:s] adv. gekruist, dwars, overdwars; aan de overkant; prep. (dwars) over, (dwars) door; aan gene zijde van, aan de overkant van.

act [ækt] sb. daad, handeling v.; wet v.; akte v., bedrijf o.; proefschrift o., verhandeling, dissertatie v.; vt. opvoeren; (v. rol) spelen; voorwenden; vi. handelen, te werk gaan, handelend optreden, doen; werken; zich gedragen; acteren.

acting ['æktiŋ] adj. werkend; tijdelijk; waarnemend; sb. handeling, daad v.; (het) toneelspelen, spel o.

action ['ækʃən] handeling, daad v.; actie v.; werking v.; aanklacht v., proces o., rechtszaak v.; (mil.) gevecht, treffen o.; werk o., mechaniek v. & o.

active ['æktiv] werkend, werkzaam, actief, bedrijvig; (gram.) bedrijvend; (v. markt) levendig.

activity [æk'tiviti] werkzaamheid, bedrijvigheid, activiteit v.; bezigheid v.

actor ['æktə] toneelspeler m.

actress ['æktris] toneelspeelster v.

actual ['æktjuəl] adj. werkelijk, wezenlijk; feitelijk; actueel.

actuality [æktju'æliti] werkelijkheid v.; bestaande toestand m.; actualiteit v.

actualize ['æktjuəlaiz] verwezenlijken.

actuate ['æktjueit] in beweging brengen, aan de gang maken; aansporen, aanzetten, (aan)drijven.

acuity [ə'kjûiti] scherpheid v.; acute toestand m.

acute(ly) [ə'kjût(li)] adj. (adv.) scherp, scherpzinnig; doordringend, schel; (v. vraagstuk) dringend; (v. ziekte) acuut; schrander.

acuteness [ə'kjûtnis] scherpte, scherpzinnigheid v.; (het) acuut zijn.

adage ['ædidʒ] spreekwoord o., spreuk v., gezegde o.

adapt [ə'dæpt] vt. geschikt maken, passend maken, aanpassen; (fig.) bewerken (from, naar); vr. — oneself to, zich aanpassen aan.

adaptability [ədæptə'biliti] aanpassingsvermogen o.

add [æd] bijvoegen, bijdoen; toevoegen; optellen, samentellen.

adder ['ædə] adder v.

addict [ə'dikt] — oneself to, zich overgeven aan; —ed to, verslaafd aan.

addition [ə'diʃən] toevoeging v.; vermeerdering v.; optelling v.

additional [ə'diʃənəl] adj. bijgevoegd aanvullend; extra.

addle ['ædl] bedorven; verward.

address [ə'dres] vt. aanspreken, toespreken; richten, adresseren; (H.) af-zenden, consigneren; verwijzen (to, naar); vr. — oneself to, zich wenden tot, zich richten tot; zich toeleggen op, aanpakken; sb. adres o.; toespraak, rede v.

addressee [ædre'sî] geadresseerde m.

addresser [ə'dresə] afzender m.; adressant m.

adduce [ə'djûs] aanhalen, aanvoeren.

adept [ə'dept] sb. ingewijde m.; deskundige m.

adequate ['ædikwit] geëvenredigd (to, aan); geschikt, gepast, doelmatig; voldoende.

adhere [əd'hîə] (aan)kleven, aanhangen.

adherence [əd'hîərəns] aankleving v.; aanhankelijkheid v.

adherent [əd'hîərənt] aanhanger m.

adhibition [ædhi'biʃən] aanhechting v.; toepassing v.; toediening v.

adit ['ædit] toegang m.; horizontale schacht v. van een mijn.

adjacent [ə'dʒeisənt] aangrenzend; nabijgelegen; (v. hoek) aanliggend.

adjective ['ædʒektiv] sb. bijvoeglijk naamwoord o.; adj. bijgevoegd.

adjoin [ə'dʒɔin] bijvoegen, toevoegen, aanhechten; grenzen aan.

adjourn [ə'dʒə:n] vt. uitstellen, verdagen, schorsen.

adjournment [ə'dʒə:nmənt] uitstel o.; verdaging, schorsing v.

adjudge [ə'dʒədʒ] toekennen, toewijzen; beslissen.

adjudication [ədʒûdi'keiʃən] toewijzing v.

adjunct ['ædʒəŋkt] adj. toegevoegd, verbonden; sb. aanhangsel, bijvoegsel o.; bijkomende omstandigheid v.; helper, adjunct m.; (v. professor) assistent m.; (gram.) bepaling v.

adjuration [ædʒuə'reiʃən] bezwering v.

adjure [ə'dʒûə] bezweren.

adjust [ə'dʒəst] regelen, in orde brengen, vereffenen; (v. instrumenten) stellen, verstellen; — oneself, zijn kleren in orde brengen.

adjustment [ə'dʒəstmənt] regeling, vereffening v.; aanpassing v.; stelling, opstelling, montering v.

adjutant ['ædʒutənt] (mil. & Dk.) adjudant m.

administer [əd'ministə] beheren, besturen; (v. wetten) uitvoeren, toepassen; (v. voedsel, enz.) toedienen.

administration [ədminis'treiʃən] beheer, bestuur o., bewind o.; regering v.; ministerie o.; toediening v.

administrator [əd'ministreitə] beheerder, bestuurder, bewindvoerder m.

admirable ['ædmirəbl] bewonderenswaardig.

admiral ['ædmirəl] admiraal m.

admiration [ædmi'reiʃən] bewondering v.

admire [əd'maiə] bewonderen.

admissible [əd'misibl] toelaatbaar, geoorloofd; aannemelijk.

admission [əd'miʃən] toelating *v.*; aanneming *v.*; toegeving, erkenning *v.*; toegang *m.*; toegangsprijs *m.*

admit [əd'mit] toelaten; erkennen; toestaan; aannemen.

admittance [əd'mitəns] toegang *m.*; toelating *v.*

admix [əd'miks] vermengen.

admonish [əd'mɔniʃ] vermanen; aanmanen; waarschuwen.

admonition [ædmə'niʃən] vermaning *v.*; waarschuwing *v.*

adnominal [æd'nɔminəl] bijvoeglijk, attributief.

ado [ə'dû] drukte, moeite *v.*, omslag, ophef *m.*

adolescence, —cy [ædə'lesəns(i)] jongelingsjaren *o. mv.*, jongelingschap *v.*

adolescent [ædə'lesənt] opgroeiend.

adopt [ə'dɔpt] aannemen; (*v. woord, gebruik, enz.*) opnemen, overnemen; ontlenen (*from,* aan); (*v. notulen, enz.*) goedkeuren.

adoptive [ə'dɔptiv] aangenomen.

adorable [ə'dɔːrəbl] aanbiddelijk.

adore [ə'dɔː] aanbidden.

adorer [ə'dɔːrə] aanbidder *m.*, aanbidster *v.*

adorn [ə'dɔːn] versieren, verfraaien, tooien.

adornment [ə'dɔːnmənt] versiering, verfraaiing *v.*, tooi *m.*

adrift [ə'drift] (*v. schip*) drijvend, driftig, vlot.

adroit (ly) [ə'drɔit(li)] *adj.* (*adv.*) handig, behendig.

adult (ə'dəlt] *adj.* volwassen; *sb.* volwassene *m. & v.*

adulterate [ə'dəltəreit] vervalsen.

adultery [ə'dəltəri] overspel, *o.*, echtbreuk *v.*; (*Bijb.*) ontucht *v.*

adumbrate ['ædəmbreit] beschaduwen; afschetsen.

adust (ə'dəst] verbrand, verschroeid, verzengd.

advance [əd'vâns] *vt.* vooruitbrengen, vooruitschuiven, naar voren brengen; (*v. argument*) aanvoeren, beweren; bevorderen, verhaasten, vervroegen; (*v. prijzen*) verhogen (*v. geld*) voorschieten; *vi.* vooruitgaan, naderen; vorderen, vooruitkomen, vorderingen maken; (*v. prijzen*) stijgen; *sb.* vordering *v.*, vooruitgang *m.*; nadering *v.*; toenadering *v.*; voorschot *o.*; (*H.*) stijging, prijsverhoging, prijsverbetering *v.*; (*mil.*) bevordering, promotie *v.*

advanced [əd'vânst] gevorderd, vergevorderd; (*v. datum*) vervroegd; (*mil.:* *v. post*) vooruitgeschoven; (*fig.:* *v. ideeën*) vooruitstrevend.

advancement [əd'vânsmənt] vordering *v.*, voortgang *m.*; bevordering, promotie *v.*; (*v. datum*) vervroeging *v.*; voorschot *o.*

advantage [əd'vântidʒ] *sb.* voordeel *o.*; voorrecht *o.*; voorrang *m.*, overwicht *o.*

advantageous (ly) [ædvən'teidʒəs(li)] *adj.* (*adv.*) voordelig; gunstig.

advent ['ædvənt] komst, nadering *r.*; (*kath.*) advent *m.*

adventure [əd'ventʃə] avontuur *o.*; voorval *o.*; waagstuk *o.*, (gevaarlijke) onderneming *v.*; speculatie *v.*; risico *o.*

adverb ['ædvəːb] bijwoord *o.*

adversary ['ædvəsəri] tegenstander; vijand *m.*

adverse ['ædvəːs] tegengesteld; nadelig, ongunstig; strijdig (met).

adversity [əd'vəːsiti] tegenspoed *m.*

advert [əd'vəːt] letten op, acht geven (*to,* op); wijzen (*to,* op).

advertise ['ædvətaiz] bekend maken, aankondigen, adverteren; waarschuwen (*of,* voor, tegen), verwittigen (*of,* van); te koop lopen met.

advertisement [əd'vəːtismənt, —tizmənt] advertentie, aankondiging *v.*; reclame *r.*

advertising [ædvətaiziŋ] (het) adverteren *o.*

advice [əd'vais] raad *m.*, advies *o.*; bericht *o.*

advisable [əd'vaizəbl] raadzaam, geraden.

advise [əd'vaiz] raden, aanraden; adviseren, berichten, kennisgeven.

adviser [əd'vaizə] raadgever, raadsman *m.*

advocate ['ædvəkit] verdediger *m.*; voorstander *m.*; (*Sc.*) advocaat, pleitbezorger *m.*

advocate ['ædvəkeit] bepleiten, voorstaan.

aerial [ei'əriəl] *adj.* bovengronds, lucht—; *sb.* antenne *v.*

aerodrome ['eiərodroum] vliegveld *o.*

aeroplane [eiərəplein] vliegmachine *v.*

aesthetic (al) [is'δetik(l)] esthetisch; schoonheids—.

aesthetics [is'δetiks] esthetica, schoonheidsleer *v.*

afar [ə'fâ] ver, in de verte.

aesthetics [is'δetiks] esthetica, schoonheidsleer *v.*

afar [ə'fâ] ver, in de verte.

affability [æfə'biliti] minzaamheid, vriendelijkheid *v.*

affable ['æfəbl] minzaam, vriendelijk.

affair [ə'fêə] zaak, aangelegenheid *v.*; kwestie *v.*; (*mil.*) treffen, gevecht *o.*, (*fam.*) ding, zaakje *o.*

affect [ə'fekt] betreffen, aangaan; raken; aandoen; (*v. ziekte, enz.*) aantasten; voorwenden; voorliefde hebben voor.

affection [ə'fekʃən] genegenheid; aandoening *v.*; neiging *v.*; invloed *m.*

affectionate [ə'fekʃənit] liefhebbend, toegenegen.

affiance [ə'faiəns] *sb.* verloving *v.*; *vt.* verloven; **—d,** verloofde.

affidavit [æfi'deivit] beëdigde verklaring.

affined [ə'faind] verwant.

affinity [ə'finiti] verwantschap *r.*; (*scheik.*) affiniteit *r.*

affirm [ə'fə:m] bevestigen, beweren, verzekeren, bekrachtigen.

affix [ə'fiks] *vt.* hechten, aanhechten, vasthechten; toevoegen, bijvoegen; (*v. salaris*) verbinden.

affix ['æfiks] *sb.* aanhangsel *o.*, toevoeging *v.*; achtervoegsel *o.*; voorvoegsel *o.*

afflict [ə'flikt] bedroeven; kwellen; bezoeken; **—ed,** diepbedroefd.

affliction [ə'flikʃən] droefheid, droefenis *v.*; leed *o.*, smart *v.*; bezoeking *v.*

affluence ['æfluəns] toevloed *m.*; overvloed, rijkdom *m.*, weelde *v.*

afford [ə'fo:d] geven.

affray [ə'frei] vechtpartij, kloppartij *v.*

affront [ə'frʌnt] *vt.* (openlijk) beledigen, affronteren; tarten, trotseren; *sb.* (openlijke) belediging *v.*, affront *o.*, hoon *m.*

afield [ə'fi:ld] op het veld; (*mil.*) te velde.

afire [ə'faiə] in brand.

afloat [ə'flout] vlot; op zee, onderweg; (*H.*) zeilend.

afoot [ə'fut] te voet, op de been.

aforecited [ə'fo:əsaitid] voornoemd.

aforesaid [ə'fo:əsed] voornoemd.

aforethought [ə'fo:əθɔ:t] voorbedacht, vooraf beraamd.

aforetime [ə'fo:ətaim] vroeger.

afraid [ə'freid] bang, bevreesd; bezorgd (*for,* voor).

afresh [ə'freʃ] opnieuw, wederom.

after ['â:ftə] *adv. & prep.* na; naar; achter; daarna, later; *conj.* nadat; *adj.* later; (*sch.*) achter.

after-crop ['â:ftəkrɔp] nagewas *o.*, naoogst, tweede oogst *m.*

after-damp ['â:ftədæmp] mijngas *o.*

aftermath ['â:ftəmæð] nagras, etgroen *o.*; (*fig.*) nasleep *m.*

afternoon ['â:ftə'nûn, 'â:ftə'nûn] middag, namiddag *m.*; (*fig.*) avond *m.*

after-pains ['â:ftəpeinz] naweeën *o. mv.*

aftertaste ['â:ftəteist] nasmaak *m.*

afterward(s) ['â:ftəwəd(z)] later, naderhand, daarna.

again [ə'gein, ə'gen] weer, opnieuw; verder, bovendien.

against [ə'geinst] *prep.* tegenover; tegen; strijdig met; *cj.* tegen de tijd dat.

agape [ə'geip] met open mond; ten hoogste verbaasd, stom verbaasd.

agate ['ægit] agaat *o. & m.*

age [eidʒ] *sb.* leeftijd, ouderdom *m.*; levensduur *m.*; eeuw *v.*; vt. verouderen, oud worden; *vt.* oud maken, doen verouderen.

agency ['eidʒənsi] agentschap *c*, agentuur *v.*

agent ['eidʒənt] agent, tussenpersoon *m.*; zaakwaarnemer *m.*

agglomerate [ə'glɔmereit] *vi.* (zich) opeenhopen.

agglutinate [ə'glûtineit] aaneenlijmen, aaneenhechten.

aggrandize ['ægrəndaiz] vergroten.

aggravate ['ægrəveit] verzwaren; verergeren.

aggregate ['ægrigeit] *vt.* opeenhopen, bijeenbrengen, verzamelen.

aggress [ə'gres] aanvallen.

aggressor [ə'gresə] aanvaller *m.*

aggrieve [ə'gri:v] bedroeven.

aghast [ə'gâst] ontzet.

agile ['ædʒail] rap, vlug, behendig.

agio ['ædʒiou, 'eidʒiou] (*H.*) agio *m.*

agitate ['ædʒiteit] bewegen, schudden; roeren, ontroeren; opwinden.

agitation [ædʒi'teiʃən] beweging *v.*; beroering *r.*; gisting, woeling, onrust *v.*; opschudding *v.*

agitator ['ædʒiteitə] volksmenner, opruier, onruststoker, agitator *m.*

agnail ['ægneil] dwangnagel, nij(d)nagel *m.*

agnate ['ægneit] verwant van vaderszijde.

ago [ə'gou] geleden.

agog [ə'gɔg] (vurig) verlangend, begerig.

agonize ['ægənaiz] *vi.* zieltogen, met de dood worstelen; doodsangsten uitstaan; *vt.* pijnigen, folteren.

agony ['ægəni] doodsstrijd *m.*; zielestrijd, zielsangst *m.*, zielepijn *v.*; foltering *r.*

agree [ə'gri] *vi.* overeenstemmen, overeenkomen; het eens zijn (worden); *vt.* in overeenstemming brengen.

agreeable [ə'griəbl] aangenaam; overeenkomstig (**to,** met).

agreement [ə'grimənt] overeenkomst, overeenstemming *v.*; akkoord *o.*, afspraak *v.*, vergelijk, verdrag *o.*; **by —,** volgens afspraak.

agriculture ['ægrikəltʃə] landbouw *m.*; landbouwkunde *r.*

aground [ə'graund] (*sch.*) aan de grond, gestrand.

ague ['eigjû] (koude) koorts *r.*; (koude) rilling, huivering *v.*

ahead [ə'hed] voorop, vooruit, vooraan; (*fig.*) in 't vooruitzicht, voor de boeg.

aheap [ə'hîp] op een hoop.

aid [eid] *vt.* helpen, bijstaan; bijdragen tot, bevorderen; *vi.* helpen; *sb.* hulp *v.*, bijstand *m.*; steun *m.*; helper *m.*; hulpmiddel *o.*

ail [eil] schelen, schorten, mankeren.

aim [eim] *vt. & vi.* mikken, doelen (**at,** op); richten (**at,** op, tegen); streven (**at,** naar); beogen; *sb.* oogmerk, doel; mikpunt *o.*

aimless(ly) ['eimlis(li)] *adj.* (*adv.*) doelloos.

air [êə] *sb.* lucht *v.*; windje *o.*; tocht *m.*; ademtocht *m.*; wijsje *o.*, melodie *v.*; voorkomen *o.*; houding *v.*; schijn *m.*; *vt.* luchten; drogen (bij 't vuur); geuren met; (*v. paarden*) afrijden; *vr.* **— oneself,** een luchtje scheppen.

air-balloon ['êəbəlûn] luchtballon *m.*

air-castle ['êəkâsl] luchtkasteel *o.*

air-cooling ['êəkûliŋ] luchtafkoeling *v.*

aircraft ['êəkrâft] luchtschip, luchtvaartuig *o.*; luchtvloot *r.*

air-cushion ['êəkuʃən] windkussen *o.*

air-force ['êəfo:s] luchtmacht, luchtvloot *v.*

air-hours ['êəauəs] *(radio)* zenduren *o. mv.*

airing ['êəriŋ] (het) luchten *o.*, (het) ventileren *o.*; wandeling *v.*; rijtoer *m.* (in openlucht).

airless ['êəlis] zonder lucht, luchtledig; bedompt; stil (zonder wind).

air-mail ['êəmeil] luchtpost *v.*

airman ['êəmən] vliegenier *m.*

air-pillow ['eəpilou] luchtkussen *o.*

airplane ['eəplein] vliegmachine *v.*

air-port ['eəpo:t] vlieghaven *v.*; patrijspoort *v.*

airship ['êəʃip] luchtschip *o.*

air-tight ['êətait] luchtdicht.

airy ['êəri] luchtig; ijl; (hoog) in de lucht; vluchtig, etherisch; luchthartig

aisle [ail] *(v. kerk)* zijbeuk *m.*; *(in kerk)* gangpad *o.*; *(Am.)* pad *o.* *(in tram, enz.)*.

ajar [ə'dʒɑ] op een kier, half open.

alabaster ['æləbɑstə] *sb.* albast *o.*; *adj.* albasten, van albast.

alarm [ə'lɑm] *sb.* alarm, alarmsein, alarmsignaal *o.*; alarmering; waarschuwing *v.*; onrust, ongerustheid *v.*; angst, schrik *m.*; alarmtoestel *o.*, alarmklok *v.*; wekker *m.*; *(sp.: schermen)* appèl *o.*; *vt.* alarmeren; waarschuwen; doen opschrikken, verontrusten.

alarm-clock [ə'lɑmklɔk] wekkerklok *v.*, wekker *m.*

alarming(ly) [ê'lɑmiŋ(li)] *adj.* *(adv.)* verontrustend, onrustbarend.

alas [ə'lɑs, ə'læs] helaas !

alb [ælb] albe *v.*, koorhemd *o.*

album ['ælbəm] album *o.*; gedenkboek *o.*; *(Am.)* vreemdelingenboek *o.*

albumen [æl'bjûmin] eiwit *o.*; eiwitstof *v.*

alcohol ['ælkəhɔl] alcohol *m.*; wijngeest *m.*

alcoholic [ælkə'hɔlik] alcoholisch.

Alcoran [ælkɔ'rân] de Koran *m.*

alcove ['ælkouv] alkoof *v.*; prieel, zomerhuisje *o.*

alder ['o:ldə] els, elzeboom *m.*

alderman ['o:ldəmən] wethouder, schepen *m.*

aldermanship ['o:ldəmənʃip] wethouderschap *o.*

aldern ['o:ldən] van elzehout, elzehouten.

ale [eil] ale, bier *o.*

aleatory ['eiliətəri] onzeker, van het toeval afhangend.

ale-house ['eilhaus] bierhuis *o.*

alert [ə'lə:t] *adj.* waakzaam, wakker, op zijn hoede; vlug; *sb.* alarm, alarmsignaal *o.*

algebra ['ældʒibrə] algebra, stelkunde, stelkunst *v.*

Algeria [æl'dʒiəriə] Algiers *o.* *(land).*

alias ['eiliəs] *adv.* alias, anders genoemd; *sb.* alias, aangenomen naam *m.*

alien ['eiliən] *adj.* vreemd *(to,* aan);

buitenlands; verschillend, anders; *sb.* vreemdeling, buitenlander *m.*; *rt.* vervreemden.

alienate ['eiljəneit] vervreemden, onttrekken *(from,* aan).

alienation [eiljə'neiʃən] vervreemding *v.*; *(mental)* —, krankzinnigheid, verstandsverbijstering.

alight [ə'lait] *adj.* aan, aangestoken; brandend; verlicht; schitterend *(with,* van).

alight [ə'lait] *ri.* uitstappen, afstappen, uitstijgen neerkomen; neerstrijken.

align [ə'lain] *vt.* richten; op één lijn plaatsen; recht maken; *ri.* zich richten.

alignment [ə'lainmənt] (het) richten *o.*; rooilijn, linie *v.*; *(mil.)* richting, richtlijn *v.*

alike [ə'laik] gelijk; evenzeer, evengoed.

alimentation [ælimən'teiʃən] voeding *v.*; onderhoud *o.*

aline [ə'lain] *vt.* op één lijn plaatsen; richten; in de rooilijn brengen; *ri.* zich richten, zich in 't gelid scharen; *vr.* — **oneself with,** zich scharen aan de zijde van.

alive [ə'laiv] in leven, levend; levendig, opgewekt.

all [o:l] *adj.* alle; geheel, gans; één en al; *adv.* heel, helemaal, geheel en al, één en al; *sb.* al, alle, allen, alles; **after —,** per slot van rekening, alles wel beschouwd.

allay [ə'lei] tot bedaren brengen, doen bedaren; verzachten, verlichten, stillen; lenigen, matigen, verminderen; *(v. dorst)* lessen.

allegation [æli'geiʃən] aanhaling, aanvoering *v.*; bewering *v.*

allegoric(al) [æli'gɔrik(l)] allegorisch, zinnebeeldig.

alleviate [ə'livieit] verlichten, verzachten, stillen, lenigen.

alleviatory [ə'liviətəri] verzachtend, lenigend.

alley ['æli] steeg, laan *v.*, pad *o.*; gang, doorgang *m.*; kegelbaan *v.*

alliance [ə'laiəns] verbond, bondgenootschap *o.*; verbintenis *v.*; huwelijk *o.*; verwantschap *v.*

allied [ə'laid] verbonden; verwant.

alligation [æli'geiʃən] verbinding, legering *v.*; *(rek.)* mengingrekening *v.*

alligator ['æligeitə] *(Dk.)* kaaiman, alligator *m.*

alliteration [əlitə'reiʃən] alliteratie *v.*, stafrijm *o.*

allocate ['æləkeit] toewijzen, toekennen, toebedelen; verdelen; aanwijzen.

allocution [ælə'kjûʃən] aanspraak, redevoering *v.*; toespraak, allocutie *v.*

allot [ə'lɔt] toekennen, toewijzen, toebedelen, toemeten; **— upon,** *(Am.)* rekenen op.

allotment [ə'lɔtmənt] toekenning, toewijzing, toebedeling *v.*; gunning *v.*; aandeel *o.*; lot, levenslot *o.*, lotsbeschikking *v.*; perceel *o.*

allow [ə'lau] *vt.* toelaten, toestaan, veroorloven; toegeven, erkennen; rekenen; (*Am.*) beweren; veronderstellen; *vi.* — **for**, in aanmerking nemen; rekening houden met.

allowance [ə'lauəns] *sb.* toelating, vergunning *v.*; aandeel *o.*, portie *v.*; toelage; toegekende som *v.*; vergoeding *v.*; korting, reductie,refactie *v.*, rabat *o.*; *vt.* een toelage verlenen; op rantsoen stellen.

alloy [ə'lɔi] *sb.* allooi, gehalte *o.*; legering, verbinding *v.*; mengsel *o.*, bijmengsel *o.*; *vt.* legeren; mengen; verminderen, temperen.

all-rounder ['o:l'raundə] veelzijdig persoon, iem. van alle markten thuis.

All-Saints' Day ['o:l'seintsdei] Allerheiligen *o.*

All-Souls' Day ['o:l'soulzdei] Allerzielen *o.*

allude [ə'ljûd] zinspelen, doelen (**to,** op).

allure [ə'ljûə] lokken, aanlokken, verlokken, verleiden.

allurement [ə'ljûəmənt] aanlokking, verlokking *v.*, lokmiddel *o.*; attractie, verleidelijkheid, bekoring *v.*

alluring [ə'ljûəriŋ] aanlokkelijk, verleidelijk.

allusion [ə'ljûȝən] zinspeling, toespeling *v.* (**to,** op).

alluvion [ə'ljûviən] alluvium *o.*, aanslibbing *v.*, aangeslibd land *o.*

ally [ə'lai] bondgenoot *m.*

almanac ['o:lmənæk] almanak *m.*

almighty ['o:l'maiti] *adj.* almachtig; *sb. the A—,* de Almachtige.

almond ['âmənd] amandel *m.*; amandelboom *m.*

almost ['o:lmoust] bijna, nagenoeg, schier; ten naaste bij.

alms [âmz] aalmoes *v.*, aalmoezen *v. mv.*

aloft [ə'lɔft] hoog, omhoog, in de hoogte; hemelwaarts.

alone [ə'loun] *adj.* alleen, eenzaam; *adv.* alléén; enkel.

along [ə'lɔŋ] *prep. & adv.* langs, langs... heen.

aloof [ə'lûf] op een afstand, ver; ontoeschietelijk, gereserveerd, afzijdig.

Alost [â'lɔst] Aalst *o.*

aloud [ə'laud] luid, luide, overluid, hardop.

alp [ælp] (hoge) berg; bergtop *m.*; bergweide *v.*; *the A—s,* de Alpen.

already [o:l'redi] reeds, al; (*dicht.*) bereids.

Alsace ['ælsæs] de Elzas *m.*

also ['o:lsou] ook, eveneens, insgelijks; bovendien.

altar ['o:ltə] altaar *o.*; (*prot.*) Avondmaalstafel *v.*

alter ['o:ltə] (zich) veranderen, wijzigen.

alterable ['o:ltərəbl] veranderlijk, voor wijziging vatbaar.

alteration [o:ltə'reiʃən] verandering, wijziging *v.*

altercate ['o:ltəkeit] twisten, kijven, kibbelen, krakelen.

altercation [o:ltə'keiʃən] twist *m.*, krakeel *o.*, woordenwisseling *v.*, gekijf *o.*

alternate ['o:ltəneit] *vt.* verwisselen, omwisselen; *vi.* elkaar afwisselen.

alternate [o:l'tə:nit] *adj.* afwisselend, verwisselend.

alternately [o:l'tə:nitli] *adv.* afwisselend, beurtelings, om de beurt.

alternation [o:ltə'neiʃən] afwisseling *v.*

alternator [o:ltəneitə] wisselstroomdynamo *m.*

although [o:l'ðou] hoewel, alhoewel, ofschoon.

altimeter [æl'timitə] hoogtemeter *m.*

altitude ['æltitjûd] hoogte *v.*; hoogtepunt *o.*

alto ['æltou] alt *v.*; altviool *v.*

altogether [o:ltə'geðə] helemaal, volkomen, in alle opzichten; allemaal, alles samengenomen.

alum ['æləm] aluin *v.*

always ['o:lwiz] altijd, steeds, altoos.

amalgamate [ə'mælgəmeit] vermengen, samensmelten.

amass [ə'mæs] ophopen, opeenhopen, opeenstapelen.

amassment [ə'mæsmənt] ophoping, opeenhoping, opeenstapeling.

amateur [æmə'tə:, æmətjuə] amateur, liefhebber, dilettant *m.*

amaze [ə'meiz] verbazen.

amazingly [ə'meiziŋli] verbazend.

ambassador [æm'bæsədə] gezant *m.*

amber ['æmbə] amber *m.*, barnsteen *o.*

ambient ['æmbiənt] omringend.

ambiguous(ly) [əm'bigjuəs(li)] *adj.* (*adv.*) dubbelzinnig.

ambition [æm'biʃən] *sb.* eerzucht *v.*; vurig verlangen *o.*, vurige wens *m.*, ideaal *o.*; *vt.* streven naar.

ambitious [æm'biʃəs] eerzuchtig; begerig (**of,** naar).

ambler ['æmblə] telganger, pasganger *m.*

ambrosia [əm'brouziə] ambrozijn *o.*, godenspijs *v.*

ambs-ace ['æmz'eis] (*fig.*) tegenslag, tegenvaller *m.*, ongeluk *o.*

ambulance ['æmbjuləns] ambulance *v.*; brancard *m.*

ambulate ['æmbjuleit] wandelen, rondwandelen, rondtrekken.

ambuscade [æmbəs'keid] **ambush** ['æmbuʃ] *sb.* hinderlaag *v.*; *vt.* in hinderlaag leggen; verdekt opstellen; **be ambushed,** in hinderlaag liggen; in een hinderlaag vallen.

ameer [ə'mîə] emir *m.*

ameliorate [ə'mîliəreit] *vt.* beter maken, verbeteren; *vi.* beter worden; (*v. prijs*) stijgen.

amelioration [əmîliə'reiʃən] verbetering *v.*; veredeling *v.*; stijging *v.*

amenable [ə'mînəbl] meegaand, gezeglijk, gedwee, handelbaar; vatbaar, ontvankelijk (**to,** voor); verantwoording schuldig (**to,** aan), verantwoordelijk.

amend [ə'mend] verbeteren; amenderen

amendable [ə'mendəbl] verbeterbaar, te verbeteren.

amendment [ə'mendmənt] verbetering, beterschap v.; amendement o., wijziging v.

amenity [ə'mîniti, ə'meniti] bevalligheid v.

amerce [ə'mə:s] beboeten (in, met); straffen, bestraffen.

American [ə'merikən] Amerikaans.

amiable ['eimiəbl] beminnelijk, vrienddelijk, liefelijk, beminnenswaardig.

amicable ['æmikəbl] vriendelijk, vriendschappelijk, minnelijk.

amicably ['æmikəbli] adv. bij minnelijke schikking.

amid [ə'mid] te midden van, onder.

amir [ə'miə] emir m.

amiss [ə'mis] verkeerd, niet in orde, niet in de haak; te onpas; mis; kwaad.

amity ['æmiti] vriendschap, vriendschappelijke verhouding v.

ammoniac [ə'mouniæk] ammoniak—.

ammunition [æmju'niʃən] sb. munitie, ammunitie v.; vt. van ammunitie voorzien.

amnesty ['æmnisti] sb. amnestie v.; vt. amnestie verlenen.

among(st [ə'məŋ(st)] onder, tussen, te midden van.

amorous ['æmərəs] verliefd (of, op).

amortization [əmo:ti'zeiʃən] overdracht (van goederen) in de dode hand; amortisatie, schulddelging v.

amortize [ə'mo:tiz] in de dode hand overdragen; amortiseren, delgen, afbetalen.

amount [ə'maunt] vi. bedragen, belopen; sb. bedrag o., som v.

amour [ə'muə] minnarij, liefdesintrige v.

amphibian [æm'fibiən] adj. tweeslachtig; sb. tweeslachtig dier o.

ample [æmpl] ruim, wijd, uitgestrekt; breedvoerig; overvloedig.

amplifier ['æmplifaiə] uitbreider m. (el.) versterker m.

amplify ['æmplifai] vt. vergroten, uitbreiden; aanvullen; uiteenzetten, uitwerken; ontwikkelen; versterken; vi. uitweiden (over), in bijzonderheden gaan; zich uitbreiden.

amply ['æmpli] adv. zie ample; ook: ruimschoots, rijkelijk.

amputate ['æmpjuteit] afzetten, amputeren.

amulet ['æmjulit] amulet v., talisman m.

amuse [ə'mjûz] vt. vermaken, amuseren; (aangenaam) bezighouden; vi. — oneself, de tijd verdrijven; zich bezighouden (by, with, met).

amusement [ə'mjûzmənt] vermaak o., vermakelijkheid v.; tijdverdrijf o.

amusing [ə'mjûziŋ] vermakelijk, amusant.

amygdala [ə'migdələ] mv.: **amygdalae** [ə'migdəlî] amandel v.

an [ən] een.

anabaptist [ænə'bæptist] wederdoper m.

anaemia [ə'nîmiə] bloedarmoede v.

analecta [ænə'lektə] **analects** ['ænəlekts] analecta, bloemlezing v.

analgesic [ænæl'dʒîsik] adj. pijnstillend; sb. pijnstillend middel o.

analogy [ə'nælədʒi] analogie, overeenkomst, overeenstemming v.; (wisk.) evenredigheid v.

analyse ['ænəlaiz] ontleden, ontbinden, analyseren.

analysis [ə'nælisis] ontleding, ontbinding, analyse v.; overzicht o.

analyst ['ænəlist] ontleder m.; scheikundige, analist m.

anarchic(al) [æ'nâkik(l)] regeringloos; anarchistisch.

anarchist ['ænəkist] sb. anarchist m.; adj. anarchistisch.

anathema [ə'næðimə] ban, banvloek, kerkban m., anathema o.

anathematize [ə'næðimətaiz] in de ban doen, de banvloek uitspreken over, vervloeken.

anatomic(al) [ænə'tomik(l)] anatomisch, ontleedkundig.

anatomize [ə'nætəmaiz] ontleden, anatomiseren.

anatomy [ə'nætəmi] ontleedkunde, anatomie v.; ontleding v.; mummie v.

ancestor ['ænsistə] voorvader, stamvader m.

anchor ['æŋkə] sb. anker o.; (fig.) plechtanker, reddingsanker o.; vt. ankeren, verankeren; vastleggen, bevestigen; vi. ankeren; zich vestigen.

anchorite ['æŋkərait] kluizenaar m.

anchovy [æn'tʃouvi] ansjovis m.

ancient ['einʃənt] adj. oud; zeer oud; sb. oude, grijsaard m.

and [ænd, ənd, ən] en; — so on, enz.

Andalusia [ændə'lûziə] Andalusië o.

anecdote ['ænikdout] anekdote v.

anemone [ə'neməni] anemoon v.

eneurism ['ænjûərizm] (gen.) slagadergezwel o.; (fig.) abnormale uitzetting v.

anew [ə'njû] opnieuw, nog eens; anders.

angel ['eindʒəl] engel m.; genius m.; oude Engelse munt v.

anger ['æŋgə] sb. gramschap, boosheid v., toorn m.; vt. vertoornen, boos maken.

angle ['æŋgl] sb. hoek m.; gezichtspunt o.; vi. met een hoek buigen, hengelen, vissen.

angler ['æŋglə] hengelaar m.

angling-rod ['æŋgliŋrod] hengel m., hengelroede v.

Anglophil(e) ['ængloufil] Engelsgezind.

angola [æŋ'goulə] angorawol.

angrily ['æŋgrili] adv. boos, toornig, verbolgen.

angry ['æŋgr] adj. boos, toornig, verbolgen; (gen.: v. wond) ontstoken, pijnlijk.

anguish ['æŋgwiʃ] sb. (ziels)angst m.,

foltering, kwelling, pijn *v.*; *rt.* kwellen, pijnigen.

angular ['æŋgjulə] hoekig.

anile ['ænail] kinds (vooral van vrouw).

animadversion [æniməd'və:ʃən] kritiek, aanmerking, afkeuring *v.*; berisping, terechtwijzing *v.*

animal ['æniməl] *sb.* dier, beest *o.*; *adj.* dierlijk· dieren—.

animate ['ænimeit] *rt.* bezielen; leven geven; opwekken, aanwakkeren, aanvuren.

animate ['ænimit] *adj.* levend, bezield, levendig.

animated ['ænimeitid] levend, bezield, levendig, opgewekt.

animation [æni'meiʃən] bezieling *v.*, leven *o.*, levendigheid *r.*; opwekking, aanmoediging *v.*

animosity [æni'mɔsiti] animositeit, verbittering, vijandigheid *r.*, wrok *m.*, vijandschap *v.*, haat *m.*

ankle ['æŋkl] enkel *m.*

annals ['ænəlz] annalen *v. mr.*, jaarboeken *o. mv.*

annex [ə'neks] *vt.* aanhechten, toevoegen, bijvoegen; inlijven, annexeren; verbinden.

annex ['æneks] *sb.* bijlage *v.*, aanhangsel *o.*; bijgebouw *o.*, aanbouw *m.*, dependance *v.*

annexation [ænek'seiʃən] aanhechting, bijvoeging *v.*; inlijving, annexatie *v.*; verbinding *v.*

annihilate [ə'nai(h)ileit] vernietigen.

anniversary [æni'və:səri] *adj.* jaarlijks; *sb.* verjaardag *m.*; jaarfeest *o.*, gedenkdag *m.*

annotate ['ænouteit] *vt.* annoteren, van verklarende aantekeningen voorzien; *ri.* aantekeningen maken (**on,** bij).

annotation [ænou'teiʃən] annotering *v.*; annotatie, (verklarende) aantekening *v.*

announce [ə'nauns] aankondigen, bekendmaken, bericht geven van.

announcement [ə'naunsmənt] aankondiging, bekendmaking *v.*

announcer [ə'naunsə] aankondiger, berichtgever *m.*; (*radio*) omroeper *m.*

annoy [ə'nɔi] ergeren, kwellen; hinderen, lastig vallen; tot last zijn; (*mil.*) bestoken; verontrusten.

annoyance [ə'nɔiəns] ergernis, kwelling *v.*; hinder, last *m.*; plaag *v.*

annoying [ə'nɔliŋ] ergerlijk; hinderlijk, lastig, vervelend.

annually ['ænjuəli] *adv.* jaarlijks.

annuity [ə'njûiti] lijfrente *v.*, jaargeld *o.*, annuïteit *v.*

annul [ə'nəl] vernietigen, te niet doen, nietig (ongeldig) verklaren; herroepen, opheffen, annuleren.

annulate(d) ['ænjuleit(id)] geringd.

annunciate [ə'nənʃieit] aankondigen.

anodyne ['ænədain] pijnstillend middel *o.*

anoint [ə'nɔint] zalven; insmeren, inwrijven; (*fam.*) afrossen, de ribben smeren.

anon [ə'nɔn] dadelijk, aanstonds; straks.

anonymous(ly) [ə'nɔniməs(li)] *adj.* (*adv.*) naamloos, anoniem.

another [ə'nʌθə] een ander; nog een; een tweede.

answer ['ânsə] *sb.* antwoord; bescheid *o.*; beslissing *v.*; (*recht*) verdediging *v.*; *in — to,* in antwoord, op; *rt.* beantwoorden, antwoorden op; beantwoorden aan; voldoen, honoreren; (*r. gebed*) verhoren; zich verantwoorden wegens; *vi.* antwoorden; baten; *— for,* verantwoorden; instaan voor; boeten voor; *— to,* antwoorden op, antwoord geven aan; zich verantwoorden tegenover; luisteren naar; beantwoorden aan.

answerable ['ânsərəbl] verantwoordelijk, aansprakelijk.

ant [ænt, ânt] mier *r.*

antagonist [æn'tægənist] tegenstander, tegenstrever *m.*; tegenpartij *v.*; (*spier*) antagonist *m.*

ant-eater ['æntitə] miereneter *m.*

antecedent [ænti'sîdənt] *adj.* voorafgaand; *sb.* (het) voorafgaande *o.*; antecedent *o.*; voorgaande term *m.*; *his —s,* zijn verleden.

antedate ['æntideit] *vt.* antedateren, te vroeg dateren; vervroegen; vooruitlopen op; *sb.* vervroegde dagtekening *v.*

antenna [æn'tenə] antenne *r.*; voelhoren, voelspriet *m.*

anterior [æn't əriə] voorafgaand, vroeger; voorste.

anthem ['ænθəm] beurtzang, tegenzang *m.*; lofzang *m.*; *national —,* volkslied.

anther ['ænθə] (*Pl.*) helmknop *m.*; *— dust,* stuifmeel.

ant-hill ['ænthil] mierenhoop *m.*, mierennest *o.*

anthology [æn'ðɔlədʒi] bloemlezing *v.*

anthracite ['ænðrəsait] antraciet *o.*

anthrax ['ænðraeks] bloedpuist, bloedzweer *r.*; miltvuur *o.*

antibilious [ænti'biljəs] galverdrijvend, tegen de gal.

anticipate [æn'tisipeit] *vt.* voorkómen, vóór zijn; vooruitlopen op; verwachten; een voorgevoel hebben van; vervroegen, verhaasten; vooraf ondervinden; *ri.* de gebeurtenissen vooruitlopen.

anticipation [æntisi'peiʃən] (het) voorkómen; (het) vooruitlopen (op iets); verwachting *v.*; voorgevoel *o.*; voorsmaak *m.*; voorschot *o.*, vooruitbetaling *v.*; *in (by) —,* bij voorbaat.

anticyclone [ænti'saikloun] anticyclone *m.*

antidote ['æntidout] tegengift *o.*

antipathy [æn'tipəðil] antipathie *r.* (*to,* voor).

antiphon ['æntifən] beurtzang, tegenzang, wisselzang *m.*

antipyretic ['æntipai'retik] *adj.* koortswerend; *sb.* koortswerend middel *o.*

antiquate ['æntikweit] doen verouderen; een oud voorkomen geven; *—d,* verouderd; ouderwets.

antiquity [æn'tikwiti] de Oudheid *r*.; antiquiteit *r*.; ouderdom *m*.
antiseptic [ænti'septik] antiseptisch, bederfwerend.
antithesis [ən'tiðisis] antithese, tegenstelling *r*.; tegengestelde *o*.
antler ['æntlə] tak *m*. (van gewei); —**s**, gewei *o*.
ant-lion ['ænt—, 'ântlaiən] mierenleeuw *m*.
anvil ['ænvil] aanbeeld *o*.
anxiety [æn'zaiiti] benauwdheid *r*.; ongerustheid, bezorgdheid, zorg *v*.; (vurig) verlangen *o*., begeerte *r*.
anxious(ly) ['æŋkʃəs(li)] *adj*. (*adv*.) ongerust, bezorgd; angstwekkend; bang, angstig; verlangend, begerig (**for**, naar).
any ['eni] enig; ieder; elk; een; welke... ook.
anybody ['enibɔdi] iedereen, eenieder; (*in vragende zin*) iemand.
anyone ['eniwən] iemand, iedereen; wie ook.
anything ['eniðiŋ] iets (wat dan ook); alles.
anyway ['eniwei] hoe dan ook, op de een of andere manier; in ieder geval, hoe het ook zij.
anywhere ['eniwêə] ergens; overal.
anywise ['eniweiz] hoe dan ook, op enige wijze, in enig opzicht.
aorta [ei'ɔ:tə] aorta, grote hartslagader *r*.
apace [ə'peis] snel, vlug.
apart [ə'pât] afzonderlijk; uiteen, uit elkaar, van elkaar; op zichzelf; terzijde, apart.
apartment [ə'pâtmənt] vertrek *o*.
apathetic(ally) [æpə'ðetik(əli)] *adj*. (*adv*.) apathisch, onverschillig, lusteloos; gevoelloos.
apathy ['æpəði] apathie, onverschilligheid, lusteloosheid; gevoelloosheid *v*.
ape [eip] *sb*. (staartloze) aap *m*.; naäper *m*.; *vt*. naäpen.
apeak [ə'pîk] (*sch*.) loodrecht.
aperient [ə'piəriənt] **aperitive** [ə'peritiv] *adj*. purgerend, laxerend; *sb*. purgeermiddel, laxeermiddel *o*.
aperture ['æpətjuə] opening, spleet *v*.
apex ['eipeks] top *m*., toppunt *o*.
aphorism ['æfərizm] kernspreuk, leerspreuk *r*.
apiarist ['eipiərist] bijenhouder, imker *m*.
apiculture ['eipikəltʃə] bijenteelt *v*.
apiece [ə'pîs] het stuk, per stuk, elk.
apogee ['æpədʒi] apogeum *o*.; hoogste punt, toppunt *o*.
apologetic [əpɔlə'dʒetik] *adj*. verontschuldigend; verdedigend, apologetisch; *sb*. —**s**, apologetiek, geloofsverdediging *v*.
apologize [ə'pɔledʒaiz] zich verontschuldigen, zich rechtvaardigen.
apology [ə'pɔlədʒi] apologie, verdediging *v*.; verweerschrift *o*.; verontschuldiging *r*.

apoplexy ['æpəpleksi] beroerte *r*.
apostasy [ə'pɔstəsi] afval *m*., afvalligheid *r*.
apostate [ə'pɔstit] *adj*. afvallig; *sb*. afvallige *m*.
apostatize [ə'pɔstətaiz] afvallen, afvallig worden.
apostle [ə'pɔsl] apostel *m*.
apostrophe [ə'pɔstrəfi] aanspraak *v*.; afkappingsteken *o*.
appal [ə'pɔ:l] doen schrikken, ontstellen, ontzetten.
appalling(ly) [ə'pɔ:liŋ(li)] *adj*. (*adv*.) verschrikkelijk, ontzettend.
apparatus [æpə'reitəs] toestel, apparaat *o*.; gereedschappen, hulpmiddelen *o*. *mv*.; organen *o*. *mr*.
apparent [ə'pæ—, ə'pêərənt] blijkbaar, klaarblijkelijk; kennelijk; ogenschijnlijk, schijnbaar, waarschijnlijk.
apparently [ə'pæ—, ə'pêərəntli] *adv*. blijkbaar, klaarblijkelijk; schijnbaar, ogenschijnlijk.
apparition [æpə'riʃən] (geest)verschijning *v*., spook *o*.; schijnsel *o*.
appeal [ə'pîl] *vi*. in beroep gaan, appelleren; — **to**, een beroep doen op; zich beroepen op; smeken; (*fig*.) spreken tot; *sb*. (*recht*) appèl, (hoger) beroep *o*.; smeekbede, smeking *v*.
appear [ə'piə] verschijnen; schijnen; lijken, blijken; optreden (**in** rol).
appearance [ə'piərəns] verschijning *v*.; schijn *m*., voorkomen *o*.; verschijnsel *o*.; optreden *o*.
appease [ə'piz] bedaren, stillen, bevredigen, sussen.
appellant [ə'pelənt] appellant *m*.; smekeling *m*.
append [ə'pend] aanhechten; aanhangen; toevoegen, bijvoegen.
appendicitis [əpendi'saitis] blindedarmontsteking *r*.
appendix [ə'pendiks] aanhangsel *o*.; bijvoegsel *o*., bijlage *v*.
appertain [æpə'tein] behoren, toebehoren (**to**, aan); behoren, passen (**to**, bij), betrekking hebben (**to**, op).
appetite ['æpitait] eetlust, trek *m*.; begeerte *v*. (**for**, naar).
appetizing ['æpitaiziŋ] appetijtelijk smakelijk; de eetlust opwekkend.
applaud [ə'plɔ:d] toejuichen, applaudisseren.
applause [ə'plɔ:z] toejuiching *r*., applaus *o*.
apple ['æpl] appel *m*.
apple-sauce ['æpl'sɔ:s] appelmoes *v*. & *o*.
apple-tree ['æpltri] appelboom *m*.
appliance [ə'plaiəns] aanwending, toepassing *v*.; toestel, hulpmiddel, middel *o*.
applicant ['æplikənt] sollicitant *m*.; inschrijver *m*. (**op** aandelen, lening).
application [æpli'keiʃən] aanwending *r*., gebruik *o*., toepassing *v*.; aanbrenging *v*.; aanvraag, sollicitatie *v*.; inschrijving *r*. (**op** aandelen); ijver *m*., vlijt, toe-

wijding *v.*; inspanning *v.*; (*gen.*) omslag *m.* & *o.*

apply [ə'plai] *vt.* aanwenden, toepassen; brengen, leggen, zetten; (*v. kleuren, enz.*) aanbrengen; *vi.* solliciteren (*for,* naar); zich wenden (*to,* tot); van toepassing zijn; betrekking hebben (*to,* op); inschrijven (*for,* op); — *for, ook;* aanvragen; *vi.* — *oneself to,* zich toeleggen op.

appoint [ə'point] *vt.* bepalen, vaststellen; voorschrijven, bestemmen; aanstellen, benoemen (tot); bescheiden, bestellen; inrichten, uitrusten; (*recht*) beschikken over; *sb.* (*H.*) saldowissel *m.*

appointment [ə'pointmənt] aanstelling, benoeming *v.*; ambt *o.*; voorschrift *o.*, bepaling *v.*; beschikking *v.*; afspraak *v.*; inrichting, uitrusting *r.*

apposite ['æpəzit] passend, geschikt; voegzaam, gepast; toepasselijk.

appraise [ə'preiz] schatten, taxeren; waarderen.

appraiser [ə'preizə] schatter, taxateur *m.*

appreciate [ə'priʃieit] *vt.* (hoog, naar waarde) schatten; waarderen, op prijs stellen; begrijpen, beseffen; verhogen in prijs; *vi.* stijgen in prijs.

appreciation [əpriʃi'eiʃən] schatting *v.*; waardering *v.*; beoordeling, kritische beschouwing *v.*; (het) stijgen *o.* in prijs.

apprehend [æpri'hend] aanhouden, gevangen nemen; begrijpen, beseffen, bevroeden; vatten; vrezen.

apprehension [æpri'henʃən] aanhouding, gevangenneming, inhechtenisneming *v.*; begrip *o.*; bevatting *v.*; bevattingsvermogen *o.*; vrees, angst, bezorgdheid *v.*

apprehensive(ly) [æpri'hensiv(li)] *adj.* (*adv.*) bevattelijk; bevattings—, begrips—; bezorgd, beducht, bevreesd, bang.

apprentice [ə'prentis] *sb.* leerjongen, leerling *m.*; *vt.* in de leer doen.

apprenticeship [ə'prentiʃip] leer *v.*, leertijd *m.*

apprise [ə'praiz] onderrichten, in kennis stellen (*of,* met), kennis geven (*of,* van).

apprize [ə'praiz] schatten; waarderen.

approach [ə'proutʃ] *vt.* naderen, nabijkomen; zich wenden tot, aanspreken; aanzoeken om; *vi.* naderen; grenzen (*to,* aan); *sb.* nadering *v.*; toegang *m.*; toenadering *v*

approachable [ə'proutʃəbl] toegankelijk; genaakbaar.

approbation [æprə'beiʃən] goedkeuring *v.*

appropriate [ə'proupriit] *adj.* passend, geschikt (*to,* voor); bestemd (*for, to,* voor); eigen (*to,* aan).

appropriate [ə'prouprieit] *vt.* zich toeëigenen; aanwijzen, toewijzen; bestemmen (*for, to,* voor).

approval [ə'prûvəl] goedkeuring *v.*, bijval *m.*

approve [ə'prûv] goedkeuren; aantonen; aanbevelen; bevestigen, bekrachtigen.

approved [ə'prûvd] bekwaam; (*v. middel, methode*) beproefd; (*algemeen*) aangenomen.

approximate [ə'proksimeit] naderen; nabijkomen; benaderen; nader brengen.

approximate [ə'proksimit] *adj.* naderend; benaderend, nabijkomend; (zeer) nabij; dicht bijeen.

approximately [ə'proksimitli] *adv.* bij benadering, ongeveer.

appurtenance [ə'pə:tinəns] aanhangsel, bijvoegsel, toevoegsel *o.*; —*s,* toebehoren.

apricot ['eiprikot] abrikoos *r.*

April ['•ipril] april *m.*

apron ['eiprən] *sb.* schort *v.* & *o.*, voorschoot *m.*; schootsvel *o.*; *vt.* een voorschoot aandoen.

apropos [æprə'pou] apropos.

apt [æpt] geschikt; gevat, juist; geneigd; bekwaam.

aptitude ['æptitjûd] geschiktheid *v.*; geneigdheid, neiging *r.*; bekwaamheid *v.*, aanleg *m.*

aquarelle [ækwə'rel] aquarel, waterverftekening *v.*

aqueduct ['ækwidəkt] waterleiding *v.*

Arab ['ærəb] Arabier *m.*

Arabia [ə'reibiə] Arabië *o.*

arable ['ærəbl] *adj.* bebouwbaar, bouw—; *sb.* bouwland *o.*

arbiter ['âbitə] scheidsrechter, scheidsman *m.*

arbitrariness ['âbitrərinis] willekeur, willekeurigheid *v.*

arbitrary ['âbitrəri] willekeurig, eigenmachtig, arbitrair.

arbitration [âbi'treiʃən] arbitrage *v.*; scheidsrechterlijke uitspraak (beslissing) *v.*

arbor ['âbo:] boom *m.*

arboreous [â'bo:riəs] boomrijk; bo(o)m(en)—.

arboriculture ['âbərikəltʃə] boomteelt *r.*

arborist ['âbərist] boomkenner *m.*; boomkweker *m.*

arbour ['âbə] prieel *o.*

arcade [â'keid] overwelfde gang, booggang *v.*; overdekte winkelgalerij *v.*

arch [âtʃ] aarts—, eerste.

arch [âtʃ] schalks, schelms, snaaks, olijk.

arch [âtʃ] *sb.* boog *m.*, gewelf *o.*; *vt.* welven, overwelven; *vi.* zich welven.

archaic [â'keiik] verouderd, oud, archaïstisch.

archangel ['âkeindʒəl] aartsengel *m.*

archbishop ['âtʃ'biʃəp] aartsbisschop *m.*

archer ['âtʃə] boogschutter *m.*

archiepiscopal [âkii'piskəpəl] aartsbisschoppelijk.

architect ['âkitekt] architect, bouwmeester.

architecture ['âkitektʃə] bouwkunde *v.*, bouwstijl *m.*

archives ['âkaivz] archief *o.*; archieven *o. mv.*

archivist ['âkivist] archivaris *m.*

archway ['âtʃwei] boog *m.*, poort, overwelfde gang *v.*

arc-lamp ['âklæmp] booglamp *v.*

ardency ['âdənsi] vurigheid *v.*, gloed, ijver *m.*

ardent(ly) ['âdənt(li)] *adj. (adv.)* brandend, vurig, volijverig.

ardour ['âdə] (*v. zonnestralen*) hitte *v.*; (*fig.*) warmte *r.*, vuur *o.*, gloed, ijver *m.*

arduous(ly) ['âdjuəs(li)] *adj. (adv.)* (*v. pad*) steil; (*v. taak*) zwaar, moeilijk; (*v. rijt*) noest.

are [â] 2e pers. enk. en 1e, 2e, 3e pers. meerv. van **to be** zijn.

are [â, eə] are *v.*

area ['êriə] vlakte *r.*; vlakteïnhoud *m.*; gebied, terrein *o.*; (open) ruimte, vrije open plaats *r.*

arena [ə'rînə] arena *r.*, strijdperk *o.*

argue ['âgjû] *rt.* beredeneren; betogen; bewijzen, duiden op; aanvoeren; tegenspreken; *ri.* redeneren; redetwisten.

argument ['âgjumənt] argument, bewijs *o.*, bewijsgrond *m.*; betoog *o.*

argumentative [âgju'mentətiv] bewijzend, betogend; beredeneerd, logisch.

aria ['âriə] aria, wijs, melodie *v.*

arid ['ærid] droog, dor, onvruchtbaar.

aridity [ə'riditi] droogte, dorheid, onvruchtbaarheid *v.*

aright [ə'rait] juist.

arise [ə'raiz] ontstaan, voortkomen, voortspruiten (*from,* uit); zich voordoen.

aristocracy [æris'tɔkrəsi] aristocratie *v.*

aristocratic(al) [æristə'krætik(l)] *adj.* aristocratisch.

arithmetic [ə'riðmətik] rekenkunde *v.*; rekenboek *o.*

arithmetical [æriδ'metikl] *adj.* rekenkundig.

ark [âk] ark *v.*

arm [âm] arm *m.*

arm [âm] *sb.* wapen *o.*; *rt.* wapenen, bewapenen; beslaan, pantseren; *vi.* zich wapenen.

armament ['âməmənt] bewapening *v.*; krijgstoerusting *r.*; krijgsmacht *r.*

armature ['âmətjuə] wapens *o. mv.*; pantser *o.*; (*v. magneet*) anker *o.*

armchair ['âmtʃêə] leuningstoel *m.*

Armenia [â'mîniə] Armenië *o.*

armistice ['âmistis] wapenstilstand *m.*

armlet ['ârmlit] armband *m.*

armory ['âməri] wapenkunde *r.*

armour ['âmə] *sb.* wapenrusting *v.*, harnas *o.*; pantser *o.*; *vt.* pantseren; blinderen.

armoury ['âməri] arsenaal *o.*; wapenzaal, wapenkamer *v.*

arm-pit ['âmpit] oksel *m.*

army [âmi] leger *o.*

aroma ə'roumə] aroma *o.*, geur *m.*

around [ə'raund] rondom, in 't rond, om en bij.

arouse [ə'rauz] wekken, wakker schudden; opwekken, aansporen, aanporren.

arow [ə'rou] in een rij.

arraign [ə'rein] beschuldigen.

arrange [ə'reindʒ] schikken, rangschikken, ordenen; in orde brengen; inrichten, regelen; afspreken; (*v. geschil, enz.*) bijleggen; (*muz.*) arrangeren.

arrangement [ə'reindʒmənt] schikking, rangschikking *v.*; inrichting; regeling *v.*; afspraak, overeenkomst *v.*; (*muz.*) arrangement *o.*; vergelijk, akkoord *o.*, minnelijke schikking *v.*

arrant ['ærənt] doortrapt, berucht.

array [ə'rei] *vt.* schikken; (*mil.*) (in slagorde) scharen; *sb.* rangschikking *v.*; rij, reeks *v.*; (*mil.*) slagorde *v.*

arrear [ə'riə] achterstand *m.*, achterstallige schuld *r.*

arrearage [ə'riəridʒ] achterstand *m.*; achterstallige schulden *v. mv.*

arrest [ə'rest] *vt.* tegenhouden; aanhouden, in hechtenis nemen, arresteren; beslag leggen op; *sb.* (het) tegenhouden; inhechtenisneming, arrestatie *v.*; beslagneming *r.*

arrival [ə'raivəl] komst, aankomst *v.*; aanvoer *m.*; aangekomene *m.*

arrive [ə'raiv] aankomen; — **at,** aankomen te; komen tot, bereiken.

arrogant(ly) ['ærəgənt(li)] *adj. (adv.)* aanmatigend, verwaand, laatdunkend.

arrogate [ærəgeit] zich aanmatigen; zich (wederrechtelijk) toeëigenen.

arrow ['ærou] pijl *m.*

arrow-head ['ærouhed] pijlspits, pijlpunt *v.*

arsenal ['âsənəl] arsenaal, tuighuis *o.*

arsenic ['âsnik] arsenicum.

art [ât] kunst *v.*; list *m.*

arterial [â'tlériél] slagaderlijk.

artery ['â əri] slagader *m.*; (*fig.*) hoofdverkeersader *m.*

artful(ly) ['âtful(i)] *adj. (adv.)* listig, geslepen, doortrapt, glad; kunstmatig.

artichoke ['âtitʃouk] artisjok *v.*

article ['âti:kl] artikel *o.*; punt *o.*; deel, onderdeel *o.*; lidwoord *o.*; —**s,** contract.

articulate [â'tikjuleit] duidelijk uitspreken, articuleren; door gewrichten verbinden.

articulation [âtikju'leiʃən] geleding; articulatie, duidelijke uitspraak *v.*

artifice ['âtifis] kunstgreep, list *m.*, listigheid *v.*, streek *m.*

artificial [âtiʃiʃél] *adj.* kunstmatig; gekunsteld, onnatuurlijk; *sb.* —**s,** kunstmeststoffen.

artillery [â'tiləri] artillerie *v.*, geschut *o.*

artisan [âti'zæn, 'âtizæn] handwerkman *m.*

artless(ly) ['âtlis(li)] *adj. (adv.)* ongekunsteld, naïef, argeloos.

Aryan ['êəriən] *adj.* Arisch; *sb.* Ariër *m.*

as [æz] *adv.* als, evenals, zoals, gelijk;

cj. als, zoals; toen, terwijl; daar, aangezien; naargelang, naarmate; — *soon* —, zodra; — *it were,* als het ware; — *it is,* zoals de zaken nu staan; — *though,* alsof; — *for,* wat betreft; *pron. such* —, zij, die; die, welke.

ascend [ə'send] beklimmen; opgaan; opvaren.

ascendancy [ə'sendənsi] overwicht *o.,* overmacht, meerderheid *r.*

ascension [ə'senʃən] bestijging *r.;* hemelvaart *r.*

ascent [ə'sent] beklimming *r.;* opgang *r.,* (opgaande) helling *c.*

ascertain [æsə'tain] nagaan, uitmaken, vaststellen, zich vergewissen van.

ascetic [ə'setik] *adj.* ascetisch, strengvroom; *sb.* asceet *m.*

ascribe [əs'kraib] toeschrijven, toekennen (*to,* aan).

nen (*to,* aan)

ascription [əs'kripsən] toeschrijving, toekenning *r.*

asexual [æ'sekʃuəl] geslachtloos.

ash [æʃ] (*mr.:* **ashes** [æʃiz] as *r.*

ash [æʃ] *sb.* es *m.;* essehout *o.; adj.* essehouten, van essehout.

ashamed [ə'ʃeimd] beschaamd (*of,* over); *be* —, zich schamen.

ashlar ['æʃlə] *sb.* hardsteen, arduinsteen *m.* & *o.; adj.* hardstenen, arduinstenen.

ashore [ə'ʃo:] aan land, aan wal.

ash-tray ['æʃtrei] asbakje *o.*

ashy ['æʃi] asachtig; askleurig, asgrauw, asblond; met as bestrooid.

Asia ['eiʃə] Azië *o.*

aside [ə'said] ter zijde, op zij, zijwaarts.

ask [âsk] vragen, verlangen, verzoeken; uitnodigen; (*r. raadsel*) opgeven; — *after,* vragen naar; — *for,* vragen om; te spreken vragen.

askew [əs'kjù] scheef, schuin; minachtend.

asleep [ə'slîp] in slaap; ter ruste.

asp [æsp] esp, espeboom, ratelpopulier *m.*

asparagus [əs'pærəgəs] asperge *r.*

aspect ['æspekt] voorkomen *o.,* aanblik *m.,* uiterlijk, uitzicht *o.;* oogpunt, gezichtspunt *o.;* zijde *r.,* kant *m.*

asperge [əs'pə:dʒ] besprenkelen.

asperity [æs'periti] scherpheid, scherpte, ruwheid *r.*

asperse [əs'pə:s] besprenkelen; belasteren, bekladden.

asphalt ['æsfælt] *sb.* asfalt *o.; adj.* van asfalt, asfalten; *rt.* asfalteren.

asphyxiate [æs'fiksieit] verstikken.

asphyxiating [æs'fiksieitiŋ] verstikkend.

aspirate ['æspireit] aspireren.

aspiration [æspi'reiʃən] aanblazing *r.;* inzuiging *r.;* geaspireerde klank *m.;* streven *o.,* aspiratie *r.*

aspire [əs'paiə] streven, dingen, trachten, haken (*after, at, to,* naar).

ass [æs, âs] ezel *m.*

assail [ə'seil] aanvallen, aanranden; bespringen; bestormen (*with,* met).

assailant [ə'seilənt], **assailer** [ə'seilə] aanrander, aanvaller *m.*

assassinate [ə'sæsineit] vermoorden.

assassination [əsæsi'neiʃən] moord, sluipmoord *m.*

assault [ə'so:lt] *rt.* aanvallen, aanranden; bestormen; *sb.* aanval *m.,* aanranding *r.;* bestorming *r.*

assay [æ'sei] *sb.* proef, essai *r.;* (*r. erts*) analyse *r.;* *rt.* toetsen, keuren, essaaieren; (*r. erts*) bij keuring opleveren.

assemblage [ə'semblidʒ] verzameling, vergadering, samenkomst *r.;* vereniging *r.*

assemble [ə'sembl] (zich) verzamelen; samenkomen, bijeenkomen; vergaderen· samenbrengen, samenvoegen; in elkaar zetten, monteren.

assembly [ə'sembli] verzameling *v.;* bijeenkomst, samenkomst *r.;* vergadering *r.;* (*mil.*) verzamelen.

assent [ə'sent] *sb.* instemming, goedkeuring *r.;* toestemming *r.;* *vi.* instemmen (*to,* met); toestemmen; toestaan.

assert [ə'sə:t] verklaren, beweren, betuigen; doen (laten) gelden; handhaven; opkomen voor.

assertion [ə'sə:ʃən] verklaring, bewering *r.;* handhaving *r.*

assess [ə'ses] belasten, aanslaan (in de belasting); beboeten; schatten, taxeren; (*r. schade, enz.*) vaststellen.

assessment [ə'sesmənt] aanslag *m.* (in belasting); schatting *r.*

assessor [ə'sesə] bijzitter, assessor *m.;* schatter *m.;* (*r. belasting*) zetter *m.*

assets ['æsits] actief *o.,* activa *o. mv.*

asseverate [ə'sevəreit] plechtig verzekeren, betuigen.

assiduity [æsi'djùiti] (onverdroten, aanhoudende) ijver *m.;* naarstigheid *v.*

assiduous(ly) [ə'sidjûəs(li)] *adj.* (*adv.*) ijverig, naarstig, volhardend.

assign [ə'sain] *rt.* toewijzen; bepalen, vaststellen, aangeven; bestemmen; aanwijzen; toeschrijven; (*r. goederen*) overdragen; *sb.* cessionaris, rechtverkrijgende *m.*

assignable [ə'sainəbl] toewijsbaar; bepaalbaar; aanwijsbaar.

assignee [æsi'ni] gevolmachtigde; procuratiehouder *m.;* rechtverkrijgende, cessionaris *m.*

assignment [ə'sainmənt] toewijzing *r.;* vaststelling *r.;* bestemming *r.;* aanwijzing *r.;* (akte van) overdracht *r.*

assimilate [ə'simileit] *rt.* opnemen, verwerken; gelijk stellen, op één lijn stellen (*to, with,* met); gelijk maken (*to, with,* aan).

assist [ə'sist] *rt.* helpen, bijstaan, ter zijde staan; *vi.* — *at,* bijwonen, tegenwoordig zijn.

assistance [ə'sistəns] hulp *r.,* bijstand *m.*

assistant [ə'sistənt] *adj.* behulpzaam, hulp—; *sb.* helper *m.*, hulp *r.*; assistent, adjunct *m.*

associate [ə'souʃiit] *sb.* kameraad, metgezel *m.*; deelgenoot, vennoot *m.*

associate [ə'souʃieit] *rt.* verenigen; verbinden, associëren.

association [əsouʃi'eiʃən] vereniging, verbinding *r.*; deelgenootschap *o.*; associatie *r.*

assort [ə'so:t] uitzoeken, sorteren.

assume [ə'sjûɪɪ] aannemen, opnemen, overnemen; in handen nemen, aanvaarden.

assuming (ly) [ə'sjûmiŋ(li)] *adj.* (*adv.*) aanmatigend.

assumptive [ə'səmtiv] aangenomen.

assurance [ə'ʃûərəns] verzekering *r.*; zekerheid *r.*; onbeschaamdheid.

assure [ə'ʃûə] verzekeren; assureren.

assurer [ə'ʃûərə] verzekeraar *m.*; verzekerde *m.*

aster ['æstə] (*Pl.*) aster *r.*

asterisk ['æstərisk] sterretje *o.* (*).

astern [ə'stə:n] (*sch.*) achteruit.

asthmatic [æsð'mætik] astmatisch.

astir [ə'stə:] in beweging; op de been.

astonish [əs'toniʃ] verbazen, verwonderen.

astonishing (ly) [əs'toniʃiŋ(li)] *adj.* (*adv.*) verbazend.

astonishment [əs'toniʃmənt] verbazing *r.*

astraddle [əs'trædl] schrijlings (*of,* op).

astray [əs'trei] verdwaald, van de weg af; op het verkeerde pad, op een dwaalspoor; **go** —, verdwalen, verdwaald raken.

astrict [əs'trikt] samentrekken; verbinden, beperken; stoppen, verstoppen.

astride [əs'traid] schrijlings (*of,* op).

astringe [əs'trin(d)ʒ] samentrekken; samenbinden.

astrologer [əs'trolədʒə] sterrenwichelaar *m.*

astronomer [əs'tronəmə] sterrenkundige *m.*

astronomy [əs'tronəmi] sterrenkunde *v.*

astute (ly) [əs'tjût(li)] *adj.* (*adv.*) slim, sluw, geslepen.

asunder [ə'səndə] gescheiden, afzonderlijk; van elkaar, uit elkaar, uiteen; in stukken.

asylum [ə'sailəm] asiel, toevluchtsoord *o.*, schuilplaats, wijkplaats *r.*

at [æt] aan, te, tot, naar, bij, van, op, om, in, ter, voor, tegen.

atheist ['eiðiist] godloochenaar, atheïst *m.*

athlete ['æðlit] atleet *m.*

athletic [æð'letik] *adj.* atletisch; *sb.* —s, atletiek.

atmosphere ['ætməsfiə] dampkring *m.*; atmosfeer *v.*

atom ['ætəm] atoom *o.*; (*fig.*) greintje, stofje *o.*

atone [ə'toun] boeten (*for,* voor);

goedmaken; in overeenstemming brengen; verzoenen.

atonement [ə'tounmənt] boete, boetedoening *v.*; vergoeding, schadeloosstelling *r.*; verzoening *r.*

atrabilious [ætrə'biliəs] zwartgallig.

atrocious (ly) [ə'trouʃəs(li)] *adj.* (*adv.*) gruwelijk, afgrijselijk.

atrocity [ə'trositi] gruwel *m.*, gruwelijkheid, gruweldaad, afgrijselijkheid *r.*

atrophy ['ætrəfi] *sb.* uittering, wegkwijning *r.*; verval *o.* van krachten; *ri.* uitteren, wegkwijnen.

attach [ə'tætʃ] *vt.* vastmaken, vasthechten, hechten aan; aan zich hechten; beslag leggen op, in beslag nemen; *ri.* verbonden zijn (*to,* aan), aankleven, kleven aan.

attachment [ə'tætʃmənt] aanhechting *r.*; gehechtheid, aanhankelijkheid, verknochtheid *v.*; verbinding *v.*, band *m.*; aanhangsel *o.*; beslag *o.*, beslaglegging *r.*

attack [ə'tæk] *vt.* aanvallen; aantasten; *sb.* aanval *m.*

attain [ə'tein] *vt.* bereiken; verkrijgen; *vi.* — **to,** komen tot, geraken tot, bereiken.

attainable [ə'teinəbl] bereikbaar, te bereiken.

attainder [ə'teində] verbeurdverklaring van goederen en verlies van burgerrechten.

attainment [ə'teinmənt] bereiking *v.*; verkrijging *v.*; (het) bereikte, (het) verworvene *o.*; talent *o.*, kundigheid *r.*

attar ['ætə] — (*of roses*), rozenolie *v.*

attemper [ə'tempə] matigen, temperen, kalmeren; geschikt maken (*to,* voor), in overeenstemming brengen (*to,* met), aanpassen (aan).

attempt [ə'tem(p)t] *rt.* pogen, trachten, beproeven; ondernemen; een aanslag doen op; *sb.* poging *r.*; aanslag *m.*

attend [ə'tend] *vt.* begeleiden, vergezellen; (*v. kerk, school*) bezoeken; (*v. colleges, enz.*) bijwonen, volgen; (*v. zieke, enz.*) verzorgen, verplegen, oppassen; (*r. klant*) bedienen.

attendance [ə'tendəns] bediening, behandeling *v.*; opkomst *v.*, bezoek, publiek *o.*, aanwezige personen *m. mv.*; bedienden *mr.*

attendant [ə'tendənt] bediende *m.*; oppasser *m.*; begeleider; volgeling *m.*; bezoeker *m.*

attention [ə'tenʃən] aandacht, oplettendheid *v.*; beleefdheid, attentie *v.*

attentive (ly) [ə'tentiv(li)] *adj.* (*adv.*) oplettend; voorkomend, gedienstig.

attenuate [ə'tenjueit] *rt.* verdunnen; vermageren; verzwakken; verzachten.

attest [ə'test] verklaren, bevestigen, betuigen; staven; (*v. rekruten*) beëdigen, de eed afnemen.

attic ['ætik] dakkamertje, zolderkamertje *o.*, vliering *r.*

attire [ə'taiə] *rt.* kleden, uitdossen, tooien; *sb.* kleding, dracht *v.*, tooi *m.*

attitude [ætitjûd] houding *v.*

attitudinize [æti'tjûdinaiz] zich aanstellen, aanstellerig doen.

attitudinizing [æti'tjûdinaizin] *adj.* aanstellerig; *sb.* aanstellerij *v.*

attorney [ə'tə:ni] procureur *m.*; gevolmachtigde, procuratiehouder *m.*; zaakwaarnemer *m.*

attract [ə'trækt] aantrekken, tot zich trekken; boeien, lokken.

attractive [ə'træktiv] *adj.* boeiend; aantrekkelijk.

attribute [ə'tribjût] *vt.* toeschrijven; toekennen; aanrekenen.

attrition [ə'trifən] wrijving *v.*; afschuring, afschaving, afslijting *v.*; (onvolmaakt) berouw *o.*

attune [ə'tjûn] stemmen; in overeenstemming brengen (*to*, met), aanpassen (*to*, aan).

auburn [o:bən] goudbruin, roodbruin, kastanjebruin.

auction [o:kfən] *sb.* openbare verkoping; veiling *v.*; *vt.* veilen.

auctioneer [o:kfə'niə] *sb.* vendumeester, afslager *m.*; *vt.* veilen, verkopen.

audacious(ly) [o:'deifəs(li)] *adj.* (*adv.*) stout, vermetel; brutaal, onbeschaamd.

audacity [o:'dæsiti] stoutheid, vermetelheid *v.*

audible [o:dibl] *adj.* hoorbaar.

audience ['o:djəns] gehoor *o.*; audiëntie *v.*

audit ['o:dit] (*v. rekeningen*) verifiëren, nazien.

auditor ['o:ditə] toehoorder *m.*; verificateur *m.*; accountant *m.*

auditory ['o:ditəri] gehoorzaal *v.*; toehoorders *m. mv.*, auditorium *o.*

augment [o:g'mənt] *vt.* vermeerderen, vergroten, verhogen; *vi.* aangroeien, vermeerderen.

augmentation [o:gmən'teifən] vermeerdering, verhoging *v.*; aangroei *m.*

August ['o:gəst] augustus *m.*

august [o:'gəst] groots, verheven, doorluchtig.

aunt [ânt] tante *v.*

aureola [o:'riələ], **aureole** ['o:rioul] aureool *v.*, stralenkrans, lichtkrans *m.*

auricle ['o:rikl] oorschelp *v.*; hartboezem *m.*

aurist ['o:rist] oorarts *m.*

aurora [o'ro:rə] dageraad *m.*, morgenrood *o.*

austere(ly) [o:s'tiə(li)] *adj.* (*adv.*) streng; stuurs, nors; sober; wrang.

Australasia [o:strə'leifə] Australië, Oceanië *o.*

Austria ['o:striə] Oostenrijk *o.*

authentic(al) [o:'ðentik(l)] *adj.* authentiek.

author ['o:ðə] schepper, voortbrenger, aanlegger, bewerker *m.*; bedrijver, dader *m.*; schrijver, auteur *m.*

authoress ['o:ðəris] bewerkster, maakster *v.*; daderes *v.*; schrijfster *v.*

authoritative [o:'ðoriteitiv] *adj.* ge-

biedend, autoritair; gezaghebbend; officieel.

authority [o:'ðoriti] autoriteit *v.*; gezag *o.*, macht *v.*; aanzien *o.*, invloed *m.*; machtiging, vergunning *v.*; bewijs *o.*, bewijsplaats, bron *v.*; zegsman *m.*

authorization [o:ðərai'zeifən] autorisatie, machtiging, bekrachtiging, volmacht *v.*

authorize [o:ðəraiz] autoriseren, machtigen, bekrachtigen, rechtvaardigen.

autocracy [o:'tokrəsi] alleenheerschappij *v.*

autocratic(al) [o:tə'krætik(l)] *adj.* autocratisch, eigenmachtig.

autographic(al) [o:tə'græfik(l)] *adj.* autografisch, eigenhandig geschreven.

automatic [o:tə'mætik] automatisch, zelfwerkend; werktuiglijk.

automaton [o:'tomətən] automaat *m.*

automobile ['o:təməbîl] auto *v.*, automobiel *m.*

automobilist [o:tə'moubilist] autorijder, automobilist *m.*

autonomy [o:'tonəmi] autonomie *v.*, zelfbestuur *o.*, zelfregering *v.*

autumn ['o:təm] herfst *m.*

auxiliary [o:g'ziliəri] *adj.* hulp—, behulpzaam; *sb.* helper, bondgenoot *m.*; hulpmiddel *o.*; (*gram.*) hulpwerkwoord *o.*

avail [ə'veil] *vt.* & *vi.* baten; *vr.* — **oneself of**, gebruik maken van, benutten, zich te nutte maken, te baat nemen; *sb.* baat, hulp *v.*, nut, voordeel *o.*

available [ə'veiləbl] beschikbaar; bruikbaar, dienstig, nuttig; geldig.

avarice ['ævəris] gierigheid, hebzucht *v.*

avaricious [ævə'rifəs] gierig, hebzuchtig; — **of**, begerig naar.

avenge [ə'ven(d)з] wreken.

avenger [ə'ven(d)зə] wreker *m.*

aver [ə'və:] beweren, verklaren; betuigen, verzekeren; (*recht*) bewijzen, waar maken.

average ['ævəridз] *sb.* gemiddelde *o.*; doorsneeprijs *m.*; (*sch.*) schade, averij *v.*; *adj.* gemiddeld.

averment [ə'və:mənt] bewering, betuiging, verzekering, bevestiging *v.*; bewijs *o.*, bewijsvoering *v.*

averse [ə'və:s] afkerig (*to, from*, van).

aversion [ə'və:fən] afkeer *m.*, afkerigheid *v.*, tegenzin, weerzin *m.*; antipathie *v.*

avert [ə'və:t] afkeren, afwenden; afkerig maken.

aviary ['eiviəri] vogelvlucht, volière *v.*

aviate ['eivieit] (*vl.*) vliegen.

aviation [eivi'eifən] (*vl.*) vliegkunst *v.*; vliegsport *v.*

aviator ['eivieitə] vlieger, vliegenier *m.*

avid ['ævid] *adj.* gretig, begerig (*of, for*, naar).

avidity [ə'viditi] gretigheid, begerigheid, begeerte *v.*

avocation [ævə'keifən] beroep *o.*; werk *o.*, werkzaamheden, bezigheden *v. mv.*

avocet, avoset ['ævouset] (*Dk.*) kluit *m.*

avoid [ə'vɔid] mijden, vermijden, ontwijken; (*recht*) ongeldig maken (verklaren), vernietigen.

avoidable [ə'vɔidəbl] vermijdbaar, te vermijden.

avow [ə'vau] belijden, erkennen, bekennen.

avowal [ə'vauəl] belijdenis, bekentenis *v.*

await [ə'weit] wachten, afwachten, wachten op; verwachten.

awake [ə'weik] *vt.* wekken, opwekken; *vi.* ontwaken, wakker worden· zich bewust worden (*to,* van), tot het besef komen (*to,* van) *adj.* wakker.

awaken [ə'weikən] *vt.* wekken; *vi.* ontwaken, wakker worden.

award [ə'wo:d] *vt.* (*v. prijs, enz.*) toekennen, toewijzen; (*v. straf*) opleggen; beslissen; *sb.* toekenning, toewijzing *v.*; uitspraak; beslissing *v.*; toegekende beloning *v.*; opgelegde straf *v.*; onderscheiding, bekroning *v.*

aware [ə'wêə] onderricht, zich bewust, gewaar.

away [ə'wei] weg, voort; verder op; er op los.

awe [o:] ontzag *o.*, eerbied *m.*; vrees *v.*

awesome ['o:səm] ontzagwekkend, ontzaglijk, vreselijk; eerbiedig.

awful ['o:ful] ontzagwekkend; ontzaglijk; schrikwekkend.

awhile [ə'wail] een poos, een tijdje.

awkward ['o:kwəd] onhandig, onbeholpen, lomp, onbehouwen; onaangenaam, vervelend; lelijk, kwaad, lastig, gevaarlijk.

awl [o:l] els *v.*, priem *m.*

awning ['o:niŋ] dekzeil, scherm *o.*, zonnetent *v.*

awry [ə'rai] scheef, schuin, krom; verkeerd; mis.

ax (e) [æks] bijl *v.*

axe-man ['æksmən] houthakker *m.*

axil ['æksil] (*Pl.*) oksel *m.*

axiom ['æksiəm] axioma *o.*, grondstelling *v.*

axis ['æksis] as, aslijn, spil *v.* draaier *m.* (*tweede halswervel*).

axle ['æksl] as, wagenas *v.*; spil *v.*

azure ['æʒə, 'eiʒə] *sb.* hemelsblauw, azuur *o.*; *adj.* hemelsblauw, azuren.

azyme ['æzaim, 'æzim] ongezuurd (ongedesemd) brood *o.*

B

Baalism ['beiəlizm] afgodendienst *m.*

babble ['bæbl] *vi.* babbelen; wauwelen; kabbelen, murmelen; *sb.* gebabbel; gewauwel *o.*; gekabbel, gemurmel *o.*

baboon [bə'bûn] baviaan *m.*

baboonery [bə'bûnəri] bavianenkolonie *v.*; aapachtig optreden *o.*

baby ['beibi] *sb.* kind (je) *o.*; (*v. dier*) jong *o.*; *adj.* kinderachtig; klein.

baby-car ['beibikâ] kinderwagen *m.*

babyhood ['beibihud] kindsheid *v.*

bachelor ['bætʃələ] vrijgezel *m.* baccalaureus *m.*

bacillus [bə'siləs] (*mv.:* **bacilli**) bacil *v.*

back [bæk] *sb.* rug *m.*; rugzijde *v.*; keerzijde *v.*; achterkant; onderkant *m.*; rugleuning *v.*; (*v. kalender*) schild *o.*; (*v. schip*) kiel *v.*; (*v. rivier*) oppervlakte *v.*; (*sp.*) achterspeler *m.*; *adj.* achter—; afgelegen, verwijderd; achterstallig; (*v. kranten, enz.*) oud; omgekeerd; *adv.* terug; achterwaarts, naar achteren, achteruit; geleden.

back [bæk] *vt.* achteruittrekken, achteruitschuiven, terugschuiven; steunen, ondersteunen, rugsteunen; endosseren; (*v. boek*) ruggen, van een rug voorzien; (*sch.: v. anker*) katten, strijken; *v. paard, enz.*) berijden, bestijgen; (*Am.*) adresseren; *vi.* teruggaan; achteruitgaan; achteruittrijden; (*sch.*) bakzeil halen; (*v. wind*) krimpen; — **out,** ergens achterwaarts uitgaan, rugwaarts heengaan.

backbite ['bækbait] lasteren, belasteren, kwaadspreken van.

backbiting ['bækbaitiŋ] achterklap, laster *m.*

backbone ['bækboun] ruggegraat *v.*; (*fig.*) wilskracht, vastheid, flinkheid *v.*

backdoor ['bæk'do:] achterdeur (tje) *v.* (*o.*).

back-fire ['bækfaiə] *sb.* (*v. motor*) terugslag; *vi.* terugslaan.

back-front ['bækfrɔnt] achtergevel *m.*

background ['bækgraund] achtergrond *m.*

back-number ['bæk'nəmbə] (*v. tijdschrift*) oud nummer *o.*; (*fig.*) uit de oude doos.

back-pass ['bækpâs] (*sp.:* *voetbal*) „hakken".

back-payment [bælpeimənt] achterstallige betaling *v.*

backroom ['bækrum] achterkamer *v.*

back-side ['bæk'said] achterste *o.*

backslider ['bæk'slaidə] afvallige *m.*; recidivist *m.*

backstairs [bæk'stêəz] *sb.* geheime trap, achtertrap *v.*; *adj.* (*ook:* **backstair**) heimelijk, slinks.

backward ['bækwəd] *adj.* achterwaarts; rugwaarts; traag, onwillig; achterlijk; schuchter; *adv.* achterwaarts, achteruit; ruggelings.

backwards ['bækwədz] *adv.* achterwaarts; rugwaarts; achteruit, terug; traag, onwillig.

backway ['bækweiJ achterweg *m*.; achteringang *m*.; omweg *m*.

bacon ['beikn] (gerookt) spek *o*.

bacteriologist [bæktiəri'ɔlədʒist] bacterioloog *m*.

bad [bæd] *adj.* slecht; kwaad, boos; ondeugend; erg; naar, onwel, ziek; (*v. lucht, enz.*) bedorven; (*v. geld*) vals, nagemaakt; *sb.* kwaad *o*.

baddish ['bædiʃ] vrij slecht, van minderwaardige hoedanighcid.

badge [bædʒ] kenteken, insigne, onderscheidingsteken, distinctief *o*.

badger ['bædʒə] das *m*.; dassehaar *o*., penseel *o*. (van dassehaar); scheerkwast *m*.

badly ['bædli] *adv.* kwalijk; slecht, erg.

badness ['bædnis] slechtheid, verdorvenheid *v*.

baffle ['bæfl] tarten; verijdelen, doen falen; ontwijken, spotten met; tegenhouden, vastzetten.

bag [bæg] *sb.* zak *m*., baal *v*.; tas, weitas *v*.; vangst *v*., buit *m*., geschoten wild *o*.; buidel *m*.; uier *m*.

bagatelle [bægə'tel] bagatel, kleinigheid *v*.

baggage ['bægidʒ] legertrein *m*.; (*Am*.) bagage *v*.

bagpipe ['bægpaip] doedelzak *m*.

bail [beil] *sb.* borg *m*.; borgtocht *m*.; borgstelling *v*.; staketsel *o*.; afsluitboom *m*., (halve) hoepel *m*.; (pot)hengsel *o*.; (*sp.: cricket*) blokje hout op wicket; *vt.* borg blijven voor; in bewaring geven; hozen.

bailer ['beilJ] borg, borgsteller *m*.; uithozer *m*.; hoosvat *o*.; (*cricket*) bal, die de bails raakt.

bailiff ['beilif] deurwaarder, gerechtsdienaar *m*.; rentmeester, zaakwaarnemer *m*.; (*gesch.*) baljuw, schout *m*.

bailment ['beilmənt] bewaargeving *v*.; borgstelling *v*.; vrijlating tegen borgstelling *v*.

bait [beit] *sb.* aas, lokaas *o*.; (het) pleisteren *o*.; (*Dk.*) witvis *m*.; *vt.* van aas (lokaas) voorzien; aanleggen; sarren, kwellen; *vi.* aanleggen, pleisteren.

baize [beiz] baai *v*. (*stof*).

bake [beik] bakken, braden; verbranden.

bakehouse ['beikhaus] bakkerij *v*.

baker ['beikə] bakker *m*.; *Am*.) bakoven *m*.

bakery ['beikəri] bakkerij *v*.

baking ['beikiŋ] (het) bakken *o*.; baksel *o*.

baking-powder ['beikiŋpaudə] bakpoeder *o*.

balance ['bæləns] *sb.* balans, weegschaal *v*.; (*sterr.*) Weegschaal *v*.; evenwicht *o*.; tegenwicht *o*.; (*in horloge*) onrust *v*.; rest *v*., overschot *o*.; (*H.*) (batig) saldo *o*.; *vt.* wegen; overwegen; in evenwicht brengen (houden); opwegen tegen; (*v. rekening*) vereffenen; (*v. begroting*) sluitend maken; (*de balans*) afsluiten; *vi.* in evenwicht zijn, balan-

ceren; (*v. rekening*) sluiten, kloppen; (*fig.*) weifelen; schommelen.

balance-sheet ['bælənsʃit] (*H.*) balans *v*.

balcony ['bælkəni] balkon *o*.; (*sch.*) galerij *v*.

bald [bɔ:ld] kaal, naakt; onopgesn:ukt, sober; armzalig.

baldhead ['bɔ:ldhed] kaalkop *m*.

bale [beil] *sb.* baal *v*.; *dicht.*) ellende *r*., ongeluk, onheil, verderf *o*.; *vt.* in balen pakken.

baleen [bə'lin] *sb.* balein *o*. & *v*.; *adj.* baleinen.

baleful ly) ['beilful'i)] *adj.* (*adv.*) noodlottig, verderfelijk, heilloos.

balk [bɔ:k] *sb.* (ruwe) balk *m*.; ongeploegde strook *v*. land; (*bilj.*) streep *v*.; struikelblo𝔨 *o*.; teleurstelling *v*.; *vt.* teleurstellen; dwarsbomen, verijdelen; ontwijken; laten voorbijgaan; *vi.* plotseling blijven steken; tegenstribbelen, bezwaren maken; (*v. paard*) uitbreken.

ball [bɔ:l] bal, bol *m*.; (kanons)kogel *m*.; kluwen *o*.; (*voor vee*) pil *v*.; bal *o*., danspartij *v*.; (*v. duim*) muis *v*.

ballad ['bæləd] ballade *v*.; lied(je) *o*.

ballet ['bælei] ballet *o*.

ball-frame ['bɔ:lfreim] telraam *o*.

balloon [bə'lūn] ballon, luchtballon *m*.; bol *m*.; (*r. distilleertoestel*) ontvanger *m*.

ballot ['bælət] *sb.* stemballetje, stembriefje *o*.; uitgebrachte stemmen *v. mv.*; geheime stemming *v*.; loting *v*.; kleine baal *v*.; *vi.* balloteren, stemmen; loten.

ballot-box ['bælətbɔks] stembus *r*.

ballot-paper ['bælətpeipə] stembriefje *o*.

ball-proof ['bɔ:lpruf] kogelvrij.

balm [bâm] *sb.* balsem *m*.; balsemgeur *m*.; balsembomen *m*.; *vt.* balsemen; verzachten, verlichten, lenigen.

balmy ['bâmi] balsemachtig; balsemend; zacht, verzachtend, kalmerend.

balsam ['bɔ:lsəm] balsem *m*.; (*Pl.*) balsemine *v*.

baluster ['bæləstə] baluster *m*., spijltje (zuiltje) *o*. van een balustrade; **—s,** trapleuning

balustrade [bæləs'treid] balustrade *v*.

bam [bæm] (*sl.*) *vt.* beetnemen, bedotten, foppen; *sb.* beetnemerij, fopperij *v*., bedrog *o*.

bamboo [bæm'bū] bamboe *m. en o*.

ban [bæn] *sb.* afkondiging *v*.; verbod *o*.; ban, banvloek *m*.; *vt.* verbieden; verbannen.

banal ['beinəl, 'bænəl] *adj.* banaal, triviaal.

banana [bə'nânə] banaan, pisang *v*.

band [bænd] *sb.* band *m*.; lint, snoer, koord *o*.; (sigaren)bandje *o*., ring *m*.; drijfriem *m*.; muziekkorps *o*., (militaire) kapel *v*., stafmuziek *v*.; troep *m*., bende *v*.; windsel *o*., zwachtel *m*.; *vt.* verenigen; verbinden; van een band voorzien.

bandage ['bændidʒ] *sb.* verband *o.*, zwachtel *m.*; blinddoek *m.*; *vt.* verbinden, zwachtelen; blinddoeken.

bandbox ['bændbɔks] hoedendoos *v.*; lintendoos *v.*

bandit ['bændit] bandiet, rover; vogelvrijverklaarde *m.*

bandmaster ['bændmâstə] kapelmeester *m.*

bandsman ['bændzmən] muzikant *m.*

baneful(ly) ['beinful(i)] *adj.* (*adv.*) giftig, vergiftig; verderfelijk.

bang [bæŋ] slaan, stompen; dichtslaan; neersmakken.

bang [bæŋ] pony (haar) *o.*

banish ['bæniʃ] bannen, verbannen.

banishment ['bæniʃmənt] verbanning, ballingschap *v.*

ban(n)ister ['bænistə] baluster *m.*, spijl *v.*, trapspijltje *o.*; **—s**, trapspijltjes; trapleuning *v.*

bank [bæŋk] *sb.* bank *v.*; speelbank *v.*; berm, dijk, dam *m.*; oever *m.*; zandbank *v.*; *vt.* op de bank zetten, deponeren; verzilveren; (*v. vuur*) inrakelen; *vi.* zijn geld beleggen; bankzaken doen; een bankrekening hebben; de bank houden; (*v. vliegtuig, auto*) naar één kant overhellen (in een bocht).

bankable ['bæŋkəbl] discontabel, betaalbaar bij een bank.

bank-book ['bæŋkbuk] rekening-courantboekje *o.*

banker ['bæŋkə] bankier; kassier *m.*; bankhouder *m.*

banking-business ['bæŋkiŋbiznis] bankierszaak *v.*; bankzaken *v. mv.*

banknote ['bæŋknout] bankbiljet *o.*

bank-rate ['bæŋkreit] bankdisconto *o.*

bankrupt ['bæŋkrəpt] bankroetier, gefailleerde, failliet *m.*

bankruptcy ['bæŋkrəpsi] bankroet, faillissement *o.*

banner ['bænə] banier *v.*, vaandel *o.*

banns [bænz] (kerkelijke) huwelijksafkondiging *v.*, geboden *o. mv.*

banquet ['bænkwit] *sb.* feestmaal, gastmaal, banket *o.*; *vt.* (feestelijk) onthalen; *vi.* banketteren, smullen.

banter ['bæntə] scherts, boert *v.*; *vt.* voor de gek houden; gekscheren met; *vi.* schertsen.

baptism ['bæptizm] doop *m.*; doopsel *o.*

baptismal [bæp'tizməl] doop—.

baptist(e)ry ['bæptist(ə)ri] doopkapel *v.*; doopvont *v.*, doopbekken *o.*

baptize [bæp'taiz] dopen.

bar [bâ] *sb.* staaf, stang, baar *v.*; afsluitboom, draaiboom, slagboom *m.*; spijl, tralie *v.*; (*wap.*) balk *m.*; (*muz.*) streep, maatstreep, maat *v.*; (*v. chocolade*) reep *m.*; rekstok *m.*; balie *v.*; rechtbank *v.*; buffet, taplokaal *o.*; (*in riviermond*) zandbank *v.*

barb [bâb] *sb.* baard *m.*; weerhaak *m.*; *m.*; *vt.* met weerhaken voorzien; (*v. wol*) scheren.

barbarian [bâ'bêəriən] *sb.* barbaar *m.*; *adj.* barbaars.

barbarous(ly) [bâbərəs(li)] *adj.* (*adv.*) barbaars.

bar-bell ['bâbel] (*sp.*) lange halter *m.*

barber ['bâbə] barbier *m.*; leervis *m.*

bare ['bââ] *adj.* bloot, kaal, naakt, ontbloot; louter; *vt.* blootleggen; ontbloten; ontdoen (**of,** van).

bareback(ed) ['bêəbæk(t)] zonder zadel, ongezadeld.

barefaced ['bêəfeist] ongebaard, met glad gezicht; ongemaskerd; onbeschaamd, schaamteloos.

barefoot(ed) ['beəfut(id)] blootsvoets, barrevoets.

bareheaded ['bêə'hedid] blootshoofds.

barely ['beəli] *adv.* open, openlijk, amper, ternauwernood, nauwelijks.

bareness ['bêənis] blootheid, naaktheid *v.*; kaalheid *v.*

bargain ['bâgin] *sb.* koop *m.*; koopje *o.*; overeenkomst, afspraak *v.*; *vi.* dingen, afdingen; onderhandelen; overeenkomen; *vt.* **— away**, verkwanselen, versjacheren, verkopen (met verlies).

barge [bâdʒ] woonschuit, woonboot *v.*

bargeman ['bâdʒmən] schuitevoerder *m.*; aakschipper *m.*

bark [bâk] *sb.* bast, schors, schil *v.*; run *v.*; kina *v.*; schuit, bark *v.*; geblaf *o.*; ontschorsen; schillen; (*v. huid*) schaven; ontvellen; met een korst bedekken; *vi.* blaffen, bassen.

barker ['bâkə] blaffer, keffer, schreeuwer *m.*; klantenlokker *m.*; (*sl.*) pistool *o.*

barley ['bâli] gerst *v.*

barm [bâm] gist *v.*

barmaid ['bâmeid] buffetjuffrouw *v.*

barn [bân] schuur *v.*

barn-floor ['bânflo:] dorsvloer *m.*

barometer [bə'rɔmitə] barometer *m.*

baron ['bærən] baron *m.*

baroness ['bærənis] barones *v.*

barrack ['bærək] *sb.* barak, keet *v.*; **—(s)**, kazerne *v.*; *vt.* (*mil.*) kazerneren.

barrage ['bærâʒ, bæ'râʒ] *sb.* (*vooral v. Nijl*) dam, afsluitdam *m.*; versperring *v.*; (*mil.*) spervuur *o.*; *vt.* met spervuur bestoken.

barrel ['bærəl] *sb.* vat *o.*, ton *v.*; (*v. speeldoos, enz.*) cilinder *m.*; (*v. vuurwapen*) loop *m.*; (*v. paard*) romp *m.*; (*v. oor, horloge*) trommel *m.*; *vt.* inkuipen; aftappen.

barrel-organ ['bærəlo:gən] draaiorgel *o.*

barren ['bærən] onvruchtbaar; kaal, dor; dom.

barrenness ['bærənnis] onvruchtbaarheid *v.*; kaalheid, dorheid *v.*

barret ['bærət] baret *v.*

barricade [bæri'keid] *sb.* barricade, versperring, hindernis *v.*; *vt.* barricaderen, versperren.

barrier ['bæriə] *sb.* slagboom, sluitboom *m.*; grenspaal *m.*; versperring hindernis *v.*, hinderpaal *m.*

barrister ['bæristə] (—-*at* —*law*), advocaat *m.*

barrow ['bærou] berrie *v.*; kruiwagen *m.*; handkar *v.*; grafheuvel *m.*

barter ['bâtə] *vi.* ruilen, ruilhandel drijven; *vt.* ruilen, verruilen; — *away*, verkwanselen; *sb.* ruil, ruilhandel *m.*

bascule ['bæskjûl] bascule, weegbrug *v.*

base [beis] *adj.* laag, gemeen; minderwaardig; (*v. metalen*) onedel; (*v. munt*) vals.

base [beis] *sb.* basis *v.*, grondslag *m.*; grondlijn *v.*; grondvlak *o.*; voetstuk *o.*; grondgetal *o.*; uitgangspunt *o.*; (*sp.*) honk *o.*; (*muz.*) bas *v.*; *vt.* baseren, gronden, grondvesten; (*mil.*, *sch.*) als basis aanwijzen.

base-born ['beisbo:n] van lage geboorte; laag, gemeen; onecht.

baseless(ly) ['beislis(li)] *adj.* (*adv.*) ongegrond.

basement ['beismənt] grondslag *m.*, fondament *o.*; souterrain *o.*

bashful(ly) ['bæʃful(i)] *adj.* (*adv.*) verlegen, bedeesd, schuchter.

bashfulness ['bæʃfulnis] verlegenheid, bedeesdheid, schuchterheid, bloheid *v.*

basin ['beisin] bekken *o.*, kom *v.*; bassin, dok *o.*; keteldal *o.*; stroomgebied *o.*

basis ['beisis] grondslag *m.*, basis *v.*; grondlijn *v.*

bask [bâsk] (zich) koesteren.

basket ['bâskit] *sb.* korf *m.*, mand *v.*; schanskorf *m.*; (*v. visser*) vangst *v.*; *vt.* in een mand pakken; in de prullemand doen; (*v. vis*) vangen.

basket-ball ['bâskitbo:l] (*sp.*) korfbal *m.*

basket-ware ['bâskitwêə] **basketwork** ['bâskitwə:k] mandewerk *o.*

bass [beis' (*muz.*) bas(stem) *v.*

bass [bæs] *Dk.*) baars *m.*; (*Am.*) lindebast *m.*

bast [bâst] (*Am.*) (linde)bast *m.*

bastard ['bæstəd] *sb.* bastaard *m.*; basterdsuiker *v.*; *adj.* bastaard—, onecht.

baste [beist] aaneenrijgen; met vet overgieten (bedruipen); afrossen, ranselen.

bastion ['bæstiən] bastion *o.*

bat [bæt] vleermuis *v.*

bat [bæt] *sb.* knuppel *m.*; (*bij cricket*) bat *o.*; slag *m.*; halve baksteen *m.*

batch [bætʃ] baksel *o.*; troep *m.*; partij *v.*

bate [beit] verminderen; aftrekken, laten vallen; laten zakken, verliezen; afstompen; sparen.

bat-fowling ['bætfaulin] lichtbakken.

bath [bâð; *mv.*; bâðz] *sb.* bad *o.*; badkuip *v.*; —*s*, badhuis *o.*; badinrichting *v.*; badplaats *v.*; *vt.* baden, een bad geven.

bathe [beiθ] *sb.* bad *o.* (*in rivier of zee*); zwembad *o.*; *vt.* baden; betten, bevochtigen; bespoelen; *vi.* zich baden.

bather ['beiθə] bader *m.*; badgast *m.*

bathing-cabin ['beiθinkæbin] (*op strand*) badhuisje *o.*

bathing-drawers ['beiθindro:əz] zwembroek *v.*

bathing-place ['beiθinpleis] badplaats *v.*; badgelegenheid *v.*

bathroom ['bâðrum] badkamer *v.*

bating ['beitin] behalve, behoudens.

batist(e) [ə'tist] batist *o.*

baton ['bætən] staf; commandostaf; maarschalksstaf *m.*; gummistok, wapenstok *m.*; dirigeerstok *m.*; vertrekstaf *m.* (*wap.*) balk *m.*

battalion [bə'tæljən] bataljon *o.*

batten ['bætn] *vt.* voeden mesten; *vi.* zich voeden; vet worden, gedijen; zich te goed doen.

batter ['bætə] *sb.* schuinte, helling *v.*; (*sp.: cricket*) batter *m.*; beslag *o.* (*voor gebak*) *vt.* beuken, rammeien; beschieten; havenen; *vi.* achterover hellen.

battery ['bætəri] (*mil.*, *el.*) batterij *v.*; keukengereedschap *o.*; koperslagerswerk *o.*; (*recht*) aanranding, geweldpleging *v.*

battle ['bætl] *sb.* slag, veldslag *m.*; strijd *m.*; *vi.* strijden, vechten, slag leveren.

battledore ['bætldo:] raket *o.*

battle-field ['bætlfîld] slagveld, gevechtsterrein *o.*

battlement ['bætlmənt] kanteel *o.*, tinne *v.*

bauble ['bo:bl] snuisterij, prul *v.*, (stuk) speelgoed *o.*; zotskolf *v.*, narrenscepter *m.*

Bavaria [bə'vêəriə] Beieren *o.*

bawdy ['bo:di] *adj.* ontuchtig.

bawdy-house [bo:dihaus] bordeel *o.*

bawl [bo:l] *vt.* schreeuwen, bulken, brullen, joelen; (*fig.*) balken; *sb.* schreeuw *m.*

bay [bei] *sb.* baai *v.*, inham *m.*; vak *o.*, ruimte *v.*; erker *m.*; uitbouw *m.*; laurierboom *m.*; lauwerkrans *m.*; geblaf, gebas *o.*; vos *m.* (*paard*).

bay [bei] *vt. & vi.* blaffen (tegen), aanblaffen; in 't nauw drijven.

bay [bei] *adj.* roodbruin, vaalbruin, voskleurig.

bayonet ['beiənit] *sb.* bajonet *v.*; *vt.* doorsteken (neersteken).

baza(a)r [bə'zâ] bazar *m.*; (Oosterse) marktplaats *v.*

be [bî] zijn, wezen; gebeuren; worden, ontstaan; liggen, staan.

beach [bîtʃ] *sb.* strand *o.*, oever, wal *m.*; grint, kiezel *o.*; *vt.* op het strand zetten (halen, trekken, drijven).

beacon ['bîkan] *sb.* baken, boei *v.*; lichttoren, vuurtoren *m.*; *vt.* bebakenen, afbakenen; verlichten; (*fig.*) voorlichten, leiden.

bead [bîd] *sb.* kraal *v.*; parel *v.*; vizierkorrel *m.*; (*bouwk.*) kraal *v.*; kraallijst *v.*; *vt.* aaneenrijgen; van kralen voorzien; *vi.* parelen.

beadle ['bîdl] pedel; bode *m.*

beagle ['bîgl] (*Dk.*) brak *m.*; (*fig.*) speurder, speurhond, spion *m.*

beak [bîk] bek, snavel *m.*

beaker ['bîkə] beker *m.*, bekerglas *o.*; bokaal *m.*

beam [bîm] *sb.* balk *m.*; ploegboom *m.*; weversboom *m.*; (*sch.*) dekbalk *m.*; grootste wijdte *v.*; (*v. balans*) juk *o.*; stam *m.* van gewei; *vt.* uitstralen; stralen van; *vi.* stralen.

bean [bîn] boon *v.*

bean-feast ['bînfîst] feest *o.*, fuif, pret *v.*

bean-fed ['bînfed] in goede conditie.

bean-goose ['bîngûs] rietgans *v.*

bean-pole ['bînpoul] bonestaak *m.*

bear [bêə] beer *m.*; (*fig.*) izegrim, ongelikte beer, bullebak *m.*; (*H.: effectenbeurs*) baissier, contramineur *m.*; *vt. & vi.* à la baisse speculeren; in prijs doen dalen.

bear [bêə] *vt.* verdragen, dulden, uitstaan; toelaten (*v.; liefde, genegenheid*) toedragen; (*v. rente*) geven; hebben, in zich sluiten; voortbrengen, baren; dragen, torsen; *vi.* dragen; (*sch.*) liggen; — **away**, (*sch.*) wegzeilen; afhouden; wegdragen; meeslepen; *vr.* — **oneself well,** zich goed gedragen.

bearable ['bêərəbl] *adj.* draaglijk, te dragen.

beard]'bîəd] baard *m.*; weerhaak *m.*

bearded ['bîədid] gebaard; met weerhaak; (*v. komeet*) met een staart.

bearer ['bêərə] drager, brenger *m.*; bode *m.*; houder *m.*; toonder *m.*; moerbalk *m.*; steunpilaar *m.*

bearing ['bêəriŋ] (het) dragen *o.*; houding *v.*, optreden, gedrag *o.*

bearish ['bêəriʃ] lomp, nors; (*effectenbeurs*) een dalende neiging vertonend.

beast [bîst] beest; dier *o.*

beastly ['bîstli] beestachtig; gemeen, smerig.

beat [bît] *vt.* slaan, kloppen; uitkloppen; beuken, stampen; (*v. vlas*) braken; smeden; verslaan; overtreffen; *vi.* slaan, kloppen; — **down**, neerslaan; omverwerpen; (*v. prijzen*) drukken; afslaan; afdingen (op); — **up,** opjagen; (*v. rekruten*) werven; (*v. geld*) bijeenbrengen; (*v. eieren*) klutsen; (*sch.*) opkruisen; *sb.* slag; klap *m.*; tik *m.*; (*muz.*) maatslag *m.*; polsslag *m.*

beat [bît] *v. t. & v. d. van beat; ook:* doodop.

beaten ['bîtn] *v. d. van beat;* geslagen, gedreven, gesmeed; veel betreden, platgetreden; afgezaagd; uitgeput.

beatification [bîætifî'keiʃən] zaligmaking *v.*; zaligverklaring.

beatify [bî'ætifai] zalig maken; zalig verklaren.

beating ['bîtiŋ] pak slaag *o.*, rammeling *v.*; afstraffing *v.*

beatitude [bî'ætitjûd] zaligheid *v.*

beau [bou] fat, modegek, pronker *m.*; galant *m.*

beautification [bjûtifî'keiʃən] verfraaiing *v.*

beautiful(ly) ['bjûtiful(i)] *adj.* (*adv.*) schoon, mooi, fraai.

beautify ['bjûtifai] mooier maken, ver fraaien, versieren.

beauty ['bjûti] schoonheid, mooiheid, fraaiheid *v.* prachtstuk.

beauty-spot ['bjûtispɔt] moesje, schoonheidspleistertje *o.*; mooi plekje *o.*

beaver ['bîvə] (*Dk.*) bever *m.*; vilt *o.*; vilten hoed *m.*

becalm [bi'kâm] stillen, bedaren.

because [bi'kɔz, bi'kɔ:z] omdat, dewijl; — **of,** wegens, van wege, om.

beck [bek] *sb.* wenk *m.*, handgebaar *o.* (als bevel); *vt. & vi.* wenken; een wenk geven.

become [bi'kəm] *vi.* worden; *rt.* passen, betamen; voegen; goed staan.

becoming(ly) [bi'kəmiŋ(li)] *adj.* (*Adv.*) gepast, betamelijk; voegzaam; (goed) passend; goed staand, bevallig, netjes.

bed [bed] *sb.* bed *o.*; leger *o.*; rustplaats *v.*; bedding *v.*; onderbouw *m.*; *vt.* (— **out**) planten, uitplanten; (*v. paard*) van een leger voorzien; vastzetten, vastleggen; (*dicht.*) naar bed brengen; *vi.* (*dicht.*) naar bed gaan; te bed liggen.

bedabble [bi'dæbl] besproeien, bespatten, bemorsen.

bed-clothes ['bedklouθz] beddegoed *o.*

bedding ['bediŋ] beddegoed *o.*; leger *o.*; ligstro *o.*; bedding *v.*; laag, onderlaag *v.*

bedevil [bi'devl] mishandelen.

bedim [bi'dim] verduisteren.

bedlam ['bedləm] krankzinnigengesticht, gekkenhuis *o.*

bed-pan ['bedpæn] steekpan *v.*; beddepan *v.*, bedwarmer *m.*

bedraggle [bi'drægl] bemodderen.

bed-rid(den) ['bedrid(n)] bedlegerig.

bedroom ['bedrum] slaapkamer *v.*

bedside ['bedsaid] (bed)sponde *v.*, bed *o.*

bedsore ['bedso:] doorgelegen plek *v.*

bed-spread ['bedspred] beddesprei *v.*

bedtime ['bedtaim] bedtijd *m.*

bee [bî] bij *v.*

beech [bîtʃ] *sb.* beuk, beukeboom *m.*; beukehout *o.*; *adj.* beuken, van beukehout.

beech-nut ['bîtʃnət] beukenoot *v.*

bee-culture ['bîkəltʃə] bijenteelt *v.*

beef [bîf] rundvlees, ossevlees *o.*

beef-tea ['bîf'tî] bouillon *m.*

bee-hive ['bîhaiv] bijenkorf *m.*

beer ['bîə] bier *o.*

beeswax [bîzwæks] *sb.* was *v.*; *vt.* (met was) boenen.

beet [bît] beetwortel *m.*, biet, kroot *v.*

beetle ['bîtl] *sb.* tor *v.*, kever *m.*; uilskuiken *o.*; (straat)stamper *m.*; heiblok *o.*; *vt.* stampen; *vi.* overhangen.

beetle-eyed ['bîtlaid] bijziende.

beetroot ['bîtrût] beetwortel *m.*, kroot *v.*

befall [bi'fo:l] *vt.* overkómen, wedervaren; *vi.* gebeuren.

befool [bi'fûl] voor de gek houden; bedotten, misleiden.

before [bi'fo:] *prep.* vóór; in het bijzijn van, in tegenwoordigheid van; boven;

adv. vooraf, vooruit, voorop; tevoren, voorheen; *cj.* voor, voordat; liever dan.
beforehand [bi'fo:hænd] van te voren, vooruit, vooraf.
beforetime [bi'fo:taim] vroeger.
beg [beg] *vi.* bedelen; (*v. hond*) opzitten; — *for,* vragen om, verzoeken om; *vt.* afbedelen; bidden, smeken, verzoeken.
beget [bi'get] verwekken; voortbrengen.
beggar ['begə] *sb.* bedelaar; schooier *m.*; kerel, vent *m.*; *vt.* tot de bedelstaf brengen; (*fig.*) spotten met.
beggary ['begəri] armoede *r.*; bedelarij *r.*
begging-friar ['beginfraiə] bedelmonnik *m.*
begin [bi'gin] beginnen, aanvangen.
beginner [bi'ginə] beginner, beginneling *m.*
beginning [bi'ginin] begin *o.*, aanvang *m.*
beguine ['begin] begijn *v.*
behalf [bi'hâf] *in* — *of,* ten behoeve van, ten voordele van, in het belang van; *on your* —, uit uw naam; om uwentwil.
behave [bi'heiv] zich gedragen; zich houden; — *oneself,* zich netjes gedragen.
behaviour [bi'heivjə] gedrag *o.*, houding *v.*, optreden *o.*
behead [bi'hed] onthoofden.
behind [bi'haind] *prep.* achter; over; na; *adv.* achter, van achteren; ten achteren; achterom; *sb.* achterste *o.*
behindhand [bi'haindhænd] achterstallig; achterblijvend, achteruit; achterlijk; bij zijn tijd ten achter; achterop.
behold [bi'hould] aanschouwen; zien, waarnemen.
being ['biin] zijnde; *sb.* wezen, bestaan, aanzijn; *in* —, bestaand; in wording.
belay [bi'lei] (*sch.*) vastmaken; vastsjorren, vastzetten, beleggen.
belch [belʃ] *vi.* oprispen; *vt.* uitbraken; *sb.* oprisping *v.*; uitbarsting, losbarsting *v.*
Belgian ['beldʒən] *adj.* Belgisch; *sb.* Belg *m.*
Belgium ['beldʒiəm] België *o.*
belie [bi'lai] logenstraffen; beliegen; belasteren; niet beantwoorden aan; niet nakomen.
belief [bi'lîf] geloof *o.*
believable [bi'lîvəbl] geloofbaar.
believe [bi'lîv] geloven.
belittle [bi'litl] kleiner maken, verkleinen; kleineren.
bell [bel] *sb.* bel, klok, schel *v.*; (*sch.*) glas *o.*; (*Pl.*) klokje *o.*; *vt.* een bel aanbinden.
bellicose ['belikous] oorlogszuchtig.
belligerent [bi—, be'lidʒərənt] *adj.* (& *sb.*) oorlogvoerend(e); strijdlustig(e).
bellman ['belmən] omroeper *m.*; nachtwacht *m.*; klokkeluider *m.*
bellow ['belou] *vi.* bulken, loeien, brul-

len; bulderen; *sb.* gebulk, geloei *o.*; gebulder *o.*
bellows ['belouz] blaasbalg *m.*; (*phot.*) balg *m.*; (*fig.*) longen *r. mv.*
bell-push ['belpuʃ] belknop *m.*
bell-wether ['belweθə] belhamel *m.*
belly ['beli] buik *m.*; schoot *m.*; buikspek *o.*
belly-ache ['belieik] buikpijn *r.*
belong [bi'lɔŋ] horen, behoren, toebehoren (*to,* aan); ergens thuishoren; — *in* (*under, with*), behoren tot (bij).
belongings [bi'lɔŋiŋz] toebehoren *o.*; hebben en houden, eigendom *o.*; bagage *v.*
beloved [bi'lɔvd] *adj.* geliefd, bemind; *sb.* geliefde, beminde *m. & v.*
below [bi'lou] onder, beneden; naar onderen, naar beneden, omlaag; in de hel.
belt [belt] *sb.* riem, gordel *m.*; (*mil.*) koppel *m.*; rand, ring *m.*
belt-saw ['beltso:] lintzaag *r.*
bench [ben(t)ʃ] *sb.* bank *r.*; werkbank, schaafbank *r.*; rechtbank *r.*; (*r. boot*) doft, roeibank *v.*
bend [bend] *sb.* bocht, kromming *r.*; (*wap.*) balk *m.*; *rt.* buigen, krommen; verbuigen; (*v. boog*) spannen; (*sch.: v. zeilen*) aanslaan; (*v. ogen, schreden*) richten; *vi.* zich buigen, krommen.
beneath [bi'nîδ] beneden, onder.
benediction [beni'dikʃən] zegening; inzegening *v.*; dankzegging *r.*
benefaction [beni'fækʃən] weldaad *r.*; schenking *v.*
benefactor [beni'fæktə] weldoener *m.*
beneficence [bi'nefisəns] liefdadigheid, weldadigheid *r.*
beneficial [beni'fiʃəl] weldadig, heilzaam; voordelig, nuttig.
benefit ['benifit] *sb.* voordeel *o.*, baat *r.*; nut *o.*, winst *v.* genot *o.*; weldaad; gunst *v.*; toelage; uitkering *r.*; benefietvoorstelling *v.*; *vt.* goeddoen, nuttig zijn voor, tot voordeel strekken; bevorderen; *vi.* voordeel trekken (*by,* uit), baat vinden bij.
benevolence [bi'nevələns] welwillendheid *v.*; vrijgevigheid, weldadigheid *v.*; weldaad *r.*; gift *v.*
benevolent [bi'nevələnt] welwillend; vrijgevig, weldadig.
benighted [bi'naitid] door de nacht overvallen; (*fig.*) verblind; onwetend, achterlijk.
bent [bent] aanleg *m.*, neiging, voorliefde *v.*; richting *v.*
benumb [bi'nəm] verkleumen; (doen) verstijven; (*fig.*) verlammen.
benzene, benzine [ben'zîn] benzine *v.*
bequeath [bi'kwiθ] vermaken, nalaten.
bequest [bi'kwest] legaat *o.*
bereave [bi'rîv] beroven (*of,* van).
bereavement [bi'rîvmənt] beroving *v.*; zwaar verlies, sterfgeval *o.*
Berlin [bə:'lin] *sb.* Berlijn *o.*; (*rijtuig*) berline *v.*; *adj.* ['bə:lin] Berlijns.
berm [bə:m] berm *m.*

berry ['beri] *sb.* bezie, bes *v.*; koffieboon *v.*; viseitje *o.*; *ri.* bessen plukken; bessen of kuit vormen; opzwellen.

berth [bə:δ] *sb. (sch.)* hut, kooi *r.*; ankerplaats, ligplaats *r.*; baantje *o.*; *rt.* een hut (kooi) geven; een ligplaats aanwijzen; een baantje bezorgen; vastleggen; *ri.* meren; voor anker gaan; de ligplaats innemen.

beseech [bi'sîtʃ] smeken (**for**, om).

beside [bi'said] naast; behalve, buiten.

besides [bi'saidz] bovendien, daarenboven, daarbij; behalve, benevens.

besiege [bi'sîdʒ] belegeren.

besmirch [bi'smətʃ] bevuilen; bekladden, besmeuren.

besom ['bîzəm] bezem *m.*

besot [bi'sɔt] verdwazen, verblinden; bedwelmen.

bespatter [bi'spætə] bespatten; bekladden, besmeuren.

best [best] *adj.* best; *adr.* het best; *sb.* **do one's —**, zijn best doen; *rt.* overtreffen, het winnen van; beetnemen, bedotten.

bestial ['bestiəl] dierlijk, beestachtig.

bestialize ['bestiəlaiz] verdierlijken.

bestir [bi'stə:] opwekken; **— oneself,** aanpakken, voortmaken, zich reppen.

best man ['best'mæn] bruidsjonker *m.*

bet [bet] *rt. & ri.* wedden, verwedden; *sb.* weddenschap *r.*; inzet *m.*

betimes [bi'taimz] bijtijds, op tijd, tijdig; weldra.

betray [bi'trei] verraden, ontrouw worden aan; misleiden; bedriegen; verleiden.

betrayal [bi'treiəl] verraad *o.*, trouwbreuk *r.*; misleiding *r.*; verleiding *r.*

betrayer [bi'treiə] verrader *m.*; verleider *m.*

betrothal [bi'trouθəl] verloving *r.*

betrothed [bi'trouθd] verloofde *m. & r.*

betrothment [bi'trouθmənt] *zie* **betrothal.**

better ['betə] *adj. & adr.* beter; *sb.* meerdere *m. (in kennis, enz.)*; *vt.* verbeteren; overtreffen; *vi.* beteren; beter worden; *vr.* **— oneself,** zijn positie verbeteren.

betterment ['betəmənt] verbetering *r.*; waardevermeerdering *v.*

between [bi'twîn] *prep.* tussen; tussen... door; *adr.* er tussen in, daartussen.

between-whiles [bi'twîn'wailz] van tijd tot tijd, af en toe.

beverage ['bevəridʒ] drank *m.*

bevy ['bevi] vlucht *r.*, troep *m.*; gezelschap, kransje *o.*

bewail [bi'weil] betreuren, bejammeren, bewenen.

beware [bi'wêə] oppassen, op zijn hoede zijn, zich in acht nemen, zich wachten (**of,** voor).

beweep [be'wîp] bewenen.

bewilder [bi'wildə] verbijsteren.

bewitch [bi'witʃ] betoveren, beheksen.

beyond [bi'jɔnd] *prep. & adr.* over, aan de andere zijde van, aan gene zijde van; voorbij, verder dan; behalve, meer dan; buiten; boven; *sb.* hiernamaals *o.*

bezel ['bezl] *(r. beitel)* schuine kant *m.*; kas *r. (ran steen in ring)*; gleufje *o.* voor horlogeglas.

bias ['baiəs] *sb.* vooroordeel *o.*, vooringenomenheid *r.*; *adj. & adr.* schuin; *rt.* doen overhellen.

bib [bib] *sb.* slabbetje *o.*; *(r. schortje)* borststuk *o.*; *(Dk.: ris)* steenbolk *m.*; *ri.* pimpelen, drinken.

bibacious [bi—, bai'beifəs] aan de drank verslaafd.

bibber ['bibə] pimpelaar, drinkebroer *m.*

bible ['baibl] bijbel *m.*

biblist ['baiblist] bijbelkenner *m.*

bibulous ['bibjuləs] opslorpend, absorᶜberend; aan de drank verslaafd.

bicipital [bai'sipitəl] tweehoofdig.

bicker ['bikə] *ri.* kibbelen; *sb.* gekibbel *o.*

biconvex [bai'kɔnveks] dubbelbol.

bicycle ['baisikl] *sb.* tweewieler *m.*, rijwiel *o.*, fiets *r.*; *ri.* fietsen.

bid [bid] *vt.* wensen; afkondigen; bieden; opbieden; *(r. goederen)* opjagen; *sb.* bod *o.*; poging *r.*

biddable ['bidəbl] gezeglijk; willig.

bidding ['bidiŋ] bod, (het) bieden *o.*; gebod, bevel *o.*, last *m.*; uitnodiging *r.*, verzoek *o.*

bide [baid] beiden, verbeiden, afwachten.

bier [biə] baar, lijkbaar *v.*

bifurcation [baifə:'keifən] splitsing, vertakking *r.*; tweesprong *m.*; vork, gaffel *r.*

big [big] dik, groot, fors, zwaar; voornaam, invloedrijk; zwanger.

bigamy ['bigəmi] bigamie *r.*

big-bellied ['bigbelid] dikbuikig.

big-boned ['bigbound] grof gebouwd, fors.

bight [bait] bocht *r.*; baai, kreek *v.*; *(r. touw)* lus *r.*

bigness ['bignis] grootte *r.*; dikte *r.*

bigot [bi'gət] kwezel(aar) *m.*

bigotry ['bigətri] kwezelachtigheid, kwezelarij *r.*

bigwig ['bigwig] *(fam.)* hoge ome, man van gewicht *m.*

bike [baik] *sb. (fam.)* fiets *v.*; *ri.* fietsen.

bilberry ['bilbəri] blauwe bosbes *r.*

bile [bail] gal *r.*

bilge [bildʒ] *sb. (v. vat)* buik *m.*; *(sch.)* kim, kielwijdte *r.*; *(sch.)* ruimwater *o.*; *rt. & ri.* een lek krijgen.

bilingual [bai'liŋwəl] tweetalig.

bill [bil] *sb.* rekening *r.*; wissel *m.*; lijst *v.*; programma *o.*; aanplakbiljet *o.*; wetsontwerp *o.*; aanklacht *v.*; *(Am.)* bankbiljet *o.*; bek, snavel *m.*; bijl *v.*; snoeimes *o.*; hellebaard *v.*; landpunt *v.*; *vt.* aanplakken; aankondigen (door biljetten); op 't programma zetten.

billet ['bilit] *sb.* inkwartieringsbiljet *o.*; *r. (mil.)* inkwartieren.

bill-hook ['bilhuk] snoeimes o.

billiard-ball ['biljədbo:l] biljartbal m.

billiards ['biljədz] biljart(spel) o.

billow ['bilou] sb. baar, golf v.; (dicht.) zee v.; vi. golven, opzwellen.

billycock ['bilikɔk] stijve ronde hoed m.

bin [bin] sb. kist v.; trog, bak m.; flessenrek o.; vt. in een kist, enz. doen.

binary ['bainəri] adj. binair, tweevoudig, tweetallig, tweeledig.

bind [baind] vt. binden; inbinden; verbinden; boorden, omboorden; (v. overeenkomst, koop) bekrachtigen; (v. darmen) verstoppen; beslaan (met metaal).

bindery ['baindəri] boekbinderij v.

binding ['baindiŋ] adj. bindend, verbindend; verplichtend; sb. (het) binden o.; band, boekband m.; verband o;. boordsel o.; omlegsel o.

binocle ['binɔkl] toneelkijker, veldkijker m.

biography [bai'ɔgrəfl] levensbeschrijving v.

bioscope ['baiəskoup] bioscoop m. & v.

biplane ['baiplein] (vl.) tweedekker m.

birch [bə:tʃ] sb. berk m.; berkehout o.; roede, tuchtroede v.; vt. de roe geven, met de roede straffen.

bird [bə:d] sb. vogel m.; patrijs m.; vi. vogels vangen.

bird-fancier ['bə:dfænsiə] vogelliefhebber m.; vogelhandelaar.

birdie ['bə:di] vogeltje o.; (fig.) lieveling m.

bird's eye ['bə:dzai] (Pl.) ereprijs m., blauwe veronica v.; tabak r. (waarvan de nerven gekorven zijn).

biretta [bi'retə] baret v.

birth [bə:ð] geboorte v.; afkomst v.

birthday ['bə:ðdei] verjaardag, geboortedag m.

birth-mark [bə:ðmâk] moedervlek v.

birth-sin ['bə:ðsin] erfzonde v.

biscuit ['biskit] beschuit v.; biscuit, koekje o.

bisect [bai'sekt] in tweeën delen, middendoor delen.

bisexual [bai'seksjuəl] tweeslachtig.

bishop ['biʃəp] bisschop m.; (in schaakspel) raadsheer m.

bishopric ['biʃəprik] bisdom o.

bissextile [bi'sekstail] schrikkeljaar o.

bit [bit] sb. beetje, stukje o., kleinigheid v.; (v. sleutel) baard m.; (v. nijptang) bek m.; schroefdraad m.; (v. toom) gebit o.; (v. boor, schaaf, enz.) ijzer o.

bitch [bitʃ] teef v.

bite [bait] vt. bijten; uitbijten; invreten; aantasten; (fam.) beetnemen; vi. bijten, toehappen; (tn.: v. raderen, enz.) pakken; sb. beet, hap m.; greep m.; vinnigheid v.; (sl.) beetnemerij v.

biter ['baitə] bijter m.

biting ['baitiŋ] bijtend, bits.

bitter ['bitə] bitter, verbitterd; bijtend, grievend; bitter koud.

bitterness ['bitənis] bitterheid v.

bituminize [bi'tjúminaiz] asfalteren.

bivouac ['bivuæk] sb. bivak o.; vi. bivakkeren, kamperen.

blab [blæb] vt. er uitflappen; verklappen, verklikken; vi. babbelen, zijn mond voorbijpraten.

black [blæk] adj. zwart; donker, duister, somber; snood; sb. zwart o.; zwartsel o.; zwarte vlek v.; brand m. (in het koren); zwarte, neger m.; vt. zwart maken; (fig.) dóórhalen.

blackbeetle ['blækbîtl] kakkerlak m.

blackberry ['blækbəri] braam, braambes v.

blackbird ['blækbə:d] merel m.

blackboard [blækbo:d] bord, schoolbord o.

black-coat ['blækkout] zwartrok m.

black-cock ['blækkɔk] korhaan m.

blacken ['blækn] vt. zwart maken; vi. zwart worden.

blackguard ['blækgâd] sb. deugniet, schurk, ploert, gemene kerel m.; adj. gemeen, schurkachtig; vt. uitschelden, zwartmaken.

black-hearted ['blækhâtid] snood.

blacking ['blækiŋ] schoensmeer o.; zwartsel o.

black-lead ['blæk'led] sb. potlood o.; vt. potloden.

blackleg ['blækleg] sb. bedrieger; oplichter m.; (bij werkstaking) onderkruiper m.; vt. onderkruipen.

blackmail ['blækmeil] sb. geldafdreiging, afpersing, chantage v.; brandschatting v.; vt. geld afdreigen, geld afpersen; brandschatten.

black-pudding ['blæk'pudiŋ] bloedbeuling m.

blacksmith ['blæksmið] smid, grofsmid m.

bladder ['blædə] blaas v.; blaar v.; (fig.) windbuil, windzak m.

blade [bleid] spriet, halm m.; blad o.; bladschijf v.; lemmet o., kling v.; (gilette)mesje o.

blain [blein] blaar, tongblaar v.

blamable ['bleiməbl] adj. laakbaar, berispelijk, afkeurenswaardig.

blame [bleim] vt. laken, berispen, afkeuren; sb. blaam, berisping, schuld v.; adj. (sl.) vervloekt.

blameless(ly) ['bleimlisli)] adj. (adv.) onberispelijk.

blameworthy ['bleimwə:ði] berispelijk laakbaar, afkeurenswaardig.

blank [blæŋk] adj. wit, blank, bleek; blanco, onbeschreven, oningevuld; rein, zuiver; louter; saai; (v. deur, muur) blind; rijmloos; sb. onbeschreven blad, blanco papier, o. open plaats v.; tin loterij) niet m.; streepje o.

blanket ['blæŋkit] (wollen) deken v.

blare ['blêə] vi. loeien, brullen; schallen; vt. uitbrullen; rondtrompetten; sb. geloei, gebrul o.

blasphemer [blæs'f mə] (gods)lasteraar m.

blasphemy ['blæsfīmi] godslastering, godslasterlijke taal *v.*

blast [blâst] *sb.* (krachtige) luchtstroom *m.*; wind, rukwind, windstoot *m.*; stoot *m.* (op blaasinstrument); springlading *v.*; ontploffing *v.* (van dynamietpatroon); *vt.* verdorren, verzengen; vernietigen, verijdelen; laten springen; bezoedelen.

blaze [bleiz] *sb.* vlam *r.*: gloed, vuurgloed *m.*; bles *v.*; *vi.* (op)vlammen, (op)-laaien; flikkeren, schitteren, lichten, gloeien.

blazon ['bleizn] *sb.* blazoen *o.*; *rt.* uitbazuinen.

bleach [blītʃ] *vt.* & *vi.* (doen) bleken; (doen) verbleken.

bleacher ['blītʃə] bleker *m.*

bleachery ['blītʃəri] blekerij *v.*

bleach-works ['blītʃwə:ks] blekerij *r.*

bleak [blīk] *adj.* bleek; guur, kil, koud; kaal, woest; open, onbeschut.

blear ['blīə] *adj.* tranend; dof, duister; wazig; vaag; *vt.* doen tranen; verduisteren; benevelen.

bleat [blīt] *vi.* blaten; *sb.* geblaat *o.*

bleed [blīd] *vi.* bloeden; *vt.* aderlaten; doen bloeden.

bleeding ['blīdiŋ] (het) bloeden *o.*; (het) aderlaten *o.*; bloeding, verbloeding *v.*

blemish ['blemiʃ] *vt.* bevlekken, besmetten, oezoedelen; bekladden; *sb.* vlek *v.*; smet, klad *v.*

blend [blend] *vt.* mengen, vermengen; (*v. wijn, enz.*) versnijden; *vi.* zich vermengen; *sb.* vermenging *v.*; mengsel *o.*

bless [blês] zegenen; loven, verheerlijken.

blessed ['blesid; blest] gezegend; zalig, gelukzalig; verwenst, vervloekt.

blessing ['blesiŋ] zegen *m.*, zegening *v.*; zegenwens *m.*

blight [blait] *sb.* meeldauw *m.*; brand *m.*; soort bladluis *v.*; bederf *o.*; ziekte *v.*; schadelijke invloed *m.*; *vt.* verderven, vernietigen; doen verdorren.

blind [blaind] *adj.* blind; verborgen; donker, duister; onduidelijk, ondoorzichtig; (*v. weg*) doodlopend; (*fig.: v. betrekking*) zonder vooruitzichten; *vt.* blind maken; verblinden; blinddoeken; verdonkeren, verduisteren; (*mil.*) blinderen; *sb.* gordijn, rolgordijn *o.*; rolluik *o.*, jaloezie *v.*; blinddoek *m.*; oogklep *v.*; (*mil.*) blindering *v.*; (*mil.*) blindganger *m.*; (*fig.*) voorwendsel *o.*

blindfold ['blaindfould] *adj.* & *adv.* geblinddoekt; blindelings.

blindly ['blaindli] *adv.* blindelings.

blindness ['blaindnis] blindheid *v.*; verblinding, verblindheid *v.*

blink [bliŋk] *vi.* knipogen; gluren; flikkeren, schitteren; *vt.* de ogen sluiten voor; (*v. kwestie, enz.*) ontduiken, ontwijken; *sb.* knipoogje *o.*; (vluchtige) blik *m.*; glimpje, schijnsel *o.*; ijsblink *m.*; ijsschots *v.*

blinker ['bliŋkə] oogklep *v.*; (*sl.*) oog *o.*; —s, bril *m.*; stofbril *m.*

bliss [blis] (geluk)zaligheid *v.*, geluk *o.*

blissful(ly) ['blisful(i)] *adj.* (*adv.*) (geluk)zalig, gelukkig, heerlijk.

blister ['blistə] blaar *v.*; trekpleister *v.*

bloated ['bloutid] gezwollen; opgeblazen.

bloater ['bloutə] verse bokking *m.*

block [blɔk] *sb.* blok *o.*; blok *o.* huizen; takelblok *o.*, katrol *v.*; hoedevorm *m.*; cliché *o.*; (*mil.*) richtbok *m.*; verkeersopstopping, (verkeers)stremming *v.*; *vt.* afsluiten, versperren, stremmen; insluiten, blokkeren; (*sp.: cricket*) tegenhouden met *bat*; (*v. stoot*) opvangen, pareren.

blockade [blɔ'keid] *sb.* blokkade, insluiting *v.*; *v.* blokkeren, insluiten.

block-calendar ['blɔkkælində] scheurkalender *m.*

blockhead ['blɔkhed] domkop *m.*

blockhouse ['blɔkhaus] blokhuis *o.*

blond(e) [blɔnd] blond.

blood [blɔd] *sb.* bloed *o.*; bloedverwantschap *v.*; temperament *o.*; ras *o.*; raspaard *o.*; volbloedpaard *o.*; *vt.* aderlaten; met bloed bevlekken (bezoedelen); tot bloedens toe bezeren.

blood-letting ['blɔdletiŋ] aderlating *v.*

blood-poisoning ['blɔdpɔizəniŋ] bloedvergiftiging *v.*

blood-relation ['blɔdri'leiʃən] bloedverwant *m.*

bloodshed(ding) ['blɔdʃed(iŋ)] bloedbad *o.*, bloedstorting *v.*, bloedvergieten *o.*

bloodshot ['blɔdʃɔt] met bloed belopen.

bloodthirsty ['blɔdðə:sti] bloeddorstig.

blood-vessel ['blɔdvesl] bloedvat *o.*

bloody ['blɔdi] bloedig; bloederig; bloeddorstig.

bloom [blūm] *sb.* bloesem *m.*; bloei *m.*; (*tn.*) puddelbal *m.*; (*fig.*) glans, gloed *m.*; blos *m.*; (*op vruchten*) waas *o.*; *vt.* (*v. ijzer*) uitwalsen; *vi.* bloeien.

bloomy ['blūmi] bloeiend, in bloei; donzig.

blossom ['blɔsəm] *sb.* bloesem *m.*; *vi.* bloeien, bloesemen.

blot [blɔt] *sb.* klad, vlek, smet *v.*; (*bij triktrak*) niet gedekte steen *m.*; *vt.* bekladden, bezoedelen; vloeien (met vloeipapier); *vi.* kladden, vlekken.

blotter ['blɔtə] vloeiblok, vloeiboek *o.*, vloeimap *v.*

blotting-paper ['blɔtiŋpeipə] vloeipapier *o.*

blouse [blauz] (werkmans)kiel *m.*; blouse *v.*

blow [blou] *sb.* slag *m.*; klap, stoot *m.*; windvlaag; stormvlaag *v.*; bloei *m.*; *vt.* blazen; aanblazen, opblazen, uitblazen, wegblazen; (*v. neus*) snuiten; (*v. vlieg*) eitjes leggen in; (*sl.*) verklikken; (*v. geld*) er doorbrengen; *vi.* blazen; waaien;

hijgen, puffen; (r. *walris*) spuiten; bloeien.

blow-hole ['blouhoul] (*in iis*) luchtgat, wak *o.*; trekgat *o.*; (r. *walris*) neusgat, spuitgat *o.*

blow-pipe ['bloupaip] (*tn.*) blaaspijp *r.*; blaasroer *o.*

blowy ['bloui] winderig.

blubber ['bləbə] grienen, huilen; snotteren.

bludgeon ['blədʒən] *sb.* knuppel, ploertendoder *m.*; *rt.* knuppelen, ranselen, slaan.

blue [blû] *adj.* blauw; landerig, neerslachtig, terneergeslagen; hopeloos; blauwkousachtig; (*fig.*) beteuterd; (r. *rerhaal, enz.*) schuin, vuil; *sb.* blauw *o.*; blauwe kleur; blauwe stof *r.*; blauwsel *o.*; azuur *o.*; blauwkous *r.*; conservatief *m.*; *rt.* blauw verven; (r. *linnen*) blauwen, blauwselen; (*sl.*: r. *geld*) wegsmijten.

blue-bottle ['blûbətl] (*Pl.*) blauwbloem, korenbloem *r.*; (*Dk.*) bromvlieg *r.*; (*sl.*) klabak, politieagent *m.*

bluff [bləf] *adj.* (*sch.*: r. *boeg*) stomp; steil; openhartig, rond, rondborstig; bruusk, bars; *sb.* steile oever *m.*; steil breed voorgebergte *o.*; (*bij poker*) bluffen *o.*; grootspraak; brutaliteit, bangmakerij *r.*; *rt.* overbluffen, overdonderen; *ri.* (*bij poker*) bluffen; ophakken.

blunder ['bləndə] *sb.* misslag, flater, bok *m.*; *ri.* een misslag begaan, een bok schieten; *rt.* verknoeien.

blunt [blənt] *adj.* stomp, bot; lomp, dom; rechtuit, rond(uit), kortaf; *sb.* stompe (korte dikke) naald *r.*; (*sl.*) duiten, moppen *mv.*; *rt.* bot maken; afstompen.

bluntly ['bləntli] *adv.* botweg, kortaf; ronduit; stomp.

blur [blə:] *sb.* vlek, smet, klad *r.*; veeg *m.*, smeer *o.*; vage verschijning *r.*; nevelachtigheid *r.*; *rt.* bevlekken; bekladden, bezoedelen; benevelen, verdoezelen, verduisteren; *ri.* kladden.

blush [bləʃ] *ri.* blozen, kleuren, rood worden; zich schamen; *adj.* rood, bleekrood, rose; *sb.* blos *m.*; kleur *r.*

bluster ['bləstə] *vi.* razen, tieren, bulderen; snoeven, zwetsen; *sb.* geraas, getier *o.*; snoeverij *v.*, gezwets *o.*

blusterer ['bləstərə] bulderbast *m.*; opsnijder, praatjesmaker, lawaaimaker *m.*

boa ['bouə] boa *v.*

board [bo:d] *sb.* plank, deel *r.*; bord *o.*; tafel *r.*; bestuurstafel *v.*, bestuur *o.*; bordpapier, karton *o.*; kost *m.*, kostgeld *o.*; *rt.* beplanken, met planken beschieten; (*sch.*) aanklampen, enteren; kartonneren; in de kost nemen (*of: doen*); *ri.* aan boord gaan; laveren; in de kost zijn (*with*, bij).

boarder ['bo:də] kostganger; kostleerling *m.*; (*sch.*) enteraar *m.*

boarding-house ['bo:diŋhaus] kosthuis, pension *o.*

board-wages ['bo:dweidʒis] kostgeld *o.*

boarish ['bo:riʃ] beestachtig, vuil, zwijnen—.

boast [boust] *ri.* bluffen, pochen, snoeven; *rt.* zich beroemen op; zich verheugen in ('t bezit van); *sb.* bluf *m.*, grootspraak *r.*; roem, trots *m.*

boaster ['boustə] bluffer, grootspreker.

boasting ['boustiŋ] *adj.* pochend, bluffend; *sb.* bluf *m.*, pocherij *r.*, gesnoef *o.*, grootspraak *r.*

boat [bout] *sb.* boot *r.*; sauskom *r.*; (*Am.*) auto *r.*; *ri.* varen, roeien; *rt.* per boot vervoeren; bevaren.

boatman ['boutmən] schipper *m.*; roeier *m.*; botenverhuurder *m.*

boat-race ['boutreis] roeiwedstrijd *m.*

bob [bəb] *sb.* slingergewicht *o.*; dieplood, schietlood *o.*; haardot *m.*; korte pruik *r.*; korte staart *m.*; peur *r.*; *rt.* kort knippen; kortstaarten; trekken, rukken aan; *ri.* op en neer gaan, dobberen; happen (*for*, naar); knikken (met); peuren.

bobbin ['bəbin] *sb.* klos, spoel *r.*; haspel *m.*; klinklichter *m.*; *rt.* (r. *kant*) klossen.

bobtail ['bəbteil] *sb.* korte staart *m.*; dier *o.* met korte staart; *rt.* kortstaarten.

bode [boud] voorspellen.

bodice ['bədis] lijfje, keurslijf *o.*; onderlijfje *o.*

bodiless ['bədilis] zonder lichaam, onlichamelijk.

bodkin ['bədkin] rijgpen *r.*; priem *m.*; lange haarspeld *r.*

body ['bədi] *sb.* lichaam, lijf *o.*, romp *m.*; lijk *o.*; (*recht*) persoon *m.*; kern *v.*, hoofdbestanddeel *o.*; hoofdmacht *v.*; (r. *kerk*) schip *o.*; *vt.* — (*forth*), belichamen.

body-guard ['bədigâd] lijfwacht *v.*

bog [bəg] *sb.* moeras *o.*; laagveen *o.*; *vt.* in de modder dompelen; in een moeras laten wegzinken.

boggle ['bəgl] *ri.* aarzelen, weifelen; (terug)schrikken (*at*, voor); bezwaren maken, tegenstribbelen; knoeien; morrelen, prutsen; *sb.* knoeierij *r.*; knoeiboel *m.*

boggy ['bəgi] moerassig, veenachtig.

bogland ['bəglænd] moerasland *o.*; veengrond *m.*

bog-trotter ['bəgtrotə] turftrapper; moerasbewoner *m.*; (*ong.*) Ier *m.*

bogus ['bougəs] nagemaakt, onecht, vals.

bogy ['bougi] duivel; boeman *m.*; spook, schrikbeeld *o.*; (*sp.*: *bij golf*) aantal punten.

Bohemia [bou'himjə] Bohemen *o.*

boil [bəil] *sb.* steenpuist *v.*; bloedzweer *r.*; (het) koken *o.*; kook *v.*; *vt.* & *ri.* koken, zieden.

boiler ['bəilə] kookketel; stoomketel; waterketel *m.*

boiler-scale ['bəiləskeil] ketelsteen *v.*

boiling-point ['bəiliŋpəint] kookpunt *o.*

boisterous(ly) ['boistəres(li)] *adj.* (*adr.*) onstuimig, rumoerig; luidruchtig.

bold [bould] stoutmoedig, stout, vermetel; vrijmoedig, vrijpostig; fors, krachtig; steil; (*v. drukletter*) vet.

bold-faced ['bouldfeist] onbeschaamd.

bole [noul] boomstam *m.*; bolus *m.*; nis *r.*

bolshevism ['bolʃivizm] bolsjewisme *o.*

bolster ['boulstə] *sb.* peluw *v.*; (*tn.*) kussen *o.*; *vt.* (onder)steunen (met kussens, enz.); opvullen.

bolt [boult] *sb.* bout, grendel *m.*; langwerpige kogel *m.*; rol *m.* (geweven stof); *rt.* grendelen; met bouten bevestigen; in boeien slaan; builen; ziften; *vi.* er van door gaan, op hol gaan; (*Pl.*) in' t zaad schieten; uitlopen; overlopen; vooruitschieten, hollen; *adv.* — **upright,** kaarsrecht.

bolter ['boultə] builmolen *m.*; overloper *m.*

bomb [bom] *sb.* bom *v.*; *vt.* bombarderen.

bombard [bom'bâd] bombarderen.

bombardment [bom'bâdmənt] bombardement *o.*

bombastic(al) [bom'bæstik(l)] *adj.* bombastisch.

bomber ['bomə] bommenwerper *m.*

bomb-proof ['bomprûf] *adj.* bomvrij; *sb.* bomvrije schuilplaats *r.*

bomb-thrower ['bomðrouə] bommenwerper *m.*

bond [bond] *sb.* band *m.*; verbintenis *v.* contract *o.*; verplichting *v.*; schuldbrief *m.*, schuldbekentenis *v.*; obligatie *v.*; verband *o.*; entrepot *o.*; *rt.* (*v. metselwerk*) verbinden; verhypothekeren; in het entrepot opslaan.

bondage ['bondidʒ] lijfeigenschap, slavernij *r.*; gevangenschap *v.*

bonded ['bondid] (in het entrepot) opgeslagen.

bondholder ['bondhouldə] obligatiehouder *m.*

bondman ['bondmən] slaaf; lijfeigene *m.*

bone [boun] *sb.* been *o.*; graat *v.*; balein *v.*; (*Am.*) dollar *m.*; beenderen; gebeente; dobbelstenen; castagnetten, klappers; streken; *adj.* benen; *vt.* uitbenen; ontgraten; baleinen zetten in.

bonfire ['bonfaiə] vreugdevuur *o.*

bonnet ['bonit] *sb.* kapothoed *m.*; kaper *m.*; muts *v.*; (*op schoorsteen, lamp*) kap *v.*; (*v. locomotief*) vonkenvanger *m.*; (*v. auto*) motorkap *v.*; (*v. herkauwers*) tweede maag *v.*

bonny ['boni] (*Sc.*) lief, aardig, knap.

bonus ['bounəs] premie; beloning *v.*; extra dividend *o.*; bijslag *m.*; gratificatie *v.*; tantième *o.*

bony ['bouni] beenachtig; benig, knokig; gratig, vol graten; beenhard.

boo [bû] *vi.* loeien; *vt.* uitjouwen.

booby ['bûbi] domkop *m.*; uilskuiken *o.*, lummel *m.*

book [buk] *sb.* boek *o.*; tekstboekje *o.*; libretto *o.*; schrijfboek *o.*; *vt.* boeken, inschrijven, noteren; (*plaats*) bespreken; een kaartje nemen (geven).

bookbinder ['bukbaində] boekbinder *m.*

book-case ['bukkeis] boekenkast *v.*

booking-office ['bukiŋɔfis] plaatsbureau *o.*

book-keeper ['bukkîpə] boekhouder *m.*

bookmark(er) [bukmâk(ə)] leeswijzer, boekenlegger *m.*

book-post ['bukpoust] drukwerkpost *r.*; *by* —, als drukwerk.

bookseller ['bukselə] boekhandelaar, boekverkoper *m.*

book-trade ['buktreid] boekhandel *m.*

boom [bûm] *sb.* (haven)boom *m.*; (*sch.*) boom *m.*, spier *v.*, spriet *m.*; gedreun, gebulder, gedonder *o.*; (*H.*) reclame; plotselinge prijsstijging *v.*; buitengewone vraag *v.*; *vi.* dreunen, bulderen, donderen; een grote vlucht nemen, opeens in de hoogte gaan; veel succes hebben; *vt.* reclame maken voor; in de hoogte steken.

boor [bûə] boer, boerenkinkel, lomperd *m.*

boorish ['bûəriʃ] boers, lomp.

boot [bût] *sb.* laars *v.*, hoge schoen *m.*; (*v. rijtuig*) bagagebak *m.*, bagageruimte *v.*; —*s*, schoenpoetser (in hotel); (*sl.*) jongste lid (*van club, enz.*); *vt.* (zijn) laarzen aantrekken; (*fam.*) trappen.

boot-black ['bûtblæk] schoenpoetser *m.*

booth [bûθ] kraam(pje) *v.* (*o.*), tent *v.*; telefooncel *r.*

boot-lace ['bûtleis] schoenveter *m.*

boot-polish ['bûtpoliʃ] schoensmeer *o.*

booty ['bûti] buit, roof *m.*

booze [bûz] *vi.* (*pop.*) zuipen, pooien; *sb.* drank *m.*; zuippartij *v.*

boracic [bo'ræsik] *adj.* boor—; — *lotion,* boorwater; *sb.* boorzuur *o.*

border ['bo:də] *sb.* rand, boord, kant *m.*; zoom *m.*; grens *v.*, grensgebied *o.*; *vt.* omranden omzomen; begrenzen; *vi.* grenzen; — (*up*) *on,* grenzen aan.

bore [bo:] *sb.* boor *v.*; boorgat *o.*; boorwijdte *v.*; (*v. kanon*) ziel *v.*; diameter *m.*; kaliber *o.*; vervelend mens *m.*; *vt.* doorboren; uitboren; (*sp.:* boksen) tegen de touwen dringen; vervelen.

boredom ['bo:dəm] verveling *v.*; vervelende lui.

borer ['bo:rə] boor *v.*; boorder *m.*; boorkever *m.*

boring ['bo:riŋ] boorgat *o.*; boorspaan *v.*

born [bo:n] geboren.

borough ['bərə] stad *v.*, vlek *o.*

borrow ['borou] *vt.* borgen; lenen van; ontlenen; *vi.* lenen.

bosh [boʃ] *sb.* onzin *m.*, dwaasheid, malligheid *v.*; *vt.* bederven; verknoeien; bedotten, verlakken, voor de mal houden.

bosk(et) [bɔsk'(it)] kreupelbos; struik-gewas o.

bosom ['bûzəm] boezem m.; borst v.; (fig.) schoot m.

boss [bɔs] knop m.; buil v., bult, knobbel m.; (Am., sl.) baas m.; kopstuk o.

botany ['bɔtəni] plantkunde, kruidkunde v.

botch [bɔtʃ] lappen, oplappen; verknoeien; samenflansen.

both [bouð] beide; zowel... als.

bother ['bɔθə] vt. lastig vallen; tot last zijn, vervelen; plagen; vi. zaniken, zeuren; drukte maken; (about, over); zich bekommeren (about, om).

bothersome [bɔθəsəm] lastig, vervelend.

bottle ['bɔtl[sb. fles v.; karaf v.; (v. hooi, stro) bos m.; vt. bottelen, in flessen doen, op flessen tappen; (fam. v. geld) oppotten; (sl.) snappen; — up, (v. woede) opkroppen; (v. vloot) insluiten.

bottle-cap ['bɔtlkæp] capsule v.

bottle-nose ['bɔtlnouz] dikke neus m.; jeneverneus m.; (Dk.) bruinvis, dolfijn m.

bottom ['bɔtəm] sb. bodem, grond m.; onderste gedeelte, benedeneinde o.; basis v., voet m.; (v. prijzen, enz.) laagste punt o.; (v. stoel) zitting, mat v.; (sch.) kiel v.; adj. onderste; laagste; laatste; vt. bodemen, een bodem inzetten; (v. stoel) een zitting inzetten, matten; gronden, grondvesten; doorgronden.

bottomless ['bɔtəmlis] bodemloos, grondeloos, peilloos; ongegrond.

bottomry ['bɔtəmri] (sch.) bodemerij v.

bough [bau] (grote) tak m.

bougie ['bûʒi] bougie v.

boulevard ['bûlvâ] boulevard m.

bounce [bauns] bonzen; stuiten; springen, opspringen; snoeven, opsnijden.

bound [baund] sb. grens v.; landpaal m.; vt. beperken; begrenzen.

bound [baund] sb. sprong m.; weeromstuit m.; vi. springen; terugkaatsen, weeromstuiten.

boundary ['baundəri] grens v.; landpaal m.; scheidspaal m.

bounder ['baundə] (sl.) ploert, poen m.

boundless (ly) ['baundlis(li)] adj. (adv.) grenzeloos; eindeloos, onbegrensd.

bountiful (ly)]'bauntiful(i)] adj. (adv.) mild, milddadig; overvloedig, rijkelijk.

bouquet ['bûkei] ruiker m., boeket o.

bourgeois ['bûəʒwâ] burgerlijk.

bourse [buəs] (H.) beurs v.

bow [bau] vt. buigen, doen buigen; doen bukken; vi. buigen, zich buigen; sb. buiging v.; (sch.) boeg m.

bow [bou] sb. boog m.; (muz.) strijkstok m.; (tn.) beugel m.; strik m.; vi. (viool) spelen, strijken.

bowel ['bauəl] sb. (gen.) darm m.; —s, ingewanden; (fig.) medelijden, hart.

bower ['bauə] prieel, tuinhuisje o.; buitenverblijf, lustoord o.; (sch.) boeganker o.; (kaartsp.) boer m.

bowl [boul] schaal, kom, bokaal v.;

bekken o.; pijpekop m.; (r. lepel, roeispaan) blad o.; (kegel)bal m.; —s, balspel o.; kegelspel o.

bowler ['boulə] (cricket) bowler m.; — (hat), dophoed m., kaasbolletje o.

bowling-alley ['boulinæli] kegelbaan v.

bowman ['boumən] boogschutter m.

bow-net ['bounet] fuik v.

bow-saw ['bauso:] spanzaag v.

bowsprit ['bousprit] (sch.) boegspriet m.

box [bɔks] sb. doos v.; kist v., koffer o.; bus v.; vt. in een doos doen; opsluiten; wegbergen; — off, in vakken verdelen; — up, opeenpakken; vi. boksen.

box-bed ['bɔksbed] alkoofbed o.

Boxing-day [b'ɔksindei] 2e Kerstdag m.

box-office ['bɔksɔfis] plaatsbureau o.

box-room ['bɔksrum] bergkamer v., tussenzolder m.

boy [bɔi] sb. jongen, knaap m.; adj. jong; jongens—; mannelijk.

boycott ['bɔikət, 'bɔikɔt] rt. boycotten; sb. boycot m.

boyish (ly) ['bɔiiʃ(li)] adj. (adv.) jongensachtig, jongens—.

boy-scout ['bɔiskaut] padvinder m.

brace [breis] sb. paar, koppel o.; riem, band m.; klamp m.; booromslag m.; vt. spannen, aantrekken; vastbinden; versterken; (v. zenuwen) stalen; verfrissen, opwekken; — oneself up, zich vermannen, zich inspannen, zich schrap zetten.

bracelet ['breislit] armband m.; (sl.) handboei v.

bracken ['brækn] (adelaars)varen(s) v. (mv.).

brackish ['brækiʃ] brak, ziltig.

brag [bræg] vi. bluffen, pochen; sb. bluf m., gepoch o.

braggart ['brægət] sb. bluffer, pocher, snoever m.; adj. bluff, blufferig.

braid [breid] sb. vlecht v.; boordsel, galon o. veterband m.; haarband m., haarlint o.; vt. vlechten; garneren; (v. haar) binden.

brain [brein] sb. hersenen mv., brein o.; verstand o.; —s, hersens; rt. de hersens inslaan.

brain-pan ['breinpæn] hersenpan v.

brainy ['breini] knap snugger, pienter.

braise [breiz] (v. vlees) smoren.

brake [breik] sb. doornbos, braambos o.; kreupelhout o.; (adelaars)varen v.; (vlas)braak v.; rem v., remtoestel o', remwagen m.; vt. remmen; (v. vlas) braken.

bramble ['bræmbl] braamstruik m.; braam v.

bran [bræn] zemelen v. mv.

branch [brân(t)ʃ] sb. arm' zijtak m.; afdeling v., vak o.; leervak o.; (v. bank) filiaal, agentschap o.; loodspatent o.; vi. zich vertakken.

branch-office ['brân(t)ʃofis] bijkantoor o.; agentschap o.

brand ['brænd] sb. brandend hout o.; verkoold stuk hout o. (dicht.) fakkel v.;

(*dicht.*) zwaard *o*.; (*Pl.*) brand *m*.; brand-merk *o*.; brandijzer *o*.; merk, merk-teken *o*.; soort, kwaliteit *v*.; *vt*. brand-merken, griffen.
brandish ['brændi] zwaaien.
brand-new ['brænd'njû] fonkelnieuw, splinternieuw.
brandy ['brændi] cognac *m*.; brande-wijn *m*.
brass [brâs] *sb*. geelkoper, messing *o*.; gedenkplaat *v*. (van koper of brons); (*muz.: in orkest*) koper *o*.; *adj*. (geel-)ko-peren; bronzen; *vt*. verkoperen.
brassard [brə'sâd] armband *m*.
brass band ['brâsbænd] fanarekorps *o*.
brass-foil ['brâsfɔil] klatergoud *o*.
brass-works ['brâswə:ks] kopergie-terij *v*.
brat [bræt] kind, jongetje *o*.; (kleine) schavuit *m*.
brave [breiv] moedig, dapper, kranig, flink; mooi (uitgedost), zwierig; statig.
bravery ['breiv(ə(ri] moed *m*., dapper-heid *v*.
brawl [bro:l] *vi*. schreeuwen, razen, tieren; kijven, twisten, krakelen; kab-belen, bruisen; *sb*. geschreeuw, getier, geraas *o*.; gekijf *o*., twist *m*., ruzie *v*.
brawler ['bro:lə] schreeuwer, lawaai-maker *m*.; ruziemaker, twistzoeker *m*.
brawn [bro:n] spieren *v*. *mv*.; spier-kracht *v*.; hoofdkaas *v*., preskop *m*.
bray [brei] *vi*. balken, schreeuwen; (*dicht.*) schallen, weergalmen; *vt*. fijn-stampen, fijnwrijven; *sb*. gebalk, ge-schreeuw *o*.; geschal *v*.
braze [breiz] bronzen; als koper kleu-ren; solderen.
brazen-faced ['breiznfeist] onbe-schaamd.
brazenly ['breiznli] *adv*. onbeschaamd, brutaal.
brazier ['breiziə] koperslager *m*.; kom-foor *o*.
Brazil [brə'zil] Brazilië *o*.
breach [britʃ] *sb*. breuk *v*.; bres *v*.; in-breuk, schending *v*.; stortzee *v*.; *vt*. doorbreken.
bread [bred] *sb*. brood *o*.
bread-cart ['bredkât] broodkar *v*.
bread-crumb ['brədkrəm] broodkrui-mel *m*.
breadless ['bredlis] brodeloos.
breadth [bredδ] breedte *v*.; (*v. stof*) baan, strook *v*.; ruime opvatting *v*.; brede blik *m*.
breadthways, breadthwise ['bredδ-weiz, '—waiz] in de breedte.
bread-winner ['bredwinə] kostwin-ner, broodwinner *m*.
break [breik] *vt*. breken; afbreken; onderbreken; verbreken; doorbreken; (*v. vlas*) braken; (*v. bank*) doen sprin-gen; *vi*. afbreken; uitbreken; (*v. weer*) veranderen; (*v. bloem*) opengaan; (*v. abces*) doorgaan; achteruitgaan; failliet gaan; — **up**, (*v. weiland*) scheuren; *sb*. breuk *v*.; afbreking *v*.; onderbreking *v*.;

verbreking *v*.; (*v. dag*) (het) aanbreken *o*.; (*v. weer*) verandering *v*.; afbrekings-teken *o*.
breakable]'breikəbl] breekbaar.
break-down ['breik'daun] defect *o*., avery *v*.; instorting *v*.; storing *v*.; mis-lukking *v*.
breaker [breikə] breker *m*.; ijsbreker *m*.; breekijzer *o*.; stortzee *v*.; (*sch.*) (water)vaatje *o*.; —**s**, branding *v*.
breakfast ['brekfəst] *sb*. ontbijt *o*.; *vi*. ontbijten.
breaking-out ['breikin'aut] uitslag *m*.
break-neck ['breiknek] halsbrekend.
break-proof ['breikprûf] onbreekbaar.
break-through ['breik'δrû] door-braak *v*.
break-up ['breik'əp] ineenstorting *v*.; verbreking *v*.; (*v. weer*) (het) omslaan *o*.; (*v. partij*) splitsing *v*.; (het) uiteenval-len *o*.
break-water ['breikwo:tə] golfbre-ker *m*.
bream [brîm] brasem *m*.
breast [brest] *sb*. borst *v*.; boezem *m*.; *vt*. het hoofd bieden (aan); ingaan tegen, worstelen tegen.
breast-plate ['brestpleit] (*mil.*) borst-harnas *o*., borstplaat *v*.; (*v. schildpad*) buikschild *o*.; (*op doodkist*) plaat *v*.
breastwork ['brestwə:k] borstwering *v*.
breath [bredδ] adem; ademtocht *m*.; lucht(je) *v*. (*o.*); windje, zuchtje *o*.
breathe [brîθ] *vi*. ademen, ademhalen; op adem komen; fluisteren; ruiken (**of**, naar); *vt*. inademen; uitademen; inbla-zen; buiten adem brengen; laten uitbla-zen, op adem laten komen; *vr*. — **one-self**, buiten adem raken; zich buiten adem lopen; even uitblazen.
breathing ['brîθin] ademhaling *v*.; li-chaamsbeweging *v*.; (*gram.*) aspiratie *v*.
breathless ['breδlis] ademloos; buiten adem; bladstil.
breeching [britʃin] (*v. paardetuig*) broek *v*.
breed [brîd] *vt*. voortbrengen, telen, fokken; grootbrengen; opleiden; op-voeden; veroorzaken; *vi*. ontstaan; zich voortplanten; jongen (krijgen); *sb*. ge-slacht, ras *o*., soort *v*.
breeding ['brîdin] (het) voortbrengen, (het) telen, (het) fokken *o*.; opleiding *v*.; opvoeding *v*.; beschaving *v*., beschaaf-de manieren *v*. *mv*.
breeze [briz] *sb*. bries *v*.; koelte *v*.; *vi*. zacht waaien.
breezy ['brîzi] *adj*. winderig; luchtig; opgewekt, vrolijk, joviaal.
breve [brîv] (pauzelijke) breve *v*.
brevet ['brevit] brevet *o*.
breviary ['brîviəri] brevier, getijden-boek *o*.
brevity ['breviti] kortheid, beknopt-heid *v*.
brew [brû] *vt*. brouwen; uitbroeden; (*v. thee*) zetten; *sb*. brouwsel *o*.
brewage ['brûidʒ] brouwsel *o*.; treksel *o*

brewery ['brûəri] **brew-house** ['brû-haus] brouwerij *v.*

bribable ['braibəbl] omkoopbaar, veil.

bribe [braib] *sb.* steekpenning *m.*, omkoopgeld *o.*; *vt.* omkopen.

bribery ['braibəri] omkoping, omkoperij *v.*

brick [brik] *sb.* steen, baksteen *m.*; blok *o.* (uit blokkendoos); *adj.* stenen, bakstenen; *vt.* met bakstenen bouwen (bekleden, plaveien); — *up,* dichtmetselen.

brick-kiln ['brikkil(n)] steenoven *m.*

brick-layer ['brikleiə] metselaar *m.*

brick-maker ['brikmeikə] steenbakker *m.*

brick-work ['brikwə:k] metselwerk *o.*; —*s,* steenbakkerij *v.*

bride [braid] bruid *v.*

bridegroom ['braidgrûm] bruidegom *m.*

bridge [bridʒ] *sb.* brug *v.*; (*r. viool*) kam *m.*; rug *m.* van de neus; (*bilj.*) linkerhand *r.* als steun; bridge *o.* (*kaartspel*); *vt.* een brug leggen; overbruggen.

bridle ['braidl] *sb.* teugel, toom *m.*; *vt.* tomen, breidelen, beteugelen.

bridle-bit ['braidlbit] bit, gebit *o.*

bridle-path, bridle-road, bridle-way ['braidlpâð, —roud, —wei] rijpad *o.*, rijweg *m.* (voor ruiters), ruiterpad *o.*

brief [brîf] *adj.* kort, beknopt; *sb.* uittreksel *o.*, samenvatting *v.*; (pauselijke) breve *v.*; (*recht*) instructie *v.*; *vt.* (*recht*) in hoofdpunten samenvatten; (een advocaat) nemen.

briefless ['brîflis] (*v. advocaat*) zonder praktijk.

briefly ['brîfli] *adv.* kort, in 't kort, beknopt.

brigade [bri'geid] brigade *v.*

brigand ['brigənd] rover, struikrover *m.*

bright [brait] *adj.* helder, licht; blinkend; opgewekt; vlug, schrander; gelukkig.

brighten ['braitn] *vt.* verhelderen; doen opklaren; doen glanzen, polijsten; opmonteren, opvrolijken; *vi.* opklaren; verhelderen; schitteren.

brightness ['braitnis] helderheid, klaarheid *v.*; glans *m.*, schittering *v.*; opgewektheid, levendigheid *v.*; vlugheid, schranderheid *v.*

brilliant ['briljənt] *adj.* schitterend; *sb.* briljant *m.*

brim [brim] *sb.* rand, boord, kant *m.*; *vt.* tot de rand vullen; *vi.* boordevol zijn; — (*over*) **with,** overvloeien van.

brimfull ['brimful] boordevol.

brimmer ['brimə] volle roemer *m.*; hoed *m.* met rand.

brindle(d) ['brindl(d)] gestreept, gespikkeld, getijgerd.

brine [brain] pekel *v.*

bring [briŋ] brengen; meebrengen; opbrengen; halen; (*v. argumenten*) aanvoeren; (*v. eis*) indienen, instellen; — *about,* teweegbrengen.

brink [briŋk] rand, kant *m.*

briny ['braini] zout, zilt.

brisk [brisk] *adj.* levendig, vlug, wakker; fris, opwekkend; *vt.* verlevendigen; — *up,* aanvuren, aanwakkeren; versnellen; *vi.* — *about,* vlug rondlopen; in de weer zijn; — *up,* vlug komen, komen aanzetten; zich optooien; opleven.

brisket ['briskit] borst *v.*, borststuk *o.* (*van dier*).

bristle ['brisl] borstels *m. mv.*

brittle ['britl] broos, bros, vergankelijk; breekbaar.

broach [broutʃ] *sb.* rijgnaald *v.*; priem *m.*; braadspit *o.*; els, stift *v.*; spits *v.*

broad [bro:d] *adj.* breed; wijd, ruim, uitgestrekt; duidelijk; ruw, grof; plat; onbekrompen, verdraagzaam; *adv.* — *awake,* klaar wakker.

broad-axe ['bro:dæks] houthakkersbijl *v.*; houweel *o.*; strijdbijl *v.*

broadcast ['bro:dkâst] *adj. & adv.* met de hand gezaaid; wijd verspreid, met milde hand uitgestrooid; draadloos verspreiden, draadloos uitzenden, omroepen; voor de microfoon spreken; *sb.* draadloze uitzending *v.* (radio-)omroep *m.*

broadcasting ['bro:dkâstiŋ] draadloze omroep, radio-omroep *m.*

broaden ['bro:dn] breed maken, verbreden, verruimen.

brochure [brɔ'ʃûə] brochure *v.*

brock [brɔk] (*Dk.*) das *m.*; (*fig.*) stinkerd *m.*, vuillik *m.*

broil [brɔil] *sb.* ruzie *v.*, twist *m.*, krakeel, tumult *o.*; gebraden vlees *o.*; *vt.* roosteren; branden; *vi.* ruzie maken; ruzie hebben.

broken ['broukn] *v. d. van* **break**; (*r. weer*) onbestendig, onvast; (*r. kistje, enz.*) aangebroken; (*r. soldaat*) invalide; (*v. water*) woelig.

broken-winded ['broukn'windid] kortademig, aamborstig.

broker ['brouk] makelaar *m.*; uitdrager *m.*; tussenpersoon *m.*

brokerage ['broukəridʒ] makelarij *v.*; courtage *v.*, makelaarsloon *o.*

bronze [brɔnz] *sb.* brons *o.*; *adj.* bronzen; *vt.* bronzen.

brooch [broutʃ] borstspeld, doekspeld, broche *v.*

brood [brûd] *sb.* broedsel *o.*; gebroed *o.*; kroost *o.*; geslacht *o.*; ras *o.*; *vt.* uitbroeden; *vi.* broeden; broeien, piekeren (**on, over,** over).

brook [bruk] *sb.* beek *v.*

broom [brûm] brem, hei *v.*; bezem *m.*

broth [brɔð] vleesnat *o.*, bouillon *m.*

brother ['brɔθə] broeder *m.*; ambtsbroeder, collega *m.*

brotherhood ['brɔθəhud] broederschap *v.*

brother-in-law ['brɔθərinlo:] schoonbroeder, zwager *m.*

brotherly ['brɔθəli] broederlijk.

brow [brau] wenkbrauw *v.*

brown [braun] adj. bruin; (dicht.) donker; sb. (het) bruin o., bruine kleur r.; duisternis r.; rt. bruinen, bruineren; ri. bruin worden.

brownie ['brauni] aardmannetje o., kabouter m.

bruise [brûz] rt. kneuzen; blutsen; fijn stampen, verpletteren; bont en blauw slaan; sb. kneuzing r.; bluts, buil, blauwe plek v.

brumal ['brûməl] winterachtig, winters.

brume [brûm] damp, mist m.

brush [brəʃ] sb. borstel, kwast m., penseel o.; vt. (af)borstelen, (af)vegen.

brushwood ['brəʃwud] kreupelhout o.; rijshout o.

Brussels ['brəslz] sb. Brussel o.; adj. Brussels.

brutal ['brûtəl] adj. beestachtig, dierlijk, bestiaal; onmenselijk, ruw, wreed; ruw, onbeschoft, grof.

brutalize ['brûtelaiz] vt. verdierlijken; wreed behandelen; ri. ontaarden.

brute [brût] sb. (redeloos) dier o.; bruut, onmens, woesteling m.; adj. dierlijk, woest, bruut.

brutish(ly) ['brûtiʃ(li)] adj. (adv.) dierlijk; dom.

bubble ['bəbl] bobbel m., waterblaas v., luchtbel, zeepbel v.; zwendel m., zwendelarij v., boerenbedrog o.

buccaneer [bəkə'niə] boekanier, zeerover m.

buck [bək] damhert o.; reebok m.; rammelaar m.; ram m., fat, modegek m.; boog m.

bucket ['bəkit] emmer m.; puts v.; (r. waterrad) schoep v.; pompzuiger m.; (tn.) schoen m.; (in mijn) kooi v.

buckle ['bəkl] sb. gesp v.; rt. gespen; aangorden; krommen; verbuigen, ontzetten.

buckler ['bəklə] beukelaar m., rond schild o.; (fig.) schild, steun m.

buckwheat ['bəkwit] boekweit v.

bud [bəd] sb. (Pl.) knop m.; kiem v.; rt. enten, oculeren; ri. uitkomen, uitbotten, knoppen, ontluiken, zich ontwikkelen.

budge [bədʒ] (zich) verroeren, bewegen.

budget ['bədʒit] sb. zak m.; voorraad m.; begroting v., budget o.; ri. de begroting opmaken; huishouden.

buff [bəf] sb. dik geelachtig leer o., zeemkleur v.; (Sc.) onzin m.; in —, spiernaakt; adj. zeemkleurig, lichtgeel.

buffalo ['bəfəlou] sb. buffel m.; karbouw m.

buffer ['bəfə] stootkussen o., buffer m.; (sl.) kerel m.

buffet ['bufei] buffet o.

buffoon [bə'fûn] grappenmaker, komiek m.

bug [bəg] wandluis, weegluis v.

bugaboo ['bəgəbû] bullebak, boeman m., spook, schrikbeeld o.

bugbear ['bəgbêə] zie **bugaboo**.

bugle ['bjûgl] jachthoorn m.

build [bild] rt. bouwen; oprichten; stichten; maken; aanleggen; — up, bouwen, opbouwen; dichtmetselen; (fig.) stichten; ri. bouwen; nestelen; sb. bouw m., bouwwijze r.; lichaamsbouw m.; vorm m., gedaante r.; (v. jas, enz.) snit m.

builder ['bildə] bouwer, bouwmeester m.; aannemer m.; stichter m.

building ['bildiŋ] gebouw o.; bouwwerk o.

bulb [bəlb] sb. bol, bloembol m.; gloeilampje o., peer r.; ri. zwellen, uitzetten.

bulge [bəldʒ] sb. uitzetting, ronding v.; (r. schip, ton, enz.) buik m.; (sl.) plotselinge stijging r. (van prijzen); ri. opbollen, opzwellen, ronden, buiken, uitpuilen; rt. doen opzwellen.

bulk [bəlk] sb. omvang m., grootte v.; meerderheid r., grootste deel o.; hoofdmacht r.; reuzengestalte v.; lading, scheepslading r.; rt. opstapelen; wegen zonder emballage.

bulk-head ['bəlkhed] (sch.) dwarsschot, waterdicht schot o.

bulky ['bəlki] groot, lijvig, omvangrijk; wichtig.

bull [bull] sb. stier m.; mannetje o. (r. olifant, enz.); (mil.) roos r. (van schijf); (H.: sl.) haussier, speculant m.; (pauselijke) bul r.; (tm.) flater m.; ri. speculeren; opdrijven.

bulldog ['buldɔg] bulhond, bullebijter m.

bullet ['bulit] (geweer)kogel m.

bullion ['buljən] staaf m., ongemunt goud of zilver o.; goudfranje r.; zilverfranje r.

bullock ['buləg] (jonge) os m.

bull's-eye ['bulzai] osseoog o.; halfbolvormige lens v.; rond venster o.; dievenlantaarn v.; (schot o. in de) roos r.; hart van de roos; (fig.) rake opmerking r.

bully ['buli] snoever, grootspreker m.; donderaar, bullebak m.; vlees o. in blik; (sp.) worsteling v.

bulwark ['bulwək] sb. bolwerk o., verschansing r.; golfbreker m.; vt. verschansen; beschermen.

bummer ['bəmə] (Am.) klaploper, vagebond, luilak m.

bump [bəmp] sb. stoot, schok, slag, bons m.; buil r., gezwel o.; knobbel m.; vt. bonzen tegen, stoten tegen; (sp.: roeien) inhalen; ri. stoten, botsen, bonzen; adv. plof, pardoes.

bumper ['bəmpə] vol glas o., volle beker m.; (r. auto) bumper, schokbreker m.

bumpkin ['bəmpkin] lomperd, boerenkinkel m.

bumpy ['bəmpi] hobbelig; hotsend, stotend; (r. wind, weer) onstuimig.

bun [bən] (krenten)broodje o.

bunch [bən(t)ʃ] sb. (v. druiven) tros m.; (r. uien, enz.) rist v.; (v. sleutels, enz) bos m.; groep r., stel o.; rt. aan bosje binden; in plooien samentrekken; *vi.* bosjes (trossen, troepen) vormen; zich in bosjes (troepen) verenigen; aan elkaar hangen.

bundle ['bəndl] *sb.* bos; bundel *m.*, pak *o.*; *vt.* samenbinden, samenvoegen, inpakken; — *away*, er van door gaan; wegjagen, wegsturen; — *out*, eruit gooien; wegsturen.

bung [bəŋ] (*v. vat*) bom, spon *v.*

bungle ['bəŋgl] *vi.* knoeien, prutsen; *vt.* verknoeien; — *up*, in elkaar flansen; *sb.* knoeiwerk *o.*

bungler ['bəŋglə] knoeier, prutser *m.*

bunk [bəŋk] rustbank, slaapbank *v.*

bunny ['bəni] konijn *o.*; eekhoorntje *o.*

buoy [bɔi] boei, ton *v.*; reddingsboei *v.*

burden ['bə:dn] *sb.* last *m.*, vracht *v.*, pak *o.*; lading *v.*; tonnemaat *v.*; refrein; hoofdthema *o.*; *vt.* beladen; belasten; bezwaren, drukken op.

burdensome ['bə:dnsəm] bezwarend, drukkend.

bureau ['bjûərou, bjûə'rou] bureau *o.*; schrijftafel *v.*; latafel *v.*; (*Am.*) toilettafel *v.*

burgess ['bə:dʒis] burger *m.*; (*gesch.*) afgevaardigde *m.* (van stad, universiteit).

burglar ['bə:glə] inbreker *m.*

burglary ['bə:gləri] (nachtelijke) inbraak *v.*

burgomaster ['bə:fəmâstə] burgemeester *m.*

burial ['beriəl] begrafenis *v.*

burin ['bjûərin] graveernaald, graveerstift *v.*

burke [bə:k] vermoorden; doen stikken, smoren; (*fig.*) doodzwijgen, in de doofpot stoppen.

burn [bə:n] *sb.* brandwond, brandplek *v.*; (*Sc.*) beek *v.*, stroompje *o.*; *vt.* verbranden; opbranden; uitbranden; (*v. stenen*) bakken; (*bij spel*) zich branden; *vi.* branden; gloeien.

burning ['bə:niŋ] *adj.* brandend; gloeiend; vurig.

burnish ['bə:niʃ] polijsten; poetsen, glanzen.

burrow ['bərou[*sb.* hol *o.* (konijnehol; vossehol; schuilplaats); *vt.* omwroeten; omwoelen; (een hol) graven.

burst [bə:st] *vt.* doen barsten; doen breken; doen springen; openbreken; verbreken; doorbreken; (*v. deur*) intrappen; *vi.* barsten; openbarsten; losbarsten; uitbarsten; openvliegen; zich ontlasten; *sb.* barst, breuk *v.*; uitbarsting; losbarsting *v.*; plotselinge verschijning; (*fam.*) fuif *v.*

bury ['beri] begraven; bedekken; verbergen.

bush [buʃ' *sb.* struik(en) *m.* (*mv.*); (*Am., Austr.*) bos *o.*; haarbos *m.*; vossestaart *m.*; (*tn.*) naafbus *v.*; *vt.* met struiken beplanten; (*tn.*) van een (naaf)bus voorzien, verbussen; *vi.* ruig groeien.

bushel ['buʃəl] schepe ?*o.*

bushranger ['buʃreindʒə] woudloper *m.*; struikrover *m.*

business ['biznis] bezigheid *v.*; zaak *v.*, zaken *v. mv.*, handel *m.*, handelszaak *v.*; bedrijf, beroep *o.*; werk, karwei *o.*

business-concern]'bizniskənsə: handelszaak, handelsonderneming *v.*

busk [bəsk] (korset)balein *v.*

bust [bəst] borstbeeld *o.*, buste, borst *v.*

bustle ['bəsl] *vi.* druk in de weer zijn, zich reppen; *vt.* aansporen; *sb.* drukte, beweging *v.*, gewoel *o.*

busy ['bizi] bezig, aan 't werk, druk bedrijvig, naarstig; rusteloos; bemoeiziek.

busybody ['bizibədi] bemoeial *m.*

but [bət] *cj.* maar; *adv.* slechts, enkel; *prep.* behalve, buiten, uitgenomen; *sb.* maar.

butcher ['butʃə] *sb.* slager, vleeshouwer *m.*; moordenaar *m.*; *vt.* slachten; vermoorden; (*fig.*) verknoeien; verminken.

butchery ['butʃəri] slagerij, vleeshouwerij *v.*; slachtplaats *v.*; slachting *v.*

butler ['bətlə] chef-huisknecht *m.*

butt [bət] *sb.* kogelvanger *m.*; doel, mikpunt *o.*, schijf *v.*; zondebok *m.*; (*v. hand*) muis *v.*; *vi.* stoten, botsen; grenzen (*on*, aan); uitsteken; — *in*, zich mengen in, zich bemoeien met; *vt.* plaatsen, zetten tegen; *adv.* pardoes.

butt-end ['bətend] stompje *o.*; uiteinde *o.*; (*v. geweer*) kolf *m.*

butter ['bətə] *sb.* boter *v.*; (*fig.*) stroop, strooplikkerij *v.*; *vt.* boteren; smeren.

butter-bean ['bətəbîn] sperzieboon *v.*

butter-boat ['bətəbout] botervlootje *o.*; sauskom *v.*; (*fig.*) stroopkwast *m.*

butter-fingered ['bətəfingəd] onhandig.

butterfly ['hətəflai] vlinder *m.*

buttermilk ['bətəmilk] karnemelk *r.*

buttock ['bətək] bil *v.*; —*s*, achterste *o.*

button ['bətn] *sb.* knoop; knop *m.*; dop *m.*; (*sl.: bij verkoping*) opjager *m.*; *vt.* knopen, vastknopen, toeknopen; van knopen voorzien, knopen aanzetten; *vi.* dichtgaan.

button-boot ['bətnbût] knooplaars *v.*

button-hole ['bətnhoul] knoopsgat *o.*

buttress ['bətris] stut, schoor, beer,; schraagpijler *m.*; (*v. boom*) wortellijst *v.*; steunpilaar *m.*

buy [bai] kopen; omkopen; — *over*, omkopen.

buyer ['baiə] koper *m.*

buzz-saw ['bəzsɔ:] cirkelzaag *v.*

by [bai' bij; door; naar; volgens; nabij; langs; voorbij; op; over; met; van; aan.

by-bidder ['baibidə] (*bij verkoping*) opjager *m.*

by-end ['baiend] bijbedoeling *v.*

by-law ['bailo:] verordening *r.*; reglement *o.*

by-purpose ['baipə:pəs] bijbedoeling v.
by-stander ['baistændə] toeschouwer m.

by-street ['baistrĭt] zijstraat, achter-
straat v.
byword ['baiwə:d] spreekwoord o;
spotnaam, schimpnaam, bijnaam m.

C

cab [kæb] huurrijtuig o., vigilant v.;
taxi v.
cabal [kə'bæl] kabaal o., kuiperij, intrige v.; kliek, partij v.
cabaret ['kæbəret] cabaret o.
cabbage ['kæbidʒ] (Pl.) kool v.
cabbage-head ['kæbidʒhed] kcolkrop
m.; uilskuiken o., domkop m.
cabbage-lettuce ['kæbidʒletis] krop-
salade v.
cabbage-worm ['kæbidʒwə:m] koolrups v.
cabin ['kæbin] hut v.; kajuit, hut v.;
(op strand) badhuisje o.
cabin-boy ['kæbinbɔi] (sch.) kajuitsjongen, scheepsjongen m.
cabinet ['kæbinit] kabinet o.; kamertje o.; raadkamer v.; ministerie o.;
ministerraad m.
cabinet-maker ['kæbinitmeikə] kas-
tenmaker, fijne schrijnwerker m.
cable ['keibl] sb. kabel m.; kabellengte
v.; telegraafkabel m., kabeltelegram o.;
vt. met een kabel vastmaken; kabelen,
telegraferen.
cablegram ['keiblgræm] kabeltelegram o.
cabman ['kæbmən] koetsier, huurkoetsier m.
caboose [kə'bûs] (sch.) kombuis,
scheepskeuken v.; veldkeuken v.
cab-stand ['kæbstænd] standplaats
voor huurrijtuigen v.
cachet ['kæʃei] stempel m., zegel o.;
(gen.) ouwel m., pastille v.
cackle ['kækl] vi. kakelen, snateren;
giechelen; sb. gekakel, gesnater; gegiechel o.
cacography [kæ'kɔgrəfi] kakografie v.
cad [kæd] poen, ploert m.; balie-
kluiver m.
cadastre [kə'dæstə] kadaster o.
caddish(ly) ['kædiʃ(li)] adj. (adv.)
ploertig, poenig, patserig.
cadence ['keidəns] cadans, maat v.,
toonval m., ritme o.
cadet [kə'det] cadet m.; jongere (jongste) zoon; jongere broeder m.
cadge [kædʒ] klaplopen; bedelen;
venten.
cadre ['kâdə] kader o.
cafe ['kæfei] koffiehuis, café o.
Caffre ['kæfə] Kaffer m.
cage [keidʒ] sb. kooi v.; gevangenis v.;
liftkooi v.; vt. in een kooi opsluiten,
gevangen zetten.
cajole [kə'dʒoul] vleien.
cake [keik] sb. gebak o., taart v.,

koek m.; (v. zeep, enz.) stuk o.; (Sc.)
haverbrood o.; havermeelkoek m.
calabash ['kæləbæʃ] (Pl.) kalebas v.,
pompoen m.
calamity [kə'læmiti] ramp, ellende v.,
onheil o.
calcify ['kælsifai] verkalken.
calcine ['kælsain] verkalken; (zich)
oxyderen.
calculable ['kælkjuləbl] berekenbaar.
calculate ['kælkjuleit] vt. berekenen,
uitrekenen, voorzicn; vi. rekenen.
calculation [kælkju'leiəʃn] berekening v.
calendar ['kælində] kalender, almanak m.
calf [kâf] kalf o.; kalfsleer o.; jong o.
van het hert; kuit v. (v. been).
calf-bound ['kâfbaund] in kalfsleren
band.
calf-skin ['kâfskin] kalfsvel o.; kalfsleer o.
caliber ['kælibə] kaliber o.; gehalte o.;
inhoud m.; gewicht o.
calico ['kælikou] sb. calico, katoen o.;
(Am.)bedrukt katoenv.; adj. (Am.)bont.
calk [ko:k] (v. paard) op scherp zetten;
breeuwen, kalefateren; calqueren.
call [ko:l] vt. roepen; bijeenroepen, oproepen, inroepen, toeroepen, uitroepen;
opbellen; noemen, heten; (als getuige)
dagvaarden; (bij kaartsp.) melden; (v.
vogels) lokken; vi. roepen; aanlopen,
aankomen; (v. trein) stoppen; (v. boot)
aandoen; opzoeken; — in, binnenroe-
pen; inzamelen; (v. geld) opvragen; invorderen, uit de circulatie terugtrekken;
(v. dokter) ontbieden, laten komen; (v.
hypotheek) opzeggen; — up, oproepen;
opbellen; — upon, een beroep doen op;
in beslag nemen; sb. roep m.; geroep o.;
roeping v.; oproeping v.; roepstem v.;
lokstem v.; navraag v.
call-bird ['ko:lbə:d] lokvogel m.
caller ['ko:lə] (tel.) aanvrager m.;
bezoeker m.
calligraphy [kə'ligrəfi] schoonschrijf-
kunst v.; schoonschrift o.
calling ['ko:liŋ] (het) roepen o.; roepstem v.; roeping v.; beroep o.
call-loan ['ko:lloun] direct opvorder-
bare lening v.
callosity [kə'lɔsiti] verharding, vereelting v., eeltknobbel m.; eeltachtig-
heid v.; (fig.) ongevoeligheid v.
callous ['kæləs] adj. verhard, vereelt;
eeltachtig; ongevoelig, gevoelloos; vi.
vereelten, verharden.

call-over ['ko:l'ouvə] appèl o.

calm [kâm] adj. kalm, rustig, bedaard; sb. kalmte v.; windstilte v.; vt. & vi. kalmeren, (doen) bedaren, stillen.

calmly ['kâmli] adv. kalm, rustig, bedaard.

calmness ['kâmnis] kalmte, rust, bedaardheid r.

calumniate [kə'ləmnieit] lasteren, belasteren.

calumny ['kæləmni] laster m., lastertaal r.

calve [kâv] kalven.

calyx ['kei—, 'kæliks] bloemkelk m.

camber ['kæmbə] sb. welving v., boog m.; (sch.) ronding v. van het dek; vt. welven; ronden.

camel ['kæməl] (Dk.) kameel m.; (sch.) scheepskameel m.; soort vliegtuig o.

camera ['kæmərə] camera v.; kamer v.

camisole ['kæmisoul] jak, morgenjak v.; korsetlijfje o.

camomile ['kæməmail] kamille v.

camouflage ['kæmûflâʒ] sb. camouflage, maskering r.; rt. camoufleren, maskeren.

camp [kæmp] sb. kamp o.; legerplaats v.; vt. & ri. kamperen, (zich) legeren.

campaign [kəm'pein] veldtocht m.; campagne v.

camp-bed ['kæmpbed] veldbed, legerbed o.

camp-chair ['kæmptʃêə] vouwstoel m.

camp-fire ['kæmpfaiə] kampvuur o.

camphor ['kæmfə] kamfer v.

campshedding ['kæmpʃediŋ] beschoeiing v.

can [kæn] sb. kan v.; (Am.) inmaakblik o.; vt. inmaken (in blik); (Am., sl.) afdanken.

can [kæn] vi. kan, kunnen.

Canada ['kænədə] Canada o.

canal [kə'næl] kanaal o.; vaart v.

canalize ['kænəlaiz] kanaliseren.

canary [kə'nêəri] sb. kanarie(vogel) m.; adj. kanariekleurig, lichtgeel.

cancel ['kænsəl] vt. doorhalen; schrappen; intrekken, herroepen; vernietigen; buiten omloop stellen; (v. uitnodiging, enz.) afschrijven; afwimpelen; (v. breuken) verkleinen; sb. doorhaling v.; schrapping v.; intrekking v.

cancer ['kænsə] kreeft m.; kanker m.

cancerous ['kænsərəs] kankerachtig.

candid ['kændid] adj. eerlijk, oprecht, openhartig.

candidate ['kændideit] kandidaat m.

candle ['kændl] kaars v.; licht o.

candlestick ['kændlstik] kandelaar m.

candour ['kændə] eerlijkheid, oprechtheid, openhartigheid v.

candy ['kændi] kandij v.; (Am.) suikergoed o.; ulevel v.

cane [kein] sb. riet o.; suikerriet o.; rotting m.; wandelstok m.;vt . afranselen, afrossen, slaan; matten (met. riet).

canister ['kænistə] busje o., trommel m.; kartets v.

canker ['kæŋkə] sb. mondkanker m.; (r. paard) voetzeer o.; (Pl.) brand m.; (Pl.) hondsroos v.; bladrups v.; (fig.) knagende worm, kanker m.; vt. aansteken, bederven; verteren, wegvreten; vi. invreten, verkankeren.

canker-worm ['kæŋkəwə:m] bladrups, spanrups v.

cannibal ['kænibəl] kannibaal m.

cannon ['kænən] sb. kanon o.; geschut o., kanonnen o. mv.; (bilj.) carambole r.; rt. beschieten, kanonneren; ri. schieten; (bilj.) caramboleren; bonzen, botsen.

cannon-fodder ['kænənfɔdə] kanonnevlees o.

canoe [kə'nû] sb. kano v.; ri. in een kano varen.

canonize ['kænənaiz] heilig verklaren, canoniseren.

canopy ['kænəpi] troonhemel, baldakijn m.; dak o., bedekking r.

cant [kænt] huichelen, huicheltaal spreken.

cant [kænt] kantelen, op zijn kant zetten; afkanten.

canteen [kæn'tîn] kantine r.; veldfles v.; veldkeuken v.; eetketeltje o. (r. soldaat).

canton ['kæntən] kanton o.

cantonal ['kæntənl] kantonnaal.

cantonment [kæntənmənt] kampement, kantonnement o.

canvas ['kænvəs] zeildoek o.; doek, schilderij o.; zeil o.

canvass ['kænvəs] rt. navorsen, onderzoeken, uitpluizen; (r. stemmen, klanten, enz.) werven; bewerken; vi. werven; sb. onderzoek o.; werving r.

canvasser ['kænvəsə] stemmenwerver, verkiezingsagent; werfagent, colporteur m.

caoutchouc ['kautʃuk, 'kûtʃuk] caoutchouc, gomelastiek o.

cap [kæp] kap v.; muts, baret, pet v;. slaghoedje o.; dop(je) m. (o.).

capability [keipə'biliti] bekwaamheid v.; gave v., aanleg m.

capable ['keipəbl] adj. bekwaam, knap; in staat (of, om, tot, te); vatbaar (of, voor).

capacious [kə'peiʃəs] ruim, veelomvattend.

capacitate [kə'pæsiteit] bekwamen, bekwaam maken, geschikt maken, in staat stellen.

capacity [kə'pæsiti] aanleg m., bekwaamheid v.; geschiktheid; bevoegdheid v.; hoedanigheid v.; inhoud m., ruimte v.; laadvermogen v.

caparison [kə'pærisən] (v. paard) vt. optuigen.

cape [keip] kaap v.; kap, pelerine v.

caper ['keipə] sb. (Pl.) kapperstruik m.; bokkesprong m., capriool v.; gril, kuur v.; vi. rondspringen, huppelen; capriolen maken.

capital ['kæpitl] sb. kapitaal o.; hoofdstad *r*.; hoofdletter, grote letter *r*.; kapiteel *o*.; *adj*. voornaamste, hoofd—; prachtig, uitmuntend; hoogst belangrijk.

capitalism ['kæpitəlizm] kapitalisme *o*.

capitulation [kəpitju'leiʃən] capitulatie *r*.

capoc [kə'pɔk] kapok *v*.

capon ['keipən] *sb*. (*Dk*.) kapoen *m*.; *vt*. snijden.

capote [kə'pout] kapotjas *r*.; lange mantel *m*.

caprice [kə'pris] gril, kuur, luim, nuk *r*.

capricious (**ly**) [kə'priʃəs(li)] *adj*. (*adv*.) grillig, wispelturig, nukkig.

capsize [kæp'saiz] (*sch*.) kapseizen, omslaan.

capstan ['kæpstən] kaapstander *m*.

cap-stone ['kæpstoun] deksteen, sluitsteen *m*.

capsule ['kæpsjûl] capsule *v*.; slaghoedje *o*.; (*Pl*.) zaaddoos *v*.; doosvrucht *r*.

captain ['kæptin] *sb*. kapitein, aanvoerder, veldheer *m*.; hoofdman *m*.; commandant, gezagvoerder *m*.; leider *m*.; meesterknecht, opzichter, ploegbaas *m*.; (*sp*.) aanvoerder *m*.; *vt*. aanvoeren, commanderen.

captious ['kæpʃəs] bedrieglijk, listig; spitsvondig; vitterig, bedillerig.

captivate ['kæptiveit] innemen, bekoren, boeien, betoveren.

captive ['kæptiv] *sb*. gevangene; krijgsgevangene *m*.; *adj*. gevangen.

captivity [kæp'tiviti] gevangenschap *v*.

capture ['kæptʃə] *sb*. prijs *m*., vangst *r*.; gevangenneming, arrestatie *r*.; verovering *r*.; *rt*. gevangen nemen, vangen; veroveren, buitmaken; innemen; pakken, boeien.

car [kâ] kar *r*., wagen *m*.; auto *v*.; tram *r*.; (*r. ballon*) schuitje *o*.; (*r. luchtschip*) gondel *v*.; (*Am*.) spoorwagen *m*.

carafe [kə'râf] karaf *r*.

carat ['kærət] karaat *o*.

caravan [kærə'væn, 'kærəvæn] karavaan *r*.; kermiswagen *m*.; woonwagen *m*.

carbine ['kâbain] karabijn *v*.

carbon ['kâbən] koolstof *v*.; koolspits *r*.; (*c. brief*) doorslag *m*.

carbuncle ['kâbəŋkl] karbonkel *m*., puist *r*.

carburettor, —er ['kâbjuretə] carburateur, vergasser *m*.

carcase, carcass ['kâkəs] geslacht, beest *o*.; lijk, kreng, karkas *o*.; geraamte *o*.; wrak *o*.; brandgranaat *r*.

card [kâd] *sb*. kaart; speelkaart *v*.; naamkaartje *o*.; balboekje *o*.; dominosteen *m*.; (*bij wedrennen, enz*.) programma *o*.

card-board ['kâdbo:d] karton, bordpapier *o*.

cardinal ['kâdinəl] *adj*. voornaamst, hoofd—; donkerrood; *sb*. kardinaal *m*.; kardinaalvogel *m*.; korte damesmantel *m*.; (*sl*.) bisschop(wijn) *m*.

card-reader ['kâdrîdə] kaartlegster *r*.

card-sharper ['kâdʃâpə] valse speler *m*.

card-table ['kâdteibl] speeltafeltje *o*.

care [kêə] *sb*. zorg, bezorgdheid *v*.; voorwerp *o*. van zorg; *vt*. & *vi*. zich bekommeren (om,) geven om; zorgen voor, verzorgen.

career [kə'rîə] *sb*. (snelle) vaart *r*.; loopbaan, carrière *v*.; *ri*. hollen; voortsnellen; rennen, draven.

care-free ['kêəfri] onbezorgd, zorgeloos.

careful ['kêəful] *adj*. zorgvuldig, nauwkeurig; omzichtig; voorzichtig; zorgvol; zuinig.

careless (**ly**) ['kêəlis(li)] *adj*. (*adv*.) zorgeloos; slordig; onverschillig, onachtzaam, nalatig.

caress [kə'res] *sb*. liefkozing *v*.; *rt*. liefkozen, strelen, aanhalen.

caretaker ['kêəteikə] huisbewaarder *m*., huisbewaarster *r*.

care-worn ['kêəwo:n] door zorgen gekweld, afgetobd.

cargo ['kâgou] (scheeps)lading, vracht *r*.

cargo-boat ['kâgoubout] vrachtschip *o*.

caricature ['kærikətjûə] *sb*. karikatuur *v*.; *rt*. een karikatuur maken van.

caricaturist [kærikə'tjûərist] karikatuurtekenaar *m*.

caries ['kêəriïz] beeneter, wolf *m*. (in tanden).

carillon ['kæriljən] klokkenspel, carillon *o*.

carmine ['kâmain] karmijn(rood).

carnage ['kânid3] bloedbad *o*., slachting *r*.

carnal ['kânəl] *adj*. vleselijk, zinnelijk.

carnation [kâ'neiʃən] *sb*. vleeskleur *v*.; (*Pl*.) anjelier *v*.; *adj*. vleeskleurig.

carnival ['kânivəl] carnaval *o*., vastenavond *m*.; (*fig*.) bacchanaal *o*., zwelgpartij *v*.

carnivorous [kâ'nivərəs] vleesetend.

carol ['kærəl] *sb*. lied *o*., zang, lofzang *m*.; *ri*. zingen, kwelen.

carousal [kə'rauzəl] drinkgelag *o*., slemppartij *v*.

carouse [kə'rauz] *ri*. zuipen, zwelgen; *sb*. drinkgelag *o*., zwelgpartij *v*.

carp [kâp] (*Dk*.) karper *m*.

carpenter ['kâpəntə] *sb*. timmerman *m*.; *ri*. timmeren; *rt*. in elkaar timmeren.

carpet ['kâpit] *sb*. tapijt, vloerkleed, karpet *o*.; loper *m*.; *rt*. met tapijten beleggen.

carpet-bag ['kâpitbæg] reiszak *m*., valies *o*.

carpet-beater ['kâpitbîtə] matteklopper *m*.

carriage ['kærid3] wagen *m*., rijtuig *o*.; wagon *m*.; affuit *o*.; (*v. wagen*) onderstel *o*.; vracht *v*., vrachtprijs *m*.; vervoer *o*.

carriage-door ['kærid3do:] portier *o*.

carrier ['kæriə] voerman, vrachtrijder *m*.; bode *m*.; vrachtvaarder *m*.; (*v. fiets*) bagagedrager *m*.

carrier-pigeon ['kæriəpidʒən] post-duif v.

carrion ['kæriən] kreng, aas o.

carrot ['kærət] (Pl.) gele wortel m., peen v.

carry ['kæri] vt. dragen; meedragen, wegdragen; brengen; meebrengen; overbrengen; vervoeren; meevoeren; wegvoeren; vi. dragen; (v. sneeuw) pakken, kleven; — on, voortzetten; doorzetten; volhouden; (v. zaak) voeren, drijven; zich aanstellen.

carry-forward ['kæri'fo:wəd] (H.) transport o.

carrying-capacity ['kæriiŋkəpæsiti] laadvermogen o.

carrying-trade ['kæriiŋtreid] goederenvervoer o.; vrachtvaart v.

cart [kât] sb. kar v., wagen m.; vt. met een kar (wagen) vervoeren; (v. oogst) binnenhalen.

cartage [kâtidʒ] vervoer o. per as; sleeploon, vrachtloon o.

carter ['kâtə] voerman, karreman m.; sleper m.

cartilage ['kâtilidʒ] kraakbeen o.

cart-load ['kâtloud] karrevracht, wagenvracht, wagenlading v.

cartridge ['kâtridʒ] patroon v.

cart-road ['kâtroud] karreweg, veldweg m.

cartwright ['kâtrait] wagenmaker m.

carve [kâv] snijden, kerven; voorsnijden; uitsnijden; beeldsnijden, beeldhouwen, graveren; splijten; verdelen.

carving ['kâviŋ] snijwerk o.; beeldsnijkunst v.

carving-knife ['kâviŋnaif] voorsnijmes o.

cascade [kæs'keid] kleine waterval m.; golvend kantwerk o.

case [keis] sb. doos v.; bus v.; kist v., koffer m.; omhulsel, foedraal, overtrek o.; trommel; koker m.; kast v.; naamval m.; geval o.; zaak, rechtszaak v.; vt. in een kist (kast, koker, enz.) doen; insluiten; overtrekken.

case-bottle ['keisbɔtl] veldfles v.; mandefles v.

casemate ['keismeit] kazemat v.

cash [kæʃ] sb. geld, contant geld; kas, kassa v.; vt. verzilveren, te gelde maken; incasseren; wisselen; — up, (fam.) opdokken.

cash-account ['kæʃəkaunt] kasrekening v.

cash-book ['kæʃbuk] kasboek o.

cash-box ['kæʃbɔks] geldkistje o.

cashier [kəʃiə] sb. kassier; kashouder m.

cashmere ['kæʃmiə] kasjmier o.; sjaal v.

casing ['keisiŋ] overtrek, omhulsel o., bekleding, verpakking v., koker m., foedraal o.; buitenband m.

casino [kə'sînou] casino o.

cask [kâsk] sb. vat, fust o., ton v.; vt. in een vat doen.

cassation [kæ'seiʃən] (recht) cassatie v.

cassock ['kæsək] toog, soutane v.

cast [kâst] vt. werpen, gooien; neerwerpen; wegwerpen; uitwerpen; afwerpen; (v. kleren) uittrekken, afleggen; (v. stem) uitbrengen; afdanken; afwijzen; verwerpen; veroordelen; rangschikken, indelen, verdelen; (tn., fig.) gieten; vi. (sch.) wenden; krom trekken; sb. worp, gooi m.; (het) uitgooien o.; hengelplaats v.; oogopslag m.; rolverdeling, bezetting v.; berekening, optelling v.; (giet)vorm m.; afgietsel o.

cast-down ['kâst'daun] terneergeslagen.

caste [kâst] kaste v.

castellan ['kæstələn] slotvoogd m.

caster ['kâstə] werper m.; rolverdeler m.; rekenaar m.; gieter m.

castigate ['kæstigeit] kastijden, tuchtigen; gispen; (v. tekst) verbeteren.

casting-net ['kâstiŋnet] werpnet o.

casting-vote ['kâstiŋ'vout] beslissende stem v.

cast-iron ['kâst'aiən] sb. gietijzer, gegoten ijzer o.; adj. ['kâstaiən] van gietijzer; (fig.) ijzersterk; onbuigzaam; meedogenloos, hardvochtig.

castle ['kâsl] sb. kasteel, slot o.; vi. (in schaakspel) rokeren.

castle-builder ['kâslbildə] dromer, fantast m.

castor ['kâstə] bevergeil o.; kastoren hoed m.; rolletje o. (onder meubel); strooier m.

casual ['kæʒuəl] adj. toevallig, terloops, casueel; vluchtig; slordig; sb. los arbeider (werkman) m.; toevallige bezoeker m.; amateur m.

casually ['kæʒuəli] adv. toevallig, terloops.

casualty ['kæʒuəlti] toeval o.; toevalligheid v.; voorval; ongeval, ongeluk o.; casualties, (mil.) doden en gewonden, verliezen.

cat [kæt] sb. kat v.; dubbele treeft v.; (sch.) kraanbalk m.

cataplasm ['kætəplæzm] (gen.) pap v., omslag m.

cataract ['kætərækt] waterval, stortvloed m.; (grauwe) staar v. (op het oog).

catastrophe [kə'tæstrəfi] ramp v., onheil o.; (v. drama) ontknoping v.

catcall]'kætko:l] sb. schel fluitje o.; (in schouwburg) gefluit o.; vt. uitfluiten.

catch [kætʃ] vt. vangen, opvangen; vatten, pakken, grijpen, aangrijpen; betrappen; raken, treffen; inhalen; (v. trein) halen; (v. ziekte) oplopen; (v. slag, enz.) toebrengen; vi. blijven haken, vastraken; (v. stem, adem) stokken; (v. schroef, enz.) pakken; zich verbreiden; besmettelijk zijn, aansteken; aanzetten, aanbranden; toevriezen, beginnen te bevriezen; sb. vangst, buit m.; greep m. & v.; aanwinst o.; voordeel o.; goede partij v.; lokmiddel o.; valstrik m., strikvraag v.; (v. stem, adem) (het) stokken o.

catching ['kætʃiŋ] *sb.* (*v. stem, adem*) (het) stokken *o.*; spiertrekking, zenuwtrekking *v.*; *adj.* aanstekelijk, besmettelijk; pakkend; aantrekkelijk; bedrieglijk; verlokkelijk.

catchword ['kætʃwə:d] leus, partijleus *v.*; mooie frase *v.*; wachtwoord *o.*

catechism ['kætikizm] catechismus *m.*

category ['kætigəri] categorie *v.*

caterpillar ['kætəpilə] rups *v.*; (*tn.*) rupsband *m.*

catgut ['kætgət] darmsnaar *v.*; (*fig.*) snaarinstrument *o.*; stramien *v. & o.*

cathedra [kə'θidrə] katheder *m.*; bisschopszetel *m.*; *ex —,* met gezag.

cathedral [kə'θidrəl] *adj.* kathedraal, bisschoppelijk; gezaghebbend; ex cathedra gegeven; *sb.* kathedraal *v.*; domkerk *v.*

catholic ['kæθəlik] *adj.* algemeen; veelzijdig; katholiek; *sb.* katholiek *m.*

cat-ice ['kætais] bomijs *o.*

cat-nap ['kætnæp] hazeslaapje, dutje *o.*

cattish ['kætiʃ] kattig.

cattle ['kætl] vee, rundvee *o.*; (*sl.*) paarden *o. mv.*

cattle-breeder ['kætlbridə] veefokker *m.*

cattle-breeding ['kætlbridiŋ] veeteelt, veefokkerij *v.*

cauliflower ['kɔliflauə] bloemkool *v.*

caulk [kɔ:k] kalefat(er)en, breeuwen.

causal ['kɔ:zəl] oorzakelijk.

cause [kɔ:z] *sb.* oorzaak, reden *v.*; zaak, aangelegenheid *v.*; rechtszaak *v.*, proces *o.*; *vt.* veroorzaken, aanrichten, teweegbrengen; doen, laten, maken dat..., zorgen dat...

causeless (ly) ['kɔ:zlis(li)] *adj.* (*adv.*) ongegrond, ongemotiveerd; zonder oorzaak.

caustic [kɔ:stik] *adj.* brandend, bijtend, scherp; (*fig.*) scherp, sarcastisch; *sb.* brandmiddel, bijtmiddel *o.*

cauterize ['kɔ:təraiz] uitbranden, toeschroeien; (*fig.*) verharden.

caution ['kɔ:ʃən] *sb.* omzichtigheid, voorzichtigheid *v.*; waarschuwing *v.*, waarschuwingscommando *v.*; berisping *v.*; (*Am., Sc.*) borgtocht *m.*; *vt.* waarschuwen (*against,* voor); berispen.

cautious (ly))'kɔ:ʃəs(li)] *adj.* (*adv.*) omzichtig, voorzichtig, behoedzaam.

cavalcade [kævəl'keid] cavalcade *v.*; ruiterstoet *m.*

cavalry ['kævəlri] ruiterij, cavalerie *v.*

cave [keiv] *sb.* hol *o.*, grot *v.*; afkalving *v.*; *vt.* uithollen; ondergraven; inslaan, indeuken; *vi.* afkalven; zich afscheiden; *— in,* instorten, inzakken; toegeven; het opgeven.

cave-dweller ['keivdwelə] holbewoner *m.*

cavern ['kævən] spelonk *v.*, hol *o.*, grot *v.*

caviar(e) [kævi'â] kaviaar *v.*

cavil ['kævil] *sb.* vitterij, haarkloverij *v.*; *vi.* vitten, haarkloven.

caviller ['kævilə] vitter, haarklover *m.*

cavity ['kæviti] holte *v.*

caw [kɔ:] *vi.* (*v. raaf*) krassen; *sb.* gekras *o.*

cayman ['keimən] (*Dk.*) kaaiman *m.*

cease [sis] *vt.* staken, beëindigen, ophouden met; *vi.* ophouden; *sb. without —,* zonder ophouden.

ceaseless (ly) ['sislis(li)] *adj.* (*adv.*) onophoudelijk.

cede [sid] afstaan, afstand doen van, overgeven; toegeven.

ceiling ['siliŋ] plafond *o.*, zoldering *v.*; (*sch.*) wegering *v.*

celebrate ['selibreit] vieren; loven, prijzen, verheerlijken; celebreren, plechtig opdragen.

celebrity [si'lebriti] vermaardheid, beroemdheid *v.*

celery ['seləri] selderij *v.*

celestial [si'lestjəl] *adj.* hemels, hemel—; *sb.* hemeling *m.*; (*fam.*) Chinees *m.*

celibacy ['selibəsi] celibaat *o.*, ongehuwde staat *m.*

celibatarian [selibə'têəriən] celibatair, ongehuwd(e).

cell [sel] cel *v.*; afdeling; kluis *v.*; (*el.*) element *o.*

cellar ['selə] *sb.* kelder *m.*; *vt.* in een kelder bewaren.

cellular ['seljulə] celvormig; cellulair; cel—.

cement ['siment] *sb.* cement *o.*; (*fig.*) band *m.*; bindmiddel *o.*; *vt.* cementeren; verbinden; (*fig.*) bevestigen.

cemetery ['semitri] begraafplaats *v.*

cense [sens] bewieroken.

censor ['sensə] *sb.* censor, zedenmeester *m.*; (kunst)criticus *m.*; *vt.* de censuur uitoefenen over, als censor nazien.

censorship ['sensəʃip] ambt *o.* van censor; censuur *v.*

censurable ['senʃərəbl] berispelijk, laakbaar, afkeurenswaardig.

censure ['senʃə] *sb.* berisping *v.*; afkeuring *v.*; censuur *v.*; *vt.* berispen; bedillen; afkeuren; critiseren.

census ['sensəs] volkstelling *v.*

cent [sent] honderd; Amerikaanse cent *m.*; *per —,* ten honderd, percent.

centenarian [senti'nêəriən] *adj.* honderdjarig; *sb.* honderdjarige *m.*

centigramme ['sentigræm] centigram *o.*

centilitre ['sentilitə] centiliter *m.*

centimetre ['sentimitə] centimeter *m.*

central ['sentrəl] centraal, midden—, middel—.

centralization [sentrəlai'zeiʃən] centralisatie *v.*

centre ['sentə] *sb.* centrum, middelpunt *o.*, spil, as *v.*; (*v. aardbeving*) haard *m.*; (*bouwk.*) boogformeel *o.*; *adj.* centraal, midden—; *vt.* het middelpunt bepalen van; in 't midden plaatsen; *vi.* zich concentreren, samenkomen (in).

centre-forward ['sentəfɔ:wəd] (*sp.: voetb.*) midden-voor *m.*

century ['sentʃuri] eeuw *r.*; (*sp.: cricket*) 100 runs; (*gesch.*) centurie *v.*

cereal ['siəriəl] *adj.* graan—; *sb.* graan *o.*

cerebro-spinal [seribrou'spainəl] — *fever*, nekkramp.

ceremonial [seri'mounjəl] *adj.* ceremonieel, vormelijk; *sb.* ceremonieel *o.*

ceremonious(ly) [seri'mounjəs(li)] *adj.*, (*adv.*) vormelijk, plechtig, plechtstatig.

ceremony ['serimeni] ceremonie, plechtigheid *v.*; vormelijkheid, plichtpleging *v.*

certain ['sə:t(i)n] *adj.* zeker, vast.

certainly ['sə:t(i)nli] *adv.* zeker, stellig, met zekerheid; voorzeker.

certainty ['sə:tinti] zekerheid *r.*

certificate [sə:'tifikit] *sb.* certificaat, getuigschrift *o.*; bewijs, attest *o.*; diploma *o.*, akte *r.*; *rt.* [sə:'tifikeit] een certificaat verlenen; diplomeren.

certify ['sə:tifai] verklaren, verzekeren; getuigen; erkennen; waarmerken.

certitude ['sə:titjûd] zekerheid *v.*

cessation [se'seiʃən] (het) ophouden *o.*, stilstand *m.*

cession ['seʃən] (boedel)afstand *m.*, cessie *v.*

cessionary ['səʃənəri] cessionaris *m.*; rechtverkrijgende *m.*

chafer ['tʃeifə] kever *m.*

chaff [tʃâf] *sb.* kaf, haksel *o.*; prulgoed *o.*, prul *v.*; plagerij *r.*; *rt.* (*r. stro*) hakken; voor de gek houden.

chaffer ['tʃæfə] *vi.* dingen, pingelen, marchanderen, sjacheren; — *away*, verkwanselen; *sb.* gepingel, gesjacher *o.*

chafing-dish ['tʃeifiŋdiʃ] komfoor *o.*

chain [tʃein] *sb.* ketting *m.*, keten *v.*; reeks, rij *v.*; (*bij 't weren*) schering *v.*; —*s*, ketenen, boeien; (*sch.*) rust; *rt.* ketenen, met ketens vastleggen; aan de ketting leggen; met een ketting sluiten; (*fig.*) boeien; — *up*, vastleggen.

chain-bridge ['tʃeinbridʒ] kettingbrug *r.*

chair [tʃêə] *sb.* stoel, zetel *m.*; voorzitterstoel *m.*; voorzitterschap *o.*; katheder, leerstoel *m.*; *rt.* op een stoel ronddragen; in triomf ronddragen; installeren (als voorzitter).

chairman ['tʃêəmən] voorzitter, president *m.*

chaise [ʃeiz] sjees *r.*

chalice ['tʃælis] kelk *m.*; avondmaalbeker *m.*

chalk [tʃo:k] *sb.* krijt *o.*; krijtstreep *v.*; *rt.* met krijt tekenen (schrijven, mengen, enz.); — *up*, aankalken, opschrijven.

chalk-bed ['tʃo:kbed] krijtlaag *r.*

chalk-pit ['tʃo:kpit] krijtgroeve *v.*

challenge ['tʃælin(d)ʒ] *sb.* uitdaging *v.*; tarting *v.*; (*mil.*) (het) aanroepen *o.*; opwekking *v.*, spoorslag *m.*; (*recht*) protest *o.*, wraking, exceptie *r.*; *vt.* uitdagen; tarten; aanroepen; betwisten, opkomen tegen; (*recht*) wraken.

chamber ['tʃeimbə] kamer *r.*; (sluis)kolk *m.*; —*s*, kamers, vertrekken; advocatenkantoor *o.*; raadkamer *v.*

chambermaid ['tʃeimbəmeid] kamenier *r.*, kamermeisje *o.*

chamois ['ʃæmwâ] gems *r.*

champagne [ʃæm'pein] champagne *m.*

champion ['tʃæmpijən] *sb.* kampioen; kampvechter *m.*; *adj.* prima; eerste klas; *rt.* vóórstaan, verdedigen, opkomen voor, strijden voor.

championship [tʃæmpjənʃip] kampioenschap *o.*

chance [tʃâns] *sb.* toeval *o.*; geluk *o.*; kans; gelegenheid *v.*; gebeurlijkheid; mogelijkheid *r.*; vooruitzicht *o.*; *adj.* toevallig; *rt.* wagen; *vi.* gebeuren, voorvallen.

chancel ['tʃânsəl] (*r. kerk*) koor *o.*

chancellery ['tʃânsələri] kanselarij *v.*; kanseliersambt, kanselierschap *o.*

chancery ['tʃânsəri] kanselarij *r.*

chancy ['tʃânsi] *adj.* onzeker, gewaagd.

chandelier [ʃændə'liə] kroonluchter *m.*

change [tʃein(d)ʒ] *sb.* verandering, wijziging *r.*; overgang *m.*; afwisseling; verwisseling *r.*; ruil *m.*; kleingeld, wisselgeld *o.*; verschoning *r.*, schoon goed *o.*; *vt.* wisselen; verwisselen, veranderen (van); ruilen, omruilen; *vi.* veranderen; verschieten; zich verkleden; overstappen; omslaan; — *over*, omschakelen; veranderen; verwisselen.

changeability [tʃein(d)ʒə'biliti] veranderlijkheid *r.*

changeable ['tʃein(d)ʒəbl] veranderlijk.

changeableness ['tʃein(d)ʒəblnis] veranderlijkheid *r.*

changeless ['tʃein(d)ʒlis] onveranderlijk.

channel ['tʃænəl] *sb.* kanaal *o.*; waterloop *m.*; vaargeul *r.*; bedding *r.*, stroombed *o.*; straatgoot *r.*; groef, voor *r.*; (*sch.*) rust *r.*; *vt.* groeven, uithollen, uitgraven.

chant [tʃânt] *sb.* lied; gezang *o.*; dreun *m.*; eentonige melodie *v.*; *vt.* zingen, bezingen; opdreunen; (*r. paarden*) tuisen; *vi.* zingen.

chanter ['tʃântə] zanger, voorzanger *m.*; (*r. doedelzak*) melodiepijp, schalmeipijp *r.*; (*sl.*) sjacheraar in paarden, tuiser *m.*

chap [tʃæp] scheur, spleet *r.*; kloof, barst *r.*

chap [tʃæp] kerel, vent, knaap *m.*

chapel ['tʃæpəl] kapel *v.*

chaplain ['tʃæplin] kapelaan *m.*; (*mil.*) aalmoezenier *m.*; (*prot.*) veldprediker *m.*

chaplet ['tʃæplit] rozenkrans *m.*, rozenhoedje *o.*; halssnoer *o.*

chappie ['tʃæpi] (*fam.*) ventje, kereltje *o.*; (*sl.*) fat *m.*

chappy ['tʃæpi] vol barsten, gebarsten, gekloofd; *zie* **chappie.**

chapter ['tʃæptə] hoofdstuk *o.*; kapittel *o.*

character ['kæriktə] *sb.* karakter *o.*, aard *m.*; kenmerk, kenteken *o.*; hoedanigheid *v.*; letter *v.*, letterteken *o.*

characteristic [kæriktə'tistik] *adj.* karakteristiek, eigenaardig, kenschetsend, kenmerkend; *be — of,* kenmerken, kenschetsen; *sb.* kenmerk *o.*

characterize [kæriktəraiz] karakterizeren, kenmerken, kenschetsen.

charcoal)'tʃâkoul] houtskool *r.*

charcoal-burner ['tʃâkoulbə:nə] kolenbrander *m.*

charge [tʃâdʒ] *sb.* lading *r.*, last *m.*, vracht *r.*; taak *r.*, plicht *m.*, opdracht *v.*; zorg *v.*; prijs *m.*, kosten, onkosten *m.* *mv.*; (*mil.*) aanval *m.*, charge *v.*; (*recht*) beschuldiging, aanklacht *v.*; *vt.* laden, beladen; belasten; bevelen, opdragen; beschuldigen; ten lasteleggen; berekenen, in rekening brengen; (*mil.*) aanvallen; *vi.* chargeren, een charge uitvoeren.

charge-man ['tʃâdʒmən] meesterknecht, ploegbaas *m.*

charge-sheet ['tʃâdʒʃit] politierol *v.*

chariot ['tʃæriət] wagen *m.*, rijtuig *o.*; strijdwagen *m.*

charitable ['tʃæritəbl]*adj.* liefdadig, menslievend, barmhartig, goedgeefs; welwillend, zacht.

charity ['tʃæriti] liefdadigheid, menslievendheid, barmhartigheid *v.*; naastenliefde *r.*; mildheid, zachtheid *v.*; aalmoes *r.*; liefdadigheidsinstelling *v.*

charity-performance ['tʃæritipə'fo:məns] liefdadigheidsvoorstelling *v.*

charlatan ['ʃâlətən] kwakzalver, charlatan *m.*

charm [tʃâm] *sb.* tovermiddel, toverformulier, toverwoord *o.*; amulet *r.*; betovering, bekoring, bekoorlijkheid *v.*; *rt.* betoveren, bekoren, verrukken.

charmer ['tʃâmə] tovenaar *m.*, tovenares *r.*, verlokker *m.*, verlokster, bekoorster *r.*; bekoorlijk wezen *o.*

charming(ly) ['tʃâmiŋ(li)] *adj.* (*adv.*) bekoorlijk; bekorend, innemend, verrukkelijk.

chart [tʃât] *sb.* tabel *v.*; zeekaart; weerkaart *v.*; *rt.* in kaart brengen.

charter ['tʃâtə] *sb.* charter *o.*, oorkonde *r.*; voorrecht, privilege *o.*; octrooi *o.*; grondwet *v.*; *rt.* bevoorrechten; octrooi verlenen aan; bevrachten, huren, charteren.

charter-party ['tʃâtəpâti] chertepartij *v.*

charwoman ['tʃâwumən] schoonmaakster, werkvrouw *v.*

chase [tʃeis] *sb.* jacht *v.*; jachtveld *o.*, jachtgrond *m.*; jachtstoet *m.*; jachtrecht *o.*; (het) gejaagde wild *o.*; vervolging *v.*; *vt.* najagen, jacht maken op; vervolgen, achtervolgen.

chaser ['tʃeisə] jager *m.*; achtervolger *m.*; (*sch.*) jaagstuk *o.*; jachtvliegtuig *o.*

chaste(ly) [tʃeist(li)] *adj.* (*adv.*) kuis, rein, zuiver; eerbaar; betamelijk; gekuist.

chastise [tʃæs'taiz] kastijden, tuchtigen, afstraffen.

chastity ['tʃæstiti] kuisheid, reinheid *v.*; eerbaarheid *v.*

chasuble ['tʃæzjubl] kazuifel *v. & o.*

chat [tʃæt] *vi.* babbelen, keuvelen, snappen; *sb.* gebabbel, gekeuvel, gesnap, gepraat *o.*; (*Dk.*) tapuit *m.*

chattel ['tʃætl] bezitting *v.*, roerend goed *o.*

chatter ['tʃætə] *vi.* klapperen, ratelen; snappen, snateren, kakelen; *sb.* gesnap, gesnater, gekakel *o.*

chatty ['tʃæti] spraakzaam; babbelziek, praatziek; (*v. stijl*) los, vlot.

chauffer ['tʃo:fə] klein fornuis *o.*

chauffeur ['ʃoufə, ʃou'fə:] chauffeur *m.*

cheap [tʃîp] goedkoop; klein, nietig; van weinig waarde, waardeloos.

cheat [tʃît] *vt.* bedriegen, beetnemen, misleiden, verschalken; *vi.* bedriegen; vals spelen; *sb.* bedrog *o.*; afzetterij *v.*; bedrieger, afzetter *m.*

cheating ['tʃîtiŋ] bedriegerij *v.*, bedrog *o.*

check [tʃek] *sb.* belemmering *v.*, oponthoud *o.*, tegenslag *m.*; beteugeling *v.*; beperking *r.*; controleur *m.*; controle *v.*; waarmerk, contramerk *o.*; (*Am.*) rekening, nota *v.*; cheque *r.*; bon *m.*; fiche *r.*; (*tn.*) knip *r.*; schaak *o.*; *rt.* belemmeren; breidelen, intomen, beteugelen; tegenhouden, tot staan brengen; controleren, nagaan; aantekenen; schaak geven.

checkmate ['tʃek'meit] *adj. & sb.* schaakmat; *vt.* schaakmat zetten.

cheek [tʃîk] *sb.* wang, kaak *v.*; (*fam.*) brutaliteit *v.*; *vt.* brutaliseren.

cheek-tooth ['tʃîktûð] maaltand *m.*, kies *v.*

cheeky ['tʃîki] *adj.* onbeschaamd, brutaal.

cheep [tʃîp] *vi.* tjilpen, piepen; *sb.* getjilp, gepiep *o.*

cheer [tʃîə] *sb.* stemming, gemoedsgesteldheid *v.*; vrolijkheid, opgeruimdheid *v.*; opbeuring *v.*, troost *m.*; aanmoediging *v.*; onthaal *o.*, spijs *v.*; bijvalsbetuiging, toejuiching *v.*, gejuich *o.*; *vt.* verheugen, opvrolijken, opmonteren; aanmoedigen, bemoedigen; begroeten, toejuichen; *vi.* juichen, hoera roepen.

cheerful(ly) ['tʃîəful(i)] *adj.* (*adv.*) vrolijk, blijmoedig, opgeruimd.

cheerless(ly) ['tʃîəlis(li)] *adj.* (*adv.*) droevig, somber, troosteloos; moedeloos; (*r. kamer*) ongezellig.

cheery ['tʃîəri] *adj.* vrolijk, blijmoedig, opgeruimd.

cheese [tʃîz] *sb.* kaas *v.*

cheese-monger ['tʃîzmʌŋgə] kaaskoper *m.*

chemise [ʃi'mîz] (vrouwen)hemd *o.*

chemist ['kemist] scheikundige *m.*; apotheker *m.*

chemistry ['kemistri] scheikunde *v.*; (*fig.*) geheimzinnige werking *v.*

cheque [tʃek] cheque v.

cheque-book ['tʃekbuk] chequeboek o.

cherish ['tʃeriʃ] liefhebben, beminnen; liefkozen; (v. hoop, enz.) voeden, koesteren.

cherry ['tʃeri] kers r.; kerseboom m.; kersenlikeur v.

chervil ['tʃə:vil] kervel v.

chess [tʃes] schaakspel o.

chess-board ['tʃesbo:d] schaakbord o.

chest [tʃest] sb. kist v., koffer m.; kas v.; borst(kas) v.; (v. paard) boeg m.; vt. in een kist (koffer) doen; opbergen.

chestnut [s'tʃetnət] sb. kastanje v.; kastanjeboom m.; kastanjebruin paard o.; adj. kastanjebruin, kastanjekleurig.

chew [tʃû] vt. & vi. kauwen, pruimen; overdenken; sb. (het) kauwen o.; (tabaks)pruim v.

chicane [ʃi'kein] sb. chicane, haarkloverij, vitterij v.; vi. chicaneren, vitten.

chicken ['tʃikin] kuiken o.; kip v. (op tafel).

chicken-hearted ['tʃikinhâtid] laf, lafhartig, vreesachtig, kleinmoedig.

chicken-pox ['tʃikinpɔks] waterpokken v. mv.

chicory ['tʃikəri] cichorei, suikerij v.

chide ['tʃaid] vt. beknorren, berispen, bekijven; vi. knorren, kijven; razen, tieren; loeien; blaffen.

chief [tʃîf] adj. voornaamste, opperste, eerste, hoofd—; sb. hoofd o., aanvoerder, leider, hoofdman, bevelhebber m.

chiefly ['tʃîfli] adv. hoofdzakelijk, voornamelijk.

chieftain ['tʃîftin] (opper)hoofd o.; hoofdman m.

chilblain ['tʃilblein] winter m. (aan handen of voeten).

child [tʃaild] kind o.

child-bed ['tʃaildbed] kraambed o.

child-birth ['tʃaildbə:δ] bevalling v.

childhood ['tʃaildhud] kindsheid v.; kinderjaren o. mv.

childish(ly) ['tʃaildiʃ(li)] adj. (adv.) kinderachtig, kinderlijk, kinder—.

childless ['tʃaildlis] kinderloos.

childlike ['tʃaildlaik] kinderlijk, kinder—.

chill [tʃil] adj. koel, kil, koud; huiverig; sb. koelheid, kilte, kilheid, koude v.; koude rilling v.; vt. afkoelen; koud maken; (v. vlees, enz.) laten bevriezen; (v. ijzer) temperen; (v. dranken) laten beslaan, de kou afnemen van.

chilli, chilly ['tʃili] Spaanse peper v.

chimb [tʃaim] (v. vat) kim v.

chime [tʃaim] sb. klokgelui o.; klokkenspel o.; samenklank m., harmonie v.; overeenstemming v.; (v. vat) kim v.; vt. luiden; spelen; samenklinken, harmoniëren; (v. klok) slaan; overeenstemmen.

chimera [kai'miərə] hersenschim v.; schrikbeeld o.

chimney ['tʃimni] schoorsteen m.; schouw v.; lampeglas o.; (nauwe) rotskloof, bergkloof v.

chin [tʃin] kin r.

china-clay ['tʃainəklei] porseleinaarde v.

china-ware ['tʃainəwêə] porselein o.

chincough ['tʃinko:f] kinkhoest m.

chine [tʃain] ruggegraat v.; ruggestuk o.; bergrug m.; kloof v., ravijn o.

chink [tʃiŋk] sb. spleet, reet, kloof v.; gerinkel o.; vi. klinken, rinkelen, rammelen; vt. rammelen met.

chintz [tʃints] sb. sits o.; adj. sitsen.

chip [tʃip] sb. spaan v.; spaander m.; snipper v.; schilfer v.; schijfje o.; reepje o.; vezel v.; (in mes) schaard v.; —s, gebakken aardappelschijfjes; (sl.) geld, duiten; vt. afkappen, afbikken; afsnijden; afbreken; afraspen; vi. afsplinteren.

chippy [tʃipi] spaanachtig; droog, saai, vervelend.

chirp [tʃə:p] vi. tjilpen, kwelen; sb. getjilp o.

chirpy ['tʃə:pi] adj. vrolijk.

chirr [tʃə:] vi. (v. krekel) sjirpen; sb. (het) sjirpen o.

chisel ['tʃizl] sb. beitel m.; vt. beitelen, uitbeitelen; beeldhouwen; (fig.: v. stijl) polijsten; (sl.) bedriegen, beetnemen.

chivalresque [ʃivəl'resk] ridderlijk.

chivalrous ['ʃivəlrəs] zie **chivalresque**

chloride ['klo:raid] chloride v.

chlorosis [klo'rousis] bleekzucht v.

chock [tʃɔk] sb. klos, klamp m.; vt. vastzetten; — up, volstoppen, volproppen.

chock-full ['tʃɔk'ful] propvol, tjokvol.

chocolate [t'ʃɔk(ə)lit] chocolade v.; chocoladekleur v.

chocolate-drop ['tʃɔk(ə)litdrɔp] flikje o.

choice [tʃɔis] sb. keus, verkiezing r.; voorkeur v.; adj. uitgelezen, keurig, prima; kieskeurig.

choir ['kwaiə] sb. koor o.; vi. in koor zingen.

choir-boy ['kwaiəbɔi] koorknaap m.

choke [tʃouk] vt. verstikken, doen stikken; versperren, verstoppen, opstoppen; smoren; vernauwen; volproppen; vi. stikken; zich verslikken; sb. benauwdheid v., verstikkingsgevoel o.; vernauwing v.; (sl.) gevangenisbrood o.

choke-damp ['tʃoukdæmp] (in mijn) stikgas, mijngas o.

choke-full ['tʃoukful] tjokvol.

choke-pear ['tʃoukpêə] prop, mondprop v.; (fig.) bittere pil v.

choose [tʃûz] kiezen, uitkiezen; verkiezen.

chop [tʃɔp] vt. kappen, hakken, kloven; afbijten; ruilen; — up, fijn hakken; vi. hakken; (v. wind) plotseling om, slaan; — about, (v. wind) draaien; van de hak op de tak springen; sb. hakhouw, slag m.; karbonade, kotelet v.; korte golfslag m.

chop-house ['tʃɔphaus] eethuis o.

chopper ['tʃɔpə] hakker m.; bijl r.; hakmes o.; hakmachine r.

chopping-block ['tʃɔpiŋblɔk] hakblok *o.*

choppy ['tʃɔpi] vol barsten, vol spleten; (*v. golfslag*) kort; (*v. wind*) veranderlijk; (*v. markt*) onvast.

choral ['kɔrəl] *sb.* koraal *o.*; *adj.* koraal—, koor— *v.*

chord [kɔ:d] snaar; pees *v.*; koorde *v.*; (*muz.*) akkoord *o.*

chorister ['kɔristə] koorzanger *m.*; koorknaap *m.*

chorus ['kɔ:rəs] *sb.* koor *o.*; refrein *o.*; *vi.* in koor zingen.

chorus-girl ['kɔ:rəsgəl] koriste *v.*

chrism [krizm 'chrisma *o.*, Heilige Olie *v.*

Christian ['kristjən] *sb.* Christen *m.*; Christin *v.*; *adj.* christen, christelijk.

Christmas ['krisməs] Kerstmis *v.*

Christmas-carol ['krisməskærəl] Kerstlied *o.*, Kerstzang *m.*

chromolithography ['kroumouli-'ðəgrəfl] kleurensteendrukkunst *v.*, kleurendruk *m.*, kleurenlithografie *v.*

chronicle ['krɔnikl] *sb.* kroniek *v.*; *vt.* boekstaven, te boek stellen.

chronicler ['krɔniklə] kroniekschrijver *m.*

chronology [krə'nɔlədʒi] tijdrekenkunde *v.*; tijdtafel *v.*

chubby ['tʃəbi] mollig, dikwangig.

chuck [tʃək] *vt.* aaien, strijken; gooien; weggooien; (*fig.*) overboord gooien; de bons geven; *vi.* klokken; *sb.* aai, streek *m.* (onder de kin); geklok *o.*; geklik *o.* (met tong); ruk *m.*

chuckle ['tʃəkl] *vi.* klokken; onderdrukt (inwendig) lachen, gnuiven; *sb.* geklok *o.*; onderdrukte lach *m.*

chum [tʃəm] *sb.* kamergenoot *m.*; maat, kameraad *m.*; *vi.* samen wonen; **— up,** goede maatjes worden.

chummy ['tʃəmi] intiem, gezellig; kameraadschappelijk.

chunk [tʃəŋk] brok, homp *v.*

church ['tʃə:tʃ] kerk *v.*

church-goer ['tʃə:tʃgouə] kerkganger *m.*

churchyard ['tʃə:tʃjâd] kerkhof *o.*

churl [tʃə:l] kinkel, boerenpummel, vlegel *m.*

cicatrice ['sikətris] litteken *o.*

cicatrize ['sikətraiz] helen, dichtgaan.

cider ['saidə] cider, appelwijn *m.*

cigar [si'gâ] sigaar *v.*

cigarette [sigə'ret] sigaret *v.*

cinchona [sin'kounə] kina *v.*; kinaboom *m.*; kinabast *m. & v.*

cinder ['sində] sintel *m.*, as *v.*

cinema ['sinimə] cinema *v.*, bioscoop *m. & v.*

cingulum ['siŋgjuləm] gordel *m.*; (*kath.*) cingel *m.*

cinnamon ['sinəmən] kaneel *v. & o.*

cipher ['saifə] *sb.* cijfer *o.*; nul *v.*; cijferschrift *o.*; monogram, naamcijfer *o.*; sleutel *m.* van cijferschrift; *vt.* in cijferschrift overbrengen; **— out,** berekenen,

becijferen; *vi.* cijferen, rekenen; (*v. orgeltoon*) naklinken.

circle ['sə:kl] *sb.* cirkel, ring, kring *m.*, ronde *v.*; cirkelgang *m.*; diadeem *m.*; *vt.* omringen, omspannen, omsingelen; zwaaien om; *vi.* draaien, ronddraaien; (*v. cavalerie*) zwenken.

circuit ['sə:kit] omloop; kringloop *m.*; omtrek *m.*; rondrit *m.*; (*vl.*) rondvlucht *v.*; (*el.*) stroombaan *v.*, stroomkring *m.*; (*recht*) arrondissement, district *o.*

circuitous [sə:'kjûitəs] *adj.* omslachtig.

circular ['sə:kjulə] *adj.* rond, cirkelvormig; rondgaand; cirkel—, kring—; *sb.* circulaire *v.*, rondschrijven *o.*

circulate ['sə:kjuleit] *vi.* in omloop zijn, circuleren; rondgaan; (*rek.*) repeteren; *vt.* laten circuleren, laten rondgaan; in omloop brengen, verspreiden.

circulation [sə:kju'leiʃən] circulatie *v.*; kringloop *m.*; (bloeds)omloop *m.*; oplaag *v.*; verspreiding *v.*

circumcision [sə:kəm'siʒən] besnijding, besnijdenis *v.*

circumference [sə'kə:mfərəns] omtrek *m.*

circumscribe [sə:kəm'skraib] omschrijven; beperken; begrenzen; (*meetk.*) beschrijven om.

circumspect ['sə:kəmspekt] omzichtig, behoedzaam.

circumstance ['sə:kəmstəns] omstandigheid *v.*; bijzonderheid *v.*; voorval *o.*, gebeurtenis *v.*, feit *o.*; omhaal *m.*; praal, drukte *v.*

circumstantial [sə:kəm'stænʃəl] *adj.* omstandig, uitvoerig; bijkomstig.

circumstantiality [sə:kəmstænʃi'æliti] omstandigheid; uitvoerigheid *v.*; bijzonderheid *v.*

circumvent [sə:kəm'vent] omgeven, omringen; beetnemen, verschalken; misleiden, om de tuin leiden; (*v. wet*) ontduiken.

circus ['sə:kəs] circus, paardenspel *o.*; rond plein *o.*; keteldal *o.*

cistern ['sistən] regenbak, waterbak *m.*

citadel ['sitədl] citadel *v.*

citation [si—, sai'teiʃən] aanhaling *v.*, citaat *o.*; (*recht*) citatie, dagvaarding *v.*; (*Am. mil.*) eervolle vermelding *v.*

cite [sait] aanhalen, citeren; dagvaarden; aanvoeren.

cither(n) ['siðə(n)] citer, luit *v.*

citizen ['sitizən] burger *m.*

citizenship ['sitizənʃip] burgerrecht; burgerschap *o.*

citron ['sitrən] citroen *m.*; citroenboom *m.*; citroenkleur *v.*

city ['siti] stad; grote stad *v.*

civic ['sivik] *adj.* burgerlijk, stedelijk, burger—, stads—; *sb.* **—s,** staatsinrichting *v.*

civil ['sivil] burgerlijk, burger—; beleefd, beschaafd.

civilization [sivilai'zeiʃən] beschaving *v.*

civilize ['sivilaiz] beschaven.

clack [klæk] *vi.* klappen, klapperen; kakelen, ratelen; *vt.* klappen met; *sb.* klap, klapper *m.*; ratel, klappermolen *m.*; *(v. klok)* klik *m.*; gesnap, geklets *o.*

claim [kleim] *sb.* vordering, aanspraak *v.*; eis *m.*; recht *o.* van voorkeur; (mijn)-concessie *v.*; *vt.* eisen, opeisen; vorderen; aanspraak maken op; beweren.

claimant ['kleimənt] eiser *m.*; pretendent *m.*

clairvoyant(e) [klêə'vɔiənt] *adj.* (*sb.*) helderziend(e).

clamber ['klæmbə] klimmen, klauteren.

clamminess ['klæminis] klamheid *v.*; kleverigheid, klefheid *r.*

clammy ['klæmi] *adj.* klam; kleverig, klef.

clamorous(ly) ['klæmərəs(li)] *adj.* (*adv.*) luid, luidruchtig, schreeuwend, tierend.

clamour ['klæmə] *sb.* geroep, geschreeuw *o.*; *vi.* roepen, schreeuwen; *vt.* — **down,** overschreeuwen.

clamp [klæmp] *sb.* klamp *m.*; klem *v.*; kram *v.*; muuranker *o.*; zware voetstap *m.*; hoop *m.*; *vt.* klampen; krammen; stevig vastgrijpen; ophopen; *vi.* zwaar stappen; klossen.

clandestine(ly) [klæn'destin(li)] *adj.* (*adv.*) heimelijk, geheim, verborgen, achterbaks, clandestien.

clang [klæŋ] *sb.* schelle klank *m.*; gekletter; gerinkel; geratel; gerammel; geschetter; geschal *o.*; *vi. & vt.* (doen, laten) kletteren; rinkelen; klinken; schetteren; schallen; galmen; *(v. tram)* bellen.

clank [klæŋk] *zie* **clang.**

clap [klæp] *sb.* slag, klap *m.*; donderslag *m.*; handgeklap *o.*; *vt.* klappen met; dichtklappen, dichtslaan; toejuichen; — **on,** *(v. kleren)* aanschieten; *(v. deksel)* dichtklappen; *vi.* klappen, slaan.

clapnet ['klæpnet] slagnet *o.*

clapper ['klæpə] klepel *m.*; ratel *m.*

claret ['klærət] *sb.* Bordeaux-wijn *m.*; *adj.* wijnkleurig.

clarify ['klærifai] *vt.* klaren, zuiveren; reinigen; verhelderen; louteren; *vi.* klaarworden, zuiver worden.

clarinet [klæri'net] klarinet *v.*

clarity ['klæriti] klaarheid, helderheid, zuiverheid *v.*

clash [klæʃ] *vi.* rammelen, ratelen, rinkelen; botsen, stoten; tegen elkaar ingaan; in strijd zijn (**with,** met); indruisen (**with,** tegen); *(v. kleuren)* vloeken (met); *sb.* gerammel, geratel *o.*, gekletter *o.*; stoot, schok *m.*; bons *m.*; tegenstrijdigheid *v.*; botsing *v.*, conflict *o.*

clasp [klâsp] *sb.* kram *v.*, haak *m.*; klamp *m.*; gesp *v.*; schakel *v.*; *vt.* vasthaken, toehaken, sluiten; grijpen; omvatten, omklemmen.

clasper ['klâspə] *(Pl.)* rank *r.*

clasp-knife ['klâspnaif] knipmes *o.*

class [klâs] *sb.* klas(se) *r.*; stand *m.*; orde *v.*; les *r.*, lesuur *o.*; cursus *m.*; promotie *v.* met lof; *(mil.)* jaarklasse, lichting *v.*; *vt.* indelen, rangschikken, classificeren.

class-hatred ['klâsheitrid] klassenhaat *m.*

classical ['klæsikl] *adj.* klassiek.

classification [klæsifi'keiʃən] classificatie *v.*

classify ['klæsifai] classificeren.

class-room ['klâsrum] klas(se) *r.*, schoollokaal *o.*

clatter ['klætə] *rt. & ri.* (doen) rammelen, klepperen, kletteren; *sb.* gerammel, geklepper, gekletter *o.*

clause [klɔ:z] clausule *v.*; passage, zinsnede *v.*; *(gram)* bijzin *m.*

clavicle ['klævikl] sleutelbeen *o.*

claw [klɔ:] *sb.* klauw *m.*; poot *m.*; *(r. kreeft, enz.)* schaar *v.*; *rt.* krabben, krauwen; grijpen; *vi.* — **off,** *(sch.)* van lager wal afwerken.

clay [klei] *sb.* klei *v.*, leem *o.*; *(fig.)* stof *o.*; *adj.* aarden; lemen; van klei; *vt.* met klei bedekken, met klei mengen.

clay-cold ['kleikould] koud, steenkoud, ijskoud.

clean [klîn] *adj.* schoon; zuiver; rein, zindelijk; knap; handig; *(vl.)* glad, zonder uitsteeksels; volslagen; rein, onschuldig, vlekkeloos; *adv.* schoon; zuiver; rein; totaal, helemaal; *vt.* schoonmaken, reinigen, zuiveren; — **out,** *(fig.)* uitschudden; *sb.* schoonmaak *v.*

cleaning ['klînin] schoonmaak *m.*; (het) schoonmaken *o.*; **—s,** veegsel.

cleaning-rod ['klîninrɔd] *(mil.)* ontlaadstok *m.*

cleanly ['klenli] *adj.* zindelijk; zuiver.

cleanly ['klînli] *adv.* schoon; zuiver, rein.

cleanness ['klînnis] zindelijkheid *v.*; zuiverheid, reinheid *v.*

cleanse ['klenz] reinigen, zuiveren; purgeren.

clear [klîə] *adj.* klaar, zuiver; helder, duidelijk; onschuldig; vrij, onbezwaard; open; vlak; *adv.* klaar; helder, enz.; totaal, volkomen; los; *sb.* licht *o.*; *vt.* klaren, helder maken; duidelijk maken, verduidelijken; *(v. lucht)* zuiveren; *(v. terrein)* vrijmaken; *(v. weg)* banen; *(v. straat, enz.)* ontruimen; *vi.* opklaren; *(H.)* opruiming houden, liquideren; weggaan.

clearance ['klîərəns] verklaring, opheldering, verheldering *v.*; vereffening *v.*; opruiming *v.*; *(H.)* netto opbrengst *r.*

clear-cut ['klîə'kɔt] scherp omlijnd.

clearing ['klîəriŋ] klaring; opheldering *v.*, enz.; gerooide plek *v.* (opengekapt terrein *o.*) in woud ter ontginning; *(H.)* verrekening *v.* van vorderingen.

clearness ['klîənis] klaarheid, helderheid, zuiverheid, duidelijkheid *r.*

cleat [klît] wig *v.*; klamp *m.*; *(sch.)* kikker *m.*

cleave [klîv] kloven, splijten, klieven.
cleaver ['klîvə] hakmes o.; kapmes o.; houthakkersbijl v.
cleft [kleft] kloof, spleet, barst, scheur v.
clement ['klemənt] adj. (v. weer) zacht; goedertieren, genadig.
clergy ['klə:dʒi] geestelijkheid v.; geestelijken m. mv.
clergyman ['klə:dʒimən] geestelijke m.; predikant, dominee m.
clerical ['klerikl] geestelijk; klerikaal; dominees—.
clerk [klâk] klerk, schrijver, kantoorbediende m.; secretaris m.; griffier m.; (Am.) winkelbediende m.
clever(**ly**) ['klevə(li)] adj. (adv.) bekwaam, knap, handig; vlug; (Am.) prettig; beminnelijk.
cleverness ['klevənis] bekwaamheid, knapheid, handigheid v.
clew [klû] kluwen o., knot m.; (sch.) schoothoorn m.
cliché ['klîʃei] cliché o.; (fig.) gemeenplaats v.
click [klîk] vi. tikken; knappen; (v. paard) aanslaan; (v. biljartballen) klotsen; vt. pakken, gappen; sb. getik; geklik o.; (v. deur) klink v.; (v. rad) pal m.; (el.) aanslag m.
click-beetle ['klikbitl] kniptor m.
clicket ['klikit] klink v.
client ['klaiənt] cliënt m.; klant, afnemer m.
clientele ['klaiəntil] cliëntele v.
cliff [klif] steile rots v., rotswand m.
cliffsman ['klifsmən] rotsbeklimmer m.
climate ['klaimit] klimaat o.; luchtstreek v.
climax ['klaimæks] climax m., opklimming v.
climb [klaim] vt. beklimmen, klimmen op (in); vi. klimmen, klauteren, stijgen; — down (fig.) inbinden, bakzeil halen, een toontje lager zingen.
climbable ['klaiməbl] beklimbaar.
climber ['klaimə] klimmer m.; klimvogel m.; klimplant v.
climbist ['klaimist] bergbeklimmer m.
clinch [klinʃ] vt. ombuigen, omklinken; klinken, vastklinken; (sp.: boksen) vastgrijpen; (v. vuisten) ballen; sb. kram v.; klinknagel m.; greep m. & v.
cling [klin] kleven; zich vastklemmen (to, aan); aankleven, aanhangen; nauw sluiten.
clinic ['klinik] klinisch onderwijs o.; kliniek v.
clink [klink] (doen) klinken.
clinker ['klinkə] klinker(steen) m.; hamerslag m.; metaalschuim o., slak v.; verharde lava v.
clip [klip] vt. (v. haar, enz.) knippen, afknippen; (v. schaap) scheren; snoeien, besnoeien; (v. woorden) afbijten; (v. letters) niet uitspreken; — off, (v. el. licht) uitdraaien; sb. (v. wol) scheersel o.; knipsel o.; knijper m., haak m.; (mil.) patroonhouder m.

clipper ['klipə] snoeier, besnoeier m.; geldsnoeier m.; schapenscheerder m.; —s, wolschaar v.
clipping ['klipin] scheerwol v., scheersel o.; snoeisel o.; knipsel, uitknipsel o.
cloak [klouk] sb. mantel m.; dekmantel m.; vt. met een mantel bedekken; bemantelen.
cloak-room ['kloukrum] kleedkamer, garderobe o.
clock [klɔk] klok v., uurwerk o.
clock-face ['klɔkfeis] wijzerplaat v.
clock-hand ['klɔkhænd] wijzer m.
clod [klɔd] sb. kluit, aardkluit m.; klonter m.; vi. kluiten, klonteren; met kluiten gooien.
clog [klɔg] sb. blok o.; holsblok o., klompschoen m.; (fig.) rem, belemmering v., blok o. aan 't been; vt. belemmeren, tegenhouden; overladen; verstoppen.
cloister ['klɔistə] klooster o.
close [klous] adj. dicht, gesloten; ingesloten; (v. jachttijd, enz.) besloten; achterhoudend, geheimhoudend; benauwd, drukkend; adv. dichtbij, vlak bij; bij elkaar; sb. omheining, ingesloten ruimte v.; speelplaats v., speelterrein o.
close [klouz] vt. sluiten; afsluiten; insluiten; besluiten, eindigen; vi. zich sluiten, dichtgaan; zich verenigen, zich aaneensluiten; (mil.) de gelederen sluiten; sb. einde, slot, besluit o.; handgemeen o.
close-fisted ['klous'fistid] gierig, vrekkig.
close-handed ['klous'hændid] zie close-fisted.
close-stool ['klousstûl] stilletje o.
closet ['klɔzit] sb. kamertje, kabinet o.; privé vertrek o., studeerkamer v.; (Am.) muurkast v.; W. C.; vt. opsluiten.
closet-bed ['klɔzitbed] slaapstee v.
close-tongued [kloustənd] gesloten.
closing ['klouzin] besluit, einde o.
closing-time ['klouzintaim] sluitingstijd m.
clot [klɔt] sb. kluit, klonter m.; vi. klonteren, stollen.
cloth [klɔð] laken o., stof v.; tafellaken o.; doek, lap m.; dweil m.; the —, de geestelijkheid, de geestelijke stand.
clothe [klouθ] kleden, aankleden; bekleden; (v. gedachten) inkleden.
clothes [klouðz] kleren o. mv., kleding v.; beddegoed o.; was v.
clothes-horse ['klouθʒho:s] droogrek o.
cloud [klaud] sb. wolk v.; vt. bewolken; overschaduwen; verduisteren; bezoedelen; benevelen; vi. betrekken; (v. hout) vlammen; (v. drukinkt) vegen.
cloudless ['klaudlis] onbewolkt.
cloudy ['klaudi] bewolkt; nevelig; betrokken; troebel; somber, duister; vaag; onduidelijk.
clough [klɔf] kloof v., ravijn o.
clove [klouv] (Pl.) bijbol m.; kruidnagel m.; anjelier v.

clover ['klouvə] klaver v.
clown [klaun] clown, hansworst m.;
(boeren)kinkel, lomperd m.
clownish(ly) ['klauniʃ(li)] adj. (adv.)
clownachtig; boers, lomp.
club [kləb] knuppel, knots m.; golfstok
m.; vereniging, club, sociëteit v.; fonds,
ziekenfonds o., bus v.; —s, (kaartsp.)
klaveren.
clubfoot ['kləb'fut] horrelvoet m.
club-house ['kləb'haus] clubgebouw o.,
sociëteit v.
cluck [klək] (v. kip) klokken, tokken.
clucker ['kləkə] klokhen, kloek v.
clump [kləmp] klomp m.; blok o., brok
v.; (v. bomen, enz.) groep v.
clumsy ['kləmzi] adj. lomp, plomp, onhandig.
cluster ['kləstə] sb. tros, bos m.; troep
m.; zwerm m.; vi. in trossen groeien;
zich verzamelen, zich groeperen; zich
scharen.
clutch [klətʃ] greep; klauw m.; (tn.)
koppeling v.; (Dk.) broedsel o.
clutter ['klətə] warboel, rommel m.;
lawaai o., herrie v.; gestommel o.; vi.
te hoop lopen; lawaai maken, herrie
maken; stommelen; klossen; vt. belemmeren; — (up), dooreengooien.
clyster ['klistə] sb. lavement o.; vt.
een lavement zetten.
coach [koutʃ] rijtuig o., koets v.; spoorwagen m.; (sch.) kapiteinshut v.; (sp.)
trainer m.
coach-box ['koutʃbɔks] bok m.
coach-builder ['koutʃbildə] rijtuigma-
ker, wagenmaker m.
coachman ['koutʃmən] koetsier m.
coact [kou'ækt] samenwerken.
coagulate [kou'ægjuleit] vi. (vt.) (doen)
stremmen, (doen) stollen.
coal [koul] sb. (steen)kool v., kolen v.
mv.; vt. van kolen voorzien; vi. kolen
innemen.
coal-bed ['koulbed] kolenlaag v.
coal-box ['koulbɔks] kolenbak m.;
(mil., sl.) brisantgranaat v.
coalition [kouə'liʃən] verbond, bondgenootschap o., coalitie v.
coarse [kɔ:s] adj. grof, ruw, lomp.
coast [koust] sb. kust v.; glijbaan v.;
vi. langs de kust varen; van een helling
affietsen, vrijwielen.
coaster ['koustə] kustvaarder m., kust-
boot v.; kustbewoner m.; flessenstan-
der m.
coaster-brake ['koustəbreik] terugtraprem v.
coat [kout] sb. jas v.; (dames)mantel m.;
bedekking; bekleding v.; vel o., huid,
vacht v., pels m.; vlies, oogvlies o.; vt.
bedekken; bekleden; verven, vernissen;
(v. pijp) doorroken.
coax [kouks] vt. vleien, strelen; —
away, meetronen, wegtronen; vi. flemen.
coaxer ['kouksə] vleier, flemer, flikflooier m.

cobble-stone ['kɔblstoun] (straat)
kei m.
cobweb ['kɔbweb] sb. spinneweb; spin-
rag o.; adj. ragfijn; broos, teer, zwak;
hersenschimmig.
cock [kɔk] sb. haan m.; mannetje o.;
weerhaan, windwijzer m.; aanvoerder,
leider m.; kraan, primus m.; vt. opto-
men, schuin zetten; opzetten, opsteken;
(v. oren) spitsen; (v. neus) optrekken;
de haan spannen van; vi. overeind
staan.
cockade [kɔ'keid] kokarde v.
cockchafer ['kɔktʃeifə] meikever m.
cockroach ['kɔkroutʃ] kakkerlak m.
cocksure ['kɔk'ʃuə] positief, zeker, volkomen zeker; zelfbewust, verwaand.
cocky ['kɔki] verwaand, eigenwijs.
coco(a) ['koukou] kokospalm, kokos-
boom m.; kokosnoot v.
coco(a)-nut ['koukənət] kokosnoot;
klappernoot v.
cod [kɔd] kabeljauw m.
cod [kɔd] vt. foppen; sb. fopperij,
verlakkerij v.
coddle ['kɔdl] vi. zacht koken; zich
vertroetelen; vt. vertroetelen, verwennen; sb. troetelkind(je) o.
code [koud] sb. wetboek o.; (telegram)code m., seinboek o.; reglement
o.; gedragslijn v.; vt. in codeschrift
overbrengen.
cod-liver oil ['kɔdlivə'rɔil] levertraan v.
coerce [kou'ə:s] dwingen, afdwingen.
coeval [kou'ivəl] adj. even oud; gelijktijdig, van gelijke duur; tijdgenoot van;
sb. tijdgenoot m.
coexist [kouig'zist] gelijktijdig bestaan.
coffee ['kɔfi] koffie v.
coffer ['kɔfə] sb. kist, geldkist v.,
koffer m.; —s, schatkist; vt. in een
koffer sluiten.
coffer-dam ['kɔfədæm] kistdam m.,
kisting v.
coffin ['kɔfin] sb. doodkist v.; peperhuisje, papieren zakje o.; (v. paardehoef) hoornschoen m.; vt. kisten; opsluiten.
cog [kɔg] sb. (v. rad) kam, tand m.;
kamrad o.; vt. vertanden.
cogent(ly) ['koudʒənt(li)] adj. (adv.)
krachtig, overtuigend; klemmend, dringend.
cogitate ['kɔdʒiteit] vi. denken; vt.
overdenken, overpeinzen; uitdenken,
verzinnen; beramen; zich een denkbeeld
vormen van.
cognac ['kɔnjæk, kounjæk] cognac m.
cognate ['kɔgneit] adj. verwant (to)
with, aan); sb. bloedverwant m.; (gram.)
verwant woord o.
cognizable ['kɔ(g)nizəbl] kenbaar,
waarneembaar; gerechtelijk vervolgbaar.
cognomen [kɔg'noumen] familienaam
m.; bijnaam m.; benaming v.
cohabit [kou'hæbit] samenwonen.

cohabitation [kouhæbi'teiʃən] samenwoning *v.*
coheir ['kou'êə] mede-erfgenaam *m.*
coherence [kou'hiərəns] samenhang *m.*
coherent [kou'hiərənt] samenhangend.
cohesion [kou'hiʒən] cohesie *v.*; samenhang *m.*
coif [kɔif] kap *v.*, mutsje *o.*
coil [kɔil] *sb.* bocht; kronkeling *v.*, kronkel *m.*; gerolde vlecht, tres *v.*; spiraal *v.*; (*v. plant*) rank *v.*; (*el.*) spoel *v.*; inductieklos *m.*; tros *m.* (kabel); *vt.* & *vi.* kronkelen, zich ineenkronkelen; oprollen; (in een bocht) opschieten.
coin [kɔin] *sb.* geldstuk *o.*, munt *v.*; muntstempel *m.*; (*v. geld*) munten, aanmunten, slaan; verzinnen.
coincide [kouin'said] samenvallen, tegelijk gebeuren; overeenstemmen; het eens zijn (*in*, met).
coke [kouk] cokes *v. mv.*
cokery ['koukri] cokesfabriek *v.*
cold [kould] *adj.* koud; koel, onhartelijk; *sb.* koude *v.*; verkoudheid *v.*
cold-livered ['kould'livəd] onaandoenlijk.
coldly ['kouldli] *adv.* koud; koel.
coldness ['kouldnis] koude *v.*; koudheid *v.*; koelheid *v.*; onverschilligheid *v.*
cole-seed ['koulsid] koolzaad *o.*
colibri ['kɔlibri] kolibrie *m.*
colic ['kɔlik] koliek, buikpijn *v.*
collaboration [kəlæbə'reiʃən] medewerking, samenwerking *v.*
collapse [kə'læps] *vi.* instorten, ineenvallen; ineenzakken, in elkaar zakken; mislukken; *sb.* instorting, invalling *v.*; ineenzinking *v.*; verval *o.* van krachten; mislukking *v.*, flasco *o.*
collar ['kɔlə] kraag *m.*; boord *m.*, boordje *o.*, halsband *m.*; ordeketen, halsketen *v.*
collar-bone ['kɔləboun] sleutelbeen *o.*
collate [kɔ'leit] collationneren, vergelijken; een kerkelijk ambt verlenen.
colleague ['kɔlig] collega, ambtgenoot *m.*
collect ['kɔlekt] *sb.* (*kath.*) collecte (*gebed*).
collect [kə'lekt] *vt.* verzamelen; ophalen; collecteren; innen, incasseren; afleiden, besluiten; *vi.* zich verzamelen.
collecting-box [kə'lektiŋbɔks] collectebus *v.*; botaniseertrommel *m.*
collection [kə'lekʃən] verzameling, collectie *v.*; collecte, inzameling *v.*; incassering *v.*; buslichting *v.*; zelfbeheersing *v.*
college ['kɔlidʒ] college *o.*; faculteit *v.*; (*sl.*) gevangenis *v.*
colligate ['kɔligeit] verbinden.
collision [kə'liʒən] botsing; aanvaring *v.*
collude [kə'l(j)ûd] het eens zijn, samenspannen.
Cologne [kə'loun] Keulen *o.*
colon ['koulən] dikke darm *m.*; dubbele punt *v.*

colonel ['kə:nəl] kolonel *m.*
colonial [kə'lounjəl] *adj.* koloniaal; *sb.* bewoner *m.* van.
colony ['kɔləni] kolonie *v.*
colorant ['kɔlərənt] kleurmiddel *o.*
colossal(ly) [kə'lɔsl(i)] *adj.* (*adv.*) kolossaal, reusachtig.
colossus [kə'lɔsəs] kolos *m.*, gevaarte *o.*
colour ['kɔlə] *sb.* verf *v.*; kleur, tint *v.*; drukinkt *m.*; —*s*, vlag *v.*, vaandel *o.*, standaard *m.*; onderscheidingskleuren *v. mv.*; gekleurde stoffen *v. mv.*; *vt.* verven; kleuren; (*v. pijp*) doorroken; *vi.* een kleur krijgen, blozen.
coloured ['kɔləd] gekleurd; geverfd; bemanteld, bewimpeld; voorgewend.
colporteur [kɔlpo:tə] colporteur *m.*
colt [koult] veulen *o.*; jonge hengst *m.*; wildzang, robbedoes *m.*; beginneling *m.*
column ['kɔləm] zuil *v.*, pilaar *m.*, kolom *v.*; (*mil.*) kolonne *v.*
comb [koum] *sb.* kam *m.*; honigraat *v.*; *vt.* kammen; roskammen; (*v. wol*) kaarden; (*v. vlas, enz.*) hekelen; doorzoeken; *vi.* (*v. golven*) omkrullen.
combat ['kɔm—, kəmbət] *sb.* gevecht *o.*, strijd *m.*; *vt.* bevechten, bestrijden; *vi.* vechten, strijden.
combatant ['kɔm—, kəmbətənt] *adj.* strijdend, strijdbaar; *sb.* strijder *m.*
combativeness ['kɔm—, 'kəmbətivnis] strijdlust *m.*, strijdlustigheid *v.*, vechtlust *m.*
combination [kɔmbi'neiʃən] combinatie *v.*; vereniging, verbinding *v.*; samenloop *m.*; (*sp.*) samenspel *o.*; samenspanning *v.*, komplot *o.*
combine [kəm'bain] combineren, verenigen, samenvoegen.
combustible [kəm'bɔstibl] *adj.* (ver)-brandbaar, ontvlambaar; *sb.* brandstof *v.*
combustion [kəm'bɔstʃən] verbranding *v.*
come [kəm] komen, naderen; aankomen; opkomen; neerkomen; uitkomen; meegaan; verschijnen; ontkiemen; worden; voortkomen (*of, from,* uit).
come-at-able [kəm'ætəbl] te bereiken, bereikbaar, toegankelijk; te krijgen, verkrijgbaar.
comedian [kə'midiən] toneelspeler *m.*; blijspelschrijver, blijspeldichter *m.*; komiek *m.*; (*fig.*) komediant *m.*
comedy ['kɔmidi] blijspel *o.*
comely ['kɔmli] bevallig, knap; gepast, welvoeglijk.
comet ['kɔmit] staartster, komeet *v.*
comfit ['kɔmfit] *sb.* suikerboon *v.*; bonbon *o.*; —*s*, suikergoed *o.*; *vt.* confijten.
comfort ['kəmfət] *sb.* troost *m.*, vertroosting *v.*; bemoediging, opbeuring *v.*, steun *m.*; welgesteldheid *v.*, welstand *m.*; geriefelijkheid *v.*, gemak, comfort *o.*; *vt.* troosten, vertroosten; opbeuren, bemoedigen; steunen.
comfortable ['kəmfətəbl] *adj.* aange-

naam, behaaglijk; gemakkelijk; geriefelijk; genoeglijk.

comic(al) ['kɔmik(l)] *adj.* komisch, grappig, kluchtig, humoristisch.

coming ['kəmiŋ] *adj.* komend, toekomstig, aanstaande; *sb.* komst, aankomst *v.*

comity ['kɔmiti] (burgerlijke) beleefdheid, hoffelijkheid *v.*

comma ['kɔmə] komma *v.*

command [kə'mând] *vt.* bevelen, gebieden; (*mil.*) aanvoeren, commanderen; (*mil.*) bestrijken; (*fig.*) beheersen; (*v. eerbied*) afdwingen; (*v. prijs*) opbrengen, halen; *vi.* het bevel voeren (over), het commando voeren (over); *sb.* bevel *o.*; gebod *o.*; order, opdracht *v.*, last *m.*; (*mil.*) commando *o.*

commandant [kɔmən'dænt] (*mil.*) commandant *m.*

commander [kə'mândə] bevelhebber; commandant *m.*; (*sch.*) gezagvoerder.

commanding [kə'mândiŋ] bevelend; bevelvoerend; (de omtrek) bestrijkend; indrukwekkend.

commandment [kə'mândmənt] bevel, gebod *o.*

commemorate [kə'meməreit] gedenken, herdenken, vieren.

commemoration [kəmemə'reiʃən] herinnering, herdenking *v.*

commencement [kə'mensmənt] begin *c.*, aanvang *m.*; promotie *v.*

commend [kə'mend] prijzen, loven; aanprijzen, aanbevelen; opdragen, toevertrouwen.

commendable [kə'mendəbl] *adj.* prijzenswaardig, lofwaardig, aanbevelenswaardig.

commendation [kɔmən'deiʃən] aanbeveling *v.*, lof *m.*

commensurate [kə'menʃərit] evenredig (*to, with,* aan); gelijkmatig; samenvallend.

comment [kɔmənt] *sb.* uitleg *m.*, commentaar *o.*; kritiek *v.*; (verklarende) aantekening *v.*; *vt.* commenteren; *vi.* (verklarende) aantekeningen maken, aanmerkingen maken.

commentary ['kɔməntəri] uitlegging *v.*, commentaar *o.*; aanmerking; opmerking *v.*

commerce ['kɔmə:s] handel *m.*; verkeer *o.*; omgang *m.*; (*kaartsp.*) kleuren *v. mv.*

commercial [kə'mə:ʃəl] *adj.* commercieel, handels—; *sb.* (*fam.*) handelsreiziger *m.*

comminute ['kɔminjût] verbrijzelen, vergruizen.

commiserate [kə'mizəreit] beklagen, medelijden hebben met.

commiseration [kəmizə'reiʃən] medelijden *o.*, deernis, deelneming *v.*

commissary ['kɔmisəri] commissaris, gemachtigde *m.*

commission [kə'miʃən] *sb.* opdracht, commissie *v.*; last, lastbrief *m.*; (offi-

ciers)aanstelling *v.*; provisie *v.*; (*v. misdaad*) (het) begaan, (het) bedrijven *o.*; *vt.* machtigen, volmacht geven; belasten, opdragen; bestellen een bestelling doen; aanstellen; (*v. schip*) in dienst stellen.

commissioner [kə'miʃənə] gevolmachtigde; gecommitteerde; commissaris; hoofdcommissaris van politie *m.*

commit [kə'mit] *vt.* begaan, plegen, bedrijven; vertrouwen, toevertrouwen; prijsgeven; verwijzen (naar een commissie); compromitteren; *vr.* — *oneself,* zich toevertrouwen aan; zich verbinden tot; zich blootgeven.

committee [kə'miti] commissie *v.*, comité *o.*; bestuur *o.*

commode [kə'moud] latafel *v.*; stilletje *o.*

commodious [kə'moudiəs] ruim; geriefelijk.

commodity [kə'mɔditi] gerief *o.*, geriefelijkheid *v.*, gemak *o.*; koopwaar *v.*, handelsartikel *o.*

common ['kɔmən] *adj.* gemeen, gemeenschappelijk; gemeenslachtig; gewoon, algemeen, alledaags; *sb.* (het) gewone *v.*; gemeenteweide *v.*

commonalty ['kɔmənəlti] gemeenschap, samenleving *v.*; burgerij *v.*, burgerstand *m.*

commonplace ['kɔmənpleis] *sb.* gemeenplaats *v.*, (afgezaagde) aanhaling *v.*, gezegde *o.*; *adj.* gewoon, alledaags, banaal, afgezaagd.

commons ['kɔmənz] burgerij *v.*, burgerstand *m.*; volk *o.*; gemeenschappelijke maaltijd *m.*; rantsoen *o.*, portie *v.*

commonwealth ['kɔmənwelθ] gemenebest *o.*; republiek *v.*

commotion [kə'mouʃən] beweging, beroering, opschudding *v.*

communal ['kɔmjunəl] gemeente—; gemeenschappelijk, gemeenschaps—.

commune ['kɔmjûn] *sb.* gemeente *v.*; omgang *m.*, gemeenschap *v.*; onderhoud *o.*; *vi.* gemeenschap hebben (*with,* met); spreken, zich onderhouden (*with,* met); overleggen; (*kath.*) communiceren.

communicate [kə'mjûnikeit] *vt.* mededelen; overbrengen; delen (*with,* met); *vi.* gemeenschap hebben, in verbinding staan (*with,* met); zich in verbinding stellen (*with,* met); (*kath.*) communiceren.

communication [kəmjûni'keiʃən] mededeling *v.*; gemeenschap *v.*; aansluiting, verbinding *v.*; verbindingsweg *m.*

communicative [kə'mjûnikeitiv] mededeelzaam; aanstekelijk.

communion [kə'mjûnjən] gemeenschap *v.*; verbinding *v.*; omgang *m.*; overeenstemming *v.*; (*kath.*) communie *v.*

communion-rails [kə'mjûnjənreilz] communiebank *v.*

communism ['kɔmjunizm] communisme *o.*

community [kə'mjûniti] gemeenschap *v.*; gemeente *v.*; maatschappij *v.*
commutable [kə'mjûtəbl] verwisselbaar, vervangbaar.
commutation [kɔmju'teiʃən] verwisseling, verandering; *v.* omzetting *v.*; (*v. straf*) verzachting *v.*; Stroomwisseling *v.*; afkoping *v.*
commute [kə'mjût] verwisselen (*for,* voor); veranderen (*into,* in); omzetten; verzachten; afkopen.
compact [kəm'pækt] dicht, compact; vast, aaneengesloten; (*v. stijl*) bondig; (*v. persoon*) gedrongen.
companion [kəm'pænjən] *sb.* gezel, metgezel, kameraad, makker *m.*; lotgenoot; deelgenoot *m.*; gezellin, gezelschapsjuffrouw *v.*; *vt.* vergezellen; gezelschap houden; *vi.* — **with,** omgaan met.
companionable [kəm'pænjənəbl] *adj.* gezellig; kameraadschappelijk.
company ['kəmpəni] gezelschap *o.*; genootschap, gilde *o.*; maatschappij, vennootschap *v.*
comparable ['kɔmpərəlb] vergelijkbaar, te vergelijken.
comparative [kəm'pærətiv] *adj.* vergelijkend; betrekkelijk; *sb.* vergrotende trap *m.*
comparatively [kəm'pærətivli] *adv.* vergelijkenderwijs; in vergelijking; betrekkelijk.
compare [kəm'pêə] *vt.* vergelijken; de trappen van vergelijking vormen van; *vi.* vergeleken kunnen worden; *sb.* vergelijking *v.*
comparison [kəm'pærisən] vergelijking *v.*
compartment [kəm'pâtmənt] afdeling *v.*, vak *o.*; (*sch.*) waterdichte afdeling *v.*, (waterdicht) schot *o.*
compass ['kəmpəs] omtrek *m.*; omvang *m.*, ruimte *v.*; gebied *o.*; grens *v.*; bereik *o.*; omweg *m.*; bestek *o.*; (*sch.*) kompas *o.*
compass-card ['kəmpəskâd] kompasroos *v.*
compasses ['kəmpəsiz] passer *m.*; *a pair of* —, een passer.
compassion [kəm'pæʃən] medelijden, mededogen, erbarmen *o.*
compassionate [kəm'pæʃənit] *adj.* medelijdend, meedogend.
compass-saw ['kəmpesso:] cirkelzaag *v.*
compatible [kəm'pætibl] bestaanbaar (*with,* met); verenigbaar.
compeer [kəm'pîə] gelijke, evenknie *m.*; makker *m.*
compel [kəm'pel] dwingen, noodzaken, verplichten; afdwingen.
compendious(ly) [kəm'pendiəs(li)] *adj.* (*adv.*) beknopt, kort.
compensate ['kɔmpenseit] opwegen (*for,* tegen); goedmaken, vergoeden; schadeloosstellen.
compensation [kɔmpən'seiʃən] ver-

goeding *v.*; schadeloosstelling *v.*; compensatie *v.*
compete [kəm'pît] wedijveren, concurreren.
competence ['kɔmpitəns] **competency** [kɔmpitənsi] bevoegdheid, bekwaamheid *v.*; welgesteldheid *v.*
competent ['kɔmpitənt] bevoegd, bekwaam, competent; toereikend; toelaatbaar, geoorloofd.
competition [kɔmpi'tiʃən] wedijver *m.*, concurrentie, mededinging *v.*; wedstrijd *m.*, competitie *v.*
competitor [kəm'petitə] concurrent *m.*; mededinger, deelnemer *m.*
compilation [kɔmpi'leiʃən] compilatie, verzameling *v.*
compile [kəm'pail] compileren, verzamelen, samenstellen.
compiler [kəm'pailə] compilator *m.*
complacence, complacency [kəm'pleisəns, —si] welgevallen *o.*; voldoening, zelfvoldoening *v.*
complain [kəm'plein] *vi.* klagen, zich beklagen (*of,* over; *to,* bij); *sb.* (*dicht.*) klacht *v.*
complainer [kəm'pleinə] klager *m.*
complaint [kəm'pleint] klacht, aanklacht *v.*; kwaal *v.*
complaisant(ly) [kəm'pleizənt(li)] *adj.* (*adv.*) voorkomend, minzaam; gedienstig, inschikkelijk.
complement ['kɔmplimənt] *sb.* aanvulling *v.*; aanvulsel, bijvoegsel *o.*; vol getal *o.*, getalsterkte *v.*; taks *m.*, vastgestelde hoeveelheid *v.*; complement *o.*; *vt.* aanvullen, voltallig maken.
complete [kəm'plît] compleet, volledig, voltallig; voltooid; volmaakt, volslagen.
completely [kəm'plîtli] *adv.* compleet, totaal, helemaal, volkomen, volslagen.
completion [kəm'plîʃən] voltooiing, voleindiging, volvoering *v.*; aanvulling *v.*
complex ['kɔmpleks] *sb.* complex, samenstel, geheel *o.*; *adj.* samengesteld, ingewikkeld.
complexion [kəm'plekʃən] gelaatskleur, teint *v.*; aanzien, voorkomen *o.*; aard *m.*
compliance [kəm'plaiəns] inwilliging *v.* (*with,* van); toestemming *v.*; nakoming *v.*
compliant(ly) [kəm'plaiənt(li)] *adj.* (*adv.*) meegaand, inschikkelijk.
complicacy ['kɔmplikəsi] ingewikkeldheid *v.*
complicate ['kɔmplikit] *adj.* ingewikkeld, gecompliceerd.
complicate ['kɔmplikeit] *vt.* ingewikkeld maken, verwikkelen.
complication [kɔmpli'keiʃən] ingewikkeldheid, verwikkeling *v.*
complicity [kəm'plisiti] medeplichtigheid *v.* (*in,* aan).
compliment ['kɔmplimənt] *sb.* compliment *o.*, plichtpleging *v.*; *vi.* [kɔm

pli'ment] plichtplegingen maken; *vt.* gelukwensen (*on,* met), complimenteren, een compliment maken; vereren (*with,* met).

comply [kəm'plai] toegeven, zich onderwerpen; berusten in, zich schikken (*with,* in).

component [kəm'pounənt] *adj.* samenstellend; *sb.* bestanddeel *o.*

comport [kəm'po:t] *vi.* overeenstemmen (*with,* met), passen (*with,* bij), zich voegen (*with,* naar); *vr.* — *oneself,* zich gedragen, optreden.

compose [kəm'pouz] *vt.* samenstellen, vormen; (*v. brief, enz.*) opstellen; regelen, schikken, in orde brengen; *vi.* (*drukk.*) zetten; (*muz.*) componeren; *vr.* — *oneself,* kalm worden, bedaren.

composed [kəm'pouzd] *adj.* kalm, bedaard, rustig.

composer [kəm'pouzə] samensteller *m.*; opsteller *m.*; (*muz.*) componist *m.*; (*drukk.*) zethaak *m.*

composing-machine [kəm'pouziŋməʃin] (*drukk.*) zetmachine *v.*

composing-stick [kəm'pouziŋstik] (*drukk.*) zethaak *m.*

composition [kɔmpə'ziʃən] samenstelling *v.*; mengsel *o.*, compositie, verbinding *v.*; (*mil.*) sas *v.*; opstel *o.*; stijloefening *v.*; (het) letterzetten *o.*

composure [kəm'pouzə] bedaardheid, bezadigdheid, kalmte *v.*

compote ['kɔmpout] compote *v.*

compound ['kɔmpaund] *adj.* (*rek.*) samengesteld; (*gen.: v. breuk*) gecompliceerd; *sb.* samenstelling *v.*; mengsel *o.*; mengdrankje *o.*

comprehend [kɔmpri'hend] begrijpen, verstaan; bevatten, omvatten, insluiten.

comprehensible [kɔmpri'hensəbl] *adj.* begrijpelijk, te begrijpen; bevattelijk.

comprehension [kɔmpri'henʃən] bevatting *v.*, bevattingsvermogen *o.*; verstand *o.*; begrip *o.*; omvang *m.*

comprehensive [kɔmpri'hensiv] *adj.* veelomvattend, uitgebreid, omvangrijk, ruim, groot.

compress ['kɔmpres] *sb.* compres *o.*

compress [kəm'pres] *vt.* samendrukken, samenpersen; verdichten, comprimeren.

compression [kəm'preʃən] samendrukking.

comprise [kəm'praiz] bevatten, omvatten; insluiten.

compromise ['kɔmprəmaiz] *sb.* vergelijk *o.*, overeenkomst, schikking *v.*, compromis *o.*; geschipper *o.*; *vt.* schikken, bijleggen; compromitteren, in opspraak brengen.

compulsion [kəm'pəlʃən] dwang *m.*

compulsory [kəm'pəlsəri] gedwongen, verplicht, dwingend, dwang—.

compunction [kəm'pəŋkʃən] berouw *o.*, spijt *v.*; wroeging, gewetensknaging *v.*

compunctious [kəm'pəŋkʃəs] berouwvol.

computable [kəm'pjûtəbl] berekenbaar.

compute [kəm'pjût[berekenen, ramen, schatten.

comrade ['kɔmrid] kameraad, makker *m.*

comradely ['kɔmridli] kameraadschappelijk.

concatenate [kɔn'kætineit] aaneenschakelen.

concatenation [kɔnkæti'neiʃən] aaneenschakeling *v.*

concave [kɔnkeiv] concaaf, hol.

concavity [kɔn'kæviti] holheid, holte *v.*

conceal [kən'sîl] verbergen; helen, verhelen; verstoppen; geheim houden, verzwijgen.

concealable [kən'sîləbl] verbergbaar.

concede [kən'sîd] toegeven; inwilligen, toestaan.

conceit [kən'sît] verbeelding *v.*; (eigen)dunk, waan *m.*, verwaandheid *v.*; gemaaktheid *v.*

conceited(ly) [kən'sîtid(li)] *adj.* (*adv.*) verwaand, eigenwijs, waanwijs.

conceitedness [kən'sîtidnis] verwaandheid *v.*, eigenwaan *m.*, waanwijsheid *v.*

conceivable [kən'sîvəbl] *adj.* denkbaar, begrijpelijk.

conceive [kən'sîv] *vt.* begrijpen, bevatten; zich voorstellen, denken, een denkbeeld vormen van; (*v. plan*) opvatten, ontwerpen; *vi.* ontvangen, zwanger worden.

concentrate ['kɔnsentreit] concentreren, samentrekken.

concentration [kɔnsen'treiʃən] concentratie, samentrekking *v.*; dichtheid *v.*; aandacht *v.*

concept ['kɔnsept] begrip *o.*; concept *o.*

conception [kən'sepʃən] begrip *o.*, opvatting *v.*; voorstelling *v.*; gedachte, mening *v.*; ontwerp *o.*

concern [kən'sə:n] *vt.* betreffen, aangaan; *vr.* — *oneself,* zich bekommeren (*about, for,* over); zich verontrusten (*about, for,* over); zich inlaten (*in, with,* met); *sb.* zaak, onderneming *v.*; aangelegenheid *v.*; deelneming, belangstelling *v.*

concerned [kən'sə:nd] bezorgd (*for,* voor), betrokken.

concerning [kən'sə:niŋ] aangaande, betreffende.

concert ['kɔnsət] *sb.* overeenstemming *v.*; (*muz.*) concert *o.*

concession [kən'seʃən] bewilliging, inwilliging, vergunning *v.*; concessie *v.*; toegeving *v.*

concessive [kən'sesiv] toegevend.

conciliate [kən'silieit] verzoenen; in overeenstemming brengen.

conciliator [kən'silieitə] verzoener; bemiddelaar *m.*

concise (ly) [kən'sais(li)] *adj.* (*adv.*) beknopt, kort.

conciseness [kən'saisnis] beknoptheid, kortheid v.

conclude [kən'klûd] besluiten, opmaken, concluderen; beslissen; besluiten, beëindigen; de gevolgtrekking maken.

conclusion [kən'klûʒən] besluit, einde, slot o.; gevolgtrekking, conclusie v.

conclusive(ly) [kən'klûsiv(li)] adj. (adv.) afdoend, beslissend.

concoction [kən'kɔkʃən] verzinsel o., beraming v.; brouwsel o.

concord ['kɔŋkoːd, 'kɔnkoːd] harmonie, eendracht, overeenstemming v.; verdrag c.

concordat [kɔn'koːdæt] concordaat o.

concourse ['kɔŋkoːs, kɔnkoːs] toeloop, samenloop m.; verzameling, menigte v.

concrete ['kɔnkrît] adj. concreet; vast, hard; samengesteld; betonnen, van beton; sb. (het) concrete; concreet begrip o.; vaste massa v.; beton o.

concubine ['kɔŋkjubain] bijzit v.

concur [kən'kəː] samenvallen; samenwerken, medewerken; overeenstemmen, het eens zijn; bijdragen (to, tot).

concurrence, concurrency [kən'kərəns(i)] (het) samenvallen o., samenloop m.; samenwerking, medewerking v.; overeenstemming v.

concussion [kən'kəʃən] schudding v., schok m., botsing v.

condemn [kən'dem] veroordelen; schuldig verklaren (of, aan); doemen, verdoemen; verbeurd verklaren; (v. ziekte) opgeven; afkeuren.

condemnable [kən'demnəbl] afkeurenswaardig, laakbaar, verwerpelijk.

condensable [kən'densəbl] verdichtbaar; samenpersbaar.

condense [kən'dens] verdichten, condenseren; samenpersen; samenvatten-bekorten.

condescend [kɔndi'send] zich verwaardigen; afdalen (to, tot).

condescending(ly) [kɔndi'sendiŋ(li)] adj. (adv.) (nederbuigend) minzaam.

condign [kən'dain] (v. straf) (wel)ver-diend.

condiment ['kɔndimənt] kruiderij v., toekruid o., toespijs v.

condition [kən'diʃən] voorwaarde v.; staat, toestand m.; gesteldheid v.; rang, stand m.

conditional [kən'diʃənəl] adj. voorwaardelijk; sb. (gram.) voorwaardelijke wijs v.

condole [kən'doul] condoleren.

condolence [kən'douləns] rouwbeklag o., condoleantie v.

condone [kən'doun] vergeven, kwijtschelden; vergoelijken; door de vingers zien; goedmaken.

conducive [kən'djûsiv] bevorderlijk (to, voor), strekkend (to, tot), dienstbaar (to, aan).

conduct ['kɔndəkt] sb. gedrag o., houding v.; optreden o.; leiding, aanvoering v.; beleid o.

conduct [kən'dəkt] vt. leiden, geleiden; aanvoeren; besturen; dirigeren; vi. (muz.) dirigeren; vr. — oneself well, zich goed gedragen.

conductor [kən'dəktə] (ge)leider, leidsman m.; bestuurder m.; (muz.) dirigent kapelmeester m.; (v. tram, enz.) conducteur m.; (el.) geleidraad m.

cone [koun] kegel m.; denappel, pijnappel m.

confectioner [kən'fekʃənə] suikerbakker, confiseur m.

confederacy [kən'fedərəsi] verbond o.; federatie v.

confederate [kən'fedərit] bondgenoot; eedgenoot m.; medeplichtige m.

confederation [kənfedə'reiʃən] verbond o.; statenbond m.

confer [kən'fəː] vt. opdragen; (v. titel, enz.) verlenen, schenken; bijdragen (to, tot); vi. beraadslagen, confereren.

conference ['kɔnfərəns] conferentie, beraadslaging v.

confess [kən'fes] erkennen, bekennen; belijden, biechten; de biecht horen.

confession [kən'feʃən] bekentenis v.; biecht v.

confessional [kən'feʃənəl] biechtstoel m.

confessor [kən'fesə] belijder m.; biechtvader m.

confidant(e) [kɔnfi'dænt] vertrouweling(e) m. (v.).

confidence ['kɔnfidəns] (zelf)vertrouwen o., vrijmoedigheid v.

confident ['kɔnfidənt] adj. (zelf)bewust, vrijmoedig, vol zelfvertrouwen; sb. vertrouweling m.

confidential [kɔnfi'denʃəl] vertrouwd; vertrouwelijk.

confine [kən'fain] begrenzen; bepalen, beperken.

confinement [kən'fainmənt] begrenzing; beperking v.; opsluiting v.; (kamer)arrest o.; bevalling v.

confirm [kən'fəːm] bevestigen, bekrachtigen; versterken; (v. notulen) arresteren, goedkeuren; (als lid) aannemen; (kath.) vormen.

confirmation [kɔnfə'meiʃən] bevestiging, bekrachtiging v.; versterking v.; aanneming v.; (kath.) vormsel o.

confiscable [kən'fiskəbl] verbeurbaar.

confiscate ['kɔnfiskeit] verbeurd verklaren, confisqueren.

confiscation [kɔnfis'keiʃən] verbeurdverklaring, confiscatie v., beslag o.

conflagration [kɔnflə'greiʃən] grote brand m.

conflict ['kɔnflikt] sb. botsing v., strijd m., geschil, conflict o.

conflict [kən'flikt] vi. botsen, strijden, in botsing komen.

conflicting [kən'fliktiŋ] tegenstrijdig.

confluence ['kɔnfluəns] samenvloeiing, vereniging v.; toeloop m.

confluent ['kɔnfluənt] adj. samenvloeiend; sb. zijrivier v., bijstroom m.

conform [kən'fɔ:m] *vt.* schikken, richten, regelen (*to*, naar); *vi.* zich schikken, zich voegen; zich gedragen (*to*, naar).

conformable [kən'fɔ:məbl] overeenkomstig, in overeenstemming (*to*, met).

conformity [kən'fɔ:miti] overeenkomst, overeenstemming *v.*

confound [kən'faund] beschamen, beschaamd doen staan; verbijsteren, versteld doen staan; verijdelen, in duigen doen vallen; verwarren, in de war sturen.

confounded [kən'faundid] *adj.* beschaamd; verward, ontsteld, onthutst, verbijsterd; verduiveld, vervloekt.

confraternity [kɔnfrə'tə:niti] broederschap *v.*

confrontation [kɔnfrən'teiʃən] vergelijking *v.* (*recht*) confrontatie *v.*

confuse [kən'fjûz] beschaamd doen staan verwarren; verbijsteren.

confused [kən'fjûz(i)d] verlegen; verward; verbijsterd.

confusion [kən'fjûzən] beschaming; verwarring; verlegenheid *v.*

confutable [kən'fjutəbl] weerlegbaar.

confute [kən'fjût] weerleggen.

congeal [kən'dzîl] (doen) stollen, stremmen, bevriezen.

congealable [kən'dzîləbl] bevriesbaar.

congelation [kɔndzi'leiʃən] stolling, stremming, bevriezing *v.*

congener ['kɔndzinə] soortgenoot, (stam)verwant *m.*, gelijksoortig iets *o.*

congenial [kən'dzîniəl] geestverwant; gelijkgestemd; sympathiek.

congenital [kən'dzenitəl] aangeboren, natuurlijk.

congest [kən'dzest] ophopen; overladen; congestie veroorzaken.

congestion [kən'dzestʃən] ophoping *v.*; (*v. verkeer*) opstopping *v.*; congestie *v.*

conglomeration ['kənglɔmə'reiʃən] samenpakking *v.*

congratulate [kən'grætjuleit] gelukwensen, feliciteren.

congratulation [kəngrætju'leiʃən] gelukwens *m.*, felicitatie *v.*

congregate ['kɔngrigeit] (zich) verzamelen, vergaderen.

congress ['kɔngres] samenkomst, bijeenkomst, vergadering *v.*, congres *o.*

congruent ['kɔngruənt] overeenstemmend.

conic(al) ['kɔnik(l)] *adj.* kegelvormig.

conjoin [kən'dzɔin] samenvoegen, verenigen.

conjoint [kən'dzɔint] verenigd.

conjugal ['kɔndzugəl] echtelijk.

conjugate ['kɔndzugeit] (*gram.*) vervoegen.

conjugation [kɔndzu'geiʃən] (*gram.*) vervoeging *v.*

conjunct [kən'dzəŋkt] gezamenlijk.

conjunction [kən'dzəŋkʃən] verbinding, vereniging *v.*; samenloop *m.*; (*v. sterren*) samenstand *m.*; (*gram.*) verbindingswoord, voegwoord *o.*

conjuncture [kən'dzəŋktʃə] samenloop *m.* (van omstandigheden).

conjuration [kɔndzu'reiʃən] samenzwering *v.*

conjure ['kəndzə] *vt.* bezweren.

conjurer, conjuror ['kəndzərə] goochelaar *m.*

connate ['kɔneit] aangeboren.

connect [kə'nekt] verbinden aansluiten.;

connection [kə'nekʃən] verbinding *v.*; samenhang *m.*; (*v. treinen, trams, enz.*) aansluiting *v.*; (familie)betrekking *v.*

connexion [kə'nekʃən] *zie* **connection.**

connive [kɔ'naiv] *vi.* oogluikend toezien; — *at*, oogluikend toelaten.

connoisseur [kɔni'sə:, kɔni'sjûə] (kunst)kenner *m.*; fijnproever *m.*

connote [kɔ'nout] insluiten; (tegelijk) betekenen.

connubial [kə'njûbiəl] echtelijk.

conquer ['kɔŋkə] veroveren; overwinnen.

conquerable ['kɔŋkərebl] overwinnelijk.

conqueror ['kɔŋkərə] veroveraar *m.*; overwinnaar *m.*

conquest ['kɔŋkwest] verovering *v.*; overwinning *v.*

consanguinity [kɔnsæŋ'gwiniti] (bloed)verwantschap *v.*

conscience ['kɔnʃəns] geweten *o.*

conscientiously [kɔn'ʃienʃəsli] nauwgezet, angstvallig.

conscious ['kɔnʃəs] bewust (*of*, van).

consciousness ['kɔnʃəsnis] bewustheid *v.*; bewustzijn *o.*

conscript ['kɔnskript] dienstplichtige, milicien *m.*

conscription [kən'skripʃən] dienstplicht *m.*, conscriptie *v.*

consecrate ['kɔnsikreit] inwijden, inzegenen.

consecration [kɔnsi'kreiʃən] wijding *v.*; inwijding, inzegening *v.*; consecratie *v.*

consecutive [kən'sekjutiv] opeenvolgend.

consent [kən'sent] *vi.* toestemmen; *sb.* toestemming.

consequence ['kɔnsikwəns] gevolg *o.*; uitwerking *v.*; gevolgtrekking *v.*; belang, gewicht *o.*, betekenis *v.*; invloed *m.*

consequently ['kɔnsikwəntli] *adv.* bijgevolg, dus.

conservation [kɔnsə'veiʃən] behoud *o.*, instandhouding *v.*

conservative [kən'sə:vətiv] behoudend, conservatief.

conservatory [kən'sə:vətri] bewaarplaats *v.*; broeikas, serre *v.*; conservatorium *o.*, muziekschool *v.*

conserve [kən'sə:v] *vt.* in stand houden, behouden; (*v. vruchten, enz.*) bewaren, inmaken; *sb.* ingemaakte groenten; ingelegd fruit.

consider [kən'sidə] beschouwen; overdenken, overwegen; in aanmerking nemen.

considerable [kən'sidərəbl] aanzienlijk, belangrijk.
considerate [kən'sidərit] adj. zorgzaam; kies.
consideration [kənsidə'reiʃən] bedenking v.; beschouwing v.; aanzien o.
consign [kən'sain] overdragen; toevertrouwen; opdragen; storten, deponeren, in deposito geven; (H.) zenden, in commissie zenden, consigneren.
consignee [kɔnsai'ni] geconsigneerde, geadresseerde m.
consigner [kən'sainə] consignatiegever, afzender m.
consignment [kən'sainmənt] overdracht v.; zending ; consignatie r.
consist [kən'sist] bestaan.
consistory [kən'sistəri] consistorie o.
consolation [kɔnsə'leiʃən] troost m.
console [kən'soul] troosten, vertroosten.
consonant ['kɔnsənənt] medeklinker m.
consort ['kɔnso:t] gemaal m.; gemalin v.
conspiracy [kən'spirəsi] komplot o., samenspanning, samenzwering v.
conspire [kən'spaiə] vi. samenzweren; vt. beramen.
constable ['kɔnstəbl] politieagent m.
constancy ['kɔnstənsi] standvastigheid.
constant ['kɔnstənt] standvastig, bestendig, vast; trouw.
constellation [kɔnsti'leiʃən] gesternte, sterrenbeeld o.
consternation [kɔnstə'neiʃən] ontsteltenis, verslagenheid v.
constipate ['kɔnstipeit] verstoppen.
constipation [kɔnsti'peiʃən] verstopping, hardlijvigheid v.
constituency [kən'stitjuənsi] kiesdistrict o.
constituent [kən'stitjuənt] adj. samenstellend; afvaardigend; constituerend; sb. lastgever m.; kiezer m.; bestanddeel o.
constitute ['kɔnstitjût] samenstellen; aanstellen (tot); instellen.
constitution [kɔnsti'tjûʃən] samenstelling v.; gestel o.; grondwet v.
constitutional [kɔnsti'tjûʃənəl] grondwettig.
constrain [kən'strein] dwingen, bedwingen; opsluiten; gevangen houden; beheersen; beperken.
constrained [kən'streind] adj. gedwongen.
constraint [kən'streint] dwang m.
constrict [kən'strikt] samentrekken.
construct [kən'strəkt] bouwen, opbouwen; oprichten; aanleggen; samenstellen.
construction [kən'strəkʃən] bouw m.; oprichting v.; aanleg m.; samenstelling v.; constructie; inrichting v.; zinsbouw m.
constructor [kən'strəktə] bouwer, maker, vervaardiger m.; (sch.) bouwopzichter.

consuetude ['kɔnswitjûd] gewoonte v., gebruik o.; gewoonterecht o.
consul ['kɔnsəl] consul m.
consular ['kɔnsjulə] consulair.
consulate ['kɔnsjulit] consulaat o.
consult [kən'səlt] vt. raadplegen, consulteren; ri. beraadslagen, overleggen, overleg plegen.
consultation [kɔnsəl'teiʃən] raadpleging v.; beraadslaging v.; (v. dokter) consult o.
consulting-room [kən'səltiŋrum] (v. dokter) spreekkamer v.
consumable [kən'sjûməbl] verteerbaar.
consume [kən'sjûm] verbruiken; verteren; nuttigen, verorberen; vernietigen.
consummate [kən'səmit] volmaakt.
consumption [kən'səm(p)ʃən] vertering v., verbruik o.; tering, uittering v.
consumptive [kən'səm(p)tiv] verterend; teringachtig.
contact ['kɔntækt] aanraking, voeling v.; (el.) contact o.
contagion [kən'teidʒən] besmetting v.
contagious(ly) [kən'teidʒəs(li)] besmettelijk; aanstekelijk.
contain [kən'tein] bevatten, inhouden.
container [kən'teinə] houder m.; doos; bus v.; vat o.; (v. lamp) peer v.
contaminate [kən'tæmineit] besmetten, bevlekken.
contemn [kən'tem] verachten, versmaden.
contemplate ['kɔntəmpleit] beschouwen, overpeinzen; denken over; voor ogen hebben; van plan zijn, beogen.
contemplative [kən'templətiv] beschouwend, bespiegelend.
contemporary [kən'tempərəri] adj. gelijktijdig; sb. tijdgenoot m.
contempt [kən'tem(p)t] minachting v.
contemptible [kən'tem(p)təbl] verachtelijk.
contemptuous [kən'tem(p)tjuəs] adj. minachtend, verachtelijk.
content [kən'tent] adj. tevreden, voldaan; sb. tevredenheid v.; genoegen o.; vt. tevreden stellen.
content ['kɔntent] sb. inhoud m., inhoudsgrootte v.; gehalte o.
contention [kən'tenʃən] twist m.
contentment [kən'tentmənt] tevredenheid, voldaanheid v.
contest ['kɔntest] sb. twist m., geschil o.; wedstrijd m.
contest [kən'test] vt. betwisten.
contestable [kən'testəbl] betwistbaar.
context ['kɔntekst] verband o., samenhang m.
contiguous [kən'tigjuəs] aangrenzend.
continence, continency ['kɔntinəns(i)] onthouding v.; kuisheid v.
continent ['kɔntinənt] adj. zich onthoudend, matig; kuis; sb. vasteland; werelddeel o.
contingence, contingency [kən'tindʒəns, —si] toeval o.; gebeurlijkheid v.

contingent [kǝn'tindʒǝnt] *adj.* toevallig; mogelijk; *sb.* gebeurlijkheid *v.*; contingent *o.*
continually [kǝn'tinjuǝl(i)] *adj.* (*adv.*) aanhoudend, gestadig, bestendig.
continuance [kǝn'tinjuǝns] voortzetting *v.*
continuation [kǝntinju'eiʃǝn] voortzetting *v.*, vervolg *o.*
continue [kǝn'tinjû] *vt.* vervolgen, voortzetten; bestendigen; verlengen; *vi.* aanhouden, voortduren; voortgaan (met).
continuous(ly) [kǝn'tinjuǝs(li)] *adj.* doorlopend; voortdurend.
contort [kǝn'toːt] verwringen.
contortionist [kǝn'toːʃǝnist] woordverdraaier *m.*; slangemens *m.*
contour ['kontûǝ] omtrek *m.*
contraband ['kontrǝbænd] smokkelhandel *m.*; contrabande.
contract ['kontrækt] *sb.* contract *o.*; overeenkomst *v.*
contract [kǝn'trækt] *vt.* samentrekken; aangaan, sluiten; contracteren; *vi.* inkrimpen; — *for,* contracteren.
contraction [kǝn'trækʃǝn] samentrekking *v.*; inkrimping *v.*
contractor [kǝn'træktǝ] aannemer *m.*
contradict [kontrǝ'dikt] tegenspreken.
contradiction [kontrǝ'dikʃǝn] tegenspraak, tegenstrijdigheid *v.*
contradictory [kontrǝ'diktǝri] tegenstrijdig.
contradistinction [kontrǝdis'tiŋkʃǝn] tegenstelling *v.*
contraposition [kontrǝpǝ'ziʃǝn] tegenstelling *v.*
contrariety [kontrǝ'rajǝti] tegenstrijdigheid *v.*; tegenslag *m.*
contrary ['kontrǝri] *adj.* tegengesteld, strijdig; tegen—; (*fam.*) dwars, koppig; *adv.* tegen; *sb.* tegengestelde *o.*
contrast ['kontræst] *sb.* contrast *o.*, tegenstelling *v.*; *vt.* [kǝn'træst] tegenover elkaar stellen; *vi.* afsteken bij.
contravention [kontrǝ'venʃǝn] overtreding *v.*
contribute [kǝn'tribjut] *vt.* bijdragen; *vi.* medewerken, helpen.
contribution [kontri'bjûʃǝn] bijdrage, contributie *v.*; belasting *v.*
contrite(ly) ['kontrait(li)] *adj.* (*adv.*) berouwvol; boetvaardig.
contrition [kǝn'triʃǝn] diep berouw *o.*; wroeging *v.*
contrivance [kǝn'traivǝns] vindingrijkheid *v.*; vernuft *o.*; list, kunstgreep *m.*
contrive [kǝn'traiv] vinden, uitvinden; verzinnen.
control [kǝn'troul] *sb.* controle *v.*, toezicht *o.*; beheersing *v.*; bedwang *o.*; (*v. machine,* enz.) leiding, bediening *v.*; *vt.* bedwingen; beheren; besturen; controleren.
controller [kǝn'troulǝ] controleur *m.*
controversy ['kontrǝvǝːsi] geschil, strijdpunt *o.*, polemiek *v.*

contumacy ['kontjumǝsi] weerspannigheid, weerbarstigheid *v.*
contumely ['kontjumili] smaad *m.*
contuse ['kǝn'tjûz] kneuzen.
contusion [kǝn'tjûʒǝn] kneuzing *v.*
convalesce [konvǝ'les] herstellende zijn.
convalescence [konvǝ'lesǝns] herstel *o.*, beterschap *v.*
convalescent [konvǝ'lesǝnt] herstellend.
convene [kǝn'vîn] *vt.* bijeenroepen; *vi.* bijeenkomen; overeenstemmen.
convenience [kǝn'vînjǝns] geschiktheid, gepastheid *v.*; geriefelijkheid *v.*
convenient(ly) [kǝn'vînjǝnt(li)] *adj.* (*adv.*) geriefelijk; gelegen komend.
convent ['konvǝnt] klooster *o.*
convention [kǝn'venʃǝn] overeenkomst *v.*; bijeenkomst *v.*
conventional [kǝn'venʃǝnǝl] overeengekomen; gebruikelijk.
converge [kǝn'vǝːdʒ] convergeren, in één punt samenkomen.
conversable [kǝn'vǝːsǝbl] spraakzaam.
conversation [konvǝ'seiʃǝn] gesprek *o.* conversatie *v.*; bespreking *v.*
converse [kǝn'vǝːs] zich onderhouden.
converse ['konvǝːs] *sb.* gesprek *o.*; omgang *m.*
converse ['konvǝːs] *adj.* omgekeerd; *sb.* (het) omgekeerde *o.*
conversion [kǝn'vǝːʃǝn] bekering *v.*; omkering; verandering *v.*
convert [kǝn'vǝːt] *vt.* bekeren; omkeren; verwisselen; herleiden.
convert ['konvǝːt] *sb.* bekeerling *m.*
converter [kǝn'vǝːtǝ] bekeerder *m.*; (*el.*) omvormer.
convertible [kǝn'vǝːtibl] omkeerbaar; verwisselbaar.
convex ['konveks] bol, bolrond, convex.
convey [kǝn'vei] overbrengen, vervoeren; overdragen.
conveyance [kǝn'veiǝns] (het) overbrengen *o.*; overdracht *v.*; vervoermiddel *o.*
conveyer [kǝn'veiǝ] vervoerder *m.*
convict ['konvikt] dwangarbeider *m.*
conviction [kǝn'vikʃǝn] overtuiging *v.*
convince [kǝn'vins] overtuigen.
convincing(ly) [kǝn'vinsiŋ(li)] *adj.* (*adv.*) overtuigend; met overtuiging.
conviviality [kǝnvivi'æliti] feestelijkheid *v.*
convocation [konvo'keiʃǝn] oproeping.
convoke [kǝn'vouk] oproepen, bijeenroepen.
convoy [kǝn'voi] *vt.* begeleiden; ['konvoi] *sb.* geleide, konvooi *o.*
convulse [kǝn'vǝls] schokken.
convulsion [kǝn'vǝlʃǝn] stuiptrekking *v.*
convulsive(ly) [kǝn'vǝlsiv(li)] *adj.* (*adv.*) krampachtig, stuipachtig.
cook [kuk] *sb.* keukenmeid *v.*; kok *m.*; *vt.* koken, bereiden; (*fig.*) verzinnen; (*v. balans,* enz.) vervalsen.

cookery ['kukəri] kookkunst v.
cool [kûl] adj. koel, fris; lauw; sb. koelte v.; vt. & vi. koelen, afkoelen.
cooler [kûlə] koeldrank m.; koelvat o.
coolly ['kûli] adv. koel, koeltjes.
coolness ['kûlnis] koelheid, koelte v.; verkoeling v.
coom [kûm] kolenstof, kolengruis o.
coop [kûp] kippemand v.; kippenhok o.
cooper ['kûpə] sb. kuiper m.; vt. inkuipen; vi. kuipen.
co-operate [kou'opəreit] samenwerken, medewerken.
co-operative [kou'opərətiv] samenwerkend; coöperatief.
coopery ['kûpəri] kuiperij v.
co-ordinate [kou'o:dinit] van dezelfde rang; nevengeschikt.
co-ordination [kouo:di'neiʃən] nevenschikking; rangschikking v.
coot [kût] (Dk.) koet m.
copal ['koupəl] kopal o.
cope [koup] koorkap v.
copper ['kopə] sb. (rood) koper o.; adj. koperen; vt. verkoperen.
coppice ['kopis] hakhout o.
copse [kops] zie **coppice**.
copy ['kopi] sb. afschrift o., kopie v.; kopij v.; exemplaar o.; vt. afschrijven; overschrijven; kopiëren; nabootsen, namaken.
copy-book ['kopibuk] schrijfboek o.
copyist ['kopiist] kopiist m.
copy-money ['kopiməni] honorarium o.
copyright ['kopirait] sb. kopijrecht o.; vt. (zich) het kopijrecht verzekeren van.
coquettish (ly) [kou'ketiʃ(li)] adj.(adv.) behaagziek, koket.
coral ['korəl] koraal o.
coralline ['korəlain] koralen.
coral-reef ['korəlrif] koraalrif o.
cord [ko:d] koord, touw, snoer o., streng v.
cordial ['ko:diəl] hartelijk; hartsterkend, opwekkend.
core [ko:] kern v., binnenste, hart o.; (v. appel) klokhuis o.
cork [ko:k] sb. kurk, stop v.; dobber m.; kurkboom, kurkeik m.; adj. kurken.
corked [ko:kt] gekurkt; naar de kurk smakend.
cork-screw ['ko:kskrû] kurketrekker m.
corm [ko:m] (Pl.) knol m.
corn [ko:n] koren, graan o.; (Sc., Ir.) haver v.; (Am.) maïs v.; korrel v.; likdoorn m., eksteroog v.
corn-cockle ['ko:nkokl] (Pl.) bolderik v.
corn-crake ['ko:nkreik] (Dk.) kwartelkoning, spriet m.
cornea ['ko:niə] hoornvlies o.
corner ['ko:nə] hoek m.
cornice ['ko:nis] lijst, kroonlijst v., lijstwerk o.
corn-loft ['ko:nloft] graanzolder m.
corn-poppy ['ko:npopi] klaproos v.
coronation [korə'neiʃən] kroning v.

coroner ['korənə] lijkschouwer m.
corporal ['ko:pərəl] sb. (mil.) korporaal m.; (kath.) corporale o.; adj. lichamelijk.
corporation [ko:pə'reiʃən] corporatie v.; rechtspersoon m.; gilde o.
corpulent ['ko:pjulənt] zwaarlijvig, corpulent.
corral [ko'ræl] kraal v.
correct [kə'rekt] adj. juist, in orde; nauwkeurig; vt. verbeteren, corrigeren; terechtwijzen.
correction [kə'rekʃən] verbetering, correctie v.; terechtwijzing v.; bestraffing v.
correctitude [kə'rektitjûd] juistheid v.; nauwkeurigheid v.; zuiverheid v.; correctheid v.
correctness [kə'rektnis] zie **correctitude**.
correspondence [koris'pondəns] correspondentie, briefwisseling v.; overeenstemming, overeenkomst v.; aansluiting v.; gemeenschap v.
corresponding (ly) [koris'pondiŋ(li)] adj. (adv.) overeenkomstig.
corridor ['korido:] gang, galerij v.
corrigible ['koridʒibl] verbeterbaar, verbeterlijk; gedwee.
corrode [kə'roud] vt. wegvreten; invreten; verteren, wegknagen; vi. verroesten; verteren.
corrosive [kə'rousiv] adj. invretend, bijtend; sb. invretend middel, bijtend middel o.
corrugate ['korugeit] rimpelen; fronsen.
corrupt [kə'rəpt] adj. bedorven, verdorven; omkoopbaar, corrupt; onecht, vervalst; verknoeid; vt.bederven;omkopen; verknoeien, verbasteren; besmetten; verontreinigen; vi. bederven, rotten, verrotten.
corruptible [kə'rəptibl] bederfelijk, aan bederf onderhevig; omkoopbaar.
corruption [kə'rəpʃən] bederf o.; verderf o., verdorvenheid v.; omkoping, corruptie, knoeierij v.
corsair ['ko:sêə] zeerover m.; kaperschip o.
corset ['ko:sit] korset o.
cortege [ko:'teiʒ] stoet m., gevolg o.
cosmographer [koz'mogrəfə] kosmograaf, wereldbeschrijver m.
cosmopolitan [kozmə'politən] adj. kosmopolitisch; sb. kosmopoliet, wereldburger m.
cosmopolite [koz'mopəlait] kosmopoliet, wereldburger m.
cost [ko:st, kost] sb. prijs m., kosten m. mv.; uitgave v.; schade v., verlies v.; vi. kosten.
costiveness ['kostivnis] hardlijvigheid v.; gierigheid v.
costly ['ko:stli, 'kostli] kostbaar; duur.
costume ['kostjûm] sb. kleding v.; kostuum o.; klederdracht v.; vt. kleden, kostumeren.

cosy ['kouzi] gezellig, behaaglijk, knus.

cot [kɔt] schaapskooi v.; hut, stulp v.; bedje o.; (hospitaal)bed o.; kooi, krib v.

cottage ['kɔtidʒ] hut v.; arbeiderswoning v.; buitentje v., paviljoen o.

cottager ['kɔtidʒə] arbeider; eenvoudige landman m.

cottier ['kɔtie] keuterboer m.

cotton ['kɔtn] sb. katoen o.; —s, katoenen stoffen, katoentjes; adj. katoenen.

cotton-mill ['kɔtnmil] katoenfabriek v.

cotton-wool ['kɔtnwul] boomwol v.; watten v. mr.

couch [kautʃ] rustbed o., rustbank v., divan m.

cough [kɔ:f, kɔf] sb. hoest m., kuch v.; vi. hoesten, kuchen.

council ['kaunsl] raad m.; raadsvergadering v.; hofraad m.; concilie o.

council-board ['kaunslbɔ:d] raadstafel, groene tafel v.

councillor ['kaunsilə] raadslid o.; raad, staatsraad m.

counsel ['kaunsil] sb. raad m., raadgeving v.; raadgever, advocaat m.; beraadslaging v., overleg o.; mening v.; vt. raden, aanraden.

counsellor ['kaunsilə] raadgever, raadsman m.; raadsheer m.

count [kaunt] sb. graaf m.

count [kaunt] vt. tellen, optellen; meetellen; aanrekenen; rekenen, achten; vi. tellen, meetellen; van belang zijn; staat maken op.

countable ['kauntəbl] telbaar.

countenance ['kauntinəns] gezicht, gelaat o., gelaatsuitdrukking v.; kalmte v.; steun m., aanmoediging v.

counter [kauntə] sb. teller m.; legpenning m., fiche v.; toonbank v.; (v. schaakspel, damspel) stuk o.

counter ['kauntə] adj. tegengesteld, tegenovergesteld; adv. tegen; integengestelde richting; sb. tegenstoot m.; tegenmaatregel m.; tegenzet m.; vt. tegenwerken; tegenspreken; weerleggen; (v. komplot) verijdelen; afslaan; vi. (sp.) een tegenstoot toebrengen, pareren.

counterbid ['kauntəbid] tegenbod o.

counterfeit ['kauntəfit] adj. nagemaakt, vals, onecht; sb. namaak m.; vt. namaken, nabootsen, vervalsen; (fig.) huichelen.

counterfoil ['kauntəfɔil] (v. cheque) souche v.; (v. postwissel) strook v.

countermand [kauntə'mând] afzeggen, afbestellen.

counterpart ['kɔntpât] (recht) tegenpartij v.; (muz.) tegenstem v.; overeenkomstig deel o.; tegenhanger m.

counterpoise ['kauntəpɔiz] tegenwicht o.; evenwicht o.

counterpoison ['kauntəpɔizən] tegengif o.

countess ['kauntis] gravin v.

countless ['kauntlis] adj. talloos, ontelbaar.

country ['kəntri] land o.; streek v. platteland o.; vaderland o.

countryman ['kəntriman] buitenman, landman m.; landsman, landgenoot m.

county ['kaunti] graafschap o.

couple ['kəpl] sb. paar o.; koppel o.; koppelband, riem m.; vt. koppelen, verenigen, verbinden; vi. paren.

coupon ['kûpən] coupon v.; bon m.

courage ['kəridʒ] moed m., dapperheid v.

courageous(ly) [kə'reidʒəs(li)] adj (adv.) moedig.

courier ['kuriə] koerier, renbode m.

course [kɔ:s] sb. loop, gang m.; koers m., richting v.; wedloop m.; bedding v., stroom m.; beloop, verloop o.; reeks, opeenvolging, rij v.; leergang, cursus m.; vt. jacht maken op; najagen; aflopen; vi. jagen; stromen.

courser ['kɔ:sə] renpaard o.

court ['kɔ:t] sb. hof o.; hofhouding v.; rechtbank v., gerechtshof o.; vt. het hof maken; de gunst zoeken van; streven naar; uitlokken.

court-day ['kɔ:tdei] (v. rechtbank) zittingsdag m.

courteous(ly) ['kə:tjəs, 'kɔ:tjəs(li)] adj. (adv.) hoffelijk, beleefd.

courtesan [kɔ:ti'zæn] courtisane v.

courtesy ['kə:tisi, 'kɔ:tisi] hoffelijkheid, vriendelijkheid v.; gunst v.

courtier ['kɔ:tjə] hoveling m.

courtly ['kɔ:tli] hoofs, hoffelijk; vleierig.

court-martial ['kɔ:t'mâʃəl] krijgsraad m.

courtship ['kɔ:tʃip] hofmakerij, vrijerij v.

cousin ['kəzn] neef m.; nicht v.

covenant ['kəvinənt] sb. overeenkomst v., contract o., akte v., verdrag, verbond o.; vt. & vi. afspreken, overeenkomen.

cover ['kəvə] vt. bedekken; dekken; overtrekken; zich uitstrekken over, beslaan, omvatten; verbergen; (mil.) bestrijken; — in, (v. huis) onder dak brengen; (v. graf, enz.) dichtgooien, vullen; sb. dekking, bedekking v.; deksel o.; beschutting v.; omhulsel o.; omslag m. & o.

covering ['kəvəriŋ] dekking v.; bedekking v.

coverlet ['kəvəlit] sprei v.; gewatteerde deken v.; dekkleed o.

covet ['kəvit] begeren.

covetous(ly) ['kəvitəs(li)] adj. (adv.) begerig, hebzuchtig.

covetousness ['kəvitəsnis] begerigheid, hebzucht v.

covey ['kəvi] vlucht v. (patrijzen); troep m.; bende v.; stel o.

cow [kau] koe v.

coward ['kauəd] sb. lafaard, bloodaard m.; adj. lafhartig, laf.

cowboy ['kaubɔi] koejongen m., (Am.) cowboy, veedrijver m.

cowherd ['kauhə:d] koeherder m.

cowl [kaul] monnikskap, monnikspij v.; schoorsteenkap v.

coxcomb ['kɔkskoum] fat, kwast m.

coy [kɔi] adj. schuchter, bedeesd, zedig; — of, karig met.

coze [kouz] vi. kouten, keuvelen; sb. praatje o.

crabbed (ly) ['kræbid(li)] adj. (adv.) kribbig, knorrig, stuurs, nors; (v. stijl) gewrongen; (v. geschrift) kriebelig.

crab-fish ['kræbfiʃ] krab v.

crack [kræk] sb. knal; slag m.; schot, o.; stoot m.; klap m.; gekraak o.; scheur; barst, breuk v.; kier m., reet, spleet v. gebrek o.; vt. & vi. breken, barsten, scheuren; (doen) kraken; doen knallen; snoeven, bluffen.

crack-brained ['krækbreind] gek, getikt.

cracked [krækt] gebarsten; getikt.

cracker ['krækə] kraker, notekraker m.; (harde) beschuit v.; voetzoeker, zevenklapper m.; knal m.

crack-jaw ['krækdʒɔ:] moeilijk uit te spreken (woord).

crackle ['krækl] vi. knetteren, knappen; sb. geknetter, geknap o.

cracknel ['kræknəl] krakeling m.

cradle ['kreidl] wieg v.; bakermat v.; spalk v.; (v. scheepshelling) slede v.

craft [krāft] handwerk, ambacht o.; vak, beroep o.; kunstnijverheid v.; gilde o.; sluwheid v.

craftiness ['krāftinis] listigheid, sluwheid v.

crafty ['krāfti] listig, sluw.

crag [kræg] rots, klip v.

cragsman ['krægsmən] rotsbeklimmer m.

cram [kræm] volstoppen, volproppen; inpompen; (voor examen) klaar stomen, drillen, africhten.

cram-full ['kræm'ful] stampvol, propvol.

cramp [kræmp] kramp, kramptrekking v.; kram v.; klemhaak m.; (muur)anker o.; (fig.) dwang m.; belemmering v.

cramp-iron ['kræmpaiən] kram v., klemhaak m., muuranker o.

cranage ['kreinidʒ] kraangeld o.

crane [krein] kraanvogel m.; kraan, hefkraan v.; hevel m.

crane-fly ['kreinflai] langpootmug v.

crank [kræŋk] sb. handvat o., kruk v.; slinger, zwengel m.; adj. licht omslaand; (sch.) rank.

crank-shaft ['kræŋkʃāft] krukas v.

cranky ['kræŋki] wankel, wrak; ziekelijk; nukkig, humeurig; excentriek; kronkelend.

crape [kreip] krip, (rouw)floers o.; rouwband m.

crash [kræʃ] vt. vermorzelen, verbrijzelen, verpletteren; vi. kraken, barsten, breken; krakend ineenstorten; (vl.) verongelukken, te pletter vallen; (v. donder) ratelen; failliet gaan; sb. gekraak o.; geratel o.; geraas o.; ineenstorting v.;

(vl.) neerstorting v., val m.; groot bankroet o., krach m.

crass [kræs] grof, lomp.

crate [kreit] krat o.; tenen mand v.

crater ['kreitə] krater m.; mijntrechter m.

cravat [krə'væt] das v.

crave [kreiv] begeren, wensen; vragen; smeken (om), bidden (om).

craving ['kreiviŋ] verlangen o., begeerte, hunkering v.

crawfish ['krɔ:fiʃ] rivierkreeft .m.

crawl [krɔ:l] kruipen; sluipen; krieuwelen, kriebelen.

crayfish ['kreifiʃ] rivierkreeft m.

crayon ['kreiən] tekenkrijt o.; pastel o., pasteltekening v.

craze [kreiz] krankzinnigheid; manie, rage v.

crazy ['kreizi] wrak, bouwvallig; ziekelijk; krankzinnig, gek.

creak [krīk] kraken, knarsen, piepen.

cream [krīm] room m.

crease [krīs] sb. kreuk, vouw, plooi v.; vt. & vi. kreukelen, vouwen, plooien.

create [kri'eit] scheppen, voortbrengen; teweegbrengen; benoemen tot, aanstellen tot.

creation [kri'eiʃən] schepping, voortbrenging v.; benoeming, aanstelling v.

creator [kri'eitə] schepper m.

creature ['krītʃə] schepsel o.

credence ['krīdəns] geloof o.; credenstafel v.

credentials [kri'denʃəlz] geloofsbrieven m. mv.

credible ['kredibl] adj. geloofwaardig.

credit ['kredit] sb. geloof, vertrouwen o.; goede naam m.; gezag, aanzien o., invloed m.; eer v.; krediet o.; credit o.; vt. geloven; crediteren; — to, toeschrijven aan.

credit-balance ['kreditbæləns] batig saldo o.

creditor ['kreditə] crediteur, schuldeiser m.

credulous (ly) ['kredjuləs(li)] adj. (adv.) lichtgelovig.

creed [krīd] geloofsbelijdenis v.

creek [krīk] kreek v., inham m., bocht v.

creep [krīp] kruipen; sluipen; krieuwelen .

creep-mouse ['krīpmaus] schuw, verlegen; stil.

creepy ['krīpi] kruipend; griezelig.

cremation [kri'meiʃən] verassing, (lijk)verbranding v.

crematory ['kremətəri] crematorium o.

crenate (d) ['krīneit(id)] (Pl., Dk.) gekarteld, getand.

crepitate ['krepiteit] knetteren.

crescent ['kresənt] adj. toenemend, wassend; halvemaanvormig; sb. wassende maan v.; halve maan v.

cress [kres] tuinkers, waterkers v.

crest [krest] kam m.; kuif v.; kruin v.; top m.; (op golven) schuimkop m.; (wap.) helmteken o.

crevice ['krevis] spleet, scheur v.

crew [krû] sb. (scheeps)bemanning v., scheepsvolk o.; troep m., bende v.; (mil.) bediening v.; gespuis o.

crib [krib] krib v.; koestal m.; hut v.; (kinder)bedje o.

crib-biter ['kribbaitə] (v. paard) kribbebijter m.; (fig.) nijdas, kankeraar, kribbebijter m.

crier ['kraiə] schreeuwer m.; omroeper m.; (bij rechtbank) deurwaarder m.

crime [kraim] misdaad v.; (mil.) overtreding.v.

criminal ['kriminəl] adj. misdadig; strafrechtelijk; crimineel; sb. misdadiger m.

criminality [krimi'næliti] misdadigheid, criminaliteit v.

criminate ['krimineit] beschuldigen; laken, gispen.

crimp [krimp] sb. ronselaar, zielverkoper m.; —s, (Am.) krullen v. mv.; adj. bros; kroes; vt. (fijn) plooien; (v. haar) krullen, friseren; (v. vis) krimp snijden; ronselen.

cringe [krindʒ] ineenkrimpen; (fig.) kruipen (to, voor).

crinkle ['kriŋkl] vt. & vi. kronkelen, rimpelen, kreukelen, ineenfrommele ; sb. kronkel, krinkel, krenkel m.

cripple ['kripl] sb. kreupele m.; vt. kreupel maken, verminken; (fig.) verlammen, belemmeren; onbruikbaar maken.

crisis ['kraisis] crisis v., keerpunt o.

crisp [krisp] adj. kroes, gekruld; bros, brokkelig; (v. papier) krakend; vt. \v. haar) krullen, friseren; doen rimpelen, doen kronkelen.

crispate ['krispeit] (Pl., Dk.) omgekruld, golvend.

critic ['kritik] criticus, beoordelaar m.; vitter, bediller m.

critical(ly) ['kritikəl(i)] adj. (adv.) kritisch, vitterig, bedillig; kritiek, hachelijk.

criticism ['kritisizm] kritiek, beoordeling, recensie v.; aanmerking v.; (mil.) bespreking v.

criticize ['kritisaiz] kritiseren, beoordelen; bekritiseren, hekelen.

croak [krouk] vi. kwaken; krassen; sb. gekwaak; gekras o.

crochet ['kroʃei, krouʃi] sb. haakwerk o.; vt. & vi. haken.

crock [krok] pot m., kan v.; potscherf v.; (sl.) kruk, sukkel m. & v.; oud meubel o.

crocodile ['krokədail] krokodil m.

crocus ['kroukəs] (Pl.) krokus m.

crony ['krouni] kameraad, boezemvriend m.

crook [kruk] sb. bocht, kromming v.; kronkel m.; vt. & vi. (zich) krommen; buigen.

crooked ['krukid] krom, gebogen, scheef, verdraaid; gebocheld; slinks, onoprecht, oneerlijk.

crop [krop] sb. krop m.; oogst m., gewas o.; stok m. (van zweep); vt. afknippen; oogsten, plukken, maaien.

cross [kro:s] sb. kruis o.; kruising v., gekruist ras o.; kruishout o.; vt. kruisen; doorkruisen; een kruis maken over; vi. elkaar kruisen; oversteken; (sp.: voetb.) van zijde verwisselen; vr. — oneself, het kruisteken maken, een kruis maken; adj. dwars, gekruist, kruiselings; tegengesteld; nijdig, boos.

cross-bar ['kro:sbâ] dwarshout o., dwarslat v.

cross-breed ['kro:sbrid] sb. gekruist ras o.; vt. (v. rassen) kruisen.

cross-country ['kro:s'kəntri] dwars over 't land, over heg en steg; (sp.) veldloop m.

cross-eyed ['kro:said] scheel.

crossing ['kro:siŋ] kruising v.; (het) oversteken o.; oversteekplaats v.; overweg m.; overvaart v.; dwarsstraat v.; kruispunt o.

crosspatch ['kro:spætʃ] (fam.) dwarsdrijver, nijdas m.

cross-road ['kro:s'roud] dwarsweg, zijweg m.; wegkruising v., tweesprong, viersprong m.

crosswise ['kro:swaiz] kruisgewijze; kruiselings.

croup [krûp] (gen.) kroep v.; (v. paard) kruis o.

crow [krou] sb. (Dk.) kraai v.; gekraai, gejubel o.; vi. kraaien, jubelen.

crowbar ['kroubâ] koevoet m., breekijzer o.

crowd [kraud] sb. menigte v.; gedrang o.; troep, hoop m.; vt. opeendringen; samenpersen; vullen, volproppen; vi. dringen, duwen; zich verdringen.

crowded ['kraudid] vol, overladen; dicht bezet; opeengepakt; (v. spoorlijn, enz.) druk; (v. stijl) gedrongen.

crown [kraun] sb. kroon v.; krans m.; kruin v.; (v. hoed) bol m.; vt. kronen; bekronen.

crown-prince ['kraun'prins] kroonprins m.

crucial ['krûsiəl] kruisvormig, kruis —; (fig.) kritiek, beslissend.

crucible ['krûsibl] smeltkroes m.; (fig.) vuurproef v.

crucifix ['krûsifiks] kruisbeeld o.

crucifixion [krûsi'fikʃən] kruisiging v.

crucify ['krûsifai] kruisen, kruisigen; (fig.) kastijden.

crude [krûd] rauw; ruw, ongezuiverd, onbereid; onrijp.

cruel ['krûil] adj. wreed, wreedaardig.

cruet-stand ['krûitstænd] olie- en azijnstelletje o.

cruise [krûz] vi. (sch.) kruisen; sb. (v. schip) kruistocht m.; zwerftocht m.

cruiser ['krûzə] kruiser m.

crumb [krəm] kruim, kruimel v.

crumble ['krəmbl] kruimelen, verbrokkelen.

crumple ['krəmpl] vt. & vi. verkreukelen.

crunch [krənʃ] *vt.* vermalen, vermorzelen; doen knarsen; *vi.* kraken, knarsen; kauwen; *sb.* gekraak; geknars *o.*

crupper ['krəpə] staartriem *m.*; kruis *o.* (*v. paard*).

crusade [krû'seid] *sb.* kruistocht *m.*; *vi.* een kruistocht ondernemen.

crusader [krû'seidə] kruisvaarder *m.*

crush [krəʃ] *vt.* samendrukken; uitpersen; verpletteren, vernietigen; onderdrukken; *sb.* uitpersing *v.*; verplettering, vernietiging *v.*; onderdrukking *v.*; schok *m.*; gedrang *o.*, menigte *v.*

crush-hat ['krəʃhæt] klakhoed *m.*; deukhoed *m.*

crush-room ['krəʃrum] foyer *m.*

crust [krəst] *sb.* korst, schaal *v.*, aanzetsel *o.*; *vt.* met een korst bedekken; *vi.* een korst vormen, aanzetten.

crustacean [krəs'teiʃən] schaaldier *o.*

crusty ['krəsti] korstig; korzelig, knorrig, kribbig, gemelijk.

crutch [krətʃ] *sb.* kruk *v.*; dwarsstuk *o.*; *vi.* steunen op een kruk.

cry [krai] *sb.* kreet, schreeuw, roep *m.*; geschreeuw, geroep *o.*; geschrei, gehuil *o.*; gejank, geblaf *o.*; gerucht *o.*; leus *v.*; openbare mening *v.*; *vt. & vi.* roepen, schreeuwen; uitroepen; omroepen; afroepen; schreien, huilen; blaffen, janken.

cryish ['kraiiʃ] huilerig, grienerig.

crypt [kript] crypt, krocht, ondergrondse gewelfde kapel *v.*

cryptogram ['kriptəgræm] stuk in geheimschrift *o.*

cryptography [krip'tɔgrəfi] geheimschrift *o.*

crystal ['kristəl] *sb.* kristal *o.*; *adj.* kristallen; kristalhelder.

cub [kəb] *sb.* jong, welp *o.*; (*fig.*) ongelikte beer, vlerk, vlegel *m.*; *vi.* 'jongen werpen.

cube [kjûb] *sb.* kubus *m.*; dobbelsteen, teerling *m.*; (*rek.*) derde macht *v.*, kubiekgetal *o.*; *vt.* tot de derde macht verheffen; de inhoud berekenen van.

cubic(**al**) ['kjûbik(l)] kubusvormig; kubiek; van de derde graad, derdemachts—.

cuckoo ['kukû] koekoek *m.*; (*fig.*) sul *m.*

cucumber ['kjûkəmbə] komkommer *v.*

cudgel ['kədʒəl] *sb.* knuppel, stok *m.*; *vt.* knuppelen, afrossen.

cue [kjû] *sb.* (*ton.*) wacht *v.*, wachtwoord *o.*; wenk *m.*, vingerwijzing, aanwijzing *v.*; (*bilj.*) keu *v.*; *vi.* (*bilj.*) stoten.

cuff [kəf] *sb.* slag, klap *m.*, oorveeg *v.*; (*v. mouw*) opslag *m.*; manchet *v.*; *vt.* slaan, klappen geven; *vi.* vechten.

cuirass [kwi'ræs] *sb.* kuras, (borst) harnas *o.*; *vt.* pantseren.

cuirassier [kwirə'stə] kurassier *m.*

cullender ['kəlində] vergiet(test) *v.*

culling ['kəliŋ] keur, keuze; bloemlezing *v.*; —**s**, uitschot *o.*

culm [kəlm] (*Pl.*) stengel, halm *m.*; steenkolenstof, kolengruis *o.*

culminate ['kəlmineit] culmineren, het toppunt bereiken.

culmination [kəlmi'neiʃən] culminatie *v.*, hoogste stand *m.*, hoogtepunt *o.*

culpable ['kəlpəbl] schuldig, misdadig.

culprit ['kəlprit] schuldige *m.*; beschuldigde *m.*

cult ['kəlt] eredienst *m.*; aanbidding; verering *v.*

cultivable ['kəltivəbl] bebouwbaar.

cultivate ['kəltiveit] bebouwen, bewerken; verbouwen, telen, kweken; beschaven.

cultivation [kəlti'veiʃən] bebouwing *v.*; verbouwing, cultuur, aankweking *v.*; aanplant *m.*; beschaving *v.*; beoefening *v.*

culture ['kəltʃə] *sb.* bebouwing *v.*; verbouw *m.*, teelt, aankweking *v.*; cultuur *v.*; beschaving; veredeling *v.*; *vt. zie* **cultivate.**

cumbersome ['kəmbəsəm] log, plomp, moeilijk te hanteren; lastig, hinderlijk.

cumulate ['kjûmjuleit] *vt.* ophopen; *adj.* opgehoopt.

cunning ['kəniŋ] *adj.* listig, sluw, geslepen; *sb.* listigheid, sluwheid, geslepenheid *v.*

cunningness ['kəniŋnis] *adv.* **cunning**!

cup [kəp] kop *m.*, kopje *o.*; beker, kroes *m.*; schaal, nap *v.*; kelk *m.*

cup-bearer ['kəpbêərə] schenker *m.*

cupboard ['kəbəd] kast *v.*; buffet *o.*

cupidity [kjû'piditi] hebzucht, begeerlijkheid *v.*

cupola ['kjûpələ] koepel *m.*, koepeldak *o.*; geschuttoren *m.*

cur [kə:] rekel *m.*; vlegel, ploert *m.*

curable ['kjûərəbl] geneeslijk.

curate ['kjûərit] (*kath.*) kapelaan *m.*; (*prot.*) (hulp)predikant *m.*

curative ['kjûərətiv] *adj.* genezend; geneeskrachtig; *sb.* geneesmiddel *o.*

curator [kju'reitə] curator, beheerder, conservator, custos *m.*

curb [kə:b] *sb.* kinketting *m.*; trottoirband *m.*; teugel, toom *m.*; omheining *v.*; (*v. paard*) spat *v.*; *vt.* een kinketting aandoen; beteugelen, in toom houden, bedwingen.

curdle [kə:dl] *vi.* klonteren, stremmen, stollen; *vt.* doen stremmen, doen stollen.

cure [kjûə] *sb.* kuur; geneeswijze *v.*; geneesmiddel *o.*; genezing *v.*; zielzorg *v.*; *vt.* genezen; verduurzamen (zouten, roken, enz.).

curfew ['kə:fjû] avondklok *v.*

curio ['kjûəriou] rariteit, curiositeit *v.*

curiosity [kjûəri'ɔsiti] nieuwsgierigheid, weetgierigheid *v.*; curiositeit *v.*

curious(**ly**) ['kjûəriəs(li)] *adj.* (*adv.*) nieuwsgierig, weetgierig; curieus, zeldzaam, raar; zonderling.

curl [kə:l] *sb.* krul *v.*, kronkel *m.*, kronkeling *v.*; *vt.* krullen, kronkelen.

curler [kə:lə] krulijzer *o.*

curl-paper ['kə:lpeipə] papillot *v.*

currant ['kərənt] krent *v.*; aalbes *v.*

currency ['kərənsi] loop *m.*; omloop *m.*, circulatie *v.*; gangbaarheid *v.*; gangbare munt *v.*, betaalmiddel *o.*; valuta *v.*, koers *m.*

current ['kərənt] *adj.* gangbaar; in omloop; *sb.* stroom *m.*; stroming *v.*; loop *m.*, richting *v.*; strekking *v.*; (*el.*) stroom *m.*

curriculum [kə'rikjuləm] programma, leerplan *o.*, cursus *m.*

curry ['kəri] (*v. leer*) bereiden, touwen; roskammen.

curry-comb ['kərikoum] roskam *m.*

curse [kə:s] *sb.* vloek *m.*; verwensing *v.*; *vt.* uitvloeken; vervloeken, verwensen; *vi.* vloeken.

curt [kə:t] *adj.* kort, beknopt, verkort; kortaf, bits, nors.

curtail [kə:'teil] korten, verkorten, inkorten; verminderen, beperken; besnoeien.

curtailment [kə:'teilmənt] verkorting, inkorting; enz.; *zie* **curtail**.

curtain ['kə:t(i)n] *sb.* overgordijn, schuifgordijn *v.* & *o.*; (*ton.*) scherm, doek *o.*; (*mil.*) courtine *v.*; *vt.* behangen met gordijnen.

curtly ['kə:tli] *adv. zie* **curt**.

curts(e)y ['kə:tsi] *sb.* (diepe) buiging *v.*; *vi.* een (diepe) buiging maken.

curvature ['kə:vətʃə] kromming, bocht *v.*

curve [kə:v] *sb.* kromming, bocht *v.*; kromme lijn *v.*; *vt.* buigen, ombuigen, krommen; *vi.* buigen, zich krommen; een bocht maken.

cushion ['kuʃən] *sb.* kussen *o.*; (*el.*) wrijfkussen *o.*; biljartband *m.*; *vt.* van kussens voorzien; steunen met kussens; (*bilj.*) bij de band brengen; in de doofpot stoppen, smoren.

cushion-tire ['kuʃəntaiə] massieve fietsband *m.*

custard ['kəstəd] vla *v.*

custodian [kəs'toudiən] bewaarder, conservator, custos *m.*

custody ['kəstədi] bewaking, bewaring, hoede *v.*; hechtenis *v.*

custom ['kəstəm] gewoonte *v.*, gebruik *o.*; klandizie, nering *v.*; —s, in- en uitgaande rechten; douane.

customable ['kəstəməbl] belastbaar; tolplichtig.

customary ['kəstəməri] gewoon, gebruikelijk.

customer ['kəstəmə] klant *m.*

custom-house ['kəstəmhaus] douanekantoor *o.*

cut [kə:t] *vt.* snijden; afsnijden, doorsnijden, opensnijden, stuksnijden, wegsnijden; afknippen; afbreken; (*v. motor*) afzetten; (*v. dijk*) doorsteken; kappen, afkappen, vellen; afschaffen; *vi.* snijden; zich laten snijden; (*v. paard*) aanslaan; *sb.* snede, knip *v.*; houw, hak *m.*; snit *m.*, fatsoen *o.*; maaksel *o.*; besnoeiing, bezuiniging *v.*; houtsnee, houtgravure *v.*; *adj.* gesneden; (*v. glas*) geslepen; (*v. bloemen*) los.

cutler ['kətlə] messenmaker *m.*

cutlet ['kətlit] kotelet, karbonade *r.*

cutter ['kətə] snijder; coupeur *m.*; mes *o.*; snijmachine *v.*; hakker *m.*; (*sch.*) kotter *m.*

cutting ['kətiŋ] *adj.* snijdend, scherp; bijtend; vinnig; *sb.* afsnijdsel *o.*; uitknipsel *o.*; (*Pl.*) afzetsel *o.*, stek *m.*; snee(wond) *v.*; doorgraving *v.*; (*v. stof*) coupon *v.*

cuttle(-fish) ['kətl(fiʃ)] inktvis *m.*

cycle ['saikl] *sb.* tijdkring, kringloop *m.*; cyclus *m.*; rijwiel *o.*, fiets *v.*; *vi.* (in een kring) ronddraaien; fietsen.

cyclist ['saiklist] wielrijder, fietser *m.*

cyclone ['saikloun] cycloon *m.* [rol *v.*

cylinder ['silində] cilinder *m.*; wals *v.*;

cylindric(al) [si'lindrik(l)] *adj.* cilindrisch, cilindervormig.

cymbal ['simbəl] cimbaal *r.*, bekken *o.*

cynical(ly) ['sinikəl(i)] *adj.* (*adv.*) cynisch.

Czecho-Slovakia ['tʃekouslou'veikiə] Tsjecho-Slowakije *o.*

D

dab [dæb] *sb.* tik *m.*, tikje *o.*; lichte klap *m.*; prik, steek *m.*; (*Dk.*) schar *v.*; *vt.* betten, bevochtigen; zacht bestrijken; strelen.

dachshund ['dækshund] (*Dk.*) taks *m.*

dactyl ['dæktil] dactylus *m.*

dactylology [dækti'lolədʒi] vingerspraak *v.* [dil *v.*

daffodil ['dæfədil] (*Pl.*) gele narcis, affodagger** ['dægə] dolk *m.*; kruisje, pijltje *o.* (†).

daily ['deili] *adj.* & *adv.* dagelijks; *sb.* dagblad *o.*; (*fam.*) dagmeisje *o.*

dainty ['deinti] *adj.* fijn, keurig; sierlijk; lekker; kieskeurig; *sb.* lekkernij *v.*

dairy ['dêəri] melkerij *v.*; melkwinkel *m.*, melkinrichting *v.*

dairy-fresh ['dêərifreʃ] roomboter *v.*

dairy-produce ['dêəriprodjûs] zuivelprodukten *o. mv.*

daisy ['deizi] *sb.* (*Pl.*) madeliefje *o.*; (*Am.*, *sl.*) snoes *m.*; iets puiks *o.*; *adj.* snoezig; puik.

dam [dæm] *sb.* dam, dijk *m.*; bovenwater, opgestuwd water *o.*; (*v. dier*) moer *v.*; *vt.* afdammen, indijken, afsluiten; stuiten.

damage ['dæmidʒ] schade *v.*, nadeel *o.*, averij *v.*; —s, schadevergoeding *v.*

damageable ['dæmidʒəbl] beschadigbaar.

damask ['dæməsk] *sb.* damast *o.*; damascering *v.*; damascusrood, lichtrood *o.*; *adj.* damasten; damascener, gedamasceerd; lichtrood; *vt.* damasceren; als damast weven; rood verven, rood kleuren.

damn [dæm] *v.* uitvloeken; vervloeken; verdoemen; veroordelen; *sb.* vloek *m.*; *adj.* & *adv.* vervloekt.

damnable ['dæmnəbl] *adv.* verdoemelijk.

damnation [dæm'neiʃən] verdoemenis *v.*

damp [dæmp] *sb.* vocht *o.*, vochtigheid *v.*; mijngas, stikgas *o.*; (*fig.*) neerslachtigheid *v.*; *adj.* vochtig, klam; *vt.* bevochtigen, vochtig maken; smoren, dempen; (*v. ijver, enz.*) doen bekoelen.

damper ['dæmpə] bevochtiger *m.*; (*muz.*) demper *m.*, sourdine *v.*; (*v. kachel*) sleutel *m.*

damsel ['dæmzəl] juffer; jongedame *v.*; (*dicht.*) jonkvrouw *v.*

damsel-fly ['dæmzəlflai] waterjuffer *v.*

damson ['dæmzn] kwets (*pruim*) *v.*

dance [dâns] *sb.* dans *m.*; danspartij *v.*, bal, dansavondje *o.*; *vt.* laten dansen; *vi.* dansen; (*v. ogen*) tintelen.

dancer ['dânsə] danser *m.*; danseres *v.*

dancing-room ['dânsiɳrum] danszaal *v.*

dandelion [dændi'laiən] (*Pl.*) paardebloem *v.*

dandle ['dændl] (*v. kind*) laten dansen (op de knie); liefkozen, vertroetelen.

dandriff ['dændrif] roos *v.* (op het hoofd).

dandruff ['dændrəf] *zie* **dandriff**.

dandy ['dændi] *sb.* fat, modegek *m.*; *adj.* fatterig; keurig.

danger ['dein(d)ʒə] gevaar *o.*

dangerous (ly) ['dien(d)ʒərəs(li)] *a lj.* (*adv.*) gevaarlijk.

dangle ['dæɳgl] *vi.* slingeren, bengelen; *rt.* laten bengelen.

dapple ['dæpl] *vt.* bespikkelen; *vi.* spikkels (vlekken) krijgen; *sb.* spikkel *m.*, vlek *v.*; *adj.* bespikkeld, gevlekt.

dare [dêə] *vt.* durven; tarten; *sb.* durf *m.*; uitdaging *v.*

dare-devil ['dêədevil] waaghals *m.*

daring ['dêəriɳ] *adj.* vermetel, koen, stout; *sb.* vermetelheid *v.*, durf *m.*

dark [dâk] *adj.* duister, donker; (*fig.*) somber, zwart; verborgen, geheimzinnig; onbekend; *sb.* donker *m.* & *o.*; duisternis *v.* (*v. schilderij*) donkere partij *v.*

darken ['dâkn] verdonkeren, verduisteren; vertroebelen.

darkness ['dâknis] donker *m.* & *o.*, duisternis.

darky ['dâki] (*fam.*) neger *m.*, zwartje *o.*; (*sl.*) dievenlantaarn *m.*

darling ['dâliɳ] *sb.* lieveling, lieverd; *adj.* geliefd, lief, geliefkoosd.

darn [dân] stoppen; mazen.

darning-needle ['dâniɳnîdl] stopnaald *v.*

dart [dât] *sb.* pijl, schicht *m.*; werpspies *v.*; angel *m.*; *vt.* schieten; werpen.

dash [dæʃ] *vt.* bespatten, besprenkelen; mengen, vermengen; smijten, gooien, smakken; *vi.* kletsen, spatten; snellen, vliegen, losstormen (*at*, op); *sb.* slag, stoot *m.*; klets, smak *m.*; botsing *v.*; bespatting, besprenkeling *v.*; tikje *o.*; scheutje *o.*

dash-board ['dæʃbo:d] spatbord *o.*; (*v. auto*) schutbord; instrumentenbord *o.*

dashing ['dæʃiɳ] kranig, flink; krachtig; haastig, onstuimig; zwierig.

dash-pot ['dæʃpɔt] slagdemper, knalpot *m.*

dashy ['dæʃi] *zie* **dashing**.

date [deit] *sb.* dadel(palm) *m.*; datum *m.*, dagtekening *v.*; jaartal, jaarcijfer *o.*; *vt.* dateren, dagtekenen.

dateless ['deitlis] ongedateerd; (*dicht.*) onheuglijk.

daub [do:b] *vt.* smeren; bekladden; kladschilderen; *sb.* pleisterkalk *v.*; pleisterwerk *o.*; smeer *o.*; kladschilderij *v.*

daughter ['do:tə] dochter *r.*

daunt [do:nt] afschrikken, ontmoedigen; (*v. haringen*) in 't vat persen.

dauntless (ly) ['do:ntlis(li)] *adj.* (*adv.*) onversaagd, onverschrokken.

daw [do:] (*Dk.*) kauw *v.*

dawdle ['do:dl] *vi.* beuzelen, treuzelen, leuteren, talmen; *vt.* — *away,* verbeuzelen; *sb.* gebeuzel, geleuter *o.*; treuzel *m.*

dawdler ['do:dlə] beuzelaar, treuzelaar *m.*

dawn [do:n] *sb.* dageraad *m.*; *vi.* licht worden; aanbreken, dagen, gloren.

day [dei] dag *m.*; daglicht *o.*

day-blush ['deibləʃ] (*dicht.*) dageraad *m.*

daylight ['deilait] daglicht *o.*

daze [deiz] *vt.* verblinden; verdoven, bedwelmen; verbijsteren; *sb.* verblinding *v.*; verdoving, bedwelming *v.*; verbijstering *v.*

dazzle ['dæzl] *vt.* verblinden, verbijsteren *sb.* verblinding *v.*; verbijstering *v.*

deacon ['dîkən] diaken *m.*

dead [ded] *adj.* dood; levenloos, onbezield; doods; doodlijk; gestorven, afgestorven; dor, verdord; *adv.* dood; totaal, volkomen; door en door; vlak; plotseling; *sb.* (het) dode *o.*; stilte, rust *v.*

dead-colouring ['dedkələriɳ] grondverven.

deaden ['dedn] verzwakken, doen verflauwen; dempen, temperen; afstompen, verstompen; mat maken.

dead-house ['dedhaus] lijkenhuis *o.*

deaf [def] doof; (*v. noot*) loos.

deafen ['defn] doof maken; verdoven, dempen.

deaf-mute ['def'mjût] doofstom.

deal [dîl] *sb.* hoeveelheid *v.*; transactie *v.*, koop *m.*; (*kaartsp.*) (het) geven *v.*

deal [dîl] *vt.* uitdelen; ronddelen; bedelen; *(v. slagen)* toebrengen; *(v. kaarten)* geven; *vi.* uitdelen; *(kaartsp.)* geven; *(H.)* handelen.

dealer ['dîlə] uitdeler *m.*; *(kaartsp.)* gever *m.*; *(H.)* koopman, handelaar *m.*

dean [dîn] deken *m.*

deanery ['dînəri] dekenaat *o.*; dekenij *v.*

dear [dîə] *adj.* lief, dierbaar, geliefd; waard; duur, kostbaar; *adv.* duur; *sb.* lieve, liefste, lieveling; schat.

dearness ['dîənis] dierbaarheid *v.*; duurte; kostbaarheid *v.*

dearth [də:δ] schaarsheid, schaarste *v.*; gebrek *o.*; duurte *v.*

death [deδ] dood *m.*; sterfgeval *o.*

death-blow ['deδblou] dodelijke slag, genadeslag *m.*

deathless ['deδli] onsterfelijk.

debase [di'beis] verlagen, vernederen; *(v. munt)* vervalsen.

debasement [di'beismənt] verlaging, vernedering *v.*; vervalsing *v.*

debate [di'beit] *sb.* debat *o.* beraadslaging *v.*; woordenstrijd *m.*; *vt.* bespreken, beredeneren; betwisten; *vi.* debatteren, beraadslagen; overleggen.

debauchery [di'bo:tʃəri] losbandigheid *v.*; uitspatting(en) *v.* *(mv.)*.

debenture [di'bentʃə] *(H.)* verklaring *v.* van uitvoer; schuldbrief *m.*; obligatie *v.*

debilitate [di'biliteit] verzwakken.

debit ['debit] *sb.* debet *o.*; debetpost *m.*; debetzijde *v.*; *vt.* debiteren.

debouch [di'bûʃ] uitkomen *(into,* op), uitlopen *(into,* in; *on,* op); uitmonden *(into,* in).

debt [det] schuld *v.*

debtor ['detə] schuldenaar, debiteur *m.*

decad(e) ['dekəd] tiental *o.* (dagen, jaren); *(v. rozenkrans)* tientje *o.*

decalitre ['dekəlîtə] decaliter *m.*

decametre ['dekəmîtə] decameter *m.*

decanter [di'kæntə] (wijn)karaf *v.*

decapitation [dikæpi'teiʃən] onthoofding *v.*

decay [di'kei] *vi.* afnemen, achteruitgaan; vervallen, in verval geraken; bederven, rotten; *(v. zijde, enz.)* verstikken; *sb.* achteruitgang *m.*; verval *o.*; bederf *o.*, verrotting *v.*

decease [di'sîs] *vi.* overlijden, sterven; *sb.* (het) overlijden *o.*

deceased [di'sîst] overledene *m. & v.*

deceit [di'sît] bedrog *o.*, bedrieglijkheid, bedriegerij; list *v.*; misleiding *v.*

deceitful(ly) [di'sîtful(i)] *adj.* *(adv.)* bedrieglijk; misleidend.

deceive [di'sîv] bedriegen; misleiden.

deceiver [di'sîvə] bedrieger *m.*

December [di'sembə] december *o.*

decency ['dîsənsi] welvoeglijkheid *v.*, fatsoen *o.*

decent(ly) ['dîsənt(li)] *adj.* *(adv.)* welvoeglijk, betamelijk, fatsoenlijk.

decide [di'said] *vt.* beslissen, bepalen; besluiten; doen besluiten, overhalen; *vi.* besluiten, een besluit (beslissing) nemen; *(recht)* uitspraak doen.

decided [di'saidid] *adj.* beslist, bepaald; vastbesloten.

decimal ['desiməl] tientallig; tiendelig.

decimate ['desimeit] decimeren.

decimetre ['desimîtə] decimeter *m.*

decipher [di'saifə] *(v. brief, enz.)* ontcijferen; ontwarren, ontraadselen.

decision [di'siʒən] beslissing *v.*, besluit *o.*, uitslag *m.*; beslistheid *v.*

decisive(ly) [di'saisiv(li)] *adj.* *(adv.)* beslissend, afdoend; beslist.

deck [dek] *(sch.)* dek *o.*; *(v. tram, enz.)* dak *o.*; *(Am.)* spel *o.* kaarten.

declaim [di'kleim] voordragen, declameren.

declaration [deklə'reiʃən] declaratie, verklaring *v.*; *(v. verkiezingsuitslag)* bekendmaking *v.*; *(v. dividend)* vaststelling *v.*; *(voor belasting)* aangifte *v.*

declare [di'klêə] verklaren; bekendmaken; vaststellen; *(bij douane)* aangeven, declareren; *(kaartsp.)* melden.

declension [di'klenʃən] afwijking; declinatie *v.*; achteruitgang *m.*, verval *o.*; helling *v.*; *(gram.)* verbuiging *v.*

declinable [di'klainəbl] verbuigbaar.

decline [di'klain] *vi.* hellen, aflopen; buigen, neigen; achteruitgaan; vervallen; afdalen *(to,* tot), zich verlagen; *vt.* verbuigen; weigeren, afslaan, van de hand wijzen, bedanken voor; *sb.* achteruitgang *m.*; verval *o.* (van krachten); (zons) ondergang *m.*; *(H.)* prijsdaling; prijsverlaging *v.*

decoction [di'kokʃən] afkooksel *o.*

decode [di'koud] ontcijferen.

decollate [di'koleit] onthalzen, onthoofden.

decolour(ize) [di'kələ(raiz)] ontkleuren.

decompose [dîkəm'pouz] *vt.* ontbinden, ontleden, oplossen; *vi.* zich oplossen; tot ontbinding overgaan.

decomposition [dîkəmpə'ziʃən] ontleding, oplossing *v.*; ontbinding *v.*, bederf *o.*

decorate ['dekəreit] versieren; decoreren; *(v. kamer)* schilderen, behangen.

decoration [dekə'reiʃən] versiering *v.*; versiersel *o.*; decoratie *v.*, ereteken *o.*

decoy [di'koi] verlokken.

decrease [di'krîs] *vt. & vi.* (doen) verminderen; *sb.* vermindering *v.*

decree [di'krî] decreet, besluit *o.*

decrepit [di'krepit] afgeleefd.

decuple [dekjupl] tienvoudig.

dedicate ['dedikeit] toewijden.

dedication [dedi'keiʃən] toewijding, opdracht *v.*

deduce [di'djûs] afleiden; ontlenen.

deduct [di'dəkt] aftrekken.

deduction [di'dəkʃən] aftrek *m.*

deed [dîd] daad; handeling *v.*

deem [dîm] oordelen, achten.

deep [dîp] diep; diepliggend; diepzinnig; snood, laag; machtig, sterk; *(v. kleur)* donker.

deep-laid ['dîp'leid] listig uitgedacht.

deer [diə] (wild) hert *o*.
deface [di'feis] beschadigen, schenden; (*v. muren, enz.*) beschrijven, bekrassen; doorhalen, uitwissen.
defalcate [di'fælkeit] *vt.* (*v. geld*) verduisteren *vi.* verduistering plegen.
defame [di'feim] (be)lasteren, smaden.
default [di'fo:lt] *sb.* gebrek *o.*, fout, feil *v.*; verzuim *o.*; (*mil.*) vergrijp *o.*; (*recht*) verstek *o.*; *vi.* falen; in gebreke blijven; (*recht*) niet verschijnen; *vt.* bij verstek veroordelen.
defeat [di'fit] *sb.* nederlaag *v.*; vernietiging *v.*; (*v. plan*) verijdeling *v.*; (*v. motie*) verwerping *v.*, *vt.* verslaan; vernietigen, nietig verklaren; verijdelen; verwerpen.
defect [di'fekt] fout *v.*, gebrek *o.*; tekort *o.*
defective [di'fektiv] gebrekkig, onvolkomen; ontbrekend; zwakzinnig; (*gram.*) defectief.
defence [di'fens] verdediging *v.*, verweer *o.*; verdedigingsrede *v.*, verweerschrift *o.*; **—s,** (*mil.*) verdedigingswerken.
defenceless (**ly**) [di'fenslis(li)] *adj.* (*adv.*) weerloos, zonder verdediging.
defend [di'fend] verdedigen; beschermen (*from,* tegen); bewaren (*from,* voor).
defendant [di'fendənt] *sb.* gedaagde, verweerder *m.*; *adj.* gedaagd.
defender [di'fendə] verdediger *m.*
defensible [di'fensibl] verdedigbaar.
defer [di'fə:] uitstellen, overdragen.
deference ['defərəns] eerbied *m.*, eerbiediging, achting *v.*
defiance [di'faiəns] uitdaging, tarting *v.*
deficiency [di'fiʃənsi] gebrek *o.*, onvolkomenheid *v.*; defect *o.*; ontoereikendheid *v.*; tekort *o.*
deficit ['defisit, 'difisit] deficit, tekort *o.*
defile [di'fail] bergkloof, bergengte *v.*, enge pas *m.*; (*mil.*) défilé *o.*
defile [di'fail] *vt.* besmetten, bezoedelen; ontwijden; onteren, schenden.
define [di'fain] begrenzen, afbakenen; bepalen, omschrijven, definiëren.
definite ['definit] *adj.* begrensd; bepaald, duidelijk omschreven.
definition [defi'niʃən] bepaling, omschrijving *v.*; (*v. kijker*) scherpte *v.*
definitive (**ly**) [di'finitiv(li)] *adj.* (*adv.*) beslissend; definitief.
deflate [di'fleit] (*v. fietsband, enz.*) lucht uitlaten; deflatie veroorzaken; (*fig.*) verminderen.
deflect [di'flekt] (doen) afwijken; buigen; afleiden.
deform [di'fo:m] misvormen.
defraud [di'fro:d] bedriegen.
defray [di'frei] betalen; bekostigen, de kosten bestrijden van.
defunct [di'fəŋkt] *adj.* overleden; *sb.* overledene *m. & v.*
defy [di'fai] trotseren, tarten; uitdagen.
degenerate [di'dʒenəreit] *vi.* ontaarden, verbasteren.

degeneration [didʒenə'reiʃən] ontaarding, verbastering *v.*
degradation [degrə'deiʃən] verlaging *v.*; vermindering; vernedering *v.*; ontaarding *v.*
degrade [di'greid] verlagen; verminderen; doen ontaarden.
degree [di'gri] graad, trap *m.*; rang, stand *m.*
degree-day [di'gridei] promotiedag *m.*
degust [di'gəst] (met aandacht) proeven.
deify ['di:ifai] vergoden, vergoddelijken.
deign [dein] zich verwaardigen.
deject [di'dʒekt] ontmoedigen, neerslachtig maken.
dejected (**ly**) [di'dʒektid(li)] *adj.* (*adv.*) ontmoedigd, neerslachtig, terneergeslagen, bedrukt.
delate [di'leit] aanbrengen, aangeven; aanklagen.
delay [di'lei] *vt.* uitstellen; vertragen; *vi.* talmen, dralen; op zich laten wachten; *sb.* uitstel *o.*; oponthoud *o.*, vertraging *v.*; (het) talmen *o.*
delectable [di'lektəbl] heerlijk, verrukkelijk, genotvol.
delegate ['deligit] gedelegeerde, afgevaardigde *m.*
delegate ['deligeit] delegeren, afvaardigen.
Delf (**t**) [delf(t)] — (*ware*), Delfts aarde werk *o.*
deliberate [di'libəreit] *vt.* overwegen; *vi.* overleggen; beraadslagen.
deliberately [di'libəritli] *adv.* weloverwogen, na rijp beraad, willens en wetens; bedaard, bezadigd.
deliberation [dilibə'reiʃən] overweging *v.*; beraadslaging *v.*; bedaardheid, bedachtzaamheid *v.*
delicacy ['delikəsi] fijnheid, keurigheid *v.*; teerheid, zwakheid *v.*; kiesheid; fijngevoeligheid *v.*
delicate (**ly**) ['delikit(li)] *adj.* (*adv.*) fijn, keurig, uitgezocht; teer, zwak; kies; fijngevoelig.
delicious (**ly**) [di'liʃəs(li)] *adj.* (*adv.*) lekker, heerlijk, aangenaam.
delight [di'lait] *sb.* genoegen, genot *o.*, verrukking *v.*; *vt.* verheugen; verrukken; strelen; *vi.* behagen scheppen; genot vinden (*in,* in).
delightful (**ly**) [di'laitful(i)] *adj.* (*adv.*) heerlijk, verrukkelijk, genotvol.
delimit [di'limit] afbakenen, de grenzen vaststellen van.
delineate [di'linieit] tekenen, schetsen.
delineation [dilini'eiʃən] tekening, schets *v.*
delinquent [di'liŋkwənt] overtreder *m.*
deliquesce [deli'kwes] vloeibaar worden, smelten.
delirious (**ly**) [di'liriəs(li)] *adj.* (*adv.*) ijlend, ijlhoofdig; dol, razend.
deliver [di'livə] bevrijden, verlossen; geven, overhandigen, ter hand stellen; overbrengen; afleveren; (*v. brieven*) bestellen; (*v. dagbladen, enz.*) bezorgen

deliverance [di'livərəns] bevrijding, verlossing v.; uitlating v.; uitspraak v., vonnis o.

deliverer [di'livərə] bevrijder, verlosser m.; bezorger m.

delivery [di'livəri] bevrijding v.; verlossing, bevalling v.; levering, aflevering v.; bestelling, bezorging v.; overhandiging v.

delude [di'l(j)ûd] misleiden, bedriegen, begoochelen.

deluge ['deljûdʒ] zondvloed m.

delusion [di'l(j)ûʒən] misleiding v., bedrog; zelfbedrog o., waan m., begoocheling v.

demand [di'mând] vt. eisen, vorderen; vragen, verlangen; sb. eis m., vordering v.; vraag v., verlangen o.

demarcate ['dîmâkeit] afbakenen, afpalen, de grenzen vaststellen van.

demean [di'mîn] vt. verlagen, vernederen; vr. — oneself, zich verlagen, zich vernederen; zich gedragen.

dement [di'ment] razend maken, krankzinnig maken.

demented [di'mentid] krankzinnig, razend.

demerit [dî'merit] fout v., gebrek o., tekortkoming v.

demilitarization [dîmilitərai'zeiʃən] demilitarisering v.

demise [di'maiz] overdracht v.; vermaking v. (bij testament); overlijden o.

demission [di'miʃən] ontslag o.; afstand m.

demit [di'mit] vt. (v. ambt) neerleggen; ontslaan; vi. zijn ambt neerleggen, aftreden, zijn ontslag nemen.

demobilization [dîmoubilai'zeiʃən] demobilisatie v.

democracy [di'mɔkrəsi] democratie v.

demolish [di'mɔliʃ] afbreken, slopen; (fig.) omverwerpen, vernietigen.

demolition [demə'liʃən] sloping, afbraak v.; vernietiging v.

demon ['dîmən] geest, genius m.; boze geest, duivel m.

demonetize [di'mɔnitaiz] buiten koers stellen, ontmunten.

demonic (ally) [di'mɔnik(əli)] adj. (adv.) demonisch.

demonstrable ['demənstrəbl] bewijsbaar.

demonstrate ['demənstreit] aantonen, bewijzen, demonstreren; aan de dag leggen; (v. gevoelens) uiten.

demonstration [demən'streiʃən] betoog o.; betoging, manifestatie v.

demur [di'mə:] aarzelen, weifelen; bezwaar maken, protesteren; (recht) excepties opwerpen.

demure (ly) [di'mjûə(li)] adj. (adv.) stemmig, bezadigd; zedig, preuts.

demurrage [di'mɔridʒ] (H.) (het) overliggen o.; overliggeld o.

den [den] hol o., kuil m.; hok o.

dengue ['dengi] (gen.) knokkelkoorts v.

deniable [di'naiəbl] loochenbaar.

denial [di'naiəl] ontkenning, loochening v.; verloochening v.; weigering v.

denigrate ['denigreit] bekladden, zwart maken; beschimpen.

denominate [di'nɔmineit] noemen, benoemen.

denomination [dinɔmi'neiʃən] benoeming, benaming v.; bedrag o.; (v. effecten) coupure v.; sekte v.

denote [di'nout] aanduiden, aanwijzen, duiden op, te kennen geven.

denounce [di'nauns] aanbrengen, aangeven, aanklagen; aankondigen, aanzeggen; wraken; aan de kaak stellen; (v. verdrag, enz.) opzeggen.

densely ['densli] adv. dicht.

dent [dent] sb. deuk v., indruk m.; vt. indeuken.

dentate (d) ['denteit(id)] (Pl., Dk.) getand.

dentifrice ['dentifris] tandpoeder o., tandpasta v.

dentist ['dentist] tandarts m.

denude [di'njûd] ontbloten, blootleggen; (v. streek) ontbossen; (v. huis) leeghalen; (v. recht, enz.) ontnemen, beroven van.

deny [di'nai] vt. ontkennen, loochenen; verloochenen; ontzeggen; onthouden; weigeren.

deodorize [dî'oudəraiz] ontsmetten; reukeloos maken.

depart [di'pât] weggaan, heengaan, vertrekken.

department [di'pâtmənt] departement o., afdeling v., werkkring m.

departure [di'pâtʃə] vertrek o.; heengaan o.; afwijking v.

depend [di'pend] hangen, neerhangen; afhangen (on, van); rekenen, vertrouwen, steunen, zich verlaten (upon, op); (v. proces, enz.) hangende zijn.

dependence [di'pendəns] afhankelijkheid v.; verband o., samenhang m.; toevlucht m.; vertrouwen o.

dependent [di'pendənt] afhangend (from, van); afhankelijk (on, upon, van); ondergeschikt.

depict [di'pikt] malen, (af)schilderen, voorstellen.

deplore [di'plo:] betreuren, bewenen bejammeren.

deploy [di'plɔi] (mil.) zich ontplooien, zich verspreiden, deployeren.

depopulate [dî'pɔpjuleit] ontvolken.

depose [di'pouz] vt. afzetten; getuigen, onder ede verklaren; vi. getuigen.

deposit [di'pɔzit] sb. deposito, gedeponeerd geld o.; bewaargeving v.; waarborgsom v.; statiegeld o.; neerslag m.; afzetting v., afzetsel o.; bezinksel o.; vt. neerleggen, plaatsen; deponeren, storten; in bewaring geven; in pand geven; afzetten, doen bezinken.

deposition [de—, dîpə'ziʃən] bewaargeving v., deposito o.; afzetting v.; bezinking v.; Kruisafneming v.; getuigenis v. & o.

depository [di'pɔzitəri] bewaarplaats *v.*; magazijn *o.*; bewaarder *m.*; (*fig.*) schatkamer *r.*

depot ['depou, 'dlpou] *sb.* depot *o.*; remise *v.*; goederenstation *o.*; (*Am.*) station *o.*; *vt.* opslaan.

deprave [di'preiv] bederven, verderven, doen ontaarden.

depravity [di'præviti] bederf *o.*, verdorvenheid, ontaarding *r.*

depreciate [di'prīſieit] doen dalen in waarde, depreciëren; kleineren, neerhalen; onderschatten.

depression [di'preſən] drukking, neerdrukking *v.*; neerlating *v.*; verlaging *v.*; indrukking *v.*; inzinking *r.* (*in zaken*) slapte, malaise *v.*; neerslachtigheid *r.*

deprivation [depri'veiſən] beroving *v.*; verlies *o.*; afzetting, ontzetting *v.* (*uit ambt*).

deprive [di'praiv] beroven; afzetten, ontzetten (uit ambt).

depth [depδ] diepte *v.*; hoogte *v.*; diepzinnigheid, scherpzinnigheid *v.*

depurative ['depjurətiv] bloedzuiverend.

depute [di'pjût] afvaardigen; overdragen.

deputy ['depjuti] afgevaardigde *m.*; gevolmachtigde *m.* plaatsvervanger *m.*

derail [di'reil] doen ontsporen, doen derailleren; **be —ed,** derailleren.

derange [di'rein(d)ʒ] storen, in de war sturen, verwarren; (*r. geest, verstand*) krenken.

derelict ['derilikt] *adj.* verlaten, onbeheerd; verwaarloosd, vervallen; (*Am.*) plichtvergeten; *sb.* verlaten schip, wrak *o.*; onbeheerd goed *o.*; zwerveling *m.*

deride [di'raid] uitlachen, bespotten, bespottelijk maken.

derision [di'riʒən] spot *m.*, bespotting *v.*

derisive [di'raisiv] *adj.* spottend, honend.

derivable [di'raivəbl] afleidbaar, af te leiden.

derivation [deri'veiſən] afleiding *v.*; afstamming *v.*; (*mil.: v. projectiel*) afwijking *v.*

derive [di'raiv] *vt.* afleiden (*from,* van, uit); ontlenen (*from,* aan); verkrijgen van, trekken uit; *vi.* afstammen, voortkomen, voortspruiten (*from,* van, uit).

derogate ['derəgeit] benadelen, te kort doen aan; afbreuk doen (*from,* aan); verkleinen.

derogation [derə'geiſən] afbreuk *v.*; verkleining *v.*; schade *v.*; verlaging *v.*; ontaarding *v.*

derrick ['derik] (*sch.*) kraan *v.*, laadboom *m.*; boortoren *m.*

descend [di'send] neerdalen, afdalen; neerstromen; naar beneden vallen, neervallen; afhellen; afstammen; overgaan (*to, on,* op); zich verlagen (*to,* tot, te).

descendant, descendent [di'sendənt] *adj.* afstammend; *sb.* afstammeling *m.*

descent [di'sent] afdaling, nederdaling *v.*; helling; afhelling *r.*; verval *o.*; afkomst, afstamming *r.*

describe [dis'kraib] beschrijven.

description [dis'kripſən] beschrijving *v.*; signalement *o.*

descry [dis'krai] ontdekken, bespeuren, gewaarworden.

desecrate ['desikreit] ontheiligen, ontwijden.

desecration [desi'kreiſən] ontheiliging, ontwijding *v.*

desert ['dezət] woestijn *v.*

desert [di'zə:t] deserteren.

desert [di'zə:t] *sb.* verdienste *v.*; verdiende loon *o.*

deserter [di'zə:tə] deserteur *m.*; afvallige *m.*

desertion [di'zə:ſən] (*mil.*) desertie *r.*

deserve [di'zə:v] verdienen.

deservingly [di'zə:viŋli] *adv.* verdienstelijk.

desiccate ['desikeit] *vt.* drogen; *vi.* droog worden, opdrogen, uitdrogen.

desiderate [di'zidəreit] verlangen.

design [di'zain] *vt.* aanwijzen, bestemmen; bedoelen, beogen; tekenen, schetsen, ontwerpen; *sb.* doel, plan, oogmerk *o.*, bedoeling *v.*; tekening *v.*, ontwerp *o.*; opzet *o.*

designate ['dezigneit] aanduiden, aanwijzen; noemen; bestemmen.

designer [di'zainə] ontwerper *m.*; ontwerp-tekenaar *m.*; intrigant *m.*

desirable [di'zaiərəbl] *adj.* wenselijk, begeerlijk.

desire [di'zaiə] *vt.* verlangen, begeren, wensen; verzoeken; *sb.* verlangen *o.*, begeerte *v.*, wens *m.*; verzoek *o.*

desirous [di'zaiərəs] begerig, verlangend (*of,* naar).

desk [desk] lessenaar *m.*; lezenaar *m.*

desolate ['desolit] *adj.* verlaten, eenzaam; woest; troosteloos.

despair [dis'pêə] *sb.* wanhoop, vertwijfeling *v.*; *vi.* wanhopen (*of,* aan), vertwijfelen.

despairing(ly) [dis'pêəriŋ(li)] *adj.* (*adv.*) wanhopig.

despatch [dis'pætſ] *zie* **dispatch.**

desperate ['despərit] *adj.* wanhopig, hopeloos, vertwijfeld.

desperation [despə'reiſən] wanhoop *r.*

despicable ['despikəbl] *adj.* verachtelijk.

despise [dis'paiz] verachten, versmaden.

despite [dis'pait] spijtigheid *r.*; (*in*) — *of,* ondanks, trots, in weerwil van.

despoil [dis'pɔil] beroven; plunderen.

despond [dis'pɔnd] moedeloos worden, wanhopen.

despot ['despɔt] despoot, dwingeland *m.*

despotic(al) [des'pɔtik(l)] *adj.* despotisch.

dessert [di'zə:t] nagerecht, dessert *o.*

destination [desti'neiſən] (plaats van) bestemming *v.*

destine ['destin] bestemmen.
destiny ['destini] bestemming *v.*, lot, noodlot *o.*
destitute ['destitjût] ontbloot, verstoken (**of,** van); behoeftig, hulpbehoevend.
destroy [dis'trɔi] vernietigen, vernielen; verwoesten; verdelgen, uitroeien; afmaken.
destroyer [dis'trɔiə] vernietiger, vernieler; verwoester *m.*; verdelger *m.*; torpedojager *m.*
destruction [dis'trɒkʃən] vernietiging, vernieling; verwoesting *v.*; verdelging *v.*; ondergang *m.*
detach [di'tætʃ] scheiden, losmaken; uitzenden; (*mil.*) detacheren.
detachment [di'tætʃmənt] scheiding, losmaking *v.*; detachement *o.*
detail ['diteil] *sb.* bijzonderheid *v.*; bijzaak *v.*; kleinigheid *v.*; opsomming *v.*; omstandig verhaal *o.*
detailed [di'teild] omstandig, uitvoerig.
detain [di'tein] achterhouden; afhouden; ophouden; vasthouden.
detect [di'tekt] bespeuren, ontdekken; betrappen (**in,** op); opsporen.
detective [di'tektiv] detective *m.*
detention [di'tenʃən] achterhouding *v.*; oponthoud *o.*; aanhouding, gevangenzetting *v.*
deter [di'tə:] afschrikken, afhouden.
deteriorate [di'tiəriəreit] *vt.* slechter maken; doen ontaarden; *vi.* ontaarden.
deterioration [ditiəriə'reiʃən] verslechting *v.*; bederf *o.*; ontaarding.
determinable [di'tə:minəbl] bepaalbaar.
determinate (**ly**) [di'tə:minit(li)] *adj.* (*adv.*) bepaald, vast, beslist, afdoend.
determination [ditə:mi'neiʃən] bepaling; vaststelling *v.*; beslissing *v.*, besluit *o.*; beslistheid, vastberadenheid *v.*; richting *v.*, koers *m.*; aandrang *m.*; einde *o.*, afloop *m.*
determine [di'tə:min] bepalen, vaststellen; beperken; beslissen, besluiten; doen besluiten; eindigen, beëindigen.
determined (**ly**) [di'tə:mind(li)] *adj.* (*adv.*) vastberaden, vastbesloten.
deterrent [di'terənt] *adj.* afschrikkend.
detest [di'test] verfoeien, verafschuwen.
detestable [di'testəbl] *adj.* verfoeilijk, afschuwelijk.
dethrone [di'δroun] onttronen.
detonate ['ditouneit, 'detouneit] (doen) ontploffen.
detonation [di—, detou'neiʃən] ontploffing *v.*; knal *m.*
detour [di'tûə] omweg *m.*
detract [di'trækt] afnemen.
detrain [di'trein] *vt.* (*v. troepen*) uitladen; *vi.* (*mil.*) uitstappen.
detriment ['detrimənt] nadeel *o.*, schade *v.*
detrimental [detri'mentəl] nadelig, schadelijk; (*sl.*) ongewenst.
detrition [di'triʃən] afslijting *v.*

deuce [djûs] (*op kaart, dobbelsteen*) twee; (*sp.: tennis*) 40 gelijk; duivel, drommel *m.*
devastation [devəs'teiʃən] verwoesting *v.*
develop [di'veləp] ontwikkelen, ontvouwen; uitbreiden; ontginnen.
development [di'veləpmənt] ontwikkeling, ontvouwing *v.*; bebouwing *v.*; verloop *o.*
deviate ['divieit] afwijken; afdwalen.
device [di'vais] plan, oogmerk *o.*; uitvinding *v.*; devies, motto *o.*, zinspreuk *v.*
devil ['devl] duivel *m.*; drukkersjongen, loopjongen *m.*; duivelstoejager *m.*; (*tn.*) wolf *m.*
devilish ['devliʃ] duivels, verduiveld.
devilment ['devlmənt] duivelarij *v.*; dolheid *v.*, dolle streken *m. mv.*
devious ['diviəs] *adj.* kronkelend; afwijkend; afdwalend; afgelegen; omslachtig, wijdlopig.
devise [di'vaiz] bedenken, verzinnen, beramen; vermaken, legateren.
deviser [di'vaizə] verzinner, beramer *m.*
devoid [di'vɔid] ontbloot; — **of,** beroofd van.
devolute ['divəl(j)ût] overdragen.
devolve [di'vɒlv] — (**up**)**on,** neerkomen op; overgaan op; toevallen aan.
devote [di'vout] (toe)wijden; bestemmen voor; overgeven, overleveren (**to,** aan).
devoted [di'voutid] *adj.* (toe)gewijd; verknocht, (aan elkaar) gehecht; gedoemd, gevloekt.
devotion [di'vouʃən] toewijding *v.*; gehechtheid, verknochtheid *v.*; vroomheid, godsvrucht *v.*
devour [di'vauə] verslinden; (*fig.*) verteren.
devout (**ly**) [di'vaut(li)] *adj.* (*adv.*) vroom, godvruchtig, godsdienstig; innig, oprecht.
devoutness [di'vautnis] vroomheid, godvruchtigheid *v.*; innigheid, oprechtheid *v.*
dew [djû] dauw *m.*
dewlap ['djûlæp] halskwabbe *v.*
dexterous ['dekstərəs] *adj.* handig, behendig; (*v. persoon*) rechts.
diabetes [daiə'bîtiz] suikerziekte *v.*
diabolic (**al**) [daiə'bɒlik(l)] *adj.* duivels.
diadem ['daiədəm] diadeem *m.*
diaeresis [dai'iərəsis] deelteken, trema *o.*
diagram ['daiəgræm] diagram *o.*, schets, tekening, schematische voorstelling *v.*
dial ['daiəl] zonnewijzer *m.*; wijzerplaat *v.*; (*v. telefoon, enz.*) schijf *v.*
dialect ['daiəlekt] dialect *o.*, tongval *m.*.
dialogue ['daiəlɔg] dialoog *m.*, samenspraak *v.*
diameter ['dai'æmitə] middellijn *v.*, diameter *m.*
diamond ['daiəmənd] *sb.* diamant *o.* & *m.*; diamantletter *v.*; ruit *v.*; (*kaartsp*) ruiten *v. mv.*; *adj.* diamanten; ruitvormig.

diamond-cutting ['daiəməndkətiŋ] diamantslijpen o.
diaphragm ['daiəfræm] middenrif o.; tussenschot o.; (v. lens) diafragma o.
diarrhœa [daiə'riə] diarree v., buikloop m.
diary ['dæiəri] dagboek o.
dibble ['dibl] sb. pootstok m., pootijzer o.; vt. met een pootijzer planten.
dice [dais] sb. dobbelstenen m. mv.; dobbelspel o.; vi. dobbelen.
dictate ['dikteit] inspraak v.
dictate [dik'teit] vt. dicteren, vóórzeggen; ingeven; voorschrijven, gebieden.
diction ['dikʃən] voordracht, dictie, wijze van zeggen v.
dictionary ['dikʃənəri] woordenboek o.
diddle ['didl] vi. waggelen, wankelen; vt. (sl.) bedotten; afzetten.
die [dai] dobbelsteen, teerling m.
die [dai] sterven; doodgaan; uitsterven; wegsterven, verflauwen; overgaan, bedaren.
die-away ['daiəwei] kwijnend; smachtend.
diet ['daiət] leefregel m., dieet o.; voedsel o., spijs v.; rijksdag m.
differ ['difə] verschillen.
difference ['difrəns] sb. verschil, onderscheid o.; (H.) koersverschil, prijsverschil o.; geschil(punt) o., onenigheid v.; vt. onderscheiden.
different ['difrənt] adj. verschillend.
difficult ['difikəlt] moeilijk, lastig.
difficulty ['difikəlti] moeilijkheid v., bezwaar o., zwarigheid v.
diffidence [difidəns] gebrek o. aan zelfvertrouwen, bedeesdheid, schroomvalligheid v.
diffident(ly) ['difidənt(li)] adj. (adv.) bedeesd, beschroomd, schroomvallig.
diffuse [di'fjûs] adj. verspreid, verstrooid; omslachtig, wijdlopig; [di'fjûz] vt. verspreiden; uitspreiden, uitgieten; diffunderen.
diffusedly [di'fjûzidli] adv. verspreid.
dig [dig] vt. graven, delven; omspitten; uitgraven; opgraven; (v.; aardappelen) rooien; vi. spitten; blokken; sb. por, stoot, stomp, duw m.; (fig.) steek m.; (sl.) blokker m.
digest [di'dʒest, dai'dʒest] verteren; verduwen; slikken, verkroppen; verwerken; in zich opnemen; rangschikken.
digestible [di'dʒestibl] (licht) verteerbaar.
digestion [di'dʒestʃən] spijsvertering v.; verwerking v.
digger ['digə] (goud)graver, delver m.
dignified ['dignifaid] waardig, vol waardigheid, deftig.
dignitary ['dignitəri] dignitaris, (kerkelijk) waardigheidsbekleder m.
dignity ['digniti] waardigheid v.
digress [dai'gres] afdwalen; uitweiden.
dike [daik] sb. sloot, gracht v.; dijk, dam m.; kloof v.; vt. indijken; met een sloot (gracht) omgeven.

dilapidated [di'læpideitid] vervallen, bouwvallig; verwaarloosd.
dilapidation [dilæpi'deiʃən] verval o., bouwvalligheid v.; verwaarlozing v.
dilatable [dai'leitəbl] uitzetbaar.
dilatation [dailei'teiʃən] uitzetting, verwijding v.; uitweiding v.
dilate [dai—, di'leit] uitbreiden; doen uitzetten.
diligence ['dilidʒəns] ijver m., naarstigheid, vlijt v.
diligent(ly) ['dilidʒənt(li)] adj. (adv.) ijverig, naarstig, vlijtig.
dilute [dai—, di'l(j)ût] vt. verdunnen; verflauwen; vervalsen; adj. [ook: 'dailjût] verdund; flauw.
dim [dim] adj. donker, duister; dof, mat; flauw, vaag; vt. verduisteren; dof maken; (v. ruit, spiegel) doen beslaan.
dimension [di'menʃən] afmeting v., omvang m., grootte v., dimensie v.
diminish [di'miniʃ] verminderen; verkleinen.
diminution [dimi'njûʃən] vermindering; verkleining v.; afname v.
diminutive [di'minjutiv] adj. klein, gering; verkleinend, verkleining —; miniatuur—; sb. verkleinwoord o.
dimming ['dimiŋ] verduistering v.; (v. glas) beslag o.
dimness ['dimnis] donkerheid, duisterheid v.; dofheid, matheid v.
dimple ['dimpl] (wang)kuiltje o.
dine [dain] dineren, middagmalen, eten.
dingy ['din(d)ʒi] adj. duister, dof, somber; goor, vuil, smerig.
dining-room ['dainiŋrum] eetkamer, eetzaal v.
dinky ['diŋki] keurig, snoezig.
dinner ['dinə] middagmaal, middageten, diner o.
dinner-set ['dinəset] eetservies o.
diocese ['daiəsis, —sis] diocees, bisdom o.
dip [dip] vt. (in)dopen, indompelen; neerlaten; verven; sb. indoping v.; onderdompeling v.; bad o.; (het) duiken o.; helling v.; buiging v.; (v. magneetnaald) inclinatie v.; vetkaars v.
diphthong [dif—, 'dipðoŋ] tweeklank m.
diploma [di'ploumə] diploma o.
diplomacy [di'plouməsi] diplomatie v.
diplomat ['dipləmæt] diplomaat m.
dip-net ['dipnet] schepnet o.
dipper ['dipə] schepper, potlepel m.; (Dk.) duiker m., waterspreeuw v.; wederdoper m.; (Am.) Grote Beer m.
dire ['daiə] ijselijk, akelig, verschrikkelijk.
direct [di—, dai'rekt] adj. direct, rechtstreeks; onmiddellijk; openhartig, ondubbelzinnig; adv. rechtstreeks; in rechte lijn; vt. richten, mikken; leiden, besturen; voorschrijven, last geven; (muz.) dirigeren.
directing-post [di'rektiŋpoust] wegwijzer m.

direction [di—, dai'rekʃən] bestuur *o.*, directie *v.*; leiding *v.*; bevel *o.*, last *m.*, opdracht, instructie *v.*; aanwijzing *v.*; voorschrift *o.*; richting *v.*

directive [di'rektiv] *adj.* regelend, leidend, besturend; *sb.* richtlijn *r.*, richtsnoer *o.*

directly [di'rektli] *adv.* rechtstreeks, direct; dadelijk, aanstonds, onmiddellijk; *cj.* zodra.

director [di'rektə] directeur, bestuurder; leider *m.*; raadsman *m.*; (*v. maatschappij*) commissaris *m.*

directory [di'rektəri] leidraad *m.*; adresboek *o.*; raad *m.* van commissarissen.

directress [di'rektris] directrice *r.*

directrix [di'rektriks] directrice *r.*

dirigible ['diridʒibl] *adj.* bestuvrbaar; *sb.* bestuurbare ballon *m.*, luchtschip *o.*

dirk [də:k] dolk, ponjaard *m.*

dirt [də:t] *sb.* vuil *o.*, vuilnis *r.* & *o.*, modder *v.*, slijk *o.*; vuiligheid *v.*; *vt.* bevuilen.

dirt-cheap ['də:t'tʃîp] spotgoedkoop.

dirty ['də:ti] *adj.* vuil, smerig; gemeen; *vt.* bevuilen, vuil maken; bezoedelen; *vi.* vuil worden.

disability [disə'biliti] onbekwaamheid *v.*, onvermogen *o.*; onbevoegdheid *v.*; diskwalificatie *v.*

disable [dis'eibl, di'zeibl] onbekwaam (onbruikbaar) maken; ontredderen; (*v. schip*) onttakelen; (*mil.*) buiten gevecht stellen; (*recht*) diskwalificeren.

disabled [dis'eibld, di'zeibld] invalide; ontredderd; buiten gevecht gesteld; gediskwalificeerd.

disaccustom [disə'kəstəm] ontwennen.

disadvantage [disəd'vântidʒ] *sb.* nadeel *o.*, verlies *o.*; *vt.* benadelen; achterstellen.

disadvantageous (**ly**) [disædvən'teidʒəs(li)] *adj.* (*adv.*) nadelig.

disagree [disə'gri] verschillen; het oneens zijn.

disagreeable [disə'grîəbl] *adj.* onaangenaam; *sb.* —**s,** onaangenaamheden.

disagreement [disə'grîmənt] meningsverschil *o.*, onenigheid *v.*

disallow [disə'lau] niet toestaan, weigeren; verwerpen.

disappear [disə'pîə] verdwijnen.

disappoint [disə'pɔint] teleurstellen.

disappointment [disə'pɔintmənt] teleurstelling *v.*

disapproval [disə'prûvəl] afkeuring *v.*

disapprove [disə'prûv] afkeuren.

disarm [dis'âm, di'zâm] (*mil.*) ontwapenen; (*sch.*) onttakelen.

disarrange [disə'reindʒ] verwarren, in de war brengen.

disarray [disə'rei] *sb.* verwarring; wanorde *v.*; *vt.* in wanorde brengen.

disaster [di'zâstə] ongeluk, onheil *o.*, ramp *v.*

disastrous (**ly**) [di'zâstrəs(li)] *adj.* (*adv.*) rampspoedig, noodlottig.

disavow [disə'vau] ontkennen, loochenen; niet erkennen.

disband [dis'bænd] (*mil.*) afdanken; ontbinden.

disbelief ['disbi'lif] ongeloof *o.*

disbeliever ['disbi'lîvə] ongelovige *m.*

disburden [dis'bədn] ontlasten; verlichten.

disburse [dis'bə:s] betalen, uitbetalen; voorschieten.

discard [dis'kâd] op zij zetten; uittrekken, afleggen, afdanken; uitsluiten, bannen.

discern [di'zə:n] onderscheiden, waarnemen, bespeuren.

discernment [di'zə:nment] onderscheidingsvermogen *o.*; doorzicht *o.*; scherpzinnigheid *v.*

discharge [dis'tʃâdʒ] *vt.* afladen, ontladen; afschieten; (*sch.*) lossen; afdoen, voldoen, betalen; ontlasten, verlichten; *vi.* zich ontlasten; (*v. wond*) dragen, etteren; *sb.* ontlading *v.*; (het) afschieten *o.*, losbranding *v.*; schot *o.*; (het) lossen *o.*; ontlasting, verlichting *v.*

disciple [di'saipl] discipel, leerling, volgeling *m.*

discipline ['disiplin] *sb.* tucht, orde *v.*; tuchtiging, kastijding *v.*; *vt.* tuchtigen, kastijden.

disclaim [dis'kleim] ontkennen; niet erkennen; afwijzen.

disclose [dis'klouz] (*fig.*) onthullen, aan het licht brengen, openbaren, blootleggen.

disclosure [dis'klouʒə] onthulling, openbaring *v.*

discolour [dis'kələ] *vt.* & *vi.* (doen) verkleuren, verbleken, verschieten.

discomfort [dis'kəmfət] *sb.* ongemak *o.*; onbehaaglijkheid *v.*; *vt.* onbehaaglijk maken; hinderen.

discommend [diskə'mend] afraden; afkeuren; berispen.

disconcert [diskən'sə:t] (doen) ontstellen, van de wijs brengen; in de war sturen, verijdelen.

disconnect [diskə'nekt] scheiden, ontbinden; losmaken; afkoppelen, loskoppelen, uitschakelen.

disconsolate (**ly**) [dis'kɔnsəlit(li)] *adj.* (*adv.*) troosteloos.

discontent [diskən'tent] *sb.* ontevredenheid *v.*; *adj.* ontevreden; *vt.* misnoegd maken.

discontented (**ly**) [diskən'tentid(li)] *adj.* (*adv.*) misnoegd, ontevreden.

discontinue [diskən'tinju] afbreken, staken, ophouden met; (*v. vergunning*) intrekken; (*v. abonnement*) opzeggen.

discord ['diskɔ:d] tweedracht, onenigheid *v.*; wanklank *m.*

discordant [dis'kɔ:dənt] disharmonisch, wanklinkend; niet overeenstemmend, tegenstrijdig.

discount ['diskaunt] *sb.* disconto *o.*; disagio *o.*; korting *v.*, rabat *o.*; discontering *r.*, (het) disconteren *o.*; [dis'kaunt] *vt.* disconteren; (*r. prijs*) iets afdoen; afbreuk doen aan, de waarde verminderen van; buiten beschouwing laten.

discourage [dis'kəridʒ] ontmoedigen; afraden; afschrikken; tegengaan.

discourse [dis'ko:s] *sb.* redevoering *v.*; toespraak *v.*; preek *v.*; *vi.* spreken, handelen (**of, upon**, over), een redevoering houden; praten, redeneren, zich onderhouden; *vt.* bespreken, beredeneren.

discourteous (ly) [dis'kə:—, dis'ko:tiəs(li)] *adj.* (*adv.*) onhoffelijk, onbeleefd.

discourtesy [dis'kə:—, dis'ko:tisi] onhoffelijkheid, onbeleefdheid *v.*

discover [dis'kəvə] ontdekken; openbaren, aan de dag leggen.

discovery [dis'kəvəri] ontdekking *v.*

discredit [dis'kredit] diskrediet *o.*

discreet (ly) [dis'krit(li)] *adj.* (*adv.*) verstandig, tactvol, oordeelkundig; omzichtig; bescheiden, discreet.

discrepancy [dis'krepənsi] tegenstrijdigheid *v.*; wanverhouding *v.*, verschil *o.*

discrepant [dis'krepənt] tegenstrijdig.

discretion [dis'kreʃən] verstand, oordeel *o.*; beleid *o.*

discrimination [diskrimi'neiʃən] onderscheiding *v.*; onderscheidingsvermogen *o.*; doorzicht *o.*

discuss [dis'kəs] bespreken, discuteren.

discussion [dis'kʊʃən] bespreking, discussie *v.*

disdain [dis'dein] minachten; versmaden.

disease [di'ziz] ziekte, kwaal *v.*

diseased [di'zizd] ziek, ziekelijk.

disembark [disim'bâk] ontschepen.

disembarkation [disəmbâ'keiʃən] ontscheping *v.*

disembarrass [disim'bærəs] bevrijden, ontdoen, ontlasten (**of,** van); ontwarren.

disembody [disim'bɔdi] van het lichaam ontdoen; (*mil.*) afdanken, ontbinden.

disembroil [disim'brɔil] ontwarren.

disenchant [disin'tʃânt] ontgoochelen, ontnuchteren.

disfavour [dis'feivə] *sb.* ongenade, ongunst *v.*; afkeuring *v.*, tegenzin *m.*; *vt.* zijn gunst onthouden aan; afkeuren; niet gaarne zien, niet genegen zijn.

disfiguration [disfigju'reiʃən] misvorming; verminking *v.*; ontsiering *v.*

disfigure [dis'figə] misvormen, verminken; ontsieren.

disgorge [dis'go:dʒ] uitbraken; ontlasten, uitstorten; teruggeven.

disgrace [dis'greis] *sb.* ongenade *v.*; schande *v.*; schandvlek *v.*; *vt.* zijn gunst onttrekken aan; tot schande strekken; schandvlekken; onteren; *vr.* — **oneself,** zich schandelijk gedragen.

disgraceful (ly) [dis'greisful(i)] *adj.* (*adv.*) schandelijk.

disguise [dis'gaiz] *vt.* vermommen; verkleden; *sb.* vermomming; verkleding *v.*; masker *o.*

disgust [dis'gəst] walging *v.*

disgusting [dis'gəstiŋ] walglijk; (*fam.*) misselijk.

dish [diʃ] *sb.* schotel *m.*; gerecht *o.*; *vt.* opscheppen; opdissen.

dishearten [dis'hâtn] ontmoedigen.

disherison [dish'herizn] onterving *v.*

dishonest (ly) [dis'ɔnist(li)] *adj.* (*adv.*) oneerlijk, onoprecht.

dishonour [dis'ɔnə] *sb.* oneer *v.*; *vt.* te schande maken; (*H.: v. wissel*) niet honoreren.

dish-towel ['diʃtauəl] vaatdoek *m.*

disillusion [disi'l(j)ûʒən] *sb.* ontgoocheling *v.*; *vt.* ontgoochelen.

disillusionize [disi'l(j)ûʒənaiz] ontgoochelen.

disincline [disin'klain] afkerig maken.

disinfect [disin'fekt] ontsmetten.

disinherit [disin'herit] onterven.

disinterested (ly) [dis'int(ə)restid(li)] *adj.* (*adv.*) onbaatzuchtig, belangeloos.

disjoin [dis'dʒɔin] scheiden, losmaken.

disjoint [dis'dʒɔint] ontwrichten, uit elkaar nemen; ontleden.

disjunct [dis'dʒən(k)t] gescheiden.

disk [disk] discus *m.*, werpschijf *v.*; (*Pl.*) schijf *v.*

dislike [dis'laik] *vt.* niet houden van; *sb.* afkeer, tegenzin *m.*

dislocate ['dislokeit] ontwrichten; uit zijn verband rukken.

dislodge [dis'lɔdʒ] losmaken; (*mil.: uit stelling, enz.*) verdrijven, verjagen; doen verhuizen.

disloyal (ly) [dis'lɔiəl(i)] *adj.* (*adv.*) ontrouw, trouweloos.

dismal ['dizməl] akelig.

dismantle [dis'mæntl] (*mil.*) ontmantelen; (*sch.*) onttakelen.

dismay [dis'mei] *vt.* ontmoedigen; *sb.* ontzetting, ontsteltenis *v.*

dismember [dis'membə] aan stukken scheuren; verbrokkelen.

dismiss [dis'mis] wegzenden; afdanken, ontslaan, afzetten; afschepen; (*recht*) afwijzen.

dismissal [dis'misəl] afdanking *v.*, ontslag *o.*

dismount [dis'maunt] afstijgen.

disobedience [diso'bidjəns] ongehoorzaamheid *v.*

disobedient (ly) [diso'bidjənt(li)] *adj.* (*adv.*) ongehoorzaam.

disoblige [diso'blaidʒ] onbeleefd zijn jegens; onheus bejegenen.

disorder [dis'o:də] *sb.* wanorde, verwarring *v.*; kwaal, ongesteldheid *v.*; *vt.* in de war brengen; van streek maken.

disordered [dis'o:dəd] verward; van streek; ziekelijk; gekrenkt.

disorderly [dis'o:dəli] wanordelijk; bandeloos.

disorganization [diso:gənai'zeiʃən] ontreddering *v.*

disown [dis'oun] verloochenen, versto] ten.

disparage [dis'pærid3] verkleinen, kleineren, geringschatten; in diskrediet brengen.

disparagement [dis'pærid3mənt] verkleining, kleinering, geringschatting v.

disparate ['dispərit] ongelijksoortig, ongelijk.

dispatch [dis'pætʃ] vt. afzenden, verzenden; vlug afdoen, afhandelen; afmaken, van kant maken; (fam.) verorberen, naar binnen spelen; sb. afzending, verzending v.; (vlugge) afdoening v.; spoedbericht o.; expeditieonderneming v.

dispensable [dis'pensəbl] vatbaar voor dispensatie.

dispensary [dis'pensəri] (armen)apotheek v.

dispeople [dis'pîpl] ontvolken.

disperse [dis'pə:s] verspreiden, verstrooien; uiteenjagen; versnipperen.

dispirited (ly) [dis'piritid(li)] adj.(adv.) ontmoedigd, moedeloos.

displace [dis'pleis] verplaatsen, verschuiven; afzetten; verdringen.

display [dis'plei] vt. ontplooien; ten toon spreiden; aan de dag leggen; sb. ontplooiing v.; tentoonspreiding v., vertoon o.

displease [dis'plîz] mishagen.

displeased [dis'plîzd] misnoegd.

displeasure [dis'pleʒə] misnoegen o.

disposable [dis'pouzəbl] beschikbaar.

disposal [dis'pouzəl] beschikking v.; schikking v.; afdoening v.; verkoop m.

dispose [dis'pouz] rangschikken, schikken; regelen; vatbaar maken (to, voor).

disposition [dispə'zisən] schikking, rangschikking, plaatsing v.; regeling v.; maatregel m., voorbereiding v.

dispossess [dispə'zes] onteigenen.

dispossession [dispə'zesən] onteigening v. [berispen.

dispraise [dis'preiz] afkeuren, laken;

disproportional (ly) [disprə'po:ʃənəl-(i)] adj. (adv.) onevenredig.

dispute [dis'pjût] vi. twisten, redetwisten, disputeren; vt. bespreken; betwisten; bestrijden; sb. dispuut o. rede twist m.; geschil o.

disqualify [dis'kwɔlifai] onbevoegd (ongeschikt) verklaren; onbekwaam (ongeschikt) maken.

disquiet [dis'kwaiət] verontrusten.

disregard [disri'gâd] vt. veronachtzamen; sb. veronachtzaming v.

disrelish [dis'reliʃ] tegenzin m.

disrepair [disri'pêə] vervallen staat m.

disrespectful (ly) [disris'pektful(i)] adj. (adv.) oneerbiedig.

disrupt [dis'rəpt] uiteenrukken, vaneenscheuren; scheiden, verbreken.

dissatisfaction [dissætis'fækʃən] ontevredenheid, onvoldaanheid v.

dissatisfied [dis'sætisfaid] ontevreden, onvoldaan.

dissect [di'sekt] ontleden.

dissecting-room [di'sektiŋrum] ontleedkamer v.

dissection [di'sekʃən] ontleding; sectie v.

disseize [dis'sîz] beroven (of, van).

dissemble [di'sembl] ontveinzen, verhelen.

dissembler [di'semblə] huichelaar m.

disseminate [di'semineit] uitstrooien.

dissension [di'senʃən] onenigheid, tweedracht v.

dissent [di'sent] verschillen (in gevoelen, van mening).

dissertation [disə'teiʃən] verhandeling v.

dissidence ['disidəns] onenigheid v.

dissimilar [di'similə] ongelijk.

dissimulation [disimju'leiʃən] veinzerij v.

dissipate ['disipeit] verstrooien; verdrijven; verkwisten, verspillen; vernietigen.

dissipation [disi'peiʃən] verstrooiing v.; verdrijving v.; verkwisting, verspilling v.; losbandigheid v.

dissoluble ['disəljubl, di'sɔljubl] oplosbaar.

dissolute (ly) ['disəl(j)ût(li)] adj. (adv.) ongebonden, losbandig, liederlijk.

dissoluteness ['disəl(j)ûtnis] ongebondenheid, losbandigheid, liederlijkheid v.

dissolution [disə'l(j)ûʃən] smelting v.; oplossing v.; ontbinding v.; dood m.

dissolvable [di'zɔlvəbl] smeltbaar; oplosbaar; ontbindbaar.

dissolve [di'zɔlv] oplossen, ontbinden; scheiden.

dissonance ['disənəns] wanklank, dissonant m.; onenigheid v.

dissuade [di'sweid] afraden, ontraden; afbrengen (from, van).

distance ['distəns] afstand m.; verte v.

distant ['distənt] ver, afgelegen.

distaste [dis'teist] afkeer, tegenzin m.

distend [dis'tend] openspalken; doen uitzetten; doen opzwellen.

distension [dis'tenʃən] uitzetting v.; omvang m.

distil [dis'til] distilleren; overhalen.

distiller [dis'tilə] distillateur m.

distillery [dis'tiləri] stokerij v.

distinct [dis'tiŋ(k)t] adj. verschillend, onderscheiden; apart; helder, duidelijk.

distinction [dis'tiŋ(k)ʃən] onderscheid o.; onderscheiding v.; voornaamheid v., aanzien o., rang m., distinctie v.

distinctive [dis'tiŋ(k)tiv] onderscheidend, kenmerkend.

distinguish [dis'tiŋwiʃ] onderscheiden.

distinguished [dis'tiŋwiʃt] aanzienlijk, voornaam.

distort [dis'to:t] verwringen.

distortionist [dis'to:ʃənist] slangemens m.

distracted [dis'træktid] verward, verbijsterd; radeloos.

distraction [dis'trækʃən] afleiding v.; ontspanning v.; beroering, verwarring v.

distrain [dis'trein] (recht) in beslag nemen, beslag leggen (upon, op).

distraint [dis'treint] *(recht)* beslaglegging *v.*

distress [dis'tres] nood *m.*, ellende *v.*; angst *m.*; droefheid *v.*; tegenspoed *m.*; *(recht)* beslag *o.*, beslaglegging *v.*

distribute [dis'tribjut] verdelen, uitdelen, ronddelen; verspreiden.

distribution [distri'bjûʃən] verdeling, uitdeling, bezorging *v.*; distributie *v.*; verspreiding *v.*

district-nurse ['distriktnə:s] wijkverpleegster *v.*

distrust [dis'trɔst] *vt.* wantrouwen; *sb.* wantrouwen *o.*

disturb [dis'təb] storen, verstoren; verontrusten.

disturbance [dis'tə:bəns] storing, verstoring *v.*; rustverstoring *v.*; verwarring *v.*

disturber [dis'tə:bə] rustverstoorder *m.*

disunite [disju'nait] scheiden.

disuse [dis'jûs] onbruik *o.*

ditch [ditʃ] sloot, gracht *v.*; schans *v.*; loopgraaf *v.*

ditto ['ditou] *adj. & adv.* dito, dergelijk, hetzelfde; evenzo.

divagate ['daivəgeit] afdwalen; uitweiden.

dive [daiv] duiken; doordringen *(to,* tot; *into,* in); zich verdiepen *(into,* in).

diver [daivə] duiker *m.*

diverge [dai—, di'və:dʒ] afwijken, uiteenlopen.

diverse [dai'və:s] onderscheiden, verschillend.

diversify [dai'və:sifai] veranderen, wijzigen; afwisselen; verschillend maken.

diversion [dai'və:ʃən] afwending *v.*; afwijking *v.*; ontspanning *v.*, vermaak *o.*; *(mil.)* schijnbeweging *v.*

diversity [dai—, di'və:siti] verscheidenheid; ongelijkheid *v.*

divert [dai—, di'və:t] afleiden, afwenden; *(v. weg, rivier)* omleggen, verleggen; afleiding bezorgen, vermaken.

diverting [dai—, di'və:tiŋ] vermakelijk.

divertissement [di'və:tizmənt] [Fr.] vermaak *o.*, uitspanning *v.*; *(muz.)* divertissement *o.*

divide [di'vaid] delen, verdelen, uitdelen; scheiden, splijten; *(rek.)* deelbaar zijn op.

dividend ['dividənd] deeltal *o.*; dividend *o.*, uitkering *v.*

divider [di'vaidə] verdeler; uitdeler *m.*; —s, steekpasser, verdeelpasser.

divine [di'vain] goddelijk; godsdienstig.

diving-dress ['daivindres] duikerpak *o.*

divining-rod [di'vainiŋrɔd] wichelroede *v.*

divinity [di'viniti] goddelijkheid, godheid *v.*; godgeleerdheid *v.*

divisible [di'vizibl] deelbaar.

division [di'viʒən] deling *v.*; verdeling *v.*; afdeling, divisie *v.*; (af)scheiding *v.*; tussenschot *o.*; verdeeldheid *v.*

divorce [di'vo:s] *sb.* echtscheiding *v.*; *vi.* scheiden.

divulgation [dai—, divəl'geiʃən] onthulling, openbaarmaking *v.*

divulge [dai—, di'vəldʒ] onthullen, openbaar maken.

dizzy ['dizi] duizelig; duizelingwekkend.

do [dû] *vt.* doen; maken; uitvoeren, verrichten; klaarmaken; afmaken; beginnen; *vi.* doen; gedijen, tieren; voldoende zijn; dienen, dienstig zijn.

docile ['dou—, dəsail] leerzaam; volgzaam, handelbaar.

docility [dou'siliti] leerzaamheid *v.*; volgzaamheid, handelbaarheid *v.*

dock [dɔk] dok *o.*; sluishaven *v.*; staartriem *m.*; *(Pl.)* wilde zuring *v.*; bank *v.* der beschuldigden.

dock-charges ['dɔktʃâdʒiz] dokgelden, havengelden *o. mv.*

docker ['dɔkə] dokwerker, bootwerker, havenarbeider *m.*

dockyard ['dɔkjâd] scheepswerf *v.*

doctor ['dɔktə] doctor, dokter *m.*

document ['dɔkjumənt] bewijsstuk, document *o.*, oorkonde *v.*

dodge [dɔdʒ] *vi.* uitwijken; heen en weer bewegen; *vt.* ontduiken; ontwijken; *sb.* ontwijkende beweging *v.*; zijsprong *m.*; kneep *v.*, kunstje, foefje *o.*

doe [dou] hinde *v.*; *(v. haas, konijn)* wijfje *o.*

doer ['dûə] dader *m.*; man *m.* van de daad.

dog [dɔg] *sb.* hond *m.*; *(v. vos, wolf, tijger)* mannetje *o.*; klemhaak, klauw *m.*; *(Dk.)* doornhaai *v.*; kerel, vent *m.*; *vt.* vervolgen; achternazitten, op de hielen zitten; nauwkeurig nagaan; iemands gangen nagaan; *(met klemhaak, enz.)* vastzetter grijpen.

dog-cheap ['dɔgtʃîp] spotgoedkoop.

dog-days ['dɔgdeiz] hondsdagen *m. mv.*

dogged ['dɔgid] *adj.* nors; koppig; vasthoudend, hardnekkig.

doggish (ly) ['dɔgiʃ(li)] *adj. (adv.)* honds.

dog-kennel ['dɔgkenəl] hondehok *o.*

dog's ear ['dɔgziə] *sb. (in boek)* ezelsoor *o.*; *vt.* omvouwen, ezelsoren maken in.

dog-tired ['dɔg'taiəd] doodmoe.

doily [d'ɔili] vingerdoekje *o.*

doing ['dûiŋ] *adj.* doend(e); *sb.* daad *v.*, werk *o.*, handelwijs *v.*; **his —s,** zijn doen en laten.

dole [doul] *sb.* aalmoes *v.*; bedeling, uitdeling *v.*; (werklozen)uitkering *v.*; *vt.* **— (out),** uitdelen, ronddelen.

doleful ['doulful] droevig, akelig.

do-little ['dûlitl] nietsdoener, leegloper *m.*

doll [dɔl] pop *v.*

dollar ['dɔlə] dollar *m.*

dolour ['doulə] *(dicht.)* smart *v.*; droefheid *v.*

dolphin ['dɔlfin] *(Dk.)* dolfijn *m.*

dolt [doult] domkop *m.*, uilskuiken *o.*, sul *m.*

domain [də'mein] domein, landgoed, gebied o.

dome [doum] koepel m.

domestic [də'mestik] adj. huiselijk, huishoudelijk; binnenlands; sb. (huis)be diende m., dienstbode v.

domesticate [də'mestikeit] aan het huiselijk leven gewennen; temmen; beschaven.

domicile ['dɔmisil, —sail] woonplaats v.

dominant ['dɔminənt] overheersend.

dominate [dɔmineit] heersen; beheersen.

domination [dɔmi'neiʃən] overheersing v.

domineer [dɔmi'niə] overheersen.

dominion [də'minjən] heerschappij v.; gebied o.; (recht) eigendomsrecht o.; dominion.

donation [dou'neiʃən] gift v., geschenk o.; schenking v.

done [dən] gedaan; gaar; klaar.

donkey ['dɔŋki] ezel m.

donor ['dounə] gever, schenker m.

doom [dûm] sb. oordeel; vonnis o.; lot, noodlot o.; ondergang m.; vt. vonnissen, veroordelen.

doomsday ['dûmzdei] dag m. des oordeels, het laatste oordeel o.

door [do:] deur v.; ingang m.

doorman ['do:mən] portier m.

doorway ['do:wei] deuropening v.; ingang m.

dormer(-window) ['do:mə('windou)] dakvenster o.

dormitory ['do:mitri] slaapvertrek o., slaapzaal v.

dose [dous] sb. dosis v.; vt. afpassen, afmeten, afwegen, doseren; toedienen; mengen, vervalsen.

dot [dɔt] sb. stip, punt v.; kindje o., dreumes m.; bruidschat m.; vt. stippen, stippelen; een punt plaatsen op.

dotdar ['doutəd] suffer m.

doting ['doutiŋ] kinds; verzot.

dotty ['dɔti] gestippeld.

double [dəbl] adj. & adv. dubbel; dubbelhartig; sb. (het) dubbele o.; duplicaat o.; dubbelganger m.; tegenhanger m.; plaatsvervanger m.; (sp.: tennis) dubbelspel o.; (mil.) looppas, stormpas m.; vt. verdubbelen; omvouwen, ombuigen; (sch.) omzeilen; vi. (zich) verdubbelen; (mil.) in de looppas marcheren; een scherpe bocht maken.

double-barrelled ['dəbl'bærəld] dubbelloops; dubbelzinnig; (v. naam) dubbel.

double-dealer ['dəbl'dîlə] dubbelzinnig mens, huichelaar m.

double-lock ['dəbl'lɔk] op het nachtslot doen.

double-minded ['dəbl'maindid] weifelend, besluiteloos.

doubt [daut] sb. twijfel m., onzekerheid, weifeling v.; vt. betwijfelen; vi. twijfelen (of, aan); weifelen.

doubtful(ly) ['dautful(i)] adj. (adv.) twijfelachtig.

doubtless(ly) ['dautlis(li)] adj. (adv.) ongetwijfeld.

dough [dou] deeg o.; (sl.) splint, geld o.

dough-nut ['dounət] oliebol m.

dove [dəv] duif(je) v. (o.).

dove-cot(e) ['dəvkot] duiventil v.

dovetail ['dəvteil] sb. zwaluwstaart m.; vt. lassen, met een zwaluwstaart verbinden.

dowager ['dauədʒə] douairière v.

dower ['dauə] weduwgoed o.; bruidsschat m.; huwelijksgift v.

down [daun] adv. (naar) beneden, neer, nederwaarts; onder; af; prep. van... af; afwaarts; langs; vt. neergooien, omvergooien; verslaan; onderdrukken; (v. vliegtuig) neerhalen, neerschieten; ontmoedigen; (sp.: boksen) leggen; sb. dons o.; duin o.; tegenslag m.

downfall ['daunfo:l] regenbui v.; val, achteruitgang m., instorting v.

down-hearted ['daun'hâtid] ontmoedigd, terneergeslagen, neerslachtig.

downhill ['daun'hil] adj. hellend; (fig.; v. werk) gemakkelijk; adv. bergafwaarts; sb. helling v.

downpour ['daunpo:] stortbui v., plasregen m.

downstairs [daun'stêəz] adv. (naar) beneden.

downstream ['daun'strim] stroomafwaarts.

downwards ['daunwədz] adv. benedenwaarts, naar beneden.

downy ['dauni] heuvelachtig; donzig, donsachtig; (sl.) uitgeslapen.

dowry ['dau(ə)ri] zie **dower**.

dowry ['dau(ə)ri] zie **dower**.

dowsing-rod ['dauziŋrod] wichelroede v.

doze [douz'] vi. dutten, soezen; suffen; — off, indutten; vt.— away, verslapen; sb. dutje o., dommeling, sluimering v.

dozen ['dəzn] dozijn o.

drab [dræb] adj. geelbruin, vaalbruin; (fig.) kleurloos, saai; sb. lichtbruine kleur v.; lichtbruine stof v.; slet; slons v.

draft [drâft] sb. ontwerp o., schets v., concept o.; (mil.) detachement o., afdeling v.; lichting v.; detachering v.; (v. geld) (het) trekken o.; (H.) wissel m., traite v.; (H.) stille uitslag m., goed gewicht o.; vt. ontwerpen, concipiëren, opstellen; (mil.) detacheren; indelen, inlijven.

drag [dræg] vt. trekken; slepen, sleuren; afdreggen; sb. dreg v.; haak m.; rem(schoen) v. (m.); (zware) eg v,

draggle ['drægl] bemodderen.

drag-net ['drægnet] sleepnet o.

dragon ['drægən] draak m.

dragon-fly ['drægənflai] waterjuffer v.

drain [drein] vt. afwateren, droogleggen; rioleren; draineren; onttrekken; aftappen; uitdrinken; uitputten; (v. aardappelen) afgieten; sb. afvoerbuis v.; afvoersloot v., afvoerkanaal o.; afwatering v.; riool o.

drain-pipe ['dreinpaip] rioolbuis, drai-neerbuis, afvoerbuis, afvoerpijp *v.*
drake ['dreik] woerd *m.*, mannetjes-eend *v.*; dagvlieg *v.*
dram [dræm] drachme *v.*; beetje *o.*, greintje *o.*; borreltje *o.*
drama ['drâmə] drama *o.*
dramatize ['dræmətaiz] dramatiseren; voor het toneel bewerken.
drape [dreip] bekleden, overtrekken, draperen.
drapery ['dreipəri] draperie *v.*
drastic(ally) ['dræstik(əli)] *adj. (adv).* drastisch, radicaal.
draught [drâft] (het) trekken *o.*; trek *m.*; slok, teug, dronk *m.*; tocht *m.*; schets *v.*, ontwerp *o.*; ontvangst, recette *v.*; (*sch.*) diepgang *m.*; stroom *m.*, zui-ging *v.*
draughty ['drâfti] tochtig.
draw [dro:] *vt.* trekken; aantrekken, dichttrekken, opentrekken, uittrekken, voortrekken, wegtrekken; slepen, mee-slepen; sleuren; rekken, uitrekken, spannen; (*v. net*) ophalen; uithalen; putten; tappen; *vi.* trekken; de sabel trekken; tekenen; — *in,* intrekken; (*v. dagen*) korten; (*v. avond*) vallen; (*v. auto, enz.*) uithalen; (*v. teugels*) aanha-len; (*v. seizoen, enz.*) ten einde lopen; zich bekrimpen; — *into,* betrekken bij; *sb.* trek *m.*; getrokken nummer (lot) *o.*; loterij *v.*; trekking *v.*; vangst *v.*; aan-trekking *v.*; succesnummer, successtuk *o.*; (*sp.*) onbesliste wedstrijd *m.*, gelijk spel *o.*
draw-bridge ['dro:bridʒ] ophaal-brug *v.*
drawee [dro:'í] (*H.*) betrokkene *m.*
drawer ['dro:ə] trekker *m.*; tekenaar. *m.*; aftapper *m.*; lade, schuiflade *v.*; (*pair of*) —**s,** onderbroek; zwembroek
drawing ['dro:iŋ] trekking *v.*; tekening *v.*; tekenkunst *v.*; —**s,** ontvangsten.
drawing-pin ['dro:iŋpin] punaise *v.*
drawing-room ['droiŋrum] salon *o.*, ontvangkamer, receptiekamer *v.*
drawl [dro:l] *vi.* temen, lijzig (lijmerig) spreken; *sb.* temerige spraak *v.*
dray [drei] sleperswagen *m.*; brouwers-wagen *m.*, brouwerskar *v.*
dread [dred] *vt.* vrezen, duchten, be-ducht zijn voor, erg opzien tegen; *adj.* gevreesd; vreselijk, verschrikkelijk, ont-zagwekkend; *sb.* vrees *v.*; schrik *m.*
dreadful ['dredful] *adj.* vreselijk, ver-schrikkelijk, ontzagwekkend.
dreadnought ['dredno:t] *adj.* onbe-schroomd, onvervaard; *sb.* onverschrok-ken kerel, durfal *m.*; dikke overjas, duffelse jas *v.*; slagschip *o.*
dream [drîm] droom *m.*
dreamer ['drîmə] dromer *m.*
dreamy ['drîmi] *adj.* dromerig; vaag; hersenschimmig.
drear ['driə] (*dicht.*) akelig, triest; woest.
dredge [dredʒ] *sb.* dreg *v.*; sleepnet *o.*;

baggermachine *v.*; *vt.* dreggen; met een sleepnet vissen; uitbaggeren; bestrooien.
dredger ['dredʒə] baggerman *m.*; bag-gernet *o.*; baggermachine *v.*; oestervis-ser *m.*; strooibus *v.*
dregs [dregz] droesem *m.*, bezinksel *o.*; (*fig.*) uitschot, schuim *o.*
drench [drenʃ] doorweken; drenken.
dress [dres] *vt.* kleden; (*v. haar*) opma-ken; bereiden; *vi.* zich kleden; (*mil.*) zich richten; *sb.* kleding *v.*; kleren *o. mv.*; japon *v.*; tenue *v. & o.*
dress-coat ['dres'kout] rok *m.*
dresser ['dresə] aankleder *m.*; kamenier *v.*; kapper *m.*
dressing ['dresiŋ] kleding, aankleding *v.*; kledij *v.*; toilet *o.*; verband *o.*, ver-bandmiddelen *o. mv.*
dressing-gown ['dresiŋgaun] kamer-japon *v.*
dressing-room ['dresiŋrum] kleedka-mer *v.*
dressmaker ['dresmeikə] naaister *v.*; dameskleermaker *m.*
dress-shoe ['dres'ʃû] lakschoen *m.*
dribble ['dribl] druppen; biggelen; kwijlen; (*sp.: voetb.*) dribbelen.
drier ['draiə] droogmachine *v.*
drift [drift] *sb.* drijfkracht *v.*; (*sch.*) drift *v.*, koers *m.*; (het) afdrijven *o.*; stroom; trek *m.*; *vi.* — *about,* rond-dobberen, rondzwalken.
driftless ['driftlis] doelloos.
drift-sand ['driftsænd] stuifzand; drijf-zand *o.*
drill [dril] *sb.* boor, drilboor *v.*; boor-machine *v.*; (*mil.*) (het) drillen *o.*, exerci-tie *v.*; drilmeester *m.*; *vt.* drillen, af-richten; boren, doorboren; in rijen zaaien.
drink [driŋk] *vt.* uitdrinken; opdrin-ken; — *down,* ineens opdrinken; (*v. zorgen, verdriet*) verdrinken; *vi.* drinken; *sb.* drank *m.*; dronk *m.*; (het) drinken *o.*; borrel *m.*
drinkable ['driŋkəbl] drinkbaar.
drinking-water ['driŋkiŋwo:tə] drink-water *o.*
drip [drip] *vi.* druipen (**with,** van), neer-druppelen; *vt.* laten druppelen; *sb.* drup *m.*; druiplijst *v.*; leksteen *m.*
drive [draiv] *vt.* drijven; aandrijven; voortdrijven; afjagen; mennen, bestu-ren; rijden; *vi.* rijden; mennen; een drijfjacht houden; *sb.* rit *m.*; rijtoer *m.*; inrij, oprij *m.*, oprijlaan *v.*; drijfjacht *v.*; (*sp.: cricket, enz.*) slag *m.*
drivel ['drivl] *vi.* wauwelen, leuteren; *sb.* gewauwel, geleuter, gebazel *o.*
driveller ['drivlə] wauwelaar, leute-raar *m.*
driver ['draivə] voerman; bestuurder; koetsier; chauffeur *m.*; (wagen-)menner *m.*; (*mil.*) stukrijder *m.*; (*bij drijfjacht*) drijver *m.*; (*tn.*) drijfwiel *o.*
driving-belt ['draiviŋbelt] drijfriem *m.*
driving-licence ['draiviŋlaisəns] rij-bewijs *o.*

driving-wheel ['draiviŋwĭl] drijfwiel *o.*; (*v. fiets*) achterwiel *o.*; (*v. auto*) stuurrad *o.*

drizzle ['drizl] motregen, stofregen *m.*

drizzly ['drizli] als stofregen.

droll [droul] *adj.* snaaks, grappig; *sb.* snaak, grappenmaker *m.*

dromedary ['drɔm—, drəmədəri] dromedaris *m.*

drone [droun] *sb.* dar *m.*, hommel *v.*; nietsdoener *m.*; *vi.* gonzen, brommen, snorren; dreunen; luieren.

droop [drûp] *vt.* laten hangen; *vi.* neerhangen; afhellen; (weg)kwijnen.

drop [drɔp] *sb.* drop, druppel *m.*; borrel *m.*; oorbel *v.*, oorknop, hanger *m.*; zuurtje *o.*; prijsdaling *v.*; *vt.* laten vallen; neerlaten; laten schieten, laten varen; opgeven; (*v. geld*) verliezen; achterwege laten; *vi.* druppelen; vallen; ophouden; sterven; (*v. wind*) gaanliggen.

drop-curtain ['drɔpkə:tin] (*ton.*) gordijn, scherm *o.*

drop-ear ['drɔpiə] hangoor *o.*

dropping-bottle ['drɔpiŋbɔtl] druppelflesje *o.*

dropsy ['drɔpsi] waterzucht *v.*; gezwollenheid *r.*

dross ['drɔs] (*v. metalen*) slakken *v. mv.*, schuim *o.*; droesem *m.*; afval *m. & o.*

drought [draut] droogte; droogheid *v.*

drove [drouv] kudde *v.*, hoop, troep *m.*, drift *r.*

drown [draun] *vt.* verdrinken; overstromen, onder water zetten; (*fig.*) smoren, overstemmen; *vi.* verdrinken.

drowse [drauz] *vi.* soezen; *vt.* slaperig maken; suf maken, doen versuffen; *sb.* dommel *m.*, dommeling *v.*; gesuf *o.*

drowsiness ['drauzinis] slaperigheid, soezerigheid *v.*

drowsy ['drauzi] slaperig, soezerig.

drubbing ['drəbiŋ] rammeling, afrossing *v.*

drudge [drədʒ] *ri.* sloven, zich afsloven, zwoegen; *vt.* afbeulen; *sb.* zwoeger, werkezel *m.*

drug [drəg] drogerij *v.*; kruid *o.*; artsenij *v.*; bedwelmingsmiddel *o.*

druggist ['drəgist] drogist *m.*; apotheker *m.*

drum [drəm] *sb.* trommel *m.*, trom *v.*; tamboer *m.*; bus *v.*; trommelholte *v.*; *vi.* trommelen; bonzen; *vt.* trommelen (met, op).

drumhead ['drəmhed] trommelvel *o.*; trommelvlies *o.*

drummer ['drəmə] trommelslager, tamboer *m.*

drumstick ['drəmstik] trommelstok *m.*; vogelbout *m.*

drunk [drəŋk] *v. d. van* **drink**; *adj.* dronken; *sb.* dronkeman, dronkaard *m.*

drunkard ['drəŋkəd] dronkaard *m.*

drunken ['drəŋkən] dronken.

drunkenness ['drəŋkənnis] dronkenschap *r.*

dry [drai] *adj.* droog; dorstig; (*r. wijn*)

niet zoet; (*r. pomp*) lens; (*v. land, stad*) drooggelegd; dor; zuiver, onvermengd; *sb.* voorstander *m.* van drankverbod; *vt.* drogen, laten drogen; afdrogen; doen uitdrogen; *vi.* uitdrogen, verdrogen; (*v. mout*) eesten.

dry-dock ['drai'dɔk] *sb.* droogdok *o.*; *vt.* dokken, in droogdok plaatsen.

dryness ['drainis] droogte, droogheid *v.*

dry-rot ['drai'rɔt] vuur *o.* (in hout).

dryshod ['drai'ʃɔd] droogvoets.

dual ['djuəl] tweevoudig.

dubious(ly) ['djûbiəs(li)] *adj.* (*adv.*) twijfelachtig, onzeker.

dubiousness ['djûbiəsnis] twijfelachtigheid *v.*

dubitative(ly) ['djûbiteitiv(li)] *adj.* (*adv.*) twijfelend, aarzelend.

duchess ['dətʃis] hertogin *r.*

duchy ['dətʃi] hertogdom *o.*

duck [dək] eend *v.*; (*sp.: cricket*) nul *v.*

duck-weed ['dəkwĭd] eendekroos *o.*

ducky ['dəki] *adj.* snoezig; *sb.* snoes *m.*

duct [dəkt] kanaal *o.*, leiding, buis *v.*

due [djû] *adj.* verplicht; schuldig, verschuldigd; (*r. schuld, wissel*) vervallen; rechtmatig, behoorlijk, gepast; *adv.* (*sch.*) vlak; *sb.* het iem. verschuldigde *o.*; schuld *v.*

due-bill ['djûbil] schuldbekentenis *v.*

due-date ['djûdeit] (*H.*) vervaldag *m.*; (*v. schip, enz.*) dag *m.* van aankomst.

duel ['djûəl] *sb.* duel, tweegevecht *o.*; *vi.* duelleren.

duet [dju'et] (*muz.*) duet *o.*

duffer ['dəfə] marskramer *m.*; bedrieger *m.*; vals geldstuk *o.*; namaaksel *o.*

duke [djûk] hertog *m.*

dukedom ['djûkdəm] hertogdom *o.*

dulcify ['dəlisfai] zoet maken, verzoeten; verzachten, vertederen.

dull [dəl] *adj.* dom; stomp, bot; dof, mat] flauw, gedrukt; loom, traag; somber, donker.

dull-brained ['dəlbreind] dom, stomp.

duly ['djûli] *adv.* behoorlijk; op tijd, stipt; terecht.

dumb-bell ['dəmbel] halter *m.*

dum(b)found(er) [dəm'faund(ə)] verstomd doen staan, verbluffen.

dummy ['dəmi] *sb.* stommerik *m.*, uilskuiken *o.*; (*ton.*) figurant *m.*; (*kaartsp.*) blinde *m.*; stroman *m.*; *adj.* onecht; nagemaakt; (*v. deur*) blind, loos.

dump(ing)-car(t) ['dəmp(iŋ)kâ(t)] stortkar *v.*, kipwagen *m.*

dumping-ground ['dəmpiŋraund] stortplaats, vuilnisbelt *v.*

dun [dən] *adj.* donkerbruin; donker, somber.

dun [dən] *sb.* (lastige) schuldeiser, maner *m.*; aanmaning *v.*; *vt.* manen, lastig vallen.

dune [djûn] duin *o.*

dung [dəŋ] *sb.* mest, drek *m.*; *vt.* bemesten.

dungeon ['dəndʒən] *sb.* kerker *m.*; *vt.* kerkeren.

dung-hill ['dɒnhil] mesthoop *m*.
duo ['djûou] duo, duet *o*.
dupe [djûp] *sb*. bedrogene, dupe *m*.;
vt. beetnemen, bedriegen, bedotten.
duplicate ['djûplikit] afschrift, duplicaat *o*.
durable ['djûərəbl] *adj*. duurzaam.
duration [dju'reiʃən] duur *m*., voortduring *v*.
duress [dju'res, 'djûəris] dwang *m*.;
gevangenschap *v*.; vrijheidsberoving *v*.
during ['djûəriŋ] gedurende.
dusk [dɒsk] schemering *v*.
dusky ['dɒski] schemerig.
dust [dɒst] *sb*. stof *o*.; stuifmeel *o*.;
(*fam*.) herrie, drukte *v*.; *vt*. afstoffen;
afkloppen; bestuiven; bestrooien; *vi*.
stuiven; stoffen, stof afnemen.
dustbin ['dɒstbin] vuilnisbak *m*.
dust-brand ['dɒstbrænd] brand *m*. (in
koren).
dust-cart ['dɒstkât] vuilniskar *v*., vuil-
niswagen *m*.
duster ['dɒstə] stoffer; stofdoek *m*.;
stofzuiger *m*.; stofjas *v*.
dust-pan ['dɒspæn] vuilnisblik *o*.
dust-proof ['dɒstprûf] stofdicht, stofvrij.

dusty ['dɒsti] stoffig, bestoven.
Dutch [dɒtʃ] *adj*. Nederlands, Hollands;
sb. Nederlands, Hollands *o*.
Dutchman ['dɒtʃmən] Nederlander
Hollander *m*.
dutiable ['djûtiəbl] belastbaar.
dutiful(ly) ['djûtiful(i)] *adj*. (*adv*.) gehoorzaam, onderdanig; plichtmatig.
duty ['djûti] plicht *m*.; dienst *m*., functie
v.; eerbied *m*.; eerbiedsbetuiging *v*.;
belasting *v*., accijns *m*., recht (en) *o*. (*mv*.).
dwarf [dwo:f] dwerg *m*.
dwell [dwel] wonen, verblijven; — **on**
(**upon**), uitweiden over, stilstaan bij;
(*v. oog*) rusten op.
dwelling ['dweliŋ] woning *v*.
dwelling-place ['dweliŋpleis] woonplaats *v*.
dwindle ['dwindl] afnemen, verminderen, achteruitgaan; inkrimpen.
dye [dai] *sb*. verf(stof), kleur, tint *v*.; *vt*.
(*v. stoffen, haar*) verven.
dyer ['daiə] verver *m*.
dye-wood ['daiwud] verfhout *o*.
dying ['daiiŋ] stervend.
dying-bed ['daiiŋbed] sterfbed *o*.
dynamite ['dainəmait] *sb*. dynamiet *o*.;
vt. in de lucht blazen.

E

each [îtʃ] elk, ieder; — **other**, elkander.
eager(ly) ['îgə(li)] *adj*. (*adv*.) gretig,
begerig; verlangend; vurig.
eagerness ['îgənis] gretigheid *v*., begeerte *v*.; verlangen *o*.; vurigheid *v*.
eagle ['îgl] arend, adelaar *m*.
ear [îə] *sb*. oor *o*.; gehoor *o*.; aar *v*.; *vi*.
aren schieten.
ear-drop ['îədrɔp] oorknopje *o*., oorbel *v*.
ear-drum ['îədrəm] trommelvlies *o*.
earl [ə:l] graaf *m*.
ear-lap ['əlæp] oorlelletje *o*.
earldom ['ə:ldəm] graafschap *o*.
early ['ə:li] vroeg; vroegtijdig; spoedig.
earn [ə:n] verdienen, verkrijgen.
earnest ['ə:nist] *adj*. ernstig; ijverig;
vurig; *sb*. ernst *m*.; handgeld *o*.; pand,
onderpand *o*.
earnestness ['ə:nistnis] ernst *m*.
earnings ['ə:niŋz] loon *o*., verdiensten,
inkomsten *v. mv*.
earth [ə:ð] *sb*. aarde *v*.; grond *m*., land
o.; (*el*.) aardsluiting *v*.; aardverbinding
r.; *vt*. met aarde bedekken; aanaarden;
(*el*.) aarden, met de aarde verbinden.
earthen ['ə:ðən] aarden, van aarde.
earthenware ['ə:ðnwêə] aardewerk *o*.
earthly ['ə:ðli] aards, stoffelijk.
earthquake ['ə:ðkweik] aardbeving *v*.
earth-work ['ə:ðwə:k] grondwerk *o*.
earthy ['ə:ði] aards, aardsgezind, wereldsgezind.
ear-wig ['îəwig] oorworm *m*.

ease [îz] *sb*. gemak *o*.; rust *v*.; gemakkelijkheid *v*.; ongedwongenheid *v*.; verlichting *v*.; *vt*. gerust stellen; sussen;
verlichten, vergemakkelijken; ontlasten;
vi. — **down** (**off**), (*H*.) flauwer (lager)
worden.
easeful(ly) ['îzful(i)] *adj*. (*adv*.) rust
gevend; rustig; traag.
easel ['îzəl] schildersezel *m*.
easement ['îzmənt] servituut *o*.
East [îst] Oosten *o*.
Easter ['îstə] Pasen *m*.
easterly ['îstəli] *adj*. oostelijk, oosten—;
adv. oostelijk, oostwaarts.
eastern ['îstən] Oosters; oostelijk,
oosten—.
eastward ['îstwəd] oostwaarts.
easy ['îzi] *adj*. & *adv*. gemakkelijk;
gemakzuchtig; behaaglijk, op zijn gemak; ongedwongen; welgesteld; gerust;
(*v. markt*) flauw, kalm; *adv*. makkelijk;
(*sch*.) langzaam!; *sb*. rust *v*.
easy-chair ['îzi'tʃêə] leuningstoel *m*.
eat [ît] *vt*. & *vi*. eten; opeten; invreten;
sb. (*fam*.) het eten *o*.; eetpartij *v*.
eatable ['îtəbl] *adj*. eetbaar; *sb*. —**s**,
eetwaren *v. mv*.
eaves-dropper ['îvzdropə] luistervink *m*.
ebb [eb] eb(be) *v*.
ebb-tide ['eb'taid] eb *v*., laag water *o*.
ebony ['ebəni] *sb*. ebbehout *o*.; *adj*.
ebbehouten.
ebullition [ebə'liʃən] koking *v*.; opbor-

reling, opbruising v.; ontboezeming, uitbarsting v.

eccentric [ek'sentrik] excentrisch; excentriek, zonderling.

ecclesiastical [iklīzi'æstikl] geestelijk; kerkelijk.

echelon ['efələn] (mil.) echelon m.

echo ['ekou] sb. echo v., weergalm m.; (fig.) weerklank m.; weerkaatsing v.; vt. weerkaatsen, terugkaatsen; herhalen; vi. weerklinken.

eclipse ['iklips] eclips, verduistering v.

economical [īkə'nɔmikl] spaarzaam, zuinig; economisch.

economization [ikɔnəmai'zeifən] besparing v.

economize [i'kɔnəmaiz] vt. sparen, besparen; spaarzaam (zuinig) zijn met; vi. bezuinigen.

economy [i'kɔnəmi] economie v.; bezuiniging v.; zuinigheid v.; beheer o.

ecstasy ['ekstəsi] opgetogenheid, geestvervoering, extase v.

edacity [i'dæsiti] gulzigheid, vraatzucht v.

eddy ['edi] sb. draaikolk, maalstroom m.; dwarrelwind m.; vi. ronddwarrelen, draaien.

edge [edʒ] sb. rand, (scherpe) kant m.; snede, snee v.; vt. scherpen, slijpen; begrenzen, omzomen; vi. — away, (sch.) afhouden; — off, (v. onweer) afdrijven; wegsluipen; vr. — oneself into, zich weten in te dringen in.

edging ['edʒiŋ] boordsel o.; rand m.

edible ['edibl] adj. eetbaar; sb. —s, eetwaren v. mv.

edict ['īdikt] edict, bevelschrift o.

edification [edifi'keifən] opbouwing v.; stichting v.

edify ['edifai] stichten, opbouwen.

edifying ['edifaiŋ] stichtelijk.

edit ['edit] uitgeven, persklaar maken.

edition [i'difən] uitgave v., druk m.

editor ['editə] redacteur m.

editorial [edi'to:riəl] adj. redactioneel; sb. hoofdartikel o.

editorship ['editəfip] bewerking v.; redacteurschap o.

educable ['edjukəbl] opvoedbaar.

educate ['edjukeit] opvoeden; onderrichten; —d, ook: ontwikkeld, beschaafd.

education [edju'keifən] opvoeding, vorming v.; onderwijs o.; ontwikkeling v.

educational [edju'keifənl] onderwijs —.

eel [īl] aal, paling m.; (azijn)aaltje o.

efface [i'feis] vt. uitwissen, uitvegen; doorhalen; (fig.) in de schaduw stellen; vr. — oneself, zich terugtrekken.

effect [i'fekt] sb. uitwerking v.; gevolg, effect o.; —s, goederen, bezittingen; vt. uitwerken, teweegbrengen; uitvoeren, ten uitvoer brengen; (v. regeling) treffen; (v. verzekering) sluiten; (v. verkoop) tot stand brengen.

effective(ly) [i'fektiv(li)] adj. (adv.) uitwerking (effect) hebbend; krachtig,

krachtdadig, werkzaam; afdoend; doeltreffend; effectief, werkelijk; sb. soldaat in werkelijke dienst m.; (v. leger) effectief o.

effectual [i'fektjuəl] krachtig; geldig, bindend; doeltreffend.

effectuate [i'fektjueit] uitvoeren, volbrengen, tot stand brengen, bewerkstelligen.

effeminate [i'feminit] adj. verwijfd; [i'femineit] vt. verwijfd maken; verwekelijken; vi. verwijfd worden.

effervesce [efə'ves] (op)bruisen, mousseren.

effervescence [efə'vesns] opbruising v., het mousseren o.

effete [e'fīt] versleten, uitgeput; krachteloos.

efficacious(ly) [efi'keiʃəs(li)] adj. (adv.) werkzaam, doeltreffend, krachtig.

efficacy ['efikəsi] werkzaamheid, doeltreffendheid; krachtdadigheid v.; uitwerking v.

efficiency [i'fiʃənsi] doeltreffendheid v.; krachtdadigheid v.; bekwaamheid, geschiktheid v.

effigy ['efidʒi] afbeeldsel o.; (v. munt) beeldenaar m., beeltenis v.

efflorescence [eflo:'resns] uitslag m.; ontluiking v.; bloei, bloeitijd m.; bloesem m.

effluence ['efluəns] uitvloeisel o.

effort ['efət] poging, krachtsinspanning v.

effrontery [e'frɔntəri] onbeschaamdheid v.

effulgence [e'fɔldʒəns] schittering v.

effuse [e'fjûz] uitgieten, uitstorten; uitstralen; verspreiden.

effusion [e'fjûʒən] uitstorting v.; uitstraling v.; (fig.) ontboezeming v.

egg [eg] ei o.; (sl.) bom m.; zeemijn v.

egg-cup ['egkəp] eierdopje o.

egg-timer ['egtaimə] zandloper m.

egoism ['egouizm] egoïsme o., zelfzucht, ikzucht v.

egotism ['egoutizm] zelfgenoegzaamheid v.; zelfzucht v.

egret ['īgrit] reiger m.

Egypt ['īdʒipt] Egypte o.

Egyptian [i'dʒipfən] adj. Egyptisch; sb. Egyptenaar m.

eider-down ['aidədaun] eiderdons o.; (donzen) dekbed o.

eight [eit] acht.

eighteen ['ei'tīn; attributief: 'eitīn] achttien.

eighth [eitδ] achtste.

eighty ['eiti] tachtig.

either ['aiδə, 'īδə] pron. beide; een van beide; cj. of.

eject [i'dʒekt] uitwerpen; (v. stralen) uitschieten, uitstralen; verdrijven, verbannen.

ejection [i'dʒekfən] uitwerping v.; uitschieting, uitstraling v.; verdrijving, verbanning v.

elaborate [i'læbərit] adj. doorwrocht,

met zorg bewerkt; nauwgezet.
elaboration [ilæbə'reiʃən] bewerking, (grondige) uitwerking *v.*
elapse [i'læps] verlopen, verstrijken.
elastic [i'læstik] *adj.* elastisch; rekbaar; (*v. geweten*) ruim; *sb.* elastiek *o.*
elasticity [ilæs'tisiti] elasticiteit, veerkracht *v.*; rekbaarheid *v.*
elate [i'leit] blij, opgetogen.
elbow ['elbou] *sb.* elleboog *m.*; *vt.* duwen, stoten.
elbow-room ['elbourum] ruimte (vrijheid) van beweging *v.*
elder ['eldə] *adj.* oudere; oudste (van twee); *sb.* oudere *m.*; ouderling *m.*
elder ['eldə] vlier *v.*, vlierstruik *m.*
elect [i'lekt] *adj.* uitverkoren; *sb.* uitverkorene *v.*; *vt.* verkiezen.
election [i'lekʃən] keus *v.*; verkiezing *v.*
elector [i'lektə] kiezer *m.*; keurvorst *m.*
electrical [i'lektrikl] elektrisch.
electricity [ilek'trisiti] elektriciteit *v.*
electrify [i'lektrifai] elektriseren; elektrificeren.
electrize [i'lektraiz] *zie* **electrify.**
elegance ['eligəns] sierlijkheid, bevalligheid *v.*; keurigheid; netheid *v.*
elegant(ly) ['eligənt(li)] *adj.* (*adv.*) sierlijk, bevallig; keurig, net; fijn.
elegy ['elidʒi] treurzang *m.*, elegie *v.*
element ['elimənt] element, bestanddeel *o.*; grondstof *v.*; beginsel *o.*
elephant ['elifənt] olifant *m.*
elevate ['eliveit] opheffen; verheffen; (*v. oogen*) opslaan; veredelen; verlichten.
elevated ['eliveitid] (*v. taal, stijl*) verheven; (*fam.*) aangeschoten.
elevation [eli'veiʃən] opheffing *v.*; verheffing *v.*; (*kath.: in de mis*) elevatie *v.*; verhevenheid, hoogte *v.*
eleven [i'levn] elf; (*sp.*) elftal *o.*
elf [elf] kabouter *m.*
elicit [i'lisit] ontlokken; aan het licht brengen.
eligible ['elidʒibl] verkiesbaar; verkieslijk; wenselijk; geschikt.
eliminate [i'limineit] verwijderen, verdrijven, uitdrijven; (*v. factor*) wegwerken; uitschakelen.
ell [el] el *v.*
elm [elm] olm, iep *m.*
elope [i'loup] weglopen.
elopement [i'loupmənt] vlucht *v.*; schaking *v.*
eloquent ['eləkwənt] welsprekend.
else [els] anders. [ders.
elsewhere ['els'wêə] elders, ergens anders.
elucidate [i'l(j)ûsideit] ophelderen, toelichten; verklaren.
elucidation [il'(j)ûsi'deiʃən] opheldering, toelichting *v.*; verklaring *v.*
elude [i'l(j)ûd] ontduiken, ontwijken; ontgaan, ontsnappen (aan).
elusive [i'l(j)ûsiv], **elusory** [i'l(j)ûsəri] ontwijkend, ontduikend; ontsnappend (aan nasporing).
emaciate [i'meiʃieit] *vi.* vermageren; *vt.* uitmergelen.

emaciation [imeiʃi'eiʃən] vermagering *v.*; uitmergeling *v.*
emanation [emə'neiʃən] uitstroming *v.*; uitstraling *v.*; emanatie *v.*
emancipation [imænsi'peiʃən] vrijmaking, bevrijding *v.*; ontvoogding, emancipatie *v.*
embalm [em'bâm] balsemen.
embankment [em'bæŋkmənt] indijking *v.*; dijk, spoordijk *m.*; kade *v.*
embargo [em'bâgou] *sb.* beslag *o.* (op schip); verbod *o.* (aan schip om haven te verlaten); *vt.* beslag leggen (op schip). ·
embark [em'bâk] *vt.* inschepen; *vi.* zich inschepen, aan boord gaan.
embarrass [em'bærəs] in verwarring brengen, verlegen maken; hinderen; bemoeilijken.
embassy ['embəsi] gezantschap *o.*
embellish [em'beliʃ] versieren, verfraaien.
embellishment [em'beliʃmənt] versiering, verfraaiing *v.*
ember-days ['embədeiz] quatertemperdagen *m. mv.*
embezzle [em'bezl] verduisteren.
embezzlement [em'bezlmənt] verduistering *v.*
embitter [em'bitə] verbitteren.
embitterment [em'bitəmənt] verbittering *v.*
emblem ['embləm] zinnebeeld, symbool *o.*
emblematic(al) [embli'mætik(l)] zinnebeeldig.
embodiment [em'bodimənt] belichaming *v.*; uitdrukking *v.*; inlijving *v.*
embody [em'bodi] belichamen; uitdrukken; inlijven.
emboss [em'bos] drijven, in reliëf maken; versieren.
embrace [em'breis] *vt.* omhelzen; omstrengelen, omsluiten; omvatten; *vi.* elkaar omhelzen; *sb.* omhelzing *v.*
embroider [em'broidə] borduren.
embroidery [em'broidəri] borduurwerk; borduursel *o.*
embroil [em'broil] verwarren, in de war brengen; (*in geschil, oorlog*) verwikkelen.
emerald ['emərəld] smaragd *o.* & *m.*
emerge [i'mə:dʒ] oprijzen, opduiken; te voorschijn komen; (*fig.*) naar voren treden; zich voordoen.
emergency [i'mə:dʒənsi] opduiking, oprijzing, verschijning *v.*; onvoorziene gebeurtenis *v.*; moeilijke omstandigheid *v.*, noodtoestand *m.*
emergency-exit [i'mə:dʒənsi'eksit] nooduitgang *m.*
emeritus [i'meritəs] emeritus, rustend.
emery ['eməri] amaril *v.*
emery-paper ['eməripeipə] schuurpapier *o.*
emetic [i'metik] braakmiddel *o.*
emigrant ['emigrənt] landverhuizer *m.*
emigrate ['emigreit] emigreren, het land verlaten.

emigration [emi'greiʃən] emigratie; landverhuizing *v.*

eminent ['eminənt] verheven; uitstekend, uitmuntend; eminent.

emission [i'miʃən] uitstraling *v.*; (*v. geluid, enz.*) uitzending *v.*; (*H.: r. bankpapier, enz.*) emissie, uitgifte *v.*; (*v. besluit, verordening*) uitvaardiging *v.*

emit [i'mit] uitstralen; uitzenden; uitgeven, in omloop brengen; uitvaardigen; (*v. klank*) uiten, uitbrengen.

emmet ['emit] (*dial.*) mier *v.*

emolument [i'mɔljumənt] emolument *o.*, bijverdienste *v.*

emotion [i'mouʃən] emotie, aandoening, ontroering *v.*

emotionable [i'mouʃənəbl] licht geroerd.

emperor ['empərə] keizer *m.*

emphasis ['emfəsis] nadruk, klemtoon *m.*

emphatic(al) [em'fætik(l)] nadrukkelijk; krachtig.

empire ['empaiə] rijk, keizerrijk *o.*; macht; heerschappij *v.*

employ [em'plɔi] *vt.* gebruiken, bezigen; aanwenden; in dienst hebben; *sb.* bezigheid *v.*, werk *o.*; dienst *m.*

employee [emplɔi'i] bediende *m.*; werknemer *m.*

employer [em'plɔiə] werkgever, patroon *m.*; (*sch.*) reder *m.*

employment [em'plɔimənt] gebruik *o.*, aanwending *v.*; bezigheid *v.*, werk *o.*; bediening *v.*, ambt *o.*

empower [em'pauə] machtigen.

empress ['empris] keizerin *v.*

empty ['em(p)ti] *adj.* ledig; leeg(hoofdig); ijdel, waardeloos; *sb.* lege kist (fles, wagon, enz.); *vt.* ledigen, leegmaken; uithalen; *vi.* leeg worden, leeglopen; zich ontlasten (*into,* in), zich uitstorten (in).

empurple [em'pə:pl] purper verven, purperrood kleuren.

emulation [emju'leiʃən] wedijver *m.*; naijver *m.*

enable [e'neibl] in staat stellen, gelegenheid geven; machtigen.

enact [e'nækt] vaststellen; bepalen (bij de wet); tot wet verheffen; bekrachtigen; (*v. toneel*) opvoeren; spelen.

enamel [e'næməl] *sb.* email *o.*, brandverf *v.*; glazuur *o.*; brandschilderwerk *o.*; *vt.* emailleren, brandschilderen; schakeren.

enameller [e'næmələ] emailleur, brandschilder *m.*

enamour [e'næmə] bekoren.

encamp [en'kæmp] kamperen.

encampment [en'kæmpmənt] kamp, kampement *o.*

encase [en'keis] omsluiten; steken in (doos, foedraal, enz.).

enchain [en'tʃein] ketenen, boeien.

enchant [en'tʃânt] betoveren; bekoren, verrukken.

enchanting(ly) [en'tʃântiŋ(li)] *adj.*

(*adv.*) betoverend, toverachtig; bekoorlijk, verrukkelijk.

enchantment [en'tʃântmənt] betovering *v.*; bekoring, verrukking *v.*

encircle [en'sə:kl] omringen, omsluiten; (*mil.*) omvatten.

enclose [en'klouz] insluiten, omsluiten; bevatten; omheinen.

enclosure [en'klouʒə] omsluiting *r.*; omheining *v.*; omsloten ruimte *v.*; bijlage *v.*

encore [ɔn'ko:] *ij.* bis; *sb.* herhaling *v.*; *vt.* bisseren.

encounter [en'kauntə] *vt.* ontmoeten, tegenkomen; aantreffen; ondervinden; het hoofd bieden (aan); *vi.* handgemeen worden; elkander ontmoeten; *sb.* ontmoeting *v.*; (*mil.*) treffen, gevecht *o.*

encourage [en'kəridʒ] aanmoedigen, aanwakkeren, aanzetten.

encouragement [en'kəridʒmənt] aanmoediging, aanwakkering, aansporing *v.*

encourager [en'kəridʒə] aanmoediger *m.*

encroach [en'kroutʃ] zich indringen; te ver gaan.

encumber [en'kəmbə] belemmeren, versperren; belasten, (met hypotheek) bezwaren.

encumbrance [en'kəmbrəns] beletsel *o.*, hindernis *v.*; hypotheek *v.*

encyclopædia [ensaiklo'pidiə] encyclopedie *v.*

end [end] *sb.* einde *o.*; slot *o.*; uitslag, afloop *m.*; (*v. touw, enz.*) eindje, stukje *o.*; doel, oogmerk *o.*; besluit *o.*; (*v. zeil*) punt *v.*; **on —,** overeind; achter elkaar, aan één stuk; *vt.* eindigen, een eind maken aan, afmaken; *vi.* eindigen, ophouden; **— in,** uitlopen op; (*v. woord*) eindigen op.

endanger [en'dein(d)ʒə] in gevaar brengen.

endearing [en'diəriŋ] innemend.

endearment [en'diəmənt] liefkozing *v.*, liefdeblijk *o.*

endeavour [en'devə] *sb.* poging, inspanning *v.*; streven *ɔ.*; *vi.* trachten, pogen; streven (*after,* naar).

ending ['endiŋ] einde *o.*; uiteinde *o.*; besluit *o.*; (*v. woord*) uitgang *m.*

endive ['endiv] andijvie *v.*

endless(ly) ['endlis(li)] *adj.* (*adv.*) eindeloos, zonder eind; onuitputtelijk.

endlong ['endlɔŋ] in de lengte, overlangs.

endmost ['endmoust] laatste, uiterste.

endorse [en'do:s] (*H.: v. wissel*) endosseren, overdragen; (*fig.: v. mening, enz.*) bevestigen, onderschrijven.

endorsee [endo:'si] (*H.*) geëndosseerde *m.*; (*v. postwissel*) gemachtigde *m.*

endorsement [en'do:smənt] endossement *o.*; bevestiging, onderschrijving *v.*

endorser [en'do:sə] endossant *m.*

endow [en'dau] begiftigen, doteren; subsidiëren.

endowment [en'daumənt] begiftiging v.; schenking, dotatie v.; talent o., begaafdheid v.

endurance [en'djûərəns] duur m.; geduld o.; lijdzaamheid v.; uithoudingsvermogen; weerstandsvermogen o.

endure [en'djûə] vt. verduren, verdragen; uithouden; dulden; vi. duren, voortduren; in stand blijven.

enema ['enimə, i'nîmə] klisteer v.

enemy ['enimi] vijand m.

energetic(al) [enə'dʒetik(l)] energiek, krachtig.

energy ['enədʒi] energie, wilskracht v.; nadruk m.; arbeidsvermogen o.

enervate ['enə:veit] vt. verslappen, verzwakken; ontzenuwen; [e'nə:vit] adj. slap, zwak.

enfeeble [en'fîbl] verzwakken.

enfeeblement [en'fîblmənt] verzwakking v.

enfold [en'fould] omwikkelen, hullen (in); omarmen, omhelzen.

enforce [en'fo:s] afdwingen, dwingen tot; (v. verzoek, enz.) kracht bijzetten; (v. wet, enz.) de hand houden aan, (streng) handhaven, (krachtig) uitvoeren.

engage [en'geidʒ] verbinden; aanwerven, in dienst nemen, engageren; beslag leggen op, in beslag nemen; (mil.) aanvallen.

engagement [en'geidʒmənt] verbintenis v., indienstneming; betrekking v.; (mil.) gevecht, treffen o.; verloving v., engagement o.

engaging(ly) [en'geidʒiŋ(li)] adj. (adv.) innemend.

engender [en'dʒendə] voortbrengen, verwekken.

engine ['endʒin] machine v.; motor·m.; locomotief v.; brandspuit v.

engine-driver ['endʒindraivə] machinist m.

engineer [endʒi'niə] sb. ingenieur m.; technicus, mecanicien, bankwerker m.; genie-officier, genie-soldaat, genist m.; vi. als ingenieur optreden; vt. als ingenieur leiden; uitvoeren, bouwen; op touw zetten; klaarspelen.

engineering [endʒi'niəriŋ] ingenieursbedrijf o.; ingenieurswezen o.; bouwkunde v.

engine-man ['endʒinmæn] machinist m.

engird(le) [en'gə:d(l)] omgorden, omringen.

England ['iŋglənd] Engeland o.

Englishman ['iŋgliʃmən] Engelsman m.

engorge [en'go:dʒ] verslinden.

engrail [en'greil] (wap.) inkerven; uitschulpen.

engrave [en'greiv] graveren; inprenten.

engraver [en'greivə] graveur m.

engraving [en'greiviŋ] graveerkunst v.; gravure v.

engross [en'grous] (v. akte, enz.) grosseren.

enhearten [en'hâtn] aanmoedigen.

enigmatic(al) [enig'mætik(l)] raadselachtig.

enjoy [en'dʒɔi] vt. genieten van; zich laten smaken; zich verheugen in.

enjoyable [en'dʒɔiəbl] genietbaar; genoeglijk, prettig.

enjoyment [en'dʒɔimənt] genoegen o.; genieting v., genot o.

enkindle [en'kindl] aansteken, ontsteken, doen ontvlammen.

enlace [in'leis] omstrengelen; ineenstrengelen.

enlarge [en'lâdʒ] vergroten; uitbreiden.

enlargement [en'lâdʒmənt] vergroting v.; uitbreiding v.

enlighten [en'laitn] verlichten; (fig.) voorlichten.

enlist [en'list] vt. inschrijven; (mil.) aanwerven; aanmonsteren; in dienst nemen; vi. (mil.) dienst nemen; zich scharen (bij), zich aansluiten (bij).

enlistment [en'listmənt] inschrijving v.; werving v.; dienstneming v.

enliven [en'laivn] verlevendigen, opvrolijken.

enlock [en'lɔk] insluiten.

enmity ['enmiti] vijandschap v.

ennoble [e'noubl] adelen, verdelen; tot de adelstand verheffen.

enormity [i'no:miti] afschuwelijkheid v.; gruweldaad v.

enormous(ly) [i'no:məs(li)] adj. (adv.) kolossaal, reusachtig, enorm; ontzettend, afschuwelijk.

enough [i'nəf] genoeg, voldoende.

enounce [i'nauns] uitdrukken; uiten, uitspreken; verklaren.

enrage [en'reidʒ] woedend maken.

enrich [en'ritʃ] verrijken; tooien; vruchtbaar maken.

enrobe [en'roub] kleden, tooien; bekleden.

enrol(l) [en'roul] inschrijven; aanwerven; aanmonsteren, in dienst nemen; registreren; oprollen; inwikkelen, inrollen.

enrolment [en'roulmənt] inschrijving v.; werving v.; aanmonstering v.; registratie v.; register o.

ensconce [en'skɔns] verschansen; verdekt opstellen; — oneself, zich nestelen.

ensign ['ensain] (onderscheidings)teken o.; (mil.) vaandel o.

ensign-bearer ['ensainbêərə] vaandrig m.

enslave [en'sleiv] tot slaaf maken, knechten.

ensnare [en'snêə] verstrikken.

ensure [en'ʃûə] verzekeren; beveiligen.

entangle [en'tæŋgl] verwarren, verstrikken, verwikkelen.

entanglement [en'tæŋglmənt] verwarring, verstrikking, verwikkeling v.; (mil.) versperring v.

enter ['entə] binnengaan, binnentreden, binnenkomen; binnenlopen; binnendringen; lid worden van; zich laten inschrijven; (*H.*) invoeren; opschrijven, boeken; — **up,** bijschrijven; (*v. boeken*) bijwerken, bijhouden.

enterprise ['entəpraiz] onderneming *v.*; ondernemingsgeest *m.*; waagstuk *o.*; speculatie *v.*

enterprising ['entəpraizin] ondernemend.

entertain [entə'tein] onderhouden; (*v. voorstel*) in overweging nemen, ingaan op; (*v. gevoelen*) koesteren; onthalen, (gastvrij) ontvangen; vermaken.

entertaining (ly) [entə'teinin(li)] *adj.* (*adv.*) onderhoudend; aangenaam, vermakelijk.

entertainment [entə'teinmənt] onthaal *o.*; feestmaal *o.*, partij *v.*; vermaak *o.*; vermakelijkheid *v.*

enthrone [en'ðroun] op de troon plaatsen; introniseren; (*v. bisschop*) installeren.

enthusiasm [en'ðjûziæzm] geestdrift, verrukking *v.*, enthousiasme *o.*

entice [en'tais] verlokken.

enticement [en'taismənt] verlokking *v.*

entire [en'taiə] geheel, algeheel; volkomen; onbeschadigd; gaaf; volledig.

entirely [en'taiəli] geheel en al.

entitle [en'taitl] betitelen.

entoil [en'tɔil] verstrikken.

entomb [en'tûm] begraven.

entrails ['entreilz] ingewanden *o. mv.*

entrance ['entrəns] ingang, toegang *m.*; intrede *v.*, intocht *m.*; aanvang *m.*, begin *o.*

entrap [en'træp] verstrikken.

entreat [en'trît] smeken.

entreaty [en'trîti] smeekbede *v.*

entrench [en'trenʃ] verschansen; — *oneself,* zich verschansen.

entrenchment [en'trenʃmənt] verschansing, schans *v.*

entrust [en'trəst] — *something,* iets toevertrouwen.

entry ['entri] binnenkomst *v.*; intocht *m.*; (*H.*) boeking *v.*, post *m.*; (*voor wedstrijd*) inschrijving *v.*

entwine [en'twain] omstrengelen.

enumerate [i'njûməreit] opsommen, opnoemen.

enumerator[i'njûməreitə] teller, volksteller *m.*

enunciate [i'nənsieit] uiten.

envelop [en'veləp] omhullen, omwikkelen; (*mil.*) omvatten; in een enveloppe doen.

envelope ['envəloup] omslag *m. & o.*

envenom [en'venəm] vergiftigen.

envier ['enviə] benijder *m.*

envious ['enviəs] afgunstig, jaloers.

enviousness ['enviəsnis] afgunst, jaloersheid *v.*

environment [en'vaiərənmənt] omgeving *v.*

environs [en'vaiərənz, 'envirənz] omstreken *v. mv.*

envoy ['envɔi] gezant, afgezant *m.*

envy ['envi] *sb.* nijd *m.*, afgunst, jaloezie *v.*; *vt.* benijden, misgunnen.

enwrap [en'ræp] wikkelen in, omhullen.

epic ['epik] *adj.* episch, verhalend; *sb.* heldendicht, epos *o.*

epidemic [epi'demik] *adj.* epidemisch; *sb.* epidemie *v.*

epigram ['epigræm] epigram, puntdicht *o.*

epilepsy ['epilepsi] vallende ziekte *v.*

epilogue ['epilɔg] epiloog *m.*, naschrift *o.*, narede *v.*

Epiphany [i'pifəni] Driekoningen *m.*

epistle [i'pisl] epistel *o.*; brief *m.*

epitaph ['epitâf, —æf] grafschrift *o.*

epitome [i'pitəmi] korte inhoud *m.*, kort begrip, uittreksel *o.*

epoch ['ipɔk, 'epɔk] tijdperk *o.*; tijdstip *o.*

epopee ['epəpî] heldendicht, epos *o.*

equable ['e—, 'îkwəbl] gelijkmatig, gelijkvormig.

equal ['îkwəl] *adj.* gelijk, gelijkvormig; gelijkmatig; onpartijdig; *sb.* gelijke *m. & v.*, weerga *v.*; *vt.* gelijkmaken; evenaren, gelijk zijn aan.

equality [i'kwɔliti] gelijkheid *v.*; gelijkstelling *v.*

equalize ['îkwəlaiz] gelijkmaken; gelijkstellen; vereffenen.

equally ['îkwəli] gelijkelijk, in gelijke mate, gelijkmatig, even(zeer).

equation [i'kweiʃən] gelijkmaking *v.*; vergelijking *v.*; (*wisk.*) equatie *v.*

equator [i'kweitə] equator, evenaar *m.*

equerry ['ekwəri] stalmeester *m.*

equilibrate [îkwi'laibreit] in evenwicht brengen (houden).

equilibrium [îkwi'libriəm] evenwicht *o.*

equip [i'kwip] uitrusten, toerusten.

equipment [i'kwipmənt] uitrusting, toerusting *v.*

equipoise ['îkwipɔiz] *sb.* evenwicht *o.*; tegenwicht *o.*; *vt.* in evenwicht brengen (houden); opwegen tegen.

equitable ['ekwitəbl] billijk; onpartijdig.

equitation [ekwi'teiʃən] rijkunst *v.*

equivalent [i'kwivələnt] gelijkwaardig, gelijkstaand (*to,* met).

equivocal [i'kwivəkl] dubbelzinnig; twijfelachtig, onzeker; verdacht.

era ['iərə] jaartelling, tijdrekening *v.*; tijdperk *o.*

eradiate [i'reidieit] uitstralen.

eradicate [i'rædikeit] ontwortelen; uitroeien.

erase [i'reiz] doorhalen, uitschrappen, uitwissen.

erasement [i'reizmənt] doorhaling, uitschrapping *v.*

eraser [i'reizə] radeermesje *o.*

erasure [i'reiʒə] *zie* **erasement**.

ere [êə] eer, voordat.

erect [i'rekt] *adj.* rechtop, overeind; *vt.* oprichten; verheffen; (*v. oren*) spitsen;

(v. *theorie*) gronden, vestigen; (*mil.*) opstellen.
erection [i'rekʃən] oprichting v.
ermine ['ə:min] (*Dk.*) hermelijn m.
erosion [i'rouʒən] wegvreting v.
err [ə:] dolen, dwalen; zich vergissen; afdwalen, zondigen.
errand ['erənd] boodschap v.
errand-boy ['erəndbɔi] loopjongen m.
erroneous [e'rounjəs] adj. foutief, verkeerd, onjuist.
error ['erə] dwaling v.; fout, vergissing v.; afdwaling, overtreding, zonde v.
erupt [i'rəpt] (v. *vulkaan*) uitbarsten; (v. *tanden*) doorkomen.
eruption [i'rəpʃən] uitbarsting v.; (*gen.*) uitslag m.; (*mil.*) uitval m.
erysipelas [eri'sipiləs] (*gen.*) roos v.
escalade [eskə'leid] beklimmen met stormladders.
escape [is'keip] sb. ontsnapping, ontvluchting v.; (v. *gas*) lek o.; vi. ontsnappen, ontvluchten, ontkomen; ontgaan, ontglippen.
eschalot ['eʃələt] sjalot v.
escheat [is'tʃit] verbeurd verklaren.
escort ['esko:t] sb. (gewapend) geleide, escorte o.; [is'ko:t] vt. begeleiden.
especially [is'peʃəli] voornamelijk, vooral, hoofdzakelijk, in het bijzonder.
essay ['essei] sb. proef v.; verhandeling v.; vt. pogen, beproeven; op de proef stellen.
essence ['esəns] wezen, wezenlijke o.; uittreksel, extract o.; vluchtige olie v.; reukwerk o.
essential [i'senʃəl] wezenlijk, werkelijk; noodzakelijk, onontbeerlijk.
establish [is'tæbliʃ] oprichten, stichten, vestigen; vaststellen; staven, bewijzen.
establishment [is'tæbliʃmənt] oprichting, stichting, vestiging v.; vaststelling v.; staving v.; handelshuis o.
estate [is'teit] staat m.; landgoed o.; plantage.
estate-duty [is'teitdjûti] successierecht o.
esteem [is'tîm] vt. achten, hoogachten, waarderen; sb. achting, waardering v.
estimable ['estiməbl] achtenswaardig.
estimate ['estimeit] vt. schatten, ramen, begroten (*at,* op); beoordelen (*b* ,naar); ['estimit] sb. schatting, raming, begroting v.; beoordeling v.; (*sch.*) bestek o.
estimation [esti'meiʃən] schatting, raming v.; waardering, achting v.; mening v., oordeel o.
estrange [is'trein(d)ʒ] vervreemden, verwijderen.
etch [etʃ] etsen.
etching ['etʃiŋ] ets v.
eternal [i'tə:nəl] eeuwig.
eternalize [i'tə:nəlaiz] vereeuwigen.
eternity [i'tə:niti] eeuwigheid v.
eternize [i'tə:naiz] zie **eternalize.**
ethics ['eðiks] ethiek, zedenkunde v.
Ethiopia [îði'oupjə] Ethiopië, Abyssinië o.

etui, etwee [e'twi] etui, foedraal o.
Eucharist ['jûkərist] Eucharistie v.
euphonic [jû'fɔnik], **euphonious** [jû-'founiəs] welluidend.
Europe ['juərəp] Europa o.
European [juərə'piən] adj. Europees; sb. Europeaan m.
evacuate [i'vækjueit] ontruimen, evacueren; ledigen, lozen; uitwerpen; lossen.
evacuation [ivækju'eiʃən] ontruiming, evacuatie v.; lediging, lozing v.; uitwerping v.; lossing v.; ontlasting v.
evade [i'veid] ontwijken; ontduiken; ontkomen, ontsnappen, ontglippen.
evaluate [i'væljueit] de waarde bepalen van, berekenen, schatten.
evaporate [i'væpəreit] verdampen, vervluchtigen; verdwijnen; (*fam.*) sterven; uitwasemen; (v. *vruchten*) drogen.
evaporation [ivæpə'reiʃən] verdamping, vervluchtiging v.; uitwaseming v.
evasion [i'veiʒən] ontduiking v.; ontwijking v.; uitvlucht m.
eve [iv] vóóravond m.
even ['iv(ə)n] adj. effen, gelijk; gelijkmatig; (v. *getal*) even; sb. (*dicht.*) avond m.; vt. effenen, gelijkmaken; gelijkstellen; adv. zelfs.
even-handed ['ivn'hændid] onpartijdig.
evening ['ivniŋ] avond, avondstond m.
evensong ['ivnsɔŋ] vesper v.
event [i'vent] gebeurtenis v.; afloop m.; gevolg o.; sportnummer o., sportwedstrijd m.
eventful [i'ventful] gewichtig; (v. *tijd*) veelbewogen.
eventuality [iventju'æliti] mogelijkheid, eventualiteit v.
ever ['evə] ooit; altijd, immer.
everlasting [evə'lâstiŋ] eeuwigdurend.
evermore [evə'mo:] altijd, voor eeuwig.
evert [i'və:t] omkeren, binnenst buiten keren.
every ['evri] ieder, elk.
everybody ['evribɔdi] iedereen.
everyday ['evridei] alledaags.
everyone ['evriwən] iedereen.
everything ['evriðiŋ] alles.
everyway ['evriwei] in elk opzicht, alleszins.
everywhere ['evriwêə] overal.
evidence ['evidəns] sb. klaarblijkelijkheid v.; getuigenis o. & v.; bewijsstuk, bewijsmiddel o.; vt. bewijzen, staven (met bewijzen); tonen.
evident ['evidənt] blijkbaar, klaarblijkelijk; duidelijk.
evil ['ivl, 'ivil] adj. & adv. kwaad, boos, slecht, snood; sb. kwaad, onheil, ongeluk o.; kwaal v.
evil-doer ['ivil'dûə] boosdoener m.
evince [i'vins] bewijzen, aantonen; aan de dag leggen.
evocate ['evokeit] oproepen.
evoke [i'vouk] oproepen; uitlokken; naar een hogere rechtbank verwijzen.

evolution [ivə'ljûʃən] evolutie, ontwikkeling v.; ontplooiing v.; (rek.) worteltrekking v.

evolve [i'vɔlv] ontvouwen, ontplooien, ontwikkelen.

ewer ['jûə] lampetkan v.

ex [eks] ex-, vroeger, gewezen; uit.

exact [ig'zækt] nauwkeurig, nauwgezet; stipt; (v. wetenschap) exact; stipt, streng.

exactitude [ig'zæktitjûd] nauwkeurigheid, nauwgezetheid; juistheid, stiptheid v.

exactly [ig'zæktli] adv. nauwkeurig, nauwgezet; juist, stipt, precies.

exactness [ig'zæktnis] zie exactitude.

exaggerate [ig'zædʒəreit] overdrijven.

exalt [ig'zɔːlt] verheffen, verhogen; verheerlijken.

exaltation [egzɔːl'teiʃən] verheffing, verhoging v.; geestvervoering v.; verheerlijking v.

exalted [ig'zɔːltid] hoog, verheven; verrukt, opgetogen, in vervoering.

examination [igzæmi'neiʃən] onderzoek o.; ondervraging v., verhoor o.; examen o.

examine [ig'zæmin] onderzoeken; ondervragen; verhoren; examineren.

example [ig'zâmpl] voorbeeld, model o.; toonbeeld o.

excavate ['ekskəveit] opgraven, uitgraven; uithollen.

exceed [ek'sîd] overtreffen, overschrijden, te boven gaan.

exceeding(ly) [ek'sîdiŋ(li)] adj. (adv.) buitengewoon, bijzonder. [munten.

excel [ek'sel] vt. overtreffen; vi. uitexcellency ['eksələnsi] excellentie v.

excellent(ly) ['eksələnt(li)] adj. (adv.) uitmuntend, uitstekend, voortreffelijk.

except [ek'sept] vt. uitzonderen; vi. een tegenwerping maken; prep. uitgezonderd, behalve.

exception [ek'sepʃən] uitzondering v.; tegenwerping v.; (recht) exceptie v.

exceptional [ek'sepʃənl] buitengewoon, exceptioneel.

excerpt [ek'səːpt] uittreksel, excerpt o.

excess [ek'ses] buitensporigheid v.; overdaad, onmatigheid v.

excessive [ek'sesiv] buitensporig; overdadig; onmatig; buitengewoon.

excessively [ek'sesivli] adv. zie excessive; ook: uiterst.

exchange [eks'tʃein(d)ʒ] sb. verwisseling v.; uitwisseling v.; ruil m.; (H.) wisselkoers m.; valuta v.; (v. dagblad, enz.) ruilnummer, ruilexemplaar o.; beurs v.; telefoonkantoor o.; vt. ruilen, verruilen, verwisselen, uitwisselen; vi. omwisselen, (van plaats) ruilen; verruild worden, ingewisseld worden.

exchangeable [eks'tʃein(d)ʒəbl] verwisselbaar, ruilbaar.

exchequer [eks'tʃekə] schatkist v.

exchequer-bond [eks'tʃekəbɔnd] schatkistobligatie v.

excisable [ek'saizəbl] accijnsplichtig.

excise [ek'saiz] accijns m.

exciseman [ek'saizmən] commies m.

excision [ek'siʒən] uitsnijding v.

excitable [ek'saitəbl] prikkelbaar.

excitation [eksi'teiʃən] prikkeling r.; opwekking v.; opwinding r.

excite [ek'sait] prikkelen; opwekken; aanhitsen.

excitement [ek'saitmənt] prikkeling v.; opwekking v.; aansporing v.; aanhitsing v.

exclaim [eks'kleim] uitroepen.

exclamation [eksklə'meiʃən] uitroep m.

exclude [eks'klûd] uitsluiten.

exclusion [eks'klûʒən] uitsluiting r.

exclusive [eks'klûsiv] uitsluitend.

excogitate [eks'kɔdʒiteit] uitdenken.

excommunication [ekskəmjûni'keiʃən] excommunicatie v., ban m.

excrement ['ekskrimənt] uitwerpsel o.

excrescence [eks'kresəns] uitwas m.

excreta [eks'krîtə] uitwerpselen o. mr.

exculpate ['ekskəlpeit] verontschuldigen, verschonen; — oneself, zich vrijpleiten.

excursion [eks'kəːʃən] uitstapje o.

excusable [eks'kjûzəbl] verschoonbaar.

excuse [eks'kjûz] vt. verontschuldigen; [eks'kjûs] verontschuldiging r.

execrate ['eksikreit] vervloeken.

execration [eksi'kreiʃən] verwensing v.

executable ['eksikjûtəbl] uitvoerbaar.

execute ['eksikjût] uitvoeren, volvoeren; (v. vonnis) ten uitvoer leggen, voltrekken; (v. akte) opmaken, passeren, verlijden; ter dood brengen.

execution [eksi'kjûʃən] uitvoering, volbrenging v.; tenuitvoerlegging, voltrekking v.; het verlijden o.; terechtstelling, executie v.

executioner [eksi'kjûʃənə] beul m.; scherprechter m.

executive [ig'zekjutiv] adj. uitvoerend; sb. uitvoerende macht v.

executor ['eksikjûtə] (recht) executeur m.

exemplar [eg'zemplə] voorbeeld, model o.; exemplaar o.

exemplary [eg'zempləri] voorbeeldig.

exemplify [eg'zemplifai] verklaren, toelichten.

exempt [eg'zem(p)t] ontheffen (from, van).

exemption [eg'zem(p)ʃən] vrijstelling, ontheffing v.

exercise ['eksəsaiz] vt. uitoefenen; beoefenen; vi. zich oefenen; (mil.) exerceren, drillen; sb. oefening v.

exercise-book ['eksəsaizbuk] schrift, schrijfboek o.

exert [eg'zəːt] inspannen; — oneself, zich inspannen.

exertion [eg'zəːʃən] inspanning v.

exhalation [eks(h)ə—, egzə'leiʃən] uitwaseming r.

exhale [eks'heil,eg'zeil] uitademen; uitwasemen; (doen) verdampen.
exhaust [eg'zo:st] uitputten.
exhausted [eg'zo:stid] uitgeput.
exhaustion [eg'zo:stʃən] uitputting v.
exhaustive(ly) [eg'zo:stiv(li)] adj. (adv.) grondig.
exhaust-pipe [eg'zo:stpaip] uitlaatpijp r.
exhibit [eg'zibit] sb. (recht) bewijsstuk o.; (op tentoonstelling) inzending v.; vt. tentoonstellen.
exhibition [eksi'biʃən] tentoonstelling v.; vertoning v.
exhibitioner [eksi'biʃənə] beursstudent m.
exhort [eg'zo:t] vermanen.
exhortation [egzo:—, ekso:'teiʃən] vermaning v.
exhorter [eg'zo:tə] vermaner m.
exhume [eks'hjûm] opgraven.
exigent ['eksidʒənt] dringend (nodig); veeleisend.
exiguity [eksi'gjûiti] geringheid v.
exile ['eksail, 'egzail] sb. verbanning; ballingschap v.; balling m.; vt. bannen, verbannen.
exist [ig'zist] bestaan.
existence [ig'zistəns] bestaan o.; (het) bestaande o.; wezen o.
exit ['eksit] (v. toneel) aftreden o.; heengaan, verscheiden o,. dood m.
exodus ['eksədəs] exodus; uittocht m.
exonerate [eg'zonəreit] (v. blaam) zuiveren; ontheffen.
exorbitant(ly) [eg'zobitənt(li)] adj. (adv.) buitensporig, overdreven.
exorcism ['ekso:sizm] geestenbezwering v.
exordium [ek'so:—, eg'zo:diəm] inleiding v., aanhef m.
exotic [ek'so—, eg'zotik] uitheems.
expand [eks'pænd] uitspreiden; uitbreiden; doen toenemen; ontplooien; ontwikkelen; (wisk.) uitwerken.
expanse [eks'pæns] uitgestrektheid v.; uitspansel o.; uitbreiding v.
expansion [eks'pænʃən] uitspreiding, uitbreiding v.; ontplooiing; ontwikkeling v.; expansie v.; uitgestrektheid v.
expansive [eks'pænsiv] uitzettend; mededeelzaam.
expatiate [eks'peiʃieit] uitweiden (on, over).
expatriate [eks'peitrieit, —pætrieit] verbannen.
expect [ek'spekt] verwachten.
expectance, expectancy [ek'spektəns(i)] verwachting v.   [ting v.
expectation [ekspek'teiʃən] verwachting v.
expectorate [ek'spektəreit] (bij het hoesten) opgeven.
expedience, expediency [eks'pidiəns(i)] gepastheid, geschiktheid v.; raadzaamheid v.
expedient [eks'pidiənt] adj. gepast, geschikt; raadzaam; sb. hulpmiddel, redmiddel o.

expedite ['ekspidait] bevorderen, bespoedigen, verhaasten; haastig verrichten.
expedition [ekspi'diʃən] vlugheid v., spoed m.; expeditie r.
expiditious(ly) [ekspi'diʃəs(li)] adj. (adv.) vlug, vaardig, snel.
expel [eks'pel] uitdrijven, wegjagen.
expend [eks'pend] uitgeven, besteden, verbruiken.
expenditure [eks'penditʃə] het uitgeven o.; uitgaven v. mv.; verbruik o.
expense [eks'pens] uitgaaf v., uitgaven v. mv.
expensive(ly) [eks'pensiv(li)] adj. (adv.) kostbaar, duur.
experience [eks'piəriəns] sb. ondervinding, ervaring v.; vt. ondervinden, ervaren; ondergaan.
experienced [eks'piəriənst] ervaren, bedreven.
experiment [eks'perimənt] sb. proef, proefneming v.; vi. een proef (proeven) nemen.
experimental [eksperi'mentəl] proefondervindelijk.
experimentation [eksperimen'teiʃən] proefneming v.
expert [eks'pə:t, 'ekspə:t] adj. bedreven (at, in, in); deskundig; ['ekspə:t] sb. deskundige m.
expertness [eks'pə:tnis] bedrevenheid v.
expiate ['ekspieit] boeten (voor); weer goedmaken.
expiatory ['ekspieitəri] boetend, boete—.
expiration [ekspi'reiʃən] uitademing v.; laatste ademtocht m.; einde o.; dood m.; afloop m.; vervaltijd m.
expire [eks'paiə] vt. uitademen; vi. de laatste adem uitblazen; (v. termijn, enz.) aflopen, verstrijken; vervallen; (v. vuur) uitgaan.
explain [eks'plein] verklaren, uitleggen.
explainable [eks'pleinəbl] verklaarbaar.
explanation [eksplə'neiʃən] verklaring, uitlegging v.
expletive [eks'plitiv, 'eksplitiv] adj. aanvullend; overtollig; sb. stopwoord o.; vloek m.
explicable ['eksplikəbl] verklaarbaar.
explicate ['eksplikeit] (v. gedachten, beginselen) ontwikkelen, ontvouwen, uiteenzetten.
explicit(ly) [eks'plisit(li)] adj. (adv.) duidelijk, uitdrukkelijk, beslist, stellig.
explode [eks'ploud] ontploffen.
exploit [eks'ploit] exploiteren; (Z. N.: uitbaten); uitbuiten.
exploitation [eksploi'teiʃən] exploitatie; uitbuiting v.
exploration [eksplo:'reiʃən] onderzoeking, navorsing v.
explore [eks'plo:] onderzoeken, navorsen.

explosion [eks'plouʒən] ontploffing *v.*; uitbarsting *v.*

explosive [eks'plousiv] *adj.* ontploffend, ontplofbaar, ontploffings—; *sb.* springstof *v.*; ontploffingsgeluid *o.*

exponent [eks'pounənt] (*rek.*) exponent *m.*; vertolker *m.*

export ['ekspo:t] *sb.* export, uitvoer *m.*; [eks'po:t] *vt.* (*H.*) uitvoeren, exporteren.

exportation [ekspo:'teiʃən] (*H.*) uitvoer *m.*

exporter ['ekspo:tə] (*H.*) exporteur *m.*

expose [eks'pouz] blootstellen; uitstallen; tentoonstellen.

exposition [ekspo'ziʃən] blootstelling *v.*; uitstalling *v.*; blootlegging; uiteenzetting, verklaring *v.*; (*Am.*) tentoonstelling *v.*

expositive [eks'pozitiv] verklarend.

exposure [eks'pouʒə] blootstelling *v.*; uitstalling *v.*

expound [eks'paund] verklaren.

express [eks'pres] *adj.* uitdrukkelijk; opzettelijk; speciaal; *adv.* per expresse; speciaal; *sb.* expresse *m.*; expres-(trein) *m.*

expression [eks'preʃən] uitdrukking *v.*

expressive [eks'presiv] expressief, vol uitdrukking; veelzeggend; (*v. taal*) krachtig.

expropriate [eks'prouprieit] onteigenen.

expropriation [eksproupri'eiʃən] onteigening *v.*

expulsion [eks'pəlʃən] uitdrijving, verdrijving *v.*; verbanning *v.*

expunge [eks'pən(d)ʒ] uitwissen.

expurgate ['ekspə:geit] zuiveren.

expurgatory [eks'pə:gətəri] zuiverend.

exquisite ['ekskwizit] uitgelezen, voortreffelijk, keurig.

extemporize [eks'tempəraiz] voor de vuist spreken, improviseren.

extend [eks'tend] (zich) uitstrekken; uitsteken, toesteken; rekken, uitrekken; spannen.

extensible [eks'tensibl] rekbaar.

extension [eks'tenʃən] uittrekking *v.*; uitstrekking *v.*; uitgebreidheid *v.*, omvang *m.*; uitgestrektheid *v.*

extensive (**ly**) [eks'tensiv(li)] *adj.* (*adv.*) uitgebreid, omvangrijk; uitgestrekt.

extent [eks'tent] uitgebreidheid *v.*, omvang *m.*; uitgestrektheid *v.*

extenuate [eks'tenjueit] vergoelijken.

exterior ['eks'tiəriə] uitwendig.

extermination [ekstə:mi'neiʃən] uitroeiing, verdelging *v.*

external [eks'tə:nəl] uitwendig, uiterlijk.

extinct [eks'tiŋkt] uitgestorven.

extinguish [eks'tiŋgwiʃ] (uit)blussen, uitdoven.

extirpate ['ekstə:peit] uitroeien.

extirpation [ekstə:'peiʃən] verdelging *v.*

extol [eks'tol] verheffen.

extort [eks'to:t] ontwringen; afpersen, afdwingen.

extortion [eks'to:ʃən] afpersing, knevelarij *v.*

extra ['ekstrə] *adj.* & *adv.* extra; *sb.* extraatje *o.*; extra uitgaaf *v.*, extra nummer *o.*

extract ['ekstrækt] uittreksel *o.*

extradition [ekstrə'diʃən] uitlevering *v.*

extraordinary [eks'tro:dinəri] *adj.* buitengewoon, ongemeen.

extravagance [eks'trævəgəns] verkwisting *v.*; buitensporigheid *v.*

extravagant (**ly**) [eks'trævəgənt(li)] *adj.* (*adv.*) verkwistend; buitensporig.

extreme [eks'trîm] *adj.* uiterst; laatst; buitengewoon; hoogst; *sb.* uiterste *o.*; uiteinde *o.*

extremely [eks'tremli] uitermate.

extremity [eks'tremiti] uiteinde *o.*

extricate ['ekstrikeit] losmaken, vrijmaken.

extrude [eks'trûd] verdrijven; wegjagen.

exuberance [eg'zjûbərəns] overvloed *m.*; weelderigheid *v.*; uitbundigheid *v.*

exuberant (**ly**) [eg'zjûbərənt(li)] *adj.* (*adv.*) overvloedig; welig; uitbundig.

exude [ig'zjûd, ek'sjûd] uitzweten.

exult [eg'zəlt] juichen, jubelen.

exultant [eg'zəltənt] juichend, triomfantelijk.

exultation [egzəl'teiʃən] gejuich *o.*

eye [ai] oog *o.*

eye-ball ['aibo:l] oogappel *m.*

eyebrow ['aibrau] wenkbrauw *v.*

eyelash ['ailæʃ] ooghaar *o.*; wimper *m.*

eyelet ['ailit] oogje *o.*; vetergaatje *o.*

eyelid ['ailid] ooglid *o.*

eye-pit ['aipit] oogholte *v.*

eye-tooth ['aitûð] oogtand *m.*

F

fable ['feibl] fabel *v.*

fabricate ['fæbrikeit] maken; namaken; bewerken; verzinnen.

fabulous (**ly**) ['fæbjuləs(li)] *adj.* (*adv.*) fabelachtig.

facade [fə'sâd] voorgevel *m.*, voorzijde *v.*

face [feis] *sb.* gezicht, aangezicht, gelaat *o.*; aanzien; voorkomen *o.*; (*v. munt*) beeldzijde *v.*; · *vt.* in het aangezicht zien; het gelaat toekeren; onder de ogen zien; het hoofd bieden; *vi.* gekeerd zijn naar.

face-paint ['feispeint] blanketsel *o.*

face-value ['feisvæljû] nominale waarde *v.*

facilitate [fə'siliteit] *rt.* vergemakkelijken.
facility [fə'siliti] gemak *o.*
fact [fækt] feit *o.*
factious (ly) ['fækʃəs(li)] *adj. (adv.)* partijzuchtig.
factory ['fæktəri] factorij *v.*
facultative ['fækəlteitiv] facultatief.
faculty ['fækəlti] vermogen *o.*; bevoegdheid *r.*; faculteit *v.*
faddle ['fædl] beuzelen.
fade [feid] verwelken; verbleken.
fadeless ['feidlis] onverwelkbaar.
fag [fæg] afmatten; afjakkeren; afbeulen.
fag-end ['fæg'end] zelfkant *m.*; rafeleind *o.*; eindje, stompje *o.*
faggot [fægət] takkenbos *m.*
faience [fei'jâŋs] plateelwerk *o.*
fail [feil] *vi.* ontbreken; mislukken; falen; *rt.* teleurstellen; in de steek laten.
failing ['feiliŋ] gebrek *o.*; tekortkoming *v.*
failure ['feiljə] (het) falen *o.*; mislukking *r.*, fiasco *o.*; gebrek *o.*, ontstentenis *r.*; gemis *o.*; (*v. el. licht*) storing *v.*; (*H.*) faillissement *o.*
faint [feint] *adj.* flauw; *sb.* flauwte, onmacht, bezwijming *v.*; *vi.* flauw vallen.
faint-heart ['feinthât] bloodaard *m.*
fainting(-fit) ['feintiŋ(fit)] bezwijming, flauwte, onmacht *v.*
faintness ['feintnis] zwakheid, flauwheid *v.*
fair ['fêə] jaarmarkt, kermis *v.*
fair ['fêə] *adj.* schoon; zuiver; eerlijk; billijk; onbelemmerd; goed; tamelijk; blond; blank.
fair-faced ['fêəfeist] met een mooi gelaat.
fair-haired ['fêə'hêəd] blond(harig):
fairly ['fêəli] *adv.* eerlijk, oprecht; billijk, billijkerwijze; behoorlijk, passend; tamelijk.
fair-spoken ['fêə'spoukn] innemend, minzaam, hoffelijk.
fairway ['fêəwei] vaarwater *o.*
fair-weather ['fêəweθə] — *friend,* schijnvriend, vriend in voorspoed.
fairy ['fêəri] fee, tovergodin *v.*
fairy-tale ['fêəriteil] sprookje *o.*
faith [feiδ] geloof *o.*; vertrouwen *o.*
faithful ['feiδful] gelovig; trouw.
faithfully ['feiδfuli] trouw, getrouw; **yours —,** uw dienstwillige.
faithfulness ['feiδfulnis] trouw *v.*
faithless (ly) ['feiδlis(li)] *adj. (adv.)* ongelovig.
faithlessness ['feiδlisnis] trouweloosheid *v.*
falcon ['fo:lkən, 'fo:kn] valk *m.*
fall [fo:l] *vi.* vallen; neervallen; dalen, verminderen, afnemen; achteruitgaan; (*v. wind*) gaan liggen; sneuvelen; *sb.* val *m.*; helling *v.*; verval *o.*; daling *v.*; prijsdaling *v.*
fallacious (ly) [fə'leiʃəs(li)] *adj. (adv.)* bedrieglijk, misleidend.

fallacy ['fæləsi] bedrog *o.*, bedrieglijkheid *r.*; dwaalbegrip *o.*
fallible]'fælibl] feilbaar.
fallow ['fælou] *adj.* braak; *sb.* braakland *o.*; *vt.* omploegen.
false [fo:ls] *adj.* vals; onecht.
falsehood ['fo:lshud] valsheid *v.*
falsify ['fo:lsifai] vervalsen; weerleggen; logenstraffen; (*v. woord, belofte*) schenden, verbreken; (*v. hoop, verwachting*) teleurstellen, beschamen.
falter ['fo:ltə] strompelen; wankelen; struikelen; stamelen, stotteren; weifelen.
fame [feim] faam, vermaardheid *v.*, roem *m.*, beroemdheid *v.*
familiar [fə'miljə] gemeenzaam; vertrouwd; vertrouwelijk.
familiarize [fə'miljəraiz] gemeenzaam maken; vertrouwd maken.
family ['fæmili] gezin, huisgezin *o.*; familie *v.*; geslacht *o.*
famine ['fæmin] hongersnood *m.*
famish ['fæmiʃ] uithongeren.
famous ['feiməs] *adj.* vermaard, beroemd; (*fam.*) fameus.
fan [fæn] *sb.* waaier *m.*; blaasbalg *m.*; ventilator *m.*; wan *v.*; *vt.* waaien; aanwakkeren; wannen.
fanatical (ly) [fə'nætikəl(i)] *adj. (adv.)* fanatiek, dweepziek.
fanaticism [fə'nætisizm] dweperij, dweepzucht *v.*, fanatisme *o.*
fanaticize [fə'nætisaiz] dwepen.
fancied ['fænsid] ingebeeld, vermeend.
fanciful (ly) ['fænsiful(i)] *adj. (adv.)* denkbeeldig, ingebeeld.
fancy ['fænsi] *sb.* verbeelding *v.*; gril *v.*; *vt.* zich verbeelden; menen, denken, geloven.
fancy-articles ['fænsiâtiklz] fantasie-artikelen *o. mv.*, galanterieën *v. mv.*
fancy price ['fænsiprais] buitensporig hoge prijs *m.*
fang [fæŋ] slagtand *m.*
far [fâ] ver, afgelegen.
farce [fâs] klucht *v.*, kluchtspel *o.*
fare [fêə] vracht *v.*; vrachtprijs *m.*; reiziger, passagier *m.*; kost *m.*, voedsel *o.*
farewell ['fêə'wel] *ij.* vaarwel! *sb.* afscheid, vaarwel *o.*
farina [fə'rainə] zetmeel *o.*
farm [fâm] *sb.* pachthoeve *v.*; verpachting *v.*; pacht *v.*; *vt.* pachten; bebouwen; — (*out*), verpachten, verhuren.
farmer ['fâmə] pachter *m.*; boer *m.*
farming ['fâmiŋ] landbouw *m.*
farmstead ['fâmsted] boerderij, boerenhofstede *v.*
far-off ['fâ'ro:f] ver, afgelegen.
farrier ['færiə] hoefsmid *m.*
farther ['fâθə] *adj. & adv.* verder.
farthermost ['fâθəmoust] verst.
farthing ['fâθiŋ] ¼ penny; (*fig.*) cent, duit *m.*
fascinate ['fæsineit] betoveren; boeien.
fascination [fæsi'neiʃən] betovering *v.*

fascism ['fæsizm] fascisme *o.*

fascist ['fæsist] *sb.* fascist *m.*; *adj.* fascistisch.

fashion ['fæʃən] *sb.* manier, wijze *r.*; maaksel, fatsoen *o.*, vorm, snit *m.*; trant; aard *m.*; *the* —, de grote wereld, de grote lui; de mode; *rt.* vormen, fatsoeneren; pasklaar maken.

fashion-monger ['fæʃənməŋgə] modegek, fat *m.*

fast [fâst] *sb.* vasten *v.*, vastentijd *m.*; *vi.* vasten.

fast [fâst] *adj.* vast, onbeweeglijk; blijvend; kleurhoudend, wasecht; snel, vlug; *(v. uurwerk)* vóór.

fast-day ['fâstdei] vastendag *m.*

fasten ['fâsn] vastmaken; vastbinden; vastdoen; vastzetten.

fastidious (ly) [fæs'tidiəs(li)] *adj. (adv.)* lastig, kieskeurig. [heid *v.*

fastness ['fâstnis] vastheid, stevigfat [fæt] *adj.* vet; vlezig; dik; *(v. boekdeel)* lijvig; rijk; *sb.* vet *o.*; (het) vette *o.*

fatal ['feitl] *adj.* rampspoedig; noodlottig, fataal; onvermijdelijk; dodelijk.

fatalism ['feitəlizm] fatalisme *v.*

fate [feit] noodlot *o.*

fateful ['feitful] fatalistisch; profetisch; noodlottig.

father ['fâðə] vader *m.*; pater *m.*

fatherhood ['fâðəhud] vaderschap *o.*

father-in-law ['fâðər-in-lo:] schoonvader *m.*

fatherland ['fâðəlænd] vaderland *o.*

fatherly ['fâðəli] vaderlijk.

fathom ['fæðəm] *sb.* vadem *m.*; *vt.* vademen; omvatten; doorgronden, peilen.

fathomless ['fæðəmlis] peilloos.

fatigue [fə'tig] *sb.* vermoeidheid, vermoeienis, afmatting *v.*; *vt.* vermoeien, afmatten.

fatten ['fætn] mesten, vet maken.

fatuity [fə'tjûiti] dwaasheid *r.*

fault [fo:lt] fout *v.*, gebrek *o.*, feil *v.*; defect *o.*; schuld *v.*

fault-finder ['fo:ltfaində] vitter *m.*

faultless (ly) ['fo:ltlis(li)] *adj. (adv.)* feilloos, onberispelijk.

faulty ['fo:lti] *adj.* gebrekkig, onvolmaakt; defect; onjuist, verkeerd.

favour ['feivə] *sb.* gunst *v.*; gunstbewijs *o.*; begunstiging *v.*; genade *v.*; *rt.* gunstig gezind zijn; begunstigen; steunen, aanmoedigen, bevorderen; bevoorrechten.

favourable ['feivərəbl] gunstig.

favourer ['feivərə] begunstiger, bevorderaar *m.*

favourite ['feivərit] *adj.* begunstigd; geliefkoosd, lievelings—; *sb.* gunsteling(e) *m.* (*v.*); lieveling(e) *m.* (*v.*); (*sp.*) favoriet *m.*

fear [fiə] *sb.* vrees *v.*, angst *m.*; *rt.* vrezen, duchten; *vi.* bang zijn.

fearful ['fiəful] vreesachtig, bang.

fearless (ly) ['fiəlis(li)] *adj. (adv.)* onbevreesd, onvervaard.

fearsome (ly) ['fiəsəm(li)] *aaj. (adv.)* vreselijk; vreesachtig.

feasible ['fizibl] uitvoerbaar, doenlijk·

feast [fist] *sb.* feest *o.*; feestmaal *o.*; *vi.* feestvieren; smullen; *rt.* onthalen; trakteren.

feast-day ['fistdei] feestdag *m.*

feat [fit] heldendaad *v.*; wapenfeit *o.*; kunststuk *o.*

feather ['feðə] *sb.* ve(d)er, pluim *v.*; pluimgedierte *o.*; *vt.* met veren bedekken (versieren); van veren voorzien; *vi.* veren krijgen; ruien.

feather-broom ['feðəbrûm] plumeau *m.*

feature ['fitʃə] *sb.* trek, gelaatstrek *m.*; hoofdtrek *m.*; *vt.* kenmerken, karakteriseren; schetsen.

febrile ['fibrail] koortsig, koorts—.

February ['februəri] februari *o.*

fecund ['fe—, 'fikənd] vruchtbaar.

fecundate ['fe—, 'fikəndeit] vruchtbaar maken, bevruchten.

federate ['fedəreit] (zich) tot een (staten)bond verenigen.

federation [fedə'reiʃən] federatie *v.* (staten)bond *m.*

fee [fi] leengoed, leen *o.*; honorarium, loon, salaris *o.*; schoolgeld *o.*

feeble ['fibl] zwak, krachteloos.

feed [fid] *vt.* voeden, spijzen; voe(de)ren; laten weiden; *vi.* zich voeden; eten; *sb.* voeder, voer *o.*; (het) voeden *o.*; maal *o.*, maaltijd *m.*; onderhoud *o.*

feeder ['fidə] voeder *m.*

feeding-bottle ['fidiŋbɔte] zuigfles *v.*

fee-farm ['fifâm] erfpacht *v.*

feel [fil] voelen; gevoelen; bevoelen, betasten; *(mil.)* verkennen.

feeler ['filə] voeler; voelhoorn *m.*

feeling ['filiŋ] *adj.* gevoelig; gevoelvol; *sb.* gevoel *o.*; gevoeligheid *v.*; gevoelen *o.*, gewaarwording *v.*

feign [fein] veinzen; huichelen.

feint [feint] veinzerij *v.*; voorwendsel *o.*

felicity [fi'lisiti] geluk *o.*; gelukzaligheid *r.*

feline ['filain] katachtig, katten—.

fell [fel] vel *o.*, huid *v.*; *vt.* vellen, neervellen.

feller ['felə] houthakker *m.*

felloe ['felou] velg *v.*

fellow ['felou] maat, kameraad *m.*; kerel, vent *m.*; (*v. genootschap*) lid *o.*; weerga *v.*, gelijke *m.* & *v.*, evenknie *v.*

fellow-citizen ['felou'sitizən] medeburger *m.*

fellowship ['felouʃip] kameraadschap *v.*; gemeenschap *v.*

felt [felt] vilt *o.*; vilten hoed *m.*

female ['fimeil] vrouwelijk.

feminine ['feminin] vrouwelijk.

feminist ['feminist] feminist, voorstander *m.* van het feminisme.

fence [fens] *sb.* schutting, omheining *v.*; haag *r.*; (het) schermen *o.*, schermkunst *v.*; *vt.* omheinen; insluiten; beschermen, beschutten; pareren.

fenceless ['fenslis] niet omsloten; *(dicht.)* onbeschermd, onbeschut.

fencer [fensə] schermer *m*.
fencing-master ['fensiŋmâstə] schermmeester *m*.
fen-pole ['fenpoul] polsstok *m*.
ferment ['fə:mənt] *sb*. gist *v*., gistmiddel *o*., giststof *v*.; gisting *v*.; [fə:'ment] *vt*. doen gisten; *vi*. gisten.
fern [fə:n] varen *r*.
ferocious(ly) [fi'rouʃəs(li)] *adj*. (*adv*.) woest, wild; verscheurend; wreed.
ferret ['ferit] *sb*. (*Dk*.) fret *c*.; *vi*. fretten; snuffelen; *rt*. met fretten vangen.
ferriferous [fe'rifərəs] ijzerhoudend.
ferruginous [fe'rûdʒinəs] ijzerhoudend.
ferry [feri] *sb*. veer *o*.; veerrecht *o*.; *vt*. overzetten; oversteken.
ferry-boat ['feribout] veerboot *v*.
fertile ['fə:tail] vruchtbaar.
fertilize ['fə:tilaiz] vruchtbaar maken; (*Pl*.) bevruchten.
fertilizer ['fə:tilaizə] bevruchter *m*.; meststof *r*.
fervency ['fə:vənsi] vuur *o*., gloed *m*., innigheid *r*.
fervent(ly) ['fə:vənt(li)] *adj*. (*adv*.) vurig, warm, innig.
fervid(ly) ['fə:vid(li)] *adj*. (*adv*.) heftig, vurig; (*dicht*.) heet, gloeiend.
festal(ly) ['festəl(i)] *adj*. (*adr*.) feestelijk, feest—.
fester ['festə] zweren, etteren.
festival ['festivəl] *adj*. feestelijk; *sb*. feest *o*., feestviering *r*.; feestdag *m*.; muziekfeest, festival *o*.
festivity [fes'tiviti] feestelijkheid *r*.; feestvreugde *v*.
festoon [fes'tûn] *sb*. festoen *v*. & *o*. slinger *m*.; *rt*. festonneren; met slingers versieren.
fetch [fetʃ] halen, behalen; brengen; (*v*. slag, enz.) toebrengen; (*v*. prijs) opbrengen; bereiken; (*v*. zucht) slaken.
fetter ['fetə] *sb*. keten, kluister, boei *v*.; belemmering *r*., blok *o*. aan 't been; *rt*. ketenen, kluisteren, boeien; binden; belemmeren.
fettle ['fetl] *sb*. **in good —,** in goede conditie; *rt*. in orde brengen; schoonmaken; afrossen, afranselen.
feud [fjûd] vijandschap *v*., twist *m*., vete *v*.; (*gesch*.) leen(goed) *o*.
feudalism ['fjûdəlizm] (*gesch*.) leenstelsel *o*.
fever ['fivə] *sb*. koorts *v*.; *v*. koortsig maken.
feverish(ly) ['fivəriʃ(li)] *adj*. (*adv*.) koortsachtig; koortsig.
few [fjû] weinig; *a* —, enkele, een paar; enige.
fiancé(e) [fi'ânsei] aanstaande, verloofde *m*. (*r*.).
fiasco [fi'æskou] fiasco *o*., mislukking *v*.
fib [fib] *sb*. leugentje, jokkentje *c*.; jokker *m*.; slag *m*.; *ri*. liegen, jokken; slaan, (af)ranselen.
fibber ['fibə] leugenaar, jokker *m*.
fibre ['faibə] vezel *v*.; bijworteltje *o*.

fibrous ['faibrəs] vezelachtig.
fickle ['fikl] wispelturig, grillig.
fiction ['fikʃən] verdichting *v*.; verdichtsel, verzinsel *o*.; verdicht verhaal *o*.
fictitious(ly) [fik'tiʃəs(li)] *adj*. (*adv*.) verdicht, verzonnen, gefingeerd; geveinsd, voorgewend; nagemaakt, onecht, vals; denkbeeldig.
fiddle ['fidl] *sb*. viool *v*.; (*dicht*.) vedel *v*.; *vi*. vioolspelen; (*fam*.) fiedelen; *vt*. — *away one's time,* zijn tijd verbeuzelen (verleuteren).
fiddler ['fidlə] vioolspeler *m*.; (*dicht*.) vedelaar *m*.; speelman *m*.
fiddlestick ['fidlstik] strijkstok *m*.
fidelity [fi'deliti] getrouwheid, trouw *v*.
fidget ['fidʒit] zenuwachtige gejaagdheid, drukte, onrust *v*. zenuwachtig persoon *m*.
fie [fai] foei! bah!
field [fild] veld *o*., akker *m*. terrein; speelterrein *o*.; slagveld *o*.
field-dressing ['filddresiŋ] (*mil*.) verbandpakje *o*.
fierce(ly) ['fiəs(li)] *adj*. (*adv*.) woest, wild; meedogenloos, wreed; onstuimig, fel, heftig; grimmig.
fiery ['faiəri] *adj*. vurig, opvliegend, licht ontvlambaar.
fife [faif] fluit, pijp *r*.
fifteen ['fif'tin 'fiftin] vijftien.
fifth [fifð] vijfde; vijfde deel *o*.; (*muz*.) kwint *v*.
fifty ['fifti] vijftig.
fig [fig] *sb*. vijg *r*.; vijgeboom *m*.; *vt*. — *out,* uitdossen.
fight [fait] *sb*. gevecht *o*., strijd *m*.; vechtpartij *v*.; strijdlust, vechtlust *m*.; *rt*. bestrijden, bekampen, bevechten; uitvechten; *ri*. vechten; strijden.
fighter ['faitə] vechter, vechtersbaas *m*.; gevechtsvliegtuig, jachtvliegtuig *o*.
figurative(ly) ['figjurətiv(li)] *adj*. (*adv*.) figuurlijk, zinnebeeldig
figure ['figə] *sb*. vorm *m*., gedaante, gestalte *v*.; figuur, afbeelding *v*.; beeld *o*.; cijfer *o*.; *vt*. vormen; afbeelden; (zinnebeeldig) voorstellen; met figuren versieren; becijferen; in cijfers uitdrukken; — *up,* optellen; *vi*. zich voorstellen, menen; figureren; rekenen, een berekening maken; voorkomen, prijken.
filament ['filəmənt] vezeltje *o*.; (*el*.) kooldraad, gloeidraad *m*.
filbert ['filbə:t] hazelaar *m*.; hazelnoot *v*.
file [fail] *sb*. vijl *v*.; rij *v*.; (*mil*.) gelid, rot *o*.; *vt*. vijlen, afvijlen; aanrijgen; rangschikken; deponeren; (*v*. aanklacht) indienen; *vi*. — *off,* (*mil*.) afmarcheren.
filial(ly) ['filjəl(i)] *adj*. (*adv*.) kinderlijk.
filigrane ['filigrein] filigraan *o*.
filings ['failiŋz] vijlsel *o*.
fill [fil] *vt*. vullen; aanvullen; invullen; (*v*. ambt) vervullen; bekleden; (*v*. plaats) innemen, beslaan; (*v*. pijp) stoppen; (*v*. bestelling*) uitvoeren; (*v*. tand) plomberen; *vi*. zich vullen; vol worden, vol

raken; (*v. zeilen*) zwellen; *sb.* vulling *v.*; bekomst; verzadiging *v.*

fillet ['fílit] haarband, hoofdband *m.*; strook *v.*; lijst *v.*; lendestuk *o.*, filet *v.* & *o.*; (*v. vis*) filet, moot *v.*

filling ['fíliŋ] vulling *v.*, vulsel, plombeersel *o.*

fillip ['fílip] *sb.* knip *m.* (met de vingers); prikkel *m.*, aansporing *v.*; opfrissing *v.*; *vt.* wegknippen (met de vingers); aansporen, aanzetten, opwekken; (*v. geheugen*) opfrissen; *vi.* knippen (met de vingers).

filly ['fíli] merrieveulen *o.*

film [film] *sb.* vlies(je) *o.*; film, rolprent *v.*; mistsluier *m.*; waas *o.*; *vt.* met een vlies bedekken; filmen, verfilmen.

filmy ['fílmi] vliezig; fijn, ragfijn; wazig, vaag.

filter ['fíltə] *sb.* filter *m.* & *o.*; (*radio*) zeefkring *m.*; *vt.* filtreren; zuiveren; *vi.* doorsijpelen, doorzijgen; doorschemeren.

filth [filθ] vuil *o.*, vuiligheid *v.*

filthy ['fílθi] *adj.* vuil; (*fig.*) smerig.

filtrate ['fíltreit] *sb.* filtraat *o.*; *vt.* filtreren.

fin [fin] (*v. vis*) vin *v.*; (*vl.*) kielvlak *o.*

finable ['fainəbl] bekeurbaar, beboetbaar.

final ['fainəl] *adj.* laatste, eind—; beslissend, afdoend; definitief; *sb.* slotletter *v.*; laatste revisie *v.*; eindexamen *o.*; (*sp.*) eindwedstrijd, beslissingswedstrijd *m.*, finale *v.*

finally ['fainəli] *adv.* ten slotte, ten laatste, eindelijk; afdoend, beslissend definitief.

financial(ly) [fi—, fai'nænʃəl(i)] *adj.* (*adv.*) financieel, geldelijk.

find [faind] *vt.* vinden; bevinden, ondervinden; bemerken, aantreffen, ontdekken; *sb.* vondst *v.*; vangst *v.*; vindplaats *v.*

findable ['faindəbl] vindbaar.

finding ['faindiŋ] vondst *v.*; (*recht*) uitspraak; toewijzing *v.*; bevinding *v.*

fine [fain] *adj.* mooi, schoon, fraai; rein, zuiver; fijn; *adv.* mooi; *sb.* mooi weer *o.*

fine [fain] *sb.* geldboete *v.*; *vt.* beboeten.

fine-draw ['fain'dro:] mazen.

finery ['fainəri] opschik, tooi *m.*

finesse [fi'nes] *sb.* sluwheid, handigheid, list *v.*; *vi.* list gebruiken.

finger ['fiŋgə] *sb.* vinger *m.*; vingerbreedte *v.*; *vt.* bevoelen, betasten; met de vingers aanraken.

finger-post ['fiŋgəpoust] handwijzer *m.*

finish ['finiʃ] *vt.* eindigen; volbrengen, voltooien, volvoeren, voleindigen; afwerken, de laatste hand leggen aan; afmaken; *vi.* ophouden, uitscheiden; *sb.* einde, slot *o.*; afwerking *v.*; voltooiing *v.*; vernis *o.*, glans *m.*

finished ['finiʃt] geëindigd, voltooid, enz.; volmaakt; afgestudeerd.

finisher ['finiʃə] voltooier *m.*; afwerker *m.*; laatste stoot *m.*; genadeslag *m.*; dooddoener *m.*

Finland ['finlənd] Finland *o.*

fir [fə:] den, denneboom *m.*; dennehout *o.*

fir-apple ['fə:ræpl] pijnappel, denneappel *m.*

fire [faiə] *sb.* vuur *o.*; brand *m.*; gloed *m.*; hitte *v.*; haard *m.*,; *vt.* verbranden; aansteken; in brand steken; (*v. stenen*) bakken; *vi.* in brand raken, vlam vatten; vuren, schieten; (*v. vuurwapen*) afgaan.

fire-ball ['faiəbo:l] vuurbol *m.*; brandbom *v.*; lichtkogel *m.*

fire-brand ['faiəbrænd] brandend stuk hout *o.*; (*fig.*) stokebrand *m.*

fire-brick ['faiəbrik] vuurvaste steen *m.*

fire-brigade ['faiəbrigeid] brandweer *v.*

fire-damp ['faiədæmp] mijngas *o.*

fire-engine ['faiərendʒin] brandspuit *v.*

fire-escape ['faiəriskeip] brandladder *v.*; reddingstoestel *o.* (bij brand).

fire-lock ['faiələk] (*mil.*) snaphaan *m.*; (slot van een) vuurroer *o.*

fireman ['faiəmən] brandweerman *m.*; stoker *m.*

fire-proof ['faiəprúf] *adj.* vuurvast; brandvrij; *vt.* brandvrij maken.

fire-raising ['faiəreiziŋ] brandstichting *v.*

fireside ['faiə'said] haard *m.*, haardstede *v.*; hoekje *o.* van de haard

firing ['faiəriŋ] brandstof *v.*; (het) vuren *o.*; geweervuur *o.*, losbranding *v.*

firm [fə:m] *sb.* firma *v.*, firmanaam *m.*

firm [fə:m] *adj.* & *adv.* vast, hecht; vastberaden; standvastig; stevig, flink; (*H.*) vast, prijshoudend, willig; *vt.* vast maken, vast zetten, bevestigen; doen stollen; *vi.* vast worden; stollen.

firmament ['fə:məmənt] firmament, uitspansel *o.*

firmly ['fə:mli] *adv.* vast, stevig, krachtig; stellig, met beslistheid.

firmness ['fə:mnis] vastheid, hechtheid *v.*; vastberadenheid *v.*; standvastigheid *v.*; stevigheid *v.*; duurzaamheid *v.*; (*H.*) willigheid *v.*

firm-set ['fə:mset] op elkaar geklemd.

fir-needle ['fə:nídl] dennenaald *v.*

first [fə:st] *adj.* eerst; voornaamst; *adv.* eerst; eerstens, ten eerste; voor het eerst; eerder, liever; *sb.* eerste *m.* & *v.*; eerste prijs *m.*; (*bij examen, enz.*) eerste plaats *v.*; (*muz.*) eerste stem *v.*

first-born ['fə:stbo:n] *adj.* eerstgeboren; *sb.* eerstgeborene *m.* & *v.*

firstcost ['fə:st'ko:st] inkoopsprijs *m.*

fir-tree ['fə:trí] denneboom, den *m.*

fisc [fisk] fiscus *m.*, schatkist *v.*

fish [fiʃ] *sb.* vis *m.* & *v.*; fiche *o.*; las *v.*; *vt.* vissen; afvissen; (*v. spoorstaven*) lassen; *vi.* vissen.

fish-bone ['fiʃboun] (vis)graat *v.*

fisherman ['fiʃəmən] visser *m.*

fishery ['fiʃəri] visserij *v.*; visplaats *v.*; visrecht *o.*

fishing-rod ['fiʃiŋrɔd] hengelroede *v.*; hengel *m.*

fishmonger ['fiʃmɔŋgə] visverkoper, vishandelaar *m*.

fishpond ['fiʃpond] visvijver *m*.

fish-trap ['fiʃtræp] visfuik *v*.

fissure ['fiʃə] *sb.* spleet, kloof, scheur *v*.; *vt.* & *vi.* splijten, kloven.

fist [fist] *sb.* vuist *v*.; *(fam.)* knuist, poot *m*.; *vt.* met de vuist slaan; *(sch.)* aanpakken.

fist-fighter ['fistfaitə] bokser *m*.

fistula ['fistjulə] fistula *v*.; *(v. insekt)* buis *v*.

fit [fit] *adj.* geschikt, bruikbaar; dienstig; gepast, betamelijk, behoorlijk; gezond, in goede conditie; *vt.* passend (geschikt) maken; stellen, monteren; uitrusten; voorzien (**with,** van); *vi.* passen; voegen; *sb.* stuip *v*., toeval *o*., beroerte *v*.; aanval *m*., vlaag, bui *v*.; gril, bevlieging *v*.

fitchet ['fitʃit] bunzing *m*.

fitchew ['fitʃû] *zie* **fitchet.**

fitful (ly) ['fitful(i)] *adj. (adv.)* afwisselend, ongeregeld; ongedurig, ongestadig; onbestendig, veranderlijk, grillig.

fitness ['fitnis] geschiktheid, bruikbaarheid *v*.; dienstigheid *v*.; gepastheid, voegzaamheid *v*.

fitting ['fitiŋ] *adj.* passend, gepast; *sb.* (het) aanzetten *o*., fitting *v*.; **—s,** benodigdheden voor het inrichten van een huis, winkel, enz.; uitrusting, installatie; bekleding, beslag.

five [faiv] vijf.

fix [fiks] *vt.* vastmaken, vasthechten, vastzetten; vastleggen; *(tn.)* aanbrengen, opstellen; bepalen, vaststellen; *(mil.: v. bajonet)* opzetten; installeren; *vi.* een vaste vorm aannemen; stollen; *vr.* **— oneself,** zich vestigen; *sb.* moeilijkheid *v*.; lastig geval *o*.

fixation [fik'seiʃən] bevestiging *v*.; vastlegging *v*.; vastzetting *v*.; aanhechting *v*.; stolling *v*.; vastheid *v*.

fixed [fikst] *adj.* vast; onbeweeglijk; niet vluchtig; *(tn.)* stationair; strak; vast aangesteld.

fizz [fiz] *vi.* sissen, bruisen; *sb.* gesis, gebruis *o*.; mousserende drank; champagne *m*.

fizzle ['fizl] *vi.* sissen, sputteren; bruisen; **— out,** met een sisser aflopen, op niets uitdraaien; *sb.* gesis, gesputter *o*.; fiasco *o*., mislukking *v*.

flag [flæg] *sb.* vlag *v*.; *vt.* bevlaggen, met vlaggen versieren; seinen (met vlaggen); (met plavuizen) bevloeren; *vi.* slap neerhangen; lusteloos worden; kwijnen; verslappen, verflauwen.

flagellate ['flædʒəleit] geselen.

flagellation [flædʒə'leiʃən] geseling *v*.

flaggy ['flægi] lusteloos, slap, hangend; kwijnend; rietachtig.

flagman ['flægmən] baanwachter *m*.; vlagseiner *m*.

flagon ['flægən] (grote) fles *v*., flacon *m*.; schenkkan *v*.

flail [fleil] *sb.* dorsvlegel *m*.; *vt.* dorsen; slaan, ranselen.

flake [fleik] vlok *v*.; schilfer *v*.; schots.

flaky ['fleiki] vlokkig, schilferachtig.

flame [fleim] *sb.* vlam *v*.; hitte *v*., vuur *o*.; *vi.* ontvlammen; opvlammen; schitteren.

Flanders ['flândəz] *sb.* Vlaanderen *o*.; *adj.* Vlaams.

flank [flæŋk] zijde *v*.; *(mil.)* flank *v*.; ribstuk *o*.

flannel ['flænl] flanel *o*.; **—s,** flanellen goederen.

flap [flæp] *sb.* lap(je) *m*. *(o.)*; *(v. enveloppe, enz.)* klep *v*.; *(v. jas)* pand *o*.; *(v. hoed)* afhangende rand *m*.; oorlel *v*.; *vt.* neerslaan, slaan tegen; (met de vleugels) slaan, klapwieken; *vi.* flappen; klapperen; fladderen.

flapper ['flæpə] klepper *m*.; vliegendoder *m*.; vin *v*.; staart *m*.

flare [flêə] flakkeren, opvlammen; flikkeren, blinken, schitteren.

flash [flæʃ] glans *m*.; vlam; opflikkering *v*.; zaklantaarn *v*.; plotselinge ingeving *v*.

flat [flæt] *adj.* vlak, plat; smakeloos; dom, onnozel; saai, afgezaagd; *(v. stem)* dof, mat; *(v. markt)* flauw, gedrukt; *sb.* vlakte *v*., vlak land, vlak terrein *o*.; ondiepte, zandbank *v*.; platte kant *m*.; plat *o*.

flat-bottomed ['flætbɔtəmd] *(sch.)* platboomd.

flat-catching ['flætkætʃiŋ] boerenbedrog *o*.

flat-foot ['flætfut] platvoet *m*.

flat-iron ['flætaiən] strijkijzer *o*.

flatly ['flætli] *adv.* vlak, plat; botweg, vierkant.

flatness ['flætnis] vlakheid *v*.

flatten ['flætn] plat (vlak) maken; flauw (smakeloos, saai, eentonig) maken; afplatten, pletten; *(muz.)* verlagen.

flatter ['flætə] vleien; strelen; flikflooien; flatteren.

flatterer ['flætərə] vleier; flikflooier *m*.)

flattering (ly) ['flætəriŋ(li)] *adj. (adv.)* vleiend.

flatting-mill ['flætiŋmil] pletmolen *m*., pletterij *v*.

flaunt [flɔ:nt] wapperen; pronken, pralen (**with,** met).

flavorous ['fleivərəs] smakelijk; geurig.

flavour ['fleivə] smaak *m*.; geur *m*., aroma *o*.; *(v. wijn)* boeket *m*.; *(fig.)* tintje *o*.

flaw [flo:] barst, scheur, breuk *v*.; fout *v*., gebrek *o*.; vlek, smet *v*.; leemte *v*.

flax [flæks] vlas *o*.

flax-seed ['flækssîd] lijnzaad *o*.

flaxy ['flæksi] vlasachtig, vlassig.

flay [flei] villen, stropen; *(fig.)* hekelen; villen.

flea [flî] vlo *v*.

fleck [flek] *sb.* vlek, smet *v*.; sproet *v*.; spatje *o*.; spikkel *m*.; *vt.* vlekken; sprenkelen; bespikkelen.

fledged ['fledʒd] *(v. jonge vogel)* vlug; *(fig.)* rijp, volwassen.

flee [fli] *vt.* ontvlieden, ontvluchten; *vi.* vlieden, vluchten.

fleece [flis] *sb.* schapevacht *v.*, vlies *o.*; schapewolkjes *o. mv.*; *vt.* scheren; (*fig.*) plukken, het vel over de oren halen; (als met een vlies) bedekken.

fleet [flit] *sb.* vloot *v.*; inham *m.*, kreek *v.*; *adj.* (*dicht.*) vlug, snel; snel heenvliedend; vergankelijk; ondiep; *vi.* vlieten; heensnellen, voorbijsnellen, voorbijgaan.

Fleming [′flemiŋ] Vlaming *m.*

Flemish [′flemiʃ] Vlaams.

flesh [fleʃ] vlees *o.*

fleshy [′fleʃi] vlezig; dik; lichamelijk.

flexible [′fleksibl] *adj.* buigzaam, soepel; handelbaar, plooibaar, inschikkelijk.

flick [flik] tik(je) *m.* (*o.*); knip *m.*; spat *v.*; scheurtje *o.*; (*sl.*) kerel *m.*

flicker [′flikə] flikkeren; fladderen, klapwieken; trillen.

flight [flait] vlucht *v.*; troep, zwerm *m.*; loop *m.*, vaart *v.*; (*v. tijd*) (het) vervliegen *o.*; vliegtuiggroep *v.*

flimsy [′flimzi] dun; nietig; zwak; ondeugdelijk; armzalig.

flinch [flinʃ] aarzelen; wankelen, wijken, terugdeinzen; krimpen, ineenkrimpen; rillen; zich ont trekken (**from**′ aan).

fling [fliŋ] gooien, werpen, smijten; afwerpen; (*fig.*) uit het zadel lichten.

flintstone [′flintstoun] vuursteen *m.*

flirt [flə:t] *sb.* ruk, zwaai *m.*; flirt *m.* & *v.*; hofmaker *m.*; *vt.* wegknippen; wegschieten; uitspreiden; *vi.* rukken, zwaaien, snel bewegen; fladderen; flirten.

flit [flit] zweven; vliegen; fladderen; (*v. tijd*) voorbijgaan; vertrekken, verhuizen.

flitter [′flitə] *sb.* lovertje *o.*; verhuizer *m.*; *vi.* fladderen.

float [flout] *sb.* vlot *o.*; houtvlot *c.*; dobber *m.*; (*in stoomketel*) vlotter *m.*; drijvende boei *v.*; (*v. vliegboot*) drijver *m.*; *vi.* vlotten, drijven; dobberen; vlot zijn; zweven; wapperen.

floating [′floutiŋ] drijvend; (*v. schuld, bevolking*) vlottend; (*v. munt*) zwevend.

flock [flɔk] *sb.* kudde *v.*; troep *m.*; (*v. wol, enz.*) vlok *v.*; pluis *v.*; *vi.* samenstromen, samenscholen, samenkomen.

flocky [′flɔki] vlokkig.

floe [flou] ijsschots *v.*, drijvend ijsveld *o.*

flog [flɔg] slaan, ranselen, afranselen.

flogging [′flɔgiŋ] slaag *m.*, pak ransel *o.*

flood [fləd] *sb.* vloed, stroom *m.*; overstroming *v.*; zondvloed *m.*; *vt.* overstromen; onder water zetten.

flood-tide [′flədtaid] vloed *m.*

floor [flo:] vloer *m.*; grond, bodem *m.*; verdieping *v.*

floor-cloth [′flo:klɔð] vloerzeil *o.*; dweil *m.*

florescence [flɔ′resəns] (*Pl.*) (het) bloeien *o.*; bloeitijd *m.*

floriculturist [flɔri′kəltʃərist] bloemkweker *m.*

florid [′flɔrid] bloemrijk; bloeiend; blozend, hoogrood; zwierig; opzichtig; praalziek.

florilegium [flo:ri′lidʒiəm] bloemlezing *v.*

florin [′flɔrin] florijn, gulden *m.*; twee-shilling-stuk *o.*

florist [′flɔrist] bloemist, bloemkweker *m.*; bloemenkenner *m.*

flotsam [′flɔtsəm] zeedrift *v.*

flounce [flauns] flap, ruk, plof *m.*; strook *v.*

flounder [′flaundə] *sb.* gespartel, geploeter *o.*; hulpeloze poging *v.*; (*Dk.*) bot *v.*; *vi.* spartelen, ploeteren; baggeren; sukkelen; hakkelen; broddelen, knoeien.

flour [′flauə] bloem *v.*, meel *o.*

flourish [′flɔriʃ] *vi.* bloeien, tieren, gedijen; in beeldrijke (bloemrijke) taal spreken; *vt.* zwaaien met; geuren met; krullen maken, met krullen versieren.

flout [flaut] *vt.* bespotten, beschimpen, honen; (*v. raadgeving*) in de wind slaan; *vi.* — **at**, bespotten, schimpen op.

flow [flou] *vi.* vloeien, stromen; overvloeien; golven; (*v. getij*) opkomen; *sb.* vloed, stroom *m.*; overstroming *v.*; golving *v.*; toevloed *m.*

flower [′flauə] bloem *v.*; bloesem *m.*; bloei *m.*

flowering-time [′flauəriŋtaim] bloeitijd *m.*

flowerpot [′flauəpɔt] bloempot *m.*

flowery [′flauəri] bloemrijk; gebloemd; bloemen—.

flu [flu] (*fam.*) influenza, griep *v.*

fluctuate [′fləktjueit] schommelen, op en neer gaan, golven; weifelen, aarzelen.

fluctuation [fləktju′eiʃən] (*v. prijzen, enz.*) schommeling *v.*; weifeling, aarzeling *v.*

fluent(ly) [′flûənt(li)] *adj.* (*adv.*) vloeiend; vloeibaar; vaardig, vlot; welbespraakt; veranderlijk.

fluff [fləf] dons *o.*; pluis *v.*

fluid [′flûid] *adj.* vloeibaar, niet vast; gasvormig; vloeiend; *sb.* vloeistof *v.*; gas *o.*; fluïdum *o.*

fluke [flûk] (*scn.*) ankerblad *o.*; leverbot *v.*, zuigworm *m.*

flush [fləʃ] *sb.* plotselinge stroom (toevloed) *m.*; (*v. riool, enz.*) doorspoeling *v.*; (*Pl.*) uitlopende blaadjes *o. mv.*; *vi.* wegvliegen; uitstromen; (*v. jonge blaadjes*) uitlopen, uitbotten; *vt.* (*v. vogels, enz.*) opjagen; doorspoelen; bespoelen; doen afvloeien; (*v. muur*) voegen; *adj.* vol, boordevol; blozend, rood; effen, vlak, gelijk; voorspoedig.

flute [flût] *sb.* fluit *v.*; fluitist *m.*; fluitbrood *o.*; fluitschip *o.*; groef *v.*; *vi.* fluiten; fluitspelen.

flutter [′flətə] *vi.* fladderen; klapwieken; zweven; dwarrelen; (*v. licht*) flikkeren, flakkeren; trillen; (*v. hart*) popelen, jagen; *vt.* zenuwachtig maken, opwinden; haasten, jachten; doen wapperen.

flux [fləks] *sb.* vloed *m.*, vloeiing *v.*; stroom, loop *m.*; buikloop *m.*; smeltmiddel *o.*; *vt.* smelten; *vi.* vloeien; stromen.

fly [flai] *sb.* vlieg *v.*; kunstvlieg *v.*; vliegwiel *o.*; vliegafstand *m.*; *vi.* vliegen; vluchten; omvliegen, voorbijsnellen; *vt.* vluchten uit; laten vliegen; (*v. vlieger*) oplaten; *adj.* uitgeslapen, glad.

flyer ['flaiə] vliegenier *m.*; hoogvlieger *m.*; vluchteling *m.*; vliegwiel *o.*

flying-bridge ['flaiiŋ'bridʒ] noodbrug *v.*; gierpont; gierbrug *v.*

flying-machine ['flaiiŋməʃîn] vliegtuig *o.*

fly-trap ['flaitræp] vliegenvanger *m.*

foal [foul] veulen *o.*

foam [foum] *sb.* schuim *o.*; *vi.* schuimen.

focus ['foukəs] brandpunt *o.*; (*v. aardbeving, ziekte, enz.*) haard *m.*

fodder ['fodəi *sb.* (droog) veevoeder *o.*; *vt.* voederen.

fog [fog] mist, nevel *m.*; (*fot.*) sluier *m.*; (*sl.*) rook *m.*; nagras *o.*

fog-bank ['fogbæŋk] mistbank *v.*

foggy ['fogi] *adj.* mistig, nevelig; (*fig.*) duister, vaag; (*fot.*) gesluierd.

foil [goil] *sb.* schermdegen *m.*; foelie *v.*, verfoeliesel *o.*; bladgoud, klatergoud *o.*; *vt.* verijdelen; verlegen maken, van zijn stuk brengen; verslaan, overtreffen, het winnen van.

fold [fould] *sb.* vouw, plooi *v.*; kronkeling *v.*; kudde *v.*; schaapskooi *v.*; schoot *m.* (der kerk); *vt.* vouwen; wikkelen (in); hullen (in); (*v. schapen*) kooien.

foldable ['fouldəbl] opvouwbaar.

folder ['fouldə] vouwer *m.*; vouwbeen *o.*; vouwblad *o.*

folding-chair ['fouldiŋtʃêə] vouwstoel *m.*

folding-doors ['fouldiŋdo:z] schuifdeur(en), dubbele deur *v.*

foliage ['fouliidʒ] gebladerte, loof *o.*; loofwerk *o.*

folk [fouk] volk(je) *o.*, mensen *m. mv.*

folklore ['fouklo:] volkskunde *v.*

folk-song ['fouksoŋ] (oud) volkslied *o.*

follow ['folou] *vt.* volgen; volgen op; nalopen, nazetten; achtervolgen; *vi.* volgen; *sb.* (*bilj.*) doorstoot *m.*

follower ['folouə] volgeling, aanhanger, leerling *m.*; (*v. heimachine*) blok *o.*; (*v. factuur*) volgblad *o.*; (*pop.*) vrijer *m.*

folly ['foli] dwaasheid *v.*; gekheid *v.*; domheid, stommiteit *v.*

fond [fond] *adj.* innig, teder; (*dicht.*) dwaas, mal; **be — of,** verzot zijn op.

fondle ['fondl] liefkozen, strelen, aanhalen.

fondling ['fondliŋ] liefkozing *v.*; lieveling *m.*

font [font] doopvont *v.*; wijwaterbakje *o.*; (*v. lamp*) oliehouder *m.*

food [fûd] spijs *v.*, voedsel, eten; voeder *o.*; **—s,** voedingsartikelen; voedingsstoffen.

food-hoarder ['fûdho:də] hamsteraar *m.*

fool [fûl] *sb.* gek, dwaas, zot *m.*; gekkin, zottin *v.*; (*gesch.*) nar *m.*; (*Bijb.*) zondaar, goddeloze *m.*; *adj.* dwaas, gek, zot; *vt.* voor de gek houden; bedotten.

foolhardiness ['fûlhâdinis] roekeloosheid, doldriestheid *v.*

foolhardy ['fûlhâdi] roekeloos, doldriest.

foolish ['fûliʃ] *adj.* dwaas, gek, zot, mal, belachelijk.

foolishness ['fûliʃnis] dwaasheid, gekheid, zotheid *v.*

foot [fut] *sb.* voet *m.*; poot *m.*; **at —,** onderaan, aan de voet der bladzijde; onderstaand; *vt.* betreden; bewandelen; (*v. kous*) aanbreien, een voet breien aan; *vi.* te voet gaan, lopen, wandelen; dansen.

football ['futbo:l] (*sp.*) voetbal *m.*

foot-board ['futbo:d] treeplank *r.*; voettrede *v.*

foot-boy ['futboi] livreiknechtje *o.*

footlights ['futlaits] voetlicht *o.*

footprint ['futprint] voetspoor *o.*, voetindruk *m.*

foot-rest ['futrest] voetbankje *o.*

footstep ['futstep] voetstap, tred *m.*

footway ['futwei] voetpad *o.*; trottoir *o.*

foot-wear ['futwêə] schoeisel *o.*

fop [fop] modegek, fat, kwast *m.*

for [fo:] *cj.* want; *prep.* voor, in plaats van; gedurende; om; uit; naar; wegens, van wege.

forage ['foridʒ] voe(de)r, fourage *v.*

forbear [fo:'bêə] *vt.* nalaten, zich onthouden; zich wachten voor; verdragen; terughouden; sparen; *vi.* geduld hebben.

forbearance [fo:'bêərəns] onthouding *v.*; verdraagzaamheid; toegevendheid *v.*, geduld *o.*

forbearing(ly) [fo:'bêəriŋ(li)] *adj.* (*adv.*) verdraagzaam, toegevend, lijdzaam.

forbid [fə—, fo:'bid] verbieden; ontzeggen.

force [fo:s] *sb.* kracht, sterkte, macht *v.*; geweld *o.*; gewicht *o.*; noodzaak *v.*; **the —,** de politie; **the —s,** de troepen, de weermacht, de krijgsmacht; *vt.* dwingen, noodzaken; geweld aandoen; afdwingen; met geweld nemen, overweldigen, bemachtigen.

forced [fo:st] *adj.* gedwongen; (*v. mars*) geforceerd; gekunsteld, gemaakt.

forceful(ly) ['fo:sful(i)] *adj.* (*adv.*) krachtig, krachtvol; heftig.

force-meat ['fo:smît] vleesvulsel, gehakt *o.*

forcing-house ['fo:siŋhaus] broeikas *v.*

ford [fo:d] *sb.* doorwaadbare plaats *v.* (in rivier); *vt.* doorwaden.

fordable ['fo:dəbl] doorwaadbaar.

forebode [fo:'boud] voorspellen; aankondigen; een voorgevoel hebben van.

forecast ['fo:kâst] voorspelling, weervoorspelling *v.*

foreclosure [fo:'klouʒə] executie *v.*

(van hypotheek), verkoping v.; uitsluiting v.

forecourt ['fo:ko:t] voorhof m. & o., voorplein o.

forefather ['fo:fâθə] voorvader m.

forefinger ['fo:fiŋgə] voorvinger, wijsvinger m.

forefront ['fo:frənt] voorgevel m.; voorzijde v.; voorste deel o.; (fig.) voorste gelid o., voorhoede v.

foregoing [fo:'gouiŋ] voorafgaand; bovenstaand, voornoemd.

foreground ['fo:graund] voorgrond m.

forehead ['fərid] voorhoofd o.

foreign ['fərin] vreemd; buitenlands, uitheems.

foreigner ['fərinə] vreemdeling, buitenlander m.; buitenlands produkt o.

foreknowledge [fo:'nɔlidʒ] (het) vooruitweten o., voorkennis v.

forelock ['fo:lɔk] voorhaar o., voorlok v.; (tn.) wig, spie v.

foreman ['fo:mən] meesterknecht, ploegbaas, voorman m.; voorwerker m.; (recht) voorzitter m. (van jury).

foremost ['fo:moust, 'fo:məst]voorste, eerste.

forenoon ['fo:nûn] voormiddag m.

fore-ordain [fo:ro:'dein] voorbeschikken, voorbestemmen.

fore-ordination ['fo:ro:di'neiʃən] voorbeschikking v.

forerunner [fo:'rənə] voorloper, voorbode m.

foresay [fo:'sei] voorzeggen, voorspellen.

foresee [fo:'sî] voorzien.

foresight ['fo:sait] (het) vooruitzien o., vooruitziendheid v.; overleg o.; (mil.) vizierkorrel v.

forest ['forist] bos, woud o.

forestall [fo:'sto:l] (v. wensen, enz.) vóór zijn, voorkomen, vooruitlopen op; (v. bezwaren) ondervangen; verhinderen, tegenhouden.

forester ['foristə] houtvester m.; boswachter m.

foretaste ['fo:teist] voorsmaak m., voorproefje o.

foretell [fo:'tel] voorzeggen, voorspellen.

forethought ['fo:θo:t] sb. voorbedachtheid v., overleg o., voorzorg v.; adj. voorbedacht, vooraf beraamd.

foreword ['fo:wə:d] voorrede v.

forfeit ['fo:fit] sb. verbeuring v.; (het) verbeurde o.; pand o.; boete v.; adj. verbeurd; vt. verbeuren, verliezen.

forge [fo:dʒ] sb. smidse, smederij v.; smidsvuur o.; smeltoven m., smelterij v.; vt. smeden; verzinnen; namaken, vervalsen; vi. valsheid in geschrifte plegen.

forger ['fo:dʒə] smeder m.; verzinner m.; vervalser, falsaris m.; valse munter m.

forgery ['fo:dʒəri] verdichting v.; verdichtsel o.; vervalsing v.; valsheid v. in geschrifte; namaak v.

forget [fə'get] vergeten.

forgetfulness [fə'getfulnis] vergeetachtigheid v.; vergetelheid v.

forget-me-not [fə'getminɔt] (Pl.) vergeet-mij-nietje o.

forgive [fə'giv] vergeven, kwijtschelden.

forgiveness [fə'givnis] vergiffenis, kwijtschelding v.; vergevensgezindheid v.

forgiving [fə'giviŋ] vergevensgezind.

fork [fo:k] vork, gaffel v.

forlorn [fə'lo:n] verloren; verlaten, troosteloos; hopeloos, wanhopig; ellendig.

form [fo:m] sb. vorm m. gedaante, gestalte v.; formaliteit v.; formule v., formulier o.; vt. vormen; (mil.) opstellen, formeren.

formal ['fo:məl] adj. formeel; bepaald, uitdrukkelijk, nadrukkelijk; vormelijk, stijf, plechtstatig; voor de vorm.

formality [fo:'mæliti] formaliteit v.; vormelijkheid.

format ['fo:mâ] formaat o.

formation [fo:'meiʃən] vorming, samenstelling, formatie v.

former ['fo:mə] vorig, vroeger, voorafgaand; eerste.

formerly ['fo:məli] adv. vroeger, eertijds.

formidable ['fo:midəbl] adj. ontzaglijk, ontzagwekkend, geducht, vreselijk.

formless ['fo:mlis] vormloos.

formula ['fo:mjulə] formule v.; formulier o.; recept o.

formulary ['fo:mjuləri] formulier o.; formulierboek o.

formulate ['fo:mjuleit] formuleren, onder woorden brengen.

forsake [fə'seik] verzaken; verlaten, in de steek laten; vaarwel zeggen; begeven.

forswear [fo:'swêə] vt. afzweren; onder ede ontkennen; vr. — oneself, een meineed doen.

fort [fo:t] fort, bolwerk o.

forth [fo:δ] voort, vooruit, voorwaarts; (naar) buiten, te voorschijn.

forthcoming [fo:δ'kəmiŋ] komend, op handen zijnd; aanstaande; ter beschikking, aanwezig; tegemoetkomend, toeschietelijk.

forthwith [fo:δ'wiδ, fo:δ'wiθ] dadelijk, aanstonds, onmiddellijk.

fortifiable ['fo:tifaiəbl] versterkbaar.

fortify ['fo:tifai] versterken.

fortitude ['fo:titjûd] (ziels)kracht, vastberadenheid, standvastigheid v.

fortnight ['fo:tnait] veertien dagen.

fortress ['fo:tris] vesting, sterkte v.

fortuitous(ly) [fo:'tjûitəs(li)]adj. (adv.) toevallig.

fortunate ['fo:tʃənit] adj. gelukkig.

fortune ['fo:tʃən] sb. geluk, fortuin, lot o.; vi. gebeuren.

fortune-teller ['fo:tʃəntelə] waarzegger m., waarzegster v.

forty ['fo:ti] veertig.

forward ['fo:wəd] adj. voorwaarts;

vooruitstrevend; gevorderd, vergevorderd; vroegtijdig; *adv.* vooruit, voorwaarts; *sb. (sp.: voetb.)* voorwaartsspeler *m.; vt.* begunstigen, bevorderen; opzenden, verzenden, doorzenden, nazenden.

forwarding ['fo:wədiŋ] bevordering *v.*; afzending *v.*; expeditie *v.*

forwardness ['fo:wədnis] vooruitstrevendheid *v.*; vroegtijdigheid *v.*; vroegrijpheid *v.*; vrijpostigheid *v.*

fossilize ['fɔsilaiz] (doen) verstenen; verstarren.

foster ['fɔstə] kweken, opkweken; aanmoedigen, bevorderen, koesteren.

foster-mother ['fɔstəmoθə] pleegmoeder *v.*; kunstmoeder *v.*; broedmachine *v.*

foul [faul] *adj.* vuil; onzuiver, onrein; gemeen, laag; smerig; oneerlijk, vals; *sb.* botsing *v.*; *(sp.)* onregelmatige (ongeoorloofde slag, stoot, enz.) *m.; vt.* bevuilen, bezoedelen; onklaar maken; versperren; in botsing komen met; *vi.* vuil worden; *(sch.)* onklaar raken; in de war raken; *(sp.)* de spelregels overtreden.

found [faund] *vt.* stichten, oprichten, grondvesten; gronden; *(v. metaal)* gieten; *vi.* — **upon,** steunen op.

foundation [faun'deiʃən] fundering *v.*, fondement *o.*; grondslag *m.*; stichting, oprichting, grondvesting *v.*

founder ['faundə] *sb.* oprichter, stichter, grondlegger *m.*; metaalgieter *m.*

founder ['faundə] *vi.* zakken, verzakken; zinken; vergaan; mislukken; in elkaar zakken; *vt.* doen vergaan; kreupel maken.

foundling ['faundliŋ] vondeling *m.*

foundry ['faundri] gieterij *v.*

fountain ['fauntin] bron, fontein *v.*

fountain-head ['fauntin'hed] bron *v.*, oorsprong *m.*

fountain-pen ['fauntinpen] vulpen *v.*

four [fo:] vier; viertal *o.*; vierriemsboot *v.*; bemanning *v.* van vier; —*s,* *(H.)* 4 percentsobligaties.

four-footed ['fo:'futid] viervoetig.

fourteen ['fo:'tin] veertien.

fourth [fo:δ] vierde.

fourway ['fo:wei] viersprong *m.*

fowl [faul] gevogelte *o.*; kip *v.*; haan *m.*

fox [fɔks] vos *m.*

fraction ['frækʃən] *(rek.)* breuk *v.*, gebroken getal *o.*; brok *v.*, brokstuk *o.*; onderdeel *o.*; fractie *v.*; *(v. het brood)* breking *v.*

fractious(ly) ['frækʃəs(li)] *adj. (adv.)* lastig, gemelijk, kribbig, twistziek.

fracture ['fræktʃə] *sb.* breuk *v.*; beenbreuk *v.*; *vt. & vi.* breken.

fragile ['frædʒail] breekbaar, broos; zwak, teer.

fragment [frægmənt] stuk, brokstuk, fragment *o.*

fragrant ['freigrənt] geurig, welriekend.

frail [freil] *sb.* vijgenmat *v.*, vijgenkorf *m.*; bies *v.*; *adj.* broos, zwak, teer.

frame [freim] *sb.* raam, geraamte *o.*; lijst *v.*; omlijsting *v.*; *vt.* bouwen; maken, vormen, samenstellen; opzetten, op touw zetten; omlijsten.

frame-saw ['freimso:] spanzaag *v.*

framework ['freimwə:k] raam, geraamte *o.*; lijstwerk *o.*, omlijsting *v.*

France [frɑns] Frankrijk *o.*

franchise ['fræn(t)ʃaiz] burgerrecht *o.*; stemrecht *o.*; *(gesch.)* vrijstelling *v.*, voorrecht *o.*

frank [fræŋk] *adj.* openhartig, oprecht, vrijmoedig.

frankincense ['fræŋkinsens] wierook *m.*

frankness ['fræŋknis] openhartigheid, oprechtheid *v.*

frantic(ally) ['fræntik(əli)] *adj. (adv.)* woest, razend, krankzinnig.

fraternal(ly) [frə'tə:nəl(i)] *adj. (adv.)* broederlijk.

fraternity [frə'tə:niti] broederschap *v.*

fraternize ['frætənaiz] zich verbroederen.

fraud [fro:d] bedrog *o.*, bedriegerij *v.*

fraudulent(ly) ['fro:djulənt(li)] *adj. (adv.)* bedrieglijk; frauduleus.

fray [frei] afslijten, verslijten; *(v. weg)* banen; *(fig.)* aantasten; — **out,** uitrafelen.

freak [frik] gril, kuur, nuk *v.*

freakish(ly) ['frikiʃ(li)] *adj. (adv.)* grillig, nukkig.

freaky ['friki] *adj.* grillig, nukkig.

freckle ['frekl] vlekje *o.*, zomersproet *v.*

freckled ['frekld] met sproeten, sproeterig.

free [fri] *adj. & adv.* vrij; vrijwillig; kosteloos, gratis; los, ongedwongen.

freedom ['fridəm] vrijdom *m.*; vrijheid *v.*; vrijpostigheid *v.*

free-handed ['fri'hændid] vrijgevig, gul, royaal.

freehold ['frihould] vrij goed, vrij leen *o.*

free-kick ['fri'kik] *(sp.: voetb.)* vrije schop *m.*

freely ['frili] *adv.* vrij, vrijelijk; vrijmoedig, openlijk.

freemason ['frimeisən] vrijmetselaar *m.*

freestone ['fristoun] zandsteen; hardsteen *m.*

freethinker ['fri'δiŋkə] vrijdenker *m.*

free-trade ['fri'treid] vrijhandel *m.*

freeze [friz] vriezen; bevriezen; stollen.

freezing ['friziŋ] vriezend, vries—; ijskoud.

freezing-point ['friziŋpoint] vriespunt *o.*

freight [freit] vracht, lading *v.*; vrachtprijs *m.*; — **paid,** franco.

freighter ['freitə] bevrachter *m.*

freight-rates ['freitreits] vrachttarief *o.*, vrachtprijzen *m. mv.*

French [fren(t)ʃ] *adj.* Frans; *sb.* (het Frans) *o.*

frenzied ['frenzid] waanzinnig, dol.

frenzy ['frenzi] waanzin *m.*, razernij *v.*

frequent ['frikwənt] *adj.* herhaald, dikwijls voorkomend; veelvuldig.

frequent [fri'kwent] vt. (dikwijls) bezoeken, omgaan met.

frequenter [fri'kwentə] bezoeker m.

frequently ['frikwəntli] adv. herhaaldelijk, dikwijls, vaak.

fresh [freʃ] adj. fris; vers; (v. water) zoet; nieuw; onervaren; sb. frisheid, koelte v.; (in rivier) plotselinge vloed m.

freshen ['freʃ(ə)n] vt. verfrissen, opfrissen; verversen; ontzouten; aanwakkeren; vi. opfrissen; (v. wind) opsteken, toenemen.

freshness ['freʃnis] frisheid, versheid v.

fret [fret] sb. kabbeling v.; ergernis v.; gisting v.; vt. invreten, wegvreten; knagen, bijten (op 't gebit); prikkelen, irriteren; vi. om zich heenvreten; kniezen, tobben; zich ergeren; vr. — oneself to death, zich doodkniezen.

friable ['fraiəbl] bros, brokkelig.

friar ['fraiə] broeder, monnik m.

fribble ['fribl] sb. beuzelaar, futselaar m.; beuzelarij v.; adj. beuzelachtig; vi. beuzelen, futselen.

friction ['frikʃən] wrijving v.

Friday ['fraidi] vrijdag m.

fried [fraid] gebakken.

friend [frend] vriend m.; vriendin v.

friendly ['frendli] adj. vriendelijk; vriendschappelijk; welwillend; goedgezind; bevriend.

friendship ['frendʃip] vriendschap v.

frieze [friz] (bouwk.) fries v.; (stof) fries o.

frigate ['frigit] (sch.) fregat o.; (Dk.) fregatvogel m.

fright [frait] sb. schrik m., vrees v.; spook o., vogelverschrikker m.; vt. (dicht.) verschrikken, doen schrikken.

frighten ['fraitn] verschrikken, doen schrikken.

frightful(ly) ['fraitful(i)] adj. (adv.) verschrikkelijk, vreselijk.

fringe [frin(d)ʒ] sb. franje v.; rand, zoom m.; vt. met franje versieren; (fig.) omzomen.

frisk [frisk] vi. springen, dartelen, huppelen; sb. dartele sprong m.; pretje o.

frisky ['friski] adj. dartel, vrolijk.

fritter ['fritə] sb. schijfje, reepje o.; poffertje o., beignet v.; vt. klein snijden, snipperen; — away, versnipperen; verkwisten, verspillen; verbeuzelen.

frivolity [fri'vɔliti] wuftheid, beuzelachtigheid v.

frivolous(ly) ['frivələs(li)] adj. (adv.) wuft, beuzelachtig.

frizzle ['frizl] krullen, friseren.

fro [frou] to and —, heen en weer.

frock [frɔk] sb. pij v.; kiel m.; jurk v.; kleed o.

frock-coat ['frɔk'kout] geklede jas v.

frog [frɔg] kikvors, kikker m.

from [frɔm] van; uit; van ... af; wegens, door; ten gevolge van; naar.

front [frɔnt] sb. voorkant m., voorzijde v.; voorste gedeelte o.; voorgevel m.; (mil.) front o.; adj. voorste; voor—; vt.

staan tegenover; het hoofd bieden; vi. — about, zich omkeren.

frontage ['frɔntidʒ] front o.; gevelbreedte v.

frontal ['frɔntəl] sb. voorgevel m.; adj. frontaal; voorhoofds—; front—.

front-door ['frɔnt'dɔ:] voordeur v.

frontier ['frɔntjə, 'frɔntjə] grens v.; grensscheiding v.

frontless ['frɔntlis] schaamteloos, onbeschaamd.

frost [frɔst] sb. vorst v.; rijm, rijp m.; (fig.) koelheid v.; vt. (v. planten) doen bevriezen; (v. glas) mat maken, mat slijpen.

frost-nail ['frɔstneil] (voor paard) ijsnagel m.

frost-work ['frɔstwə:k] ijsbloemen v. mv.

frosty ['frɔsti] adj. vriezend, vorstig kil, koud, ijzig; bevroren; berijpt.

froth [frɔð] sb. schuim o.; gebazel o.; vt. doen schuimen; vi. schuimen; schuimbekken.

frown [fraun] het voorhoofd fronsen; dreigend (stuurs) kijken.

fructify ['frʌktifai] bevruchten; vruchtbaar maken.

fructuous ['frʌktjuəs] vruchtbaar; vruchtdragend; voordelig.

frugal ['frûgəl] adj. matig, sober; zuinig, spaarzaam.

frugality [fru'gæliti] matigheid, soberheid v.; zuinigheid, spaarzaamheid v.

fruit [frût] vrucht v.; vruchten v. mv., fruit o.

fruitful(ly) ['frûtful(i)] adj. (adv.) vruchtbaar.

fruition [frû'iʃən] genot, vruchtgebruik o.; rijpheid v.; vervulling, verwezenlijking v.

fruitless(ly) ['frûtlis(li)] adj. (adv.) zonder vrucht(en); vruchteloos, nutteloos.

fruit-tree ['frûttri] vruchtboom, fruitboom m.

frustrate [frʌs'treit] verijdelen, doen mislukken, te niet doen; dwarsbomen; teleurstellen.

fry [frai] sb. broedsel o.; school v. (van jonge vissen); vt. bakken, braden; vi. braden.

fudge [fʌdʒ] sb. klets v., onzin m.; verzinsel o.; knoeierij v.; vt. samenflansen; verzinnen; vervalsen; vi. onzin praten; knoeien; opsnijden.

fuel ['fjûil] sb. brandstof v.; (fig.) voedsel o.; vt. van brandstof voorzien; (v. vuur, enz.) voeden; vi. brandstof opdoen; benzine innemen.

fugitive ['fjûdʒitiv] adj. vluchtig; kortstondig, voorbijgaand; voortvluchtig; sb. vluchteling; uitgewekene m.

fulfil [ful'fil] volbrengen, vervullen; uitvoeren; beantwoorden aan.

fulfilment [ful'filmənt] volbrenging, vervulling; uitvoering v.

full [ful] adj. vol, gevuld; volledig;

voltallig; verzadigd; *adv.* vol, ten volle, helemaal; volmaakt, in alle opzichten; vlak; *sb.* volheid *v.*; volle maat *v.*

full-blown ['ful'bloun] in volle bloei; geheel ontwikkeld; volleerd; volslagen.

full-grown ['ful'groun] volwassen.

full-hearted ['ful'hâtid] moedig; gevoelvol.

full-speed ['ful'spîd] in volle vaart.

fumble ['fəmbl] *vt.* bevoelen, betasten; — **up,** verfrommelen; *vi.* voelen, tasten; frommelen; — **for,** zoeken naar.

fume [fjûm] *sb.* damp *m.*, uitwaseming *r.*; lucht *v.*, reuk *m.*; vlaag *v.* van woede; *vt.* beroken; uitroken; bewieroken; luchten; *vi.* roken; dampen; (*v. damp*) opstijgen; luchten; (*v. woede*) koken, zieden.

fumigator ['fjûmigeitə] ontsmetter *m.*; ontsmettingstoestel *o.*

fun [fən] *sb.* grap, aardigheid *v.*; pret *v.*, plezier *o.*; *vi.* grappen maken, gekheid maken.

function ['fəŋkʃən] ambt *o.*, bediening, functie *v.*

functionary ['fəŋkʃənəri] ambtenaar, functionaris *m.*; beambte *m.*

fund [fənd] fonds *o.*; kapitaal *o.*; voorraad *m.*; —**s,** fondsen, geldmiddelen, contanten.

fundament ['fəndəmənt] fondement *o.*

fundamental [fəndə'mentl] *adj.* fundamenteel, ten grondslag liggend, oorspronkelijk, grond—; *sb.* grondslag *m.*, basis *v.*; grondbeginsel *o.*; grondwaarheid *v.*; grondnoot *v.*, grondtoon *m.*

fund-holder ['fəndhouldə] bezitter van effecten, houder *m.* van staatspapieren.

funeral ['fjûnərəl] begrafenis *v.*; begrafenisstoet, lijkstoet *m.*; lijkdienst *m.*

fungus ['fəŋgəs] zwam *v.*; paddestoel *m.*

funnel ['fənəl] trechter *m.*; schoorsteenpijp *v.*; luchtkoker *m.*

funny ['fəni] grappig, aardig, kluchtig; vreemd, raar.

fur [fə:] *sb.* bont, bontwerk, pelswerk *o.*; pels *m.*, pelsjas *v.*; pelsdieren *o. mv.*; (*gen.*) beslag *o.* (op de tong); *adj.* bonten, bont—, met bont gevoerd; *vi.* (*v. tong*) beslaan; (*v. ketelsteen, enz.*) aanzetten.

furious (ly) ['fjûəriəs(li)] *adj.* (*adv.*) woedend, dol, razend.

furl [fə:l] opvouwen, oprollen; (*sch.: v. zeil*) vastmaken; (*v. hoop*) opgeven.

furlough ['fə:lou] *sb.* (*mil.*) verlof *o.*; *vt.* verlof geven.

furnace ['fə:nis] *sb.* fornuis *o.*; oven *m.*; (*fig.*) broeinest *o.*; *vt.* verhitten.

furnish ['fə:niʃ] verschaffen, verstrekken, leveren; uitrusten; meubileren; voorzien (**with,** van).

furniture ['fə:nitʃə] meubelen *o. mv.*, huisraad *o.*; stoffering *v.*; uitrusting, toerusting *v.*; montering *v.*

furrier ['fəriə] bontwerker *m.*; bonthandelaar *m.*

furriery ['fəriəri] bontwerk, pelswerk *o.*

furrow ['fərou] *sb.* voor, groef *v.*; rimpel *m.*; *vt.* doorploegen; groeven, rimpelen.

furry ['fə:ri] met bont gevoerd; zacht.

furstone ['fə:stoun] ketelsteen *m.*

further ['fə:θə] *adj.* verder; (*fig.*) nader; **the — side,** de overzijde; *adv.* verder; *vt.* bevorderen.

furthermore ['fə:θəmo:] verder, bovendien.

furtive ['fə:tiv] *adj.* heimelijk; steels; gestolen.

fury ['fjûəri] woede, razernij, furie *v.*

fuse [fjûz] smelten; versmelten, samensmelten.

fuse [fjûz] *sb.* (*el.*) zekering, veiligheid *v.*; (*v. bom*) lont *v.*; (*v. granaat*) buis *v.*

fuss [fəs] *sb.* (onnodige) drukte, herrie *v.*, ophef *m.*; opwinding *v.*; overdreven bezorgdheid *v.*; *vi.* drukte maken; zich druk maken; zenuwachtig maken.

fustigate ['fəstigeit] geselen, ranselen.

fusty ['fəsti] *adj.* muf, duf.

futile ['fjûtail] onbeduidend, onbetekenend, nietig; vergeefs, nutteloos; beuzelachtig.

futility [fju'tiliti] onbeduidendheid, nietigheid *v.*; nutteloosheid *v.*; beuzelachtigheid, beuzelarij *v.*

future ['fjûtʃə] *adj.* toekomstig, aanstaand; toekomend; *sb.* toekomst *v.*; aanstaande *m.* & *v.*; (*gram.*) toekomende tijd *m.*

fy [fai] foei!

G

gab [gæb] *vi.* snappen, kakelen; *sb.* gesnap, gekakel *o.*

gabble ['gæbl] *vi.* kakelen, snappen, snateren; *vt.* — (**over**), (*v. les, enz.*)aframmelen, opdreunen; *sb.* gekakel, gesnap, gesnater *o.*

gable ['geibl] gevelspits *v.*; puntgevel *m.*

gadabout ['gædəbaut] uitloper, straatslijper, lanterfanter *m.*

gad-fly ['gædflai] brems, horzel *v.*

gag [gæg] *sb.* (mond)prop *v.*; (*v. toneel*) (door toneelspeler) ingelaste woorden; *vt.* knevelen; de mond snoeren; (*v. pers*) muilbanden; (woorden) inlassen.

gain [gein] *sb.* winst *v.*, voordeel *o.*; aanwinst *v.*; *vt.* winnen; verdienen; verkrijgen, verwerven; bereiken; (*v. overwinning, enz.*) behalen.

gainer ['geinə] winner *m.*

gainful ['geinful] winstgevend; voordelig.

gainless ['geinlis] onvoordelig.

gainly ['geinli] bevallig; innemend.

gait [geit] gang, loop, pas *m.*

gaiter ['geitə] slobkous *r*.

galaxy ['gæləksi] (*sterr*.) melkweg *m*.

Galilee ['gælili] Galilea *o*.

gall [go:l] *sb*. gal *v*.; bitterheid *v*.; galnoot *v*.; *vt*. (*v. huid*) afschaven; verbitteren; ergeren; kwetsen; (*mil*.) bestoken.

gallant ['gælənt] *adj*. dapper, kranig; fier; schitterend. statig; smaakvol.

gall-bladder ['go:lblædə] galblaas *v*.

gallery ['gæləri] galerij *v*., gaanderij *v*., zuilengang *m*.; tribune *v*.

galley ['gæli] (*sch*.) galei *v*.; kombuis *v*.; kapiteinssloep *v*.; (*drukk*.) galei *v*.

galloon [gə'lûn] *sb*. galon, boordsel *o*.; *vt*. galonneren.

gallop ['gæləp] *sb*. galop *m*.; *vi*. (*vt*.) (laten) galopperen.

gallows-tree ['gælouztri] galg *v*.

gall-stone ['go:lstoun] galsteen *m*.

galosh [gə'loʃ] (gummi-)overschoen *m*.

galvanize ['gælvənaiz] galvaniseren.

gamble ['gæmbl] *vi*. spelen, dobbelen, gokken; — *away*, verspelen, verdobbelen; *sb*. dobbelarij *v*., gokje *o*.; (*fig*.) loterij, speculatie *v*.

gambling-den ['gæmbliŋden] speelhol *o*.

game [geim] *sb*. spel *o*.; spelletje *o*.; wild *o*.; wildbraad *o*.; *adj*. dapper, moedig, flink, kranig; (*v. arm, been*) lam, kreupel; *vi*. spelen, dobbelen.

game-bag ['geimbæg] weitas *v*.

game-licence ['geimlaisəns] jachtakte *v*. [fel *v*

gaming-table ['geiminteibl] speeltagamut** ['gæmət] gamma, toonladder, toonschaal *v*.

gang [gæŋ] bende *v*., troep *m*., kliek *v*.; (*v. werklieden*) ploeg *v*.; (*v. gereedschap, werktuigen*) stel *o*.

gang-board ['gæŋbo:d] (*sch*.) loopplank *v*.

gangrene ['gæŋgrin] *sb*. koudvuur *o*.; (*fig*.) kanker *m*., bederf *o*.; *vi*. (*vt*.) het koudvuur (doen) krijgen.

gangster ['gæŋstə] bendelid *o*., bandiet *m*.

gangway ['gæŋwei] pad *o*. (tussen stoelen, enz.); doorgang *m*.; (*in Lagerhuis*) middenpad, dwarspad *o*.; (*sch*.) gangboord *o*.; loopplank *v*.; overloop *m*.

gaol(er) [dʒeil(ə)] cipier *m*.

gap [gæp] gat *o*., opening *v*.; hiaat *o*.; leemte *v*.; kloof *v*.; (*v. mes*) schaard *v*.; (*aardk*.) gaping *v*.

gape [geip] *vi*. gapen, geeuwen; — *after*, snakken naar; *sb*. gaping *v*.; gaap *m*.; —*s*, gaapziekte.

garage ['gæridʒ] *sb*. garage *v*.; *vt*. stallen (in garage).

garb [gâb] *sb*. gewaad, kleed *o*.; dracht, kleding *v*.; *vt*. kleden; inkleden.

garbage ['gâbidʒ] afval (v. dier) *o*;. (*fig*.) vuil, uitschot *o*.

garble ['gâbl] verdraaien, verminken; verknoeien; ziften.

garden ['gâdn] *sb*. tuin, hof *m*.; *vi*. tuinieren.

gardener ['gâdnə] tuinman, tuinier, hovenier *m*.

garden-frame ['gâdnfreim] broeibak *m*.

garden-peas ['gâdnpîz] doperwten *v. mv*.

garden-shears ['gâdnʃiəz] snoeischaar *v*.

gargle ['gâgl] *vi*. gorgelen; *sb*. gorgeldrank *m*.

garland ['gâlənd] *sb*. guirlande *v*., krans *m*.; *vt*. omkransen, bekransen.

garlic ['gâlik] knoflook *o*.

garment ['gâmənt] *sb*. kledingstuk, gewaad *o*.; *vt*. (*dicht*.) kleden.

garnet ['gânit] granaat(steen) *m*.

garnish ['gâniʃ] *vt*. versieren, garneren; voorzien (*with*, van); (*recht*) waarschuwen; dagvaarden; *sb*. versiering, garnering *v*.

garret ['gærit] vliering *v*., zolderkamertje *o*.

garrison ['gærisən] *sb*. garnizoen *o*.; bezetting *v*.; *vt*. garnizoen leggen in; bezetten; in garnizoen leggen.

garrulous(ly) ['gæruləs(li)] *adj*. (*adv*.) praatgraag, praatziek.

garter ['gâtə] *sb*. kouseband *m*.; (*Am*.) sokophouder *m*.; *vt*. met een kouseband vastmaken; de orde van de Kouseband verlenen.

gas [gæs] *sb*. gas *o*.; bluf *m*.; geklets *o*.; (*Am*.) benzine *v*.; *vt*. met gas verlichten (bedwelmen, behandelen); van gas voorzien; *vi*. bluffen, opsnijden; kletsen; (*Am*.) benzine innemen.

gas-bag ['gæsbæg] (*tn*.) gaszak *m*.; (*fig*.) windbuil, windzak *m*.; (*sl*.) luchtballon *m*., luchtschip *o*.

gas-bill ['gæsbil] gasrekening *r*.

gas-bracket ['gæsbrækit] gasarm *m*.

gaseous ['gæsiəs, 'geiziəs] gasachtig, gas—; vluchtig.

gash [gæʃ] *sb*. houw *m*., snede *v*.; *vt*. een wond (snede) toebrengen, snijden.

gas-helmet ['gæshelmit] brandweerhelm *m*., (helm met) gasmasker *o*.

gasp [gâsp] *vi*. (naar adem) snakken; hijgen; *vt*. — *life awa* ' (*out*), de laatste adem uitblazen; *sb*. snik; ademtocht *m*.

gas-ring ['gæsriŋ] gasstel *o*.

gas-station ['gæssteiʃən] (*Am*.) benzinelaadstation *o*.

gastronome ['gæstrənoum], **gastronomer** [gæs'trənəmə] gastronoom, lekkerbek, fijnproever *m*.

gate [geit] poort, deur *v*.; toegang *m*.; hek *o*.; slagboom, afsluitboom *m*.; (*bij voetbalwedstrijd*) betalende bezoekers *m. mv*.; entreegeld *o*.; (*Sc*.) weg *m*., straat *v*.

gate-keeper ['geitkipə] portier *m*.; baanwachter, overwegwachter *m*.

gather ['gæθə] *vt*. verzamelen, vergaren; bijeenbrengen; plukken; (*v. koren, enz.*) oogsten, binnenhalen; (*v. kleed*) plooien, innemen; *vi*. zich verzamelen; bijeenkomen, vergaderen; (*v. onweer, enz.*)

opkomen; (*r. kracht, omvang*) toenemen, aangroeien; (*c. zweer*) rijp worden; *sb.* **—s,** plooisel; opnaaisel *o.*

gathering ['gæθəriŋ] verzameling *v.* inzameling *r.*; pluk *m.*; oogst *m.*; bijeenkomst *r.*; abces *o.*

gauche [gouʃ] links, onhandig.

gaudy ['goːdi] *adj.* opzichtig, opgesmukt, bont; *sb.* feestmaal *o.*, fuif.

gauge [geidʒ] (standaard)maat *v.*; peilstok *m.*, peilglas *o.*; (*sch.*) diepgang *m.*; (*mil.*) kaliber *o.*; spoorwijdte *v.*

gauger ['geidʒə] peiler, meter *m.*

gauging-rod ['geidʒiŋrɔd] peilstok *m.*

gaunt [gɔːnt] schraal, mager; (*r. kamer*) hol.

gauntlet ['gɔːntlit] (*gesch.*) pantserhandschoen *m.*; werkhandschoen *m.*; (lange) dameshandschoen *m.*; sport-, schermhandschoen *m.*

gauntree ['gɔːntri] steiger *m.*, stelling *v.*

gauze [gɔːz] *sb.* gaas *o.*; waas *o.*; lichte nevel *m.*; *adj.* gazen.

gauzy ['gɔːzi] gaasachtig; wazig; nevelig.

gawk [gɔːk] *sb.* lummel, sul, slungel *m.*, uilskuiken *o.*; (*Dk.*) koekoek *m.*; *vi.* staan gapen.

gay [gei] vrolijk, opgewekt; luchtig; luchthartig; losbandig, licht (van zeden); kleurig, bont, schitterend.

gaze [geiz] *ri.* staren, turen; *sb.* starende blik *m.*

gear [giə] *sb.* tuig, gareel *o.*; toestel *o.*; gereedschap *o.*; uitrusting *r.*; versnelling *v.*; (*tn.*) overbrengwerk *o.*; *vt.* tuigen, optuigen *ri.* **— into,** (*r. tandrad*) grijpen in.

gearing-wheel ['giəriŋwil] tandrad *o.*; (*r. fiets*) kettingwiel *o.*

gem [dʒem] *sb.* edelsteen *m.*, juweel, kleinood *o.*; *rt.* met edelgesteenten versieren.

gender ['dʒendə] *sb.* geslacht *o.*; *rt.* (*dicht.*) voortbrengen, telen.

genealogic(al) [dʒiniə'lɔdʒik(l)] genealogisch; **— tree,** stamboom *m.*

general ['dʒenərəl] *adj.* algemeen; gewoon; *sb.* het algemeen *o.*; (*mil.*) generaal, veldheer *m.*

generalissimo [dʒenərə'lisimou] opperbevelhebber *m.*

generally ['dʒenərəli] *adv.* algemeen, in 't algemeen; gewoonlijk.

generate ['dʒenəreit] voortbrengen, verwekken; (*r. elektriciteit*) opwekken; (*r. gas*) ontwikkelen.

generosity [dʒenə'rɔsiti] mildheid, milddadigheid *r.*; edelmoedigheid *v.*

generous(ly) ['dʒenərəs(li)] *adj.* (*adv.*) mild, milddadig; edelmoedig; rijk, overvloedig.

Genesis ['dʒenisis] Genesis *r.*; wording *r.*, ontstaan *o.*

genial ['dʒiniəl] levenwekkend; groeizaam, vruchtbaar; opwekkend; opgewekt, levendig.

geniality [dʒini'æliti] groeizaamheid, vruchtbaarheid *r.*; opgewektheid,

genius ['dʒiniəs] geest, genius *m.*; genie, talent *o.*, aanleg *m.*; beschermgeest *m.*

genteel [dʒen'til] beschaafd, deftig, fatsoenlijk.

gentile ['dʒentail] *adj.* heidens *sb.* heiden *m.* & *v.*

gentle ['dʒentl] *adj.* aanzienlijk, voornaam; vriendelijk, minzaam; zacht, zachtzinnig; vreedzaam; *sb.* made *v.* (als aas); **—s,** (*pop.*) voorname lui; *vt.* verzachten; temmen, africhten; temperen, dempen.

gentleman ['dʒentlmən] heer *m.*; man van eer, fatsoenlijk man *m.*

gentlemanlike ['dʒentlmənlaik], **gentlemanly** ['dʒentlmənli] fatsoenlijk, beschaafd.

gentleman player ['dʒentlmən'pleiə] amateur *m.*

gentleness ['dʒentlnis] voornaamheid *r.*; vriendelijkheid, minzaamheid *v.*; zachtheid, zachtzinnigheid *r.*

gently ['dʒentli] *adv.* zacht; vriendelijk.

genuflexion [dʒenju'flekʃən] kniebuiging *v.*, knieval *m.*

genuine ['dʒenjuin] *adj.* echt, onvervalst.

geography [dʒi'ɔgrəfi] aardrijkskunde *v.*

geometer [dʒi'ɔmitə] meetkundige *m.*; landmeter *m.*; (*Dk.*) spanrups *r.*

geometry [dʒi'ɔmətri] meetkunde *v.*

germ [dʒəːm] *sb.* kiem *r.*; *vi.* kiemen, ontkiemen.

German [dʒəːmən] *sb.* Duitser-Germaan *m.*; Duits *o.*; *adj.* Duits.

Germanophil(e) [dʒəː'mænoufil] Duitsgezind.

Germany ['dʒəːməni] Duitsland *o.*

germicidal ['dʒəːmisaidəl] kiemdodend.

germinate ['dʒəːmineit] *vi.* (*rt.*) (doen) ontkiemen, ontspruiten.

gestation [dʒes'teiʃən] zwangerschap *v.*; dracht, drachtigheid *r.*

gesticulate [dʒes'tikjuleit] gesticuleren, gebaren maken.

gesture ['dʒestʃə] *sb.* gebaar *o.*, beweging *v.*; daad *v.*; stap *m.*; *ri.* gebaren maken, gesticuleren.

get [get] *vt.* krijgen, verkrijgen; verdienen; (*v. hooi, enz.*) binnenhalen; verschaffen, bezorgen; bemachtigen; overhalen (tot); (*sl.*) snappen, begrijpen; *vi.* komen; worden; (ge-)raken; **— off** (**by heart**), van buiten leren; **— through,** er door komen, slagen; (*v. telef.*) aansluiting krijgen; (*v. wetsontwerp*) aangenomen worden; **— up,** opstaan; (*r. wind*) opsteken; (*v. haar, linnen*) opmaken; (*v. onderwerp*) bestuderen; (*v. spel*) monteren; (*v. werk, enz.*) uitvoeren; in elkaar zetten, op touw zetten; **— at,** bereiken; te pakken krijgen; (*fig.*) knoeien met, omkopen; (*Am.*) iem. op zijn nummer zetten; *vt.* **— oneself up,** zich opdirken, zich mooi maken; *sb.* nest *o.*, worp *m.*; jong(en) *o.* (*mv.*); opbrengst *v.*

gettable ['getəbl] te krijgen.

get-up [get'ɒp] uitrusting *v.*; toneelschikking *v.*; (*v. toneelstuk*) aankleding, montering *v.*; (*v. boek*) uitvoering *v.*

ghastly ['gâstli] doodsbleek; akelig, afgrijselijk; grimmig.

gherkin ['gâkin] augurkje *o.*

ghetto ['getou] ghetto *o.*, jodenbuurt *v.*, jodenkwartier *o.*

ghost [goust] geest *m.*; spook *o.*, schim *r.*; schijntje *o.*, zweem *m.*; iem. die een werk uitvoert, waarvan een ander de eer krijgt.

ghostly ['goustli] spookachtig.

ghoul [gûl] (*fig.*) grafschender *m.*

giant ['dʒaiənt] *sb.* reus *m.*; *adj.* reusachtig.

gibberish ['giberiʃ] brabbeltaal *v.*, koeterwaals *o.*

gibe [dʒaib] *vt. & vi.* spotten (met), honen, (be)schimpen; *sb.* hatelijkheid, spotternij; schimpscheut *v.*

giber ['dʒaibə] spotter, (be)schimper *m.*

giddy ['gidi] *adj.* duizelig, draaierig; duizelingwekkend; onbezonnen, lichtzinnig; *vi.* (*vt.*) (doen) duizelen.

gift [gift] *sb.* gift, gave *v.*, geschenk *o.*; (recht *o.* van) begeving *v.*; *vt.* schenken; begiftigen.

gifted ['giftid] begiftigd; begaafd.

gig [gig] *sb.* sjees, cabriolet *v.*; (*sch.*) giek *v.*; harpoen *m.*; *vt.* harpoeneren.

gigantic(ally) [dʒai'gæntik(əli)] *adj.* (*adv.*) reusachtig, reuzen—.

giggle ['gigl] *vi.* giechelen; *sb.* gegiechel *o.*

gild [gild] vergulden, versieren, verfraaien, smukken.

gill [gill] *sb.* kieuw *v.*; kaak *v.*; ravijn *o.*; bergstroom *m.*; *vt.* (*v. vis*) uithalen; (*v. haring*) kaken.

gillyflower ['dʒiliflauə] anjelier *v.*; muurbloem *v.*

gilt [gilt] *sb.* verguldsel *o.*; (*sl.*) geld, goud *o.*; *adj.* verguld.

gilt-edged ['giltedʒd] verguld op snee.

gin [dʒin] *sb.* jenever *v.*; (*Am.*) sterke drank *m.*; strik, valstrik *m.*; kraan *v.*, windas *o.*; *vt.* strikken, vangen; (*v. katoen*) ontkorrelen.

ginger ['dʒindʒə] *sb.* gember *v.*; (*sl.*) fut *v.*; (*sl.*) prikkel *m.*, opwekking *r.*; *vt.* met gember bereiden (kruiden); (*sl.*) — (*up*), opkikkeren; aanporren.

gingerbread ['dʒindʒəbred] *sb.* peperkoek *m.*; (*fig.*) prullerij *v.*; (*sl.*) geld *o.*, duiten *m. mv.*; *adj.* prullerig; opzichtig.

gipsy ['dʒipsi] *sb.* zigeuner(in) *m.* (*v.*); heiden *m.*; zigeunertaal *v.*; (*fam.*) heks *v.*; *vi.* picknicken; leven als zigeuners; *adj.* zigeunerachtig.

gipsy-cart ['dʒipsikât] woonwagen *m.*

giraffe [dʒi'râf] giraffe *v.*

gird [gâd] *vt.* omgorden omringen, omsingelen, insluiten; uitrusten; *vi.* — *at*, spotten met, schimpen op; *sb.* spotternij; hatelijkheid *v.*, steek *m.*

girdle ['gâdl] *sb.* gordel *m.*; *vt.* omgorden; omringen, omgeven.

girl [gâl] meisje; dienstmeisje *o.*

girl-guide ['gâ:lgaid] padvindster *v.*

girlish ['gâ:liʃ] meisjesachtig; meisjes—.

girth [gâ:θ] *sb.* buikriem, singel *m.*; gordel *m.*; omvang; omtrek *m.*; *vt.* (*v. paard*) singelen; (*v. zadel*) vastmaken; (*v. omvang*) meten.

gist [dʒist] hoofdpunt *o.*, hoofdzaak *v.*; kern *v.*

give [giv] *vt. & ri.* geven; verlenen, schenken; (*bilj.*) vóórgeven; (*v. werk*) opgeven; — *away*, weggeven; (*fig.*) verklikken, verraden; — *out*, aankondigen, uitstrooien; uitdelen; (*v. licht*) uitgaan; — *in*, inleveren; (*v. instemming*) betuigen; toegeven; zich gewonnen geven; *sb.* (het) meegeven *o.*

give-away [givə'wei] (het) verklappen, (het) verraden *o.*

given ['givn] gegeven; verslaafd (*to, aan*); geneigd (*to,* tot).

giver ['givə] gever, schenker *m.*; (*H.: v. wissel*) trekker *m.*

gizzard ['gizəd] spiermaag *r.*; (*fig.*) strot *m.*

glacial ['gleisiəl, 'glæsiəl] ijzig; ijs—.

glad [glæd] *adj.* blij, verheugd.

gladden ['glædn] verblijden, verheugen.

gladiator ['glædieitə] gladiator, zwaardvechter *m.*

gladly ['glædli] *adv.* blij; blijmoedig, met blijdschap; gaarne, met genoegen.

gladness ['glædnis] blijheid, blijdschap, blijmoedigheid *v.*

glair [glêə] *sb.* eiwit *o.*; *vt.* met eiwit bestrijken.

glance [glâns] *sb.* oogopslag, (vluchtige) blik *m.*; flikkering *v.*; schampschot *o.*; (*tn.*) glans *m.*; *vt.* — *one's eyes at* (*over, upon*), een blik werpen op; *vi.* blinken, glinsteren, schitteren, (even) kijken.

gland [glænd] klier *v.*; (*wet.*) eikel *m.*, (*tn.*) drukring *m.*, drukstuk *o.*

glandular ['glændjulə] klierachtig; klier—.

glare [glêə] *sb.* verblindende glans *m.*; schittering *v.*; fel licht *o.*; felle gloed *m.*; woeste blik *m.*; *vi.* schitteren, hel flikkeren; woest kijken (staren).

glaring(ly) ['glêəriŋ(li)] *adj.* (*adv.*) (*v. licht*) hel, schel, verblindend; (*v. ogen*) vlammend, vurig; (*v. onrecht*) schreeuwend; (*v. tegenstelling*) schril.

glass [glâs] *sb.* glas *o.*; glaswerk *o.*; broeikas *v.*; verrekijker *m.*; vergrootglas *o.*; (*pair of*) —*es*, bril *m.*; lorgnet *o.*; *adj.* glazen; *vt.* verglazen; afspiegelen, weerkaatsen.

glass-bell ['glâsbel] stolp *r.*

glasscase ['glâs'keis] glazen uitstalkast, vitrine *v.*

glass-paper ['glâspeipə] schuurpapier *o.*

glassy ['glâsi] glasachtig, glazig; (*spiegel*) glad.

glaze [gleiz] *rt.* van glazen (ruiten) voorzien; in glas zetten; verglazen; glanzen, polijsten; *vi.* glazig worden; (*v. ogen*) breken; *sb.* glazuur *o.*; glans *m.*; vernis *o.*

glazier ['gleiziǝ] glazenmaker *m.*

gleam [glîm] *sb.* glans *m.*; schijnsel *o.*; glimp, straal *m.*; *vi.* glanzen, blinken, stralen; glimmen; flikkeren.

glean [glîn] *vt.* bijeenlezen, verzamelen; opvangen, oppikken. *vi.* aren lezen.

gleaner ['glînǝ] arenlezer *m.* (*fig.*) samenlezer, sprokkelaar *m.*

glib(ly) ['glib(li)] *adj.* (*adv.*) vloeiend; rad van tong, welbespraakt; glad, glibberig.

glibness ['glibnis] radheid van tong, welbespraaktheid *v.*; gladheid, glibberigheid *v.*

glide [glaïd] *vi.* glijden; zweven; sluipen; (*vl.*) planeren; — *into,* ongemerkt overgaan in; *sb.* het glijden *o.*; glijvlucht, zweefvlucht *v.*

glider ['glaïdǝ] glijder *m.*; glijvliegtuig, zweefvliegtuig *o.*; zweefvlieger *m.*

glimmer ['glimǝ] *vi.* flikkeren, schemeren, zacht schijnen; *sb.* flikkering *v.*, schijnsel *o.*; glimp *m.*; straaltje *o.*; flauw begrip *o.*

glimpse [glim(p)s] *sb.* glimp, straal *m.*; schijnsel *o.*; vluchtige blik *m.*; *vt.* vluchtig (even) zien.

glint [glint] *sb.* schijnsel *o.*, flikkering *v.*; glimp; vluchtige blik *m.*; *vi.* glinsteren, schitteren, flikkeren.

glitter ['glitǝ] *vi.* flikkeren, fonkelen, schitteren, blinken; *sb.* flikkering, schittering *v.*; glans, luister *m.*

gloaming ['gloumiŋ] schemering *v.*

globe [gloub] *sb.* bol; aardbol, wereldbol *m.*; (*v. lamp*) ballon *m.*; *vt.* tot een bol vormen.

globe-trotter ['gloubtrotǝ] wereldreiziger *m.*

globular ['globjulǝ] bolvormig.

gloom [glûm] *sb.* donkerte; schemering *v.*; somberheid, droefgeestigheid *v.*; *vt.* verdonkeren, donker maken; somber maken, met droefgeestigheid vervullen; *ri.* er somber, droefgeestig uitzien; donker kijken, kniezen; (*v. lucht*) verduisteren, betrekken.

gloomy ['glûmi] duister; somber; droefgeestig, neerslachtig.

glorification [glo:rifi'keiʃǝn] verheerlijking *v.*

glorious ['glo:riǝs] roemrijk, glorierijk; heerlijk, prachtig, glansrijk.

glory ['glo:ri] *sb.* roem *m.*, glorie *v.*; lof *m.*, eer *v.*; heerlijkheid, zaligheid *v.*; stralenkrans *m.*, aureool *v.*; *vi.* — *in,* zich beroemen op; zich verheugen in.

gloss [glos] *sb.* glans, luister *m.*; valse schijn *m.*; glosse, toelichting, kanttekening *v.*; *vt.* glanzend maken; doen schitteren; — *over,* verbloemen, vergoelijken, bemantelen; glossen maken (*upon,* op); verdraaien.

glove [glov] handschoen *m.*

glow [glou] *sb.* gloed *m.*, vuur *o.*; *vi.* gloeien, branden.

glowing(ly) ['glouiŋ(li)] *adj.* (*adv.*) gloeiend, vurig, met gloed, met vuur; (*Am.*) aangeschoten.

glowworm ['glouwǝ:m] glimworm *m.*

gloze [glouz] *vt.* verbloemen, bewimpelen, vergoelijken; vleien; *sb.* vleierij, vleitaal *v.*; schijn *m.*

glucose ['glûkous] druivesuiker *v.*

glue [glû] *sb.* lijm *v.*; *vt.* lijmen; plakken, kleven.

glum(ly) [glom(li)] *adj.* (*adv.*) somber, nors, triest, stuurs.

glut [glot] *vt.* (over)verzadigen; (*v. markt*) overvoeren, overladen; *sb.* (over)verzadiging *v.*; overvoering, overlading *v.*

glutinous(ly) ['glûtinǝs(li)] *adj.* (*adv.*) lijmachtig, lijmig, kleverig.

glutton ['glotn] *sb.* gulzigaard, schrokker *m.*; (*v. dier*) veelvraat *m.*; *adj.* gulzig, schrokkerig.

gluttonous(ly) ['glotnǝs(li)] *adj.* (*adv.*) gulzig; *be* — *of,* verslinden.

gnash [næʃ] knarsen.

gnat [næt] mug *v.*

gnat-strainer ['nætstreinǝ] muggezifter *m.*

gnaw [no:] knagen, knabbelen, afknagen.

gnome [noum] aardmannetje *o.*; kabouter *m.*; zinspreuk *v.*

go [gou] *vi.* gaan, lopen; voorbijgaan; (*v. geld*) gangbaar zijn; verdwijnen; *sb.* het gaan *o.*; gang *m.*; vaart *v.*; vuur *o.*, fut, bezieling *v.*; mode *v.*; beurt *v.*

goad [goud] *sb.* prikkel *m.*; *vt.* prikkelen, aansporen, aanzetten.

goal [goul] eindpaal *m.*, bestemming *v.*; (*sp.*) goal *m.*, doelpunt *o.*

goal-keeper ['goulkîpǝ] doelverdediger, doelman *m.*

goat [gout] geit *v.*

goatee [gou'tî] sik(je) *v.* (*o.*).

go-between ['goubitwîn] bemiddelaar, tussenpersoon *m.*

goblin ['goblin] kabouter, (boze) geest *m.*

God, god [god] God; afgod *m.*

god-child ['godtʃaild] petekind *o.*

goddess ['godis] godin *v.*

godfather ['godfâθǝ] peet(oom) *m.*

god-fearing ['godfîriŋ] godvrezend.

godless(ly) ['godlis(li)] *adj.* (*adv.*) goddeloos.

godmother ['godmǝθǝ] petemoei *v.*

godsend ['godsend] buitenkansje *o.*, meevaller *m.*

goggle ['gogl] *vt.* & *vi.* met de ogen rollen; scheel kijken; uitpuilen; *adj.* uitpuilend; *sb.* stofbril; autobril; zonnebril *m.*; oogkleppen *v. mv.*

going ['gouiŋ] (het) gaan *o.*; gang *m.*; stap *m.*

goitre ['goitǝ] kropgezwel *o.*

gold [gould] *sb.* goud *o.*; (*v. schijf*) roos *v.*; *adj.* gouden.

golden ['gouldn] gouden; gulden; goudkleurig; goud—.

gold-leaf ['gouldlif] bladgoud o.

goldsmith ['gouldsmiδ] goudsmid m.

golf [gɔ(l)f] sb. golfspel o.; vi. golf spelen.

gondola ['gɔndələ] gondel v.

good [gud] adj. goed; knap, sterk; (v. kind) zoet; braaf; fatsoenlijk, eerbaar; **make** —, (v. schade, enz.) goedmaken, vergoeden; (v. tekort) aanvullen, aanzuiveren; (v. belofte) houden, nakomen; (v. beweringen, enz.) bewijzen; adv. (Am.) goed, terdege; sb. goed o.; welzijn o.; voordeel o.

good-bye ['gud'bai] goedendag! adieu! sb. [gud'bai] afscheid, vaarwel o.

goodish ['gudiʃ] goedig; tamelijk goed.

good-looking ['gud'lukiŋ] knap, mooi.

goodly ['gudli] knap, mooi; flink; uitnemend.

good-natured(ly) ['gud'neitʃəd(li)] adj. (adv.) goedaardig; welwillend.

goodness ['gudnis] goedheid v.; deugd v.; voortreffelijkheid v.

goods [gudz] goederen o. mv.; waren v. mv.; (fam.) goederentrein m.; (sp., sl.) renpaarden o. mv.

goods van ['gudzvæn] goederenwagen m.

goody ['gudi] sb. bonbon o., lekkernij v.; (Am.) sul m.; adj. goed(ig), sullig.

goody-goody ['gudi'gudi] goed, braaf, sullig; zoetsappig.

goose [gûs] gans v.; (fig.) eend v., uilskuiken o.; (v. kleermaker) persijzer o.

gooseberry ['guzbəri] kruisbes v.; kruisbessestruik m.

gooseberry-season ['guzbərisizn]
gooseberry-time ['guzbəritaim] komkommertijd m.

goose-flesh ['gûsfleʃ] ganzevlees o.; (fig.) kippevel o.

gorge [gɔ:dʒ] sb. keel v., strot m.; ravijn o., bergkloof v.; zwelgpartij v.; vt. opslokken, inzwelgen, verzwelgen; volproppen, volstoppen; vi. schrokken.

gorgeous(ly) ['gɔ:dʒəs(li)] adj. (adv.) prachtig, schitterend.

gormandize ['gɔ:məndaiz] sb. gulzigheid v.; vt. verslinden; vi. schrokken, zwelgen.

goshawk ['gɔshɔ:k] havik, patrijsvalk m.

gospel ['gɔspəl] evangelie o.

gossip ['gɔsip] sb. babbelaar(ster) m. (v.), kletskous v.; gepraat, gebabbel o., praatjes o. mv.; vi. babbelen, kletsen, kwebbelen.

gourd [guəd, gɔ:d] pompoen m., kalebas v. ver m.

gourmet ['guəmei] lekkerbek, fijnproever m.

gout [gaut] jicht v.; druppel m.

govern ['gəvən] vt. & vi. regeren, besturen; leiden; beheersen; vr. — oneself, zich beheersen.

governess ['gəvənis] gouvernante v.

government ['gəvənmənt] regering v., bestuur o.; leiding v.; gouvernement o.

governmental [gəvən'mentl] regerings—, rijks—.

governor ['gəvənə] gouverneur, landvoogd m.; bestuurder, bewindvoerder m.

gown [gaun] sb. japon v., kleed o., jurk v.; tabberd m., toga v.; vt. (zich) kleden; de toga aantrekken.

grabble ['græbl] grabbelen, tasten (for, naar); spartelen.

grace [greis] sb. genade; gunst v.; gratie, bevalligheid v.; beleefdheid, betamelijkheid v.; uitstel, respijt o.; vt. (ver)sieren, tooien; opluisteren; begunstigen.

graceful(ly) ['greisful(i)] adj. (adv.) bevallig, gracieus, sierlijk.

gracious ['greiʃəs] adj. genadig, goeder tieren; goedgunstig; minzaam; hoffelijk.

gradation [grə'deiʃən] gradering v.; gradatie v.; schakering v.; onmerkbare overgang m.

grade [greid] sb. graad; rang m.; kwaliteit v., gehalte o.; stap, trap m.; vt. graderen; rangschikken.

gradual ['grædjuəl] adj. geleidelijk; trapsgewijze opklimmend (afdalend); sb. (kath.) graduale o.

gradually ['grædjuəli] geleidelijk, trapsgewijze; langzamerhand.

graduation [grædju'eiʃən] geleidelijke opklimming, progressie v.; graduatie v.; promotie v.; gradering v.

graft [grâft] sb. ent v.; enting v.; spit o., spadesteek m.; (sl.) werk, karwei o.; vt. enten; vi. (Am.) knoeien.

grain [grein] graan, koren o.; (graan)-korrel m.; greintje o.; (v. leer) nerf v.; (v. hout, vlees) draad m.

grammar ['græmə] spraakkunst, spraakleer v.

grammatical(ly) [grə'mætikəl(i)] adj. (adv.) spraakkunstig, taalkundig.

gramme [græm] gram o.

granary ['grænəri] graanschuur v., graanzolder m.

grand [grænd] groot; groots, verheven; belangrijk, voornaam; (fam.) prachtig, heerlijk.

grandchild ['grændtʃaild] kleinkind o.

grand-daughter ['grænddɔ:tə] kleindochter v.

grand-duchy ['grænd'dətʃi] groothertogdom; grootvorstendom o.

grandfather ['græn(d)fâðə] grootvader m.

grandiose ['grændious] groots, weids, grandioos.

grandmother ['grændmɔθə] grootmoeder v.

grand-nephew ['grændnevjû] achterneef m.

grand-parents ['grændpêərənts] grootouders m. mv.

grandson ['grændsən] kleinzoon m.

granite ['grænit] graniet o.

granny ['græni] grootje o.

grant [grânt] vt. toestaan, inwilligen, vergunnen; schenken; (v. rechten) verlenen; toegeven; toestemmen; sb. inwilliging, vergunning *v.*; schenking *v.*; gift, bijdrage *v.*, subsidie *o.* & *v.*

granular ['grænjulə] korrelachtig, korrelig.

granulate ['grænjuleit] korrelen, granuleren, greineren.

grape [greip] druif *v.*; (*mil.*) schroot *o.*

grape-fruit ['greipfrût] pompelmoes *v.*

grape-shot ['greipʃɔt] schroot *o.*

grape-stone ['greipstoun] druivepit *v.*

grape-vine ['greipvain] wijnstok *m.*

graphic(al) ['græfik(l)] *adj.* grafisch; schrift—, schrijf—; tekenachtig, aanschouwelijk.

grapnel ['græpnəl] enterdreg *v.*, enterhaak *m.*

grapple ['græpl] *sb. zie* **grapnel**; greep *m.*, omvatting, worsteling *v.*; *vt.* enteren; aanklampen; beetpakken; *vi.* — *with,* worstelen met, zich meten met.

grasp [grâsp] *vt.* grijpen, vastgrijpen; omvatten; begrijpen; omklemmen, vasthouden; *vi.* — *at,* grijpen naar; *sb.* greep *m.*; bereik *o.*; macht *v.*; houvast *o.*; beheersing *v.*

grasping(ly) ['grâspiŋ(li)] *adj.* (*adv.*) inhalig, hebzuchtig.

grass [grâs] gras *o.*; weiland *o.*

grass-blade ['grâsbleid] grashalm *m.*

grass-court ['grâskɔ:t] (*sp.:* tennis) grasveld *o.*

grasshopper ['grâshɔpə] sprinkhaan *m.*

grassland ['grâslænd] grasland, weiland *o.*

grassplot ['grâsplɔt] grasperk, grasveld *o.*

grass-widow ['grâswidou] onbestorven weduwe *v.*

grate [greit] *sb.* rooster *m.*; traliewerk *o.*; haard *m.*; *vt.* traliën; raspen; *vi.* knarsen; krassen; schuren, wrijven (tegen).

grateful(ly) ['greitful(i)] *adj.* (*adv.*) dankbaar, erkentelijk; aangenaam; weldadig; behaaglijk.

grater ['greitə] rasp *v.*

gratification [grætifi'keiʃən] bevrediging, voldoening *v.*; genoegen, genot *o.*; beloning, gratificatie *v.*

gratify ['grætifai] bevredigen, voldoen; behagen; belonen; omkopen.

grating ['greitiŋ] *sb.* traliewerk *o.*; *adj.* knarsend; krassend.

gratis ['greitis] gratis, om niet, kosteloos.

gratitude ['grætitjûd] dankbaarheid, erkentelijkheid *v.*

gratuitous(ly) [græ'tjûitəs(li)] *adj.* (*adv.*) gratis, kosteloos, vrij; ongemotiveerd, ongegrond; niet gerechtvaardigd.

gratuity [græ'tjûiti] gift *v.*; fooi *v.*; gratificatie *v.*

grave [greiv] *sb.* graf *o.*; kuil *m.*; *vt.* beitelen, graveren.

grave [greiv] *adj.* ernstig, gewichtig; deftig; plechtig; (*v. kleur*) somber, donker; (*v. toon*) diep.

grave-digger ['greivdigə] doodgraver *m.*

gravel ['grævəl] grind, kiezel, steengruis *o.*; graveel *o.*, niersteen *m.*

gravel-court ['grævəlkɔ:t] (*sp.:* tennis) grindbaan *v.*

gravestone ['greivstoun] grafsteen *m.*

graveyard ['greivjâd] kerkhof *o.*

gravitation [grævi'teiʃən] aantrekkingskracht *v.*; zwaartekracht *v.*

gravity ['græviti] ernst *m.*; gewicht *o.*; gewichtigheid *v.*; deftigheid *v.*; zwaarte, zwaartekracht *v.*; (*v. toon*) diepte *v.*

gravy ['greivi] vleesnat *o.*, saus *v.*

gray [grei] *zie* **grey.**

graze [greiz] grazen, weiden; laten grazen; hoeden.

grazing-shot ['greiziŋʃɔt] schampschot *o.*

grease [grîs] *sb.* vet, smeer *o.*; mok(ziekte) *v.*; [grîz] *vt.* smeren, insmeren, invetten, oliën; de handen smeren, omkopen.

greasy ['grîzi] *adj.* vettig, vuil; zalvend.

great [greit] groot; lang; voornaam, belangrijk.

great-aunt ['greitânt] oudtante *v.*

Great Britain [greit'britn] Groot-Brittannië *o.*

greatcoat ['greit'kout] overjas *v.*; (*mil.*) kapotjas *v.*

great-grandfather ['greit'grændfâθə] overgrootvader *m.*

great-grandson ['greit'græn(d)sən] achterkleinzoon *m.*

greatly ['greitli] grotelijks; groots, op grootste wijze; zeer, hoog.

greatness ['greitnis] grootte *v.*; grootheid *v.*

great-uncle ['greitəŋkl] oudoom *m.*

Greece [grîs] Griekenland *o.*

greed [grîd], **greediness** ['grîdinis] hebzucht, begerigheid; gulzigheid *v.*

greedy ['grîdi] *adj.* hebzuchtig, begerig; gulzig; belust (*for,* op).

Greek [grîk] *adj.* Grieks; *sb.* Griek *m.*; Grieks *o.*; (*sl.*) bedrieger, valse speler *m.*

green [grîn] groen; onrijp; nieuw, vers, fris; (*v. huiden*) ongelooid.

greenery ['grînəri] groen *o.* (ter versiering); serre, broeikas *v.*

greengrocer ['grîngrousə] groenteboer, groentehandelaar *m.*

green-sickness ['grînsiknis] (*gen.*) bleekzucht *v.*

greet [grît] groeten; begroeten; (*Sc.*) schreien.

greeting ['grîtiŋ] groet *m.*; begroeting *v.*

grenade [gri'neid] (hand)granaat *v.*

grewsome ['grûsəm] *zie* **gruesome.**

grey [grei] *adj.* grijs, grauw; (*fig.*) donker, somber; *sb.* grijs, grauw *o.*; schimmel *m.*; *vi.* (*vt.*) grijs worden (maken).

grey-beard ['greibîəd] grijsaard *m.*

grey-haired ['grei'hêəd], **grey-headed** ['grei'hedid] grijs, met grijs haar; vergrijsd.

grey-hound ['greihaund] hazewind *m.*

grid [grid] rooster; braadrooster *m.*

griddle ['gridl] *sb.* koekeplaat *v.*; mijnwerkerszeef *v.*; rooster *m.*; *vt.* bakken (op rooster).

gridiron ['gridaiən] (braad)rooster *m.*; traliewerk *o.*

grief [grif] droefheid *v.*; leed, hartzeer, verdriet *o.*

grievance ['grivəns] grief *v.*

grieve [griv] *vt.* bedroeven; leed doen; betreuren, berouwen; *vi.* treuren over.

grievous(ly) ['grivəs(li)] *adj.* (*adv.*) smartelijk, pijnlijk; snood, afschuwelijk; zwaar, drukkend.

grill [grill] *sb.* rooster *m.*; geroosterd vlees *o.*; *vt.* roosteren, braden.

grill-room ['grilrum] restaurant *o.* (waar vlees geroosterd wordt).

grim [grim] grimmig, akelig, bars; bar, streng; onverbiddelijk, wreed; verwoed.

grimace [gri'meis] *sb.* grimas *v.*, grijns *m.*; gemaaktheid *v.*; *vi.* grijnzen, grimassen maken.

grime [graim] vuil *o.*; roet *o.*

grimness ['grimnis] grimmigheid, verwoedheid, felheid *v.*; strengheid *v.*

grimy ['graimi] vuil, smerig.

grind [graind] malen, vermalen; slijpen, scherpen; (*v. orgel*) draaien.

grinder ['graində] slijper *m.*; scharenslijper *m.*; slijpsteen *m.*; maaltand, kies *m.*; (*fig.*) verdrukker, uitzuiger *m.*

grindstone ['graindstoun] slijpsteen *m.*; —, iem. afbeulen.

grip [grip] *sb.* greep *m.*; houvast *o.*; begrip *o.*; macht *v.*, meesterschap *o.*; voor *v.*, greppel *m.*; *vt.* grijpen, vastgrijpen, beetpakken; (*fig.*) boeien, pakken.

gripe [graip] *sb.* greep *m.*; houvast *o.*; handvat *o.*; (*v. honger, pijn*) knaging *v.*; (*fig.*) klauw *m.*, vuist, macht *v.*; —s, kramp, koliek *v.*; *vt.* & *vi.* grijpen, vastgrijpen, beetpakken; koliek veroorzaken.

griper ['graipə] grijper *m.*; uitzuiger *m.*; afperser *m.*

grisly ['grizli] akelig, griezelig.

gristle ['grisl] kraakbeen *o.*

grit [grit] *sb.* steengruis *o.*; grove zandsteen *m.*; korrel *m.* (van steen); (*fam.*) flinkheid, vastberadenheid, fut, pit *v.*; —s, grutten *v. mv.*; *vt.* malen; wrijven; *vi.* knarsen; krassen.

groan [groun] *vi.* kreunen, steunen, kermen; zuchten; (*v. houtwerk*) kraken; *sb.* gesteun, gekreun *o.*

groats [grouts] grutten *v. mv.*

grocer ['grousə] kruidenier *m.*

grocery ['grousəri] kruidenierswaren *v. mv.*; kruidenierswinkel *m.*

groom [grum] stalknecht *m.*; rijknecht *m.*; kamerheer *m.*; bruidegom *m.*

groove [gruv] groef, voor, gleuf, sponning *v.*; (*v. geweer, kanon*) trek *m.*; (*v. hoefijzer*) rits *v.*; (*fig.*) sleur *m.*

grope [group] (rond)tasten (*for, after, naar*); zoeken.

gross [grous] *adj.* dik; grof, lomp;

ruw, onbeschoft; (*v. gewicht*) bruto; *sb.* gros *o.* (twaalf dozijn).

grotto ['grotou] grot *v.*

ground [graund] *sb.* grond; bodem *m.*; grondkleur, grondverf *v.*; grondtoon *m.*; achtergrond *m.*; terrein *o.*; *vt.* gronden; grondvesten; in de grondverf zetten; (*mil.*: *v. geweer*) afzetten; (*el.*) naar de aarde afleiden, met de grond verbinden; *vi.* (*sch.*) stranden, aan de grond raken; (*v. vliegtuig*) landen; aan de grond lopen.

ground-floor ['graund'flo:] benedenverdieping *v.*

groundless(ly) ['graundlis(li)] *adj.* (*adv.*) grondeloos; ongegrond.

ground-plan ['graundplæn] platte grond *m.*

group [grup] *sb.* groep *m.*; *vt.* groeperen.

grouse [graus] mopperen.

grow [grou] groeien, aangroeien, wassen; ontstaan; worden.

growl [graul] *vi.* snauwen; brommen, knorren; *sb.* snauw, grauw *m.*; gebrom, geknor *o.*

growler ['graulə] brompot, knorrepot *m.*; (*fam.*) huurrijtuig *o.*, vigilante *v.*

grown-up ['groun'əp] volwassen.

growth [grouð] groei, wasdom *m.*; toeneming, vermeerdering *v.*; aanwas *m.*; uitwas *m.*, gezwel *o.*

grub [grəb] larve, made *v.*; engerling *m.*; werkezel, zwoeger *m.*

grubby ['grəbi] vol maden; vuil, vies, smerig.

grudge [grədʒ] *sb.* wrok *m.*; afgunst *v.*; *vt.* misgunnen, niet gunnen; met tegenzin toestaan.

gruesome(ly) ['grusəm(li)] *adj.* (*adv.*) ijselijk, griezelig, akelig, huiveringwekkend.

gruff(ly) ['grəf(li)] *adj.* (*adv.*) nors, bars, ruw.

grumble ['grəmbl] *vi.* brommen, grommen; mopperen; rommelen; *sb.* gebrom *o.*; gemopper *o.*; gerommel *o.*

grumbler ['grəmblə], **grumbletonian** ['grəmbl'touniən] knorrepot, brompot, mopperaar *m.*

grume [grum] klonter *m.*; fluim *v.*

grumpy ['grəmpi] *adj.* mopperig, brommerig, knorrig; *sb.* brompot, brombeer *m.*

grunt [grənt] *vi.* knorren; *sb.* geknor *o.*

guarantee [gærən'ti] *sb.* waarborg *m.*, garantie *v.*; borg, garant *m.*; (*v. wissel*) aval *o.*; *vt.* waarborgen, garanderen; borg staan voor, instaan voor; (*v. wissel*) voor aval tekenen, avaleren.

guard [gâd] *sb.* wacht *v.*; hoede *v.*; bewaking *v.*; beschutting; bescherming *v.*; wachter, bewaker *m.*; *vt.* bewaken; behoeden; beschermen.

guard-duty ['gâdd ûti] wachtdienst *m.*

guardian ['gâdjən] bewaker; bewaarder *m.*; curator, opziener *m.*; voogd(es) *m.* (*v.*); (*v. klooster*) gardiaan *m.*

guardianship ['gâdjənʃip] bewaking; hoede *v.*; bescherming *v.*; voogdij-schap *v.*

guardless ['gâdlis] onbeschermd; onvoorzichtig.

guess [ges] *vt. & vi.* raden, gissen; (*Am.*) denken, geloven; *sb.* gis(sing) *v.*; raadsel *o.*

guesser ['gesə] rader, gisser *m.*

guest [gest] gast *m.*; logé, logeergast *m.*; genodigde *m.*

guidable ['gaidəbl] bestuurbaar; (*fig.*) handelbaar, meegaand, volgzaam.

guidance ['gaidəns] leiding *v.*; bestuur *o.*; geleide *o.*; richtsnoer *o.*

guide [gaid] *sb.* gids *m.*; geleider *m.*; bestuurder *m.*; reisgids *m.*; *vt.* leiden; geleiden; besturen; tot gids dienen, rondleiden.

guide-post ['gaidpoust] handwijzer *m.*

guild [gild] gilde *v.*; vereniging *v.*

guilder ['gildə] gulden *m.*

guildhall ['gild'ho:l] gildehuis *o.*

guile [gail] *sb.* bedrog *o.*; list, valsheid, veinzerij *v.*; *vt.* bedriegen; verstrikken.

guilt [gilt] schuld *v.*; misdaad *v.*

guiltless ['giltlis] onschuldig, schuldeloos.

guilty ['gilti] schuldig, misdadig; schuldbewust.

guinea-pig ['ginipig] Guinees biggetje, marmotje *o.*; proefkonijn *o.*; (*H.*) commissaris (van maatschappij) *m.*

guitar [gi'tâ] gitaar *r.*

gulf [gəlf] golf *v.*, zeeboezem *m.*; draaikolk *m.*; afgrond *m.*; (*fig.*) kl:of, klove *v.*

gullet ['gelit] slokdarm *m.*, keel *v.*

gullible ['gəlibl], **gullish** ['gəliʃ] onnozel, lichtgelovig.

gully ['gəli] geul *r.*; riool *o.* (*Z. N.:* goot *v.*).

gulp [gəlp] *vt.* inslikken; inslokken; *r.*, slokken; *sb.* slok *m.*

gum [gəm] gom *v.*; gomboom *m.*; (*Am.*) kauwgom *v.*; —**s**, tandvlees *o.*; (*fam.*) overschoenen *m. mv.*

gummy ['gəmi] gomachtig, kleverig; opgezet, gezwollen.

gun [gən] *sb.* kanon *o.*; (jacht)geweer *o.*; jager *m.*; *vi.* schieten.

gun-carriage ['gənkæridʒ] affuit *o.*

gun-cotton ['gənkɔtn] schietkatoen *o.*

gunner ['gənə] kanonnier, artillerist *m.*; (*marine*) konstabel *m.*

gun-powder ['gənpaudə] buskruit *o.*

gurgle ['gəgl] klokken; (*v. beekje, enz.*) murmelen, klateren; (*v. stervende*) rochelen; gorgelen.

gush [gəʃ] *vi.* (uit)stromen, gutsen; uitstorten; dwepen (*about, over,* met); *sb.* stroom *m.*; uitstroming *v.*; uitstorting; uitbarsting *v.*; opwelling, ontboezeming *v.*; dweperij *v.*

gust [gəst] vlaag, windvlaag *v.*; (*dicht.*) smaak *m.*

gustation [gəs'teiʃən] het proeven *o.*; smaak *m.*

gut [gət] darm *m.*; darmsnaar *v.*; engte; nauwte, vernauwing *v.*; —**s**, ingewanden *o. mv.*; inhoud *m.*

gutter ['gətə] groef, geul *v.*

gutter-snipe ['gətəsnaip] straatkind *o.*, straatjongen *m.*; voddenraper *m.*

guttle [gətl] (*pop.*) schrokken, slokken.

guttural ['gətərəl] *adj.* keel—; *sb.* keelklank *m.*; keelletter *v.*

guzzle ['gəzl] *vt. & vi.* opschrokken; zuipen, zwelgen, brassen; *sb.* drank *m.*; zwelgpartij *v.*

gymnastic [dʒim'næstik] *adj.* gymnastisch, gymnastiek—; (—**s**), gymnastiek *v.*

H

haberdashery ['hæbədæʃeri] ellewaren *v. mv.*, garen en band *o.*; garen en bandwinkel *m.*

habit ['hæbit] *sb.* gewoonte *v.*, aanwensel *o.*, hebbelijkheid *v.*; gesteldheid; geaardheid *v.*; rijkleed *o.*; *vt.* kleden.

habitable ['hæbitəbl] *adj.* bewoonbaar.

habitation [hæbi'teiʃən] bewoning *v.*; woning, woonplaats *v.*

habituate [hə'bitjueit] wennen, gewennen (**to,** aan).

habitude ['hæbitjûd] gewoonte *v.*, aanwensel *o.*, hebbelijkheid *v.*; gesteldheid *v.*, karakter *o.*, geaardheid *v.*

hack [hæk] *sb.* houweel *o.*; hakmes *o.*; houw *m.*, snede, kerf *v.*; (*bij voetbal*) verwonding, trapwond *v.*; *vt.* hakken, afhakken, houwen, inkerven; (*bij voetbal*) een scheentrap geven.

hackle ['hækl] *sb.* (vlas)hekel *m.*; nek-veer *v.* (van haan, pauw, duif); *vt.* (*r* *vlas, hennep*) hekelen; stuk hakken.

hackney ['hækni] *sb.* rijpaard, huurpaard *o.*; huurrijtuig *o.*; loonslaaf *m.*; *vt.* verhuren.

hack-writer ['hækraitə] broodschrijver *m.*

haddock ['hædək] schelvis *m.*

haemorrhoids ['hemərɔidz] aambeien *v. mv.*

haft [hæft] *sb.* heft, handvat *o.*; *vt.* van een heft (handvat) voorzien.

hag [hæg] heks, toverkol *v.*

haggard ['hægəd] verwilderd, ontdaan; bleek en vervallen; (*v. valk*) ongetemd.

haggle ['hægl] *vi.* knibbelen, kibbelen; afdingen; *sb.* gekibbel *o.*, kibbelpartij *v.*

haggler ['hæglə] knibbelaar, kibbelaar *m.*; afdinger *m.*

hail [heil] *sb.* hagel *m.*; roep, aanroep,

welkomstgroet *m.*; *vi.* hagelen; — *from,* komen van, afkomstig zijn van; *vt.* aanroepen; (*sch.*) praaien; begroeten (als); verwelkomen; *ij.* heil.

hailstone ['heilstoun] hagelsteen, hagelkorrel *m.*

hair [hêə] haar, haartje *o.*

hair-clippers ['hêə'klipəz] tondeuse *v.*

hair-clipping ['hêəklipiŋ] (het) haarknippen *o.*

hair-curler ['hêəkə:lə] krultangetje, krulijzer *o.*

hairdress ['hêədres] haartooi *m.*

hairdresser ['hêədresə] kapper *m.*

hairless ['hêəlis] *adj.* onbehaard.

hairy ['hêəri] harig, behaard; haren.

hake [heik] stokvis *m.*

half [hâf] *adj.* & *adv.* half; *sb.* helft *v.*; (*fam.*) half jaar *o.*; halve mijl *v.*, enz.

half-baked ['hâf'beikt] *adj.* halfgaar.

half-pay ['hâfpei] *sb.* wachtgeld; nonactiviteitstraktement *o.*; *adj.* nonactief, op nonactiviteitstraktement.

half-pence ['heip(ə)ns] *meerv. van:*

half-penny ['heipəni] halve stuiver *m.*

half-seas-over ['hâfsiz'ouvə] aangeschoten, half dronken.

hall [ho:l] hal, vestibule *v.*; zaal *v.*; rechtszaal *v.*; eetzaal *v.*

hall-mark ['ho:lmâk] *sb.* stempel *m.*; waarmerk *o.*; (*op goud, zilver*) keur *v.*; (*op maten en gewichten*) ijk *m.*; *vt.* stempelen; keuren; ijken.

hallucination [həl(j)ûsi'neiʃən] hallucinatie, zinsbegoocheling *v.*, zinsbedrog *o.*

halo ['heilou] *sb.* halo *v.* (kring om zon of maan); stralenkrans *m.*; *vt.* met een stralenkrans omgeven.

halt [ho:lt] *ij.* halt! *sb.* halt *v.*, stilstand *m.*; *vi.* halt houden; mank gaan; (*v. gesprek, enz.*) hokken; *vt.* halt doen houden.

halter ['ho:ltə] halster; strik, strop *m.*

ham [hæm] bil, dij *v.*; ham *v.*

hamlet ['hæmlit] gehucht *o.*

hammer ['hæmə] *sb.* hamer *m.*; *vi.* hameren; *vt.* smeden; — *out,* uitvissen, uitvorsen; uitdenken, verzinnen.

hammock ['hæmək] hangmat *v.*

hamper ['hæmpə] *sb.* pakmand; sluitmand *v.*, sluitkorf *m.*; *vt.* in een mand doen; bemoeilijken, belemmeren, hinderen.

hand [hænd] *sb.* hand *v.*; handtekening *v.*; handschrift *o.*; handbreedte *v.*; (*v. uurwerk, enz.*) wijzer *m.*; *vt.* overhandigen, aanreiken, overreiken; (*v. geld, enz.*) overmaken; (bij de hand) geleiden; aanpakken.

handbag ['hændbæg] handtas(je) *v.* (*o.*).

handbill ['hændbil] strooibiljet *o.*; affiche *v.*; snoeimes *o.*

handbook ['hændbuk] handboek *o.*

handcuff ['hændkəf] *sb.* handboei *v.*; *vt.* de handboeien aanleggen, boeien.

handful ['hændful] handvol *o.*; (*fig.*) lastig portret *o.*

handhold ['hændhould] houvast *o.*

handicap ['hændikæp] *sb.* (*sp.*) handicap *o.*, wedstrijd *m.* met voorgift; bezwarende voorwaarde *v.*; belemmering *v.*, nadeel *o.*; *vt.* aan bezwarende voorwaarden onderwerpen; handicappen, belemmeren, benadelen.

handicraft ['hændikrâft] handwerk *o.*, handenarbeid *m.*

handkerchief ['hæŋkətʃif] zakdoek *m.*; halsdoek *m.*

handle ['hændl] *sb.* handvat; hengsel *o.*; handgreep *v.*; (*tn.*) handel *m.*, kruk *v.*, zwengel *m.*; (*v. degen, enz.*) gevest *o.*; deurkruk *v.*, deurknop *m.*; *vt.* betasten, bevoelen; hanteren; (*mil.: v. kanon*) bedienen; (*sch.*) manœuvreren; behandelen.

hand-made ['hændmaid] *adj.* met de hand gemaakt, handwerk.

handmaid(en) ['hændmeid(ən)] (*dicht.*) dienstmaagd *v.*; (*fig.*) dienares *v.*

hand-post ['hændpoust] wegwijzer *m.*

handrail(ing) ['hændreil(iŋ)] leuning *v.*

han(d)sel ['hæns(ə)l] *sb.* handgift *v.*; handgeld *o.*; nieuwjaarsgift *v.*; (*fig.*) voorproefje *o.*; *vt.* een handgift geven; inwijden.

handshake ['hændʃeik] *sb.* handdruk *m.*; *vt.* (elkaar) de hand drukken.

handsome ['hænsəm] *adj.* mooi, schoon, knap; mild; grootmoedig, edel; (*v. prijs*) flink.

handwork ['hændwə:k] handenarbeid *m.*

handwriting ['hændraitiŋ] handschrift *o.*

handy ['hændi] handig; bij de hand.

hang [hæŋ] *vt.* hangen, ophangen; behangen; laten hangen; *vi.* hangen, afhangen; talmen, aarzelen, weifelen.

hangdog ['hændɔg] *sb.* galgebrok *m.*; *adj.* gemeen, gluiperig.

hanging ['hæŋiŋ] *sb.* ophanging, verhanging *v.*; het hangen *o.*; behang; wandtapijt *o.*; *adj.* hangend, afhangend; hang—.

hangman ['hæŋmən] beul *m.*

hang-nail ['hæŋneil] nijnagel *m.*

hanker ['hæŋkə] verlangen, hunkeren (*after, for,* naar).

happen ['hæpn] gebeuren, plaats hebben; (*fam.*) toevallig verschijnen (ontstaan, enz.); — (*up*)*on,* toevallig ontmoeten (aantreffen).

happiness ['hæpinis] geluk *o.*

happy ['hæpi] *adj.* gelukkig; blij, tevreden.

harangue [hə'ræŋ] aanspraak *v.*; heftige toespraak *v.*

harass ['hærəs] kwellen, teisteren; afmatten.

harbour ['hâbə] *sb.* haven *v.*; schuilplaats, wijkplaats *v.*; herberg *v.*; *vt.* (*v. vluchteling, enz.*) herbergen; (*v. gedachten, verdenkingen*) koesteren.

hard [hâd] hard; moeilijk, zwaar; bezwaarlijk; vermoeiend; hardvochtig, verhard, wreed.

harden ['hàdn] *vt.* harden; verharden; hardvochtig maken; *vi.* hard worden; gehard (verhard) worden; (*v. markt, prijzen*) vaster (hoger) worden; (*v. mening*) veld winnen.

hard-got(ten) ['hâd'gɔt(n)] *adj.* met moeite verworven; zuur verdiend.

hard-handed ['hâd'hændid] *adj.* hardhandig; streng.

hard-headed ['hâd'hedid] *adj.* nuchter, praktisch.

hardly ['hâdli] *adv.* hard; met moeite, moeilijk, bezwaarlijk; nauwelijks, ternauwernood, bijna niet.

hardness ['hâdnis] hardheid, gestrengheid *v.*

hardware ['hâdwêə] ijzerwaren *v. mv.*

hardy ['hâdi] onversaagd, stoutmoedig; onbeschaamd; gehard.

hare [h ə] haas *m.*

hare-brained ['hêəbreind] *adj.* onnadenkend, onbesuisd.

harlequin ['hâlik(w)in] harlekijn, hansworst *m.*

harm [hâm] *sb.* kwaad *o.*; schade *v.*, nadeel *o.*; leed, letsel *o.*; *vt. & vi.* schaden, schade toebrengen, benadelen; kwaad doen.

harmful(ly) ['hâmful(i)] *adj.* (*adv.*) nadelig, schadelijk.

harmless(ly) ['hâmlis(li)] *adj.* (*adv.*) onschadelijk; argeloos, onschuldig; onbeschadigd.

harmonious(ly) [hâ'mounjəs(li)] *adj.* (*adv.*) harmonisch; eensgezind, eenstemmig; welluidend, harmonieus.

harmonize ['hâmənaiz] harmoniëren, overeenstemmen.

harmony ['hâməni] harmonie, overeenstemming, eensgezindheid *v.*

harness ['hânis] *sb.* (paarde)tuig, gareel *o.*; harnas *o.*; *vt.* (*v. paard*) optuigen; inspannen, in het gareel spannen.

harp [hâp] harp *v.*

harpoon [hâ'pûn] *sb.* harpoen *m.*; *vt.* harpoeneren.

harrow ['hærou] *sb.* eg(ge) *v.*; *vt.* eggen; openrijten, (open)scheuren; kwellen, pijnigen, folteren.

harvest ['hâvist] *sb.* oogst *m.*; oogsttijd *m.*; *vt.* oogsten; vergaren, inzamelen.

hash [hæʃ] *vt.* hakken, klein hakken, fijn hakken, fijn maken; *sb.* hachee *o.*; (*fig.*) mengelmoes *o.*, poespas *m.*; opgewarmde kost *m.*

hasp [hâsp] *sb.* knip; beugel *m.*; grendel *m.*; met een grendel (knip, enz.) sluiten.

haste [heist] *sb.* haast *v.*, spoed *m.*; overhaasting, overijling *v.*; *vi.* zich haasten.

hasten ['heisn] *vi.* zich haasten; *vt.* verhaas'en, bespoedigen.

hastily ['heistili] *adv. zie* **hasty**.

hasty ['heisti] *adj.* haastig; overhaast, overijld; (*v. groenten*) vroeg; driftig, heetgebakerd.

hat [hæt] hoed *m.*; kardinaalshoed *m.*; (*mil.: sl.*) helm *m.*

hatch [hætʃ] *sb.* halve deur, onderdeur

v.; (*sch.*) luik *o.*; het broeden *o.*; broedsel *o.*; *vt.* uitbroeden; (*v. complot*) smeden; beramen; *vi.* broeden; uitkomen.

hatchet ['hætʃit] bijl *v.*; bijltje *o.*

hate [heit] haten; een hekel hebben aan.

hateful(ly) ['heitful(i)] *adj.* (*adr.*) hatelijk; gehaat; haatdragend; (*fam.*) akelig; weerzinwekkend.

hater ['heitə] hater *m.*

hatred ['heitrid] haat *m.*, vijandschap *r.*

haughtiness ['hɔ:tinis] hoogmoed, trots *m.*, hooghartigheid *v.*

haughty ['hɔ:ti] *adj.* hoogmoedig, trots; hooghartig.

haul [hɔ:l] *vt.* trekken, slepen; (*sch.*) aanhalen, verhalen, wenden; *vi.* trekken, rukken (*at, upon,* aan); (*v. wind*) draaien, omslaan; *sb.* trek, haal *m.*; vangst *v.*; winst, verdienste *r.*

haulm [hɔ:m] (*v. bonen, erwten*) halm, stengel *m.*; (*v. aardappelen*) loof *o.*

haunch [hɔ:n(t)ʃ] lendestuk *o.*; (*r. paard*) dij, bil *v.*; bout *m.*

haunt [hɔ:nt] *vt.* geregeld (veelvuldig) bezoeken; zich ophouden bij (in); (*v. gedachten*) kwellen, vervolgen, niet loslaten; *vi.* spoken; *sb.* veel bezochte plaats *v.*; verblijfplaats *v.*; (*v. dieren*) hol, leger *o.*

haunter ['hɔ:ntə] vaste bezoeker, stamgast *m.*

have [hæv, (h)əv] *vt. & ri.* hebben; bezitten; houden; krijgen; (*v. bericht, enz.*) ontvangen.

haversack ['hævəsæk] (*mil.*) broodzak *m.*

haw [hɔ:] *sb.* haagdoorn *m.*; haagappel *m.*; (*gesch.*) haag, omheining *v.*; aarzeling, hapering *v.*; *vi.* aarzelen, haperen, stotteren.

hawbuck ['hɔ:bək] lomperd, boerenkinkel *m.*

hawk [hɔ:k] *sb.* valk *m.*; havik *m.*; (*fig.*) haai *m.*; keelschraping *v.*; (*v. metselaar*) kalkbord *o.*; *vi.* met valken jagen; zich de keel schrapen; *vt.* venten, rondventen; verspreiden, uitstrooien.

hawker ['hɔ:kə] valkenier *m.*; venter, marskramer *m.*

hawser ['hɔ:zə] kabel, tros *m.*

hay [hei] *sb.* hooi *o.*; **make —,** hooien; (*fig.*) de boel in de war sturen; *vi.* hooien.

hay-cock ['heikɔk] hooiopper *m.*

hay-maker ['heimeikə] hooier *m.*; hooister *v.*; hooimachine *v.*

hazard ['hæzəd] *sb.* toeval *o.*; kans *v.*; gevaar, risico *o.*; wisselvalligheid *v.*; hazardspel *o.*; *vt.* wagen, riskeren, op het spel zetten.

hazardous(ly) ['hæzədəs(li)] *adj.* (*adv.*) gewaagd, riskant, gevaarlijk; toevallig, onzeker.

haze [heiz] *sb.* waas *o.*, damp, nevel *m.*; *vt.* benevelen, met een waas bedekken.

hazel-nut ['heizlnət] hazelnoot *v.*

hazy ['heizi] *adj.* dampig, wazig, nevelig, vaag; beneveld, aangeschoten.

he [hi] *pron.* hij; *sb.* mannetje *o.*; *ij.* he!

head [hed] *sb.* hoofd *o.*; kop *m.*; kruin *v.*, top *m.*; (*v. rijtuig, enz.*) kap *v.*; (*mil.*) spits *v.*; opperhoofd *o.*; hoofdman, leider, bestuurder *m.*; hoofdeinde *o.*; *vt.* aan het hoofd staan van; aanvoeren; zich aan het hoofd stellen van; (*v. gevaar, enz.*) het hoofd bieden; overtreffen; (*sp.: voetbal.*) koppen; *vi.* aansturen (*at, for, towards,* op); (*v. sla*) kroppen, een krop vormen; (*fig.*) ontspringen.
headache ['hedeik] hoofdpijn *v.*
head-clerk ['hedklâk] (*H.*) eerste bediende *m.*
head-collar ['hedkɔlə] halster *m.*
head-dress ['heddres] kapsel *o.*; hoofdtooi *m.*
head-gear ['hedgiə] hoofddeksel *o.*; hoofdtooisel *o.*
heading ['hediŋ] hoofd *o.*, titel *m.*, opschrift *o.*
headman ['hed'mæn] hoofdman *m.*; meesterknecht; werkbaas *m.*; dorpshoofd; stamhoofd *o.*
head-master ['hed'mâstə] hoofd ener school *o.*; directeur; rector *m.*
head-mistress ['hed'mistris] hoofdonderwijzeres; directrice *v.*
head-office ['hed'ɔfis] (*H.*) hoofdkantoor *o.*
headshake ['hedʃeik] hoofdschudden.
headstrong ['hedstrɔŋ] *adj.* koppig, eigenzinnig, hardhoofdig, onhandelbaar.
head-wind ['hedwind] tegenwind *m.*
heady ['hedi] *adj.* onbesuisd, onstuimig, opvliegend; (*v. wijn, enz.*) koppig.
heal [hîl] *vt.* helen, genezen, gezond maken; *vi.* genezen, beter worden.
healable ['hîləbl] *adj.* heelbaar.
health [helδ] gezondheid *v.*; heil, welzijn *o.*
health-resort ['helδrizo:t] herstellingsoord *o.*
healthy ['helδi] *adj.* gezond.
heap [hîp] *sb.* hoop, stapel *m.*; menigte *v.*; *vt.* opkopen, opstapelen; — **upon,** overladen met, overstelpen met.
hear [hîə] *vt.* horen; (*v. gebed*) verhoren; (*v. les, enz.*) overhoren; *vi.* horen, luisteren; gehorig zijn.
hearing ['hîəriŋ] gehoor *o.*; gehoorsafstand *m.*; (*recht*) verhoor, onderzoek *o.*; (*muz.*) auditie *v.*
heart [hât] *sb.* hart *o.*; binnenste *o.*, kern *v.*; moed *m.*; *vi.* (*v. sla, enz.*) kroppen.
heartache ['hâteik] hartzeer, harteleed *o.*, zielesmart *v.*
heart-beat ['hâtbît] hartslag *m.*, hartklopping *v.*
heart-break ['hâtbreik] hartzeer *o.*
heartburn ['hâtbə:n] zuur (in de maag) *o.*
heart-failure ['hâtfeiljə] hartverlamming *v.*
hearth [hâδ] haard *m.*, haardstede *v.*
heartless(ly) ['hâtlis(li)] *adj.* (*adv.*) harteloos; lafhartig; kleinmoedig; moedeloos; flauw.

heart-rending ['hâtrendiŋ] *adj.* hartverscheurend.
heartsore ['hâtso:] *sb.* hartzeer, harteleed *o.*; *adj.* bedroefd.
heartstrings ['hâtstriŋz] hartzenuwen *v. mv.*; innigste gevoel *o.*
heart-to-heart ['hâttə'hât] openhartig.
heart-whole ['hâthoul] *adj.* gezond van harte; oprecht; onversaagd; vrij.
hearty ['hâti] *adj.* hartelijk; innig; oprecht.
heat [hît] *sb.* hitte, warmte *v.*; gloed *m.*, vuur *o.*; prikkeling *v.*; *vt.* verhitten, warm (heet) maken; aanhitsen, ophitsen.
heater ['hîtə] verwarmer *m.*; verwarmingstoestel *o.*
heath [hîδ] heide *v.*
heathen ['hîθən] *sb.* heiden *m.*; *adj.* heidens.
heather ['heθə] heidekruid *o.*, heideplant *v.*; heidestruik *m.*
heating ['hîtiŋ] verwarming *v.*
heave [hîv] *vt.* opheffen, optillen, ophijsen; (*v. anker*) lichten; (*v. zucht*) slaken; *vi.* rijzen; zich verheffen; op- en neergaan; (*v. borst*) zwoegen.
heaven ['hevn] hemel *m.*; —**s,** hemelen; uitspansel *o.*
heavenly ['hevnli] *adj.* hemels, goddelijk.
heavenward(s) ['hevnwəd(z)] *adj.* & *adv.* hemelwaarts.
heaviness ['hevinis] zwaarte *v.*; zwaarmoedigheid *v.*; loomheid, traagheid *v.*
heavy ['hevi] zwaar; zwaarmoedig; loom, traag; (*v. lucht*) drukkend.
hebdomadal [heb'dɔmədəl], **hebdomadary** [heb'dɔmədəri] *adj.* wekelijks.
heckle ['hekl] *sb.* hekel *m.*; *vt.* hekelen; lastige vragen stellen.
hectare ['hektêə, 'hektâ] hectare *v.*
hectolitre ['hektəlitə] hectoliter *m.*
hectometre, hectometer ['hektəmîtə] hectometer *m.*
hedge [hedʒ] *sb.* heg, haag *v.*; (*fig.*) belemmering *v.*; afsluiting *v.*; *vt.* omheinen, afsluiten; belemmeren; (*v. weddenschap*) blokkeren, dekken.
hedgehog ['hedʒhɔg] egel *m.*; zeeegel *m.*
heedless ['hîdlis] *adj.* onachtzaam, achteloos, zorgeloos.
heel [hîl] hiel, hak *m.*; (*v. brood, kaas*) korst *v.*; (*sch.*) hieling, overhelling *v.*
heel-piece ['hîlpîs] hielstuk *o.*, achterlap *m.*; (*fig.*) einde *o.*
heifer ['hefə] vaars *v.*
height [hait] hoogte *v.*; verhevenheid *v.*; top *m.*, toppunt *o.*
heighten ['haitn] verhogen; ophogen; (*v. verhaal*) opsmukken.
heinous(ly) ['heinəs(li)] *adj.* (*adv.*) snood, afschuwelijk.
heir [êə] erfgenaam *m.*
hell [hel] hel *v.*; speelhol *o.*
hell-cat ['helkæt] feeks, helleveeg *v.*

hellish ['heliʃ] *adj.* hels.

helm [helm] helmstok *m.*, roerpen *v.*; (*fig.*) roer *o.*

helmet ['helmit] helm *m.*

help [help] *vt.* helpen, bijstaan, hulp verlenen; ondersteunen; (aan tafel) bedienen; ronddienen; *vr.* **— oneself,** zichzelf helpen; zich bedienen; *sb.* hulp *v.*, bijstand, steun *m.*; ondersteuning *v.*; helper *m.*; helpster *v.*

helpful(ly) ['helpful(i)] *adj.* (*adv.*) behulpzaam, hulpvaardig; nuttig, dienstig; bevorderlijk.

helping ['helpiŋ] *adj.* helpend; *sb.* (*v. eten*) portie *v.*

helpless(ly) ['helplis(li)] *adj.* (*adv.*) hulpeloos; machteloos; onbeholpen; hulpbehoevend.

helve [helv] *sb.* (*v. bijl, enz.*) steel *m.*; *vt.* van een steel voorzien.

Helvetia [hel'viʃiə] Helvetië: Zwitserland *o.*

hem [hem] *sb.* zoom, boord, kant *m.*; kuchje *o.*; *vt.* (om)zomen, omboorden.

hemisphere ['hemisfiə] halfrond *o.*, halve bol *m.*

hemp [hemp] hennep *m.*; strop *m.*

hen [hen] hen, kip *v.*; (*v. vogel*) pop *v.*; (*in samenstellingen*) wijfjes—.

hence [hens] *adv.* van hier, hier vandaan; vandaar; daarom.

henceforth ['hens'fo:δ], **henceforward** ['hens'fo:wəd] *adv.* van nu af, voortaan.

hen-house ['henhaus] kippenhok, hoenderhok *o.*

henpecked ['henpekt] *adj.* onder de pantoffel zittend.

heptagon ['heptəgən] zevenhoek *m.*

her [hə:] *pron.* haar.

herald ['herəld] *sb.* heraut *m.*; (*fig.*) bode; voorbode, voorloper *m.*; *vt.* aankondigen, melden; (**— in**), inleiden, inluiden.

herb [hə:b] kruid *o.*

herd [hə:d] *sb.* kudde *v.*; troep *m.*; herder; hoeder *m.*; *vi.* in kudden leven; te zamen leven; in kudden weiden; **— together,** samenscholen; zich in kudden verzamelen; hokken; *vt.* hoeden.

herd-book ['hə:dbuk] rundveestamboek *o.*

herdsman ['hə:dzmən] veehoeder *m.*

here [hiə] *adv.* hier; (*mil.*) present! **hereabout(s)** ['hiərəbaut(s)] hieromtrent, hier in de buurt.

hereafter [hiə'râftə] *adv.* hierna; later, voortaan, (*in boek, enz.*) verderop; hiernamaals; *sb.* toekomst *v.*; (het) hiernamaals *o.*

hereby ['hiə'bai] hierbij; hierdoor.

hereditary [hi'reditəri] erfelijk; overgeërfd.

hereof ['hiə'rəv] hiervan.

heresy ['herisi] ketterij *v.*

heretic ['heretik] ketter *m.*

hereto ['hiə'tû] nevensgaand, hierbij (behorende); hiertoe.

heretofore ['hiətu'fo:] voorı :n, eertijds, vóór deze(n).

herewith ['hiə'wiθ] hiermede, hierbij, bij deze(n).

heritᵃ le ['heritəbl] erfelijk; overerfelijk; erfgerechtigd.

heritage ['heritidʒ] erfenis *v.*; erfdeel *o.*; erfgoed *o.*; onroerend goed *o.*

heritor ['heritə] erfgenaam *m.*

hermetic(al) [hə:'metik(l)] hermetisch, luchtdicht.

hermit ['hə:mit] kluizenaar *m.*

hermitage ['hə:mitidʒ] kluis *v.*; hermitage, Franse wijnsoort *v.*

hernia ['hə:niə] (*gen.*) breuk, liesbreuk *v.*

hero ['hiərou] held *m.*; halfgod, heros *m.*

heroic [hi'rouik] heldhaftig; helden—; hoogdravend; (*v. maatregelen*) drastisch.

heroine ['herouin] heldin *v.*

heroism ['herouizm] heldhaftigheid *v.*, heldenmoed *m.*

heron ['herən] (*Dk.*) reiger *m.*

herring ['heriŋ] haring *m.*

herring-bone ['heriŋboun] haringgraat *v.*; (*bouwk.*) visgraatverband *o.*

hesitate ['heziteit] aarzelen, weifelen; haperen, stamelen.

hesitating(ly) ['heziteitiŋ(li)] *adj.* (*adv.*) aarzelend, weifelend.

hesitation [hezi'teiʃən] aarzeling, weifeling *v.*; hapering *v.*

heterogeneous(ly) [hetərо'dʒiniəs(li)] *adj.* (*adv.*) ongelijksoortig, heterogeen.

hew [hjû] *vt.* houwen; uithouwen; hakken; vellen; *ri.* houwen, hakken.

hewer ['hjûə] hakker, houwer, steenhouwer *m.*

hexahedron [heksə'hidrən] zesvlak *o.*

hiatus [hai'eitəs] gaping, leemte *v.*; hiaat *o.*

hibernal [hai'bə:nəl] winters, winter—.

hibernation [haibə:'neiʃən] overwintering *v.*; winterslaap *m.*

hiccough, hiccup ['hikəp] *vi.* hikken, de hik hebben; *sb.* hik *m.*

hide [haid] *sb.* huid *v.*, vel *o.*; leren zweep *v.*; (*fam.*) hachje *o.*; *vt.* (*fam.*) afrossen, afranselen.

hide [haid] *vt.* verbergen, wegstoppen, verstoppen; *vi.* zich verbergen, zich verschuilen; *sb.* schuilplaats *v.*; geheime bergplaats *v.*

hide-and-seek ['haidən'sik] verstoppertje *o.*

hidebound ['haidbaund] strak; (*fig.*) bekrompen, kleingeestig.

hideous(ly) ['hidiəs(li)] *adj.* (*adv.*) afschuwelijk, afzichtelijk.

hiding-place ['haidiŋpleis] schuilplaats *v.*

hierarch ['haiərə:k] opperpriester, kerkvoogd *m.*; aartsbisschop *m.*

higgle ['higl] *vi.* dingen, afdingen, pingelen; *vt.* rondventen.

higgledy-piggledy ['higldi'pigldi] *adv.* ondersteboven; door elkander, verward, overhoop; *sb.* warboel, rommel *m.*

higgler ['higlə] afdinger, pingelaar *m.*

high [hai] *adj*. hoog; verheven; machtig; (*v. wind*) krachtig; sterk,luid; *adv.* hoog; krachtig, hevig; grof.

high-day ['haidei] hoogdag, feestdag *m.*

higher ['haiə] *adj.* hoger; *vt.* verhogen.

high-flyer ['haiflaiə] hoogvlieger *m.*; fantast *m.*; (*sl.*) zwendelaar *m.*

high-handed ['hai'hændid] aanmatigend, eigenmachtig, autoritair.

high-hearted ['hai'hâtid] moedig; fier.

high-life ['hai'laif] *sb.* de grote wereld *v.*; *adj.* van de grote wereld.

high-lived ['hai'laivd] voornaam, tot de grote wereld behorend.

high-minded ['hai'maindid] edel, grootmoedig; (*Bijb.*) hoogmoedig.

highness ['hainis] hoogheid, verhevenheid *v.*; hoogte *v.*

high-sounding ['hai'saundiŋ] (*fig.*) hoogdravend; holklinkend; (*v. titel*) klinkend.

high-spirited ['hai'spiritid] vurig; fier; vermetel, stoutmoedig.

high-strung ['hai'strəŋ] hooggespannen; overprikkeld.

highwayman ['haiweimən] struikrover *m.*

hilarious (**ly**) [hi'lêəriəs(li)] *adj.* (*adv.*) vrolijk.

hill [hil] *sb.* heuvel, berg *m.*; *vt.* ophopen; — (*up*), aanaarden.

hilly ['hili] bergachtig, heuvelachtig.

hilt [hilt] gevest, hecht *o.*

him [him] hem; (*fam.*) hij.

hind [haind] *sb.* hinde *v.*; boer; boerenknecht, boerenarbeider *m.*; *adj.* achterste; achter—.

hinder ['hində] hinderen; verhinderen, belemmeren, beletten.

hindrance ['hindrəns] hindernis *v.*,hinderpaal *m.*, belemmering *v.*, beletsel *o.*

hinge [hin(d)ʒ] *sb.* hengsel *o.*, scharnier *v.*; (*fig.*) spil *v.*; *vt.* van hengsels voorzien, met scharnieren verbinden; *vi.* draaien; steunen.

hinny ['hini] *sb.* muilezel *m.*; *vi.* hinniken.

hint [hint] *sb.* wenk *m.*; zinspeling, toespeling *v.*; *vt.* aanduiden; te kennen geven; laten doorschemeren; opperen; *vi.* — *at,* zinspelen op.

hinterland ['hintəlænd] achterland *o.*

hip [hip] *sb.* heup *v.*; (*v. dak*) graatbalk *m.*, graatspar *v.*; zwaarmoedigheid *v.*; (*Pl.*) rozebottel *v.*; *vt.* gedrukt maken.

hip-bath ['hipbâδ] zitbad *o.*

hippopotamus [hipə'potəməs] nijlpaard *o.*

hire ['haiə] *sb.* huur *v.*; loon *o.*; beloning *v.*; *vt.* huren; in dienst nemen; — *out,* verhuren.

hireling ['haiəliŋ] *sb.* huurling *m.*; *adj.* gehuurd; huurlingen—.

hirer ['haiərə] huurder *m.*

hirsute ['hə:sjût] ruig, harig, behaard.

his [hiz] zijn; van hem; het zijne, de zijnen.

hiss [his] *vi.* sissen; fluiten; *vt.* uitfluiten,

uitjouwen; — *at,* ophitsen tegen; *sb.* gesis *o.*; gefluit *o.*; sisklank *m.*

historic [his'tɔrik] historisch; beroemd, gewichtig.

historical [his'tɔrikl] historisch, geschiedkundig.

history ['histəri] geschiedenis *v.*; verhaal *o.*

hit [hit] *vt.* slaan; stoten; raken, treffen; grijpen; gissen, raden; *vi.* slaan; raken, treffen; *sb.* stoot, slag *m.*; houw *m.*; tref *m.*; rake opmerking *v.*, gelukkige zet *m.*; (*mil.*) treffer *m.*; steek *m.* (onder water).

hitch [hitʃ] *vt.* vastmaken; aanhaken, vasthaken; een weinig verplaatsen; *vi.* geduring in beweging zijn; zich vasthechten (*to,* aan); blijven haken, blijven steken, blijven vastzitten; (*v. paard*) aanslaan; *sb.* ruk *m.*; haak, steek *m.*; hapering *v.*, beletsel *o.*, storing *v.*, defect *o.*

hitcher ['hitʃə] haak, boothaak, schippershaak *m.*

hither ['hiθə] hier, hierheen, herwaarts.

hitherto ['hiθə'tû] tot nu toe, tot dusver.

hoard [ho:d] *sb.* hoop *m.*; voorraad *m.*; schat *m.*; spaarpot *m.*, spaargeld *o.*; omheining *v.*; *vt.* vergaren, opsparen, oppotten; hamsteren.

hoarding ['ho:diŋ] (het) opsparen, (het) potten *o.*; houten schutting *v.*; advertentiebord *o.*

hoar-frost ['ho:'frɔst] rijp, rijm *m.*

hoarse (**ly**) [ho:s(li)] *adj.* (*adv.*) hees, schor.

hob [hɔb] haardplaat *v.*; pin *v.*; dikkopspijker *m.*

hobble ['hɔbl] strompelen, hobbelen; hinken, kreupel lopen.

hobby-horse ['hɔbi'ho:s] hobbelpaard *o.*; stokpaardje *o.*; paard *o.* (van draaimolen).

hod-carrier ['hɔdkæriə] opperman *m.*

hodge-podge ['hɔdʒpɔdʒ] hutspot *m.*, mengelmoes, allegaartje *o.*

hodman ['hɔdmən] opperman *m.*; (*fig.*) helper *m*

hodometer [hɔ'dɔmitə] afstandsmeter *m.*

hoe [hou] *sb.* schoffel, hak *v.*; *vt.* schoffelen, hakken.

hog [hg] *sb.* (*Dk.*) varken *o.*, barg *m.*; lam, schaap *o.* (vóór het eerste scheren); (*fig.*) zwijn *o.*; vraat *m.*; (*sch.*) hog, schrobber *m.*; *vt.* (*v. manen*) kort knippen; naar boven krommen, doen doorbuigen; (*sch.*) hoggen, varkenen, schrobben; *vi.* vreten, schrokken; woest rijden.

hoggish (**ly**) ['hɔgiʃ(li)] *adj.* (*adv.*) zwijnachtig; beestachtig; vuil; gulzig.

hogshead ['hɔgzhed] okshoofd *o.*

hoist [hɔist] *vt.* hijsen, ophijsen; lichten, optillen; *sb.* hijstoestel *o.*; elevator *m.*; lift *m.*

hold [hould] *vt.* houden; behouden, achterhouden, inhouden, vasthouden;

terughouden; inhouden, bevatten; in zijn bezit hebben; *vi.* stilhouden; ophouden; doorgaan; van kracht blijven; niet loslaten; (*v. vorst. enz.*) aanhouden blijven duren; — *in,* (zich) inhouden; tegenhouden; beteugelen; aanhouden; *vr.* — *oneself (in),* zich inhouden, zich bedwingen; *sb.* houvast *o.*; vat *m.,* greep *v.*; steun *m.*; steunpunt *o.*; macht *v.,* invloed *m.*

holder ['houldə] houder *m.*; aandeelhouder *m.*; bezitter *m.*

holdfast ['houldfâst] houvast *o.*; kram *v.,* klemhaak *m.*

holding ['houldiŋ] houvast *o.*; invloed *m.*; macht *v.*; bezit *o.*; pachthoeve *v.*

hole [houl] *sb.* gat, hol *o.,* kuil *m.*; opening *v.*; hok, krot *o.*; *vt.* een gat (gaten) maken in; (*v. tunnel*) graven; (*sp.: v. bal*) stoppen.

holiday ['holidei] feestdag *m.*; vakantiedag *m.*; heiligedag *m.*; —s, vakantie.

holiness ['houlinis] heiligheid *v.*; *His H—,* Zijne Heiligheid (de Paus).

Holland ['holənd] Holland, Nederland *o.*

Hollands ['holəndz] Hollandse jenever *m.*

hollow ['holou] *adj. & adv.* hol, uitgehold; vals, geveinsd, onoprecht; ondeugdelijk; *sb.* holte *v.*; uitholling *v.*; hol *o.*; laagte *v.*; *vt.* uithollen; uitboren; (*v. hand*) hol maken.

holly ['holi] hulst *m.*; steeneik *m.*

holy ['houli] heilig, gewijd.

holy-day ['houlidei] heiligedag *m.*

homage ['homidʒ] *sb.* hulde, huldiging, huldebetuiging *v.*; *vt.* huldigen.

home [houm] *sb.* huis *o.*; tehuis *o.*; verblijf *o.*; (*v. dier*) leger *o.*; land, geboorteland, vaderland *o.*; geboorteplaats *v.*; bakermat *v.*; honk *o.*; *at —,* thuis; in het vaderland; *adj.* huiselijk, huis—; binnenlands; krachtig; raak; gevoelig; *adv.* huiswaarts, naar huis; thuis; bij (naar) honk; vast, stevig; raak; *vi.* wonen; (*vooral v. duif*) naar huis gaan; *vt.* huisvesten.

home-born ['houm'bo:n, 'houmbo:n] inlands; aangeboren.

home-coming ['houmkəmiŋ] thuiskomst *v.*

home-freight ['houmfreit] (*sch.*) retourvracht *v.*

homeless ['houmlis] dakloos.

homely ['houmli] huiselijk; eenvoudig, alledaags, gewoon; (*Am.*) lelijk.

home-made ['houm'meid; 'hoummeid] eigengemaakt; eigengebakken; van inlands fabrikaat.

home-match ['hoummætʃ] (*sp.*) thuiswedstrijd *m.*

homer ['houmə] — (*pigeon*), reisduif, postduif *v.*

Home-Rule ['houmrûl] zelfbestuur *o.*

home-sickness ['houmsiknis] heimwee *o.*

homeward(s) ['houmwəd(z)] huiswaarts.

home worker ['houmwə:kə] dienstbode *v.*

homey, *zie* **homi.**

homicide ['homisaid] doodslag, manslag *m.*; doodslager; moordenaar *m.*

homily ['homili] predikatie, zedepreek, leerrede *v.*

homing-pigeon ['houmiŋpidʒən] reisduif, postduif *v.*

homogeneous(ly) [houmə'dʒiniəs(li)] *adj.* (*adv.*) homogeen, gelijksoortig.

homologate [ho'moləgeit] homologeren; bekrachtigen, goedkeuren.

homonymous [ho'moniməs] gelijkluidend, homoniem.

homy ['houmi] huiselijk, gezellig.

honest ['onist] *adj.* eerlijk; eerbaar, deugdzaam; rechtschapen; braaf; oprecht; onvervalst.

honey ['honi] *sb.* honi(n)g *m.*; *vt.* zoet maken; met honi(n)g smeren; *vi.* flikflooien, zoete woordjes gebruiken.

honeycomb ['honikoum] honingraat *v.*; raatvormig patroon *o.*

honeyed ['honid] honingachtig; honingzoet; honing—.

honeymoon ['honimûn] *sb.* wittebroodsweken *v. mv.*; huwelijksreis *v.*; *vi.* de wittebroodsweken doorbrengen; op huwelijksreis zijn.

honey-suckle ['honisəkl] (*Pl.*) kamperfoelie *v.*; rode klaver *v.*

honorary ['onərəri] *adj.* honorair, ere—; onbezoldigd; *sb.* honorarium *o.*

honour ['onə] *sb.* eer *v.*; eerbewijs *o.*; ereteken *o.*; eergevoel *o.*; erewoord *o.*; *vt.* eren; vereren; (*v. wissel*) honoreren; (*v. verplichtingen*) nakomen.

honourable ['onərəbl] *adj.* eervol; eerzaam, achtbaar; eerwaardig; voornaam, aanzienlijk; rechtschapen.

hood [hud] kap *v.*; huif *v.*; muts *v.*; doctorshoed *m.*; (*v. gondel*) tent *v.*

hoof [hûf] hoef *v.*; stuk vee *o.*; (*fam.*) voet, poot *m.*

hook [huk] *sb.* haak *m.*; vishaak, angel *m.*; snoeimes *o.*; sikkel *v.*; (*tn.*) duim *m.,* kram *o.*; scherpe bocht *v.*; *vt.* aanhaken; dichthaken; van haken voorzien, haken zetten aan; aan de haak slaan; *vi.* haken, blijven haken.

hoop [hûp] *sb.* hoepel *m.*; hoepelrok *m.*; band, ring, beugel *m.*; *vt.* met hoepels (banden) beslaan; omvatten, omringen; samenbinden.

hooping-cough ['hûpiŋko:f] kinkhoest *m.*

hoop-iron ['hûpaiən] bandijzer *o.*

hoot [hût] *vi.* jouwen; (*v. uil*) krassen, schreeuwen; (*v. auto, enz.*) toeteren; (*v. stoomfluit*) toeten; *vt.* uitjouwen; *sb.* gejouw *o.*; (*v. uil*) gekras, geschreeuw *o.*

hooter ['hûtə] stoomfluit; sirene *v.*; toeter, (auto)hoorn *m.*

hop [hop] *vi.* springen, huppelen; hinken; (*fam.*) dansen; — *it,* ophoepelen, 'm smeren; *vt.* huppelend (hinkend) afleggen; *sb.* sprongetje *o.*; (*fam.*) dansje o.; danspartij v.; (v. vliegtuig) sprong m.; vlucht v.; etappe v.

hop [hɔp] sb. (Pl.) hop v.; hopplant v.; (Am.) bedwelmend middel o.; **—s,** hopbellen; vt. hoppen; vi. hop voortbrengen; hop plukken.

hope [houp] sb. hoop; verwachting v.; vt. (vi.) hopen (for, op); verwachten (of, van).

hopeful(ly) ['houpful(i)] adj. (adv.) hoopvol; veelbelovend.

hopeless(ly) ['houplis(li)] adj. (adv.) hopeloos.

hopper ['hɔpə] springer m.; danser m.; sprinkhaan m.; (v. molen) tremel, hopper m.

horde [hɔ:d] sb. horde, bende v., troep m.; vi. in benden leven; zich in benden verenigen.

horizon [ho'raizn] sb. gezichtskring; horizon, gezichtseinder m.; vt. begrenzen.

horizontal [hɔri'zɔntl] horizontaal.

horn [hɔ:n] sb. hoorn m.; voelhoorn m.; drinkhoorn m.; landpunt v.; adj. hoornen.

hornet ['hɔ:nit] horzel v.; hoornaar m.

horny ['hɔ:ni] hoornachtig; eeltig, vereelt; hoorn—.

horrible ['hɔribl] adj. afschuwelijk, afgrijselijk, verschrikkelijk, gruwelijk.

horrid ['hɔrid] adj. afschuwelijk, afgrijselijk; (dicht.) borstelig, rechtopstaand.

horrify ['hɔrifai] afschuw inboezemen, ontzetten; aanstoot geven.

horror ['hɔrə] afschuw m., afgrijzen o.; gruwel m., verschrikking v.; huivering, rilling v.; **the —s,** delirium tremens.

horse [hɔ:s] sb. paard o.; ruiterij v., paardenvolk o., cavalerie v.; schraag v.; (droog)rek o.; vt. van paarden (van een rijdier) voorzien; berijden; te paard zetten; inspannen.

horseback ['hɔ:sbæk] **on —,** te paard.

horse-breaker ['hɔ:sbreikə] pikeur, paardendresseur m.

horseman ['hɔ:smən] ruiter, paardrijder m.

horsemanship ['hɔ:smənʃip] rijkunst v.

horse-pond ['hɔ:spɔnd] paardewed o.

horse-race ['hɔ:sreis] wedren m.

horse-sense ['hɔ:ssens] gezond verstand, boerenverstand v.

horse-shoe ['hɔ:sʃû] sb. hoefijzer o.; adj. hoefijzervormig; vt. beslaan.

hortation [hɔ:'teiʃən] vermaning; aansporing v.

horticulture ['hɔ:tikəltʃə] tuinbouw m.

hose [houz] sb. (v. brandspuit, enz.) slang v.; huls, schede v.; kous(en) v. (mv.); (korte) broek v.; vt. bespuiten.

hoseman ['houzmən] spuitgast; pijpleider m.

hose-pipe ['houzpaip] brandslang; tuinslang v.

hospice ['hɔspis] hospitium; gasthuis o.

hospitable ['hɔspitəbl] adj. herbergzaam, gastvrij.

hospital ['hɔspitəl] hospitaal, ziekenhuis, gasthuis o.; godshuis o.

host [houst] gastheer m.; waard, herbergier m.; menigte v.; (op plant) gast m.; leger, heir o. hostie v.

hostage ['hɔstidʒ] gijzelaar m. onderpand o.

hostess ['houstis] gastvrouw v.; waardin, herbergierster v.; (in vliegtuig) hofmeesteres v.

hostile(ly) ['hɔstail(li)] adj. (adv.) vijandig, vijandelijk.

hostility [hɔs'tiliti] vijandigheid, vijandige gezindheid v.; vijandelijkheid v.

hot [hɔt] adj. heet, warm; (v. as) warmgelopen; hevig, vurig, heftig; vt. heet (warm) maken; opwarmen.

hot-bed ['hɔtbed] broeibak m.; broeinest o.

hot-brained ['hɔtbreind] heethoofdig.

hotchpot(ch) ['hɔtʃpɔt(ʃ)] hutspot m., mengelmoes o.

hotfoot ['hɔtfut] in aller ijl.

hothause ['hɔthaus] broeikas v.; droogkamer v.

hotspurred ['hɔtspə:d] doldriftig, onstuimig.

hot-tempered ['hɔt'tempəd] opvliegend.

hound [haund] hond; jachthond m.

hour [auə] uur o.; (dicht.) stonde v.

hour-glass ['auəglâs] zandloper m.

hour-hand ['auəhænd] uurwijzer m.

hourly ['auəli] ieder uur, alle uren; van uur tot uur; om het uur; gestadig, voortdurend.

house [haus; mv.: 'hauziz] sb. huis o., woning v.; handelshuis o.; [hauz] vt. huisvesten; onder dak brengen; stallen; (v. oogst) binnenhalen; vi. huizen, wonen.

house-breaker ['hausbreikə] inbreker m.; huizensloper m.

household ['haushould] sb. gezin, huisgezin o.; huishouden o.; huishouding v.; adj. huiselijk; huishoudelijk.

housekeeper ['hauskîpə] huishoudster v.; huisbewaarder m.; huisbewaarster v.

housemaid ['hausmeid] werkmeid v.

housemate ['hausmeit] huisgenoot m.

housewife ['hauswaif] sb. huisvrouw v.; vi. huishouden, het huishouden doen.

housework ['hauswə:k] huishoudelijk werk o.

housing ['hauziŋ] huisvesting v.; onderdak o.; (sch.) huizing v.; paardedek o.

hover ['hɔvə, 'hʌvə] vi. fladderen; zweven, hangen; weifelen, aarzelen; sb. gefladder o.; onzekerheid v.

how [hau] hoe.

however [hau'evə] evenwel, echter; niettemin; hoe... ook.

howitzer ['hauitsə] (mil.) houwitser m.

howl [haul] vi. huilen, janken; vt. uitbrullen; sb. gehuil, gejank o.

howler ['haulə] huiler, janker m.; huile-

balk *m.*; brulaap *m.*; (*jam.*) stommiteit *v.*
howling ['haulin] *sb.* gehuil, gejank, geschreeuw *o.*; *adj.* huilend, jankend, schreeuwend.   [wit *o.*
hub [hǝb] naaf *v.*; uitsteeksel *o.*; doelhubbub ['hǝbǝb] herrie *v.*, geraas, rumoer, kabaal *o.*
huckster ['hǝkstǝ] *sb.* venter, (mars)-kramer *m.*; sjacheraar *m.*; *vt.* venten, in 't klein verkopen; vervalsen; *vi.* afdingen, pingelen; sjacheren.
huddle ['hǝdl] *vt.* opeenhopen, op een hoop smijten; dooreengooien, door elkander smijten; opeendringen; *vi.* — (*together*), zich opeenhopen; samenhokken; *sb.* opeenhoping *v.*; (verwarde) hoop *m.*; troep *m.*; warboel *m.*; verwarring *v.*
hue [hjû] kleur *v.*; tint, schakering *v.*
huff [hǝf] *sb.* boze (nijdige) bui *v.*; geraaktheid, drift *v.*; (plotselinge) vlaag *r.* van woede; *vt.* nijdig maken; beledigen; uit de hoogte behandelen; *vi.* razen, tieren, uitvaren; nijdig worden, zich beledigd voelen; zich dik maken.
huffy ['hǝfi] *adj.* opgeblazen; lichtgeraakt.
hug [hǝg] *vt.* omhelzen, omknellen; liefkozen; (*v. gedachte, vooroordeel*) koesteren; *sb.* omhelzing; omknelling *v.*
huge [hjûdʒ] *adj.* zeer groot, kolossaal, reusachtig.
hull [hǝl] *sb.* schil, pel *v.*, dop *m.*; omhulsel *o.*; (*v. schip*) romp *m.*; *vt.* schillen, ' .... *ers*) openmaken; (*v. schip*) in de romp treffen.
hum [hǝm] *vt.* neuriën; *vi.* gonzen, zoemen, snorren; *sb.* geneurie *o.*; gegons, gezoem, gesnor *o.*
humane [hju'mein] *adj.* humaan, menslievend, goedhartig; humanistisch.
humanism ['hjûmǝnizm] humanisme *o.*
humanity [hju'mæniti] mensdom *o.*; mensheid *v.*; menselijkheid *v.*; menslievendheid *v.*
humanize ['hjûmǝnaiz] beschaven, veredelen; menselijk(er) maken.
humankind ['hjûmǝn'kaind] mensdom *o.*, mensheid *v.*
humble ['hǝmbl] *adj.* nederig, ootmoedig; bescheiden; onderdanig; gering onaanzienlijk; *vt.* vernederen, verootmoedigen.
humble-bee ['hǝmblbi] hommel *m.*
humbleness ['hǝmblnis] nederigheid *v.*
humbug ['hǝmbǝg] zwendel *m.*, bedrog *o.*; humbug, bluf *m.*; onzin *m.*, larie *v.*
humid ['hjûmid] vochtig, nattig.
humidity [hju'miditi] vocht *o.*, vochtigheid, nattigheid *v.*
humiliate [hju'milieit] **vernederen**, verootmoedigen.
humiliation [hjûmili'eiʃǝn] vernedering, verootmoediging *v.*
humility [hju'militi] nederigheid *v.* ootmoed *m.*

hummer ['hǝmǝ] neuriër *m.*; gonzer, brommer *m.*; gonzend insekt *o.*
humming-bird ['hǝminbǝ:d] kolibrie *v.*
humorous(**ly**) ['hjûmǝrǝs(li)] *adj.* (*adv.*) luimig, grappig; grillig.
humour ['hjûmǝ] humeur *o.*; stemming *v.*; luim, gril *v.*; humor *m.*
hump [hǝmp] bult, bochel *m.*, uitsteeksel *o.*
humpback ['hǝmpbæk] bochel *m.*; gebochelde, bultenaar *m.*
humus ['hjûmǝs] humus *m.*, teelaarde *v.*
hunch [hǝn(t)ʃ] *vt.* krommen, buigen; optrekken; duwen; *sb.* bult, bochel *m.*; homp, klomp *m.*; wenk *m.*; voorgevoel *o.*
hundred ['hǝndrǝd] honderd; honderdtal.
hundredweight ['hǝndrǝdweit] centenaar *m.*
hunger ['hǝngǝ] *sb.* honger *m.*; hunkering *v.*; *vi.* hongeren; hunkeren (*after, for,* naar); *vt.* uithongeren.
hunger-bit(**ten**) ['hǝngǝbit(n)] uitgehongerd.
hungry ['hǝngri] *adj.* hongerig; hunkerend; (*v. grond*) schraal.
hunt [hǝnt] *vi.* jagen; op de jacht gaan; zoeken, snuffelen; *vt.* najagen, nazetten; afjagen, afzoeken; jacht maken op; nastreven; — **down,** in 't nauw brengen; opsporen, achterhalen; *sb.* (vosse)-jacht *v.*; jachtclub *v.*, jachtgezelschap *o.*; jachtgebied, jachtveld *o*
hunter ['hǝntǝ] jager *m.*; jachtpaard *o.*; jachthond *m.*; jachtvliegtuig *o.*
hunting ['hǝntin] jacht *v.*; (het) jagen *o.*
hunting-field ['hǝntinfîld] jachtgebied, jachtveld *o.*
hurdle [hǝ:dl] *sb.* (tenen) horde *v.*; (*bij wedrennen*) hek *o.*; *vt.* met horden afsluiten.
hurl [hǝ:l] slingeren, werpen, smijten.
hurricane ['hǝrikǝn] orkaan *m.*
hurried(**ly**) ['hǝrid(li)] *adj.* (*adv.*) haastig, gehaast, overijld; inderhaast.
hurry ['hǝri] *sb.* (grote) haast *v.*; verwarring *v.*; gewoel *o.*; *vi.* zich haasten; *vt.* (*v. persoon*) haasten, jachten, drijven; (*v. zaak*) verhaasten, haast maken met; *vr.* — **oneself,** zich haasten.
hurt [hǝ:t] *sb.* wonde *v.*, letsel *o.*; kwaad, nadeel *o.*, schade *v.*; slag *m.*; pijn *v.*; *vt.* wonden, verwonden; kwetsen, krenken, beledigen; pijn doen, zeer doen; benadelen; beschadigen; *vi.* schaden; *vr.* — **oneself,** zich zeer doen.
hurtful ['hǝ:tful] schadelijk, nadelig (**to,** voor).
hurtless ['hǝ:tlis] ongedeerd; onschadelijk.
husband ['hǝzbǝnd] echtgenoot, man *m.*
hush [hǝʃ] *sb.* stilte, rust *v.*; (het) zwijgen *o.*; (het) sussen *o.*; *vt.* tot zwijgen brengen; sussen; — **up,** in de doofpot

stoppen; *vi.* zwijgen; stil worden; *adj.* stil; zwijgend.
hush-money ['həʃməni] steekpenning *m.*
husk [həsk] *sb.* schil *v.*, bolster, dop *m.*; omhulsel *o.*; *vt.* schillen, pellen, doppen.
husky ['həski] schor, hees.
hussar [hu'zâ] huzaar *m.*
hut [hət] hut *v.*; (*mil.*) barak *v.*
hydraulic [hai'drɔ:lik] *adj.* hydraulisch; *sb.* —s, hydraulica, waterwerktuigkunde *r.*
hydro-aeroplane ['haidrou'eiərəplein] watervliegtuig *o.*
hydrochloric ['haidrou'klɔrik] — *acid,* zoutzuur.
hydrocycle ['haidrousaikl] waterfiets *v.*
hydrodynamics ['haidroudai'næmiks] hydrodynamica, waterwerktuigkunde *v.*
hydro-electric ['haidroui'lektrik] — *station,* waterkrachtcentrale.
hydrogen ['haidridʒən] waterstof *v.*
hydrophobia [haidrə'foubiə] watervrees, hondsdolheid *v.*
hydropic [hai'drɔpik] waterzuchtig.

hydroplane ['haidrouplein] watervliegtuig *o.*; glijboot *v.*
hygiene ['haidʒ(i)in] gezondheidsleer *v.*
hygienic [hai'dʒinik] *adj.* hygiënisch; *sb.* —s, gezondheidsleer *r.*
hymn [him] *sb.* gezang *o.*, lofzang *m.*, loflied *o.*; *vt.* & *vi.* zingen, bezingen, loven.
hyphen ['haifən] *sb.* koppelteken *o.*; *vt.* door een koppelteken verbinden.
hypnotic [hip'nɔtik] *adj.* slaapwekkend, hypnotisch; *sb.* slaapwekkend middel, slaapmiddel *o.*; gehypnotiseerde *m.*
hypocrisy [hi'pɔkrisi] veinzerij, huichelarij *v.*; huichelachtigheid *v.*
hypocrite ['hipəkrit] huichelaar, veinzer *m.*
hypocritic(al) [hipə'kritik(l)] *adj.* huichelachtig, geveinsd, schijnheilig.
hypothecate [hai'pɔðikeit] verhypothekeren; verpanden.
hypothesis [hai'pɔðisis] hypothese, veronderstelling *v.*
hysteric(al) [his'terik(l)] *adj.* hysterisch; zenuwachtig.
histerics [his'teriks] zenuwaanval *m.*

I

1 [ai] ik; *the* —, het ik.
ibex ['aibeks] steenbok *m.*
ice [ais] *sb.* ijs *o.*; ijsmassa *v.*, ijsveld *o.*; *vt.* met ijs bedekken; (doen) bevriezen; (*v. dranken*) in ijs zetten, afkoelen, frapperen; (*v. gebak*) glaceren.
iceberg ['aisbə:g] ijsberg *m.*
ice-bound ['aisbaund] *adj.* ingevroren.
ice-cream ['ais'krim] roomijs *o.*
ice-drift ['aisdrift] ijsgang *m.*
Iceland ['aislənd] IJsland *o.*
ice-safe ['aisseif] ijskast *v.*
icicle ['aisikl] ijskegel *m.*
icon ['aikɔn] beeld *o.*; heiligenbeeld *o.*
iconoclastic [aikɔno'klæstik] beeldenstormend.
icy ['aisi] *adj.* ijsachtig; ijzig, ijskoud; met ijs bedekt; ijs—.
idea [ai'diə] denkbeeld, begrip *o.*; plan, ontwerp *o.*
ideal [ai'diəl] *adj.* ideaal; denkbeeldig, ideëel; *sb.* ideaal *o.*
identic(al) [ai'dentik(l)] *adj.* gelijk, gelijkwaardig, volkomen hetzelfde, identiek.
identification [aidentifi'keiʃən] vereenzelviging, gelijkstelling *v.*; identificatie *v.*
identity [ai'dentiti] volkomen gelijkheid, overeenstemming *v.*; persoonlijkheid, individualiteit *v.*; identiteit *v.*; (*Z. N.*) eenzelvigheid *v.*
idiot ['idiət] *adj.* idioot, stompzinnig; *sb.* idioot, stompzinnige *m.*; (*fig.*) domkop, stommerik *m.*
idiotic(al) [idi'ɔtik(l)] *adj.* idioot.

idle ['aidl] *adj.* ijdel, nutteloos; nietswaardig; nietsdoend, werkloos; (*v. gerucht, enz.*) ongegrond; *vi.* leeglopen; leegzitten; lanterfanten; luieren; *vt.* (*v. tijd*) verbeuzelen. [lak *m.*
idler ['aidlə] leegloper, nietsᵈ ner, lui**idol** ['aidl] afgod *m.*; afgoᵤsoeeld *o.*; dwaalbegrip *o.*
idolater [i'dɔlətə] afgodendienaar *m.*; aanbidder, vergoder *m.*
idolize ['aidəlaiz] vergoden; verafgoden.
idyllic(ally) [ai'dilik(əli)] *adj.* (*adv.*) idyllisch.
if [if] indien, als, zo, ingeval.
ignite [ig'nait] *vt.* in brand steken; doen ontbranden; *vi.* in brand raken; ontbranden.
ignition [ig'niʃən] ontbranding; ontsteking *v.*; gloeiing; gloeihitte *v.*
ignominious(ly) [igno'miniəs(li)] *adj.* (*adv.*) schandelijk, onterend; smadelijk, oneervol.
ignoramus [igno'reiməs] domkop, weetniet *m.*
ignorance ['ignərəns] onwetendheid *v.*; onkunde, onbekendheid *v.* (*of,* met).
ignorant ['ignərənt] *adj.* onwetend; onkundig, onbekend (*of,* met).
ignore [ig'no:] niet weten; niet willen weten (*of:* kennen), negeren, opzettelijk miskennen.
ill [il] *adj.* slecht, kwaad; ziek; misselijk; *adv.* slecht; kwalijk; met moeite; *sb.* kwaad *o.*; kwaal *v.*; ramp *v.*
ill-considered ['ilkən'sidəd] onbezonnen, onberaden, onbedacht.

ill-disposed ['ildis'pouzd] slechtgezind; kwaadwillig.

illegal [i'ligəl] *adj.* onwettig; wederrechtelijk, onrechtmatig.

illegible [i'ledʒibl] *adj.* onleesbaar.

illegitimate [ili'dʒitimit] *adj.* onwettig; onecht; *sb.* bastaard *m.*

illegitimize [ili'dʒitimaiz] onwettig (onecht) verklaren.

ill-famed ['il'feimd] *adj.* berucht.

ill-fated ['il'feitid] *adj.* ongelukkig, rampspoedig, noodlottig.

ill-favoured ['il'feivəd] *adj.* lelijk, mismaakt, misvormd; onaangenaam.

ill-gotten ['il'gɔtn] *adj.* onrechtvaar-.dig verkregen.

illicit (ly) [i'lisit(li)] *adj.* (*adv.*) onwettig; verboden, ongeoorloofd.

illimitable [i'limitəbl] *adj.* onbegrensd.

illiterate [i'litərit] ongeletterd, ongeleerd.

ill-luck ['il'lək] ongeluk *o.*, tegenspoed *m.*

ill-mannered ['il'mænəd] *adj.* ongemanierd.

ill-natured ['il'neitʃəd] *adj.* kwaadaardig, boosaardig.

illness ['ilnis] ziekte, ongesteldheid *v.*

illogical [i'lɔdʒikl] *adj.* onlogisch.

ill-omened ['il'oumend] *adj.* ongelukkig; ongeluks—; onheilspellend.

ill-starred ['il'stâd] ongelukkig; onder een kwaad gesternte geboren.

ill-tempered ['il'tempəd] knorrig, humeurig; kwaadgeluimd.

ill-treat ['il'trît] slecht behandelen; mishandelen.

illuminate [i'l(j)ûmineit] verlichten; belichten; voorlichten; opluisteren; (*v. boek, enz.*) verluchten.

illumination [il(j)ûmi'neiʃən] verlichting *v.*; voorlichting *v.*; verluchting *v.*; lichtsterkte *v.*; glans, luister *m.*; illuminatie *v.*

illusion [i'l(j)ûʒən] zinsbegoocheling *v.*, zinsbedrog *o.*, illusie *v.*; hersenschim *v.*

illusive, illusory [i'l(j)ûsiv, —əri] *adj.* denkbeeldig, hersenschimmig; bedrieglijk.

illustrate ['iləstreit] ophelderen, toelichten; (*v. boek, tijdschrift*) illustreren.

illustration [iləs'treiʃən] toelichting *v.*; illustratie *v.*; geïllustreerd tijdschrift *o.*; aanschouwing *v.*

illustrious (ly) [i'ləstriəs(li)] *adj.* (*adv.*) doorluchtig; beroemd, vermaard; roemrijk.

ill-will ['il'wil] kwaadwilligheid *v.*; onwil *m.*; tegenzin *m.*

image ['imidʒ] *sb.* beeld; evenbeeld *o.*; beeltenis *v.*; afbeeldsel *o.*; *vt.* afbeelden; voorstellen.

imaginable [i'mædʒinəbl] denkbaar.

imaginary [i'mædʒinəri] denkbeeldig, ingebeeld.

imagination [imædʒi'neiʃən] verbeelding; voorstelling *v.*; verbeeldingskracht *v.*, voorstellingsvermogen *o.*

imagine [i'mædʒin] *vt.* zich verbeelden, zich voorstellen; *vi.* denkbeelden vormen; fantaseren.

imaginable [i'mædʒinəbl] denkbaar.

imaginary [i'mædʒinəri] denkbeeldig, ingebeeld.

imagination [imædʒi'neiʃən] verbeelding; voorstelling *v.*; verbeeldingskracht *v.*, voorstellingsvermogen *o.*

imagine [i'mædʒin] *vt.* zich verbeelden, zich voorstellen; *vi.* denkbeelden vormen; fantaseren.

imbecile ['imbisil, —sail] *adj.* zwakhoofdig; idioot; *sb.* zwakhoofdige, idioot *m.*

imbibe [im'baib] inzuigen, opnemen; opslorpen.

imitable ['imitəbl] navolgbaar; navolgenswaardig.

imitate ['imiteit] navolgen, nabootsen; (*ong.*) naäpen.

imitation [imi'teiʃən] navolging, nabootsing *v.*; namaak *v.*, namaaksel *o.*

immaculate [i'mækjulit] *adj.* onbevlekt, vlekkeloos; onberispelijk; (*Dk.* & *Pl.*) ongevlekt.

immaterial [imə'tiəriəl] *adj.* onstoffelijk; onbelangrijk, van geen betekenis; onverschillig.

immature [imə'tjûə] *adj.* onrijp, onvolkomen, onvolwassen.

immeasurable [i'meʒərəbl] onmeetbaar; onmetelijk, oneindig.

immediate [i'midjət] *adj.* onmiddelijk, dadelijk; (*op brief, enz.*) spoed, dringend.

immediately [i'midjətli] *adv.* onmiddelijk, ogenblikkelijk.

immemorial (ly) [imi'mo:riəl(i)] *adj.* (*adv.*) onheuglijk; eeuwenoud.

immense (ly) [i'mens(li)] *adj.* (*adv.*) oneindig, onmetelijk; (*fam.*) reusachtig, kolossaal.

immensurable [i'menʃurəbl] *adj.* onmeetbaar.

immerse [i'mə:s] onderdompelen; indopen.

immigration [imi'greiʃən] immigratie *v.*

imminent ['iminənt] *adj.* dreigend, nakend.

immission [i'miʃən] inspuiting *v.*

immitigable [i'mitigəbl] niet te verzachten, niet te lenigen; onvermurwbaar.

immobile [i'moubil] *adj.* onbeweeglijk.

immoderate (ly) [i'mɔdərit(li)] *adj.* (*adv.*) onmatig; buitensporig; overdreven, onredelijk.

immodest (ly) [i'mɔdist(li)] *adj.* (*adv.*) onbescheiden; onbehoorlijk, onbetamelijk, onwelvoeglijk.

immoral [i'mɔrəl] *adj.* onzedelijk; zedeloos.

immortal [i'mo:təl] *adj.* onsterfelijk; onvergankelijk.

immortalize [i'mo:təlaiz] onsterfelijk maken, vereeuwigen.

immovable [i'mûvəbl] adj. onbeweeglijk; onveranderlijk, onwrikbaar; (recht) onroerend, vast; sb. **—s**, onroerende goederen.

immune [i'mjûn] immuun, onvatbaar (**from**, voor).

immunity [i'mjûniti] immuniteit, onvatbaarheid v.; vrijstelling, ontheffing v. (**from**, van).

immure [i'mjûə] opsluiten, insluiten, tussen vier muren zetten.

immutable [i'mjûtəbl] adj. onveranderlijk.

imp [imp] (kleine) schelm, deugniet m.

impact ['impækt] sb. stoot, slag m.; schok m.; botsing v.; [im'pækt] vt. stoten; indrijven.

impair [im'pêə] benadelen, beschadigen; aantasten; verzwakken.

impalpable [im'pælpəbl] adj. ontastbaar, onvoelbaar.

imparity [im'pæriti] ongelijkheid v.

impart [im'pât] mededelen; geven, schenken, verlenen.

impartial [im'pâʃəl] adj. onpartijdig.

impartible [im'pâtibl] adj. mededeelbaar; onverdeelbaar.

impassable [im'pâsəbl] adj. onbegaanbaar; ontoegankelijk; onoverkomelijk.

impassible [im'pæsibl] adj. ongevoelig, gevoelloos; onaandoenlijk; onvatbaar (**to**, voor).

impassioned [im'pæʃənd] adj. hartstochtelijk, vurig.

impassive(ly) [im'pæsiv(li)] adj. (adv.) ongevoelig; gevoelloos; onverstoorbaar.

impatience [im'peiʃəns] ongeduld o.; afkeer (van), hekel (aan) m.

impatient [im'peiʃənt] adj. ongeduldig; vurig verlangen (**for**, naar).

impawn [im'po:n] verpanden.

impeach [im'pîtʃ] in twijfel trekken; in diskrediet brengen, verdacht maken; aanklagen, beschuldigen.

impeachment [im'pîtʃmənt] het in twijfel trekken o., verdachtmaking v.; beschuldiging, aanklacht v. (wegens hoogverraad e. d.).

impecunious [impi'kjûniəs] adj. zonder geld, in geldverlegenheid; onbemiddeld, onvermogend, arm.

impede [im'pîd] belemmeren, bemoeilijken, verhinderen.

impediment [im'pedimənt] belemmering, verhindering v., beletsel o.

impedimenta [impedi'mentə] (mil.) legerbagage v.

impend [im'pend] boven het hoofd hangen, dreigen, ophanden zijn.

impenetrable [im'penitrəbl] adj. ondoordringbaar; ondoorgrondelijk.

imperator [impə'reitə] keizer m.

imperceptible [impə'septibl] adj. onmerkbaar; onwaarneembaar.

imperfect [im'pə:fikt] adj. onvolmaakt, onvolkomen; sb. (gram.) onvoltooid verleden tijd m.

imperial [im'piəriəl] keizerlijk.

imperious(ly) [im'piəriəs(li)] adj. (adv.) heerszuchtig; aanmatigend; gebiedend; dringend.

imperishable [im'periʃəbl] adj. onvergankelijk; duurzaam; onverslijtbaar; (H.: v. waren) niet aan bederf onderhevig.

impermeable [im'pe:miəbl] adj. ondoordringbaar.

impersonal [im'pə:sənəl] adj. onpersoonlijk, niet persoonlijk; sb. onpersoonlijk werkwoord o.

impersonate [im'pə:səneit] verpersoonlijken, belichamen; (v. rol) spelen, vertolken.

impertinent(ly) [im'pə:tinənt(li)] adj. (adv.) ongepast; vrijpostig, onbeschaamd; dwaas, ongerijmd; niet ter zake dienend.

imperturbable [impə'tə:bəbl] adj. onverstoorbaar.

impetuous(ly) [im'petjuəs(li)] adj. (adv.) onstuimig, heftig.

impiety [im'paiəti] goddeloosheid v., ongeloof o.; oneerbiedigheid v.

impinge [im'pindʒ] stoten, botsen (**on**; **upon**, tegen); raken, treffen.

impious ['impiəs] goddeloos, profaan.

implacable [im'pleikəbl, im'plækəbl] adj. onverzoenlijk, onverzettelijk, onverbiddelijk.

implicit [im'plisit] adj. stilzwijgend (er in begrepen, aangenomen); onvoorwaardelijk.

implore [im'plo:] smeken, bidden; afsmeken.

impolite(ly) [impo'lait(li)] adj. (adv.) onbeleefd, onwellevend.

impoliteness [impo'laitnis] onbeleefdheid, onwellevendheid v.

imponderable [im'pondərəbl] adj. onweegbaar.

import ['impo:t] sb. invoer, import m.; invoerartikel o.; belang, gewicht o.; [im'po:t] vt. invoeren, importeren; van belang zijn (voor); betekenen, inhouden; te kennen geven.

importable [im'po:təbl] invoerbaar.

importance [im'po:təns] belang o., betekenis v.; belangrijkheid v.

important [im'po:tənt] belangrijk, van betekenis; gewichtig doende.

importation [impo:'teiʃən] invoer m.; invoerartikel o.; invoering v.

importunate [im'po:tjunit] lastig, opdringerig.

importune [impo:'tjûn, im'po:tjun] lastig vallen; voortdurend aandringen.

impose [im'pouz] vt. opleggen; (v. zetsel) opmaken; vi. **— on**, imponeren, indruk maken; **— upon**, beetnemen, bedriegen.

imposing [im'pouziŋ] adj. imponerend; indrukwekkend; bedrieglijk, veeleisend.

impossible [im'posibl] adj. onmogelijk.

impost ['impoust] belasting v.; impost m.

impostor [im'postə] bedrieger m.

impotence, impotency ['impotens(i)] onmacht, machteloosheid *v.*; onvermogen *o.*

impotent ['impotent] onmachtig, machteloos; onvermogend.

impoverish [im'pɔvəriʃ] verarmen; (*v. land*) uitputten.

impracticable [im'præktikəbl] *adj.* onuitvoerbaar, ondoenlijk; onhandelbaar; (*v. weg*) onbegaanbaar.

imprecation [impri'keiʃən] verwensing, vervloeking *v.*

impregnable [im'pregnəbl] *adj.* onneembaar; onaantastbaar; onverzettelijk, onwrikbaar.

impregnate [im'pregnit] *adj.* doortrokken, doordrongen (*with*, van); [im-'pregneit] *vt.* bezwangeren, bevruchten; doortrekken, verzadigen (*with*, van).

impression [im'preʃən] indruk *m.*; afdruk *m.*; het afdrukken *o.*; stempel *m.*; druk *m.*, oplage *v.*

impressive(ly) [im'presiv(li)] *adj.* (*adv.*) indrukwekkend, treffend.

imprint ['imprint] *sb.* indruk *m.*, spoor *o.*; afdruk *o.*; stempel *m.*; [im'print] *vt.* indrukken; afdrukken; stempelen; inprenten.

imprison [im'prizn] gevangen zetten.

imprisonment [im'priznmənt] gevangenzetting *v.*; gevangenschap *v.*

improbable [im'prɔbəbl] onwaarschijnlijk.

improbity [im'prɔbiti] oneerlijkheid *v.*

improper(ly) [im'prɔpə(li)] *adj.* (*adv.*) ongeschikt; ongepast, onwelvoeglijk; onjuist; (*v. breuk*) onecht.

improvable [im'prûvəbl] *adj.* vatbaar voor verbetering; bebouwbaar.

improve [im'prûv] *vt.* verbeteren, beter maken; veredelen; gebruik maken van, zich ten nutte maken; *vi.* beter worden, vooruitgaan; meevallen.

improvement [im'prûvmənt] verbetering *v.*; vooruitgang *m.*, vordering *v.*; beterschap *v.*

improvident [im'prɔvidənt] zorgeloos; ondoordacht.

imprudent(ly) [im'prûdənt(li)] *adj.* (*adv.*) onvoorzichtig.

impudence ['impjudəns] onbeschaamdheid, schaamteloosheid *v.*

impudent(ly) ['impjudənt(li)] *adj.* (*adv.*) onbeschaamd, schaamteloos.

impugn [im'pjûn] betwisten, bestrijden, bekampen.

impulse ['impʌls], **impulsion** [im-'pʌlʃən] stoot, druk *m.*; aandrang *m.*, aandrift, aansporing *v.*; prikkel, spoorslag *m.*

impunity [im'pjûniti] straffeloosheid *v.*; *with* —, ongestraft, straffeloos.

impure(ly) [im'pjûə(li)] *adj.* (*adv.*) onrein, onzuiver; onkuis.

imputable [im'pjûtəbl] toe te schrijven, te wijten (aan); toerekenbaar.

impute [im'pjût] toeschrijven, ten laste leggen, aanwrijven.

in [in] *prep.* in; bij; op; naar, volgens; voor; uit; over; *adv.* (*v. boot, trein*) binnen; aan (het bewind, de regering); thuis.

inadvertence, inadvertency [inəd-'və:təns(i)] onachtzaamheid, onoplettendheid *v.*

inanimate [i'nænimit] *adj.* onbezield, levenloos; (*H.*) flauw.

inanition [inə'niʃən] (*gen.*) uitputting, zwakte *v.*; (*bij gesprek*) gebrek aan stof *o.*

inappeasable [inə'pîzəbl] niet te stillen, onbevredigbaar.

inasmuch [inəz'mʌtʃ] aangezien.

inaugural [i'nɔ:gjurəl] inaugureel; inwijdings-, openings—; — *address*, openingsrede.

inaugurate [i'nɔ:gjureit] inhuldigen; inwijden.

inauguration [inɔ:gju'reiʃən] inhuldiging *v.*; inwijding *v.*

inauspicious(ly) [inɔ:s'piʃəs(li)] *adj.* (*adv.*) onheilspellend; ongunstig, ongelukkig.

inborn ['in'bɔ:n] aangeboren.

incandescent [inkæn'desnt] *adj.* gloeiend; gloei—; *sb.* gloeilamp *v.*

incapability [inkeipə'biliti] onbekwaamheid *v.*; (*recht*) onbevoegdheid *v.*

incapacity [inkə'pæsiti] *zie* **incapability.**

incarcerate [in'kâsəreit] gevangen zetten; opsluiten.

incarnation [inkâ'neiʃən] vleeswording *v.*; belichaming *v.*

incendiary [in'sendjəri] *adj.* brandstichtend; opruiend, oproerig; *sb.* brandstichter *m.*; opruier *m.*

incense ['insens] *sb.* wierook *m.*; bewieroking; vleierij *v.*; *vt.* bewieroken.

incensory ['insensəri] wierookvat *o.*

incentive [in'sentiv] *adj.* aansporend, opwekkend, prikkelend; *sb.* aansporing *v.*, prikkel *m.*, drijfveer *v.*, motief *o.*

incessant(ly) [in'sesənt(li)] *adj.* (*adv.*) aanhoudend, onophoudelijk voortdurend.

inch [in(t)ʃ] *sb.* (Engelse) duim *m.* (1|12 voet, 2,54 cm.); kleinigheid *v.*; *vi.* zich voetje voor voetje bewegen.

incident ['insidənt] (onvoorziene) gebeurtenis *v.*, voorval *o.*; storend voorval, incident *o.*

incidentally [insi'dentəli] *adv.* toevallig; terloops; tussen twee haakjes.

incinerate [in'sinəreit] (tot as) verbranden; verassen.

incise [in'saiz] insnijden, (in)kerven, graveren.

incite [in'sait] aansporen; aanhitsen; opwekken, prikkelen.

incitement [in'saitmənt] aansporing *v.*; prikkel *m.*

incivism ['insivizm] gebrek aan burgerzin *o.*

inclement [in'klemənt] guur, bar, ruw; onmeedogend, onbarmhartig.

inclinable [in'klainəbl] geneigd, genegen.

inclination [inkli'neiʃən] helling v., hellingshoek m.; (hoofd) buiging v.; neiging, geneigdheid v.; genegenheid v.

incline [in'klain] buigen, neigen; hellen, overhellen; geneigd zijn.

include [in'klûd] insluiten; bevatten, omvatten, in zich sluiten; meerekenen, meetellen.

inclusive [in'klûsiv] adj. insluitend; omvattend; ingesloten; inclusief.

income ['inkəm] inkomen o., inkomsten v. mv.

incomparable [in'kɔmpərəbl] adj. onvergelijkelijk, weergaloos.

inconsequence [in'kɔnsikwəns] het onlogische o.; onlogische gevolgtrekking v.

incontrovertible [inkɔntrə'və:təbl] onbetwistbaar.

inconvenience [inkən'vînjəns] sb. ongerief, ongemak o., ongelegenheid v.; vt. last veroorzaken, in ongelegenheid brengen; lastig vallen.

incorporate [in'kɔ:pərit] adj. als rechtspersoon erkend; nauw verenigd, tot één lichaam verbonden; belichaamd; [in'kɔ:pəreit] vt. tot één lichaam verenigen; indelen, inlijven (bij); rechtspersoonlijkheid verlenen, als rechtspersoon erkennen; vi. zich verbinden, zich verenigen (with, met).

incorporation [inkɔ:pə'reiʃən] vereniging v. tot één lichaam; inlijving, opneming v.; erkenning v. als rechtspersoon.

increase [in'krîs] vi. toenemen, vermeerderen; vooruitgaan; (bij het breien) meerderen; vt. doen toenemen, vermeerderen; vergroten; verhogen; versterken.

increase ['inkrîs] sb. toeneming, vermeerdering v.; aanwas, groei m.; (v. loon) verhoging v.; kroost o.

incredulous(ly) [in'kredjuləs(li)] adj. (adv.) ongelovig.

increment ['inkrimənt] vermeerdering, toeneming v.; aanwas m.; opslag m., loonsverhoging v.

incriminate [in'krimineit] beschuldigen.

incrust(ate) [in'krəst(eit)] omkorsten; inleggen.

incubate ['inkjubeit] vt. & vi. broeden; uitbroeden.

inculcate [in'kəlkeit, 'inkəlkeit] inprenten.

incult [in'kəlt] onbebouwd; onbeschaafd, ruw.

incur [in'kə:] oplopen, zich op de hals halen.

incurable [in'kjûərəbl] adj. ongeneeslijk; sb. ongeneeslijke zieke m.

incursion [in'kə:ʃən] inval m.

indebted [in'detid] verschuldigd, schuldig; verplicht.

indebtedness [in'detidnis] schuld v.; verplichting v.

indecision [indi'siʒən] besluiteloosheid v.

indecisive [indi'saisiv] besluiteloos, weifelend; niet beslissend, niet afdoend.

indeclinable [indi'klainəbl] onverbuigbaar.

indeed [in'dîd] aav. inderdaad; voorwaar, voorzeker; werkelijk; in werkelijkheid: eigenlijk.

indefatigable [indi'fætigəbl] adj. onvermoeibaar; onvermoeid; onverdroten.

indefeasible [indi'fîzəbl] onschendbaar, onaantastbaar; onvervreemdbaar.

indefectible [indi'fektibl] adj. onvergankelijk; onfeilbaar, feilloos.

indefinite(ly) [in'definit(li)] adj. (adv.) onbepaald, onbegrensd.

indelible [in'delibl] onuitwisbaar.

indelicate [in'delikit] onkies; grof.

indemnification [indemnifi'keiʃən] schadeloosstelling, vergoeding v.

indemnify [in'demnifai] schadeloosstellen; vrijwaren (against, from, voor).

indent [in'dent] tanden; insnijden, inkerven; (drukk.) inspringen.

indentation [inden'teiʃən] uittanding v.; insnijding, inkerving v.; (drukk.) inspringing v.

independent [indi'pendənt] adj. onafhankelijk; zelfstandig; sb. (in politiek) onafhankelijke, wilde m.

indescribable [indis'kraibəbl] onbeschrijfelijk.

indeterminate [indi'tə:minit] onbepaald; onbestemd, vaag; onbeslist; besluiteloos.

index ['indeks] wijsvinger m.; aanwijzing v., leidraad m.; alfabetisch register o., bladwijzer m.; (v. instrument) wijzer m.; (kath.) index m., lijst v. van verboden boeken.

india-rubber ['indjə'rəbə] gummi, gom-elastiek o.

indicate ['indikeit] aanwijzen, aanduiden; wijzen op; aantonen.

indication [indi'keiʃən] aanwijzing, aanduiding v.; teken o.

indicator ['indikeitə] aanwijzer m.; (tn.: v. machine) verklikker m.; spanningmeter m.; nummerbord o.

indict [in'dait] aanklagen, beschuldigen.

indictment [in'daitmənt] aanklacht v.; (akte van) beschuldiging v.

Indies ['indiz] the —, Indië o.

indifferent [in'difrənt] adj. onverschillig; middelmatig; onbeduidend; (el.) indifferent; sb. onverschillige m.

indigence ['indidʒəns] behoeftigheid v., gebrek o., armoede v.

indigene ['indidʒîn] inboorling m.

indigenous [in'didʒinəs] inheems; inlands; aangeboren.

indigent ['indidʒənt] behoeftig, arm.

indignant(ly) [in'dignənt(li)] adj. (adv.) verontwaardigd.

indignation [indig'neiʃən] verontwaardiging v.

indirect ['ind(a)i'rekt] adj. indirect, niet rechtstreeks; zijdelings; onoprecht, slinks.

indiscreet [indis'krit] onbezonnen, onberaden; onvoorzichtig; onbescheiden, indiscreet; loslippig.

indiscriminate(ly) [indis'kriminit(li)] adj. (adv.) zonder onderscheid, door elkaar; algemeen.

indispensable [indis'pensəbl] onvermijdelijk; onmisbaar, noodzakelijk.

indisposed [indis'pouzd] adj. ongesteld; ongenegen; afkerig; ongunstig gestemd.

indisposition [indispə'ziʃən] ongesteldheid v.; ongeneigdheid; afkerigheid v.

indisputable [in'dispjutəbl] adj. onbetwistbaar.

indissoluble [indi'sɔljubl, in'disəljubl] adj. onoplosbaar; onverbreekbaar.

indite [in'dait] opstellen, (neer) schrijven.

individual [indi'vidjuəl] adj. individueel, afzonderlijk, persoonlijk, op zich zelf staand; sb. enkeling m.; individu o.

indolence ['indoləns] vadsigheid, traagheid, lusteloosheid v.; (gen.: v. gezwel) pijnloosheid v.

indolent(ly) ['indolənt(li)] adj. (adv.) vadsig, traag, lusteloos; pijnloos.

indomitable [in'dɔmitəbl] ontembaar, onbedwingbaar; onverzettelijk.

indoors [in'do:z] adv. binnen, binnenshuis; thuis.

indubitable [in'djûbitəbl] ontwijfelbaar.

induce [in'djûs] bewegen, er toe brengen; nopen; leiden tot, veroorzaken, te weeg brengen; afleiden, besluiten; (nat.) induceren.

inducement [in'djûsmənt] aanleiding, beweegreden, drijfveer v.; lokmiddel o.

induct [in'dəkt] in ambt bevestigen, installeren; (fig.) inwijden (in), bekend maken met.

induction [in'dəkʃən] bevestiging (in ambt), installatie v.; (v. feiten, enz.) aanvoering v.; gevolgtrekking v., besluit o.; (el.) inductie v.

indulge [in'dəldʒ] toegeven (aan), zich overgeven (aan); toegeeflijk behandelen, verwennen; koesteren.

indulgence [in'dəldʒəns] toegevendheid, inschikkelijkheid v.; gunst v., gunstbewijs o.; het toegeven, het zich overgeven aan o.; genoegen, genot o.; aflaat m.

indulgent(ly) [in'dəldʒənt(li)] adj. (adv.) toegeeflijk, inschikkelijk; goedgunstig.

indurate ['indjureit] vi. verharden, verhard worden; verstokken; (v. gewoonte) zich vastwortelen; vt. verharden, verhard maken.

industrial [in'dəstriəl] adj. industrieel, nijverheids—; sb. industrieel m.; industrie-arbeider m.; **—s,** (H.) industrie-aandelen, industriële waarden.

industrious [in'dəstriəs] adj. arbeidzaam, nijver, ijverig, vlijtig.

industry ['indəstri] arbeidzaamheid, naarstigheid, vlijt v., ijver m.; nijverheid, industrie v.

inebriate [i'nibriit] dronken, beschonken.

ineffaceable [ini'feisəbl] adj. onuitwisbaar.

inefficient [ini'fiʃənt] ondoeltreffend, zonder voldoende uitwerking; ongeschikt, onbruikbaar; onbekwaam.

inert [i'nə:t] adj. traag, log, loom; bewegingloos.

inescapable [inis'keipəbl] onontkoombaar.

inestimable [i'nestiməbl] onschatbaar, onberekenbaar.

inevitable [i'nevitəbl] adj. onvermijdelijk.

inexhaustible [inig'zo:stibl], **inexhaustive** [inig'zo:stiv] onuitputtelijk.

inexorable [i'neksərəbl] adj. onverbiddelijk.

inexpiable [i'nekspiəbl] niet te boeten, niet goed te maken, onverzoenlijk.

inexpressible [iniks'presibl] adj. onuitsprekelijk.

infallible [in'fælibl] adj. onfeilbaar, zeker, stellig, onbedrieglijk.

infamous(ly) ['infəməs(li)] adj. (adv.) schandelijk, berucht, (recht) eerloos.

infamy ['infəmi] schandelijkheid, schande v., schanddaad v.; eerloosheid v.

infant ['infənt] sb. zuigeling m.; kind o.; minderjarige, onmondige m.; adj. jong, jeugdig; kinder—.

infantile ['infəntail], **infantine** ['infəntain] kinderlijk; kinderachtig; kinder—.

infantry ['infəntri] infanterie v., voetvolk o.

infant-school ['infəntskûl] bewaarschool v.

infatuate [in'fætjueit] verzot maken; verdwazen; verblinden.

infatuation [infætju'eiʃən] verzotheid v.; verdwaasdheid v.; dwaze ingenomenheid v.; dwaze verliefdheid v.

infect [in'fekt] besmetten, aansteken; verpesten.

infection [in'fekʃən] besmetting, aansteking, infectie v.; verpesting v.

infectious [in'fekʃəs] besmettelijk, aanstekelijk.

infelicity [infi'lisiti] ongeluk o., rampspoed m.; ongelukkige keuze, ongelukkig gekozen uitdrukking v.

infer [in'fə:] afleiden, besluiten; insluiten, betekenen.

inference ['infərəns] gevolgtrekking v.

inferior [in'fiəriə] adj. lager; minder, ondergeschikt; minderwaardig, inferieur; (Pl.) onderstandig; onder—; sb. mindere, ondergeschikte m.

inferiority [infiəri'oriti] minderheid, ondergeschiktheid v.; minderwaardigheid v.

infernal [in'fə:nəl] hels, duivels; (fam.) afschuwelijk, beroerd.

infest [in'fest] onveilig maken; kwellen, verontrusten; verpesten.

infidel ['infidəl] *adj.* ongelovig; *sb.* ongelovige *m.*

infinite ['infinit] oneindig; eindeloos, onbegrensd.

infirm [in'fə:m] zwak, ziekelijk, gebrekkig; onvast, onzeker, weifelend.

infirmary [in'fə:məri] ziekenhuis *o.*; (*in school, klooster*) ziekenzaal *v.*

inflame [in'fleim] *vt.* doen ontvlammen; in gloed zetten; aanvuren; (*v. bloed*) verhitten; *vi.* ontvlammen, ontbranden, vuur vatten; (*gen.*) ontsteken.

inflammable [in'flæməbl] ontvlambaar, brandbaar.

inflammation [inflə'meiʃən] ontbranding *v.*; ontsteking *v.*

inflate [in'fleit] opblazen; (*v. fiets*) oppompen; (*v. ballon*) vullen; (*v. prijzen*) opdrijven.

inflation [in'fleiʃən] het opblazen *o.*; het oppompen *o.*; vulling *v.* opdrijving *v.*; inflatie, vermeerdering *v.* van papiergeld.

inflexible [in'fleksibl] *adj.* onbuigbaar; onbuigzaam; onverzettelijk, onwrikbaar.

inflict [in'flikt] (*v. straf*) opleggen; (*v. slag, wond*) toebrengen; (*fam.*) opknappen (met), opschepen (met), lastig vallen (met).

inflow ['inflou] instroming, binnenstroming *v.*; toevloed *m.*

influence ['influəns] *sb.* invloed *m.* (**on, upon, over,** op); inwerking *v.*; protectie *v.*; (*el.*) inductie *v.*; *vt.* invloed hebben (*of:* oefenen) op, beïnvloeden; inwerken op.

influential [influ'enʃəl] *adj.* invloedrijk.

influenza [influ'enzə] griep *v.*; influenza *v.*

influx ['infləks] *zie* **inflow.**

inform [in'fo:m] *vt.* melden, mededelen, berichten; bezielen; doordringen; *vi.* bericht zenden; onderrichten; *adj.* vormeloos.

informant [in'fo:mənt] zegsman *m.*; (*recht*) aanklager *m.*

information [info:'meiʃən] mededeling *v.*, bericht *o.*; kennisgeving *v.*; inlichting *v.*; aanklacht *v.*

informer [in'fo:mə] aanklager *m.*

infraction [in'frækʃən] inbreuk, schending, schennis *v.*

infrangible [in'fræn(d)ʒibl] *adj.* onbreekbaar, onverbreekbaar.

infringe [in'frin(d)ʒ] inbreuk maken op, schenden, overtreden.

infringement ['in'frin(d)ʒmənt] inbreuk, schennis, overtreding *v.*

infuriate [in'fjûəriit] *adj.* woedend, razend; [in'fjûərieit] *vt.* woedend (razend) maken.

infusion [in'fjûʒən] ingieting *v.*; inprenting *v.*; instorting *v.*; aftreksel *o.*

ingeminate [in'dʒemineit] verdubbe-

len; herhalen; bij herhaling aandringen op.

ingenious (**ly**) [in'dʒinjəs(li)] *adj.* (*adv.*) vindingrijk, vernuftig.

ingeniousness [in'dʒinjəsnis] *zie* **ingenuity.**

ingenuity [indʒi'njûiti] vindingrijkheid *v.*; vernuftigheid *v.*, vernuft *o.*

ingestion [in'dʒestʃən] (*v. voedsel*) opneming *v.*

ingot ['ingət] (*v. goud, zilver, enz.*) baar staaf *v.*

ingratitude [in'grætitjûd] ondankbaarheid *v.*

inhabit [in'hæbit] bewonen, wonen in.

inhabitable [in'hæbitəbl] bewoonbaar.

inhabitant [in'hæbitənt] bewoner; inwoner *m.*

inhale [in'heil] inademen, inhaleren.

inhere [in'hiə] onafscheidelijk verbonden zijn aan (met), een bestanddeel vormen van; eigen zijn aan.

inherit [in'herit] erven.

inheritance [in'heritəns] overerving *v.*; erfenis *v.*

inhibition [inhi'biʃən] verbod *o.*; verhindering *v.*; schorsing *v.*

inhuman [in'hjûmən] *adj.* onmenselijk.

inhume [in'hjûm] begraven.

inimical [i'nimikl] vijandelijk; vijandig; nadelig, schadelijk.

iniquity [i'nikwiti] onrechtvaardigheid, onbillijkheid *v.*; ongerechtigheid, zonde *v.*; boosheid, snoodheid.

initial [i'niʃəl] *adj.* aanvangs—, begin—, eerste; *sb.* beginletter; voorletter, initiaal *v.*

initiate [i'niʃieit] *vt.* inwijden; inleiden; aanvangen, beginnen; [i'niʃiit] a) *adj.* ingewijd; b) *sb.* ingewijde *m.*

initiative [i'niʃiətiv] *sb.* eerste stap *m.*, begin, initiatief *o.*; *adj.* inleidend, aanvangs—.

injection [in'dʒekʃən] inspuiting *v.*

injure ['in(d)ʒə] beledigen, kwetsen; verongelijken, onrecht aandoen; benadelen, kwaad doen.

injurious [in'dʒûəriəs] beledigend, kwetsend, krenkend; nadelig, schadelijk.

injury ['in(d)ʒəri] belediging, krenking *v.*; verongelijking *v.*, onrecht *o.*; nadeel *o.*, schade *v.*, letsel *o.*

ink [iŋk] *sb.* inkt *m.*; *vt.* inkten.

inkstand ['iŋkstænd] inktkoker *m.*, inktstel *o.*

inlaid ['inleid] ingelegd.

inland ['inlənd] *adj.* binnenlands; *adv.* landwaarts, het binnenland in.

inlet ['inlet] ingang, toegang *m.*, opening *v.*; inham *m.*; inzetsel *o.*

inmate ['inmeit] (mede)bewoner, huisgenoot *m.*; inzittende *m.*

inn [in] *sb.* herberg *v.*, logement *o.*; *vt.* huisvesten, herbergen.

innate ['ineit, i'neit] aangeboren, ingeboren.

inner ['inə] inwendig, innerlijk, binnenste; verborgen.

innermost ['inəmoust] binnenste.

inn-keeper ['inkîpə] herbergier, waard *m.*

innocence ['inəsəns] onschuld *v.*; onnozelheid *v.*

innocent ['inəsənt] *adj.* onschuldig, schuldeloos; onschadelijk; onnozel; *sb.* onschuldige *m.*

innovation [ino'veiʃən] invoering van nieuwigheden *v.*; nieuwigheid *v.*

innoxious [i'nɔkʃəs] onschadelijk.

innumerable [i'njûmərəbl], **innumerous** [i'njûmərəs] ontelbaar, talloos.

innutrition [inju'triʃən] ondervoeding *v.*

inoculate [i'nɔkjuleit] (in)enten.

inodorous [i'noudərəs] reukeloos.

inoffensive [inə'fensiv] onschadelijk, onschuldig; geen aanstoot gevend, niet beledigend.

inopportune [i'nɔpətjûn] ongelegen, ontijdig.

inquest ['inkwest] onderzoek *o.*

inquire [in'kwaiə] *vt.* vragen naar; onderzoeken; *vi.* navraag doen, informeren.

inquiry [in'kwaiəri] onderzoek *o.*, navorsing *v.*; vraag, navraag *v.*

inquisitive(ly) [in'kwizitiv(li)] *adj.* (*adv.*) nieuwsgierig; onderzoekend.

inquisitiveness [in'kwizitivnis] nieuwsgierigheid *v.*

inroad ['inroud] vijandelijke inval *m.*; inbreuk *v.*; (*v. gezondheid, enz.*) aantasting *v.*

insane [in'sein] krankzinnig.

insanity [in'sæniti] krankzinnigheid *v.*

inscribe [ins'kraib] inschrijven, opschrijven; graveren; inprenten; (*v. boek*) opdragen; (*meetk.*) beschrijven in.

inscription [ins'kripʃən] inschrijving *v.*; inschrift, opschrift *o.*; opdracht *v.*

inscrutable [ins'krûtəbl] ondoorgrondelijk, onnaspeurlijk.

insect ['insekt] insekt *o.*

insensate [in'sens(e)it] gevoelloos; onverstandig, dom, onzinnig, zinneloos.

insensible [in'sensibl] *adj.* ongevoelig; gevoelloos; bewusteloos; onverschillig; onmerkbaar.

insert [in'sə:t] *vt.* invoegen; inzetten; inlassen; (*in dagblad, tijdschrift*) plaatsen, opnemen; *sb.* inlassing *v.*

insertion [in'sə:ʃən] invoeging *v.*; inlassing *v.*; plaatsing, opname *v.*

inside ['insaid] *adj.* binnenste, binnen—; *prep.* in, binnenin; binnen; ['in'said] *sb.* binnenkant *m.*, binnenzijde *v.*; (*v. trottoir*) huizenkant *m.*; het inwendige *o.*; *adv.* binnen.

insidious(ly) [in'sidiəs(li)].*adj.* (*adv.*) arglistig; verraderlijk.

insight ['insait] inzicht *o.*

insignia [in'signiə] onderscheidingstekenen, ordetekenen *o. mv.*

insinuate [in'sinjueit] (ongemerkt) indringen, inbrengen; (bedekt) te kennen geven, te verstaan geven, insinueren.

insinuation [insinju'eiʃən] het indringen *o.*; zijdelingse aanduiding, bedekte toespeling, insinuatie *v.*

insipid [in'sipid] smakeloos, flauw, geesteloos.

insist [in'sist] aandringen; aanhouden, volhouden; blijven bij; met nadruk beweren.

insobriety [inso'braiəti] onmatigheid *v.*; drankzucht, dronkenschap *v.*

insolent(ly) ['insələnt(li)] *adj.* (*adv.*) onbeschaamd.

insolvent [in'sɔlvənt] *adj.* onvermogend om te betalen, insolvent; *sb.* insolvente schuldenaar *m.*

inspect [in'spekt] in ogenschouw nemen; inspecteren; nagaan, nazien, onderzoeken.

inspection [in'spekʃən] inspectie *v.*; onderzoek *o.*; inzage *v.*

inspector [in'spektə] opziener, inspecteur *m.*

inspectorate [in'spektərit] inspecteurschap *o.*; inspectie *v.*

inspiration [inspi'reiʃən] inademing *v.*; ingeving, inspiratie *v.*

inspire [in'spaiə] inademen; ingeven, inboezemen; inspireren; bezielen.

install [in'stoːl] (*v. licht, enz.*) plaatsen, aanleggen; (*in ambt*) bevestigen, installeren; — *oneself,* zich vestigen; zich inrichten.

instalment [in'stoːlmənt] (*v. betaling*) termijn *m.*; (*v. artikel, betaling, enz.*) gedeelte *o.*

instance ['instəns] *sb.* aandrang *m.*, dringend verzoek *o.*; voorbeeld *o.*; (*recht*) instantie *v.*, aanleg *m.*; *vt.* als voorbeeld aanhalen; met voorbeelden bewijzen.

instantaneous [instən'teinjəs] ogenblikkelijk.

instantly ['instəntli] *adv.* ogenblikkelijk, onmiddellijk, op staande voet; dringend; zodra.

instate [in'steit] plaatsen, installeren.

instead [ins'ted] in plaats daarvan; — *of,* in plaats van.

instep ['instep] wreef *v.* (van voet).

instigate ['instigeit] aansporen, aanzeggen (tot); ophitsen, aanhitsen.

instigator ['instigeitə] aanzetter *m.*; ophitser, aanhitser *m.*; aanstichter, aanstoker *m.*

instinct ['instiŋkt] *sb.* instinct *o.*, natuurdrift *v.*; intuïtie *v.*

institute ['institjût] *vt.* instellen, oprichten, stichten; aanstellen, installeren; bevestigen (in ambt); *sb.* instituut *o.*, instelling *v.*; genootschap *o.*

institution [insti'tjûʃən] instituut *o.*, instelling *v.*; gesticht *o.*; installatie, bevestiging (in ambt) *v.*

instruct [ins'trɔkt] onderrichten; last geven; voorschrijven.

instruction [ins'trɔkʃən] onderricht *o.*; last *m.*, opdracht *v.*; voorschrift *o.*

instrument ['instrumənt] (*muz.*) speel-

tuig, instrument *o.*; (*tn.*) werktuig, gereedschap *o.*
insubordination [insəbo:di'neiʃən] weerspannigheid *v.*
insulator ['insjuleitə] (*el.*) isolator *m.*
insult ['insəlt] *sb.* belediging *v.*, hoon *m.*; [in'səlt] *vt.* beledigen, honen.
insulting (ly) [in'səltiŋ(li)] *adj.* (*adv.*) beledigend.
insurance [in'ʃûərəns] verzekering, assurantie *v.*
insure [in'ʃûə] verzekeren, assureren.
insured [in'ʃûəd] *adj.* verzekerd; *sb.* verzekerde *m.*
insurer [in'ʃûərə] verzekeraar, assuradeur *m.*
insurgent [in'sə:dʒənt] *adj.* oproerig; *sb.* oproerling, opstandeling *m.*
insurmountable [insə'mauntəbl] *adj.* onoverkomelijk.
insurrection [insə'rekʃən] opstand *m.*, oproer *o.*
intact [in'tækt] intact, ongerept, ongeschonden.
intangibility [intændʒə'biliti] ontastbaarheid *v.*
integral ['intigrəl] *adj.* integrerend; geheel, volledig, integraal; integraal *v.*
intellect ['intilekt] intellect, verstand *o.*
intellectual [inti'lektjuəl] *adj.* verstandelijk, intellectueel; geestelijk, verstands—; *sb.* intellectueel *m.*
intelligence [in'telidʒəns] verstand; oordeel *o.*; schranderheid, vlugheid van begrip *v.*; nieuws, bericht *o.*, inlichting *v.*
intelligence-service [in'telidʒənssə:vis] inlichtingsdienst *m.*
intelligent [in'telidʒənt] *adj.* verstandig, vlug van begrip, schrander.
intelligible [in'telidʒibl] begrijpelijk.
intend [in'tend] van plan zijn, voornemens zijn, voorhebben; menen, bedoelen; bestemmen (**for,** voor).
intended [in'tendid] *adj.* voorgenomen, aanstaande; opzettelijk; *sb.* aanstaande *v.*
intense (ly) [in'tens(li)] *adj.* (*adv.*) krachtig, sterk, hevig, intens; ingespannen.
intensify [in'tensifai] versterken, verhogen.
intensive [in'tensiv] *adj.* krachtig, intensief; (*gram.*) versterkend; *sb.* versterkend woord *o.*
intention [in'tenʃən] voornemen *o.*, bedoeling *v.*, doel, oogmerk *o.*; (*kath.*) intentie *v.*; begrip *o.*, conceptie *v.*
intentional (ly) [in'tenʃənl(i)] *adj.* (*adv.*) opzettelijk, met opzet, voorbedacht.
inter [in'tə:] begraven, ter aarde bestellen.
interaction [intə'rækʃən] wisselwerking *v.*
intercalate [in'tə:keleit] inlassen, invoegen, tussenvoegen.
intercalation [intə:kə'leiʃən] inlassing, tussenvoeging *v.*

intercede [intə'sid] tussenbeide komen, voorspreken, (iemands) voorspraak zijn.
intercept [intə'sept] onderscheppen, opvangen, (de pas) afsnijden.
intercession [intə'seʃən] tussenkomst, bemiddeling *v.*; voorspraak, voorbede *v.*
intercessor [intə'sesə] bemiddelaar *m.*; voorspraak *m.*
interchange [intə'tʃein(d)ʒ] *vt.* wisselen, uitwisselen, ruilen; afwisselen; *sb.* wisseling *v.*, ruil *m.*; ruilhandel *m.*, ruilverkeer *o.*; afwisseling *v.*
intercourse ['intəko:s] omgang *m.*, verkeer *o.*, gemeenschap *v.*
interdict ['intədikt] *sb.* verbod *o.*; ontzegging *v.*; (*kath.*) interdict *o.*, kerkelijke ban *v.* (over een land of streek); [intə'dikt] *vt.* verbieden; ontzeggen; het interdict uitspreken over.
interdiction [intə'dikʃən] verbod *o.*; ontzegging *v.*; interdict *o.*
interest ['int(ə)rest] *sb.* belang *o.*; voordeel *o.*; aandeel *o.*; rente *v.*, interest *m.*; *vt.* belang (belangstelling) inboezemen; belang doen stellen in; betreffen, raken; *vr.* — **oneself in** (*for*), belang stellen in, zich interesseren voor.
interesting (ly) ['int(ə)restiŋ(li)] *adj.* (*adv.*) belangwekkend, interessant.
interfere [intə'fiə] tussenbeide komen; zich inlaten, zich bemoeien (met); (*v. dokter*) ingrijpen.
interference [intə'fiərəns] tussenkomst *v.*; inmenging, bemoeiing *v.*; het ingrijpen *o.*
interim ['intərim] *sb.* tussentijd *m.*; **in the** —, intussen; *adj.* tussentijds; tijdelijk; (*v. dividend*) voorlopig.
interior [in'tiəriə] *adj.* inwendig; innerlijk; binnenste; binnen—; binnenlands; *sb.* inwendige *o.*; innerlijke *o.*; binnenste *o.*; binnenland *o.*
interjection [intə'dʒekʃən] tussenwerpsel *o.*
interline [intə'lain] tussen de regels schrijven; interliniëren.
interlope [intə'loup] onderkruipen.
interlude ['intəl(j)ûd] pauze *v.*; tussenbedrijf, tussenspel *o.*; intermezzo *o.*
intermeddle [intə'medl] zich mengen in, zich bemoeien (**with,** met).
intermediary [intə'midiəri] *adj.* tussenliggend, tussen—; bemiddelend; *sb.* tussenpersoon, bemiddelaar *m.*; bemiddeling *v.*
intermediate [intə'midiit] *adj.* tussenliggend, tussen—; *sb.* tussenpersoon *m.*; tussenvorm, overgangsvorm *m.*
interment [in'tə:mənt] begrafenis, teraardebestelling *v.*
interminable [in'tə:minəbl] *adj.* oneindig, eindeloos.
intermingle [intə'miŋgl] *vt.* mengen, vermengen; *vi.* zich vermengen.
intermission [intə'miʃən] tussenpoos, pauze *v.*; afbreking, onderbreking *v.*
intermix [intə'miks] (zich) vermengen.
intern [in'tə:n] interneren.

internal [in'tə:nəl] *adj.* inwendig, innerlijk; binnenlands.

international [intə'næʃənəl] *adj.* internationaal; *sb.* internationale *v.*; (*sp.*) internationaal *m.*

internee [intə:'nî] geïnterneerde *m.*

internment [in'tə:nmənt] internering *v.*

interpellation [intəpe'leiʃən] interpellatie *v.*

interplay ['intəplei] tussenspel o.; wisselwerking *v.*

interpolation [intə:po'leiʃən] invoeging, tussenvoeging, inlassing *v.*

interpose [intə'pouz] *vt.* tussenplaatsen; in 't midden brengen; *vi.* tussenbeide komen.

interpret [in'tə:prit] verklaren, uitleggen, vertolken.

interpretation [intə:pri'teiʃən] uitlegging, verklaring, vertolking, interpretatie *v.*

interpreter [in'tə:pritə] uitlegger, vertolker *m.*; tolk *m.*

interrogate [in'terəgeit] (onder)vragen.

interrogation [interə'geiʃən] ondervraging *v.*; vraag *v.*

interrupt [intə'rəpt] *vt.* afbreken; onderbreken; in de rede vallen; (*v. uitzicht*) belemmeren; storen; *vi.* hinderen, storen.

interruptor [intə'rəptə] onderbreker *m.*; (*el.*) stroombreker *m.*

intersection [intə'sekʃən] doorsnijding *v.*; snijpunt o.; kruispunt o.

interspace ['intəspeis] tussenruimte *v.*

interstice [in'tə:stis] tussenruimte; spleet *v.*

intertwine [intə'twain], **intertwist** [intə'twist] dooreenvlechten, ineenstrengelen.

interval ['intəvəl] tussenruimte *v.*; tussentijd *m.*, tussenpoos *v.*; (*muz.*) toonafstand *m.*, interval o.

intervene [intə'vîn] tussenbeide komen; (*gen.*) ingrijpen; gebeuren, zich voordoen; (*H.: v. wissel*) interveniëren.

intervention [intə'venʃən] tussenkomst, interventie *v.*; bemiddeling *v.*

interview ['intəvjû] *sb.* samenkomst *v.*; vraaggesprek, interview o.; *vt.* interviewen.

interviewee [intəvju'î] geïnterviewde *m.*

interviewer ['intəvjûə] interviewer *m.*

intestine [in'testin] *adj.* inwendig; binnenlands; *sb.* darm *m.*; —s, ingewanden o. mv.

intimate ['intimit] *adj.* vertrouwelijk, intiem; innig; innerlijk; *sb.* boezemvriend(in) *m.* (*v.*); [intimeit] *vt.* bekend maken; te kennen geven.

intimation [inti'meiʃən] kennisgeving *v.*; aanduiding *v.*; wenk *m.*

into ['intu; vóór medeklinker: 'intə] in; tot.

intolerable [in'tolərəbl] on(ver)draaglijk.

intolerant [in'tolərənt] onverdraagzaam.

intonation [into(u)'neiʃən] intonatie, stembuiging *v.*; aanheffing *v.*; toonaangeving *v.*

intoxicate [in'toksikeit] bedwelmen; dronken maken.

intractable [in'træktəbl] onhandelbaar; (*v. ziekte*) hardnekkig.

intrench [in'trenʃ] *zie* **entrench.**

intrepid [in'trepid] onverschrokken, onversaagd.

intricate ['intrikit] ingewikkeld, verward.

intrigue [in'trig] *sb.* kuiperij *v.*, gekonkel o.; *vi.* intrigeren, kuipen, konkelen.

intriguer [in'trigə] intrigant, konkelaar *m.*

intrinsic(al) [in'trinsik(l)] *adj.* innerlijk, wezenlijk.

introduce [intrə'djûs] inleiden; binnenleiden; invoeren; (*v. persoon*) voorstellen, introduceren.

introduction [intrə'dəkʃən] inleiding *v.*; invoering *v.*; (*v. persoon*) voorstelling, introductie *v.*

intrude [in'trûd] *vt.* indringen; opdringen; *vi.* zich indringen; storen, ongelegen komen.

intruder [in'trûdə] indringer; ongenode gast *m.*

intrusive(ly) [in'trûsiv(li)] *adj.* (*adv.*) indringend; indringerig; ingevoegd.

inundate ['inəndeit] onder water zetten; overstromen.

inundation [inən'deiʃən] overstroming *v.*; (*fig.*) stroom, stortvloed *m.*

inure [i'njûə] *vt.* gewennen (*to, aan*); harden (*to, tegen*), *vi.* (*recht*) van kracht worden; ten goede komen (*to, aan*).

invade [in'veid] binnendringen, binnenvallen, inbreuk maken op, schenden, aangrijpen.

invalid ['invəlid] *adj.* gebrekkig, gebrekkelijk, hulpbehoevend, ziekelijk, *sb.* zieke, gebrekkige, hulpbehoevende *m.*; (*mil.*) invalide *m.*

invalidate [in'vælideit] krachteloos (ongeldig) maken; (*v. argument*) ontzenuwen.

invalidity [invə'liditi] zwakte; invaliditeit *v.*; krachteloosheid; ongeldigheid *v.*

invaluable [in'væljuəbl] onschatbaar.

invariable [in'vêəriəbl] *adj.* onveranderlijk, standvastig.

invasion [in'veiʒən] inval *m.*; inbreuk, schending, aanranding *v.*; (*v. ziekte, enz.*) optreden o.

inveigh [in'vei] uitvaren, schelden, schimpen.

inveigle [in'vigl] verlokken, verleiden.

invent [in'vent] uitvinden; verzinnen, verdichten.

invention [in'venʃən] uitvinding *v.*; verzinsel, uitvindsel, bedenksel o.

inventive(ly) [in'ventiv(li)] *adj.* (*adv.*) vindingrijk.

inventiveness [in'ventivnis] vindingrijkheid v.

inventor [in'ventə] uitvinder m.; verzinner m.

inventory ['invəntri] sb. inventaris m.; vt. inventariseren.

inverse [in'və:s] omgekeerd.

inversion [in'və:ʃən] omkering v.; omzetting, inversie v.

invert [in'və:t] omkeren; omzetten.

invertebrate [in'və:tibrit] (Dk.) ongewerveld; (fig.) slap, zwak, karakterloos, zonder ruggegraat.

invest [in'vest] kleden; bekleden; (mil.) insluiten, omsingelen; (v. geld) beleggen; (in ambt) installeren.

investigate [in'vestigeit] onderzoeken, navorsen, nasporen.

investigation [investi'geiʃən] (nauwkeurig) onderzoek o., navorsing, nasporing v.

investment [in'vestmənt] (geld)belegging v.; (mil.) insluiting, omsingeling v.

inveterate [in'vetərit] ingeworteld, ingekankerd; (v. zondaar, dronkaard) verstokt, onverbeterlijk; (v. kwaal, ziekte) verouderd; (pop.) verbitterd, gebeten (against, op).

invidious(ly) [in'vidiəs(li)] adj. (adv.) hatelijk; aanstotelijk; hachelijk, netelig.

invigilate [in'vidʒileit] (bij examen) surveilleren.

invigorate [in'vigəreit] kracht geven, kracht bijzetten, versterken.

invincible [in'vinsibl] adj. onoverwinnelijk; onoverkomelijk.

inviolable [in'vaiələbl] onschendbaar.

invisible [in'vizibl] onzichtbaar.

invitation [invi'teiʃən] uitnodiging v.

invite [in'vait] uitnodigen; (beleefd) verzoeken.

invoice ['invɔis] sb. (H.) factuur v.; vt. factureren.

invoke [in'vouk] aanroepen; inroepen; afsmeken; oproepen.

involuntary [in'vɔləntəri] adj. onwillekeurig.

involve [in'vɔlv] wikkelen in; verwikkelen (in), betrekken (in, bij); met zich brengen, na zich slepen.

invulnerable [in'vɔlnərəbl] onkwetsbaar.

inward ['inwəd] adj. inwendig; innerlijk; binnenwaarts.

inwards ['inwədz] adv. inwendig; innerlijk; sb. ingewanden o. mv.

iodine ['aiod(a)in] jodium o.

irascible [(a)i'ræsibl] lichtgeraakt, oplopend, opvliegend.

Ireland ['aiələnd] Ierland o.

iris ['aiəris] regenboog m.; (v. oog) regenboogvlies o.; (Pl.) zwaardlelie v.

iron ['aiən] sb. ijzer o.; strijkijzer o.; brandijzer o.; —s, boeien v. mv.; adj. ijzeren; ijzerhard; vt. met ijzer beslaan; boeien, kluisteren; strijken.

iron-bound ['aiənbaund] met ijzer beslagen; ijzerhard; (fig.) zeer streng.

ironclad ['aiənklæd] adj. gepantserd; sb. pantserschip o.

ironer ['aiənə] strijk(st)er m. (v.).

ironing-board ['aiəninbo:d] strijkplank v.

ironmonger ['aiənmʌŋgə] handelaar in ijzerwaren m.

irony ['airəni] sb. ironie v.

irrational [i'ræʃənəl] redeloos; onredelijk; ongerijmd, dwaas; (rek.) onmeetbaar.

irreclaimable [iri'kleiməbl] onverbeterlijk, verstokt; onherstelbaar.

irregular [i'regjulə] adj. onregelmatig; ongeregeld; ongelijk; sb. —s, (mil.) ongeregelde troepen.

irreparable [i'repərəbl] onherstelbaar.

irrepressible [iri'presibl] onbedwingbaar.

irreproachable [iri'proutʃəbl] adj. onberispelijk.

irresistible [iri'zistibl] adj. onweerstaanbaar.

irresolute(ly) [i'rezəl(j)ût(li)] adj. (adv.) besluiteloos.

irretrievable [iri'trivəbl] adj. onherstelbaar.

irrevocable [i'revəkəbl] onherroepelijk.

irrigate ['irigeit] bevochtigen, besproeien, bevloeien.

irrigation [iri'geiʃən] bevochtiging, bevloeiing, besproeiing v.

irritable ['iritəbl] adj. prikkelbaar.

irritant ['iritənt] prikkelend.

irritate ['iriteit] prikkelen; wrevelig maken, verbitteren.

irruption [i'rʌpʃən] inval m.

isinglass ['aizinglâs] vislijm v.

island ['ailənd] eiland o.

islander ['ailəndə] eilandbewoner m.

isle [ail] eiland o.

isolated ['aisəleitid] alleenstaand, afgezonderd; eenzaam.

isolation [aisə'leiʃən] afzondering v.; eenzaamheid v.

issue ['isjû, 'iʃu] sb. uitstroming, uitstorting v.; uittocht m.; uitgang m.; uitkomst v.; kroost o.; (v. dagblad) nummer o.; (v. bankbiljetten, enz.) uitgifte v.; vt. (v. bankbiljetten, enz.) uitgeven, in omloop brengen; (v. uitnodigingen) verzenden; uitvaardigen; verlenen; vi. uitkomen, uitstromen; zich uitstorten; voortkomen (from, uit).

issueless ['isjûlis] adj. kinderloos; zonder resultaat.

isthmus ['isðməs, 'istməs, 'isməs] landengte v.

it [it] het; hij, zij.

italic [i'tælik] adj. cursief; sb. cursieve letter v.; —s, cursieve druk m.

italicize [i'tælisaiz] cursiveren.

Italy ['iteli] Italië o.

itch [itʃ] sb. schurft v.; jeukte, jeuking v.; hunkering, zucht (from, naar); vi. jeuken; hunkeren.

itchy ['itʃi] jeukerig; schurftig.

item ['aitəm] *adv.* item; eveneens; *sb.* (*op programma*) nummer *o.*; (*op agenda*) punt, artikel *o.*; (*op rekening*) post *m.*
itinerant [(a)i'tinərənt] reizend, rondtrekkend.
itinerary [(a)i'tinərəri] reisroute *v.*,

reisweg *m.*; reisgids *m.*; reisplan *o.*; reisbeschrijving *v.*
itself [it'self] zich(zelf).
ivory ['aivəri] *sb.* ivoor, elpenbeen *o.*; *adj.* ivoren, elpenbenen.
ivy ['aivi] (*Pl.*) klimop *o.*

J

jab [dʒæb] *vt.* & *vi.* steken; *sb.* prik, steək, por *m.*
jabber ['dʒæbə] *vt.* & *vi.* babbelen; uitkramen; *sb.* gebabbel *o.*
jack [dʒæk] *sb.* (*kaartsp.*) boer *m.*; zaagbok *m.*, schraag *v.*; (*el.*) stopcontact *o.*; dommekracht, vijzel *v.*; *vt.* & *vi.* opvijzelen; opdraaien (met dommekracht).
jackal ['dʒæko:l] jakhals *m.*
jackdaw ['dʒækdo:] kauw, kerkkauw *v.*
jacket ['dʒækit] jekkertje, jasje *o.*; (*v. boek*) kaft *v.* & *o.*, omslag *m.* & *o.*; omhulsel *o.*; pels *m.*, vacht *v.*; (*v. aardappel*) schil *v.*
Jack-plane ['dʒækplein] (*tn.*) rijschaaf *v.*
jack-screw ['dʒækskrû] dommekracht, vijzel *v.*
Jack-tar ['dʒæk'tâ] (*fam.*) pikbroek *m.*, Jantje *o.*
jack-towel ['dʒæktauəl] handdoek op rol *m.*
jade [dʒeid] *sb.* knol *m.*, oud paard *o.*; feeks *v.*; *vt.* afrijden, afjakkeren; afmatten.
jail [dʒeil] *sb.* gevangenis *v.*, kerker *m.*; *vt.* gevangen zetten.
jail-bird ['dʒeilbə:d] (gevangenis)-boef *m.*
jailer ['dʒeilə] cipier *m.*
jam [dʒæm] *sb.* jam, vruchtengelei *v.*; gedrang *o.*; klemming *v.*; *vt.* vastzetten, klemmen, knellen; samendrukken; (*v. radio*) storen, hinderen; versperren.
jamb [dʒæm] stijl (*v. deur, enz.*), post *m.*; steenlaag *v.*
jamboree [dʒæmbo'rî] (*sl.*) fuif, pretmakerij *v.*; samenkomst *v.*; jamboree *v.*
jamming ['dʒæmiŋ] *sb.* het knellen *o.*, knelling *v.*; (*el., radio*) storing *v.*; *adj.* knellend; klemmend.
janitor ['dʒænitə] portier, deurwachter *m.*
January ['dʒænjuəri] januari *m.*
japan [dʒə'pæn] *sb.* vernislak *o.*; lakwerk *o.*; *vt.* lakken, verlakken; (*v. schoenen*) poetsen.
jar [dʒâ] *sb.* pot *m.*, kruik, fles *v.*; wanklank *m.*, vals geluid *o.*; (*fig.*) wanklank *m.*; *vi.* vals klinken, een wanklank voortbrengen; knarsen; *vt.* doen trillen.
jaunt [dʒo:nt] *vi.* een uitstapje maken; *sb.* uitstapje, tochtje, plezierreisje *o.*
jaunty ['dʒo:nti] zwierig, luchtig.

javelin ['dʒævlin] werpspies *v.*
jaw [dʒo:] *sb.* kaak *v.*; (*tn.*: *v. tang, gaffel*) klauw *m.*; (*v. sleutel*) bek *m.*; praat *m.*; *vi.* kletsen, zwammen; schelden; de les lezen.
jaw-breaker ['dʒo:breikə] moeilijk uit te spreken woord *o.*
jazz [dʒæz] herrie *v.*, lawaai *o.*, drukte *v.*; (*sl.*) rommel *m.*; (*muz.*) jazz *v.*
jealous(ly) ['dʒeləs(li)] *adj.* (*adv.*) jaloers, afgunstig; bezorgd, angstvallig; waakzaam.
jealousy ['dʒeləsi] jaloersheid *v.*, afgunst *v.*; (*angstvallige*) bezorgdheid *v.*
jeer [dʒiə] *sb.* hoon *m.*, spotternij *v.*; *vt.* honen, bespotten; beschimpen; *vi.* spotten met; schimpen op.
jejune [dʒi'dʒûn] schraal, schamel; (*v. opsomming, enz.*) dor, droog; nuchter.
jelly ['dʒeli] gelei *v.*; (*v. vlees*) dril *m.*
jelly-fish ['dʒelifiʃ] kwal *v.*
jemmy ['dʒemi] (toebereide) schaapskop *m.*; (*sl.*) breekijzer *o.*; overjas *v.*
jeopard ['dʒepəd], **—ize** ['dʒepədaiz] in gevaar brengen, wagen.
jerk [dʒə:k] *sb.* ruk, stoot *m.*; schok *m.*; zenuwtrekking *v.*; *vi.* rukken, stoten; schokken.
jerkin ['dʒə:kin] buis, wambuis *o.*, kolder *m.*
jerry-building ['dʒeribildiŋ] revolutiebouw *m.*
jersey ['dʒə:zi] trui, (wollen) sporttrui *v.*; jersey *v.*, damesmanteltje *o.*
jessamine ['dʒesəmin] jasmijn *v.*
jest [dʒest] *sb.* scherts, grap, mop, gekheid *v.*; spot *m.*, spotternij *v.*; *vi.* schertsen, gekheid maken.
jester ['dʒestə] spotvogel, grappenmaker *m.*; hofnar *m.*
jet [dʒet] *sb.* waterstraal *v.*; rookwolk *v.*; (*gas*)vlam *v.*; gaspit *v.*; (*v. spuit*) mondstuk *o.*; git *o.*; *adj.* gitten; *vt.* uitspuiten; *vi.* uitschieten, omhoogschieten.
jetsam ['dʒetsəm] overboord geworpen lading *v.*; strandgoed *o.*
jettison ['dʒetisn] (uit nood) overboord werpen.
jetty ['dʒeti] *sb.* havenhoofd *o.*, pier *m.*; steiger *m.*; uitsprong *m.*
Jew [dʒû] jood *m.*
jewel ['dʒûil] juweel, kleinood *o.*; (*in uurwerk*) steen *m.*; edelgesteente *o.*
jeweller ['dʒûilə] juwelier *m.*
Jewess ['dʒûis] jodin *v.*
Jewish ['dʒûiʃ] joods.

jingle ['dʒingl] *vt.* (& *vi.*) (laten) rinkelen; klingelen; klinken met; (*v. verzen*) rammelen; *sb.* gerinkel *o.*; klinkklank *m.*; rijmklank *m.*

job [dʒɔb] *sb.* karwei, werk *o.*; baantje, zaakje *o.*; sjachelarij; knoeierij *v.*; *vt.* uitvoeren (van aangenomen werk); handelen in; huren; verhuren; *vi.* karweien aannemen; op stuk werken; sjacheren; knoeien.

jobbery ['dʒɔbəri] (politieke) knoeierij *v.*, geknoei *o.*

jobmaster ['dʒɔbmâstə] stalhouder *m.*

job-work ['dʒɔbwəːk] aangenomen werk *o.*; smoutwerk *o.*

jockey ['dʒɔki] *sb.* jockey; rijknecht *m.*; jongen; ondergeschikte *m.*; bedrieger *m.*; *vt.* bedriegen, beetnemen; berijden; *vi.* knoeien, konkelen; in zijn eigen voordeel intrigeren.

jocular ['dʒɔkjulə] *adj.* grappig, boertig, snaaks; schertsend.

joggle ['dʒɔgl] *sb.* duwtje *o.*; sukkeldrafje *o.*; (*tn.*) vertanding *v.*; las *v.*; *vt.* schudden; (*tn.*) vertanden; lassen; *vi.* horten; sjokken.

John [dʒɔn] Jan *m.*

join [dʒɔin] *vt.* verenigen, samenvoegen; bij elkaar brengen; bijvoegen, toevoegen; zich aansluiten bij; toetreden tot; *vi.* zich verenigen; samenvoegen; zich associëren; (— *up*), (*fam.*) dienst nemen; — *in*, (*muz.*) invallen; meedoen, meezingen; deelnemen aan; *sb.* aaneenvoeging, verbinding *v.*; verbindingsplaats; verbindingslijn *v.*

joiner ['dʒɔinə] schrijnwerker *m.*

joint [dʒɔint] *sb.* gewricht *o.*; gelid *o.*; (*Pl.*) knoop, knobbel *m.*; voeg *v.*; las *v.*; *adj.* verenigd, verbonden; gezamenlijk; *vt.* verbinden, samenvoegen; voegen; lassen; (*v. vlees*) verdelen.

joint-heir ['dʒɔint'êə] mede-erfgenaam *m.*

jointly ['dʒɔintli] gezamenlijk.

joist [dʒɔist] dwarsbalk *m.*; rib *v.*

joke [dʒouk] *sb.* scherts, grap *v.*, kwinkslag *m.*; gekheid *v.*; *vt.* voor de gek houden, plagen met; *vi.* schertsen, gekheid maken.

joker ['dʒoukə] grappenmaker *m.*

jolly ['dʒɔli] *adj.* vrolijk, jolig, lollig; (*fam.*) aardig, leuk; kostelijk; *adv.* (*fam.*) aardig; kostelijk.

jolly-boat ['dʒɔlibout] (*sch.*) jol *v.*

jolt [dʒoult] *vi.* schokken, horten, stoten; *vt.* doen schudden; *sb.* schok, hort, stoot, ruk *m.*

jostle ['dʒɔsl] *vt.* stoten, duwen (met elleboog); verdringen; *vi.* dringen; *sb.* stoot, duw *m.*; gedrang *o.*

jot [dʒɔt] *sb.* jota *v.*; *vt.* (even) aantekenen, (vlug) opschrijven, noteren.

journal ['dʒəːnəl] dagboek, journaal *o.*; dagblad; tijdschrift *o.*; (*tn.*) tap *m.*

journalist ['dʒəːnəlist] dagbladschrijver *m.*

journey ['dʒəːni] *sb.* reis *v.*; *vi.* reizen.

joust [dʒûst] steekspel, toernooi *o.*

Jove [dʒouv] Jupiter *m.*

jovial ['dʒouvjəl] vrolijk, opgewekt, blijgeestig; gulhartig, joviaal.

joviality [dʒouvi'æliti] vrolijkheid, opgewektheid *v.*; gulhartigheid, jovialiteit *v.*

joy [dʒɔi] *sb.* vreugde, blijdschap *v.*; genoegen *o.*; *vi.* zich verheugen, blij zijn; *vt.* (*dicht.*) verblijden.

joyful(ly) ['dʒɔiful(i)] *adj.* (*adv.*) blijde, verheugd; verblijdend, heerlijk; blij te moede.

joyless ['dʒɔilis] vreugdeloos, treurig, somber.

jubilate ['dʒûbileit] juichen, jubelen.

jubilee ['dʒûbili] jubeljaar *o.*; jubelfeest *o.*; jubileum *o.*; gejubel, gejuich *o.*

Judaic [dʒu'deiik] joods.

judge [dʒədʒ] *sb.* rechter *m.*; (*gesch.*) richter *m.*; kenner *m.*; (*bij tentoonstelling, enz.*) jurylid *o.*; *vt.* oordelen; beoordelen; veroordelen; (*v. afstand*) schatten; *vi.* rechtspreken; uitspraak doen (over).

judge-advocate ['dʒədʒ'ædvəkit] (*mil.*) auditeur-militair, krijgs-auditeur *m.*

judg(e)ment ['dʒədʒmənt] oordeel *o.*, oordeelvelling *v.*; vonnis *o.*, uitspraak *v.*

judicature ['dʒûdikətʃə] rechtspleging *v.*; rechterlijke macht *v.*; rechtersambt *o.*; rechtbank *v.*, gerechtshof *o.*

judicial [dʒu'diʃəl] *adj.* rechterlijk, gerechtelijk.

judicious(ly) [dʒu'diʃəs(li)] *adj.* (*adv.*) oordeelkundig, verstandig.

jug [dʒəg] *sb.* kruik; kan *v.*; (*sl.*) gevangenis *v.*; (*v. nachtegaal*) slag *m.*; *vi.* slaan (*v. nachtegaal*).

juggle ['dʒəgl] *vi.* goochelen; *vt.* begoochelen; bedotten; *sb.* goocheltoer *m.*; bedriegerij *v.*, bedrog *o.*

juggler ['dʒəglə] goochelaar *m.*; bedrieger *m.*

Jugo-Slavia ['jûgous'lâviə] Joegoslavië *o.*

juice [dʒûs] sap; vocht *o.*; vruchtesap; druivesap *o.*

juicy ['dʒûsi] *adj.* sappig, saprijk; (*v. stijl, verhaal*) sappig, smakelijk.

July [dʒû'lai] juli *m.*

jumble ['dʒəmbl] *vt.* dooreengooien, dooreenhaspelen; samenflansen; rondspartelen; *sb.* mengelmoes *o.*; warboel, rommel *m.*

jump [dʒəmp] *sb.* sprong *m.*; plotselinge beweging *v.* (*v. schrik, verbazing*); *vi.* springen; opspringen; stijgen; *vt.* laten springen; doen opspringen; (*v. hoofdstuk, enz.*) overslaan.

umping-pole ['dʒəmpiŋpoul] springstok, polsstok *m.*

junction ['dʒəŋkʃən] verbinding *v.*; verbindingspunt, aansluitingspunt *o.*; (*v. spoorwegen*) knooppunt *o.*

juncture ['dʒəŋktʃə] verbinding, aansluiting *v.*; voeg *v.*; naad *m.*; aanhechtingspunt *o.*; kritiek ogenblik *o.*

June [dʒûn] juni *m.*
jungle ['dʒɒŋgl] tropische wildernis *v.*; (*fig.*) warboel *m.*
juniper ['dʒûnipə] jeneverstruik *m.*; (*sl.*) jenever *v.*
junketing ['dʒɒŋkitiŋ] smulpartij, fuif *v.*
juridical (**ly**) [dʒû'ridikəl(i)] *adj.* (*adv.*) gerechtelijk, juridisch.
jurisdiction [dʒûəris'dikʃən] rechtspraak *v.*; rechtsbevoegdheid *v.*; rechtsgebied *o.*; jurisdictie *v.*
jurisprudence [dʒûəris'prûdəns] rechtsgeleerdheid *v.*; rechtsopvatting, jurisprudentie *v.*
jurist ['dʒûərist] rechtsgeleerde, jurist *m.*
juror ['dʒûərə] gezworene *m.*; jurylid *o.*
jury ['dʒûəri] gezworenen *m. mv.*, jury *v.*
just [dʒɒst] *adj.* rechtvaardig; gegrond, gerechtvaardigd; rechtmatig; juist;

adv. juist; zoëven; enkel, alleen maar; — *as,* evenals, zoals.
justice ['dʒɒstis] rechtvaardigheid *v.*; gerechtigheid *v.*; recht *o.*; billijkheid *v.*; rechtspleging *v.*; justitie *v.*; *in* —, billijkheidshalve, naar recht en billijkheid; van rechtswege.
justification [dʒɒstifi'keiʃən] rechtvaardiging; verantwoording *v.*; wettiging *v.*
justifier ['dʒɒstifaiə] verdediger *m.*; justeerder *m.*
justify ['dʒɒstifai] rechtvaardigen, verdedigen; verantwoorden; wettigen.
justness ['dʒɒstnis] rechtvaardigheid; billijkheid *v.*; juistheid, nauwkeurigheid *v.*
juvenescence [dʒûvi'nesəns] verjonging *v.*; jeugd *v.*
juvenile ['dʒûvinail] jeugdig; jong; voor de jeugd, kinder—.

K

keel [kîl] *sb.* (*sch.*) kiel *v.*; kolenschuit *v.*; praam *v.*; (*fig.*) in evenwicht; *vi.* kantelen; — *over,* overhellen; omslaan, omvallen; — *round,* kapseizen.
keen [kîn] scherp; scherpzinnig; bits, vinnig; (*v. belangstelling*) levendig.
keen-eyed ['kîn'aid] scherp van gezicht.
keenness ['kînnis] scherpte; scherpheid *v.*; bitsheid *v.*; hevigheid *v.*
keen-witted ['kîn'witid] scherpzinnig.
keep [kîp] *vt.* houden; behouden; bewaren; tegenhouden; nakomen; onderhouden; (*v. eetwaren, vruchten*) goed blijven; (*fam.*; *Am.*) wonen, zich ophouden; doorgaan met, blijven —; — *away,* wegblijven; op een afstand houden; — *down,* onderdrukken; weren; (*kosten*) laag houden; bedwingen, in bedwang houden; (*v. tranen*) inhouden; — *out,* (er)buiten houden; buiten blijven; *sb.* bewaking *v.*; hoede *v.*; onderhoud *o.*, kost *m.*
keeper ['kîpə] bewaarder *m.*; oppasser *m.*; opzichter *m.*; cipier *m.*
keeping ['kîpiŋ] bewaring *v.*; hoede *v.*; onderhoud *o.*
keepsake ['kîpseik] herinnering *v.*, aandenken *o.*
keeve [kîv] kuip *v.*, brouwvat *o.*
kennel ['kenəl] hondehok *o.*; troep *m.* (koppel *o.*) jachthonden; (*v. vossen*) hol, leger *o.*; hok, krot *o.*
kernel ['kə:nəl] korrel *o.*; pit, kern *v.*
kettle ['ketl] ketel *m.*
kettledrum ['ketldrəm] keteltrom, pauk *v.*
key [kî] *sb.* sleutel *m.*; toon, toonaard *m.*; klavier *o.*, toets *v.*; (*tn.*) spie, pin, wig *v.*; sluitsteen *m.*; *vt.* spannen; (met

wig, enz.) bevestigen; — *up,* opschroeven; opwekken; (*muz.*) stemmen.
keyboard ['kîbo:d] klavier *o.*; toetsenbord *o.*
keyhole ['kîhoul] sleutelgat *o.*
keystone ['kîstoun] sluitsteen, hoeksteen *m.*
kick [kik] *sb.* schop, trap *m.*; slag (van paard) *m.*; *vi.* schoppen, trappen; achteruitslaan; *vt.* voortschoppen, wegtrappen; — *off,* (*v. schoenen*) uitgooien; (*voetb.*) aftrappen; (*sl.*) het hoekje omgaan, kreperen.
kick-off ['kik'o:f] (*voetb.*) aftrap *m.*
kid [kid] jonge geit *v.*, geitje *o.*; geiteleer *o.*; glacé (handschoen) *m.*; (*fam.*) kleuter *m.*
kidnap ['kidnæp] (een kind) stelen, ontvoeren; pressen.
kidnapper ['kidnæpə] kinderdief, ontvoerder *m.*; zielverkoper *m.*
kidney ['kidni] nier *v.*; aard *m.*, soort *v.*
kill [kil] *vt.* doden, ter dood brengen; slachten; — *off,* afmaken; slachten; — *out,* uitroeien, verdelgen; *vi.* zich laten doden; dodelijk zijn.
kill-time ['kiltaim] tijdverdrijf *o.*
kilogram (**me**) ['kiləgræm] kilogram *o.*
kilometre, kilometer ['kiləmîtə] kilometer *m.*
kin [kin] *sb.* maagschap, bloedverwantschap *v.*; familie *v.*, geslacht *o.*; *adj.* verwant (*to,* aan).
kind [kaind] *sb.* aard *m.*, natuur *v.*; soort, slag *o.*; *adj.* vriendelijk, minzaam; welwillend; goed.
kindergarten ['kindəgâtn] fröbelschool *v.*
kind-hearted ['kaind'hâtid, 'kaindhâtid] goed, goedhartig, goedaardig.
kindle ['kindl] *vt.* ontsteken, aansteken;

doen ontvlammen, doen ontbranden; *vi.* ontvlammen, ontbranden; beginnen te gloeien; vlammen schieten.

kindly ['kaindli] vriendelijk; goed, goedaardig; vriendschappelijk; welwillend; aangenaam, weldadig; (*v. weer, enz.*) prettig.

kindred ['kindrid] *sb.* verwantschap *v.*; verwanten *m. mv.*; *adj.* verwant.

king [kiŋ] koning, vorst *m.*; (*in spel*) koning, heer *m.*

kingdom ['kiŋdəm] koninkrijk *o.*

kingly ['kiŋli] koninklijk.

kink [kiŋk] *sb.* kink (in de kabel) *v.*; (*in touw*) slag, kronkel *m.*; (*in haar*) krul *v.*; *vi.* kinken.

kinless ['kinlis] zonder familie.

kinsman ['kinzmən] bloedverwant *m.*

kiosk [ki'ɔsk] kiosk *v.*

kipper ['kipə] *sb.* gezouten en gedroogde (gerookte) haring *m.*; *vt.* zouten en drogen (roken).

kiss [kis] *sb.* kus, zoen *m.*; *vt.* kussen, zoenen.

kit [kit] vaatje *o.*; tobbe *v.*; uitrusting *v.*, uitzet *m.*

kitchen ['kitʃin] keuken *v.*; (*sch.*) kombuis *v.*

kitchener ['kitʃinə] keukenfornuis *o.*; keukenmeester *m.*

kitchen-garden ['kitʃin'gâdn] moestuin *m.*

kitchen-utensils ['kitʃinjû'tensilz] keukengereedschap, keukengerei *o.*

kite [kait] (*Dk.*) kiekendief, wouw *m.*; (*fig.*) haai, grijpgier, schraper *m.*; vlieger *m.*

kite-balloon ['kaitbəlûn] kabelballon, observatieballon *m.*

knack [næk] slag *m.*, handigheid *v.*; behendigheid *v.*

knag [næg] (*in hout*) kwast, knoest *m.*

knapsack ['næpsæk] ransel, knapzak *m.*

knave [neiv] schurk, schelm *m.*; (*in kaartspel*) boer *m.*; (*oud*) knecht *m.*

knavish ['neiviʃ] schurkachtig, schelmachtig.

knead [nîd] kneden; masseren.

knee [nî] knie *v.*

kneel [nîl] knielen (**to**, voor).

knell [nel] *sb.* doodsklok *v.*; *vi.* de doodsklok luiden.

knickers ['nikəz] wijde kniebroek *v.*

knick-knack ['niknæk] snuisterij *v.*; beuzeling; beuzelarij *v.*; snoeperij, lekkernij *v.*

knife [naif] *sb.* mes *o.*; *vt.* doorsteken.

knife-rest ['naifrest] messelegger *m.*

knight [nait] ridder *m.*; (*schaakspel*) paard *o.*

knighthood ['naithud] ridderschap *o.*

knightlike ['naitlaik], **knightly** ['naitli] ridderlijk.

knit [nit] *vt.* breien; knopen; (*v. wenkbrauwen*) fronsen; samenvlechten.

knitter ['nitə] breier *m.*; breister *v.*; breimachine *v.*

knitting-needle ['nitiŋnidl] breinaald *v.*

knitwear ['nitwêə] gebreide goederen *o. mv.*

knob [nɔb] (*v. deur of stok*) knop *m.*; knobbel, knoest *m.*; (*v. boter, enz.*) kluit *m.*, klontje *o.*

knock [nɔk] *vi.* slaan; kloppen; — **about,** rondslingeren; rondslenteren; toetakelen; — **down,** neerslaan, neervellen; omver gooien, aanrijden; (*v. prijs*) verlagen, verminderen; (*op veiling*) toeslaan, toewijzen; — **off,** afslaan; ophouden, uitscheiden (met); opgeven, laten; klaarspelen; (*r. werkman*) gedaan geven; — **over,** omgooien, omver gooien; overrijden; neervellen; (*fam.*) sterven; *sb.* slag, klop *m.*; tik, stoot *m.*; geklop *o.*

knocker ['nɔkə] klopper *m.*; (*in de mijnen*) klopgeest *m.*

knocker-up [nɔkə'rəp] porder *m.*

knock-out ['nɔk'aut] slag, genadeslag *m.*; het niet tegen elkaar opbieden *o.* (bij veiling).

knot [nɔt] knoop *m.*; (*v. sajet, garen*) knot *v.*; knobbel, knoest *m.*

knotty ['nɔti] *adj.* knoestig, kwastig; vol knopen; (*fig.*) netelig, lastig.

know [nou] *vt.* kennen; herkennen; onderscheiden; verstaan, begrijpen. *vi.* weten

knowable ['nouəbl] te weten; te kennen; herkenbaar; — **of,** bekend met.

knowledge ['nɔlidʒ] kennis *v.*; bekendheid (**of,** met); geleerdheid, wetenschap *v.*

knuckle ['nəkl] *sb.* knokkel *m.*; knook *m.*; schenkel *m.*; *vt.* met de knokkels slaan (tikken); *vi.* — **down** (**under**), zich gewonnen geven; zwichten, toegeven.

knuckle-duster ['nəkldəstə] boksijzer *o.*, boksbeugel *m.*

kobold ['koubɔld] kabouter *m.*

kohlrabi ['koul'râbi] (*Pl.*) koolraap *v.*

koran [ko'rân, 'ko:ræn] koran *m.*

L

label ['leibl] *sb.* etiket *o.*; naambordje, naamplaatje *o.*; strookje *o.*; *o. w.* etiketteren, van een etiket voorzien.

laboratory ['læbərətəri] laboratorium *o.*

laborious(ly) [lə'bo:riəs(li)] *adj.* (*adv.*) werkzaam, arbeidzaam; moeilijk, zwaar.

labour ['leibə] *sb.* arbeid *m.*, werk *o.*; moeite *v.*; arbeiders *m. mv.*, arbeidskrachten *v. mv.*; *vi.* arbeiden, werken, zwoegen; zich inspannen; zich moeite geven; *vt.* bewerken; uitwerken; bebouwen.

labourer ['leibərə] arbeider, werkman *m.*

labour-pains ['leibəpeinz] barensweeën *o. mv.*

laburnum [lə'bə:nəm] (*Pl.*) goudenregen *m.*

labyrinth ['læbirinδ] doolhof *m.*

lace [leis] *sb.* veter *m.*, snoer *o.*; galon *o.*; boordsel *o.*; kant *v.*, kantwerk *o.*; *adj.* kanten; *vt.* rijgen, snoeren; galonneren; omboorden; met kant afzetten; afranselen; — *up,* rijgen, vastrijgen.

lace-maker ['leismeikə] kantwerkster *v.*; passementwerker *m.*

lacerate ['læsəreit] vaneenscheuren, openscheuren, verscheuren.

lachrymatory ['lækrimətəri] *adj.* traan—; tranenverwekkend; *sb.* (*mil.*) traangranaat *v.*; (*gesch.*) tranenkruikje *o.*

lack [læk] *sb.* gebrek, gemis, tekort *o.*, behoefte *v.*; *vt.* missen, ontberen, gebrek hebben aan; *vi.* gebrek lijden.

lacquer ['lækə] *sb.* lak, vernis *o.*; lakwerk *o.*; *vt.* lakken, vernissen.

lad [læd] knaap, jongen, jongeling *m.*

ladder ['lædə] ladder *v.*

lade [leid] laden; beladen.

ladle ['leidl] *sb.* pollepel, soeplepel *m.*; (*mil.*) laadlepel *m.*; (*v. molenrad*) schoep *v.*; *vt.* — (*out*), opscheppen; uitscheppen.

lady ['leidi] dame *v.*; vrouw (des huizes) *v.*; (*dicht.*) mevrouw *v.*

ladybird ['leidibə:d], **lady-bug** ['leidibəg] lieveheersbeestje *o.*

Ladyday ['leididei] Maria-Boodschap.

lady-killer ['leidikilə] don Juan, hartenveroveraar *m.*

laggard ['lægəd] *adj.* achterblijvend, traag, treuzelig; *sb.* talmer; achterblijver *m.*

laic ['leiik] *adj.* wereldlijk, leken; *sb.* leek *m.*

lake [leik] meer *o.*; vijver *m.*; lakverf *v.*

lake-settlement ['leiksetlmənt] paaldorp *o.*

lamb [læm] lam *o.*

lame [leim] *adj.* kreupel, mank; (*fig.*) gebrekkig; onvoldoende; (*v. verontschuldiging*) armzalig; *vt.* kreupel maken; (*fig.*) verminken; verlammen.

lament [lə'ment] *sb.* weeklacht, jammerklacht *v.*; klaaglied *o.*; *vi.* weeklagen, jammeren; *vt.* bejammeren; betreuren, bewenen.

lamentable ['læməntəbl] *adj.* betreurenswaardig; jammerlijk.

lamentation [læmen'teiʃən] weeklacht, jammerklacht *v.*; klaaglied *o.*

lamp [læmp] lamp *v.*; lantaarn *m.*; —*s,* (*sl.*) ogen.

lampoon [læm'pûn] *sb.* schotschrift, pamflet *o.*; *vt.* in schotschriften hekelen.

lamp-post ['læmppoust] lantaarnpaal *m.*

lance [lâns] *sb.* lans *v.*; lansier *m.*; *vt.'* (met een lans) doorsteken.

lancinating ['lænsineitiŋ] *adj.* (*v. pijn*) scherp, vlijmend, snijdend.

land [lænd] *sb.* land *o.*; landerij(en) *v.* (*mv.*), grondbezit *o.*; landstreek *v.*; *vt.* aan land (aan wal) zetten, afzetten; (*v. geld*) opstrijken; (*v. prijs*) binnenhalen; (*v. vis*) ophalen; (*vi.*) landen; (*v. vliegtuig*) neerkomen; (*sp.*) het eerst aankomen.

land-agent ['lændeidʒənt] rentmeester *m.*

landforce(s) ['lændfo:s(iz)] landmacht *v.*

landing ['lændiŋ] landing *v.*; lossing *v.*; landingsplaats; aanlegplaats *v.*; portaal *o.*

landing-net ['lændiŋnet] schepnet *o.*

landlady ['lændleidi] kostjuffrouw, hospita *v.*; waardin *v.*; huiseigenares *v.*

landlord ['lændlo:d] landheer *m.*; huisbaas *m.*; kostbaas, hospes *m.*; waard, herbergier *m.*

land-registry ['lænd'redʒistri] kadaster *o.*

landscape ['lændskeip] landschap *o.*

land-slide ['lændslaid], **land-slip** ['lændslip] aardverschuiving *v.*

lane [lein] landweg *m.* (tussen twee heggen); laantje *o.*; steeg *v.*

language ['læŋgwidʒ] taal; spraak *v.*

languid(ly) ['læŋgwid(li)] *adj.* (*adv.*) loom, traag; mat, lusteloos; kwijnend, smachtend; (*v. markt*) flauw.

languish ['læŋgwiʃ] kwijnen, wegkwijnen; verzwakken; verflauwen; smachtend kijken; smachten (*for,* naar).

lank [læŋk] *adj.* schraal, lang en mager; (*v. haar*) sluik.

lantern ['læntən] lantaarn *m.*

lap [læp] *sb.* schoot *m.*; pand *o.*, slip *v.*; (*sp.: bij wedstrijd*) ronde, baanronde *v.*; *vt.* omwikkelen, inwikkelen; omhullen, omgeven; opslorpen; *vi.* kabbelen; (*v. vlammen*) lekken; slorpen.

lapidate ['læpideit] stenigen.

lappet ['læpit] slip *v.*, pand *o.*; oorlel *v.*

lapse [læps] *sb.* fout, vergissing *v.*; afval *m.*, afvalligheid *v.*; misslag, misstap *m.*, afdwaling *v.*; (*v. tijd*) loop *m.*, verloop *o.*; *vi.* afvallen; afdwalen; voorbijgaan, verlopen; (*v. contract*) aflopen.

larboard ['lâbo:d] (*sch.*) bakboord *o.*

lard [lâd] *sb.* varkensreuzel *v.*; *vt.* larderen; (*fig.*) doorspekken (*with,* met).

larder ['lâdə] provisiekamer, provisiekast *v.*

large [lâdʒ] *adj.* groot; omvangrijk, veelomvattend; ruim, wijd, uitgestrekt.

largely ['lâdʒli] *adv.* op grote schaal, in ruime mate, ruimschoots; grotendeels.

largeness ['lâdʒnis] grootte *v.*; omvang *m.*; uitgestrektheid, ruimte, wijdte *v.*; onbekrompenheid *v.*

lark [lâk] *sb.* (*Dk.*) leeuwerik *m.*; pret *v.*, grapje *o.*; dwaze streek *m.*; *vt.* voor de gek houden; *vi*. pret maken; streken uithalen.

larva ['lâvə] *mv*.: **larvae** ['lâvi] larve *v*.

larynx ['lærinks] strottehoofd *o*.

lascivious (ly) [lə'sivjəs(li)] *adj*. (*adv*.) wulps, wellustig.

lash [læʃ] *sb*. zweepslag *m*.; geseling *v*.; geselroede *v*.; wimper *m*., ooghaartje *o*.; *vt*. zwepen; geselen; slaan.

lass (ie) ['læs(i)] deerntje, meisje *o*.

last [lâst] leest *v*.; (*H*.) last *m*.

last [lâst] *adj*. laatst; vorig, verleden; jongstleden; uiterste, hoogste; *sb*. laatste; einde *o*.

last [lâst] *sb*. uithoudingsvermogen *o*.; duur *m*.; *vi*. duren, voortduren; het uithouden.

lasting ['lâstiŋ] blijvend, voortdurend, bestendig; duurzaam.

lastly ['lâstli] *adv*. ten laatste, ten slotte.

latch [lætʃ] *sb*. klink *v*.; (*v. deur*) veerslot *o*.; *vt*. op de klink doen.

late [leit] *adj*. laat; te laat; vergevorderd; wijlen, overleden; gewezen, vroeger, ex—; *adv*. laat; te laat; in de laatste tijd; laatst, onlangs; voorheen.

lately ['leitli] *adv*. laatst, onlangs, kort geleden; in de laatste tijd.

lateness ['leitnis] laatheid *v*.

lateral ['lætərəl] *adj*. zijdelings; *sb*. zijtak *m*.

latest ['leitist] laatste.

lath [lâð] lat *v*.

lathe [leiθ] draaibank *v*.

lather ['læθə] *sb*. zeepsop *o*.; schuim *o*.; *vt*. inzepen; met schuim bedekken; *vi*. schuimen.

lather-brush ['læθəbrəʃ] scheerkwast *m*.

latitude ['lætitjûd] (geografische) breedte *v*.; luchtstreek, hemelstreek *v*.; omvang *m*.; vrijheid (van handelen), speelruimte *v*.

lattice ['lætis] traliewerk, open latwerk *o*.

lattice-window ['lætiswindou] tralievenster *o*.; venster met glas in lood *o*.

laud [lo:d] *sb*. loflied *o*., lofzang *m*.; —**s**, (*kath*.) lauden *v. mv*.; *vt*. loven, prijzen.

laudable ['lo:dəbl] *adj*. lofwaardig, prijzenswaardig, loffelijk.

laugh [lâf] *vt*. & *vi*. lachen; — **at**, lachen om; lachen tegen; uitlachen; *sb*. lach *m*.; gelach *o*.

laughable ['lâfəbl] *adj*. belachelijk; lachwekkend.

laughter ['lâftə] gelach *o*.

launch [lo:nʃ, lânʃ] *vt*. slingeren; werpen; (*v. slag, enz*.) toebrengen; (*v. schip*) te water laten, van ɛ Japel laten lopen; *vi*. van stapel lopen; — **forth**, (*fig*.) in zee steken; — **out**, van wal steken; zich laten gaan; uitweiden, uitpakken; het er van nemen; *sb*. (*sch*.) het te water laten, het van stapel laten lopen; barkas *v*.

laundress ['lo:ndris, [lândris] wasvrouw *v*.; schoonmaakster *v*.

laundry ['lo:ndri, 'lândri] wasserij *v*.; washuis *o*.; was *v*.; wasgoed *o*.

laurel ['lorəl] laurier *m*.; lauwerkrans *m*.

lavatory ['lævətəri] wasplaats *v*., wasvertrek *o*.; toilet *o*., retirade *v*.

lavish ['læviʃ] *adj*. verkwistend; kwistig (**of**, met); *vt*. kwistig zijn met; verkwisten, verspillen.

law [lo:] wet *v*.; recht *o*.; gerecht *o*.; rechtspleging *v*.; (*sp*.) voorsprong *m*.

law-costs ['lo:ko:stz] gerechtskosten *m. mv*.; (*bij koop van huis*) overschrijvingskosten *m. mv*.

lawful (ly) ['lo:ful(i)] *adj*. (*adv*.) wettelijk; wettig, rechtmatig.

lawless (ly) ['lo:lis(li)] *adj*. (*adv*.) wetteloos; bandeloos; losbandig.

law merchant ['lo:'mə:tʃənt] handelsrecht *o*.

lawn [lo:n] grasperk *o*.; kamerdoek, batist *o*.

lawsuit ['lo:sjût] proces, rechtsgeding *o*.

lawyer ['lo:jə] rechtgeleerde; advocaat *m*.

lax [læks] *adj*. los, slap; laks, slordig; loslijvig.

laxative ['læksətiv] *adj*. laxerend; *sb*. laxerend middel *o*.

lay [lei] *adj*. wereldlijk, leken—.

lay [lei] *vt*. leggen; beleggen, bekleden; aanleggen; (*v. tafel*) dekken; *vi*. leggen; dekken; — **down**, neerleggen, neerzetten; (*v. hoop, enz*.) opgeven; afstand doen van; (*v. wegen, enz*.) aanleggen; (*v. schip*) bouwen, op stapel zetten; (*v. regels*) vaststellen; (*v. voorraad*) opslaan; (*v. leven*) geven; — **off**, afleggen; afbakenen; (*4m*.: *v. werkvolk*) gedaan geven; — **on**, opleggen; (*v. gas, enz*.) aanleggen; (*v. slag, stoot*) toebrengen; — **out**, (*v. tuin, enz*.) aanleggen; (*v. dode*) afleggen.

lay [lei] *sb*. leg *m*., het leggen *o*.; ligging *v*.; (*v. dier*) leger *o*.; winstaandeel *o*.; (*sl*.) werk, karwei *o*.

layer ['leiə] leghen *v*.; (*Pl*.) aflegger *m*.; laag *v*.

lay-out ['lei'aut] (*v. tuin, park*) aanleg *m*.

lazy ['leizi] *adj*. traag, lui, vadsig.

lazy-bones ['leizibounz], **lazy-boots** ['leizibûts] luilak, !niwammes *m*.

lead [led] *sb*. lood *o*.; potlood *o*.; peillood, dieplood *o*.; *adj*. loden; *vt*. met lood bedekken; loden; in lood vatten; (*v. douane*) plomberen.

lead [lid] *vt*. leiden; aanvoeren; (*v. kaart*) uitspelen; (*muz*.) dirigeren; *vi*. voorgaan; de leiding hebben, de toon aangeven; (*bij kaartsp*.) uitkomen; (*muz*.) dirigeren; *sb*. leiding *v*.; voorsprong *m*.; (*sch*.) vaargeul *v*.; hoofdrol *v*.

leader ['lidə] leider, leidsman, aanvoerder, gids *m*.; (*muz*.) dirigent *m*.

leading ['lidiŋ] *adj*. leidend; eerste, voornaamste; vooraanstaand; hoofd—; *sb*. leiding *v*., bestuur *o*.

leaf [lif] blad *o*.; (*v. deur*) vleugel *m*.

leaflet ['liflit] blaadje o.; traktaatje o.
leaf-metal ['lifmetl] klatergoud o.; bladmetaal o.
league [lig] sb. bond m., verbond o., verbintenis r.; (sp.: voetb.) competitie v.; vt. (& vi.) een verbond aangaan, (zich) in een verbond verenigen.
leak [lik] sb. lek o.; lekkage v.; vi. lekken, lek zijn.
lean [lin] vi. overhellen, neigen, scheef staan; leunen (on, upon, op); (fig,) steunen (op), zich verlaten (op); vt. doen (laten) leunen op; sb. overhelling v.; schuine stand m.
lean [lin] adj. mager, schraal; sb. mager vlees o.
leanness ['linnis] magerheid, schraalheid v.
leap [lip] vi. springen, opspringen; vt. laten springen over; (v. woord, tekst, enz.) overslaan; sb. sprong m.
leaping-pole ['lipinpoul] polsstok m.
leap-year ['lipjiə] schrikkeljaar o.
learn [lə:n] leren; vernemen.
learned ['lə:nid] adj. geleerd.
learning ['lə:nin] geleerdheid, kunde, wetenschap v.
lease [lis] sb. huurcontract o., huurceel v.; huurtijd m.; pacht v.; vt. huren; pachten; verhuren; verpachten.
leaseholder ['lishouldə] pachter m.
leash [liʃ] koppel(riem), koppelband m.
least [list] kleinst; minst, geringst.
leather ['leθə] sb. leder, leer o.; zeemleer o., zeemlap m.; (v. kraan, enz.) leertje o.; (sl.) voetbal m.; —s, leren kledingstukken o. mv.; adj. leren van leer.
leathern ['leθən] adj. leren, van leer.
leave [liv] sb. verlof o.; vt. nalaten; achterlaten; laten liggen, laten staan; verlaten; in de steek laten; — about, laten slingeren; — off, (v. kleren) afleggen; uitlaten; ophouden met; — out, uitlaten, weglaten; voorbijgaan; overslaan; vi. ophouden; vertrekken, heengaan.
leave-man ['livmæn] (mil.) verlofganger m.
leaven ['leyn] sb. zuurdeeg o., zuurdesem m.; vt. desemen; doortrekken, doordringen.
leavings ['livinz] overblijfsel, overschot o.; afval m.
lecherous ['letʃərəs] adj. wellustig.
lecture ['lektʃə] sb. lezing, verhandeling v.; voordracht v.; college o.; vermaning, berisping v.; vt. de les lezen; onderrichten; spreken voor; vi. college geven.
lecturer ['lektʃərə] spreker m.; lector m.; hulppredikant m.
led captain ['ledkæptin] klaploper, parasiet m.
ledge [ledʒ] richel, rand, scherpe kant m.
ledger ['ledʒə] grootboek o.; dwarsbalk m. (plank v.) van steiger.
leech [litʃ] sb. bloedzuiger m.; (sch.: v. zeil) lijk o.; rt. aderlaten.

leek [lik] prei v., look o.
lees [liz] droesem m., grondsop o.
leeward ['liwəd] (sch.) lijwaarts, onder de wind.
left [left] adj. links, linker; adv. links; sb. linkerhand v.; linkerzijde v.
left-off ['left'o:f, 'lefto:f] afgelegd; —s, afleggers m. mv.
leg [leg] sb. been o.; poot m.; schenkel m.; (broeks)pijp v.; vt. — it, (fam.) zijn benen gebruiken, lopen.
legacy ['legəsi] erfmaking v., legaat o.; nalatenschap v.
legal ['ligəl] adj. wettelijk; wettig; rechterlijk; rechtskundig; rechtsgeldig.
legality [li'gæliti] wettelijkheid; wettigheid v.; rechtsgeldigheid v.
legalize ['ligəlaiz] wettigen; legaliseren.
legally ['ligəli] adv. zie legal.
legate ['legit] legaat, pauselijk gezant m.
legate [li'geit] vermaken, legateren.
legation [li'geiʃən] legatie v., gezantschap o.
legend ['ledʒənd] legende, overlevering v.; randschrift, omschrift o.
legible ['ledʒibl] adj. leesbaar, duidelijk.
legion ['lidʒən] legioen o., krijgsbende, krijgsmacht v.; legio o.
legislation [ledʒis'leiʃən] wetgeving v.
legitimate [li'dʒitimit] adj. wettig; rechtmatig; echt; [li'dʒitimeit] wettigen; wettig verklaren, als wettig (echt) erkennen.
leisure ['leʒə, 'liʒə] sb. vrije tijd m.; adj. vrij, onbezet.
lemon ['lemən] citroen m.
lend [lend] vt. lenen; uitlenen; verlenen, geven; vr. — oneself to, zich lenen tot.
lending-library ['lendinlaibrəri] leesbibliotheek, uitleenbibliotheek v.
length [lenδ] lengte v.; (lange) duur m.; grootte v.; hoogte v.; afstand m.
lengthen ['lenδən] vt. verlengen, langer maken; vi. lengen, langer worden.
lengthening ['lenδnin] verlenging v.; verlengstuk o.
lengthways ['lenδweiz], **lengthwise** ['lenδwaiz] in de lengte.
lenience, leniency ['liniəns(i)] zachtheid, zachtzinnigheid v.; toegevendheid v.
lenient (ly) ['liniənt(li)] adj. (adv.) zacht; toegevend.
Lent [lent] vasten(tijd) m.
leopard ['lepəd] luipaard m.
leprous ['leprəs] melaats.
less [les] adj. minder, geringer; min, minus.
lessee [le'si] huurder, pachter m.
lessen [lesn] vt. verminderen; verkleinen; vi. verminderen; kleiner worden, afnemen.
lesson ['lesn] sb. les v.; vt. de les lezen.
lest [lest] opdat niet, uit vrees dat.
let [let] vt. laten; toelaten, toestaan; verhuren; vi. verhuren; to —, te huur; — be, zich niet inlaten met; op zijn

beloop laten; — **down**, neerlaten; in de steek laten; verraden; vernederen; (*tn.*) ontlaten, afkoelen; — **off**, vrijlaten, vrijstellen; kwijtschelden; vrijstellen (van); *sb.* verhuring *v.*; plaatsbespreking *v.*, kaartenverkoop *m.*

letter ['letə] letter *v.*; brief *m.*; ingezonden stuk *o.*; —**s**, letteren *v. mv.*

letter-carrier ['letəkæriə] postbode *m.*

letter-press ['letəpres] copieerpers *v.*; tekst *m.*, bijschrift *o.*; pressepapier *o.*

levee ['levi] receptie, partij *v.*; (*Am.*) rivierdijk *m.*; landingsplaats *v.*

level ['levl] *sb.* waterpas, paslood *o.*; peil *o.*, stand *m.*, hoogte *v.*; vlak *o.*, oppervlakte *v.*; *adj.* horizontaal, waterpas; vlak, effen; gelijkmatig; *vt.* gelijk maken (met de grond), slechten; nivelleren, waterpas maken; (*mil.*) richten, aanleggen; — **up**, (*v. weg, enz.*) ophogen; (*v. bedrag*) naar boven afronden; op hoger peil brengen; verheffen; *vi.* aanleggen, mikken.

level-crossing ['levl'krosin] overweg *m.*

level-headed ['levl'hedid] bezadigd, evenwichtig, met een gezond verstand.

levelling ['levlin] gelijkmaking *v.*; nivellering *v.*

lever ['livə] *sb.* hefboom *m.*; (*v. auto*) manet *v.*; *vt.* optillen, opvijzelen.

levitate ['leviteit] (*v. geesten*) (doen) zweven.

levy ['levi] *sb.* heffing, inning *v.*; (*mil.*) lichting; werving *v.*; *vt.* heffen; (*mil.*) lichten, werven.

lewd (**ly**) ['ljûd(li)] *adj.* (*adv.*) ontuchtig, wulps.

liability [laiə'biliti] verantwoordelijkheid *v.*; aansprakelijkheid *v.*; (geldelijke) verplichting *v.*; *mv.*; **liabilities**, passiva *o. mv.*, passief *o.*

liable ['laiəbl] *adj.* verantwoordelijk; aansprakelijk; blootgesteld (**to**, aan); onderhevig (**to**, aan).

liar ['laiə] leugenaar *m.*

libation [lai'beiʃən] plengoffer *o.*

libel ['laibəl] *sb.* (*recht*) (schriftelijke, aanklacht *v.*; smaadschrift, schotschrift *o.*; hoon, smaad *m.*; laster *m.*; *vt.* aanklagen; een schotschrift schrijven op; belasteren.

libellous ['laibələs] lasterlijk.

liberal ['libərəl] mild, vrijgevig; ruim, overvloedig; vrijzinnig, liberaal.

liberate ['libəreit] bevrijden; vrijlaten, in vrijheid stellen; (*el.*) uitschakelen.

liberation [libə'reiʃən] bevrijding, vrijlating *v.*; uitschakeling *v.*

liberator ['libəreitə] bevrijder *m.*

liberty ['libəti] vrijheid *v.*

libra ['laibrə] pond *o.*; (*sterr.: in Dierenriem*) de Weegschaal *v.*

librarian [lai'brêəriən] bibliothecaris *m.*

library ['laibrəri] bibliotheek, boekerij *v.*

librate ['laibreit] schommelen; zich in evenwicht houden.

licence ['laisəns] *sb.* verlof *o.*, vergunning *v.*; vrijheid *v.*; losbandigheid *v.*; rijbewijs *o.*; patent *o.*

licensee [laisən'si] licentie-houder *m.*; vergunninghouder *m.*

licenser ['laisənsə] vergunning-gever; patent-gever *m.*

licentious (**ly**) [lai'senʃəs(li)] *adj.* (*adv.*) losbandig, ongebonden.

licentiousness [lai'senʃəsnis] losbandigheid, ongebondenheid *v.*

lich-house ['litʃhaus] lijkenhuisje *o.*

lick [lik] *vt.* likken; aflikken; oplikken; (*sl.*) afranselen, er van langs geven; *vi.* likken; (*sl.*) lopen, rennen; *sb.* lik *m.*; klap, veeg *m.*; (*Am.*) poging, inspanning *v.*

lid [lid] deksel *o.*; lid; ooglid *o.*

lie [lai] *sb.* leugen *v.*; *vi.* liegen.

lie [lai] *vi.* liggen; gaan liggen; blijven liggen; staan; rusten; slapen; — **by**, liggen, rusten; rust nemen; zich schuil houden; (*v. geld*) uitstaan; — **up**, gaan liggen, naar bed gaan; (*sch.*) dokken; *sb.* ligging *v.*; ligplaats *v.*; (*v. dier*) leger *o.*

lie-a-bed ['laiəbed] langslaper *m.*

lieutenant [lef—, lif'tenənt] luitenant *m.*

life [laif] leven *o.*; levenswijze *v.*; levensbeschrijving *v.*

life-boat ['laifbout] reddingsboot *v.*

lifeless (**ly**) ['laiflis(li)] *adj.* (*adv.*) levenloos.

life-rent ['laifrent] (*Sc.*) vruchtgebruik *o.*, lijfrente *v.*

lift [lift] *vt.* opheffen, optillen, oplichten; (*v. ogen*) opslaan; (*v. hand*) opsteken; verheffen; verhogen; *vi.* zich opheffen; ophouden; (*v. mist*) optrekken; omhooggaan, rijzen; *sb.* opheffing *v.*; het oplichten, het optillen *o.*; stijging, rijzing *v.*; lift *v.*

lifter ['liftə] lichter *m.*

lift-pump ['liftpəmp] zuigpomp *v.*

ligature ['ligətʃə] *sb.* band *m.*; verband *o.*; *vt.* (*gen.*) afbinden.

light [lait] *sb.* licht *o.*; daglicht *o.*; levenslicht *o.*; belichting *v.*; *vt.* verlichten; bijlichten; voorlichten; aansteken; opsteken; *vi.* lichten, schijnen; vuur vatten, aangaan; schitteren, stralen; *adj.* & *adv.* licht, helder, klaar; licht (*niet zwaar*); licht, gemakkelijk.

lighten ['laitn] *vt.* verlichten; verhelderen, opklaren; lossen; *vi.* weerlichten, bliksemen; lichter worden.

light-footed ['lait'futid] vlug ter been.

light-hearted ['lait'hâtid] luchthartig; opgeruimd, onbezorgd.

lighthouse ['laithaus] vuurtoren *m.*

lighting ['laitin] verlichting *v.*

lightning ['laitnin] *sb.* bliksem *m.*, weerlicht *o.*; *adj.* bliksemsnel; snel—.

lightship ['laitʃi] (*sch.*) lichtschip, vuurschip *o.*

ligneous ['ligniəs] houtachtig; houten.

lignite ['lignait] bruinkool *v.*

like [laik] adj. gelijk; dergelijk, soort- gelijk, overeenkomstig; gelijkend; zo- als; prep. zo, als, zoals; adv. ietwat; cj. zoals; sb. gelijke m., weerga v.; **the —,** iets dergelijks.

like [laik] vt. houden van, geven om; (graag) willen; sb. voorliefde v.

likely ['laikli] waarschijnlijk, vermoe- delijk; geschikt(lijkend); in aanmerking komend; aannemelijk.

likeness ['laiknis] gelijkenis v.; vorm m., gedaante v., uiterlijk o.; portret o.

likewise ['laikwaiz] adv. evenzo; even- eens, ook, insgelijks.

liking ['laikiŋ] lust, zin, smaak m.; welgevallen o., ingenomenheid v.

lilac ['lailək] sb. sering v.; seringestruik m.; adj. lila, lichtpaars.

lily ['lili] sb. lelie v.; adj. (lelie)wit.

limb [lim] sb. lid o.; been o.; vt. ontle- den; vaneenscheuren.

limber ['limbə] adj. buigzaam, lenig; (fig.) meegaand; vt. & vi. lenig maken (worden); sb. (mil.: v. kanon) vóór- wagen m.

lime [laim] sb. lijm, vogellijm v.; kalk v.; linde v., lindeboom m.; vt. lijmen; met lijm bestrijken; met kalk be- mesten (behandelen), kalken.

limit ['limit] sb. grens,grenslijn; afschei- ding v.; begrenzing; beperking v.; limiet n.; vt. begrenzen; beperken; limiteren.

limitation [limi'teiʃən] begrenzing v.; beperking v.; grens v.

limited ['limitid] begrensd; beperkt; bekrompen.

limitless (ly) ['limitlis(li)] adj. (adv.) onbegrensd, onbeperkt.

limp [limp] adj. slap, buigzaam, lenig; lusteloos.

limp [limp] vi. mank gaan, kreupel lopen; hinken.

limpid ['limpid] adj. helder, klaar, doorschijnend.

line [lain] sb. lijn v.; streep, schreef v.; spoorlijn v.; stoomvaartlijn v.; tele- foon—, telegraaflijn v.; vt. liniëren; strepen; aftekenen; (v. weg,enz.)afzetten.

linen ['linin] sb. linnen (goed), lijnwaad o.; adj. linnen.

liner-company ['lainəkɔmpəni] stoom- vaartmaatschappij v.

linesman ['lainzmən] liniesoldaat m.; (sp.) grensrechter m.

linger ['liŋgə] vi. toeven, talmen, dra- len; weifelen; kwijnen; verwijlen, ver- toeven; vt. **— away,** (v. tijd) verbeu- zelen; **— out,** rekken; voortslepen.

lingering ['liŋgəriŋ] adj. drälend, tal- mend; langzaam, slepend, langgerekt; sb. gedraal, getalm o.; kwijning v.

linguistic [liŋ'gwistik] adj. taalkundig; taal—; sb. **—s,** taalwetenschap v.

liniment ['linimənt] smeersel o.

lining ['lainiŋ] voering, bekleding v.

link [liŋk] sb. schakel v.; (pek)toorts, fakkel v.; vt. verbinden, aaneenschake- len; (v. handen) ineenslaan.

linnet ['linit] vlasvink m., kneu v.

linseed ['linsid] lijnzaad o.

lint [lint] pluksel o.

lion ['laiən] leeuw m.; (fig.) beroemd- heid, merkwaardigheid v.

lip [lip] sb. lip v.; rand m.; brutale praat m.; vt. met de lippen aanraken.

lip-deep ['lip'dip] onoprecht, niet ge- meend.

liquefy ['likwifai] smelten; oplossen.

liquid ['likwid] adj. vloeibaar; vloeiend; (H.) beschikbaar; gemakkelijk los te maken; sb. vloeistof v.; (gram.) vloeien- de letter v.

liquidate ['likwideit] vereffenen, af- betalen; liquideren.

liquor ['likə] sb. vocht o., vloeistof v.; (sterke) drank m.; vt. nat maken; laten trekken.

liquorice ['likəris] zoethout o.; drop v.

list [list] sb. lijst, naamlijst v.; cata- logus m.; rand, zelfkant m.; (recht) rol v.; vt. een lijst opmaken van; catalogi- seren.

listen ['lisn] vi. luisteren (**to,** naar); **— in,** (v. radio) luisteren; sb. **be up)on the —,** luisteren.

listener ['lisnə] luisteraar m.; luister- vink m. en v.; (sl.) oor o.

listless (ly) ['listlis(li)] adj. (adv.) luste- loos, traag.

literal ['litərəl] letterlijk; woordelijk; letter—; prozaïsch, nuchter.

literary ['litərəri] letterkundig, literair; geletterd.

literate ['litərit] adj. geletterd; sb. ge- letterde m.

lithography [li'ðɔgrəfi] lithografie v., steendruk m.; steendrukkunst v.

litigate ['litigeit] vi. procederen; vt. betwisten.

litigious [li'tidʒəs] pleitziek, proces- ziek; betwistbaar; recht(s)—.

litre ['litə] liter m.

litter ['litə] sb. draagbaar v., draagstoel m.; (stal)stro, strooisel o.; stalmest m.; rommel, warboel m.; vt. van stro voor- zien, strooien; met stro bedekken; door- eengooien; bezaaien (**with,** met); vi. door elkaar liggen.

little ['litl] adj. klein; gering, luttel; kleingeestig; onaanzienlijk; adj. weinig; sb. weinig(e) o.; kleinigheid v., beetje o.

little-minded ['litlmaindid] kleinzie- lig.

liturgy ['litədʒi] liturgie v.

live [liv] leven; bestaan; wonen; (in storm, enz.) het uithouden; in het leven blijven; doorleven; **— out,** uitwonend zijn, niet intern zijn; overleven.

live [laiv] adj.levend, in leven; levendig; druk.

livelihood ['laivlihud] levensonderhoud o., kostwinning v.

lively ['laivli] levendig; vrolijk; be- drijvig.

liver ['livə] lever v.; leverziekte v.

living ['liviŋ] adj. levend; levendig

wakker; (v. *water*) stromend; *sb.* leven *o.*; levenswijze *v.*; levensonderhoud, bestaan *o.*

living-room ['liviŋrum] huiskamer, woonkamer *v.*, woonvertrek *o.*

lizard ['lizəd] hagedis *v.*

load [loud] *sb.* vracht *v.*, last *m.*; lading *v.*; (*tn.*) belasting *v.*; (*fig.*) last *m.*, gewicht *o.*; *vt.* inladen, opladen; bevrachten; bezwaren, belasten.

loading-berth ['loudiŋbə:δ] ladingsplaats *v.*

loaf [louf] *sb.* brood *o.*; (*v. sla, enz.*) krop *m.*; *vi.* (*v. sla, kool, enz.*) kroppen.

loam [loum] *sb.* leem *o.*; *vt.* met leem bestrijken (bedekken).

loan [loun] *sb.* lening *v.*; het geleende *o.*; het ontleende *o.*; het lenen *o.*; het uitlenen *o.*; *vt.* lenen, uitlenen.

loan-office ['lounɔfis] leenbank *v.*; (*Am.*) lommerd *m.*

loathe [louθ] walgen van, verfoeien, verafschuwen.

loathsome(ly) ['louθsəm(li)] *adj.* (*adv.*) walglijk, afschuwelijk.

lobby ['lɔbi] portaal *o.*, hal, voorzaal *v.*; gang, wandelgang *v.*, couloir *m.*

lobe [loub] lob *v.*; lel *v.*; kwab *v.*

lobster ['lɔbstə] (*Dk.*) zeekreeft *m.*

lob-worm ['lɔbwə:m] pier *m.*

local ['loukəl] *adj.* plaatselijk, lokaal; plaats; *sb.* plaatselijk nieuws *o.*; (*Am.*) lokaaltrein *m.*

locate [lou'keit] *vt.* de plaats bepalen van; vaststellen; plaatsen; (*Am.: v. weg*) afbakenen, aanleggen; *vi.* (*Am.*) zich vestigen.

loch [lɔx, lɔk] (*Sc.*) meer *o.*

lock [lɔk] *sb.* lok *v.*; (*v. wol, enz.*) vlok *v.*; slot *o.*; sluis, kolk *v.*; *vt.* sluiten, op slot doen; opsluiten; insluiten; van sluizen voorzien; — *up*, opsluiten; (*v. kapitaal*) vastleggen; afsluiten.

lock-chamber ['lɔktʃeimbə] sluiskolk, schutkolk *v.*

locker ['lɔkə] kastje *o.*, kist *v.*

lock-jaw ['lɔkdʒɔ:] (*gen.*) mondklem *v.*

lock-out ['lɔk'aut] uitsluiting *v.*

locksman ['lɔksmən] sluiswachter *m.*

locksmith ['lɔksmiδ] slotenmaker *m.*

locust ['loukəst] sprinkhaan *m.*

lodge [lɔdʒ] *sb.* portierswoning *v.*; (vrijmetselaars(loge *m.*; (*v. dier*) leger *o.*; *vt.* huisvesten, herbergen; indienen, inleveren; *vi.* wonen; (*mil.*) liggen; — *with*, inwonen bij.

lodger ['lɔdʒə] kamerbewoner, huurder *m.* (van kamers).

lodging ['lɔdʒiŋ] huisvesting *v.*, verblijf, logies *o.*; (*mil.*) kwartier *o.*

lodging-house ['lɔdʒiŋhaus] logement *o.*

loft [lɔ:ft] zolder *m.*; vliering *v.*; duiventil *v.*, duivenhok *o.*; galerij, tribune *v.*

lofty ['lo:fti] *adj.* hoog, verheven; fier, trots, hooghartig; voornaam.

log [lɔg] blok (hout) *o.*; (*sch.*) logboek, (scheeps)journaal *o.*

loggerhead ['lɔgəhed] domkop *m.*

logical ['lɔdʒikl] *adj.* logisch.

loin [lɔin] lende *v.*; lendestuk *o.*

loiter ['lɔitə] *vi.* talmen, dralen, treuzelen; — *about*, rondslenteren; *vt.* — *away one's time,* zijn tijd verbeuzelen.

loiterer ['lɔitərə] talmer, draler, treuzelaar; slenteraar *m.*

lonely ['lounli], **lonesome** ['lounsəm] eenzaam, verlaten.

long [lɔŋ] *adj.* lang; langdurig; (*v. gezin*) groot; (*v. prijs*) hoog; *adv.* lang, al lang; *sb.* lange klinker *m.*; lange lettergreep *v.*; *vi.* verlangen (*for,* naar).

long-ago [lɔŋə'gou] *adj.* van lang geleden; *sb.* the —, het verre verleden *o.*

longboat ['lɔŋbout] sloep *v.*

longevity ['lɔn'dʒeviti] lang leven *o.*, hoge ouderdom *m.*

longing ['lɔŋiŋ] verlangen *o.*, hunkering *v.*

longing(ly) ['lɔŋiŋ(li)] *adj.* (*adv.*) (erg) verlangend.

longitude ['lɔn(d)ʒitjûd] geografische lengte *v.*

long-sighted ['lɔŋ'saitid] vèrziend; (*fig.*) vooruitziend.

long-winded ['lɔŋ'windid] lang van adem; langdradig.

looby ['lûbi] lummel, lomperd *m.*; kwast *m.*

look [luk] *vi.* & *vt.* kijken, zien; uitzien; er uitzien; lijken; — *after,* nakijken; letten op; zorgen voor; — *down,* neerzien, neerkijken (*upon,* op); (*H.: v. prijzen*) naar beneden gaan, dalen; —*downwards,* (in prijs) dalen; — *for,* uitzien naar; verwachten, tegemoet zien; — *in,* (even) aanlopen (*upon,* bij); — *up,* opzien, opkijken; (*v. prijzen*) omhooggaan; (*v. zaken*) beter worden, opleven; *sb.* blik *m.*; uitzicht; uiterlijk *o.*; gelaatsuitdrukking *v.*; schijn *m.*

looker ['lukə] kijker *m.*

looking-glass ['lukiŋglâs] spiegel *m.*; spiegelglas *o.*

look-out ['luk'aut] uitkijk, uitkijkpost *m.*; uitzicht *o.*

loom [lûm] *sb.* weefgetouw *o.*; handvat *o.*; *vi.* opdoemen, (dreigend) oprijzen.

loop [lûp] *sb.* lus *v.*, strop *m.*; bocht *v.*; beugel *m.*; schietgat *o.*; *vi.* een bocht maken; zich in een lus kronkelen; *vt.* met een lus vastmaken.

loophole ['lûphoul] kijkgat, schietgat *o.*; (*fig.*) uitvlucht *v.*

loose [lûs] *adj.* los; ruim, wijd; slap; (*v. definitie*) onnauwkeurig, vaag; onsamenhangend; *sb.* **give a — to,** de vrije teugel geven aan; *vt.* losmaken; loslaten; (*sch.*) losgooien.

loot [lût] *sb.* buit, roof *m.*, plundering *v.*; *vt.* buitmaken, roven, uitplunderen; *vi.* plunderen, stelen.

lop [lɔp] *sb.* snoeihout, snoeisel *o.*; *vt.* afkappen; wegkappen; snoeien; laten hangen; *vi.* slap neerhangen; rondslenteren.

loppings ['lɔpiŋz] snoeibout, snoeisel *o*.
loquacious [lo'kweiʃəs] *adj*. spraakzaam; praatziek.
lord [lo:d] heer, meester *m*.; lord *m*.
lordly ['lo:dli] voornaam, vorstelijk;
ʰoogʰartig.
lordship ['lo:dʃip] heerschappij, macht
v. (*of, over,* over); adellijk goed *o*.,
heerlijkheid *v*.; lordschap *o*.
lorry ['lɔri] lorrie *v*.
lose [lûz] *vt*. verliezen; kwijtraken, verspelen; (*v. kans*) verzuimen, laten voorbijgaan; (*v. trein*) missen; *be lost,* omkomen; vergaan; wegraken, te loor
gaan, verloren gaan; *vr.* — *oneself,*
verdwalen; zich verdiepen in.
loss [lo:s] verlies; nadeel *o*., schade *v*.;
ondergang *m*.; *be at a* —, (*jacht*) het
spoor bijster zijn; geen raad weten.
lot [lɔt] *sb*. lot *o*.; deel *o*., portie *v*.;
partij, kaveling *v*.; (*fam*.) hoop, boel
m.; perceel, stuk grond *o*.; *vt.* — *out,*
verkavelen.
lotion ['louʃən] wasmiddel *o*.; (schoonheids)watertje *o*.
lottery ['lɔtəri] loterij *v*.
loud [laud] *adj*. luid; luidruchtig; (*v.
kleuren*) schreeuwend, opvallend; (*v.
reuk*) sterk.
lounge [laun(d)ʒ] *vi*. slenteren, kuieren,
lanterfanten; luieren; *sb*. slentergang *m*.;
ligstoel *m*., rustbank *v*.; wandeling *v*.
louse [laus] *sb*. luis *v*.; *vt.* (ont)luizen.
lout [laut] lomperd, pummel *m*.
lovable ['lɒvəbl] *adj*. beminnelijk, lief.
love [lɒv] *sb*. liefde *v*.; lieveling, liefste
m.; geliefde *m*.; *vt*. beminnen, liefhebben, houden van; gaarne hebben.
loveliness ['lɒvlinis] beminnelijkheid,
lieftalligheid *v*.
lovely ['lɒvli] *adj*. beminnelijk, lieftallig;
(*v. geur*) heerlijk.
lover ['lɒvə] (be)minnaar, liefhebber *m*.;
—*s,* verliefden *m*. *mv*., paartje *o*.
loving ['lɒviŋ] *adj*. liefhebbend; lief-
derijk; hartelijk, teder.
low [lou] *adj*. laag; (*v. kleed*) laag uitge-
sneden; (*v. buiging*) diep; minderwaardig, gemeen; *adv*. laag, diep; zachtjes;
(*H*.) tegen lage prijs; *sb*. laagterecord *o*.;
laag terrein *o*.; gebied *o*. van lage druk;
be —, laag staan; aan lager wal zijn;
(*v. zieke*) minnetjes zijn.
low [lou] *vi*. loeien, bulken; *sb*. geloei,
gebulk *o*.
lower ['louə] *adj*. lager; dieper; zwak-
ker; slapper; *vt*. neerlaten, laten zakken;
(*v. gas, enz*.) lager draaien; (*v. prijs*)
verlagen, verminderen; *vi*. zakken; lager worden, afhellen; afnemen.
lower ['lauə] *vi*. dreigend (nors, somber)
zien; (*v. wolken*) dreigen; *sb*. sombere
(norse)blik *m*.
low-grade ['lougreid] van minder gehalte, van slechte kwaliteit.
lowland ['loulənd] laagland *o*.
lowly ['louli] nederig, ootmoedig, dee-
moedig, bescheiden; laag; gering.

low-minded ['lou'maindid] *adj*. onedel•
gemeen, laag (van geest).
low-priced ['lou'praist] goedkoop.
low-spirited ['lou'spiritid] neerslachtig.
loyal ['lɔiəl] *adj*. trouw; eerlijk, oprecht;
loyaal.
loyalty ['lɔiəlti] trouw *v*.; eerlijkheid,
oprechtheid *v*.; loyaliteit *v*.
lozenge ['lɔzindʒ] (*in raam*) ruitje *o*.;
(*wap*.) ruit *v*.; tablet *v*.
lubricate ['l(j)ûbrikeit] smeren, oliën.
lubricator ['l(j)ûbrikeitə] smeerpot,
oliepot *m*.; smeermiddel, smeersel *o*.
lubricous ['l(j)ûbrikəs] glad, glibberig; ongestadig; geil.
lucent ['l(j)ûsənt] glanzend, blinkend;
doorschijnend.
lucid ['l(j)ûsid] *adj*. schitterend, glanzend, stralend; helder, klaar; duidelijk.
lucidity [ljû'siditi] schittering *v*., glans
m.; helderheid, klaarheid *v*.
luck [lɒk] toeval *o*.; geluk, succes *o*.
luckless ['lɒklis] *adj*. ongelukkig.
lucky ['lɒki] *adj*. gelukkig.
lucrative (ly) ['l(j)ûkrətiv(li)] *adj*. (*adv*.)
winstgevend, voordelig.
lucre ['l(j)ûkə] winst *v*., voordeel *o*.;
winstbejag *o*.
ludicrous (ly) ['l(j)ûdikrəs(li)] *adj*.
(*adv*.) belachelijk, bespottelijk; koddig.
luggage ['lɒgidʒ] bagage *v*., reisgoed *o*.;
passagiersgoed *o*.
lugubrious (ly) [l(j)u'gjûbriəs(li)] *adj*.
(*adv*.) somber, akelig, treurig.
lukewarm ['l(j)ûkwo:m] lauw.
lumbago [lɒm'beigou] lendepijn *v*.,
spit (in de rug) *o*.
lumber ['lɒmbə] rommel *m*., oud goed
o.; ruwe planken *v*. *mv*., timmerhout *o*.
luminous ['l(j)ûminəs] lichtgevend,
lichtend; helder, stralend.
lump [lɒmp] *sb*. stuk *o*., klomp *m*.;
buil *v*., knobbel *m*.; hoop, boel *m*.;
(*v. suiker*) klontje *o*.; *adj. a* — *sum,*
een ronde som; *vt*. bijeengooien; tot
een klomp versmelten; — *together,*
over een kam scheren; *vi*. klonteren;
knobbels vormen.
lunacy ['l(j)ûnəsi] krankzinnigheid *v*.
lunatic ['l(j)ûnətik] *adj*. maanziek; gek,
krankzinnig; *sb*. krankzinnige *m*.
lunch [lɒnʃ] *sb*. lunch *v*., tweede ontbijt *o*., twaalfuurtje *o*.; *vi*. lunchen; een
lunch aanbieden.
lung ['lɒŋ] long *v*.
lungy ['lɒŋi] teringachtig.
lupin(e) ['l(j)ûpin] (*Pl*.) lupine, wolfs-
boon *v*.
lurch [lə:tʃ] *sb*. plotselinge slingering
v.; (*Am*.) neiging *v*.; aanleg *m*.; *vi*. slingeren; over stag gaan.
lurk [lə:k] loeren, op de loer liggen;
zich schuil houden; schuilen.
luscious ['lɒʃəs] lekker, smakelijk, sappig; erg zoet.
lush [lɒʃ] *adj*. (*v. gras*) sappig, mals.

weelderig; *sb. (sl.)* sterke drank *m.*; drinkgelag *o.*
lust [ləst] *sb.* begeerlijkheid *v.*, lust, wellust *m.*; zucht (*of*, naar), begeerte (*of*, naar) *v.*; *vi.* dorsten (*after, for*, naar), haken (naar).
lustful ['ləstful] wellustig.
lustration [ləs'treiʃən] reiniging *v.*; reinigingsoffer *o.*
lustre ['ləstə] *sb.* schittering *v.*; luister, glans *m.*; luchter, kroonkandelaar *m.*; (*stof*) lustre *o.*; *vt. & vi.* glanzen.
lustrum ['ləstrəm] lustrum *o.*

lusty ['ləsti] *adj.* krachtig, gezond, flink; (*v. maal, slag, enz.*) stevig, ferm.
luxuriance [ləg'ʒûəriəns], **luxuriancy** [ləg'ʒûəriənsi] weelderigheid, weligheid *v.*
luxuriant(ly) [ləg'ʒûəriənt(li)] *adj.* (*adv.*) weelderig, welig.
luxurious(ly) [ləg'ʒûəriəs(li)] *adj.* (*adv.*) weelderig; wellustig.
luxury ['ləkʃəri] weelde, luxe *v.*; weelderige levenswijze *v.*; weeldeartikel *o.*; genotmiddel *o.*; lekkernij *v.*; wellust *m.*
lying-in ['laiin'in] bevalling *v.*

M

macabre [mæ'kâbə] *adj.* griezelig, akelig, somber.
macadam [mək'ædəm] macadam, steenslag *o.*
macaroni [mækə'rouni] macaroni *v.*; mengelmoes *o.*
mace [meis] foelie *v.*; staf, scepter *m.*; (*gesch.*) strijdknots, goedendag *m.*
mace-bearer ['meisbêərə] stafdrager, pedel *m.*
macerate ['mæsəriet] vermageren; kastijden; weken, laten weken.
machinate ['mækineit] *vi.* kuipen, konkelen, samenspannen; *vt.* (*v. plan, enz.*) ontwerpen; (*v. aanslag, komplot*) beramen, smeden.
machination [mæki'neiʃən] kuiperij, machinatie *v.*
machinator ['mækineitə] intrigant *m.*
machine [mə'ʃin] machine *v.*; werktuig, toestel *o.*; rijwiel *o.*, fiets *v.*; auto *v.*; naaimachine *v.*
machine-gun [me'ʃingən] *sb.* (*mil.*) machinegeweer *o.*, mitrailleur *m.*; *vt.* met mitrailleur beschieten; *vi.* met mitrailleur schieten.
mackerel ['mækrəl] makreel *m.*
mackle ['mækl] *sb.* misdruk *m.*, maculateur *v.*; *vt.* (*bij het drukken*) doubleren.
mad [mæd] *adj.* gek, dol (*after, about,* op); krankzinnig; razend (*at, about,* over); (*Am.*) boos, nijdig; *vt.* dol maken, razend maken; *vi.* razend zijn.
madam ['mædəm] mevrouw, mejuffrouw *v.*
madder ['mædə] *sb.* meekrap *v.*; *vt.* met meekrap verven.
made [meid] *v. t. & v. d. van* **make**; verzonnen; (*v. paard*) afgericht; kunstmatig in elkaar gezet.
made-up ['meidəp] verzonnen; voorgewend; kunstmatig.
madhouse ['mædhaus] gekkenhuis :.
madman ['mædmən] gek, krankzinnige, dolleman *m.*
madness ['mædnis] gekheid, krankzinnigheid, dolheid *v.*
magazine [mægə'zîn] magazijn wa

penmagazijn, kruitmagazijn *o.*; tijdschrift *o.*
maggot ['mægət] made *v.*; (*fig.*) gril, luim *v.*
maggoty ['mægəti] vol maden; wormstekig; (*fig.*) grillig.
magic ['mædʒik] *sb.* toverij, toverkunst, toverkracht *v.*; betovering *v.*; *adj.* magisch, toverachtig, betoverend.
magician [mə'dʒiʃən] tovenaar *m.*
magistral [mæ'dʒistrəl] meesterachtig; gezaghebbend.
magistrate ['mædʒistr(e)it] magistraat, overheidspersoon *m.*; politierechter *m.*
magnanimous [mæg'næniməs] grootmoedig.
magnate ['mægneit] magnaat *m.*
magnet ['mægnit] magneet, magneetstaaf *m.*
magnific [mæg'nifik] groots, verheven, prachtig, heerlijk.
magnificence [mæg'nifisəns] pracht *v.*, luister *m.*, heerlijkheid *v.*
magnificent(ly) [mæg'nifisənt(li)] *adj.* (*adv.*) prachtig, heerlijk; groots, luisterrijk.
magnify ['mægnifai] vergroten, groter maken; verheerlijken; ophemelen.
magpie ['mægpai] ekster *v.*; (*fig.*) babbelkous *v.*
mahogany [mə'hɔgəni] mahoniehout *o.*; mahonieboom *m.*
maid [meid] meid *v.*; meisje *o.*; maagd *v.*; kamenier *v.*
maiden ['meidn] *sb.* meisje *o.*, maagd *v.*; jongejuffrouw *v.*; *adj.* maagdelijk; meisjes—, ongetrouwd.
maidenhood ['meidnhud] maagdelijkheid *v.*
maidenish ['meidniʃ] maagdelijk.
maid-servant ['meidsə:vənt] dienstmeid *v.*
mail [meil] *sb.* postzak *m.*; brievenmaal *v.*; mail *v.*, mailtrein *m.*; postwagen *m.*; *vt.* met de post verzenden.
mail [meil] *sb.* maliënkolder *m.*, pantserhemd *o.*; *vt.* bepantseren, pantseren.

mail-box ['meilbɔks] (*Am.*) brievenbus *v.*; postbus *v.*
maim [meim] *vt.* verminken; *sb.* verminking *v.*
main [mein] *adj.* voornaamste, grootste, hoofd—; *sb.* kracht *v.*, geweld *o.*; (*v. gas, enz.*) hoofdkraan, hoofdleiding *v.*; (*v. spoorweg*) hoofdleiding *v.*; (*v. spoorweg*) hoofdlijn *v.*; **in the —,** in hoofdzaak, over 't algemeen genomen.
mainland ['mein'lænd] vasteland *o.*
mainly ['meinli] *adv.* voornamelijk, hoofdzakelijk.
mainmast ['meinmâst] (*sch.*) grote mast *m.*
mainprize ['meinpraiz] borgtocht *m.*
mainstay ['meinstei] (*sch.*) grootstag *o.*; (*fig.*) voornaamste steun, steunpilaar *m.*
maintain [mein—, mən'tein] handhaven, in stand houden, verdedigen, steunen; beweren, volhouden, staande houden.
maintainable [mein—, mən'teinəbl] houdbaar, verdedigbaar, te handhaven.
maintenance ['maintinəns] handhaving *v.*; onderhoud *o.*; verdediging *v.*
maize [meiz] maïs *v.*
majestic(ally) [me'dʒestik(əli)] *adj.* (*adv.*) majestueus.
majesty ['mædʒisti] majesteit *v.*
major ['meidʒə] *adj.* groot, groter, grootste; hoger; hoofd—; (*muz.*) majeur; meerderjarig; *sb.* (*mil.*) majoor *m.*; meerderjarige *m.* & *v.*
majority [mə'dʒɔ:riti] meerderheid *v.*; meerderjarigheid *v.*; (*mil.*) majoorschap *o.*, majoorsrang *m.*
make [meik] *vt.* maken, vervaardigen; voortbrengen, scheppen; vormen; (*v. geld*) verdienen; *vi.* maken, doen; zich begeven (**for,** naar); **— against,** benadelen, schaden; **— at,** afkomen op, afstuiven op; **— in favour of,** bijdragen tot; pleiten voor; **— up,** (*v. lijst, rekening*) opmaken; (*v. brief*) opstellen; (*v. recept*) klaarmaken; (*v. vuur*) aanleggen; (*v. leemte*) aanvullen; (*v. geschil*) bijleggen; (*v. geld*) bijeenbrengen; (*v. verhaal*) verzinnen, uit zijn duim zuigen; (*v. verlies*) vergoeden; (*v. getij*) opkomen; (*sch.: v. zeil*) beslaan; (*fig.*) komedie spelen; *sb.* maaksel, fabrikaat *o.*; constructie *v.*; bouw, lichaamsbouw *m.*; aard *m.*, natuur *v.*; soort *v.*
makepeace ['meikpîs] vredestichter *m.*
maker ['meikə] maker, vervaardiger, schepper; fabrikant *m.*
makeshift ['meikʃift] *sb.* hulpmiddel, redmiddel *o.*; uitvlucht *v.*; *adj.* geïmproviseerd.
makeweight ['meikweit] toegift *v.*; tegenwicht *o.*
making ['meikiŋ] vervaardiging; vorming *v.*; maak *m.*, maaksel *o.*
malady ['mælədi] ziekte *v.*
malaise ['mæ'leiz] onbehaaglijkheid *v.*, onbehaaglijk gevoel *o.*; malaise *v.*

malapropos ['mælæprə'pou] ongelegen; te onpas.
malcontent ['mælkəntent] *adj.* ontevreden, misnoegd; *sb.* ontevredene *m.*
male [meil] *adj.* mannelijk, mannen—, mans—; van het mannelijk geslacht; *sb.* (*Dk.*) mannetje *o.*; manspersoon *m.*
malediction [mæli'dikʃən] vervloeking, verwensing *v.*
maledictory [mæli'diktəri] vervloekend, vloek—.
malefaction [mæli'fækʃən] misdaad *v.*
malefactor [mæli'fæktə] misdadiger, boosdoener *m.*
maleficence [mə'lefisns] verderfelijkheid, schadelijkheid; boosaardigheid *v.*
maleficent [mə'lefisnt] verderfelijk, schadelijk, boosaardig.
malevolence [mə'levələns] kwaadwilligheid, boosaardigheid *v.*
malevolent(ly) [mə'levələnt(li)] *adj.* (*adv.*) kwaadwillig, boosaardig.
malfeasant [mæl'fîzənt] *adj.* kwaaddoend; *sb.* misdadiger *m.*
malformed [mæl'fo:md] misvormd.
malice ['mælis] boosheid, boosaardigheid, kwaadaardigheid *v.*; plaagzucht *v.*; arglist *v.*; (*recht*) boos opzet *o.*
malicious [mə'liʃəs] *adj.* boos, boosaardig, slecht, kwaadwillig; plaagziek; arglistig; (*recht*) opzettelijk, voorbedacht.
malign [mə'lain] *adj.* verderfelijk, slecht, ongunstig, schadelijk, noodlottig; (*v. ziekte*) kwaadaardig; *vt.* kwaad spreken van, belasteren; benadelen.
malignant [mə'lignənt] *adj.* boos, boosaardig, kwaadwillig; kwaadaardig; *sb.* kwaadwillige *m.*
maligner [mə'lainə] kwaadwillige *m.*; kwaadspreker *m.*
Malines [mə'lîn] Mechelen *o.*
malleable ['mæliəbl] smeedbaar, pletbaar; (*fig.*) kneedbaar, gedwee.
malleate ['mælieit] smeden, uithameren.
mallet ['mælit] houten hamer *m.*; slaghamer *m.*
malnutrition [mælnju'triʃən] slechte voeding, ondervoeding *v.*
malodorous [mæ'loudərəs] kwalijk riekend.
malodour ['mæ'loudə] stank *m.*
malpractice ['mæl'præktis] verkeerde behandeling *v.*; kwade praktijk(en) *v.* (*mv.*); malversatie *v.*; wangedrag *o.*
malt [mɔ:lt] *sb.* mout *o.*; (*sl.*) bier *o.*; *vt. & vi.* mouten.
malt-house ['mo:lthaus] mouterij *v.*
maltreat [mæl'trît] mishandelen, slecht behandelen.
maltreatment [mæl'trîtmənt] mishandeling, slechte behandeling *v.*
maltster ['mo:ltstə] mouter *m.*
mammal ['mæməl] zoogdier *o.*
mammon ['mæmən] mammon *m.*
mammy ['mæmi] maatje *o.*
man [mæn] *sb.* man *m.*; mens *m.*;

knecht, werkman, bediende *m*.; (*mil.*) mindere *m*.; (*mv*.: manschappen *m. mv*.); *adj*. mannelijk, van het mannelijk geslacht; *vt*. bemannen; bezetten; bedienen; *vr*. — *oneself*, zich vermannen.

manacle ['mænəkl] *sb*. handboei *v*.; *vt*. de handboeien aandoen, boeien, kluisteren.

manage ['mænidʒ] *vt*. besturen, beheren; leiden; hanteren; regeren, naar zijn hand zetten; *ri*. — *for oneself*, zich redden; op eigen wielen drijven.

manageable ['mænidʒəbl] handelbaar, gedwee, meegaand.

management ['mænidʒmənt] bestuur, beheer *o*.; leiding *r*.; administratie *v*.; directie *v*.

manager ['mænidʒə] bestuurder, beheerder; directeur, administrateur *m*.; leider *m*.; zetbaas, gerant *m*.

manageress ['mænidʒəris] bestuurster, directrice; administratrice *r*.; leidster *v*.; hoofd *o*.

mandarine ['mændərin] mandarijntje *o*.

mandate ['mændeit] *sb*. mandaat, bevelschrift *o*., opdracht *v*.; (*kath*.) mandement *o*.; [mæn'deit] *vt*. onder mandaat stellen.

manducate ['mændjukeit] kauwen, eten.

mane [mein] manen *v. mr*.

man-eater ['mænitə] menseneter *m*.

manege [mæ'neiʒ] rijschool *v*.; rijkunst *v*.

manful(**ly**) ['mænful(i)] *adj*. (*adv*.) moedig, dapper, manhaftig.

mange [mein(d)ʒ] schurft *v*. & *o*.

manger ['mein(d)ʒə] krib *v*., trog, voerbak *m*.

mangle ['mæŋgl] *sb*. mangel *m*.; *rt*. mangelen.

mangy ['mein(d)ʒi] schurftig.

mania ['meiniə] manie *v*., waanzin *m*.

maniac ['meiniək] *adj*. waanzinnig; *sb*. maniak, waanzinnige *m*.

manicure ['mænikjuə] *sb*. manicure *m*. & *v*.; handen- en nagelverzorging *v*.; *vt*. manicuren, de handen en nagels verzorgen.

manifest ['mænifest] *adj*. duidelijk, kennelijk, klaarblijkelijk; *sb*. scheepsmanifest *o*.; manifest *o*.; *vt*. openbaren, aan de dag leggen; bewijzen; (*v. goederen*) aangeven; *ri*. manifesteren; — (*itself*), zich manifesteren.

manifestation [mænifes'teiʃən] openbaring, openbaarmaking *v*.; betoging, manifestatie *v*.

manifold ['mænifould] *adj*. menigvuldig; veelvuldig; onderscheiden; — *writer*, hectograaf; *vt*. vermenigvuldigen, verveelvoudigen, hectograferen.

manikin ['mænikin] mannetje *o*., dwerg *m*.; ledepop *v*.; (*gen*.) fantoom *o*.

manipulate [mə'nipjuleit] *vt*. behandelen, hanteren, manipuleren; (*v. pers, enz.*) bewerken; knoeien met; *ri*. manipuleren.

manipulation [mænipju'leiʃən] behandeling, hantering *v*.; manipulatie, betasting *v*.

mankind [mæn'kaind] het mensdom *o*., de mensheid *v*.; ['mænkaind] de mannen *m. mv*.

manly ['mænli] mannelijk, manhaftig.

manner ['mænə] manier, wijze *v*.; gewoonte *r*.; aanstellerij *v*.; soort *v*.

mannered ['mænəd] gemanierd; geaffecteerd.

mannerless ['mænəlis] ongemanierd.

mannerly ['mænəli] welgemanierd, beleefd.

mannish ['mæniʃ] manachtig; als een man.

manœuvre [mə'n(j)ûvə] *sb*. manœuver *v*.; kunstgreep *m*.; *vi*. manœuvreren; kuipen, intrigeren; *rt*. — *away*, wegwerken.

man-of-war ['mænə(v)'wo:] oorlogsschip *v*.

manorial [mə'no:riəl] van een (ambachts)heerlijkheid.

mansard(**roof**) ['mænsəd(rûf)] mansardedak, gebroken dak *o*.

mansion ['mænʃən] herenhuis *o*., (*block of*) — *s*, flatgebouw.

manslaughter ['mænslo:tə] (onvrijwillige) manslag, doodslag *m*.

mansuetude ['mænswitjûd] zachtaardigheid, zachtmoedigheid, zachtheid *v*.

mantel(**piece**) ['mæntlpis] schoorsteenmantel *m*.

mantelshelf ['mæntlʃelf] schoorsteenwand *m*.

mantle ['mæntl] *sb*. mantel *m*.; (*fig.*) dekmantel *m*.; gloeikousje *o*.; *vt*. bedekken, bemantelen, verbergen; *vi*. (*v. wangen*) rood worden; (*v. bloed*) naar de wangen stijgen; schuimen.

mantrap ['mæntræp] voetangel *m*., klem, val *v*.

manual ['mænjuəl] *adj*. hand—, handen—, met de hand; *sb*. (*v. orgel*) manuaal *o*.; handboek *o*.; handspuit *v*.; *the* — *s*, (*mil.*) de handgrepen.

manufacture [mænju'fæktʃə] *sb*. fabrikaat *o*.; vervaardiging, fabricage *v*.; *vt*. vervaardigen, fabriceren.

manure [mə'njûə] *sb*. mest *m*.; *vt*. bemesten.

manuscript ['mænjuskript] *adj*. (met de hand) geschreven; *sb*. manuscript, handschrift *o*.

many ['meni] veel, vele; — *a man*, menigeen; *a great* —, heel veel; *a good* —, heel wat.

many-coloured ['menikələd] veelkleurig.

many-sided ['menisaidid] veelzijdig.

map [mæp] *sb*. landkaart; hemelkaart *v*.; *vt*. in kaart brengen; — (*out*), ontwerpen.

mar [mâ] bederven.

maraud [mə'ro:d] plunderen, stropen.

marauder [mə'ro:də] plunderaar, stroper *m*.

marauding [mə'rɔːdiŋ] plundering *r.*

marble ['mâbl] *sb.* marmer *o.*; marmeren beeld *o.*; knikker *m.*; *adj.* marmeren; *vt.* marmeren.

marble-hearted ['mâblhâtid] hardvochtig.

marbly ['mâbli] marmerachtig; koud als marmer.

March [mâtʃ] *sb.* maart *m.*; *adj.* maarts.

march [mâtʃ] *sb.* (*mil.*, *muz.*) mars *m.*; opmars *m.*; (*v. gebeurtenissen, enz.*) loop *m.*, verloop *o.*; (*v. wetenschap*) vooruitgang *m.*; *vi.* marcheren; opmarcheren; afmarcheren; oprukken; *rt.* laten marcheren; laten oprukken.

marching-order ['mâtʃiŋɔːdə] (*mil.*) marstenue, veldtenue *v.* & *o.*; **—s,** marsorder(s).

marchpane ['mâtʃpein] marsepein *v.* & *o.*

march-past ['mâtʃ'pâst] (*mil.*) defilé *o.*

marconigram [mâ'kounigræm] draadloos telegram, radiogram *o.*

mare [mêə] merrie *r.*; nachtmerrie *v.*

margin ['mâdʒin] *sb.* rand, kant *m.*; marge *v.*; (*H.*) overschot, saldo *o.*, winst *v.*; *vt.* van een rand voorzien, een marge laten; van kanttekeningen voorzien; in de marge vermelden.

marginal ['mâdʒinəl] *adj.* kant—, rand—, marginaal; op de grens gelegen.

margrave ['mâgreiv] markgraaf *m.*

marigold ['mærigould] goudsbloem *v.*

marine [mə'rîn] *adj.* zee—; marine—; scheeps—; *sb.* vloot, handelsvloot *v.*; marinier, zeesoldaat *m.*; zeestuk *o.*

mariner ['mærinə] zeeman, matroos *m.*

maritime ['mæritaim] zee—; kust—; maritiem; **— law,** zeerecht; **— power,** zeemogendheid.

mark [mâk] *sb.* merk, merkteken *o.*; stempel *m.*; spoor *o.*; kruisje *o.* (als handtekening); litteken *o.*; *vt.* merken; tekenen; kenmerken, onderscheiden; optekenen, aantekenen, noteren.

marked [mâkt] *adj.* merkbaar; opvallend, in het oog lopend; gemarkeerd.

market ['mâkit] *sb.* markt *v.*; afzetgebied *o.*; aftrek *m.*, vraag *v.*; marktprijs *m.*; handel *m.*; *vt.* kopen (op de markt); ter markt brengen, verkopen (op de markt); handelen in; *vi.* markten, inkopen doen.

market-day ['mâkitdei] marktdag *m.*

marketer ['mâkitə] marktganger *m.*

market-price ['mâkitpreis] marktprijs *m.*

market-stall ['mâkitstoːl] marktkraam *v.*

market-trot ['mâkittrɔt] sukkeldrafje *o.*

market-vendor ['mâkitvendə] marktkramer *m.*

marking ['mâkiŋ] (het) merken *o.*; (*v. dier*) tekening *v.*; (*Beurs*) notering *v.*

marksman ['mâksmən] schutter, scherpschutter *m.*; (*sp.*) doelschutter *m.*

marl [mâl] *sb.* mergel *v.*; *vt.* (met mergel) bemesten; (*sch.*) marlen.

marmalade ['mâməleid] marmelade *r.*

marmot ['mâmət] marmot *r.*

marquee [mâ'kî] grote veldtent *v.*

marquess ['mâkwis] markies *m.*

marquet(e)ry ['mâkitri] inlegwerk *o.*

marquis ['mâkwis] markies *m.*

marquise [mâ'kîz] markiezin *v.*; luifel, overdekking *r.*

marriage ['mæridʒ] huwelijk *o.*; echt *m.*; **by —,** aangetrouwd.

marriageable ['mæridʒəbl] huwbaar.

marriage-portion ['mæridʒpɔːʃən] huwelijksgoed *o.*, bruidsschat *m.*

marriage-settlement ['mæridʒsetlmənt] huwelijksvoorwaarden *r. mv.*

married ['mærid] getrouwd, gehuwd; echtelijk, huwelijks—.

marrow ['mærou] *sb.* merg *o.*; (*fig.*) pit, fut *r.*; *rt.* met merg vullen.

marrow-bone ['mærouboun] mergpijp *r.*

marry ['mæri] *rt.* trouwen, tot vrouw nemen; in de echt verbinden; uithuwelijken; paren; nauw verbinden; **— off,** aan de man brengen; *ri.* trouwen.

marsh [mâʃ] moeras *o.*

marshal ['mâʃəl] *sb.* maarschalk *m.*; *vt.* rangschikken, ordenen; opstellen; geleiden.

marsh-fire ['mâʃfaiə] dwaallicht *o.*

marshy ['mâʃi] moerassig, drassig.

mart [mât] markt *r.*; handelscentrum *o.*; verkooplokaal *o.*

marten ['mâtin] marter *m.*; marterbont *o.*

martial ['mâʃəl] *adj.* krijgshaftig, krijgs—.

martyr ['mâtə] *sb.* martelaar *m.*; *vt.* pijnigen, martelen; de marteldood doen sterven.

martyrdom ['mâtədəm] martelaarschap *o.*; marteldood *m.*; marteling *v.*

martyrize ['mâtəraiz] martelen; (*fig.*) tot martelaar maken.

marvel ['mâvəl] *sb.* wonder *o.*; verwondering, verbazing *v.*; *vi.* zich verwonderen, zich verbazen (*at,* over), verbaasd staan; zich afvragen.

marvellous(ly) ['mâv(ə)ləs(li)] *adj.* (*adv.*) wonderbaar, verbazend.

marzipan [mâzi'pæn] marsepein *v.* & *o.*

mascot ['mæskət] mascotte *v.*, talisman *m.*, gelukbrengend voorwerp *o.*

masculine ['mâs—, 'mæskjulin] mannelijk.

mash [mæʃ] *sb.* (*in brouwerij*) beslag, moutbeslag *o.*; mengvoer *o.*; mengelmoes *o.*; *vt.* fijnmaken, fijnstampen; (*v. mout*) mengen, aanmengen.

mask [mâsk] *sb.* masker *o.*; gemaskerde *m.*; *vt.* maskeren, vermommen; maskeren, verbergen; *vi.* zich vermommen; een masker voordoen.

mason ['meisn] *sb.* steenhouwer *m.*; vrijmetselaar *m.*; *vt.* metselen.

masonry ['meisnri] metselwerk *o.*; vrijmetselarij *v.*

masquerade [mæskə'reid] *sb.* mas-

kerade v.; vermomming v.; ri. zich ver
mommen; vermomd zijn.
mass [mæs, mas] mis v.
mass [mæs] sb. massa v.; (grote) hoop
m., merendeel o.; menigte v.; **in the —,**
in massa, in zijn geheel, samengenomen;
vt. bijeenbrengen, verzamelen; groeperen; opkopen; (mil.: v. troepen) samentrekken; vi. zich ophopen; zich verzamelen.
massacre ['mæsəkə] sb. bloedbad o.,
slachting, moordpartij v.; vt. vermoorden, uitmoorden.
massage [mæ'sâʒ, 'mæsâʒ] sb. massage v.; vt. masseren.
massive (ly) ['mæsiv(li)] adj. (adv.)
massief, zwaar.
mast [mâst] sb. mast m.; vt. masten.
master ['mâstə] sb. meester m.; heer
des huizes m.; bezitter, eigenaar m.;
baas, chef m.; gezagvoerder, kapitein
m.; vt. overmeesteren, zich meester
maken van; onder de knie krijgen; te
boven komen; besturen; de baas spelen
over; **— oneself,** zich beheersen.
master-builder ['mâstəbildə] bouwmeester m.; meester-metselaar, patroon
m. in 't bouwvak.
master-key ['mâstəki] loper.
masterly ['mâstəli] meesterlijk.
master-man ['mâstəmən] patroon,
baas m.
master-piece ['mâstəpis] meesterstuk o.
mastery ['mâstəri] meesterschap o.;
heerschappij v.; overhand, overmacht v.
mast-head ['mâsthed] top m. van de
mast.
masticate ['mæstikeit] kauwen.
mat [mæt] sb. mat v., matje o.; kleedje
o.; verwarde (dooreengestrengelde) massa v.; vt. met matten beleggen; dooreenvlechten, samenvlechten; vi. in de
war raken; samenkleven.
mat [mæt] adj. mat, dof; sb. matte rand
m.; vt. mat maken.
match [mætʃ] sb. lucifer m.; lont v.; vt.
zwavelen.
match [mætʃ] sb. gelijke m., evenknie
v., partuur o.; tegenhanger m.; wedstrijd, kamp m.; partij v., huwelijk o.;
vt. paren; schikken, sorteren; evenaren;
— oneself against, zich meten met;
vi. bij elkaar passen (komen); een paar
vormen; zich paren.
matchless ['mætʃlis] onvergelijkelijk,
weergaloos.
match-maker ['mætʃmeikə] lucifer-
maker m.; koppelaar(ster) m. (v.).
mate [meit] sb. maat, kameraad, makker m.; gezel m.; helper m.; levensgezel-
(lin), echtvriend(in) m. (v.); (sch.) stuurman m.; vt. paren, verenigen; in de echt
verbinden, trouwen; vi. samengaan
(met); omgaan (met); zich paren, zich
verenigen.
material [mə'tiəriəl] adj. stoffelijk,
materieel; lichamelijk, zinnelijk; be-

langrijk; sb. materiaal o., bouwstof v.;
grondstof v., bestanddeel o.
materialism [mə'tiəriəlizm] materia-
lisme o.
maternal [mə'tə:nəl] adj. moederlijk,
moeder—; van moederszijde.
maternity [mə'tə:niti] moederschap o.;
moederlijkheid v.; kraaminrichting v.
mathematical [mæði'mætikl] adj.
wiskundig, mathematisch.
mathematician [mæðimə'tiʃən] wiskundige m.
mathematics [mæði'mætiks] wiskunde v.
matie ['meiti] maatjesharing m.
matricide ['meitrisaid] moedermoord
m.; moedermoordenaar m.
matriculate [mə'trikjuleit] vt. inschrijven (als student); vi. zich laten inschrijven.
matriculation [mətrikju'leiʃən] inschrijving v. als student; **— (examination),** toelatingsexamen.
matrimony ['mætriməni] huwelijk o.;
huwelijke staat m.
matrix ['meitriks] matrijs v., gietvorm m.
matron ['meitrən] matrone, getrouw-
de dame v.; (v. inrichting) hoofd o. van
de huishouding; (v. ziekenhuis) directrice v., huismoeder v.
matter ['mætə] sb. stof, materie v.;
aangelegenheid v.; aanleiding, reden v.;
inhoud m.; vi. van belang zijn; betekenen.
matterful ['mætəful] zaakrijk.
matter-of-course [mætərəv'ko:s] van-
zelfsprekend, natuurlijk.
mattock ['mætək] houweel o.
mattress ['mætris] matras v.
mature [mə'tjûə] adj. rijp; (v. wissel,
enz.) vervallen; vt. rijp maken; vi. rijpen,
rijp worden; (v. wissel) vervallen; in vervulling gaan, verwezenlijkt worden.
maturity [mə'tjûəriti] rijpheid v.; (v.
wissel) vervaltijd, vervaldag m.; **at —,** in
volle rijpheid; (v. wissel) op de vervaldag.
maul [mo:l] sb. beukhamer, moker, m.;
vt. beuken, slaan; ranselen, toetakelen;
kneuzen.
Maundy Thursday ['mo:ndiðə:zdi]
Witte Donderdag m.
mausoleum [mo:sə'liəm] mausoleum,
praalgraf o.
mauve [mouv] mauve, lichtpaars.
maw [mo:] pens, maag v.; bek, muil m.
mawkish (ly) ['mo:kiʃ(li)] adj. (adv.)
walglijk zoet, walglijk flauw van smaak;
sentimenteel.
maxim ['mæksim] stelregel m.; leerspreuk v.; grondstelling v.
May [mei] mei m.
may [mei] mogen, kunnen, kunnen zijn.
maybe ['meibi] misschien, mogelijk,
wellicht.
mayor ['mêə] burgemeester m.
maypole ['meipoul] meiboom m.; (fig.)
bonestaak m.

maze [ineiz] *sb.* doolhof *m.*; verbijstering *v.*; *vt.* verbijsteren.
mazy ['meizi] *adj.* verward.
me [mi] mij; (*fam.*) ik.
mead [mid] mee, mede *v.*; (*dicht.*) weide *v.*, beemd *m.*
meadow ['medou] weiland *o.*, weide *v.*, hooiland *o.*
meagre ['migə] mager, schraal.
meagreness ['migənis] magerheid, schraalheid *v.*
meal [mil] *sb.* maal *o.*, maaltijd *m.*; meel *o.*; *at* —*s*, aan tafel; bij de maaltijd; *vi.* eten, middagmalen.
mealy ['mili] meelachtig; melig.
mealy-mouthed ['mili'mauθd] zoetsappig, zalvend; schijnheilig.
mean [min] *adj.* gering; laag, gemeen, verachtelijk; gierig, krenterig; schriel.
mean [min] *adj.* gemiddeld; middelbaar; middelste; middel—; *in the* — *time,* middelerwijl, ondertussen; *sb.* middelmaat *v.*; middelweg *m.*; gemiddelde *o.*; midden *o.*
mean [min] menen, bedoelen; in de zin hebben, voornemens zijn; betekenen; bestemmen (*for,* voor).
mean-born ['minbo:n] laaggeboren.
meander [mi'ændə] *sb.* kronkeling *v.*; kronkelpad *o.*; doolhof *m.*; *vi.* kronkelen, zich slingeren; dolen.
meaning ['minin] *adj.* veelbetekenend; *sb.* bedoeling *v.*; betekenis *v.*
meaningless ['mininlis] zonder zin, zinledig, zonder betekenis.
meanness ['minnis] geringheid *v.*; onaanzienlijkheid *v.*; laagheid, gemeenheid *v.*; gierigheid *v.*
means [minz] middelen *o. mv.*, inkomsten *v. mv.*; middel *o.*; *by* — *of,* door middel van, door toedoen van.
meantime ['min'taim] ondertussen, middelerwijl.
measles ['mizlz] mazelen *v. mv.*
measly ['mizli] lijdend aan de mazelen; (*sl.*) armzalig, miezerig.
measurable ['meʒərəbl] *adj.* meetbaar; afzienbaar.
measure ['meʒə] *sb.* maat *v.*; maatstaf *m.*; maatregel *m.*; *vt.* meten; afmeten, opmeten; toemeten; de maat nemen.
measurement ['meʒəmənt] afmeting *v.*; maat *v.*
measurer ['meʒərə] meter *m.*
meat [mit] vlees *o.*; spijs *v.*, kost *m.*, voedsel *o.*
meaty ['miti] vlezig; vleesachtig; vlees—; degelijk, stevig.
mechanic [mi'kænik] *adj.* mechanisch; *sb.* handwerksman *m.*; werktuigkundige, mecanicien *m.*; —*s,* mechanica, werktuigkunde.
mechanical [mi'kænikl] *adj.* machinaal, werktuiglijk; werktuigkundig.
mechanism ['məkenizm] mechanisme *o.*, mechaniek *v.* & *o.*
mechanist ['mekənist] machinebouwer *m.*

medal ['medl] medaille *v.*; penning *m.*
meddle ['medl] zich bemoeien, zich inlaten (*with,* met); zich mengen (*in,* in); tornen (*with,* aan).
meddler ['medlə] bemoeial *m.*
meddlesome ['medisəm] bemoeiziek.
mediaeval [medi'ivəl] middeleeuws.
mediate ['midiit] *adj.* middellijk, indirect; tussenliggend, gemiddeld.
mediate ['midieit] *vt.* bemiddelen; *vi.* bemiddelen, als bemiddelaar optreden, tussen beide treden.
mediation [midi'eiʃən] bemiddeling *v.*; voorspraak *v.*; middelaarschap *o.*
mediatize ['midiətaiz] annexeren.
mediator ['midieitə] (be)middelaar *m.*
mediatorial [midiə'to:riəl] bemiddelend, bemiddelings—.
mediatrix [midi'eitriks] bemiddelaarster *v.*
medical ['medikl] geneeskundig, medisch; — *man,* dokter, medicus.
medicaster ['medikæstə] kwakzalver *m.*
medicate ['medikeit] geneeskundig behandelen; genezen; medicinaal bereiden, bemiddelings—.
medicinal [mi'disinəl] *adj.* geneeskundig; geneeskrachtig, genezend, medicinaal.
medicine ['medsn] geneeskunde *v.*; geneesmiddel *o.*, medicijn *v.*; artsenij *v.*
mediocre ['midioukə] middelmatig.
meditate ['mediteit] *vt.* overdenken, bepeinzen, denken over; beramen; *vi.* nadenken, peinzen (*on, over,* over); (*kath.*) mediteren.
meditation [medi'teiʃən] overdenking, overpeinzing *v.*; (*kath.*) meditatie *v.*
medium ['midiəm] *sb.* midden *o.*; middenweg *m.*; middelsoort *v.*; tussenpersoon *m.*; medium *o.*; *adj.* middelmatig; gemiddeld.
medlar ['medlə] mispel *v.*
medley ['medli] *sb.* mengelmoes *o.*; mengeling *v.*; (*muz.*) potpourri *m.* & *o.*; *adj.* gemengd, bont; *vt.* mengen, dooreenmengen.
meed [mid] (*dicht.*) beloning *v.*, prijs *m.*, loon *o.*
meek(ly) ['mik(li)] *adj.* (*adv.*) zachtmoedig, zachtzinnig, gedwee.
meekness ['miknis] zachtmoedigheid, zachtzinnigheid, gedweeheid *v.*
meerschaum ['miəʃəm] meerschuim *o.*; meerschuimen pijp *v.*
meet [mit] *vt.* tegenkomen, ontmoeten, aantreffen; tegemoet gaan; tegemoet komen (aan); (*v. wensen*) voldoen (aan); *vi.* elkaar ontmoeten; bijeenkomen, samenkomen.
meeting ['mitin] ontmoeting *v.*; bijeenkomst, vergadering, meeting *v.*; wedstrijd *m.*
megalomania [megəlo(u)'meinjə] grootheidswaanzin *m.*; (*fig.*) grootdoenerij *v.*
megrim ['migrim] (schele) hoofdpijn

v.; gril *v.*; **—s,** (*bij paarden*) duizeligheid *v.*

melancholy ['melənkəli] *adj.* zwaarmoedig, melancholiek; droefgeestig; *sb.* zwaarmoedigheid, melancholie; droefgeestigheid *v.*

meliorate ['mīliəreit] *vt.* verbeteren; (*v. gewassen*) veredelen; *vi.* beter worden.

melioration [mīliə'reiſən] verbetering; veredeling *v.*

mellifluent [me'lifluənt] zoetvloeiend; honigzoet.

mellow ['melou] *adj.* rijp; zacht, murw, mals, sappig; (*v. toon*) zachtsmeltend, mollig; hartelijk, joviaal; (*fam.*) lichtelijk aangeschoten, half dronken; *vi.* rijpen, rijp worden; zacht worden; *vt.* doen rijpen; zacht (mals, enz.) maken; benevelen.

mellowness ['melounis] rijpheid; zachtheid, malsheid, sappigheid *v.*

melodious (ly) [mi'loudjəs(li)] *adj.* (*adv.*) welluidend, melodieus, zangerig.

melody ['melədi] melodie *v.*

melon ['melən] meloen *m.*

melt [melt] *vi.* smelten; **—** (*away*), wegsmelten, versmelten; vertederd worden; **— into,** versmelten tot; ongemerkt overgaan in; *vt.* smelten; vertederen, vermurwen; *sb.* gesmolten metaal *o.*; smelting *v.*

melting-point ['meltiŋpoint] smeltpunt *o.*

melting-pot ['meltiŋpot] smeltkroes *m.*

member ['membə] lid *o.*; lidmaat *o.*; afgevaardigde *m.*

membership ['membəſip] lidmaatschap *o.*

membrane ['membrein] vlies *o.*

membranous ['membrənəs] vliezig.

memento [mi'mentou] herinnering *v.*, aandenken *o.*

memorable ['memərəbl] *adj.* gedenkwaardig, heuglijk.

memorandum [memə'rændəm] memorandum *o.*; aantekening, notitie *v.*; nota *v.*

memorial [mi'mo:riəl] herinnering, gedachtenis *v.*, aandenken *o.*; herdenking *v.*; gedenkschrift *o.*; gedenkteken *o.*; adres, verzoekschrift *o.*, petitie *v.*

memorize ['memərаiz] optekenen; vermelden, memoreren; in de herinnering bewaren.

memory ['memǝri] geheugen *o.*; gedachtenis *v.*, aandenken *o.*, herinnering *v.*

menace ['menis] *sb.* bedreiging *v.*; *vt.* dreigen, bedreigen.

mend [mend] *vt.* verbeteren, beter maken; herstellen, repareren, opknappen; (*v. kousen*) stoppen; (*v. netten*) boeten; *vi.* beteren, beter worden; zich beteren; (*v. ziekte*) vooruitgaan; *sb.* verstelde plaats *v.*; **on the —,** aan de beterhand.

mendable ['mendəbl] herstelbaar; verstelbaar.

mendacious [men'deiſəs] leugenachtig.

mender ['mendə] hersteller; versteller *m.*, verstelster *v.*

mendicity [men'disiti] bedelarij *v.*; bedelstand *m.*

menial ['mīniəl] *adj.* dienstbaar; in dienst, dienend; slaven—, slaafs; *sb.* knecht, bediende, lakei, huurling *m.*

mensurable ['menſurəbl] meetbaar.

mental ['mentl] geestelijk, geestes—, verstandelijk.

mentation [men'teiſən] geestesgesteldheid *v.*

mention ['menſən] *sb.* melding, vermelding *v.*, gewag *o.*; *vt.* melden, vermelden, melding maken van.

mentionable ['menſənəbl] te vermelden, noembaar, noemenswaard.

menu ['men(j)û] menu *o.*, spijslijst, spijskaart *v.*

mercantile ['mə:kəntail] koopmans—, handels—; mercantiel, winzuchtig.

mercenary ['mə:sinəri] *adj.* veil, te koop; mercantiel, baatzuchtig, winzuchtig; huur—, huurlings—; *sb.* huurling *m.*

merchandize ['mə:tſəndaiz] koopwaar *v.*, waren *v. mv.*

merchant ['mə:tſənt] koopman, groothandelaar *m.*; (*Am.*) winkelier *m.*

merchant-man ['mə:tſəntmən] koopvaardijschip *o.*

merchant-marine ['mə:tſəntmə'rīn] koopvaardijvloot *v.*

merchant-service ['mə:tſəntsə:vis] handelsvloot, koopvaardijvloot *v.*; koopvaardijvaart *v.*

merciful (ly) ['mə:siful(i)] *adj.* (*adv.*) genadig, barmhartig.

merciless (ly) ['mə:silis(li)] *adj.* (*adv.*) meedogenloos, onbarmhartig.

mercury ['mə:kjuri] kwik, kwikzilver *o.*

mercy ['mə:si] genade, barmhartigheid *v.*; weldaad *v.*, geluk *o.*, zegening *v.*

mere [mīə] *adj.* louter, zuiver, bloot, enkel; maar.

merely ['mīəli] *adv.* louter, enkel, alleen.

merge [mə:dʒ] *vt.* samensmelten (**in, into,** met); doen opgaan (in); laten samenvloeien; (*soms:*) indompelen; **be —d in,** opgaan in; *vi.* samenvloeien; zinken opgaan in; (*recht*) vervallen.

meridian [mi'ridiən] meridiaan *m.*, middaglijn *v.*, middagcirkel *m.*; hoogtepunt, culminatiepunt; toppunt *o.*

merit ['merit] *sb.* verdienste *v.*; **—s,** ook: (het) eigenlijke, (het) essentiële; *vt.* verdienen; *vi.* **— well of,** zich verdienstelijk maken jegens.

meritorious (ly) [meri'to:riəs(li)] *adj.* (*adv.*) verdienstelijk.

mermaid ['mə:meid] meermin *v.*

merriment ['merimənt] vrolijkheid *v.*

merry ['meri] *adj.* vrolijk; prettig; lichtelijk aangeschoten; **make —,** pret maken; vrolijk zijn.

merry-andrew ['meri'ændrû] hansworst, paljas, clown *m.*

merry-go-round ['merigouraund] draaimolen, mallemolen *m.*

merry-maker ['merimeikə] pretmaker *m.*

mesh [meʃ] *sb.* maas *v.*; net, netwerk *o.*; (*fig.*) strik *m.*; *vt.* verstrikken; in de mazen van een net vangen; *vi.* verstrikt raken; (*v. tandraderen*) in elkaar grijpen.

mess [mes] *sb.* gerecht *o.*, schotel *m.*; spijs *v.*, voer *o.*; (*mil.*) menage *v.*; kantine *v.*; (*sch.*) bak *m.*; *vt.* bemorsen; bederven, verknoeien; te eten geven; *vi.* morsen; knoeien.

message ['mesidʒ] boodschap *v.*; tijding *v.*, bericht *o.*; officiële mededeling *v.*

messenger ['mesindʒə] boodschapper, koerier *m.*; bode *m.*; voorbode *m.*

messing-allowance ['mesiŋəlauəns] (*mil.*) menagegeld, tafelgeld *o.*

mess-mate ['mesmeit] tafelgenoot, disgenoot *m.*; (*sch.*) bakgast *m.*

mess-room ['mesrum] (*mil.*, *sch.*) eetzaal, eetkamer, eetkajuit *v.*

metabolism [me'tæbəlizm] stofwisseling *v.*

metal ['metl] *sb.* metaal *o.*; steenslag *o.*; glasspijs, glasspecie *v.*; scheepsgeschut *o.*; **—s**, spoorstaven; *vt.* (*v. schip*) bekleden; met metaal bedekken; (*v. weg*) verharden, begrinten; *adj.* metalen.

metallic [mi'tælik] metaalachtig; metalen, metaal—.

metalliferous [metə'lifərəs] metaalhoudend.

metallize ['metəlaiz] (*v. hout*) metalliseren; (*v. rubber*) vulcaniseren.

metallurgy [me'tælə:dʒi] metallurgie, metaalkunde *v.*; metaalbewerking *v.*

metamorphose [metə'mo:fouz] *vt.* herscheppen; van gedaante doen veranderen; *vi.* van gedaante veranderen.

metamorphosis [metə'mo:fəsis] gedaanteverwisseling *v.*

metaphor ['metəfə] beeldspraak, overdrachtelijke uitdrukking, metafoor *v.*

mete [mit] *sb.* maat *v.*; grens *v.*; *vt.* meten.

metempsychosis [metempsi'kousis] zielsverhuizing *v.*

meteor ['mitjə] meteoor *m.*

meteorologic(al) [mitjərə'lodʒik(l)] *adj.* meteorologisch, weerkundig.

methane ['meðein] methaan, moerasgas, mijngas *o.*

method ['meðəd] methode, werkwijze *v.*; orde, regelmaat *v.*

methodic(al) [mi'ðədik(l)] *adj.* methodisch.

methodize ['meðədaiz] methodisch behandelen.

meticulous(ly) [mi'tikjuləs(li)] *adj.* (*adv.*) erg precies, angstvallig nauwgezet.

metis ['mitis] mesties, halfbloed *m.*

metre ['mitə] dichtmaat, versmaat *v.*, metrum *o.*; meter *m.*

metropolis [mi'trəpəlis] hoofdstad *v.*; wereldstad *v.*

metropolitan [metrə'politən] *adj.* van de hoofdstad (wereldstad); metropolitaans, aartsbisschoppelijk; *sb.* metropolitaan, aartsbisschop *m.*

mettle ['metl] vuur *o.*, moed *m.*; aard *m.*, temperament *o.*; energie *v.*

Meuse [mjûz] Maas *v.*

mew [mjû] *sb.* meeuw *v.*

mew [mjû] *sb.* ruikooi *v.*; schuilplaats *v.*; gevangenis *v.*; *vt.* opsluiten; *vi.* ruien.

mew [mjû] *vi.* miauwen; *sb.* gemiauw *o.*

miaow [mi'au] *sb.* gemiauw *o.*; *vi.* miauwen.

miaul [mi'o:l] *sb.* gemiauw *o.*; *vi.* miauwen.

mica ['maikə] mica, glimmer *o.*

microbe ['maikroub] microbe *v.*

microphone ['maikrəfoun] microfoon *v.*

midday ['middei] middag *m.*

middle ['midl] *adj.* midden—, middel—, middelst, middelbaar, tussen—; *sb.* midden *o.*; (*v. lichaam*) middel *o.*; middelpunt *o.*; *vt.* in 't midden plaatsen; doormidden delen.

middle-class ['midl'klâs; 'midlklâs] *sb.* burgerklasse *v.*, middenstand *m.*; *adj.* van de middenstand, van de burgerklasse, burgerlijk.

middleman ['midlmæn] tussenpersoon *m.*

middlemost ['midlmoust] middelste.

middle-sized ['midlsaizd] van middelbare grootte.

middle-weight ['midlweit] (*sp.*: bokser, jockey*) middelgewicht *o.*

middling ['midliŋ] *adj.* & *adv.* middelmatig, redelijk, tamelijk; *sb.* **—s**, (*v. goederen*) middelsoort, middelmaat *v.*; (*veevoeder*) (rogge)meel en zemelen.

midge [midʒ] mug *v.*; (*fig.*) dwerg *m.*

midland ['midlənd] *sb.* binnenland, (het) midden *o.* van een land; *adj.* binnenlands.

mid-lent ['midlent] halfvasten *v.*

midnight ['midnait] *sb.* middernacht *m.*; *adj.* middernachtelijk.

midriff ['midrif] middenrif *o.*

midsea ['midsi] (*sch.*) volle zee *v.*

midshipman ['midʃipmən] (*sch.*) adelborst *m.*

midst [midst] *sb.* midden *o.*; *prep.* (*dicht.*) te midden van.

midstream ['midstrim] *sb.* midden *o.* van de stroom; *adv.* op stroom.

midway ['mid'wei] halfweg; halverwege, in 't midden.

midwife ['midwaif] vroedvrouw *v.*

miff [mif] *sb.* ruzietje *o.*; boze (nijdige) bui *v.*; *vi.* nijdig worden.

might [mait] macht, kracht *v.*, vermogen *o.*

mighty ['maiti] *adj.* machtig, sterk, vermogend; (*fam.*) kolossaal; **— works**, (*Bijb.*) wonderen; *adv.* ontzaglijk, verbazend, kolossaal, (alle)machtig; *sb.* machtige, grote *m.*

mignonette [minjə'net] reseda *v.*

migrate [mai'greit, [maigreit] verhuizen; trekken; zwerven.

migration [mai'greiʃən] verhuizing v.; trek m.

milch-cow ['miltʃkau] melkkoe v.

mild [maild] adj. zacht, zachtaardig; (v. ziekte) goedaardig; (v. middel) zachtwerkend; (v. sigaar, bier, enz.) licht; zwak, flauw.

mildew ['mildjû] sb. meeldauw m.; schimmel v.; vt. met meeldauw bedekken (besmetten); (doen) beschimmelen.

mildness ['maildnis] zachtheid, zachtaardigheid v.; goedaardigheid v.

mile [mail] (Engelse) mijl v.

milestone ['mailstoun] mijlsteen; mijlpaal m.

militancy ['militənsi] strijdlust m.

militant ['militənt] adj. strijdend, strijdlustig; sb. strijder m.

militarily ['militərili] adv. op soldatenmanier; gewapenderhand.

militarism ['militərizm] militarisme o.

military ['militəri] adj. militair; man, soldaat, krijgsman; sb. the —, de militairen, het leger.

milk [milk] sb. melk v.; vt. melken; melk doen in.

milk-glass ['milkglâs] matglas o.

milkman ['milkmən] melkboer m.

milksop ['milksɔp] lafbek, melkmuil m.

milky ['milki] melkachtig; (fig.) zoetsappig; zacht, teder.

mill [mil] sb. molen m.; tredmolen m.; fabriek; spinnerij v.; bokspartij v.; vt. malen, vermalen; vollen; (v. munt) kartelen; (sl.) ranselen, afranselen; vi. in het rond lopen.

millennial [mi'leniəl] duizendjarig; langdurig; blijvend.

miller ['milə] molenaar m.

milligram(me) ['miligræm] milligram o.

millilitre ['mililîtə] milliliter m.

millimetre ['milimîtə] millimeter m.

milliner ['milinə] modemaakster, hoedenmaakster, modiste v.

millinery ['milinəri] modevak o.; modezaak v.; (fig.) opschik m.

million ['miljən] miljoen o.

millstone ['milstoun] molensteen m.

milt [milt] milt, hom v.

mime [maim] sb. gebarenspel o.; gebarenspeler, mimicus m.; nabootser m.; vi. als gebarenspeler optreden, pantomime spelen; vt. door gebaren voorstellen; nabootsen.

mimic ['mimik] adj. mimisch, nabootsend; nagebootst; geveinsd, voorgewend, gehuicheld; sb. mimicus m.; nabootser m.; naäper m.; vt. mimeren; nabootsen; naäpen.

mimicry ['mimikri] mimiek v.; nabootsing v.; naäping v.; aanpassing v. (in kleur, enz.) aan de omgeving.

minacious [mi'neiʃəs] dreigend.

mince [mins] sb. fijn gehakt vlees o.; adj. fijngehakt; vt. fijn hakken; aan stukjes snijden, verdelen; bewimpelen,

verbloemen, vergoelijken; vi. gemaakt spreken; gemaakt lopen, trippelen.

mincing-machine ['minsiŋməʃîn] vleesmolen m.

mind [maind] sb. geest m., verstand o.; neiging, gezindheid v., lust m.; mening v.; gemoed o.; vt. bedenken, denken om; passen op, oppassen, verzorgen, zorgen voor; acht slaan op; in acht nemen; (v. machine) bedienen; vi. zich in acht nemen, op zijn tellen passen; om iets denken; vr. — oneself, zich in acht nemen.

minded ['maindid] gezind, geneigd; van zins; aangelegd, georiënteerd.

mindful ['maindful] indachtig; oplettend, opmerkzaam; behoedzaam, voorzichtig; be — of, denken om.

mindless ['maindlis] onoplettend, achteloos, nonchalant; geesteloos.

mine [main] pron. de mijne, het mijne; de mijnen; van mij; mijn.

mine [main] sb. mijn v.; (fig.) bron, schatkamer v.; vt. uithollen, uitgraven, ondermijnen; ontginnen, exploiteren; (v. steenkool, enz.) winnen; mijnen leggen; in de lucht laten vliegen; vi. delven, in de mijn(en) werken; mijnen leggen.

mine-field ['mainfîld] mijnenveld o.

miner ['mainə] mijnwerker m.; mijnenlegger m.; (mil.) mineur m.

mineral ['minərəl] adj. mineraal, delfstoffen—; sb. delfstof v., mineraal o.

mine-sweeper ['mainswîpə] mijnenveger m.

mingle ['miŋgl] mengen, vermengen; zich (ver)mengen.

miniate ['minieit] meniën.

miniature ['minjətʃə] sb. miniatuur v.; vt. in miniatuur voorstellen.

minify ['minifai] verkleinen, kleineren.

minimize ['minimaiz] tot een minimum herleiden (terugbrengen); verkleinen; geringachten; vergoelijken.

mining ['mainin] sb. mijnbouw, bergbouw m.; mijnwezen o.; mijnarbeid m.

mining-engineering ['maininendʒi'nîariŋ] mijnbouwkunde v.

mining-industry ['mainiŋindəstri] mijnbedrijf o., mijnbouw m.

minister ['ministə] sb. minister m.; dienaar m.; predikant m.; vt. verlenen; toedienen; (v. troost, enz.) verschaffen; vi. dienen; de dienst verrichten; — to, bijdragen tot; bevorderlijk zijn aan; verzorgen.

ministry ['ministri] ministerie o.; bediening v., dienst m.; evangeliebediening v.; medewerking, tussenkomst v.

minium ['miniəm] menie v.

minor ['mainə] adj. minder, geringer, kleiner; jonger; junior; minderjarig; (muz.) mineur; sb. minderjarige m.; mineur v. & m.; minderterm m.

minority [mai—, mi'nɔriti] minderheid v.; minderjarigheid v.

mint [mint] sb. (Pl.) munt, kruizemunt v.

mint [mint] *sb.* munt *v.*; *vt.* munten, aanmunten; smeden; fabriceren; verzinnen; *vi.* — *at*, munten op.

mint-drop ['mint'drɔp] pepermunt(je) *v.* (*o.*).

minuet [minju'et] menuet *o.*

minuscule [mi'nəskjûl] *adj.* klein; gering; *sb.* kleine letter *v.*

minute [mai'njût] *adj.* (zeer) klein; gering; minutieus, erg precies.

minute ['minit] *sb.* minuut *v.*; ogenblik *o.*; minuut *v.*, origineel *o.* (v. akte, enz.); memorandum *o.*; —*s*, notulen; *vt.* notuleren, in de notulen opnemen; ontwerpen; de tijd opnemen van.

minute-book ['minitbuk] notulenboek *o.*; kladboek *o.*

minute-hand ['minithænd] minuutwijzer *m.*

miracle ['mirəkl] wonder, mirakel *o.*

miracle-monger ['mirəklmɔŋgə] wonderdoener *m.*

miracle-play ['mirəklplei] mysteriespel *o.*

miracle-worker ['mirəklwə:kə] wonderdoener *m.*

miraculous (**ly**) [mi'rækjuləs(li)] *adj.* (*adv.*) wonderbaarlijk, wonderdadig, miraculeus.

mire [maiə] *sb.* modder *v.*, slik, slijk *o.*; *vt.* bemodderen; in moeilijkheden brengen; *vi.* in de modder zakken.

mirror ['mirə] *sb.* spiegel *m.*; toonbeeld *o.*; afspiegeling *v.*; *vt.* weerspiegelen, afspiegelen, weerkaatsen.

mirth [mə:ð] vrolijkheid, opgewektheid, lustigheid *v.*

mirthful (**ly**) ['mə:ðful(i)] *adj.* (*adv.*) vrolijk, opgewekt, lustig.

miry ['maiəri] modderig, slijkerig.

misadventure ['misəd'ventʃə] ongeluk *o.*, tegenspoed *m.*, ramp *v.*

misalliance ['misə'laiəns] ongelijk huwelijk *o.*, mesalliance *v.*

misanthrope ['mizənðroup] mensenhater *m.*

misapply ['misə'plai] verkeerd toepassen; (*v. geld*) verduisteren.

misapprehend ['misæpri'hend] misverstaan, verkeerd begrijpen.

misapprehension ['misæpri'henʃən] misverstand *o.*, misvatting *v.*

misbehave ['misbi'heiv] zich misdragen; —*d*, onopgevoed.

miscalculation ['miskælkju'leiʃən] misrekening; verkeerde berekening *v.*

miscall ['mis'kɔ:l] verkeerd noemen; (*dial.*) uitschelden.

miscarriage [mis'kærid3] mislukking *v.*; miskraam *v.*; (het) wegraken, (het) verloren gaan *o.*

miscarry [mis'kæri] mislukken, niet slagen; wegraken, verloren gaan.

miscellaneous [misi'leinjəs] gemengd; veelsoortig; afwisselend; veelzijdig.

mischance [mis'tʃâns] ongeluk *o.*

mischief ['mistʃif] onheil *o.*; kwaad, kattekwaad *o.*, streken *m. mv.*; rekel,

rakker *m.*; (*fam.*) duivel, drommel *m.*

mischief-maker ['mistʃifmeikə] onruststoker, tweedrachtzaaier; onheilstichter *m.*

mischievous (**ly**) ['mistʃivəs(li)] *adj.* (*adv.*) schadelijk, nadelig; ondeugend, boosaardig, moedwillig; noodlottig.

miscible ['misibl] (ver)mengbaar.

miscomprehend ['miskɔmpri'hend] verkeerd begrijpen.

misconception ['miskən'sepʃən] verkeerde opvatting, misvatting *v.*, misverstand *o.*; dwaalbegrip *o.*

misconduct ['miskən'dəkt] *vt.* slecht besturen, slecht beheren; verkeerd leiden; *vr.* — *oneself*, zich misdragen.

misconduct ['mis'kɔndəkt] *sb.* slecht bestuur, wanbeheer *o.*; wangedrag *o.*; overspel *o.*

miscount ['mis'kaunt] *vt.* verkeerd (op)tellen; *vi.* zich vertellen, zich verrekenen; *sb.* verkeerde telling *v.*

miscreant ['miskriənt] *adj.* ongelovig; laag, gemeen; *sb.* ongelovige *m.*; onverlaat, schurk *m.*

misdeal ['mis'dîl] *vi.* de kaarten verkeerd geven; *sb.* (het) verkeerd geven *o.*

misdemeanour ['misdi'mînə] vergrijp, misdrijf *o.*; wangedrag *o.*, wandaad *v.*

misdoubt ['mis'daut] wantrouwen, verdenken; betwijfelen; vrezen, vermoeden.

misemploy ['misem'plɔi] misbruiken.

miser ['maizə] gierigaard, vrek *m.*

miserable ['mizərəbl] *adj.* ellendig, rampzalig, diep ongelukkig; droevig, jammerlijk, beroerd; *sb.* rampzalige, ongelukkige *m.*

miserliness ['maizəlinis] gierigheid, vrekkigheid *v.*

misery ['mizɔri] ellende, rampzaligheid *v.*; (*kaartsp.*) misère *v.*

misfire ['mis'faiə] *sb.* ketsschot *o.*; *vi.* ketsen, weigeren; (*v. motor*) overslaan; (*v. komplot, enz.*) mislukken.

misfit ['mis'fit] *sb.* slecht (niet) passend kledingstuk *o.*; (het) niet passen *o.*; *adj.* niet passend; ongeschikt; *vi.* niet passen.

misform ['mis'fo:m] misvormen.

misfortune [mis'fo:tʃən] ongeluk *o.*

misgiving [mis'giviŋ] bange twijfel *m.*, angstig voorgevoel *o.*, bezorgdheid *v.*; argwaan *m.*

misguide ['mis'gaid] verkeerd leiden; misleiden, op een dwaalspoor brengen.

mishap ['mis'hæp] ongeluk, ongeval *o.*

mishmash ['miʃmæʃ] mengelmoes *o.*, hutspot *v.*

misintelligence ['misin'telid3əns] verkeerde inlichting *v.*; verkeerde opvatting *v.*, misverstand *o.*

misjudge ['mis'd3əd3] *vt.* verkeerd beoordelen; *vi.* verkeerd oordelen.

mislead [mis'lîd] misleiden, op een dwaalspoor brengen; bedriegen.

misogynist [mai—, mi'sɔd3inist] vrouwenhater *m.*

misplace ['mis'pleis] verkeerd plaatsen, misplaatsen.
misprint ['mis'print] *vt.* verkeerd drukken; *sb.* drukfout *r.*
misprize ['mis'praiz] onderschatten.
misproportion ['mispra'po:ʃən] wanverhouding *v.*
misrepresent ['misrepri'zent] verkeerd voorstellen (uitleggen).
miss [mis] *sb.* (me)juffrouw *v.*
miss [mis] *vt.* missen; misslaan; mislopen; (*v. school, gelegenheid, enz.*) verzuimen; *vi.* missen; mis schieten; verzuimen; (*v. motor*) haperen; *sb.* misslag *m.*; misstoot *m.*; misschot *o.*; gemis *o.*
mis-shapen ['mis'ʃeipn] misvormd, mismaakt, wanstaltig.
mission ['miʃən] zending, missie *v.*; zendingspost *m.*; gezantschap *o.*; boodschap *v.*; roeping *v.*
missionary ['miʃənər] missionaris, zendeling *m.*
missish ['misiʃ] jongedamesachtig, juffertjesachtig, preuts.
missive ['misiv] missive *v.*, zendbrief *m.*
mist [mist] *sb.* mist, nevel *m.*; motregen *m.*; waas *o.*; *vt.* benevelen.
mistake [mis'teik] *vt.* misverstaan, verkeerd verstaan (begrijpen, opvatten); zich vergissen in; **— for,** ten onrechte aanzien voor; *vi.* zich vergissen; *sb.* vergissing *v.*; misslag *m.*, dwaling, fout *v.*; misverstand *o.*
mistaken [mis'teikn] *adj.* verkeerd, onjuist; foutief; misplaatst; verkeerd begrepen; mislukt.
mistakenly [mis'teiknli] *adv.* verkeerdelijk; bij vergissing.
mister ['mistə] mijnheer; (geschreven: **Mr.**).
mistletoe ['misltou, 'mizltou] maretak *m.*, vogellijm *v.*
mistress ['mistris] meesteres *v.*; gebiedster, heerseres *v.*; onderwijzeres *v.*; minnares *v.*; mevrouw *v.*
mistrust ['mis'trəst] *vt.* wantrouwen; *sb.* wantrouwen *o.*
misty ['misti] *adj.* mistig, nevelachtig; beneveld, wazig.
misunderstanding ['misəndə'stændiŋ] misverstand *o.*, misvatting *v.*, geschil *o.*
misuse [mis'jûs] *sb.* verkeerd gebruik *o.*; misbruik *o.*; *vt.* [mis'jûz] verkeerd gebruiken; misbruiken; mishandelen.
mite [mait] mijt, kaasmijt *v.*; penning *m.*; kleinigheid *v.*, ziertje *o.*
mitigate ['mitigeit] verzachten, lenigen, verlichten; **—d,** (*v. ziekte*) goedaardig.
mitre ['maitə] *sb.* mijter *m.*; (*bouwk.*) verstek *o.*, hoek *m.* van 45°; schoorsteenkap *v.*; *vt.* de mijter opzetten; in 't verstek (be)werken.
mitt(en) ['mit(n)] want *v.*, vuisthandschoen *m.*
mix [miks] *vt.* mengen, vermengen; (*v. salade*) aanmaken; (*v. medicament, enz.*) klaarmaken; door elkaar gooien;

vi. zich vermengen; **— with,** ook: omgaan met; *sb.* mengsel *o.*
mixture ['mikstʃə] mengsel *o.*, mengeling *v.*; drankje *o.*
mizzle ['mizl] *sb.* motregen *m.*; *vi.* motregenen.
moan [moun] *vi.* kreunen, kermen, steunen; jammeren; *vt.* betreuren, bejammeren; *sb.* gekreun, gekerm *o.*; geklaag, gejammer *o.*
moat [mout] gracht *v.* (om kasteel, enz.).
mob [mɔb] *sb.* gepeupel, janhagel, gespuis *o.*; troep *m.*, bende *v.*; volkshoop *m.*, volksmenigte *v.*; *vt.* hinderlijk volgen, nalopen; omstuwen, omringen, zich verdringen om; *vi.* samenscholen.
mobile ['moub(a)il] beweeglijk; (*mil.*) mobiel; (*v. kapitaal*) vlottend.
mobilization [moubilai'zeiʃən] mobilisatie *v.*
mobilize ['moubilaiz] mobiliseren.
mock [mɔk] *sb.* bespotting *v.*, voorwerp *o.* van spot; nabootsing, naäping *v.*; *adj.* nagemaakt, onecht, vals; voorgewend, huichelachtig; zogenaamd; *vt.* bespotten, spotten met; tarten; naäpen; voor de gek houden.
mocker ['mɔkə] spotter *m.*; spotvogel *m.*
mockery ['mɔkəri] spotternij, bespotting *v.*, spot *m.*
mocking-bird ['mɔkiŋbə:d] (*Dk.*) spotvogel *m.*
mock-orange ['mɔk'ɔrindʒ] (*Pl.*) boerenjasmijn *v.*
mock-velvet ['mɔkvelvit] trijpfluweel *o.*
mode [moud] wijze, manier *v.*; vorm *m.*; mode *v.*; (*muz.*) toonaard *m.*, toonsoort *v.*
mode-book ['moudbuk] modejournaal *o.*
model ['mɔdl] *sb.* model, voorbeeld, toonbeeld *o.*; (*tn.*) mal *m.*, patrijs *v.*; *adj.* model—; *vt.* modelleren, boetseren; vormen (naar een bepaald model).
moderate ['mɔdərit] *adj.* matig, gematigd; middelmatig; *sb.* gematigde *m.*; ['mɔdəreit] *vt.* matigen, stillen, doen bedaren; presideren; *vi.* zich matigen, bedaren; kalmer worden; presideren.
modern ['mɔdən] modern, nieuw, nieuwerwets, hedendaags.
modest(ly) [mɔdist(li)] *adj.* (*adv.*) bescheiden, ingetogen, zedig, eerbaar.
modesty ['mɔdisti] bescheidenheid, ingetogenheid, zedigheid, eerbaarheid *v.*
modification [mɔdifi'keiʃən] wijziging, verandering *v.*; matiging, verzachting *v.*; beperking *v.*
modifier ['mɔdifaiə] wijziger *m.*; (*gram.*) beperkend bijwoord *o.*
modify ['mɔdifai] wijzigen, veranderen; matigen, verzachten; beperken; (*gram.*) bepalen.
modish ['moudiʃ] modisch, modieus; fatterig.
modist ['moudist] modeheer, fat *m.*

modulate ['mɔdjuleit] (*muz.*) moduleren; regelen.

moil [moil] zwoegen, sloven.

moist [moist] vochtig, nattig, klam.

moisten ['moisn] bevochtigen.

moisture ['moistfə] vochtigheid *v.*, vocht *o.*

molar ['moulə] *adj.* malend; *sb.* maaltand *m.*

molasses [mə'kesiz] melasse, suikerstroop *v.*

mole [moul] *sb.* mol *m.*; moedervlek *v.*; havendam *m.*; keerdam *m.*; *ct.* ondergraven.

mole-cricket ['moulkrikit] veenmol, aardkrekel *m.*

molecule ['moulikjûl] molecule *v.* & *o.* stofdeeltje *o.*

mole-hill ['moulhil] molshoop *m.*

moleskin ['moulskin] mollevel *o.*; Engels leer *o.*

molest [mo'lest] molesteren, lastig vallen, overlast aandoen.

mollify ['mɔlifai] verzachten, week maken; vertederen, vermurwen.

mollusc ['mɔləsk] weekdier *o.*

moment ['moumənt] ogenblik, moment *o.*; gewicht, belang *o.*; **this —,** ogenblikkelijk; daarnet, zoëven, een minuut geleden.

momentary ['mouməntəri] *adj.* kortstondig, vluchtig; van een ogenblik, een ogenblik durend.

momentous [mou'mentəs] gewichtig, van belang.

monachism ['mɔnəkizm] kloosterleven, monniksleven *o.*; kloosterwezen *o.*

monarch ['mɔnək] monarch; vorst *m.*, vorstin *v.*; koning *m.*, koningin *v.*

monarchal [mo'nâkl] vorstelijk.

monarchie(al) [mo'nâkik(l)] *adj.* monarchaal.

monarchy ['mɔnəki] monarchie; eenhoofdige regering *v.*

monastery ['mɔnəstri] (mannen)klooster *o.*

Monday ['məndi] maandag *m.*

monetary ['mənitəri] geldelijk; munt—.

monetize ['mɔnitaiz] aanmunten.

money ['məni] *sb.* geld *o.*; *ct.* munten; te gelde maken.

money-box ['mənibɔks] spaarpot *m.*; collectebus *v.*

money-grub(ber) ['mənigrʌd(ə)] geldwolf, schraper *m.*

money-lender ['mənilendə] geldschieter *m.*

moneyless ['mənilis] geldeloos, zonder geld.

money-order ['mənio:də] postwissel *m.*

mongrel ['mɔngrəl] *sb.* (*Dk.*, *Pl.*) bastaard *m.*; *adj.* van gemengd ras, bastaard —.

monition [mou'nifən] vermaning *v.*; waarschuwing *v.*; dagvaarding *v.*

monitor ['mɔnitə] vermaner *m.*; monitor *v.*

monk [mɔŋk] monnik *m.*; (*Dk.*) zeeduivel *m.*

monkey ['mɔŋki] *sb.* (*Dk.*) aap *m.*; apekop *m.*; heiblok, heitoestel *o.*; *vt.* naäpen; voor de gek houden; *ri.* morrelen; streken uithalen; zich bemoeien (**with,** met).

monkey-meat ['mɔŋkimit] (*Am.*, *sl.*) vlees *o.* in blik.

monkey-spanner ['mɔŋkispænə] Engelse sleutel *m.*

monocle ['mɔnəkl] monocle *v.*, oogglas *o.*

monologue ['mɔnələg] alléénspraak *v.*

monoplane ['mɔnəplein] (*vl.*) ééndekker *m.*

monopolize [mə'nɔpəlaiz] monopoliseren; geheel in beslag nemen.

monopoly [mə'nɔpəli] monopolie *o.*, alleenhandel *m.*

monotone ['mɔnətoun] *adj.* eentonig; *sb.* eentonigheid *v.*

monotonous(ly) [mə'nɔtənəs(li)] *adj.* (*adv.*) eentonig.

monotony [mə'nɔtəni] eentonigheid *v.*

monotype ['mɔnətaip] zetmachine *v.*

monster ['mɔnstə] monster, gedrocht *o.*

monstrance ['mɔnstrəns] monstrans *m.*

monstrosity [mɔns'trɔsiti] monster, wangedrocht *o.*; monsterachtigheid *v.*

monstrous ['mɔnstrəs] *adj.* monsterachtig, gedrochtelijk, afschuwelijk.

month [mənð] maand *v.*

monthly ['mənðli] *adj.* maandelijks; *adv.* maandelijks; *sb.* maandblad, maandschrift *o.*

monument ['mɔnjumənt] monument, gedenkteken *o.*

mood [mûd] stemming, luim *v.*, humeur *o.*; wijze *v.*; (*gram.*) wijs *v.*

moody ['mûdi] *adj.* humeurig, gemelijk; somber gestemd, zwaarmoedig.

moon [mûn] *sb.* maan *v.*; (*dicht.*) maand *v.*; *ri.* dromen, (zitten) suffen; **about** rondslenteren; *rt.* **— away one's time,** zijn tijd versuffen (verdromen).

moonlight ['mûnlait] maanlicht *o.*, maneschijn *m.*

moonshiner ['mûnʃainə] dranksmokkelaar, clandestiene jeneverstoker *m.*

moon-struck ['mûnstrək] maanziek.

moor [muə] *sb.* heide *v.*; *rt.* (*sch.*) vastmeren, vastleggen, vertuien.

moorage ['muəridʒ] ankerplaats *v.*; ankergeld *o.*

moor-fowl ['muəfaul] korhoen(ders) *o.* (*mv.*).

mooring-mast ['muəriŋmâst] (*v. luchtschip*) ankermast, landingsmast *m.*

moot [mût] *sb.* dispuut, debat *o.*; *adj.* betwistbaar; *rt.* ter sprake brengen; (*v. vraag*) opwerpen.

mop [mɔp] *sb.* stokdweil, zwabber *m.*; *rt.* dweilen, zwabberen; vegen; afwissen.

mop [mɔp] *sb.* grimas *v.*; *ri.* gezichten trekken.

mope [moup] *ri.* kniezen, druilen, mokken; *rt.* **— away one's life,** zijn leven verkniezen; *vr.* — *oneself to death,* zich dood kniezen; *sb.* kniesoor, druiloor *m.*

mope-eyed ['moup'aid] bijziende.

moral ['mɔrəl] *adj.* moreel, zedelijk; zedenkundig; zeden—; *sb.* zedenles, moraal *v.*; zedenleer *v.*; (*pop.*) evenbeeld *o.*; (*sl.*) zekerheid, uitgemaakte zaak *v.*; —**s,** zeden; zedelijk gedrag.

morality [mɔ'ræliti] zedelijkheid *v.*; zedenleer *v.*; zedelijk gedrag *o.*; zinnespel *o.*, moraliteit *v.*

morass [mə'ræs] moeras *o.*

morbid ['mo:bid] *adj.* ziekelijk; ziekte—.

morbific [mo:'bifik] ziekteveroorzakend; ziekte—.

mordacious [mo:'deiʃəs] bijtend, scherp, vinnig.

mordacity [mo:'dæsiti] bijtendheid, scherpheid, vinnigheid *v.*

mordant ['m:dənt] *adj.* bijtend, scherp, sarcastisch; *sb.* bijtmiddel; beitsmiddel *o.*; (*bij 't vergulden*) fixeermiddel, hechtmiddel *o.*; *vt.* beitsen.

more [mo:] meer, meerder; *no* —, niet meer, niet langer; — *and* —, meer en meer; hoe langer hoe meer; *once* —, nog eens.

morello [mo'relou] morel, zure kers *v.*

moreover [mo:'rouvə] bovendien, daarenboven.

moribund ['mɔribənd] *adj.* zieltogend, stervend; *sb.* stervende, zieltogende *m.*

morning ['mo:niŋ] morgen, ochtend; morgenstond *m.*; vóórmiddag *m.*

morning-dress ['mo:niŋ'dres] jacquetcostuum, colbertcostuum *o.*

morning-gown ['mo:niŋgaun] sjamberloek *m.*; ochtendjapon *v.*

morning-prayer ['mo:niŋprêə] morgengebed *o.*; (*prot.: anglicaans*) voormiddagdienst *m.*

morocco [mə'rɔkou] marokijn(leder) *o.*

morose(ly) [mə'rous(li)] *adj.* (*adv.*) knorrig, gemelijk.

morphia ['mo:fje] morfine *v.*

morphine ['mo:fin] morfine *v.*

morrow ['mɔrou] volgende dag.

morsel ['mo:səl] beet *m.*, hapje, stukje, brokje *o.*

mortal ['mo:tl] *adj.* sterfelijk; dodelijk; *adv.* (*pop.*) verschrikkelijk, ontzettend; *sb.* sterveling *m.*

mortality [mo:'tæliti] sterfelijkheid *v.*; sterfte *v.*; sterftecijfer *o.*; stoffelijk overschot *o.*

mortar ['mo:tə] *sb.* vijzel *m.*; (*mil.*) mortier *m.*; mortel, metselkalk *v.*; *vt.* met mortel pleisteren.

mortgage ['mo:gidʒ] *sb.* hypotheek *v.*; *vt.* (ver)hypothekeren; verpanden.

mortgage-bank ['mo:gidʒbæŋk] hypotheekbank *v.*

mortgage-bond ['mo:gidʒbɔnd] pandbrief *m.*

mortgagee [mo:gi'dʒi] hypotheekhouder, hypothecaire crediteur *m.*

mortgager ['mo:gidʒə] hypotheeknemer, hypothecaire debiteur *m.*

mortification [mo:tifi'keiʃən] (zelf)kastijding, (zelf)tuchtiging *v.*; versterving *v.*; grievende vernedering *v.*

mortify ['mo:tifai] *vt.* kastijden, tuchtigen; vernederen, verootmoedigen; ergeren; *vi.* afsterven; door koudvuur aangetast worden.

mosaic [mo'zeiik] mozaiek *o.*

mosque [mɔsk] moskee *v.*

mosquito [mɔs'kitou] muskiet *v.*

mosquito-bar [mɔs'kitoubâ] muskietengordijn, muskietennet *o.*

mosquito-craft [mɔs'kitoukrâft] kleine lichte oorlogsschepen.

mosquito-net [mɔs'kitounet] muskietennet *o.*

moss [mɔs] *sb.* mos *o.*; moeras *o.*; laagveen *o.*; *vt.* met mos bedekken.

moss-clad ['mɔsklæd] met mos begroeid, bemost.

moss-litter ['mɔslitə] turfstrooisel *o.*

moss-rose ['mɔs'rouz] mosroos *v.*

most [moust] *adj.* meest; grootst; *adv.* meest; hoogst; zeer.

mostly ['moustli] *adv.* meestal, meestendeels, grotendeels, voornamelijk.

moth [mɔθ] mot *v.*

mother ['mʌθə] moeder *v.*; moer *v.*, droesem *m.*

mother-country ['mʌθəkʌntri] moederland *o.*

motherhood ['mʌθəhud] moederschap *o.*

mother-in-law ['mʌθərinlo:] schoonmoeder *v.*

motherly ['mʌθəli] moederlijk, als een moeder.

mother-tongue ['mʌθətɔŋ] moedertaal *v.*; stamtaal, grondtaal *v.*

motif [mou'tif] motief *o.*

motion ['mouʃən] *sb.* beweging *v.*; voorstel *o.*, motie *v.*; gebaar *o.*, wenk *m.*; *vt.* wenken; door een beweging te kennen geven (dat); *vi.* wenken; bewegingen maken.

motionless ['mouʃənlis] bewegingloos, onbeweeglijk.

motion-pictures ['mouʃənpiktʃez] bioscoop *m.* & *v.*

motivate ['moutiveit] motiveren; aanzetten, aandrijven.

motive ['moutiv] *sb.* beweegreden *v.*, beweeggrond *m.*, motief *o.*; *adj.* bewegend, beweeg—, bewegings—; *vt.* motiveren; gronden, rechtvaardigen.

motley ['mɔtli] *adj.* bont, geschakeerd; gemengd; *sb.* bonte mengeling *v.*; narrenpak *o.*

motor ['moutə] *sb.* motor *m.*; beweger *m.*; beweegkracht *v.*; drijfkracht *v.*; auto *v.*; bewegende spier *v.*; motorische zenuw *v.*; *adj.* bewegend, bewegings—; *vi.* auto rijden; *vt.* met een auto vervoeren.

motor-bicycle ['moutəbaisikl] motorfiets *v.*

motor-bike ['moutəbaik] (*fam.*) motorfiets *v.*

motor-car ['moutəkâ] auto *v.*, automobiel *m.*; (*v. tram*) motorwagen *m.*

motor-cyclist ['moutəsaiklist] motorrijder *m.*

motorist ['moutərist] automobilist *m.*

motor-lorry ['moutələri] vrachtauto *v.*

motor-man ['mountəmæn] chauffeur *m.*; (*v. el. tram of trein*) wagenbestuurder *m.*

motor-spirit ['moutəspirit] benzine *v.*

motor-truck ['moutətrɔk] vrachtauto *v.*

motor-van ['moutəvæn] vrachtauto *v.*

motto ['mɔtou] motto *o.*, zinspreuk *v.*; (*wap.*) devies *o.*, wapenspreuk *v.*

mould [mould] *sb.* losse aarde, teelaarde, pootaarde *v.*; (*dicht.*) stof *o.*; schimmel *v.*; *vt.* aanaarden, met teelaarde bedekken; doen beschimmelen; *vi.* beschimmelen.

mould [mould] *sb.* vorm, gietvorm *m.*; matrijs *v.*; vorming *v.*; aard *m.*, gesteldheid *v.*; *vt.* vormen; modelleren; kneden; boetseren; gieten; lijsten.

moulder ['mouldə] *sb.* vormer; kneder; gieter *m.*

moulder ['mouldə] *vi.* verbrokkelen, verkruimelen, vermolmen, tot stof vergaan.

mouldy ['mouldi] *adj.* beschimmeld; vermolmd, half vergaan; (*fig.: v. mop*, enz.) afgezaagd; beroerd, vervelend; *sb.* (*sl.*) torpedo *v.*

moult [moult] *vi.* ruien, verharen; vervellen; *sb.* (het) ruien, (het) verharen *o.*; vervelling *v.*

mount [maunt] *sb.* berg *m.*; (*v. hand*) muis *v.*; rijpaard, rijdier *o.*; (*sp.: bij wedren*) rit *m.*; montuur *v. & o.*; *vt.* bestijgen, beklimmen; opgaan; opvaren; (*v. diamant*) zetten; (*v. kanon, enz.*) opstellen; monteren; *vi.* klimmen, stijgen; rijzen; opstijgen, de hoogte ingaan; (*v. mist*) optrekken; — (*up*), (*v. uitgaven, enz.*) oplopen.

mountable ['mauntəbl] beklimbaar, bestijgbaar.

mountain ['mauntin] berg *m.*

mountaineer [maunti'niə] *sb.* bergbewoner *m.*; bergbeklimmer *m.*; *vi.* bergen beklimmen.

mountainous ['mauntinəs] bergachtig; berg—; hemelhoog, kolossaal.

mountebank ['mauntibæŋk] kwakzalver *m.*

mounting ['mauntiŋ] montering, opstelling *v.*; montuur *v.*; beslag *o.*; affuit *o.*

mourn [mɔ:n] *vi.* treuren, rouwen, rouw dragen; *vt.* betreuren, bewenen.

mournful (**ly**) ['mɔ:nful(i)] *adj.* (*adv.*) treurig, droevig.

mourning ['mɔ:niŋ] (het) treuren *o.*; droefheid *v.*; rouw *m.*, rouwgewaad *o.*, rouwkleding *v.*

mourning-wear ['mɔ:niŋwêə] rouwkleding *v.*

mouse [maus] *sb.* muis *v.*; (*sl.*) blauw oog *o.*, buil *v.*; [mauz] *vi.* muizen, muizen vangen; snuffelen.

mouser ['mauzə] muizevanger *m.*, muiskat *v.*

mousetrap ['maustræp] muizeval *v.*

moustache [məs—, mus'tâʃ] snor *v.*, knevel *m.*

mouth [mauδ] *sb.* mond *m.*; muil, bek *m.*; monding *v.*; opening *v.*; woordvoerder *m.*; *vt.* in de mond nemen; met de bek grijpen; uitgalmen, declameren; (*fig.*) aanblaffen; *vi.* schetteren, galmen, declameren; gezichten trekken.

mouthful ['mauδful] mondvol *m.*

mouth-piece ['mauδpis] mondstuk *o.*; (*tel.*) hoorn *m.*; woordvoerder *m.*, spreekbuis *v.*

mouthy ['mauθi] galmend, schetterend, bombastisch.

movable ['mûvəbl] *adj.* beweeglijk, beweegbaar; (*v. rib*) zwevend; *sb.* meubelstuk *o.*; —**s**, roerende goederen.

move [mûv] *sb.* beweging *v.*; (*bij spel*, enz.) zet *m.*; slag *m.*; stap *m.*; verhuizing *v.*; *vt.* bewegen, in beweging brengen; verzetten, verschuiven; verleggen, verplaatsen; *vi.* zich bewegen; in beweging komen, zich in beweging zetten; verhuizen.

movement ['mûvmənt] beweging *v.*; voortgang *m.*; (*mil.*) afmars *m.*

movies ['mûviz] (*fam.*) bioscoop *m. & v.*; (*mil.*) zoeklichten *o. mv.*

moving ['mûviŋ] *adj.* bewegend; beweegbaar; aandoenlijk, roerend.

mow [mau] *sb.* hooiberg, opper *m.*; plaats *v.* in schuur voor hooi, graan, enz.

mow [mou] *vt.* maaien; *sb.* hooischelf *v.*

mower ['mouə] maaier *m.*

much [mətʃ] veel; zeer, erg; verreweg; — *the same*, vrijwel hetzelfde; *nothing* —, niet veel bijzonders.

muck [mək] (natte) mest *m.*; vuiligheid, smeerlapperij *v.*; rommel *m.*; *vt.* bemesten; — (*up*), bevuilen; (*sl.*) verknoeien.

mucous ['mjûkəs] slijmig.

mucus ['mjûkəs] slijm *o.*

mud [məd] *sb.* modder *v.*, slijk *o.*; leem *o.*; *vt.* bemodderen; vertroebelen.

mud-bath ['mədbâδ] modderbad *o.*

muddle ['mədl] *sb.* modder *v.*; warboel, janboel *m.*; *vt.* benevelen, bedwelmen; vertroebelen; verknoeien; *vi.* modderen; ploeteren.

muddle-head ['mədlhed] warhoofd *o.*, domkop *m.*

muddy ['mədi] modderig; bemodderd; troebel; dof, wazig; onduidelijk.

mud-flat ['mədflæt] modderbank *v.*, wad *o.*; baggerboot *v.*

mud-guard ['mədgâd] spatbord *o.*

mud-scraper ['mədskreipə] voetenschrapper *m.*

muff [məf] *sb.* mof *m.*; sul, suffer, sufkop *m.*, uilskuiken *o.*; *vt.* bederven, verknoeien.

muffle ['məfl] *sb.* moffel; moffeloven *m.*; bokshandschoen *m.*; dwanghandschoen *m.*; klankdemper *m.*; *vt.* inwikkelen, inpakken; inbakeren; instoppen, toedekken; dempen; *vi.* mompelen.

muffler ['məflə] das *v.*; sluier *m.*; omslagdoek *m.*; bokshandschoen *m.*; geluiddemper *m.*

mufti ['məfti] *in* —, in burgerkleren.

muggy ['məgi] drukkend, zwoel, broeierig, benauwd; duf.

mulberry ['məlbəri] moerbezie *v.*; moerbezieboom *m.*

mulct [məlkt] *sb.* geldboete *v.*; *vt.* beboeten; — *of,* beroven van.

mule [mjûl] muildier *o.*; (*Dk., Pl.*) bastaard *m.*; (*fig.*) stijfkop, dwarskop *m.*; muiltje *o.*, pantoffel *v.*

mullein ['məlin] (*Pl.*) koningskaars *v.*

multifarious [məlti'fêəriəs] veelsoortig, velerlei, verscheiden.

multilateral [məlti'lætərəl] veelzijdig.

multiple ['məltipl] *adj.* veelvuldig; veelvoudig, veelsoortig, velerlei; *sb.* veelvoud *o.*

multiplex ['məltipleks] meervoudig, veelvoudig; veelvuldig.

multiplication [məltipli'keiʃən] vermenigvuldiging *v.*

multiply ['məltiplai] *vt.* vermenigvuldigen *vi.* zich vermenigvuldigen.

multitude ['məltitjûd] menigte, massa *v.*, groot aantal *o.*; *the* —, de grote hoop.

mumble ['məmbl] *vi.* mompelen; mummelen; *vt.* prevelen; knauwen (aan); *sb.* gemompel *o.*

mumbler ['məmblə] mompelaar *m.*; prevelaar *m.*

mummy ['məmi] mummie *v.*; moes *o.*, pulp *v.*; (*fam.*) maatje, moesje *v.* & *o.*

munch ['mənʃ] knabbelen, knauwen; smakkend eten, hoorbaar kauwen.

mundane ['məndein] werelds, mondain; aards; kosmisch, van 't heelal.

municipal [mju'nisipəl] gemeentelijk, stedelijk.

municipality [mjunisi'pæliti] gemeente *v.* gemeentebestuur *o.*

munificence [mju nifisəns] mildheid, milddadigheid, vrijge vigheid *v.*

munificent (ly) [mju nifisənt(li)] *adj.* (*adv.*) mild, milddadig, vrijgevig.

muniment-room ['mjûniməntrum] archief *o.*

munition [mju'niʃən] *sb.* munitie *v.*, krijgsvoorraad *m.*; *vt.* van munitie voorzien; *vi.* munitie maken.

murder ['mə:də] *sb.* moord *m.*; *vt.* vermoorden; verknoeien.

murderer ['mə:dərə] moordenaar *m.*

murderous ['mə:dərəs] moorddadig.

mure [mjûə] ommuren; — (*up*), opsluiten (tussen vier muren); — *up,* dichtmetselen.

muriatic [mjûəri'ætik] (*H.*) zout—.

murky ['mə:ki] duister, donker, somber; triest.

murmur ['mə:mə] *vi.* mompelen; mop-

peren, morren; murmelen; ruisen; suizen; *sb.* gemompel *o.*; gemopper, gemor *o.*; gemurmel; geruis; gesuis *o.*

murmurer ['mə:mərə] mopperaar *m.*

muscadel [məskə'del] muskadeldruif *v.*; muskadelpeer *v.*; muskaatwijn *m.*

muscle ['məsl] spier *v.*; spierkracht *v.*

muscular ['məskjulə] gespierd.

muse [mjûz] muze, zanggodin *v.*

muse [mjûz] *vi.* peinzen, mijmeren; — *on,* overpeinzen, overdenken; *sb.* gemijmer *o.*

musette [mju'zet] doedelzak *m.*

museum [mju'ziəm, mju'zîəm] museum *o.*

mush [məʃ] moes *o.*, pulp *v.*; (*Am.*) (maïs)pap *v.*

mushroom ['məʃrum] paddestoel *m.*; parvenu *m.*; (*sl.*) paraplu *v.*; *adj.* parvenuachtig; nieuwbakken.

mushroom-company ['məʃrumkəmpəni] zwendelmaatschappij *v.*

music [mjûzik] muziek *v.*

musical ['mjûzikl] muzikaal; welluidend; muziek—.

musically ['mjûzikəli] *adv.* muzikaal, in muzikaal opzicht.

music-case ['mjûzikkeis] muziektas *v.*; muziekkastje *o.*

music-hall ['mjûzikho:l] variététheater *o.*; (*Am.*) concertzaal *v.*

musician [mju'ziʃən] toonkunstenaar, musicus; muzikant *m.*

music-master ['mjûzikmâstə] muziekleraar, muziekmeester *m.*

music-room ['mjûzikrum] muzieksalon *o.*; concertzaal *v.* [je *o.*

music-stool ['mjûzikstûl] pianokrukmusk [məsk] *sb.* muskus *v.*; muskusdier *o.*; *vt.* met muskus parfumeren.

musket ['məskit] musket *o.*, snaphaan *m.*; geweer *o.*

musk-rat ['məsk'ræt] muskusrat, bisamrat *v.* [neteldoek *o.*

muslin ['məzlin] mousseline *v.* & *o.*,

musquash ['məskwoʃ] muskusrat *v.*

mussel ['məsl] mossel *v.*

mussy ['məsi] wanordelijk; rommelig; slordig, vuil.

must [məst] moet, moeten; moest, moesten.

mustard ['məstəd] mosterd *m.*

muster ['məstə] *sb.* monstering *v.*; (*mil.*) inspectie, wapenschouwing *v.*; monsterrol *v.*; (*H.*) monster *o.*; verzameling, opkomst *v.*; *vt.* monsteren; oproepen; verzamelen; bij elkaar brengen (krijgen).

musty ['məsti] *adj.* beschimmeld; schimmelig; muf, duf; suf (van ouderdom); verouderd, afgezaagd.

mutable ['mjûtəbl] veranderlijk, ongedurig, wispelturig, onbestendig.

mutation [mju'teiʃən] verandering *v.*; klankwijziging *v.*; (*wet.*) mutatie *v.*

mute [mjût] *adj.* stom, sprakeloos, zwijgend; *sb.* stomme *m.*; stomme letter *v.*, stemloze medeklinker *m.*; figurant *m.*

muteness ['mjûtnis] stomheid v., zwijgen, stilzwijgen o.
mutilate ['mjûtileit] verminken.
mutilation [mjûti'leifən] verminking v.
mutineer [mjûti'niə] sb. muiter, muiteling, oproermaker, oproerling m.; vi. aan 't muiten slaan.
mutinous(**ly**) ['mjûtinəs(li)] adj. (adv.) muitziek, oproerig, opstandig.
mutiny ['mjûtini] sb. muiterij v., oproer o., opstand m.; vi. muiten, aan 't muiten slaan, in opstand komen.
mutter ['mətə] vt. mompelen, prevelen; vi. mompelen; mopperen, preutelen; (v. donder) rommelen; sb. gemompel o.; gemopper o.
mutton ['mətn] schapevlees o.; (scherts.) schaap o.
mutual ['mjûtjuəl] adj. onderling, wederkerig; wederzijds.
muzzle ['məzl] sb. muil, bek, snuit m.; muilband, muilkorf m.; (v. vuurwapen)

mond m.; rt. muilbanden; **besnuffelen**, beruiken; (v. zeil) innemen.
muzzy ['məzi] beneveld, suf; saai.
my [mai] mijn.
mylord [mai'lo:d, mi'lo:d] milord m.
myopic [mai'ɔpik] bijziend.
myosotis [maiə'soutis] vergeet-mijnietje o.
myrrh [mə:] mirre v.
myrtle-berry ['mə:tlberi] mirtbes v.; blauwe bosbes v.
myself [mai'self] ikzelf, mijzelf, zelf.
mysterious(**ly**) [mis'tiəriəs(li)] adj. (adv.) geheimzinnig; verborgen.
mystery ['mistəri] geheim, mysterie o.; verborgenheid, geheimzinnigheid v.; mysteriespel o.   [verborgen.
mystic(**al**) ['mistik(l)] adj. mystiek, **mysticism** ['mistisizm] mysticisme o.; mystiek v.   [bedotten.
mystify ['mistifai] mystificeren, foppen, **mythology** [mi'ðɔlədʒi] mythologie v.

N

nacre ['neikə] paarlemoer o.
nag [næg] sb. hit m.; (fam.) paard o.; (Am.) a) oude auto v.; b) gevit o.; vt. vitten op, bevitten; treiteren, sarren; vi. zaniken, zeuren.
naiad ['neiæd] waternimf v.; (Pl.) fonteinkruid o.; zoetwatermossel v.
nail [neil] sb. nagel, spijker m.; klauw m.; **on the** —, dadelijk, onverwijld; contant, met gereed geld; vt. spijkeren, vastspijkeren; (sl.) snappen, betrappen; gappen, zich meester maken van; — **up,** dichtspijkeren.
nail-brush ['neilbrəf] nagelborstel m.
naive(**ly**) [nâ'îv(li)] adj. (adv.) naïef, ongekunsteld.
naked ['neikid] naakt, bloot; (v. paard) ongezadeld; weerloos; (v. elekt. draad) niet geïsoleerd; onopgesmukt.
name [neim] sb. naam m.; benaming v.; vt. noemen; benoemen; (v. schip) dopen; (in parlement) tot de orde roepen.
nameable ['neiməbl] noembaar.
name-child ['neimtfaild] naamgenoot m.
name-day ['neimdei] naamdag m.
nameless ['neimlis] naamloos; onbekend; onnoemelijk.
namely ['neimli] namelijk, te weten.
name-plate ['neimpleit] naambordje o.
namesake ['neimseik] naamgenoot m.
nap [næp] sb. dutje o.; nop v.; haar o.; vi. dutten, soezen; vt. noppen.
nape [neip] nek m.
napery ['neipəri] tafellinnen o.
napkin ['næpkin] servet o.; luier m.
narcissus [nâ'sisəs] narcis v.
narcotic [nâ'kɔtik] adj. (& sb.) bedwelmend, verdovend, slaapverwekkend (middel).

narrate [nə'reit] verhalen, vertellen.
narration [nə'reifən] verhaal o., vertelling v.; het verhalen o.
narrow ['nærou] adj. nauw, eng, smal; bekrompen, kortzichtig, kleingeestig; (v. onderzoek) nauwkeurig, scherp; karig, schriel; sb. —s, zee-engten; vt. vernauwen; beperken, begrenzen; — **down,** (v. aantal) verminderen; in het nauw drijven; vi. nauwer worden; (bij breien) minderen.
narrow-minded ['nærou'maindid] kleingeestig.
nasal ['neizəl] neusklank m.; neusletter v.; (v. helm) neusstuk o.
nasty ['nâsti] morsig, vuil, smerig; akelig, gemeen, lelijk; onbeschoft; kwaadaardig; hatelijk.
natality [nə'tæliti] geboortecijfer o.
natation [nei'teifən] zwemkunst v., het zwemmen o.
nation ['neifən] volk o., natie v.
national ['næfənəl] adj. nationaal; vaderlands (gezind); volks—, staats—, lands—; sb. —s, landgenoten (in het buitenland).
nationality [næfə'næliti] nationaliteit v.; volkskarakter o.; volksbestaan o.
native ['neitiv] adj. aangeboren, natuurlijk; (Pl., Dk.) inheems; geboorte—; (v. mineralen) gedegen; sb. inboorling, inlander m.; inheems dier o.; inheemseplant v.
natural ['nætfrəl] natuurlijk; aangeboren; menselijk.
naturalize ['nætfrəlaiz] naturaliseren; inburgeren; (v. planten, enz.) acclimatiseren — **oneself,** zich laten naturaliseren zich inburgeren.
nature ['neitfə] natuur v.; aard m., karakter o., natuur v.

naught [no:t] niets, nul.
naughty ['no:ti] *adj.* ondeugend, stout; *sb.* (*v. kind*) ondeugd *v.*
nauseate ['no:sieit, 'no:ʃieit] *vt.* misselijk maken, doen walgen; verafschuwen; *vi.* misselijk worden, walgen (*at,* van).
nauseous ['no:siəs, 'no:ʃiəs] walgingwekkend.
nautic(al) ['no:tik(l)] zee—, scheepvaart—, zeevaartkundig.
naval ['neivəl] zee—, scheepvaart—; scheeps—, vloot—, marine—.
nave [neiv] (*v. wiel*) naaf *v.*; (*v. kerk*) schip *o.*
navel ['neivl] navel *m.*
navigable ['nævigəbl] bevaarbaar; zeewaardig; bestuurbaar.
navigate ['nævigeit] *vt.* bevaren, varen op; besturen; *vi.* varen.
navigation [nævi'geiʃən] scheepvaart, navigatie *v.*; stuurmanskunst *v.*
navigator ['nævigeitə] zeevaarder *m.*; (*v. vliegtuig*) navigator *m.*
navy ['neivi] marine, zeemacht, vloot *v.*; marineblauw *o.*
navy-blue [neivi'blû] marineblauw.
navy-office ['neiviɔfis] admiraliteit *v.*
near [niə] *adj.* dichtbijzijnd; naverwant; (*v. vriend*) dierbaar, intiem; (*v. vertaling*) nauwkeurig; *adv.* dichtbij, nabij; bijna; schriel, krenterig; *prep.* nabij; *vi.* naderen.
near-by ['niəbai] naburig, nabijgelegen.
nearly ['niəli] bijna, haast; van nabij; nauwkeurig; ten nauwste, innig.
near-sighted ['niə'saitid] bijziend.
neat [nit] *sb.* rund *o.*; rundvee, hoornvee *o.*
neat [nit] *adj.* net(jes), keurig, ordelijk; zuiver, zindelijk; smakelijk; handig; (*H.*) netto.
neat-handed ['nit'hændid] behendig, handig.
neat-herd ['nithə:d] veehoeder *m.*
neat's-leather ['nitsleðə] runderleer *o.*
neb [neb] neb *v.*, bek *m.*; tuit *v.*; (*v. pet*) klep *v.*
necessary ['nesisəri] *adj.* noodzakelijk, noodwendig, nodig; *sb.* het noodzakelijke *o.*
necessitate [ni'sesiteit] noodzakelijk maken; noodzaken, dwingen.
necessitous(ly) [ni'sesitəs(li)] *adj.* (*adv.*) behoeftig, nooddruftig, noodlijdend.
necessity [ni'sesiti] noodzakelijkheid, noodzaak *v.*; behoefte *v.*, nooddruft *m.*
neck [nek] hals *m.*; halsstuk *o.*; (*sp.*) halslengte *v.*
neck-tie ['nektai] das *v.*; (*sl.*) strop *m.*
necropsy ['nekrɔpsi], **necroscopy** [ne'krɔskəpi] (*gen.*) lijkschouwing *v.*
necrosis [ne'krousis] (*gen.*) beeneter *m.*, koudvuur *o.*; (*Pl.*) brand, kanker *m.*
nectar ['nektə] nectar, godendrank *m.*; honing *m.*
need [nid] *sb.* nood *m.*, noodzaak *v.*;

noodzakelijkheid *v.*; behoefte *v.*; *vt.* nodig hebben, behoeven; *vi.* gebrek lijden.
needful ['nidful] *adj.* nodig, noodzakelijk; *sb.* het nodige *o.*; **the —,** (*fam.*) de nodige fondsen, de duiten.
needle ['nidl] *sb.* naald *v.* (*ook:* dennenaald, gedenknaald, kompasnaald, magneetnaald, enz.); rotspunt *v.*; *vt.* naaien; doorprikken (met een naald).
needle-case ['nidlkeis] naaldenkoker *m.*
needless(ly) ['nidlis(li)] *adj.* (*adv.*) onnodig, nodeloos.
needlewoman ['nidlwumən] naaister *v.*
needlework ['nidlwə:k] naaldwerk *o.*; naaiwerk *o.*; handwerk *o.*
needy ['nidi] behoeftig, armoedig, nooddruftig.
ne'er [nêə] (*dicht.*) nooit.
ne'er-do-well ['nêədûwel] deugniet *m.*
nefarious(ly) [ni'fêəriəs(li)] *adj.* (*adv.*) schandelijk, afschuwelijk, snood.
negate [ni'geit] ontkennen, loochenen.
negation [ni'geiʃən] ontkenning *v.*; weigering *v.*
negative ['negətiv] *adj.* ontkennend; weigerend; *sb.* ontkenning *v.*; weigering *v.*, weigerend antwoord *o.*; (*r. foto*) negatief *o.*; (*el.*) negatieve pool *v.*; *vt.* ontkennen; (*v. wet*) verwerpen, afstemmen; weerleggen; ongedaan maken.
neglect [ni'glekt] *sb.* verzuim *o.*; veronachtzaming *v.*; verwaarlozing *v.*; *vt.* verzuimen, nalaten; veronachtzamen; verwaarlozen.
neglectful [ni'glektful] achteloos, nalatig; verwaarloosd.
negligence ['neglidʒəns] nalatigheid, achteloosheid *v.*; veronachtzaming *v.*
negligent ['neglidʒənt] nalatig, achteloos; onachtzaam; ongedwongen.
negligible ['neglidʒəbl] te verwaarlozen, niet noemenswaard.
negotiable [ni'gouʃiəbl] verhandelbaar.
negotiate [ni'gouʃieit] *vt.* verhandelen; tot stand brengen; (*v. lening, huwelijk, enz.*) sluiten; *vi.* onderhandelen; handel drijven.
negotiation [nigouʃi'eiʃən] verhandeling *v.*; totstandbrenging *v.*; sluiting *v.*; discontering, verhandeling *v.*; onderhandeling *v.*
negotiator [ni'gouʃieitə] onderhandelaar *m.*; verhandelaar *m.*
negress ['nigris] negerin *v.*
negro ['nigrou] *sb.* neger *m.*; *adj.* neger—, zwart.
neigh [nei] *vi.* hinniken; *sb.* gehinnik *o.*
neighbour ['neibə] *sb.* buur, buurman *m.*, buurvrouw *v.*, natuur *m.*; (*Bijb.*) naaste *m.*; *vt.* grenzen aan, begrenzen; als buren omgaan; *vi.* **— upon,** grenzen aan; **— with,** passen bij.
neighbourhood ['neibəhud] buurt, buurtschap *v.*; nabijheid *v.*; nabuurschap *v.*

neighbouring ['neibəriŋ] naburig, nabijgelegen; aangrenzend.

neither ['naiθə, 'niθə] *adj.* & *pron.* geen van beide(n); geen, geen van alle(n); *cj.* & *adv.* ook... niet; — *... nor,* noch... noch.

neophyte ['nîo(u)fait] pas bekeerde, nieuwgedoopte *m.*; (*Prot.*) nieuw lidmaat der gemeente *o.*; nieuweling *m.*

nephew ['nevju] neef (oomzegger) *m.*

nervate ['nə:veit] (*Pl.*) generfd.

nerve [nə:v] *sb.* zenuw *v.*; nerf *v.*; pees *v.*; kracht, spierkracht *v.*; geestkracht *v.*; moed, durf *m.*; *vt.* stalen, sterken, kracht geven; *vz.* — *oneself,* zich vermannen.

nervous ['nə:vəs] *adj.* zenuwachtig; zenuw—; gespierd, sterk, krachtig.

nervy ['nə:vi] sterk, gespierd; (*fam.*) zenuwachtig.

nest [nest] *sb.* nest *o.*; broeinest *o.*; ziektehaard *m.*; *vi.* nestelen, een nest bouwen; *vr.* — *oneself,* zich nestelen.

nestle ['nesl] *vi.* zich nestelen; nestelen; — *down,* zich neervlijen; *vt.* omstrengelen; koesteren; *vr.* — *oneself,* zich neervlijen.

net [net] *sb.* net *o.*; strik; valstrik *m.*; netje, haarnetje *o.*; *vt.* in (met) een net vangen; afvissen met een net; (*fig.*) in zijn netten vangen; knopen; *vi.* (*sp.: voetbal*) doelpunten.

net [net] *adj.* (*H.*) netto; *vt.* (*H.*) netto opbrengen.

netting ['netiŋ] netwerk *o.*

nettle ['netl] *sb.* (*Pl.*) brandnetel *v.*; *vt.* netelen, steken (met brandnetels); (*fig.*) ergeren, prikkelen.

nettle-rash ['netlræʃ] (*gen.*) netelroos *v.*

neurotic [nju'rɔtik] *adj.* zenuw—; *sb.* zenuwmiddel *o.*; zenuwlijder(es) *m.* (*v.*).

neuter ['njûtə] *adj.* onzijdig; *sb.* onzijdig geslacht *o.*; onzijdig woord *o.*; geslachtloos insekt *o.*

neutral ['njûtrəl] *adj.* onzijdig, neutraal; vaag, onbestemd; kleurloos; geslachtloos; *sb.* onzijdige, neutrale *m.*; onzijdig land (schip, enz.) *o.*

never ['nevə] nooit, nimmer; in 't geheel niet, volstrekt niet.

nevertheless [nevəθə'les] niettemin, niettegenstaande dat.

new [njû] nieuw; (*v. brood, enz.*) vers; onervaren.

new-build ['njûbild] verbouwen.

new-comer ['njûkəmə] pas aangekomene, nieuweling *m.*

newel ['njûəl] spil *v.* van een wenteltrap.

new-fledged ['njûfledʒd] pas gevederd; (*fig.*) nieuw.

new-laid ['njû'leid] (*v. eieren*) vers, vers gelegd.

newly ['njûli] pas kort geleden, onlangs; nieuw.

new-made ['njûmeid] pas gemaakt, nieuw; (*fig.*) nieuwbakken.

news [njûz] nieuws, bericht *o.*, tijding *v.*

news-boy ['njûzbɔi] krantenjongen *m.*

newspaper ['njûzpeipə] krant *v.*, dagblad *o.*

news-reel ['njûzrîl] filmjournaal *o.*

new-year ['njûjîə] nieuwjaar *o.*

next [nekst] *adj.* naast; volgend (op), eerstvolgend; toekomend, aanstaande; *adv.* & *prep.* naast; vervolgens.

nib [nib] *sb.* neb *v.*, snavel *m.*; punt, spits *v.*; *vt.* punten, aanpunten.

nibble ['nibl] *vi.* knabbelen, bijten (aan); vitten; *vi.* afknabbelen; (*sl.*) gappen; te pakken krijgen; *sb.* geknabbel *o.*; (*v. vis*) beet *m.*

nibbler ['niblə] knabbelaar *m.*; vitter *m.*

nice [nais] *adj.* lief, aardig; lekker, heerlijk, smakelijk; kieskeurig; nauwgezet, stipt; fijn, nauwkeurig.

nicely ['naisiti] lekkernij *v.*; nauwgezetheid, stiptheid *v.*; fijne smaak *m.*

niche [nitʃ] *sb.* nis *v.*; (*fig.*) plaatsje *o.*; *vt.* in een nis plaatsen; een plaatsje geven.

nick [nik] *sb.* keep, kerf, insnijding *v.*; kerfstok *m.*; *vt.* inkepen, inkerven; afsnijden, afknippen.

nickel ['nikl] *sb.* nikkel *o.*; nikkelen geldstuk *o.*; *adj.* nikkelen; *vt.* vernikkelen.

nickname ['nikneim] *sb.* bijnaam *m.*; roepnaam *m.*; *vt.* een bijnaam geven; —*d,* bijgenaamd.

niece [nis] nicht *v.*

niggard ['nigəd] *sb.* vrek, gierigaard *m.*; *adj.* vrekkig, gierig; zuinig, krenterig.

nigger ['nigə] neger *m.*

niggle ['nigl] peuteren; beuzelen, vitten.

niggling ['nigliŋ] *adj.* peuterig, pietluttig; *sb.* gepeuter *o.*

night [nait] nacht *m.*; avond *m.*, duisternis *v.*; *at* —, 's nachts; 's avonds; *good* —*!* wel te rusten! *to*-—, heden-avond; *last* —, gisterenavond.

night-bell ['naitbel] nachtbel *v.*

nightcap ['naitkæp] slaapmuts *v.*; (*fam.*) slaapmutsje *o.*

night-cellar ['naitselə] nachtkroeg *v.*

night-class ['naitklâs] avondles *v.*; avondschool *v.*

night-dress ['naitdres] nachtgewaad, nachtgoed *o.*; nachtjapon *v.*

nightfall ['naitfo:l] (het) vallen van de avond *o.*

night-gown ['naitgaun] nachtjapon *v.*

nightjar ['naitdʒâ] nachtzwaluw *v.*, geitenmelker *m.*

nightingale ['naitiŋgeil] nachtegaal *m.*

night-light ['naitlait] nachtkaars *v.*, nachtlichtje *o.*

nightly ['naitli] *adj.* nachtelijk; avond—; *adv.* 's nachts; elke nacht; elke avond.

nightmare ['naitmêə] nachtmerrie *v.*

night-school ['naitskûl] avondschool *v.*

nightshade ['naitʃeid] (*Pl.*) nachtschade *v.*

night-stand ['naitstænd] nachtkastje *o.*

nightwalker ['naitwo:kə] nachtloper; slaapwandelaar *m*.

nihilism ['nai(h)ilizm] nihilisme *o*.

nihility [nai'hiliti] nietigheid, nulliteit *v*.; het niets-zijn *o*.

Nile [nail] de Nijl *m*.

nimble ['nimbl] *adj*. vlug, rap, lenig.

nimbleness ['nimblnis] vlugheid, lenigheid *v*.

nimbus ['nimbəs] lichtkrans, stralenkrans *m*.; regenwolk *v*.

Nimeguen [ni'meigən] Nijmegen *o*.

nine [nain] negen.

ninepins ['nainpinz] kegelspel *o*.; kegels *m. mv*.

nineteen ['naintîn] negentien.

ninety ['nainti] negentig.

ninny ['nini] uilskuiken *o*.; sul *m*.

ninth [nainδ] negende; (*muz*.) none *v*., 9ᵉ toontrap *m*.

nip [nip] *vt*. nijpen, knijpen; klemmen; (*v. planten: door de kou*) doden, beschadigen; wegpakken; —*ped*, (*v. handen, enz*.) verkleumd; (*v. plant*) bevroren; *sb*. kneep *v*.; beet *m*.; nijpende koude, vinnigheid *v*. (van koude); (*v. plant*) beschadiging (door koude) *v*.

nip [nip] *sb*. borrel *m*., hartversterking *v*., slokje *o*.; *vi*. borrelen, pimpelen.

nippers ['nipəz] kniptang; ijzerdraadschaar *v*.; knijper, pince-nez *m*.

nipple ['nipl] tepel *m*.; speen *v*.; (*tn*.) nippel *m*.

nitrate ['naitre(i)t] *sb*. nitraat, salpeterzuurzout *o*.; *vt*. met salpeterzuurzout behandelen.

nitre ['naitə] salpeter *o*.

nitric ['naitrik] salpeter—.

nitrogen ['naitrədʒən] stikstof *v*.

no [nou] *adj*. geen; zonder; *adv*. neen; niet; *sb*. neen; tegenstemmer *m*.

nobiliary [nou'biliəri] adellijk, adel—.

nobility [nou'biliti] adel *m*.; adelstand; adeldom *m*.; edelheid *v*.

noble ['noubl] *adj*. edel; adellijk, van adel; edelaardig; nobel; groots; *sb*. edele, edelman *m*.

noble-minded ['noubl'maindid] edelmoedig, grootmoedig.

nobody ['noubədi] niemand; (*fig*.) nul.

nock [nɔk] keep, inkeping *v*.; (*sch*.) nok *v*.

nocturnal [nɔk'tə:nl] nachtelijk, nacht.

nod [nɔd] *vi*. knikken; ja knikken; knikkebollen; — *off*, in slaap vallen, indutten; *vt*. knikken; *sb*. knik, hoofdknik *m*.; wenk *m*.

node [noud] knobbel, knoest *m*.; knoop *m*.; knooppunt *o*.; jichtknobbel *m*.; knobbelgezwel *m*.

noise [nɔiz] *sb*. leven, lawaai *o*.; geraas, gerucht *o*.; *vt*. — abroad (*about*), ruchtbaar maken, uitbazuinen; *vi*. geraas maken.

noiseless(*ly*) ['nɔizlis(li)] *adj*. (*adv*.) geruisloos, stil.

noisome ['nɔisəm] schadelijk, ongezond; walglijk, stinkend.

noisy ['nɔizi] *adj*. luidruchtig, lawaaierig; (*v. kleuren, enz*.) druk, schreeuwend; gehorig; *be* —, drukte (leven) maken.

nomad ['nɔməd] *sb*. zwerver *m*.; *adj*. zwervend; nomadisch.

nominal ['nɔminəl] *adj*. nominaal; in naam; (*gram*.) naamwoordelijk.

nominate ['nɔmineit] benoemen; op de voordracht zetten, voordragen, kandidaat stellen; (*soms:*) noemen.

nomination [nɔmi'neiʃən] benoeming *v*.; voordracht, kandidaatstelling *v*.

nonchalant(*ly*) ['nɔnʃələnt(li)] *adj*. (*adv*.) onverschillig, nonchalant.

non-commissioned ['nɔnkə'miʃənd] — *office.*, onderofficier *m*.

nonconformist ['nɔnkən'fɔ:mist] afgescheidene (v. Engelse kerk) *m*.

none [nən] *pron. & adj*. geen; niemand; niets; *adv*. niets; volstrekt niet.

nonentity [nɔ'nentiti] het niet-bestaan *o*.; niet-bestaand iets *o*.; onbeduidend persoon *m*.; onding *o*.

non-pareil ['nɔnpərel] *adj*. onvergelijkelijk, weergaloos; *sb*. pareldrukletter *v*.

nonsense ['nɔnsəns] onzin *m*., dwaasheid, gekheid *v*.

nonsensical(*ly*) [nɔn'sensikəl(i)] *adj*. (*adv*.) onzinnig, ongerijmd, gek.

non-sexual ['nɔn'sekʃuəl] geslachtloos.

non-stop ['nɔn'stɔp] (*v. trein*) doorgaand; (*v. vlucht*) zonder tussenlanding.

non-union ['nɔn'jûnjən] (*v. arbeider*) niet aangesloten, ongeorganiseerd.

noodle ['nûdl] sul *m*., uilskuiken *o*.; meelbal, knoedel *m*.

nook [nuk] *sb*. hoekje, (gezellig) plekje *o*.; uithoek *m*.

noon [nûn] *sb*. middag, noen *m*.; middaghoogte *v*.; *vi*. (*Am*.) het middagmaal gebruiken; een middagdutje doen.

noose [nûs] *sb*. lus *v*., strik *m*.; strop *m*.; *vt*. strikken; in een strik vangen, verstrikken; opknopen.

normal ['no:məl] normaal, gewoon; loodrecht.

normality [no:'mæliti] normaliteit *v*.

north [no:δ] *sb*. Noorden *o*.; noordenwind *m*.; *adj*. noordelijk, noord(er)—; *adv*. noordwaarts; noordelijk; *vi*. (*v. wind*) naar 't noorden gaan.

north-east ['noδ'îst] *sb*. noord-oosten *o*.; *adj*. noord-oostelijk.

northern ['no:θən] noordelijk, noord—.

north light ['no:δlait] noorderlicht *o*.

north-pole ['no:δpoul] noordpool *v*.

North Sea ['no:δsi] Noordzee *v*.

north-west ['no:δ'west] noord-west; noord-westen.

Norway ['no:wei] Noorwegen *o*.

nose [nouz] *sb*. neus *m*.; geur, reuk *m*.; tuit *v*.; *vt*. ruiken; — *out*, uitvissen, er achter komen; — *at*, besnuffelen; — *down*, (*vl*.) duikvliegen; *vi*. snuffelen; zijn neus in andermans zaken steken.

nose-bleed ['nouzblîd] neusbloeding v.; (Pl.) duizendblad o.

nose-dive ['nouzdaiv] vi. (v. vliegtuig) in steile stand dalen; met de kop naar voren omlaag storten; sb. steile daling v.; kopbuiteling v.

nosegay ['nouzgei] ruiker m.

nostalgia [nɔs'tældʒiə] heimwee o.

nostril ['nɔstril] neusgat o.

not [nɔt] niet.

notability [noutə'biliti] merkwaardigheid v.; notabele m.

notable ['noutəbl] adj. merkwaardig; belangrijk, aanzienlijk; (v. huisvrouw) flink, bedrijvig, werkzaam; sb. aanzienlijk persoon, notabele m.

notarial(ly) [nou'têəriəl(i)] adj. (adv.) notarieel.

notary ['noutəri] notaris m.

notch [nɔtʃ] sb. keep, inkeping v.; (in mes, enz.) schaarde v.; gleuf, spleet v.; vt. inkepen, kerven.

note [nout] sb. noot v.; toets v.; toon, grondtoon m.; teken, merk o.; vt. nota nemen van, notitie nemen van; opmerken; noteren, aantekenen; van aantekeningen voorzien.

note-book ['noutbuk] aantekenboek-(je), notitieboekje o.

note-case ['noutkeis] zakportefeuille v.

noted ['noutid] bekend, befaamd, vermaard.

note-paper ['noutpeipə] postpapier o.

noteworthy ['noutwə:θi] opmerkenswaardig; merkwaardig.

nothing ['nəðiŋ] pron. & sb. niets; adv. in 't geheel niet, helemaal niet.

notice ['noutis] sb. bericht o., kennisgeving, aankondiging v.; waarschuwing v.; aandacht, opmerkzaamheid, oplettendheid v.; convocatiebiljet o.; vt. opmerken; acht slaan op, notitie nemen van; vermelden.

noticeable ['noutisəbl] adj. merkbaar, waarneembaar; opmerkelijk, merkwaardig; in het oog vallend.

notification [noutifi'keiʃən] kennisgeving, bekendmaking, aanschrijving, aanzegging v.

notify ['noutifai] kennis geven van, bekend maken, aankondigen. [notie v.]

notion ['nouʃən] begrip, denkbeeld o.,

notorious [nou'to:riəs] (algemeen) bekend, welbekend; befaamd, berucht.

notwithstanding [nɔtwið'stændiŋ] prep. niettegenstaande, ondanks; adv. desniettegenstaande, desondanks, ondanks dat.

nought [nɔ:t] niets; nul.

noun [naun] zelfstandig naamwoord o.

nourish ['nəriʃ] voeden; aankweken; koesteren; aanwakkeren; (v. overlevering) onderhouden, hooghouden.

nourisher ['nəriʃə] voeder; (aan)kweker m.

nourishing ['nəriʃiŋ] voedzaam.

nourishment ['nəriʃmənt] voeding v.; voedsel o.

novel ['nɔvəl] sb. roman m.; (recht) novelle v.; adj. nieuw, ongewoon, nieuw uitgevonden.

novelty ['nɔvəlti] nieuwigheid v.; nieuwheid v., het nieuwe o.; nieuw artikel o.

November [nou'vembə] november o.

novice ['nɔvis] novice m. & v.; nieuweling, beginner m.

noviciate, novitiate [nou'viʃiit] noviciaat o.; leertijd, proeftijd m.

now [nau] adv. nu, thans; prep. nu; sb. het tegenwoordige; nu o.

nowadays ['nauədeiz] tegenwoordig, heden ten dage.

nowhere ['nouwêə] nergens; be —, (v. renpaard) helemaal achteraan komen.

noxious ['nɔkʃəs] schadelijk, verderfelijk.

nozzle ['nɔzl] tuit v., mondstuk o.

nubile ['njûbil] huwbaar.

nude [njûd] adj. naakt, bloot; (v. contract, ong.) eenzijdig; sb. het naakt (model) o.

nudge [nədʒ] vt. zachtjes aanstoten (met de elleboog); sb. duwtje o.

nudist ['njûdist] naaktloper m.

nuisance ['njûsəns] plaag v., hinder, last, overlast m.; lastpost m.; burengerucht o.

null [nəl] adj. nietig, ongeldig; krachteloos; nietswaardig; onbeduidend; sb. nul v.

nullify ['nəlifai] krachteloos maken; (recht) vernietigen, nietig (ongeldig) verklaren.

number ['nəmbə] sb. nummer o.; getal, aantal o.; (vers) maat v.; vt. nummeren; tellen; — with (in, among), rekenen onder; vi. tellen; — off, (mil.) zich nummeren.

numberless ['nəmbəlis] talloos, zonder tal.

numbness ['nəmnis] verkleumdheid, verstijving v.; verdoving v.

numeral ['njûmərəl] adj. getal—, nummer—, getalaanduidend; sb. telwoord o.; getalletter v., getalteken o.

numerator ['njûməreitə] (v. breuk) teller m.

numeric(al) [nju'merik(l)] getal—, numeriek.

numerous ['njûmərəs] talrijk, vele, tal van; overvloedig.

nun [nən] non v.; (Dk.) nonnetje o.; pimpelmees v.

nunciature ['nənʃiətʃə] nuntiatuur v., pauselijk gezantschap o.

nuncio ['nənʃiou] nuntius, pauselijk gezant m.

nunnery ['nənəri] nonnenklooster o.

nuptial ['nəpʃəl] adj. huwelijks—, bruilofts—; sb. —s, bruiloft v.

nurse [nə:s] sb. baker v.; min v.; kindermeisje o., kinderjuffrouw v.; verpleegster, pleegzuster v.; verzorger m.; vt. zogen; verplegen, verzorgen, oppassen; grootbrengen; vi. zogen; uit verplegen gaan.

nursery ['nə:sri] kinderkamer *v.*; kinderbewaarplaats *v.*; kweekschool *v.*; planten—, boomkwekerij *v.*; kweekvijver *m.*

nursery-garden ['nə:srigâdn] kwekerij *v.*

nurseryman ['nə:srimən] boomkweker *m.*

nursery-school ['nə:sriskûl] bewaarschool, kleuterschool *o.*

nursing-mother ['nə:siŋməθə] pleegmoeder *v.*

nurture ['ne:tfə] *sb.* voeding *v.*, voedsel *o.*; opvoeding *v.*; verzorging *v.*; *vt.* voeden; opvoeden; verzorgen; koesteren.

nut [nət] *sb.* noot, hazelnoot *v.*; (*v. schroef*) moer *v.*; (*v. anker*) neut *v.*; (*mil.*; *v. geweer*) tuimelaar *m.*; —s,

nootjeskolen; —s! (*Am.*) onzin ! *vi.* noten plukken.

nut-cracker ['nətkrækə] notenkraker *m.*

nuthatch ['nəthætʃ] (*Dk.*) boomklever *m.*

nutmeg ['nətmeg] notemuskaat *v.*

nutriment ['njûtrimənt] voedsel *o.*

nutrition [nju'trifən] voeding *v.*; voedsel *o.*

nutritious [nju'trifəs], **nutritive** ['njûtritiv] *adj.* voedend, voedzaam; *sb.* voedingsartikel *o.*

nutshell ['nətfel] notedop *m.*

nuzzle ['nəzl] *vt.* koesteren; omwroeten; *vi.* snuffelen; wroeten in; zich nestelen.

nymph [nimf] nimf *v.*; (*Dk.*: *v. insekt*) pop *v.*

O

oak [ouk] *sb.* eik *m.*; eikehout *o.*; eikeloof *o.*; *adj.* eikehouten.

oak-apple ['oukæpl] galnoot *v.*

oaken ['ouk(ə)n] eikehouten.

oak-fig ['oukfig] galnoot *v.*

oakum [oukəm] werk, uitgeplozen touw *o.*

oar [o:] *sb.* lange roeiriem *m.*; roeier *m.*; *vt. & vi.* roeien.

oasis [o(u)'eisis] oase *v.*

oat [out] haver *v.*

oath [ouδ] eed *m.*; vloek *m.*

oath-breaking ['ouδbreikiŋ] eedbreuk *v.*

oatmeal ['outmîl] havermeel *o.*

obduracy ['obdjurəsi] verstoktheid, halsstarrigheid, verharding *v.*

obdurate(ly) ['obdjurit(li)] *adj.* (*adv.*) verstokt, halsstarrig, verhard.

obedience [o(u)'bîdjəns] gehoorzaamheid *v.*

obedient [o(u)'bîdjənt] gehoorzaam.

obediently [o(u)'bîdjəntli] *adv.* gehoorzaam; **yours —,** uw dienstwillige.

obese [o(u)'bîs] zwaarlijvig, corpulent.

obey [o(u)'bei] gehoorzamen; gehoor geven aan; luisteren naar.

obfuscate ['obfəskeit] verduisteren, overschaduwen; (*v. verstand*) benevelen; verbijsteren.

obituary [o'bitjuəri] dodenlijst *v.*; doodsbericht *o.*

object ['obdʒikt] *sb.* voorwerp *o.*; doel *o.*, bedoeling *v.*, plan *o.*; [əb'dʒekt] *vt.* tegenwerpen; *vi.* tegenwerpingen maken; bezwaar maken; op iets tegen hebben.

objection [əb'dʒekfən] tegenwerping *v.*; bezwaar *o.*

objectionable [əb'dʒekfənəbl] *adj.* betwistbaar, aanvechtbaar, aan bedenking onderhevig; laakbaar, berispelijk; afkeurenswaardig, verwerpelijk; aanstotelijk.

objective [əb'dʒektiv] *adj.* objectief; (*gram.*) voorwerps—; *sb.* (*v. kijker*) objectief *o.*; (*mil.*) object, militair doel *o.*; voorwerpsnaamval *m.*

oblation [ə'bleifən] offerande *v.*; gave, offergave *v.*

obligation [obli'geifən] verplichting, verbintenis *v.*; (*H.*) obligatie, schuldbekentenis *v.*

obligatory ['obligətəri] verplicht, verbindend.

oblige [ə'blaidʒ] *vt.* verbinden, verplichten; aan zich verplichten; gerieven; **be —d to,** moeten, verplicht zijn; *vi.* van dienst zijn, aan zich verplichten; iets ten beste geven.

obliging [ə'blaidʒiŋ] voorkomend, vriendelijk, gedienstig, dienstvaardig.

obligingness [ə'blaidʒiŋnis] voorkomendheid, gedienstigheid, dienstvaardigheid *v.*

oblique [ə'blîk] scheef, schuin; zijdelings, onrechtstreeks; (*v. handelwijze*) slinks.

obliterate [ə'blitəreit] uitwissen, doorhalen; (*v. postzegel*) afstempelen; vernietigen.

oblivion [ə'blivian] vergetelheid *v.*

oblivious [ə'bliviəs] *adj.* vergeetachtig; **— of (to),** vergetend.

oblong ['oblɔŋ] *adj.* langwerpig; *sb.* rechthoek *m.*

obscene(ly) [ob'sîn(li)] *adj.* (*adv.*) ontuchtig, vuil, gemeen.

obscuration [obskju'reifən] verdonkering, verduistering *v.*

obscure [əb'skjûə] *adj.* duister, donker; onbekend, verborgen; onduidelijk; *sb.* duisternis *v.*; vaagheid *v.*; *vt.* verduisteren, verdonkeren; onduidelijk maken, doen vervagen.

obscurity [əb'skjûəriti] duisternis, donkerte *v.*; duisterheid, donkerheid *v.*

obsequies ['obsikwiz] uitvaart *v.*; lijk.

plechtigheden *v. mv.*; lijkstaatsie *v.*; teraardebestelling *v.*

observable [əb'zə:vəbl] waarneembaar, merkbaar; opmerkelijk.

observant [əb'zə:vənt] oplettend, opmerkzaam; nalevend.

observation [ɔbzə'veiʃən] waarneming, observatie *v.*; opmerking *v.*

observatory [əb'zə'vətri] sterrenwacht *v.*

observe [əb'zə:v] *vt.* waarnemen, gadeslaan; in acht nemen, nakomen; opmerken; *vi.* — (*up*)*on*, opmerkingen maken over.

observer [əb'zə:və] waarnemer *m.*; opmerker *m.*; observator *m.*

obsess [ɔb'ses] kwellen, niet loslaten, geen rust laten; (*v. gedachte, enz.*) achtervolgen.

obsession [ɔb'seʃən] kwelling, kwellende gedachte *v.*; steeds achtervolgende gedachte, obsessie *v.*

obsolete ['ɔbsəlit] verouderd, in onbruik geraakt.

obstacle ['ɔbstəkl] hinderpaal *m.*, hindernis *v.*, beletsel *o.*

obstetric [ɔb'stetrik] *adj.* verloskundig, vroedkundig; *sb.* —*s*, verloskunde, vroedkunde *v.*

obstinacy ['ɔbstinəsi] halsstarrigheid, stijfhoofdigheid, hardnekkigheid *v.*

obstinate(ly) ['ɔbstinit(li)] *adj.* (*adv.*) halsstarrig, stijfhoofdig, hardnekkig.

obstruct [əb'strɔkt] verstoppen; versperren; tegenhouden, (de voortgang) belemmeren; obstructie voeren tegen.

obstruction [əb'strɔkʃən] verstopping *v.*; versperring *v.*; belemmering *v.*; obstructie *v.*

obtain [əb'tein] *vt.* verkrijgen, bekomen, verwerven; verschaffen; *vi.* heersen, van kracht zijn, gelden, algemene regel zijn.

obtainable [əb'teinəbl] verkrijgbaar.

obtest [əb'test] bidden, smeken, bezweren; aanroepen; verzekeren, plechtig verklaren.

obtrude [əb'trûd] *vt.* opdringen (*upon*, aan); — *one's company*, zich opdringen; *vi.* zich indringen; lastig zijn.

obtruder [əb'trudə] indringer *m.*

obtuse(ly) [əb'tjûs(li)] *adj.* (*adv.*) stomp, bot; stompzinnig.

obverse ['ɔbvə:s] *adj.* (*Pl.*) omgekeerd; toegekeerd; tegengesteld; *sb.* (*v. munt, medaille*) vóórzijde *v.*; (*v. stelling*) omkering *v.*, tegengestelde *o.*

obversion [ɔb'və:ʃən] omkering *v.*

obviate ['ɔbvieit] voorkomen, afwenden; uit de weg ruimen.

obvious(ly) ['ɔbviəs(li)] duidelijk, klaar, klaarblijkelijk, voor de hand liggend.

occasion [ə'keiʒən] *sb.* gelegenheid *v.*; aanleiding *v.*; reden *v.*; *vt.* veroorzaken; aanleiding geven tot.

occasionally [ə'keiʒənəli] *adv.* nu en dan, af en toe, van tijd tot tijd.

occident ['ɔksidənt] westen *o.*

occidental [ɔksi'dentəl] westelijk, westers, west—.

occult [ɔ'kɔlt] *adj.* verborgen, geheim; *vt.* verbergen, verduisteren.

occupant ['ɔkjupənt] bezitnemer *m.*; bezitter *m.*; bewoner *m.*; (*v. ambt*) bekleder *m.*

occupation [ɔkju peiʃən] bezitneming *v.*; (*mil.*) bezetting *v.*; bezigheid *v.*; beroep *o.*

occupy ['ɔkjupai] *vt.* bezetten; bezighouden; (*v. ruimte*) innemen, beslaan; (*v. tijd*) in beslag nemen; *vr.* — *oneself in*, zich bezighouden met.

occur [ə'kə:] vóórkomen; zich voordoen; voorvallen, gebeuren; invallen, opkomen (*to*, bij).

occurrence [ə'kɔrəns] gebeurtenis *v.*, voorval *o.*

ocean ['ouʃən] oceaan *m.*, wereldzee *v.*

Oceania [ouʃi'einiə] Oceanië *o.*

ochre ['oukə] oker *v.*; (*sl.*) geld *o.*, duiten, moppen *m. mv.*

ochr(e)ous ['oukr(i)əs], **ochry** ['oukri] okerachtig, okergeel, okerhoudend.

o'clock [ə'klɔk] op de klok; *it is five* —, het is vijf uur.

octave ['ɔktiv] achttal *o.*; octet *o.*; ['ɔkteiv] (*kath.*) octaaf *o.*; octaafdag *m.*

October [ɔk'toubə] october *m.*

oculist ['ɔkjulist] oogarts *m.*

odd [ɔd] *adj.* oneven; enkel, ongepaard; overblijvend (na deling door 2); vreemd, zonderling.

oddments ['ɔdmənts] restanten, ongeregelde goederen *o. mv.*

odious(ly) ['oudjəs(li)] *adj.* (*adv.*) hatelijk, verfoeilijk, afschuwelijk.

odontalgic [ɔdɔn'tældʒik] *adj.* tandpijnstillend; *sb.* tandpijnstillend middel *o.*

odontalgy [ɔdɔn'tældʒi] tandpijn *v.*

odoriferous(ly) [oudə'rifərəs(li)] *adj.* (*adv.*) welriekend, geurig.

odour ['oudə] reuk, geur *m.*; (*fig.*) luchtje, zweempje *o.*

odourless ['oudəlis] reukeloos.

of [ɔv, əv] van.

off [o:f] *adv.* af, eraf; weg, van hier, van daar; verwijderd, ver; *be* —, weggaan; indutten, in slaap zijn; in zwijm liggen; (*v. verloving, enz.*) af zijn; (*v. wedstrijd, enz.*) niet doorgaan; *prep.* van (... af); (*sch.*) op de hoogte van; in de buurt van, nabij; *adj.* vérder, verder gelegen; rechter, rechts; *vt.* (*v. contract, onderhandelingen*) afbreken; (*fam.*) afleggen, uittrekken; — *it*, opstappen, er vandoorgaan; *ij.* weg !

offal ['ɔfəl] afval *m.* (vooral van geslacht dier); bedorven vlees *o.* (afval); (*fig.*) uitschot, bocht *o.*

off-chance ['o:ftʃâns] mogelijkheid *v.*, klein kansje *o.*, twijfelachtige kans *v.*

offence [ə'fens] belediging *v.*; ergernis *v.*, aanstoot *m.*; overtreding *v.*, vergrijp *o.*

offend [ə'fend] beledigen; ergeren, aanstoot geven; overtreden.

offender [ə'fendə] belediger *m.*; overtreder; zondaar *m.*

offensive [ə'fensiv] *adj.* beledigend; aanstotelijk, ergerlijk; onaangenaam, hinderlijk, weerzinwekkend; aanvallend, aanvals—; *sb.* offensief *o.*

offer ['ɔfə] *vt.* bieden, aanbieden; offeren, ten offer brengen; (*v. opmerkingen, enz.*) maken, ten beste geven; (*v. redenen*) aanvoeren; (*v. prijs*) uitloven; *vi.* zich aanbieden; *sb.* aanbod *o.*, aanbieding *v.*; (*H.*) offerte *v.*; bod *o.*

offering ['ɔfəriŋ] offer *o.*; offerande *v.*

off-hand ['o:f'hænd] *adv.* onvoorbereid, voor de vuist weg; ineens, op stel en sprong, op staande voet; *adj.* ['o:fhænd] hooghartig.

off-hours ['o:fauəz] vrije uren.

office ['ɔfis] ambt *o.*, betrekking *v.*; taak *v.*; dienst *m.*; godsdienstoefening *v.*; bureau, kantoor *o.*; ministerie *v.*; —s, keuken *v.*; bediendenkamer *v.*; bijgebouw *o.*

officer ['ɔfisə] officier *m.*; ambtenaar, beambte *m.*

official [ə'fiʃəl] *adj.* ambtelijk, officieel; *sb.* ambtenaar, beambte *m.*

officiant [ə'fiʃənt] (*kath.*) celebrant *m.*

offing ['o:fiŋ] het ruime sop *o.*, volle zee *v.*

off-print ['o:fprint] afdruk *m.*; overdrukje *o.*

offspring ['o:fspriŋ] kroost *o.*, nakomelingen *m. mv.*, nakomelingschap *v.*

off-street ['o:fstrit] zijstraat *v.*

often ['o:fn, 'o:ftn] dikwijls, vaak.

oil [ɔil] *sb.* olie *v.*; petroleum *v.*; *vt.* oliën; met olie insmeren; in olie inleggen; met olie bereiden; *vi.* olie worden; stookolie innemen.

oilcake ['ɔil'keik] lijnkoek *m.*

oil-colour ['ɔilkələ] olieverf *v.*

oil-field ['ɔilfild] petroleumveld *o.*

oil-steamer ['ɔilstimə] olieboot *v.*, tankschip *o.*

oil-tank ['ɔiltæŋk] petroleumtank *v.*

ointment ['ɔintmənt] zalf *v.*, smeersel *o.*

old [ould] *adj.* oud; ouderwets; vroeger; *sb. of* —, van oudsher; in (van) oude tijden.

old-age ['ouldeidʒ] ouderdom, hoge leeftijd *m.*

old-fangled ['ould'fæŋgld], **old-fashioned** ['ould'fæʃənd] ouderwets.

oldness ['ouldnis] ouderdom *m.*; oudheid *v.*

old-timer ['ould'taimə] iem. van de oude stempel *m.*; oudgediende *m.*

oleander [ouli'ændə] (*Pl.*) oleander *m.*

olive ['ɔliv] olijf *m.*; olijftak *m.*; olijfkleur *v.*

olive-tree ['ɔlivtri] olijfboom *m.*

omelet(te) ['ɔmlit] omelet, eierstruif *v.*

omen ['oumən] *sb.* voorteken *o.*; *vt.* aankondigen, voorspellen.

ominous ['ɔminəs] *adj.* onheilspellend; voorspellend.

omission [o(u)'miʃən] weglating, uitlating *v.*; verzuim *o.*, nalatigheid *v.*

omit [o(u)'mit] weglaten, uitlaten; verzuimen, nalaten.

omnipotent [ɔm'nipətənt] almachtig.

omnipresent [ɔmni'prezənt] alomtegenwoordig.

omniscient [ɔm'nif(i)ənt] alwetend.

on [ɔn] *prep.* op; te; in; aan; bij; om; over; met; na; *adv.* aan; op, erop; voort, verder; **be** —, aan de beurt zijn; (*v. rechtszaak*) in behandeling zijn; meedoen; (*bilj.*) aan stoot zijn.

once [wɔns] *adv.* eens, eenmaal; *at* —, tegelijk; dadelijk; *conj.* — (*that*), zodra; *sb.* (*for*) *this* —, (voor) deze keer.

one [wɔn] een; een enkele; dezelfde; enig; een zekere; men.

one-eyed ['wɔn'aid, 'wɔnaid] éénogig; (*sl.*) eenzijdig, partijdig; onbillijk.

onerous(ly) ['ɔnərəs(li)] *adj.* (*adv.*) zwaar, drukkend; lastig, bezwaarlijk; (*v. eigendom, enz.*) bezwaard.

one-seater ['wɔnsitə] éénpersoonsauto *v.*; éénpersoons-vliegtuig *o.*

one-sided(ly) ['wɔn'saidid(li)] *adj.* (*adv.*) eenzijdig; partijdig.

one-way ['wɔnwei] — *traffic,* éénrichtingsverkeer.

onion ['ɔnjən] ui *m.*

onion ['ɔnjən] ui *m.*

only ['ounli] *adj.* enig, enkel; enigst; *adv.* alleen, enkel, maar; pas, eerst; *conj.* alleen (maar); — *that,* behalve dat, ware het niet dat.

onset ['ɔnset] aanval *m.*; aanvang *m.*, begin *o.*

onwards ['ɔnwədz] *adv.* voorwaarts, vooruit.

ooze [ûz] *sb.* modder *v.*, slijk *o.*; looiwater *o.*; sijpeling *v.*; *vi.* sijpelen, doorsijpelen; lekken, uitlekken; — *out,* doorsijpelen; (*fig.*) uitlekken; *vt.* uitzweten.

oozy ['ûzi] modderig, slijkerig; vochtig, klam.

opaque [o(u)'peik] ondoorschijnend; ondoorzichtig; donker, duister; niet helder, onbevattelijk.

open ['oup(ə)n] *adj.* open; openlijk; openhartig; onverholen; blootgesteld (aan); toegankelijk (voor); *sb.* opening *v.*; het open veld, het vrije veld *o.*; (*tn.*) speelruimte *v.*; *vt.* openen, openmaken; openleggen; blootleggen; (*v. fles*) aanbreken; (*v. onderwerp, rechtszaak*) inleiden; *vi.* opengaan, zich openen; (*sch.*) in zicht komen; (*v. persoon*) loskomen.

open-handed(ly) ['oup(ə)n'hændid(li)] *adj.* (*adv.*) mild, royaal.

open-hearted(ly) ['oup(ə)n'hâtid(li)] *adj.* (*adv.*) openhartig; ontvankelijk; hartelijk.

opening ['oup(ə)niŋ] *adj.* openend; inleidend; *sb.* opening *v.*; begin *o.*; inleiding v.; gelegenheid v.; (vooral mv.) vooruitzicht o.

openly ['oup(ə)li] adv. openlijk; openhartig.

open-minded (ly) ['oup(ə)n'maindid-(li)] adj. (adv.) onbevangen, onbevooroordeeld; ontvankelijk.

opera ['ɔpərə] opera v.

opera-glass ['ɔpərəglâs] toneelkijker m.

operate ['ɔpəreit] vi. (v. geneesmiddel, enz.) werken; uitwerking hebben; (mil.; H.: aan beurs) opereren; (gen.) een operatie doen, opereren; vt. bewerken, uitwerken; teweegbrengen, veroorzaken, ten gevolge hebben; (v. machine) bedienen; in werking brengen, drijven.

operating-expenses ['ɔpəreitiŋekspensiz] bedrijfskosten m. mv.

operation [ɔpə'reiʃən] operatie v.; werking, uitwerking v.; bewerking; verrichting v.

operetta [ɔpə'retə] operette v.

opinion [ə'pinjən] opinie, mening v., gevoelen o.; denkwijze v.; (rechtskundig, geneeskundig) advies o.

opinionated ['ə'pinjəneitid], **opinionative** [ə'pinjəneitiv] eigenzinnig, koppig; stijfhoofdig; eigenwijs.

opium-den ['oupjəmden] opiumkit v.

opium-smoker ['oupjəmsmoukə] opiumschuiver m.

opponent [ə'pounənt] adj. tegenstrevend; sb. tegenstrever; tegenstander, bestrijder m.

opportune ['ɔpətjûn, ɔpə'tjûn] gelegen, geschikt, gunstig, juist van pas (op tijd) komend.

opportunity [ɔpə'tjûniti] (gunstige) gelegenheid v.

oppose [ə'pouz] vt. stellen tegenover, tegenover elkaar stellen; zich kanten tegen, zich verzetten tegen, bestrijden; dwarsbomen, tegenwerken; vi. tegenwerpingen maken, opponeren.

opposer [ə'pouzə] tegenstrever, opponent m.; bestrijder m.

opposite ['ɔpəzit] adj. tegen(over)-gesteld; tegenovergelegen; (v. hoeken) overstaand; (Pl.) tegenoverstaand; sb. tegen(over)gestelde, tegendeel o.; adv. & prep. tegenover; daartegenover; aan de overkant.

opposition [ɔpə'ziʃən] tegenstand m., verzet o., oppositie v.; tegenstelling v.

oppress [ə'pres] onderdrukken, verdrukken; drukken (op); bezwaren, benauwen.

oppression [ə'preʃən] onderdrukking, verdrukking v.; druk m., benauwing v.

oppressor [ə'presə] onderdrukker, verdrukker m.

opprobrious (ly) [ə'proubriəs(li)] adj. (adv.) smadelijk, smalend, honend, beledigend, smaad—.

optician [ɔp'tiʃən] opticien m.

option ['ɔpʃən] keus, verkiezing v.; voorkeur, optie v.; (H.) premie v.

optional ['ɔpʃənl] adj. facultatief, ter keuze, naar eigen verkiezing.

opulence ['ɔpjuləns], **opulency** ['ɔpjulənsi] rijkdom m.; weelde v., overvloed m.; weelderigheid v.

opulent ['ɔpjulənt] rijk; overvloedig; weelderig.

or [ɔ:] of: — else, of wel, anders.

oracle ['ɔrəkl] sb. orakel o.; godsspraak v.; vi. orakelen.

oral ['o:rəl] adj. mondeling; mond—, sb. mondeling examen o.

orange ['ɔrin(d)ʒ] oranjeappel; sinaasappel m.; oranjeboom m.; oranje (kleur) v.

orangeade [ɔrin'(d)ʒeid] orangeade, sinaasappellimonade v.

orange-blossom ['ɔrin(d)ʒblɔsəm] oranjebloesem m.

oration [o'reiʃən] rede, redevoering, oratie v.

orbit ['o:bit] (v. hemellichaam) baan, loopbaan v.; oogkas, oogholte v.; (fig.) kring m., sfeer v.

orchard ['o:tʃəd] boomgaard m.

orcharding ['o:tʃədiŋ] ooftbouw m.

orchestra ['o:kistrə] orkest o.

ordain [o:'dein] vt. (tot priester) wijden; bepalen, voorschrijven; bestemmen; bevelen, verordenen; vi. verordenen.

order ['o:də] sb. stand m., klasse, soort v.; orde; rangorde v.; ridderorde v.; order v., bevel o., lastgeving v.; bestelling v.; (H.) order v.; vt. bevelen, gelasten, verordenen; bestellen; ordenen, schikken, rangschikken; regelen, inrichten; vi. commanderen.

order-book ['o:dəbuk] (H.) orderboek o.

order-form ['o:dəfo:m] (H.) bestelbiljet, bestelformulier o.

orderly ['o:dəli] adj. ordelijk, geregeld; ordelievend; sb. (mil.) ordonnans; oppasser m.; hospitaalsoldaat m.

ordinal ['o:dinəl] adj. rangschikkend; sb. rangtelwoord o.; ritueal, wijdingsboek o.

ordinance ['o:dinəns] verordening, ordonnantie v.; ritus m.

ordinary ['o:d(i)nəri] adj. gewoon, alledaags; sb. het gewone o.; (kath.) ordinaris m.; ordinarium o., gewone misgebeden o. mv.

ordination [o:di'neiʃən] ordening, rangschikking v.; (priester)wijding v.; (v. Voorzienigheid) beschikking v., raadsbesluit o.

ordure ['o:djuə] drek m., vuilnis v.; vuile taal v.

ore [o:] erts o.

organ ['o:gən] sb. (muz.) orgel o.; werktuig; orgaan o.; vi. op het orgel spelen.

organ-blower ['o:gənblouə] orgeltrapper m.

organ-grinder ['o:gəngraində] orgeldraaier m.

organic (al) [o:'gænik(l)] adj. organisch, bewerktuigd.

organism ['o:gənizm] organisme *o.*
organist ['o:gənist] organist *m.*
organization [o:gənai'zeifən] organisatie *v.*; bewerktuiging *v.*
organize [o:'gənaiz] organiseren; bewerktuigen.
orgy ['o:dʒi] braspartij *v.*, drinkgelag *o.*, slemppartij, orgie *v.*
Orient ['o:ri'ənt] (het) Oosten *o.*
orient ['o:riənt] *adj.* oostelijk; opgaand; *vr.* — **oneself,** zich oriënteren.
oriental [o:ri entəl] oostelijk; oosters.
orifice ['orifis] opening *v.*; mond *m.*
origin ['oridʒin] oorsprong *m.*, afkomst, afstamming, herkomst *v.*; begin *o.*; oorzaak *v.*
original [ə'ridʒinəl] *adj.* oorspronkelijk, origineel; *sb.* origineel (mens) *m.*; oorspronkelijk stuk *o.*; oorsprong *m.*, afkomst *v.*
originate [ə'ridʒineit] *vt.* voortbrengen; *vi.* ontstaan, voortkomen (*from,* uit); opkomen (*with,* bij).
originator [ə'ridʒineitə] ontwerper *m.*; schepper, verwekker *m.*
oriole ['o:rioul] (*Dk.*) goudmerel *v.*, wielewaal *m.*
ornament ['o:nəmənt] *sb.* ornament, versiersel *o.*; sieraad *o.*; ['o:nəment] *vt.* versieren, tooien.
ornamental [o:nə'mentəl] *adj.* versierend, ter versiering dienend, decoratief.
ornate (**ly**) [o:'neit(li)] *adj.* (*adv.*) te veel (kwistig) versierd, overladen; (*v. stijl*) beeldrijk, bloemrijk.
orphan ['o:fən] *sb.* wees *m.* & *v.*, weeskind *o.*; *adj.* verweesd, ouderloos.
orphanage ['o:fənidʒ] verweesdheid *v.*; weeshuis *o.*
orthodox ['o:ðədɔks] orthodox, rechtzinnig; hecht, solied, degelijk.
orthography [o:'ðɔgrəfi] spellingleer *v.*; (juiste) spelling *v.*
oscillate ['ɔsileit] slingeren, schommelen; (*v. radio*) oscilleren.
oscillation [ɔsi'leifən] slingering, schommeling *v.*; oscillatie *v.*
osier ['ouʒə] *sb.* katwilg, waterwilg *m.*; rijs *o.*; teen *v.*; *adj.* tenen.
osseous ['ɔsiəs] beenachtig, beender—.
ossify ['ɔsifai] *vt.* doen verbenen; *vi.* verbenen, in been veranderen; (*fig.: v. gevoel*) verharden, afstompen.
ossuary ['ɔsjuəri] knekelhuis(je), dodenhuis *o.*
ostensible [ɔs'tensibl] ogenschijnlijk; schijnbaar, voorgewend; zichtbaar, in 't oog vallend.
ostentation [ɔsten'teifən] (uiterlijk) vertoon *o.*, pronkerij, praal *v.*
ostentatious [ɔsten'teifəs] *adj.* pronkziek, praalziek; opzichtig; (sterk) in 't oog lopend; blufferig.
ostrich ['ɔstritf] struisvogel *m.*
other ['ʌðə] *adj.* ander; anders, verschillend; nog (een, meer); *sb.* andere *o.*
otherwhere ['ʌðəwêə] elders.

otherwhile(**s**) ['ʌðəwail(z)] op een andere tijd.
otherwise ['ʌðəwaiz] anders, op een andere manier; anderszins.
otter ['ɔtə] (zee)otter *m.*; otterbont *o.*
ought [o:t] behoren, moeten.
ounce [auns] ons *o.*
our ['auə] ons, onze.
out [aut] *adv.* uit, buiten, erbuiten; (*mil.*) te velde; onder de wapenen; uit de mode; uitgedoofd; (*bij spel*) af; *prep.* **from** —, uit; *vt.* eruit zetten; (*Am.*) uit de weg ruimen; *vi.* te voorschijn halen; *ij.* weg (met); *sb.* uitstapje *o.*; **the** —**s,** de niet regerende partij.
outbuilding ['autbildiŋ] bijgebouw *o.*
outburst ['autbə:st] uitbarsting *v.*; (*fig.*) ontboezeming *v.*; uitval *m.*
outcast ['autkâst] *sb.* verworpeling, verschoppeling, verstoteling *m.*; *adj.* verworpen, verstoten; verbannen.
outcome ['autkəm] uitslag *m.*, resultaat; gevolg *o.*
outdated [aut'deitid] verouderd.
oudo [aut'dû] overtreffen.
outdoor ['autdo:] buiten—; buitenshuis; openlucht—.
outdoors ['aut'do:z] buitenshuis.
outfit ['autfit] uitrusting *v.*, uitzet *o.*
outflank [aut'flæŋk] (*mil.*) overvleugelen, omtrekken; (*fig.*) beetnemen.
outgrowth ['autgrouð] uitgroeisel *o.*; uitkomst *v.*, resultaat *o.*
outing ['autiŋ] uitgang, uitgaansdag *m.*; uitstapje *o.*
outlander ['autlændə] buitenlander, vreemdeling *m.*
outlandish [aut'lændif] buitenlands; vreemd, zonderling, vreemdsoortig; afgelegen.
outlaw ['autlo:] *sb.* vogelvrij verklaarde; balling *m.*; *vt.* vogelvrij verklaren, buiten de wet stellen.
outlay ['autlei] *sb.* uitgave(n) *v.* (*mv.*), onkosten *m. mv.*; [aut'lei] *vt.* uitgeven.
outlet ['autlet, 'autlit] uitgang, uitweg *m.*; afvoerkanaal *o.*; (*v. rivier*) mond *m.*; (*fig.*) veiligheidsklep *v.*; (*H.*) afzetgebied *o.*
outline ['autlain] *sb.* omtrek *m.*, schets *v.*; **the** —**s,** (*ook:*) de hoofdlijnen, de hoofdpunten; *vt.* in (ruwe) omtrek schetsen, met enkele lijnen tekenen; de hoofdlijnen aangeven.
outlive ['aut'liv] langer leven dan, overleven.
outlook ['autluk] uitkijk *m.*; uitzicht, vooruitzicht *o.*; schildwacht *m.*
outlying ['autlaiiŋ] verwijderd, afgelegen.
outness ['autnis] uitwendigheid *v.*; objectiviteit *v.*
out-of-date ['autəv'deit] verouderd, ouderwets.
out-of-work ['autəv'wə:k] *adj.* werkloos; *sb.* werkloze *m.*
outpost ['autpoust] buitenpost *m.*; (*mil.*) voorpost *m.*

output ['autput] opbrengst, produktie *v.*; (*tn.*) effect, vermogen *o.*

outrage ['autreidʒ, 'autridʒ] *vt.* beledigen, krenken; geweld aandoen, verkrachten; *sb.* belediging *v.*, smaad *m.*; aanranding, gewelddaad, verkrachting *v.*

outrageous(ly) [aut'reidʒəs(li)] *adj.* (*adv.*) beledigend, krenkend; gewelddadig; schandelijk; uitbundig, bovenmate.

outrun [aut'rən] harder lopen dan; voorbij lopen; (*fig.*) voorbijstreven.

outset ['autset] aanvang *m.*, begin *o.*

outside ['aut'said] *sb.* buitenkant *m.*, buitenzijde *v.*; buitenste, uitwendige *o.*; uiterste *o.*; *adj.* buitenste; uiterste, maximum; *adv.* buiten; naar buiten, van buiten; buitenop; *prep.* buiten; (*Am.*) behalve.

outsider ['aut'saidə] niet ingewijde, buitenstaander *m.*

outskirt ['autske:t] zoom, buitenkant, rand *m.*; **—s**, buitenwijken *v. mv.*

outspoken(ly) [aut'spoukn(li)] *adj.* (*adv.*) openhartig, vrijmoedig.

outspread ['aut'spred] uitspreiden.

outstanding [aut'stændiŋ] uitstaand; uitstekend; onafgedaan; onuitgemaakt, onbeslist; opvallend, in 't oog lopend.

outstrip [aut'strip] voorbijstreven; achter zich laten; overtreffen.

outturn ['autto:n] produktie *v.*

outvote [aut'vout] overstemmen.

outward ['autwəd] *adj.* uitwendig, uiterlijk; buitenwaarts; buiten—; *adv.* naar buiten; *sb.* uiterlijk *o.*

outwit [aut'wit] verschalken, te slim af zijn.

outwork ['autwə:k] (*mil.*) buitenwerk *o.*; werk *o.* buiten de fabriek, enz. verricht.

outworn ['aut'wo:n] versleten; afgezaagd; uitgeput.

oval ['ouvəl] *adj.* ovaal, eirond.

ovation [ou'veifən] ovatie, hulde *v.*

oven ['əvn] oven *m.*

over ['ouvə] *prep. & adv.* over, boven; over... heen; bij; betreffende, aangaande; *sb.* overschot *o.*; het springen over *o.*; *vt.* springen over.

overall ['ouvəro:l] stofjas *v.*; morskiel *m.*; **—s**, werkbroek *v.*; werkpak *o.*

overarch [ouvə'râtʃ] overwelven.

overarm ['ouvərâm] (*sp.*) bovenarms.

overboard ['ouvəbo:d] overboord.

overbold [ouvə'bould] al te vrijmoedig.

overburden [ouvə'bə:dn] overladen.

over-busy ['ouvə'bizi] al te druk.

overcare ['ovə'kêə] te grote zorg *v.*

overcast ['ouvə'kâst] *vt.* verduisteren, verdonkeren, een schaduw werpen op; te hoog aanslaan, te hoog schatten; *adj.* (*v. lucht*) betrokken.

overcharge ['ouvə'tʃâdʒ] *vt.* overladen, te zwaar laden; overdrijven; (*H.*) overvragen; ['ouvətʃâdʒ] *sb.* overbelasting *v.*; (*H.*) overvraging *v.*; overdreven prijs *m.*; (*mil.*) te sterke lading *v.*

overcloud [ouvə'klaud] bewolken, verdonkeren.

overcoat ['ouvəkout] overjas *v.*

overcome [ouvə'kəm] *vt.* overwinnen; te boven komen; *adj.* onder de indruk; overmand; overstelpt; (*fam.*) beneveld, dronken.

overcrowd [ouvə'kraud] overladen (met bijzonderheden, enz.).

overdo [ouvə'dû] overdrijven; afmatten, uitputten; te gaar koken (braden, enz.).

overdone [ouvə'dən] overdreven; afgemat, uitgeput; te gaar.

overdrive [ouvə'draiv] afjakkeren, afbeulen.

overdue ['ouvə'djû] (*v. trein, boot*) te laat, over zijn tijd; (*v. schuld*) achterstallig; (*v. wissel*) vervallen, over de vervaltijd.

overestimate [ouvə'restimeit] *vt.* te hoog aanslaan; overschatten; ['ouvə'restimit] *sb.* overschatting *v.*; te hoge schatting *v.*

overexert ['ouvəreg'zə:t] (**— oneself**), (zich) te zeer inspannen.

overfeed [ouvə'fîd] (zich) te sterk voeden.

overflow ['ouvəflou] *sb.* overstroming *v.*; overvloed *m.*; [ouvə'flou] *vt. & vi.* overstromen; overlopen, overvloeien.

overfull ['ouvə'ful] (al) te vol.

overgrown ['ouvə'groun] begroeid, bedekt (met gras, enz.); (*v. tuin*) verwilderd; uit zijn kracht gegroeid, opgeschoten.

overhasty ['ouvə'heisti] overijld.

overhaul [ouvə'ho:l] *vt.* (*v. machine*) nazien; grondig nagaan; onderzoeken, inspecteren; (*sch.*) inhalen; *sb.* het nazien *o.*; inspectie *v.*

overhear [ouvə'hiə] toevallig horen, opvangen; afluisteren.

overleaf [ouvə'lîf] aan ommezijde.

overlive [ouvə'liv] overleven, langer leven dan.

overload ['ouvə'loud] *vt.* overladen; overbelasten, te zwaar laden; ['ouvəloud] te zware last *m.*

overlook [ouvə'luk] overzien; uitzien op; door de vingers zien; over het hoofd zien; toezien op, in 't oog houden.

overlooker [ouvə'lukə] opzichter *m.*; bespieder *m.*

overman ['ouvəmæn] opzichter, ploegbaas *m.*   [toegift *v.*

over-measure ['ouvəmeʒə] overmaat,

overpay ['ouvə, pei] te veel betalen.

overpower [ouvə'pauə] overstelpen, overweldigen.

overprint [ouvə'print] *vt.* (*v. foto*) te donker afdrukken; ['ouvəprint] *sb.* overdrukje *o.*; (*op postzegel*) opdruk *m.*

overproduction ['ouvəprə'dəkfən] overproduktie *v.*

overrate [ouvə'reit] overschatten.

overreach ['ouvəritʃ] *vt.* verder reiken dan; beetnemen, bedriegen; *vi.* (*v. paard*) aanslaan; *vr.* **— oneself**, te ver reiken, zich verrekken; (*fig.*) het doel voorbijstreven.

override [ouvə'raid] omverrijden; onder de voet lopen; met voeten treden; vernietigen; (*v. paard*) afjakkeren, afbeulen.
overripe ['ouvə'raip] overrijp.
oversea ['ouvəsi] *adj.* overzees; ['ouvə'si] *adv.* overzee.
oversee [ouvə'si] overzien; toezicht houden op.
overseer ['ouvəsiə] opziener, opzichter *m.*, inspecteur *m.*; controleur *m.*
overshadow [ouvə'ʃædou] overschaduwen; verduisteren.
overshoe ['ouvəʃû] overschoen *m.*
oversight ['ouvəsait] vergissing *v.*, abuis *o.*; onachtzaamheid *v.*; toezicht *o.*
oversleep [ouvə'slîp] *vt.* langer slapen dan; *vr.* — *oneself,* zich verslapen, te lang slapen.
oversleeve ['ouvəslîv] morsmouw *v.*
overspill ['ouvəspil] *sb.* het overtollige *o.*; overbevolking *v.*; *vi.* overlopen.
overstrain ['ouvə'strein] *vt.* al te zeer inspannen, overspannen; overdrijven; *vr.* — *oneself,* zich verrekken.
overstrung [ouvə'strʌŋ] overspannen, overprikkeld; ['ouvəstrʌŋ] (*v. piano*) kruissnarig.
overtake [ouvə'teik] inhalen; achterhalen; (*v. onweer, enz.*) overvallen, verrassen; (*v. achterstand*) bijwerken.
overtask ['ouvə'tâsk] met werk overladen; te veel vergen van.
overthrow [ouvə'ðrou] *vt.* omwerpen, omverwerpen; doen vallen, ten val brengen; verslaan; ['ouvəðrou] *sb.* omverwerping *v.*; (*v. ministerie, enz.*) val *m.*; nederlaag *v.*
overtime ['ouvə'taim] overuren *o. mv.*; overwerk *o.*
overture ['ouvətjuə] voorstel, aanbod *o.* (*bij onderhandelingen*); (*muz.*) ouverture *v.*; (*v. gedicht*) inleiding *v.*
overturn [ouvə'tə:n] *vt.* omwerpen, omverwerpen; vernietigen; te gronde richten, ten val brengen; *vi.* omslaan, omvallen; *sb.* ['ouvətə:n] omverwerping *v.*; vernietiging *v.*
overvalue ['ouvə'vælju] *vt.* te hoog schatten, overschatten; ['ouvəvælju] overwaarde *v.*
overweight [ouvə'weit] *vt.* te zwaar belasten, overbelasten; *sb.* ['ouvəweit] overwicht *o.*; *adj.* te zwaar.
overwhelm [ouvə'welm] overstelpen (*with,* met); verpletteren.
overwork ['ouvə'wə:k] *vt.* te hard laten werken; uitputten; *vi.* zich overwerken; ['ouvəwə:k] *sb.* overwerk *o.*; te grote inspanning *v.*
overworn ['ouvə'wo:n] afgedragen; afgezaagd; afgemat.
overwrought ['ouvə'ro:t] overspannen, overwerkt; (*fig.*) overladen; te zeer uitgewerkt.
owe [ou] *vt.* schuldig zijn, verschuldigd zijn; te danken hebben, te wijten hebben (aan); *vi.* schuld(en) hebben.
owing ['ouiŋ] *adj.* te betalen, verschuldigd; *sb.* —*s,* schulden *v. mv.*
owl [aul] uil *m.*; (*fig.*) uilskuiken *o.*
own [oun] eigen.
own [oun] *vt.* bezitten, hebben; erkennen, toegeven; *vi.* eigendom bezitten; — *up,* bekennen, opbiechten; door de mand vallen.
owner ['ounə] bezitter *m.*; reder *m.*
ownerless ['ounəlis] onbeheerd.
ownership ['ounəʃip] eigendomsrecht *o.*; bezit *o.*
ox [ɔks] os *m.* [binding *v.*
oxide ['ɔksaid] oxyde *o.*, zuurstofver-
oxo ['ɔksou] vleesextract *o.*
oxygen ['ɔksidʒən] zuurstof *v.*; bleekpoeder *m.*
oyster ['ɔistə] oester *v.*
oyster-bank ['ɔistəbæŋk] oesterplaat oesterbank *v.*

P

pace [peis] *sb.* pas *m.*; schrede *v.*, stap *m.*; (*v. paard*) gang *m.*; *vi.* stappen, stapvoets gaan; *vt.* afpassen, afstappen; op en neer stappen in.
pace-maker ['peismeikə] (*sp.*) gangmaker *m.*
pacific [pə'sifik] vredelievend, vreedzaam; *P*— (*Ocean*), Stille Zuidzee.
pacify ['pæsifai] stillen, bedaren; bevredigen.
pack [pæk] *sb.* pak *o.*; last *m.*; bepakking; mars *v.*; (— *of cards*), spel kaarten *o.*; *vt.* inpakken; verpakken; bepakken, beladen; *vi.* pakken; zich samenpakken; samenscholen.
package ['pækidʒ] verpakking *v.*; pak *o.*; pakgoed *o.*; verpakkingskosten *m. mv.*; —*s,* colli.
packet ['pækit] *sb.* pakje, pakket *o.*; pakketboot *v.*; (*sl.*) projectiel *o.*; *vt.* inpakken.
packet-boat ['pækitbout] pakketboot *v.*
packing ['pækiŋ] (het) inpakken *o.*; verpakking *v.*; (*tn.*) pakking, vulling *v.*; (*Am.*) (het) verduurzamen *o.* van levensmiddelen.
packing-paper ['pækiŋpeipə] pakpapier *o.*
packman ['pækmən] pakkendrager *m.*; marskramer *m.*
pact [pækt] verdrag, verbond *o.*, overeenkomst *v.*
pad [pæd] *sb.* stootkussen *o.*; vulsel *o.*; onderlegger *m.*, vloeiboek *o.*; zacht zadel *o.*; beenkap *v.*; weg *m.*; *vt.* op-

vullen, volstoppen; bekleden, capiton-
neren; betreden; *vi.* te voet gaan, stappen.
padding ['pædiŋ] vulsel *o.*; vulling,
bladvulling *v.*
paddle ['pædl] *sb.* pagaai *v.*; (*v. roeiriem*) blad *o.*; (*v. scheprad*) schoep *v.*;
vi. roeien, pagaaien; waggelen; (in
't water) plassen.
paddle-wheel ['pædlwîl] scheprad *o.*
padlock ['pædlɔk] *sb.* hangslot *o.*; (*fig.*)
slot *o.*; *rt.* met een hangslot sluiten.
pagan ['peigən] *sb.* heiden *m.*; *adj.* heidens.
page [peidʒ] *sb.* page, livreiknecht *m.*;
rokophouder *m.*; bladzijde *v.*; *vt.* pa-
gineren.
pageant ['pædʒənt] praal, vertoning *v.*;
(groots) schouwspel *o.*; (historische)
optocht *m.*
paillasse [pæl'jæs] stromatras *v.*
pain [pein] *sb.* pijn *v.*, lijden *o.*, smart
v., leed *o.*; straf *v.*; **—s,** pijnen, weeën;
moeite, inspanning *v.*; *vt.* pijn doen; pijn
veroorzaken; pijnigen; leed doen, bedroeven.
painful(ly) ['peinful(i)] *adj.* (*adv.*) pijnlijk; moeilijk, lastig.
pain-killer ['peinkilə] pijnstillend middel *o.*
painless(ly) ['peinlis(li)] *adj.* (*adv.*)
pijnloos.
paint [pcint] *sb.* verf *v.*; kleurstof *v.*;
blanketsel *o.*; *vt.* schilderen; verven; (*v.
wond, enz.*) penselen, aanstrijken (met
penseel); *vi.* schilderen; zich verven.
painter ['peintə] schilder *m.*; (*sch.*)
vanglijn *v.*
painting ['peintiŋ] schilderkunst *v.*;
schilderij *v.* & *o.*; schildering *v.*
pair [pêə] *sb.* paar *o.*; *vt.* paren; paarsgewijze rangschikken; verenigen (in de
echt, tot een paar); *vi.* (zich) paren;
een paar vormen; samengaan.
pairing-season ['pêəriŋsîzn] paartijd *m.*
palace ['pælis] paleis *o.*
palatable ['pælətəbl] *adj.* smakelijk.
palate ['pælit] verhemelte *o.*; (*fig.*)
smaak *m.*
palaver [pə'lâvə] *sb.* bespreking *v.*, onderhoud *o.*, conferentie *v.*; gewauwel
o.; vleitaal *v.*; *vt.* bepraten; vleien; *vi.*
confereren; wauwelen.
pale [peil] *sb.* paal *m.*; grens *v.*, grenzen
v. mv., grenspaal *m.*; *vt.* ompalen,
omheinen, insluiten.
pale [peil] *adj.* bleek, dof, mat; flauw,
fiets; *vt.* bleek maken; *vi.* bleek worden,
verbleken.
paleness ['peilnis] bleekheid, dofheid,
matheid *v.*
paletot ['pæltou] losse overjas *v.*; mantel *m.*
palette ['pælit] palet *o.*
paling ['peiliŋ] omheining, omrastering
v., staketsel *o.*
palisade [pæli'seid] *sb.* palissade *v.*,

paalwerk, staketsel *o.*; (*mil.*) schans-
paal *m.*; *vt.* ompalen, palissaderen.
pallet ['pælit] palet *o.*; verguldmesje *o.*;
spaantje *o.*; (*v. orgel*) windklep *v.*; strozak *m.*; strobed *o.*, stromatras *v.*
palliasse [pæl'jæs] stromatras *v.*
palliate ['pælieit] lenigen, verzachten,
verlichten; verbloemen, bemantelen,
vergoelijken.
pallid ['pælid] *adj.* bleek, doodsbleek,
ziekelijk bleek.
pallor ['pælə] bleekheid *v.*
palm [pâm] *sb.* palm *m.*; palmboom
m.; palmtak *m.*; (*v. hand*) palm *v.*; *vt.*
betasten; aaien; (in de hand) verbergen;
omkopen, de hand smeren.
palmer ['pâmə] pelgrim *m.*; koolrups *v.*
palm-oil ['pâmɔil] palmolie *v.*; omkoopgeld *o.*, fooi *v.*, steekpenning *m.*
Palm-Sunday ['pâm'sɵndi] Palmzondag *m.*
palp [pælp] voeler, taster, voelhoorn *m.*
palpable ['pælpəbl] *adj.* tastbaar.
palpate ['pælpeit] betasten.
palpitation [pælpi'teiʃən] hartklopping *v.*; popeling, trilling *v.*
palsy ['po:lzi] *sb.* verlamming *v.*; *vt.*
verlammen.
paltry ['po:ltri] armzalig, nietig.
pamper ['pæmpə] volproppen, volstoppen, overvoeren; vertroetelen, verwennen.
pamphlet ['pæmflit] vlugschrift *o.*,
brochure *v.*
pan [pæn] pan *v.*; hersenpan *r.*; (*v.
weegschaal*) schaal *v.*; bodem, harde ondergrond *m.*; ijsschots *v.*
Pan-American ['pænə'merikən] Pan-
Amerikaans.
pancake ['pænkeik] *sb.* pannekoek *m.*;
vi. (*vl.*) doorzakken.
pander ['pændə] *sb.* koppelaar *m.*; handlanger *m.*; *vi.* koppelen, voor koppelaar
spelen; **— to,** ter wille zijn, toegeven aan.
pane [pein] (glas)ruit, vensterruit *v.*;
(*v. deur*) paneel *o.*; muurvak *o.*; vlakke
zijde *v.*; (*v. hamer*) pen *v.*
panel ['pænl] *sb.* paneel *o.*; tussenschot
o.; vak *o.*; luik *o.*; *vt.* lambrizeren; in
vakken verdelen.
panic ['pænik] *sb.* paniek *v.*; panische
schrik *m.*; *adj.* panisch; *vi.* door een panische schrik aangegrepen worden.
panicle ['pænikl] (*Pl.*) pluim *v.*; samengestelde aar *v.*
panic-monger ['pænikmɵŋə] alarmist *m.*
panorama [pæn'ərâmə] panorama *o.*
pant [pænt] *vi.* hijgen, snakken, haken
(*for, after,* naar); (*v. bloed, enz.*) hevig
kloppen; *vt.* hijgend uitbrengen; *sb.* hij-
ging *v.*
pantalet(te)s [pæntə'lets] damespanta-
lon *v.*; fietsbroek *v.*
panther ['pændə] panter *m.*
pantile ['pæntail] (gewelfde) dakpan,
nokpan *v.*; (*sl.*) hoge hoed *m.*, kachelpijp *v.*; scheepsbeschuit *r.*

pantograph ['pæntəgrâf, —græf] tekenaap m.

pantomime ['pæntəmaim] sb. pantomime v., gebarenspel o.; gebarenspeler m.; vi. (zich) door gebaren uitdrukken.

pantry ['pæntri] provisiekamer v.; provisiekast v.

pants ['pænts] (fam.) broek v.; onderbroek v.

pap [pæp] pap v.; vleesvrucht v.; (sl.) bijverdiensten v. mv.; tepel m.

papal ['peipəl] pauselijk.

paper ['peipə] sb. papier o.; blad, nieuwsblad, dagblad o., krant v.; behangselpapier o.; adj. papieren; (fig.) op papier; vt. in papier pakken; (v. kamer, enz.) behangen.

paper currency ['peipəkərənsi] papieren geld o.

paper-folder ['peipəfouldə] vouwbeen o.

paper-hanger ['peipəhæŋə] behanger m.

paper-knife ['peipənaif] papiersnijder m.; vouwbeen o.

paper-warfare ['peipəwu:fêə] papieren oorlog, krantenoorlog m.

paper-weight ['peipəweit] pressepapier o.

par [pâ] gelijkheid v.; (H.) parikoers m.; normaalstand m.

parable ['pærəbl] parabel, gelijkenis v.

parachute [pærə'ʃût, 'pærəʃût] sb. valscherm o., parachute v.; vt. & vi. (zich) in een valscherm neerlaten.

parachutist [pærə'ʃûtist, [pærəʃûtist] valschermspringer, parachutist m.

parade [pə'reid] sb. parade v.; (fig.) vertoon o.; schijn m.; (mil.) exercitieplein o., paradeplaats v.; vt. inspecteren, parade laten maken; (v. kennis, enz.) pronken met, luchten; vi. marcheren; trots stappen; in optocht marcheren; (mil.) aantreden.

paradise ['pærədais] paradijs o.

paraffin(e) ['pærəfin] paraffine v.; — oil, gezuiverde petroleum.

paragraph ['pærəgrâf] sb. paragraaf, alinea v.; (kort) nieuwsbericht, krantebericht o.; vt. paragraferen.

parallel ['pærəlel] adj. evenwijdig, parallel; overeenkomstig; sb. evenwijdige lijn, parallel v.; (mil.) evenwijdige loopgraaf v.; vt. evenwijdig plaatsen; evenwijdig lopen met; vergelijken; op één lijn stellen; evenaren.

paralyse ['pærəlaiz] verlammen.

paralysis [pə'rælis!s] verlamming v.

paralytic [pærə'litik] adj. lam, verlamd; aanleg hebbend voor verlamming; sb. lamme, verlamde m.

paramount ['pærəmaunt] adj. hoogste, opperste; overwegend, overheersend; sb. opperheer, opperste m.

parapet ['pærəpit] borstwering v.; (v. brug, enz.) (stenen) leuning v.

paraph ['pæræf] sb. paraaf v.; vt. paraferen.

paraphrase ['pærəfreiz] sb. parafrase, omschrijving v.; vrije overzetting v.; vt. parafraseren, omschrijven, in eigen woorden weergeven.

parasite ['pærəsait] parasiet, klaploper m.; woekerplant v.; woekerdier o.

parasol ['pærəsɔl] parasol m., zonnescherm o.

parcel ['pâsl] sb. deel, stuk o.; partij v.; perceel o., kaveling v.; pak(je), pakket o.; adj. & adv. gedeeltelijk, half; vt. verdelen, kavelen; inpakken.

parcel-office ['pâslɔfis] bestelkantoor o., bestelgoederenbureau o.

parch [pâtʃ] vt. & vi. roosteren; schroeien, verzengen; (doen) verdrogen; verdorren.

parchment ['pâtʃmənt] sb. perkament o.; diploma o.; (v. koffieboon) hoornschil v.; adj. perkamenten.

pardon ['pâdn] sb. vergiffenis, vergeving v.; begenadiging, gratie v.; aflaat m.; vt. vergeven, vergiffenis schenken; begenadigen; — me, neem mij niet kwalijk.

pardonable ['pâdnəbl] adj. vergeeflijk.

pare [pêə] (v. appel, enz.) schillen; afsnijden, afknippen; afschaven; wegsnijden; besnoeien; beknibbelen.

parent ['pêərənt] ouder m.; vader m., moeder v.; (fig.) oorzaak v., wortel m., bron v.; —s, ouders.

parental(ly) [pə'rentəl(i)] adj. (adv.) ouderlijk; vaderlijk; moederlijk.

parenthood ['pêərənthud] ouderschap o.

parentless ['pêərəntlis] ouderloos.

parent-ship ['pêərəntʃip] moederschip o.

parents-in-law ['pêərəntzinlo:] schoonouders mv.

parget ['pâdʒit] sb. pleisterkalk v.; vt. pleisteren, bepleisteren.

pargeting ['pâdʒitiŋ] pleistering v.; pleisterwerk o.

pariah ['pæriə, 'pêəriə] paria, uitgeworpene m.

paring ['pêəriŋ] schil v.; afknipsel o.; afschaafsel o.; (het) afknippen o.

paris ['pæris] sb. Paris m.; Parijs o.; adj. Parijs.

parish ['pæriʃ] parochie v., kerspel o., kerkelijke gemeente v.

parishioner [pə'riʃənə] parochiaan m.

parity ['pæriti] gelijkheid; overeenkomst v.; (H.) pariteit v.

park [pâk] sb. park o.; artilleriepark o.; oesterpark o.; parkeerterrein o.; vt. in een park sluiten; aanleggen als park; parkeren; stallen, opbergen.

purley ['pâli] sb. gesprek, onderhoud o.; onderhandeling v.; vi. onderhandelen, parlementeren; babbelen, praten.

parliament ['pâləmənt] parlement o.

parlour ['pâlə] woonkamer, huiskamer; zitkamer v.; spreekkamer v.; (v. kapper, enz.) salon o.; (v. fotograaf) atelier o.

parole ['pə'roul] *sb.* erewoord *o.*; *(mil.)* wachtwoord, parool *o.*; *vt.* op erewoord vrijlaten; *(Am.)* onder borgtocht vrijlaten.

paronym ['pærənim] verwant woord *o.*

parquet ['pâkit] *sb.* parket *o.*; parketvloer *m.*; *vt.* van een parketvloer voorzien, parketteren.

parrot ['pærət] *sb.* papegaai *m.*; *vt.* napraten; nadoen; drillen.

parry ['pæri] *vt.* afweren, pareren; ontwijken; *vi.* pareren; *sb.* afwering *v.*; ontwijking *v.*; *(schermen)* parade *v.*

parse [pâs] taalkundig ontleden.

parsimonious(**ly**) [pâsi'mounjəs(li)] *adj.* (*adv.*) spaarzaam, zuinig; karig, schriel, gierig.

parsing ['pâsiŋ] taalkundige ontleding *v.*

parsley ['pâsli] peterselie *v.*

parsnip ['pâsnip] pastinaak, witte peen *v.*

part [pât] *sb.* part, gedeelte *o.*; aandeel *o.*; partij *v.*; rol *v.*; **—s,** bekwaamheid, talent; *vt.* verdelen; indelen; scheiden; afscheiden; schiften; *vi.* scheiden; uiteen gaan, uit elkaar gaan; breken, afbreken, doorbreken.

partable ['pâtəbl] deelbaar, scheidbaar.

partake [pâ'teik] deelnemen, deel hebben (**of, in,** aan, in); *(v. maaltijd, enz.)* gebruiken; **— of,** iets hebben van, niet vrij zijn van.

partial ['pâʃəl] *adj.* gedeeltelijk, partieel; partijdig, eenzijdig.

partiality [pâʃi'æliti] voorliefde *v.*; partijdigheid, eenzijdigheid *v.*

participate [pâ'tisipeit] delen (in); deel hebben, deel nemen (**in, of,** in, aan); zijn medewerking verlenen.

participation [pâtisi'peiʃən] deelneming *v.*; aandeel *o.*

participle ['pâtisipl] deelwoord *o.*

particular [pə'tikjələ] *adj.* speciaal, afzonderlijk, eigen; bijzonder; nauwkeurig; *sb.* bijzonderheid *v.*; bijzondere omstandigheid *v.*; bijzonder geval *o.*

particularity [pətikju'læriti] bijzonderheid; eigenaardigheid *v.*

parting ['pâtiŋ] *sb.* scheiding *v.*; splitsing *v.*; afscheid *o.*; vertrek *o.*; *adj.* afscheids—.

partisan [pâti'zæn] *sb.* aanhanger, voorstander *m.*; partijganger, partijgenoot *m.*; partizaan *v.*; *adj.* partijdig; partij—; partijgangers—.

partition [pâ'tiʃən] *sb.* deling, verdeling *v.*; scheiding *v.*; beschot, tussenschot *o.*; *vt.* verdelen; afscheiden, afschutten.

partly ['pâtli] *adv.* gedeeltelijk; deels.

partner ['pâtnə] *sb.* deelgenoot *m.*; compagnon, vennoot *m.*; makker, maat, gezel *m.*; *vt.* koppelen.

partnership ['pâtnəʃip] vennootschap *v.*, deelgenootschap *o.*

part-payment ['pâtpeimənt] **in —,** op afbetaling.

partridge ['pâtridʒ] patrijs *m.*

part-song ['pâtsɔŋ] meerstemmig lied (gezang) *o.*

party ['pâti] partij *v.*; deelnemer *m.*; troep *m.*, gezelschap *o.*; aanhang *m.*, factie *v.*

party-spirit ['pâtispirit] partijgeest *m.*

parvenu ['pâvənjû] *sb.* parvenu *m.*; *adj.* parvenuachtig.

pass [pâs] *vi.* voorbijgaan, passeren; voorbijtrekken; voorbijstromen; doorlopen; aflopen; *vt.* voorbijgaan; voorbijlopen; voorbijtrekken; overgaan; oversteken, overtrekken; overslaan; *(v. tijd)* doorbrengen; doormaken; *sb.* pas, bergpas *m.*; doorgang *m.*; vaargeul *v.*; reispas; verlofpas *m.*; toegangsbewijs; vrijbiljet *o.*

passable ['pâsəbl] *adj.* begaanbaar; berijdbaar; doorwaadbaar; gangbaar; draaglijk, vrij goed.

passage ['pæsidʒ] doorgang *m.*; doortocht *m.*; doorvaart *v.*; overtocht *m.*; overgang *m.*

passenger ['pæsindʒə] passagier *m.*; passagiersboot *v.*; voorbijganger *m.*

passer-by ['pâsə'bai] voorbijganger *m.*

passing ['pâsiŋ] *adj.* voorbijgaand; doortrekkend; *adv.* zeer, buitengewoon, in hoge mate, ongemeen; *sb.* voorbijgang *m.*; overlijden *o.*; *(v. wet)* (het) aannemen *o.*; *(v. examen)* (het) slagen *o.*; **in —,** in 't voorbijgaan, terloops.

passion ['pæʃən] lijden *o.*; hartstocht *m.*, passie *v.*

Passion-Sunday ['pæʃən'sʊndi] Passiezondag *m.*

Passion-week ['pæʃənwik] lijdensweek, Goede Week *v.*

passive ['pæsiv] *adj.* lijdelijk; lijdend, passief; *sb.* *(gram.)* lijdende vorm; lijdend werkwoord.

Passover ['pâsouvə] joods Paasfeest *o.*

passport ['pâspo:t] paspoort *o.*

pass-word ['pâswə:d] parool, wachtwoord *o.*

past [pâst] *adj.* verleden, voorbij; voorbijgegaan; geleden; *sb.* verleden *o.*; verleden tijd *m.*; (het) gebeurde *o.*; *adv.* voorbij; *prep.* voorbij, langs; over, na; buiten.

paste [peist] *sb.* deeg *o.*; smeersel *o.*; stijfsel *o.*, pap *v.* (om te plakken); plaksel *o.*; pasta *o.*; *vt.* plakken, beplakken; *(sl.)* ranselen; **— up,** aanplakken; dichtplakken.

paste-board ['peistbo:d] *sb.* deegplank *v.*; bordpapier *o.*; *adj.* bordpapieren.

pastil(**le**) ['pâstil] pastille *v.*

pastime ['pâstaim] tijdverdrijf *o.*

pastor ['pâstə] zielenherder, zielverzorger *m.*

pastry ['peistri] gebak, gebakje *o.*

pastry-cook ['peistrikuk] pasteibakker *m.*

pasture ['pâstʃə] weide *v.*; gras *o.*

pasty ['peisti] *adj.* deegachtig; **— (- faced),** slap en bleek.

pasty ['pæsti, 'pâsti] (vlees)pastei *v.*
pat [pæt] *sb.* tikje, klapje *o.*; (*v. boter*) stukje, klompje *o.*, kluit *m.*; *vt.* tikken, kloppen; een (goedkeurend) tikje geven; *adj. & adv.* geschikt, toepasselijk; net van pas; raak, ad rem; klaar, bij de hand.
patch [pætʃ] *sb.* lap *m.*, stuk *o.*; stukje (lapje) *o.* grond; plek *v.*; moesje *o.*; *vt.* lappen, oplappen, een lap zetten op; samenflansen.
patcher ['pætʃə] lapper *m.*; knoeier *m.*
patchwork ['pætʃwɑːk] lapwerk *o.*; knoeiwerk *o.*
patent ['peitənt] *adj.* openbaar; duidelijk; zichtbaar; patent, voortreffelijk; gepatenteerd; *sb.* patent, octrooi *o.*; vergunning *v.*; gepatenteerd artikel *o.*; *vt.* patenteren; patent nemen op.
patentee [pei—, pætən'tî] patenthouder *m.*
paternal(ly) [pə'təːnəl(i)] *adj.* (*adv.*) vaderlijk; van vaderszijde.
paternity [pə'təːniti] vaderschap *o.*
path [pâð] pad *o.*, weg *m.*, baan *v.*
pathetic [pə'ðetik] pathetisch, aandoenlijk, gevoelvol.
path-finder ['pâðfaində] padvinder *m.*; baanbreker, pionier *m.*
pathway ['pâðwei] pad, voetpad *o.*; (*fig.*) weg *m.*
patience ['peiʃəns] geduld *o.*, lijdzaamheid, lankmoedigheid *v.*
patient ['peiʃənt] *adj.* geduldig, lijdzaam, lankmoedig; **be — of**, geduldig verdragen; *sb.* patiënt, lijder, zieke *m.*
patriarchal(ly) [peitri'âkəl(i)] *adj.* (*adv.*) aartsvaderlijk, patriarchaal.
patrimony ['pætriməni] vaderlijk erfdeel *o.*; erfgoed *o.*
patriotic(ally) [pætri'ɔtik(əli)] *adj.* (*adv.*) vaderlandlievend.
patrol [pə'troul] *sb.* patrouille, ronde *v.*; *vt.* afpatrouilleren; *vi.* patrouilleren, de ronde doen.
patron [pei—, 'pætrən] patroon, beschermheilige *m.*; beschermer, beschermheer *m.*
patronage ['pætrənidʒ] bescherming *v.*; patronaat, beschermheerschap *o.*
patronize ['pætrənaiz] beschermen; begunstigen; steunen.
patter ['pætə] *vi.* trappelen, trippelen; ritselen; ratelen; (*v. hagel*) kletteren; *vt.* doen kletteren; (*v. taal, enz.*) praten, babbelen, kakelen; (*v. gebeden, enz.*) prevelen, aframmelen; *sb.* getrippel *o.*; geritsel *o.*; geratel *o.*; gekletter *o.*; gebabbel, gesnap *o.*
pattern ['pætən] *sb.* model, voorbeeld *o.*; toonbeeld *o.*; staal, patroon *o.*; *adj.* model—; *vt.* vormen, modelleren; naar een model (volgens patroon) maken; monsteren; tot voorbeeld nemen; **— out**, namaken, kopiëren.
paucity ['pɔːsiti] geringheid *v.*, gering aantal *o.*; schaarste *v.*, gebrek *o.*
paunch [pɔːn(t)ʃ] *sb.* buik *m.*, pens *v.*; *vt.* ontweien.

pause [pɔːz] *sb.* rust, verpozing *v.*; onderbreking, pauze *v.*; *ri.* pauseren, even rusten; zich bedenken, nadenken, weifelen.
pave [peiv] bestraten, plaveien; bevloeren.
pavement ['peivmənt] bestrating *v.*; plaveisel *o.*; stenen vloer *m.*; trottoir *o.*
paver ['peivə] straatmaker, plaveier *m.*; plaveihamer, straatstamper *m.*
pavilion [pə'viljən] paviljoen *o.*
paving ['peiviŋ] bestrating *v.*; plaveisel *o.*
paving-beetle ['peiviŋbîtl] straatstamper *m.*
paving-stone ['peiviŋstoun] vloersteen *m.*
paw [pɔː] *sb.* poot, klauw *m.*; (*fam.*) pootje; schrift *o.*; *vt.* betasten; ruw beetpakken; *vi.* (met voorpoot) kappen, krabben.
pawky ['pɔːki] *adj.* (*Sc.*) slim, listig.
pawn [pɔːn] *sb.* pand, onderpand *o.*; *vt.* verpanden, belenen.
pawnee [pɔː'nî] pandhouder *m.*
pawner ['pɔːnə] verpander, pandgever *m.*
pawnshop ['pɔːnʃɔp] lommerd *m.*, pandjeshuis *o.*
pay [pei] *sb.* betaling, uitbetaling *v.*; loon, salaris *o.*, bezoldiging *v.*, traktement *o.*; (*mil.*) soldij *v.*; *vt.* betalen; uitbetalen, uitkeren; voldoen; vereffenen; vergoeden; *vi.* betalen; (de moeite) lonen; voordeel afwerpen.
payable ['peiəbl] betaalbaar, te betalen; lonend.
payee [pei'î] te betalen persoon; (*v. wissel*) nemer *m.*
paymaster ['peimâstə] betaler *m.*; betaalmeester *m.*
payment ['peimənt] betaling *v.*; (*fig.*) loon *o.*
pay-warrant ['peiwɔrənt] betalingsmandaat *o.*
pea [pî] erwt *v.*
peace [pîs] vrede *m.*; rust, kalmte *v.*
peaceable ['pîsəbl] *adj.* vreedzaam; vredelievend.
peace-breaker ['pîsbreikə] vredebreker *m.*; rustverstoorder *m.*
peaceful(ly) ['pîsful(i)] *adj.* (*adv.*) vreedzaam; vredig, kalm.
peach [pîtʃ] perzik *v.*; perzikboom *m.*
peacock ['pîkɔk] pauw *m.*; (*vlinder*) pauwoog *m.*
pea-fowl ['pîfaul] pauw *m.*
peak [pîk] punt, spits *v.*; top *m.*, hoogtepunt *o.*; (*v. berg*) piek *v.*; (*v. pet*) klep *v.*
pear [pêə] (*Pl.*) peer *v.*
pearl [pəːl] parel *v.*; diamantletter *v.*; staar *v.* (op het oog).
pearl-oyster ['pəːlɔistə] pareloester *v.*
pearl-powder ['pəːlpaudə] parelwit.
peasant ['pezənt] boer, landman *m.*
peasantry ['pezəntri] boerenstand *m.*, landvolk *o.*
pea-soup ['pîsûp] erwtensoep *r.*

peat [pît] turf *m.*; veen *o.*
peat-cutter ['pîtkətə] turfsteker *m.*
peatery ['pîtəri] veenderij *v.*
peat-litter ['pîtlitə] turfstrooisel *o.*
peat-moor ['pîtmuə] hoogveen *o.*
peck [pek] *sb.* pik *m.* (met snavel); *vt.* pikken, oppikken; bikken.
pecker ['pekə] pikker *m.*; specht *m.*
peculate ['pekjuleit] (geld) verduisteren.
peculiar [pi'kjûliə] *adj.* bijzonder; eigenaardig; — *to,* eigen aan; *sb.* eigenaardigheid *v.*
pecuniary [pi'kjûniəri] *adj.* geldelijk.
pedagogic(al) [pedə'gogik(l), —god-ʒik(l)] *adj.* opvoedkundig, pedagogisch.
pedal ['pedəl] *sb.* pedaal *o.*; *vi.* het pedaal gebruiken; peddelen, fietsen.
pedant ['pædənt] schoolmeester, schoolvos, pedant *m.*
pedantic(al) [pi'dæntik(l)] *adj.* schoolmeesterachtig, schoolvossig, pedant, verwaand.
peddle ['pedl] *vi.* venten, in de mars lopen; beuzelen, prutsen; knoeien; *vt.* rondventen; rondvertellen.
pedestal ['pedistl] *sb.* voetstuk *o.*; nachtkastje *o.*; *vt.* op een voetstuk plaatsen.
pedestrian [pi'destriən] *adj.* voet—; te voet; wandel—; (*fig.*) alledaags, laag bij de gronds; *sb.* voetganger *m.*; hardloper *m.*; beoefenaar *m.* van de wandelsport.
pedigree ['pedigrî] stamboom, geslachtsboom *m.*
pedlar ['pedlə] marskramer *m.*
peel [pîl] *sb.* schil *v.*; *vt.* schillen, pellen; — *off,* schillen; afschillen; ontschorsen.
peep [pîp] *vi.* gluren, kijken; (*v. dag*) gloren; piepen; — (*out*), zich laten zien; *sb.* blik *m.*; kijkje *o.*; gepiep *o.*; (*v. bladeren*) (het) uitbotten *o.*
peeper ['pîpə] bespieder, begluurder, loervogel *m.*; (*sl.*) kijker *m.* (oog); jong kuiken, piepkuiken *o.*
peep-hole ['pîphoul] kijkgat *o.*
peer [piə] *vi.* turen, kijken; gluren; zich vertonen.
peer [piə] *sb.* gelijke *m.*, weerga *v.*; pair, edelman *m.*; *vi.* — (*with*), evenaren.
peerless ['piəlis] weergaloos.
peevish(ly) ['pîviʃ(li)] *adj.* (*adv.*) knorrig, gemelijk, korzelig, verdrietig.
peevishness ['pîviʃnis] knorrigheid, gemelijkheid, korzeligheid *v.*
peg [peg] *sb.* pin, houten pen *v.*; klemhoutje *o.*; kapstok *m.*; *vt.* met een pin vastmaken; (*H.: v. markt*) stabiliseren; *vi.* ploeteren; zich afjakkeren.
pegtop ['pegtop] priktol *m.*
pelican ['pelikən] pelikaan *m.*
pellet ['pelit] *sb.* balletje; propje *o.*; pilletje *o.*; kogeltje *o.*; hagelkorrel *v.*; *vt.* met proppen schieten naar.
pellicle ['pelikl] vliesje, huidje *o.*
pell-mell ['pel'mel] *adj.* verward; *adv.*

door elkaar; hals over kop; *sb.* verwarring *v.*; handgemeen *o.*; warboel *m.*
pelt [pelt] *sb.* vel *o.*, huid, vacht *v.*; (het) gooien *o.*; (het) slaan *o.*; slagregen *m.*; *vt.* beschieten; bestormen; gooien met; *vi.* (*v. regen, enz.*) slaan, kletteren.
peltry ['peltri] pelterij *v.*, huiden *v. mv.*
pen [pen] *sb.* pen *v.*; (*dicht.*) slagpen *v.*; (*Dk.*) wijfjeszwaan *v.*; *vi.* schrijven, pennen; neerpennen.
pen [pen] *sb.* schaapskooi *v.*, perk, hok *o.*; *vt.* opsluiten; perken.
penal ['pînəl] strafbaar.
penalty ['pen(ə)lti] straf; boete *v.*
penance ['penəns] *sb.* boete; boetedoening *v.*; *vt.* straffen; doen boeten.
pencil ['pens(i)l] *sb.* potlood *o.*; griffel *v.*; stift *v.*; penseel *o.*; *vt.* tekenen; optekenen; opschrijven; penselen; *vi.* met potlood schrijven; tekenen.
pending ['pendin] *adj.* hangende, onafgedaan, nog onbeslist; *prep.* gedurende; in afwachting van.
pendulum ['pendjuləm] slinger *m.*
penetrable ['penitrəbl] doordringbaar; toegankelijk, ontvankelijk; te doorgronden.
penetrate ['penitreit] *vt.* doortrekken, doordringen; doorgronden, doorzien; *vi.* binnendringen (*into, through,* in).
penetrating ['penitreitin] doordringend; scherpzinnig; diepgaand.
penetration [peni'treiʃən] (het) doordringen *o.*; (het) binnendringen *o.*; doordringingsvermogen *o.*; doorzicht *o.*
penholder ['penhouldə] pennehouder *m.*
peninsula [pi'ninʃulə] schiereiland *o.*
penitence ['penitəns] berouw *o.*, boete, boetvaardigheid *v.*
penitent ['penitənt] *adj.* berouwvol, boetvaardig; *sb.* boetvaardige, boeteling(e) *m.* (*v.*); biechteling(e) *m.* (*v.*).
penknife ['pennaif] pennemes, zakmesje *o.*
penman ['penmən] schoonschrijver *m.*; schrijver *m.*
penmanship ['penmənʃip] (schoon-) schrijfkunst *v.*; schrijftrant *m.*
pen-name ['penneim] schuilnaam *m.*, pseudoniem *o.*
penniless ['penilis] geldeloos, zonder geld, arm.
penny ['peni] stuiver *m.*
pension ['penʃən] *sb.* pensioen, jaargeld *o.*; *vt.* een jaargeld toekennen; — *off,* op pensioen stellen, pensioneren.
pentagon ['pentəgən] vijfhoek *m.*
pentagraph ['pentəgrâf] tekenaap *m.*
Pentecost ['pentikost] Pinksterfeest *o.*
penthouse ['penthaus] afdak, hellend dak *o.*, luifel *v.*
pent-up ['pent'əp] opgesloten, ingesloten; (*fig.*) opgekropt, lang ingehouden.
penultimate [pi'nəltimit] *adj.* voorlaatste; *sb.* voorlaatste lettergreep *v.*

penury ['penjuri] armoede, behoeftigheid v., (volkomen) gebrek (*of*, aan).
penwiper ['penwaipə] inktlap m.
peony ['pïəni] pioen(roos) v.
people ['pïpl] *sb*. volk o.; mensen, lieden, personen m. mv.; vt. bevolken.
pepper ['pepə] *sb*. peper v.; (*fam.*) rammel, slaag m.; vt. peperen; (*sl.*) ranselen, afrossen.
pepper-box ['pepəbɔks] peperbus v.
pepper-caster ['pepəkâstə] peperbus v.
peppermint ['pepəmint] (*Pl.*) pepermunt v.; pepermuntje o.
per [pə:] per.
perambulator [pə'ræmbjuleitə] kinderwagen m.; melkkarretje o.
perceive [pə'sïv] waarnemen, (be)merken, bespeuren; ontwaren.
per cent [pə'sent] ten honderd, percent.
percentage [pə'sentidʒ] percentage o.; commissieloon o.
perceptible [pə'septibl] adj. waarneembaar; (be)merkbaar.
perception [pə'sepʃən] waarneming, perceptie v.; gewaarwording v.; inning, invordering v.
perch [pə:tʃ] *sb*. baars m.; rek o.; (v. vogel) stang v., roest v. & o.; vi. neerstrijken; (v. vogel) roesten, gaan zitten; vt. plaatsen; doen zitten.
percolate ['pə:kəleit] vi. & vt. (laten) doorzijgen, filtreren, doordringen, uitlekken.
percolator ['pə:kəleitə] filter m.; filtreerkan v.
percussion-cap [pə'kəʃənkæp] slaghoedje o.
perdition [pə:'diʃən] verderf o., ondergang m.; verdoemenis v.
perdurable [pə:'djûərəbl] adj. langdurig, duurzaam; eeuwig(durend).
perfect ['pə:fikt] adj. volmaakt, volkomen, perfect; volslagen; voortreffelijk; *sb*. (*gram.*) voltooid tegenwoordige tijd m.; [pə'fekt, 'pə:fikt] vt. volmaken, verbeteren, perfectioneren; voltooien; volvoeren.
perfection [pə'fekʃən] volmaaktheid, volkomenheid, perfectie v.; vervolmaking v.
perfidious(ly) [pə'fïdiəs(li)] adj. (adv.) trouweloos, verraderlijk, vals.
perfidy ['pə:fidi] trouweloosheid, valsheid v.; ontrouw, trouwbreuk v.
perforate ['pə:fəreit] vt. doorboren, perforeren; ['pə:fərit] adj. geperforeerd.
perforation [pə:fə'reiʃən] doorboring, perforatie v.; gat, gaatje o.
perform [pə'fo:m] vt. uitvoeren; (v. toneelstuk) vertonen; (v. functie) verrichten; vi. een voorstelling geven, spelen, optreden.
performance [pə'fo:məns] uitvoering v.; spel o., voorstelling v.; nakoming, vervulling v.; prestatie v.
perfume ['pə:fjûm] *sb*. geur, reuk m.; reukwerk o.; [pə'fjûm] vt. geurig maken, doorgeuren.

perhaps [pə'hæps, præps] misschien.
peril ['peril] *sb*. gevaar o.; vt. in gevaar brengen.
perilous(ly) ['periləs(li)] adj. (adv.) gevaarlijk, gevaarvol, hachelijk.
perimeter [pə'rimitə] omtrek m. (van figuur).
period ['pïəriəd] tijdvak, tijdperk o., tijdkring m.; periode v.; (v. planeet) omloopstijd m.; volzin m., zinsnede v.
periodical [pïəri'ɔdikl] adj. periodiek; *sb*. tijdschrift, periodiek o.
periphrasis [pə'rifrəsis] omschrijving v.
periscope ['periskoup] periscoop m.
perish ['periʃ] vi. omkomen; sterven; vergaan; ten onder gaan, te gronde gaan; vt. doen omkomen; te gronde richten, vernietigen.
perishable ['periʃəbl] adj. vergankelijk; bederfelijk, aan bederf onderhevig; *sb*. —s, aan bederf onderhevige waren.
peritoneum [peritə'nïəm] buikvlies o.
peritonitis [peritə'naitis] (*gen.*) buikvliesontsteking v.
periwig ['periwig] pruik v.
periwinkle ['periwiŋkl] alikruik v.; (*Pl.*) maagdepalm m.
perjure ['pə:dʒə] — oneself, een meineed doen.
perjurer ['pə:dʒərə] meinedige m.
perjury ['pə:dʒəri] meineed m.; woordbreuk v.
perky ['pə:ki] adj. parmantig; verwaand, eigenwijs; astrant, brutaal.
permanent ['pə:mənənt] adj. voortdurend, bestendig, duurzaam, vast, blijvend.
permeable ['pə:miəbl] doordringbaar.
permeate ['pə:mieit] doordringen, doortrekken.
permission [pə'miʃən] vergunning v., verlof o.
permit [pə'mit] vt. veroorloven, toestaan, toelaten, vergunnen; — of, toelaten, veroorloven; dulden; ['pə:mit] *sb*. (schriftelijke) vergunning v.; verlof o.; geleibiljet o.; consent o.
permutation [pə:mjû'teiʃən] verwisseling, omzetting, permutatie v.
permute [pə'mjût] verwisselen, omzetten.
pernicious(ly) [pə:'niʃəs(li)] adj. (adv.) verderfelijk, schadelijk; (v. koorts, enz.) kwaadaardig.
pernickety [pə'nikiti] (*fam.*) kieskeurig; peuterig, pietluttig; kittelorig; netelig, teer.
peroration [pero'reiʃən] peroratie v., slot van een redevoering, slotwoord o.; oratie v.
perpendicular [pə:pən'dikjulə] adj. loodrecht, rechtop, steil; *sb*. loodlijn v.; schietlood o.; loodrechte stand m. (houding, enz.).
perpetrate ['pə:pitreit] bedrijven, begaan, plegen.
perpetrator ['pə:pitreitə] bedrijver, dader m.

perpetual [pə'petjuəl] *adj.* eeuwig, eeuwigdurend, altijddurend; levenslang; (*v. ambt*) vast; (*v. lening*) onaflosbaar.

perpetuate [pə'petjueit] bestendigen, doen voortduren; vereeuwigen.

perplexed [pə'plekst] *adj.* verward, verlegen, verslagen.

perquisite ['pə:kwizit] bijverdienste *v.*; fooi *v.*; (*fig.*) uitsluitend bezit, — recht *o.*; —*s*, emolumenten; verval.

persecute ['pə:sikjût] vervolgen; lastig vallen (*with*, met).

persecution [pə:si'kjûʃən] vervolging *v.*

persecutor ['pə:sikjûtə] vervolger *m.*

perseverance [pə:si'viərəns] volharding *v.*

persevere [pə:si'viə] volharden, volhouden.

persist [pə'sist] volharden, hardnekkig volhouden; aanhouden, voortduren.

persistence, persistency [pə'sistəns(i)] volharding *v.*, (het) hardnekkig volhouden *o.*; koppigheid *v.*; (het) aanhouden, (het) voortduren *o.*

persistent(ly) [pə'sistənt(li)] *adj.* (*adv.*) volhardend, hardnekkig; aanhoudend, blijvend.

person ['pə:sn] persoon; mens *m.*; figuur, voorkomen, uiterlijk *o.*

personable ['pə:sənəbl] knap (van uiterlijk), welgemaakt.

personal ['pə:sənəl] *adj.* persoonlijk; lichamelijk; *sb.* persoonlijk voornaamwoord *o.*; —*s*, persoonlijkheden, personaliteiten; (*in dagblad, enz.*) personalia; persoonlijk eigendom; roerende goederen.

personate ['pə:səneit] voorstellen, uitbeelden, de rol spelen van; zich uitgeven voor.

personify [pə'sonifai] verpersoonlijken.

personnel [pə:sə'nel] personeel *o.*

perspective [pə'spektiv] *sb.* doorzichtkunde *v.*, perspectief *o.*; perspectieftekening *v.*; (*fig.*) verschiet, vooruitzicht *o.*; *adj.* perspectivisch.

perspicacious(ly) [pə:spi'keiʃəs(li)] *adj.* (*adv.*) scherpziend, scherpzinnig, schrander.

perspicuous(ly) [pə'spikjuəs(li)] *adj* (*adv.*) duidelijk, helder, klaar.

perspiration [pə:spi'reiʃən] uitwaseming *v.*; transpiratie *v.*, zweet *o.*

perspire [pəs'paiə] uitwasemen; transpireren, zweten.

persuade [pə'sweid] *vt.* overreden, overhalen; overtuigen; *vi.* — *into,* overhalen tot; — *from,* afbrengen van; *vr.* — *oneself,* zich overtuigen; — *oneself of something,* zich iets wijsmaken.

persuasion [pə'sweiʒən] overreding, overtuiging *v.*; richting *v.*, geloof *o.*

persuasiveness [pə'sweisivnis] overredingskracht *v.*

pert [pə:t] vrijpostig, brutaal, onbeschaamd.

pertain [pə:'tein] behoren (*to,* tot); betrekking hebben (*to,* op).

pertinacious(ly) [pə:ti'neiʃəs(li)] *adj.* (*adv.*) hardnekkig, vasthoudend, volhardend.

pertinent ['pə:tinənt] *adj.* toepasselijk, zakelijk, van pas.

perturb [pə'tə:b] verstoren, in beroering brengen, verontrusten.

peruke [pə'rûk] pruik *v.*

perusal [pə'rûzəl] (nauwkeurige) lezing *v.*

peruse [pə'rûz] (nauwkeurig) lezen, doorlezen, nagaan.

perverse(ly) [pə'və:s(li)] *adj.* (*adv.*) slecht, verdorven, verkeerd, pervers; onhandelbaar, onredelijk, koppig.

pervert [pə'və:t] *vt.* (*v. feit, woord*) verdraaien; bederven, verleiden; (ver)storen; misbruiken; afvallig maken.

pessimism ['pesimizm] pessimisme *o.*

pessimistic(al) [pesi'mistik(l)] *adj.* pessimistisch.

pest [pest] pest *v.*; plaag *v.*; lastpost, plaaggeest *m.*

pestilence ['pestiləns] pest, pestziekte, pestilentie *v.*

pestle ['pes(t)l] *sb.* stamper *m.*; *vt.* stampen.

pet [pet] *sb.* kwade luim, boze bui *v.*; (*fig.*) lieveling *m.*; *adj.* geliefd, vertroeteld; *vt.* vertroetelen, aanhalen, liefkozen.

petition [pi'tiʃən] *sb.* verzoekschrift, smeekschrift *o.*, petitie *v.*; bede *v.*; *vt.* verzoeken; smeken; *vi.* een petitie indienen; een verzoek richten tot.

petitioner [pi'tiʃənə] verzoeker, adressant *m.*

petrify ['petrifai] verstenen.

petrol ['petrəl] benzine *v.*

petroleum [pi'trouljəm] petroleum *v.*

petticoat ['petikout] rok; onderrok *m.*; (*fam.*) vrouw *v.*

pettiness ['petinis] kleinheid, geringheid, nietigheid *v.*; kleinzieligheid *v.*

pettishly ['petiʃ(li)] *adj.* (*adv.*) korzelig, gemelijk, nukkig, humeurig; prikkelbaar.

petty ['peti] *adj.* klein, gering, nietig; kleinzielig.

petulance, petulancy ['petjuləns(i)] gemelijkheid, knorrigheid, kribbigheid; prikkelbaarheid *v.*

petulant(ly) ['petjulənt(li)] *adj.* (*adv.*) gemelijk, knorrig, kribbig; prikkelbaar.

pew [pjû] kerkbank *v.*; (*sl.*) stoel *m.*, zitplaats *v.*

pewit ['piwit] kievit *m.*

phantasm ['fæntæzm] droombeeld *o.*, hersenschim, illusie *v.*; geestverschijning *v.*

phantasy ['fæntəsi] fantasie *v.*

phantom ['fæntəm] *sb.* spook *o.*, schim, geestverschijning *v.*; droombeeld *o.*; *adj.* denkbeeldig; geheimzinnig.

pharisee ['færisî] farizeeër, schijnheilige *m.*

pharmaceutic(al) [fâmə'sjûtik l)] artsenijkundig; — *chemist,* apotheker.

pharmacy ['fâməsi] artsenijbereid-kunde v.; apotheek v.

pheasant ['fezənt] fazant m.

phenomenon [fi'nɔmənən] verschijn-sel o.; fenomeen, wonderkind o., wondermens m.

philanderer [fi'lændərə] flirter m.

philanthropic al) [filən'ðrɔpik l)] adj. menslievend, filantropisch; liefdadig-heids—.

philanthropy [fi'lændrəpi] mensen-liefde v.; menslievendheid v., liefdadig-heidszin m.

philologic al) [filə'lɔdʒik,l)] adj. filo-logisch, taalkundig.

philosopher [fi'lɔsəfə] filosoof, wijs-geer m.

philosophy [fi'lɔsəfi] filosofie, wijsbe-geerte v.

phlegm [flem] slijm o., fluim v.; flegma o., onaandoenlijkheid, koelheid v.

phlegmatic [fleg'mætik] adj. slijm-achtig, slijmerig; flegmatisch, flegma-tiek, onaandoenlijk, koel, nuchter.

phlegmy ['flemi] slijmachtig, —slijm.

phonetic [fo'netik] adj. fonetisch; sb. —s, fonetiek, klankleer v.

phonofilm ['founoufilm] klankfilm v.

phonograph ['founəgráf] sb. fono-graaf m.; vt. fonografisch opnemen.

phosphate ['fɔsfit] fosfaat o.

phosphor ['fɔsfə] fosfor o.

phosphorate ['fɔsfəreit] met fosfor verbinden.

phosphoresce [fɔsfə'res] fosforesceren, lichten.

photograph ['foutəgráf, —græf] sb. fotografie, foto v.; portret o.; vt. foto-graferen.

photographer [fo'tɔgrəfə] fotograaf m.

phrase [freiz] sb. frase v.; uitdrukking, spreekwijze, zegswijze v.; bewoording v.; vt. (v. gedachten, enz.) uitdrukken, onder woorden brengen, inkleden.

phtisis ['ðai—, 'fðai—, 'taisis] tering, longtering v.

physic ['fizik] sb. geneeskunde v.; ge-neesmiddel o.; purgeermiddel o.; —s, natuurkunde v.; vt. geneeskundig be-handelen; geneesmiddelen toedienen; laten purgeren; (sl.) geducht toeta-kelen.

physical (ly) ['fizikəl(i)] adj. (adv.) natuurkundig; natuurwetenschappelijk; fysiek, lichamelijk.

physician [fi'ziʃən] dokter, genees-heer m.

physicist ['fizisist] natuurkundige m.

piano ['pjænou] piano v.

pick [pik] sb. punthouweel o.; pikhamer m.; tandestoker m.; haaksleutel m.; (v. hennep, enz.) pluk m.; keus v.; keur v., het beste o.; vt. hakken; pikken; prik-ken; (v. slot) opensteken; (v. bloemen, gerogelte, enz.) plukken; kiezen, uitkie-zen; vi. bikken; kluiven.

pickax (e)]'pikæks] sb. houweel o.; vt. met een houweel bewerken.

picked [pikt] uitgelezen, uitgezocht, uitgekozen; puntig.

picket ['pikit] sb. paal, staak m.; (mil.) piket o.; (bij staking) post m.; vt. met palen omheinen (afzetten); aan een paal binden (vastmaken); posten plaatsen bij; (als piket) stationeren; vi. (bij staking) posten.

picking ['pikiŋ] (het) hakken (pikken; krabben; kluiven) o.; pluk m.; pro-fijtje, voordeeltje o.; —s, restantjes o. mv.; bijverdiensten v. mv., emolumen-ten o. mv.

pickle ['pikl] sb. pekel v.; azijn m. (voor inmaak); (ingemaakt) zuur o.; beits o.; vt. pekelen, inmaken; met pekel be-handelen; beitsen.

pickpocket ['pikpɔkit] zakkenroller m.

picksome ['piksəm] kieskeurig.

pick-up ['pikəp] (fam.) koopje o.; vondst v.; (radio) (grammofoon)op-nemer m.

picture ['piktʃə] sb. schilderij v. & o.; plaat, prent v.; afbeelding, beeltenis v.; tafereel o., schildering v.; schilder-kunst v.; vt. afbeelden, schilderen; — (to oneself), zich voorstellen.

picture-book ['piktʃəbuk] prenten-boek o.

picture-gallery ['piktʃəgæləri] schil-derijenmuseum o.; schilderijzaal v.

picture-goer ['piktʃəgouə] bioscoop-bezoeker m.

picturesque (ly) [piktʃə'resk(li)] adj. (adv.) schilderachtig.

piddle ['pidl] een plasje doen; beuzelen, prutsen; kieskauwen.

pie [pai] sb. taart, pastei v.; ekster v.; warboel m.; vt. door elkaar gooien, in de war gooien.

piece [pis] sb. stuk o.; (mil.) stuk o. (geschut); stukje, staaltje o.; (H.) eind o., lap m.; —s, (sl.) duiten; vt. lap-pen, verstellen; aaneenhechten, verbin-den; samenvoegen, in elkaar zetten; — in, invoegen.

piece goods ['pisgudz] manufacturen v. mv., geweven goederen o. mv.

piecemeal ['pismil] adv. bij gedeelten, bij stukken en brokken; adj. samen-gelapt; stuksgewijze gedaan.

piece-wage ['pisweidʒ] stukloon o.

piece-work ['piswə:k] stukwerk o.

pied [paid] bont, gevlekt, gespikkeld.

pier [piə] (brug)pijler m.; pier m.; havenhoofd o.; penant v.

pierce [piəs] doordringen; doorboren, ðoorsteken; doorgronden; doorsnijden; (v. vat) opensteken; vi. binnendringen (into, in); doordringen (to, tot); zich een weg banen.

piercing (ly) ['piəsiŋ(li)] adj. (adv.) doordringend.

piety ['paiəti] vroomheid, piëteit v.

pig [pig] sb. varken, zwijn o.; varkens-vlees o.; wild zwijn o.; smeerlap; beroer-ling m.; (tn.) gieteling m.; schuitje o.; klomp m. ruw ijzer; vi. biggen werpen, biggen; (samen)hokken; bij elkaar stoppen.

pigeon ['pidʒ(i)n] (*Dk.*) duif *v.*

pigeon-breast ['pidʒənbrest] kippeborst *v.*

pigeon-fancier ['pidʒənfænsiə] duivenmelker, duivenfokker *m.*

pig-eyed ['pigaid] met varkensoogjes.

piggery ['pigəri] varkensfokkerij *v.*; zwijnestal *m.*; varkenshok *o.*; zwijnerij *v.*

pig-headed ['pig'hedid] koppig; eigenwijs.

pigmy ['pigmi] *sb.* dwerg *m.*; *adj.* dwergachtig, dwergen—.

pigskin ['pigskin] varkenshuid *v.*; varkensleer *o.*

pigsty ['pigstai] varkenskot, varkenshok *o.*

pigtail ['pigteil] haarvlecht *v.*

pike [paik] piek, spies *v.*; tolboom *m.*; snoek *m.*

pile [pail] *sb.* paal, heipaal *m.*; (*mil.: v. geweren*) rot *o.*; stapel, hoop *m.*; *vt.* opstepelen, ophopen; beladen; aan rotten zetten.

pile-house ['pailhaus] paalwoning *v.*

pilfer ['pilfə] kapen, ontfutselen, gappen.

pilferer ['pilfərə] gapper; langvinger *m.*

pilgrim ['pilgrim] *sb.* pelgrim *m.*; *vi.* een bedevaart doen; zwerven.

pilgrimage ['pilgrimidʒ] *sb.* bedevaart *v.*, pelgrimstocht *m.*; (*fig.*) levensreis *v.*; *vi.* een bedevaart ondernemen.

pill [pil] *sb.* pil *v.*; (*fig.*) bittere pil *v.*; (*v. tennis, enz.*) bal *m.*; **play —s,** (*sl.*) biljarten; *vt.* pillen ingeven; deballoteren; plunderen; beroven.

pillage ['pilidʒ] *sb.* roof *m.*, plundering *v.*; *vt.* roven, plunderen.

pillar ['pilə] pilaar *m.*, zuil *v.*, pijler *m.*; stut, stijl *m.*

pillory ['piləri] *sb.* kaak *v.*, schandpaal *m.*; *vt.* aan de kaak stellen.

pillow ['pilou] *sb.* oorkussen *o.*; (*tn.*) kussen *o.*; *vt.* op een kussen leggen; met kussens ondersteunen.

pillow-case ['piloukeis] kussensloop *v.*

pillow-slip ['pilouslip] kussensloop *v.*

pilose ['pailous] behaard, harig; langharig.

pilot ['pailət] *sb.* loods, gids *m.*; (*vl.*) bestuurder, piloot *m.*; *vt.* loodsen; besturen, sturen; geleiden.

pilotage ['pailətidʒ] loodsgeld *o.*; loodswezen *o.*; (het) loodsen *o.*

pilot-balloon ['pailətbəlûn] proefballon *m.*

pilot-bread ['pailətbred] scheepsbeschuit *v.*

pimple ['pimpl] puist *v.*, blaasje *o.*

pin [pin] *sb.* speld *v.*; pin, pen *v.*; stift *v.*; kegel *m.*; **—s,** (*sl.*) benen; *vt.* vastspelden; vastklemmen; opsluiten; doorsteken; **— up,** dichtspelden; vastspelden; opsluiten.

pinafore ['pinəfo:] (kinder)schort *v.* & *o.*, voorspeldertje *o.*

pincers ['pinsəz] nijptang *v.*; (*v. kreeft, enz.*) schaar *v.*

pinch [pin(t)ʃ] *sb.* kneep *m.*; klem, knel *v.*; uiterste nood *m.*; snuifje *o.*; *vt.* knijpen, knellen, klemmen; beknibbelen, krap houden; gebrek laten lijden; *vi.* knijpen, knellen; zich bekrimpen; gebrek lijden; gierig zijn.

pin-cushion ['pinkuʃən] speldenkussen *o.*

pine [pain] *sb.* pijn (boom), grove den *m.*; grenehout, vurehout *o.*; ananas *v.*; *vi.* smachten (***after, for,*** naar); kwijnen, verkwijnen.

pine-cone ['painkoun] pijnappel *m.*

pine-tree ['paintri] pijnboom, mastboom *m.*

pinion ['pinjən] *sb.* (*v. vleugel*) slagpen *v.*; vleugelpunt *v.*; (*dicht.*) vleugel *m.*, wiek *v.*; vlerk *v.*; (*tn.*) rondsel, klein tandrad *o.*; *vt.* kortwieken; vastbinden, boeien; omklemmen.

pink [pink] *sb.* anjelier *v.*; roserood *o.*; vossenjager *m.*; toppunt *o.*; (*Dk.*) jonge zalm *m.*; (*sch.*) pink *v.*; *adj.* rose, rosekleurig; *vt.* doorboren, doorsteken; prikken; perforeren, uittanden; versieren, opsieren; rose maken; *vi.* (*v. motor*) kloppen; rose worden.

pinnacle ['pinəkl] pinakel *o.*; spits torentje *o.*; top *m.*; (*fig.*) toppunt *o.*, hoogtepunt *o.*

pint [paint] pint *v.*

pioneer [paiə'niə] *sb.* (*mil.*) schansgraver *m.*; pionier, baanbreker, wegbereider; voortrekker *m.*; *vi.* pionierswerk doen voor, de weg bereiden voor; baanbrekerswerk verrichten; invoeren, het eerst aanpakken.

pious (ly) ['paiəs(li)] *adj.* (*adv.*) godvruchtig, vroom; trouw; teder; vol piëteit.

pip [pip] *sb.* (*vogelziekte*) pip *v.*; (*op dobbelsteen, enz.*) oog *o.*; (*v. appel, enz.*) pit *v.*; *vt.* deballoteren; (*mil.*) raken (met kogel); *vi.* piepen.

pipe [paip] *sb.* pijp *v.*; buis *v.*; fluitje *o.*; (fluit)signaal *o.*; gefluit *o.*; luchtpijp *v.*; **the —s,** de doedelzak; de ademhalingsorganen; *vi.* pijpen, fluiten, piepen; *vt.* van buizen voorzien; door buizen leiden; stekken.

pipe-line ['paiplain] buisleiding *v.*

piping ['paipiŋ] *adj.* pijpend, fluitend, piepend; *sb.* buizenstelsel *o.*; bies(versiering) *v.*; (*Pl.*) stek *m.*; galonkoord *o.*

pirate ['paiərit] *sb.* zeerover, piraat *m.*; zeeroversschip *o.*; nadrukker, letterdief *m.*; *vt.* roven; nadrukken; *vi.* zeeroof plegen.

pismire ['pismaiə] mier *v.*

pistil ['pistil] (*Pl.*) stamper *m.*

pistol ['pistəl] pistool *o.*; revolver *v.*

piston ['pistən] zuiger *m.*; klep *v.*, ventiel *o.*

pit [pit] *sb.* kolenput *m.*, (kolen)mijn, mijnschacht *v.*; kuil *m.*, kuiltje, putje *o.*; *vt.* inkuilen; uitgraven.

pitch [pitʃ] *sb.* pik, pek *o.*; (*v. schip*) (het) stampen *o.*; (*sp.*) worp *m.*; trap, graad *m.*; hoogte *v.*; *vt.* vastmaken, bevestigen; (*v. tent, enz.*) opslaan, opstellen, opzetten; (*v. waren, enz.*) uitstallen; *vi.* vallen, voorovervallen, tuimelen; neerkomen; neerstrijken; (*v. schip*) stampen.

pitcher ['pitʃə] pik *v.*, houweel *o.*; werper *m.*; straatventer *m.* (met vaste standplaats); kruik, kan, waterkruik *v.*

pitchfork ['pitʃfo:k] hooivork *v.*

piteous (ly) ['pitiəs(li)] *adj.* (*adv.*) jammerlijk, beklagenswaardig, erbarmelijk, deerlijk; armzalig.

pith [piθ] pit *v.*; merg, ruggemerg *o.*; (*fig.*) kern *v.*: kracht, sterkte *v.*

pithless ['piθlis] zonder pit, krachteloos, futloos.

pithy ['piθi] pittig, kernachtig, bondig, krachtig.

pitiable ['pitiəbl] jammerlijk, beklagenswaardig, deerniswaardig.

pitiful (ly) ['pitiful(i)] *adj.* (*adv.*) medelijdend; jammerlijk, erbarmelijk, armzalig, deerniswekkend.

pitiless (ly) ['pitilisnis] onbarmhartig, meedogenloos.

pity ['piti] *sb.* medelijden *o.*; (*dicht.*) deernis *v.*; —*!* jammer! *vt.* medelijden hebben met, beklagen; *vi.* medelijden tonen.

pivot ['pivət] *sb.* spil *v.*; tap *m.*; *vt.* doen draaien (om een spil); *vi.* draaien (**upon**, om).

placable ['plei—, 'plækəbl] verzoenlijk, vergevensgezind.

placard ['plækâd] *sb.* plakkaat, aanplakbiljet *o.*; *vt.* aanplakken; door aanplakken bekend maken.

place [pleis] *sb.* plaats *v.*; plek *v.*; ambt *o.*, positie, betrekking *v.*; buitenplaats *v.*; buiten *o.*; (*rek.*) decimaal *v.*; *vt.* plaatsen, zetten, stellen; aanstellen; uitzetten, beleggen; — **out,** uitbesteden.

place-hunter ['pleishəntə] baantjesjager *m.*

plagiarize ['pleidʒiəraiz] *vi.* plagiaat plegen, plagiëren; *vt.* plagiëren, naschrijven.

plague [pleig] *sb.* pest *v.*; plaag *v.*; — (**up**)**on** **him!** de drommel (de duivel) hale hem! *vt.* bezoeken (met ramp of plaag); kwellen, pesten.

plain [plein] *adj.* vlak; glad, effen; duidelijk, klaar; eenvoudig; onopgesmukt, ongekunsteld; ongekleurd, onversierd; *adv.* duidelijk, ronduit; *sb.* vlakte *v.*; (*dicht.*) slagveld *o.*; *vi.* jammeren, klagen, weeklagen.

plain-clothes ['pleinklouθz] burgerkleren.

plain-dealing ['pleindilin] *adj.* oprecht, eerlijk, rond; *sb.* oprechtheid, eerlijkheid, rondheid *v.*

plainly ['pleinli] *adv.* duidelijk; gewoon, eenvoudig; rondborstig, ronduit.

plaint [pleint] klaagtoon *m.*; klaagzang

m.; klacht, weeklacht *v.*; (*recht*) aanklacht *v.*

plaintiff ['pleintif] (*recht*) klager, aanklager, eiser *m.*

plait [plæt] *sb.* vouw, plooi *v.*; vlecht *v.*; *vt.* vouwen, plooien; vlechten.

plan [plæn] *sb.* plan *o.*; ontwerp *o.*; vlak *o.*; stelsel *o.*; *vt.* een plan maken van; schetsen; inrichten; ordenen; plannen maken (smeden) voor.

plane [plein] *sb.* (*Pl.*) plataan *m.*; schaaf *v.*; (plat) vlak *o.*; (draagvlak *o.* van) vliegmachine *v.*; *adj.* vlak, effen; *vt.* schaven; — **away** (**down**), afschaven, wegschaven; *vi.* (*vl.*) vliegen; (*vl.*) glijden; — **down,** (*vl.*) dalen.

planet ['plænit] planeet *v.*

planish ['plæniʃ] (*v. hout*) gladschaven; (*v. metaal*) planeren, pletten; glad maken, polijsten; (*v. papier*) glanzen.

plank [plæŋk] *sb.* dikke plank *v.*; punt *o.* van een (partij)programma, verkiezingsleus *v.*; *vt.* met planken beleggen, bevloeren.

plank-bed ['plæŋkbed] brits *r.*

plank-bridge ['plæŋkbridʒ] vonder *m.*

plant [plânt] *sb.* plant *v.*, gewas *o.*; spruit *v.*; (*tn.*) installatie *v.*; *vt.* planten, poten; beplanten; aanleggen; — **out,** uitplanten, verplanten.

plantation [plæn'teiʃən] beplanting *v.*, aanplant *m.*; plantage *v.*; plantsoen *o.*

planter ['plântə] planter *m.*; stichter *m.*

plash [plæʃ] *vi.* plassen; plonzen, kletteren; (*v. takken, enz.*) in elkaar vlechten; *sb.* geplas *o.*; geplons, gekletter *o.*; poel, plas *m.*

plaster ['plâstə] *sb.* pleister *v.*; pleisterkalk *v.*; gips *o.*; *adj.* gipsen; *vt.* pleisteren, bepleisteren; een pleister leggen op; beplakken; besmeren.

plasterer ['plâstərə] pleisteraar, stukadoor, gipswerker *m.*

plastic ['plæstik] plastisch, beeldend; (*fig.*) kneedbaar; — **art,** plastiek, beeldende kunst.

plate [pleit] *sb.* plaat *v.*; bord *o.*; naambord(je) *o.*; (*voor collecte*) schaal *v.*; *vt.* platteren; vergulden, verzilveren, vertinnen; pantseren.

plate-basket ['pleitbâskit] messenbak *m.*

plate-glass ['pleitglâs] spiegelglas *o.*

platform ['plætfo:m] *sb.* terras *o.*; perron *o.*; podium *o.*; (*v. tram*) balkon.

platinum ['plætinəm] platina *o.*

platoon [plə'tûn] (*mil.*) peloton *o.*

platter ['plætə] platte schotel *m.*; (*Am., sl.*) grammofoonplaat *v.*

plaudit ['plo:dit] toejuiching(en) *v.* (*mv.*), applaus *o.*

plausible ['plo:zibl] *adj.* aannemelijk, geloofwaardig; innemend, aangenaam (in de omgang); glad (van tong).

play [plei] *vi.* spelen; speelruimte hebben, zich vrij bewegen; (*v. fontein*) werken; *vt.* spelen (op), bespelen; (*v. kaart*) uitspelen; (*v. grammofoonplaat*) afdraaien; laten spelen; (*v. vis*) laten uitspartelen; (*sl.*) wedden op; *sb.* spel *o.*; speling, speelruimte, vrijheid van beweging *v.*; toneelstuk *o.*; werking *v.*

play-actor ['pleiæktə] toneelspeler *m.*; komediant *m.*

play-bill ['pleibil] affiche *v.*; programma *o.*

play-debt ['pleidet] speelschuld *v.*

player ['pleiə] speler; toneelspeler *m.*

play-fellow ['pleifelou] speelmakker, speelkameraad *m.*

playful(ly) ['pleiful(i)] *adj.* (*adv.*) speelziek; speels, dartel.

play-house ['pleihaus] schouwburg *m.*

playing-card ['pleiiŋkâd] speelkaart *v.*

playmate ['pleimeit] speelmakker, speelkameraad *m.*

plaything ['pleiðiŋ] (stuk) speelgoed *o.*; (*fig.*) speelbal *m.*

playtime ['pleitaim] speeltijd *m.*; speelseizoen *o.*

playwright ['pleirait], **play-writer** ['pleiraitə] toneelschrijver *m.*

plea [pli] verontschuldiging *v.*, voorwendsel *o.*; betoog *o.*; pleit, pleidooi, verweer *o.*; dringend verzoek *o.*

plead [plid] *vt.* bepleiten, verdedigen; aanvoeren; voorwenden; *vi.* zich verdedigen, zijn zaak uiteenzetten; pleiten; — *for,* smeken om.

pleadable ['plidəbl] aanvoerbaar, rechtsgeldig.

pleader ['plidə] pleiter, verdediger *m.*

pleading ['plidiŋ] (het) pleiten *o.*; pleidooi *o.*; uiteenzetting *v.*

pleasant(ly) ['plezənt(li)] *adj.* (*adv.*) aangenaam, prettig; vrolijk, opgeruimd; grappig.

pleasantry ['plezəntri] scherts, grap, aardigheid *v.*

please [pliz] aanstaan, bevallen, behagen; believen; voldoen; —*!* als het u belieft; om u te dienen.

pleasing(ly) ['pliziŋ(li)] *adj.* (*adv.*) behaaglijk; aangenaam; innemend.

pleasurable ['pleʒərəbl] *adj.* aangenaam, prettig, genoeglijk.

pleasure ['pleʒə] *sb.* genoegen, genot *o.*; vermaak, plezier *o.*, pret *v.*; welbehagen *o.*; welgevallen, believen, goedvinden *o.*; *vt.* een genoegen doen, iem. een dienst bewijzen; behagen; *vi.* behagen scheppen (*in,* in), plezier hebben (*in,* in).

pleasure-ground ['pleʒəgraund] lusthof *m.*, park *o.*

pleat [plit] *sb.* plooi *v.*; vlecht *v.*; *vt.* plooien; vlechten.

plebiscite ['plebisit] plebisciet *o.*, volksstemming *v.*

pledge [pledʒ] *sb.* pand, onderpand *o.*, zekerheid *v.*; borgtocht *m.*; belofte; gelofte *v.*; toóst *m.*; *vt.* verpanden, in pand geven, belenen; plechtig beloven; *vr.* — *oneself,* zich borg stellen.

pledget ['pledʒit] propje *o.*; plukselverband *o.*

plenary ['plinəri] volkomen, volledig, geheel.

plentiful(ly) ['plentiful(i)] *adj.* (*adv.*) overvloedig.

plenty ['plenti] *sb.* overvloed *m.*; *adj.* overvloedig; *adv.* ruimschoots, overvloedig, rijkelijk.

pleura ['plûərə] borstvlies *o.*

pleurisy ['pluərisi] (*gen.*) pleuris, borstvliesontsteking *v.*

pliability [plaiə'biliti] buigzaamheid *v.*; (*fig.*) plooibaarheid, volgzaamheid *v.*

pliable ['plaiəbl] buigzaam; (*fig.*) plooibaar, volgzaam.

pliant ['plaiənt] buigzaam, plooibaar, gedwee, soepel, handelbaar.

plicate(d) ['plaikit, —eitid] geplooid.

plight [plait] *sb.* staat, toestand *m.*, conditie, positie *v.*; belofte, verbintenis *v.*; *vt.* verpanden; beloven.

plop [plɔp] *sb.* plons, plof *m.*; *vi.* plonsen, ploffen.

plot [plɔt] *sb.* stukje (plekje) *o.* grond; komplot *o.*, samenzwering *v.*; (*Am.*) plattegrond *m.*; *vt.* ontwerpen, in tekening brengen; afbakenen, aanleggen; beramen, smeden; (*v. tijd, enz.*) indelen; *vi.* samenspannen, samenzweren; plannen smeden, intrigeren.

plotter ['plɔtə] ontwerper *m.*; samenzweerder *m.*; intrigant *m.*

plough [plau] *sb.* ploeg *m.*; ploegschaaf *v.*; ploegmes *o.*; omgeploegd land *o.*; (*drukk.*) snijmachine *v.*, boekbindersploeg *m.*; *vt.* ploegen, omploegen; (*v. gelaat*) doorploegen; (*v. golven*) doorklieven; *vi.* ploegen.

ploughman ['plaumən] ploeger *m.*; boerenknecht *m.*; boer *m.*

plover ['plʌvə] pluvier *v.*; (*fam.*) kievit *m.*

pluck [plʌk] *vt.* afrukken; plukken, afplukken; trekken (aan); (*v. snaarinstrument*) tokkelen; *sb.* ruk, trek *m.*; moed, durf *m.*; (*v. dier*) hart, long en lever; (*sl.*) afwijzing *v.*

plug [plʌg] *sb.* plug, prop, pin *v.*; tap *m.*; stop *m.*; (*el.*) stekker *m.*; *vt.* pluggen; dichtstoppen, vullen; plomberen.

plug-connection ['plʌgkə'nekʃən] (*el.*) stopcontact *o.*

plum [plʌm] pruim *v.*; rozijn *v.*; bonbon *o.*

plumb [plʌm] *sb.* schietlood *o.*; dieplood *o.*; *adj.* loodrecht; in het lood; volkomen, volmaakt; *adv.* loodrecht; precies, vlak; (*Am.*) volslagen, helemaal, totaal; *vt.* loodrecht maken (plaatsen); peilen, loden; plomberen.

plumber ['plʌmə] loodgieter, loodwerker *m.*

plumb-rule ['plʌmrûl] timmermanswaterpas *o.*

plume [plûm] *sb.* veer, pluim *v.*; vederbos *m.*; *vt.* van veren voorzien, met

veren versieren; (*v. veren*) gladstrijken;
— *oneself,* (*v. vogel*) de veren gladstrijken; (*fig.*)zich met andermans veren
tooien; zich laten voorstaan op.
plum-loaf ['pləm'louf] rozijnenbrood *o.*
plummet ['pləmit] schietlood; dieplood *o.;* gewichtje *o.* aan dobber; (*fig.*)
last *m.*
plump [pləmp] *adj.* mollig, poezelig,
dik, rond, gevuld, vlezig; *vt.* mollig
(rond, gevuld) maken; doen uitzetten;
vi. gevuld(er) (mollig(er)) worden; uitzetten, zwellen.
plump ['pləmp] *vi.* ploffen, neerploffen,
plompen; *vt.* neerploffen, neerkwakken;
sb. plof, bons *m.;* (*Sc.*) stortbui *v.; adj.*
bot, vierkant.
plunder ['pləndə] *vt.* plunderen; beroven, bestelen; *vi.* plunderen, roven;
sb. buit *m.;* (*sl.*) winst *v.;* (*Am.*) bagage
v.; huisraad *o.*
plunge [plən(d)ʒ] *vt.* indompelen, onderdompelen; stoten in, storten in;
vi. duiken, zich storten; (*v. schip*)
stampen; (*v. prijzen*) kelderen; (*v.
paard*) de achterpoten omhoog gooien;
achteruitspringen en slaan; *sb.* indompeling, onderdompeling *v.;* onderdui-
king *v.;* benedenwaartse slag *m.*
plunger ['plən(d)ʒə] duiker; dompelaar *m.;* (*v. pomp*) zuiger *m.*
plural ['plûərəl] *adj.* meervoudig; *sb.*
meervoud *o.*
plurality [plu'ræliti] meervoud *o.;*
meervoudigheid *v.;* menigte *v.;* meerderheid *v.;* (het) merendeel *o.*
plus-fours ['pləsfo:z] wijde sportbroek
(golfbroek) *v.*
plush [pləʃ] pluche *v.*
plutocracy [plû'tokrəsi] plutocratie,
geldheerschappij *v.*
pluvious ['plûviəs] regenachtig, regen-
—.
ply [plai] *sb.* plooi, vouw *v.;* (*v. garen*)
draad *m.;* richting, neiging *v.;* karaktertrek *m.*
ply [plai] *vt.* gebruiken, hanteren; beoefenen; (*v. beroep*) uitoefenen; (*v.
zaak*) drijven; *vi.* bezig zijn met; in de
weer zijn, werken; (*sch.*) laveren; (heen
en weer) varen; zijn beroep uitoefenen.
plywood ['plaiwud] triplex, multiplex *o.*
poach [poutʃ] stropen; (*v. land*) gaten
krijgen.
poacher ['poutʃə] stroper, wilddief *m.*
pochard ['pou-, 'potʃəd] tafeleend *v.*
pocket ['pokit] *sb.* zak *m.;* baal *v.;* beurs
v.; tasje *o.;* map *v.; vt.* in de zak steken;
bij zich steken; kapen; gappen; opsluiten; insluiten.
pocket-book ['pokitbuk] zakboekje *o.;*
portefeuille *v.*
pocket-knife ['pokitnaif] zakmes, pennemes *o.*
pocket-piece ['pokitpis] gelukspen-
ning *m.*

pock-marked ['pokmâkt] pokdalig,
van de pokken geschonden.
pod [pod] *sb.* dop *m.,* schil, peul *v.;*
fuik *v.; vt.* doppen, peulen; *vi.* peulen,
vormen, peulen zetten.
podagra ['podəgrə, pə'dægrə] podagra,
pootje *o.*
podded ['podid] (*Pl.*) peul—; (*sl.*)
welgesteld; — *ware,* peulvruchten.
podware ['podwêə] peulvruchten *v. mr.*
poem ['pouim] gedicht *o.*
poet ['pouit] dichter *m.*
poetaster [poui'tæstə] rijmelaar *m.*
poetic(al) [pou'etik(l)] *adj.* dichterlijk,
poëtisch.
poetry ['pouitri] dichtkunst, poëzie *v.*
point [point] *sb.* punt *o.;* stip *v.,* puntje
o.; decimaalteken *o.;* leesteken *o.;* spits
v.; (kompas)streek *v.; vt.* punten, aanpunten, scherpen; interpuncteren; (*tn.*)
stellen; (*mil.*) richten, mikken; de nadruk leggen op, doen uitkomen, onderstrepen; *vi.* wijzen (*at, to,* op); (*v.
jachthond*) blijven staan; aansturen
(*towards,* op); (*v. barometer*) staan op.
point-blank ['point'blæŋk] (*mil.*) à
bout portant; (*fig.*) zonder omwegen,
rechtstreeks, op de man af.
pointed ['pointid] *adj.* puntig, scherp,
spits; nadrukkelijk.
pointer ['pointə] wijzer *m.;* aanwijsstok
m.; graveerstift, etsnaald *v.;* aanwijzing *v.,* wenk *m.*
pointless ['pointlis] zonder punt,
stomp; onbeduidend.
pointsman ['pointsmən] wisselwachter *m.*
poison ['poizn] *sb.* vergif, gif *o.;* (*sl.*)
sterke drank *m.; vt.* vergeven, vergiftigen; vergallen, bederven; verbitteren.
poisoner ['poiznə] vergiftiger *m.;* giftmenger *m.;* giftmengster *v.*
poison-gas ['poizngæs] giftgas *o.*
poisonous ['poiznəs] vergiftig.
poke [pouk] *sb.* zak, buidel *m.;* stoot,
por, duw *m.;* (*Am.*)suffer *m.;* luilak *m.;*
vt. duwen, stoten, steken; voelen,
tasten; oppoken; opporren; *vi.* snuffelen, scharrelen.
poker ['poukə] *sb.* pook *v.;* (*fig.*) stijve
hark *v.;* (*sl.*) pedel *m.; vt.* met brand-
werk versieren.
poky ['pouki] *adj.* bekrompen, nauw,
benepen; slonzig; peuterig; hokkerig.
Poland ['poulənd] Polen *o.*
polar ['poulə] van de polen, pool—.
polder ['pouldə] polder *m.*
pole [poul] *sb.* pool *v.;* paal, staak, stok
m.; balanceerstok *m.; vt.* van palen
(staken) voorzien; (*sch.*) bomen.
polemic [po'lemik] *adj.* polemisch; *sb.*
polemiek *v.,* pennestrijd *m.;* polemist,
polemicus *m.;* —*s,* polemiek.
police [pə'lis] *sb.* politie *v.; vt.* onder
politietoezicht stellen; bewaken, toezicht houden op.
policeman [pə'lismən] politieagent *m.*

police-station [pə'lïssteiʃən] politiepost *m*.

policlinic [pɔli'klinik] polikliniek *v*.

policy ['pɔlisi] staatsbeleid *o*., politiek *v*.; staatkunde, staatsmanswijsheid *v*.; overleg *o*., omzichtigheid *r*.; polis *v*.

polish ['pɔliʃ] *vt*. polijsten, politoeren; poetsen, boenen; afvegen, afwrijven; (*v. glas*) slijpen; beschaven; — *off*, (*fam*.) (*v. werk*) opknappen; *sb*. politoersel *o*.; beschaving, beschaafdheid *v*., glans *m*.

polite [pə'lait] beleefd; beschaafd.

politeness [pə'laitnis] beleefdheid *v*.

politic ['pɔlitik] *adj*. staatkundig, politiek; handig, slim; *sb*. —*s*, politiek, staatkunde *v*.

political [pə'litikl] *adj*. politiek, staatkundig; *sb*. —*s*, politici *m*. *mv*.

politician [pɔli'tiʃən] politicus, staatsman *m*.; staatkundige *m*.

poll [poul] *sb*. hoofd *o*., kop *m*.; nek *m*.; ongehoornd rund *o*.; kiezerslijst *v*.; stembus *v*.; stembureau *o*.; *vt*. (*v. boom*) toppen, knotten; de horens afsnijden; laten stemmen; zijn stem uitbrengen op.

pollard ['pɔləd] *sb*. getopte boom *m*.; ongehoornd rund *o*.; hert *o*. dat zijn gewei verloren heeft; *vt*. (*v. boom*) knotten.

pollen ['pɔlin] *sb*. stuifmeel *o*.; *vt*. bestuiven.

pollinate ['pɔlineit] bestuiven.

pollute [pə'l(j)ût] bezoedelen, bevlekken, bevuilen, besmetten, verontreinigen; ontwijden, ontheiligen.

poltroon [pɔl'trûn] bloodaard, lafaard *m*.

polygamy [pɔ'ligəmi] veelwijverij *v*.

polyglot ['pɔliglɔt] veeltalig.

polyp(e) ['pɔlip] poliep *v*.

polypus ['pɔlipəs] poliep *v*.

pomade [pə—, po'mâd] *sb*. pommade *v*.; *vt*. pommaderen.

pomatum [pə'meitəm] *sb*. pommade *v*.; *vt*. pommaderen.

pommel ['pɔməl] *sb*. degenknop *m*.; zadelknop *m*.; *vt*. beuken, stompen, (bont en blauw) slaan.

pomp [pɔmp] pracht, praal *v*., luister *m*.

pomposity [pɔm'pɔsiti] praalzucht *v*.; gezwollenheid; hoogdravendheid *v*.

pompous(ly) ['pɔmpəs(li)] *adj*. (*adv*.) statig, deftig, gewichtigdoend; gezwollen, hoogdravend.

pond [pɔnd] *sb*. plas, vijver *m*.; *vi*. een plas vormen; *vt*. — *back* (*up*), ophouden, afdammen.

ponder ['pɔndə] *vt*. overwegen, overpeinzen, overdenken; *vi*. peinzen.

ponderable ['pɔndərəbl] weegbaar.

ponderous(ly) ['pɔndərəs(li)] *adj*. (*adv*.) zwaar; zwaarwichtig, zwaar op de hand.

poniard ['pɔnjəd] *sb*. ponjaard, dolk *m*.; *vt*. doorsteken.

pontiff ['pɔntif] hogepriester, opperpriester *m*.

pontifical [pɔn'tifikl] *adj*. pontificaal, pauselijk; *sb*. pontificaal, bisschoppelijk ceremonieboek *o*.; —*s*, bisschoppelijk gewaad.

pontoon [pɔn'tûn] *sb*. ponton *v*.; kiellichter *m*.; *vt*. in een ponton (in pontons) oversteken.

pony ['pouni] *sb*. hit *m*.; *vi*. — (*up*), opdokken.

poodle ['pûdl] poedel *m*.

pool [pûl] *sb*. poel, plas *m*.; (zwem)bassin *o*.; (*bij spel*) pot *m*.; trust *v*., syndicaat *o*.; *vt*. (*v. kapitaal*) samenleggen, bij elkaar doen; verenigen, samensmelten, onder één beheer brengen; *vi*. samendoen; gemene zaak maken.

poop [pûp] *sb*. (*sch*.) achterschip, achterdek *o*., kampanje *v*.; *vi*. be —*ed*, (*sch*.) een stortzee over de achtersteven krijgen.

poor [pûə, pɔə] *adj*. arm, behoeftig; armoedig; (*v. grond, enz*.) schraal, dor, mager.

poorly ['pêəli] *adr*. arm, armelijk; armoedig; erbarmelijk; armzalig, ellendig.

poor-spirited ['pûə'spiritid] lafhartig, zonder durf, stumperachtig.

pop [pɔp] *sb*. plof, klap, knal *m*.; schot *o*.; plek *v*.; (*sl*.) pistool *o*.; *adj*. *a* — *visit*, een onverwacht bezoek; *vi*. poffen, paffen, knallen; klappen, smakken; schieten; *vt*. doen knallen; afschieten; (*Am*.: *v. maïs*) poffen; — *across*, overwippen; — *away*, hard weglopen; — *in*, binnenwippen; — *off*, wegwippen; (*v. geweer*) afschieten; — *out*, (*v. licht*) opeens uitdoen; — *up*, ineens opduiken; *adv*. & *ij*. pof, paf, floep; *go* —, op de fles gaan, over de kop gaan; (*v. fietsband, enz*.) barsten.

pope [poup] paus *m*.

pope's head ['poupshed] raagbol *m*.

pop-gun ['pɔpgən] proppeschieter *m*.; kinderpistooltje *o*.; prulgeweer *o*.

poplar ['pɔplə] populier *m*.

poppy ['pɔpi] papaver, klaproos *v*.

populace ['pɔpjulis] gepeupel, grauw *o*.; gewone volk *o*.

popular ['pɔpjulə] volksgezind, volks; populair; gewoon, algemeen.

popularity ['pɔpju'læriti] populariteit, volksgunst *v*.

populate ['pɔpjuleit] bevolken; bewonen.

population [pɔpju'leiʃən] bevolking *v*.

populous(ly) ['pɔpjuləs(li)] *adj*. (*adv*.) volkrijk, dicht bevolkt.

porcelain ['pɔːslin] porselein *o*.

porch [pɔːtʃ] portaal, portiek *o*.; zuilengang *v*.; (*Am*.) veranda *v*.

porcupine ['pɔːkjupain] stekelvarken *o*.

pore [poː] porie *v*.; — *at* (*on*), turen naar, staren op; — *over* (*upon*), ijverig bestuderen; zich verdiepen in.

pork [pɔːk] varkensvlees *o*.

pork-butcher ['pɔːkbutʃə] varkensslager *m*.

porker ['po:kə] mestvarken, gemest (jong) varken *o.*
porous ['po:rəs] poreus.
porpoise ['po:pəs] bruinvis *m.*
porridge ['poridʒ] (meel)pap *v.*
port [po:t] *sb.* haven, havenplaats *v.;* poort *r.,* ingang *m.; (sch.)* geschutspoort *v.; (sch.)* patrijspoort *v.; (sch.)* bakboord *o.;* — *of call,* aanloophaven; — *of distress,* noodhaven; — *of refuge,* vluchthaven; *adj. (sch.)* bakboords—; *vt. (sch.)* het roer links omleggen.
portable ['po:təbl] *adj.* draagbaar; verplaatsbaar; — *goods,* roerende goederen; *sb.* roerende goederen.
portal ['po:təl] *sb.* poort, deur *v.,* ingang *m.;* portaal *o.; adj.* — *vein,* poortader.
port-dues ['po:tdjûz] havengelden *o. mv.*
porter ['po:tə] portier *m.;* drager, kruier, besteller *m.*
portfolio [po:t'fouliou] portefeuille *v.*
port-hole ['po:thoul] *(sch.)* patrijspoort *v.;* geschutspoort *v.*
portion ['po:ʃən] *sb.* portie *v.,* deel, aandeel *o.;* erfdeel *o.;* bruidsschat *m.; vt.* verdelen, uitdelen; begiftigen met een bruidsschat (erfdeel) toewijzen; — *out,* uitdelen, verdelen; — *off,* afscheiden, afschutten.
portliness ['po:tlinis] deftigheid *v.;* gezetheid, welgedaanheid *v.*
portmanteau [po:t'mæntou] valies *o.*
portray [po:'trei] portretteren, schilderen.
pose [pouz] *sb.* houding, pose *v.;* aanstellerij *v.; vt. (v. vraag)* stellen; plaatsen, opstellen; een houding doen aannemen; *vi.* poseren, zich aanstellen.
posit ['pozit] poneren, veronderstellen, (als waar) aannemen; plaatsen.
position [pə'ziʃən] *sb.* positie *v.;* rang, stand *m.;* houding *v.;* ligging *v.;* standpunt *o.; vt.* plaatsen, opstellen; de plaats bepalen van.
position-war [pə'ziʃənwo:ə] stellingoorlog *m.*
positive ['pozitiv] *adj.* bepaald, stellig, zeker; positief, volstrekt; dogmatisch; *sb.(gram.)* stellende trap *m.;* positiefgetal *o.;* werkelijkheid *v.; (fot.)* positief *o.*
possess [pə'zes] bezitten, hebben; bezit nemen van; *(v. taal, enz.)* beheersen.
possession [pə'zeʃən] bezitting *v.;* bezit, eigendom *o.;* bezetenheid *v.*
possessor ['pə'zesə] bezitter, eigenaar *m.*
possibility [posi'biliti] mogelijkheid *v.*
possible ['posəbl] *adj.* mogelijk; *if —,* zo mogelijk; *sb.* (het) mogelijke *o.;* mogelijkheid *v.*
post [poust] *sb.* post *v.;* postdienst *m.;* postkantoor *o.;* postbode *m.;* brievenbesteller *m.;* postpapierformaat *o.;* brievenbus *v.;* standplaats *v.;* betrekking *v.; (mil.)* wachtpost *m.; by —,* er post, over de post; *by return of —,*

— *for —,* per omgaande; *vt.* posten, op de post doen; *(mil.)* uitzetten, posteren, op post zetten; boeken; aanplakken; — *off,* met de post verzenden; uitste' len.
post [poust] in samenstellingen: na, achter.
postage ['poustidʒ] port *o.; additional* —, strafport; — *due stamp,* strafportzegel; — *stamp,* postzegel; — *paid,* franco.
postal ['poustəl] *adj.* van de post, post—; — *article,* poststuk; — *delivery,* postbestelling; — *order,* postbewijs; — *collection order,* postkwitantie; — *parcel,* postpakket; — *rates,* posttarief; — *system,* postwezen; — *card,* *(Am)* briefkaart; *sb.* poststuk *o.;* brief *m.;* briefkaart *v.*
post-box ['poustboks] postbus *v.;* brievenbus *v.*
post-boy ['poustboi] postbode, postrijder, postiljon *m.*
postcard ['poustkâd] briefkaart *v.*
post-entry ['poust'entri] latere boeking *v.*
poster ['poustə] renbode *m.;* postpaard *o.;* aanplakker *m.;* aanplakbiljet *o.*
posterity [pos'teriti] nakomelingschap *v.,* nageslacht *o.*
post-free ['poust'fri] franco.
posthumous ['postjuməs] na de dood geboren; nagelaten.
postlude ['poustljûd] naspel *o.*
postman ['pous(t)mən] brievenbesteller, postbode *m.*
postmark ['pous(t)mâk] *sb.* postmerk *o.; vt.* stempelen.
postmaster ['pous(t)mâstə] postmeester, postdirecteur *m.*
post-office ['poustofis] postkantoor *o.*
post-office order ['poustofiso:də] postwissel *m.*
post-paid ['poustpeid] gefrankeerd, franco.
postpone [pous(t)'poun] *vt.* uitstellen, verschuiven, opschorten; achterstellen *(to,* bij); *vi.* uitstellen; *(v. koorts)* later opkomen.
postponement [pous(t)'pounmənt] uitstel *o.;* achterstelling *v.*
postscript ['pous(t)skript] postscriptum *o.*
postulant ['postjulənt] postulant, sollicitant *m.;* kandidaat *m.* (in de theologie, voor geestelijke orde).
postulate ['postjulit] *sb.* postulaat *o.,* hypothese *v.,* axioma *o.;* ['postjuleit] *vt.* postuleren; veronderstellen; (als bewezen) aannemen; verzoeken, eisen.
posture ['postʃə] *sb.* houding *v.;* gestalte *v.;* staat, toestand *m.; vt.* plaatsen; *vi.* een zekere houding aannemen.
pot [pot] *sb.* pot *m.;* kan *v.;* bloempot *m.;* kroes, beker *m.; (sp.)* pot, inzet *m.;* prijs *m.; vt. (v. planten)* potten, overplanten, in potten doen; inleggen, zulten.

potable ['poutǝbl] *adj.* drinkbaar; *sb.*
—*s,* drinkwaren *v. mv.*
potato [pǝ'teitou] aardappel *m.;* (*sl.*)
knol *m.*
potato-flour [pǝ'teitouflauǝ] aardappelmeel *o.*
potence, potency ['poutǝns(i)]
kracht, macht, sterkte *v.;* invloed *m.*
potent ['poutǝnt] *adj.* krachtig, machtig, sterk; invloedrijk.
potentate ['poutǝnteit] potentaat,
vorst *m.*
potential [pǝ'tenʃǝl] *adj.* potentieel,
mogelijk, eventueel; latent (aanwezig);
(*gram.*) mogelijkheid uitdrukkend; *sb.*
potentieel *o.;* mogelijkheid *v.*
pot-house ['pɔthaus] bierhuis *o.,*
kroeg *v.*
potion ['pouʃǝn] drankje *o.*
pot-ladle ['pɔtleidl] pollepel *m.*
potpourri ['pou'puri] (*muz.*) potpourri *o.;* mengeling *v.,* mengelmoes *o.;*
mengsel *o.* van gedroogde kruiden en
bloembladen.
potsherd ['pɔtʃǝ:d] potscherf *v.*
potted ['pɔtid] ingemaakt; (*fig.*) gekunsteld; stereotiep; in 't kort, verkort.
potter ['pɔtǝ] *sb.* pottenbakker *m.*
potter ['pɔtǝ] *vi.* beuzelen; strompelen;
sukkelen; snuffelen; *vt.* — *away,*
verbeuzelen.
pottery ['pɔtǝri] aardewerk *o.,* potten
en pannen *mv.;* pottenbakkerij *v.*
pouch [pautʃ] *sb.* beurs *o.;* tas *v.;* patroontas *v.;* zak; tabakszak *m.;* buidel
m.; vt. in een zak doen; in de zak steken.
poulterer ['poultǝrǝ] poelier *m.*
poultry ['poultri] gevogelte, pluimgedierte, pluimvee *o.*
poultry-farm ['poultrifâm] hoenderpark *o.*
poultry-house ['poultrihaus] kippenhok *o.*
pounce [pauns] *sb.* klauw *m.* (van roofvogel); greep *m.;* sprong *m.;* neerschie-
tende beweging *v.;* fijn poeder, radeer-
poeder *o.; vt.* met de klauwen grijpen;
neerschieten op; *vi.* — (*up*)*on,* zich
werpen op, neerschieten op; *adv.* pardoes.
pound [paund] *sb.* pond *o.;* pond sterling *o.;* schutstal *m.;* omsloten ruimte
v.; vt. schutten; insluiten; fijnstampen;
stompen, beuken; *vi.* stampen; beuken;
(*v. motor*) kloppen; (*v. hart*) bonzen.
poundage ['paundidʒ] schutgeld *o.;*
postwisselrecht *o.;* aandeel *o.* in de opbrengst.
pounder ['paundǝ] stamper *m.;* vijzel
m.; schutmeester *m.*
pour [po:] *vt.* gieten, uitgieten; schenken, inschenken, uitschenken; doen
stromen; *vi.* gieten; stortregenen; in
stromen neerkomen; *sb.* stortbui *v.,*
stortregen *m.;* stroom *m.;* (het) gieten *o.*
pout [paut] *sb.* (*Dk.: vis*) steenbolk;

lamprei *v.;* gepruil *o.; vt.* (*v. lippen*)
vooruitsteken; *vi.* pruilen.
poverty ['pɔvǝti] armoede *v.;* armoe-
digheid *v.;* behoefte *v.,* gebrek *o.;*
schraalheid *v.*
powder ['paudǝ] *sb.* poeier, poeder *o.;*
buskruit *o.;* (*fig.*) kracht *v.; vt.* fijn
maken (stampen); poeieren, bestrooien;
besprenkelen; bezaaien; *vi.* zich poeieren; tot poeder worden.
powder-blue ['paudǝblû] blauwsel *o.*
powder-box ['paudǝbɔks] poeierdoos
v.; kruitkist *v.*
powder-puff ['paudǝpɔf] poeder-
kwastje, poederdoosje *o.*
power ['pauǝ] macht, kracht *v.;* vermogen *o.;* gezag *o.;* mogendheid *v.;* (*v. lens*)
sterkte *v.*
powerful(ly) ['pauǝful(i)] *adj.* (*adv.*)
machtig, krachtig, sterk; vermogend;
indrukwekkend.
powerless(ly) ['pauǝlis(li)] *adj.* (*adv.*)
machteloos, krachteloos.
practicable ['præktikǝbl] uitvoerbaar,
doenlijk; begaanbaar; bruikbaar.
practical ['præktikl] *adj.* praktisch,
werkdadig; werkelijk, feitelijk.
practice ['præktis] praktijk *v.;* beoefening, uitoefening *v.;* gebruik *o.,* toepassing, aanwending *v.*
practice-flight ['præktisflait] oefen-
vlucht *v.*
practise ['præktis] *vt.* beoefenen; uitoefenen; in praktijk brengen, in toepassing brengen; (*v. muziek, enz.*) instuderen; zich oefenen in; *vi.* oefenen; zich
oefenen; praktizeren; — *upon,* beetnemen.
practitioner [præk'tiʃǝnǝ] man *m.* van
de praktijk; praktizerend geneesheer
m.; beoefenaar *m.*
praise [preiz] *sb.* lof *m.,* lofspraak *v.;*
vt. prijzen, loven; — *up,* ophemelen.
praiseful ['preizful] prijzend, lovend.
praiseworthy ['preizwǝːθi] loffelijk,
lofwaardig, prijzenswaardig.
praline ['prâlîn] praline *v.*
prance [prâns] steigeren.
prank [præŋk] poets *v.;* streek *m.*
prankish ['præŋkiʃ] guitig, schelms.
prate [preit] *vi.* babbelen, wauwelen;
sb. gebabbel, gewauwel *o.*
prater ['preitǝ] babbelaar, wauwelaar *m.*
prattle ['prætl] *vi.* babbelen, snappen;
sb. gesnap *o.*
prattler ['prætlǝ] babbelaar, snapper *m.*
pravity ['præviti] bedorven toestand
m., slechte kwaliteit *v.;* verdorvenheid *v.*
pray [prei] verzoeken, bidden, smeken.
prayer ['preiǝ] biddende, bidder *m.*
prayer [prêǝ] gebed *o.;* verzoek *o.;*
—(*s*), godsdienstoefening *v.*
prayer-book ['prêǝbuk] gebedenboek *o.*
preach [pritʃ] *vt. & vi.* prediken; *sb.*
preek *v.*
preacher ['pritʃǝ] prediker; predikant *m.*

preamble [pri'æmbl] inleiding v.
preambulatory [pri'æmbjulətəri] voorafgaand, inleidend.
prebendary ['prebəndəri] domheer m.
precarious(ly) [pri'kêəriəs(li)] adj. (adv.) onzeker, onbestendig, wisselvallig, hachelijk, precair.
precaution [pri'ko:ʃən] sb. voorzorg v., voorzorgsmaatregel m.; voorbehoedmiddel o.; vt. vooraf waarschuwen.
precautionary [pri'ko:ʃənəri] uit voorzorg gedaan; waarschuwend.
precautious(ly) [pri'ko:ʃəs(li)] adj. (adv.) omzichtig, vol voorzorg.
precede [pri'sid] voorafgaan; vóórgaan; de voorrang hebben boven.
precedence ['presidəns, pri'sidəns] voorrang m.; prioriteit v.
precedent [pri'sidənt] adj. voorafgaand, vroeger; ['presidənt] sb. precedent o.
precent [pri'sent] voorzingen.
precentor [pri'sentə] voorzanger m.
precept ['prisept] voorschrift o.; stelregel, grondregel m.; bevel, mandaat o.; schoolgeld o.
precious ['preʃəs] adj. kostbaar; dierbaar; kostelijk, mooi; (v. metalen) edel; adv. drommels, verduiveld.
precipice ['presipis] steilte v., steile rotswand m.; (fig.) afgrond m.
precipitancy, precipitancy [pri'sipitəns(i)] haast, overhaasting, overijling v.
precipitation [prisipi'teiʃən] neerstorting v.; haast, overhaasting, overijling v.; neerslag m.
precipitous(ly) [pri'sipitəs(li)] adj. (adv.) (zeer) steil; overijld, overhaastig.
precise(ly) [pri'sais(li)] adj. (adv.) juist, nauwkeurig, precies; stipt, nauwgezet.
precision [pri'siʒən] juistheid, nauwkeurigheid v.
precursor [pri'kə:sə] voorloper, voorbode m.
predatory ['predətəri] adj. rovend, plunderend; roofzuchtig; rovers—, roof—.
predecessor [pridi'sesə] voorganger m.; voorvader m.
predestination [pridesti neiʃən] voorbestemming, voorbeschikking v.
predestine [pri'destin] voorbestemmen, voorbeschikken.
predicate ['predikit] sb. predikaat o., eigenschap v.; (gram.) gezegde o.; ['predikeit] vt. zeggen, beweren, uiten; bevestigen; insluiten; toekennen.
predict [pri'dikt] voorzeggen, voorspellen.
prediction [pri'dikʃən] voorzegging, voorspelling v.; profetie v.
predilection [pridi'lekʃən] voorliefde, voorkeur, vooringenomenheid v.
predominate [pri'domineit] overheersen, de overhand hebben; de doorslag geven, overwegen; sterk uitkomen, op de voorgrond treden.

pre-eminently [pri'eminəntli] a tv. uitmuntend, uitstekend; bij uitstek.
preface ['prefis] sb. voorrede v., voorbericht o.; inleiding v.; (v. de mis) prefatie v.; vt. van een voorrede (inleiding) voorzien; inleiden; laten voorafgaan (with, door).
prefer [pri'fə:] verkiezen, de voorkeur geven; bevorderen (to, tot); (v. rekwest) aanbieden, voordragen; (v. wetsontwerp) indienen, voorleggen; (v. klacht) inbrengen.
preferable ['prefərəbl] adj. verkieslijk, te verkiezen (to, boven).
preference ['prefərəns] voorkeur, voorliefde; verkiezing v.; (H.) preferentie, prioriteit v.
preferential [prefə'renʃəl] preferentieel; prioriteits—, voorkeurs—.
prefix ['prifiks] voorvoegsel o.
pregnable ['pregnəbl] (in)neembaar.
pregnancy ['pregnənsi] zwangerschap v.
pregnant ['pregnənt] adj. zwanger; veelzeggend, veelbetekenend, betekenisvol.
prejudice ['predʒudis] sb. vooroordeel o.; vooringenomenheid v.; nadeel o., schade v.; without —, onder voorbehoud, alle rechten voorbehouden; zonder verantwoordelijkheid, zonder obligo; vt. voorinnemen; innemen tegen; benadelen, kwaad doen, afbreuk doen, schaden.
prejudicial [predʒu'diʃəl] schadelijk, nadelig.
prelate ['prelit] prelaat, kerkvoogd m.
preliminary [pri'liminəri] adj. voorafgaand, inleidend; sb. voorbereiding, inleiding v.
prelude ['preljûd] sb. voorspel o.; inleiding v.; vt. inleiden, een inleiding vormen tot; inzetten (met een voorspel); inluiden; vi. preluderen, een voorspel spelen.
premature(ly) [premə'tjûə(li), 'premətjuə(li)] adj. (adv.) te vroeg rijp; ontijdig, voorbarig.
premeditate [pri'mediteit] vooraf bedenken, vooraf beramen (overleggen).
premeditation [primedi'teiʃən] opzet o., voorbedachtheid v., voorafgaand overleg o.
premier ['premjə] adj. eerste, voornaamste; sb. eerste minister, ministerpresident m.
premise [pri'maiz] vt. vooraf laten gaan, vooropstellen; ['premis] sb. premisse, voorafgaande stelling v.; —s, (recht) bovengenoemd pand (huis, eigendom); huis en erf.
premium ['primjəm] premie v.; toeslag m.; prijs m., beloning v.; leergeld o.; (H.) agio o., waarde v. boven pari.
preoccupied [pri'okjupaid] bezorgd; in gedachten verzonken; verstrooid.
prepaid ['pri'peid] vooruitbetaald, franco.

preparation [prepə'reiʃən] voorbereiding *v.*, voorbereidsel, toebereidsel *o.*; (het) klaarmaken *o.*, bereiding *v.*
preparative [pri'pærətiv] *adj.* voorbereidend; *sb.* voorbereidsel, toebereidsel *o.*
prepare [pri'pêə] *vt.* voorbereiden; bereiden, toebereiden; *(voor examen)* opleiden, klaarmaken; *vi.* zich gereed maken, zich klaar maken; *vr.* — *oneself for (to)*, zich voorbereiden om.
prepay ['pri'pei] vooruitbetalen, vooraf betalen; frankeren.
prepense [pri'pens] voorbedacht.
preponderance [pri'pɔndərəns] overwicht *o.*
preponderant [pri'pɔndərənt] overwegend, van overwegend belang.
preposition [prepə'ziʃən] voorzetsel *o.*
prepossess [pripə'zes] innemen *(for, in favour of,* voor); gunstig stemmen; beïnvloeden; *(soms:)* vooraf in bezit men.
preposterous(ly) [pri'pɔstərəs(li)] *adj.* *(adv.)* ongerijmd, onzinnig, dwaas; verkeerd, averechts.
prerogative [pri'rɔgətiv] *sb.* recht, voorrecht; prerogatief *o.*; *adj.* bevoorrecht.
presage ['presidʒ] *sb.* voorteken *o.*; voorgevoel *o.*; [pri'seidʒ, presidʒ] *vt.* voorspellen, voorzeggen, aankondigen; een voorgevoel hebben van.
presageful [pri'seidʒful] voorspellend; onheilspellend; vol (bange) vermoedens.
presbyopic [prezbi'ɔpik] vèrziend.
presbytery ['prezbitəri] raad van ouderlingen, kerkeraad *m.*; *(kath.)* priesterkoor *o.*; pastorie *v.*
prescience ['preʃiəns] voorwetenschap *v.*; vooruitziendheid *v.*
prescind [pri'sind] afsnijden, afzonderen.
prescribe [pris'kraib] *vt.* voorschrijven; *vi.* voorschriften geven.
prescript ['priskript] voorschrift, bevel *o.*
prescription [pris'kripʃən] voorschrijving *v.*; voorschrift, recept *o.*; *(recht)* verjaring *v.*
prescriptive [pris'kriptiv] voorschrijvend; *(recht)* verjaard.
presence ['prezəns] aanwezigheid, tegenwoordigheid *v.*; bijzijn *o.*, voorkomen, uiterlijk *o.*
present ['prezənt] *adj.* aanwezig, tegenwoordig, present; hedendaags; onderhavig; in kwestie; *sb.* tegenwoordige tijd *m.*, (het) heden *o.*; geschenk, cadeau *o.*
present [pri'zent] *vt.* voorstellen; voorleggen, overleggen; *(v. geweer)* presenteren; *(v. klacht)* indienen; *(v. cheque)* aanbieden; *vi.* de voordracht opmaken; *(v. gelegenheid)* zich voordoen; *vr.* — *oneself*, verschijnen, opdagen; *(v. gedachte)* opkomen; *(v. gelegenheid, enz.)* zich voordoen; zich aanbieden.

presentable [pri'zentəbl] *adj.* toonbaar, presentabel; goed om aan te bieden.
presentation [prezən'teiʃən] voorstelling *v.*; voorlegging, overlegging *v.*; indiening *v.*; aanbieding *v.*
presentiment [pri'zentimənt] voorgevoel *o.*
presently ['prezntli] *adv.* aanstonds, dadelijk, zo meteen; dadelijk daarop.
presentment [pri'zəntmənt] aanbieding *v.*; voorstelling *v.*; aanklacht *v.*; voorkomen *o.*
preservation [prezə'veiʃən] bewaring *v.*; bescherming *v.*; behoud *o.*, redding *v.*; inmaak *m.*
preservative [pri'zə:vətiv] *adj.* voorbehoedend; conserverend; *sb.* bederfwerend (conserverend) middel *o.*; voorbehoedmiddel *o.*
preserve [pri'zə:v] *vt.* bewaren, behoeden; inmaken; behouden; *sb.* ingemaakte vruchten *v. mv.*, jam *v.*, enz.
preserver [pri'zə:və] bewaarder, behoeder; beschermer *m.*; *(v. vruchten, enz.)* inmaker *m.*; conserverend middel *o.*
preside [pri'zaid] voorzitten, presideren.
president ['prezidənt] president, voorzitter *m.*
press [pres] *sb.* pers *v.*; drukpers, drukkerij *v.*; drukproef *v.*; gedrang *o.*; *vt.* samenpersen; uitpersen; oppersen; uitdrukken; uitknijpen; *vi.* drukken; knellen; zich verdringen; *(v. menigte)* opdringen; dringen, presseren.
press-agency ['preseidʒənsi] persbureau *o.*
press-agent ['preseidʒənt] publiciteitsagent *m.*
press-button ['presbʌtn] drukknopje *o.*
press-campaige ['preskəmpein] perscampagne *v.*
pressing ['presiŋ] *adj.* dringend; nijpend, dreigend; *sb.* persing *v.*; druk, drang; aandrang *m.*
pressman ['presmən] (handpers)drukker *m.*; dagbladschrijver, journalist, persman *m.*
press-reader ['presri:də] corrector *m.*
press-room ['presrum] drukkerij *v.*
press-stud ['presstəd] drukknoopje *o.*
pressure ['preʃə] drukking *v.*; druk *m.*, spanning *v.*; dwang *m.*
press-work ['preswə:k] drukwerk *o.*
prestige [pres'tiʒ] aanzien *o.*, invloed *m.*, gezag, prestige *o.*
presumable [pri'zjûməbl] *adj.* vermoedelijk.
presume [pri'zjûm] vermoeden, veronderstellen; aannemen; zich inbeelden; durven, zich vermeten.
presuming(ly) [pri'zjûmiŋ(li)] *adj.* *(adv.)* ᴌaanmatigend, verwaand.
presumption [pri'zəm(p)ʃən] vermoeden *o.*, veronderstelling *v.*; aanmatiging, verwaandheid *v.*

presumptuous(**ly**) [pri'zǝm(p)tjuǝs-(li)] *adj*. (*adv*.) aanmatigend, verwaand, ingebeeld, arrogant, ont>eschaamd.

pretence [pri'tens] voorwendsel, voorgeven *o*.; schijn *m*., uiterlijk vertoon *o*.

pretend [pri'tend] *vt*. voorwenden, voorgeven; (ten onrechte) beweren; *vi*. doen alsof, huichelen; — *to*, aanspraak maken op; zich aanmatigen.

pretended (**ly**) [pri'tendid(li)] *adj*. (*adv*.) voorgewend; vermeend; — *to*, zogenaamd om.

pretender [pri'tendǝ] pretendent *m*.; veinzer, huichelaar *m*.

pretension [pri'tenʃǝn] aanspraak *v*.; aanmatiging, pretentie *v*.; voorwendsel *o*.

pretentious(**ly**) [pri'tenʃǝs(li)] *adj*. (*adv*.) aanmatigend, pretentieus; onbescheiden.

pretext [pri'tekst] *sb*. voorwendsel *o*.; [pri'tekst] *vt*. voorwenden.

pretty [pri'ti] *adj*. lief, aardig, mooi; *adv*. tamelijk, redelijk, vrij; *vt*. (*vr*.) — (*oneself*) *up*, (zich) mooi maken.

pretty-pretty [pri'ti'priti] *adj*. gemaakt, geaffecteerd; poeslief; popperig; *sb*. **prett -pretties**, snuisterijen *v*. *mv*.

pretty-spoken [pri'tispoukn] aangenaam (in de omgang); aardig gezegd.

prevail [pri'veil] de overhand hebben, zegevieren; heersen, overheersend zijn, algemeen zijn.

prevalence, prevalency [pri'velǝns(i)] overwicht *o*.; invloed *m*., gezag *o*.; (*v. ziekte, enz.*) (het) heersen *o*.; (het) algemeen voorkomen *o*.

prevent [pri'vent] beletten, verhinderen, verhoeden; voorkomen.

preventive [pri'ventiv] *adj*. voorkomend; verhinderend; *sb*. voorbehoedmiddel *o*.

previous [pri'vjǝs] *adj*. voorafgaand, vorig, vroeger; (*sl*.) voorbarig.

previously [pri'vjǝsli] *adv*. vroeger, (van) te voren, vóór die tijd.

previse [pri'vaiz] voorzien, vooruitzien.

prey [prei] *sb*. prooi *v*., buit *m*.; *vi*. — (*up*)*on*, roven, plunderen; azen op; (*fig*.) knagen aan.

price [prais] *sb*. prijs *m*.; (*v. effecten*) koers *m*.; waarde *v*.; — *of issue*, koers van uitgifte; *vt*. (*v. artikelen*) prijzen; de prijs vaststellen (bepalen, noemen, aangeven).

price-current [praiskǝrǝnt] (*H*.) prijscourant, prijslijst *v*.

price-cutter [praiskǝtǝ] (*H*.) onderkruiper *m*.

price-list [praislist] (*H*.) prijscourant, prijslijst *v*.

prick [prik] *sb*. prik, *m*., stip, punt *v*.; stekel *m*.; prikkel *m*.; (*v. tabak, garen*) rolletje *o*.; *vt*. prikken (in), doorprikken, steken; opensteken, doorsteken; prikkelen; — *in*, inplanten; poten; — *off*, uitpoten; *vi*. prikken, steken; (*v. geweten*) knagen; de sporen geven.

prick-eared [prikiǝd] met opstaande oren.

pricker [prikǝ] prikkel, priem *m*.; ruimnaald *v*.; prikstok *m*.

prickle [prikl] *sb*. prikkel; stekel *m*.; dorentje *o*.; tenen mandje *o*.; *vt*. prikkelen, steken.

pickly [prikli] prikkend, stekelig; netelig.

pride [praid] *sb*. trots *m*.; hoogmoed *m*.; luis:er *m*.; *vr*. — *oneself on*, zich beroemen op; trots zijn op.

priest [prist] priester *m*.; (*Dk*.) pauwstaart:duif *v*.

prig [prig] *sb*. kwast, fat, pedant persoon *m*.; (*sl*.) dief *m*.; *vt*. (*sl*.) gappen, kapen. ont:futselen.

priggish(**ly**) [prigiʃ(li)] *adj*. (*adv*.) eigenwijs, ingebeeld, pedant.

primary [praimǝri] *adj*. eerst, oorspronkelijk; elementair, grond—; grootste, voornaamste; — *education*, lager onderwijs; — *school*, lagere school; *sb*. hoofdzaak *v*.; beginsel *o*.

primate [praimit] primaat, opperkerkvoogd *m*.

prime [praim] *adj*. eerste, voornaamste; oorspronkelijk, grond—; (*v. kwaliteit*) prima, uitstekend, puik; *sb*. begin *o*.; aanvang *m*.; oorspronkelijke toestand *m*.; *vt*. in de grondverf zetten; (*fig*.) voorbereiden; inlichten, instrueren; africhten.

primeval [prai'mivǝl] oorspronkelijk, oer—.

primitive [primitiv] *adj*. oorspronkelijk, oer—; primitief; *sb*. grondwoord, stamwoord *o*.; oorspronkelijk bewoner *m*.; een der Primitieven.

primrose [primrouz] sleutelbloem *v*.

primula [primjulǝ] sleutelbloem *v*.

prince [prins] prins; vorst *m*.

princely [prinsli] prinselijk, vorstelijk.

princess [prin'ses; prinses] prinses; vorstin *v*.

principal [prinsip(ǝ)l] *adj*. voornaamste, hoofd—; *sb*. hoofd *o*.; directeur *m*.; hoofdpersoon *m*.; patroon *m*.; principaal *m*.

principality [prinsi'pæliti] vorstelijke (prinselijke) waardigheid *v*.; vorstendom, prinsdom *o*.

principle [prinsipl] beginsel *o*., bron *v*., oorsprong *m*.; grondbeginsel, principe *o*.; stelregel *m*.; element, bestanddeel *o*.

principled [prinsipld] met... beginselen.

print [print] *sb*. teken, merk *o*., indruk *m*.; afdruk *m*.; plaat, prent *v*.; *in* —, ter perse; nog te verkrijgen, nog in de handel; *adj*. gedrukt; *vt*. drukken; bedrukken; afdrukken.

printer [printǝ] drukker *m*.

printing [printiŋ] (het) drukken *o*.; (boek)drukkunst *v*.; oplaag *v*.

printing-press [printiŋpres] drukpers *v*.

prior ['praiə] *adj*. eerste, oudste; vroeger, voorafgaand; *prep*. — *to*, voor, voordat, alvorens te; *sb*. prior *m*.

prioress ['praiəris] priores *v*.

priority [prai'ɔriti] prioriteit *v*., voorrang *m*.

prison ['prizn] *sb*. gevangenis *v*.; *vt*. gevangen zetten (houden).

prisoner ['priznə] gevangene *m*.; beklaagde *m*.

privacy ['praivəsi, privəsi] eenzaamheid, afzondering *v*.; geheimhouding *v*.

private ['praivit] *adj*. privaat, privé; persoonlijk, particulier; (*v. verkoop, inschrijving*) onderhands; *sb*. gemeen soldaat *m*.; *in* —, onder vier ogen; in 't geheim, in stilte; alleen, in afzondering; in 't particuliere leven.

privateer [praivə'tiə] kaper *m*., kaperschip *o*.

privately ['praivitli] *adv*. in stilte; heimelijk; voor eigen rekening, op eigen kosten.

privation [prai'veiʃən] ontbering *v*., gebrek, gemis *o*.; beroving *v*.

privilege ['privilidʒ] *sb*. privilege *o*.; voorrecht *o*., gunst *v*.; *vt*. bevoorrechten; vrijstellen (*from*, van); verontschuldigen; machtigen.

privy ['privi] *adj*. geheim, heimelijk, verborgen; ingewijd (*to*, in), bekend (*to*, met); *sb*. privaat *o*., (*recht*) belanghebbende, deelhebber *m*.

prize [praiz] *sb*. prijs *m*.; beloning *v*.; buit *m*.; voordeel, buitenkansje *o*.; *adj*. bekroond; eersteklas, prima; *vt*. op prijs stellen, waarderen; bekronen (met een prijs).

prize-court ['praizkɔ:t] prijsgerecht, prijzenhof *o*.

prize-fighting ['praizfaitiŋ] (het) boksen *o*.

pro [prou] vóór; — *and con*, het voor en tegen.

probability [prɔbə'biliti] waarschijnlijkheid *v*.

probable ['prɔbəbl] *adj*. waarschijnlijk, vermoedelijk; aannemelijk.

probation [prɔ'beiʃən] proef *v*., onderzoek *o*.; proeftijd *m*.; voorwaardelijke veroordeling; voorwaardelijke invrijheidstelling *v*.

probity ['prɔbiti] eerlijkheid, oprechtheid, rechtschapenheid *v*.

problem ['prɔblim] vraagstuk, probleem *o*.; opgave *v*.

problematic(al) [prɔbli'mætik(l)] *adj*. twijfelachtig, problematisch; onzeker; raadselachtig.

procedure [prə'sidʒə] werkwijze, methode, handelwijze *v*.; (*legal*), — rechtspleging, rechtspraktijk *v*.

proceed [prə'sid] gaan; voortgaan, verder gaan; vorderen; te werk gaan.

proceeding [prə'sidiŋ] handeling *v*.; verrichting *v*.; handelwijze, gedragslijn *v*.

process ['prouses, 'prɔses] *sb*. gang *m*., verloop *o*.; voortgang *m*.; bereidings-

wijze *v*.; werkwijze *v*., procédé *o*.; *vt* (machinaal) reproduceren; conserveren, verduurzamen; gerechtelijk vervolgen.

procession [prə'seʃən] optocht, stoet *m*.; (*kath*.) processie *v*.

proclaim [pro'kleim] afkondigen, bekendmaken; verkondigen; proclameren, uitroepen.

proclamation [prɔklə'meiʃən] proclamatie *v*.; bekendmaking *v*.; afkondiging *v*.; (*v. oorlog*) verklaring *v*.

procreate ['proukrieit] voortbrengen, scheppen, verwekken, telen.

procurable [pro'kjûərəbl] verkrijgbaar, te krijgen.

procuration [prɔkju'reiʃən] verschaffing *v*.; bezorging *v*.; aanschaffing *v*.; volmacht, procuratie *v*.

procure [pro'kjûə] verschaffen; bezorgen; (zich) aanschaffen.

procurer [pro'kjûərə] verschaffer *m*.; bezorger *m*.; bewerker *m*.; koppelaar *m*.

prodigal ['prɔdigəl] *adj*. verkwistend; — *of*, kwistig met; *sb*. verkwister, doorbrenger *m*.

prodigious(ly) [pro'didʒəs(li)] *adj*. (*adv*.) wonderbaar(lijk); geweldig, verbazend, ontzaglijk.

prodigy ['prɔdidʒi] wonder *o*.

produce ['prɔdjûs] *sb*. voortbrengsel(en), produkt(en) *o*. (*mv*.); produktie, opbrengst *v*.; [prə'djûs] *vt*. opbrengen, opleveren, voortbrengen; produceren; bijbrengen; (*v. papieren, enz*.) overleggen, voor de dag halen; (*v. indruk*) teweegbrengen.

producer [prə'djûsə] producent, voortbrenger *m*.; (*ton*.) spelleider, toneelleider, regisseur *m*.

product ['prɔdəkt] voortbrengsel, produkt *o*.; vrucht *v*., resultaat *o*.

production [prə'dəkʃən] produktie, voortbrenging *v*.; voortbrengsel, produkt *o*.

productive [prə'dəktiv] *adj*. voortbrengend, producerend; vruchtbaar, produktief.

profanation [prɔfə'neiʃən] ontheiliging, ontwijding, (heilig)schennis, profanatie *v*.

profane [prə'fein] *adj*. ongewijd; oningewijd; werelds; goddeloos; *vt*. ontwijden, ontheiligen, schenden, profaneren; ijdellijk gebruiken; (*v. tijd*) misbruiken.

profaner [pro'feinə] ontheiliger, ontwijder, heiligschender *m*.; misbruiker *m*.

profess [pro'fes] *vt*. belijden; betuigen; verklaren, beweren; beoefenen; *vi*. doceren; zijn godsdienstplichten vervullen; de kloostergeloften afleggen.

professed [pro'fest] *adj*. openlijk, verklaard; van beroep, beroeps—; voorgewend, beweerd; zogenaamd; geprofest.

professedly [pro'fesidli] *adv*. openlijk, onverholen; ogenschijnlijk.

profession [pro'feʃən] belijdenis *v*.; verklaring, betuiging, bekentenis *v*.; stand *m*., beroep *o*.; professie *v*.

professional [pro'feʃənəl] *adj.* vak—, beroeps—: van beroep; ambts—; *sb.* vakman *m.*; beroepsspeler *m.*

professor [pro'fesə] belijder *m.*; professor, hoogleraar *m.*; vakman *m.*

proficient [prə'fiʃənt] *adj.* vaardig; bedreven, bekwaam; *sb.* vergevorderde; meester (*in,* in).

profile ['proufil] *sb.* profiel *o.*; (verticale) doorsnede *v.*; omtrek *m.*; *vt.* in profiel tekenen.

profit ['profit] *sb.* voordeel, nut *o.*; winst, baat *v.*; *vt.* voordeel afwerpen voor, baten, van nut zijn; helpen; *vi.* zijn voordeel doen (*bv,* met), profiteren (*by,* van), gebruik maken (*by,* van).

profitable ['profitəbl] *adj.* winstgevend, voordelig; heilzaam, nuttig.

profiteer [profi'tiə] *vi.* woekerwinst (oorlogswinst) maken; *sb.* woekerwinstmaker; afzetter *m.*

profiteering [profi'tiəriŋ] woekerwinst-bejag *o.*; afzetterij *v.*

profitless ['profitlis] onvoordelig; zonder nut.

profit-sharing ['profitʃêəriŋ] met aandeel in de winst.

profligate ['profligit] *adj.* losbandig, zedeloos; *sb.* losbol *m.*

profound [pro'faund] *adj.* diep; diepzinnig; grondig, diepgaand; *sb.* (*dicht.*) onmetelijke diepte *v.*, afgrond *m.*

profuse [pro'fjûs] *adj.* kwistig; verkwistend; rijk, overvloedig.

profusion [pro'fjûʒən] kwistigheid *v.*; verkwisting *v.*; overvloed *m.*

progenitor [prou'dʒenitə] voorvader, stamvader, voorzaat *m.*; (*fig.*) voorganger *m.*; verwekker *m.*

progeny ['prodʒini] kroost, nageslacht *o.*, nakomelingen *m. mv.*

prognostication [prognosti'keiʃən] voorspelling *v.*; voorteken *o.*

program(**me**) ['prougræm] programma *o.*

progress ['prougres] *sb.* vooruitgang *m.*, vordering *v.*, voortgang *m.*; toeneming *v.*; (*v. ziekte*) verloop *o.*; [prə'gres] *vi.* vooruitgaan, vooruitkomen; vorderingen maken, opschieten; aan de gang zijn.

progressive [prə'gresiv] voortgaand, vooruitgaand; opklimmend; toenemend; vooruitstrevend.

prohibit [prə'hibit] verbieden; beletten.

prohibition [proui'biʃən] verbod, drankverbod *o.*

project ['prodʒekt] *sb.* ontwerp, plan *o.*; (*Am.*) onderneming *v.*; [prə'dʒekt] *vt.* ontwerpen, beramen; projecteren; werpen, slingeren; (*v. stralen*) uitschieten; *vi.* vooruitsteken, uitspringen.

projectile [prə'dʒektail] *adj.* voortdrijvend; voortwerpend; *sb.* [ook: prodʒiktail] (*mil.*) projectiel *o.*

projection [pro'dʒekʃən] projectie *v.*; ontwerp *o.*; uitstek, vooruitspringend deel *o.*; projectietekening *v.*

prolapse [prou'læps] *sb.* (*gen.*) verzakking *v.*; *vi.* verzakken.

proletarian [prouli'têəriən] *adj.* proletarisch; *sb.* proletariër, proleet *m.*

proletariat [prouli'têəriæt] proletariaat *o.*

proletary ['prolitəri] *adj.* proletarisch; *sb.* proletariër *m.*

prolix ['prouliks] langdradig, breedsprakig, wijdlopig.

prologue ['proulog] proloog *m.*, voorspel *o.*; inleiding, voorrede *v.*

prolong [pro'loŋ] verlengen, rekken; (*v. noot*) aanhouden; (*H.*) prolongeren; —*ed,* ook: langdurig.

prolongation [prouloŋ'geiʃən] verlenging *v.*; (*H.*) prolongatie *v.*

prolusion [prə'l(j)ûʒən] voorspel *o.*; proeve *v.*

prominent ['prominənt] *adj.* vooruitstekend; uitstekend, eminent; vooraanstaand, op de voorgrond tredend.

promise ['promis] *sb.* belofte, toezegging *v.*; *vt.* beloven, toezeggen; *vi.* beloven, zijn woord geven.

promising ['promisiŋ] veelbelovend.

promissory ['promisəri] belovend.

promote [prə'mout] verwekken; aankweken; bevorderen, begunstigen.

promotion [prə'mouʃən] bevordering, promotie *v.*

promotional [prə'mouʃənl] bevorderend, bijstand verlenend.

prompt [prom(p)t] *adj.* vlug, vaardig, stipt, prompt; (*H.*) contant; *adv.* precies; *sb.* betalingstermijn, ontvangsttermijn, betalingsdatum *m.*; (het) souffleren *o.*; *vt.* voorzeggen, souffleren; inblazen, ingeven; aanmoedigen.

prompter ['prom(p)tə] vóórzegger *m.*; souffleur *m.*

promulgate ['proməlgait] afkondigen, uitvaardigen, verkondigen, openbaar maken.

promulgator ['proməlgeitə] afkondiger *m.*, verkondiger *m.*

prone [proun] hellend, (voorover, naar beneden) gebogen, vooroverliggend, steil — *to,* vatbaar voor; geneigd tot.

prong [proŋ] priem *v.*; hooivork, gaffel *v.*; (*v. vork*) tand *m.*

pronoun ['prounaun] voornaamwoord.

pronounce [prə'nauns] *vt.* uitspreken; uiten, uitbrengen; zeggen, verklaren; *vi.* zich uitspreken; uitspraak doen.

pronounced [prə'naunst] *adj.* sterk sprekend, beslist, geprononceerd.

pronunciation [prənənsi'eiʃən] uitspraak *v.*; voordracht *v.*

proof [prûf] *sb.* bewijs, blijk *o.*; proef, drukproef *v.*; proefblad *o.*; (*v. alcohol*) sterktegraad *m.*; *adj.* beproefd; bestand (*against,* tegen); *vt.* ondoordringbaar maken, waterdicht maken; vuurvast maken.

proofless ['prûflis] onbewezen.

proof-reader ['prûfridə] corrector *m.*

prop [prop] *sb.* stut, steun *m.*; steunpilaar *m.*; *vt.* stutten, steunen, schragen, schoren.

propagate ['propageit] *vt.* voortplanten, verbreiden, verspreiden; *vi.* zich voortplanten.

propagation [propə'geiʃən] voortplanting, verbreiding, verspreiding *v.*

propel [pro'pel] voortbewegen, voortdrijven, voortstuwen.

propeller [pro'pelə] schroef *v.*

proper ['propə] *adj.* eigen; geschikt, passend, gepast; behoorlijk, betamelijk, voegzaam; fatsoenlijk.

property ['propəti] bezit *o.*, bezitting *v.*, eigendom *o.*; landgoed *o.*; eigendomsrecht *o.*; hoedanigheid, eigenschap; eigenaardigheid *v.*

property-tax ['propətitæks] vermogensbelasting *v.*

prophecy ['profisi] voorspelling, voorzegging, profetie *v.*

prophet ['profit] profeet *m.*

propitiate [pro'piʃieit] gunstig stemmen; verzoenen.

propitious (ly) [pro'piʃəs(li) *adj.* (*adv.*) genadig; gunstig.

proportion [prə'po:ʃən] *sb.* evenredigheid *v.*; verhouding *v.*; afmeting *v.*; *in — as,* naarmate; naar gelang; *vt.* evenredig maken; afmeten; afwegen.

proportional [prə'po:ʃənəl] *adj.* evenredig, geëvenredigd (**to,** aan); *sb.* evenredige *v.*, term *m.* van evenredigheid.

proportionally [prə'po:ʃənəli] *adv.* evenredig; naar evenredigheid, in verhouding.

proportionate [prə'po:ʃənit] *adj.* evenredig, geëvenredigd (**to,** aan); [prə'po:ʃəneit] *vt.* evenredig maken.

proposal [prə'pouzl] voorstel *o.*; aanbod *o.*

propose [prə'pouz] *vt.* voorstellen; voorleggen; aanbieden; *vi.* van plan zijn, zich voorstellen, zich voornemen.

proposition [propə'ziʃən] voorstel *o.*; (*wisk.*) stelling *v.*

proprietor [pro'praiətə] eigenaar *m.*; huisbaas *m.*; patenthouder *m.*

propriety [pro'praiəti] juistheid *v.*; gepastheid *v.*; behoorlijkheid, welvoeglijkheid *v.*, fatsoen *o.*

prorogue [pro'roug] verdagen, opschorten; uitstellen; (*v. parlement*) sluiten.

proscribe [pros'kraib] verbannen, in de ban doen; vogelvrij verklaren, buiten de wet stellen; te velde trekken tegen.

proscription [pros'kripʃən] verbanning *v.*; vogelvrijverklaring *v.*; veroordeling *v.*; verbod *o.*

prosecute ['prosikjût] *vt.* (*recht*) vervolgen; (*v. studie, enz.*) voortzetten; (*v. plan*) doorzetten; (*v. beroep*) uitoefenen; *vi.* een gerechtelijke vervolging instellen.

prosecution [prosi'kjûʃən] (gerechtelijke) vervolging *v.*; voortzetting *v.*; doorzetting *v.*; uitoefening *v.*

prosecutor ['prosikjûtə] (*recht*) aanklager, eiser *m.*; voortzetter *m.*

proselyte ['prosilait] proseliet, bekeerling *m.*

prospect ['prospekt] verschiet *o.*; uitzicht *o.*; vooruitzicht *o.*, verwachting *v.*

prospectus [prəs'pektəs] prospectus *o.*

prosper ['prospə] *vt.* begunstigen, bevorderen; *vi.* bloeien, gedijen; voorspoed hebben, geluk hebben.

prosperity [pros'periti] voorspoed *m.*, welvaart *v.*, bloei *m.*

prosperous (ly) ['prospərəs(li)] *adj.* (*adv.*) voorspoedig, welvarend, bloeiend; gelukkig; (*v. wind, enz.*) gunstig.

prostitution [prosti'tjûʃən] prostitutie, ontucht; veilheid *v.*

prostrate ['prostreit] *adj.* ter aarde geworpen, uitgestrekt; voorovergebogen; verootmoedigd; verslagen, gebroken; machteloos, uitgeput; [pros'treit] *vt.* neerwerpen, omverwerpen, ter aarde werpen; verootmoedigen, vernederen, in het stof doen buigen; uitputten; vernietigen; verslaan; *vr.* — *oneself,* een knieval doen, in het stof buigen.

protect [prə'tekt] beschermen, behoeden; beschutten; vrijwaren (**from,** voor); (*v. wissel*) dekken, honoreren.

protection [prə'tekʃən] bescherming; beschutting *v.*; (*v. wissel, enz.*) protectie *v.*; protectionisme *o.*; vrijgeleide *o.*; gunst *v.*

protective [prə'tektiv] beschermend.

protector [prə'tektə] beschermer, protector *m.*

protectorate [prə'tektərit] protectoraat *o.*

protest ['proutest] *sb.* protest, verzet *o.*; betuiging *v.*; [prə'test] *vt.* betuigen, openlijk verklaren; (*H.*) laten protesteren; *vi.* protesteren.

Protestant ['protistənt] protestant *m.*

protract [prə'trækt] rekken, verlengen; op schaal tekenen; uitstellen, op de lange baan schuiven.

protrude [pro'trûd] *vt.* vooruitduwen; (voor)uitsteken; *vi.* uitpuilen, uitsteken; (*fig.*) opdringen.

protuberance [pro'tjûbərəns] gezwel, uitwas *o.*, knobbel *m.*; uitpuiling, opzwelling *v.*

proud [praud] *adj.* trots, fier, hovaardig; (*v. rivier, enz.*) gezwollen; prachtig, indrukwekkend.

proud-hearted ['praud'hâtid] hooghartig, trots.

provable ['prûvəbl] bewijsbaar, te bewijzen.

prove [prûv] *vt.* bewijzen, aantonen; op de proef stellen; proberen; (*v. plaat*) een afdruk nemen van, een proef trekken van; *vi.* blijken (te zijn); *vz.* **you must — · ourself,** ge moet laten zien wat ge kunt.

proverb ['provəb] spreekwoord; spreekwoordelijk gezegde *o.*

proverbial [prə'və:biəl] *adj.* spreek-woordelijk.

provide [pro'vaid] *vt.* bezorgen, ver-schaffen; zorgen voor; voorzien (van); (*recht*) bepalen, voorschrijven; *vi.* — *for,* zorgen voor; verzorgen.

provided [pro'vaidid] — *school,* open-bare lagere school; — (*that*), mits, onder voorwaarde dat, onder voorbehoud dat.

providence ['prɔvidəns] vooruitziend-heid *v.*; voorzorg *v.*; zuinigheid *v.*

provider [pro'vaidə] verzorger *m.*; leverancier *m.*

province ['prɔvins] provincie *v.*; depar-tement, gebied *o.*; ambt: ;ebied *o.*; landschap, gewest; wingewest *o.*

provincial [prə'vinʃəl] provinciaal; ge-westelijk.

provision [prə'viʒən] *sb.* voorziening; voorzorg *v.*; voorzorgsmaatregel *m.*; voorraad *m.*, proviand *o.*; provisie *v.*; (*v. wissel*) dekking *v.*; *vt.* provianderen, van levensmiddelen (leeftocht) voor-zien.

provisional(ly) [prə'viʒənəl(i)] *adj.* (*adv.*) voorlopig, tijdelijk.

proviso [prə'vaizou] voorbehoud, be-ding *o.*; voorwaarde, bepaling *v.*

provocation [prɔvo'keiʃən] uitdaging, tarting, provocatie *v.*; terging *v.*; prikkel *m.*; aanleiding *v.*

provoke [prə'vouk] wekken, opwekken, gaande maken; veroorzaken; uitlokken; aansporen, aanzetten, aanhitsen; prik-kelen; tergen.

provost ['prɔvəst] (*v. universiteit*) rector *m.*; (*Sc.*) burgemeester *m.*; [prə'vou] (*mil.*) provoost *v.*

prow [prau] (*sch.*) voorsteven, boeg *m.*

prowl [praul] rondzwerven. rondsluipen.

proximity [prɔk'simiti] nabijheid *v.*

proxy ['prɔksi] volmacht *v.*; gevol-machtigde, procuratiehouder *m.*

prude [prûd] *adj.* preuts; *sb.* preuts meisje *o.*

prudence ['prûdəns] voorzichtigheid, omzichtigheid *v.*; beleid *o.*

prudent ['prûdənt] *adj.* voorzichtig, omzichtig; beleidvol; oordeelkundig; verstandig.

prudish(ly) ['prûdiʃ(li)] *adj.* (*adv.*) preuts.

prune [prûn] *sb.* pruimedant *v.*

prune [prûn] *vt.* snoeien; besnoeien.

pruner ['prûnə] snoeier *m.*; snoei-schaar *v.*

pruning-knife ['pruniŋnaif] snoei-mes *o.*

pry [prai] *vi.* gluren, loeren; turen; snuffelen; *sb.* blik *m.*, kijkje *o.*; loervo-gel, loerder *m.*

psalm [sâm] psalm *m.*

pseudonym ['sjûdənim] pseudoniem *m. & o.*

pub [pəb] (*fam.*) herberg, kroeg *v.*

public ['pəblik] *adj.* openbaar, publiek; algemeen; staats—, volks—; *sb.* pu-bliek *o.*; (*pop.*) herberg *v.*

publication [pəbli'keiʃən] afkondiging, openbaarmaking *v.*; publikatie *v.*; uit-gave *v.*. blad, nummer *o.*

public-house ['pəblikhaus] herberg *v.*

publicity [pə'blisiti] openbaarheid, (al-gemene) bekendheid, publiciteit *v.*; openbaarmaking; ruchtbaarheid *v.*

publish ['pəbliʃ] openbaar maken, be-kend maken; afkondigen; (*v. boek, enz.*) uitgeven, publiceren; (*v. vals bankpa-pier*) in omloop brengen.

publisher ['pəbliʃə] uitgever *m.*

puck [pək] kabouter *m.*, kabouter-mannetje *o.*; kwelduivel *m.*; rakker, snaak *m.*

pucker ['pəkə] *vi.* rimpelen, plooien, kreuken; zich fronsen; *vt.* kreuken, doen rimpelen; fronsen; *sb.* rimpel *m.*, plooi, kreuk *v.*; (*fam.*) zenuwachtigheid *v.*

puckish ['pəkiʃ] snaaks, ondeugend.

pudding ['pudiŋ] pudding *m.*; beu-ling *v.*

puddle ['pədl] *sb.* (modder)plas, mod-derpoel *m.*; vulklei *v.*; knoeiboel, war-boel *m.*; *vi.* plassen, ploeteren; knoeien.

puddly ['pədli] modderig.

pudgy ['pədʒi] dik, pafferig.

puerile ['pjûərail] kinderachtig.

puff [pəf] *sb.* windstoot, rukwind *m.*; (*aan pijp*) haal *m.*, trekje *o.*; reclame *v.*, bluf *m.*; *vi.* blazen, snuiven; (*v. trein*) puffen; (*aan pijp*) paffen; opzwellen; *vt.* opblazen; bol laten staan; in de hoogte steken; reclame maken voor; uitblazen.

puff-box ['pəfbɔks] poeierdoos *v.*

puff-cake ['pəfkeik] soes *v.*

puffy ['pəfi] *adj.* puffend; kortademig; winderig; opgeblazen; pafferig; bol; bombastisch, gezwollen.

pug-dog ['pəgdɔg] mopshond *m.*

pugnacity [pəg'næsiti] strijdlustigheid *v.*, vechtlust *m.*

pull [pul] *vt.* trekken, rukken; scheuren; plukken; (*v. proef, enz.*) trekken, af-drukken; (*v. spier*) verrekken; *vi.* trek-ken; roeien; — *down,* neerhalen; (*v. regering*) omverwerpen; (*v. prijzen*) om-laag brengen (*v. huis*) afbreken; (*fig.*) drukken; — *in,* intrekken; (zich) inhou-den; (*v. riemen*) innemen; (*v. trein*) bin-nenkomen; zich bekrimpen; (*sl.*) inre-kenen; — *out,* uittrekken; (*v. auto*) uithalen; (*v. trein*) vertrekken; weggaan; — *round,* er doorheen komen, er zich doorheen slaan; er weer bovenop ko-men; *sb.* (het) trekken *o.*; ruk *m.*; teug *m.*; (*aan pijp*) trek *m.*; aantrekkings-kracht *v.*

pull-bell ['pulbel] trekbel *v.*

pulley ['puli] *sb.* katrol *v.*, katrolblok *o.*; riemschijf *v.*; *vt.* ophijsen met een katrol.

pull-up ['pul'əp] (het) stilhouden *o.*; pleisterplaats *v.*

pulmonary ['pəlmənəri] *adj.* long—; longziek; *sb.* (*Pl.*) longkruid *o.*

pulp [pəlp] weke massa *v.*; merg *o.*;

vruchtvlees *o.*; moes *o.*, pulp *v.*; papierbrij *v.*

pulpit ['pulpit] kansel, preekstoel, katheder *m.*

pulpous ['pɒlpəs] zacht, vlezig, moesachtig, pappig.

pulpy ['pɒlpi] *zie* **pulpous**; (*fig.*) slap.

pulsation [pɒl'seiʃən] klopping *v.*, (het) slaan *o.*; trilling *v.*; (schroef)slag *m.*

pulse [pɒls] *sb.* pols; polsslag *m.*, klopping *v.*; trilling *v.*; peulvrucht(en) *v.* (*mv.*); *vi.* kloppen, slaan.

pulverize ['pɒlvəraiz] *vt.* fijnstampen, fijnwrijven; doen verstuiven; (*fig.*) vermorzelen; *vi.* tot poeder (stof) worden; in gruis vallen.

pumice ['pɒmis] *sb.* puimsteen *m.*; *vt.* puimen, ·afpuimen.

pump [pɒmp] *sb.* pomp *v.*; pompslag *m.*; gebons *o.*; balschoen *m.*; (het) uithoren *o.*; *vt.* uitpompen, leegpompen; uithoren; *vi.* pompen; (*v. hart*) bonzen.

pun [pɒn] *sb.* woordspeling *v.*; *vi.* woordspelingen maken; *vt.* (*v. aarde*) vaststampen.

punch [pɒnʃ] *sb.* (*tn.*) pons, doorslag, drevel *m.*; stoot, stomp, por, slag *m.*; (munt)stempel *m.*; kaartjesknipper *m.*; *adj.* kort en dik; *vt.* ponsen, doorslaan; (*v. kaartjes*) knippen; (*v. leder*) uitslaan; (*fam.*) stompen.

punctate ['pɒŋktit] gestippeld.

punctual ['pɒŋktjuəl] stipt, nauwgezet; precies (op tijd).

punctuality [pɒŋkju'æliti] stiptheid, nauwgezetheid *v.*

puncture ['pɒŋktʃə] *sb.* prik *m.*, gaatje *o.*; (*in fietsband*) lek *o.*; *vt.* prikken; (*v. bewijs*) ontzenuwen.

pungent(ly) [('pɒndʒənt(li)] *adj.* (*adv.*) scherp, bitter, vinnig.

punish ['pɒniʃ] straffen, kastijden; afstraffen; verbeteren; ranselen; (*v. bokser*) toetakelen.

punishable ['pɒniʃəbl] strafbaar.

punishment ['pɒniʃmənt] straf, kastijding; afstraffing *v.*

punitive ['pjùnitiv] *adj.* straffend, straf—.

punitively ['pjùnitivli] *adv.* voor straf, bij wijze van straf.

punting-pole ['pɒntiŋpoul] vaarboom *m.*

puny ['pjùni] klein, nietig, zwak.

pupa ['pjùpə] (*mv.* **pupae** [pjùpi] pop *r.* (van insekt).

pupil ['pjùpil] oogappel *m.*; leerling *m.*; (*H.*) volontair *m.*; (*recht*) pupil *m.*

pupil(l)age ['pjùpilidʒ] minderjarigheid, onmondigheid *v.*; leertijd *m.*

pupil-teacher ['pjùpiltitʃə] kwekeling *m.*

puppet ['pɒpit] marionet, pop *v.*; (*fig.*) speelpop *m.*

puppet-show ['pɒpitʃou] poppenspel *o.*, poppenkast *v.*

purblind ['pə:blaind] *adj.* bijziend, slecht van gezicht; (*fig.*) kortzichtig; *vt.* bijziend maken; benevelen.

purchasable ['pə:tʃəsəbl] te koop; omkoopbaar.

purchase ['pə:tʃəs] *sb.* koop *m.*; aankoop, inkoop *m.*; aanschaffing *v.*; (*recht*) verwerving *v.*; (*tn.*) hefkracht *v.*; *vt.* kopen, aankopen; (*recht*) verwerven; (*tn.*) opheffen, tillen; (*v. anker*) lichten.

purchase-money ['pə:tʃəsmɒni] koopsom *v.*, kooppenningen *m. mv.*; inkoopsprijs *m.*

purchaser ['pə:tʃəsə] koper; afnemer *m.*

purchasing-power ['pə:tʃəsiŋpauə] koopkracht *v.*

pure [pjùə] *adj.* zuiver, rein, kuis; onvermengd; puur.

pure-bred ['pjùəbred] rasecht.

purée ['pjùərei] puree *v.*

purgation [pə:'geiʃən] zuivering *v.*; purgatie *v.*

purgative ['pə:gətiv] *adj.* zuiverend; purgerend; *sb.* purgeermiddel *o.*

purgatory ['pə:gətəri] *sb.* vagevuur *o.*; *adj.* zuiverend, reinigend.

purge [pə:dʒ] *vt.* zuiveren, reinigen; laten purgeren, een purgatie toedienen; verwijderen, uitwissen; (*tn.*) spuien; *sb.* purgatie *v.*, purgeermiddel *o.*; zuivering, reiniging *r.*

purification [pjurifi'keiʃən] zuivering, reiniging *v.*

purify ['pjùərifai] *vt.* zuiveren, reinigen; louteren; klaren; afschuimen; *vi.* zuiver worden; helder worden.

purity ['pjueriti] zuiverheid, reinheid *v.*

purl [pə:l] *sb.* boordsel *o.*; gestikte rand *m.*; kabbeling *v.*; tuimeling *v.*; *vi.* averechts breien; kabbelen; tuimelen.

purple ['pə:pl] *adj.* purper, purperrood; purperen; *sb.* purper *o.*; *vt.* purperen, purperkleurig verven, purper (rood) maken.

purplish ['pə:pliʃ] purperachtig.

purport ['pə:pət] *sb.* inhoud *m.*; strekking, bedoeling *v.*; zin *m.*, betekenis *v.*; *vt.* beweren, voorgeven; (*soms:*) inhouden, behelzen; te kennen geven; van plan zijn.

purpose ['pə:pəs] *sb.* doel, doeleinde, oogmerk *o.*; bedoeling *v.*; strekking *v.*; *vt.* van plan zijn, voornemens zijn, zich voornemen· *ri.* plannen maken.

purposeful(ly) ['pə:pəsful(i)] *adj.* (*adv.*) doelbewust; opzettelijk; betekenisvol.

purposeless ['pə:pəslis] doelloos; nutteloos.

purr [pə:] (*v. kat*) snorren, spinnen; (*fig.*) gonzen, murmelen.

purse [pə:s] *sb.* beurs *v.*; portemonnaie *v.*; buidel *m.*; (*onder ogen*) wal *m.*; premie *v.*, geldprijs *m.*; *vt.* samentrekken; rimpelen, fronsen; (*soms:*) in de beurs steken. [ler *m.*

purse-cutter ['pə:skətə] zakkenrol-

purseless ['pə:slis] zonder beurs, arm.
purser ['pə:sə] (op schip) administrateur m.
purslane ['pə:slin] (Pl.) postelein v.
pursuance [pə'sjûəns] voortzetting v.; vervolging v.; uitvoering v.; (het) najagen, (het) nastreven o.
pursue [pə'sjû] vt. vervolgen, voortzetten; achtervolgen; (v. weg, enz.) volgen; nastreven, najagen; vi. doorgaan, verder gaan; — after, najagen.
pursuit [pə'sjût] vervolging v.; najaging v.; jacht v. (of, op); (het) streven o. (of, naar); beoefening v.; —s, bezigheden v. mv., werk o.
purulent ['pjûərulənt] etterend, etterig, etterachtig.
purveyance [pə:'veiəns] verschaffing, levering, voorziening v.; proviandering v.; voorraad m.
pus [pəs] etter m.
push [puʃ] vt. stoten, duwen; drijven, aandrijven, voortdrijven; schuiven; (v. paard) aanzetten; (v. bedrijf) uitbreiden; aanprijzen, aan de man brengen; (met kracht) doorzetten; aandringen op; vi. stoten, duwen; dringen; zich inspannen; — in, naar de kust varen; zich indringen; — off, afstoten; (v. trein) zich in beweging zetten; (v. goed) van de hand doen; (fig. & eig.) van wal steken; (fam.) heengaan, opstappen; — over, omverstoten; vr. — oneself forward, zich naar voren dringen; sb. stoot, duw m.; stuwkracht v.; drang, druk m.; (mil.) aanval, opmars m.; offensief o.; energie, fut v.; drukknop m.
pushing ['puʃiŋ] stotend; energiek, vooruitstrevend, ondernemend; voortvarend; eerzuchtig.
pusillanimous [pjusi'læniməs] kleinmoedig, blohartig, lafhartig.
puss [pus] poes, kat v.; haas m.
pussy-cat ['pusikæt] poesje o.
pustule ['pəstjûl] puistje, blaartje o.
put [put] vt. zetten, plaatsen, leggen, stellen; bergen; doen; steken; zeggen, uitdrukken; — away, wegleggen; (v. geld) op zij leggen; (v. gedachten) van zich afzetten; stallen; (sl.) van kant

maken; in de lommerd zetten; verklikken; — by, ter zijde leggen; (v. geld) overleggen, op zij leggen; van de hand wijzen; (v. persoon) afschepen; (v. slag) pareren; — forth, uitzenden; (v. boek) uitgeven; (v. hand) uitsteken; (v. theorie) verkondigen; (v. plant) uitlopen; (v. krachten) inspannen; ontplooien; uitvaardigen; (v. mening) opperen, te berde brengen; — forward, vooruitzetten; (v. mening) opperen; — in, invoegen; aanstellen; (v. document) overleggen; (v. vordering) indienen; (v. artikel) opnemen, plaatsen; (v. paarden) aanspannen, inspannen; (v. schip) binnenlopen; binnenloodsen; binnengaan; (bij verkoop) inzetten; (v. stukken) inzenden; (v. brief) posten; (v. licht, gas, enz.) aanleggen; — off, (v. kleren) uittrekken; afleggen; afzetten; (v. vals geld) in omloop brengen; (v. persoon, vergadering, enz.) afschrijven, afzeggen; afschepen; (bij operatie) wegmaken; afschrikken; een tegenzin doen krijgen in; — on, (v. kleren) aantrekken, aandoen; opzetten; (ton.) opvoeren, op de planken brengen; (v. persoon) aan het werk zetten; (v. schip) in de vaart brengen; (v. spoorwegwagen) aanhaken; (v. trein) inleggen; (v. klok) vóórzetten, vooruitzetten; — up, (v. paraplu, haar, enz.) opsteken; in zijn zak steken; opstellen; (v. versiering) aanbrengen; (v. huis, enz.) bouwen; optrekken; (v. prijs) verhogen, opslaan; (v. boter, enz.) inmaken; (v. auto) stallen; (v. wild) opjagen; (ton.) op de planken brengen; (v. bekendmaking) aanplakken; (v. gebed) opzenden; (v. prijs) uitloven; sb. (H.) baissepremie v.
put-up ['put'əp] geconserveerd; afgesproken.
puzzle ['pəzl] sb. moeilijkheid, niet op te lossen kwestie, lastige vraag v.; raadsel o.; verlegenheid v.; legkaart, puzzel v.; vt. in de war brengen, verbijsteren; verlegen maken; vi. piekeren, zich het hoofd breken; vr. — oneself with, zich het hoofd breken over.
pylon ['pailən] ingang m.; (v. draadloos station) mast m.

Q

quack [kwæk] sb. gekwaak o.; kwakzalver; marktschreeuwer m.; adj. kwakzalvers—; — doctor, kwakzalver; vi. kwaken; kwakzalveren; vt. met kwakzalversmiddelen behandelen; kwakzalverachtig ophemelen, aanprijzen.
quadrangle [kwɔ'dræŋgl] vierkant o., vierhoek m.; (v. school, paleis, enz.) binnenplaats v., binnenplein o.; vierkant huizenblok o.
quadrangular [kwɔ'dræŋgjulə] vierkant, vierhoekig.

quadrant ['kwɔdrənt] kwadrant o., hoekmeter, graadboog m.; kwartcirkel m.
quadrate ['kwɔdrit] adj. & sb. vierkant.
quadrille [k(w)ə'dril] (dans; kaartspel) quadrille v.
quadripartite [kwɔdri'pâtait] vierdelig.
quadruped ['kwɔdruped] adj. viervoetig; sb. viervoetig dier o.
quadruple ['kwɔdrupl] adj. viervoudig;

sb. viervoud, vierdubbele *o.*; *vt.* verviervoudigen; *vi.* zich verviervoudigen.

quaff [kwâf] *vt. & vi.* (met grote teugen) leegdrinken, zwelgen; *sb.* teug *m.*

quagmire ['kwægmaiǝ] moeras, drasland *o.*, modderpoel *m.*

quail [kweil] *sb.* (*Dk.*) kwartel *m.*; *vi.* de moed laten zinken, versagen, bang worden; zwichten, wijken (**to, before,** voor); *vt.* de moed benemen, vrees aanjagen.

quaint(ly) ['kweint(li)] *adj.* (*adv.*) vreemd, vreemdsoortig, eigenaardig, zonderling.

quake [kweik] *vi.* schudden, beven, trillen; *sb.* beving trilling *v.*; aardbeving *v.*

quaker ['kweikǝ] Kwaker *m.*

quaky ['kweiki] bevend; beverig.

qualified ['kwɔlifaid] beperkt, niet zonder voorbehoud; bevoegd, bekwaam, geschikt; gediplomeerd; niet onverdeeld gunstig.

qualify ['kwɔlifai] *vt.* kwalificeren, kenschetsen, aanduiden, betitelen; (*gram.*) (nader) bepalen; bevoegd (bekwaam, geschikt) maken; *vi.* zich bekwamen, de bevoegdheid verwerven voor; *vr.* —**oneself for,** zich bekwamen voor, de bevoegdheid verwerven voor.

quality ['kwɔliti] kwaliteit, hoedanigheid *v.*; (goede) eigenschap *v.*; karaktertrek *m.*; aanleg *m.*, bekwaamheid *v.*

qualmish(ly) ['kwâmiʃ(li)] *adj.* (*adv.*) misselijk, onbehaaglijk.

quantify ['kwɔntifai] de hoeveelheid bepalen van.

quantity ['kwɔntiti] kwantiteit, hoeveelheid *v.*; (*fam.*) een boel, heel wat.

quarantine ['kwɔrǝntîn] *sb.* quarantaine *v.*; quarantaineplaats *v.*; *vt.* in quarantaine plaatsen; onder quarantaine stellen.

quarrel ['kwɔrǝl] *sb.* twist *m.*, krakeel *o.*, ruzie *v.*; geschil *o.*, onenigheid *v.*; reden *v.* tot onenigheid (twist); *vi.* twisten, krakelen, ruzie maken; —**with,** ook: bezwaar hebben tegen, aanmerkingen maken op.

quarreller ['kwɔrǝlǝ] twister, twistzoeker *m.*

quarrelsome(ly) ['kwɔrǝlsǝm(li)] *adj.* (*adv.*) twistziek, ruzieachtig.

quarry ['kwɔri] *sb.* steengroeve *v.*; (*fig.*) mijn, bron *v.*; *vt.* uitgraven, opdelven; (*fig.*) opdelven; *vi.* graven, delven; (*fig.*) vorsen.

quarter ['kwo:tǝ] *sb.* vierde, vierdedeel, vierendeel, kwart *o.*; (*v. stad*) wijk, buurt *v.*; (*wap.*) kwartier *o.*; (*v. paard, enz.*) achterdeel *o.*; (*v. schoen*) hielstuk, achterstuk *o.*; kwartaal *o.*, kwartaalrekening *v.*; *vt.* in vieren delen; vierendelen; (*mil.*) inkwartieren; (*wap.*) kwartieren, vierendelen; *vi.* verblijf houden; (*sch.*) van de wind zeilen; (*v. hond, enz.*) heen en weer lopen.

quartering ['kwo:tǝriŋ] verdeling in

vieren *v.*; vierendeling *v.*; (*mil.*) inkwartiering *v.*

quarterly ['kwo:tǝli] *adj.* driemaandelijks; (*wap.*) gevierendeeld; *adv.* driemaandelijks; *sb.* driemaandelijks tijdschrift *o.*

quartermaster ['kwo:tǝmâstǝ] (*bij de marine*) kwartiermeester *m.*; (*mil.*) kwartiermeester, officier van administratie *m.*

quartet(te) [kwo:'tet] kwartet *o.*; viertal *o.*; vierregelig vers *o.*

quash ['kwɔʃ] (*v. plannen, enz.*) verijdelen; (*v. opstand*) dempen, onderdrukken; (*recht: v. vonnis*) vernietigen, casseren; verbrijzelen, verpletteren.

quaver ['kweivǝ] *sb.* (*muz.*) triller *m.*; achtste noot *v.*; trilling *v.*; *vi.* trillen, beven; (*muz.*) vibreren.

quay [ki] kaai, kade *v.*

queasy ['kwîzi] misselijk; kieskeurig; preuts.

queen [kwin] koningin *v.*; (*in kaartsp.*) vrouw *v.*

queen-bee ['kwinbî] bijenkoningin *v.*

queer [kwiǝ] *adj.* wonderlijk, vreemd, zonderling; raar, gek; verdacht; (*v. geld*) vals; onlekker, draaierig; (*sl.*) dronken; *vt.* (*sl.*) beetnemen, bedotten; bederven, in de war sturen; van streek brengen.

quell [kwel] (*dicht.*) (*v. opstand*) onderdrukken, dempen, bedwingen, de kop indrukken.

quench [kwenʃ] blussen, uitdoven; lessen; dempen; afkoelen, verkoelen; (*sl.*) de mond snoeren.

quenchless ['kwenʃlis] onblusbaar; onlesbaar, onverzadelijk.

query ['kwîǝri] *sb.* vraag *v.*; vraagteken *o.*; *vt.* ondervragen, vragen naar; een vraagteken zetten bij; (*fig.*) in twijfel trekken; *vi.* vragen.

question ['kwestʃǝn] *sb.* vraag *v.*; vraagstuk *o.*, kwestie *v.*; interpellatie *v.*; examenopgaaf *v.*; *vt.* vragen, ondervragen; interpelleren; betwijfelen, in twijfel trekken.

questionable ['kwestʃǝnǝbl] *adj.* twijfelachtig, onzeker; bedenkelijk; verdacht.

queue [kjû] vlecht *v.*, (haar)staart *m.*; file, queue *v.*

quibble ['kwibl] woordspeling *v.*; spitsvondigheid *v.*; voorwendsel *o.*

quick [kwik] *adj.* levend, levendig; vlug, snel, haastig; (*v. oog, oor*) scherp; (*v. gevoel, reuk*) fijn; (*v. begrip, bevatting*) vlug; *adv.* vlug, gauw, snel; *sb.* levend vlees *o.*; levende haag *v.*

quicken ['kwikn] *vt.* levend maken; verlevendigen; bezielen, aanvuren, aanmoedigen; verhaasten; *vi.* levend worden; opleven.

quick-firer ['kwikfaiǝrǝ] (*mil.*) snelvuurkanon *o.*

quicklime ['kwiklaim] ongebluste kalk *v.*

quicksand ['kwiksænd] drijfzand, loopzand *o*.

quicksilver ['kwiksilvə] kwikzilver *o*.

quick-tempered ['kwik'tempəd] opvliegend, oplopend, driftig.

quick-witted ['kwik'witid] vlug van begrip, gevat, scherpzinnig.

quid [kwid] *sb*. (*sl*.) pond (sterling) *o*.; tabakspruim *v*.; *vi*. pruimen.

quiet ['kwaiət] *adj*. rustig, kalm, stil; bedaard; (*v. kleding, enz*.) stemmig, niet opzichtig; *sb*. rust, stilte, kalmte *v*.; bedaardheid *v*.; *vt*. kalmeren, tot bedaren brengen, stillen, tot rust brengen.

quill [kwil] schacht *v*.; veren pen *v*.; tandestoker *m*.; (*voor garen, enz*.) spoel *v*.; (*muz*.) pijp *v*.; (*Dk*.: *v. stekelvarken*) stekel *m*.

quince [kwins] kwee(peer) *v*.

quinine [kwi'nîn, kwi'nain] kinine *v*.

quinquina [kin'kînə, kwiŋ'kwainə] kina *v*.

quintal ['kwintl] 100 pond; 100 kg., centenaar *m*.

quintessence [kwin'tesəns] kwintessens *v*.

quip [kwip] *sb*. schimpscheut, steek *m*.; geestigheid *v*.; kwinkslag *m*.; spitsvondigheid, chicane *v*.; gril *v*.; *vi*. schimpen.

quirk [kwə:k] spitsvondigheid *v*., uit-

vlucht *m*.; kwinkslag *m*.; grap, spotternij *v*.; (*v. letter*) krul *v*.

quit [kwit] *adj*. vrij; ontslagen (*of*, van); *vt*. verlaten; opgeven, laten varen; overlaten (*to*, aan); voldoen, kwijten; vereffenen; (*Am*.) ophouden (met).

quite [kwait] geheel, helemaal, heel, volkomen; bepaald.

quiver ['kwivə] *sb*. pijlkoker *m*.; trilling *v*.; *vi*. trillen; beven, sidderen.

quiz [kwiz] *sb*. vreemde snaak, rare snuiter *m*.; spotvogel, grappenmaker *m*.; spotternij *v*., bespotting *v*.; *vt*. voor de gek houden, de draak steken met; begluren.

quizzical ['kwizikl] spotziek; guitig, snaaks; grappig, mal.

quod [kwɔd] gevangenis, nor, doos *v*.

quoit [kɔit] werpring *m*.; (*gesch*.) werpschijf *v*.; —**s**, ringwerpen *o*.

quota ['kwoutə] evenredig deel, aandeel *o*.; kiesdeler *m*.

quotation [kwou'teiʃən] aanhaling *v*., citaat *o*.; (*H*.) prijsnotering *v*.

quote [kwout] *vt*. aanhalen, citeren; (*H*.: *v. prijzen*) noteren; *sb*. aanhaling *v*., citaat *o*.; —**s**, aanhalingstekens.

quotidian [kwou'tidiən] dagelijks; alledaags.

quotient ['kwouʃənt] quotiënt *o*., uitkomst (van deling) *v*.

R

rabbet ['ræbit] sponning, groeve *v*.

rabbin ['ræbin] rabbijn *m*.

rabbit ['ræbit] konijn *o*.; (*sp*.) onbetrouwbaar paard *o*.; (*sl*.) slecht speler, kruk, stumperd *m*.

rabid(**ly**) ['ræbid(li)] *adj*. (*adv*.) woedend, woest, razend; dol, krankzinnig.

rabies ['reibiiz] hondsdolheid; razernij *v*.

race [reis] *sb*. wedloop, wedren *m*.; loopbaan *v*.; levensloop *m*.; loop, stroom *m*.; ras, geslacht *o*., afkomst *v*.; *vi*. rennen.

race-course ['reisko:s] renbaan *v*.

race-ground ['reisgraund] renbaan *v*.

race-horse ['reisho:s] renpaard *o*., harddraver *m*.

raceme [rə'sîm] (*Pl*.) tros *m*.

racer ['reisə] renner; hardloper *m*.; renpaard *o*., harddraver *m*.; renwagen *m*.; race-fiets *v*.; race-auto *v*.

racial ['reiʃəl] rassen—, ras—.

rack [ræk] *sb*. pijnbank *v*.; rek *o*.; ruif *v*.; rooster *m*.; *vt*. op de pijnbank leggen; spannen; (*fig*.) folteren, kwellen, pijnigen; (*v. vloeistof*) klaren; *vi*. (*v. wolken*) jagen, drijven.

racket ['rækit] *sb*. raket *o*.; —**s**, raketspel *o*.; sneeuwschoen *m*.; leven *o*., drukte, herrie *v*., kabaal *o*.; *vi*. lawaai maken, herrie maken; er op los leven.

racy ['reisi] pittig, pikant, gekruid; sappig; (*v. wijn*) geurig; echt, rasecht.

radiate ['reidiit] *adj*. gestraald, stervormig; *sb*. straaldier *o*.; ['reidieit] *vt*. uitstralen; draadloos uitzenden.

radical ['rædikl] *adj*. radicaal, grondig, ingrijpend; wezenlijk, essentieel; ingeworteld; *sb*. (*gram*.) grondwoord *o*.; stamletter *v*.; (*rek*.) wortel *m*.; (*in politiek*) radicaal *m*.

radio ['reidiou] *sb*. radio *v*.; radiotelegrafie *v*.; radiotelefonie *v*.; radiotelegram *o*.; *vt*. & *vi*. draadloos telegraferen; radiotelegrafisch seinen (uitzenden); met radium behandelen.

radioscopy [reidi'ɔskəpi] X-stralenonderzoek *o*.

radiotelegram ['reidiou'teligræm] radiotelegram *o*.

radish ['rædiʃ] (*Pl*.) radijs *v*.

radius ['reidiəs] straal, radius *m*.; spaakbeen *o*.

raffle ['ræfl] *sb*. loterij, verloting *v*.; rommel *m*.; *vt*. verloten; *vi*. loten.

raft [râft] *sb*. vlot, houtvlot *o*.; *vt*. vlotten, op een vlot vervoeren.

rafter ['râftə] dakspar, spanrib *v*.

rag [ræg] lomp, vod *v*.; lapje *o*.; prul *v*.; zakdoek *m*.; (*sch*.) doek, zeil *o*.

ragamuffin ['rægəmɔfin] schobbejak, schooier, smeerlap *m*.; boefje *o*.

rag-dealer ['rægdilə] voddenkoopman *m.*

rage [reidʒ] *sb.* woede, razernij *v.*; manie *v.*; vuur *o.*, geestdrift *v.*; *vi.* woeden, razen (**at, against,** tegen).

rag-fair ['rægfêə] voddenmarkt *v.*

rag-gatherer ['ræggæθərə] voddenraper *m.*

ragged ['rægid] *adj.* voddig, gescheurd, in lompen; haveloos; ruw, ruig; ongelijk, knoestig; onregelmatig, slordig.

raging ['reidʒiŋ] woedend.

ragman ['rægmən] voddenraper, voddenman *m.*

rag-picker ['rægpikə] voddenraper *m.*

raid [reid] *sb.* (vijandelijke) inval *m.*; aanval *m.* (met vliegtuig); klopjacht *v.*; rooftocht, strooptocht *m.*; *vt.* een inval doen in; plunderen.

raider ['reidə] iemand die een inval doet; plunderaar; stroper *m.*; kaperschip *o.*

rail [reil] *sb.* leuning *v.*; hek *o.*, omheining *v.*, rasterwerk *o.*; slagboom *m.*; (*v. stoel*) sport *v.*; dwarsbalk *m.*, dwarshout *o.*; plank, lat *v.*; rail, spoorstaaf *v.*; *vt.* omrasteren; per spoor verzenden; — **off,** afrasteren; *vi.* sporen, met het spoor reizen; schelden, schimpen; uitvaren.

railing ['reiliŋ] leuning, reling *v.*; traliewerk, stakethel, hek *o.*, rastering *v.*; schimp, spot, hoon *m.*

raillery ['reiləri] boert, scherts, grap *v.*

railroad ['reilroud] spoorweg *m.*

railway ['reilwei] *sb.* spoorweg *m.*, spoorbaan *v.*; *vi.* sporen, per spoor reizen.

railway-bond ['reilweibɔnd] spoorwegobligatie *v.*

railway-porter ['reilweipo:tə] witkiel, kruier *m.*

railway-sleeper ['reilweislîpə] dwarsligger *m.*

railway-wag(g)on ['reilweiwægən] goederenwagen *m.*

rain [rein] *sb.* regen *m.*; *vi.* regenen; *vt.* doen regenen, doen neerkomen, doen neerdalen.

rain-bird ['reinbə:d] groene specht *m.*

rainbow ['reinbou] regenboog *m.*

rain-coat ['reinkout] regenjas *v.*

rain-glass ['reinglâs] weerglas *o.*, barometer *m.*

rain-proof ['reinprûf] regendicht, waterdicht.

rain-shower ['reinʃauə] regenbui *v.*

rainy ['reini] regenachtig, regen—.

raise [reiz] *vt.* oprichten, overeind zetten; ophalen; doen opstaan, wakker maken; (*v. ogen*) opslaan; (*v. stem*) verheffen; (*v. loon, enz.*) verhogen; *sb.* verhoging *v.*, opslag *m.*

raisin ['reizn] rozijn *v.*

rake [reik] *sb.* hark, rijf *v.*; krabber *m.*; (*v. schoorsteen, mast, enz.*) valling, helling *v.*; losbol, lichtmis *m.*; *vt.* harken; krabben; aanharken; schrapen,

bijeenschrapen; doorsnuffelen; — **out,** opscharrelen; — **up,** oprakelen.

rakish ['reikiʃ] losbandig, ongebonden, liederlijk; zwierig; (*v. schip*) slank gebouwd.

rally ['ræli] *vt.* verzamelen; weer verzamelen; verenigen; herenigen; weer doen opleven; *sb.* verzameling *v.*; hereniging *v.*; (*v. prijzen*) verbetering *v.*; beterschap *v.*, herstel *o.* (van krachten).

ram [ræm] *sb.* ram *m.*; (*mil.*) stormram *m.*; heiblok *o.*; straatstamper *m.*; *vt.* aanstampen, vaststampen; instampen; heien; (*gesch.*) rammeien.

ramble ['ræmbl] *vi.* zwerven, rondzwerven, (rond)dolen, dwalen; afdwalen; bazelen, ijlen; *sb.* zwerftocht *m.*; uitstapje *o.*; gebazel *o.*

ramification [ræmifi'keiʃən] vertakking *v.*

rammer ['ræmə] aanzetter *m.*; heiblok *o.*; straatstamper *m.*; laadstok *m.*

ramp [ræmp] glooiing, helling *v.*; oprit *m.*; bocht *v.*; sprong *m.*; (*sl.*) afzetterij *v.*; zwendel *m.*

rampageous [ræm'peidʒəs] dol, uitgelaten, luidruchtig.

rampart ['ræmpât, 'ræmpət] wal *m.*, bolwerk *o.*

ramshackle, ramshackly ['ræmʃækl(i)] bouwvallig, vervallen; waggelend, rammelend, wankel.

rancid ['rænsid] ranzig, garstig; (*v. boter*) sterk.

rancour ['ræŋkə] ingewortelde haat, wrok *m.*, rancune *v.*

random ['rændəm] *sb.* **at —,** op goed geluk af, in 't wilde weg; *adj.* op goed geluk; lukraak (in 't wilde) afgeschoten.

range [rein(d)ʒ] *vt.* rangschikken; scharen; zeilen langs, gaan langs; overzien; doorzwerven, aflopen; (*mil.*) bestrijken; inschieten; *vi.* zich uitstrekken; zich bewegen, lopen; zwerven; reiken; (*v. vuurwapen, enz.*) dragen; *vr.* — **oneself on the side of,** zich scharen aan de zijde van; *sb.* rij, reeks *v.*; aaneenschakeling *v.*; (*v. bergen*) keten *v.*; (*v. aardlagen*) ligging, richting *v.*; (*v. kanon*) draagwijdte *v.*; (*vl.*) actieradius *v.*

range-finder ['rein(d)ʒfaində] (*mil.*) afstandsmeter *m.*

ranger ['rein(d)ʒə] zwerver *m.*; speurhond *m.*; (*mil.*) jager *m.* te paard; houtvester *m.*

rank [ræŋk] *sb.* rij *v.*, gelid *o.*; rang, graad *m.*; stand *m.*; (*voor auto's, huurrijtuigen*) standplaats *v.*; *vt.* opstellen, ordenen, scharen; in 't gelid plaatsen; indelen; schatten.

rank [ræŋk] *adj.* (*v. groei, enz.*) (te) weelderig, (te) welig; (*v. grond*) te vet, geil; ranzig, sterk (riekend); vuil, gemeen.

ransack ['rænsæk] doorzoeken, doorsnuffelen; plunderen; beroven.

ransom ['rænsəm] *sb.* losgeld *o.*, losprijs *m.*; afkoopsom *v.*; verlossing; bevrijding *v.*; geldafpersing *v.*; *vt.* vrijkopen, loskopen; verlossen; vrijlaten tegen losgeld; geld afpersen.

rant [rænt] *vi.* uitvaren, bulderen, schetteren; oreren, declameren; hoogdravende taal voeren; *sb.* gebulder, geschetter *o.*; bombast *m.*

ranter ['ræntə] schreeuwer *m.*; volksredenaar *m.*

ranunculus [rə'nəŋkjuləs] ranonkel *v.*

rap [ræp] *sb.* tik *m.*; slag *m.*; knip *m.*; geklop *o.*; (*sl.*) stuiver, duit *m.*; *vt.* tikken (op); kloppen (op); slaan; (*Am.*) afkeuren.

rapacious(ly) [rə'peiʃəs(li)] *adj.* (*adv.*) hebzuchtig, roofgierig, roofzuchtig.

rapacity [rə'pæsiti] hebzucht, roofzucht, roofgierigheid *v.*

rape [reip] *vt.* verkrachten, onteren; (*dicht.*) ontvoeren, schaken; *sb.* verkrachting; ontering *v.*; (*dicht.*) ontvoering, schaking *v.*; koolzaad, raapzaad *o.*

rape-seed ['reipsid] raapzaad *o.*

rapid ['ræpid] *adj.* snel, vlug; steil; *sb.* stroomversnelling *v.*; (*mil.*, *fam.*) snelvuur *o.*

rapidity [rə'piditi] snelheid, vlugheid *v.*

rapprochement [ræ'prɔʃmɔ:ŋ] toenadering *v.*

rapture ['ræptʃə] opgetogenheid, vervoering, verrukking *v.*

rare [rêə] *adj.* zeldzaam, ongewoon; buitengewoon mooi; (*v. lucht*) dun, ijl; *adv.* (*pop.*) zeldzaam; bijzonder.

rarefy ['rêərifai] *vt.* verdunnen; verfijnen, zuiveren; *vi.* zich verdunnen, ijler worden.

rarely ['rêəli] *adj.* zeldzaam; bijzonder; *adv.* zelden; zeldzaam.

rascal ['râskəl] *sb.* schelm, schurk *m.*; *adj.* gemeen.

rash [ræʃ] *sb.* (huid)uitslag *m.*

rash [ræʃ] *adj.* overijld, overhaast; onbezonnen, onbedachtzaam; vermetel, roekeloos; lichtvaardig.

rasher ['ræʃə] sneetje *o.* spek of ham.

rashness ['ræʃnis] overijling, overhaasting *v.*; onbezonnenheid *v.*; roekeloosheid; lichtvaardigheid *v.*

rasp [râsp] *sb.* rasp *v.*; gerasp: gekras *o.*; framboos *v.*; *vt.* raspen; (af)schrappen; krassend schuren over; onaangenaam aandoen; *vi.* krassen.

raspberry ['râzb(ə)ri] framboos *v.*; (*sl.*) klets *v.*; uitbrander *m.*

rat [ræt] *sb.* rat *v.*; (*sl.*) overloper; onderkruiper, werkwillige *m.*; (*Am.*) kikspaan; gluiperd *m.*; *vi.* ratten vangen; overlopen; de onderkruiper spelen.

ratable ['reitəbl] schatbaar; belastbaar; belastingplichtig, cijnsplichtig.

ratch(et) ['rætʃ(it)] pal *m.*; palrad *o.*

rate [reit] *sb.* tarief *o.*; verhouding *v.*, maatstaf *m.*; prijs, koers *m.*; vaart, snelheid *v.*, spoed *m.*; (gemeente)belasting *v.*; *vt.* aanslaan; bepalen, schatten, taxeren; rekenen (*among*, onder); *vi.* gerekend worden; geschat worden; de

rang hebben van; *vr.* — *oneself with*, zich op één lijn stellen met.

rate-payer ['reitpeiə] belastingschuldige, belastingbetaler *m.*

rather ['râθə] eer(der), veeleer, liever; vrij, nogal, tamelijk; enigszins; heel wat.

ratify ['rætifai] bekrachtigen, goedkeuren.

ration ['ræʃən] *sb.* rantsoen *o.*, portie *v.*; *vt.* rantsoeneren, op rantsoen stellen.

rational ['ræʃənl] redelijk; rationeel; verstandig, met verstand begaafd; verstandelijk, op de rede gegrond.

ratsbane ['rætsbein] rattekruid *o.*

ratten ['rætn] saboteren, sabotage plegen; hinderlijk volgen.

rattle ['rætl] *vi.* rammelen; ratelen, klepperen, kletteren; reutelen, rochelen; *vt.* doen rammelen, doen ratelen; rammelen met; (*sl.*) zenuwachtig maken, in de war (van streek) maken, bang maken; *sb.* gerammel, geratel, geklepper *o.*; ratel, rammelaar *m.*; kletser *m.*, rammelkous *v.*; (het) reutelen *o.*; *the* —*s*, de kroep.

rattletrap ['rætltræp] rammelkast *v.*; —*s*, snuisterijen.

rat-trap ['rættræp] ratteval *v.*; getand fietspedaal *o.*

ravage ['rævidʒ] *vt.* verwoesten, plunderen; *sb.* verwoesting, plundering *v.*

rave [reiv] *vi.* ijlen, raaskallen; razen, tieren; — *about* (*of, over, upon*), dwepen met, dol zijn op, in verrukking zijn over; *vt.* uitkramen, uitslaan, — (*out*) *nonsense*, onzin uitkramen.

ravel ['rævl] *vt.* verwarren, in de war brengen; ontwarren, uitrafelen; — *out*, losrafelen, ontrafelen; *vi.* in de war raken; rafelen; *sb.* verwikkeling *v.*; ingewikkeldheid *v.*; wirwar *m.*; verwarde massa *v.*; rafel *v.*, rafeldraad *m.*

raven ['reivn] *sb.* raaf *v.*; *adj.* ravezwart.

raven ['rævn] *vt.* verslinden, opslokken; *vi.* (gulzig) schrokken; plunderen, roven.

ravenous(ly) ['rævinəs(li)] *adj.* (*adv.*) roofzuchtig, vraatzuchtig; verslindend; uitgehongerd.

ravine [rə'vin] ravijn *o.*, kloof *v.*; holle weg *m.*

raving ['reiviŋ] ijlend; razend, tierend; (*Am.*) buitengewoon.

ravish ['ræviʃ] ontroven; ontvoeren, wegvoeren; verrukken, in vervoering brengen; verkrachten.

ravishing(ly) ['ræviʃiŋ(li)] *adj.* (*adv.*) verrukkelijk.

ravishment ['ræviʃmənt] roof *m.*, ontvoering, wegvoering *v.*; verrukking *v.*; verkrachting *v.*

raw [ro:] rauw; ruw, onbewerkt; (*v. melk*) ongekookt; ongelooid; grof; (*v. dranken*) onvermengd, puur.

ray [rei] *sb.* straal *m.*; krans *m.* van samengestelde bloem; (*Dk.*) rog *m.*; *vi.* stralen schieten; straalsgewijs uitlopen; schitteren.

raze [reiz] doorhalen, uitkrabben; uitwissen; slechten; met de grond gelijk maken; (*v. huid*) schaven.

razor ['reizə] scheermes *o.*

razor-edge ['reizə'redʒ] scherp *o.* (*v. scheermes*); scherpe kant *m.*; bergrug *m.*

razor-strop ['reizəstrɔp] scheerriem, aanzetriem *m.*

razzle (-**dazzle**) ['ræzl('dæzl)] herrie, drukte *v.*; braspartij *v.*

reach [rîtʃ] *vt.* bereiken; aanreiken, overreiken, toereiken, overhandigen; uitsteken, toesteken; uitstrekken; nemen, pakken; *vi.* reiken; zich uitstrekken; (*sp.*) bij de wind zeilen; *sb.* bereik *o.*; omvang *m.*, uitgestrektheid *v.*; (*sp.: boksen*) armlengte *v.*, reikvermogen *o.*

reach-me-down [rîtʃmi'daun] *adj.* gemaakt, confectie—; tweedehands; (*fig.*) stereotiep; — **suit**, confectiepakje; *sb.* —**s**, gemaakte kleren *o. mv.*, confectiekleding *v.*; gedragen kleren, tweedehands kleren *o. mv.*

react [ri'ækt] *vi.* reageren, terugwerken; (*H.*) in reactie zijn.

reaction [ri'ækʃən] reactie, terugwerking *v.*; inwerking *v.*; (*radio*) terugkoppeling *v.*

read [rîd] *vt.* lezen; aflezen; oplezen; (*v. droom, enz.*) uitleggen; (*v. rol, muz.*) vertolken, interpreteren; *vi.* lezen; studeren; een lezing houden; (*v. telegram, enz.*) luiden; klinken; zich laten lezen; (*v. thermometer*) aanwijzen.

readable ['rîdəbl] *adj.* lezenswaardig; leesbaar.

reader ['rîdə] lezer *m.*, lezeres *v.*; voorlezer *m.*; lector *m.*; corrector *m.*; adviseur *m.* (van uitgever); (*v. gasmeter, enz.*) opnemer *m.*; leesboek *o.*

readily ['redili] *adv.* geredelijk; gaarne; gemakkelijk; dadelijk; vlug.

reading-book ['rîdiŋbuk] leesboek *o.*

ready ['redi] gereed, klaar; bereid; bereidvaardig, bereidwillig; vaardig, bij de hand; snel, vlug; gevat; (*v. tong*) glad.

ready-made ['redi'meid] *adj.* klaar (voor 't gebruik); (*v. kleren*) gemaakt, confectie—; *sb.* confectiepakje *o.*

ready-witted ['redi'witid] gevat.

real ['riəl] *adj.* wezenlijk, werkelijk; echt, onvervalst; waar; (*v. recht*) zakelijk; (*v. eigendom*) vast; *sb.* **the** —, de werkelijkheid; —**s**, werkelijke dingen, feiten.

realism ['riəlizm] realisme *o.*

realization [riəlai'zeiʃən] verwezenlijking *v.*; besef *o.*; (*H.*)realisatie, te-gelde-making *v.*

realize ['riəlaiz] *vt.* verwezenlijken, tot werkelijkheid maken; beseffen; zich voorstellen; realiseren, te gelde maken; (*v. winst*) maken; (*v. prijs*) opbrengen, halen; *vi.* realiseren; winst maken.

really ['riəli] *adv.* werkelijk, in werkelijkheid; waarlijk, wezenlijk; inderdaad.

ream [rîm] riem *m.* (papier).

reanimate [ri'ænimeit] weer bezielen, doen herleven, weer doen opleven.

reap [rîp] maaien, oogsten, inoogsten.

reaper ['rîpə] maaier, oogster *m.*

reaping-hook ['rîpiŋhuk] sikkel *v.*

rear [riə] *sb.* achterhoede *v.*; achterkant *m.*, achterste gedeelte *o.*; achtergrond *m.*; (*fam.*) privaat *o.*; *adj.* achterste, achter—; *vt.* oprichten; opsteken, opheffen, verheffen; kweken, grootbrengen; verbouwen; *vi.* steigeren; *vr.* — **oneself**, zich verheffen.

rear-admiral ['riə'rædmirəl] schout-bij-nacht *m.*

rear-guard ['riəgâd] (*mil.*) achterhoede *v.*

rearwards ['riəwədz] *adv.* achterwaarts, naar achteren.

reason ['rîzn] *sb.* rede *v.*; verstand *o.*; reden, oorzaak *v.*; grond *m.*; redelijkheid *v.*; recht *o.*, billijkheid *v.*; evenredigheid *v.*; *vt.* redeneren over, beredeneren; bespreken, bepraten; — **away**, wegredeneren; *vi.* redeneren, spreken over; — **from**, uitgaan van.

reasonable ['rîznəbl] *adj.* redelijk; voor redenering vatbaar; matig; behoorlijk; (*v. prijs*) billijk, matig.

reasonless ['rîznlis] redeloos; zinloos; onverstandig; onlogisch.

reassure [riə'ʃûə] opnieuw verzekeren; herverzekeren; geruststellen.

rebate [ri'beit] *sb.* vermindering *v.*; (*H.*) korting *v.*, rabat *o.*; *vt.* verminderen; verzwakken.

rebel ['rebl] *sb.* oproerling, opstandeling, oproermaker, rebel *m.*; muiter *m.*; *adj.* oproerig, opstandig; rebels, muitend; [ri'bel] *vi.* oproer maken, in opstand komen, muiten.

rebellion [ri'beljən] oproer *o.*, opstand *m.*

rebellious (**ly**) [ri'beljəs(li)] *adj.* (*adv.*) oproerig, opstandig; weerspannig; (*v. ziekte*) hardnekkig.

re-birth ['ri'bə:ð] wedergeboorte; herleving *v.*

rebound [ri'baund] terugstuiten, terugspringen; terugkaatsen; afstoten; (*fig.*) terugwerken; neerkomen (**upon**, op); weerklinken.

rebuff [ri'bʌf] *sb.* terugstoot *m.*; tegenslag *m.*; afwijzing, weigering *v.*; onheuse bejegening *v.*; *vt.* terugstoten; afwijzen, weigeren; afstoten; voor 't hoofd stoten.

rebuild [ri'bild] herbouwen, weer opbouwen; verbouwen.

rebuke [ri'bjûk] *vt.* berispen; (*Bijb.*) straffen; *sb.* berisping *v.*; standje *o.*; (*Bijb.*) tuchtiging *v.*

rebut [ri'bət] *vt.* terugslaan, terugstoten, afweren; weerleggen; *vi.* afstuiten; repliceren, van repliek dienen.

recalcitrant [ri'kælsitrənt] *adj.* weerspannig, tegenstrevend, tegenstribbelend, recalcitrant; *sb.* weerspannige *m.*

recalcitrate [ri'kælsitreit] weerspannig zijn, tegenstribbelen.

recall [ri'ko:l] *vt.* terugroepen; herroepen; terugnemen; weer in 't geheugen roepen; *sb.* terugroeping *v.*; herroeping *v.*; rappel *o.*; *(ton.)* bis *o.*

recapitulate [rĭkə'pĭtjuleit] *vt.* in 't kort herhalen, (kort) samenvatten; *vi.* recapituleren, resumeren.

recapture [rĭ'kæptʃə] hernemen; heroveren.

recede [ri'sĭd] teruggaan, terugwijken; achteruitgaan; *(v. prijzen enz.)* teruglopen; *(v. getij)* afgaan; *(van de kust, enz.)* zich verwijderen.

receipt [ri'sĭt] ontvangst *v.*; kwitantie *v.*; bewijs van ontvangst, reçu *o.*; voorschrift, recept *o.*

receipt-note [ri'sĭtnout] ontvangstbewijs *o.*

receipt-stamp [ri'sĭtstæmp] plakzegel *o.*

receive [ri'sĭv] *vt.* ontvangen; in ontvangst nemen, aannemen; krijgen, bekomen; *(in familiekring, enz.)* opnemen; *vi.* ontvangen, recipiëren; *(recht)* helen.

receiver [ri'sĭvə] ontvanger *m.*; *(bij faillissement)* curator, bewindvoerder *m.*; *(v. telefoon)* hoorn *m.*; *(tel., radio)* ontvangtoestel *o.*; heler *m.*

recent ['rĭsnt] *adj.* van de laatste tijd, recent, van recente datum; nieuw, vers, fris.

recently ['rĭsntli] *adv.* onlangs, kortgeleden; in de laatste tijd.

receptacle [ri'septəkl] vergaarbak *m.*; schuilplaats *v.*; *(Pl.)* vruchtbodem *m.*

reception [ri'sepʃən] ontvangst *v.*, onthaal *o.*; receptie *v.*; opneming; opname *v.*; heling *v.*

receptive [ri'septiv] ontvankelijk; vatbaar; (in zich) opnemend.

recess [ri'ses] *sb.* terugwijking, terugtrekking *v.*; *(v. gevel)* terugstand *m.*; inham *m.*; nis; alkoof *v.*; *vt.* doen terugwijken; achteruit plaatsen; *vi.* *(Am.)* op reces gaan; de zitting verdagen.

recessive [ri'sesiv] terugwijkend.

recidivism [ri'sidivizm] recidive *v.*

recipe ['resipi] recept *o.*

recipient [ri'sipiənt] *adj.* ontvangend, opnemend; ontvankelijk; *sb.* ontvanger, recipiënt *m.*

reciprocal [ri'siprəkl] wederzijds, wederkerig.

reciprocate [ri'siprəkeit] *vt.* vergelden; *(v. gevoelens, enz.)* beantwoorden; teruggeven; *(v. beleefdheden)* wisselen; *vi.* *(tn.)* heen en weer gaan; een wederdienst bewijzen; bewezen gunsten beantwoorden; verwisselbaar zijn.

reciprocity [resi'prɔsiti] wederkerigheid *v.*; wisselwerking *v.*

recital [ri'saitl] optelling, opsomming *v.*; verhaal *o.*, vertelling *v.*; voordracht *v.*; concert *o.*

recite [ri'sait] voordragen, opzeggen, reciteren; verhalen, vertellen; opsommen.

reckless ['reklis] *adj.* zorgeloos; onbesuisd, roekeloos, vermetel; *(v. motorrijder)* woest, niets ontziend.

recklessness ['reklisnis] zorgeloosheid *v.*; roekeloosheid, vermetelheid *v.*

reckon ['rekn] *vt.* tellen, rekenen; schatten; achten, houden voor, beschouwen (als); denken, geloven; veronderstellen; *(sch.)* gissen; *vi.* rekenen; — (*up*)*on,* rekenen op, vertrouwen op, staat maken op; — *with,* rekening houden met; afrekenen met.

reckoner ['reknə] rekenaar *m.*

reckoning ['reknɪŋ] rekening; afrekening *v.*; berekening *v.*; schatting *v.*; achting, waardering *v.*; tijdrekening *v.*; *(sch.)* gissing *v.*

reclaim [ri'kleim] *vt.* terugeisen; terugroepen; terugbrengen op het rechte pad; verbeteren; *vi.* protesteren, in verzet komen (*against,* tegen); *sb.* verbetering *v.*

reclamation [reklə'meiʃən] terugvordering *v.*; vordering *v.*, eis *m.*; terugroeping *v.*; reclame *v.*, protest *o.*

recluse [ri'klûs] *adj.* eenzaam, afgezonderd; *sb.* kluizenaar *m.*

recognizable ['rekəgnaizəbl] te herkennen, herkenbaar; kennelijk.

recognize ['rekəgnaiz] herkennen; erkennen; *(v. beginsel)* huldigen; *(prot.: als predikant)* bevestigen.

recoil [ri'kɔil] *vi.* terugdeinzen; terugspringen; *(v. geweer)* stoten, terugstoten; *(v. kanon)* teruglopen; *sb.* terugsprong *m.*; terugstoot *m.*; terugloop *m.*; terugslag *m.*; hevige weerzin *m.*

recommend [rekə'mend] aanbevelen, aanprijzen; aanraden, adviseren.

recommandable [rekə'mendəbl] aan te bevelen, aanbevelenswaardig.

recommendation [rekəmen'deiʃən] aanbeveling, aanwijzing *v.*; advies *o.*

recompense ['rekəmpens] *vt.* belonen; vergelden; schadeloosstellen, vergoeden; *sb.* beloning *v.*; vergelding; schadeloosstelling, vergoeding *v.*

reconciliable ['rekənsailəbl] verzoenbaar; verenigbaar, bestaanbaar.

reconcile ['rekənsail] *vt.* verzoenen (*to, with,* met); overeenbrengen, verenigen (*with,* met); *(v. geschil)* bijleggen, beslechten; *vr.* — *oneself to,* zich schikken in, berusten in, zich verzoenen met.

reconciliation [rekənsili'eiʃən] verzoening *v.*

reconnoitring-party [rekə'nɔitrɪŋpâti] verkenningsdetachement *o.*

reconquer [ri'kɔŋkə] heroveren, herwinnen, weer overwinnen.

reconsider [rĭkən'sidə] opnieuw overwegen (in overweging nemen).

reconstruct ['rĭkəns'trɔkt] opnieuw samenstellen; opnieuw bouwen, weer opbouwen; reconstrueren.

reconstruction ['rĭkəns'trɔkʃən] nieuwe samenstelling *v.*; wederopbouw *m.*; reconstructie *v.*

record [ri'ko:d] *vt.* aantekenen, optekenen; registreren; vermelden, boekstaven, te boek stellen; verhalen; (*op grammofoonplaat*) opnemen; (*v. stem*) uitbrengen; (*v. thermometer*) aanwijzen; ['reko:d] *sb.* aantekening, optekening *v.*; vermelding *v.*; verhaal *o.*; document *o.*; grammofoonplaat *v.*; (*sp.*) record *o.*; **—s**, archief; annalen; (*Am.*) notulen.

recorder [ri'ko:də] griffier *m.*; archivaris *m.*; (stedelijk) rechter *m.*; rapporteur *m.*; registreertoestel *o.*

recount [ri'kaunt] *vt.* verhalen; opsommen; ['ri'kaunt] *vt.* opnieuw rekenen; opnieuw tellen, overtellen.

recoup [ri'kûp] *vt.* schadeloosstellen; (*v. verlies*) vergoeden; (*v. geld*) inhouden; aftrekken; opbrengen; herkrijgen, weer goed maken; *vr.* **— oneself,** zich schadeloos stellen, zijn verlies goedmaken.

recourse [ri'ko:s] toevlucht *m.*; (*H.*) regres *o.*

recover [ri'kəvə] *vt.* terugkrijgen, herkrijgen, herwinnen; heroveren; (*v. fout*) goedmaken; (*v. wrak, enz.*) bergen; (*v. tijd*) weer inhalen; *vi.* zich herstellen; (*v. ziekte*) beter worden, herstellen; weer bijkomen; (*H.*) weer de hoogte ingaan; (*recht*) zijn eis toegewezen krijgen; *vr.* **— oneself,** zich herstellen; weer bijkomen, weer op zijn verhaal komen; zijn kalmte herkrijgen; *sb.* terugkeer *m.* tot de vroegere positie; (*v. wapen*) herstel *o.*

recovery [ri'kəvəri] (het) terugkrijgen, (het) herwinnen *o.*; wederverkrijging *v.*; verhaal *o.*; (*v. gezondheid*) herstel *o.*

recreate ['rekrieit] *vt.* verkwikken, vermaken, ontspannen; *vi.* zich vermaken.

recreate ['ri'kri'eit] *vt.* herscheppen.

recreation [rekri'eiʃən] ontspanning, uitspanning *v.*, vermaak *o.*; pauze *v.*, vrij kwartier *o.*, speeltijd *m.*

recruit [ri'krût] *sb.* rekruut *m.*; nieuweling *m.*; aanwinst *v.*; *vt.* (aan)werven, rekruteren; versterken, nieuwe kracht geven; aanvullen; *vi.* herstellen, weer op krachten komen, aansterken.

recruiting-office [ri'krûtiŋɔfis] werfbureau *o.*

recruitment [ri'krûtmənt] (aan)werving, rekrutering *v.*; versterking *v.*; herstel *o.* (van krachten).

rectangular (ly) [rek'tæŋgjulə(li)] *adj.* (*adv.*) rechthoekig.

rectifiable ['rektifaiəbl] te herstellen, te verbeteren; (*wisk.*) tot een rechte lijn te herleiden.

rectify ['rektifai] verbeteren, rectificeren; herstellen; (*bij distillatie*) opnieuw overhalen, zuiveren; (*wisk.*) tot een rechte lijn herleiden.

rectory ['rektəri] predikantsplaats *v.*; pastorie *v.*

recuperate [ri'kjûpəreit] *vi.* herstellen, opknappen; er weer bovenop komen; *vt.* — **one's health,** zijn gezondheid herkrijgen.

recur [ri'kə:] terugkeren, terugkomen;

(*wisk.*) repeteren; zijn toevlucht nemen (**to**, tot).

red [red] rood; (*fig.*) bloedig.

redact [ri'dækt] opstellen; bewerken.

redactor [ri'dæktə] opsteller; bewerker *m.*

redbreast ['redbrest] roodborstje *o.*

redden ['redn] *vt.* rood maken, rood kleuren; doen blozen; (*v. bokking*) roken; *vi.* rood worden; blozen.

reddish ['rediʃ] roodachtig, rossig.

reddition [re'diʃən] teruggave *v.*; uiteenzetting *v.*; uitlevering *v.*

redeem [ri'dîm] terugkopen; loskopen, vrijkopen; verlossen; redden, bevrijden; terugwinnen; (*v. hypotheek, enz.*) aflossen.

redeemable [ri'dîməbl] afkoopbaar; aflosbaar; uitlootbaar.

redeemer [ri'dîmə] bevrijder *m.*

redemand ['ridi'mând] *vt.* terugvorderen, terugeisen; *sb.* terugvordering *v.*

redemption [ri'dem(p)ʃən] terugkoop *m.*; loskoping *v.*; verlossing *v.*; aflossing *v.*

red-haired ['redhêəd] roodharig, rossig.

red-handed ['redhændid] **catch (take) —,** op heterdaad betrappen.

red-hot ['red'hɔt] roodgloeiend; gloeiend heet; (*fig.*) vurig, heftig; (*v. toorn, enz.*) gloeiend; kersvers.

redirect ['ridi'rekt] (*v. brieven*) opzenden; (*v. telegram*) naseinen.

red-lead ['redled] *sb.* menie *v.*; *vt.* meniën.

redolent ['redələnt] geurig, welriekend.

redouble [ri'dəbl] *vt.* verdubbelen; *vi.* zich verdubbelen, toenemen.

redoubt [ri'daut] *sb.* (*mil.*) redoute *v.*; *vt.* duchten.

redoubtable [ri'dautəbl] te duchten, geducht, gevreesd.

redress [ri'dres] *vt.* herstellen; vergoeden, goedmaken; verhelpen; weer in orde brengen; schadeloos stellen; *sb.* (*v. grieven, enz.*) herstel *o.*; verhaal *o.*, vergoeding *v.*

redskin ['redskin] roodhuid *m.*

reduce [ri'djûs] brengen; terugbrengen, herleiden, reduceren; (*v. been*) zetten; verminderen, verjagen.

reducible [ri'djûsibl] herleidbaar, enz.

reducing-diet [ri'djûsiŋdaiət] vermageringsdieet *o.*

reduction [ri'dəkʃən] terugbrenging *v.*; herleiding *v.*; verkleining *v.*; vermindering *v.*; verlaging *v.*

redundant (ly) [ri'dəndənt(li)] *adj.* (*adv.*) overtollig; overvloedig; weelderig.

re-echo [ri'ekou] *vt.* weerkaatsen; herhalen; *vi.* weergalmen, weerklinken.

reed [rîd] *sb.* (*Pl.*) riet *o.*; (*in klarinet, hobo, enz.*) rietje *o.*; *vt.* met riet dekken; (*muz.*) van een rietje (tongetje) voorzien.

reed-babbler ['rîdbæblə] rietzanger *m.*

reedy ['rîdi] volriet; rieten; riet—; (*v. stem*) schel, schraal, krassend.

reef [riff] klip *v.*; rif *o.*; ertsader *v.* van goudhoudend kwarts; (*sch.*) reef *o.*

re-elect ['rii'lekt] herkiezen.

re-enforce ['riin'fo:s] versterken.

re-engage ['riin'geidʒ] opnieuw dienst nemen; bijtekenen.

refashion ['ri'fæʃən] opnieuw vormen, vervormen, omwerken.

refection [ri'fekʃən] verkwikking, verversing *v.*

refectory [ri'fektəri] refter *m.*, eetzaal *v.*

refer [ri'fə:] *vt.* terugbrengen, terugvoeren (*to*, tot); onderwerpen (*to*, aan); toeschrijven (*to*, aan); verwijzen (*to*, naar); in handen stellen (*to*, van); doorzenden (*to*, naar); *vi.* — *to*, zich beroepen op; zich wenden tot; zinspelen op; betrekking hebben op; *vr.* — *oneself to*, zich beroepen op; zich toevertrouwen aan.

referee [refə'rí] *sb.* scheidsrechter, referent *m.*; *vi.* als scheidsrechter optreden.

reference ['refərəns] verwijzing *v.*; betrekking *v.*, verband *o.*; zinspeling, toespeling *v.*; referentie *v.*, getuige *m.* & *v.*; verwijzingsteken *o.*; (scheidsrechterlijke) beslissing *v.*; (*H.*) referte *v.*

referendary [refə'rendəri] referendaris; adviseur *m.*

refine [ri'fain] *vt.* raffineren, zuiveren, klaren, louteren; verbeteren; verfijnen; veredelen; beschaven; *vi.* zuiverder worden; beschaafder worden; spitsvondig redeneren (*upon*, over).

refinement [ri'fainmənt] zuivering, loutering *v.*; verfijning; veredeling *v.*; beschaving *v.*; geraffineerdheid *v.*

refit ['ri'fit] *vt.* weder aanpassen; herstellen, repareren; opnieuw uitrusten; *sb.* herstel *o.*, reparatie *v.*

reflect [ri'flekt] *vt.* terugkaatsen, terugwerpen; weerkaatsen, weerspiegelen; weergeven; bedenken; *vi.* zich weerspiegelen; nadenken; — (*up*)*on*, nadenken over; aanmerkingen maken op; zich ongunstig uitlaten over; een blaam werpen op.

reflection [ri'flekʃən] terugkaatsing *v.*; weerkaatsing, weerspiegeling *v.*; weerschijn *m.*; overdenking *v.*; aanmerking, blaam *v.*; hatelijkheid *v.*; verdachtmaking *v.*

reflex ['rifleks] weerkaatsing *v.*; weerkaatst beeld *o.*; spiegelbeeld *o.*; afspiegeling, afstraling *v.*; reflexbeweging *v.*

reflexible [ri'fleksibl] weerkaatsbaar.

reflexive [ri'fleksiv] (*gram.*) wederkerend; (*Pl.*) omgebogen.

reform [ri'fo:m] *vt.* hervormen; verbeteren; bekeren; (*v. misbruiken*) afschaffen, wegnemen; *vi.* zich bekeren, zijn leven beteren; *sb.* hervorming *v.*; verbetering *v.*; bekering *v.*; afschaffing *v.*

reformatory [ri'fo:mət(ə)ri] *adj.* hervormend; verbeterings—; *sb.* verbeteringsgesticht, opvoedingsgesticht *o.*, tuchtschool *v.*

refractable [ri'fræktəbl] breekbaar.

refraction [ri'frækʃən] straalbreking *v.*

refractory [ri'fræktəri] *adj.* weerspannig, weerbarstig; hardnekkig; moeilijk smeltbaar; vuurvast; — *to*, (*gen.*) ongevoelig voor; immuun tegen.

refrain [ri'frein] *sb.* refrein *o.*; *vt.* inhouden, in bedwang houden, in toom houden, beteugelen; *vi.* zich inhouden, zich bedwingen; zich onthouden (*from*, van).

refresh [ri'freʃ] *vt.* verversen, verfrissen; verkwikken; (*v. geheugen, enz.*) opfrissen; *vi.* zich verfrissen; nieuwe voorraad innemen.

refreshment [ri'freʃmənt] verversing, verfrissing; verkwikking *v.*

refrigerant [ri'fridʒərənt] verkoelend, afkoelend.

refrigerate [ri'fridʒəreit] koel maken, verkoelen, afkoelen.

refrigerator [ri'fridʒəreitə] koelapparaat *o.*; koelvat *o.*; koelkamer, vrieskamer *v.*; ijskast *v.*

refuge ['refjûdʒ] toevlucht *m.*, toevluchtsoord *o.*, wijkplaats, schuilplaats *v.*; uitvlucht *v.*; hulpmiddel, redmiddel *o.*; vluchtheuvel *m.*

refugee [refjû'dʒí] vluchteling, uitgewekene *m.*

refuge-shelter ['refjûdʒʃeltə] schuilkelder *m.*

refund [ri'fond] *vt.* teruggeven, terugbetalen; schadeloosstellen; *sb.* terugbetaling *v.*; schadeloosstelling *v.*

refusal [ri'fjûzəl] weigering *v.*

refuse ['refjûs] *sb.* afval *m.*, uitschot *o.*; vuil, vuilnis *o.*; *adj.* afgedankt, waardeloos.

refuse [ri'fjûz] *vt.* weigeren, afwijzen, van de hand wijzen; afslaan; afkeuren; *vi.* weigeren; *vr.* — *oneself*, belet geven.

refutable ['refjutəbl] weerlegbaar.

refute [ri'fjût] weerleggen.

regain [ri'gein] herwinnen, herkrijgen; weer bereiken.

regal ['rigəl] koninklijk, vorstelijk; konings—.

regale [ri'geil] *sb.* gastmaal, feestmaal *o.*; onthaal *o.*, traktatie *v.*; *vt.* vergasten, onthalen, trakteren; (*v. oor, enz.*) strelen; *vr.* — *oneself on*, zich te goed doen aan.

regard [ri'gâd] *vt.* aanzien, kijken naar; beschouwen; achten, hoogachten; houden voor; zich bekommeren om; acht geven op; aangaan, betreffen; *sb.* aanzien *o.*; blik *m.*; achting *v.*; aandacht, zorg *v.*; —*s*, groeten.

regarding [ri'gâdiŋ] betreffende, ten aanzien van, met betrekking tot.

regardless [ri'gâdlis] *adj.* onoplettend, onachtzaam, achteloos; verachtelijk; — *of*, onverschillig voor, zich niet bekommerend om.

regency ['ridʒənsi] regentschap *o.*

regenerate [ri'dʒenərit] *adj.* herboren, wedergeboren; [ri'dʒenəreit] *vt.* tot nieuw leven brengen, doen herleven;

herscheppen; *vi.* herboren worden; zich vernieuwen.

regeneration [ridʒenə'reiʃən] herleving, herschepping, vernieuwing, verjonging, wedergeboorte *v.*

regimen ['redʒimən] leefregel *m.*, dieet *o.*; stelsel *o.*; *(gram.)* regering *v.*

regiment ['redʒimənt] regiment *o.*

regimental [redʒi'mentəl] *adj.* regiments—; *sb.* —(**s**), (militair) uniform *o.*; *(sl.)* gevangeniskleren *o. mv.*

region ['ridʒən] gewest *o.*, streek, landstreek *v.*; *(fig.)* gebied *o.*, sfeer *v.*

register ['redʒistə] *sb.* register *o.*, lijst *v.*; kiezerslijst *v.*; *(muz.)* orgelregister; stemregister *o.*; *(v. kachelpijp)* sleutel *m.*; *vt.* inschrijven, registreren; *(v. thermometer)* aanwijzen; *(v. brief)* (laten) aantekenen; nota nemen van.

registration [redʒis'treiʃən] registratie *v.*; inschrijving *v.*; *(v. brief)* aantekening *v.*

regnal ['regnəl] regerings—.

regret [ri'gret] *vt.* betreuren, spijt hebben van, berouw hebben over; *sb.* spijt, leedwezen, berouw *o.*; verontschuldiging *v.*

regrettable [ri'gretəbl] *adj.* betreurenswaardig.

regular ['regjulə] regelmatig, geregeld; *(v. klant)* vast, trouw; behoorlijk, in orde; oppassend, ordelijk; behoorlijk opgeleid.

regulate ['regjuleit] regelen, schikken, ordenen; reglementeren; *(v. uurwerk)* reguleren.

regulation [regju'leiʃən] *sb.* regeling, schikking, ordening *v.*; voorschrift; reglement *o.*; the —**s**, het reglement; *adj.* voorgeschreven, reglementair; gewoon; vast; *(mil.)* model—.

regulator ['regjuleitə] regelaar *m.*; regulateur *m.*; *(v. uurwerk)* onrust *v.*, slinger *m.*

rehabilitation [ri(h)əbili'teiʃən] eerherstel *o.*, rehabilitatie *v.*

rehearsal [ri'hə:səl] herhaling *v.*; *(ton., enz.)* repetitie *v.*

rehearse [ri'hə:s] herhalen; opzeggen; verhalen; opsommen; *(ton.)* instuderen, repeteren.

reheat ['ri'hi:t] opnieuw verhitten; opwarmen.

reign [rein] *sb.* regering *v.*; bestuur, bewind *o.*; *vi.* regeren, heersen.

rein [rein] *sb.* teugel *m.*, leidsel *o.*; *vt.* intomen, breidelen, beteugelen.

reindeer ['reindiə] rendier(en) *o.* *(mv.).*

reinforce [riin'fo:s] *vt.* versterken; *sb.* versterking *v.*

reinforcement [riin'fo:smənt] versterking *v.*

reiterate [ri'itəreit] herhalen.

reject [ri'dʒekt] verwerpen; afkeuren; afwijzen, van de hand wijzen; ter zijde leggen; uitwerpen, uitbraken.

rejectable [ri'dʒektəbl] verwerpelijk.

rejection [ri'dʒekʃən] verwerping *v.*;

afkeuring *v.*; afwijzing *v.*; uitwerping *v.*

rejoice [ri'dʒɔis] *vt.* verheugen, verblijden; *vi.* zich verheugen, blij zijn.

rejoicing [ri'dʒɔisiŋ] vreugde *v.*, gejubel, gejuich *o.*; —**s**, feestelijkheden, vreugdebetoon.

rejoin [ri'dʒɔin] *vt.* beantwoorden; zich weer voegen bij; *vi.* antwoorden; *(recht)* dupliceren.

rejoin ['ri'dʒɔin] *vt.* opnieuw (weer) verenigen; *vi.* zich opnieuw verenigen.

rejuvenate [ri'dʒûvineit] verjongen.

relapse [ri'læps] *vi.* terugvallen, weer vervallen (**into,** in, tot); *(v. zieke)* weer instorten; *sb.* *(v. zieke)* instorting *v.*; *(tot kwaad, enz.)* terugval *m.*

relate [ri'leit] verhalen; in verband brengen met; toeschrijven aan.

related [ri'leitid] verwant (**to,** aan, met).

relation [ri'leiʃən] betrekking, relatie; verhouding *v.*; familiebetrekking, verwantschap *v.*; bloedverwant *m.*, familielid *o.*; verhaal *o.*

relationship [ri'leiʃənʃip] verwantschap *v.*; verhouding *v.*

relative ['relətiv] *adj.* betrekkelijk, relatief; — **to,** betrekking hebbend op; met betrekking tot; evenredig aan; *sb.* verwant, bloedverwant *m.*; betrekkelijk voornaamwoord *o.*; relatief begrip *o.*

relax [ri'læks] doen verslappen, verzachten; ontspannen; doen afnemen; matigen.

relaxation [rilæk'seiʃən] verslapping *v.*; ontspanning; uitspanning *v.*; *(v. wet)* verzachting *v.*; *(v. straf, enz.)* gedeeltelijke kwijtschelding *v.*

release [ri'lis] *sb.* ontslag *o.*; bevrijding, verlossing *v.*; ontheffing *v.*; *vt.* vrijlaten, loslaten, bevrijden; ontslaan; ontheffen; *(v. recht)* afstaan.

relentless (ly) [ri'lentlis(li)] *adj.* *(adv.)* onmeedogend, meedogenloos.

reliable [ri'laiəbl] *adj.* te vertrouwen; betrouwbaar.

relic ['relik] relikwie *v.*; overblijfsel *o.*; —**s**, ook: stoffelijk overschot.

relief [ri'lif] verlichting *v.*; leniging *v.*; ondersteuning *v.*; aflossing *v.*; *(v. stad)* ontzet *o.*; reliëf *o.*

relief-committee [ri'lifkə'miti] steuncomité *o.*

relieve [ri'liv] helpen, steunen; verlichten; opbeuren; *(mil.)* ontzetten; aflossen.

religion [ri'lidʒən] godsdienst *m.*; godsdienstplechtigheid *v.*; vroomheid, godsvrucht *v.*

religious [ri'lidʒəs] godsdienstig, godvruchtig, vroom.

relinquish [ri'liŋkwiʃ] verlaten; *(v. plan, enz.)* laten varen, opgeven; afstand doen van; loslaten; *(v. schuld)* kwijtschelden.

relish ['reliʃ] *vt.* smakelijk maken; kruiden; zich laten smaken; genieten van; *vi.* — **of,** smaken naar; — **well,**

goed smaken; *sb.* smaak *m.*; bijsmaakje *o.*: zweem *m.*; genot *o.*; bekoring *v.*

relishable ['relifəbl] smakelijk.

reluctance, reluctancy [ri'ləktəns(i)] weerzin, tegenzin *m.*; tegenkanting *v.*, verzet *o.*

reluctantly [ri'ləktəntli] *adv.* met tegenzin, node, ongaarne, schoorvoetend.

rely [ri'lai] — *upon,* vertrouwen op, zich verlaten op, steunen op.

remain [ri'mein] *vi.* blijven; overblijven, overschieten; *sb.* overblijfsel *o.*; ruïne *v.*; —*s,* ook: (stoffelijk) overschot; nagelaten werken.

remainder [ri'meində] overblijfsel, restant *o.*; (stoffelijk) overschot *o.*; (*v. aftrekking*) rest *v.*

remand [ri'mând] *vt.* terugzenden; terugroepen; (*v. beklaagde*) terugzenden in voorarrest; *sb.* terugzending *v.*; terugroeping *v.*; (verlengd) voorarrest *o.*

remanet ['remənet] restant *o.*; uitgestelde zaak *v.*; uitgesteld wetsontwerp *o.*

remark [ri'mâk] *vt.* bemerken, bespeuren: opmerken; aanmerken; *vi.* — *on,* opmerkingen maken over; *sb.* opmerking *v.*: aanmerking *v.*

remarkable [ri'mâkəbl] *adj.* opmerkelijk; opmerkenswaardig, merkwaardig.

remediable [ri'mïdiəbl] herstelbaar, te verhelpen.

remediless ['remidilis] (*dicht.*) onherstelbaar, ongeneeslijk.

remedy ['remidi] *sb.* middel, geneesmiddel *o.*, remedie *v.*; hulpmiddel *o.*; *vt.* genezen; verhelpen; voorzien in.

remember [ri'membə] zich herinneren; denken aan; onthouden, niet vergeten; gedenken.

remembrance [ri'membrəns] herinnering *v.*; aandenken *o.*, gedachtenis *v.*; geheugen *o.*; —*s,* groeten.

remind [ri'maind] herinneren, doen denken (*of,* aan).

reminder [ri'maində] herinnering *v.*; waarschuwing, aanschrijving *v.*

remiss [ri'mis] *adj.* nalatig, lui, traag; slap, zwak; onachtzaam.

remissible [ri'misibl] vergeeflijk; toegeeflijk.

remission [ri'mifən] verslapping, verzwakking *v.*; afneming, vermindering *v.*; kwijtschelding *v.*; vergeving, vergiffenis *v.*

remit [ri'mit] *vt.* verzachten, verminderen; doen afnemen; kwijtschelden; vergeven; (*v. beleg*) opheffen; (*H.*) overmaken, remitteren; *vi.* verflauwen, verslappen; verminderen; afnemen.

remittance [ri'mitəns] overmaking, remise, geldzending *v.*; overgemaakt bedrag *o.*

remnant ['remnənt] overblijfsel *o.*; overschot, restant *o.*; (*v. stof*) coupon *v.*; lap *m.*

remodel ['ri'mɔdl] vervormen, omwerken; opnieuw modelleren.

remonstrance [ri'mɔnstrəns] protest *o.*; remonstrantie *v.*, vertoog *o.*; vermaning, berisping; terechtwijzing *v.*

remonstrate [ri'monstreit] *vt.* betogen, aanvoeren, tegenwerpen; *vi.* protesteren; tegenwerpingen maken.

remorse [ri'mo:s] wroeging *v.*, berouw *o.*; medelijden *o.*

remorseful (ly) [ri'mo:sful(i)] *adj.* (*adv.*) berouwvol.

remorseless (ly) [ri'mo:slis(li)] *adj.* (*adv.*) meedogenloos, onbarmhartig.

remote [ri'mout] *adj.* afgelegen, ver, verwijderd; afgezonderd; dromerig; (*v. gelijkenis*) flauw, gering.

removable [ri'mûvəbl] verplaatsbaar; afneembaar; afzetbaar.

removal [ri'mûvəl] verplaatsing; verwijdering *v.*; verhuizing *v.*; afzetting *v.*

remove [ri'mûv] *vt.* verplaatsen, verzetten; verwijderen; ontslaan, afdanken; wegzenden; afzetten; *vi.* verhuizen; *sb.* (*op school*) bevordering *v.*; (*v. bloedverwantschap, enz.*) graad *m.*, trap *v.*; (*op spijskaart*) gerecht *o.*, gang *m.*; verwijdering *v.*; verhuizing *v.*

remover [ri'mûvə] — (*of furniture*), verhuizer *m.*

remunerate [ri'mjûnəreit] belonen, vergelden; vergoeden.

remuneration [rimjûnə'reifən] beloning, vergelding *v.*; vergoeding *v.*

remunerative [ri'mjûnərətiv] lonend, winstgevend.

renal ['rînəl] nier—; — *calculus,* niersteen.

rend [rend] scheuren; doorklieven; doen splijten.

render ['rendə] geven; overgeven; teruggeven; (*v. dienst*) bewijzen; (*v. dank*) betuigen; vertolken; (*v. reden*) opgeven; — *up,* overgeven; teruggeven; uitleveren.

rendezvous ['râㅇdivû] verzamelplaats, (plaats van) samenkomst *v.*

renegade ['renigeid] *sb.* renegaat, afvallige *m.*; overloper *m.*; *vi.* afvallig worden; overlopen.

renew [ri'njû] vernieuwen; verversen; hervatten, weer opvatten; verjongen; doen herleven; (*v. wissel*) prolongeren.

renewable [ri'njûəbl] vernieuwbaar.

renewal [ri'njûəl] vernieuwing *v.*

rennet ['renit] kaasstremsel *o.*; (*appel*) renet *v.*

renounce [ri'nauns] afstand doen van; afzien van; vaarwel zeggen, opgeven, laten varen; verwerpen; verloochenen.

renouncement [ri'naunsmənt] verloochening *v.*; verzaking *v.*; afstand *m.*

renovate ['renoveit] vernieuwen, herstellen, restaureren.

renovation [reno'veifən] vernieuwing, restauratie *v.*

renown [ri'naun] vermaardheid, befaamdheid *v.*; beroemdheid *v.*, roem *m.*

renowned [ri'naund] vermaard, befaamd, beroemd.

rent [rent] *sb.* scheur *v.*; scheuring *v.*
rent [rent] *sb.* huur, pacht *v.*; *vt.* huren, in huur hebben, pachten; verhuren; huur (pacht) laten betalen.
rent-day ['rentdei] betaaldag *m.* (*v. huur*).
renter ['rentə] *sb.* huurder, pachter *m.*
rent-free ['rentfri] vrijgesteld van huur, pachtvrij.
renunciation [rinənsi'eiʃən] verzaking *v.*; (akte *v.* van) afstand *m.*; verwerping *v.*; zelfverloochening *v.*
reorganization ['riɔ:gənai'zeiʃən] reorganisatie *v.*
reorganize ['ri'ɔ:gənaiz] reorganiseren.
repair [ri'pêə] *vt.* herstellen; vergoeden; verstellen, repareren; *vi.* — *to*, zich begeven naar; *sb.* herstel *o.*; herstelling, reparatie *v.*; onderhoud *o.*
reparation [repə'reiʃən] herstel *o.*; herstelling, reparatie *v.*; voldoening, genoegdoening *v.*; schadeloosstelling *v.*; —*s*, herstelbetalingen.
repartee [repâ'tî] gevat antwoord *o.*; gevatheid *v.*
repast [ri'pâst] maal *o.*; maaltijd *m.*
repayable [ri'peiəbl] terugbetaalbaar.
repayment [ri'peimənt] terugbetaling *v.*
repeal [ri'pîl] *vt.* intrekken, herroepen; afschaffen; *sb.* intrekking, herroeping, afschaffing *v.*
repeat [ri'pît] *vt.* herhalen; overdoen; nazeggen, nabouwen; navertellen; oververtellen, verder vertellen; (*op school*) (over)leren, repeteren; *vi.* repeteren; oprispen; *vr.* — *oneself*, in herhalingen vervallen; *sb.* herhaling *v.*; bis *o.*; (*muz., ton.*) reprise *v.*; (*muz.*) herhalingsteken *o.*; (*H.*) nabestelling *v.*
repeatedly [ri'pîtidli] *adv.* herhaaldelijk, bij herhaling.
repeat-order [ri'pîtɔ:də] (H.) nabestelling *v.*
repel [ri'pel] *vt.* terugdrijven; terugslaan, terugwerpen; weerstaan, afwenden; afweren; afstoten; *vi.* afstoten.
repent [ri'pent] berouw hebben over, spijt voelen over.
repentance [ri'pentəns] berouw *o.*
repentant [ri'pentənt] berouwvol; boetvaardig.
repertory ['repətəri] repertoire *o.*
repetition [repi'tiʃən] herhaling, repetitie *v.*; (het) opzeggen *o.*; voordracht *v.*: (*op school*) les *v.*
repine [ri'pain] morren, klagen (*at, against*, over).
replace [ri'pleis] terugplaatsen; terugleggen, terugzetten; de plaats innemen van.
replenish [ri'pleniʃ] weer vullen; bijvullen; aanvullen (v. voorraad).
replete [ri'plît] *adj.* vol; overladen (*with*, met); verzadigd (*with*, van); *vt.* vullen, aanvullen.
reply [ri'plai] *vi.* repliceren; antwoorden, hernemen; — *to*, antwoorden op,

beantwoorden; *sb.* antwoord; wederantwoord *o.*; (*Sc.*) repliek *v.*; *in* — *to*, in antwoord op.
reply-paid ['ri'plaipeid] met betaald antwoord.
report [ri'pɔ:t] *vt.* melden, rapporteren, berichten, overbrengen; verslag geven van, rapport maken van; *vi.* verslag geven, rapport uitbrengen; zich melden (*to*, bij); reporterswerk doen, verslaggever zijn; *vr.* — *oneself*, zich melden (*to*, bij); *sb.* rapport, verslag *o.*; bericht *o.*; gerucht *o.*; faam, reputatie *v.*; slag; knal *m.*, schot *o.*
reporter [ri'pɔ:tə] verslaggever, berichtgever *m.*
repose [ri'pouz] *vi.* rusten; uitrusten; be-usten (*on*, op); *vr.* — *oneself*, uitrusten; *sb.* rust; kalmte *v.*
reposer [ri'pouzə] (*fam.*) afzakkertje *o.*
repository [ri'pɔzitəri] bewaarplaats, opslagplaats *v.*; magazijn *o.*; begraafplaats *v.*; graf *o.*
reprehend [repri'hend] berispen.
reprehensible [repri'hensibl] *adj.* berispelijk, laakbaar.
represent [repri'zent] voorstellen, afbeelden: vertegenwoordigen.
representation [reprizen'teiʃən] voorstelling, afbeelding *v.*; vertegenwoordiging *v.*; (*ton.*) opvoering, voorstelling *v.*; vertoog; protest *o.*
representative [repri'zentətiv] *adj.* voorstellend; vertegenwoordigend, representatief; typisch: *sb.* vertegenwoordiger; plaatsvervanger *m.*
reprieve [ri'prîv] *vt.* uitstellen, uitstel verlenen; gratie verlenen; *sb.* uitstel *o.*, opschorting *v.*; (*recht*) gratie *v.*
reprimand ['reprimând] *sb.* (officiële) berisping, reprimande *v.*; *vt.* berispen, een berisping geven.
reprint ['ri'print] *sb.* herdruk *m.*; [ri'print] *vt.* herdrukken.
reprisal [ri'praiz(ə)l] weerwraak, vergelding *v.*
reproach [ri'proutʃ] *vt.* verwijten; berispen; *sb.* verwijt *o.*; schande *v.*; blaam *v.*
reproachable [ri'proutʃəbl] berispelijk, laakbaar.
reprobate ['reprəbit] *adj.* verworpen, verdoemd; goddeloos; snood; gewetenloos; *sb.* verworpeling, verdoemeling *m.*; snoodaard, onverlaat *m.*; ['reprəbeit] *vt.* verwerpen, verdoemen; afkeuren.
reproduce [riprə'djûs] weer voortbrengen; weergeven; reproduceren; (zich) voortplanten, vermenigvuldigen.
reproof [ri'prûf] terechtwijzing, berisping *v.*, verwijt *o.*
reptile ['reptail] *sb.* kruipend dier, reptiel *o.*; (*fig.*) lage kruiper *m.*; *adj.* kruipend: kruiperig.
repudiate [ri'pjûdieit] verwerpen, verstoten; (*v. verantwoordelijkheid, enz.*) afwijzen; loochenen; verloochenen; (*v. schuld*) niet erkennen.

repugnance [ri'pagnəns] afkeer *m.*, afkerigheid *v.*; weerzin *m.*; tegenstrijdigheid *v.*

repulse [ri'pəls] terugstoten, terugslaan; terugdrijven; afslaan; afwijzen.

repulsion [ri'pəlʃən] (het) terugstoten *o.*, (het) terugslaan *o.*; afstoting *v.*; afkeer, tegenzin, weerzin *m.*

repulsive(ly) [ri'pəlsiv(li)] *adj. (adv.)* afstotend, terugstotend; walglijk, weerzinwekkend; *(dicht.)* weerstrevend.

reputable ['repjutəbl] *adj.* achtenswaardig, fatsoenlijk, eervol.

reputation [repju'teiʃən] reputatie *v.*, (goede) naam *m.*, faam *v.*

repute [ri'pjût] *sb.* reputatie *v.*, (goede) naam *m.*; *vt.* houden voor, beschouwen als.

request [ri'kwest] *sb.* verzoek *o.*; aanvraag *v.*; navraag *v.*; *vt.* verzoeken, vragen (om).

requirable [ri'kwaiərəbl] vereist.

require [ri'kwaiə] eisen, vorderen, verlangen; vereisen; nodig hebben; behoeven.

requirement [ri'kwaiəmənt] eis *m.*; vereiste, behoefte *v.*

requisite ['rekwizit] *adj.* vereist, nodig; *sb.* vereiste *v.*

requital [ri'kwaitəl] beloning, vergelding *v.*; wraak, weerwraak *v.*

rescue ['reskjû] *vt.* redden, verlossen, bevrijden; (met geweld) terugnemen; *sb.* redding, verlossing, bevrijding *v.*; terugneming *v.*

research [ri'sə:tʃ] *sb.* (nauwkeurig, wetenschappelijk) onderzoek *o.*; nasporing, navorsing *v.*; onderzoekingswerk *o.*; *vt.* (nauwkeurig) onderzoeken.

resemblance [ri'zembləns] gelijkenis, overeenkomst *v.* (**to**, met).

resemble [ri'zembl] gelijken (op).

resent [ri'zent] kwalijk nemen; zich beledigd voelen door; wrok koesteren over; wraak nemen over.

resentful [ri'zentful] *adj.* lichtgeraakt; gebelgd; wrokkend, haatdragend.

resentment [ri'zentmənt] boosheid, verbolgenheid *v.*; wrevel, wrok; haat *m.*

reservation [rezə'veiʃən] voorbehoud *o.*; terughouding *v.*

reserve [ri'zə:v] *vt.* bewaren; reserveren, in reserve houden; inhouden, achterhouden; *(v. plaats)* bespreken; *(v. oordeel)* opschorten; openhouden; zich voorbehouden; *sb.* reserve *v.*; terughouding *v.*; voorbehoud *o.*; invaller, reservespeler *m.*

reserved [ri'zə:vd] *adj.* gereserveerd; terughoudend.

reserve-price [ri'zə:vprais] *(bij verkoop)* limiet *v.*

reside [ri'zaid] wonen, verblijven, verblijf houden; zetelen; berusten (**in**, bij).

residence ['rezidəns] verblijf *o.*, verblijfplaats, woonplaats *v.*; residentie *v.*

resident ['rezidənt] *adj.* woonachtig;

inwonend, intern; *(v. bevolking)* vast; *sb.* inwoner *m.*

resign [ri'zain] *vt.* afstaan; overgeven, overlaten; opgeven, afstand doen van; *(v. ambt)* neerleggen; *vi.* aftreden, zijn ontslag nemen; *(voor betrekking)* bedanken; *(kaartsp.)* passen; *vr.* — **one-self**, berusten.

resignation [rezig'neiʃən] afstand *m.*; ontslag *o.*; berusting, gelatenheid; overgave *v.*

resigned [ri'zaind] *adj.* gelaten.

resin ['rezin] hars *o.* & *v.*

resinous ['rezinəs] harsachtig.

resist [ri'zist] weerstaan, weerstand bieden aan; zich verzetten tegen; bestand zijn tegen.

resistance [ri'zistəns] weerstand, tegenstand *m.*, verzet *o.*; weerstandsvermogen *o.*

resistible [ri'zistibl] weerstaanbaar.

resistless [ri'zistlis] geen weerstand biedend; onweerstaanbaar.

resoluble ['rezəljubl] oplosbaar, smeltbaar; ontleedbaar.

resolute ['rezəl(j)ût] beslist, vastberaden, vastbesloten, resoluut; onversaagd, doortastend.

resolution [rezəl'(j)ûʃən] oplossing, ontbinding *v.*; *(v. gezwel, enz.)* verdwijning *v.*; besluit *o.*, beslissing *v.*; resolutie *v.*; beslistheid *v.*; doortastendheid *v.*

resolve [ri'zɔlv] oplossen, ontbinden; besluiten; doen besluiten, een besluit doen nemen; *(v. twijfel)* wegnemen.

resonance ['rezənəns] weerklank *m.*, resonantie *v.*

resort [ri'zo:t] *vi.* — **to,** zijn toevlucht nemen tot; zich begeven naar; *sb.* toevlucht *m.*; hulpmiddel, redmiddel *o.*; toevloed, samenloop *m.*; druk bezochte plaats *v.*

resound [ri'zaund] *vi. (vt.)* (doen) weerklinken, weergalmen; weerkaatsen.

resource [ri'so:s] hulpbron *v.*, hulpmiddel *o.*; toevlucht *v.*; uitkomst *v.*, redmiddel *o.*; vindingrijkheid *v.*; —**s,** geldmiddelen; middelen van bestaan.

respect [ris'pekt] *sb.* achting *v.*, aanzien *o.*, eerbied *m.*; opzicht *o.*; *vt.* eerbiedigen, respecteren; achten, hoogachten; ontzien; betrekking hebben op, aangaan, betreffen.

respectable [ris'pektəbl] achtenswaardig, achtbaar; fatsoenlijk, eerzaam.

respectful [ris'pektful] *adj.* eerbiedig.

respectfully [ris'pektfəli] *adv.* eerbiedig; **yours** —, hoogachtend, Uw dw.

respective [ris'pektiv] *adj.* respectief.

respirable [ris'paiərəbl] inadembaar.

respiration [respi'reiʃən] ademhaling *v.*

respire [ris'paiə] ademen, ademhalen; weer op adem komen.

respite ['respit] *sb.* uitstel, respijt *o.*; schorsing *v.*; verademing; verpozing *v.*; *vt.* uitstellen, opschorten; uitstel verlenen aan; *(mil.: v. soldij)* inhouden.

respond [ris'pɔnd] antwoorden (*to,* op); gehoor geven (*to,* aan); reageren (*to,* op).

response   [ris'pɔns]   antwoord   *o.*; responsorium *o.,* tegenzang *m.*; (*fig.*) weerklank *m.*

responsibility [rispɔnsi'biliti] verantwoordelijkheid; aansprakelijkheid *v.*

responsible [ris'pɔnsibl] verantwoordelijk, aansprakelijk; (*H.*) solied.

rest [rest] *vi.* rusten, uitrusten; rust hebben; berusten (*on, upon,* op); zich verlaten (*on, upon,* op); vertrouwen stellen (*in,* in); *vt.* laten rusten; rust geven; gronden, baseren (*on, upon,* op); *vr.* **— oneself,** uitrusten; rust nemen; *sb.* rust *v.*; pauze *v.*; (*muz.*) rustteken *o.*; rustpunt *o.,* steun *m.*

rest [rest] *vi.* blijven; overblijven, overschieten; *sb.* rest *v.,* overschot *o.*; (het) overige *o.,* de overigen *mv.*; saldo *o.*; (*v. bank*) reservefonds *o.*; inventarisatie *v.*

rest-cure ['restkjûə] rustkuur *v.*

restful(**ly**) ['restful(i)] *adj.* (*adv.*) rustig, stil, kalm; gerust; rustgevend, rustig stemmend, kalmerend.

restitution [resti'tjûəʃn] vergoeding, schadeloosstelling; teruggave *v.,* herstel *o.*

restive ['restiv] *adj.* weerspannig, koppig; onwillig, onhandelbaar; prikkelbaar, kriebelig, ongeduldig.

restless(**ly**) ['restlis(li)] *adj.* (*adv.*) rusteloos, onrustig; woelig.

restlessness ['restlisnis] rusteloosheid, onrustigheid; woeligheid *v.*

restoration [restə'reiʃən] herstel *o.,* herstelling, restauratie *v.*; teruggave *v.*

restore [ris'to:] *vt.* herstellen, restaureren; teruggeven, terugbrengen; terugplaatsen.

restrain [ris'trein] in bedwang houden, in toom houden, bedwingen, beteugelen; beperken; opsluiten.

restrict [ris'trikt] beperken, begrenzen.

result [ri'zəlt] *vi.* voortkomen, voortvloeien (*from,* uit); volgen (*from,* uit); uitlopen (*in,* op); *sb.* uitslag *m.,* uitkomst *v.*; resultaat *o.*; gevolg *o.*; besluit *o.,* slotsom *v.*

resume [ri'zjûm] hernemen, hervatten; herkrijgen; weer opvatten; weer beginnen; samenvatten, resumeren; (*v. vriendschap*) weer aanknopen.

resurrection [rezə'rekʃən] opstanding, verrijzenis *v.*; herleving *v.*

resuscitate [ri'səsiteit] weer opwekken; doen herleven; vernieuwen; weer bijbrengen.

ret [ret] (*v. vlas*) roten, weken; (*v. hooi*) (doen) rotten.

retail ['riteil] *sb.* kleinhandel *m.*; [ri'teil] *vt.* in 't klein verkopen; omstandig verhalen, rondvertellen.

retail-trade ['riteiltreid] kleinhandel *m.*

retain [ri'tein] houden, behouden; onthouden; tegenhouden; vasthouden.

retaining-wall [ri'teiniŋwo:l] steunmuur; kademuur *m.*

retake ['ri'teik] *vt.* hernemen, terugnemen; heroveren; *sb.* (*v. film*) herhaalde opname *v.*

retaliation [ritæli'eiʃən] wedervergelding *v.*; wraak, weerwraak *v.*

retaliatory [ri'tælieitəri] vergeldings—; wraakzuchtig.

retard [ri'tâd] *vt.* vertragen, uitstellen; tegenhouden; *sb.* vertraging *v.*

retardation [ritâ'deiʃən] vertraging *v.*; uitstel *o.*

retardment [ri'tâdmənt] *zie* **retardation.**

reticent(**ly**) ['retisənt(li)] *adj.* (*adv.*) zwijgzaam, gesloten, niet erg spraakzaam; achterhoudend.

retina ['retinə] netvlies *o.*

retinue ['retinjû] gevolg *o.,* stoet *m.*; aanhang *m.*

retire [ri'taiə] *vt.* terugnemen, terugtrekken; intrekken; ontslaan; (*v. wissel*) aan de circulatie onttrekken; *vi.* zich terugtrekken; terugwijken; zich verwijderen, heengaan; uittreden, aftreden, zijn ontslag nemen; stil gaan leven.

retired [ri'taiəd] *adj.* teruggetrokken; afgezonderd; eenzaam; afgelegen; gepensioneerd; rentenierend.

retirement [ri'taiəmənt] terugtrekking *v.*; teruggetrokkenheid *v.*; afzondering *v.*; ontslag *o.,* ontslagneming *v.*; aftreden *o.*

retiring [ri'taiəriŋ] terugtrekkend; aftredend; teruggetrokken; ingetogen.

retouch ['ri'tətʃ] *vt.* weer aanraken; opwerken, retoucheren; *sb.* bijwerking, opwerking, retouche *v.*

retract [ri'trækt] intrekken, herroepen; terugtrekken.

retreat [ri'trit] *vt.* (*bij schaakspel*) terugzetten; *vi.* (zich) terugtrekken, terugwijken; *sb.* aftocht, terugtocht *m.*; sein *o.* tot de aftocht; afzondering *v.*; retraite *v.*; rustoord *o.*

retrench [ri'trenʃ] *vt.* afsnijden, wegsnijden; beperken; verkorten; (*v. uitgaven*) besnoeien; *vi.* bezuinigen, zich bekrimpen, zich beperken.

retribution [retri'bjûʃən] vergelding, vergoeding, beloning *v.*

retrievable [ri'trivəbl] terug te vinden; te redden; herstelbaar.

retrieve [ri'triv] *vt.* terugvinden; terugkrijgen, herkrijgen; (*v. eer, enz.*) redden; herstellen, weer goedmaken; *sb.* herstel *o.*

retroaction [ritrou'ækʃən] terugwerking *v.*; terugwerkende kracht *v.*

retroactive [ritrou'æktiv] terugwerkend.

retrocession [ritrou'seʃən] teruggang *m.,* terugwijking *v.*; wederafstand *m.,* teruggave *v.*

retrograde ['retrougreid] *adj.* achterwaarts; achteruitgaand, teruggaand; reactionair; *sb.* achteruitgang *m.*; reac-

tionair *m.*; *vi.* teruggaan, achteruitgaan.
retrogress [rîtrou'gres] teruggaan, achteruitgaan.
retrospect ['rîtrouspekt] terugblik *m.*
retrospective [rîtrou'spektiv] terugziend; terugwerkend.
return [ri'tə:n] *vi.* weerkeren, terugkomen: terugkeren; antwoorden; *vt.* teruggeven; terugbetalen; terugzenden; terugslaan; beantwoorden; *sb.* terugkeer *m.*, terugkomst *v.*; terugreis *v.*; terugweg *m.*; thuiskomst *v.*; terugbetaling *v.*; teruggave *v.*; *by — of post,* per omgaande.
returning-officer [ri'tə:ninɔfîsə] voorzitter *m.* van het stembureau.
return-ticket [ri'tə:ntikit] retourkaartje *o.*
return-visit [ri'tə:nvizit] tegenbezoek *o.*
reveal [ri'vîl] *vt.* openbaren, onthullen, blootleggen, bekendmaken; *vr. — oneself,* (ook:) zich ontpoppen als.
reveille [ri'veli] *(mil.)* reveille *v.*
revel ['revəl] *vi.* brassen, zwelgen, zwieren; pret maken; *sb.* braspartij *v.*; feestelijkheid, festiviteit *v.*
revelation [revi'leiʃən] openbaring, onthulling *v.*
reveller ['revələ] brasser, zwelger, zwierbol *m.*; pretmaker *m.*
revenge [ri'ven(d)ʒ] *vt.* wreken; *vr. — oneself for,* zich wreken over; *sb.* wraak, wraakneming *v.*; wraakzucht *v.*; revanche *v.*
revengeful(ly) [ri'ven(d)ʒful(i)] *adj.* *(adv.)* wraakgierig, wraakzuchtig.
revengefulness [ri'ven(d)ʒfulnis] wraakgierigheid, wraakzucht *v.*
revenue ['revinjû] inkomsten *v. mv.*
revenue-officer ['revinjûɔfîsə] belastingambtenaar *m.*
reverberate [ri'və:bəreit] weerkaatsen, terugkaatsen.
revere [ri'viə] eren, vereren; eerbiedigen.
reverence ['revərəns] *sb.* eerbied *m.*, (diepe) verering *v.*; ontzag *o.*; buiging *v.*; *vt.* eerbiedigen, eerbied hebben voor.
reverend ['revərənd] *adj.* eerwaard, eerwaardig; *sb.* dominee; geestelijke *m.*
reverent ['revərənt] *adj.* eerbiedig.
reversal [ri'və:səl] omkering *v.*; ommekeer *m.*, kentering *v.*; *(recht: v. vonnis)* vernietiging, herroeping *v.*; *(tn.: v. machine)* omzetting *v.*
reverse [ri'və:s] *adj.* omgekeerd; tegengesteld; *— current,* tegenstroom; *sb.* omgekeerde, tegengestelde *o.*; keerzijde *v.*; ommekeer *m.*; tegenspoed *m.*; *vt.* omkeren, het onderste boven keren; *(recht: v. vonnis)* vernietigen, nietig verklaren; *(v. besluit)* intrekken, herroepen; *(tn.)* omschakelen, omzetten; *vi.* achteruitrijden.
revert [ri'və:t] *vt.* terugstellen; omkeren; *vi.* terugkeren; terugkomen; vervallen *(to,* aan); terugvallen *(to,* op); verwilderen.

review [ri'vjû] *sb.* overzicht *o.*, terugblik *m.*; *(mil.)* wapenschouwing, parade, revue *v.*; herziening *v.*; boekbeoordeling, recensie *v.*; tijdschrift *o.*; maandschrift *o.*; *vt.* een overzicht geven van; overzien, terugzien op; herzien.
reviewer [ri'vjûə] boekbeoordeler, recensent *m.*
revile [ri'vail] smaden, smalen op, beschimpen.
revilement [ri'vailmənt] smaad *m.*; beschimping *v.*, geschimp *o.*
revisal [ri'vaizəl] herziening, revisie *v.*
revise [ri'vaiz] *vt.* herzien; nazien, verbeteren; *(v. les, enz.)* repeteren, nazien; *sb.* herziening, herziene uitgaaf *v.*; revisie, tweede proef *v.*
revision [ri'viʒən] herziening, revisie *v.*; correctie *v.*; herziene uitgaaf *v.*
revival [ri'vaivəl] herleving, wederopleving *v.*; *(ton.)* wederopvoering, reprise *v.*; godsdienstige opleving *v.*; herstel *o.*
revive [ri'vaiv] *vi.* herleven, nieuw leven krijgen; weer opleven; weer bijkomen; *vt.* doen herleven, nieuw leven geven; weer doen opleven; weer bijbrengen; oprakelen; opknappen; vernieuwen.
revocable ['revəkəbl] herroepbaar.
revoke [ri'vouk] *vt.* herroepen; intrekken; *vi.* *(kaartsp.)* kleur verzaken, niet bekennen; *sb.* kleurverzaking, renonce *v.*
revolt [ri'voult] *vi.* opstaan, in opstand komen; *vt.* in opstand brengen, in opstand doen komen; doen walgen; *sb.* opstand *m.*, oproer *o.*; walging *v.*
revolter [ri'voultə] oproerling, opstandeling *m.*
revolting(ly) [ri'voultin(li)] *adj. (adv.)* oproerig weerzinwekkend, walglijk.
revolution [revə'l(j)ûʃən] omwenteling, revolutie *v.*; kring; omloop *m.*; *(v. motor)* toer *m.*, omwenteling *v.*
revolve [ri'vɔlv] omwentelen omdraaien; overdenken, overpeinzen.
revolver [ri'vɔlvə] revolver *v.*
revue [ri'vjû] *(ton.)* revue *v.*
revulsion [ri'vɔlʃən] *(v. ziekte)* afleiding *v.*; *(v. gevoelens, enz.)* (plotselinge) ommekeer *m.*; reactie *v.*; *(v. kapitaal)* onttrekking *v.*
reward [ri'wo:d] *sb.* beloning, vergelding *v.*; loon *o.*; *vt.* belonen, vergelden.
rewarder [ri'wo:də] beloner, vergelder *m.*
rhapsodic(al) [ræp'sɔdik(l)] *adj.* rapsodisch.
rhetorician [retə'riʃən] retor *m.*; redenaar *m.*
rheumatism ['rûmətizm] reumatiek *o.*
rhinoceros [rai'nɔsərəs] rinoceros *m.*, neushoorndier *o.*
rhomb [rɔm] ruit *v.*
rhubarb ['rûbâb] rabarber *v.*
rhyme [raim] *sb.* rijm *o.*; *vt.* rijmen.
rhymeless ['raimlis] rijmloos.
rhymer ['raimə], **rhymester** ['raimstə], **rhymist** ['raimist] rijmelaar, rijmer *m.*

rhythmic(al) ['riθ—, 'riðmik(l)] *adj.* ritmisch.

rib [rib] rib *v.*; ribstuk *o.*; richel *v.*; ertsader *v.*; (*v. paraplu*) balein *v.*

ribbon ['ribən] *sb.* lint *o.*, band *m.*, strook *v.*; (*sch.*) sent *o.*; *vt.* met linten versieren.

rice [rais] rijst *v.*

rice-field ['raisfîld] rijstveld *o.*, rijstakker *m.*

rice-milk ['raismilk] rijstepap *v.*

rich [ritʃ] *adj.* rijk; (*v. voedsel*) machtig, krachtig; vruchtbaar, overvloedig; kostelijk.

richness ['ritʃnis] rijkdom *m.*

rick [rik] *sb.* hoop *m.*; mijt *v.*; opper; hooiberg *m.*; *vt.* ophopen, aan hopen zetten.

rickety ['rikiti] *adj.* lijdend aan Engelse ziekte, rachitisch; wrak; wankel, waggelend.

rid [rid] bevrijden, verlossen; uit de weg ruimen, opruimen.

ridable ['raidəbl] berijdbaar.

riddle ['ridl] *sb.* raadsel *o.*; grove zeef *v.*; *vt.* raden, oplossen, ontraadselen; ziften, uitziften; doorzeven.

ride [raid] *vi.* rijden; paardrijden; varen, zeilen; *vt.* berijden, rijden op; (*v. land, streek*) afrijden, doorrijden; laten rijden; (*fam.*) regeren, beheersen, tiranniseren; *sb.* rit *m.*, rijtoertje *o.*

rider ['raidə] rijder, ruiter *m.*; berijder *m.*; jockey *m.*; (*in wagen, enz.*) passagier *m.*; (*aan officieel document, wetsontwerp, enz.*) toegevoegde clausule *v.*

ridge [ridʒ] bergrug *m.*; bergketen, heuvelketen *v.*; nok, vorst *v.*

ridge-tile ['ridʒtail] vorstpan, nokpan *v.*

ridicule ['ridikjûl] *sb.* spot *m.*, bespotting, belachelijkmaking *v.*; belachelijkheid *v.*; *vt.* belachelijk maken, bespotten.

ridiculous(ly) [ri'dikjuləs(li)] *adj.* (*adv.*) belachelijk, bespottelijk.

riding-boot ['raidiŋbût] rijlaars *v.*

riding-horse ['raidiŋho:s] rijpaard *o.*

riding-school ['raidiŋskûl] rijschool, manege *v.*

riding-whip ['raidiŋwip] rijzweep *v.*

rifle [raifl] geweer *o.*; buks *v.*; *the —s,* (*mil.*) de jagers.

rifle-club ['raiflkləb] schietvereniging *v.*

rifleman ['raiflmən] scherpschutter *m.*; (*mil.*) jager; fuselier *m.*

rig [rig] *sb.* (*sch.*) tuig *o.*, tuigage, takelage *v.*; optuiging *v.*; (*sl.*) kleding, plunje *v.*, kostuum *o.*; grap, poets *v.*; streek *m.*; *vt.* optuigen, optakelen; uitrusten; in elkaar zetten; voor de gek houden; bewerken, beïnvloeden.

rigging ['rigiŋ] uitrusting, tuigage *v.*; want *o.*

right [rait] *adj.* goed, juist, in orde; billijk, rechtvaardig, recht; rechtmatig; echt, waar; rechts; rechter; *adv.* goed; juist; billijk, recht; zoals 't hoort; be-

hoorlijk; (*naar*) rechts; vlak; precies; zeer, heel; *sb.* rechterkant *m.*, rechterzijde *v.*; (*mil.*) rechtervleugel *m.*; recht *o.*; *vt.* rechtop zetten, overeind zetten; (*v. boot, enz.*) weer oprichten; herstellen, verbeteren, corrigeren; in orde maken; recht verschaffen.

right-down ['raidaun] echt, door en door.

righteous(ly) ['raitʃəs(li)] *adj.* (*adv.*) rechtvaardig, gerecht, rechtschapen.

rightful(ly) ['raitful(i)] *adj.* (*adv.*) rechtvaardig; rechtmatig.

right-handed ['rait'hændid] rechts.

right-hearted ['rait'hâtid] rechtgeaard, rechtschapen.

rightless ['raitlis] rechteloos.

rightly ['raitli] *adv.* rechtvaardig; goed, juist; terecht.

right-minded ['rait'maindid] rechtgeaard.

rightness ['raitnis] juistheid *v.*; billijkheid, rechtvaardigheid *v.*; gepastheid *v.*; rechtmatigheid *v.*

rigid ['ridʒid] stijf; stug, star; streng; onbuigzaam.

rigorous(ly) ['rigərəs(li)] *adj.* (*adv.*) streng; hard, onbuigzaam.

rigour ['rigə] strengheid *v.*; hardheid, onbuigzaamheid *v.*

rig-out ['rigaut] (*fam.*) uirusting *v.*; plunje *v.*

rig-up ['rigəp] *zie* **rig-out.**

rill [ril] *sb.* beek *v.*, vliet *m.*; *vi.* vlieten.

rim [rim] (*v. kom, enz.*) rand *m.*; (*v. bril*) montuur *v.*, garnituur *o.*; (*v. wiel*) velg *v.*

rime [raim] *sb.* rijm, rijp *m.*; *vt.* met rijm (rijp) bedekken.

rind [raind] *sb.* schors *v.*, bast *m.*; schil *v.*; (*v. kaas*) korst *v.*; (*v. spek*) zwoerd *o.*; *vt.* ontschorsen; schillen.

rinderpest ['rindəpest] veepest, runderpest *v.*

ring [riŋ] *sb.* ring *m.*; kring *m.*, kringetje *o.*; arena *v.*, circus *o.*; renbaan *v.*; boksstrijdperk *o.*; *the —,* de boksers, de bokserswereld; *vt.* een ring aandoen; (*v. boom, duif, enz.*) ringen; (*v. appels, enz.*) aan schijven (ringen) snijden.

ring [riŋ] *vi.* klinken, weergalmen; luiden; bellen; (*v. bel*) overgaan; *vt.* luiden; laten klinken; (*tel.*) opbellen; *sb.* klank *m.*, geluid *o.*; gelui; gerinkel *o.*; klokkenspel *o.*

ring-finger ['riŋfiŋgə] ringvinger *m.*

ring-leader ['riŋlidə] belhamel, roervink *m.*

rinse [rins] *vt.* spoelen, omspoelen; *sb.* spoeling, mondspoeling *v.*

riot ['raiət] *sb.* uitgelatenheid, buitensporigheid; uitspatting, braspartij *v.*; lawaai, tumult *o.*; relletje, opstootje *o.*; *vi.* brassen, zwelgen, zwieren; oproerig worden; oproer maken.

riotous(ly) ['raiətəs(li)] *adj.* (*adv.*) uitgelaten; buitensporig; ongebonden, bandeloos, losbandig; verkwistend; rumoerig; oproerig.

rip [rip] *sb.* scheur, torn *v.*; deugniet, losbol *m.*; slet *v.*; (*v. paard*) knol *m.*; *vt.* scheuren, openscheuren, openrijten; lostornen; *vi.* losgaan, uit de naad gaan; met vliegende vaart gaan (rijden).

ripe [raip] rijp; (*v. kaas, wijn*) belegen, oud.

ripeness ['raipnis] rijpheid *v.*

ripple ['ripl] *sb.* rimpeling *v.*; gekabbel, gemurmel *o.*; *vi.* rimpelen; kabbelen, murmelen.

rise [raiz] *vi.* rijzen, stijgen; oprijzen, opstaan; boven komen; (*v. vogel*) opvliegen; (*v. zon, enz.*) opgaan, opkomen; zich verheffen, uitsteken (**above**, boven); *vt.* (*v. vogels*) opjagen, doen opvliegen; (*v. vis*) aan de oppervlakte lokken, doen bijten; (*v. schip*) zien opdoemen; (in prijs) verhogen; *sb.* rijzing *v.*; helling *v.*; opklimming *v.*; opkomst *v.*; (*v. zon*) opgang *m.*; (*v. vis*) (het) bovenkomen *o.*; (*v. prijs*) stijging *v.*; (*v. loon, prijs*) verhoging *v.*, opslag *m.*; (*H.*) hausse *v.*

risk [risk] *sb.* gevaar, risico *o.*; *vt.* wagen, riskeren, op het spel zetten.

riskful ['riskful] gewaagd, riskant; gevaarlijk; gedurfd.

risky ['riski] *adj. zie* **riskful.**

rite [rait] kerkgebruik *o.*, (godsdienstige) plechtigheid *v.*, ritus *m.*; plichtpleging *v.*

rival ['raiv(ə)l] *sb.* mededinger; medeminnaar *m.*; *adj.* mededingend, concurrerend, wedijverend; *vt.* wedijveren met.

rivality [ri'væliti] wedijver *m.*, concurrentie *v.*; medeminnaarschap *o.*

rivalry ['raiv(ə)lri] *zie* **rivality.**

river ['rivə] *sb.* rivier *v.*, stroom *m.*

rivet ['rivit] *sb.* klinknagel *m.*; *vt.* klinken, met klinknagels bevestigen; (*fig.*) vastklinken; vastleggen; bestendigen.

rixdollar ['riks'dolə] rijksdaalder *m.*

road [roud] weg, rijweg *m.*, straat *v.*; rede *v.*

road-mender ['roudmendə] wegwerker *m.*

roadside ['roud'said] kant *m.* van de weg.

roadstead ['roudsted] rede, ree *v.*

roadway ['roudwei] rijweg *m.*; brugdek *o.*

roam [roum] ronddolen, zwerven, omzwerven.

roar [ro:ə] *vi.* schreeuwen, razen; brullen, bulderen, loeien; (*v. donder*) rollen; (*v. motor*) ronken; weergalmen; (*v. dampig paard*) snuiven; *vt.* — **down,** overschreeuwen, brullend overstemmen; *sb.* geschreeuw, geraas *o.*; gebrul, gebulder, geloei *o.*; geronk *o.*; geschater *o.*

roast [roust] *vt.* braden, roosteren; (*v. koffie*) branden; *sb.* (het) braden *o.*; (het) roosteren *o.*; gebraad; gebraden vlees *o.*; *adj.* gebraden.

rob [rob] *vt.* bestelen, beroven; uitplunderen; roven, stelen, plunderen; *ri.* roven, stelen.

robber ['robə] rover, dief *m.*

robbery ['robəri] roof *m.*, roverij, beroving *v.*; diefstal *m.*

robe [roub] *sb.* toga *v.*; tabberd *m.*; mantel *m.*; ambtsgewaad *o.*; *vt.* kleden, aankleden; bekleden.

robot [roubot] machinemens *m.*; automatisch verkeerssein *o.*

robust [rou'bəst] *adj.* krachtig, fors, sterk, gespierd; (*v. oefeningen*) inspannend.

rock [rok] *sb.* rots, klip *v.*, rif *o.*; rotsblok, gesteente *o.*; ketelsteen *o.*; *vt.* schommelen, doen schudden, heen en weer schudden; wiegen; *vi.* schommelen, waggelen, wankelen.

rock-bottom ['rokbotəm] rotsbodem, rotsgrond *m.*

rock-bound ['rokbaund] door rotsen ingesloten.

rocker ['rokə] hobbelpaard *o.*

rocket ['rokit] raket *v.*, vuurpijl *m.*; (*Pl.*) raket *v.*

rocking-chair ['rokintʃêə] schommelstoel *m.*

rocking-horse ['rokinho:s] hobbelpaard *o.*

rock-salt ['rokso:lt] klipzout *o.*

rocky ['roki] rotsachtig.

rod [rod] roede *v.*; staaf; staf *m.*; (*tn.*) stang *v.*; hengelroede *v.*

rodent ['roudənt] *adj.* knagend; *sb.* knaagdier *o.*

roe [rou] reebok *m.*; ree, hinde *v.*; (vis)kuit *v.*

rogation [rou'geiʃən] verzoek *o.*, smeekbede *v.*

rogue [roug] schurk, schelm *m.*; guit, snaak, schalk *m.*

roguish(ly) ['rougiʃ(li)] *adj.* (*adv.*) schurkachtig, schelmachtig; guitig, snaaks, schalks.

roll [roul] *sb.* rol *v.*; wals *v.*; cilinder *m.*; lijst *v.*, register *o.*, monsterrol *v.*; (*mil.*) roffel *m.*; *vt.* doen rollen; wentelen; oprollen; voortrollen; walsen; pletten; (*mil.*) roffelen op; *vi.* rollen; zich rollen, zich wentelen; schommelen, waggelen; (*v. schip*) slingeren.

roller ['roulə] rol *v.*; rolletje *o.*; inktrol *v.*; cilinder *m.*; wals *v.*; rolstok *m.*

roller-blind ['rouləblaind] rolgordijn *o.*

roller-skate ['rouləskeit] rolschaats *r.*

rolling ['roulin] rollend; wentelend; enz.; (*v. terrein*) golvend.

rolling-mill ['roulinmil] pletmolen, pletterij *v.*; walswerk *o.*

Roman ['roumən] *sb.* Romein *m.*; romein, gewone drukletter *v.*; roomskatholiek *m.*; *adj.* Romeins; rooms.

romance [ro'mæns] romance *v.*

romp [romp] *vi.* stoeien, dartelen; (*sl.*) hollen, rennen; — **off,** er vandoor gaan; — **in,** (*sl.*) op zijn gemak winnen; *sb.* stoeipartij *v.*; wildzang, wildebras *m.*, wilde meid *v.*

rood [rûd] roede *v.*; kruis *o.*

roof [rûf] *sb.* dak *o.*; gewelf *o.*; (*v. rijtuig*) tent *v.*; (*v. mond*) verhemelte *o.*;

vt. van een dak voorzien, met een dak bedekken; onder dak brengen; overdekken; overwelven.

roofer ['rûfə] dakwerker; leidekker *m.*

roofless ['rûflis] dakloos.

room [rûm, rum] ruimte, plaats *v.*; kamer *v.*, vertrek *o.*; zaal *v.*; aanleiding, reden, oorzaak.

roomy ['rûmi] ruim; wijd; breed.

roost [rûst] rek *o.*, roest *v.* & *o.*; roeststok *m.*; slaapplaats *v.*; troep *m.* vogels.

root [rût] *sb.* wortel *m.*; wortelgewas *o.*; (*fig.*) grondvest, basis *v.*; grondtoon *m.*; *vt.* inplanten; wortel doen schieten; (*dicht.*) uitroeien; omwroeten, omwoelen; doorsnuffelen; — *out* (*up*), ontwortelen, uitroeien; *vi.* wortel schieten; geworteld zijn (*in*, in); wroeten, woelen; (*fig.*) snuffelen.

rooted ['rûtid] *adj.* ingeworteld, diep geworteld.

rope [roup] *sb.* touw, koord *o.*; strik, strop *m.*; (*v. paarlen*) snoer *o.·* (*in bier, enz.*) draad *m.*; *vt.* binden, vastbinden; insluiten, afsluiten; (*sch.: v. zeil*) lijken; (*v. uien*) risten; met een lasso vangen; — *in*, in de strik lokken; inpalmen; (*v. winst*) binnenhalen; (*v. geld*) opstrijken; — *up*, vastbinden; *vi.* (*v. vloeistof*) draderig worden; zich rekken.

rope-dancer ['roupdânsə] koorddanser(es) *m.* (*v.*).

rope-maker ['roupmeikə] touwslager *m.*

rosary ['rouzəri] rozenkrans *m.*; rosarium, rozenpark *o.*, rozentuin *m.*

rose [rouz] *sb.* roos *v.*; rozet *v.*; rozetvenster *o.*; rozetsteen *m.*; rozekleur *v.*; rose *o.*; (*v. gieter, enz.*) sproeier *m.*; *adj.* rooskleurig, rose.

rose-bud ['rouzbəd] rozeknop *m.*; (*fig.*) jong meisje *o.*; (*Am.*) debutante *v.*

rose-bush ['rouzbuʃ] rozestruik, rozelaar *m.*

rose-knot ['rouznət] rozet *v.*

rosemary ['rouzməri] (*Pl.*) rosmarijn *m.*

rosette [rou'zet] rozet *v.*

rosin ['rɔzin] *sb.* hars, vioolhars *o.* & *v.*; *vt.* met hars bestrijken.

roster ['rɔstə] rooster *o.*, lijst *v.*

rosy ['rouzi] *adj.* rooskleurig; blozend.

rot [rot] *sb.* rotheid *v.*; verrotting *v.*; (*v. schapen*) leverziekte *r.*; (*in 't hout*) vuur *o.*; (*sl.*) onzin *m.*, klets *v.*; *vi.* rotten, verrotten, vergaan; (*sl.*) kletsen, leuteren, onzin praten; *vt.* doen rotten; (*v. vlas*) roten; (*sl. v.: plannen, enz.*) in de war sturen, in duigen doen vallen; van streek brengen; kwellen, plagen, voor de gek houden.

rotary ['routəri] *adj.* rondgaand, draaiend, rotatie—; *sb.* rotatiepers *v.*

rotate [rou'teit] draaien, omwentelen; afwisselen, rouleren.

rotation [rou'teiʃən] draaiing, omdraaiing, omwenteling *v.*; rotatie *v.*;

afwisseling *v.*; — (*of crops*), wisselbouw *m.*; *by* (*in*) —, om de beurt.

rotten ['rɔtn] *adj.* rot, verrot, bedorven; (*sl.*) beroerd, akelig, treurig.

rotter ['rɔtə] (*sl.*) snertvent, vent *m.* van niks.

rotundity [rou'tənditi] rondheid, bolvormigheid *v.*; omvangrijkheid *v.*; volheid *v.*; gezwollenheid, hoogdravendheid *v.*

rouble ['rûbl] roebel *m.*

rouge [rûʒ] *adj.* rood; *sb.* rode verf *v.*; rood blanketsel *o.*; rood poetspoeder *o.*; (*in politiek*) rode *m.*; *vt.* (*vi.*) (zich) blanketten, (zich) schminken.

rough [rʌf] *adj.* ruw, grof, ruig; ongeslepen, onbehouwen; onafgewerkt; (*v. weg*) oneffen, hobbelig; (*v. rijst*) ongepeld; (*v. zee*) onstuimig, woest, wild; (*v. wijn*) wrang; (*v. tijd*) moeilijk, hard; nors, bars, streng; guur; *sb.* ruwe kant *m.*; (*v. stoffen*) ruwe toestand *m.*; oneffen terrein *o.*; woesteling, ruwe kerel, ruwe klant *m.*; (*v. paard*) ijsnagel *m.*; moeilijkheden *v. mv.*; *vᵗ.* ruw bewerken; ruw bekappen; ruw maken; prikkelen; (*v. paard*) op scherp zetten; — *it*, zich er door heen slaan; — *out*, ontwerpen; ruw bewerken; — *off*, ruw fatsoeneren.

round [raund] *adj.* rond; *adv.* rond; rondom; in de rondte; in de omtrek; *prep.* om, rond, rondom, om... heen; (*Am.*) omstreeks; *sb.* bol *m.*; kring *m.*; cirkel, ring *m.*; omtrek *m.*; omwenteling *v.*; kringloop *m.*; bocht *v.*; rondreis *v.*; *vt.* rond maken; afronden; omringen; (*sch.*) omzeilen; — *up*, (*v. vee*) bijeendrijven; gevangen nemen; omsingelen; verzamelen; *vi.* rond worden; vol worden; rondlopen; zich omdraaien; — *on*, zich keren tegen; — *to*, (*sch.*) bijdraaien.

roundabout ['raundəbaut] *adj.* gezet; om de zaak heendraaiend; wijdlopig; *sb.* omweg *m.*; omhaal *m.*; omschrijving *v.*; draaimolen *m.*

rounding ['raundiŋ] ronding *v.*

roundish ['raundiʃ] rondachtig.

roundly ['raundli] *adv.* rond, cirkelvormig; ronduit, onbewimpeld, vierkant, botweg; flink, krachtig.

roundness ['raundnis] rondheid, enz.

round trip ['raund'trip] rondreis *v.*

round-up ['raund'əp] (*v. vee*) (het) bijeendrijven *o.*; omsingeling *v.*; klopjacht, razzia *r.*

rouse [rauz] *vt.* wekken, wakker maken, doen ontwaken; opwekken; aanporren, opporren; (*sch.*) aanhalen, inhalen; (*v. wild*) opjagen; boos maken, prikkelen; (*v. haring, enz.*) zouten; *vi.* wakker worden, ontwaken; — *out*, (*sch.*) rijzen, opstaan; *vr.* — *oneself*, wakker worden; zich vermannen; *sb.* (*mil.*) reveille *v.*; (*sch.*) dagwaak *v.*

rout [raut] *sb.* leven, lawaai, rumoer *o.*, herrie *v.*; (*rumoerige*) troep *m.*, wanordelijke bende *v.*; *vt.* op de vlucht drijven; geheel verslaan.

rout [raut] *vt.* omwoelen, omwroeten.

routine [rû'tin] sleur, routine *v.*

rove [rouv] *vi.* zwerven, omzwerven; (*v. ogen*) dwalen; *sb.* zwerftocht *m.*

rover ['rouvə] zwerver; vagebond *m.*; — (*of the seas*), zeerover, zeeschuimer *m.*; voortrekker; padvinder *m.*

row [rou] *sb.* rij, reeks *v.*; huizenrij *v.*; straat *v.*

row [rou] *vi.* roeien; — *in*, naar de wal roeien; *sb.* (het) roeien *o.*; roeitochtje *o.*

row [rau] herrie, ruzie *v.*, kabaal, spektakel *o.*; standje *o.*

row-boat ['roubout] roeiboot *v.*

row-de-dow ['raudi'dau] herrie *v.*, lawaai, kabaal *o.*

rowdy ['raudi] *sb.* herriemaker, ruwe kerel *m.*; *adj.* ruw, lawaaierig.

royal ['rɔiəl] koninklijk, vorstelijk; van koninklijken bloede; eerste klas, prima.

royalist ['rɔiəlist] *adj.* koningsgezind; *sb.* koningsgezinde, royalist *m.*

royalty ['rɔiəlti] koningschap *o.*; koninklijke familie *v.*; vorstelijke personen *m. mv.*; recht *o.* der Kroon; tantième *o.*

rub [rəb] *vt.* (*v. meubelen, enz.*) afwrijven; boenen; poetsen; polijsten; (*v. smeersel*) inwrijven; (*v. ogen*) wrijven, uitwrijven; *vi.* wrijven; schuren (langs); — *along*, voortscharrelen, voortsukkelen; (*fig.*) slijten; *sb.* (het) wrijven *o.*; wrijving *v.*; onaangenaamheid, moeilijkheid *v.*; steek *m.* (onder water), hatelijkheid *v.*; wederwaardigheid *v.*; botsing, hindernis *v.*

rubber ['rəbə] wrijver, polijster *m.*; wrijflap; wrijfborstel *m.*; badhanddoek *m.*; rubber *m.*, gummi *o.*; gummiband *m.*; (*kaartsp.*) robber *m.*; (*el.*) wrijfkussen *o.*; slijpsteen *m.*

rubbish ['rəbiʃ] puin *o.*; bocht *o.*, prullen *v. mv.*; afval *m.*, uitschot *o.*; kletspraat, onzin *m.*

rubbishy ['rəbiʃi] prullig, prullerig; vol rommel.

rubble ['rəbl] puin *o.* (van afbraak); steenslag *m.*; breuksteen, (ruwe) natuursteen *m.*

Rubicon ['rûbikən] Rubicon *m.*

rubric ['rûbrik] rubriek, afdeling *v.*; (*kath.*) rubriek *v.*, liturgisch voorschrift *o.*; kerkregel *m.*

rubstone ['rəbstoun] slijpsteen, wetsteen *m.*

ruby ['rûbi] robijn *m.*; robijnkleur *v.*; karbonkel *m.*, rode puist *v.*

ruck [rək] *sb.* troep *m.*, menigte *v.*; grote hoop *m.*; kreukel, plooi *v.*, rimpel *m.*; vouw *v.*; *vt. & vi.* kreukelen, plooien, rimpelen.

ruckle ['rəkl] *vi.* kreukelen; rochelen; *sb.* (doods)gerochel *o.*

rucksack ['ruksæk] rugzak, ransel *m.*

rudder ['rədə] roer; roerblad *o.*

rudderless ['rədəlis] (*sch.*) roerloos.

ruddle ['rədl] *sb.* roodaarde *v.*, roodsel *o.*; *vt.* merken (kleuren) met rood.

ruddy ['rədi] rood, blozend, met frisse kleur; rossig.

rude [rûd] *adj.* ruw; grof; onopgevoed, onbeleefd, onbeschaafd, lomp; primitief; streng, hard; krachtig; (*v. landschap*) woest.

rudiment ['rûdimənt] grondbeginsel, eerste begin *o.*; onvolkomen ontwikkeld orgaan *o.*

rue [rû] betreuren, berouw hebben over.

rue-bargain ['rûbâgin] rouwkoop *m.*

rueful(**ly**) ['rûful(i)] *adj.* (*adv.*) treurig, droevig.

ruff [rəf] *sb.* plooi *v.*, geplooide kraag *m.*; (*vis*) pos *m.*; kemphaan *m.*; (*kaartsp.*) (het) troeven *o.*; roffel *m.*; *vt.* (af)troeven.

ruffian ['rəfjən] *sb.* bandiet, schurk *m.*; woesteling *m.*; *adj.* gemeen; woest.

ruffle ['rəfl] *vt.* plooien, rimpelen, kreukelen; verstoren, verstoord maken, uit zijn humeur brengen; (*v. tekst, brieven, enz.*) vlug doorlopen; (*v. bladz. v. boek*) snel omslaan; in de war brengen; — (*up*, (*v. veren*) opzetten; roffelen; *vi.* zich fronsen; snoeven, opscheppen, opsnijden; *sb.* rimpeling, fronsing *v.*; plooi *v.*; geplooide kraag *m.*; herrie, ruzie *v.*; worsteling, schermutseling *v.*; roffel *m.*

rug [rəg] reisdeken *v.*; kleedje, vloerkleedje, haardkleedje *o.*

rugged(**ly**) ['rəgid(li)] *adj.* (*adv.*) ruw, ruig; oneffen, hobbelig; rimpelig; streng, nors; grof, lomp; stoer; onwelluidend; (*v. tabak*) zwaar; (*Am.*) krachtig, sterk.

ruin ['rûin] *sb.* val *m.*, vernietiging *v.*, ondergang *m.*, verderf *o.*; puin *o.*, puinhoop *m.*; bouwval *m.*; (*fig.*) wrak *o.*; *vt.* vernielen, verwoesten, ruïneren, te gronde richten, in 't verderf storten; ten val brengen; (*v. ogen*) geheel bederven; (*v. meisje*) verleiden; *vi.* te gronde gaan; instorten.

ruination [rûi'neiʃən] ruïne *v.*; ondergang *m.*, verderf *o.*; vernieling *v.*

ruinous(**ly**) ['rûinəs(li)] *adj.* (*adv.*) bouwvallig, vervallen; verderfelijk.

rule [rûl] *sb.* regel *m.*; levensregel *m.*; bestuur, bewind *o.*, heerschappij *v.*; regering *v.*; (*recht*) uitspraak, rechterlijke beslissing *v.*; duimstok, dubbele decimeter *m.*; *vt.* regeren, heersen (*over*, over); beheersen; besturen; liniëren; (*recht*) beslissen, bepalen; — *out*, uitschakelen; uitsluiten.

ruler ['rûlə] regeerder, bestuurder *m.*; liniaal *v.*

rum [rəm] *sb.* rum *v.*; (*Am.*) sterke drank *m.*; *adj.* raar, gek, zonderling, vreemd.

rumble ['rəmbl] *vi.* rommelen; dreunen; *vt.* doen rommelen; (*sl.*) doorzien; *sb.* gerommel, gestommel; gedreun *o.*; (*v. rijtuig*) kattebak *m.*

ruminant ['rûminənt] *adj.* herkauwend; *sb.* herkauwend dier *o.*, herkauwer *m.*

rummage ['rəmidʒ] *vt.* doorzoeken, doorsnuffelen; (*v. vloeistoffen*) omroe-

ren; — **out** (**up**), opsnorren; *sb.* doorzoeking *v.*, gesnuffel *o.*; rommel *m.*
rummer ['rəmə] roemer *m.*
rumour ['rûmə] *sb.* gerucht *o.*, praatje(s) *o.* (*mv.*); *vt.* (*v. praatjes*) rondstrooien, uitstrooien.
rump [rəmp] stuitbeen *o.*, stuit *m.*; staartstuk *o.*; achterste *o.*; restant, overschot *o.*
rumple ['rəmpl] *sb.* vouw, kreuk(el) *v.*; *vt.* vouwen, kreuken, verkreuk(el)en; verfrommelen; (*v. haar*) in de war maken.
rumpsteak ['rəmpsteik] biefstuk *m.*
run [rən] *vi.* lopen; hard lopen, hollen, rennen; (*v. bloed*) vloeien, stromen; (*v. kleuren*) doorlopen, in elkaar lopen; (*v. kaars*) aflopen; (*v. inkt*) vloeien; (*v. melk*) schiften; (*v. plant*) klimmen, kruipen; varen, stomen, zeilen; smelten; lekken; in omloop zijn, geldig zijn, gangbaar zijn; verlopen; etteren; (*v. brief, tekst*) luiden; (*v. zalm*) de rivier opgaan; meedoen, meedingen; *vt.* afleggen; doorzwerven; (*v. loop, enz.*) vervolgen; (*v. paard*) laten draven; (*v. trein, enz.*) laten lopen; (*v. rekening*) laten oplopen; (*v. vee*) in de wei sturen; (*v. drank, wapens*) smokkelen; (*v. blokkade*) doorbreken; (*v. touw*) vieren, laten schieten; (*v. vos, enz.*) najagen, achtervolgen; (*v. zaak*) drijven, besturen; rijgen, los in elkaar naaien; (*v. blik, enz.*) laten dwalen; — **down**, (*v. uurwerk*) aflopen; (*v. fietsband*) leeglopen; opraken, uitgeput raken; afnemen; (*v. getij*) vallen; — **in**, (*v. nieuwe auto*) inrijden; (*v. motor*) inlopen; (*v. trein*) binnenlopen; (*v. dief, enz.*) inrekenen; — **on**, (*v. tijd*) voorbijgaan; (*v. rekening*) oplopen; — **out**, lekken; uitsteken; (*v. plant*) uitlopen; (*v. voorraad*) opraken; (*v. contract, termijn*) aflopen; (*v. touw, kabel*) afrollen, aflopen; (*v. fortuin*) doorbrengen, er door lappen; — **over**, overvloeien (**with**, van); (*v. vloeistof*) overlopen; (*v. rekening, enz.*) doorlopen, nagaan; — **through**, lopen door; (*v. tekst, enz.*) doorlopen; (*bilj.*) doorstoten; (*v. ervaring*) doormaken; (*v. inkt*) doorvloeien; (*v. fortuin*) er door jagen; (*v. boek: herdrukken*) beleven; — **up**, oplopen; opgroeien; opschieten; (*v. prijzen*) opdrijven; (*bij verkoping*) opjagen; (*v. geschut*) opstellen, in positie brengen; (*v. muur*) optrekken; (*v. vlag*) hijsen; (*v. scheur*) aanhalen; samenstellen; krimpen; optellen; (*Am.*) opknopen; *sb.* loop *m.*; aanloop *m.*; geloop *o.*; verloop *o.*; (*v. klanten, enz.*) toeloop *m.*; wedloop, wedren *m.*; uitstapje *o.*, reis *v.*; tochtje *o.*; (*bij 't zeilen*) vaart *v.*; richting *v.*; vrije toegang *m.*; (*in mijn*) luchtgang *v.*; waterpijp *v.*; stroompje, beekje *o.*; (*in zee*) stroom *m.*, stroming *v.*; uitgestrektheid *v.*; (*muz.*) loopje *o.*; roulade *v.*; vrije beschikking *v.* (**of**, over); reeks, serie, periode *v.*; (*kaartsp.*) volgkaarten *v. mv.*; (*v. toneelstuk, film*)

onafgebroken speeltijd *m.*; kippenren *v.*
run [rən] *v. d. van* **run**; *adj.* (*v. boter*) afgeklaard, uitgesmolten; (*v. goederen, drank*) gesmokkeld.
runabout ['rənəbout] *adj.* rondzwervend; *sb.* zwerver, landloper *m.*; loopjongen *m.*; loopmeisje *o.*; kruipplant *v.*
runaway ['rənəwei] *sb.* vluchteling; deserteur *m.*; hollend paard *o.*; vlucht; schaking *v.*; *adj.* weggelopen; (*v. paard*) op hol.
rung [rəŋ] *sb.* spijl *v.*; (*v. ladder*) sport *v.*
runner ['rənə] loper *m.*; hardloper *m.*; boodschapper; bode *m.*; bankloper *m.*; loopvogel *m.*
rupture ['rəptʃə] *sb.* breuk *v.*; vredebreuk *v.*; scheuring *v.*; verbreking *v.*; *vt.* doen barsten, doen springen; verbreken; (*v. grasland*) scheuren; *vi.* barsten, springen; breken.
rural ['rûərəl] landelijk.
rush [rəʃ] *sb.* (*Pl.*) bies *v.*; haast *v.*, spoed *m.*; stormloop *m.*; bestorming *v.*; grote toeloop *m.*, plotselinge drukte *v.*; paniek *v.*; gedrang *o.*, aandrang *m.*; (*v. mensen*) hoop *m.*; (*v. vogels*) vlucht *v.*; vlaag *v.*; geraas, geruis *o.*; levendige vraag *v.* (**for**, naar); *vt.* (*v. stoelen*) matten; met biezen bestrooien; bestormen; losstormen op; stormenderhand (in stormloop) nemen; overrompelen, verrassen; snel vervoeren; afroffelen; haast maken met, overijld te werk gaan met; (*sl.*) afzetten; *vi.* rennen, vliegen, snellen; dringen; zich storten, zich werpen; — **after**, nasnellen; *adj.* **the —hours**, de spitsuren.
rush-bottomed ['rəʃbɔtəmd] met matten zitting.
rushlight ['rəʃlait] nachtpitje *o.*; (*fig.*) flauw licht *o.* [ling *v.*
rush-order ['rəʃo:də] spoedbestel
rusk [rəsk] beschuit; scheepsbeschuit *v.*
Russia ['rəʃə] Rusland *v.*
rust [rəst] *sb.* roest *o.*; *vi.* roesten, verroesten; roestkleurig worden; afstompen.
rustic ['rəstik] *adj.* landelijk, plattelands, boers; (*v. brug, enz.*) rustiek; *sb.* plattelander, landbewoner, landman *m.*; boer, kinkel, pummel *m.*
rustle ['rəsl] *vi.* ritselen, ruisen; (*Am.*) er vaart achter zetten; *vt.* doen ritselen; (*Am.*) stelen; aanpakken, doorzetten; haastig doen; *sb.* geritsel, geruis *o.*
rustless ['rəstlis] roestvrij.
rustling ['rəsliŋ] geritsel *o.*, ritseling *v.*
rust-proof ['rəstprûf] *adj.* roestvrij; *vt.* roestvrij maken.
rusty ['rəsti] *adj.* roestig; (*v. kleren, enz.: van ouderdom*) rood, vaal; ouderwets; stram, stijf; (*v. stem*) krassend, knorrig, ruw; ransig, garstig; weerspannig.
rut [rət] *sb.* wagenspoor *o.*; spoor *o.*; groef, voor *v.*; sleur, routine *v.*; *vt.* sporen maken in, met sporen doorsnijden.
ruthless (**ly**) ['rûθlis(li)] *adj.* (*adv.*) meedogenloos, onmeedogend, onbarmhartig.
rye [rai] rogge *v.*

S

sable ['seibl] *sb.* (*Dk.*) sabeldier *o.*; sabelbont *o.*; *adj.* zwart, donker.

sabotage ['sæbətidʒ] *sb.* sabotage *v.*; *vt.* saboteren.

sabre ['seibə] (cavalerie)sabel *v.*

sack [sæk] *sb.* zak *m.*; *vt.* in zakken doen, in een zak stoppen; de bons geven; (*bij wedstrijd*) verslaan, kloppen.

sack [sæk] *sb.* plundering *v.* (*v. stad*); *vt.* uitplunderen.

sack-race ['sækreis] (*sp.*) zaklopen.

sacrament ['sækrəmənt] (*kath.*) sacrament *o.*; (*Prot.*) Avondmaal *o.*

sacred ['seikrid] heilig; geheiligd; gewijd; geestelijk, kerk—.

sacrifice ['sækrifais] *sb.* offer *o.*, offerande *v.*; opoffering *v.*; *vt.* offeren, opofferen; slachtofferen; *vr.* — *oneself*, zich opofferen.

sacrilege ['sækrilidʒ] heiligschennis; kerkschenderij *v.*, kerkroof *m.*

sacristan ['sækristən] koster *m.*

sad [sæd] *adj.* bedroefd, droevig, verdrietig, treurig, somber; donker; jammerlijk; (*v. brood*) kleverig; zwaar.

sadden ['sædn] *vt.* bedroeven, bedroefd (droevig) maken; somber maken, versomberen; donker tinten; *vi.* droevig (somber) worden.

saddle ['sædl] *sb.* zadel *m.*; stut *m.*, schraag *v.*; beugel *m.*; rugstuk, lendestuk, ribstuk *o.*; *vt.* zadelen; *vi.* — *up*, opzadelen; *vr.* — *oneself with*, op zich nemen.

saddle-cloth ['sædlklɔδ] zadeldek, zadelkleed *o.*, sjabrak *v.*

saddler ['sædlə] zadelmaker *m.*

safe [seif] *adj.* zeker, veilig; behouden, ongedeerd; betrouwbaar, vertrouwd; (*H.*) solied; gerust; *sb.* brandkast, kluis *v.*; provisiekast, vliegenkast *v.*

safe-conduct ['seif'kɔndəkt] vrijgeleide *o.*

safe-deposit [seifdi'pɔzit] (brand)-kluis *v.*

safeguard ['seifgåd] *sb.* vrijgeleide *o.*; waarborg *m.*, beveiliging, bescherming *v.*; voorzorgsmaatregel *m.*; (*aan locomotief*) baanschuiver *m.*; *vt.* beveiligen, beschermen.

safety ['seifti] veiligheid; zekerheid *v.*; betrouwbaarheid *v.*

safety-belt ['seiftibelt] reddingsgordel *m.*

safety-brake ['seiftibreik] noodrem *v.*

safety-pin ['seiftipin] veiligheidsspeld *v.*

saffron ['sæfrən] *sb.* saffraan *v.*; *adj.* saffraankleurig, saffraangeel, lichtgeel.

sag [sæg] *vi.* doorbuigen, overhellen; verzakken, inzakken; doorzakken; slap hangen; afnemen; (in prijs) dalen; (*fig.*) versagen; *vt.* doen doorzakken; *sb.* verzakking *v.*; doorzakking *v.*; overhelling *v.*

sagacious (**ly**) [sə'geiʃəs(li)] *adj.* (*adv.*) scherpzinnig, schrander.

sagacity [sə'gæsiti] scherpzinnigheid, schranderheid *v.*

sage [seidʒ] *adj.* wijs, verstandig; *sb.* wijze, wijsgeer *m.*; (*Pl.*) salie *o.*

Sagittarius [sædʒi'têəriəs] (*sterr.*) de Schutter *m.*

sail [seil] *sb.* (*sch.*) zeil *o.*; zeilschip *o.*, zeiltocht *m.*; (molen)wiek *v.*; vleugel *m.*; —*s*, (*sch.*) zeilmaker; *vi.* zeilen; uitzeilen; afvaren; — *into*, aanpakken, onderhanden nemen.

sail-arm ['seilâm] molenroede *v.*

sailcloth ['seilklɔδ] *sb.* zeildoek *o.*; (*v. molen*) wiek *v.*; *adj.* van zeildoek.

sailer ['seilə] (*sch.*) zeiler *m.*, zeilschip *o.*; (*vl.*) motorloos glijvliegtuig *o.*

sailing ['seiliŋ] (het) zeilen *o.*; afvaart *v.*

sailing-vessel ['seiliŋvesəl] zeilschip *o.*

sailor ['seilə] matroos, zeeman *m.*; matelothoed *m.*; zeilschip *o.*

sail-plane ['seilplein] zweefvliegtuig *o.*

saint [seint] *adj.* heilig, sint; *sb.* heilige *m.*; *vt.* heilig verklaren, canoniseren.

sake [seik] *for goodness'* —, in 's hemels naam; *for the* — *of*, ter wille van.

salable ['seiləbl] verkoopbaar; gewild, goed van de hand gaand.

salacious [sə'leiʃəs] geil, wulps, wellustig.

salad ['sæləd] salade, sla *v.*

salamander ['sæləmændə] (*Dk.*) salamander *m.*

salary ['sæləri] *sb.* salaris *o.*, bezoldiging *v.*; *vt.* salariëren, bezoldigen.

sale [seil] verkoop *m.*; verkoping, veiling *v.*; —(*s*), uitverkoop *m.*

sale-room ['seilrum] verkooplokaal *o.*

saleswoman ['seilzwumən] verkoopster *v.*

saline ['seilain, sə'lain] *adj.* zout, zilt; zoutachtig; zouthoudend; *sb.* zoutpan *v.*; zoutmeer *o.*; zoutoplossing *v.*; purgeerzout *o.*

saliva [sə'laivə] speeksel *o.*

sallow ['sælou] waterwilg *m.*

sallow ['sælou] *adj.* ziekelijk bleek (geel); vuilgeel; *sb.* vuilgele tint, vale kleur *v.*

sally ['sæli] *sb.* uitval *m.*; inval, geestige zet, kwinkslag *m.*; sprong *m.*; opwelling, uitbarsting *v.*; (*bouwk.*) uitstek *o.*; uitstapje *o.*; *vi.* een uitval doen, uitvallen; opeens te voorschijn komen.

salmon ['sæmən] *sb.* zalm *m.*; zalmkleur *v.*; *adj.* zalmkleurig.

saloon [sə'lûn] zaal *v.*; salon *m.* & *o.*

salsify ['sælsifi] (wilde) schorseneer *v.*

salt [so:lt, sɔlt] *sb.* zout *o.*; zoutvaatje *o.*; (*fig.*) Attisch zout *o.*, geestigheid *v.*; (*fam.*) zeerob *m.*; zoutmoeras *o.*; —*s*, Engels zout; reukzout; *adj.* zout, zilt;

gezouten; (*fig.*) pittig, gekruid; (*v. rekening*) gepeperd; (*Bijb.*) dor, onvruchtbaar; *vt.* zouten; inzouten, pekelen; met zout behandelen; (*fig.*) kruiden; (*v. rekening*) peperen; (*v. boeken*) vervalsen.
salt-cellar ['so:ltselə] zoutvaatje *o.*
saltish ['so:ltiʃ] zoutachtig, zilt, brak.
salt-marsh ['so:ltmâʃ] zoutmoeras *o.*, zouttuin *m.*
salt-mine ['so:ltmain] zoutmijn *v.*
saltpetre ['so:lt'pîtə] salpeter *o.*
salt-water ['so:lt'wo:tə] zoutwater *o.*; (*fam.*) zeerob *m.*
salt-work(s) ['so:ltwə:k(s)] zoutkeet, zoutziederij *v.*
salty ['so:ltj] zout, zoutachtig, zilt, ziltachtig; pikant.
salubrious [sə'l(j)ûbriəs] gezond, heilzaam.
salutary ['sæljutəri] *adj.* heilzaam, weldadig.
salutation [sælju'teiʃən] groet *m.*, begroeting *v.*; (*in brief*) aanspreking *v.*
salute [sə'l(j)ût] *vt.* groeten, begroeten; (*mil.*) salueren, aanslaan voor; *sb.* groet *m.*, begroeting *v.*; saluut, saluutschot(en) *o.* (*mv.*).
salvable ['sælvəbl] te redden; (*sch.*) te bergen, bergbaar.
salvage ['sælvidʒ] *sb.* redding *v.*; (*sch.*) berging *v.*; (*sch.*) bergloon *o.*; *vt.* bergen.
salvage-money ['sælvidʒməni] bergloon *o.*
salvation [sæl'veiʃən] redding, verlossing, zaligheid, zaligmaking *v.*
salve [sâv] *sb.* zalf *v.*, balsem *m.*; *vt.* insmeren; zalven; (*fig.*) verbloemen; (*v. geweten*) sussen; — (*over*), (*fig.*) een pleister leggen op.
salver ['sælvə] presenteerblad; schenkbord *o.*
same [seim] zelfde; genoemde, bovengenoemde; eentonig; *all the* —, precies hetzelfde; hoe dan ook, met dat al, toch, niettegenstaande dat: *at the* — *time,* terzelfdertijd; niettemin, toch.
sameness ['seimnis] gelijkheid, eenvormigheid *v.*; eentonigheid *v.*
sample ['sâmpl] *sb.* monster, staal *o.*; (*fig.*) staaltje, proefje *o.*; *vt.* bemonsteren; proeven, keuren; monsters trekken uit; proberen; tot voorbeeld dienen van; ondervinding opdoen van.
sample-order ['sâmplo:də] proeforder *v.*
sanative ['sænətiv] geneeskrachtig, genezend, heilzaam.
sanatorium [sænə'to:riəm] sanatorium *o.*
sanctification [sæŋktifi'keiʃən] heiligmaking; heiliging *v.*
sanctify ['sæŋktifai] heiligen, heilig maken.
sanctimonious [sæŋkti'mouniəs] *adj.* schijnheilig.
sanction ['sæŋkʃən] *sb.* sanctie *v.*; bekrachtiging, goedkeuring wettiging *v.*; (*H.*) homologatie *v.*; *vt.* sanctionneren;

bekrachtigen, bevestigen, wettigen; (*H.*) homologeren.
sanctuary ['sæŋktjuəri] heiligdom *o.*; allerheiligste, sanctuarium *o.*; wijkplaats, vrijplaats *v.*, toevluchtsoord *o.*
sand [sænd] *sb.* zand *o.*; zandgrond *m.*; zandbank *v.*; zandkorrel *v.*; *the* —*s*, het strand; de woestijn.
sandal ['sændəl] sandaal *v.*
sandalwood ['sændəlwud] sandelhout *o.*
sand-bag ['sændbæg] zandzak *m.*
sand-bar ['sændbâ] zandbank *v.*, drempel *m.*
sand-glass ['sændglâs] zandloper *m.*
sand-paper ['sændpeipə] schuurpapier *o.*
sand-pit ['sændpit] zandgroeve, zanderij *v.*; (*voor kinderen*) zandkuil *m.*
sand-shoes ['sændʃûz] strandschoenen *m. mv.*
sandstone ['sændstoun] zandsteen *m.*
sandwich-man ['sændwitʃmæn] loper *m.* met reclamebord.
sandy ['sændi] zandig; zand—; rossig; los, onvast; (*Am.*) flink, ferm.
sane [sein] gezond (van geest); verstandig; bij zijn volle verstand.
sanguinariness ['sæŋgwinərinis] bloedigheid *v.*; bloeddorstigheid *v.*
sanguinary ['sæŋgwinəri] bloedig; bloeddorstig.
sanguine ['sæŋgwin] volbloedig; bloedig; bloedrood; vol vertrouwen, hoopvol, optimistisch.
sanguineous [sæŋ'gwiniəs] volbloedig, bloedrijk; bloedrood.
sanitary ['sænitəri] sanitair, gezondheids—; hygiënisch; — *board,* gezondheidscommissie.
sanitate ['sæniteit] assaineren, gezond maken, hygiënisch inrichten.
sanity ['sæniti] gezond verstand *o.*; gezondheid *v.* (van geest); toerekenbaarheid *v.*
sap [sæp] *sb.* sap, vocht *o.*; plantensap *o.*; (*v. boom*) spint *o.*; levenssap *o.*, kracht *v.*; (*sl.*) onnozele hals *m.*, groentje *o.*; (*mil.*) sappe; naderingsloopgraaf *v.*; sappering *v.*; (*fig.*) ondermijning *v.*; (*sl.*) blokker *m.*; karwei *o.*; *vt.* het sap ontrekken aan; het spint verwijderen van; (*fig.*) ondermijnen, uitputten, slopen; (*mil.*) ondergraven, ondermijnen; *vi.* sapperen, sappen graven; (*sl.*) blokken, vossen.
sapience ['seipiəns] wijsheid *v.*
sapper ['sæpə] (*mil.*) sappeur *m.*
sapphire ['sæfaiə] *sb.* saffier *m.* & *o.*; *adj.* saffierblauw.
sappy ['sæpi] sappig, saprijk; (*fig.*) onnozel, groen.
sarcastic(al) [sâ'kæstik(l)] *adj.* sarcastisch, spottend.
sardine [sâ'dîn] sardien, sardine *v.*
sash [sæʃ] sjerp *v.*; gordel *m.*; ceintuur *v.*; raam; schuifraam *o.*
sash-door ['sæʃdo:] glazen deur *v.*

sash-fastener ['sæʃfâsnə] raam-klink v.
satanic(al) [sə'tænik(l)] adj. satanisch, duivels.
satchel ['sætʃəl] zakje o.; boekentas v.
sateen [sə'tîn] satinet o.
satiable ['seiʃiəbl] verzadigbaar.
satiate ['seiʃiit] adj. verzadigd; beu; ['seiʃieit] vt. verzadigen.
satin ['sætin] sb. satijn o.; adj. satijnen; vt. satineren.
satire ['sætaiə] satire v., hekeldicht, hekelschrift o.
satirist ['sætirist] satiricus, hekeldichter m.
satirize ['sætiraiz] hekelen, over de hekel halen, doorhalen.
satisfaction [sætis'fækʃən] voldoening, genoegdoening v.; genoegen, tevredenheid v.
satisfactory [sætis'fæktəri] adj. bevredigend, voldoening schenkend.
satisfy ['sætisfai] vt. voldoen, voldoening geven; (v. nieuwsgierigheid, enz.) bevredigen; (v. honger, dorst) verzadigen, stillen: overtuigen; geruststellen; vr. — oneself, zijn genoegen eten; zich overtuigen, zich zekerheid verschaffen.
saturate ['sætʃəreit] verzadigen; doortrekken.
Saturday ['sætədi] zaterdag m.
sauce [so:s] sb. saus v.; tabakssaus v.; (Am.) groente v.; vruchten v. mv., moes o.; (fam.) brutaliteit v.; vt. sausen; kruiden; (fam.) brutaliseren.
sauce-boat ['so:sbout] sauskom v.
saucer ['so:sə] schoteltje, bordje o.
sauce-tureen ['so:stju'rîn] sauskom v.
saunter ['so:ntə] vi. drentelen, slenteren; sb. wandeling v., kuier m.; gedrentel o.; drentelpas, drentelgang m.
sausage ['sosidʒ] worst, saucijs v.; (mil.) observatieballon m.
sausage-roll ['sozidʒroul] saucijzebroodje o.
savage ['sævidʒ] adj. wild; woest; wreed, barbaars; (fam.) woest, woedend, razend; (wap.) naakt; sb. wilde m.; barbaar m.; woestaard m.; vt. wild (woest, woedend) maken; (fam.) mishandelen.
save [seiv] vt. redden, verlossen, zalig maken; behoeden behouden, bewaren; vrijhouden; vi. sparen, bezuinigen, zuinig zijn; sb. besparing, bezuiniging v.; prep. uitgezonderd. behalve; cj. tenzij.
saveloy ['sæviloi] cervelaatworst v.
saving ['seivin] adj. reddend, verlossend, zaligmakend; behoedend; spaarzaam, zuinig; sb. redding; verlossing v.; behoud o.; besparing v.; voorbehoud o.; uitzondering v.; —s, spaarpenningen; prep. behoudens, behalve, uitgezonderd.
savings-bank ['seivinbænk] spaarbank v.
Saviour ['seivjə] Zaligmaker, Heiland m.

savour ['seivə] sb. smaak m.; smakelijkheid v.; geur m., geurigheid v., aroma o.; bijsmaak m.; vt. kruiden; proeven, smaken, smaak vinden in; vi. — of, rieken naar; smaken naar; doen denken aan.
savourless ['seivəlis] smakeloos, flauw.
savoury ['seivəri] smakelijk; geurig; aangenaam; pikant.
savoy [sə'voi] savooiekool v.
saw [so:] sb. zaag v.; vt. zagen; doorzagen.
saw-bones ['so:bounz] (sl.) chirurg m.
sawdust ['so:dəst] zaagsel, zaagmeel o.
saw-horse ['so:ho:s] zaagbok m., zaagpaard o.
sawyer ['so:jə] zager m.
say [sei] vt. zeggen; opzeggen; vi. zeggen: (v. brief, enz.) luiden.
saying ['seiin] (het) zeggen o.; gezegde o., spreuk v.; spreekwoord o.
scab [skæb] sb. roof(je) v. (o.); schurft v.; (sl.) gemene kerel, ploert m.; (sl.) onderkruiper m.; vi. een roof vormen, korsten; (sl.) onderkruipen.
scabbard ['skæbəd] sb. schede v.; vt. in de schede steken, opsteken.
scabby ['skæbi] schurftig; (pop.) gemeen, schooierig.
scaffold ['skæfəld] sb. schavot o.; steiger m., stellage v.; vt. van een steiger voorzien; schragen, schoren.
scalawag ['skæləwæg] deugniet, rakker m.; schobbejak, schooier m.; intrigant m.; (sl.) werkschuwe m.
scald [sko:ld] sb. brandwond v.; hoofdzeer o.; vt. broeien, schroeien; met heet water branden; bijna tot het kookpunt verhitten.
scale [skeil] sb. schub, schilfer v.; tandsteen o.; ketelsteen o.; aanslag m.; vt. afschilferen; schubben, schrappen; pellen, doppen; (v. stoomketel) bikken, van ketelsteen ontdoen; (v. kanon) afblazen; vi. schilferen; — off, afbladderen.
scale [skeil] sb. weegschaal v.; vt. wegen.
scale [skeil] sb. schaal v.; toonschaal, toonladder v.; (rek.) talstelsel o.; maatstaf m.; graadverdeling v.; reeks v.; vt. beklimmen (met ladders); overklimmen; meten; op schaal tekenen.
scallop ['skoləp] sb. kammossel v.; schulp, schulpwerk o.; (voor pasteitje, enz.) schelp v.; vt. uitschulpen; in een schelp bakken.
scalpel ['skælpəl] ontleedmes o.
scamp [skæmp] rakker, deugniet m.; schelm, schurk m.
scamper ['skæmpə] vi. hollen, rennen; — away (off), er van door gaan; sb. geren o. galop m.
scandal ['skændl] schandaal o., schande v.; aanstoot m., ergernis v.; laster, achterklap m.
scandalize ['skændəlaiz] aanstoot geven, ergernis geven; belasteren.
scandal-monger ['skændəlmɔŋgə] kwaadspreker m.

scandalous(ly) ['skændələs(li)] *adj.* (*adv.*) schandelijk; lasterlijk; aanstootgevend, ergerlijk.

scant [skænt] *adj.* gering; schraal, karig, krap toegemeten; *vt.* bekrimpen, verminderen; krap houden.

scantling ['skæntliŋ] beetje *o.*, kleine hoeveelheid *v.*; staaltje, proefje *o.*; (voorgeschreven) maat, afmeting *v.*; kleine balk *m.*; (*sch.*) profiel *o.*

scanty ['skænti] *adj.* schraal, karig, krap, bekrompen, schaars.

scapegoat ['skeipgout] zondebok *m.*

scapegrace ['skeipgreis] rakker, (onverbeterlijke) deugniet *m.*

scar [skå] *sb.* schram *v.*; litteken *o.*; insnijding *v.*; (*fig.*) smet *v.*; papegaaivis *m.*; steile rotswand *m.*; klip *v.*; *vt.* schrammen; met littekens bedekken; *vi.* een litteken vormen; (*v. wond*) dichtgaan.

scarab ['skærəb] kever *m.*, tor *v.*

scarce [skêəs] *adj.* schaars, zeldzaam; *adv. zie* **scarcely.**

scarcely ['skêəsli] *adv.* nauwelijks, bijna niet, ternauwernood.

scarcity ['skêəsiti] schaarsheid, zeldzaamheid *v.*; schaarste *v.*, gebrek (**of**, **aan**).

scare [skêə] *vt.* doen schrikken, verschrikken, bang maken; afschrikken; **— away**, wegjagen; **— up**, opjagen; opsnorren, opscharrelen; *vi.* schrikken; *sb.* (plotselinge) schrik *m.*, paniek *v.*; bangmakerij *v.*

scarecrow ['skêəkrou] vogelverschrikker *m.*

scaremonger ['skêəmʌŋgə] alarmist *m.*

scarf [skåf] *sb.* sjaal, sjerp *v.*; ceintuur *v.*; (heren)das *v.*; las *m.*; lassing *v.* (van hout); *vt.* een sjaal (sjerp) omslaan (aandoen); (*v. hout*) lassen.

scarf-pin ['skåfpin] dasspeld *v.*

scarf-skin ['skåfskin] opperhuid *v.*

scarlatina [skålə'tinə] roodvonk *o.*, scharlakenkoorts *v.*

scarlet ['skålit] *sb.* scharlaken *o.*; *adj.* scharlakens, scharlakenrood.

scarp [skåp] *sb.* steile helling, glooiing *v.*

scathe ['skeiθ] *vt.* schaden, deren, beschadigen, letsel toebrengen; (*fig.*) vernietigen; *sb.* letsel *o.*

scatter ['skætə] *vt.* verstrooien, verspreiden; uitstrooien, rondstrooien; verdrijven, uiteendrijven, uiteenjagen; (*fig.: v. hoop, verwachting*) verijdelen, de bodem inslaan; *vi.* zich verstrooien, zich verspreiden; uiteengaan; *sb.* spreiding, uiteenspreiding; verspreiding *v.*; kleine verspreide hoeveelheid *v.*

scatter-brain ['skætəbrein] warhoofd *o.*

scavenger ['skævin(d)ʒə] straatveger, straatreiniger *m.*; aaskever *m.*; spoelpomp *v.*

scene [sin] toneel, tafereel *o.*; scherm *o.*; scène *v.*

scent [sent] *vt.* ruiken, de lucht krijgen van; doorgeuren, met geur vervullen; parfumeren; beruiken; *vi.* rieken; **— of,** rieken naar; doen denken aan; *sb.* reuk, geur *m.*; reukzin *m.*; (*v. wild*) lucht *v.*, spoor *o.*; (*fig.*) flair, fijne neus *m.*

scent-bottle ['sentbɔtl] reukflesje *o.*

scentless ['sentlis] reukeloos, zonder reuk.

sceptic ['skeptik] *adj.* sceptisch, twijfelend, twijfelzuchtig; *sb.* scepticus, twijfelaar *m.*

sceptre ['septə] schepter, staf *m.*

scheme [skim] *sb.* schema *o.*, schets *v.*, ontwerp *o.*; plan *o.*; oogmerk, voornemen *o.*; diagram *o.*; *vt.* ontwerpen, beramen; *vi.* plannen maken; intrigeren.

schism ['sizm] schisma *o.*, scheuring *v.*; afgescheiden sekte *v.*

scholar ['skɔlə] geleerde *m.*; scholier, leerling *m.*; beursstudent *m.*

scholarship ['skɔləʃip] geleerdheid *v.*; wetenschap *v.*; studiebeurs *v.*

scholastic [skɔ'læstik] scholastisch, schools; schoolmeesterachtig.

school [skûl] *sb.* school *v.*; schoolgebouw; schoollokaal *o.*; schooltijd *m.*; examenlokaal *o.*; *vt.* onderrichten, onderwijzen, leren; oefenen; (*v. paard*) africhten; vermanen, bestraffen, een lesje geven; **—ed,** geschoold; *vi.* (*v. vissen*) scholen, scholen vormen.

school-board ['skûlbo:d] schoolcommissie *v.*

school-fee(s) ['skûlfi(z)] schoolgeld *o.*

schooner ['skûnə] (*sch.*) schoener *m.*

science ['saiəns] wetenschap, kennis, kunde *v.*; natuurwetenschap(pen) *v.* (*mv.*); wis- en natuurkunde *v.*

scion ['saiən] ent, spruit *v.*

scissors ['sizəz] schaar *v.*; **a pair of —,** een schaar.

scoff [sko:f] *sb.* spot *m.*, bespotting, beschimping *v.*; schimpscheut *m.*; *vi.* spotten (**at,** met), schimpen (**at,** op); *vt.* (*sl.*) eten, verslinden, verorberen; (*sl.*) stelen; bespotting.

scoffer ['sko:fə] spotter *m.*

scoffing(ly) ['sko:fiŋ(li)] *adj.* (*adv.*) spottend.

scold [skould] *vi.* kijven (**at,** op); *vt.* bekijven, een standje maken, een uitbrander geven; *sb.* helleveeg, feeks *v.*

scolding ['skouldiŋ] standje *o.*, uitbrander *m.*

scoop [skûp] *sb.* (*v. waterrad*) schoep *v.*; (*v. baggermachine*) emmer, schepemmer *m.*; hoosvat *o.*; kaasboor *v.*; spatel *v.*; holte *v.*; (het) scheppen *o.*; (*sl.*) winstje, buitenkansje *o.*; *vt.* uitscheppen, uithozen; uithollen; bijeenschrapen; (*sl.: v. geld*) opstrijken, binnenhalen.

scooper ['skûpə] hozer *m.*; uitholler *m.*; schep *m.*; (*Dk.*) kluit *m.*

scope [skoup] speelruimte, vrijheid *v.* van beweging; (*v. voorstel, enz.*) strekking *v.*; gebied, terrein *o.*; gezichtskring *m.*, veld *o.* van werkzaamheid; (soms:) doel *o.*, bedoeling *v.*, oogmerk *o.*

scorch [skɔ:tʃ] *vt.* schroeien, verschroeien, verzengen; *vi.* schroeien; (*fig.: v. spot, enz.*) bijten; (*v. fietser, enz.*) woest rijden; *sb.* verzenging *v.*; verschroeide plek *v.*; woeste rit *m.*

score [skɔ:] *sb.* kerf, insnijding, keep *v.*; lijn, streep *v.*, dwarsstreepje *o.*; schram. kras; striem *v.*; rekening *v.*, gelag *o.*; (*muz.*) partituur *v.*; behaald aantal *o.* punten; (*fam.*) overwinning *v.*, succes *o.*; twintig, twintigtal *o.*; *vt.* inkerven, inkepen; opschrijven, optekenen, aantekenen; (*v. woord, enz.*) onderstrepen; doorhalen; (*muz.*) op noten zetten; boeken; schrammen, krassen; afschaven; (*sp.: v. punten*) behalen; *vi.* punten maken (behalen); succes behalen; het winnen.

scorn [skɔːn] *sb.* hoon *m.*, verachting, versmading *v.*; *vt.* verachten, versmaden.

scornful ['skɔːnful] *adj.* minachtend, verachtend, honend.

Scorpio ['skɔːpiou] (*sterr.*) Schorpioen *m.*

scorpion ['skɔːpiən] (*Dk.*) schorpioen *m.*; schorpioenvis *m.*

scorzonera [skɔːzo'nɪərə] schorseneer *v.*

scot [skɔt] (*gesch.*) belasting *v.*

scoundrel ['skaundrəl] *sb.* deugniet, fielt, schurk *m.*; *adj.* fieltachtig, schurkachtig, gemeen.

scour ['skauə] *vt.* schuren, wrijven; reinigen, zuiveren, schoonmaken; doorspoelen; (*v. wol*) wassen, ontvetten; (*v. bos, zee*) doorkruisen; (*v. zee*) schoonvegen; varen langs; doorzoeken, afzoeken; beschieten; *sb.* (het) schuren, enz.; (*in rivierbedding*) uitschuring; uitgeschuurde plaats *v.*; reinigingsmiddel *o.*

scourge [skə:dʒ] *sb.* roede *v.*, gesel *m.*, zweep *v.*; plaag *v.*; *vt.* tuchtigen, kastijden, geselen; teisteren.

scouring ['skauəriŋ] (het) schuren *o.*; reiniging, enz., zie **scour**; (*v. vee*) buikloop *m.*; **—s**, afschuursel *o.*; uitschot *o.*

scouring-drops ['skauəriŋdrɔps] vlekkenwater *o.*

scout [skaut] *sb.* verkenner, padvinder *m.*; spion *m.*; verkenningsvaartuig *o.*; verkenningsvliegtuig *o.*; verkenning *v.*; (*Dk.*) zeekoet *m.*, duikerhoen *o.*; papegaaiduiker *m.*; *vt.* verkennen; verachtelijk afwijzen (verwerpen); *vi.* op verkenning uitgaan; spieden.

scouting ['skautiŋ] verkenningsdienst *m.*; bespieding *v.*

scow [skau] *sb.* (*sch.*) schouw *v.*; *vt.* in een schouw vervoeren.

scowl [skaul] *vi.* het voorhoofd fronsen; boos kijken; *sb.* dreigende blik *m.*

scrabble ['skræbl] *vi.* krabben, krabbelen; scharrelen; schuifelen; grabbelen; klauteren; *vt.* krabbelen; *sb.* gekrabbel *o.*; gegrabbel *o.*; geklauter *o.*

scramble ['skræmbl] *vi.* grabbelen; klauteren; scharrelen; zich verdringen (**for**, om); *vt.* te grabbel gooien; *sb.*

gegrabbel *o.*; geklauter *o.*; gescharrel *o.*; gedrang *o.*; (*fig.*) wedloop *m.*

scrap [skræp] *sb.* brokje, stukje, beetje *o.*; snipper, vezel *m.*; uitknipsel *o.*; plakplaatje *o.*; oud ijzer, oud roest *o.*; (*vl.*) luchtgevecht *o.*; (*sl.*) ruzie, kloppartij *v.*; **—s**, afval; kliekjes; *vt.* afkeuren, afdanken, buiten dienst stellen; aan kant zetten; (*v. schip*) slopen; *vi.* vechten, bakkeleien.

scrape [skreip] *vt.* schrapen, afkrabben; schrappen, uitschrappen; (*op viool*) krassen, zagen; *vi.* schrapen; schuren; (*muz.*) krassen; **— along**, met moeite rondkomen, er door scharrelen; *sb.* gekrab *o.*; gekras *o.*; schram *v.*; kras *v.*; strijkvoetje *o.*; verlegenheid, moeilijkheid *v.*; (*pop.*) kloppartij *v.*

scrap-heap ['skræphip] hoop *m.*, oud roest, afval *m.*

scraping ['skreipiŋ] *adj.* schrapend; *sb.* geschraap *o.*; gekras *o.*; **—s**, afkrabsel *o.*; samenraapsel *o.*; (het) bijeengeschraapte *o.*; strijkvoetjes *o. mv.*

scratch [skrætʃ] *vt.* krabben; schrammen; terugtrekken; schrappen, doorhalen; bekrabbelen; (*v. lucifer*) aanstrijken; *vi.* krabben, krassen; krassen krijgen; (*bilj.*) beesten; (*v. scheermes*) trekken; *sb.* krab, krabbel, schram *v.*; gekras *o.*; (*sp.*) streep, meet *v.*; krassend geluid *o.*; (*bilj.*) beest *o.*; pruik *v.*; (*fam.*) kloppartij *v.*; schermutseling *v.*; *adj.* samengeraapt, bijeengeraapt, bijeengescharreld.

scratcher ['skrætʃə] krabber *m.*, krabijzer *o.*

scratch-wig ['skrætʃwig] pruik *v.*

scream [skrim] *vi.* gillen; gieren; het uitgillen, het uitschreeuwen; *vt.* gillen; **— out**, uitgillen; *sb.* gil *m.*

screamer ['skrimə] schreeuwer *m.*; (*Dk.*) gierzwaluw *v.*

screamy ['skrimi] *adj.* gillend; om te gieren: schreeuwerig, schril.

screech [skritʃ] *vi.* gillen, schreeuwen, krijsen; knarsen; *sb.* gil, schreeuw *m.*; gegil, geschreeuw *o.*

screech-owl ['skritʃaul] kerkuil *m.*; (*fig.*) ongeluksprofeet *m.*

screen [skrin] *sb.* scherm; schut *o.*; (*v. bioscoop*) doek *o.*, film *v.*; (*v. auto*) voorruit *v.*; koorhek *o.*; (*drukk.*) raster *m.*; grove zeef *v.*; traliewerk *o.*; beschutting, maskering *v.*; *vt.* beschermen, beschutten (**from**, voor, tegen); maskeren; ziften; schiften; (*radio*) afschermen; (*mil.*) dekken; verbergen; (*in bioscoop*) op het doek brengen, vertonen.

screw [skrû] *sb.* schroef *v.*; schroefboot *v.*; (*bilj.*) effect *o.*; kurketrekker *m.*; peperhuisje *o.* (vooral voor tabak); vrek, pingelaar *m.*; (*sl.*) loon, salaris *o.*; (*sl.*) loper *m.* (sleutel); (*sl.*) oude knol *m.*; **—s**, duimschroeven; *vt.* aanschroeven, vastschroeven; (*v. gezicht*) vertrekken, verwringen, verdraaien; uitzuigen, afzetten; afpersen; **— up**, vastschroeven, dichtschroeven; aanzetten; inrijgen; opschroeven, opvijzelen; (*fig.: v. huur, prijzen, enz.*) opdrijven; (*v. lippen*) samentrekken; (*v. gezicht*) vertrekken; *vi.* schroefsgewijs draaien; (*bilj.*) effect geven; schrapen, potten; afdingen.

screw-driver ['skrûdraivə] schroevedraaier *m.*

screw-eye ['skrûai] oogbout *m.,* schroefoog *o.*

screw-spanner ['skrûspænə] schroefsleutel, Engelse sleutel *m.*

screw-wrench ['skrûrenʃ] schroefsleutel, Engelse sleutel *m.*

scribble ['skribl] *vt.* krabbelen; bekrabbelen; (*v. wol*) schrobbelen, grof kaarden; *vi.* kribbelen, pennen; *sb.* gekribbel, krabbelschrift *o.*; (*fam.*) kattebelletje *o.*

script [skript] schrift *o.*; geschrift *o.*; (*ton.: v. rol*) manuscript, handschrift *o.*; (*drukk.*) schrijfletter *v.*; blokschrift *o.*

scrofulous ['skrofjuləs] klierachtig.

scroll [skroul] *sb.* rol *v.*; krul; krulversiering *v.*; (*aan zuil*) volute *v.*; *vt.* op de rol zetten (*v. akte*) grosseren; met krultrekken versieren.

scrub [skrəb] *sb.* struikgewas, kreupelhout *o.*; boender, schrobborstel, luiwagen *m.* stumper, stakker *m.*; dreumes *m.*; dwergplant *v.*; prul, vod *v.*; *vt.* schrobben, schuren, boenen dweilen; *vi.* zwoegen, ploeteren.

scrubber ['skrəbə] boender, schrobber, luiwagen *m.*

scrubby['skrəbi] *adj.* armzalig, miezerig, klein; borstelig; met struikgewas bedekt.

scruple ['skrûpl] *sb.* gemoedsbezwaar, gewetensbezwaar *o.*; angstvalligheid *v.*; scrupel *o.*; (*fig.*) greintje *o.*; *vi.* gewetensbezwaren hebben, zwarigheid maken; terugdeinzen voor; aarzelen, er tegen opzien.

scrupulosity [skrûpju'lositi] nauwgezetheid, angstvalligheid *v.*

scrupulous(ly) ['skrûpjuləs(li)] *adj.* (*adv.*) nauwgezet, angstvallig.

scrutinize['skrûtinaiz] nauwkeurig onderzoeken, navorsen.

scud [skəd] *vi.* hard lopen; wegsnellen; (*sch.*) lenzen; (*v. wolken*) ijlen, jagen; *sb.* vlucht *v.*, snelle loop *m.*, vaart *v.*; wolkenjacht *v.*; windvlaag *v.*; (*sl.*) hardloper *m.*

scuffle ['skəfl] *vi.* vechten, plukharen, bakkeleien; *sb.* vechtpartij, kloppartij *v.*, handgemeen *o.*

scull [skəl] *sb.* wrikriem *m.*; *vt.* & *vi.* wrikken.

scullery ['skələri] bijkeuken, achterkeuken *v.*

sculptor ['skəlptə] beeldhouwer *m.*

scum [skəm] *sb.* metaalschuim *o.*; (*fig.*) heffe *v.*, uitschot, schuim *o.*; *vt.* afschuimen; *vi.* schuim vormen.

scurf [skə:f] (*op hoofd*) roos *v.*; schilfertje *o.*; roofje *o.*; ketelsteen *o.*; (*sl.*) schooier *m.*; (*sl.*) onderkruiper *m.*

scurvy ['skə:vi] *sb.* scheurbuik *v.*; *adj.* aan scheurbuik lijdend; gemeen, schunnig, min.

scut [skət] stompstaartje *o.*; (*Am., sl.*) vent; lammeling *m.*

scutch [skətʃ] (*v. vlas*) zwingelen.

scutcheon ['skətʃən] (*wap.*) wapenschild *o.*; sleutelschild *o.*; naamplaat(je) *v.* (*o.*); (*sch.*) naambord *o.*

scuttle ['skətl] *sb.* kolenbak *m.*; (platte) mand *v.*; luik *o.*, klep *v.*; (*v. auto*) schulp *v.*; ren *m.*; overhaaste vlucht *v.*; *vt.* (*v. schip*) gaten boren in; aanboren; de kleppen openzetten; *vi.* hard lopen; er van door gaan; zich haastig terugtrekken.

scuttle-port ['skətlpo:t] (*sch.*) patrijspoort *v.*

scythe [saiθ] *sb.* zeis *v.*; *vt.* maaien.

sea [si] zee *v.*; stortzee *v.*; zeewater *o.,* *at* —, op zee.

sea-bank ['sibæŋk] zeedijk *m.*

sea-damaged ['sidæmidʒd] (*H.*) door zeewater beschadigd.

sea-dog ['sidog] hondshaai, zeehond *m.*; zeerob *m.*

sea-drome ['sidroum] drijvende luchthaven *v.*

sea-gull ['sigəl] kokmeeuw, zeemeeuw *v.*

sea-hog ['sihog] bruinvis *m.*; (*sl.*) snelvarende boot *v.*

seal [si:l] *sb.* zeehond, rob *m.*; robbevel *o.*; *vi.* op de robbevangst gaan (zijn).

seal [si:l] *sb.* zegel *o.*; stempel *m.*; (*op brief*) lak *o.*; bezegeling *v.*; (*v. riool*) afsluiting *v.*; *vt.* zegelen, verzegelen; stempelen; (*v. brief*) lakken; —*ed,* (*Am., sl.*) getrouwd.

sealing-wax ['si:liŋwæks] lak, zegellak *o.*

seal-ring ['si:lriŋ] zegelring *m.*

seam [si:m] *sb.* naad *m.*; litteken *o.,* diepe rimpel *m.*; dunne kolenlaag; mijnader *v.*; *vt.* aaneennaaien; met littekens bedekken; rimpelen; doorsnijden.

seaman ['si:mən] zeeman, matroos *m.*

sea-mew ['si:mjû] zeemeeuw *v.*

seamstress ['semstris] naaister *v.*

seamy ['si:mi] met naad, vol naden.

sea-plane ['si:plein] watervliegtuig *o.*

sea-port ['si:po:t] zeehaven *v.*

search [sə:tʃ] *vt.* onderzoeken, nasporen, navorsen; doorzoeken, visiteren, fouilleren; (*v. wond*) peilen, sonderen; onderzoekend aankijken; — *out,* uitvorsen; *vi.* zoeken; — *after,* zoeken (vorsen) naar; — *into,* onderzoeken, navorsen; *sb.* onderzoek *o.*; doorzoeking; visitatie *v.*; (*v. wind, enz.*) doordringendheid *v.*

search-light ['sə:tʃlait] zoeklicht *o.*

search-warrant ['sə:tʃwɔrənt] machtiging *v.* tot huiszoeking.

sea-rover ['si:rouvə] zeeschuimer *m.,* kaperschip *o.*

sea-salt ['si:so:lt] zeezout *o.*

sea-shore ['si:ʃo:] zeekust *v.*

seasick ['si:sik] zeeziek.

season ['sizn] *sb.* seizoen, jaargetijde *o.*; tijdperk *o.*; (geschikte) tijd *m.*; *vt.* toebereiden; kruiden, smakelijk maken; (*v. hout, enz.*) (laten) drogen; temperen; gewennen, acclimatiseren; (*v. pijp*) doorroken; *vi.* drogen; rijp worden.

seasonable ['siznəbl] *adj.* tijdig; geschikt, gepast; actueel.

seasonal ['siznəl] van 't seizoen, seizoen—.

seasoned ['siznd] toebereid; gekruid; gekonfijt; (*v. wijn, sigaren, enz.*) belegen; (*v. speler*) verstokt; (*v. persoon*) gehard; volleerd.

seasoning ['siznin] toebereiding *v.*; kruiderij *v.*

season-ticket ['sizn'tikit] abonnementskaart *v.*

seat [sit] *sb.* zitplaats *v.*; stoel, zetel *m.*; bank *v.*; zitting *v.*; (*v. W.C.*) bril *m.*; (*v. broek*) kruis *o.*; (*fam.*) zitvlak *o.*; ligging *v.*; *vt.* plaatsen, een plaats geven; neerzetten, doen zitten; (*v. stoel*) van een zitting voorzien; van zitplaatsen voorzien; (*v. broek*) een kruis zetten in; *vr.* — **oneself,** gaan zitten.

seaward(s) ['siwəd(z)] zeewaarts.

seaweed ['siwid] zeegras, zeewier *o.*

seaworthy ['siwə:θi] zeewaardig.

secant ['sikənt] *adj.* snijdend; *sb.* snijlijn *v.*

secede [si'sid] zich afscheiden, zich terugtrekken.

secession [si'seʃən] scheiding, afscheiding *v.*

secluded [si'klûdid] afgesloten; afgezonderd.

seclusion [si'klûʒən] uitsluiting *v.*; afzondering *v.*; eenzame plaats; afgesloten ligging *v.*

second ['sekənd] *adj.* tweede; ander; *adv.* in de tweede plaats, ten tweede; *sb.* nummer twee; (*H.*) secundawissel *m.*; (*muz.*) tweede stem *v.*; secondant; getuige *m.*; seconde *v.*; ogenblikje *o.*; *vt.* helpen, bijstaan, steunen; (*v. motie, enz.*) ondersteunen; (*bij duel*) seconderen; de tweede stem zingen bij.

secondary ['sekəndəri] *adj.* ondergeschikt, bijkomend; (*v. kleuren, enz.*) secundair; *sb.* afgevaardigde, gedelegeerde *m.*; satelliet *m.*; secondaire kleur *v.*

second-childish ['sekənd'tʃaildiʃ] kinds.

second-hand ['sekəndhænd] *adj.* tweedehands, gebruikt, oud; opgewarmd; *sb.* secondewijzer *m.*

second-rate ['sekəndreit] van de tweede rang, tweederangs—.

seconds-hand ['sekəndzhænd] secondewijzer *m.*

secrecy ['sikrəsi] stilzwijgen *o.*, geheimhouding *v.*; verborgenheid, heimelijkheid *v.*; geheim *o.*; eenzaamheid, afzondering *v.*

secret ['sikrit] *adj.* geheim; heimelijk, verborgen; geheimhoudend; vertrouwelijk; eenzaam; *sb.* geheim *o.*

secretary ['sekritəri] secretaris, geheimschrijver *m.*; minister *m.*; secretaire, schrijftafel *v.*; (*Dk.*) secretaris(vogel) *m.*

secrete [si'krit] verbergen, verhelen; verduisteren, ontfutselen; geheimhouden; verheimelijken; afscheiden (uit het bloed, enz.); afzonderen.

secretion [si'kriʃən] verberging, heling *v.*; verduistering *v.*; geheimhouding *v.*; afscheiding *v.*

secretive(ly) [si'kritiv(li)] *adj. (adv.)* heimelijk; geheimhoudend, gesloten; geheimzinnig (doend); afscheidend, de afscheiding bevorderend; (*v. ogen*) sluw.

secretly ['sikritli] *adv.* in 't geheim; heimelijk; in stilte.

sect [sekt] secte *v.*

section ['sekʃən] *sb.* opensnijding, sectie *v.*; onderdeel *o.*, afdeling, paragraaf *v.*; doorsnede *v.*, profiel *o.*; baanvak, traject *o.*; (*Beurs*) hoek *m.*; *vt.* in secties verdelen.

sector ['sektə] sector *m.*; hoekmeter *m.*

secular ['sekjulə] *adj.* seculair; honderdjarig; eeuwenoud; eens in een eeuw plaatshebbend; eeuwen durend; (*v. roem*) onvergankelijk; wereldlijk, nietkerkelijk; (*v. geestelijke*) wereldlijk, seculier; *sb.* wereldgeestelijke, seculier priester *m.*; leek *m.*

secure [si'kjûə] *adj.* zeker; veilig; vast, stevig, verzekerd; *vt.* beveiligen; in veiligheid brengen; vastleggen; (*v. kisten, enz.*) versterken; waarborgen, verzekeren; (*v. plaats*) bespreken; zich verschaffen, sluiten, grendelen; opsluiten; *vr.* — **oneself against,** zich vrijwaren voor.

security [si'kjûəriti] veiligheid *v.*; bescherming *v.*; waarborg *m.*; pandbrief *m.*; **securities,** ook: obligaties, effecten, fondsen.

sedate(ly) [si'deit(li)] *adj. (adv.)* rustig, kalm, bezadigd.

sedative ['sedətiv] *adj.* kalmerend, pijnstillend; *sb.* kalmerend (pijnstillend) middel *o.*

sediment ['sedimənt] droesem *m.*, bezinksel *o.*, neerslag *m.*

sedition [si'diʃən] opruiing *v.*; opstand *m.*; muiterij *v.*

seditious(ly) [si'diʃəs(li)] *adj. (adv.)* opruiend; oproerig.

seduce [si'djûs] verleiden; verlokken.

seducer [si'djûsə] verleider *m.*

seducing(ly) [si'djûsin(li)] *adj. (adv.)* verleidelijk, aanlokkelijk.

seduction [si'dəkʃən] verleiding, verlokking *v.*; verleidelijkheid *v.*

seductive(ly) [si'dəktiv(li)] *adj. (adv.)* verleidend, verlokkend; verleidelijk.

sedulous ['sedjuləs] *adj.* ijverig, naarstig, nijver.

see [si] *sb.* (aarts)bisschopszetel *m.*

see [si] *vt.* zien; inzien; begrijpen; bezoeken, opzoeken; ontvangen; zich

voorstellen; beleven; (*v. dokter*) raadplegen; (*mil.*) bestrijken. *vi.* zien, kijken;
seed [sid] *sb.* zaad *o.*; zaadje *o.*; (*v. vis*)
kuit *v.*; (*fig.*) kiem *v.*, zaad *o.*; (*fig.*)
verlopen, in verval geraken; (*v. tuin,
enz.*) verwilderen; *vt.* zaaien, bezaaien;
van de zaden ontdoen; *vi.* in het zaad
schieten.
seed-cake ['sidkeik] kruidkoek *m.*;
lijnkoek *m.*
seedless ['sidlis] zaadloos.
seed-time ['sidtaim] zaaitijd *m.*
seek [sik] *vt.* zoeken; opzoeken; afzoeken, doorzoeken; trachten; — *out,*
opzoeken, opsporen; *vi.* zoeken.
seem [sim] schijnen, lijken.
seeming ['simiŋ] *sb.* schijn *m.*; *adj.*
schijnbaar, ogenschijnlijk.
seemly ['simli] *adj.* betamelijk, gepast;
bevallig, statig, mooi.
seer ['siə] ziener, profeet *m.*
seesaw ['si'so:] *adj.* op- en neer-
gaand; schommelend; afwisselend: *sb.*
op- en neergaande beweging; schommeling *v.*; wip, wipplank *v.*; *vi.* wippen;
op- en neer gaan; (*fig.*) schommelen.
seethe [siθ] *vt.* & *vi.* zieden, koken;
sb. (het) zieden, (het) koken *o.*
segment ['segmənt] *sb.* segment, deel
o.; (*v. insekt*) lid *o.*; *vt.* verdelen; *vi.*
zich splijten.
seizable ['sizəbl] grijpbaar, te vatten.
seize [siz] *vt.* grijpen, vatten, pakken;
beslag leggen op, in beslag nemen; begrijpen, snappen; bemachtigen, in bezit
nemen; (*v. stad*) nemen; (*v. schip*) opbrengen; (*sch.*) sjorren; *vi.* (*v. motor*)
vastlopen.
seizure ['sizə] beslaglegging *v.*; arrestatie *v.*; bezitneming *v.*; (*v. ziekte*) plotselinge aanval *m.*; beroerte *v.*; vlaag *v.*;
overmeestering, overrompeling *v.*
seldom ['seldəm] zelden.
select [si'lekt] *adj.* uitgelezen, uitgekozen, uitgezocht; keurig; kieskeurig; *vt.*
kiezen, uitkiezen.
selection [si'lekʃən] keur, keus *v.*; se-
lectie *v.*; teeltkeus *v.*
selective(ly) [si'lektiv(li)] *adj.* (*adv.*)
uitkiezend, uitzoekend; (*radio*) selectief, vrij van storingen.
selectivity [silek'tiviti] (het) uitkiezen,
(het) uitzoeken *o.*; (*radio*) selectiviteit *v.*
self [self] *adj.* zelfde; (*v. kleur*) uniform;
sb. persoon; eigen persoon *m.*; het „ik";
zelfzucht, eigenliefde *v.*
self-acting ['selfæktiŋ] automatisch.
self-command ['selfkə'mând] zelfbeheersing *v.*
self-conceit ['selfkən'sit] eigendunk
m., laatdunkendheid, verwaandheid *v.*
self-conceited ['selfkən'sitid] laatdunkend, verwaand.
self-conscious ['self'kənʃəs] bedeesd,
verlegen; (soms:) zelfbewust.
self-control ['selfkən'troul] zelfbeheersing *v.*

self-defence ['selfdi'fens] zelfverdediging *v.*; (*recht*) noodweer *v.*
self-denial ['selfdi'naiəl] zelfverloochening *v.*; zelfonthouding *v.*
self-determination ['selfditə:mi'nei-
ʃən] zelfbeschikking, zelfbestemming *v.*
self-esteem ['selfis'tim] gevoel *o.* van
eigenwaarde.
self-evident ['self'evidənt] vanzelf-
sprekend; klaarblijkelijk.
self-government ['self'gəvənmənt]
zelfbestuur *o.*
self-interest ['self'int(ə)rist] eigenbelang *o.*
selfish ['selfiʃ] zelfzuchtig, egoïstisch,
baatzuchtig.
selfishness ['selfiʃnis] zelfzucht *v.*,
egoïsme *o.*, baatzucht *v.*
self-love ['self'lʌv] eigenliefde *v.*
self-made ['self'meid; *attr.*: 'selfmeid]
eigengemaakt.
self-possession ['selfpə'zeʃən] zelfbeheersing, kalmte *v.*
self-praise ['self'preiz] eigenlof *m.*
self-styled ['self'staild] zich noemend,
zogenaamd, voorgewend.
self-supporting ['selfsə'po:tiŋ] in eigen behoeften voorziend.
self-will ['self'wil] eigenzinnigheid, koppigheid *v.*
self-willed ['self'wild] eigenzinnig, koppig.
sell [sel] *vt.* verkopen; uitverkopen;
verraden; (*sl.*) bedriegen, beetnemen,
verlakken; (*Am.*) aanpraten; *vi.* verkopen; verkocht worden, van de hand
gaan; — *off,* liquideren; *sb.* (*sl.*) beetnemerij, verlakkerij, afzetterij *v.*
selling-off ['seliŋ'o:f] uitverkoop *m.*;
liquidatie *v.*
selvage, selvedge ['selvidʒ] *sb.* zelfkant *m.*; *vt.* van een zelfkant voorzien.
semblance ['sembləns] schijn *m.*, voorkomen *o.*; gelijkenis *v.*
semen ['simən] (*Dk.*) zaad, sperma *o.*
semi ['semi] half—.
semicolon ['semi'koulən] puntkom-
ma *v.*
seminary ['seminəri] seminarie *o.*;
kweekschool *v.*; (*fig.*) broeinest *o.*
semolina [semə'linə] griesmeel *o.*
senate ['senit] senaat; raad *m.*; (*Am.*)
Hogerhuis *o.*
send [send] *vt.* & *vi.* zenden, sturen;
afzenden, verzenden; *sb.* golfbeweging
v.; stuwkracht *v.*
sender ['sendə] zender *m.*; afzender *m.*;
inzender *m.*; (*telegr.*) seingever *m.*;
(*telef.*) microfoon *v.*
senile ['sinail] seniel, van de oude dag,
ouderdoms—.
sensation [sen'seiʃən] gevoel *o.*, gewaarwording, aandoening *v.*; opschudding,
beroering *v.*, opzien *o.*, sensatie *v.*
sensational [sen'seiʃənəl] *adj.* gewaar-
wordings—, zinnelijk; sensationeel, opzienbarend.
sense [sens] *sb.* gevoel *o.*; begrip, besef

o.; zin *m.*; verstand *o.*; gevoelen *o.*; onderscheidingsvermogen *o.*; *vt.* voelen, gewaar worden; merken, zich bewust worden van; begrijpen.

senseless(ly) ['senslis(li)] *adj.* (*adv.*) gevoelloos, bewusteloos; onverstandig, dwaas, onzinnig, redeloos.

sense-organ ['senso:gən] zintuig *o.*

sensible ['sensibl] gevoelig; merkbaar, waarneembaar; verstandig; bij (volle) kennis, bij zijn verstand; zich bewust (*of*, van).

sensitive ['sensitiv] *adj.* gevoelig; fijngevoelig, teergevoelig; gevoels—; *sb.* sensitief persoon, overgevoelige *m.*

sensitiveness ['sensitivnis] gevoeligheid *v.*

sensual ['senʃuəl] *adj.* zinnelijk; wellustig; sensualistisch; materialistisch.

sensualism ['senʃuəlizm] zinnelijkheid *v.*; sensualisme *o.*

sensuality [senʃu'æliti] zinnelijkheid *v.*

sensuous(ly) ['senʃuəs(li)] *adj.* (*adv.*) van de zinnen, zinnelijk; tot de zinnen sprekend; de zinnen strelend.

sentence ['sentəns] *sb.* vonnis; oordeel *o.*, uitspraak *v.*; zin, volzin *m.*; spreuk, zinspreuk *v.*; *vt.* vonnissen, veroordelen.

sentiment ['sentimənt] gevoel *o.*; gevoelen *o.*, gedachte *v.*; gevoeligheid, sentimentaliteit *v.*; (*op de Beurs*) stemming *v.*; toost *m.*

sentimental [senti'mentəl] *adj.* (overdreven) gevoelig, sentimenteel; gevoels—.

sentinel ['sentinəl] *sb.* (*mil.*) schildwacht *m.*; *vt.* bewaken; laten bewaken (door een schildwacht); (als schildwacht) plaatsen, op post zetten.

sentry ['sentri] schildwacht *m.*

sentry-box ['sentriboks] schilderhuisje *o.*

sentry-go ['sentrigou] (het) schilderen *o.*, wacht *v.*; *do —*, schilderen; (*fig.*) ijsberen.

separable ['sepərəbl] *adj.* scheidbaar.

separate ['sepərit] *adj.* afgescheiden, afzonderlijk; *sb.* (afzonderlijke) afdruk *m.*; ['sepəreit] *vt.* scheiden; afscheiden; afzonderen; verdelen; (*in factoren, enz.*) ontbinden; *vi.* scheiden (*from*, van); uiteengaan, vaneengaan; weggaan, heengaan; zich afscheiden.

separately ['sepəritli] *adv.* afzonderlijk, apart.

separation [sepə'reiʃən] scheiding *v.*; afscheiding *v.*; afzondering *v.*

separatum [sepə'reitəm] (afzonderlijke) afdruk *m.*

September [sep'tembə] september *m.*

septum ['septəm] (*Pl., Dk.*) tussenschot *o.*

sequacious [si'kweiʃəs] volgzaam; logisch, samenhangend.

sequel ['sikwəl] vervolg *o.*; gevolg, resultaat *o.*; afloop *m.*; naspel *o.*; nawerking *v.*

sequence ['sikwəns] opeenvolging *v.*;

volgorde *v.*; reeks, serie *v.*; (*kath.*) sequentie *v.*; (*muz.*) sequens *v.*; diatonische toonladder *v.*; (*gram.: v. tijden*) overeenstemming *v.*; (*kaartsp.*) volgkaarten *v. mv.*

serenade [seri'neid] *sb.* serenade *v.*; *vt.* een serenade brengen.

serene(ly) [si'rin(li)] *adj.* (*adv.*) helder, klaar; onbewolkt; rustig, kalm, bedaard; doorluchtig.

serenity [si'reniti] helderheid, klaarheid *v.*; kalmte *v.*; doorluchtigheid *v.*

serge [sə:dʒ] serge *v.*

sergeant ['sâdʒənt] (*mil.*) sergeant *m.*

series ['siər(i)iz] reeks, serie, opeenvolging *v.*

serious ['siəriəs] *adj.* ernstig; bedenkelijk; vroom, godsdienstig; stemmig; degelijk, solide.

sermon ['sə:mən] preek, predikatie; leerrede *v.*; vermaning *v.*

serpent ['sə:pənt] slang *v.*; (*muz.*) serpent *o.*; voetzoeker, zwermer *m.*

servant ['sə:vənt] knecht, bediende *m.*; dienaar *m.*; meid, dienstbode *v.*; dienares *v.*; (*mil.*) oppasser *m.*; beambte, ambtenaar *m.*

servant-girl ['sə:vəntgə:l] dienstmeisje *o.*, dienstmeid *v.*

serve [sə:v] *vt.* dienen; bedienen; helpen, baten, dienstig zijn; voldoen aan; (*v. maaltijden*) opdienen, opdoen; (*v. dranken*) schenken; (*sch.: v. touw*) bekleden, omwoelen; behandelen; (*v. dagvaarding*) betekenen; dagvaarden; (*sp.: tennis, enz.*) serveren; *vi.* dienen; dienstig zijn; (*sp.*) serveren.

service ['sə:vis] *sb.* dienst *m.*; dienstbaarheid *v.*; tak *m.* van dienst; dienstverrichting *v.*; bediening *v.*; kerkdienst *m.*; *vt.* dienen; bedienen; (*v. auto, enz.*) verzorgen.

serviceable ['sə:visəbl] *adj.* dienstig, bruikbaar; geschikt, nuttig; dienstvaardig.

serviette [sə:vi'et] servet *v.*

servile ['se:vail] slaafs, onderworpen, kruiperig.

servitude ['sə:vitjûd] dienstbaarheid, slavernij *v.*; (*recht*) servituut *o.*

session ['seʃən] zitting *v.*; zittingstijd *m.*

set [set] *vt.* zetten, plaatsen; leggen; schikken; (*v. klok*) gelijkzetten; (*v. scheermes*) aanzetten; (*v. zeil*) bijzetten; (*v. toon, maat, enz.*) aangeven; (*v. tijd, enz.*) vaststellen, bepalen; (*v. taak, enz.*) opgeven; aanhitsen, aanzetten; (*v. wacht, netten*) uitzetten; (*v. tafel*) dekken; zaaien; planten, poten; (*v. eieren*) laten uitbroeden; (*v. steen*) vatten, zetten; *vi.* dik worden, vast worden, stollen; (*v. karakter*) zich vormen; (*v. boom*) vruchten vormen; (*v. vrucht, bloesem*) zich zetten; (*v. zon*) ondergaan; (*v. roem*) tanen; (*v. gezicht*) een harde uitdrukking aannemen; (*v. jachthond*) staan, blijven staan voor; (*v. kledingstuk*) zitten, vallen; *— about,* beginnen,

aanpakken; (*v. geruchten, enz.*) verspreiden; — *in*, (*v. vloed*) opkomen; (*v. dooi, duisternis*) invallen; (*v. jaargetijde, enz.*) intreden; — *off*, aan de gang maken; (*v. kleur, schoonheid, enz.*) doen uitkomen, verhogen; (*v. vuurwapen*) doen afgaan; (*v. geld*) afzonderen; (*drukk.*) beginnen te zetten; (*v. honden*) loslaten; — *up*, plaatsen; opstellen, oprichten, overeind zetten; instellen; (*v. zieke*) weer op de been helpen; (*v. ziekte*) veroorzaken; (*v. verontschuldiging*) aanvoeren; (*v. boek, enz.*) zetten; (*v. kreet*) aanheffen; (*v. wagen, enz.*) zich aanschaffen; aanplakken; uitrusten; *vr.* — *oneself against,* zich verzetten tegen; — *oneself up to,* zich opwerpen om; *sb.* stel *o.*; span *o.*; garnituur *o.*; bende, ploeg *v.*; reeks *v.*; partij *v.*; (*v. ketels*) batterij *v.*; toestel *o.*; installatie *v.*; stek, loot, jonge plant *v.,* zaailing *m.*, afzetsel *o.*; kring *m.*; vruchtknop *m.*; (*v. getij, enz.*) richting *v.*; (*v. zon*) ondergang *m.*; (*v. grond*) verzakking *v.*; het (zich) zetten *o.*; (*v. kleding*) (het) zitten *o.*, snit *m.*; (*v. hoofd, enz.*) houding *v.*; vierkante straatsteen *m.*; (*ton.*) toneelschikking *v.*; vaste gewoonte *v.*; geestesrichting *v.*; *adj.* gezet; vast; vastgesteld; star, strak, onveranderlijk; (*v. gelaat*) strak, onbeweeglijk; (*v. lippen*) op elkaar geklemd; (*v. bezoek, enz.*) formeel, officieel; voorgeschreven; (*Am.*) koppig, hardnekkig.
set-back [ˈsetbæk, setˈbæk] terugzetting, achteruitzetting *v.*; teruggang, achteruitgang *m.*; tegenslag *m.*
set-down [ˈsetˈdaun] standje *o.*, uitbrander *m.*
set-off [ˈsetˈoːf] versiering *v.*, versiersel *o.*; tegenstelling *v.*, contrast *o.*; tegenhanger *m.*; tegenvordering *v.*; vergoeding, compensatie *v.*; korting *v.*
settee [seˈtiː] zitbank, canapé, sofa *v.*
setter-on [setəˈrɔn] aanhitser, opstoker *m.*
setting [ˈsetiŋ] zetting, invatting *v.*; montering *v.*; montuur *v.*; omgeving, omlijsting *v.*, achtergrond *m.*; toonzetting *v.*
settele [ˈsetl] *sb.* zitbank *v.* met hoge leuning; *vt.* vestigen, stichten; vastzetten; (*v. land*) koloniseren; (*v. kamer*) op orde brengen; (*v. zaak*) beklinken, regelen, oplossen; tot bedaren brengen, doen bedaren; (*v. vloeistof*) klaren: doen bezinken; (*v. rekening*) vereffenen, afdoen; (*v. geschil*) bijleggen; (*v. dochters*) aan de man brengen; besluiten; beslissen; (*v. kleren*) in orde schikken, terecht schikken; de mond snoeren; *vi.* zich vestigen; zich neerzetten, gaan zitten (liggen); tot rust komen; verzakken; neerdalen, neerstrijken (**on,** op); een vaste vorm aannemen; (*v. schip*) langzaam zinken; afrekenen; *vr.* — *oneself,* gaan zitten; zich vestigen.
settlement [ˈsetlmənt] vestiging, volks-

planting *v.*; nederzetting *v.*; kolonisatie *v.*; regeling *v.*; (*Beurs*) rescontre *o.*; uitkering *v.*, jaargeld *o.*, lijfrente *v.*; schenking *v.*; bezinking *v.*; aardschuiving, verzakking *v.*; liquidatie *v.*; vaste woonplaats *v.*
settler [ˈsetlə] kolonist *m.*; (*tn.*) klaarpan *v.*; beslissend woord *o.*, dooddoener *m.*; (*fam.*) afzakkertje *o.*
settlings [ˈsetliŋz] bezinksel *o.*, droesem *m.*
seven [ˈsevn] zeven.
seventeen [ˈsevnˈtin; sevntin] zeventien.
seventy [ˈsevnti] zeventig.
sever [ˈsevə] *vt.* scheiden, afscheiden; afsnijden, afhakken; afscheuren; verdelen; *vi.* uit elkaar gaan; *vr.* — *oneself from,* zich afscheiden van.
several [ˈsevrəl] *adj.* verscheiden; onderscheiden; afzonderlijk; respectief; eigen; *pron.* verscheidene, velen.
severance [ˈsevərəns] scheiding, afscheiding; losmaking *v.*; scheuring *v.*; verdeling *v.*; afzondering *v.*
severe [siˈviə] *adj.* streng, gestreng; (*v. pijn*) hevig; (*v. slag, verlies*) zwaar; (*v. stijl*) sober; (*v. concurrentie*) scherp.
severity [siˈveriti] strengheid, enz.
sew [sou] naaien; aannaaien, aanzetten; (*v. boek*) brocheren; — *up,* (*v. wond*) dichtnaaien.
sewer [ˈsouə] *sb.* kleermaker *m.*; naaister *v.*
sewer [ˈsjûə] *sb.* riool *o.*; waterlozing *v.*; *vt.* rioleren.
sewing-bee [ˈsouiŋbī] naaikransje *o.*
sewing-machine [ˈsouiŋməʃīn] naaimachine *v.*
sex [seks] geslacht *o.*, sekse, kunne *v.*
sexton [ˈsekstən] koster *m.*; doodgraver *m.*
sexual [ˈsekʃuəl] *adj.* geslachtelijk, seksueel.
shabby [ˈʃæbi] *adj.* kaal, haveloos; schraal; armzalig; krenterig; gemeen, schandelijk; (*v. polsslag*) zwak.
shabrack [ˈʃæbræk] sjabrak *v.*
shackle [ˈʃækl] *sb.* (*tn.*) beugel *m.*, koppeling; schakel *v.*; (*sch.*) sluiting, ankersluiting *v.*; —(**s**), boei(en), kluister(s) *v.* (*mv.*); (*fig.*) belemmering *v.*; *vt.* (*tn.*) koppelen; boeien, kluisteren; (*fig.*) belemmeren.
shad [ʃæd] elft *m.* & *v.*
shade [ʃeid] *sb.* schaduw *v.*; lommer *v.* & *o.*; schaduwzijde *v.*; schim *v.*; schakering, tint *v.*; zweem *m.*; kap, lampekap *v.*; stolp *v.*; scherm, oogscherm *o.*; (*Am.*) gordijn *o.*; —**s,** ook de schimmenrijk *o.*; duisternis *v.*; *vt.* schaduwen; beschaduwen; overschaduwen; in de schaduw stellen; verduisteren; arceren; beschutten, beschermen; temperen; van een scherm voorzien; *vi.* — *off into,* (*v. kleuren, enz.*) onmerkbaar (langzaam) overgaan in.
shadiness [ˈʃeidinis] schaduwrijkheid,

lommerrijkheid v.; (fig.) dubbelzinnigheid v.

shadow ['ʃædou] sb. schaduw v.; schaduwbeeld o.; afschaduwing v., evenbeeld o.; schim v., geest m.; schijn m., spoor o., zweem m.; vt. schaduwen; als een schaduw volgen; beschaduwen, overschaduwen; afschaduwen.

shadowgraph ['ʃædougrâf, —græf] schaduwbeeld o.

shady ['ʃeidi] adj. schaduwrijk, beschaduwd; lommerig, belommerd; (fig.) verdacht, twijfelachtig, onbetrouwbaar.

shaft [ʃâft] schacht v.; mijnschacht v.; pijl m.; werpspies v.; lamoenstok, lamoenboom m.; vlaggestok m.; (tn.) drijfas v.; liftkoker m.

shaggy ['ʃægi] adj. ruig, ruigharig, borstelig.

shagreen ['sʃəgrîn] sb. segrijnleder o.; adj. segrijnen.

shake [ʃeik] vt. schudden, schokken; (fig.) schokken, doen wankelen; roeren, indruk maken op; wakker schudden; uitschudden; uitslaan; van zich afschudden; (Am.: v. gewoonle, enz.) opgeven; (v. persoon) laten schieten; vi. schudden, wankelen; beven, trillen, vibreren; — **together,** (goed) met elkaar opschieten, met elkaar overweg kunnen; sb. (het) schudden o.; handdruk m.; schok m.; beving v.; ruk m.; (muz.) triller m.; (v. stem) trilling v.

shaky ['ʃeiki] adj. beefachtig, beverig; onvast, wankel; onzeker, onbetrouwbaar; (fig.) zwak; (v. hout) vol scheuren.

shall [ʃæl, ʃəl] zal, zullen; moet, moeten.

shallop ['ʃæləp] sloep v.

shallot [ʃə'lɔt] sjalot v.

shallow ['sælou] adj. ondiep; laag; (fig.) oppervlakkig; hol; sb. ondiepte, ondiepe plaats, zandbank v.; (platte) venterskar; platte mand v.; vt. (vi.) ondiep(er) maken (worden).

shallow-brained ['sæloubreind] hersenloos, leeghoofdig, oppervlakkig, dom.

sham [ʃæm] vt. voorwenden, veinzen, simuleren; bedriegen; misleiden; vi. simuleren, doen alsof; zich aanstellen; sb. voorwendsel o.; schijn m., komedie v.; bedotterij v.; veinzer, simulant, komediant m.; bedrieger m.; adj. voorgewend, gefingeerd; nagemaakt; (v. deur) blind; (v. cheque) vals.

shamble ['ʃæmbl] vi. sloffen, schuifelend lopen; waggelend gaan; sb. sloffende gang m., geslof o.

shame [ʃeim] sb. schaamte v.; schande v.; vt. beschamen, beschaamd maken; te schande maken; vi. zich schamen.

shamefaced ['ʃeimfeist] adj. schaamachtig; beschaamd, verlegen, bedeesd, beschroomd.

shameful(ly) ['ʃeimful(i)] adj. (adv.) schandelijk.

shameless(ly) ['ʃeimlis(li)] adj. (adv.) schaamteloos, onbeschaamd.

sham-fight ['ʃæmfait] spiegelgevecht o.

shammer ['ʃæmə] veinzer; komediant; simulant m.

shammy ['ʃæmi] sb. gemzeleer, zeemleer o.; adj. zeemleren.

shank [ʃæŋk] been; scheenbeen o.; beenpijp v.; (Pl.) steel, stengel m.; (v. zuil, anker, enz.) schacht v.; (v. sleutel) pijp, schacht v.

shanty ['ʃænti] hut v.; loods, keet v.; kroeg v.

shape [ʃeip] vt. vormen; maken; modelleren, fatsoeneren; pasklaar maken; inrichten, regelen; vi. zich vormen: zich fatsoeneren; een zekere vorm aannemen; zich ontwikkelen; sb. vorm m.; gedaante, gestalte v.; leest v.; model, fatsoen o.; blok o.

shapeless ['ʃeiplis] vormeloos; wanstaltig.

share [ʃêə] sb. deel o.; aandeel o.; portie v.; ploegschaar v.; vt. delen (**with,** met); verdelen (**between,** onder); vi. delen (**in,** in), deelnemen (**in,** aan).

shareholder ['ʃêəhouldə] aandeelhouder m.

share-out ['ʃêəaut] verdeling v.; uitkering v.

sharer ['ʃêərə] deelnemer, deelhebber m.

shark [ʃâk] sb. (Dk.) haai v.; (fig.) afzetter; gauwdief m.; zwendelaar m.; vt. opslokken; kapen; gappen; afzetten, bedriegen; — **up,** bijeenscharrelen.

sharp [ʃâp] adj. scherp, puntig, spits; hevig, vinnig; bits; bijtend; vlug, gezwind; pienter, glad, slim; scherpzinnig; schel, snijdend; adv. scherp; vlug, gauw; plotseling; sb. (muz.) kruis o., noot v. met een kruis; scherpe medeklinker m.; —**s,** fijne naalden v. mv.; grintmeel o.; vt. scherp maken; (muz.) een halve toon verhogen; afzetten; vi. stelen, gappen; (bij spel) bedriegen.

sharpen ['ʃâpn] scherpen, scherp maken.

sharper ['ʃâpə] bedrieger, afzetter; gauwdief m.

sharpness ['ʃâpnis] scherpte, scherpheid v.

sharp-shooter ['ʃâpʃûtə] scherpschutter m.

sharp-sighted ['ʃâp'saitid] scherp van gezicht, scherpziend, scherpzinnig.

sharp-witted ['ʃâp'witid] scherpzinnig, schrander.

shatter ['ʃætə] vt. verbrijzelen, verpletteren, versplinteren; (fig.) vernietigen; in de war brengen; ontredderen; (v. gestel) ondermijnen; (v. zenuwen) schokken; (v. vijand) verstrooien, uiteenjagen; vi. in stukken vallen, uiteenvallen; versplinteren.

shattery ['ʃætəri] broos, licht breekbaar.

shave [ʃeiv] vt. scheren; afscheren; schaven; snijden, afsnijden; (v. voortbrengst) beperken, verminderen; vi. zich scheren;

— *through,* er net doorkomen; de dans ontspringen; *sb.* (het) scheren *o.*; sneetje *o.*; spaander *m.*; schaafmes *o.*; afzetterij *v.*

shaving ['ʃeiviŋ] (het) scheren *o.*; afscheersel *o.*; snipper, spaander *m.*; **—s,** schavelingen, krullen.

shaving-bowl ['ʃeiviŋboul] scheerbakje *o.*

shaving-brush ['ʃeiviŋbrəʃ] scheerkwast *m.*

shaving-set ['ʃeiviŋset] scheergerei *o.*

shaving-soap ['ʃeiviŋsoup] scheerzeep *v.*

shawl [ʃɔ:l] sjaal *v.*, omslagdoek *m.*

sheaf [ʃif] schoof *v.*; bundel *m.*

shear [ʃiə] (*v. dieren, laken*) scheren; (*v. metalen*) knippen.

shears ['ʃiəz] grote schaar *v.*

sheath [ʃiθ] schede *v.*; (*Pl.*) bladschede *v.*

she-bear ['ʃi'bêə] berin *v.*

shed [ʃed] *sb.* loods *v.*, schuurtje *o.*, keet *v.*; afdak *o.*; kooi, schaapskooi *v.*

shed [ʃed] *vt.* (*v. bloed*) vergieten; (*v. tranen*) storten; (*v. haar, enz.*) verliezen; (*v. kuit*) schieten; (*v. licht*) verspreiden, werpen; (*v. horens, enz.*) afwerpen; (*v. tanden*) wisselen; (*v. geur, enz.*) afgeven, verspreiden; (*v. kennissen, enz.*) laten schieten; *vi.* afvallen; uitvallen.

sheen [ʃin] *sb.* glans *m.*, schittering, glinstering *v.*; pracht *v.*, luister *m.*; *vi.* glanzen, schijnen, glinsteren.

sheeny ['ʃini] *adj.* glanzend, glinsterend, blinkend.

sheep [ʃip] schaap *o.*; schapen *mv.*

sheep-dog ['ʃipdɔg] herdershond *m.*

sheep-fold ['ʃipfould] schaapstal *m.*

sheepish(ly) ['ʃipiʃ(li)] *adj.* (*adv.*) schaapachtig, onnozel, sullig, bedeesd.

sheepskin ['ʃipskin] schaapsvacht *v.*, schaapsvel *o.*; schaapsleer *o.*; perkament *o.*

sheer [ʃiə] *adj.* zuiver, helder, rein; (*v. wijn*) onverdund; enkel, louter, niet anders dan; steil, loodrecht; (*Am.: v. stoffen*) doorschijnend; *adj.* steil, loodrecht; regelrecht, pardoes; plotseling.

sheet [ʃit] laken, beddelaken *o.*; doodskleed *o.*; (*v. papier*) blad, vel *o.*; blaadje *o.*, krant *v.*; (*v. metaal*) plaat *v.*; (*v. mist, enz.*) gordijn *o.*; (*sch.*) schoot *m.*

sheet-anchor ['ʃitæŋkə] plechtanker *o.*

sheet-iron ['ʃitaiən] plaatijzer *o.*

sheet-lightning ['ʃitlaitniŋ] weerlicht *o.*, zeebrand *m.*

shelf [ʃelf] (*v. rek, enz.*) plank *v.*; boekenplank *v.*; vak *o.*; vooruitstekende rand *m.*; blinde klip, zandbank, plaat *v.*; ertsbank *v.*; terras *o.*

shell [ʃel] *sb.* schil; peul; bolster *v.*; dop *m.*, schaal *v.*; schelp, schulp *v.*; huis *v.*, omhulsel *o.*; (*mil.*) granaat *v.*; *vt.* schillen; ontbolsteren; doppen; met schelpen bedekken; (*mil.*) beschieten, bombarderen; omhullen; (*v. gezwel*) uitnemen; *vi.* uit de bolster vallen; (*v.*

---

graan, enz.) uitvallen; (*fam.*) betalen, opdokken.

shell-hole ['ʃelhoul] granaattrechter *m.*

shelter ['ʃeltə] *sb.* beschutting, bescherming *v.*; schuilplaats *v.*; onderdak *o.*; *vt.* beschermen, beschutten; behoeden (*from,* voor); in bescherming nemen (*from,* tegen); huisvesting verlenen; *vr.* zich verschuilen.

shepherd ['ʃepəd] herder, schaapherder *m.*; zielenherder *m.*

shepherdess ['ʃepədis] herderin *v.*

sherbet ['ʃə:bət] sorbet *o.*

shield [ʃild] *sb.* schild *o.*, beukelaar *m.*; wapenschild *o.*; *vt.* beschermen, beschutten; de hand boven 't hoofd houden, dekken.

shift [ʃift] *vt.* veranderen; verleggen, verplaatsen, verschuiven; (*v. schip*) verhalen; (*v. roer*) omleggen; overplaatsen; verwisselen; verruilen; *vi.* zich verplaatsen; (*v. wind*) omlopen, van richting veranderen; (*v. lading*) werken, losraken; zich verkleden; zich verschonen; *sb.* verandering *v.*; verwisseling; afwisseling *v.*; hulpmiddel, redmiddel *o.*; list, uitvlucht *v.*; verschoning *v.*

shifting ['ʃiftiŋ] *adj.* veranderend, zich verplaatsend; *sb.* verandering *v.*; verplaatsing *v.*; list, uitvlucht. *v.*

shiftless ['ʃiftlis] onbeholpen, hulpeloos, weinig vindingrijk.

shilling ['ʃiliŋ] shilling *m.*

shimmer ['ʃimə] *vi.* glinsteren, flikkeren, glimmen; *sb.* glinstering, flikkering *v.*; glans *m.*

shin [ʃin] scheen *v.*, scheenbeen *o.*

shin-bone ['ʃinboun] scheenbeen *o.*

shine [ʃain] *vi.* schijnen; blinken, schitteren, glinsteren; uitblinken; *vt.* doen glimmen, doen blinken; laten schijnen; poetsen; *sb.* zonneschijn *m.*; glans *m.*; schijnsel *o.*; blink *m.*, schoensmeer *o.*

shingle ['ʃiŋgl] dakspaan *o.*, plank *v.*; (*Am.*) naambord *o.*; klein uithangbord *o.*; keisteen, kiezelsteen *m.*

shin-guard ['ʃingâd] scheenkap, *v.* scheenbedekking *v.*

shiny ['ʃaini] glimmend, blinkend.

ship [ʃip] *sb.* schip *o.*; (*sp.*) boot *v.*; *vt.* inschepen; innemen, laden; binnenkrijgen; (*v. stortzee*) overkrijgen; aanmonsteren; verschepen.

ship-boy ['ʃipbɔi] scheepsjongen *m.*

ship-broker ['ʃipbroukə] scheepsmakelaar *m.*; cargadoor *m.*

ship-building ['ʃipbildiŋ] scheepsbouw *m.*

ship-canal ['ʃipkənæl] scheepvaartkanaal *o.*

shipload ['ʃiploud] scheepslading, scheepsvracht *v.*

shipment ['ʃipmənt] verscheping, verzending *v.*; lading *v.*

ship-owner ['ʃipounə] reder *m.*

shipper ['ʃipə] verscheper, aflader *m.*; exporteur *m.*

shipping ['ʃipiŋ] inscheping *v.*; versche-

ping *v.*; (gezamenlijke) schepen *o. mv.* (v. land, haven, enz.); scheepvaart *v.*

shipping-agent [ˈʃipiŋeidʒənt] expediteur *m.*

shipwreck [ˈʃiprek] schipbreuk *v.*

ship-yard [ˈʃipjâd] scheepstimmerwerf *v.*

shire [ˈʃaiə] graafschap *o.*

shirk [ʃəːk] verzuimen; ontduiken, ontwijken, zich onttrekken aan; opzien tegen.

shirt [ʃəːt] (mans)hemd, overhemd *o.*; kiel *m.*

shiver [ˈʃivə] *sb.* schijfje, plakje *o.*; schilfer *v.*; leirots *v.*; rilling, trilling, siddering, huivering *v.*; *vt.* verbrijzelen; (*sch.: v. zeilen*) doen killen; *vi.* aan gruzelementen vallen; (*mil.*) stukspringen; rillen, sidderen, huiveren; griezelen; (*sch.: v. zeil*) killen.

shivery [ˈʃivəri] rillend, huiverend; rillerig, beverig; huiverig; bros, brokkelig.

shoal [ʃoul] *sb.* (*v. haringen, enz.*) school *v.*; troep *m.*, menigte *v.*, hoop *m.*; ondiepte, zandbank, zandplaat *v.*; —**s**, (*fig.*) klippen; *vi.* samenscholen; ondiep(er) worden.

shock [ʃɔk] *sb.* schok *m.*, botsing *v.*; zenuwschok *m.*; aanval *m.*; aanstoot *m.*; schrik *m.*, ontzetting *v.*; *vt.* schokken; botsen tegen; aanstoot geven.

shocker [ˈʃɔkə] sensatieroman, gruwelroman *m.*

shocking [ˈʃɔkiŋ] aanstoot gevend, aanstotelijk, ergerlijk, stuitend; gruwelijk.

shock-troops [ˈʃɔktrûps] stormtroepen *m. mv.*

shoe [ʃû] *sb.* schoen *m.*; remschoen *m.*; hoefijzer *o.*; *vt.* schoeien; beslaan.

shoeblack [ˈʃûblæk] schoenpoetser *m.*

shoe(ing)-horn [ˈʃû(iŋ)hoːn] schoenaantrekker, schoenhoorn *m.*

shoeing-smith [ˈʃûiŋsmiθ] hoefsmid *m.*

shoe-last [ˈʃûlâst] schoenleest *v.*

shoemaker [ˈʃûmeikə] schoenmaker *m.*

shoot [ʃût] *vt.* afschieten, neerschieten; doodschieten; fusilleren; voorbijschieten; uitsteken; (*voor film*) opnemen; (*v. boot*) te water laten; (*v. anker, netten*) uitwerpen; (*v. puin*) storten; (*v. zak*) leeggooien; (*v. beschrijving, enz.*) doorspekken, doorweven (**with,** met); *vi.* schieten; (*v. ster*) verschieten; jagen; (*v. pijn*) steken; uitlopen, uitbotten; *sb.* jacht; jachtpartij *v.*; jachtveld *o.*; jachtrecht *o.*; schietwedstrijd *m.*; beschieting *v.*, bombardement *o.*; scheut *v.*, uitloper *m.*; stroomversnelling *v.*; stortplaats *v.*; losplaats *v.*; (*voor graan, enz.*) stortkoker *m.*; goot *v.*, kanaal *o.*

shooting [ˈʃûtiŋ] jacht *v.*

shooting-licence [ˈʃûtiŋlais(ə)ns] jachtakte *v.*

shooting-range [ˈʃûtiŋrein(d)ʒ] schietbaan *v.*, schietterrein *o.*

shop [ʃɔp] *sb.* winkel *m.*; werkplaats

v.; (*sl.*) kantoor *o.*; zaak *v.*; (*ton.*) baantje *o.*; (*op school; mil.*) hok *o.*; *vi.* winkelen; *vt.* verklikken; laten inrekenen; (*sl.*) in de doos stoppen.

shop-assistant [ʃɔpəˈsistənt] winkelbediende *m.*; winkeljuffrouw *v.*

shop-front [ˈʃɔpfrənt] winkelpui *v.*

shop-girl [ˈʃɔpgəːl] winkeljuffrouw *v.*

shopkeeper [ˈʃɔpkîpə] winkelier *m.*; (*fig.*) winkelknecht *m.*, winkeldochter *v.*

shoplifter [ˈʃɔpliftə] winkeldief, ladenlichter *m.*

shopman [ˈʃɔpmən] winkelier *m.*; winkelknecht *m.*; werker *m.* in vɛ plaats.

shop-window [ˈʃɔpwindou] winkelraam *o.*; (*fig.*) vertoning *v.*

shop-worn [ˈʃɔpwoːn] (*v. goederen*) verlegen.

shore [ʃoː] *sb.* kust *v.*, oever *m.*; strand *o.*; *vt.* op 't strand zetten; *vi.* op 't strand lopen; landen.

shore [ʃoː] *sb.* schoor, stut *m.*; schraag *v.*; *vt.* schoren, stutten; schragen.

short [ʃɔːt] *adj. & adv.* kort; te kort; (*v. gestalte*) klein; (*v. leerboek*) beknopt; (*v. gebak, enz.*) bros, brokkelig; (*v. portie, rantsoen*) karig, krap; (*H.*) krap gemeten; bits, kortaf, kort aangebonden; (*v. zee*) met korte golfslag; (*v. vlees*) mals; (*sl.*) onverdund, niet met water aangemengd; *sb.* korte klinker *m.*; korte lettergreep *v.*; kort begrip *o.*; (*el.*) kortsluiting *v.*; baissier *m.*; —**s**, korte broek; grof meel met zemelen.

shortage [ˈʃɔːtidʒ] tekort *o.*, schaarste *v.*

short-breathed [ʃɔːtˈbreθt] kortademig.

short-circuiting [ʃɔːtˈsəːkitiŋ] kortsluiting *v.*

shortcoming [ʃɔːtˈkəmiŋ] tekortkoming *v.*; gebrek *o.*

shorten [ˈʃɔːtn] *vt.* verkorten, korter maken; verminderen, beperken; bros maken; (*v. munt*) snoeien; *vi.* korten, korter worden; afnemen.

shorthand [ˈʃɔːthænd] *sb.* stenografie *v.*, snelschrift, kortschrift *o.*; — **typist,** steno-typiste; — **writer,** stenograaf; *adj.* stenografisch.

short-handed [ʃɔːtˈhændid] met te weinig personeel.

shortly [ˈʃɔːtli] *adv.* in 't kort; kort daarop, kort daarna; binnenkort; kortaf.

shortness [ˈʃɔːtnis] kortheid, enz.; *zie* **short.**

short-pass(ing) [ˈʃɔːtpâs(iŋ)] (*sp.: voetb.*) kort samenspel *o.*

short-sighted [ʃɔːtˈsaitid] bijziend; kortzichtig.

short-tempered [ʃɔːtˈtempəd] kort aangebonden, oplopend.

short-winded [ʃɔːtˈwindid] kortademig.

short-witted [ʃɔːtˈwitid] bekrompen, dom.

shot [ʃɔt] schot *o.*; bereik *o.*; (*voetb.*

schop *m.*; (*tennis*) slag *m.*; (*bilj.*) stoot *m.*; opname *v.*, kiekje *o.*; schroot *o.*, hagel *m.*; (kanons)kogel *m.*; schutter, scherpschutter *m.*; gelag *o.*, rekening *v.*

shot-proof ['ʃɔtprûf] kogelvrij.

shoulder ['ʃouldə] schouder *m.*; schoft *v.*; schouderstuk *o.*; schoor, stut *m.*; (*v. fles*) verwijding *v.*

shoulder-belt ['ʃouldəbelt] draagband, bandelier *m.*

shoulder-blade ['ʃouldəbleid] schouderblad *o.*

shoulder-knot ['ʃouldənɔt] schouderbedekking *v.*; (*mil.*) schouderkwast *m.*, epaulet *v.*

shout [ʃaut] *vi.* schreeuwen; roepen, juichen; (*sl.*) trakteren; *vt.* uitroepen; *sb.* geschreeuw *o.*; geroep, gejuich *o.*; schreeuw, kreet *m.*

shove [ʃʌv] *vt.* schuiven; duwen, stoten; (*in zak, enz.*) steken, stoppen; (*v. vals geld*) uitgeven; *vi.* stoten, duwen; hossen; *sb.* duw, stoot *m.*

shovel ['ʃʌvl] *sb.* schop *v.*; schuithoed *m.*; *vt.* scheppen; opscheppen; — *in,* (*v. geld*) opstrijken.

shovelful ['ʃʌvlful] schopvol *v.*

shoveller ['ʃʌvlə] schepper *m.*; (*Dk.*) slobeend *v.*

show [ʃou] *vt.* tonen, laten zien; vertonen; ten toon stellen; wijzen; (*v. thermometer, enz.*) aanwijzen; bewijzen; betonen; aantonen; leiden, brengen; *vi.* zich vertonen; voor de dag komen; uitkomen; (*v. artikel*) aan de markt komen; (*ton.*) optreden; *vr.* — *oneself,* zich tonen; *sb.* vertoning *v.*; vertoon *o.*; tentoonstelling *v.*; schouwspel *o.*; geurmakerij *v.*; schijn, zweem *m.*; (*sl.*) komedie *v.*; kraam *v.*

show-box ['ʃoubɔks] kijkkast *v.*

show-case ['ʃoukeis] uitstalkast, vitrine *v.*

shower ['ʃauə] *sb.* bui, regenbui, stortbui *v.*; (*fig.*) stroom, vloed; regen *m.*; *vt.* beregenen, begieten; doen neerkomen, doen neerdalen; uitstorten; *vi.* stortregenen; neerstromen.

shower-bath ['ʃauəbâð] stortbad *o.*; (*fig.*) stortvloed *m.*

showery ['ʃauəri] regenachtig, buiig.

show-girl ['ʃougə:l] mannequin *v.*; figurante *v.*

show-place ['ʃoupleis] bezienswaardigheid *v.*

show-window ['ʃouwindou] uitstalvenster, winkelraam *o.*

showy ['ʃoui] *adj.* opzichtig, opvallend; pronkerig, praalziek.

shrapnel ['ʃræpnəl] (*mil.*) granaatkartets *v.*

shred [ʃred] *sb.* stukje, reepje, lapje *o.*; flard *m.*; (*fig.*) ziertje *o.*; schijn; zweem *m.*; *vt.* aan repen snijden; klein snijden; (*v. tabak*) kerven; — *off,* afknippen; *vi.* rafelen; afschilferen.

shrew [ʃrû] helleveeg, feeks, haaibaai *v.*; spitsmuis *v.*

shriek [ʃrîk] *vi.* gillen, gieren; *sb.* gil, schreeuw *m.*; alarmkreet *m.*

shrill [ʃril] *adj.* schel; schril; (*fig.*) scherp, snerpend; *vi.* schel klinken; gillen, snerpen; *vt.* — *out,* uitgillen.

shrimp [ʃrimp] garnaal *v.*

shrine [ʃrain] reliquieënkastje *o.*; altaar *o.*; heilige plaats *v.*, heiligdom *o.*; grafteken *o.*

shrink [ʃriŋk] *vi.* krimpen; ineenkrimpen; verschrompelen; slinken; afnemen, verminderen; *vt.* (doen) krimpen.

shrinkage ['ʃriŋkidʒ] inkrimping *v.*; opkrimping *v.*; slinking *v.*; (*v. waarde, enz.*) vermindering *v.*; bekrimping, bezuiniging *v.*

shrinkless ['ʃriŋklis] krimpvrij.

shrivel ['ʃrivl] *vi.* (*vt.*) (doen) rimpelen; (doen) verschrompelen.

Shrovetide ['ʃrouvtaid] vastenavond *m.*

shrub [ʃrʌb] heester, struik *m.*

shrug [ʃrʌg] *vt.* ophalen; de schouders ophalen; *sb.* schouderophalen *o.*

shrunken ['ʃrʌŋkn] (ineen)gekrompen, verschrompeld; (*v. gelaat*) vervallen.

shuck [ʃʌk] *sb.* dop, bolster *m.*, schaal *v.*, bast *m.*; prul *v.*, bocht *o.*; —*s* ! larie! onzin! *vt.* doppen.

shudder ['ʃʌdə] *vi.* huiveren, rillen; *sb.* huivering, rilling *v.*

shuddery ['ʃʌdəri] griezelig.

shuffle ['ʃʌfl] *vt.* schudden, dooreenschudden; mengen, dooreenmengen; (*v. kaarten*) wassen; — *off,* (*v. verplichting, verantwoordelijkheid*) van zich afschuiven; *vi.* sloffen, strijkvoeten; schuifelen; draaien, uitvluchten zoeken; niet recht door zee gaan; een slag om de arm houden; — *along,* voortsloffen, voortsjokken; aansloffen; — *off,* heensloffen, heenslenteren; doodgaan; — *together,* samenflansen.

shun [ʃʌn] *vt.* schuwen, vermijden, ontvlieden.

shunt [ʃʌnt] *vt.* (*v. trein*) op een zijspoor brengen, rangeren; (*el.*) aftakken; (*fig.*) op zij schuiven, op de lange baan schuiven; op zij gaan; *vi.* rangeren; *sb.* (het) rangeren *o.*; zijspoor *o.*; spoorwegwissel *m.*; (*el.*) aftakking, nevensluiting *v.*

shunting-engine ['ʃʌntiŋendʒin] rangeerlocomotief *v.*

shut [ʃʌt] *vt.* sluiten, toedoen, dichtdoen, dichtmaken; afsluiten; insluiten; *vi.* (zich) sluiten; dichtgaan; (*v. dag*) eindigen; (*v. winter*) voor goed invallen; *vr.* — *oneself up from,* zich afzonderen van; *sb.* sluiting *v.*; (*v. dag*) einde *o.*

shuttle ['ʃʌtl] schietspoel *v.*; (*v. naaimachine*) schuitje *o.*

shuttle-cock ['ʃʌtlkɔk] pluimbal *m.*

shut-up ['ʃʌt'ɔp] gesloten.

shy [ʃai] *adj.* schuw, verlegen, bedeesd, beschroomd; achterdochtig; (*v. vruchtboom*) slecht dragend; (*v. plaats*) afgezonderd; (*sl.*) verdacht; schunnig; *be* — *of,* vermijden, zich niet inlaten met; huiverig zijn om; *vt.* schuwen, ontwijken,

vermijden, links laten liggen; *vi.* schuw
worden, schichtig worden, schrikken,
op zij springen; terugschrikken (*at*,
from, voor): *sb.* zijsprong *m.*
shyness ['ʃainis] schuwheid, enz.; *zie*
shy.
sick [sik] ziek; misselijk; zeeziek; beu,
moe; bleek; moedeloos, angstig; (*sl.*)
verdrietig; geërgerd.
sick-bed ['sikbed] ziekbed *o.*
sick-call ['sikko:l] ziekenbezoek *o.*;
(*mil.*) doktersappel, ziekenrapport *o.*
sick-club ['sikkləb] ziekenfonds *o.*
sickening ['sikniŋ] misselijk (makend),
walglijk.
sickle ['sikl] sikkel *v.*
sick-leave ['siklîv] ziekteverlof *o.*
sickly ['sikli] *adj.* ziekelijk; ongezond;
misselijk; bleek; (*v. glimlach*) flauw; (*v.
reuk*) walglijk.
sickness ['siknis] ziekte *v.*; misselijkheid *v.*
side [said] zijde *v.*, kant *m.*; kantje,
zijdje *o.*, bladzijde *v.*; (*bilj.*) effect *o.*;
(*sp.*) elftal *o.*, ploeg *v.*; partij *v.*; coulisse
v.; (*fam.*) bijgerecht *o.*; (*sl.*) air *o.*
side-aisle ['saidail] zijbeuk *m.*
sideboard ['saidbo:d] buffet *o.*; aan-
recht *o.*; zijplank *v.*; —*s,* (*sl.*) staande
boord; bakkebaarden, tochtlatjes.
side-car ['saidkâ] zijspanwagen *m.*
side-dish ['saiddiʃ] bijgerecht, tussen-
gerecht *o.*
side-issue ['saidiʃû] bijzaak *v.*
side-light ['saidlait] kantlicht, zijlicht
o.; zijraam, zijvenster *o.*; (*sch.*) zijlan-
taarn *v.*; (*fig.*) toelichting; zijdelingse
illustratie *v.*
sidelong ['saidloŋ] *adv.* (*adj.*) zijdelings.
side-rail ['saidreil] wisselspoor *o.*
side-scene ['saidsîn] coulisse *v.*
side-slip ['saidslip] (*v. auto,* enz.)
slippen; (*vl.*) dwars afglijden; een misstap begaan.
side-street ['saidstrît] zijstraat *v.*
side-table ['saidteibl] zijtafel, wand-
tafel *v.*
side-walk ['saidwo:k] trottoir *o.*
sideward(s) ['saidwəd(z)] zijwaarts.
siding ['saidiŋ] zijspoor, wisselspoor,
rangeerspoor *o.*
siege [sîdʒ] *sb.* beleg *o.*, belegering *v.*;
vt. belegeren.
sieve [siv] *sb.* zeef *v.*; grove mand *v.*;
vt. zeven, ziften.
sift [sift] *vt.* zeven, ziften, uitziften;
onderzoeken, uitvorsen, uitpluizen; uitvragen, uithoren; (*v. suiker*) strooien;
vi. vallen (als door een zeef); doorzijgen; poeieren.
sigh [sai] *vi.* zuchten; smachten (*for,*
naar): *sb.* zucht *m.*
sight [sait] *sb.* gezicht *o.*; aanblik *m.*,
schouwspel *o.*; gezichtspunt *o.*; visioen
o.; bezienswaardigheid, merkwaardigheid *v.*; (*v. geweer*) korrel *v.*, vizier *o.*;
(*v. instrument*) kijkspleet *v.*; (*met instrument*) waarneming *v.*; (*fam.*) hoop,

boel *m.*; *vt.* in 't gezicht krijgen; te zien
krijgen; waarnemen; (*v. geweer*) richten,
stellen; (*H.: v. wissel*) presenteren; bezichtigen; van vizier(en) voorzien; *vi.*
mikken.
sight-bill ['saitbil] zichtwissel, wissel
m. op zicht.
sightless ['salitis] blind; (*dicht.*) onzichtbaar.
sign [sain] *sb.* teken *o.*; gebaar *o.*; wenk
m.; kenteken, voorteken *o.*; uithangbord *o.*; gevelplaat *v.*; wonderteken *o.*;
(*mil.*) wachtwoord *o.*; reclame *v.*; *vt.*
tekenen, ondertekenen; een teken
geven; door een teken te kennen geven;
— *away,* (*v. eigendom, rechten*) overdragen, afstand doen van.
signal ['signəl] *sb.* signaal, teken, sein
o.; *adj.* uitstekend, voortreffelijk; buitengewoon, opmerkelijk; luisterrijk,
schitterend; *vt.* seinen; te kennen geven;
melden, aankondigen; van signalen
voorzien.
signal-box ['signəlbɔks] seinhuisje *o.*
signal-gun ['signəlgən] seinschot *o.*
signaller ['signələ] seiner *m.*
signalman ['signəlmən] seiner *m.*;
seinwachter *m.*; baanwachter *m.*
signature ['signətʃə] handtekening, ondertekening *v.*; teken, kenmerk *o.*;
(*muz.*) voortekening *v.*; (*drukk.*) signatuur *v.*
sign-board ['sainbo:d] uithangbord *o.*;
(*Am.*) advertentiebord *o.*
signet ['signit] zegel *o.*; zegelring *m.*
significant [sig'nifikənt] *adj.* veelbetekenend, betekenisvol; veelzeggend; gewichtig; *sb.* aanduiding *v.*
signification [signifi'keiʃən] betekenis
v.; aanduiding *v.*; betekening, gerechtelijke aanzegging *v.*
signify ['signifai] *vt.* betekenen, beduiden; aanduiden; te kennen geven; aankondigen; *vi.* van betekenis zijn.
sign-language ['sainlæŋgwidʒ] gebarentaal *v.*
sign-post ['sainpoust] handwijzer,
wegwijzer *m.*
silence ['sailəns] *sb.* zwijgen, stilzwijgen *o.*; stilzwijgendheid *v.*; geheimhouding *v.*; stilte *v.*; *vt.* tot zwijgen
brengen.
silencer ['sailənsə] geluiddemper *m.*;
schokdemper *m.*; knalpot *m.*; (*fig.*)
dooddoener *m.*, afdoend antwoord *o.*
silent ['sailənt] *adj.* zwijgend, stilzwijgend; stil; (*v. letter*) stom; (*tn.*) geruisloos.
siliceous [si'liʃəs] kiezelachtig, kiezel-
houdend.
silk [silk] *sb.* zijde *v.*; zijden japon (of
toga) *v.*; —*s,* zijden stoffen; zijden kleren; *adj.* zijden, van zijde; *vt.* met zijde
voeren.
sliken ['silkn] zijden; zijdeachtig; zacht
als zijde; zoetvloeiend.
silk-worm ['silkwə:m] zijdeworm *m.*
silky ['silki] *zie* *silken.*

silly ['sili] adj. onnozel, dwaas, sullig, dom; kinderachtig, flauw; adv. — **drunk,** stomdronken; sb. onnozele hals, sul m.

silo ['sailou] sb. silo v.; bewaarplaats v. voor groenvoer; graanpakhuis o.; vt. inkuilen.

silt [silt] sb. slib, slik o., verzanding v.; vt. & vi. (doen) dichtslibben, (doen) verzanden; — **through,** doorsijpelen.

silver ['silvə] sb. zilver o.; zilvergeld o.; tafelzilver o.; zilverwerk o.; adj. zilveren; zilverachtig; vt. verzilveren; foeliën· vi. zilverwit worden, een zilverglans aannemen.

silver-fox ['silvəfɔks] zilvervos m.

silverware ['silvəwêə] tafelzilver, zilverwerk o.

similar ['similə] adj. dergelijk, soortgelijk; gelijksoortig; gelijkvormig; overeenkomstig; sb. gelijke, evenknie m. & v.

similarity [simi'læriti] gelijkheid, gelijksoortigheid v.; gelijkvormigheid v.; overeenkomst v.

simmer ['simə] vi. eventjes (zachtjes) koken, pruttelen; (fig.) gisten, smeulen; vt. zacht laten koken; — **down,** bedaren; sb. gepruttel; (het) zacht koken o.

simple ['simpl] adj. enkel, enkelvoudig, niet samengesteld; gewoon, eenvoudig; onnozel, simpel· sb. eenvoudige, onnozele m.; artsenijkruid o.; vi. (geneeskundige) kruiden zoeken.

simple-minded ['simpl'maindid] eenvoudig· zwakzinnig.

simpleton ['simpltən] onnozele bloed, sul m.

simplify ['simplifai] vereenvoudigen.

simply ['simpli] adv. eenvoudig, eenvoudigweg, gewoonweg; enkel, alleen.

simulate ['simjuleit] vt. veinzen, voorwenden, simuleren; (bedrieglijk) nabootsen; ['simjulit] adj. nagebootst.

simultaneous(ly) [siməl'teinjəs(li)] adj. (adv.) gelijktijdig.

sin [sin] sb. zonde v.; vi. zondigen.

since [sins] adv. sedert, sinds, sindsdien; geleden; prep. sedert, sinds; cj. sedert, sinds; aangezien; (dicht.) dewijl.

sincere [sin'sîə] adj. oprecht, ongeveinsd; zuiver, onvervalst, onvermengd.

sincerely [sin'sîəli] adv. oprecht; **yours** —, uw dienstwillige.

sincerity [sin'seriti] oprechtheid v.

sinew ['sinjû] sb. zenuw, pees, spier v.; vt. sterken, stalen.

sinful(ly) ['sinful(i)] adj. (adv.) zondig, verdorven.

sing [sin] vi. zingen; (v. bij) gonzen; (v. oren) suizen, tuiten; (v. wind, kogels) fluiten; krijsen; sissen; kraaien; — **off,** van 't blad zingen; — **out,** hardop zingen; luid zingen; hard roepen, schreeuwen; vt. zingen; bezingen; sb. (het) zingen o.; (v. kogel) (het) fluiten o.; (Am.) zangbijeenkomst.

singe [sin(d)ʒ] vt. zengen, verzengen,

schroeien, verschroeien; (v. haar) branden; vi. verzengen, schroeien; sb. verzenging; verschroeiing v.; verschroeide plek v.

singer ['sinə] zanger m.; zangvogel m.

singing ['sinin] adj. zingend· zangerig; sb. (het) zingen o.; (het) suizen o.; zangkunst v.

singing-bird ['sininbə:d] zangvogel m.

single ['singl] adj. enkel, enkelvoudig; eenvoudig; afzonderlijk; enig, alleen; ongehuwd; vt. (v. planten) dunnen; — (**out**), uitkiezen.

single-breasted ['singlbrestid] met één rij knopen.

single-eyed ['singlaid] éénogig; (fig.) met één doel voor ogen, doelbewust.

single-handed ['singl'hændid] met (voor) één hand; alleen, zonder (iemands) hulp.

single-hearted(ly) ['singl'hâtid(li)] adj. (adv.) oprecht, eerlijk.

single-minded ['singl'maindid] doelbewust, recht op zijn doel afgaand; oprecht, eerlijk.

single-seater ['singlsîtə] éénpersoonsauto v.; éénpersoonsvliegtuig o.

singly ['singli] adv. afzonderlijk, één voor één; op zichzelf; alléén.

singsong ['sinsɔn] eentonig; zangerig.

singular ['singjulə] adj. enkelvoudig; enig (in zijn soort), uniek; zeldzaam; eigenaardig, zonderling, bijzonder; sb. op zichzelf staand (afzonderlijk) **geval** o. (persoon m.); (gram.) enkelvoud o.

sinister ['sinistə] onheilspellend; (v. uiterlijk) ongunstig; noodlottig; snood.

sink [sink] vi. zinken; dalen, zakken, vallen; (fig.) afnemen, verflauwen; ondergaan; te gronde gaan; vt. doen zinken; tot zinken brengen; in de grond boren; neerlaten, laten zakken; vernietigen, te gronde richten; sb. gootsteen m.; afwasbakje o.; zinkput m.; riool o.

sinking ['sinkin] (het) zinken o.; amortisatie v.; mijnschacht v.

sink-stone ['sinkstoun] gootsteen m.

sinless(ly) ['sinlis(li)] adj. (adv.) zondeloos, zonder zonde.

sinner ['sinə] zondaar m.

sinuous ['sinjuəs] bochtig, kronkelig, kronkelend, krom.

sip [sip] vt. lepperen, slurpen, oplepelen, met kleine teugjes drinken; sb. teugje o.

sir [sə:] heer m.; mijnheer m.

siren ['sairən] sirene v.

siskin ['siskin] sijsje o.

sister ['sistə] zuster v.

sister-in-law ['sistərinlo:] schoonzuster v.

sisterly ['sistəli] zusterlijk; zuster—.

sit [sit] vi. zitten; liggen, zich bevinden; (voor portret) poseren; zitting hebben; zitting houden; vt. zitten op; doen zitten, neerzetten; vr. — **oneself (down),** gaan zitten; zich neerzetten; sb. (het) zitten o.; zitvlak o.

site ['sait] ligging *v.*; (bouw)terrein *o.*; plekje *o.*
sitting ['sitiŋ] *adj.* zittend; zitting hebbend; *sb.* zitting *v.*; zittijd *m.*; (*in kerk*) vaste zitplaats *v.*; broedtijd *m.*; stel *o.* broedeieren.
sitting-room ['sitiŋrum] huiskamer; zitkamer *v.*; zitplaats(en) *v.* (*mv.*).
situated ['sitjueitid] geplaatst, gelegen.
situation [sitju'eiʃən] ligging *v.*; stand *m.*, positie *v.*; toestand *m.*, situatie *v.*; betrekking, plaats *v.*
sitz-bath ['sitsbâð] zitbad *o.*
six ['siks] zes.
sixteen ['siks'tîn; 'sikstîn] zestien.
sixth [siksð] zesde (deel, klas); (*muz.*) sext.
sixty ['siksti] zestig.
sizable ['saizəbl] tamelijk groot, van tamelijke omvang, flink, behoorlijk.
size [saiz] *sb.* grootte *v.*; omvang *m.*; afmeting *v.*, formaat *o.*; (*v. schoenen, enz.*) maat *v.*, nummer *o.*; kaliber *o.*; *vt.* rangschikken, sorteren; passend maken; op de juiste maat brengen; meten; ijken; (*v. ertsen*) ziften.
size-stick ['saizstik] schoenmakersmaatstok *m.*
skate [skeit] *sb.* schaats *v.*; *vi.* schaatsenrijden.
skater ['skeitə] schaatsenrijder *m.*
skating-club ['skeitiŋkləb] ijsclub *v.*
skein [skein] streng *v.*; kluwen *o.*
skeleton ['skelitən] geraamte; skelet *o.*; (*fig.*) schets *v.*, schema, geraamte *o.*; (*mil.*) kader *o.*
sketch [sketʃ] *sb.* schets *v.*; *vt. & vi.* schetsen.
skew [skjû] *adj.* scheef, schuin.
ski [ʃî, skî] *sb.* ski, sneeuwschaats *v.*; *vi.* skilopen, skiën.
skid [skid] *sb.* remschoen, remketting *m.*, slof *v.*; (*sch.*) slee *v.*; glijplank *v.*; *vt.* de remschoen aanleggen; laten glijden; (*fig.*) remmen; *vi.* (*v. auto, enz.*) slippen.
skilful(ly) ['skilful(i)] *adj.* (*adv.*) handig, bekwaam, bedreven, ervaren.
skill [skil] *sb.* handigheid, bekwaamheid, bedrevenheid, ervarenheid *v.*
skilled [skild] handig, bekwaam, bedreven.
skim [skim] *vt.* schuimen, afschuimen, afscheppen; afromen; ondiep ploegen; met een dun laagje bedekken; vluchtig doorlopen, even inkijken.
skimmer ['skimə] schuimspaan *v.*
skim-milk ['skimmilk] taptemelk *v.*
skin [skin] *sb.* huid *v.*; vel *o.*, pels *m.*; vlies(je) *o.*; (*v. vrucht*) schil, schaal, pel *v.*; leren zak *m.*; *vt.* met een vel (vliesje) bedekken; villen, stropen; (*fig.*) afzetten pellen; *vi.* dichtgaan; spieken.
skinflint ['skinflint] schrielhannes, vrek *m.*
skinner [s'kinə] vilder *m.*; huidenkoper *m.*; bonthandelaar *m.*; afzetter *m.*
skip [skip] *vi.* springen, huppelen;

(*fam.*) er van doorgaan; *vt.* laten springen; (*bij 't lezen*) overslaan; overspringen; (*v. steentjes, enz.*) keilen.
skirmish ['skə:miʃ] *sb.* schermutseling *v.*; *vi.* schermutselen; (*mil.*) tirailleren.
skirmisher ['skə:miʃə] schermutselaar *m.*; tirailleur *m.*
skirt [skə:t] *sb.* (vrouwen)rok *m.*; rand, zoom, boord *m.*; pand *o.*, slip *v.*; uiteinde *o.*; grens *v.*; (*v. dier*) middenrif *o.*; (*tn.*) mantel *m.*; —**s**, (*v. bos*) zoom, rand; (*v. stad*) buitenwijken; *vt.* omzomen, omboorden; begrenzen; langs de rand lopen; langs de kust varen; *vi.* — *along*, lopen langs; grenzen aan.
skit [skit] *sb.* schimpscheut; stekelige zet *m.*; parodie *v.*; schotschrift *o.*
skittish ['skitiʃ] (*v. paard*) schichtig; dartel, uitgelaten; grillig.
skittle ['skitl] *sb.* kegel *m.*; —**s**, kegelspel: *vi.* kegelen.
skittle-alley ['skitlæli] kegelbaan *v.*
skive [skaiv] (*v. leer*) snijden, splitsen; afschaven; afslijpen.
skulk [skəlk] *vi.* loeren, gluipen, sluipen; zich verschuilen, zich schuil houden; lijntrekken, malengeren; *vt.* ontwijken, uit de weg gaan.
skull [skəl] schedel *m.*, hersenkas *v.*; doodskop *m.*
skunk [skəŋk] stinkdier *o.*; skunksbont *o.*; (*fig.*) smeerlap, stinkerd *m.*
sky [skai] lucht *v.*, hemel *m.*, uitspansel *o.*; luchtstreek *v.*, klimaat *o.*; hemelsblauw *o.*
sky-blue ['skaiblû] *adj.* hemelsblauw; *sb.* hemelsblauw *o.*; (*sl.*) waterachtige melk *v.*
skyline ['skailain] gezichteinder, horizon *m.*
skyscraper ['skaiskreipə] wolkenkrabber *m.*, torengebouw *o.*
slab [slæb] (marmeren) plaat *v.*; platte steen *m.*; gedenksteen *m.*; schaal *v.*; slik *o.*
slack [slæk] *adj.* slap, los; laks, traag; (*v. weer*) maf, loom; *sb.* (*v. touw*) loos *v.*; (*v. broek*) kruis *o.*; (*in handel*) slapte *v.*; (*tn.*) speling *v.*; steenkoolgruis *o.*; —**s**, (*sl.*) lange broek; *vi.* verslappen; treuzelen, lijntrekken; slabbakken; *vt.* doen afnemen; (*v. plicht*) verwaarlozen; (*v. kalk*) blussen.
slack-baked ['slækbeikt] slecht doorbakken, half gaar, klef.
slacken ['slækn] *vt.* doen verslappen; vertragen; (*v. vaart*) verminderen; (*in kracht, enz.*) doen afnemen; (*v. teugels*) vieren; *vi.* slap worden, verslappen; afnemen, verminderen.
slacker ['slækə] treuzelaar, luilak *m.*; (*sl.*) lijntrekker *m.*
slackness ['slæknis] slapheid, losheid *v.*; laksheid, traagheid *v.*; loomheid *v.*
slag [slæg] (metaal)slak *v.*, sintel *m.*
slake [sleik] lessen; (*v. kalk*) blussen; (*v. nieuwsgierigheid*) bevredigen; verkwikken.

slam [slæm] *vt.* dichtslaan, dichtgooien; (*fig.*) totaal verslaan, het winnen van; — *down,* neersmakken; *vi.* (*kaarts p.*) slem maken; *sb.* harde slag, bons *m.*; (*kaartsp.*) slem *o.*; (*Am.*) vitterij *v.*

slander ['slândə] *sb.* laster, achterklap *m.*; *vt.* lasteren, belasteren.

slang [slæn] niet als beschaafd Engels beschouwde taal *v.*; taal *v.* van bepaald beroep of bedrijf; dieventaal *v.*, argot *o.*; scheldwoorden *o. mv.*

slant [slânt] *vi.* hellen; schuin gaan (lopen, vallen); *vt.* doen hellen; schuin houden; afschuimen; *adj.* hellend, schuin; *sb.* helling *v.*; schuine richting *v.*

slanting ['slântin] *adj.* hellend, schuin.

slap [slæp] *vt.* slaan, een klap geven; dichtslaan; *vi.* — *at,* slaan naar; (*fam.*) schieten op; *sb.* klap, slag, mep *m.*; (*fig.*) veeg *m.* uit de pan.

slash [slæʃ] *vt.* snijden, een jaap geven; slaan, ranselen; splitsen; (*fig.*) er van langs geven; afmaken, ongenadig kritiseren; *vi.* om zich heen slaan; hakken, houwen (*at,* naar); *sb.* houw, jaap *m.*, snee *v.*; slag, veeg *m.*; mouwsplit *o.*

slate [sleit] lei *v.*; leisteen *m.*; —*s,* leien dak.

slate-pencil ['sleitpens(i)l] griffel *v.*

slater ['sleitə] leidekker *m.*

slattern ['slætən] *sb.* slons, morsebel *v.*; *adj.* slonzig, slordig.

slaternly ['slætənli] slonzig, slordig.

slaughter ['slo:tə] *sb.* (het)slachten *o.*; slachting *v.*; bloedbad *o.*; enorme prijsverlaging *v.*; *vt.* afmaken, vermoorden, slachten; tegen afbraakprijzen verkopen.

slaughterer ['slo:tərə] slachter *m.*

slaughterhouse ['slo:təhaus] slachthuis *o.*

slaughterous ['slo:tərəs] moorddadig, bloedig.

slave [sleiv] *sb.* slaaf *m.*, slavin *v.*; *vi.* slaven, sloven, zwoegen, zich afbeulen.

slaver ['slævə] *sb.* kwijl *v.*; gekwijl, gezever *o.*; *vi.* kwijlen, zeveren.

slavery ['sleivəri] slavernij *v.*

slavish ['sleiviʃ] *adj.* slaafs.

slay [slei] doden, doodslaan, vermoorden, afmaken.

sled [sled] slede *v.*, sleetje *o.*

sledge [sledʒ] *sb.* voorhamer *m.*

sleep [slîp] *sb.* slaap *m.*; *put to* —, naar bed brengen; in slaap maken; (*fig.*) in slaap sussen, in slaap wiegen; *vi.* slapen; inslapen; sluimeren, rusten; (*v. tol*) staan; — *in,* (*v. dienstbode, enz.*) in huis slapen; — *out,* buitenshuis slapen; in de open lucht slapen; uitslapen; *vt.* laten slapen; in slaap brengen.

sleepiness ['slîpinis] slaperigheid *v.*

sleeping-draught ['slîpindrâft] slaapdrank *m.*

sleeping-partner ['slîpin'pâtnə] stille vennoot *m.*

sleepless(ly) ['slîplis(li)] *adj.* (*adv.*) slapeloos.

sleep-walker ['slîpwo:kə] slaapwandelaar *m.*

sleepy ['slîpi] *adj.* slaperig; slaapwekkend; (*v. stad, enz.*) doods; (*v. peer*) beurs; melig.

sleeve [slîv] mouw *v.*; (*tn.*) huls, mof *v.*

sleigh [slei] *sb.* (arre)slede *v.*; *vi.* arren.

slender ['slendə] *adj.* slank, rank; tenger, mager, spichtig; gering, onbeduidend; karig.

sleuth-hound ['slûðhaund] speurhond *m.* [stuk *o.*

slice [slais] sneetje, schijfje *o.*; deel,

slide [slaid] *vi.* glijden; glippen; afglijden; uitglijden; afdwalen; een misstap begaan; *vt.* laten glijden; laten glippen; laten schieten; — *back,* terugschuiven; *sb.* het glijden *o.*; glijbaan *v.*; glijplank *v.*; hellend vlak *o.*; afdwaling *v.*; (*v. boot*) glijbank *v.*; chassis *o.*; (*v. toverlantaarn*) plaat *v.*; schuifraampje *o.*

sliding ['slaidin] glijdend, glippend, enz.; glij—, schuif—; veranderlijk; voorbijgaand.

sliding-rule ['slaidinrûl] rekenliniaal *v.*

sliding-valve ['slaidinvælv] schuifklep *v.*; (*v. stoommachine*) bakschuif *v.*

slight [slait] *adj.* gering; onbeduidend; vluchtig, oppervlakkig; licht; luchtig; tenger; *sb.* minachting, geringschatting; kleinering *v.*; *vt.* geringschatten, minachten, met geringschatting behandelen; buiten beschouwing laten; ter zijde leggen; versmaden.

slim [slim] *adj.* rank, slank, schraal; tenger; dun, smal; (*v. kans*) gering; slim, sluw, listig.

slime [slaim] slib, slik, slijk *o.*; (*v. aal*) slijm *o.*; (*v. slang*) spog *o.*, zwadder *m.*; aardpek *o.*

slimming-course ['slimin'ko:s] vermageringskuur *v.*

slimy ['slaimi] *adj.* glibberig; kleverig; vuil, schuin.

sling [slin] *vt.* gooien, werpen, smijten; slingeren, zwaaien (met); ophangen; ophijsen; (*sch.*) aanslaan, vastsjorren; *sb.* slinger *m.*; slingerverband *o.*, draagband; doek *m.*; (*v. geweer, enz.*) riem *m.*; (*sch.*) leng *v.*, strop *m.*

slink [slink] sluipen, wegsluipen.

slip [slip] *vi.* glibberen, glijden; slippen; uitglijden; sluipen, wegsluipen; — *away,* wegsluipen, uitknijpen; (*v. tijd*) voorbijvliegen; — *down,* (*v. kousen, enz.*) afzakken; *vt.* laten glijden; laten glippen, laten schieten; (*v. hond*) losslaten; ontvallen, ontglippen; stilzwijgend voorbijgaan; (*v. gelegenheid*) laten voorbijgaan; (*v. les*) verzuimen; *sb.* uitglijding *v.*; stek *m.*, loot, spruit *v.*; (*vis*) kleine tong *v.*; (*v. papier*) reepje *o.*, strook *v.*

slip-board ['slipbo:d] schuifplank *v.*

slipper ['slipə] pantoffel, slof *v.*; remschoen *m.*

slipperiness ['slipərinis] gladheid, glibberigheid *v.*

slippery ['slipəri] glad, glibberig.
slit [slit] *vt.* doorsnijden; aan repen snijden; splijten, kloven; *vi.* splijten; *sb.* spleet, gleuf, lange snede *v.*
slither ['sliðə] *(fam.)* glibberen, glijden, slieren.
slithery ['sliðəri] glibberig.
slobber ['slɔbə] *vi.* kwijlen; grienen, huilen; *vt.* bekwijlen, bemorsen, bevuilen; opslobberen; afroffelen; verknoeien; *sb.* kwijl *v.*; gekwijl, gezever *o.*; slik *o.*
slogan ['slougən] oorlogskreet; strijdkreet *m.*; *(fig.)* leus, strijdleus *v.*; slagzin *m.*
sloop [slûp] sloep *v.*
slop-basin ['slɔpbeisin] spoelkom *v.*
slope [sloup] *sb.* helling, glooiing, schuinte *v.*; *(mil.)* talud *o.*; *(v. rivier)* verval *o.*; *vi.* glooien, hellen, aflopen; *(sl.)* er vandoor gaan; *vt.* afschuinen; schuin maken; schuin houden; doen hellen.
sloppy ['slɔpi] *adj.* drassig, slikkig; slordig; flodderig; morsig; *(fig.)* sentimenteel, zoetelijk.
slop-shop ['slɔpʃɔp] goedkope confectiewinkel *m.*
slot [slɔt] gleuf *v.*; sponning *v.*; *(op toneel)* valdeur *v.*; *(v. hert, enz.)* spoor *o.*
slot-machine ['slɔtməʃîn] (verkoop)-automaat *m.*
slough [slau] modderpoel *m.*, moeras *o.*
sloughy ['slaui] modderig, drassig, moerassig.
sloven ['slʌvn] slons *v.*
slovenly ['slʌvənli] slonzig, slordig.
slow [slou] *adj.* traag; langzaam, langzaam werkend; loom; *(v. zaken)* flauw, slap; saai, vervelend; achterlijk, niet vlug; *adv.* langzaam; *vi.* zijn vaart (gang) verminderen; langzamer rijden; *vt.* vertragen; *(v. trein)* langzamer laten lopen; *(v. machine)* langzamer laten werken.
slow-belly ['sloubeli] treuzelaar *m.*, treuzelkous *v.*; saaie vent *m.*
slow-coach ['sloukoutʃ] *zie* **slow-belly.**
slow-gaited ['slou'geitid] langzaam, traag.
slowness ['slounis] traagheid; langzaamheid *v.*; loomheid *v.*; slapte *v.*; saaiheid *v.*
slug [slʌg] (naakte) slak *v.*; luiaard, luilak *m.*; klomp *m.* ruw metaal; kogel, schrootkogel *m.*
sluggard ['slʌgəd] luiaard, luilak *m.*
sluice [slûs] *sb.* sluis *v.*; overlaat *m.*; afvoerbuis; inlaatbuis *v.*; sluiswater *o.*; *vt.* laten uitstromen; laten aflopen; afspoelen; *vi.* uitstromen; neerstromen, in stromen neerkomen.
slum [slʌm] slop *o.*, achterbuurt *v.*
slumber ['slʌmbə] *vi.* sluimeren; *sb.* sluimer *m.*, sluimering *v.*
slump [slʌmp] *sb.* plotselinge prijsda-

ling *v.*; achteruitgang *m.*; instorting *v.*; *vi.* plotseling zakken; ineenstorten.
slur [slə:] *vt.* onduidelijk uitspreken (of schrijven); losjes heenlopen over; onduidelijk maken, doen vervagen, verdoezelen; *(muz.)* slepen; besmetten, bezoedelen; besmeuren, bekladden; *sb.* blaam; kleinering *v.*; smet, schandvlek *v.*
slut [slʌt] slons, morsebel *v.*
sly [slai] slim, sluw, listig, geslepen; heimelijk.
slyboots ['slaibûts] slimmerd, leperd *m.*
slyness ['slainis] slimheid, sluwheid, listigheid, geslepenheid *v.*
smack [smæk] *sb.* *(schip)* smak *v.*; smak, mep, klap *m.*; *vt.* slaan op, meppen; doen knallen, doen klappen; smakken met; *vi.* smakken; klappen; knallen; — **of,** smaken naar; rieken naar; doen denken aan; *adv.* & *ij.* vlak, vierkant; pats! pardoes!
small [smo:l] *adj.* klein; weinig, gering; fijn, smal; *(v. bier, enz.)* dun, slap; min; kleingeestig, kleinzielig; *sb.* dun gedeelte *o.*; *(kaartsp.)* kleintje *o.*; **—s,** korte broek, kniebroek; klein brood, broodjes; klein soort.
small-arms ['smo:lâmz] handvuurwapenen, draagbare vuurwapenen *o. mv.*
small-holding ['smo:l'houdiŋ] klein boerenbedrijf, boerderijtje *o.*
small-minded ['smo:l'maindid] benepen, kleinzielig.
smallpox ['smo:lpɔks] pokken *v. mv.*
smart [smât] *adj.* pijnlijk; scherp, vinnig, bits; vlug, levendig, wakker, flink; knap, bijdehand, gewiekst; gevat, snedig; geestig; elegant, zwierig, chic; *sb.* (gewilde) geestigheid *v.*; fat, kwast, dandy *m.*
smart [smât] *vi.* pijn doen, zeer doen; lijden; boeten; *sb.* schrijnende pijn *v.*; smart *v.*
smarten ['smâtn] — **(up),** mooi maken, optooien, opknappen; opmonteren.
smart-money ['smâtmǝni] rouwkoop *m.*; smartgeld *o.*
smash [smæʃ] *vt.* stukgooien, kapot gooien, kapot smijten; *(v. ruiten)* inslaan, ingooien; verbrijzelen, verpletteren, vermorzelen; vernietigen, totaal vernielen; *vi.* breken; bankroet gaan: op de fles gaan, over de kop gaan; kapot gaan (vallen); *(sl.)* vals geld uitgeven; *sb.* slag, kwak, smak *m.*; botsing *v.*; vernieling *v.*; bankroet *o.*, krach *m.*; verpletterende nederlaag *v.*
smasher ['smæʃə] breek-al *v.*; vernietigende slag *m.*; verpletterend argument *o.*, dooddoener *m.*; vernietigende kritiek *v.*
smash-up ['smæʃ'ʌp] botsing *v.*; verbrijzeling, vermorzeling *v.*; bankroet *o.*, krach *m.*
smear [smîə] *vt.* insmeren, besmeren; bevuilen, besmeuren; bezoedelen, bezwalken; *sb.* vlek, smet *v.*; smeersel *o.*
smell [smel] *sb.* reuk, geur *m.*, lucht-

(je) v. (o.); vt. ruiken; beruiken, ruiken aan; — **out**, uitvorsen, opsporen, achter iets komen; vi. ruiken, rieken; stinken; snuffelen; — **about**, rondsnuffelen; — **at**, ruiken aan; — **of**, rieken naar.

smelling-bottle ['smelinbɔtl] reukflesje o.

smelt [smelt] sb. spiering m.; zandaal m.; vt. (v. erts) smelten.

smelting-furnace ['smeltinfə:nis] smeltoven m.

smelting-works ['smeltinwə:ks] smelterij v.

smile [smail] vi. lachen, glimlachen (**at, on, to**, tegen); vt. lachen; door een glimlach uitdrukken; sb. lachje o., glimlach m.; (Am.) slokje o.

smirk [smə:k] gemaakt lachen, meesmuilen.

smite [smait] vt. smijten; slaan, treffen; straffen, kastijden; verslaan; (v. harp, enz.) tokkelen; vi. slaan; botsen; sb. slag m.; (fig.) gooi m.

smith [smiδ] smid m.

smithy ['smiθi, 'smiδi] smidse, smederij v.

smock-frock ['smɔkfrɔk] boerenkiel, werkmanskiel m.

smokable ['smoukəbl] adj. rookbaar.

smoke [smouk] sb. rook; damp m.; mist m.; rookwolk v.; vi. roken; dampen; (v. lamp) walmen; vt. roken, beroken; uitroken; lucht krijgen van; voor de gek houden; afranselen; — **out**, (v. sigaar) oproken; (v. pijp) uitroken; door rook verdrijven; uitroeien; (fig.) uitvissen.

smoke-dry ['smoukdrai] (v. vis, enz.) roken, in de rook hangen.

smokeless ['smouklis] rokeloos, zonder rook.

smoker ['smoukə] roker m.; rookcoupé m.

smoke-room ['smoukrum] rookkamer v.

smoking-room ['smoukinrum] rookkamer v.

smoky ['smouki] rokerig; walmend; berookt.

smooth [smûθ] adj. & adv. glad, vlak, gelijk, effen; smedig; zacht; (v. gezicht) uitgestreken; (v. stijl, enz.) vlot, vloeiend; vriendelijk, minzaam, vleiend; (v. rad) ongetand; (Am., sl.) fijn, chic; vt. glad maken, gladstrijken; gladschaven; polijsten; afvlakken; (v. misstap) bemantelen, bewimpelen; verzachten, bedaren; — **over**, (v. fouten) bemantelen, vergoelijken; (v. moeilijkheden) uit de weg ruimen, vereffenen; sb. gladstrijking v.; gladde oppervlakte v.; kalm water o.

smoothing-iron ['smûθinaiən] strijkijzer o.

smoothness ['smûθnis] gladheid, enz.

smother ['smʌδə] sb. damp, (dikke) rook, walm m.; (wolk van) stof o.; (fig.) smeuling, gisting v.; vt. smoren, versmo-

ren, verstikken, doen stikken; dempen; (v. lach, geeuw) onderdrukken; in de doofpot stoppen; (met geschenken, enz.) overladen; vi. smoren, stikken; smeulen.

smoulder ['smouldə] vi. smeulen; sb. smeulend vuur o.; walm m.

smudge [smʌdʒ] vt. besmeren; bevuilen, besmeuren, bezoedelen; verknoeien; vi. vlekken, smetten; sb. vlek, smet v.; veeg m.; verwarde massa v.; verstikkende rook m.; rokend vuur o.

smudgy ['smʌdʒi] adj. vuil, smerig, smoezelig.

smuggle ['smʌgl] smokkelen; (mil., sl.) stelen; — **away**, wegmoffelen; verdonkeremanen; — **off**, er heimelijk vandoor gaan; — **out**, over de grenzen smokkelen.

smuggler ['smʌglə] smokkelaar m.

smut [smʌt] sb. roetvlok v., roetdeeltje o.; zwarte vlek, roetvlek v.; vuiltje o., vuiligheid v.; vuile taal v.; (in koren) brand m.; vt. vuil maken; bevuilen, bezoedelen; (v. koren) brandig maken.

smutty ['smʌti] adj. vuil, vies, smerig; berookt; (v. koren) brandig.

snack [snæk] sb. haastige maaltijd m.; klein slokje o.; deel o.; vi. lunchen.

snaffle ['snæfl] trens v.

snail [sneil] huisjesslak v.

snail slow ['sneil'slou] (zo traag) als een slak.

snake [sneik] slang v.

snake-charmer ['sneiktʃâmə] slangenbezweerder m.

snap [snæp] vi. snappen, happen (**at**, naar); toehappen; snauwen; knippen; dichtklappen; afknappen; breken; knetteren; vt. doen afknappen; dichtklappen; toesnauwen; (v. vuurwapen) aftrekken, overhalen; op de kop tikken; (fam.) kieken; sb. hap m., hapje o., beet m.; klap; knak, krak m.; knip m. (v. beurs; met vingers); breuk v.; barst v.; snauw m.; adj. plotseling, overijld.

snappish(**ly**) ['snæpiʃ(li)] adj. (adv.) snibbig, bits, vinnig, kortaf.

snappy ['snæpi] adj. knappend; pittig; kranig; elegant; snibbig, bits.

snap-shot ['snæpʃɔt] sb. schot o. op de aanslag; kiek m., momentopname v.; vt. kieken.

snare ['snêə] sb. strik m.; (v. trommel) snaar v.; (fig.) valstrik m.; vt. (v. vogels) strikken; (fig.) verstrikken.

snarl [snâl] vi. grommen, brommen; grauwen, snauwen; vt. toesnauwen; verwarren, in de war maken; verstrikken; sb. grauw, snauw m.; verwikkeling v., warboel m.

snatch [snætʃ] vt. grijpen, pakken; aangrijpen; wegrukken, afrukken; — **off**, afrukken; (v. jas, enz.) uitgooien; vi. — **at**, grijpen naar; aangrijpen; sb. ruk, greep m.; vlaag v.; ogenblikje, tijdje o.; stuk, brokstuk o.

sneak [snîk] vi. sluipen, gluipen; (Am.) wegsluipen; (sl.) klikken; vt. (sl.) gappen; ontfutselen; *sb.* gluiperd *m.*; kruiper *m.*; gauwdief *m.*

sneaky ['sniki] *adj.* gluipend, gluiperig.

sneer [snîə] *vi.* spottend lachen, grijnslachen; *sb.* spotlach, grijns, spottende grijnslach *m.*

sneeze [snîz] niezen.

sniff [snif] *vi.* snuiven; snuffelen; *vt.* ruiken; opsnuiven; *sb.* gesnuif, gesnuffel *o.*; reuk *m.*; luchtje *o.*

snigger ['snigə] *vi.* giechelen, grinniken, gnuiven; *sb.* gegiechel, gegrinnik *o.*

snip [snip] *vt.* afsnijden, afknippen; doorknippen; *vi.* knippen; *sb.* snipper *m.*, stukje *o.*; knip *m.*, sneetje *o.*

snipe [snaip] snip(pen) *v.* (*mv.*); (*Am.*) half opgerookte sigaar (sigaret) *v.*

snobbish (ly) ['snɔbiʃ(li)] *adj.* (*adv.*) snobachtig, poenig.

snoop [snûp] (*Am.*) *vi.* snoepen; snuffelen, neuzen; loeren, gluren; zijn neus in andermans zaken steken; *vt.* gappen, kapen; *sb.* bemoeial *m.*

snore [sno:] *vi.* snorken, snurken; *vt.* verslapen; *sb.* gesnurk, gesnork *o.*

snort [sno:t] *vi.* snuiven, blazen; briesen; ronken; *sb.* gesnuif *o.*; geronk *o.*

snot [snɔt] snot *o.*; snotneus *m.*

snotty ['snɔti] *adj.* snotterig; (*sl.*) gemeen; *sb.* snotneus *m.*

snout [snout] *sb.* snoet, snuit *m.*; tuit *v.*; *vi.* wroeten.

snow [snou] *sb.* sneeuw *v.*; geklopt schuim *o.* van eieren; **—s,** sneeuw; sneeuwvelden; *vi.* sneeuwen; *vt.* besneeuwen; laten sneeuwen, laten neerdalen (als sneeuw); bestrooien; sneeuwwit maken.

snow-drift ['snoudrift] sneeuwjacht *v.*; sneeuwbank *v.*

snow-drop ['snoudrɔp] (*Pl.*) sneeuwklokje *o.*

snow-flake ['snoufleik] sneeuwvlok *v.*

snow-man ['snoumæn] sneeuwman *m.*

snowy ['snoui] sneeuwachtig; sneeuwwit· besneeuwd; sneeuw—.

snub [snʌb] *vt.* afsnauwen, toegrauwen; bits (minachtend) afwijzen; de mond snoeren; *sb.* snauw *m.*; terechtwijzing *v.*; onheuse bejegening *v.*; afwijzing *v.*; *adj.* (*v. neus*) stomp; stompneuzig.

snuff [snʌf] *vt.* (*v. kaars*) snuiten; opsnuiven; besnuffelen; beruiken; *vi.* snuiven.

snuff-box ['snʌfbɔks] snuifdoos *v.*

snuffer ['snʌfə] snuiver *m.*; (*Dk.*) bruinvis *m.*, zeevarken *o.*; **—s,** snuiter *m.* (*voor kaars*).

snuffle ['snʌfl] snuiven; snuffelen; door de neus spreken.

snug [snʌg] gezellig, behaaglijk, knus; lekker (warm, beschut); netjes, knap; nauwsluitend; zeewaardig.

so [sou] *adv.* zo, alzo, aldus; zodanig; zozeer; zulks; dat; *cj.* als, indien, zo; dus, derhalve; (*Am.*) zodat, opdat.

soak [souk] *vt.* week maken, weken, in de week zetten; soppen; opslorpen,

inzuigen; (laten) trekken; drenken, doordringen; *vi.* in de week staan; trekken; sijpelen; (*pop.*) zuipen.

soap [soup] *sb.* zeep *v.*; mooipraterij, lekkermakerij *v.*; *vt.* zepen, inzepen; (*sl.*) vleien, honig om de mond smeren.

soap-boiler ['soupbɔilə] zeepzieder *m.*

soap-dish ['soupdiʃ] zeepbakje *o.*

soap-works ['soupwə:ks] zeepfabriek, zeepziederij *v.*

soar [so:] omhoog vliegen; opstijgen, de lucht ingaan; hoog vliegen, zich verheffen; (*vl.*) zeilen.

sob [sɔb] *vi.* snikken; *vt.* uitsnikken; *sb.* snik *m.*

sober ['soubə] *adj.* sober, matig; ernstig, bezadigd; nuchter, verstandig; bescheiden; bedaard; (*v. kleding*) stemmig; *vt.* bedaren, doen bedaren; ernstig stemmen; ontnuchteren; *vi.* bedaren; **— off,** nuchter worden.

sober-headed ['soubəhedid] bezadigd, nuchter, bedaard.

soberness ['soubənis] soberheid, enz.

sober-suited ['soubə'sjûtid] stemmig gekleed.

sobriety [sou'braiəti] soberheid, matigheid *v.*; bezadigdheid *v.*; bescheidenheid *v.*; bedaardheid *v.*; stemmigheid *v.*

sobriquet ['soubrikei] bijnaam; scheldnaam, spotnaam *m.*

so-called ['sou'ko:ld] zogenaamd.

social ['souʃəl] maatschappelijk, sociaal; gezellig.

socialism ['souʃəlizm] socialisme *o.*

socialization [souʃəlai'zeiʃən] socialisatie *v.*

society [sə'saiəti] maatschappij *v.*; (de) samenleving *v.*; genootschap *o.*, vereniging *v.*; de (grote) wereld *v.*; gezelschap *o.*, omgang *m.*

sock [sɔk] *sb.* sok *v.*; losse binnenzool *v.*; lichte toneellaars *v.*; (*fig.*) (het) blijspel *o.*; (*sl.*) mep *m.*, pak slaag *o.*; *vt.* gooien, smijten; (*sl.*) raken, ranselen; *vi.* (*sl.*) snoepen; *adv.* vlak, pardoes.

sockdologer [sɔk'dɔlədʒə] (*sl.*) opstopper, oplazer *m.*; genadeslag *m.*

socket ['sɔkit] (*v. kandelaar*) pijp *v.*; (*v. tand*) holte *v.*; (*tn.*) sok, mof *v.*; (*el.*) stopgat *o.*; houder, koker *m.*

sod [sɔd] zode *v.*; grasveld *o.*

sodality [sou'dæliti] broederschap *v.*

soda-water ['soudəwo:tə] spuitwater *o.*

sodden ['sɔdn] *adj.* doorweekt, doortrokken; pafferig; (*v. groenten*) waterig; (*v. brood*) klef, nattig, niet doorbakken; (*v. vlees*) te gaar; *vt.* weken, doorweken; *vi.* weken, doorweekt worden.

soft [so:ft] *adj.* zacht, week; mals; (*v. boord*) slap; (*v. leven, werk, enz.*) gemakkelijk; (*fig.*) week, verwijfd; zoetsappig, sentimenteel; verliefd; *adv.* zachtjes.

soften [so:fn] *vt.* zacht maken, verzachten; vermurwen, vertederen; lenigen; temperen; verwekelijken; *vi.* zacht worden, week worden; vertederd worden.

soft-hearted ['so:fthâtid] weekhartig, teerhartig.

softness ['so:ftnis] zachtheid, enz.

soft-soap ['so:ftsoup] groene zeep v.

soft-spoken ['so:ftspoukn] zacht vriendelijk; zacht gesproken, zacht gezegd.

softy ['so:fti] sukkel, sul, onnozele bloed, halve gare m.

soggy ['sogi] drassig, vochtig, nat; (v. brood) klef; sullig; zwoel.

soil [soil] sb. grond, bodem m.; land, stuk land o.; teelaarde v.; smet, vlek v.; vuiligheid, vuilnis v.; vuil o., drek m.; vt. besmetten, bevuilen, bezoedelen; besmeuren; vi. smetten, vuil worden.

soilless ['soillis] smetteloos, vlekkeloos.

sojourn ['sodʒə:n] sb. (tijdelijk) verblijf o.; verblijfplaats v.; vi. vertoeven, zich ophouden, (tijdelijk) verblijven.

solace ['soləs, 'solis] sb. troost m., vertroosting v.; verlichting v.; vt. troosten, vertroosten; verlichten, lenigen.

solar ['soulə] van de zon, zonne—.

solder ['soldə, 'so:də] sb. soldeersel o.; (fig.) cement o., band m.; vt. solderen; (fig.) cementeren, verbinden, bevestigen; herstellen.

soldier ['souldʒə] soldaat, militair, krijgsman m.; lieveheersbeestje o.; rode spin v.

sole [soul] sb. zool v.; bodem m., ondervlak o.; voet m.; (Dk.: vis) tong o.; vt. verzolen; adj. enig; enkel; (recht) ongehuwd.

solely ['soulli] adv. alleen, enkel, uitsluitend.

solemn ['soləm] adj. plechtig, deftig, plechtstatig.

solemnity [so'lemniti] plechtigheid, statigheid, solemniteit v.

solicitation [səlisi'teiʃən] verzoek, aanzoek o.

solicitor [sə'lisitə] verzoeker, aanzoeker m.; (recht) procureur; zaakwaarnemer m.

solicitous(ly) [sə'lisitəs(li)] adj. (adv.) bezorgd, bekommerd (about, for, concerning, over); verlangend, begerig (of, naar); nauwgezet.

solicitude [sə'lisitjûd] bezorgdheid, bekommernis v.; angst, kommer m.; nauwgezetheid v.

solid ['solid] vast; stevig, duurzaam; sterk, flink; solidair, aaneengesloten; massief.

solidary ['solidəri] solidair.

soliloquy [sə'liləkwi] alleenspraak v.

solitaire [soli'têə] alleen gezette diamant (steen) m.

solitary ['solitəri] adj. eenzaam, verlaten; afgelegen, afgezonderd; op zichzelf staand; sb. kluizenaar m.

soloist ['soulouist] solist m.

soluble ['soljubl] oplosbaar.

solution [sə'l(j)ûʃən] oplossing v.

solvability [solvə'biliti] oplosbaarheid v.; (H.) soliditeit, kredietwaardigheid v.

solvable ['solvəbl] oplosbaar; solvent, solvabel.

solve [solv] oplossen; ontbinden; ontwarren, ontraadselen; (v. schuld) afbetalen; (v. belofte) inlossen.

solvency ['solvənsi] solvabiliteit, soliditeit, kredietwaardigheid v.

solvent ['solvənt] oplossend, ontbindend; solvabel, solvent, in staat om te betalen.

sombre ['sombə] adj. somber, donker; vt. versomberen, verdonkeren, verduisteren.

some [som, səm] pron. enige; sommige; iets, wat; (Am.) heel wat; adj. enige, sommige; wat, een beetje; ettelijke; een zeker(e), de een of ander; ongeveer, om en bij, zowat; adv. (sl.) enigszins, nogal; iets, een beetje, ietwat; verbazend veel; niet gering ook.

somebody ['sombodi] iemand; een zeker iemand.

someone, some one ['somwən] zie somebody.

somersault ['soməso:lt] sb. buiteling v., sprong m.; vi. buitelen.

something ['somðin] sb. & pron. iets, wat; het een of ander; adv. iets, ietwat, enigszins.

sometimes ['somtaimz, səm'taimz] soms, somtijds.

somewhat ['somwot] enigszins, ietwat, iets.

somewhere ['somwêə] ergens.

somnambulist [som'næmbjulist] slaapwandelaar m.

son [sən] zoon m.

song [son] zang m., lied o.; gezang o.; poëzie v.

song-bird ['sonbə:d] zangvogel m.

songster ['sonstə] zanger m.

son-in-law ['səninlo:] schoonzoon m.

sonnet ['sonit] sonnet o.

sonority [sə'noriti] klankrijkheid, klankvolheid, sonoriteit v.

sonorous [sə'no:rəs] adj. geluidgevend; (helder)klinkend, diepklinkend, klankrijk, klankvol; (v. titel) weids.

soon [sûn] weldra, spoedig, gauw, vlug; vroeg.

soot [sut] roet o.; roetvlok v.

soothe [sûθ] verzachten, kalmeren, sussen; bevredigen, tevredenstellen.

soothing(ly) ['sûθin(li)] adj. (adv.) verzachtend.

soothsayer ['sûðseiə] waarzegger m.

sophism ['sofizm] sofisme o., drogrede v.

sophisticate [so'fistikeit] vervalsen verdraaien; misleiden.

soporific [soupə'rifik] adj. slaapwekkend; sb. slaapwekkend middel o.

soppy ['sopi] sopperig, drassig, doorweekt, kletsnat; (fig.) slap, futloos, flauw, week, sentimenteel.

soprano [sə'prânou] sopraan v.

sorbet ['so:bət] sorbet o.

sorcerer ['so:sərə] tovenaar m.

sordid(ly) ['so:did(li)] *adj.* (*adv.*) vuil, smerig, vies; onsmakelijk; gemeen, laag; gierig, inhalig, vrekkig.

sore [so:] *adj.* pijnlijk; (*v. lichaamsdeel*) rauw; bekommerd; bedroefd; prikkelbaar, gevoelig; nijdig, boos; gekrenkt; zwaar, hevig, erg; moeilijk; *adv.* zeer; *sb.* pijnlijke plek; rauwe plek *v.*

sorrel ['sorəl] *sb.* (*Pl.*) zuring *v.*

sorrel ['sorəl] *adj.* rossig, rosachtig; *sb.* roodbruin *o.*, roskleur *v.*; (*Dk.: paard*) vos *m.*

sorrow ['sorou] *sb.* droefheid, smart *v.*, leed *o.*; weeklacht *v.*; leedwezen *o.*; *vi.* treuren, bedroefd zijn; pijn doen; leedwezen gevoelen (*at, for, over,* over).

sorrowful(ly) ['sorouful(i)] *adj.* (*adv.*) droevig, treurig; jammerlijk.

sorry ['sori] *adj.* smartelijk; bedroefd, droevig; ellendig, armzalig; min.

sort [so:t] *sb.* soort *v.* & *o.*; slag *o.*; klasse *v.*; *vt.* sorteren, rangschikken, indelen; uitzoeken; *vi.* — **with,** omgaan met; passen bij, stroken met; (*Sc.*) voorzien van.

sough [sof] *sb.* (*v. wind*) gesuis *o.*, zucht *v.*; zoevend geluid *o.*; gerucht *o.*; *vi.* suizen, zuchten; zoeven.

soul [soul] ziel *v.*; geest *m.*

soulless ['soullis] zielloos.

sound [saund] *sb.* geluid *o.*, klank, toon *m.*; geschal *o.*; (*sch.*) peiling, loding *v.*; sonde *v.*; zeeëngte *v.*; zwemblaas *v.*; *adj.* gezond; gaaf; flink, krachtig; grondig; solied, degelijk, solvent; betrouwbaar, te vertrouwen; oprecht; zuiver in de leer; (*v. slaap*) vast; *adv.* **sleep —,** vast slapen; — **asleep,** vast in slaap; *vt.* doen (weer)klinken; doen schallen; uitbazuinen; uitspreken; (*v. waarschuwing, enz.*) doen horen; (*v. wielen, enz.*) kloppen op; bekloppen, ausculteren; sonderen, peilen; *vi.* klinken, weerklinken; luiden; galmen; schallen.

sounder ['saundə] (*telegr.*) klopper *m.*; (*telegr.*) weergever *m.*; dieplood *o.*

sounding-lead ['saundinled] dieplood *o.*

soundless ['saundlis] geluidloos; onpeilbaar.

soundness ['saundnis] gezondheid, enz.

soup [sûp] soep *v.*

soup-plate ['sûppleit] soepbord, diep bord *o.*

sour ['sauə] *adj.* zuur; wrang; (*v. weer*) guur; knorrig, nors; *sb.* zuur *o.*; *vt.* zuur maken; verbitteren; *vi.* zuur worden, verzuren.

source [so:s] bron *v.*; (*fig.*) bron *v.*, oorsprong *m.*

sour-crout ['sauəkraut] zuurkool *v.*

sourish ['sauərif] zuurachtig, zuur, rins.

soutane [sû'tân] soutane, toog *v.*

south [sauð] *sb.* zuiden *o.*; *adj.* zuidelijk; zuid—; *adv.* zuidelijk, zuidwaarts, in zuidelijke richting.

southerly ['seðəli] zuidelijk.

southern ['seðən] zuidelijk.

south-pole ['sauðpoul] zuidpool *v.*

southward(ly) ['sauðwəd(li)] zuidelijk, zuidwaarts.

sovereign ['sovrin] *adj.* souverein, opperst; oppermachtig; (*v. middel*) afdoend, probaat; onovertroffen; *sb.* souverein, vorst *m.*; goudstuk *o.* van 20 shilling.

sovereignty ['sovrinti] oppermacht, opperheerschappij *v.*; onafhankelijke staat *m.*

sow [sau] *sb.* (*Dk.*) zeug *v.*; geus, gieteling *m.*, schuitje tin *o.*

sow [sou] *vt.* zaaien, bezaaien; (*v. oesters*) poten; (*v. evangelie*) verspreiden.

sow-bug ['saubəg] keldermot, kelderpissebed *v.*

sower ['souə] zaaier *m.*; zaaimachine *v.*

space [speis] *sb.* ruimte, wijdte *v.*, afstand *m.*; tijdruimte *v.*; tijdje *o.*; spatie *v.*; *vt.* (in ruimten) verdelen; — (*out*), spatiëren.

spacious(ly) ['speifəs(li)] *adj.* (*adv.*) groot, ruim, wijd, uitgestrekt.

spade [speid] *sb.* spade, schop *v.*; (*kaartsp.*) schoppen *v. mv.*; (*v. affuit*) spoor *o.*; *vt.* spitten, omspitten.

Spain [spein] Spanje *o.*

spall [spo:l] *sb.* splinter *m.*; *vt.* versplinteren; *vi.* splinteren, afsplinteren.

span [spæn] *sb.* span *o.*; (*v. brug, boog*) spanwijdte *v.*; spanne tijds *v.*, korte duur *m.*; (*v. vliegtuig*) vleugelbreedte *v.*; *vt.* spannen; afspannen, omspannen; overspannen.

span-new ['spænnjû] fonkelnieuw, splinternieuw.

spar [spâ] *sb.* dakspar *v.*; paal *m.*; (*sch.*) rondhout *o.*; (*v. vliegtuig*) langsligger *m.*; spaat *o.*; vuistgevecht *o.*, kloppartij, bokspartij *v.*; hanengevecht *o.*; *vi.* met de vuist vechten; met de armen uitslaan, er op los slaan; (*v. haan*) met de sporen slaan.

spare ['spêə] *adj.* schraal, mager; dun; zuinig, karig; *sb.* reservedeel *o.*; *vt.* sparen, besparen; zuinig zijn met, bezuinigen; ontzien; geven, afstaan; missen, het stellen zonder; verschonen van; *vi.* zuinig zijn, het spaarzaam aanleggen; *vr.* — *oneself,* zich ontzien.

sparerib ['spêərib, 'spæərib] krap *v.*

sparing(ly) ['spêərin(li)] *adj.* (*adv.*) spaarzaam, zuinig; schraal; matig; (*met woorden, enz.*) karig.

spark [spâk] *sb.* vonk *v.*, vonkje *o.*; sprankje, greintje *o.*; *vi.* vonken, vonken spatten; het hof maken.

sparking-plug ['spâkinpləg] (*el.*) (ontstekings)bougie *v.*

sparkle ['spâkl] *vi.* vonken schieten; fonkelen, glinsteren, schitteren; tintelen; (*v. wijn*) parelen, schuimen, mousseren; *sb.* vonk, sprank *v.*; fonkeling, glinstering *v.*; tinteling *v.*; pareling *v.*; geestigheid *v.*

sparkless ['spâklis] vonkvrij.

sparrow ['spærou] mus v.

sparrow-hawk ['spærouho:k] sperwer m.

spasm [spæzm] kramp v.; (fig.) opwelling, vlaag v.

spasmodic(ally) [spæz'mɔdik(əli)] adj. (adv.) krampachtig.

spat [spæt] slobkous v.

spatter ['spætə] vt. bespatten; bespuwen; bekladden, bezoedelen; vi. spatten; sputteren; sb. spat v.; gesputter o.

spatterdashes ['spætədæʃiz] slobkousen v. mv.

spavin ['spævin] spat, aderspat v.

spawn [spo:n] sb. kuit v.; broed o.; (fig.) produkt, broedsel o.; zaad o.; vi. kuit schieten; (eieren) leggen; wemelen (with, van); vt. uitbroeden, voortbrengen.

speak [spîk] vi. spreken; praten; (v. instrument) geluid geven, aanslaan, aanspreken; (v. hond) spreken; aanslaan; zich declareren; (v. testament) van kracht zijn; vt. spreken; uitspreken, uiten; uitdrukken; opzeggen; (sch.) praaien.

speaker ['spîkə] spreker m.

speaking ['spîkiŋ] sprekend; spreek—.

speaking-tube ['spîkiŋtjûb] spreekbuis v.

spear [spîə] speer, lans v.

special ['speʃəl] bijzonder, speciaal; extra.

specialist ['speʃəlist] specialiteit v. (in bepaald vak).

species ['spiʃ(i)îz] soort(en) v. (mv.); geslacht(en) o. (mv.).

specific [spe'sifîk] soortelijk, specifiek; soort—; bijzonder, bepaald; eigenaardig, eigen.

specification [spesifi'keiʃən] specificatie, nauwkeurige opgaaf v.; —s (and conditions), bestek.

specify ['spesifai] specificeren, in bijzonderheden opgeven (vermelden).

specimen ['spesimin] specimen o., proef v.; voorbeeld, staaltje o.; (fam.) exemplaar, type o.

specious(ly) ['spiʃəs(li)] adj. (adv.) schoonschijnend; zich mooi voordoend; bevallig.

speck [spek] sb. vlek(je), smet(je) v.(o.); spatje o.; spikkel m.; nietigheid v.; vt. vlekken; spikkelen

speckle ['spekl] sb. spikkel m., spikkeling v.; vt. spikkelen.

spectacle ['spektəkl] schouwspel o., vertoning v., toneel o.; (pair of) —s, bril.

spectacle-case ['spektəklkeis] brilledoos v.

spectator [spek'teitə] toeschouwer, aanschouwer m.

spectral ['spektrəl] spookachtig; spook—; spectraal; van het spectrum.

speculate ['spekjuleit] bespiegelingen houden; mijmeren, peinzen; speculeren (on, in, in).

speculation [spekju'leiʃən] bespiege-

ling, beschouwing v.; overpeinzing v.; (H.) speculatie v.

speculative ['spekjulətiv] adj. bespiegelend, beschouwend; zuiver theoretisch; speculatief.

speech [spîtʃ] spraak, taal v.; rede, redevoering, toespraak v.; gesprek o.; (op school) voordracht v.

speechless(ly) ['spîtʃlis(li)] adj. (adv.) sprakeloos, stom.

speed [spîd] sb. spoed m., haast, snelheid v.; versnelling v.; (at) full —, met volle kracht; in volle vaart, spoorslags; vi. zich spoeden, haast maken, voortmaken; woest rijden; vt. bespoedigen; bevorderen, begunstigen; een bepaalde snelheid geven aan; (v. paard) aanzetten; afmaken.

speedy ['spîdi] snel, vlug, spoedig; voortvarend.

spell [spel] sb. toverformule v., tovermiddel o.; toverij; betovering v.; tovermacht, toverkracht v.; bekoring v.; vt. spellen; betekenen, voorspellen; ontcijferen, uitvorsen.

spellbound ['spelbaund] als betoverd, aan de grond genageld.

spelling ['speliŋ] spelling v.

spelter ['speltə] zink o.

spend [spend] vt. uitgeven, besteden; (v. tijd) doorbrengen; verspillen, verkwisten; vi. uitgaven doen; verteerd worden; vr. — oneself, zich uitputten, zich afmatten.

spendthrift ['spendθrift] sb. verkwister, doorbrenger m.; adj. verkwistend.

sperm [spə:m] sperma, zaad o.; kuit v.

spew [spjû] vt. uitspuwen, uitbraken; vi. spuwen, braken.

sphere ['sfîə] sfeer v.; bol, bal m.; hemelbol m., globe v.; (dicht.) hemelgewelf o.; kring m., gebied o.; werkkring m., arbeidsveld o.

spheric(al) ['sferik(l)] bolrond, bolvormig; bol—; hemels.

spice [spais] sb. specerij, kruiderij v.; geur m.; zweempje, tikje o.; vt. kruiden.

spick and span ['spikən'spæn] (spik)-splinternieuw; keurig, netjes, piekfijn.

spider ['spaidə] spin, spinnekop v.

spike [spaik] sb. aar v.; maïskolf v.; spijl v.; (Pl.) spijk v.; (v. kam) tand m.; (v. haar) piek v.; lange spijker; nagel m.; vt. vastspijkeren, dichtspijkeren.

spiky ['spaiki] puntig, met scherpe punten; (v. haar) piekerig; bits, scherp.

spile [spail] spil v.; pin v., zwikje o.; staak, paal m.

spill [spil] sb. spil, spijl v.; staaf m.; splinter m.; fidibus m.; val m.; tuimeling v.; plasregen m., stortbui v.; vt. (v. melk, enz.) morsen; (v. bloed) vergieten, storten; verstrooien; (v. ruiter) afwerpen; omgooien.

spin [spin] vt. spinnen; uitspinnen, rekken; (v. tol) opzetten; snel laten draaien; (vl.) in vrille doen gaan; — out,

uitspinnen; tot in het oneindige rekken;
vi. spinnen; snel draaien, in de rondte
draaien; (v. bloed) gutsen; snel lopen
(rijden); (vl.) in vrille gaan.
spinach, spinage ['spinidʒ] spinazie v.
spinal ['spainəl] ruggegraats—.
spindle ['spindl] spil, as v.; spoel v.,
klos m.; staaf m., spijl, stang v.
spindle-legs ['spindllegz] spillebenen
o. mv.
spine [spain] (Pl.) witte doorn m.; (v.
egel, enz.) stekel m.; ruggegraat m.;
(heuvel)rug m.; kernhout o.
spinning-wheel ['spiniŋwil] spinnewiel o.; draaibord o.
spinous ['spainəs] doornig; stekelig;
(fig.) lastig, netelig.
spiny ['spaini] zie **spinous.**
spiral ['spaiərəl] adj. spiraalvormig,
schroefvormig; kronkelend; sb. spiraal v.
spire ['spaiə] grashalm, grasspriet m.;
(v. toren) spits v.; piek, punt v.; (v. hert)
spiets v.; tak m. van gewei; kronkeling
v.; spiraal v.
spirit ['spirit] sb. geest m.; geestkracht,
levenskracht v.s wilskracht, energie, fut
v.; moed, durf m.; aard m., temperament o.; ziel, bezieling v.; gevoel o., zin
m.; spiritus, sterke drank m.; —s, levensgeesten, bewustzijn; stemming, gemoedsgesteldheid; sterke drank, spiritualiën; brandewijn; vt. aanmoedigen,
aanwakkeren, aanvuren, bezielen.
spirited(ly) ['spiritid(li)] adj. (adv.)
levendig, bezield, geanimeerd; geestrijk;
vurig; pittig; energiek.
spiritual ['spiritjuəl] onstoffelijk,
geestelijk; geestes—; intellectueel.
spiritualistic(ally) [spiritjuə'listik(ə-
li)] adj. (adv.) spiritualistisch; spiritis-
tisch.
spirituous ['spiritjuəs] geestrijk, alcoholisch.
spit [spit] sb. spit, braadspit o.; land-
tong v.; (fam.) slakkesteker m., sabel
v., degen m.; speeksel, spuug o.; spadesteek m.; vt. aan het spit steken; doorsteken, spietsen, aan de degen rijgen;
spitten; vi. spuwen, spugen; (v. kat)
blazen.
spit-box ['spitbɔks] spuwbak m.
spite [spait] sb. boosaardigheid, kwaadaardigheid v.; wrok, wrevel m.; in — of,
trots, ten spijt van, in weerwil van;
vt. ergeren, het land opjagen; dwarsbomen.
spiteful(ly) ['spaitful(i)] adj. (adv.)
boosaardig, kwaadaardig; spijtig; hatelijk; afgunstig.
spittle ['spitl] speeksel, spuug o.
spittoon [spi'tûn] spuwbak, kwispe-
door m.
spitz [spits] spits, spitshond, keeshond m.
splash [splæʃ] vt. bespatten, bemodderen; doen spatten; spikkelen; onregelmatig kleuren; vi. (in water) plassen,

ploeteren; plonzen; spatten, uit elkaar
spatten; klateren; sb. geplas, geploeter;
geplons o.; geklater o.; spat v.; vlek,
plek v.; (v. verf, enz.) klad; klets v.
splash-board ['splæʃbo:d] spatbord,
slijkbord o.
splatter ['splætə] vi. plassen, klateren;
vt. doen spatten; bespatten; sputteren;
sb. geplas; geklater o.
spleen [splin] milt, miltzucht v.; zwaarmoedigheid, gemelijkheid v., spleen o.
spleenful ['splinful] zwaarmoedig, gemelijk.
spleeny ['splini] zie **spleenful.**
splendid(ly) ['splendid(li)] adj. (adv.).
prachtig, schitterend, luisterrijk; weelderig.
splendour ['splendə] pracht v., luister
m., praal v.
splenetic [spli'netik] van de milt; gemelijk, humeurig, verdrietig.
splenic ['splenik] van de milt, milt—.
splice [splais] vt. splitsen, ineendraaien;
verbinden; (sl.) trouwen; sb. splitsing v.;
verbinding v.; (sl.) huwelijk o.
splint [splint] sb. spalk v.; splinter m.;
spaan v.; (op paardepoot) spat v.; vt.
spalken.
splinter ['splintə] sb. splinter, spaander
m.; (v. glas, granaat, enz.) scherf v.;
rotspunt v.; vt. versplinteren; vi. splinteren.
splinter-proof ['splintəprûf] adj.
scherfvrij; sb. (granaat)scherfvrije
schuilplaats v.
split [split] vt. splijten, klieven, doorklieven; splitsen; samen delen; verdelen;
versnipperen; vi. splijten; springen
scheuren, barsten; zich splitsen; uiteenvallen; — up, (sl.) uit elkaar gaan (met
ruzie); vr. — oneself, splijten; barsten;
adj. gesplitst, gespleten; (v. schip) uit-
eengeslagen, verpletterd (op rots);
sb. scheur, spleet, kloof v.; (v. partijen)
splitsing, scheuring v.; afgescheiden
partij v.; stokvis, klipvis m.
splutter ['splatə] vi. (v. pen) sputteren,
spatten; brabbelen; vt. doen spatten;
bespatten; sb. gesputter; gespat o.;
dispuut o.
spoil [spɔil] vt. roven, stelen, plunderen;
ontroven; bederven; verijdelen; vi. bederven; verrotten; schaden; sb. roof
m.; buit; oorlogsbuit m.; bagger v.
spoil-trade ['spɔiltreid] marktbeder-
ver, onderkruiper m.; spelbederver m.
spoke [spouk] spaak, sport v.
spokesman ['spouksmən] woordvoe -
der m.
spoliate ['spoulieit] vt. roven; beroven,
uitplunderen; vi. roven, plunderen.
sponge [spən(d)ʒ] sb. spons v.; spons-
diertje o.; gebakdeeg o.; (mil.) (kanon)-
wisser m.; vt. afwissen, uitwissen; af-
sponsen; (v. deeg) doen rijzen; (mil.)
wissen; opzuigen; (fig.) de spons halen
over; vi. sponsen; vocht opzuigen;
(v. deeg) rijzen.

sponger ['spɒn(d)ʒə] klaploper, tafelschuimer *m.*; sponsvisser *m.*

spongy ['spɒn(d)ʒi] sponsachtig.

sponsor ['spɒnsə] *sb.* peter, peetoom *m.*; meter, peettante *v.*; borg *m.*; helper, steun *m.*; *vt.* peet zijn over, ten doop houden; borg staan voor; krachtig steunen.

spontaneous [spɒn'teinjəs] *adj.* spontaan, ongedwongen, vrijwillig; natuurlijk, in 't wild groeiend.

spool [spûl] *sb.* spoel *v.*, klos *m.*; *vt.* spoelen, op een spoel winden.

spoon [spûn] *sb.* lepel *m.*, lepeltje *o.*; (*sp.*) lepelvormige golfstok *m.*; holbladige roeiriem *m.*; *vt.* lepelen, scheppen; *vi.* met een lepel eten.

spoonful ['spûnful] lepelvol, lepel *m.*

spoon-meat ['spûnmît] lepelkost *m.*; (*fig.*) kinderkost *m.*

sport [spɒːt] *sb.* spel, vermaak, tijdverdrijf *o.*, uitspanning, pret *v.*; speelbal *m.*; sport *v.* (*vooral jagen, vissen, enz.*); scherts, grap *v.*; **—s**, sport; sportwedstrijden; *vi.* spelen, dartelen, zich vermaken, zich ontspannen, schertsen, gekscheren; (*v. dier, plant*) afwijkingen vertonen; — *with*, spelen met; spotten met; *vt.* geuren met, pronken met; ten toon spreiden; houden, er op na houden; zich uitdossen met; (*v. geld*) stuksla ın

sportful ['spɒːtful] speels, dartel, vrolijk.

sportsman ['spɔːtsmən] sportliefhebber *m.*; flinke (eerlijke) kerel *m.*; (*Am,*) gokker; zwendelaar *m.*

spot [spɒt] *sb.* vlek; smet, plek *v.*; stip *v.*, spikkel *m.*; moedervlek *v.*; druppel *m.*; (*op das, enz.*) bolletje *o.*; gespikkelde stof *v.*; **—s**, (*H.*) locogoederen, goederen voor loco-levering; gevlekte panter; **on the —**, (*H.*) loco, ter plaatse; op staande voet; op de plaats zelf; **be on the —**, goed op de hoogte zijn, zijn vak kennen; accuraat zijn; bij de pinken zijn; *vt.* plekken; bevlekken, bezoedelen, een smet werpen op; marmeren; stippelen; *vi.* plekken; smetten; druppelen.

spot-cash ['spɒtkæʃ] contante betaling *v.*

spotless(**ly**) ['spɒtlis(li)] *adj.* (*adv.*) vlekkeloos, smetteloos.

spotted ['spɒtid] gevlekt, gespikkeld, bont; (*fig.*) niet zuiver, bezoedeld.

spotter ['spɒtə] verkenningsvlieger *m.*; verkenningsvliegtuig *o.*

spouse [spauz] echtgenoot *m.*; echtgenote, gade *v.*

spout [spaut] *vi.* spatten, gutsen; (*fam.*) oreren, declameren; *vt.* bespuiten; uitspuiten; opspuiten; (*fam.*) declameren; verkondigen, uitbazuinen; *sb.* spuit, tuit, pijp *v.*; dakgoot *v.*; (*v. bloed*) straal *m.*; (*voor graan, enz.*) glijkoker *m.*

sprag [spræg] *sb.* remblok *o.*; (*in mijn*) stut, schoor *m.*; *vt.* remmen; schoren.

sprain [sprein] *vt.* verrekken; verstuiken; *sb.* verrekking; verstuiking *v.*

sprat [spræt] *sb.* sprot *v.*; *vi.* sprot vissen.

sprawl [sprɔːl] *vi.* nonchalant (gaan) liggen; spartelen; (*mil.*) uitzwermen; (*v. huizen, enz.*) verspreid liggen; wijd uit elkaar schrijven; *vt.* onregelmatig bedekken (*with*, met); *sb.* nonchalante houding *v.*; spartelende beweging *v.*

spray [sprei] *sb.* takje, rijsjc **o.**; rijshout *o.*; stuifwater, spattend water *o.*; stofregen *m.*; sproeier; pulverisator *m.*; *vt.* besproeien; besprenkelen; verstuiven; afspuiten.

sprayer ['spreiə] sproeier *m.*

spread [spred] *vt.* spreiden; uitspreiden; verspreiden; uitstrooien, verbreiden; (*v. slag, banier*) ontplooien; (*v. vleugels*) uitslaan; (*v. brood*) (be)smeren; *vi.* zich uitspreiden; zich verspreiden; zich uitstrekken; uiteen (gaan) staan; zich ontplooien; *vr.* — *oneself*, zich verspeiden; zich uitstrekken; (*s(l)*) zich uitsloven; uitweiden (*upon*, over); *sb.* uitspreiding *v.*; verspreiding, verbreiding *v.*; (*mil.*) spreiding *v.*; ontplooiing *v.*

spreader ['spredə] verspreider; verbreider *m.*; uitstrooier *m.*; sproeier *m.*; spatel *v.*; (*el., tel.*) uithouder *m.*

spree [sprî] *sb.* fuif *v.*, pret(je) *v.* (*o.*), lolletje *o.*; braspartij *v.*; *vi.* pierewaaien; *vt.* (*v. geld*) verboemelen.

sprig [sprig] *sb.* takje, twijgje, rijsje *o.*; stift *v.*, spijkertje *o.* (zonder kop); *vt.* met twijgvormige figuren versieren; spijkeren.

spring [sprin] *vi.* springen; opspringen; ontspringen; (*v. plant*) opkomen; (*v. hout*) kromtrekken; (*v. dag*) aanbreken; (*v. zon*) opkomen; verrijzen; ontstaan, voortkomen (*from, out of,* uit); afstammen (*from, of, out of,* van); *vt.* doen springen; doen barsten; (*v. mijn, enz.*) laten springen; (*v. wild*) opjagen; plotseling voor de dag komen met; (*v. val*) plotseling laten toespringen; van veren voorzien; *sb.* sprong *m.*; (*v. boog, enz.*) terugsprong *m.*; bron *v.*; oorsprong *m.*; (*v. horloge, enz.*) veer *v.*; veerkracht, elasticiteit *v.*; elastiekje *o.*; opgewektheid; energie *v.*; drijfveer *v.*; lente *v.*

spring-bolt ['springboult] veergrendel *m.*

spring-mattress ['sprin'mætris] springmatras *v.*

springy ['sprini] *adj.* veerkrachtig, elastisch; bronrijk.

sprinkle ['sprinkl] *vt.* besprenkelen; (met zout) sprengen; bestrooien; uitstrooien (*over,* over); *vi.* stofregenen; *sb.* sprenkeling *v.*; sprengkwast *m.*; stofregen *m.*; buitje *o.*; klein aantal *o.*, kleine hoeveelheid *v.*

sprinkler ['sprinklə] sprenkelaar *m.*; sprengkwast *m.*; sproeier *m.*; strooibus *v.*

sprit [sprit] (*sch.*) spriet *m.*; spruit *v.*
sprout [spraut] *vi.* spruiten, uitspruiten, ontluiken, uitlopen, opschieten; *vt.* doen uitspruiten, doen opschieten; *sb.* spruitje *o.*, scheut *v.*; —*s,* spruitjes, spruitkool.
spruce [sprûs] *adj.* keurig, net, knap; opgedirkt, zwierig; *vt.* net aankleden, opknappen, opdirken; *vr.* — *oneself,* zich opdirken, zich mooi maken.
spruce-fir ['sprûsfə:] sparreboom, spar *m.*
spry [sprai] wakker, monter, vlug, kwiek.
spume [spjûm] *sb.* schuim *o.*; *vi.* schuimen.
spunk [spʌŋk] tonder, zwam *v.*; (*fam.*) fut *v.*, pit *o.*; (*fam.*) lef, durf, moed *m.*; (*Sc.*) vonk *v.*, sprankje *o.*
spur [spə:] *sb.* spoor *o.*; klimspoor *o.*; spoorslag, prikkel *m.*, aansporing *v.*; (*v. gebergte*) uitloper, zijtak *m.*; (*v. spoorweg*) zijlijn *v.*; (*v. boom*) hoofdwortel *m.*; (*in rogge*) brand *m.*; *vt.* (*v. paard*) de sporen geven; aansporen; van sporen voorzien; — *on,* aansporen, aanzetten.
spurious (ly) ['spjûəriəs(li)] *adj.* (*adv.*) onecht, vals, nagemaakt.
spurn [spə:n] *vt.* wegtrappen, wegschoppen; met verachting afwijzen; verachten, versmaden; *vi.* — *at,* met verachting afwijzen; *sb.* verachting, versmading *v.*
spurry ['spʌri] (*Pl.*) spurrie *v.*
sputter ['spʌtə] *vi.* sputteren; spatten; knetteren; brabbelen, rammelen; *vt.* rabbelen, brabbelen; *sb.* gesputter *o.*; geknetter *o.*; gebrabbel *o.*
spy [spai] *sb.* bespieder, spion *m.*; *vt.* bemerken, bespeuren, ontdekken; afloeren, bespieden; — *out,* uitvissen, uitvorsen; *vi.* spioneren; loeren; zitten gluren.
spy-glass ['spaiglâs] verrekijker *m.*
spy-hole ['spaihoul] kijkgat *o.*
spy-mirror ['spaimirə] spionnetje *o.*
squabble ['skwɔbl] *vi.* kibbelen, krakelen; *vt.* (*drukk.: v. zetsel*) door elkaar gooien; *sb.* gekibbel, gekrakeel *o.*; ruzie *v.*
squad [skwɔd] (*mil.*) escouade *v.*, rot *o.*; troep *m.*, ploeg, kliek *v.*; (*sch.*, *fam.*) eskader *o.*
squadron ['skwɔdrən] (*mil.*) eskadron *o.*; (*sch.*) eskader, smaldeel *o.*; (*vl.*) escadrille, eskader *o.*
squall [skwɔ:l] *sb.* gil, schreeuw *m.*, geschreeuw *o.*; bui, windvlaag *v.*; herrie, kijfpartij *v.*; *vi.* schreeuwen, gillen.
squander ['skwɔndə] verspillen, verkwisten, opmaken, doorbrengen.
square [skwêə] *sb.* vierkant, kwadraat *o.*; (*mil.*) carré *o.*; kazerneplein *o.*; exercitieplein *o.*; vierkant blok *o.* huizen; ruit *v.*; in de war; *adj.* vierkant; in het vierkant; rechthoekig; effen, op gelijke hoogte; eerlijk, openhartig; *adv.* vierkant; rechthoekig; (*fig.*) eer-

lijk; ronduit; *vt.* vierkant maken; kanten, kanthouwen, kantrechten; (*wisk.*) in 't kwadraat brengen; rechthoekig plaatsen; *vi.* overeenstemmen, kloppen; vierkant worden; — (*up*), zich in postuur zetten; — *up,* afrekenen.
square-built ['skwêəbilt] vierkant, breedgebouwd, breedgeschouderd.
squash ['skwɔʃ] *vt.* kneuzen; verpletteren; tot moes maken; (*fig.*) de mond snoeren, de kop indrukken; (*recht*) vernietigen; *vi.* moezen; plassen; *sb.* pulp *v.*, moes *o.*; zachte massa *v.*; kwak *m.*; gedrang *o.*, menigte *v.*; verbrijzeling *v.*
squat [skwɔt] *vi.* hurken, neerhurken; op de hurken gaan zitten; (*op land*) zich neerzetten; *vt.* doen hurken; (*v. dier: staart*) laten hangen; *adj.* hurkend; gehurkt; kort en dik, gedrongen; plomp.
squeak [skwîk] *vi.* piepen, krassen, knarsen, kraken; *sb.* gepiep, gekras, geknars *o.*; gilletje *o.*; klein kansje *o.*
squeal [skwîl] *vi.* knarsen, piepen, krassen; krijsen; gillen, schreeuwen, gieren; *vt.* gillen, uitgillen; *sb.* gepiep; geknars *o.*; gil *m.*
squeamish (ly) ['skwîmiʃ(li)] *adj.* (*adv.*) licht misselijk; overdreven kieskeurig; preuts.
squeeze [skwîz] *vt.* drukken, samendrukken; uitknijpen, uitpersen, persen; uitbuiten, uitzuigen; duwen; omarmen, omhelzen; druk uitoefenen op; *vi.* drukken, duwen; dringen; (*v. drukinkt*) ketsen; *sb.* druk *m.*, drukking *v.*; pressie *v.*; afdruk, wasafdruk *m.*; handdruk *m.*; stevige omhelzing *v.*; gedrang *o.*; afpersing *v.*
squeezer ['skwîzə] drukker *m.*; pers; citroenpers *v.*; drukje *o.*
squib [skwib] *sb.* voetzoeker *m.*; schotschrift *o.*; schotschrijver *m.*; *vi.* voetzoekers afsteken; schotschriften maken.
squint [skwint] *vi.* scheel zien, loensen; schuin oversteken; zinspelen (*at, upon, op*; overhellen (*at, towards,* naar); *vt.* scheel kijken naar; *sb.* (het) scheelzien *o.*; schele blik; loense (steelse) blik *m.*; kijkgat *o.*, spleet *v.*; verdraaiing *v.*; oogmerk *o.*; neiging *v.*; *adj.* scheel; scheef.
squire ['skwaiə] landedelman, grondbezitter *m.*; (*gesch.*) schildknaap *m.*
squirm [skwə:m] *vi.* wriggelen; kronkelen; zich in allerlei bochten wringen; liggen krimpen (*v. pijn*); kruipen (*to,* voor).
squirrel ['skwirəl] eekhoorntje *o.*
squirt [skwə:t] *vi.* spuiten; *vt.* uitspuiten; spuwen; *sb.* spuit *v.*, spuitje *o.*; straal *m.*; (*fig.*) opwelling, vlaag *v.*; (*fam.*) praatjesmaker, kwast *m.*
stab [stæb] *vt.* doorsteken, doorboren; doodsteken; de doodsteek geven; prikken; *sb.* steek, dolksteek, dolkstoot *m.*; (*Am.*) poging *v.*
stability [stə'biliti] stabiliteit, duurzaamheid, bestendigheid *v.*; standvastigheid *v.*

stabilize ['stæbilaiz] stabiliseren.
stable ['steibl] *adj.* stabiel, duurzaam, bestendig; standvastig; *sb.* stal *m.*; *vt.* stallen; *vi.* op stal staan; *(fig.)* huizen.
stable-boy ['steiblbɔi] staljongen *m.*
stable-man ['steiblmən] stalknecht *m.*
stack [stæk] *sb.* hoop, stapel *m.*; mijt *v.*; hooiberg *m.*; schoorsteen(pijp) *m. (v.)*; groep *v.*, schoorstenen; *(mil.: v. geweren)* rot *o.*; *vt.* opstapelen; aan mijten zetten; *(v. auto)* parkeren.
stad(t)holder ['stæd—, 'stæthouldə] *(gesch.)* stadhouder *m.*
staff [stɑːf] *sb.* staf *m.*; schacht *v.*; *(v. vlag)* stok *m.*; notenbalk *m.*; personeel *o.*; *(fig.)* steun, stut *m.*; *vt.* van personeel voorzien; stutten.
stag [stæg] (mannetjes) hert, damhert *o.*; hertshoorn *m.*; (kalkoense) haan *m.*
stage [steidʒ] *sb.* steiger *m.*, stellage *v.*; toneel *o.*; pleisterplaats *v.*; traject *o.*; laag *v.*; *(fig.)* graad *m.*, stadium *o.*, trap *v.*; *vt.* opvoeren, ten tonele voeren; monteren, ensceneren; tentoonstellen; *(fig.)* op touw zetten.
stage-fright ['steidʒfrait] plankenkoorts, plankenvrees *v.*
stag-evil ['stægivl] *(bij paarden)* klem *v.*
stagger ['stægə] *vi.* waggelen, wankelen; omtuimelen; weifelen, twijfelen; *vt.* doen waggelen, doen wankelen; versteld doen staan; *sb.* wankeling *v.*; omtuimeling *v.*; schok *m.*; *(vl.)* voorsprong *m.*; **—s,** duizeligheid; draaiziekte, kolder.
staggering ['stægəriŋ] *adj.* waggelend, wankelend.
staging ['steidʒiŋ] stellage, tribune *v.*; *(v. toneelstuk)* montering *v.*
stagnant(ly) ['stægnənt(li)] *adj. (adv.)* stilstaand; stil.
stagnate ['stægneit] *vi.* stilstaan; *vt.* doen stilstaan; stremmen.
staid [steid] *adj.* bezadigd, stemmig, ernstig.
stain [stein] *vt.* vlekken; bevlekken, bezoedelen, onteren; verven, kleuren; *(v. hout)* beitsen; *(v. glas)* beschilderen, branden; *vi.* vlekken, smetten, vlekken geven; *(v. stof)* afgeven; schilderen, glasschilderen; *sb.* vlek, smet *v.*; smaad *m.*, schande *v.*; schandvlek *v.*; verf *v.*; kleurstof *v.*; beits *o.*
stainless(ly) ['steinlis(li)] smetteloos, vlekkeloos, onbesmet; *(v. staal)* vlekvrij.
stair [stêə] trede *v.*; trap *v.*; **—s,** trap *v.*; steiger, aanlegsteiger *m.*
stair-carpet ['stêəkɑːpit] traploper *m.*
staircase ['stêəkeis] trap *v.*
stair-rod ['stêərɔd] traproede *v.*
stake [steik] *sb.* staak, paal *m.*; brandstapel *m.*; inzet *m.*; **—s,** inzet, pot *m.*; staketsel *o.*; *vt.* afpalen, afbakenen; aan een paal binden; stutten; inzetten, op het spel zetten; verwedden, wagen.
stake-money ['steikmʌni] inleggeld *o.*
stale [steil] *adj.* vunzig, muf, verschaald,

oudbakken; *(v. goederen)* verlegen; afgezaagd, saai; *vt.* muf maken; oudbakken maken; doen verschalen; *(v. belangstelling)* doen verflauwen; *(v. grond)* uitmergelen; *vi.* muf worden; oudbakken worden; verschalen; verflauwen; uitgeput raken.
stalemate ['steil'meit] schaakmat.
stalk [stɔːk] *sb.* steel, stengel *m.*; schacht *v.*; hoge schoorsteen *m.*; *(v. hert, enz.)* besluiping *v.*; *vi.* statig (trots) stappen; sluipen; voortschrijden; *vt. (v. wild, vijand)* besluipen; van stelen ontdoen.
stall [stɔːl] *sb.* stal *m.*; *(in stal, restaurant, enz.)* afdeling *v.*; stalletje *o.*, kraam *v.*; koorstoel *m.*; *(in schouwburg)* parketplaats, stallesplaats *v.*; *vt.* stallen, op stal zetten; van koorstoelen voorzien; *(fig.)* van zich afschuiven; *vi.* vastzitten, blijven steken; *(v. machine)* vastlopen; *(vl.)* afglijden.
stallage ['stɔːlidʒ] stalgeld *o.*; staangeld, marktgeld *o.*
stallion ['stæljən] (dek)hengst *m.*
stamen ['steimən] *(Pl.)* meeldraad *m.*
stammer ['stæmə] *vi.* stamelen, stotteren; *sb.* gestamel, gestotter *o.*
stamp [stæmp] *vt.* stampen, trappen; instampen; fijnstampen; stempelen; een postzegel plakken op, frankeren; *(fig.)* brandmerken; **— out,** *(v. vuur)* uittrappen; *(r. misbruiken)* uitroeien; *(v. opstand)* dempen, de kop indrukken; *vi.* stampen, trappen; *(Am.)* woedend zijn; *sb.* (het) stampen *o.*; stamp *m.*; stempel *m.*, zegel *o.*; postzegel *o.*; merk *o.*; *(tn.)* stamper, stampmolen *m.*
stamp-duty ['stæmpdjûti] zegelrecht *o.*
stamper ['stæmpə] stamper *m.*; stempel *m.*; stempelaar *m.*
stamp-paper ['stæmppeipə] gezegeld papier *o.*
stanch [stɑːnʃ] stelpen, stremmen; waterdicht maken; *(v. ziekte)* tot staan brengen.
stand [stænd] *vi.* staan; gaan staan, zich plaatsen; blijven staan; stilstaan; halt houden; stand houden; *(v. stad, enz.)* liggen; *(v. rekening)* laten staan; koers houden (naar); **— by,** er bij staan, staan bij; *(v. overtuiging, beginselen)* trouw blijven aan, vasthouden aan; *(v. persoon)* ter zijde staan, bijstaan, het opnemen voor; **— down,** naar beneden stappen; *(recht: v. getuige)* gaan zitten, naar zijn plaats gaan; *(bij verkiezing)* zich terugtrekken, zijn kandidatuur intrekken; *(bij wedstrijd)* zich terugtrekken; *(mil.)* zich verspreiden; *(sch.)* voor de wind varen; **— for,** *(v. betrekking)* dingen naar; *(sch.)* koers zetten naar, aankoersen op; *vt.* neerzetten, plaatsen; doen staan; opstellen; uitstaan, verdragen; *(v. proef, aanval)* doorstaan; uithouden; weerstaan; trakteren; zich onderwerpen aan; *sb.* stand *m.*; stilstand *m.*, halt *v.*; oponthoud *o.*;

(het) staan *o*.; standplaats *v*.; kraampje, stalletje *o*.; (*v. bomen*) opstand *m*.; (*v. graan*) gewas *o*.; positie; stelling *v*.; tribune *v*., podium *o*.; standaard *m*.; weerstand *m*.; lessenaar *m*.; stellage *v*.; onderstel *o*.; stel *o*.; plaats *v*. voor taxis (huurrijtuigen); (*Am.: v. gebouw*) stand *m*.; (*Am.*) te velde staande oogst *m*.

standard ['stændəd] *sb*. standaard *m*., vlag *v*., vaandel *o*.; standaard, maatstaf *m*., richtsnoer *o*., norm *m*.; gehalte *o*.; muntvoet *m*.; (*in lagere school*) klas *v*.; stijl; paal *m*.; stander *m*.; standaardwerk *o*.; hoogstammige boom *m*.; stamroos *v*.; hoge kandelaar *m*.; *adj*. standaard—; eenheids—, normaal—; staand; (*Pl*.)alleenstaand; hoogstammig)

standard-bearer ['stændədbêərə] vaandeldrager *m*.

stand-by ['stændbai] steun, stut *m*.; houvast *o*.; hoofdmiddel *o*. van bestaan; stevige maaltijd *m*.; trouw aanhanger *m*.; reserve *v*.; (*sch*.) vergezellend schip *o*. (voor hulp bij ongelukken).

stander ['stændə] wie staat, staande persoon *m*.

standing ['stændiŋ] *adj*. staand; stilstaand; (*v. kleuren, enz*.) vast; duurzaam, bestendig; (*v. offerte*) blijvend; (*v. bedreiging*) voortdurend; (*v. gewassen*) te velde staand; stereotiep; *sb*. (het) staan *o*.; staanplaats *v*.; positie *v*., rang, stand *m*.; aanzien *o*.; dienst, diensttijd *m*.; standaard *m*., peil *o*.; duur *m*.; (*v. boom*) ouderdom *m*.

standing-room ['stændiŋrum] staanplaats *v*.

stand-point ['stændpɔint] standpunt *o*.
stand-still ['stændstil] stilstand *m*.
stand-up ['stæn'dəp] (*v. boord, receptie, enz*.) staand.

stanza ['stænzə] stanza *v*., couplet *o*.

staple ['steipl] *sb*. produkt, hoofdprodukt *o*.; hoofdbestanddeel *o*.; stapelplaats, markt *v*., handelscentrum *o*.; (*fig*.) hoofdschotel *m*.; (*v. wol, katoen, enz*.) draad *m*., vezel *v*.; (*tn.: grendel, enz*.) kram *v*.; *adj*. voornaamste, hoofd—; *vt*. krammen, met krammen vastzetten; (*v. wol*) sorteren.

star [stâ] *sb*. ster *v*.; sterretje *o*.; gesternte *o*.; (*fig*.) geluksster *v*.; kol *v*.; *adj*. prima, eersterangs, eersteklas; *vt*. met sterren versieren; met een sterretje aanduiden.

starch [stâtʃ] *sb*. zetmeel *o*.; stijfsel *o*.; (*fig*.) stijfheid, vormelijkheid *v*.; *adj*. stijf; vormelijk; *vt*. (*v. linnen*) stijven.

stare ['stêə] *vi*. grote ogen opzetten, met grote ogen kijken; staren, strak kijken naar; gapen; in 't oog springen; (*v. haar*) overeind staan; *vt*. — *down*, de ogen doen neerslaan; *sb*. starre (starende) blik *m*.

stark [stâk] *adj*. stijf, strak; star; onbuigzaam; spiernaakt; (*v. landschap*) naakt, kaal; bar, grimmig; kras; *adv*. gans, geheel en al, absoluut.

starling ['stâliŋ] spreeuw *v*.; stroom—ijsbreker *m*.

start [stât] *vt*. doen opschrikken; beginnen; oprichten; (*v. gezang*) aanheffen; in beweging brengen, aan de gang maken; (*v. kwestie*) opwerpen; te berde brengen; wegzenden; (*v. wild*) opjagen; (*sch*.) storten; (*op veiling*) inzetten; (*v. motor*) aanzetten; ledigen, leeggieten; *vi*. opspringen; (op)schrikken; ontstellen; weggaan, vertrekken; afrijden; afvaren; (*v. plant*) uitlopen; beginnen, ontstaan; (*v. motor*) aanslaan; losgaan, losspringen; — *from,* vertrekken van; (*v. beginsel, onderstelling*) uitgaan van; — *up,* (*fam*.) op de proppen komen; (*v. motor*) aanslaan; *sb*. (het) opspringen *o*.; sprong *m*.; ruk, schok *m*.; voorsprong *m*., voordeel *o*.; (*sp*.) start, afrit *m*.; vertrek *o*.; plaats *v*. van vertrek; begin *o*., aanloop *m*.

starting-point ['stâtiŋpɔint] uitgangspunt *o*.

startle ['stâtl] *vt*. doen schrikken, doen ontstellen; verbazen, verrassen, doen opkijken; *sb*. schrik *m*., ontsteltenis *v*.; schok *m*.

startling ['stâtliŋ] verrassend, verbazend; ontstellend; schrikaanjagend; opzienbarend.

starvation [stâ'veiʃən] hongerlijden *o*., verhongering *v*.; uithongering *v*.; hongerdood *m*.; gebrek *o*.

starve [stâv] *vi*. honger lijden; verhongeren, van honger omkomen; gebrek lijden; kwijnen; — *for,* hunkeren naar; *vt*. honger laten lijden, laten verhongeren; uithongeren; gebrek laten lijden; doen kwijnen; door een hongerkuur genezen.

state [steit] *sb*. staat, toestand *m*.; stemming *v*.; staat *m*., rijk *o*.; rang, stand *m*.; *vt*. aangeven, opgeven; mededelen; vermelden; uiteenzetten; stellen.

state-aid ['steiteid] rijkssubsidie *v*.
stately ['steitli] statig, deftig, groots.
statement ['steitmənt] verklaring, bewering, uiteenzetting *v*.; mededeling *v*., bericht *o*.; verslag *o*.; staat *m*., lijst, opgaaf *v*.

statesman ['steitsmən] staatsman *m*.
station ['steiʃən] *sb*. plaats, standplaats *v*., post *m*.; (*spoorw*.) station *o*.; (*v. kruisweg*) statie *v*.; observatiepost *m*.; *at —*, (*H*.) franco station; *vt*. plaatsen, zetten, stationeren.

stationary ['steiʃnəri] stationair, stilstaand, op één plaats blijvend; op dezelfde hoogte blijvend.

stationer ['steiʃnə] handelaar *m*. in kantoor- en schrijfbehoeften.

station-master ['steiʃənmâstə] stationschef.

statistic [stə'tistik] *adj*. statistisch; *sb*. statistiek *v*.; statisticus *m*.
statuary ['stætjuəri] beeldhouwer *m*.
statue ['stætjû] standbeeld, beeld *o*.

stature ['stætʃə] gestalte, lengte, grootte v.

status ['steitəs] toestand, staat m.; rang, stand m., positie v.; rechtspositie v.

statute ['stætjût] wet v.; verordening v.; statuut o.

statute-book ['stætjûtbuk] gezamenlijke landswetten.

statute-labour ['stætjûtleibə] (verplichte) herendiensten m. mv.

statutory ['stætjutəri] wettelijk (voorgeschreven), volgens de wet, wets—.

staunch [stoːn(t)ʃ, stân(t)ʃ] hecht, sterk; trouw, betrouwbaar; verknocht, onwrikbaar; waterdicht; luchtdicht.

stay [stei] vi. blijven, wachten, toeven, talmen; wonen, vérblijven; logeren; (sp.) het uithouden, volhouden; vt. tegenhouden, terughouden; stuiten; tot staan brengen; uitstellen, opschorten; (tn.) verankeren; (sch.) staggen, overstag gooien; — up, stutten, steunen, schragen, schoren; sb. stilstand m.; verblijf, oponthoud o.; schorsing, opschorting v., uitstel o.; belemmering r.; uithoudingsvermogen o.; steun, stut m.

stay-at-home ['steiəthoum] thuiszittend, hokvast, huiselijk; (v. vogels) in 't land blijvend.

staying-power ['steiɳpauə] uithoudingsvermogen, weerstandsvermogen o.

stays [steiz] korset, keurslijf o.; a pair of —, een korset.

steadfast ['stedfəst] standvastig, trouw, onwrikbaar; vastberaden.

steadfastness ['stedfəstnis] standvastigheid, onwrikbaarheid; vastberadenheid v.

steady ['stedi] adj. vast, vaststaand; gestadig, bestendig; standvastig, trouw; geregeld, gelijkmatig; kalm, bezadigd; oppassend, solied; —! bedaard! kalm! kalmpjes aan! sb. steun m.; (tn.: v. draaibank) bril m.; vt. steunen, vastheid geven aan; geregeld (bestendig) maken; kalmeren, tot bedaren brengen; de koers doen houden; vi. bestendig (vast) worden; oppassend worden; tot rust komen.

steady-going ['stedigouɳ] solied (levend); oppassend; kalm, bedaard.

steal [stil] vt. stelen, roven; op slinkse wijze verkrijgen; vi. stelen; sluipen; glijden; — awa ', wegsluipen; (v. tijd) (ongemerkt) voorbijgaan; sb. (fam.) diefstal m., dieverij v.; (het) gestolene o.; (Am.) zwendel m.

stealth [stelθ] sluipende manier, heimelijkheid v.; by —, tersluiks, steelsgewijze.

stealthily ['stelθili] adv. tersluiks, steelsgewijze.

steam [stiːm] sb. stoom, damp m.; uitwaseming v.; vt. stomen, dampen; uitwasemen; uitstomen; gaar (laten) stomen; (door stoom) losweken; vi. stomen, dampen; (v. venster, enz.) beslaan; stoom maken.

steam-engine ['stiːmendʒin] stoommachine v.; stoombrandspuit v.

steamer ['stiːmə] stoomboot v.; stoomkoker m.; stoomketel m.; stoombrandspuit v.

steam-meat ['stiːmhit] sb. stoomverwarming, centrale verwarming v.; vt. door stoom verwarmen.

steatite ['stiːətait] speksteen m.

steed [stid] ros, strijdros o.

steel [stil] sb. staal o.; staalmiddel o.; wetstaal o.; vuurslag m.; (sp.) uithoudingsvermogen o.; —s, schaatsen; staalwaarden; adj. stalen, van staal; staalachtig; vt. stalen, verstalen; verharden, hard maken; harden, ongevoelig maken, pantseren (against, tegen).

steely ['stiːli] stalen; staalachtig, staalblank, staalhard, sterk als staal; onbuigzaam.

steep [stip] adj. steil; (v. prijs) (buitensporig) hoog; (v. verhaal, enz.) ongelooflijk, overdreven; kras; sb. steilte, (steile) helling v.

steep [stip] vt. indopen, indompelen, onderdompelen; doorweken; in de week zetten; laten doortrekken; vi. weken; (v. thee) trekken; sb. bad o., loog v.; kaasstremsel o.; (het) indopen o., (het) indompelen o.

steeple ['stipl] (spitse) toren m.; torenspits v.

steepness ['stipnis] steilte r.

steer [stiə] vt. sturen, richten; — (one's course) for, koers zetten naar; vi. sturen; naar het roer luisteren; zeilen, varen; (Am.) lokken.

steerable ['stiərəbl] bestuurbaar.

steerage ['stiəridʒ] (het) sturen o.; stuurmanskunst v.; stuurinrichting v.; tussendek o.

steering-wheel ['stiəriɳwil] (sch.) stuurrad o.

steersman ['stiəzmən] stuurman m.

stem [stem] sb. stam, stengel m.; (v. bloem, pijp, enz.) steel m.; schacht v.; (v. letter) neerhaal m.; (fig.) tak m., loot v.; geslacht o.; (sch.) boeg, voorsteven m.; vt. (v. tabak) strippen; (v. bloed) stelpen; stuiten, tegenhouden; het hoofd bieden aan.

stench [stenʃ] stank m.

stencil ['stensl] sb. sjabloon v., mal m.; vt. mallen.

stenographer [ste'nɔgrəfə] stenograaf m.

step [step] vi. stappen, treden, gaan; trappen; dansen, passen maken; (fam.) opstappen; — aside, op zij gaan, uitwijken; (fig.) zich terugtrekken; een misstap begaan, zich op zijpaden begeven; (van onderwerp) afdwalen; — between, tussenbeide komen; — down, (el.) neertransformeren; — out, (v. afstand) afstappen, afpassen; (mil.) de pas verlengen; — up, (el.) optransformeren; *vt. (v. afstand)* afpassen, afstappen; *(sch.: v. mast, enz.)* inzetten, vastzetten; laten stappen; *sb.* stap, pas, tred *m.*; voetstap *m.*; trap, trede *v.*; *(v. ladder)* sport *v.*; drempel *m.*, stoep *v.*; *(sch.: v. mast)* spoor *o.*; *(mil.)* promotie *v.*; **—s,** stappen, enz.; stoep *v.*; trapladder *v.*; *(mil.)* promotie *v.*

step-brother ['stepbrɔθə] stiefbroeder *m.*

step-father ['stepfâθə] stiefvader *m.*

step-ladder ['steplædə] trap, trapladder *v.*

steppe [step] steppe *v.*

sterile ['sterail] onvruchtbaar; *(fig.)* nutteloos; klemvrij, bacteriënvrij, steriel.

sterlet ['stə:lit] *(Dk.)* kleine steur *m.*

stern [stə:n] *sb. (sch.)* achtersteven *m.*, achterschip *o.*, spiegel *m.*, hek *o.*; staart *m.*; *adj.* ernstig; streng, hardvochtig, bars; ongastvrij.

stew [stjû] *vt.* stoven, smoren; *vi.* stoven, smoren; *(sl.)* blokken, vossen; *sb.* gestoofd vlees *o.*; visvijver *m.*

steward ['stjuəd] *sb.* hofmeester, keukenmeester, bottelier *m.*; *(aan boord)* kellner, bediende *m.*; hofmeester *m.*; *(bij feestmaal)* ceremoniemeester *m.*; rentmeester, beheerder *m.*; winkelchef, winkelopzichter *m.*; *vt.* beheren.

stick [stik] *vt.* steken; insteken; doorsteken; vaststeken; vastmaken; aanplakken, vastplakken; opsteken, opprikken; *(v. planten)* stokken zetten bij; *(fam.)* vastzetten, in de war brengen; *(sl.)* afzetten; *(sl.)* opschepen; *vi.* blijven steken; blijven zitten, blijven hangen; niet verder kunnen; (in rede) stokken; *(v. deur, raam)* klemmen; *(fig.)* beklijven; **— up,** overeind staan; *vr.* **— oneself up,** een hoge borst zetten, een air aannemen; *sb.* stok *m.*; stokje *o.*; wandelstok *m.*; dirigeerstok; strijkstok; trommelstok *m.*; maatstokje *o.*; *(spoorw.)* vertrekstaf *m.*; *(sch.)* mast *m.*, ra *v.*; *(v. vliegtuig)* knuppel *m.*; *(v. drop, lak, enz.)* pijp *v.*; zethaak *m.*; biljartkeu *v.*; kandelaar *m.*; *(fam.)* houten Klaas *m.*; *(sl.)* pistool *o.*; *(sl.)* breekijzer *o.*

sticker ['stikə] aanplakker *m.*; plakbroek; huismus *v.*; *(sp.)* volhouder, doorzetter *m.*; *(fam.)* steekwapen *o.*; *(H.: fam.)* winkelknecht *m.*, winkeldochter *v.*

sticking-plaster ['stikiŋplâstə] hechtpleister *v.*

stick-in-the-mud ['stikinθəməd] *adj.* treuzelachtig; achterlijk; sullig; *sb.* treuzel, treuzelaar *m.*, treuzelkous *v.*; achterlijk persoon, sul *m.*; achterblijver *m.*

sticky ['stiki] *adj.* kleverig, plakkerig; *(v. brood)* klef; taai; niet vlottend; weifelend; houterig, stokkerig; *(sl.)* beroerd.

sticky-fingered ['stikifiŋgəd] langvingerig, gapperig.

stiff [stif] *adj.* stijf; stram; stevig, strak; stroef; *(v. examen, enz.)* moeilijk, lastig, streng· stijfhoofdig, onbuigzaam; vastberaden; *(v. gevecht)* hardnekkig; verstijfd; *(v. akkergrond)* taai; *sb. (sl.) (H.)* handelspapier *o.*, wissel *m.*, document *o.*; geld *o.*; lijk *o.*; lummel *m.*

stiffen ['stifn] *vt.* (met stijfsel) stijven; stijf maken, doen verstijven; *(fig.)* moed inspreken; *(mil.)* het moreel opwekken; *(v. wet, enz.)* verscherpen; *vi.* hard worden; stijf worden, verstijven; *(v. wind)* aanwakkeren; een vastere vorm aannemen; *(v. markt)* vaster worden.

stifle ['staifl] smoren, verstikken; onderdrukken; blussen.

stifling(ly) ['staifliŋ(li)] *adj. (adv.)* verstikkend.

stigma ['stigmə] brandmerk *o.*; vlek, blaam *v.*; *(kath.)* stigma, wondteken *o.*; *(Pl.: v. bloem)* stempel *m.*

still [stil] *adj.* stil; rustig; *(v. wijn)* niet schuimend, niet mousserend; *(v. geluid)* zacht; *sb.* stilte *v.*; *vt.* stillen, doen bedaren, kalmeren; stilhouden; *vi.* bedaren.

still [stil] *adv.* nog altijd, nog; toch; steeds, altijd.

stillborn ['stilbo:n] doodgeboren.

stillness ['stilnis] stilte *v.*

stilt [stilt] stelt *v.*

stilted ['stiltid] op stelten; *(fig.)* hoogdravend.

stilt-walker ['stiltwo:kə] steltloper *m.*; *(Dk.)* steltloper; steltkluit *m.*

stimulate ['stimjuleit] prikkelen, aansporen, aanzetten.

stimulus ['stimjuləs] prikkel *m.*, aansporing *v.*; *(Pl.)* brandhaar *o.*

sting [stiŋ] *vi.* steken; prikken, prikkelen; *(v. netels, enz.)* branden; *(op de tong)* bijten; *(fig.)* smarten; pijndoen, pijnlijk treffen; grieven; *(v. geweten)* knagen; *sb.* angel *m.*; stekel *m.*; prikkel *m.*; *(v. netel)* brandhaar *o.*; steek *m.*; wroeging, knaging *v.*; pittigheid, stekeligheid *v.*

sting-fish ['stiŋfiʃ] *(Dk.)* pieterman *m.*

stinginess ['stin(d)ʒinis] zuinigheid *v.*; gierigheid, vrekkigheid *v.*

stinging-nettle [stiŋiŋnetl] brandnetel *v.*

stingy ['stiŋi] *adj.* stekend, brandend.

stingy ['stin(d)ʒi] *adj.* zuinig; gierig, inhalig, vrekkig.

stink [stiŋk] *vi.* stinken; *(sl.)* ruiken; *vt.* doen stinken; *sb.* stank *m.*

stint [stint] *vt.* beperken; beknibbelen, bekrimpen; karig toemeten, karig (zuinig) zijn met; sparen, ontzien; terughouden; *vi.* zuinig zijn; zich bekrimpen; *vr.* **— oneself,** zich bekrimpen; *sb.* beperking *v.*; bekrimping *v.*; karigheid *v.*

stipend ['staipənd] jaarwedde, bezolding *v.*

stipulate ['stipjuleit] *vt.* bepalen, vaststellen, overeenkomen, bedingen, stipuleren; (soms:) beloven, garanderen; *vi.* afspreken; — *for,* bedingen.

stipulation [stipju'leiʃən] bepaling, vaststelling *v.*; beding *o.*, voorwaarde *v.*; afspraak, overeenkomst *v.*

stir [stə:] *vt.* bewegen, in beweging brengen; roeren, omroeren; verroeren; (*v. vuur*) opporren, oppoken; (*fig.*) opwekken; aanzetten; aandoen, treffen; *vi.* zich bewegen, zich verroeren; in de weer zijn, zich roeren; in beweging komen; ('*s morgens*) opstaan; *sb.* beweging *v.*; drukte *v.*; opwinding, opschudding, beroering *v.*; por *m.*; opwekking *v.*; (het) roeren *o.*

stirless ['stə:lis] onbeweeglijk, bladstil, roerloos.

stirring ['stə:riŋ] *adj.* bewegend; in beweging; bedrijvig actief; roerig, levendig; (*v. drama, enz.*) roerend; emotievol; veelbewogen; *sb.* (het) bewegen *o.*; (het) roeren *o.*; beweging *v.*; teken *o.* van leven; (innerlijke) aandrang *m.*

stirrup ['stirəp] stijgbeugel *m.*; spanriem *m.*

stitch [stitʃ] *sb.* steek *m.*; wondhechting *v.*; steek *m.* in de zij; *vt.* stikken; bestikken, borduren; innaaien, brocheren; dichtnaaien; hechten.

stitcher ['stitʃə] stikster *v.*; stikmachine *v.*

stoat [staut] (*Dk.*) hermelijn *m.*

stock [stɔk] *sb.* stam *m.*; blok *o.*; (wortel)stok *m.*; (geweer)lade *v.*; (*v. zweep, enz.*) steel *m.*; ankerstok *m.*; (*v. aambeeld*) voet *m.*; (*v. schaats, schaaf*) hout *o.*; stapelblok *o.*; familie *v.*, geslacht *o.*; afkomst *v.*; stamvader *m.*; kapitaal, fonds *o.*; voorraad *m.*, goederen *o. mv.*, inventaris *m.*; materiaal *o.*; (*v. boerderij, enz.*) gereedschappen *o. mv.*; veestapel *m.*; stropdas *v.*; stokroos *v.*; (*fig.*) uilskuiken *o.*, damkap *m.*; —s, effecten, staatspapieren; (*sch.*) stapel *m.*; (*gesch.*) voetblok *o.*; (*Am.*) aandelen; *adj.* voorhanden; vast; stereotiep; traditioneel; *vt.* (*v. voorraad*) opdoen, inslaan; (*H.*) hebben, in voorraad hebben, er op na houden; van het nodige voorzien, van voorraad voorzien; uitrusten; (*v. schip*) provianderen; (*gesch.*) in 't blok zetten.

stock-breeder ['stɔkbridə] veefokker *m.*

stock-broker ['stɔkbroukə] (*H.*) makelaar in effecten, commissionnair *m.*

stock-exchange ['stɔkekstʃein(d)ʒ] effectenbeurs *v.*

stockfish ['stɔkfiʃ] stokvis *m.*

stock-gillyflower ['stɔkdʒiliflauə] violier *v.*

stocking ['stɔkiŋ] kous *v.*

stock-in-trade ['stɔkintreid] voorraad, goederenvoorraad; inventaris *m.*; (*v. werklieden*) gereedschap *o.*; geestelijk kapitaal *o.*, (geestelijke) uitrusting *v.*

stock-jobbing ['stɔkdʒɔbiŋ] effecten-

handel *m.*; beursspeculatie *v.*, windhandel *m.* in effecten.

stock-list ['stɔklist] (*H.*) fondsenlijst, beursnotering *v.*

stock-still ['stɔkstil] stokstil, doodstil.

stoic ['stouik] *sb.* stoïcijn *m.*; *adj.* stoïcijns.

stoical(ly) ['stouikəl(i)] *adj.* (*adv.*) stoïcijns.

stoke [stouk] (*v. machine*) stoken; — *up,* aanstoken, aanwakkeren.

stolid ['stɔlid] *adj.* onaandoenlijk, gevoelloos, flegmatiek; traag, stompzinnig.

stomach ['stəmək] *sb.* maag *v.*; buik *m.*; lust, eetlust, honger *m.*; aard *m.*, geaardheid *v.*, temperament *o.*; *vt.* trek hebben in; verduwen, slikken, verkroppen.

stomach-ache ['stəməkeik] maagpijn *v.*; buikpijn *v.*

stone [stoun] *sb.* steen *m.*; (*v. vrucht*) pit *v.*; edelsteen *m.*; hagelsteen *m.*; niersteen, galsteen *m.*, graveel *o.*; schuursteen *m.*; *adj.* stenen, van steen; *vt.* stenigen, met stenen gooien; met stenen beleggen, bedekken, plaveien; van pitten (stenen) ontdoen; slijpen (schuren) met steen.

stone-blind ['stoun'blaind] stekeblind.

stone-cutter ['stounkətə] steenbikker, steenhouwer *m.*

stone-dead ['soun'ded] morsdood.

stone-deaf ['stoun'def] stokdoof, potdoof.

stone-pit ['stounpit] steengroeve *v.*

stony ['stouni] *adj.* steenachtig, steenhard; onaandoenlijk; hardvochtig; (*v. toon*) ijskoud; (*v. blik*) koud, strak.

stool [stûl] *sb.* stoeltje *o.*, kruk, kantoorkruk *v.*; bankje, voetenbankje *o.*; vensterbank *v.*; boomstomp *m.*; bestekamer *v.*; (*gen.*) stoelgang *m.*, ontlasting *v.*; (*Dk.*) lokduif *v.*; *vi.* (*Pl.*) stoelen; stoelgang hebben.

stoop [stûp] *vi.* bukken, zich bukken; voorover lopen, gebukt lopen; (*fig.*) zich vernederen, zich verlagen; *vt.* buigen; vooroverbuigen; *sb.* buiging *v.*; (*fig.*) nederbuiging *v.*

stop [stɔp] *vt.* stoppen, dichtstoppen, dichtmaken; (*v. tand*) vullen, plomberen; (*v. gas, enz.*) afsnijden, afsluiten; (*v. weg*) versperren; (*v. bloed*) stelpen; (*v. werk, enz.*) staken; (*v. fabriek*) stopzetten; opschorten; (*v. klok*) laten stilstaan; (*v. loon*) inhouden; tegenhouden, tot staan brengen; aanhouden; ophouden; verhinderen; een eind maken aan; (*v. vogel*) neerschieten; interpungeren; (*fot.*) diafragmeren; (*v. stoot*) pareren; (*v. vioolsnaar*) neerdrukken; *vi.* stilhouden; (*v. horloge*) blijven stilstaan; (*v. trein*) stoppen; uitscheiden met, ophouden; overblijven, logeren; blijven; niet doorgaan; *sb.* (het) stoppen, enz.; onthoud *o.*; halte *v.*; pauze; pauzering *v.*; leesteken *o.*; (*v. blaasinstrument*) klep *v.*, gat *o.*; (*v. orgel*) register *o.*; (*klankl.*) ontploffingsgeluid *o.*; klamp, haak *m.*, pen *v.*

stop-gap ['stɔpgæp] *sb.* stoplap *m.*; vulwoord; stopwoord *o.*; bladvulling *v.*; tijdvulling *v.*; invaller *m.*, noodhulp *v.*; *adj.* tijdelijk, als noodhulp gebruikt.

stoppage ['stɔpidʒ] (het) stoppen *o.*; stopzetting *v.*; verstopping *v.*; oponthoud *o.*; (*v. bedrijf, enz.*) stilstand *m.*; (*v. loon*) inhouding *v.*; korting *v.*; (*v. betaling*) staking *v.*

stopper ['stɔpə] *sb.* stopper *m.*; stop *v.*; *vt.* een stop doen op, met een stop dichtmaken.

stopping-place ['stɔpiŋpleis] halte *v.*

stopple ['stɔpl] *sb.* stop *v.*; *vt.* met een stop sluiten.

storage ['stɔ:ridʒ] opberging, opstapeling *v.*; bergruimte, pakhuisruimte *v.*; pakhuishuur *v.*

storage-battery ['stɔ:ridʒbætəri] accumulator *m.*

store [stɔ:] *sb.* grote hoeveelheid *v.*, (grote) voorraad *m.*; pakhuis *o.*, opslagplaats *v.*; meubelbewaarplaats *v.*; warenhuis *o.*, bazaar *m.*; (*Am.*) winkel *m.*; overvloed *m.*; (*fig.*) rijkdom *m.*; mestdier *o.*; **—s**, voorraad; proviand; legerbehoeften; warenhuis, bazaar; *vt.* (*v. voorraad*) opdoen, inslaan; (*v. goederen*) opslaan; (*v. meubelen, enz.*) opbergen; (*v. voorraad*) bergen; (*v. oogst*) binnenhalen; verzamelen, bewaren; provianderen, voorzien (*with*, van); uitrusten (*with*, met); **— away,** opbergen, wegbergen.

store-house ['stɔ:haus] pakhuis, magazijn *o.*; voorraadschuur *v.*; (*fig.*) schatkamer *v.*

store-room ['stɔ:rum] bergplaats, bergruimte *v.*; provisiekamer *v.*

storey ['stɔ:ri] verdieping *v.*

stork [stɔ:k] ooievaar *m.*

storm [stɔ:m] *sb.* storm *m.*; onweer *o.*; vlaag *v.*; regenbui; sneeuwbui, hagelbui *v.*; (*mil.*) bestorming *v.*; (*fig.*) vlaag *v.*, aanval *m.*; *by* **—,** stormenderhand; *vi.* stormen; woeden, razen, bulderen; (*mil.*) storm lopen; **— at,** uitvaren tegen; *vt.* (*mil.*) bestormen, stormlopen op.

stormy ['stɔ:mi] stormachtig, storm—; onstuimig.

story ['stɔ:ri] geschiedenis *v.*; verhaal *o.*, vertelling *v.*; legende, overlevering *v.*; sprookje *o.*; leugentje *o.*; (*Am.*) artikel *o.* (in tijdschrift).

stout [staut] *sb.* stout, donker bier *o.*; *adj.* stevig, sterk; flink, dapper, kloek; dik, gezet; (*v. weerstand*) krachtig.

stout-hearted ['staut'hâtid] moedig, onverschrokken, kordaat.

stove [stouv] *sb.* kachel *v.*, fornuis *o.*; droogoven *m.*; stoof *v.*; *vt.* stoven; drogen.

stow [stou] stuwen, stouwen; bergen, opbergen; plaatsen; **— away,** wegleggen; bergen, opbergen; (*fig.*; *v. eten*)

verorberen, verduwen; zich versteken aan boord.

stowaway ['stouwəwei] blinde passagier, verstekeling *m.*

straddle-legged ['strædllegd] wijdbeens; schrijlings.

straggle ['strægl] dwalen, zwerven; verstrooid liggen; verspreid groeien; (*mil.*) uit het gelid marcheren; achterblijven.

straggler ['stræglə] zwerver; landloper *m.*; achterblijver *m.*; deserteur *m.*; (*Pl.*) wilde loot *v.*

straight [streit] *adj.* recht; glad; (*v. haar*) sluik; (*fig.*) eerlijk, openhartig; rechtschapen; betrouwbaar; in orde; op orde; (*v. rekening*) vereffend; (*Am.*) echt, onvermengd; *adv.* recht; rechtuit; rechtstreeks, direct; juist, raak; eerlijk, openlijk; **— on,** rechtuit, rechtdoor.

straighten ['streitn] recht maken; recht zetten; recht trekken; (*v. benen*) strekken; vereffenen; (*v. kamer*) opredderen.

strain [strein] *vt.* spannen, rekken, uittrekken; persen; (*v. spier, gewricht*) verrekken; (*v. stem*) forceren; (*v. feiten, woorden*) verdraaien; (*v. stem*) forceren; (*v. waarheid, geweten*) geweld aandoen; uitbuiten, het uiterste vergen van; uitzijgen; (*v. krachten, ogen*) te veel inspannen; *vi.* spannen; trekken; zwoegen; *sb.* spanning *v.*; inspanning *v.*; overspanning *v.*; (*v. spier*) verrekking *v.*; (*v. feit, waarheid*) verdraaiing *v.*; streven *o.*; druk *m.*; trant, stijl *m.*; toon *m.*; karakter *o.*; wijs, melodie *v.*; lied *o.*; gedicht *o.*

strained [streind] (*v. uitlegging*) verdraaid, gewrongen; (*v. vrolijkheid, lach*) gedwongen, gemaakt; (*v. verhoudingen*) gespannen.

strainer ['streinə] zijgdoek *m.*; vergiet *o.*, zeef *v.*

strait [streit] *adj.* eng, nauw; bekrompen; streng; nauwgezet; *sb.* engte, zeeëngte, zeestraat *v.*; bergpas *m.*; moeilijkheid; verlegenheid *v.*

straiten ['streitn] nauw(er) maken, vernauwen; knellen, spannen, insluiten; (*v. touw*) strak aanhalen; in verlegenheid brengen.

strand [strænd] *sb.* strand *o.*, kust *v.*, oever *m.*; (*v. paarlen*) snoer *o.*; (*v. touw*) streng *v.*; lok, haarlok *v.*; vezel *v.*; *vt.* doen stranden, op het strand zetten; (*v. touw*) doen knappen; *vi.* stranden, op het strand lopen.

strange [strein(d)ʒ] *adj.* vreemd, onbekend; ongewoon, vreemdsoortig, zonderling, raar; opvallend; wonderlijk.

stranger ['strein(d)ʒə] *sb.* vreemdeling, vreemde, onbekende *m.*; nieuweling *m.*; *adj.* vreemd.

strangle ['stræŋgl] worgen; smoren, onderdrukken; (*v. debat*) afsnijden.

strangler ['stræŋglə] worger *m.*

strap [stræp] *sb.* riem *m.*; drijfriem *m.*;

aanzetriem *m.*; (*mil.*) schouderbedekking *v.*; schouderriem *m.*; (*v. stoommachine*) beugel *m.*; (*in tram*) lus *v.*; scheerriem *m.*; *vt.* vastmaken (met een riem); aanzetten (op een riem); ranselen; opknopen.

strategy ['strætidʒi] strategie, krijgswetenschap *v.*

stratum ['streitəm] laag, aardlaag *v.*; gesteentelaag *v.*

straw [stro:] *sb.* stro *o.*; strootje *o.*; strohalm *m.*; strohoed *m.*; *adj.* van stro; strooien. ˙

strawberry ['stro:b(ə)ri] aardbei, aardbezie *v.*

straw-board ['stro:bo:d] strokarton *o.*

straw-bottomed ['stro:bɔtəmd] (*v. stoel*) met strooien zitting.

stray [strei] *vi.* zwerven; rondzwerven; dwalen, verdwalen, dolen; afdwalen; de slechte weg opgaan; kronkelen; (*el.*) strooien; *sb.* zwerver, zwerveling *m.*; verdoolde *m.*; verdwaald dier *o.*; **—s**, luchtstoringen, atmosferische storingen; *adj.* afgedwaald, verdwaald; (*v. klant, bezoeker*) toevallig; verspreid; sporadisch (voorkomend); onbeheerd.

streak [strik] *sb.* streep *v.*; laag, kolenlaag *v.*; ader, metaalader *v.*; *vt.* strepen; *vi.* strepen krijgen; ijlen, rennen; **— off,** er vandoor gaan.

streaked [strikt] gestreept; geaderd; (*v. spek*) doorregen; (*Am.*) verlegen, niet op zijn gemak.

stream [strim] *sb.* stroom *m.*; (*fig.*) stroming, richting *v.*; *vt.* doen stromen; *vi.* stromen, vloeien; wapperen, fladderen; golven.

streamer ['strimə] wimpel *m.*; lamfer *m.*; lang lint *o.*; loshangende veer *v.*

street [strit] straat *v.*

street-arab ['stritæerəb] straatjongen *m.*, boefje *o.*

street-door ['stritdo:] voordeur *v.*

street-walker ['stritwo:kə] straatmeid, straatmadelief *v.*

strength [streŋð] sterkte, kracht, macht *v.*; (*v. stof*) soliditeit *v.*; (*v. tabak*) zwaarte *v.*

strenghten ['streŋð(ə)n] *vt.* versterken, sterk maken; (*v. wet*) verscherpen; *vi.* aansterken, sterk worden; in kracht toenemen.

strenghtless ['streŋðlis] krachteloos; machteloos.

strenuosity [strenju'ɔsiti] (aanhoudende) inspanning, vlijt *v.*; energie *v.*

strenuous ['strenjuəs] *adj.* inspannend; krachtig, ijverig, energiek.

stress [stres] *sb.* nadruk *m.*, klem *v.*; aandrang *m.*; klemtoon *m.*, accent *o.*; inspanning *v.*; beslommering *v.*; (*tn.*) spanning *v.*, druk *m.*; kracht *v.*, gewicht *o.*; *vt.* de nadruk leggen op; de klemtoon leggen op, accentueren.

stretch [stretʃ] *vt.* rekken, oprekken; strekken; uitstrekken, uitspreiden; (*v. armen, handen*) uitsteken; (*v. metalen*) uitsmeden, uithameren; (*v. vleugels*) uitslaan; (*v. ogen*) opensperren; overdrijven; (*v. waarheid*) geweld aandoen; (*v. krachten*) inspannen; (*v. macht*) te buiten gaan; *vi.* zich uitstrekken; flink stappen; met volle zeilen varen; (*fig.*) met spek schieten, overdrijven; *vr.* **— oneself,** zich uitrekken; zich inspannen; benen maken; *sb.* strekking, uitstrekking *v.*; spanning *v.*; inspanning *v.*; (*v. macht*) misbruik *o.*; (*v. rivier*) rak *o.*; uitgestrektheid *v.*; traject *o.*; wandeling *v.*; (*sch.: bij 't zeilen*) slag *m.*

stretcher ['stretʃə] rekker *m.*; spanraam *o.*; strekijzer *o.*; (*bouwk.*) strekse steen *m.*; (*mil.*) draagbaar *v.*; veldbed *o.*, brits *v.*; (*fam.*) leugen *v.*

strew [strû] *vt.* uitstrooien; bestrooien; bezaaien; *vi.* verspreid liggen op.

strickle ['strikl] strijkhout *o.*, afstrijkstok *m.*; (*voor zeisen*) wetsteen *m.*

strict [strikt] *adj.* strikt, stipt, nauwkeurig, nauwgezet, precies, streng.

strictness ['striktnis] striktheid, stiptheid, nauwkeurigheid, nauwgezetheid, strengheid *v.*

stride [straid] *vi.* schrijden, grote stappen nemen; **— out,** flink stappen, aanstappen; *vt.* stappen over, schrijden over; afpassen; *sb.* schrede *v.*, (grote) stap *m.*

strident(ly) ['straidənt(li)] *adj.* (*adv.* schel, schril, doordringend, krassend.

strideways ['straidweiz] schrijlings.

strife [straif] strijd, twist *m.*; tweedracht *v.*

strike [straik] *vt.* slaan; slaan op (tegen, met); stoten (tegen, op); treffen, raken; (*v. toon, enz.*) aanslaan; (*v. weg*) inslaan; (*v. slag*) toebrengen; (*v. vis*) aan de haak slaan; (*v. lucifer*) aansteken, aanstrijken; (*v. planten*) stekken; (*v. lijn, enz.*) trekken; (*v. vlag, zeil*) strijken; (*v. kolen, olie, enz.*) aanboren; ontmoeten; (*v. jury, enz.*) vormen; *vi.* slaan; (*v. lucifer*) aangaan, vuur vatten; wortel schieten; (*v. bliksem*) inslaan; zich overgeven, de vlag strijken; stranden, op een rots lopen; staken; (links, rechts) afslaan; **— in,** (*muz.*) invallen; (*v. mazelen, enz.*) naar binnen slaan; **— off,** (*v. artikelen, enz.*) uit zijn mouw schudden; (*v. exemplaren*) drukken, afdrukken; (*v. bedrag, prijs*) laten vallen; (*v. gelijkenis*) juist treffen; **— out,** (*v. woord*) doorhalen, schrappen; (*v. plan*) bedenken, smeden; (*bij boksen*) van zich afslaan; (*bij zwemmen, enz.*) de armen uitslaan; **— up,** (*muz.*) inzetten, beginnen te spelen; (*v. lied*) aanheffen; (*v. verdrag*) sluiten, aangaan; *sb.* slag *m.*; staking, werkstaking *v.*; strijkhout *o.*; vangst *v.*; (*v. olie, goud, enz.*) vondst *v.*

striker ['straikə] wie (wat) slaat, treffer *m.*; staker, werkstaker *m.*; (*bij korenmaat*) strijkhout *o.*, strijkstok *m.*; (*v. klok*) slagwerk *o.*; slagpin *v.*; harpoen *m.*

striking ['straikiŋ] *adj.* slaand; treffend; opvallend, markant; stakend.
string [striŋ] *sb.* koord, touw *o.*; band *m.*, lint *o.*; snoer *o.*; draad *m.*, vezel *v.*; snaar *v.*; pees *v.*; rist, sliert *v.*; streng *v.*; rij, reeks *v.*; aaneenschakeling *v.*; riem *m.*; (*v. paarden*) koppel *o.*; —*s*, strijkinstrumenten; *vt.* rijgen (*aan snoer, enz.*); (*v. bonen*) afhalen; risten, afristen; (*v. boog, zenuwen*) spannen; (*v. instrument*) stemmen; besnaren, met snaren bespannen; (*v. raket*) bespannen; (*fam.*) aan 't lijntje houden; — *up,* spannen, veerkracht geven; (*fam.*) ophangen, opknopen; *vi.* (*v. vloeistoffen*) draderig worden; zich uitstrekken.
stringed [striŋd] besnaard; snaar—.
stringy ['striŋi] vezelig, draderig, zenig.
strip [strip] *vt.* stropen, afstropen, villen; afrijgen, afrissen; (*v. tabak*) strippen; schillen, ontschorsen; afscheuren, aftrekken; (*v. bed*) afhalen; (*sch.*) onttakelen; ontmantelen; (*v. geweer*) uit elkaar nemen; uitkleden; ontbloten, beroven (*of,* van); (*v. schroef*) doldraaien, doen afslijten; — *off,* (*v. tabak*) strippen; — *up,* (*v. mouwen*) opstropen; *vi.* zich uitkleden; losgaan, loslaten; afschilferen; (*v. schroef*) afslijten; *vr.* — *oneself,* zich uitkleden; *sb.* strook, reep *v.*; (*Sc.*) streep *v.*
stripe [straip] *sb.* streep *v.*; (*mil.*) chevron *m.*; strook *v.*; striem *v.*; —*s*, streepjesgoed, gestreept laken; *vt.* strepen; striemen.
striped [straipt] gestreept; streepjes—.
strip-leaf ['striplif] strippeling *v.*
strive [straiv] zich inspannen, moeite doen (*to,* om); streven (*after, for,* naar); worstelen, strijden (*against, with,* tegen).
stroke [strouk] *sb.* slag *m.*; stoot *m.*; trek, haal *m.*; streep *v.*; (*v. ziekte*) aanval *m.*; beroerte *v.*; (*sp.*) slagroeier *m.*
stroke [strouk] *vt.* strelen, aaien; gladstrijken; *sb.* streling *v.*, aai *m.*
stroll [stroul] *vi.* slenteren, rondslenteren, wandelen, kuieren; dolen, ronddwalen, omzwerven; *vt.* (*v. toneelspelers*) doortrekken; *sb.* wandeling *v.*, kuier *m.*; zwerftocht *m.*
stroller ['stroulə] slenteraar *m.*; zwerver; (*Sc.*) landloper *m.*; rondreizend toneelspeler *m.*
strong [stroŋ] *adj.* sterk; krachtig; (*v. koorts*) hevig; (*v. bier, sigaren*) zwaar; (*mil.*) versterkt; (*v. maatregel*) kras; vurig; (*v. prijs*) hoog; (*v. boter, enz.*) ranzig; (*v. adem*) riekend.
strong-bodied [stroŋ'bodid] sterk, fors (gebouwd); (*v. wijn*) krachtig, pittig.
stronghold ['stroŋhould] sterkte *v.*, bolwerk *o.*, burcht *v.*
strongly ['stroŋli] *adv.* met kracht; sterk, enz.
strong-minded ['stroŋ'maindid] krachtig van geest; resoluut, energiek.

strong-room ['stroŋrum] kluis, bankkluis *v.*
strop [strop] *sb.* aanzetriem, scheerriem *m.*; (*sch.*) strop *m.*; *vt.* (*v. scheermes*) aanzetten.
structure ['strəktʃə] bouw *m.*, structuur, samenstelling *v.*; gebouw *o.*
struggle ['strəgl] *vi.* worstelen, kampen; strijden; zwoegen, zich afsloven, zich veel moeite geven; tegenspartelen; *sb.* worsteling *v.*, kamp; strijd *m.*; krachtinspanning *v.*, pogingen *v. mv.*
stub [stəb] *sb.* (*v. boom*) stronk *m.*, stobbe *v.*; (*v. sigaar*) stompje, eindje *o.*; oude hoefnagel *m.*; (*Am.: v. cheque*) souche *v.*; *vt.* — *one's toe,* zijn teen stoten; — *up,* opgraven; rooien; uitroeien.
stubble ['stəbl] stoppel(s) *m.* (*mv.*).
stubble-field ['stəblfild] stoppelveld *o.*
stubborn (ly) ['stəbən(li)] *adj.* (*adv.*) hardnekkig, halsstarrig; weerspannig, onverzettelijk.
stucco ['stəkou] *sb.* pleisterkalk *v.*; pleisterwerk; stukadoorswerk *o.*; *vt.* pleisteren, stukadoren.
stuck [stək] *adj.* verbaasd; verwaand.
stud [stəd] *sb.* stoeterij *v.*; renstal *m.*; knop(je) *m.* (*o.*); overhemdsknoopje; manchetknoopje *o.*; tapeinde *o.*; beslagnagel *m.*; (*voor verkeer*) wegpunaise *v.*; *vt.* met knopjes beslaan (versieren); het knoopje steken in.
stud-book ['stədbuk] paardenstamboek *o.*
student ['stjûdənt] student *m.*; leerling; studerende *m.*; navorser *m.*
stud-farm ['stədfâm] stoeterij *v.*
stud-horse ['stədho:s] hengst *m.*
studio ['stjûdiou] (*v. kunstenaar*) atelier *o.*; (*radio*) studio, klankzaal, zendzaal *v.*
studious ['stjûdiəs] *adj.* vlijtig, ijverig; leergierig; studerend; begerig, verlangend; bestudeerd, opzettelijk; nauwgezet, angstvallig.
study ['stədi] *sb.* studie *v.*; (*muz.*) étude *v.*; studeerkamer *v.*; (*fig.*) streven, doel *o.*; *vt.* studeren; bestuderen; studeren in; zich toeleggen op; zich beijveren (*to,* om); streven naar; (*ton.: v. rol*) instuderen; (*v. persoon*) opnemen; *vi.* studeren.
stuff [stəf] *sb.* stof *v.*; materiaal *o.*, grondstof(fen) *v.* (*mv.*); goederen *o. mv.*, waar *v.*; lading *v.*; (*sch.*) tuig *o.*; (*fam.*) rommel *m.*, bocht *o.*; (*fam.*) fut *v.*, pit *o.*; (*fam.*) klets, onzin *m.*, gebazel *o.*; *vt.* volstoppen, volproppen; opvullen; opzetten; farceren; dichtstoppen; stoppen (*into,* in); *vi.* zich volproppen, schransen; *adj.* stoffen.
stuffer ['stəfə] opvuller *m.*; (*v. dieren, enz.*) opzetter *m.*
stuffing ['stəfiŋ] vulsel, opvulsel *o.*; pakking *v.*; (*v. neus, enz.*) verstopping *v.*
stuffy ['stəfi] benauwd, bedompt, dom-

pig, duf; (sl.) boos; (v. neus, enz.) verstopt; saai.

stumble ['stəmbl] vi. struikelen; strompelen; stamelen, hakkelen; (Bijb.) zich ergeren; vt. — **a person,** iem. versteld doen staan; sb. struikeling v.; blunder, misstap m.

stumbling-block ['stəmbliŋblɔk] struikelblok o., hinderpaal m.; steen des aanstoots m.

stump [stəmp] sb. stomp, stronk, tronk m.; (v. persoon) prop(je) m. (o.); doezelaar m.; zware stap m., geklos o.; eindje (sigaar) o.; (sp.: cricket) paaltje o.; (v. cheque) souche v.; houten been o.; **—s,** (fam.) onderdanen, benen; haarstoppels; vt. knotten, afknotten; afstompen; (v. bomen) rooien; (v. land) van boomstronken zuiveren; doezelen; (sp.: v. wicket) omslaan; (schoolt.) laten zakken; (fig.) in verlegenheid brengen, in 't nauw drijven, vastzetten; — **up,** (v. paard) afjakkeren; (v. bomen) rooien; vi. hompelen, strompelen; stommelen; klossen; adj. stomp; propperig; afgesleten.

stumper ['stəmpə] doezelaar m.

stump-foot ['stəmpfut] horrelvoet m.

stump-speech ['stəmpspitʃ] verkiezingsrede v.

stumpy ['stəmpi] stomp, afgestompt; afgeknot; kort en dik, propperig; (v. borstel) versleten; (Am.) vol stronken.

stun [stən] vt. verdoven, bedwelmen, bewusteloos slaan; verbazen, verbluffen, versteld doen staan; sb. verdoving, bedwelming v.; verbluffing v.

stunt [stənt] in de groei belemmeren.

stupefaction [stjûpi'fækʃən] verdoving, bedwelming v.; verbazing, verbijstering v.

stupefier ['stjûpifaiə] verdovend (bedwelmend) middel o.

stupefy ['stjûpifai] verdoven, bedwelmen; verbluffen, verstomd doen staan; verstompen, afstompen.

stupendous (ly) [stju'pendəs(li)] adj. (adv.) verbazend, verbazingwekkend, verbluffend, overweldigend, kolossaal.

stupid ['stjûpid] adj. dom, stom, onzinnig; wezenloos; suf, versuft; saai; sb. (fam.) domkop, stommerik m.

stupidity [stju'piditi] domheid, stomheid v.; stommiteit v.

stupor ['stjûpə] stomme verbazing v.; verdoving, bedwelming; gevoelloosheid v.; stompzinnigheid v.

sturdy ['stə:di] adj. sterk, stoer, stevig.

sturgeon ['stə:dʒən] (Dk.) steur m.

stutter ['stətə] vi. stotteren, stamelen, hakkelen; sb. gestotter, gestamel o.

sty [stai] varkenshok, kot o.

style [stail] sb. (gesch.) stilus m., schrijfstift v.; (v. zonnewijzer) stift v., wijzer m.; graveerstift, etsnaald v.; stijl, trant, schrijftrant m.; (Pl.: v. bloemstamper) stijl m.; tijdrekening v.; titel m., titulatuur v.; (firma)naam m.; wijze, manier v. (van leven, enz.); sonde v.; vt. noemen, betitelen.

stylish (ly) ['stailiʃ(li)] adj. (adv.) naar de mode, elegant, zwierig; deftig.

styptic ['stiptik] adj. bloedstelpend, samentrekkend; sb. bloedstelpend middel o.

suable ['sjûəbl] vervolgbaar (in rechten).

suave (ly) ['sweiv(li)] adj. (adv.) minzaam, vriendelijk; zacht, aangenaam.

subconscious ['səb'kɔnʃəs] onderbewust.

subdivide ['səbdivaid] vt. onderverdelen; vi. zich weer verdelen.

subdivision ['səbdiviʒən] onderverdeling v.; onderafdeling v.; (mil.) peloton o.

subdue [səb'djû] onderwerpen; klein krijgen; ten onder brengen; (v. hartstochten) beheersen, bedwingen, beteugelen; (v. licht, enz.) verzachten, temperen, inhouden; (v. land) ontginnen; **—d,** ook: stil, zacht; zich zelf meester; ingetogen; ingehouden; berustend; (v. kleding) stemmig; (v. toon) gedempt.

subject ['səbdʒikt] adj. onderworpen, onderdanig; blootgesteld, onderhevig (to, aan); vatbaar (to, voor); afhankelijk (to, van); sb. onderdaan m.; onderwerp o.; vak, leervak o.; persoon m., individu, sujet o.; (muz.) thema o.; aanleiding, reden v.; patiënt m.; proefpersoon m., proefdier o.

subject [səb'dʒekt] vt. onderwerpen; blootstellen (to, aan).

subjection [səb'dʒekʃən] onderwerping v.; afhankelijkheid v.

subjective [səb'dʒektiv] adj. subjectief; onderwerps—; sb. eerste naamval m.

subject-matter ['səbdʒiktmætə] (v. boek, enz.) stof v., inhoud m., onderwerp o.

subjoin [səb'dʒɔin] bijvoegen; (er aan) toevoegen.

subjugate ['səbdʒugeit] onderwerpen.

sublease [səb'lîs] sb. onderverhuring v.; onderverpachting v.; vt. onderverhuren, onderverpachten.

sublessee ['səble'sî] onderhuurder; onderpachter m.

sublet ['səb'let] onderverhuren; onderaanbesteden.

sublettee ['səble'tî] zie **sublessee.**

sublimity [sə'blimiti] verhevenheid, hoogheid v.

submarine ['səbmərîn] adj. onderzees; onderzee—; sb. onderzeeboot, duikboot v., onderzeeër m.; onderzeese mijn v.; zeedier o.; zeeplant v.; vt. torpederen.

submerge [səb'mə:dʒ] onderdompelen; onder water zetten, overstromen; bedelven; (fig.) verzwelgen.

submersible [səb'mə:sibl] adj. overstroombaar; sb. duikboot v.

submission [səb'miʃən] onderwerping v.; overlegging v.; onderworpenheid, onderdanigheid, nederigheid v.

submissive (ly) [səb'misiv(li)] adj.

(adv.) onderdanig, onderworpen, nederig, ootmoedig.

submit [səb'mit] onderwerpen; voorleggen, onderwerpen (aan oordeel); óverleggen.

sub-office ['səb'ɔfis] bijkantoor o.

subordinate [sə'bo:dinit] adj. ondergeschikt; (gram.) onderschikkend; sb. ondergeschikte m.; [sə'bo:dineit] vt. ondergeschikt maken (to, aan).

subordination [səbo:di'neiʃən] ondergeschiktheid v.; (gram.) onderschikking v.

suborn [sə'bo:n] omkopen; door omkoping verkrijgen.

suborner [sə'bo:nə] omkoper m.

subscribe [səb'skraib] vt. tekenen, ondertekenen; inschrijven, intekenen voor; vi. tekenen; intekenen.

subscriber [səb'skraibə] ondertekenaar m.; intekenaar m.; abonnee m.

subscription [səb'skripʃən] onderschrift o.; ondertekening v.; intekening, inschrijving v.; abonnement o.; (v. vereniging, enz.) contributie v.; (Am.) colportage v.

subsection ['səb'sekʃən] onderafdeling v.

subserve [səb'sə:v] dienen, bevorderlijk zijn aan, dienstig zijn voor.

subside [səb'said] zinken, zakken; inzakken, verzakken, bedaren, tot bedaren komen, tot rust komen; (v. wind) gaan liggen, luwen; (v. gezwel) afnemen, slinken.

subsidence [səb'saidəns, 'səbsidəns] (het) zinken, (het) zakken o.; (v. muur, gebouw) verzakking; (v. bodem) inzinking v.; afneming v.; (v. wind) (het) gaan liggen o.

subsidiary [səb'sidjəri] adj. helpend, hulp—; tijdelijk vervangend, plaatsvervangend; bijkomstig, ondergeschikt; sb. noodhulp v.; helper, assistent m.; hulpmiddel o.

subsidize ['səbsidaiz] subsidiëren, geldelijk steunen; (v. troepen) huren; omkopen.

subsidy ['səbsidi] subsidie; bijdrage v.

subsist [səb'sist] vi. bestaan, leven ((up)on, van); voortbestaan, blijven bestaan; vt. proviandeeren, van leeftocht voorzien.

subsistence [səb'sistəns] bestaan o.; middel van bestaan o.; broodwinning v.; leeftocht m., proviandering v.; (sch.) voeding v., onderhoud o.

substance ['səbstəns] stof, zelfstandigheid, substantie v.; wezen o., wezenlijkheid, werkelijkheid v.; zakelijke inhoud; hoofdinhoud m., hoofdzaak v.; degelijkheid v.; vermogen o.

substantial [səb'stænʃəl] adj. wezenlijk, echt, werkelijk (bestaand); stoffelijk; degelijk, deugdelijk, solied; lijvig; gezeten, welgesteld, vermogend; aanzienlijk, belangrijk; sb. —s, (het) wezenlijke o.; wezenlijke bestanddelen o. mv.,

hoofdzaken v. mv.; hoofdschotels m. mv., stevige spijzen v. mv.

substantiate [səb'stænʃieit] verwezenlijken; belichamen; met bewijzen staven; bevestigen; stevig maken; effectief maken.

substantiation [səbstænʃi'eiʃən] verwezenlijking v.; staving v.; bewijs o.

substantive ['səbstəntiv] adj. zelfstandig; onafhankelijk; wezenlijk, essentieel; (mil.) effectief; (v. betrekking, enz.) vast, definitief; aanzienlijk, gewichtig; sb. zelfstandig naamwoord o.

substitute ['səbstitjût] sb. plaatsvervanger; substituut m.; vervangmiddel, surrogaat o.; vt. vervangen, in de plaats stellen, substitueren; de plaats vervullen van.

substitution [səbsti'tjûʃən] vervanging, plaatsvervanging v.; substitutie, in-de-plaatsstelling v.

subtenant ['səb'tenənt] onderhuurder m.

subterfuge ['səbtəfjûdʒ] uitvlucht v.

subterranean [səbtə'reiniən] onderaards.

subtle ['sətl] adj. ijl; subtiel, (ontastbaar) fijn; fijnbesnaard; vernuftig, spitsvondig, listig, sluw.

subtlety ['sətlti] ijlheid v.; subtiliteit, fijnheid, ontastbaarheid v.; haarkloverij v.; spitsvondigheid, list, listigheid v.

subtract [səb'trækt] aftrekken; onttrekken.

subtraction [səb'trækʃən] aftrekking v.; vermindering v.

suburb ['səbə:b] voorstad v.

subvene [səb'vîn] bijspringen, te hulp komen.

subvention [səb'venʃən] sb. hulp v., bijstand m.; subsidie, bijdrage v.; vt. subsidiëren.

subway ['səbwei] onderaardse doorgang; (perron)tunnel m.

succedaneum [səksi'deiniəm] vervangmiddel, surrogaat o.

succeed [sək'sîd] vt. opvolgen; volgen op, komen na; vi. opvolgen; slagen, succes hebben, goed aflopen, gelukken; (v. planten) gedijen.

success [sək'ses] succes o.; goede afloop, gunstige uitslag m.

successful [sək'sesful] adj. voorspoedig, gelukkig, succes hebbend, geslaagd.

succession [sək'seʃən] opvolging, successie, erfopvolging, troonopvolging v.; reeks, volgreeks, opeenvolging, volgorde v.; nakomelingschap v.

successively [sək'sesivli] adv. achtereenvolgens, successievelijk.

successor [sək'sesə] opvolger; troonopvolger m.

succinct [sək'siŋkt] adj. bondig, kort, beknopt.

succour ['səkə] vt. helpen, bijstaan, te hulp komen, helpen; sb. hulp v., bijstand, steun m.; helper m.

succulent ['søkjulənt] sappig.
succumb [sə'kəm] bezwijken (*to,* voor).
such [sətʃ] *adj.* zulk, zo, zodanig; dergelijk; *pron.* dezulken; degenen, zij; dezelve; zulks, dergelijke dingen; — *as,* degenen die, zij die; zoals bijv.
suchlike ['søtʃlaik] dergelijk(e).
suck [søk] *vt.* zuigen (aan, op); inzuigen; opzuigen; uitzuigen; *vi.* zuigen; (*v. pomp*) lens zijn; *sb.* (het) zuigen *o.*; zuiging *v.*; (*sl.*) slokje, teugje *o.*; (*sl.*) beetnemerij *v.*; flasco *o.*; —**s**, (*schoolterm*) snoep, lekkers.
sucker ['søkə] zuiger *m.*; zuigleer *o.*; (*Dk.*) zuignapje *o.*; zuigvis *m.*; walvisjong *o.*; zuigbuis *v.*; (*Pl.*) uitloper *m.*, spruit *v.*
sucking-bag ['søkiŋbæg] zuigdot *m.*
sucking-pig ['søkiŋpig] speenvarken *o.*
suckle ['søkl] zogen; (*fig.*) opkweken, grootbrengen.
suckling ['søkliŋ] zuigeling *m.*; (*Dk.*) jong *o.*
suction-cleaner ['søkʃənklinə] stofzuiger *m.*
suction-pump ['søkʃənpəmp] zuigpomp *v.*
sudden ['sødn] *adj.* plotseling, schielijk, onverhoeds; haastig, overijld; (*all*) *of a* —, *on the* —, schielijk, plotseling, eensklaps.
suddenly ['sødnli] *adv.* schielijk, plotseling, eensklaps.
sudorific [sjûdə'rifik] *adj.* zweetverwekkend, zweetdrijvend; *sb.* zweetmiddel *o.*, zweetdrank *m.*
suds [sødz] zeepsop *o.*; schuim *o.*
sue [s(j)û] *vt.* in rechten aanspreken, vervolgen; verzoeken, smeken.
suffer ['søfə] *vt.* lijden; te lijden hebben; (*v. straf*) ondergaan; toelaten; dulden, verdragen, uitstaan, uithouden; *vi.* lijden; het kind van de rekening zijn; boeten; de marteldood sterven.
sufferable ['søf(ə)rəbl] te verdragen; uit te houden; toelaatbaar, te dulden.
sufferer ['søf(ə)rə] lijder; patiënt *m.*; slachtoffer *o.*; martelaar *m.*
suffice [sə'fais] genoeg (voldoende, toereikend) zijn.
sufficient [sə'fiʃənt] *adj.* genoeg, voldoende, toereikend; zelfgenoegzaam; bekwaam.
suffix ['søfiks] *sb.* achtervoegsel *o.*; [sə'fiks] *vt.* achtervoegen.
suffocate ['søfəkeit] *vt.* verstikken, doen stikken, smoren; *vi.* stikken, smoren.
suffrage ['søfridʒ] stem *v.*; kiesrecht, stemrecht *o.*; stemming *v.*; goedkeuring *v.*; smeekbede *v.*, smeekgebed *o.*
suffuse [sə'fjûz] overgieten, overdekken, overspreiden; stromen langs.
sugar ['ʃugə] *sb.* suiker *v.*; (*fig.*) vleierij, lekkermakerij *v.*, zoete woordjes *o. mv.*; *vt.* suikeren, besuikeren; suiker doen in; (*fig.*) verzoeten, verbloemen; (*fam.*) honig om de mond smeren; vervalsen, knoeien met.

sugar-basin ['ʃugəbeisin] suikerpot *m.*
sugar-cane ['ʃugəkein] suikerriet *o.*
sugary ['ʃugəri] suikerachtig, suikerzoet.
suggest [sə'dʒest] suggereren, op de gedachte brengen; voorstellen, opperen, in overweging geven; ingeven, inblazen, influisteren; aanduiden, wijzen op, doen denken aan; voor de geest roepen.
suggestion [sə'dʒestʃən] suggestie *v.*; voorstel *o.*; overweging *v.*; ingeving, inblazing, influistering *v.*; wenk *m.*; aanduiding *v.*; aansporing *v.*
suicide ['sjûisaid] zelfmoord *m.*; zelfmoordenaar *m.*
suit [s(j)ût] *sb.* verzoek *o.*; aanzoek, huwelijksaanzoek *o.*; verzoekschrift *o.*; aanklacht *v.*; proces, rechtsgeding *o.*; rij, reeks, opeenvolging *v.*; stel, garnituur *o.*; kostuum, pak *o.*; (*kaartsp.*) kleur *v.*, volgkaarten *v. mv.*; *vt.* passen, schikken; aanpassen, geschikt maken; voorzien (*with,* van); *vi.* gelegen komen; geschikt zijn voor; (*v. kleuren*) komen bij, bijeenkomen; — *with,* overeenkomen met; (*v. kleuren*) goed passen bij; *vr.* — *oneself,* doen wat men wil, naar eigen goeddunken handelen; zijn eigen gang gaan; iets naar zijn gading vinden.
suitable ['s(j)ûtəbl] *adj.* gepast, voegzaam; geschikt.
suite [swit] (*v. vorst, enz.*) gevolg *o.*; stoet *m.*; reeks, rij *v.*; stel *o.*; (*muz.*) suite *v.*
suitor ['s(j)ûtə] (*in proces*) klager, eiser *m.*; vrijer, minnaar *m.*; verzoeker; aanzoeker *m.*
sulk [sølk] *sb.* boze luim *v.*; gemok, gepruil *o.*, pruilerij *v.*; landerigheid *v.*; *vi.* pruilen, mokken; het land hebben.
sullen ['sølən] gemelijk, nors, stuurs, knorrig, korzelig; somber, akelig, naargeestig; traag; weerspannig; (*v. geluid*)
sulphur ['sølfə] zwavel *v.*
sultan ['søltən] sultan *m.*
sultry ['søltri] *adj.* zwoel, drukkend; (*fig.*) onfris; wellustig.
sum [søm] *sb.* som *v.*; totaal *o.*; hoeveelheid *v.*, aantal *o.*; in één woord, om kort te gaan; *vt.* optellen, samentellen; sommeren; *vi.* sommen maken.
summarily ['sømərili] *adv.* in 't kort, summier; beknopt, in beknopte vorm; zonder vorm van proces.
summarize ['søməraiz] resumeren, (kort) samenvatten.
summary ['søməri] *adj.* beknopt, kort; *sb.* samenvatting *v.*, kort begrip, kort overzicht *o.*
summer ['sømə] zomer *m.*; dwarsbalk, schoorbalk *m.*; bovendrempel *m.*; opteller *m.*; (*fam.*) rekenaar *m.*
summer-house ['søməhaus] tuinhuis, priëel *o.*; zomerhuisje *o.*; zomerverblijf *o.*
summery ['søməri] zomers, zomerachtig.

summit ['semit] top *m.*, kruin *v.*; toppunt *o.*

summon ['semən] dagvaarden; sommeren; bekeuren; oproepen, ontbieden; (*v. vergadering*) bijeenroepen; (*v. stad*) opeisen.

summons ['semənz] *sb.* dagvaarding; sommatie *v.*; oproep *m.*, oproeping *v.*; opvordering *v.*; *vt.* dagvaarden; bekeuren, proces-verbaal opmaken tegen.

sumptuous(ly) ['semptjuəs(li)] *adj.* (*adv.*) kostbaar, weelderig, prachtig, rijk, weids.

sun [sen] *sb.* zon *v.*; zonneschijn *m.*; *see the* —, (*dicht.*) het daglicht zien; in leven zijn; *vt.* zonnen, aan de zon blootstellen; in de zon drogen; *vi.* zich zonnen; *vr.* — *oneself*, zich zonnen, zich in de zon koesteren.

sun-beam ['senbîm] zonnestraal *m.*

sun-blind ['senblaind] *adj.* zonneblind; *sb.* zonnescherm, zonneblind *o.*, jaloezie *v.*

Sunday ['sendi] zondag *m.*

sunder ['sendə] *vt.* scheiden; uiteenrukken; verdelen, splijten; (*v. touw*) doorsnijden; (*v. ledematen*) afhouwen; *vi.* (van elkaar) scheiden.

sun-dial ['sendaiəl] zonnewijzer *m.*

sundown ['sendaun] zonsondergang *m.*

sundry ['sendri] diverse, allerlei, allerhande.

sun-helmet ['senhelmit] zonnehelm *m.*

sunny ['seni] *adj.* zonnig; (*fig.*) vrolijk, zonnig.

sunset ['senset] zonsondergang *m.*

sunshade ['senʃeid] parasol *v.*, zonnescherm *o.*; zonneklep *v.*; zonnetent *v.*

sunshine ['senʃain] zonneschijn *m.*; voorspoed *m.*; vrolijkheid *v.*

sunshiny ['senʃaini] zonnig.

sun-spot ['senspɔt] zonnevlek *v.*; sproet *v.*

sun-stroke ['senstrouk] zonnesteek *m.*

sup [sep] *vi.* het avondmaal gebruiken, souperen; *vt.* een souper geven aan; *sb.* slokje *o.*

superabundance [s(j)ûpərə'bendəns] (grote) overvloed *m.*

superabundant(ly) [s(j)ûpərə'bendənt(li)] *adj.* (*adv.*) te overvloedig, meer dan genoeg.

superannuate [s(j)ûpə'rænjueit] *vt.* op pensioen stellen, pensioneren, ontslaan wegens de leeftijd; *vi.* de dienst verlaten (wegens de leeftijd); —*d*, ook: afgedankt, op stal gezet, aan de dijk gezet; te oud; versleten.

superficial [s(j)ûpə'fiʃəl] *adj.* oppervlakkig, aan de oppervlakte; ondiep; — *measure*, vlaktemaat.

superficies [s(j)ûpə'fiʃiz] oppervlakte *v.*; vlak *o.*

superfluous(ly) [s(j)û'pə:fluəs(li)] *adj.* (*adv.*) overvloedig; overbodig, overtollig.

superintendence, superintenden-

cy [s(j)ûpərin'tendəns(i)] toezicht, oppertoezicht *o.*

superintendent [(s(j)ûpərin'tendənt] opziener, opzichter, inspecteur *m.*; directeur *m.*

superior [s(j)û'piəriə] *adj.* voortreffelijk, superieur; hoger, beter; boven—, hoofd—, opper—, opperst; voornaam, deftig; hooghartig, arrogant, uit de hoogte; (*Pl.*) bovenstandig; (*v. moeilijkheden*) te boven komen; *sb.* meerdere, superieur *m.*; kloosteroverste *m.* & *v.*

superiority [s(j)ûpiəri'ɔriti] meerderheid, superioriteit *v.*; meerdere bekwaamheid *v.*; overmacht *v.*; voorrang *m.*

superlative [s(j)û'pə:lətiv] *adj.* voortreffelijk, van de hoogste graad; van de beste soort; ongemeen, alles overtreffend; hoogste; *sb.* overtreffende trap, superlatief *m.*

supermundane [s(j)ûpə'məndein] bovenaards.

supernumerary [s(j)ûpə'njûmərəri] boven het bepaalde aantal, boventallig; extra.

supernutrition [s(j)ûpənjû'triʃən] overvoeding *v.*

superscription [s(j)ûpə'skripʃən] opschrift *o.*; (*v. brief*) adres *o.*

supersede [s(j)ûpə'sîd] vervangen, in de plaats treden van; op zij zetten, verdringen; afzetten, ontzetten; afschaffen, te niet doen, opheffen; (*v. moeilijkheid*) uit de weg ruimen, te boven komen.

superstition [s(j)ûpə'stiʃən] bijgeloof *o.*; bijgelovigheid *v.*

superstitious(ly) [s(j)ûpə'stiʃəs(li)] *adj.* (*adv.*) bijgelovig.

supervision [s(j)ûpə'viʒən] opzicht, toezicht *o.*

supervisor [s(j)ûpə'vaizə] opziener, opzichter, inspecteur *m.*; corrector *m.*

supper ['sepə] *sb.* avondeten, avondmaal, souper *o.*; *vt.* een souper geven aan.

supplanter [sə'plântə] verdringer, onderkruiper *m.*

supple ['sepl] buigzaam, lenig, soepel; elastisch; (*fig.*) gedwee, plooibaar.

supplement ['seplimənt] *sb.* supplement, bijvoegsel, toevoegsel *o.*, aanvulling *v.*; *vt.* aanvullen.

supplemental [sepli'mentəl] aanvullend, aanvullings—; suppletoir.

suppleness ['seplnis] buigzaamheid, lenigheid, soepelheid *v.*; (*fig.*) gedweeheid, plooibaarheid *v.*

suppliant ['sepliənt] *adj.* smekend; *sb.* smekeling *m.*

supplicate ['seplikeit] *vi.* smeken (*for*, om); *vt.* afsmeken; aanroepen.

supplication [sepli'keiʃən] smeking *v.*, nederig verzoek *o.*, bede, smeekbede *v.*

supplier [sə'plaiə] leverancier *m.*; verschaffer *m.*

supply [sə'plai] *vt.* (*v. tekort*) aanvullen; (*v. goederen*) verstrekken, verschaffen, leveren; (v. *verlies*) vergoeden; (v. *vacature*) vervullen; vervangen; voorzien; (**with,** van); invullen; *sb.* aanvulling *v.*; verschaffing, levering, verstrekking *v.*; vervanging *v.*; voorziening *v.*; plaatsvervanger *m.*; (*mil.*) verpleging, proviandering *v.*; aanvoer; voorraad *m.*; (*H.: v. goederen*) partij *v.*; — **and demand,** vraag en aanbod.

support [sə'po:t] *vt.* ondersteunen, schragen; steunen, bijstaan; onderhouden; (v. *bewering, enz.*) volhouden; (v. *theorie, enz.*) staven; verdragen; zich staande houden; in zijn eigen onderhoud voorzien; *sb.* steun *m.*, ondersteuning *v.*; onderstand *m.*; stut *m.*, steunsel *o.*; bestaan, levensonderhoud *o.*; broodwinning *v.*; broodwinner *m.*

supportable [sə'po:təbl] draaglijk, duldbaar; houdbaar, verdedigbaar.

supporter [sə'po:tə] ondersteuner *m.*; medestander, voorstander, verdediger *m.*; aanhanger *m.*; begeleider *m.*

supposable [sə'pouzəbl] denkbaar, onderstelbaar, te veronderstellen.

suppose [sə'pouz] (ver)onderstellen, stellen, aannemen; vermoeden, menen, geloven.

supposedly [sə'pouzidli] *adv.* vermoedelijk, naar men vermoeden mag, naar men veronderstelt.

supposition [səpə'ziʃən] veronderstelling *v.*; vermoeden *o.*

suppress [sə'pres] onderdrukken, bedwingen; (v. *bijzonderheden*) verzwijgen, weglaten; (v. *boek, dagblad, enz.*) verbieden; stelpen, stoppen, stuiten; achterhouden.

suppressive [sə'presiv] onderdrukkend.

suppurate ['sʌpjureit] (*gen.*) etteren, etter vormen, dragen; rijp worden.

supremacy [sju'preməsi] oppermacht *v.*, oppergezag *o.*, suprematie *v.*

supreme [s(j)u'prîm] hoogste, opperste, allerhoogste; voortreffelijk, uitmuntend; verheven; souverein, oppermachtig.

surcharge [sə:'tʃâdʒ] *sb.* toeslag *m.*, extra betaling *v.*; extra belasting *v.*; strafport *o.*; (v. *postzegel*) opdruk *m.*; overlading; overbelasting *v.*; overvraging *v.*; oververhitting *v.*; *vt.* extra belasting opleggen; overvragen, te veel laten betalen; (v. *schip*) overladen, overbeladen; oververzadigen; (v. *postzegel*) van opdruk voorzien; overstelpen; (v. *stoom*) oververhitten.

sure [ʃûə, ʃo:ə] *adj.* zeker, gewis, verzekerd; vast, stellig, onfeilbaar; veilig; *adj.* zeker, voorzeker.

surely ['ʃûəli] *adv.* zeker, voorzeker, met zekerheid; toch.

surety ['ʃûəti] borg *m.*; borgtocht *m.*; onderpand *o.*; veiligheid, zekerheid *v.*

surf [sə:f] branding *v.*

surface ['sə:fis] *sb.* oppervlakte *v.*; (v. *water, enz.*) vlak *o.*; buitenkant *m.*; *adj.* oppervlakkig; uiterlijk; ogen-

schijnlijk; geveinsd; (v. *mijnarbeid*) bovengronds; *vt.* planeren, glad maken, polijsten; aan de oppervlakte brengen; beleggen (**with,** met); *vi.* (v. *duikboot*) bovenkomen.

surfaceman ['sə:fismæn] (*spoorw.*) wegwerker *m.*

surfeit ['sə:fit] *sb.* overlading *v.* (van de maag); oververzadiging *v.*; *vt.* (de maag) overladen; oververzadigen.

surge [sə:dʒ] *vi.* golven, hoog gaan; zwellen, deinen; (*sch.: v. touw*) schrikken; dringen, stuwen; *sb.* baar, golf, stortzee *v.*; (*fig.*) golving, deining *v.*; opwelling *v.*

surgeon ['sə:dʒən] heelmeester, chirurg *m.*

surgery ['sə:dʒəri] heelkunde, chirurgie *v.*; (v. *dokter*) spreekkamer *v.*

surly ['sə:li] *adj.* nors, bokkig, stuurs, gemelijk, knorrig, korzelig.

surmise [sə:'maiz] *sb.* vermoeden, gissing *v.*; *vt.* vermoeden, gissen.

surmount [sə:'maunt] te boven komen, overwinnen; beklimmen; overklimmen; staan boven (op), liggen op.

surname ['sə:neim] bijnaam, toenaam *m.*; familienaam, achternaam *m.*; —**d...,** bijgenaamd...

surpass [sə:'pâs] overtreffen, te boven gaan.

surplus ['sə:pləs] *sb.* overschot, teveel *o.*; *adj.* overtollig.

surprise [sə'praiz] *sb.* verrassing; overrompeling *v.*; verwondering, verbazing *v.*; *vt.* verrassen; overrompelen, overvallen; verwonderen, verbazen; betrappen.

surprising [sə'praiziŋ] *adj.* verwonderlijk, verbazingwekkend.

surrender [sə'rendə] *vt.* overgeven; inleveren; uitleveren; opgeven, afstand doen van; afstaan; *vi.* zich overgeven; *sb.* (het) overgeven *o.*, overgave *v.*; uitlevering *v.*; afstand *m.*

surreptitious(ly [sərəp'tiʃəs(li)] *adj.* (*adv.*) heimelijk, clandestien; onecht, vervalst; sluw, geniepig; nagedrukt.

surround [sə'raund] *vt.* omringen, insluiten, omsingelen; *sb.* omsingeling, insluiting *v.*; rand *m.*, omranding *v.*

surroundings [sə'raundiŋz] omgeving *v.*

surtax ['sə:tæks] *sb.* extra-belasting *v.*, toeslag *m.*; *vt.* extra belasten.

survey [sə:'vei] *vt.* bezien, bezichtigen; opnemen; overzien; (*dicht.*) schouwen; opmeten, opnemen; (*sch.*) pellen; ['sə:vei] *sb.* bezichtiging, inspectie *v.*; overzicht *o.*; schouwing *v.*; (v. *land*) opmeting, opneming *v.*; rapport, verslag *o.*

surveyor [sə:'veiə] opziener, opzichter, inspecteur *m.*; landmeter; opnemer *m.*; (*bij verzekering*) taxateur, expert *m.*; spanrups *v.*; onderzoeker; beschouwer *m.*

survival [sə:'vaivəl] overleving *v.*;

voortbestaan o.; langst overgeblevene m.; overblijfsel o.

survive [sə:'vaiv] vt. overléven; vi. nog leven, nog in leven zijn; blijven leven, voortleven, voortbestaan; het er levend afbrengen.

susceptible [sə'septibi] adj. vatbaar (of, voor); gevoelig (to, voor); ontvankelijk; lichtgeraakt; blootgesteld (to, aan).

suspect [səs'pekt] vt. vermoeden; bevroeden; verdenken, wantrouwen; ['səs-pekt, səs'pekt] adj. verdacht; sb. verdachte m.

suspend [səs'pend] onderbreken; (v. vijandelijkheden) staken; (v. oordeel) opschorten; ophangen; laten afhangen (upon, van); (v. vergunning, enz.) tijdelijk in'rekken.

suspender [səs'pendə] ophanger m.; sokophouder, kousophouder m.; bretel v.

suspension [səs'penʃən] onderbreking; afbreking v.; opschorting v.; schorsing v.; ophanging v.; uitstel o.

suspicion [səs'piʃən] sb. achterdocht v., argwaan m.; verdenking v., schijnt j o., zweem m.; vt. wantrouwen; verdenken; vermoeden.

suspicious [səs'piʃəs] verdacht; achterdochtig, argwanend, wantrouwend.

sustain [səs'tain] ondersteunen, schragen, stutten, dragen; staande houden; (v. bewering) staven, bewijzen; (v. gesprek) gaande houden; (v. briefwisseling) onderhouden, (v. verlies) lijden; (v. koude) verduren; (v. vergelijking, aanval) doorstaan; (muz.: v. noot) aanhouden; (v. gezag) hooghouden; (v. beweging, enz.) volhouden.

suture ['s(j)utjuə] sb. (v. wond) hechting v.; (v. been) naad m.; vt. hechten.

svelte [svelt] slank.

swab [swɔb] sb. zwabber m., wis v.; (mil.) loopborstel m.; (sl.) (v. zee-officier) epaulet v.; vt. zwabberen, dweilen.

swagger ['swægə] geur maken, wind maken, opscheppen, snoeven, pochen, zwetsen.

swallow ['swɔlou] sb. zwaluw v.

swallow ['swɔlou] vt. slikken; inslikken, doorslikken; opslokken; verslinden; verzwelgen; (v. trots) op zij zetten; (v. woorden) terugnemen; onderdrukken; vi. slikken; sb. slok; dronk m.; slokdarm m.; keel v.; afgrond, draaikolk m.

swallow-tail ['swɔlouteil] (Dk.) zwaluwstaart m.; (tn.) zwaluwstaart m., verbindingsstuk o.; (Dk.: vlinder) koninginnepage v.

swamp [swɔmp] sb. moeras o.; drasland o.; vi. zinken (in een moeras); (v. boot) vol water lopen; vt. vol water doen (laten) lopen; overstromen, onder water zetten; verzwelgen; opslokken; (met woorden, enz.) overstelpen; (radio) overstemmen; ruïneren.

swampy ['swɔmpi] moerassig, drassig.

swan [swɔn] zwaan v.

swank [swæŋk] vi. geuren, bluffen, opsnijden; zich aanstellen; blokken, vossen; sb. bluf m., opsnijderij v.; aanstellerij v.

sward [swɔːd] grasperk, grasveld o.; zwoerd o.

swarm [swɔːm] sb. zwerm m.; vi. zwermen, krioelen, wemelen; klauteren (in).

sway [swei] vi. zwaaien, slingeren, wiegelen, schommelen, zwenken; hellen, overhellen; regeren, heersen; invloed hebben; vt. doen zwaaien; beheersen, besturen, regeren; (v. zwaard) hanteren; (sch.) hijsen, ophalen; sb. zwaai m.; schommeling v.; heerschappij v., gezag o., macht v.; invloed m., overwicht o.

swear [swêə] vi. zweren, de eed afleggen; vloeken; (v. kat) blazen; vt. zweren, onder ede bevestigen; bezweren; doen zweren, de eed afnemen, beëdigen; sb. eed m.; vloek m., vloekwoord o.; (v. kat) geblaas o.

sweat [swet] sb. zweet o.; zweting, uitzweting v.; zweetkuur v.; opwinding v., ongeduld o.; (fam.) inspanning v., koeliewerk o.; vi. zweten; (fig.) zwoegen; werken voor een hongerloon; vt. doen zweten; laten uitzweten; (v. werkvolk) uitzuigen, uitbuiten, tegen een hongerloon laten werken.

sweater ['swetə] wollen sporttrui v.; zweetmiddel o.; uitbuiter, uitzuiger m.; (fam.) zware karwei v.

sweating-system ['swetiŋsistəm] uitzuiging v. van arbeiders.

Sweden ['swidn] Zweden o.

sweep [swip] vi. vegen; (zich) snel bewegen; zich uitstrekken; zwenken; vt. vegen, aanvegen, wegvegen; schoonvegen; (v. land) doorkruisen; afjagen; afvissen; (v. rivier, enz.) dreggen, afdreggen; afzoeken; slepen over; strijken langs; (v. winst) opstrijken; (mil.) bestrijken; meeslepen; teisteren; sb. veeg m.; draai, zwaai m.; zwenking v.; riemslag m.; (v. schip) beloop o.; (v. ziekte) verspreiding v.; (mil.) bestrijkingshoek m.; opruiming v.; omvang m., bereik, gebied o.; uitgestrektheid v.; vaart v.; golving, deining v.; molenwiek v.; golflijn, bocht v.; oprit m., oprijlaan v.; trek, slag m.; schoorsteenveger m.; straatveger m.; veegsel o.; pompzwengel m.; (sl.) ploert, smeerlap, schurk m.; (kaartsp.) slem o.

sweeper ['swipə] veger m.; schuier m.; schoorsteenveger m.; straatveger m.; straatveegmachine v.; (sch.) mijnenveger m.; (v. locomotief) baanruimer m.

sweeping ['swipiŋ] adj. vegend; vèrstrekkend, vèrreikend, ingrijpend; (v. maatregelen) doortastend; overweldigend; sb. —s, veegsel o.; (fig.) uitvaagsel o.

sweet [swit] adj. zoet; welriekend, geurig, lekker; aangenaam, liefelijk; aanvallig, bevallig; vers, fris; (v. bewe-

ging) zacht; *adv.* zoet; lekker; *sb.* zoetheid *r.*; zoetigheid *v.*, suikertje, lekkers *o.*; zoete spijs *v.*, toetje *o.*; lieveling *m.*
sweetbread ['swîtbred] zwezerik *m.*
sweeten ['swîtn] *rt.* zoet maken; aanzoeten, verzoeten; verzoeten, veraangenamen; verzachten, verlichten; (*v. lucht*) ververschen; (*v. licht*) temperen; (*v. kamer*) luchten; *ri.* zoet(er) worden.
sweetheart ['swîthât] *sb.* geliefde *m.* & *v.*; meisje, liefje *o.*; lieveling *m.*; *vi.* (*vt.*) vrijen (met).
sweetmeat ['swîtmît] bonbon; suikertje *o.*; —(**s**), suikergoed *o.*
sweet-natured ['swît'neitʃəd] goedaardig, zacht van aard.
sweet-scented ['swît'sentid] geurig, welriekend.
sweet-smelling ['swît'smeliŋ] *zie* **sweet-scented.**
sweet-tooth ['swîttûð] zoetekauw *m.* & *v.*
swell [swel] *vi.* zwellen; aanzwellen, opzwellen; uitzetten, opbollen, buiken; (*fig.*) aangroeien, toenemen, oplopen; zich opblazen; (*fam.*) de grote heer uithangen; *vt.* doen zwellen; (*fig.*) doen aangroeien, verhogen; hovaardig maken, opblazen; *sb.* (het) zwellen *o.*, zwelling *v.*; deining *v.*; gezwollenheid *v.*; (*v. orgel*) zwelkast *v.*; (*sl.*) fat, pronker *m.*; grote meneer *m.*; *adj.* (*fam.*) prachtig, fijn, chic, voornaam.
swelling ['sweliŋ] *adj.* zwellend; uitzettend, enz.; *zie* **swell**; *sb.* (het) opzwellen; (het) aanzwellen *o.*; uitzetting *v.*; gezwel *o.*; uitwas *o.*; verhevenheid *v.*; (*fig.*) opgeblazenheid *v.*
sweltering ['swelteriŋ] smoorheet, snikheet, broeiend, zwoel.
swerve [swə:v] *vi.* afwijken, afdwalen; uitwijken, op zij gaan; zwerven, rondzwerven; *vt.* doen afwijken; op zij doen gaan; *sb.* zwenking *v.*, zwaai *m.*
swift [swift] *adj.* snel, vlug; vaardig; *sb.* gierzwaluw, muurzwaluw *v.*; kleine hagedis *v.*; watersalamander *m.*; soort nachtvlinder *m.*; haspel *m.*; *vt.* (*sch.*) zwichten; vastsjorren.
swift-footed ['swift'futid] snelvoetig, vlug ter been.
swiftness ['swiftnis] snelheid, vlugheid *v.*
swig [swig] *sb.* (*sl.*) grote slok *m.*; *vt.* & *vi.* (*sl.*) met grote teugen drinken, zuipen; leegdrinken.
swill [swil] *vt.* doorspoelen; opzuipen; inzwelgen; (*v. geld*) verzuipen; volop te drinken geven; *vi.* zuipen, zich bedrinken.
swim [swim] *vi.* zwemmen; drijven; draaien, duizelen; glijden, zweven; *vt.* overzwemmen; laten zwemmen (drijven); om het hardst zwemmen met; *sb.* (het) zwemmen *o.*; (het) drijven *o.*; visrijke plaats *v.*; zwemblaas *v.*
swimmer ['swimə] zwemmer *m.*; zwemvogel *m.*; waterspin *v.*; dobber *m.*

swimming-bell ['swimiŋbel] (*v. kwal*) scherm *o.*
swimming-bladder ['swimiŋblædə] zwemblaas *v.*
swindle ['swindl] *vt.* afzetten, oplichten; *vi.* zwendelen; *sb.* afzetterij, oplichterij *v.*, zwendel *m.*, zwendelarij *v.*
swindler ['swindlə] afzetter, oplichter, zwendelaar *m.*
swine [swain] varken(s), zwijn(en) *o.* (*mr.*).
swine-herd ['swainhə:d] zwijnenhoeder *m.*
swing [swiŋ] *vi.* schommelen, slingeren; zwaaien; bengelen; zwenken; met veerkrachtige pas lopen; — **to**, (*v. deur*) dichtslaan, dichtvliegen; *vt.* doen (laten) schommelen (slingeren, enz.); slingeren met; zwaaien met; doen (laten) zwenken; (*Am.*) beheersen; besturen; *vr.* — **oneself**, zich slingeren; zich draaien; *sb.* zwaai *m.*, zwenking, schommeling *v.*; schommel *m.*; slingering *v.*; veerkrachtige gang *m.*; bezieling *v.*, vuur *o.*
swing-boat ['swiŋbout] schommelbootje *o.*; —(**s**), (*op kermis*) Russische schommel *m.*
swing-gate ['swiŋgeit] draaiboom *m.*, draaihek *o.*
swingle ['swiŋgl] *sb.* zwingel *m.*; zwingelstok *m.*; *vt.* zwingelen.
swish [swiʃ] *vi.* zwiepen; (*v. kogel*) fluiten; (*v. zijde*) ruisen; slaan met; *vt.* afranselen, met de roe geven; *sb.* gezwiep *o.*; gefluit *o.*; geruis, geritsel *o.*, ritseling *r.*; zwierigheid *v.*; *adj.* ruisend; *ij.* zwiep!
Swiss [swis] Zwitser *m.*
switch [switʃ] *sb.* teentje, rijsje *o.*; roede *v.*; karwats *v.*; (*el.*) schakelaar, omschakelaar, stroomwisselaar *m.*; (*spoorw.*) wissel *m.*; valse vlecht *v.*; verandering *v.*, draai, omkeer *m.*; (*met karwats, enz.*) slag, zwiep *m.*; (*mil.*) versterkte linie *v.*; *vt.* slaan, ranselen; uitkloppen; (*el.*) omschakelen; op een ander spoor brengen; snoeien; (*v. licht*) uitdraaien; (*v. telefoon*) afzetten; (*fig.*: *v. aandacht*) afleiden, op iets anders brengen; *vi.* zwiepen; (*el.*) schakelen; overstag gaan, een andere richting inslaan; (*sl.*) ophouden, eindigen.
switch-board ['switʃbo:d] (*el.*) schakelbord *o.*
switchman ['switʃmən] wisselwachter *m.*
Switzerland ['switsələnd] Zwitserland *o.*
swivel ['swivl] wervel *m.*
swoon [swûn] *vi.* bezwijmen, in zwijm vallen; (*fig.*) kwijnen, wegsterven; *sb.* bezwijming *v.*
sword [so:d] zwaard *o.*, degen *m.*; sabel *v.*; (*sl.*) bajonet *v.*
symbol ['simbəl] *sb.* symbool, zinnebeeld, teken *o.*; symbolum *o.*, geloofsbelijdenis *v.*; *vt.* symboliseren, zinnebeeldig voorstellen.

symbolic(al) [sim'bɔlik(l)] *adj.* symbolisch, zinnebeeldig.
symmetric(al) [si'metrik(l)] *adj.* symmetrisch.
sympathize ['simpəðaiz] sympathiseren (*with*, met); medegevoelen, medelijden hebben (*with*, met); deelnemen (*in*, in).
sympathy ['simpəði] sympathie *v.*; medegevoel *o.*, deelneming *v.*, medelijden *o.*
symphony ['simfəni] symfonie *v.*
symptom ['sim(p)təm] symptoom, verschijnsel, teken *o.*
synagogue ['sinəgɔg] synagoge *v.*
synchronous ['siŋkrənəs] gelijktijdig, synchronisch.
syndicate ['sindikit] *sb.* syndicaat, consortium *o.*; ['sindikeit] *vt.* tot een syndicaat (consortium) verenigen.

synod ['sinəd] synode, kerkvergadering *v.*
synonym ['sinənim] synoniem *o.*
synonymous(ly) [si'nɔniməs(li)] *adj.* (*adv.*) synoniem, zinverwant, gelijkbetekenend.
synopsis [si'nɔpsis] overzicht, kort begrip *o.*
syringe ['sirin(d)ʒ] *sb.* spuit(je) *v.* (*o.*); *vt.* bespuiten; inspuiten; uitspuiten.
syrup ['sirəp] siroop, stroop *v.*; stroopje *o.*
system ['sistim] systeem, stelsel *o.*; samenstel *o.*, inrichting *v.*; lichaam, lichaamsgestel *o.*, constitutie *v.*; (*aardk.*) formatie *v.*
systematic(al) [sisti'mætik(l)] *adj.* systematisch, stelselmatig, methodisch.

T

tab [tæb] (*v. jas, enz.*) lus *v.*; schoenleertje *o.*; label *v.*; (*v. pet, muts*) oorklep *v.*
tabard ['tæbəd] tabberd, tabbaard *m.*
table ['teibl] *sb.* tafel *v.*; speeltafel *v.*; tabel *v.*, register *o.*; tafelland *o.*; kost *m.*; —*s*, tafels (van vermenigvuldiging) *v.*; logaritmentafel *v.*; *vt.* voeden, te eten geven; rangschikken; ter tafel brengen; (*v. motie, enz.*) indienen, voorstellen; (*Am.*) voor kennisgeving aannemen, onder 't loodje leggen; *vi.* in de kost zijn; eten.
table-cover ['teiblkʌvə] tafelkleed *o.*
table-runner ['teiblrʌnə] tafelloper *m.*
table-service ['teiblsə:vis] eetservies *o.*
tablet ['tæblit] tablet *v.*; plakje *o.*; plaat, gedenkplaat *v.*; —*s*, notitieboekje *o.*
tabouret ['tæbərit] krukje, stoeltje *o.*; borduurraam *o.*; naaldenkussen *o.*
tachometer [tæ'kɔmitə] snelheidsmeter *m.*; (*v. machine*) slagenteller *m.*
tacit(ly) ['tæsit(li)] *adj.* (*adv.*) stilzwijgend.
taciturn ['tæsitə:n] zwijgend, stil, stilzwijgend.
taciturnity [tæsi'tə:niti] stilzwijgendheid *v.*
tack [tæk] *sb.* spijkertje *o.*; rijgsteek *m.*; (*sch.: v. zeil*) hals *m.*; (*v. schip*) koers, gang *m.*; (*v. blikje*) tong *v.*; aanhechtsel, aanhangsel *o.*; kleverigheid *v.*; (*mil., sch , sl.*) kost *m.*, eten, brood *o.*; *soft* —, brood; lekker eten, lekkere kost; *vt.* (*v. vloerkleed, enz.*) vastspijkeren; rijgen, hechten, vastmaken; (*sch.*) bij de wind omwenden; *vi.* (*sch.*) overstag gaan, laveren; het over een andere boeg gooien.
tackle ['tækl] *sb.* takel *m.*; talie *v.*; tuig *o.*; gerei *o.*; (*sl.*) kost *m.*, eten *o.*; *vt.*

grijpen, pakken; vastmaken; (*v. paard*) tuigen; aanvallen op; aanpakken, onder handen nemen; (*sp.: voetb.*) takkelen; *vi.* — *to*, de handen uit de mouwen steken, flink aanpakken.
tact [tækt] tact *m.*; (*muz.*) slag, maatslag *m.*
tactful(ly) ['tæktful(i)] *adj.* (*adv.*) tactvol.
tactic ['tæktik] tactiek *v.*
tactless(ly) ['tæktlis(li)] *adj.* (*adv.*) tactloos.
taffeta ['tæfitə], **taffety** ['tæfiti] taf *v.*
tag [tæg] *sb.* malle *v.*, veterbeslag *o.*; (*v. lakei, enz.*) nestel *m.*; kwastje *o.*; (*v. laars*) lus *v.*; (*v. lint, enz.*) rafel *v.*; uiteinde *o.*; aanhangsel *o.*; brokstuk *o.*, aanhaling *v.*; stereotiep gezegde *o.*; refrein *o.*; epiloog *m.*; leus *v.*; (*v. staart*) punt *v.*, tip *m.*; adreskaart *v.*; bagageetiket *o.*; *vt.* aanhechten, vasthechten, vastknopen; aaneenrijgen, samenflansen; achternalopen, op de voet volgen; (*Am.*) noemen, bestempelen (als); *vi.* — *after*, overal nalopen.
tail [teil] *sb.* staart *m.*; vlecht *v.*; rij *v.*, slier *m.*; (*v. jas*) pand *o.*, slip *v.*; (*v. japon*) sleep *m.*; gevolg *o.*; nasleep *m.*; uiteinde, laatste gedeelte *o.*; (*v. munt*) keerzijde *v.*; (*v. hark, enz.*) steel *m.*; *head*(*s*) *or* —(*s*), kruis of munt; *vt.* van een staart voorzien; van staart ontdoen, kortstaarten; bij de staart grijpen (trekken); (*v. vruchten*) van stelen ontdoen; (*Am., sl.*) in 't oog houden, volgen; *vi.* in een staart uitlopen, een staart vormen; achter elkaar aan komen; achteraan komen, achter blijven.
tail-board ['teilbo:d] (*v. wagen*) achterschot, krat *o.*; voeteneindplank *v.*
tail-light ['teillait] (*v. trein, enz.*) achterlicht, sluitlicht *o.*

tailor ['teilə] *sb.* kleermaker *m.*; *vi.* kleermaker zijn; *vt.* kleren maken voor; op kleermakerswijze maken.

taint [teint] *sb.* (*v. rotheid, enz.*) plek *v.*; vlek, smet *v.*; (*fig.*) smet, blaam *v.*; besmetting *v.*, bederf *o.*; (*fig.*) kanker *m.*; *vt.* besmetten, bezoedelen; aansteken; (*v. vlees, enz.*) bederven; *come of a —ed stock*, erfelijk belast zijn.

taintless ['teintlis] vlekkeloos, smetteloos, onbesmet, zuiver.

take [teik] *vt.* nemen; aannemen; innemen; opnemen; overnemen; in behandeling nemen; meenemen; (*v. loon*) trekken; (*v. ziekte, enz.*) krijgen; (*v. tijd*) in beslag nemen; (*v. prijs, enz.*) behalen; (*v. slag*) toebrengen; raken, treffen; (*v. koffie, thee*) drinken, gebruiken; (*v. boodschap*) brengen, overbrengen; (*v. kou*) vatten; betrappen; opvatten, beschouwen (*as*, als); vatten, snappen; (*v. gevolgen*) aanvaarden; (*v. gelegenheid*) waarnemen; (*v. temperatuur*) opnemen; bemachtigen; bezielen; *vi.* pakken; treffen; inslaan, succes hebben; (*v. vis*) bijten; wortel schieten; gaan, lopen; (*Am.*) vlam vatten; — *after,* aarden naar; nazetten; nalopen; — *down,* neerhalen; naar beneden halen; (*v. schilderij, enz.*) afnemen; (*v. boek, enz.*) van de plank nemen, uit het rek nemen; (*v. huis, enz.*) afbreken, slopen; (*v. tent, enz.*) uit elkaar nemen, afbreken; voorbijstreven, achter zich laten; innemen, slikken; vernederen, verootmoedigen, een toontje lager doen zingen, op zijn plaats zetten; optekenen, opschrijven, noteren; (*v. haar*) losmaken; (*v. boom*) omhalen; — *in,* innemen; binnenleiden; (*v. water*) binnenkrijgen; (*v. gasten*) houden, ontvangen; (*v. leugen, verhaal*) slikken; (*v. woord*) opvangen; (*v. schip*) opbrengen; in zich opnemen, begrijpen, beseffen; omvatten; (*v. geld*) beuren; verdienen; (*v. persoon*) beetnemen; zich toeëigenen; afsluiten, omheinen; — *off,* afnemen, wegnemen; verwijderen; (*v. kleren*) afleggen, uittrekken; (*v. hoed*) afdoen, afzetten; uit de weg ruimen; nabootsen; afdrukken, een afdruk maken van; (*v. embargo, enz.*) opheffen; (*v. de prijs*) aflaten, laten vallen; (*vl.*) opstijgen, starten; (*v. zijrivier*) zich afscheiden; ontlasten van; weggaan; — *on,* aan boord nemen; (*v. taak, verantwoordelijkheid*) op zich nemen; (*v. werkvolk, enz.*) aannemen; (*v. zaak*) overnemen; (*fam.*) pakken, opgang maken, succes hebben; dienst nemen; zich verbinden; te keer gaan; erg bedroefd zijn (*about,* over); — *out,* nemen uit, te voorschijn halen; (*v. vlek*) verwijderen, wegmaken; uit de zak nemen; wegbrengen; (*v. pand*) inlossen; (*v. patent, enz.*) nemen; (*v. paarden*) uitspannen, afspannen; — *over,* (*v. zaak, enz.*) overnemen; (*met boot*) overzetten, overbrengen; (*mil.*) de wacht overnemen; — *over to,*

(*radio*) verbinden met; — *up,* opnemen; oppakken; oppikken; inrekenen, arresteren; (*v. tijd, plaats*) in beslag nemen; (*v. plaats*) innemen; (*v. houding*) aannemen; (*v. ader*) afbinden; (*v. straat*) opbreken; (*met rijtuig*) komen afhalen; (*v. voorwerp*) in ontvangst nemen; (*v. wissel*) betalen, in disconto nemen; ter hand nemen; ingaan op; terechtwijzen; een standje maken, onder handen nemen; (*v. aandelen, lening*) inschrijven op; (*v. weer*) beter worden; (*v. refrein, enz.*) overnemen; (*Am.*) beginnen; *vr.* — *oneself away,* heengaan, er van door gaan; — *oneself off,* zich wegpakken; *sb.* vangst *v.*; (*v. schouwburg, enz.*) ontvangst, recette *v.*

take-in ['teik'in] beetnemerij, bedotterij *v.*

take-off ['teik'o:f] springplaats *v.*; (*bij 't springen*) afzet *m.*; (*het*) afspringen *o.*; vermindering *v.*; schaduwzijde *v.*; karikatuur *v.*; start *m.*, opstijging *v.*

taking ['teikiŋ] *adj.* innemend, aantrekkelijk, aanlokkelijk; (*v. stijl*) boeiend; (*v. titel, melodie*) pakkend; besmettelijk; *sb.* (het) nemen *o.*, *enz.*; inneming, inname *v.*; vangst *v.*; opgewonden toestand *m.*, zenuwachtigheid *v.*; — *s,* ontvangsten, recette.

talc [tælk] talk, talkaarde *v.*; mica *o.*

tale [teil] verhaal, vertelsel *o.*; sprookje *o.*; praatje, smoesje *o.*; getal, aantal *o.*; bedrag *o.*; rekening *v.*

tale-bearer ['teilbêərə] klikspaan, aanbrenger, verklikker *m.*

talent ['tælənt] talent *o.*, gave, bekwaamheid, begaafdheid *v.*

talented ['tæləntid] talentvol, begaafd.

talisman ['tælizmən] talisman *m.*

talk [to:k] *vi.* praten, spreken; *vt.* praten, spreken; spreken over; — *oneself out,* uitgepraat raken; *sb.* gepraat *o.*; praat *m.*, praatje *o.*; gesprek *o.*; onderhoud *o.*, bespreking *v.*

talkative ['to:kətiv] praatgraag, praatziek, babbelachtig.

talkee-talkee ['to:ki'to:k] koeterwaals *o.*, brabbeltaal *v.*; gepraat, geklets, gewauwel *o.*, kletspraat *m.*

talking ['to:kiŋ] *adj.* pratend; (*v. film, ogen*) sprekend; *sb.* praat *m.*; gepraat *o.*

tall [to:l] *adj.* lang, hoog; (*v. persoon*) groot, lang, rijzig; (*fig.*) hoogdravend, bombastisch; blufferig, opsnijerig; (*Am.*) overdreven, opgesmukt; *adv. talk —,* snoeven, opsnijden.

tallish ['to:liʃ] vrij lang, nogal hoog, *enz.*; *zie tall.*

tallow ['tælou] talk *v.*; kaarsvet *o.*

tallow-dip ['tæloudip] vetkaars *v.*

tally ['tæli] *sb.* kerfstok *m.*; kerf, inkeping *v.*; rekening, verantwoording *v.*; overeenstemming *v.*; andere helft *v.*, overeenkomstig deel *o.*; getal, aantal *o.*; naamhoutje *o.* (aan een plant); merk, etiket *o.*; duplicaat *o.*; *vt.* inkepen

(op de kerfstok); aanstrepen, aantekenen; natellen, nagaan, controleren; merken, van een etiket voorzien; *vi.* overeenstemmen, kloppen.
talon ['tælən] klauw *m.*; (*v. kaarten*) stok *m.*; (*v. sabel*) hiel *m.*; (*bouwk.*) talaan *m.*; nok *v.*, uitsteeksel *o.*; (*v. effecten*) talon *m.*
tamarind ['tæmərind] tamarinde *v.*
tame [teim] *vt.* temmen, tam maken; temperen; *adj.* tam, getemd; mak, gedwee; saai, kleurloos, flauw, futloos, vervelend.
tamer ['teimə] temmer, dierentemmer *m.*
tamper ['tæmpə] *sb.* stamper *m.*; *vi.* — *with,* knoeien met; verknoeien, vervalsen; zich bemoeien met; heulen met; (*v. getuigen, enz.*) bewerken, trachten om te kopen.
tan [tæn] *sb.* run; taan *v.*; taankleur *v.*; **—s,** (bruin)gele schoenen; *adj.* runkleurig, tankleurig; *vt.* looien, tanen; bruinen; *vi.* tanen; (*v. de huid, door de zon*) bruinen, bruin worden.
tandem ['tændəm] tandem *v.*
tang [tæŋ] *sb.* (*v. gesp*) tong *v.*; (*v. mes, enz.*) doorn *m.*; wortel *m.*; (*aan zeis*) arend *m.*; (*v. bij*) angel *m.*; (*v. vork*) tand *m.*; smaakje *o.*, bijsmaak, nasmaak *m.*; luchtje, geurtje *o.*, scherpe lucht *v.*; (*fig.*) zweem *m.*, tikje *o.*; (*Pl.*) plaatwier *o.*; klank *m.*, geluid *o.*; *vt.* een eigenaardig smaakje geven; doen klinken; *vi.* klinken.
tangible ['tændʒibl] *adj.* voelbaar, tastbaar.
tangle ['tæŋgl] *vt.* in de war maken; verwarren; verwikkelen, verstrikken; *vi.* in de war raken; *sb.* verwarring, verwikkeling *v.*; warboel *m.*; verwarde massa *v.*; wirwar, knoop *m.*; soort zeewier *o.*
tank [tæŋk] *sb.* waterbak *m.*; (vis)kaar *v.*; (petroleum)tank *v.*; (*mil.*) tank *v.*, gevechtswagen *m.*; *vt.* in een tank doen; in een tank bewaren; *vi.* — (**up**), benzine innemen; (*Am.*) zuipen.
tanner ['tænə] looier, leertouwer *m.*
tap [tæp] *sb.* (houten) kraan *v.*; (*v. vat*) tap *m.*, spon *v.*; tapperij, gelagkamer *v.*; brouwsel *o.*; schroefboor *v.*; tik(je) *m.* (*o.*); *vt.* van een kraan voorzien; een kraan slaan in; (*v. vat*) aansteken, opsteken; tappen, aftappen; (*v. fles*) aanbreken, opentrekken; een schroefgat boren in; (*fig.*) uithoren; (*v. bankbiljet*) wisselen; (*v. mijn*) exploiteren; zachtjes kloppen op; pikken tegen; (*Am.: v. schoenen*) lappen; *vi.* — *against* (**at**), tikken tegen, kloppen op.
tape [teip] *sb.* lint *o.*; band *m.*; strook *v.* papier (aan telegraaftoestel); telegrafisch koersbericht *o.*; (*gen.*) lintworm *m.*; (*sl.*) sterke drank *m.*; *white* **—,** jenever; *red* **—,** cognac; *vt.* met linten (ver)binden.
taper ['teipə] *sb.* waspit *v.*; zwak licht

o.; (*fig.*) toorts *v.*; spits *v.*; geleidelijke vermindering (afneming) *v.*; *adj.* spits toelopend; geleidelijk afnemend; *vi.* (& *vt.*) spits (doen) toelopen; geleidelijk (doen) afnemen.
tapestry ['tæpistri] geweven behangsel, tapijtwerk, wandtapijt *o.*
tar [tâ] *sb.* teer *o.*; (*sl.*) pikbroek, matroos *m.*; *vt.* teren, beteren; (*fig.*) zwartmaken.
tardy ['tâdi] *adj.* traag, langzaam; laat; achterlijk; dralend.
tare [tê̯ə] *sb.* tarra *v.*; (*Pl.*) dolik *v.*; voederwikke *v.*
target ['tâgit] schietschijf *v.*; mikpunt, doelwit *o.*; schietwedstrijd *m.*; spoorwegsein *o.*; beukelaar *m.*, schild *o.*
tariff ['tærif] *sb.* tarief; toltarief *o.*; *vt.* tariferen, in tarief brengen, een tarief opmaken voor.
tarnish ['tâniʃ] *vt.* (*v. metalen*) laten aanlopen; dof maken, mat maken; ontglanzen; ontluisteren; doen tanen; (*fig.*) bezoedelen, bezwalken; *vi.* (*v. metalen*) aanlopen; dof worden, mat worden; verbleken, tanen; *sb.* dofheid, matheid *v.*; ontluistering *v.*; verbleking *v.*; bezoedeling, smet *v.*
tarpaulin [tâ'po:lin] (*v. wagen*) dekkleed *o.·* (*sch.*) presenning *v.*, geteerd zeildoek *o.·* matrozenhoed *m.*; (*fam.*) pikbroek, matroos *m.*
tarry ['tæri] *vi.* dralen, toeven; *vt.* wachten op.
tart [tât] *adj.* wrang, zuur; bits, scherp, vinnig.
tart [tât] *sb.* taart *v.*, vruchtentaart(je) *v.* (*o.*).
tartlet ['tâtlit] taartje *o.*
task [tâsk] *sb.* taak *v.*; huiswerk *o.*; karwei *v.*; *vt.* een taak opgeven; werk (een taakwerk) opleggen; hard laten werken, veel vergen van; op de proef stellen.
tassel ['tæsl] kwast *m.*, franje *v.*; lint *o.* (als bladwijzer in boek); (*Pl.*) katje *o.*, bloesem *m.*
taste ['teist] *vt.* proeven; smaken; ondervinden; beproeven; keuren; smaak vinden in, genieten van; *vi.* smaken; — *of,* smaken naar; *sb.* smaak *m.*; bijsmaak *m.*; voorsmaak *m.*; proefje, voorproefje *o.*; slokje *o.*; ietsje, zweempje *o.*
tasteful (**ly**) ['teistful(i)] *adj.* (*adv.*) smakelijk; smaakvol.
tasteless (**ly**) ['teistlis(li)] *adj.* (*adv.*) smakeloos.
taster ['teistə] (*v. wijn, thee, enz.*) proever *m.*; voorproever *m.*; (*v. wijnproever*) proefbekertje, proefglaasje *o.*; kaasboor *v.*; (*fig.*) beoordelaar, criticus *m.*
tatter ['tætə] *sb.* lap *m.*, vod, lomp, flard; *vt.* aan flarden scheuren, verscheuren; *vi.* aftakelen; **—ed,** ook; haveloos; gehavend.
tattle ['tætl] *vi.* babbelen, snappen; klikken; uit de school klappen; *sb.* gebabbel, gesnap *o.*; geklik *o.*

tattoo [tə'tû] *sb.* (*mil.*) taptoe *v.*, avondappèl *o.*; tatoeëring *v.*; (*E.I.*) hit, pony *m.*; *vt.* tatoeëren.

taunt [to:nt] *vt.* beschimpen, smaden, honen; *vi.* schimpen (*at*, op); *sb.* schimp, smaad, hoon, spot *m.*, spotternij *v.*

Taurus ['to:rəs] (*sterr.: in dierenriem*) de Stier.

taut [to:t] strak, gespannen; in goede toestand; stipt, nauwgezet, streng.

tavern ['tævən] herberg, kroeg *v.*, wijnhuis *o.*; logement *o.*

taw [to:] *sb.* (grote) knikker, alikas *m.*; knikkerspel *o.*; meet, streep *v.* (bij 't knikkerspel).

tawny ['to:ni] tanig, taankleurig, getaand, geelbruin.

tax [tæks] *sb.* (rijks)belasting *v.*; schatting *v.*; last *m.*; (zware) proef *v.*; *vt.* belasten, belasting (schatting) opleggen; op een zware proef stellen; veel vergen van; beslag leggen op; (*recht*) schatten, taxeren, vaststellen; beschuldigen; berispen, de les lezen; (*Am.*) vragen, berekenen, in rekening brengen.

taxable ['tæksəbl] belastbaar.

tax-collector ['tækskəlektə] ontvanger *m.* der belastingen.

tax-form ['tæksfo:m] belastingbiljet; belastingformulier *o.*

tax-free ['tæksfri] vrij van belasting.

taxi-cab ['tæksikæb] taxi(auto) *v.*

tea [ti] *sb.* thee *v.*; theemaaltijd *m.*; theeroos *v.*; (*sl.*) sterke drank *m.*; *make* —, thee zetten; *vi.* (*fam.*) thee drinken; op thee onthalen.

teach [titʃ] onderwijzen, leren; les geven, onderricht geven (in).

teachable ['titʃəbl] te onderwijzen, geschikt om onderwezen te worden; bevattelijk, leerzaam.

teacher ['titʃə] onderwijzer(es) *m.* (*v.*); leraar *m.*, lerares *v.*

tea-cosy ['tikouz] theemuts *v.*

tea-cup ['tikəp] theekopje *o.*

teal [til] (*Dk.*) taling *m.*

team [tim] *sb.* (*v. werklieden*) ploeg *v.*; (*sp.: voetb.*) elftal *o.*; (*v. paarden, ossen*) span *o.*; (*v. varkens, kippen*) toom *m.*; (*v. wilde eenden, enz.*) vlucht *v.*; (*v. kanon*) bediening *v.*; (*fig.*) span, stelletje *o.*; (*Am.*) wagen *m.*; *vt.* aanspannen, inspannen; (*Am.: v. werk*) uitbesteden; door ploegen laten verrichten.

team-work ['timwə:k] (*in ploeg*) samenwerking *v.*; (*sp.*) samenspel *o.*

tea-pot ['tipɔt] theepot; trekpot *m.*

tear [tiə] *sb.* traan *m.*; droppel *m.*

tear [têə] *vt.* scheuren, verscheuren, stukscheuren; ontrukken; rijten, openrijten; ontrukken (*from*, aan); (*v. haar*) uitdrukken; *vi.* scheuren; razen, tieren; rennen, stormen, vliegen; — *down*, (*v. biljet, enz.*) afscheuren; (*v. huis*) afbreken; — *up*, verscheuren, stukscheuren; *vr.* — *oneself away*, zich losrukken, zich (met moeite) losmaken (*from*, van); *sb.* scheur *v.*;

haast *v.*; woede *v.*; (*Am.*)* dolle fuif *v.*

tearful ['tiəful] *adj.* vol tranen; schreiend; beschreid; huilerig.

tear-gas ['tiəgæs] (*mil.*) traangas *o.*

tease [tiz] *vt.* plagen, kwellen; sarren; lastig vallen; (*v. wol, enz.*) kammen, kaarden; — *out*, ontwarren; *vi.* plagen; zeuren, dwingen; *sb.* plaaggeest, plager *m.*

teaser ['tizə] plager, plaaggeest *m.*; kaarder *m.*; kaardmachine *v.*; (*fig.*) lastig geval *o.*, puzzel *v.*; (*sp.: boksen*) lastige tegenpartij *v.*

teasing (**ly**) ['tiziŋ(li)] *adj.* (*adv.*) plagend, plagerig.

tea-spoon ['tispûn] theelepeltje *o.*

teat [tit] tepel, uier *m.*; speen *v.*

technician [tek'niʃən] technicus *m.*

technicist ['teknisist] technicus *m.*

tedious (**ly**) ['tidiəs(li)] *adj.* (*adv.*) vervelend, saai; langdradig.

teething ['titθiŋ] (het) tanden krijgen *o.*

teetotal (**l**)**er** [ti'toutlə] geheelonthouder *m.*

telegram ['teligræm] telegram *o.*

telegraph ['teligrâf] *sb.* telegraaf *v.*; *vt. & vi.* telegraferen.

telegrapher ['teligrâfə] telegrafeerder *m.*; telegrafist *m.*

telegraphic [teli'græfik] *adj.* telegrafisch; — *address*, telegramadres.

telephone ['telifoun] *sb.* telefoon *v.*; *vt. & vi.* telefoneren.

telephonist [ti'lefənist] telefonist(e) *m.* (*v.*).

telescope ['teliskoup] *sb.* verrekijker *m.*, telescoop *v.*; *vt.* inéénschuiven; in elkaar schuiven; *vi.* in elkaar geschoven kunnen worden.

tell [tel] *vt.* zeggen, mededelen; vertellen, verhalen; onderrichten; bevelen; zien; kennen, herkennen; onderscheiden; tellen; *vi.* vertellen, verhalen; het oververtellen, klikken; indruk maken; effect hebben, uitwerking hebben; pleiten (*against*, tegen); — *up*, (*v. rekening*) oplopen.

teller ['telə] verteller *m.*; teller *m.*; (*v. bank*) kassier *m.*; stemopnemer *m.*

telling ['teliŋ] (*v. woord, enz.*) krachtig, kernachtig; (*v. rede*) pakkend, indrukwekkend; (*v. antwoord, schot*) raak.

telltale ['telteil] *sb.* babbelaar *m.*; aanbrenger, verklikker *m.*; *adj.* verraderlijk.

temerarious [temə'rêəriəs] vermetel, roekeloos.

temerity [ti'meriti] vermetelheid, roekeloosheid *v.*

temper ['tempə] *vt.* temperen, matigen; verzachten; in toom houden; doen bedaren; (*muz.*) tempereren; (*v. kalk*) aanmaken; laten beslaan; (*v. kleuren*) mengen, temperen; (*v. staal*) harden, blauw laten aanlopen; *sb.* aard *m.*, geaardheid, natuur *v.*; temperament *o.*, gemoedsgesteldheid *v.*, gemoedstoestand *m.*; kalmte, bedaardheid; ge-

moedrust *v.*; boze luim *v.*, slecht humeur *o.*; drift, opvliegendheid *v.*; (*v. staal, enz.*) graad *m.* van hardheid, vastheid *v.*; middelweg *m.*; vermenging *v.*

temperament ['temp(ə)rəmənt] temperament *o.*; (*muz.*) temperatuur *v.*

temperate ['temp(ə)rit] *adj.* matig; gematigd.

temperature ['tempritʃə] temperatuur *v.*, warmtegraad *m.*; (*gen.*) verhoging *v.*

tempest ['tempist] *sb.* (hevige) storm *m.*; vloed *m.*; *vi.* stormen; *vt.* in beroering brengen.

tempestuous(ly) [tem'pestjuəs(li)] *adj.* (*adv.*) stormachtig, onstuimig.

temple ['templ] tempel *m.*; (*prot.*) kerk *v.*; (*aan 't hoofd*) slaap *m.*

temporal ['temp(ə)rəl] *adj.* tijdelijk; wereldlijk, seculier; *sb.* iets tijdelijks; iets wereldlijks; **—s,** wereldse zaken; temporaliën.

temporary ['temp(ə)rəri] *adj.* tijdelijk, voorlopig; niet blijvend, niet vast; *sb.* tijdelijk aangestelde, tijdelijk beambte; los werkman *m.*

temporize ['tempəraiz] zich naar tijd en omstandigheden schikken.

tempt [tem(p)t] verzoeken, in verzoeking brengen; verleiden, verlokken; beproeven.

temptation [tem(p)'teiʃən] verzoeking, bekoring *v.*; verleiding, verlokking *v.*; aanvechting.

ten [ten] tien; tiental.

tenable ['ti—, 'tenəbl] te houden, houdbaar, verdedigbaar.

tenacious [ti'neiʃəs] *adj.* vasthoudend; taai; kleverig, plakkerig; hardnekkig; (*v. geheugen*) sterk.

tenacity [ti'næsiti] vasthoudendheid *v.*; taaiheid *v.*; hardnekkigheid, onverzettelijkheid *v.*; (*v. geheugen*) sterkte *v.*

tenancy ['tenənsi] huur, pacht *v.*; verblijf *o.*; (*v. bezit*) genot *o.*

tenant ['tenənt] *sb.* huurder, pachter *m.*; bewoner *m.*; *vt.* in huur (in pacht) hebben; als huurder bewonen; (*v. ruimte*) innemen.

tenantless ['tenəntlis] onverhuurd; leegstaand; onbewoond.

tench [tenʃ] (*Dk.: vis*) zeelt *v.*

tend [tend] *vi.* zich uitstrekken; zich richten; gaan, zich bewegen (in zekere richting); bijdragen; streven; leiden, strekken (**to,** tot); (*sch.*) om zijn anker draaien; *vt.* passen op; (*v. ziekte*) oppassen; (*v. vee*) hoeden; (*v. klanten, machine*) bedienen; (*Am.*) bezoeken.

tendance ['tendəns] oppassing, verzorging; zorg *v.*; bediening *v.*; gevolg *o.*

tendency ['tendənsi] strekking *v.*; neiging *v.*; aanleg *m.*; (*beurs*) stemming *v.*

tendentious [ten'denʃəs] tendentieus.

tender ['tendə] *sb.* oppasser *m.*; oppasster *v.*; (*v. locomotief*) tender, kolenwagen *m.*

tender ['tendə] *vt.* aanreiken; (*v. diensten, telegram, enz.*) aanbieden; (*v.*

ontslag*) indienen; *vi.* **— for, (*v. lening, werk*) inschrijven op; *sb.* aanbieding, offerte *v.*; aanbod *o.*; inschrijving *v.*; inschrijvingsbiljet *o.*; betaalmiddel *o.*; **by —,** bij inschrijving.

tender ['tendə] *adj.* teder; teergevoelig, teerhartig; liefhebbend; zacht, mals; gevoelig, pijnlijk; **be — of,** bezorgd zijn voor; naijverig zijn op; gesteld zijn op.

tender-hearted(ly) ['tendəhâtid(li)] *adj.* (*adv.*) teerhartig, teergevoelig.

tendon ['tendən] pees *v.*

tendril ['tendril] (*Pl.*) hechtrank *v.*; (*in sierkunst*) rank *v.*

tenement ['tenimənt] pachtgoed *o.*, pachthoeve *v.*; woning *v.*, huis *o.*

tenfold ['tenfould] *adj.* & *adv.* tienvoudig, tiendubbel; *vt.* vertiendubbelen.

tennis ['tenis] tennis *o.*

tenon ['tenən] *sb.* (*tn.*) tap *m.*, pen *v.*; *vt.* met een tap lassen.

tenor ['tenə] gang, loop *m.*; richting *v.*; strekking *v.*, geest, zin, inhoud *m.*; (*muz.*) tenor *m.*; tenorstem *v.*; altviool *v.*

tense [tens] *sb.* (*gram.*) tijd *m.*

tense [tens] *adj.* strak, gespannen; ingespannen; in spanning; *vt.* spannen, strak maken.

tension ['tenʃən] *sb.* spanning, gespannenheid *v.*; spankracht *v.*; inspanning *v.*; *vt.* spannen.

tent [tent] tent *v.*; wiek *v.* (*van pluksel*); Spaanse wijn *m.*

tenth [tenθ] *adj.* tiende; *sb.* tiende (deel) *o.*; tiend *o.*; (*muz.*) decime *v.*

term [tə:m] *sb.* grens *v.*; einde *o.*; termijn *m.*, periode *v.*; betaaldag *m.*; (*v rechtbank*) zittingstijd *m.*; uitdrukking *v.*, term *m.*; schooltrimester *m.*; kwartaal *o.*; **—s,** voorwaarden, condities; prijzen; schoolgeld; honorarium; verstandhouding; *vt.* noemen.

terminal ['tə:minəl] *adj.* grens—, eind—, slot—; in termijnen betaalbaar; (*Pl.*) eindstandig, terminal; (*v. betalingen*) periodiek; *sb.* einde, eindpunt; uiterste *o.*; eindstation *o.*; eindlettergreep *v.*; (*el.*) klem, poolklem, klemschroef *v.*

terminate ['tə:minit] *adj.* (*rek.: v. tiendelige breuk*) opgaand, eindigend; ['tə:mineit] *vt.* begrenzen; beëindigen, een eind maken aan; (*v. contract*) opzeggen, laten aflopen; *vi.* eindigen, ophouden; (*v. contract*) aflopen; **— in,** uitlopen op; (*v. woord*) eindigen op.

termination [tə:mi'neiʃən] begrenzing *v.*; grens *v.*; (*v. contract*) afloop *m.*; (*v. woord*) uitgang *m.*; besluit, slot; einde *o.*

terrace ['teris] *sb.* terras *o.*; *vt.* tot terras vormen; van een terras voorzien.

terrestrial [ti'restriəl] *adj.* aards, ondermaans; *sb.* aardbewoner *m.*

terrible ['teribl] *adj.* verschrikkelijk, vreselijk.

terrific(ally) [tə'rifik(əli)] *adj.* (*adv.*) schrikwekkend; verschrikkelijk.

terrify ['terifai] verschrikken, met schrik vervullen; schrik aanjagen.

territorial [teri'to:riəl] adj. territoriaal; land—, grond—; sb. soldaat m. van het territoriale leger.

territory ['teritəri] gebied, grondgebied o.; landstreek v.; (fig.) gebied o., sfeer v.

terror ['terə] angst, schrik m., vrees v.; schrikbeeld o.; voorwerp van schrik o.

terrorism ['terərizm] schrikbewind o.

terrorize ['terəraiz] vt. schrik aanjagen, terroriseren, een schrikbewind voeren over; vi. — over, terroriseren.

terse(ly) ['tə:s(li)] adj. (adv.) beknopt, kort (en bondig), pittig.

tertiary ['tə:ʃiəri] adj. tertiair; van de derde rang; van de derde orde; sb. lid o. van de derde orde, tertiaris m.; tertiaire formatie v.

test [test] sb. toetssteen m., toets v.; proef, beproeving v.; reagens o.; criterium o.; proefwerk o.; (v. schaaldier) schaal v., schild; pantser o.; vt. toetsen, beproeven, op de proef stellen; keuren, onderzoeken; attesteren.

testament ['testəmənt] testament o.

tester ['testə] keurder m.; proefmiddel o.; (v. ledikant) hemel m.; klankbord o.; baldakijn m. & o.

test-examination ['testigzæmineiʃən] overgangsexamen o.

test-flight ['testflait] (vl.) proefvlucht v.

test-fly ['testflai] (vl.) invliegen.

testify ['testifai] getuigen (van); getuigenis afleggen van; belijden; betuigen.

testimonial [testi'mounjəl] testimonium, getuigschrift o.; verklaring v.; getuigenis v. & o.; huldeblijk o.

testimony ['testiməni] getuigenis v. & o.; getuigenverklaring v.; bewijs o.

test-paper ['testpeipə] reageerpapier o.; (op school) proefwerk o.; (Am.) handschrift o. als bewijsstuk.

test-tube ['testtjûb] reageerbuisje o.

testy ['testi] adj. prikkelbaar, kribbig, gemelijk, knorrig.

tetanus ['tetənəs] (gen.) stijfkramp, wondkramp v.

text [tekst] tekst m.; onderwerp o.

textile ['tekstail] adj. weef—; textiel; (v. stof) geweven; sb. geweven stof v.; weefmateriaal o.

textual ['tekstjuəl] adj. letterlijk, woordelijk, tekstueel, volgens de tekst; tekst—.

texture ['tekstʃə] weefsel o.; bouw m., structuur v., samenstel o.

than [ðæn] dan (na vergrotende trap).

thank [ðæŋk] vt. danken, bedanken, dank zeggen; sb. —s, dank m.; dankzegging v.

thankful(ly) ['ðæŋkful(i)] adj. (adv.) dankbaar.

thankfulness ['ðæŋkfulnis] dankbaarheid v.

thankless(ly) ['ðæŋklis(li)] adj. (adv.) ondankbaar. ,

thanklessness ['ðæŋklisnis] ondankbaarheid v.

that [ðæt] pron. (aanwijzend) dat, die; (betrekkelijk) die, dat, welke, hetwelk, wat; all —, dat alles; before —, daarvóór; after —, daarna; upon —, daarop; adv. zó; cj. dat; opdat.

thatch [ðætʃ] sb. stro, riet o.; rieten dak o.; hut, met riet gedekte woning v.; (sl.) haar o.; vt. met riet dekken.

thaw [ðo:] vi. dooien; ontdooien; (fig.) loskomen; ontdooien; vt. doen dooien, ontdooien; sb. dooi m.

the [onbeklemtoond: ðə, ði; beklemtoond: ði] de, het.

theatre ['ðiətə] schouwburg m.; toneel o.; podium o., estrade v.; (v. universiteit, enz.) gehoorzaal, aula v.; operatiezaal v.

theft [ðeft] diefstal m.

their [ðɛə] hun, haar.

them [ðem, ð(ə)m] hen, hun, haar, ze; (pop.) die.

theme [ðîm] thema, onderwerp o.; (gram.) stam m.

themselves [ðəm'selvz] zich(zelf); zelf; zijzelf.

then [ðen] adv. dan, alsdan; toen; daarop, dan; verder; bovendien; — and there, op staande voet, onmiddellijk; adj. toenmalig; van dat ogenblik; cj. dan, dus.

thence [ðens] vandaar, daardoor, daaruit.

theologian [ðiə'loudʒiən] godgeleerde m.

theorem ['ðiərem, —rəm] theorema o., stelling v.

theory ['ðiəri] theorie v.

there [ðɛə] adv. daar, aldaar, er; vandaar, daarvandaan; daarheen, derwaarts; daarin; sb. by —, daarlangs; from —, daarvandaan.

thereabout(s) [ðɛərə'baut(s)] daar in de buurt; daaromtrent.

thereafter [ðɛə'râftə] daarna; daarnaar.

thereby ['ðɛə'bai] daardoor; daarbij, daarnevens.

therefore ['ðɛəfo:] daarom; derhalve, bijgevolg.

thereof [ðɛə'ro:v] hiervan, daarvan.

thereon [ðɛə'rɔn] daarop, daarna.

thereto [ðɛə'tû] daaraan; daartoe; daarenboven, bovendien.

thereunder [ðɛə'rəndə] daaronder.

therewithal [ðɛəwi'ðo:l] daarmede, daarbij; daarenboven, bovendien.

thesis ['ðisis] stelling v.; thesis, dissertatie v.

they [ðei] zij, ze; men.

thick [ðik] adj. dik; dicht, dicht bezet; dicht begroeid; goed gevuld; mistig; troebel; onduidelijk; dom, stompzinnig; (fam.) kras; adv. dik; dicht; dicht op elkaar; sb. (het) dikke o., (de) dikte v.; het dikste (dichtste) gedeelte o. van iets; (*sl.*) botterik, stommerd, stomme-ling *m.*

thicken ['ðikn] *vt.* dik(ker) maken, ver-dikken; verdichten; opvullen, aanvullen; (*v. saus, enz.*) binden; *vi.* dikker (dichter) worden; talrijker worden, toe-nemen, zich ophopen; zich samenpak-ken; ingewikkeld worden.

thicket ['ðikit] bosje, kreupelbosje, struikgewas *o.*

thickly ['ðikli] *adv.* dik; dicht, enz.

thick-set ['ðikset] *adj.* dicht beplant; dicht opééngroeiend; dicht bijeen ge-plaatst; gezet; sterk gebouwd; *sb.* dichte heg *v.*; dicht struikgewas *o.*; soort bombazijn *o.*

thief [ðif] dief *m.*

thievish(ly) ['ðiviʃ(li)] *adj.* (*adv.*) dief-achtig.

thigh [ðai] dij *v.*

thigh-bone ['ðaiboun] dijbeen *o.*

thimble ['ðimbl] vingerhoed *m.*; (*sch.*) kous *v.*; (*tn.*) dopmoer *v.*

thin [ðin] *adj.* dun, dunnetjes; mager, schraal; ijl; doorzichtig; (*v. grap, enz.*) flauw; *vt.* dunner maken, verdunnen; *vi.* dun worden; vermageren; uit elkaar gaan; — *off* (*out*), geleidelijk (doen) afnemen.

thing [ðin] ding *o.*; zaak(je) *v.* (*o.*); schepsel *o*

think [ðiŋk] *vt.* denken; menen, geloven; vinden, achten; bedenken, zich herin-neren; van plan zijn; zich voorstellen; overdenken, overwegen; *vi.* denken; nadenken; — *of*, denken aan (over); denken van; bedenken, vinden; zich te binnen brengen; — *out*, bedenken, uit-denken; ontwerpen; overdenken, over-wegen; — *up*, bedenken, uitdenken, verzinnen; ontwerpen; *sb.* (*fam.*) ge-dachte *v.*

thinker ['ðinkə] denker *m.*

thinking-faculty ['tinkinfækəlti] denkvermogen *o.*

third [ðə:d] *adj.* derde; *sb.* derde deel, derde *o.*; derde man *m.*; (*muz.*) terts *v.*; (*H.*) tertiawissel *m.*; 1-60 seconde; (*gram.*) derde persoon *m.*

third-rate ['ðə:dreit] derderangs—, minderwaardig.

thirst [ðə:st] *sb.* dorst *m.*; *vi.* dorsten.

thirteen ['ðə:'tîn, 'ðə:tîn] dertien.

thirty ['ðə:ti] dertig.

this [ðis] dit, deze.

thither ['θiðə] *adv.* derwaarts, daar-heen, daar naartoe; *adj.* gene.

thong [ðɔŋ] riem *m.*

thorax ['ðo:ræks] borst, borstkas *v.*; (*v. insekt*) borststuk *o.*

thorn [ðo:n] *sb.* doorn, stekel *m.*; doornstruik *m.*; *vt.* (soms:) prikken.

thornback ['ðo:nbæk] stekelrog *m.*; grote zeespin *v.*

thorn-bush ['to:nbuʃ] doornstruik *m.*

thorny ['ðo:ni] doornachtig, doornig, stekelig; met doornen bezaaid; (*fig.*) lastig, netelig.

thorough ['ðərə] *adj.* volledig; volko-men, volmaakt; flink, degelijk; grondig; doortastend, ingrijpend; echt; door-trapt; *sb.* doortastendheid *v.*

thoroughbred ['ðərəbred] *adj.* vol-bloed, rasecht; (*v. persoon*) welopgevoed, zeer beschaafd; *sb.* volbloed paard *o.*; zeer beschaafd persoon *m.*

thoroughfare ['ðərəfêə] doorgang *m.*; hoofdstraat *v.*; hoofdverkeersweg *m.*

thoroughly ['ðərəli] *adv.* door en door; grondig, degelijk.

thorough-paced ['ðərəpeist] vol-maakt, volleerd, doortrapt; geheel ge-schoold.

those [ðouz] die, degenen, zij; — *who*, zij die.

though [ðou] *cj.* hoewel, ofschoon; al; *as* —, alsof, als; *adv.* evenwel, echter, maar, (en) toch.

thought [ðo:t] gedachte *v.*, gepeins *o.*; overweging *v.*; overleg *o.*; inval *m.*; idee, opinie *v.*; denkvermogen *o.*; oor-deel *o.*

thoughtful ['ðo:tful] *adj.* denkend; na-denkend, peinzend; (*v. boek, enz.*) tot nadenken stemmend; bedacht, bedacht-zaam; bezonnen; attent, denkend om anderen.

thoughtless(ly) ['ðo:tlis(li)] *adj.* (*adv.*) gedachteloos; zorgeloos; onattent.

thought-reader ['ðo:tridə] gedachten-lezer *m.*

thought-transfer ['ðo:t'trænsfə:] ge-dachtenoverbrenging, telepathie *v.*

thousand ['ðauzənd] duizend.

thousand-feet ['ðauzəndfît] duizend-poot *m.*

thousandfold ['ðauzəndfould] dui-zendvoudig.

thrash [ðræʃ] *vt.* beuken, slaan; dorsen; afranselen, afrossen; verslaan; (*fig.*) doorziften; *vi.* (*in bed*) woelen rollen.

thrashing ['ðræʃin] (het) dorsen *o.*; afranseling *v.*, pak ransel *o.*, ramme-ling *v.*

thrashing-floor ['ðræʃinflo:] dors-vloer *m.*

thread [ðred] *sb.* draad *m.*; *vt.* een draad steken in; (*v. kralen*) aanrijgen; doorboren; van een draad (schroef-draad) voorzien; draden spannen over.

threadbare ['ðredbêə] kaal, versleten; (*fig.*) afgezaagd.

thread-worn ['ðredwo:n] versleten, kaal; (*fig.*) afgezaagd.

threat [ðret] *sb.* bedreiging *v.*, dreige-ment *o.*; *vt.* bedreigen.

threaten ['ðretn] *vt.* bedreigen; drei-gen met.

three [ðri] drie; drietal.

threefold ['ðrifould] drievoudig.

three-four ['ðri'fo:] — *time*, drie-kwartsmaat.

three-handed ['ðri'hændid, 'ðri-hændid] driehandig, met drie handen.

threepence ['ðripəns] driestuiverstuk-je *o.*

threepenny ['ðripəni] driestuivers—; (fig.) goedkoop; gering; armoedig.

threnody ['ðri—, 'ðrenədi] klaaglied o., lijkzang m.

thresh [ðreʃ] dorsen; afranselen, afrossen.

threshing-floor ['ðreʃiŋflo:] dorsvloer m.

threshold ['ðreʃould] drempel, dorpel m.; (fig.) begin o.; grenslijn, grens v.

thrice ['ðrais] driemaal, driewerf.

thrill [ðril] vt. doordringen; doorboren; doen rillen, doen huiveren; doortintelen, doortrillen; met ontroering vervullen, ontroeren; aangrijpen; vi. rillen, trillen, huiveren, sidderen; sb. trilling v.; rilling, huivering v.; ontroering v.; sensatie v.; schok m.; krachttoer m.; (muz.) triller m.

thrive [ðraiv] gedijen, vooruitkomen, voorspoed hebben, floreren; (Pl.) (welig) tieren.

thriving ['ðraiviŋ] adj. opkomend, voorspoedig, bloeiend, florerend; sb. groei m., gedijen o.

throat [ðrout] keel v., strot m.; keelgat o.; hals m.; ingang m., monding v.; nauwe doorgang m.; (sch.: v. gaffelzeil) klauw m.

throb [ðrɔb] vi. (v. hart, enz.) kloppen; bonzen; (v. machine) puffen; sb. klop m. klopping v.

throne [ðroun] sb. troon m.; vt. op de troon plaatsen (verheffen); vi. tronen.

throng [ðrɔŋ] sb. gedrang o., menigte v., toeloop m.; vt. zich verdringen; volproppen (with, met); vi. dringen, opdringen, elkaar verdringen; toestromen, samenstromen.

throttle ['ðrɔtl] sb. luchtpijp v., strot m.; keel v.; (tn.) smoorklep v.; vt. worgen, verstikken, doen stikken, de keel dichtknijpen; smoren; (fig.: v. handel, enz.) verlammen.

through [ðrû] prep. door; door... heen; uit; adv. door; uit; tot het einde toe; adj. doorgaand.

throw [ðrou] vt. werpen, gooien, smijten; afwerpen; weggooien; uitgooien; neerwerpen; (v. net) uitwerpen; (v.zijde twijnen; (v. hout) draaien; (v. trots, enz.) overwinnen; (v. ministerie) doen vallen; verslaan; (sp.: worstelen) leggen; (v. aardewerk) vormen; (Sc.) dwarsbomen; (Am.: v. wedren, enz.) opzettelijk verliezen; vi. werpen, gooien, smijten, enz.; aanraking komen; — away, wegwerpen, weggooien; (v. aanbod, enz.) verwerpen; afslaan; (v. kans) laten voorbijgaan; — off, afwerpen, wegwerpen; uitgooien; verwerpen; (v. werklieden) afdanken; (v.: eren) aanschieten; — open, (v. deur, openzetten, openwerpen; (v. wedstrijd, lening) openstellen; — together, bijeengooien, bij elkaar gooien; (v. personen) samenbrengen, met elkaar in aanraking brengen; vr. — oneself, zich neerwerpen; — oneself

upon, zijn toevlucht nemen tot, een beroep doen op; sb. worp, gooi m.; pottenbakkersschijf v.

throw-outs ['ðrou'auts] uitschot o.; strooibiljetten o. mv.

thrust [ðrʌst] vt. duwen, stoten; steken; werpen; vi. dringen; een uitval doen; vr. — oneself forward, zich naar voren dringen; sb. stoot, duw m.; steek m.; voortstuwingskracht v.; (bouwk.) zijwaartse druk m.; (bij schermen) uitval m.; aanval m.

thud [ðʌd] sb. doffe slag, plof, smak m.; gedreun; gestamp o.; (v. geschut) geboem o.; slag m.; vi. ploffen; dreunen; stampen; bonzen; vt. (om de oren) slaan; ij. plof!

thumb [ðʌm] sb. duim m.; vt. betasten met de duim, met de duim voelen; beduimelen; met de duim induwen; (muz.) knoeierig spelen, onhandig bespelen; doorbladeren.

thumb-tack ['ðʌmtæk] punaise v.

thump [ðʌmp] vt. stompen, stoten, slaan, ploffen; (fam.) er van langs geven, op zijn kop geven; vt. stampen, bonken, bonzen; sb. stomp, stoot m.; bonk, plof, bons m.; adv. pardoes, met een bons.

thunder ['ðʌndə] sb. donder m.; donderslag m.; (v. kanonnen) (het) donderen o.; (fig.) bliksem, banbliksem m.; vi. donderen; bulderen; vt. — forth (out), met donderende stem uitroepen.

thunderbolt ['ðʌndəboult] donderslag m.; donderkeil m.; bliksemflits, bliksemschicht v.; (fig.) banbliksem m.; ijzervreter m.

thunder-cloud ['ðʌndəklaud] onweerswolk v.

Thursday ['ðə:zdi] donderdag m.

thus [ðʌs] adv. dus; aldus, zo; as —, als volgt; — far, tot zover, tot hiertoe, tot dusverre.

thwart [ðwo:t] adv. & prep. dwars; adj. dwarsliggend; (fig.) dwars, koppig; vt. kruisen; (fig.) dwarsbomen, tegenwerken; verijdelen; sb. (r. boot) (dwarsscheepse) doft v.; tegenwerking, belemmering v.

thyroid ['ðairoid] schildvormig.

tic [tik] zenuwtrekking v.; gril v.

tick [tik] vi. tikken; vt. doen tikken; stippelen; puncteren; sb. tikje o.; getik o.; stip v., tekentje o.; streepje o.; (bedde)tijk o.; teek v.

tick [tik] sb. (sl.) krediet o., pof m.; ri. krediet geven, poffen.

ticket ['tikit] sb. kaartje, plaatsbewijs, toegangsbewijs, biljet o.; (prijs)etiket o.; loterijbriefje o.; lommerdbriefje o.; (mil.) ontslagbriefje o.; (Am.) stembiljet, stembriefje o.; (sl.) visitekaartje o.; (sl.) diploma o.; get one's —, (mil., sl.) zijn paspoort krijgen; vt. van een etiket voorzien, etiketteren; prijzen; (fig.) aanduiden.

ticket-office ['tikitɔfis] loket, plaatskaartenbureau o.

tickle ['tikl] *vt.* kietelen, kittelen; prikkelen; (*v. gehemelte*) strelen; aangenaam aandoen; kastijden; *vi.* kietelen, kriebelen; *sb.* kieteling *v.*; gekietel *o.*

ticklish (ly) ['tikliʃ(li)] *adj.* (*adv.*) kittelachtig; kittelig; lichtgeraakt, kittelorig; wankel, onvast; netelig, kies, teer, delicaat; lastig, gevaarlijk.

tide [taid] *sb.* tij, getij *o.*; stroom *m.*; stroming *v.*; vloed *m.*; hoogtepunt *o.*; kerkelijk feest *θ.*; *vi.* met de stroom meevaren (meedrijven), door de stroom meegevoerd worden; (*fig.*) voortsjokken.

tide-gauge ['taidgeidʒ] peilschaal *v.*, getijmeter *m.*

tidiness ['taidinis] zindelijkheid, netheid, properheid *v.*

tidings ['taidiŋz] tijding(en) *v.* (*mv.*), bericht(en) *o.* (*mv.*).

tidy ['taidi] *adj.* zindelijk, net, proper; flink; (*fam.*) tamelijk goed; *sb.* antimakassar *m.*; werkmandje *o.*; spons- en zeepbakje *o.*; schortje *o.*; *vt.* opruimen, aanvegen, in orde brengen; *vr.* — *oneself,* zich wat opknappen.

tie [tai] *vt.* binden; vastbinden, vastmaken, vastknopen; (*v. ader*) afbinden; (*bouwk.*) verankeren; klemmen; (*Am.*) van dwarsliggers voorzien; *vi.* binden; zich laten binden; (*in wedstrijd*) gelijkstaan; *sb.* knoop *m.*; band *m.*; das(je) *v.* (*o.*), strik(je) *m.* (*O.*); verbinding *v.*; verbindingsteken *o.*; (*muz.*) verbindingsteken *o.*; (*muz.*) verbindingsbalk *m.*; onbesliste wedstrijd *m.*; (*bouwk.*) ankerbout *m.*; lage rijgschoen *m.*; (*Am.*) dwarsligger *m.*

tie-pin ['taipin] dasspeld *v.*

tierce ['tɪəs] derde; driekaart *v.*; (*muz.*) terts *v.*; (*kath.*) tertia, terts *v.*; (*bij schermen*) derde positie *v.*; (*wap.*) drielingsbalk *m.*

tiff [tif] *sb.* teugje, slokje *o.*; boze bui *v.*; ongenoegen *o.*; *vt.* slurpen; *vi.* ruzie hebben; een boze bui hebben.

tiffin ['tifin] *sb.* (*E.I.*) lunch *m.*; rijsttafel *v.*; *vi.* lunchen; rijsttafelen.

tiger ['taigə] tijger *m.*; (*Z. A.*) panter, luipaard *m.*; (*sl.*) palfrenier *m.*, livreiknechtje *o.*; donderaar, bullebak *m.*; (*sp.*) goed speler *m.*; *buck* (*fight*) *the* —, dobbelen, gokken.

tight [tait] *adj. & adv.* strak, nauwsluitend; gespannen; krap, nauw; dicht, waterdicht; erg zuinig, gierig; (*v. geld*) schaars; benauwd, beklemd; flink, kranig; kort en bondig; (*sl.*) dronken; (*sl.*) blut; *sb.* —*s,* spanbroek *v.*; (*v. acrobaat*) tricot *o.*

tighten ['taitn] *vt.* spannen; aanhalen, toehalen; (*v. schroef*) aandraaien; samensnoeren, samentrekken; *vi.* (zich) spannen; strakker worden; (*v. geldmarkt*) krap worden; (*v. ijsschotsen*) samenpakken; vaster klemmen.

tight-fisted ['taitfistid] vasthoudend, schriel, vrekkig.

tight-lipped ['taitlipt] met opeengeklemde lippen; (*fig.*) gesloten, niets uitlatend.

tilbury ['tilbəri] tilbury *v.*

tile [tail] *sb.* pan, dakpan *v.*; tegel *m.*; draineerbuis *v.*; (*sl.*) hoge hoed *m.*; *vt.* met pannen dekken; betegelen, met tegels bekleden (bevloeren); plaveien.

tile-maker ['tailmeikə] pannenbakker *m.*

tile-works ['tailwə:ks] pannenbakkerij *v.*

till [til] *sb.* (*in winkel, enz.*) geldlade *v.*; *vt.* bebouwen, beploegen, omploegen; *prep.* tot, tot aan; totdat.

till-money ['tilmoni] kasgeld *o.*

tilt [tilt] *sb.* huif *v.*, dekzeil *o.*; regentent, zonnetent *v.*; overhelling *v.*; steekspel, toernooi *o.*; toernooiveld *o.*; (*tn.*) staarthamer *m.*; *full* —, in volle vaart; *on the* —, op zijn kant; *vt.* met een zeil overdekken; een (dek)zeil spannen over; schuin zetten, scheef zetten, op zijn kant zetten; smeden; kantelen; kippen; (*v. lans*) vellen; *vi.* hellen; omslaan; toernooien, aan een steekspel deelnemen; met de lans steken; (*dicht.*) wiegelen.

tilt-car ['tiltkâ] kipkar *v.*; huifkar *v.*

timber ['timbə] *sb.* timmerhout *o.*; boomstam *m.*; opgaand hout *o.*; (*sch.*) spant *v.*, kromhout *o.*; bekisting *v.*; balk *m.*; (*sl., bij wedren*) hek *o.*; (*sl.*) houten been *o.*; (*fig.*) materiaal *o.*; *adj.* houten; *vt.* van spanten voorzien; met hout beschieten.

timber-legged ['timbəlegd] (*sl.*) met houten been.

timber-yard ['timbəjâd] houtloods *v.*, houttuin *m.*, houtstapelplaats *v.*

time [taim] *sb.* tijd *m.*; maal *v.*, keer *m.*; gelegenheid *v.*; (*muz.*) maat *v.*, tempo *o.*; *keep* —, de maat houden; in de pas blijven; op tijd zijn; mettertijd, op de duur; in de maat; in de pas; op zijn tijd; *out of* —, te onpas; (*muz.*) uit de maat, niet in de maat; (*mil.*) uit de pas; te laat; *vt.* een tijd kiezen voor, de tijd regelen van, het juiste tijdstip kiezen voor; de tijd berekenen (aangeven, bepalen) van; (*v. klok, enz.*) regelen, repasseren; dateren; (*mil.*) temperen; (*sp.*) de tijd opnemen; (*muz.*) de maat slaan (aangeven) bij; in de maat spelen (zingen); *vi.* — *to,* in de maat blijven met; zich regelen naar; *vr.* — *oneself,* zijn tijd afmikken; nagaan hoeveel tijd men voor iets nodig heeft.

time-bargain ['taimbâgin] (*H.*) termijnzaak, termijnaffaire *v.*

time-clock ['taimklɔk] controleklok *v.*; chronometer, tijdmeter *m.*; (*bij wedstrijd*) tijdopnemer *m.*; (*muz.*) metronoom *m.*

time-killer ['taimkilə] lanterfanter *m.*; tijdkorting *v.*

time-lag ['taimlæg] vertraging *v.*

timeless ['taimlis] ontijdig: aan geen tijd gebonden: eeuwig, oneindig.

timely ['taimli] adj. juist van pas komend: actueel; adv. tijdig, bijtijds; op de juiste tijd.

time-payment ['taimpeimənt] termijnbetaling, betaling v. in termijnen; betaling v. per uur.

timepiece ['taimpis] uurwerk o.

time-pleaser ['taimplizə] die de huik naar de wind hangt, weerhaan m.

time-server ['taimsə:və] zie **time-pleaser.**

time-table ['taimteibl] dienstregeling v.; spoorboekje o.; spoorweggids m.; lesrooster o.; (muz.) maattabel v.

time-worn ['taimwo:n] oud, verouderd. versleten; (fig.) afgezaagd.

timidity [ti'miditi] beschroomdheid, verlegenheid, schuchterheid v.

Timon ['taimən] Timon m.; (fig.) mensenhater m.

timorous(ly) ['timərəs(li) adj. (adv.) bang, schroomvallig, angstvallig, beschroomd.

tin [tin] sb. tin o.; blik o.; (inmaak)blikje o., bus v.; (sl.) geld. splint o.; (mil.) eetketeltje o.; adj. tinnen: blikken, van blik; (fig.) nietig, prullig; vt. vertinnen; inmaken in blik, verduurzamen.

tin-bank ['tinbæŋk] spaarpot m.

tinder ['tində] tonder v.; zwam v.

tine [tain] (v. vork, eg) tand m.; (v. gewei) tak m.

tinge [tin(d)ʒ] sb. tint, kleur; verf v.; (fig.) tikje o., zweem m.; bijsmaakje o.; vt. kleuren, verven.

tingle ['tingl] vi. tintelen, prikkelen; jeuken; (v. wangen) gloeien; sb. tinteling, prikkeling v.

tin-hat ['tinhæt] (mil.) stalen helm m.; (sl.) stafofficier m.

tinman ['tinmən] tinnegieter m.; blikslager m.

tin-plate ['tinpleit] blik o.

tinsel ['tinsəl] sb. klatergoud o.; adj. schijnmooi, schoonschijnend, oppervlakkig, opzichtig: onecht, vals, schijn—; vt. met klatergoud versieren.

tint [tint] sb. tint v.; vt. tinten.

tiny ['taini] adj. (heel) klein: miniem: *a — bit,* een heel klein beetje; sb. kleintje o.

tip [tip] sb. tip m., eind(je) o.; spits v.; (v. vinger) top m.; (v. neus) punt(je) v. (o.); (v. sigaar) puntje o.; (v. sigaret) mondstuk o.; (aan stok, enz.) beslag, dopje o.; (v. biljartkeu) pomerans v.; verguldpenseel o.; vt. beslaan (aan de punt): omranden.

tip [tip] vt. tikken, even aanraken; schuin zetten, schuin houden; omvergooien; (sl.) een fooi geven; (sl.) een wenk geven; vi. kantelen, kippen; fooien geven; — (up), afdokken, in de bus blazen; sb. tikje o.; schuine stand m., overhelling v.; kipkar v.; vuilnisbelt,

stortplaats v.: (fam.) wenk m., inlichting v.: (sl.) drinkgeld o., fooi v.: waarschuwing v., raad m.; voorspelling v.; foefje, examenfoefje o.

tip-car(t) ['tipkâ(t)] kipkar v.

tippet ['tipit] pelskraag m.; schoudermanteltje o.

tippy ['tipi] handig, knap, vernuftig; keurig, chic: (v. thee) vol bladknopjes; (v. zee) woelig.

tipsy ['tipsi] adj. aangeschoten, dronken, beschonken· wankel.

tip-tilted ['tiptiltid] opgewipt.

tire ['taiə] sb. (v. fiets) band m.: (v. wiel) band, hoepel m.; dos, tooi: hoofdtooi m.; (Am.) schort v. & o.: (fam.) vermoeidheid v.: vt. een band leggen om; tooien, uitdossen: vermoeien, moe maken· vervelen: vi. moe worden.

tired ['taiəd] adj. vermoeid, moe.

tiredness ['taiədnis] vermoeidheid, moeheid v.

tireless(ly) ['taiəlis(li)) adj. (adv.) onvermoeid.

tiresome(ly) ['taiəsəm(li)] adj. (adv.) vermoeiend: vervelend.

tiresomeness ['taiəsəmnis] vermoeiendheid v.; vervelendheid v.

tissue ['tisjû, 'tiʃû] sb. weefsel o.: goudlaken, zilverlaken o.; vt. weven, doorweven.

tit [tit] zie **teat**; mees v.; graspieper m.; paardje o., hit m.; tikje o.

titbit ['titbit] lekker beetje, lekker hapje o.; (fig.) belangrijk nieuwtje o.

tithe [taiθ] adj. tiende; sb. tiend o.; tiende (deel) o.; vt. vertienden, tienden heffen van.

title ['taitl] sb. titel: eretitel m.; naam m., benaming v., opschrift o.: (v. goud) gehalte o.; recht o., aanspraak v.; eigendomsrecht o., eigendomsbewijs o.; vt. titelen, betitelen; noemen; een titel verlenen (aan).

titmouse ['titmaus] mees v.

titular ['titjulə] adj. titulair, in naam; een titel dragend; sb. titularis m.; schutspatroon m.

to [vóór klinker: tu; vóór medekl.: tu, tə: alleen: tû] prep. tot, aan: naar: tot aan: tegen: bij, in vergelijking met, vergeleken bij: te, om te: voor· tot op; over: adv. dicht, toe; — *and fro,* heen en weer.

toad [toud] (Dk.) pad v.; (fig.) beroerling: vuilik m.

toadstool ['toudstûl] paddestoel m.

toast [toust] sb. geroosterd brood o.; heildronk, toost m.; vt. roosteren: warmen; een dronk instellen op: vi. toosten; vr. — *oneself,* zich warmen.

tobacco [tə'bækou] tabak v.

tocsin ['toksin] alarmklok, noodklok v.: alarmgelui o.

to-day, today [tə—, tu'dei] vandaag, heden; tegenwoordig, op de huidige dag.

toddle ['tɔdl] *vi.* dribbelen, trippelen, waggelen, waggelend gaan; (*v. klein kind*) met onvaste stapjes lopen; kuieren; — *off*, opstappen; — *round*, rondkuieren; eens aanlopen; *vt.* — *one's way*, verder kuieren, voortkuieren; *sb.* kuier *m.*; slentergangetje *o.*; dribbelaar, kleine peuter, dreumes *m.*

toddler ['tɔdlə] dribbelaar, kleuter, kleine dreumes *m.*; kruipjurk *v.*

toe [tou] *sb.* teen *m.*; voorhoef *v.*; (*v. schoen*) neus *m.*; punt *v.*, uitsteeksel *o.*; (*sl.*) in de lorum; *stick in one's* —*s*, zich er mee gaan bemoeien; *vt.* (*v. kous*) een teen aanzetten (aanbreien); (*v. schoen*) een neus aanzetten; met de tenen aanraken; (*sl.*) schoppen, een schop geven; — *the line*, (*bij wedstrijd*) met de tenen aan de streep gaan staan; (*fig.*) een uitdaging aannemen; het aandurven.

toe-cap ['toukæp] (*v. schoen*) neus *m.*

toga ['tougə] toga *v.*, tabberd *m.* ,

together [tə'geθə] samen, te zamen; tegelijk; achtereen; aaneen, aan elkaar; één geheel vórmend.

toil [tɔil] *sb.* zware arbeid *m.*, inspanning *v.*, gezwoeg *o.*; —*s*, netten, strikken; *vi.* hard werken, arbeiden, zwoegen, zware arbeid verrichten; *vt.* laten zwoegen, afbeulen.

toilet-table ['tɔilitteibl] toilettafel *v.*

toilful ['tɔilful] moeilijk, zwaar, afmattend; zwoegend.

toilsome ['tɔilsəm] *zie* **toilful.**

toil-worn ['tɔilwɔːn] afgewerkt.

token ['toukn] *sb.* teken, kenteken *o.*; blijk, bewijs *o.*; aandenken *o.*; *vt.* betekenen, voorstellen.

tolerable ['tɔlərəbl] *adj.* te verdragen, draaglijk, duldbaar; tamelijk, redelijk.

tolerance ['tɔlərəns] verdraagzaamheid *v.*; toelating, vergunning *v.*; (*tn.*) speling *v.*; remedie *v.* (*toegestane afwijking in gehalte en gewicht van munten*).

tolerant ['tɔlərənt] *adj.* verdraagzaam.

tolerate ['tɔləreit] verdragen, gedogen, dulden, tolereren; toelaten.

toll [toul] *sb.* tol *m.*, tolgeld *o.*; staangeld, marktgeld *o.*; schatting *v.*; (*gesch.*) maalloon *o.*; (*fig.*) bijdrage *v.*, aandeel *o.*; *vi.* tol heffen; tol betalen.

toll [toul] *vi.* kleppen, luiden; de doodsklok luiden voor; *vt.* kleppen, slaan; door geklep aankondigen; door gelui oproepen; *sb.* geklep, gelui *o.*; klokslag *m.*

toll-bar ['toulbâ] tolboom *m.*

toll-gate ['toulgeit] tolhek *o.*

tolling ['toulin] geklep, getamp *o.*

Tom [tɔm] Tom, Thomas *m.*; *t*—, (*v. dier*) mannetje *o.*; kater *m.*; (*sl.*) jenever *m.*; — *Thumb*, Klein Duimpje; *long* —, lang kanon van groot kaliber.

tomato [tə'mâtou] tomaat *v.*

tomb [tûm] *sb.* graf *o.*; grafstede, graftombe *v.*; *vt.* begraven, bijzetten (in een graftombe).

tomboy ['tɔmbɔi] robbedoes *m.* & *v.*, wildebras, wildzang (van een meisje).

tomcat ['tɔm'kæt] kater *m.*

tome [toum] boekdeel *o.*

to(-)morrow [tə—, tu'mɔro(u)] morgen, de dag van morgen; de volgende dag.

tomtit ['tɔm'tit] meesje *o.*, koolmees, pimpelmees *v.*

ton [tɔn] *sb.* ton *v.*

ton [tɔːn, tɔːŋ] *sb.* goede toon *m.*; mode *v.*

tone [toun] *sb.* toon, klank *m.*; klemtoon *m.*; toon *m.*, tint, (kleur)schakering *v.*; geest; gemoedstoestand *m.*; stemming *v.*; spanning *v.*; veerkracht *v.*; *vt.* stemmen, de rechte toon geven aan; een kleurtoon geven; (op zekere toon) lezen, voordragen, zingen; doen harmoniëren; *vi.* harmoniëren (*with*, met).

toneless ['tounlis] toonloos, klankloos; kleurloos; slap, krachteloos.

toneless(ly) ['tounlis(li)] *adv.* met klankloze stem.

tongs [tɔnz] tang *v.*

tongue [tɔn] *sb.* tong *v.*; taal, spraak *v.* (*v. balans, gesp*) tongetje *o.*; (*v. klok*) klepel *m.*; (*v. plank*) messing *o.*; (*v. schoen*) leertje *o.*; (*v. jachthond*) aanslag *m.*, geblaf *o.*; (*holle*) woorden *o. mv.*; *vt.* van een messing voorzien, een messing maken aan; (*muz.*) staccato blazen; doorhalen; *vi.* zijn tong laten gaan; kletsen; schelden; (*v. hond*) aanslaan; likken; in een tong uitlopen.

tongueless ['tɔnlis] zonder tong; (*fig.*) sprakeloos, stom.

to(-)night [tə—, tu'nait] van avond, heden avond; van nacht, deze nacht.

tonnage ['tɔnidʒ] (*sch.*) tonnemaat, scheepsruimte, laadruimte *v.*; tonnegeld *o.*

tonsil ['tɔnsil] (keel)amandel *v.*

tonsure ['tɔnʃə] *sb.* tonsuur, kruinschering *v.*; *vt.* de tonsuur geven, de kruin scheren van.

too [tû] ook, insgelijks, eveneens; ook nog, nog wel; te, al te.

tool [tûl] *sb.* gereedschap *o.*; werktuig *o.*; (*v. draaibank*) beitel *m.*; tandhamer *m.*; groot penseel *o.*, kwast *m.*; (*boekbinderij*) stempelversiering *v.*; *vt.* bewerken; behouwen (met een tandhamer); (*v. boekomslag*) van geperste versieringen voorzien, met blinddruk versieren; (*sl.*) mennen, rijden; *vi.* (*sl.*) rijden (in rijtuig); fletsen.

tooth [tûθ] *sb.* tand, kies *m.*; *vt.* van tanden voorzien, tanden; de tanden zetten in; *vi.* in elkaar grijpen.

tooth-ache ['tûθeik] kiespijn, tandpijn *v.*

tooth-brush [tûθbrɔʃ] tandenborstel *m.*; (*sl.*) geknipte snor *m.*

tooth-cutting ['tûθkɔtin] (het) tandenkrijgen *o.*

toothed [tûðt] getand, tand.

toothless ['tûðlis] tandeloos.
toothpick ['tûðpik] tandestoker m.
tooth-powder ['tûðpaudə] tandpoeder o.
top [tɔp] sb. top m.; spits, kruin v.; bovenste, bovenstuk o.; (v. tafel) hoofd, boveneinde o.; (v. schip) mars v.; (v. rijtuig, laars) kap v.; (v. ledikant) hemel m.; (v. vulpen, enz.) dop m.; (v. schoen) bovenleer o.; bovenvlak o., oppervlakte v.; (v. gezin, enz.) hoofd o.; (mil.) borstwering v. van loopgraaf; (fig.) toppunt o.; adj. bovenste; hoogste; voornaamste; prima; vt. bedekken; van een top voorzien; bekronen; beklimmen; (v. bomen) toppen, van de top ontdoen; afmaken, voltooien; (sp.: golfbal) van boven raken; staan op de top van; (fig.) overtreffen, zich verheffen boven, overheersen; (sl.) opknopen; vi. zich verheffen; — off (up), besluiten, er een eind aanmaken.
topaz ['toupæz] topaas m.
top-boots [tɔp'bûts] kaplaarzen v. mv.
top-coat [tɔp'kout] overjas v.
top-full ['tɔp'ful] boordevol.
top-heavy ['tɔp'hevi] topzwaar.
topic ['tɔpik] onderwerp o. (van gesprek); thema o.; plaatselijk geneesmiddel o.
top-note ['tɔp'nout] hoogste noot v.
topping ['tɔpiŋ] adj. hoog; bovenste; eerste, voornaamste; prima; (sl.) heerlijk, verrukkelijk; (Am.) zelfbewust, bazig; uit de hoogte; sb. (v. bomen, enz.) (het) toppen o.
topple ['tɔpl] vi. kantelen, omvallen, tuimelen; dreigen te vallen, dreigend overhangen; vt. doen omvallen, doen tuimelen, omgooien.
top-speed ['tɔpspîd] sb. grootste snelheid v.; adv. work —, met volle kracht werken.
topsyturvy ['tɔpsi'tə:vi] adv. onderste boven, op zijn kop; turn —, onderste boven gooien (keren); op zijn kop zetten; in de war raken; adj. omgekeerd, op zijn kop staand; in de war; ongerijmd; sb. verkeerde wereld, chaotische verwarring v., chaos m.; vt. het onderste boven keren, op zijn kop zetten.
top-up ['tɔpəp] (sl.) afzakkertje o.
torch [to:tʃ] fakkel, toorts v.; electric —, elektrische zaklantaarn.
torch-lily ['to:tʃlili] (Pl.) vuurpijl m.
toreador ['to:riədo:] toreador m.
torment ['to:mənt] sb. kwelling, marteling, foltering v.; plaag v.; folterwerktuig o.; [to:'ment] vt. kwellen, martelen, folteren; plagen.
torpedo [to:'pîdou] sb. torpedo v.; zeemijn v.; (op spoorbaan) knalsignaal o.; (Dk.) sidderrog, krampvis m.; knalklapper m., knalpatroon v.; vt. torpederen; (fig.) de doodsteek geven.
torpedo-boat [to:'pîdoubout] torpedoboot v.
torpor ['to:pə] verstijving, verstijfd-

heid v.; verdoving v.; loomheid, traagheid v.
torrefy ['torifai] branden; roosteren; drogen; verzengen.
torrent ['torənt] (berg)stroom m.; vloed, stortvloed m.
torrid ['torid] verzengd, verzengend, brandend, heet.
torsion ['to:ʃən] draaiing, wringing, torsie v.
tortious ['to:ʃəs] (recht) onrechtmatig, onrechtvaardig.
tortoise ['to:təs] (land)schildpad v.; (gesch.) schilddak o.
tortuous(ly) ['to:tjuəs(li)] adj. (adv.) bochtig, kronkelig, gekronkeld; gedraaid; krom; (meetk.) gebogen; (v. stijl) gewrongen; (fig.) slinks, niet recht door zee; draaiend.
torture ['to:tʃə] sb. pijniging, kwelling v.; foltering, marteling v.; (v. woorden) verdraaiing v.; vt. pijnigen, kwellen; folteren, martelen; (v. woorden, enz.) verdraaien v.
toss [to:s] vt. opgooien, omhooggooien; heen en weer gooien, heen en weer slingeren; toegooien, toesmijten, toewerpen; (sp.) tossen; (v. hooi) keren, omwerpen; — off, in één teug uitdrinken; — out, uitgooien; opdirken; — up, opgooien; haastig klaarmaken; vi. heen en weer rollen; (in bed) woelen; geslingerd worden, dobberen; om iets opgooien; — about, (in bed) woelen; sb. (het) opgooien o.; (sp.) opgooi, toss m.; (met dobbelsteen) gooi, worp m.; slingering, slingerende beweging v.; (sl.) wippertje o., borrel m.
total ['toutl] adj. geheel, totaal, volkomen, volslagen; sb. totaal o.; gezamenlijk bedrag o.; vt. optellen; (in totaal) bedragen, een totaal vormen van.
totally ['toutəli] adv. totaal, helemaal, geheel en al.
tote [tout] (pop.) geheelonthouder m.; (fam.) totalisator m.; (dial.) geheel, totaal o.
totter ['totə] vi. waggelen, wankelen; sb. waggeling, wankeling v.; onvaste gang m.
touch [tɔtʃ] vt. aanraken; aanroeren; aanstrijken; (v. haven) aandoen; raken; aantasten; roeren, treffen; kwetsen; (muz.) aanslaan, spelen (op); bespelen; (v. geld, enz.) ontvangen, innen; (v. goud) toetsen; (fam.) evenaren, halen bij; (fam.) opstrijken; (sl.) stelen; (sl.) beetnemen, bedriegen; — up, opknappen; bijwerken; (v. schilderij) restaureren; (fot.) optoetsen, retoucheren; (v. paard) aanzetten; bijwerken, polijsten, mooier maken; vi. elkaar raken (aanraken); (sch.) op een zandbank stoten; sb. aanraking v.; betasting v.; gevoel o., tastzin m.; (muz.) aanslag m.; toets v.; (karakter)trek m.; (met penseel) streek m.; (mil.) voeling v., contact o.; zet, steek m.; (v. ziekte) lichte aanval m.;

tikje, zweempje o.; toetssteen m.; waarmerk o., keur v.; gehalte o., soort v.; (sl.) diefstal m., zakkenrollen o.; (sp.; voetb.) (het) raken o. van de grond achter het doel; veld o. achter de zijlijnen.

touch-and-go ['tətʃən(d)'gou] adj. los; oppervlakkig; haastig; onbetrouwbaar; gewaagd; sb. krijgertje, nalopertje o.

touching ['tətʃiŋ] adj. roerend, treffend, aandoenlijk; prep. betreffende, aangaande.

touch-me-not ['tətʃminot] kruidje roer-me-niet o.; springzaad o.

touchstone ['tətʃstoun] toetssteen m.

touchy ['tətʃi] adj. lichtgeraakt, kittelorig.

tough adj. taai; onverzettelijk; (v. strijd) hardnekkig; (v. werk) moeilijk, lastig; (v. bries) stevig; (Am.) hard, ruw, zonder gevoel; misdadig; gemeen.

tour [tûə] sb. reis v., uitstapje, tochtje o.; rondreis v.; kunstreis v.; vt. een rondreis maken door; afreizen; bezoeken; vi. een reisje maken.

tournament ['tûə—, 'tə:'—, 'toənəmənt] steekspel, toernooi o.

tourney ['tûəni, 'tə:ni] sb. toernooi, steekspel o.; vi. aan een toernooi deelnemen.

tousle ['tauz] vt. in wanorde brengen; verfomfaaien; heen en weer trekken, stoeien met; vi. stoeien; sb. (v. haar) ragebol m.; pruik v.; warklomp m.; stoeipartij v.

tout [taut] vt. klanten lokken; (be)spioneren; klanten werven voor; sb. klantenlokker m.; handelsreiziger m.; spion m.

tow [tou] sb. werk o. (van touw); (fig.) vlasbaar o.; touw, sleeptouw o.; sleepboot v.; gesleept schip o.; (het) slepen o.; vt. slepen, boegseren.

toward ['touəd] adj. aanstaande, op til; leerzaam, gewillig.

toward [to:d, tə'wo:d] ˉprep. zie towards.

towards [to:dz, tə'wo:dz] tegen, tegenover, jegens; omtrent; naar... toe, in de richting van.

tow-boat ['toubout] sleepboot v.

towel ['tauəl] sb. handdoek m.; vt. afdrogen (met een handdoek); (sl.) afdrogen, afranselen; vi. zich afdrogen.

towel-horse ['tauəlho:s] handdoekenrekje o.

tower ['touə] sb. boegseerder, sleper m.

tower ['tauə] sb. toren m.; burcht v., kasteel o.; (gesch.) hoog kapsel o.; vi. zich verheffen, (hoog) uitsteken (above, boven); (v. aangeschoten vogel) hoog opvliegen.

towing-line ['touiŋlain] sleeptouw o., sleeptros m., jaagtouw o., jaaglijn v.

towing-rope ['touiŋroup] zie **towing-line.**

town [taun] stad v.; gemeente v.; Londen o.

town-council ['taunkaunsl] gemeenteraad m.

town-dweller ['taundwelə] stadsbewoner, stedeling m.

townish ['tauniʃ] steeds.

town-major ['taunmeidʒə] (mil.) plaatscommandant m.

townman ['taunmən] stedeling m.

towny ['tauni] adj. stads; sb. stedeling m.; (sl.) stadgenoot m.

tow-path ['toupâδ] jaagpad o.

toxin(e) ['toksin] toxine, giftstof v.

toy [toi] sb. (stuk) speelgoed o.; (fig.) speelbal m.; beuzelarij, snuisterij, prul v.; spelletje o.; vi. spelen, dartelen, mallen.

toy dog ['toidog] schoothondje o.; (speelgoed) hondje o.

trace [treis] sb. spoor, voetspoor o.; schets v., ontwerp o.; (v. fort) tracé o.; (v. paard) streng v.; draagriem m., draagzeel o.; vt. nasporen, opsporen, nagaan; tekenen, ontwerpen, schetsen; overtrekken, natrekken, calqueren; (v. weg) afbakenen; (v. woorden, enz.) neerschrijven; (v. gedragslijn) aangeven; — out, nagaan, opsporen; traceren, afbakenen, uitstippelen; — over, natrekken.

traceable ['treisəbl] naspeurbaar, na te gaan; terug te brengen (to, tot).

traceless ['treislis] spoorloos.

trachea ['treikjə, trə'kiə] (v. mens) luchtpijp v.; (v. insekt) luchtbuis v.; (v. plant) luchtvat o.

tracing-paper ['treisiŋpeipə] calqueerpapier o.

tracing-pen ['treisiŋpen] trekpen v.

track [træk] sb. spoor, voetspoor, wagenspoor o.; bospad o., ongebaande weg, landweg m.; spoorbaan, spoorlijn v.; spoorwijdte v.; (v. komeet, enz.; bij weastrijd) baan v.; (v. torpedo) bellenbaan v.; rupsband m.; make —s, (sl.) er van door gaan, de plaat poetsen; make —s for, (sl.) koers zetten naar, zich begeven naar; nazetten; vt. nasporen, opsporen; (v. spoor, voetstappen) volgen; (v. weg, pad) plattreden; (sch.) slepen, op sleeptouw hebben; vi. (v. wielen) in het spoor rijden, gelijk lopen.

trackless ['træklis] spoorloos; geen spoor achterlatend; zonder spoor; niet op rails lopend; ongebaand, onbetreden.

tractable ['træktəbl] adj. handelbaar, volgzaam, meegaand.

trade [treid] sb. handel, koophandel m.; bedrijf, beroep, vak, ambacht o.; ruilgoederen o. mv.; (politieke) transactie v.; the —, de handelaars, de wederverkopers; de boekhandel; het drankbedrijf, de handel in dranken; (sch., sl.) de onderzeebootdienst; vt. verhandelen, verruilen; vi. handelen; handel drijven; (sch.) varen (to, op).

trade-board ['treidbo:d] arbeidsraad; nijverheidsraad m.

trader ['treidə] koopman, handelaar

m.; handelsvaartuig, koopvaardijschip *o.*
trade-secret ['treidsīkrit] fabrieksgeheim *o.*
tradesman ['treidzmən] neringdoende; winkelier, kleinhandelaar *m.*; handwerksman *m.*
trades-union ['treidz'jūnjən] *zie trade-union.*
trade-treaty ['treidtrīti] handelsverdrag *o.*
trade-union ['treid'jūnjən] vakvereniging *v.*
trade-unionism ['treid'jūnjənizm] vakverenigingswezen *o.*, vakbeweging *v.*
trade-wind ['treidwind] pnssaatwind *m.*
trading-company ['treidiŋkəmpəni] handelmaatschappij *v.*
tradition [trə'difən] overlevering, traditie *v.*
traduce [trə'djūs] lasteren, belasteren, kwaadspreken van.
traducer [trə'djūsə] lasteraar *m.*
traduction [trə'dəkfən] overdracht, overbrenging; voortplanting *v.*; vertaling *v.*; laster *m.*, belastering *v.*
traffic ['træfīk] *sb.* handel, koophandel *m.*; verkeer *o.*; *vt.* verhandelen; verkwanselen; *vi.* handel drijven, handelen (*in*, in); schacheren; intrigeren, samenspannen, heulen (*with*, met).
tragedy ['trædʒidi] treurspel *o.*, tragedie *v.*
trail [treil] *sb.* sleep, sliert *m.*; (*v. komeet*) staart *m.*; affuitstaart *m.*; spoor *o.*; sleepnet *o.*; reeks *v.*; kruipende rank *v.* (tak *m.*); (*Sc.*) slons *v.*; *vt.* (laten) slepen; plat treden; met ranken versieren; (*v. woorden*) rekken; (*v. gras*) plattreden; opsporen, nasporen; *vi.* slepen; (*Pl.*) kruipen.
trailer ['treilə] (*Pl.*) kruipplant *v.*; aanhangwagen *m.*; sleepwiel *o.*; speurder, speurhond *m.*
train [trein] *vt.* grootbrengen, opvoeden; opleiden; oefenen, africhten, drillen; (*sp.*) trainen; (*v. boom, enz.*) leiden; (*v. kanon*) richten; *vi.* zich oefenen, zich trainen; (*fam.*) per spoor reizen; *sb.* (*v. kleed, enz.*) sleep *m.*; nasleep *m.*; gevolg *o.*, stoet *m.*; gang, loop *m.*; (*v. komeet, affuit*) staart *m.*; reeks, aaneenschakeling *v.*; (*mil.*) loopvuur *o.*; raderwerk *o.*; (*fig.*) lokaas *o.*; krijgslist *v.*; (*Canada*) slede *v.*
trained [treind] geoefend, afgericht, getraind; geschoold, ervaren.
trainer ['treinə] africhter, drilmeester, trainer *m.*; oefenvliegtuig *o.*
training ['treiniŋ] oefening, africhting *v.*; opleiding *v.*; training *v.*; (*mil.*) exercitie *v.*; (*v. bomen*) leiding *v.*
training-college ['treiniŋkɔlidʒ] kweekschool *v.*
train-oil ['treinɔil] (walvis)traan *v.*
train-sick ['treinsik] treinziek, wagenziek.
trait [trei] haal, trek *m.*; toets *v.*

traitorous (ly) ['treitərəs(li)] *adj.* (*adv.*) verraderlijk.
traitress ['treitris] verraadster *v.*
tram [træm] *sb.* tram *v.*, tramwagen *m.*; rail, spoorrail *v.*; (*in mijn*) kolenwagen *m.*; inslag *m.*; *vi.* trammen, in een tram reizen; *vt.* per tram vervoeren; (*in mijn*) per kolenwagen vervoeren.
tramp [træmp] *vt.* treden, vertreden, plattreden; aanstampen, vaststampen; afzwerven, aflopen; *vi.* treden, trappen, stampen; stappen, lopen, marcheren; rondtrekken, rondzwerven; vagebonderen; *sb.* zware tred, stap *m.*; gestamp *o.*; zwerftocht *m.*, omzwerving *v.*; lange tocht *m.*, voetreis *v.*; zwerver, vagebond, landloper *m.*; (*sch.*) wilde boot *v.*, vrachtzoeker *m.*
trample ['træmpl] *vi.* treden, trappen, trappelen, stampen; *vt.* trappen op, vertrappen, vertreden, met voeten treden.
tramway ['træmwei] tram *v.*
tranquil ['træŋkwil] *adj.* rustig, kalm, stil.
tranquillity [træŋ'kwiliti] rust, rustigheid, kalmte *v.*
tranquillize ['træŋkwilaiz] kalmeren, tot bedaren brengen, bedaren.
transact [træns'ækt, trân'zækt] *vt.* verrichten, tot stand brengen; verhandelen, afdoen; (*v. afstand*) afleggen; *vi.* zaken doen; onderhandelen; schipperen, transigeren.
transaction [træns'ækfən, trân'zækfən] transactie, handeling, zaak *v.*; verrichting, afdoening, uitvoering *v.*; vergelijk *o.*, schikking, overeenkomst *v.*
transcend [trân'send] te boven gaan, overtreffen, uitsteken boven.
transcribe [trân'kraib] *vt.* overschrijven, afschrijven; in gewoon schrift overbrengen; (*muz.*) zetten, overschrijven (voor een ander instrument, enz.); *vi.* afschrijven, naschrijven.
transfer [trâns'fə:] *vt.* overdragen, overbrengen, transporteren; overmaken, overschrijven; overboeken; verplaatsen, overplaatsen; overdrukken, calqueren; *vi.* overstappen; overgaan; ['trânsfə:] *sb.* overbrenging, overdracht *v.*, transport *o.*; overmaking, remise *v.*; overschrijving *v.*; overdruk *m.*; overstapkaartje *o.*; (*v. spoor, tram*) verbindingspunt, verenigingspunt, verbindingsspoor *o.*; overgeplaatste *m.*
transferor ['trænsfərə:] overdrager, cedent *m.*
transfer-paper ['trânsfə:peipə] overdrukpapier *o.*
transfiguration [trânsfigju'reifən] herschepping, gedaanteverwisseling *v.*; (*van Jezus*) verheerlijking, transfiguratie *v.*
transfix [trâns'fiks] doorboren, doorsteken.
transform [trânsafo:m] vervormen, omvormen; van gedaante (doen) veranderen; transformeren; (*wisk.*) herleiden.

transformable [trâns'fo:'məbl] te veranderen, vervormbaar.

transformation [trânsfo:'meiʃən] vervorming, omvorming v.; verandering, gedaanteverwisseling v.; transformatie; omzetting v.; (rek.) reductie v.; valse haartooi m., pruik v.

transgress [trâns'gres] vt. overtreden, zondigen tegen; overschrijden, te buiten gaan; vi. zondigen.

transgression [trâns'greʃən] overtreding v.

tranship [trân'ʃip] overschepen; overladen; op een andere boot overgaan.

transit ['trânsit] sb. transito, doorvoer m.; vervoer o.; doorgang, doortocht m.; overgang m.; in —, onderweg, gedurende het vervoer; doortrekkend; transito—; vt. doortrekken, gaan door; transiteren.

transition [træn—, trân'siʒən] sb. overgang m., overgangsperiode v.; adj. overgangs—.

transitory ['trânsitəri] vergankelijk, kortstondig, voorbijgaand, van voorbijgaande aard.

translate [trâns'leit] vertalen, overzetten; uitleggen, vertolken; (v. stoffelijk overschot) overbrengen; (v. bisschop) verplaatsen, overplaatsen; (v. ziekte, enz.) overbrengen; (v. telegram) doorseinen; vervormen; veranderen; herleiden; (sl.: v. oude schoenen) oplappen, weer opknappen.

translation [trâns'leiʃən] vertaling, overzetting v.; uitlegging, vertolking v.; overbrenging; overplaatsing, verplaatsing v.; (v. eigendom) overdracht v.; vervorming, verandering v.; naar schilderij bewerkte ets v.; (sl.: v. oude schoenen) (het) opknappen o.

transmarine [trânzmə'rin] overzees.

transmission [trânz'miʃən] overbrenging v.; overseining v.; overzending v.; overlevering v.; geleiding, voortplanting v.; (v. licht) doorlating v.; (v. bezitting) overdracht v.; overerving v.; (v. auto) gangwissel m.; overbrengwerk o.

transmit [trânz'mit] overbrengen; overseinen; overzenden; overleveren; geleiden, voortplanten; (v. licht) doorlaten; (v. bezitting) overdragen; overerven.

transmitter [trânz'mitə] overzender m.; doorseiner, seingever m.; (v. telefoon) spreekbuis v.; (omroep)zender m.

transmutable [trânz'mjûtəbl] verwisselbaar; veranderbaar; omzetbaar.

transmute [trânz'mjût] verwisselen; veranderen; omzetten.

transparent [trâns'pêərənt] adj. doorschijnend, doorzichtig; (fig.) open, oprecht.

transpierce [trâns'piəs] doorboren, doorsteken.

transpire [trâns'paiə] vt. uitwasemen, uitdampen, uitzweten; vi. (Pl.) zweten; uitwasemen; zweten, transpireren; (fig.) uitlekken, ruchtbaar worden.

transplant [træns—, trâns'plânt] verplanten, overplanten; overbrengen.

transport [træns'po:t] vt. overbrengen, verplaatsen, transporteren; vervoeren, overvoeren; deporteren; (fig.) verrukken, in vervoering brengen, meeslepen; ['trænspo:t] sb. overbrenging v., vervoer, transport o.; vervoering, verrukking; geestvervoering v.; transportschip o., transportmiddelen o. mv.; gedeporteerde m.

transpose [trâns'pouz] verplaatsen, verschikken; omzetten, verwisselen; (muz.) transponeren; (algebra) overbrengen.

transposition [trânspə'ziʃən] verplaatsing, verschikking v.; omzetting, verwisseling v.; (muz.) transpositie v.; (algebra) overbrenging v.

transversal [trânz'vəsəl] adj. dwars, dwarslopend, overdwars; sb. transversaal, dwarslijn v.

trap [træp] sb. val v., strik, valstrik m.; knip v.; valdeur v., luik o.; (v. duivenslag) klep, val v.; autoval, hinderlaag v.; (v. riool, enz.) stankafsluiting v.; strikvraag v.; (fam.) (tweewielig) wagentje o.; (fam.) bedriegerij v.; (sl.) politieagent m.; vt. in de val laten lopen, verstrikken, vangen; ri. vallen zetten, strikken spannen.

trap [træp] vt. optooien, opsmukken, optuigen; sb. —s, (fam.) spullen, bullen.

trapdoor ['træpdo:] valdeur v., luik o.; (in kleren) winkelhaak m.

trapeze [trə'pîz] trapeze v., zweefrek o.

trapezium [trə'pîziəm] trapezium o.

trapper ['træpə] strikkenspanner, strikkenzetter m.; pelsjager m.; (in kolenmijn) valdeurwachter m.; (fam.) rijtuigpaard o.

trappings ['træpiŋz] sjabrak v.; opschik, tooi m., praal v.

trappy ['træpi] (fam.) verraderlijk, vol valstrikken.

trash [træʃ] sb. uitschot o., afval m.; ampas v., uitgeperst suikerriet o.; (fig.) bocht o., prul(len) v. (mv.); vodderij v.; onzin m., geklets o.; vt. snoeien; (dial.) afmatten.

trashy ['træʃi] adj. prullig, prullerig, voddig.

travel ['trævl] vi. reizen; heen en weer gaan; zich verplaatsen, zich bewegen; (v. licht, geluid) zich voortplanten; (fam.) rennen, vliegen; vt. (v. land) doorreizen, afreizen; doortrekken; (v. pad) begaan; (v. afstand) afleggen; laten trekken; (v. vee, enz.) vervoeren; sb. (het) reizen o.; reis v.; reisbeschrijving v., reisverhaal o.; (v. zuiger, enz.) beweging v., slag m.

traveller ['trævlə] reiziger m.; (tn.) loopkraan; loopkat v.; (Am.) rondtrekkend prediker m.

traverse ['trævəs] adj. dwars; dwars—; sb. dwarsbalk m., dwarshout o., dwarslat v., dwarsstuk o.; (v. paard) dwarsgang *m.*; (*sch.*) koppelkoers, dwarskoers *m.*; (*mil.*) dwarswal *m.*; (*v. ladder*) sport *v.*; doortocht, overtocht *m.*; doorgang *m.*; tussenschot *o.*; (*meetk.*) transversaal *v.*; (*recht*) exceptie *v.*; wederwaardigheid *v.*; tegenspoed *m.*; *vt.* doortrekken, oversteken; doorkruisen, doorsnijden; bestrijden, betwisten; tegenwerken, dwarsbomen; (*mil.: v. kanon*) draaien; (*recht*) excepties opwerpen tegen; *vi.* draaien; (*v. paard*) traverseren, dwarsgaan, overschenkelen.

trawler ['tro:lə] treiler *m.*

tray [trei] schenkblaadje; presenteerblaadje *o.*; (*voor penhouders, enz.*) legbakje *o.*; (*in koffer, enz.*) houten bak *m.*; dienbak *m.*

treacherous(**ly**) ['tretʃərəs(li)] *adj.* (*adv.*) verraderlijk.

treachery ['tretʃəri] verraad *o.*; trouweloosheid, ontrouw *v.*

treacle['trikl] *sb.* stroop *v.*; (*fig.*) stroopsmeerderij *v.*, honig *m.* om de mond; *vt.* met stroop besmeren.

tread [tred] *vi.* treden, trappen, lopen, stappen; *vt.* betreden; bewandelen; (*v. weg*) volgen; vervolgen; lopen over; *sb.* tred, stap *m.*, schrede *v.*; trap *m.*; trede, sport *v.*; hanetred *m.*; (*v. voet, schoen*) zool *v.*; (*v. rail, enz.*) loopvlak *o.*

treadle ['tredl] *sb.* (*v. fiets, naaimachine*) trapper *m.*; (*v. orgel*) voetklavier, pedaal *o.*; (*Dk.*) hanetred *m.*; *vt.* trappen.

treason ['trizn] verraad *o.*

treasure['treʒə] *sb.* schat(ten) *m.* (*mv.*); schat(je) *m.* (*o.*); juweeltje *o.*; *vt.* waarderen, erg op prijs stellen; — (*up*), verzamelen, vergaren.

treasurer ['treʒərə] schatbewaarder, schatmeester *m.*; penningmeester *m.*

treasury ['treʒəri] schatkamer *v.*; schatkist *v.*; ministerie *o.* van financiën; (*sl.*) gage *v.* van toneelspelers.

treat [trit] *vt.* behandelen, bejegenen; onthalen, trakteren; (*v. onderwerp, enz.*) behandelen; *vi.* onderhandelen; onderhandelingen aanknopen (*for*, over); een verdrag sluiten; trakteren; *vr.* — **oneself to,** zich de weelde veroorloven van, zich aanschaffen; zich zelf eens trakteren op; *sb.* onthaal *o.*, traktatie *v.*; feest *o.*

treatise ['tritiz, —is] verhandeling *v.*

treatment ['tritmənt] behandeling *v.*; bejegening *v.*; onthaal *o.*

treaty['triti] verdrag, traktaat *o.*; overeenkomst *v.*, contract *o.*

treble ['trebl] *adj.* drievoudig; driedubbel; sopraan—; hoog, schel; *sb.* (het) drievoudige *o.*; sopraan; *vt.* verdrievoudigen; *vi.* zich verdrievoudigen.

tree [tri] *sb.* boom *m.*; stamboom *m.*; leest *v.*; galg *v.*; (*sch.*) spier *v.*; kruishout *o.*; *vt.* met bomen beplanten; (*v. dier, enz.*) in een boom jagen; op de leest zetten; (*fig.: v. persoon*) in het nauw brengen; *vi.* in een boom vluchten.

tree-nursery ['trinə:sri] boomkwekerij *v.*

trellis ['trelis] *sb.* tralie *v.*, traliewerk, latwerk *o.*; *vt.* van traliewerk (latwerk) voorzien; (*v. boom*) leiden langs latten.

trellis-work ['treliswə:k] traliewerk, rasterwerk *o.*

tremble ['trembl] *vi.* beven, sidderen, rillen; (*v. geluid*) trillen; *sb.* beving, siddering, rilling *v.*; (*v. stem*) trilling *v.*; **—s,** rillingen; delirium tremens.

tremendous(**ly**) [tri'mendəs(li)] *adj.* (*adv.*) verschrikkelijk, vreselijk, geducht, kolossaal, vervaarlijk.

tremulous(**ly**) ['tremjuləs(li)] *adj.* (*adv.*) bevend, sidderend, huiverend; schroomvallig.

trench [trenʃ] *vt.* snijden, doorsnijden; graven; (*diep*) omspitten, ploegen; verschansen, met loopgraven versterken; *vi.* — **upon,** inbreuk maken op; grenzen aan, raken; betrekking hebben op; *sb.* greppel, sloot *v.*; loopgraaf *v.*; rimpel *m.*, groef *v.*

trenchant ['trenʃənt] *adj.* scherp, snijdend; bits; sarcastisch; beslist, krachtig, doortastend; scherp omlijnd.

trench-coat ['trenʃkout] waterdichte overjas *v.*

trencher ['trenʃə] graver, loopgraafmaker *m.*; broodplank *v.*; (*fig.*) tafel *v.*

trend [trend] *vi.* lopen, gaan (in zekere richting); zich ombuigen; zich uitstrekken; *sb.* richting *v.*; neiging, strekking *v.*; stroming *v.*; (*sch.: v. anker*) kruis *o.*

trespass ['trespəs] *vi.* op verboden terrein komen; zich vergrijpen, zondigen; — (*up*)**on,** misbruik maken van; *sb.* overtreding *v.*; vergrijp *o.*; misbruik *o.*; zonde *v.*

tress [tres] *sb.* lok, haarlok, krul *v.*; haarvlecht *v.*; rank *v.*, (bloeiende) tak *m.*; *vt.* vlechten.

trestle ['tresl] schraag *v.*, bok *m.*, onderstel *o.*

trews [trûz] (*Sc.*) broek *v.*

trial ['traiəl] proef, proefneming *v.*; proeftocht *m.*; (*vl.*) proefvlucht *v.*; beproeving, bezoeking *v.*; (*recht*) onderzoek, verhoor *o.*; openbare behandeling *v.*; (*soms*) poging *v.*

trial-ascent ['traiələsent] (*vl.*) proefvlucht *v.*

triangle ['traiæŋgl] driehoek *m.*; (*muz.*) triangel *m.*; (*sch.*) bok *m.*

tribe [traib] stam *m.*, geslacht *o.*, familie *v.*; soort *v.*, slag *o.*; (*Dk., Pl.*) onderorde *v.*

tribulation [tribju'leiʃən] beproeving *v.*, tegenspoed, rampspoed *m.*, wederwaardigheid *v.*, leed *o.*

tribunal [tri'bjûnəl] rechtbank *v.*, rechterstoel *m.*

tribune ['tribjûn] (*gesch.*) tribuun *m.*; tribune *v.*, spreekgestoelte, podium *o.*

tributary ['tribjutəri] *adj.* schatplichtig, cijnsbaar; *sb.* schatplichtige *m.*; zijrivier *v.*

tribute ['tribjût] schatting *v.*, cijns, tol *m.*; bijdrage *v.*; hulde, huldebetuiging *v.*, huldeblijk *o.*

trice [trais] *sb. in a* —, in een ommezien, in een wip, in één-twee-drie; *vt.* (*sch.*) trijsen, ophijsen.

trick [trik] *sb.* streek *m.*, poets, grap *v.*; list *v.*, foefje *o.*, kneep *v.*, kunstgreep *m.*; truc *m.*; kunstje *o.*, goochelarij *v.*; (*kaartspel*) slag, trek *m.*; eigenaardigheid *v.*; hebbelijkheid *v.*, eigenaardig aanwensel *o.*; *vt.* bedotten, bedriegen, een loer draaien; verrassen; *vi.* streken uithalen, kunsten uithalen; op bedriegerij uit zijn.

tricky ['triki] *adj.* bedrieglijk; vol streken; sluw, verraderlijk; (*v. dier*) kwaadaardig; (*fam.*) lastig, netelig, gewaagd.

tricolour ['traikələ] *adj.* driekleurig; *sb.* driekleur, driekleurige vlag *v.*

tricot ['trikou] tricot *o.*

tricycle ['traisikl] *sb.* driewieler *m.*; *vi.* op de driewieler rijden.

trier ['traiə] onderzoeker *m.*; rechter *m.*; proef *v.*; toetssteen *m.*

trifle ['traifl] *sb.* beuzeling, beuzelarij *v.*; kleinigheid, bagatel *v.*; snuisterij *v.*; halfhard tin *o.*; *vi.* beuzelen, zich met beuzelarijen ophouden; spelen; spotten, gekscheren (*with*, met); *vt.* — *away*, verbeuzelen, verspillen, vermorsen.

trifling(ly) ['traifliŋ(li)] *adj.* (*adv.*) beuzelachtig; nietig, onbeduidend, onbelangrijk, onbetekenend.

trigger ['trigə] (*mil.*) trekker *m.*; remblok *o.*

trill [tril] *sb.* (*v. stem*) trilling *v.*; trilklank *m.*, met trilling uitgesproken letter *v.* (bv. r); (*muz.*) triller *m.*; *vi.* trillend (met trillende stem) zingen (spreken); trillers maken; vloeien, kabbelen; biggelen; *vt.* trillend uitspreken (zingen).

trilling ['triliŋ] één van een drieling; —*s*, drieling.

trim [trim] *adj.* net, netjes, keurig, proper; (*v. kleren*) goed passend, goed zittend; keurig in orde, goed onderhouden; *vt.* in orde maken (brengen); (*v. haar, enz.*) bijknippen, gelijkknippen; mooi maken, opsmukken, opknappen, versieren; (*v. hoed, enz.*) garneren; (*v. kolen*) tremmen; (*v. hout, enz.*) behouwen; (*v. kaars*) snuiten; (*v. booglamp*) nieuwe koolspitsen zetten in; (*sch.: v. zeilen*) opzetten; snoeien, besnoeien; (*v. scheepslading*) stuwen; (*fig.*) de mantel uitvegen, afrossen, aftroeven; (*sl.*) afzetten; *vi.* (*v. schip*) liggen; (*fig.*) schipperen, laveren; *vr.* — *oneself up*, zich mooi maken; *sb.* toestand, (goede) staat *m.*, gesteldheid *v.*; voorkomen *o.*; aard *m.*, manier van doen *v.*; tooi, opschik *m.*; kostuum *o.*, kledij, uitrusting *v.*; (*sch.*) stuwage *v.*, zeilvaardigheid *v.*; (*Am.*) winkeluitstalling *v.*

trimming ['trimiŋ] garneersel; belegsel, oplegsel *o.*; draaierij *v.*, geschipper *o.*; uitbrander *m.*, schrobbering *v.*; pak slaag, pak ransel *o.*; snoeisel, afknipsel *o.*; toebehoren *o.*; uiterlijkheden *v. mv.*

trinket ['triŋkit] kleinood, sieraad, juweel *o.*

trip [trip] *vi.* trippelen, huppelen; struikelen; een fout begaan, een misstap doen; zich verspreken; een uitstapje maken; *vt.* doen struikelen, doen vallen; een beentje lichten; de voet lichten; erin laten lopen; (op een fout) betrappen; (*sch.: v. anker*) lichten; *sb.* trippelpas *m.*, getrippel *o.*; struikeling *v.*; fout *v.*, misstap *m.*; uitstapje, tochtje, reisje *o.*; (*sch.: bij 't lareren*) gang, slag *m.*; (*v. vis*) vangst *v.*; (*tn.*) uitkoppeling *v.*

tripe [traip] pens *v.*; darmen *m. mv.*, ingewanden *o. mv.*; (*sl.*) prulleboel *m.*, prullaria *o. mv.*; (*sl.*) onzin, kletspraat *m.*, larie *v.*

triplane ['traiplein] (*vl.*) driedekker *m.*

triplex ['tripleks] *sb.* drievoud *o.*; *adj.* drievoudig.

tripod ['traipod] drievoet *m.*; (*fot.*) statief *o.*

triptyck ['triptik] triptiek, drieluik *o.*; (*fam.*) internationaal paspoort *o.* voor automobilist.

trite(ly) [trait(li)] *adj.* (*adv.*) afgezaagd, banaal, alledaags; versleten, afgesleten.

triumph ['traiəmf] *sb.* triomf *m.*, overwinning, zegepraal, zege *v.*; zegetocht *m.*; *vi.* zegevieren, zegepralen, triomferen; victorie kraaien; een zegetocht houden.

triumphal [trai'əmfəl] *adj.* zegevierend, zegepralend, triomferend.

trivial ['triviəl] *adj.* onbeduidend, onbelangrijk, nietig; alledaags, plat; afgezaagd.

trombone ['trɔm'boun] schuiftrompet, trombone *v.*

troop [trûp] *sb.* troep *m.*, menigte, bende *v.*, hoop *m.*; (*mil.*) half eskadron *o.*; marssignaal *o.*; ritmeestersplaats *v.*; *vt.* (*mil.*) troepsgewijs formeren, in troepen formeren; *vi.* zich verzamelen, samenscholen, te hoop lopen; afmarcheren, aftrekken.

trooper ['trûpə] cavalerist *m.*; cavaleriepaard *o.*; transportschip *o.*; (*Austr.*) bereden politieagent *m.*; (*Am.*) staatspolitieagent *m.*

trophy ['troufi] trofee *v.*, zegeteken *o.*

tropic ['trɔpik] *sb.* keerkring *m.*

tropical ['trɔpikl] *adj.* tropisch, keerkrings—, van de keerkringen; figuurlijk, zinnebeeldig, overdrachtelijk.

trot [trɔt] *sb.* draf *m.*, drafje *o.*; leireep *v.*; (*fam.*) dribbeltje, hummeltje *o.*; treuzelaar *m.*; zetlijn *v.*; (*Am.*) dans(je) *m.* (*o.*); op stap gaan, een eind omstappen; *vi.* draven, op een drafje lopen; tippelen; opstappen; *vt.* laten draven; in draf brengen (zetten); laten rijden (op de knie); (*v. land, enz.*) afreizen; — **up,** (*sl.*) (*v. prijs*) opjagen; (*v. wijn, enz.*) laten aanrukken; (*v. kwestie*) weer ter sprake brengen.

trotting-match ['trɔtiŋmætʃ] draverij, harddraverij *v.*

trouble ['trɔbl] *vt.* verontrusten, beroeren, in beroering brengen; kwellen, verdriet doen, leed doen; beangstigen; lastig vallen, last veroorzaken, moeite veroorzaken, storen; troebel maken, vertroebelen; *vi.* moeite doen, de moeite nemen; zich ongerust maken; *vr.* — **oneself,** zich moeite geven; zich bekommeren, zich het hoofd breken (**about,** over); — **oneself with,** zich bemoeien met; *sb.* moeite *v.*, last *m.*, ongemak *o.*; onrust, verwarring *v.*; verdriet *o.*, droefheid *v.*; zorg; verlegenheid *v.*; ongeluk *o.*; lastpost *m.*; kwaal *v.*; (*Am., fam.*) openbare feestelijkheid *v.*; —**s,** tegenspoed, troebelen, onlusten.

troubled ['trɔbld] ongerust, beangst; onrustig; verontrust, gestoord; (*v. tijden, leven*) veelbewogen; gekweld.

trouble-mirth ['trɔblmə:ð] spelbederver *m.*

trough [trɔ:f] *sb.* trog, bak *m.*; pijp, buis, goot *v.*; laagte, diepte *v.*; *vt.* in een trog bewerken.

troupe [trûp] (*v. toneelspelers, enz.*) troep *m.*

trouser ['trauzə] *sb.* broek *v.*; (**pair of**) —**s,** (lange) broek; *vt.* de broek aantrekken, in de broek steken; (*sl.*) in de broekzak steken.

trousseau ['trûsou] (*v. bruid*) uitzet *m.*

trout [traut] *sb.* forel(len) *v.* (*mv.*); *vi.* naar forellen vissen.

trowel ['trauəl] *sb.* troffel *m.*; tuinschopje *o.*; *vt.* pleisteren.

truce [trûs] wapenstilstand *m.*, bestand *o.*; — **of God,** Godsvrede.

truck [trɔk] *sb.* (*v. spoorwagen*) onderste-*o.*; blokwagen *m.*; lorrie *v.*; handkar *v.*, steekwagentje *o.*; open goederenwagen, veewagen *m.*; vrachtauto *v.*; (*v. vlaggestok*) bol, knop *m.*; *vt.* per vrachtauto, enz. vervoeren.

truck [trɔk] *sb.* ruil *m.*, ruiling *v.*, ruilhandel *m.*; omgang *m.*; bocht, tuig *o.*; gedwongen winkelnering *v.*; ruilwaren *v. mv.*; (*Am.*) groente(n) *o.* (*mv.*); *vt.* ruilen (**against, for,** tegen); *vi.* ruilen; ruilhandel drijven; sjacheren.

truckle ['trɔkl] *sb.* wieltje, rolletje *o.*; rolbed *o.*; *vi.* zich slaafs onderwerpen.

truckler ['trɔklə] kruiper *m.*

true [trû] *adj.* waar, echt; rechtmatig; oprecht; trouw, getrouw (**to,** aan); glad, gelijk, effen; (*v. lijn*) recht; (*v. wind*) vast, bestendig; zeker; juist, zuiver; goed gericht, juist gericht; *sb.* **be out of the** —, niet zuiver recht zijn, niet zuiver passen; *vt.* haaks maken (zetten), juist doen passen, in de juiste stand brengen.

true-blue ['trû'blû] *adj.* echt, onver-

valst; oprecht, trouw, rechtschapen; *sb.* eerlijke kerel *m.*, oprechte ziel *v.*, man *m.* van beginselen.

true-born ['trûbo:n] echt, rechtgeaard, rasecht.

true-hearted ['trûhâtid] eerlijk, trouwhartig.

truffle ['trɔfl] *sb.* truffel *v.*; *vt.* trufferen.

trull [trɔl] slet *v.*; bijzit *v.*

truly ['trûli] *adv.* waarlijk, werkelijk, in waarheid, voorwaar; oprecht, trouw; terecht.

trump [trɔmp] *sb.* troef, troefkaart *v.*; beste vent, kranige kerel *m.*; trompet; bazuin *v.*; trompetgeschal *o.*; (*Sc.*) mondharmonica *v.*; **turn up** —**s,** goed uitvallen; geluk hebben, boffen; *vt.* aftroeven; overtroeven, uitbazuinen; — **up,** verzinnen; ophemelen; *vi.* troef uitspelen, troeven.

trumpet ['trɔmpit] *sb.* trompet; bazuin *v.*; trompetgeschal *o.*; scheepsroeper *m.*; (*v. olifant, enz.*) (het) trompetten *o.*; *vt.* met trompetgeschal aankondigen; uitbazuinen; *vi.* op de trompet blazen; trompetten.

trumpeter ['trɔmpitə] (*mil.*) trompetter *m.*; (*Dk.*) trompetvogel *m.*; trompetduif *v.*; trompetvis *m.*; dampig paard *o.*; (*fig.*) voorbode *m.*

trundle ['trɔndl] *sb.* rolletje, wieltje *o.*; rolwagen(tje) *m.* (*O.*); rolbed *o.*

trunk [trɔŋk] stam, boomstam *m.*; (*v. zuil*) schacht *v.*; (*v. lichaam*) romp *m.*; (*v. olifant*) slurf *v.*, snuit *m.*; koffer; bak *m.*; viskaar *v.*; hoofdader; hoofdzenuw *v.*; (*tel.*, *v. spoorweg*) hoofdlijn *v.*; koker *m.*; blaaspijp *v.*; (*sl.*) neus *m.*; —**s,** zwembroek *v.*; kniebroek *v.*; — **airline,** hoofdluchtvaartweg.

trunk-call ['trɔŋkko:l] (*tel.*) interlokaal gesprek *o.*

trunnion ['trɔnjən] (*v. kanon, enz.*) tap *m.*

truss [trɔs] *sb.* (*v. hooi, enz.*) bundel, bos *m.*; draagsteen *m.*, console *v.*; bint *o.*; dakstoel *m.*, hangwerk *o.*; (*sch.*) rak *o.*; breukband *m.*; *vt.* opbinden, samenbinden; (*v. vogel, vóór 't braden*) pennen; (*bouwk.*) verankeren, versterken; knevelen.

trust [trɔst] *sb.* (goed) vertrouwen *o.*; hoop *v.*; (*H.*) krediet *o.*; toevertrouwd pand *o.*; trust *v.*; stichting *v.*; *adj.* — **money,** toevertrouwd geld; *vt.* vertrouwen; toevertrouwen; geloven; hopen; krediet geven, borgen; *vi.* vertrouwen; (*H.*) op krediet geven.

trustable ['trɔstəbl] te vertrouwen.

trustee [trɔs'tî] beheerder, bewindvoerder, commissaris, gevolmachtigde, curator, boedelberedderaar *m.*; (*v. weeshuis, enz.*) regent *m.*

trustful (**ly**) ['trɔstful(i)] *adj.* (*adv.*) vol vertrouwen, goed van vertrouwen, vertrouwend.

trustless ['trɔstlis] trouweloos; niet et vertrouwen.

trustworthy ['trəstwə:0i] te vertrouwen, betrouwbaar.

trusty ['trəsti] adj. betrouwbaar, te ₓvertrouwen; getrouw; sb. (Am.) wegens goed gedrag bevoorrechte gevangene.

truth [trûð] waarheid v.; waarheidsliefde v.; oprechtheid v.; nauwkeurigheid r.; echtheid v.

truthful ['trûðful] adj. waarheidlievend; waar; (v. portret) getrouw.

try [trai] vt. beproeven, pogen, trachten, proberen; op de proef stellen, de proef nemen met; aan een proef onderwerpen; proefstomen, proefstoken; (v. ogen, enz.) veel vergen van, vermoeien; (v. metalen) zuiveren; verhoren, in verhoor nemen; onderzoeken; berechten; aanpakken; (met roffelschaaf) roffelen; (v. traan) koken; vi. (het) proberen; sb. (fam.) poging v.; (Rugbyvoetb.) recht o. om te proberen een goal te maken.

trying ['traiiŋ] moeilijk, lastig; vermoeiend; pijnlijk, smartelijk; (v. toestand) benard; (v. klimaat) afmattend.

tryst [trist] afspraak, bijeenkomst, (plaats van) samenkomst v., rendezvous o.

tsar, etc. zie **czar,** etc.

T-square ['tiskwêə] tekenhaak m.

tub [təb] sb. tobbe v.; ton v., vat o.; trog m.; bak m., kuip v.; bad o, ĺĺadkuip v.; zitbad o.; (fam.) schuit, boot v.; roeiboot v.; (fam.) kansel, preekstoel m.; (fam.) auto v. wagen m.; vt. in de tobbe wassen; baden, een bad geven; in een kuip planten; (v. mijnschacht) bekleden; (v. boter) tonnen, vaten; vi. een (zit)bad nemen.

tube [tjûb] sb. buis, pijp v., koker m.; (gummi)slang v.; binnenband m.; luchtdrukbuis v.; ondergrondse elektrische spoorweg m.; vlampijp v.; reageerbuisje o.; vt. van buizen (pijpen, enz.) voorzien; in een tube doen; vi. met de ondergrondse elektrische spoorweg gaan.

tuber ['tjûbə] (Pl.) knol m.; gezwel o.; (fam.) aardappel m.

tubercular [tju'bə:kjulə] knobbelachtig; tuberculeus, vol tuberkels, vol knobbels.

tuberculous [tju'bə:kjuləs] tuberculeus.

tuck [tək] sb. (v. broek) omslag m.; opnaaisel o., plooi v.; (sl.) lekkers o., snoep m., suikergoed o.; trommelslag m.; rapier o.; (het) instoppen o.; vt. (v. mouwen) omslaan, opschorten, opstroppen; (v. rok) opnemen; plooien; instoppen; innemen, inslaan; verstoppen, wegstoppen; in de mond proppen; — in, innemen, inleggen; instoppen; (v. benen) intrekken; (sl.) (v. eten) verorberen, naar binnen slaan; naar binnen werken; vi. — into, (sl.) zich te goed doen aan.

tuck-in ['tək'in] (sl.) stevig maal o.; smulpartij v.

tuck-out ['tokaut] zie **tuck-in.**

Tuesday ['tjûzdi] dinsdag m.

tuft [təft] sb. bosje o.; kwastje o.; sik v.; kuif v.; groepje o. bomen; vt. met een kwastje versieren; (v. matras) doorsteken; in bosjes groeien.

tug [təg] vi. trekken, rukken (at, aan); zwoegen; zich voortslepen; vt. trekken aan; voorttrekken, voortslepen; sb. ruk, trek, haal m.; (v. trekdier) streng v.; (voor bomen van wagen) riem m.; sleepboot v.; krachtige inspanning v.

tug-boat ['təgbout] sleepboot v.

tulip ['tjûlip] tulp v.

tulle [t(j)ûl] sb. tule v.; adj. tulen.

tumble ['təmbl] vi. vallen, tuimelen, storten; buitelen, buitelingen maken; duikelen; in elkaar vallen, instorten; (in bed) woelen; (sl.: v. effecten) kelderen; vt. gooien; doen vallen, neergooien, het onderste boven gooien; (v. vogels, enz.) neerschieten; verfomfaaien, verfrommelen, in de war maken; ruw aanpakken; sb. tuimeling, buiteling v.; val m.; warboel m.

tumbledown ['təmbldaun] bouwvallig; vervallen.

tumbler ['təmblə] buitelaar, kunstenmaker, acrobaat m.; duikelaar m.; glas zonder voet, bekerglas o., tumbler m.; (v. slot: duif) tuimelaar m.

tumefaction [tjûmi'fækʃən] opzwelling v., gezwel o.

tumour ['tjûmə] gezwel o.; gezwollenheid v.

tumult ['tjûməlt] lawaai, rumoer, tumult o., herrie v.; beroering, opschudding v.; oproer o.

tumulus ['tjûmjuləs] grafheuvel m.

tun [tən] sb. ton v., vat o.; (gist)kuip v.; vt. tonnen, in een vat (in vaten doen).

tune [tjûn] sb. liedje, wijsje, deuntje o.; melodie v.; stemming, gestemdheid v.; toon, klank m.; (radio) resonantie v.; vt. (v. piano) stemmen; (radio, enz.) afstemmen; (v. machine) instellen; in overeenstemming brengen met, doen harmoniëren met; in zekere stemming brengen; (v. lied) zingen; (dicht.) aanheffen; vi. samenstemmen; — in, een woordje gaan meespreken, een woordje in het midden brengen.

tuneful ['tjûnful] welluidend, zangerig, melodieus; muzikaal.

tuneless ['tjûnlis] onwelluidend; zonder melodie; geen geluid gevend, geen muziek makend, zwijgend, stom.

tunnel ['tənəl] sb. tunnel m.; schacht v.; trechter m.; pijp v.; vt. een tunnel maken onder (door); (tunnelvormig) uithollen; trechtervormig uitgraven.

tunny ['təni] (Dk.) tonijn m.

tuppence ['təpəns] zie **twopence.**

turban ['tə:bən] tulband m.

turbid ['tə:bid] adj. drabbig, troebel; (v. rook) dicht, dik; (v. stijl) duister, verward.

turbot ['tə:bət] tarbot v.

turbulent(ly) ['tə:bjulənt(li)] adj. (adv.)

onstuimig, woelig, roerig, rumoerig.
turf [təːf] *sb.* zode *v.*; plag *v.*; grastapijt *o.*; (*Ir.*) turf *m.*; renbaan *v.*; wedren *m.*, harddraverij *v.*; rensport, renpaarde-sport *v.*; *vt.* met zoden bedekken; onder de zoden leggen, begraven; *vi.* (*dial.*) zoden steken; turf graven.
Turkey ['təːki] *sb.* Turkije *o.*; *adj.* Turks.
turkey ['təːki] kalkoen *m.*
turmoil ['təːmoil] *sb.* rumoer, lawaai, gewoel *o.*; opwinding, onrust, beroering, gisting, agitatie *v.*; verwarring *v.*, chaos *m.*; *vt.* kwellen, lastig vallen, pla-gen; in beroering brengen; *vi.* in onrust verkeren, in beroering zijn.
turn [təːn] *vt.* draaien omdraaien, om-keren, omwenden; doen keren, een andere wending geven; (*v. blad*) om-slaan; omwoelen; (*mil.*) omtrekken; (*v. slag*) afwenden; op de vlucht drijven; vormen, fatsoeneren; (*v. sinaasappel, enz.*) aan één stuk schillen; aanwenden; veranderen (*into, to,* in); (*tn.*) tornen; (*v. weg, rivier*) verleggen; (*snede v. mes, enz.*) omzetten; (*fig.*) afstompen, de scherpte wegnemen van; (*v. kaap*) om-zeilen, omgaan; overzetten, vertalen; verzetten; doen schiften, zuur doen worden; overdenken; (*v. persoon*) weg-sturen; van kleur doen veranderen; geen spier vertrekken; kalm blijven; geen haar krenken; *vi.* draaien; zich keren, zich wenden; gisten, zuur wor-den; (*v. bladeren*) geel worden; van kleur veranderen, kenteren, een keer nemen; (*drukk.*) blokkeren; — *after,* aarden naar; *vr.* — *oneself,* zich draaien; *sb.* draai *m.*, draaiing *v.*; bocht, kromming *v.*; kentering *v.*, keerpunt *o.*; zwenking *v.*; (*v. touw, spiraal*) slag *m.*; winding *v.*; draaibank *v.*; draaiziekte *v.*; wande-lingetje, toertje *o.*; tochtje, ritje *o.*; (*v. balans*) doorslag *m.*; (*v. woede, enz.*) vlaag *v.*; (*v. ziekte*) aanval *m.*; (*v. fortuin*) wisseling, verandering *v.*; neiging *v.*, aanleg *m.*; slag *o.*, soort *v.*; (*op programma*) nummer *o.*; (*muz.*) dubbelslag *m.*; zinswending *v.*, stijl *m.*; betekenis, uit-legging *v.*; beurt *v.*; werktijd *m.*
turnagain ['təːnə'gein] refrein *o.*
turncoat ['təːnkout] afvallige, rene-gaat *m.*
turning ['təːniŋ] (het) draaien *o.*; (het) kunstdraaien *o.*; draai *m.*, kronkeling, bocht *v.*; kentering *v.*, keerpunt *o.*; vouw *v.*; omgeslagen deel *o.*; zijstraat *v.*; (*mil.*) omtrekkende beweging *v.*; (*v. weegschaal*) doorslag *m.*
turning-point ['təːniŋpoint] keer-punt *o.*
turnip ['təːnip] raap *v.*, knol *m.*; (*fam.*) kale knikker *m.*; (*mil., sl.*) granaat *v.*; *get* —*s,* de bons krijgen.
turnip-cabbage ['təːnipkæbidʒ] kool-raap *v.*
turnover ['təːnouvə] omkering *v.*; ken-tering *v.*, ommekeer *m.*; omkanteling *v.*; omverwerping *v.*; omgeslagen boord

o.; (*v. kous, enz.*) omslag *m.*; (*H.*) omzet, verkoop *m.*; — *tax,* omzetbelasting.
turn-sick ['təːnsik] *adj.* draaiziek; *sb.* draaiziekte *v.*
turnsole ['təːnsoul] heliotroop *v.*; zonnebloem *v.*
turnspit ['təːnspit] spitdraaier *m.*
turn-up ['təːnəp] *adj.* (*v. broekspijp*) omgeslagen; (*v. kraag*) opstaand; *sb.* (*v. broekspijp*) omslag *m.*; (*v. dobbelsteen*) worp *m.*; bloot toeval *o.*; (*fam.*) buiten-kansje *o.*; (*sl.*) ruzie, herrie *v.*
turpentine ['təːpəntain] *sb.* terpen-tijn *v.*; *vt.* met terpentijn bestrijken (behandelen).
turquoise ['təːkwəːz, 'təːkoiz] tur-koois *m. & o.*
turtle ['təːtl] *b.* tortelduif *v.*; zeeschild-pad *v.*; schildpadsoep *v.*; *vt.* doen om-slaan; (*v. nek*) vooruitsteken; *vi.* schild-padden vangen.
turtle-dove ['təːtldəv] tortelduif *v.*
tusk [təsk] *sb.* slagtand *m.*; (*v. eg, enz.*) tand *m.*; (*Dk.: vis*) lom *m.*; *vt.* door-boren (met de slagtanden).
tussle ['təsl] *sb.* worsteling *v.*; vinnige strijd *m.*; *vi.* vechten, worstelen, bakke-leien.
tut [tət] *ij.* och kom! komaan! *vi.* och kom! roepen.
tutelage ['tjûtilidʒ] voogdij *v.*, voogdij-schap *o.*
tutelar(**y**) ['tjûtiləˈri]) beschermend.
tutor ['tjûrə] *sb.* leermeester, huisonder-wijzer *m.*; leerboek *o.*, handleiding *v.*; (*recht*) voogd *m.*; *vt.* onderwijzen; af-richten, dresseren; berispen; (*v. getui-gen*) bewerken; bedillen.
tutoress ['tjûtəris] leermeesteres, gou-vernante *v.*
tuxedo [tək'sidou] (*Am.*) smoking *v.*
twaddle ['twɔdl] *vi.* wauwelen, bazelen, kletsen, beuzelen; *sb.* gewauwel, geklets *o.*, beuzelpraat *m.*, gebazel *o.*
tweak [twik] katapult *v.*
tweaker ['twikə] katapult *v.*
tweezers ['twizəz] haartangetje *o.*
twelfth [twelfθ] twaalfde.
Twelfth-day ['twelfθdei] Driekonin-gen(dag) *m.*
twelve [twelv] twaalf; *in* —*s,* in duo-decimo.
twentieth ['twentiiθ] twintigste; twin-tigste deel *o.*
twenty ['twenti] twintig.
twice [twais] tweemaal, twee keer; dub-bel.
twice-told ['twaistould] (*v. verhaal, enz.*) tweemaal verteld; welbekend.
twig [twig] *sb.* takje, twijgje *o.*; wichel-roede *v.*; *in good* (*prime*) —, (*sl.*) keu-rig gekleed; in uitstekende conditie; *vt.* begrijpen, snappen; bemerken.
twilight ['twailait] schemering *v.*
twill [twil] *sb.* keper *m.*; *vt.* keperen.
twin [twin] *adj.* tweeling(s)—; ge-paard; paarsgewijze voorkomend (*of:* geplaatst); dubbel; *sb.* tweeling *m.*; dubbelganger *m.*; tweelingbroeder *m.*;

tweelingzuster *v*.; (*fig*.) tegenhanger *m*.; *vi*. bevallen van een tweeling; een paar vormen; zich paren (*with,* aan); evenaren; weerspiegelen; *vt*. (*fig*.) paren.

twin-brother ['twinbrəθə] tweelingbroeder *m*.

twine [twain] *sb*. tweern, twijn *m*., getwijnd garen, bindgaren *o*., twijndraad *m*.; kronkel *m*., kronkeling, bocht *v*., draai *m*.; omstrengeling *v*.; warboel *m*.; *vt*. twijnen, tweernen; vlechten; strengelen, omstrengelen; *vi*. zich kronkelen.

twinkle ['twiŋkl] *vi*. tintelen, flikkeren, fonkelen, schitteren; snel heen en weer gaan; fladderen; knipogen; *vt*. seinen, overseinen; (*v. licht*) uitzenden; *sb*. tinteling, flikkering *v*.; (*met ogen*) knip *m*.

twinkling ['twiŋkliŋ] tintelend, flikkerend.

twirl [twə:l] *vi*. draaien, ronddraaien; *vt*. doen draaien, ronddraaien; (*v. tolletje*) opzetten.

twist [twist] *sb*. draai *m*.; verdraaiing *v*.; kronkel, strengel *m*.; kronkel *m*. in de hersens; (*sch*.: *v. touw*) streng *v*.; poetskatoen *o*.; (*bilj*.) trekeffect *o*.; wrong *m*., wringing *v*.; krul, lok *v*.; roltabak *v*.; gedraaid broodje, stengelbrood *o*.; bocht, kromming, kronkeling *v*.; verrekking *v*.; katoengaren, twist *o*.; (*sl*.) trek, eetlust *m*.; (*sl.*: *v. drank*) half-omhalf *o*., gemengde drank *m*.; (*v. schroefdraad*) helling *v*.; (*v. gezicht*) vertrekking *v*.; bedriegerij *v*.; *vt*. draaien, samendraaien; winden; vlechten, strengelen; verdraaien; (*v. gelaat*) vertrekken; (*v. tabak*) spinnen; (*fig*.) samenstrengelen; (*sl*.) verorberen; (*sl*.) bedriegen; *vi*. zich wringen, kronkelen; slingeren, draaien.

twister ['twistə] twijnder, vlechter *m*.; bedrieger *m*.; uitvluchtenzoeker *m*.; (*bilj*.) trekbal *m*.; steunbalk *m*.; (*sl*.) flink karwei *o*.; (*sl*.) geduchte leugen *v*.; (*Am*.) wervelwind, cycloon *m*.

twitch [twitʃ] *vt*. trekken, rukken (aan); *vi*. zenuwachtig bewegen, trekken; tokkelen; *sb*. ruk *m*.; zenuwtrekking *v*.; (*v. pijn*) scheut, steek *m*.

twitter ['twitə] *ri*. tjilpen, sjilpen, kwetteren; (*v. opwinding, zenuwachtigheid*) trillen; (*dial*.) giechelen; *sb*. getjilp, gekwetter *o*.; trilling *v*.; zenuwachtigheid *v*.

two [tû] twee; tweetal *o*.

two-edged ['tûedʒd] tweesnijdend.

twofold ['tûfould] dubbel, tweevoudig, tweeledig; (*v. garen*) tweedraads.

two-pence ['təpəns] twee stuivers; (*N. Ned*.) dubbeltje *o*.

twopenny ['təpəni] *adj*. van twee stuivers; van weinig waarde; onbeduidend; goedkoop; prullig; *sb*. soort dun bier *o*.; kleine dreumes *m*.; (*sl*.) kop *m*.

twosome ['tûsəm] *adj*. door twee personen uitgevoerd; twee aan twee; *sb*. tweetal *o*.; door twee personen gespeelde wedstrijd *m*.

tympan ['timpən] (*drukk*.) timpaan, persraam *o*.; trommelvlies *o*.

type [taip] *sb*. type, voorbeeld; toonbeeld; zinnebeeld *o*.; staaltje *o*.; lettervorm *m*., lettersoort *v*.; drukletter *v*.; zetsel *o*.; *vt*. (*op schrijfmachine*) typen, tikken; symboliseren, een voorbeeld zijn van.

typewrite ['taiprait] typen, tikken (op de schrijfmachine).

typewriter ['taipraitə] schrijfmachine *v*.

typhoid ['taifɔid] *adj*. tyfeus; *sb*. tyfuskoorts *v*.; buiktyfus, darmtyfus *m*.; tyfuslijder *m*.

typhoon [tai'fûn] wervelstorm, tyfoon *m*.

typist ['taipist] typist(e) *m*. (*v*.).

typographer [tai—, ti'pogrəfə] typograaf, boekdrukker *m*.

tyrant ['tairənt] tiran, dwingeland *m*.

tyre ['taiə] *sb*. fietsband, wielband *m*. *vt*. een band (banden) leggen om.

U

U-boat ['jûbout] onderzeeboot *v*.

udder ['ədə] uier *m*.

uglify ['əglifai] lelijk maken, verlelijken.

ugly ['əgli] *adj*. lelijk; vervelend, beroerd; bedenkelijk, verdacht; (*v. stilte*) dreigend.

uhlan ['ûlân, 'jûlən] ulaan *m*.

ulcer ['əlsə] zweer *v*., ettergezwel *o*.; (*fig*.) kanker *m*.

ulcerate ['əlsəreit] *vi*. zweren, verzweren; etteren; *vt*. doen zweren; (*fig*.) verbitteren.

ulcerous ['əlsərəs] zwerend, etterend; vol zweren.

ullage ['əlidʒ] *sb*. wan *o*.; restant *o*.; uitschot *o*.; doorgesijpelde vloeistof *v*.;

(*sl*.: *in wijnglas*) staartje *o*.; *vt*. een weinig aftappen; (*v. vat*) aanvullen.

ultimatum [əlti'meitəm] ultimatum *o*.; einddoel *o*.; uiterste grens *v*.; grondbeginsel *o*.; grondstelling *v*.

ultra ['əltrə] *adj*. uiterst, uiterst radicaal; *sb*. (*in politiek, enz*.) ultra *m*.

ululate ['jûljuleit] huilen; jammeren, weeklagen.

umbel ['əmbəl] (*Pl*.) (bloem)scherm *o*.

umbrage ['əmbridʒ] schaduw *v*., lommer *o*.; ergernis *v*.

umbrella [əm'brelə] regenscherm *o*., paraplu *v*.; zonnescherm *o*.; (*v. kwal*) scherm *o*.; (*sl*.) parachute *v*.

umpire ['əmpaiə] *sb*. scheidsrechter

m.; (*H.*) derde *m.*; *vi.* als scheidsrechter optreden, arbitreren; *vt.* arbitreren bij.

unasbashed ['ənə'bæʃt] onbeschaamd, schaamteloos; niet verlegen, niet uit het veld geslagen.

unabated ['ənə'beitid] onverminderd, onverzwakt, onverflauwd.

unable ['ə'neibl] onbekwaam, niet in staat.

unabridged ['ənə'bridʒd] onverkort.

unaccented ['ənək'sentid] onbetoond, toonloos, zonder klemtoon.

unacceptable ['ənək'septəbl] onaannemelijk; onaangenaam, niet welkom.

unaccessible ['ənək'sesibl] ontoegankelijk, ongenaakbaar.

unaccustomed ['ənə'kɔstəmd] ongewoon; ongebruikelijk; niet gewend (*to, aan*).

unadmittable [ənəd'mitəbl] niet toelaatbaar; onaannemelijk.

unadulterated [ənə'dɔltəreitid] onvervalst, zuiver, echt.

unadvisable ['ənəd'vaizəbl] ongeraden, onraadzaam.

unaffected (ly) ['ənə'fektid (li)] *adj.* (*adv.*) natuurlijk, ongedwongen, ongekunsteld; onaangedaan; ongeroerd.

unallowed ['ənə'laud] niet goedgekeurd; ongepermitteerd, ongeoorloofd.

unalloyed ['ənə'lɔid] onvermengd, zuiver.

unaltered ['ə'nɔ:ltəd] onveranderd, ongewijzigd.

unambiguous (ly) ['ənəm'bigjuəs (li)] *adj.* (*adv.*) ondubbelzinnig.

unanimity [jûnə'nimiti] eenstemmigheid *v.*; eensgezindheid *v.*

unanimous (ly) [ju'næniməs (li)] *adj.* (*adv.*) eenstemmig; eensgezind.

unanswerable [ə'nânsərəbl] *adj.* niet te beantwoorden; onweerlegbaar; niet verantwoordelijk.

unapproachable ['ənə'proutʃəbl] *adj.* ontoegankelijk; ongenaakbaar; weergaloos.

unawares [ənə'wêəz] *adv.* onbewust, zonder het te weten; ongemerkt; plotseling, onverwachts, onverhoeds.

unbearable [ən'bêərəbl] *adj.* ondraaglijk, onuitstaanbaar.

unbeaten ['ən'bîtn] niet verslagen, ongeslagen; (*v. weg*) ongebaand, onbetreden.

unbecoming ['ənbi'kəmiŋ] *adj.* ongepast; onwelvoeglijk, onbetamelijk.

unbend ['ən'bend] *vt.* ontspannen; losmaken; ontplooien, ontvouwen; (*sch.: v. zeil*) afslaan.

unbending ['ən'bendiŋ] *adj.* ook: stijf, strak; onbuigzaam, ontoegevend, hardnekkig, halsstarrig.

unbidden [ən'bidn] ongenood, ongevraagd: vanzelf. [lijk.

unblamable ['ən'bleiməbl] onberispe-

unbleached [ən'blîtʃt] ongebleekt.

unblest ['ən'blest] ongezegend; ongelukkig, ellendig, onzalig.

unbound ['ən'baund] (*v. boek*) niet gebonden, oningebonden; (*v. haar*) loshangend, niet opgebonden.

unbounded ['ən'baundid] onbegrensd, onbeperkt, grenzeloos; teugelloos, onbedwongen.

unbridgeable [ən'bridʒəbl] onoverbrugbaar.

unbridled [ən'braidld] teugelloos, tomeloos, onbeteugeld.

unburden [ən'bə:dn] *vt.* ontlasten; verlichten; *vr.* — **oneself,** zijn hart uitstorten.

unbury [ən'beri] opgraven.

unceasing [ən'sîsiŋ] *adj.* onophoudelijk, voortdurend.

uncertain (ly) [ən'sə:tin (li)] *adj.* (*adv.*) onzeker; onbepaald, onbestemd, vaag; onbestendig; onduidelijk, dubbelzinnig.

uncertainty [ən'sə:tinti] onzekerheid *v.*; enz.

unchain ['ən'tʃein] ontketenen; loslaten, bevrijden.

uncle ['əŋkl] oom *m.*; (*sl.*) ome Jan *m.*

uncleared-up ['ən'klîədəp] onopgehelderd.

unclouded ['ən'klaudid] onbewolkt, helder.

uncomfortable [ən'kəmfətəbl] *adj.* ongemakkelijk; ongerieflijk; onbehaaglijk; onaangenaam; niet op zijn gemak.

uncommon [ən'kɔmən] *adj.* ongewoon, ongemeen.

uncommonly [ən'kɔmənli] *adv. not —* niet zelden.

unconcealed ['ənkən'sîld] niet verborgen, onverholen.

unconditionally ['ənkən'diʃənəli] *adv.* onvoorwaardelijk; (*mil.*) op genade of ongenade.

unconformable ['ənkən'fo:məbl] niet overeenkomstig; zich niet schikkend (*to,* naar).

unconfutable ['ənkən'fjûtəbl] onweerlegbaar.

unconquerable [ən'kɔŋkərəbl] onoverwinnelijk, onverwinbaar.

unconscious [ən'kɔnʃəs] *adj.* onbewust; onkundig (*of,* van): bewusteloos.

unconstrained ['ənkən'streind] *adj.* ongedwongen, los; vrijwillig, vrij; onbeperkt.

unconsumable ['ənkən'sjûməbl] *adj.* onverteerbaar.

uncontroverted [ən'kɔntrəvə:tid] onbetwist.

uncooked ['ən'kukt] ongekookt; niet toebereid.

uncorrupt (ed) ['ənkə'rəpt (id)] onbedorven, onvervalst; onomkoopbaar.

uncover [ən'kəvə] *vt.* het deksel afnemen van, ontdekken; ontbloten · blootleggen; (*mil.*) de dekking wegnemen van, zonder dekking laten; *vi.* zijn hoed afzetten.

unction ['əŋkʃən] zalving *v.*; zalf *v.*, balsem *m.*

uncultivated ['ən'kəltiveitid] onbebouwd; onontwikkeld, onbeschaafd.

undamaged ['ən'dæmidʒd] onbeschadigd.

undaunted [ən'do:ntid] *adj.* onversaagd, onverschrokken; niet afgeschrikt (*by,* door).

undecaying ['əndi'keiiŋ] onveranderlijk; onvergankelijk; onverwelkbaar.

undeceive ['əndi'siv] (iem.) de ogen openen, ontgoochelen, uit een dwaling helpen.

undecided(ly) ['əndi'saidid(li)] *adj.* (*adv.*) onbeslist, onbeslecht; besluiteloos, weifelend.

undefined [əndi'faind] onbepaald, onbestemd.

undemonstrable ['əndi'mɔnstrəbl] onbewijsbaar.

undeniable [əndi'naiəbl] *adj.* onloochenbaar, onbetwistbaar, ontegenzeggelijk; onberispelijk.

undepraved ['əndi'preivd] onbedorven, onverdorven.

underage ['əndə'reidʒ(d)] minderjarig, onmondig; te jong.

underbred ['əndə'bred] onopgevoed, ongemanierd.

under-carriage ['əndəkæridʒ] onderstel *o.*

underdone ['əndə'dən] niet gaar, niet genoeg gebraden.

underfed ['əndə'fed] ondervoed.

undergo ['əndə'gou] ondergaan; verduren, lijden.

underground [əndə'graund] *adv.* onder de grond; (*fig.*) in 't geheim; ['əndəgraund] a) *adj.* onderaards, ondergronds; (*fig.*) heimelijk, geheim; b) *sb.* ondergrondse spoorweg *m.*

undergrowth ['əndəgrouδ] kreupelhout *o.*

underhand [əndə'hænd] *adv.* onder de hand, heimelijk, in 't geniep; ['əndəhænd] *adj.* onderhands, heimelijk, achterbaks, slinks.

underlease ['əndəliz] *zie* **sublease.**

undermentioned ['əndə'menʃənd] onderstaand, hierondergenoemd, navolgend.

undermine [əndə'main] ondermijnen, ondergraven.

undermost ['əndəmoust] *adj.* onderste, benedenste.

underneath [əndə'niδ] *prep.* onder, beneden; *adv.* daaronder, hieronder, beneden.

underpaid ['əndə'peid] *v. t.* & *v. d. van* **underpa .**

underrate [əndə'reit] onderschatten; te laag schatten.

undersign [əndə'sain] ondertekenen.

underskirt ['əndəskə:t] onderrok *m.*

understand [əndə'stænd] verstaan, begrijpen; vatten; verstand hebben van; de kunst verstaan van; vernemen, horen. [begrijpelijk.

understandable [əndə'stændəbl] *adj.*

understanding [əndə'stændiŋ] *adj.* bevattelijk, verstandig, schrander; *sb.* verstand; begrip *o.*; verstandhouding *v.*; schikking *v.*; **—s,** (*fam.*) onderdanen (benen); schoeisel *o.*

undertake [əndə'teik] *vt.* ondernemen, op zich nemen; zich belasten met; (*v. werk*) aannemen; *vi.* (*fam.*) begrafenissen bezorgen.

undertaking [əndə'teikiŋ] onderneming *v.*; verbintenis; plechtige belofte *v.*; begrafenisonderneming, lijkbezorging *v.*

undervalue ['əndə'væljû] onderschatten; te laag schatten.

undervest ['əndəvest] borstrok *m.*

underwood ['əndəwud] kreupelhout, hakhout *o.*

underwriter ['əndəraitə] assuradeur *m.*

undetermined ['əndi'tə:mind] onbepaald; onbeslist; onzeker weifelend.

undiminished [əndi'miniʃt] onverminderd.

undisguised [əndis'gaizd] *adj.* onvermomd; (*fig.*) openlijk, onbewimpeld, onverholen.

undismayed [əndis'meid] onverschrokken, onvervaard.

undisturbed [əndis'tə:bd] ongestoord, onverstoord.

undivided(ly) [əndi'vaidid(li)] *adj.* (*adv.*) onverdeeld.

undo [ən'dû] losmaken; losrijgen; losknopen; (*v. pakje, enz.*) openmaken; ongedaan maken weer goed maken: te niet doen, vernietigen; te gronde richten, in 't verderf storten.

undoubted [ən'dautid] *adj.* ontwijfelbaar; onverdacht; stellig, zeker, onbetwist.

undraw [ən'dro:] opentrekken.

undress [ən'dres] *vt.* ontkleden, uitkleden; (*v. wond, enz.*) ontzwachtelen, het verband afnemen van; *vi.* zich uitkleden; *sb.* ochtendkleed, huisgewaad, négligé *o.*; (*mil.*) klein tenue *o.*

undue ['ən'dû] ongepast, onbehoorlijk, onbetamelijk; bovenmatig, overdreven; (*v. schuld*) nog niet vervallen; niet verschuldigd.

undulating ['əndjuleitiŋ] (*v. terrein, enz.*) golvend; (*v. haar*) geonduleerd; gegolfd.

undulation [əndju'leiʃən] golving *v.*; (*muz.: v. toon*) het vibreren *o.*

unearth [ə'nə:δ] opgraven; (*v. aardappelen*) rooien; (*tn.*) opdelven; opdiepen, aan 't licht brengen.

uneasiness [ə'nîzinis] onbehaaglijkheid *v.*; ongerieflijkheid *v.*; ongemak *o.*; onrust, ongerustheid, bezorgdheid *v.*

uneasy [ə'nîzi] onbehaaglijk; ongemakkelijk; ongerust, bezorgd; onrustig.

unemployed [ənim'plɔid] ongebruikt; werkloos, zonder werk; (*mil.*) ter beschikking.

unencumbered [ənin'kəmbəd] (*v. eigendommen*) onbelast, onbezwaard.

unendurable ['ʌnin'djûərəbl] ondraaglijk.

unequal [ə'nîkwəl] *adj.* ongelijk, oneffen; ongelijkmatig; oneven; (*v. pols*) onregelmatig; — *to the task*, niet opgewassen tegen (niet berekend voor) de taak.

unequalled [ə'nîkwəld] ongeëvenaard, onvergelijkelijk.

unequivocal(ly) [əni'kwivəkəl(i)] *adj.* (*adv.*) ondubbelzinnig.

unestimable [ə'nestiməbl] onschatbaar, onwaardeerbaar.

uneven [ə'nîvən] *adj.* ongelijk, oneffen; ongelijkmatig.

unexpected [əniks'pektid] *adj.* onverwacht, onvoorzien; onberekenbaar.

unfailing [ən'feiliŋ] onfeilbaar, zeker; onuitputtelijk.

unfair [ən'fêə] *adj.* onbillijk, onredelijk; oneerlijk; (*v. wind*) ongunstig.

unfaithful(ly) [ən'feiðful(i)] *adj.* (*adv.*) ontrouw, trouweloos; (*v. vertaling*) niet getrouw.

unfaltering [ən'fo:ltəriŋ] *adj.* niet weifelend, onwankelbaar.

unfamiliar ['ənfə'miljə] ongemeenzaam; niet vertrouwd (*with*, met).

unfamiliarity ['ənfəmili'æriti] ongemeenzaamheid *v.*; onbekendheid (*with*, met) *v.*

unfathomable [ən'fæθəməbl] onpeilbaar, ondoorgrondelijk.

unfeasible [ən'fîzəbl] ondoenlijk.

unfeeling(ly) [ən'fîliŋ(li)] *adj.* (*adv.*) ongevoelig, hardvochtig, wreed.

unfeigned [ən'feind] *adj.* ongeveinsd, oprecht.

unfit [ən'fit], *adj.* ongeschikt, onbekwaam, ongepast; in slechte conditie; *vt.* ongeschikt maken.

unfitting ['ən'fitiŋ] *adj.* ongeschikt; ongepast; onbetamelijk.

unfix [ən'fiks] losmaken.

unfold [ən'fould] *vt.* ontvouwen, ontplooien, uitspreiden; blootleggen, openbaren, onthullen; *vi.* zich ontplooien, zich uitspreiden.

unfordable [ən'fo:dəbl] ondoorwaadbaar.

unforgivable [ənfə'givəbl] onvergeeflijk.

unfortified [ən'fo:tifaid] onversterkt; (*v. stad ook:*) open.

unfortunate [ən'fo:tʃənit] *adj.* ongelukkig; *sb.* ongelukkige *m.*

unfounded [ən'faundid] *adj.* ongegrond.

unfriend ['ən'frend] vijand *m.*

unfriendly ['ən'frendli] onvriendelijk, onvriendschappelijk; (*v. weer*) ongunstig.

unfurl [ən'fə:l] *vt.* uitspreiden; (*v. vlag*) ontplooien; *vi.* zich uitspreiden.

ungear [ən'gîə] (*v. paard*) uitspannen; (*tn.*) ontkoppelen.

ungovernable [ən'gʌvənəbl] onhandelbaar, niet te regeren, ontembaar.

ungracious [ən'greiʃəs] *adj.* onbevallig; onvriendelijk, onaardig, onhoffelijk.

ungrateful [ən'greitful] (*v. za cen, grond, enz.*) ondankbaar; (*v. spijzen, enz.*) onaangenaam.

unguent ['əngwənt] zalf *v.*

unhandily [ən'hændili] *adv.* onhandig.

unhandy [ən'hændi] *adj.* onhandig.

unharmed [ən'hâmd] onbeschadigd, ongedeerd.

unharness [ən'hânis] (*v. paard*) uitspannen.

unhealable ['ən'hîləbl] ongeneeslijk.

unhealthful ['ən'helðful] ongezond.

unhealthily [ən'helðili] *adv.* ongezond.

unheard [ən'hə:d] niet gehoord; ongehoord; (*recht*) onverhoord.

unhurriedly [ən'həridli] *adv.* bedaard, zonder zich te haasten.

unhurt ['ən'hə:t] ongedeerd.

unification [jûnifi'keiʃən] unificatie, éénmaking *v.*

uniform ['jûnifo:m] *adj.* eenvormig; gelijkvormig; (*tn.*) constant, onveranderlijk; (*v. versnelling*) eenparig; *sb.* uniform *o.*; *vt.* uniform maken; in uniform kleden.

unify ['jûnifai] verenigen, één maken.

unimpaired [ənim'pêəd] ongeschonden, onverzwakt.

unimpeachable [ənim'pîtʃəbl] onberispelijk; onbetwistbaar, onwraakbaar.

unimpeded [ənim'pîdid] onbelemmerd, ongehinderd.

unimprovable [ənim'prûvəbl] onverbeterlijk.

uninjured [ə'nindʒəd] *adj.* onbeschadigd, ongeschonden; ongedeerd.

unintelligible ['ənin'telidʒibl] *adj.* onverstaanbaar, onbegrijpelijk.

unintentional(ly) ['ənin'tenʃənəl(i)] *adj.* (*adv.*) onopzettelijk.

uninteresting [ə'nintristiŋ] *adj.* niet interessant.

uninterrupted [əNintə'rəptid] *adj.* onafgebroken, onverpoosd.

union ['jûnjən] vereniging, verbinding *v.*; verbintenis *v.*; eendracht, eensgezindheid *v.*; (*v. wond*) heling *v.*

union-man ['jûnjənmən] lid *o.* van een arbeidersvereniging.

unique [ju'nîk] *adj.* énig, ongeëvenaard; *sb.* unicum *o.*

unit ['jûnit] eenheid *v.*

unitable [ju'naitəbl] verenigbaar.

unite [ju'nait] *vt.* verenigen, verbinden; *vi.* zich verenigen (*with*, met); samenwerken (*to*, om); aaneengroeien.

united [ju'naitəd] verenigd, verbonden; eendrachtig.

unity ['jûniti] eenheid, overeenstemming; eendracht *v.*

universal [jûni'və:səl] *adj.* algemeen, universeel; (*v. verstand*) alzijdig; *sb.* algemeen begrip *o.*, algemene stelling *v.*

universe ['jûnivə:s] heelal *o.*, wereld *v.*

university [jûni'və:siti] *sb.* hogeschool,

universiteit v.; adj. universiteits—, universitair, academisch.

unjust [ən'dʒəst] adj. onrechtvaardig, onbillijk; (v. gewicht, weegschaal) onzuiver.

unjustifiable [ən'dʒəstifaiəbl] adj. niet te rechtvaardigen, onverantwoordelijk.

unknown ['ən'noun] adj. onbekend; ongekend; sb. (wisk.) onbekende v.; het onbekende o.

unlawful(ly) ['ən'lɔ:ful(i)] adi. (adv.) onwettig, ongeoorloofd.

unlearn ['ən'lə:n] verleren, afleren.

unless [ən'les] conj. tenzij, indien... niet: prep. behalve.

unlighted [ən'laitid] niet verlicht; niet aangestoken.

unlike [ən'laik] niet gelijkend op, verschillend van; ongelijk.

unlikely [ən'laikli] onwaarschijnlijk.

unlimited [ən'limitid] adj. onbegrensd, onbeperkt; vrij, ongelimiteerd.

unload [ən'loud] vt. ontlasten, ontladen; aan de man brengen; (v. aandelen) spuien, in grote hoeveelheid op de markt brengen; vi. lossen, afladen.

unlock [ən'lɔk] ontsluiten, opensluiten; (v. geheim) onthullen.

unlooked for [ən'luktfo:] onverwacht; onverhoopt.

unlucky [ən'ləki] adj. ongelukkig; onvoorspoedig.

unmake ['ən'meik] te niet doen, vernietigen; (uit ambt, enz.) afzetten.

unmanageable [ən'mænidʒəbl] adj. (sch.) onbestuurbaar; niet te regeren; onhandelbaar.

unmannerly [ən'mænəli] ongemanierd, onhebbelijk.

unmarked ['ən'mâkt] ongemerkt.

unmask [ən'mâsk] vt. ontmaskeren, het masker afrukken; vi. het masker afleggen.

unmastered [ən'mâstəd] onbedwongen.

unmeasurable [ən'meʒərəbl] onmetelijk, onbegrensd.

u=mentioned [ən'menʃənd] onvermeld.

unmerchantable [ən'mə:tʃəntəbl] onverkoopbaar.

unmerciful(ly) [ən'mə:siful(i)] adj. (adv.) onbarmhartig; (fam.) onmogelijk, onmenselijk.

unmerited [ən'meritid] onverdiend.

unminded [ən'maindid] onopgemerkt; onverzorgd, verwaarloosd.

unmistak(e)able ['ənmis'teikəbl] adj. onmiskenbaar.

unmixed ['ən'mikst] ongemengd, onvermengd.

unmolested [ənmo'lestid] ongehinderd, ongestoord.

unmounted [ən'mauntid] (mil.) onbereden; (tn.) niet gemonteerd.

unmoved [ən'mûvd] onbewogen, ongeroerd; onbeweeglijk.

unnecessary [ən'nesisəri] adj. niet noodzakelijk, nodeloos, onnodig.

unnerve [ən'nə:v] ontzenuwen, verlammen.

unnoticed [ən'noutist] ongemerkt; onopgemerkt.

unoccupied [ə'nɔkjupaid] zonder bezigheid; ongebruikt; (v. stoel, tijd, enz.) vrij, onbezet; (v. huis, enz.) onbewoond.

unoffending ['ənə'fendiŋ] niet aanstotelijk; onschadelijk, onschuldig.

unofficious ['ənə'fiʃəs] ongedienstig.

unopposed [ənə'pouzd] ongehinderd; zonder verzet, zonder tegenstand; zonder tegenkandidaat.

unorderly [ə'no:dəli] onordelijk, wanordelijk.

unowned ['ə'nound] onbeheerd; zonder eigenaar; niet erkend.

unpack ['ən'pæk] uitpakken, afladen; (v. hart) uitstorten.

unpaid ['ən'peid] onbetaald; onbezoldigd; ongefrankeerd.

unpainful [ən'peinful] pijnloos, zonder pijn.

unpalatable [ən'pælitəbl] onsmakelijk; (v. waarheid) onaangenaam, minder aangenaam; onverkwikkelijk.

unparented ['ən'pɛərəntid] ouderloos.

unpaved ['ən'peivd] (v. straat) opgebroken; onbestraat; ongeplaveid.

unpayable ['ən'peiəbl] onbetaalbaar; niet renderend.

unpeople [ən'pîpl] ontvolken.

unpeopled [ən'pîpld] ontvolkt; onbevolkt.

unperceived [ənpə'sîvd] ongemerkt.

unperturbed [ənpə'tə:bd] onverstoord.

unpitiful [ən'pitiful] onbarmhartig, onmeedogend.

unpleasant(ly) [ən'plezənt(li)] adj. (adv.) onprettig, onplezierig; onaangenaam, onbehaaglijk.

unpleased [ən'plizd] misnoegd.

unpractised [ən præktist] niet gebruikelijk; onervaren, onbedreven.

unprejudiced [ən'predʒudist] onbevooroordeeld, onpartijdig.

unpretending ['ənpri'tendiŋ], **unpretentious** [ənpri'tenʃəs] niet aanmatigend, bescheiden. [lig.

unprofitable [ən'prɔfitəbl] onvoordelig.

unprotected [ənprə'tektid] onbeschermd, weerloos.

unprovided [ənprə'vaidid] onvoorzien.

unquailing [ən'kweiliŋ] onversaagd.

unqualified [ən'kwɔlifaid] onbevoegd, ongeschikt; (v. wijn, enz.) onvermengd, onversneden; (v. bijval, enz.) onverdeeld.

unquenched [ən'kwenʃt] ongeblust, ongelest.

unquestionable [ən'kwestʃənəbl] adj. ontwijfelbaar, onbetwistbaar.

unquiet [ən'kwaiət] adj. ongerust; onrustig; woelig; sb. rusteloosheid v.; onrust v.

unravel [ən'rævl] uitrafelen; ontwarren, ontknopen, ophelderen.
unreadable [ən'rîdəbl] onleesbaar, niet te lezen.
unreal [ən'rîəl] onwezenlijk, onwerkelijk.
unreasonable [ən'rîznəbl] *adj.* onredelijk, onbillijk.
unrecoverable [ənri'kəvərəbl] onherstelbaar.
unreformable ['ənri'fo:məbl] onverbeterlijk; niet te veranderen.
unrefutable ['ənri'fjûtəbl] onweerlegbaar.
unrelenting [ənri'lentiŋ] onverbiddelijk; meedogenloos; onbuigzaam; niet verslappend.
unreliable [ənri'laiəbl] onbetrouwbaar.
unremarkable ['ənri'mâkəbl] alledaags, heel gewoon, weinig opmerkelijk.
unremitting (ly) [ənri'mitiŋ(li)] *adj.* (*adv.*) aanhoudend, onverpoosd.
unrepair [ənri'pêə] verval *o.*, slechte staat *m.*
unrest ['ən'rest] onrust; rusteloosheid *v.*
unrestrained ['ənri'streind] onbeperkt; teugelloos.
unridden [ən'ridn] onbereden.
unriddle [ən'ridl] ontraadselen, oplossen.
unrig [ən'rig] (*sch.*) onttuigen, aftakelen.
unripe ['ən'raip] onrijp.
unrivalled [ən'raivəld] ongeëvenaard, weergaloos.
unrobe [ən'roub] *vt.* ontkleden, uitkleden; van een (ambts)gewaad ontdoen; de toga afnemen; *vi.* zich uitkleden; zijn ambtsgewaad (de toga, enz.) afleggen.
unroll [ən'roul] *vt.* ontrollen, afrollen; *vi.* zich ontrollen; (*fig.*) zich ontplooien.
unruly [ən'rûli] lastig, weerbarstig, weerspannig; onordelijk.
unsafe [ən'seif] onveilig; onbetrouwbaar; gevaarlijk, gewaagd.
unsatisfied ['ən'sætisfaid] onvoldaan, onbevredigd; ontevreden.
unsavoury [ən'seivəri] onsmakelijk; onaangenaam; onverkwikkelijk.
unsealed [ən'sîld] ongezegeld; ontzegeld.
unsearchable [ən'sə:tʃəbl] *adj.* ondoorgrondelijk, onnaspeurlijk.
unseasonable [ən'sîznəbl] *adj.* ontijdig; ongelegen; ongeschikt; ongepast.
unseat [ən'sît] uit het zadel werpen; (*fig.*) van zijn zetel beroven; (*v. minister*) wippen.
unsectarian [ənsek'têəriən] neutraal.
unsecured ['ənsi'kjuəd] ongedekt, niet verzekerd, niet beveiligd.
unseemly [ən'sîmli] onbetamelijk, ongepast, onvoegzaam; onooglijk, lelijk.
unselfish (ly) ['ən'selfiʃ(li)] *adj.* (*adv.*) onbaatzuchtig, onzelfzuchtig.
unservice [ən'sə:vis] dienstverzuim *o.*
unsettled [ən'setld] weifelend, beslui-

teloos; ongeordend, onzeker; (*v. weer*) onvast, onbestendig; ongedurig; overstuur, van streek, in de war; (*v. rekening*) onbetaald; onuitgemaakt; zonder vaste woonplaats.
unshackle [ən'ʃækl] losmaken, ontkluisteren, vrijmaken.
unshakable [ən'ʃeikəbl] onwankelbaar, onwrikbaar.
unsightly [ən'saitli] onooglijk, lelijk.
unskilful (ly) [ən'skilful(i)] *adj.* (*adv.*) onbekwaam, onbedreven, onervaren.
unslacked ['ən'slækt], **unslaked** ['ən'sleikt] ongelest; (*v. kalk*) ongeblust.
unsociable ['ən'souʃəbl] *adj.* ongezellig.
unsocial ['ən'souʃəl] onmaatschappelijk; eenzelvig.
unsolicited [ənsə'lisitid] ongevraagd.
unsolvable [ən'səlvəbl] onoplosbaar.
unsouled ['ən'sould] zielloos.
unsound ['ən'saund] ongezond; aangetast, aangestoken; ondeugdelijk; onbetrouwbaar; wrak; zwak; niet zuiver (in de leer), niet rechtzinnig.
unspeakable [ən'spîkəbl] *adj.* onuitsprekelijk, onzeglijk; onbeschrijfelijk.
unspecified [ən'spesifaid] niet nader aangeduid, ongespecificeerd.
unspoiled [ən'spoild] onbedorven.
unstable [ən'steibl] onvast, onbestendig wankelbaar.
unstaid [ən'steid] onstandvastig, onbestendig; onbeteugeld.
unstained [ən'steind] onbesmet, onbevlekt; ongekleurd, ongeverfd.
unstamped ['ən'stæm(p)t, 'ən'stæm(p)t] ongestempeld; ongezegeld.
unstatutable ['ən'stætjutəbl] onwettelijk; onwettig.
unsteadfast [ən'stedfâst] onbestendig, onstandvastig, wispelturig.
unsteady [ən'stedi] *adj.* onvast; ongestadig, onbestendig; wispelturig; (*v. leefwijze*) onsolide; *vt.* onvast (enz.) maken.
unstinted [ən'stintid] onbekrompen, onbeperkt.
unstressed [ən'strest] onbetoond, toonloos.
unsubmission [ənsəb'miʃən] ongehoorzaamheid, weerspannigheid *v.*
unsubstantial [ənsəb'stænʃəl] onstoffelijk, onlichamelijk; (*v. gebouw*) onsolide; (*v. voedsel, enz.*) ondegelijk; op niets berustend, zonder vaste ondergrond.
unsuccess ['ənsək'ses] mislukking *v.*
unsuitable [ən'sjûtəbl] ongeschikt; ongepast.
unsure [ən'ʃûə] onvast, onzeker, wisselvallig.
unsuspecting (ly) ['ənsəs'pektiŋ(li)] *adj.* (*adv.*) argeloos, zonder argwaan; geen kwaad vermoedend; zonder erg.
unsustainable [ənsəs'teinəbl] onhoudbaar.
unsweet ['ən'swît] onaangenaam; niet zoet.

untam(e)able [ən'teiməbl] ontembaar.

untamed [ən'teimd] ongetemd, wild.

untaught [ən'tɔːt] onwetend, onge-leerd.

untaxed ['ən'tækst] onbelast, vrij(ge-steld) van belasting; onbeschuldigd.

unteach [ən'tiːtʃ] afleren.

untellable ['ən'teləbl] onuitsprekelijk.

untenable [ən'tinəbl] onhoudbaar; on-verdedigbaar.

untended [ən'tendid] onverzorgd.

unterrified [ən'terifaid] onvervaard, onverschrokken.

unthinkable [ən'ðiŋkəbl] adj. ondenk-baar.

unthinking [ən'ðiŋkiŋ] adj. onnaden-kend, onbezonnen, onbedachtzaam; (v. ogenblik) onbewaakt.

unthorough(ly) [ən'ðərə(li)] adj. (adv.) ondegelijk.

unthriftiness [ən'ðriftinis] verkwis-ting v.

untidiness [ən'taidinis] onordelijkheid, slordigheid v.

untidy [ən'taidi] adj. onordelijk, slordig.

untie ['ən'tai] losmaken, losknopen, ontbinden.

until [ən'til, ən'til] prep. tot.

untimely [ən'taimli] adj. ontijdig; vroegtijdig; ongelegen; voorbarig, te vroeg; adv. vóór zijn tijd, te vroeg; ter ongelegener ure.

untirable [ən'taiərəbl] onvermoeibaar.

untiring(ly) [ən'taiəriŋ(li)] adj. (adv.) onvermoeid.

unto ['əntu] tot, tot aan.

untold ['ən'tould] onverteld, onver-meld; ongeteld; talloos, onnoemelijk veel.

untouched [ən'tətʃt] onaangeraakt; (fig.) onaangedaan, ongeroerd, onbewo-gen.

untoward [ən'touəd] weerbarstig, weer-spannig, eigenzinnig, onhandelbaar; on-aangenaam; ongelukkig, onvoorspoe-dig.

untractable [ən'træktəbl] onhandel-baar.

untrained ['ən'treind] ongeoefend, on-afgericht, ongetraind.

unusual(ly) [ən'jûʒuəl(i)] adj. (adv.) ongewoon.

unutterable [ə'nətərəbl] adj. onuit-sprekelijk, onbeschrijfelijk.

unveil [ən'veil] vt. ontsluieren; ont-hullen; aan het licht brengen; vi. zich ontsluieren; onthuld worden.

unwarranted [ən'wɔrəntid] ongewet-tigd, ongerechtvaardigd; onverant-woord; ongeoorloofd; niet gewaarborgd.

unweakened [ən'wikənd] onverzwakt.

unwearying [ən'wiərliŋ] adj. onver-moeibaar; onvermoeid.

unwell [ən'wel] onwel, onpasselijk, on-gesteld.

unwieldy [ən'wildi] adj. log, zwaar, moeilijk te hanteren.

unwilling [ən'wiliŋ] adj. onwillig; on-

genegen; **be — to,** geen lust (zin) heb-ben om te, niet genegen zijn te.

unwillingly [ən'wiliŋli] adv. onwillig; ongaarne, met tegenzin; tegen wil en dank.

unwillingness ['ənwiliŋnis] onwillig-heid v.

unwind [ən'waind] vt. loswinden; los-wikkelen; vi. losgaan; zich loswinden.

unwise(ly) ['ən'waiz(li)] adj. (adv.) on-wijs, onverstandig.

unwontedness [ən'wountidnis] onge-woonheid, ongewoonte v.; (het) ongewo-ne o.

unworkable [ən'wəːkəbl] onuitvoer-baar; niet te bewerken; niet te exploi-teren.

unworthiness [ən'wəːθinis] onwaar-digheid v.

unyielding [ən'jildiŋ] niet meegevend; onbuigzaam; onverzettelijk, halsstarrig.

unyoke [ən'jouk] vt. het juk afnemen, uitspannen; van het juk bevrijden; vi. het juk afwerpen; (fig.) ophouden met werken.

up [əp] adv. op, naar boven, omhoog, in de hoogte, opwaarts; (v. rivier) ge-zwollen, buiten haar oevers getreden; in rep en roer; verstreken, voorbij; **be —,** op zijn; (v. prijzen) hoger zijn, ge-stegen zijn; (v. tijd) om zijn; (v. spreker) aan het woord zijn, het woord hebben; **be — against,** staan tegenover; in conflict komen met; sb. **—s and downs,** hoog en laag o., terreingolvingen v. mv.; (fig.) vóór- en tegenspoed m., wisselval-ligheden v. mv.; vt. opnemen; vi. op-staan; opspringen.

upbraid [əp'breid] verwijten; verwij-tingen doen.

uphill [əp'hil; 'əphil] adj. opwaarts, bergop; (fig.: v. werk, enz.) moeilijk, zwaar.

uphold [əp'hould] steunen, ondersteu-nen, schragen; handhaven; verdedigen.

upholster [əp'houlstə] bekleden, stof-feren.

upholsterer [əp'houlstərə] stoffeerder, behanger m.

upkeep ['əp'kiːp] (kosten m. mv. van) onderhoud o.

uplift [əp'lift] vt. optillen; opheffen, verheffen; ['əplift] sb. bodemverheffing v.; (v. ziel, enz.) verheffing v.; opwek-king v.

upon [ə'pɔn] prep. zie **on.**

upper ['əpə] adj. bovenste, boven—, opper—; sb. bovenleer o.; bovenkaak v.; (Am.) slobkous v.

upright ['əp'rait; 'əprait] adj. recht, rechtopstaand, rechtstandig; (fig.) op-recht, rechtschapen; adv. rechtop, overeind; sb. ['əprait] stijl, post m.; stander m.; (fam.) pianino v.

uprightness ['əpraitnis] verticale stand m.; oprechtheid, rechtschapenheid v.

uproar ['əproː] lawaai, rumoer, tumult o., herrie v.

uproot [ɒp'rût] ontwortelen.
upset [ɒp'set] vt. omverwerpen, omgooien; (fig.) ten val brengen; (v. plannen) verijdelen, in de war sturen; van streek maken, overstuur maken; (v. testament) vernietigen; be —, omslaan, omvallen; van streek zijn; sb. omkanteling v., het omslaan o.; (v. gezag, enz.) omverwerping v.; verwarring, ontsteltenis v.; adj. ['ɒpset] — price, inzet m.
upside ['ɒpsaid] bovenzijde v., bovenkant m.; — down, 't onderste boven; op zijn kop.
upstairs ['ɒp'stêəz] adv. de trap op, naar boven, boven; ['ɒpstêəz] adj. boven—.
upstart ['ɒpstât] sb. parvenu m.; (Pl.) herfsttijloos v.; adj. parvenuachtig.
up-stream ['ɒp'strîm] adv. stroomopwaarts; ['ɒpstrîm] adj. tegen de stroom ingaand, tegen de stroom oproeiend; aan de bovenstroom gelegen.
upwards ['ɒpwədz] adv. opwaarts, naar boven.
urban ['ə:bən] adj. stedelijk, stads—.
urge [ədʒ] vt. aandrijven, voortdrijven; aanzetten, aansporen; dringend verzoeken; (v. argument, enz.) aanvoeren; vi. aandringen; dringen; sb. aandrang, prikkel m.
urgency ['ədʒənsi] urgentie, dringende noodzakelijkheid v.; urgentieverklaring v.; drang, aandrang m.
urinal ['jûərinəl] urineglas o.; urinoir o.
urinate ['jûərineit] urineren.
urn [ə:n] urn, vaas v.; lijkbus v.; kan, kruik v.
usable ['jûzəbl] adj. bruikbaar.
usage ['jûzidʒ] gebruik o., gewoonte v.
use [jûs] sb. gebruik o.; gewoonte v.; ritueel o.; aanwending, toepassing v.;
nut o.; for — of, ten gebruike van; out of —, buiten gebruik; [jûz] vt. gebruiken, gebruik maken van; aanwenden; behandelen, bejegenen; (doen) gewennen aan; — oneself, zich gedragen.
useful ['jûsful] adj. nuttig, bruikbaar; (sl.) knap, bedreven (at, in).
useless ['jûslis] adj. nutteloos; (sl.) a) onlekker; b) tot niets nut.
usher ['əʃə] sb. portier m.; deurwaarder m.; ceremoniemeester m.; suppoost m.; (ong.) ondermeester m.; bruidsjonker, paranimf m.; vt. binnenleiden, binnenbrengen.
usual ['jûzuəl] adj. gebruikelijk, gewoon.
usufruct ['jûsjufrəkt] sb. vruchtgebruik o.; vt. in vruchtgebruik hebben.
usurer ['jûʒərə] woekeraar m.
usurious (ly) [ju'zjûəriəs(li)] adj. (adv.) woekerend, woekerachtig, woeker—.
usurp [ju'zə:p] zich wederrechtelijk toeëigenen; (v. troon) overweldigen.
usurper [ju'zə:pə] overweldiger, usurpator m.
usury ['jûzəri] woeker m., woekerrente v.
utility [ju'tiliti] nut o., nuttigheid, bruikbaarheid v.
utilize ['jûtilaiz] benutten, nuttig aanwenden, goed gebruiken.
utmost ['ɒtmoust] adj. uiterste, hoogste.
utter ['ɒtə] adj. algeheel, volkomen, volstrekt, volslagen; uiterst; vt. uiten, uitdrukken, uitspreken; (v. bankpapier) uitgeven, in omloop brengen.
utterance ['ɒtərəns] uiting v.; uitspraak v.; uitlating v.; spreektrant m., wijze van uitdrukken v.; voordracht v.
utterly ['ɒtəli] adv. volkomen, volstrekt, volslagen.
uvula ['jûvjulə] huig v.

V

vacancy ['veikənsi] ledigheid, onbezetheid v., het onbezet zijn o.; leegte, ledige ruimte v.; leemte, gaping v., hiaat o.; openstaande betrekking, vacature v.
vacant ['veikənt] vacant, openstaand, onbezet; (v. huis, enz.) leegstaand, onbewoond; (v. blik) wezenloos; (v. rivieren, enz.) ijsvrij; leeghoofdig; gedachteloos; ijl.
vacate [və'keit] vt. (v. plaats) ontruimen; (v. betrekking) neerleggen; (v. troon) afstand doen van; (recht) nietig verklaren, vernietigen; vi. wegtrekken, er uittrekken (uit huis); (Am.) vrijaf nemen, vakantie nemen.
vaccinate ['væksineit] inenten, vaccineren.
vaccination act, vaccination law [væksi'neiʃənækt, —lo:] wet op de vaccinatie v.
vaccinia [væk'siniə] koepokken v. mv.
vacillate ['væsileit] schommelen, wankelen; weifelen, besluiteloos zijn.
vacillating (ly) ['væsileitin(li)] adj. (adv.) schommelend, wankelend; weifelend, besluiteloos.
vacillation [væsi'leiʃən] schommeling, wankeling v.; weifeling, besluiteloosheid v.
vacuity [væ'kjûiti] ledige ruimte, leegte, ledigheid v.; wezenloosheid, gedachteloosheid v.; afwezigheid v.
vacuous ['vækjuəs] wezenloos, nietszeggend, onbenullig; leeg, leeghoofdig, leeg, ijl.
vacuum ['vækjuəm] sb. (lucht)ledige ruimte v.; vt. (fam.) met stofzuiger schoonmaken.
vagabond ['vægəbənd] adj. zwervend, rondzwervend; vagebonderend, heen en weer trekkend; boefachtig, schooierig; sb. zwerver m.; vagebond, landloper

m.; boef, schelm, schooier *m.*; *vi.* zwerven, rondzwerven; vagebonderen.

vagrant ['veigrənt] *adj.* zwervend, rondzwervend, rondtrekkend; (*fig.*) afdwalend; ongestadig, ongedurig; wild groeiend; *sb.* zwerver, landloper *m.*

vague [veig] onbepaald, onbestemd; vaag.

vail [veil] *sb.* sluier *m.*; *vt.* sluieren, bedekken; (*v. vlag*) strijken, neerlaten; (*v. ogen*) neerslaan; (*v. hoed*) afnemen; *vi.* zich onderwerpen, toegeven (*to*, aan); hulde brengen (*to*, aan).

vain [vein] ijdel; vergeefs, nutteloos.

vainglory ['vein'glo:ri] ijdelheid *v.*; blufferigheid *v.*

vale [veil] (*dicht.*) dal *o.*, vallei *v.*

valet ['vælit, 'vælei] *sb.* bediende, kamerdienaar, lijfknecht *m.*; *vi.* als lijfknecht dienen.

valiant (ly) ['væljənt (li)] *adj.* (*adv.*) dapper, heldhaftig, moedig.

valid ['vælid] (*v. argument, enz.*) deugdelijk; (*recht*) geldig, rechtsgeldig, van kracht; gezond (van lijf en leden).

validation [væli'deiʃən] bevestiging, bekrachtiging *v.*; geldigverklaring *v.*

validity [və'liditi] deugdelijkheid *v.*; geldigheid, rechtsgeldigheid *v.*

Valkyrie ['vælkiri, væl'kîəri] Walkure *v.*

valley ['væli] dal *o.*, vallei *v.*; (*v. dak*) kiel *v.*

valorous (ly) ['vælərəs(li)] *adj.* (*adv.*) dapper, moedig, kloekmoedig, koen.

valour ['vælə] dapperheid *v.*, moed *m.*, kloekmoedigheid, koenheid *v.*

valuable ['væljuəbl] *adj.* waardevol, van grote waarde, kostbaar; *sb.* —s, zaken van waarde, kostbaarheden *v. mv.*

valuation [vælju'eiʃən] schatting, taxatie, waardering *v.*; geschatte waarde *v.*; taxatieprijs *m.*

valuator ['væljueitə] schatter, taxateur *m.*

value ['væljû] *sb.* waarde *v.*, prijs *m.*; (*v. schilderij*) lichtverdeling *v.*, effect *o.*; *vt.* schatten, taxeren, waarderen; op prijs stellen; *vr.* — **oneself for** (**on, upon**) **a thing,** zich op iets laten voorstaan; *vi.* — **on a person,** (*H.*) op iem. trekken, op iem. disponeren.

valueless ['væljûlis] waardeloos.

valuer ['væljûə] schatter, taxateur *m.*

valve [vælv] *sb.* klep *v.*, ventiel *o.*; (*v. deur*) vleugel *m.*; (*v. schelp*) schaal *v.*; (radio)lamp *v.*; *vt.* (*v. gas*) uitlaten (door klep).

vamp [væmp] *sb.* bovenleer, overleer *o.*; voorstuk *o.*; lapwerk *o.*; (*muz.*) geïmproviseerd accompagnement *o.*; *vt.* van nieuw bovenleer (nieuwe voorschoenen) voorzien; lappen, oplappen; (*fig.*) in elkaar flansen, verzinnen; *vi.* (een accompagnement) improviseren; (*dial., sl.*) lopen, stappen.

vamp [væmp] (*Am.*) (vrouwelijke) vampier *v.*

vampire ['væmpaiə] vampier *m.*; (*fig.*) bloedzuiger, uitzuiger *m.*

van [væn] *sb.* wan *v.*; vleugel *m.*, wiek *v.*; molenwiek *v.*; (*mil., sch.*) voorhoede *v.*; (*fig.*) de eerste gelederen *o. mv.*, de pioniers *m. mv.*, de voormannen *m. mv.*; (*v. optocht, enz.*) kop *m.*, spits *v.*; *vt.* wannen.

van [væn] *sb.* verhuiswagen, meubelwagen *m.*; (*v. trein*) goederenwagen *m.*; bestelwagen *m.*; gevangenwagen *m.*; *vt.* in een wagen vervoeren.

vandalism ['vændəlizm] vandalisme *o.*, vernielzucht *v.*

vane [vein] weerhaan *m.*, windvaan *v.*; molenwiek *v.*; (*v. weer*) slag *v.*, baard *m.*; (*v. schroef, enz.*) blad *o.*; (*v. kwadrant, nivelleerstok, enz.*) vizier *o.*

vanguard ['vængâd] voorhoede, spits *v.*

vanilla [və'nilə] vanille *v.*

vanish ['væniʃ] *vi.* verdwijnen; wegsterven; *vt.* laten (doen) verdwijnen.

vanity ['væniti] ijdelheid *v.*; vruchteloosheid, nietigheid *v.*

vanquish ['væŋkwiʃ] overwinnen; (*v. argumenten, enz.*) weerleggen.

vapid ['væpid] verschaald, vervlogen; flauw, geesteloos, onbenullig; laf.

vaporizable ['veipəraizəbl] verdampbaar.

vaporizer ['veipəraizə] vaporisator, verstuiver *m.*

vaporous (ly) ['veipərəs(li)] *adj.* (*adv.*) dampig, nevelig; (*fig.*) vluchtig, ijl, onbeduidend.

vapour ['veipə] *sb.* damp, wasem *m.*; (*fig.*) ijdele waan *m.*; *vi.* dampen, wasemen; bluffen, snoeven, pochen.

variable ['vêəriəbl] *adj.* veranderlijk; onbestendig, ongestadig, ongedurig; *sb.* veranderlijke grootheid *v.*

variance ['vêəriəns] verschil *o.*, afwijking *v.*; tegenspraak, tegenstrijdigheid *v.*; geschil *o.*, onenigheid *v.*; verschil van mening *o.*; **be at** —, het oneens zijn; in onmin zijn; in strijd zijn, in tegenspraak zijn (**with,** met).

variant ['vêəriənt] *adj.* afwijkend, verschillend; veranderlijk; afwisselend; *sb.* variant *v.*

variation [vêəri'eiʃən] verandering *v.*; afwisseling *v.*; afwijking *v.*; verscheidenheid *v.*; (*Pl.*) variëteit *v.*

varicose [væri'kous] spatader—.

variegation [vêəri'geiʃən] afwisseling, verscheidenheid *v.*; veelkleurigheid, kleurschakering *v.*

variety [və'raiiti] verscheidenheid *v.*; afwisseling *v.*; verandering *v.*; soort, variëteit *v.*

variety-store [və'raiitisto:ə] (*Am.*) bazaar *m.*

various (ly) ['vêəriəs(li)] *adj.* (*adv.*) verscheiden, afwisselend, vol verscheidenheid; verschillend, onderscheiden, van elkaar afwijkend.

varix ['vêəriks] spatader, *v.*

varmint ['vâmint] (pop.) deugniet! rakker!

varnish ['vâniʃ] sb. vernis, lak, glazuur o.; (fig.) vernisje o.; schijn m.; vt. vernissen, lakken, verlakken, verglazen; (fig.) bemantelen, verbloemen; opsmukken.

varsity ['vâsiti] (fam.) universiteit v.

vary ['vêəri] vt. veranderen, wijzigen, verandering brengen in; afwisselen, variëren; (muz.) variaties maken op; vi. afwijken, verschillen van; afwisselen, variëren.

vase [vâz, vo:z] vaas, pul v.; vat o.; (Pl.) bloemkelk m.

vassal ['væsəl] (gesch.) leenman, vazal m.; (fig.) handlanger, knecht, slaaf m.

vast [vâst] adj. uitgestrekt, onmetelijk; ontzaglijk; omvangrijk; (fam.) kolossaal; veelomvattend; sb. wijde uitgestrektheid, uitgestrekte vlakte, onmetelijkheid v.

vat [væt] sb. vat o., kuip v.; vt. in een vat doen; (v. wijn, enz.) mengen.

Vatican ['vætikən] Vaticaan o.

vault [vo:lt] sb. gewelf, verwulf o.; kelder m.; sprong m.; vt. verwelven, overwelven; springen (over).

vaulter ['vo:ltə] springer, acrobaat m.

vaulting-horse ['vo:ltiŋho:s] (in gymnastiek) (spring)paard o.

vaunter ['vo:ntə] pocher, bluffer, snoever m.

veal [vil] kalfsvlees o.

veer [viə] vi. vieren; (v. wind) draaien, omlopen; uitschieten, ruimen; vt. vieren; doen draaien; sb. wending v., draai m.

vegetable ['vedʒitəbl] adj. plantaardig, planten—; sb. plant v., gewas o.; groente v.

vegetal ['vedʒitəl] adj. plantaardig, planten—; vegetatief, groei—; sb. plant v., gewas o.

vegetarian [vedʒi'têəriən] vegetariër m.

vegetation [vedʒi'teiʃən] groei, wasdom m.; plantengroei m.; plantenrijk o., plantenwereld v.; uitwas o., woekering, vegetatie v.; het vegeteren, plantenleven o.

vehement (ly) ['viimənt(li)] adj. (adv.) hevig, heftig, onstuimig, driftig.

vehicle ['viikl] voertuig, rijtuig o.; (v. geluid, enz.) geleider m.; voertaal v.; (gen.) oplosmiddel; bindmiddel o.

veil [veil] sb. sluier m.; volle v.; (v. tempel) voorhang m.; zachte verhemelte o.; (fig.) dekmantel m., mom, masker o.; vt. sluieren, met een sluier bedekken; (fig.) bemantelen, bewimpelen.

vein [vein] sb. ader v.; stemming, luim v.; (v. karakter) trek m.; vt. aderen; marmeren.

vellum ['veləm] velijn, kalfsperkamento.

velocity [vi'lositi] snelheid v.

velvet ['velvit] sb. fluweel o.; winst v., voordeel o.; adj. fluwelen.

venal ['vinəl] omkoopbaar, te koop, veil; (soms:) aderlijk.

veneer [vi'niə] vt. fineren, met fineerhout beleggen; (fig.) een vernisje geven; sb. fineerhout o.; (fig.) vernisje o.

venerable ['venərəbl] eerbiedwaardig, eerwaardig, achtbaar.

venerate ['venəreit] (diep) vereren.

veneration [venə'reiʃən] (diepe) verering v.

Venetian [vi'niʃən] adj. Venetiaans; sb. Venetiaan m.; Venetiaanse v.; jaloezie v.

vengeance ['ven(d)ʒəns] wraak v.

venial ['viniəl] vergeeflijk.

venison ['ven(i)zn] wildbraad o.

venom ['venəm] vergif, venijn o.

venomous (ly) ['venəməs(li)] adj. (adv.) vergiftig, venijnig; (fig.) venijnig.

vent [vent] sb. opening v., luchtgat o.; (v. jas) split o.; (tn.: v. kogel, enz.) speelruimte v.; (v. vis, vogel, enz.) anus m.; (v. vuurwapen) zundgat o.; vt. lucht geven aan, uiting geven aan, uiten; verkondigen, ruchtbaar maken.

ventil ['ventil] (muz.: v. orgel) ventiel o., klep v.

ventilate ['ventileit] ventileren, luchten, verse lucht toevoeren; (fig.) ruchtbaar maken; (v. grieven, enz.) luchten.

ventilator ['ventileitə] ventilator m.

ventriloquist [ven'triləkwist] buikspreker m.

venture ['ventʃə] sb. waagstuk, waagspel o.; gewaagde onderneming v.; risico o.; speculatie v.; op speculatie verzonden goederen o. mv.; vt. wagen; op het spel zetten; (H.) op speculatie verzenden (verschepen); vi. zich wagen; het erop wagen.

venturer ['ventʃərə] waaghals; avonturier m.

veracious (ly) [vi'reiʃəs(li)] adj. (adv.) waarheidlievend; waar, waarachtig.

veranda (h) [və'rændə] veranda v.

verb [və:b] werkwoord o.

verbal ['və:bəl] adj. in woorden uitgedrukt; slechts in woorden bestaande; woordelijk, letterlijk; mondeling; werkwoordelijk; sb. zelfstandig gebruikt werkwoord, verbaal substantief o.

verbiage ['və:biidʒ] woordenvloed, omhaal van woorden m., breedsprakigheid v.

verbose [və:'bous] woordenrijk, breedsprakig.

verbosity [və:'bositi] woordenrijkheid, breedsprakigheid v.

verdant ['və:dənt] groen.

verdict ['və:dikt] uitspraak (van de jury) v.; (fig.) oordeel, vonnis o., beslissing v.

verdure ['və:djə] groen, gebladerte o.; groenheid v.

verge [və:dʒ] sb. roede v., staf m.; rand, zoom m.; grasrand m.; vi. hellen (naar); neigen (naar); grenzen (aan).

verger ['və:dʒə] stafdrager, pedel m.; kerkeknecht m.

verify ['verifai] waar maken, staven, bewijzen; bewaarheiden; bekrachtigen;

nazien, verifiëren; (*v. belofte, voorwaarde*) vervullen.
vermicelli [və:mi′seli] vermicelli *v*.
vermilion [və′miljən] *sb.* vermiljoen *o.*; *adj.* vermiljoen (rood); *vt.* vermiljoenrood verven (kleuren).
vermin-killer [′və:minkilə] insektenpoeder *o.*
vernacular [və′nækjulə] *adj.* inlands, inheems; de landstaal sprekend; *sb.* landstaal, moedertaal *v*.
versatile [′vəsətail] veranderlijk, onstandvastig, ongestadig; (*v. talent*) veelzijdig; draaibaar.
versatility [və:sə′tiliti] veranderlijkheid, onstandvastigheid *v.*; veelzijdigheid *v*.
verse [və:s] *sb.* vers *o.*, versregel *m.*; strofe *v.*, couplet *o.*; poëzie *v.*; *vi.* dichten, verzen maken; *vt.* bezingen (in verzen); berijmen.
versificator [′və:sifikeitə], **versifier** [′və:sifaiə] verzenmaker; rijmelaar *m*.
version [′və:ʃən] overzetting, vertaling *v.*; (*v. zaak*) verklaring, voorstelling, lezing *v*.
versus [′və:səs] (*recht*) tegen.
vertebra [′və:tibrə] wervel *m.*, wervelbeen *o.* (*meerv.* **vertebrae**).
vertex [′və:təks] hoogste punt, zenit *o.*; toppunt *o*.
vertical [′və:tikl] *adj.* loodrecht, rechtstandig, verticaal; (*v. druk*) opwaarts; **— angle,** tophoek; tegenoverstaande hoek; *sb.* loodlijn *v.*; loodrechte stand *m.*; toppuntshoek *m*.
vertiginous [və:′tidʒinəs] draaierig, duizelig; duizelingwekkend; (*fig.*) onbestendig, wispelturig.
very [′veri] *adj.* waar, werkelijk, echt; (*voor vergrotende trap*) aller—; *adv.* zeer, erg.
vesicant [′vesikənt], **vesicatory** [′vesikeitəri] *adj.* blaartrekkend; *sb.* blaartrekkend middel *o*.
vesper [′vespə] avondster *v.*; (*dicht.*) avond *m.*; **—s,** vesper *v*.
vespiary [′vespiəri] wespennest *o*.
vessel [′vesəl] vat *o.*; (*sch.*) vaartuig, schip *o*.
vest [vest] *sb.* borstrok *m.*; vest, vestje *o.* (v. japon); (*dicht.*) dracht *v.*; kleed, gewaad *o.*; *vt.* kleden; bekleden (**with,** met); (*v. geld*) beleggen; *vi.* **— in,** (*v. macht*) berusten bij.
vestibule [′vestibjûl] vestibule *v.*, voorhuis, portaal *o.*; (*v. oor*) voorhof *o. & m.*; (*v. spoorwagen*) harmonika *v*.
vestige [′vestidʒ] spoor; overblijfsel *o*.
veteran [′vetərən] *sb.* oudgediende, oudsoldaat, oudstrijder *m.*; *adj.* oudgediend; beproefd, ervaren.
veterinary [′vetərinəri] veeartsenij—, veeartsenijkundig.
vex [veks] *vt.* kwellen, plagen, tergen; hinderen, lastig vallen; ergeren; verontrusten; *vr.* **— oneself,** tobben.

vexation [vek′seiʃən] kwelling, plagerij *v.*; ergernis *v*.
vexatious(ly) [vek′seiʃəs(li)] *adj.* (*adv.*) lastig, hinderlijk; kwellend, plagerig; ergerlijk.
via [′vaiə] *sb.* weg *m.*; (*H.: v. wissel*) exemplaar *o.*; *prep.* via, over.
viaduct [′vaiədəkt] viaduct *o*.
viand [′vaiənd] spijs *v.*, voedsel *o.*; gerecht *o.*; **—s,** levensmiddelen *o. mv.*, voedsel *o*.
vibrate [vai′breit] *vi.* trillen, vibreren; slingeren, schommelen; *vt.* doen slingeren (schommelen; trillen).
vibration [vai′breiʃən] trilling *v.*; slingering, schommeling *v*.
vicar [′vikə] plaatsvervanger, vicaris *m.*; predikant, dominee *m.*; (*kath.*) kapelaan *m*.
vice [vais] ondeugd *v.*; gebrek *o.*, fout *v.*; (*v. paard, enz.*) kuur *v*.
vice [vais] *sb.* schroef, bankschroef *v.*; *vt.* vastzetten, vastklemmen.
vice [vais] *adj.* onder—; vervangend, plaatsvervangend.
vice [′vaisi] *prep.* in plaats van.
vice-chairman [′vais′tʃêəmən] ondervoorzitter, vice-president *m*.
viceroy [′vaisrɔi] onderkoning *m*.
vicinage [′visinidʒ] buurt, nabijheid *v.*; nabuurschap *v*.
vicinity [vi′siniti] *zie* **vicinage.**
vicious(ly) [′viʃəs(li)] *adj.* (*adv.*) slecht, verdorven, met ondeugden behept; verkeerd; boosaardig, nijdig; (*v. hond, enz.*) vals.
vicissitude [vi′sisitjûd] wisselvalligheid, wederwaardigheid *v.*; (soms:) afwisseling *v*.
victim [′viktim] slachtoffer *o.*; dupe *m. & v*.
victorious [vik′to:riəs] *adj.* overwinnend, zegevierend.
victory [′viktəri] overwinning, zegepraal *v*.
victual [′vitl] *sb.* voedsel *o.*; **—s,** levensmiddelen *o. mv.*; mondbehoeften *v. mv.*; *vt.* van levensmiddelen (mondbehoeften) voorzien, provianderen.
view [vjû] *sb.* gezicht, uitzicht *o.*; voorkomen *o.*; aanschouwing *v.*; mening *v.*, oordeel *o.* (over); kijk *m.* (op); bedoeling *v.*, oogmerk *o.*; vooruitzicht *o.*, verwachting *v.*; kiekje *o.*; blik *m.*; overzicht *o*.
view-point [′vjûpɔint] uitzichtpunt *o.*; gezichtspunt, standpunt *o*.
vigilant(ly) [′vidʒilənt(li)] *adj.* (*adv.*) waakzaam.
vigorous(ly) [′vigərəs(li)] *adj.* (*adv.*) krachtig, sterk, flink; (*fig.: v. stijl*) gespierd.
vile [vail] laag, gemeen, verachtelijk; snood, laaghartig; (*v. weer*) slecht, gemeen.
vilify [′vilifai] lasteren, belasteren; kwaadspreken; honen.
village [′vilidʒ] dorp *o*.

villager ['vilidʒə] dorpsbewoner, dorpeling m.
villain ['vilin] schelm, schurk m.; (in toneelstuk, roman) verrader, booswicht m.
vindictive(ly) [vin'diktiv(li)] adj. (adv.) wraakgierig, wraakzuchtig.
vindictiveness [vin'diktivnis] wraakgierigheid, wraakzucht v.
vine [vain] wijnstok; wijngaard m.; klimplant v.
vine-culture ['vainkəltʃə] wijnbouw m.
vine-dresser ['vaindresə] wijngaardenier m.
vinegar ['vinigə] sb. azijn m.; adj. zuur; vt. in het zuur leggen, in azijn inmaken; verzuren, zuur maken.
vineyard ['vinjəd, 'vinjâd] wijngaard m.
vinous ['vainəs] wijnachtig; wijn—; aan wijn verslaafd; wijnkleurig.
vintage ['vintidʒ] wijnoogst m.; (wijn)gewas o., jaargang m. (v. wijn).
violable ['vaiələbl] schendbaar.
violate ['vaiəleit] (v. eed, belofte) breken; (v. wet) overtreden, schenden; (v. tempel) ontwijden; onteren, verkrachten; geweld aandoen.
violation [vaiə'leiʃən] verbreking v.; overtreding, schending v.; ontering, verkrachting v.
violence ['vaiələns] geweld o., gewelddadigheid v.; geweldpleging v.; hevigheid; heftigheid v.; (v. woorden, enz.) verdraaiing v.
violent ['vaiələnt] hevig, heftig; gewelddig, krachtig; gewelddadig; (v. kleuren) hel.
violet ['vaiəlit] sb. (Pl.) viooltje o.; violet o.; adj. paars, violet(kleurig).
violin [vaiə'lin] viool v.
violinist [vaiə'linist] violist, vioolspeler m.
viper ['vaipə] adder v.; (fig.) slang v., serpent o.
viperous ['vaipərəs] adderachtig; giftig, venijnig.
virago [vi'reigou] helleveeg, feeks v., manwijf o.
virgin ['və:dʒin] sb. maagd v.; maagdenpeer v.; adj. maagdelijk, onbevlekt, zuiver; (v. metaal) gedegen; (v. honig) ongepijnd.
virginal ['və:dʒinl] adj. maagdelijk; (fig.) rein, onbevlekt.
virtue ['və:tjû] deugd v.; deugdzaamheid v.; kracht; geneeskracht v.
virtuoso [və:tju'ouzou] virtuoos m.; kunstkenner, kunstminnaar m.
virtuous(ly) ['və:tjuəs(li)] adj. (adv.) deugdzaam.
visa ['vîzə] sb. visum o.; vt. viseren, voor gezien tekenen.
viscous ['viskəs] kleverig, lijmerig, taai.
visibility [vizi'biliti] zichtbaarheid v.; (op zee) zicht o.
visible ['vizibl] adj. zichtbaar; voor het oog waarneembaar; sb. (meestal

mv.) —s, zichtbare dingen o. mv.
vision ['viʒən] sb. visioen o., verschijning v., droombeeld o.; gezicht, het zien o.: vt. in een droom zien; voor ogen toveren.
visit ['vizit] vt. bezoeken; bezoeken, beproeven, teisteren; visiteren, inspecteren; bezichtigen; vi. bezoeken afleggen; huisbezoek doen; sb. bezoek o.; huisbezoek o.; op bezoek; te logeren.
visitation [vizi'teiʃən] bezoek o.; ziekenbezoek o.; huisbezoek o.; beproeving, bezoeking v.; visitatie v.
visiting-card ['vizitiŋkâd] visitekaartje o.
visitor ['vizitə] bezoeker; logé m.; inspecteur m.
visor ['vaizə] (v. helm) klep v., vizier o.; (Am.: v. pet) klep v.; (fig.) mom v., masker o.
vista ['vistə] uitzicht, vergezicht o.; verschiet o.; laan v.
vital ['vaitəl] adj. vitaal, levens—; levensgevaarlijk; essentieel, gebiedend noodzakelijk; sb. (meestal mv.) edele delen o. mv.; het essentiële o.
vitiate ['viʃieit] (v. lucht, bloed, enz.) bederven; (v. waarheid) vervalsen; (v. contract, verkiezing) ongeldig maken; besmetten, verontreinigen.
vitrify ['vitrifai] vt. verglazen, tot glas maken; vi. verglazen, tot glas worden.
vitrine ['vitrin] uitstalkast v.
vitriol ['vitriəl] vitriool v. & o., zwavelzuur o.
vivid ['vivid] adj. levendig; helder.
vivisection [vivi'sekʃən] vivisectie, ontleding v. van levende dieren.
vixen ['viksn] (Dk.) wijfjesvos v.; (fig.) feeks, helleveeg v.
viz [viz] namelijk, te weten.
vizier [vi'zîə] vizier m.
vocabulary [və'kæbjuləri] woordenlijst v.; woordenschat m.
vocalist [vou'kəlist] zanger m.; zangeres v.
vocation [vou'keiʃən] roeping v.; beroep o.
voice [vois] sb. stem v.; geluid o.; spraak v.; stemhebbende klank m.; (fig.) spreekbuis v.; vt. uiten; uitdrukking geven aan; vertolken; (klankl.) stemhebbend maken; (muz.: v. orgel) stemmen.
void [void] adj. ledig; (v. plaats, enz.) onbezet, vacant; (v. verkiezing, enz.) nietig, ongeldig; sb. leegte, ledige ruimte v.; leemte v.; vt. ledigen, ruimen; ontlasten, lozen; (recht) vernietigen, ongeldig maken, nietig (ongeldig) verklaren.
volatile ['volətail] vluchtig, vervliegend (fig.) wuft; wispelturig.
volatilize [vo'lætilaiz] vt. vluchtig maken, vervluchtigen, doen vervliegen; vi. vluchtig worden, vervliegen.
volcano [vol'keinou] vulkaan m.
volley ['voli] sb. salvo o.; (fig.: v. woorden, enz.) stroom m.; (v. pijlen, enz.)

regen *m.*; (*cricket, tennis*) terugslag *m.*
vóór de bal stuit; *vt.* een salvo afvuren;
(*fig.*) uitbraken.
voltage ['voultidʒ] (*el.*) spanning,
stroomspanning *v.*
voluble ['vɔljubl] rad van tong, woordenrijk; rollend; beweeglijk, vlug.
volume ['vɔljum] deel, boekdeel, *o.*;
omvang *m.*, grootte *v.*; massa *v.*
voluminous [və'ljûminəs] uit vele
boekdelen bestaande; omvangrijk, lijvig.
voluntary ['vɔləntəri] *adj.* vrijwillig,
vrij; moedwillig; opzettelijk; willekeurig; *sb.* (*muz.: v. orgelspel*) fantasie
v., voorspel, naspel *o.*; vrijwilliger *m.*
volunteer [vɔlən'tîə] *sb.* vrijwilliger
m.; *adj.* vrijwillig, vrijwilligers—; *vt.*
vrijwillig op zich nemen; (*v. opmerking,
verklaring, enz.*) geven, opperen; *ri.*
(*mil.*) vrijwillig dienstnemen; zich aanbieden.
voluptuary [və'ləptjuəri] *adj.* wellustig; *sb.* wellusteling *m.*
voluptuous(ly) [və'ləptjuəs(li)] *adj.*
(*adv.*) wellustig; weelderig.
voluptuousness [və'ləptjuəsnis] wellust *m.*
vomit ['vɔmit] *vt.* & *vi.* braken, overgeven; uitbraken; *sb.* braaksel; uitbraaksel *o.*; braakmiddel *o.*
vomitory ['vɔmitəri] *adj.* braakwekkend; *sb.* braakmiddel *o.*
voracious(ly) [və'reiʃəs(li)] *adj.* (*adv.*)
gulzig, vraatzuchtig.
voracity [və'ræsiti] gulzigheid, vraatzucht *v.*
vortex ['vo:teks] (*mv.: vortices*) werveling, dwarreling *v.*; draaikolk *v.*,
maalstroom *m.*; wervelwind *m.*

votary ['voutəri] *sb.* aanhanger, volgeling *m.*; vereerder, aanbidder *m.*; *adj.*
— *church,* votiefkerk.
vote [vout] *sb.* stem *v.*; stemming *v.*;
stembriefje *o.*; stemrecht *o.*; *vt.* stemmen voor (op); bij stemming verkiezen
(aannemen, enz.); *vi.* stemmen; tot
stemming overgaan.
voter ['voutə] kiezer, stemgerechtigde *m.*
voting-paper ['voutiŋpeipə] stembiljet *o.*
vouch [vautʃ] *vt.* getuigen, bevestigen,
staven; bewijzen, met bewijzen staven,
de bewijsstukken overleggen bij; *vi.*
— *for,* instaan voor, borg staan voor.
vouchsafe [vautʃ'seif] zich verwaardigen; (genadig) toestaan.
vow [vau] *sb.* eed *m.*, belofte *v.*; gelofte
v.; *vt.* zweren, (plechtig) beloven; toewijden, wijden aan; *vi.* een gelofte doen.
vowel ['vauəl] *sb.* klinker *m.*; klinkerteken *o.*; *vt.* van vocaaltekens voorzien.
voyage ['vɔiidʒ] *sb.* reis, zeereis, luchtreis *v.*; *vt.* bereizen, bevaren; *vi.* reizen.
voyager ['vɔiidʒə] (zee)reiziger *m.*;
ontdekkingsreiziger *m.*
vulgar ['vʌlgə] *adj.* gemeen, plat, grof;
gewoon, alledaags algemeen; *sb. the —,*
het gemeen *o.*; de grote hoop *m.*
vulgarian [vʌl'gêəriən] parvenu, proleet, ordinaire vent *m.*
vulgarism ['vʌlgərizm] platte uitdrukking *v.* platheid *v.*
vulgarity [vʌl'gæriti] platheid, grofheid *v.*
vulture ['vʌltʃə] (*Dk.*) gier *m.*; (*fig.*)
grijpgier *m.*

W

wad [wɔd] *sb.* (*v. papier, watten, enz.*)
prop *v.*; (*v. bankbiljetten*) rolletje, pakje
o.; vulsel *o.*; *vt.* tot een prop maken;
watteren, met watten voeren; opvullen.
wadable ['weidəbl] *adj.* doorwaadbaar.
waddle ['wɔdl] *vi.* schommelen, waggelen; *sb.* schommelende (waggelende)
gang, schommelgang *m.*
wade [weid] *vi.* waden; — *through,*
doorwaden; (*fig.*) doorworstelen; *vt.*
laten waden; doorwaden; *sb.* het
waden *o.*
wader ['weidə] wader *m.*; (*Dk.*) waadvogel *m.*; —*s,* waterlaarzen *v. mv.*
wafer ['weifə] *sb.* wafeltje *o.*; ouwel *m.*;
vt. met een ouwel dichtmaken.
wafer-iron ['weifəraiən], **wafertongs** ['weifətɔŋz] wafelijzer *o.*
waffle ['wɔfl] (*Am.*) wafel *v.*
wag [wæg] grappenmaker, spotvogel *m.*
wag [wæg] *vt.* schudden; kwispelen
met; heen en weer bewegen; verroeren;

vi. zich bewegen, in beweging zijn;
schommelen, heen en weer gaan; schudden; kwispelen; *sb.* schudding *v.*;
kwispeling, kwispelende beweging *v.*
wage [weidʒ] *sb.* loon, arbeidsloon *o.*;
huur *v.*; (*mil.*) soldij *v.*; —*s,* loon; *vt.*
— *battle,* slag leveren; — *war,* oorlog
voeren.
wage-earner ['weidʒə:nə] loontrekker
m.; kostwinner *m.*
wager ['weidʒə] *sb.* weddenschap *v.*;
waagstuk *o.*; *vt.* wedden om, verwedden; wedden met; op het spel zetten; *vi.*
wedden.
wage-rate ['weidʒreit] loonstandaard *m.*
wages-sheet ['weidʒizʃit] loonstaat *m.*,
loonlijst *v.*
waggish ['wægiʃ] *adj.* schalks, snaaks,
guitig, ondeugend.
waggon ['wægən] *sb.* vrachtwagen; boerenwagen *m.*; wagon, goederenwagon
m.; dientafeltje *o.*; *the W—,* (*sterr.*) de

Grote Beer; *vt.* (*Am.*) in een wagen vervoeren.

wagtail ['wægteil] (*Dk.*) kwikstaartje *o.*; lichtekooi *v.*

waif [weif] onbeheerd goed, strandgoed *o.*; zwerver, dakloze *m.*; verwaarloosd kind *o.*; **—s and strays,** zwervers, daklozen, verlaten kinderen; rommel, brokstukken.

wailing ['weiliŋ] weeklacht *v.*, gejammer *o.*

wainscot ['weinskət] *sb.* wagenschot *o.*; beschot *o.*, lambrizering *v.*; *vt.* bekleden, betimmeren, lambrizeren; beschieten (met wagenschot).

wainscoting ['weinskətiŋ] wagenschot *o.*; beschot *o.*, lambrizering *v.*

waist [weist] middel *o.*, leest *v.*; lijfje *o.*; keurslijf *o.*; gordel *m.* (om 't middel); (*Am.*) blouse *v.*; (*sch.*) kuil *m.*, middeldek *o.*

waist-band ['weistbænd] broeksband *m.*, roksband *m.*; gordel *m.*, ceintuur *v.*

waistcoat ['weis(t)kout, 'weskət] vest *o.*

wait [weit] *vi.* wachten, afwachten; staan te wachten; tafeldienen; bedienen; zijn opwachting maken bij; wachten op; volgen op, gepaard gaan met; (*v. persoon*) begeleiden, vergezellen; *vt.* afwachten; wachten op; wachten met; *sb.* (het) wachten *o.*; wachttijd *m.*; oponthoud *o.*; pauze, rust *v.*

waiter ['weitə] *sb.* wachtende *m.*; kelner *m.*; stommeknecht *m.*; presenteerblad *o.*

waiting ['weitiŋ] *adj.* wachtend, afwachtend; bedienend.

waiting-room ['weitiŋrum] wachtkamer *v.*

waitress ['weitris] kelnerin *v.*

waive [weiv] afzien van, afstand doen van, opgeven, laten varen; in de steek laten; ter zijde stellen, op zij zetten; (*v. discussie*) vermijden.

wake [weik] *sb.* (*sch.*) kielwater, zog *o.*; (*v. torpedo*) bellenbaan *v.*; (*fig.*) spoor *o.*

wake [weik] *vi.* wakker worden, ontwaken; wakker zijn, waken; (uit dood) opstaan; opvlammen; *vt.* wekken; wakker maken; (*fig.*) wakker schudden; opwekken; *sb.* (het) waken *o.*; nachtwake *v.* (bij een lijk); kerkwijdingsfeest *o.*; kermis *v.*

wakeful ['weikful] *adj.* wakker, wakend; waakzaam; slapeloos.

walk [wo:k] *vi.* lopen, gaan; wandelen; stappen, stapvoets lopen (rijden); slaapwandelen; rondwaren, spoken; (*sl.*) doodgaan; *vt.* betreden; bewandelen; aflopen; laten (doen) lopen; stapvoets laten gaan; *sb.* gang, loop *m.*; wandeling *v.*; toertje *o.*; voetpad *o.*; dreef *v.*, wandelweg *m.*, wandelplaats *v.*; levenswandel *m.*; kippenloop *m.*, kippenren *v.*; (*v. nachtwaker, melkboer, enz.*) wijk *v.*; werkkring *m.*; gebied *o.*, sfeer *v.*, terrein *o.*; (*sp.*) ronde *v.*; schapeweide *v.*; weigrond *m.*

walker ['wo:kə] voetganger, wandelaar *m.*; loper, loopbode, colporteur *m.*; loopvogel *m.*

walking-stick ['wo:kiŋstik] wandelstok *m.*; (*Dk.*) wandelende tak *m.*

wall [wo:l] *sb.* muur, wand *m.*; wal, waldijk *m.*; *vt.* ommuren; **— up,** dichtmetselen, toemetselen; inmetselen.

wallet ['wɔlit] knapzak *m.*; bedelzak *m.*; ransel *m.*; gereedschapstasje *o.*; zadeltas *v.*; portefeuille *v.*

wallop ['wɔləp] *vt.* (*sl.*) slaan, afranselen, afrossen; troef geven; *vi.* koken, opborrelen; hollen; zich log bewegen; fladderen; *sb.* logge beweging *v.*; (*sl.*) opstopper, mep *m.*; *adv.* pardoes.

wall-paper ['wo:lpeipə] behangsel(papier) *o.*; **make —,** (*jam.: op bal*) als muurbloempje blijven zitten.

wall-plate ['wo:lpleit] muurplaat *v.*

Wall Street ['wo:lstrit] (te New York) effectenbeurs en geldmarkt, centrum van de geldhandel.

walnut ['wo:lnət] noot, walnoot *v.*; notehout *o.*; (*sl.*) geweer *o.*

waltz [wo:ls] *sb.* wals *v.*; *vi.* walsen; (*fig.*) ronddraaien; zweven.

wan [wɔn] *adj.* bleek, flets, ziekelijk; *vi.* bleek worden, er bleek (ziekelijk) gaan uitzien.

wander ['wɔndə] *vi.* zwerven, rondzwerven, (rond)dolen; afdwalen; van de hak op de tak springen; (*v. lichaamsdeel: nier, enz.*) wandelen; ijlen, raaskallen; *vt.* afzwerven, zwerven over; *sb.* (het) lopen *o.*; zwerftocht *m.*

wanderer ['wɔndərə] zwerver, zwerveling *m.*; landloper *m.*; dwaler *m.*; zwerfvogel *m.*; zwerfspin *v.*

want [wɔnt] *sb.* gebrek *o.*, armoede *v.*, nood *m.*; gemis *o.*; *vt.* nodig hebben, moeten hebben, behoeven; verlangen, wensen, willen; missen, gebrek hebben aan; te kort komen, mankeren; *vi.* gebrek hebben, gebrek lijden.

wanton ['wɔntən] *adj.* speels, dartel, uitgelaten; wulps, wellustig; baldadig, brooddronken, moedwillig; *sb.* lichtekooi *v.*; lichtmis *m.*; (*v. kind*) wildebras, robbedoes *m.*; *vi.* spelen, dartelen, stoeien.

war [wo:ə] *sb.* oorlog *m.*; krijg *m.*; strijd *m.*; *vi.* oorlog voeren, strijd voeren (**on, against,** tegen); *vt.* beoorlogen.

warble ['wo:bl] *vi.* & *vt.* kwelen, kwinkeleren, zingen, slaan; (*Am.*) jodelen; (*v. stroom*) murmelen; *sb.* gekweel, gekwinkeleer *o.*, slag *m.*; lied *o.*

ward [wo:d] *sb.* bewaking, wacht *v.*; voogdijschap, curatele *v.*; verzekerde bewaring, gevangenschap *v.*; pupil, beschermeling *m.*; bezetting *v.*, garnizoen *o.*; (stads)wijk *v.*; (*in ziekenhuis, gevangenis*) afdeling, zaal *v.*; (*bij schermen*) (het) pareren *o.*; (*v. slot*) werk *o.*; *vt.* bewaken; de wacht houden bij; waken over; beschermen; **— (off),** pareren, afweren.

warden ['wo:dn] bewaker *m.*; opzichter *m.*; portier; bewaarder *m.*; marktmeester; havenmeester *m.*; voogd *m.*; schildwacht *m.*; (*Am.: v. gevangenis*) directeur *m.*: soort stoofpeer *v.*

wardrobe ['wo:droub] kleerkast *v.*; garderobe *v.*

wardship ['wo:dʃip] voogdij *v.*; bescherming *v.*

ware [wêə] *adj.* voorzichtig, op zijn hoede; gewaar, zich bewust; *vt.* op zijn hoede zijn voor, zich wachten voor.

warehouse ['wêəhaus] *sb.* pakhuis *o.*, opslagplaats *v.*: magazijn *o.*

warfare ['wo:fêə] *sb.* oorlog, krijg, strijd *m.*; oorlogvoering *v.*; *vi.* oorlog voeren.

war-footing ['wo:futiŋ] oorlogsvoet *m.*

warily ['wêərili] *adv.* omzichtig, voorzichtig, behoedzaam.

war-law ['wêəlo:] oorlogsrecht *o.*

warlike ['wo:laik] krijgshaftig, oorlogszuchtig, strijdbaar; oorlogs—, krijgs—.

warm [wo:m] *adj.* warm, heet; vurig, gloeiend; verhit; heetgebakerd; (*v. spoor*) vers; (*fam.: v. rekening*) gepeperd; rijk, gegoed, er warm in zittend; *vt.* warmen, verwarmen, warm maken; opwarmen; (*sl.*) afrossen; *vi.* warm worden; — **over,** (*Am.*) opwarmen; — **up,** opwarmen; warm worden; op temperatuur komen (brengen); *vr.* — **oneself,** zich warmen; *sb.* warmte *v.*; (*fam.*) warme jas *v.*

warm-hearted ['wo:m'hâtid] hartelijk.

warming ['wo:miŋ] (het) warmen *o.*; verwarming *v.*; (*fam.*) pak slaag, pak ransel *o.*, afstraffing *v.*

warmth [wo:mδ] warmte *v.*

warn [wo:n] waarschuwen; verwittigen; — **of,** aankondigen, inlichten omtrent; onder het oog brengen.

warner ['wo:nə] waarschuwer *m.*

warning ['wo:niŋ] waarschuwing; verwittiging *v.*; aanzegging *v.*; aankondiging; kennisgeving *v.*; opzegging *v.*; (*v. klok*) voorslag *m.*

War-office ['wo:rofis] Ministerie *o.* van Oorlog.

warp [wo:p] *vi.* kromtrekken, scheeftrekken; (*jongen*) werpen; *vt.* (*doen*) kromtrekken; een verkeerde richting geven aan; (*v. feiten*) verdraaien, scheef voorstellen; doen afdwalen van, op een dwaalspoor brengen; (*v. land*) bevloeien; (*bij 't weven*) scheren; (*sch.*) verhalen; werpen; *sb.* kromtrekking, kromming *v.*; afwijking *v.*; verdraaiing *v.*; vooroordeel *o.*; (*sch.*) werptros, verhaaltros *m.*; bezinksel, slib *o.*; (*v. weefgetouw*) schering *v.*

warrant ['worənt] *sb.* machtiging, volmacht *v.*; waarborg *m.*, garantie *v.*; verzekering *v.*; ceel *v.*; bevoegdheid *v.*, recht *o.*; aanstelling *v.*; (*betalings*)mandaat *o.*; bevelschrift *o.*; grond *m.*, rechtvaardiging *v.*; motivering *v.*; *vt.* mach-

tigen, machtiging geven tot; waarborgen, garanderen, instaan voor; rechtvaardigen, motiveren; wettigen; bekrachtigen.

warrantee [worən'ti] wie iets gewaarborgd wordt; gevolmachtigde *m.*; aan wie een bevelschrift betekend wordt.

warranter ['worəntə] waarborger *m.*; volmachtgever *m.*; verkoper *m.*

warranty ['worənti] waarborg *m.*, garantie *v.*; zekerheidstelling *v.*; grond *m.*, rechtvaardiging *v.*; machtiging, volmacht *v.*

warrior ['woriə] *sb.* krijgsman, soldaat *m.*; *adj.* krijgshaftig; krijgs—.

wart [wo:t] wrat *v.*; uitwas *o.*; (*mil., sl.*) jong luitenantje *o.*; jonge adelborst *m.*

wary ['wêəri] *adj.* omzichtig, voorzichtig, behoedzaam.

wash [woʃ] *vt.* wassen; afwassen, schoonwassen; uitwassen; spoelen, afspoelen, omspoelen; uitspoelen; dweilen; bespoelen, besproeien; bevochtigen, betten; *vi.* wassen; zich wassen; (*v. stoffen*) wasecht zijn, zich laten wassen; *vr.* — **oneself,** zich wassen; *sb.* was *v.*; wassing, spoeling *v.*; spoelwater *o.*; haarwater *o.*; waterverf *v.*; kleurtje; vernisje *o.*; golfslag *m.*; deining *v.*; kielwater *o.*; poel *m.*; ondiepte, zandbank *v.*

washerwoman ['woʃəwumən] wasvrouw *v.*

wash-hand basin ['woʃhændbeisin] waskom *v.*, fonteintje *o.*

wash-hand stand ['woʃhændstænd] wastafel *v.*

washy ['woʃi] waterig; (*v. drank*) slap, dun; (*v. kleur*) bleek, mat, flets; (*v. stijl*) kleurloos; verwaterd.

wasp [wosp] wesp *v.*; (*fig.*) (nijdige) spin *v.*

wastage ['weistidʒ] verspilling *v.*; verbruik *o.*, slijtage *v.*; (het) verspilde, afgesletene *o.*; (verlies *o.* door) slinking, indroging *v.*

waste [weist] *adj.* onbebouwd, braak; ongebruikt, leeg, onnut; dor; onvruchtbaar; waardeloos; overtollig; *vt.* verspillen, verkwisten; weggooien; vermorsen, verknoeien; verwoesten, vernielen; verbruiken; (*recht*) verwaarlozen, laten vervallen; *vi.* verteren, uitteren, wegkwijnen, vermageren; slinken, afnemen; slijten; opraken; *sb.* verspilling, verkwisting *v.*; verwoesting, vernieling *v.*; verbruik *o.*, slijtage *v.*; verlies *o.*, vermindering, indroging *v.*; verwaarlozing *v.*, verval *o.*; woestijn, woestenij *v.*; onbebouwd land *o.*, woeste grond *m.*; wildernis *v.*; afval, puin *o.*; misdruk *m.*; poetskatoen *o.*; afvoerpijp *v.*

wasteful ['weistful] *adj.* verkwistend, spilziek; overdadig.

waste-paper ['weistpeipə] scheurpapier *o.*; misdruk *m.*

waste-pipe ['weistpaip] afvoerpijp, loospijp *v.*

watch [wɔtʃ] *sb.* nachtwake *v.*; (het) waken *o.*, wacht *v.*; waakzaamheid *v.*; horloge *o.*; *vt.* bewaken; gadeslaan, in 't oog houden, letten op; hoeden; nagaan, volgen, naogen; *vi.* waken; wacht doen, op wacht staan; uitkijken, op zijn hoede zijn, waakzaam zijn.

watcher [′wɔtʃə] waker, bewaker *m.*; waarnemer; bespieder *m.*; (*bij staking*) poster *m.*

watchful [′wɔtʃful] *adj.* waakzaam, waaks.

watchmaker [′wɔtʃmeikə] horlogemaker *m.*; (*sl.*) horlogedief *m.*

watchman [′wɔtʃmən] wachter *m.*; waker, nachtwaker *m.*

watchword [′wɔtʃwə:d] wachtwoord *o.*

water [′wɔ:tə] *sb.* water *o.*; vaarwater *o.*; tranen *m. mv.*; waterverf *v.*; (*fam.: Beurs*) verwaterd kapitaal *o.*; scheep gaan; te water gaan, zich te water begeven; van stapel lopen; *vt.* (*v. paarden, vee*) drenken; (*v. troepen, schip*) van water voorzien; (*v. schip*) water laten innemen; (*v. land, enz.*) besproeien; (*v. bloemen*) begieten; (*rivier*) bespoelen; (*v. melk, enz.*) aanlengen, verdunnen; (*H.: v. kapitaal*) verwateren; (*v. zijde*) moireren; (*v. vlas*) roten; bevochtigen, doorweken; (*v. tabak*) sausen; (*mil., sl.*) met granaatvuur beschieten; *vi.* wateren; (*v. ogen*) tranen, lopen; (*v. schip*) water innemen.

water-bottle [′wɔ:təbɔtl] karaf *v.*; veldfles *v.*; (*v. vogelkooi*) fonteintje *o.*

water-cart [′wɔ:təkât] sproeiwagen *m.*

water-cock [′wɔ:təkɔk] waterkraan *v.*; brandkraan *v.*

water-colour [′wɔ:təkələ] waterverf *v.*; waterverfschilderij *v.*

waterfall [′wɔ:təfɔ:l] waterval *m.*; waterafloop *m.*; slipdas *v.*

water-famine [′wɔ:təfæmin] watergebrek *o.*, waternood *m.*

water-ga(u)ge [′wɔ:təgeidʒ] peilglas *o.*; watermeter *m.*

watering-place [′wɔ:təriŋpleis] wed *o.*, drinkplaats *v.*; plaats *v.* om water in te nemen; badplaats *v.*

watering-pot [′wɔ:təriŋpɔt] gieter *m.*

water-level [′wɔ:tələvəl] waterstand *m.*; waterpas *o.*

water-line [′wɔ:təlain] waterlijn *v.*; watermerk *o.*

water-ordeal [′wɔ:tərɔ:′diəl] waterproef *v.*

water-pot [′wɔ:təpɔt] waterkan *v.*; gieter *m.*

waterproof [′wɔ:təprûf] *adj.* waterdicht; *sb.* waterdichte jas (mantel, stof); *vt.* waterdicht maken.

watershed [′wɔ:təʃed] waterscheiding *v.*; stroomgebied *o.*

water-supply [′wɔ:təsəplai] wateraanvoer *m.*; watervoorziening *v.*; watervoorraad *m.*

water-tank [′wɔ:tətæŋk] waterbak *m.*, waterreservoir *o.*

water-tight [′wɔ:tətait] *adj.* waterdicht; (*fig.*) sluitend als een bus; *sb.* —s, waterdichte laarzen.

waterway [′wɔ:təwei] waterweg *m.*; (*v. schip*) watergang *m.*; vaarwater *o.*

water-works [′wɔ:təwə:ks] waterleiding *v.*

watery [′wɔ:təri] waterachtig, waterig; regenachtig; water—; (*fig.*) verwaterd, flauw, slap.

wattle-work [′wɔtlwə:k] hordenwerk, teenwerk *o.*

wave [weiv] *vi.* golven; wapperen; wuiven, zwaaien; *vt.* doen golven; (*v. haar*) onduleren; (*v. zijde*) wateren, moireren; wuiven met, zwaaien met; toewuiven; *sb.* golf; baar *v.*; golving *v.*; (*mil.*) aanvalsgolf *v.*; (*v. zijde, enz.*) golflijn, vlam *v.*; wuivend gebaar, gewuif *o.*; (*fig.*) opwelling *v.*; golf *v.*, vloed *m.*

wave-length [′weivleŋθ] golflengte *v.*

waver [′weivə] *vi.* wankelen, waggelen; onvast zijn; weifelen, aarzelen; flikkeren; schommelen; bengelen; zweven; (*v. stem*) beven; (*v. troepen*) wijken; *sb.* weifeling, aarzeling *v.*; flikkering *v.*

waverer [′weivərə] weifelaar *m.*

wavering [′weivəriŋ] *adj.* wankel, wankelbaar; wankelend, wankelmoedig; *sb.* geweifel *o.*, weifeling *v.*, gewankel *o.*

waving [′weiviŋ] *adj.* golvend, gegolfd; *sb.* golving *v.*; gewapper *o.*; gewuif, (het) wuiven *o.*

wavy [′weivi] *adj.* golvend, gegolfd; veranderlijk, weifelend.

wax [wæks] *sb.* was *o.*; boenwas *o.*; oorsmeer *o.*; lak *o.*; (*sl.*) woede *v.*; *vt.* wassen, met was bestrijken; boenen; *vi.* wassen, toenemen; groeien; (*v. dagen*) lengen.

wax-candle [′wækskændl] waskaars *v.*

waxen [′wæksn] wassen, van was; wasachtig; wasgeel; week als was.

wax-end [′wæksend] *sb.* pikdraad *m.*; *vt.* met pikdraad omwikkelen.

way [wei] *sb.* weg *m.*; baan *v.*; straat *v.*; (*fig.*) pad *o.*; richting *v.*, kant *m.*, zijde *v.*; gang *m.*, vaart, snelheid *v.*; afstand *m.*; eind weegs *o.*; wijze, manier *v.*; handelwijze *v.*; gewoonte *v.*, gebruik *o.*; aanwensel *o.*, hebbelijkheid *v.*; *adv.* (*Am.*) — *back in A.*, daar ginds in A.; — *back in 1935*, reeds in 1935; — *down East*, ver van hier in 't Oosten.

way-bill [′weibil] geleibiljet, vervoerbiljet *o.*; passagierslijst *v.*

wayfarer [′weifêərə] voetganger, (voet)reiziger *m.*; zwerver *m.*

waylay [wei′lei] belagen, loeren op, hinderlagen leggen.

wayless [′weilis] ongebaand, zonder weg(en).

wayward [′weiwəd] dwars, eigenzinnig, weerspannig; grillig; onberekenbaar.

we [wî] wij.

weak [wik] *adj.* zwak; slap, krachteloos; (*v. markt, koffie, enz.*) slap; toonloos; niet op volle sterkte.

weaken ['wîkn] *vt.* verzwakken; verslappen, verdunnen; *vi.* zwak(ker) worden.

weakening ['wîkniŋ] verzwakking *v.*

weak-headed ['wîk'hedid] zwakhoofdig.

weakness ['wîknis] zwakte *v.*; zwakheid *v.*; zwak punt *o.*, zwakke plaats *v.*; zwak *o.*

wealth [welθ] weelde, pracht *v.*; rijkdom, overvloed *m.*

wealthy ['welθi] *adj.* rijk.

wean [wîn] spenen.

weapon ['wepən] wapen *o.*

wear [wêə] *vt.* (*v. kleren, enz.*) dragen, aanhebben; doen slijten, afslijten, uitslijten; (*v. voorkomen, enz.*) hebben, vertonen; afmatten, uitputten; (*sch.*) laten ophalzen; *vi.* slijten, verslijten; (*in gebruik*) zich goed houden; zich laten dragen; (*v. tijd*) voorbijgaan; (*sch.*) ophalzen; *sb.* (het) dragen *o.*; dracht *v.*; gebruik *o.*; slijtage *v.*; (*v. stof, enz.*) sterkte, soliditeit *v.*

weariness ['wîərinis] vermoeidheid, moeheid *v.*; afmatting *v.*; verveling *v.*

weary ['wîəri] *adj.* moe, vermoeid; vermoeiend; moeizaam; mat, lusteloos; vervelend, langdradig, langwijlig; *vt.* vermoeien, afmatten; vervelen; *vi.* moe worden (*of,* van).

weasel ['wîzl] *sb.* (*Dk.*) wezel *v.*; *vt.* *Am.*: *v. woord*) de betekenis (kracht) ontnemen aan.

weather ['weθə] *sb.* weer, weder *o.*; (*Am.*; *sch.*) slecht weer *o.*; (*sch.*) loefzijde *v.*; *vt.* aan de lucht blootstellen; luchten; (*fig.*) te boven komen; doorstaan; (*sch.*) te boven zeilen; de loef afsteken; (*sl.*) in de luren leggen; *vi.* laveren; verweren.

weather-beaten ['weθəbîtn] door stormen geteisterd; verweerd.

weather-glass ['weθəglâs] weerglas *o.*; barometer *m.*; (*Pl.*) guichelheil *v.*

weather-vane ['weθəvein] windwijzer *m.*, windvaan *v.*

weave [wîv] *vt.* weven; vlechten; *vi.* weven; waggelen, schommelen; zich heen en weer bewegen; *sb.* weefsel *o.*; weeftrant *m.*

weaver ['wîvə] wever *m.*; (*Dk.*) wevervogel *m.*; (*tn.*) weverbok *m.*

weaving-loom ['wîviŋlûm] weefgetouw *o.*, weefstoel *m.*

weaving-mill ['wîviŋmil] weverij *v.*

web [web] *sb.* web, spinneweb *o.*; weefsel *o.*; bindweefsel *o.*; zwemvlies *o.*; (*v. oog*) nagelvlies *o.*; (*v. veer*) baard *m.*, vlag *v.*; (*tn.*) wang *v.*; lange papierrol *v.*; (*v. sleutel*) baard *m.*; (*v. spanzaag*) zaagblad *o.*; *vt.* weven, inweven; (als) met een netwerk bedekken; (als) in een web verstrikken.

wed [wed] trouwen (met), huwen (met); in de echt verbinden; (*fig.*) verenigen, paren (*to,* aan).

wedding ['wediŋ] huwelijk *o.*, huwelijksplechtigheid; bruiloft *v.*

wedge [wed3] *sb.* wig, keg *v.*, keil *m.*; (*v. taart*) punt *v.*; (*voor raam, enz.*) klemmetje *o.*; *vt.* een wig slaan in, een wig insteken.

wedlock ['wedlɔk] huwelijk *o.*, huwelijke staat *m.*

Wednesday ['wenzdi] woensdag *m.*

weed [wîd] *sb.* onkruid *o.*; wier, zeegras *o.*; (*fam.*) tabak; sigaar *v.*; (*sl.,v. paard*) knol *m.*; rouwgewaad; rouwfloers *o.*; rouwband *m.*; *vt.* wieden; (*fig.*) zuiveren, ontdoen (*of,* van).

weeding-hook ['wîdiŋhuk] wiedijzer *o.*

week [wîk] week *v.*

weekly ['wîkli] *adj.* wekelijks, week—; *adv.* wekelijks, per week; *sb.* wekelijks tijdschrift, weekblad *o.*

weep [wîp] *vi.* wenen, schreien; druppelen, sijpelen; (*v. wond*) dragen; *vt.* bewenen, betreuren.

weeping-willow ['wîpiŋ'wilou] treurwilg *m.*

weever ['wîvə] (*Dk.*: *vis*) pieterman *m.*

weigh [wei] *vt.* wegen; overwegen; lichten, tillen; *vi.* wegen; gewicht in de schaal leggen, van gewicht zijn; zich laten wegen; het anker lichten; *sb.* (het) wegen *o.*; (*sch.*) vaart *v.*

weighage ['wêid3] weegloon, waaggeld *o.*

weigh-house ['weihaus] waag *v.*

weighing-machine ['weiiŋməʃin] weegtoestel *o.*; weegbrug, bascule *v.*

weight [weit] *sb.* gewicht *o.*; zwaarte *v.*, last *m.*; druk *m.*, pressie *v.*; (*v. renpaard*) belasting *v.*; (*Am.*) pond *o.*; *vt.* bezwaren; zwaarder maken, belasten.

weighty ['weiti] *adj.* zwaar; zwaarwegend, zwaarwichtig; gewichtig; invloedrijk.

weir [wîə] weer *v.*; waterkering *v.*, stuwdam *m.*

welcome ['welkəm] *ij.* welkom; *sb.* welkom *o.*, welkomst, verwelkoming *v.*; ontvangst *v.*; *adj.* welkom; *vt.* welkom heten, verwelkomen; vriendelijk ontvangen.

weld [weld] *sb.* (*Pl.*) wouw *v.*; welnaad *m.*, las *v.*; *vt.* wellen, aaneensmeden, lassen.

welfare ['welfêə] welvaart *r.*, welzijn *o.*, voorspoed *m.*

well [wel] *sb.* put *m.*; wel, bron *v.*; petroleumbron *v.*; liftkoker *m.*; trappenhuis *o.*; wagenbak *m.*; viskaar, bun *v.*; (*in lessenaar*) inktpot *m.*; diepe ruimte *v.*; (*fig.*) bron *v.*; *vi.* opwellen, ontspringen.

well [wel] *adv.* goed, wel; eerlijk; *as —,* eveneens, ook; even goed, net zo goed; *as — as,* even goed als; zoveel als; evenzeer als; *adj.* wel, gezond; goed, in orde; *sb.* welzijn *o.*; (het) goede *o.*; *ij.* wel! goed!

well-behaved ['welbi'heivid] oppassend, zich goed gedragend, fatsoenlijk.

well-being ['wel'Lîiŋ] welzijn *o.*

well-beloved ['welbi'ləvd] dierbaar, teergeliefd.

well-bred ['wel'bred] welopgevoed, beschaafd; van goed ras.

well-connected ['welkə'nektid] van goede familie, van goeden huize; met goede relaties.

well-doing ['wel'dûiŋ] *adj.* rechtschapen; weldoend; (*Sc.*) welvarend; *sb.* rechtschapenheid *v.*; welvaart *v.*, welzijn *o.*

well-fed ['wel'fed] goed gevoed, doorvoed, welgedaan.

well-founded ['wel'faundid] gegrond

well-informed ['welin'fo:md] goed ingelicht, goed op de hoogte; zaakkundig; (*v. artikel, enz.*) zakelijk.

well-known ['wel'noun] bekend, welbekend.

well-meant ['wel'ment] welgemeend, goed bedoeld.

well-nigh ['welnai] bijna, nagenoeg.

well-off ['wel'o:f] welgesteld, in goede doen.

well-read ['wel'red] belezen.

well-set ['wel'set] goed geplaatst; welgevormd; stevig gebouwd.

well-spent ['wel'spent] goed besteed; goed doorgebracht.

well-spoken ['wel'spoukn] goed (treffend) gezegd; welbespraakt, beschaafd ter taal.

well-to-do ['weltə'dû] welgesteld.

well-tried ['wel'traid] beproefd.

well-worn ['welwo:n] veel gedragen, afgedragen; versleten; (*fig.*) afgezaagd.

welter ['weltə] *vi.* (zich) wentelen; baden (**in,** in); (*v. golven*) rollen; zwalken; *vt.* (*sl.*) afranselen; (*Sc.*) omverwerpen; *sb.* (het) wentelen *o.*; (*v. golven, enz.*) (het) rollen *o.*; verwarring *v.*, chaos *m.*; mengelmoes *o.*

wench [wen(t)ʃ] meid, deern *r.*; (*Am.*) negerin *v.*

wentletrap ['wentltræp] (*schelp*) wenteltrap *v.*

west [west] *sb.* westen *o.*; westenwind *m.*; *adj.* westelijk, west—, wester—; *adv.* westelijk, westwaarts; **go —,** (*sl.*) naar de maan gaan, verloren gaan, verdwijnen; om zeep gaan; het hoekje omgaan; de kraaienmars blazen.

westerly ['westəli] *adj.* westelijk, westen—; *sb.* (heersende) westenwind *m.*

western ['westən] westelijk, westers.

wet [wet] *adj.* nat, vochtig; (*v. vis*) vers; (*sl.*) aangeschoten, dronken; *sb.* nat *o.*, nattigheid *v.*; vochtigheid *v.*; regen, neerslag *m.*; (*sl.*) slokje *o.*; (*Am., sl.*) anti-onthouder *m.*; *vt.* nat maken, bevochtigen.

wether ['weθə] (*Dk.*) hamel *m.*

wettish ['witiʃ] nattig, vochtig.

whack [wæk] *vt.* ranselen, afranselen, klop geven; verdelen; *vi.* (*sl.*) delen; *sb.* mep, slag, smak *m.*; deel, aandeel *o.*; (*v. geld*) hoop *m.*; borrel *m.*; *adv.* & *ij.* pats!

whale [weil] *sb.* walvis *m.*; (*Am.*) hoge ome *m.*; *vi.* op de walvisvangst zijn (gaan), walvissen vangen; *vt.* (*Am.*) ranselen.

whalebone ['weilboun] balein *o.*

whale-fishery ['weilfiʃəri] walvisvangst *v.*

whaling ['weiliŋ] *sb.* walvisvangst *v.*; (*Am.*) pak slaag *o.*; *adj.* (*Am., sl.*) reusachtig.

wharfage ['wo:fidʒ] kaaigeld *o.*; kaairuimte *v.*

what [wɔt] (*vragend*) wat, wat voor, wat voor een; welk(e), welk een; (*in uitroep*) wat (een); (*betrekkelijk*) wat, dat wat, hetgeen, datgene wat; al wat.

whatever [wɔt'evə] *pron.* wat; wat ook; welke ook; al wat.

wheat [wit] tarwe *v.*; **—s,** tarwesoorten.

wheedling ['widliŋ] *adj.* flikflooiend; *sb.* geflikflooi *o.*

wheel [wil] *sb.* wiel, rad *o.*; stuurrad *o.*; rijwiel *o.*; spinnewiel *o.*; (*v. vuurwerk*) zon *v.*; pottenbakkersschijf *v.*; (*mil.*) zwenking *v.*; omwenteling, draaiende beweging *v.*; (*Am.*) dollar *m.*; (*sl.*) achterwiel *o.*; rolletje *o.*; *vt.* per as vervoeren; voortrollen; van wielen voorzien; (*mil.*) laten zwenken; *vi.* draaien; zwenken; cirkelen; zich omkeren; zich afwenden; (*fam.*) wielrijden.

wheelman ['wilmən] wielrijder *m.*; (*Am.*) roerganger *m.*

wheel-work ['wilwə:k] raderwerk *o.*

whelp [welp] *sb.* welp *o.*; jonge hond *m.*; kwajongen, brak *m.*; *vi.* werpen, jongen; *vt.* werpen.

when [wen] *adv.* wanneer; *cj.* als, toen, wanneer; waarop; en daarop; in welk geval; *sb.* **the — and where,** plaats en tijd.

whence [wens] *adv.* vanwaar, waarvandaan; waaruit; *sb.* **the — and whither of humanity,** de oorsprong en bestemming der mensheid.

whencesoever [wenssou'evə] waar ook vandaan, vanwaar ook.

whenever [we'nevə] wanneer ook; telkens als.

where [wêə] *adv.* waar, alwaar; waarheen; waarin; *sb.* **a better —,** (*dicht.*) een betere plaats, betere gewesten.

whereabout ['wêərə'baut] *adv.* zie **whereabouts.**

whereabouts ['wêərə'bauts] *adv.* waar; waaromtrent; waar ergens; waar ongeveer; *sb.* verblijfplaats *v.*, adres *o.*

whereas [wêə'ræz] terwijl (daarentegen); aangezien, vermits, nademaal.

whereby [wêə'bai] waarbij, waardoor.

wherefore [wêə'fo:] waarom, waarvoor; zodat, weshalve.

whereof [wêə'rov] waarvan.

whereon [wêə'ron] waarop.

whereto [wêə'tû] waartoe, met welk doel; waarheen.

whereupon [wêərə'pon] *zie* **whereon.**

wherever [wêə'revə] waar ook, overal waar; (*fam.*) waar... toch.

wherewithal [wêǝwi'θo:l] *adv.* waarmede; ['wêǝwiθo:l] *sb.* middel(en) *o.* (*mv.*).

whet [wet] *vt.* wetten, scherpen, slijpen; (*fig.: v. eetlust*) prikkelen, opwekken; *sb.* (het) wetten, (het) slijpen *o.*: (*fig.*) prikkel *m.*, prikkeling *v.*: (*fam.*) opwekkertje *o.*, borrel *m.*; appetijthapje *o.*

whether ['weθǝ] *pron.* wie van beiden, welke van de twee; *cj.* of.

whetstone ['wetstoun] wetsteen, slijpsteen *m.*

which [witʃ] (*vragend*) welk(e), wie, wat: (*betrekkelijk*) die, dat, wat, hetwelk.

while [wail] wijl *v.*, tijd(je) *m.* (*o.*), poos *v.*

whilst [wailst] terwijl.

whim [wim] gril, kuur, nuk *v.*; inval *m.*: (*in mijn*) kaapstander *m.*

whimsical ['wimzikl] *adj.* grillig, nukkig; eigenaardig, zonderling; fantastisch; grappig.

whine [wain] *vi.* temen, jengelen, janken, jammeren; *sb.* geteem, gejengel, enz.; klagend geluid *o.*

whinny ['wini] *adj.* vol gaspeldoorns; *vi.* hinniken; *sb.* gehinnik *o.*

whip [wip] *sb.* zweep *v.*; gesel *m.*; twijg *v.*, rijs *o.*; (*sch.*) wimpel *m.*; molenwiek *v.*; (*fam.*) koetsier *m.*; overhandse steek *m.*; *vt.* met de zweep geven, er van langs geven; afrossen, ranselen, tuchtigen, kastijden; (*v. eieren*) kloppen, slaan; dorsen; overhands naaien; (*sch.*) takelen, betakelen, omwoelen; (*sl.*) snel nemen, gappen, grissen; (*Am., sl.*) verslaan, kloppen, de baas zijn; (*v. rivier*) afvissen; *vi.* met de zweep klappen; wippen; zich vlug bewegen.

whip-cord ['wipko:d] zweepkoord *v.* & *o.*; soort snaar *v.*; soort kamgaren *o.*

whip-lash ['wiplæʃ] zweepkoord *v.* & *o.*; zweepslag *m.*

whipper-snapper ['wipǝsnæpǝ] kereltje, ventje *o.*; praatjesmaker, verwaande kwast *m.*

whip-saw ['wipso:] *sb.* trekzaag *v.*; *vt.* met de trekzaag bewerken; (*Am., sl.*) geheel verslaan.

whir [wǝ:] *vi.* snorren, gonzen, brommen; *sb.* gesnor, gegons, gebrom *o.*

whirl [wǝ:l] *vt.* snel ronddraaien, omdraaien, doen draaien; doen dwarrelen; *vi.* (*in rijtuig, enz.*) snorren; slingeren; *sb.* dwarreling *v.*, gedwarrel *o.*; (*v. schelp*) winding *v.*; spiraal *v.*; (*tn.*) wartelblok *o.*; haspel *m.*; wervel *m.*; maalstroom, draaikolk *m.*; (*v. opwinding, enz.*) roes *m.*

whirlpool ['wǝ:lpûl] draaikolk, maalstroom *m.*

whirlwind ['wǝ:lwind] dwarrelwind, wervelwind *m.*

whisk [wisk] *sb.* borstel; stoffer *m.*; bosje *o.* stro (gras, enz.); vliegenmepper *m.*; eierklopper, roomklopper *m.*; veeg, slag *m.*; snelle beweging *v.*; *vt.* afborstelen, stoffen, vegen; (*v. eieren*)

kloppen; wippen; snel bewegen; *vi.* — *about*, fladderen.

whisker ['wiskǝ] borsteltje *o.*; eierklopper *m.*; (*v. kat, enz.*) snor *v.*; —(**s**), bakkebaard(en) *m.* (*mv.*).

whisper ['wispǝ] *vi.* fluisteren; *rt.* fluisteren, influisteren, toefluisteren; fluisterend toespreken; *sb.* gefluister *o.*, fluistering *v.*

whist [wist] *ij.* st! stil! *sb.* whist *o.*; (*Ir.*) stilte *v.*

whistle ['wisl] *vi.* (*v. wind, enz.*) fluiten, gieren, huilen, blazen; suizen; (*v. dampig paard*) snuiven; (*sl.*) in de wind praten; afschepen; *vt.* fluiten; *sb.* (het) fluiten, gefluit *o.*; fluit(je) *v.* (*o.*); (*scherts.*) keel *v.*, keelgat *o.*

whit [wit] **not a** —, geen zier, geen jota; **every** —, in elk opzicht.

white [wait] *adj.* wit, blank; spierwit, doodsbleek; (*v. haar*) grijs; (*v. glas, enz.*) doorzichtig, kleurloos; (*sch.*) ongeteerd; (*fig.*) vlekkeloos, zuiver, rein, onbezoedeld, onschuldig; (*v. dag, enz.*) gelukkig; (*fam.*) eerlijk, nobel; wit tussen de regels; witte verkeerslijn; (*vl.*) krijtstreep; *sb.* (het) wit *o.*; witheid; witte kleur *v.*; blankheid *v.*; reinheid, zuiverheid *v.*; eiwit *o.*; (*Dk.: vlinder*) witje *o.*; doelwit *o.*; (*Am.*) alcohol *m.*; —**s**, wit (van de ogen); (*v. landschap*) witte partijen; witte goederen; witte kleren; fijn tarwemeel; witte suiker; *vt.* wit maken; witten.

whitebait ['waitbeit] witvis *m.*

white-hot ['wait'hɔt, 'waithɔt] witgloeiend.

whiten ['waitn] *vt.* wit maken, bleek maken; witten; bleken; (*fig.*) zuiveren, schoonwassen.

whitener ['waitnǝ] bleker *m.*; bleekwater; bleekpoeder *o.*

whitesmith ['waitsmiδ] blikslager *m.*; metaalbewerker *m.*

whitewash ['waitwɔʃ] *sb.* witsel *o.*, witkalk *v.*; (*sl.*) blanketsel *o.*; (*fig.*) vergoelijking; verschoning *v.*; rehabilitatie *v.*; *vt.* witten; (*fig.*) van blaam zuiveren; schoonwassen; (*H.*) homologeren; *vi.* gerehabiliteerd worden.

whitewasher ['waitwɔʃǝ] witter *m.*; (*fig.*) schoonwasser *m.*

whither ['wiθǝ] werwaarts, waarheen.

whitlow ['witlou] fijt *v.*

Whitsun ['witsn] Pinkster—; (soms: Pinksteren *o.*

whiz(**z**) [wiz] *vi.* sissen, suizen, snorren, fluiten; *sb.* gesis, gesuis, gesnor, gefluit *o.*; (*Am.*) afspraak *v.*

who [hû, hu] wie, die.

whoever [hû'evǝ] wie ook, alwie.

whole [houl] *adj.* heel, geheel; volledig, volmaakt; gaaf, ongeschonden; gezond; ongedeerd; *sb.* geheel *o.*

wholesale ['houlseil] *sb.* groothandel *m.*; *adj.* in het groot, en gros; *adv.* in 't groot; op grote schaal; zonder onderscheid; *vi.* in 't groot verkopen.

wholesaler ['houlseilə] groothandelaar *m*.

wholesome(ly) ['houlsəm(li)] *adj.* (*adv.*) gezond, heilzaam.

whooping-cough ['hûpiŋko:f] kinkhoest *m*.

why [wai] *adv.* waarom; *ij.* wel, welnu; *sb.* **the —**, het waarom, de reden.

wick [wik] (*v. lamp, enz.*) wiek, pit *v*.

wicked ['wikid] *adj.* zondig, verdorven, slecht, gemeen; goddeloos; boos, boosaardig; (*v. dier*) woest, vals; ondeugend, snaaks; *sb.* **the —**, de goddelozen.

wicker-work ['wikəwə:k] vlechtwerk, mandewerk *o*.

wide [waid] *adj.* wijd, breed; wijd open; uitgebreid, uitgestrekt, ruim; ruim van opvatting; (*v. verschil*) groot; (*v. term*) rekbaar; (*sl.*) er naast, niet raak; de plank mis; (*sl.*) uitgeslapen; (*sl.: v. prijs*) buitensporig; *adv.* wijd, wijd uiteen, wijdbeens; *sb.* wijde ruimte *v*.; (*sp.*) niet rake bal *m*.

wide-awake ['waidə'weik] *adj.* klaar wakker; uitgeslapen; (*fig.*) uitgeslapen, wakker, bijdehand, snugger; *sb.* ['waidəweik] flaphoed, flambard *m*.

wide-minded ['waid'maindid] ruim van opvatting.

widen ['waidn] *vt.* verwijden, verruimen, verbreden, breder maken; *vi.* wijder worden, breder worden; zich verwijden.

wide-spread ['waidspred] uitgestrekt; uitgebreid; vèrstrekkend; algemeen verspreid; (*v. komplot*) wijdvertakt, wijd verspreid.

widow ['widou] *sb.* weduwe *v*.; *vt.* tot weduwe maken; (*dicht.*) beroven (**of,** van).

widower ['widouə] weduwnaar *m*.

width [widθ] wijdte, breedte; uitgestrektheid *v*.; (*v. japon*) baan *v*.

wield [wild] hanteren; (*v. scepter*) zwaaien; (*v. pen*) voeren; (*v. macht, invloed*) uitoefenen.

wife [waif] vrouw, huisvrouw, echtgenote, gade *v*.

wig [wig] *sb.* pruik *v*.; (*fam.*) uitbrander *m*.; *vt.* een uitbrander geven.

wigging ['wigiŋ] uitbrander *m*., standje *o*., schrobbering *v*.

wild [waild] *adj.* wild, woest; verwilderd; losbandig, loszinnig; (*v. weer*) ruw; (*v. geruchten*) los, ongegrond; (*v. verhalen*) fantastisch; schuw; *adv.* in 't wild; *sb.* woestenij; wildernis *v*.

wilderness ['wildənis] woestenij, wildernis *v*.; (*fig.*) menigte, massa *v*., hoop *m*.

wilful ['wilful] *adj.* moedwillig; koppig, eigenzinnig, halsstarrig.

will [wil] *sb.* wil, wens *m*.; wilskracht *v*.; willekeur *v*.; laatste wil *m*., testament *o*.; *vi.* (*hulpwerkwoord*) willen, wensen; zullen; plegen; *vt.* (*zelfstandig werkwoord*) willen; (*v. hypnotiseur, enz.*) suggereren, door zijn wil oproepen, door

wilskracht dwingen; (*bij testament*) vermaken, testeren, legateren.

will-o'-the-wisp ['wiləθə'wisp] dwaallichtje *o*.

willow ['wilou] *sb.* (*Pl.*) wilg *m*.; (*tn.: in spinnerij*) wolf *m*.; cricketbat *o*.; *vt.* (*tn.: v. wol, enz.*) wolven.

will-power ['wilpauə] wilskracht *v*.

willy-nilly ['wili'nili] of hij (zij) wil of niet, goedschiks of kwaadschiks.

wilt [wilt] 2' *pers. enk. van* **will**.

wilt [wilt] *vi.* verwelken, kwijnen, verleppen, verschrompelen; verslappen; *vt.* verslappen, slap maken.

win [win] *vt.* winnen; verdienen; behalen, verkrijgen; verwerven; (*v. eerbied, enz.*) afdwingen; bereiken; (*v. persoon*) overhalen, bewegen; bezorgen; (*sl.*) gappen; *vi.* het winnen, zegevieren; *sb.* (*fam.*) overwinning; gewonnen partij *v*.; succes *o*.

wind [wind; *in poëzie*: waind] *sb.* wind *m*.; windstreek *v*.; lucht *v*.; tocht, trek *m*., luchtzuiging *v*.; adem *m*.; blaasinstrumenten *o. mv.*; (*v. orkest*) (de) blazers *m. mv.*; (*sl.*) maagstreek *v*.; *vt.* in de wind hangen, in de wind laten drogen; luchten, laten doorwaaien; buiten adem brengen; op adem laten komen; (*v. paard*) afrijden, afdraven; de lucht krijgen van.

wind [waind] *vt.* winden, opwinden; omwikkelen, omsluiten; sluiten in; (*v. steenkool*) delven, naar boven halen; (*v. hoorn, enz.*) blazen op; *vi.* wenden; draaien, bochten maken; zich kronkelen, zich slingeren; **— up,** (*H.*) in liquidatie gaan, liquideren zich afwikkelen; zijn rede beëindigen; *sb.* bocht *v*., draai *m*.; (*bij opwinden, enz.*) slag *m*.

wind-bag ['windbæg] *sb.* windzak, windbuil, snoever, opsnijder *m*.; *vi.* ophakken, pochen.

windfall ['windfo:l] *sb.* afgewaaid ooft *o*., afgewaaide vruchten *v. mv.*; omgewaaide boom *m*.; (*fig.*) buitenkansje, meevallertje *o*.; *adj.* (*v. vruchten*) afgewaaid; (*v. bomen*) omgewaaid.

winding ['waindiŋ] *adj.* bochtig, kronkelend, slingerend; (*v. verhaal*) wijdlopig; *sb.* bocht, kronkeling *v*., draai *m*.

windlass ['windləs] *sb.* windas *o*.; *vt.* (*met een windas*) opwinden.

window ['windou] *sb.* venster, raam *o*.; loket *o*.; opening *v*.; *vt.* van vensters (ramen) voorzien.

window-frame ['windoufreim] vensterkozijn *o*.

wind-screen ['windskrin] windscherm *o*.; (*v. auto*) voorruit *v*.

windy ['windi] winderig; wind verwekkend; (*fig.*) opgeblazen; ijdel, onbeduidend; (*sl.*) bang.

wine [wain] *sb.* wijn *m*.; (*fam.*) wijnfuif *v*.; **—s,** wijnen, wijnsoorten; wijnglazen; *vi.* wijn drinken; een wijnfuif geven; *vt.* op wijn trakteren; wijn laten drinken.

wine-cellar ['wainselə] wijnkelder *m.*
wing [wiŋ] *sb.* vleugel *m.*; vlerk *v.*; wiek, molenwiek *v.*; (*v. auto*) spatbord *o.*; (*v. boord*) omgeslagen punt *v.*; (*sp.*: *voetb.*) vleugelspeler *m.*; (*vl.*) vliegtuiggroep *v.*; bataljon *o.* vliegers; (*scherts.*) arm *m.*; *vt.* van vleugels voorzien; (*v. pijl*) van veren voorzien; (*v. lucht*) (vliegend) doorklieven; afschieten; (*fam.*) aanschieten; vleugellam maken; *vi.* vliegen.
wing-beat ['wiŋbit] vleugelslag *m.*
wing-spread ['wiŋspred] (*v. vogel*) vlucht *r.* (afstand tussen de toppen der uitgespreide vleugels); (*vl.*) vleugelspanning *v.*, afstand *m.* der zweefvlakuiteinden.
wink [wiŋk] *vi.* knippen, knipogen; flikkeren; — *at*, door de vingers zien; een knipoogje geven; *vt.* — *one's eyes,* knipperen met de ogen; — *away a tear,* een traan wegpinken; *sb.* knipoogje *o.*; wenk *m.* (van verstandhouding); geknipper *o.* met de ogen; oogwenk *m.*
winner ['winə] winner *m.*; winnende partij *v.*; (*v. loterij*) winnend nummer *o.*; successtuk *o.*
winnow ['winou] wannen, ziften, uitziften, schiften; (*dicht.*) toewuiven.
winter ['wintə] *sb.* winter *m.*; *vi.* overwinteren, de winter doorbrengen; *vt.* (*v. planten*) de winter overhouden; de winter op stal houden; (*fig.*) koud maken; doen bevriezen.
winter-coat ['wintəkout] (*v. dier*) wintervacht *v.*
wipe [waip] *vt.* vegen, afvegen, wegvegen; afwissen, uitwissen; (*sl.*) afdrogen, afranselen; iem. iets afhandig maken, iem. een vlieg afvangen, iem. de loef afsteken; iem. verlakken; iem. een blauw oog slaan; *sb.* veeg *m.*; (*sl.*) veeg *m.* uit de pan; schrobbering *v.*, uitbrander *m.*; (*fam.*) zakdoek *m.*
wiper ['waipə] veger *m.*; afneemdoek *m.*; handdoek *m.*; zakdoek, neusdoek *m.*
wire ['waiə] *sb.* (metaal)draad *m.*; ijzerdraad; staaldraad *m.*; (*sch.*) draadkabel *m.*; telegraafdraad *m.*; telegram, draadbericht *o.*; (*sl.*) zakkenroller *m.*; *vt.* met ijzerdraad vastmaken; met ijzerdraad omvlechten; aan metaaldraad rijgen; (*v. vogels*) strikken; met prikkeldraad afsluiten (versperren); (over)seinen, telegraferen, per draad melden; (*v. geld*) telegrafisch overmaken; elektrische leiding aanbrengen in; *vi.* seinen, telegraferen.
wire-bridge ['waiəbridʒ] hangbrug *v.*
wire-edge ['waiəredʒ] (*v. mes, enz.*) braam *v.*
wireless ['waiəlis] *adj.* draadloos; — *operator,* radiotelegrafist, marconist; *sb.* draadloze telegrafie *v.*; draadloos bericht, draadloos telegram *o.*; draadloze installatie *v.*; *vt. & vi.* draadloze installatie *v.*; *vt. & vi.* draadloos telegraferen.
wire-nail ['waiəneil] draadnagel *m.*

wire-stitched ['waiəstitʃt] (*v. boek*) met metaaldraad genaaid.
wiry ['waiəri] *adj.* van ijzerdraad; draad—; (*fig.*) taai, mager en gespierd.
wisdom ['wizdəm] wijsheid *v.*
wise [waiz] *adj.* wijs, verstandig; *vt.* (*vi.*) (*Am., sl.*) op de hoogte brengen (komen).
wise [waiz] *sb.* wijze *v.*
wiseacre ['waizeikə] betweter, wijsneus, waanwijze *m.*
wish [wiʃ] *vt.* wensen, begeren, verlangen; toewensen; *vi.* wensen; verlangen; *vr.* — *oneself dead,* wensen, dat men dood was; *sb.* wens *m.*, verlangen *o.*
wispish ['wispiʃ] piekerig; spichtig, schraal; in bosjes; in wolkjes.
wispy ['wispi] *zie* **wispish.**
wit [wit] *sb.* verstand, vernuft *o.*; wijsheid *v.*; geest *m.*, geestigheid *v.*; geestig man *m.*; —*s,* verstand; *vt.* weten.
witch [witʃ] *sb.* heks, tovenares, toverkol *v.*; feeks *v.*; ondeugend nest *o.*, kleine heks *v.*; *vt.* beheksen, betoveren.
witchery ['witʃəri] toverij, hekserij, betovering *v.*
with [wiθ] met; bij; van; door.
withdraw [wiθ'drɔ:] *vt.* terugtrekken; (*v. woorden, geld, enz.*) terugnemen; (*v. voorstel, enz.*) intrekken; (*v. school*) afnemen, wegnemen; (*v. woorden*) herroepen; (*bij verkoping*) ophouden; *vi.* zich terugtrekken; heengaan, zich verwijderen; (*v. minister*) aftreden.
withdrawal [wiθ'drɔ:əl] (het) terugtrekken, enz.; *zie* **withdraw.**
wither ['wiθə] *vt.* doen verwelken, doen verdorren, doen verschrompelen; doen verkwijnen; (*v. theeblaren*) drogen; (*fig.*: met blik) vernietigen; *vi.* verwelken, verdorren, verschrompelen; verkwijnen.
withers ['wiθəz] (*v. paard, enz.*) schoft *v.* (*v. harpoen*) weerhaken *m.*
withhold [wiθ'hould] onthouden, onttrekken; terugtrekken, terughouden, weerhouden.
within [wi'θin] *prep.* binnen, in; tot op; binnen de perken van; *adv.* binnen, van binnen.
without [wi'θaut] *prep.* zonder; buiten; *adv.* buiten; daarbuiten; *cj.* als niet, tenzij.
withstand [wiθ'stænd] *vt.* weerstaan; *vi.* weerstand bieden, zich verzetten.
withstander [wiθ'stændə] tegenstander *m.*
witness ['witnis] *sb.* getuige *m. & v.*; getuigenis *o. & v.*; *vt.* getuigen (van), getuigenis afleggen van; getuige zijn van; bijwonen, beleven; betuigen; (als getuige) tekenen; *vi.* getuigen.
witty ['witi] geestig.
wobble ['wɔbl] *vi.* waggelen, wiebelen; (*v. prijzen, enz.*) schommelen; weifelen; (*v. stem*) beven; *sb.* wiebeling, waggeling *v.*; schommeling *v.*
woe [wou] wee; —*s,* ellende, smart, rampen.
woeful(ly) ['wouful(i)] *adj.* (*adv.*) droe-

vig, treurig, ongelukkig, ellendig; jammerlijk, pijnlijk; kommervol, zorgvol.
wolf [wulf] *sb.* (*Dk.*, *gen.*, *muz.*, *tn.*) wolf *m.*; (*fig.*) haai *m.*; *vt.* verslinden, opschrokken, naar binnen schrokken; nodeloos alarmeren, misleiden met vals alarm; *vi.* gulzig eten, schrokken, vreten.
woman ['wumən] *sb.* vrouw *v.*, vrouwspersoon *o.*; kamenier *v.*; (*ong.*) wijf *o.*; mens *o.*; *adj.* vrouwelijk; van 't vrouwelijk geslacht; *vt.* als vrouw behandelen; met vrouw aanspreken; van vrouwelijk personeel voorzien.
woman-hater ['wumenheitə] vrouwenhater *m.*
womanish (ly) ['wuməniʃ(li)] *adj.* (*adv.*) vrouwachtig; als (van) een vrouw; verwijfd.
womanly ['wumənli] vrouwelijk.
womb [wûm] *sb.* schoot *m.*
wonder ['wəndə] *sb.* wonder *o.*, mirakel; wonderwerk *o.*; verwondering, verbazing, verbaasdheid *v.*; (*Am.*) knijpkoekje *o.*; *vi.* zich verwonderen, zich verbazen, verbaasd zijn; *vt.* nieuwsgierig zijn, benieuwd zijn (te weten), wel eens willen weten; zich afvragen.
wonderful (ly) ['wəndəful(i)] *adj.* (*adv.*) verwonderlijk, wonderbaarlijk; wonderschoon.
wondering (ly) ['wəndəriŋ(li)] *adj.* (*adv.*) verwonderd, verbaasd, vol verbazing; met verbazing.
wonder-worker ['wəndəwə:kə] wonderdoener *m.*
wood [wud] *sb.* hout *o.*; bos *o.*; (*sp.*) bal *m.*; cricketbat *o.*; houten blaasinstrumenten *o. mv.*; **—s**, bossen; houtsoorten; *vt.* bebossen; van hout voorzien; met hout laden.
woodcut ['wudkət] houtsnee *v.*
wood-cutter ['wudkətə] houthakker *m.*; houtgraveur, houtsnijder *m.*
wooded ['wudid] bebost, met bos bedekt (begroeid); bosrijk, houtrijk.
wooden ['wudn] houten, van hout; (*fig.*) stijf, houterig, harkerig; dom, stom, suf, wezenloos; ongevoelig, onaandoenlijk.
woodland ['wudlənd] *sb.* bosland *o.*, bosgrond *m.*; *adj.* met bos begroeid; bosachtig.
wood-louse ['wudlaus] houtluis *v.*; doodskloppertje *o.*; keldermot, kelderpissebed *v.*; witte mier *v.*
wood-notes ['wudnouts] wildzang *m.*, gekwinkeleer *o.*; (*fig.*) ongekunstelde poëzie *v.*
woodpecker ['wudpekə] specht *m.*
woodruff ['wudrəf] (*Pl.*) lievevrouwebedstro *o.*
woodsman ['wudzmən] bosbewoner; woudloper *m.*; houthakker *m.*
wood-stack ['wudstæk] houtmijt *v.*
woody ['wudi] houtachtig; hout—; bosachtig; bosrijk; (*Am.*) dom; gek.
wooer ['wûə] vrijer *m.*

woof [wûf] inslag *m.*; weefsel *o.*
woof [wuf] *ij.* (*v. hond*) woef! *vi.* blaffen; *sb.* geblaf *o.*
wool [wul] *sb.* wol *v.*; boomwol *v.*; dons *o.*; wollen garen *o.*, sajet *v.* & *o.*; (*scherts.*) haar *o.*; *adj.* wollen.
woollen ['wulən] *adj.* wollen, van wol; *sb.* wollen artikel, wollen goed *o.*
woolly ['wuli] *adj.* wollig, wolachtig; (*Pl.*: *v. radijs*, *appel*, *enz.*) voos; (*v. peer*) melig; vaag, doezelig; (*v. stem*) dof, dofklinkend; (*v. atmosfeer*) zwoel; (*v. roman*) taai; (*sl.*) gek, dwaas; *sb.* wollen sporttrui *v.*; wolletje *o.*; **woollies**, wollen onderkleren.
word [wə:d] *sb.* woord *o.*; wachtwoord, parool *o.*; motto *o.*; bevel *o.*; bericht *o.*; *vt.* onder woorden brengen, uitdrukken, formuleren.
wording ['wə:diŋ] (*v. zin*, *enz.*) bewoordingen *v. mv.*, redactie, inkleding *v.*
wordy ['wə:di] *adj.* woordenrijk, langdradig; woorden—.
work [wə:k] *sb.* (*alg.*) werk *o.*; bezigheid *v.*, arbeid *m.*; (*sp.*) oefening, training *v.*; **—s**, (*v. horloge*, *enz.*) werk *o.*; fabriek(en); werkplaats(en); (*mil.*) vestingwerk(en); *vi.* werken; in beweging zijn, in beroering zijn; gisten; effect hebben, effect sorteren; een handwerkje doen; (*v. schip*) stampen; *vt.* bewerken, bearbeiden; vervaardigen; kneden; bereiden; laten werken; uitrekenen, uitcijferen; in beweging brengen (houden); (*v. orders*) uitvoeren; (*v. moord*) bedrijven; (*v. mijn*, *enz.*) exploiteren; hanteren, bedienen; vormen, smeden; (*v. dienst*, *enz.*) onderhouden; borduren; *vr.* — **oneself into favour**, in de gunst zien te komen.
work-box ['wə:kbɔks] werkdoos *v.*
worker ['wə:kə] werker *m.*; werkster *v.*; bewerker *m.*; werkman, arbeider *m.*; (*Dk.*) werkbij *v.*; werkmier *v.*
work-fellow ['wə:kfelou] werkmakker; maat *m.*; medearbeider *m.*
work-girl ['wə:kgə:l] werkmeisje; fabrieksmeisje *o.*
working ['wə:kiŋ] *adj.* werkend; werk—, arbeids—; werkzaam; bruikbaar; praktisch; *sb.* (het) werken *o.*; werking *v.*; bewerking *v.*; exploitatie, ontginning *v.*; bedrijf *o.*; mijn *v.*; groeve *v.*; (*v. plan*) uitvoering *v.*; (*v. vraagstuk*) uitwerking *v.*
working-capital ['wə:kiŋkæpitl] bedrijfskapitaal *o.*
working-class ['wə:kiŋklâs] *sb.* arbeidersklasse *v.*, arbeidersstand *m.*; *adj.* arbeiders—.
workless ['wə:klis] werkloos, zonder werk.
workmanship ['wə:kmənʃip] bewerking, afwerking, uitvoering *v.*; techniek *v.*; bekwaamheid, vaardigheid *v.*; werk, produkt *o.*
workshop ['wə:kʃop] werkplaats *v.*
world [wə:ld] *sb.* wereld *v.*; (*fig.*)

hoop *m.*, menigte *v.*; *adj.* werelds; wereld—.

world-famed ['wə:ldfeimd] wereldberoemd.

worldling ['wə:ldliŋ] wereldling; wereldse mens *m.*

worldly ['wə:ldli] werelds, aards; wereldsgezind.

world-shaking ['wə:ldʃeikiŋ] wereldschokkend.

world-wide ['wə:ldwaid] over de hele wereld verspreid, wereld—.

worm [wə:m] *sb.* worm *m.*; (*v. hond*) tongbandje *o.*, tongriem *m.*; (*tn.*) schroefdraad *m.*; (*mil.*) krasser, patroontrekker *m.*; (*v. distilleertoestel*) koelslang *v.*; (*fig.*) aardworm *m.*; stumper(d) *m.*; (*fam.*) vetpuistje *o.*; *vi.* kruipen; kronkelen (als een worm); wormen zoeken; *vt.* van wormen zuiveren; (*v. hond*) van de tongriem (het tongbandje) snijden; (*mil.*) met de krasser schoonmaken; (*sch.*) trenzen.

wormwood ['wə:mwud] (*Pl.*) alsem *m.*

wormy ['wə:mi] wormachtig; wormvormig; wormstekig, vol wormen; (*fig.*) laag, kruiperig.

worn [wo:n] *v. d. van **wear**; *adj.* versleten; afgedragen; vermoeid, doodop, uitgeput, afgetobd; verweerd; afgezaagd.

worry ['wori] *vt.* rukken aan, scheuren; kwellen, plagen, geen rust laten; het lastig maken, in 't vaarwater zitten, narijden; *vi.* tobben, piekeren, kniezen, zich zorgen maken; (*v. vee, enz.*) onrustig zijn; *vr.* — **oneself,** zich bezorgd maken; zich nodeloos kwellen; *sb.* geruk *o.*; bezorgdheid, ongerustheid *v.*; kwelling, plagerij *v.*

worse [wə:s] *adj.* erger, slechter; (*v. koers*) minder, lager, lager genoteerd; snoder; *adv.* erger, slechter; *sb.* iets ergers, iets slechters; *vt.* slechter maken, erger maken.

worsen ['wə:sn] *vt.* slechter maken, erger maken; (*v. prijs*) doen dalen; *vi.* slechter worden, erger worden; (*v. prijs*) lager worden.

worship ['wə:ʃip] *sb.* aanbidding; verering *v.*; godsdienst, eredienst *m.*; godsdienstoefening *v.*; waardigheid *v.*, aanzien *o.*, achting *v.*; *vt.* aanbidden; *vi.* bidden; in aanbidding verzonken zijn; zijn godsdienstplichten vervullen; ter kerke gaan.

worshipper ['wə:ʃipə] aanbidder; vereerder *m.*; biddende *m.*; kerkganger *m.*

worst [wə:st] *adj.* ergst; slechtst; snoodst; *adv.* het ergst; het slechtst; *sb.* **the** — (*of it*), het ergste; *vt.* verslaan, het winnen van, het onderspit doen delven; in de luren leggen; slechter maken.

worsted ['wə:stid] *v. t. & v. d.* van **worst.**

worsted ['wustid] *sb.* sajet *v. & o.*; kamgaren *o.*; *adj.* sajetten; kamgaren.

worth [wə:ð] *adj.* waard; *sb.* waarde *v.*; innerlijke waarde; verdienste *v.*; deugdelijkheid, voortreffelijkheid *v.*

worthiness ['wə:θinis] waardigheid *v.*; verdienste, (innerlijke) waarde *v.*; deugdzaamheid *v.*

worthless (**ly**) ['wə:ðlis(li)] *adj.* (*adv.*) waardeloos; nietswaardig; verachtelijk.

worthy ['wə:ði] *adj.* waard, waardig; achtenswaardig; braaf; *sb.* achtenswaardig (braaf) man; verdienstelijk man *m.*; beroemdheid *v.*

would-be ['wudbi] zogenaamd, zogezegd; voorgewend; bedoeld als; aanstaand.

wound [waund] *v. t. & v. d. van **wind.**

wound [wûnd] *sb.* wond(e), kwetsuur *v.*; *vt.* wonden, kwetsen; krenken.

wrack [ræk] wrak *o.*; aangespoeld zeegras, zeewier *o.*; spoor *o.*

wrangle ['ræŋgl] *vi.* kijven, twisten, kibbelen, krakelen, ruzie hebben; *vt.* (*Am.: v. paarden*) bijeendrijven; *sb.* gekijf, gekibbel, gekrakeel *o.*

wrangling ['ræŋgliŋ] (het) kibbelen, gekibbel, gekrakeel, gekijf *o.*

wrap [ræp] *vt.* omhullen, inpakken, wikkelen, oprollen; (*v. randen van kledingstuk*) over elkaar heen slaan; *vi.* zich inpakken; *sb.* omhulsel *o.*; omwikkeling *v.*; omslagdoek *m.*, sjaal *v.*; kamerjapon *v.*; overmantel *m.*; reisdeken *v.*

wrapper ['ræpə] *sb.* inwikkelaar; inpakker *m.*; omslag *m. & o.*, kaft *v. & o.*; (*v. sigaar*) dekblad *o.*; (*v. paraplu, enz.*) overtrek *o.*; ochtendjapon *v.*; stoflaken *o.*; (*voor dagblad*) kruisband *m.*; (*Am.*) sigaar *v.*; pakpapier *o.*; *vt.* van een omslag (kaft, enz.) voorzien.

wrapping-paper ['ræpiŋpeipə] pakpapier *o.*

wrath [ro:ð] toorn *m.*, gramschap *v.*

wrathful (**ly**) ['ro:ðful(i)] *adj.* (*adv.*) toornig, vertoornd, vergramd.

wreath [rið] krans, slinger *m.*, festoen *v. & o.*; winding *v.*, rimpel *m.*; (*v. rook*) kronkel, kring *m.*; (*in glas*) streep *v.*; (*wap.*) wrong *v.*; (*van hoef*) kroon *v.*

wreathe [riθ] *vt.* winden, draaien, vlechten; strengelen; omstrengelen; ineenstrengelen; omkransen; *vi.* zich strengelen, kronkelen.

wreck [rek] *sb.* wrak *o.*; wrakhout *o.*, wrakgoederen *o. mv.*; schipbreuk *v.*; vernieling, vernietiging, verwoesting *v.*; ondergang *m.*; *vt.* schipbreuk doen lijden, doen stranden; vernielen, verwoesten, te gronde richten; doen mislukken; (*v. trein*) doen verongelukken; saboteren; *vi.* wrakhout zoeken, wrakgoederen roven, stranddieverij plegen.

wreckage ['rekidʒ] schipbreuk *v.*; wrakhout *o.*, wrakstukken *o. mv.*; wrakgoederen *o. mv.*; puin *o.*, overblijfselen *o. mv.*

wrench [renʃ] *sb.* ruk, draai *m.*; verrekking, verzwikking, verstuiking *v.*; verdraaiing, verwringing *v.*; schroefsleutel, schroevedraaier *m.*; (*fig.*) pijnlijke operatie; pijnlijke scheiding *v.*; *vt.* rukken, draaien, wringen; verdraaien, verwringen; verrekken, verzwikken, verstuiken.

wrestle ['resl] *vi.* worstelen; *vt.* — *a person,* met iem. worstelen; *sb.* worsteling *v.*; (*sp.*) worstelwedstrijd *m.*

wrestler ['reslǝ] worstelaar *m.*; strijder; kampvechter *m.*

wretch [retʃ] arme (ongelukkige) stakker *m.*; ellendeling, schelm *m.*

wrick [rik] *vt.* verrekken; verdraaien; *sb.* verrekking; verdraaiing *v.*

wriggle ['rigl] *vi.* wriggelen; draaien; wriemelen; (*v. worm*) kronkelen; (op stoel) zitten draaien; er omheen draaien; zich in allerlei bochten wringen; tegenstribbelen; *vt.* wrikken; *vr.* — *oneself into a person's favour,* zich in iemands gunst weten te dringen; *sb.* wriggelende beweging *v.*; gewriemel *o.*; gekronkel *o.*

wring [riŋ] *vt.* wringen; uitwringen; uitknijpen; toeknijpen; draaien; omdraaien; (*v. Schrift*) verdraaien; knellen, drukken; *vi.* zich wringen; zich kronkelen; *sb.* wringing *v.*, wrong *m.*; kaaspers; wijnpers *v.*

wrinkle ['riŋkl] *sb.* rimpel *m.*, plooi, kreuk *v.*; vouw *v.*; wenk *m.*; idee *o.*; kneep *m.*, foefje, kunstje *o.*; *vt.* (*vi.*) (zich) rimpelen, plooien.

wrist [rist] pols *m.*, polsgewricht *o.*

wristband ['ris(t)bænd, 'rizbǝnd] (vaste) manchet *v.*

wristlet ['ristlit] polsarmband *m.*; (*sl.*) handboei *v.*

writ [rit] *v. t.* & *v. d. van* **write.**

writ [rit] *sb.* schrift, geschrift *o.*; bevelschrift *o.*; dagvaarding *v.*

write [rait] *vt.* schrijven; uitschrijven; opschrijven; *vr.* — *oneself down,* zijn reputatie als schrijver door minderwaardig werk schaden.

writer ['raitǝ] schrijver *m.*; schrijfster *v.*; klerk *m.*; (*Sc.*) procureur *m.*

writhe [raiθ] *vt.* verwringen, verdraaien; *vi.* zich wringen, zich kronkelen, zich draaien; ineenkrimpen; *sb.* verwringing, verdraaiing *v.*

writing ['raitiŋ] (het) schrijven *o.*; schrift, geschrift *o.*; schrijftrant, stijl *m.*; opschrift *o.*

writing-book ['raitiŋbuk] schoonschrift, schrijfboek *o.*

writing-materials ['raitiŋmǝtiǝriǝlz] schrijfbehoeften *v. mv.*, schrijfgereedschap *o.*

writing-pad ['raitiŋpæd] onderlegger *m.*, vloeimap *v.*

writing-table ['raitiŋteibl] schrijftafel *v.*

wrong [rɔn] *adj.* verkeerd; niet in orde, niet in de haak; in de war; onjuist; mis; slecht; *adv.* verkeerd, mis; de verkeerde kant uit; *sb.* kwaad *o.*; iets verkeerds; onrecht *o.*; ongelijk *o.*; *vt.* onrecht aandoen, verongelijken; onbillijk beoordelen (behandelen), onbillijk zijn tegenover.

wrongly ['rɔnli] *adv.* onrechtvaardig; ten onrechte; verkeerd(elijk).

wrong-timed ['rɔntaimd] ontijdig.

wroth [ro:ð, rɔð] vertoornd, toornig, vergramd, verbolgen.

wrought [ro:t] *v. t.* & *v. d. van* **work**; *adj.* bewerkt; geslagen; gesmeed; behouwen; geborduurd.

wrought-up ['ro:t'ǝp] opgewonden, geprikkeld, overprikkeld, overspannen.

wry [rai] *adj.* scheef, verdraaid, verkeerd; verwrongen, krom getrokken; *vt.* verdraaien; verwringen.

wrymouthed ['raimauθd] met een scheve mond; (*fig.*) ironisch vleiend.

wry-necked ['rainekt] met een scheve hals.

X

xebec ['zibek] chebek, kleine driemaster *m.*

X-ray ['eks'rei] met X-stralen behandelen.

xylophone ['zailǝfoun] xylofoon *v.*

Y

yacht [jɔt] *sb.* jacht, zeiljacht, plezierjacht *o.*; *vi.* zeilen in een jacht.

yap [jæp] *sb.* gekef *o.*; (*dial.*) keffer *m.*; *vi.* keffen; kletsen; snauwen.

yard [jâd] *sb.* (Engelse) el *v.*; (*o,* 914m.), yard *m.*; (*sch.*) ra *v.*; (*bij huis, enz.*) plaats *v.*, plaatsje *o.*; (*v. gevangenis*) binnenplaats *v.*; (*v. spoorweg*) emplacement *o.*; erf *o.*; (*dial., Am.*) moestuin *m.*; *vt.*

(*Am.: v. vee*) op afgesloten terrein opsluiten.

yarn [jân] *sb.* garen *o.*, draad *m.*; (*fam.*) praatje *o.*; *vt.* een (ongelooflijk) verhaal opdissen.

yawl [jo:l] *sb.* jol *v.*; klein zeiljacht *o.*; gejank *o.*; *vi.* (*fam.*) (*v. hond*) huilen, janken.

yawn [jo:n] *sb.* geeuw, gaap *m.*; *vi.*

geeuwen, gapen; zich wijd openen.
year [jîə] jaar *o.*; jaartal *o.*; (*v. wijnsoort*) jaargang *m.*
year-book ['jîəbuk] jaarboek *o.*
yearly ['jîəli] *adj.* jaarlijks, jaar—; *adv.* jaarlijks.
yearn [jə:n] vurig verlangen, smachtend verlangen (*after, for,* naar); — *to,* er naar smachten om; zich aangetrokken voelen tot.
yeast [jîst] gist *v.*; (*fig.*) zuurdesem *m.*; (*op de golven*) schuim *o.*
yell [jel] *sb.* gil, angstkreet *m.*; *vi.* gillen, schreeuwen; *vt.* (uit)gillen, (uit)schreeuwen.
yellow ['jelou] *adj.* geel; vergeeld; *sb.* geel *o.*; geelsel *o.*; gele stof (Aint. enz.) *v.*; knolraap *v.*; geel van een ei *o.*; *vt.* geel maken; *vi.* geel worden.
yelp [jelp] *sb.* gekef, gejank *o.*; *vi.* keffen, janken.
yes [jes] *adv.* ja, jawel; wel?; *vi.* (*fam.*) ja zeggen; *vt.* — *a person,* iem. gelijk geven.
yesterday ['jestədi] gisteren.
yet [jet] *adv.* nog; tot nog toe; alsnog; nog steeds; toch, nochtans; *cj.* maar, doch, nochtans.
yield [jîld] *vt.* (*v. vruchten, enz.*) voortbrengen; (*v. voordeel, winst*) opleveren,

afwerpen; (*v. stad, vesting*) overgeven; (*v. touw*) vieren; geven, verlenen; *vi.* (*bij druk*) meegeven; toegeven (*to,* aan); wijken, zwichten (*to,* voor); plaats maken (*to,* voor); *vr.* — *oneself prisoner,* zich gevangen geven; *sb.* opbrengst *v.*; oogst *m.*; (*onder druk*) het meegeven *o.*
yielding ['jîldiŋ] vrechtbaar; voordelig; toegeeflijk, inschikkelijk, meegaand; buigzaam; meegevend.
yodel ['joudəl] *vt. & vi.* jodelen; *sb.* gejodel *o.*
yoke [jouk] *sb.* juk *o.*; (*v. ossen*) koppel, span, juk *o.*; *vt.* het juk opleggen (aandoen); onder het juk brengen; verenigen, verbinden.
yolk [jouk] (eier)dooier *m.*; wolvet *o.*
you [jû, ju] gij, u, gijlieden, ulieden, jullie; je, men.
young [jəŋ] *adj.* jong; (*fam.*) klein; *sb.* (*v. dier*) jong *o.*; jongen *o. mv.*
youngish ['jəŋiʃ] vrij jong, nog jong, jeugdig.
your [jûə, jo:ə, jə] uw; (*fam.*) je, jouw.
youth [jûð] jeugd *v.*; jeugdigheid *v.*; jonkheid *v.*; jongeling *m.*; jongelieden, jongelui *m. mv.*; jongelingschap *v.*
youthful(ly) ['jûðful(i)] *adj.* (*adv.*) jeugdig, jong.

Z

zeal [zîl] ijver, dienstijver *m.*, vuur *o.*
zealot ['zelət] ijveraar, dweper, zeloot *m.*
zealous(ly) ['zeləs(li)] *adj.* (*adv.*) ijverig, vurig.
zenith ['zenið] zenit, toppunt *o.*
zephyr ['zefə] zefier *m.*, koeltje *o.*, zachte wind *m.*
zero ['zîərou] nul *v.*; nulpunt *o.*; laagste punt *o.*; beginpunt *o.*
zest [zest] *sb.* smaak *m.*, genot *o.*; kruiderij *v.*, iets pikants *o.*; oranjeschil; snipper *m.*; *vt.* kruiden, iets pikants geven aan, de smaak verhogen.
zigzag ['zigzæg] *sb.* zigzag *m.*, zigzaglijn *v.*; *adj.* zigzag—, zigzagsgewijze lopend; *adv.* zigzagsgewijze; *vi.* zigzagsgewij-

ze lopen; (*fig.*) heen en weer gaan.
zinc [ziŋk] *sb.* zink *o.*; *vt.* met zink bekleden; galvaniseren.
zodiac ['zoudiæk] dierenriem, zodiak *m.*
zone [zoun] *sb.* gordel *m.*, zone, luchtstreek *v.*; *vt.* omgorden; in zonen verdelen.
zoography [zou'ɔgrəfl] dierenbeschrijving *v.*
zoolatry ['zou'ɔlətri] dierenaanbidding *v.*
zoological ['zou'əlɔdʒikl] dierkundig, zoölogisch.
zoology [zou'ɔlədʒi] dierkunde *v.*
zoom [zûm] *vi.* (*v. vliegtuig*) plotseling de lucht ingaan onder een steile hoek.

Other Hippocrene Dictionaries
and Language Books of Interest . . .

DUTCH-ENGLISH/ENGLISH-DUTCH
CONCISE DICTIONARY
418 pages 4 x 6 14,000 entries
0-87052-910-2 $11.95pb (361)

DUTCH HANDY DICTIONARY
120 pages 5 x 7¾
0-87052-049-0 $8.95pb (323)

DUTCH-ENGLISH/ ENGLISH-DUTCH
STANDARD DICTIONARY
578 pages 5½ x 8¼ 35,000 entries
0-7818-0541-4 $16.95pb (629)

DANISH-ENGLISH/ENGLISH-DANISH
PRACTICAL DICTIONARY
601 pages 4⅜ x 7 32,000 entries
0-7818-0823-8 $14.95pb (198)

MASTERING FRENCH
288 pages 5½ x 8½
0-87052-055-5 $14.95pb (511)
2 Cassettes:
0-87052-060-1 $12.95 (512)

MASTERING ADVANCED FRENCH
348 pages 5½ x 8½
0-7818-0312-8 $14.95pb (41)
2 Cassettes:
0-7818-0313-6 $12.95 (54)

FRENCH HANDY DICTIONARY
120 pages 5 x 7¾
0-7818-0010-2 $8.95pb (155)

FRENCH-ENGLISH/ ENGLISH-FRENCH
PRACTICAL DICTIONARY, with Larger Print
386 pages 5½ x 8¼ 35,000 entries
0-7818-0178-8 $9.95pb (199)

GERMAN-ENGLISH/ ENGLISH-GERMAN
PRACTICAL DICTIONARY
New Edition Larger Print
400 pages 5½ x 8¼ 35,000 entries
0-7818-0355-1 $9.95pb (200)

GERMAN HANDY DICTIONARY
120 pages 5 x 7¾
0-7818-0014-5 $8.95pb (378)

MASTERING GERMAN
340 pages 5½ x 8½
0-87052-056-3 $11.95pb (514)
2 Cassettes:
0-87052-061-X $12.95 (515)

INDONESIAN-ENGLISH/ ENGLISH-INDONESIAN
PRACTICAL DICTIONARY
289 pages 4¼ x 7 17,000 entries
0-87052-810-6 $11.95pb (127)

ENGLISH-NEW NORWEGIAN
PRACTICAL DICTIONARY
422 pages 5½ x 8½
0-7818-0466-3 $29.95hc (654)

NORWEGIAN-ENGLISH/ ENGLISH-NORWEGIAN
COMPREHENSIVE DICTIONARY
1400 pages 6 x 9 100,000 entries
0-7818-0544-9 $45.00hc

SWEDISH-ENGLISH/ ENGLISH-SWEDISH
STANDARD DICTIONARY, Revised Edition
804 pages 5½ x 8½ 70,000 entries
0-7818-0379-9 $19.95pb (242)

SWEDISH HANDY DICTIONARY
120 pages 5 x 7¾
0-87052-054-7 $8.95pb (345)

SWEDISH-ENGLISH
COMPREHENSIVE DICTIONARY
888 pages 6 x 9 75,000 entries
0-7818-0462-0 $60.00hc (437)
0-7818-0474-4 $39.50pb (553)

ENGLISH-SWEDISH
COMPREHENSIVE DICTIONARY
957 pages 6 x 9 75,000 entries
0-7818-0463-9 $60.00hc (439)
0-7818-0475-2 $39.50pb (552)

All prices subject to change. **TO PURCHASE HIPPOCRENE BOOKS** contact your local bookstore, call (718) 454-2366, or write to: HIPPOCRENE BOOKS, 171 Madison Avenue, New York, NY 10016. Please enclose check or money order, adding $5.00 shipping (UPS) for the first book and $.50 for each additional book.